WORLD ATLAS

Philip's are grateful to the following for acting as specialist geography consultants on 'The World in Focus' front section:

Professor D. Brunsden, Kings College, University of London, UK
Dr C. Clarke, Oxford University, UK
Dr I. S. Evans, Durham University, UK
Professor P. Haggett, University of Bristol, UK
Professor K. McLachlan, University of London, UK
Professor M. Monmonier, Syracuse University, New York, USA
Professor M-L. Hsu, University of Minnesota, Minnesota, USA
Professor M. J. Tooley, University of St Andrews, UK
Dr T. Unwin, Royal Holloway, University of London, UK

THE WORLD IN FOCUS
Cartography by Philip's

Picture Acknowledgements:
Cover photography left, Best View Stock/Alamy Stock Photo; centre, Timothy Hodgkinson/Alamy Stock Photo; right, Siempreverde2/iStock
Robin Scagell/Galaxy Picture Library page 3
Thinkstock/iStockphoto page 7 (bottom left & bottom right), /Digital Vision page 7 (centre)

WORLD CITIES
Cartography by Philip's

Page 11, Edinburgh, and page 15, London:
This product includes mapping data licensed from Ordnance Survey® with the permission of the Controller of Her Majesty's Stationery Office. © Crown copyright 2019. All rights reserved. Licence number 100011710.

All satellite images in this section courtesy of NPA Satellite Mapping, CGG Services (UK) Ltd, Edenbridge, Kent, UK (www.npa.cgg.com).

Published in Great Britain in 2019 by Philip's,
a division of Octopus Publishing Group Limited
(www.octopusbooks.co.uk)
Carmelite House, 50 Victoria Embankment, London EC4Y 0DZ
An Hachette UK Company (www.hachette.co.uk)

Copyright © 2019 Philip's

Cartography by Philip's

HARDBACK EDITION: ISBN 978–1–84907–517–6
PAPERBACK EDITION: ISBN 978–1–84907–516–9

A CIP catalogue record for this book is available from the British Library.

Printed in Malaysia

Details of other Philip's titles and services can be found on our website at:
www.philips-maps.co.uk

PHILIP'S

WORLD ATLAS

Royal Geographical Society
with IBG

In association with
The Royal Geographical Society
with The Institute of British Geographers

Contents

World Statistics

Countries	vi
Physical Dimensions	vii
User Guide	viii

The World in Focus

Planet Earth	2–3
Restless Earth	4–5
Landforms	6–7
Oceans	8–9
Climate	10–11
Water and Vegetation	12–13
Environment	14–15
Population	16–17
The Human Family	18–19
Wealth	20–21
Quality of Life	22–23
Energy	24–25
Production	26–27
Trade	28–29
Travel and Tourism	30–31

World Cities

Amsterdam	2
Athens	2
Atlanta	3
Baghdad	3
Bangkok	3
Barcelona	4
Beijing	4
Berlin	5
Boston	6
Brussels	6
Budapest	7
Buenos Aires	7
Cairo	7
Cape Town	8
Copenhagen	8
Chicago	9
Dallas–Fort Worth	9
Dubai	9
Delhi	10
Edinburgh	11
Guangzhou (Canton)	11
Helsinki	11
Hong Kong	12
Istanbul	12
Jakarta	12
Jerusalem	13
Johannesburg	13
Karachi	13
Kolkata (Calcutta)	14
Lagos	14
Las Vegas	14
Lima	14
London	15
Lisbon	16
Los Angeles	16
Madrid	17
Manila	17
Melbourne	18
Mexico City	18
Milan	18
Miami	19
Moscow	19
Montréal	20
Mumbai (Bombay)	20
Munich	21
New Orleans	21
New York	22
Orlando	23
Osaka	23
Oslo	23
Paris	24
Prague	25
Rio de Janeiro	25
Rome	26
San Francisco	26
St Petersburg	27
Santiago	27
São Paulo	27
Seoul	27
Shanghai	28
Singapore	28
Stockholm	29
Sydney	29
Tokyo	30
Tehran	31
Toronto	31
Venice	32
Vienna	32
Warsaw	33
Washington	33
Index to City Maps	34–39
World Cities Satellite Images	40–48

World Maps

Map Symbols	1
The World: Political 1:95 000 000	2–3
Arctic Ocean 1:35 000 000	4
Antarctica 1:35 000 000	5

Europe

Europe: Physical 1:20 000 000	6
Europe: Political 1:20 000 000	7
Scandinavia 1:6 000 000 Iceland 1:6 000 000 Færoe Islands 1:6 000 000	8–9
Ireland 1:2 000 000	10
Scotland 1:2 000 000	11
England and Wales 1:2 000 000	12–13
British Isles 1:5 000 000	14

Netherlands, Belgium and Luxembourg 1:2 500 000	15
Central Europe 1:5 000 000	16–17
Eastern Europe and Turkey 1:10 000 000	18–19
France 1:5 000 000	20
Spain and Portugal 1:5 000 000	21
Italy and the Balkan States 1:5 000 000	22–23

Asia

Asia: Physical 1:47 000 000	24
Asia: Political 1:47 000 000	25
Russia and Northern Asia 1:20 000 000	26–27
Japan 1:5 000 000	28–29

China and the Far East 1:15 000 000 Hong Kong, Macau and Shenzhen 1:1 000 000	30–31
Northern China and Korea 1:6 000 000	32–33
Southern China 1:6 000 000	34–35
Indonesia and the Philippines 1:12 500 000 Java and Madura 1:7 500 000 Bali 1:2 000 000	36–37
Mainland South-east Asia 1:6 000 000 Ko Phuket 1:1 000 000 Ko Samui 1:1 000 000 Pinang 1:1 000 000 Singapore 1:1 000 000	38–39
South Asia 1:10 000 000	40–41
Northern India, Pakistan and Nepal 1:6 000 000 Jammu and Kashmir 1:6 000 000	42–43

Southern India and Sri Lanka
1:6 000 000
Andaman and Nicobar Islands
1:6 000 000

44–45

The Middle East
1:7 000 000

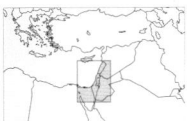

46–47

The Near East 1:2 500 000

48

**Arabia and the Horn
of Africa** 1:15 000 000

49

Africa

Africa: Physical
1:42 000 000   50

Africa: Political
1:42 000 000   51

Northern Africa
1:15 000 000
Azores 1:15 000 000
Cape Verde Islands 1:10 000 000

52–53

Central and Southern Africa
1:15 000 000
Comoros 1:8 000 000
Seychelles 1:2 500 000
Réunion 1:2 500 000
Mauritius 1:2 500 000
Madagascar 1:15 000 000

54–55

Southern Africa
1:8 000 000

56–57

Australia and Oceania

**Australia and Oceania:
Physical and Political**
1:50 000 000   58

New Zealand 1:6 000 000
Fiji 1:6 000 000
Samoan Islands 1:6 000 000
Tonga 1:6 000 000
Tahiti and Moorea 1:1 000 000

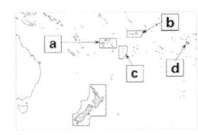

59

Western Australia
1:8 000 000

60–61

Eastern Australia
1:8 000 000
Torres Strait 1:8 000 000
Whitsunday Islands 1:2 500 000
Tasmania 1:8 000 000

62–63

Pacific Ocean
1:54 000 000   64–65

North America

North America: Physical
1:35 000 000   66

North America: Political
1:35 000 000   67

Canada 1:15 000 000

68–69

Western Canada 1:7 000 000

70–71

Eastern Canada 1:7 000 000

72–73

United States 1:15 000 000
Hawai'i 1:15 000 000
Alaska 1:15 000 000

74–75

United States – West
1:6 700 000

76–77

**Central and Southern
California and Western
Washington**
1:2 500 000

78–79

**United States – Midwest and
North-east**
1:6 700 000

80–81

North-eastern United States
1:2 500 000

82–83

United States – South
1:6 700 000

84–85

Mexico 1:8 000 000

86–87

**Central America and the
West Indies** 1:8 000 000
Jamaica 1:3 000 000
Guadeloupe 1:2 000 000
Martinique 1:2 000 000
Puerto Rico 1:3 000 000
Virgin Islands 1:2 000 000
St Lucia 1:1 000 000
Barbados 1:1 000 000

88–89

South America

South America: Physical
1:35 000 000   90

South America: Political
1:35 000 000   91

South America – North
1:16 000 000
Trinidad and Tobago 1:2 500 000

92–93

Central South America
1:8 000 000

94–95

South America – South
1:16 000 000

96

Index to World Maps

97–176

World Statistics: Countries

This alphabetical list includes the principal countries and territories of the world. If a territory is not completely independent, the country it is associated with is named. The area figures give the total area of land, inland water and ice. The population figures are 2017 estimates where available. The annual income is the Gross Domestic Product per capita (ppp) in US dollars. The figures are the latest available, usually 2017 estimates.

Country/Territory	Area km² Thousands	Area miles² Thousands	Population Thousands	Capital	Annual Income US $
Afghanistan	652	252	34,125	Kabul	1,900
Albania	28.7	11.1	3,048	Tirana	12,500
Algeria	2,382	920	40,969	Algiers	15,100
American Samoa (US)	0.20	0.08	52	Pago Pago	13,000
Andorra	0.47	0.18	86	Andorra La Vella	49,900
Angola	1,247	481	29,310	Luanda	6,800
Anguilla (UK)	0.10	0.04	17	The Valley	12,200
Antigua & Barbuda	0.44	0.17	95	St John's	26,300
Argentina	2,780	1,074	44,293	Buenos Aires	20,700
Armenia	29.8	11.5	3,045	Yerevan	9,100
Aruba (Netherlands)	0.19	0.07	115	Oranjestad	25,300
Australia	7,741	2,989	23,232	Canberra	49,900
Austria	83.9	32.4	8,754	Vienna	49,200
Azerbaijan	86.6	33.4	9,961	Baku	17,400
Azores (Portugal)	2.2	0.86	246	Ponta Delgada	15,197
Bahamas	13.9	5.4	330	Nassau	25,100
Bahrain	0.69	0.27	1,411	Manama	51,800
Bangladesh	144	55.6	157,827	Dhaka	4,200
Barbados	0.43	0.17	292	Bridgetown	17,500
Belarus	208	80.2	9,550	Minsk	18,600
Belgium	30.5	11.8	11,491	Brussels	46,300
Belize	23.0	8.9	360	Belmopan	8,300
Benin	113	43.5	11,039	Porto-Novo	2,200
Bermuda (UK)	0.05	0.02	71	Hamilton	85,700
Bhutan	47.0	18.1	758	Thimphu	8,700
Bolivia	1,099	424	11,138	La Paz/Sucre	7,500
Bosnia-Herzegovina	51.2	19.8	3,856	Sarajevo	11,400
Botswana	582	225	2,215	Gaborone	18,100
Brazil	8,514	3,287	207,353	Brasília	15,500
Brunei	5.8	2.2	444	Bandar Seri Begawan	76,700
Bulgaria	111	42.8	7,102	Sofia	21,600
Burkina Faso	274	106	20,108	Ouagadougou	1,900
Burundi	27.8	10.7	11,467	Bujumbura	800
Cabo Verde	4.0	1.6	561	Praia	6,900
Cambodia	181	69.9	16,204	Phnom Penh	4,000
Cameroon	475	184	24,995	Yaoundé	3,400
Canada	9,971	3,850	35,624	Ottawa	48,100
Canary Is. (Spain)	7.2	2.8	2,105	Las Palmas/Santa Cruz	19,900
Cayman Is. (UK)	0.26	0.10	58	George Town	43,800
Central African Republic	623	241	5,625	Bangui	700
Chad	1,284	496	12,076	Ndjaména	2,400
Chile	757	292	17,789	Santiago	24,600
China	9,597	3,705	1 379,303	Beijing	16,600
Colombia	1,139	440	47,699	Bogotá	14,500
Comoros	2.2	0.86	808	Moroni	1,600
Congo	342	132	4,955	Brazzaville	6,700
Congo (Dem. Rep. of the)	2,345	905	83,301	Kinshasa	800
Cook Is. (NZ)	0.24	0.09	9	Avarua	12,300
Costa Rica	51.1	19.7	4,930	San José	17,200
Côte d'Ivoire (Ivory Coast)	322	125	24,185	Yamoussoukro	3,900
Croatia	56.5	21.8	4,292	Zagreb	24,100
Cuba	111	42.8	11,147	Havana	11,900
Curaçao (Netherlands)	0.44	0.17	150	Willemstad	15,000
Cyprus	9.3	3.6	1,222	Nicosia	36,600
Czechia	78.9	30.5	10,675	Prague	35,200
Denmark	43.1	16.6	5,606	Copenhagen	49,600
Djibouti	23.2	9.0	865	Djibouti	3,600
Dominica	0.75	0.29	74	Roseau	12,000
Dominican Republic	48.5	18.7	10,734	Santo Domingo	17,000
Ecuador	284	109	16,291	Quito	11,000
Egypt	1,001	387	97,041	Cairo	13,000
El Salvador	21.0	8.1	6,172	San Salvador	8,900
Equatorial Guinea	28.1	10.8	778	Malabo	34,900
Eritrea	118	45.4	5,919	Asmara	1,400
Estonia	45.1	17.4	1,252	Tallinn	31,500
Eswatini (Swaziland)	17.4	6.7	1,467	Mbabane	9,900
Ethiopia	1,104	426	105,350	Addis Ababa	2,100
Falkland Is. (UK)	12.2	4.7	3	Stanley	96,200
Faroe Is. (Denmark)	1.4	0.54	51	Tórshavn	40,000
Fiji	18.3	7.1	921	Suva	9,900
Finland	338	131	5,518	Helsinki	44,000
France	552	213	67,106	Paris	43,600
French Guiana (France)	90.0	34.7	250	Cayenne	8,300
French Polynesia (France)	4.0	1.5	281	Papeete	17,000
Gabon	268	103	1,772	Libreville	19,300
Gambia, The	11.3	4.4	2,051	Banjul	1,700
Georgia	69.7	26.9	4,926	Tbilisi	10,600
Germany	357	138	80,594	Berlin	50,200
Ghana	239	92.1	27,500	Accra	4,600
Gibraltar (UK)	0.006	0.002	29	Gibraltar Town	61,700
Greece	132	50.9	10,768	Athens	27,800
Greenland (Denmark)	2,176	840	58	Nuuk	37,600
Grenada	0.34	0.13	112	St George's	14,700
Guadeloupe (France)	1.7	0.66	402	Basse-Terre	7,900
Guam (US)	0.55	0.21	167	Agana	30,500
Guatemala	109	42.0	15,461	Guatemala City	8,200
Guinea	246	94.9	12,414	Conakry	2,000
Guinea-Bissau	36.1	13.9	1,792	Bissau	1,800
Guyana	215	83.0	738	Georgetown	8,300
Haiti	27.8	10.7	10,647	Port-au-Prince	1,800
Honduras	112	43.3	9,039	Tegucigalpa	5,500
Hungary	93.0	35.9	9,851	Budapest	28,900
Iceland	103	39.8	340	Reykjavik	52,100
India	3,287	1,269	1,281,936	New Delhi	7,200
Indonesia	1,905	735	260,581	Jakarta	12,400
Iran	1,648	636	82,022	Tehran	20,000
Iraq	438	169	39,192	Baghdad	17,000
Ireland	70.3	27.1	5,011	Dublin	72,600
Israel	20.6	8.0	8,300	Jerusalem	36,200
Italy	301	116	62,138	Rome	38,000
Jamaica	11.0	4.2	2,991	Kingston	9,200
Japan	378	146	126,451	Tokyo	42,700
Jordan	89.3	34.5	10,248	Amman	12,500
Kazakhstan	2,725	1,052	18,557	Astana	26,100
Kenya	580	224	47,616	Nairobi	3,500
Kiribati	0.73	0.28	108	Tarawa	1,900
Korea, North	121	46.5	25,248	Pyo˘ngyang	1,700
Korea, South	99.3	38.3	51,181	Seoul	39,400
Kosovo	10.9	4.2	1,895	Pristina	10,400
Kuwait	17.8	6.9	2,875	Kuwait City	69,700
Kyrgyzstan	200	77.2	5,789	Bishkek	3,700
Laos	237	91.4	7,127	Vientiane	7,400

*OPT 5 Occupied Palestinian Territory

Country/Territory	Area km² Thousands	Area miles² Thousands	Population Thousands	Capital	Annual Income US $
Latvia	64.6	24.9	1,945	Riga	27,300
Lebanon	10.4	4.0	6,230	Beirut	19,500
Lesotho	30.4	11.7	1,958	Maseru	3,900
Liberia	111	43.0	4,689	Monrovia	900
Libya	1,760	679	6,653	Tripoli	9,800
Liechtenstein	0.16	0.06	38	Vaduz	139,100
Lithuania	65.2	25.2	2,824	Vilnius	31,900
Luxembourg	2.6	1.0	594	Luxembourg	109,100
Macedonia (FYROM)	25.7	9.9	2,104	Skopje	15,200
Madagascar	587	227	25,054	Antananarivo	1,600
Madeira (Portugal)	0.78	0.30	289	Funchal	25,800
Malawi	118	45.7	19,196	Lilongwe	1,200
Malaysia	330	127	31,382	Kuala Lumpur/Putrajaya	28,900
Maldives	0.30	0.12	393	Malé	19,200
Mali	1,240	479	17,885	Bamako	2,200
Malta	0.32	0.12	416	Valletta	42,500
Marshall Is.	0.18	0.07	75	Majuro	3,400
Martinique (France)	1.1	0.43	371	Fort-de-France	14,400
Mauritania	1,026	396	3,759	Nouakchott	4,500
Mauritius	2.0	0.79	1,356	Port Louis	21,600
Mayotte (France)	0.37	0.14	213	Mamoudzou	4,900
Mexico	1,958	756	124,575	Mexico City	19,500
Micronesia, Fed. States of	0.70	0.27	104	Palikir	3,400
Moldova	33.9	13.1	3,474	Kishinev	5,700
Monaco	0.002	0.0008	31	Monaco	115,700
Mongolia	1,567	605	3,068	Ulan Bator	12,600
Montenegro	14.0	5.4	643	Podgorica	17,400
Montserrat (UK)	0.10	0.39	5	Brades	8,500
Morocco	447	172	33,987	Rabat	8,600
Mozambique	802	309	26,574	Maputo	1,300
Myanmar (Burma)	677	261	55,124	Rangoon/Naypyidaw	6,300
Namibia	824	318	2,485	Windhoek	11,500
Nauru	0.02	0.008	10	Yaren	12,200
Nepal	147	56.8	29,384	Katmandu	2,700
Netherlands	41.5	16.0	17,085	Amsterdam/The Hague	53,600
New Caledonia (France)	18.6	7.2	279	Nouméa	31,100
New Zealand	271	104	4,510	Wellington	38,500
Nicaragua	130	50.2	6,026	Managua	5,800
Niger	1,267	489	19,245	Niamey	1,200
Nigeria	924	357	190,632	Abuja	5,900
Northern Mariana Is. (US)	0.46	0.18	52	Saipan	13,300
Norway	324	125	5,320	Oslo	70,600
Oman	310	119	3,424	Muscat	45,500
Pakistan	796	307	204,925	Islamabad	5,400
Palau	0.46	0.18	21	Melekeok	16,700
Panama	75.5	29.2	3,753	Panamá	24,300
Papua New Guinea	463	179	6,910	Port Moresby	3,800
Paraguay	407	157	6,944	Asunción	9,800
Peru	1,285	496	31,037	Lima	13,300
Philippines	300	116	104,256	Manila	8,200
Poland	323	125	38,476	Warsaw	29,300
Portugal	88.8	34.3	10,840	Lisbon	30,300
Puerto Rico (US)	8.9	3.4	3,352	San Juan	37,900
Qatar	11.0	4.2	2,314	Doha	124,900
Réunion (France)	2.5	0.97	845	St-Denis	6,200
Romania	238	92.0	21,530	Bucharest	24,000
Russia	17,075	6,593	142,258	Moscow	27,900
Rwanda	26.3	10.2	11,901	Kigali	2,100
St Kitts & Nevis	0.26	0.10	52	Basseterre	26,800
St Lucia	0.54	0.21	164	Castries	13,500
St Vincent & Grenadines	0.39	0.15	102	Kingstown	11,600
Samoa	2.8	1.1	200	Apia	5,700
San Marino	0.06	0.02	34	San Marino	59,500
São Tomé & Príncipe	0.96	0.37	201	São Tomé	3,200
Saudi Arabia	2,150	830	28,572	Riyadh	55,300
Senegal	197	76.0	14,669	Dakar	2,700
Serbia	77.5	29.9	7,111	Belgrade	15,200
Seychelles	0.46	0.18	94	Victoria	28,900
Sierra Leone	71.7	27.7	6,163	Freetown	1,800
Singapore	0.68	0.26	5,889	Singapore City	90,500
Slovakia	49.0	18.9	5,446	Bratislava	32,900
Slovenia	20.3	7.8	1,972	Ljubljana	34,100
Solomon Is.	28.9	11.2	648	Honiara	2,100
Somalia	638	246	11,031	Mogadishu	400
South Africa	1,221	471	54,842	Cape Town/Pretoria	13,400
Spain	498	192	48,958	Madrid	38,200
Sri Lanka	65.6	25.3	22,409	Colombo	13,000
Sudan	1,886	728	37,346	Khartoum	4,600
Sudan, South	620	239	13,026	Juba	1,500
Suriname	163	63.0	592	Paramaribo	13,900
Sweden	450	174	9,960	Stockholm	51,300
Switzerland	41.3	15.9	8,236	Bern	61,400
Syria	185	71.5	18,029	Damascus	2,900
Taiwan	36.0	13.9	23,508	Taipei	49,800
Tajikistan	143	55.3	8,469	Dushanbe	3,100
Tanzania	945	365	53,951	Dodoma	3,300
Thailand	513	198	68,414	Bangkok	17,800
Timor-Leste	14.9	5.7	1,291	Dili	5,000
Togo	56.8	21.9	7,965	Lomé	1,600
Tonga	0.65	0.25	106	Nuku'alofa	5,600
Trinidad & Tobago	5.1	2.0	1,218	Port of Spain	31,200
Tunisia	164	63.2	11,404	Tunis	12,000
Turkey	775	299	80,845	Ankara	26,500
Turkmenistan	488	188	5,351	Ashkhabad	18,700
Turks & Caicos Is. (UK)	0.43	0.17	53	Cockburn Town	29,100
Tuvalu	0.03	0.01	11	Fongafale	3,800
Uganda	241	93.1	39,570	Kampala	2,400
Ukraine	604	233	44,034	Kiev	8,700
United Arab Emirates	83.6	32.3	5,927	Abu Dhabi	68,200
United Kingdom	242	93.4	64,769	London	43,600
United States of America	9,629	3,718	326,626	Washington, DC	59,500
Uruguay	175	67.6	3,361	Montevideo	22,400
Uzbekistan	447	173	29,749	Tashkent	7,000
Vanuatu	12.2	4.7	283	Port-Vila	2,800
Vatican City	0.0004	0.0002	1	Vatican City	
Venezuela	912	352	31,304	Caracas	12,400
Vietnam	332	128	96,160	Hanoi	6,900
Virgin Is. (UK)	0.15	0.06	35	Road Town	42,300
Virgin Is. (US)	0.35	0.13	107	Charlotte Amalie	36,100
Yemen	528	204	28,037	Sana'	2,300
Zambia	753	291	15,972	Lusaka	4,000
Zimbabwe	391	151	13,805	Harare	2,300

World Statistics: Physical Dimensions

Each topic list is divided into continents and within a continent the items are listed in order of size. The bottom part of many of the lists is selective in order to give examples from as many different countries as possible. The order of the continents is the same as in the atlas, beginning with Europe and ending with South America. The figures are rounded as appropriate.

World, Continents, Oceans

	km²	miles²	%
The World	509,450,000	196,672,000	–
Land	149,450,000	57,688,000	29.3
Water	360,000,000	138,984,000	70.7
Asia	44,500,000	17,177,000	29.8
Africa	30,302,000	11,697,000	20.3
North America	24,241,000	9,357,000	16.2
South America	17,793,000	6,868,000	11.9
Antarctica	14,100,000	5,443,000	9.4
Europe	9,957,000	3,843,000	6.7
Australia & Oceania	8,557,000	3,303,000	5.7
Pacific Ocean	155,557,000	60,061,000	46.4
Atlantic Ocean	76,762,000	29,638,000	22.9
Indian Ocean	68,556,000	26,470,000	20.4
Southern Ocean	20,327,000	7,848,000	6.1
Arctic Ocean	14,056,000	5,427,000	4.2

Ocean Depths

	m	ft
Atlantic Ocean	m	ft
Puerto Rico (Milwaukee) Deep	8,605	28,232
Cayman Trench	7,680	25,197
Gulf of Mexico	5,203	17,070
Mediterranean Sea	5,121	16,801
Black Sea	2,211	7,254
North Sea	660	2,165
Indian Ocean	m	ft
Java Trench	7,450	24,442
Red Sea	2,635	8,454
Pacific Ocean	m	ft
Mariana Trench	11,022	36,161
Tonga Trench	10,882	35,702
Japan Trench	10,554	34,626
Kuril Trench	10,542	34,587
Arctic Ocean	m	ft
Molloy Deep	5,608	18,399
Southern Ocean	m	ft
South Sandwich Trench	7,235	23,737

Mountains

		m	ft
Europe		m	ft
Elbrus	*Russia*	5,642	18,510
Dykh-Tau	*Russia*	5,205	17,076
Shkhara	*Russia/Georgia*	5,201	17,064
Koshtan-Tau	*Russia*	5,152	16,903
Kazbek	*Russia/Georgia*	5,047	16,558
Pushkin	*Russia/Georgia*	5,033	16,512
Katyn-Tau	*Russia/Georgia*	4,979	16,335
Shota Rustaveli	*Russia/Georgia*	4,860	15,945
Mont Blanc	*France/Italy*	4,808	15,774
Monte Rosa	*Italy/Switzerland*	4,634	15,203
Dom	*Switzerland*	4,545	14,911
Liskamm	*Switzerland*	4,527	14,852
Weisshorn	*Switzerland*	4,505	14,780
Taschorn	*Switzerland*	4,490	14,730
Matterhorn/Cervino	*Italy/Switzerland*	4,478	14,691
Grossglockner	*Austria*	3,797	12,457
Mulhacén	*Spain*	3,478	11,411
Zugspitze	*Germany*	2,962	9,718
Olympus	*Greece*	2,917	9,570
Galdhøpiggen	*Norway*	2,469	8,100
Ben Nevis	*UK*	1,345	4,411
Asia		m	ft
Everest	*China/Nepal*	8,850	29,035
K2 (Godwin Austen)	*China/Kashmir*	8,611	28,251
Kanchenjunga	*India/Nepal*	8,598	28,208
Lhotse	*China/Nepal*	8,516	27,939
Makalu	*China/Nepal*	8,481	27,824
Cho Oyu	*China/Nepal*	8,201	26,906
Dhaulagiri	*Nepal*	8,167	26,795
Manaslu	*Nepal*	8,156	26,758
Nanga Parbat	*Kashmir*	8,126	26,660
Annapurna	*Nepal*	8,078	26,502
Gasherbrum	*China/Kashmir*	8,068	26,469
Broad Peak	*China/Kashmir*	8,051	26,414
Xixabangma	*China*	8,012	26,286
Kangbachen	*Nepal*	7,858	25,781
Trivor	*Pakistan*	7,720	25,328
Pik Imeni Ismail Samani	*Tajikistan*	7,495	24,590
Demavend	*Iran*	5,604	18,386
Ararat	*Turkey*	5,165	16,945
Gunong Kinabalu	*Malaysia (Borneo)*	4,101	13,455
Fuji-San	*Japan*	3,776	12,388
Africa		m	ft
Kilimanjaro	*Tanzania*	5,895	19,340
Mt Kenya	*Kenya*	5,199	17,057
Ruwenzori (Margherita)	*Ug./Congo (D.R.)*	5,109	16,762
Meru	*Tanzania*	4,565	14,977
Ras Dashen	*Ethiopia*	4,553	14,937
Karisimbi	*Rwanda/Congo (D.R.)*	4,507	14,787
Mt Elgon	*Kenya/Uganda*	4,321	14,176
Batu	*Ethiopia*	4,307	14,130
Toubkal	*Morocco*	4,165	13,665
Mt Cameroun	*Cameroon*	4,070	13,353
Oceania		m	ft
Puncak Jaya	*Indonesia*	4,884	16,024
Puncak Trikora	*Indonesia*	4,730	15,518
Puncak Mandala	*Indonesia*	4,702	15,427
Mt Wilhelm	*Papua New Guinea*	4,508	14,790
Mauna Kea	*USA (Hawai'i)*	4,205	13,796
Mauna Loa	*USA (Hawai'i)*	4,169	13,678
Aoraki Mt Cook	*New Zealand*	3,724	12,218
Mt Kosciuszko	*Australia*	2,228	7,310
North America		m	ft
Denali (Mt McKinley)	*USA (Alaska)*	6,168	20,237
Mt Logan	*Canada*	5,959	19,551
Pico de Orizaba	*Mexico*	5,610	18,405
Mt St Elias	*USA/Canada*	5,489	18,008
Popocatépetl	*Mexico*	5,452	17,887
Mt Foraker	*USA (Alaska)*	5,304	17,401
Iztaccihuatl	*Mexico*	5,286	17,342
Mt Lucania	*Canada*	5,226	17,146
Mt Steele	*Canada*	5,073	16,644
Mt Bona	*USA (Alaska)*	5,005	16,420
Mt Whitney	*USA*	4,418	14,495
Tajumulco	*Guatemala*	4,220	13,845
Chirripó Grande	*Costa Rica*	3,837	12,589
Pico Duarte	*Dominican Rep.*	3,175	10,417
South America		m	ft
Aconcagua	*Argentina*	6,962	22,841
Bonete	*Argentina*	6,872	22,546
Ojos del Salado	*Argentina/Chile*	6,863	22,516
Pissis	*Argentina*	6,779	22,241
Mercedario	*Argentina/Chile*	6,770	22,211
Huascarán	*Peru*	6,768	22,204
Llullaillaco	*Argentina/Chile*	6,723	22,057
Nevado de Cachi	*Argentina*	6,720	22,047
Yerupaja	*Peru*	6,632	21,758
Sajama	*Bolivia*	6,520	21,391
Chimborazo	*Ecuador*	6,267	20,561
Pico Cristóbal Colón	*Colombia*	5,800	19,029
Pico Bolivar	*Venezuela*	5,007	16,427
Antarctica		m	ft
Vinson Massif		4,897	16,066
Mt Kirkpatrick		4,528	14,855

Rivers

		km	miles
Europe		km	miles
Volga	*Caspian Sea*	3,700	2,300
Danube	*Black Sea*	2,850	1,770
Ural	*Caspian Sea*	2,535	1,575
Dnieper	*Black Sea*	2,285	1,420
Kama	*Volga*	2,030	1,260
Don	*Black Sea*	1,990	1,240
Petchora	*Arctic Ocean*	1,790	1,110
Oka	*Volga*	1,480	920
Dniester	*Black Sea*	1,400	870
Vyatka	*Kama*	1,370	850
Rhine	*North Sea*	1,320	820
N. Dvina	*Arctic Ocean*	1,290	800
Elbe	*North Sea*	1,145	710
Asia		km	miles
Yangtse	*Pacific Ocean*	6,380	3,960
Yenisey–Angara	*Arctic Ocean*	5,550	3,445
Huang He	*Pacific Ocean*	5,464	3,395
Ob–Irtysh	*Arctic Ocean*	5,410	3,360
Mekong	*Pacific Ocean*	4,500	2,795
Amur	*Pacific Ocean*	4,442	2,760
Lena	*Arctic Ocean*	4,402	2,735
Irtysh	*Ob*	4,250	2,640
Yenisey	*Arctic Ocean*	4,090	2,540
Ob	*Arctic Ocean*	3,680	2,285
Indus	*Indian Ocean*	3,100	1,925
Brahmaputra	*Indian Ocean*	2,900	1,800
Syrdarya	*Aralkum Desert*	2,860	1,775
Salween	*Indian Ocean*	2,800	1,740
Euphrates	*Indian Ocean*	2,700	1,675
Amudarya	*Aralkum Desert*	2,540	1,575
Africa		km	miles
Nile	*Mediterranean*	6,695	4,160
Congo	*Atlantic Ocean*	4,670	2,900
Niger	*Atlantic Ocean*	4,180	2,595
Zambezi	*Indian Ocean*	3,540	2,200
Oubangi/Uele	*Congo (D.R.)*	2,250	1,400
Kasai	*Congo (D.R.)*	1,950	1,210
Shaballe	*Indian Ocean*	1,930	1,200
Orange	*Atlantic Ocean*	1,860	1,155
Cubango	*Okavango Delta*	1,800	1,120
Limpopo	*Indian Ocean*	1,770	1,100
Senegal	*Atlantic Ocean*	1,640	1,020
Australia		km	miles
Murray–Darling	*Southern Ocean*	3,750	2,330
Darling	*Murray*	3,070	1,905
Murray	*Southern Ocean*	2,575	1,600
Murrumbidgee	*Murray*	1,690	1,050
North America		km	miles
Mississippi–Missouri	*Gulf of Mexico*	5,971	3,710
Mackenzie	*Arctic Ocean*	4,240	2,630
Missouri	*Mississippi*	4,088	2,540
Mississippi	*Gulf of Mexico*	3,782	2,350
Yukon	*Pacific Ocean*	3,185	1,980
Rio Grande	*Gulf of Mexico*	3,030	1,880
Arkansas	*Mississippi*	2,340	1,450
Colorado	*Pacific Ocean*	2,330	1,445
Red	*Mississippi*	2,040	1,270
Columbia	*Pacific Ocean*	1,950	1,210
Saskatchewan	*Lake Winnipeg*	1,940	1,205
South America		km	miles
Amazon	*Atlantic Ocean*	6,450	4,010
Paraná–Plate	*Atlantic Ocean*	4,500	2,800
Purus	*Amazon*	3,350	2,080
Madeira	*Amazon*	3,200	1,990
São Francisco	*Atlantic Ocean*	2,900	1,800
Paraná	*Plate*	2,800	1,740
Tocantins	*Atlantic Ocean*	2,750	1,710
Orinoco	*Atlantic Ocean*	2,740	1,700
Paraguay	*Paraná*	2,550	1,580
Pilcomayo	*Paraná*	2,500	1,550
Araguaia	*Tocantins*	2,250	1,400

Lakes

		km²	miles²
Europe		km²	miles²
Lake Ladoga	*Russia*	17,700	6,800
Lake Onega	*Russia*	9,700	3,700
Saimaa system	*Finland*	8,000	3,100
Vänern	*Sweden*	5,500	2,100
Asia		km²	miles²
Caspian Sea	*Asia*	371,000	143,000
Lake Baikal	*Russia*	30,500	11,780
Tonlé Sap	*Cambodia*	20,000	7,700
Lake Balqash	*Kazakhstan*	18,500	7,100
Aral Sea	*Kazakhstan/Uzbekistan*	6,800	2,620
Africa		km²	miles²
Lake Victoria	*East Africa*	68,000	26,300
Lake Tanganyika	*Central Africa*	33,000	13,000
Lake Malawi/Nyasa	*East Africa*	29,600	11,430
Lake Chad	*Central Africa*	25,000	9,700
Lake Bangweulu	*Zambia*	9,840	3,800
Lake Turkana	*Ethiopia/Kenya*	8,500	3,290
Australia		km²	miles²
Lake Eyre	*Australia*	8,900	3,400
Lake Torrens	*Australia*	5,800	2,200
Lake Gairdner	*Australia*	4,800	1,900
North America		km²	miles²
Lake Superior	*Canada/USA*	82,350	31,800
Lake Huron	*Canada/USA*	59,600	23,010
Lake Michigan	*USA*	58,000	22,400
Great Bear Lake	*Canada*	31,800	12,280
Great Slave Lake	*Canada*	28,500	11,000
Lake Erie	*Canada/USA*	25,700	9,900
Lake Winnipeg	*Canada*	24,400	9,400
Lake Ontario	*Canada/USA*	19,500	7,500
Lake Nicaragua	*Nicaragua*	8,200	3,200
South America		km²	miles²
Lake Titicaca	*Bolivia/Peru*	8,300	3,200
Lake Poopo	*Bolivia*	2,800	1,100

Islands

		km²	miles²
Europe		km²	miles²
Great Britain	*UK*	229,880	88,700
Iceland	*Atlantic Ocean*	103,000	39,800
Ireland	*Ireland/UK*	84,400	32,600
Novaya Zemlya (N.)	*Russia*	48,200	18,600
Sicily	*Italy*	25,500	9,800
Corsica	*France*	8,700	3,400
Asia		km²	miles²
Borneo	*Southeast Asia*	744,360	287,400
Sumatra	*Indonesia*	473,600	182,860
Honshu	*Japan*	230,500	88,980
Celebes	*Indonesia*	189,000	73,000
Java	*Indonesia*	126,700	48,900
Luzon	*Philippines*	104,700	40,400
Hokkaido	*Japan*	78,400	30,300
Africa		km²	miles²
Madagascar	*Indian Ocean*	587,040	226,660
Socotra	*Indian Ocean*	3,600	1,400
Réunion	*Indian Ocean*	2,500	965
Oceania		km²	miles²
New Guinea	*Indonesia/Papua NG*	821,030	317,000
New Zealand (S.)	*Pacific Ocean*	150,500	58,100
New Zealand (N.)	*Pacific Ocean*	114,700	44,300
Tasmania	*Australia*	67,800	26,200
Hawai'i	*Pacific Ocean*	10,450	4,000
North America		km²	miles²
Greenland	*Atlantic Ocean*	2,175,600	839,800
Baffin Is.	*Canada*	508,000	196,100
Victoria Is.	*Canada*	212,200	81,900
Ellesmere Is.	*Canada*	212,000	81,800
Cuba	*Caribbean Sea*	110,860	42,800
Hispaniola	*Dominican Rep./Haiti*	76,200	29,400
Jamaica	*Caribbean Sea*	11,400	4,400
Puerto Rico	*Atlantic Ocean*	8,900	3,400
South America		km²	miles²
Tierra del Fuego	*Argentina/Chile*	47,000	18,100
Falkland Is. (E.)	*Atlantic Ocean*	6,800	2,600

User Guide

The reference maps which form the main body of this atlas have been prepared in accordance with the highest standards of international cartography to provide an accurate and detailed representation of the Earth. The scales and projections used have been carefully chosen to give balanced coverage of the world, while emphasizing the most densely populated and economically significant regions. A hallmark of Philip's mapping is the use of hill shading and relief colouring to create a graphic impression of landforms: this makes the maps exceptionally easy to read. However, knowledge of the key features employed in the construction and presentation of the maps will enable the reader to derive the fullest benefit from the atlas.

Map sequence

The atlas covers the Earth continent by continent: first Europe; then its land neighbour Asia (mapped north before south, in a clockwise sequence), then Africa, Australia and Oceania, North America and South America. This is the classic arrangement adopted by most cartographers since the 16th century. For each continent, there are maps at a variety of scales. First, physical relief and political maps of the whole continent; then a series of larger-scale maps of the regions within the continent, each followed, where required, by still larger-scale maps of the most important or densely populated areas. The governing principle is that by turning the pages of the atlas, the reader moves steadily from north to south through each continent, with each map overlapping its neighbours.

Map presentation

With very few exceptions (for example, for the Arctic and Antarctica), the maps are drawn with north at the top, regardless of whether they are presented upright or sideways on the page. In the borders will be found the map title; a locator diagram showing the area covered; continuation arrows showing the page numbers for maps of adjacent areas; the scale; the projection used; the degrees of latitude and longitude; and the letters and figures used in the index for locating place names and geographical features. Physical relief maps also have a height reference panel identifying the colours used for each layer of contouring.

Map symbols

Each map contains a vast amount of detail which can only be conveyed clearly and accurately by the use of symbols. Points and circles of varying sizes locate and identify the relative importance of towns and cities; different styles of type are employed for administrative, geographical and regional place names. A variety of pictorial symbols denote features such as glaciers and marshes, as well as man-made structures including roads, railways, airports and canals.

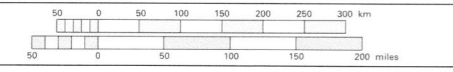

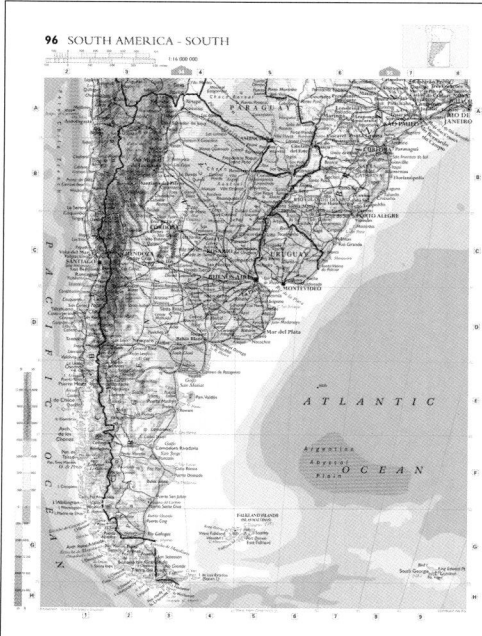

International borders are shown by red lines. Where neighbouring countries are in dispute, for example in the Middle East, the maps show the de facto boundary between nations, regardless of the legal or historical situation. The symbols are explained on the first page of the World Maps section of the atlas.

Map scales

The scale of each map is given in the numerical form known as the 'representative fraction'. The first figure is always one, signifying one unit of distance on the map; the second figure, usually in millions, is the number by which the map unit must be multiplied to give the equivalent distance on the Earth's surface. Calculations can easily be made in centimetres and kilometres, by dividing the Earth units figure by 100 000 (i.e. deleting the last five 0s). Thus 1:1 000 000 means 1 cm = 10 km. The calculation for inches and miles is more laborious, but 1 000 000 divided by 63 360 (the number of inches in a mile) shows that the ratio 1:1 000 000 means approximately 1 inch = 16 miles. The table below provides distance equivalents for scales down to 1:50 000 000.

LARGE SCALE		
1:1 000 000	1 cm = 10 km	1 inch = 16 miles
1:2 500 000	1 cm = 25 km	1 inch = 39.5 miles
1:5 000 000	1 cm = 50 km	1 inch = 79 miles
1:6 000 000	1 cm = 60 km	1 inch = 95 miles
1:8 000 000	1 cm = 80 km	1 inch = 126 miles
1:10 000 000	1 cm = 100 km	1 inch = 158 miles
1:15 000 000	1 cm = 150 km	1 inch = 237 miles
1:20 000 000	1 cm = 200 km	1 inch = 316 miles
1:50 000 000	1 cm = 500 km	1 inch = 790 miles
SMALL SCALE		

Measuring distances

Although each map is accompanied by a scale bar, distances cannot always be measured with confidence because of the distortions involved in portraying the curved surface of the Earth on a flat page. As a general rule, the larger the map scale (i.e. the lower the number of Earth units in the representative fraction), the more accurate and reliable will be the distance measured. On small-scale maps such as those of the world and of entire continents, measurement may only be accurate along the 'standard parallels', or central axes, and should not be attempted without considering the map projection.

Latitude and longitude

Accurate positioning of individual points on the Earth's surface is made possible by reference to the geometrical system of latitude and longitude. Latitude *parallels* are drawn west–east around the Earth and numbered by degrees north and south of the Equator, which is designated 0° of latitude. Longitude *meridians* are drawn north–south and numbered by degrees east and west of the *prime meridian*, 0° of longitude, which passes through Greenwich in England. By referring to these co-ordinates and their subdivisions of minutes ($1/60$th of a degree) and seconds ($1/60$th of a minute), any place on Earth can be located to within a few hundred metres. Latitude and longitude are indicated by blue lines on the maps; they are straight or curved according to the projection employed. Reference to these lines is the easiest way of determining the relative positions of places on different maps, and for plotting compass directions.

Name forms

For ease of reference, both English and local name forms appear in the atlas. Oceans, seas and countries are shown in English throughout the atlas; country names may be abbreviated to their commonly accepted form (for example, Germany, not The Federal Republic of Germany). Conventional English forms are also used for place names on the smaller-scale maps of the continents. However, local name forms are used on all large-scale and regional maps, with the English form given in brackets only for important cities – the large-scale map of Russia and Central Asia thus shows Moskva (Moscow). For countries which do not use a Roman script, place names have been transcribed according to the systems adopted by the British and US Geographic Names Authorities. For China, the Pin Yin system has been used, with some more widely known forms appearing in brackets, as with Beijing (Peking). Both English and local names appear in the index, the English form being cross-referenced to the local form.

THE
WORLD
IN FOCUS

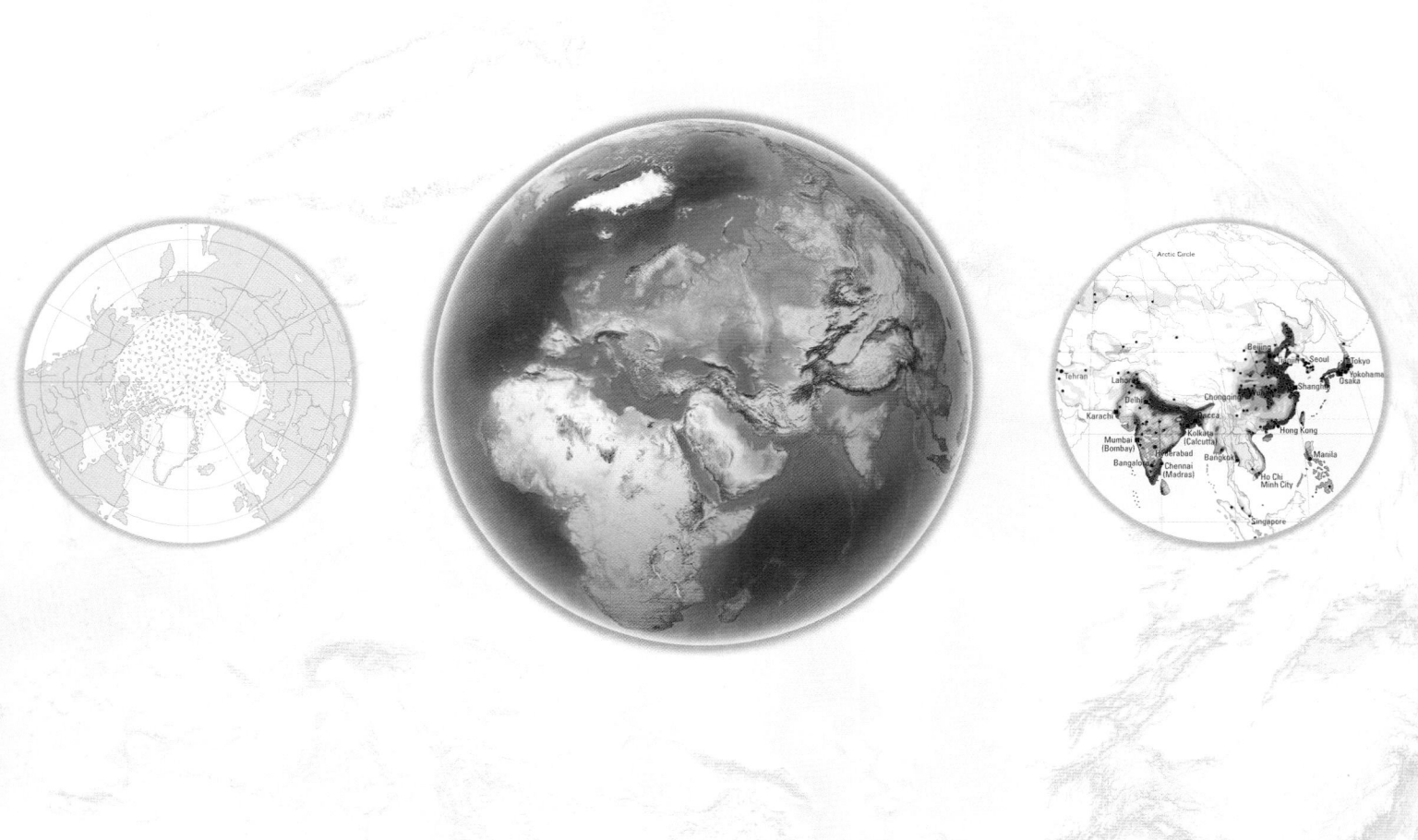

PLANET EARTH	2	WATER AND VEGETATION	12	QUALITY OF LIFE	22
RESTLESS EARTH	4	ENVIRONMENT	14	ENERGY	24
LANDFORMS	6	POPULATION	16	PRODUCTION	26
OCEANS	8	THE HUMAN FAMILY	18	TRADE	28
CLIMATE	10	WEALTH	20	TRAVEL AND TOURISM	30

Planet Earth

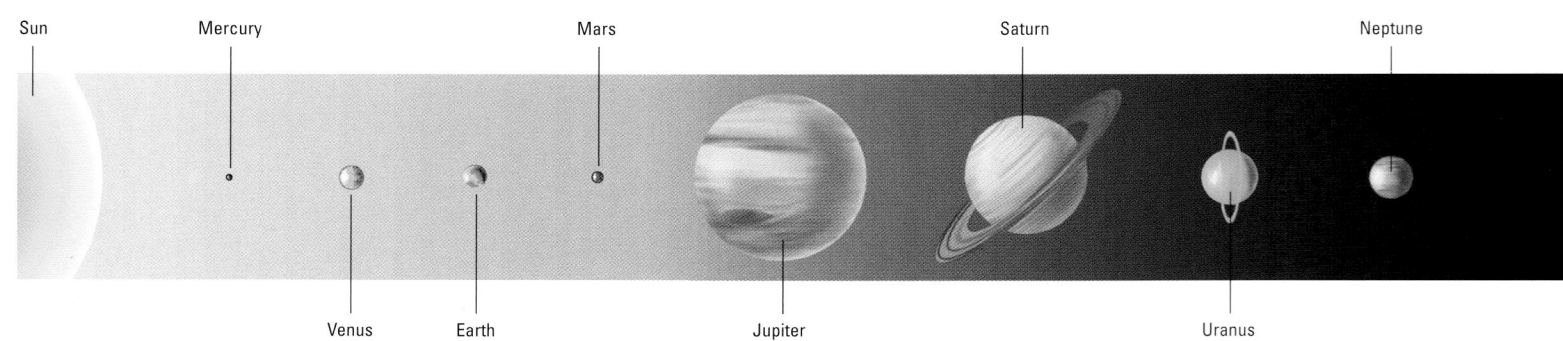

Sun   Mercury   Mars   Saturn   Neptune

Venus   Earth   Jupiter   Uranus

THE SOLAR SYSTEM

A minute part of one of the billions of galaxies (collections of stars) that populate the Universe, the Solar System lies about 26,000 light-years from the centre of our own Galaxy, the 'Milky Way'. Thought to be about 5 billion years old, it consists of a central Sun with eight planets and their moons revolving around it, attracted by its gravitational pull. The planets orbit the Sun in the same direction – anti-clockwise when viewed from above the Sun's north pole – and almost in the same plane. Their orbital distances, however, vary enormously.

The Sun's diameter is 109 times that of the Earth, and the temperature at its core – caused by continuous thermonuclear fusions of hydrogen into helium – is estimated to be 15 million degrees Celsius. It is the Solar System's source of light and heat.

PROFILE OF THE PLANETS

	Mean distance from Sun (million km)	Mass (Earth = 1)	Period of orbit (Earth days/years)	Period of rotation (Earth days)	Equatorial diameter (km)	Number of known satellites*
Mercury	57.9	0.06	87.97 days	58.65	4,879	0
Venus	108.2	0.82	224.7 days	243.02	12,104	0
Earth	149.6	1.00	365.3 days	1.00	12,756	1
Mars	227.9	0.11	687.0 days	1.029	6,792	2
Jupiter	778	317.8	11.86 years	0.411	142,984	67
Saturn	1,427	95.2	29.45 years	0.428	120,536	62
Uranus	2,871	14.5	84.02 years	0.720	51,118	27
Neptune	4,498	17.2	164.8 years	0.673	49,528	14

Number of known satellites at mid-2018

All planetary orbits are elliptical in form, but only Mercury follows a path that deviates noticeably from a circular one. In 2006, Pluto was demoted from its former status as a planet and is now regarded as a member of the Kuiper Belt of icy bodies at the fringes of the Solar System.

THE SEASONS

Seasons occur because the Earth's axis is tilted at an angle of approximately 23½°. When the northern hemisphere is tilted to a maximum extent towards the Sun, on 21 June, the Sun is overhead at the Tropic of Cancer (latitude 23½° North). This is midsummer, or the summer solstice, in the northern hemisphere.

On 22 or 23 September, the Sun is overhead at the Equator, and day and night are of equal length throughout the world. This is the autumnal equinox in the northern hemisphere. On 21 or 22 December, the Sun is overhead at the Tropic of Capricorn (23½° South), the winter solstice in the northern hemisphere. The overhead Sun then tracks north until, on 21 March, it is overhead at the Equator. This is the spring (vernal) equinox in the northern hemisphere.

In the southern hemisphere, the seasons are the reverse of those in the north.

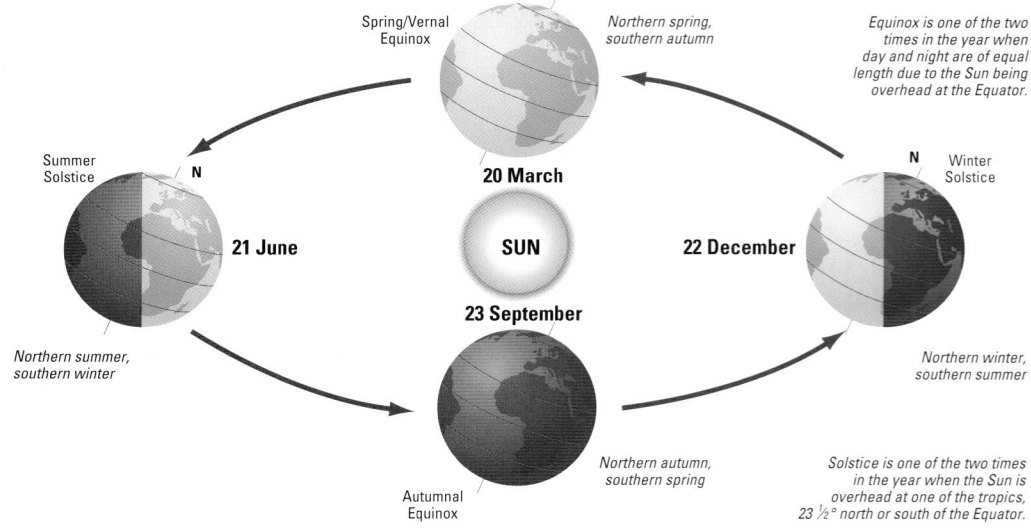

DAY AND NIGHT

The Sun appears to rise in the east, reach its highest point at noon, and then set in the west, to be followed by night. In reality, it is not the Sun that is moving but the Earth rotating from west to east. The moment when the Sun's upper limb first appears above the horizon is termed sunrise; the moment when the Sun's upper limb disappears below the horizon is sunset.

At the summer solstice in the northern hemisphere (21 June), the Arctic has total daylight and the Antarctic total darkness. The opposite occurs at the winter solstice (21 or 22 December). At the Equator, the length of day and night are almost equal all year.

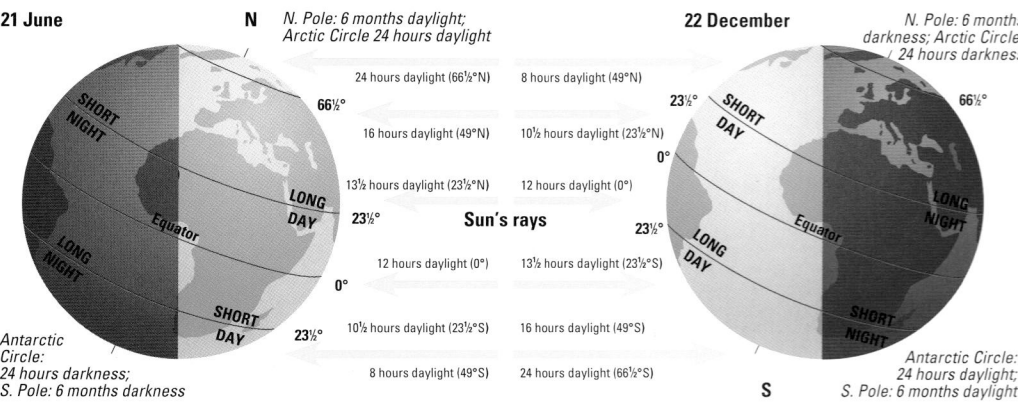

TIME

Year: The time taken by the Earth to revolve around the Sun, or 365.24 days.

Leap Year: A calendar year of 366 days, 29 February being the additional day. It offsets the difference between the calendar and the solar year.

Month: The 12 calendar months of the year are approximately equal in length to a lunar month.

Week: An artificial period of 7 days, not based on astronomical time.

Day: The time taken by the Earth to complete one rotation on its axis.

Hour: 24 hours make one day. The day is divided into hours a.m. (ante meridiem or before noon) and p.m. (post meridiem or after noon), although most timetables now use the 24-hour system, from midnight to midnight.

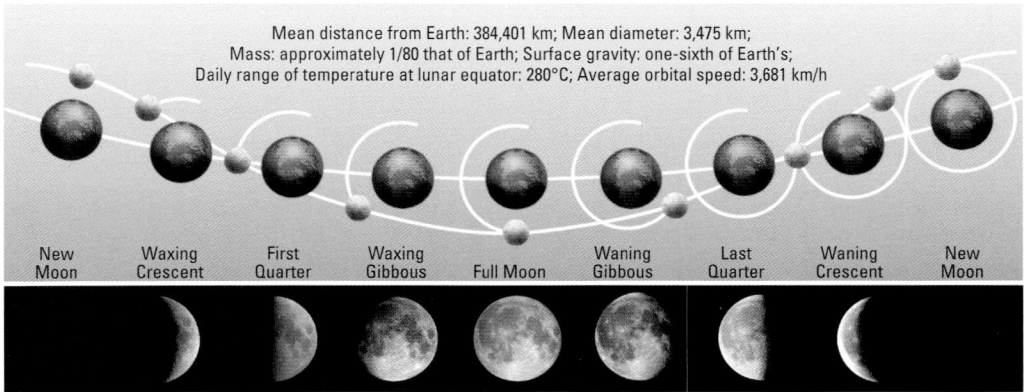

THE MOON

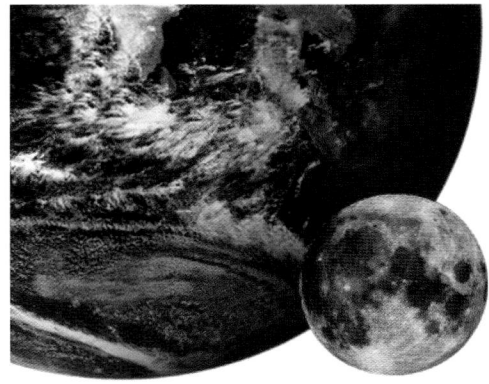

The Moon rotates more slowly than the Earth, taking just over 27 days to make one complete rotation on its axis. This corresponds to the Moon's orbital period around the Earth, and therefore the Moon always

PHASES OF THE MOON

Mean distance from Earth: 384,401 km; Mean diameter: 3,475 km; Mass: approximately 1/80 that of Earth; Surface gravity: one-sixth of Earth's; Daily range of temperature at lunar equator: 280°C; Average orbital speed: 3,681 km/h

| New Moon | Waxing Crescent | First Quarter | Waxing Gibbous | Full Moon | Waning Gibbous | Last Quarter | Waning Crescent | New Moon |

presents the same hemisphere towards us; some 41% of the Moon's far side is never visible from the Earth. The interval between one New Moon and the next is 29½ days – this is called a lunation, or lunar month.

The Moon shines only by reflected sunlight, and emits no light of its own. During each lunation the Moon displays a complete cycle of phases, caused by the changing angle of illumination from the Sun.

ECLIPSES

When the Moon passes between the Sun and the Earth, the Sun becomes partially eclipsed (1). A partial eclipse becomes a total eclipse if the Moon proceeds to cover the Sun completely (2) and the dark central part of the lunar shadow touches the Earth. The broad geographical zone covered by the Moon's outer shadow (P) has only a very small central area (often less than 100 km wide) that experiences totality. Totality can never last for more than 7½ minutes at maximum, but is usually much briefer than this. Lunar eclipses take place when the Moon moves through the shadow of the Earth, and can be partial or total. Any single location on Earth can experience a maximum of four solar and three lunar eclipses in any single year, while a total solar eclipse occurs an average of once every 360 years for any given location.

TIDES

The daily rise and fall of the ocean's tides are the result of the gravitational pull of the Moon and that of the Sun, though the effect of the latter is not as strong as that of the Moon. This effect is greatest on the hemisphere facing the Moon and causes a tidal 'bulge'.

Spring tides occur when the Sun, Earth and Moon are aligned; high tides are at their highest, and low tides fall to their lowest. When the Moon and Sun are furthest out of line (near the Moon's First and Last Quarters), neap tides occur, producing the smallest range between high and low tides.

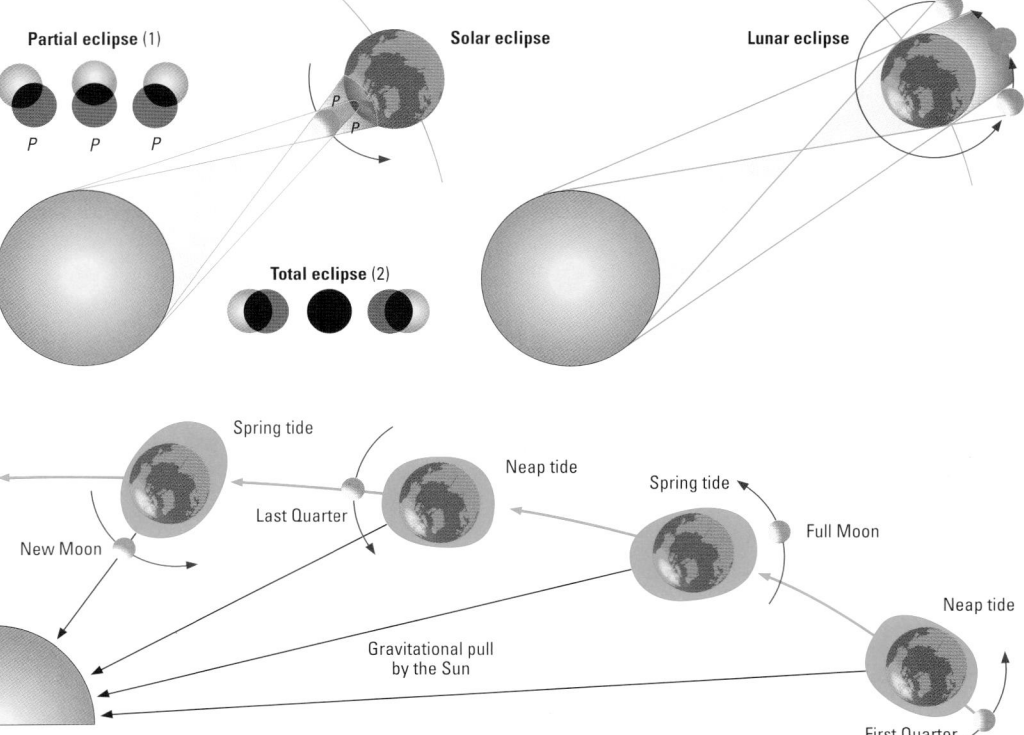

Restless Earth

THE EARTH'S STRUCTURE

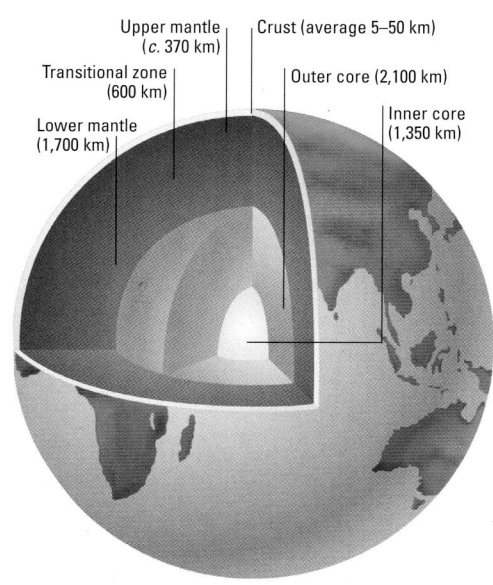

Upper mantle (c. 370 km)
Crust (average 5–50 km)
Transitional zone (600 km)
Outer core (2,100 km)
Lower mantle (1,700 km)
Inner core (1,350 km)

CONTINENTAL DRIFT

About 200 million years ago the original Pangaea landmass began to split into two continental groups, which further separated over time to produce the present-day configuration.

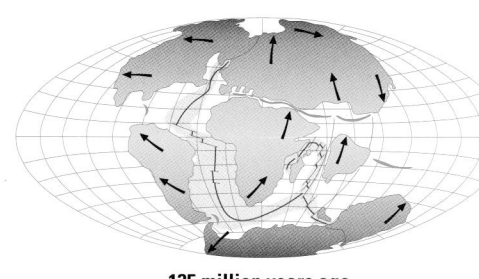

135 million years ago

Trench
Rift
New ocean floor
Zones of slippage

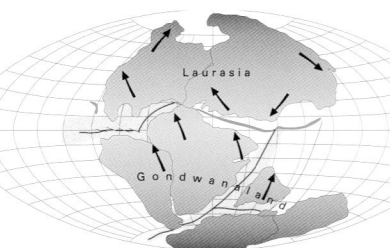

180 million years ago

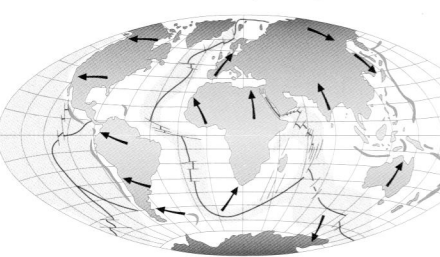

Present day

NOTABLE EARTHQUAKES SINCE 1900

Year	Location	Richter Scale	Deaths
1906	San Francisco, USA	8.3	3,000
1906	Valparaiso, Chile	8.6	22,000
1908	Messina, Italy	7.5	83,000
1915	Avezzano, Italy	7.5	30,000
1920	Gansu (Kansu), China	8.6	180,000
1923	Yokohama, Japan	8.3	143,000
1927	Nan Shan, China	8.3	200,000
1932	Gansu (Kansu), China	7.6	70,000
1934	Bihar, India/Nepal	8.4	10,700
1935	Quetta, India (now Pakistan)	7.5	60,000
1939	Chillan, Chile	8.3	28,000
1939	Erzincan, Turkey	7.9	30,000
1960	S. W. Chile	9.5	2,200
1960	Agadir, Morocco	5.8	12,000
1962	Khorasan, Iran	7.1	12,230
1964	Anchorage, USA	9.2	125
1970	N. Peru	7.8	70,000
1972	Managua, Nicaragua	6.2	5,000
1976	Guatemala	7.5	22,500
1976	Tangshan, China	8.2	255,000
1978	Tabas, Iran	7.7	25,000
1980	El Asnam, Algeria	7.3	20,000
1985	Mexico City, Mexico	8.1	4,200
1988	N.W. Armenia	6.8	55,000
1990	N. Iran	7.7	36,000
1993	Maharashtra, India	6.4	30,000
1994	Los Angeles, USA	6.6	51
1995	Kobe, Japan	7.2	5,000
1998	Rostaq, Afghanistan	7.0	5,000
1999	Izmit, Turkey	7.4	15,000
2001	Gujarat, India	7.7	14,000
2003	Bam, Iran	6.6	30,000
2004	Sumatra, Indonesia	9.0	250,000
2005	N. Pakistan	7.6	74,000
2006	Java, Indonesia	6.4	6,200
2008	Sichuan, China	7.9	70,000
2010	Haiti	7.0	230,000
2011	Christchurch, New Zealand	6.3	182
2011	N. Japan	9.0	20,000
2015	Nepal	7.8	8,500
2016	Ecuador	7.8	668
2017	Chiapas, Mexico	8.2	98

EARTHQUAKES

Earthquake magnitude is usually rated according to either the Richter or the Modified Mercalli scale, both devised by seismologists in the 1930s. The Richter scale measures absolute earthquake power with mathematical precision: each step upwards represents a tenfold increase in shockwave amplitude. Theoretically, there is no upper limit, but most of the largest earthquakes measured have been rated at between 8.8 and 8.9. The 12–point Mercalli scale, based on observed effects, is often more meaningful, ranging from I (earthquakes noticed only by seismographs) to XII (total destruction); intermediate points include V (people awakened at night; unstable objects overturned), VII (collapse of ordinary buildings; chimneys and monuments fall), and IX (conspicuous cracks in ground; serious damage to reservoirs).

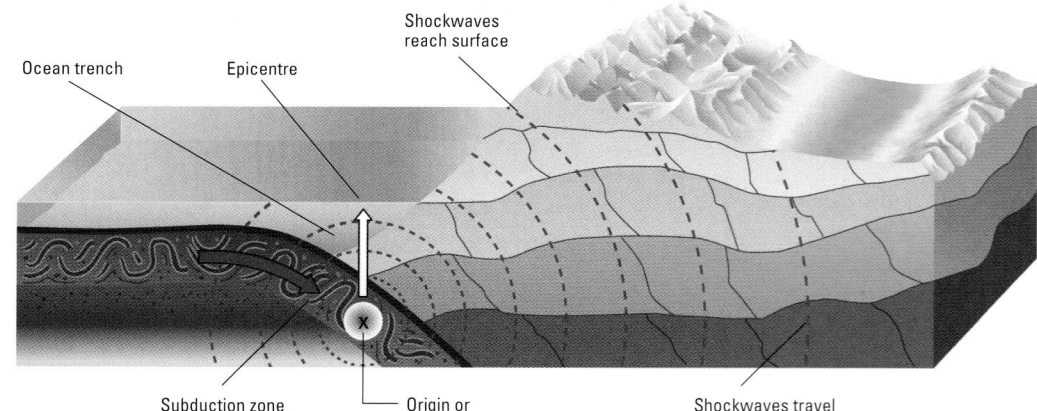

Shockwaves reach surface
Ocean trench
Epicentre
Subduction zone
Origin or focus
Shockwaves travel away from focus

DISTRIBUTION OF EARTHQUAKES

Mobile land areas
Submarine zones of mobile land areas
Stable land platforms
Submarine extensions of stable land platforms

• 1995 Principal earthquakes and dates (since 1900)

Earthquakes are a series of rapid vibrations originating from the slipping or faulting of parts of the Earth's crust when stresses within build up to breaking point. They usually happen at depths varying from 8 km to 30 km. Severe earthquakes cause extensive damage when they take place in populated areas, destroying structures and severing communications. Most initial loss of life occurs due to secondary causes such as falling masonry, fires and flooding.

Projection: Interrupted Mollweide

PLATE TECTONICS

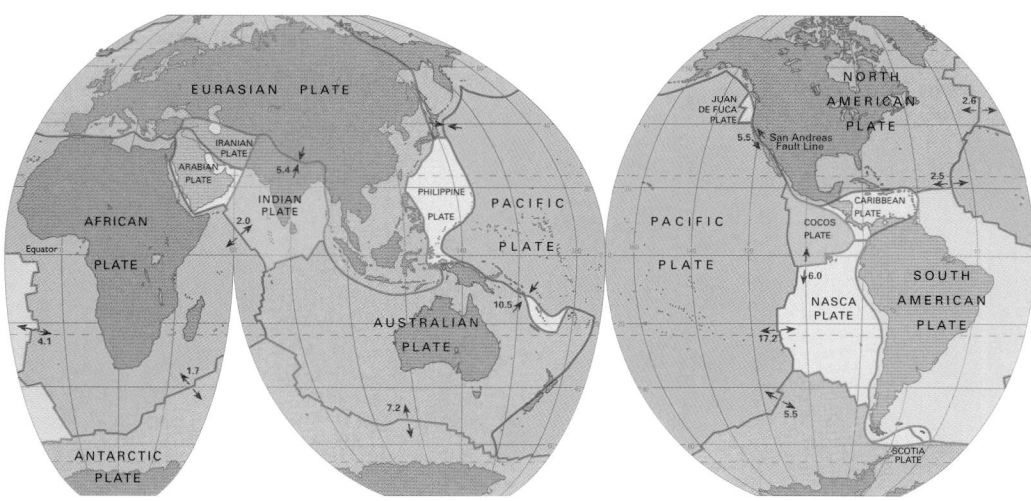

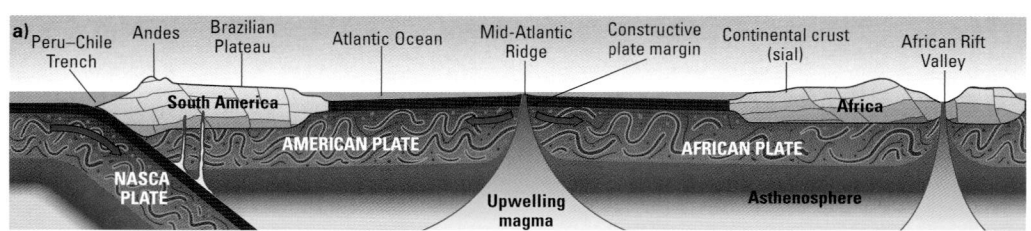

a) Peru–Chile Trench | Andes | Brazilian Plateau | Atlantic Ocean | Mid-Atlantic Ridge | Constructive plate margin | Continental crust (sial) | African Rift Valley

South America | AMERICAN PLATE | AFRICAN PLATE | Africa

NASCA PLATE | Upwelling magma | Asthenosphere

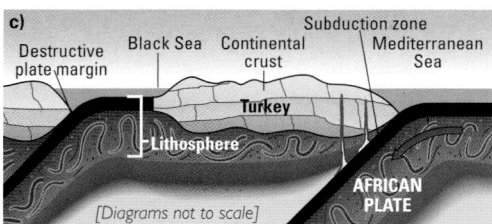

b) Tibetan Plateau | Collision zone | Indian Ocean
Himalayas | Oceanic crust (sima) | Mid-Indian Ocean Ridge

Asia | India | INDIAN PLATE

c) Subduction zone
Destructive plate margin | Black Sea | Continental crust | Mediterranean Sea

Turkey

Lithosphere

AFRICAN PLATE

[Diagrams not to scale]

—— Plate boundaries

↙ Direction of plate movements and rate of movement (cm/year)

The drifting of the continents is a feature that is unique to planet Earth. The complementary, almost jigsaw-puzzle fit of the coastlines on each side of the Atlantic Ocean inspired Alfred Wegener's theory of continental drift in 1915. The theory suggested that the ancient supercontinent, which Wegener named Pangaea, incorporated all of the Earth's landmasses and gradually split up to form today's continents.

The original debate about continental drift was a prelude to a more radical idea: plate tectonics. The basic theory is that the Earth's crust is made up of a series of rigid plates which float on a soft layer of the mantle and are moved about by continental convection currents within the Earth's interior. These plates diverge and converge along margins marked by seismic activity. Plates diverge from mid-ocean ridges where molten lava pushes upwards and forces the plates apart at rates of up to 40 mm [1.6 in] a year.

The three diagrams, left, give some examples of plate boundaries from around the world. Diagram (a) shows sea-floor spreading at the Mid-Atlantic Ridge as the American and African plates slowly diverge. The same thing is happening in (b) where sea-floor spreading at the Mid-Indian Ocean Ridge is forcing the Indian plate to collide into the Eurasian plate. In (c) oceanic crust (sima) is being subducted beneath lighter continental crust (sial).

VOLCANOES

Volcanoes occur when hot liquefied rock beneath the Earth's crust is pushed up by pressure to the surface as molten lava. Some volcanoes erupt in an explosive way, throwing out rocks and ash, whilst others are effusive and lava flows out of the vent. There are volcanoes which are both, such as Mount Fuji. An accumulation of lava and cinders creates cones of variable size and shape. As a result of many eruptions over centuries, Mount Etna in Sicily has a circumference of more than 120 km [75 miles].

Climatologists believe that volcanic ash, if ejected high into the atmosphere, can influence temperature and weather for several years afterwards. The 1991 eruption of Mount Pinatubo in the Philippines ejected more than 20 million tonnes of dust and ash 32 km [20 miles] into the atmosphere and is believed to have accelerated ozone depletion over a large part of the globe.

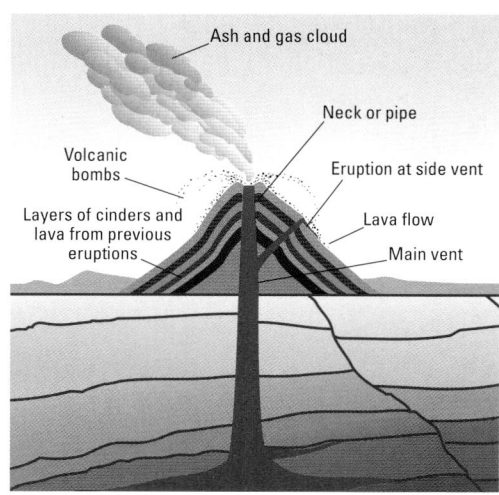

DISTRIBUTION OF VOLCANOES

Volcanoes today may be the subject of considerable scientific study but they remain both dramatic and unpredictable: in 1991 Mount Pinatubo, 100 km [62 miles] north of the Philippines capital Manila, suddenly burst into life after lying dormant for more than six centuries. Most of the world's active volcanoes occur in a belt around the Pacific Ocean, on the edge of the Pacific plate, called the 'ring of fire'. Indonesia has the greatest concentration with 90 volcanoes, 12 of which are active. The most famous, Krakatoa, erupted in 1883 with such force that the resulting tidal wave killed 36,000 people, and tremors were felt as far away as Australia.

▬▬ 'Ring of Fire'

○ Submarine volcanoes

▲ Land volcanoes active since 1700

—— Boundaries of tectonic plates

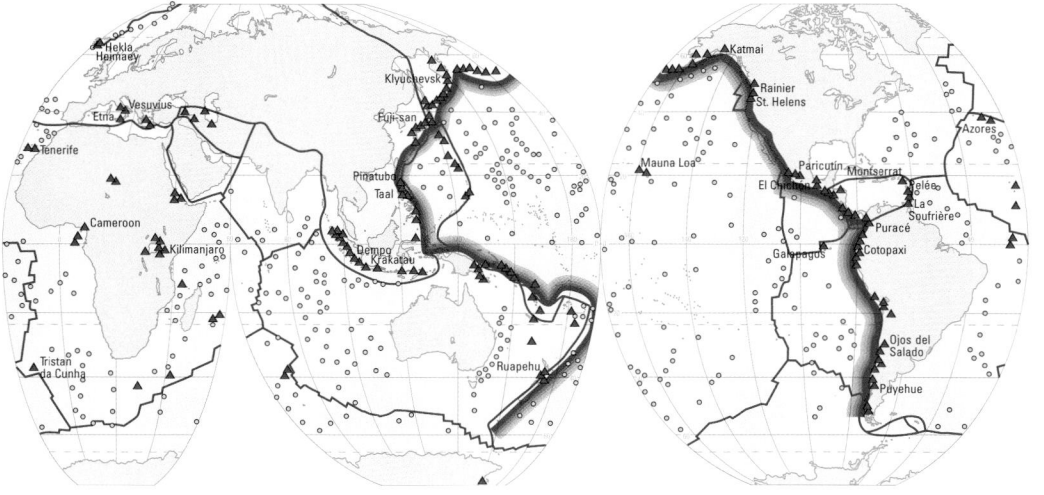

Landforms

THE ROCK CYCLE

James Hutton first proposed the rock cycle in the late 1700s after he observed the slow but steady effects of erosion.

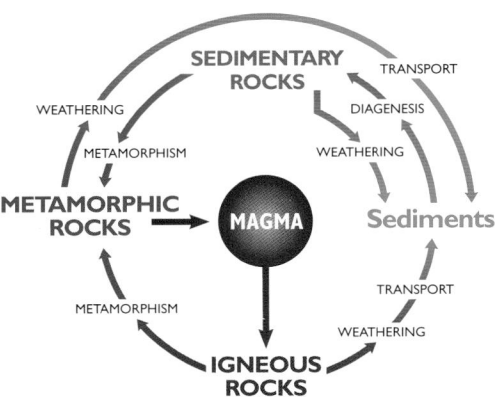

Above and below the surface of the oceans, the features of the Earth's crust are constantly changing. The phenomenal forces generated by convection currents in the molten core of our planet carry the vast segments or 'plates' of the crust across the globe in an endless cycle of creation and destruction. A continent may travel little more than 25 mm [1 in] per year, yet in the vast span of geological time this process throws up giant mountain ranges and creates new land.

Destruction of the landscape, however, begins as soon as it is formed. Wind, water, ice and sea, the main agents of erosion, mount a constant assault that even the most resistant rocks cannot withstand. Mountain peaks may dwindle by as little as a few millimetres each year, but if they are not uplifted by further movements of the crust they will eventually be reduced to rubble and transported away.

Water is the most powerful agent of erosion – it has been estimated that 100 billion tonnes of sediment are washed into the oceans every year.

Three Asian rivers account for 20% of this total: the Huang He, in China, and the Brahmaputra and the Ganges in Bangladesh.

Rivers and glaciers, like the sea itself, generate much of their effect through abrasion – pounding the land with the debris they carry with them. But as well as destroying they also create new landforms, many of them spectacular: vast deltas like those of the Mississippi and the Nile, or the deep fjords cut by glaciers in British Columbia, Norway and New Zealand.

Geologists once considered that landscapes evolved from 'young', newly uplifted mountainous areas, through a 'mature' hilly stage, to an 'old age' stage when the land was reduced to an almost flat plain, or peneplain. This theory, called the 'cycle of erosion', fell into disuse when it became evident that so many factors, including the effects of plate tectonics and climatic change, constantly interrupt the cycle, which takes no account of the highly complex interactions that shape the surface of our planet.

MOUNTAIN BUILDING

Mountains are formed when pressures on the Earth's crust caused by continental drift become so intense that the surface buckles or cracks. This happens where oceanic crust is subducted by continental crust or, more dramatically, where two tectonic plates collide: the Rockies, Andes, Alps, Urals and Himalayas resulted from such impacts. These are all known as fold mountains because they were formed by the compression of the rocks, forcing the surface to bend and fold like a crumpled rug. The Himalayas were formed from the folded former sediments of the Tethys Sea, which was trapped in the collision zone between the Indian and Eurasian plates.

The other main mountain-building process occurs when the crust fractures to create faults, allowing rock to be forced upwards in large blocks; or when the pressure of magma within the crust forces the surface to bulge into a dome, or erupts to form a volcano. Large mountain ranges may reveal a combination of these features; the Alps, for example, have been compressed so violently that the folds are fragmented by numerous faults and intrusions of molten igneous rock.

Over millions of years, even the greatest mountain ranges can be reduced by the agents of erosion (most notably rivers) to a low rugged landscape known as a peneplain.

Types of faults: Faults occur where the crust is being stretched or compressed so violently that the rock strata break in a horizontal or vertical movement. They are classified by the direction in which the blocks of rock have moved. A normal fault results when a vertical movement causes the surface to break apart; compression causes a reverse fault. Horizontal movement causes shearing, known as a strike-slip fault. When the rock breaks in two places, the central block may be pushed up in a horst fault, or sink (creating a rift valley) in a graben fault.

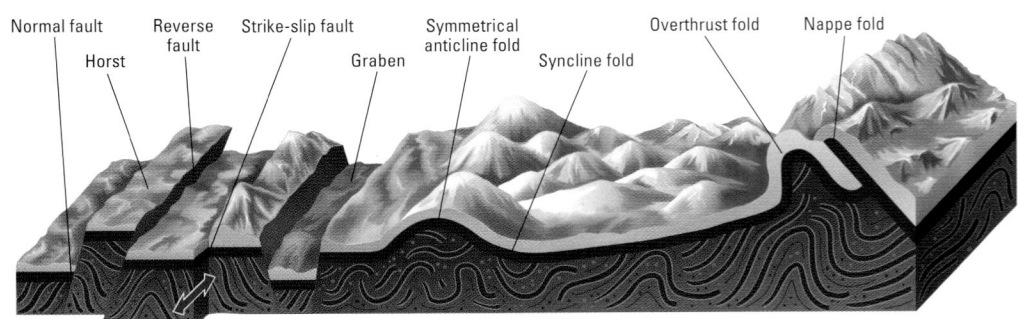

Types of fold: Folds occur when rock strata are squeezed and compressed. They are common, therefore, at destructive plate margins and where plates have collided, forcing the rocks to buckle into mountain ranges. Geographers give different names to the degrees of fold that result from continuing pressure on the rock. A simple fold may be symmetric, with even slopes on either side, but as the pressure builds up, one slope becomes steeper and the fold becomes asymmetric. Later, the ridge or 'anticline' at the top of the fold may slide over the lower ground or 'syncline' to form a recumbent fold. Eventually, the rock strata may break under the pressure to form an overthrust and finally a nappe fold.

CONTINENTAL GLACIATION

Ice sheets were at their greatest extent about 200,000 years ago. The maximum advance of the last Ice Age was about 18,000 years ago, when ice covered virtually all of Canada and reached as far south as the Bristol Channel in Britain.

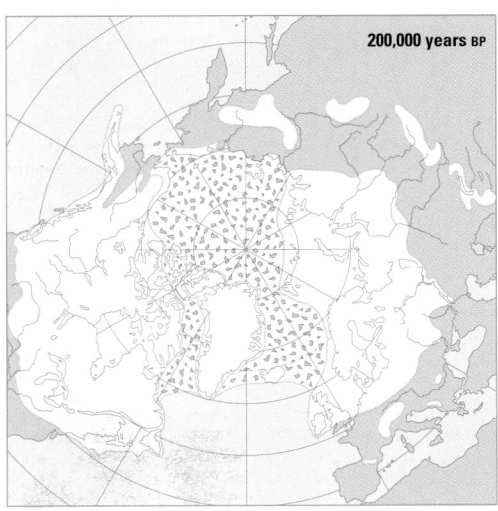

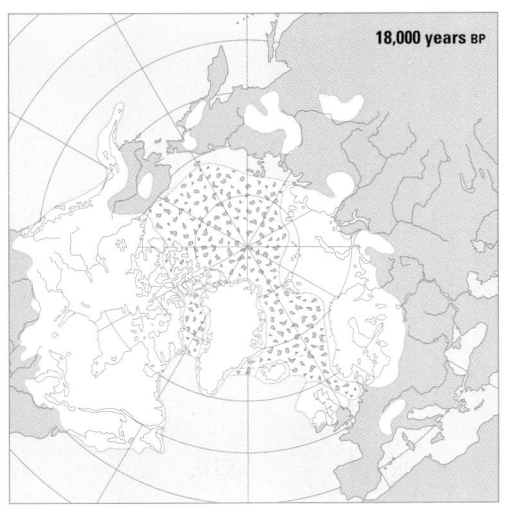

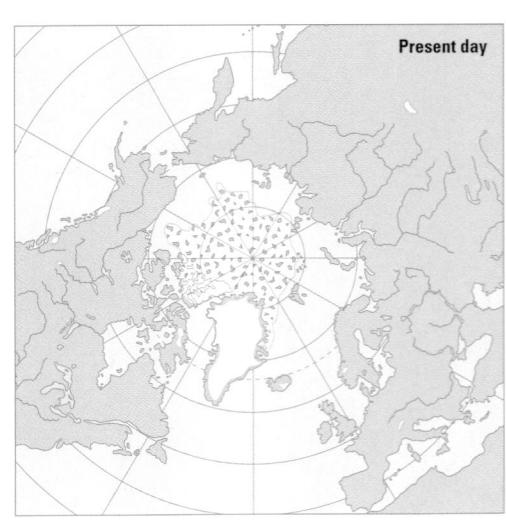

NATURAL LANDFORMS

A stylized diagram to show some of the major natural landforms found in the mid-latitudes.

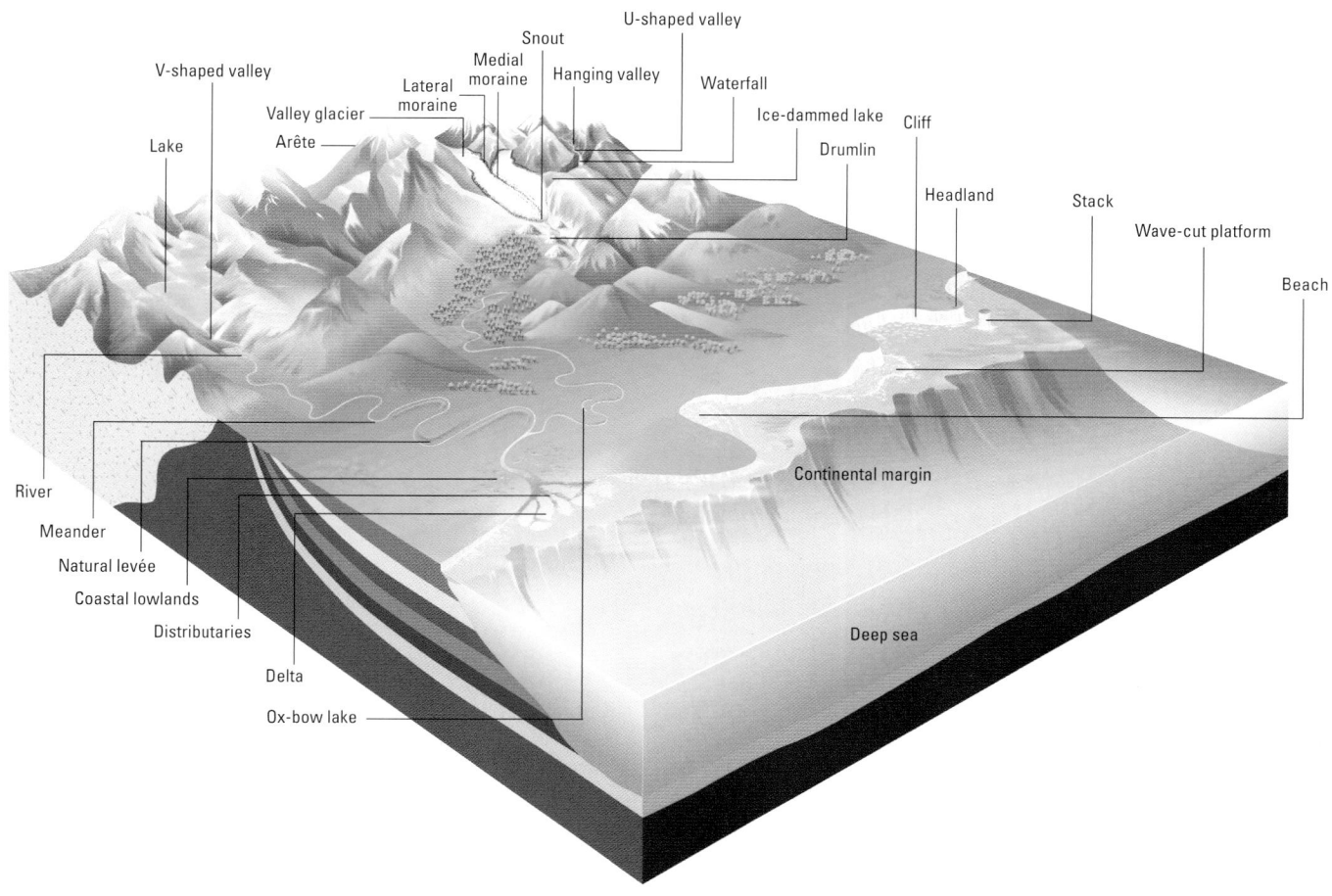

DESERT LANDSCAPES

The popular image that deserts are all huge expanses of sand is wrong. Despite harsh conditions, deserts contain some of the most varied and interesting landscapes in the world. They are also one of the most extensive environments – the hot and cold deserts together cover almost 40% of the Earth's surface.

The three types of hot desert are known by their Arabic names: sand desert, called *erg*, covers only about one-fifth of the world's desert; the rest is divided between *hammada* (areas of bare rock) and *reg* (broad plains covered by loose gravel or pebbles).

In areas of *erg*, such as the Namib Desert, the shape of the dunes reflects the character of local winds. Where winds are constant in direction, crescent-shaped *barchan* dunes form. In areas of bare rock, wind-blown sand is a major agent of erosion. The erosion is mainly confined to within 2 m [6.5 ft] of the surface, producing characteristic mushroom-shaped rocks.

Erg

Hammada

Reg

SURFACE PROCESSES

Catastrophic changes to natural landforms are periodically caused by such phenomena as avalanches, landslides and volcanic eruptions, but most of the processes that shape the Earth's surface operate extremely slowly in human terms. One estimate, based on a study in the United States, suggested that 1 m [3 ft] of land was removed from the entire surface of the country, on average, every 29,500 years. However, the time-scale varies from 1,300 years to 154,200 years depending on the terrain and climate.

In hot, dry climates, mechanical weathering, a result of rapid temperature changes, causes the outer layers of rock to peel away, while in cold mountainous regions, boulders are prised apart when water freezes in cracks in rocks. Chemical weathering, at its greatest in warm, humid regions, is responsible for hollowing out limestone caves and decomposing granites.

The erosion of soil and rock is greatest on sloping land and the steeper the slope, the greater the tendency for mass wasting – the movement of soil and rock downhill under the influence of gravity. The mechanisms of mass wasting (ranging from very slow to very rapid) vary with the type of material, but the presence of water as a lubricant is usually an important factor.

Running water is the world's leading agent of erosion and transportation. The energy of a river depends on several factors, including its velocity and volume, and its erosive power is at its peak when it is in full flood. Sea waves also exert tremendous erosive power during storms when they hurl pebbles against the shore, undercutting cliffs and hollowing out caves.

Glacier ice forms in mountain hollows and spills out to form valley glaciers, which transport rocks shattered by frost action. As glaciers move, rocks embedded into the ice erode steep-sided, U-shaped valleys. Evidence of glaciation in mountain regions includes cirques, knife-edged ridges, or arêtes, and pyramidal peaks.

Oceans

THE GREAT OCEANS

Relative sizes of the world's oceans

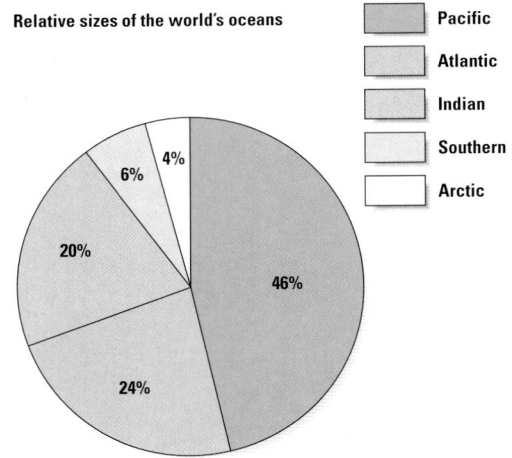

Legend:
- Pacific
- Atlantic
- Indian
- Southern
- Arctic

From ancient times to about the 15th century, the legendary 'Seven Seas' comprised the Red Sea, Mediterranean Sea, Persian Gulf, Black Sea, Adriatic Sea, Caspian Sea and Indian Sea.

The Earth is a watery planet: more than 70% of its surface – over 360,000,000 sq km [140,000,000 sq miles] – is covered by the oceans and seas. The mighty Pacific alone accounts for nearly 36% of the total, and more than 46% of the sea area. Gravity holds in around 1,400 million cubic km [320 million cubic miles] of water, of which over 97% is saline.

The vast underwater world starts in the shallows of the seaside and plunges to depths of more than 11,000 m [36,000 ft]. The continental shelf, part of the landmass, drops gently to around 200 m [650 ft]; here the seabed falls away suddenly at an angle of 3° to 6° – the continental slope. The third stage, called the continental rise, is more gradual with gradients varying from 1 in 100 to 1 in 700. At an average depth of 5,000 m [16,500 ft] there begins the aptly-named abyssal plain – massive submarine depths where sunlight fails to penetrate and few creatures can survive.

From these plains rise volcanoes which, taken from base to top, rival and even surpass the tallest continental mountains in height. Mauna Kea, on Hawai'i, reaches a total of 10,203 m [33,400 ft], some 1,355 m [4,500 ft] higher than Mount Everest, though scarcely 40% is visible above sea level.

In addition, there are underwater mountain chains up to 1,000 km [600 miles] across, whose peaks sometimes appear above sea level as islands, such as Iceland and Tristan da Cunha.

OCEAN DEPTHS

Average and maximum depths of the world's great oceans, in metres

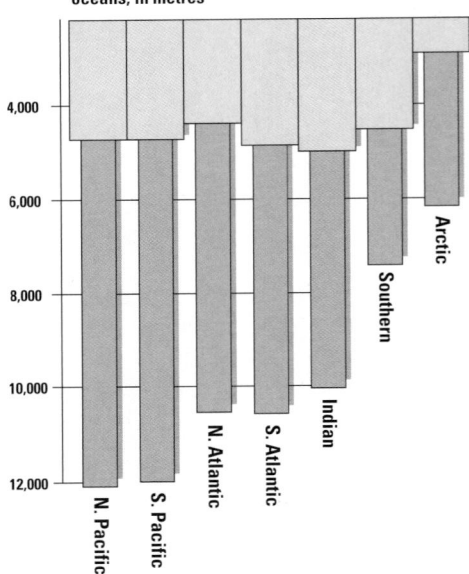

OCEAN CURRENTS

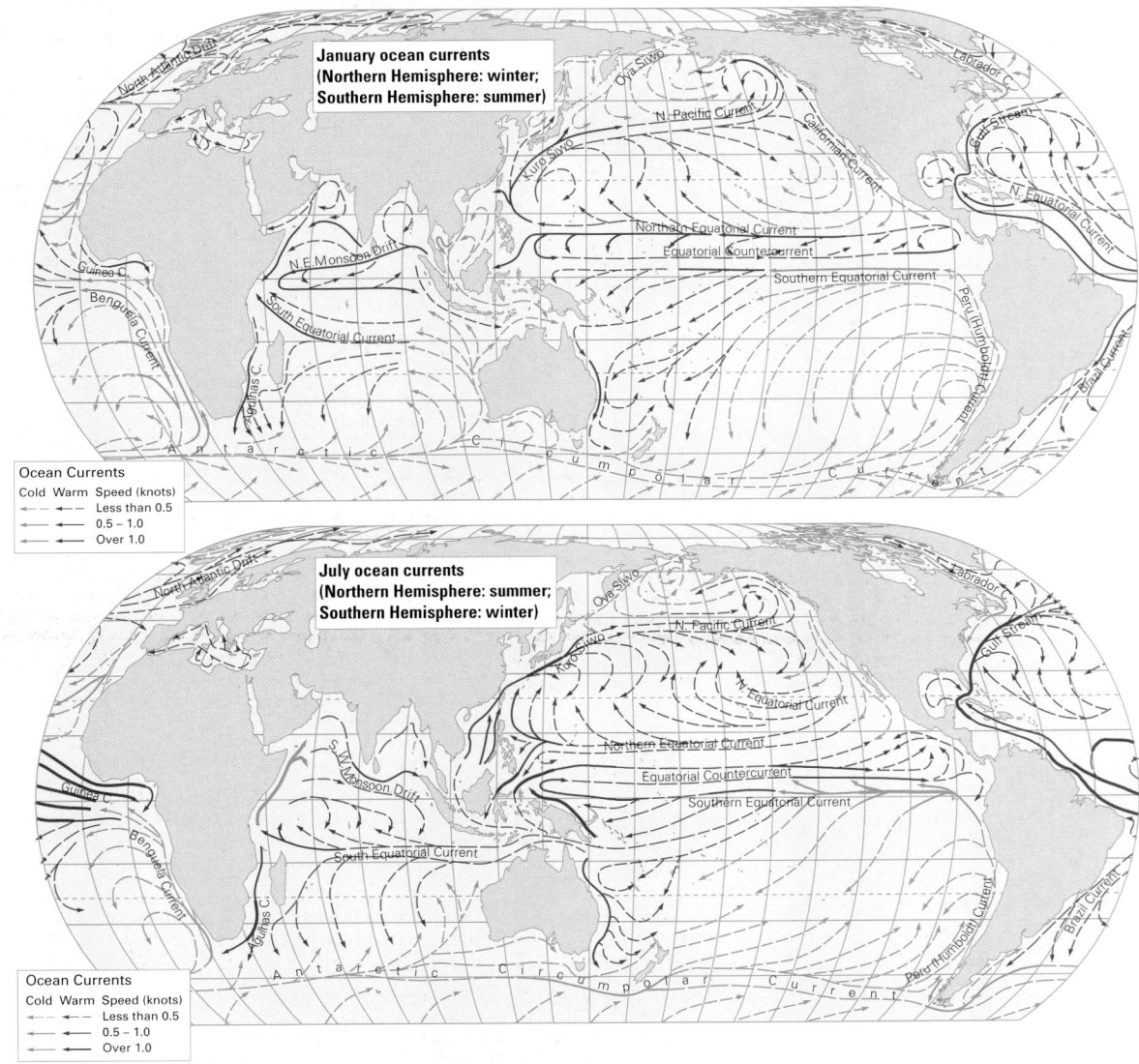

January ocean currents (Northern Hemisphere: winter; Southern Hemisphere: summer)

Ocean Currents
Cold Warm Speed (knots)
- Less than 0.5
- 0.5 – 1.0
- Over 1.0

July ocean currents (Northern Hemisphere: summer; Southern Hemisphere: winter)

Ocean Currents
Cold Warm Speed (knots)
- Less than 0.5
- 0.5 – 1.0
- Over 1.0

Moving immense quantities of energy as well as billions of tonnes of water every hour, the ocean currents are a vital part of the great heat engine that drives the Earth's climate. They themselves are produced by a twofold mechanism. At the surface, winds push huge masses of water before them; in the deep ocean, below an abrupt temperature gradient that separates the churning surface waters from the still depths, density variations cause slow vertical movements.

The pattern of circulation of the great surface currents is determined by the displacement known as the Coriolis effect. As the Earth turns beneath a moving object – whether it is a tennis ball or a vast mass of water – it appears to be deflected to one side. The deflection is most obvious near the Equator, where the Earth's surface is spinning eastwards at 1,700 km/h [1,050 mph]; currents moving polewards are curved clockwise in the northern hemisphere and anti-clockwise in the southern.

The result is a system of spinning circles known as 'gyres'. The Coriolis effect piles up water on the left of each gyre, creating a narrow, fast-moving stream that is matched by a slower, broader returning current on the right. North and south of the Equator, the fastest currents are located in the west and in the east respectively. In each case, warm water moves from the Equator and cold water returns to it. Cold currents often bring an upwelling of nutrients with them, supporting the world's most economically important fisheries.

Depending on the prevailing winds, some currents on or near the Equator may reverse their direction in the course of the year – a seasonal variation on which Asian monsoon rains depend, and whose occasional failure can bring disaster to millions of people.

WORLD FISHING AREAS

Total world fish catch in metric tonnes, inland and marine fishing (2015)

- Over 10 million
- 1 million – 10 million
- 100,000 – 1 million
- 10,000 – 100,000
- Under 10,000
- No data available

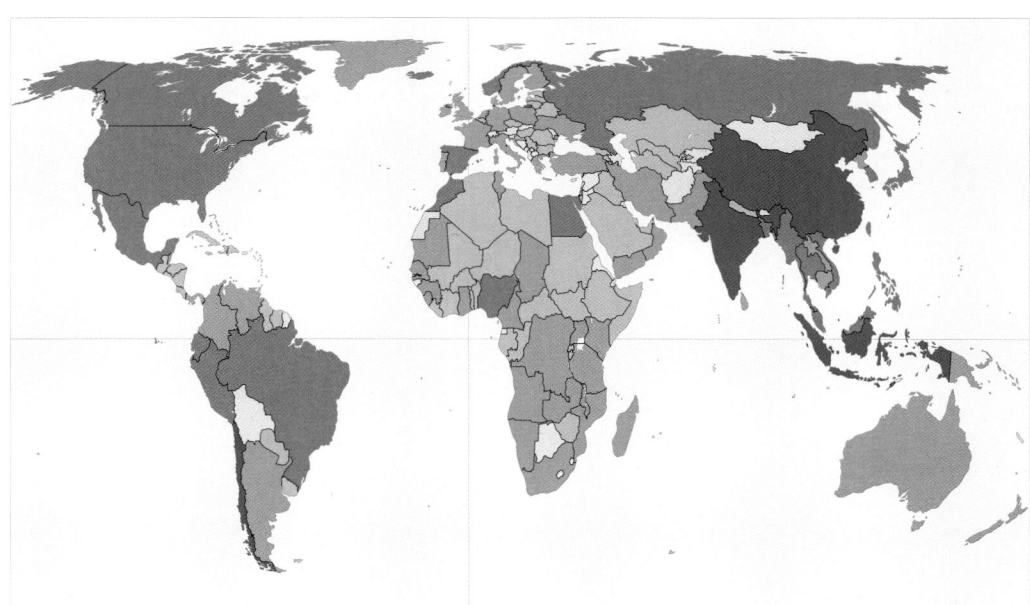

Leading fishing nations

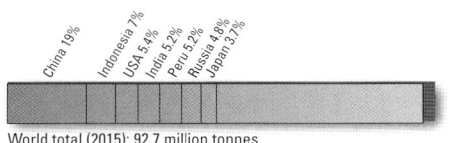

China 19% | Indonesia 7% | USA 5.4% | India 5.2% | Peru 5.2% | Russia 4.8% | Japan 3.7%

World total (2015): 92.7 million tonnes
(Marine catch 88% : Inland catch 12%)

MARINE POLLUTION

Sources of marine oil pollution

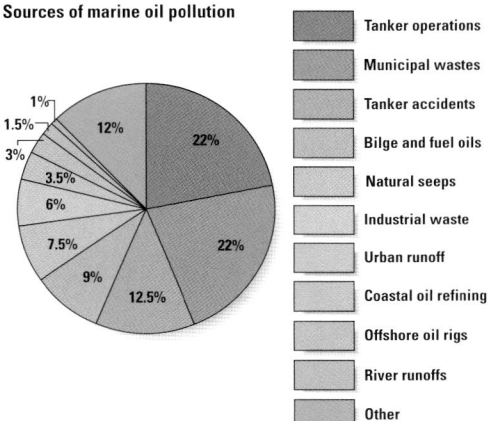

22% — Tanker operations
22% — Municipal wastes
12.5% — Tanker accidents
9% — Bilge and fuel oils
7.5% — Natural seeps
6% — Industrial waste
3.5% — Urban runoff
3% — Coastal oil refining
1.5% — Offshore oil rigs
1% — River runoffs
12% — Other

OIL SPILLS

Major oil spills from tankers and combined carriers

Year	Vessel	Location	Spill (barrels)*	Cause
1979	Atlantic Empress	West Indies	1,890,000	collision
1983	Castillo de Bellver	South Africa	1,760,000	fire
1978	Amoco Cadiz	France	1,628,000	grounding
1991	Haven	Italy	1,029,000	explosion
1988	Odyssey	Canada	1,000,000	fire
1967	Torrey Canyon	UK	909,000	grounding
1972	Sea Star	Gulf of Oman	902,250	collision
1977	Hawaiian Patriot	Hawaiian Is.	742,500	fire
1979	Independenta	Turkey	696,350	collision
1993	Braer	UK	625,000	grounding
1996	Sea Empress	UK	515,000	grounding
2002	Prestige	Spain	463,250	storm

Other sources of major oil spills

1983	Nowruz oilfield	Persian Gulf	4,250,000†	war
1979	Ixtoc 1 oilwell	Gulf of Mexico	4,200,000	blow-out
2010	Deepwater Horizon	Gulf of Mexico	3.6 – 4,610,000	blow-out

* 1 barrel = 0.136 tonnes/159 lit./35 Imperial gal./42 US gal. † estimated

RIVER POLLUTION

Sources of river pollution, USA

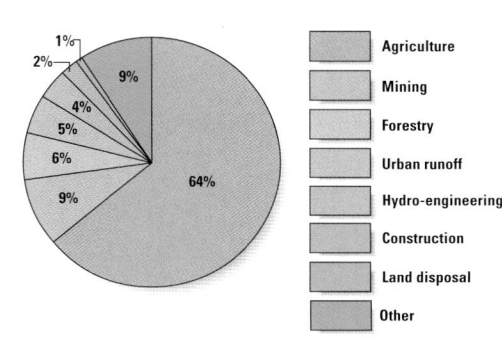

64% — Agriculture
9% — Mining
9% — Forestry
6% — Urban runoff
5% — Hydro-engineering
4% — Construction
2% — Land disposal
1% — Other

EL NIÑO

El Niño, 'The Little Boy' in Spanish, was originally the name given by local fishermen to the warm current that can appear off the Pacific coast of South America. In a normal year, south-easterly trade winds drive surface waters westwards off the coast of South America, drawing cold, nutrient-rich water up from below. In an El Niño year, warm water from the west Pacific suppresses upwelling in the east, depriving the region of nutrients and driving the fish away. The water is warmed by as much as 7°C, disturbing the tropical atmosphere circulation. During an intense El Niño, the south-east trade winds change direction and become equatorial westerlies, resulting in climatic extremes in many regions of the world, such as drought in parts of Australia and India, and heavy rainfall in south-eastern USA.

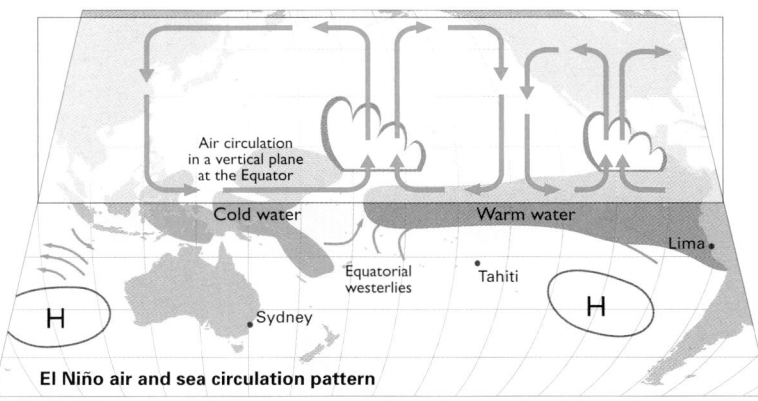

Air circulation in a vertical plane at the Equator

Cold water | Warm water

Equatorial westerlies | Tahiti | Lima

Sydney | H | H

El Niño air and sea circulation pattern

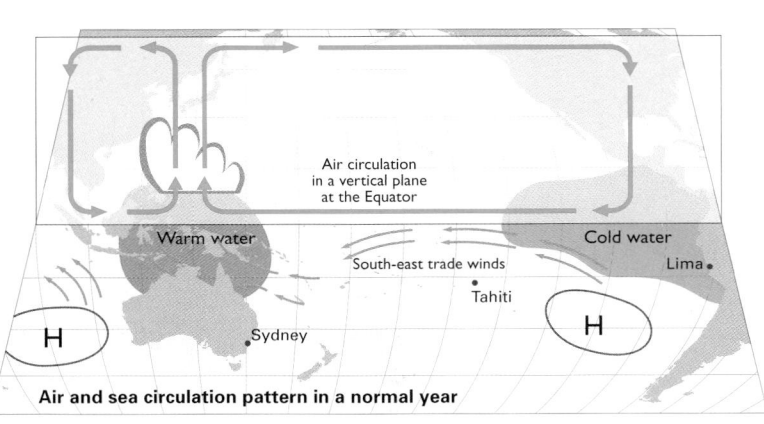

Air circulation in a vertical plane at the Equator

Warm water | Cold water

South-east trade winds | Tahiti | Lima

Sydney | H | H

Air and sea circulation pattern in a normal year

El Niño events occur about every 4 to 7 years and typically last for around 12 to 18 months. El Niño usually results in reduced rainfall across northern and eastern Australia. This can lead to widespread and severe drought, as well as increased temperatures and bushfire risk. However, each El Niño event is unique in terms of its strength as well as its impact. It is measured by the Southern Oscillation Index (SOI) and the changes in ocean temperatures.

La Niña, or 'The Little Girl', is associated with cooler waters in the central and eastern Pacific. A La Niña year can result in cooler land temperatures across the tropics and subtropics, and more storms in the North Atlantic.

Climate

Colour of climate region on map

Name of place

SINGAPORE

Average monthly temperature

Average monthly daily maximum temperature

Average monthly daily minimum temperature

Temperature

Average annual precipitation
2413mm/95in

Precipitation

Average monthly precipitation

Months of the year

J F M A M J J A S O N D

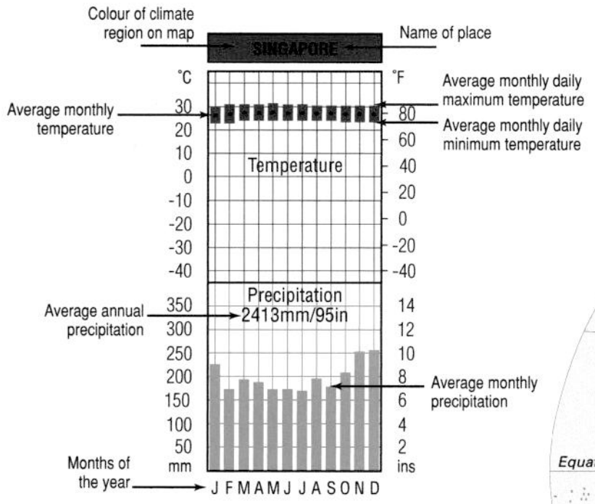

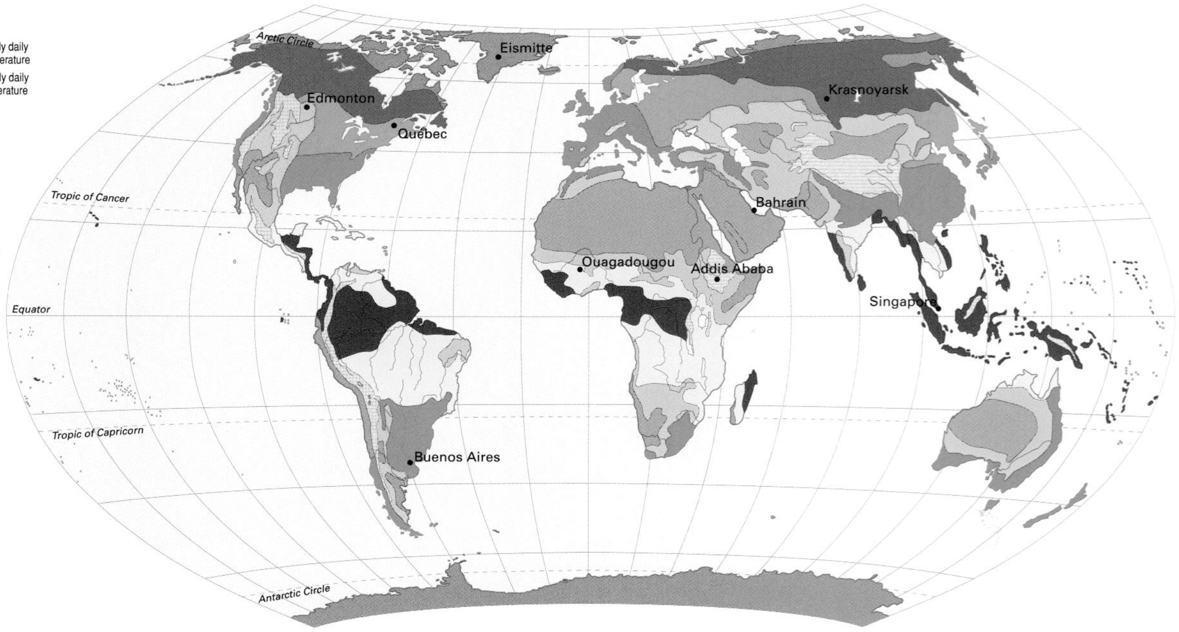

- ■ Tropical climate (hot with rain all year)
- ■ Desert climate (hot and very dry)
- □ Savanna climate (hot with dry season)

- □ Steppe climate (warm and dry)
- ■ Mild climate (warm and wet)
- ■ Continental climate (wet with cold winter)

- ■ Subarctic climate (very cold winter)
- ■ Polar climate (very cold and dry)
- □ Mountainous climate (altitude affects climate)

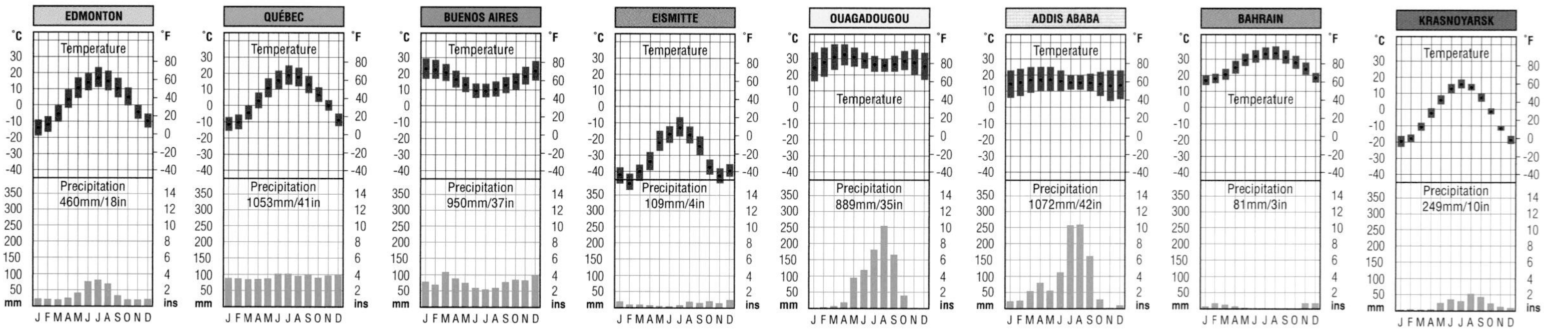

Arctic Circle

Eismitte

Krasnoyarsk

Edmonton

Québec

Bahrain

Tropic of Cancer

Ouagadougou · Addis Ababa

Equator

Singapore

Tropic of Capricorn

Buenos Aires

Antarctic Circle

EDMONTON	QUÉBEC	BUENOS AIRES	EISMITTE	OUAGADOUGOU	ADDIS ABABA	BAHRAIN	KRASNOYARSK
Temperature	Temperature	Temperature	Temperature	Temperature	Temperature	Temperature	Temperature
Precipitation 460mm/18in	Precipitation 1053mm/41in	Precipitation 950mm/37in	Precipitation 109mm/4in	Precipitation 889mm/35in	Precipitation 1072mm/42in	Precipitation 81mm/3in	Precipitation 249mm/10in
J F M A M J J A S O N D	J F M A M J J A S O N D	J F M A M J J A S O N D	J F M A M J J A S O N D	J F M A M J J A S O N D	J F M A M J J A S O N D	J F M A M J J A S O N D	J F M A M J J A S O N D

THE MONSOON

Monthly rainfall

mm		mm	
■ 400		□ 50	
■ 200		□ 25	
■ 100		□ 0	

→ Wind direction

━ ITCZ (intertropical convergence zone)

In early March, which normally marks the end of the subcontinent's cool season and the start of the hot season, winds blow outwards from the mainland. But as the overhead sun and the ITCZ move northwards, the land is intensely heated, and a low-pressure system develops. The south-east trade winds, which are drawn across the Equator, change direction and are sucked into the interior, bringing heavy rain. By November, the overhead sun and the ITCZ have again moved southwards and the wind directions are again reversed. Cool winds blow from the Asian interior to the sea, losing any moisture on the Himalayas before descending to the coast.

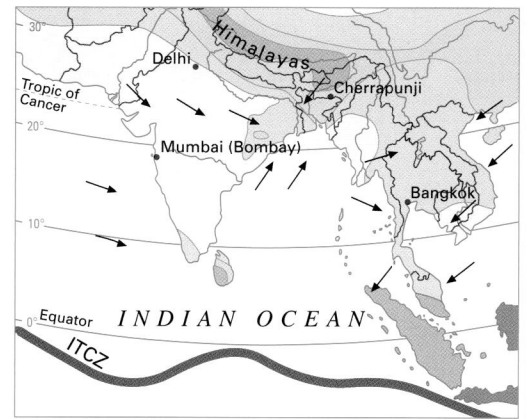

March – Start of the hot, dry season, the ITCZ is over the southern Indian Ocean.

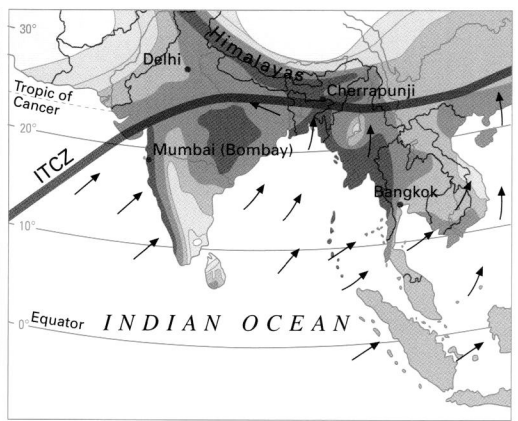

July – The rainy season, the ITCZ has migrated northwards; winds blow onshore.

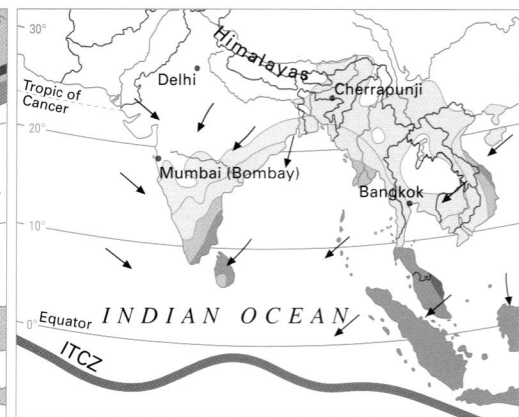

November – The ITCZ has returned south, the offshore winds are cool and dry.

CLIMATE

Climate is weather in the long term: the seasonal pattern of hot and cold, wet and dry, averaged over time (usually 30 years). At the simplest level, it is caused by the uneven heating of the Earth. Surplus heat at the Equator passes towards the poles, levelling out the energy differential. Its passage is marked by a ceaseless churning of the atmosphere and the oceans, further agitated by the Earth's diurnal spin and the motion it imparts to moving air and water. The heat's means of transport – by winds and ocean currents, by the continual evaporation and recondensation of water molecules – is the weather itself. There are four basic types of climate, each of which can be further subdivided: tropical, desert (dry), temperate and polar.

COMPOSITION OF DRY AIR

Nitrogen	78.09%	Sulphur dioxide	trace
Oxygen	20.95%	Nitrogen oxide	trace
Argon	0.93%	Methane	trace
Water vapour	0.2–4.0%	Dust	trace
Carbon dioxide	0.03%	Helium	trace
Ozone	0.00006%	Neon	trace

CLIMATE RECORDS

Temperature
Highest recorded shade temperature: Death Valley, USA, 56.7°C [134.1°F], 10 July 1913.

Highest mean annual temperature: Dallol, Ethiopia, 34.4°C [94°F], 1960–66.

Longest heatwave: Marble Bar, W. Australia, 162 days over 38°C [100°F], 23 October 1923 to 7 April 1924.

Lowest recorded temperature (outside poles): Verkhoyansk, Siberia, –68°C [–93.6°F], 7 February 1982.

Lowest mean annual temperature: Polus Nedostupnosti, Pole of Cold, Antarctica, –57.8°C [–72°F].

Precipitation
Driest place: Quillagua, Chile, mean annual rainfall 0.5 mm [0.02 in], 1964–2001.

Wettest place (average): Mt Wai-ale-ale, Hawai'i, USA, mean annual rainfall 11,680 mm [459.8 in].

Wettest place (12 months): Cherrapunji, Meghalaya, N. E. India, 26,461 mm [1,042 in], August 1860 to July 1861. Cherrapunji also holds the record for the most rainfall in one month: 2,930 mm [115 in], July 1861.

Wettest place (24 hours): Fac Fac, Réunion, Indian Ocean, 1,825 mm [71.9 in], 15–16 March 1952.

Heaviest hailstones: Gopalganj, Bangladesh, up to 1.02 kg [2.25 lb], 14 April 1986 (killed 92 people).

Heaviest snowfall (continuous): Bessans, Savoie, France, 1,730 mm [68 in] in 19 hours, 5–6 April 1969.

Heaviest snowfall (season/year): Mt Baker, Washington, USA, 28,956 mm [1,140 in], June 1998 to June 1999.

Pressure and winds
Highest barometric pressure: Agata, Siberia (at 262 m [862 ft] altitude), 1,083.8 mb, 31 December 1968.

Lowest barometric pressure: Typhoon Tip, Guam, Pacific Ocean, 870 mb, 12 October 1979.

Highest recorded wind speed: Bridge Creek, Oklahoma, USA, 512 km/h [318 mph], 3 May 1999. Measured by Doppler radar monitoring a tornado.

Windiest place: Port Martin, Antarctica, where winds of more than 64 km/h [40 mph] occur for not less than 100 days a year.

Conversions
°C = (°F − 32) × 5/9; °F = (°C × 9/5) + 32; 0°C = 32°F
1 in = 25.4 mm; 1 mm = 0.0394 in; 100 mm = 3.94 in

TEMPERATURE

Average temperature in January

Average temperature

- 30°C
- 20°C
- 10°C
- 0°C
- −10°C
- −20°C
- −30°C
- −40°C

Average temperature in July

Average temperature

- 30°C
- 20°C
- 10°C
- 0°C
- −10°C

PRECIPITATION (RAINFALL AND SNOW)

Average annual precipitation

- 3,000 mm
- 2,000 mm
- 1,000 mm
- 500 mm
- 250 mm

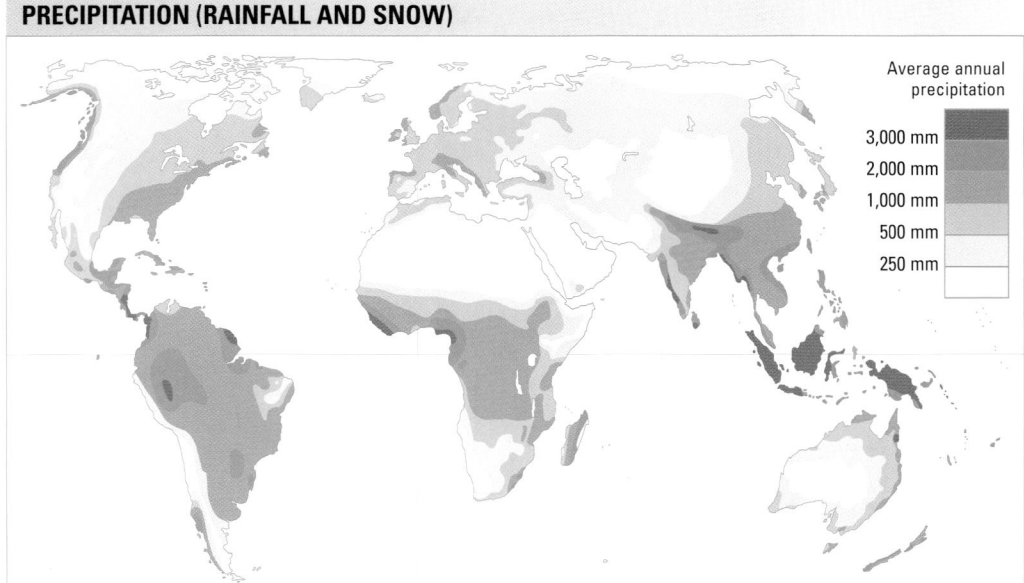

Water and Vegetation

THE HYDROLOGICAL CYCLE

The world's water balance is regulated by the constant recycling of water between the oceans, atmosphere and land. The movement of water between these three reservoirs is known as the hydrological cycle. The oceans play a vital role in the hydrological cycle: 74% of the total precipitation falls over the oceans and 84% of the total evaporation comes from the oceans.

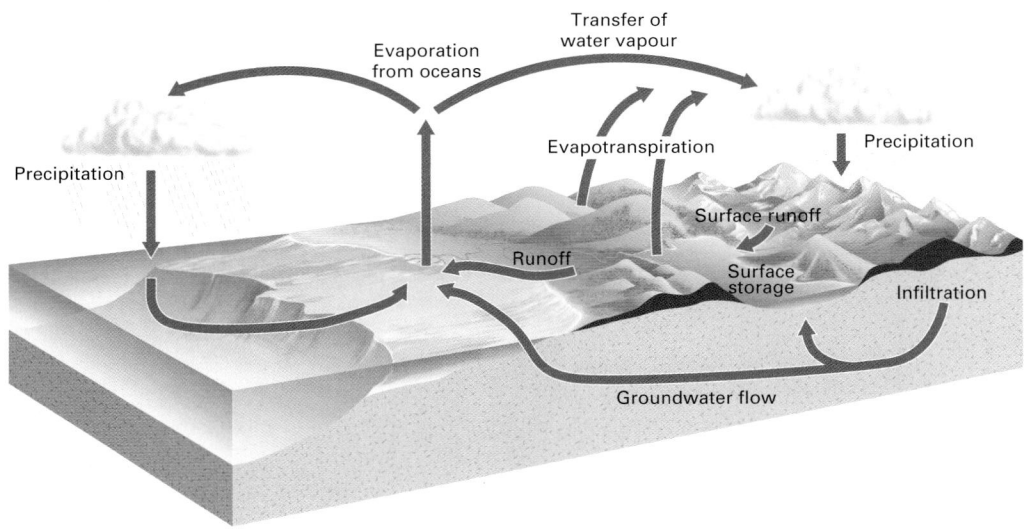

WATER DISTRIBUTION

The distribution of planetary water, by percentage. Oceans and ice caps together account for more than 99% of the total; the breakdown of the remainder is estimated.

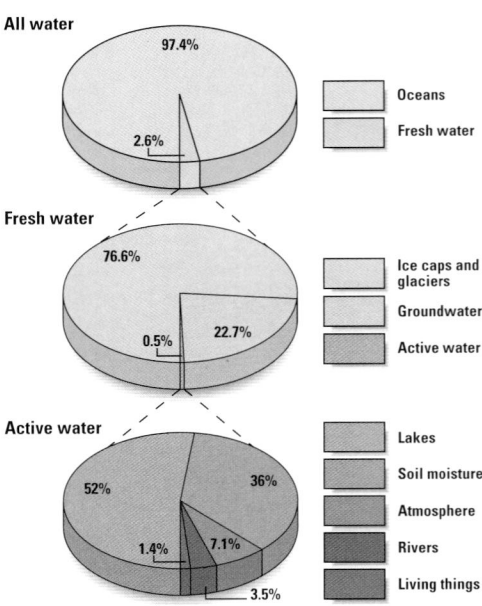

All water
- 97.4%
- 2.6%
- Oceans
- Fresh water

Fresh water
- 76.6%
- 22.7%
- 0.5%
- Ice caps and glaciers
- Groundwater
- Active water

Active water
- 52%
- 36%
- 1.4%
- 7.1%
- 3.5%
- Lakes
- Soil moisture
- Atmosphere
- Rivers
- Living things

WATER UTILIZATION

The percentage breakdown of water usage by sector, selected countries

Domestic — Industrial — Agriculture

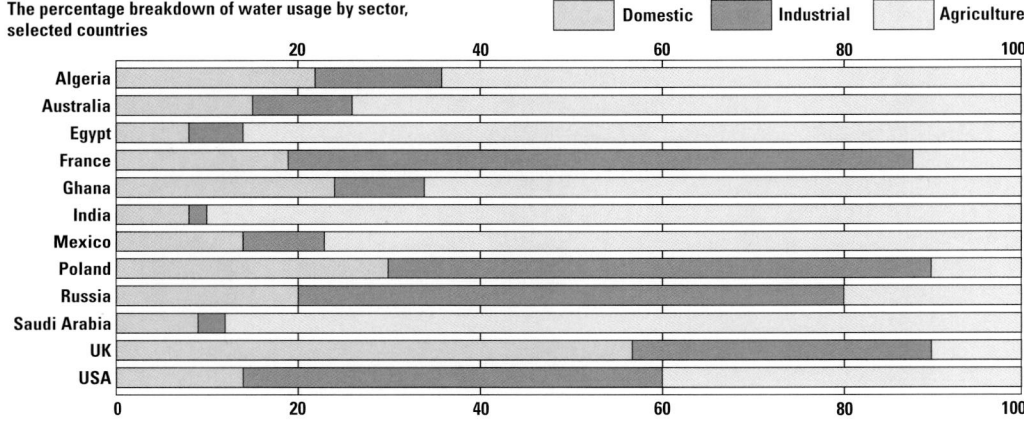

Algeria, Australia, Egypt, France, Ghana, India, Mexico, Poland, Russia, Saudi Arabia, UK, USA

WATER USAGE

Almost all the world's water is 3,000 million years old, and all of it cycles endlessly through the hydrosphere, though at different rates. Water vapour circulates over days or even hours, deep ocean water circulates over millennia, and ice-cap water remains solid for millions of years.

Fresh water is essential to all terrestrial life. Humans cannot survive more than a few days without it, and even the hardiest desert plants and animals could not exist without some water. Agriculture requires huge quantities of fresh water: without large-scale irrigation most of the world's people would starve. In the USA, agriculture uses 40% and industry 46% of all water withdrawals.

According to the latest figures, the average North American uses 1.5 million litres of water per year. This is more than six times the average African, who uses just 186,000 litres of water each year. Europeans and Australians use 694,000 litres per year.

WATER SUPPLY

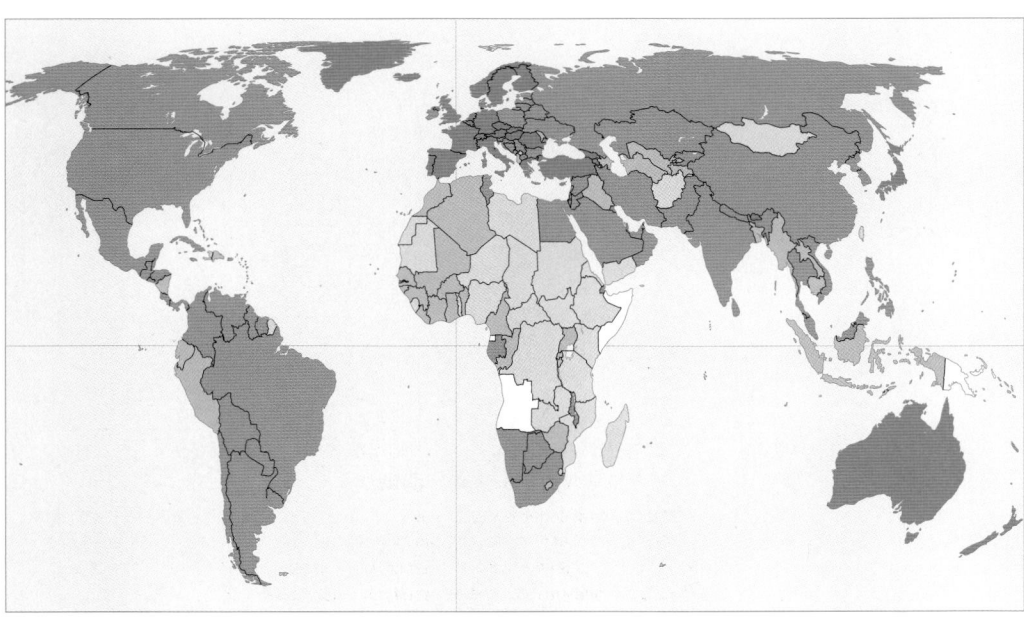

Percentage of total population with access to safe drinking water (2015)

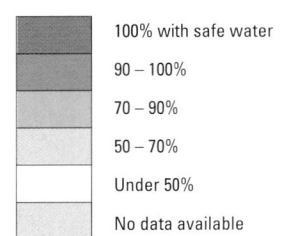

- 100% with safe water
- 90 – 100%
- 70 – 90%
- 50 – 70%
- Under 50%
- No data available

Least well-provided countries

Somalia	32%	Mozambique	51%
Papua New Guinea	40%	Madagascar	52%
Equatorial Guinea	48%	Congo (Dem. Rep.)	52%
Angola	49%	Libya	54%
Chad	51%	Yemen	55%

NATURAL VEGETATION

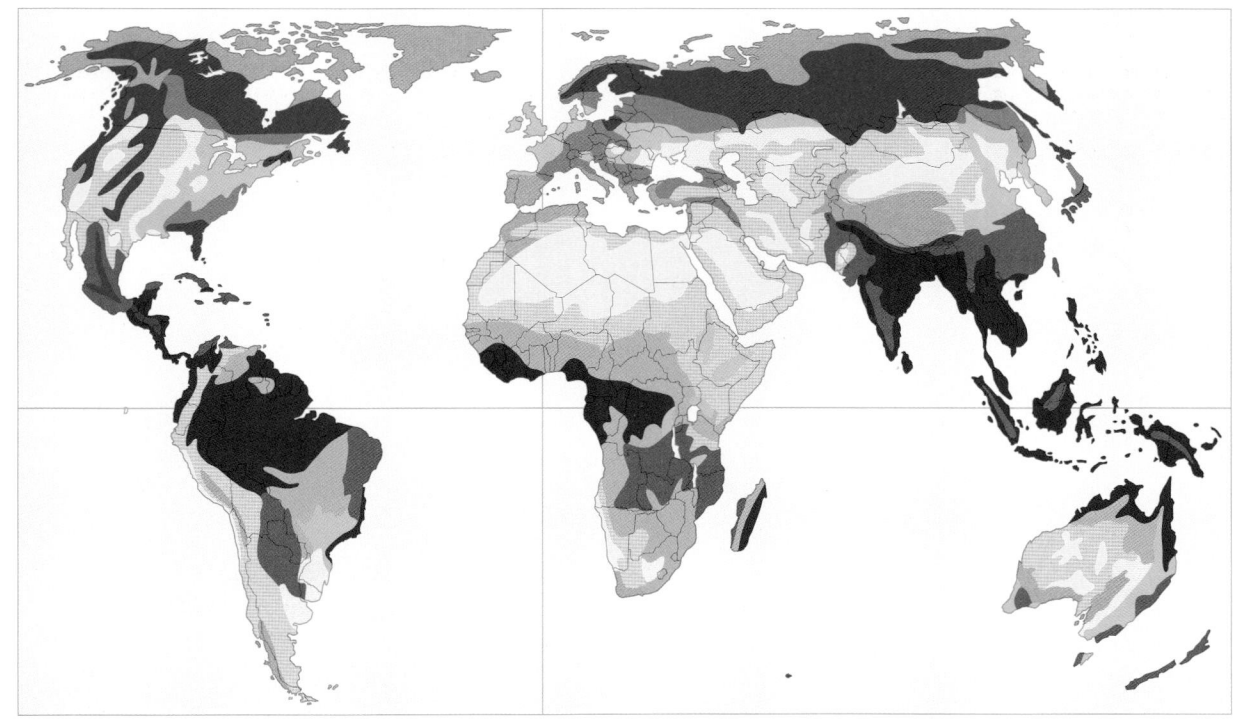

Regional variation in vegetation

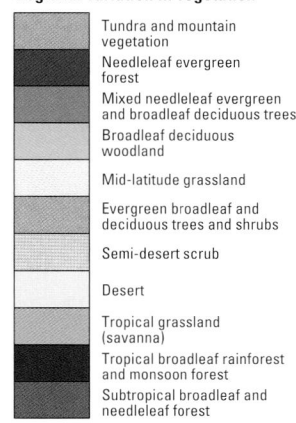

- Tundra and mountain vegetation
- Needleleaf evergreen forest
- Mixed needleleaf evergreen and broadleaf deciduous trees
- Broadleaf deciduous woodland
- Mid-latitude grassland
- Evergreen broadleaf and deciduous trees and shrubs
- Semi-desert scrub
- Desert
- Tropical grassland (savanna)
- Tropical broadleaf rainforest and monsoon forest
- Subtropical broadleaf and needleleaf forest

The map shows the natural 'climax vegetation' of regions, as dictated by climate and topography. In most cases, however, agricultural activity has drastically altered the vegetation pattern. Western Europe, for example, lost most of its broadleaf forest many centuries ago, while irrigation has turned some natural semi-desert into productive land.

LAND USE BY CONTINENT

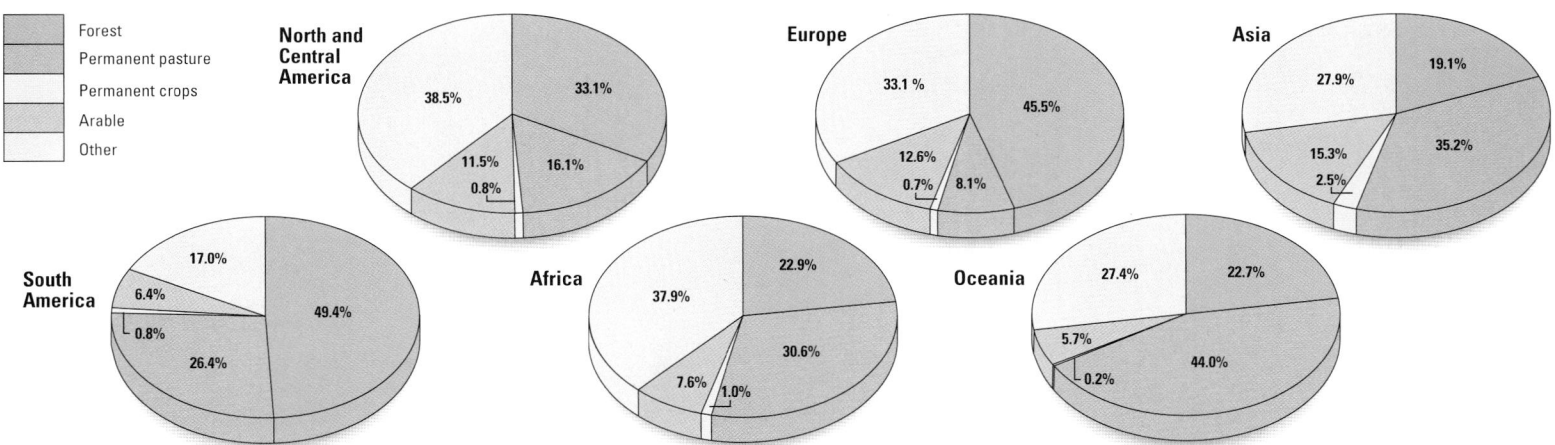

- Forest
- Permanent pasture
- Permanent crops
- Arable
- Other

North and Central America: 33.1%, 16.1%, 0.8%, 11.5%, 38.5%

Europe: 45.5%, 8.1%, 0.7%, 12.6%, 33.1%

Asia: 19.1%, 35.2%, 2.5%, 15.3%, 27.9%

South America: 49.4%, 26.4%, 0.8%, 6.4%, 17.0%

Africa: 22.9%, 30.6%, 1.0%, 7.6%, 37.9%

Oceania: 22.7%, 44.0%, 0.2%, 5.7%, 27.4%

FORESTRY: PRODUCTION

Fuelwood
Top producers (2016)

(million cubic metres)

India	306
China	169
Brazil	112
Ethiopia	109
Congo, Dem. Rep.	84
World	1,863

Industrial roundwood*
Top producers (2016)

(million cubic metres)

USA	357
Russia	198
China	164
Canada	158
Brazil	145
World	1,874

* roundwood is timber as it is felled

Paper and Board
Top producers (2016)

(million tonnes)

China	113
USA	72
Japan	26
Germany	23
India	15
World	409

Top exporters (2016)

(million tonnes)

Germany	13
USA	11
Sweden	10
Finland	10
China	8

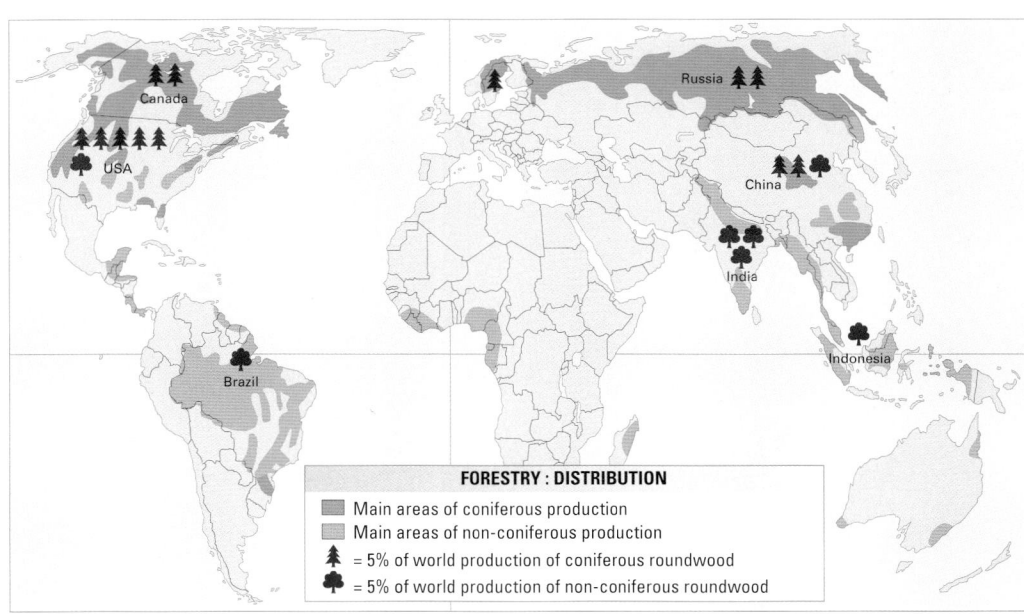

FORESTRY : DISTRIBUTION

- Main areas of coniferous production
- Main areas of non-coniferous production
- ♠ = 5% of world production of coniferous roundwood
- ♣ = 5% of world production of non-coniferous roundwood

13

Environment

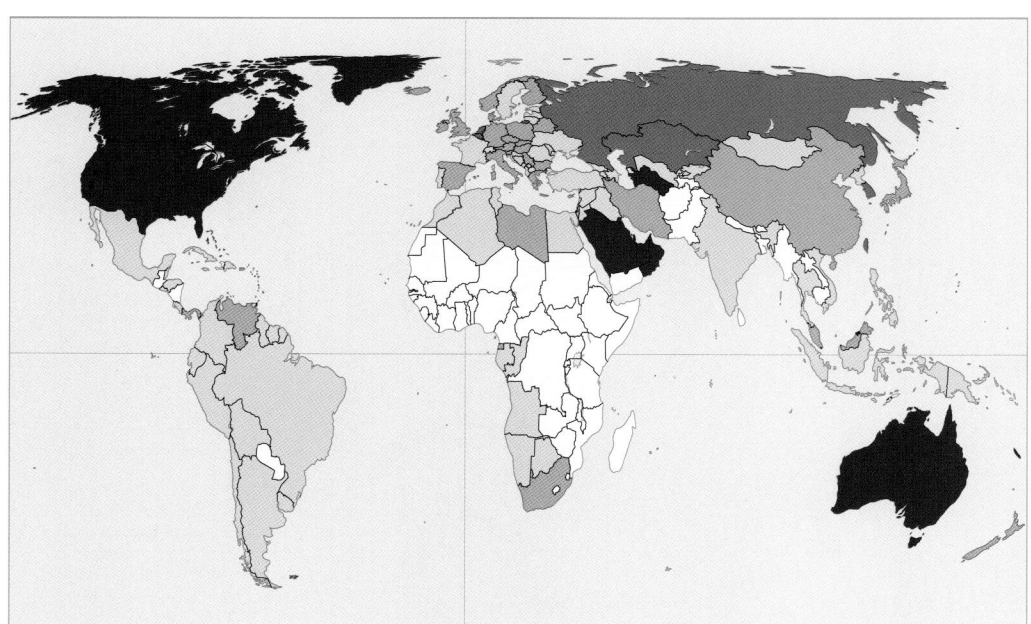

CARBON DIOXIDE EMISSIONS

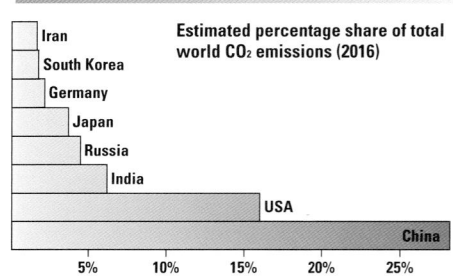

Estimated percentage share of total world CO_2 emissions (2016)

- Iran
- South Korea
- Germany
- Japan
- Russia
- India
- USA
- China

5%   10%   15%   20%   25%

PREDICTED CHANGE IN PRECIPITATION

The difference between actual annual average precipitation, 1960–1990, and the predicted annual average precipitation, 2070–2100. It should be noted that these predicted annual mean changes mask quite significant seasonal detail.

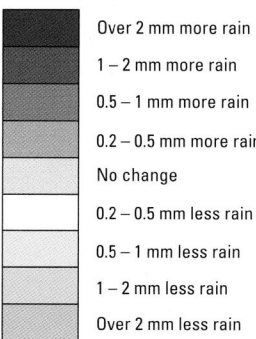

- Over 2 mm more rain
- 1 – 2 mm more rain
- 0.5 – 1 mm more rain
- 0.2 – 0.5 mm more rain
- No change
- 0.2 – 0.5 mm less rain
- 0.5 – 1 mm less rain
- 1 – 2 mm less rain
- Over 2 mm less rain

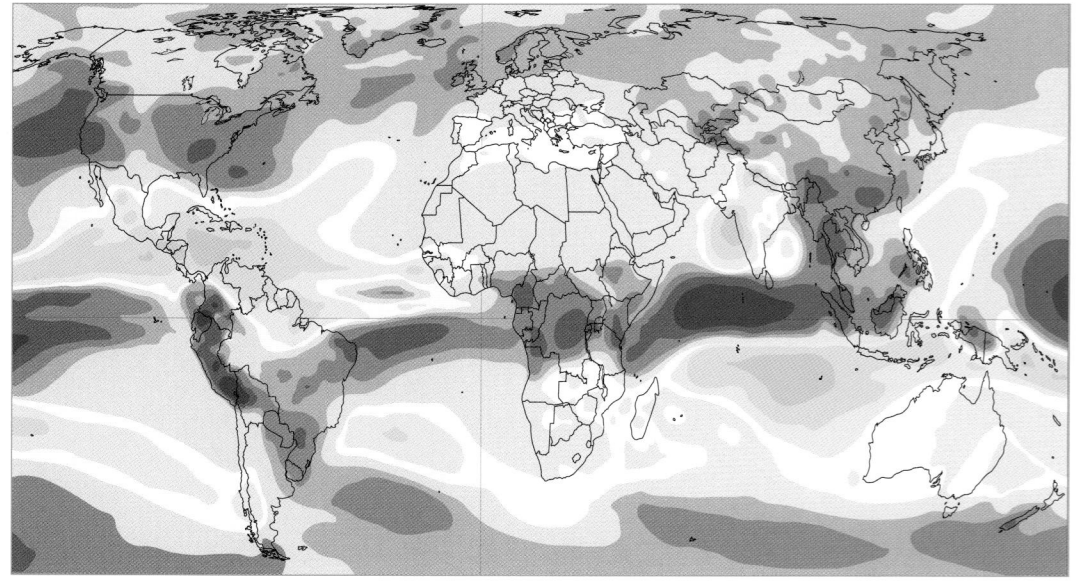

PREDICTED CHANGE IN TEMPERATURE

The difference between actual annual average surface air temperature, 1960–1990, and the predicted annual average surface air temperature, 2070–2100. This map shows the predicted increase, assuming a 'medium growth' of global economy and assuming that no measures are taken to combat the emission of greenhouse gases.

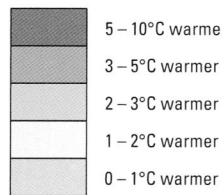

- 5 – 10°C warmer
- 3 – 5°C warmer
- 2 – 3°C warmer
- 1 – 2°C warmer
- 0 – 1°C warmer

Source: The Hadley Centre of Climate Prediction and Research, The Met. Office

GLOBAL WARMING PROJECTIONS

Projected Change in Global Warming

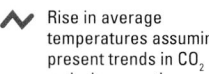 Rise in average temperatures assuming present trends in CO_2 emissions continue

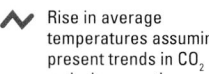 Assuming some cuts are made in emissions

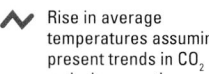 Assuming drastic cuts are made in emissions

Climate models are used to provide the best scientifically-based estimates of the future global climate. A typical method is to run the models for some decades ahead and then to compare the predicted average with a past 30-year period. A range of climate models are used, run with different scenarios that express the breadth of possibilities of, for example, industrial development and the degree of atmospheric pollution 'clean-up' by industrial nations.

The diagram on the right shows global observed and predicted surface mean temperature change from 1950 to 2070 with three prediction scenarios. The first (red) assumes rapid economic growth and continued population increases. The second (blue) assumes some attempts are made to cut greenhouse gas emissions, while the green line involves the greater use of cleaner technologies, with global population peaking mid-century then declining.

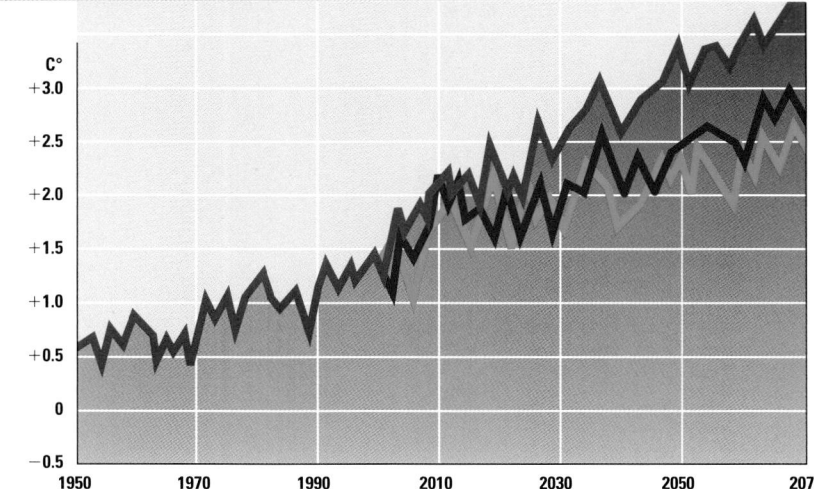

GREENHOUSE EFFECT

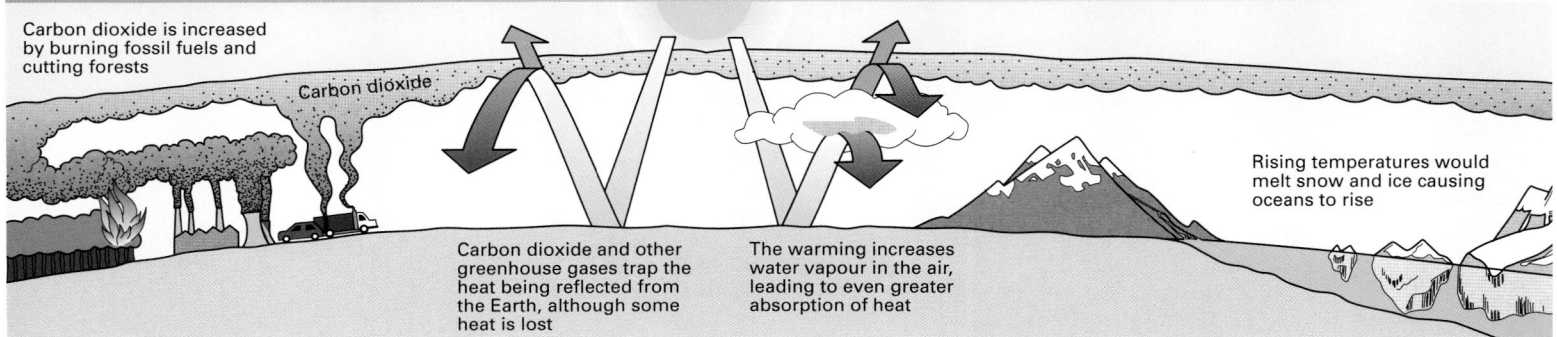

Carbon dioxide is increased by burning fossil fuels and cutting forests

Carbon dioxide

Carbon dioxide and other greenhouse gases trap the heat being reflected from the Earth, although some heat is lost

The warming increases water vapour in the air, leading to even greater absorption of heat

Rising temperatures would melt snow and ice causing oceans to rise

DEFORESTATION 1990–2015

	Total forest cover in 1000 sq kms 1990	Total forest cover in 1000 sq kms 2015	% change 1990-2015
Venezuela	520	148	-71.5
Togo	7	2	-71.4
Nigeria	172	70	-59.3
Uganda	48	21	-56.3
Pakistan	25	15	-40.0
North Korea	82	50	-39.0
Sudan	307	192	-37.5
Zimbabwe	222	141	-36.5
Nicaragua	45	31	-31.1
Timor-Leste	10	7	-30.0
Paraguay	212	153	-27.8
Myanmar	392	290	-26.0
Ethiopia	167	125	-25.1
Nepal	48	36	-25.0
Indonesia	1,185	910	-23.2
Somalia	83	64	-22.9
Cameroon	243	188	-22.6
Namibia	88	69	-21.6
Tanzania	559	461	-17.5
Ecuador	146	125	-14.4
Bolivia	628	548	-12.7
Mozambique	434	379	-12.7
Senegal	93	83	-10.8
Brazil	5,467	4,935	-9.7
Madagascar	137	125	-8.8
Zambia	528	486	-8.0
Mexico	698	660	-5.4
Peru	779	740	-5.0
Australia	1,285	1,248	-2.9
Congo	227	223	-1.8

DESERTIFICATION AND DEFORESTATION

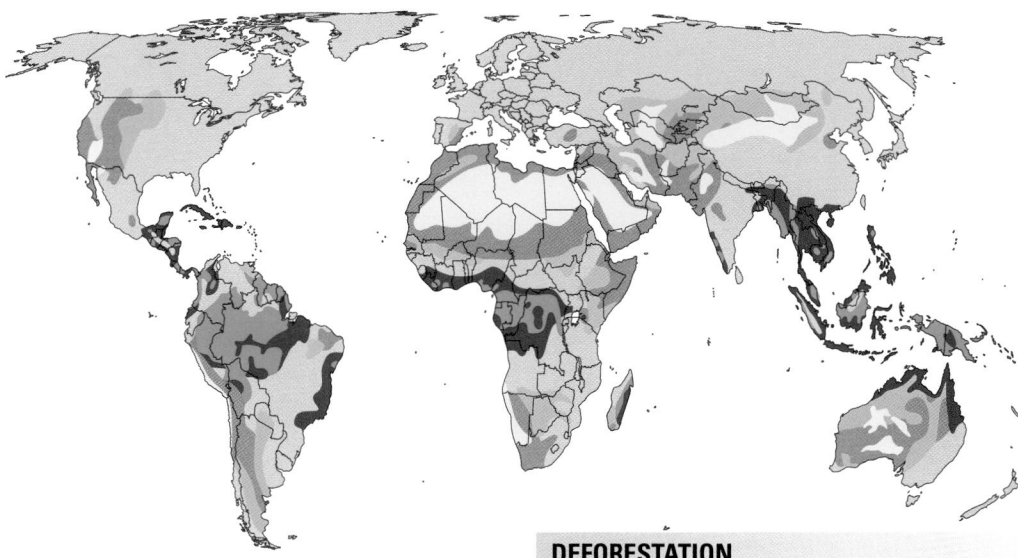

Existing deserts

Areas with a high risk of desertification

Areas with a moderate risk of desertification

Former areas of rainforest

Existing rainforest

DEFORESTATION

The Earth's remaining forests are under attack from three directions: expanding agriculture, logging, and growing consumption of fuelwood, often in combination. Sometimes deforestation is the direct result of government policy, as in the efforts made to resettle the urban poor in some parts of Brazil; just as often, it comes about despite state attempts at conservation. Loggers, licensed or unlicensed, blaze a trail into virgin forest, often destroying twice as many trees as they harvest. Landless farmers follow, burning away most of what remains to plant their crops, completing the destruction. However, some countries such as Vietnam, Philippines and Costa Rica have successfully implemented reafforestation programmes.

Population

DEMOGRAPHIC PROFILES

Developed nations such as the UK have populations evenly spread across the age groups and, usually, a growing proportion of elderly people. The great majority of the people in developing nations, however, are in the younger age groups, about to enter their most fertile years. In time, these population profiles should resemble the world profile (even Nigeria has made recent progress by reducing its birth rate), but the transition will come about only after a few more generations of rapid population growth.

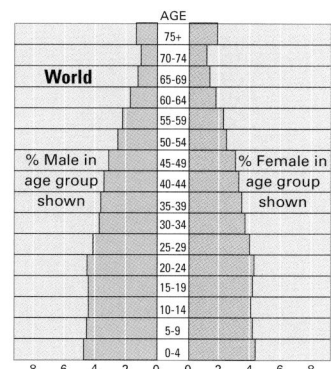

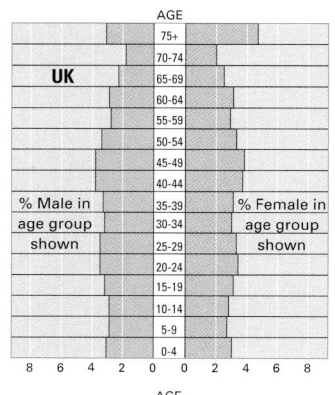

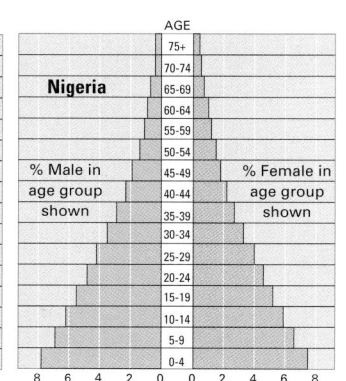

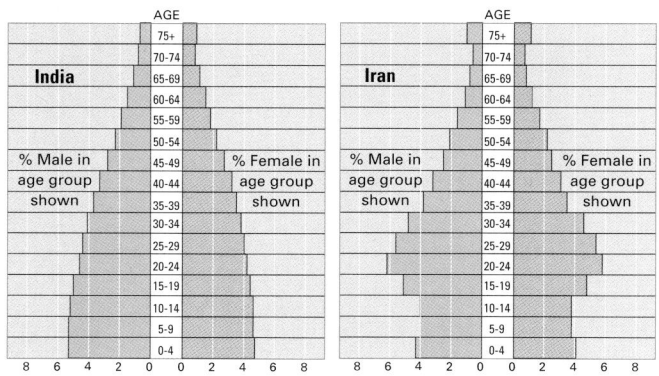

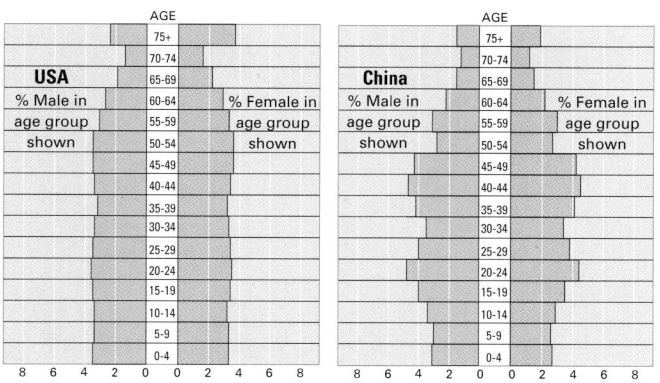

MOST POPULOUS NATIONS

Totals in millions (2017 estimates)

1. China 1,379	9. Russia 142	17. Iran 82
2. India 1,282	10. Japan 126	18. Turkey 81
3. USA 327	11. Mexico 125	19. Germany 81
4. Indonesia 261	12. Ethiopia 105	20. Thailand 68
5. Brazil 207	13. Philippines 104	21. France 67
6. Pakistan 205	14. Egypt 97	22. UK 65
7. Nigeria 191	15. Vietnam 96	23. Italy 62
8. Bangladesh 158	16. Congo (Dem. Rep.) 83	24. Myanmar (Burma) 55

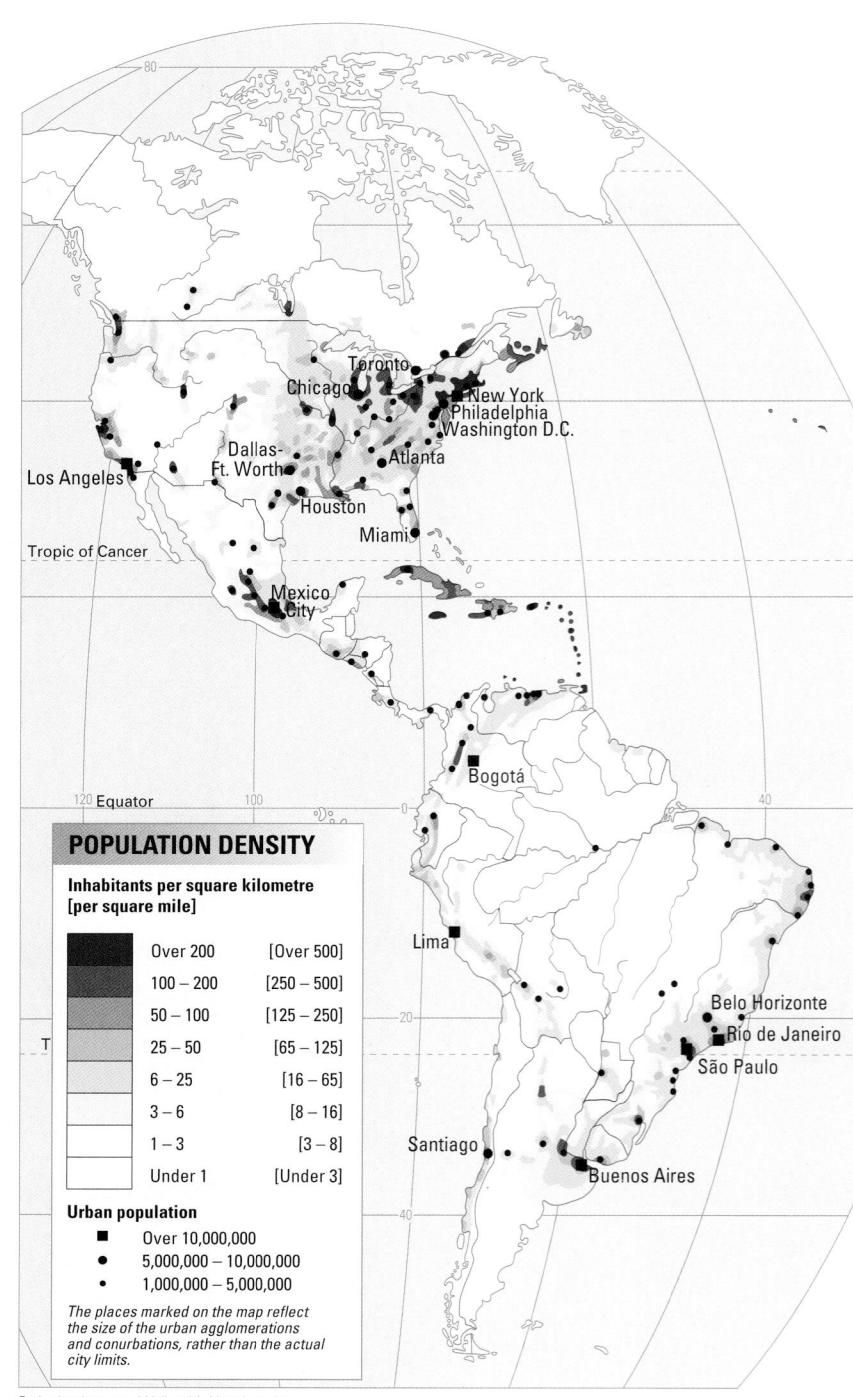

POPULATION DENSITY

Inhabitants per square kilometre [per square mile]

Over 200	[Over 500]
100 – 200	[250 – 500]
50 – 100	[125 – 250]
25 – 50	[65 – 125]
6 – 25	[16 – 65]
3 – 6	[8 – 16]
1 – 3	[3 – 8]
Under 1	[Under 3]

Urban population

■ Over 10,000,000
● 5,000,000 – 10,000,000
· 1,000,000 – 5,000,000

The places marked on the map reflect the size of the urban agglomerations and conurbations, rather than the actual city limits.

Projection: *Interrupted Mollweide's Homolographic*

CONTINENTAL COMPARISONS

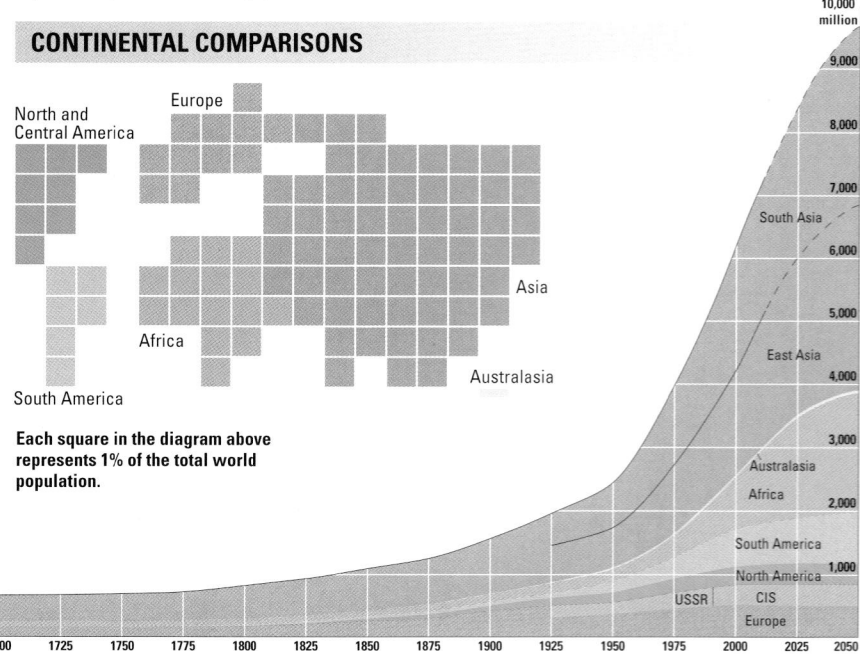

Each square in the diagram above represents 1% of the total world population.

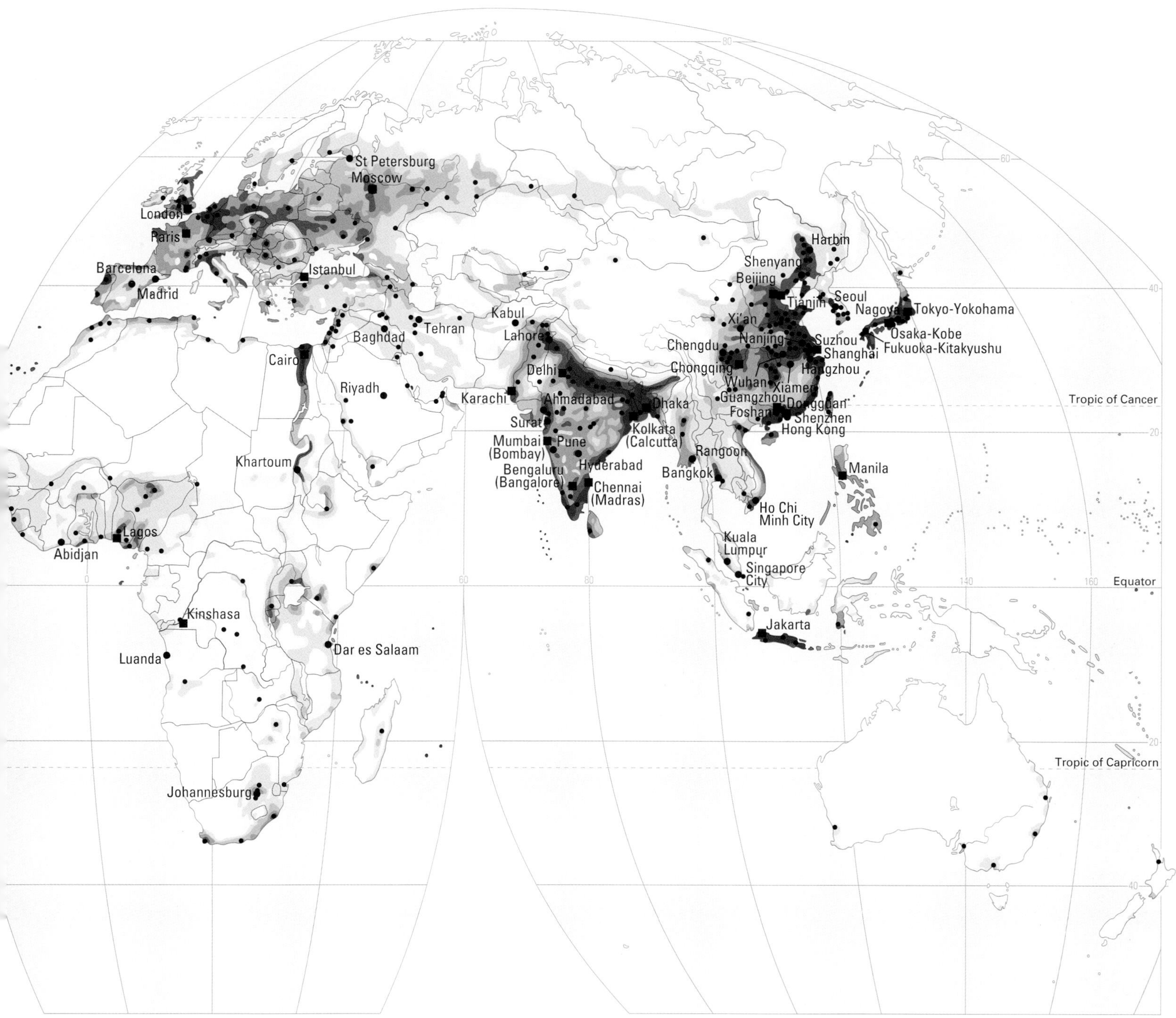

St Petersburg
Moscow
London
Paris
Barcelona
Madrid
Istanbul
Kabul
Baghdad
Tehran
Lahore
Cairo
Riyadh
Karachi
Delhi
Ahmadabad
Dhaka
Surat
Kolkata
(Calcutta)
Mumbai Pune
(Bombay)
Bengaluru Hyderabad
(Bangalore)
Chennai
(Madras)
Khartoum
Khartoum
Lagos
Abidjan
Kinshasa
Luanda
Dar es Salaam
Johannesburg

Harbin
Shenyang
Beijing
Xi'an
Chengdu
Chongqing
Wuhan
Nanjing
Tianjin
Seoul
Nagoya Tokyo-Yokohama
Osaka-Kobe
Suzhou
Shanghai Fukuoka-Kitakyushu
Hangzhou
Xiamen
Guangzhou Dongguan
Foshan Shenzhen
Hong Kong
Rangoon
Bangkok
Manila
Ho Chi
Minh City
Kuala
Lumpur
Singapore
City
Jakarta

Tropic of Cancer

Equator

Tropic of Capricorn

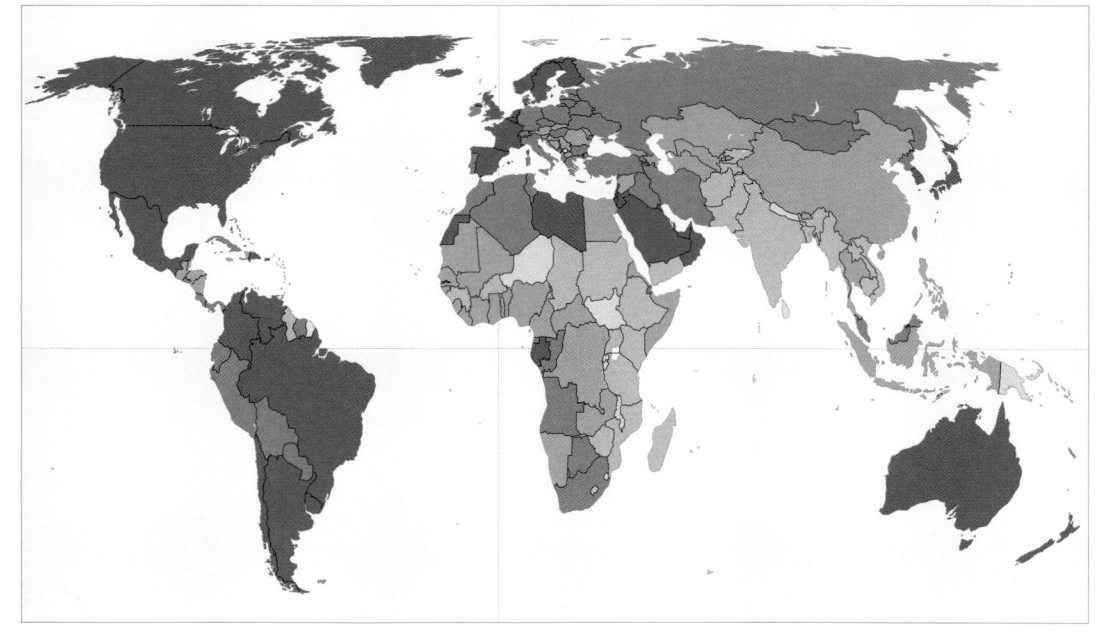

URBAN POPULATION

Percentage of total population living in towns and cities
(2018)

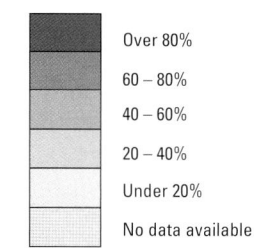

Over 80%

60 – 80%

40 – 60%

20 – 40%

Under 20%

No data available

Most urbanized		Least urbanized	
Singapore	100%	Burundi	13%
Kuwait	100%	Papua New Guinea	13%
Monaco	100%	Liechtenstein	14%
Kuwait	100%	Niger	16%
Qatar	99%	Malawi	17%

The Human Family

PREDOMINANT LANGUAGES

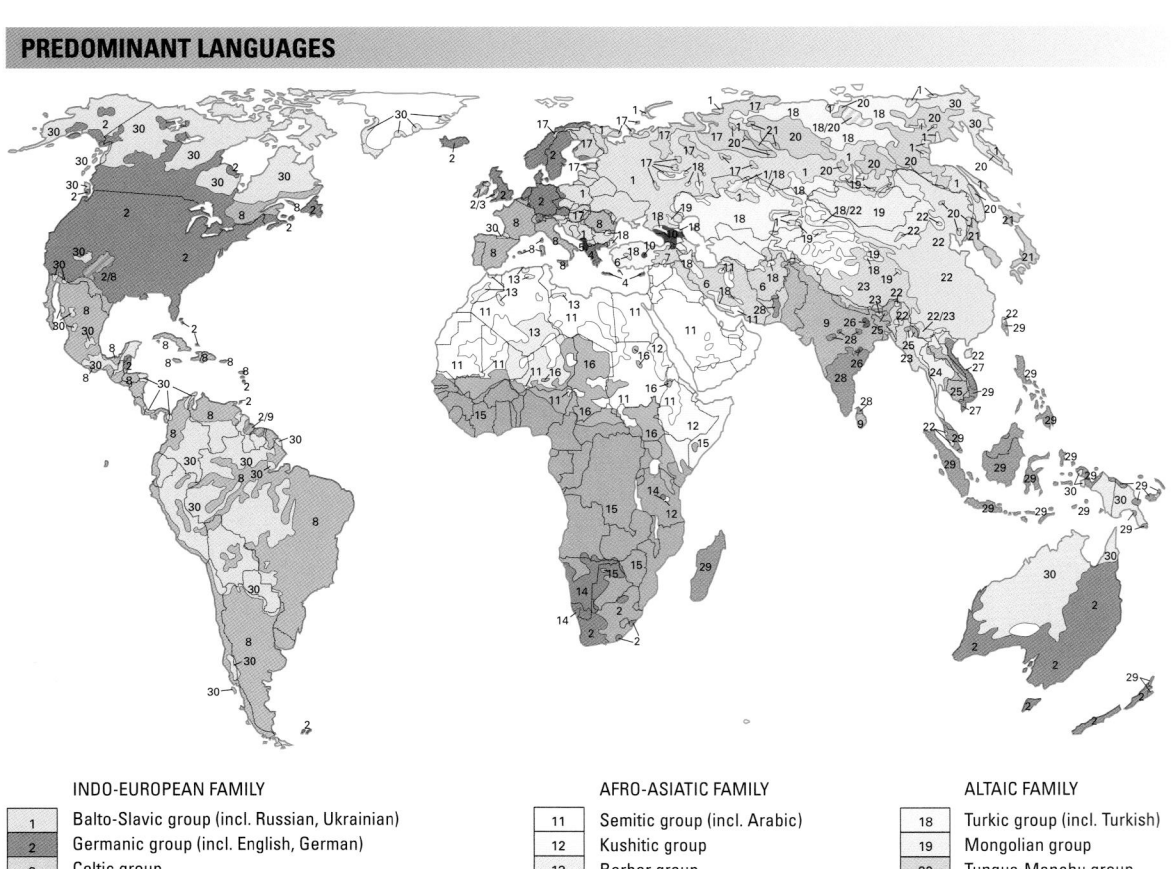

INDO-EUROPEAN FAMILY

1	Balto-Slavic group (incl. Russian, Ukrainian)
2	Germanic group (incl. English, German)
3	Celtic group
4	Greek
5	Albanian
6	Iranian group
7	Armenian
8	Romance group (incl. Spanish, Portuguese, French, Italian)
9	Indo-Aryan group (incl. Hindi, Bengali, Urdu, Punjabi, Marathi)
10	CAUCASIAN FAMILY

AFRO-ASIATIC FAMILY

11	Semitic group (incl. Arabic)
12	Kushitic group
13	Berber group
14	KHOISAN FAMILY
15	NIGER-CONGO FAMILY
16	NILO-SAHARAN FAMILY
17	URALIC FAMILY

ALTAIC FAMILY

18	Turkic group (incl. Turkish)
19	Mongolian group
20	Tungus-Manchu group
21	Japanese and Korean

SINO-TIBETAN FAMILY

22	Sinitic (Chinese) languages (incl. Mandarin, Wu, Yue)
23	Tibetic-Burmic languages
24	TAI FAMILY

AUSTRO-ASIATIC FAMILY

25	Mon-Khmer group
26	Munda group
27	Vietnamese
28	DRAVIDIAN FAMILY (incl. Telugu, Tamil)
29	AUSTRONESIAN FAMILY (incl. Malay-Indonesian, Javanese)
30	OTHER LANGUAGES

LANGUAGES OF THE WORLD

Language can be classified by ancestry and structure. For example, the Romance and Germanic groups are both derived from an Indo-European language believed to have been spoken 5,000 years ago.

First-language speakers, in millions
Mandarin Chinese 850, Spanish 430, English 340, Hindi 260, Arabic 240, Portuguese 215, Bengali 190, Russian 160, Japanese 130, Javanese 84, French 80, German 78, Wu Chinese 77, Korean 77, Telugu 74, Marathi 72, Tamil 69, Vietnamese 68, Italian 64, Punjabi 63.

Distribution of Living Languages

The figures refer to the number of languages currently in use in the regions shown

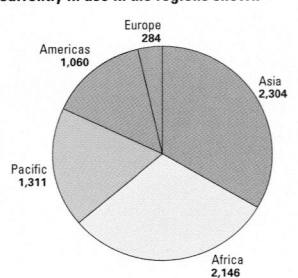

Europe 284
Americas 1,060
Asia 2,304
Pacific 1,311
Africa 2,146

PREDOMINANT RELIGIONS

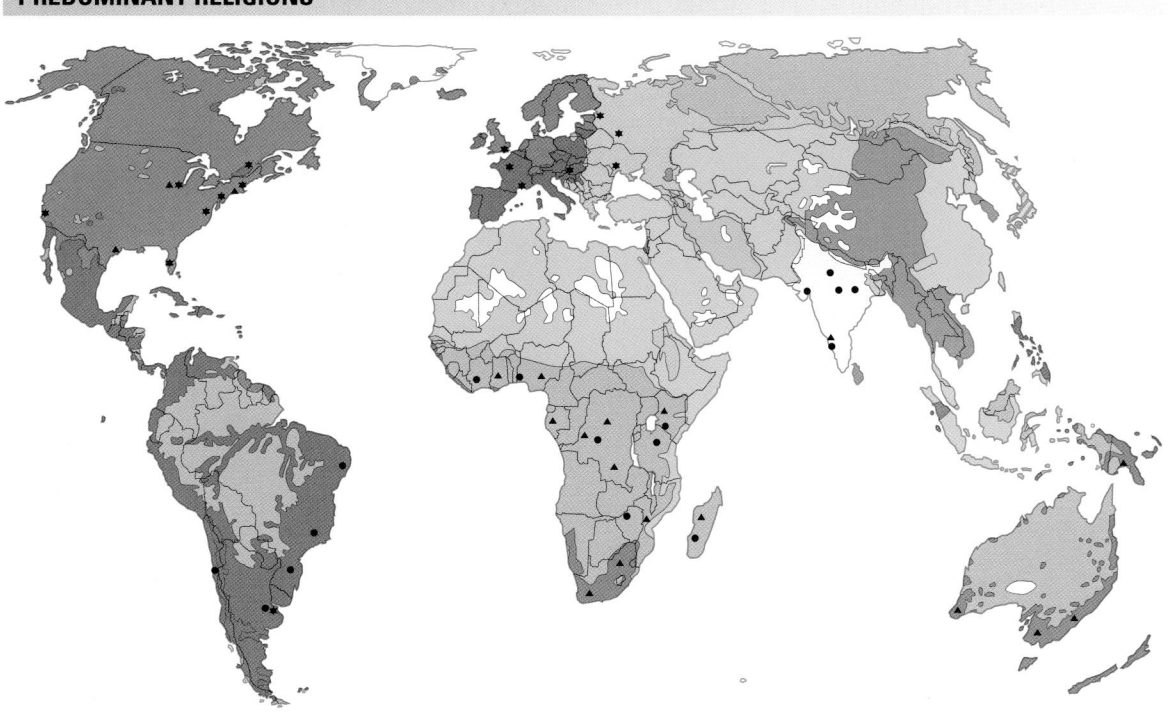

RELIGIOUS ADHERENTS

Religious adherents in millions

Christianity	2,000	Chinese traditional	394
Roman Catholic	*1,500*	Buddhism	360
Orthodox	*225*	Sikhism	23
Anglican	*70*	Taoism	20
Lutheran	*66*	Judaism	14
Methodist	*8*	Mormonism	12
Islam	1,300	Spiritism	11
Sunni	*940*	Baha'i	6
Shi'ite	*120*	Confucianism	5
Non-religious	1,100	Jainism	4
Hinduism	900	Shintoism	4

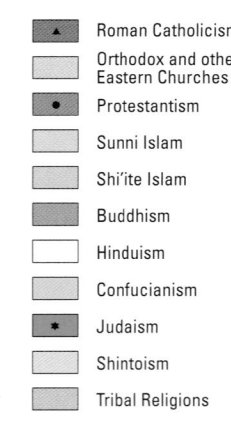

▲ Roman Catholicism

Orthodox and other Eastern Churches

● Protestantism

Sunni Islam

Shi'ite Islam

Buddhism

Hinduism

Confucianism

★ Judaism

Shintoism

Tribal Religions

UNITED NATIONS

Created in 1945 to promote peace and co-operation, and based in New York, the United Nations is the world's largest international organization, with 193 members and an annual budget of US $5.4 billion (2018-19). Each member of the General Assembly has one vote, while the five permanent members of the 15-nation Security Council – China, France, Russia, the UK and the USA – each hold a veto. The Secretariat is the UN's principal administrative arm. The 54 members of the Economic and Social Council are responsible for economic, social, cultural, educational, health and related matters. The UN has 16 specialized agencies – based in Canada, France, Switzerland and Italy, as well as the USA – which help members in fields such as education (UNESCO), agriculture (FAO), medicine (WHO) and finance (IFC). By the end of 1994, all the original 11 trust territories of the Trusteeship Council had become independent.

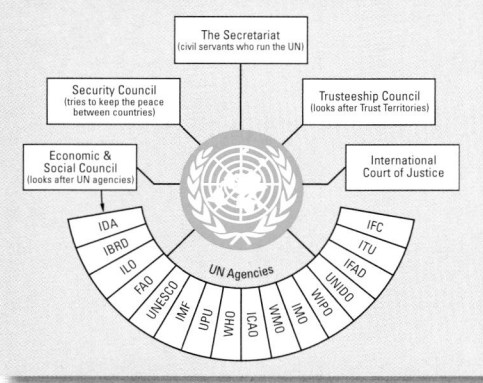

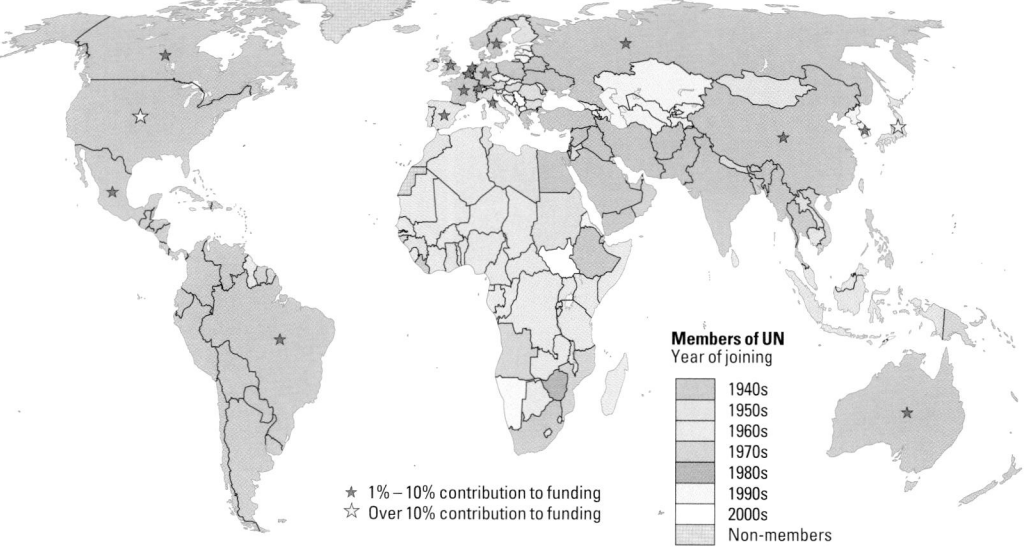

Members of UN
Year of joining

- 1940s
- 1950s
- 1960s
- 1970s
- 1980s
- 1990s
- 2000s
- Non-members

★ 1% – 10% contribution to funding
☆ Over 10% contribution to funding

MEMBERSHIP OF THE UN From the original 51, membership of the UN has now grown to 193. Recent additions include Switzerland, Montenegro and South Sudan. There are only two independent states which are not members of the UN – Taiwan and the Vatican City. All the successor states of the former USSR had joined by the end of 1992. The official languages of the UN are Chinese, English, French, Russian, Spanish and Arabic.

FUNDING The UN budget for 2018-19 was US $5.4 billion. Contributions are assessed by the members' ability to pay, with the maximum 22% of the total (USA's share), and the minimum 0.001%. The 28-member EU pays 35% of the budget.

PEACEKEEPING The UN has been involved in 67 peacekeeping operations worldwide since 1948.

INTERNATIONAL ORGANIZATIONS

ACP African-Caribbean-Pacific (formed in 1963). Members have economic ties with the EU.

APEC Asia-Pacific Economic Co-operation (formed in 1989). It aims to enhance economic growth and prosperity for the region and to strengthen the Asia-Pacific community. APEC is the only intergovernmental grouping in the world operating on the basis of non-binding commitments, open dialogue, and equal respect for the views of all participants. There are 21 member economies.

ARAB LEAGUE (formed in 1945). The League's aim is to promote economic, social, political and military co-operation. There are 22 member nations. Syria's membership was suspended in 2011.

ASEAN Association of South-east Asian Nations (formed in 1967). Cambodia joined in 1999.

AU The African Union replaced the Organization of African Unity (formed in 1963) in 2002. Its 55 members represent over 94% of Africa's population. Arabic, English, French and Portuguese are recognized as working languages.

COLOMBO PLAN (formed in 1951). Its 27 members aim to promote economic and social development in Asia and the Pacific.

COMMONWEALTH The Commonwealth of Nations evolved from the British Empire. Pakistan was suspended in 1999, but reinstated in 2004. Zimbabwe was suspended in 2002 and, in response to its continued suspension, Zimbabwe left the Commonwealth in 2003. Fiji was suspended in 2006 following a military coup. Rwanda joined the Commonwealth in 2009, as the 54th member state. The Gambia left in 2013. There are currently 53 members.

EU European Union (evolved from the European Community in 1993). Cyprus, Czechia, Estonia, Hungary, Latvia, Lithuania, Malta, Poland, Slovakia and Slovenia joined the EU in May 2004; Bulgaria and Romania joined in 2007; Croatia joined in 2013. The other 15 members of the EU are Austria, Belgium, Denmark, Finland, France, Germany, Greece, Ireland, Italy, Luxembourg, Netherlands, Portugal, Spain, Sweden and the UK. There are currently 28 members: the UK is scheduled to leave the EU in 2019.

LAIA Latin American Integration Association (1980). Its aim is to promote freer regional trade.

NATO North Atlantic Treaty Organization (formed in 1949). It continues despite the winding-up of the Warsaw Pact in 1991. Bulgaria, Estonia, Latvia, Lithuania, Romania, Slovakia and Slovenia became members in 2004, Albania and Croatia in 2009. Montenegro joined in 2017.

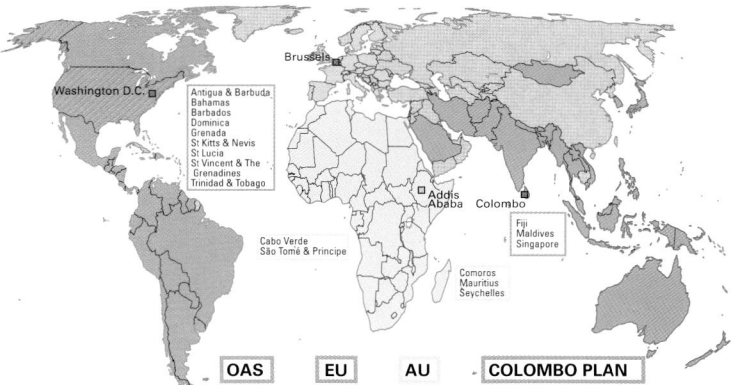

OAS Organization of American States (formed in 1948). It aims to promote social and economic co-operation between countries in developed North America and developing Latin America.

OECD Organization for Economic Co-operation and Development (formed in 1961). It comprises 35 major free-market economies. Chile, Estonia, Israel and Slovenia joined in 2010. The 'G7' is its 'inner group' of leading industrial nations, comprising Canada, France, Germany, Italy, Japan, the UK and the USA.

OPEC Organization of Petroleum Exporting Countries (formed in 1960). It controls about three-quarters of the world's oil supply. Gabon rejoined in 2016.

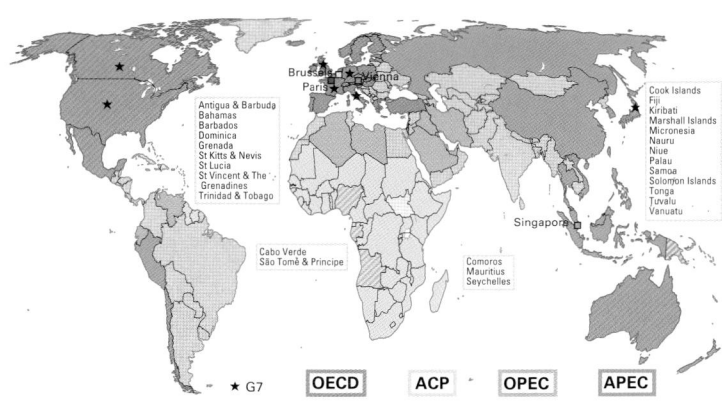

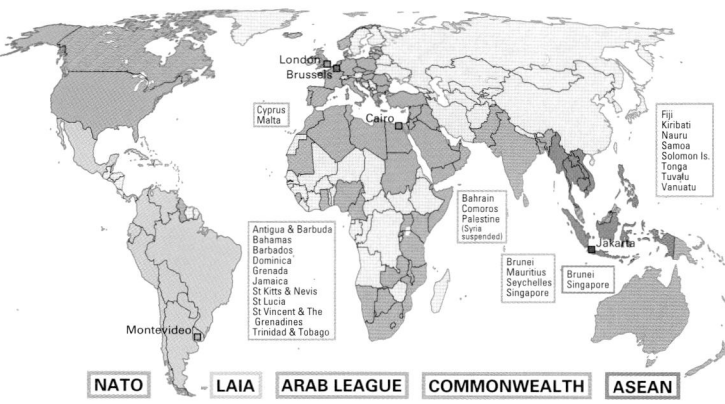

Wealth

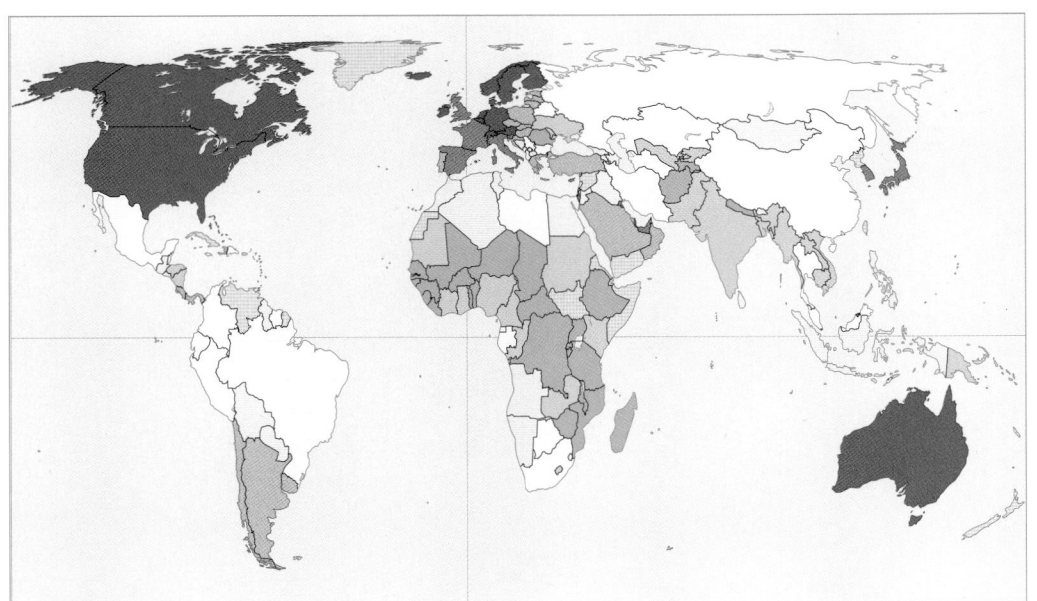

LEVELS OF INCOME

Gross National Income per capita: the value of total production divided by the population (2017)

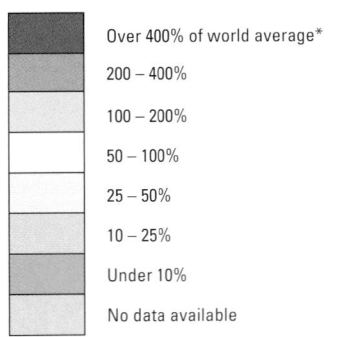

- Over 400% of world average*
- 200 – 400%
- 100 – 200%
- 50 – 100%
- 25 – 50%
- 10 – 25%
- Under 10%
- No data available

*World average = US$ 10,366 (2017)

WEALTH CREATION

The Gross National Income (GNI) of the world's largest economies, US $ million (2017)

#	Country	GNI	#	Country	GNI
1.	USA	18,980,259	21.	Argentina	577,148
2.	China	12,042,906	22.	Sweden	529,460
3.	Japan	4,888,124	23.	Poland	482,526
4.	Germany	3,596,610	24.	Belgium	475,205
5.	UK	2,675,928	25.	Iran	438,368
6.	France	2,548,257	26.	Thailand	411,731
7.	India	2,430,837	27.	Norway	401,390
8.	Italy	1,878,330	28.	Austria	400,263
9.	Brazil	1,796,487	29.	Nigeria	397,525
10.	Canada	1,573,492	30.	Philippines	383,509
11.	South Korea	1,460,492	31.	UAE	367,821
12.	Russia	1,355,593	32.	Hong Kong (China)	342,344
13.	Spain	1,265,880	33.	Israel	324,678
14.	Australia	1,263,489	34.	Denmark	318,623
15.	Mexico	1,112,530	35.	Pakistan	311,667
16.	Indonesia	934,365	36.	South Africa	308,189
17.	Turkey	882,852	37.	Singapore	306,048
18.	Netherlands	791,270	38.	Malaysia	305,051
19.	Switzerland	682,059	39.	Egypt	293,380
20.	Saudi Arabia	661,495	40.	Colombia	286,066

THE WEALTH GAP

The world's richest and poorest countries, by Gross National Income (GNI) per capita in US $ (2017)

Richest countries		Poorest countries	
1. Switzerland	80,560	1. Malawi	270
2. Norway	75,990	2. Burundi	280
3. Luxembourg	70,260	3. Central African Rep.	320
4. Qatar	61,070	4. Congo (Dem. Rep.)	400
5. Iceland	60,830	5. Liberia	410
6. USA	58,270	6. Niger	410
7. Ireland	55,290	7. Madagascar	440
8. Denmark	55,220	8. Guinea	460
9. Singapore	54,530	9. Ethiopia	470
10. Sweden	52,590	10. Eritrea	490
11. Australia	51,360	11. Gambia, The	510
12. Netherlands	46,180	12. Uganda	510
13. Austria	45,440	13. Guinea-Bissau	520
14. Finland	44,580	14. Togo	530
15. Germany	43,490	15. Mozambique	590
16. Canada	42,870	16. Rwanda	620
17. Belgium	41,790	17. Tanzania	630
18. UK	40,530	18. Burkina Faso	670
19. UAE	39,130	19. Mali	670
20. Japan	38,550	20. Sierra Leone	680

CONTINENTAL SHARES

Shares of population and of wealth (GNI) by continent

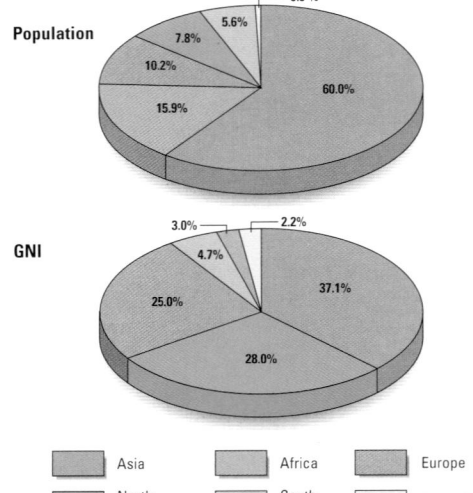

Population
- 0.5 %
- 5.6 %
- 7.8 %
- 10.2 %
- 15.9 %
- 60.0 %

GNI
- 2.2 %
- 3.0 %
- 4.7 %
- 25.0 %
- 37.1 %
- 28.0 %

Legend:
- Asia
- Africa
- Europe
- North America
- South America
- Australia

INFLATION

Average annual rate of inflation (2017)

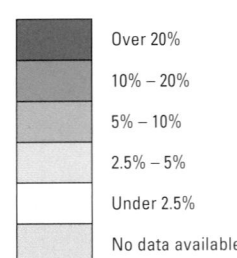

- Over 20%
- 10% – 20%
- 5% – 10%
- 2.5% – 5%
- Under 2.5%
- No data available

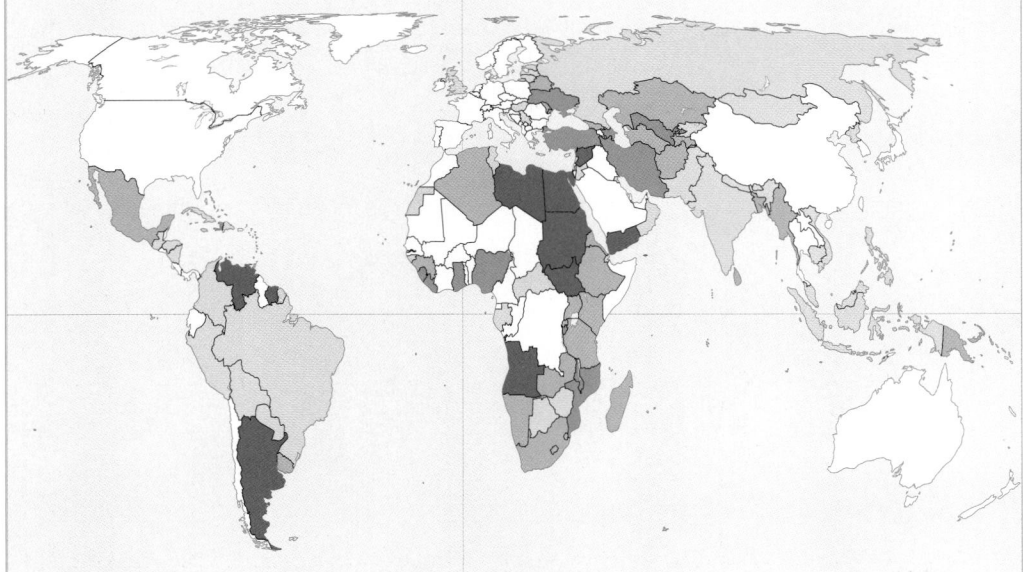

Highest average inflation		Lowest average inflation	
Venezuela	652%	Andorra	-0.9%
South Sudan	182%	Solomon Islands	-0.5%
Libya	33%	Liechtenstein	-0.4%

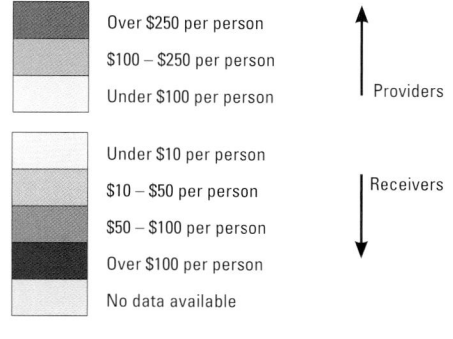

INTERNATIONAL AID

Official Development Assistance (ODA) provided and received, per capita (2016)

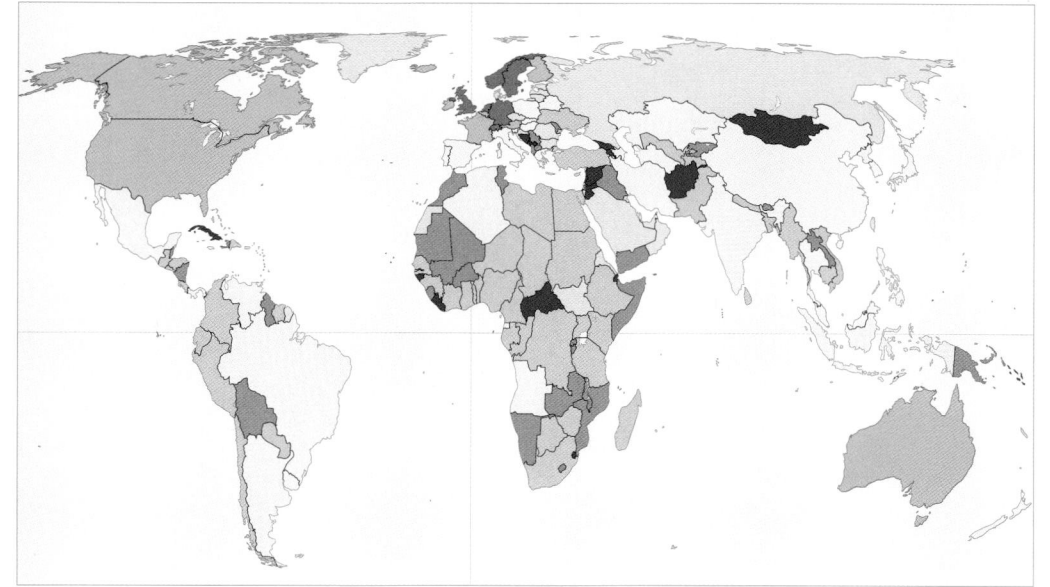

Over $250 per person
$100 – $250 per person
Under $100 per person
Providers

Under $10 per person
$10 – $50 per person
$50 – $100 per person
Over $100 per person
Receivers

No data available

DEBT AND AID

International debtors and the aid they receive

Although aid grants make a vital contribution to many of the world's poorer countries, they are usually dwarfed by the burden of debt that the developing economies are expected to repay. It is estimated that the total debt burden of developing countries has increased by 60% between 2014 and 2017. It is now at its highest level since 2004..

Debt, US$ per capita (2016)

Aid, US$ per capita (2016)

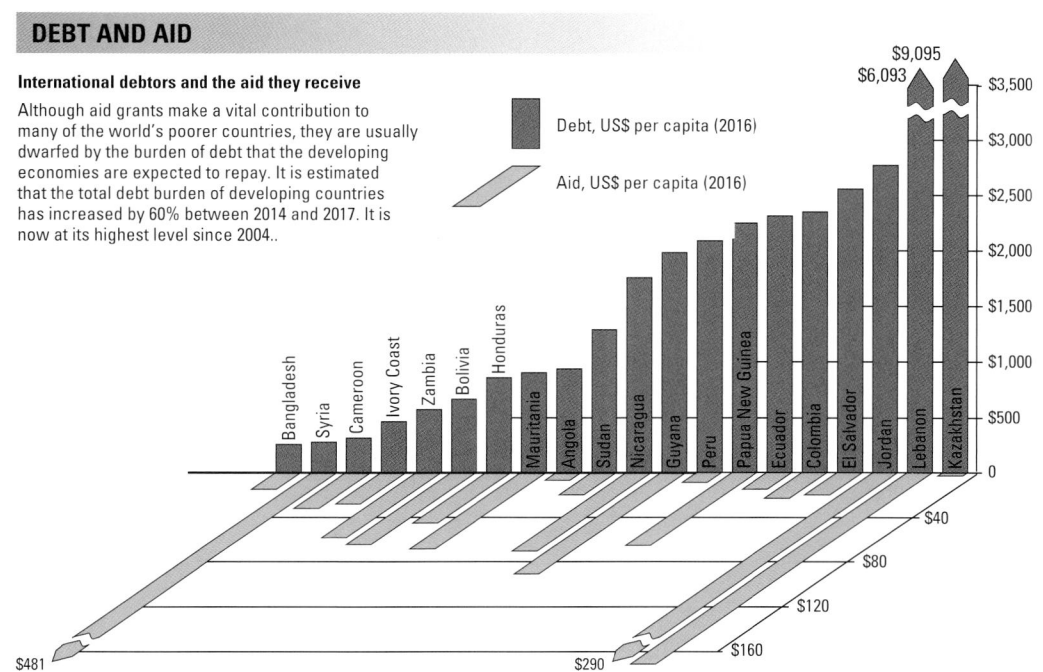

DISTRIBUTION OF SPENDING

Percentage share of household spending, selected countries

Food
Clothing
Energy & Housing
Medicine & Education
Transport
Other

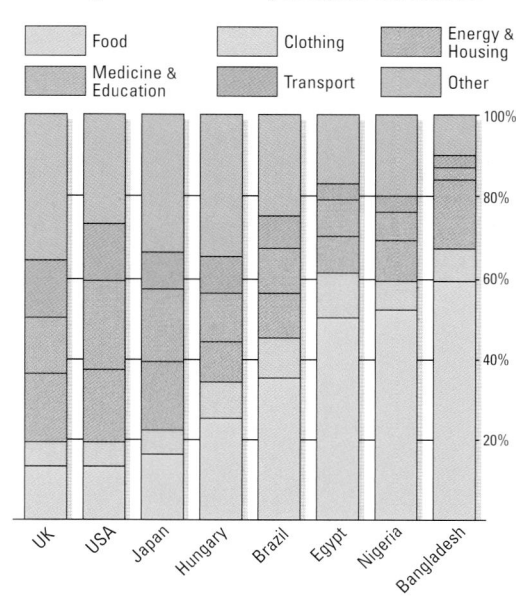

UK   USA   Japan   Hungary   Brazil   Egypt   Nigeria   Bangladesh

WEALTH INDICATORS

Number of motor vehicles, Internet users and mobile phones for each 1,000 people, selected countries (2016)

Motor vehicles   Internet users   Mobile phones

High Income

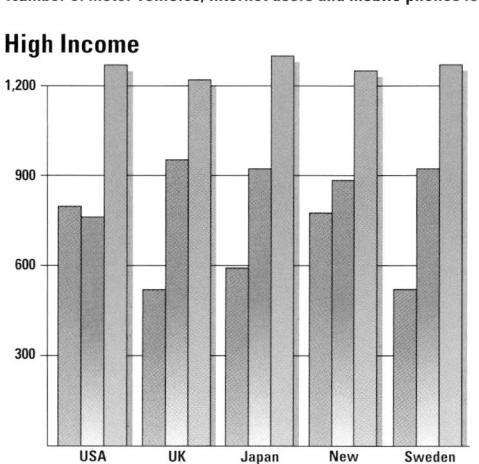

USA   UK   Japan   New Zealand   Sweden

Middle Income

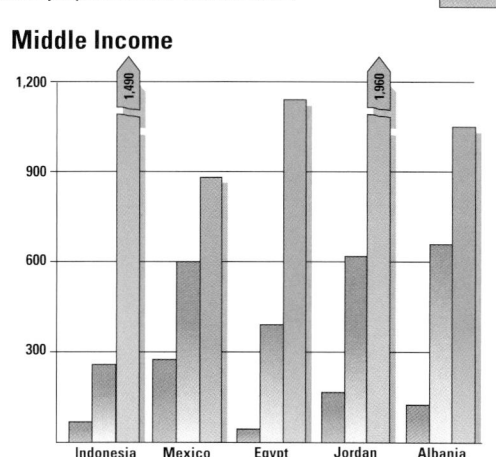

Indonesia   Mexico   Egypt   Jordan   Albania

Low Income

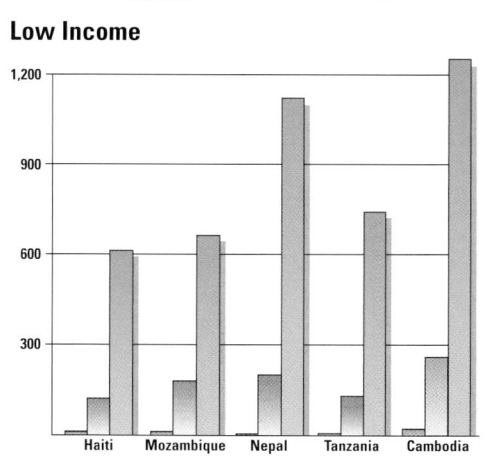

Haiti   Mozambique   Nepal   Tanzania   Cambodia

21

Quality of Life

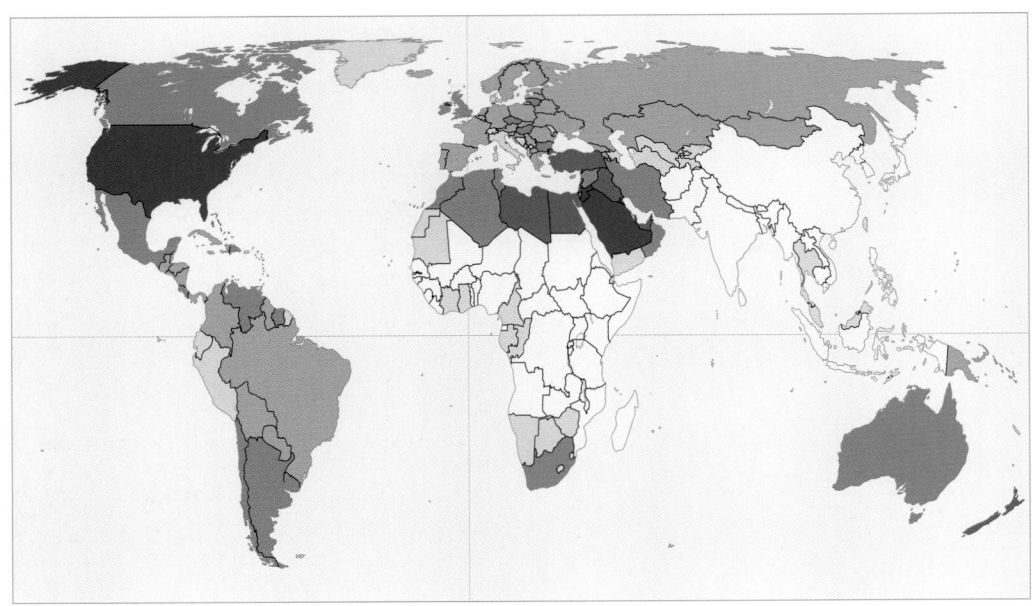

LEVEL OF OBESITY

Percentage of total adult population considered to be obese (2016)*

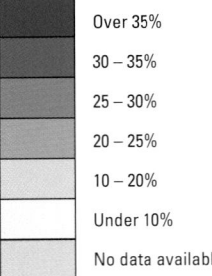

- Over 35%
- 30 – 35%
- 25 – 30%
- 20 – 25%
- 10 – 20%
- Under 10%
- No data available

*Obesity is defined as an adult having a Body Mass Index (BMI) greater than 30.0

HOSPITAL CAPACITY

Hospital beds available for each 1,000 people (2015)

Highest capacity		Lowest capacity	
Monaco	13.8	Mali	0.1
Japan	13.4	Madagascar	0.2
North Korea	13.2	Iran	0.2
South Korea	11.5	Senegal	0.3
Belarus	11.0	Niger	0.3
Ukraine	8.8	Guinea	0.3
Somalia	8.7	Ethiopia	0.3
Germany	8.3	Mauritania	0.4
Russia	8.2	Côte d'Ivoire	0.4
Austria	7.6	Chad	0.4
Turkmenistan	7.4	Burkina Faso	0.4
Liechtenstein	7.3	Uganda	0.5
Lithuania	7.3	Nigeria	0.5
Hungary	7.0	Benin	0.5
Mongolia	7.0	Afghanistan	0.5

Although the ratio of people to hospital beds gives a good approximation of a country's health provision, it is not an absolute indicator. Raw numbers may mask inefficiency and other weaknesses: the high availability of beds in Belarus, for example, has not prevented infant mortality rates over twice as high as in the United States.

LIFE EXPECTANCY

Years of life expectancy at birth, selected countries (2017)

The chart shows combined data for both sexes. On average, women live longer than men worldwide, even in developing countries with high maternal mortality rates. Overall, life expectancy is steadily rising, though the difference between rich and poor nations remains dramatic.

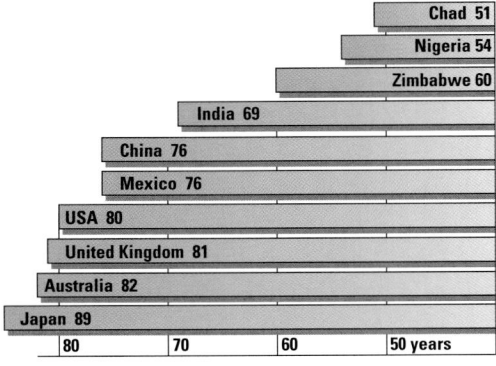

- Chad 51
- Nigeria 54
- Zimbabwe 60
- India 69
- China 76
- Mexico 76
- USA 80
- United Kingdom 81
- Australia 82
- Japan 89

80   70   60   50 years

CAUSES OF DEATH

Causes of death for selected countries by percentage

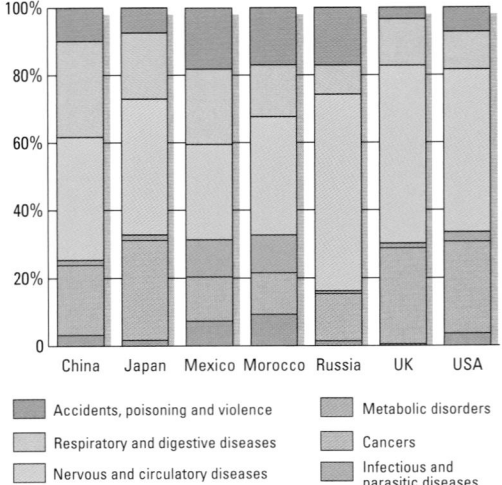

China Japan Mexico Morocco Russia UK USA

- Accidents, poisoning and violence
- Respiratory and digestive diseases
- Nervous and circulatory diseases
- Metabolic disorders
- Cancers
- Infectious and parasitic diseases

INFANT MORTALITY

Number of babies who died under the age of one, per 1,000 live births (2017)

- Over 75 deaths per 1,000 births
- 50 – 75 deaths per 1,000 births
- 25 – 50 deaths per 1,000 births
- 10 – 25 deaths per 1,000 births
- Under 10 deaths per 1,000 births
- No data available

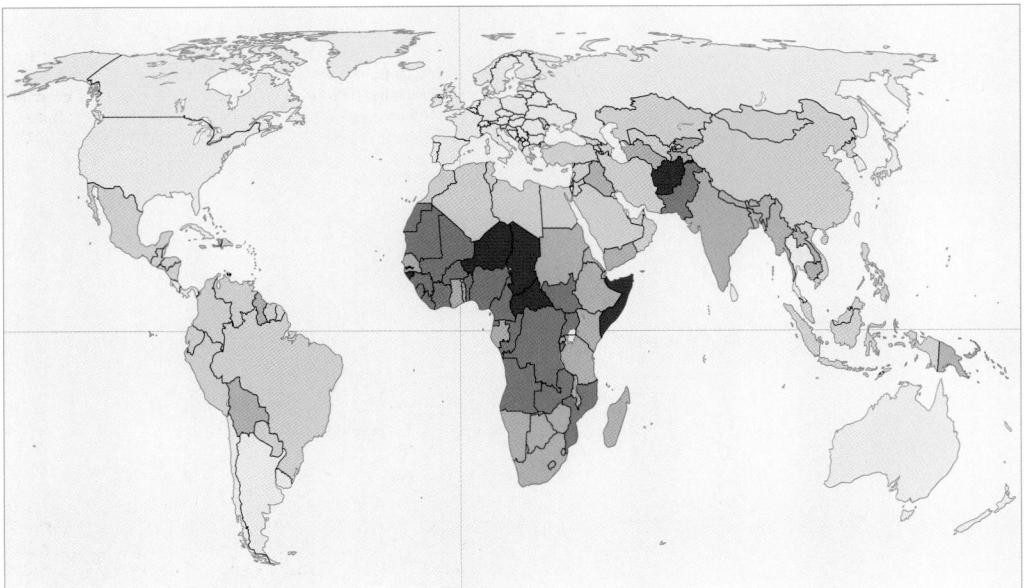

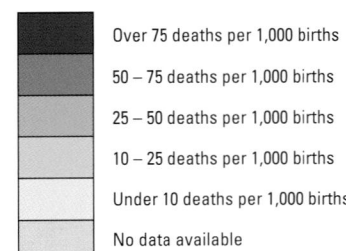

Highest infant mortality		Lowest infant mortality	
Afghanistan	111 deaths	Monaco	1.8 deaths
Somalia	95 deaths	Japan	2.0 deaths
CAR	86 deaths	Iceland	2.1 deaths

ILLITERACY

Percentage of the total adult population unable to read or write (2015)

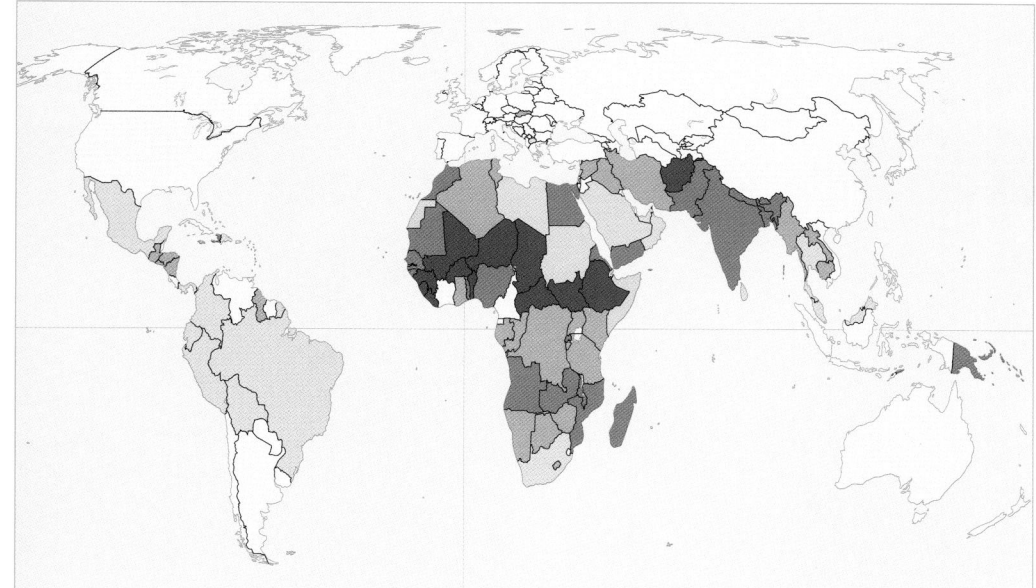

■	Over 50% of population illiterate
■	25 – 50% of population illiterate
■	10 – 25% of population illiterate
▨	5 – 10% of population illiterate
□	Under 5% of population illiterate
▨	No data available

Countries with the highest illiteracy rates as percentage of population

Niger	81%	Burkina Faso	64%
Chad	78%	CAR	63%
South Sudan	73%	Afghanistan	62%
Guinea	70%	Benin	62%
Mali	67%	Liberia	52%

FERTILITY AND EDUCATION

Fertility rates compared with female education, selected countries

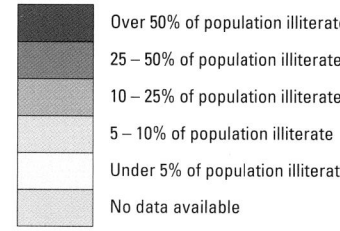

| | Percentage of females aged 12–17 in secondary education | | Fertility rate: average number of children borne per woman |

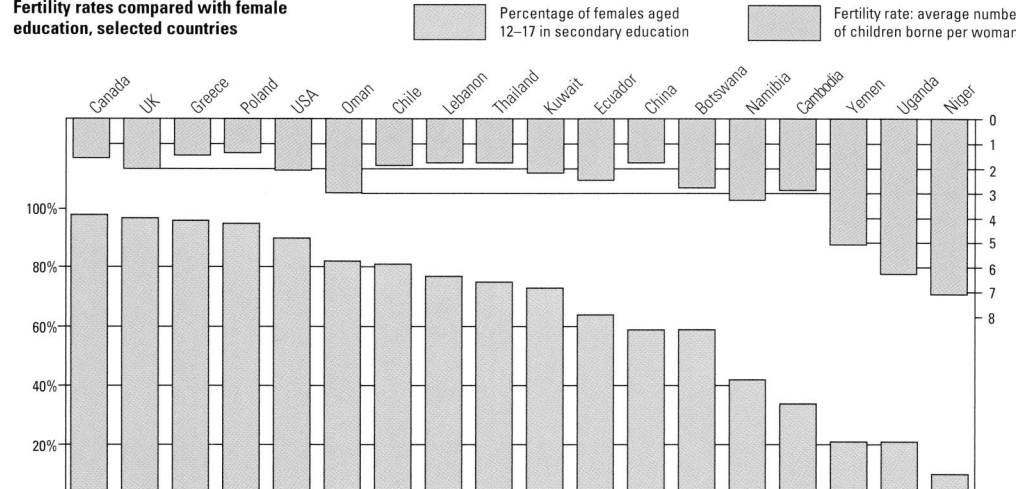

LIVING STANDARDS

At first sight, most international contrasts in living standards are swamped by differences in wealth. The rich not only have more money, they have more of everything, including years of life. Those with only a little money are obliged to spend most of it on food and clothing, the basic maintenance costs of their existence; air travel and tourism are unlikely to feature on their expenditure lists. However, poverty and wealth are both relative: slum dwellers living on social security payments in an affluent industrial country have far more resources at their disposal than an average African peasant, but feel their own poverty nonetheless. A middle-class Indian lawyer cannot command the earnings of a counterpart living in New York, London or Rome; nevertheless, he rightly sees himself as prosperous.

The rich not only live longer, on average, than the poor, they also die from different causes. Infectious and parasitic diseases, all but eliminated in the developed world, remain a scourge in the developing nations. On the other hand, more than two-thirds of the populations of OECD nations eventually succumb to cancer or circulatory disease.

HUMAN DEVELOPMENT INDEX

The Human Development Index (HDI), calculated by the UN Development Programme (UNDP), gives a value to countries using indicators of life expectancy, education and standards of living (2015). Higher values show more developed countries.

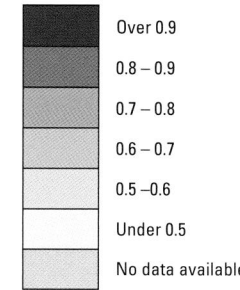

■	Over 0.9
■	0.8 – 0.9
■	0.7 – 0.8
▨	0.6 – 0.7
□	0.5 –0.6
□	Under 0.5
▨	No data available

Highest values

Norway	0.949
Australia	0.939
Switzerland	0.939
Germany	0.926
Denmark	0.925

Lowest values

Central African Rep.	0.352
Niger	0.353
Chad	0.396
Burkina Faso	0.402
Burundi	0.404

Energy

ENERGY PRODUCTION

Each square represents 1% of world primary energy production, by region

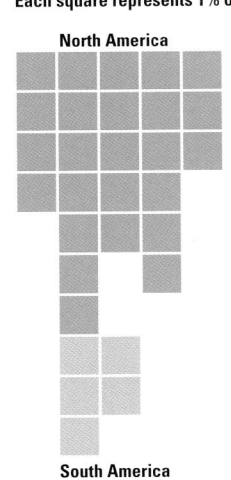

North America Western Europe Eastern Europe & Russia

Middle East

Africa

Asia

South America

Oceania

ENERGY CONSUMPTION

Each square represents 1% of world primary energy production, by region

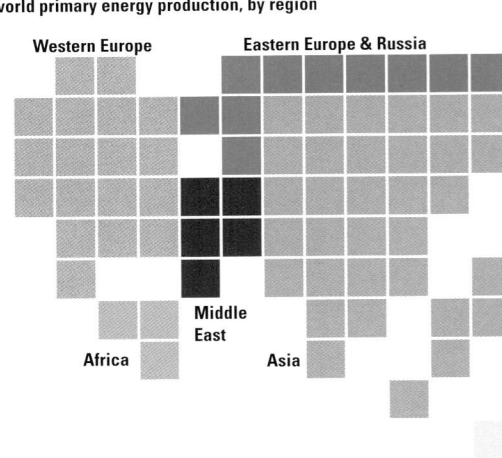

North America Western Europe Eastern Europe & Russia

Middle East

Africa

Asia

South America

Oceania

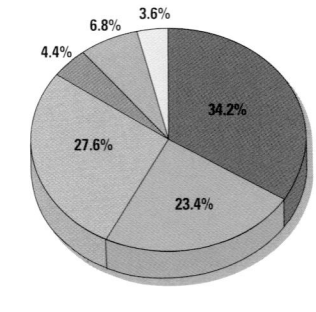

ENERGY BALANCE

Difference between energy production and consumption in millions of tonnes of oil equivalent (MtOe)

Energy surplus

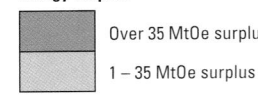

Over 35 MtOe surplus

1 – 35 MtOe surplus

Between 1 deficit – 1 surplus (approx. balance)

1 – 35 MtOe deficit

Over 35 MtOe deficit

No data available

Energy deficit

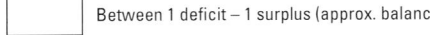

- ● Principal oilfields
- ● Secondary oilfields
- ▼ Principal gasfields
- ▽ Secondary gasfields
- ∧ Principal coalfields
- △ Secondary coalfields

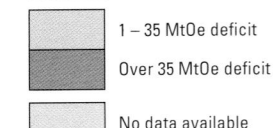

WORLD ENERGY CONSUMPTION

Energy consumed by world regions, measured in million tonnes of oil equivalent (2017)
Total world consumption was 13,513 MtOe. Only energy from oil, natural gas, coal, nuclear and hydroelectric sources are included. Excluded are biomass fuels such as wood, peat and animal waste, and wind, solar and geothermal energy which, though important locally in some countries, are not always reliably documented statistically.

World energy consumption, by source (2017)

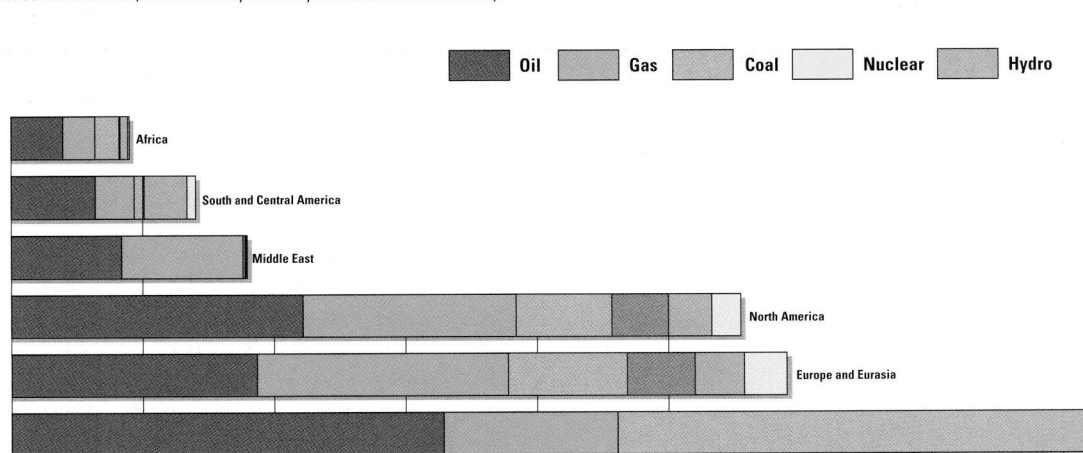

Oil   Gas   Coal   Nuclear   Hydro

Africa

South and Central America

Middle East

North America

Europe and Eurasia

Asia Pacific

0   500   1,000   1,500   2,000   2,500   3,000   3,500   4,000   4,500   5,000   5,500

million tonnes of oil equivalent

Source: BP Statistical Review of World Energy 2018

3.6%
6.8%
4.4%
34.2%
27.6%
23.4%

ENERGY

Energy is used to keep us warm or cool, fuel our industries and our transport systems, and even feed us; high-intensity agriculture, with its use of fertilizers, pesticides and machinery, is heavily energy-dependent. Although we live in a high-energy society, there are vast discrepancies between rich and poor; for example, a North American consumes six times as much energy as a Chinese person. But even developing nations have more power at their disposal than was imaginable a century ago.

The distribution of energy supplies, most importantly fossil fuels (coal, oil and natural gas), is very uneven. In addition, the diagrams and map opposite show that the largest producers of energy are not necessarily the largest consumers. The movement of energy supplies around the world is therefore an important component of international trade.

As the finite reserves of fossil fuels are depleted, renewable energy sources, such as solar, hydro-thermal, wind, tidal and biomass, will become increasingly important around the world.

NUCLEAR POWER

Major producers by percentage of world total and by percentage of domestic electricity generation (2016)

Country	% of world total production	Country	% of nuclear as proportion of domestic electricity
1. USA	32.5%	1. France	73.3%
2. France	15.6%	2. Slovakia	54.1%
3. China	8.0%	3. Ukraine	52.3%
4. Russia	7.4%	4. Belgium	51.7%
5. South Korea	6.2%	5. Hungary	51.3%
6. Canada	3.9%	6. Sweden	40.0%
7. Germany	3.2%	7. Slovenia	35.2%
8. Ukraine	3.1%	8. Bulgaria	35.9%
9. UK	2.6%	9. Switzerland	34.4%
10. Sweden	2.4%	10. Finland	33.7%

Although the 1980s were a bad time for the nuclear power industry (fears of long-term environmental damage were heavily reinforced by the 1986 disaster at Chernobyl), the industry picked up in the early 1990s. Despite this, growth has recently been curtailed whilst countries review their energy mix, in light of the March 2011 Japanese earthquake and tsunami which seriously damaged the Fukushima nuclear power station.

HYDROELECTRICITY

Major producers by percentage of world total and by percentage of domestic electricity generation (2015)

Country	% of world total production	Country	% of hydroelectric as proportion of domestic electricity
1. China	28.4%	1. Albania	100.0%
2. Brazil	9.6%	2. Paraguay	100.0%
3. Canada	9.5%	3. Nepal	99.7%
4. USA	6.3%	4. Tajikistan	99.7%
5. Russia	4.0%	5. Zambia	99.7%
6. Norway	3.5%	6. Congo (Dem. Rep.)	99.6%
7. India	3.2%	7. Mozambique	97.7%
8. Japan	2.3%	8. Norway	96.0%
9. Venezuela	2.0%	9. Ethiopia	95.6%
10. Sweden	1.9%	10. Namibia	95.6%

Countries heavily reliant on hydroelectricity are usually small and non-industrial: a high proportion of hydroelectric power more often reflects a modest energy budget than vast hydroelectric resources. The USA, for instance, produces only 6% of its power requirements from hydroelectricity; yet that 6% amounts to almost half the hydropower generated by most of Africa.

ELECTRICITY PRODUCTION

Percentage of electricity generated by source (latest available data)

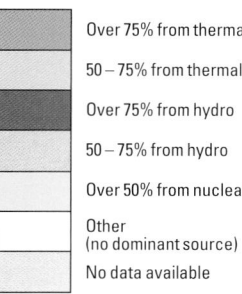

- Over 75% from thermal
- 50 – 75% from thermal
- Over 75% from hydro
- 50 – 75% from hydro
- Over 50% from nuclear
- Other (no dominant source)
- No data available

● Selected geothermal plants

◇ Selected hydroelectric plants

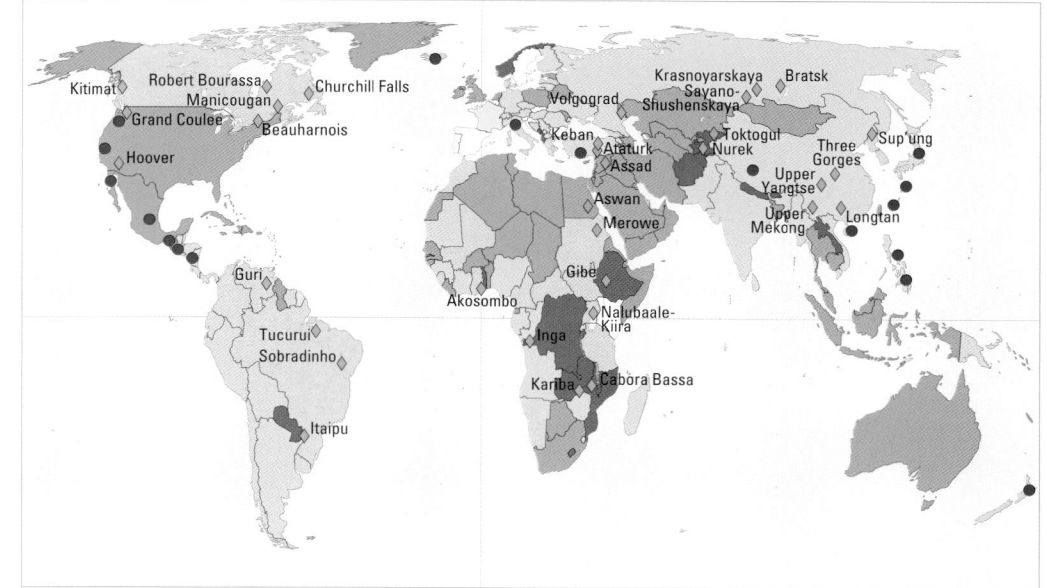

Conversion Rates

1 barrel = 0.136 tonnes or 159 litres or 35 Imperial gallons or 42 US gallons

1 tonne = 7.33 barrels or 1,185 litres or 256 Imperial gallons or 261 US gallons

1 tonne oil = 1.5 tonnes hard coal or 3.0 tonnes lignite or 12,000 kWh

1 Imperial gallon = 1.201 US gallons or 4.546 litres or 277.4 cubic inches

Measurements
For historical reasons, oil is traded in 'barrels'. The weight and volume equivalents (shown right) are all based on average-density 'Arabian light' crude oil.

The energy equivalents given for a tonne of oil are also somewhat imprecise: oil and coal of different qualities will have varying energy contents, a fact usually reflected in their price on world markets.

ENERGY RESERVES

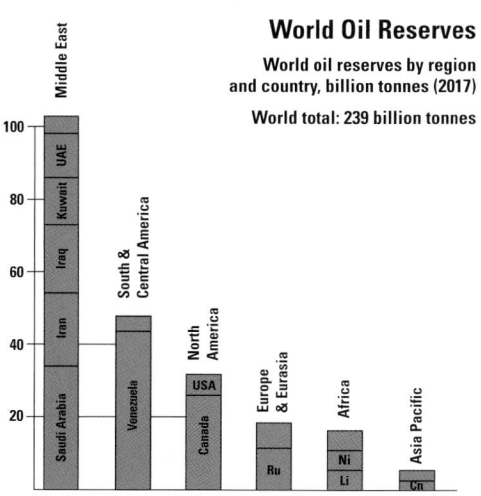

World Oil Reserves
World oil reserves by region and country, billion tonnes (2017)
World total: 239 billion tonnes

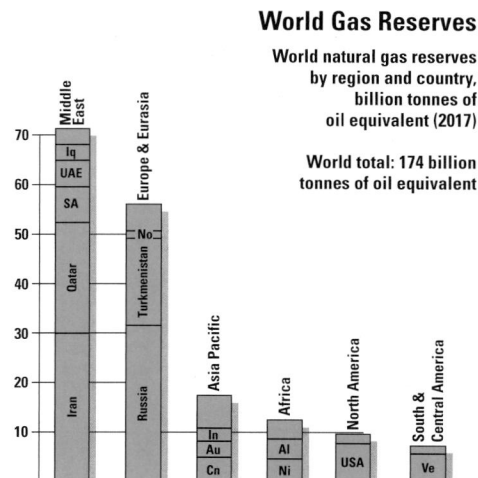

World Gas Reserves
World natural gas reserves by region and country, billion tonnes of oil equivalent (2017)
World total: 174 billion tonnes of oil equivalent

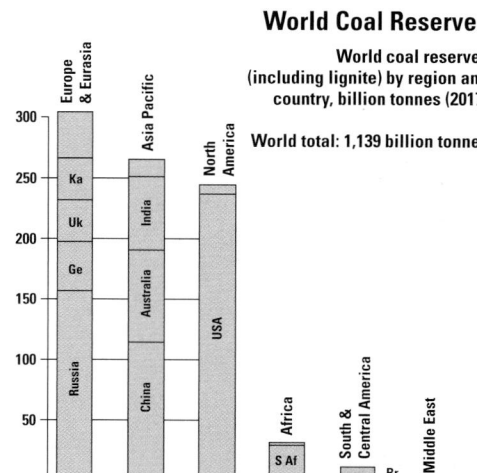

World Coal Reserves
World coal reserves (including lignite) by region and country, billion tonnes (2017)
World total: 1,139 billion tonnes

Production

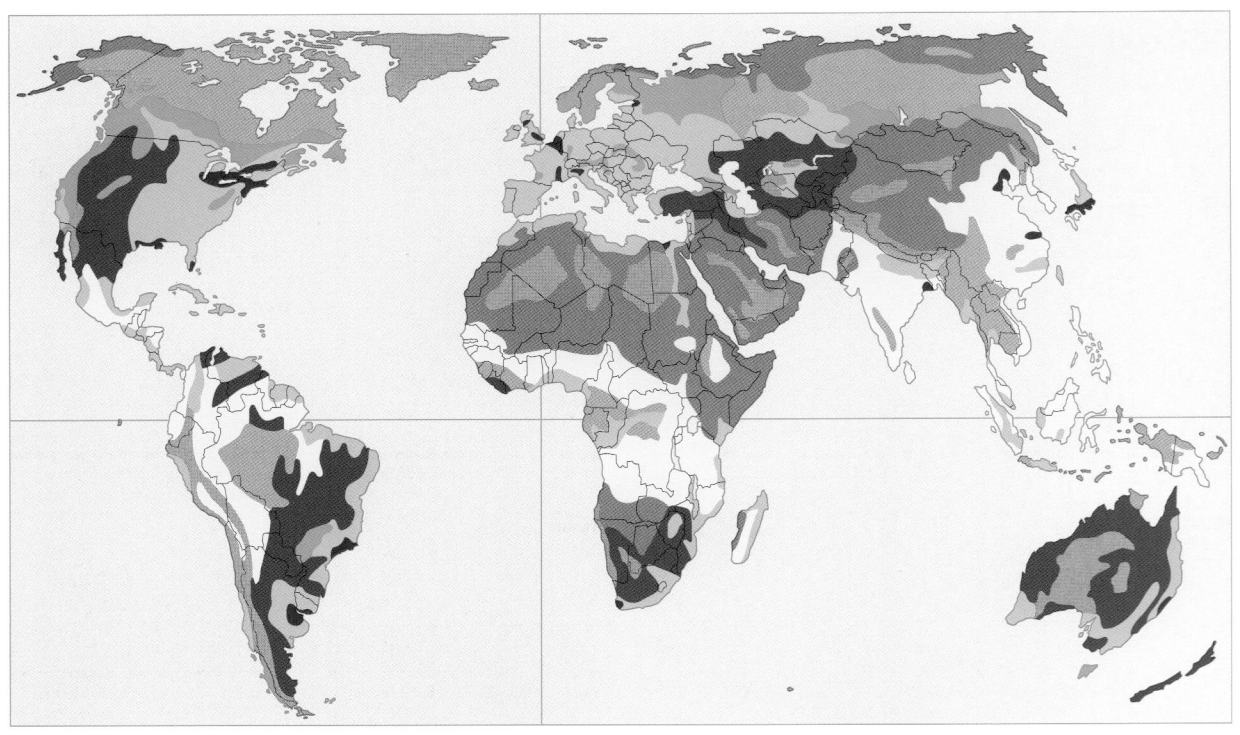

AGRICULTURE

Predominant type of farming or land use

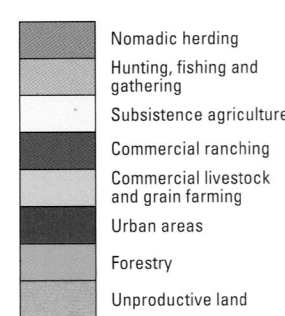

- Nomadic herding
- Hunting, fishing and gathering
- Subsistence agriculture
- Commercial ranching
- Commercial livestock and grain farming
- Urban areas
- Forestry
- Unproductive land

The development of agriculture has transformed human existence more than any other. The whole business of farming is constantly developing: due mainly to the new varieties of rice and wheat, world grain production has more than doubled since 1965. New machinery and modern agricultural techniques enable farmers to produce food for the world's developed economies, but the poorer third world relies very much on subsistence agriculture.

STAPLE CROPS

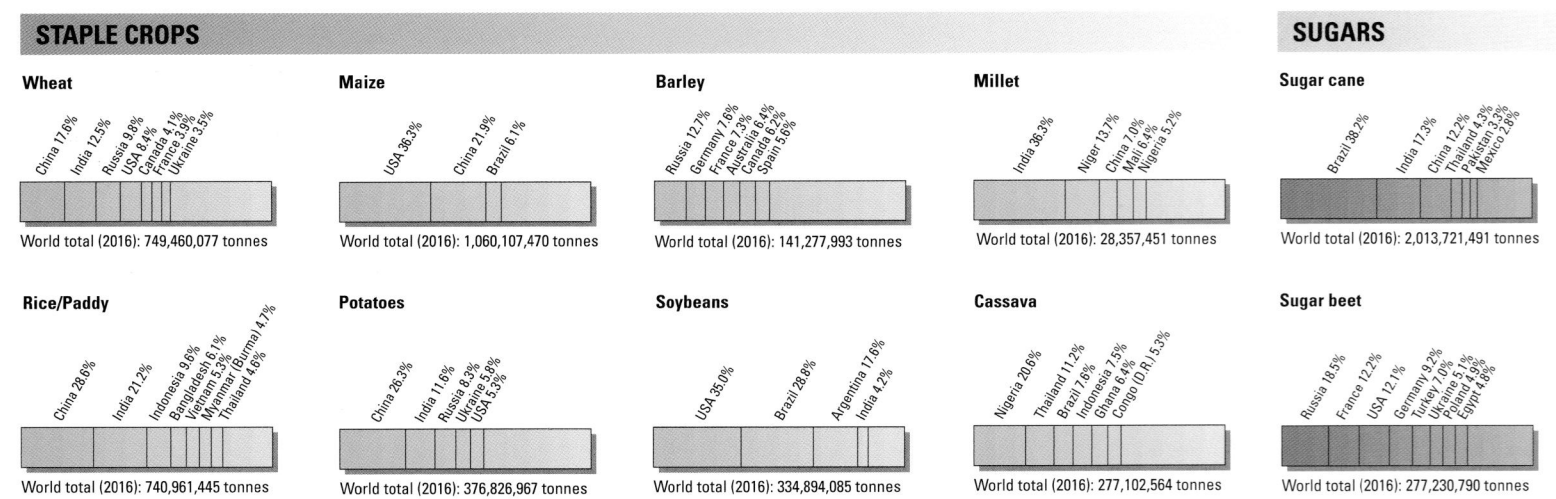

Wheat

China 17.6% | India 12.5% | Russia 9.8% | USA 8.4% | Canada 4.1% | France 3.9% | Ukraine 3.5%

World total (2016): 749,460,077 tonnes

Maize

USA 36.3% | China 21.9% | Brazil 6.1%

World total (2016): 1,060,107,470 tonnes

Barley

Russia 12.7% | Germany 7.6% | France 7.3% | Australia 6.4% | Canada 6.2% | Spain 5.6%

World total (2016): 141,277,993 tonnes

Millet

India 36.3% | Niger 13.7% | China 7.0% | Mali 6.4% | Nigeria 5.2%

World total (2016): 28,357,451 tonnes

Rice/Paddy

China 28.6% | India 21.2% | Indonesia 9.6% | Bangladesh 6.1% | Vietnam 5.3% | Myanmar (Burma) 4.7% | Thailand 4.6%

World total (2016): 740,961,445 tonnes

Potatoes

China 26.3% | India 11.5% | Russia 8.3% | Ukraine 5.8% | USA 5.5%

World total (2016): 376,826,967 tonnes

Soybeans

USA 35.0% | Brazil 28.8% | Argentina 17.6% | India 4.2%

World total (2016): 334,894,085 tonnes

Cassava

Nigeria 20.6% | Thailand 11.2% | Brazil 7.6% | Indonesia 7.5% | Ghana 6.4% | Congo (D.R.) 5.3%

World total (2016): 277,102,564 tonnes

SUGARS

Sugar cane

Brazil 38.2% | India 17.3% | China 12.2% | Thailand 4.3% | Pakistan 3.3% | Mexico 2.8%

World total (2016): 2,013,721,491 tonnes

Sugar beet

Russia 18.5% | France 12.2% | USA 12.1% | Germany 9.2% | Turkey 7.0% | Ukraine 5.1% | Poland 4.9% | Egypt 4.6%

World total (2016): 277,230,790 tonnes

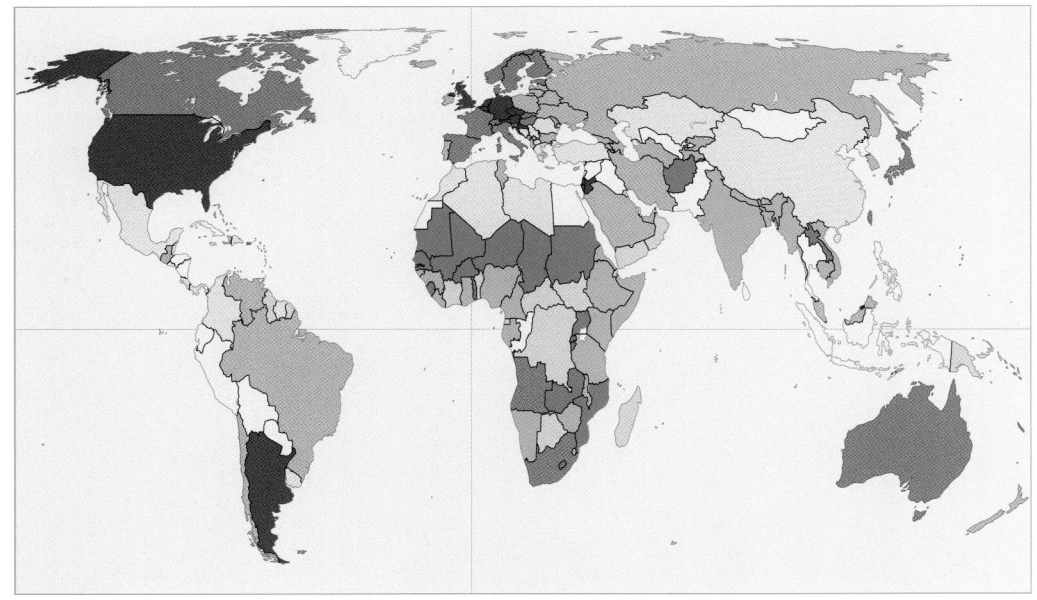

EMPLOYMENT

The number of workers employed in industry for every 100 workers engaged in agriculture (2017)

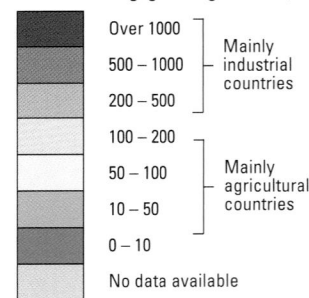

- Over 1000 — Mainly industrial countries
- 500 – 1000
- 200 – 500
- 100 – 200
- 50 – 100 — Mainly agricultural countries
- 10 – 50
- 0 – 10
- No data available

Countries with the highest number of workers employed in industry per 100 workers engaged in agriculture (2017)

1. Argentina	4,960	6. St Kitts & Nevis	2,727
2. Liechtenstein	4,613	7. Luxembourg	1,818
3. Austria	3,614	8. Germany	1,729
4. Bahrain	3,200	9. Israel	1,573
5. USA	2,900	10. Singapore	1,550

COPYRIGHT PHILIP'S

MINERAL PRODUCTION

Aluminium
China 54.3% · Russia 6.0% · Canada 5.5% · India 4.3% · UAE 4.3% · Australia 2.5% · Norway 2.0% · Bahrain 1.6% · USA 1.2%
World total (2017): 60,000,000 tonnes

Bauxite
Australia 27.7% · China 22.7% · Guinea 15.0% · Brazil 12.0% · India 9.0% · Jamaica 2.7% · Russia 1.9% · Kazakhstan 1.7%
World total (2017): 300,000,000 tonnes

Chromium
South Africa 48.4% · Kazakhstan 17.4% · India 10.3% · Turkey 9.0%
World total (2017): 31,000,000 tonnes

Copper
Chile 27.1% · Peru 12.1% · USA 6.4% · China 6.4% · Congo (Dem. Rep.) 4.7% · Australia 4.3% · Zambia 3.8% · Mexico 3.8%
World total (2017): 19,700,000 tonnes

Diamonds
Congo (Dem. Rep.) 30.6% · Russia 29.0% · Australia 22.6% · Botswana 9.7% · Zimbabwe 3.2% · South Africa 1.7%
World total (2017): 62,000,000 carats

Gold
China 14.0% · Australia 9.5% · Russia 8.1% · USA 7.8% · Canada 5.7% · Peru 4.9%
World total (2017): 3,150,000 kg (metal content)

Iron Ore
Australia 36.7% · Brazil 18.3% · China 14.2% · India 7.9% · Russia 4.4% · South Africa 2.8% · Ukraine 2.6%
World total (2017): 2,400,000 tonnes

Lead
China 51.1% · Australia 9.6% · USA 6.7% · Peru 6.4% · Russia 5.3%
World total (2017): 4,700,000 tonnes

Manganese
South Africa 33.1% · China 15.6% · Australia 13.8% · Gabon 10.0% · Brazil 7.5% · India 4.9%
World total (2017): 16,000,000 tonnes

Mercury
China 80.0% · Mexico 12.0% · Kyrgyzstan 2.0% · Peru 1.6
World total (2017): 2,500,000 tonnes (metal content)

Nickel
Indonesia 19.0% · Philippines 11.0% · Canada 10.0% · New Caledonia 10.0% · Australia 9.0% · Russia 8.6% · Brazil 6.7% · China 4.7%
World total (2017): 2,100,000 tonnes

Silver
Mexico 22.4% · Peru 18.0% · China 10.0% · Russia 6.4% · Poland 5.6% · Chile 4.8% · Australia 4.8% · Bolivia 4.8%
World total (2017): 25,000 tonnes (metal content)

Tin
China 34.5% · Indonesia 17.2% · Myanmar 17.2% · Brazil 8.8% · Peru 6.2% · Bolivia 6.2% · Australia 2.4%
World total (2017): 290,000 tonnes

Uranium
Kazakhstan 39.4% · Canada 22.5% · Australia 10.1% · Namibia 5.9% · Niger 5.0% · Russia 4.8%
World total (2016): 63,366 tonnes

Zinc
China 38.6% · Peru 10.6% · India 9.8% · Australia 7.6% · USA 5.5% · Mexico 5.2% · Bolivia 3.8%
World total (2017): 13,200,000 tonnes

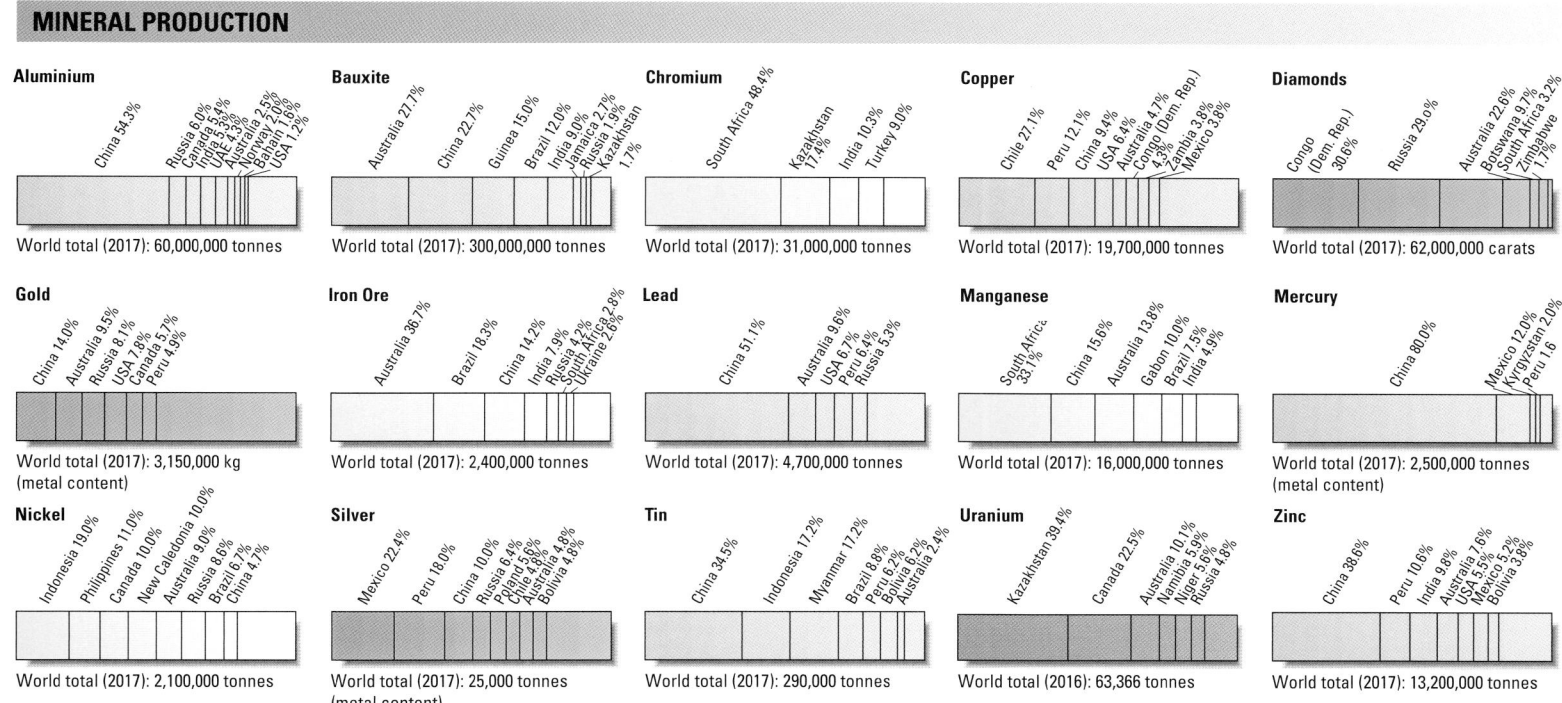

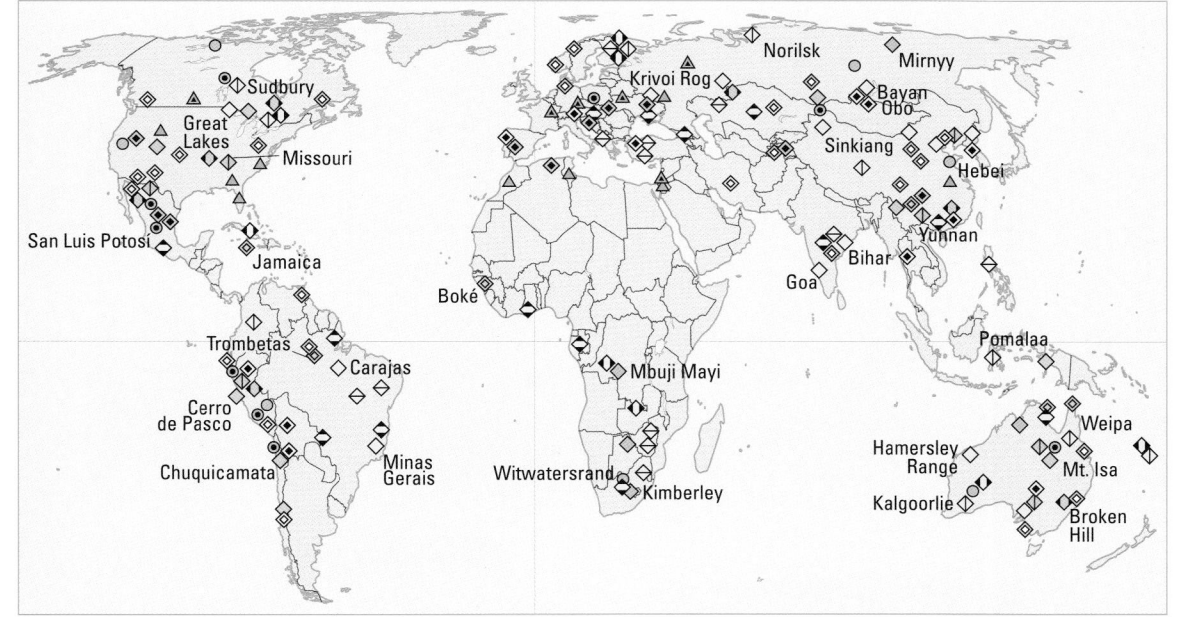

MINERAL DISTRIBUTION

The map shows the richest sources of the most important minerals

Precious metals
◇ Diamonds
○ Gold
◉ Silver

Iron and ferro-alloys
⇔ Chromium
◇ Cobalt
◇ Iron ore
◈ Manganese
◈ Molybdenum
◇ Nickel ore
◈ Tungsten

Non-ferrous metals
◈ Bauxite
   (◈ Aluminium)
◇ Copper
◇ Lead
◈ Mercury
◇ Zinc

Fertilizers
△ Phosphates
▲ Potash

The map does not show undersea deposits, most of which are currently inaccessible.

INDUSTRIAL PRODUCTION

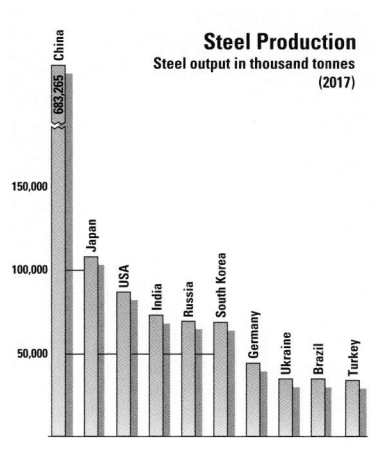

Steel Production
Steel output in thousand tonnes (2017)

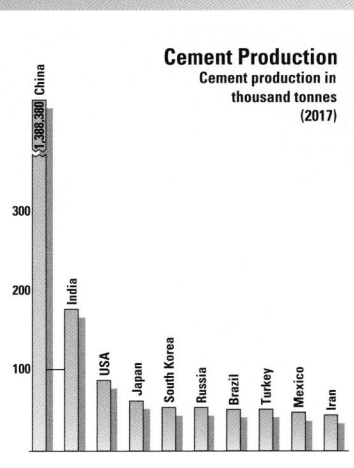

Cement Production
Cement production in thousand tonnes (2017)

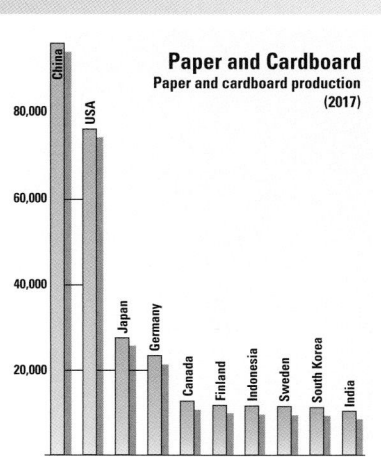

Paper and Cardboard
Paper and cardboard production (2017)

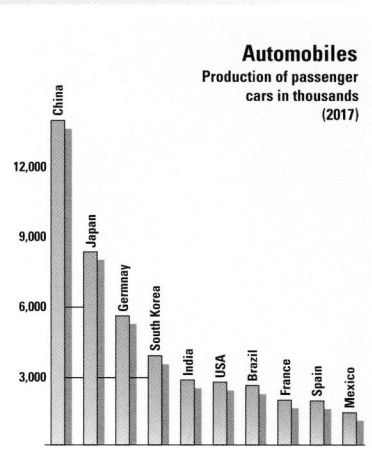

Automobiles
Production of passenger cars in thousands (2017)

Trade

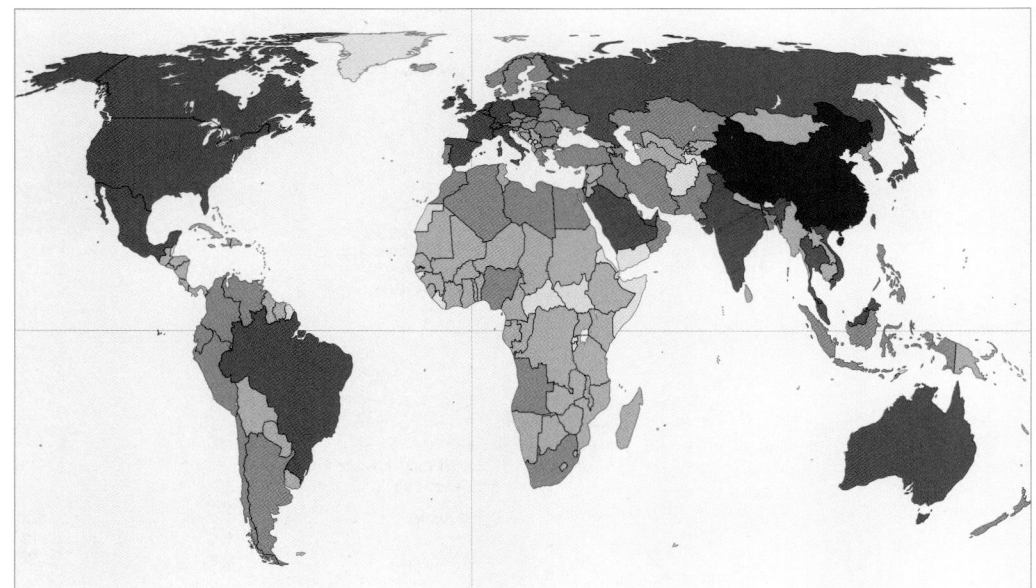

Countries with the largest share of world trade (2017)

1. China	12.4%	6. France	3.1%
2. USA	9.1%	7. Netherlands	3.0%
3. Germany	8.1%	8. Italy	2.9%
4. Japan	3.9%	9. UK	2.5%
5. South Korea	3.2%	10. Canada	2.5%

THE MAIN TRADING NATIONS

The imports and exports of the top ten trading nations as a percentage of world trade (2016). Each country's trade in manufactured goods is shown in dark blue

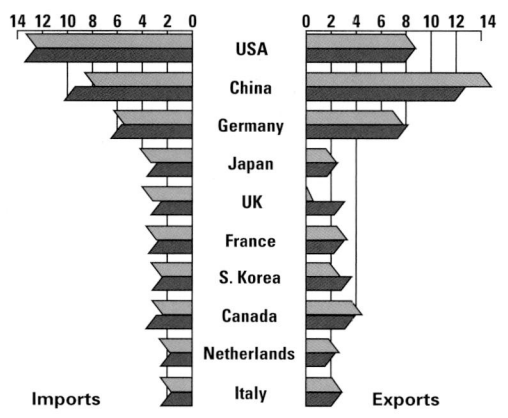

MAJOR EXPORTS

Leading manufactured items and their exporters

Motor Vehicles
World total (2017): US$ 1,259,747 million

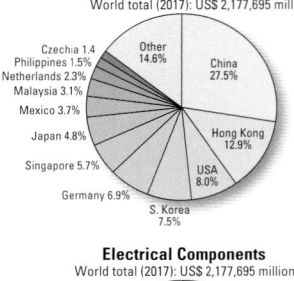

Telecommunications Gear
World total (2017): US$ 2,177,695 million

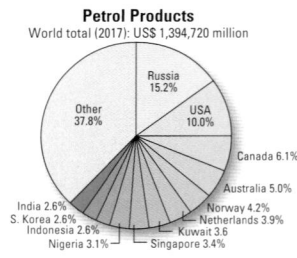

Petrol Products
World total (2017): US$ 1,394,720 million

Computers
World total (2017): US$ 305,907 million

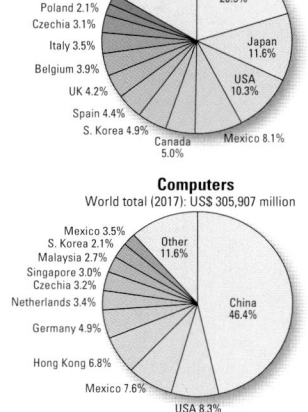

Electrical Components
World total (2017): US$ 2,177,695 million

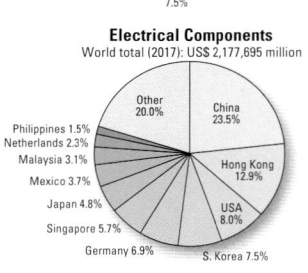

Pharmaceuticals
World total (2017): US$ 415,632 million

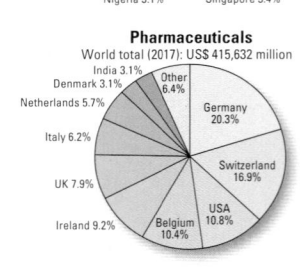

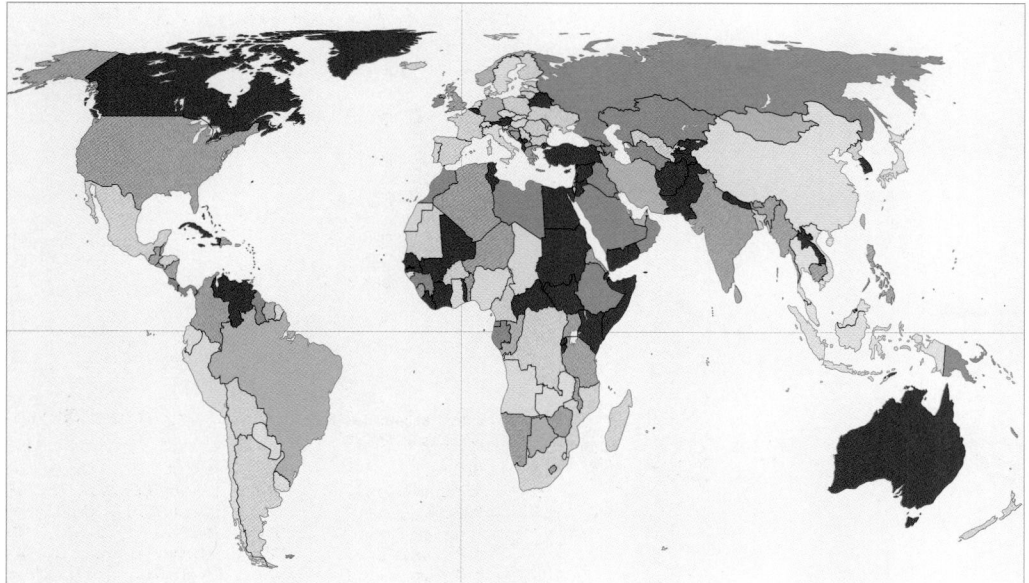

BALANCE OF TRADE

Value of exports in proportion to the value of imports (2017)

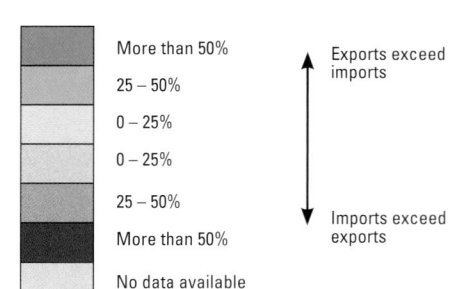

- More than 50%
- 25 – 50%
- 0 – 25%
- 0 – 25%
- 25 – 50%
- More than 50%
- No data available

Exports exceed imports

Imports exceed exports

The total world trade balance should amount to zero, since exports must equal imports on a global scale. In practice, at least $100 billion in exports go unrecorded, leaving the world with an apparent deficit and many countries in a better position than public accounting reveals. However, a favourable trade balance is not necessarily a sign of prosperity: many poorer countries must maintain a high surplus in order to service debts, and do so by restricting imports below the levels needed to sustain successful economies.

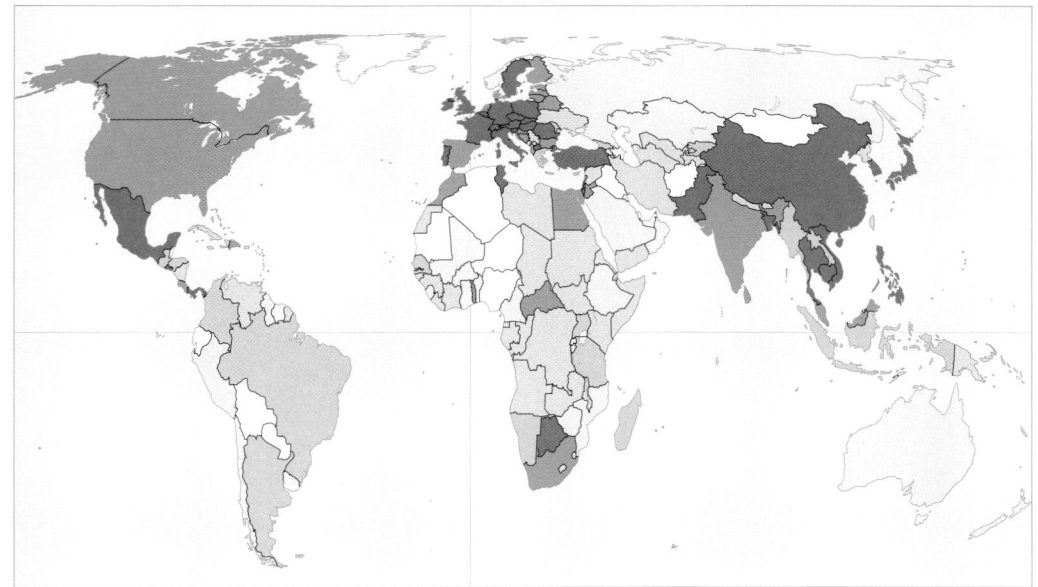

INDUSTRY AND TRADE

Manufactured goods as a percentage of total exports (2016))

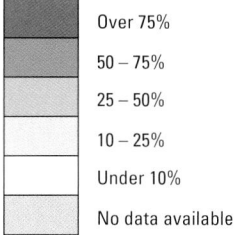

Over 75%

50 – 75%

25 – 50%

10 – 25%

Under 10%

No data available

Countries most dependent on the export of manufactured goods (2016)

1. Botswana	94%	4. Israel	93%
2. China	94%	5. Switzerland	91%
3. Cambodia	93%	6. Czechia	90%

MERCHANT FLEETS

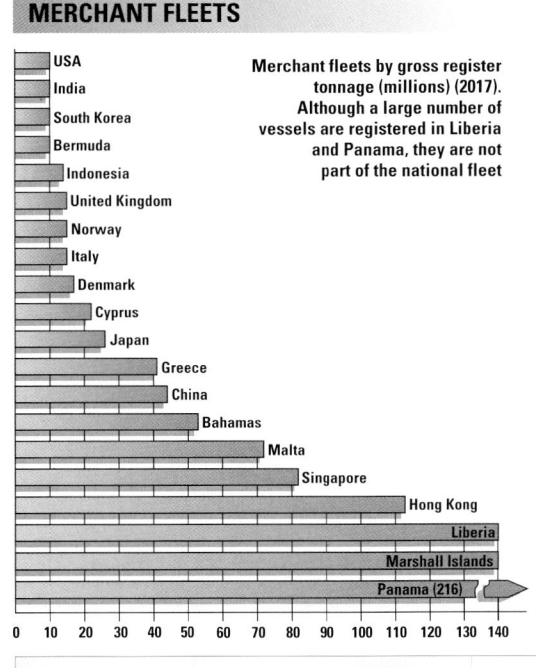

Merchant fleets by gross register tonnage (millions) (2017). Although a large number of vessels are registered in Liberia and Panama, they are not part of the national fleet

USA, India, South Korea, Bermuda, Indonesia, United Kingdom, Norway, Italy, Denmark, Cyprus, Japan, Greece, China, Bahamas, Malta, Singapore, Hong Kong, Liberia, Marshall Islands, Panama (216)

0 10 20 30 40 50 60 70 80 90 100 110 120 130 140

TOP TEN PORTS

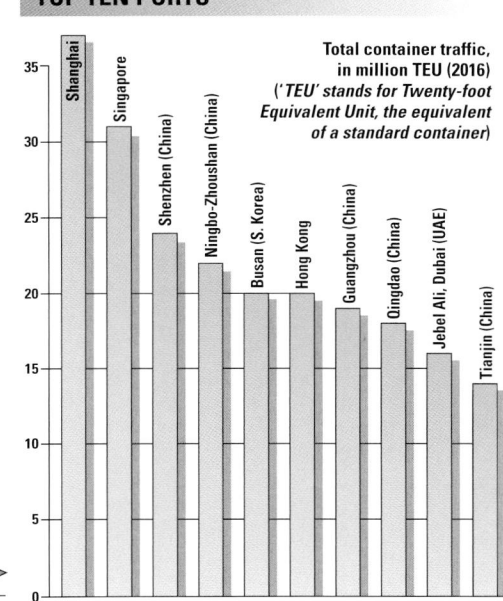

Total container traffic, in million TEU (2016) ('TEU' stands for Twenty-foot Equivalent Unit, the equivalent of a standard container)

Shanghai, Singapore, Shenzhen (China), Ningbo-Zhoushan (China), Busan (S. Korea), Hong Kong, Guangzhou (China), Qingdao (China), Jebel Ali, Dubai (UAE), Tianjin (China)

TYPES OF VESSELS

World fleet by type of vessel (2017)

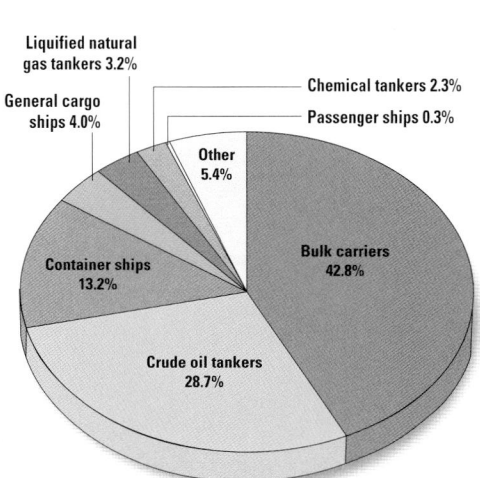

Liquified natural gas tankers 3.2%

General cargo ships 4.0%

Chemical tankers 2.3%

Passenger ships 0.3%

Other 5.4%

Container ships 13.2%

Bulk carriers 42.8%

Crude oil tankers 28.7%

IMPORTANCE OF SERVICE SECTOR

Percentage of total GDP from service sector (2017)

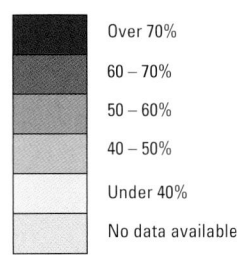

Over 70%

60 – 70%

50 – 60%

40 – 50%

Under 40%

No data available

Countries with the highest and lowest percentage of GDP from services (2017)

Highest		Lowest	
1. Bahamas	90%	1. Timor-Leste	14%
2. Malta	88%	2. Chad	27%
3. Luxembourg	88%	3. Angola	28%
4. Barbados	87%	4. Austria	31%
5. Cyprus	87%	5. Somalia	33%

Travel and Tourism

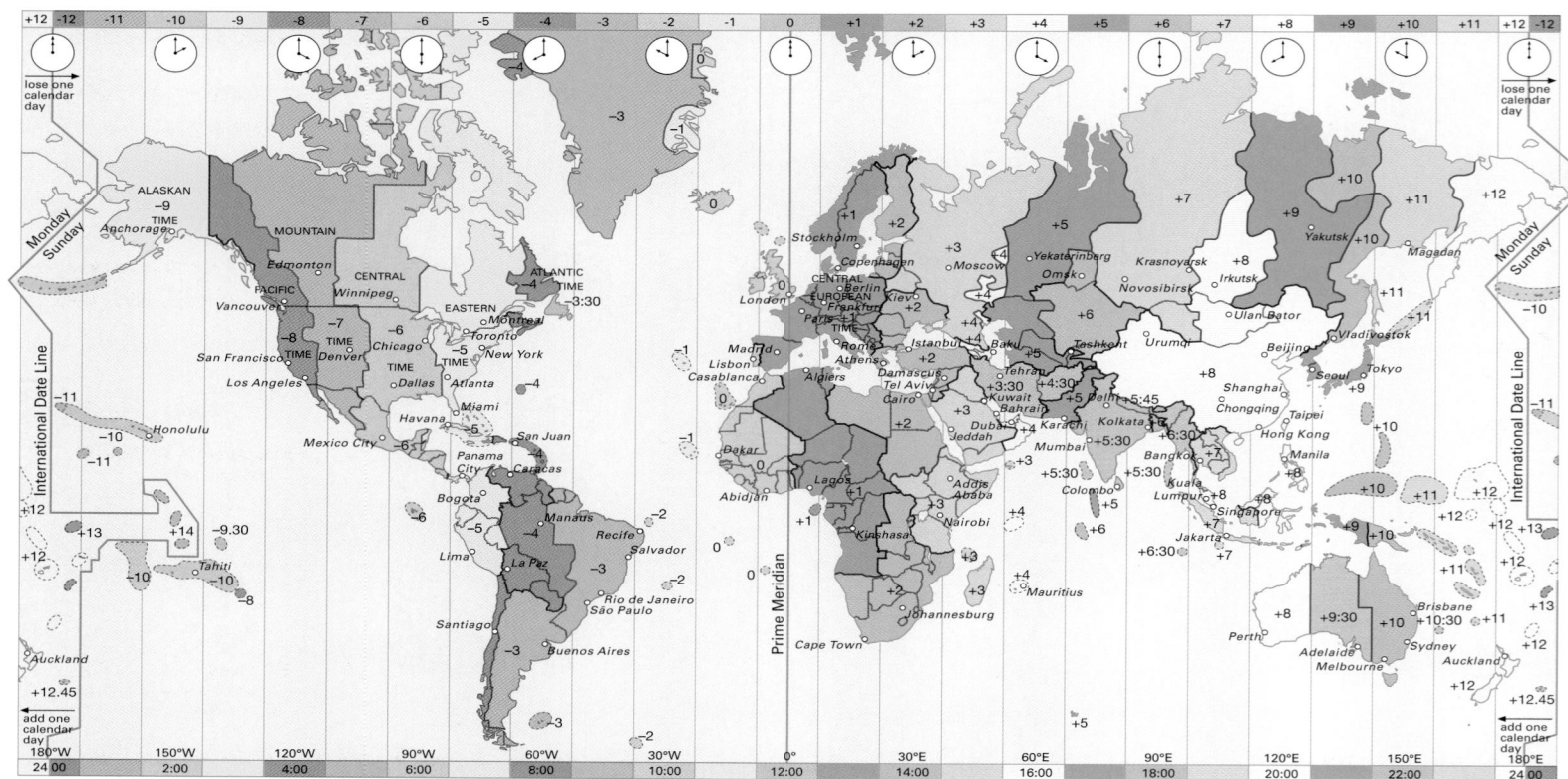

TIME ZONES

Zones using UT (GMT)	Zones ahead of UT (GMT)
Zones behind UT (GMT)	Half-hour zones
International boundaries	Time-zone boundaries
10 — Hours fast or slow of UT or Co-ordinated Universal Time	International Date Line

Certain time zones are affected by the incidence of daylight saving time in countries where it is adopted.

Actual solar time, when it is noon at Greenwich, is shown along the top of the map.

The world is divided into 24 time zones, each centred on meridians at 15° intervals, which is the longitudinal distance the sun travels every hour. The meridian running through Greenwich, London, passes through the middle of the first zone.

RAIL AND ROAD: THE LEADING NATIONS

Total rail network ('000 km)		Passenger km per head per year		Total road network ('000 km)		Vehicle km per head per year		Number of vehicles per km of roads	
1. USA	293.5	Switzerland	2,430	USA	6,586.6	Peru	38,553	Monaco	388
2. China	124.0	Japan	1,995	India	4,699.0	USA	34,560	Portugal	278
3. Russia	87.2	Denmark	1,329	China	4,106.4	Tunisia	25,225	Hong Kong	271
4. Canada	77.9	France	1,298	Brazil	1,580.9	Pakistan	25,199	UAE	230
5. India	68.5	Austria	1,245	Russia	1,282.3	Ecuador	23,570	Singapore	230
6. Germany	43.5	Russia	1,220	Japan	1,218.7	Chile	22,671	Macau	228
7. Australia	37.0	Ukraine	1,150	Canada	1,042.3	South Korea	21,763	Japan	222
8. Argentina	36.9	Belarus	1,030	France	1,028.4	Singapore	21,563	Kuwait	217
9. Brazil	29.9	Belgium	1,009	Australia	832.2	Morocco	18,455	South Korea	174
10. France	29.6	UK	981	South Africa	737.0	Croatia	17,723	Bulgaria	157
11. Japan	27.3	Germany	959	Spain	683.1	Finland	17,639	Jordan	152
12. Ukraine	21.7	Netherlands	940	Germany	645.0	Canada	17,498	Israel	138
13. South Africa	21.0	Kazakhstan	880	Sweden	579.5	Denmark	16,903	Bahrain	112
14. Italy	20.2	Italy	780	Indonesia	496.6	Thailand	16,823	Mauritius	107
15. Poland	19.2	India	777	Italy	487.6	Isreal	16,721	Puerto Rico	92

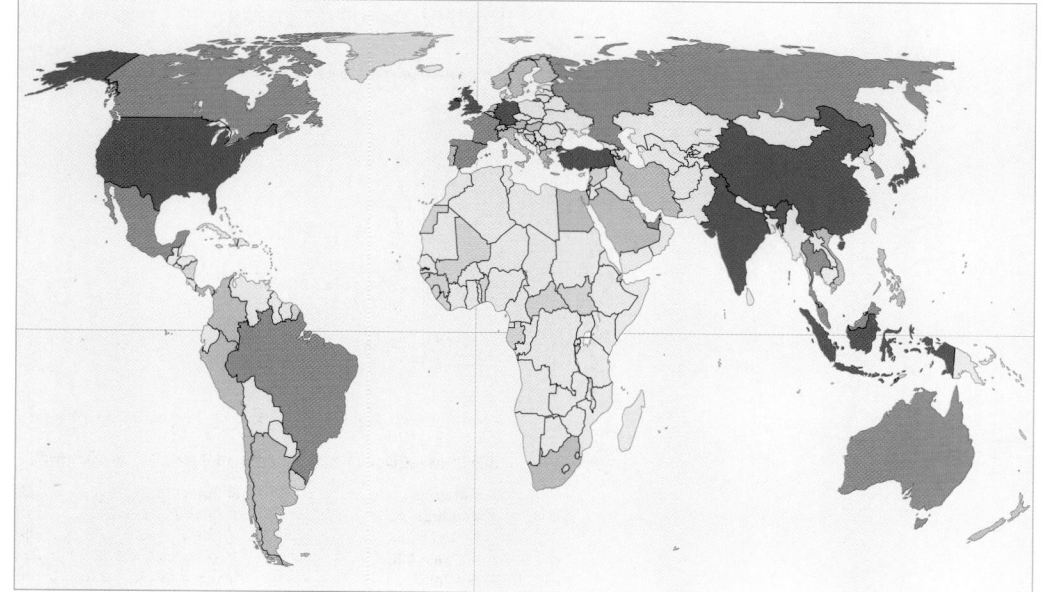

AIR TRAVEL

Number of air passengers carried (2016)

	Over 100 million
	50 – 100 million
	10 – 50 million
	Under 10 million
	No data available

World's busiest airports (2017) – total passengers in millions

1. Atlanta Hartsfield International (ATL) 103.9
2. Beijing Capital International (PEK) 95.8
3. Dubai International (DXB) 88.2
4. Tokyo Haneda (HND) 85.4
5. Los Angeles International (LAX) 84.6
6. Chicago O'Hare International (ORD) 79.8
7. London Heathrow (LHR) 78.0
8. Hong Kong International (HKG) 72.7
9. Shanghai Pudong International (PVG) 70.0
10. Paris Charles de Gaulle (CDG) 69.5

TOURIST CENTRES

- ■ Cultural and historical centres
- □ Coastal resorts
- ■ Ski resorts
- ■ Centres of entertainment
- ■ Places of pilgrimage
- ■ Places of great natural beauty
- — Popular holiday cruise routes

VISITORS TO THE USA

Overseas arrivals to the USA, in thousands (2016)

1.	Canada	19,302
2.	Mexico	18,730
3.	UK	4,574
4.	Japan	3,577
5.	China	2,972
6.	Germany	2,034
7.	South Korea	1,973
8.	Brazil	1,693
9.	France	1,628
10.	Australia	1,346

TOURIST SPENDING

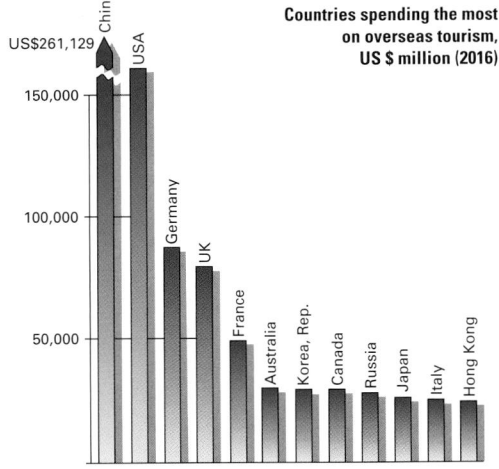

Countries spending the most on overseas tourism, US $ million (2016)

TOURISTS

International tourist arrivals

		millions (2016)
1.	France	82.6
2.	United States of America	75.6
3.	Spain	75.6
4.	China	59.3
5.	Italy	52.4
6.	United Kingdom	35.8
7.	Germany	35.6
8.	Mexico	35.0
9.	Thailand	32.6
10.	Austria	28.1

The UNWTO (United Nations World Tourism Organization) ranks countries by international tourism receipts (see bar chart right) and international tourist arrivals as table above. France has remained at the top of the list of main destinations for several years, with the USA in second place.

TOURIST EARNINGS

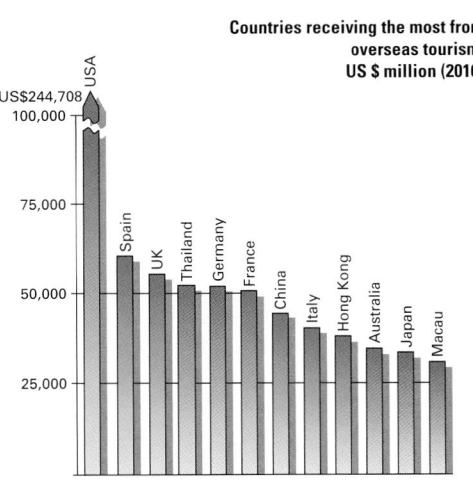

Countries receiving the most from overseas tourism, US $ million (2016)

IMPORTANCE OF TOURISM

Tourism receipts as a percentage of Gross National Income (2016)

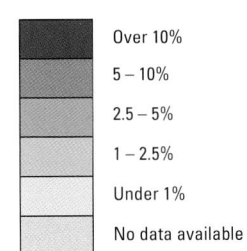

- Over 10%
- 5 – 10%
- 2.5 – 5%
- 1 – 2.5%
- Under 1%
- No data available

Countries with the highest tourism receipts as % of GNI (2016)

1.	Palau	75	6.	Vanuatu	39
2.	Grenada	52	7.	St Kitts & Nevis	39
3.	St Lucia	52	8.	Seychelles	35
4.	Antigua & Barbuda	51	9.	St Vincent & Grenadines	28
5.	Dominica	45	10.	Bahamas	25

WORLD CITIES

AMSTERDAM	2	GUANGZHOU	11	MOSCOW	19	SYDNEY	29
ATHENS	2	HELSINKI	11	MONTRÉAL	20	TOKYO	30
ATLANTA	3	HONG KONG	12	MUMBAI	20	TEHRAN	31
BAGHDAD	3	ISTANBUL	12	MUNICH	21	TORONTO	31
BANGKOK	3	JAKARTA	12	NEW ORLEANS	21	VENICE	32
BARCELONA	4	JERUSALEM	13	NEW YORK	22	VIENNA	32
BEIJING	4	JOHANNESBURG	13	ORLANDO	23	WARSAW	33
BERLIN	5	KARACHI	13	OSAKA	23	WASHINGTON	33
BOSTON	6	KOLKATA	14	OSLO	23		
BRUSSELS	6	LAGOS	14	PARIS	24	INDEX	34–39
BUDAPEST	7	LAS VEGAS	14	PRAGUE	25		
BUENOS AIRES	7	LIMA	14	RIO DE JANEIRO	25	WORLD CITIES	
CAIRO	7	LONDON	15	ROME	26	SATELLITE IMAGES	
CAPE TOWN	8	LISBON	16	SAN FRANCISCO	26	BANGKOK	40
COPENHAGEN	8	LOS ANGELES	16	ST PETERSBURG	27	BOSTON	41
CHICAGO	9	MADRID	17	SANTIAGO	27	ISTANBUL	42
DUBAI	9	MANILA	17	SÃO PAULO	27	LAS VEGAS	43
DALLAS–		MELBOURNE	18	SEOUL	27	MELBOURNE	44
FORT WORTH	10	MEXICO CITY	18	SHANGHAI	28	MEXICO CITY	45
DELHI	10	MILAN	18	SINGAPORE	28	NEW ORLEANS	46
EDINBURGH	11	MIAMI	19	STOCKHOLM	29	ROME	47
						ST PETERSBURG	48

CITY MAPS

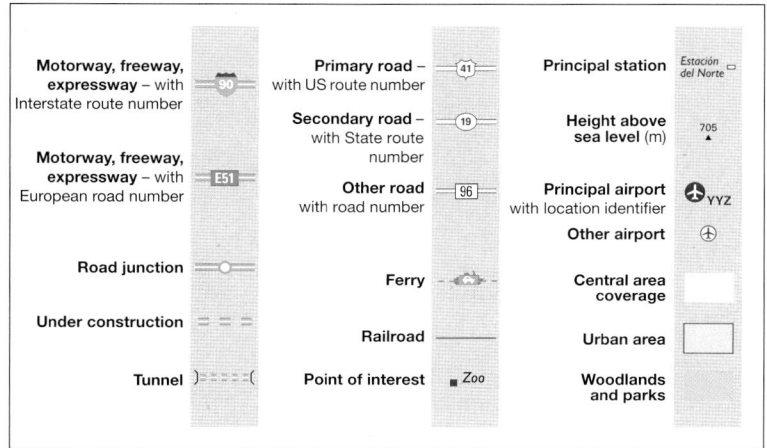

Motorway, freeway, expressway – with Interstate route number	**Primary road** – with US route number	**Principal station**
Motorway, freeway, expressway – with European road number	**Secondary road** – with State route number	**Height above sea level** (m)
	Other road with road number	**Principal airport** with location identifier
		Other airport
Road junction	**Ferry**	**Central area coverage**
Under construction	**Railroad**	**Urban area**
Tunnel	**Point of interest**	**Woodlands and parks**

CENTRAL AREA MAPS

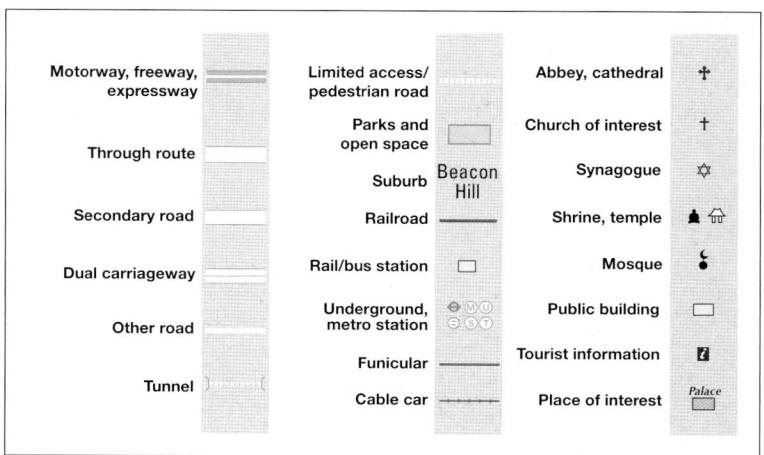

Motorway, freeway, expressway	**Limited access/ pedestrian road**	**Abbey, cathedral**
	Parks and open space	**Church of interest**
Through route	**Suburb**	**Synagogue**
Secondary road	**Railroad**	**Shrine, temple**
Dual carriageway	**Rail/bus station**	**Mosque**
	Underground, metro station	**Public building**
Other road	**Funicular**	**Tourist information**
Tunnel	**Cable car**	**Place of interest**

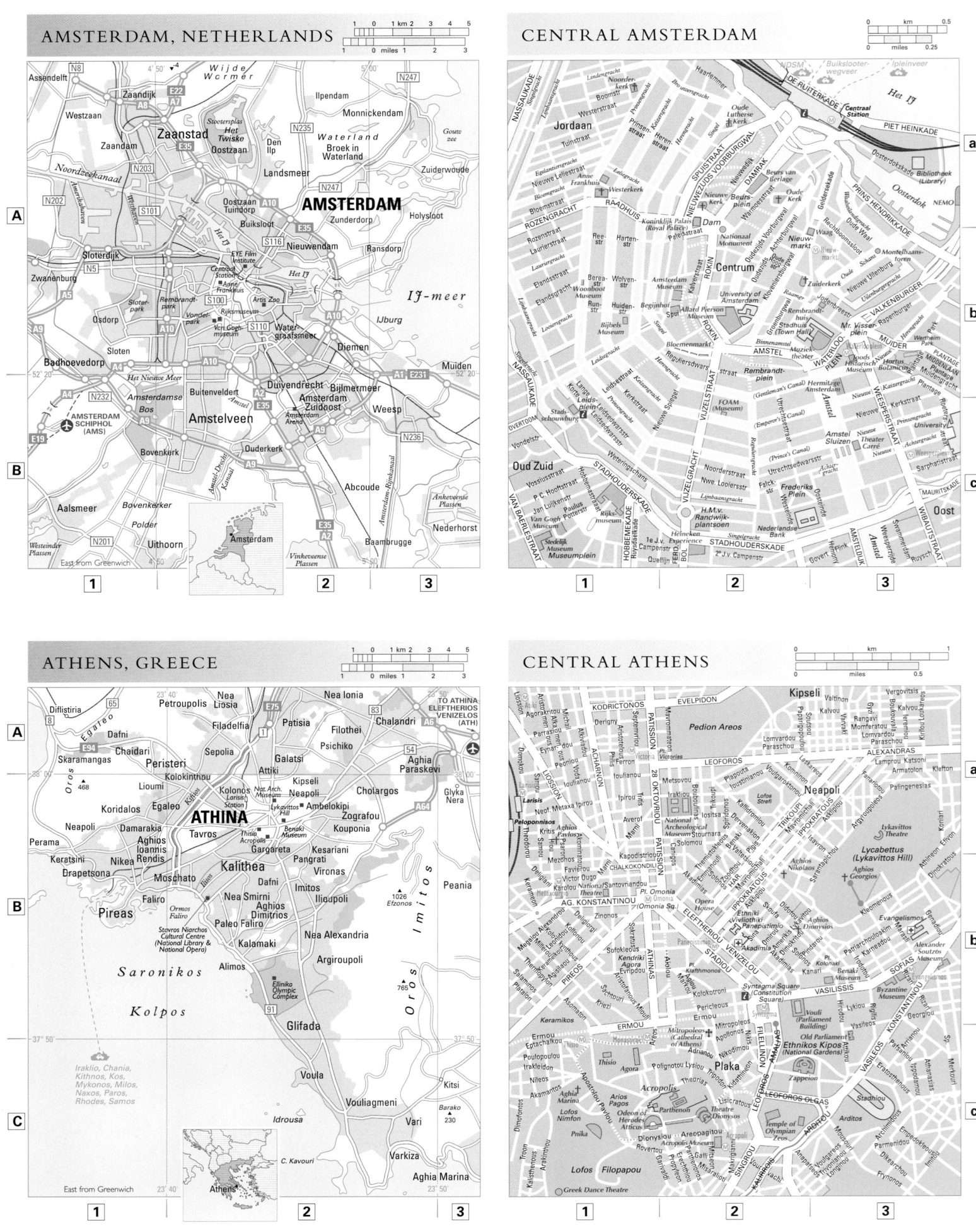

AMSTERDAM, NETHERLANDS

CENTRAL AMSTERDAM

ATHENS, GREECE

CENTRAL ATHENS

Tram Route

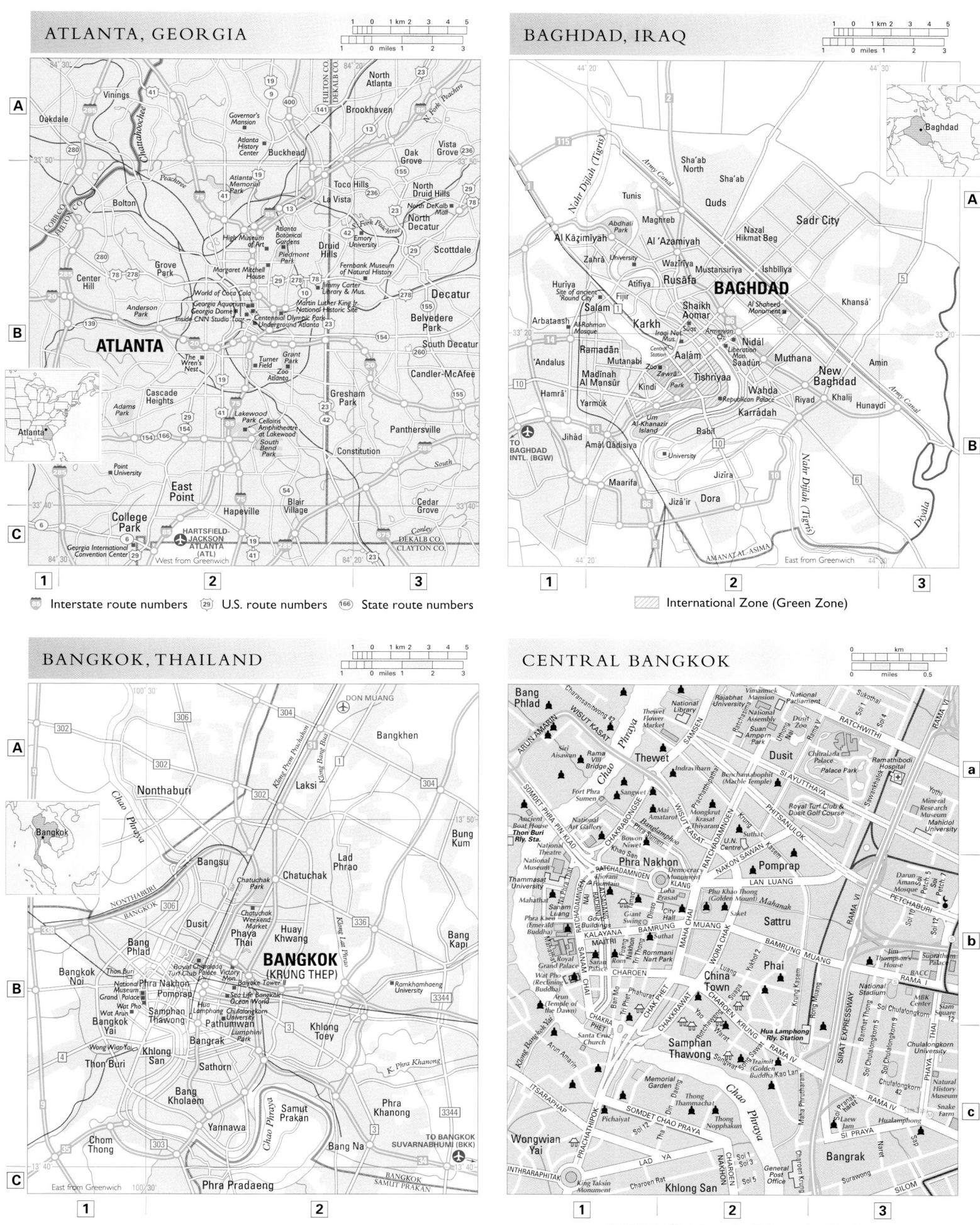

BERLIN, GERMANY

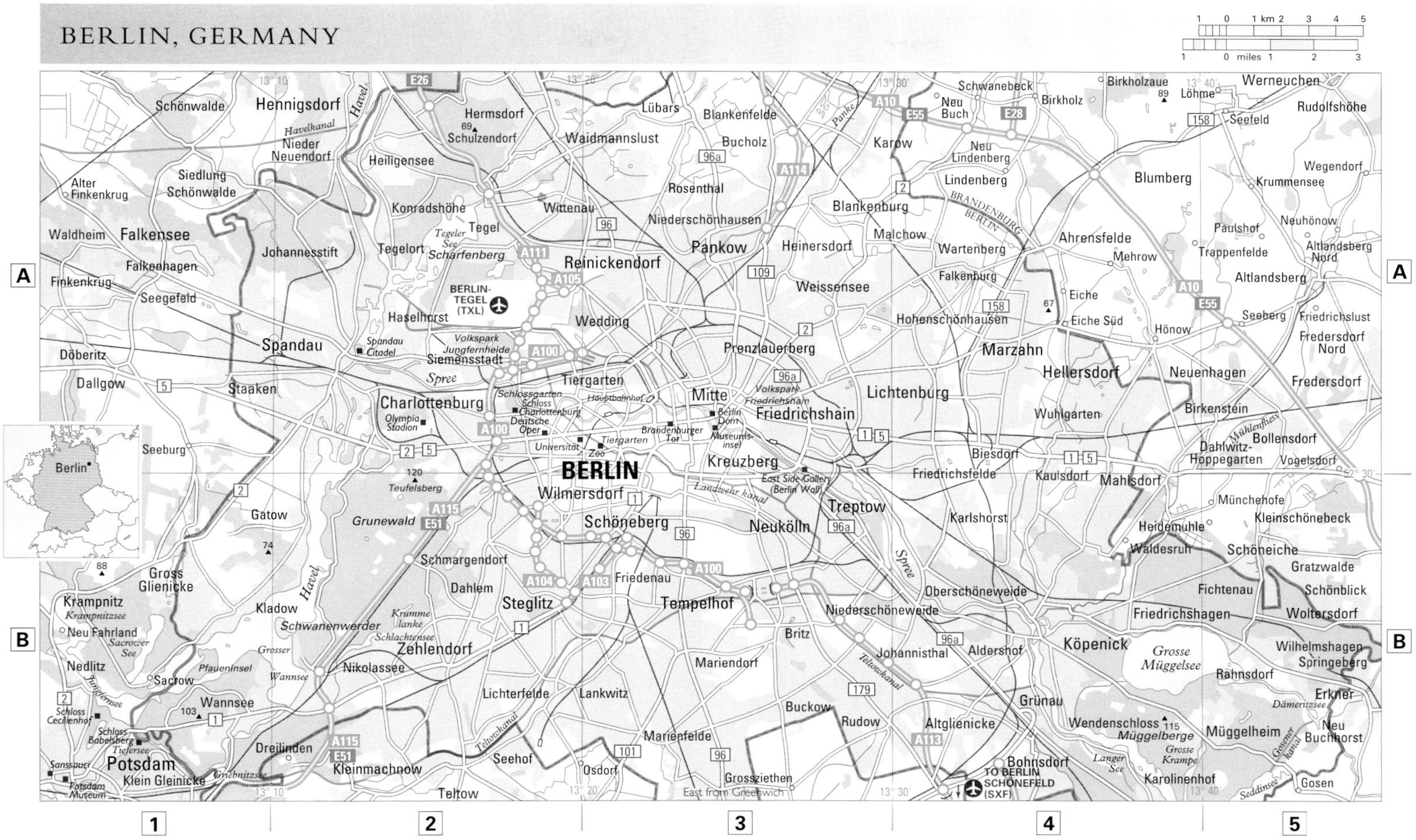

Schönwalde Hennigsdorf Hermsdorf Blankenfelde Buchholz Schwanebeck Birkholzaue Birkholz Löhme Werneuchen
Havelkanal Waidmannslust Karow Neu Buch Seefeld Rudolfshöhe
Nieder Neuendorf Schulzendorf Rosenthal Lindenberg Wegendorf
Alter Finkenkrug Siedlung Schönwalde Heiligensee Niederschönhausen Blankenburg Malchow Neu Lindenberg Blumberg Krummensee
Waldheim Falkensee Tegeler See Tegel Konradshöhe Wittenau Pankow Heinersdorf Wartenberg Ahrensfelde Mehrow Paulshof Neuhönow Altlandsberg Nord
Finkenkrug Falkenhagen Tegelort Scharfenberg Reinickendorf Weissensee Falkenburg Hohenschönhausen Eiche Seeberg Friedrichslust
Seegefeld BERLIN-TEGEL (TXL) Wedding Prenzlauerberg Eiche Süd Altlandsberg
Döberitz Spandau Haselhorst Volkspark Jungfernheide Siemensstadt Tiergarten Marzahn Hellersdorf Neuenhagen
Dallgow Staaken Spree Schloss Charlottenburg Mitte Friedrichshain Lichtenburg Wuhlgarten Birkenstein Fredersdorf
Charlottenburg Deutsche Oper Hauptbahnhof Berliner Dom Museumsinsel Biesdorf Dahlwitz-Hoppegarten Bollensdorf Vogelsdorf
Olympia Stadion Universität Tiergarten Brandenburger Tor Kreuzberg Friedrichsfelde Kaulsdorf Mahlsdorf
BERLIN Treptow Münchehofe Kleinschönebeck
Teufelsberg Wilmersdorf Schöneberg Neukölln Karlshorst Heidemühle Schöneiche
Grunewald East Side Gallery (Berlin Wall) Waldesruh Gratzwalde
Landwehr kanal Oberschöneweide Fichtenau Schönblick
Gross Glienicke Schmargendorf Neuköln Niederschöneweide Friedrichshagen Wolterdorf
Krampnitz Grunewald Dahlem Friedenau Tempelhof Köpenick Grosse Müggelsee Rahnsdorf Wilhelmshagen Springeberg
Neu Fahrland Steglitz Britz Johannisthal Dämeritz Erkner
Nedlitz Schwanenwerder Nikolassee Lichterfelde Lankwitz Mariendorf Adlershof Müggelheim Neu Buchhorst
Sacrow Pfaueninsel Wannsee Grünau Wendenschloss Müggelberge Grosse Krampe Müggelheim Gosen
Schloss Cecilienhof Babelsberg Dreilinden Kleinmachnow Buckow Rudow Altglienicke Bohnsdorf Karolinenhof Langer See
Potsdam Klein Gleinicke Teltow Seehof Osdorf Grossziethen Grossbeeren TO BERLIN SCHÖNEFELD (SXF)

East from Greenwich

CENTRAL BERLIN

Charlottenburg Tiergarten Hauptbahnhof Scheunenviertel Alexanderplatz
Kaiserin-Augusta-Allee Turmstrasse Hannoversche Str. Volksbühne
Deutsche Oper Bellevue Schlosspark Schloss Bellevue Siegessäule Tiergarten Mitte Museumsinsel
Savignypl. Zoologischer Garten Kaiser Wilhelm Gedächtniskirche Europa-Center Brandenburger Tor (Brandenburg Gate) Unter den Linden Fernsehturm (T.V. Tower)
Wilmersdorf Kurfürstendamm Potsdamer Platz Checkpoint Charlie Kreuzberg
Anhalter Bf. Jüdisches Museum (Jewish Museum)
Deutsches Technikmuseum Berlin Yorckstrasse

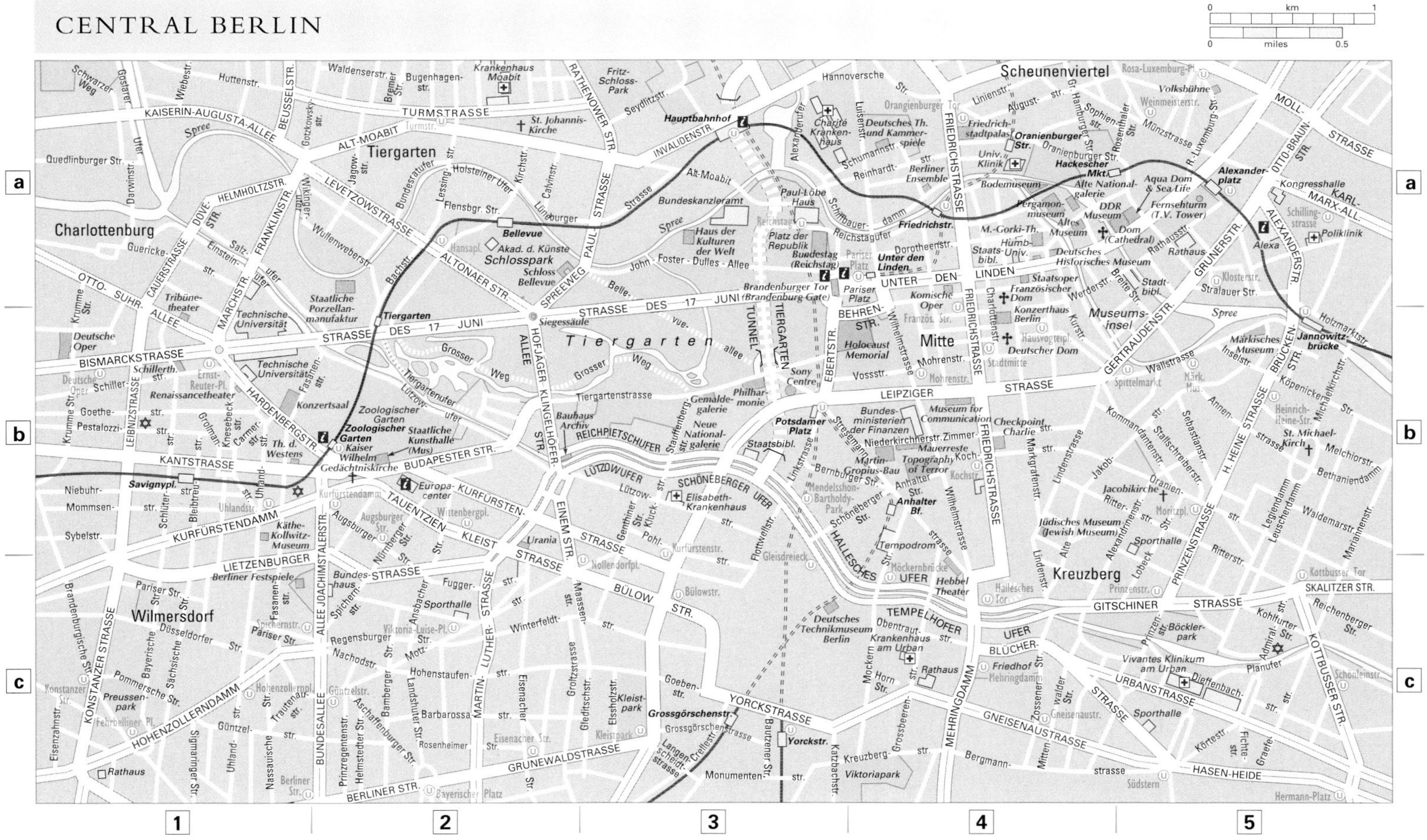

COPYRIGHT PHILIP'S

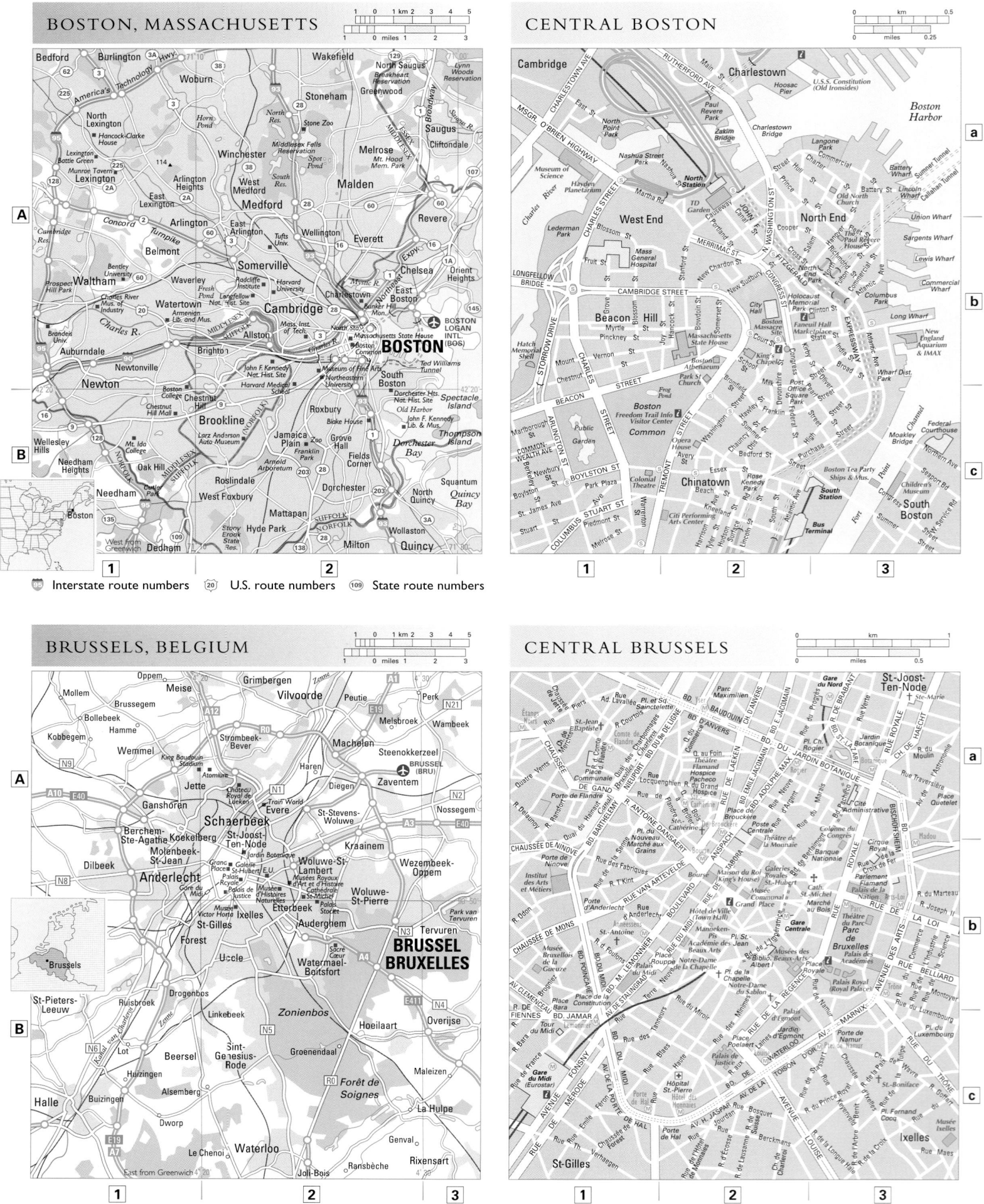

BOSTON, MASSACHUSETTS

CENTRAL BOSTON

BRUSSELS, BELGIUM

CENTRAL BRUSSELS

Interstate route numbers   U.S. route numbers   State route numbers

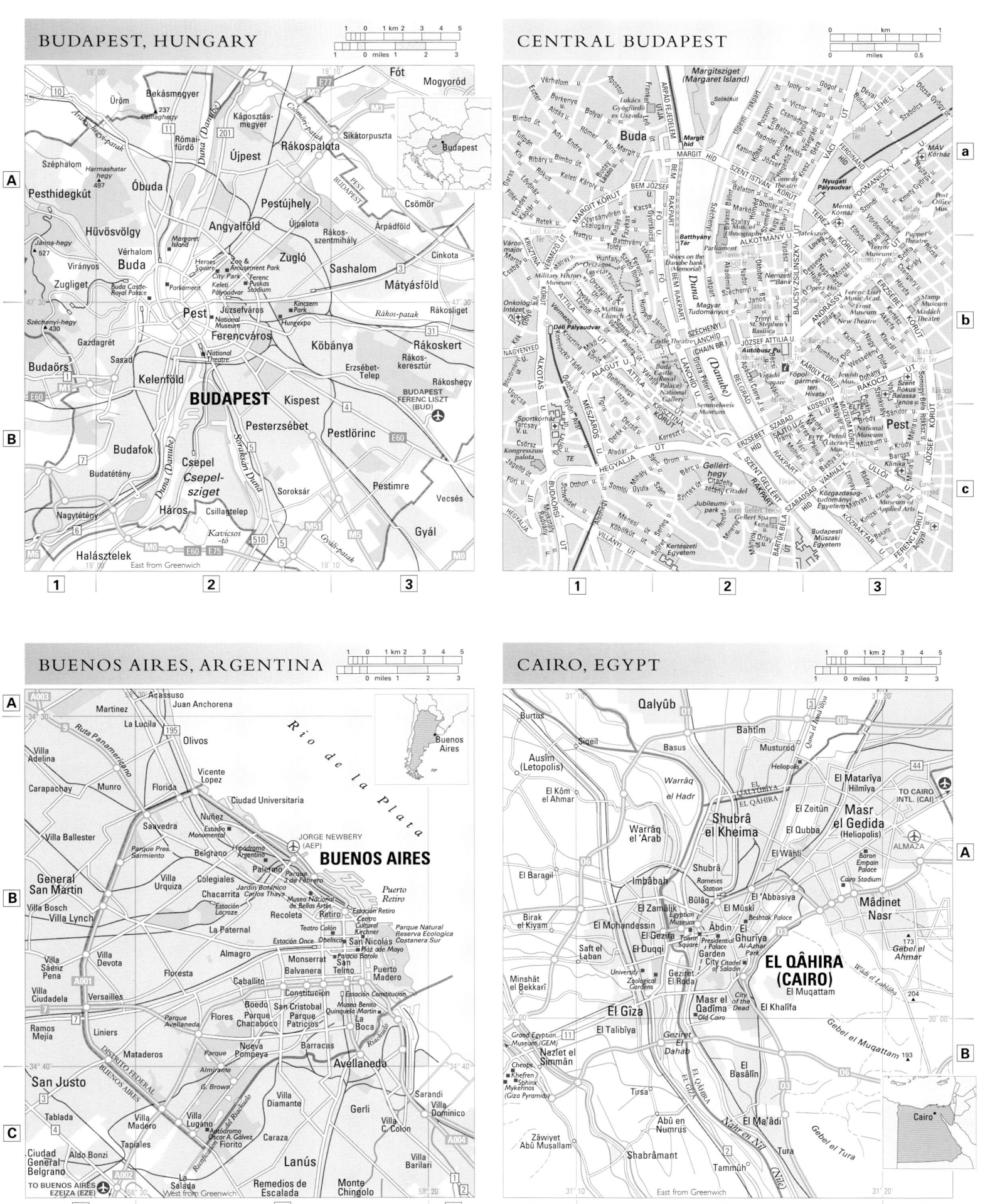

BUDAPEST, HUNGARY

Békásmegyer, Üröm, Fót, Mogyoród, Csillaghegy, Káposztás-megyer, Sikátorpuszta, Rómaifürdő, Újpest, Rákospalota, Széphalom, Harmashatar hegy 497, Óbuda, Csömör, Pesthidegkút, Angyalföld, Pestújhely, Úpalota, Rákosszentmihály, Árpádföld, Cinkota, Hüvösvölgy, Vérhalom, Margaret Island, Zugló, Sashalom, Mátyásföld, János-hegy 527, Virányos, Buda, Heroes Square, Zoo & Amusement Park, City Park, Ferenc Puskás Stadium, Kincsem Park, Rákosliget, Zugliget, Buda Castle-Royal Palace, Parlament, Keleti Pályaudvar, Hungexpo, Rákos-patak, Széchenyi-hegy 430, Gazdagrét, Pest, Józsefváros, National Museum, Köbánya, Rákos-keresztúr, Rákoshegy, Sasad, National Theatre, Ferencváros, Erzsébet-Telep, Budaörs, Kelenföld, BUDAPEST, Kispest, BUDAPEST FERENC LISZT (BUD), Budafok, Pesterzsébet, Pestlörinc, Budatétény, Csepel, Soroksár, Péstimre, Vecsés, Nagytétény, Csepel-sziget, Háros, Csillagtelep, Kaviccsos-tó, Gyál, Halásztelek

CENTRAL BUDAPEST

Margitsziget (Margaret Island), Vérhalom, Buda, Margit hid, MARGIT HID, ARPAD FEJEDELEM ÚTJA, Nyugati Pályaudvar, MÁV Kórház, Batthyány Tér, Parliament, Shoes on the Danube bank (Memorial), Military History Museum, Mattias Church, Buda Castle Royal Palace, National Gallery, Magyar Tudományos, Nemzeti Bank, Opera Ho., Ferenc Liszt Music Acad., New Theatre, Déli Pályaudvar, Castle Theatre, SZÉCHENYI LÁNCHID (CHAIN BR.), JÓZSEF ATTILA U., Autóbusz Pu., Vigadó Square, Pest, St. Stephen's Basilica, Jewish Cemetery, Dohany, RÁKÓCZI, Sportkórház, Semmelweis Museum, National Museum, Gellért-hegy, Citadella, Gellert Citadel, Szabadság, KÖRÚT, Budapesti Müszaki Egyetem, Gellert Spa, Jubileumi-park, Közgazdaságtudományi Egyetem, Museum of Applied Arts, Budapesti Müszaki Egyetem, Kertészeti Egyetem

BUENOS AIRES, ARGENTINA

Acassuso, Martinez, Juan Anchorena, La Lucila, Olivos, Villa Adelina, Vicente Lopez, Carapachay, Munro, Florida, Ciudad Universitaria, Río de la Plata, Buenos Aires, Saavedra, Nuñez, Estadio Monumental, JORGE NEWBERY (AEP), Villa Ballester, Parque Pres. Sarmiento, Hipódromo Argentino, Belgrano, BUENOS AIRES, General San Martín, Villa Urquiza, Palermo, Parque 3 de Febrero, Villa Bosch, Villa Lynch, Colegiales, Jardín Botánico Carlos Thays, Chacarita, Puerto Retiro, Estación Lacroze, Recoleta, Museo Nacional de Bellas Artes, Estación Retiro, Villa Devota, La Paternal, Teatro Colón, Centro Cultural Kirchner, Parque Natural Reserva Ecologica Costanera Sur, Villa Sáenz Pena, Almagro, Estación Once, Obelisco, San Nicolás, Villa Ciudadela, Versailles, Monserrat, Palacio Barolo, Plaza de Mayo, Puerto Madero, Ramos Mejia, Floresta, Caballito, Balvanera, San Telmo, Liniers, Boedo, San Cristobal, Parque Patricios, Museo Benito Quinquela Martin, La Boca, Mataderos, Flores, Parque Chacabuco, Nueva Pompeya, Barracas, Riachuelo, Avellaneda, Parque Avellaneda, Almirante G. Brown, Villa Diamante, Gerli, Villa Colón, Sarandi, Villa Dominico, San Justo, Tablada, Villa Madero, Villa Lugano, Caraza, Lanús, Villa Barilari, Ciudad General Belgrano, Aldo Bonzi, Tapiales, Autódromo Oscar A. Gálvez Fiorito, La Salada, Remedios de Escalada, Monte Chingolo, TO BUENOS AIRES EZEIZA (EZE)

CAIRO, EGYPT

Burtus, Qalyûb, Bahtîm, Siqeil, Basus, Musturud, Ausim (Letopolis), Heliopolis, El Kôm el Ahmar, Warrâq el Hadr, El Zeitûn, El Matarîya, Hilmîya, Shubrâ el Kheima, El Qubba, Masr el Gedida (Heliopolis), ALMAZA, Warrâq el 'Arab, El Wâhli, Baron Empain Palace, Cairo Stadium, El Baragil, Imbâbah, Shubrâ, Rameses Station, El 'Abbasiya, Mâdinet Nasr, Birak el Kiyam, Bûlâq, El Zamâlik, El Mûskî, Egyptian Museum, Beshtok Palace, El Mohandessin, Abdin, El Ghuriya, Al-Azhar Park, Gebel el Ahmar, El Gezira, Tahrir Square, Presidential Palace, Citadel of Saladin, El Duqqi, City Garden, Saft el Laban, EL QÂHIRA (CAIRO), El Muqattam, Minshât el Bekkarî, University, Zoological Gardens, Geziret El Roda, Masr el Qadîma, Old Cairo, City of the Dead, El Khalifa, El Gîza, Grand Egyptian Museum (GEM), El Talibîya, Geziret El Dahab, El Basâtîn, Gebel el Muqattam, Nazlet el Simmân, Cheops, Khefren, Sphinx, Mykerinos (Giza Pyramids), Tirsa, El Qâhira, El Ma'âdi, Abû en Numrus, Nahr en Nîl, Tura, Zâwiyet Abû Musallam, Shabrâmant, Tammûh, Gebel el Tura, Cairo

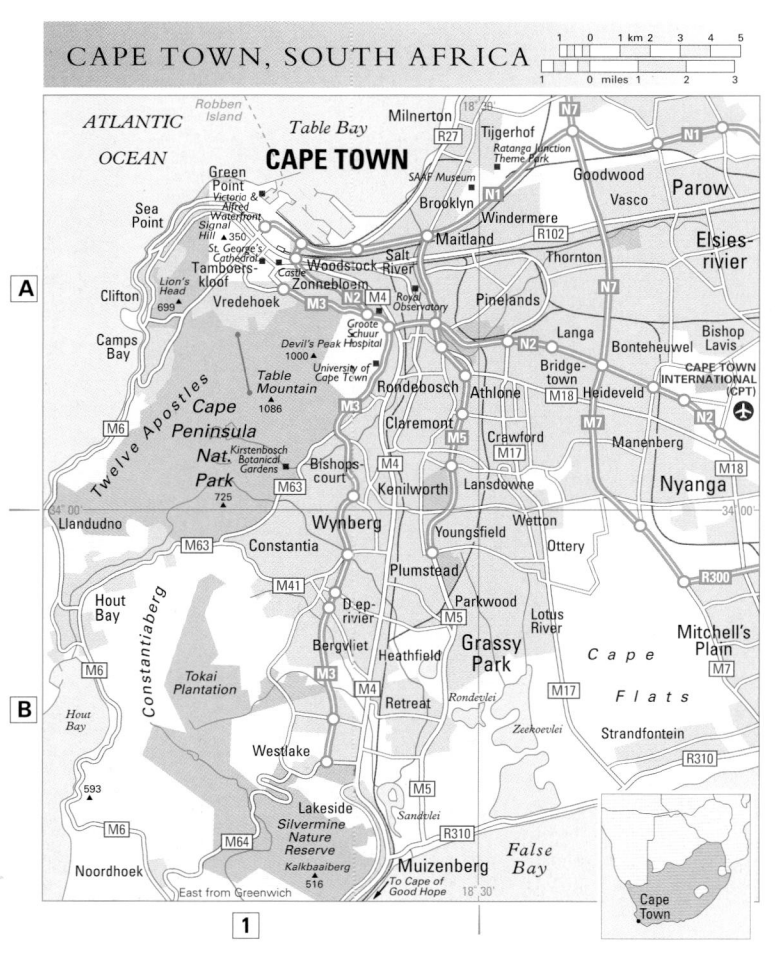

CAPE TOWN, SOUTH AFRICA

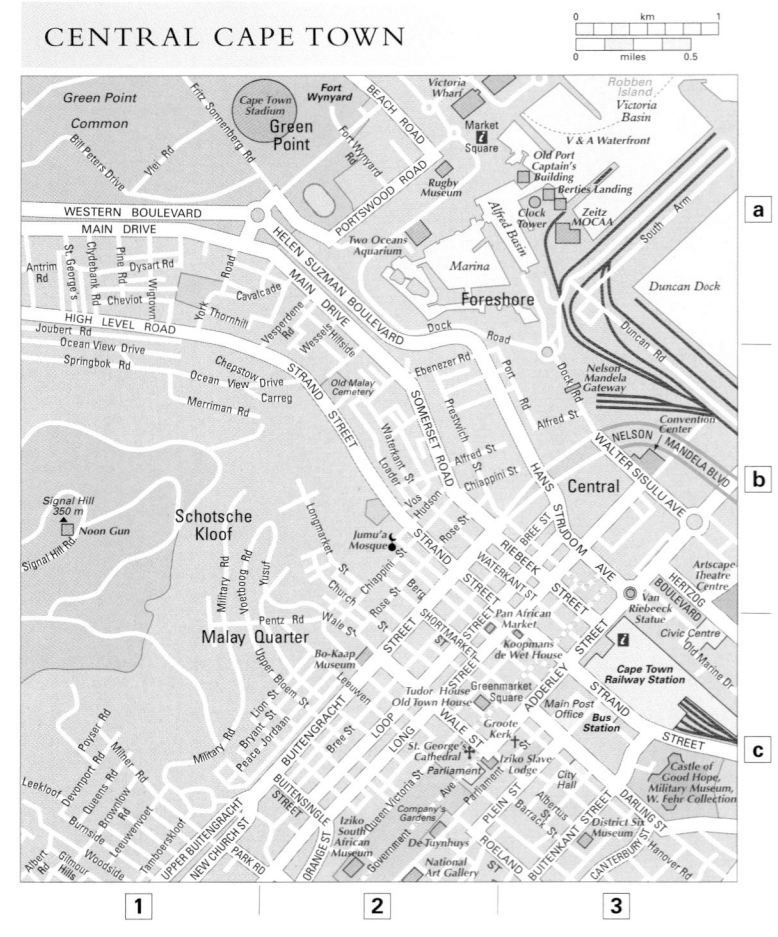

CENTRAL CAPE TOWN

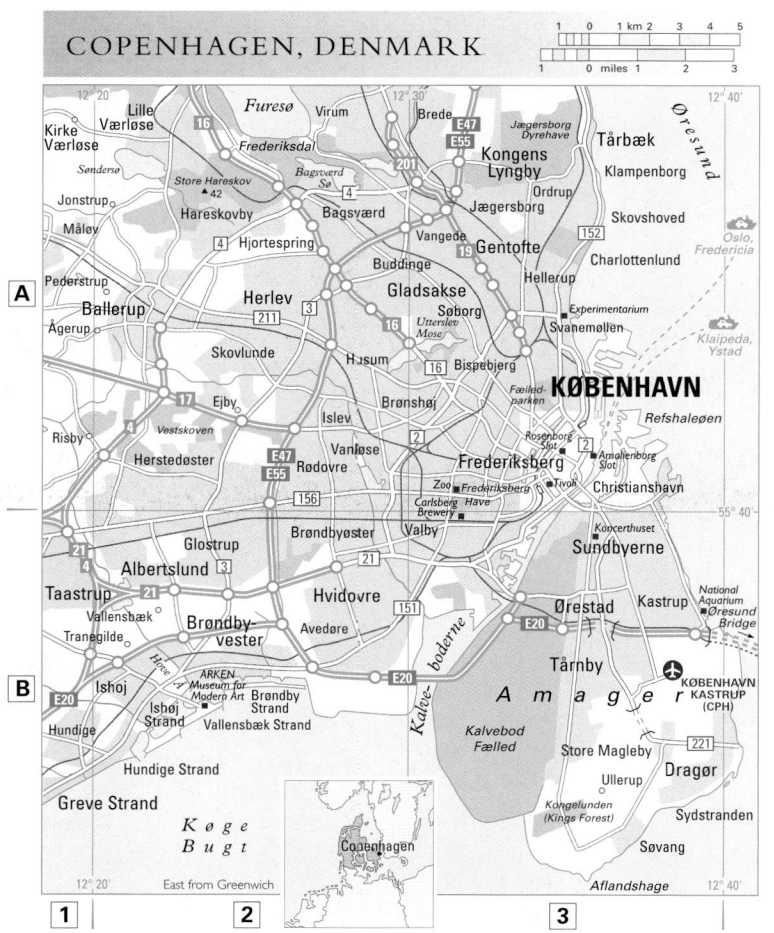

COPENHAGEN, DENMARK

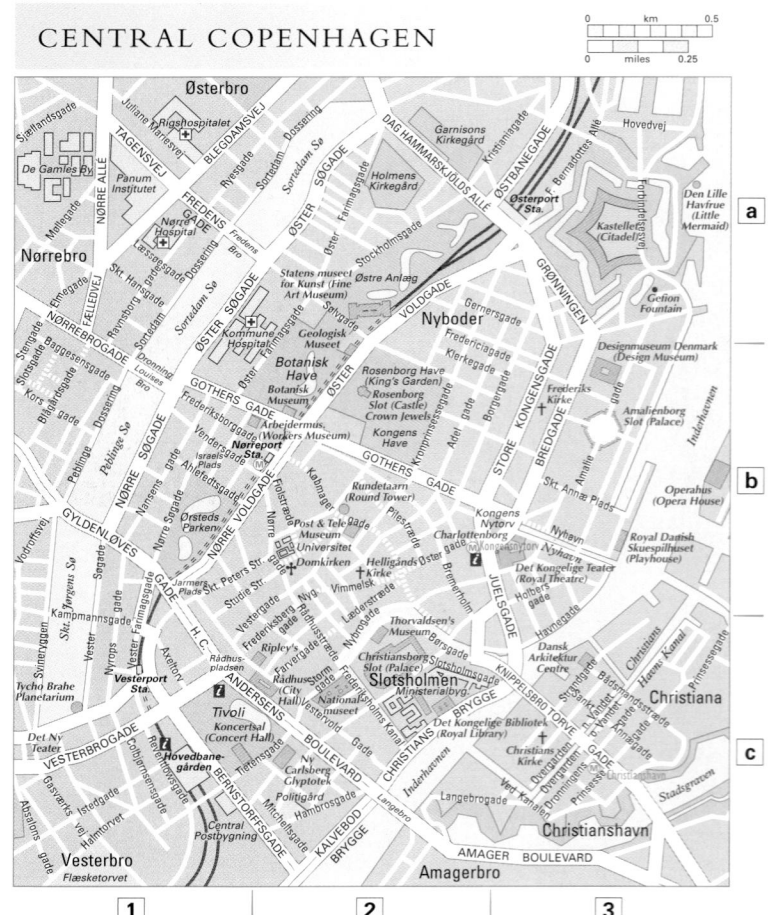

CENTRAL COPENHAGEN

CENTRAL CHICAGO

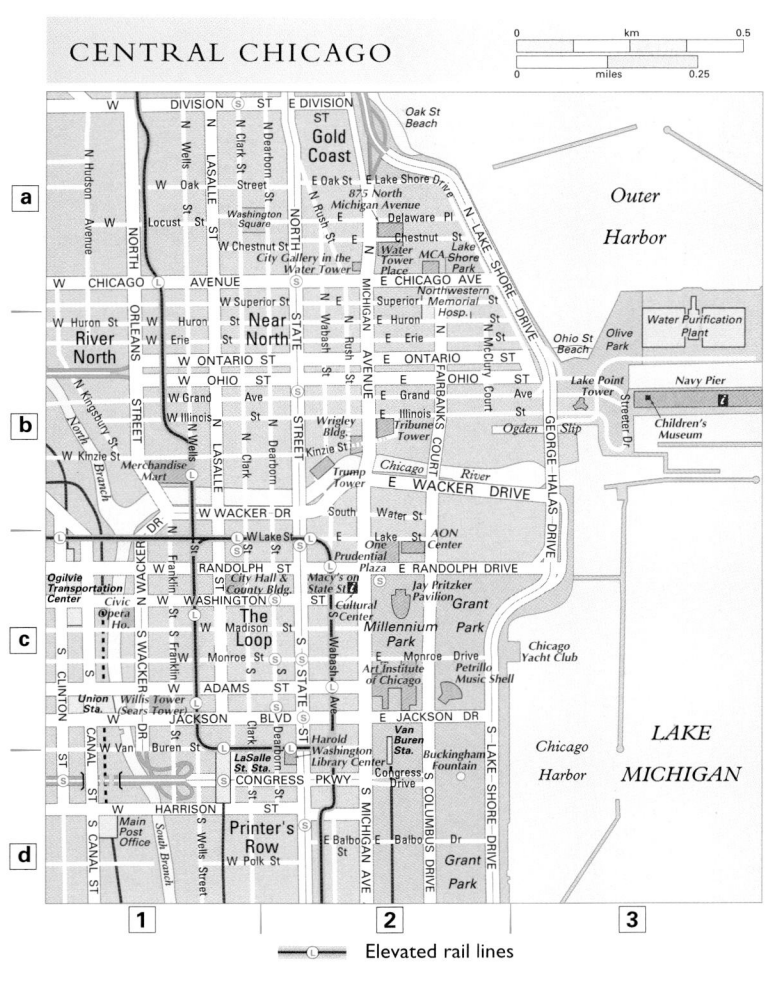

Elevated rail lines

DUBAI, U.A.E.

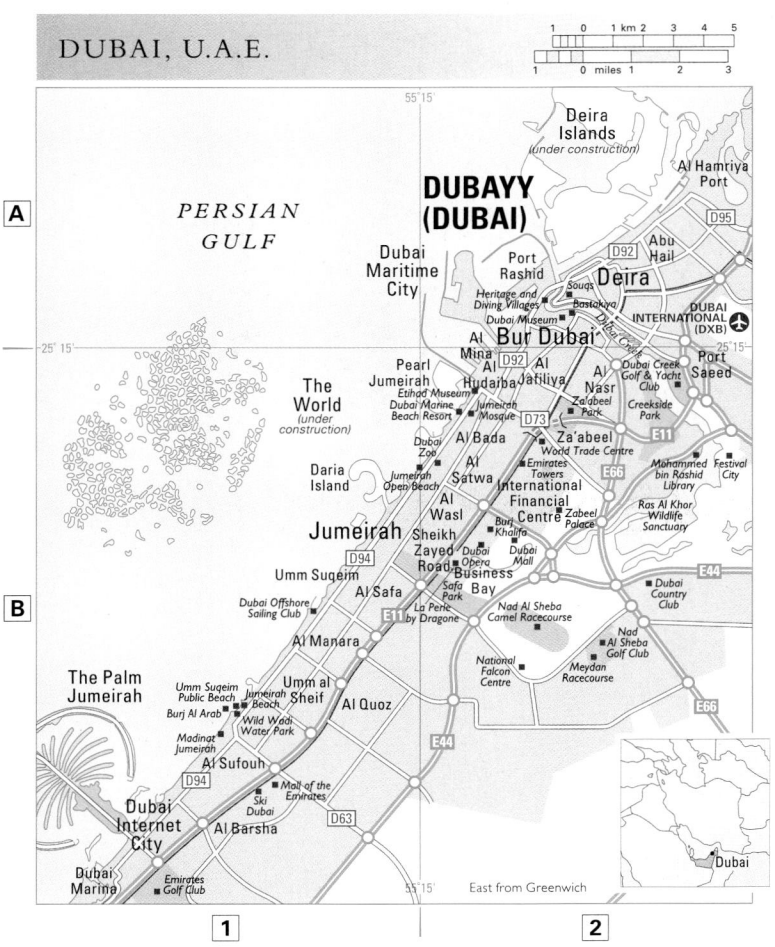

PERSIAN GULF

East from Greenwich

CHICAGO, ILLINOIS

West from Greenwich

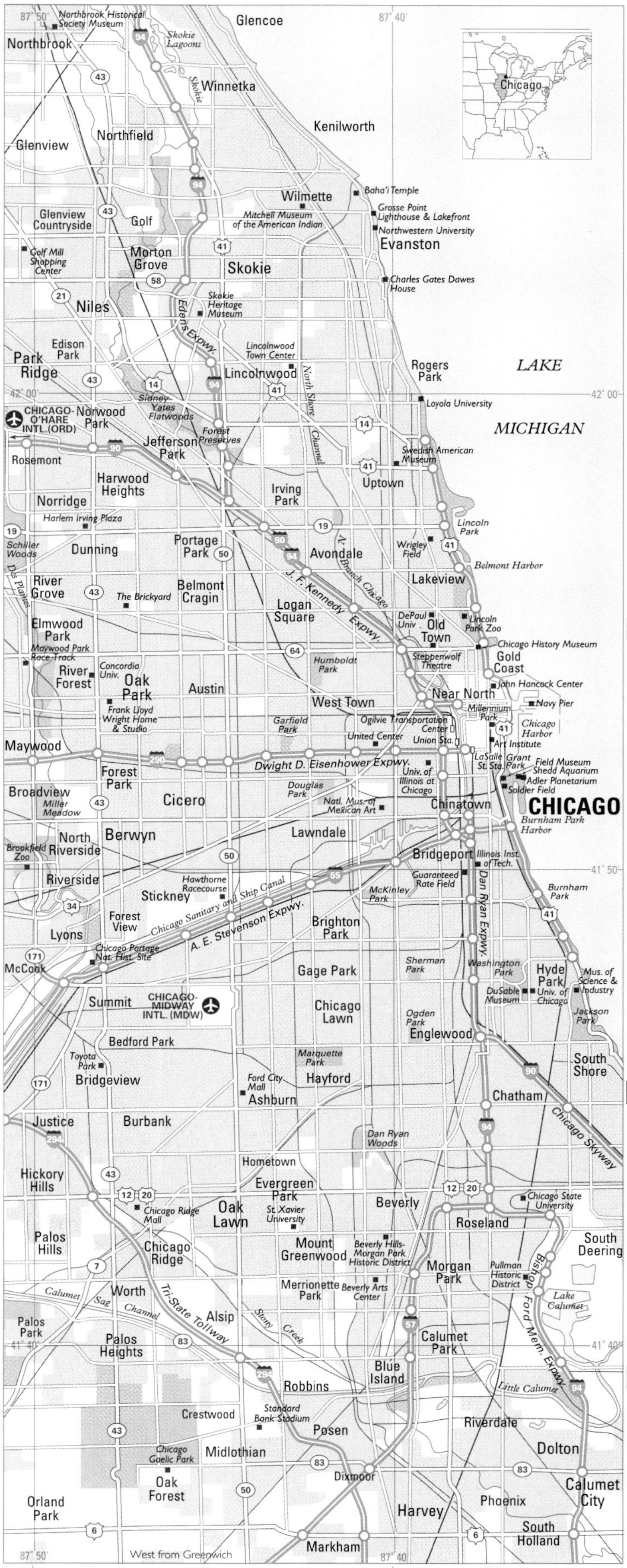

Interstate route numbers   U.S. route numbers   State route numbers

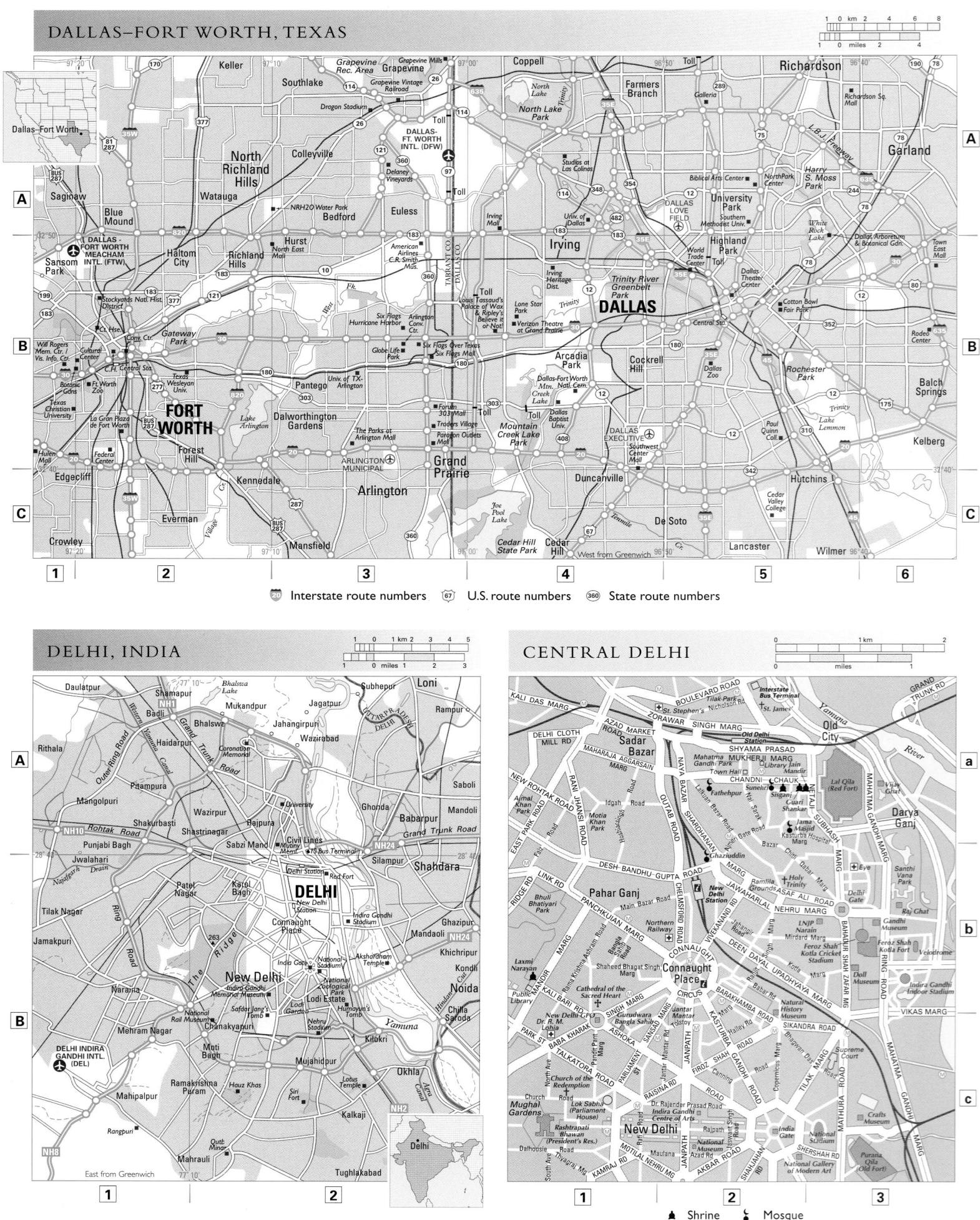

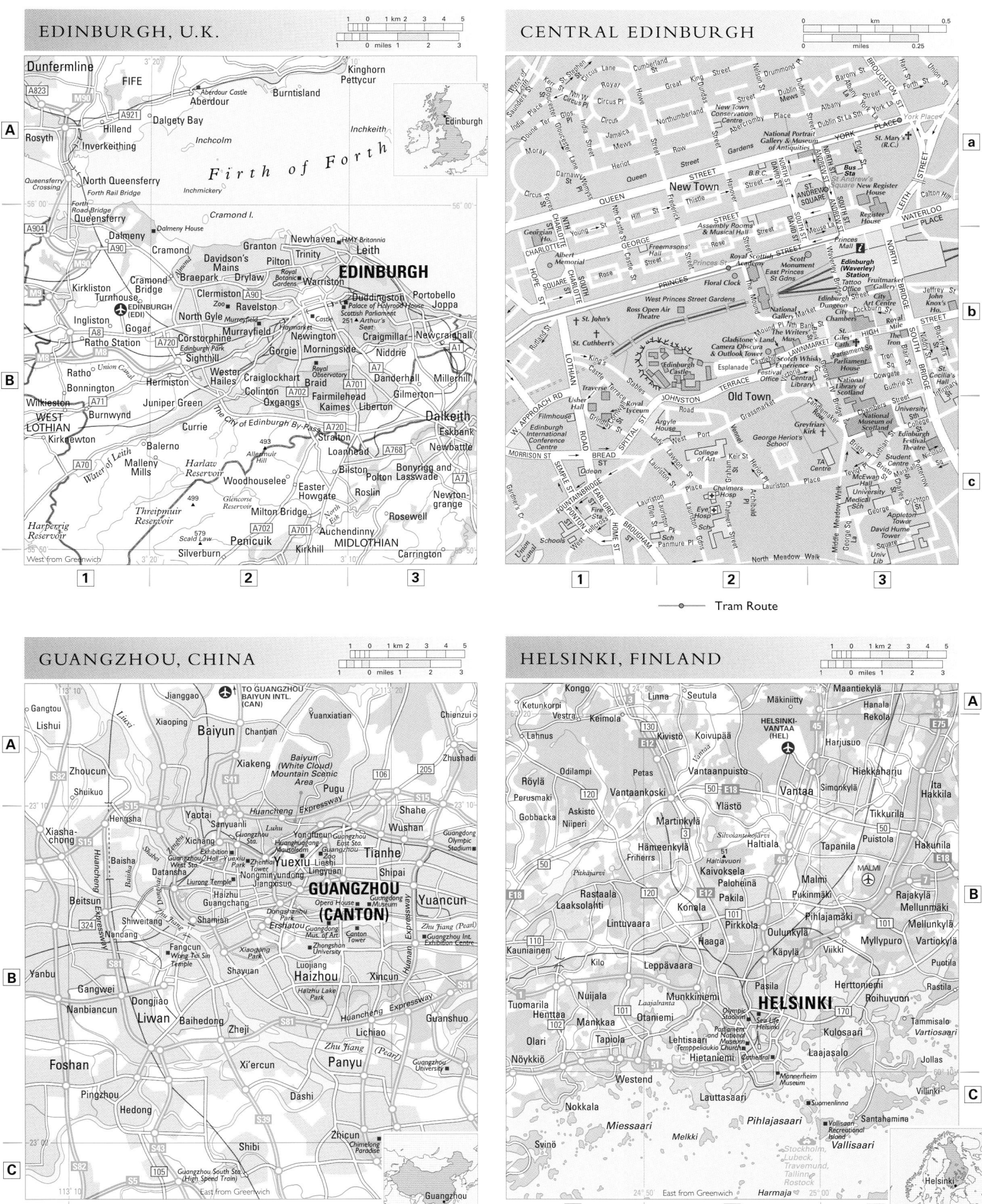

HONG KONG, CHINA

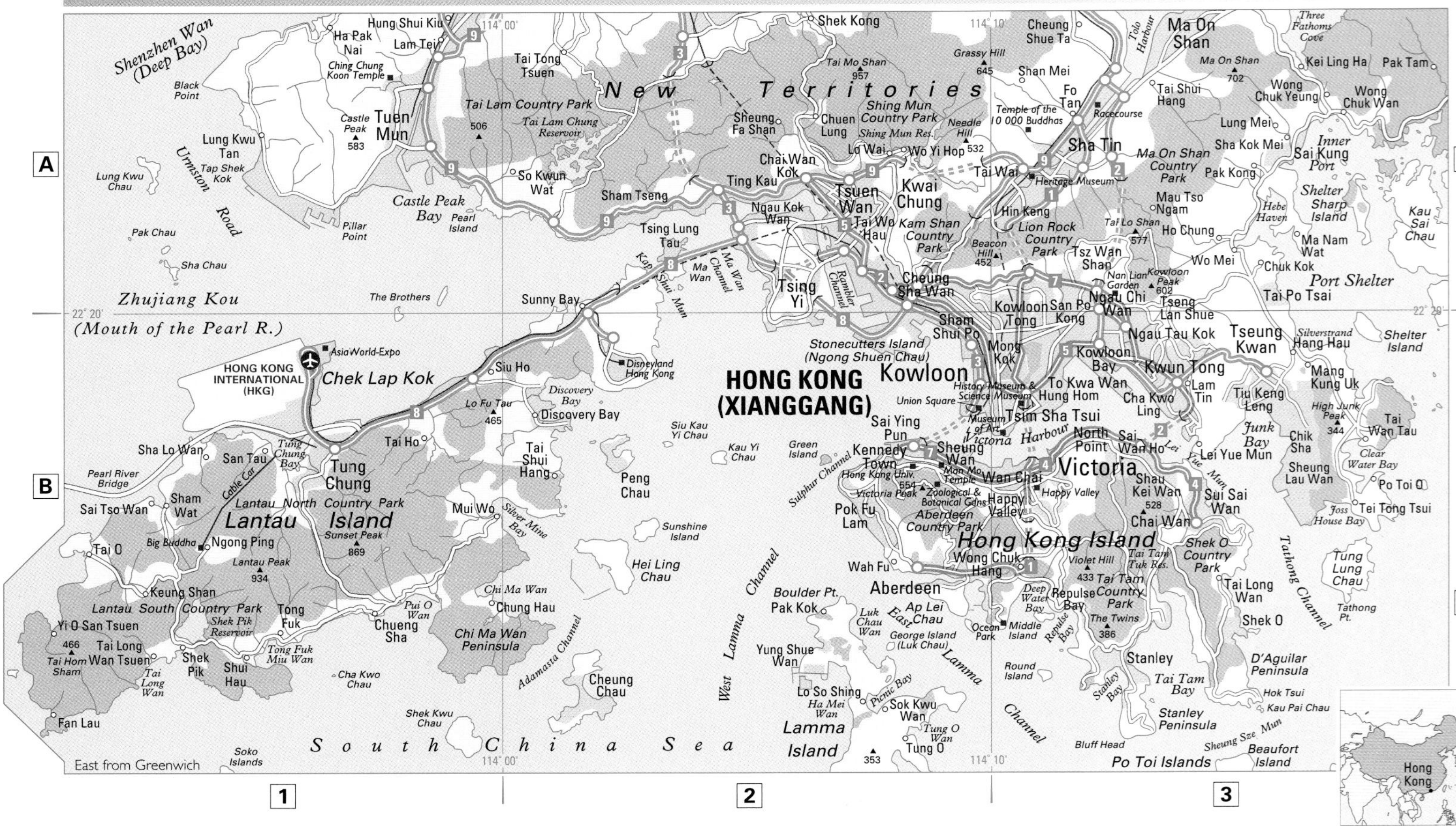

ISTANBUL, TURKEY

JAKARTA, INDONESIA

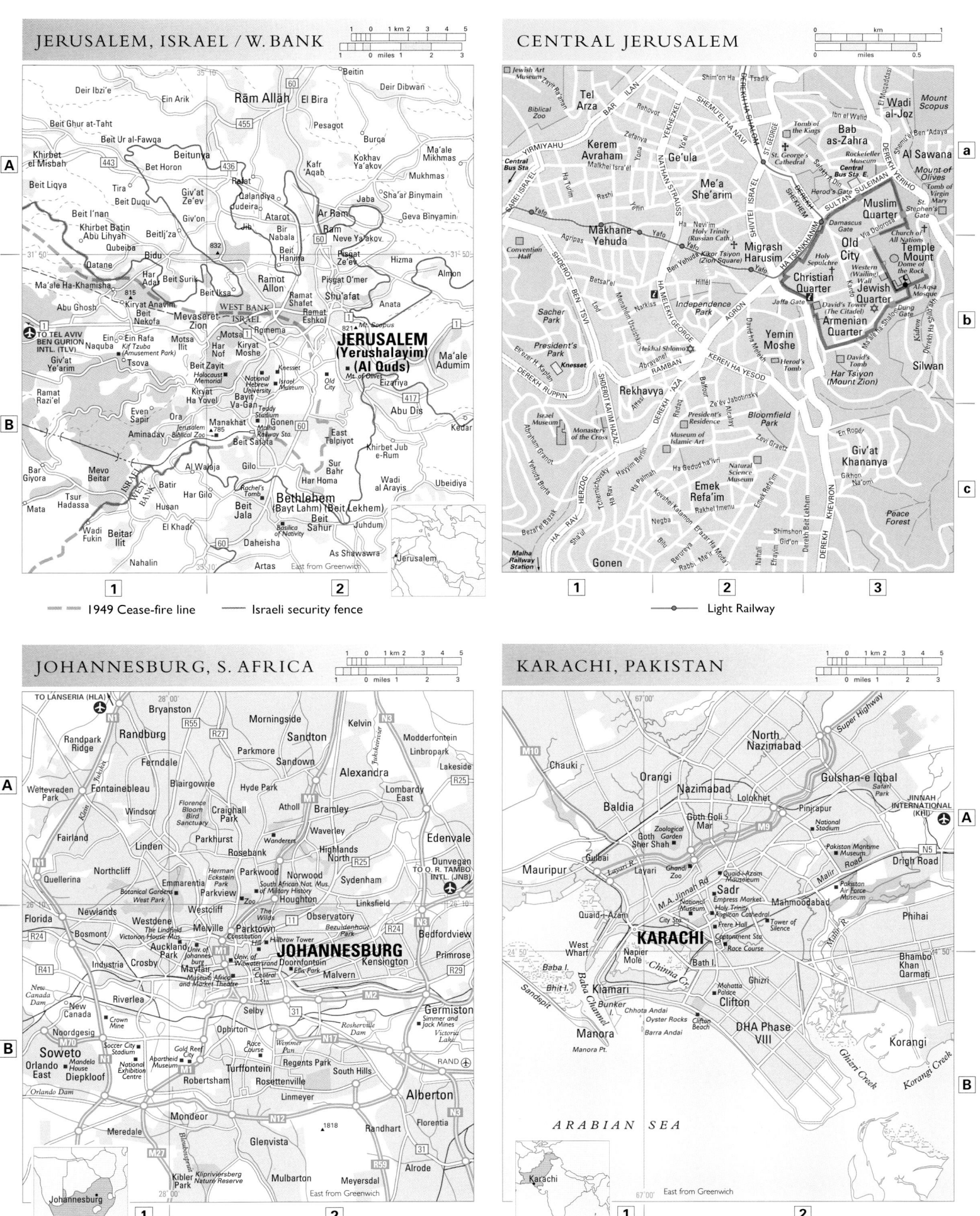

KOLKATA, INDIA

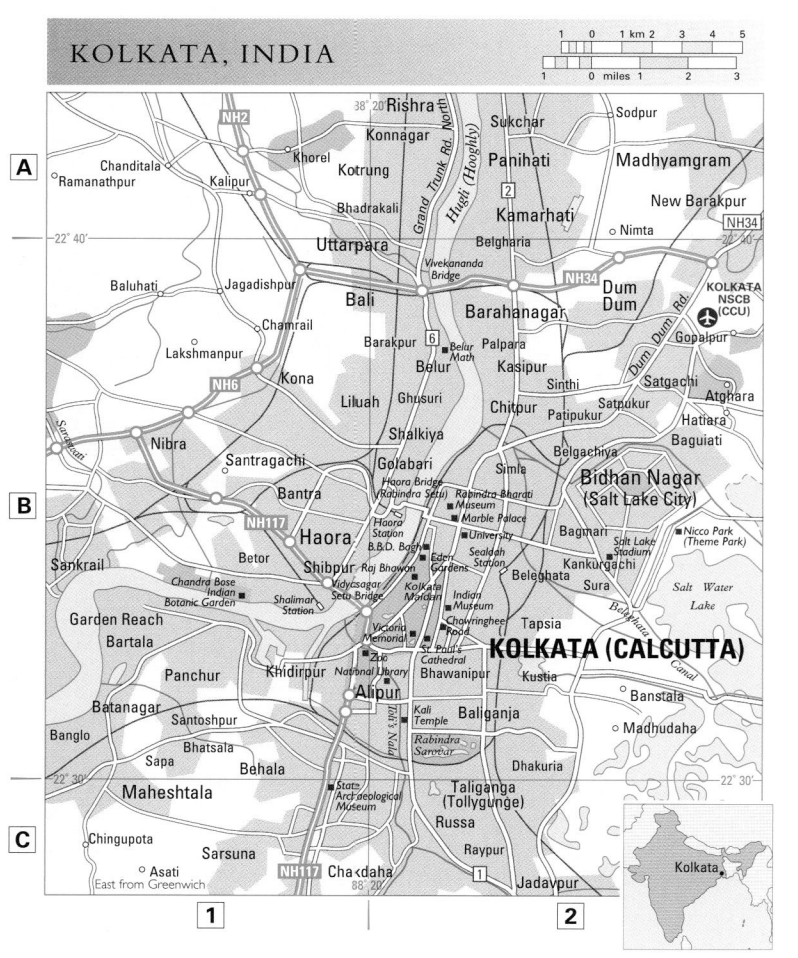

LAGOS, NIGERIA

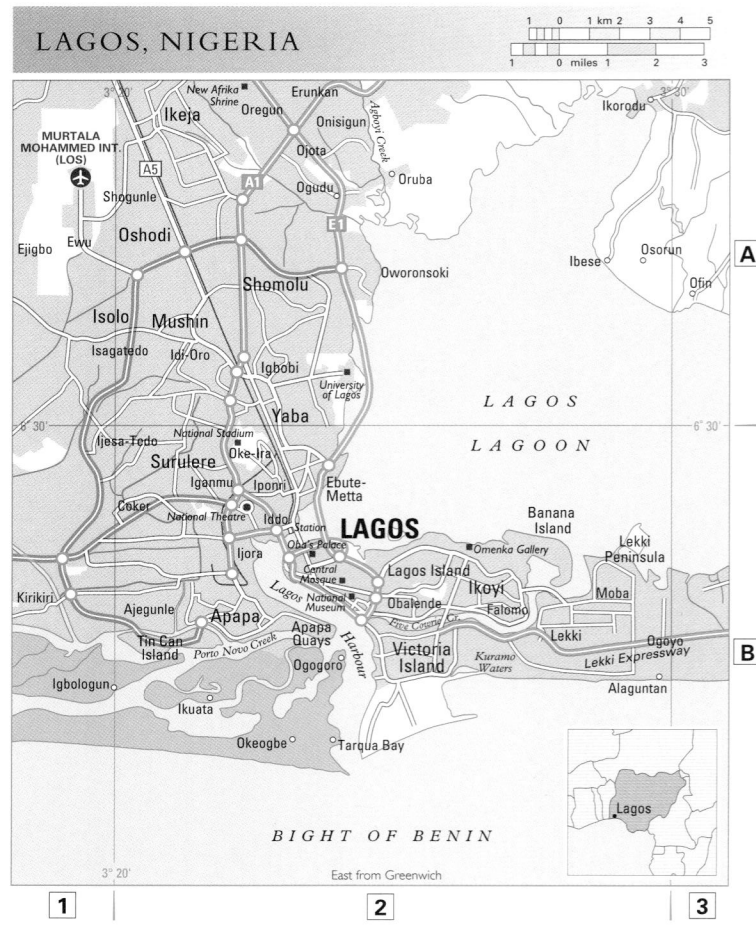

LAS VEGAS, NEVADA

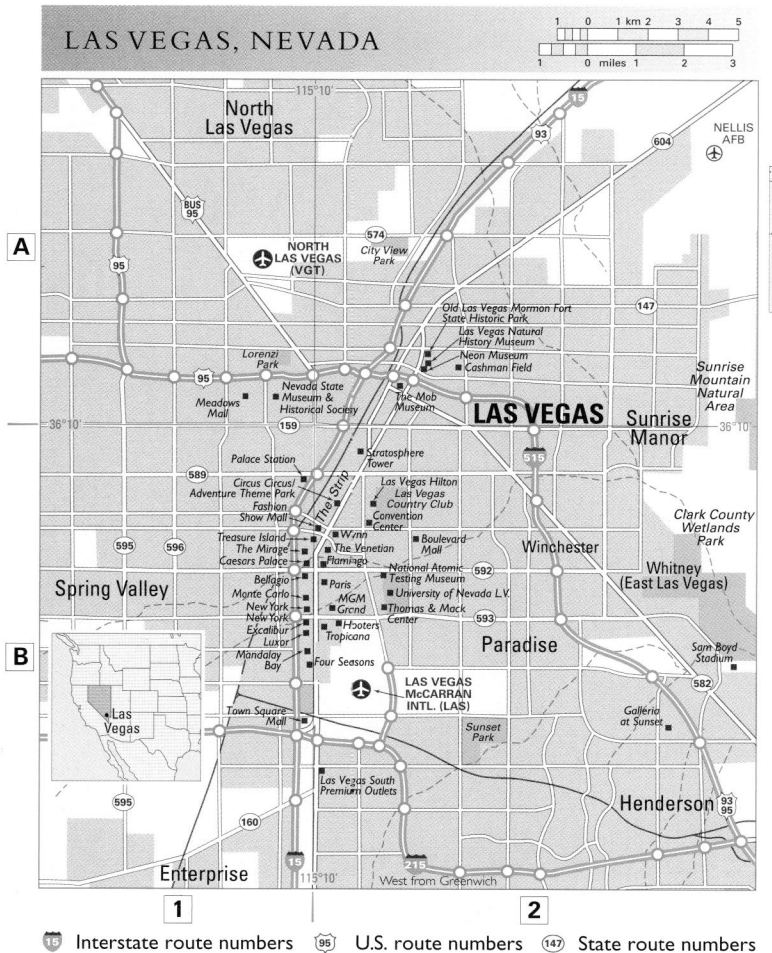

LIMA, PERU

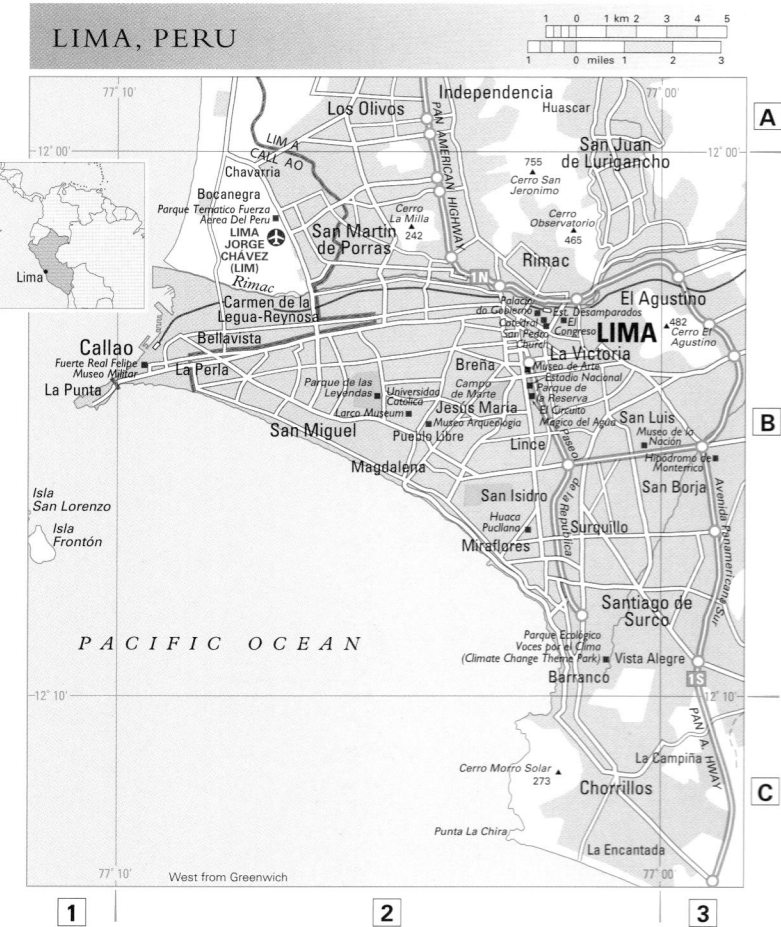

Interstate route numbers   U.S. route numbers   State route numbers

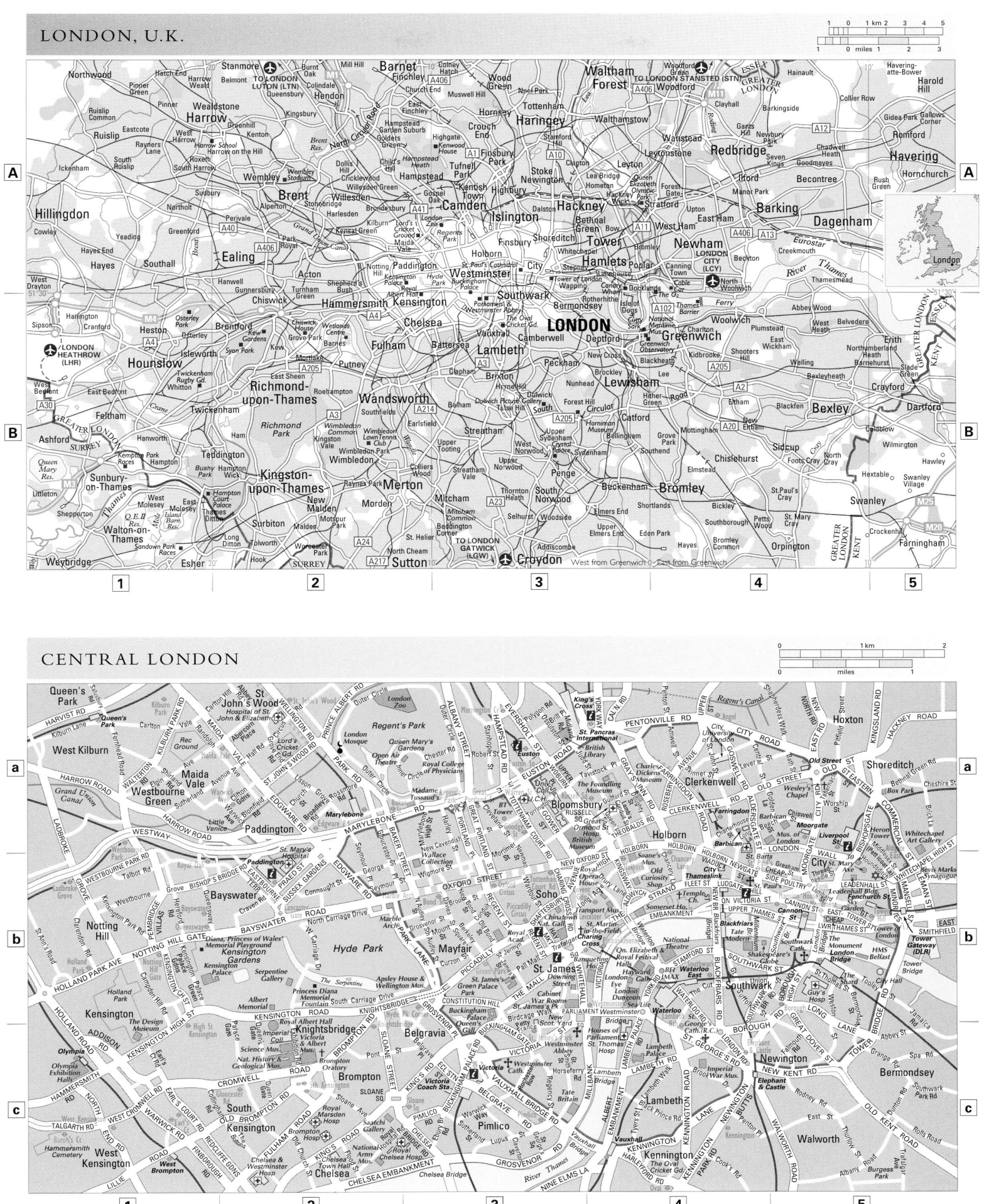

LONDON, U.K.

CENTRAL LONDON

Congestion Charging Zone

LISBON, PORTUGAL

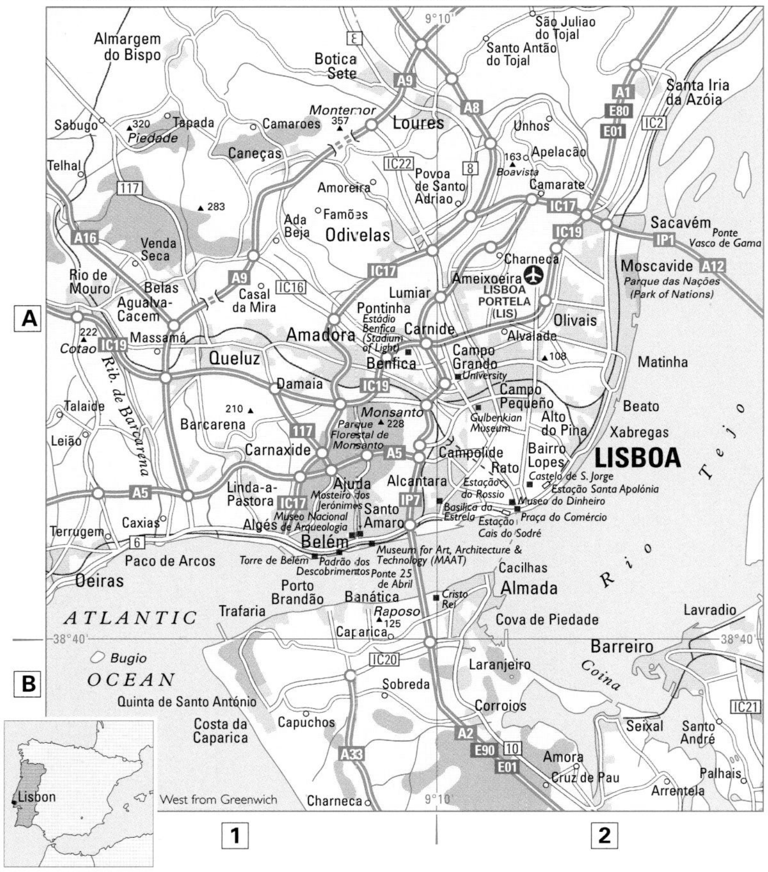

1 km 2 3 4 5
0 miles 3

Almargem do Bispo
Botica Sete
São Julião do Tojal
Santo Antão do Tojal
Sabugo
Telhal
▲320 Tapada Piedade
Camaroes 357
Loures
Monteror
Caneças
Unhos
Santa Iria da Azóia
163 Boavista
Apelação
Amoreira
Ada Beja
Famões
Camarate
Povoa de Santo Adrião
Sacavém
Ponte Vasco da Gama
Moscavide
Venda Seca
Rio de Mouro
Odivelas
Charneca
Ameixoeira
LISBOA PORTELA (LIS)
Parque das Nações (Park of Nations)
Belas
Aguala-Cacem
Lumiar
Pontinha
Carnide
Estádio Benfica (Stadium of Light)
Olivais
Alvalade
Massamá
Queluz
Amadora
Benfica
Campo Grande
University
Matinha
Damaia
Campo Pequeno
Alto do Pina
Beato
Xabregas
Talaide
Barcarena
Monsanto Parque Florestal de Monsanto
Campolide
Gulbenkian Museum
Bairro Lopes
Leião
▲210
Carnaxide
▲228
Rato
Castelo de S. Jorge
Cotao
Ajuda Mosteiro dos Jerónimos
Linda-a-Pastora
Museu Nacional de Arqueologia
Alcântara
Santo Amaro
Estação do Rossio
Basilica da Estrela
Estação Santa Apolónia
LISBOA
Terrugem
Caxias
Algés
Belém
Torre de Belém
Padrão dos Descobrimentos
Ponte 25 de Abril
Cristo Rei
Estação Cais do Sodré
Praça do Comércio
Museum for Art, Architecture & Technology (MAAT)
Cacilhas
Oeiras
Paco de Arcos
Porto Brandão
Banática
Raposo
▲125
Almada
Lavradio
ATLANTIC
Trafaria
Cova de Piedade
OCEAN
Bugio
Quinta de Santo António
Capricar
Barreiro
Costa da Caparica
Sobreda
Laranjeiro
Coina
Capuchos
Corroios
Seixal
Santo André
Amora
Cruz de Pau
Arrentela
Palhais
Charneca
West from Greenwich

CENTRAL LISBON

km
miles 0.5

Palácio de Justiça
Penitenciária
S. Sebastião
Instituto Superior Técnico
Estefânia
Amoreiros
Marquês de Pombal
Parque Eduardo VII
Pavilhão Carlos Lopes
Penha de França
Rato
Museu Nacional de História Natural e de Ciência
Jardim Botânico
Anjos
Igreja d. Anjos
Bairro Lopes
Hospital de Santa Marta
Hospital dos Capuchos
Graça
Palácio de Assembleia Nacional
Instituto de Medicina Legal
Hospital de S. José
Igreja de Graça
Bairro Alto
Estação do Rossio
Museu Arqueológico do Carmo
Castelo de São Jorge (St. George's Castle)
Igreja Sta. Engrácia
Estação Santa Apolónia
Hospital de Jesus
Praça Rossio
Teatro Nac. de São Carlos
Elevador da Glória
Alfama
Museu Antoniano (St. Anthony Mus.)
Military Trigo Museum
Museu de Arte Contemporânea
Biblioteca Nacional
Museu do Dinheiro
Museu de Arte Decorativas
Baixa
Estação Cais do Sodré
Praça do Comércio
Dom José I
Terreiro do Paço
Estação Fluvial
Rio Tejo (Tagus)
AV. VINTE E QUATRO DE JULHO
AV. RIBEIRA DAS NAUS
R. DA ALFÂNDEGA
INFANTE DOM HENRIQUE
Seixal
Montijo, Barreiro

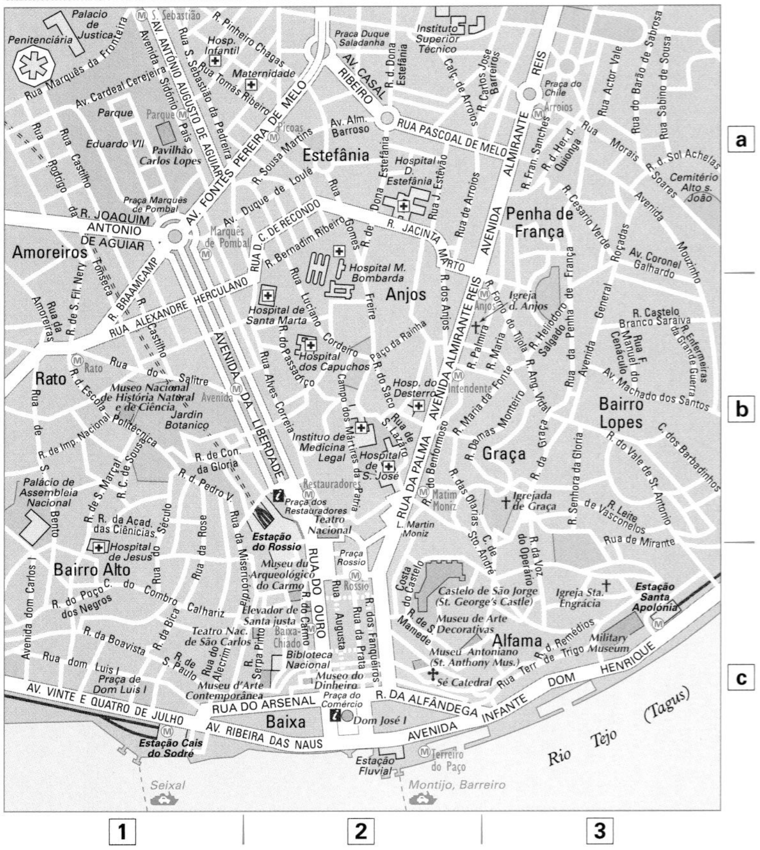

LOS ANGELES, CALIFORNIA

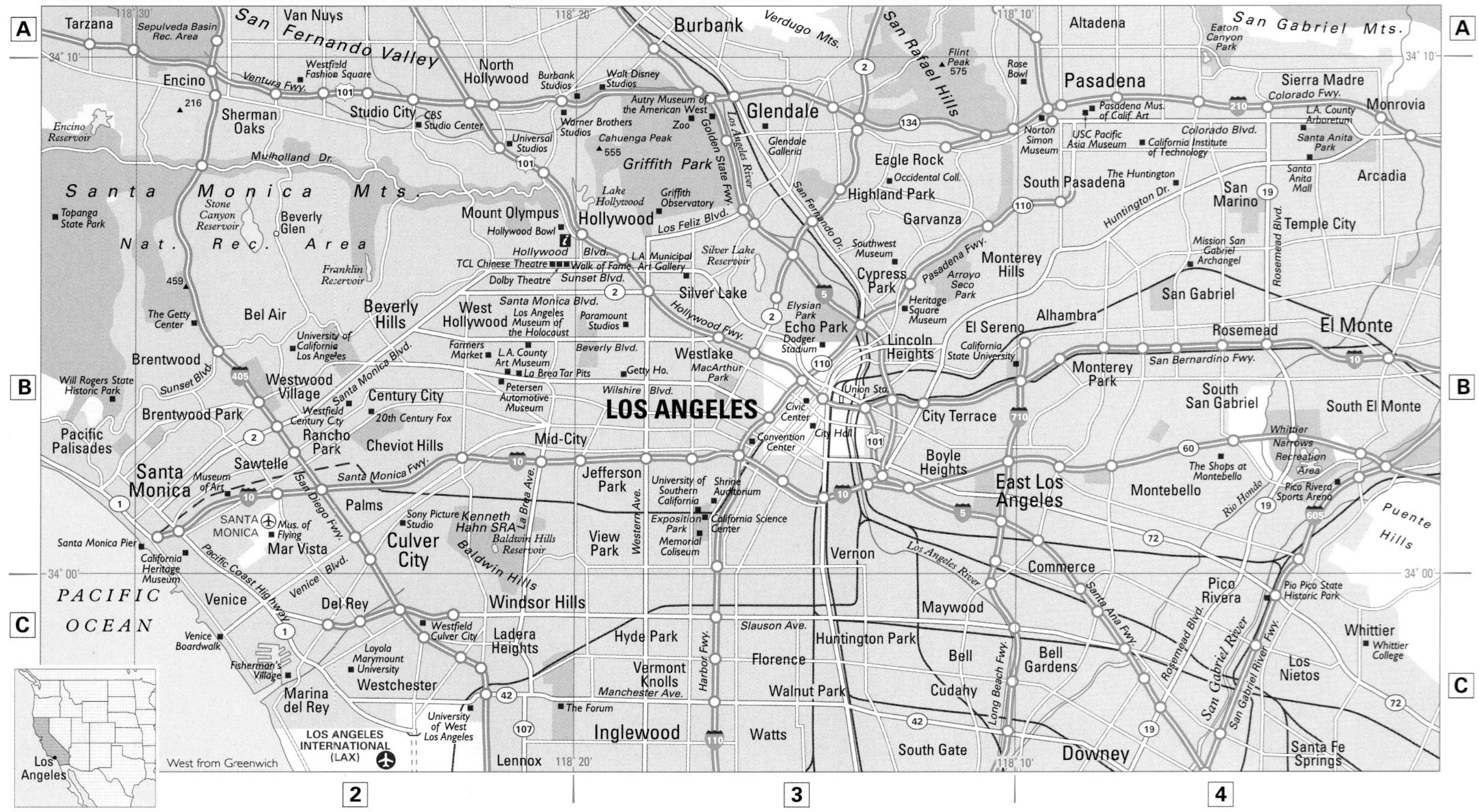

1 0 1 km 2 3 4 5
1 0 miles 1 2 3

Tarzana
Sepulveda Basin Rec. Area
Van Nuys
San Fernando Valley
Burbank
Verdugo Mts.
Altadena
San Gabriel Mts.
Eaton Canyon Park
Encino
Westfield Fashion Square
North Hollywood
Burbank Studios
Walt Disney Studios
Flint Peak
Rose Bowl
Pasadena
Sierra Madre
▲216
Ventura Fwy.
Studio City
CBS Studio Center
Autry Museum of the American West
Zoo
Glendale
Norton Simon Museum
Pasadena Mus. of Calif. Art
Colorado Fwy.
Monrovia
Encino Reservoir
Sherman Oaks
Universal Studios
Warner Brothers Studios
Cahuenga Peak
555
Griffith Park
Glendale Galleria
USC Pacific Asia Museum
Colorado Blvd.
California Institute of Technology
L.A. County Arboretum
Santa Anita Park
Mulholland Dr.
Griffith Observatory
Eagle Rock
Occidental Coll.
South Pasadena
The Huntington
San Marino
Arcadia
Santa Anita Mall
Santa Monica Mts.
Lake Hollywood
Highland Park
Garvanza
Stone Canyon Reservoir
Beverly Glen
Mount Olympus
Hollywood Bowl
Hollywood
Los Feliz Blvd.
Southwest Museum
Monterey Hills
Mission San Gabriel Archangel
Temple City
Topanga State Park
Nat. Rec. Area
Franklin Reservoir
TCL Chinese Theatre
Dolby Theatre
Hollywood Blvd.
Walk of Fame
L.A. Municipal Art Gallery
Silver Lake Reservoir
Cypress Park
Pasadena Fwy.
Arroyo Seco Park
San Gabriel
459
Sunset Blvd.
Silver Lake
Heritage Square Museum
Alhambra
Rosemead
The Getty Center
Bel Air
Beverly Hills
West Hollywood
Los Angeles Museum of the Holocaust
Paramount Studios
Echo Park
Dodger Stadium
Elysian Park
Lincoln Heights
California State University
Brentwood
University of California Los Angeles
Farmers Market
Century City
L.A. County Art Museum
La Brea Tar Pits
Beverly Blvd.
Getty Ho.
Union Sta.
Civic Center
City Terrace
El Sereno
Monterey Park
Will Rogers State Historic Park
Sunset Blvd.
Westwood Village
Westfield Century City
20th Century Fox
Petersen Automotive Museum
Wilshire Blvd.
LOS ANGELES
City Hall
Boyle Heights
South San Gabriel
South El Monte
El Monte
Pacific Palisades
Brentwood Park
Rancho Park
Cheviot Hills
Mid-City
Convention Center
Jefferson Park
University of Southern California
Shrine Auditorium
East Los Angeles
Montebello
The Shops at Montebello
Whittier Narrows Recreation Area
Santa Monica
Museum of Art
Santa Monica Blvd.
Sawtelle
Santa Monica Fwy.
Palms
Sony Picture Studio
Kenneth Hahn SRA
Baldwin Hills Reservoir
View Park
Exposition Park
California Science Center
Memorial Coliseum
Vernon
Commerce
Pico Rivera
Pico Rivera Sports Arena
Puente Hills
SANTA MONICA
Mus. of Flying
California Heritage Museum
Mar Vista
Culver City
Baldwin Hills
Windsor Hills
Maywood
Pio Pico State Historic Park
Santa Monica Pier
Del Rey
Venice Blvd.
Venice
Venice Boardwalk
Westfield Culver City
Ladera Heights
Hyde Park
Vermont Knolls
Manchester Ave.
Slauson Ave.
Harbor Fwy.
Huntington Park
Florence
Bell
Bell Gardens
Cudahy
Commerce
Santa Fe Springs
PACIFIC OCEAN
Fisherman's Village
Loyola Marymount University
Marina del Rey
Westchester
University of West Los Angeles
The Forum
Inglewood
Watts
Walnut Park
South Gate
Downey
Los Nietos
Whittier
Whittier College
LOS ANGELES INTERNATIONAL (LAX)
Lennox
West from Greenwich
Los Angeles

🔵 15 Interstate route numbers ⬭ 101 U.S. route numbers ⬭ 147 State route numbers

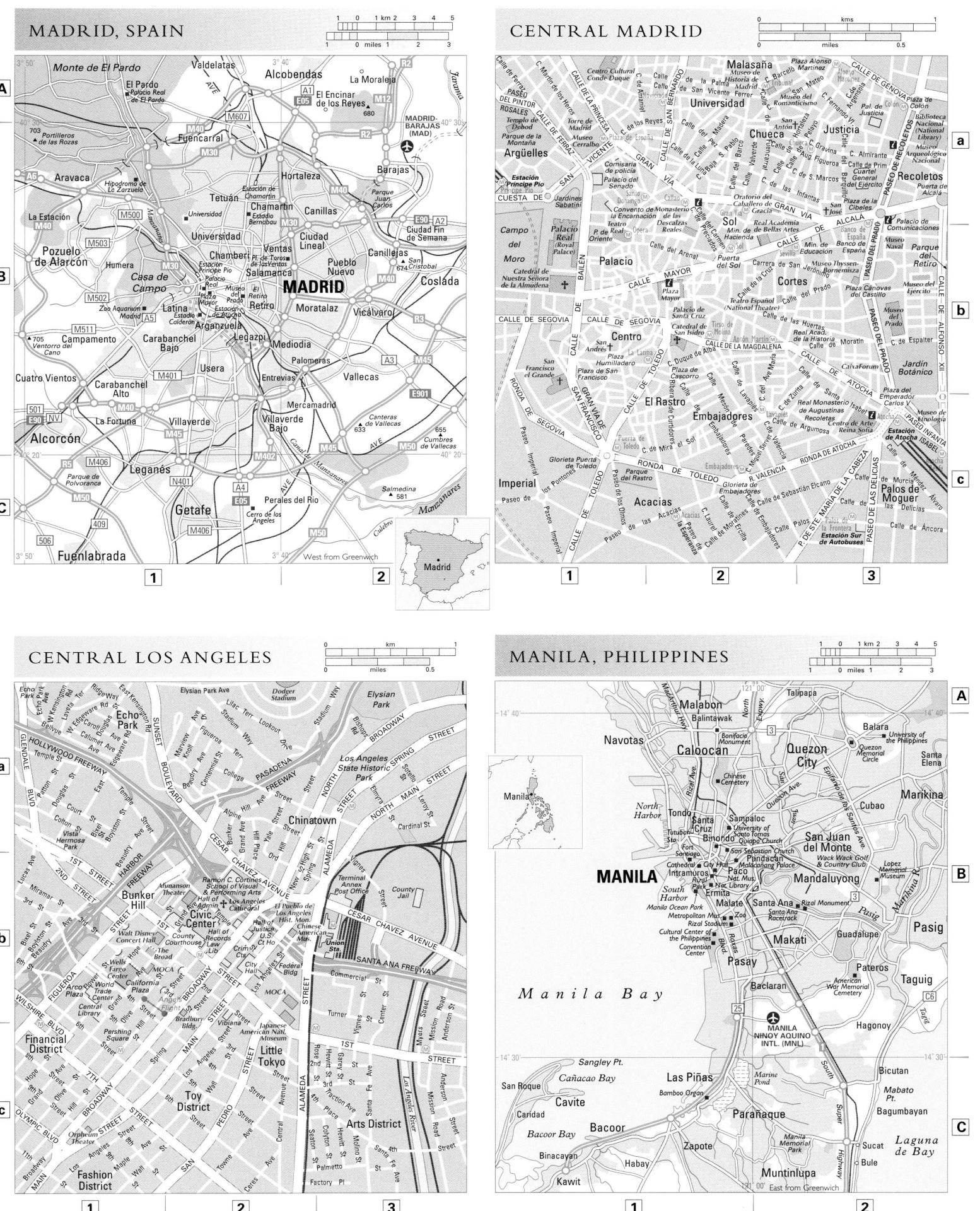

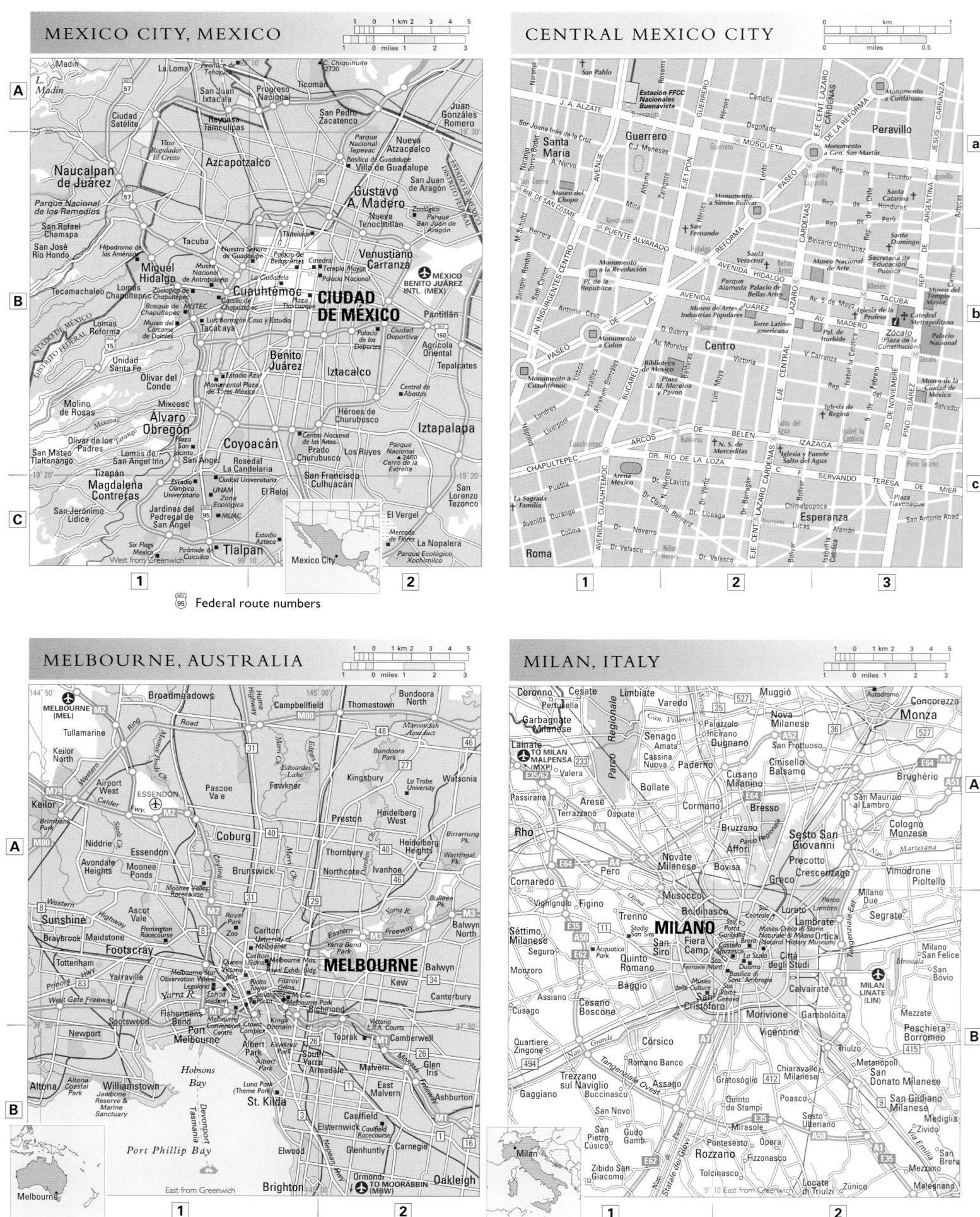

MEXICO CITY, MEXICO

1 0 1 km 2 3 4 5
0 miles 1 2 3

L. Madín
Madín
La Loma
Pirámides de Tehuacán
C. Chiquihuite 2730
Ticomán
San Juan Ixtacala
Progreso Nacional
San Pedro Zacatenco
Juan Gonzáles Romero
Ciudad Satélite
Reynosa Tamaulipas
Parque Nacional Tepeyac
Nueva Atzacoalco
Vaso Regulador El Cristo
Azcapotzalco
Basílica de Guadalupe
Villa de Guadalupe
San Juan de Aragón
Gustavo A. Madero
Naucalpan de Juárez
Parque Nacional de los Remedios
Nueva Tenochtitlán
Zoológico
Parque San Juan de Aragón
San Rafael Chamapa
Tacuba
Tlatelolco
Venustiano Carranza
Hipódromo de las Américas
Nuestra Señora de Guadalupe
Palacio de Bellas Artes
Catedral
Plaza Tlaxcoaque
San José Río Hondo
Miguel Hidalgo
Museo Nacional de Antropología
La Ciudadela
Templo Mayor
Palacio Nacional
Pantitlán
Tecamachalco
Lomas Chapultepec
Zoológico de Chapultepec
Castillo de Chapultepec
MUTEC
Cuauhtémoc
CIUDAD DE MÉXICO
MÉXICO BENITO JUÁREZ INTL. (MEX)
Bosque de Chapultepec
Luis Barragán Casa y Estudio
Museo del Carcamo de Dolores
Tacubaya
Palacio de los Deportes
Ciudad Deportiva
ESTADO DE MÉXICO
Lomas Reforma
Agrícola Oriental
Tepalcates
Unidad Santa Fe
Olivar del Conde
Benito Juárez
Estadio Azul
Iztacalco
DISTRITO FEDERAL
Molino de Rosas
Monumental Plaza de Toros México
Central de Abastos
Mixcoac
Álvaro Obregón
Olivar de los Padres
Plaza San Jacinto
Coyoacán
Rosedal La Candelaria
Centro Nacional de las Artes
Prado Churubusco
Los Reyes
Parque Nacional Cerro de la Estrella 2460
Iztapalapa
San Mateo Tlaltenango
Lomas de San Ángel Inn
San Ángel
San Francisco Culhuacán
San Lorenzo Tezonco
Tizapán
Magdalena Contreras
Estadio Olímpico Universitario
Ciudad Universitaria
UNAM Zona Ecológica
El Reloj
San Jerónimo Lídice
Jardines del Pedregal de San Ángel
MUAC
El Vergel
Six Flags México
Pirámide de Cuicuilco
Estadio Azteca
Mercado de Flores
La Nopalera
Tlalpan
Parque Ecológico Xochimilco
West from Greenwich
Mexico City

Federal route numbers

1   2

CENTRAL MEXICO CITY

0 km 1
0 miles 0.5

San Pablo
Estación FFCC Nacionales Buenavista
Monumento a Cuitláhuac
J. A. ALZATE
Rosario
Naranjo
Camelia
EJE CENT LÁZARO CÁRDENAS
Peravillo
Sor Juana Inés de la Cruz
Guerrero
C.J. Menesas
Guerrero
MOSQUETA
PASEO DE LA REFORMA
JESÚS CARRANZA
Santa María
A. Nervo
Rep.
de
Ecuador
Museo del Chopo
Mina
Monumento a Simón Bolívar
Garibaldi Lagunilla
Chile
Santa Catarina
Honduras
Perú
ARGENTINA
Lagunilla
RIO DE SAN COSME
Revolución
San Fernando
REFORMA
Santo Domingo
PUENTE ALVARADO
Hidalgo
Belisario Domínguez
AVENIDA HIDALGO
Santa Veracruz
Bellas Artes
Museo Nacional de Arte
Secretaría de Educación Pública
Monumento a la Revolución
Pl. de la República
Parque Alameda Palacio de Bellas Artes
JUÁREZ
Allende
TACUBA
Museo del Templo Mayor
Antonio Caso
DE
AVENIDA
Torre Latinoamericana
Av. 5 de Mayo
Iglesia de la Profesa
Catedral Metropolitana
Museo de Artes e Industrias Populares
MADERO
Monumento a Colón
D. Guerra
Juárez
Pal. de Iturbide
Zócalo (Plaza de la Constitución)
Palacio Nacional
PASEO
Centro
Victoria
Isabel la Católica
V. Carranza
Museo de la Ciudad de México
Monumento a Cuauhtémoc
BUCARELI
J. M. Morelos y Pavón
Plaza
Salvador
Londres
Abraham González
Luis Moya
5 de Febrero
20 DE NOVIEMBRE
Liverpool
Versalles
Iglesia de Regina
PINO SUÁREZ
Nápoles
ARCOS
BELÉN
Baldeías
N. S. de Merceditas
Iglesia y Fuente Salto del Agua
IZAZAGA
Salto del Agua
CHAPULTEPEC
DR. RÍO DE LA LOZA
Cuauhtémoc
SERVANDO
TERESA
DE
MIER
Arena México
AVENIDA CUAUHTÉMOC
Dr. Lavista
Dr. Vertiz
Dr. Barragán
Bolívar
Chimalpopoca
Plaza Tlaxcoaque
La Sagrada Familia
Puebla
Dr. Liceaga
EJE CENT LÁZARO CÁRDENAS
Esperanza
Roma
Avenida Durango
Colima
Dr. Navarro
Dr. Claudio Bernard
Dr. Lucas
Doctores
Afamán
San Antonio Abad
Dr. Velasco
Dr. Velasco
Niños Héroes
Bolívar
Isabel la Católica

a   b   c

1   2   3

MELBOURNE, AUSTRALIA

1 0 1 km 2 3 4 5
1 0 miles 1 2 3

144° 50'   145° 00'
MELBOURNE (MEL)
M2
Broadmeadows
Campbellfield
Thomastown
Bundoora North
Tullamarine
Ring
Road
Hume Highway
M80
Maroondah Aqueduct
48
46
Keilor North
Airport West
Calder Fwy.
ESSENDON
M2
31
Edgars Ck.
Bundoora Park
27
La Trobe University
Watsonia
Keilor
M79
Brimbank Park
Pascoe Vale
Fawkner
Kingsbury
M80
Niddrie
Essendon
Coburg
40
Preston
Heidelberg West
Birrarrung Pk.
Avondale Heights
Moonee Ponds
Brunswick
31
Thornbury
Heidelberg Heights
Warringal Pk.
Moonee Valley Racecourse
40
Northcote
Ivanhoe
46
Sunshine
Western Highway
Ascot Vale
M2
Royal Park Zoo
Carlton
University of Melbourne
29
Bullen Pk.
M3
Balwyn North
Braybrook
Maidstone
8
Flemington Racecourse
31
Carlton Gardens
Melbourne Mus.
Royal Exhib. Bldg.
Eastern Freeway
Footscray
8
Melbourne Star Observation Wheel
Queen Victoria Mkt.
MELBOURNE
Balwyn
Tottenham
Princes Hwy
83
Etihad Stadium
Fitzroy Grdns.
M1
Kew
Canterbury
Yarraville
West Gate Freeway
Yarra R.
Legoland
Southbank
M.C.G.
Melbourne Park
Richmond
34
Fishermens Bend
Melbourne Convention Centre
Crown Casino Complex
Kings Domain
Toorak
M1
Camberwell
Port Melbourne
Albert Park
Kowkner Pk.
South Yarra
Armadale
Glen Iris
26
Ashburton
Newport
Spotswood
Luna Park (Theme Park)
Malvern
26
East Malvern
Altona
Williamstown
Jawbone Reserve & Marine Sanctuary
St. Kilda
Caulfield
Caulfield Racecourse
Elsternwick
3
M1
Altona Coastal Park
Hobsons Bay
Devonport Tasmania
Elwood
Glenhuntly
Carnegie
16
Port Phillip Bay
East from Greenwich
Ormond
TO MOORABBIN (MBW)
Oakleigh
Brighton
37° 50'
145° 00'
Melbourne

1   2

MILAN, ITALY

1 0 1 km 2 3 4 5
1 0 miles 1 2 3

Coronno
Cesate
Limbiate
Muggiò
Autodromo
Concorezzo
Pertusella
Varedo
35
527
Nova Milanese
36
527
Monza
Garbagnate Milanese
Senago
Incirano
Dugnano
San Frottuoso
Lainate
TO MILAN MALPENSA (MXP)
233
Amata
Cassina Nuova
Paderno
A52
Cusano Milanino
Ciniselle Balsamo
E64
A4
Passirana
E35/62
Valera
Arese
Ospiate
Bollate
Cormano
E64
Bruzzano
Affori
Sesto San Giovanni
Precotto
Crescenzago
Vimodrone
Pioltello
Brughério
A51
A
San Maurizio al Lambro
Cologno Monzese
Rho
Novate Milanese
Pero
Bovisa
Greco
Milano Due
Cornaredo
Vighignolo
Figino
Trenno
Musocco
Sta. Centrale
Loreto
Lambrate
Parco Lambro
Segrate
Milano San Felice
Séttimo Milanese
E35
11
Stadio San Siro
MILANO
San Siro
Fiera Camp.
A50
Museo Civico di Storia Naturale di Milano
Ortica
Assiano
Ferrovie Nord
La Scala
Città degli Studi
MILAN LINATE (LIN)
San Bóvio
Monzoro
A50
E62
Acquatica Park
Quinto Romano
Duomo
Basilica di Sant'Ambrogio
Calvairate
Mezzate
Cusago
Museo delle Culture
San Cristóforo
Morivione
Gambolóita
Peschiera Borromeo
Baggio
Quartiere Zingone
Assiano
Cesano Boscone
Córsico
Vigentino
415
Naviglio Grande
B
494
Romano Banco
Trezzano sul Naviglio
Buccinasco
412
Chiaravalle Milanese
Metanopoli
Gaggiano
Assago
Gratósoglio
Poasco
San Donato Milanese
San Novo
Tangenziale Ovest
Quinto de Stampi
Sesto Ulteriano
9
San Giuliano Milanese
San Pietro Cúsico
Gudo Gamb.
E35
Zividio
Mediglia
Zibido San Giacomo
E62
Rozzano
Opera
Fizzonasco
A1
San Brera
E35
Tolcinasco
Puntesesto
Locate di Triulzi
Zúnico
Melegnano
Mezzano
9° 10' East from Greenwich
Milan

1   2

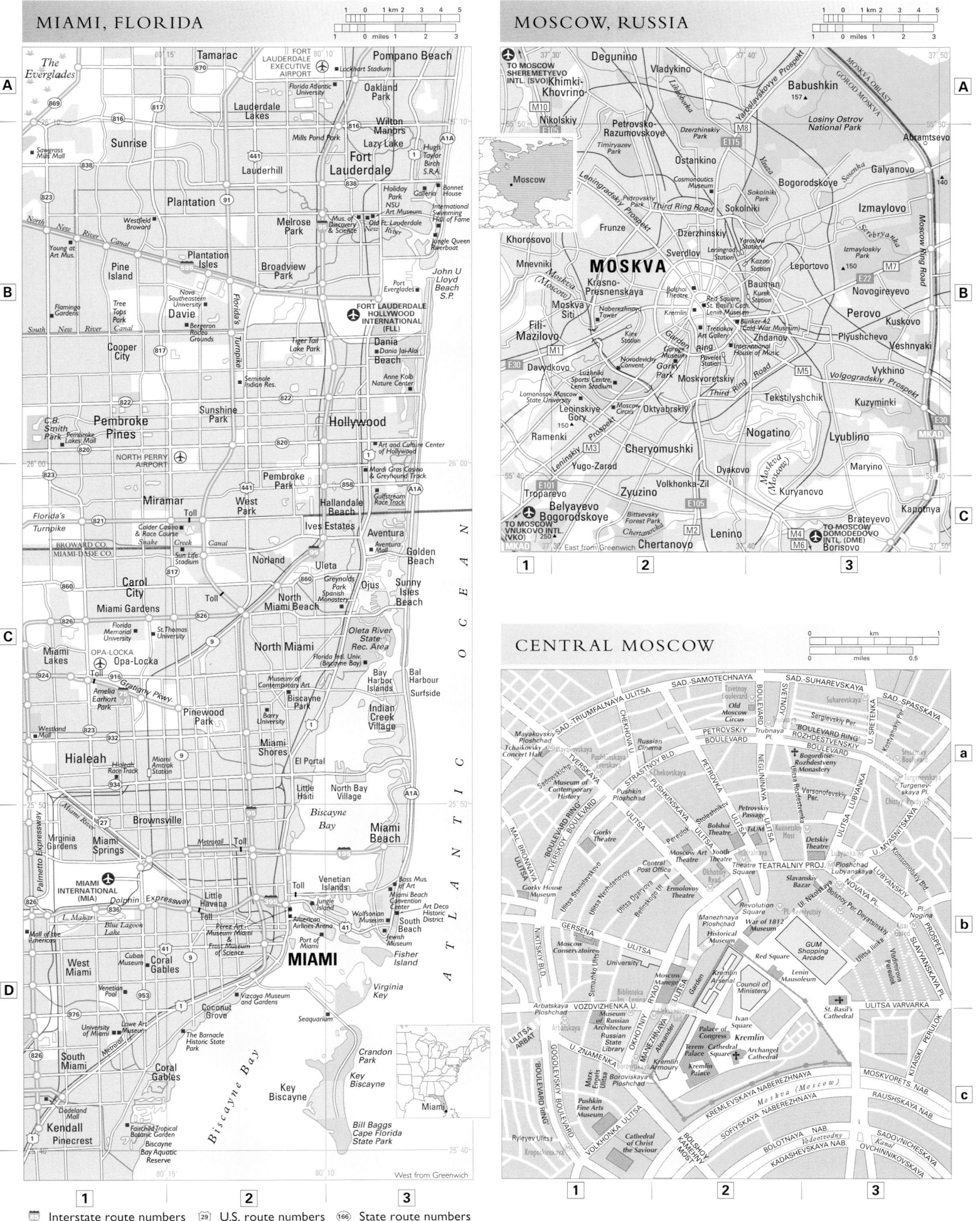

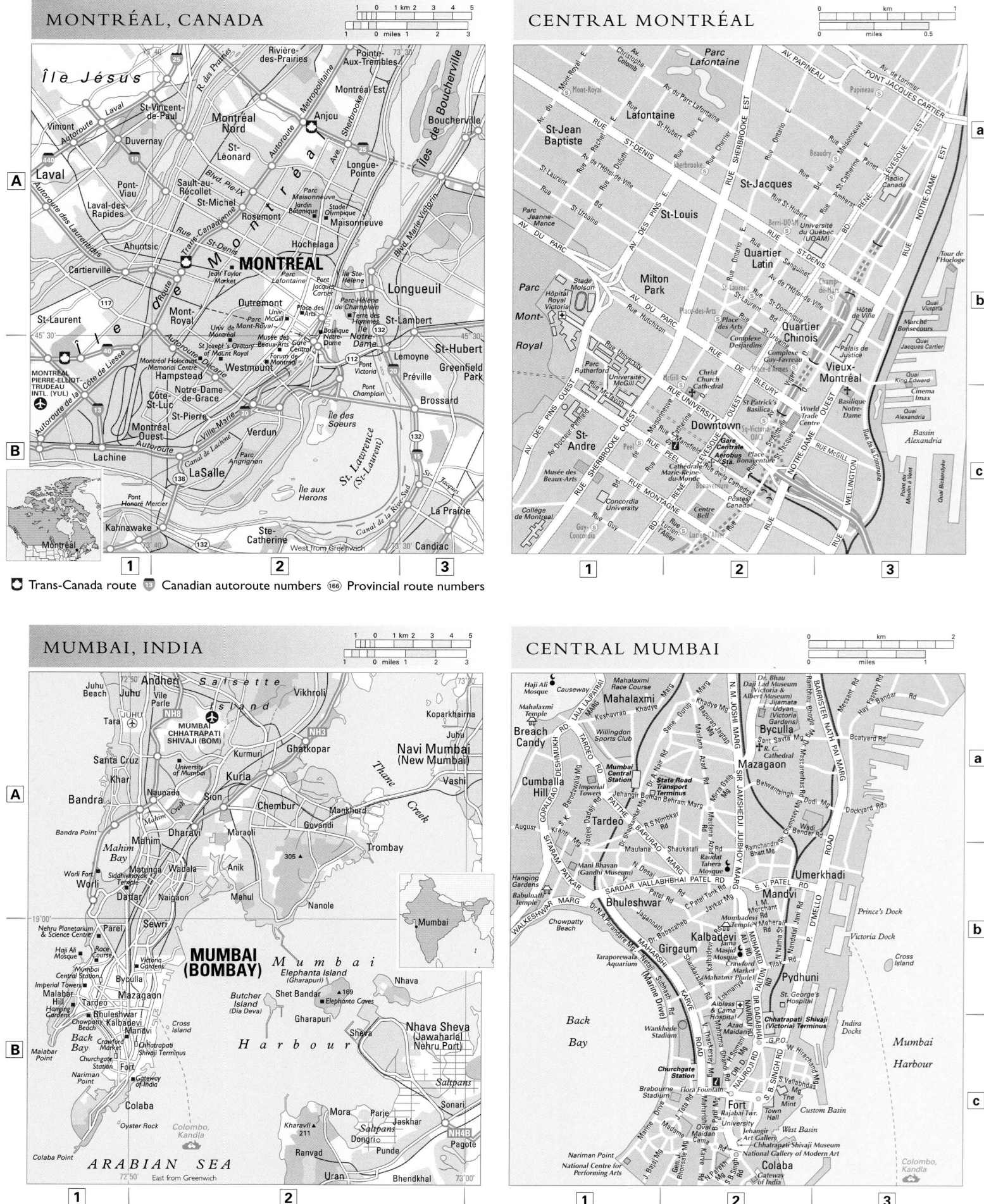

MONTRÉAL, CANADA

CENTRAL MONTRÉAL

Trans-Canada route   Canadian autoroute numbers   Provincial route numbers

MUMBAI, INDIA

CENTRAL MUMBAI

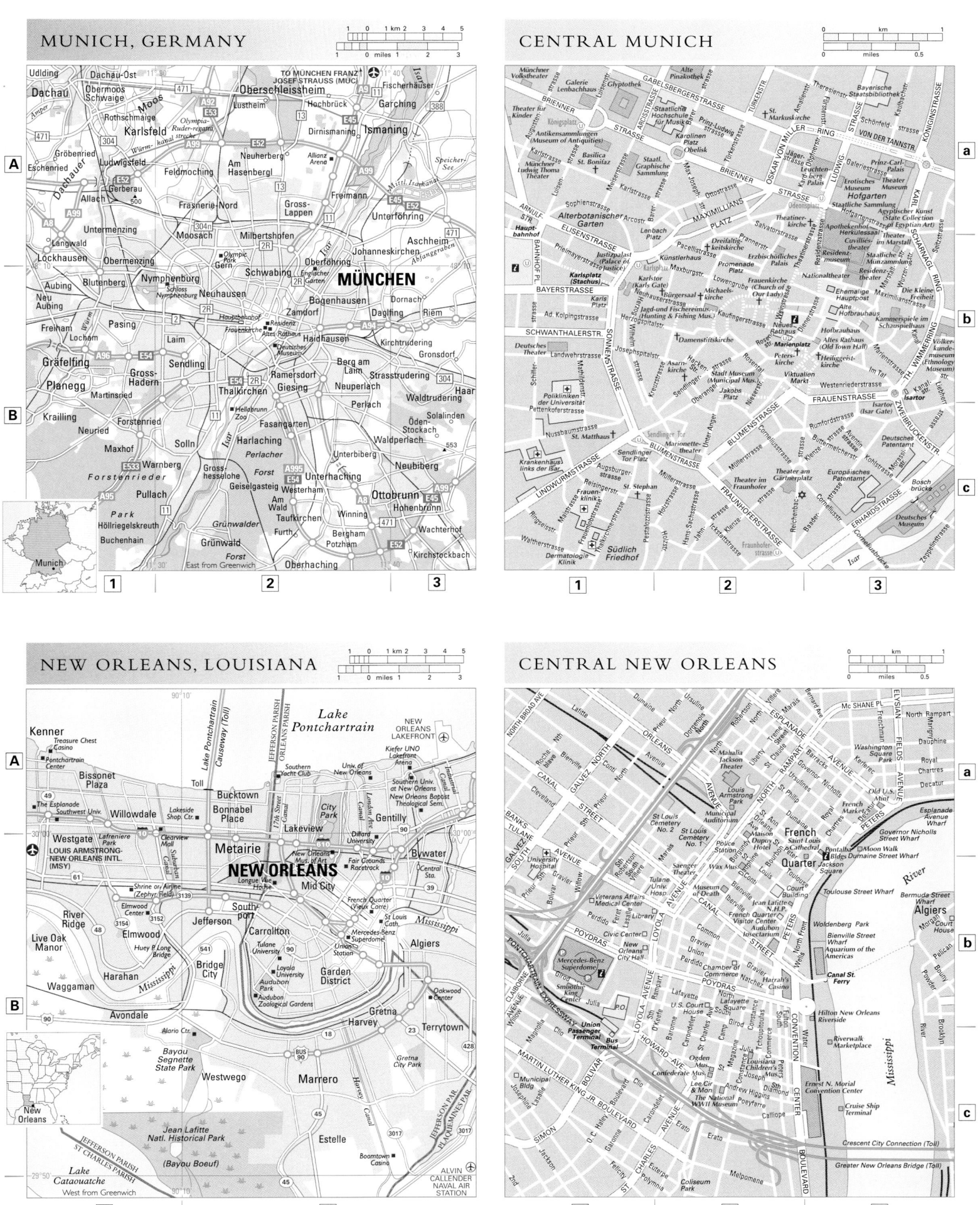

Interstate route numbers U.S. route numbers 17 State route numbers 417

COPYRIGHT PHILIP'S

NEW YORK, NEW YORK

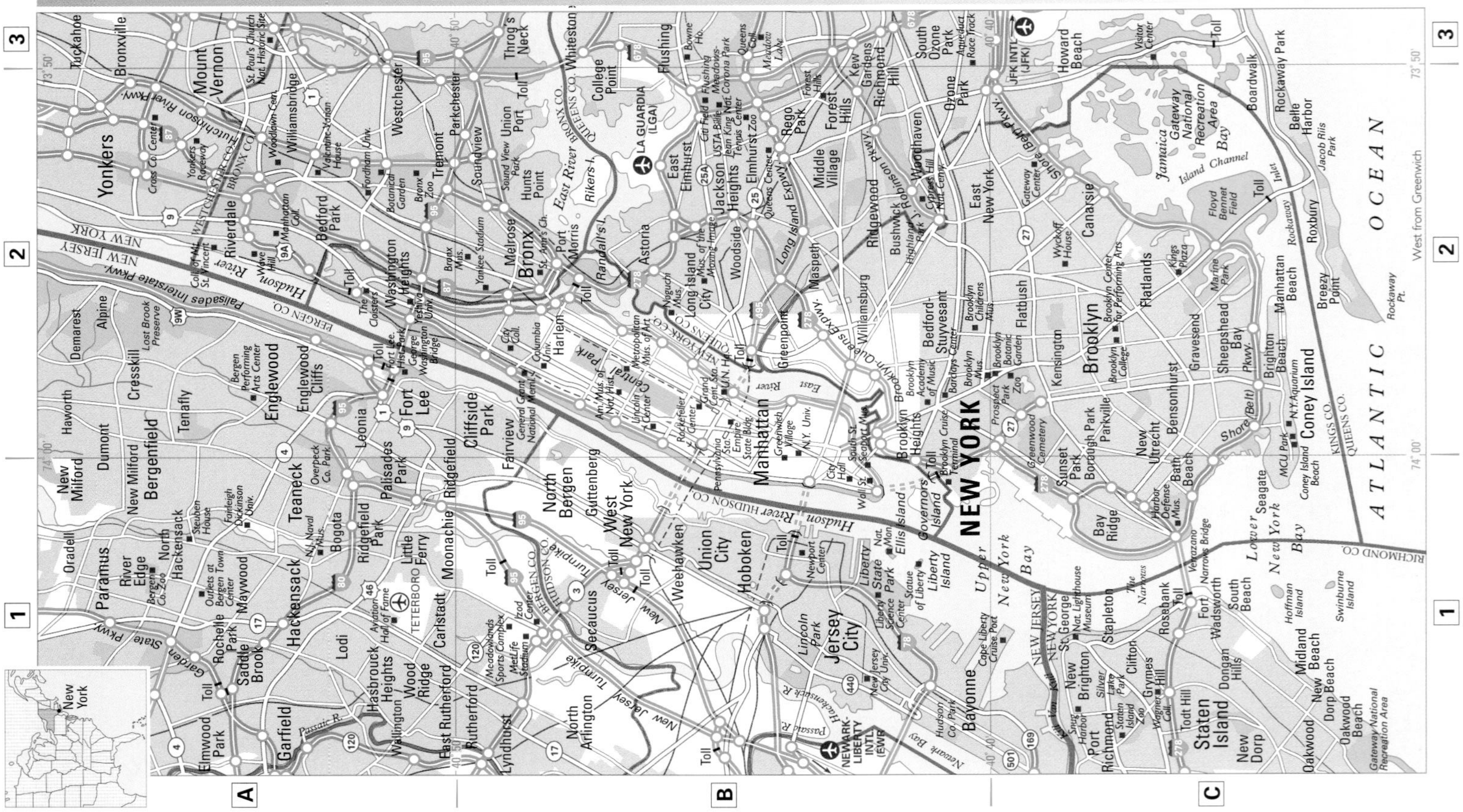

1 0 1 km 2 3 4 5
1 0 miles 1 2 3

West from Greenwich

ATLANTIC OCEAN

Yonkers · Mount Vernon · Bronxville · Tuckahoe · Bronxville · St. Paul's Church Nat. Historic Site · Williamsbridge · Westchester · Throg's Neck · Whitestone · College Point · Flushing · Queens · Kew Gardens · Forest Hills · Rego Park · South Ozone Park · Richmond Hill · Howard Beach · JFK INTL (JFK) · Rockaway Park · Boardwalk · Belle Harbor

Riverdale · Bedford Park · Washington Heights · Tremont · Soundview · Hunts Point · Bronx · Melrose · Morris Hts · Randall's I. · Astoria · Long Island City · Woodside · Elmhurst · Jackson Heights · Maspeth · Middle Village · Ridgewood · Bushwick · Forest Park

La Guardia (LGA) · East River · Rikers I. · East Elmhurst · Corona · USTA Billie Jean King Nat. Tennis Center · Flushing Meadows Corona Park

Englewood · Englewood Cliffs · Fort Lee · Leonia · Palisades Park · Ridgefield · Cliffside Park · Fairview · North Bergen · Guttenberg · West New York · Union City · Weehawken · Hoboken

Harlem · Central Park · Manhattan · Metropolitan Mus. of Art · Mus. of the City of N.Y. · Columbia Univ. · Rockefeller Center · Empire State Bldg · Greenwich Village · N.Y. Univ. · Brooklyn Bridge · Brooklyn Cruise Terminal

Greenpoint · Williamsburg · Bedford-Stuyvesant · Brooklyn · Brooklyn Heights · Brooklyn Navy Yard · Brooklyn Academy of Music · Prospect Park · Brooklyn Botanic Garden · Flatbush · Flatlands · Canarsie · Marine Park · Mill Basin · Sheepshead Bay · Brighton Beach · Coney Island · Gravesend · Bensonhurst · Bath Beach · New Utrecht · Borough Park · Sunset Park · Bay Ridge · Fort Hamilton

NEW YORK · Governors Island · Ellis Island · Liberty Island · Statue of Liberty · Upper New York Bay · Jersey City · Bayonne · Jacob Riis Park · Floyd Bennett Field · Breezy Point · Rockaway Pt

New Jersey · Newark · NEWARK LIBERTY INTL (EWR) · Elizabeth · Kearny · Secaucus · Lyndhurst · North Arlington · East Rutherford · Rutherford · Wood Ridge · Hasbrouck Heights · Teterboro · Wallington · Garfield · Lodi · Hackensack · Bogota · Teaneck · Maywood · Paramus · River Edge · New Milford · Bergenfield · Dumont · Haworth · Demarest · Alpine · Cresskill · Tenafly

Staten Island · New York Bay · St. George · New Brighton · Stapleton · Clifton · Rosebank · South Beach · Midland Beach · New Dorp · Oakwood · Gateway National Recreation Area

New York (inset)

A · B · C
1 · 2 · 3

CENTRAL NEW YORK

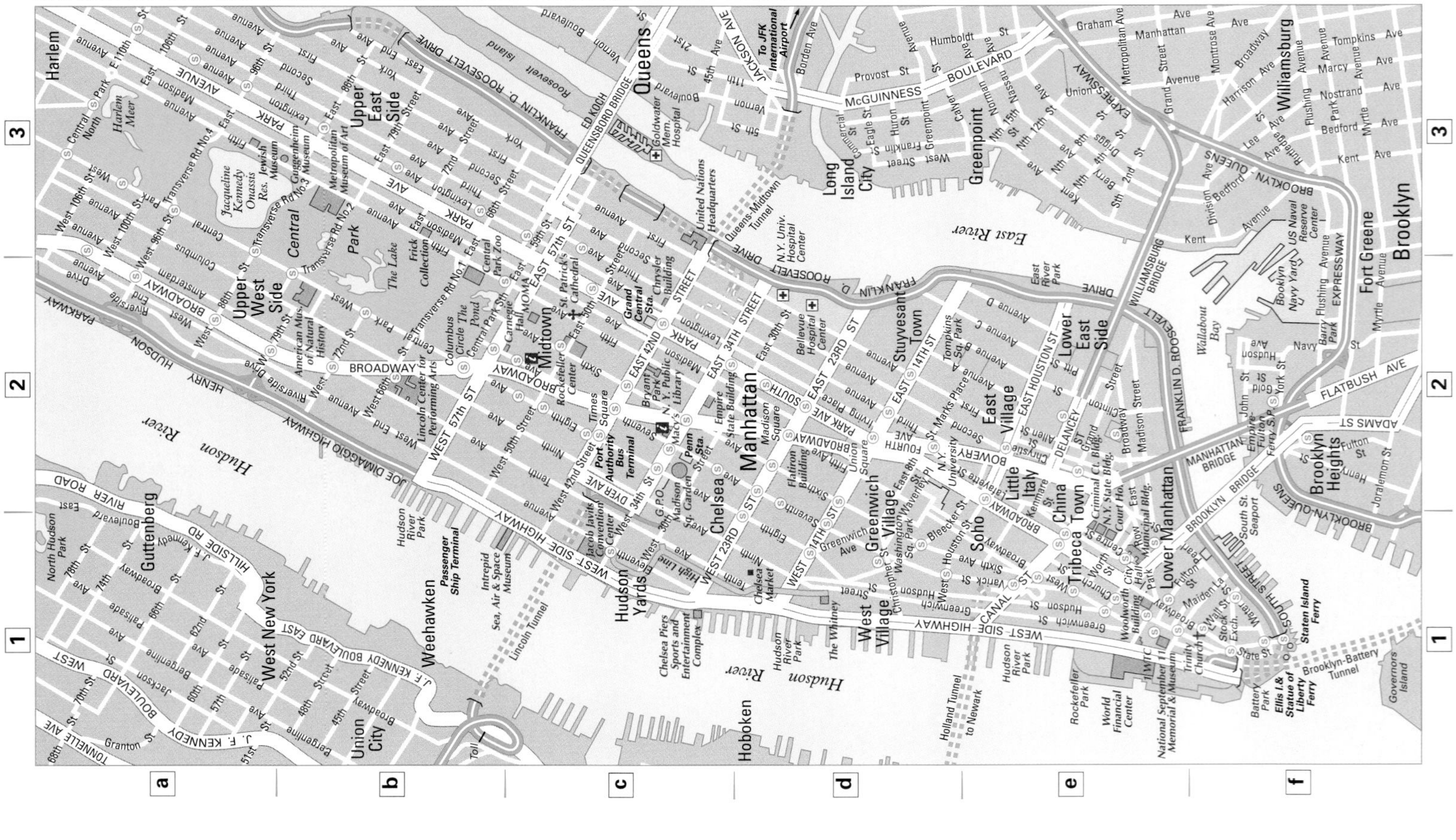

0 1 km 2
0 miles 1

Harlem · Central Park · Jacqueline Kennedy Onassis Res. · Metropolitan Museum of Art · Guggenheim Museum · Upper East Side · Upper West Side · American Museum of Natural History · The Lake · Frick Collection · Columbus Circle · Carnegie Hall · MoMA · St. Patrick's Cathedral · Grand Central Sta. · Chrysler Building · Midtown · Times Square · Port Authority Bus Terminal · Penn Sta. · Macy's · N.Y. Public Library · Bryant Park · Empire State Building · Madison Square · Flatiron Building · Bellevue Hospital Center · Stuyvesant Town · Tompkins Sq. Park · East Village · Gramercy Park · Greenwich Village · Washington Square · Little Italy · China Town · Soho · Tribeca · Lower East Side · Lower Manhattan · Bowery · Manhattan Bridge · Brooklyn Bridge · World Financial Center · Trinity Church · National September 11 Memorial & Museum · Battery Park · Ellis I. & Statue of Liberty Ferry · Staten Island Ferry · Brooklyn-Battery Tunnel

Hudson River · East River · Roosevelt Island · Queensboro Bridge · Williamsburg Bridge · Queens · Long Island City · Greenpoint · Williamsburg · Fort Greene · Brooklyn · Brooklyn Heights · US Naval Reserve Center · Wallabout Bay · Navy Yard · Governors Island

Weehawken · West New York · Union City · Hoboken · Guttenberg · North Hudson Park · Passenger Ship Terminal · Intrepid Sea, Air & Space Museum · Hudson Yards · Chelsea · Chelsea Piers Sports and Entertainment Complex · Jacob Javits Convention Center · Lincoln Tunnel · Holland Tunnel · to Newark · The Whitney · West Village · Hudson River Park

United Nations Headquarters · To JFK International Airport · Franklin D. Roosevelt Drive · Joe DiMaggio Highway · West Side Highway · Henry Hudson Parkway · West End Ave · Broadway · Fifth Ave · Park Ave · Lexington Ave · Madison Ave · Canal St · Houston St · Delancey St · 14th Street · 23rd St · 34th Street · 42nd St · 57th St

a · b · c · d · e · f
1 · 2 · 3

ORLANDO, FLORIDA

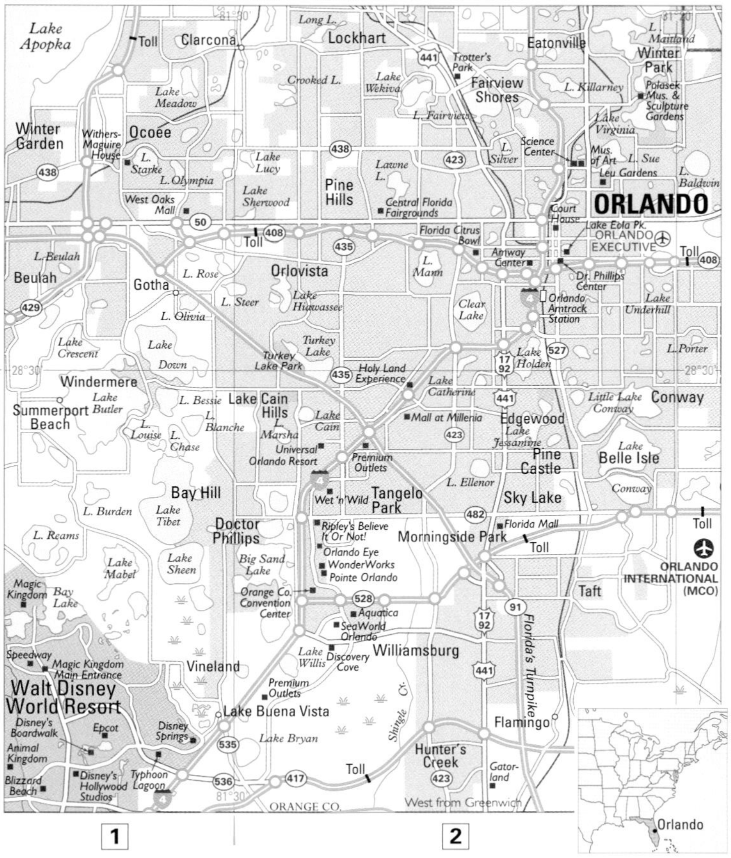

OSAKA, JAPAN

Interstate route numbers   U.S. route numbers   State route numbers

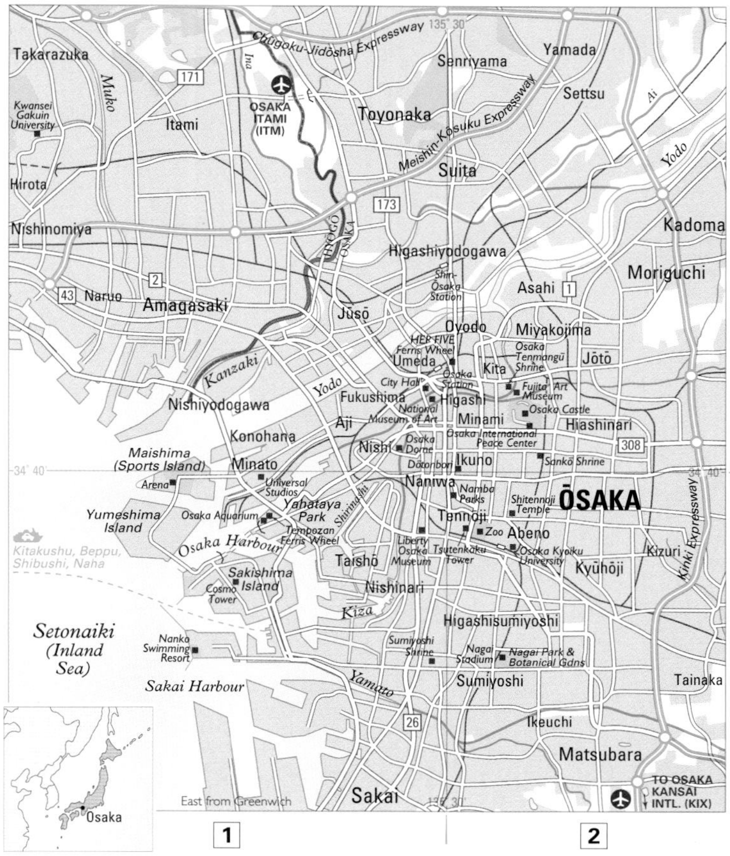

OSLO, NORWAY

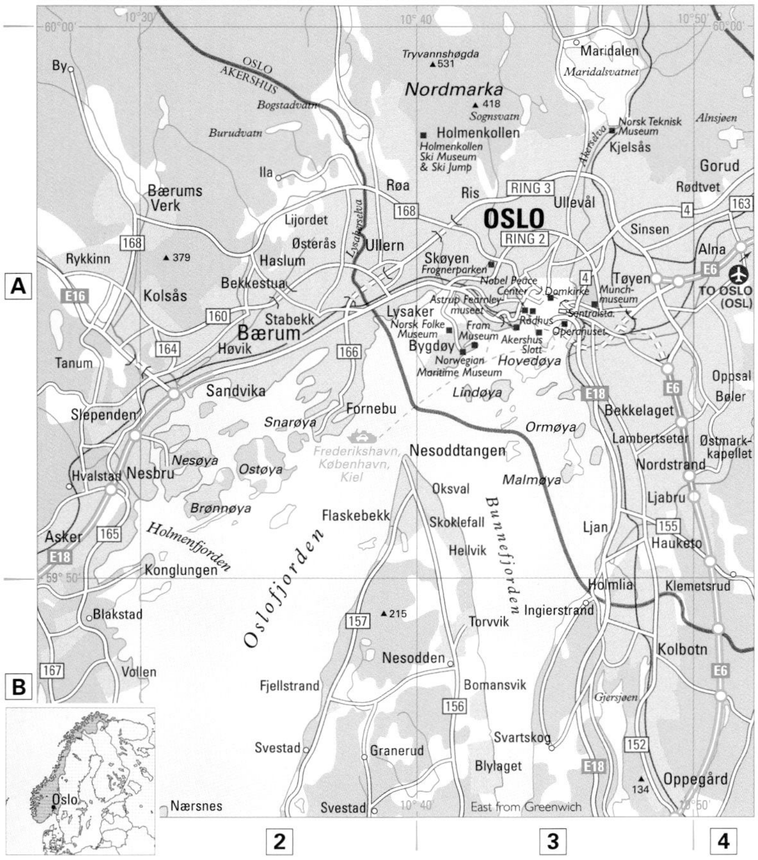

CENTRAL OSLO

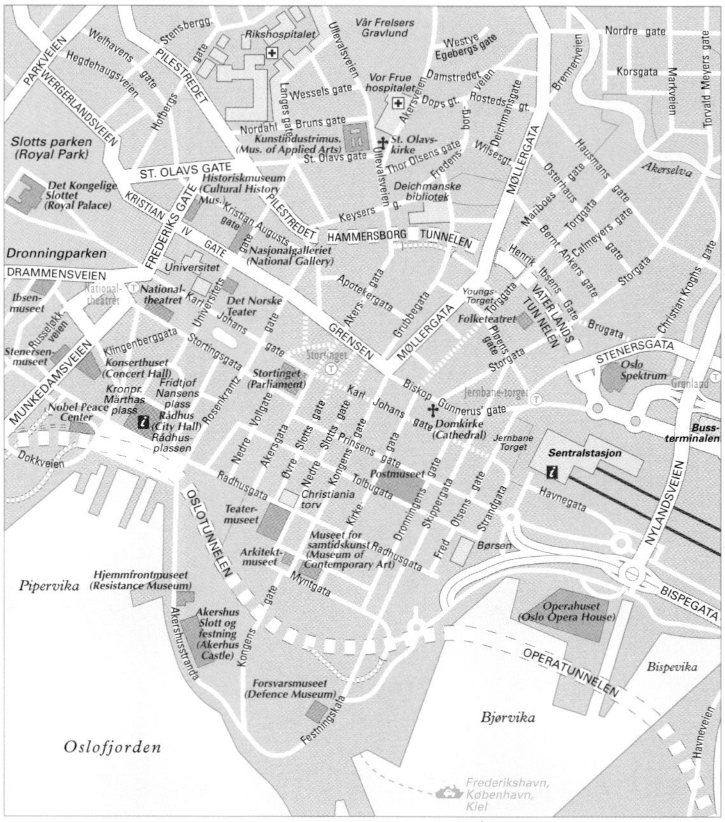

PARIS, FRANCE

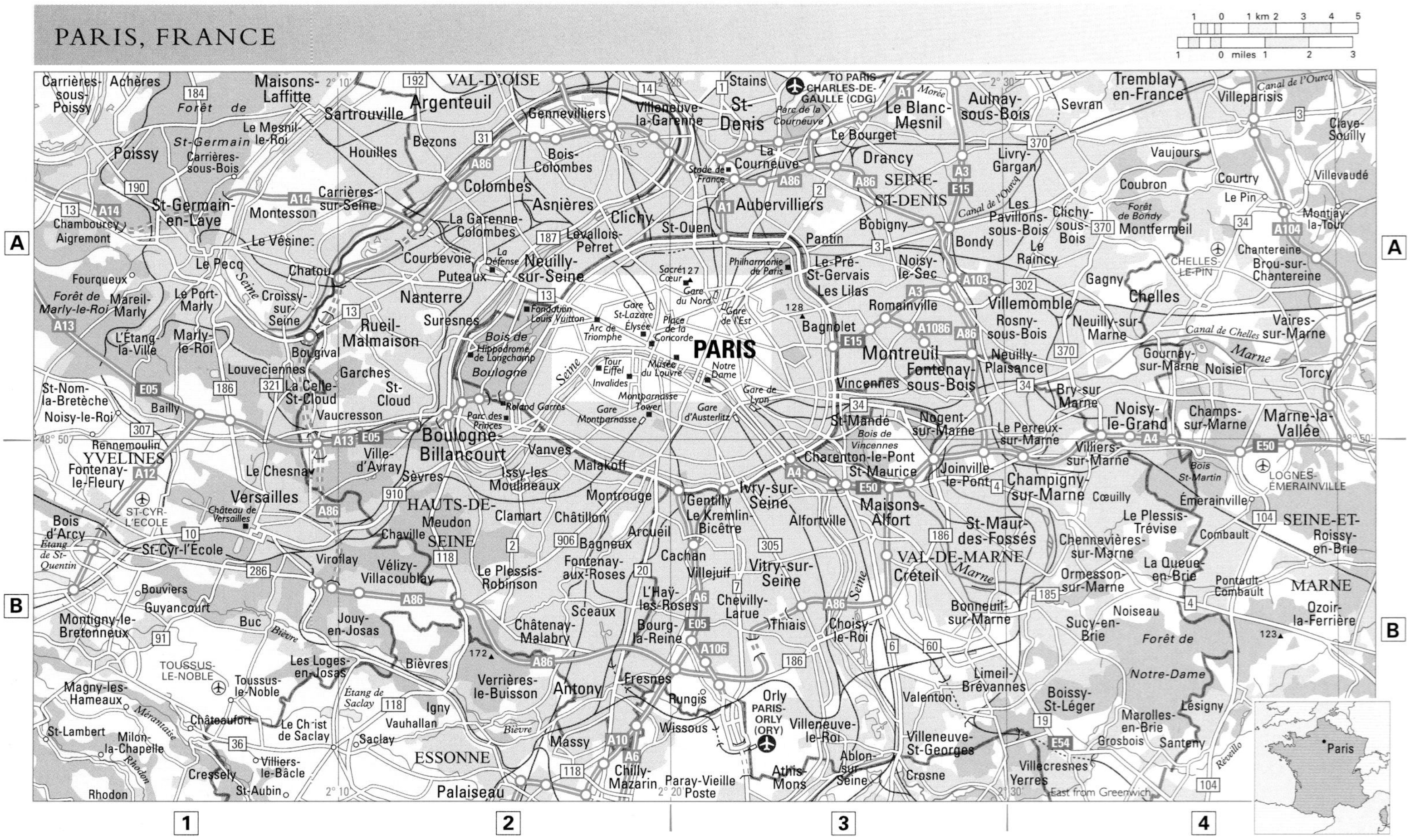

1 0 1 km 2 3 4 5
1 0 miles 1 2 3
A
B
1
2
3
4
Carrières-sous-Poissy
Achères
Maisons-Laffitte
VAL-D'OISE
Argenteuil
Sartrouville
Gennevilliers
Villeneuve-la-Garenne
Stains
St-Denis
TO PARIS CHARLES-DE-GAULLE (CDG)
Le Blanc-Mesnil
Aulnay-sous-Bois
Sevran
Tremblay-en-France
Villeparisis
Claye-Souilly
Canal de l'Ourcq
Forêt de St-Germain
Le Mesnil-le-Roi
Poissy
Carrières-sous-Bois
Houilles
Bezons
Bois-Colombes
Colombes
Stade de France
La Courneuve
Le Bourget
Drancy
Livry-Gargan
Vaujours
Coubron
Courtry
Villevaudé
St-Germain-en-Laye
Montesson
Carrières-sur-Seine
Asnières
Clichy
Aubervilliers
SEINE-ST-DENIS
Les Pavillons-sous-Bois
Clichy-sous-Bois
Montfermeil
Le Pin
Montjay-la-Tour
Chambourcy
Aigremont
Le Vésinet
La Garenne-Colombes
Levallois-Perret
St-Ouen
Pantin
Bobigny
Bondy
Le Raincy
Chelles
Chantereine
Brou-sur-Chantereine
Le Pecq
Chatou
Courbevoie
La Défense
Puteaux
Neuilly-sur-Seine
Sacré Cœur
Gare du Nord
Gare de l'Est
Philharmonie de Paris
Le-Pré-St-Gervais
Les Lilas
Noisy-le-Sec
Romainville
Villemomble
Gagny
Fourqueux
Forêt de Marly-le-Roi
Mareil-Marly
Le Port-Marly
Croissy-sur-Seine
Nanterre
Rueil-Malmaison
Suresnes
Fondation Louis Vuitton
Bois de Boulogne
Hippodrome de Longchamp
Gare St-Lazare
Arc de Triomphe
Place de la Concorde
PARIS
Bagnolet
Montreuil
Rosny-sous-Bois
Neuilly-sur-Marne
Vaires-sur-Marne
Canal de Chelles
L'Étang-la-Ville
Marly-le-Roi
Bougival
Louveciennes
Garches
St-Cloud
La Celle-St-Cloud
Vaucresson
Tour Eiffel
Invalides
Musée du Louvre
Notre Dame
Gare de Lyon
Montparnasse Tower
Gare Montparnasse
Gare d'Austerlitz
Roland Garros
Parc des Princes
Vincennes
Fontenay-sous-Bois
Neuilly-Plaisance
Bry-sur-Marne
Gournay-sur-Marne
Noisiel
Torcy
St-Nom-la-Bretèche
Noisy-le-Roi
Bailly
Rennemoulin
YVELINES
Fontenay-le-Fleury
Le Chesnay
Versailles
Château de Versailles
Ville-d'Avray
Boulogne-Billancourt
Sèvres
Issy-les-Moulineaux
Vanves
Malakoff
St-Mandé
Bois de Vincennes
Nogent-sur-Marne
Le Perreux-sur-Marne
Noisy-le-Grand
Champs-sur-Marne
Marne-la-Vallée
Villiers-sur-Marne
Charenton-le-Pont
St-Maurice
Joinville-le-Pont
Champigny-sur-Marne
Bois St-Martin
LOGNES-EMERAINVILLE
Émerainville
ST-CYR-L'ÉCOLE
Bois d'Arcy
Étang de St-Quentin
St-Cyr-l'École
HAUTS-DE-SEINE
Meudon
Clamart
Châtillon
Montrouge
Gentilly
Le Kremlin-Bicêtre
Ivry-sur-Seine
Alfortville
Maisons-Alfort
St-Maur-des-Fossés
Chennevières-sur-Marne
Cœuilly
Le Plessis-Trévise
Combault
SEINE-ET-MARNE
Roissy-en-Brie
Viroflay
Chaville
Vélizy-Villacoublay
Bagneux
Arcueil
Cachan
Villejuif
Vitry-sur-Seine
VAL-DE-MARNE
Créteil
Ormesson-sur-Marne
La Queue-en-Brie
Pontault-Combault
Bouviers
Guyancourt
Montigny-le-Bretonneux
Buc
Le Plessis-Robinson
Fontenay-aux-Roses
L'Haÿ-les-Roses
Chevilly-Larue
Thiais
Choisy-le-Roi
Bonneuil-sur-Marne
Sucy-en-Brie
Noiseau
Ozoir-la-Ferrière
Jouy-en-Josas
Sceaux
Bourg-la-Reine
Châtenay-Malabry
Forêt de Notre-Dame
TOUSSUS-LE-NOBLE
Toussus-le-Noble
Les Loges-en-Josas
Bièvres
Verrières-le-Buisson
Antony
Fresnes
Rungis
Orly
PARIS-ORLY (ORY)
Limeil-Brévannes
Valenton
Boissy-St-Léger
Marolles-en-Brie
Lésigny
Magny-les-Hameaux
Châteaufort
Étang de Saclay
Igny
Vauhallan
Le Christ de Saclay
Saclay
Wissous
Villeneuve-le-Roi
Villeneuve-St-Georges
Grosbois
Santeny
St-Lambert
Milon-la-Chapelle
Villiers-le-Bâcle
ESSONNE
Massy
Chilly-Mazarin
Paray-Vieille Poste
Athis-Mons
Ablon-sur-Seine
Crosne
Villecresnes
Yerres
Cressely
St-Aubin
Rhodon
Palaiseau
East from Greenwich
Paris

CENTRAL PARIS

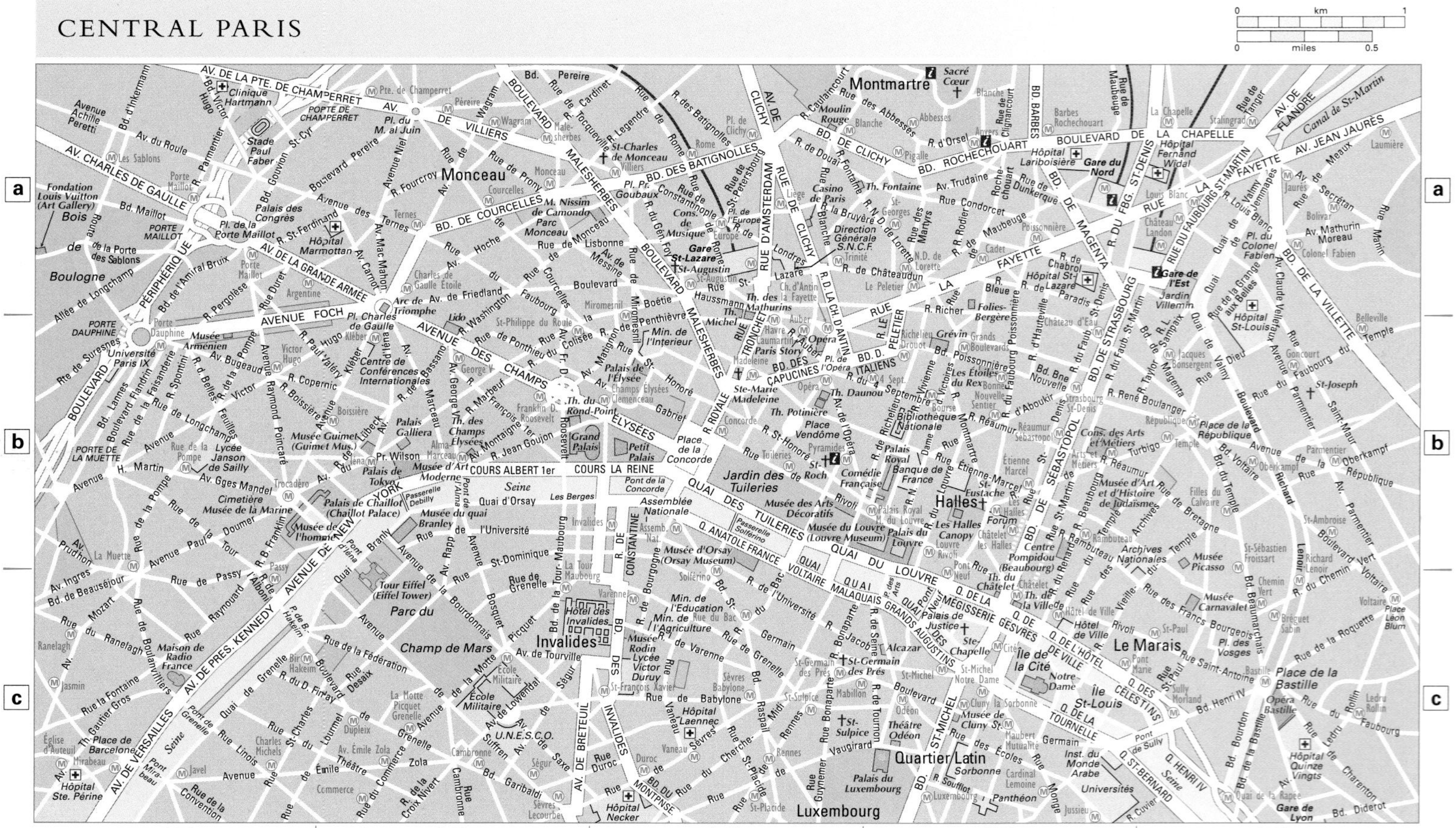

0 km 1
0 miles 0.5
a
b
c
1
2
3
4
5
Montmartre
Sacré Cœur
AV. DE LA PTE. DE CHAMPERRET
PORTE DE CHAMPERRET
Clinique Hartmann
Stade Paul Faber
Pereire
Wagram
BOULEVARD MALESHERBES
Monceau
Parc Monceau
Musée Nissim de Camondo
BD. DES BATIGNOLLES
Pl. de Clichy
BD. DE CLICHY
BD. ROCHECHOUART
Moulin Rouge
Pigalle
Abbesses
Barbès Rochechouart
BOULEVARD DE LA CHAPELLE
Gare du Nord
Hôpital Lariboisière
Hôpital Fernand Widal
Stalingrad
Canal de St-Martin
AV. JEAN JAURÈS
AV. DE FLANDRE
AV. CHARLES DE GAULLE
Fondation Louis Vuitton (Art Gallery)
Bois de Boulogne
PORTE MAILLOT
Palais des Congrès
Hôpital Marmottan
BD. DE COURCELLES
Gare St-Lazare
St-Augustin
Casino de Paris
Direction Générale S.N.C.F.
Trinité
N.D. de Lorette
Rue Condorcet
Rue de Maubeuge
BD. DE MAGENTA
Hôpital St-Lazare
Gare de l'Est
Jardin Villemin
Pl. du Colonel Fabien
BD. DE LA VILLETTE
AV. DE LA GRANDE ARMÉE
Arc de Triomphe
Pl. Charles de Gaulle
AVENUE FOCH
PORTE DAUPHINE
Musée Arménien
Université Paris IX
Centre de Conférences Internationales
AVENUE DES CHAMPS ÉLYSÉES
Palais de l'Élysée
Min. de l'Intérieur
BOULEVARD HAUSSMANN
Opéra
Paris Story
Th. des Mathurins
BD. DES CAPUCINES
BD. DES ITALIENS
Folies-Bergère
Grévin
RUE LA FAYETTE
BD. DE STRASBOURG
BD. DE SÉBASTOPOL
Hôpital St-Louis
BD. DE LA VILLETTE
Musée Guimet (Guimet Mus.)
Palais Galliera
Grand Palais
Petit Palais
Place de la Concorde
Ste-Marie Madeleine
Place Vendôme
Bibliothèque Nationale
Place de la République
Lycée Janson de Sailly
Cimetière Musée de la Marine
Palais de Chaillot (Chaillot Palace)
Musée de l'Homme
Palais de Tokyo
Musée d'Art Moderne
COURS ALBERT 1er
COURS LA REINE
Jardin des Tuileries
Musée des Arts Décoratifs
Comédie Française
Palais Royal
Banque de France
Halles
Les Halles Canopy
Forum
Cons. des Arts et Métiers
Musée d'Art et d'Histoire du Judaïsme
Archives Nationales
Musée Picasso
Assemblée Nationale
Musée du quai Branly
QUAI D'ORSAY
Invalides
Musée d'Orsay (Orsay Museum)
QUAI ANATOLE FRANCE
QUAI DES TUILERIES
QUAI DU LOUVRE
Musée du Louvre (Louvre Museum)
Pompidou (Beaubourg) Centre
Musée Carnavalet
Tour Eiffel (Eiffel Tower)
Parc du Champ de Mars
Hôtel des Invalides
Min. de l'Agriculture
Min. de l'Education
QUAI MALAQUAIS
QUAI DE LA MÉGISSERIE
QUAI DE GESVRES
Hôtel de Ville
Le Marais
Pl. des Vosges
Place de la Bastille
AV. DE PRES. KENNEDY
Maison de Radio France
École Militaire
Musée Rodin
Lycée Victor Duruy
St-Germain des Prés
St-Sulpice
Théâtre Odéon
Musée de Cluny
Ste-Chapelle
Notre Dame
Île de la Cité
Île St-Louis
Opéra Bastille
Place de Barcelone
Hôpital Ste. Périne
AV. DE VERSAILLES
U.N.E.S.C.O.
AV. DE BREUIL
BD. DES INVALIDES
Hôpital Laennec
Hôpital Necker
BD. DU MONTPARNASSE
Palais du Luxembourg
Quartier Latin
Sorbonne
Panthéon
Luxembourg
Inst. du Monde Arabe
Universités
Hôpital Quinze Vingts
Gare de Lyon
Bd. Diderot
BD. ST-MICHEL
BD. ST-GERMAIN
QUAI DES CÉLESTINS
QUAI DE LA TOURNELLE
QUAI ST-BERNARD
BD. HENRI IV
Seine

PRAGUE, CZECHIA

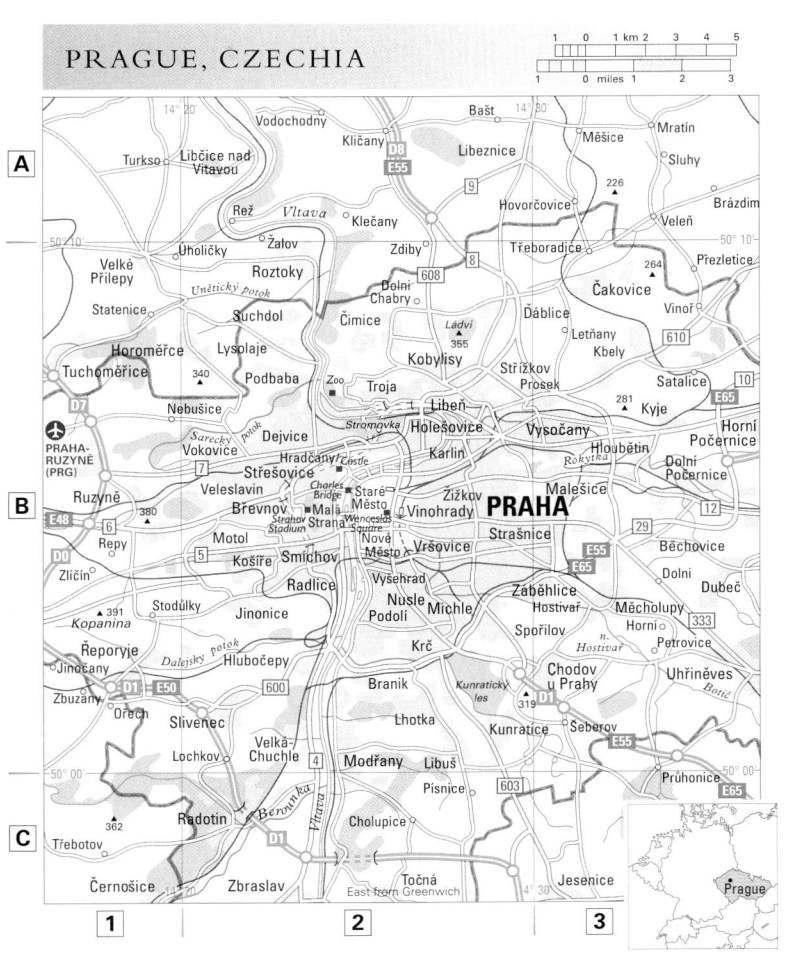

CENTRAL PRAGUE

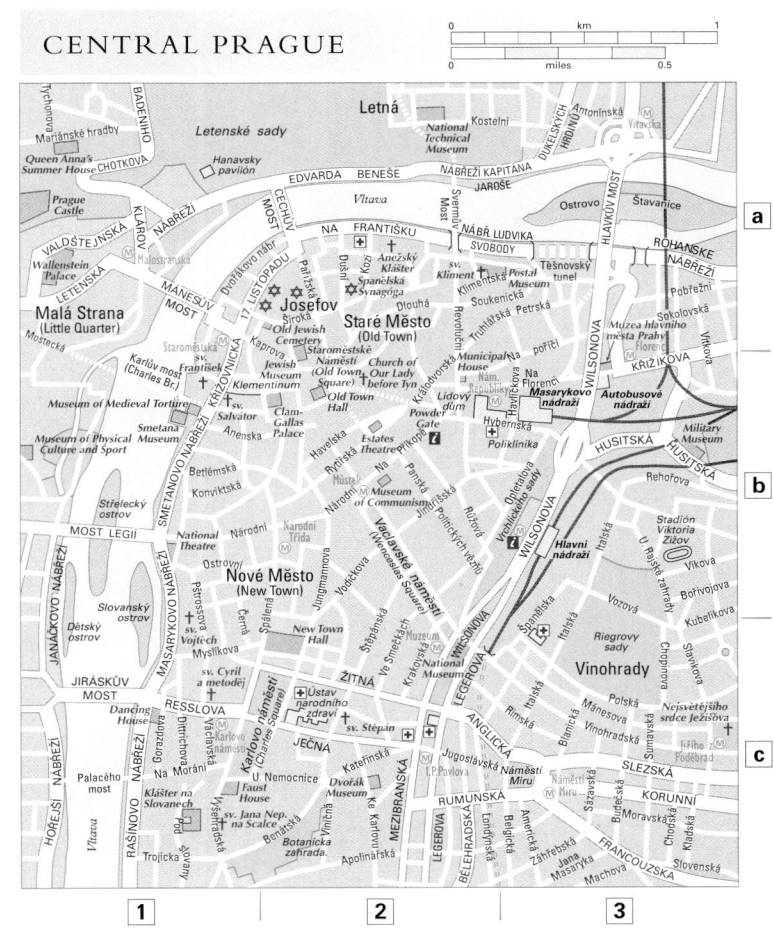

RIO DE JANEIRO, BRAZIL

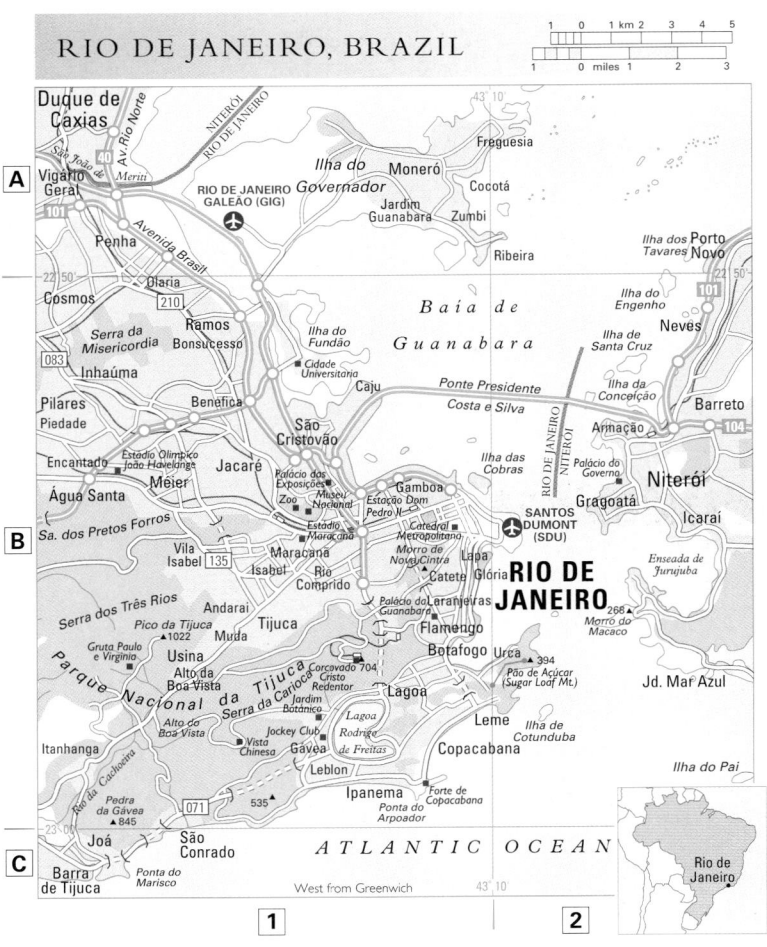

CENTRAL RIO DE JANEIRO

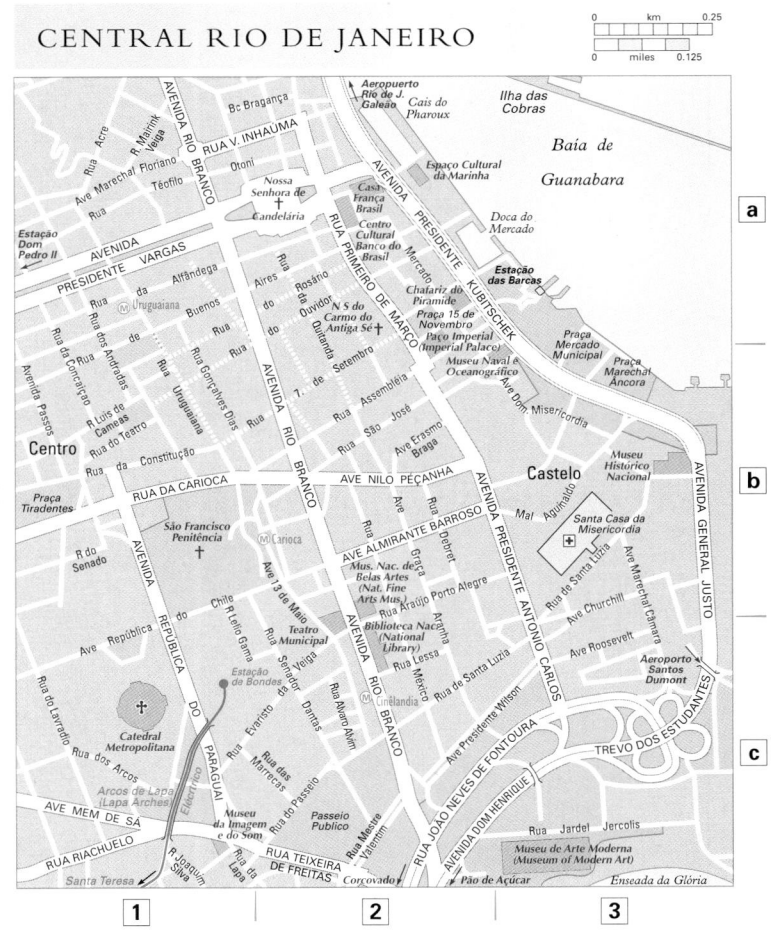

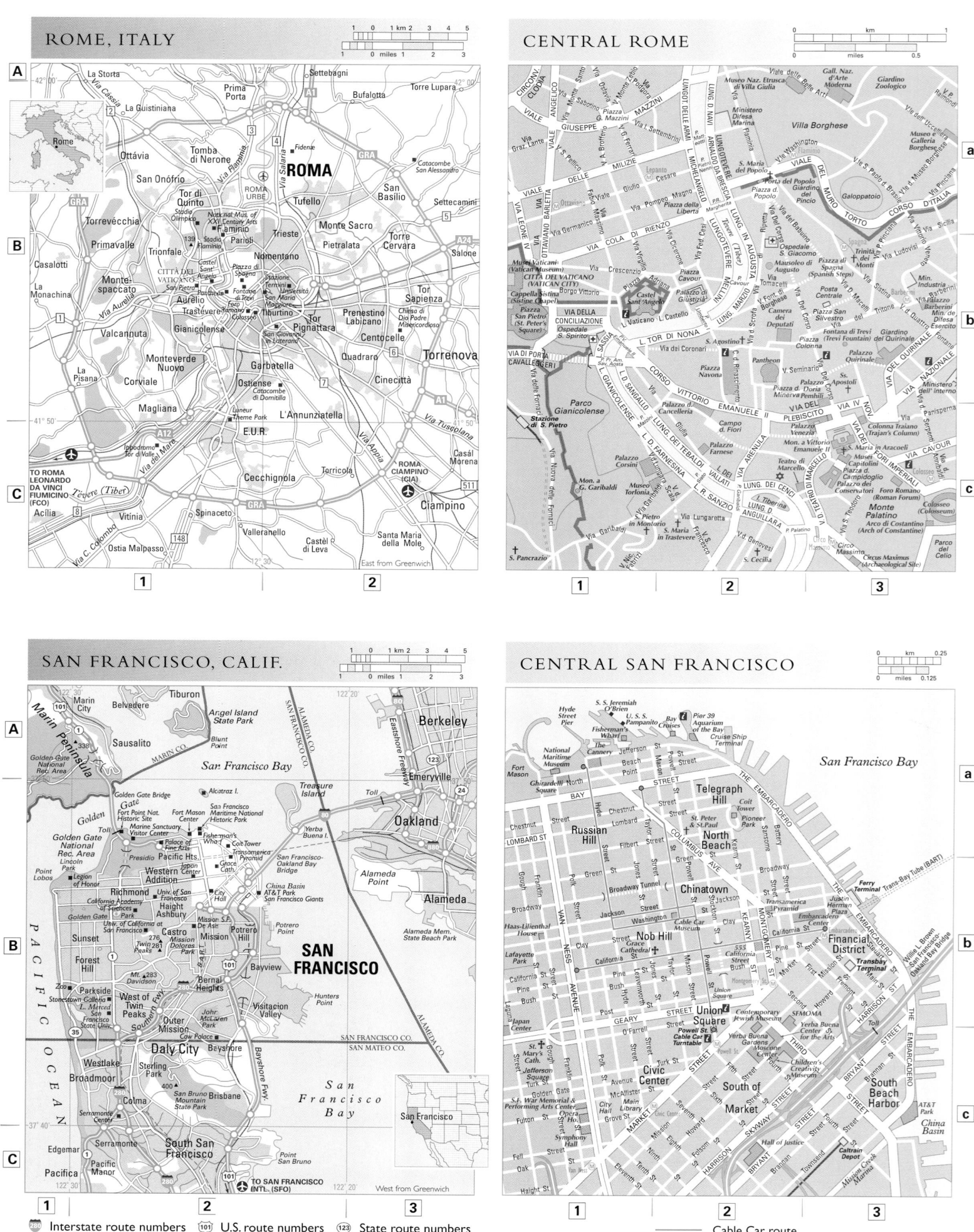

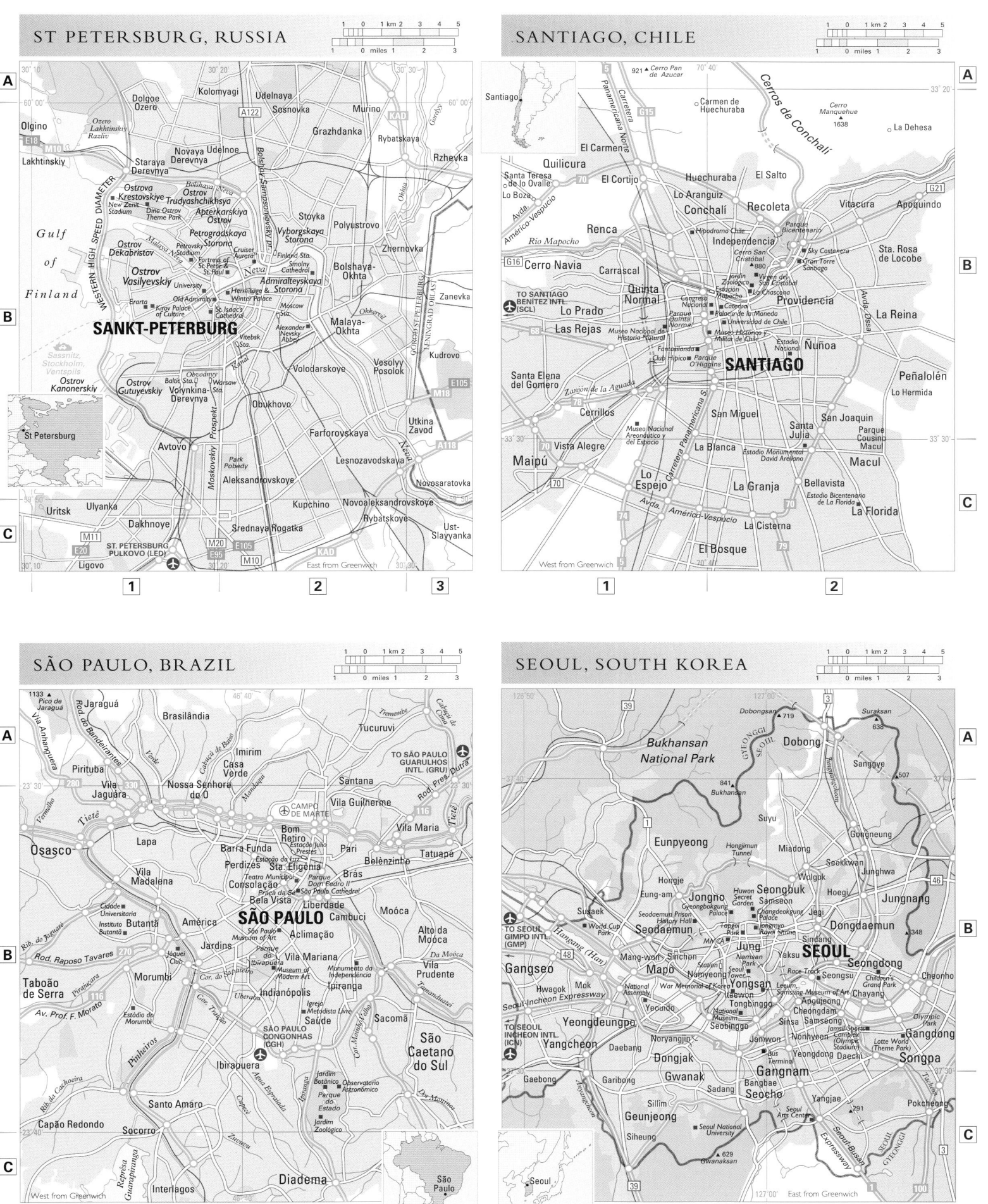

ST PETERSBURG, RUSSIA

1 0 1 km 2 3 4 5
1 0 miles 1 2 3

Olgino
Dolgoe Ozero
Kolomyagi
Udelnaya
Sosnovka
Murino
Rybatskaya
KAD
Lakhtinskiy
Staraya Derevnya
Novaya Udelnoe
Grazhdanka
Rzhevka
Ostrova Krestovskiye
Ostrov Trudyashchikhsya
Apterkarskiya Ostrov
Stóyka
Vyborgskaya Storona
Polyustrovo
New Zenit Stadium
Dina Ostrov Theme Park
Petrovsky Stadium
Petrogradskaya Storona
Zhernovka
Ostrov Dekabristov
Erarta
Kirov Palace of Culture
Old Admiralty
University
Neva
Admiralteyskaya & Storona
Bolshaya-Okhta
Ostrov Vasilyevskiy
Fortress of St Peter & St. Paul
Cruiser Aurora
Hermitage & Winter Palace
Finland Sta.
Smolny Cathedral
Moscow Sta.
Zanevka
Malaya-Okhta
St. Isaac's Cathedral
Vitebsk Sta.
Alexander Nevsky Abbey
Okkervil
Kudrovo
SANKT-PETERBURG
Obvodnyy Canal
Warsaw Sta.
Baltic Sta.
Volodarskoye
Vesolyy Posolok
Ostrov Gutuyevskiy
Volynkina-Derevnya
Obukhovo
Farforovskaya
Utkina Zavod
Avtovo
Park Pobedy
Aleksandrovskoye
Lesnozavodskaya
Novosaratovka
Uritsk
Ulyanka
Dakhnoye
Kupchino
Novoaleksandrovskoye
Rybatskoye
Ligovo
Srednaya Rogatka
Ust-Slavyanka
ST. PETERSBURG PULKOVO (LED)

Gulf of Finland

Sassnitz, Stockholm, Ventspils
Ostrov Kanonerskiy
St Petersburg

East from Greenwich

SANTIAGO, CHILE

1 0 1 km 2 3 4 5
1 0 miles 1 2 3

Santiago

Cerro Pan de Azucar
Carretera Panamericana Norte
Cerros de Conchali
Carmen de Huechuraba
Cerro Manquehue 1638
La Dehesa
El Carmen
Quilicura
Santa Teresa de lo Ovalle
Lo Boza
El Cortijo
Huechuraba
El Salto
Recoleta
Vitacura
Apoquindo
Avda. Américo-Vespucio
Renca
Conchalí
Hipodromo Chile
Independencia
Parque Bicentenario
Sky Costanera
Gran Torre Santiago
Sta. Rosa de Locobe
Río Mapocho
Cerro Navia
Carrascal
Cerro San Cristóbal 880
Virgen del San Cristóbal
Jardín Zoológico
La Chascona
Providencia
Avda. Ossa
Quinta Normal
Estación Mapocho
Museo Historico y Militar de Chile
La Reina
Lo Prado
Congreso Nacional
Catedral
Palacio de la Moneda
Ñuñoa
Las Rejas
Museo Nacional de Historia Natural
Universidad de Chile
Fantasilandia
Estadio Nacional
Peñalolén
Santa Elena del Gomero
Club Hípico
Parque O'Higgins
Parque Quinta Normal
Lo Hermida
Cerrillos
Zanjón de la Aguada
San Miguel
Santa Julia
San Joaquin
Parque Cousiño Macul
SANTIAGO
Museo Nacional Aeronáutico y del Espacio
Vista Alegre
La Blanca
Estadio Monumental David Arellano
Macul
Maipú
Avda. Américo-Vespucio
Bellavista
Estadio Bicentenario de La Florida
Lo Espejo
La Granja
La Florida
La Cisterna
El Bosque

West from Greenwich

SÃO PAULO, BRAZIL

1 0 1 km 2 3 4 5
1 0 miles 1 2 3

Pico de Jaraguá 1133
Jaraguá
Brasilândia
Tremembé
Cabeça de China
Via Anhanguera
Rod. do Bandeirantes
Imirim
Tucuruvi
Cabeça de Porco
Piritúba
Casa Verde
Santana
TO SÃO PAULO GUARULHOS INTL. (GRU)
Vila Jaguára
Nossa Senhora do Ó
Vila Guilherme
Rod. Pres. Dutra
Tietê
Osasco
Lapa
Barra Funda
Bom Retiro
Estação da Luz
Estação Júlio Prestes
Pari
Vila Maria
Tatuapé
Perdizes
Sta. Efigênia
Belênzinho
Brás
Vila Madalena
Teatro Municipal
Consolação
Parque Dom Pedro II
São Paulo Cathedral
Praça da Sé
Liberdade
Móoca
Cidade Universitária
Bela Vista
Cambuci
Instituto Butantã
Butantã
América
Aclimação
Alto da Móoca
Jóquei Club
Jardins
Vila Mariana
Da Móoca
São Paulo Museum of Art
Parque do Ibirapuera
Vila Prudente
Rod. Raposo Tavares
Morumbi
Museum of Modern Art
Monumento da Independência
Ipiranga
SÃO PAULO
Taboão de Serra
Estádio do Morumbi
Indianópolis
Igreja Metodista Livre
Saúde
Sacomã
Av. Prof. F. Morato
Capela
SÃO PAULO CONGONHAS (CGH)
São Caetano do Sul
Santo Amáro
Ibirapuera
Jardim Botânico
Observatório Astronômico
Represa Guarapiranga
Capão Redondo
Parque do Estado
Jardim Zoológico
Socorro
São Paulo
Interlagos
Diadema

West from Greenwich

SEOUL, SOUTH KOREA

1 0 1 km 2 3 4 5
1 0 miles 1 2 3

Dobongsan 719
Suraksan 638
Bukhansan National Park
Dobong
Sanggye 507
Bukhansan 841
Suyu
Gongneung
Eunpyeong
Hongjimun Tunnel
Miadong
Seokkwan
Junghwa
Hongje
Wolgok
Jongno
Huwon Secret Garden
Seongbuk
Hoegi
Jungnang
Eung-am
Seodaemun Prison History Hall
Gyeongbokgung Palace
Changdeokgung Palace
Jongmyo Royal Shrine
Jegi
Dongdaemun 348
Susaek
World Cup Park
Seodaemun
MMCA
Topgol Park
Sindang
TO SEOUL GIMPO INTL. (GMP)
Hangang (Han)
Mang-won
Sinchon
Namsan Park
Yaksu
Gangseo
Mapo
Jung
Seoul Station
Seoul Namsan Tower
SEOUL
Seongdong
Cheonho
Race Track
Seongsu
Children's Grand Park
Hwagok
Mok
War Memorial of Korea
Yongsan
Itaewon
Leeum Samsung Museum of Art
Chayang
Seoul-Incheon Expressway
National Assembly
Yeoudo
Tongbinggo
National Museum
Seobinggo
Sinsa
Samseong
Apgujeong
Cheongdam
Jamsil Sports Complex
Olympic Stadium
Olympic Park
Yeongdeungpo
TO SEOUL INCHEON INTL. (ICN)
Yangcheon
Daebang
Noryangjin
Bus Terminal
Jomwon
Nonhyeon
Yeongdong Daechy
Gangdong
Lotte World (Theme Park)
Songpa
Gaebong
Dongjak
Gwanak
Gangnam
Bangbae
Seocho
Sadang
Yangjae
Pokcheong
Sillim
Seoul Arts Center
Geunjeong
Seoul-Busan Expressway
Seoul National University
Siheung
Gwanaksan 629
Seoul
291
100

East from Greenwich

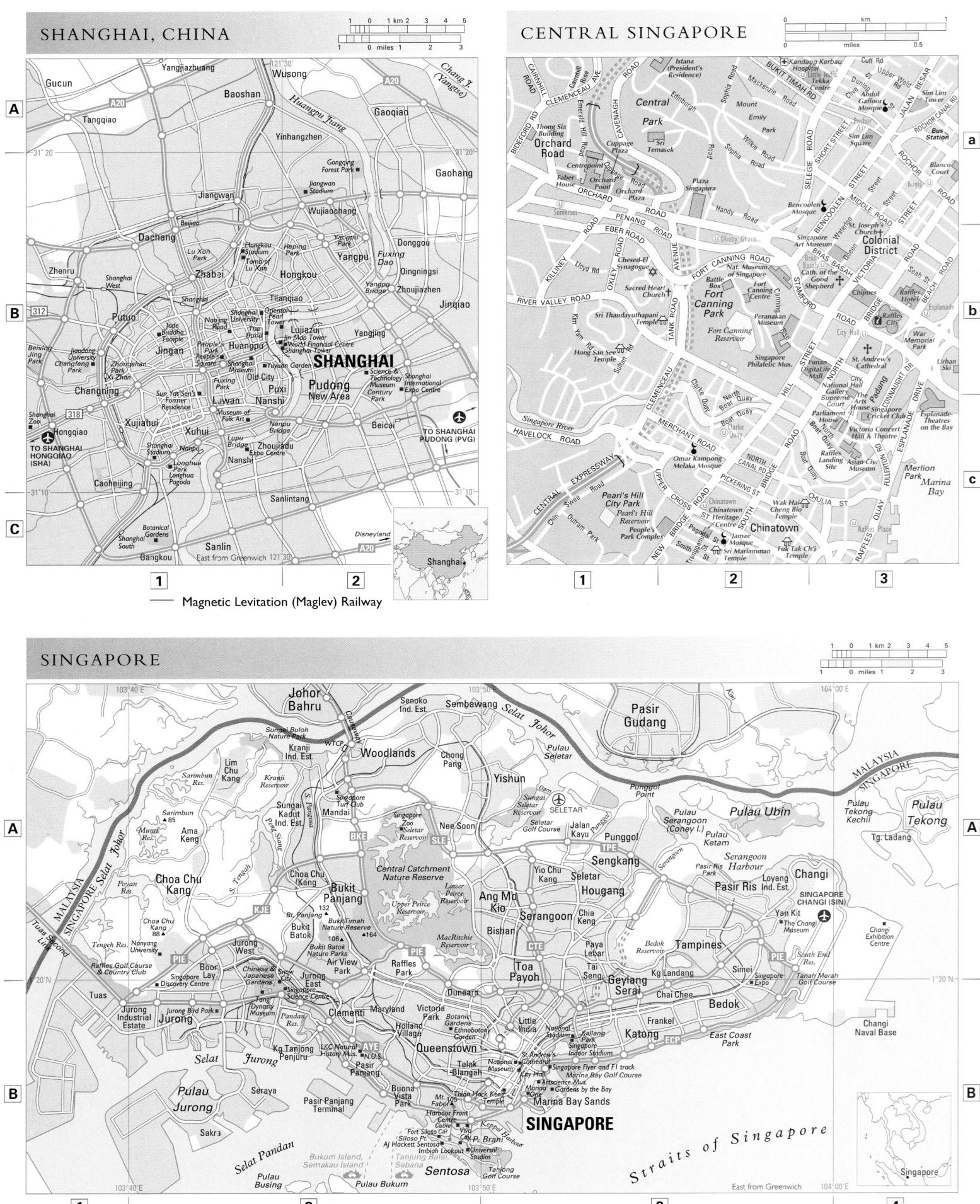

STOCKHOLM, SWEDEN

CENTRAL STOCKHOLM

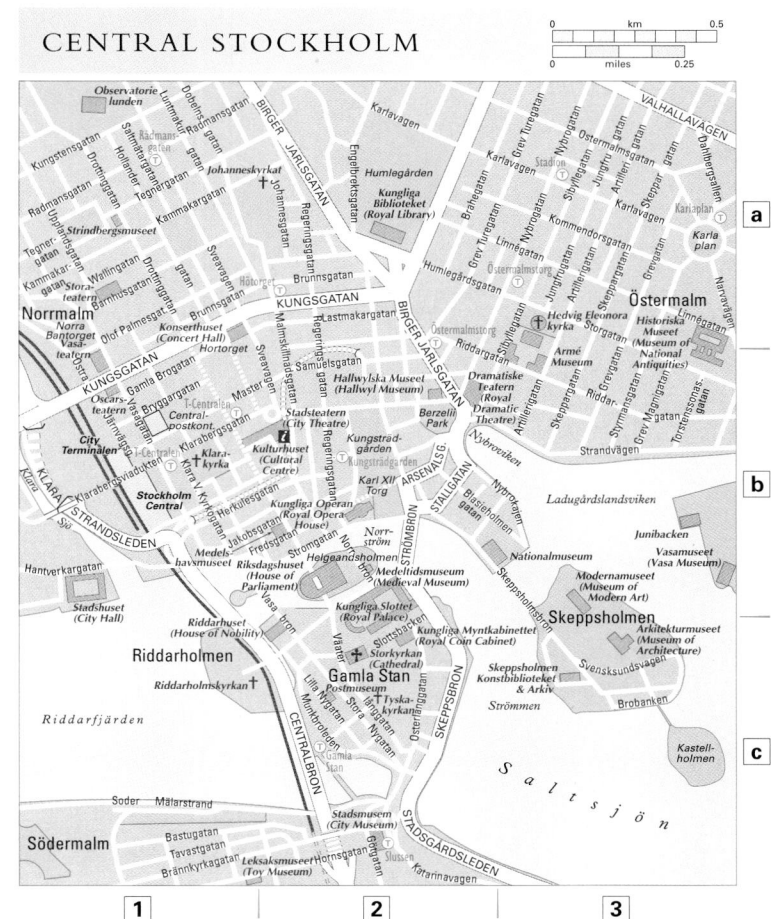

SYDNEY, AUSTRALIA

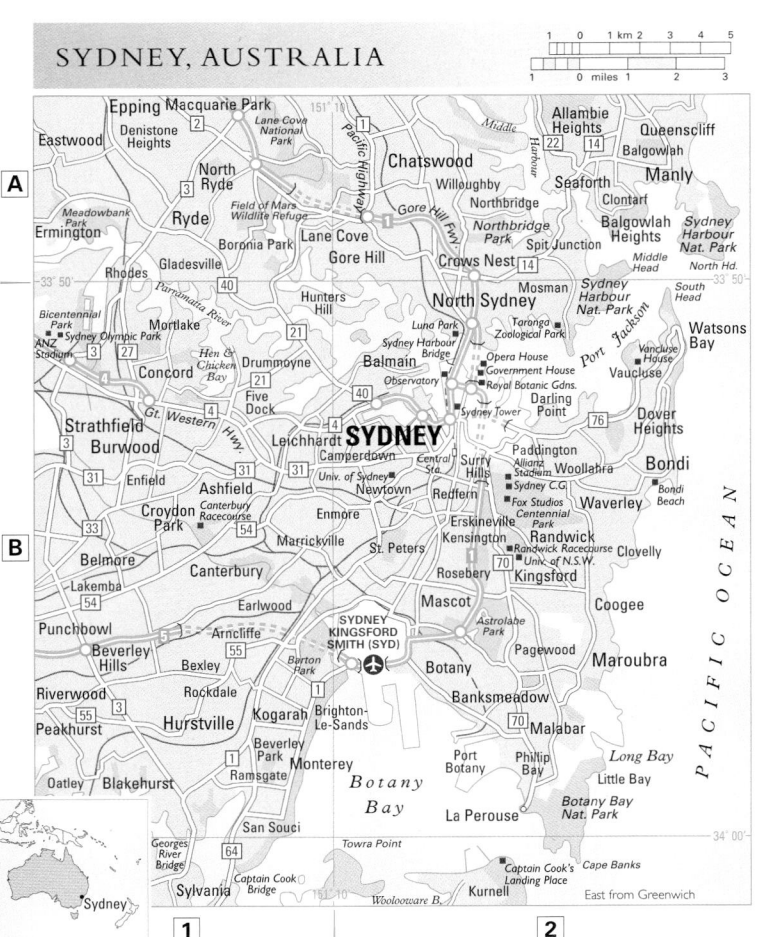

CENTRAL SYDNEY

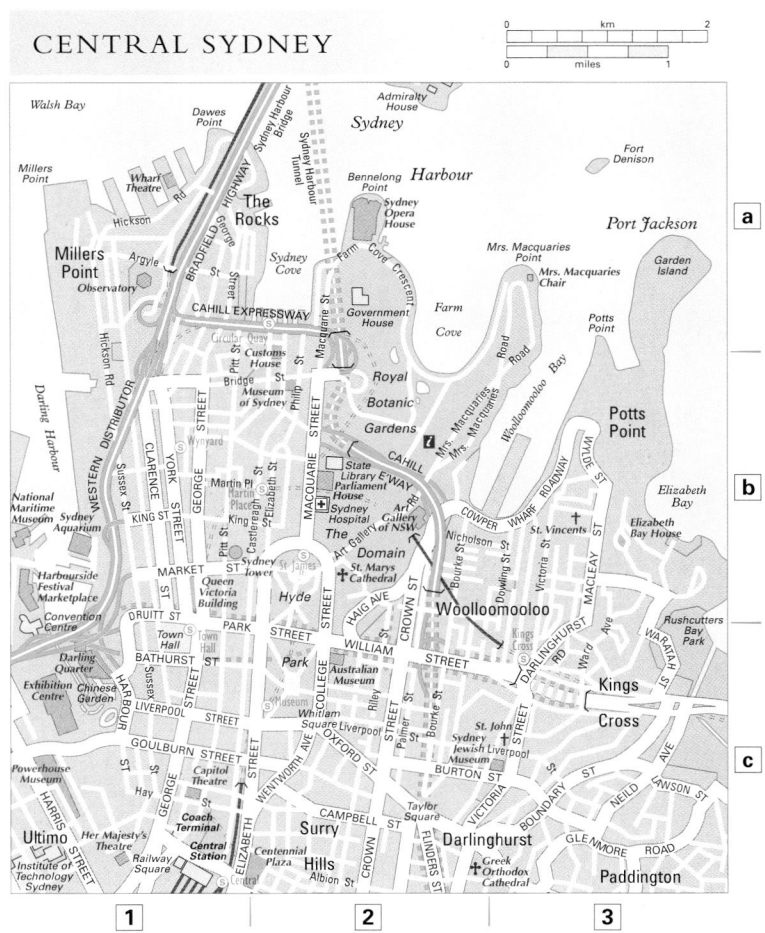

COPYRIGHT PHILIP'S

TOKYO, JAPAN

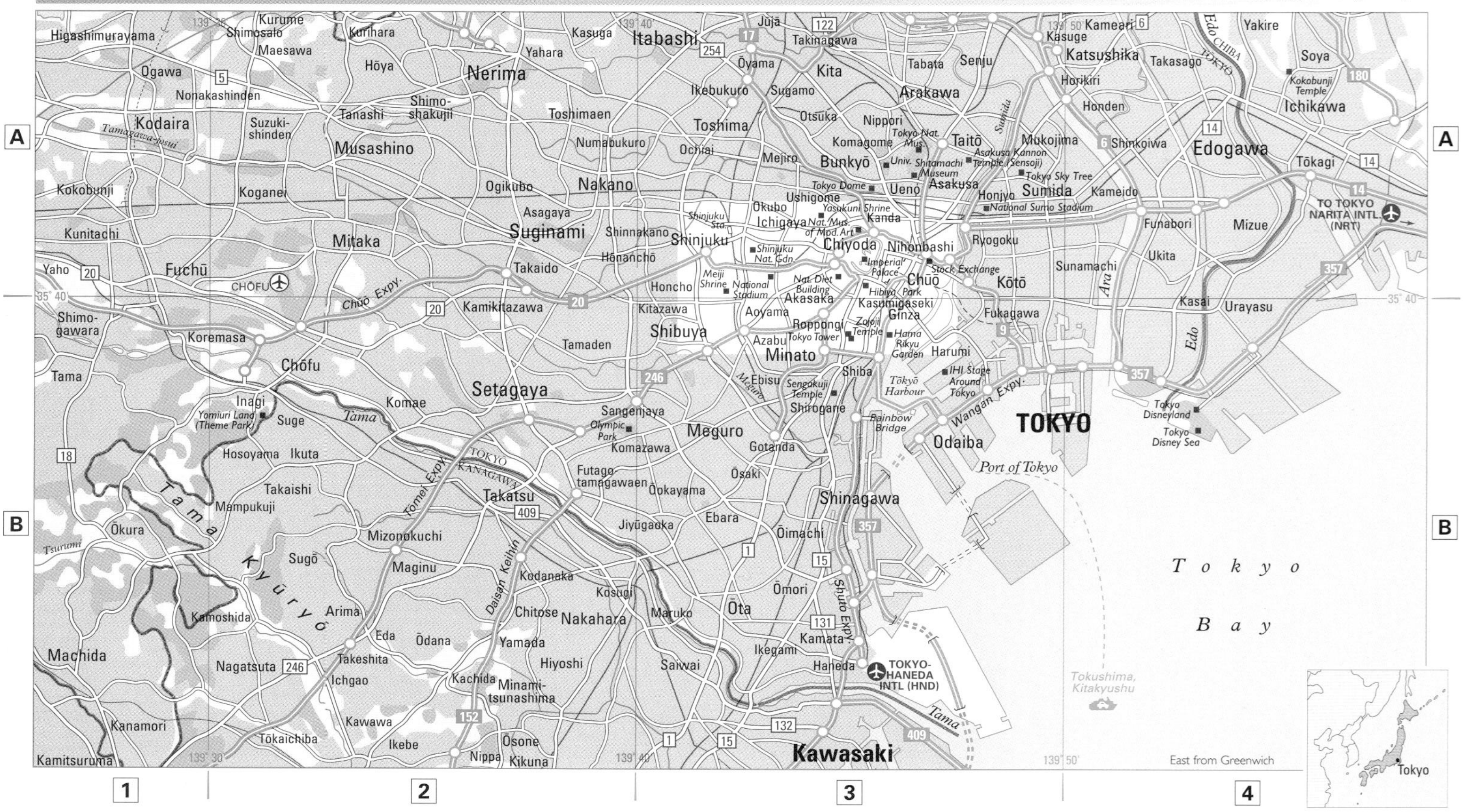

Higashimurayama, Kurume, Shimosato, Kurihara, Kasuga, Jūjō, Takinagawa, Itabashi, Ōyama, Kita, Tabata, Senju, Katsushika, Takasago, Kokubunji Temple, Ichikawa, Soya, Yakire

Ogawa, Shimosaki, Maesawa, Hōya, Yahara, Ikebukuro, Sugamo, Ōtsuka, Nippori, Honden, Horikiri, Takasago, Mukojima, Shinkoiwa, Edogawa, Tōkagi

Kodaira, Suzuki-shinden, Tanashi, Shimo-shakuji, Toshimaen, Toshima, Mejiro, Bunkyō, Univ. Shigomori, Asakusa Kannon, Tokyo Sky Tree, Sumida

Musashino, Nakano, Ogikubo, Asagaya, Shinnakano, Shinjuku Sta, Shinjuku, Ushigome, Ueno, Asakusa, National Sumo Stadium, Kameido, Mizue

Kokubunji, Mitaka, Takaido, Honcho, Honchō, Chiyoda, Nihonbashi, Ryogoku, Funabori, Ukita, Kasai, Urayasu

Kunitachi, Fuchū, Kamikitazawa, Kitazawa, Shibuya, Aoyama, Akasaka, Chūō, Kōtō, Fukagawa

Yaho, Chōfu, Koremasa, Tamaden, Minato, Shiba, Harumi, TOKYO

Shimogawara, Inagi, Suge, Komae, Setagaya, Sangenjaya, Meguro, Gotanda, Odaiba, Tokyo Disneyland, Tokyo Disney Sea

Tama, Hosoyama, Ikuta, Komazawa, Ōsaki, Port of Tokyo

Ōkura, Takaishi, Mizonokuchi, Maginu, Takatsu, Jiyūgaoka, Ebara, Ōimachi, Shinagawa

Machida, Sugō, Arima, Kamoshida, Eda, Ōdana, Chitose, Yamada, Nakahara, Maruko, Ōta, Ōmori, Kamata

Kanamori, Nagatsuta, Takeshita, Ichgao, Kachida, Minami-tsunashima, Hiyoshi, Saiwai, Ikegami, Haneda, TOKYO-HANEDA INTL (HND)

Kamitsuruma, Tōkaichiba, Ikebe, Ōsone, Nippa, Kikuna, Kawasaki

Tokyo Bay

CENTRAL TOKYO

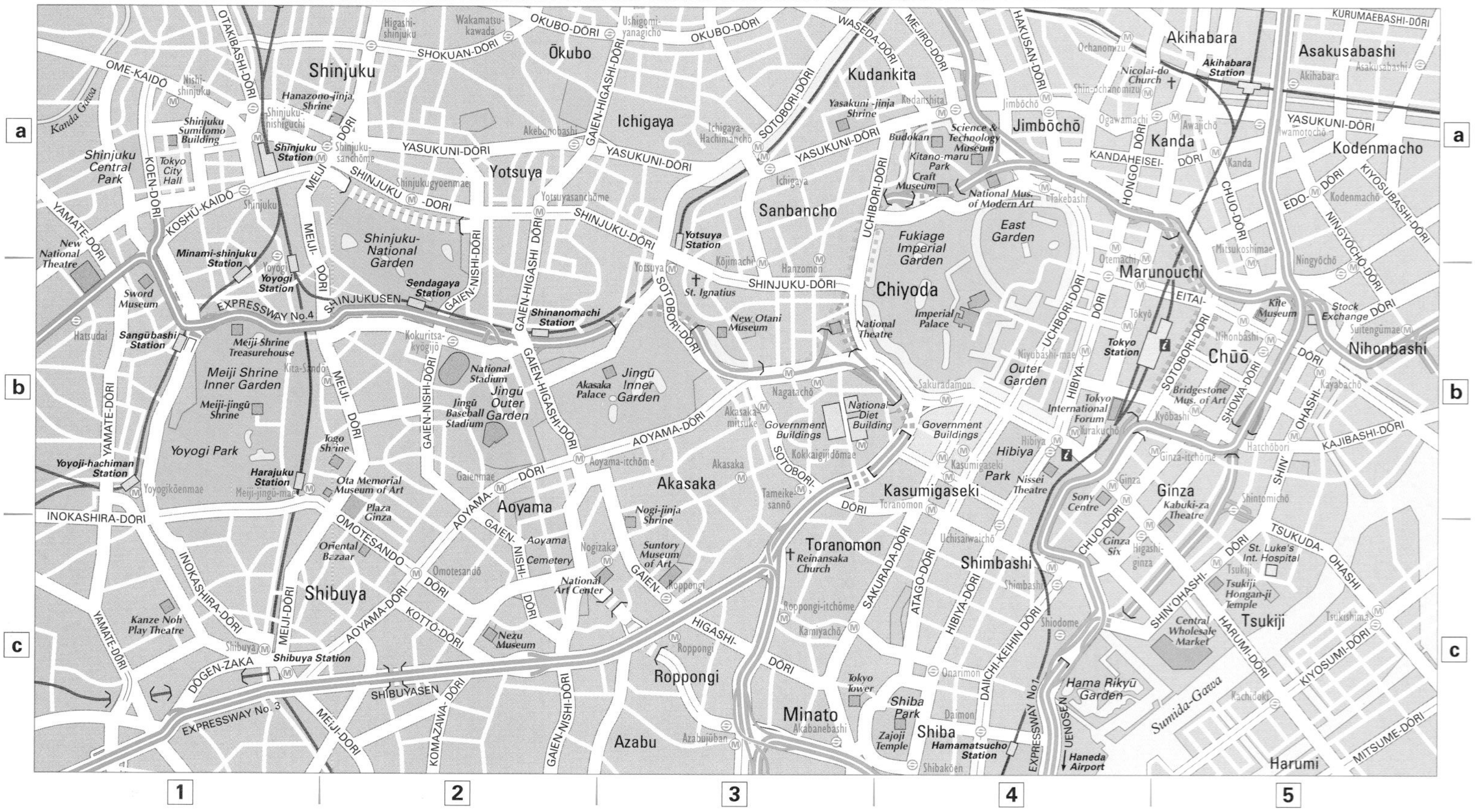

Shinjuku, Ōkubo, Kudankita, Akihabara, Asakusabashi, Kodenmacho

Shinjuku Central Park, Tokyo City Hall, Shinjuku Station, Yotsuya, Ichigaya, Sanbancho, Jimbōchō, Kanda

New National Theatre, Minami-shinjuku Station, Yoyogi Station, Shinjuku National Garden, Sendagaya Station, Fukiage Imperial Garden, East Garden, National Mus. of Modern Art, Marunouchi

Sword Museum, Sangubashi Station, Meiji Shrine Treasurehouse, Shinanomachi Station, Chiyoda, Imperial Palace, Tokyo Station

Meiji Shrine Inner Garden, Meiji-jingū Shrine, National Stadium, Jingū Baseball Stadium, Jingū Outer Garden, Akasaka Palace, Jingū Inner Garden, New Otani Museum, National Theatre, Outer Garden, Chūō, Nihonbashi

Yoyogi Park, Kato Shrine, Harajuku Station, Ota Memorial Museum of Art, Government Buildings, National Diet Building, Government Buildings, Hibiya Park, Ginza

Yoyogi-hachiman Station, Plaza Ginza, Akasaka, Nogi-jinja Shrine, Kasumigaseki, Nissei Theatre, Sony Centre, Kabuki-za Theatre

Oriental Bazaar, Aoyama, Aoyama Cemetery, Suntory Museum of Art, Toranomon, Reinanzaka Church, Shimbashi, Tsukiji Hongan-ji Temple

Kanze Noh Play Theatre, Shibuya, Nezu Museum, National Art Center, Roppongi, Minato, Tokyo Tower, Shiba Park, Zojoji Temple, Shiba, Hamamatsucho Station, Hama Rikyū Garden, Tsukiji, Central Wholesale Market

Shibuya Station, Azabu, Harumi

Toei Subway | Tokyo Metro

COPYRIGHT PHILIP'S

TEHRAN, IRAN

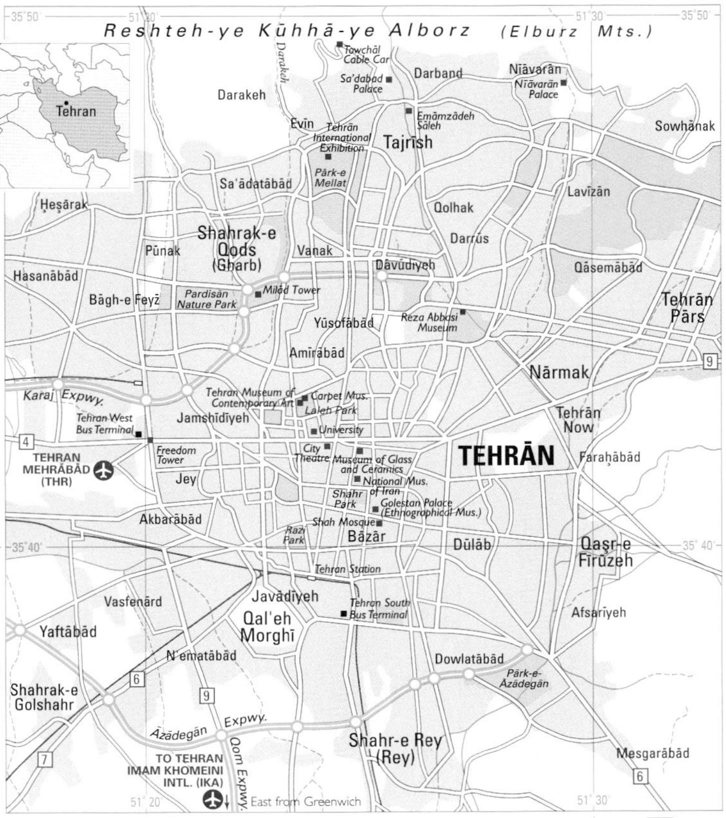

Reshteh-ye Kūhhā-ye Alborz (Elburz Mts.)

Tehran

1 0 1 km 2 3 4 5
1 0 miles 1 2 3

Tochāl Cable Car
Darakeh
Sa'dābād Palace
Darband
Darakeh
Niāvarān
Niāvarān Palace
Evīn
Tehrān International Exhibition
Emāmzādeh Sāleh
Sowhānak
Sa'ādatābād
Tajrīsh
Pārk-e Mellat
Lavīzān
Shahrak-e Qods (Gharb)
Vanak
Qolhak
Pūnak
Dāvūdīyeh
Darrūs
Qāsemābād
Hasanābād
Milād Tower
Tehrān Pārs
Bāgh-e Feyż
Pardīsān Nature Park
Yūsofābād
Reza Abbasi Museum
Akbarābād
Amīrābād
Nārmak
Karaj Expwy.
Tehran Museum of Contemporary Art
Carpet Mus.
Laleh Park
Tehrān Now
Tehran West Bus Terminal
Jamshīdīyeh
University
Farahābād
TEHRAN MEHRĀBĀD (THR)
Freedom Tower
City Theatre
Museum of Glass and Ceramics
National Mus. of Iran
Golestan Palace (Ethnographical Mus.)
TEHRĀN
Jey
Shahr Park
Shah Mosque
Akbarābād
Rāzī Park
Bāzār
Dūlāb
Qasr-e Fīrūzeh
Vasfenārd
Tehran Station
Javādīyeh
Tehran South Bus Terminal
Afsarīyeh
Yaftābād
Qal'eh Morghī
Shahrak-e Golshahr
N'ematābād
Dowlatābād
Pārk-e Āzādegān
Mesgarābād
Āzādegān Expwy.
Shahr-e Rey (Rey)
Qom Expwy.
TO TEHRAN IMAM KHOMEINI INTL. (IKA)
East from Greenwich
Heşārak

1 2 3

CENTRAL TORONTO

0 km 0.5
0 miles 0.25

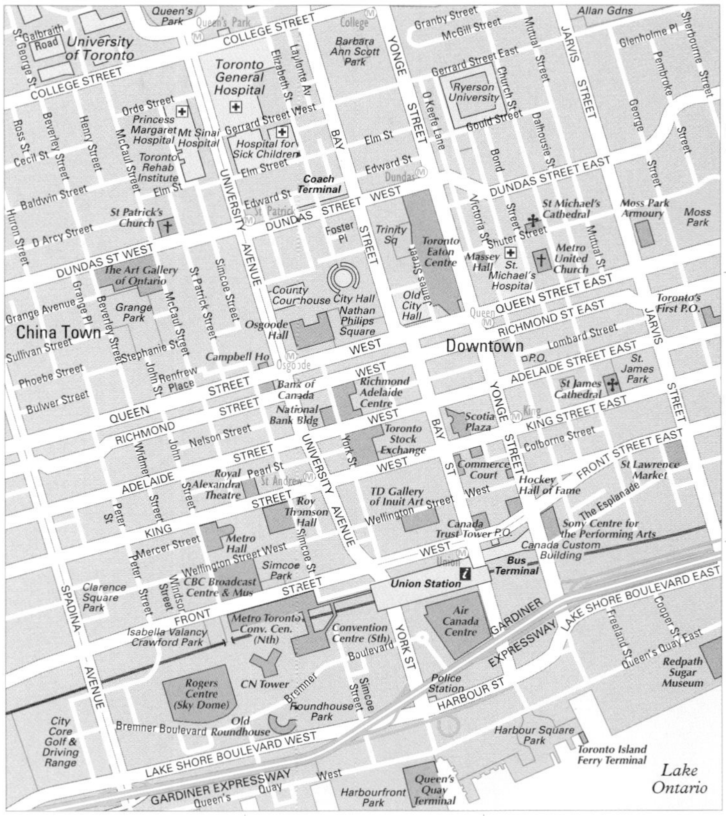

Queen's Park
University of Toronto
College
Granby Street
Allan Gdns
COLLEGE STREET
Barbara Ann Scott Park
YONGE
Glenholme Pl
Galbraith Road
McGill Street
Gerrard Street East
Sherbourne Street
Pembroke
COLLEGE STREET
Toronto General Hospital
Orde Street
Princess Margaret Hospital
Mt Sinai Hospital
Gerrard Street West
Elm St
JARVIS
George
Ross St
Cecil St
Henry Street
McCaul Street
Hospital for Sick Children
Elm Street
O'Keefe Lane
Gould Street
Ryerson University
STREET
Baldwin Street
Toronto Rehab Institute
Edward St
Edward Street
DUNDAS STREET EAST
a
St Patrick's Church
Coach Terminal
DUNDAS
Dundas Sq
St Michael's Cathedral
Moss Park Armoury
Moss Park
D'Arcy Street
STREET WEST
Foster Pl
Trinity Sq
Toronto Eaton Centre
Victoria Street
Metro United Church
DUNDAS ST WEST
The Art Gallery of Ontario
St Patrick's Street
Simcoe Street
St. Michael's Hospital
Masey Hall
St.
Grange Avenue
Grange Pl
County Courthouse
City Hall
Nathan Philips Square
QUEEN STREET EAST
A
China Town
Grange Park
McCaul Street
Osgoode Hall
Old City Hall
Downtown
Toronto's First P.O.
Sullivan Street
Stephanie St
Campbell Ho
RICHMOND ST EAST
Phoebe Street
Renfrew Pl
Bank of Canada
Richmond Adelaide Centre
P.O.
Lombard Street
St James Park
Butwer Street
QUEEN
STREET
National Bank Bldg
Toronto Stock Exchange
Scotia Plaza
ADELAIDE STREET EAST
St James Cathedral
St. James Park
RICHMOND
Nelson Street
WEST
YONGE
Colborne Street
b
ADELAIDE
Royal Alexandra Theatre
Pearl St
St Andrew
Commerce Court
KING STREET EAST
Hockey Hall of Fame
St Lawrence Market
KING
Mercer Street
Roy Thomson Hall
TD Gallery of Inuit Art
FRONT STREET EAST
UNIVERSITY AVENUE
Wellington
West
Canada Trust Tower P.O.
Som Centre for the Performing Arts
SPADINA
Clarence Square Park
CBC Broadcast Centre & Mus
Simcoe Park
WEST
Canada Custom Building
FRONT
STREET
Metro Toronto Conv. Cen. (Nth)
Union Station
Bus Terminal
LAKE SHORE BOULEVARD EAST
c
AVENUE
Isabella Valancy Crawford Park
Convention Centre (Sth)
YORK ST
Air Canada Centre
GARDINER
EXPRESSWAY
Freeland Street
Cooper St East
Queen's Quay East
Redpath Sugar Museum
Rogers Centre (Sky Dome)
CN Tower
Bremner
Simcoe Street
Police Station
HARBOUR ST
City Core Golf & Driving Range
Bremner Boulevard
Old Roundhouse
Roundhouse Park
Harbour Square Park
Toronto Island Ferry Terminal
Lake Ontario
LAKE SHORE BOULEVARD WEST
West
Queen's Quay
Harbourfront Park
Harbourfront Terminal
GARDINER EXPRESSWAY
Queen's Quay

1 2 3

TORONTO, CANADA

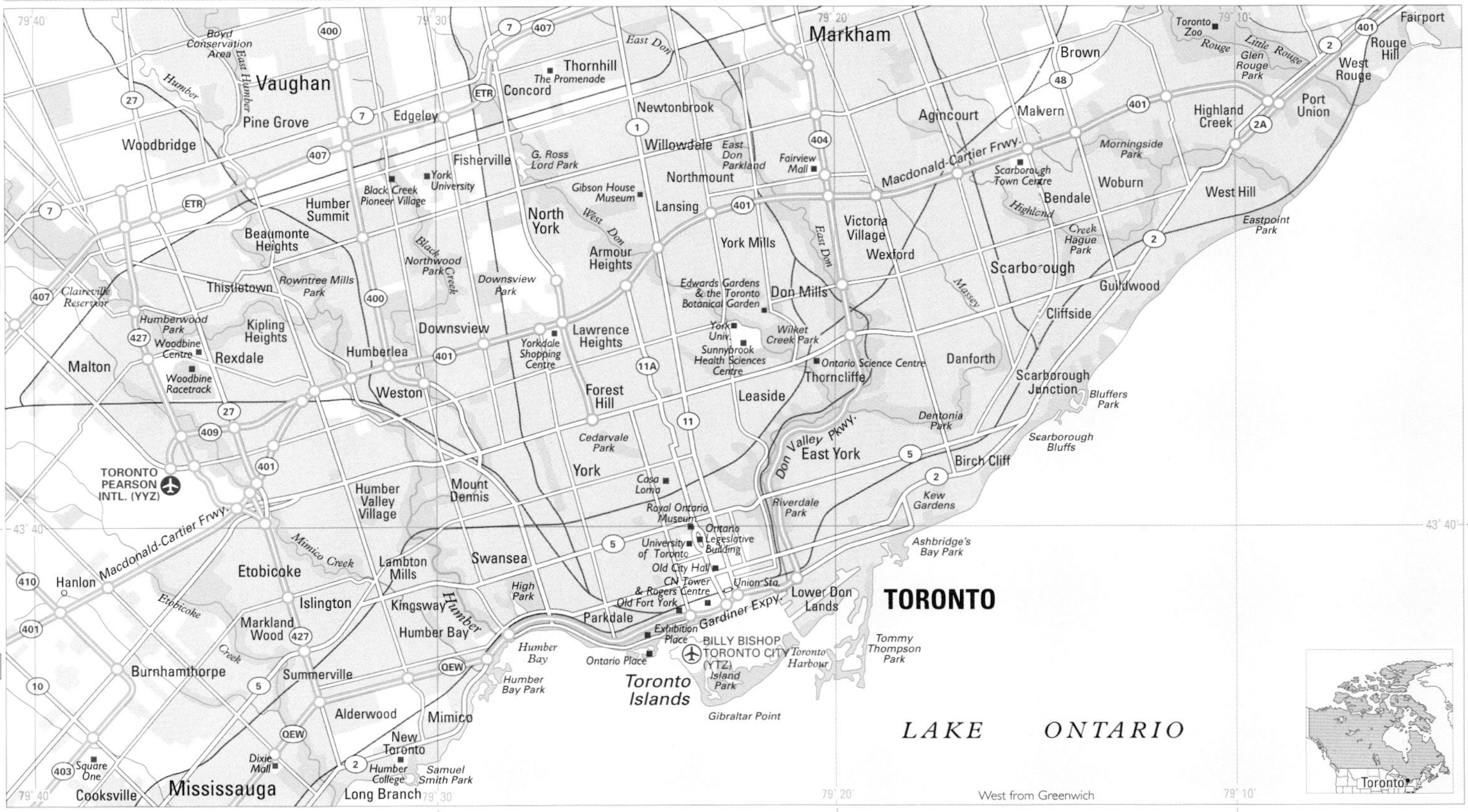

1 0 1 km 2 3 4 5
1 0 miles 1 2 3

79°40
79°30
79°20
79°10
Fairport
Boyd Conservation Area
400
7
407
East Don
Markham
Toronto Zoo
Rouge
Little Rouge
401
Rouge Hill
27
Humber
ETR
Thornhill
The Promenade
Concord
Brown
Glen Rouge Park
West Rouge
Vaughan
Pine Grove
7
Edgeley
Newtonbrook
48
Port Union
Woodbridge
407
Fisherville
G. Ross Lord Park
Willowdale
East Don Parkland
Fairview Mall
404
Agincourt
Malvern
401
Highland Creek
2A
7
ETR
York University
Black Creek Pioneer Village
1
Gibson House Museum
Northmount
Macdonald-Cartier Frwy
Scarborough Town Centre
Morningside Park
Humber Summit
Beaumonte Heights
Black Creek
Northwood Park
North York
West Don
Lansing
401
York Mills
East Don
Victoria Village
Woburn
Bendale
West Hill
A
Claireville Reservoir
407
Thistletown
Rowntree Mills Park
400
Downsview Park
Armour Heights
Wexford
Highland
Scarborough
Guildwood
Humberwood Park
427
Woodbine Centre
Kipling Heights
Rexdale
Humberlea
401
Downsview
Lawrence Heights
Edwards Gardens & the Toronto Botanical Garden
Don Mills
York Univ.
Wilket Creek Park
Ontario Science Centre
Cliffside
Malton
Woodbine Racetrack
27
Weston
11A
Forest Hill
Sunnybrook Health Sciences Centre
Thorncliffe
Danforth
Scarborough Junction
Bluffers Park
409
401
Cedarvale Park
11
Leaside
Dentonia Park
Scarborough Bluffs
TORONTO PEARSON INTL. (YYZ)
Humber Valley Village
York
Casa Loma
Don Valley Pkwy
East York
5
Birch Cliff
43°40
410
Macdonald-Cartier Frwy
Humber
Royal Ontario Museum
Ontario Legislative Building
Riverdale Park
Kew Gardens
43°40
Hanlon
Etobicoke
Lambton Mills
Swansea
University of Toronto
Old City Hall
Ashbridge's Bay Park
401
Islington
Kingsway
High Park
CN Tower & Rogers Centre
Old Fort York
Union Sta.
Gardiner Expwy
Lower Don Lands
TORONTO
427
Markland Wood
Humber Bay
Parkdale
Tommy Thompson Park
B
10
Burnhamthorpe
Summerville
OEW
Exhibition Place
BILLY BISHOP TORONTO CITY (YTZ)
Toronto Island
Toronto Harbour
Mimico Creek
Humber Bay
Humber Bay Park
Ontario Place
Toronto Islands
Etobicoke Creek
403
Square One
Dixie Mall
New Toronto
2
Gibraltar Point
LAKE ONTARIO
Toronto
Cooksville
Mississauga
Alderwood
Mimico
Humber College
Samuel Smith Park
Long Branch
79°40
79°30
West from Greenwich
79°20
79°10

1 2 3 4

427 Provincial route numbers

COPYRIGHT PHILIP'S

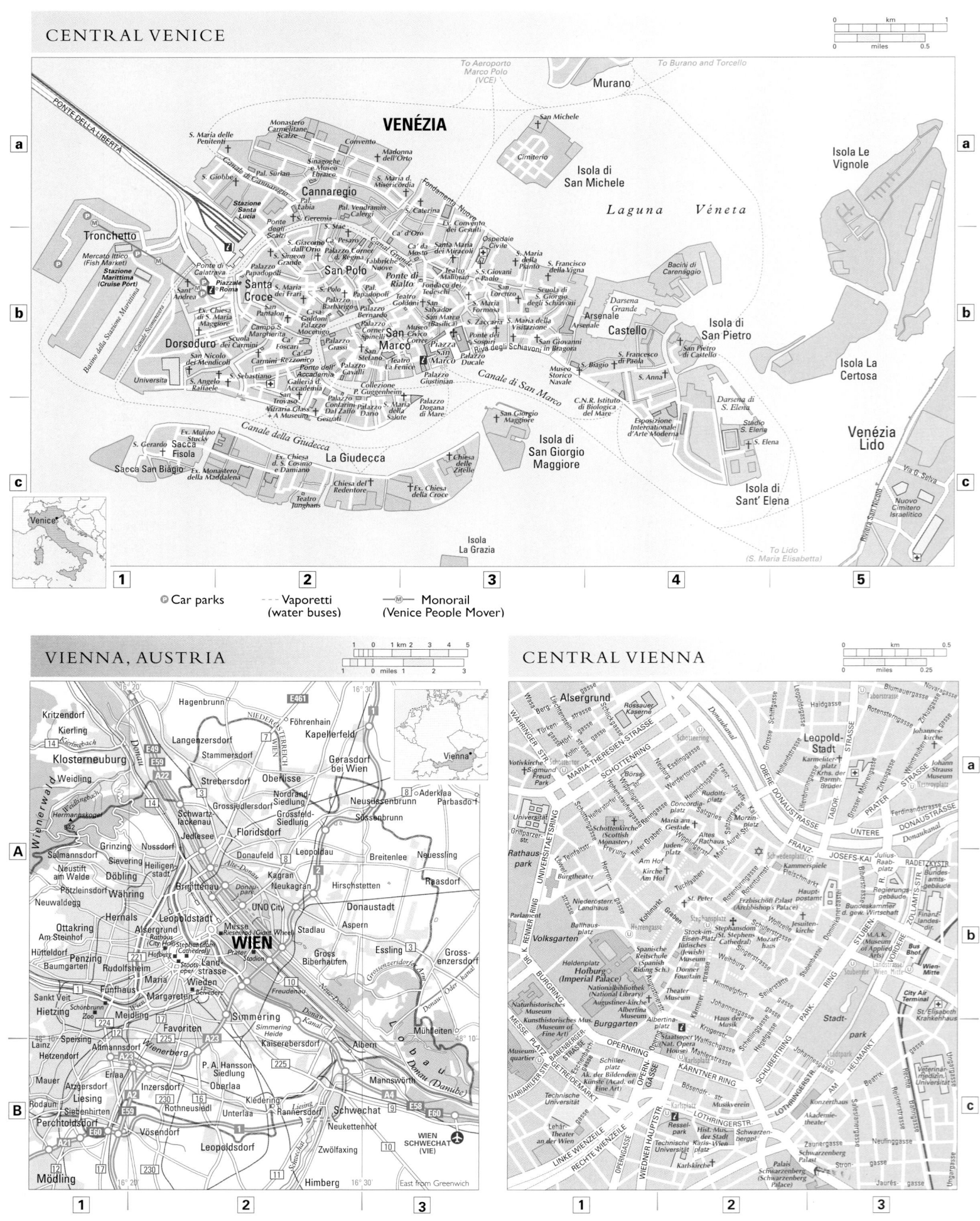

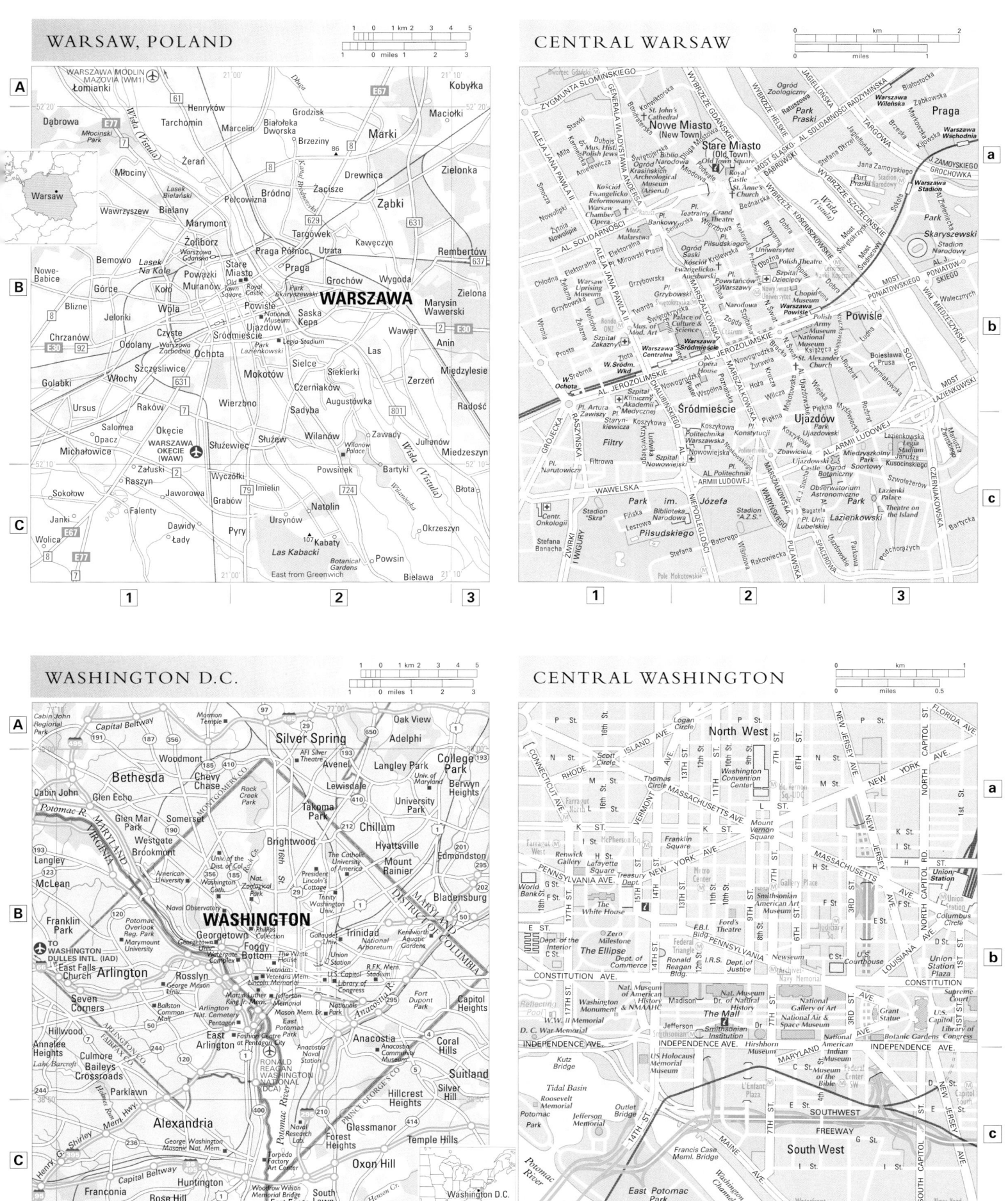

Interstate route numbers (29) U.S. route numbers (166) State route numbers

COPYRIGHT PHILIP'S

INDEX TO CITY MAPS

The index contains the names of all the principal places and features shown on the City Maps. Each name is followed by an additional entry in italics giving the name of the City Map within which it is located.

The number in bold type which follows each name refers to the number of the City Map page where that feature or place will be found.

The letter and figure which are immediately after the page number give the grid square on the map within which the feature or place is situated.

The letter represents the latitude and the figure the longitude. The full geographic reference is provided in the border of the City Maps.

The location given is the centre of the city, suburb or feature and is not necessarily the name. Rivers, canals and roads are indexed to their name. Rivers carry the symbol → after their name.

An explanation of the alphabetical order rules and a list of the abbreviations used are to be found at the beginning of the World Map Index.

A

A.N.Z. Stadium *Sydney* **29** B1
Aalām *Baghdad* **3** B2
Aalsmeer *Amsterdam* **2** B1
Abbey Wood *London* **15** B4
Abcoude *Amsterdam* **2** B2
Âbdin *Cairo* **7** A2
Abeno *Osaka* **23** B2
Aberdeen *Hong Kong* **12** B2
Aberdeen Country Park ⌓ *Hong Kong* **12** B2
Aberdour *Edinburgh* **11** A2
Aberdour Castle *Edinburgh* **11** A2
Abfanggraben → *Munich* **21** A3
Ablon-sur-Seine *Paris* **24** B3
Abramtsevo *Moscow* **19** B3
Abu Dis *Jerusalem* **13** B2
Abû en Numrus *Cairo* **7** B2
Abu Ghosh *Jerusalem* **13** B1
Abu Hail *Dubai* **9** A2
Acassuso *Buenos Aires* **7** A2
Achères *Paris* **24** A1
Acília *Rome* **26** C1
Aclimação *São Paulo* **27** B2
Acropolis *Athens* **2** B2
Acton *London* **15** A2
Açúcar, Pão de *Rio de Janeiro* **25** B2
Ada Beja *Lisbon* **16** A1
Adamasta Channel *Hong Kong* **12** B2
Adams Park *Atlanta* **3** B2
Addiscombe *London* **15** B3
Adelphi *Washington* **33** A3
Aderklaa *Vienna* **32** A3
Adler Planetarium *Chicago* **9** B3
Admiralteyskaya Storona *St. Petersburg* **27** B2
Áffori *Milan* **18** A2
Aflandshage *Copenhagen* **8** B3
Afsarīyeh *Tehran* **31** B2
Agboyi Cr. → *Lagos* **14** A2
Ågerup *Copenhagen* **8** A1
Ågesta *Stockholm* **29** B2
Aghia Marina *Athens* **2** C3
Aghia Paraskevi *Athens* **2** A2
Aghios Dimitrios *Athens* **2** B2
Aghios Ioannis Rendis *Athens* **2** B1
Agincourt *Toronto* **31** A3
Agra Canal *Delhi* **10** B2
Agricola Oriental *Mexico City* **18** B2
Água Espraiada → *São Paulo* **27** B2
Agualva-Cacem *Lisbon* **16** A1
Ahrensfelde *Berlin* **5** A4
Ahuntsic *Montreal* **20** A1
Ai → *Osaka* **23** A2
Aigremont *Paris* **24** A1
Air View Park *Singapore* **28** A2
Airport West *Melbourne* **18** A1
Ajegunle *Lagos* **14** B2
Aji *Osaka* **23** A1
Ajuda *Lisbon* **16** A1
Akalla *Stockholm* **29** A1
Akasaka *Tokyo* **30** A3
Akbarābād *Tehran* **31** A2
Akershus Slott *Oslo* **23** A3
Al 'Aẓamīyah *Baghdad* **3** A2
Al Bada *Dubai* **9** B2
Al Barsha *Dubai* **9** B1
Al Hamriya Port *Dubai* **9** A2
Al Hudaiba *Dubai* **9** B2
Al Jafiliya *Dubai* **9** B2
Al Manara *Dubai* **9** B1
Al Mina *Dubai* **9** B2
Al Nasr *Dubai* **9** B2
Al Quds = Jerusalem *Jerusalem* **13** B2
Al Quoz *Dubai* **9** B1
Al Safa *Dubai* **9** B1
Al Satwa *Dubai* **9** B2
Al Sufouh *Dubai* **9** B1
Al Walaja *Jerusalem* **13** B1
Al Wasl *Dubai* **9** B2
Alaguntan *Lagos* **14** B2
Alameda *San Francisco* **26** B3
Alameda Memorial State Beach Park *San Francisco* **26** B3
Albern *Vienna* **32** B2
Albert Park *Melbourne* **18** B1
Alberton *Johannesburg* **13** B2
Albertslund *Copenhagen* **8** B2
Alcantara *Lisbon* **16** A1
Alcatraz I. *San Francisco* **26** B2
Alcobendas *Madrid* **17** A2
Alcorcón *Madrid* **17** B1
Aldershof *Berlin* **5** B4
Alderwood *Toronto* **31** B1
Aldo Bonzi *Buenos Aires* **7** C1
Aleksandrovskoye *St. Petersburg* **27** B2
Alexander Nevsky Abbey *St. Petersburg* **27** B2
Alexandra *Johannesburg* **13** A2
Alexandra *Singapore* **28** B2
Alexandria *Washington* **33** C2
Alfortville *Paris* **24** B3
Algés *Lisbon* **16** A1
Algiers *New Orleans* **21** B2
Alhambra *Los Angeles* **16** B4
Alibey → *Istanbul* **12** B1
Alibey Barajı *Istanbul* **12** B1
Alibeyköy *Istanbul* **12** B1
Alimos *Athens* **2** B2
Alipur *Kolkata* **14** B1
Allach *Munich* **21** A1
Allambie Heights *Sydney* **29** A2
Allermuir Hill *Edinburgh* **11** B2
Allianz Arena *Munich* **21** A2
Allston *Boston* **6** A2
Almada *Lisbon* **16** A2
Almagro *Buenos Aires* **7** B2
Almargem do Bispo *Lisbon* **16** A1
Almirante G. Brown, Parque *Buenos Aires* **7** C2
Almon *Jerusalem* **13** B2
Almond → *Edinburgh* **11** B2
Alna *Oslo* **23** A4
Alnsjøen *Oslo* **23** A4
Alperton *London* **15** A2
Alpine *New York* **22** A2
Alrode *Johannesburg* **13** B2
Alsemberg *Brussels* **6** B2
Alsergrund *Vienna* **32** A2
Alsip *Chicago* **9** C2
Ålsten *Stockholm* **29** B1
Älta *Stockholm* **29** B3
Altadena *Los Angeles* **16** A4
Alte-Donau → *Vienna* **32** A2
Alter Finkenkrug *Berlin* **5** A1
Altes Rathaus *Munich* **21** B2
Altglienicke *Berlin* **5** B4
Altlandsberg *Berlin* **5** A5
Altlandsberg Nord *Berlin* **5** A5
Altmannsdorf *Vienna* **32** B1
Alto da Boa Vista *Rio de Janeiro* **25** B1
Alto da Moóca *São Paulo* **27** B2
Alto do Pina *Lisbon* **16** A2
Altona *Melbourne* **18** B1
Alvalade *Lisbon* **16** A2
Alvik *Stockholm* **29** B1
Alvin Callendar Naval Air Station *New Orleans* **21** B2
Älvsjo *Stockholm* **29** B2
Älvvik *Stockholm* **29** A3
Am Hasenbergl *Munich* **21** A2
Am Steinhof *Vienna* **32** A1
Am Wald *Munich* **21** B2
Ama Keng *Singapore* **28** A2
Amadora *Lisbon* **16** A1
Amagasaki *Osaka* **23** A1
Amager *Copenhagen* **8** B3
Amāl Qādisiya *Baghdad* **3** B2
Amalienborg Slot *Copenhagen* **8** A3
Amata *Milan* **18** A1
Ambelokipi *Athens* **2** B2
Ameixoeira *Lisbon* **16** A2
Amelia Earhart Park *Miami* **19** C1
América *São Paulo* **27** B1
American Univ. *Washington* **33** B2
Amin *Baghdad* **3** B2
Aminadav *Jerusalem* **13** B1
Amīrābād *Tehran* **31** A2
Amora *Lisbon* **16** B2
Amoreira *Lisbon* **16** A1
Amper → *Munich* **21** A1
Amstel-Drecht-Kanaal *Amsterdam* **2** B2
Amstelveen *Amsterdam* **2** B2
Amsterdam *Amsterdam* **2** A2
Amsterdam ✈ (AMS) *Amsterdam* **2** B1
Amsterdam Arena *Amsterdam* **2** B2
Amsterdam-Rijnkanaal *Amsterdam* **2** B3
Amsterdam Zuidoost *Amsterdam* **2** B2
Amsterdamse Bos *Amsterdam* **2** B1
Anacostia *Washington* **33** B3
Anacostia → *Washington* **33** B3
Anadoluhisarı *Istanbul* **12** B2
Anadolukavağı *Istanbul* **12** A2
Anata *Jerusalem* **13** B2
Ancol *Jakarta* **12** A1
'Andalus *Baghdad* **3** B1
Andaraí *Rio de Janeiro* **25** B1
Anderlecht *Brussels* **6** A1
Anderson Park *Atlanta* **3** B2
Andingmen *Beijing* **4** B2
Ang Mo Kio *Singapore* **28** A3
Ängby *Stockholm* **29** A1
Angel I. *San Francisco* **26** A2
Angel Island State Park ⌓ *San Francisco* **26** A2
Angke, Kali → *Jakarta* **12** A1
Angyalföld *Budapest* **7** A2
Anik *Mumbai* **20** A2
Anin *Warsaw* **33** B2
Anjou *Montreal* **20** A2
Annalee Heights *Washington* **33** B1
Anne Frankhuis *Amsterdam* **2** A2
Antonio Carlos Jobim Int. ✈ (GIG) *Rio de Janeiro* **25** A1
Antony *Paris* **24** B2
Aoyama *Tokyo* **30** B3
Ap Lei Chau *Hong Kong* **12** B2
Apapa *Lagos* **14** B2
Apapa Quays *Lagos* **14** B2
Apelacão *Lisbon* **16** A2
Apgujeong *Seoul* **27** B2
Apopka, L. *Orlando* **23** A1
Apoquindo *Santiago* **27** B2
Apterkarskiy Ostrov *St. Petersburg* **27** B2
Ar Kazimiyah *Baghdad* **3** B1
Ar Ram *Jerusalem* **13** A2
Ara → *Tokyo* **30** A4
Arakawa *Tokyo* **30** A3
Arany-hegyi-patak → *Budapest* **7** A2
Aravaca *Madrid* **17** B1
Arbataash *Baghdad* **3** A1
Arc de Triomphe *Paris* **24** A2
Arcadia *Los Angeles* **16** B4
Arcadia Park *Dallas-Fort Worth* **10** B4
Arcueil *Paris* **24** B2
Arese *Milan* **18** A1
Arganzuela *Madrid* **17** B1
Argenteuil *Paris* **24** A2
Argiroupoli *Athens* **2** B2
Arima *Tokyo* **30** B2
Arken *Copenhagen* **8** B2
Arlanda, Stockholm ✈ (ARN) *Stockholm* **29** A1
Arlington *Boston* **6** A1
Arlington *Dallas-Fort Worth* **10** C3
Arlington *Washington* **33** B2
Arlington, L. *Dallas-Fort Worth* **10** B2
Arlington Heights *Boston* **6** A1
Arlington Municipal ✈ (JLH) *Dallas-Fort Worth* **10** B3
Arlington Nat. Cemetery *Washington* **33** B2
Armação *Rio de Janeiro* **25** B2
Armadale *Melbourne* **18** B2
Armour Heights *Toronto* **31** A2
Arncliffe *Sydney* **29** B1
Arnold Arboretum *Boston* **6** B2
Árpádföld *Budapest* **7** A3
Arrentela *Lisbon* **16** B2
Arroyo Seco Park *Los Angeles* **16** B3
Årsta *Stockholm* **29** B2
Artas *Jerusalem* **13** B2
Arthur's Seat *Edinburgh* **11** B3
Arts, Place des *Montreal* **20** A2
As Shawawra *Jerusalem* **13** B2
Asagaya *Tokyo* **30** A2
Asahi *Osaka* **23** A2
Asakusa *Tokyo* **30** A3
Asati *Kolkata* **14** C1
Aschheim *Munich* **21** A3
Ascot Vale *Melbourne* **18** A1
Ashbridge's Bay Park *Toronto* **31** B3
Ashburn *Chicago* **9** C2
Ashburton *Melbourne* **18** B2
Ashfield *Sydney* **29** B1
Ashford *London* **15** B1
AsiaWorld-Expo *Hong Kong* **12** B1
Askisto *Helsinki* **11** B1
Askrikefjärden *Stockholm* **29** A3
Asnières *Paris* **24** A2
Aspern *Vienna* **32** A2
Assago *Milan* **18** B1
Assendelft *Amsterdam* **2** A1
Assiano *Milan* **18** B1
Astoria *New York* **22** B2
Astrolabe Park *Sydney* **29** B2
Atarot *Jerusalem* **13** A2
Atarot ✈ (JRS) *Jerusalem* **13** A2
Atghara *Kolkata* **14** B2
Athens = Athina *Athens* **2** B2
Athina *Athens* **2** B2
Athina ✈ (ATH) *Athens* **2** A3
Athínai = Athina *Athens* **2** B2
Athis-Mons *Paris* **24** B3
Athlone *Cape Town* **8** A2
Atholl *Johannesburg* **13** A2
Atīfiya *Baghdad* **3** A2
Atişalen *Istanbul* **12** B1
Atlanta *Atlanta* **3** B2
Atlanta Hartsfield-Jackson Int. ✈ (ATL) *Atlanta* **3** C2
Atlanta History Center *Atlanta* **3** B2
Atlanta Zoo *Atlanta* **3** B2
Atomium *Brussels* **6** A2
Attiki *Athens* **2** A2
Atzgersdorf *Vienna* **32** B1
Aubervilliers *Paris* **24** A3
Aubing *Munich* **21** B1
Auburndale *Boston* **6** A1
Auchendinny *Edinburgh* **11** B2
Auckland Park *Johannesburg* **13** B2
Auderghem *Brussels* **6** B2
Audubon Park *New Orleans* **21** B2
Augustówka *Warsaw* **33** B2
Aulnay-sous-Bois *Paris* **24** A3
Aurelio *Rome* **26** B1
Ausîm *Cairo* **7** A1
Austerlitz, Gare d' *Paris* **24** A3
Austin *Chicago* **9** B2
Autry Museum of the American West *Los Angeles* **16** B3
Avedøre *Copenhagen* **8** B2
Avellaneda *Buenos Aires* **7** C2
Avenel *Washington* **33** B3
Aventura *Miami* **19** C3
Avondale *Chicago* **9** B2
Avondale *New Orleans* **21** B1
Avondale Heights *Melbourne* **18** A1
Avtovo *St. Petersburg* **27** B1
Ayazağa *Istanbul* **12** B1
Ayer Chawan, Pulau *Singapore* **28** B2
Ayer Merbau, Pulau *Singapore* **28** B2
Azabu *Tokyo* **30** B3
Azcapotzalco *Mexico City* **18** B1
Azteca, Estadia *Mexico City* **18** C2
Azucar, Cerro Pan de *Santiago* **27** A1

B

Baambrugge *Amsterdam* **2** B2
Baba Channel *Karachi* **13** B1
Baba I. *Karachi* **13** B1
Babarpur *Delhi* **10** A2
Babushkin *Moscow* **19** A3
Back B. *Mumbai* **20** B1
Baclaran *Manila* **17** B2
Bacoor *Manila* **17** C1
Bacoor B. *Manila* **17** C1
Badalona *Barcelona* **4** A2
Badhoevedorp *Amsterdam* **2** A1
Badli *Delhi* **10** A1
Bærum *Oslo* **23** A2
Bağcılar *Istanbul* **12** B1
Bággio *Milan* **18** B1
Bāgh-e-Feyz *Tehran* **31** A1
Baghdād *Baghdad* **3** A2
Baghdad Int. ✈ (BGW) *Baghdad* **3** B1
Bagmari *Kolkata* **14** B2
Bagneux *Paris* **24** B2
Bagnolet *Paris* **24** A3
Bagsværd *Copenhagen* **8** A2
Bagsværd Sø *Copenhagen* **8** A2
Baguiati *Kolkata* **14** B2
Bagumbayan *Manila* **17** C2
Baha'i Temple *Chicago* **9** A2
Bahçeköy *Istanbul* **12** A1
Bahçelıevler *Istanbul* **12** B1
Bahtîm *Cairo* **7** A2
Baihedong *Guangzhou* **11** B2
Baileys Crossroads *Washington* **33** B2
Bailly *Paris* **24** A1
Bairro Lopes *Lisbon* **16** A2
Baisha *Guangzhou* **11** B2
Baiyun *Guangzhou* **11** A2
Baiyun Mountain Scenic Area ⌓ *Guangzhou* **11** A2
Bakırköy *Istanbul* **12** C1
Bal Harbor *Miami* **19** C3
Balara *Manila* **17** B2
Balch Springs *Dallas-Fort Worth* **10** B6
Baldia *Karachi* **13** A1
Baldwin, L. *Orlando* **23** A3
Baldwin Hills *Los Angeles* **16** B2
Baldwin Hills Res. *Los Angeles* **16** B2
Balgowlah *Sydney* **29** A2
Balgowlah Heights *Sydney* **29** A2
Balham *London* **15** B3
Bali *Kolkata* **14** B1
Baliganja *Kolkata* **14** B2
Balingsnäs *Stockholm* **29** B2
Balingsta *Stockholm* **29** B2
Balintawak *Manila* **17** B1
Ballerup *Copenhagen* **8** A2
Balmain *Sydney* **29** B2
Baluhati *Kolkata* **14** B1
Balvanera *Buenos Aires* **7** B2
Balwyn *Melbourne* **18** A2
Balwyn North *Melbourne* **18** A2
Banana Island *Lagos* **14** B2
Banática *Lisbon* **16** A1
Bandra *Mumbai* **20** A1
Bandra Pt. *Mumbai* **20** A1
Bang Kapi *Bangkok* **3** B2
Bang Na *Bangkok* **3** B2
Bangbae *Seoul* **27** C1
Bangkhen *Bangkok* **3** A2
Bangkok *Bangkok* **3** B2
Bangkok Don Muang Int. ✈ (BKK) *Bangkok* **3** A2
Bangkok Noi *Bangkok* **3** B1
Bangkok Yai *Bangkok* **3** B1
Banglo *Kolkata* **14** B1
Bangrak *Bangkok* **3** B2
Bangsu *Bangkok* **3** B2
Banks, C. *Sydney* **29** C2
Banksmeadow *Sydney* **29** B2
Banstala *Kolkata* **14** B2
Bantra *Kolkata* **14** B1
Baoshan *Shanghai* **28** A1
Bar Giyora *Jerusalem* **13** B1
Barahanagar *Kolkata* **14** B2
Barajas *Madrid* **17** B2
Barajas, Madrid ✈ (MAD) *Madrid* **17** B2
Barakpur *Kolkata* **14** A2
Barcarena *Lisbon* **16** A1
Barcarena, Rib. de → *Lisbon* **16** A1
Barcelona *Barcelona* **4** A2
Barcelona, El Prat ✈ (BCN) *Barcelona* **4** B1
Barcroft, L. *Washington* **33** B2
Barking *London* **15** A4
Barkingside *London* **15** A4
Barnes *London* **15** B2
Barnet *London* **15** A2
Baron Empain Palace *Cairo* **7** A2
Barra Andai *Karachi* **13** B2
Barra Funda *São Paulo* **27** B2
Barracas *Buenos Aires* **7** B2
Barrackpur = Barakpur *Kolkata* **14** A2
Barranco *Lima* **14** B2
Barreiro *Lisbon* **16** B2
Barreto *Rio de Janeiro* **25** B2
Bartala *Kolkata* **14** B1
Barton Park *Sydney* **29** B1
Bartyki *Warsaw* **33** C2
Basus *Cairo* **7** A2
Batanagar *Kolkata* **14** B1
Bath Beach *New York* **22** C1
Bath I. *Karachi* **13** B2
Batir *Jerusalem* **13** B1
Batok, Bukit *Singapore* **28** A2
Battersea *London* **15** B3
Bauman *Moscow* **19** B3
Baumgarten *Vienna* **32** A1
Bay, L. *Orlando* **23** A2
Bay Harbor Islands *Miami* **19** C3
Bay Hill *Orlando* **23** B1
Bay Ridge *New York* **22** C1
Bayit Va-Gan *Jerusalem* **13** B2
Bayonne *New York* **22** B1
Bayou Boeuf *New Orleans* **21** B1
Bayou Segnette State Park ⌓ *New Orleans* **21** B2
Bayrampaşa *Istanbul* **12** B1
Bayshore *San Francisco* **26** B2
Bayt Lahm *Jerusalem* **13** B2
Bayview *San Francisco* **26** B2
Bāzār *Tehran* **31** A2
Beacon Hill *Hong Kong* **12** A3
Beato *Lisbon* **16** A2
Beaumonte Heights *Toronto* **31** A1
Bebek *Istanbul* **12** B2
Běchovice *Prague* **25** B3
Beckenham *London* **15** B3
Beckton *London* **15** A4
Becontree *London* **15** A4
Beddington Corner *London* **15** B3
Bedford *Boston* **6** A1
Bedford *Dallas-Fort Worth* **10** A3
Bedford Park *Chicago* **9** C2
Bedford Park *New York* **22** A2
Bedford Stuyvesant *New York* **22** B2
Bedford View *Johannesburg* **13** B2
Bedok *Singapore* **28** B3
Bedok, Res. *Singapore* **28** A3
Beersel *Brussels* **6** B1
Behala *Kolkata* **14** B1
Bei Hai *Beijing* **4** B2
Beicai *Shanghai* **28** B2
Beijing *Beijing* **4** B1
Beit Duqu *Jerusalem* **13** A1
Beit Ghur at-Taht *Jerusalem* **13** A1
Beit Ghur el-Fawqa *Jerusalem* **13** A1
Beit Hanina *Jerusalem* **13** B2
Beit Ij'za *Jerusalem* **13** A1
Beit Iksa *Jerusalem* **13** B2
Beit I'nan *Jerusalem* **13** A1
Beit Jala *Jerusalem* **13** B2
Beit Lahm = Bayt Lahm *Jerusalem* **13** B2
Beit Liqya *Jerusalem* **13** A1
Beit Nekofa *Jerusalem* **13** B1
Beit Sahur *Jerusalem* **13** B2
Beit Sofafa *Jerusalem* **13** B2
Beit Surik *Jerusalem* **13** B1
Beit Ur al-Fawqa *Jerusalem* **13** A1
Beit Zayit *Jerusalem* **13** B1
Beitaipingzhuan *Beijing* **4** B1
Beitar Ilit *Jerusalem* **13** B1
Beitin *Jerusalem* **13** A2
Beitsun *Guangzhou* **11** B2
Beitunya *Jerusalem* **13** A2
Beixing Jing Park *Shanghai* **28** B1
Békásmegyer *Budapest* **7** A2
Bekkelaget *Oslo* **23** A3
Bekkestua *Oslo* **23** A2
Bel Air *Los Angeles* **16** B2
Bela Vista *São Paulo* **27** B2
Bélanger *Montreal* **20** A1
Belas *Lisbon* **16** A1
Beleghata *Kolkata* **14** B2
Belém *Lisbon* **16** A1
Belém, Torre de *Lisbon* **16** A1
Belènzinho *São Paulo* **27** B2
Belgachiya *Kolkata* **14** B2
Belgharia *Kolkata* **14** B2
Belgrano *Buenos Aires* **7** B2
Bell *Los Angeles* **16** C3
Bell Gardens *Los Angeles* **16** C4
Bellavista *Lima* **14** B2
Bellavista *Santiago* **27** C2
Belle Harbor *New York* **22** C2
Bellingham *London* **15** B3
Belmont *Boston* **6** A1
Belmont *London* **15** A2
Belmont Cragin *Chicago* **9** B2
Belmont Harbor *Chicago* **9** B3
Belmore *Sydney* **29** B1
Belur *Kolkata* **14** B2
Belvedere *London* **15** B4
Belvedere *San Francisco* **26** A2
Belvedere Park *Atlanta* **3** B3
Belyayevo Bogorodskoye *Moscow* **19** C2
Bemowo *Warsaw* **33** B1
Benaki Museum *Athens* **2** B2
Bendale *Toronto* **31** A3
Benefica *Rio de Janeiro* **25** B1
Benfica *Lisbon* **16** A1
Benítez Int. ✈ (SCL) *Santiago* **27** B1
Benito Juárez Int. ✈ (MEX) *Mexico City* **18** B2
Bensonhurst *New York* **22** C2
Berchem-Ste-Agathe *Brussels* **6** A1
Berg am Laim *Munich* **21** B2
Bergenfield *New York* **22** A2
Bergham *Munich* **21** B2
Bergvliet *Cape Town* **8** B1
Beri *Barcelona* **4** A1
Berkeley *San Francisco* **26** A3
Berlin *Berlin* **5** A3
Berlin Brandenburg ✈ (BER) *Berlin* **5** B4
Berlin Dom *Berlin* **5** A3
Berlin Tegel ✈ (TXL) *Berlin* **5** A2
Bermondsey *London* **15** B3
Bernabeu, Estadio *Madrid* **17** B1
Bernal Heights *San Francisco* **26** B2
Berwyn *Chicago* **9** B2
Berwyn Heights *Washington* **33** B3
Besiktas *Istanbul* **12** B2
Besós → *Barcelona* **4** A2
Bessie, L. *Orlando* **23** B1
Bet Horon *Jerusalem* **13** A1
Bethesda *Washington* **33** B2
Bethlehem = Bayt Lahm *Jerusalem* **13** B2
Bethnal Green *London* **15** A3
Betor *Kolkata* **14** B1
Beulah *Orlando* **23** A1
Beulah, L. *Orlando* **23** A1
Beverley Hills *Sydney* **29** B1
Beverley Park *Sydney* **29** B1
Beverly *Chicago* **9** C3
Beverly Arts Center *Chicago* **9** C2
Beverly Glen *Los Angeles* **16** B2
Beverly Hills *Los Angeles* **16** B2
Beverly Hills -Morgan Park Historic District *Chicago* **9** C2
Bexley *Sydney* **29** B1
Bexley □ *London* **15** B4
Bexleyheath *London* **15** B4
Beykoz *Istanbul* **12** B2
Beylerbeyi *Istanbul* **12** B2
Beyoğlu *Istanbul* **12** B1
Bezons *Paris* **24** A2
Bezuidenhout Park *Johannesburg* **13** B2
Bhadrakali *Kolkata* **14** A2
Bhalswa *Delhi* **10** A2
Bhambo Khan Qarmati *Karachi* **13** B2
Bhatsala *Kolkata* **14** B1
Bhawanipur *Kolkata* **14** B2
Bhendkhal *Mumbai* **20** B2
Bhit I. *Jerusalem* **13** B1
Bhuleshwar *Mumbai* **20** B1
Białołeka Dworska *Warsaw* **33** B2
Bicentennial Park *Los Angeles* **16** B4
Bicentennial Park *Sydney* **29** B1
Bickley *London* **15** B4
Bicutan *Manila* **17** C2
Bidhan Nagar *Kolkata* **14** B2
Bidu *Jerusalem* **13** B1
Bielany *Warsaw* **33** B1
Bielawa *Warsaw* **33** C2
Biesdorf *Berlin* **5** A4
Bièvre → *Paris* **24** B1
Bièvres *Paris* **24** B2
Big Buddha *Hong Kong* **12** B1
Big Sand L. *Orlando* **23** B2
Bijlmermeer *Amsterdam* **2** B2
Bill Baggs Cape Florida State Recr. Area ⌓ *Miami* **19** D3
Bilston *Edinburgh* **11** B2
Binacayan *Manila* **17** C1
Binondo *Manila* **17** B1
Bintaro Jaya *Jakarta* **12** B1
Bir Nabala *Jerusalem* **13** A2
Birak el Kiyam *Cairo* **7** A1
Birch Cliff *Toronto* **31** A3
Birkenstein *Berlin* **5** A5
Birkholz *Berlin* **5** A4
Birkholzaue *Berlin* **5** A4
Birrarrung Park *Melbourne* **18** A2
Biscayne Bay Aquatic Reserve *Miami* **19** E2
Biscayne Park *Miami* **19** C2
Bishop Lavis *Cape Town* **8** A2
Bishopscourt *Cape Town* **8** A1
Bispebjerg *Copenhagen* **8** A3
Bissonet Plaza *New Orleans* **21** A1
Bittsevsky Forest Park *Moscow* **19** C2
Björknas *Stockholm* **29** B3
Black Cr. → *Toronto* **31** A2
Black Creek Pioneer Village *Toronto* **31** A1
Blackfen *London* **15** B4
Blackheath *London* **15** B4
Bladensburg *Washington* **33** B3
Blair Village *Atlanta* **3** C2
Blairgowrie *Johannesburg* **13** A2
Blake House *Boston* **6** B2
Blakehurst *Sydney* **29** B1
Blakstad *Oslo* **23** B1
Blanche, L. *Orlando* **23** B1
Blankenburg *Berlin* **5** A3
Blankenfelde *Berlin* **5** A3
Blizne *Warsaw* **33** B1
Błota *Warsaw* **33** C3
Blue Island *Chicago* **9** D2
Blue Lagoon L. *Miami* **19** D1
Blue Mosque = Sultanahme Camil *Istanbul* **12** B1
Blue Mound *Dallas-Fort Worth* **10** A2
Bluff Hd. *Hong Kong* **12** B3
Bluffers Park *Toronto* **31** A3
Blumberg *Berlin* **5** A4
Blunt Pt. *San Francisco* **26** A2
Blutenberg *Munich* **21** B1
Blylaget *Oslo* **23** B3
Boa Vista, Alto do *Rio de Janeiro* **25** B1
Boardwalk *New York* **22** C3
Boavista *Lisbon* **16** A2
Bobigny *Paris* **24** A3
Bocanegra *Lima* **14** B2
Boedo *Buenos Aires* **7** B2
Bogenhausen *Munich* **21** B2
Bogorodskoye *Moscow* **19** B3
Bogota *New York* **22** A1
Bogstadvatnet *Oslo* **23** A2
Bohnsdorf *Berlin* **5** B4
Bois-Colombes *Paris* **24** A2
Bois-d'Arcy *Paris* **24** B1
Boissy-St-Léger *Paris* **24** B4
Boldinasco *Milan* **18** B1
Bøler *Oslo* **23** A4
Bollate *Milan* **18** A1
Bollebeek *Brussels* **6** A1
Bollensdorf *Berlin* **5** A5
Bollmora *Stockholm* **29** B3
Bolshaya Okhta *St. Petersburg* **27** B2
Bolton *Atlanta* **3** B2
Bom Retiro *São Paulo* **27** B2
Bombay = Mumbai *Mumbai* **20** B2
Bondi *Sydney* **29** B2
Bondy *Paris* **24** A3
Bondy, Forêt de *Paris* **24** A4
Bonifacio Monument *Manila* **17** B1
Bonnabel Place *New Orleans* **21** A2
Bonneuil-sur-Marne *Paris* **24** B4
Bonnington *Edinburgh* **11** B1
Bonnyrigg and Lasswade *Edinburgh* **11** B3
Bonsucesso *Rio de Janeiro* **25** B1
Bonteheuwel *Cape Town* **8** A2
Boo *Stockholm* **29** A3
Borisovo *Moscow* **19** C3
Borle *Mumbai* **20** A2
Boronia Park *Sydney* **29** A1
Bosmont *Johannesburg* **13** B1
Bosön *Stockholm* **29** A3
Bosporus = İstanbul Boğazı *Istanbul* **12** B2
Bostancı *Istanbul* **12** C2
Boston *Boston* **6** A2
Boston Common *Boston* **6** A2
Boston Logan Int. ✈ (BOS) *Boston* **6** A2
Botafogo *Rio de Janeiro* **25** B1
Botany *Sydney* **29** B2
Botany B. *Sydney* **29** B2
Botany Bay △ *Sydney* **29** B2
Botič → *Prague* **25** B3
Botica Sete *Lisbon* **16** A1
Boucherville *Montreal* **20** A3
Boucherville, Îs. de *Montreal* **20** A3
Bougival *Paris* **24** A1
Boulder Pt. *Hong Kong* **12** B2
Boulogne, Bois de *Paris* **24** A2
Boulogne-Billancourt *Paris* **24** A2
Bourg-la-Reine *Paris* **24** B2
Bouviers *Paris* **24** B1
Bovenkerk *Amsterdam* **2** B2
Bovenkerker Polder *Amsterdam* **2** B2
Bovisa *Milan* **18** A2
Bow *London* **15** A3
Boyacıköy *Istanbul* **12** B2
Boyd Conservation Area *Toronto* **31** A1
Boyle Heights *Los Angeles* **16** B3
Braepark *Edinburgh* **11** B2
Braid *Edinburgh* **11** B2
Bramley *Johannesburg* **13** A2
Brandeis Univ. *Boston* **6** A1
Brandenburger Tor *Berlin* **5** A3
Brani, Pulau *Singapore* **28** B3
Branik *Prague* **25** B2
Brännkyrka *Stockholm* **29** B2
Brás *São Paulo* **27** B2
Brasilândia *São Paulo* **27** A1
Brateyevo *Moscow* **19** C3
Braybrook *Melbourne* **18** A1
Brázdim *Prague* **25** A3
Breakheart Reservation *Boston* **6** A2
Brede *Copenhagen* **8** A3
Breezy Point *New York* **22** C2
Breitenlee *Vienna* **32** A3
Breña *Lima* **14** B2
Brent □ *London* **15** A2
Brent Res. *London* **15** A2
Brentford *London* **15** B2
Brentwood *Los Angeles* **16** B2
Brentwood Park *Los Angeles* **16** B2
Brera *Milan* **18** B2
Bresso *Milan* **18** A2
Brevik *Stockholm* **29** A3
Břevnov *Prague* **25** B2
Brickyard, The *Chicago* **9** B2
Bridge City *New Orleans* **21** B2
Bridgeport *Chicago* **9** B3
Bridgetown *Cape Town* **8** A2
Bridgeview *Chicago* **9** C2
Brighton *Boston* **6** A2
Brighton *Melbourne* **18** B1
Brighton Beach *New York* **22** C2
Brighton-Le-Sands *Sydney* **29** B1
Brighton Park *Chicago* **9** C2
Brightwood *Washington* **33** B2
Brigittenau *Vienna* **32** A2
Brimbank Park *Melbourne* **18** A1
Brisbane *San Francisco* **26** B2
Britz *Berlin* **5** B3
Brixton *London* **15** B3
Broadmeadows *Melbourne* **18** A1
Broadmoor *San Francisco* **26** B2
Broadview *Chicago* **9** B1
Broadview Park *Miami* **19** B2
Brockley *London* **15** B3
Bródno *Warsaw* **33** B2
Bródnowski, Kanal *Warsaw* **33** B2
Broek *Amsterdam* **2** A2
Bromley □ *London* **15** B4
Bromley Common *London* **15** B4
Bromma *Stockholm* **29** A1
Bromma ✈ (BMA) *Stockholm* **29** A1
Brøndby Strand *Copenhagen* **8** B2
Brøndbyøster *Copenhagen* **8** B2
Brøndbyvester *Copenhagen* **8** B2
Brondesbury *London* **15** A2
Brønnøya *Oslo* **23** A2
Brønshøj *Copenhagen* **8** A2
Bronxville *New York* **22** A3
Brookfield Zoo *Chicago* **9** B1
Brookhaven *Atlanta* **3** A2
Brookline *Boston* **6** B2
Brooklyn *Cape Town* **8** A1
Brooklyn *New York* **22** C2
Brooklyn Heights *New York* **22** B2
Brookmont *Washington* **33** B2
Brossard *Montreal* **20** B3
Brothers, The *Hong Kong* **12** A1
Brou-sur-Chantereine *Paris* **24** A4
Brown *Toronto* **31** A3
Brownsville *Miami* **19** D1
Brughério *Milan* **18** A2
Brunswick *Melbourne* **18** A1
Brussegem *Brussels* **6** A1
Brussel *Brussels* **6** A2
Brussel ✈ (BRU) *Brussels* **6** A2
Brussels = Brussel *Brussels* **6** A2
Bruxelles = Brussel *Brussels* **6** A2
Bruzzano *Milan* **18** A2
Bry-sur-Marne *Paris* **24** A4
Bryan, L. *Orlando* **23** B2
Bryanston *Johannesburg* **13** A1
Brzeziny *Warsaw* **33** B2
Bubeneč *Prague* **25** B2
Buc *Paris* **24** B1
Buchenhain *Munich* **21** B1
Buchholz *Berlin* **5** A3
Buckhead *Atlanta* **3** A2
Buckingham Palace *London* **15** A3
Buckow *Berlin* **5** B3
Bucktown *New Orleans* **21** A2
Buda *Budapest* **7** A2
Buda Castle = Budaváripalota *Budapest* **7** A2
Budafok *Budapest* **7** B2
Budaörs *Budapest* **7** B1
Budapest *Budapest* **7** B2
Budapest Ferenc Liszt ✈ (BUD) *Budapest* **7** B3
Budatétény *Budapest* **7** B2
Budaváripalota *Budapest* **7** A2
Buddinge *Copenhagen* **8** A3
Buenos Aires *Buenos Aires* **7** B2
Buenos Aires Ezeiza ✈ (EZE) *Buenos Aires* **7** C1
Bufalotta *Rome* **26** B2
Bugio *Lisbon* **16** B1
Buiksloot *Amsterdam* **2** A2
Buitenveldert *Amsterdam* **2** B2
Buizingen *Brussels* **6** B1
Bukhansan *Seoul* **27** B1
Bukit Batok *Singapore* **28** A2
Bukit Panjang *Singapore* **28** A2
Bukit Panjang Nature Reserve ⌓ *Singapore* **28** A2
Bukit Timah Nature Reserve ⌓ *Singapore* **28** A2
Bukum, Pulau *Singapore* **28** B2
Bûlâq *Cairo* **7** A2
Bule *Manila* **17** C2
Bullen Park *Melbourne* **18** A2
Bund, The *Shanghai* **28** B1
Bundoora North *Melbourne* **18** A2
Bundoora Park *Melbourne* **18** A2
Bunker Hill Memorial *Boston* **6** A2
Bunker I. *Karachi* **13** B1
Bunkyō *Tokyo* **30** A3
Bunnefjorden *Oslo* **23** A3
Buona Vista Park *Singapore* **28** B2
Bur Dubai *Dubai* **9** A2
Burbank *Chicago* **9** C2
Burbank *Los Angeles* **16** A3
Burden, L. *Orlando* **23** B1
Burj Al Arab *Dubai* **9** B1
Burj Khalifa *Dubai* **9** B2
Burlington *Boston* **6** A1
Burnham Park *Chicago* **9** C3
Burnham Park Harbor *Chicago* **9** B3
Burnhamthorpe *Toronto* **31** B1
Burnt Oak *London* **15** A2
Burntisland *Edinburgh* **11** A2
Burnwynd *Edinburgh* **11** B1
Burqa *Jerusalem* **13** A2
Burtus *Cairo* **7** A1
Burudvatn *Oslo* **23** A2
Burwood *Sydney* **29** B1
Bushwick *New York* **22** B2
Bushy Park *London* **15** B1
Business Bay *Dubai* **9** B2
Butantã *São Paulo* **27** B1
Butcher I. *Mumbai* **20** B2
Butler, L. *Orlando* **23** B1
Büyükdere *Istanbul* **12** B2
Byculla *Mumbai* **20** B2
Bygdøy *Oslo* **23** A3
Bywater *New Orleans* **21** B2

C

C.B.S. Fox Studios *Los Angeles* **16** B2
C.N. Tower *Toronto* **31** B2
Caballito *Buenos Aires* **7** B2
Cabin John *Washington* **33** B1
Cabin John Regional Park ⌓ *Washington* **33** A1
Cabuçú de Baixo → *São Paulo* **27** A1
Cabuçú de Cima → *São Paulo* **27** A2
Cachan *Paris* **24** B2
Cachoeira, Rib. da → *São Paulo* **27** B1
Cacilhas *Lisbon* **16** A2
Cahuenga Pk. *Los Angeles* **16** B3
Cain, L. *Orlando* **23** B2
Cairo = El Qâhira *Cairo* **7** A2
Cairo Int. ✈ (CAI) *Cairo* **7** A3
Caju *Rio de Janeiro* **25** B1
Čakovice *Prague* **25** B3
Calcutta = Kolkata *Kolkata* **14** B2
California Institute of Technology *Los Angeles* **16** B4
California Los Angeles, Univ. of *Los Angeles* **16** B2
California State Univ. *Los Angeles* **16** B3
Callao *Lima* **14** B2
Caloocan *Manila* **17** B1

Calumet, L. *Chicago* 9 C3
Calumet City *Chicago* 9 D3
Calumet Park *Chicago* 9 C3
Calumet Sag Channel → *Chicago* 9 C2
Calvairate *Milan* 18 B2
Camarate *Lisbon* 16 A2
Camaroes *Lisbon* 16 A1
Camberwell *London* 15 B3
Camberwell *Melbourne* 18 B2
Cambridge *Boston* 6 A2
Cambuci *São Paulo* 27 B2
Camden □ *London* 15 A3
Çamlıca *Istanbul* 12 B2
Camp Nou F.C. Barcelona *Barcelona* 4 A1
Camp Springs *Washington* 33 C3
Campamento *Madrid* 17 B1
Campbellfield *Melbourne* 18 A1
Camperdown *Sydney* 29 B2
Campo, Casa de *Madrid* 17 B1
Campo Grando *Lisbon* 16 A2
Campo Pequeño *Lisbon* 16 A2
Campolide *Lisbon* 16 A2
Camps Bay *Cape Town* 8 A1
C'an San Joan *Barcelona* 4 A2
Cañacao B. *Manila* 17 C1
Canarsie *New York* 22 C2
Canary Wharf *London* 15 A3
Candiac *Montreal* 20 B3
Candler-McAfee *Atlanta* 3 B3
Caneças *Lisbon* 16 A1
Canillas *Madrid* 17 B2
Canillejas *Madrid* 17 B2
Canning Town *London* 15 A4
Canteras de Vallecas *Madrid* 17 B2
Canterbury *Melbourne* 18 A2
Canterbury *Sydney* 29 B1
Canton = Guangzhou *Guangzhou* 11 B2
Canton Tower *Guangzhou* 11 B2
Caoheijing *Shanghai* 28 B1
Capão Redondo *São Paulo* 27 B1
Caparica *Lisbon* 16 A2
Caparica, Costa da *Lisbon* 16 B1
Cape Flats *Cape Town* 8 B2
Cape Town *Cape Town* 8 A1
Cape Town Int. ✕ (CPT) *Cape Town* 8 A2
Capitol Heights *Washington* 33 B3
Captain Cook Bridge *Sydney* 29 C1
Captain Cook Landing Place Park *Sydney* 29 C2
Capuchos *Lisbon* 16 B1
Carabanchel Alto *Madrid* 17 B1
Carabanchel Bajo *Madrid* 17 B1
Carapachay *Buenos Aires* 7 B1
Caraza *Buenos Aires* 7 C2
Caridad *Manila* 17 C1
Carioca, Sa. da *Rio de Janeiro* 25 B1
Carlstadt *New York* 22 A1
Carlton *Melbourne* 18 A1
Carlton Gardens *Melbourne* 18 A1
Carmen de Huechuraba *Santiago* 27 B1
Carmen de la Legua -Reynosa *Lima* 14 B2
Carnaxide *Lisbon* 16 A1
Carnegie *Melbourne* 18 B2
Carnide *Lisbon* 16 A1
Carol City *Miami* 19 C1
Carollton *New Orleans* 21 B2
Carrascal *Santiago* 27 B1
Carrières-sous-Bois *Paris* 24 A1
Carrières-sous-Poissy *Paris* 24 A1
Carrières-sur-Seine *Paris* 24 A2
Cartierville *Montreal* 20 A1
Casa Loma *Toronto* 31 A2
Casa Verde *São Paulo* 27 A1
Casal da Mira *Lisbon* 16 A1
Casal Morena *Rome* 26 C2
Casalotti *Rome* 26 B1
Cascade Heights *Atlanta* 3 B2
Castèl di Leva *Rome* 26 C2
Castèl Sant' Angelo *Rome* 26 B1
Castle Peak B. *Hong Kong* 12 A1
Castle Pk. *Hong Kong* 12 A1
Castleton Corners *New York* 22 C1
Cataouatche, L. *New Orleans* 21 B1
Catete *Rio de Janeiro* 25 B1
Catford *London* 15 B3
Catherine, L. *Orlando* 23 B2
Caulfield *Melbourne* 18 B2
Cavite *Manila* 17 C1
Caxias *Lisbon* 16 A1
Cebecci *Istanbul* 12 B1
Cecchignola *Rome* 26 C2
Cecilienhof, Schloss *Berlin* 5 B1
Cedar Grove *Atlanta* 3 C3
Cedar Hill *Dallas-Fort Worth* 10 C4
Cedar Hill State Park ⌂ *Dallas-Fort Worth* 10 C4
Cedarvale Park *Toronto* 31 A2
Cempaka Putih *Jakarta* 12 B2
Çengelköy *Istanbul* 12 B2
Cengkareng *Jakarta* 12 A1
Centennial Olympic Park *Atlanta* 3 B2
Centennial Park *Sydney* 29 B2
Center Hill *Atlanta* 3 B2
Centocelle *Rome* 26 B2
Central, Gare *Montreal* 20 B2
Central Park *New York* 22 B2
Century City *Los Angeles* 16 B2
Cerdanyola del Vallès *Barcelona* 4 A1
Cerillos *Santiago* 27 B1
Cerro de la Estrella △ *Mexico City* 18 B2
Cerro de los Angeles *Madrid* 17 C1
Cerro Navia *Santiago* 27 B1
Cesano Boscone *Milan* 18 B1
Cesate *Milan* 18 A1
Cha Kwo Ling *Hong Kong* 12 B3
Chacarita *Buenos Aires* 7 B2
Chadwell Heath *London* 15 A4
Chai Chee *Singapore* 28 B3
Chai Wan *Hong Kong* 12 B3
Chai Wan Kok *Hong Kong* 12 A2
Chaidari *Athens* 2 A1
Chakdaha *Kolkata* 14 C1
Chalandri *Athens* 2 A2
Chamartin *Madrid* 17 B1
Chamberi *Madrid* 17 B1
Chambourcy *Paris* 24 A1
Champigny-sur-Marne *Paris* 24 B4
Champlain, Pont *Montreal* 20 B2
Champs-sur-Marne *Paris* 24 A4
Chamrail *Kolkata* 14 B1
Chanakyapuri *Delhi* 10 B2
Chanditala *Kolkata* 14 A1
Changfeng Park *Shanghai* 28 B1
Changhai = Shanghai *Shanghai* 28 B2
Changi *Singapore* 28 A3
Changi, Singapore ✕ (SIN) *Singapore* 28 A3
Changning *Shanghai* 28 B1
Chantereine *Paris* 24 A4
Chantian *Guangzhou* 11 A2
Chaoyang *Beijing* 4 B2
Chaoyangmen *Beijing* 4 B2
Chapultepec, Bosque de *Mexico City* 18 B1
Chapultepec, Castillo de *Mexico City* 18 B1
Charenton-le-Pont *Paris* 24 B3
Charleroi, Kanal de → *Brussels* 6 B1
Charles Bridge = Karlův most *Prague* 25 B2
Charles Gates Dawes House *Chicago* 9 A2
Charlestown *Boston* 6 A2
Charlottenburg *Berlin* 5 A2
Charlottenburg, Schloss *Berlin* 5 A2
Charlottenlund *Copenhagen* 8 A3
Charlton *London* 15 B4
Charneca *Lisbon* 16 A2
Charneca *Lisbon* 16 B1
Chase, L. *Orlando* 23 B1
Châteaufort *Paris* 24 B1
Châtenay-Malabry *Paris* 24 B2
Chatham *Chicago* 9 C3
Châtillon *Paris* 24 B2
Chatou *Paris* 24 A1
Chatpur *Kolkata* 14 B2
Chatswood *Sydney* 29 A2
Chatuchak *Bangkok* 3 B2
Chatuchak Park *Bangkok* 3 B2
Chauki *Karachi* 13 A1
Chavarria *Lima* 14 B2
Chaville *Paris* 24 B2
Chayang *Seoul* 27 B2
Chek Lap Kok *Hong Kong* 12 B1
Chek Lap Kok ✕ (HKG) *Hong Kong* 12 B1
Chelles *Paris* 24 A4
Chelles, Canal de *Paris* 24 A4
Chelles-le-Pin ✕ *Paris* 24 A4
Chelsea *Boston* 6 A2
Chelsea *London* 15 B2
Chembur *Mumbai* 20 A2
Chengshousi *Beijing* 4 C2
Chennevières-sur-Marne *Paris* 24 B4
Cheongdam *Seoul* 27 B2
Cheonho *Seoul* 27 B2
Cheops *Cairo* 7 B1
Chertanovka → *Moscow* 19 C2
Chertanovo *Moscow* 19 C2
Cheryomushki *Moscow* 19 B2
Chestnut Hill *Boston* 6 B1
Cheung Chau *Hong Kong* 12 B2
Cheung Sha *Hong Kong* 12 B1
Cheung Sha Wan *Hong Kong* 12 B1
Cheung Shue Tan *Hong Kong* 12 A3
Cheverly *Washington* 33 B3
Chevilly-Larue *Paris* 24 B3
Cheviot Hills *Los Angeles* 16 B2
Chevy Chase *Washington* 33 B2
Chhatrapati Shivaji Int., Mumbai ✕ (BOM) *Mumbai* 20 A2
Chhatrapati Shivaji Terminus *Mumbai* 20 B2
Chi Ma Wan Pen. *Hong Kong* 12 B1
Chia Keng *Singapore* 28 A3
Chiaravalle Milanese *Milan* 18 B2
Chicago *Chicago* 9 B3
Chicago, Univ. of *Chicago* 9 C3
Chicago Harbor *Chicago* 9 B3
Chicago Lawn *Chicago* 9 C2
Chicago Ridge *Chicago* 9 C2
Chicago River, North Branch → *Chicago* 9 B2
Chicago Sanitary and Ship Canal *Chicago* 9 C2
Chicago State Univ. *Chicago* 9 C3
Chienzui *Guangzhou* 11 A3
Chik Sha *Hong Kong* 12 B3
Child's Hill *London* 15 A2
Chile, Univ. de *Santiago* 27 B2
Chilla Saroda *Delhi* 10 B2
Chillum *Washington* 33 B3
Chilly-Mazarin *Paris* 24 B2
Chinese Theatre *Los Angeles* 16 B2
Chingupota *Kolkata* 14 C1
Chinna Cr. → *Karachi* 13 B2
Chiquihuite, Cerro *Mexico City* 18 A2
Chislehurst *London* 15 B4
Chiswick *London* 15 B2
Chiswick House *London* 15 B2
Chitose *Tokyo* 30 B2
Chitralada Palace *Bangkok* 3 B2
Chiyoda *Tokyo* 30 A3
Choa Chu Kang *Singapore* 28 A2
Chodov u Prahy *Prague* 25 B3
Chōfu *Tokyo* 30 B2
Choisy-le-Roi *Paris* 24 B3
Cholargos *Athens* 2 B2
Cholupice *Prague* 25 C2
Chom Thong *Bangkok* 3 B1
Chong Pang *Singapore* 28 A2
Chongwen *Beijing* 4 B2
Chorrillos *Lima* 14 C2
Chowpatty Beach *Mumbai* 20 B1
Christianshavn *Copenhagen* 8 A3
Chrzanów *Warsaw* 33 B1
Chuen Lung *Hong Kong* 12 A2
Chuk Kok *Hong Kong* 12 A3
Chulalongkorn Univ. *Bangkok* 3 B2
Chung Hau *Hong Kong* 12 B2
Chuō *Tokyo* 30 A3
Church End *London* 15 A2
Church of our Lady = Frauenkirche *Munich* 21 B2
Ciampino *Rome* 26 C2
Ciampino ✕ (CIA) *Rome* 26 C2
Cicero *Chicago* 9 B2
Cilandak *Jakarta* 12 B1
Cilincing *Jakarta* 12 A2
Ciliwung → *Jakarta* 12 B2
Čimice *Prague* 25 B2
Cinecittà *Rome* 26 B2
Cinisello Bálsamo *Milan* 18 A2
Cinkota *Budapest* 7 A3
Cipete *Jakarta* 12 B1
Città degli Studi *Milan* 18 B2
Città del Vaticano = Vatican City ■ *Rome* 26 B1
City, The *London* 15 A3
City Hall = Rådhus *Oslo* 23 A3
City Hall = Stadshuset *Stockholm* 29 B2
City of the Dead *Cairo* 7 A2
City Park *New Orleans* 21 A2
City Terrace *Los Angeles* 16 B3
Ciudad de México *Mexico City* 18 B2
Ciudad Deportiva *Mexico City* 18 B2
Ciudad Fin de Semana *Madrid* 17 B2
Ciudad General Belgrano *Buenos Aires* 7 C1
Ciudad Lineál *Madrid* 17 B2
Ciudad Satélite *Mexico City* 18 A1
Ciudad Universitaria *Buenos Aires* 7 B2
Ciudad Universitaria *Mexico City* 18 C1
Claireville Res. *Toronto* 31 A1
Clamart *Paris* 24 B2
Clapham *London* 15 B3
Clapton *London* 15 A3
Claremont *Cape Town* 8 A1
Clayhall *London* 15 A4
Clear, L. *Orlando* 23 A2
Clear Water B. *Hong Kong* 12 B3
Clermiston *Edinburgh* 11 B2
Clichy *Paris* 24 A2
Clichy-sous-Bois *Paris* 24 A4
Cliffside *Toronto* 31 A3
Cliffside Park *New York* 22 B2
Clifton *Cape Town* 8 A1
Clifton *Karachi* 13 B2
Clifton *New York* 22 C1
Clifton Beach *Karachi* 13 B2
Cliftondale *Boston* 6 A2
Clontarf *Sydney* 29 A2
Clovelly *Sydney* 29 B2
CNN Center *Atlanta* 3 B2
Cobras, I. das *Rio de Janeiro* 25 B2
Coburg *Melbourne* 18 A1
Cockrell Hill *Dallas-Fort Worth* 10 B4
Coconut Grove *Miami* 19 D2
Cocotá *Rio de Janeiro* 25 A1
Cœuilly *Paris* 24 B4
Coina *Lisbon* 16 B2
Coker *Lagos* 14 B2
Colaba *Mumbai* 20 B1
Colaba Pt. *Mumbai* 20 B1
Colegiales *Buenos Aires* 7 B2
Colindale *London* 15 A2
Colinton *Edinburgh* 11 B2
College Park *Atlanta* 3 C2
College Park *Washington* 33 B3
College Point *New York* 22 B2
Collégien *Paris* 24 A4
Colleyville *Dallas-Fort Worth* 10 A3
Collier Row *London* 15 A4
Colliers Wood *London* 15 B2
Colma *San Francisco* 26 B2
Colney Hatch *London* 15 A3
Cologno Monzese *Milan* 18 A2
Colombes *Paris* 24 A2
Colonia Güell *Barcelona* 4 A1
Colosseo *Rome* 26 B1
Colosseum = Colosseo *Rome* 26 B1
Combault *Paris* 24 B4
Comércio, Praça do *Lisbon* 16 A2
Commerce *Los Angeles* 16 B4
Conceição, I. da *Rio de Janeiro* 25 B2
Conchali *Santiago* 27 B2
Concord *Sydney* 29 B1
Concord *Toronto* 31 A2
Concorde, Place de la *Paris* 24 A2
Concorezzo *Milan* 18 A2
Condet *Jakarta* 12 A2
Coney I. = Serangoon, Pulau *Singapore* 28 A3
Coney Island *New York* 22 C2
Congonhas, São Paulo ✕ (CGH) *São Paulo* 27 B2
Conley → *Atlanta* 3 C3
Connaught Place *Delhi* 10 B2
Consolação *São Paulo* 27 B2
Constantia *Cape Town* 8 B1
Constitución *Buenos Aires* 7 B2
Constitution *Atlanta* 3 B2
Conway *Orlando* 23 B2
Conway, L. *Orlando* 23 B2
Coogee *Sydney* 29 B2
Cooksville *Toronto* 31 B1
Cooper City *Miami* 19 B1
Copacabana *Rio de Janeiro* 25 B1
Copenhagen = København *Copenhagen* 8 A2
Coppell *Dallas-Fort Worth* 10 A4
Coral Gables *Miami* 19 D1
Coral Hills *Washington* 33 B3
Corcovado, Cristo Redentor *Rio de Janeiro* 25 B1
Cormano *Milan* 18 A2
Cornaredo *Milan* 18 A1
Córsico *Milan* 18 B1
Corstorphine *Edinburgh* 11 B2
Corviale *Rome* 26 B1
Coslada *Madrid* 17 B2
Cosmonautics Museum *Moscow* 19 B2
Cossigny *Paris* 24 B4
Cotao *Lisbon* 16 A1
Côte-St-Luc *Montreal* 20 B2
Cotunduba, I. de *Rio de Janeiro* 25 B2
Coubron *Paris* 24 A4
Courbevoie *Paris* 24 A2
Courtry *Paris* 24 A4
Cowley *London* 15 A1
Coyoacán *Mexico City* 18 B2
Craighall Park *Johannesburg* 13 A2
Craiglockhart *Edinburgh* 11 B2
Craigmillar *Edinburgh* 11 B3
Cramond *Edinburgh* 11 B2
Cramond Bridge *Edinburgh* 11 B1
Cramond I. *Edinburgh* 11 B2
Crandon Park *Miami* 19 D3
Cranford *London* 15 B1
Crawford *Cape Town* 8 A2
Crayford *London* 15 B5
Creekmouth *London* 15 A4
Crescent, L. *Orlando* 23 A1
Crescenzago *Milan* 18 A2
Cressely *Paris* 24 B1
Cresskill *New York* 22 A2
Crestwood *Chicago* 9 D2
Créteil *Paris* 24 B3
Cricklewood *London* 15 A2
Cristo Redentor, Corcovado *Rio de Janeiro* 25 B1
Crockenhill *London* 15 B4
Croissy-Beaubourg *Paris* 24 B4
Croissy-sur-Seine *Paris* 24 A1
Crosby *Johannesburg* 13 B1
Crosne *Paris* 24 B3
Cross I. *Mumbai* 20 B2
Crouch End *London* 15 A3
Crowley *Dallas-Fort Worth* 10 C1
Crown Mine *Johannesburg* 13 B1
Crows Nest *Sydney* 29 A2
Croydon *London* 15 B3
Croydon Park *Sydney* 29 B1
Cruz de Pau *Lisbon* 16 B2
Crystal Palace *London* 15 B3
Csepel *Budapest* 7 B2
Csepelsziget *Budapest* 7 B2
Csillaghegy *Budapest* 7 A2
Csillagtelep *Budapest* 7 B2
Csömör *Budapest* 7 A3
Csömöri-patak → *Budapest* 7 A3
Cuatro Vientos *Madrid* 17 B1
Cuauhtémoc *Mexico City* 18 B2
Cuban Museum *Miami* 19 D1
Cubao *Manila* 17 B2
Çubuklu *Istanbul* 12 B2
Cudahy *Los Angeles* 16 C3
Cuicuilco, Pirámide de *Mexico City* 18 C1
Culmore *Washington* 33 B2
Culver City *Los Angeles* 16 B2
Cupecé → *São Paulo* 27 B1
Currie *Edinburgh* 11 B2
Cusago *Milan* 18 B1
Cusano Milanino *Milan* 18 A2
Cutler Park *Boston* 6 B1
Çuvuşabaşi → *Istanbul* 12 B1
Cuwei *Beijing* 4 B1
Cypress Hills *New York* 22 B2
Cypress Park *Los Angeles* 16 B3
Czerniaków *Warsaw* 33 B2
Czyste *Warsaw* 33 B1

D

D.H.A. Phase VIII *Karachi* 13 B2
Da Moóca → *São Paulo* 27 B2
Ďáblice *Prague* 25 B2
Dąbrowa *Warsaw* 33 B1
Dachang *Shanghai* 28 B1
Dachang ✕ *Shanghai* 28 B1
Dachau *Munich* 21 A1
Dachau-Ost *Munich* 21 A1
Dachauer Moos *Munich* 21 A1
Dadar *Mumbai* 20 A1
Daebang *Seoul* 27 B1
Daechi *Seoul* 27 B2
Dafni *Athens* 2 B2
Dagenham *London* 15 A4
Daglfing *Munich* 21 B2
D'Aguilar Pen. *Hong Kong* 12 B2
Dahab, Gezîret el *Cairo* 7 B2
Daheisha *Jerusalem* 13 B2
Dahlem *Berlin* 5 B2
Dahlwitz-Hoppegarten *Berlin* 5 A5
Dahongmen *Beijing* 4 C2
Daiba = Odaiba *Tokyo* 30 B3
Dajiaoting *Beijing* 4 B2
Dakhnoye *St. Petersburg* 27 C1
Dalejsky potok → *Prague* 25 B2
Dalgety Bay *Edinburgh* 11 A1
Dalkeith *Edinburgh* 11 B3
Dallas *Dallas-Fort Worth* 10 B4
Dallas-Fort Worth Int. ✕ (DFW) *Dallas-Fort Worth* 10 A3
Dallas-Fort Worth Meacham Int. ✕ (FTW) *Dallas-Fort Worth* 10 B1
Dallgow *Berlin* 5 A1
Dalmeny *Edinburgh* 11 B1
Dalston *London* 15 A3
Dalworthington Gardens *Dallas-Fort Worth* 10 B3
Daly City *San Francisco* 26 B2
Damaia *Lisbon* 16 A1
Damarakia *Athens* 2 B1
Dämeritzsee *Berlin* 5 B5
Dan Ryan Woods *Chicago* 9 C2
Danderhall *Edinburgh* 11 B3
Danderyd *Stockholm* 29 A2
Danforth *Toronto* 31 A3
Dania Beach *Miami* 19 B3
Darakeh *Tehran* 31 A2
Darband *Tehran* 31 A2
Darling Point *Sydney* 29 B2
Darrūs *Tehran* 31 A2
Dartford *London* 15 B5
Dashi *Guangzhou* 11 B2
Datansha *Guangzhou* 11 B2
Datun *Beijing* 4 B2
Daulatpur *Delhi* 10 A1
Davidson, Mt. *San Francisco* 26 B2
Davidson's Mains *Edinburgh* 11 B2
Davie *Miami* 19 B2
Dāvūdīyeh *Tehran* 31 A2
Davydkovo *Moscow* 19 B1
Dawidy *Warsaw* 33 C1
Daxing *Beijing* 4 C2
De Soto *Dallas-Fort Worth* 10 C5
Decatur *Atlanta* 3 B3
Dedham *Boston* 6 B1
Deep Water B. *Hong Kong* 12 B3
Degunino *Moscow* 19 A2
Deir Dibwan *Jerusalem* 13 A2
Deir Ibzi'e *Jerusalem* 13 A1
Deira *Dubai* 9 A2
Deira Is. *Dubai* 9 A2
Dejvice *Prague* 25 B2
Dekabristov, Ostrov *St. Petersburg* 27 B1
Del Rey *Los Angeles* 16 C2
Delhi *Delhi* 10 B2
Delhi Indira Gandhi Int. ✕ (DEL) *Delhi* 10 B1
Demarest *New York* 22 A2
Den Ilp *Amsterdam* 2 A2
Denistone Heights *Sydney* 29 A1
Dentonia Park *Toronto* 31 A3
DePaul Univ. *Chicago* 9 B3
Deptford *London* 15 B3
Desert Wetlands Park *Las Vegas* 14 B2
Deutsche Oper *Berlin* 5 A2
Deutsches Museum *Munich* 21 B2
Devil's Peak *Cape Town* 8 A1
Dhakuria *Kolkata* 14 B2
Dharavi *Mumbai* 20 A2
Dia Deva = Butcher I. *Mumbai* 20 B2
Diadema *São Paulo* 27 C2
Diegen *Brussels* 6 A2
Diemen *Amsterdam* 2 A2
Diepkloof *Johannesburg* 13 B1
Dieprivier *Cape Town* 8 B1
Dilbeek *Brussels* 6 A1
Dilli = Delhi *Delhi* 10 B2
Dirnismaning *Munich* 21 A2
Discovery B. *Hong Kong* 12 B2
Disney-M.G.M. Studios *Orlando* 23 B1
Disney Studios *Los Angeles* 16 B3
Disneyland Hong Kong *Hong Kong* 12 B2
Disneyland Tōkyō *Tokyo* 30 B4
Dixmoor *Chicago* 9 D2
Djakarta = Jakarta *Jakarta* 12 A2
Djursholm *Stockholm* 29 A2
Döberitz *Berlin* 5 A1
Döbling *Vienna* 32 A2
Dobong *Seoul* 27 B2
Dobongsan *Seoul* 27 A2
Docklands *London* 15 A3
Doctor Phillips *Orlando* 23 B2
Dodger Stadium *Los Angeles* 16 B3
Dogs, Isle of *London* 15 B3
Dolgoe Ozero *St. Petersburg* 27 A1
Dollis Hill *London* 15 A2
Dolni *Prague* 25 B3
Dolni Chabry *Prague* 25 B2
Dolni Počernice *Prague* 25 B3
Dolton *Chicago* 9 D3
Dom Pedro II, Parque *São Paulo* 27 B2
Don Mills *Toronto* 31 A2
Don Muang Int. ✕ (BKK) *Bangkok* 3 A2
Donau-Oder Kanal *Vienna* 32 A3
Donaufeld *Vienna* 32 A2
Donaupark *Vienna* 32 A2
Donaustadt *Vienna* 32 A2
Dongan Hills *New York* 22 C1
Dongcheng *Beijing* 4 B2
Dongdaemung *Seoul* 27 B2
Donggou *Shanghai* 28 B2
Dongjak *Seoul* 27 B1
Dongshanhu Park *Guangzhou* 11 B2
Dongri *Mumbai* 20 B2
Dongzhimen *Beijing* 4 B2
Doornfontein *Johannesburg* 13 B2
Dora *Baghdad* 3 A2
Dorchester *Boston* 6 B2
Dorchester B. *Boston* 6 B2
Dorchester Heights Nat. Historical Site ⌂ *Boston* 6 B2
Dornach *Munich* 21 B3
Dorval Int., Montréal ✕ (YUL) *Montreal* 20 B1
Dos Moninos → *São Paulo* 27 B2
Douglas Park *Chicago* 9 B2
Dover Heights *Sydney* 29 B2
Dowlatābād *Tehran* 31 B2
Down, L. *Orlando* 23 A1
Downey *Los Angeles* 16 C4
Downsview *Toronto* 31 A2
Downsview Park *Toronto* 31 A2
Dragør *Copenhagen* 8 B3
Drancy *Paris* 24 A3
Drapetsona *Athens* 2 B1
Dreilinden *Berlin* 5 B2
Drewnica *Warsaw* 33 B2
Drigh Road *Karachi* 13 A2
Drogenbos *Brussels* 6 B1
Drottningholm *Stockholm* 29 B1
Druid Hills *Atlanta* 3 B2
Drummoyne *Sydney* 29 B1
Drylaw *Edinburgh* 11 B2
Dubai = Dubayy *Dubai* 9 A2
Dubai Creek *Dubai* 9 A2
Dubai Int. ✕ (DXB) *Dubai* 9 A2
Dubai Int. Financial Centre *Dubai* 9 B2
Dubai Internet City *Dubai* 9 B1
Dubai Marina *Dubai* 9 B1
Dubai Maritime City *Dubai* 9 A2
Dubayy *Dubai* 9 A2
Dubeč *Prague* 25 B3
Duddingston *Edinburgh* 11 B3
Dugnano *Milan* 18 A2
Duivendrecht *Amsterdam* 2 B2
Dūlāb *Tehran* 31 B2
Dulwich *London* 15 B3
Dum Dum *Kolkata* 14 B2
Dumont *New York* 22 A2
Duncanville *Dallas-Fort Worth* 10 C4
Dunearn *Singapore* 28 B2
Dunning *Chicago* 9 B2
Dunvegan *Johannesburg* 13 A2
Duomo *Milan* 18 B2
Duque de Caxias *Rio de Janeiro* 25 A1
Duren Sawit *Jakarta* 12 B2
Dusit *Bangkok* 3 B2
Dworp *Brussels* 6 B1
Dyakovo *Moscow* 19 B2
Dyker Beach Park *New York* 22 C1
Dzerzhinskiy *Moscow* 19 B2
Dzerzhinskiy Park *Moscow* 19 B2

E

E.U.R. = Esposizione Universale di Roma *Rome* 26 C1
Eagle Rock *Los Angeles* 16 B3
Ealing □ *London* 15 A2
Earlsfield *London* 15 B2
Earlwood *Sydney* 29 B1
East Arlington *Boston* 6 A2
East Arlington *Washington* 33 B2
East Bedfont *London* 15 B1
East Boston *Boston* 6 A2
East Don → *Toronto* 31 A2
East Don Parkland *Toronto* 31 A2
East Elmhurst *New York* 22 B2
East Falls Church *Washington* 33 B2
East Finchley *London* 15 A2
East Flatbush *New York* 22 C2
East Ham *London* 15 A4
East Humber → *Toronto* 31 A1
East Lamma Channel *Hong Kong* 12 B2
East Las Vegas = Whitney *Las Vegas* 14 B2
East Lexington *Boston* 6 A1
East Los Angeles *Los Angeles* 16 B3
East Molesey *London* 15 B1
East New York *New York* 22 B2
East Pines *Washington* 33 B3
East Point *Atlanta* 3 B2
East Potomac Park *Washington* 33 B2
East River → *New York* 22 B2
East Rutherford *New York* 22 A1
East Sheen *London* 15 B2
East Talpiyot *Jerusalem* 13 B2
East Wickham *London* 15 B4
East York *Toronto* 31 A2
Eastcote *London* 15 A1
Easter Howgate *Edinburgh* 11 B2
Eastpoint Park *Toronto* 31 A4
Eastwood *Sydney* 29 A1
Eaton Canyon Park *Los Angeles* 16 A4
Ebara *Tokyo* 30 B3
Ebisu *Tokyo* 30 B3
Ebute-Metta *Lagos* 14 B2
Eda *Tokyo* 30 B2
Eden Gardens *Kolkata* 14 B2
Edendale *Johannesburg* 13 A2
Edgars Cr. → *Melbourne* 18 A1
Edgecliff *Dallas-Fort Worth* 10 C1
Edgeley *Toronto* 31 A1
Edgemar *San Francisco* 26 C2
Edgewater *New York* 22 B2
Edgewood *Orlando* 23 B2
Edinburgh *Edinburgh* 11 B2
Edinburgh ✕ (EDI) *Edinburgh* 11 B1
Edinburgh Castle *Edinburgh* 11 B2
Edison Park *Chicago* 9 A2
Edmondston *Washington* 33 B3
Edo → *Tokyo* 30 B4
Edogawa *Tokyo* 30 A4
Edsberg *Stockholm* 29 A1
Edwards L. *Melbourne* 18 A1
Efzonos *Athens* 2 B2
Egaleo *Athens* 2 B1
Egaleo, Oros *Athens* 2 B1
Eiche *Berlin* 5 A4
Eiche Süd *Berlin* 5 A4
Eiffel, Tour *Paris* 24 A2
Ein Arik *Jerusalem* 13 A1
Ein Naquba *Jerusalem* 13 B1
Ein Rafa *Jerusalem* 13 B1
Eizariya *Jerusalem* 13 B2
Ejby *Copenhagen* 8 A2
Ejigbo *Lagos* 14 A1
Ekeberg *Oslo* 23 A3
Eknäs *Stockholm* 29 B3
El 'Abbasiya *Cairo* 7 A2
El Agustino *Lima* 14 B2
El Agustino, Cerro *Lima* 14 B3
El Baragil *Cairo* 7 A1
El Basâtîn *Cairo* 7 B2
El Bira *Jerusalem* 13 A2
El Bosque *Santiago* 27 C2
El Carmen *Santiago* 27 B1
El Cortijo *Santiago* 27 B1
El Cristo, Vaso Regulador *Mexico City* 18 B1
El Duqqi *Cairo* 7 A2
El Encinar de los Reyes *Madrid* 17 A2
El Gezira *Cairo* 7 A2
El Ghurîya *Cairo* 7 A2
El Giza *Cairo* 7 B2
El Khadr *Jerusalem* 13 B1
El Khalîfa *Cairo* 7 A2
El Kôm el Ahmar *Cairo* 7 A2
El Ma'âdi *Cairo* 7 B2
El Matarîya *Cairo* 7 A2
El Mohandessin *Cairo* 7 A2
El Monte *Los Angeles* 16 B4
El Muqattam *Cairo* 7 A2
El Mûskî *Cairo* 7 A2
El Pardo *Madrid* 17 A1
El Pobleneu *Barcelona* 4 A2
El Portal *Miami* 19 C2
El Prat Barcelona ✕ (BCN) *Barcelona* 4 B1
El Prat de Llobregat *Barcelona* 4 B1
El Qâhira *Cairo* 7 A2
El Qubba *Cairo* 7 A2
El Reloj *Mexico City* 18 C2
El Retiro *Madrid* 17 B1
El Salto *Santiago* 27 B2
El Sereno *Los Angeles* 16 B3
El Talibîya *Cairo* 7 B2
El Vergel *Mexico City* 18 C2
El Wâhli *Cairo* 7 A2
El Zamâlik *Cairo* 7 A2
El Zeitûn *Cairo* 7 A2
Eleftherios Venizelos ✕ (ATH) *Athens* 2 A3
Elephanta Caves *Mumbai* 20 B2
Elephanta I. *Mumbai* 20 B2
Ellboda *Stockholm* 29 A3
Ellenor, L. *Orlando* 23 B2
Elliniko Olympic Complex *Athens* 2 B2
Ellis I. *New York* 22 B1
Elmers End *London* 15 B3
Elmhurst *New York* 22 B2
Elmstead *London* 15 B4
Elmwood *New Orleans* 21 B1
Elmwood Park *Chicago* 9 B2
Elmwood Park *New York* 22 A1
Elsiesrivier *Cape Town* 8 A2
Elsternwick *Melbourne* 18 B2
Eltham *London* 15 B4
Elwood *Melbourne* 18 B1
Élysée *Paris* 24 A2
Elysian Park *Los Angeles* 16 B3
Emāmzādeh Sāleh *Tehran* 31 A2
Émerainville *Paris* 24 B4
Emeryville *San Francisco* 26 A3
Eminönü *Istanbul* 12 B1
Emirates, Mall of the *Dubai* 9 B1
Emirgan *Istanbul* 12 B2
Emmarentia *Johannesburg* 13 A2
Empire State Building *New York* 22 B2
Encantado *Rio de Janeiro* 25 B1
Encino *Los Angeles* 16 B2
Encino Res. *Los Angeles* 16 B1
Enebyberg *Stockholm* 29 A1
Enfield *Sydney* 29 B1
Engenho, I. do *Rio de Janeiro* 25 B2
Englewood *Chicago* 9 C3
Englewood *New York* 22 A2
Englewood Cliffs *New York* 22 A2
Enmore *Sydney* 29 B2
Enskede *Stockholm* 29 B2
Enterprise *Las Vegas* 14 B1
Entrevias *Madrid* 17 B1
Epcot *Orlando* 23 B1
Epping *Sydney* 29 A1
Erenköy *Istanbul* 12 C2
Erith *London* 15 B5
Erlaa *Vienna* 32 B1
Ermington *Sydney* 29 A1
Ermita *Manila* 17 B1
Ershatou *Guangzhou* 11 B2
Erskineville *Sydney* 29 B2
Erunkan *Lagos* 14 A2
Erzsébet-Telep *Budapest* 7 B3
Eschenried *Munich* 21 A1
Esenler *Istanbul* 12 B1
Esher *London* 15 B1
Eskbank *Edinburgh* 11 B3
Esplanade *Shanghai* 28 C3
Esplugas *Barcelona* 4 A1
Esposizione Universale di Roma *Rome* 26 C1
Essendon *Melbourne* 18 A1
Essendon ✕ (MEB) *Melbourne* 18 A1
Essingen *Stockholm* 29 B1
Essling *Vienna* 32 A3
Est, Gare de l' *Paris* 24 A3
Estado, Parque do *São Paulo* 27 B2
Estelle *New Orleans* 21 B2
Estrela, Basílica da *Lisbon* 16 A2
Etobicoke *Toronto* 31 B1
Etobicoke Cr. → *Toronto* 31 B1
Etterbeek *Brussels* 6 B2
Euless *Dallas-Fort Worth* 10 A3
Eung-am *Seoul* 27 B1
Eunpyeong *Seoul* 27 B1
Evanston *Chicago* 9 A2
Even Sapir *Jerusalem* 13 B1
Evere *Brussels* 6 A2
Everett *Boston* 6 A2
Evergreen Park *Chicago* 9 C2
Everman *Dallas-Fort Worth* 10 C2
Evīn *Tehran* 31 A2
Ewu *Lagos* 14 A1
Exhibition Place *Toronto* 31 B2
Experimentarium *Copenhagen* 8 A3
Expo Centre *Shanghai* 28 B1
Exposições, Palácio das *Rio de Janeiro* 25 B1
Eyüp *Istanbul* 12 B1
Ezeiza ✕ (EZE) *Buenos Aires* 7 C1

F

Faber, Mt. *Singapore* 28 B2
Fælledparken *Copenhagen* 8 A3
Fågelön *Stockholm* 29 B1
Fagersjö *Stockholm* 29 B2
Fairland *Johannesburg* 13 A1
Fairmilehead *Edinburgh* 11 B2
Fairport *Toronto* 31 A4
Fairview *New York* 22 B2
Fairview, L. *Orlando* 23 A2
Falenty *Warsaw* 33 C1
Faliro *Athens* 2 B1
Faliro, Ormos *Athens* 2 B2
Falkenburg *Berlin* 5 A4
Falkenhagen *Berlin* 5 A1
Falkensee *Berlin* 5 A1
Falomo *Lagos* 14 B2
False Bay *Cape Town* 8 B2
Famões *Lisbon* 16 A1
Fan Lau *Hong Kong* 12 B1
Fangcun *Guangzhou* 11 B2
Farahābād *Tehran* 31 A2
Farforovskaya *St. Petersburg* 27 B2
Farmers Branch *Dallas-Fort Worth* 10 A4
Farningham *London* 15 B5
Farsta *Stockholm* 29 B2
Fasanerie-Nord *Munich* 21 A2
Fasangarten *Munich* 21 B2
Fatih *Istanbul* 12 B1
Favoriten *Vienna* 32 B2
Fawkner *Melbourne* 18 A1
Fawkner Park *Melbourne* 18 B1
Feldkirchen *Munich* 21 B3
Feldmoching *Munich* 21 A2
Feltham *London* 15 B1
Fener *Istanbul* 12 B1
Fenerbahçe *Istanbul* 12 C2
Fengtai *Beijing* 4 C1
Fengtai Stadium *Beijing* 4 B1
Ferenc Liszt, Budapest ✕ (BUD) *Budapest* 7 B3
Ferencváros *Budapest* 7 B2
Ferndale *Johannesburg* 13 A2
Fichtenau *Berlin* 5 B5
Field Museum of Natural History *Chicago* 9 B3
Fields Corner *Boston* 6 B2
Fiera Camp *Milan* 18 B1
Figino *Milan* 18 B1
Fijir *Baghdad* 3 A2
Filadelfia *Athens* 2 A2
Fili-Mazilovo *Moscow* 19 B1
Filothei *Athens* 2 A2
Finchley *London* 15 A2
Fine Arts, Museum of *Boston* 6 A2
Finsbury *London* 15 A3
Finsbury Park *London* 15 A3
Fiorito *Buenos Aires* 7 C2
Fischerhäuser *Munich* 21 A3
Fisher I. *Miami* 19 D3
Fishermans Bend *Melbourne* 18 A1
Fisherman's Village *Los Angeles* 16 C2
Fisherville *Toronto* 31 A2
Fisksätra *Stockholm* 29 B3
Fitzroy Gardens *Melbourne* 18 A1
Five Cowrie Cr. → *Lagos* 14 B2
Five Dock *Sydney* 29 B1
Fjellstrand *Oslo* 23 B2
Flamengo *Rio de Janeiro* 25 B1
Flamingo *Orlando* 23 B2
Flaminio *Rome* 26 B1
Flaskebekk *Oslo* 23 A2
Flatbush *New York* 22 C2
Flaten *Stockholm* 29 B2
Flatlands *New York* 22 C2
Flemington Racecourse *Melbourne* 18 A1
Flint Pk. *Los Angeles* 16 B3
Florence *Los Angeles* 16 C3
Florence Bloom Bird Sanctuary ⌂ *Johannesburg* 13 A2
Florentia *Johannesburg* 13 B2
Flores *Buenos Aires* 7 B2
Flores, Mercado de *Mexico City* 18 C2
Floresta *Buenos Aires* 7 B2
Florida *Buenos Aires* 7 B2
Florida *Johannesburg* 13 B1
Floridsdorf *Vienna* 32 A2
Flushing *New York* 22 B3
Flushing Meadows Corona Park *New York* 22 B2
Flysta *Stockholm* 29 A1
Fo Tan *Hong Kong* 12 A3
Foggy Bottom *Washington* 33 B2
Föhrenhain *Vienna* 32 A2
Fontainebleau *Johannesburg* 13 A1
Fontenay-aux-Roses *Paris* 24 B2
Fontenay-le-Fleury *Paris* 24 B1
Fontenay-sous-Bois *Paris* 24 A3
Foots Cray *London* 15 B4
Footscray *Melbourne* 18 A1
Forbidden City = Imperial Palace Museum *Beijing* 4 B2
Forest *Brussels* 6 B1
Forest Gate *London* 15 A4
Forest Heights *Washington* 33 C2
Forest Hill *Dallas-Fort Worth* 10 B2
Forest Hill *London* 15 B3
Forest Hill *Toronto* 31 A2
Forest Hills *New York* 22 B2
Forest Park *Chicago* 9 B2
Forest Park *New York* 22 B2
Forest View *Chicago* 9 C2
Fornebu *Oslo* 23 A2
Foro Romano *Rome* 26 B1
Forstenried *Munich* 21 B1
Forstenrieder Park *Munich* 21 B1
Fort *Mumbai* 20 B1
Fort Dupont Park *Washington* 33 B3
Fort Foote Village *Washington* 33 C2
Fort Lauderdale *Miami* 19 B3
Fort Lauderdale Executive ✕ (FXE) *Miami* 19 A2
Fort Lauderdale-Hollywood Int. ✕ (FLL) *Miami* 19 B3
Fort Lee *New York* 22 A2
Fort Worth *Dallas-Fort Worth* 10 B2
Forth, Firth of *Edinburgh* 11 A3
Forth Rail Bridge *Edinburgh* 11 A1
Forth Road Bridge *Edinburgh* 11 A1
Forum, The *Los Angeles* 16 C2
Foshan *Guangzhou* 11 B1
Föt *Budapest* 7 A3
Fourqueux *Paris* 24 A1
Fox Studios *Sydney* 29 B2
Fram Museum *Oslo* 23 A3
Franconia *Washington* 33 C2
Frank Lloyd Wright Home *Chicago* 9 B2
Frankel *Singapore* 28 B3
Franklin Park *Boston* 6 B2
Franklin Park *Washington* 33 B2
Franklin Res. *Los Angeles* 16 B2
Franz Josef Strauss ✕ (MUC) *Munich* 21 A3
Frauenkirche *Munich* 21 B2
Frederiksberg *Copenhagen* 8 A3
Frederiksdal *Copenhagen* 8 A2
Fredersdorf *Berlin* 5 A5
Freguesia *Rio de Janeiro* 25 A1
Freidrichshain, Volkspark *Berlin* 5 A3
Freiham *Munich* 21 B1
Freimann *Munich* 21 A2
French Quarter *New Orleans* 21 B2
Fresh Pond *Boston* 6 A2
Fresnes *Paris* 24 B3
Freudenau *Vienna* 32 B2
Friedenau *Berlin* 5 B3
Friedrichsfelde *Berlin* 5 B4
Friedrichshagen *Berlin* 5 B4
Friedrichshain *Berlin* 5 A3
Friedrichslust *Berlin* 5 A5
Friends Arena *Stockholm* 29 A2
Friherrs *Helsinki* 11 B1
Frilufts Museum *Helsinki* 11 B2
Frontón, I. *Lima* 14 B1
Frunze *Moscow* 19 B2
Fuchū *Tokyo* 30 A1
Fuencarral *Madrid* 17 B1
Fuenlabrada *Madrid* 17 C1
Fukagawa *Tokyo* 30 B3
Fukushima *Osaka* 23 A1
Fulham *London* 15 B2
Funabori *Tokyo* 30 A4
Fundão, I. do *Rio de Janeiro* 25 B1
Fünfhaus *Vienna* 32 A2
Furesø *Copenhagen* 8 A2
Fürth *Munich* 21 B2
Futago-tamagawaen *Tokyo* 30 B2
Fuxing Dao *Shanghai* 28 B2
Fuxing Park *Shanghai* 28 B1
Fuxinglu *Beijing* 4 B1

G

G. Ross Lord Park *Toronto* 31 A2
Gaebong *Seoul* 27 C1
Gage Park *Chicago* 9 C2
Gagny *Paris* 24 A4
Galata *Istanbul* 12 B1
Galata Tower *Istanbul* 12 B1
Galatsi *Athens* 2 A2
Galeão Int. ✕ (GIG) *Rio de Janeiro* 25 A1
Galyanovo *Moscow* 19 B3
Gambir *Jakarta* 12 A1
Gamboa *Rio de Janeiro* 25 B1
Gambolóita *Milan* 18 B2
Gamlebyen *Oslo* 23 A3
Gangdong *Seoul* 27 B2
Gangnam *Seoul* 27 B1
Gangseo *Seoul* 27 B1
Gangtou *Guangzhou* 11 A1
Gangwei *Guangzhou* 11 B2
Ganjiakou *Beijing* 4 B1
Ganshoren *Brussels* 6 A1
Gants Hill *London* 15 A4
Gaohang *Shanghai* 28 B2
Gaoqiao *Shanghai* 28 A2
Garbagnate Milanese *Milan* 18 A1
Garbatella *Rome* 26 B2
Garches *Paris* 24 A2
Garching *Munich* 21 A3
Garden City *Cairo* 7 A2
Garden District *New Orleans* 21 B2
Garden Reach *Kolkata* 14 B1
Garder *Oslo* 23 B2
Garfield *New York* 22 A1
Garfield Park *Chicago* 9 B2
Gargareta *Athens* 2 B2
Garibong *Seoul* 27 C1
Garland *Dallas-Fort Worth* 10 A6
Garvanza *Los Angeles* 16 B3
Gåshaga *Stockholm* 29 A3
Gateway → *New York* 22 C2
Gateway of India *Mumbai* 20 B2
Gateway Park *Dallas-Fort Worth* 10 B2
Gatow *Berlin* 5 B1
Gavà *Barcelona* 4 B1
Gavamar *Barcelona* 4 B1
Gávea *Rio de Janeiro* 25 B1
Gávea, Pedra da *Rio de Janeiro* 25 B1
Gazdagrét *Budapest* 7 B1
Gaziosmanpaşa *Istanbul* 12 B1
Gebel el Ahmar *Cairo* 7 A3
Gebel el Muqattam *Cairo* 7 A2
Gebel el Tura *Cairo* 7 B2
Geiselgasteig *Munich* 21 B2
Gelora Bung Karno *Stadium Jakarta* 12 B1
General San Martín *Buenos Aires* 7 B1
Gennevilliers *Paris* 24 A2
Gentilly *New Orleans* 21 A2
Gentilly *Paris* 24 B3
Gentofte *Copenhagen* 8 A3
Genval *Brussels* 6 B2
George I. *Hong Kong* 12 B2
Georges River Bridge *Sydney* 29 C1
Georgetown *Washington* 33 B2
Georgia Aquarium *Atlanta* 3 B2
Georgia Dome *Atlanta* 3 B2
Gerasdorf bei Wien *Vienna* 32 A2
Gerberau *Munich* 21 A1
Gerli *Buenos Aires* 7 C2
Germiston *Johannesburg* 13 B2
Gern *Munich* 21 B2
Getafe *Madrid* 17 C1
Getty Center, The *Los Angeles* 16 B2
Geumjeong *Seoul* 27 C1
Geva Binyamin *Jerusalem* 13 A2
Geylang Serai *Singapore* 28 B3
Gharapuri = Elephanta I. *Mumbai* 20 B2
Gharb = Shahrak-e Qods *Tehran* 31 A2
Ghatkopar *Mumbai* 20 A2
Ghazipur *Delhi* 10 B2
Ghizri *Karachi* 13 B2
Ghizri Cr. → *Karachi* 13 B2
Ghonda *Delhi* 10 A2
Ghusuri *Kolkata* 14 B2
Gianicolense *Rome* 26 B1
Giant Wheel = Riesenrad *Vienna* 32 A2
Gibraltar Pt. *Toronto* 31 B2
Gidea Park *London* 15 A5
Giesing *Munich* 21 B2
Gilmerton *Edinburgh* 11 B3
Gilo *Jerusalem* 13 B2
Gimmersta *Stockholm* 29 B3
Ginza *Tokyo* 30 B3
Giv'at Ram *Jerusalem* 13 B2
Giv'at Ye'arim *Jerusalem* 13 B1
Giv'at Ze'ev *Jerusalem* 13 A2
Giv'on *Jerusalem* 13 A1
Giza = El Gîza *Cairo* 7 A2
Giza Pyramids *Cairo* 7 B1
Gjersjøen *Oslo* 23 B3
Gladesville *Sydney* 29 B1
Gladsakse *Copenhagen* 8 A2
Glassmanor *Washington* 33 C3
Glen Iris *Melbourne* 18 B2
Glen Mar Park *Washington* 33 B2
Glen Rouge Park *Toronto* 31 A4
Glencoe *Chicago* 9 A2
Glencorse Res. *Edinburgh* 11 B2
Glendale *Los Angeles* 16 B3
Glenhuntly *Melbourne* 18 B2
Glenview *Chicago* 9 A2
Glenview Countryside *Chicago* 9 A2
Glenvista *Johannesburg* 13 B2
Glifada *Athens* 2 B2
Glostrup *Copenhagen* 8 B2
Glyfada = Glifada *Athens* 2 B2
Gogar *Edinburgh* 11 B2

Göktürk Istanbul 12 A1
Golabari Kolkata 14 B2
Golabki Warsaw 33 B1
Gold Coast Chicago 9 B3
Golden Beach Miami 19 C3
Golden Gate San Francisco 26 B2
Golden Gate ⌓ San Francisco 26 A2
Golden Gate Bridge San Francisco 26 B2
Golden Gate Park San Francisco 26 B2
Golden Horn = Haliç Istanbul 12 B1
Golders Green London 15 A2
Golestan Palace Tehran 31 A2
Golf Chicago 9 A2
Gonen Jerusalem 13 B2
Gongneung Seoul 27 B2
Goodmayes London 15 A4
Goodwood Cape Town 8 A2
Gopalpur Kolkata 14 B2
Górce Warsaw 33 B1
Gore Hill Sydney 29 A2
Gorelyy → St. Petersburg 27 A3
Gorgie Edinburgh 11 B2
Gorky Park Moscow 19 B2
Gosen Berlin 5 B5
Gosener kanal Berlin 5 B5
Gospel Oak London 15 A3
Gotanda Tokyo 30 B3
Goth Goli Mar Karachi 13 A2
Goth Sher Shah Karachi 13 A1
Gotha Orlando 23 A1
Gournay-sur-Marne Paris 24 A4
Governador, I. do Rio de Janeiro 25 A1
Governors I. New York 22 B1
Grabów Warsaw 33 C1
Gràcia Barcelona 4 A2
Gräfelfing Munich 21 B1
Gragoatá Rio de Janeiro 25 B2
Grand Bazaar = Kapali Carsi Istanbul 12 B1
Grand Central Station New York 22 B2
Grand Palace Bangkok 3 B1
Grand Place Brussels 6 A2
Grand Prairie Dallas-Fort Worth 10 B3
Grande Place Brussels 6 A2
Grankulla = Kauniainen Helsinki 11 B1
Grant Park Chicago 9 B3
Granton Edinburgh 11 B2
Grapevine Dallas-Fort Worth 10 A3
Grapevine Recr. Area Dallas-Fort Worth 10 A3
Grassy Park Cape Town 8 B2
Gratosóglio Milan 18 B2
Gratzwalde Berlin 5 B5
Gravesend New York 22 C2
Grazhdanka St. Petersburg 27 B2
Greco Milan 18 A2
Green I. Hong Kong 12 B2
Green Point Cape Town 8 A1
Greenfield Park Montreal 20 B3
Greenford London 15 A1
Greenhill London 15 A2
Greenwich □ London 15 B3
Greenwich Observatory London 15 B3
Greenwich Village New York 22 B2
Greenwood Boston 6 A2
Grefsen Oslo 23 A3
Gresham Park Atlanta 3 B2
Gretna New Orleans 21 B2
Gretna City Park New Orleans 21 B2
Greve Strand Copenhagen 8 B1
Greynolds Park Miami 19 C3
Griebnitzsee Berlin 5 B1
Griffith Park Los Angeles 16 B3
Grimbergen Brussels 6 A2
Grinzing Vienna 32 A2
Gröbenried Munich 21 A1
Grochów Warsaw 33 B2
Grodzisk Warsaw 33 B2
Groenendaal Brussels 6 B2
Grogol Petamburin Jakarta 12 A1
Gronsdorf Munich 21 B3
Grorud Oslo 23 A4
Gross Glienicke Berlin 5 B1
Gross-Hadern Munich 21 B1
Gross-Lappen Munich 21 A2
Grosse Krampe Berlin 5 B5
Grosse Müggelsee Berlin 5 B4
Grosse Point Lighthouse Chicago 9 A2
Grossenzersdorf Vienna 32 A3
Grossenzersdorfer Arm → Vienna 32 A3
Grosser Biberhaufen Vienna 32 A2
Grosser Wannsee Berlin 5 B2
Grossfeld-Siedlung Vienna 32 A2
Grosshesselohe Munich 21 B2
Grossjedlersdorf Vienna 32 A2
Grossziethen Berlin 5 B3
Grove Hall Boston 6 B2
Grove Park Atlanta 3 B2
Grove Park London 15 B4
Grove Park London 15 B2
Groveton Washington 33 C2
Grünau Berlin 5 B4
Grunewald Berlin 5 B2
Grünwald Munich 21 B2
Grünwalder Forst Munich 21 B2
Grymes Hill New York 22 C1
Guadalupe Manila 17 B2
Guadalupe, Basilica de Mexico City 18 B2
Guanabara, B. de Rio de Janeiro 25 B1
Guanabara, Jardim Rio de Janeiro 25 A1
Guanabara, Palácio da Rio de Janeiro 25 B1
Guang'anmen Beijing 4 B1
Guangdong Olympic Stadium Guangzhou 11 B3
Guangqumen Beijing 4 B2
Guangzhou Guangzhou 11 B2
Guanshuo Guangzhou 11 B3
Gucun Shanghai 28 A1
Gudö Stockholm 29 B3
Güell, Parque de Barcelona 4 A2
Guildwood Toronto 31 A3
Guinardó Barcelona 4 A2
Gulbai Karachi 13 A1
Gulshan-e Iqbal Jerusalem 13 A2
Güngören Istanbul 12 B1
Gunnersbury London 15 B2
Guomao Beijing 4 B2
Gustavo A. Madero Mexico City 18 B2
Guttenberg New York 22 B1
Gutuyevskiy, Ostrov St. Petersburg 27 B1
Guyancourt Paris 24 B1
Gwanak Seoul 27 C1
Gwanaksan Seoul 27 C1
Gyál Budapest 7 B3
Gyáli-patak → Budapest 7 B2

H

Haaga Helsinki 11 B2
Haar Munich 21 B3
Habay Manila 17 C1
Hackbridge London 15 B3
Hackensack New York 22 A1
Hackensack → New York 22 B1
Hackney □ London 15 A3
Hackney Wick London 15 A3
Hadr, Warrâq el Cairo 7 A2
Haga Stockholm 29 A2
Hagenbrunn Vienna 32 A2
Hägersten Stockholm 29 B1
Häggvik Stockholm 29 A1
Hagonoy Manila 17 B2
Hague Park Toronto 31 A3
Haidari = Chaidari Athens 2 A1
Haidarpur Delhi 10 A1
Haidhausen Munich 21 B2
Haidian Beijing 4 B1
Haight-Ashbury San Francisco 26 B2
Hainault London 15 A4
Haizhou Guangzhou 11 B2
Haizhu Guangchang Guangzhou 11 B2
Hakunila Helsinki 11 B3
Halandri = Chalandri Athens 2 A2
Halásztelek Budapest 7 B1
Haliç Istanbul 12 B1
Halim Perdana Kusuma Int. ✈ (HLP) Jakarta 12 B2
Hallandale Beach Miami 19 C3
Halle Brussels 6 B1
Haltiala Helsinki 11 B2
Haltiavuori Helsinki 11 B2
Haltom City Dallas-Fort Worth 10 B2
Ham London 15 B2
Hämeenkylä Helsinki 11 B1
Hammarby Stockholm 29 B2
Hamme Brussels 6 A1
Hammersmith London 15 B2
Hampstead London 15 A2
Hampstead Montreal 20 B2
Hampstead Garden Suburb London 15 A2
Hampstead Heath London 15 A2
Hampton London 15 B1
Hampton Court Palace London 15 B1
Hampton Wick London 15 B2
Hamrā' Baghdad 3 B1
Hanala Helsinki 11 A3
Haneda Tokyo 30 B3
Haneda, Tōkyō ✈ (HND) Tokyo 30 B3
Hang Hau Hong Kong 12 B3
Hanging Gardens Mumbai 20 B1
Hanlon Toronto 31 B1
Hanwell London 15 A1
Hanworth London 15 B1
Haora Kolkata 14 B1
Hapeville Atlanta 3 C2
Happy Valley Hong Kong 12 B3
Har Adar Jerusalem 13 B1
Har Gilo Jerusalem 13 B2
Har Homa Jerusalem 13 B2
Har Nof Jerusalem 13 B2
Harahan New Orleans 21 B1
Harbour Front Centre Singapore 28 B2
Haren Brussels 6 A2
Hareskovby Copenhagen 8 A2
Haringey □ London 15 A3
Harjusuo Helsinki 11 B3
Harlaching Munich 21 B2
Harlaw Res. Edinburgh 11 B2
Harlem New York 22 B2
Harlesden London 15 A2
Harlington London 15 B1
Harmaja Helsinki 11 C2
Harmashatar hegy Budapest 7 A2
Háros Budapest 7 B2
Harperrig Res. Edinburgh 11 B1
Harrow □ London 15 A1
Harrow on the Hill London 15 A1
Harrow School London 15 A1
Harrow Weald London 15 A1
Harry S. Moss Park Dallas-Fort Worth 10 A5
Hartsfield-Jackson Atlanta Int. ✈ (ATL) Atlanta 3 C2
Harumi Tokyo 30 B3
Harvard Univ. Boston 6 A2
Harvey Chicago 9 D3
Harvey New Orleans 21 B2
Harwood Heights Chicago 9 B2
Ḩasanābād Tehran 31 A1
Hasbrouck Heights New York 22 A1
Haselhorst Berlin 5 A2
Hasköy Istanbul 12 B1
Hasle Oslo 23 B2
Haslum Oslo 23 A2
Hästhagen Stockholm 29 B2
Hatch End London 15 A1
Hatiara Kolkata 14 B2
Hauketo Oslo 23 A3
Hauz Khas Delhi 10 B2
Havel → Berlin 5 A2
Havelkanal Berlin 5 A2
Havering □ London 15 A5
Havering-atte-Bower London 15 A5
Haworth New York 22 A2
Hawthorne Racecourse Chicago 9 C2
Hayes London 15 B4
Hayes London 15 A1
Hayes End London 15 A1
Hayford Chicago 9 C2
Heathfield Cape Town 8 B1
Heathrow, London ✈ (LHR) London 15 B1
Hebe Haven Hong Kong 12 A3
Hedong Guangzhou 11 B2
Hei Ling Chau Hong Kong 12 B2
Heidelberg Heights Melbourne 18 A2
Heidelberg West Melbourne 18 A2
Heidemühle Berlin 5 B5
Heideveld Cape Town 8 A2
Heiligensee Berlin 5 A2
Heiligenstadt Vienna 32 A2
Heinersdorf Berlin 5 A3
Hélène de Champlain, Parc ⌓ Montreal 20 A2
Helenelund Stockholm 29 A1
Heliopolis = Masr el Gedida Cairo 7 A2
Hellersdorf Berlin 5 A4
Hellerup Copenhagen 8 A3
Helsingfors = Helsinki Helsinki 11 B2
Helsinki Helsinki 11 B2
Helsinki-Vantaa ✈ (HEL) Helsinki 11 B2
Hen and Chicken B. Sydney 29 B1
Henderson Las Vegas 14 B2
Hendon London 15 A2
Hengsha Guangzhou 11 B2
Hennigsdorf Berlin 5 A2
Henryków Warsaw 33 B1
Henson Cr. → Washington 33 C3
Henttaa Helsinki 11 B1
Heping Park Shanghai 28 B2
Hepingli Beijing 4 B2
Herlev Copenhagen 8 A2
Herman Eckstein Park Johannesburg 13 A2
Hermannskogel Vienna 32 A1
Hermiston Edinburgh 11 B2
Hermitage and Winter Palace St. Petersburg 27 B2
Hermsdorf Berlin 5 A2
Hernals Vienna 32 A2
Herne Hill London 15 B3
Héroes de Churubusco Mexico City 18 B2
Herons, Î. aux Montreal 20 B2
Herstedøster Copenhagen 8 A2
Herttoniemi Helsinki 11 B3
Ḩeşārak Tehran 31 A1
Heston London 15 B1
Hetzendorf Vienna 32 B1
Hextable London 15 B5
Hialeah Miami 19 C1
Hialeah Race Track Miami 19 C1
Hiawassa, L. Orlando 23 A2
Hickory Hills Chicago 9 C2
Hiekkaharju Helsinki 11 B3
Hietaniemi Helsinki 11 B2
Hietzing Vienna 32 A1
Higashi Osaka 23 A2
Higashimurayama Tokyo 30 A1
Higashinari Osaka 23 A2
Higashisumiyoshi Osaka 23 B2
Higashiyodogawa Osaka 23 A1
High Junk Pk. Hong Kong 12 B3
High Park Toronto 31 B2
Highbury London 15 A3
Highgate London 15 A3
Highland Cr. → Toronto 31 A3
Highland Creek Toronto 31 A3
Highland Park Dallas-Fort Worth 10 B5
Highland Park Los Angeles 16 B3
Highlands North Johannesburg 13 A2
Hillbrow Tower Johannesburg 13 B2
Hillcrest Heights Washington 33 C3
Hillend Edinburgh 11 A1
Hillingdon □ London 15 A1
Hillwood Washington 33 B2
Hilmîya Cairo 7 A2
Hin Keng Hong Kong 12 A3
Hirota Osaka 23 A1
Hirschstetten Vienna 32 A2
Hither Green London 15 B3
Hiyoshi Tokyo 30 B2
Hizma Jerusalem 13 B2
Hjortekær Copenhagen 8 A3
Hjortespring Copenhagen 8 A2
Hlubočepy Prague 25 B2
Ho Chung Hong Kong 12 A3
Hoboken New York 22 B1
Hobsons B. Melbourne 18 B1
Hochbrück Munich 21 A2
Hochelaga Montreal 20 A2
Hoegi Seoul 27 B2
Hoeilaart Brussels 6 B2
Hofburg Vienna 32 A2
Hoffman I. New York 22 C1
Hohenbrunn Munich 21 B3
Hohenschönhausen Berlin 5 A4
Hok Tsui Hong Kong 12 B3
Holargos = Cholargos Athens 2 B2
Holborn London 15 A3
Holden, L. Orlando 23 B2
Holešovice Prague 25 B2
Holiday Park Miami 19 B3
Holland Village Singapore 28 B2
Höllriegelskreuth Munich 21 B1
Hollywood Los Angeles 16 B3
Hollywood Miami 19 B3
Hollywood Bowl Los Angeles 16 B2
Holmenkollen Oslo 23 A3
Holmgård Stockholm 29 B1
Holmlia Oslo 23 B3
Holocaust Memorial Jerusalem 13 B2
Holyrood House, Palace of Edinburgh 11 B3
Holysloot Amsterdam 2 A3
Homerton London 15 A3
Hometown Chicago 9 C2
Hōnanchō Tokyo 30 A2
Honcho Tokyo 30 A3
Honden Tokyo 30 A4
Hondo, Rio → Los Angeles 16 B4
Hong Kong I. Hong Kong 12 B3
Hong Kong Int. ✈ (HKG) Hong Kong 12 B1
Hong Kong Univ. Hong Kong 12 B2
Hongje Seoul 27 B1
Hongjimun Tunnel Seoul 27 B1
Hongkou Shanghai 28 B1
Hongqiao Shanghai 28 B1
Honjyo Tokyo 30 A3
Honoré Mercier, Pont Montreal 20 B1
Hönow Berlin 5 A4
Hook London 15 B2
Horikiri Tokyo 30 A4
Horn Pond Boston 6 A1
Hornchurch London 15 A5
Horni Prague 25 B3
Horni Počernice Prague 25 B3
Hornsey London 15 A3
Horoměřice Prague 25 B1
Hortaleza Madrid 17 B2
Hosoyama Tokyo 30 B2
Hostafranchs Barcelona 4 A1
Hostivař Prague 25 B3
Houbětin Prague 25 B3
Hougang Singapore 28 A3
Houghton Johannesburg 13 B2
Houilles Paris 24 A2
Hounslow □ London 15 B1
Hout Bay Cape Town 8 B1
Hove Å → Copenhagen 8 B2
Hovedøya Oslo 23 A3
Høvik Oslo 23 A2
Hovorčovice Prague 25 A3
Howard Beach New York 22 C2
Howrah = Haora Kolkata 14 B1
Hōya Tokyo 30 A2
Hradčany Prague 25 B2
Huanghuagang Mausoleum Guangzhou 11 B2
Huangpu Shanghai 28 B2
Huangpu Jiang → Shanghai 28 B1
Huangtugang Beijing 4 C1
Huascar Lima 14 A2
Huay Khwang Bangkok 3 B2
Huddinge Stockholm 29 B2
Huechuraba Santiago 27 B1
Hugh Taylor Birch State Recr. Area ⌓ Miami 19 B3
Huizingen Brussels 6 B1
Humayun's Tomb Delhi 10 B2
Humber → Toronto 31 A1
Humber B. Toronto 31 B2
Humber Bay Toronto 31 B2
Humber Bay Park Toronto 31 B2
Humber College Toronto 31 B1
Humber Summit Toronto 31 A1
Humber Valley Village Toronto 31 A1
Humberlea Toronto 31 A1
Humberwood Park Toronto 31 A1
Humboldt Park Chicago 9 B2
Humera Madrid 17 B1
Hunaydī Baghdad 3 B2
Hundige Copenhagen 8 B1
Hundige Strand Copenhagen 8 B2
Hung Hom Hong Kong 12 B3
Hunters Hill Sydney 29 B1
Hunters Pt. San Francisco 26 B2
Huntington Washington 33 C2
Huntington Park Los Angeles 16 C3
Hurīya Baghdad 3 A1
Hurst Dallas-Fort Worth 10 B3
Hurstville Sydney 29 B1
Husan Jerusalem 13 B1
Husby Stockholm 29 A1
Husum Copenhagen 8 A2
Hutchins Dallas-Fort Worth 10 C5
Hütteldorf Vienna 32 A1
Hüvösvölgy Budapest 7 A2
Huwon Secret Garden Seoul 27 B1
Hvalstad Oslo 23 A1
Hvalstrand Oslo 23 A2
Hvidovre Copenhagen 8 B2
Hwagok Seoul 27 B1
Hyattsville Washington 33 B3
Hyde Park Boston 6 B2
Hyde Park Chicago 9 C3
Hyde Park Johannesburg 13 A2
Hyde Park London 15 A2
Hyde Park Los Angeles 16 C3

I

Ibese Lagos 14 A2
Ibirapuera São Paulo 27 B1
Ibirapuera, Parque do São Paulo 27 B2
Icarai Rio de Janeiro 25 B2
Içerenköy Istanbul 12 C2
Ichgao Tokyo 30 B2
Ichigaya Tokyo 30 A3
Ichikawa Tokyo 30 A4
Ickenham London 15 A1
Iddo Lagos 14 B2
Idi-Oro Lagos 14 A2
Iganmu Lagos 14 B2
Igbobi Lagos 14 A2
Igbologun Lagos 14 B1
Igny Paris 24 B2
IJ, Het → Amsterdam 2 A2
IJ-meer Amsterdam 2 A3
IJburg Amsterdam 2 A3
Ijesa-Tedo Lagos 14 B1
Ijora Lagos 14 B2
Ikebe Tokyo 30 B2
Ikebukuro Tokyo 30 A3
Ikegami Tokyo 30 B3
Ikeja Lagos 14 A2
Ikeuchi Osaka 23 B2
Ikorodu Lagos 14 A2
Ikoyi Lagos 14 B2
Ikuata Lagos 14 B2
Ikuno Osaka 23 A2
Ikuta Tokyo 30 B2
Ila Oslo 23 A2
Ilford London 15 A4
Ilioupoli Athens 2 B2
Illinois at Chicago, Univ. of Chicago 9 B3
Illinois Institute of Technology Chicago 9 B3
Ilpendam Amsterdam 2 A2
Ilsos → Athens 2 B2
Imbâbah Cairo 7 A2
Imbiah Lookout Singapore 28 B2
Imielin Warsaw 33 C2
Imirim São Paulo 27 A2
Imitos Athens 2 B2
Imitos, Oros Athens 2 B2
Imperial Palace Museum Beijing 4 B2
Inagi Tokyo 30 B2
Inchcolm Edinburgh 11 A2
Inchkeith Edinburgh 11 A3
Inchmickery Edinburgh 11 A2
Incirano Milan 18 A1
Independencia Lima 14 A2
Independencia Santiago 27 B2
India Gate Delhi 10 B2
Indian Creek Village Miami 19 C3
Indianópolis São Paulo 27 B2
Indira Gandhi Int. ✈ (DEL) Delhi 10 B1
Indira Gandhi Memorial Museum Delhi 10 B2
Industria Johannesburg 13 B1
Industrial Canal New Orleans 21 A2
Ingierstrand Oslo 23 B3
Inglewood Los Angeles 16 C3
Ingliston Edinburgh 11 B1
Inhaúma Rio de Janeiro 25 B1
Inner Port Shelter Hong Kong 12 A3
Interlagos São Paulo 27 C1
Intramuros Manila 17 B1
Invalides Paris 24 A2
Inverkeithing Edinburgh 11 A1
Inzersdorf Vienna 32 B2
Ipanema Rio de Janeiro 25 B1
Ipiranga São Paulo 27 B2
Ipiranga → São Paulo 27 B2
Iponri Lagos 14 B2
Irving Dallas-Fort Worth 10 B4
Irving Park Chicago 9 B2
Isabel Rio de Janeiro 25 B1
Isagatedo Lagos 14 A1
Isar → Munich 21 A3
Ishbīlīya Baghdad 3 A2
Ishøj Strand Copenhagen 8 B2
Island Park Toronto 31 B2
Islev Copenhagen 8 A2
Isleworth London 15 B2
Islington Toronto 31 B1
Islington □ London 15 A3
Ismâ'ilîya, Qanâ el Cairo 7 A2
Ismaning Munich 21 A3
Ismayloskiy Park Moscow 19 B3
Isolo Lagos 14 A1
Issy-les-Moulineaux Paris 24 B2
İstanbul Istanbul 12 C1
İstanbul Boğazı Istanbul 12 B2
İstinye Istanbul 12 B2
Itä Hakkila Helsinki 11 B3
Itaewon Seoul 27 B1
Itami Osaka 23 A1
Itanhanga Rio de Janeiro 25 B1
Ivanhoe Melbourne 18 A2
Ives Estates Miami 19 C2
Ivry-sur-Seine Paris 24 B3
Ixelles Brussels 6 B2
Izmaylovo Moscow 19 B3
Iztacalco Mexico City 18 B2
Iztapalapa Mexico City 18 B2

J

Jaba Jerusalem 13 A2
Jabotabek = Jakarta Jakarta 12 A2
Jacaré Rio de Janeiro 25 B1
Jackson Heights New York 22 B2
Jackson Park Chicago 9 C3
Jacques-Cartier Montreal 20 A3
Jacques-Cartier, Pont Montreal 20 A2
Jadavpur Kolkata 14 C2
Jade Buddha Temple Shanghai 28 B1
Jægersborg Copenhagen 8 A3
Jægersborg Dyrehave Copenhagen 8 A3
Jagadishpur Kolkata 14 B1
Jagatpur Delhi 10 A2
Jaguaré, Rib. do → São Paulo 27 B1
Jahangirpur Delhi 10 A2
Jakarta Jakarta 12 A2
Jakarta, Teluk Jakarta 12 A1
Jakarta Halim Perdana Kusuma Int. ✈ (HLP) Jakarta 12 B2
Jalan Kayu Singapore 28 A3
Jamaica B. New York 22 C3
Jamaica Plain Boston 6 B2
Jamakpuri Delhi 10 B1
Jamshīdīyeh Tehran 31 A2
Jamsil Seoul 27 B2
Jamwon Seoul 27 B2
Janki Warsaw 33 C1
Jaraguá São Paulo 27 A1
Jaraguá, Pico de São Paulo 27 A1
Jardim Paulista São Paulo 27 B1
Järvatältet Stockholm 29 A1
Jaskhar Mumbai 20 B2
Jatinegara Jakarta 12 B2
Javādīyeh Tehran 31 B2
Jawaharlal Nehru Port = Nhava Sheva Mumbai 20 B2
Jaworowa Warsaw 33 C1
Jean Lafitte Nat. Historical Park ⌓ New Orleans 21 B1
Jedlesee Vienna 32 A2
Jefferson New Orleans 21 B2
Jefferson Memorial Washington 33 B2
Jefferson Park Chicago 9 B2
Jefferson Park Los Angeles 16 B3
Jegi Seoul 27 B2
Jelambar Jakarta 12 A1
Jelonki Warsaw 33 B1
Jerónimos, Mosteiro dos Lisbon 16 A1
Jersey City New York 22 B1
Jerusalem Jerusalem 13 B2
Jessamine, L. Orlando 23 B2
Jésus, Î. Montreal 20 A1
Jesús Maria Lima 14 B2
Jette Brussels 6 A1
Jey Tehran 31 B2
Jianggao Guangzhou 11 A2
Jiangwan Shanghai 28 B1
Jib Jerusalem 13 A2
Jihād Baghdad 3 B1
Jingan Shanghai 28 B1
Jinnah Int. ✈ (KHI) Karachi 13 A2
Jinočany Prague 25 B1
Jinonice Prague 25 B2
Jinqiao Shanghai 28 B2
Jiulong = Kowloon Hong Kong 12 B3
Jiyūgaoka Tokyo 30 B3
Jizā'ir Baghdad 3 B2
Jizīra Baghdad 3 B2
Joe Pool Lake Dallas-Fort Worth 10 C4
Joglo Jakarta 12 B1
Johannesburg Johannesburg 13 B2
Johannesburg, Univ. of Johannesburg 13 B2
Johanneskirchen Munich 21 A2
Johannesstift Berlin 5 A2
Johannisthal Berlin 5 B4
John F. Kennedy Nat. Historic Site ⌓ Boston 6 A2
John McLaren Park San Francisco 26 B2
John U. Lloyd Beach ⌓ Miami 19 B3
Joinville-le-Pont Paris 24 B3
Joli-Bois Brussels 6 B2
Jollas Helsinki 11 B3
Jongmyo Royal Shrine Seoul 27 B1
Jongno Seoul 27 B1
Jonstrup Copenhagen 8 A2
Joppa Edinburgh 11 B3
Jorge Chavez Int. ✈ (LIM) Lima 14 B2
Jorge Newbery ✈ (AEP) Buenos Aires 7 B2
Józefa Piłsudskiego Park Warsaw 33 B1
Joss House B. Hong Kong 12 B3
Jōtō Osaka 23 A2
Jouy-en-Josas Paris 24 B2
Juan Anchorena Buenos Aires 7 A2
Juan González Romero Mexico City 18 A2
Juárez Int. ✈ (MEX) Mexico City 18 B2
Judeira Jerusalem 13 A2
Juhdum Jerusalem 13 B2
Juhu Mumbai 20 A2
Jūjā Tokyo 30 A3
Jukskeirivier → Johannesburg 13 A2
Julianów Warsaw 33 B2
Jumeirah Dubai 9 B1
Jung Seoul 27 B1
Jungfernheide, Volkspark Berlin 5 A2
Jungfernsee Berlin 5 B1
Junghwa Seoul 27 B2
Jungnang Seoul 27 B2
Jungnangcheon → Seoul 27 B1
Juniper Green Edinburgh 11 B2
Junk B. Hong Kong 12 B3
Jurong Singapore 28 B2
Jurong, Selat Singapore 28 B2
Jurong Industrial Estate Singapore 28 B1
Jurujuba, Enseada de Rio de Janeiro 25 B2
Jūsō Osaka 23 A1
Justice Chicago 9 C2
Jwalahari Delhi 10 B1

K

Kaapstad = Cape Town Cape Town 8 A1
Kabaty Warsaw 33 C2
Kadıköy Istanbul 12 C2
Kadoma Osaka 23 A2
Kafr 'Aqab Jerusalem 13 A2
Kâğıthane Istanbul 12 B1
Kâğıthane → Istanbul 12 B1
Kagran Vienna 32 A2
Kahnawake Montreal 20 B1
Kaimes Edinburgh 11 B2
Kaiserebersdorf Vienna 32 B2
Kaivoksela Helsinki 11 B2
Kalamaki Athens 2 B2
Kalbadevi Mumbai 20 B1
Kalipur Kolkata 14 A1
Kalithea Athens 2 B2
Kalkaji Delhi 10 B2
Kalookan = Caloocan Manila 17 B1
Kalvebod Fælled Copenhagen 8 B3
Kalveboderne Copenhagen 8 B3
Kam Shan Country Park ⌓ Hong Kong 12 A2
Kamarhati Kolkata 14 A2
Kamata Tokyo 30 B3
Kameari Tokyo 30 A4
Kameido Tokyo 30 A4
Kami-Itabashi Tokyo 30 A3
Kamikitazawa Tokyo 30 B2
Kamitsuruma Tokyo 30 B1
Kamoshida Tokyo 30 B2
Kampong Landang Singapore 28 A3
Kampong Tanjong Penjuru Singapore 28 B2
Kampung Bali Jakarta 12 B1
Kanamori Tokyo 30 B1
Kanda Tokyo 30 A3
Kandilli Istanbul 12 B2
Kankurgachi Kolkata 14 B2
Kanlıca Istanbul 12 B2
Kanonerskiy, Ostrov St. Petersburg 27 B1
Kansai Int. ✈ (KIX) Osaka 23 B2
Kanzaki → Osaka 23 A1
Kapali Carsi Istanbul 12 B1
Kapellerfeld Vienna 32 A2
Káposztásmegyer Budapest 7 A2
Kapotnya Moscow 19 C3
Käppala Stockholm 29 A3
Kapuk Jakarta 12 A1
Käpylä Helsinki 11 B2
Karachi Karachi 13 A2
Karkh Baghdad 3 A2
Karlin Prague 25 B2
Karlsfeld Munich 21 A1
Karlshorst Berlin 5 B4
Karlův most Prague 25 B2
Karol Bagh Delhi 10 B2
Karolinenhof Berlin 5 B4
Karow Berlin 5 A3
Karrādah Baghdad 3 B2
Kärsön Stockholm 29 B1
Kasai Tokyo 30 B4
Kasipur Kolkata 14 B2
Kastrup Copenhagen 8 B3
Kastrup, København ✈ (CPH) Copenhagen 8 B3
Kasuga Tokyo 30 A2
Kasuge Tokyo 30 A3
Kasumigaseki Tokyo 30 B3
Katong Singapore 28 B3
Katsushika Tokyo 30 A4
Kau Pai Chau Hong Kong 12 B3
Kau Sai Chau Hong Kong 12 A3
Kau Yi Chau Hong Kong 12 B2
Kaulsdorf Berlin 5 B4
Kauniainen Helsinki 11 B1
Kawasaki Tokyo 30 B3
Kawawa Tokyo 30 B2
Kawęczyn Warsaw 33 B2
Kayu Putih Jakarta 12 B2
Kbely Prague 25 B3
Kebayoran Baru Jakarta 12 B1
Kebayoran Lama Jakarta 12 B1
Kebon Jeruk Jakarta 12 B1
Kedar Jerusalem 13 B2
Kedoya Jakarta 12 B1
Kei Ling Ha Hong Kong 12 A3
Keilor Melbourne 18 A1
Keilor North Melbourne 18 A1
Keimola Helsinki 11 A1
Kelapa Gading Jakarta 12 A2
Kelberg Dallas-Fort Worth 10 B6
Kelenföld Budapest 7 B2
Keller Dallas-Fort Worth 10 A2
Kelvin Johannesburg 13 A2
Kemang Jakarta 12 B1
Kemayoran Jakarta 12 B2
Kemerburgaz Istanbul 12 B1
Kempton Park Races London 15 B1
Kendall Miami 19 D1
Kenilworth Cape Town 8 A1
Kenilworth Chicago 9 A2
Kennedale Dallas-Fort Worth 10 C2
Kennedy Town Hong Kong 12 B2
Kenner New Orleans 21 A1
Kenneth Hahn State Recreation Area ⌓ Los Angeles 16 B2
Kensal Green London 15 A2
Kensington Johannesburg 13 B2
Kensington London 15 B2
Kensington New York 22 C2
Kensington Sydney 29 B2
Kensington Palace London 15 A2
Kentish Town London 15 A3
Kenton London 15 A2
Kenwood House London 15 A3
Kepa Warsaw 33 B2
Keppel Harbour Singapore 28 B2
Kesariani Athens 2 B2
Keung Shan Hong Kong 12 B1
Kew London 15 B2
Kew Melbourne 18 A2
Kew Gardens London 15 B2
Kew Gardens Toronto 31 A3
Key Biscayne Miami 19 D3
Khalīj Baghdad 3 B2
Khansā' Baghdad 3 A2
Kharavli Mumbai 20 B2
Khefren Cairo 7 B1
Khichripur Delhi 10 B2
Khidirpur Kolkata 14 B1
Khimki-Khovrino Moscow 19 A2
Khirbet Batin Abu Lihyah Jerusalem 13 A1
Khirbet el-Misbah Jerusalem 13 A1
Khirbet Jub e-Rum Jerusalem 13 B2
Khlong San Bangkok 3 B2
Khlong Toey Bangkok 3 B2
Khorel Kolkata 14 A1
Khorosovo Moscow 19 B1
Kiamari Karachi 13 B1
Kierling Vienna 32 A1
Kierlingbach → Vienna 32 A1
Kifisos → Athens 2 B2
Kikuna Tokyo 30 B2
Kilburn London 15 A2
Kilo Helsinki 11 B1
Kilokri Delhi 10 B2
Kincsem Park Budapest 7 B2
Kindi Baghdad 3 B2
Kinghorn Edinburgh 11 A2
Kings Domain Melbourne 18 A1
Kings Forest = Kongelunden Copenhagen 8 B3
Kingsbury London 15 A2
Kingsbury Melbourne 18 A2
Kingsford Sydney 29 B2
Kingsford Smith, Sydney ✈ (SYD) Sydney 29 B2
Kingston-upon-Thames □ London 15 B2
Kingston Vale London 15 B2
Kingsway Toronto 31 B1
Kipling Heights Toronto 31 A1
Kipseli Athens 2 B2
Kirchstockbach Munich 21 B3
Kirchtrudering Munich 21 B3
Kirikiri Lagos 14 B1
Kirke Værløse Copenhagen 8 A1
Kirkhill Edinburgh 11 B2
Kirkliston Edinburgh 11 B1
Kirknewton Edinburgh 11 B1
Kirov Palace of Culture St. Petersburg 27 B1
Kiryat Anavim Jerusalem 13 B1
Kiryat Ha Yovel Jerusalem 13 B1
Kısıklı Istanbul 12 B2
Kispest Budapest 7 B2
Kista Stockholm 29 A1
Kita Osaka 23 A2
Kita Tokyo 30 A3
Kitazawa Tokyo 30 B3
Kivistö Helsinki 11 B2
Kiza → Osaka 23 B1
Kızıltoprak Istanbul 12 C2
Kizuri Osaka 23 B2
Kjelsås Oslo 23 A3
Kladow Berlin 5 B1
Klampenborg Copenhagen 8 A3
Klečany Prague 25 A2
Kledering Vienna 32 B2
Klein Jukskei → Johannesburg 13 A1
Kleinmachnow Berlin 5 B2
Kleinschönebeck Berlin 5 B5
Klemetsrud Oslo 23 A4
Klender Jakarta 12 A2
Kličany Prague 25 A2
Klipriviersberg Nature Reserve ⌓ Johannesburg 13 B2
Klosterneuburg Vienna 32 A1
Köbánya Budapest 7 B2
Kobbegem Brussels 6 A1
København Copenhagen 8 A2
København ✈ (CPH) Copenhagen 8 B3
Kobylisy Prague 25 B2
Kobyłka Warsaw 33 A3
Kodaira Tokyo 30 A1
Kodanaka Tokyo 30 B2
Koekelberg Brussels 6 A1
Koganei Tokyo 30 A2
Kogarah Sydney 29 B1
Koivupää Helsinki 11 B2
Koja Jakarta 12 A2
Koja Utara Jakarta 12 A2
Kokhav Ya'akov Jerusalem 13 A2
Kokobunji Tokyo 30 A1
Kokobunji-Temple Tokyo 30 A4
Kolarängen Stockholm 29 B3
Kolbotn Oslo 23 B3
Kolkata Kolkata 14 B2
Kolkata Maidan Kolkata 14 B1
Kolkata Netaji Subhash Chandra Bose Int. ✈ (CCU) Kolkata 14 B2
Koło Warsaw 33 B1
Kolokinthou Athens 2 B2
Kolomyagi St. Petersburg 27 A1
Kolonos Athens 2 B2
Kolsås Oslo 23 A2
Komae Tokyo 30 B2
Komagome Tokyo 30 A3
Komazawa Tokyo 30 B3
Kona Kolkata 14 B1
Konala Helsinki 11 B2
Kondli Delhi 10 B2
Kongelunden Copenhagen 8 B3
Kongens Lyngby Copenhagen 8 A3
Kongo Helsinki 11 A1
Konnagar Kolkata 14 A2
Konohana Osaka 23 A1
Konradshöhe Berlin 5 A2
Kopanina Prague 25 B1
Koparkhairna Mumbai 20 A2
Köpenick Berlin 5 B4
Korangi Karachi 13 B2
Koremasa Tokyo 30 B1
Koridalos Athens 2 B1
Kosino Moscow 19 B4
Kosugi Tokyo 30 B2
Kota Jakarta 12 A1
Kōtō Tokyo 30 A3
Kotrung Kolkata 14 A2
Kouponia Athens 2 B2
Kowloon Hong Kong 12 B3
Kowloon Peak Hong Kong 12 A3
Kowloon Tong Hong Kong 12 B3
Kraainem Brussels 6 A2
Krailling Munich 21 B1
Krampnitz Berlin 5 B1
Krampnitzsee Berlin 5 B1
Kranji Industrial Estate Singapore 28 A2
Kranji Res. Singapore 28 A2
Krasno-Presnenskaya Moscow 19 B2
Krč Prague 25 B2
Kremlin Moscow 19 B2
Krestovskiye, Ostrov St. Petersburg 27 B1
Kreuzberg Berlin 5 A3
Kritzendorf Vienna 32 A1
Krumme Lanke Berlin 5 B2
Krummensee Berlin 5 A5
Krung Thep = Bangkok Bangkok 3 B2
Krusboda Stockholm 29 B3
Kuangchou = Guangzhou Guangzhou 11 B2
Küçükköy Istanbul 12 B1
Küçüksu Istanbul 12 B2
Kudrovo St. Petersburg 27 B3
Kulosaari Helsinki 11 B3
Kumla Stockholm 29 B3
Kungens kurva Stockholm 29 B1
Kungliga Slottet Stockholm 29 B2
Kungshatt Stockholm 29 B1
Kungsholmen Stockholm 29 A2
Kuningan Jakarta 12 B1
Kunitachi Tokyo 30 A1
Kunming Hu Beijing 4 B1
Kunratice Prague 25 B2
Kupchino St. Petersburg 27 B2
Kuramo Waters Lagos 14 B2
Kurbağalı → Istanbul 12 C2
Kurihara Tokyo 30 A2
Kurla Mumbai 20 A2
Kurmuri Mumbai 20 A2
Kurume Tokyo 30 A2
Kuryanovo Moscow 19 C3
Kuskovo Moscow 19 B3
Kustia Kolkata 14 B2
Kuzguncuk Istanbul 12 B2
Kuzyminki Moscow 19 B3
Kwai Chung Hong Kong 12 A2
Kwangchow = Guangzhou Guangzhou 11 B2
Kwun Tong Hong Kong 12 B3
Kyje Prague 25 B3
Kyūhōji Osaka 23 B2

L

L.A. County Art Museum Los Angeles 16 B2
La Barceloneta Barcelona 4 A2
La Blanca Santiago 27 C2
La Boca Buenos Aires 7 B2
La Bretèche Paris 24 A1
La Campiña Lima 14 C2
La Celle-St-Cloud Paris 24 A1
La Cisterna Santiago 27 C2
La Courneuve Paris 24 A3
La Dehesa Santiago 27 B2
La Encantada Lima 14 C2
La Estación Madrid 17 B1
La Floresta Barcelona 4 A1
La Florida Santiago 27 C2
La Fortuna Madrid 17 B1
La França Barcelona 4 A1
La Garenne-Colombes Paris 24 A2
La Giustiniana Rome 26 B1
La Granja Santiago 27 C2
La Guardia, New York ✈ (LGA) New York 22 B2
La Hulpe Brussels 6 B2
La Llacuna Barcelona 4 A2
La Loma Mexico City 18 A1
La Lucila Buenos Aires 7 B2
La Maladrerie Paris 24 A1
La Milla, Cerro Lima 14 B2
La Monachina Rome 26 B1
La Moraleja Madrid 17 A2
La Nopalera Mexico City 18 C2
La Paternal Buenos Aires 7 B2
La Perla Lima 14 B2
La Perouse Sydney 29 B2
La Pisana Rome 26 B1
La Prairie Montreal 20 B3
La Punta Lima 14 B1
La Puntigala Barcelona 4 A2
La Queue-en-Brie Paris 24 B4
La Reina Santiago 27 B2
La Ribera Barcelona 4 A1
La Sagrera Barcelona 4 A2
La Salada Buenos Aires 7 C2
La Scala Milan 18 B2
La Storta Rome 26 A1
La Taxonera Barcelona 4 A2
La Victoria Lima 14 B2
La Vista Atlanta 3 B2
Laajalahti Helsinki 11 B1
Laajasalo Helsinki 11 B3
Laaksolahti Helsinki 11 B1
Labagou Nat. Forest Park ⌓ Beijing 4 A2
Lablâba, W. el → Cairo 7 A2
Lachine Montreal 20 B1
Lachine, Canal de Montreal 20 B2
Lad Phrao Bangkok 3 B2
Ladera Heights Los Angeles 16 C2
Ládvi Prague 25 B2
Łady Warsaw 33 C1
Lafontaine, Parc Montreal 20 A2
Lagoa Rio de Janeiro 25 B1
Lagos Lagos 14 B2
Lagos Harbour Lagos 14 B2
Lagos-Ikeja ✈ (LOS) Lagos 14 A1
Lagos Island Lagos 14 B2
Lagos Lagoon Lagos 14 B2
Laguna de B. Manila 17 C2
Lai Chi Wo Hong Kong 12
Laim Munich 21 B2
Lainate Milan 18 A1
Lainz Vienna 32 B1
Lake Buena Vista Orlando 23 B1
Lake Cain Hills Orlando 23 B2
Lakemba Sydney 29 B1
Lakeside Cape Town 8 B1
Lakeside Johannesburg 13 A2
Lakeview Chicago 9 B3
Lakeview New Orleans 21 A2
Lakewood Park Atlanta 3 B2
Lakhtinskiy St. Petersburg 27 B1
Lakhtinskiy Razliv, Oz. St. Petersburg 27 B1
Lakshmanpur Kolkata 14 B1
Laksi Bangkok 3 A2
Lal Qila Delhi 10 B2
Lam Tin Hong Kong 12 B3
Lambert Oslo 23 A3
Lambeth □ London 15 B3
Lambrate Milan 18 B2
Lambro, Parco Milan 18 B2
Lambton Mills Toronto 31 B1
Lamma I. Hong Kong 12 B2
Lancaster Dallas-Fort Worth 10 C5
Landianchang Beijing 4 B1
Landsmeer Amsterdam 2 A2
Landstrasse Vienna 32 A2
Landwehr kanal Berlin 5 B3
Lane Cove Sydney 29 A1
Lane Cove Nat. Park △ Sydney 29 A1
Langa Cape Town 8 A2
Langenzersdorf Vienna 32 A2
Langer See Berlin 5 B4
Langley Washington 33 B1
Langley Park Washington 33 B3
Langwald Munich 21 A1
Lankwitz Berlin 5 B3
L'Annunziatella Rome 26 C2
Lansdowne Cape Town 8 A2
Lansing Toronto 31 A2
Lantau I. Hong Kong 12 B1
Lantau Pk. Hong Kong 12 B1
Lanus Buenos Aires 7 C2
Lapa Rio de Janeiro 25 B1
Laranjeiras Rio de Janeiro 25 B1
Las Warsaw 33 B2
Las Corts Barcelona 4 A1
Las Kabacki Warsaw 33 C2
Las Pinas Manila 17 C1
Las Rejas Santiago 27 B1
Las Vegas Las Vegas 14 A2
Las Vegas McCarran Int. ✈ (LAS) Las Vegas 14 B2
LaSalle Montreal 20 B2
LaSalle Street Station Chicago 9 B3
Lasek Bielański Warsaw 33 B1
Lasek Na Kole Warsaw 33 B1
Latina Madrid 17 B1
Lauderdale Lakes Miami 19 B1
Lauderhill Miami 19 B2
Lauttasaari Helsinki 11 C2
Laval-des-Rapides Montreal 20 A1
Lavīzān Tehran 31 A2
Lavradio Lisbon 16 A2
Lawndale Chicago 9 B2
Lawne L. Orlando 23 A2
Lawrence Heights Toronto 31 A2
Layari Karachi 13 A2
Layari → Karachi 13 A1
Łazienkowski Park Warsaw 33 B2
Lazy Lake Miami 19 B3
Le Blanc-Mesnil Paris 24 A3
Le Bourget Paris 24 A3
Le Chenoi Brussels 6 B2
Le Chesnay Paris 24 B1
Le Christ de Saclay Paris 24 B2
Le Kremlin-Bicêtre Paris 24 B3
Le Mesnil-le-Roi Paris 24 A1
Le Pecq Paris 24 A1
Le Perreux Paris 24 A3

Le Pin Paris 24 A4
Le Plessis-Robinson Paris 24 B2
Le Plessis-Trévise Paris 24 B4
Le Port-Marly Paris 24 A1
Le Pré-St-Gervais Paris 24 A3
Le Raincy Paris 24 A4
Le Vésinet Paris 24 A1
Lea Bridge London 15 A3
Leaside Toronto 31 A2
Leblon Rio de Janeiro 25 B1
Lee London 15 B4
Leganés Madrid 17 C1
Legazpi Madrid 17 B1
Lehtisaari Helsinki 11 B2
Lei Yue Mun Hong Kong 12 B3
Leião Lisbon 16 A1
Leichhardt Sydney 29 B1
Leith Edinburgh 11 B3
Lekki Lagos 14 B2
Lekki Peninsula Lagos 14 B2
Leme Rio de Janeiro 25 B1
Lemmon, L.
Dallas-Fort Worth 10 B5
Lemoyne Montreal 20 B3
Lenino Moscow 19 C2
Leninskiye Gory Moscow 19 B2
Lennox Los Angeles 16 C2
Leonia New York 22 A2
Leopoldau Vienna 32 A2
Leopoldsdorf Vienna 32 B2
Leopoldstadt Vienna 32 A2
Leportovo Moscow 19 B3
Leppävaara Helsinki 11 B1
Les Lilas Paris 24 A3
Les Loges-en-Josas Paris 24 B1
Les Pavillons-sous-Bois
Paris 24 A4
Lésigny Paris 24 B4
Lesnozavodskaya
St. Petersburg 27 B2
Lester B. Pearson Int.,
Toronto ✕ (YYZ) Toronto 31 A1
L'Étang-la-Ville Paris 24 A1
Letňany Prague 25 B3
Letopolis = Ausîm Cairo 7 A1
Levallois-Perret Paris 24 A2
Levent Istanbul 12 B2
Lewisdale Washington 33 B3
Lewisham □ London 15 B3
Lexington Boston 6 A1
Leyton London 15 A3
Leytonstone London 15 A4
L'Haÿ-les-Roses Paris 24 B3
L'Hospitalet de Llobregat
Barcelona 4 A1
Lhotka Prague 25 B2
Liangshui He → Beijing 4 C2
Lianhua Chi Beijing 4 B1
Lianhua He → Beijing 4 B1
Libčice nad Vitavou Prague 25 A2
Libeň Prague 25 B2
Liberdade São Paulo 27 B2
Liberton Edinburgh 11 B3
Liberty I. New York 22 B1
Liberty Ōsaka Museum
Osaka 23 B1
Liberty State Park ⌂
New York 22 B1
Libeznice Prague 25 A2
Libuš Prague 25 B2
Lichiao Guangzhou 11 B2
Lichtenburg Berlin 5 A4
Lichterfelde Berlin 5 B2
Lidingö Stockholm 29 A2
Lieshi Lingyuan Guangzhou 11 B2
Liesing Vienna 32 B1
Liesing → Vienna 32 B2
Ligovo St. Petersburg 27 C1
Lijordet Oslo 23 A2
Likhoborka → Moscow 19 A2
Lilla Värtan Stockholm 29 A3
Lille Værløse Copenhagen 8 A2
Liluah Kolkata 14 B1
Lim Chu Kang Singapore 28 A2
Lima Lima 14 B2
Lima Jorge Chavez Int. ✕
(LIM) Lima 14 B2
Limbiate Milan 18 A1
Limehouse London 15 A3
Limeil-Brévannes Paris 24 B3
Linate, Milano ✕ (LIN)
Milan 18 B2
Linbropark Johannesburg 13 A2
Lincoln Center for
Performing Arts
New York 22 B2
Lincoln Heights Los Angeles 16 B3
Lincoln Memorial
Washington 33 B2
Lincoln Park Chicago 9 B3
Lincoln Park New York 22 B1
Lincoln Park San Francisco 26 B1
Lincoln Park Zoo Chicago 9 B3
Lincolnwood Chicago 9 A2
Linda-a-Pastora Lisbon 16 A1
Linden Johannesburg 13 A2
Lindenberg Berlin 5 A4
Lindøya Oslo 23 A3
Liniers Buenos Aires 7 B1
Linkebeek Brussels 6 B2
Linksfield Johannesburg 13 A2
Linmeyer Johannesburg 13 B2
Linna Helsinki 11 A2
Lintuvaara Helsinki 11 B1
Lion Rock Country
Park ⌂ Hong Kong 12 A3
Lion's Head Cape Town 8 A1
Lioumi Athens 2 B2
Lisboa Lisbon 16 A2
Lisboa ✕ (LIS) Lisbon 16 A2
Lisbon = Lisboa Lisbon 16 A2
Lishui Guangzhou 11 A1
Little B. Sydney 29 B2
Little Calumet → Chicago 9 D3
Little Ferry New York 22 A1
Little Haiti Miami 19 C2
Little Havana Miami 19 D1
Little India Singapore 28 B3
Little Lake Conway Orlando 23 B2
Little Rouge → Toronto 31 A4
Liuhang Shanghai 28 A1
Liurong Temple Guangzhou 11 B2
Live Oak Manor
New Orleans 21 B1
Livry-Gargan Paris 24 A4
Liwan Guangzhou 11 B2
Ljan Oslo 23 A3
Llano de Can Gineu
Barcelona 4 A2
Lo Aranguiz Santiago 27 B2
Lo Boza Santiago 27 B1
Lo Espejo Santiago 27 C1
Lo Hermida Santiago 27 B2
Lo Prado Santiago 27 B1
Lo Sho Shing Hong Kong 12 B2
Lo Wai Hong Kong 12 A2
Loanhead Edinburgh 11 B3
Lobau Vienna 32 A3
Lobos, Pt. San Francisco 26 B1
Locham Munich 21 B1
Lochkov Prague 25 B2
Lockhausen Munich 21 A1
Lodi New York 22 A1
Lodi Estate Delhi 10 B2
Logan Int., Boston ✕
(BOS) Boston 6 A2
Logan Square Chicago 9 B2
Lognes-Émerainville ✕
(XLG) Paris 24 B4
Löhme Berlin 5 A5
Lolokhet Karachi 13 A2
Lomas Chapultepec
Mexico City 18 B1
Lomas de San Angel Inn
Mexico City 18 B1
Lombardy East Johannesburg 13 A2
Lomianki Warsaw 33 A1
Lomus Reforma Mexico City 18 B1
London London 15 B3
London Avenue Canal
New Orleans 21 A2
London City ✕ (LCY)
London 15 A4
London Heathrow ✕
(LHR) London 15 B1
London Zoo London 15 A3
Long B. Sydney 29 B2
Long Branch Toronto 31 B1
Long Ditton London 15 B2
Long Island City New York 22 B2
Longchamp, Hippodrome
de Paris 24 A2
Longhua Pagoda Shanghai 28 B1
Longhua Park Shanghai 28 B1
Longtan Hu → Beijing 4 B2
Longue-Pointe Montreal 20 A2
Longueuil Montreal 20 A3
Loni Delhi 10 A2
Lord's Cricket Ground
London 15 A2
Loreto Milan 18 B2
Los Angeles Los Angeles 16 B3
Los Angeles Int. ✕ (LAX)
Los Angeles 16 C2
Los Angeles Museum of
the Holocaust Los Angeles 16 B2
Los Cerrillos ✕ (ULC)
Santiago 27 B1
Los Nietos Los Angeles 16 C4
Los Olivos Lima 14 A2
Los Remedios △ Mexico City 18 B1
Los Reyes Mexico City 18 B2
Losiny Ostrov △ Moscow 19 A3
Lot Brussels 6 B1
Lotus River Cape Town 8 B2
Lotus Temple Delhi 10 B2
Louis Armstrong New
Orleans Int. ✕ (MSY)
New Orleans 21 B1
Louise, L. Orlando 23 B1
Louisiana Superdome =
Mercedes-Benz
Superdome New Orleans 21 B2
Loures Lisbon 16 A1
Louveciennes Paris 24 A1
Louvre, Musée du Paris 24 A3
Lower B. New York 22 C1
Lower Don Lands Toronto 31 B2
Lower New York B. =
Lower B. New York 22 C1
Lower Peirce Res. Singapore 28 A2
Loyola Univ. Chicago 9 B3
Lu Xun, Tomb of Shanghai 28 B1
Lu Xun Park Shanghai 28 B1
Lübars Berlin 5 A3
Lucy, L. Orlando 23 A2
Ludwigsfeld Munich 21 A1
Luhu Guangzhou 11 B2
Luk Chau = George I.
Hong Kong 12 B2
Lumiar Lisbon 16 A2
Lundtofte Copenhagen 8 A3
Lung Kwu Chau Hong Kong 12 A1
Lung Kwu Tan Hong Kong 12 A1
Lung Mei Hong Kong 12 A3
Luojiang Guangzhou 11 B2
Lustheim Munich 21 A2
Luwan Shanghai 28 B1
Luz, Estádio da Lisbon 16 A1
Luzhniki Sports Centre
Moscow 19 B2
Lyndhurst New York 22 B1
Lynn Woods Res. Boston 6 A2
Lyon, Gare de Paris 24 A3
Lyons Chicago 9 C2
Lysaker Oslo 23 A2
Lysakerselva → Oslo 23 A2
Lysolaje Prague 25 B2
Lyublino Moscow 19 B3

M

Ma Nam Wat Hong Kong 12 A3
Ma On Shan Hong Kong 12 A3
Ma On Shan Country
Park ⌂ Hong Kong 12 A3
Ma Wan Hong Kong 12 A2
Ma Wan Channel
Hong Kong 12 A2
Ma'ale Adumim Jerusalem 13 B2
Ma'ale Ha Khamisha
Jerusalem 13 B1
Ma'ale Mikhmas Jerusalem 13 A2
Maantiekylä Helsinki 11 A3
Maarifa Baghdad 3 B2
Mabato Pt. Manila 17 C2
Mabel, L. Orlando 23 B1
Macacо, Morro do
Rio de Janeiro 25 B2
McCarran Int., Las
Vegas ✕ (LAS) Las Vegas 14 B2
McCook Chicago 9 C2
McGill Univ. Montreal 20 A2
Machelen Brussels 6 A2
Machida Tokyo 30 B1
Maciołki Warsaw 33 B2
McKinley Park Chicago 9 C2
McLean Washington 33 B1
Macopocho → Santiago 27 B1
MacRitchie Res. Singapore 28 A2
Macul Santiago 27 C2
Madhudaha Kolkata 14 B2
Madhyamgram Kolkata 14 A2
Madin Mexico City 18 A1
Madin, L. Mexico City 18 A1
Madinah Al Mansûr
Baghdad 3 B2
Mâdinet Nasr Cairo 7 A2
Madrid Madrid 17 B1
Madrid Barajas ✕ (MAD)
Madrid 17 B2
Madrona Barcelona 4 A1
Maesawa Tokyo 30 A2
Magdalena Lima 14 B2
Magdalena Contreras
Mexico City 18 C1
Magelungen Stockholm 29 B2
Maghreb Baghdad 3 A2
Maginu Tokyo 30 B2
Magliana Rome 26 B1
Magny-les-Hameaux Paris 24 B1
Mahar, L. Miami 19 D1
Maheshtala Kolkata 14 C1
Mahim Mumbai 20 A2
Mahim B. Mumbai 20 A1
Mahipalpur Delhi 10 B1
Mahlsdorf Berlin 5 A4
Mahmoodabad Karachi 13 A2
Mahrauli Delhi 10 B2
Mahul Mumbai 20 A2
Maida Vale London 15 A2
Maidstone Melbourne 18 A1
Maipú Santiago 27 C1
Maisonneuve, Parc
Montreal 20 A2
Maisons-Alfort Paris 24 B3
Maisons-Laffitte Paris 24 A1
Maissoneuve Montreal 20 A2
Maitland Cape Town 8 A1
Makasar Jakarta 12 A2
Makati Manila 17 B2
Mäkiniitty Helsinki 11 A2
Malá Strana Prague 25 B2
Malabar Sydney 29 B2
Malabar Hill Mumbai 20 B1
Malabar Pt. Mumbai 20 B1
Malabon Manila 17 B1
Malacañang Palace Manila 17 B1
Malakoff Paris 24 B2
Mälarhöjaen Stockholm 29 B1
Malate Manila 17 B1
Malaya Neva St. Petersburg 27 B1
Malaya Okhta
St. Petersburg 27 B2
Malchow Berlin 5 A3
Malden Boston 6 A2
Malden London 15 B2
Maleizen Brussels 6 B3
Malešice Prague 25 B3
Malir → Karachi 13 B2
Malleny Mills Edinburgh 11 B2
Malmi Helsinki 11 B2
Malmøya Oslo 23 A3
Målov Copenhagen 8 A1
Malpense, Milano ✕
(MXP) Milan 18 A1
Malton Toronto 31 A1
Malvern Johannesburg 13 B2
Malvern Melbourne 18 B2
Malvern Toronto 31 A3
Mampang Prapatan Jakarta 12 B1
Mampukuji Tokyo 30 B2
Man Budrukh Mumbai 20 A2
Man Khurd Mumbai 20 A2
Manakhat Jerusalem 13 B2
Mandai Singapore 28 A2
Mandaluyong Manila 17 B2
Mandaoli Delhi 10 B2
Mandaqui → São Paulo 27 A2
Mandoli Delhi 10 A2
Mandvi Mumbai 20 B2
Manenberg Cape Town 8 A2
Mang Kung Uk Hong Kong 12 B3
Mang-won Seoul 27 B1
Mangolpuri Delhi 10 A1
Manhattan New York 22 B2
Manhattan Beach
New York 22 C2
Manila Manila 17 B1
Manila Ninoy Aquino
Int. ✕ (MNL) Manila 17 B2
Mankkaa Helsinki 11 B1
Manly Sydney 29 A2
Mann, L. Orlando 23 A2
Mannswörth Vienna 32 B3
Manor Park London 15 A4
Manora Karachi 13 B1
Manora Pt. Karachi 13 B1
Manquehue, Cerro Santiago 27 B2
Mansfield Dallas-Fort Worth 10 C3
Manzanares, Canal de
Madrid 17 C2
Mapo Seoul 27 B1
Mar Vista Los Angeles 16 B2
Maracanã, Estádio
Rio de Janeiro 25 B1
Maraoli Mumbai 20 A2
Marcelin Warsaw 33 B1
Mareil-Marly Paris 24 A1
Margaret I. = Margitsziget
Budapest 7 A2
Margareten Vienna 32 A2
Margitsziget Budapest 7 A2
Maria Vienna 32 A2
Maridalen Oslo 23 A3
Maridalsvatnet Oslo 23 A3
Mariendorf Berlin 5 B3
Marienfelde Berlin 5 B3
Marikina Manila 17 B2
Marikina → Manila 17 B2
Marin City San Francisco 26 A1
Marin Pen. San Francisco 26 A1
Marina Bay Sands
Singapore 28 B3
Marina del Rey Los Angeles 16 C2
Marisco, Ponta do
Rio de Janeiro 25 C1
Markham Chicago 9 D2
Markham Toronto 31 A2
Marki Warsaw 33 B2
Markland Wood Toronto 31 B1
Marly, Forêt de Paris 24 A1
Marly-le-Roi Paris 24 A1
Marne-la-Vallée Paris 24 A4
Marolles-en-Brie Paris 24 B4
Maroubra Sydney 29 B2
Marquette Park Chicago 9 C2
Marrero New Orleans 21 B2
Marrickville Sydney 29 B1
Marsfield Sydney 29 A1
Marsha, L. Orlando 23 B2
Marte, Campo de São Paulo 27 B2
Martesana, Naviglio della
Milan 18 A2
Martin Luther King Nat.
Historic Site ⌂ Atlanta 3 B2
Martinez Buenos Aires 7 A1
Martinkylä Helsinki 11 B2
Martinsried Munich 21 B1
Maruko Tokyo 30 B3
Maryino Moscow 19 B3
Maryland Singapore 28 B2
Marymont Warsaw 33 B1
Marysin Wawerski Warsaw 33 B2
Marzahn Berlin 5 A4
Mascot Sydney 29 B2
Masmo Stockholm 29 B1
Maspeth New York 22 B2
Masr el Gedida Cairo 7 A2
Masr el Qadîma Cairo 7 A2
Massachusetts Inst. of
Tech. Boston 6 A2
Massamá Lisbon 16 A1
Massey → Toronto 31 A3
Massy Paris 24 B2
Mata Jerusalem 13 B1
Matinha Lisbon 16 A2
Matramam Jakarta 12 B2
Matsubara Osaka 23 B2
Mattapan Boston 6 B2
Mátyásföld Budapest 7 A3
Mau Tso Ngam Hong Kong 12 A3
Mauer Vienna 32 B1
Mauripur Karachi 13 A1
Maxhof Munich 21 B1
MAXXI National Museum
of 21st Century Arts
Rome 26 B1
Mayfair Johannesburg 13 B2
Maywood Chicago 9 B1
Maywood Los Angeles 16 C3
Maywood New York 22 A1
Maywood Park Race
Track Chicago 9 B1
Mazagaon Mumbai 20 B2
Meadowbank Park Sydney 29 A1
Meadowlands Sports
Complex New York 22 B1
Měcholupy Prague 25 B3
Měčice Prague 25 A3
Mecidiyeköy Istanbul 12 B2
Medford Boston 6 A2
Mediodia Madrid 17 B2
Meguro Tokyo 30 B3
Meguro → Tokyo 30 B3
Mehrābād ✕ (THR) Tehran 31 A1
Mehram Nagar Delhi 10 B1
Mehrow Berlin 5 A4
Meidling Vienna 32 A2
Méier Rio de Janeiro 25 B1
Meiji Shrine Tokyo 30 A3
Meise Brussels 6 A1
Mejiro Tokyo 30 A3
Melbourne Melbourne 18 A1
Melbourne ✕ (MEL)
Melbourne 18 A1
Melkki Helsinki 11 C2
Mellunkylä Helsinki 11 B3
Mellunmäki Helsinki 11 B3
Melrose Boston 6 A2
Melrose New York 22 B2
Melrose Park Miami 19 B3
Melsbroek Brussels 6 A2
Melville Johannesburg 13 B2
Menteng Jakarta 12 B1
Mérantaise → Paris 24 B1
Mercamadrid Madrid 17 B2
Merced, L. San Francisco 26 B2
Mercedes-Benz
Superdome New Orleans 21 B2
Meredale Johannesburg 13 B1
Merlimau, Pulau Singapore 28 B2
Merri Cr. → Melbourne 18 A1
Merrionette Park Chicago 9 C2
Merton □ London 15 B2
Mesgarābād Tehran 31 B3
Messe Vienna 32 A2
Metairie New Orleans 21 A2
Metanópoli Milan 18 B2
MetLife Stadium New York 22 B1
Metro Toronto Zoo Toronto 31 A3
Metropolitan Museum of
Art New York 22 B2
Meudon Paris 24 B2
Mevaseret Zion Jerusalem 13 B1
Mevo Beitar Jerusalem 13 B1
México, Ciudad de
Mexico City 18 B2
Mexico City Int. ✕ (MEX)
Mexico City 18 B2
Meyersdal Johannesburg 13 B2
Mezzate Milan 18 B2
Miadong Seoul 27 B2
Miami Miami 19 D2
Miami → Miami 19 D1
Miami Beach Miami 19 D3
Miami Gardens Miami 19 C1
Miami Int. ✕ (MIA) Miami 19 D1
Miami Lakes Miami 19 C1
Miami Shores Miami 19 C2
Miami Springs Miami 19 D1
Miasto Warsaw 33 B2
Michałowice Warsaw 33 B1
Michle Prague 25 B2
Mid-City Los Angeles 16 B2
Mid City New Orleans 21 B2
Middle Harbour Sydney 29 A2
Middle Hd. Sydney 29 A2
Middle Park Melbourne 18 B1
Middle Village New York 22 B2
Middlesex Fells
Reservation Boston 6 A2
Midland Beach New York 22 C1
Midlothian Chicago 9 D2
Midwood New York 22 C2
Miedzeszyn Warsaw 33 B3
Międzylesie Warsaw 33 B3
Miessaari Helsinki 11 C1
Miguel Hidalgo Mexico City 18 B1
Milan = Milano Milan 18 B1
Milanese, Parco
Regionale ⌂ Milan 18 A1
Milano Milan 18 B1
Milano Due Milan 18 B2
Milano Linate ✕ (LIN)
Milan 18 B2
Milano Malpense ✕
(MXP) Milan 18 A1
Milano San Felice Milan 18 B2
Milbertshofen Munich 21 A2
Mill Hill London 15 A2
Millennium Dome London 15 A4
Miller Meadow Chicago 9 B2
Millerhill Edinburgh 11 B3
Milnerton Cape Town 8 A1
Milon-la-Chapelle Paris 24 B1
Milton Boston 6 B2
Milton Bridge Edinburgh 11 B2
Mimico Toronto 31 B2
Mimico Creek → Toronto 31 B1
Minami Osaka 23 A2
Minamitsunashima Tokyo 30 B2
Minato Osaka 23 B1
Minato Tokyo 30 B3
Minshât el Bekkari Cairo 7 A1
Miraflores Lima 14 B2
Miramar Miami 19 C1
Misericordia, Sa. da
Rio de Janeiro 25 B1
Mission San Francisco 26 B2
Mississauga Toronto 31 B1
Mitaka Tokyo 30 A2
Mitcham London 15 B2
Mitcham Common London 15 B3
Mitchell Museum of the
American Indian Chicago 9 A2
Mitchell's Plain Cape Town 8 B2
Mitte Berlin 5 A3
Mittel Isarkanal → Munich 21 A3
Mixcoac Mexico City 18 B1
Miyakojima Osaka 23 A2
Mizonokuchi Tokyo 30 B2
Mizue Tokyo 30 A4
Mlocinski, Park Warsaw 33 B1
Mlociny Warsaw 33 B1
Mnevniki Moscow 19 B1
Moba Lagos 14 B2
Moczydło Warsaw 33 C2
Modderfontein Johannesburg 13 A2
Modřany Prague 25 B2
Mogyoród Budapest 7 A3
Moinho Velho, Cor. →
São Paulo 27 B2
Mok Seoul 27 B1
Mokotów Warsaw 33 B2
Molenbeek-St-Jean Brussels 6 A1
Molino de Rosas
Mexico City 18 B1
Mollem Brussels 6 A1
Mollins de Rey Barcelona 4 A1
Mondeor Johannesburg 13 B2
Moneda, Palacio de la
Santiago 27 B2
Monerò Rio de Janeiro 25 A1
Mong Kok Hong Kong 12 B3
Monnickendam Amsterdam 2 A3
Monrovia Los Angeles 16 B4
Monsanto Lisbon 16 A1
Monsanto, Parque
Florestal de Lisbon 16 A1
Mont-Royal Montreal 20 A2
Mont-Royal, Parc Montreal 20 A2
Montcada i Reixac Barcelona 4 A2
Monte Chingolo Buenos Aires 7 C2
Montebello Los Angeles 16 B4
Montemor Lisbon 16 A1
Monterey Hills Los Angeles 16 B3
Monterey Park Los Angeles 16 B4
Montespaccato Rome 26 B1
Montesson Paris 24 A1
Monteverde Nuovo Rome 26 B1
Montfermeil Paris 24 A4
Montigny-le-Bretonneux
Paris 24 B1
Montjay-la-Tour Paris 24 A4
Montjuïc Barcelona 4 A2
Montparnasse, Gare Paris 24 A2
Montréal Montreal 20 A2
Montréal, Î. de Montreal 20 A2
Montréal, Univ. de Montreal 20 B2
Montréal Est Montreal 20 A2
Montréal Nord Montreal 20 A2
Montréal Ouest Montreal 20 B1
Montréal Trudeau Int. ✕
(YUL) Montreal 20 B1
Montreuil Paris 24 A3
Montrouge Paris 24 B2
Montserrat Buenos Aires 7 B2
Monza Milan 18 A2
Monzoro Milan 18 B1
Moóca São Paulo 27 B2
Moonachie New York 22 B1
Moonee Ponds Melbourne 18 A1
Moonee Valley
Racecourse Melbourne 18 A1
Moosach Munich 21 A2
Mora Mumbai 20 B2
Moratalaz Madrid 17 B2
Mörby Stockholm 29 A2
Morden London 15 B2
Morée → Paris 24 A3
Morgan Park Chicago 9 C3
Moriguchi Osaka 23 A2
Morivione Milan 18 B2
Morningside Edinburgh 11 B2
Morningside Johannesburg 13 A2
Morningside Park Orlando 23 B2
Morningside Park Toronto 31 A3
Morro Solar, Cerro Lima 14 C2
Mortlake London 15 B2
Mortlake Sydney 29 B1
Morton Grove Chicago 9 A2
Morumbi São Paulo 27 B1
Moscavide Lisbon 16 A2
Moschato Athens 2 B2
Moscow = Moskva Moscow 19 B2
Moscow Sheremetyevo
Int. ✕ (SVO) Moscow 19 A1
Moskva Moscow 19 B2
Moskvoretskiy Moscow 19 B2
Mosman Sydney 29 B2
Moti Bagh Delhi 10 B1
Motol Prague 25 B2
Motsa Jerusalem 13 B2
Motsa Illit Jerusalem 13 B1
Motspur Park London 15 B2
Mottingham London 15 B4
Mount Dennis Toronto 31 A2
Mount Greenwood Chicago 9 C2
Mount Hood Memorial
Park ⌂ Boston 6 A2
Mount Olympus Los Angeles 16 B2
Mount Rainier Washington 33 B3
Mount Vernon New York 22 A3
Mountain Creek L.
Dallas-Fort Worth 10 B4
Mountain Creek Lake
Park Dallas-Fort Worth 10 B4
Müggelberge Berlin 5 B4
Müggelheim Berlin 5 B5
Muggiò Milan 18 A2
Mühleiten Vienna 32 A3
Mühlenfliess → Berlin 5 A5
Mui Wo Hong Kong 12 B1
Muiden Amsterdam 2 A3
Muizenberg Cape Town 8 B1
Mujahidpur Delhi 10 B2
Mukandpur Delhi 10 A2
Mukhmas Jerusalem 13 A2
Muko → Osaka 23 A1
Mukojima Tokyo 30 A3
Mulbarton Johannesburg 13 B2
Mumbai Mumbai 20 B2
Mumbai Chhatrapati
Shivaji Int. ✕ (BOM)
Mumbai 20 A2
Mumbai Harbour Mumbai 20 B2
Munch-museum Oslo 23 A3
Münchehofe Berlin 5 B5
München Munich 21 B2
München Franz Josef
Strauss ✕ (MUC) Munich 21 A2
Munich = München
Munich 21 B2
Munkkiniemi Helsinki 11 B2
Munro Buenos Aires 7 B1
Muntinlupa Manila 17 C2
Murai Res. Singapore 28 A2
Muranów Warsaw 33 B1
Murino St. Petersburg 27 A2
Murrayfield Edinburgh 11 B2
Murtala Mohammed
Int. ✕ (LOS) Lagos 14 A1
Musashino Tokyo 30 A2
Museumsinsel Berlin 5 A3
Mushin Lagos 14 A2
Musocco Milan 18 B1
Mustansiriya Baghdad 3 A2
Musturud Cairo 7 A2
Muswell Hill London 15 A3
Mutanabi Baghdad 3 B2
Muthana Baghdad 3 B2
Myllypuro Helsinki 11 B3
Mystic → Boston 6 A2

N

N.S.C.B. Int. ✕ (CCU)
Kolkata 14 B2
Naberezhnaya Tower
Moscow 19 B2
Nacka Stockholm 29 B3
Nærsnes Oslo 23 B1
Nagatsuta Tokyo 30 B2
Nagytétény Budapest 7 B1
Nahalin Jerusalem 13 B1
Najafgarh Drain → Delhi 10 B1
Nakahara Tokyo 30 B2
Nakano Tokyo 30 A2
Namsan Park Seoul 27 B1
Namyeong Seoul 27 B1
Nanbiancun Guangzhou 11 B1
Nanchang He → Beijing 4 B1
Nandang Guangzhou 11 B2
Nangal Dewat Delhi 10 B1
Naniwa Osaka 23 B1
Nanole Mumbai 20 A2
Nanpu Bridge Shanghai 28 B2
Nanshi Shanghai 28 B1
Nanterre Paris 24 A2
Napier Mole Karachi 13 B1
Naraina Delhi 10 B1
Nariman Pt. Mumbai 20 B1
Nārmak Tehran 31 A2
Naruo Osaka 23 A1
Näsby Stockholm 29 A2
Näsbypark Stockholm 29 A2
National Arboretum
Washington 33 B2
National Atomic Testing
Museum Las Vegas 14 B2
National Maritime
Museum London 15 B3
National University
(N.U.S.) Singapore 28 B2
National Zoological Park
Washington 33 B2
Nationals Park Washington 33 B2
Nativity, Basilica of
Jerusalem 13 B2
Natolin Warsaw 33 C2
Naucalpan de Juárez
Mexico City 18 B1
Naupada Mumbai 20 A2
Navi Mumbai Mumbai 20 A2
Naviglio di Pavia Milan 18 B1
Naviglio Grande Milan 18 B1
Navotas Manila 17 B1
Navy Pier Chicago 9 B3
Nazal Hikmat Beg Baghdad 3 A2
Nazimabad Karachi 13 A2
Nazlet el Simmân Cairo 7 B1
Nea Alexandria Athens 2 B2
Nea Ionia Athens 2 A2
Nea Liosia Athens 2 A2
Nea Smirni Athens 2 B2
Neapoli Athens 2 B2
Near North Chicago 9 B3
Nebušice Prague 25 B1
Nederhorst Amsterdam 2 B3
Nedlitz Berlin 5 B1
Nee Soon Singapore 28 A2
Needham Boston 6 B1
Needham Heights Boston 6 B1
Nellis Air Force Base ✕
(LSV) Las Vegas 14 A2
N'emātābād Tehran 31 B2
Nerima Tokyo 30 A3
Nesodden Oslo 23 B3
Nesoddtangen Oslo 23 A3
Nesøya Oslo 23 A2
Netaji Subhash Chandra
Bose Int. ✕ (CCU) Kolkata 14 B2
Neu Aubing Munich 21 B1
Neu Buch Berlin 5 A4
Neu Buchhorst Berlin 5 B5
Neu Fahrland Berlin 5 B1
Neu Lindenberg Berlin 5 A4
Neubiberg Munich 21 B3
Neuenhagen Berlin 5 A4
Neuessling Vienna 32 A3
Neuhausen Munich 21 B2
Neuherberg Munich 21 A2
Neuhönow Berlin 5 A5
Neuilly-Plaisance Paris 24 A4
Neuilly-sur-Marne Paris 24 A4
Neuilly-sur-Seine Paris 24 A2
Neukagran Vienna 32 A2
Neukettenhof Vienna 32 B2
Neukölln Berlin 5 B3
Neuperlach Munich 21 B2
Neuried Munich 21 B1
Neustift am Walde Vienna 32 A1
Neusüssenbrunn Vienna 32 A2
Neuwaldegg Vienna 32 A1
Neve Ya'akov Jerusalem 13 A2
Neves Rio de Janeiro 25 B2
New Baghdād Baghdad 3 B2
New Barakpur Kolkata 14 A2
New Brighton New York 22 C1
New Canada Johannesburg 13 B1
New Canada Dam
Johannesburg 13 B1
New Cross London 15 B3
New Delhi Delhi 10 B2
New Dorp New York 22 C1
New Dorp Beach New York 22 C1
New Malden London 15 B2
New Milford New York 22 A1
New Mumbai = Navi
Mumbai Mumbai 20 A2
New Orleans New Orleans 21 B2
New Orleans Int. ✕ (MSY)
New Orleans 21 B1
New River → Miami 19 B3
New Territories Hong Kong 12 A2
New Toronto Toronto 31 B1
New Utrecht New York 22 C2
New York New York 22 B2
New York La Guardia ✕
(LGA) New York 22 B2
Newark B. New York 22 B1
Newbattle Edinburgh 11 B3
Newbury Park London 15 A4
Newcraighall Edinburgh 11 B3
Newham □ London 15 A4
Newhaven Edinburgh 11 B2
Newington Edinburgh 11 B2
Newlands Johannesburg 13 B1
Newport Melbourne 18 B1
Newton Boston 6 B1
Newtonbrook Toronto 31 A2
Newtongrange Edinburgh 11 B3
Newtonville Boston 6 A1
Newtown Sydney 29 B2
Ngau Chi Wan Hong Kong 12 B3
Ngau Tau Kok Hong Kong 12 B3
Ngong Ping Hong Kong 12 B1
Ngong Shuen Chau =
Stonecutters I. Hong Kong 12 B2
Ngua Kok Wan Hong Kong 12 A2
Nhava Sheva Mumbai 20 B2
Niāvarān Tehran 31 A2
Nibra Kolkata 14 B1
Nidāl Baghdad 3 B2
Niddrie Edinburgh 11 B3
Niddrie Melbourne 18 A1
Nieder Neuendorf Berlin 5 A2
Niederschöneweide Berlin 5 B3
Niederschönhausen Berlin 5 A3
Niemeyer Rio de Janeiro 25 B1
Nieuwendam Amsterdam 2 A2
Nihonbashi Tokyo 30 A3
Niipperi Helsinki 11 B1
Nikea Athens 2 B1
Nikolassee Berlin 5 B2
Nikolskiy Moscow 19 B1
Niles Chicago 9 A2
Nimta Kolkata 14 A2
Ninoy Aquino Int. ✕
(MNL) Manila 17 B2
Nippa Tokyo 30 B2
Nippori Tokyo 30 A3
Nishi Osaka 23 A1
Nishinari Osaka 23 B1
Nishinomiya Osaka 23 A1
Nishiyodogawa Osaka 23 A1
Niterói Rio de Janeiro 25 B2
Nockeby Stockholm 29 B1
Noel Park London 15 A3
Nogatino Moscow 19 B3
Nogent-sur-Marne Paris 24 A3
Noida Delhi 10 B2
Noiseau Paris 24 B4
Noisiel Paris 24 A4
Noisy-le-Grand Paris 24 A4
Noisy-le-Roi Paris 24 A1
Noisy-le-Sec Paris 24 A3
Nokkala Helsinki 11 C1
Nomentano Rome 26 B2
Nonakashinden Tokyo 30 A2
Nongminyundong
Jiangxisuo Guangzhou 11 B2
Nonhyeon Seoul 27 B2
Nonthaburi Bangkok 3 A1
Noordgesig Johannesburg 13 B1
Noordzeekanaal Amsterdam 2 A1
Nord, Gare du Paris 24 A3
Nordmarka Oslo 23 A3
Nordrand-Siedlung Vienna 32 A2
Nordstrand Oslo 23 A3
Norland Miami 19 C2
Norridge Chicago 9 B2
Norrmalm Stockholm 29 A2
North Arlington New York 22 B1
North Atlanta Atlanta 3 A3
North Bay Village Miami 19 C3
North Bergen New York 22 B1
North Cheam London 15 B2
North Cray London 15 B4
North Decatur Atlanta 3 B3
North Druid Hills Atlanta 3 B3
North Esk → Edinburgh 11 B2
North Gyle Edinburgh 11 B2
North Hackensack
New York 22 A1
North Harbor Manila 17 B1
North Hd. Sydney 29 A2
North Hollywood
Los Angeles 16 B2
North L. Dallas-Fort Worth 10 A4
North Lake Park
Dallas-Fort Worth 10 A4
North Las Vegas Las Vegas 14 A1
North Las Vegas ✕ (VGT)
Las Vegas 14 A1
North Lexington Boston 6 A1
North Miami Miami 19 C2
North Miami Beach Miami 19 C2
North Nazimabad Karachi 13 A2
North Perry ✕ (HWO)
Miami 19 B2
North Point Hong Kong 12 B3
North Queensferry
Edinburgh 11 A1
North Quincy Boston 6 B2
North Res. Boston 6 A2
North Richland Hills
Dallas-Fort Worth 10 A2
North Riverside Chicago 9 B2
North Saugus Boston 6 A2
North Shore Channel →
Chicago 9 B2
North Station Boston 6 A2
North Sydney Sydney 29 B2
North Woolwich London 15 A4
North York Toronto 31 A2
Northbridge Sydney 29 A2
Northbridge Park Sydney 29 A2
Northbrook Chicago 9 A2
Northcliff Johannesburg 13 A1
Northcote Melbourne 18 A2
Northeastern Univ. Boston 6 A2
Northfield Chicago 9 A2
Northmount Toronto 31 A2
Northolt London 15 A1
Northumberland Heath
London 15 B5
Northwestern Univ. Chicago 9 A2
Northwood London 15 A1
Northwood Park Toronto 31 A1
Norwood Johannesburg 13 A2
Norwood Park Chicago 9 B2
Noryangjin Seoul 27 B1
Nossa Senhora do Ó
São Paulo 27 B1
Nossegem Brussels 6 A3
Notre-Dame Paris 24 A3
Notre-Dame, Basilique
Montreal 20 B2
Notre-Dame, Bois Paris 24 B4
Notre-Dame-de-Grace
Montreal 20 B2
Notting Hill London 15 A2
Nova Milanese Milan 18 A2
Novate Milanese Milan 18 A1
Novaya Derevnya
St. Petersburg 27 A1
Nové Město Prague 25 B2
Novoaleksandrovskoye
St. Petersburg 27 B2
Novodevichy Convent
Moscow 19 B2
Novogireyevo Moscow 19 B3
Novosaratovka
St. Petersburg 27 B3
Nowe-Babice Warsaw 33 B1
Nöykkiö Helsinki 11 B1
Nueva Atzacoalco
Mexico City 18 B2
Nueva Pompeya Buenos Aires 7 C2
Nueva Tenochtitlán
Mexico City 18 B2
Nuijala Helsinki 11 B1
Numabukuro Tokyo 30 A2
Nuñez Buenos Aires 7 B2
Nunhead London 15 B3
Ñuñoa Santiago 27 B2
Nusle Prague 25 B2
Nussdorf Vienna 32 A2
Nyanga Cape Town 8 A2
Nymphenburg Munich 21 B2
Nymphenburg, Schloss
Munich 21 B2

O

Oak Forest Chicago 9 D2
Oak Grove Atlanta 3 A3
Oak Hill Boston 6 B1
Oak Lawn Chicago 9 C2
Oak Park Chicago 9 B2
Oak View Washington 33 A3
Oakdale Atlanta 3 A2
Oakland San Francisco 26 B3
Oakland Park Miami 19 A3
Oaklawn Washington 33 C3
Oakleigh Melbourne 18 B2
Oakwood Beach New York 22 C1
Oatley Sydney 29 B1
Obalende Lagos 14 B2
Oba's Palace Lagos 14 B2
Oberföhring Munich 21 B2
Oberhaching Munich 21 B2
Oberlaa Vienna 32 B2
Oberlisse Vienna 32 A2
Obermenzing Munich 21 A1
Obermoos Schwaige
Munich 21 A1
Oberschleissheim Munich 21 A2
Oberschöneweide Berlin 5 B4
Observatory Johannesburg 13 B2
Óbuda Budapest 7 A2
Obukhovo St. Petersburg 27 B2
Obvodnyy Kanal
St. Petersburg 27 B1
Ocean Park Hong Kong 12 B3
Ochota Warsaw 33 B1
Ocoee Orlando 23 A1
Odaiba Tokyo 30 B3
Ōdana Tokyo 30 B2
Ōden-Stockach Munich 21 B3
Odilampi Helsinki 11 B1
Odivelas Lisbon 16 A1
Odolany Warsaw 33 B1
Oeiras Lisbon 16 A1
Ofin Lagos 14 A3
Ogawa Tokyo 30 A1
Ogden Park Chicago 9 C2
Ogikubo Tokyo 30 A2
Ogilvie Transportation
Center Chicago 9 B3
Ogogoro Lagos 14 B2
Ogoyo Lagos 14 B2
Ogudu Lagos 14 A2
O'Higgins, Parque Santiago 27 B2
Ōimachi Tokyo 30 B3
Ojota Lagos 14 A2
Ojus Miami 19 C3
Oke-Ira Lagos 14 B2
Okęcie Warsaw 33 B1
Okęcie, Warszawa ✕
(WAW) Warsaw 33 B1
Okeogbe Lagos 14 B2
Okhla Delhi 10 B2
Okhta → St. Petersburg 27 B2
Okkervil → St. Petersburg 27 B2
Okrzeszyn Warsaw 33 C2
Oksval Oslo 23 A3
Oktyabrskiy Moscow 19 B2
Ōkubo Tokyo 30 A3
Ōkura Tokyo 30 B1
Olari Helsinki 11 B1
Olaria Rio de Janeiro 25 B1
Old Admiralty St. Petersburg 27 B1
Old City Jerusalem 13 B2
Old City Shanghai 28 B1
Old Ford Fort Worth Toronto 31 B2
Old Harbor Boston 6 B2
Old Town = Stare Miasto
Warsaw 33 B2
Old Town Chicago 9 B3
Old Town Hall = Altes
Rathaus Munich 21 B2
Oleta River State Rec.
Area Miami 19 C3
Olgino St. Petersburg 27 B1
Olimpico, Estadio
Mexico City 18 C1
Olivais Lisbon 16 A2
Olivar de los Padres
Mexico City 18 B1
Olivar del Conde
Mexico City 18 B1
Olives, Mt. of Jerusalem 13 B2
Olivia, L. Orlando 23 A1
Olivos Buenos Aires 7 B2
Olona → Milan 18 B1
Olympia, L. Orlando 23 A1
Olympic Green Beijing 4 B2
Olympic Stadium =
Turner Field Atlanta 3 B2
Olympic Stadium Beijing 4 B2
Olympic Stadium Helsinki 11 B2
Olympique, Stade Montreal 20 A2
Ōmori Tokyo 30 B3
One World Trade Center
New York 22 e1
Onisigun Lagos 14 A2
Ontario Science Centre
Toronto 31 A2
Ōokayama Tokyo 30 B3
Oostzaan Tuindorp
Amsterdam 2 A2
Opa-Locka Miami 19 C1
Opa-Locka ✕ (OPF) Miami 19 C1
Opacz Warsaw 33 B1
Opera House Sydney 29 B2
Ophirton Johannesburg 13 B2
Oppegård Oslo 23 B3
Oppem Brussels 6 A1
Oppsal Oslo 23 A4
Ora Jerusalem 13 B1
Oradell New York 22 A1
Oradell Res. New York 22 A1
Orangi Karachi 13 A2
Ordrup Copenhagen 8 A3
Ořech Prague 25 B1
Oregun Lagos 14 A2
Ørestad Copenhagen 8 B3
Orient Heights Boston 6 A3
Oriental Pearl Tower
Shanghai 28 B2
Orland Park Chicago 9 D2
Orlando Orlando 23 A2
Orlando Dam Johannesburg 13 B1
Orlando East Johannesburg 13 B1
Orlando Executive ✕
(ORL) Orlando 23 A2
Orlando Int. ✕ (MCO)
Orlando 23 B3
Orlovista Orlando 23 A2
Orly Paris 24 B3
Orly, Paris ✕ (ORY) Paris 24 B3
Ormesson-sur-Marne Paris 24 B4
Ormond Melbourne 18 B2
Ormøya Oslo 23 A3
Orpington London 15 B4
Ortaköy Istanbul 12 B2
Ortica Milan 18 B2
Oruba Lagos 14 A2
Ōsaka Osaka 23 B2
Ōsaka Castle Osaka 23 A2
Ōsaka Harbour Osaka 23 A1
Ōsaka Itami Int. ✕ (ITM)
Osaka 23 A1
Ōsaka Kansai Int. ✕ (KIX)
Osaka 23 B2
Ōsaki Tokyo 30 B3
Osasco São Paulo 27 B1
Osdorf Berlin 5 B3
Osdorp Amsterdam 2 A1
Oshodi Lagos 14 A2
Oslo Oslo 23 A3
Oslo ✕ (OSL) Oslo 23 A4
Ōsone Tokyo 30 B2
Osorun Lagos 14 A2
Ospiate Milan 18 A1
Ostankino Moscow 19 B2
Osterley London 15 B1
Osterley Park London 15 B1
Östermalm Stockholm 29 A2
Österskär Stockholm 29 A3
Ostia Malpasso Rome 26 C1
Ostiense Rome 26 B1
Østmarkkapellet Oslo 23 A4
Østøya Oslo 23 A2
Ōta Tokyo 30 B3
Otaniemi Helsinki 11 B1
Otsuka Tokyo 30 A3
Ottakring Vienna 32 A1
Ottávia Rome 26 B1
Ottery Cape Town 8 B2
Ottobrunn Munich 21 B3
Ouderkerk Amsterdam 2 B2
Oulunkylä Helsinki 11 B2
Ourcq, Canal de l' Paris 24 A3
Outer Mission San Francisco 26 B2
Outremont Montreal 20 A2
Overijse Brussels 6 B3
Oworonsoki Lagos 14 A2
Oxgangs Edinburgh 11 B2
Oxon Hill Washington 33 C3
Oyodo Osaka 23 A1
Oyster Rock Mumbai 20 B1
Oyster Rock Karachi 13 B2
Ozoir-la-Ferrière Paris 24 B4
Ozone Park New York 22 B2

P

Pacific Heights *San Francisco* 26 B2
Pacific Manor *San Francisco* 26 C2
Pacific Palisades *Los Angeles* 16 B1
Pacifica *San Francisco* 26 C2
Paco *Manila* 17 B1
Paco de Arcos *Lisbon* 16 A1
Paddington *London* 15 A2
Paddington *Sydney* 29 B2
Paderno *Milan* 18 A1
Pagewood *Sydney* 29 B2
Pagote *Mumbai* 20 B2
Pai, I. do *Rio de Janeiro* 25 B2
Pak Kok *Hong Kong* 12 B2
Pak Kong *Hong Kong* 12 A3
Pak Tam *Hong Kong* 12 A3
Pakila *Helsinki* 11 B2
Palacio Real *Madrid* 17 B1
Palaiseau *Paris* 24 B2
Palazzolo *Milan* 18 A1
Paleo Faliro *Athens* 2 B2
Palermo *Buenos Aires* 7 B2
Palhais *Lisbon* 16 B2
Palisades Park *New York* 22 A1
Palm Jumeirah, The *Dubai* 9 B1
Palms *Los Angeles* 16 B2
Paloheinä *Helsinki* 11 B2
Palomeras *Madrid* 17 B2
Palos Heights *Chicago* 9 D2
Palos Hills *Chicago* 9 C2
Palos Park *Chicago* 9 C1
Palpara *Kolkata* 14 B2
Panchur *Kolkata* 14 B1
Pandacan *Manila* 17 B2
Pandan, Selat *Singapore* 28 B2
Pandan Res. *Singapore* 28 B2
Pangrati *Athens* 2 B2
Pangsua, Sungei → *Singapore* 28 A2
Panihati *Kolkata* 14 A2
Panjang, Bukit *Singapore* 28 A2
Panke → *Berlin* 5 A3
Pankow *Berlin* 5 A3
Pantego *Dallas-Fort Worth* 10 B3
Pantheon *Rome* 26 B1
Panthersville *Atlanta* 3 B3
Pantin *Paris* 24 A3
Pantitlán *Mexico City* 18 B2
Panyu *Guangzhou* 11 B2
Papiol *Barcelona* 4 A1
Paradise *Las Vegas* 14 B2
Paramount Studios *Los Angeles* 16 B3
Paramus *New York* 22 A1
Paranaque *Manila* 17 B1
Paray-Vieille-Poste *Paris* 24 B3
Parc des Princes *Paris* 24 A2
Pardisān Nature Park *Tehran* 31 A2
Parel *Mumbai* 20 B1
Pari *São Paulo* 27 B2
Parioli *Rome* 26 B1
Paris *Paris* 24 A3
Paris Orly ✕ (ORY) *Paris* 24 B3
Parje *Mumbai* 20 B2
Pārk-e Āzādegān *Tehran* 31 B2
Pārk-e Mellat *Tehran* 31 A2
Park Ridge *Chicago* 9 A1
Park Royal *London* 15 A2
Parkchester *New York* 22 B2
Parkdale *Toronto* 31 B2
Parkhurst *Johannesburg* 13 A2
Parklawn *Washington* 33 B2
Parkmore *Johannesburg* 13 A2
Parkside *San Francisco* 26 B2
Parktown *Johannesburg* 13 B2
Parkview *Johannesburg* 13 A2
Parkville *New York* 22 C2
Parkwood *Cape Town* 8 B1
Parkwood *Johannesburg* 13 A2
Parow *Cape Town* 8 A2
Parque Chacabuco *Buenos Aires* 7 B2
Parque Patricios *Buenos Aires* 7 B2
Parramatta → *Sydney* 29 A1
Paşabahçe *Istanbul* 12 B2
Pasadena *Los Angeles* 16 B4
Pasar Minggu *Jakarta* 12 B1
Pasay *Manila* 17 B1
Pascoe Vale *Melbourne* 18 A1
Pasig *Manila* 17 B2
Pasig → *Manila* 17 B2
Pasila *Helsinki* 11 B2
Pasing *Munich* 21 B1
Pasir Panjang *Singapore* 28 B2
Pasir Ris *Singapore* 28 A3
Passaic *New York* 22 A1
Passaic → *New York* 22 B1
Passirana *Milan* 18 A1
Patel Nagar *Delhi* 10 B1
Pateros *Manila* 17 B2
Pathumwan *Bangkok* 3 B2
Patipukur *Kolkata* 14 B2
Patisia *Athens* 2 A2
Paulo E. Virginia, Gruta *Rio de Janeiro* 25 B1
Paulshof *Berlin* 5 A5
Paya Lebar *Singapore* 28 A3
Peakhurst *Sydney* 29 B1
Peania *Athens* 2 B3
Pearson Int. Toronto ✕ (YYZ) *Toronto* 31 A1
Peckham *London* 15 B3
Pederstrup *Copenhagen* 8 A2
Pedralbes *Barcelona* 4 A1
Pedregal de San Angel, Jardines del *Mexico City* 18 C1
Peip'ing = Beijing *Beijing* 4 B1
Peking = Beijing *Beijing* 4 B1
Pelcowizna *Warsaw* 33 B2
Pembroke Park *Miami* 19 C2
Pembroke Pines *Miami* 19 B1
Peñalolén *Santiago* 27 B2
Peng Chau *Hong Kong* 12 B2
Peng Siang → *Singapore* 28 A2
Penge *London* 15 B3
Penha *Rio de Janeiro* 25 A1
Penicuik *Edinburgh* 11 B2
Penjaringan *Jakarta* 12 A1
Pentagon *Washington* 33 B2
Penzing *Vienna* 32 A1
People's Park *Shanghai* 28 B1
People's Square *Shanghai* 28 B1
Perales del Rio *Madrid* 17 C2
Perchtoldsdorf *Vienna* 32 B1
Perdizes *São Paulo* 27 B2
Peristeri *Athens* 2 A2
Perivale *London* 15 A2
Perk *Brussels* 6 A2
Perlach *Munich* 21 B2
Perlacher Forst *Munich* 21 B2
Pero *Milan* 18 A1
Peropok, Bukit *Singapore* 28 B2
Perovo *Moscow* 19 B3
Pertusella *Milan* 18 A1
Pesagot *Jerusalem* 13 A2
Pesanggrahag, Kali → *Jakarta* 12 B1
Peschiera Borromeo *Milan* 18 B2
Pesek, Pulau *Singapore* 28 B2
Pest *Budapest* 7 B2
Pesterzsébet *Budapest* 7 B2
Pesthidegkút *Budapest* 7 A1
Pestimre *Budapest* 7 B3
Pestlőrinc *Budapest* 7 B3
Pestújhely *Budapest* 7 A2
Petas *Helsinki* 11 B2
Petrogradskaya Storona *St. Petersburg* 27 B2
Petroupoli *Athens* 2 A2
Petrovice *Prague* 25 B3
Petrovskiy Park *Moscow* 19 B2
Petrovsko-Razumovskoye *Moscow* 19 B2
Petrovsky Stadium *St. Petersburg* 27 B1
Pettycur *Edinburgh* 11 A2
Peutie *Brussels* 6 A2
Pfaueninsel *Berlin* 5 B1
Phaya Thai *Bangkok* 3 B2
Phihai *Karachi* 13 A2
Phillip B. *Sydney* 29 B2
Phoenix *Chicago* 9 D3
Phra Khanong *Bangkok* 3 B2
Phra Nakhon *Bangkok* 3 B2
Phra Pradaeng *Bangkok* 3 C2
Picnic B. *Hong Kong* 12 B2
Pico Rivera *Los Angeles* 16 C4
Piedade *Lisbon* 16 A1
Piedade *Rio de Janeiro* 25 B1
Piedade, Cova da *Lisbon* 16 A2
Piedmont Park *Atlanta* 3 B2
Pierre Elliott Trudeau Int. ✕ (YUL) *Montreal* 20 B1
Pietralata *Rome* 26 B2
Pihlajamäki *Helsinki* 11 B2
Pihlajasaari *Helsinki* 11 C2
Pilares *Rio de Janeiro* 25 B1
Pilton *Edinburgh* 11 B2
Pine Castle *Orlando* 23 B2
Pine Grove *Toronto* 31 A1
Pine Hills *Orlando* 23 A2
Pine Island *Miami* 19 B1
Pinecrest *Miami* 19 D1
Pinewood Park *Miami* 19 C2
Pingzhou *Guangzhou* 11 B2
Pinheiros → *São Paulo* 27 B1
Pinjrapur *Karachi* 13 A2
Pinner *London* 15 A1
Pinner Green *London* 15 A1
Pioltello *Milan* 18 A2
Piræus = Pireas *Athens* 2 B1
Piraiévs = Pireas *Athens* 2 B1
Pirajuçara → *São Paulo* 27 B1
Pireas *Athens* 2 B1
Pirinççi *Istanbul* 12 B1
Pirituba *São Paulo* 27 A1
Pirkkola *Helsinki* 11 B2
Pisgat O'mer *Jerusalem* 13 B2
Pisgat Ze'ev *Jerusalem* 13 B2
Pisnice *Prague* 25 C2
Pitampura *Delhi* 10 A1
Pitkäjärvi *Helsinki* 11 B1
Planegg *Munich* 21 B1
Plantation *Miami* 19 B2
Plantation Isles *Miami* 19 B2
Plaza Mayor *Madrid* 17 B1
Pleasure Island *Orlando* 23 B1
Plumstead *Cape Town* 8 B1
Plumstead *London* 15 B4
Plyushchevo *Moscow* 19 B3
Po Toi Is. *Hong Kong* 12 B3
Po Toi O *Hong Kong* 12 B3
Poasco *Milan* 18 B2
Podbaba *Prague* 25 B2
Podoli *Prague* 25 B2
Pointe-Aux-Trembles *Montreal* 20 A2
Poissy *Paris* 24 A1
Pok Fu Lam *Hong Kong* 12 B2
Pokcheong *Seoul* 27 C2
Polton *Edinburgh* 11 B3
Polvoranca, Parque de *Madrid* 17 C1
Polyustrovo *St. Petersburg* 27 B2
Pompano Beach *Miami* 19 A3
Pomprap *Bangkok* 3 B2
Pondok Gede *Jakarta* 12 A2
Pondok Indah *Jakarta* 12 B1
Pont-Viau *Montreal* 20 A1
Pontault-Combault *Paris* 24 B4
Pontinha *Lisbon* 16 A1
Poplar *London* 15 A3
Port Botany *Sydney* 29 B2
Port Melbourne *Melbourne* 18 B1
Port Rashid *Dubai* 9 A2
Port Richmond *New York* 22 C1
Port Saeed *Dubai* 9 B2
Port Shelter *Hong Kong* 12 A3
Port Union *Toronto* 31 A4
Portage Park *Chicago* 9 B2
Portela, Lisboa ✕ (LIS) *Lisbon* 16 A2
Porter, L. *Orlando* 23 A3
Porto Brandão *Lisbon* 16 A1
Pôrto Novo *Rio de Janeiro* 25 A2
Porto Novo Cr. → *Lagos* 14 B2
Portobello *Edinburgh* 11 B3
Portrero *San Francisco* 26 B3
Posen *Chicago* 9 D2
Potomac Overlook Reg. Park ⌂ *Washington* 33 B2
Potrero Pt. *San Francisco* 26 B2
Potsdam *Berlin* 5 B1
Potzham *Munich* 21 B2
Pötzleinsdorf *Vienna* 32 A1
Póvoa de Santo Adriao *Lisbon* 16 A2
Powązki *Warsaw* 33 B1
Powiśle *Warsaw* 33 B2
Powsin *Warsaw* 33 C2
Powsinek *Warsaw* 33 C2
Poyan Res. *Singapore* 28 A2
Pozuelo de Alarcón *Madrid* 17 B1
Prado, Museo del *Madrid* 17 B1
Prado Churubusco *Mexico City* 18 B2
Praga *Warsaw* 33 B2
Prague = Praha *Prague* 25 B2
Praha *Prague* 25 B2
Praha ✕ (PRG) *Prague* 25 B1
Praires, R. des → *Montreal* 20 A2
Prater *Vienna* 32 A2
Precotto *Milan* 18 A2
Prenestino Labicano *Rome* 26 B2
Prenzlauerberg *Berlin* 5 A3
Preston *Melbourne* 18 A1
Pretos Forros, Sa. dos *Rio de Janeiro* 25 B1
Préville *Montreal* 20 B3
Přezletice *Prague* 25 B3
Prima Porta *Rome* 26 B1
Primavalle *Rome* 26 B1
Primrose *Johannesburg* 13 B2
Progreso Nacional *Mexico City* 18 A2
Prosek *Prague* 25 B3
Prospect Hill Park *Boston* 6 A1
Providencia *Santiago* 27 B2
Průhonice *Prague* 25 C3
Psichiko *Athens* 2 A2
Pudong New Area *Shanghai* 28 B2
Pueblo Libre *Lima* 14 B2
Pueblo Nuevo = El Poblenou *Barcelona* 4 A2
Pueblo Nuevo *Madrid* 17 B2
Puerto Madero *Buenos Aires* 7 B2
Pugu *Guangzhou* 11 A2
Puhuangyu *Beijing* 4 B2
Pui O Wan *Hong Kong* 12 B1
Puistola *Helsinki* 11 B3
Pukinmäki *Helsinki* 11 B2
Pulkovo Int. ✕ (LED) *St. Petersburg* 27 C1
Pullach *Munich* 21 B1
Pullman Historic District *Chicago* 9 C3
Pulo Gadung *Jakarta* 12 B2
Pūnak *Tehran* 31 A2
Punchbowl *Sydney* 29 B1
Punde *Mumbai* 20 B2
Punggol *Singapore* 28 A3
Punggol, Sungei → *Singapore* 28 A3
Punggol Pt. *Singapore* 28 A3
Punjabi Bagh *Delhi* 10 A1
Puotila *Helsinki* 11 B3
Puteaux *Paris* 24 A2
Putney *London* 15 B2
Putuo *Shanghai* 28 B1
Putxet *Barcelona* 4 A1
Puxi *Shanghai* 28 B1
Pyramids *Cairo* 7 B1
Pyry *Warsaw* 33 C1

Q

Qalandiya *Jerusalem* 13 A2
Qal'eh Morghī *Tehran* 31 B2
Qāsemābād *Tehran* 31 A3
Qasr-e Fīrūzeh *Tehran* 31 B3
Qatane *Jerusalem* 13 B1
Qianmen *Beijing* 4 B2
Qinghuayuan *Beijing* 4 B1
Qingningsi *Shanghai* 28 B2
Qolhak *Tehran* 31 A2
Quadraro *Rome* 26 B2
Quaid-i-Azam *Karachi* 13 A1
Quartiere Zingone *Milan* 18 B1
Qubeiba *Jerusalem* 13 A1
Quds *Baghdad* 3 A2
Queen Elizabeth Olympic Park *London* 15 A3
Queen Mary Res. *London* 15 B1
Queen Victoria Market *Melbourne* 18 A1
Queensbury *London* 15 A2
Queenscliffe *Sydney* 29 A2
Queensferry *Edinburgh* 11 B1
Queenstown *Singapore* 28 B2
Quellerina *Johannesburg* 13 A1
Queluz *Lisbon* 16 A1
Quezon City *Manila* 17 B2
Quilicura *Santiago* 27 B1
Quincy *Boston* 6 B2
Quincy B. *Boston* 6 B3
Quinta Normal *Santiago* 27 B1
Quinto de Stampi *Milan* 18 B2
Quinto Romano *Milan* 18 B1
Quirinale *Rome* 26 B1
Qutb Minar *Delhi* 10 B2

R

R.F.K. Memorial Stadium *Washington* 33 B3
Raasdorf *Vienna* 32 A3
Radcliffe College *Boston* 6 A2
Rådhus *Oslo* 23 A3
Radlice *Prague* 25 B2
Radość *Warsaw* 33 B3
Radotín *Prague* 25 C2
Rafat *Jerusalem* 13 A2
Raffles Park *Singapore* 28 B2
Rahnsdorf *Berlin* 5 B5
Rajakylä *Helsinki* 11 B3
Rajpura *Delhi* 10 A2
Rákos-patak → *Budapest* 7 B3
Rákoshegy *Budapest* 7 B3
Rákoskeresztúr *Budapest* 7 B3
Rákoskert *Budapest* 7 B3
Rákosliget *Budapest* 7 B3
Rákospalota *Budapest* 7 A2
Rákosszentmihály *Budapest* 7 A2
Raków *Warsaw* 33 B1
Ram *Jerusalem* 13 A2
Rām Allāh *Jerusalem* 13 A2
Ramadān *Baghdad* 3 B2
Ramakrishna Puram *Delhi* 10 B1
Rāmallāh = Rām Allāh *Jerusalem* 13 A2
Ramanathpur *Kolkata* 14 A1
Ramat Allon *Jerusalem* 13 B2
Ramat Eshkol *Jerusalem* 13 B2
Ramat Razi'el *Jerusalem* 13 B1
Ramat Shafet *Jerusalem* 13 B2
Rambler Channel *Hong Kong* 12 A2
Ramenki *Moscow* 19 B1
Ramersdorf *Munich* 21 B2
Rameses Station *Cairo* 7 A2
Ramos *Rio de Janeiro* 25 B1
Ramos Mejía *Buenos Aires* 7 B1
Ramot *Jerusalem* 13 B2
Rampur *Delhi* 10 A2
Ramsgate *Sydney* 29 B1
Rancho Park *Los Angeles* 16 B2
Rand ✕ (QRA) *Johannesburg* 13 B2
Randalls I. *New York* 22 B2
Randburg *Johannesburg* 13 A1
Randhart *Johannesburg* 13 B2
Randpark Ridge *Johannesburg* 13 A1
Randwick *Sydney* 29 B2
Rangpuri *Delhi* 10 B1
Rannersdorf *Vienna* 32 B2
Ransbèche *Brussels* 6 B2
Ransdorp *Amsterdam* 2 A2
Ranvad *Mumbai* 20 B2
Raposo *Lisbon* 16 A1
Rastaala *Helsinki* 11 B1
Rastila *Helsinki* 11 B3
Raszyn *Warsaw* 33 C1
Ratho *Edinburgh* 11 B1
Ratho Station *Edinburgh* 11 B1
Rato *Lisbon* 16 A2
Ravelston *Edinburgh* 11 B2
Rawamangun *Jakarta* 12 B2
Rayners Lane *London* 15 A1
Raynes Park *London* 15 B2
Raypur *Kolkata* 14 C2
Real Felipe, Fuerte *Lima* 14 B2
Reams, L. *Orlando* 23 B1
Reclining Buddha = Wat Pho *Bangkok* 3 B1
Recoleta *Buenos Aires* 7 B2
Recoleta *Santiago* 27 B2
Red Fort = Lal Qila *Delhi* 10 B2
Red Square *Moscow* 19 B2
Redbridge □ *London* 15 A4
Redfern *Sydney* 29 B2
Refshaleøen *Copenhagen* 8 A3
Regents Park *Johannesburg* 13 B2
Regent's Park *London* 15 A3
Rego Park *New York* 22 B2
Reinickendorf *Berlin* 5 A3
Rekola *Helsinki* 11 B3
Rembertów *Warsaw* 33 B2
Rembrandtpark *Amsterdam* 2 A2
Remedios de Escalada *Buenos Aires* 7 C2
Rémola, Estany del *Barcelona* 4 B1
Renca *Santiago* 27 B1
Rennemoulin *Paris* 24 A1
Řeporyje *Prague* 25 B1
Repulse Bay *Hong Kong* 12 B3
Repy *Prague* 25 B1
Residenz *Munich* 21 B2
Retiro *Buenos Aires* 7 B2
Retiro *Madrid* 17 B1
Retiro, Puerto *Buenos Aires* 7 B2
Retreat *Cape Town* 8 B1
Reutov *Moscow* 19 B4
Réveillon → *Paris* 24 B4
Revere *Boston* 6 A2
Rexdale *Toronto* 31 A1
Reynosa Tamaulipas *Mexico City* 18 A1
Rho *Milan* 18 A1
Rhodes *Sydney* 29 A1
Rhodon *Paris* 24 B1
Rhodon → *Paris* 24 B1
Rialto Towers *Melbourne* 18 A1
Ribeira *Rio de Janeiro* 25 A1
Ricarda, Estany de la *Barcelona* 4 B1
Richardson *Dallas-Fort Worth* 10 A5
Richland Hills *Dallas-Fort Worth* 10 B2
Richmond *Melbourne* 18 A2
Richmond *San Francisco* 26 B2
Richmond Hill *New York* 22 B2
Richmond Park *London* 15 B2
Richmond-upon-Thames □ *London* 15 B2
Ridge, The *Delhi* 10 B2
Ridgefield *New York* 22 B1
Ridgefield Park *New York* 22 A1
Ridgewood *New York* 22 B2
Riem *Munich* 21 B3
Riesenrad *Vienna* 32 A2
Rijksmuseum *Amsterdam* 2 A2
Rikers I. *New York* 22 B2
Rimac *Lima* 14 B2
Rinkeby *Stockholm* 29 A1
Rio Comprido *Rio de Janeiro* 25 B1
Rio de Janeiro *Rio de Janeiro* 25 B1
Rio de Janeiro Galeão ✕ (GIG) *Rio de Janeiro* 25 A1
Rio de Mouro *Lisbon* 16 A1
Ripollet *Barcelona* 4 A1
Ris *Oslo* 23 A3
Risby *Copenhagen* 8 A1
Rishra *Kolkata* 14 A2
Rithala *Delhi* 10 A1
Rive Sud, Canal de la *Montreal* 20 B2
River Edge *New York* 22 A1
River Forest *Chicago* 9 B2
River Grove *Chicago* 9 B1
River Ridge *New Orleans* 21 B1
Riverdale *Chicago* 9 D3
Riverdale *New York* 22 A2
Riverdale *Washington* 33 B3
Riverdale Park *Toronto* 31 A2
Riverlea *Johannesburg* 13 B1
Riverside *Chicago* 9 C2
Riverwood *Sydney* 29 B1
Rivière-des-Praires *Montreal* 20 A2
Rixensart *Brussels* 6 B3
Riyad *Baghdad* 3 B2
Rizal Park *Manila* 17 B1
Rizal Stadium *Manila* 17 B1
Røa *Oslo* 23 A2
Robbins *Chicago* 9 D2
Robertsham *Johannesburg* 13 B2
Rochelle Park *New York* 22 A1
Rochester Park *Dallas-Fort Worth* 10 B5
Rock Cr. → *Washington* 33 B2
Rock Creek Park *Washington* 33 B2
Rockaway Beach *New York* 22 C3
Rockaway Pt. *New York* 22 C2
Rockdale *Sydney* 29 B1
Rockefeller Center *New York* 22 B2
Roda, Gezîret el *Cairo* 7 A2
Roda I. = Roda, Gezîret el *Cairo* 7 A2
Rodaon *Vienna* 32 B1
Rødovre *Copenhagen* 8 A2
Rodrigo de Freitas, L. *Rio de Janeiro* 25 B1
Roehampton *London* 15 B2
Rogers Park *Chicago* 9 A3
Roihuvuori *Helsinki* 11 B3
Roissy-en-Brie *Paris* 24 B4
Rokytka → *Prague* 25 B3
Roland Garros *Paris* 24 A2
Roma *Rome* 26 B1
Roma Urbe ✕ *Rome* 26 B2
Római-Fürdő *Budapest* 7 A2
Romainville *Paris* 24 A3
Roman Forum = Foro Romano *Rome* 26 B1
Romano Banco *Milan* 18 B1
Rome = Roma *Rome* 26 B1
Romema *Jerusalem* 13 B2
Romford *London* 15 A5
Ronald Reagan Nat. Washington ✕ (DCA) *Washington* 33 B2
Rondebosch *Cape Town* 8 A1
Roppongi *Tokyo* 30 B3
Rose, L. *Orlando* 23 A1
Rose Bowl *Los Angeles* 16 B4
Rose Hill *Washington* 33 C2
Rosebank *Johannesburg* 13 A2
Rosebank *New York* 22 C1
Rosebery *Sydney* 29 B2
Rosedal La Candelaria *Mexico City* 18 B2
Roseland *Chicago* 9 C3
Rosemead *Los Angeles* 16 B4
Rosemont *Chicago* 9 B1
Rosemont *Montreal* 20 A2
Rosenborg Slot *Copenhagen* 8 A3
Rosenthal *Berlin* 5 A3
Rosettenville *Johannesburg* 13 B2
Rosewell *Edinburgh* 11 B3
Rosherville Dam *Johannesburg* 13 B2
Rösjön *Stockholm* 29 A2
Roslags-Näsby *Stockholm* 29 A2
Roslin *Edinburgh* 11 B3
Roslindale *Boston* 6 B2
Rosny-sous-Bois *Paris* 24 A4
Rosslyn *Washington* 33 B2
Rosyth *Edinburgh* 11 A1
Rotherhithe *London* 15 B3
Rothneusiedl *Vienna* 32 B2
Rothschmaige *Munich* 21 A1
Rouge Hill *Toronto* 31 A4
Round I. *Hong Kong* 12 B3
Roxbury *Boston* 6 B2
Roxeth *London* 15 A1
Royal Botanic Gardens *Edinburgh* 11 B2
Royal Exhibition Building *Melbourne* 18 A1
Royal Observatory *Edinburgh* 11 B2
Royal Palace = Kungliga Slottet *Stockholm* 29 B2
Royal Palace = Palacio Real *Madrid* 17 B1
Royal Park *Melbourne* 18 A1
Röylä *Helsinki* 11 B1
Rozas, Portilleros de las *Madrid* 17 B1
Roztoky *Prague* 25 B2
Rozzano *Milan* 18 B1
Rubí → *Barcelona* 4 A1
Rudolfsheim *Vienna* 32 A2
Rudolfshöhe *Berlin* 5 A5
Rudow *Berlin* 5 B3
Rueil-Malmaison *Paris* 24 A2
Ruisbroek *Brussels* 6 B1
Ruislip *London* 15 A1
Rumelihisarı *Istanbul* 12 B2
Rungis *Paris* 24 B3
Rusāfa *Baghdad* 3 A2
Rush Green *London* 15 A5
Russa *Kolkata* 14 C2
Rutherford *New York* 22 B1
Ruzyně *Prague* 25 B1
Ruzyně, Praha ✕ (PRG) *Prague* 25 B1
Rybatskaya *St. Petersburg* 27 B2
Rydboholm *Stockholm* 29 A3
Ryde *Sydney* 29 A1
Ryogoku *Tokyo* 30 A3
Rzhevka *St. Petersburg* 27 B3

S

Sa'ādatābād *Tehran* 31 A2
Saadūn *Baghdad* 3 B2
Saavedra *Buenos Aires* 7 B2
Saboli *Delhi* 10 A2
Sabugo *Lisbon* 16 A1
Sabzi Mand *Delhi* 10 A2
Sacavém *Lisbon* 16 A2
Saclay *Paris* 24 B2
Saclay, Étang de *Paris* 24 B1
Sacomã *São Paulo* 27 B2
Sacré Cœur *Paris* 24 A3
Sacrow *Berlin* 5 B1
Sacrower See *Berlin* 5 B1
Sadang *Seoul* 27 C1
Saddle → *New York* 22 A1
Saddle Brook *New York* 22 A1
Sadr *Karachi* 13 A2
Sadr City *Baghdad* 3 A2
Sadyba *Warsaw* 33 B2
Safdar Jang's Tomb *Delhi* 10 B2
Saft el Laban *Cairo* 7 A2
Sagene *Oslo* 23 A3
Saginaw *Dallas-Fort Worth* 10 A1
Sagrada Familia, Templo de *Barcelona* 4 A2
Sahar, Mumbai ✕ (BOM) *Mumbai* 20 A2
Sai Kung *Hong Kong* 12 A3
Sai Tso Wan *Hong Kong* 12 B1
Sai Wan Ho *Hong Kong* 12 B3
Sai Ying Pun *Hong Kong* 12 B2
St-Aubin *Paris* 24 B1
St-Cloud *Paris* 24 A2
St-Cyr-l'École *Paris* 24 B1
St-Cyr-l'École ✕ *Paris* 24 B1
St-Denis *Paris* 24 A3
St-Germain, Forêt de *Paris* 24 A1
St-Germain-en-Laye *Paris* 24 A1
St-Gilles *Brussels* 6 B2
St. Helier *London* 15 B2
St-Hubert *Montreal* 20 B3
St-Hubert, Galeries Royales *Brussels* 6 A2
St. Isaac's Cathedral *St. Petersburg* 27 B1
St-Jacques → *Montreal* 20 B3
St-Joost-Ten-Node *Brussels* 6 A2
St. Kilda *Melbourne* 18 B1
St-Lambert *Montreal* 20 A3
St-Lambert *Paris* 24 B1
St-Laurent *Montreal* 20 A1
St-Léonard *Montreal* 20 A2
St-Mandé *Paris* 24 A3
St-Martin, Bois *Paris* 24 B4
St. Mary Cray *London* 15 B4
St-Maur-des-Fossés *Paris* 24 B3
St-Maurice *Paris* 24 B3
St-Michel *Montreal* 20 A2
St-Ouen *Paris* 24 A3
St. Paul's Cray *London* 15 B4
St. Peters *Sydney* 29 B2
St. Peter's Square = San Pietro, Piazza *Rome* 26 B1
St. Petersburg = Sankt-Peterburg *St. Petersburg* 27 B1
St. Petersburg Pulkovo Int. ✕ (LED) *St. Petersburg* 27 C1
St-Pierre *Montreal* 20 B2
St-Pieters Leew *Brussels* 6 B1
St-Quentin, Étang de *Paris* 24 B1
St. Stephen's Cathedral = Stephansdom *Vienna* 32 A2
St-Stevens-Woluwe *Brussels* 6 A2
St-Vincent-de-Paul *Montreal* 20 A2
St. Xavier Univ. *Chicago* 9 C2
Ste-Catherine *Montreal* 20 B2
Ste-Hélène, Î. *Montreal* 20 A2
Saiwai *Tokyo* 30 B3
Sakai *Osaka* 23 B1
Sakai Harbour *Osaka* 23 B1
Sakra, Pulau *Singapore* 28 B2
Salam *Baghdad* 3 A2
Salamanca *Madrid* 17 B1
Salmannsdorf *Vienna* 32 A1
Salmedina *Madrid* 17 C2
Salomea *Warsaw* 33 B1
Salsette I. *Mumbai* 20 A2
Salt Lake City = Bidhan Nagar *Kolkata* 14 B2
Salt Lake Stadium *Kolkata* 14 B2
Salt River *Cape Town* 8 A1
Salt Water L. *Kolkata* 14 B2
Saltsjö-Duvnäs *Stockholm* 29 B3
Samatya *Istanbul* 12 C1
Sampaloc *Manila* 17 B1
Samphan Thawong *Bangkok* 3 B2
Samseon *Seoul* 27 B2
Samseong *Seoul* 27 B2
Samuel Smith Park *Toronto* 31 B1
Samut Prakan *Bangkok* 3 B2
San Andrés *Barcelona* 4 A2
San Angel *Mexico City* 18 B1
San Basilio *Rome* 26 B2
San Borja *Lima* 14 B3
San Bóvio *Milan* 18 B2
San Bruno, Pt. *San Francisco* 26 C2
San Bruno Mountain State Park ⌂ *San Francisco* 26 B2
San Cristóbal *Buenos Aires* 7 B2
San Cristóbal *Madrid* 17 B2
San Cristóbal, Cerro *Santiago* 27 B2
San Cristóbal, Virgen del *Santiago* 27 B2
San Cristoforo *Milan* 18 B1
San Donato Milanese *Milan* 18 B2
San Francisco *San Francisco* 26 B2
San Francisco B. *San Francisco* 26 B3
San Francisco Culhuacán *Mexico City* 18 C2
San Fruttuoso *Milan* 18 A2
San Gabriel *Los Angeles* 16 B4
San Gabriel → *Los Angeles* 16 C4
San Giuliano Milanese *Milan* 18 B2
San Isidro *Lima* 14 B2
San Jerónimo Lídice *Mexico City* 18 C1
San Joaquín *Santiago* 27 B2
San José Rio Hondo *Mexico City* 18 B1
San Juan → *Manila* 17 B2
San Juan de Aragón *Mexico City* 18 B2
San Juan de Aragón, Parque *Mexico City* 18 B2
San Juan de Lurigancho *Lima* 14 A2
San Juan del Monte *Manila* 17 B2
San Juan Ixtacala *Mexico City* 18 A1
San Just Desvern *Barcelona* 4 A1
San Justo *Buenos Aires* 7 C1
San Lorenzo Tezonco *Mexico City* 18 C2
San Luis *Lima* 14 B2
San Marino *Los Angeles* 16 B4
San Martín *Barcelona* 4 A2
San Martín de Porras *Lima* 14 B2
San Mateo Tlaltenango *Mexico City* 18 B1
San Miguel *Lima* 14 B2
San Miguel *Santiago* 27 B2
San Nicolás *Buenos Aires* 7 B2
San Onófrio *Rome* 26 B1
San Pedro Mártir *Barcelona* 4 A1
San Pedro Zacatenco *Mexico City* 18 A2
San Pietro, Piazza *Rome* 26 B1
San Po Kong *Hong Kong* 12 B3
San Rafael Chamapa *Mexico City* 18 B1
San Rafael Hills *Los Angeles* 16 A3
San Roque *Manila* 17 B2
San Siro *Milan* 18 B1
San Souci *Sydney* 29 B1
San Tau *Hong Kong* 12 B1
San Telmo *Buenos Aires* 7 B2
San Vicenç dels Horts *Barcelona* 4 A1
Sandown *Johannesburg* 13 A2
Sandown Park Races *London* 15 B1
Sandton *Johannesburg* 13 A2
Sandvika *Oslo* 23 A2
Sangenjaya *Tokyo* 30 B2
Sanggye *Seoul* 27 B2
Sangley Pt. *Manila* 17 C1
Sankrail *Kolkata* 14 B1
Sankt-Peterburg *St. Petersburg* 27 B1
Sankt Veit *Vienna* 32 A1
Sanlihe *Beijing* 4 B1
Sanlin *Shanghai* 28 C1
Sanlintang *Shanghai* 28 C1
Sans *Barcelona* 4 A1
Sansom Park *Dallas-Fort Worth* 10 B1
Sanssouci *Berlin* 5 B1
Sant Ambrogio, Basilica di *Milan* 18 B2
Sant Boi de Llobregat *Barcelona* 4 A1
Sant Cugat *Barcelona* 4 A1
Sant Feliu de Llobregat *Barcelona* 4 A1
Sant Joan Despi *Barcelona* 4 A1
Santa Ana *Manila* 17 B2
Santa Anita Park *Los Angeles* 16 B4
Santa Coloma de Gramenet *Barcelona* 4 A2
Santa Cruz *Manila* 17 B1
Santa Cruz *Mumbai* 20 A1
Santa Cruz, I. de *Rio de Janeiro* 25 B2
Santa Cruz de Olorde *Barcelona* 4 A1
Santa Efigénia *São Paulo* 27 B2
Santa Elena *Manila* 17 B2
Santa Elena del Gomero *Santiago* 27 B1
Santa Eulalia *Barcelona* 4 A2
Santa Fe Springs *Los Angeles* 16 C4
Santa Iria da Azóia *Lisbon* 16 A2
Santa Julia *Santiago* 27 C2
Santa Monica *Los Angeles* 16 B2
Santa Monica Mts. *Los Angeles* 16 B2
Santa Rosa de Locobe *Santiago* 27 B2
Santa Teresa de la Ovalle *Santiago* 27 B1
Santahamina *Helsinki* 11 C3
Santana *São Paulo* 27 A2
Santeny *Paris* 24 B4
Santiago *Santiago* 27 B2
Santiago Benítez Int. ✕ (SCL) *Santiago* 27 B1
Santiago de Surco *Lima* 14 B2
Santo Amaro *Lisbon* 16 A1
Santo Amaro *São Paulo* 27 B1
Santo André *Lisbon* 16 B2
Santo Antão do Tojal *Lisbon* 16 A2
Santo Antônio, Qta. de *Lisbon* 16 B1
Santo Tomas, Univ. of *Manila* 17 B1
Santos Dumont ✕ (SDU) *Rio de Janeiro* 25 B2
Santoshpur *Kolkata* 14 B1
Santragachi *Kolkata* 14 B1
Sanyuanli *Guangzhou* 11 B2
São Caetano do Sul *São Paulo* 27 B2
São Conrado *Rio de Janeiro* 25 B1
São Cristóvão *Rio de Janeiro* 25 B1
São Jorge, Castelo de *Lisbon* 16 A2
São Julião do Tojal *Lisbon* 16 A2
São Paulo *São Paulo* 27 B2
São Paulo Congonhas ✕ (CGH) *São Paulo* 27 B2
Sapa *Kolkata* 14 B1
Sapateiro, Cor. do → *São Paulo* 27 B1
Sarandi *Buenos Aires* 7 C2
Saraswati → *Kolkata* 14 A1
Sarecky potok → *Prague* 25 B2
Sarimbun *Singapore* 28 A2
Sarimbun Res. *Singapore* 28 A2
Sarıyer *Istanbul* 12 A2
Sarriá *Barcelona* 4 A1
Sarsuna *Kolkata* 14 C1
Sartrouville *Paris* 24 A2
Sasad *Budapest* 7 B2
Sashalom *Budapest* 7 A3
Saska *Warsaw* 33 B2
Satalice *Prague* 25 B3
Satgachi *Kolkata* 14 B2
Satpukur *Kolkata* 14 B2
Sätra *Stockholm* 29 B1
Saúde *São Paulo* 27 B2
Saugus *Boston* 6 A2
Saugus → *Boston* 6 A2
Sault-au-Récollet *Montreal* 20 A2
Sausalito *San Francisco* 26 A2
Sawah Besar *Jakarta* 12 A1
Sawtelle *Los Angeles* 16 B2
Scald Law *Edinburgh* 11 B2
Scarborough *Toronto* 31 A3
Scarborough Bluffs *Toronto* 31 A3
Scarborough Junction *Toronto* 31 A3
Sceaux *Paris* 24 B2
Schaerbeek *Brussels* 6 A2
Scharfenberg *Berlin* 5 A2
Schiller Woods *Chicago* 9 B1
Schiphol, Amsterdam ✕ (AMS) *Amsterdam* 2 B1
Schlachtensee *Berlin* 5 B2
Schlossgarten *Berlin* 5 A2
Schmargendorf *Berlin* 5 B2
Schönblick *Berlin* 5 B5
Schönbrunn *Vienna* 32 A1
Schöneberg *Berlin* 5 B3
Schönefeld *Berlin* 5 B4
Schöneiche *Berlin* 5 B5
Schönwalde *Berlin* 5 A1
Schulzendorf *Berlin* 5 A2
Schwabing *Munich* 21 B2
Schwanebeck *Berlin* 5 A4
Schwanenwerder *Berlin* 5 B2
Schwarzlackenau *Vienna* 32 A2
Schwechat *Vienna* 32 B2
Schwechat, Wien ✕ (VIE) *Vienna* 32 B3
Science and Industry, Museum of *Chicago* 9 C3
Scopus, Mt. *Jerusalem* 13 B2
Scottdale *Atlanta* 3 B3
Scottish Parliament *Edinburgh* 11 B2
Scutari = Üsküdar *Istanbul* 12 B2
Sea Point *Cape Town* 8 A1
Seacliff *San Francisco* 26 B2
Seaforth *Sydney* 29 A2
Seagate *New York* 22 C1
SeaWorld *Orlando* 23 B2
Seberov *Prague* 25 B3
Secaucus *New York* 22 B1
Seddinsee *Berlin* 5 B5
Seeberg *Berlin* 5 A5
Seeburg *Berlin* 5 A1
Seefeld *Berlin* 5 A5
Seegefeld *Berlin* 5 A1
Seehof *Berlin* 5 B2
Segeltorp *Stockholm* 29 B1
Segrate *Milan* 18 B2
Seguro *Milan* 18 B1
Seixal *Lisbon* 16 B2
Selby *Johannesburg* 13 B2
Seletar *Singapore* 28 A3
Seletar, Pulau *Singapore* 28 A3
Seletar Hills *Singapore* 28 A3
Seletar Res. *Singapore* 28 A2
Selhurst *London* 15 B3
Sembawang *Singapore* 28 A2
Senago *Milan* 18 A1
Senayan Stadium = Gelora Bung Karno Stadium *Jakarta* 12 B1
Sendling *Munich* 21 B2
Senju *Tokyo* 30 A3
Senkang *Singapore* 28 A3
Senriyama *Osaka* 23 A2
Sentosa *Singapore* 28 B2
Seobinggo *Seoul* 27 B1
Seocho *Seoul* 27 C1
Seodaemun *Seoul* 27 B1
Seokkwan *Seoul* 27 B2
Seongbuk *Seoul* 27 B2
Seongdong *Seoul* 27 B2
Seongsu *Seoul* 27 B2
Seoul *Seoul* 27 B2
Seoul Nat. Univ. *Seoul* 27 C1
Seoul Tower *Seoul* 27 B1
Sepolia *Athens* 2 A2
Sepulveda Dam Rec. Area ⌂ *Los Angeles* 16 A2
Serangoon *Singapore* 28 A3
Serangoon, Pulau *Singapore* 28 A3
Serangoon, Sungei → *Singapore* 28 A3
Serangoon Harbour *Singapore* 28 A3
Seraya, Pulau *Singapore* 28 B2
Serebryanka → *Moscow* 19 B3
Serramonte *San Francisco* 26 C2
Sesto San Giovanni *Milan* 18 A2
Sesto Ulteriano *Milan* 18 B2
Setagaya *Tokyo* 30 B2
Seter *Oslo* 23 A3
Setia Budi *Jakarta* 12 B1
Settebagni *Rome* 26 A2
Settecamini *Rome* 26 B2
Séttimo Milanese *Milan* 18 B1
Settsu *Osaka* 23 A2
Seutula *Helsinki* 11 A2
Seven Corners *Washington* 33 B2
Seven Kings *London* 15 A4
Seventeenth Street Canal *New Orleans* 21 A2
Sévesco → *Milan* 18 A1
Sevran *Paris* 24 A4
Sèvres *Paris* 24 B2
Sewri *Mumbai* 20 B2
Sforzesco, Castello *Milan* 18 B2
Sha Chau *Hong Kong* 12 A1
Sha Kok Mei *Hong Kong* 12 A3
Sha Lo Wan *Hong Kong* 12 B1
Sha Tin *Hong Kong* 12 A3
Sha'ab *Baghdad* 3 A2
Sha'ab North *Baghdad* 3 A2
Sha'ar Binyamin *Jerusalem* 13 A2
Shabrāmant *Cairo* 7 B2
Shah Mosque *Tehran* 31 A2
Shahdara *Delhi* 10 A2
Shahe *Guangzhou* 11 B2
Shahr-e Rey *Tehran* 31 B2
Shahrak-e Golshahr *Tehran* 31 B1
Shahrak-e Qods *Tehran* 31 A2
Shaikh Aomar *Baghdad* 3 A2
Shakurbasti *Delhi* 10 A1
Shalkiya *Kolkata* 14 B2
Sham Shui Po *Hong Kong* 12 B2
Sham Tseng *Hong Kong* 12 A2
Sham Wat *Hong Kong* 12 B1
Shamapur *Delhi* 10 A1
Shamian *Guangzhou* 11 B2
Shan Mei *Hong Kong* 12 A3
Shanghai *Shanghai* 28 B1
Shanghai Hongqiao Int. ✕ (SHA) *Shanghai* 28 B1
Shanghai Pudong Int. ✕ (PVG) *Shanghai* 28 B2
Sharp I. *Hong Kong* 12 A3
Shastrinagar *Delhi* 10 A2
Shau Kei Wan *Hong Kong* 12 B3
Shawocun *Beijing* 4 B1
Shayuan *Guangzhou* 11 B2
Sheen, L. *Orlando* 23 B1
Sheepshead Bay *New York* 22 C2
Sheikh Zayed Road *Dubai* 9 B2
Shek Kong *Hong Kong* 12 A2
Shek Kwu Chau *Hong Kong* 12 B1
Shek O *Hong Kong* 12 B3
Shek O Country Park ⌂ *Hong Kong* 12 B3
Shek Pik *Hong Kong* 12 B1
Shek Pik Res. *Hong Kong* 12 B1
Shelter I. *Hong Kong* 12 B3
Shepherds Bush *London* 15 A2
Shepperton *London* 15 B1
Sheremetyevo Int., Moscow ✕ (SVO) *Moscow* 19 A1
Sherman Oaks *Los Angeles* 16 B2
Sherman Park *Chicago* 9 C2
Sherwood, L. *Orlando* 23 A2
Shet Bandar *Mumbai* 20 B2
Sheung Fa Shan *Hong Kong* 12 A2
Sheung Lau Wan *Hong Kong* 12 B3
Sheung Wan *Hong Kong* 12 B2
Sheva *Mumbai* 20 B2
Sheva Nhava *Mumbai* 20 B2
Shiba *Tokyo* 30 B3
Shibpur *Kolkata* 14 B1
Shibuya *Tokyo* 30 B3
Shilihe *Beijing* 4 B2
Shimogawara *Tokyo* 30 B1
Shimosalo *Tokyo* 30 A2
Shimoshakujii *Tokyo* 30 A2
Shinagawa *Tokyo* 30 B3
Shing Mun Country Park ⌂ *Hong Kong* 12 A2
Shing Mun Res. *Hong Kong* 12 A2
Shinjuku *Tokyo* 30 A3
Shinjuku Nat. Garden *Tokyo* 30 A3
Shinkoiwa *Tokyo* 30 A4
Shinnakano *Tokyo* 30 A3
Shipai *Guangzhou* 11 B3
Shirinashi → *Osaka* 23 B1
Shirogane *Tokyo* 30 B3
Shitennoji Temple *Osaka* 23 B2
Shiweitang *Guangzhou* 11 B2
Shogunle *Lagos* 14 A2
Shomolu *Lagos* 14 A2
Shooters Hill *London* 15 B4
Shoreditch *London* 15 A3
Shortlands *London* 15 B4
Shu'afat *Jerusalem* 13 B2
Shubra *Cairo* 7 A2
Shubrā el Kheima *Cairo* 7 A2
Shui Hau *Hong Kong* 12 B1
Shuikuo *Guangzhou* 11 A2
Sidcup *London* 15 B4
Siebenhirten *Vienna* 32 B1
Siedlung *Berlin* 5 A1
Siekierki *Warsaw* 33 B2
Sielce *Warsaw* 33 B2
Siemensstadt *Berlin* 5 A2
Sierra Madre *Los Angeles* 16 B4
Sievering *Vienna* 32 A2
Sighthill *Edinburgh* 11 B2
Signal Hill *Cape Town* 8 A1
Siheung *Seoul* 27 C1
Sikátorpuszta *Budapest* 7 A3
Silampur *Delhi* 10 B2
Sillim *Seoul* 27 C1
Silver, L. *Orlando* 23 A2
Silver Hill *Washington* 33 B3
Silver Lake *Los Angeles* 16 B3
Silver Mine B. *Hong Kong* 12 B2
Silver Spring *Washington* 33 A2
Silvermine Nature Reserve *Cape Town* 8 B1
Silverstrand *Hong Kong* 12 B3
Silvolantekojärvi *Helsinki* 11 B2
Simei *Singapore* 28 A3
Simla *Kolkata* 14 B2
Simmering *Vienna* 32 A2
Simmeringer Heide *Vienna* 32 A2
Simonkylä *Helsinki* 11 B3
Sinchon *Seoul* 27 B1
Sindang *Seoul* 27 B2
Singapore ■ *Singapore* 28 B3
Singapore Changi ✕ (SIN) *Singapore* 28 A3
Sinki, Selat *Singapore* 28 B2
Sinsa *Seoul* 27 B2
Sint-Genesius-Rode *Brussels* 6 B2
Sion *Mumbai* 20 A2
Sipson *London* 15 B1
Siqeil *Cairo* 7 A1
Şişli *Istanbul* 12 B1
Siu Kau Yi Chau *Hong Kong* 12 B2
Skansen *Stockholm* 29 B2
Skärholmen *Stockholm* 29 B1
Skarpäng *Stockholm* 29 A2
Skarpnäck *Stockholm* 29 B2
Skaryszewski, Park *Warsaw* 33 B2
Skogskyrkogården *Stockholm* 29 B2
Skokie *Chicago* 9 A2
Skokie → *Chicago* 9 A2
Skokie Heritage Museum *Chicago* 9 A2
Skoklefall *Oslo* 23 A3
Sköndal *Stockholm* 29 B2
Skovlunde *Copenhagen* 8 A2
Skovshoved *Copenhagen* 8 A3
Skuru *Stockholm* 29 B3
Sky Lake *Orlando* 23 B2
Slade Green *London* 15 B5
Slependen *Oslo* 23 A2
Slipi *Jakarta* 12 B1
Slivenec *Prague* 25 B2
Sloten *Amsterdam* 2 A1
Sloterdijk *Amsterdam* 2 A1
Sloterpark *Amsterdam* 2 A1
Sluhy *Prague* 25 A3
Służew *Warsaw* 33 B2
Służewiec *Warsaw* 33 B2
Smíchov *Prague* 25 B2
Smith Forest Preserve *Chicago* 9 B2
Smolny *St. Petersburg* 27 B2
Smolny Cathedral *St. Petersburg* 27 B2
Snake Creek Canal *Miami* 19 C2
Snarøya *Oslo* 23 A2
Snättringe *Stockholm* 29 B1
So Kwun Wat *Hong Kong* 12 A2
Søborg *Copenhagen* 8 A2
Sobreda *Lisbon* 16 B1
Soccer City Stadium *Johannesburg* 13 B1
Söderby *Stockholm* 29 A3
Södermalm *Stockholm* 29 B2
Sodpur *Kolkata* 14 A2
Soeurs, Î. des *Montreal* 20 B2
Sognsvatn *Oslo* 23 A3
Soignes, Forêt de *Brussels* 6 B2
Sok Kwu Wan *Hong Kong* 12 B2
Soko Is. *Hong Kong* 12 B1
Sokolniki *Moscow* 19 B3
Sokolniki Park *Moscow* 19 B3
Sokołów *Warsaw* 33 C1
Solalinden *Munich* 21 B3
Sollentuna *Stockholm* 29 A1
Solln *Munich* 21 B2
Solna *Stockholm* 29 A1
Somerset *Washington* 33 B2
Somerville *Boston* 6 A2
Sonari *Mumbai* 20 B2
Sønderso *Copenhagen* 8 A2
Songpa *Seoul* 27 B2

Sony Picture Studio Los Angeles 16 B2
Soroksár Budapest 7 B2
Soroksari Duna → Budapest 7 B2
Sosenka → Moscow 19 B3
Sosnovka St. Petersburg 27 B2
Sŏul = Seoul Seoul 27 B2
Soundview New York 22 B2
South African National Museum of Military History Johannesburg 13 A2
South Beach Miami 19 D3
South Beach New York 22 C1
South Bend Park Atlanta 3 B2
South Boston Boston 6 A2
South Decatur Atlanta 3 B3
South Deering Chicago 9 C3
South El Monte Los Angeles 16 B4
South Gate Los Angeles 16 C3
South Harbor Manila 17 B1
South Harrow London 15 A1
South Hd. Sydney 29 B2
South Hills Johannesburg 13 B2
South Holland Chicago 9 D3
South Lawn Washington 33 C2
South Miami Miami 19 D1
South Norwood London 15 B3
South of Market San Francisco 26 B2
South Ozone Park New York 22 B3
South Pasadena Los Angeles 16 B4
South Res. Boston 6 A2
South Ruislip London 15 A1
South San Francisco San Francisco 26 C2
South San Gabriel Los Angeles 16 B4
South Shore Chicago 9 C3
Southall London 15 A1
Southborough London 15 B4
Southend London 15 B3
Southern California, Univ. of Los Angeles 16 B3
Southfields London 15 B2
Southlake Dallas-Fort Worth 10 A3
Southport New Orleans 21 B2
Southwark □ London 15 B3
Southwest Museum Los Angeles 16 B3
Søvang Copenhagen 8 B3
Soweto Johannesburg 13 B1
Sowhānak Tehran 31 A3
Soya Tokyo 30 A4
Spandau Berlin 5 A1
Spånga Stockholm 29 A1
Spectacle I. Boston 6 A3
Speicher-See Munich 21 A3
Speising Vienna 32 B1
Sphinx Cairo 7 B1
Spinaceto Rome 26 C1
Spit Junction Sydney 29 A2
Spořilov Prague 25 B3
Spot Pond Boston 6 A2
Spotswood Melbourne 18 B1
Spring Valley Las Vegas 14 B1
Springeberg Berlin 5 B5
Springfield Washington 33 C1
Squantum Boston 6 B2
Srednaya Rogatka St. Petersburg 27 C2
Środmieście Warsaw 33 B2
Staaken Berlin 5 A1
Stabekk Oslo 23 A2
Stade de France Paris 24 A3
Stadlau Vienna 32 A2
Stadshuset Stockholm 29 B2
Stains Paris 24 A3
Stamford Hill London 15 A3
Stammersdorf Vienna 32 A2
Stanley Hong Kong 12 B3
Stanley B. Hong Kong 12 B3
Stanley Pen. Hong Kong 12 B3
Stanmore London 15 A2
Stapleton New York 22 C1
Staraya Derevnya St. Petersburg 27 B1
Staré Město Prague 25 B2
Stare Miasto Warsaw 33 B2
Starke, L. Orlando 23 A1
Staten Island Zoo New York 22 C1
Staten Islands Ferry Terminal New York 22 C1
Statenice Prague 25 B1
Stavros Niarchos Cultural Centre Athens 2 B2
Steele Creek Melbourne 18 A1
Steenokkerzeel Brussels 6 A2
Steer, L. Orlando 23 A2
Steglitz Berlin 5 B2
Stephansdom Vienna 32 A2
Stepney London 15 A3
Sterling Park San Francisco 26 B2
Sticklinge udde Stockholm 29 A2
Stickney Chicago 9 C2
Stockholm Stockholm 29 B2
Stockholm Arlanda ✕ (ARN) Stockholm 29 A1
Stocksund Stockholm 29 A2
Stoclet, Palais Brussels 6 B2
Stodůlky Prague 25 B1
Stoke Newington London 15 A3
Stone Canyon Res. Los Angeles 16 B2
Stone Zoo Boston 6 A2
Stonebridge London 15 A2
Stonecutters I. Hong Kong 12 B2
Stoneham Boston 6 A2
Stony Brook Res. Boston 6 B2
Stony Creek → Chicago 9 C2
Stora Värtan Stockholm 29 A2
Store Hareskov Copenhagen 8 A2
Store Magleby Copenhagen 8 B3
Storholmen Stockholm 29 A2
Stoyka St. Petersburg 27 B2
Straiton Edinburgh 11 B3
Strandfontein Cape Town 8 B2
Strašnice Prague 25 B2
Strasstrudering Munich 21 B3
Stratford London 15 A4
Strathfield Sydney 29 B1
Streatham London 15 B3
Streatham Vale London 15 B3
Strebersdorf Vienna 32 A2
Střešovice Prague 25 B2
Strip, The Las Vegas 14 B2
Střížkov Prague 25 B2
Strombeek-Bever Brussels 6 A2
Stromovka Prague 25 B2
Studio City Los Angeles 16 B2
Stureby Stockholm 29 B2
Stuvsta Stockholm 29 B2
Subhepur Delhi 10 A2
Suburban Canal New Orleans 21 B1
Sucat Manila 17 C2
Suchdol Prague 25 B2
Sucy-en-Brie Paris 24 B4
Sue, L. Orlando 23 B2
Sugamo Tokyo 30 A3
Sugar Loaf Mt. = Açúcar, Pão de Rio de Janeiro 25 B2
Suge Tokyo 30 B2
Suginami Tokyo 30 A2
Sugō Tokyo 30 B2
Sui Sai Wan Hong Kong 12 B3
Suita Osaka 23 A2
Suitland Washington 33 B3
Sukchar Kolkata 14 A2
Sulphur Channel Hong Kong 12 B2
Sultanahme Camii Istanbul 12 B1
Sumida Tokyo 30 A3
Sumida → Tokyo 30 A3
Sumiyoshi Osaka 23 B2
Sumiyoshi Shrine Osaka 23 B1
Summerville Toronto 31 B1
Summit Chicago 9 C2
Sunamachi Tokyo 30 A4
Sunbury-on-Thames London 15 B1
Sundbyberg Stockholm 29 A1
Sundbyerne Copenhagen 8 B3
Sungei Kadut Industrial Estate Singapore 28 A2
Sungei Selatar Res. Singapore 28 A3
Sunny Bay Hong Kong 12 B1
Sunny Isles Beach Miami 19 C3
Sunrise Miami 19 B2
Sunrise Manor Las Vegas 14 A2
Sunrise Mountain Natural Area ⌂ Las Vegas 14 A2
Sunset Park Las Vegas 14 B2
Sunset Park New York 22 C2
Sunset Peak Hong Kong 12 B1
Sunshine I. Hong Kong 12 B2
Sunshine Park Miami 19 B2
Sunter Jakarta 12 A2
Sunter, Kali → Jakarta 12 B2
Suomenlinna Helsinki 11 C2
Sur Bahr Jerusalem 13 B2
Sura Kolkata 14 B2
Suraksan Seoul 27 A2
Surbiton London 15 B2
Suresnes Paris 24 A2
Surfside Miami 19 C3
Surquillo Lima 14 B2
Surrey Hills Sydney 29 B2
Surulere Lagos 14 B2
Susaek Seoul 27 B1
Süssenbrunn Vienna 32 A2
Sutton London 15 B2
Suyu Seoul 27 B2
Suzukishinden Tokyo 30 A2
Svanemøllen Copenhagen 8 A3
Sveaborg = Suomenlinna Helsinki 11 C2
Sverdlov Moscow 19 B2
Svestad Oslo 23 B2
Svinö Helsinki 11 C1
Swanley London 15 B4
Swansea Toronto 31 B2
Swinburne I. New York 22 C1
Sydenham Johannesburg 13 A2
Sydney Sydney 29 B2
Sydney, Univ. of Sydney 29 B2
Sydney Harbour △ Sydney 29 B2
Sydney Harbour Bridge Sydney 29 B2
Sydney Kingsford Smith ✕ (SYD) Sydney 29 B2
Sydstranden Copenhagen 8 B3
Sylvania Sydney 29 C1
Syon Park London 15 B2
Szczęśliwice Warsaw 33 B1
Széchenyi-hegy Budapest 7 B1
Széphalom Budapest 7 A1

T

Taastrup Copenhagen 8 B1
Tabata Tokyo 30 A3
Tablada Buenos Aires 7 C1
Table B. Cape Town 8 A1
Table Mountain △ Cape Town 8 A1
Table Mt. Cape Town 8 A1
Taboão da Serra São Paulo 27 B1
Täby Stockholm 29 A2
Tacuba Mexico City 18 B1
Tacubaya Mexico City 18 B1
Tafelbaai = Table B. Cape Town 8 A1
Taft Orlando 23 B2
Tagig → Manila 17 B2
Taguig Manila 17 B2
Tahrir Square Cairo 7 A2
Tai Ho Hong Kong 12 B1
Tai Lam Chung Res. Hong Kong 12 A2
Tai Lam Country Park ⌂ Hong Kong 12 A2
Tai Lo Shan Hong Kong 12 A3
Tai Long Wan Tsuen Hong Kong 12 B1
Tai Mo Shan Hong Kong 12 A2
Tai O Hong Kong 12 B1
Tai Po Tsai Hong Kong 12 A3
Tai Seng Singapore 28 A3
Tai Shui Hang Hong Kong 12 A3
Tai Tam B. Hong Kong 12 B3
Tai Tam Country Park ⌂ Hong Kong 12 B3
Tai Tam Tuk Res. Hong Kong 12 B3
Tai Wai Hong Kong 12 A3
Tai Wan Tau Hong Kong 12 B3
Tai Wo Hau Hong Kong 12 A2
Tai Yue Shan = Lantau I. Hong Kong 12 B1
Tainaka Osaka 23 B2
Taishō Osaka 23 B1
Tajrīsh Tehran 31 A2
Takaido Tokyo 30 A2
Takaishi Tokyo 30 B2
Takarazuka Osaka 23 A1
Takasago Tokyo 30 A4
Takatsu Tokyo 30 B2
Takeshita Tokyo 30 B2
Takinegawa Tokyo 30 A3
Takoma Park Washington 33 B2
Taksim Istanbul 12 B1
Talaide Lisbon 16 A1
Taliganga Kolkata 14 B2
Talipapa Manila 17 A2
Tallkrogen Stockholm 29 B2
Tama Tokyo 30 B1
Tama → Tokyo 30 B2
Tama Kyūryō Tokyo 30 B2
Tamaden Tokyo 30 B2
Tamagawa-josui → Tokyo 30 A1
Taman Sari Jakarta 12 A1
Tamanduateí → São Paulo 27 B2
Tamarac Miami 19 A1
Tamboerskloof Cape Town 8 A1
Tambora Jakarta 12 A1
Tammisalo Helsinki 11 B3
Tammūh Cairo 7 B2
Tampines Singapore 28 A3
Tanah Abang Jakarta 12 B1
Tanah Kusir Jakarta 12 B1
Tangelo Park Orlando 23 B2
Tanjung Duren Jakarta 12 B1
Tanjung Priok Jakarta 12 A2
Tanum Oslo 23 A1
Tap Shek Kok Hong Kong 12 A1
Tapada Lisbon 16 A1
Tapanila Helsinki 11 B3
Tapiales Buenos Aires 7 C1
Tapiola Helsinki 11 B1
Tapsia Kolkata 14 B2
Tara Mumbai 20 A1
Tarabya Istanbul 12 B2
Tårbæk Copenhagen 8 A3
Tarchomin Warsaw 33 B1
Tardeo Mumbai 20 B1
Targówek Warsaw 33 B2
Tårnby Copenhagen 8 B3
Tarqua Bay Lagos 14 B2
Tathong Channel Hong Kong 12 B3
Tathong Pt. Hong Kong 12 B3
Tatuapé São Paulo 27 B2
Taufkirchen Munich 21 B2
Tavares, I. dos Rio de Janeiro 25 A2
Tavros Athens 2 B2
Teaneck New York 22 A1
Tebet Jakarta 12 B2
Tecamachalco Mexico City 18 B1
Ted Williams Tunnel Boston 6 A2
Teddington London 15 B1
Tegel Berlin 5 A2
Tegel, Berlin ✕ (TXL) Berlin 5 A2
Tegeler See Berlin 5 A2
Tegelort Berlin 5 A2
Teheran = Tehrān Tehran 31 A2
Tehrān Tehran 31 A2
Tehrān Mehrābād ✕ (THR) Tehran 31 A1
Tehrān Pārs Tehran 31 A3
Tei Tong Tsui Hong Kong 12 B3
Tejo, Rio → Lisbon 16 A2
Tekstilyshchik Moscow 19 B3
Telhal Lisbon 16 A1
Telok Blangah Singapore 28 B2
Teltow Berlin 5 B2
Teltow kanal Berlin 5 B3
Tempelhof Berlin 5 B3
Temple City Los Angeles 16 B4
Temple Hills Washington 33 C3
Temple of Heaven Beijing 4 B2
Temppeliaukio Church Helsinki 11 B2
Tenafly New York 22 A2
Tenayuca, Piramide de Mexico City 18 A1
Tengah → Singapore 28 A2
Tennoji Osaka 23 B2
Tepalcates Mexico City 18 B2
Tepeyac △ Mexico City 18 B2
Terrazzano Milan 18 A1
Terre des Hommes Montreal 20 A2
Terrugem Lisbon 16 A1
Terrytown New Orleans 21 B2
Tervuren Brussels 6 B3
Tervuren, Park van Brussels 6 B3
Tetuán Madrid 17 B1
Teufelsberg Berlin 5 B2
Thalkirchen Munich 21 B2
Thames Ditton London 15 B1
Thamesmead London 15 A4
Thana Cr. → Mumbai 20 A2
Thiais Paris 24 B3
Thisio Athens 2 B2
Thistletown Toronto 31 A1
Thomastown Melbourne 18 A2
Thompson I. Boston 6 B3
Thon Buri Bangkok 3 B1
Thornbury Melbourne 18 A2
Thorncliffe Toronto 31 A2
Thornhill Toronto 31 A2
Thornton Cape Town 8 A2
Thornton Heath London 15 B3
Three Fathoms Cove Hong Kong 12 A3
Threipmuir Res. Edinburgh 11 B2
Throg's Neck New York 22 B3
Tian Tan Buddha = Big Buddha Hong Kong 12 B1
Tiancun Beijing 4 B1
Tianhe Guangzhou 11 B2
Tibet, L. Orlando 23 B1
Tibidabo Barcelona 4 A1
Tiburon San Francisco 26 A2
Tiburtino Rome 26 B2
Ticomán Mexico City 18 A2
Tiefersee Berlin 5 B1
Tiergarten Berlin 5 A3
Tijgerhof Cape Town 8 A2
Tijuca Rio de Janeiro 25 B1
Tijuca, Pico da Rio de Janeiro 25 B1
Tijuca △ Rio de Janeiro 25 B1
Tikkurila Helsinki 11 B3
Tilak Nagar Delhi 10 B1
Tilanqiao Shanghai 28 B1
Timah, Bukit Singapore 28 A2
Timiryazev Park Moscow 19 B2
Tin Can I. Lagos 14 B2
Ting Kau Hong Kong 12 A2
Tira Jerusalem 13 A1
Tirsa Cairo 7 B2
Tishrīyaa Baghdad 3 B2
Tiu Keng Leng Hong Kong 12 B3
Tizapán Mexico City 18 C1
Tlalnepantla → Mexico City 18 A1
Tlalpan Mexico City 18 C2
To Kwa Wan Hong Kong 12 B3
Toa Payoh Singapore 28 A3
Točná Prague 25 C2
Toco Hills Atlanta 3 B2
Todt Hill New York 22 C1
Tōkagi Tokyo 30 A4
Tokai Plantation Cape Town 8 B1
Tōkaichiba Tokyo 30 B2
Tōkyō Tokyo 30 B3
Tōkyō B. = Tōkyō-Wan Tokyo 30 B4
Tōkyō Haneda ✕ (HND) Tokyo 30 B3
Tōkyō Harbour Tokyo 30 B3
Tōkyō Sky Tree Tokyo 30 A3
Tōkyō-Wan Tokyo 30 B4
Tollygunge = Taliganga Kolkata 14 B2
Tolo Harbour Hong Kong 12 A3
Tolworth London 15 B2
Tomba di Nerone Rome 26 B1
Tommy Thompson Park Toronto 31 B3
Tondo Manila 17 B1
Tong Fuk Hong Kong 12 B1
Tongbinggo Seoul 27 B1
Tongqiao Shanghai 28 A1
Toorak Melbourne 18 B2
Topanga State Park ⌂ Los Angeles 16 B1
Topkapı Istanbul 12 B1
Topkapı Palaca Istanbul 12 B1
Tor di Quinto Rome 26 B1
Tor Pignattara Rome 26 B2
Tor Sapienza Rome 26 B2
Torcy Paris 24 A4
Toronto Toronto 31 B2
Toronto, Univ. of Toronto 31 B2
Toronto City Centre ✕ (YTZ) Toronto 31 B2
Toronto Harbour Toronto 31 B2
Toronto I. Toronto 31 B2
Toronto Lester B. Pearson Int. ✕ (YYZ) Toronto 31 A1
Torre Lupara Rome 26 B2
Torre Nova Rome 26 B2
Torrellas → Barcelona 4 A1
Torrevècchia Rome 26 B1
Toshima Tokyo 30 A3
Toshimaen Tokyo 30 A2
Tottenham London 15 A3
Tottenham Melbourne 18 A1
Toussus-le-Noble Paris 24 B1
Toussus-le-Noble ✕ (TNF) Paris 24 B1
Towchāl Cable Car Tehran 31 A2
Tower Hamlets □ London 15 A3
Tower of London London 15 A3
Towra Pt. Sydney 29 C2
Tøyen Oslo 23 A3
Toyonaka Osaka 23 A1
Trafaria Lisbon 16 A1
Traição, Cor. → São Paulo 27 B2
Tranegilde Copenhagen 8 B2
Trångsund Stockholm 29 B2
Trappenfelde Berlin 5 A4
Trastévere Rome 26 B1
Treasure I. San Francisco 26 B2
Třeboradice Prague 25 B3
Třebotov Prague 25 C1
Tree Tops Park Miami 19 B1
Tremblay-en-France Paris 24 A4
Tremembe → São Paulo 27 A2
Tremont New York 22 A2
Trenno Milan 18 B1
Treptow Berlin 5 B3
Três Rios, Sa. dos Rio de Janeiro 25 B1
Trevi, Fontana di Rome 26 B1
Trezzano sul Naviglio Milan 18 B1
Trieste Rome 26 B2
Trinidad Washington 33 B3
Trinity Edinburgh 11 B2
Trinity River Greenbelt Park Dallas-Fort Worth 10 B4
Trionfale Rome 26 B1
Triulzo Milan 18 B2
Troja Prague 25 B2
Trollbäcken Stockholm 29 B3
Trombay Mumbai 20 A2
Troparevo Moscow 19 C1
Trudeau Int., Montréal ✕ (YUL) Montreal 20 B1
Trudyashchikhsya, Ostrov St. Petersburg 27 B1
Tryvasshøgda Oslo 23 A3
Tseng Lan Shue Hong Kong 12 B3
Tseung Kwan Hong Kong 12 B3
Tsim Sha Tsui Hong Kong 12 B3
Tsing Lung Tau Hong Kong 12 A2
Tsing Yi Hong Kong 12 A2
Tsova Jerusalem 13 B1
Tsuen Wan Hong Kong 12 A2
Tsur Hadassa Jerusalem 13 B1
Tsurumi → Tokyo 30 B3
Tsz Wan Shan Hong Kong 12 A3
Tuas Singapore 28 B1
Tuchoměřice Prague 25 B1
Tuckahoe New York 22 A3
Tucuruvi São Paulo 27 A2
Tuen Mun Hong Kong 12 A1
Tufello Rome 26 B2
Tufnell Park London 15 A3
Tufts Univ. Boston 6 A2
Tughlakabad Delhi 10 B2
Tullamarine Melbourne 18 A1
Tulse Hill London 15 B3
Tung Chung Hong Kong 12 B1
Tung Lung Chau Hong Kong 12 B3
Tung O Hong Kong 12 B2
Tunis Baghdad 3 A2
Tuomarila Helsinki 11 B1
Tureberg Stockholm 29 A1
Turffontein Johannesburg 13 B2
Türk Telekom Arena Istanbul 12 B1
Turkey L. Orlando 23 A2
Turkey Lake Park Orlando 23 A2
Turner Field Atlanta 3 B2
Turnham Green London 15 B2
Turnhouse Edinburgh 11 B1
Tuscolana, Via Rome 26 B2
Twelve Apostles Cape Town 8 A1
Twentieth Century Fox Studios Los Angeles 16 B2
Twickenham London 15 B1
Twickenham Rugby Ground London 15 B1
Twin Peaks San Francisco 26 B2
Twins, The Hong Kong 12 B3

U

U.S. Capitol Washington 33 B2
U.S. Cellular Field Chicago 9 C3
Ubeidiya Jerusalem 13 B2
Uberaba → São Paulo 27 B2
Ubin, Pulau Singapore 28 A3
Uccle Brussels 6 B2
Udelnaya St. Petersburg 27 A2
Udelnoe St. Petersburg 27 B1
Udlding Munich 21 A1
Ueno Tokyo 30 A3
Úholičky Prague 25 B1
Uhříněves Prague 25 B3
Uithoorn Amsterdam 2 B1
Ujazdów Warsaw 33 B2
Újpalota Budapest 7 A2
Újpest Budapest 7 A2
Ukita Tokyo 30 A4
Uleta Miami 19 C2
Ullerup Copenhagen 8 B3
Ullevål Oslo 23 A3
Ulriksdal Stockholm 29 A1
Ulyanka St. Petersburg 27 B1
Um Al Khanazir I. Baghdad 3 B2
Umeda Osaka 23 A1
Umm al Sheif Dubai 9 B1
Umm Suqeim Dubai 9 B1
Ümraniye Istanbul 12 B2
Underground Atlanta Atlanta 3 B2
Underhill, L. Orlando 23 A3
Unětický potok → Prague 25 B2
Unhos Lisbon 16 A2
Unidad Santa Fe Mexico City 18 B1
Union City New York 22 B1
Union Port New York 22 B2
Union Square Hong Kong 12 B2
Union Station Toronto 31 B2
United Center Chicago 9 B2
United Nations Headquarters New York 22 B2
Universal Studios Los Angeles 16 B2
Universal Studios Orlando 23 B2
Universidad Madrid 17 B1
University Park Dallas-Fort Worth 10 A5
University Park Washington 33 B3
Unterbiberg Munich 21 B2
Unterföhring Munich 21 A3
Unterhaching Munich 21 B2
Unterlaa Vienna 32 B2
Untermenzing Munich 21 A1
Upper B. New York 22 C1
Upper Elmers End London 15 B3
Upper New York B. = Upper B. New York 22 C1
Upper Norwood London 15 B3
Upper Peirce Res. Singapore 28 A2
Upper Sydenham London 15 B3
Upper Tooting London 15 B3
Upton London 15 A4
Uptown Chicago 9 B2
Uran Mumbai 20 B2
Urayasu Tokyo 30 B4
Urbe ✕ Rome 26 B2
Urca Rio de Janeiro 25 B2
Uritsk St. Petersburg 27 C1
Urmston Road Hong Kong 12 A1
Üröm Budapest 7 A2
Ursus Warsaw 33 B1
Ursvik Stockholm 29 A1
Usera Madrid 17 B1
Ushigome Tokyo 30 A3
Usina Rio de Janeiro 25 B1
Üsküdar Istanbul 12 B2
Ust-Slavyanka St. Petersburg 27 C3
Uteke Stockholm 29 A3
Utrata Warsaw 33 B2
Uttarpara Kolkata 14 B1
Utterslev Mose Copenhagen 8 A2

V

Vaclavské náměstí Prague 25 B2
Vadaul Mumbai 20 A2
Vaires-sur-Marne Paris 24 A4
Valby Copenhagen 8 B2
Valcannuta Rome 26 B1
Valdelatas Madrid 17 A1
Valenton Paris 24 B3
Valera Milan 18 A1
Vallcarca Barcelona 4 A1
Valldoreix Barcelona 4 A1
Vallecas Madrid 17 B2
Vallecas, Cumbres de Madrid 17 B2
Vallensbæk Copenhagen 8 B2
Vallensbæk Strand Copenhagen 8 B2
Vallentunasjön Stockholm 29 A2
Valleranello Rome 26 C1
Vallisaari Helsinki 11 C3
Vallvidrera Barcelona 4 A1
Valvidrera → Barcelona 4 A1
Van Gogh Museum Amsterdam 2 A2
Vanak Tehran 31 A2
Vanda = Vantaa Helsinki 11 B2
Vangede Copenhagen 8 A3
Vaniköy Istanbul 12 B2
Vanløse Copenhagen 8 A2
Vantaa Helsinki 11 B2
Vantaankoski Helsinki 11 B2
Vantaanpuisto Helsinki 11 B2
Vanves Paris 24 B2
Varedo Milan 18 A1
Varkiza Athens 2 C2
Vartiokylä Helsinki 11 B3
Vartiosaari Helsinki 11 B3
Vasamuseet Stockholm 29 B2
Vasco Cape Town 8 A2
Vasfenārd Tehran 31 B2
Vashi Mumbai 20 A2
Vasilyevskiy, Ostrov St. Petersburg 27 B1
Vatican City ■ Rome 26 B1
Vaucluse Sydney 29 B2
Vaucluse House Sydney 29 B2
Vaucresson Paris 24 A1
Vaughan Toronto 31 A1
Vauhallan Paris 24 B2
Vaujours Paris 24 A4
Vauxhall London 15 B3
Vecsés Budapest 7 B3
Veleň Prague 25 A3
Veleslavín Prague 25 B2
Vélizy-Villacoublay Paris 24 B2
Velka-Chuchle Prague 25 B2
Velké Přílepy Prague 25 B1
Venda Seca Lisbon 16 A1
Venetian Islands Miami 19 D3
Venice Los Angeles 16 C2
Ventas Madrid 17 B1
Ventorro del Cano Madrid 17 B1
Venustiano Carranza Mexico City 18 B2
Verde → São Paulo 27 A1
Verdugo Mts. Los Angeles 16 A2
Verdun Montreal 20 B1
Vérhalom Budapest 7 A2
Vermelho → São Paulo 27 B1
Vermont Knolls Los Angeles 16 C3
Vernon Los Angeles 16 B3
Verrières-le-Buisson Paris 24 B2
Versailles Buenos Aires 7 B1
Versailles Paris 24 B1
Veshnyaki Moscow 19 B3
Vesolyy Posolok St. Petersburg 27 B2
Vestra Helsinki 11 B1
Vestskoven Copenhagen 8 A2
Vicálvaro Madrid 17 B2
Vicente Lopez Buenos Aires 7 B2
Victoria Hong Kong 12 B2
Victoria, Pont Montreal 20 B2
Victoria and Alfred Waterfront Cape Town 8 A1
Victoria Gardens Mumbai 20 B2
Victoria Harbour Hong Kong 12 B3
Victoria Island Lagos 14 B2
Victoria L. Johannesburg 13 B2
Victoria Lawn Tennis Courts Melbourne 18 B2
Victoria Park Singapore 28 B2
Victoria Peak Hong Kong 12 B2
Victoria Terminus = Chhatrapati Shivaji Terminus Mumbai 20 B2
Victoria Village Toronto 31 A3
Vienna = Wien Vienna 32 A2
Vietnam Veterans Memorial Washington 33 B2
Vieux Carré = French Quarter New Orleans 21 B2
View Park Los Angeles 16 B3
Vigário Geral Rio de Janeiro 25 A1
Vigentino Milan 18 B2
Viggbyholm Stockholm 29 A2
Vighignolo Milan 18 B1
Viikki Helsinki 11 B3
Vikhroli Mumbai 20 A2
Vila Guilherme São Paulo 27 B2
Vila Isabel Rio de Janeiro 25 B1
Vila Jaguára São Paulo 27 B1
Vila Madalena São Paulo 27 B1
Vila Maria São Paulo 27 B2
Vila Mariana São Paulo 27 B2
Vila Prudente São Paulo 27 B2
Viladecans Barcelona 4 A1
Vile Parle Mumbai 20 A2
Villa Adelina Buenos Aires 7 B1
Villa Ballester Buenos Aires 7 B1
Villa Barilari Buenos Aires 7 C2
Villa Bosch Buenos Aires 7 B1
Villa C. Colon Buenos Aires 7 C2
Villa Ciudadela Buenos Aires 7 B1
Villa de Guadalupe Mexico City 18 B2
Villa Devoto Buenos Aires 7 B1
Villa Diamante Buenos Aires 7 C2
Villa Dominico Buenos Aires 7 C3
Villa Lugano Buenos Aires 7 C2
Villa Lynch Buenos Aires 7 B1
Villa Madero Buenos Aires 7 C1
Villa Sáenz Pena Buenos Aires 7 B1
Villa Urquiza Buenos Aires 7 B2
Villaverde Madrid 17 B1
Villaverde Bajo Madrid 17 B1
Ville-d'Avray Paris 24 B2
Villecresnes Paris 24 B4
Villejuif Paris 24 B3
Villemomble Paris 24 A4
Villeneuve-la-Garenne Paris 24 A2
Villeneuve-le-Roi Paris 24 B3
Villeneuve-St-Georges Paris 24 B3
Villeparisis Paris 24 A4
Villevaudé Paris 24 A4
Villiers-le-Bâcle Paris 24 B1
Villiers-sur-Marne Paris 24 B4
Villinki Helsinki 11 C3
Villoresi, Canale Milan 18 A1
Vilvoorde Brussels 6 A2
Vimodrone Milan 18 A2
Vimont Montreal 20 A1
Vincennes Paris 24 A3
Vincennes, Bois de Paris 24 B3
Vineland Orlando 23 B1
Vinings Atlanta 3 A2
Vinohrady Prague 25 B2
Vinoř Prague 25 B3
Violet Hill Hong Kong 12 B3
Virányos Budapest 7 A1
Virginia, L. Orlando 23 A2
Virginia Gardens Miami 19 D1
Virginia Key Miami 19 D3
Viroflay Paris 24 B2
Vironas Athens 2 B2
Virum Copenhagen 8 A2
Visitacion Valley San Francisco 26 B2
Vista Alegre Lima 14 B3
Vista Alegre Santiago 27 C1
Vista Grove Atlanta 3 A3
Vitacura Santiago 27 B2
Vitinia Rome 26 C1
Vitry-sur-Seine Paris 24 B3
Vladykino Moscow 19 A2
Vokovice Prague 25 B2
Volgelsdorf Berlin 5 B5
Volkhonka-Zil Moscow 19 C2
Vollen Oslo 23 B1
Volodarskoye St. Petersburg 27 B2
Volynkina-Derevnya St. Petersburg 27 B1
Vondelpark Amsterdam 2 A2
Vösendorf Vienna 32 B2
Voula Athens 2 C2
Vouliagmeni Athens 2 C2
Vredehoek Cape Town 8 A1
Vršovice Prague 25 B2
Vyborgskaya Storona St. Petersburg 27 B2
Vykhino Moscow 19 B3
Vyšehrad Prague 25 B2

W

Wachterhof Munich 21 B3
Wadala Mumbai 20 A2
Wadi al-Arayis Jerusalem 13 B2
Wadi Fukin Jerusalem 13 B1
Waduk Pluit Jakarta 12 A1
Waggaman New Orleans 21 B1
Wah Fu Hong Kong 12 B2
Wahda Baghdad 3 B2
Währing Vienna 32 A2
Waidmannslust Berlin 5 A3
Wakefield Boston 6 A2
Waldesruh Berlin 5 B4
Waldperlach Munich 21 B3
Waldtrudering Munich 21 B3
Wall Street New York 22 B1
Walt Disney World Resort Orlando 23 B1
Waltham Boston 6 A1
Waltham Forest □ London 15 A3
Walthamstow London 15 A3
Walton-on-Thames London 15 B1
Wambeek Brussels 6 A3
Wan Chai Hong Kong 12 B3
Wandle → London 15 B2
Wandsworth □ London 15 B2
Wangjing Beijing 4 B2
Wannsee Berlin 5 B1
Wansdorf Berlin 5 A1
Wanstead London 15 A4
Wapping London 15 A3
Wards I. New York 22 B2
Warnberg Munich 21 B2
Warner Brothers Studios Los Angeles 16 B2
Warrâq el 'Arab Cairo 7 A2
Warringal Park Melbourne 18 A2
Warriston Edinburgh 11 B2
Warsaw = Warszawa Warsaw 33 B2
Warsaw Chopin ✕ (WAW) Warsaw 33 B1
Warszawa Warsaw 33 B2
Wartenberg Berlin 5 A4
Washington Washington 33 B2
Washington Heights New York 22 A2
Washington Park Chicago 9 C3
Washington Ronald Reagan Nat. ✕ (DCA) Washington 33 B2
Wat Pho Bangkok 3 B1
Watauga Dallas-Fort Worth 10 A2
Water of Leith → Edinburgh 11 B1
Watergraafsmeer Amsterdam 2 A2
Waterland Amsterdam 2 A2
Waterloo Brussels 6 B2
Watermeal-Boitsfort Brussels 6 B2
Watertown Boston 6 A1
Watsonia Melbourne 18 A2
Watts Los Angeles 16 C3
Waverley Boston 6 A1
Waverley Johannesburg 13 A2
Waverley Sydney 29 B2
Wawer Warsaw 33 B2
Wawrzyszew Warsaw 33 B1
Wazirabad Delhi 10 A2
Wazīrīya Baghdad 3 A2
Wazirpur Delhi 10 A2
Wealdstone London 15 A1
Wedding Berlin 5 A3
Weehawken New York 22 B1
Weesp Amsterdam 2 B3
Weidling Vienna 32 A1
Weidlingbach Vienna 32 A1
Weissensee Berlin 5 A3
Wellesley Hills Boston 6 B1
Welling London 15 B4
Wellington Boston 6 A2
Weltevreden Park Johannesburg 13 A1
Wembley London 15 A2
Wemmel Brussels 6 A1
Wemmer Pan Johannesburg 13 B2
Wenceslas Square = Vaclavské náměstí Prague 25 B2
Wendenschloss Berlin 5 B4
Wennington London 15 A5
Werneuchen Berlin 5 A5
West Don → Toronto 31 A2
West Drayton London 15 A1
West Ham London 15 A4
West Harrow London 15 A1
West Heath London 15 B4
West Hill Toronto 31 A3
West Hollywood Los Angeles 16 B2
West Lamma Channel Hong Kong 12 B2
West Los Angeles, Univ. of Los Angeles 16 C2
West Medford Boston 6 A2
West Miami Miami 19 D1
West Molesey London 15 B1
West New York New York 22 B1
West of Twin Peaks San Francisco 26 B2
West Park Johannesburg 13 A1
West Park Miami 19 C2
West Rouge Toronto 31 A4
West Roxbury Boston 6 B2
West Town Chicago 9 B2
West Wharf Karachi 13 B1
Westchester Los Angeles 16 C2
Westchester New York 22 A2
Westcliff Johannesburg 13 B2
Westdene Johannesburg 13 B1
Westend Helsinki 11 C1
Wester Hailes Edinburgh 11 B2
Westerham Munich 21 B2
Western Addition San Francisco 26 B2
Westgate New Orleans 21 A1
Westgate Washington 33 B2
Westlake Cape Town 8 B1
Westlake Los Angeles 16 B3
Westlake San Francisco 26 B2
Westminster London 15 A3
Westmount Montreal 20 B2
Weston Toronto 31 A1
Westwego New Orleans 21 B2
Westwood Village Los Angeles 16 B2
Westzaan Amsterdam 2 A1
Wetton Cape Town 8 B2
Wexford Toronto 31 A3
Weybridge London 15 B1
Wezembeek-Oppem Brussels 6 A2
White Cloud Hill = Baiyun Mountain Scenic Area ⌂ Guangzhou 11 A2
White House, The Washington 33 B2
White Rock L. Dallas-Fort Worth 10 A5
Whitechapel London 15 A3
Whitney Las Vegas 14 B2
Whittier Los Angeles 16 C4
Whittier Narrows Recreation Area ⌂ Los Angeles 16 B4
Whitton London 15 B1
Wieden Vienna 32 A2
Wien Vienna 32 A2
Wien-Schwechat ✕ (VIE) Vienna 32 B3
Wienerberg Vienna 32 B2
Wierzbno Warsaw 33 B2
Wijde Wormer Amsterdam 2 A2
Wilanów Warsaw 33 B2
Wilanówka → Warsaw 33 C2
Wilds, The Johannesburg 13 B2
Wilhelmshagen Berlin 5 B5
Wilket Creek Park Toronto 31 A2
Wilkieston Edinburgh 11 B1
Will Rogers State Historical Park ⌂ Los Angeles 16 B1
Willesden London 15 A2
Willesden Green London 15 A2
Williamsbridge New York 22 A2
Williamsburg New York 22 B2
Williamsburg Orlando 23 B2
Williamstown Melbourne 18 B1
Willis, L. Orlando 23 B2
Willoughby Sydney 29 A2
Willowdale New Orleans 21 A1
Willowdale Toronto 31 A2
Wilmer Dallas-Fort Worth 10 C5
Wilmersdorf Berlin 5 B2
Wilmette Chicago 9 A2
Wilmington London 15 B5
Wilton Manors Miami 19 B3
Wimbledon London 15 B2
Wimbledon Common London 15 B2
Wimbledon Park London 15 B2
Wimbledon Tennis Ground London 15 B2
Winchester Boston 6 A2
Winchester Las Vegas 14 B2
Windermere Cape Town 8 A2
Windermere Orlando 23 B1
Windsor Johannesburg 13 A1
Windsor, Gare Montreal 20 B2
Windsor Hills Los Angeles 16 C2
Winnetka Chicago 9 A2
Winning Munich 21 B2
Wissous Paris 24 B2
Wittenau Berlin 5 A2
Witwatersrand, Univ. of Johannesburg 13 B2
Włochy Warsaw 33 B1
Wo Mei Hong Kong 12 A3
Wo Yi Hop Hong Kong 12 A2
Woburn Boston 6 A2
Woburn Toronto 31 A3
Wola Warsaw 33 B1
Wolgok Seoul 27 B2
Wolica Warsaw 33 C1
Wollaston Boston 6 B2
Woltersdorf Berlin 5 B5
Woluwe-St-Lambert Brussels 6 A2
Woluwe-St-Pierre Brussels 6 A2
Wong Chuk Hang Hong Kong 12 B2
Wong Chuk Wan Hong Kong 12 A3
Wong Chuk Yeung Hong Kong 12 A3
Wood Green London 15 A3
Wood Ridge New York 22 A1
Woodbine Race Track Toronto 31 A1
Woodbridge Toronto 31 A1
Woodford London 15 A4
Woodford Bridge London 15 A4
Woodford Green London 15 A4
Woodhaven New York 22 B2
Woodhouselee Edinburgh 11 B2
Woodlands Singapore 28 A2
Woodmont Washington 33 B2
Woodside London 15 B3
Woodside New York 22 B2
Woodstock Cape Town 8 A1
Woollahra Sydney 29 B2
Woolooware B. Sydney 29 C1
Woolwich London 15 B4
Worker's Stadium Beijing 4 B2
World Financial Centre Shanghai 28 B2
Worli Mumbai 20 A1
Worth Chicago 9 C2
Wren's Nest Atlanta 3 B2
Wrigley Field Chicago 9 B3
Wuhlgarten Berlin 5 A4
Wujiaochang Shanghai 28 B2
Würm → Munich 21 B1
Würm-kanal Munich 21 A1
Wushan Guangzhou 11 B3
Wusong Shanghai 28 A1
Wyczółki Warsaw 33 C1
Wygoda Warsaw 33 B2
Wynberg Cape Town 8 B1

X

Xabregas Lisbon 16 A2
Xiakeng Guangzhou 11 A2
Xiaogang Park Guangzhou 11 B2
Xiaoping Guangzhou 11 A2
Xiashachong Guangzhou 11 B1
Xichang Guangzhou 11 B2
Xicheng Beijing 4 B1
Xidan Beijing 4 B2
Xi'ercun Guangzhou 11 B2
Xincun Guangzhou 11 B2
Xizhimen Beijing 4 B1
Xochimilco, Parque Ecológico Mexico City 18 C2
Xuanwu Beijing 4 B1
Xuhui Shanghai 28 B1
Xujiahui Shanghai 28 B1

Y

Yaba Lagos 14 A2
Yaftābād Tehran 31 B1
Yahara Tokyo 30 A2
Yaho Tokyo 30 A1
Yakire Tokyo 30 A4
Yaksu Seoul 27 B2
Yamada Osaka 23 A2
Yamada Tokyo 30 B2
Yamato → Osaka 23 B1
Yan Kit Singapore 28 A3
Yanbu Guangzhou 11 B1
Yangcheon Seoul 27 B1
Yanghuayuan Beijing 4 C1
Yangjae Seoul 27 C2
Yangjiazhuang Shanghai 28 A1
Yangjing Shanghai 28 B2
Yangpu Shanghai 28 B2
Yangpu Park Shanghai 28 B2
Yannawa Bangkok 3 B2
Yaotai Guangzhou 11 B2
Yarmūk Baghdad 3 B1
Yarra Bend Park Melbourne 18 A2
Yarraville Melbourne 18 A1
Yauza → Moscow 19 B4
Yeading London 15 A1
Yedikule Istanbul 12 C1
Yenikapı Istanbul 12 B1
Yeniköy Istanbul 12 B2
Yeongdeungpo Seoul 27 B1
Yeongdong Seoul 27 B2
Yeouido Seoul 27 B1
Yerba Buena I. San Francisco 26 B2
Yerres Paris 24 B4
Yerushalayim = Jerusalem Jerusalem 13 B2
Yi O San Tsuen Hong Kong 12 B1
Yiheyuan Beijing 4 B1
Yıldız Park Istanbul 12 B2
Yinhangzhen Shanghai 28 A2
Yishun Singapore 28 A3
Ylästö Helsinki 11 B2
Yodo → Osaka 23 A2
Yongdingman Beijing 4 B2
Yongfucun Guangzhou 11 B2
Yongsan Seoul 27 B2
Yonkers New York 22 A2
York Toronto 31 A2
York Mills Toronto 31 A2
York Univ. Toronto 31 A1
You'anmen Beijing 4 B1
Youngsfield Cape Town 8 B1
Yuancun Guangzhou 11 B3
Yuanmingyuan Park Beijing 4 A1
Yuanxiatian Guangzhou 11 A2
Yuexiu Guangzhou 11 B2
Yuexiu Park Guangzhou 11 B2
Yugo-Zarad Moscow 19 B2
Yung Shue Wan Hong Kong 12 B2
Yūsofābād Tehran 31 A2

Z

Za'abeel Dubai 9 B2
Zaandam Amsterdam 2 A1
Zaandijk Amsterdam 2 A1
Zaanstad Amsterdam 2 A1
Záběhlice Prague 25 B2
Zabki Warsaw 33 B2
Zacisze Warsaw 33 B2
Zahrā Baghdad 3 A1
Žalov Prague 25 A2
Załuski Warsaw 33 C1
Zamdorf Munich 21 B2
Zanevka St. Petersburg 27 B3
Zapote Manila 17 C1
Zaventem Brussels 6 A2
Zawady Warsaw 33 B2
Zāwiyet Abū Musallam Cairo 7 B1
Zawrā' Park Baghdad 3 B2
Zbraslav Prague 25 C2
Zbuzany Prague 25 B1
Zdiby Prague 25 B2
Zeekoevlei Cape Town 8 B2
Zehlendorf Berlin 5 B2
Zenne → Brussels 6 A2
Zephyr Field New Orleans 21 B1
Żerań Warsaw 33 B1
Zerzeń Warsaw 33 B2
Zeytinburnu Istanbul 12 C1
Zhabei Shanghai 28 B1
Zhdanov Moscow 19 B3
Zheji Guangzhou 11 B2
Zhenru Shanghai 28 B1
Zhernovka St. Petersburg 27 B2
Zhicun Guangzhou 11 B1
Zhongguancun Beijing 4 B1
Zhongshan Park Shanghai 28 B1
Zhoucun Guangzhou 11 A2
Zhoujiadu Shanghai 28 B1
Zhoujiazhen Shanghai 28 B2
Zhouzhuangzi Beijing 4 B1
Zhulebino Moscow 19 B4
Zhushadi Guangzhou 11 A3
Zielona Warsaw 33 B3
Zielonka Warsaw 33 B2
Zizhuyuan Park Beijing 4 B1
Žižkov Prague 25 B2
Zličín Prague 25 B1
Zografou Athens 2 B2
Żoliborz Warsaw 33 B2
Zonnebloem Cape Town 8 A1
Zugliget Budapest 7 B1
Zugló Budapest 7 A2
Zuiderwoude Amsterdam 2 A3
Zumbi Rio de Janeiro 25 A1
Zunderdorp Amsterdam 2 A2
Zuvuvu → São Paulo 27 C1
Zwanenburg Amsterdam 2 A1
Zwölfaxing Vienna 32 B2

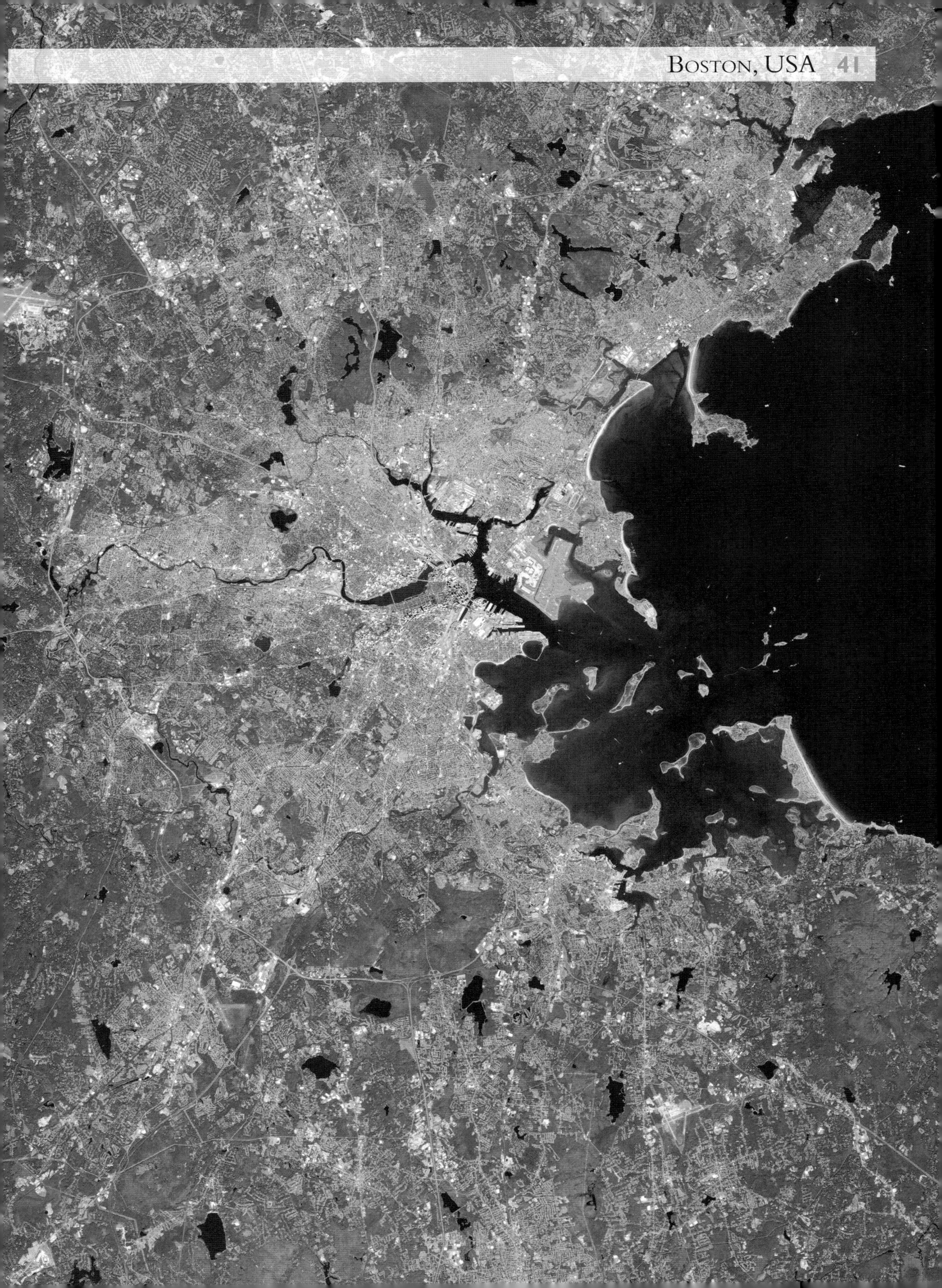

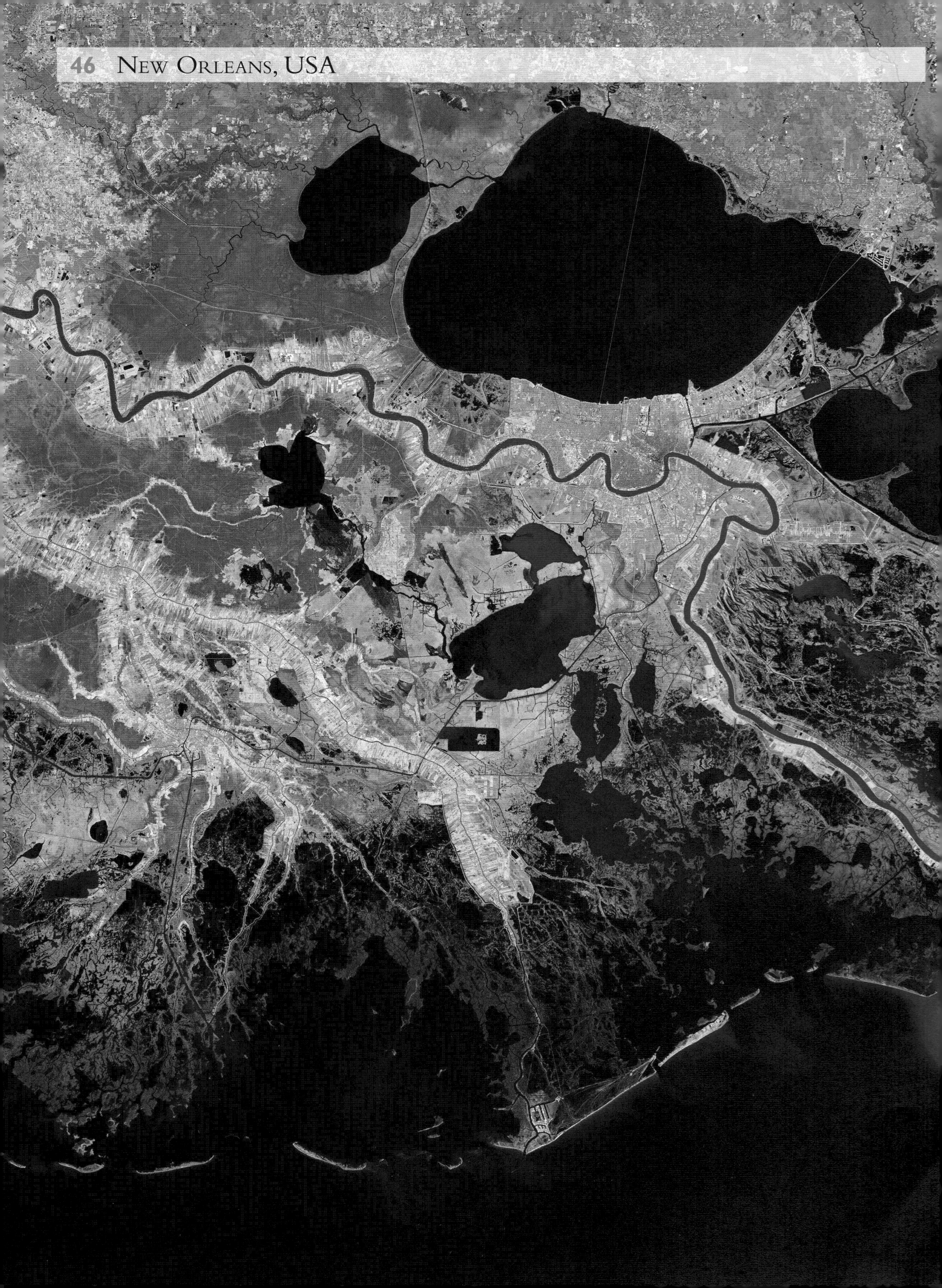

46 New Orleans, USA

WORLD
MAPS

SETTLEMENTS

■ **PARIS**   ◉ Rotterdam   ◉ **Livorno**   ◉ **Brugge**   ◎ Exeter   ○ *Torremolinos*   ○ *Oberammergau*   ○ *Thira*

Settlement symbols and type styles vary according to the scale of each map and indicate the importance
of towns on the map rather than specific population figures

● *Vaduz*   Capital cities have red infills   ∴   Ruins or archaeological sites

⬠   Urban agglomerations   ⌣   Wells in desert

ADMINISTRATION

———— International boundaries   ·········· Internal boundaries   PERU   Country names

– – – · International boundaries
(undefined or disputed)   ⬡ National parks   KENT   Administrative
area names

International boundaries show the *de facto* situation where there are rival claims to territory

COMMUNICATIONS

═══ Motorways, freeways
and expressways   —— Principal railways   LHR ✈   Principal airports

———— Principal roads   – – – – Railways
under construction   ⊕   Other airports

—— Other roads   —— Other railways   ············· Principal canals

+ - - + Road tunnels   + - - + Railway tunnels   ⨝   Passes

PHYSICAL FEATURES

〜〜 Perennial streams   ⬭ Intermittent lakes   ▲ 8850   Elevations in metres

– – – Intermittent streams   ⬭ Swamps and marshes   ▾ 8500   Sea depths in metres

⬭ Perennial lakes   ⬭ Permanent ice
and glaciers   *1134*   Height of lake surface
above sea level in metres

⬚ Sand deserts

ELEVATION AND DEPTH TINTS

Height of land above sea level   Land below sea level   Depth of sea

in metres	6000	4000	3000	2000	1500	1000	400	200	0						in feet
in feet	18 000	12 000	9000	6000	4500	3000	1200	600		6000	12 000	15 000	18 000	24 000	
									0	200	2000	4000	5000	6000	8000	in metres

Some of the maps have different contours to highlight and clarify the principal relief features

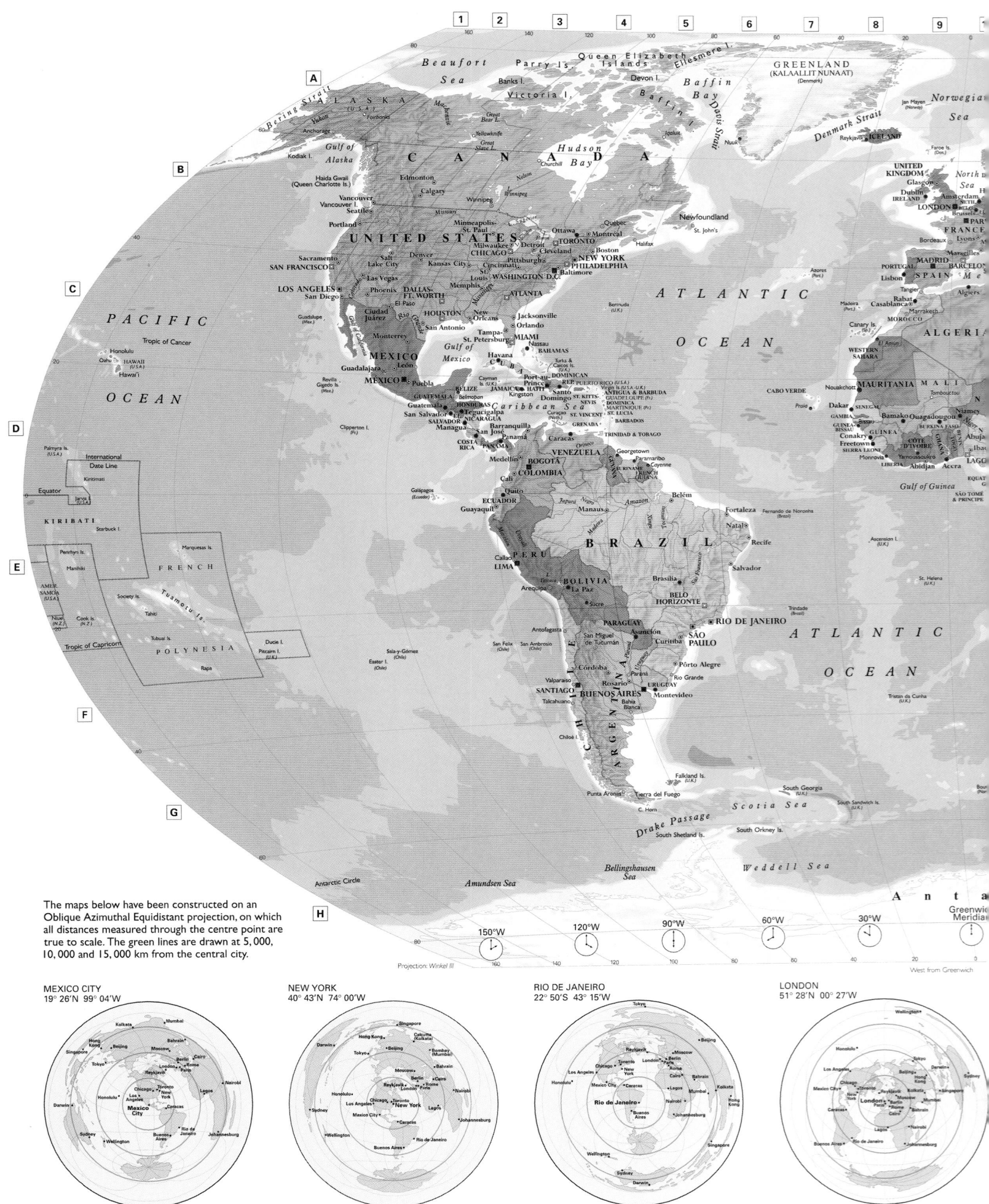

The maps below have been constructed on an Oblique Azimuthal Equidistant projection, on which all distances measured through the centre point are true to scale. The green lines are drawn at 5,000, 10,000 and 15,000 km from the central city.

Projection: Winkel III

West from Greenwich

MEXICO CITY
19° 26'N 99° 04'W

NEW YORK
40° 43'N 74° 00'W

RIO DE JANEIRO
22° 50'S 43° 15'W

LONDON
51° 28'N 00° 27'W

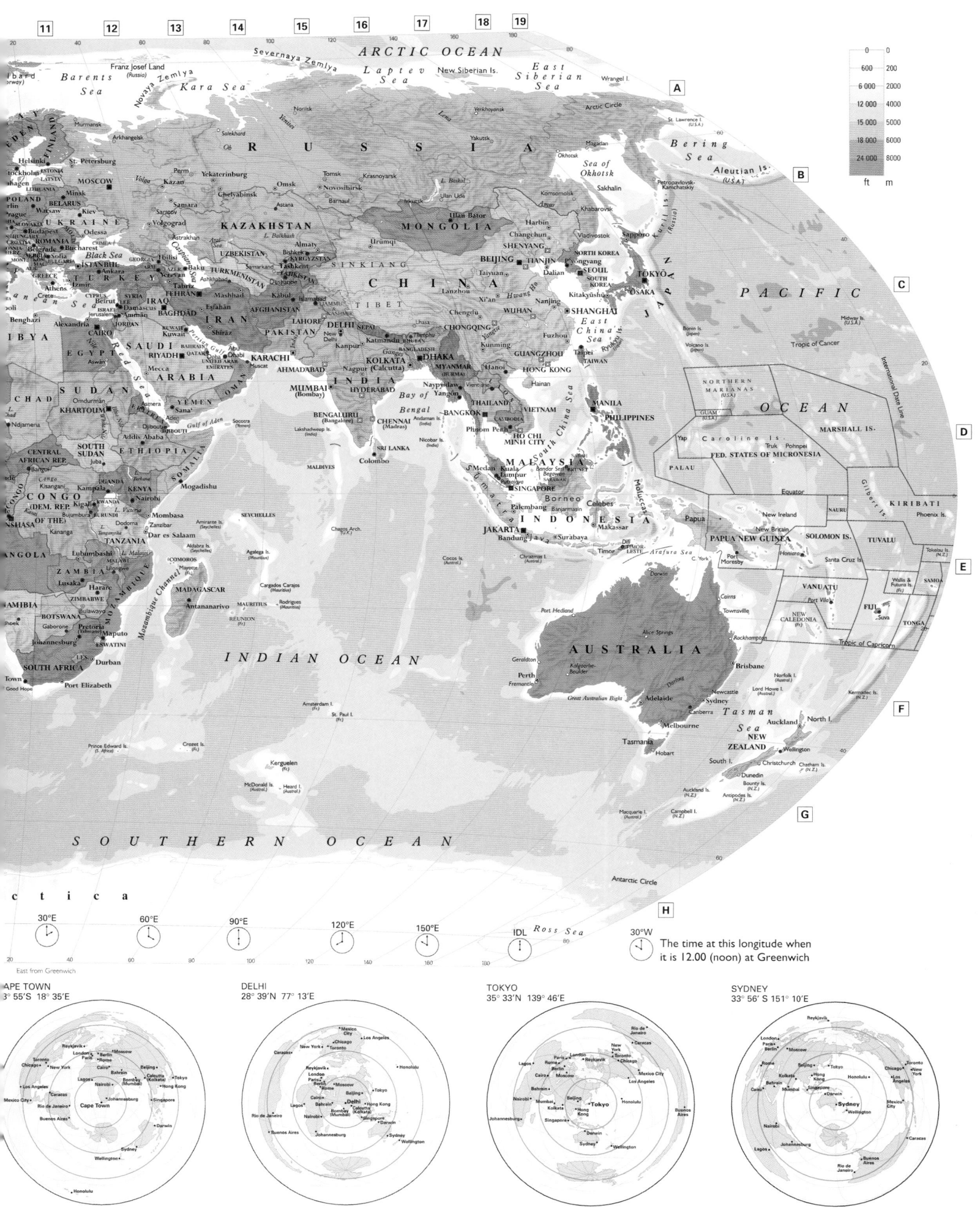

11 12 13 14 15 16 17 18 19

ARCTIC OCEAN

Franz Josef Land (Russia) Severnaya Zemlya *Laptev Sea* New Siberian Is. *East Siberian Is.* Wrangel I.

Barents Sea Novaya Zemlya *Kara Sea* Norilsk Yenisey Lena Verkhoyansk Arctic Circle St. Lawrence I. (U.S.A.)

0   0
600   200
6 000   2000
12 000   4000
15 000   5000
18 000   6000
24 000   8000
ft   m

A

Murmansk Arkhangelsk Ob R U S S I A Yakutsk Magadan *Bering Sea*

Salekhard Tomsk Krasnoyarsk Okhotsk Petropavlovsk-Kamchatskiy *Aleutian Is. (U.S.A.)*

Helsinki St. Petersburg MOSCOW Yekaterinburg Omsk Novosibirsk L. Baikal Irkutsk Ulan Ude Sea of Okhotsk Sakhalin Kuril Is. (Russia)

B

Stockholm ESTONIA LATVIA Perm Chelyabinsk Barnaul Komsomolsk Khabarovsk

Minsk LITHUANIA Volga Kazan KAZAKHSTAN Astana MONGOLIA Ulan Bator Amur Harbin Vladivostok Sapporo

POLAND BELARUS Samara Aral Sea Almaty Ürümqi SINKIANG Changchun NORTH KOREA SHENYANG

Warsaw Kiev UKRAINE Saratov L. Balkhash Bishkek Beijing TIANJIN P'yongyang Dalian SEOUL TŌKYŌ

Prague Volgograd UZBEKISTAN KYRGYZSTAN C H I N A Taiyuan SOUTH KOREA ŌSAKA

SLOVAKIA ROMANIA Budapest Astrakhan Caspian Sea TAJIKISTAN Hwang Kitakyūshū

CROATIA Bucharest CRIMEA Black Sea GEORGIA Tbilisi Baku TURKMENISTAN Lanzhou Xi'an Nanjing SHANGHAI

SERBIA Belgrade Sofia Ankara AZER. Ashkhabad Samarkand Tashkent TIBET WUHAN

GREECE Istanbul ARMENIA Yerevan Mashhad Kābul Islamabad Lhasa CHONGQING East China Sea

Athens Izmir T U R K E Y Tabriz AFGHANISTAN JAMMU Chengdu Fuzhou TAIWAN

Crete CYPRUS SYRIA Damascus FEHRĀN Esfahān LAHORE KASHMIR SEPAL Kunming GUANGZHOU Taipei

Beirut IRAQ I R A N Shiraz PAKISTAN DELHI Katmandu BANGLADESH Hanoi HONG KONG

Alexandria ISRAEL Jerusalem Amman BAGHDĀD KUWAIT Kuwait Abu New Delhi Kanpur Ganges DHAKA Hainan

JORDAN Persian Gulf Dhabi KARACHI Nagpur KOLKATA (Calcutta) MYANMAR (BURMA)

LIBYA EGYPT SAUDI RIYADH QATAR UNITED ARAB EMIRATES AHMADABAD I N D I A Naypyidaw Yangon *South China Sea*

CAIRO BAHRAIN Muscat MUMBAI (Bombay) HYDERABAD *Bay of Bengal* THAILAND VIETNAM MANILA NORTHERN MARIANAS (U.S.A.)

Benghazi Aswan Red Sea Mecca OMAN Andaman Is. (India) BANGKOK CAMBODIA PHILIPPINES GUAM (U.S.A.)

C

D

CHAD SUDAN Omdurman YEMEN Gulf of Aden Socotra (Yemen) Lakshadweep Is. (India) CHENNAI (Madras) Nicobar Is. (India) Phnom Penh HO CHI MINH CITY Vientiane MARSHALL IS.

Tropic of Cancer

Ndjamena KHARTOUM Sana'a DJIBOUTI SRI LANKA Yap Caroline Is. Truk Pohnpei FED. STATES OF MICRONESIA

CENTRAL AFRICAN REP. Addis Ababa ETHIOPIA MALDIVES Colombo PALAU

Bangui SOUTH SUDAN Juba SOMALIA Mogadishu Equator New Ireland NAURU KIRIBATI Phoenix Is.

CONGO UGANDA KENYA Kisangani Kampala L. Victoria Nairobi Medan Kuala Lumpur Bandar Seri Begawan BRUNEI SARAWAK Celebes Papua New Britain

CONGO (DEM. REP. OF THE) Kigali RWANDA BURUNDI Bujumbura Amirante Is. (Seychelles) SEYCHELLES MALAYSIA SINGAPORE Borneo Makassar Moluccas PAPUA NEW GUINEA SOLOMON IS. TUVALU

Kinshasa Kananga TANZANIA Dar es Salaam Aldabra Is. (Seychelles) Palembang I N D O N E S I A Santa Cruz Is. Tokelau (N.Z.)

E

ANGOLA Lubumbashi L. Malawi MALAWI COMOROS Cargados Carajos (Mauritius) JAKARTA Java Surabaya Dili TIMOR-LESTE *Arafura Sea* Port Moresby C. York Honiara VANUATU Wallis & Futuna Is. (Fr.) SAMOA

ZAMBIA Lusaka Harare Antananarivo MAURITIUS Rodrigues (Mauritius) Timor Darwin Cairns NEW CALEDONIA Port Vila FIJI Suva TONGA

NAMIBIA ZIMBABWE Bulawayo MADAGASCAR REUNION (Fr.) Agalega Is. (Mauritius) Mayotte (Fr.) Port Hedland Townsville Tropic of Capricorn

BOTSWANA Gaborone Pretoria ESWATINI Maputo Mozambique Channel *INDIAN OCEAN* A U S T R A L I A Alice Springs Rockhampton Kermadec Is. (N.Z.)

Johannesburg LESOTHO Durban Geraldton Kalgoorlie-Boulder Darling Brisbane Norfolk I. (Austral.) Lord Howe I. (Austral.)

F

SOUTH AFRICA Town Port Elizabeth Good Hope Perth Fremantle Great Australian Bight Adelaide Sydney Newcastle Canberra *Tasman Sea* Auckland North I.

Amsterdam I. (Fr.) St. Paul I. (Fr.) Melbourne NEW ZEALAND Wellington

Prince Edward Is. (S. Africa) Crozet Is. (Fr.) Tasmania Hobart South I. Christchurch Chatham Is. (N.Z.)

G

Kerguelen (Fr.) Dunedin Bounty Is. (N.Z.) Antipodes Is. (N.Z.)

McDonald I. (Austral.) Heard I. (Austral.) Macquarie I. (Austral.) Campbell I. (N.Z.)

S O U T H E R N   O C E A N

H

Antarctic Circle

ctica

Ross Sea

30°E 60°E 90°E 120°E 150°E IDL 30°W The time at this longitude when it is 12.00 (noon) at Greenwich

East from Greenwich

CAPE TOWN
33° 55'S 18° 35'E

DELHI
28° 39'N 77° 13'E

TOKYO
35° 33'N 139° 46'E

SYDNEY
33° 56' S 151° 10'E

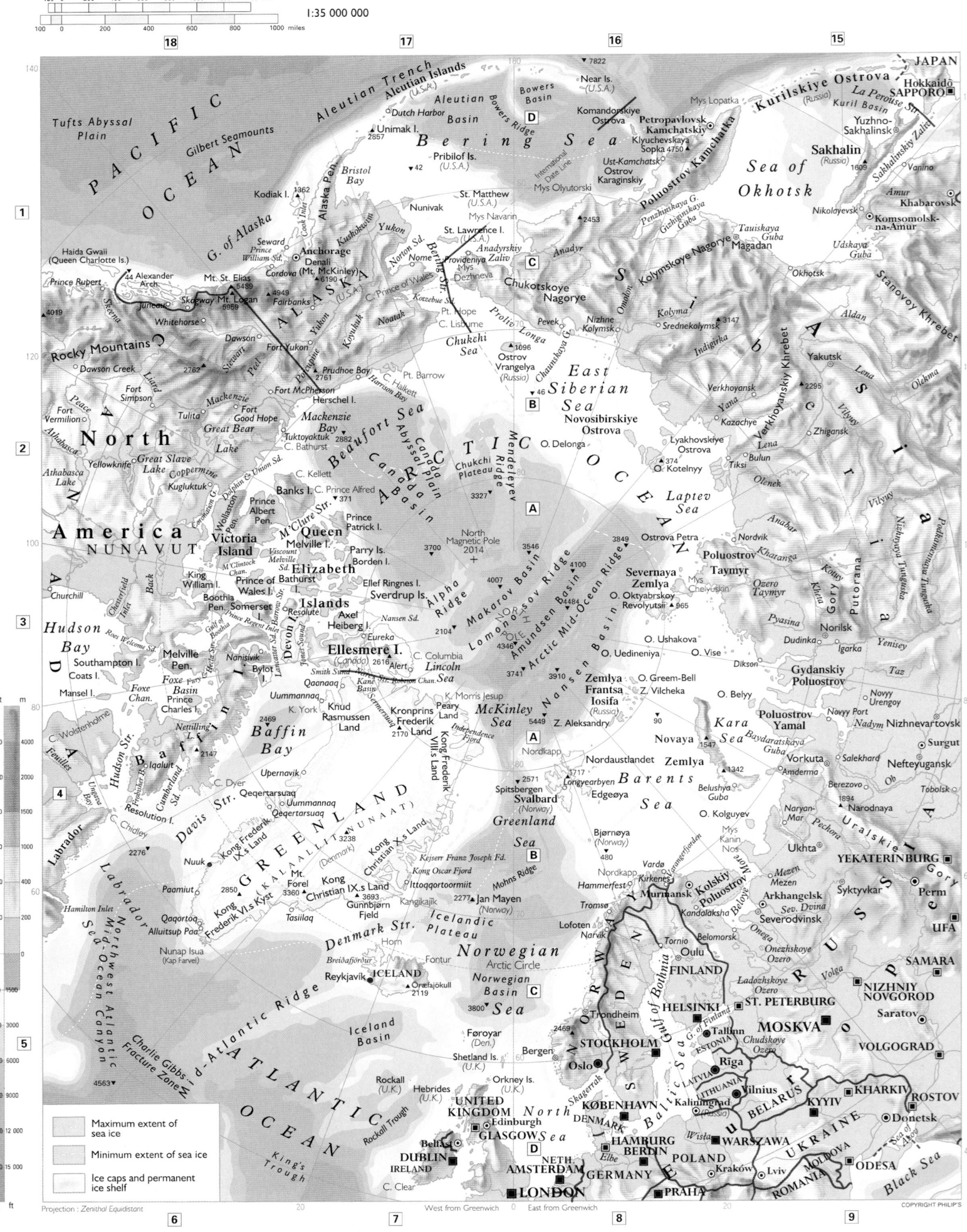

1:35 000 000

100 0 200 400 600 800 1000 1200 1400 km

100 0 200 400 600 800 1000 miles

18   17   16   15

JAPAN

PACIFIC

Tufts Abyssal
Plain

Gilbert Seamounts

Aleutian Trench
Aleutian Islands
(U.S.A.)

Bowers
Basin

Near Is.
(U.S.A.)

▽ 7822

Hokkaidō
SAPPORO

Kurilskiye Ostrova
(Russia)

La Perouse Str.

Kuril Basin

Mys Lopatka

Yuzhno-
Sakhalinsk

OCEAN

Aleutian
Basin

Bowers
Ridge

Bering   Sea

Dutch Harbor

Komandorskiye
Ostrova

Petropavlovsk-
Kamchatskiy

Sakhalin
(Russia)

1609

Sakhalinskiy Zaliv

Vanino

Unimak I.
2857

Pribilof Is.
(U.S.A.)

International Date Line

Ust-Kamchatsk
Ostrov
Karaginskiy

 Klyuchevskaya
Sopka 4750

**Sea of
Okhotsk**

Amur

Bristol
Bay

Kodiak I.   1362

St. Matthew
(U.S.A.)

▽ 42

Mys Olyutorski

Poluostrov Kamchatka

Khabarovsk

G. of Alaska

Seward
Prince
William Sd.

Anchorage

Nunivak

St. Lawrence I.
(U.S.A.)

Mys Navarin

▲ 2453

Penzhinskaya G.
Gizhiginskaya
Guba

Komsomolsk-
na-Amur

Haida Gwaii
(Queen Charlotte Is.)

Cordova (Mt. McKinley)
6190

Denali

Norton Sd.

Nome

Anadyrskiy
Zaliv

Anadyr

Tauiskaya
Guba

Magadan

Udskaya
Guba

Nikolayevsk

Prince Rupert

44 Alexander
Arch.

Mt. St. Elias
5489

4949

Fairbanks

ALASKA
(U.S.A.)

Bering   Str.

Prince of Wales

Provideniya
Mys
Dezhneva

Chukotskoye
Nagorye

Omolon

Kolymskoye Nagorye

Okhotsk

Skagway Mt. Logan
5959

Juneau

Yukon

Pt. Hope
C. Lisburne

Pevek

Srednekolymsk

Kolyma
3147

Stanovoy Khrebet

4019

Whitehorse

Yukon

Kuskokwim

Noatak

Chukchi
Sea

1096

Nizhne
Kolymsk

Indigirka

Yakutsk

Lena

Olekma

Dawson

Kuyukuk

C. Pt. Barrow

Ostrov
Vrangelya
(Russia)

▽ 46

Chaunskaya

**East
Siberian
Sea**

Verkhoyansk

Yana

2295

Aldan

North

2762

Fort Yukon

Peel

Porcupine

Prudhoe Bay
2761

C. Halkett

Harrison Bay

Pt. Barrow

Novosibirskiye
Ostrova

Verkhoyanskiy Khrebet

Kazachye

Zhigansk

Dawson Creek

Stewart

Fort McPherson

Herschel I.

Beaufort Sea

374

Lyakhovskiye
Ostrova

Lena

Olenek

Fort
Simpson

Liard

Mackenzie

Tulita

Fort
Good Hope

Mackenzie
Bay

Tuktoyaktuk   2882

C. Bathurst

**Canada
Abyssal Plain**

374

O. Kotelnyy

Bulun

Olenek

Tiksi

Fort
Vermilion

Peace

Great Bear
Lake

C. Kellett

Banks I.

C. Prince Alfred

**Canada
Basin**

Chukchi
Plateau

Mendeleyev Ridge

**Laptev
Sea**

Vilyuy

America

NUNAVUT

Yellowknife

Great Slave
Lake

Coppermine

Coronation G.

Dolphin & Union Str.

Prince
Albert
Pen.

371

Victoria
Island

M'Clure Str.

Prince
Patrick I.

3327

A

3849

Ostrova Petra

Nordvik

Khatanga

Anabar

Nizhnyaya Tunguska

Athabasca
Lake

Kugluktuk

Wollaston Pen.

M'Clintock
Chan.

Melville I.

Parry Is.

North
Magnetic Pole
2014
+

3700

3546

4007

4100

Norway Ridge

Amundsen Basin

1484

Poluostrov
Taymyr

Mys
Chelyuskin

Ozero
Taymyr

Putorana

Rocky Mountains

Churchill

Queen

Viscount
Melville Sd.

Borden I.

3546

**Alpha
Ridge**

Makarov Basin

Lomonosov Ridge

Arctic Mid-Ocean Ridge

**Severnaya
Zemlya**

O. Oktyabrskoy
Revolyutsii

965

Gory

Kheta

Pyasina

Norilsk

Yenisey

A

King
William I.

**Prince of
Wales I.**

Prince of Bathurst

Ellef Ringnes I.

4007

POLE

4346

2104

O. Ushakova

O. Uedineniya

O. Vise

Dudinka

Igarka

Chatterton Inlet

Boothia
Pen.

Somerset

Resolute

Elizabeth

Sverdrup Is.

Axel
Heiberg I.

Nansen Sd.

2104

3910

Zemlya
Frantsa
Iosifa
(Russia)

O. Greem-Bell

Z. Vilcheka

O. Belyy

Gydanskiy
Poluostrov

Taz

Hudson

Bay

Southampton I.

Coats I.

Melville
Pen.

Back

Gulf of Boothia

Prince Regent Inlet

Devon

Islands

Eureka

2616

Alert

C. Columbia

**Lincoln
Sea**

3741

K. Morris Jesup

Peary
Land

5449

Z. Aleksandry

90

Novaya

1547

Kara
Sea

Baydaratskaya
Guba

Poluostrov
Yamal

Novyy Port

Novyy
Urengoy

Nadym

Nizhnevartovsk

Ob

Surgut

Mansel I.

Foxe
Chan.

Roes Welcome Sd.

Baffin

Bylot

Lancaster Sound

Jones Sound

Kennedy Ch.

Ellesmere I.
(Canada)

Smith Sd.

Kane
Basin

Robeson Chan.

K. York

Knud
Rasmussen
Land

Kronprins
Frederik
Land

2170

**McKinley
Sea**

Independence Fjord

Kong Frederik
VIII s Land

Zemlya

Nordaustlandet

1342

Salekhard

Anderma

Neftyugansk

Foxe
Basin

Prince
Charles I.

2147

Nettilling

2469

Uummannaq

Qaanaaq

Land

Kronprins
Frederik

2170

3910

3741

Nordkapp

Spitsbergen

Svalbard

Edgeøya

2571

1717

Longyearbyen

**Barents
Sea**

Belushya
Guba

Vorkuta

Berezovo

Tobolsk

Iqaluit

Hudson Str.

C. Wolstenholme

Frobisher Bay

Resolution I.

**Baffin
Bay**

Upernavik

Uummannaq
Qeqertarsuaq

Uummannaq

3238

Kong Frederik
IX s Land

Kong Christian X s Land

Kejser Franz Joseph Fd.

Kong Oscar Fjord

Greenland

Bjørnøya
(Norway)

480

Nordkapp

Vardø

Kirkenes

Mys
Kanin
Nos

O. Kolguyev

Naryan-
Mar

Pechora

1894

Narodnaya

Uralskie

YEKATERINBURG

Perm

UFA

C. Chidley

Davis Str.

Paamiut

GREENLAND
(KALAALLIT NUNAAT)
(Denmark)

Mt.
Forel
3360

Ittoqqortoormiit

2277

**Greenland
Sea**

Hammerfest

Tromsø

Murmansk

Kandalaksha

Arkhangelsk

Severodvinsk

Sev. Dvina

Kolskiy
Poluostrov

Belyy

Mezen

Syktyvkar

Labrador

2276

Nuuk

2850

Kong
Frederik VI s Kyst

Kong
Christian IX s Land

3693

Gunnbjørn
Fjeld

Kangikajik

**Icelandic
Plateau**

Mohns Ridge

Jan Mayen
(Norway)

Lofoten

Narvik

Tornio

Onega

Belomorsk

Onezhskoye
Ozero

SAMARA

Hamilton Inlet

Qaqortoq

Alluitsup Paa

Nunap Isua
(Kap Farvel)

Breiðafjörður

Horn

Fontur

**Icelandic
Plateau**

Norwegian
Basin

3800

Trondheim

2469

Oulu

Finland

Ladozhskoye
Ozero

Volga

**NIZHNIY
NOVGOROD**

Saratov

RUSSIA

**Northwest Atlantic
Mid-Ocean Canyon**

Mid-Atlantic Ridge

Reykjavík

ICELAND

Öræfajökull
2119

Norwegian

Sea

Bergen

HELSINKI

ST. PETERBURG

Chudskoye
Ozero

MOSKVA

VOLGOGRAD

5

Charlie Gibbs Fracture Zone

4563

**Iceland
Basin**

Føroyar
(Den.)

Shetland Is.
(U.K.)

STOCKHOLM

Oslo

Tallinn

ESTONIA

Riga

LATVIA

LITHUANIA

Vilnius

KHARKIV

ROSTOV

Mid-Atlantic Ridge

King's
Trough

ATLANTIC

Rockall
(U.K.)

Hebrides
(U.K.)

Orkney Is.
(U.K.)

**North
Sea**

KØBENHAVN

DENMARK

Kaliningrad
(Russia)

BELARUS

KYYIV

Donetsk

Rockall Trough

**UNITED
KINGDOM**

Edinburgh

GLASGOW

Skagerrak

HAMBURG

BERLIN

Wisła

WARSZAWA

UKRAINE

ODESA

OCEAN

Belfast

DUBLIN

IRELAND

Elbe

NETH.
AMSTERDAM

GERMANY

POLAND

Kraków

Lviv

MOLDOVA

ROMANIA

C. Clear

LONDON

PRAHA

Black Sea

Sea of Azov

COPYRIGHT PHILIPS

Projection : Zenithal Equidistant

West from Greenwich   0   East from Greenwich

6   7   8   9

ft   m

12 000   4000

6000   2000

4500   1500

3000   1000

600   200

0   0

500   1500

1000   3000

2000   6000

3000   9000

4000   12 000

5000   15 000

m   ft

Maximum extent of
sea ice

Minimum extent of
sea ice

Ice caps and permanent
ice shelf

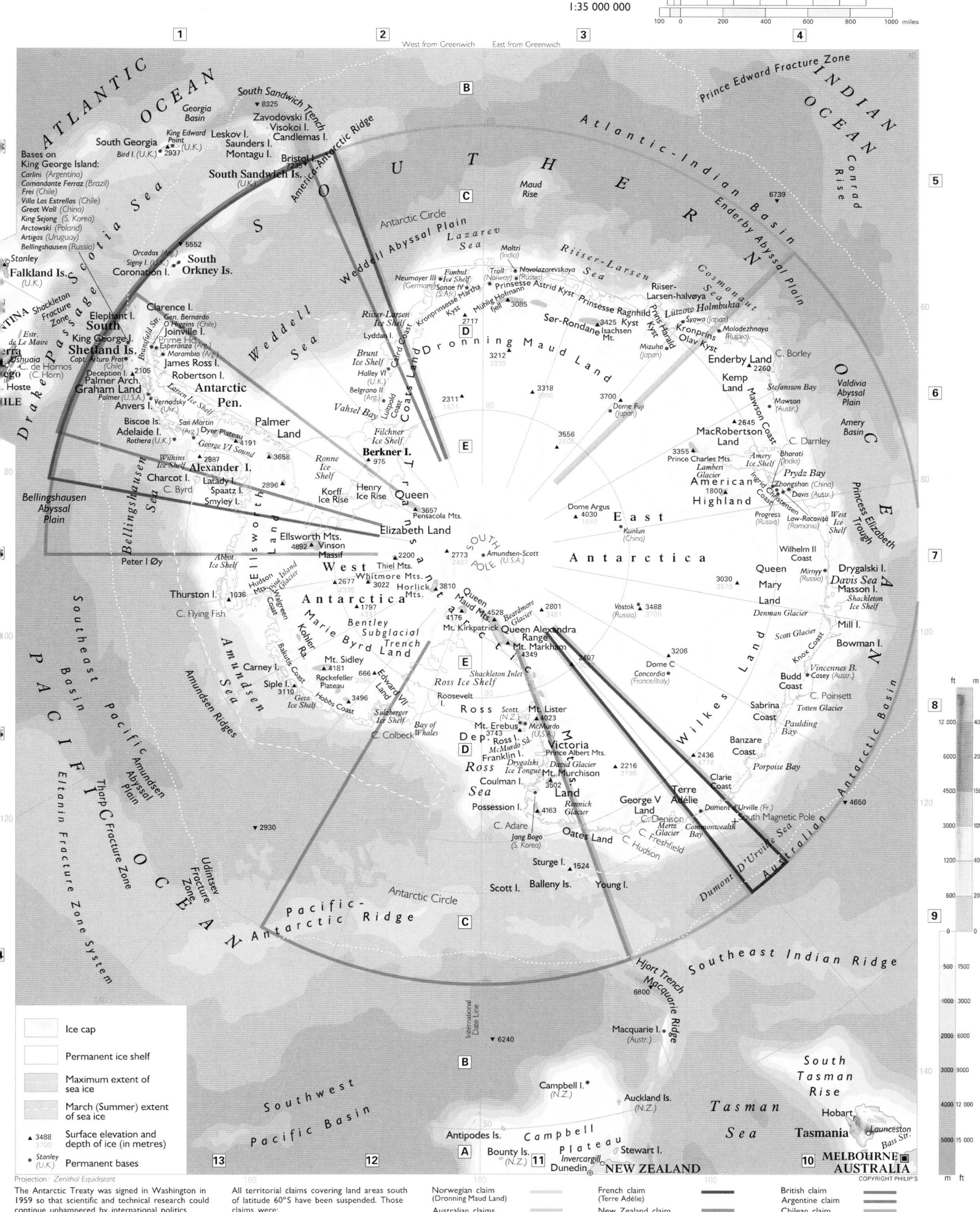

ANTARCTICA 5

1:35 000 000

100 0 200 400 600 800 1000 1200 1400 km

100 0 200 400 600 800 1000 miles

West from Greenwich   East from Greenwich

ATLANTIC OCEAN

SOUTHERN OCEAN

INDIAN OCEAN

Prince Edward Fracture Zone

Atlantic-Indian Ridge

Atlantic-Indian Basin

Conrad Rise

Enderby Abyssal Plain

Cosmonaut

6739

Georgia Basin

South Sandwich Trench

Zavodovski I.
Visokoi I.
Candlemas I.

8325

Leskov I.
Saunders I.
Montagu I.

Bristol I.
7235

South Sandwich Is.
(U.K.)

Maud Rise

Antarctic Circle

Lazarev Sea

Weddell Abyssal Plain

Maitri (India)

Riiser-Larsen Sea

American-Antarctic Ridge

South Georgia
Bird I. (U.K.)
King Edward Point 2937 (U.K.)

Bases on
King George Island:
Carlini (Argentina)
Comandante Ferraz (Brazil)
Frei (Chile)
Villa Las Estrellas (Chile)
Great Wall (China)
King Sejong (S. Korea)
Arctowski (Poland)
Artigas (Uruguay)
Bellingshausen (Russia)

Scotia Sea

5552

Orcadas (Arg.)
Signy I. (U.K.)
Coronation I.

South Orkney Is.

Neumayer III (Germany)
Sanae IV (S. Afr.)

Fimbul Ice Shelf

Troll (Norway)

Novolazarevskaya (Russia)

Prinsesse Astrid Kyst

Prinsesse Ragnhild Kyst

Sør-Rondane

Lützow Holmbukta

Syowa (Japan)

Riiser-Larsen-halvøya

Mühlig Hofmann fjell 3085

Isachsen Mt.

3425

Prins Harald Kyst

Kronprins Olav Kyst

Molodezhnaya (Russia)

Stanley
Falkland Is. (U.K.)

Clarence I.

Gen. Bernardo O'Higgins (Chile)
Joinville I.

Elephant I.
South Shetland Is.

King George I.
Prime Hd.
Esperanza (Arg.)

Brabant Str.

Deception I.

Capt. Arturo Prat (Chile)

Marambio (Arg.)

James Ross I.
Robertson I.

Mizuho (Japan)

Enderby Land

C. Borley

Kemp Land

Stefansson Bay

Mawson (Austr.)

2260

Valdivia Abyssal Plain

Dronning Maud Land

Lyddan I.

Riiser-Larsen Ice Shelf

2717

3212
3039

3318

Dome Fuji (Japan)

3700

MacRobertson Land

C. Darnley

Amery Basin

ARGENTINA
Shackleton Fracture Zone

Sierra

Estr. de Le Maire

Tierra del Fuego

Ushuaia

C. de Hornos (C. Horn)

Hoste

CHILE

Palmer Arch.
Graham Land
Palmer (U.S.A.)

Anvers I.

Vernadsky (U.K.)

2105

Antarctic Pen.

San Martin (Arg.)
Dyer Plateau

Weddell Sea

Brunt Ice Shelf

Halley VI (U.K.)

Belgrano II (Arg.)

Coats Land

Luitpold Coast

Vahsel Bay

3556

2311
1431

3355

Prince Charles Mts.

Lambert Glacier

Amery Ice Shelf

Bharati (India)

American Highland

1800

Prydz Bay

Zhongshan (China)

Davis (Austr.)

Princess Elizabeth Trough

Biscoe Is.
Adelaide I.
Rothera (U.K.)

George VI Sound

Alexander I.

Latady I.
Spaatz I.
Smyley I.

Palmer Land

4191

3658

Ronne Ice Shelf

Filchner Ice Shelf

Berkner I. 975

Korff Ice Rise

Henry Ice Rise

Queen

4030
1040

Dome Argus

East Antarctica

Kunlun (China)

West Ice Shelf

Progress (Russia)

Law-Racoviță (Romania)

Ingrid Christensen Coast

Wilkins Ice Shelf

Charcot I.
C. Byrd

2987

2896

Ellsworth Land

Transantarctic

Elizabeth Land

3657

Pensacola Mts.

2773

Amundsen-Scott (U.S.A.)

2407
3700

SOUTH POLE

Wilhelm II Coast

Queen Mary Land

3030
2570

Mirnyy (Russia)

Drygalski I.

Davis Sea

Masson I.

Shackleton Ice Shelf

Bellingshausen Abyssal Plain

Peter I Øy

Thurston I.

Abbot Ice Shelf

1036

Hudson Mts.

2200

Ellsworth Mts.
4892

Vinson Massif

Thiel Mts.

West Antarctica

Whitmore Mts.
2677
4335

3022

Horlick Mts.

3810

Vostok (Russia) 3488
3700

Denman Glacier

Mill I.

Bowman I.

C. Flying Fish

1797

Marie Byrd Land

Bentley Subglacial Trench

Beardmore Glacier

4176

Mt. Kirkpatrick 4528

2801

Queen Alexandra Range

3206

Dome C Concordia (France/Italy)

Knox Coast

Vincennes B.
Casey (Austr.)

Budd Coast

C. Poinsett

Totten Glacier

Amundsen Sea

Carney I.

Kohler Ra.

Bakutis Coast

Mt. Sidley 4181

Siple I. 3110

Rockefeller Plateau

666
2080

Getz Ice Shelf

3496

Hobbs Coast

Edward VII Land

Sulzberger Ice Shelf

C. Colbeck

Queen Maud Mts.

Mt. Markham 4349

2407

Ross Ice Shelf

Roosevelt I.

Shackleton Inlet

Scott (N.Z.)

Mt. Lister 4023

Sabrina Coast

Banzare Coast

Porpoise Bay

Paulding Bay

Clarie Coast

2436
4776

Wilkes Land

Amundsen Ridges

Ross Sea

Bay of Whales

Mt. Erebus 3743
Ross I.

McMurdo (U.S.A.)

McMurdo Sd.

Franklin I.

Victoria Land

Prince Albert Mts.

Drygalski Ice Tongue

Mt. Murchison

David Glacier

2216
2798

Terre Adélie

George V Land

Dumont d'Urville (Fr.)

+ South Magnetic Pole

4650

Australian Basin

Dep.

Coulman I.

3502

Rennick Glacier

Mertz Glacier

C. Denison

Commonwealth Bay

C. Freshfield

C. Hudson

Dumont D'Urville Sea

Southeast Basin

Pacific Basin

Eltanin Fracture Zone System

Tharp Fracture Zone

Amundsen Abyssal Plain

Udintsev Fracture Zone

Possession I.

4163

C. Adare

Jang Bogo (S. Korea)

Oates Land

Sturge I. 1524

2930

Pacific-Antarctic Ridge

Antarctic Circle

Scott I.

Balleny Is.

Young I.

Hjort Trench

Macquarie Ridge

Southeast Indian Ridge

6800

International Date Line

6240

Macquarie I. (Austr.)

South Tasman Rise

PACIFIC OCEAN

Southwest Pacific Basin

Campbell I. (N.Z.)

Auckland Is. (N.Z.)

Tasman Sea

Hobart

Launceston

Bass Str.

Tasmania

Antipodes Is.
Bounty Is. (N.Z.)

Campbell Plateau

Stewart I.

Invercargill
Dunedin

NEW ZEALAND

MELBOURNE
AUSTRALIA

COPYRIGHT PHILIP'S

Projection: Zenithal Equidistant

Legend

	Ice cap
	Permanent ice shelf
	Maximum extent of sea ice
	March (Summer) extent of sea ice
▲ 3488 3700	Surface elevation and depth of ice (in metres)
• Stanley (U.K.)	Permanent bases

ft   m
12 000 — 4000
6000 — 2000
4500 — 1500
3000
1200 — 400
600 — 200
0 — 0
500 — 1500
1000 — 3000
2000 — 6000
3000 — 9000
4000 — 12 000
5000 — 15 000
m   ft

The Antarctic Treaty was signed in Washington in 1959 so that scientific and technical research could continue unhampered by international politics.

All territorial claims covering land areas south of latitude 60°S have been suspended. Those claims were:

Norwegian claim (Dronning Maud Land)
Australian claims
French claim (Terre Adélie)
New Zealand claim (Ross Dependency)
British claim
Argentine claim
Chilean claim

1:20 000 000

Projection: Bonne

1:20 000 000

100 0 100 200 300 400 500 600 700 800 km
100 0 100 200 300 400 500 miles

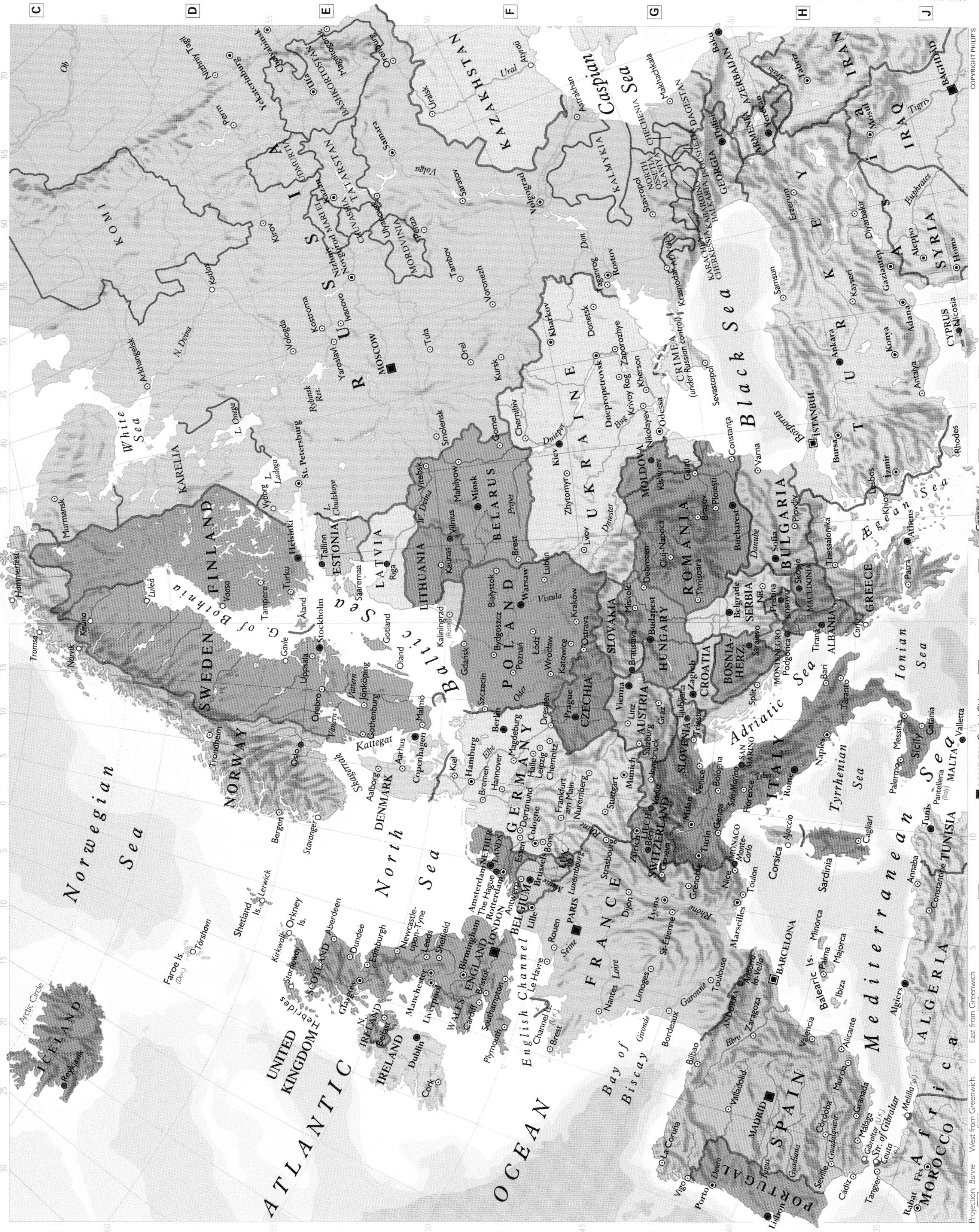

■ LONDON Capital Cities

Projection: Bonne   West from Greenwich   East from Greenwich   COPYRIGHT PHILIP'S

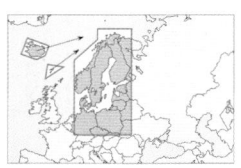

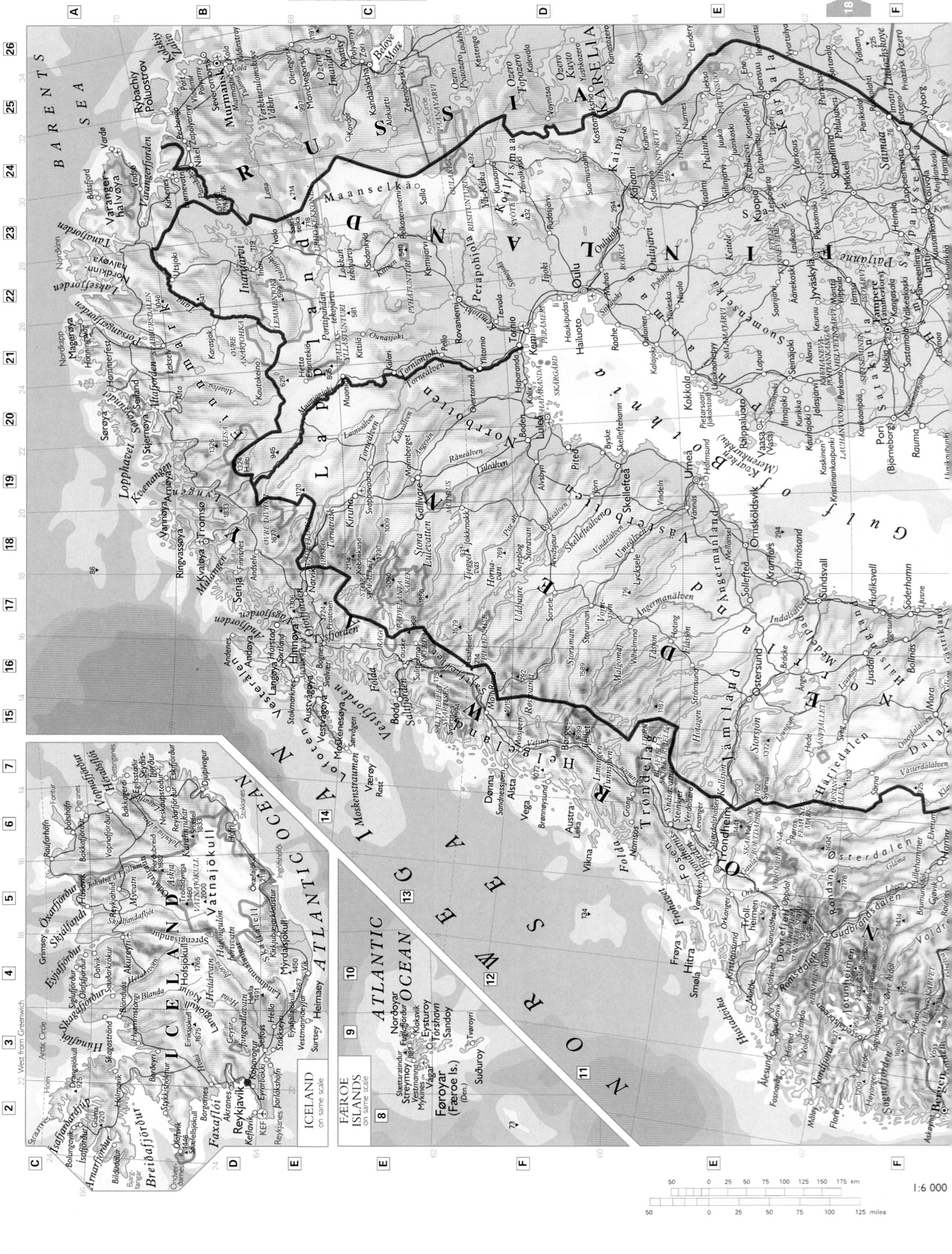
BARENTS SEA
NORWEGIAN SEA
ATLANTIC OCEAN
Gulf of Bothnia
ICELAND on same scale
FÆROE ISLANDS on same scale
1:6 000 000
0 25 50 75 100 125 150 175 km
0 25 50 75 100 125 miles

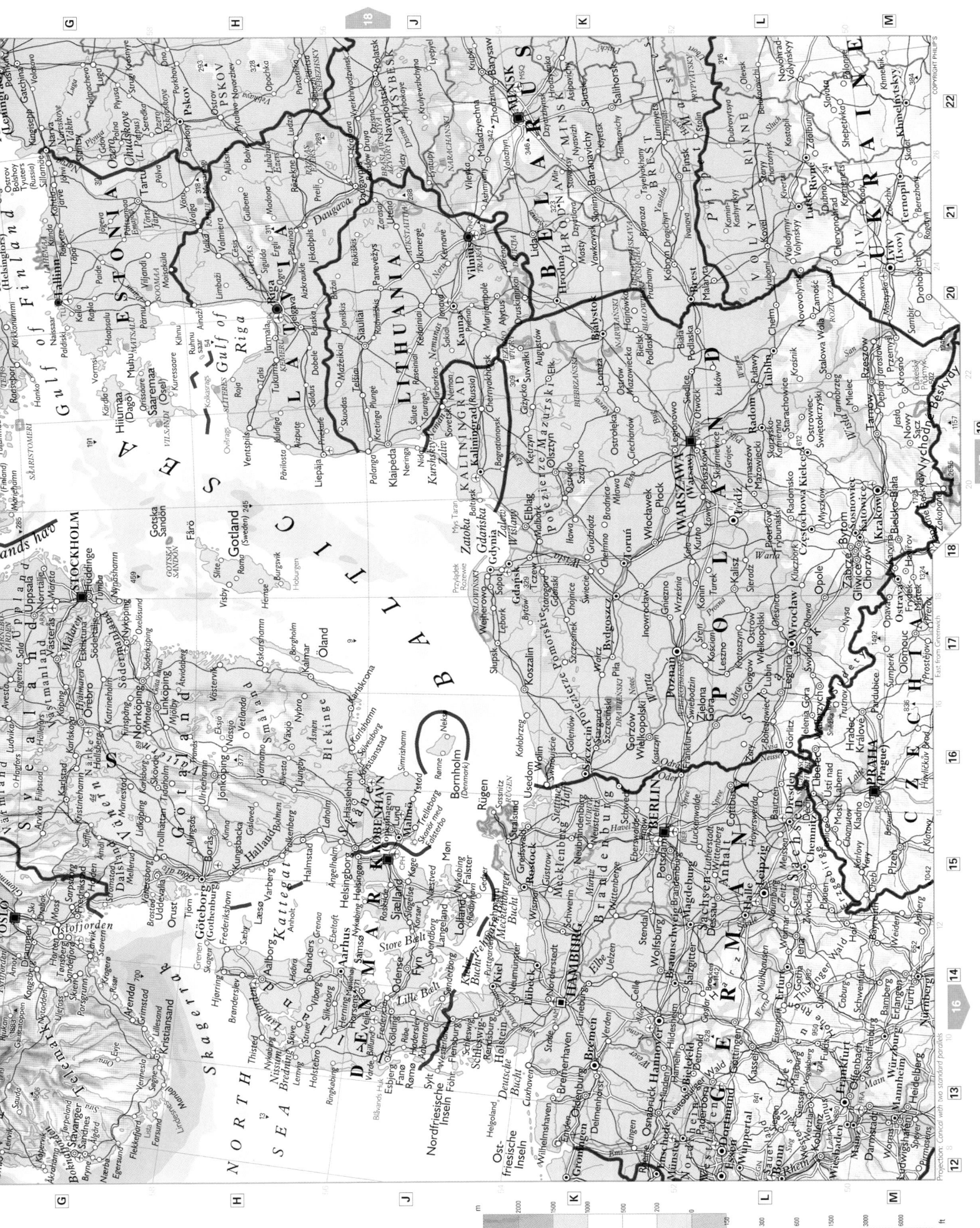

1:2 000 000

10 0 10 20 30 40 50 60 70 80 km
10 0 10 20 30 40 50 miles

ATLANTIC OCEAN

SCOTLAND
Kintyre
Brodick
Arran
Campbeltown
Mull of Oa
Mull of Kintyre
Ailsa Craig
Firth of Clyde
North Channel
Stranraer
Cairnryan
Portpatrick
L. Ryan

NORTHERN IRELAND

Mull of Oa
Malin Hd.
Inishtrahull
Trawbreaga B.
Malin
Inishowen Pen.
Carndonagh
Moville
Glengad Hd.
Giants Causeway
Rathlin I.
Fair Hd.
Garron Pt.
Cushendall
Ballycastle
Portrush
Portstewart
Coleraine
Limavady
Ballymoney
Ballymena
Larne
Carncastle
Carnlough

Tory I.
Horn Hd.
Sheep Haven
Mulroy B.
Fanad Hd.
Lough Swilly
Dunfanaghy
Buncrana
L. Foyle
Derry/Londonderry
Dungiven
Trostan
554
Sperrin Mts.
Garvagh
Maghera
Magherafelt
Antrim
Randalstown
Ballyclare
Newtownabbey
Belfast L.
Holywood
Bangor
Donaghadee
Newtownards
Ards Pen.
Portaferry
Strangford

Bloody Foreland
Gweedore
Errigal 752
Derryveagh Mts.
GLENVEAGH
Rathmelton
Letterkenny
Lifford
Strabane
Sion Mills
Newtownstewart
Omagh
TYRONE
Cookstown
Dungannon
Moneymore
L. Neagh
Craigavon
Lurgan
Portadown
Lisburn
Lagan
Belfast
BFS
BHD
DOWN
Ballynahinch
Downpatrick
Dundrum B.
St. John's Pt.
Dundrum
Newcastle
852
Slieve Donard

Inishfree B.
Arranmore
The Rosses
Dunglow
Crohy Hd.
683
Gweebarra B.
Dawros Hd.
Ardara
Glenties
Rossan Pt.
Glencolumbkille
601
Killybegs
Slieve League
St. John's Pt.
DONEGAL
Glenties
Lavagh More 676
Finn
Castlederg
Derg
ULSTER
Manorhamilton
Lough Melvin
Lower L. Erne
Enniskillen
FERMANAGH
Upper Erne
Clones
MONAGHAN
Castleblaney
Monaghan
Aughnacloy
Blackwater
ARMAGH
Armagh
Middletown
Keady
Newry
577 Slieve Gullion
Mourne Mts.
Warrenpoint
Greenore
Carlingford L.
Kilkeel

Donegal
Ballyshannon
Bundoran
Donegal Bay
Inishmurray
Sligo Bay
Sligo
Dromore West
Killala B.
Lenadoon Pt.
Downpatrick Hd.
Lackagh Hills
Shannon
Belturbet
Ballyconnell
Annalee
Cavan
Cootehill
Carrickmacross
Castlebellingham
Dundalk (Dún Dealgan)
Louth
LOUTH
Dundalk Bay
Ardee
Dunleer
Clogher Hd.

Broad Haven
Erris Hd.
Portacloy
Belmullet
Mullet Pen.
380
Crossmolina
Ballina
Killala
Inishkea North
Inishkea South
BALLYCROY
Blacksod Bay
Nephin Beg Range
Slieve Gamph
544
SLIGO
Tobercurry
Collooney
L. Arrow
L. Key
L. Gara
Boyle
Carrick-on-Shannon
LEITRIM
Leitrim
L. Allen
L. Oughter
L. Gowna
L. Sheelin
CAVAN
Baileborough
Kingscourt
Oldcastle
Kells (Ceanannus Mor)
Blackwater
Navan
Trim
MEATH
Balbriggan
Skerries
Lambay I.
Rush
Swords
Malahide
Howth Hd.

Achill Hd.
Achill I.
461
Clare I.
Clew Bay
Croagh Patrick 765
Westport
Newport
Castlebar
Corraun Pen.
Louisburgh
Mweelrea 819
Killary Harbour
Inishturk
Inishbofin
Inishshark
Partry Mts.
683
L. Cara
L. Mask
Ballinrobe
Claremorris
Knock
Ballyhaunis
MAYO
Swinford
Charlestown
Foxford
672
Nephin
806 L. Conn
Ballaghaderreen
ROSCOMMON
Castlerea
Strokestown
Roscommon
LONGFORD
Longford
Granard
Castlepollard
Mullingar
WESTMEATH
Moate
Kilbeggan
Trim
Dunshaughlin
Maynooth
Leixlip
Lucan
Celbridge
DUBLIN (Baile Átha Cliath)
Dún Laoghaire
Dalkey
Killiney
Bray
Greystones

1. DUBLIN
2. FINGAL
3. SOUTH DUBLIN
4. DÚN LAOGHAIRE - RATHDOWN

Connaught
CONNEMARA
Clifden
Slyne Hd.
Roundstone
Bertraghboy B.
Kilkieran B.
Oughterard
L. Corrib
Cong
Glennamaddy
Tuam
Mount Bellew Bridge
GALWAY
Athenry
Loughrea
Ballinasloe
Shannonbridge
Banagher
Ferbane
Tullamore
OFFALY
Clara
Daingean
Edenderry
Grand Canal
Bog of Allen
KILDARE
Naas
Newbridge
Kildare
Monasterevin
Portarlington
Rathangan
Athy
WICKLOW
WICKLOW MTS.
Lugnaquilla 926

Galway (Gaillimh)
Spiddle
Galway Bay
Black Hd.
Aran Is.
Inishmore
Inishmaan
Inisheer
Burren
BURREN
Lisdoonvarna
345
Cliffs of Moher
Hags Hd.
368
Gort
Kinvara
Slieve Aughty
Portumna
Lough Derg
Birr
Borrisokane
Roscrea
Mountrath
Slieve Bloom 527
Portlaoise
Mountmellick
LAOIS
Abbeyleix
Durrow
Stradbally
Athy
Baltinglass
Hollywood
Blessington
Poulaphouca Res.
Wicklow
Wicklow Hd.
Rathdrum
Avoca
Arklow
123

Liscannor Bay
Ennistimon
Crusheen
Mal Bay
Mutton I.
Milltown Malbay
Feakle
Tulla
Ennis
SNN
Shannon
CLARE
Sixmilebridge
Silvermine Mts.
694
Keeper Hill
Nenagh
Killaloe
Templemore
Thurles
TIPPERARY
Johnstown
Durrow
Castlecomer
KILKENNY
Kilkenny
Callan
Thomastown
Bagenalstown (Muine Bheag)
CARLOW
Carlow
Tullow
Shillelagh
Gorey
Bunclody
Ballycanew
Cahore Pt.

Loop Hd.
Kilkee
Kilrush
Mouth of the Shannon
Tarbert
Foynes
Ballybunion
LIMERICK
Adare
Rathkeale
Limerick (Luimneach)
Golden Vale
Golden
Tipperary
Cashel
Cahir
Galtymore 920
Galty Mts.
Slievenamon 722
Clonmel
Carrick-on-Suir
Comeragh Mts.
792
New Ross
WEXFORD
Enniscorthy
Mt. Leinster 796
Blackstairs Mt. 734
Barrow
Nore
Suir
Wexford Harbour
Wexford
Rosslare Harbour
Rosslare (Rosslare Europort)
Greenore Pt.
Carnsore Pt.
Saltee Is.

Kerry Hd.
Brandon B.
Tralee B.
Smerwick Harbour
Brandon Mt. 953
Dingle Pen.
Dingle
Great Blasket I.
Slea Hd.
Inishvickillane
Dingle Bay
Slieve Mish 853
Castlegregory
Castleisland
Newmarket
Listowel
Feale
Abbeyfeale
Newcastle West
Charleville (Ráth Luirc)
519
Kilmallock
Kanturk
Buttevant
Mitchelstown
Knockmealdown Mts. 795
WATERFORD
Lismore
Dungarvan
Tramore
Tramore B.
Dunmore East
Hook Hd.
Waterford (Port Láirge)
Passage East
Waterford Harbour

Valencia I.
Puffin I.
Great Skellig
Ballinskelligs B.
Cahirciveen
Iveragh Pen.
Glenbeigh
Killorglin
Killarney
Carrauntoohil 1041
Macgillycuddy's Reeks
KILLARNEY
KERRY
Castlemaine
Milltown
Milltown
Castleisland
Rathmore
Laune
Kenmare
Sneem
Kenmare River
707
Caha Mts. 686
Glengarriff
Bantry
Bantry Bay
Dursey I.
Crow Hd.
Castletown Bearhaven
Bear I.
Whiddy I.
Dunmanus B.
Mizen Hd.
Dunmanway
Sheep's Hd.
Skull
Ballydehob
Clonakilty
Clonakilty B.
Long I.
Baltimore
Sherkin I.
Clear I.
C. Clear
Galley Hd.
Fastnet Rock

Boggeragh Mts. 646
Macroom
Blarney
Nagles Mts. 429
Mallow
Millstreet
Fermoy
Blackwater
Lee
CORK
Cork (Corcaigh)
Midleton
Youghal
Youghal B.
Carrigaline
Crosshaven
Cork Harbour
Carrigaline
Passage West
Kinsale
Old Head of Kinsale
Timoleague
Bandon
Bandon
Ballincollig

IRELAND
Leinster
Munster

CELTIC SEA

IRISH SEA

St. George's Channel

WALES
St. David's Hd.
St. David's
St. Brides Bay
115

ft m
1500 500
600 200
300 100
0 0
50 150
100 300
200 600
500 1500
1000 3000
2000 6000
m ft

Projection: Lambert's Conformal Conic
West from Greenwich
COPYRIGHT PHILIP'S

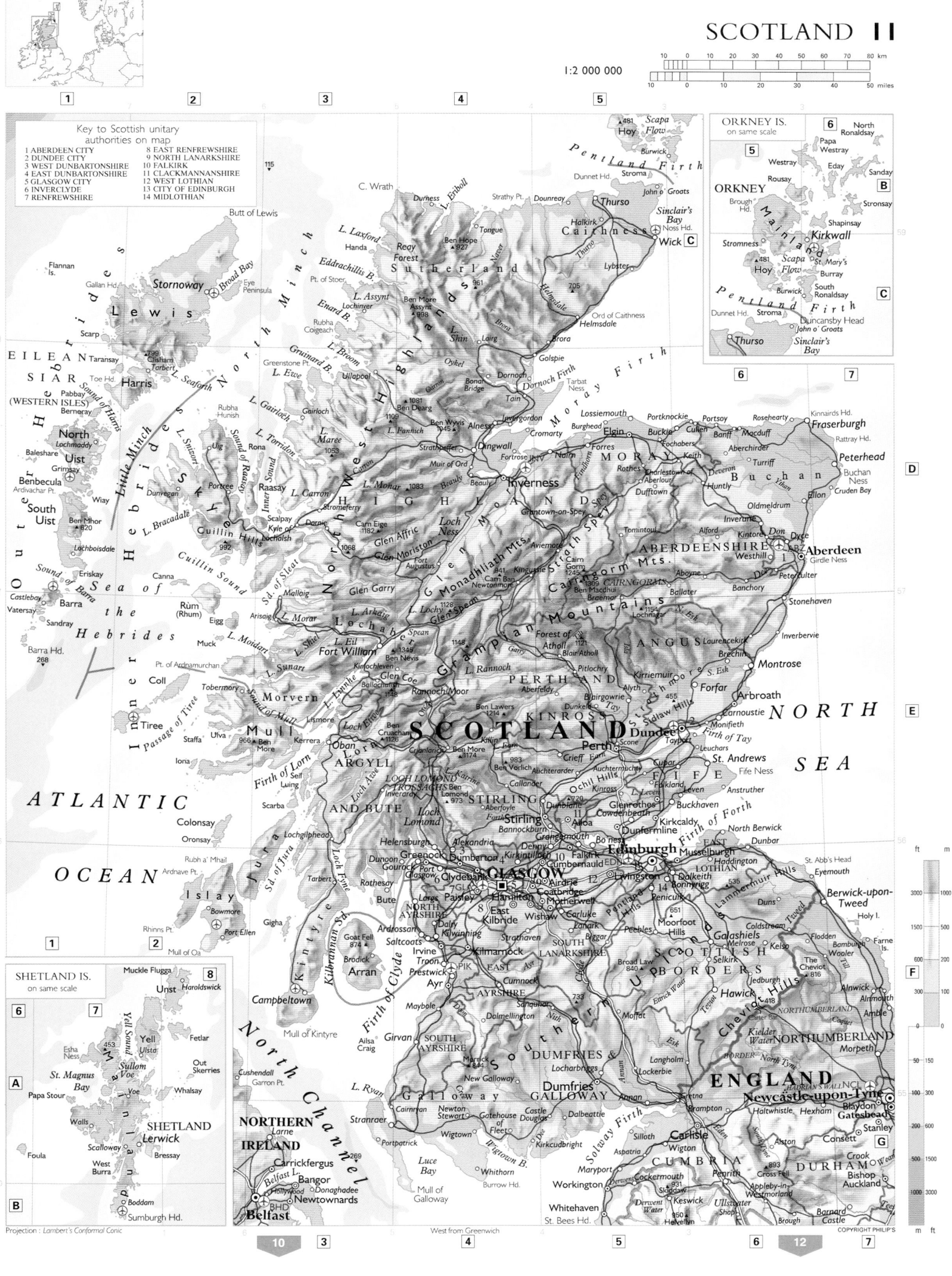

1:2 000 000

10 0 10 20 30 40 50 60 70 80 km
10 0 10 20 30 40 50 miles

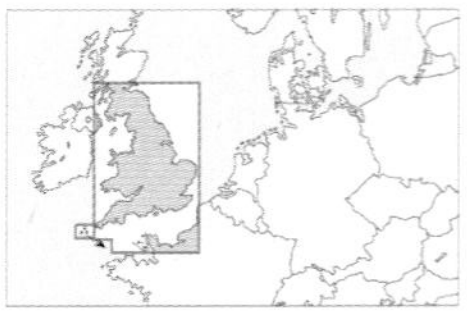

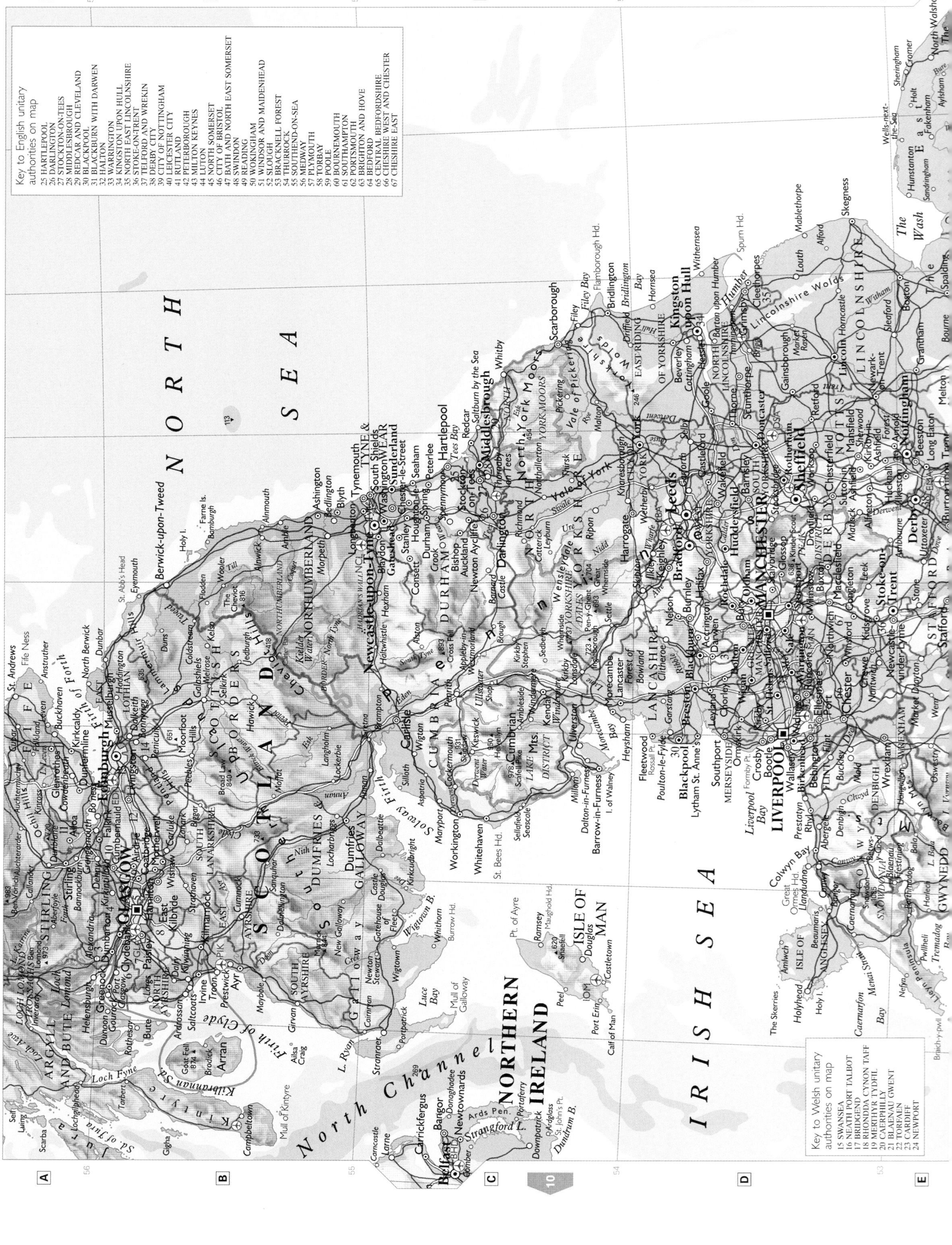

Key to English unitary authorities on map

25 HARTLEPOOL
26 DARLINGTON
27 STOCKTON-ON-TEES
28 MIDDLESBROUGH
29 REDCAR AND CLEVELAND
30 BLACKPOOL
31 BLACKBURN WITH DARWEN
32 HALTON
33 WARRINGTON
34 KINGSTON UPON HULL
35 NORTH EAST LINCOLNSHIRE
36 STOKE-ON-TRENT
37 TELFORD AND WREKIN
38 DERBY CITY
39 CITY OF NOTTINGHAM
40 LEICESTER CITY
41 RUTLAND
42 PETERBOROUGH
43 MILTON KEYNES
44 LUTON
45 NORTH SOMERSET
46 CITY OF BRISTOL
47 BATH AND NORTH EAST SOMERSET
48 SWINDON
49 READING
50 WOKINGHAM
51 WINDSOR AND MAIDENHEAD
52 SLOUGH
53 BRACKNELL FOREST
54 THURROCK
55 MEDWAY
56 SOUTHEND-ON-SEA
57 PLYMOUTH
58 TORBAY
59 POOLE
60 BOURNEMOUTH
61 SOUTHAMPTON
62 PORTSMOUTH
63 BRIGHTON AND HOVE
64 BEDFORD
65 CENTRAL BEDFORDSHIRE
66 CHESHIRE WEST AND CHESTER
67 CHESHIRE EAST

Key to Welsh unitary authorities on map

15 SWANSEA
16 NEATH PORT TALBOT
17 BRIDGEND
18 RHONDDA CYNON TAFF
19 MERTHYR TYDFIL
20 CAERPHILLY
21 BLAENAU GWENT
22 TORFAEN
23 CARDIFF
24 NEWPORT

NORTH SEA

IRISH SEA

North Channel

NORTHERN IRELAND

SCOTLAND

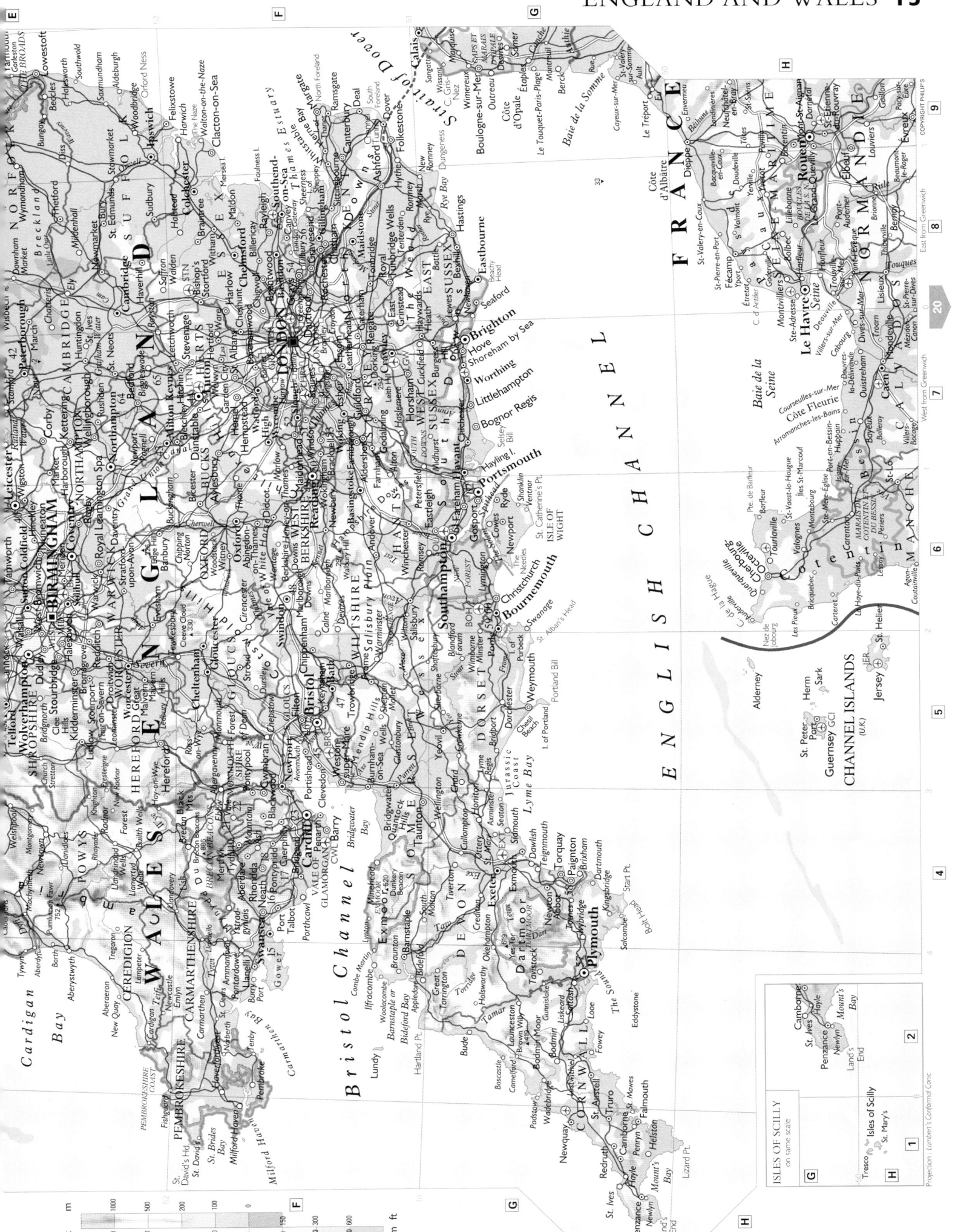

1:5 000 000

1:2 500 000

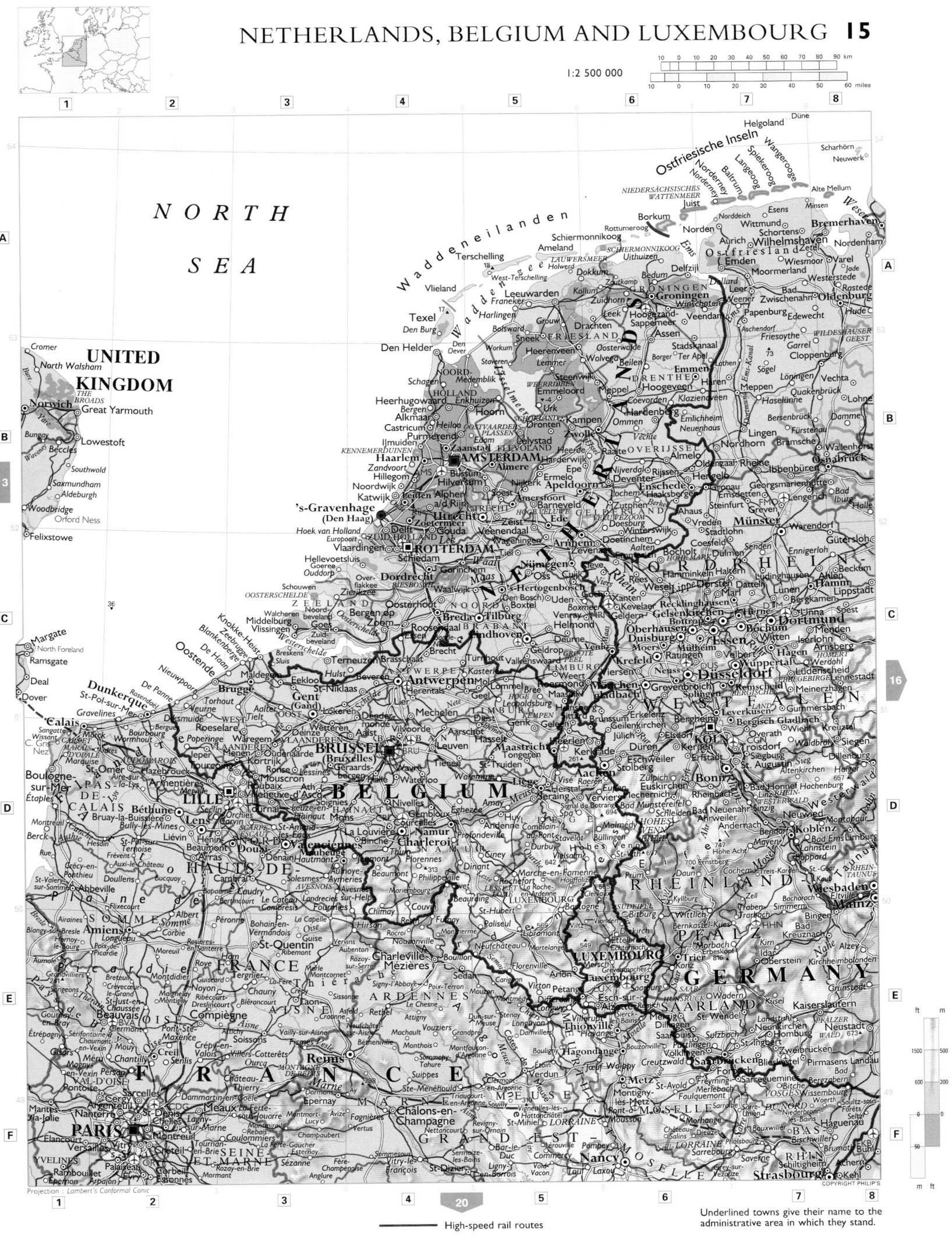

Projection : Lambert's Conformal Conic

━━━ High-speed rail routes

Underlined towns give their name to the
administrative area in which they stand.

COPYRIGHT PHILIP'S

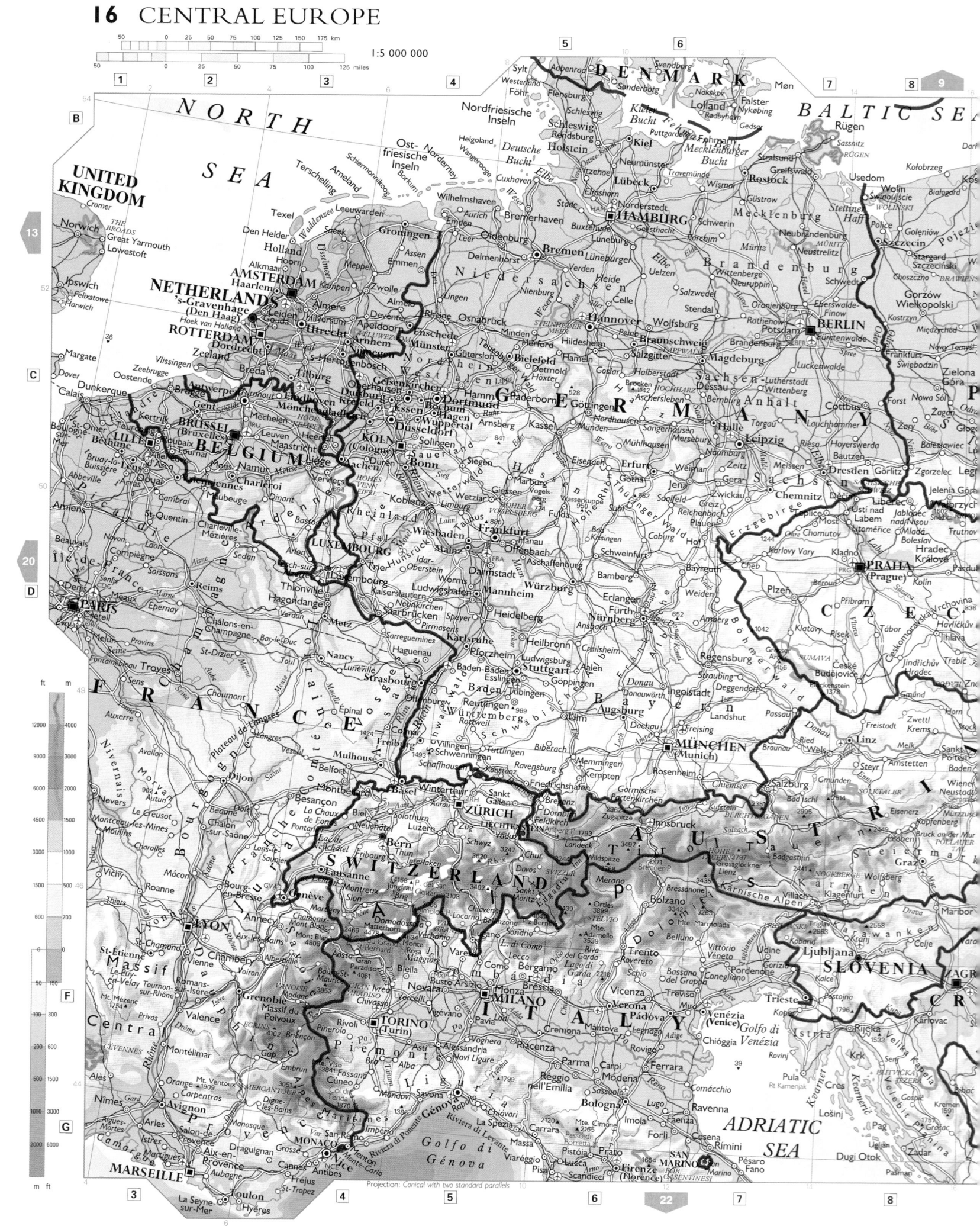

1:5 000 000

Projection: Conical with two standard parallels

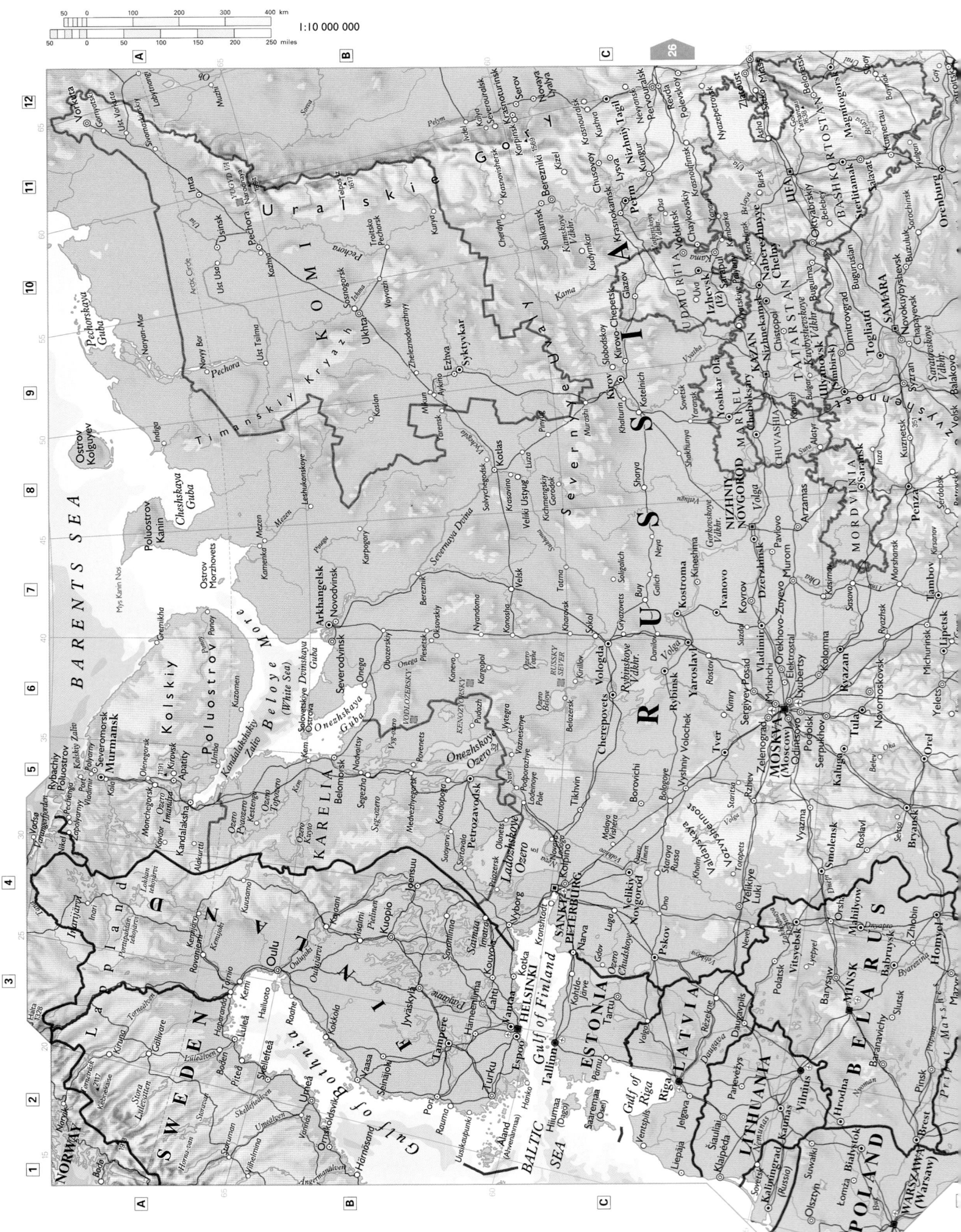

1:10 000 000

26

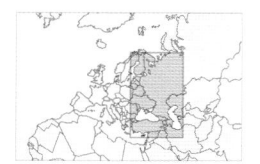

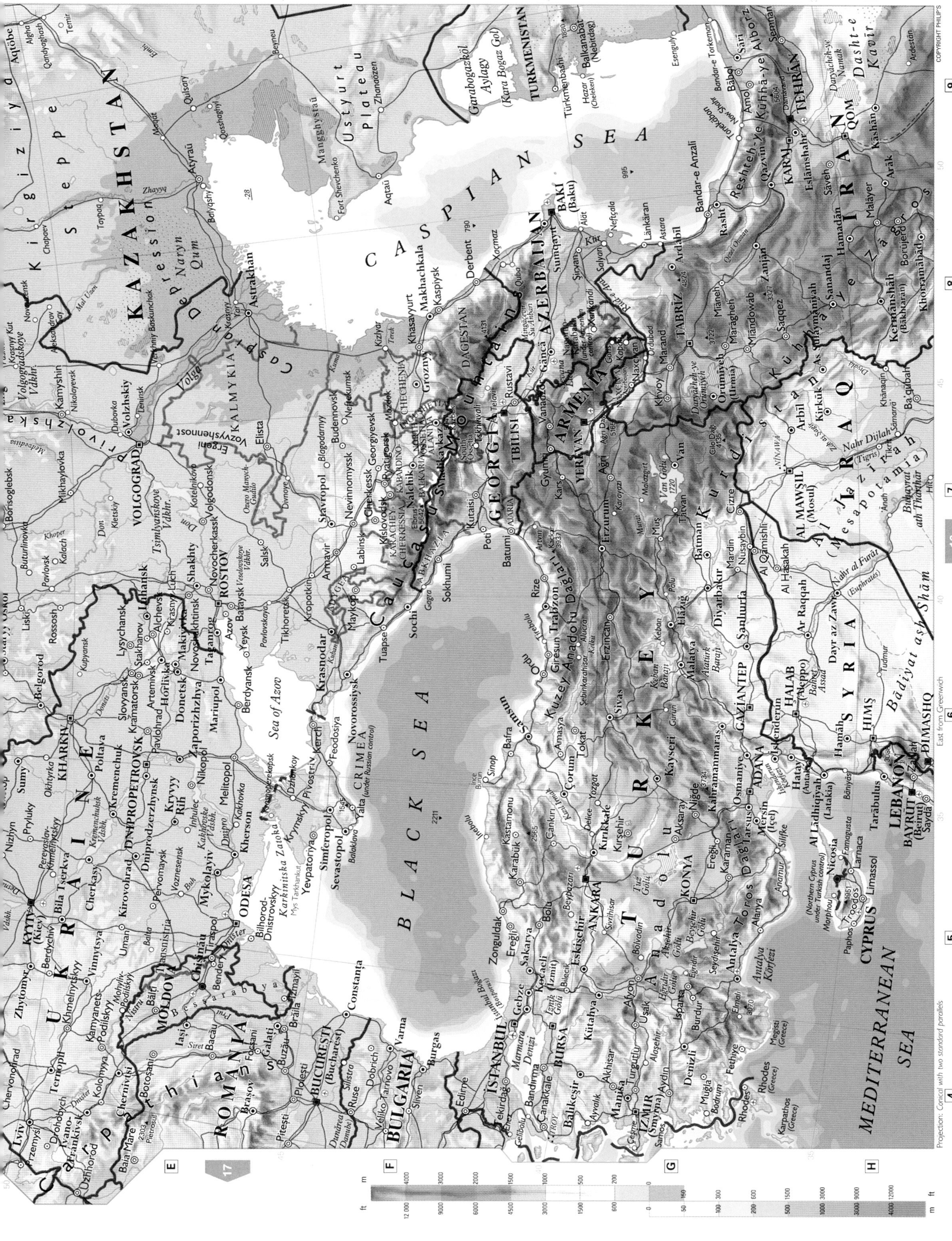
BLACK SEA
CASPIAN SEA
MEDITERRANEAN SEA
Sea of Azov
KAZAKHSTAN
UKRAINE
ROMANIA
MOLDOVA
BULGARIA
GEORGIA
ARMENIA
AZERBAIJAN
TURKMENISTAN
TURKEY
SYRIA
IRAQ
IRAN
CYPRUS
LEBANON
CRIMEA
Caspian Depression
Ustyurt Plateau
Anadolu
Kurdistan
Mesopotamia
Projection: Conical with two standard parallels
East from Greenwich
COPYRIGHT PHILIP'S

1:5 000 000

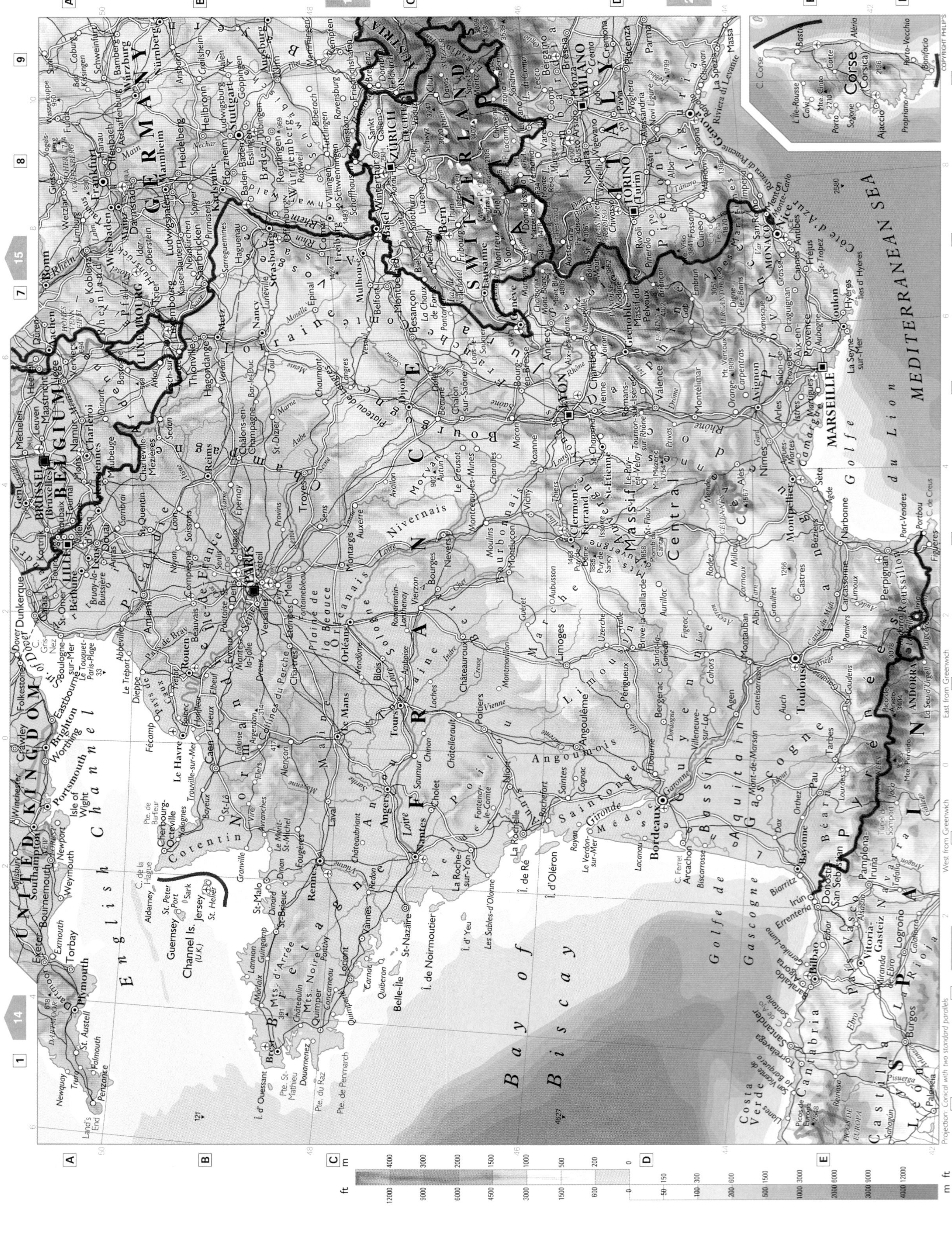

50 0 25 50 75 100 125 150 175 km
50 0 25 50 75 100 125 miles

GERMANY

UNITED KINGDOM

BELGIUM

LUXEMBOURG

SWITZERLAND

AUSTRIA

ITALY

ANDORRA

SPAIN

FRANCE

PARIS

BRUXELLES
BRUSSEL

LILLE

LYON

MARSEILLE

MONACO

TORINO (Turin)

MILANO

ZURICH

Bern

Corse (Corsica)

English Channel

Bay of Biscay

MEDITERRANEAN SEA

Golfe du Lion

Golfe de Gascogne

Normandie

Bretagne

Aquitaine

Provence

Pyrénées

Massif Central

Alpes

Côte d'Azur

1:5 000 000

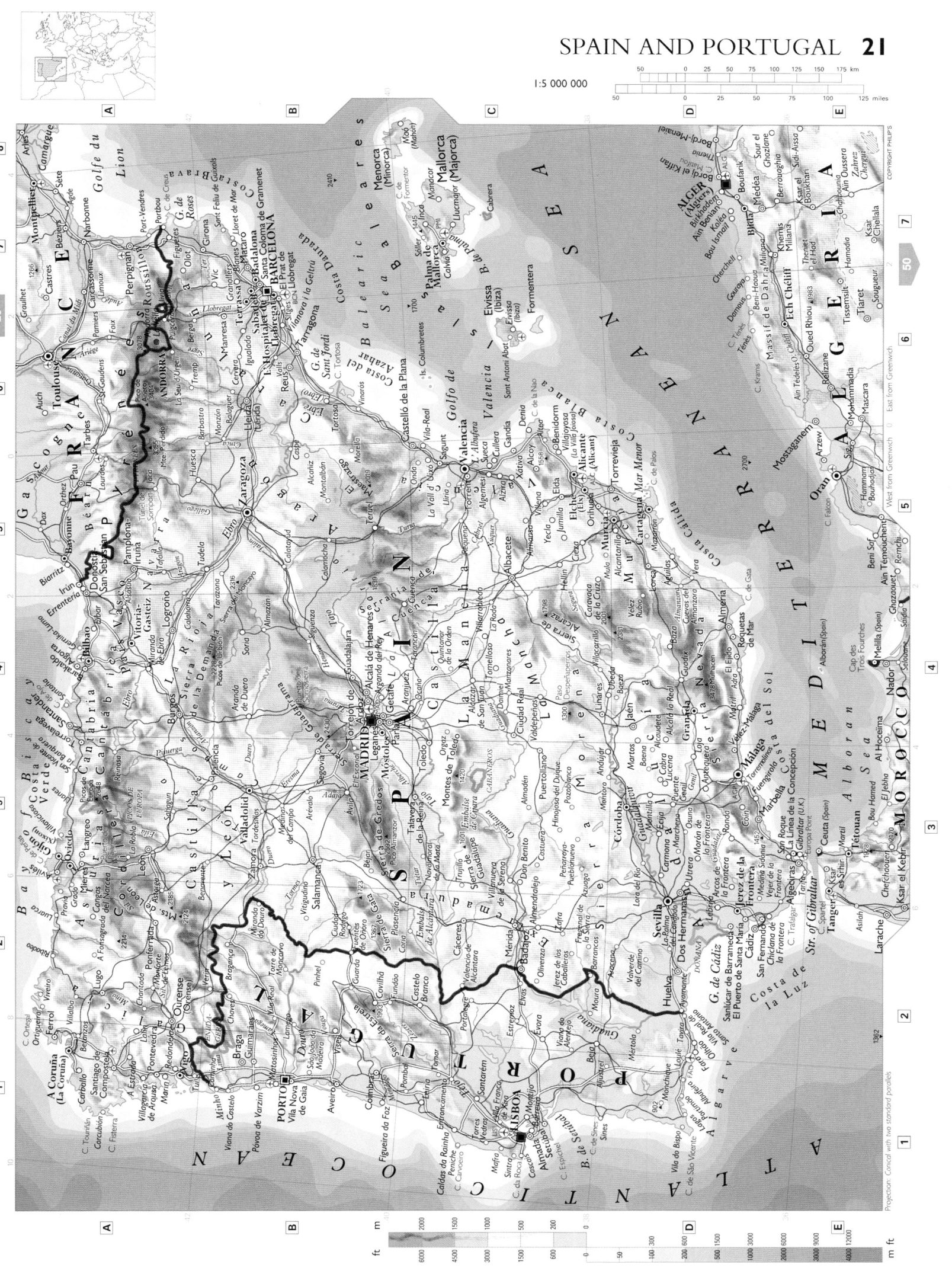

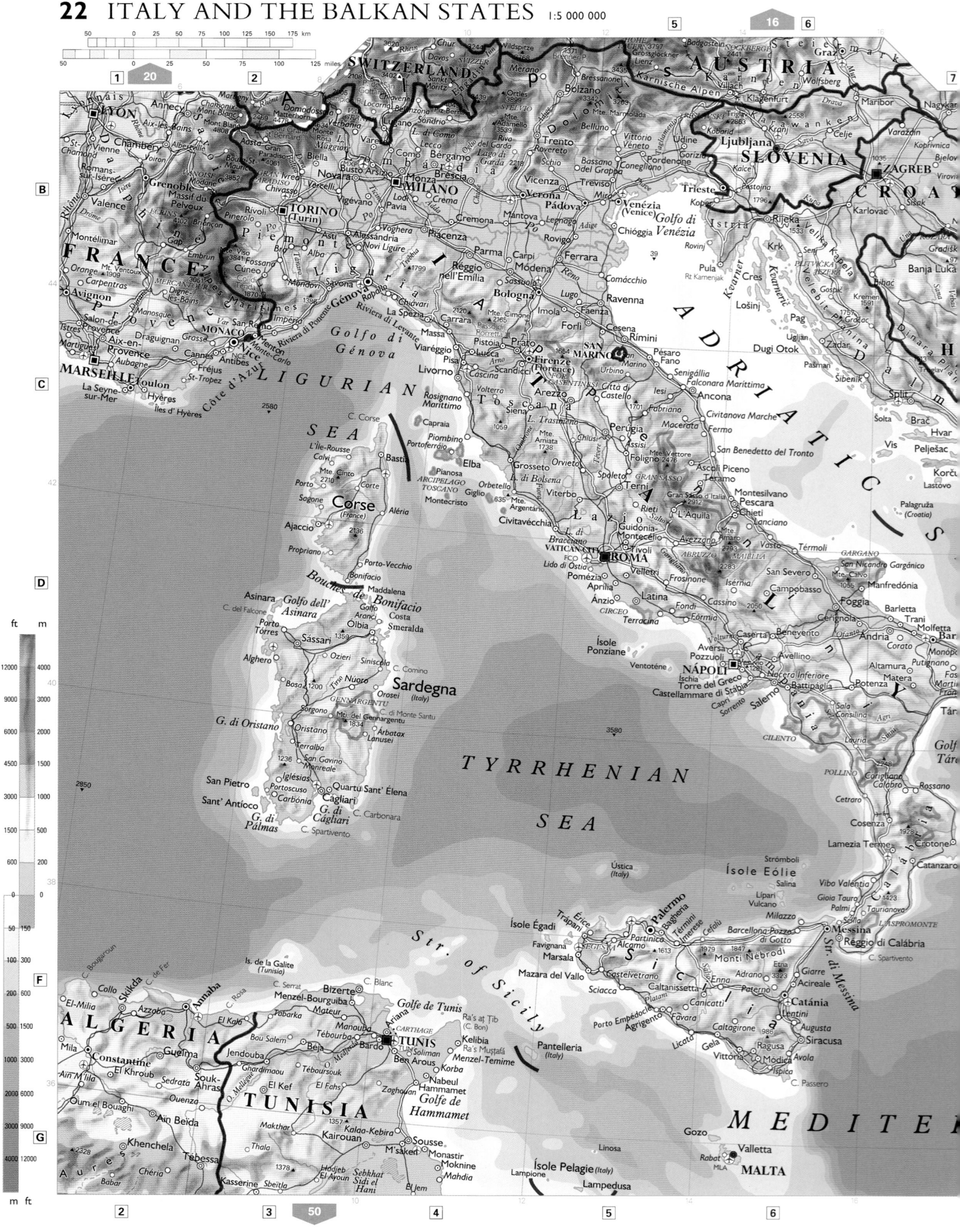

COPYRIGHT PHILIP'S

1:47 000 000

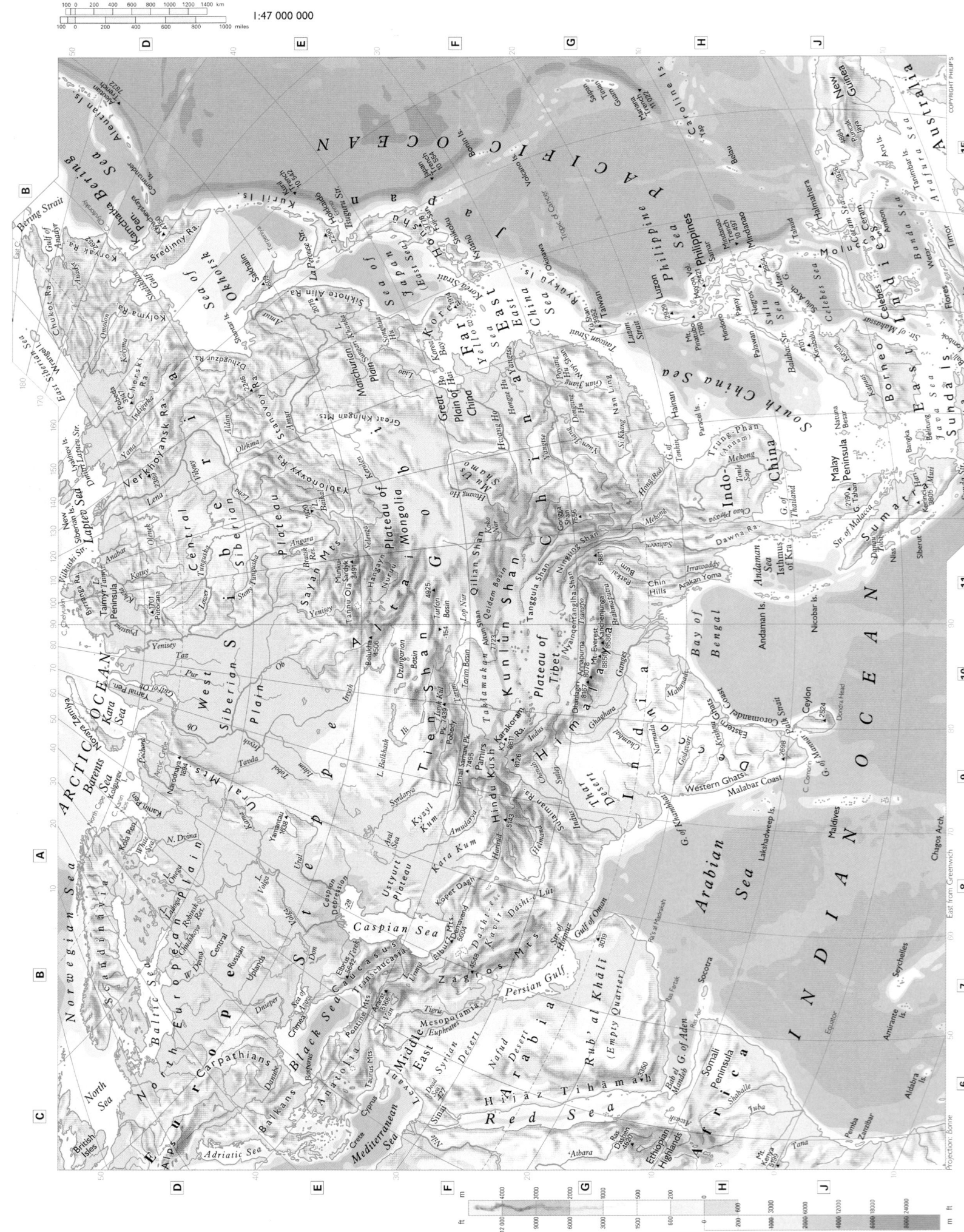

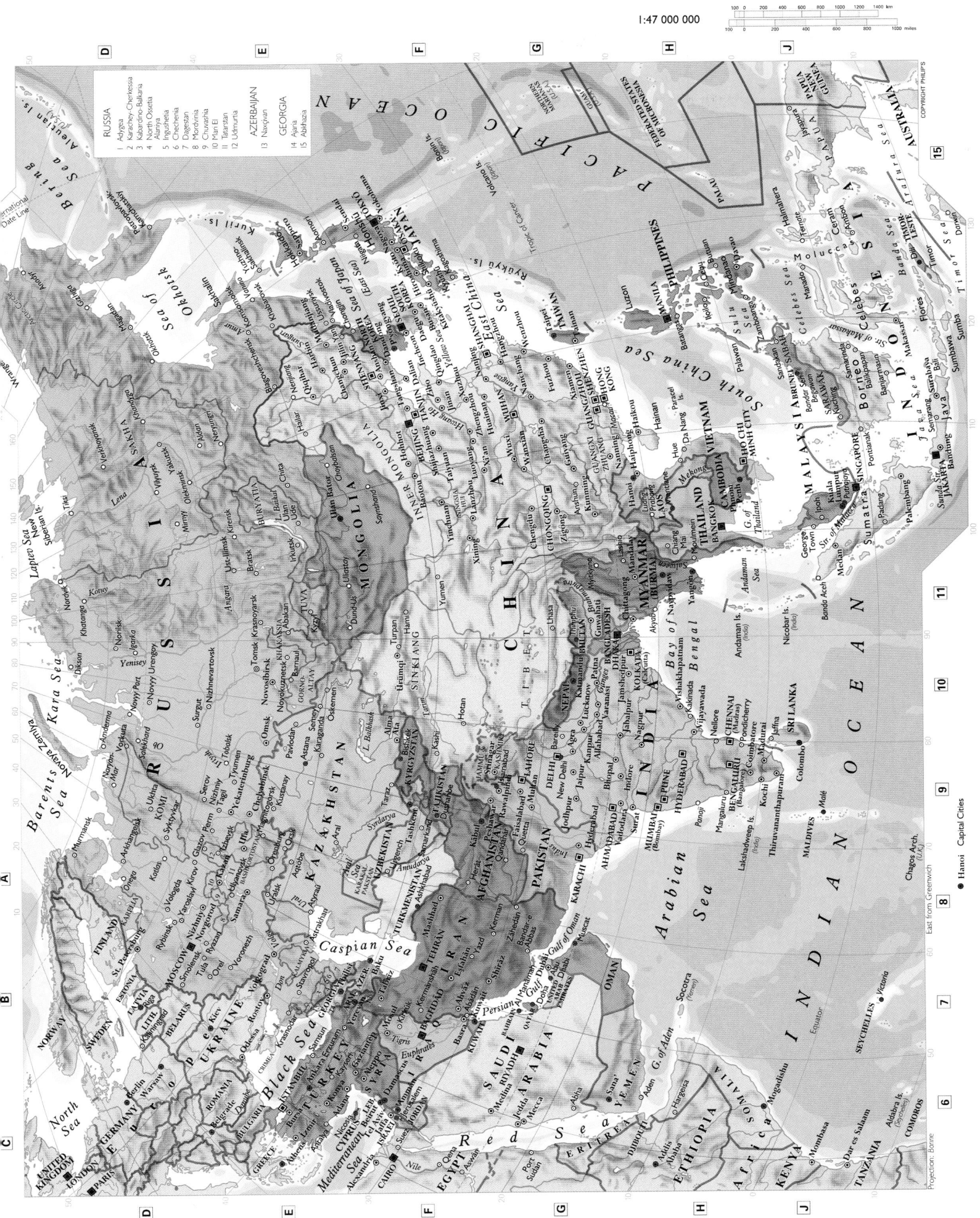

1:47 000 000

Projection: Bonne

COPYRIGHT PHILIPS

● Hanoi Capital Cities

1:20 000 000

Projection: Conical Orthomorphic with two standard parallels

East from Greenwich

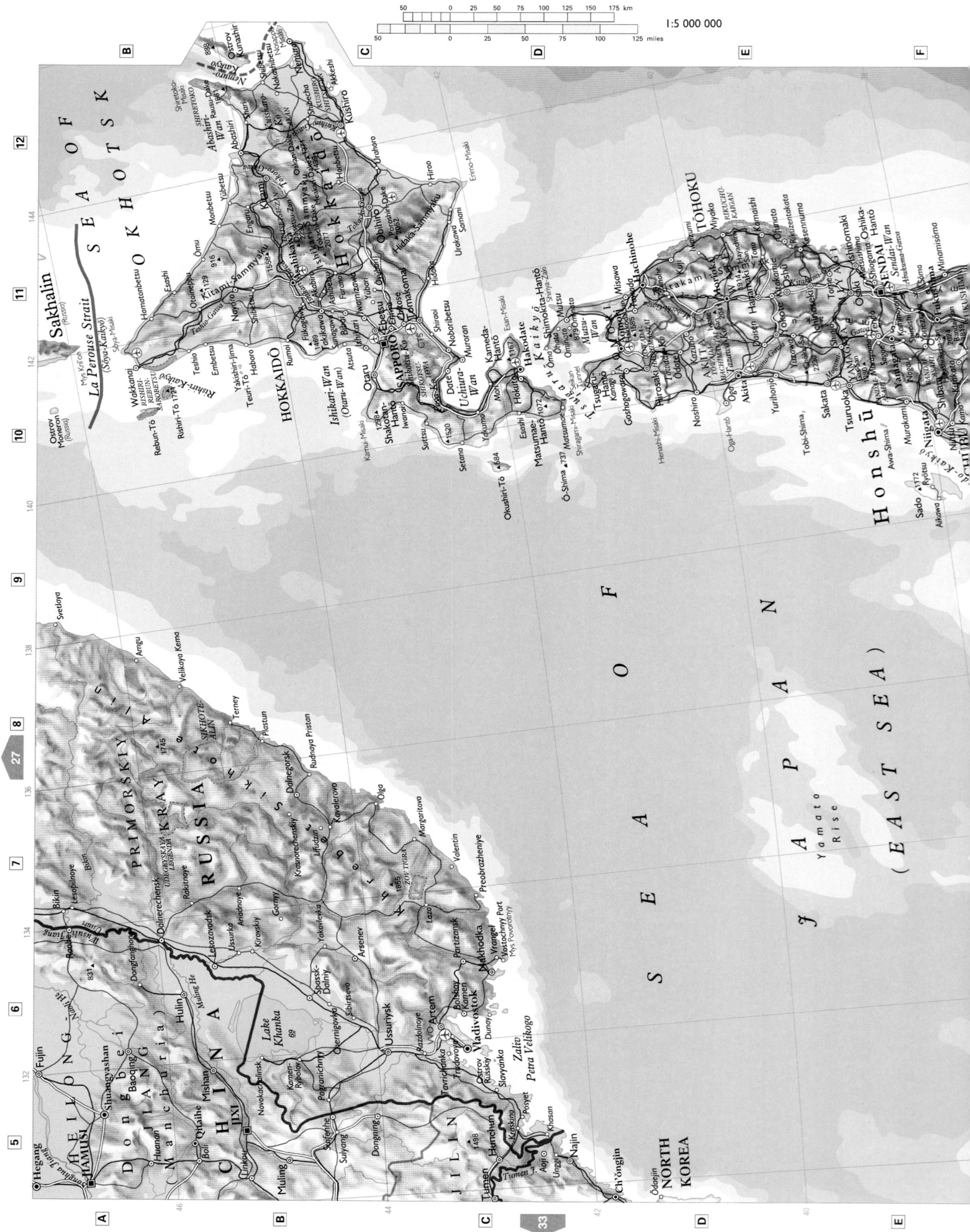

1:5 000 000

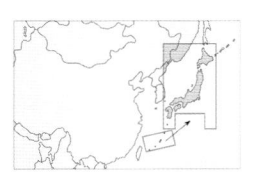

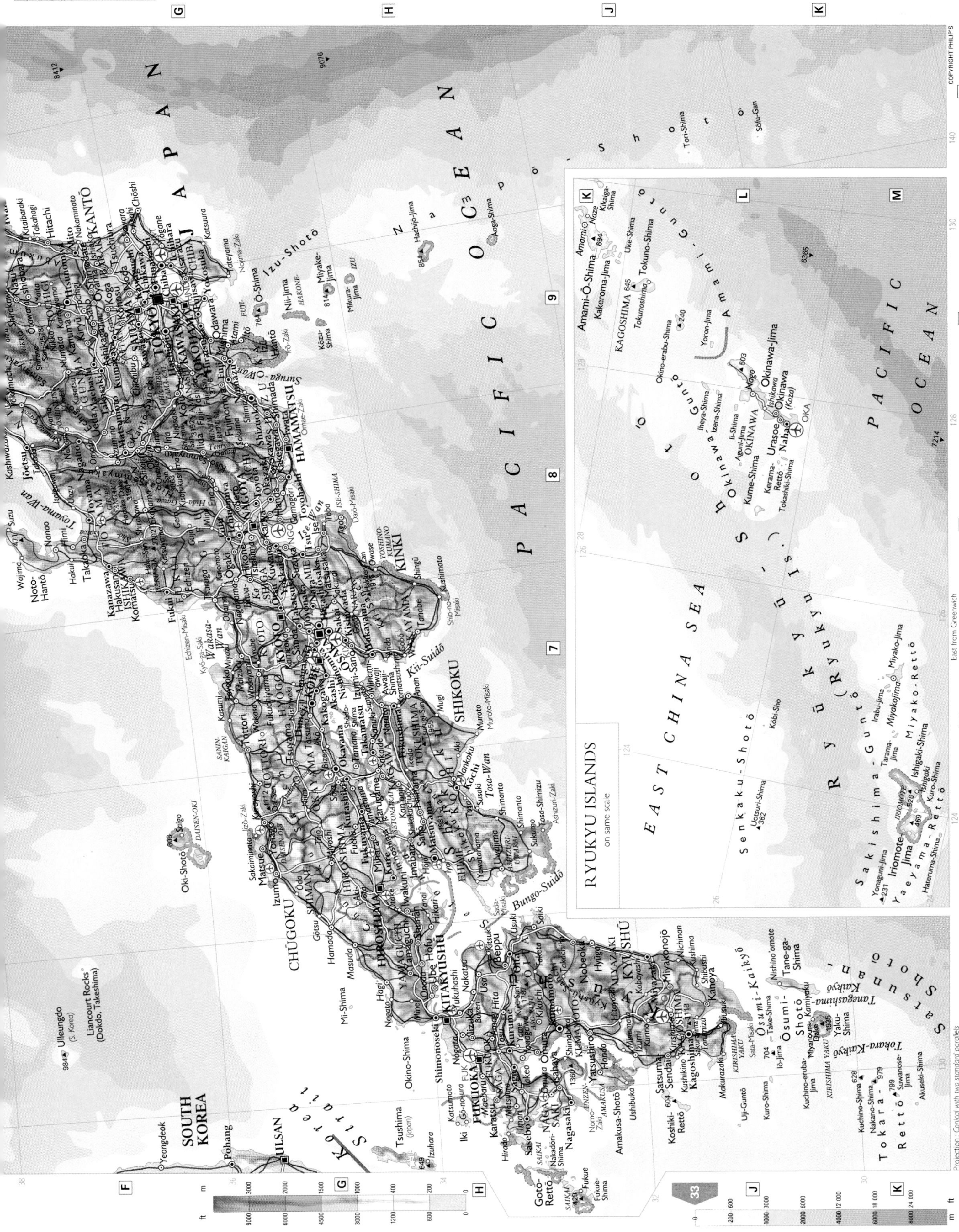

G   H   J   K

J A P A N

P A C I F I C   O C E A N

SOUTH KOREA

Yeongdeok
Pohang
ULSAN

Ulleungdo (S. Korea)
Liancourt Rocks (Dokdo, Takeshima)

Tsushima (Japan)

Korea Strait

CHŪGOKU

KANTŌ

TŌKYŌ
YOKOHAMA
HAMAMATSU
NAGOYA

KINKI
KŌCHI
SHIKOKU
KYŪSHŪ

FUKUOKA
KITAKYUSHU
NAGASAKI
Kagoshima
HIROSHIMA
Shimonoseki

Izu-Shotō
Hachijō-Jima
Miyake-Jima
Aoga-Shima
Sōfu-Gan
Tori-Shima

EAST CHINA SEA

RYUKYU ISLANDS
on same scale

Senkaku-Shotō
Sakishima-Guntō
Iriomote
Ishigaki-Shima
Miyako-Rettō
Miyako-Jima

R y ū k y ū   I s.   (Ryukyu)

Amami-Guntō
Amami-Ō-Shima
Amami
Naze
Kikaiga-Shima
Kakeroma-Jima
Uke-Shima
Tokuno-Shima

KAGOSHIMA
Okino-erabu-Shima
Yoron-Jima

Okinawa-Guntō
Iheya-Shima
Izena-Shima
Ie-Jima
Aguni-Jima
OKINAWA
Okinawa-Jima
Urasoe
Naha
Ishikawa
OKA
(Koza)
Kume-Shima
Kerama-Rettō
Tokashiki-Shima

P A C I F I C   O C E A N

Tanegashima YAKU
Ōsumi-Kaikyō
Tane-ga-shima
Nishino-omote
Ōsumi Shotō
Yaku-Shima
Tokara-Kaikyō
Satsunan-Shotō
Tokara-Rettō
Nakano-Shima
Kuchino-Shima
Suwanose-Jima
Akuseki-Shima

Satsuma-Hantō
Amakusa-Shotō
Kuro-Shima
Koshiki-Rettō
Uji-Guntō

Gotō-Rettō
Fukue-Shima

K   L   M

East from Greenwich

Projection: Conical with two standard parallels

ft
9000
6000
4500
3000
1500
600
0
m
3000
2000
1500
1000
400
200
0

ft
24 000
18 000
12 000
6000
3000
0
m
6000
4000
2000
1000
200
0

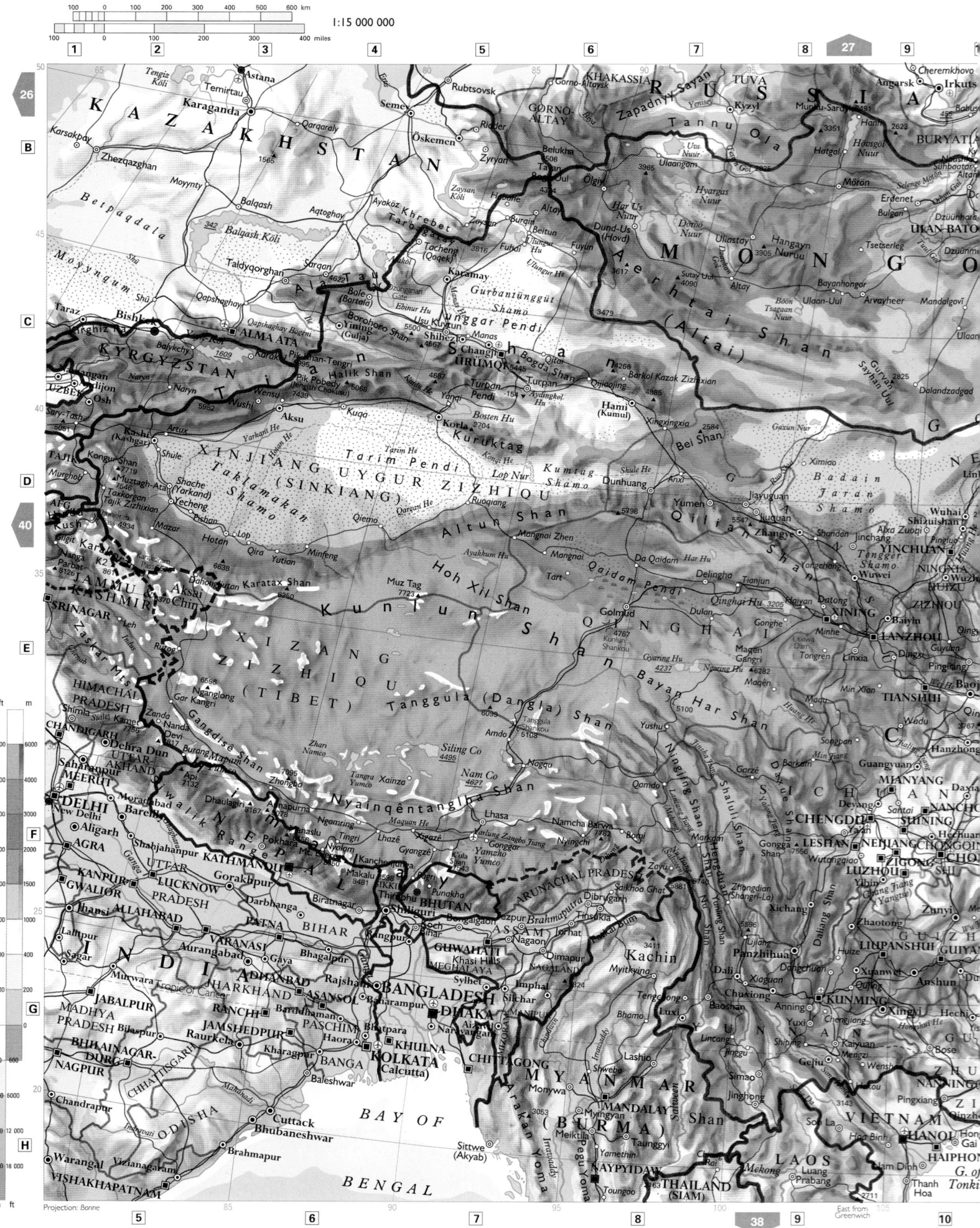

Projection: Bonne

East from Greenwich

RUSSIA

MONGOLIA (INNER MONGOLIA)

Sakhalin

HOKKAIDO
SAPPORO

SEA OF

JAPAN
(EAST SEA)

TOKYO
KAWASAKI
YOKOHAMA
NAGOYA
OSAKA
KYOTO
KOBE
HAMAMATSU

J A P A N

QIQIHAR
DAQING
HARBIN
MUDANJIANG
CHANGCHUN
JILIN
CHIFENG
SHENYANG
ANSHAN

NORTH
KOREA

P'YONGYANG
NAMP'O

SOUTH
KOREA
SEOUL
INCHEON
DAEJEON
GWANGJU
BUSAN
ULSAN
DAEGU

HOHHOT
DATONG
BEIJING
(Peking)
BEIJING SHI
TANGSHAN
TIANJIN SHI
TIANJIN
BAODING
SHIJIAZHUANG
TAIYUAN
HANDAN
ANYANG
ZIBO
JINAN
QINGDAO
YANTAI
WEIFANG

YELLOW
SEA

HIROSHIMA
KITAKYUSHU
FUKUOKA
SHIKOKU
Kyūshū

DALIAN

ZHENGZHOU
LUOYANG
XI'AN
NANYANG
WUHAN
HEFEI
NANJING
SHANGHAI
HANGZHOU
NINGBO

EAST CHINA
SEA

PACIFIC

OCEAN

CHANGSHA
NANCHANG
WENZHOU

GUANGZHOU
(Canton)
FOSHAN
SHENZHEN
HONG KONG
(Xianggang)
Macau
ZHUHAI

TAIPEI
TAICHUNG
TAINAN
KAOHSIUNG
TAIWAN

Tropic of Cancer

SOUTH CHINA
SEA

PHILIPPINES

HAIKOU
Hainan Dao
HAINAN

COPYRIGHT PHILIP'S

HONG KONG, MACAU AND SHENZHEN
1:1 000 000

GUANGDONG

SHENZHEN
ZHONGSHAN
Tuen Mun
Kowloon
HONG KONG
(Xianggang)
Hong Kong Island
ZHUHAI
Macau
(Aomen)
Lantau Island
(Tai Yue Shan)

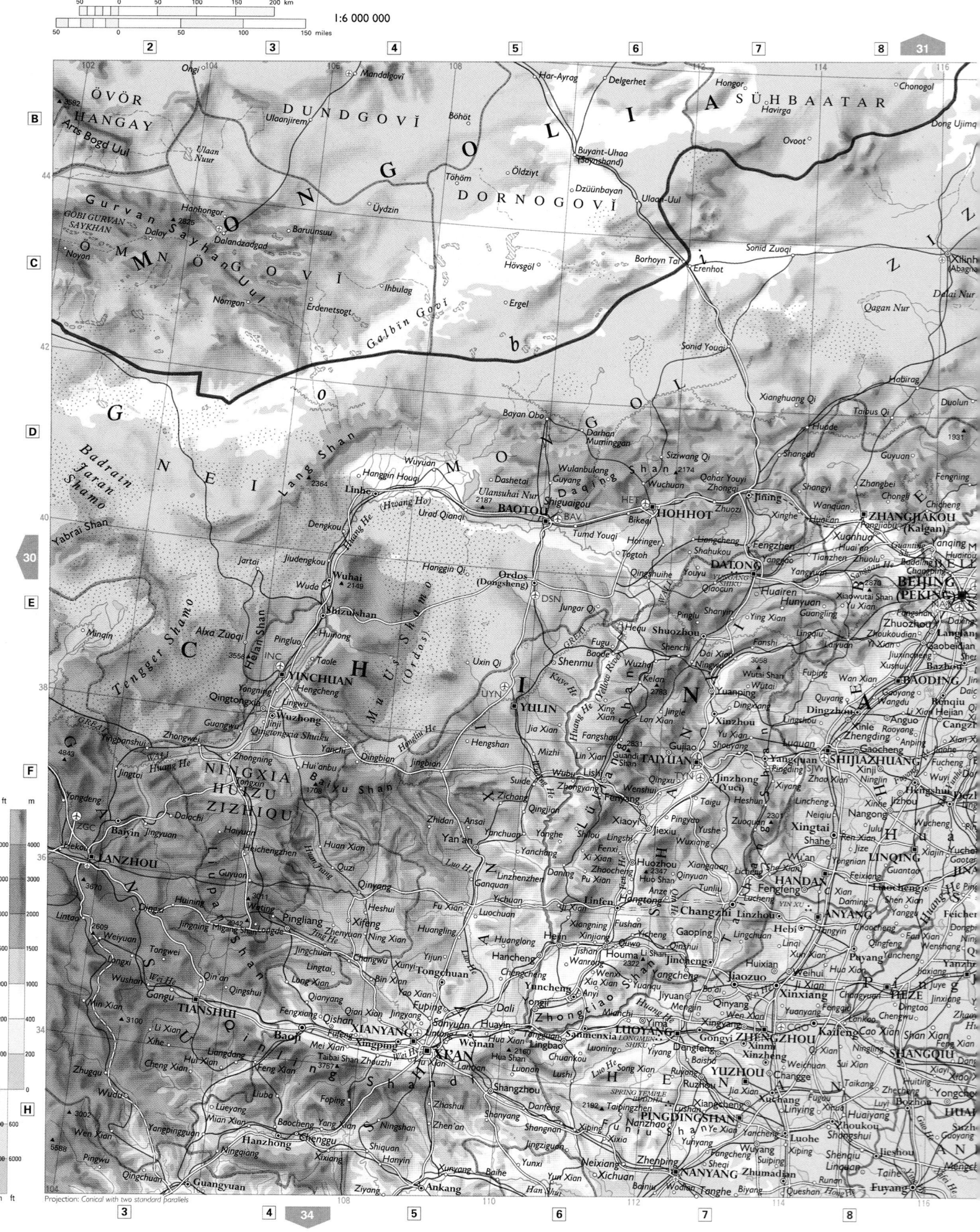

1:6 000 000

50 0 50 100 150 200 km
50 0 50 100 150 miles

B

C

D

E

F

H

ÖVÖR
HANGAY
Arts Bogd Uul
▲3582

GÖBI GURVAN
SAYKHAN
▲2825

Ö
M
N
Ö
G
O
V
Ï

Noyon

Gurvan Saykhan Gui

Hanhongor

Dalay

Dalandzadgad

Baruunsuu

Nömgön

Ihbulag

Erdenetsogt

Galbin Govi

Ulaan
Nuur

Ulaanjirem

Üydzin

Töhöm

Böhöt

Hövsgöl

Ergel

o

b

Mandalgovï

DUNDGOVÏ

DORNOGOVÏ

Öldziyt

Dzüünbayan

Ulaan-Uul

Borhoyn Tal

M O N G O L I A

Delgerhet

Buyant-Uhaa
(Saynshand)

Hongor

Har-Ayrag

Havirga

Ovoot

SÜHBAATAR

Chonogol

Dong Ujimq

Erenhot

Sonid Zuoqi

Sonid Youqi

Xilinh

Abagha

Delai Nur

Qagan Nur

Z
I
Z

G
U
N
E
I
M
O
N
G
O
L

Badrain
Jaran
Shamo

Yabrai Shan

Lang Shan
▲2364

Hanggin Houqi

Wuyuan

Linhe

Huang He (Hwang Ho)

Urad Qianqi

Dengkou

BAOTOU

Bayan Obo

Darhan
Muminggan

Dashetai

Ulansuhai Nur
▲2187

Shiguaigou

BAV

Daqing Shan

Guyang
Wulanbulang

Siziwang Qi
▲2174

Qahar Youyi
Zhongqi

Shangdu

Guyuan

HET

HOHHOT

Jining

Xinghe

Wanquan

Zhangbei

Chongli

Fengning

Chigheng

1931

Xianghuang Qi

Taibus Qi

Huade

Zhuozi

Bikeqi

Tumd Youqi

Horinger

Togtoh

Liangcheng

Shahukou

Fengzhen

Huai'an
Tianzhen

Xuanhua

Zhuolu

Guanting
Badaling

Changping

Z

E

Zhangbei

ZHANGJIAKOU
Xiahuayuan (Kalgan)

anqing

B E I

BEIJING
(PEKING)

Badrain
Jaran Shamo

Jartai

Jiudengkou

Wuda

Wuhai
▲2149

Hanggin Qi

Ordos
(Dongsheng)

Qingshuihe

Youyu

DSN

Jungar Qi

Pinglu

Hequ

Shuozhou

Shenchi

Baode

Fugu

Wuzhai

Kelan
▲2788

Xing
Xian

GREAT

Datong

Qiaocun

Huairen

Hunyuan

Guangling

Yu Xian

Ying Xian

Shanyin

Fanshi

Dai Xian
▲3058

Wutai Shan
▲2870

Yangyuan

Xiaowutai Shan

Zhuozhou

Laiyuan

Lanping

Gaobeidian

Xushui

Zhoukoudian

Langfang

Fuping

Jiuxianghe

Bazhou

Wan Xian

BAODING

Tengger Shamo

Minqin

Alxa Zuoqi
▲3556

Helan Shan

Shizuishan

Huinong

YINCHUAN

Hengcheng

INC

Taole

Pingluo

Mu Us Shamo
(Ordos)

Uxin Qi

UYN

YULIN

Jia Xian

Mizhi

Huang He (Yellow River)

Kuye He

Lin Xian

Lishi

TAIYUAN

LYN

Jinzhong
(Yuci)

Yangquan

Pingding
Ringding

SJW

SHIJIAZHUANG

Gaoyang

Lixian

Zhao Xian

Wuqiang

Anping

Xian
Lin

Cang

C

Qingtongxia

Yongning

Wuzhong

Yinji

Guangwu

Qingtongxia Shuiku

Shenmu

Hengshan

Jingbian

Jia Xian

Guandi
Shan
▲2831

Fenyang

Jiexiu

Pingyao

Taigu

Shouyang

Yu Xian

Heshun

Xiyang

Gujiao

Linchen

Neiqiu

Nangong

N I N G X I A
H U I Z U
Z I Z H I Q U

Zhongwei

Zhongning

Tongxin
▲1708

Baiyu Shan

Hui'anbu

Yanchi

Dingbian

Suide

Wubu

Zhongyang

Wenshui

Wuxiang

Zuoquan
▲2301

Xingtai

Shahe

Jize

Linqing

JIN

▲4843
ZGC

Jingtai

Huang
Jiang

Guyuan

Haiyuan

Heichengzhen

Zichang

Ansai

Yanchuan

Yonghe

Shilou

Xi Xian

Fenxi

Huozhou

Xiangyuan

Tunliu

Gaoping

Lucheng

HANDAN

Cheng Xian

Daming

Feixiang

ANYANG

Pu Xian

Daning

Linzhenzhen

YIN XU

Hebi

Baiyin
Jingyuan

Dalachi

▲3670

Heshui

Huan Xian

Quzi

Luo He

Ganquan

Yan'an

Yichuan

Huangling

Luochuan

Huo Shan
▲2347

Qinyuan

Changzhi
Linzhou

Lingshou

Hebi

Weihui

Ji Xian

Huaxian

Huojia

Puyang

P

Fan Xian

Feichen

LANZHOU

Hekou

Longxi
▲3011

Weiyuan

Tongwei

Jingning
Migang Shan
▲2609

Pingliang

Zhenyuan
Ning Xian

Xifeng

Fu Xian

Huangling

Hancheng

Jishan
▲2322

Houma

Yangcheng

Huixian

Jiaozuo

Xinxiang

Qinyang

Mengjin

Yima

Gongyi

ZHENGZHOU

Kaifeng
Cao Xian

Shan Xian

Huangang

Changyuan

Yanzhou

Juye

g

Jinxiang

HEZE

SHANGQIU

Tianshui

Gangu

Wushan

Longxi

Qin'an

Qingshui

Chongwu

Xunyi

Tongchuan

Long Xian

Bin Xian

Lintai

Jingchuan

Qian Xian

Qianyang

Qishan

Xia Xian
Wenxi

Yuncheng

Anyi

Wanrong

Linfen

Hongtong

Fushan
Yicheng

Xinjiang

Hejin

Yongji

Zhongtiao Shan

Huang He

Jiyuan

Sanmenxia
LONGMEN

Luoyang

Xin'an

Luoning

Yiyang

Dengfeng

Xinzheng

Yuzhou

Xuchang

Linying

Weichuan

Ling

SHANGQIU

Xiayi

Yongcheng

Menglu

Li Xian
Xihe

Liangdang

Tianshui

Baoji

Fufeng
Xingping

Mei Xian
Taibai Shan
▲3767

XIANYANG

Feng Xian

Zhouzhi

Weinan

Hua Xian

XI'AN

XAN

Lianhu

Hua Shan
▲2162

Lingbao

Chuankou

Luonan

Lushi

Song Xian

Ruyang

Jia Xian

Baisha

Yuzhou

Xinzheng

SPRING TEMPLE
BUDDHA

Changge

Xiangcheng

Linying

Luohe

Shangqiu

Xiangzhou

Xiping

Suiping

Linquan

H

E
N
A
N

Zhugqu

Wudu

▲3002

Lueyang

Mian Xian

Chenggu

Ningqiang

▲5588
Pingwu

Qinchuan

Guangyuan

Hanzhong

Ningqiang

Zhashui

Shanyang

Danfeng

Shangnan

Xixia

Neixiang
Xichuan

Zhenping

Yunxi

Shangzhou

▲2192

Taipingzhen

Funiu Shan

Nanzhao

PINGDINGSHAN

Lushan

Ye Xian
Fangcheng

Yucheng

Biyang

Tanghe

Wuyang

NANYANG
Zhumadian

Runan

Baiquan

Taihe

Foping

Ningshan

Shiquan

Hanyin

Ankang

Xunyang

Baihe

Yun Xian

Han Shui

Yunxi

Danjiangkou

Wudian

Tanghe

Queshan

HUA

Yangpingguan

Chenggu

Baoqeng

Yang Xian

Zhen'an

Jingziguan

Gangu

Qinchuan

Zhuging

Han Shui

Zitong

Ankang

Guangyuan

Projection: Conical with two standard parallels

ft m
12 000 4000
9000 3000
6000 2000
4500 1500
3000 1000
1200 400
600 200
0 0
200 600
2000 6000
m ft

30

34

HARBIN
HEILONGJIANG
RUSSIA
Lake Khanka
Ussuriysk
Vladivostok

CHANGCHUN
JILIN
Tumen
Hunchun

SHENYANG   FUSHUN
LIAONING
ANSHAN
Haicheng

CHIFENG
(Ulanhad)

NORTH
KOREA
P'YONGYANG
NAMP'O

SEA OF
JAPAN
(EAST SEA)

Liaodong
Wan

BO HAI
Bo Hai Haixia

DALIAN
(Lüda)

Korea
Bay

SOUTH
KOREA
SEOUL
INCHEON   SEONGNAM
SUWON
DAEJEON
DAEGU
ULSAN

YANTAI
Weihai

WEIFANG

QINGDAO

YELLOW   SEA
(HUANG HAI)

GWANGJU
BUSAN

Korea Strait
Tsushima
(Japan)

Jeju Haehyop
Jeju-do (S. Korea)
Hallasan

JAPAN
Nagasaki

East from Greenwich

1:6 000 000

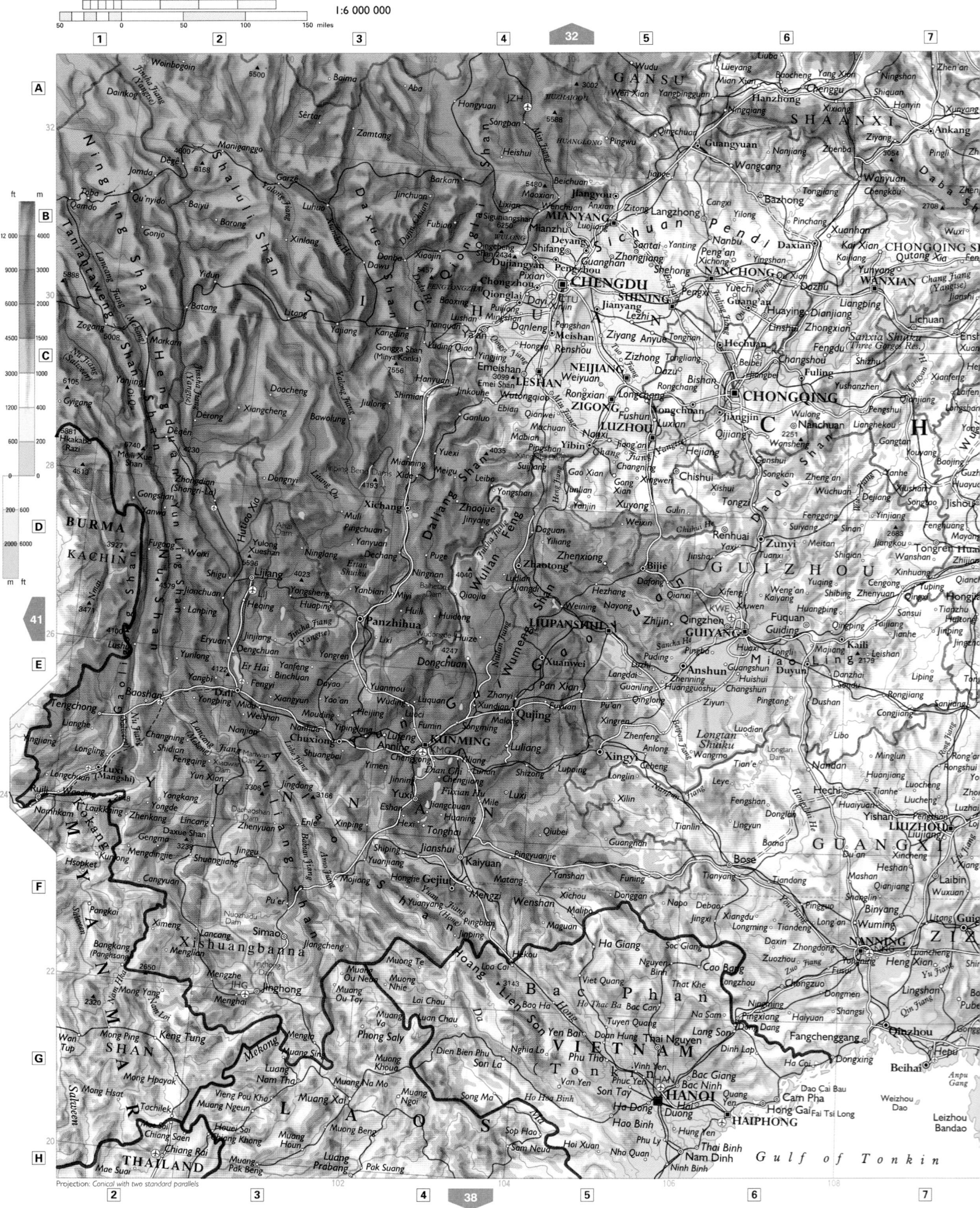

Projection: Conical with two standard parallels

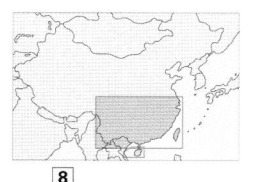

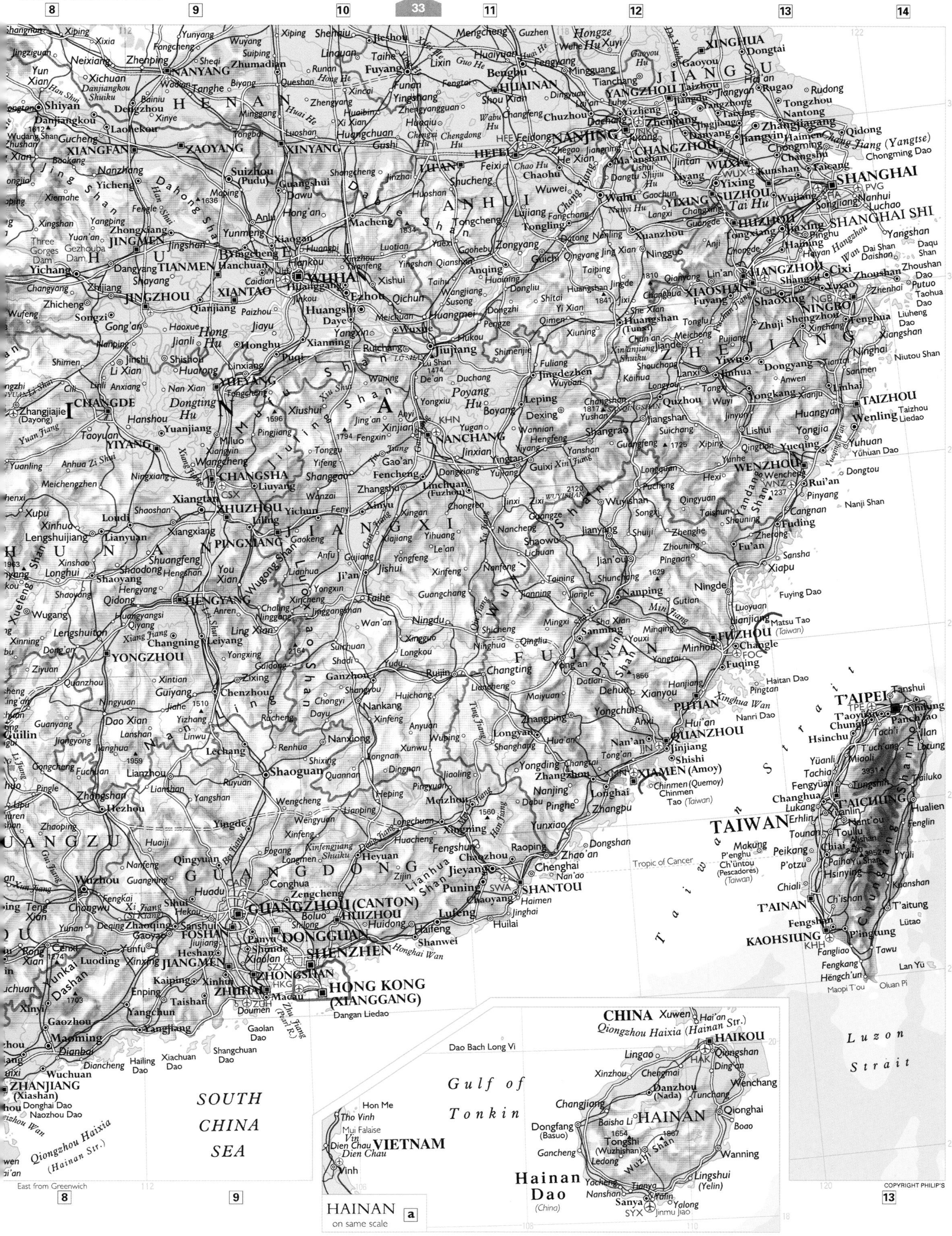

1:12 500 000

Projection: Mercator

East from Greenwich

JAVA AND MADURA
1:7 500 000

BALI
1:2 000 000

COPYRIGHT PHILIP'S

KO SAMUI
1:1 000 000

Gulf of Thailand

Ko Samui

KO PHUKET
1:1 000 000

AO PHANGNGA

Ko Phuket

ANDAMAN SEA

PINANG
1:1 000 000

Pulau Pinang

SINGAPORE
1:1 000 000

Straits of Singapore

SINGAPORE

MALAYSIA

INDONESIA

SOUTH CHINA SEA

PENINSULAR MALAYSIA

MALAYSIA

Gulf of Thailand

Kho Khot Kra (Isthmus of Kra)

Mergui Archipelago

Kyunzu

Straits of Malacca

INDONESIA

RIAU

SUMATERA UTARA

ACEH

Projection: Conical with two standard parallels

1:10 000 000

Projection: Conical with two standard parallels

continuation southwards
on same scale

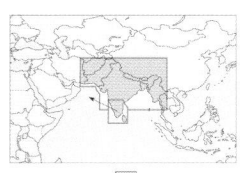

13 14 **30** 15 16 17 18 19 20 21 22

B

XIN JIANG UYGUR ZIZHIQU (SINKIANG) Muz Tag Kun Lun Shan Hoh Xil Shan Kunlun Shankou QINGHAI Huang He Maqên Gangri Maqu

C

XIZANG CHINA Yushu Nangqên Dêgê Garzê

ZIZHIQU TIBET Tanggula (Dangla) Shan Tanggula Shankou Amdo Baqên Dêngqên Qamdo Baiyu Xinlong SICHUAN

D

Kangrinboqê Feng (Kailash) Mapam Yumco Gang Shan Dongco Siling Co Nagqu Nu Jiang Lhorong Zhaxizê Markam Yidun Litang Yajiang

Namco Gyaring Co Xainza Nam Co Lhari Gongbo'gyamda Namcha Bomi Zayū Zhongdian

E

NEPAL Simikot Mugu Jumla Saga Ngamring Xigazê Lhasa Nyingchi Gogên Weixi Lijiang

Maquan He (Tsangpo) Yamzho Yumco Yarlung Zangbo Jiang (Brahmaputra) Nang Xian ARUNACHAL PRADESH Jianchuan Dali

F

Dhaulagiri Pokhara KATHMANDU Everest Kanchenjunga SIKKIM Thimphu BHUTAN Punakha Tongsa Dzong ASSAM KACHIN Baoshan Tengchong

G

Gorakhpur Darbhanga BIHAR PATNA Shiliguri Jalpaiguri Rangpur GUWAHATI NAGALAND Kohima MANIPUR Imphal Tropic of Cancer

VARANASI Ghazipur Gaya Bhagalpur Bogra BANGLADESH Mymensingh SYLHET Silchar MIZORAM SHAN MANDALAY

H

JHARKHAND DHANBAD ASANSOL RANCHI JAMSHEDPUR DHAKA Narayanganj TRIPURA Agartala Aizawl CHIN

Durgapur KOLKATA Haora Khulna BARISAL CHITTAGONG MYANMAR (BURMA)

J

CHHATTISGARH RAIPUR BHILAINAGAR-DURG Kharagpur Medinipur The Sundarbans Mouths of the Ganges Cox's Bazar Sittwe (Akyab) RAKHINE NAYPYIDAW

K

ODISHA Cuttack Bhubaneshwar Puri Chilka L. THAILAND Chiang Mai Lampang

Brahmapur BAY OF BENGAL Cheduba I. BAGO YANGON (Rangoon) Mawlamyine MON

L

VISHAKHAPATNAM Arakan Coast Pathein AYEYAWADI G. of Mottama

38

M

Kakinada INDIAN OCEAN Preparis North Channel Pariparit Kyun (Burma) Preparis South Channel Koko Kyunzu (Burma) Mouths of the Irrawaddy Moscos Is. Maungmagan Is. Launglon Bok Dawei

COPYRIGHT PHILIP'S

ARABIAN SEA

Projection: Conical with two standard parallels

1:6 000 000

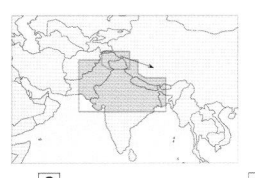

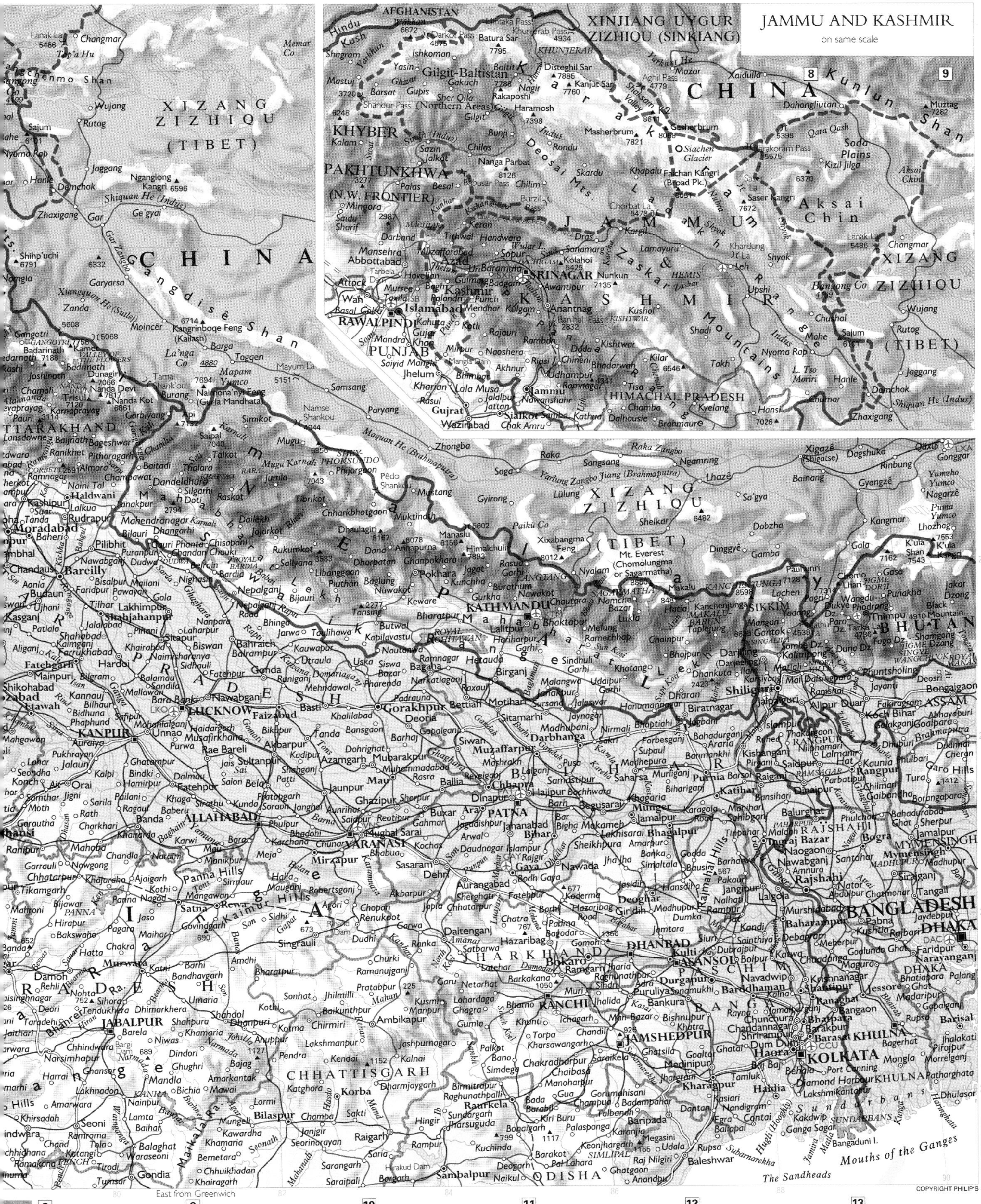
JAMMU AND KASHMIR
on same scale
XINJIANG UYGUR
ZIZHIQU (SINKIANG)
AFGHANISTAN
CHINA
Gilgit-Baltistan
KHYBER
PAKHTUNKHWA
(N.W. FRONTIER)
JAMMU & KASHMIR
SRINAGAR
Islamabad
RAWALPINDI
PUNJAB
HIMACHAL PRADESH
Aksai Chin
XIZANG ZIZHIQU (TIBET)
Kunlun Shan
Karakoram Range
Ladakh Range
Zaskar Mountains
Gangdisê Shan
UTTARAKHAND
UTTAR PRADESH
NEPAL
KATHMANDU
Mt. Everest
(Chomolungma
or Sagarmatha)
SIKKIM
BHUTAN
Thimphu
BIHAR
PATNA
LUCKNOW
KANPUR
ALLAHABAD
VARANASI
JHARKHAND
RANCHI
JAMSHEDPUR
DHANBAD
ASANSOL
PASCHIM BANGA
KOLKATA
Haora
BANGLADESH
DHAKA
KHULNA
RAJSHAHI
ASSAM
MADHYA PRADESH
JABALPUR
CHHATTISGARH
ODISHA
Mouths of the Ganges
The Sandheads
East from Greenwich
COPYRIGHT PHILIP'S

1:6 000 000

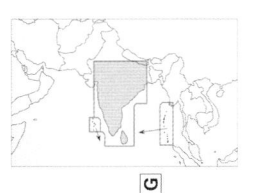

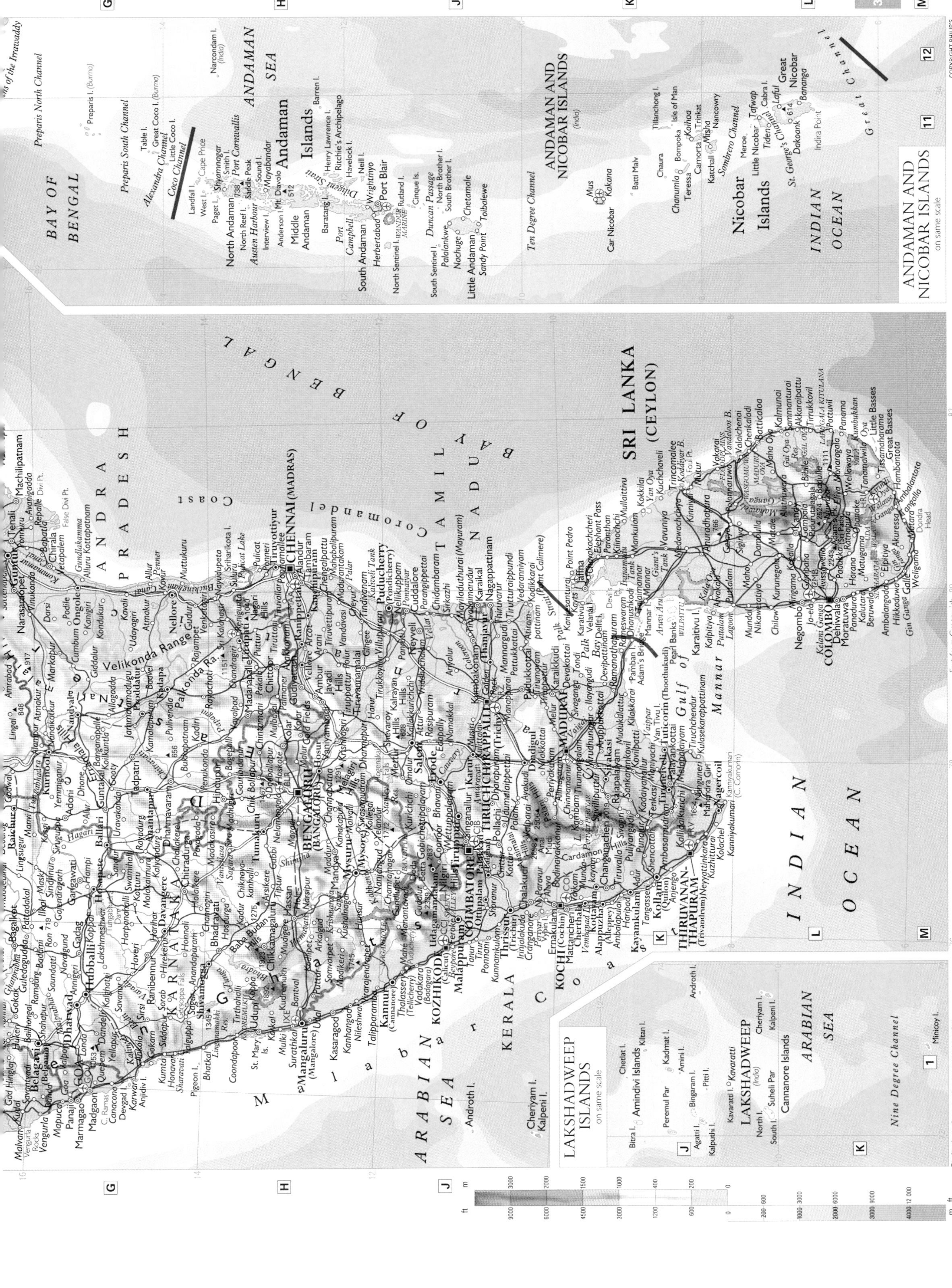

BAY OF BENGAL
ARABIAN SEA
INDIAN OCEAN
ANDAMAN SEA
SRI LANKA (CEYLON)
ANDHRA PRADESH
TAMIL NADU
KARNATAKA
KERALA
Coromandel Coast
Gulf of Mannar
Palk Strait
Palk Bay
CHENNAI (MADRAS)
BENGALURU (BANGALORE)
COLOMBO
KOCHI (Cochin)
THIRUVANANTHAPURAM (Trivandrum)
MADURAI
TIRUCHCHIRAPPALLI (Trichy)
COIMBATORE
Puducherry (Pondicherry)
Mangaluru (Mangalore)
Mysuru (Mysore)
KOZHIKODE (Calicut)
GOA
Jaffna
Trincomalee
Kandy
Galle
ANDAMAN AND NICOBAR ISLANDS (India)
Andaman Islands
Nicobar Islands
Port Blair
Ten Degree Channel
Great Channel
LAKSHADWEEP ISLANDS on same scale
LAKSHADWEEP (India)
ANDAMAN AND NICOBAR ISLANDS on same scale
Nine Degree Channel
East from Greenwich
Projection: Conical with two standard parallels
COPYRIGHT PHILIP'S

1:7 000 000

Projection: Conical with two standard parallels

Underlined towns in Iraq give their name
to the administrative area in which they stand

Lava fields

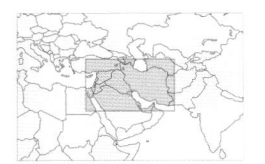

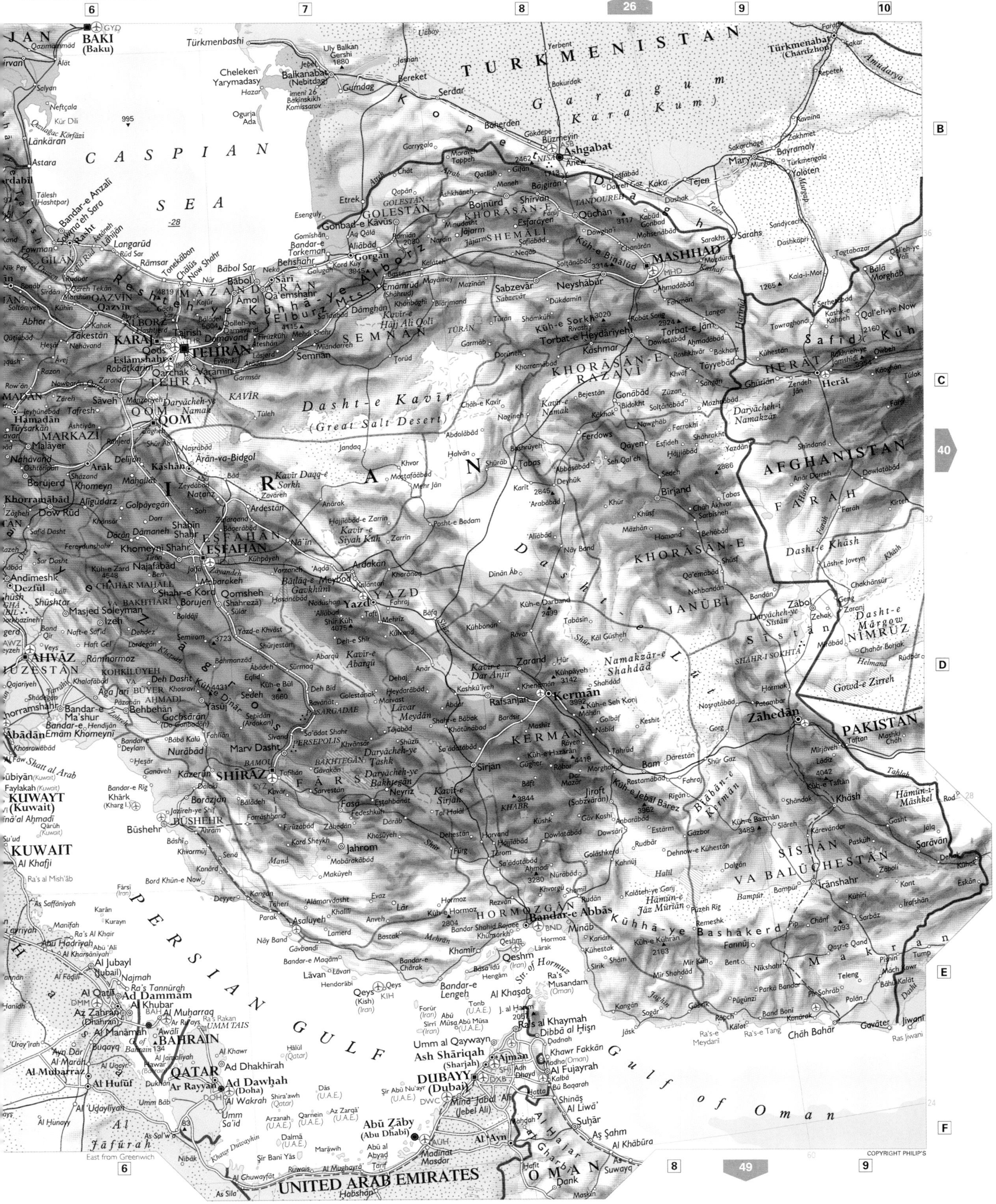

TURKMENISTAN
Garagum (Kara Kum)
Kopet Dagh
CASPIAN SEA
BAKI (Baku)
Türkmenbashi
Ashgabat
Mary
Türkmenabat (Chardzhou)
Tejen
Sarahs
GOLESTĀN
KHORĀSĀN-E SHEMĀLĪ
KHORĀSĀN-E RAZAVĪ
KHORĀSĀN-E JANŪBĪ
MĀZANDARĀN
GĪLĀN
QAZVĪN
ALBORZ
TEHRĀN
SEMNĀN
QOM
MARKAZĪ
ESFAHAN
YAZD
KERMĀN
FĀRS
HORMOZGĀN
SĪSTĀN VA BALŪCHESTĀN
Reshteh-ye Kūhhā-ye Alborz (Elburz Mts.)
Dasht-e Kavīr (Great Salt Desert)
Dasht-e Lūt
IRAN
Zagros
Kūhhā-ye Bashākerd
Makran
Mashhad
Neyshābūr
Sabzevār
Gorgān
Rasht
Qazvin
Karaj
Qom
Kāshān
Esfahān
Yazd
Kermān
Bam
Zāhedān
Shīrāz
Būshehr
Bandar-e Abbās
Ahvāz
Ābādān
AFGHANISTAN
Herāt
Safīd Kūh
FARĀH
NIMRŪZ
PAKISTAN
KUWAIT
BAHRAIN
QATAR
Ad Dawhah (Doha)
PERSIAN GULF
Gulf of Oman
Str. of Hormuz
DUBAYY (Dubai)
Abū Ẓaby (Abu Dhabi)
UNITED ARAB EMIRATES
OMAN
Al Jāfūrah
Ad Dammām
COPYRIGHT PHILIP'S

26
40
49

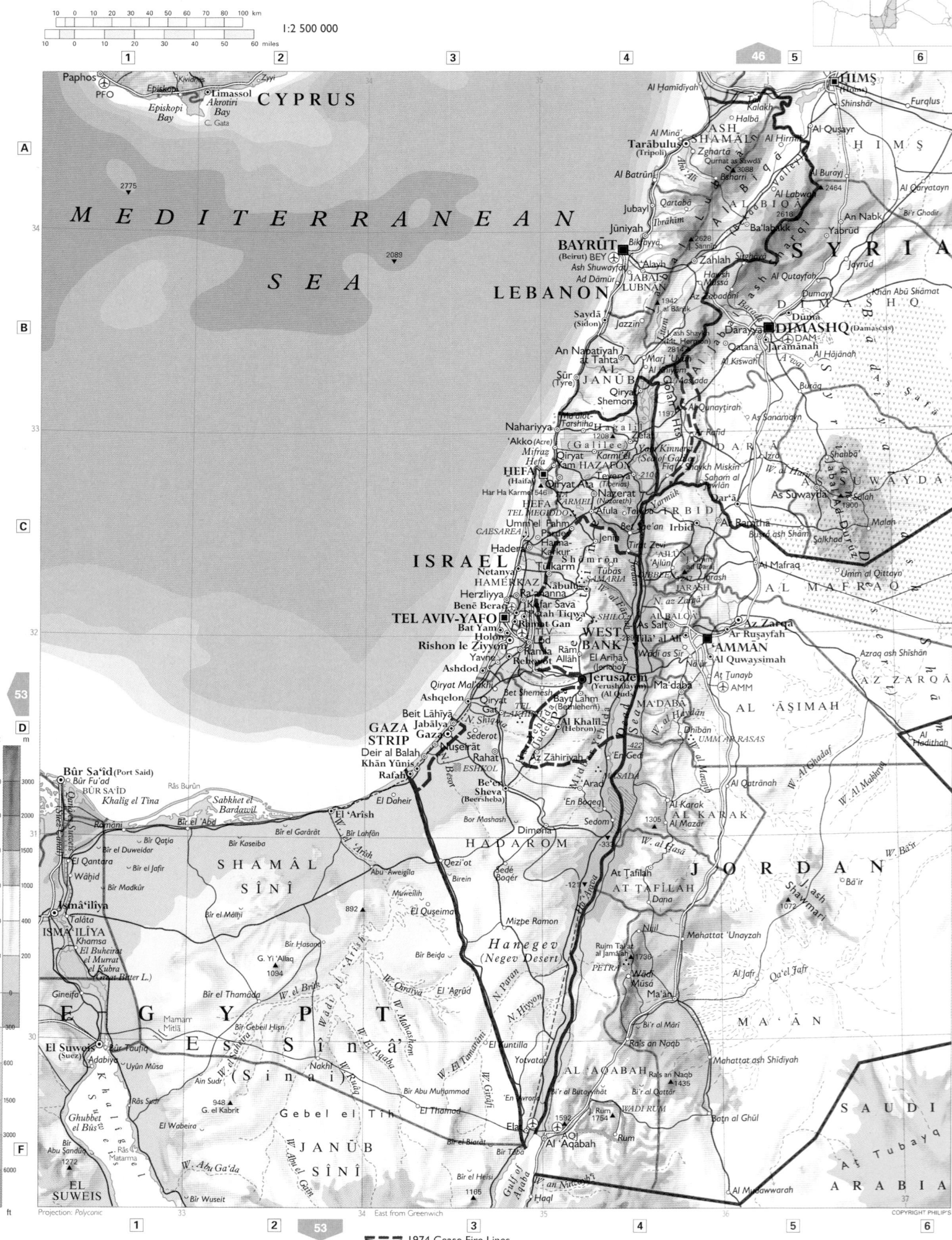

1:2 500 000

1974 Cease Fire Lines

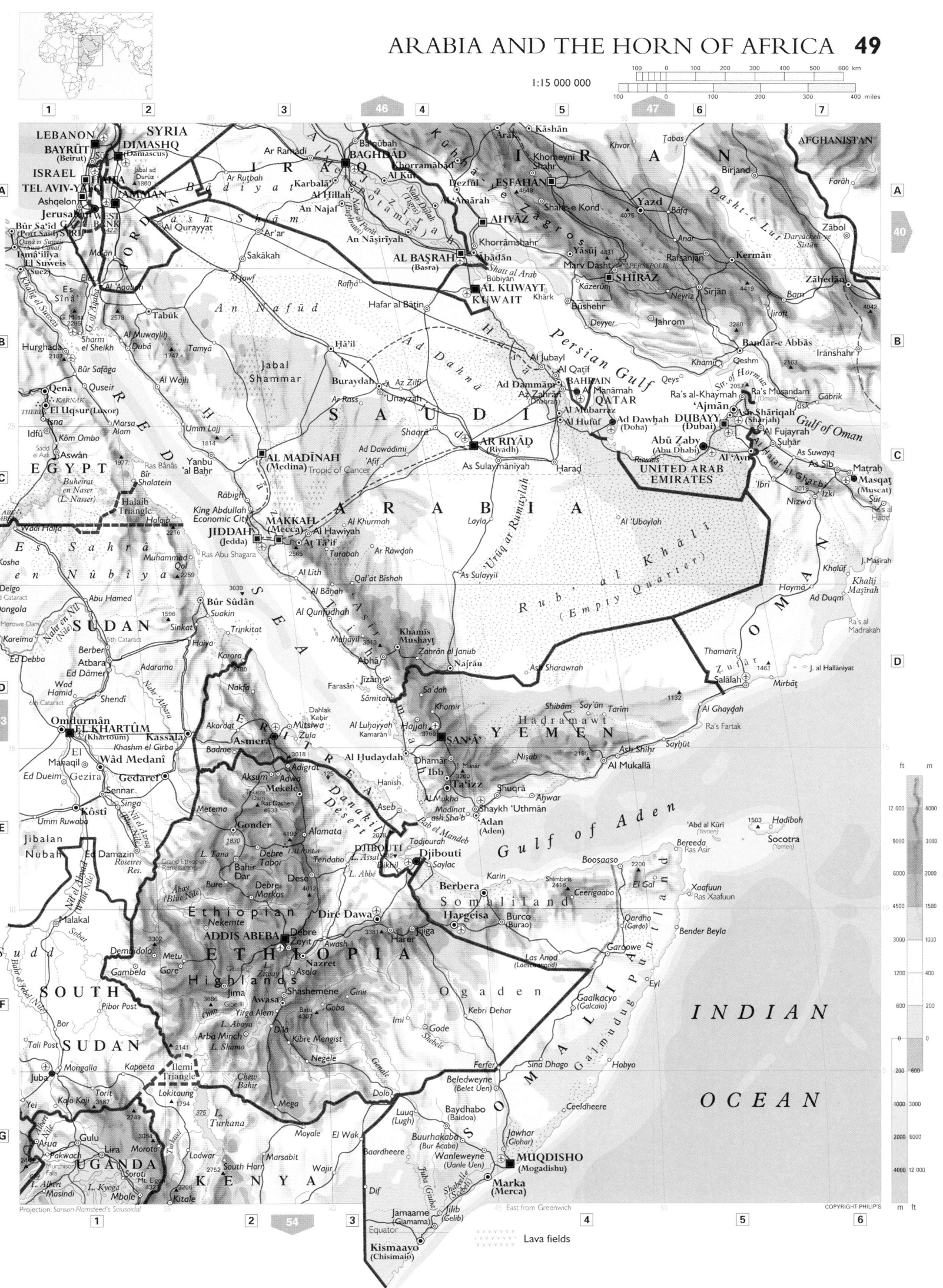

1:15 000 000

Lava fields

Projection: Sanson-Flamsteed's Sinusoidal

COPYRIGHT PHILIP'S

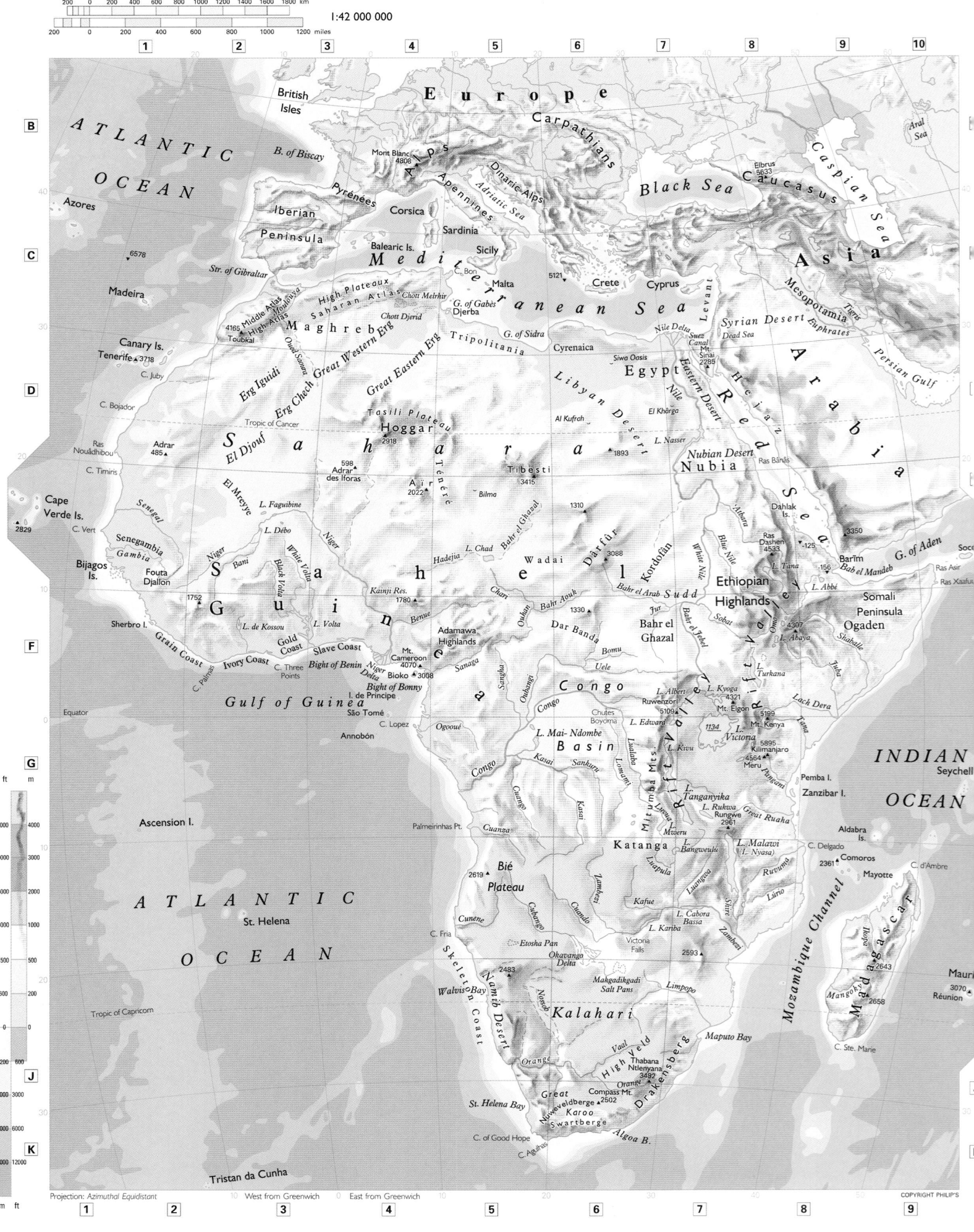

200 0 200 400 600 800 1000 1200 1400 1600 1800 km

1:42 000 000

200 0 200 400 600 800 1000 1200 miles

Projection: *Azimuthal Equidistant*

10 West from Greenwich 0 East from Greenwich 10

COPYRIGHT PHILIP'S

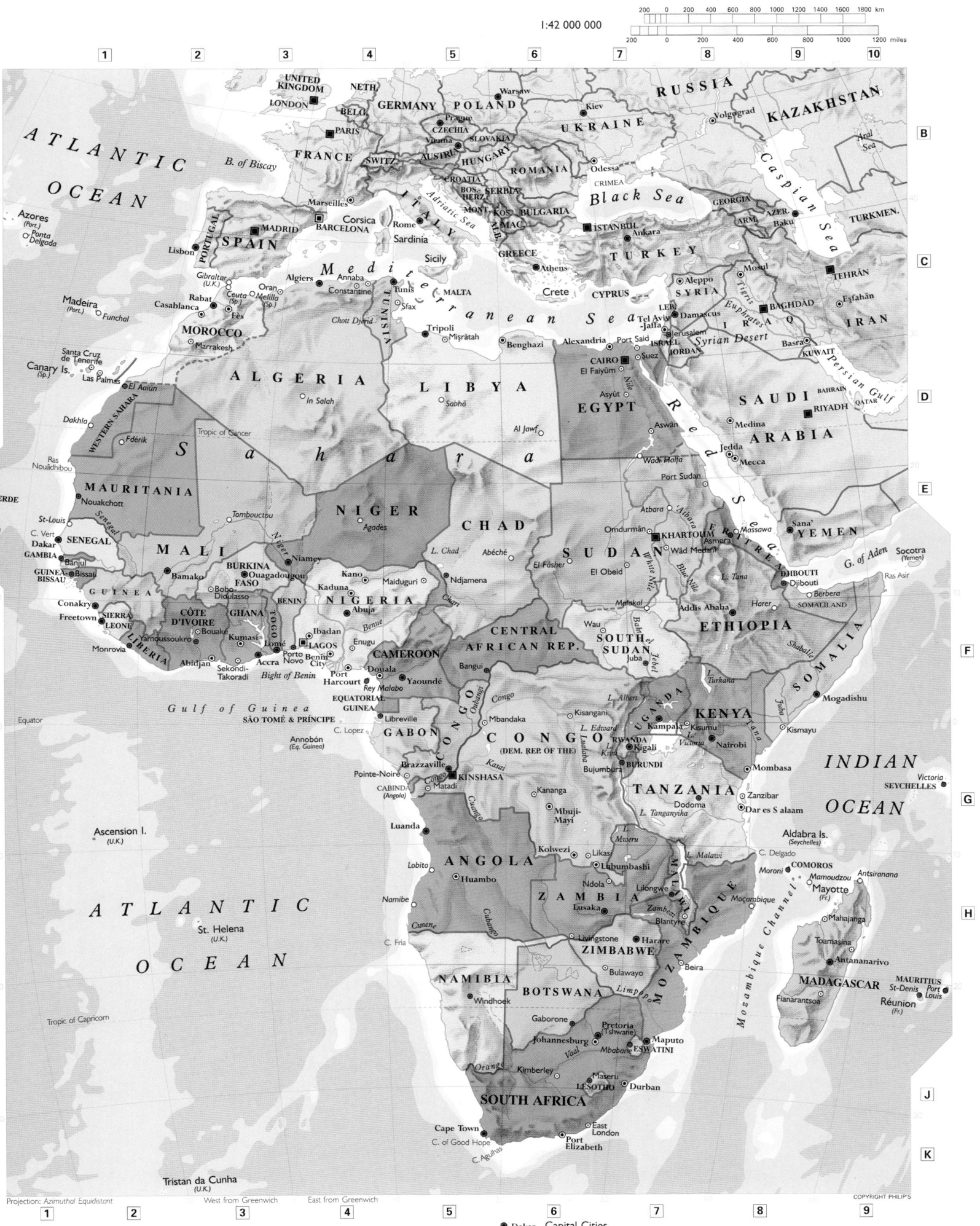

1:42 000 000

Projection: Azimuthal Equidistant

West from Greenwich   East from Greenwich

● Dakar   Capital Cities

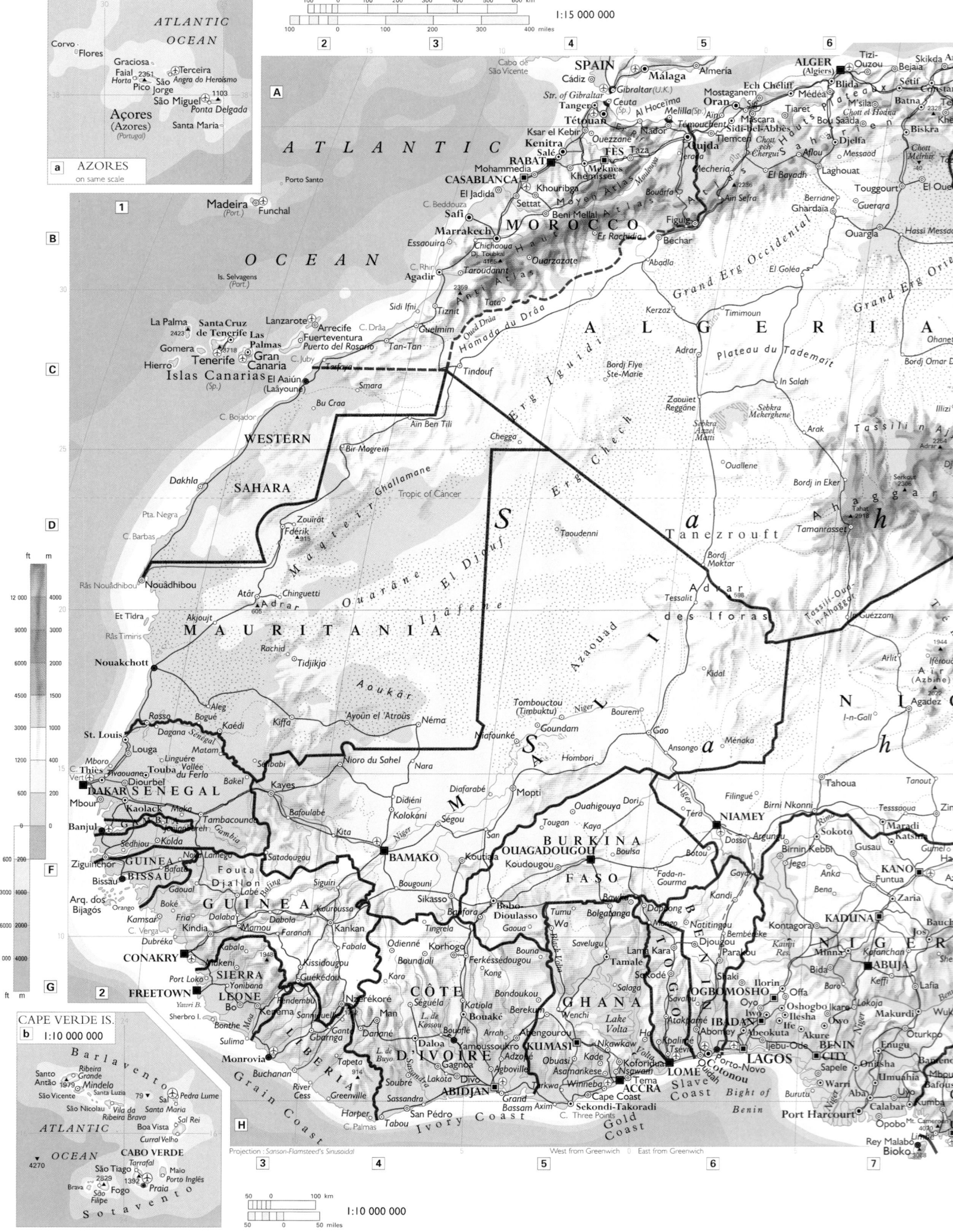

8   **9**   **10**   **11**   **12**   **13**   **14**

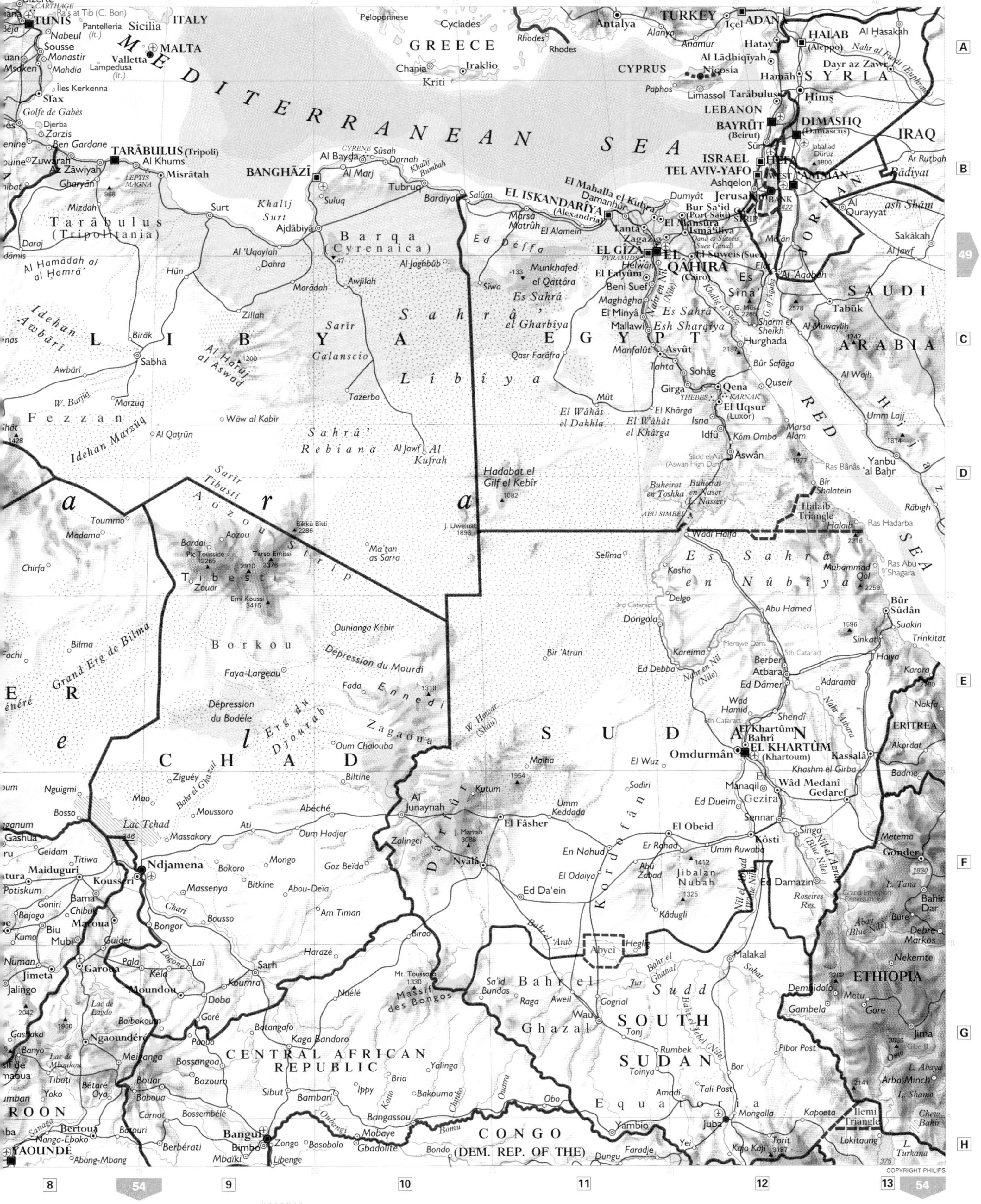

Bizerte
CARTHAGE
Ra's at Tib (C. Bon)
TUNIS
Pantelleria Sicilia **ITALY**
Nabeul (It.)
Sousse
Monastir
Mahdia   Valletta
Lampedusa (It.)
Sfax
Golfe de Gabès
Zarzis
Ben Gardane
Zuwārah **TARĀBULUS** (Tripoli)
Az Zāwiyah   Al Khums   Misrātah
Gharyān   LEPTIS MAGNA
Mizdah   968

Peloponnese   Cyclades
GREECE   Rhodes
Chania   Iraklio   Rhodes
Kriti

TURKEY   İçel **ADANA**
Antalya   **HALAB** Al Hasakah
Alanya   Anamur   Hatay   (Aleppo)
  Al Lādhiqīyah   Nahr al Furāt (Euphrates)
CYPRUS   Nicosia   Dayr az Zawr
Paphos   Hamāh   **SYRIA**
Limassol Tarābulus   Himş

A

M E D I T E R R A N E A N   S E A

A

Al Bayda   Sūsah
BANGHĀZĪ   Al Marj   Darnah
Suluq   Tubruq   Bumbah
CYRENE
Khalīj

LEBANON
BAYRŪT (Beirut)   **DIMASHQ** (Damascus)
ISRAEL   **AMMÂN**
TEL AVIV-YAFO   Jabal ad Durūz   1800
Ashqelon   **JERUSALEM**   Al Qurayyāt
WEST BANK   1422   ash Shām

B

Surt
TARĀBULUS
(Tripolitania)
Daraj
Al Hamādah al al Ḥamrā'
Mizdah
Ḥūn

Khalīj Surt
Ajdābiyā
Al 'Uqaylah
Dahra
Marādah
Awjilah

Barqa
(Cyrenaica)
-47
Al Jaghbūb
Sīwa

Ed Déffa
Bardīyah   Salūm
Marsā   Sīdi
Matrūh   Barrāni
El Alamein

EL ISKANDARIYA
(Alexandria)
El Mahalla el Kubra
Damanhûr   Dumyât
Tanta   Bur Sa'id (Port Said)
Zagazig   Ismā'ilīya
El Mansūra

Saddat
Es Sīnā'
Al 'Aqabah
Ma'ān
Sakākah
Al Jawf

B

SAUDI

49

Zillah
Sarīr
L I B Y A
Birāk
Galanscio
Sabhā
Al Harūj al Aswad   1200
Tazerbo
Marzūq
Wāw al Kabīr
W. Barjūj
Fezzan   Idehan Marzūq
1428   Al Qaţrūn

S a h r ā'
L î b î y a
Sahrā' Rebiana
Al Jawf Al Kufrah

E G Y P T
El Gîza PYRAMIDS **EL QAHIRA** (Cairo)
Helwân
El Faiyûm   El Suveis (Suez)
Beni Suef
Maghâgha
El Minyâ   Es Sahrâ
Mallawi   Esh Sharqîya
Manfalût   Asyût   2187
Tahta   2285
Sohâg

Es Sahrā' el Gharbîya
Qasr Farâfra
Qasr Farâfra
Mût
El Wâhât el Dakhla
El Khârga
El Wâhât el Khârga

Hurghada
Bûr Safâga
Umm Lajj
Tabûk
A R A B I A
1747

C

Munkhafed el Qattâra
-133
El Alamein

Girga
Qena KARNAK
THEBES El Uqsur (Luxor)
Isna
Idfû
Kôm Ombo
Aswân

Quseir
Marsa Alam
1977
Ras Bânâs
Yanbu al Baḥr
1814

D

Ma'tan
as-Sarra
Hadabat el
Gilf el Kebîr
1082
J. Uweinat
1893

Sadd el Aali
(Aswan High Dam)
Buheirat en Toshka
Buheirat en Naser
(L. Nasser)
ABU SIMBEL
Wadi Halfa
Selima
Bîr Shalatein
Halaib Triangle
Halaib   2216
Râbigh
Ras Hadarba
Ras Abu Shagara   2259

RED

D

Sarīr Tibastī
Aozou Strip
Toummo
Madama
Bardai   Aozou
Pic Toussidé 3265
Chirfa
Tarso Emissi 3376
Zouar 2910
Tibesti
Emi Koussi 3415
Bikkū Bītī 2286

Borkou
Ounianga Kébir
Faya-Largeau
Dépression du Bodélé
Fada   Ennedi   1310
Erg du Djourab
Zagaoua

Es Sahrâ
en Nûbîya
Delgo
Kosha
Dongola
3rd Cataract
Bir 'Atrun
Abu Hamed
Kareima
Merowe Dam
Ed Debba   1696
Berber   Sinkat
Atbara   5th Cataract

Bûr Sûdân
Suakin
Trinkitat
Haiya
Karora
2480
Nakfa

E

N I G E R
Grand Erg de Bilma
Bilma
Nguigmi
Bosso
Lac Tchad   246
Geidam
Maiduguri
Massakory
Kousséri

Moussoro
Mao
Ati
Abéché
Biltine
Zalingei
Al Junaynah
Kutum   1954
J. Marrah 3088
Nyâlâ

Malha
Umm Keddada
El Fâsher
En Nahud
El Odaiya

Sodiri
Ed Dueim
El Obeid
Er Rahad
Umm Ruwaba

SUDAN
Ed Dâmer
Wad Hamid   Shendî
6th Cataract
EL KHARTÛM (Khartoum)
Omdurmân
Manaqil   Wâd Medanî
Gezira   Gedaref
Sennar
Kôsti   Singa
Khashm el Girba
Kassalâ   Badme
Gonder
1830
Metema

ERITREA
Akordat
Nahr al 'Aţbara

F

C H A D
Ziguéy
Bahr el Ghazal
Massenya
Bitkine
Bokoro
Mongo
Goz Beïda
Am Timan
Abou-Deïa
Oum Hadjer

Darfur
Kordofân
Abû Zabad
Jibalan Nubah   1412
1325

Nîl el Azraq (Blue Nile)
Ed Damazin
Roseires Res.
Grand Ethiopian Renaissance Dam
L. Tana
Bahir Dar

F

ETHIOPIA
3202
Demidolo
Metu   Nekemte
Gambela
Gore

G

Ndjamena
Chari
Bongor
Laï
Sarh
Koumra
Moundou
Doba
Goré
Batangafo
Kaga Bandoro
Birao
Bahr el 'Arab
Abyei
Heglig
Jur
Bahr el Ghazal
Sudd
Malakal
Sôbat

Bahr el Jebel (Nile)
3686
Jima
L. Abaya

G

CENTRAL AFRICAN
REPUBLIC
Bossangoa
Bouar
Bozoum
Ndélé
Massif des Bongos
Bria
Yalinga
Ippy
Bambari

Sa'id Bundas
Raga
Aweil
Wau
Gogrial
Tonj
Rumbek
Bor
Pibor Post
2141
Arba Minch
L. Shamo

S O U T H
S U D A N
Bahr el Ghazal
Toinya
Amadi
Tali Post
Mongalla
Juba
Kajo Kaji
Torit
Ilemi Triangle
L. Turkana
Cheu Bahir

H

CAMEROON
Garoua
Ngaoundéré
YAOUNDÉ
Bertoua
Bétaré Oya
Batouri
Carnot
Berbérati
Bangui
Bimbo
Mbaïki

Bakouma
Chinko
Bangassou
Obo
Bosobolo
Zongo
Libenge
Gbadolite
Bondo
Dungu
Yei
Faradje
Yambio

CONGO
(DEM. REP. OF THE)

H

Lava fields

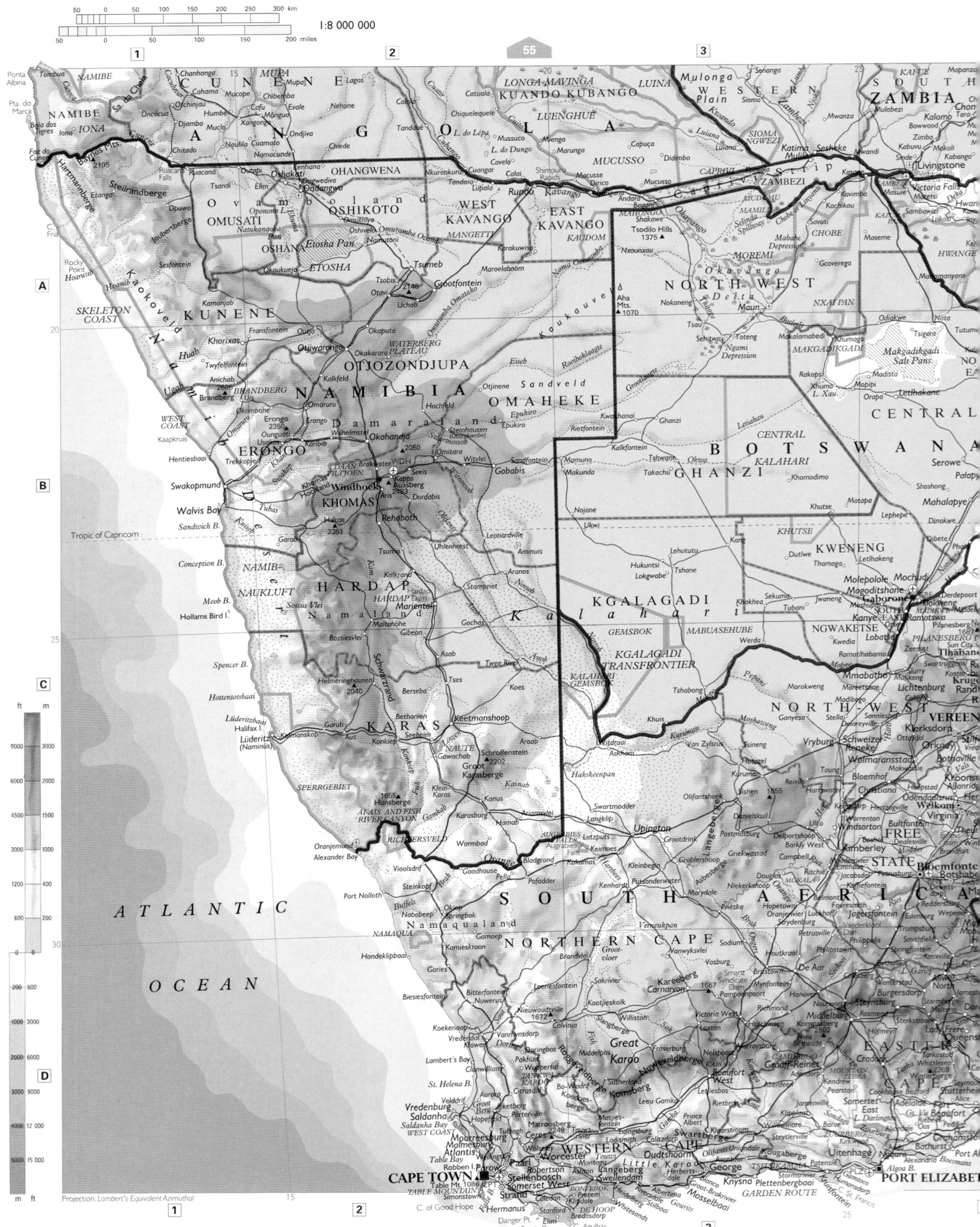

1:8 000 000

Projection: Lambert's Equivalent Azimuthal

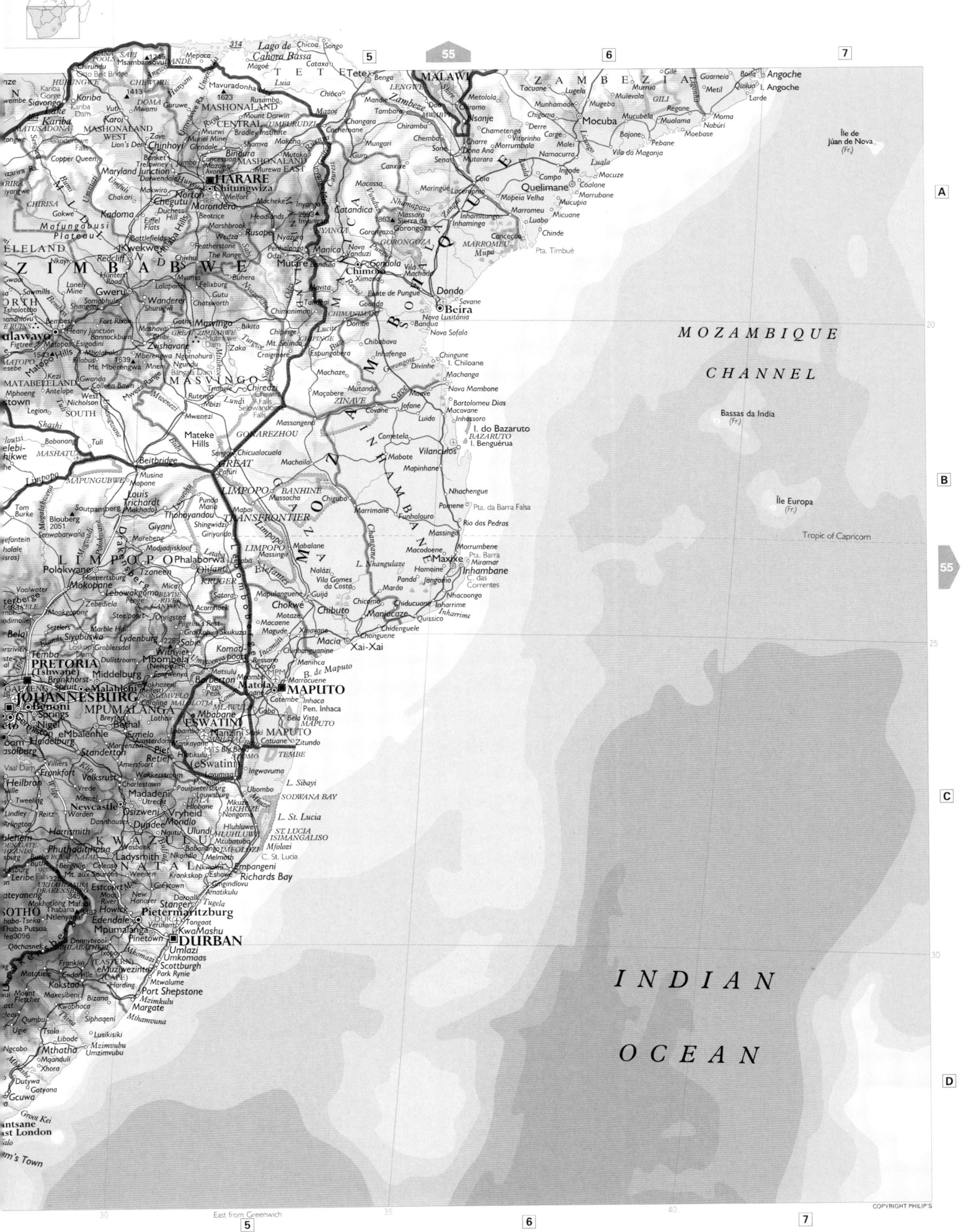

A

B

C

D

MOZAMBIQUE

CHANNEL

Tropic of Capricorn

INDIAN

OCEAN

Île de
Júan de Nova
(Fr.)

Bassas da India
(Fr.)

Île Europa
(Fr.)

55

20

25

30

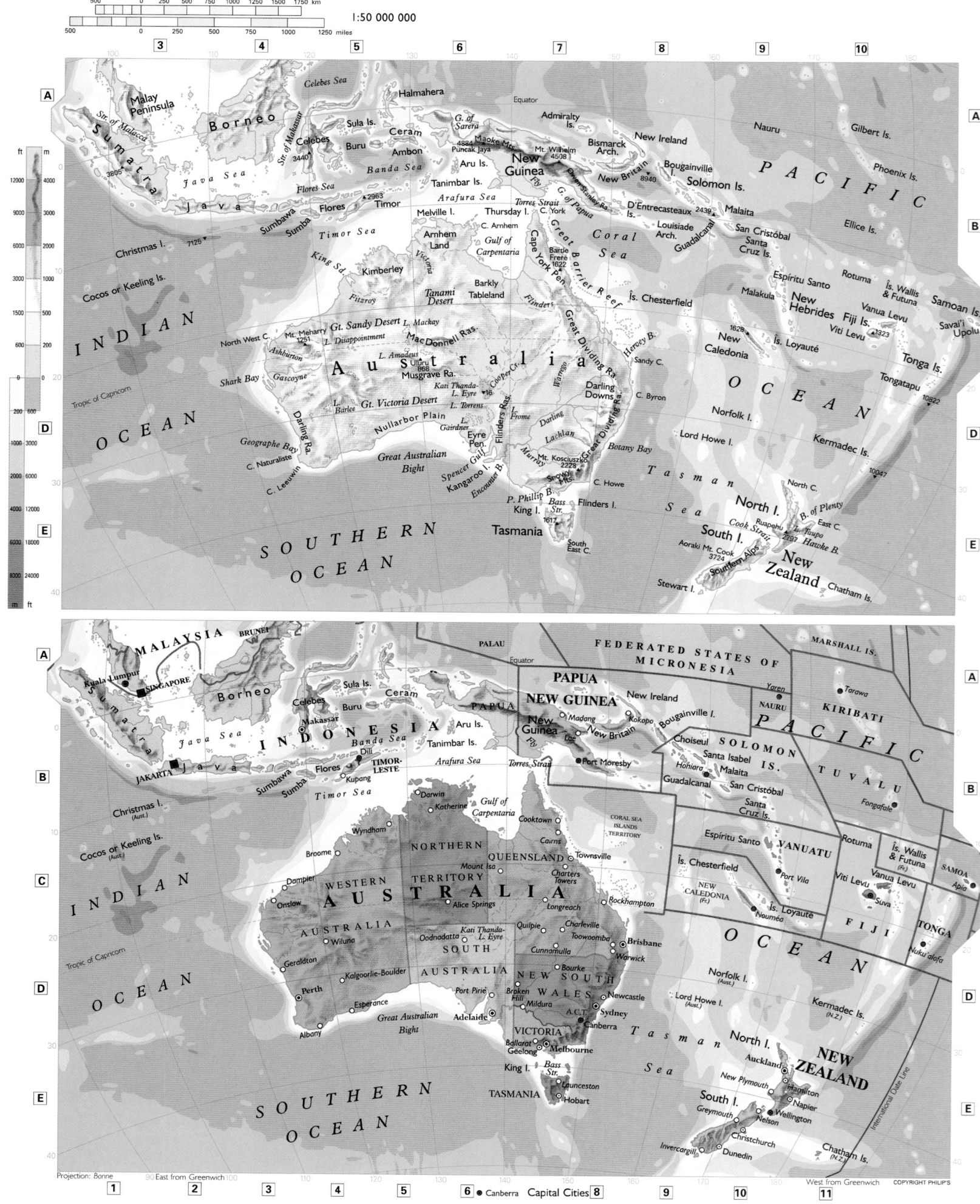

Scale bar: 500 0 250 500 750 1000 1250 1500 1750 km
500 0 250 500 750 1000 1250 miles
1:50 000 000

Physical map (top)

Malay Peninsula · *Borneo* · *Celebes Sea* · Halmahera · Admiralty Is. · New Ireland · Nauru · Gilbert Is.

Sumatra · *Str. of Malacca* · Celebes · 3440 · Ceram · Buru · Ambon · Maoke Mts. · 4884 Puncak Jaya · Mt. Wilhelm 4508 · Bismarck Arch. · Bougainville · Solomon Is. · Phoenix Is.

3805 · *Java Sea* · *Str. of Makassar* · Sula Is. · *Banda Sea* · Aru Is. · New Guinea · New Britain 8940 · D'Entrecasteaux Is. · 2439 · Malaita · Ellice Is.

Christmas I. · 7125 · *Java* · Sumbawa · Sumba · Flores · *Flores Sea* · 2963 · Timor · Tanimbar Is. · *Arafura Sea* · Torres Strait · G. of Papua · Owen Stanley Ra. · Coral · Malaita · San Cristóbal · Santa Cruz Is.

Cocos or Keeling Is. · *Timor Sea* · Melville I. · Thursday I. · C. York · Great Barrier Reef · *Sea* · Îs. Chesterfield · Espíritu Santo · Rotuma · Îs. Wallis & Futuna · Samoan Is.

King Sd. · Arnhem Land · C. Arnhem · Gulf of Carpentaria · Cape York Pen. · Bartle Frere 1622 · Malakula · New Hebrides · Fiji Is. · Vanua Levu · Savai'i · Upolu

INDIAN · Kimberley · *Victoria* · Barkly Tableland · Flinders · Great Dividing Ra. · Viti Levu · 1323

Fitzroy · *Tanami Desert* · 1628 · New Caledonia · Tonga Is.

Mt. Meharry 1251 · Gt. Sandy Desert · L. Mackay · MacDonnell Ras. · Hervey B. · Sandy C. · Îs. Loyauté · Tongatapu · 10822

North West C. · Ashburton · L. Disappointment · Uluru 868 · Musgrave Ra. · **Australia** · Warrego · C. Byron · Norfolk I. · *OCEAN*

Shark Bay · Gascoyne · L. Amadeus · Kati Thanda- · L. Eyre · 16 · Cooper Cr. · Darling Downs

OCEAN · Darling Ra. · L. Barlee · Gt. Victoria Desert · L. Torrens · L. Frome · Darling · Lachlan · Lord Howe I. · Kermadec Is.

Geographe Bay · Nullarbor Plain · L. Gairdner · Eyre Pen. · Flinders Ras. · Murray · Mt. Kosciuszko 2228 · Botany Bay · *Tasman* · 10047

C. Naturaliste · Great Australian Bight · Spencer Gulf · Kangaroo I. · Encounter B. · Snowy Mts. · C. Howe · North C.

C. Leeuwin · P. Phillip B. · Bass Str. · Flinders I. · *Sea* · North I. · Ruapehu · B. of Plenty

King I. · 1617 · Tasmania · South East C. · South I. · Cook Strait · 2797 L. Taupo · Hawke B. · East C.

SOUTHERN OCEAN · Aoraki Mt. Cook 3724 · Southern Alps · New Zealand · Chatham Is.

Tropic of Capricorn · Stewart I.

Elevation key (left):
ft / m
12000 / 4000
9000 / 3000
6000 / 2000
3000 / 1000
1500 / 500
600 / 200
0 / 0
200 / 600
1000 / 3000
2000 / 6000
4000 / 12000
6000 / 18000
8000 / 24000
m / ft

Political map (bottom)

MALAYSIA · BRUNEI · PALAU · **FEDERATED STATES OF MICRONESIA** · MARSHALL IS.

Kuala Lumpur · SINGAPORE · Borneo · Celebes · Sula Is. · Ceram · **PAPUA NEW GUINEA** · New Ireland · Yaren · Tarawa

Sumatra · *Java Sea* · *Makassar* · Buru · **INDONESIA** · PAPUA · Madang · Kokopo · Bougainville I. · **NAURU** · **KIRIBATI**

JAKARTA · *Java* · *Banda Sea* · Aru Is. · New Guinea · Lae · New Britain · Choiseul · **SOLOMON IS.** · **PACIFIC**

Christmas I. (Aust.) · Dili · **TIMOR-LESTE** · Tanimbar Is. · *Arafura Sea* · Torres Strait · Port Moresby · Santa Isabel · Malaita · **TUVALU**

Sumbawa · Flores · Kupang · *Timor Sea* · Darwin · Katherine · Gulf of Carpentaria · Honiara · Guadalcanal · San Cristóbal · Fongafale

Cocos or Keeling Is. (Aust.) · Wyndham · Cooktown · CORAL SEA ISLANDS TERRITORY · Santa Cruz Is. · Rotuma · Îs. Wallis & Futuna · **SAMOA**

Broome · **NORTHERN TERRITORY** · Cairns · Espíritu Santo · **VANUATU** · Apia

INDIAN · Dampier · **WESTERN** · Mount Isa · **QUEENSLAND** · Townsville · Îs. Chesterfield · Port Vila · Vanua Levu

Onslow · **AUSTRALIA** · Alice Springs · Charters Towers · **NEW CALEDONIA** (Fr.) · Îs. Loyauté · Viti Levu · Suva · **TONGA**

OCEAN · Wiluna · SOUTH · Oodnadatta · Kati Thanda- L. Eyre · Longreach · Rockhampton · Nouméa · **FIJI** · Nuku'alofa

Geraldton · Kalgoorlie-Boulder · Quilpie · Charleville · Toowoomba · Brisbane · **OCEAN**

Perth · **AUSTRALIA** · Port Pirie · Cunnamulla · Warwick · Norfolk I. (Aust.)

Esperance · Broken Hill · **NEW SOUTH WALES** · Bourke · Newcastle · Lord Howe I. (Aust.) · Kermadec Is. (N.Z.)

Adelaide · Mildura · A.C.T. · Sydney · *Tasman*

Albany · Great Australian Bight · Ballarat · Canberra · North I. · Auckland

VICTORIA · Geelong · Melbourne · *Sea* · New Plymouth · Hamilton · **NEW ZEALAND**

King I. · Bass Str. · Napier

TASMANIA · Launceston · South I. · Wellington

Hobart · Greymouth · Nelson

SOUTHERN OCEAN · Invercargill · Christchurch · Chatham Is. (N.Z.)

Dunedin

Tropic of Capricorn · International Date Line

1:6 000 000

50   0   50   100   150   200 km
50   0   50   100   150 miles

FIJI a
on same scale

PACIFIC OCEAN

Great Sea Reef   Kia   Udu Pt.   Ringgold Is.
Yaqaga   Labasa   Natewa Bay   Rabi
Yasawa Group   Yasawa   Yadua   Bua   Savusavu Bay   **Taveuni**
Naviti   **Vanua Levu** ▲1031   Somosomo   Qamea
Nacula   Nabouwalu   BUMA   Kanacea   Naitaba
Viwa   Waya   Vomo   Tavua   Rakiraki   Namenalala   Nasau   Koro   Vanua Balavu
Lautoka   Tomanivi ▲1323   Lawaki   Vatu   Mago   Lomaloma
Mamanuca Group   Nadi   VICORYANITU   Navai   Levuka   Wakaya   Vara   Cicia   Tuvuca
Malolo   Keiyasi   Korovou   Yunidawa   **Ovalau**   Nairai   Batiki   Sawaleke
Sigatoka   Korolevu   Navua   Nausori   Gau   Nayau   Northern Lau Group
Yanuca   **Suva**   Lakeba Passage   Lakeba   Tubou
FIJI   Beqa   Moala   Vanua Vatu   Oneata   Moce
Vatulele   Ono   Totoya   Kabara   Yagasa Cluster
Kadavu   Matuku   Fulaga   Ogea Levu
Kadavu Passage   Tavuki   Vunisea   Ogea Driki
18 S   KORO SEA   Lau Group
East from Greenwich   180   West from Greenwich

SAMOA
Asau   Safune   Pu'apu'a
Falelima   ▲1858   Salelologa
Savai'i   Satoalepai   Saleimoa   **Apia**   Falefa
Taga   Manono   Faleolu   ▲410   Amaile
OLE PUPU PUE   Safata Bay   **'Upolu**
SAMOAN ISLANDS b
on same scale
14 S

PACIFIC OCEAN

AMERICAN SAMOA (U.S.A.)
Ofu   Olosega
AMERICAN SAMOA   Lumo   Ta'u   AMERICAN SAMOA
Tutuila   Pago Pago   Manu'a Is.
Leone   Vaitogi
172 W   West from Greenwich

TONGA c
on same scale
18 S

PACIFIC OCEAN
Fonualei   Toku
Vava'u   Late   Vava'u Group   'Neiafu
Home Reef
Disney Reef
Ofolanga
Tofua   Kao   Ha'ano   Foa   Ha'apai
Fonuafo'ou   Nomuka   Lifuka   Uiha   Group
Hunga Ha'apai   Nomuka Group   Mango   Oto Tolu Group   Tonumea
20 S
TONGA
Nuku'alofa   **Tongatapu**
Tongatapu Group   Eua
West from Greenwich

TASMAN SEA

PACIFIC OCEAN

North Island
(Te Ika-a-Māui)

C. Reinga   North C.
C. Maria van Diemen   Rangaunu B.   Doubtless B.
Houhora Heads   Mangonui   Whangaroa Harb.
Ahipara B.   Kaitaia   C. Brett
Tauroa Pt.   Okaihau   Waitangi   Opua
Rawene   Hikurangi
Hokianga Harbour   Waipoua Forest   **Whangarei**   Whangarei Harb.   Bream Hd.
Dargaville   Waipu   Little Barrier I.
Kaipara Harbour   Warkworth   C. Rodney   Great Barrier I.
Helensville   C. Colville   Cuvier I.
Takapuna   Hauraki Gulf   Coromandel   Whitianga
AUCKLAND   Whangamata   Mayor I.
Manukau   Papakura   Thames   Whakatane
Waiuku   Pukekohe   Mercer   Paeroa   Waihi   Tauranga Harb.
Waikato   Huntly   Te Aroha   Mount Maunganui   Whakaari (White I.)
Hamilton   Morrinsville   Te Puke   Bay of Plenty   Runaway
Raglan   Cambridge   **Tauranga**   Whakatane   East C.
Kawhia   Te Awamutu   Matamata   **Rotorua**   Kawerau   Taneatua   **Hikurangi** ▲1763
Kawhia Harbour   Otorohanga   Putaruru   L. Rotorua   Murupara   TE UREWERA   Waipiro
Waitomo   Te Kuiti   Tokoroa   L. Taupo   Ruatahuna   Ruatoria
North Taranaki Bight   Mokau   Mokai   Wairakei   Ongarue   Waikaremoana   Tolaga Bay
Waitara   Mangaweka   Taumarunui   L. Taupo   Rangitaiki Pts.   **Gisborne**
New Plymouth   Inglewood   WHANGANUI   Whangamomona   Turangi   Wairoa   Poverty Bay
Mt. Taranaki or Mt. Egmont ▲2518   Stratford   ▲2797   Ohakune   **TONGARIRO**   Tarawera   Waikokopu
Opunake   Eltham   Raetihi   **Napier**   Mahia Pen.
Kapuni   Hawera   Taihape   Waiouru   Ruahine Ra.   C. Kidnappers
South Taranaki Bight   Waverley   Mangaweka   **Hastings**   Hawke Bay
Patea   **Wanganui**   Marton   Hunterville   Waipawa
Bulls   Halcombe   Dannevirke
Feilding   Waipukurau
Palmerston North   Woodville   C. Turnagain
Foxton   Shannon   Pahiatua
Levin   Eketahuna
Paraparaumu   Kapiti I.   Otaki   Masterton
Pelorus Sd.   Featherston   Carterton
Upper Hutt   Greytown   Martinborough
Petone   **Lower Hutt**   Eastbourne   L. Wairarapa
Wellington   Cook Strait

C. Farewell
Collingwood   Golden B.   ABEL TASMAN   D'Urville I.
KAHURANGI   Takaka   Tasman B.   Motueka
Karamea   Tasman Mts.   Havelock   Picton
Karamea Bight   Tadmor   **Nelson**   Wakefield   Richmond
Seddonville   Matiri Ra.   Murchison   NELSON LAKES   Seddon   Ward
Granity   Lyell   Inangahua   **Blenheim**
Westport   L. Rotoiti   Mt. Travers ▲2885   Tapuae-o-Uenuku
Punakaiki   Reefton   Spenser Mts.   ▲2337   Clarence
PAPAROA   Blackball   Lewis Pass   Kaikoura
Runanga   Hanmer Springs   Waiau
Greymouth   Kumara   Stillwater   L. Brunner   Culverden   Waiau
Hokitika   Jacksons   ARTHUR'S PASS   Waikari   Amberley
Ross   Arthur's Pass   Waipara
Abut Hd.   Oxford   Pegasus Bay
WESTLAND TAI POUTINI   Springfield   Rangiora   **New Brighton**
Mt. Cook   Methven   Whitecliffs   Riccarton   **Christchurch**
Aoraki   ▲3724   Staveley   Lincoln   Lyttelton
Mount Cook   AORAKI MT. COOK   L. Coleridge   Rakaia   L. Ellesmere   Banks Pen.
Jackson B.   Okuru   Rolleston   Little River   Akaroa
MOUNT ASPIRING   Haast   Fairlie   Ashburton   Rakaia
Mt. Aspiring ▲3033   L. Tekapo   Temuka   Canterbury Bight
Earnslaw ▲2819   Ohau   Pukaki   **Timaru**
Milford Sd.   Wanaka   St. Andrews   Canterbury Bight
Sutherland Falls   L. Wanaka   Omarama   Waimate
Bligh Sound   Milford   Arrowtown   Kurow   Tokarahi
George Sound   Cromwell   Naseby   Maheno   **Oamaru**
Queenstown   Clyde   Alexandra   Hampden
Secretary I.   L. Wakatipu   Roxburgh   Danback
Doubtful Sd.   Te Anau   Kingston   Waikouaiti
FIORDLAND   L. Manapouri   Edievale   Tapanui   Port Chalmers
Manapouri   Mossburn   Waipahi   Otago Harbour
Breaksea Sd.   Lumsden   Kelso   Milton   **Dunedin**
Resolution I.   Ohai   Nightcaps   Gore   Mataura   Balclutha   Mosgiel
Dusky Sd.   Winton   Clinton   C. Saunders
Chalky Inlet   Tuatapere   Riverton   Mataura   Lawrence   Kaitangata
Preservation Inlet   Orepuki   Wyndham   Owaka
Te Waewae B.   **Invercargill**   Gore   Tahakopa   Nugget Pt.
Solander I.   Foveaux Str.   Bluff   Invercargill
Halfmoon Bay   Ruapuke I.
Stewart I.
(Rakiura)   RAKIURA
South West C.   Port Pegasus

South Island
(Te Waipounamu)

Southern Alps   Tiritiri (Aorangi)   Canterbury Plains
Westland Bight

TASMAN SEA

PACIFIC OCEAN

Projection : Conical with two standard parallels
East from Greenwich

COPYRIGHT PHILIP'S

TAHITI & MOOREA
1:1 000 000

Pte. Aroa
Papetool   B. de Matavai   Pte. Vénus   Mahina
Paopao   Arué   Pirae   Papenoo
Mt. Tohiea ▲1207   **Papeete**   Tiarei
Haapiti   Faaa   Afareaitu   **Tahiti** (France)
Moorea (France)   Mt. Aorai ▲2060   Mt. Orohena ▲2241   Hitiaa
Punaauia   Faaone
Mt. Teturea ▲1799   Lac Vaihiria   Faaone
Paea   Afaahiti   Pte. Tatatua
Maraa   Papara   Taravao   Isthme de Taravao
Atimaono   Papeari   Pueu   Tautira
Maraa   Mataiea   Vairao
Mt. Rooniu ▲1332
Teahupoo   Presqu'île de Taiarapu
West from Greenwich

10   0   10 km
10   0   10 miles
1:1 000 000

ft   m
9000   3000
6000   2000
3000   1000
1200   400
600   200
0   0
200   600
2000   6000
4000   12 000
6000   18 000
m   ft

1:8 000 000

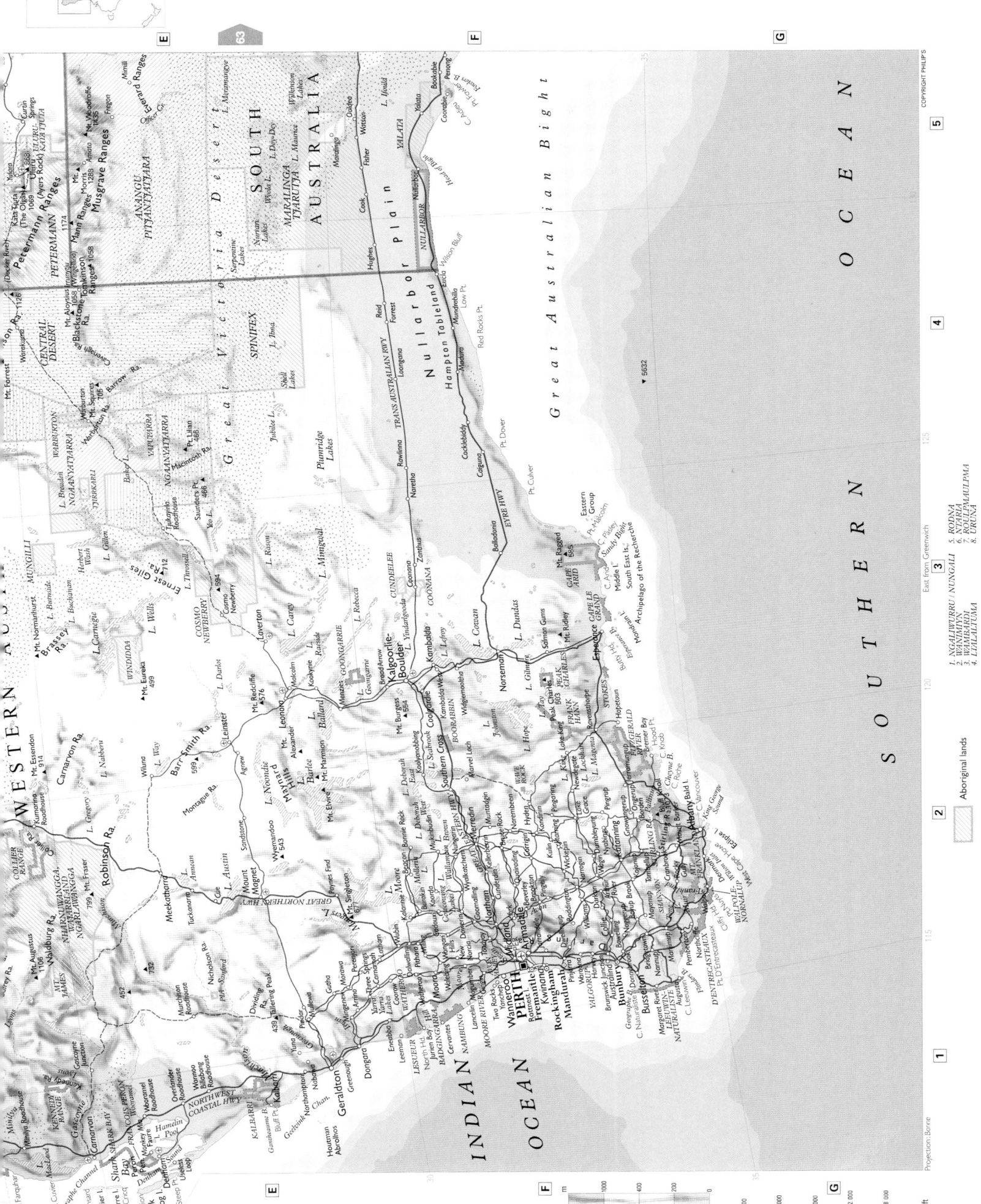

SOUTH AUSTRALIA

WESTERN AUSTRALIA

INDIAN OCEAN

SOUTHERN OCEAN

OCEAN

Great Australian Bight

Great Victoria Desert

Nullarbor Plain

Hampton Tableland

PERTH

Kalgoorlie-Boulder

Geraldton

Albany

Esperance

Bunbury

Aboriginal lands

1. NGALIWURRU / NUNGALI
2. WANMIYN
3. WAMBARDI
4. LIALALTUMA
5. RODNA
6. NTARIA
7. ROULPMAULPMA
8. URUNA

East from Greenwich

Projection: Bonne

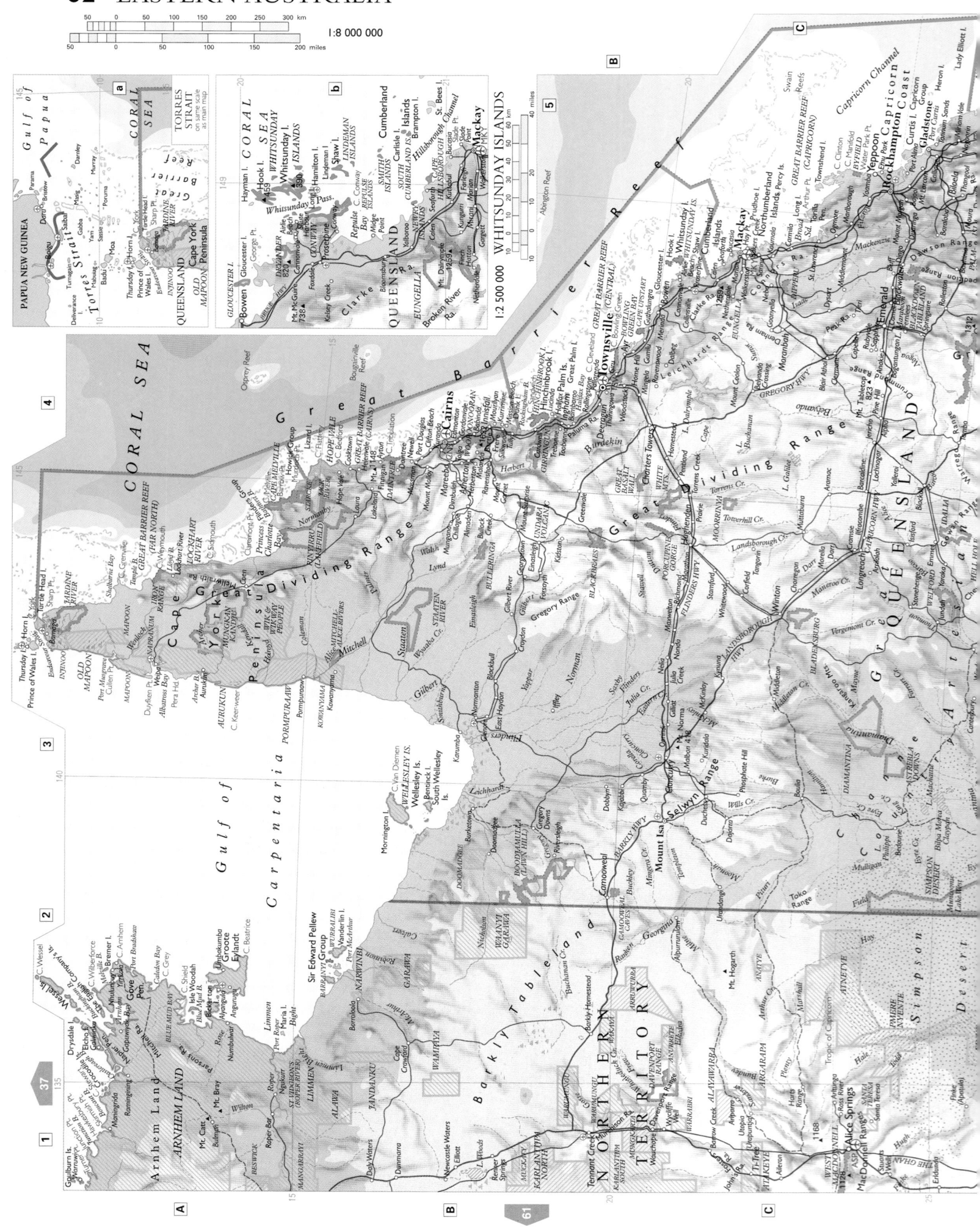

TASMAN SEA

NEW SOUTH WALES

SOUTH AUSTRALIA

TASMANIA

BRISBANE
SYDNEY
Newcastle
Wollongong
Canberra
MELBOURNE
ADELAIDE
Hobart

Gold Coast
Sunshine Coast
Toowoomba
Armidale
Tamworth
Dubbo
Orange
Bathurst
Wagga Wagga
Albury
Broken Hill
Port Augusta
Whyalla
Port Lincoln
Geelong
Ballarat
Bendigo
Warrnambool
Mount Gambier
Launceston

Darling River
Murray River
Murrumbidgee R.
Lake Eyre
Lake Torrens
Lake Gairdner
Lake Frome
Spencer Gulf
Gulf St Vincent
Kangaroo I.
Eyre Peninsula
Yorke Peninsula
Flinders Ranges
Bass Strait
King Island
Flinders Island
Furneaux Group
Cape Barren I.
Wilsons Promontory

Simpson Desert
Sturt Stony Desert
Strzelecki Desert
Barrier Range
Grey Range
Great Dividing Range

Bass Strait
on same scale

Aboriginal lands

East from Greenwich

Projection Bonne

COPYRIGHT PHILIP'S

m
ft
4500 3000 1500 1200 1000 600 400 200 0
6000 3000 2000 1000 400 200 0 12 000

7   8   9

6

1   2   3   4   5

B

R U S S I A

Yekaterinburg

Tomsk

Moskva
Volga

Novosibirsk

Okhotsk

Sea of Okhotsk

Aleutian
Basin

Ber

Astana
(Aqmola)

Semey

Irkutsk

Oz. Baykal   Chita

Blagoveshchensk

Poluostrov Kamchatka

Komandorskiye
Ostrova
(Russia)

Near I.
(U.S.A.)

Andrea

KAZAKHSTAN
Balqash Köl

Ulaanbaatar

Khabarovsk

Amur

Sakhalin

Petropavlovsk
-Kamchatskiy

Aleutian

U.S.A.

C

Aral Sea

Almaty

Ürümqi

MONGOLIA
Altai

Changchun

Sapporo

Kuril'skiye Ostrova
(Russia)

La Perouse Str.

7822

Aleutian Trench

Toshkent

KYRGYZSTAN

Harbin

Shenyang

Vladivostok

Hakodate

10,542

Kurile-Kamchatka Trench

Chinook R

TAJIKISTAN

Beijing

Taiyuan

Tianjin

**NORTH
KOREA**

Dalian

Seoul

*Sea of
Japan*

Sendai

Northwest

Emperor Trough

D

AFGHANISTAN

Kabul

Srinagar

Kunlun Shan

Lanzhou

C H I N A

Qingdao

**SOUTH
KOREA**

Nagoya

Kyōto

Fuji-San 3776

Tōkyō

*Shatsky
Rise*

Pacific

Seamount Chain

Lahore

Delhi

Himalaya

XIZANG

Xi'an

Huang He

Kitakyūshū

Osaka **JAPAN**

Yokohama

*Tamu
Massif* 1980

Basin

H

Kanpur

8848 Everest

Lhasa

NEPAL

Chongqing

Wuhan

Nanjing

Yellow Sea

Shikoku

10,554

Kyūshū

*Japan
Trench*

Midway I.
(U.S.A.)

Ganga

Brahmaputra

Changsha

Shanghai

Hangzhou

*East
China*

Okinawa

Iwo-Jima
(Japan)

Ogasawara Gunto
(Japan)

Lisianski I.
(U.S.A.)

E

INDIA

Kolkata
(Calcutta)

Dhaka

BANGLADESH

Mandalay

Irrawaddy

MYANMAR

Kunming

Fuzhou

Guangzhou

Macau

Hong
Kong

Taipei

TAIWAN

Ryūkyū-rettō
(Japan)

Sea

Kyūshū-Palau Ridge

Kazan-Rettō
(Japan)

Minami-Tori-Shima
(Japan)

Mid-

Wake I. (U.S.A.)

Pacific

Mou

P

A

F

Hyderabad

Chennai
(Madras)

*Bay of
Bengal*

Yangôn

THAILAND

Bangkok

LAOS

Hanoi

VIETNAM

Mekong

Salween

Hainan

C. Engano

Luzon

Paracel Is.

Manila

*Philippine
Sea*

*West
Mariana
Basin*

**NORTHERN
MARIANAS**
(U.S.A.)

Tinian   Saipan

*East
Mariana
Basin*

MARSHALL IS.

Enewetak
Atoll

Bikini
Atoll

Kwajalein

Ralik Chain

Rarik Chain

International Date Line

G

SRI LANKA

Colombo

Andaman Is.
(India)

CAMBODIA

Phnom
Penh

*G. of
Thailand*

Nicobar Is.
(India)

Thanh Pho
Ho Chi
Minh

South

China

Mindoro

Palawan

Samar

10,497

*Sulu
Sea*

Mindanao

Davao

Mindanao Trench

Melekeok

Yap

GUAM
(U.S.A.)

Challenger 11,022
Deep

Mariana Trench

M *i* *c* *r* *o* *n*

Caroline Is.

Chuuk

PALAU

**FED. STATES
OF MICRONESIA**

Pohnpei

Palikir

Jaluit I.

e *s* *i*

Majuro

Pacif

MALAYSIA

Kuala
Lumpur

MALAYSIA

Singapore

Sea 4101

BRUNEI

SABAH

*Celebes
Sea*

Maluku

Butaritari

Tarawa

Gilbert Is.

Howland I. (U.S.A.)
Baker I. (U.S.A.)

Pacif

O

H

Sumatera

Sunda Ridge

Ninety East Ridge

Palembang

Java Sea

Borneo

Sulawesi

Halmahera

Buru

Seram

PALAU

*West
Caroline
Basin*

*Eauripik
Rise*

*East Caroline
Basin*

M *e* *l*

*Solomon
Rise*

*Melanesian
Basin*

n

Yaren

Banaba

Abariring

Phoenix
Is.

Enderbur

K I

Jakarta

Makassar

*Banda
Sea* 7440

Flores

Puncak Jaya 4884

PAPUA

New
Guinea

PAPUA NEW GUINEA

Admiralty
Is.

Bismarck
Arch.

New Ireland

Kokopo

i *a*

NAURU

a

S *i*

a

I

Jawa

Surabaya

*Flores
Sea*

Bali

Sumbawa

Dili

**TIMOR-
LESTE**

Timor

Arafura Sea

Lae

8940

Bougainville

New Britain

SOLOMON IS.

Fongafale

Tokelau
(N.Z.)

*Selat
Sunda*

Java Trench

Sumba

Christmas I.
(Austral.)

Cocos Is.
(Austral.)

Torres Strait

C. York

Port Moresby

Honiara

Guadalcanal

Santa
Cruz I.
9165

Rotuma

TUVALU

*Is. Wallis
& Futuna*
(Fr.)

SAMO

Api

INDIAN

*North
Australian
Basin*

C. Arnhem

Darwin

*Gulf of
Carpentaria*

Louisiade
Arch.

*Coral Sea
Basin*

Espiritu
Santo

VANUATU

Port
Vila

*West
Fiji
Basin*

Vanua Levu

Viti
Levu

Suva

FIJI

Nuku'alofa

TON

L

*Wharton
Basin*

*Exmouth
Plateau*

Broome

Cairns

Coral Sea

Great Barrier Reef

Is. Chesterfield

**NEW
CALEDONIA**
(Fr.)

7670

Is. Loyauté

Nouméa

*Norfolk
Ridge*

Lord

Howe

Trough

10,822

Tonga Trench

OCEAN

Broken Ridge

Perth
Basin

Geraldton

*North
West C.*

Townsville

Rockhampton

AUSTRALIA

Mount Isa

Alice Springs

Brisbane

Middleton
Basin

New Caledonia Trough

Norfolk I.
(Austral.)

*South
Fiji
Basin*

Kermadec Is.
(N.Z.)

*Kermadec
Trench*
10,047

Mid-

Indian

Nouvelle Amsterdam
I. St. Paul (Fr.)

Perth

*Naturaliste
Plateau*

Albany

*Great
Australian Bight*

*Kati Thanda-
L. Eyre*

Adelaide

Darling

Murray

Canberra

Sydney

Mt. Kosciuszko
2228

Lord
Howe I.
(Austral.)

*Tasman
Sea*

Auckland

**NEW
ZEALAND**

M

Ridge

Is. Crozet
(Fr.)

S O U T H E R N

Bass Str.

Melbourne

Tasmania

Hobart

*East
Tasman
Plateau*

Tasman

Basin

South Tasman Rise

Aoraki Mt. Cook
3724

*Chatham
Rise*

Wellington

Christchurch

Chatha
(N.Z.)

Kerguelen
(Fr.)

Heard I.
(Austral.)

O C E A N

Dunedin

*Bounty
Trough*

Bounty Is.
(N.Z.)

Invercargill

Antipodes Is.
(N.Z.)

Auckland Is.
(N.Z.)

*Campbell
Plateau*

Macquarie I.
(N.Z.)

Campbell I.
(N.Z.)

N

1   2   3   4   5   6   7   8   9   10

ft	m
12 000	4000
9000	3000
6000	2000
3000	1000
1500	500
600	200
0	0
200	600
1000	3000
2000	6000
4000	12 000
6000	18 000
8000	24 000

m ft

1 12 13 14 15 16 17 18 19 20

Arctic Circle

ALASKA
(U.S.A.)
Anchorage
5959

Bristol Bay
Gulf of Alaska
Juneau
R
S. (U.S.A.)
Prince of Wales I.
(U.S.A.) Prince Rupert
Haida Gwaii
(Queen Charlotte Is.)
(Canada)
Tufts
Vancouver
Vancouver I. Victoria
Seattle
Portland
Boise
Snake
Edmonton
Calgary
Regina
Winnipeg
L. Winnipeg
O C E A N
C A N A D A
Newfoundland

B

Northeast
Mendocino Fracture Zone C. Mendocino
Tufts
Abyssal
Plain
Pacific
6741
San Francisco
Sacramento
Murray Fracture Zone
4418
Salt Lake
City
Denver
Kansas City
St. Louis
Minneapolis
Chicago
Detroit
Pittsburgh
Cincinnati
Toronto
Ottawa
Buffalo
L. Superior
L. Michigan
L. Huron
L. Ontario
L. Erie
Montréal
Québec
St. Lawrence
Boston
New York
Philadelphia
Baltimore
Washington D.C.
St. John's
Appalachian Mts.
ATLANTIC

C

D

Tropic of Cancer
Molokai Fracture Zone
Basin
UNITED STATES
Los Angeles
San Diego
Phoenix
Oklahoma City Memphis
Dallas
Houston
San Antonio
Ciudad
Juárez
Guadalupe
(Mex.)
Baja California
Golfo de California
M E X I C O
New
Orleans
Gulf of Mexico
Jacksonville
C. Hatteras
Tampa
Miami
BAHAMAS
Bermuda
(U.K.)
Sargasso Sea
OCEAN

E

Honolulu
Maui
Kauai
Oahu
4205
Hilo
Hawaii
HAWAIIAN IS.
(U.S.A.)
C. San Lucas
Clarion Fracture Zone Is. Revilla Gigedo
(Mex.)
Guadalajara
Mexico
Puebla
Acapulco
Mérida
Canal de Yucatán
7680
8605
C U B A
La Habana
JAMAICA
Kingston
HAITI
DOMINICAN REP.
PUERTO
RICO
(U.S.A.)
Leeward
Is.
West Indies
Caribbean Sea

F
C I F I C
F
Palmyra Is.
(U.S.A.)
Middle America Trench 6662
GUATEMALA
Guatemala
San Salvador
EL SALVADOR
HONDURAS
NICARAGUA
Managua
Barranquilla
San José
BARBADOS
Windward Is.
Maracaibo
Caracas
Orinoco
VENEZUELA

Î. Clipperton
(Fr.)
Guatemala
Basin
Clipperton Fracture Zone
COSTA
RICA
Colón
PANAMA
Panamá
Panama
Basin
I. del Coco
(Costa Rica)
Cocos Ridge
Medellín
Bogotá
Cali
COLOMBIA

G
Teraina
Tabuaeran
Kiritimati
Cooper Ridge
I. de Malpelo
(Colombia)
G

Equator
Galápagos Fracture Zone
Galápagos
(Ecuador)
Carnegie Ridge
Quito
ECUADOR
Amazonas
BRAZIL

Jarvis I.
(U.S.A.)
E A N
Line Islands
Malden I.
Starbuck I.
Guayaquil
C. Palinas
Iquitos

H
B A T I
Penrhyn
(Tongareva)
Manihiki
Pukapuka
Manihiki
Plateau
Suwarrow Is.
Vostok I.
Caroline I.
(Millennium I.)
Flint I.
Nuku Hiva
Hiva Oa
Îs. Marquises
Marquesas Fracture Zone
Trujillo
6369
PERU
East Pacific Ridge
Galápagos Fracture Zone
Yupanqui
Basin
Mendaña
Peru Basin
H

J
Îs. de la
Société
Bora Bora
Huahine
Raiatea
Tahiti
Papeete
Rangiroa
Îs. Tuamotu
Pacific Ridge
Lima
Cusco
Arequipa
6866
Peru-
Arica
L. Titicaca
Nevado Ancohuma
6550
La Paz
BOLIVIA
J

Cook Is.
(N.Z.)
Aitutaki
Atiu
Rarotonga
Mangaia
Austral
FRENCH POLYNESIA
Îs. Gambier
Mururoa
Îs. Tubuai
Seamount Chain
Oeno I.
Henderson I.
Pitcairn I. Ducie I.
(U.K.)
Rapa
Tropic of Capricorn
Easter Fracture Zone
Sala-y-Gómez
(Chile)
Sala-y-Gómez Ridge
I. de Pascua
(Chile)
San Felix
(Chile)
San Ambrosio
(Chile)
Iquique
Chile
Antofagasta
8050
Trench
Nazca Ridge
PARAGUAY
Asunción
San Miguel
de Tucumán
Pôrto
Alegre

K

Challenger Fracture Zone
Chile Rise
Roggeveen
Basin
Arch. de
Juan Fernández
(Chile)
Valparaíso
Santiago
Concepción
Córdoba
Aconcagua
6962
Rosario
Buenos
Aires
URUGUAY
Montevideo
Río de la Plata
ARGENTINA

L

Southwest
Pacific
Basin
Pacific-Antarctic Ridge
East
Menard Fracture
Zone
Patagonia
ATLANTIC
6212
OCEAN

M
Ridge
M

Southeast
Pacific Basin
Punta Arenas
C. de Hornos
Tierra del Fuego
Drake Passage
Est. de Magallanes
Falkland Is.
(U.K.)
South Georgia
(U.K.)

N

West from Greenwich
COPYRIGHT PHILIP'S

11 12 13 14 15 16 17 18 19 20

1:35 000 000

Projection: Bonne

West from Greenwich

COPYRIGHT PHILIP'S

1:35 000 000

| 100 | 0 | 200 | 400 | 600 | 800 | 1000 | 1200 | 1400 km |
| 100 | 0 | 200 | | 400 | | 600 | | 800 | 1000 miles |

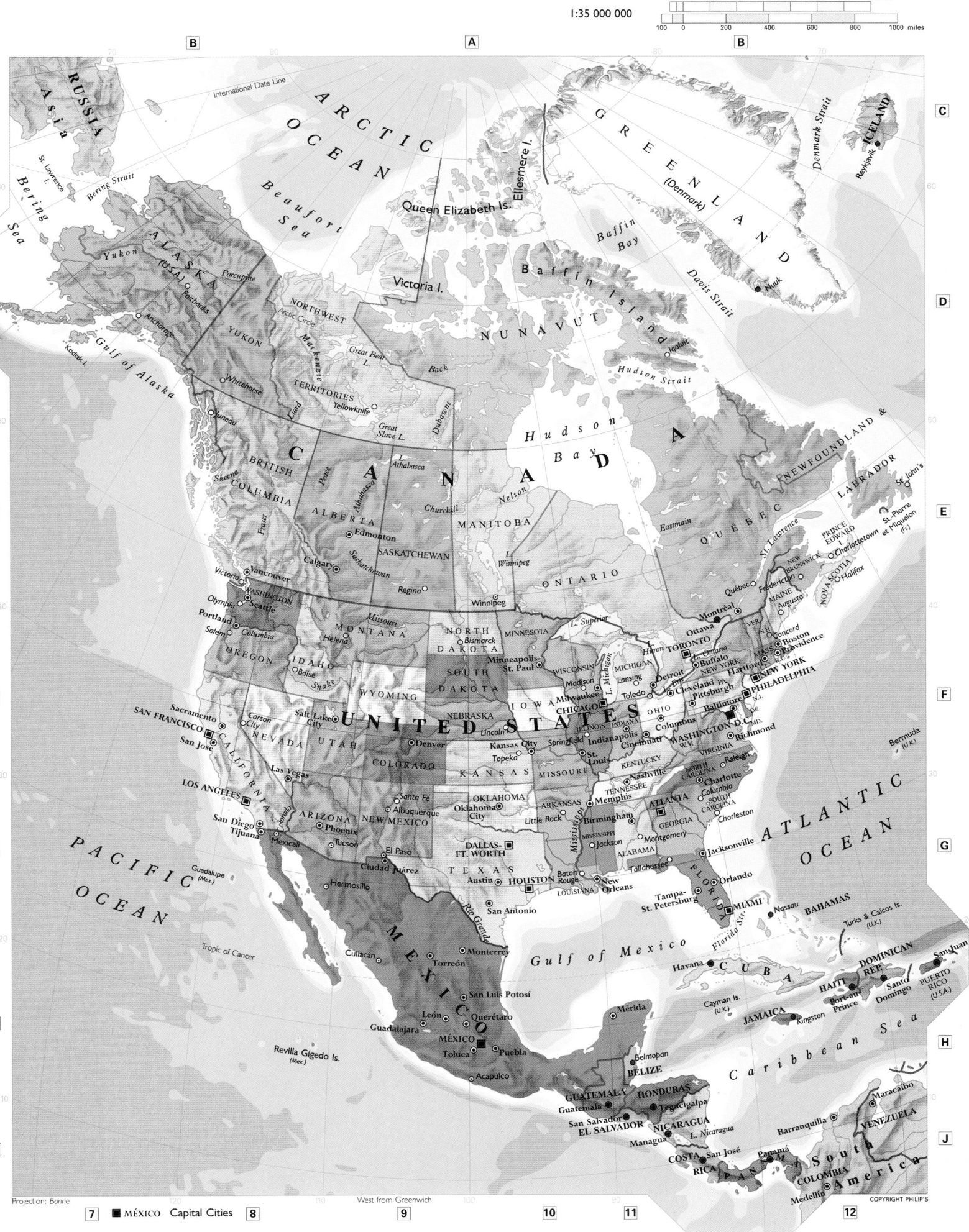

RUSSIA
Asia
St. Lawrence I.
Bering Strait
Bering Sea

ARCTIC OCEAN
International Date Line
Beaufort Sea
Queen Elizabeth Is.
Ellesmere I.

GREENLAND (Denmark)
Denmark Strait
ICELAND
Reykjavik

Baffin Bay

ALASKA (U.S.A.)
Yukon
Porcupine
Fairbanks
Anchorage
Gulf of Alaska
Kodiak I.

NORTHWEST
Arctic Circle
Mackenzie
YUKON
Whitehorse
Juneau
Skeena
Liard

Victoria I.
Great Bear L.
Back
Nunavut

TERRITORIES
Yellowknife
Great Slave L.
Dubawnt

Baffin Island
Davis Strait
Nuuk

Hudson Strait

CANADA
BRITISH COLUMBIA
Fraser
ALBERTA
Edmonton
Calgary
Peace
Athabasca
Athabasca
SASKATCHEWAN
Saskatchewan

Churchill
MANITOBA
Nelson
Hudson Bay

QUÉBEC
Eastmain
St. Lawrence
NEWFOUNDLAND & LABRADOR
St. John's
St. Pierre et Miquelon (Fr.)

Hudson Bay

Vancouver
Victoria
WASHINGTON
Seattle
Olympia
Portland
Salem
OREGON

MONTANA
Helena
Missouri
IDAHO
Boise
Snake
WYOMING

NORTH DAKOTA
Bismarck
SOUTH DAKOTA
MINNESOTA
Minneapolis-St. Paul

Regina
Winnipeg
L. Winnipeg

ONTARIO
L. Superior
WISCONSIN
Madison
Milwaukee
CHICAGO
ILLINOIS

L. Huron
MICHIGAN
Lansing
L. Michigan
Detroit
Toledo

Ottawa
TORONTO
Ontario
Buffalo
NEW YORK
Cleveland
PA.
Pittsburgh

Montréal
Québec
Fredericton
NEW BRUNSWICK
MAINE
Augusta
Concord
Boston
Providence
Hartford
NEW YORK
PHILADELPHIA
N.J.

PRINCE EDWARD I.
Charlottetown
NOVA SCOTIA
Halifax
VER.

Sacramento
SAN FRANCISCO
San Jose
CALIFORNIA
NEVADA
Carson City
Salt Lake City
UTAH
Las Vegas

COLORADO
Denver
NEBRASKA
Lincoln
IOWA
Kansas City
St. Louis
Topeka
Springfield
INDIANA
Indianapolis
OHIO
Columbus
Cincinnati

WASHINGTON D.C.
W.V.
Richmond
VIRGINIA
DEL.
MD.

LOS ANGELES
San Diego
Tijuana
ARIZONA
Phoenix
Tucson
Mexicali
El Paso
NEW MEXICO
Santa Fe
Albuquerque
Colorado

UNITED STATES
KANSAS
OKLAHOMA
Oklahoma City
ARKANSAS
Little Rock
Memphis
TENNESSEE
Nashville
KENTUCKY
MISSOURI

NORTH CAROLINA
Raleigh
Charlotte
SOUTH CAROLINA
Charleston
ATLANTA
GEORGIA
Birmingham

Bermuda (U.K.)

DALLAS-FT. WORTH
TEXAS
Austin
HOUSTON
San Antonio
Ciudad Juárez
Rio Grande

MISSISSIPPI
Jackson
ALABAMA
Montgomery
Baton Rouge
LOUISIANA
New Orleans

Jacksonville
Tallahassee
Orlando
FLORIDA
Tampa-St. Petersburg
MIAMI

ATLANTIC OCEAN

PACIFIC OCEAN
Guadalupe (Mex.)
Tropic of Cancer
Revilla Gigedo Is. (Mex.)

Hermosillo
Culiacán
Monterrey
Torreón
MÉXICO
San Luis Potosí
León
Querétaro
Guadalajara
MÉXICO
Toluca
Puebla
Acapulco

Gulf of Mexico
Florida Str.
Havana
CUBA
Nassau
BAHAMAS
Turks & Caicos Is. (U.K.)

Mérida
BELIZE
Belmopan

Cayman Is. (U.K.)
JAMAICA
Kingston
HAITI
Port-au-Prince
DOMINICAN REP.
Santo Domingo
San Juan
PUERTO RICO (U.S.A.)

Caribbean Sea

GUATEMALA
Guatemala
San Salvador
EL SALVADOR
HONDURAS
Tegucigalpa
NICARAGUA
Managua
L. Nicaragua
COSTA RICA
San José
PANAMA
Panamá

Maracaibo
VENEZUELA
Barranquilla
COLOMBIA
Medellín
South America

Projection: Bonne
West from Greenwich
COPYRIGHT PHILIP'S

7 ■ MÉXICO Capital Cities 8 9 10 11 12

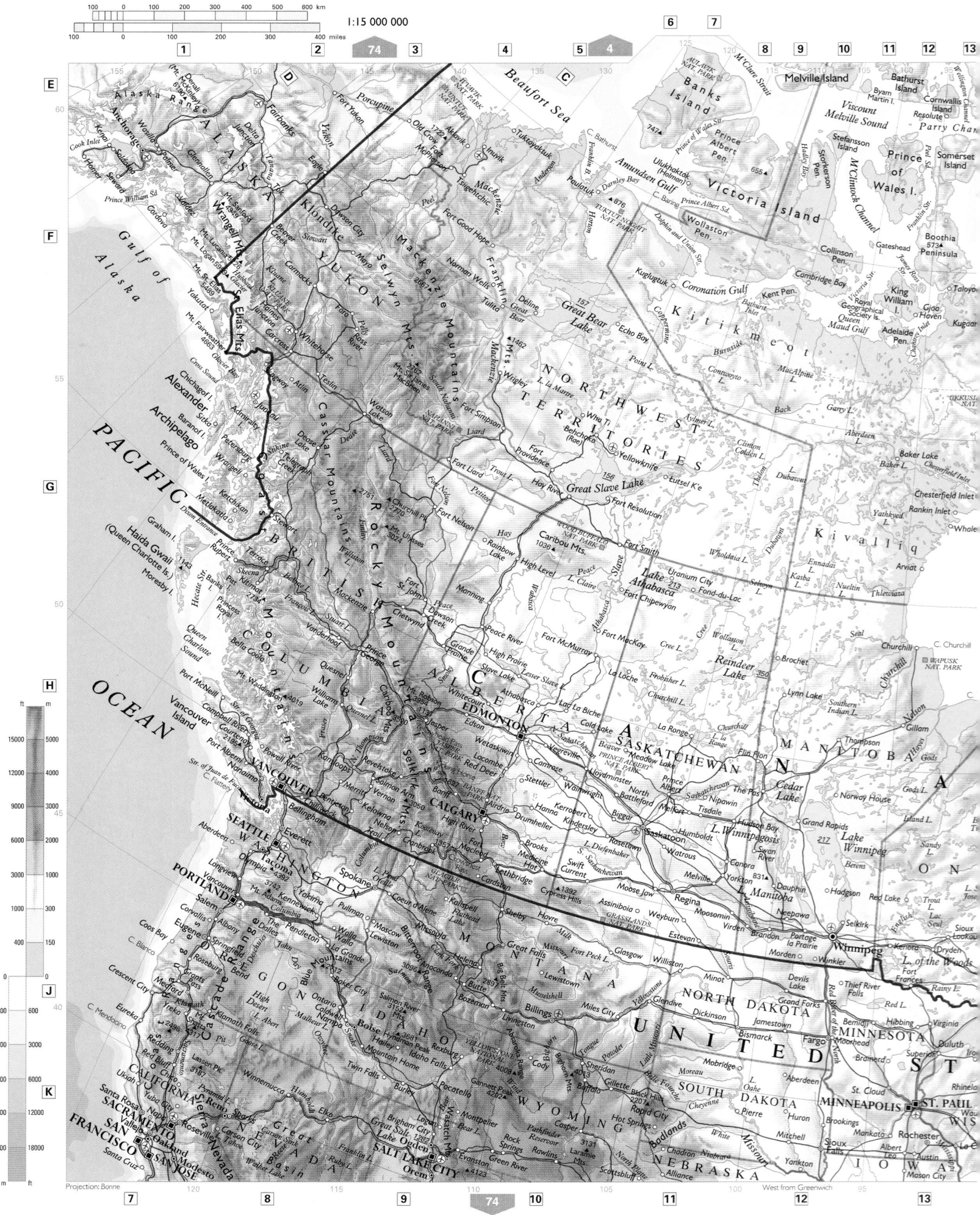

NORTHERN CANADA
continuation northwards on same
scale as main map

8 9 10 11 12 13 14 15 16 17 18 19

A R C T I C

O C E A N

G R E E N L A N D
(KALAALLIT NUNAAT)

Kronprins
Frederik
Land

Ellesmere Island

N U N A V U T

N.W.T.

Queen Elizabeth Islands

Parry Islands

Devon Island

Baffin Bay

Prince
of
Wales I.

Somerset
Island

Lancaster Sound

B a f f i n   B a y

GREENLAND
(Denmark)

Nunavik

Lancaster Sound

B
a
f
f
i
n
(Q
i
k
i
q
t
a
a
l
u
k)
I
s
l
a
n
d

D
a
v
i
s
S
t
r
a
i
t

Cumberland
Peninsula

Frobisher Bay

N U N A V U T

Foxe
Basin

Foxe
Channel

Southampton
I.

Hudson   Strait

Péninsule
d'Ungava

Ungava
Bay

L a b r a d o r

S e a

A
T
L
A
N
T
I
C

O
C
E
A
N

James Bay

Hudson

Bay

N
u
n
a
v
i
k

Labrador

NEWFOUNDLAND
& LABRADOR

Q
u
e
b
e
c

P
l
a
t
e
a
u
d
e

Newfoundland

Gulf of
St. Lawrence

PRINCE EDWARD

NEW
BRUNSWICK

NOVA SCOTIA

MAINE

VERMONT

NEW
HAMPSHIRE

MASS.

CONN. R.I.

PENNSYLVANIA

MONTRÉAL

OTTAWA

Québec

TORONTO

Hamilton

BUFFALO

ROCHESTER

NEW YORK

BOSTON

PROVIDENCE

HARTFORD

DETROIT

CLEVELAND

Lake   Huron

Lake   Erie

Georgian
Bay

L. Michigan

L. Ontario

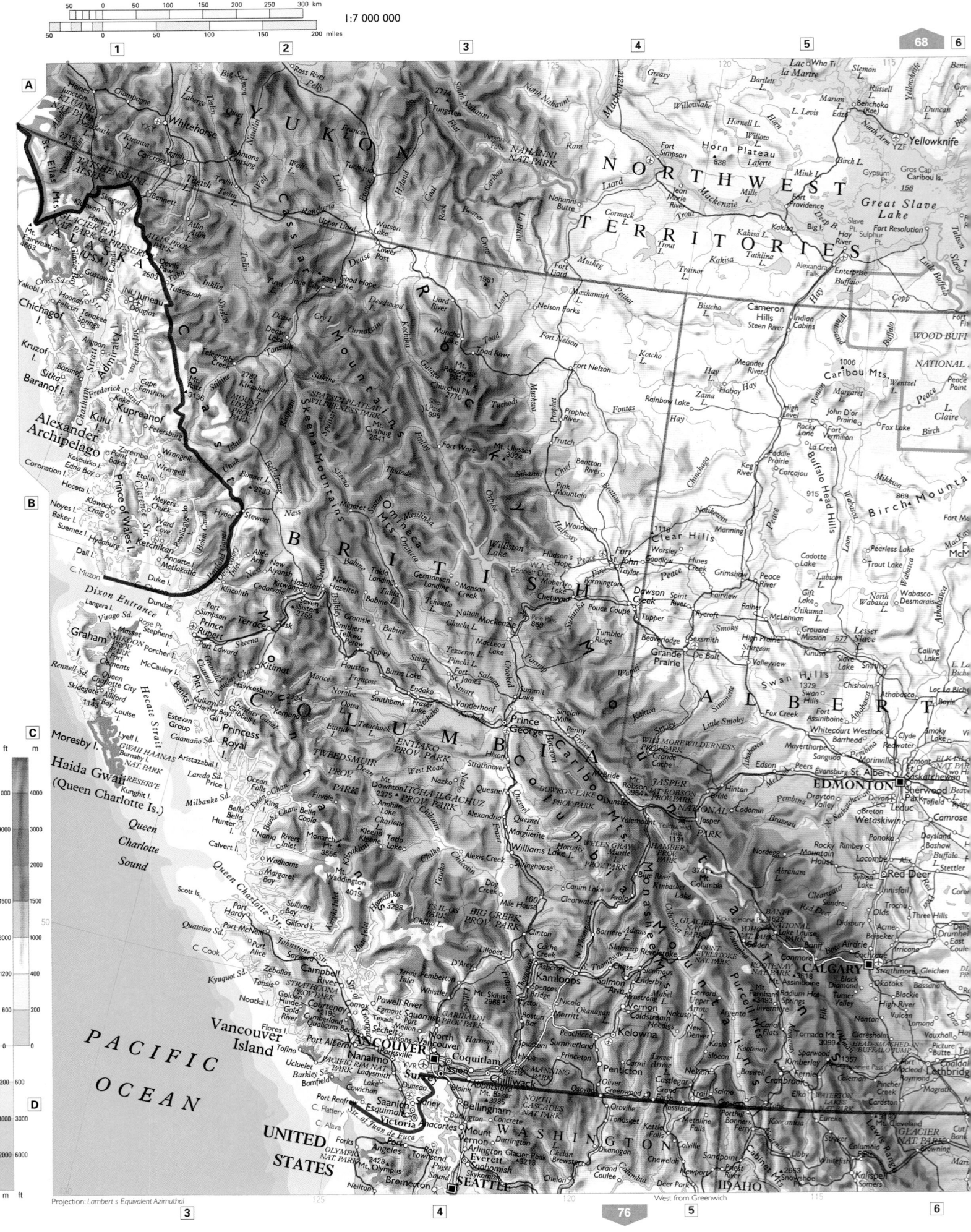

1:7 000 000

Projection: Lambert's Equivalent Azimuthal

West from Greenwich

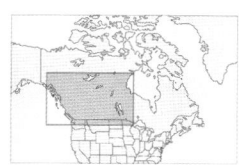

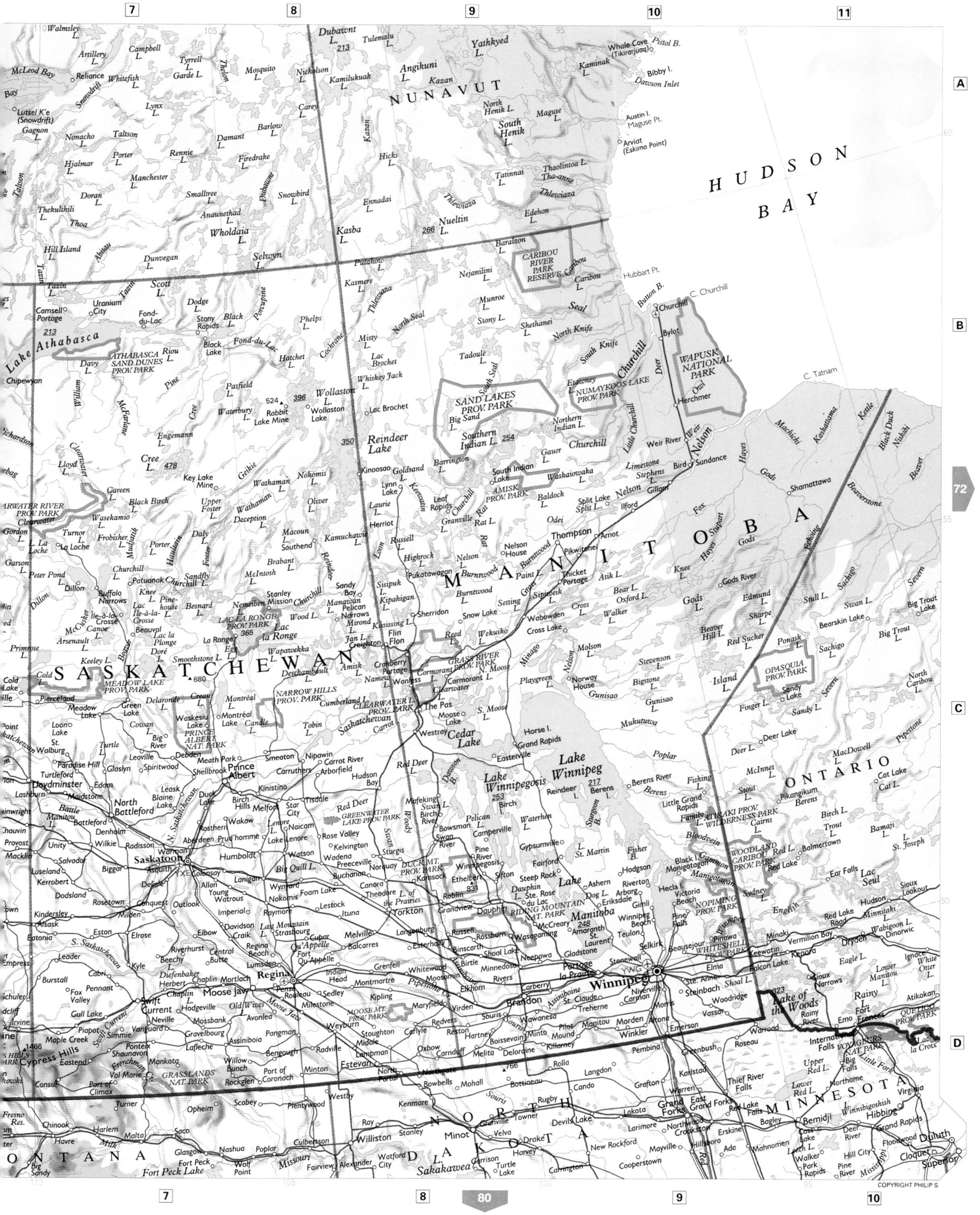
NUNAVUT
HUDSON BAY
MANITOBA
SASKATCHEWAN
ONTARIO
MINNESOTA
NORTH DAKOTA
MONTANA
Lake Athabasca
Reindeer Lake
Wollaston L.
Lake Winnipeg
Lake Winnipegosis
Lake Manitoba
Cedar Lake
Lake of the Woods
WAPUSK NATIONAL PARK
SAND LAKES PROV. PARK
PRINCE ALBERT NAT. PARK
RIDING MOUNTAIN NAT. PARK
GRASSLANDS NAT. PARK
VOYAGEURS NAT. PARK
Churchill
Thompson
The Pas
Flin Flon
Prince Albert
Saskatoon
Regina
Moose Jaw
Swift Current
North Battleford
Yorkton
Brandon
Winnipeg
Dauphin
Grand Forks
Minot
Bemidji
Duluth
Kenora
Dryden
72
80
COPYRIGHT PHILIP S

1:7 000 000

Projection: Lambert's Equivalent Azimuthal

6 69 7 8 9

LABRADOR
SEA
NEWFOUNDLAND &
LABRADOR
Newfoundland
Labrador
Nunatsiavut
Smallwood Reservoir
Churchill Falls
Happy Valley-Goose Bay
Labrador City
Schefferville
Fermont
Sept-Îles
Port-Cartier
Havre-St-Pierre
Île d'Anticosti
GULF OF
ST. LAWRENCE
St. Lawrence
Baie-Comeau
Matane
Rimouski
Gaspé
Pén. de la Gaspésie
Chicoutimi
Jonquière
Rivière-du-Loup
Lévis
Québec
Sherbrooke
Edmundston
Bathurst
Campbellton
NEW
BRUNSWICK
Fredericton
Moncton
Saint John
Bay of Fundy
Sackville
Amherst
Truro
Halifax
Dartmouth
Yarmouth
NOVA
SCOTIA
PRINCE EDWARD
ISLAND
Charlottetown
Summerside
Îs. de la Madeleine
Cape Breton
Island
Sydney
Cabot Strait
Channel-Port
aux Basques
Corner Brook
Stephenville
Deer Lake
Grand Falls
Windsor
Gander
Long Range Mts.
St. John's
Mount Pearl
ST-PIERRE-
ET-MIQUELON
(France)
Sable I.
(Nova Scotia)
ATLANTIC
OCEAN
MAINE
Bangor
Augusta
Portland
Portsmouth
Manchester
Lowell
BOSTON
UNITED
STATES
Mts. Otish
Mts. Groulx
Rés. Manicouagan
St. Lawrence
Str. of Belle Isle
Mealy Mts.

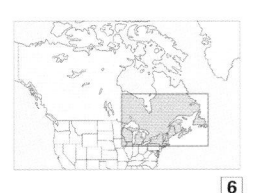

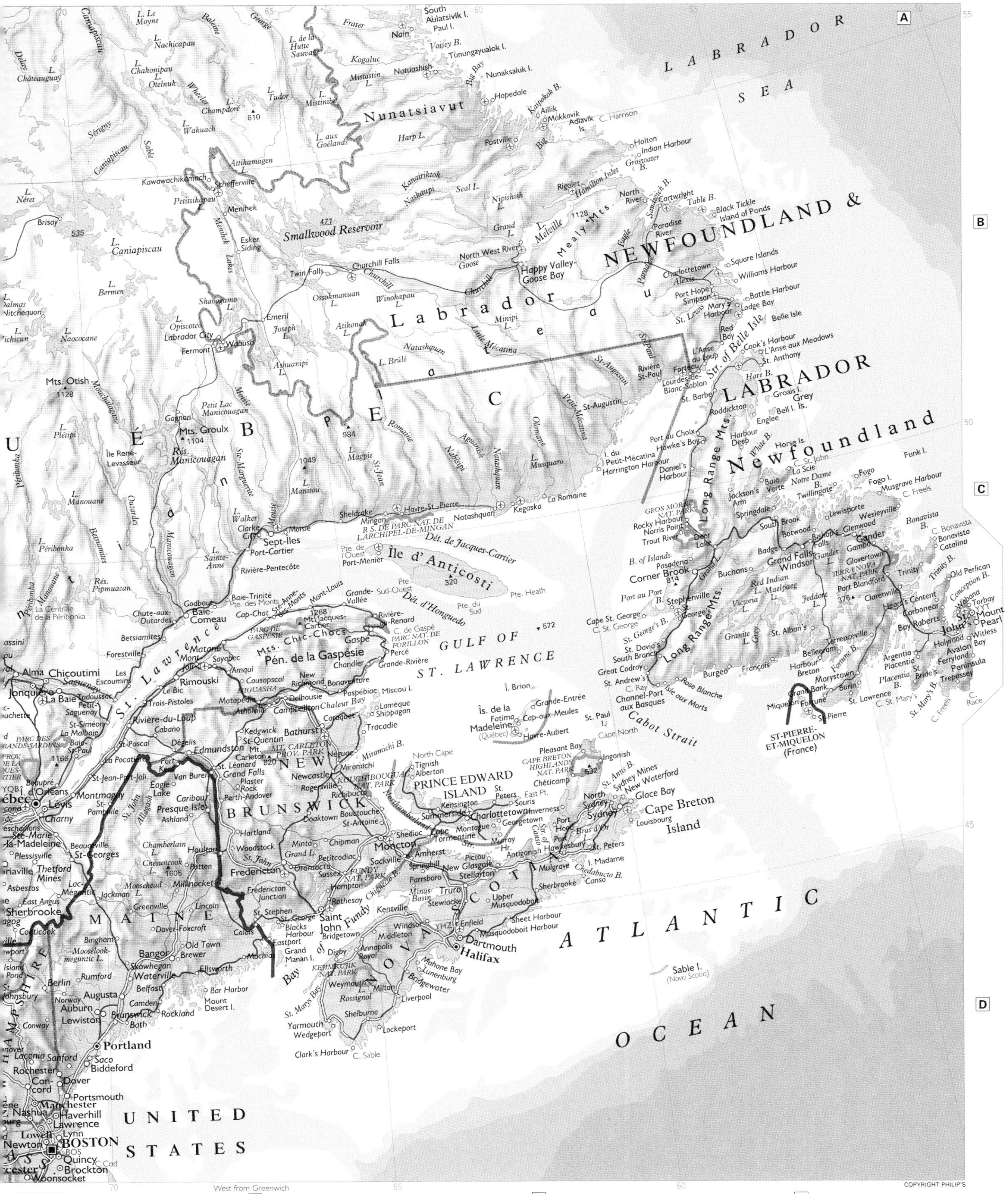

74 UNITED STATES

1:15 000 000

100 0 100 200 300 400 500 600 km
100 0 100 200 300 400 miles

11   12   13   14   16   68   17

G   H   J   K

Anchorage   3363 miles 5412 km   Washington D.C.
2010 miles 3234 km
2438 miles 3923 km
San Francisco
2785 miles 4482 km
2395 miles 3854 km
Honolulu
Tropic of Cancer

P A C I F I C   O C E A N

West from Greenwich

Washington / Oregon / California region

BRITISH COLUMBIA
VANCOUVER   Kelowna   Penticton   Trail   Cranbrook   ALBERTA
Str. of Georgia   Vancouver I.   Chilliwack   Franklin D. Roosevelt L.   Townsend   Shelby
C. Flattery   Victoria   Bellingham   Milk
Mt. Olympus 2428   Puget Sd.   Everett   Spokane   Kalispell   Flathead Lake
W A S H I N G T O N   SEATTLE   Tacoma   Wenatchee   Coeur d'Alene   Missoula   Helena
Grays Hbr.   Aberdeen   Olympia   Mt. Rainier 4392   Ellensburg   Pullman   Moscow   Lewiston   Clark Fork
C. Disappointment   Centralia   Yakima   Walla Walla   Grangeville   Anaconda
Astoria   Longview   Mt. St. Helens 2550   Richland   Kennewick   Butte   Bozeman   Livingston
PORTLAND   Vancouver   Columbia   Pendleton   La Grande   YELLOWSTONE NATIONAL PARK
McMinnville   Mt. Hood 3426   The Dalles   I D A H O   Grand Teton 4196   W
Corvallis   Salem   Day   Payette   Caldwell   Boise   Rexburg   PARK 4009
O R E G O N   Albany   Bend   Nampa   Idaho Falls   Pocatello
Eugene   Springfield   Harney L.   Mountain Home   Twin Falls   Montpelier   Bear L.
Coos Bay   Malheur L.   Hailey   Rupert   Burley   Brigham City   Logan
C. Blanco   Roseburg   Summer L.   Goose L.   Winnemucca   Humboldt   Ogden   SALT LAKE CITY
Grants Pass   Upper Klamath L.   L. Abert   Elko   Great Salt L.   Orem   Uinta   Evanston
Crescent City   Medford   Klamath Falls   Ruby L.   Salt Desert   Provo   Nephi
Eureka   Yreka   Mt. Shasta 4317   NEVADA   Great Basin   U T A H   Richfield   Moab
C. Mendocino   Redding   Lassen Pk. 3187   Pyramid L.   Carson Sink   Sevier   Grand Junction
Red Bluff   Chico   Reno   Sparks   Carson City   Hawthorne   3710
Pt. Arena   Ukiah   Honey L.   L. Tahoe   Walker Lake   Tonopah   Cedar City   ZION NAT. PARK
SACRAMENTO   Santa Rosa   Roseville   Ely   Wheeler Pk. 4342   Page
Napa   Vallejo   Stockton   YOSEMITE NAT. PARK   St. George   GRAND CANYON NAT. PARK
SAN FRANCISCO   Oakland   Concord   Modesto   Merced   Colorado Plateau   2989
SAN JOSE   Santa Cruz   Fresno   Mt. Whitney 4418   Las Vegas   Lake Mead   Gallup
Salinas   Monterey   Hanford   Visalia   SEQUOIA NAT. PARK   Henderson   Hoover Dam   Flagstaff   Humphreys Peak 3851   Winslow
Paso Robles   Bakersfield   Ridgecrest   Bullhead   Mojave Desert   Lake Havasu   A R I Z O N A   Payson
San Luis Obispo   Santa Maria   Santa Clarita   Barstow   Prescott   Baldy Pk. 3476
Pt. Conception   Oxnard   Pasadena   San Bernardino   Riverside   Mesa   PHOENIX   Globe
Channel Islands   LOS ANGELES   Glendale   Palm Springs   Yuma   Sonoran Desert   Safford
Long Beach   Anaheim   Mission Viejo   Salton Sea   Gila   Tucson
SAN DIEGO   Oceanside   El Centro   Grande   Nogales
TIJUANA   Mexicali   SONORA   Agua Prieta   Douglas

ALASKA on same scale

R U S S I A   Penzhino   Anadyr   Arctic Circle   Chukotskoye Nagorye   ARCTIC OCEAN   Barrow   Pt. Barrow
Koryakskoye Nagorye 2455   Ugolnye Kopi   Egvekinot   CHUKCHI SEA   Cape Lisburne   Wainwright   North Slope   Prudhoe Bay
Tilichiki   Anadyr   Beringovskiy   Anadyrskiy Zaliv   Mys Dezhneva (East Cape)   Point Hope   De Long Mts. 1489   Colville   Harrison Bay
Kovacha   Khatyrka   Providenya   Mys Chukotskiy 1194   Uelen   Ostrov Ratmanova (Russia)   Little Diomede I. (U.S.A.)   Kotzebue   Baird Mts. 2781   Brooks   Range   Endicott Mts.   Davidson Mts.
Mys Olyutorski   Mys Navarin   Bering Strait   Cape Prince of Wales   Kobuk   Schwatka Mts. 2682   Philip Smith Mts. 2446   British Mts.
St. Lawrence I. (U.S.A.) 533   556   Shungnak   Selawik L.   Wiseman   Old Crow   Fort McPh
St. Matthew I.   Teller   Seward Peninsula   Koyukuk   Yukon Flats   Fort Yukon   Porcupine
International Date Line   Nome   Council   Nulato   A L A S K A   Ray Mts.   Circle
B E R I N G   S E A   17   Stuart I.   Norton Sound 1040   Kaltag   Kaiyuh Mts.   Tanana   College   Fairbanks   Eagle
Emmonak   Kotlik   Unalakleet   Nenana   Eielson   Delta Junction 1994   Mt. Harper
Cape Romanzof   Hooper Bay   Yukon Delta   U.S.A.   Denali (Mt. McKinley) 6190   Mt. Hayes 4216   Tok   Klondike
Nunivak I. 511   Eidra Str.   Yukon   Holy Cross   Kuskokwim   Mt. Foraker 5304   Alaska   Range   Dawson City
St. Paul I.   Bethel   Kuskokwim Mts. 1266   Mt. Gerdine 3431   Palmer   Copper Center 4949   Beaver Creek   YUKON
St. George I.   Pribilof Is.   Kuskokwim Bay   Kilbuck Mts.   Wasilla   Anchorage   Mt. Marcus Baker 4016   Mt. Sanford 4949   Carmacks
95   C. Newenham   Hagemeister I.   Tikchik Lakes   Iliamna Lake   Redoubt Volcano 3109   Whittier   Chugach Mts.   Mt. Blackburn 4996   Lucania   Kluane
Near Islands   Attu I. 945   Agattu I.   Dillingham   Bristol Bay   Becharof Lake 2153   Kenai Mts.   Valdez   Cordova   Mt. St. Elias 5489   Hubbard Glacier
Buldir I.   Kiska I.   Semisopochnoi I.   Amchitka I.   Rat Islands   Homer   Seward   Prince William Sound   Bering Glacier   Yakutat
A l e u t i a n   I s l a n d s   3621   Montague I.   Kayak I.   Malaspina Glacier 5951
Kanaga I.   Tanaga I.   Adak   Atka I.   Seguam I.   Amlia I.   Shelikof Strait   Kodiak   Chichagof I.
Andreanof Islands   Islands of Four Mountains   Umnak I.   Unalaska   Fox Islands   Afognak I.   1362   Middleton I.   Cross Sound
Amchitka Pass   Ulak I.   Amukta Pass   Makushin Volcano 2036   Dutch Harbor   Unimak I.   Unimak Pass 2587   Kodiak I.   Gulf of Alaska   Alexander
Samalga Pass 2149   Umnak I.   Shishaldin Volcano   Sanak I.   Sutwik I.   Chirikof I.   Trinity Is.   Kodiak   Alaska Peninsula 2507   Shumagin Is.   Bararof   Arc

Projection: Albers' Equal Area with two standard parallels   West from Greenwich

27

3   4   5   6   7   8   9   10   11   12

A   B   C   D   E

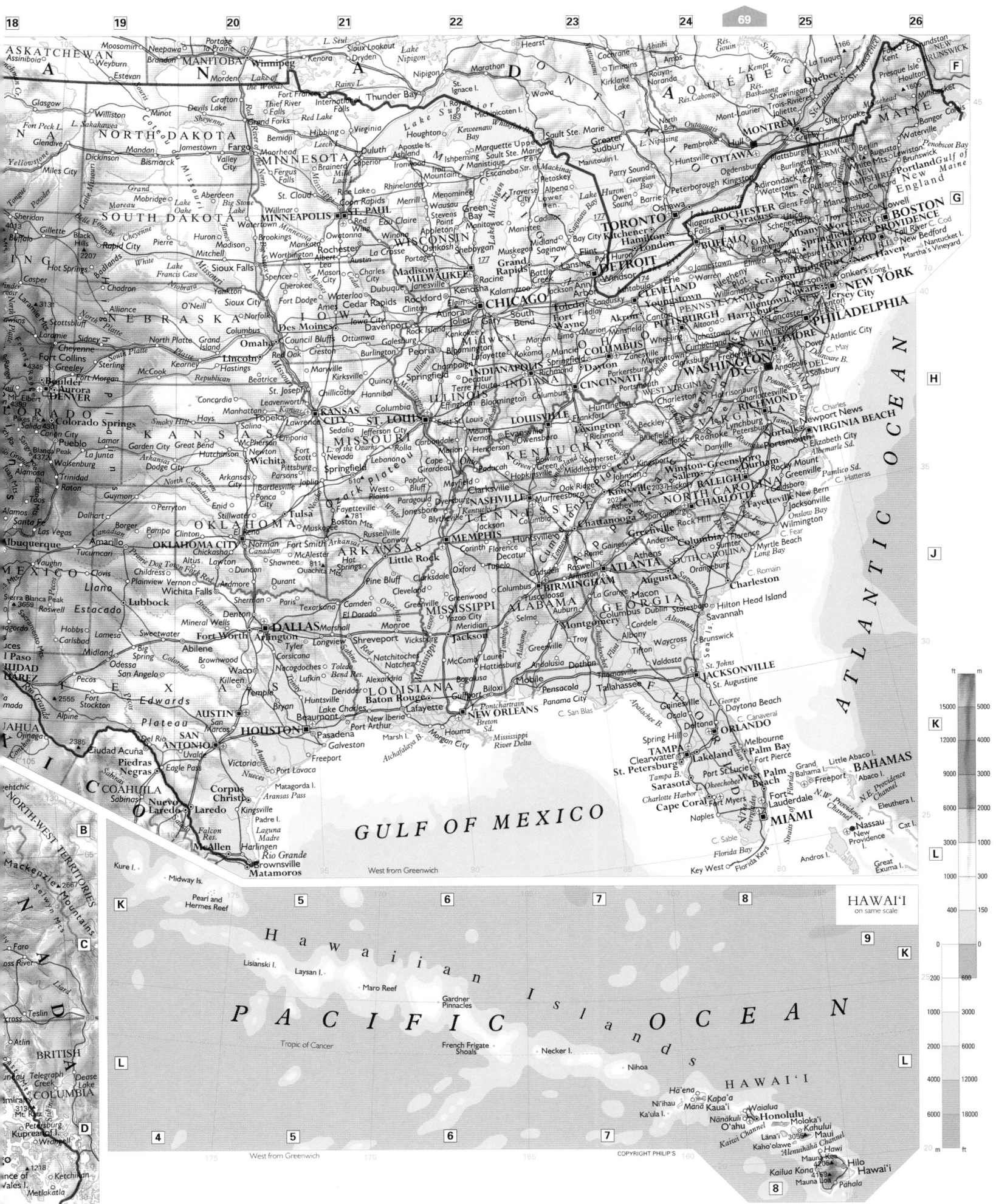

GULF OF MEXICO

ATLANTIC OCEAN

PACIFIC OCEAN

HAWAI'I
on same scale

West from Greenwich

COPYRIGHT PHILIP'S

1:6 700 000

1:2 500 000

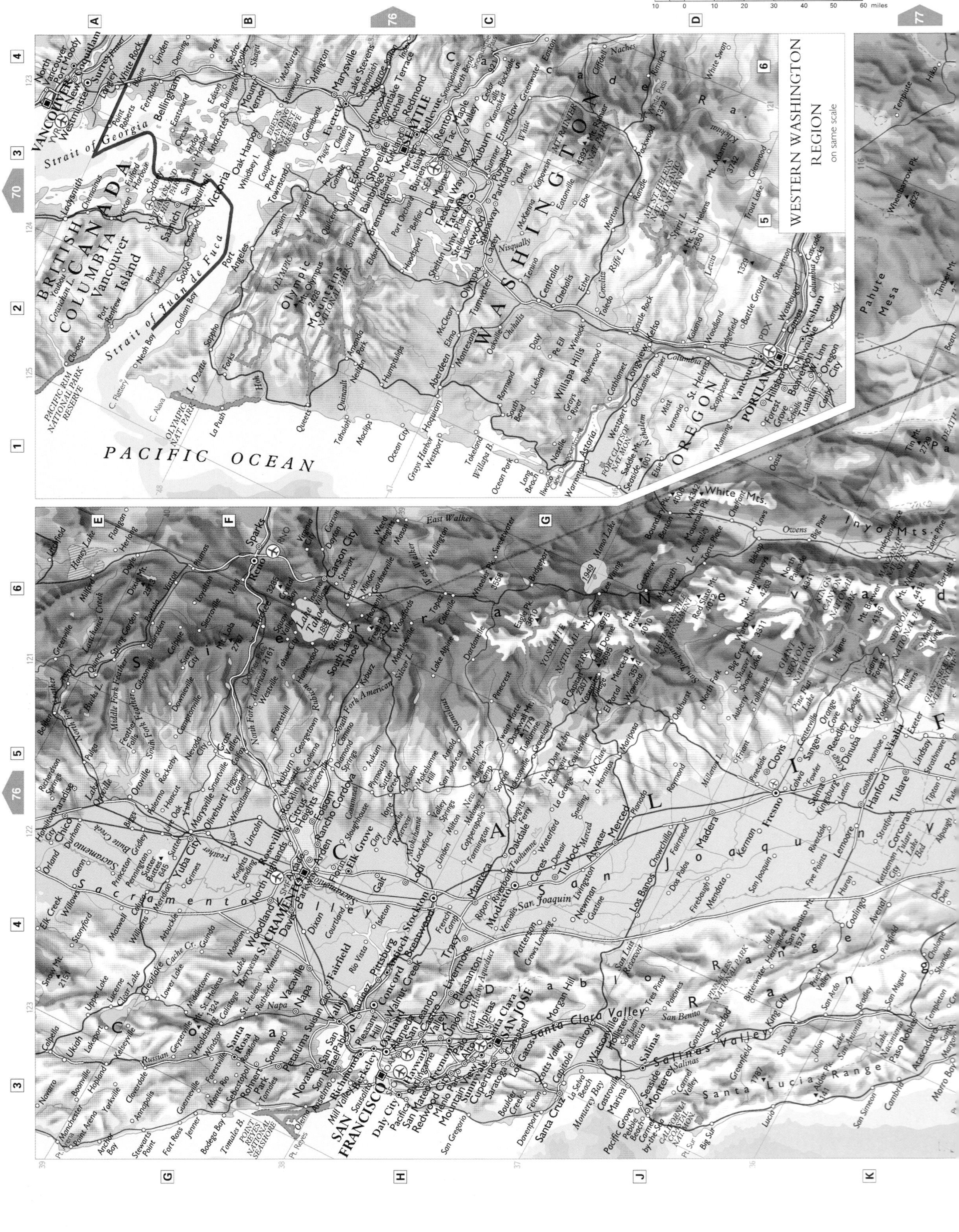
10 0 10 20 30 40 50 60 70 80 90 km
10 0 10 20 30 40 50 60 miles
WESTERN WASHINGTON REGION
on same scale
PACIFIC OCEAN
BRITISH COLUMBIA
CANADA
Vancouver Island
Strait of Georgia
Strait of Juan de Fuca
WASHINGTON
OREGON
Olympic Mountains
OLYMPIC NATIONAL PARK
VANCOUVER
Victoria
Bellingham
Everett
SEATTLE
Tacoma
Olympia
Aberdeen
PORTLAND
Vancouver
Mt. Rainier
MT. RAINIER NAT. PARK
Mt. St. Helens
Mt. Adams
Columbia
Puget Sound
Sierra Nevada
Lake Tahoe
Reno
Carson City
Mono Lake
YOSEMITE NATIONAL PARK
KINGS CANYON NATIONAL PARK
SEQUOIA NATIONAL PARK
White Mts.
Inyo Mts.
Owens
Sacramento
SACRAMENTO
Stockton
Modesto
Merced
Fresno
Visalia
Tulare
Hanford
San Joaquin
Diablo Range
Santa Lucia Range
SAN FRANCISCO
Oakland
SAN JOSE
Santa Clara Valley
Salinas Valley
Salinas
Monterey
Santa Cruz
Monterey Bay
Napa
Santa Rosa
Pahute Mesa

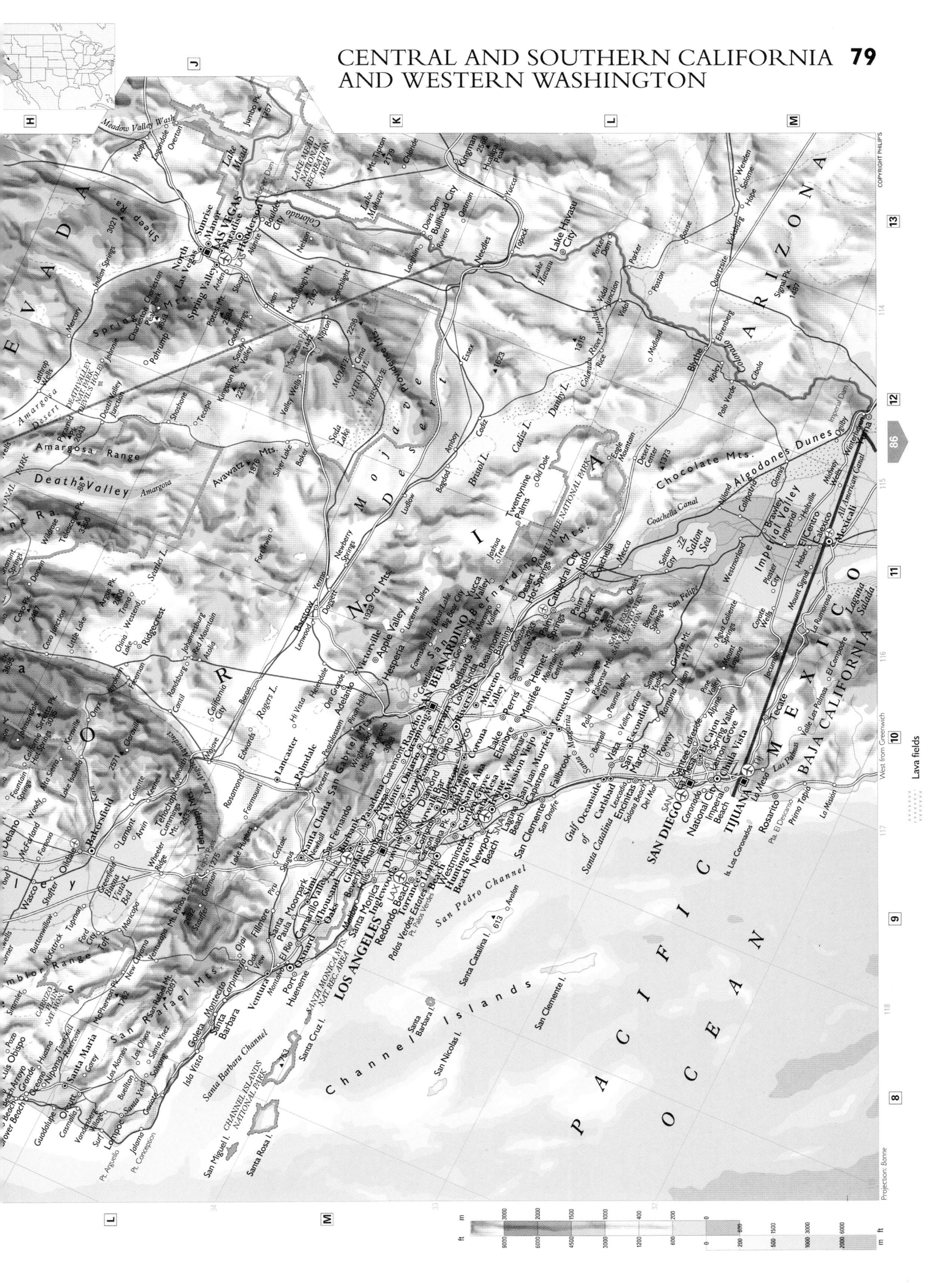

Lava fields

West from Greenwich

Projection Bonne

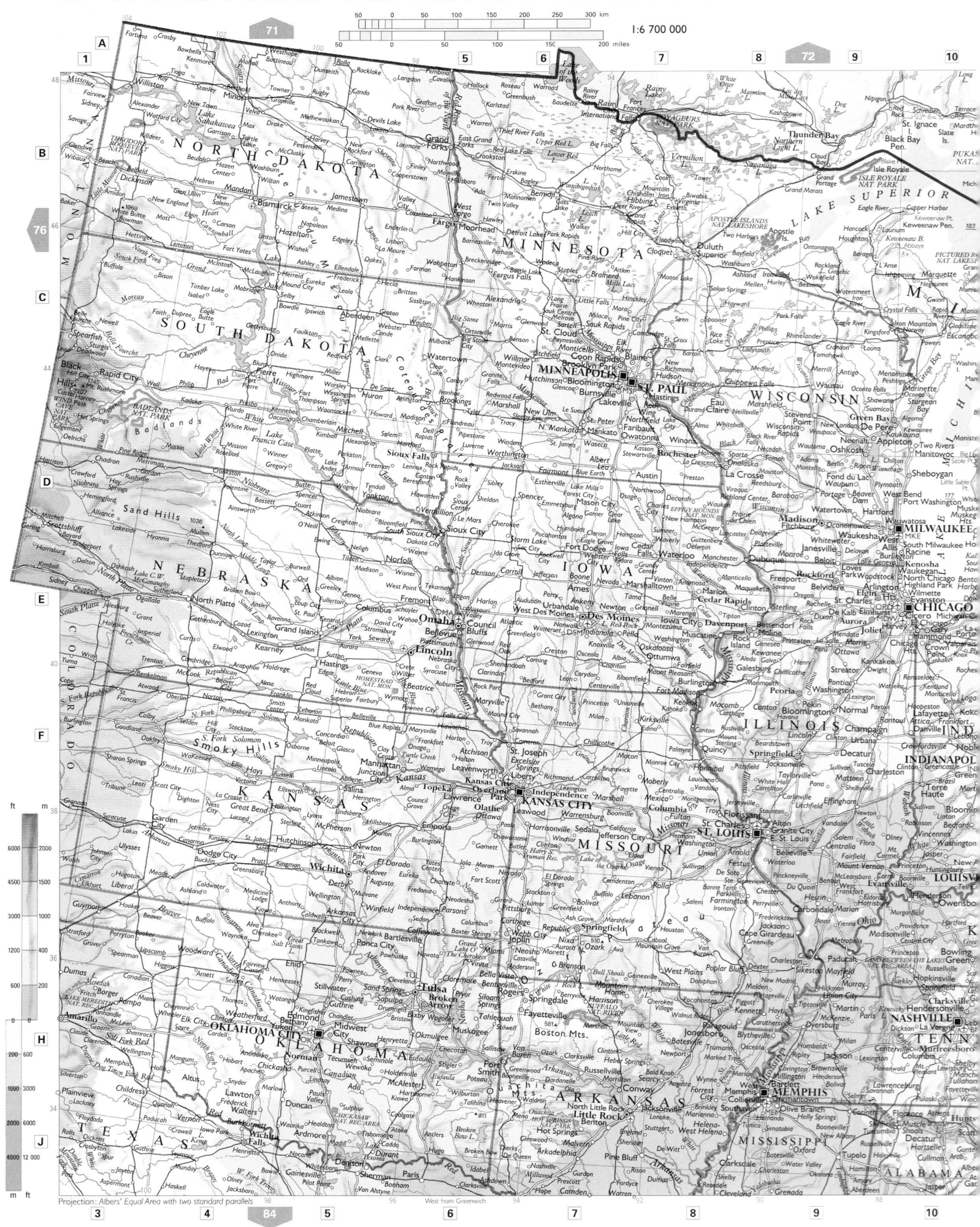

1:6 700 000

Projection: Albers' Equal Area with two standard parallels
West from Greenwich

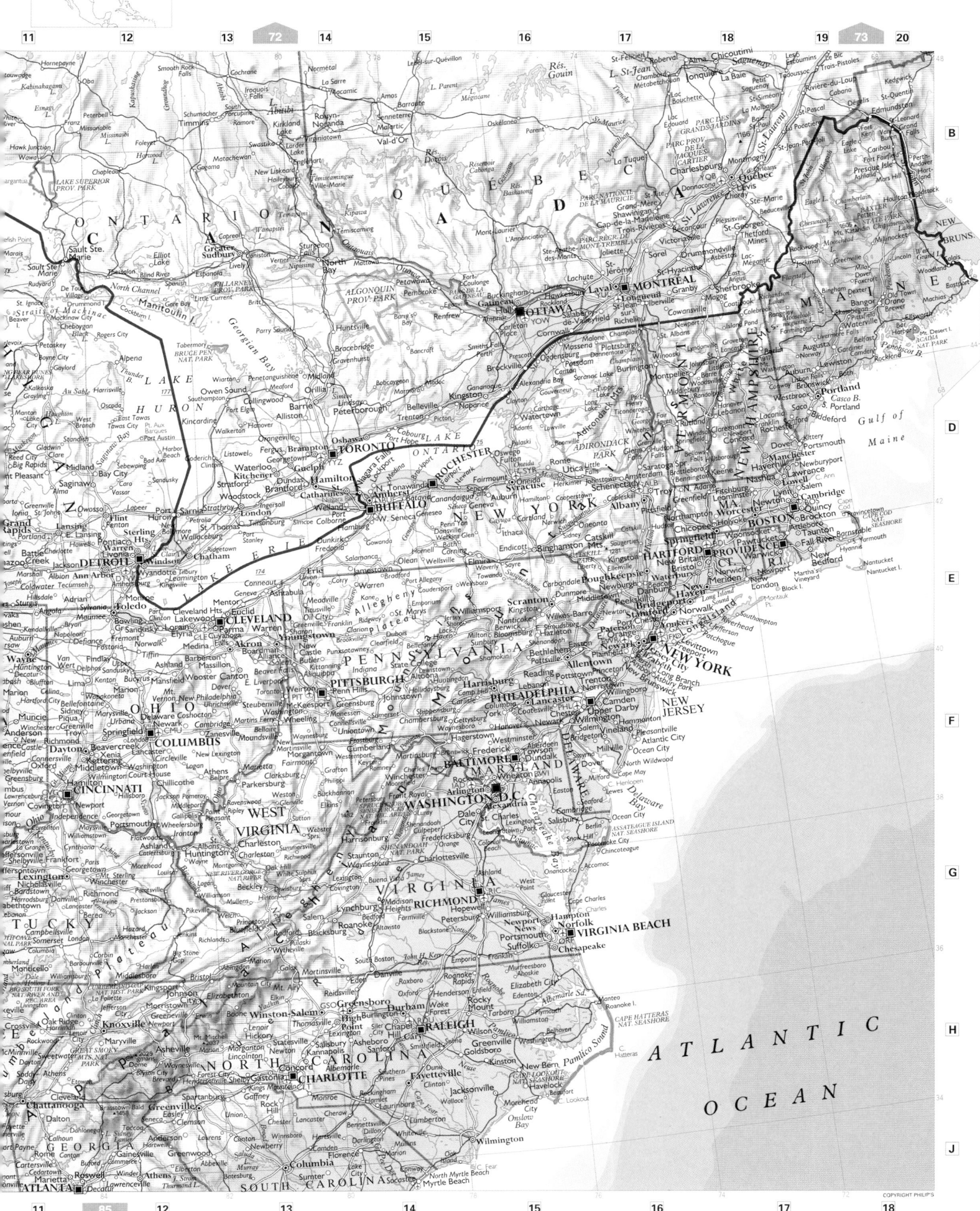

1:2 500 000

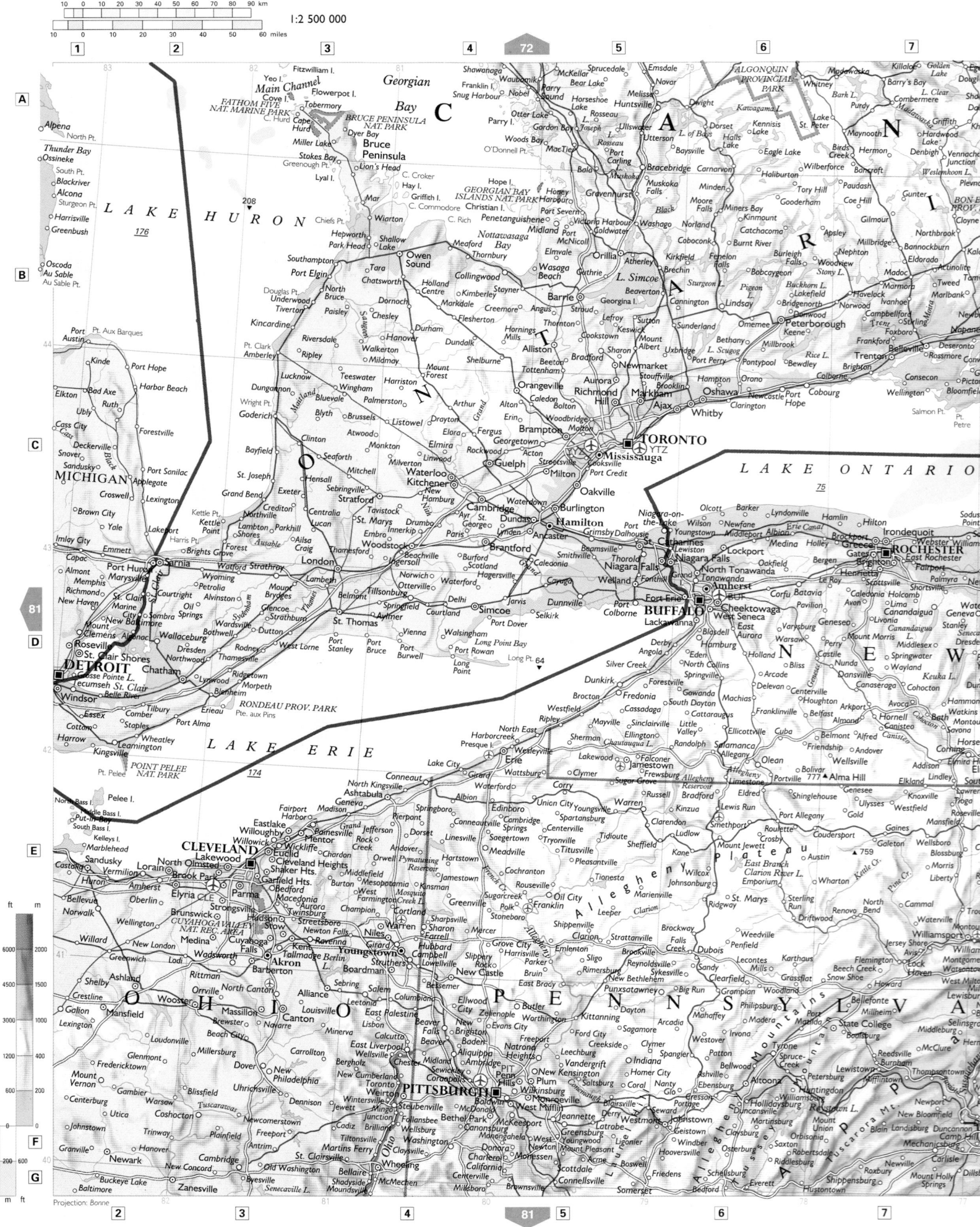

Projection: Bonne

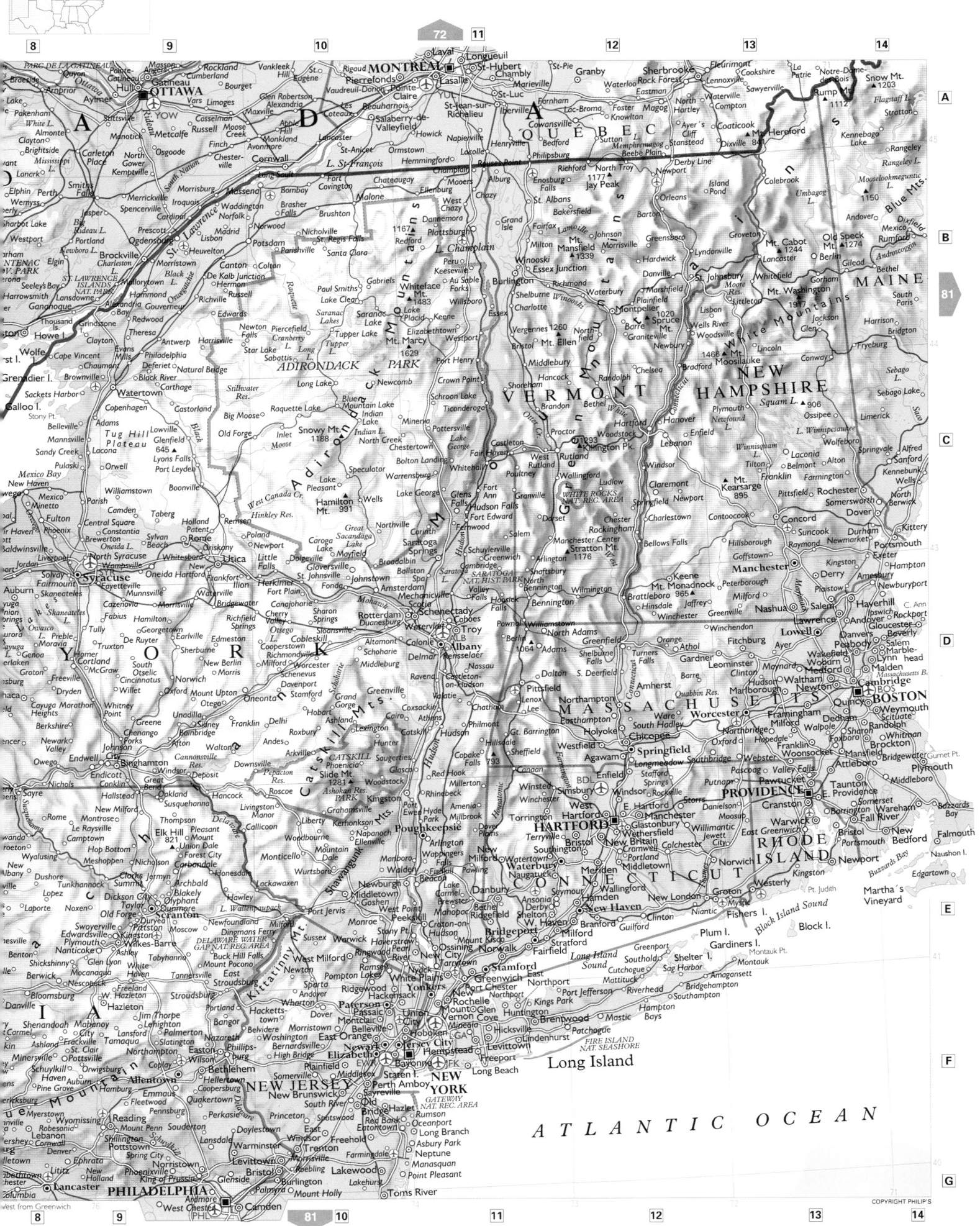

ATLANTIC OCEAN

1:6 700 000

1:8 000 000

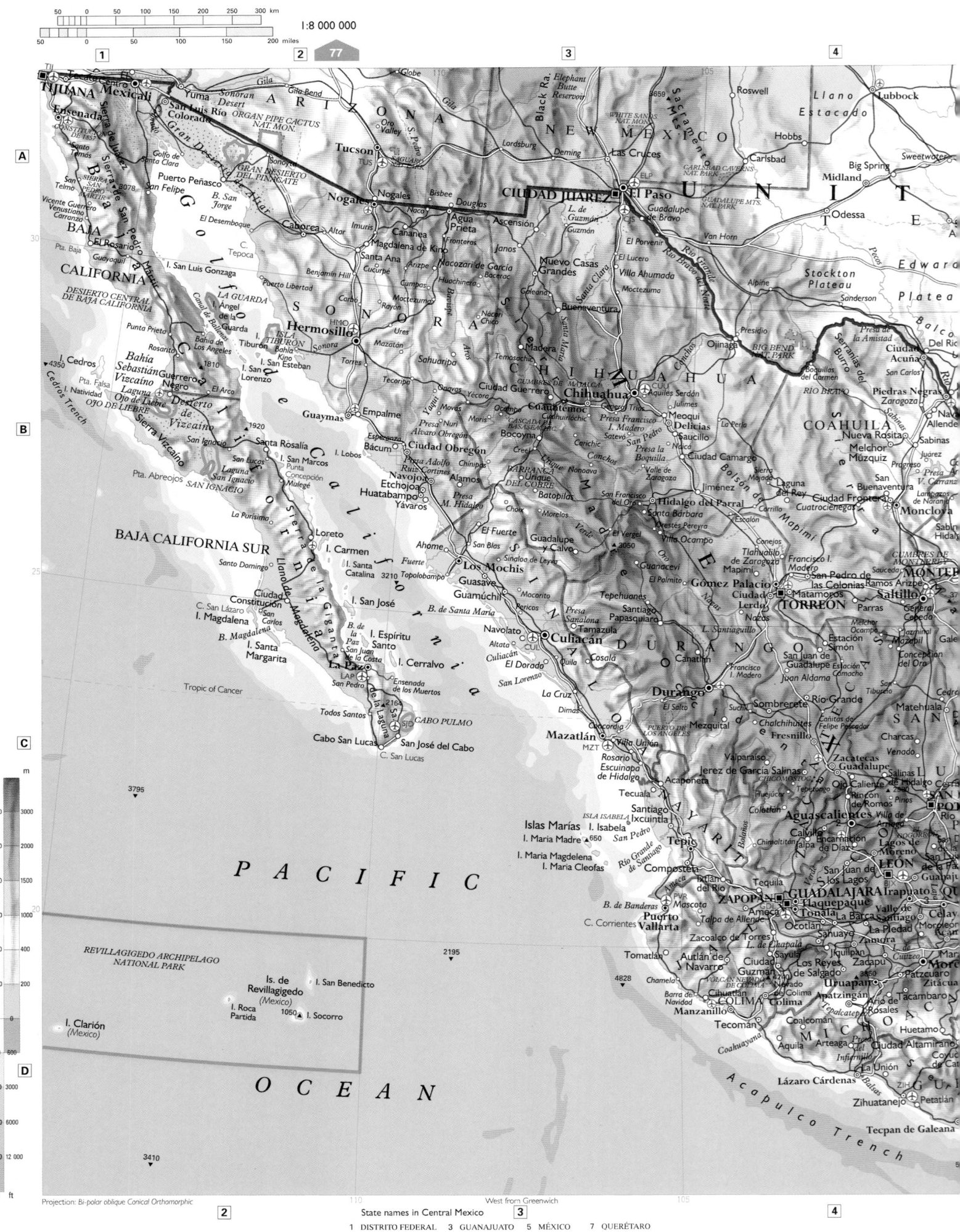

Projection: Bi-polar oblique Conical Orthomorphic

West from Greenwich

State names in Central Mexico

1 DISTRITO FEDERAL   3 GUANAJUATO   5 MÉXICO   7 QUERÉTARO
2 AGUASCALIENTES   4 HIDALGO   6 MORELOS   8 TLAXCALA

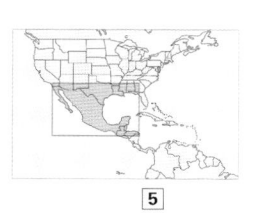

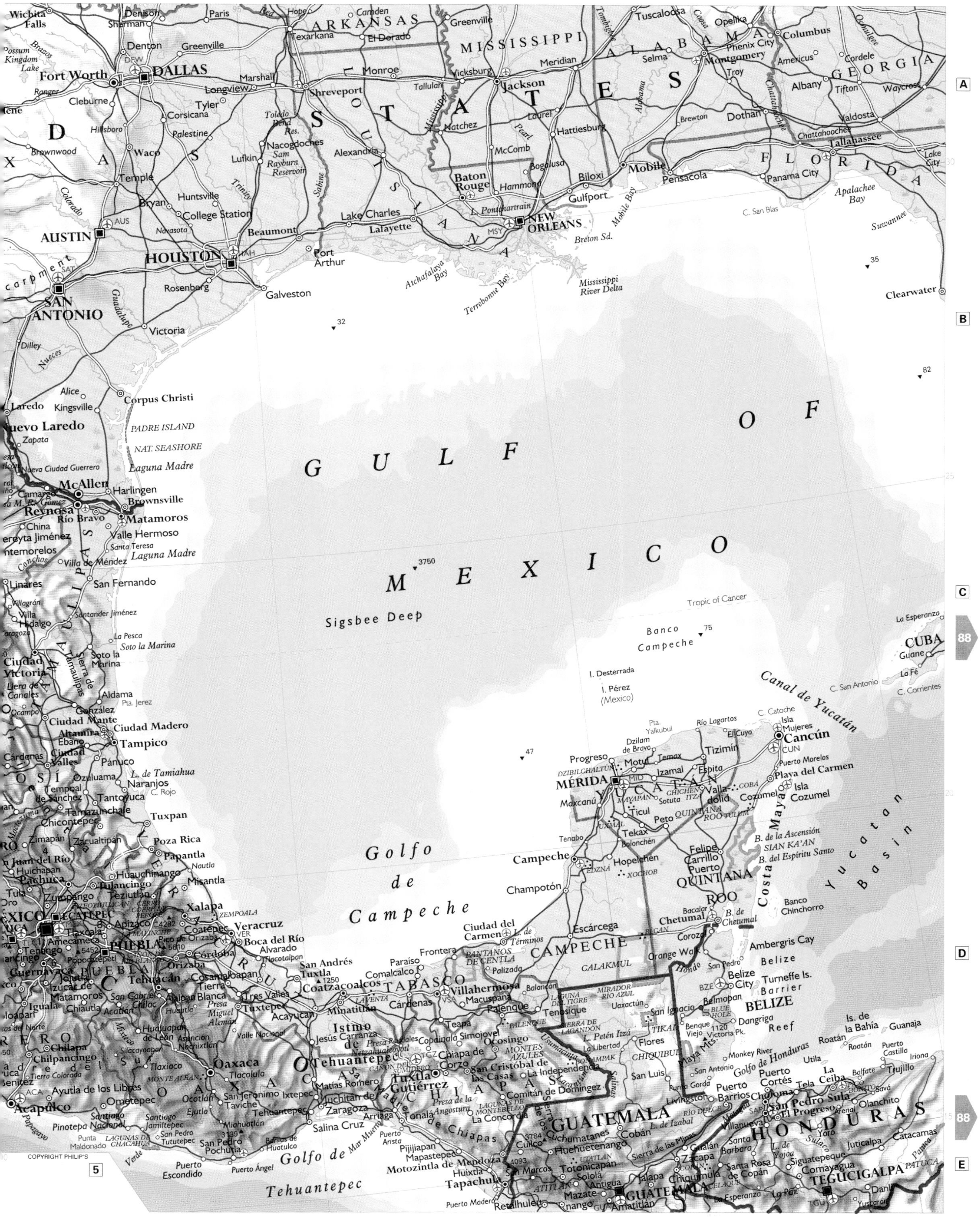

Wichita
Falls
Sherman
Denison
Paris
Red
Hope
Camden
ARKANSAS
Greenville
MISSISSIPPI
Tuscaloosa
Opelika
Columbus
A

Possum Kingdom Lake
Denton
Greenville
Texarkana
El Dorado
Monroe
Vicksburg
Meridian
Selma
Phenix City
Montgomery
Americus
Cordele
Tifton
GEORGIA

Ranger
DALLAS
DFW
Marshall
Longview
Jackson
Troy
Albany
Waycross

Fort Worth
Cleburne
Tyler
S
T
A
T
E
S
Laurel
Dothan
Valdosta

D
Hillsboro
Corsicana
LOUISIANA
Shreveport
Tallulah
Natchez
Hattiesburg
Brewton
FLORIDA
Chattahoochee
Tallahassee
Lake City

Brownwood
Waco
Palestine
Nacogdoches
Sam Rayburn Reservoir
Alexandria
McComb
Bogalusa
Mobile
Pensacola
Panama City
Apalachee Bay

Temple
Bryan
Huntsville
Lufkin
Lake Charles
Baton Rouge
Hammond
Biloxi
Gulfport
Mobile Bay
C. San Blas
Suwannee

AUSTIN
AUS
College Station
Beaumont
Lafayette
L. Pontchartrain
MSY
NEW ORLEANS
Breton Sd.
Apalachee Bay
35

HOUSTON
IAH
Rosenberg
Port Arthur
Atchafalaya Bay
Terrebonne Bay
Mississippi River Delta
Clearwater

SAN ANTONIO
Galveston
32

Victoria
Guadalupe

Dilley
Nueces

Alice
Kingsville
Corpus Christi
PADRE ISLAND
NAT. SEASHORE
82

Laredo
Nuevo Laredo
Zapata

G   U   L   F   O   F

Nueva Ciudad Guerrero
Laguna Madre

McAllen
Harlingen
Reynosa
Río Bravo
Brownsville
Matamoros
Valle Hermoso

China
Jiménez
Santa Teresa
Laguna Madre

morelos
Villa de Méndez
San Fernando
M   E   X   I   C   O

Linares
Villagrán
Villa Hidalgo
La Pesca
Sigsbee Deep
3750
Tropic of Cancer
La Esperanza

Ciudad Victoria
Soto la Marina
Banco Campeche
75
CUBA
Guane

Llera de Canales
La Fé

Ciudad Mante
I. Desterrada
C. San Antonio
C. Corrientes

Altamira
Tampico
Ciudad Madero
I. Pérez
(Mexico)
Canal de Yucatán

Ebano
Ciudad Valles
Pánuco
47
Pta. Yalkubul
Río Lagartos
C. Catoche
Isla Mujeres
Cancún

Ozuluama
L. de Tamiahua
Naranjos
Progreso
Dzilam de Bravo
Motul
Temax
El Cuyo
Tizimín
Espita
CUN
Puerto Morelos

Temapal de Sánchez
Tantoyuca
DZIBILCHALTUN
MID
Izamal
Valladolid
Playa del Carmen

Chicontepec
Tuxpan
MÉRIDA
MAYAPAN
CHICHEN ITZA
Sotuta
Isla Cozumel

Zimapán
Zacualtipán
Poza Rica
Papantla
Maxcanú
Ticul
QUINTANA
COBÁ
Cozumel

Juan del Río
Huichapan
Nautla
Tekax
Peto
ROO
TULUM

Pachuca
Tulancingo
Huauchinango
Misantla
YUCATÁN
UXMAL
Bolonchén
B. de la Ascensión
SIAN KA'AN

Zumpango
Teziutlán
Xalapa
ZEMPOALA
Tenabo
Felipe
Carrillo
B. del Espíritu Santo
Yucatan Basin

MEXICO
ECATEPEC
Apizaco
Xalapa
Campeche
EDZNA
Hopelchén
XOCHOB
Puerto
Banco
Chinchorro

Tlaxcala
Coatepec
Veracruz
VER
Golfo
Champotón
QUINTANA
Bacalar
Costa Maya

PUEBLA
Pico de Orizaba
Orizaba
Boca del Río
Alvarado
de
Chetumal
B. de Chetumal

Popocatépetl
Córdoba
ROO
Corozal
Ambergris Cay

Cuernavaca
Tehuacán
San Andrés
Tuxtla
Campeche
Ciudad del Carmen
L. de Términos
Orange Walk
San Pedro
Belize
D

Iguala
Chiauta
Cosamaloapan
Paraíso
Frontera
BANTANOS DE CENTLA
CALAKMUL
Hondo
BZE
Belize City
Turneffe Is.
Barrier

Matamoros
San Gabriel
Blanca
Comalcalco
Palizada
TABASCO
Balancán
BELIZE
Belmopan
Dangriga
Reef

Chilapa
Oaxaca
Tierra Blanca
Presa Miguel Alemán
Coatzacoalcos
Villahermosa
Macuspana
Palenque
Tenosique
Flores
BLUE HOLE
Is. de la Bahía
Guanaja

Chilpancingo
Tlaxiaco
MONTE ALBÁN
Tres Valles
Minatitlán
Cárdenas
PALENQUE
SIERRA DE LACANDÓN
Petén Itzá
TIKAL
Benque
Roatán
Roatán
Puerto Castilla

Acapulco
ACA
Ayutla de los Libres
Tuxtepec
Acayucan
Istmo de Tehuantepec
Teapa
Comitán de Domínguez
Uaxactún
GUATEMALA
Puerto Barrios
La Ceiba
Trujillo

Ometepec
Ocotlán
San Jerónimo Ixtepec
Jesús Carranza
Copainalá
Simojovel
MONTES AZULES
CHIQUIBUL
San Ignacio
Livingston
San Pedro Sula
Olanchito

Pinotepa Nacional
Santiago
Ejutla
Juchitán de
Tuxtla Gutiérrez
Chiapa de Corzo
San Cristóbal de las Casas
CHIAPAS
LAGUNA DE MONTEBELLO
MIRADOR RÍO AZUL
El Progreso
HONDURAS

Puerto Escondido
Santiago Pochutla
Salina Cruz
Tonalá
Arriaga
Angostura
La Concordia
RÍO DULCE
L. de Izabal
Zacapa
TEGUCIGALPA

Golfo de Tehuantepec
Pijijiapan
Mapastepec
3784
Cuilco
Huehuetenango
Cobán
San Antonio
Comayagua

Motozintla de Mendoza
Huixtla
4093
San Marcos
Totonicapán
Quetzaltenango
Sololá
ATITLÁN
Antigua
GUATEMALA
Amatitlán
La Esperanza

Tapachula
Puerto Madero
Retalhuleu
Mazatenango
Chiquimula
Copán
Santa Rosa de Copán
La Paz

1:8 000

JAMAICA
1:3 000 000

CARIBBEAN SEA

Montego Bay
Lucea
Falmouth
Runaway Bay
St. Ann's Bay
Galina Point
South Negril Pt.
Negril
Cambridge
Wakefield
Ocho Rios
Port Maria
Dry Harbour
Moneague
Annotto Bay
The Cockpit Country
Mount Denham 985▲
Mountains
Port Antonio
Savanna-la-Mar
Maggotty
Don Figueroroa Mts.
Linstead
Blue Mountains
2256▲ Blue Mountain Peak
John Crow Mts.
Black River
Mandeville
Santa Cruz Mts.
Spanish Town
Portmore
Kingston
Port Morant
Great Pedro Bluff
Alligator Pond
May Pen
Old Harbour
Morant Bay
Port Morant
Portland Point
Portland Bight

Gulf of Mexico

MÉRIDA
Progreso
Dzilam de Bravo
Rio Lagartos
El Cuyo
C. Catoche
Isla Mujeres
Motul
Temax
Tizimin
Cancún
Maxcanú
Espita
Playa del Carmen
Calkiní
Ticul
Valladolid
Cozumel
Campeche
Tenabo
Sotuta
Peto
Isla Cozumel
Champotón
Bolonchén
Hopelchén
Felipe Carrillo Puerto
Ciudad del Carmen
MEXICO
Escárcega
Bacalar
CAMPECHE
Chetumal
QUINTANA ROO
Orange Walk
Ambergris Cay
San Pedro
BELIZE
Belize City
Turneffe Is.
Belmopan
Belize Barrier Reef
GUATEMALA
Flores
Dangriga
Monkey River
Roatán
Is. de la Bahía
Guanaja
Puerto Cortés
HONDURAS
Trujillo
La Ceiba
TEGUCIGALPA
SAN SALVADOR
EL SALVADOR
NICARAGUA
MANAGUA
Lago de Nicaragua
COSTA RICA
SAN JOSÉ
PANAMÁ

CUBA
LA HABANA (Havana)
Matanzas
Santa Clara
Camagüey

Cayman Islands (U.K.)
George Town
Grand Cayman

Pedro Bank
Pedro Cays (Jamaica)

CARIBBEAN

FLORIDA
U.S.A.
Miami
West Palm Beach
Fort Lauderdale
Naples
Key West
Nassau

GUADELOUPE
Grande-Terre
Pointe-à-Pitre
Basse-Terre
Soufrière 1467
Marie-Galante

MARTINIQUE
Fort-de-France
Montagne Pelée 1483
St-Pierre

PACIFIC OCEAN

GUADELOUPE AND MARTINIQUE
1:2 000 000

Isthmus of Panama
Golfo de Panamá
Golfo del Darién

ATLANTIC OCEAN

PUERTO RICO
d
1:3 000 000

PUERTO RICO
(U.S.A.)

Pta. Aguijereada
Aguadilla
Isabela
Barceloneta
Arecibo
Manati
Vega Baja
Rio Grande
SAN JUAN
SJU
Dewey
Mayagüez
San Sebastian
Utuado
Bayamón
Carolina
Sierra de Luquillo
Fajardo
Culebra
San German
Adjuntas
Cordillera Central
Cerro
Caguas
Humacao
Naguabo
Puerca
Vieques
1338 de Punta
Coamo
Yauco
Uroyan
Cayey
Yabucoa
Esperanza
Ponce
Guayama
Pta. Aguila
Guanica
I. Caja de Muertos

VIRGIN ISLANDS
e
1:2 000 000

Virgin Islands
(U.K.)

Rufling Pt.
The Settlement
Anegada
East Pt.
Great Camanoe
Virgin Is.
(U.S.A.)
Jost Van Dyke I.
Guana I.
Beef I.
Virgin Gorda
Hans Lollik I.
521
Tortola
Spanish Town
STT
Cruz Bay
Road Town
Charlotte Amalie
St. Thomas I.
St. John I.
VIRGIN IS.
Peter I.

ST. LUCIA
f
1:1 000 000

Cap Point
Pte. Hardy
Gros Islet
Esperance Bay
Castries
Marquis
Girard
Anse la Raye
Canaries
Millet
Dennery
Soufrière
Mt. Gimie
950
Trou Gras Pt.
Soufrière Bay
1.750
Petit Piton
Micoud
796
Gros Piton Pt.
Gros Piton
Vierge Pt.
Choiseul
UVF
Laborie
C. Moule à Chique
ST. LUCIA
Vieux Fort

ATLANTIC OCEAN

Crab Hill
North Point
Spring Hall
Fustic
Boscobelle
Portland
245
Belleplaine
Speightstown
Bathsheba
BARBADOS
Westmoreland
Mt. Hillaby
Hillcrest
Alleynes Bay
840
Martin's Bay
Holetown
Massiah Street
Jackson
Bridgefield
Six Cross Roads
Black Rock
Ellerton
Edey
Ragged Pt.
The Crane
Bridgetown
Ivy
St. Martins
Carlisle Bay
Worthing
Oistins
Chancery Lane
Oistins Bay
BGI
South Point

BARBADOS
g
1:1 000 000

ATLANTIC OCEAN

Tropic of Cancer

Crooked I. Passage
Samana Cay
Crooked I.
Plana Cays
Albert Town
Acklins I.
Snug Corner
Mayaguana I.
Mira por vos Cay
Caicos Passage
Hogsty Reef
Turks & Caicos Is.
(U.K.)
PLS
Caicos Is.
Little Inagua I.
Cockburn Town
Lake Rose
Turks Is.
INAGUA
Turks Island Passage
Silver Bank Passage
Matthew Town
Mouchoir Bank
Silver Bank
Great Inagua I.
Navidad Bank

Monte Cristi
LA ISABELA
Cap-Haïtien
Puerto Plata
Santiago de los Caballeros
San Francisco de Macoris
Milwaukee Deep 8605
Puerto Rico Trench
Fort Liberté
Cord.
La Vega
Nagua
Samana
Cap-à-Foux
G. de la Gonâve
Gonaïves
Hinche
Central
3175
Pico Duarte
Sánchez
Sabana de la Mar
St-Marc
HAITIAN
Bayamón
SAN JUAN
Virgin Gorda
Anegada
Jérémie
Î. de la Gonâve
PORT-AU-PRINCE
HAITI
DOMINICAN REP.
San Pedro de Macoris
Hato Mayor
Aguadilla
Arecibo
Carolina
St. Thomas
Tortola
Virgin Is. (U.K.)
Sombrero (U.K.)
Î. de la Tortue

Dame Marie
Petit
San Juan
Higüey
C. Engaño
Fajardo
STT
Road Town
Anguilla (U.K.)
Les Cayes
Jacmel
2680
San Cristóbal
SANTO DOMINGO
La Romana
Yuma
PUERTO RICO (U.S.A.)
Mayagüez
Ponce
Caguas
Guayama
Charlotte Amalie
Virgin Is. (U.S.A.)
Christiansted
St.-Martin (Fr.)
St. Maarten (Neth.)
St.-Barthélemy (Fr.)
Pointe-à-Gravois
Î. à Vache
Pedernales
Barahona
Compostela
Isla Saona
Mona Passage
Isla Mona (U.S.A.)
Frederiksted
St. Croix (U.S.A.)
St. Eustatius (Neth.)
Saba (Neth.)
Barbuda
ANTIGUA & BARBUDA

Hispaniola
Antilles
I. Beata
C. Beata
5500
Muertas Trough
Muertas Trough
Basseterre
St. John's
Nevis
ST. KITTS & NEVIS
Antigua
Redonda
Soufrière
Montserrat
1156
ANU
(U.K.)
Hills
914
Guadeloupe Passage

4530
Venezuelan
Ste-Rose
PTP
Le Moule
La Désirade
GUADELOUPE
(Fr.)
1467
Pointe-à-Pitre
Marie-Galante (Fr.)
Basse-Terre
Grand-Bourg
Î. des Saintes (Fr.)
Dominica Passage

Beata Ridge
SEA
Basin
I. de Aves
(Venezuela)
Portsmouth
DOMINICA
Morne
DOM
Roseau
Diablotin
MORNE
TROIS PITONS
Martinique Passage
5420
Mt. Pelée
Ste-Marie
1397
Le Robert
Fort-de-France
Rivière-Pilote
FDF
MARTINIQUE
St. Lucia Channel (Fr.)
Castries
ST. LUCIA
Soufrière
UVF

ABC Lesser Islands
Aruba
(Neth.)
Oranjestad
Curaçao
(Neth.)
Willemstad
Bonaire
(Neth.)
AUA
CUR
ARC. LOS ROQUES
I. de Aves
Aves Ridge
St. Vincent Passage
Soufrière
1234
St. Vincent
Speightstown
SVD
BGI
340
Kingstown
Bridgetown
Bequia
BARBADOS
Tobago
ST. VINCENT & THE GRENADINES
Canouan
The Grenadines
Carriacou
840
GRENADA
St. George's
GND

COLOMBIA
Pta. Gallinas
GUAJIRA
Puerto Bolívar
Pen. de la Guajira
Uribia
Punto Fijo
Pta. Espada
Maicao
C. San Román
MAGURIA
Pen. de Paraguaná
Punta Cardón
MÉDANOS DE CORO
Puerto Cumarebo
Coro
La Vela
I. Las Aves (Ven.)
I. Orchila (Ven.)
Is. Los Roques (Ven.)
I. Blanquilla (Ven.)
Is. Los Hermanos (Ven.)
Is. Los Testigos (Ven.)
Tobago
TAB
Scarborough
Galera Pt.

Santa Marta
TAYRONA
Riohacha
ISLA DE SALAMANCA
SA. NEVADA DE STA MARTA
5775
Golfo de Venezuela
FALCÓN
CUEVA DE LA QUEBRADA DEL TORO
Tucacas
NUEVA ESPARTA
I. de Margarita
I. La Tortuga (Ven.)
La Asunción
Porlamar
PMV
Pen. de Paria
Port of Spain
940
Trinidad
Galera Pt.

Soledad
Cienaga
Sierra Nevada de Sta Marta
MARACAIBO
MAR
Santa Rita
Altagracia
Mene de Mauroa
Baragua
Coro
San Felipe
Maiquetía
La Guaira
MARACAY
CARACAS
Petare
C. Codera
Higuerote
Rio Chico
Puerto La Cruz
Cumaná
SUCRE
Carúpano
Rio
Güiria
G. de Paria
San Fernando
TRINIDAD & TOBAGO
POS
Rio Claro
Serpent's Mouth

Valledupar
CÉSAR
Villa del Rosario
Ciudad Ojeda
Cabimas
LARA
Carora
BARQUISIMETO
YARACUY
VALENCIA
CARABOBO
Villa de Cura
San Juan de los Morros
Aragua de Barcelona
Barcelona
Anaco
MONAGAS
Maturín
MARIUSA
DELTA
AMACURO
Tucupita

Fundación
MAGDALENA
Plato
Zambrano
Agustín Codazzi
La Concepción
TRUJILLO
Mene Grande
ARAGUA
Altamira
Valera
El Guache
PORTUGUESA
Araure
Acarigua
COJEDES
San Carlos
Calabozo
GUÁRICO
Santa María de Ipire
El Sombrero
Valle de la Pascua
El Tigre
ANZOÁTEGUI
Soledad
Los Barrancos
Ciudad Guayana
Sierra Imataca

El Banco
Mompós
ZULIA
PERIJA
CIÉNAGAS DEL CATATUMBO
San Carlos del Zulia
MÉRIDA
4981
Pico Bolívar
BARINAS
Barinas
Libertad
Guanare
Portuguesa
El Baúl
Aguaro Guariquito
San Fernando de Apure
Mapire
Cantaura
Pariaguán
Ciudad Bolívar
Embalse de Guri
Guasipati
El Callao
Tumeremo

Ocaña
NORTE DE SANTANDER
Cúcuta
TACHIRA
San Cristóbal
San Antonio
Santa Bárbara
VENEZUELA
BARINAS
Bruzual
Ciudad de Nutrias
Achaguas
Apure
Caicara
San Fernando
Orinoco
Ciudad Bolívar
Upata

BOLÍVAR
Simití
Caucasia
Ayapel
Majagual
COPYRIGHT PHILIP'S

West from Greenwich

100 0   200   400   600   800 1000 1200 1400 km

1:35 000 000

100 0   200   400   600   800   1000 miles

Projection: Lambert's Azimuthal Equal Area

COPYRIGHT PHILIP'S

1:35 000 000

100 0 200 400 600 800 1000 1200 1400 km
100 0 200 400 600 800 1000 miles

1 ■ LIMA Capital Cities **2**

Projection: Lambert's Azimuthal Equal Area

COPYRIGHT PHILIP'S

West from Greenwich

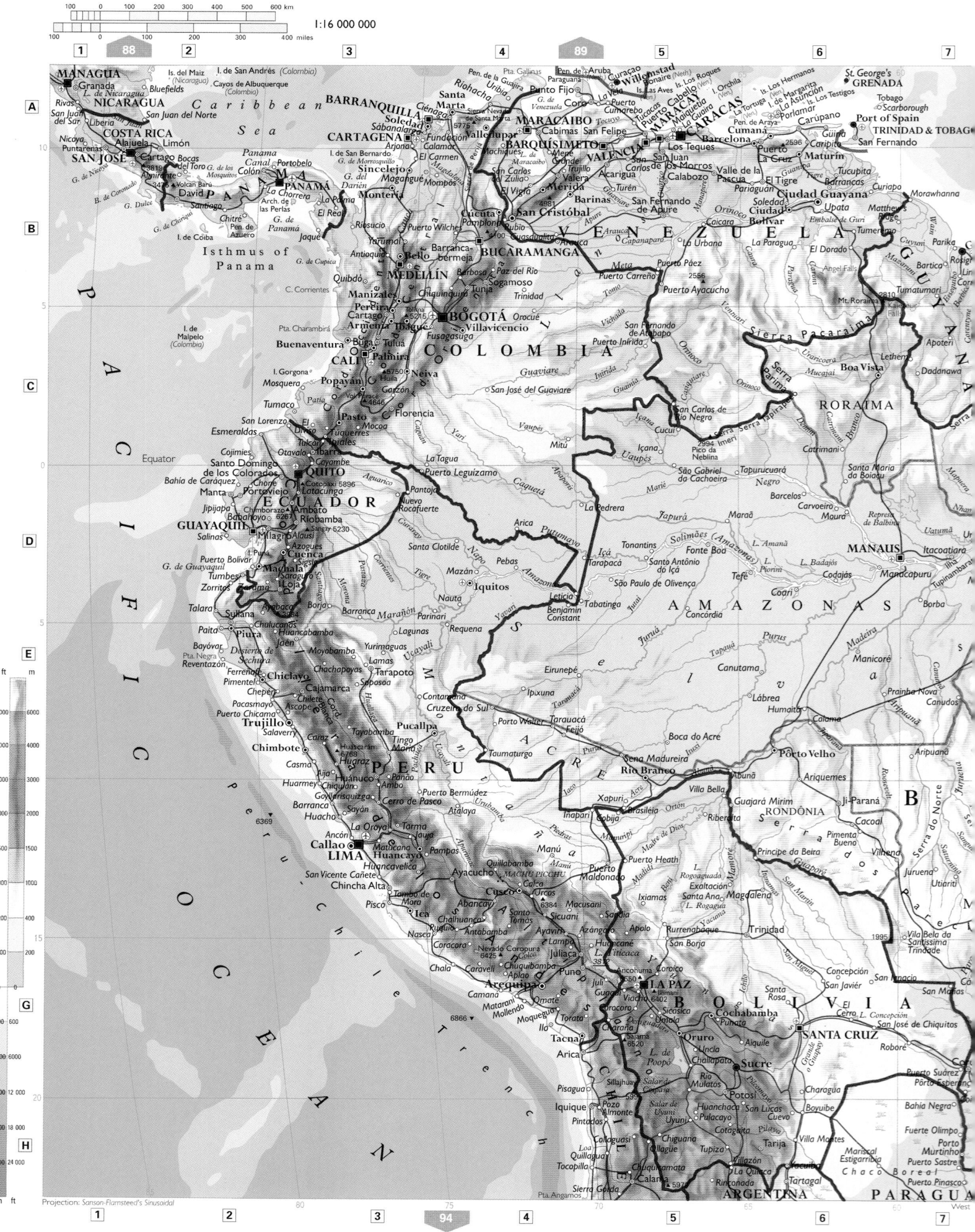

100 0 100 200 300 400 500 600 km
1:16 000 000
100 0 100 200 300 400 miles

Projection: Sanson-Flamsteed's Sinusoidal

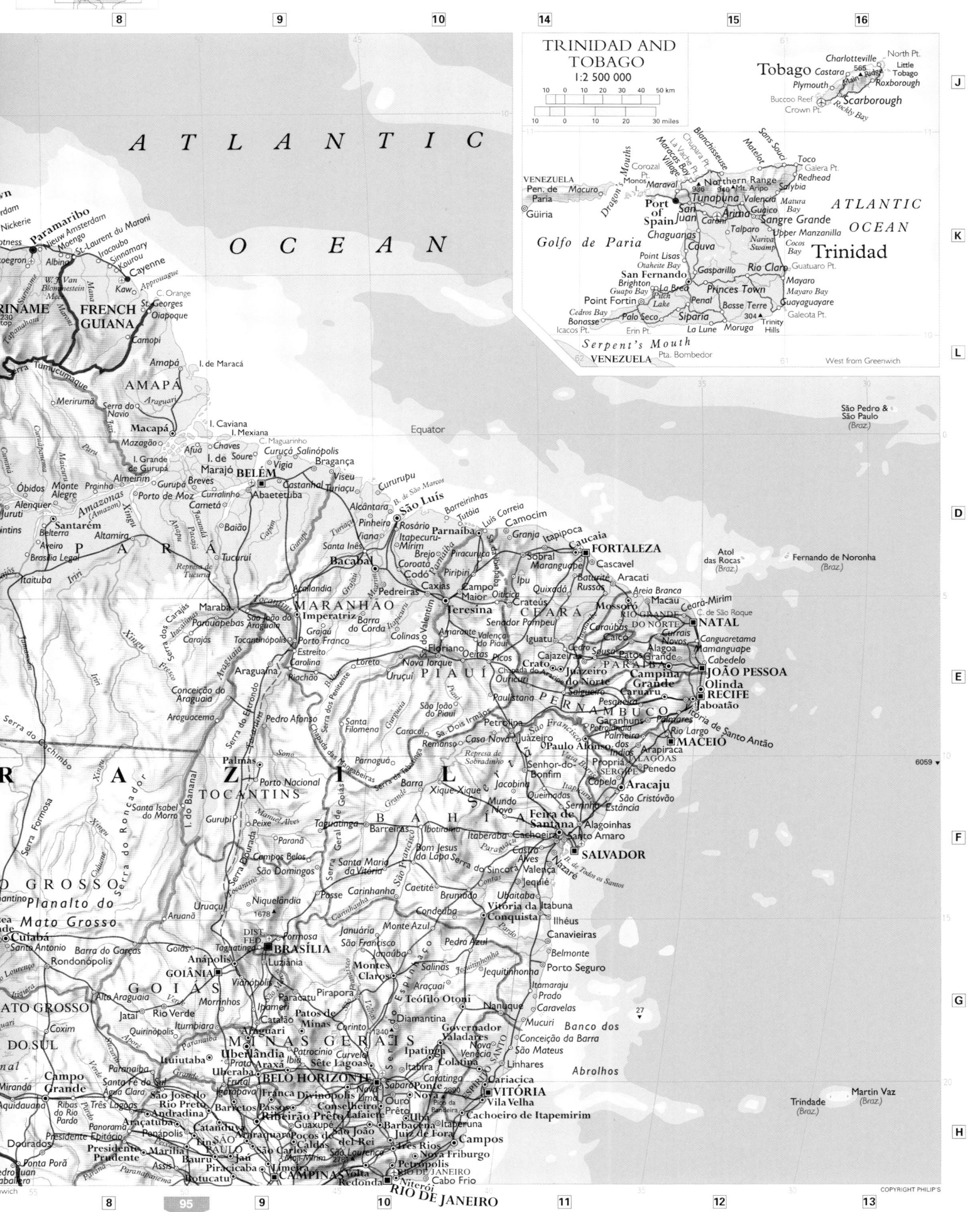

ATLANTIC

OCEAN

TRINIDAD AND TOBAGO
1:2 500 000

10   0   10   20   30   40   50 km
10   0   10   20   30 miles

Tobago
Charlotteville North Pt.
Castara 565 Roxborough Little Tobago
Plymouth ▲ Main Ridge
Buccoo Reef Scarborough
Crown Pt. Rockly Bay

VENEZUELA
Pen. de Paria
Macuro
Güiria

La Vache Pt.
Chupara Pt.
Maraval
Monos I.
Corozal Pt.
Blanchisseuse
Maracas Village
Matelot
Sans Souci
Toco
Galera Pt.
Redhead
Salybia
Toco

Dragon's Mouths

Port of Spain
San Juan
Chaguanas

Northern Range
940 ▲ Mt. Aripo
Tunapuna Valencia
Arima Guanapo
Caroni Talparo Upper Manzanilla
Couva Sangre Grande
Matura Bay
Nariva Swamp

ATLANTIC
OCEAN

Golfo de Paria

Point Lisas
Otaheite Bay
San Fernando
Brighton
Guapo Bay La Brea
Point Fortin Penal
Cedros Bay Pitch Lake
Bonasse Palo Seco
Icacos Pt. La Lune
Erin Pt. Moruga

Gasparillo
Rio Claro Guatuaro Pt.
Princes Town
Basse Terre
Siparia 304 ▲ Guayaguayare
Trinity Hills
Cocos Bay
Mayaro
Mayaro Bay
Galeota Pt.

Trinidad

Serpent's Mouth
VENEZUELA Pta. Bombedor

West from Greenwich

Equator

São Pedro & São Paulo (Braz.)

Paramaribo
Nieuw Amsterdam
Moengo
Nickerie
Albina
W.J. Van Blommestein Meer
Serra Tumucumaque

Cayenne
St-Laurent du Maroni
Iracoubo
Sinnamary
Kourou
Kaw
C. Orange
St-Georges
Oiapoque
Camopi

FRENCH GUIANA

SURINAME

Amapá
Serra do Navio
Araguari
Merirumã

AMAPÁ

I. de Maracá

Macapá
Mazagão
I. Caviana
I. Mexiana
C. Maguarinho
Chaves
Afuá
Soure
Curuçá Salinópolis
Vigia
Bragança

Monte Alegre
Óbidos
Alenquer
Juruti
Santarém
Belterra
Aveiro
Altamira
Brasília Legal
Itaituba

PARÁ

Prainha
I. Grande de Gurupá
Almeirim
Breves
Gurupá
Porto de Moz
Cametá
BELÉM
Marajó
Castanhal Turiaçu
Abaetetuba
Viseu
Cururupu
B. de São Marcos
São Luís
Barreirinhas
Luís Correia
Tutóia
Granja Itapipoca
Camocim

Parnaíba
Piracuruca
Piripiri
Sobral
Marangaupe
Caucaia
FORTALEZA
Cascavel
Ipu Quixadá
Baturité Aracati

Atol das Rocas (Braz.)

Fernando de Noronha (Braz.)

Tucuruí
Represa de Tucuruí
Itacaiúnas
Marabá
São João do Araguaia
Parauapebas
Carajás
Serra dos Carajás

Pinheiro
Rosário
Itapecuru-Mirim
Viana
Santa Inês
Bacabal
Coroatá Codó
Pedreiras

Caxias
Timbiras
Campo Maior
Teresina
Senador Pompeu
Crateús
Mossoró
Russas
Areia Branca
Macau
Ceará-Mirim
C. de São Roque

MARANHÃO

Imperatriz
Barra do Corda
Colinas
Floriano
Amarante
Oeiras
Picos
Iguatu
Carolina
Estreito
Porto Franco
Tocantinópolis
Loreto
Nova Iorque
Riachão

CEARÁ

RIO GRANDE DO NORTE

NATAL

Caraúbas
Caicó

Conceição do Araguaia
Araguaína

PIAUÍ
Uruçuí
São João do Piauí

Cajazeiras
Crato
Juazeiro do Norte
Souza
Cedro
Salgueiro
Ouricuri
Paulistana

Patos
Currais Novos
Alagoa Grande
Canguaretama
Mamanguape
Cabedelo
JOÃO PESSOA
Campina Grande
Olinda
RECIFE
Jaboatão

PARAÍBA

PERNAMBUCO

TOCANTINS

Palmas
Porto Nacional

Gurupi
Peixe
Paranã
Taguatinga
Barreiras
Campos Belos
São Domingos

BAHIA

Xique-Xique
Barra
Ibotirama

Aracaju
São Cristóvão
Estância

Garanhuns
Palmeira dos Índios
Arapiraca
MACEIÓ
Penedo
Propriá
Capela
Alagoinhas

Petrolina
Juazeiro
Remanso
Casa Nova
Senhor do Bonfim
Jacobina
Mundo Novo
Queimadas
Serrinha
Feira de Santana
Santo Amaro
Cachoeira
SALVADOR

Represa de Sobradinho
Paulo Afonso

ALAGOAS

SERGIPE

6059 ▼

Cuiabá
Santo Antônio
Barra do Garças
Rondonópolis
Goiás

MATO GROSSO
planalto do
Mato Grosso

DIST. FED.
BRASÍLIA
Luziânia
Anápolis
GOIÂNIA
Vianópolis
Niquelândia
Aruanã

GOIÁS

Formosa
São Francisco
Januária
Juazeiro
Monte Azul
Carinhanha
Condeúba
Brumado
Livramento
Vitória da Conquista
Ilhéus
Canavieiras
Itaberaba
Jequié
Valença
Nazaré
Ubaitaba
Caetité
Santa Maria da Vitória
Bom Jesus da Lapa
Castro Alves
Serra do Sincorá
Bananal

MATO GROSSO DO SUL
Campo Grande
Coxim
Aquidauana
Miranda

Jataí
Rio Verde
Itumbiara
Quirinópolis
Catalão
Ipameri
Paracatu
Unaí
Arinos
Patos de Minas
Diamantina
Teófilo Otoni
Nanuque
Mucuri
Caravelas
Prado
Itamaraju
Belmonte
Porto Seguro
Conceição da Barra
Pedra Azul
Jequitinhonha
Itaúna
Salinas

Banco dos Abrolhos

Trindade (Braz.)
Martin Vaz (Braz.)

27 ▼

MINAS GERAIS

Araguari
Ituiutaba
Uberlândia
Uberaba
Frutal
Araxá
Patrocínio
Curvelo
Sete Lagoas
Ipatinga
Itabira
Governador Valadares
São Mateus
Linhares
Aracruz

Presidente Epitácio
Três Lagoas
Andradina
Araçatuba
Penápolis
Birigui
Lins
Catanduva
São José do Rio Preto
Barretos
Ribeirão Prêto
Franca
Passos
Poços de Caldas
Guaxupé
Divinópolis
Conselheiro Lafaiete
Barbacena
São João del Rei
Juiz de Fora
Campos
Itaperuna
Nova Friburgo
BELO HORIZONTE
Ouro Prêto
Ponte Nova
Sabará
VITÓRIA
Vila Velha
Cachoeiro de Itapemirim
Colatina

Dourados
Ponta Porã

Presidente Prudente
Marília
Assis
Bauru
Jaú
Piracicaba
Limeira
CAMPINAS
SÃO PAULO
São Carlos
Araraquara
Mococa
São Lourenço
Volta Redonda
Petrópolis
Niterói
RIO DE JANEIRO
Cabo Frio
Três Rios

BRASIL / BRAZIL

COPYRIGHT PHILIP'S

1:8 000 000

Projection : Lambert's Equivalent Azimuthal

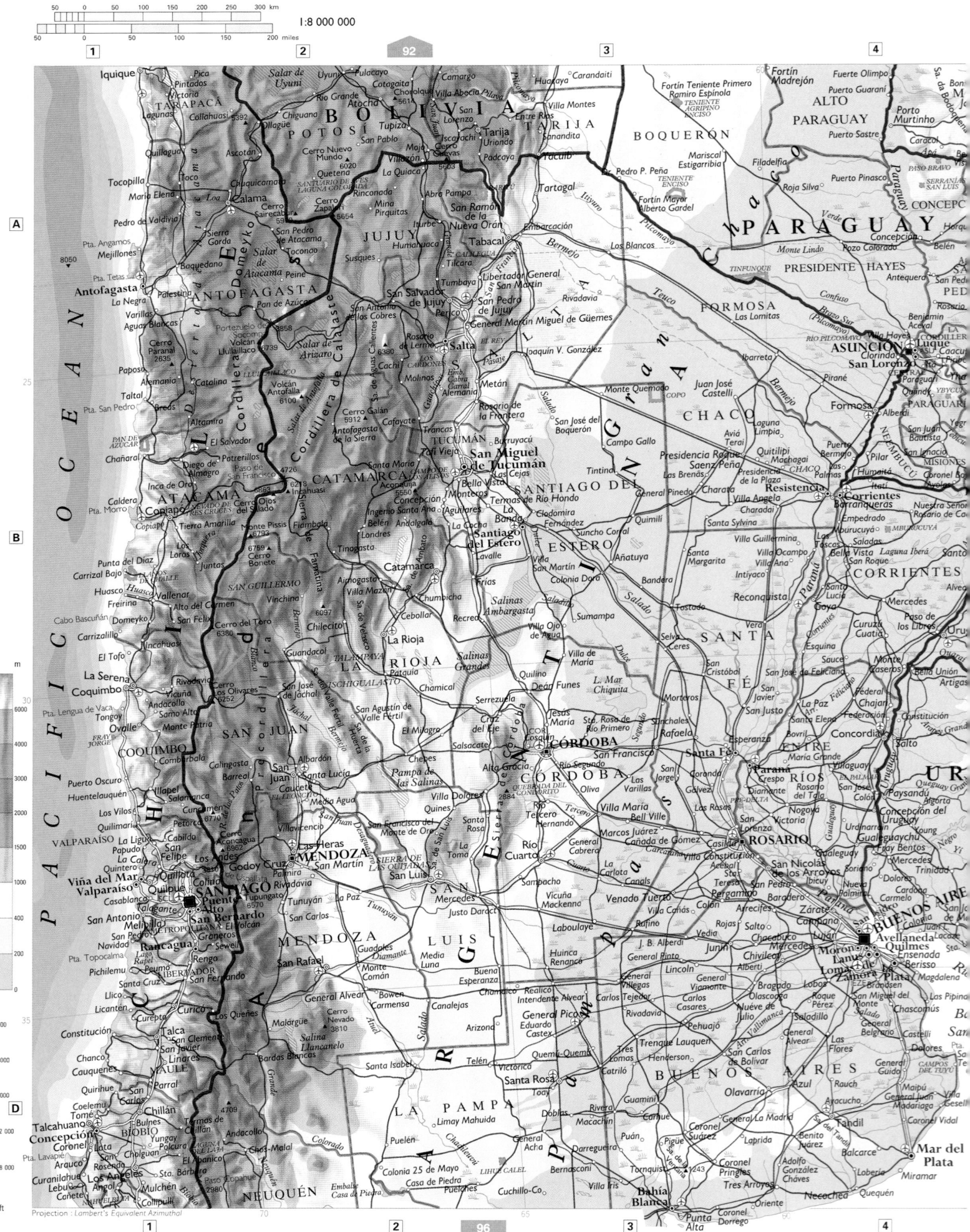

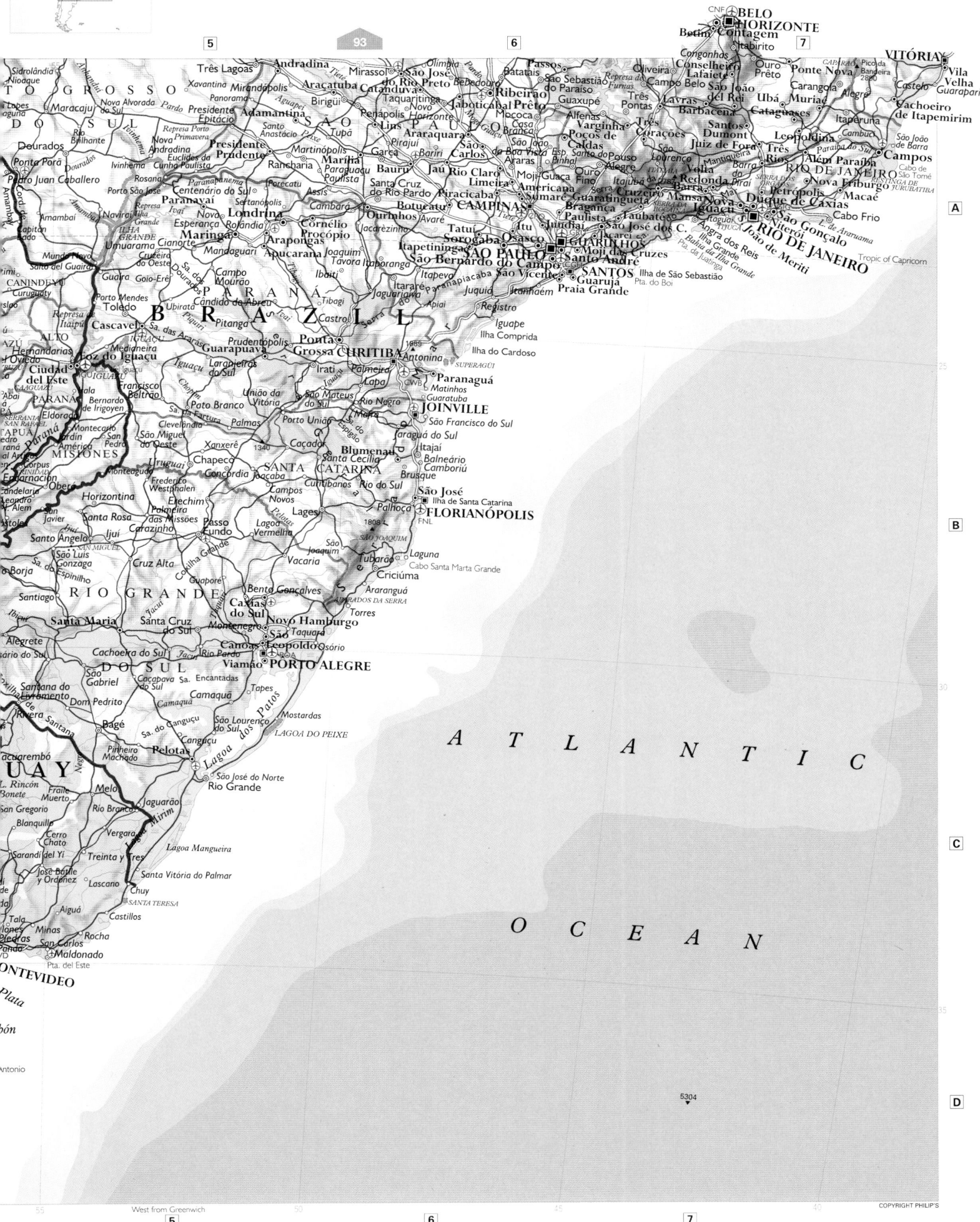

100 0 100 200 300 400 500 600 km
100 0 100 200 300 400 miles

1:16 000 000

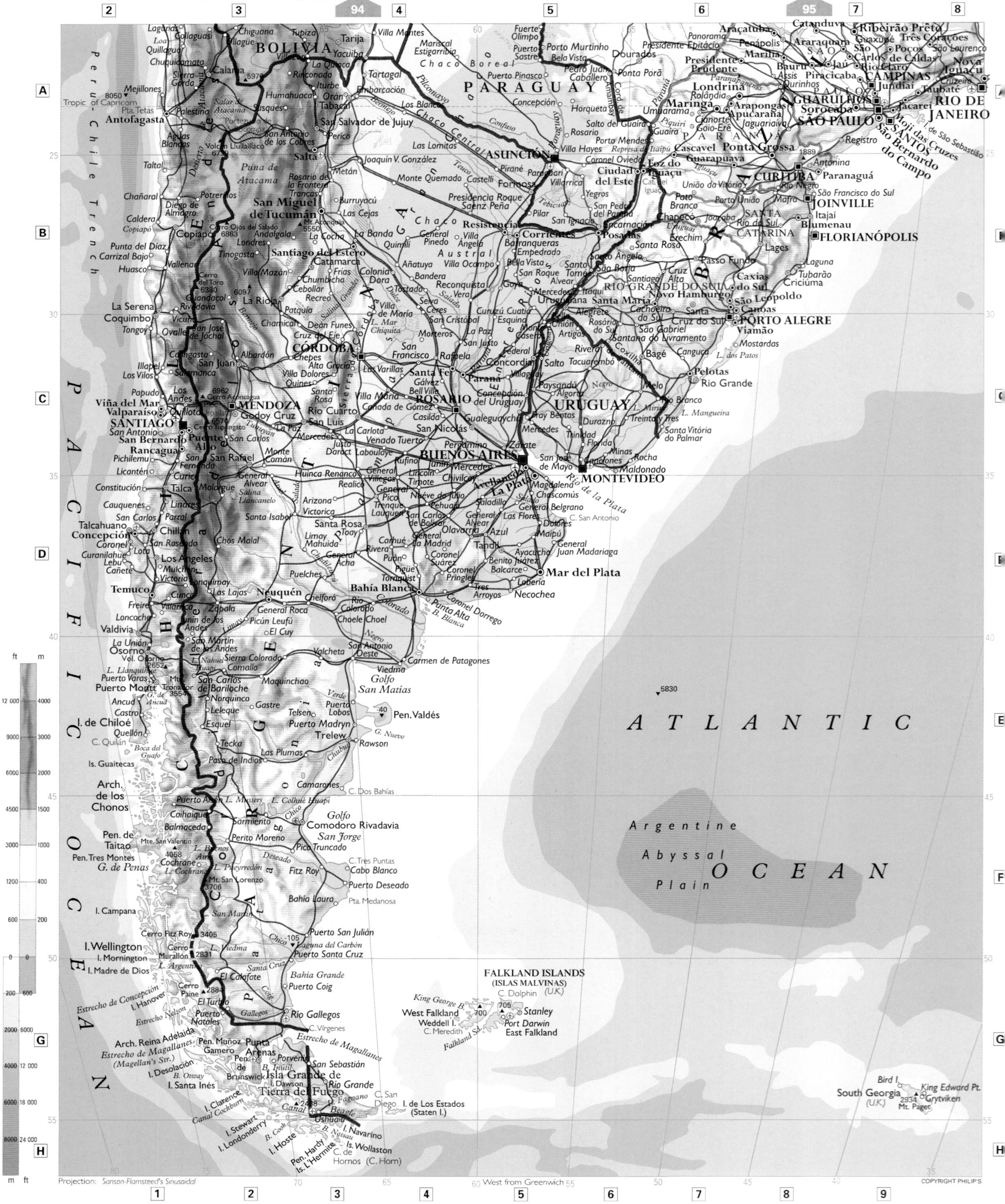

BOLIVIA

PARAGUAY

ASUNCIÓN

URUGUAY

MONTEVIDEO

BUENOS AIRES

CÓRDOBA

ROSARIO

MENDOZA

SANTIAGO

RIO DE JANEIRO

SÃO PAULO

GUARULHOS

CAMPINAS

CURITIBA

FLORIANÓPOLIS

PORTO ALEGRE

Mar del Plata

Bahía Blanca

Neuquén

Temuco

Valdivia

Puerto Montt

Comodoro Rivadavia

Río Gallegos

Punta Arenas

Isla Grande de Tierra del Fuego

Ushuaia

Hornos (C. Horn)

FALKLAND ISLANDS
(ISLAS MALVINAS)
(U.K.)
West Falkland
East Falkland
Stanley
Port Darwin

South Georgia
(U.K.)
Mt. Paget
King Edward Pt.
Grytviken

ATLANTIC

OCEAN

Argentine
Abyssal
Plain

PACIFIC OCEAN

Peru–Chile Trench

Tropic of Capricorn

Estrecho de Magallanes
(Magellan's Str.)

Projection: Sanson-Flamsteed's Sinusoidal

West from Greenwich

COPYRIGHT PHILIP'S

INDEX TO WORLD MAPS

The index contains the names of all the principal places and features shown on the World Maps. Each name is followed by an additional entry in italics giving the country or region within which it is located. The alphabetical order of names composed of two or more words is governed primarily by the first word, then by the second, and then by the country or region name that follows. This is an example of the rule:

Mīr Kūh *Iran*	26°22N 58°55E	**47** E8
Mīr Shahdād *Iran*	26°15N 58°29E	**47** E8
Mira *Italy*	45°26N 12°8E	**22** B5
Mira por vos Cay *Bahamas*	22°9N 74°30W	**89** B5

Physical features composed of a proper name (Erie) and a description (Lake) are positioned alphabetically by the proper name. The description is positioned after the proper name and is usually abbreviated:

Erie, L. *N. Amer.*	42°15N 81°0W	**82** D4

Where a description forms part of a settlement or administrative name, however, it is always written in full and put in its true alphabetical position:

Mount Morris *U.S.A.*	42°44N 77°52W	**82** D7

Names beginning with M' and Mc are indexed as if they were spelled Mac. Names beginning St. are alphabetized under Saint, but Sankt, Sint, Sant', Santa and San are all spelt in full and are alphabetized accordingly. If the same place name occurs two or more times in the index and all are in the same country, each is followed by the name of the administrative subdivision in which it is located.

The geographical co-ordinates which follow each name in the index give the latitude and longitude of each place. The first co-ordinate indicates latitude – the distance north or south of the Equator. The second co-ordinate indicates longitude – the distance east or west of the Greenwich Meridian. Both latitude and longitude are measured in degrees and minutes (there are 60 minutes in a degree).

The latitude is followed by N(orth) or S(outh) and the longitude by E(ast) or W(est).

The number in bold type which follows the geographical co-ordinates refers to the number of the map page where that feature or place will be found. This is usually the largest scale at which the place or feature appears.

The letter and figure that are immediately after the page number give the grid square on the map page, within which the feature is situated. The letter represents the latitude and the figure the longitude. A lower-case letter immediately after the page number refers to an inset map on that page.

In some cases the feature itself may fall within the specified square, while the name is outside. This is usually the case only with features that are larger than a grid square.

Rivers are indexed to their mouths or confluences, and carry the symbol ➔ after their names. The following symbols are also used in the index: ■ country, ☑ overseas territory or dependency, ☐ first-order administrative area, △ national park, ⌂ other park (provincial park, nature reserve or game reserve), ✖ (LHR) principal airport (and location identifier), ☼ Australian aboriginal land.

Abbreviations used in the index

A.C.T. – Australian Capital Territory
A.R. – Autonomous Region
Afghan. – Afghanistan
Afr. – Africa
Ala. – Alabama
Alta. – Alberta
Amer. – America(n)
Ant. – Antilles
Arch. – Archipelago
Ariz. – Arizona
Ark. – Arkansas
Atl. Oc. – Atlantic Ocean
B. – Baie, Bahía, Bay, Bucht, Bugt
B.C. – British Columbia
Bangla. – Bangladesh
Barr. – Barrage
Bos.-H. – Bosnia-Herzegovina
C. – Cabo, Cap, Cape, Coast
C.A.R. – Central African Republic
C. Prov. – Cape Province
Calif. – California
Cat. – Catarata
Cent. – Central
Chan. – Channel
Colo. – Colorado
Conn. – Connecticut
Cord. – Cordillera
Cr. – Creek
D.C. – District of Columbia
Del. – Delaware
Dem. – Democratic
Dep. – Dependency
Des. – Desert
Dét. – Détroit
Dist. – District
Dj. – Djebel
Dom. Rep. – Dominican Republic
E. – East

El Salv. – El Salvador
Eq. Guin. – Equatorial Guinea
Est. – Estrecho
Falk. Is. – Falkland Is.
Fd. – Fjord
Fla. – Florida
Fr. – French
G. – Golfe, Golfo, Gulf, Guba, Gebel
Ga. – Georgia
Gt. – Great, Greater
Guinea-Biss. – Guinea-Bissau
H.K. – Hong Kong
H.P. – Himachal Pradesh
Hants. – Hampshire
Harb. – Harbor, Harbour
Hd. – Head
Hts. – Heights
I.(s). – Île, Ilha, Insel, Isla, Island, Isle
Ill. – Illinois
Ind. – Indiana
Ind. Oc. – Indian Ocean
J. – Jabal, Jebel
Jaz. – Jazīrah
Junc. – Junction
K. – Kap, Kapp
Kans. – Kansas
Kep. – Kepulauan
Ky. – Kentucky
L. – Lac, Lacul, Lago, Lagoa, Lake, Limni, Loch, Lough
La. – Louisiana
Ld. – Land
Liech. – Liechtenstein
Lux. – Luxembourg
Mad. P. – Madhya Pradesh
Madag. – Madagascar
Man. – Manitoba
Mass. – Massachusetts
Md. – Maryland
Me. – Maine

Medit. S. – Mediterranean Sea
Mich. – Michigan
Minn. – Minnesota
Miss. – Mississippi
Mo. – Missouri
Mont. – Montana
Mozam. – Mozambique
Mt.(s) – Mont, Montaña, Mountain
Mte. – Monte
Mti. – Monti
N. – Nord, Norte, North, Northern, Nouveau, Nahal, Nahr
N.B. – New Brunswick
N.C. – North Carolina
N. Cal. – New Caledonia
N. Dak. – North Dakota
N.H. – New Hampshire
N.I. – North Island
N.J. – New Jersey
N. Mex. – New Mexico
N.S. – Nova Scotia
N.S.W. – New South Wales
N.W.T. – North West Territory
N.Y. – New York
N.Z. – New Zealand
Nac. – Nacional
Nat. – National
Nebr. – Nebraska
Neths. – Netherlands
Nev. – Nevada
Nfld & L. – Newfoundland and Labrador
Nic. – Nicaragua
O. – Oued, Ouadi
Occ. – Occidentale
Okla. – Oklahoma
Ont. – Ontario
Or. – Orientale
Oreg. – Oregon
Os. – Ostrov

Oz. – Ozero
P. – Pass, Passo, Pasul, Pulau
P.E.I. – Prince Edward Island
Pa. – Pennsylvania
Pac. Oc. – Pacific Ocean
Papua N.G. – Papua New Guinea
Pass. – Passage
Peg. – Pegunungan
Pen. – Peninsula, Péninsule
Phil. – Philippines
Pk. – Peak
Plat. – Plateau
Prov. – Province, Provincial
Pt. – Point
Pta. – Ponta, Punta
Pte. – Pointe
Qué. – Québec
Queens. – Queensland
R. – Rio, River
R.I. – Rhode Island
Ra. – Range
Raj. – Rajasthan
Recr. – Recreational, Récréatif
Reg. – Region
Rep. – Republic
Res. – Reserve, Reservoir
Rhld-Pfz. – Rheinland-Pfalz
S. – South, Southern, Sur
Si. Arabia – Saudi Arabia
S.C. – South Carolina
S. Dak. – South Dakota
S.I. – South Island
S. Leone – Sierra Leone
Sa. – Serra, Sierra
Sask. – Saskatchewan
Scot. – Scotland
Sd. – Sound
Sev. – Severnaya
Sib. – Siberia
Sprs. – Springs
St. – Saint

Sta. – Santa
Ste. – Sainte
Sto. – Santo
Str. – Strait, Stretto
Switz. – Switzerland
Tas. – Tasmania
Tenn. – Tennessee
Terr. – Territory, Territoire
Tex. – Texas
Tg. – Tanjung
Trin. & Tob. – Trinidad & Tobago
U.A.E. – United Arab Emirates
U.K. – United Kingdom
U.S.A. – United States of America
Ut. P. – Uttar Pradesh
Va. – Virginia
Vdkhr. – Vodokhranilishche
Vdskh. – Vodoskhovyshche
Vf. – Vîrful
Vic. – Victoria
Vol. – Volcano
Vt. – Vermont
W. – Wadi, West
W. Va. – West Virginia
Wall. & F. Is. – Wallis and Futuna Is.
Wash. – Washington
Wis. – Wisconsin
Wlkp. – Wielkopolski
Wyo. – Wyoming
Yorks. – Yorkshire

A

A Coruña Spain 43°20N 8°25W 21 A1
A Estrada Spain 42°43N 8°27W 21 A1
A Fonsagrada Spain 43°8N 7°4W 21 A2
A Shau Vietnam 16°6N 107°22E 38 D6
Aabenraa Denmark 55°3N 9°25E 9 J13
Aachen Germany 50°45N 6°6E 16 C4
Aalborg Denmark 57°2N 9°54E 9 H13
Aalen Germany 48°51N 10°6E 16 D6
Aalst Belgium 50°56N 4°2E 15 D4
Aalten Neths. 51°56N 6°35E 15 C6
Aalter Belgium 51°5N 3°28E 15 C3
Äänekoski Finland 62°36N 25°44E 8 E21
Aarau Switz. 47°23N 8°4E 20 C8
Aare → Switz. 47°33N 8°14E 20 C8
Aarhus Denmark 56°8N 10°11E 9 H14
Aarschot Belgium 50°59N 4°49E 15 D4
Aba China 32°59N 101°42E 34 A3
Aba Nigeria 5°10N 7°19E 52 G7
Abaco I. Bahamas 26°25N 77°10W 88 A4
Ābādān Iran 30°22N 48°20E 47 D6
Ābādeh Iran 31°8N 52°40E 47 D7
Abadla Algeria 31°2N 2°45W 52 B5
Abaetetuba Brazil 1°40S 48°50W 93 D9
Abagnar Qi = Xilinhot
  China 43°52N 116°2E 32 C9
Abah, Tanjung Indonesia 8°46S 115°38E 37 K18
Abai Paraguay 25°58S 55°54W 95 B4
Abakan Russia 53°40N 91°10E 27 D10
Abancay Peru 13°35S 72°55W 92 F4
Abang, Gunung
  Indonesia 8°16S 115°25E 37 J18
Abariringa Kiribati 2°50S 171°40W 64 H10
Abarqū Iran 31°10N 53°20E 47 D7
Abashiri Japan 44°0N 144°15E 28 B12
Abashiri-Wan Japan 44°0N 144°30E 28 C12
Ābay = Nîl el Azraq →
  Sudan 15°38N 32°31E 53 E12
Abay Kazakhstan 49°38N 72°53E 26 E8
Abaya, L. Ethiopia 6°30N 37°50E 49 F2
Abaza Russia 52°39N 90°6E 26 D10
'Abbāsābād Iran 33°34N 58°23E 47 C8
Abbay = Nîl el Azraq →
  Sudan 15°38N 32°31E 53 E12
Abbaye, Pt. U.S.A. 46°58N 88°8W 80 B9
Abbé, L. Ethiopia 11°8N 41°47E 49 E3
Abbeville France 50°6N 1°49E 20 A4
Abbeville Ala., U.S.A. 31°34N 85°15W 85 F12
Abbeville La., U.S.A. 29°58N 92°8W 84 G8
Abbeville S.C., U.S.A. 34°11N 82°23W 85 D13
Abbeyfeale Ireland 52°23N 9°18W 10 D2
Abbeyleix Ireland 52°54N 7°22W 10 D4
Abbot Ice Shelf Antarctica 73°0S 92°0W 5 D16
Abbotsford Canada 49°5N 122°20W 70 D4
Abbottabad Pakistan 34°10N 73°15E 42 B5
ABC Islands W. Indies 12°15N 69°0W 89 D6
Abd al Kūrī Yemen 12°5N 52°20E 49 E5
Ābdar Iran 30°16N 55°19E 47 D7
'Abdolābād Iran 34°12N 56°30E 47 C8
Abdulpur Bangla. 24°15N 88°59E 43 G13
Abéché Chad 13°50N 20°35E 53 F10
Abel Tasman △ N.Z. 40°59S 173°3E 59 D4
Abengourou Côte d'Ivoire 6°42N 3°27W 52 G5
Åbenrå = Aabenraa
  Denmark 55°3N 9°25E 9 J13
Abeokuta Nigeria 7°3N 3°19E 52 G6
Aberaeron U.K. 52°15N 4°15W 13 E3
Aberayron = Aberaeron
  U.K. 52°15N 4°15W 13 E3
Aberchirder U.K. 57°34N 2°37W 11 D6
Abercorn Australia 25°12S 151°5E 63 D5
Aberdare U.K. 51°43N 3°27W 13 F4
Aberdaugleddau = Milford Haven
  U.K. 51°42N 5°7W 13 F2
Aberdeen Australia 32°9S 150°56E 63 E5
Aberdeen Canada 52°20N 106°8W 71 C7
Aberdeen S. Africa 32°28S 24°2E 56 D3
Aberdeen U.K. 57°9N 2°5W 11 D6
Aberdeen Idaho, U.S.A. 42°57N 112°50W 76 E7
Aberdeen Md., U.S.A. 39°31N 76°10W 81 F15
Aberdeen Miss., U.S.A. 33°49N 88°33W 85 E10
Aberdeen S. Dak., U.S.A. 45°28N 98°29W 80 C4
Aberdeen Wash., U.S.A. 46°59N 123°50W 78 D3
Aberdeen City □ U.K. 57°10N 2°10W 11 D6
Aberdeen L. Canada 64°30N 99°0W 68 E12
Aberdeenshire □ U.K. 57°17N 2°36W 11 D6
Aberdovey = Aberdyfi
  U.K. 52°33N 4°3W 13 E3
Aberdyfi U.K. 52°33N 4°3W 13 E3
Aberfeldy U.K. 56°37N 3°51W 11 E5
Aberfoyle U.K. 56°11N 4°23W 11 E4
Abergavenny U.K. 51°49N 3°1W 13 F4
Abergele U.K. 53°17N 3°35W 12 D4
Abergwaun = Fishguard
  U.K. 52°0N 4°58W 13 F3
Aberhonddu = Brecon
  U.K. 51°57N 3°23W 13 F4
Abermaw = Barmouth
  U.K. 52°44N 4°4W 12 E3
Abernathy U.S.A. 33°50N 101°51W 84 E4
Aberpennar = Mountain Ash
  U.K. 51°40N 3°23W 13 F4
Abert, L. U.S.A. 42°38N 120°14W 76 E3
Abertawe = Swansea
  U.K. 51°37N 3°57W 13 F4
Aberteifi = Cardigan U.K. 52°5N 4°40W 13 E3
Aberystwyth U.K. 52°25N 4°5W 13 E3
Abhā Si. Arabia 18°0N 42°34E 49 D3
Abhar Iran 36°9N 49°13E 47 B6
Abhayapuri India 26°24N 90°38E 43 F14
Abidjan Côte d'Ivoire 5°26N 3°58W 52 G5
Abilene Kans., U.S.A. 38°55N 97°13W 80 F5
Abilene Tex., U.S.A. 32°28N 99°43W 84 E5
Abingdon U.K. 36°43N 81°59W 81 G13
Abingdon-on-Thames
  U.K. 51°40N 1°17W 13 F6
Abington Reef Australia 18°0S 149°35E 62 B4
Abisko △ Sweden 68°18N 18°44E 8 B18
Abitau → Canada 59°53N 109°3W 71 B7

Abitibi → Canada 51°3N 80°55W 72 B3
Abitibi, L. Canada 48°40N 79°40W 72 C4
Abkhaz Republic = Abkhazia □
  Georgia 43°12N 41°5E 19 F7
Abkhazia □ Georgia 43°12N 41°5E 19 F7
Abminga Australia 26°8S 134°51E 63 D1
Åbo = Turku Finland 60°30N 22°19E 9 F20
Abohar India 30°10N 74°10E 42 D6
Abomey Benin 7°10N 2°5E 52 G6
Abong-Mbang Cameroon 4°0N 13°8E 54 D2
Abou-Deïa Chad 11°20N 19°20E 53 F9
Aboyne U.K. 57°4N 2°47W 11 D6
Abra Pampa Argentina 22°43S 65°42W 94 A2
Abraham L. Canada 52°15N 116°35W 70 C5
Abreojos, Pta. Mexico 26°50N 113°40W 86 B2
Abrolhos, Banco dos Brazil 18°0S 38°40W 90 E7
Abrud Romania 46°19N 23°5E 17 E12
Absaroka Range U.S.A. 44°45N 109°50W 76 D9
Abu India 24°41N 72°50E 42 G5
Abū al Abyad U.A.E. 24°11N 53°50E 47 E7
Abū al Khaṣīb Iraq 30°25N 48°0E 46 D5
Abū 'Alī Si. Arabia 27°20N 49°27E 47 E6
Abū 'Alī → Lebanon 34°25N 35°50E 48 A4
Abu Dhabi = Abū Ẓāby
  U.A.E. 24°28N 54°22E 47 E7
Abū Du'ān Syria 36°25N 38°15E 46 B3
Abu el Gaïn, W. → Egypt 29°35N 33°30E 48 F2
Abu Ga'da, W. → Egypt 29°15N 32°53E 48 F1
Abū Ḥadrīyah Si. Arabia 27°20N 48°58E 47 E6
Abū Hamed Sudan 19°32N 33°13E 53 E12
Abū Kamāl Syria 34°30N 41°0E 46 C4
Abū Madd, Ra's Si. Arabia 24°50N 37°7E 46 E3
Abū Mūsā U.A.E. 25°52N 55°3E 47 E7
Abū Qaşr Si. Arabia 30°21N 38°34E 46 D3
Abu Shagara, Ras Sudan 21°4N 37°19E 53 D13
Abu Simbel Egypt 22°18N 31°40E 53 D12
Abū Şukhayr Iraq 31°54N 44°30E 46 D5
Abu Zabad Sudan 12°25N 29°10E 53 F11
Abū Ẓāby U.A.E. 24°28N 54°22E 47 E7
Abū Zeydābād Iran 33°54N 51°45E 47 C6
Abuja Nigeria 9°5N 7°32E 52 G7
Abukuma-Gawa →
  Japan 38°6N 140°52E 28 E10
Abukuma-Sammyaku
  Japan 37°30N 140°45E 28 F10
Abunã Brazil 9°40S 65°20W 92 E5
Abunã → Brazil 9°41S 65°20W 92 E5
Abut Hd. N.Z. 43°7S 170°15E 59 E3
Abyei ☑ Sudan 9°30N 28°30E 53 G11
Åbyek Iran 36°9N 50°33E 47 B6
Acadia △ U.S.A. 44°20N 68°13W 81 C19
Açailândia Brazil 4°57S 47°30W 93 D9
Acajutla El Salv. 13°36N 89°50W 88 D2
Acámbaro Mexico 20°2N 100°44W 86 D4
Acaponeta Mexico 22°30N 105°22W 86 C3
Acapulco Mexico 16°51N 99°55W 87 D5
Acapulco Trench Pac. Oc. 12°0N 88°0W 86 D4
Acaraí, Serra Brazil 1°50N 57°50W 92 C7
Acaraí Mts. = Acaraí, Serra
  Brazil 1°50N 57°50W 92 C7
Acarigua Venezuela 9°33N 69°12W 92 B5
Acatlán Mexico 18°12N 98°3W 87 D5
Acayucán Mexico 17°57N 94°55W 87 D6
Accomac U.S.A. 37°43N 75°40W 81 G16
Accra Ghana 5°35N 0°6W 52 G5
Accrington U.K. 53°45N 2°22W 12 D5
Acebal Argentina 33°20S 60°50W 94 C3
Aceh □ Indonesia 4°15N 97°30E 36 D1
Achalpur India 21°22N 77°32E 44 D3
Acharnes Greece 38°5N 23°44E 23 E10
Acheloos → Greece 38°19N 21°7E 23 E9
Acher India 23°10N 72°32E 42 H5
Acheng China 45°30N 126°58E 33 B14
Achill Hd. Ireland 53°58N 10°15W 10 C1
Achill I. Ireland 53°58N 10°1W 10 C1
Achinsk Russia 56°20N 90°20E 27 D10
Acireale Italy 37°37N 15°10E 22 F6
Ackerman U.S.A. 33°19N 89°11W 85 E10
Acklins I. Bahamas 22°30N 74°0W 89 B5
Acme Canada 51°33N 113°30W 70 C6
Aconcagua, Cerro
  Argentina 32°39S 70°0W 94 C2
Aconquija, Mt. Argentina 27°0S 66°0W 94 B2
Açores, Is. dos Atl. Oc. 38°0N 27°0W 52 a
Acornhoek S. Africa 24°37S 31°2E 57 B5
Acraman, L. Australia 32°2S 135°23E 63 E2
Acre = 'Akko Israel 32°55N 35°4E 48 C4
Acre □ Brazil 9°1S 71°0W 92 E4
Acre → Brazil 8°45S 67°22W 92 E5
Actinolite Canada 44°32N 77°19W 82 B7
Acton Canada 43°38N 80°3W 82 C4
Ad Dahnā Si. Arabia 24°30N 48°10E 49 C4
Ad Dammām Si. Arabia 26°20N 50°5E 47 E6
Ad Dāmūr Lebanon 33°43N 35°27E 48 B4
Ad Dawādimī Si. Arabia 24°35N 44°15E 46 E5
Ad Dawḥah Qatar 25°15N 51°35E 47 E6
Ad Dawr Iraq 34°27N 43°47E 46 C4
Ad Dhakhīrah Qatar 25°44N 51°33E 47 E6
Ad Dir'īyah Si. Arabia 24°44N 46°35E 46 E5
Ad Dīwānīyah Iraq 32°0N 45°0E 46 D5
Ad Dujayl Iraq 33°51N 44°14E 46 C5
Ad Duwayd Si. Arabia 30°15N 42°17E 46 D4
Ada Minn., U.S.A. 47°18N 96°31W 80 B5
Ada Okla., U.S.A. 34°46N 96°41W 84 D6
Adabiya Egypt 29°53N 32°28E 48 F1
Adair, C. Canada 71°30N 71°34W 69 C17
Adaja → Spain 41°32N 4°52W 21 B3
Adak U.S.A. 51°45N 176°45W 74 E4
Adak I. U.S.A. 51°45N 176°45W 74 E4
Adama = Nazret Ethiopia 8°32N 39°22E 49 F2
Adamaoua, Massif de l'
  Cameroon 7°20N 12°20E 53 G8
Adamawa Highlands =
  Adamaoua, Massif de l'
  Cameroon 7°20N 12°20E 53 G8
Adamello, Mte. Italy 46°9N 10°30E 20 C9
Adaminaby Australia 36°0S 148°45E 63 F4
Adams Mass., U.S.A. 42°38N 73°7W 83 D11
Adams N.Y., U.S.A. 43°49N 76°1W 83 C8

Adams Wis., U.S.A. 43°57N 89°49W 80 D9
Adams, Mt. U.S.A. 46°12N 121°30W 78 D5
Adam's Bridge Sri Lanka 9°15N 79°40E 45 K4
Adam's Peak Sri Lanka 6°48N 80°30E 45 L5
'Adan Yemen 12°45N 45°0E 49 E4
Adana Turkey 37°0N 35°16E 46 B2
Adang, Ko Thailand 6°33N 99°18E 39 J2
Adapazarı = Sakarya
  Turkey 40°48N 30°25E 19 F5
Adarama Sudan 17°10N 34°52E 53 E12
Adare Ireland 52°34N 8°47W 10 D3
Adare, C. Antarctica 71°0S 171°0E 5 D11
Adaut Indonesia 8°8S 131°7E 37 F8
Adavale Australia 25°52S 144°32E 63 D3
Adda → Italy 45°8N 9°53E 20 B8
Addatigala India 17°31N 82°3E 44 F6
Addis Ababa = Addis Abeba
  Ethiopia 9°2N 38°42E 49 F2
Addis Abeba Ethiopia 9°2N 38°42E 49 F2
Addison U.S.A. 42°1N 77°14W 82 D7
Addo S. Africa 33°32S 25°45E 56 D4
Addo △ S. Africa 33°30S 25°50E 56 D4
Ādeh Iran 37°42N 45°11E 46 B5
Adel U.S.A. 31°8N 83°25W 85 F13
Adelaide Australia 34°52S 138°30E 63 E2
Adelaide S. Africa 32°42S 26°20E 56 D4
Adelaide I. Antarctica 67°15S 68°30W 5 C17
Adelaide Pen. Canada 68°15N 97°30W 68 D12
Adelaide River Australia 13°15S 131°7E 60 B5
Adelaide Village Bahamas 25°0N 77°31W 88 A4
Adelanto U.S.A. 34°35N 117°22W 79 L9
Adele I. Australia 15°32S 123°9E 60 C3
Adélie, Terre Antarctica 68°0S 140°0E 5 C10
Adelie Land = Adélie, Terre
  Antarctica 68°0S 140°0E 5 C10
Aden = 'Adan Yemen 12°45N 45°0E 49 E4
Aden, G. of Ind. Oc. 12°30N 47°30E 49 E4
Adendorp S. Africa 32°15S 24°30E 56 D3
Adh Dhayd U.A.E. 25°17N 55°53E 47 E7
Adhoi India 23°26N 70°32E 42 H4
Adi Indonesia 4°15S 133°30E 37 E8
Adieu, C. Australia 32°0S 132°10E 61 F5
Adieu Pt. Australia 15°14S 124°35E 60 C3
Adige → Italy 45°9N 12°20E 22 B5
Adigrat Ethiopia 14°20N 39°26E 49 E2
Adilabad India 19°33N 78°20E 44 E4
Adirondack △ U.S.A. 44°0N 74°20W 83 C10
Adirondack Mts. U.S.A. 44°0N 74°0W 83 C10
Adis Abeba = Addis Abeba
  Ethiopia 9°2N 38°42E 49 F2
Adjuntas Puerto Rico 18°10N 66°43W 89 d
Adlavik Is. Canada 55°0N 58°40W 73 B8
Admiralty G. Australia 14°20S 125°55E 60 B4
Admiralty Gulf ☺
  Australia 14°16S 125°52E 60 B4
Admiralty I. U.S.A. 57°30N 134°30W 70 B2
Admiralty Inlet Canada 72°30N 86°0W 69 C14
Admiralty Is. Papua N. G. 2°0S 147°0E 58 B7
Adolfo González Chaves
  Argentina 38°2S 60°5W 94 D3
Adolfo Ruiz Cortines, Presa
  Mexico 27°15N 109°6W 86 B3
Adonara Indonesia 8°15S 123°5E 37 F6
Adoni India 15°33N 77°18E 45 G3
Adour → France 43°32N 1°32W 20 E3
Adra Indonesia 23°30N 86°42E 43 H12
Adra Spain 36°43N 3°3W 21 D4
Adrano Italy 37°40N 14°50E 22 F6
Adrar Algeria 27°51N 0°19W 52 C6
Adrar Mauritania 20°30N 7°30W 52 D3
Adrar des Iforas Africa 19°40N 1°40E 52 E6
Adrian Mich., U.S.A. 41°54N 84°2W 81 E11
Adrian Tex., U.S.A. 35°16N 102°40W 84 D3
Adriatic Sea Medit. S. 43°0N 16°0E 22 C6
Adua Indonesia 1°45S 129°50E 37 E7
Adur India 9°8N 76°40E 45 K3
Adwa Ethiopia 14°15N 38°52E 49 E2
Adygea □ Russia 45°0N 40°0E 19 F7
Adzhar Republic = Ajaria □
  Georgia 41°30N 42°0E 19 F7
Adzopé Côte d'Ivoire 6°7N 3°49W 52 G5
Ægean Sea Medit. S. 38°30N 25°0E 23 E11
Aerhtai Shan Mongolia 46°40N 92°45E 30 B7
Afaahiti Tahiti 17°45S 149°17W 59 d
'Afak Iraq 32°4N 45°15E 46 C5
Afareaitu Moorea 17°33S 149°47W 59 d
Afghanistan ■ Asia 33°0N 65°0E 40 C4
Aflou Algeria 34°7N 2°3E 52 B6
Afognak I. U.S.A. 58°15N 152°30W 74 D9
Africa 10°0N 20°0E 50 E6
'Afrīn Syria 36°32N 36°50E 46 B3
Afton N.Y., U.S.A. 42°14N 75°32W 83 D9
Afton Wyo., U.S.A. 42°44N 110°56W 76 E8
Afuá Brazil 0°15S 50°20W 93 D8
'Afula Israel 32°37N 35°17E 48 C4
Afyon Turkey 38°45N 30°33E 19 G5
Afyonkarahisar = Afyon
  Turkey 38°45N 30°33E 19 G5
Ağa Jarī Iran 30°42N 49°50E 47 D6
Agadès = Agadez Niger 16°58N 7°59E 52 E7
Agadez Niger 16°58N 7°59E 52 E7
Agadir Morocco 30°28N 9°55W 52 B4
Agalega Is. Mauritius 11°0S 57°0E 3 E12
Agar India 23°40N 76°2E 42 H7
Agar → India 21°0N 82°57E 44 D6
Agartala India 23°50N 91°23E 41 H17
Agassiz Canada 49°14N 121°46W 70 D4
Agassiz Icecap Canada 80°15N 76°0W 69 A16
Agats Indonesia 5°33S 138°0E 37 F9
Agatti I. India 10°50N 72°12E 45 J1
Agawam U.S.A. 42°5N 72°37W 83 D12
Agboville Côte d'Ivoire 5°55N 4°15W 52 G5
Ağdam Azerbaijan 40°0N 46°58E 46 B5
Agde France 43°19N 3°28E 20 E5
Agen France 44°12N 0°38E 20 D4
Āgh Kand Iran 37°15N 48°4E 47 B6
Aghios Efstratios Greece 39°34N 24°58E 23 E11
Aghiou Orous, Kolpos
  Greece 40°6N 24°0E 23 D11

Aginskoye Russia 51°6N 114°32E 27 D12
Agnew Australia 28°1S 120°31E 61 E3
Agori India 24°33N 82°57E 43 G10
Agra India 27°17N 77°58E 42 F7
Ağrı Turkey 39°44N 43°3E 19 G7
Agri → Italy 40°13N 16°44E 22 D7
Ağrı Dağı Turkey 39°50N 44°15E 46 B5
Ağrı Karakose = Ağrı
  Turkey 39°44N 43°3E 19 G7
Agrigento Italy 37°19N 13°34E 22 F5
Agrinio Greece 38°37N 21°27E 23 E9
Agua Caliente Mexico 32°29N 116°59W 79 N10
Agua Caliente Springs
  U.S.A. 32°56N 116°19W 79 N10
Água Clara Brazil 20°25S 52°45W 93 H8
Agua Fria △ U.S.A. 34°14N 112°0W 77 J8
Agua Hechicera
  Mexico 32°38N 116°15W 79 N10
Agua Prieta Mexico 31°18N 109°34W 86 A3
Aguadilla Puerto Rico 18°26N 67°10W 89 d
Aguadulce Panama 8°15N 80°32E 88 E3
Aguanga U.S.A. 33°27N 116°51W 79 M10
Aguanish Canada 50°14N 62°2W 73 B7
Aguanish → Canada 50°13N 62°5W 73 B7
Aguapey → Argentina 29°7S 56°36W 94 B4
Aguaray Guazú →
  Paraguay 24°47S 57°19W 94 A4
Aguarico → Ecuador 0°59S 75°11W 92 D3
Aguaro-Guariquito △
  Venezuela 8°20N 66°35W 89 E6
Aguas Blancas Chile 24°15S 69°55W 94 A2
Aguas Calientes, Sierra de
  Argentina 25°26S 66°40W 94 B2
Aguascalientes Mexico 21°53N 102°18W 86 C4
Aguascalientes □
  Mexico 22°0N 102°20W 86 C4
Aguila, Punta Puerto Rico 17°57N 67°13W 89 d
Aguilares Argentina 27°26S 65°35W 94 B2
Águilas Spain 37°23N 1°35W 21 D5
Aguja, C. de la Colombia 11°18N 74°12W 90 B3
Agujereada, Pta.
  Puerto Rico 18°30N 67°8W 89 d
Agulhas, C. S. Africa 34°52S 20°0E 56 D3
Agung, Gunung
  Indonesia 8°20S 115°28E 37 J18
Aguni-Jima Japan 26°30N 127°10E 29 L3
Agusan → Phil. 9°0N 125°30E 37 C7
Aha Mts. Botswana 19°45S 21°0E 56 B3
Ahaggar Algeria 23°0N 6°30E 52 D7
Ahai Dam China 27°21N 100°30E 34 D3
Ahar Iran 38°35N 47°0E 46 B5
Ahipara B. N.Z. 35°5S 173°5E 59 A4
Ahiri India 19°30N 80°0E 44 E5
Ahmad Wal Pakistan 29°18N 65°58E 42 E1
Ahmadabad Iran 35°3N 60°50E 47 C9
Ahmadābād Khorāsān, Iran 35°3N 60°50E 47 C9
Ahmadābād Khorāsān,
  Iran 35°49N 59°42E 47 C8
Ahmadī Iran 27°56N 56°42E 47 E8
Ahmadnagar India 19°7N 74°46E 44 E2
Ahmadpur India 18°40N 76°57E 44 E3
Ahmadpur East Pakistan 29°12N 71°10E 42 E4
Ahmadpur Lamma
  Pakistan 28°19N 70°3E 42 E4
Ahmedabad = Ahmadabad
  India 23°0N 72°40E 42 H5
Ahmednagar = Ahmadnagar
  India 19°7N 74°46E 44 E2
Ahome Mexico 25°55N 109°11W 86 B3
Ahoskie U.S.A. 36°17N 76°59W 85 C16
Ahram Iran 28°52N 51°16E 47 D6
Ahuachapán El Salv. 13°54N 89°52W 88 D2
Ahvāz Iran 31°20N 48°40E 47 D6
Ahvenanmaa = Åland
  Finland 60°15N 20°0E 9 F19
Ahwar Yemen 13°30N 46°40E 49 E4
Ai → India 26°26N 90°44E 43 F14
Ai-Ais Namibia 27°54S 17°59E 56 C2
Ai-Ais and Fish River Canyon △
  Namibia 24°45S 17°15E 56 B2
Aichi □ Japan 35°0N 137°15E 29 G8
Aigrettes, Pte. des Réunion 21°3S 55°13E 55 c
Aiguá Uruguay 34°13S 54°46W 95 C5
Aigues-Mortes France 43°35N 4°12E 20 E6
Aihui = Heihe China 50°10N 127°30E 31 A14
Aija Peru 9°50S 77°45W 92 E3
Aikawa Japan 38°2N 138°15E 28 E9
Aiken U.S.A. 33°34N 81°43W 85 E14
Ailao Shan China 24°0N 101°20E 34 F3
Aileron Australia 22°39S 133°20E 62 C1
Aillik Canada 55°11N 59°18W 73 A8
Ailsa Craig Canada 43°8N 81°33W 82 C3
Ailsa Craig U.K. 55°15N 5°6W 11 F3
Aim Russia 59°0N 133°55E 27 D14
Aimogasta Argentina 28°33S 66°50W 94 B2
Aïn Ben Tili Mauritania 25°59N 9°27E 52 C4
Aïn Sefra Algeria 32°47N 0°37W 52 B5
Ain Sudr Egypt 29°50N 33°6E 48 F2
Aïn Témouchent Algeria 35°16N 1°8W 52 A5
Ainaži Latvia 57°50N 24°24E 9 H21
Ainsworth U.S.A. 42°33N 99°52W 80 D4
Aiquile Bolivia 18°10S 65°10W 92 G5
Aïr Niger 18°30N 8°0E 52 E7
Air Force I. Canada 67°58N 74°5W 69 D17
Air Hitam Malaysia 1°55N 103°11E 39 M4
Airdrie Canada 51°18N 114°2W 70 C6
Airdrie U.K. 55°52N 3°57W 11 F5
Aire → U.K. 53°43N 0°55W 12 D7
Airlie Beach Australia 20°16S 148°43E 62 b
Aisne → France 49°26N 2°50E 20 B5
Ait India 25°54N 79°14E 43 G8
Aitkin U.S.A. 46°32N 93°42W 80 B7
Aitutaki Cook Is. 18°52S 159°45W 65 J12
Aiud Romania 46°19N 23°44E 17 E12
Aix-en-Provence France 43°32N 5°27E 20 E6
Aix-la-Chapelle = Aachen
  Germany 50°45N 6°6E 16 C4
Aix-les-Bains France 45°41N 5°53E 20 D6
Aizawl India 23°40N 92°44E 41 H18
Aizkraukle Latvia 56°36N 25°11E 9 H21

Aizpute Latvia 56°43N 21°40E 9 H19
Aizuwakamatsu Japan 37°30N 139°56E 28 F9
Ajaccio France 41°55N 8°40E 20 F8
Ajaigarh India 24°52N 80°16E 43 G9
Ajalpan Mexico 18°22N 97°15W 87 D5
Ajanta India 20°30N 75°48E 44 D2
Ajanta Ra. India 20°28N 75°50E 44 D2
Ajari Rep. = Ajaria □
  Georgia 41°30N 42°0E 19 F7
Ajaria □ Georgia 41°30N 42°0E 19 F7
Ajax Canada 43°50N 79°1W 82 C5
Ajdābiyā Libya 30°54N 20°4E 53 B10
Ajitgarh India 30°47N 76°41E 42 D7
Ajka Hungary 47°4N 17°31E 17 E9
'Ajlūn Jordan 32°18N 35°47E 48 C4
'Ajlūn □ Jordan 32°18N 35°47E 48 C4
'Ajmān U.A.E. 25°25N 55°30E 47 E7
Ajmer India 26°28N 74°37E 42 F6
Ajnala India 31°50N 74°48E 42 D6
Ajo U.S.A. 32°22N 112°52W 77 K7
Ajo, C. de Spain 43°31N 3°35W 21 A4
Akabira Japan 43°33N 142°5E 28 C11
Akalkot India 17°30N 76°13E 44 F3
Akan △ Japan 43°20N 144°20E 28 C12
Akaroa N.Z. 43°49S 172°59E 59 E4
Akashi Japan 34°45N 134°58E 29 G7
Akbarpur Bihar, India 24°39N 83°58E 43 G10
Akbarpur Ut. P., India 26°25N 82°32E 43 F10
Akçakale Turkey 36°41N 38°56E 46 B3
Akelamo Indonesia 1°35N 129°40E 37 D7
Akeru → India 17°25N 80°5E 44 F5
Aketi Dem. Rep. of the Congo 2°38N 23°47E 54 D4
Akhisar Turkey 38°56N 27°48E 23 E12
Akhnur India 32°52N 74°45E 43 C6
Akhtyrka = Okhtyrka
  Ukraine 50°25N 35°0E 19 D5
Aki Japan 33°30N 133°54E 29 H6
Akimiski I. Canada 52°50N 81°30W 72 B3
Akiōta Japan 34°36N 132°19E 29 G6
Akita Japan 39°45N 140°7E 28 E10
Akita □ Japan 39°40N 140°30E 28 E10
Akjoujt Mauritania 19°45N 14°15W 52 E3
Akkaraipattu Sri Lanka 7°13N 81°51E 45 L5
Akkeshi Japan 43°2N 144°51E 28 C12
'Akko Israel 32°55N 35°4E 48 C4
Aklavik Canada 68°12N 135°0W 68 D4
Aklera India 24°26N 76°32E 42 G7
Akō Japan 34°45N 134°24E 29 G7
Akola Maharashtra, India 20°42N 77°2E 44 D3
Akola Maharashtra, India 19°32N 74°3E 44 E2
Akordat Eritrea 15°30N 37°40E 49 D2
Akot India 21°10N 77°10E 44 D3
Akpatok I. Canada 60°25N 68°8W 69 E18
Åkrahamn Norway 59°15N 5°10E 9 G11
Akranes Iceland 64°19N 22°5W 8 D2
Akron Colo., U.S.A. 40°10N 103°13W 76 F12
Akron Ohio, U.S.A. 41°5N 81°31W 82 E3
Aksai Chin China 35°15N 79°55E 43 B8
Aksaray Turkey 38°25N 34°2E 46 B2
Aksay = Aqsay Kazakhstan 51°11N 53°0E 19 D9
Akşehir Turkey 38°18N 31°30E 46 B1
Akşehir Gölü Turkey 38°30N 31°25E 19 G5
Aksu China 41°5N 80°10E 30 C5
Aksum Ethiopia 14°5N 38°40E 49 E2
Aktsyabrski Belarus 52°38N 28°53E 17 B15
Aktyubinsk = Aqtöbe
  Kazakhstan 50°17N 57°10E 19 D10
Akure Nigeria 7°15N 5°5E 52 G7
Akureyri Iceland 65°40N 18°6W 8 D4
Akuseki-Shima Japan 29°27N 129°37E 29 K4
Akyab = Sittwe
  Myanmar 20°18N 92°45E 41 J18
Al 'Adan = 'Adan Yemen 12°45N 45°0E 49 E4
Al Aḥsā = Hasa Si. Arabia 25°50N 49°0E 47 E6
Al Ajfar Si. Arabia 27°26N 43°0E 46 E4
Al Amādīyah Iraq 37°5N 43°30E 46 B4
Al 'Amārah Iraq 31°55N 47°15E 46 D5
Al Anbār □ Iraq 33°25N 42°0E 46 C4
Al 'Aqabah Jordan 29°31N 35°0E 48 F4
Al 'Aqabah □ Jordan 29°40N 35°5E 48 F4
Al Arak Syria 34°38N 38°35E 46 C3
Al 'Aramah Si. Arabia 25°30N 46°0E 46 E5
Al 'Arṭāwīyah Si. Arabia 26°31N 45°20E 46 E5
Al 'Āşimah □ Jordan 31°40N 36°30E 48 D5
Al 'Assāfiyah Si. Arabia 28°17N 38°59E 46 D3
Al 'Awdah Si. Arabia 25°32N 45°41E 46 E5
Al 'Ayn Si. Arabia 25°4N 38°6E 46 E3
Al 'Ayn U.A.E. 24°15N 55°45E 47 E7
Al 'Azīzīyah Iraq 32°54N 45°4E 46 C5
Al Bāb Syria 36°23N 37°29E 46 B3
Al Bad' Si. Arabia 28°28N 35°1E 46 D2
Al Bada'i' Si. Arabia 26°2N 43°33E 46 E4
Al Bāḍī Iraq 35°56N 41°32E 46 C4
Al Bāhah Si. Arabia 20°1N 41°28E 49 D3
Al Bahral Mayyit = Dead Sea
  Asia 31°30N 35°30E 48 D4
Al Balqā' □ Jordan 32°5N 35°45E 48 C4
Al Bārūk, J. Lebanon 33°39N 35°40E 48 B4
Al Başrah Iraq 30°30N 47°50E 46 D5
Al Baṭḥā Iraq 31°6N 45°53E 46 D5
Al Batrūn Lebanon 34°15N 35°40E 48 A4
Al Bayḍā Libya 32°50N 21°44E 53 B10
Al Biqā Lebanon 34°10N 36°10E 48 A5
Al Bi'r Si. Arabia 28°51N 36°16E 46 D3
Al Bukayrīyah Si. Arabia 26°9N 43°40E 46 E4
Al Buraij Syria 33°15N 36°46E 48 B5
Al Fadilī Si. Arabia 26°55N 49°10E 47 E6
Al Fallūjah Iraq 33°20N 43°55E 46 C4
Al Fāw Iraq 30°0N 48°30E 47 D6
Al Fujayrah U.A.E. 25°7N 56°18E 47 E8
Al Ghadaf, W. → Jordan 31°26N 36°43E 48 D5
Al Ghammās Iraq 31°45N 44°37E 46 D5
Al Ghazālah Si. Arabia 26°48N 41°19E 46 E4
Al Ghuwayfāt U.A.E. 24°10N 51°38E 47 E6
Al Ḥadīthah Iraq 34°0N 42°30E 46 C4
Al Ḥadīthah Si. Arabia 31°28N 37°8E 46 D3
Al Ḥaḍr Iraq 35°35N 42°44E 46 C4
Al Hājānah Syria 33°20N 36°33E 48 B5

Al Ḥajar al Gharbī *Oman* 24°10N 56°15E **47** E8
Al Ḥāmad *Si. Arabia* 31°30N 39°30E **46** D3
Al Ḥamdānīyah *Syria* 35°25N 36°50E **46** C3
Al Ḥamīdīyah *Syria* 34°42N 35°57E **48** A4
Al Ḥammār *Iraq* 30°57N 46°51E **46** D5
Al Ḥamrā' *Si. Arabia* 24°2N 38°55E **46** E3
Al Ḥamzah *Iraq* 31°43N 44°58E **46** D5
Al Ḥanākīyah *Si. Arabia* 24°51N 40°31E **46** E4
Al Ḥarūj al Aswad *Libya* 27°0N 17°10E **53** C9
Al Ḥasakah *Syria* 36°35N 40°45E **46** B4
Al Ḥayy *Iraq* 32°5N 46°5E **46** C5
Al Ḥillah *Iraq* 32°30N 44°25E **46** C5
Al Hindīyah *Iraq* 32°30N 44°10E **46** C5
Al Hirmil *Lebanon* 34°26N 36°24E **48** A5
Al Hoceïma *Morocco* 35°8N 3°58W **52** A5
Al Ḥudaydah *Yemen* 14°50N 43°0E **49** E3
Al Ḥudūd ash Shamālīyah □ *Si. Arabia* 29°10N 42°30E **46** D4
Al Hufūf *Si. Arabia* 25°25N 49°45E **47** E6
Al Ḥumaydah *Si. Arabia* 29°14N 34°56E **46** D2
Al Ḥunayy *Si. Arabia* 25°58N 48°45E **47** E6
Al Īsāwīyah *Si. Arabia* 30°43N 37°59E **46** D3
Al Jafr *Jordan* 30°18N 36°14E **48** E5
Al Jāfūrah *Si. Arabia* 25°0N 50°15E **47** E7
Al Jaghbūb *Libya* 29°42N 24°38E **53** C10
Al Jahrah *Kuwait* 29°25N 47°40E **46** D5
Al Jalāmīd *Si. Arabia* 31°20N 40°6E **46** D3
Al Jamalīyah *Qatar* 25°37N 51°5E **47** E6
Al Janūb □ *Lebanon* 33°20N 35°20E **48** B4
Al Jawf *Libya* 24°10N 23°24E **53** D10
Al Jawf □ *Si. Arabia* 29°30N 39°30E **46** D3
Al Jazair = Algeria ■ *Africa* 28°30N 2°0E **52** C6
Al Jazirah *Iraq* 33°30N 44°0E **46** C5
Al Jithāmīyah *Si. Arabia* 27°41N 41°43E **46** E4
Al Jubayl *Si. Arabia* 27°0N 49°50E **47** E6
Al Jubaylah *Si. Arabia* 24°55N 46°25E **46** E5
Al Jubb *Si. Arabia* 27°11N 42°17E **46** E4
Al Junaynah *Sudan* 13°27N 22°45E **53** F10
Al Kabā'ish *Iraq* 30°58N 47°0E **46** D5
Al Karak *Jordan* 31°11N 35°42E **48** D4
Al Karak □ *Jordan* 31°0N 36°0E **48** E5
Al Kāẓimīyah *Iraq* 33°22N 44°18E **46** C5
Al Khābūrah *Oman* 23°57N 57°5E **47** F8
Al Khafji *Si. Arabia* 28°24N 48°29E **47** E6
Al Khalīl *West Bank* 31°32N 35°6E **48** D4
Al Khāliṣ *Iraq* 33°49N 44°32E **46** C5
Al Kharsānīyah *Si. Arabia* 27°13N 49°18E **47** E6
Al Khaṣab *Oman* 26°14N 56°15E **47** E8
Al Khawr *Qatar* 25°41N 51°30E **47** E6
Al Khiḍr *Iraq* 31°12N 45°33E **46** D5
Al Khiyām *Lebanon* 33°20N 35°36E **48** B4
Al Khubar *Si. Arabia* 26°17N 50°12E **47** E6
Al Khums *Libya* 32°40N 14°17E **53** B8
Al Khurmah *Si. Arabia* 21°54N 42°3E **49** C3
Al Kiswah *Syria* 33°23N 36°14E **48** B5
Al Kūfah *Iraq* 32°2N 44°24E **46** C5
Al Kufrah *Libya* 24°17N 23°15E **53** D10
Al Kuhayfiyah *Si. Arabia* 27°12N 43°3E **46** E4
Al Kūt *Iraq* 32°30N 46°0E **46** C5
Al Kuwayt *Kuwait* 29°30N 48°0E **46** D5
Al Labwah *Lebanon* 34°11N 36°20E **48** A5
Al Lādhiqīyah *Syria* 35°30N 35°45E **46** C2
Al Līth *Si. Arabia* 20°9N 40°15E **49** C3
Al Liwā' *Oman* 24°31N 56°36E **47** E8
Al Luḥayyah *Yemen* 15°45N 42°40E **49** D3
Al Madīnah *Iraq* 30°57N 47°16E **46** D5
Al Madīnah *Si. Arabia* 24°35N 39°52E **46** E3
Al Mafraq *Jordan* 32°17N 36°14E **48** C5
Al Mafraq □ *Jordan* 32°17N 36°15E **48** C5
Al Maghreb = Morocco ■ *N. Afr.* 32°0N 5°50W **52** B4
Al Maḥmūdīyah *Iraq* 33°3N 44°21E **46** C5
Al Majma'ah *Si. Arabia* 25°57N 45°22E **46** E5
Al Makhruq, W. → *Jordan* 31°28N 37°0E **48** D6
Al Makḥūl *Si. Arabia* 26°37N 42°39E **46** E4
Al Manāmah *Bahrain* 26°10N 50°30E **47** E6
Al Maqwa' *Kuwait* 29°10N 47°59E **46** D5
Al Marāḥ *Si. Arabia* 25°35N 49°35E **47** E6
Al Marj *Libya* 32°25N 20°30E **53** B10
Al Maṭlā *Kuwait* 29°24N 47°40E **46** D5
Al Mawṣil *Iraq* 36°15N 43°5E **46** B4
Al Mayādin *Syria* 35°1N 40°27E **46** C4
Al Mazār *Jordan* 31°4N 35°41E **48** D4
Al Midhnab *Si. Arabia* 25°50N 44°18E **46** E5
Al Minā' *Lebanon* 34°24N 35°49E **48** A4
Al Miqdādīyah *Iraq* 34°0N 45°0E **46** C5
Al Mubarraz *Si. Arabia* 25°30N 49°40E **47** E6
Al Mudawwarah *Jordan* 29°19N 36°0E **48** F5
Al Mughayrā' *U.A.E.* 24°5N 53°32E **47** E7
Al Muḥarraq *Bahrain* 26°15N 50°40E **47** E6
Al Mukallā *Yemen* 14°33N 49°2E **49** E4
Al Mukhā *Yemen* 13°18N 43°15E **49** E3
Al Musayjīd *Si. Arabia* 24°5N 39°5E **46** E3
Al Musayyib *Iraq* 32°49N 44°20E **46** C5
Al Muthannā □ *Iraq* 30°30N 45°15E **46** D5
Al Muwayliḥ *Si. Arabia* 27°40N 35°30E **46** E2
Al Qādisīyah □ *Iraq* 32°0N 45°0E **46** D5
Al Qā'im *Iraq* 34°21N 41°7E **46** C4
Al Qalībah *Si. Arabia* 28°24N 37°42E **46** D3
Al Qāmishlī *Syria* 37°2N 41°14E **46** B4
Al Qaryatayn *Syria* 34°12N 37°13E **48** A6
Al Qaṣīm □ *Si. Arabia* 26°0N 43°0E **46** E4
Al Qaṭ'ā *Syria* 34°40N 40°48E **46** C4
Al Qaṭīf *Si. Arabia* 26°35N 50°0E **47** E6
Al Qatrānah *Jordan* 31°12N 36°6E **48** D5
Al Qaṭrūn *Libya* 24°56N 15°3E **53** D9
Al Qayṣūmah *Si. Arabia* 28°20N 46°7E **46** D5
Al Qunayṭirah *Syria* 33°5N 35°45E **48** B4
Al Qunfudhah *Si. Arabia* 19°3N 41°4E **49** D3
Al Qurayyāt *Si. Arabia* 31°20N 37°20E **46** D3
Al Qurnah *Iraq* 31°1N 47°25E **46** D5
Al Quṣayr *Iraq* 30°39N 45°50E **46** D5
Al Quṣayr *Syria* 34°31N 36°34E **48** A5
Al Quṭayfah *Syria* 33°44N 36°36E **48** B5
Al Quwaysimah *Jordan* 31°55N 35°57E **48** D4
Al 'Ubaylah *Si. Arabia* 21°59N 50°57E **49** C5
Al 'Uḍaylīyah *Si. Arabia* 25°8N 49°18E **47** E6
Al 'Ulā *Si. Arabia* 26°35N 38°0E **46** E3
Al 'Uqayr *Si. Arabia* 25°40N 50°15E **47** E6
Al 'Uwaynid *Si. Arabia* 24°50N 46°0E **46** E5
Al 'Uwayqīlah *Si. Arabia* 30°30N 42°10E **46** D4
Al 'Uyūn *Ḥijāz, Si. Arabia* 24°33N 39°35E **46** E3
Al 'Uyūn *Najd, Si. Arabia* 26°30N 43°50E **46** E4
Al 'Uzayr *Iraq* 31°19N 47°25E **46** D5
Al Wajh *Si. Arabia* 26°10N 36°30E **46** E3
Al Wakrah *Qatar* 25°10N 51°40E **47** E6
Al Waqbah *Si. Arabia* 28°48N 45°33E **46** D5
Al Wari'āh *Si. Arabia* 27°51N 47°25E **46** E5
Al Yaman = Yemen ■ *Asia* 15°0N 44°0E **49** E3
Ala Dağ *Turkey* 37°44N 35°9E **46** B2
Ala Tau *Asia* 45°30N 80°40E **30** B5
Ala Tau Shankou = Dzungarian Gate *Asia* 45°10N 82°0E **30** B5
Alabama □ *U.S.A.* 33°0N 87°0W **85** E11
Alabama → *U.S.A.* 31°8N 87°57W **85** F11
Alabaster *U.S.A.* 33°15N 86°49W **85** E11
Alaçam Dağları *Turkey* 39°18N 28°49E **23** E13
Alacant = Alicante *Spain* 38°23N 0°30W **21** C5
Alachua *U.S.A.* 29°47N 82°30W **85** G13
Alagoa Grande *Brazil* 7°3S 35°35W **93** E11
Alagoas □ *Brazil* 9°0S 36°0W **93** E11
Alagoinhas *Brazil* 12°7S 38°20W **93** F11
Alaheaieatnu = Altaelva → *Norway* 69°54N 23°17E **8** B20
Alajuela *Costa Rica* 10°2N 84°8W **88** D3
Alaknanda → *India* 30°8N 78°36E **43** D8
Alakurtti *Russia* 66°58N 30°25E **8** C24
Alamarvdasht *Iran* 27°37N 52°59E **47** E7
Alameda *U.S.A.* 35°11N 106°37W **77** J10
Alamo *U.S.A.* 37°22N 115°10W **79** H11
Alamogordo *U.S.A.* 32°54N 105°57W **77** K11
Alamos *Mexico* 27°1N 108°56W **86** B3
Alamosa *U.S.A.* 37°28N 105°52W **77** H11
Alampur *India* 15°55N 78°6E **45** G4
Åland *Finland* 60°15N 20°0E **9** F19
Aland *India* 17°36N 76°35E **44** F3
Ålands hav *Europe* 60°0N 19°30E **9** G18
Alandur *India* 13°0N 80°15E **45** H5
Alaniya = North Ossetia-Alaniya □ *Russia* 43°30N 44°30E **19** F7
Alanya *Turkey* 36°38N 32°0E **46** B1
Alapayevsk *Russia* 57°52N 61°42E **26** D7
Alappuzha *India* 9°30N 76°28E **45** K3
Alaşehir *Turkey* 38°23N 28°30E **23** E13
Alaska □ *U.S.A.* 64°0N 154°0W **74** C9
Alaska, G. of *Pac. Oc.* 58°0N 145°0W **68** F3
Alaska Peninsula *U.S.A.* 56°0N 159°0W **74** D8
Alaska Range *U.S.A.* 62°50N 151°0W **68** E1
Älät *Azerbaijan* 39°58N 49°25E **47** B6
Alatau Shan = Ala Tau *Asia* 45°30N 80°40E **30** B5
Alatyr *Russia* 54°55N 46°35E **18** D8
Alausi *Ecuador* 2°0S 78°50W **92** D3
Alava, C. *U.S.A.* 48°10N 124°44W **78** B2
Alavo = Alavus *Finland* 62°35N 23°36E **8** E20
Alavus *Finland* 62°35N 23°36E **8** E20
Alawa ☼ *Australia* 15°42S 134°39E **62** B1
Alawoona *Australia* 34°45S 140°30E **63** E3
Alayawarra ☼ *Australia* 22°0S 134°30E **62** C1
'Alayh *Lebanon* 33°46N 35°33E **48** B4
Alba *Italy* 44°42N 8°2E **20** D8
Alba-Iulia *Romania* 46°8N 23°39E **17** E12
Albacete *Spain* 39°0N 1°50W **21** C5
Albacutya, L. *Australia* 35°45S 141°58E **63** F3
Albanel, L. *Canada* 50°55N 73°12W **72** B5
Albania ■ *Europe* 41°0N 20°0E **23** D9
Albany *Australia* 35°1S 117°58E **61** G2
Albany *Ga., U.S.A.* 31°35N 84°10W **85** F12
Albany *N.Y., U.S.A.* 42°39N 73°45W **83** D11
Albany *Oreg., U.S.A.* 44°38N 123°6W **76** D2
Albany *Tex., U.S.A.* 32°44N 99°18W **84** E5
Albany → *Canada* 52°17N 81°31W **72** B3
Albardón *Argentina* 31°20S 68°30W **94** C2
Albatross B. *Australia* 12°45S 141°30E **62** A3
Albemarle *U.S.A.* 35°21N 80°12W **85** D14
Albemarle Sd. *U.S.A.* 36°5N 76°0W **85** C16
Alberche → *Spain* 39°58N 4°46W **21** C3
Alberdi *Paraguay* 26°14S 58°20W **94** B4
Alberga → *Australia* 27°6S 135°33E **63** D2
Albert, L. *Africa* 1°30N 31°0E **54** D6
Albert, L. *Australia* 35°30S 139°10E **63** F2
Albert Edward Ra. *Australia* 18°17S 127°57E **60** C4
Albert Lea *U.S.A.* 43°39N 93°22W **80** D7
Albert Nile → *Uganda* 3°36N 32°2E **54** D6
Albert Town *Bahamas* 22°37N 74°33W **89** B5
Alberta □ *Canada* 54°40N 115°0W **70** C6
Alberti *Argentina* 35°1S 60°16W **94** D3
Albertinia *S. Africa* 34°11S 21°34E **56** D3
Alberton *Canada* 46°50N 64°0W **73** C7
Albertville *France* 45°40N 6°22E **20** D7
Albertville *U.S.A.* 34°16N 86°13W **85** D11
Albi *France* 43°56N 2°9E **20** E5
Albia *U.S.A.* 41°2N 92°48W **80** E7
Albina *Suriname* 5°37N 54°15W **93** B8
Albina, Ponta *Angola* 15°52S 11°44E **56** A1
Albion *Mich., U.S.A.* 42°15N 84°45W **81** D11
Albion *Nebr., U.S.A.* 41°42N 98°0W **80** E4
Albion *Pa., U.S.A.* 41°53N 80°22W **82** E4
Alborán *Medit. S.* 35°57N 3°0W **21** E4
Ålborg = Aalborg *Denmark* 57°2N 9°54E **9** H13
Alborz □ *Iran* 36°0N 50°50E **47** B6
Alborz, Reshteh-ye Kūhhā-ye *Iran* 36°0N 52°0E **47** C7
Albufeira *Portugal* 37°5N 8°15W **21** D1
Albuquerque *U.S.A.* 35°5N 106°39W **77** J10
Albuquerque, Cayos de *Caribbean* 12°10N 81°50W **88** D3
Alburg *U.S.A.* 44°59N 73°18W **83** B11
Albury *Australia* 36°3S 146°56E **63** F4
Alcalá de Henares *Spain* 40°28N 3°22W **21** B4
Alcalá la Real *Spain* 37°27N 3°57W **21** D4
Álcamo *Italy* 37°59N 12°55E **22** F5
Alcañiz *Spain* 41°2N 0°8W **21** B5
Alcântara *Brazil* 2°20S 44°30W **93** D10
Alcántara, Embalse de *Spain* 39°44N 6°50W **21** C2
Alcantarilla *Spain* 37°59N 1°12W **21** D5
Alcaraz, Sierra de *Spain* 38°40N 2°20W **21** C4
Alcaudete *Spain* 37°35N 4°5W **21** D3
Alcázar de San Juan *Spain* 39°24N 3°12W **21** C4
Alchevsk *Ukraine* 48°30N 38°45E **19** E6
Alcira = Alzira *Spain* 39°9N 0°30W **21** C5
Alcova *U.S.A.* 42°34N 106°43W **76** E10
Alcoy *Spain* 38°43N 0°30W **21** C5
Aldabra Is. *Seychelles* 9°22S 46°28E **51** G8
Aldama *Mexico* 22°55N 98°4W **87** C5
Aldan *Russia* 58°40N 125°30E **27** D13
Aldan → *Russia* 63°28N 129°35E **27** C13
Aldeburgh *U.K.* 52°10N 1°37E **13** E9
Alder Pk. *U.S.A.* 35°53N 121°22W **78** K5
Alderney *U.K.* 49°42N 2°11W **13** H5
Aldershot *U.K.* 51°15N 0°44W **13** F7
Aledo *U.S.A.* 41°12N 90°45W **80** E8
Aleg *Mauritania* 17°3N 13°55W **52** E3
Alegre *Brazil* 20°50S 41°30W **95** A7
Alegrete *Brazil* 29°40S 56°0W **95** B4
Aleksandriya = Oleksandriya *Ukraine* 50°37N 26°19E **17** C14
Aleksandrov Gay *Russia* 50°9N 48°34E **19** D8
Aleksandrovsk-Sakhalinskiy *Russia* 50°50N 142°20E **31** A17
Aleksandry, Zemlya *Russia* 80°25N 48°0E **26** A5
Além Paraíba *Brazil* 21°52S 42°41W **95** A7
Alemania *Argentina* 25°40S 65°30W **94** B2
Alemania *Chile* 25°10S 69°55W **94** B2
Alençon *France* 48°27N 0°4E **20** B4
Alenquer *Brazil* 1°56S 54°46W **93** D8
'Alenuihähä Channel *U.S.A.* 20°30N 156°0W **75** L8
Aleppo = Ḥalab *Syria* 36°10N 37°15E **46** B3
Aléria *France* 42°5N 9°26E **20** E9
Alert *Canada* 83°2N 60°0W **69** A20
Alert *India* 17°39N 79°3E **44** F4
Alès *France* 44°9N 4°5E **20** D6
Alessándria *Italy* 44°54N 8°37E **20** D8
Ålesund *Norway* 62°28N 6°12E **8** E12
Aleutian Basin *Pac. Oc.* 57°0N 177°0E **64** B9
Aleutian Is. *Pac. Oc.* 52°0N 175°0W **64** B10
Aleutian Range *U.S.A.* 60°0N 154°0W **74** D9
Aleutian Trench *Pac. Oc.* 48°0N 180°0E **4** D17
Alexander *U.S.A.* 47°51N 103°39W **80** B2
Alexander, Mt. *Australia* 28°58S 120°16E **61** E3
Alexander Arch. *U.S.A.* 56°0N 136°0W **68** F4
Alexander Bay *S. Africa* 28°40S 16°30E **56** C2
Alexander City *U.S.A.* 32°56N 85°58W **85** E12
Alexander I. *Antarctica* 69°0S 70°0W **5** C17
Alexandra *Australia* 37°8S 145°40E **63** F4
Alexandra *N.Z.* 45°14S 169°25E **59** F2
Alexandra Channel *Myanmar* 14°7N 93°13E **45** G11
Alexandra Falls *Canada* 60°29N 116°18W **70** A5
Alexandria = El Iskandarîya *Egypt* 31°13N 29°58E **53** B11
Alexandria *B.C., Canada* 52°35N 122°27W **70** C4
Alexandria *Ont., Canada* 45°19N 74°38W **83** A10
Alexandria *Romania* 43°57N 25°24E **17** G13
Alexandria *S. Africa* 33°38S 26°28E **56** D4
Alexandria *U.K.* 55°59N 4°35W **11** F4
Alexandria *La., U.S.A.* 31°18N 92°27W **84** F8
Alexandria *Minn., U.S.A.* 45°53N 95°22W **80** C6
Alexandria *S. Dak., U.S.A.* 43°39N 97°47W **80** D5
Alexandria Bay *U.S.A.* 44°20N 75°55W **83** B9
Alexandrina, L. *Australia* 35°25S 139°10E **63** F2
Alexandroupoli *Greece* 40°50N 25°54E **23** D11
Alexis → *Canada* 52°33N 56°8W **73** B8
Alexis Creek *Canada* 52°10N 123°20W **70** C4
Aleysk *Russia* 52°40N 83°0E **26** D9
Alfenas *Brazil* 21°20S 46°10W **95** A6
Alford *Aberds., U.K.* 57°14N 2°41W **11** D6
Alford *Lincs., U.K.* 53°15N 0°10E **12** D8
Alfred *Maine, U.S.A.* 43°29N 70°43W **83** C14
Alfred *N.Y., U.S.A.* 42°16N 77°48W **82** D7
Alfreton *U.K.* 53°6N 1°24W **12** D6
Ålgård *Norway* 58°46N 5°53E **9** G11
Algarve *Portugal* 36°58N 8°20W **21** D1
Algeciras *Spain* 36°9N 5°28W **21** D3
Algemesí *Spain* 39°11N 0°27W **21** C5
Alger *Algeria* 36°42N 3°8E **52** A6
Algeria ■ *Africa* 28°30N 2°0E **52** C6
Algha *Kazakhstan* 49°53N 57°20E **19** E10
Alghero *Italy* 40°33N 8°19E **22** D3
Algiers = Alger *Algeria* 36°42N 3°8E **52** A6
Algoa B. *S. Africa* 33°50S 25°45E **56** D4
Algodones Dunes *U.S.A.* 32°50N 115°5W **79** N11
Algoma *U.S.A.* 44°36N 87°26W **80** C10
Algona *U.S.A.* 43°4N 94°14W **80** D6
Algonac *U.S.A.* 42°37N 82°32W **82** D2
Algonquin ⌂ *Canada* 45°50N 78°30W **72** C4
Algorta *Spain* 43°21N 2°59W **21** A4
Algorta *Uruguay* 32°25S 57°24W **94** C4
Algorta *Uruguay* 32°25S 57°23W **95** C5
Alhucemas = Al Hoceïma *Morocco* 35°8N 3°58W **52** A5
'Alī al Gharbī *Iraq* 32°30N 46°45E **46** C5
'Alī ash Sharqī *Iraq* 32°7N 46°44E **46** C5
Äli Bayramlı = Şirvan *Azerbaijan* 39°59N 48°52E **47** B6
'Alī Khēl *Afghan.* 33°57N 69°43E **42** C3
Alī Shāh *Iran* 38°9N 45°50E **46** B5
'Alīābād *Golestān, Iran* 36°40N 54°33E **47** B7
'Alīābād *Khorāsān, Iran* 32°30N 57°30E **47** C8
'Alīābād *Kordestān, Iran* 35°4N 46°58E **46** C5
'Alīābād *Yazd, Iran* 31°41N 53°49E **47** D7
Aliağa *Turkey* 38°47N 26°59E **23** E12
Aliakmonas → *Greece* 40°30N 22°36E **23** D10
Alibag *India* 18°38N 72°56E **44** E1
Alicante *Spain* 38°23N 0°30W **21** C5
Alice *S. Africa* 32°48S 26°55E **56** D4
Alice *U.S.A.* 27°45N 98°5W **84** H5
Alice → *Queens., Australia* 24°2S 144°50E **62** C3
Alice → *Queens., Australia* 15°35S 142°20E **62** B3
Alice Arm *Canada* 55°29N 129°31W **70** B3
Alice Springs *Australia* 23°40S 133°50E **62** C1
Alicedale *S. Africa* 33°15S 26°4E **56** D4
Aliceville *U.S.A.* 33°8N 88°9W **85** E10
Aliganj *India* 27°30N 79°10E **43** F8
Aligarh *Raj., India* 25°55N 76°15E **42** G7
Aligarh *Ut. P., India* 27°55N 78°10E **42** F8
Alīgūdarz *Iran* 33°25N 49°45E **47** C6
Alingsås *Sweden* 57°56N 12°31E **9** H15
Alipur *Pakistan* 29°25N 70°55E **42** E4
Alipur Duar *India* 26°30N 89°35E **41** F16
Aliquippa *U.S.A.* 40°37N 80°15W **82** F4
Alishan *Taiwan* 23°31N 120°48E **35** F13
Alitus = Alytus *Lithuania* 54°24N 24°3E **9** J21
Aliwal North *S. Africa* 30°45S 26°45E **56** D4
Alix *Canada* 52°24N 113°11W **70** C6
Aljustrel *Portugal* 37°55N 8°10W **21** D1
Alkhanay △ *Russia* 51°0N 113°30E **27** D12
Alkmaar *Neths.* 52°37N 4°45E **15** B4
All American Canal *U.S.A.* 32°45N 115°15W **79** N11
Allagadda *India* 15°8N 78°30E **45** G4
Allagash → *U.S.A.* 47°5N 69°3W **81** B19
Allah Dad *Pakistan* 25°38N 67°34E **42** G2
Allahabad *India* 25°25N 81°58E **43** G9
Allan *Canada* 51°53N 106°4W **71** C7
Allanridge *S. Africa* 27°45S 26°40E **56** C4
Allegany *U.S.A.* 42°6N 78°30W **82** D6
Allegheny → *U.S.A.* 40°27N 80°1W **82** F5
Allegheny Mts. *U.S.A.* 38°15N 80°10W **81** F13
Allegheny Plateau *U.S.A.* 41°30N 78°30W **81** E14
Allegheny Res. *U.S.A.* 41°50N 79°0W **82** E6
Allègre, Pte. *Guadeloupe* 16°22N 61°46W **88** b
Allen, Bog of *Ireland* 53°15N 7°0W **10** C5
Allen, L. *Ireland* 54°8N 8°4W **10** B3
Allendale *U.S.A.* 33°1N 81°18W **85** E14
Allende *Mexico* 28°20N 100°51W **86** B4
Allentown *U.S.A.* 40°37N 75°29W **83** F9
Alleppey = Alappuzha *India* 9°30N 76°28E **45** K3
Aller → *Germany* 52°56N 9°12E **16** B5
Alleynes B. *Barbados* 13°13N 59°39W **89** g
Alliance *Nebr., U.S.A.* 42°6N 102°52W **80** D2
Alliance *Ohio, U.S.A.* 40°55N 81°6W **82** F3
Allier → *France* 46°57N 3°4E **20** C5
Alliford Bay *Canada* 53°12N 131°58W **70** C2
Alligator Pond *Jamaica* 17°52N 77°34W **88** a
Allinagaram *India* 10°2N 77°30E **45** J3
Alliston *Canada* 44°9N 79°52W **82** B5
Alloa *U.K.* 56°7N 3°47W **11** E5
Allora *Australia* 28°2S 152°0E **63** D5
Alluitsup Paa *Greenland* 60°30N 45°35W **4** C5
Allur *India* 14°40N 80°4E **45** G5
Alluru Kottapatnam *India* 15°24N 80°7E **45** G5
Alma *Canada* 48°35N 71°40W **73** C5
Alma *Ga., U.S.A.* 31°33N 82°28W **85** F13
Alma *Kans., U.S.A.* 39°1N 96°17W **80** F5
Alma *Mich., U.S.A.* 43°23N 84°39W **81** D11
Alma *Nebr., U.S.A.* 40°6N 99°22W **80** E4
Alma *Wis., U.S.A.* 44°20N 91°55W **80** C8
Alma Ata = Almaty *Kazakhstan* 43°15N 76°57E **30** C4
Alma Hill *U.S.A.* 42°2N 78°0W **82** D7
Almaden *Australia* 17°22S 144°40E **62** B3
Almadén *Spain* 38°49N 4°52W **21** C3
Almalyk = Olmaliq *Uzbekistan* 40°50N 69°35E **26** E7
Almanor, L. *U.S.A.* 40°14N 121°9W **76** F3
Almansa *Spain* 38°51N 1°5W **21** C5
Almanzor, Pico *Spain* 40°15N 5°18W **21** B3
Almanzora → *Spain* 37°14N 1°46W **21** D5
Almaty *Kazakhstan* 43°15N 76°57E **30** C4
Almazán *Spain* 41°30N 2°30W **21** B4
Almeirim *Brazil* 1°30S 52°34W **93** D8
Almelo *Neths.* 52°22N 6°42E **15** B6
Almendralejo *Spain* 38°41N 6°26W **21** C2
Almere *Neths.* 52°20N 5°15E **15** B5
Almería *Spain* 36°52N 2°27W **21** D4
Almirante *Panama* 9°10N 82°30W **88** E3
Almond *U.S.A.* 42°19N 77°44W **82** D7
Almont *U.S.A.* 42°55N 83°3W **82** D1
Almonte *Canada* 45°14N 76°12W **83** A8
Almora *India* 29°38N 79°40E **43** E8
Alness *U.K.* 57°41N 4°16W **11** D4
Alnmouth *U.K.* 55°24N 1°37W **12** B6
Alnwick *U.K.* 55°24N 1°42W **12** B6
Alon *Myanmar* 22°12N 95°5E **41** H19
Alor *Indonesia* 8°15S 124°30E **37** F6
Alor Setar *Malaysia* 6°7N 100°22E **39** J3
Alot *India* 23°56N 75°40E **42** H6
Aloysius, Mt. *Australia* 26°0S 128°38E **61** E4
Alpaugh *U.S.A.* 35°53N 119°29W **78** K7
Alpena *U.S.A.* 45°4N 83°27W **82** A1
Alpha *Australia* 23°39S 146°37E **62** C4
Alpha Ridge *Arctic* 84°0N 118°0W **4** A2
Alphen aan den Rijn *Neths.* 52°7N 4°40E **15** B4
Alpine *Ariz., U.S.A.* 33°51N 109°9W **77** K9
Alpine *Calif., U.S.A.* 32°50N 116°46W **79** N10
Alpine *Tex., U.S.A.* 30°22N 103°40W **84** F3
Alps *Europe* 46°30N 9°30E **16** E5
Alpurrurulam *Australia* 20°59S 137°50E **62** C2
Alsace *France* 48°15N 7°25E **20** B7
Alsask *Canada* 51°21N 109°59W **71** C7
Alsasua *Spain* 42°54N 2°10W **21** A4
Alsek → *U.S.A.* 59°10N 138°12W **70** B1
Alsta *Norway* 65°58N 12°40E **8** D15
Alston *U.K.* 54°49N 2°25W **12** C5
Alta *Norway* 69°57N 23°10E **8** B20
Alta Gracia *Argentina* 31°40S 64°30W **94** C3
Alta Sierra *U.S.A.* 35°42N 118°33W **79** K8
Altaelva → *Norway* 69°54N 23°17E **8** B20
Altafjorden *Norway* 70°5N 23°5E **8** A20
Altai = Aerhtai Shan *Mongolia* 46°40N 92°45E **30** B7
Altai = Gorno-Altay □ *Russia* 51°0N 86°0E **26** D9
Altamaha → *U.S.A.* 31°20N 81°20W **85** F14
Altamira *Brazil* 3°12S 52°10W **93** D8
Altamira *Chile* 25°47S 69°51W **94** B2
Altamira *Mexico* 22°24N 97°55W **87** C5
Altamont *U.S.A.* 42°42N 74°2W **83** D10
Altamura *Italy* 40°49N 16°33E **22** D7
Altanbulag *Mongolia* 50°16N 106°30E **30** A10
Altar *Mexico* 30°43N 111°44W **86** A2
Altar, Gran Desierto de *Mexico* 31°50N 114°10W **86** B2
Altata *Mexico* 24°40N 107°55W **86** C3
Altavista *U.S.A.* 37°6N 79°17W **81** G14
Altay *China* 47°48N 88°10E **30** B6
Altay *Mongolia* 46°22N 96°15E **30** B8
Altea *Spain* 38°38N 0°2W **21** C5
Altiplano *Bolivia* 17°0S 68°0W **92** G5
Alto Araguaia *Brazil* 17°15S 53°20W **93** G8
Alto Cuchumatanes = Cuchumatanes, Sierra de los *Guatemala* 15°35N 91°25W **88** C1
Alto del Carmen *Chile* 28°46S 70°30W **94** B1
Alto Molocue *Mozam.* 15°50S 37°35E **55** H7
Alto Paraguay □ *Paraguay* 21°0S 58°30W **94** A4
Alto Paraná □ *Paraguay* 25°30S 54°50W **95** B5
Alton *Canada* 43°54N 80°5W **82** C4
Alton *U.K.* 51°9N 0°59W **13** F7
Alton *Ill., U.S.A.* 38°53N 90°11W **80** F8
Alton *N.H., U.S.A.* 43°27N 71°13W **83** C13
Altona *Canada* 49°6N 97°33W **71** D9
Altoona *U.S.A.* 40°31N 78°24W **82** F6
Altsasu = Alsasua *Spain* 42°54N 2°10W **21** A4
Altun Kupri *Iraq* 35°45N 44°9E **46** C5
Altun Shan *China* 38°30N 88°0E **30** D6
Alturas *U.S.A.* 41°29N 120°32W **76** F3
Altus *U.S.A.* 34°38N 99°20W **84** D5
Alucra *Turkey* 40°22N 38°47E **19** F6
Alūksne *Latvia* 57°24N 27°3E **9** H22
Alunite *U.S.A.* 35°59N 114°55W **79** K12
Alur *India* 15°24N 77°15E **45** E3
Alusi *Indonesia* 7°35S 131°40E **37** F8
Alutgama *Sri Lanka* 6°26N 79°59E **45** L4
Alutnuwara *Sri Lanka* 7°19N 80°59E **45** L5
Aluva *India* 10°8N 76°24E **45** J3
Alva *U.S.A.* 36°48N 98°40W **84** C5
Alvarado *Mexico* 18°46N 95°46W **87** D5
Alvarado *U.S.A.* 32°24N 97°13W **84** E6
Alvaro Obregón, Presa *Mexico* 27°52N 109°52W **86** B3
Alvear *Argentina* 29°5S 56°30W **94** B4
Alvesta *Sweden* 56°54N 14°35E **9** H16
Alvinston *Canada* 42°49N 81°52W **82** D3
Älvkarleby *Sweden* 60°34N 17°26E **9** F17
Alvord Desert *U.S.A.* 42°30N 118°25W **76** E4
Älvsbyn *Sweden* 65°40N 21°0E **8** D19
Alwar *India* 27°38N 76°34E **42** F7
Alwaye = Aluva *India* 10°8N 76°24E **45** J3
Alxa Zuoqi *China* 38°50N 105°40E **32** E3
Alyangula *Australia* 13°55S 136°30E **62** A2
Alyata = Älät *Azerbaijan* 39°58N 49°25E **47** B6
Alyth *U.K.* 56°38N 3°13W **11** E5
Alytus *Lithuania* 54°24N 24°3E **9** J21
Alzada *U.S.A.* 45°2N 104°25W **76** D11
Alzamay *Russia* 55°33N 98°39E **27** D10
Alzira *Spain* 39°9N 0°30W **21** C5
Am Timan *Chad* 11°0N 20°10E **53** F10
Amadeus, L. *Australia* 24°54S 131°0E **61** D5
Amadi *South Sudan* 5°29N 30°25E **53** G12
Amadjuak L. *Canada* 65°0N 71°8W **69** E17
Amagansett *U.S.A.* 40°59N 72°9W **83** F12
Amagi *Japan* 33°25N 130°39E **29** H5
Amahai *Indonesia* 3°20S 128°55E **37** E7
Amaile *Samoa* 13°59S 171°22W **59** b
Amakusa = Hondo *Japan* 32°27N 130°12E **29** H5
Amakusa-Shotō *Japan* 32°15N 130°10E **29** H5
Åmål *Sweden* 59°3N 12°42E **9** G15
Amalapuram *India* 16°35N 81°55E **45** F5
Amaliada *Greece* 37°47N 21°22E **23** F9
Amalner *India* 21°5N 75°5E **44** D2
Amamapare *Indonesia* 4°53S 136°38E **37** E9
Amambaí *Brazil* 23°5S 55°13W **95** A4
Amambaí → *Brazil* 23°22S 53°56W **95** A5
Amambay □ *Paraguay* 23°0S 56°0W **95** A4
Amambay, Cordillera de *S. Amer.* 23°0S 55°45W **95** A4
Amami *Japan* 28°22N 129°27E **29** K4
Amami-Guntō *Japan* 27°16N 129°21E **29** L4
Amami-Ō-Shima *Japan* 28°16N 129°21E **29** K4
Aman, Pulau *Malaysia* 5°16N 100°24E **39** c
Amaná, L. *Brazil* 2°35S 64°40W **92** D6
Amanat → *India* 24°7N 84°4E **43** G11
Amanda Park *U.S.A.* 47°28N 123°55W **78** C3
Amankeldi *Kazakhstan* 50°10N 65°10E **26** D7
Amapá *Brazil* 2°5N 50°50W **93** C8
Amapá □ *Brazil* 1°40N 52°0W **93** C8
Amarante *Brazil* 6°14S 42°50W **93** E10
Amaranth *Canada* 50°36N 98°43W **71** C9
Amaravati → *India* 11°0N 78°15E **45** J4
Amargosa → *U.S.A.* 36°14N 116°51W **79** J10
Amargosa Desert *U.S.A.* 36°40N 116°30W **79** J10
Amargosa Range *U.S.A.* 36°20N 116°45W **79** J10
Amarillo *U.S.A.* 35°13N 101°50W **84** D4
Amarkantak *India* 22°40N 81°45E **43** H9
Amarnath *India* 19°12N 73°22E **44** E1
Amaro, Mte. *Italy* 42°5N 14°5E **22** C6
Amarpur *India* 25°5N 87°0E **43** G12
Amarwara *India* 22°18N 79°10E **43** H8
Amasya *Turkey* 40°40N 35°50E **19** F6
Amata *Australia* 26°9S 131°9E **61** E5
Amatikulu *S. Africa* 29°3S 31°33E **57** C5
Amatitlán *Guatemala* 14°29N 90°38W **88** D1
Amay *Belgium* 50°33N 5°19E **15** D5
Amazon = Amazonas → *S. Amer.* 0°5S 50°0W **93** D8
Amazonas □ *Brazil* 5°0S 65°0W **92** E6
Amazonas → *S. Amer.* 0°5S 50°0W **93** D8
Ambad *India* 19°38N 75°50E **44** E2
Ambagarh Chowki *India* 20°47N 80°43E **44** D5
Ambah *India* 26°43N 78°13E **42** F8
Ambajogal *India* 18°44N 76°23E **44** E3
Ambala *India* 30°23N 76°56E **42** D7
Ambalangoda *Sri Lanka* 6°15N 80°5E **45** L5

Ambalantota Sri Lanka 6°7N 81°1E 45 L5
Ambalapulai India 9°25N 76°25E 45 K3
Ambalavao Madag. 21°50S 46°56E 55 J9
Ambanja Madag. 13°40S 48°27E 55 G9
Ambarchik Russia 69°40N 162°20E 27 C17
Ambasamudram India 8°43N 77°25E 45 K3
Ambato Ecuador 1°5S 78°42W 92 D3
Ambato, Sierra de Argentina 28°25S 66°10W 94 B2
Ambatolampy Madag. 19°20S 47°35E 55 H9
Ambatondrazaka Madag. 17°55S 48°28E 55 H9
Amberg Germany 49°26N 11°52E 16 D6
Ambergris Cay Belize 18°0N 87°55W 87 D7
Amberley Canada 44°2N 81°42W 82 B3
Amberley N.Z. 43°9S 172°44E 59 E4
Ambikapur India 23°15N 83°15E 43 H10
Ambilobé Madag. 13°10S 49°3E 55 G9
Amble U.K. 55°20N 1°36W 12 B6
Ambleside U.K. 54°26N 2°58W 12 C5
Ambo Peru 10°5S 76°10W 92 F3
Ambohitra Madag. 12°30S 49°10E 55 G9
Amboise France 47°24N 1°2E 20 C4
Ambon Indonesia 3°43S 128°12E 37 E7
Ambositra Madag. 20°31S 47°25E 55 J9
Ambovombe Madag. 25°11S 46°5E 55 K9
Amboy U.S.A. 34°33N 115°45W 79 L11
Amboyna Cay S. China Sea 7°50N 112°50E 36 C4
Ambridge U.S.A. 40°36N 80°14W 82 F4
Ambriz Angola 7°48S 13°8E 54 F2
Ambur India 12°48N 78°43E 45 H4
Amchitka I. U.S.A. 51°32N 179°0E 74 E3
Amderma Russia 69°45N 61°30E 26 C7
Amdhi India 23°51N 81°27E 43 H9
Amdo China 32°20N 91°40E 30 E7
Ameca Mexico 20°33N 104°2W 86 C4
Ameca → Mexico 20°41N 105°18W 86 C3
Amecameca de Juárez Mexico 19°8N 98°46W 87 D5
Amed Indonesia 8°19S 115°39E 37 J18
Ameland Neths. 53°27N 5°45E 15 A5
Amenia U.S.A. 41°51N 73°33W 83 E11
America-Antarctica Ridge S. Ocean 59°0S 16°0W 5 B2
American Falls U.S.A. 42°47N 112°51W 76 E7
American Falls Res. U.S.A. 42°47N 112°52W 76 E7
American Fork U.S.A. 40°23N 111°48W 76 F8
American Highland Antarctica 73°0S 75°0E 5 D6
American Samoa ⊿ Pac. Oc. 14°20S 170°0W 59 b
American Samoa △ Amer. Samoa 14°15S 170°28W 59 b
Americana Brazil 22°45S 47°20W 95 A6
Americus U.S.A. 32°4N 84°14W 85 E12
Amersfoort Neths. 52°9N 5°23E 15 B5
Amersfoort S. Africa 26°59S 29°53E 57 C4
Amery Basin S. Ocean 68°15S 74°30E 5 C6
Amery Ice Shelf Antarctica 69°30S 72°0E 5 C6
Ames U.S.A. 42°2N 93°37W 80 D7
Amesbury U.S.A. 42°51N 70°56W 83 D14
Amet India 25°18N 73°56E 42 G5
Amga Russia 60°50N 132°0E 27 C14
Amga → Russia 62°38N 134°32E 27 C14
Amgaon India 21°22N 80°22E 44 D5
Amgu Russia 45°45N 137°15E 28 B8
Amgun → Russia 52°56N 139°38E 27 D14
Amherst Canada 45°48N 64°8W 73 C7
Amherst Mass., U.S.A. 42°23N 72°31W 83 D12
Amherst N.Y., U.S.A. 42°59N 78°48W 82 D6
Amherst Ohio, U.S.A. 41°24N 82°14W 82 E2
Amherst I. Canada 44°8N 76°43W 83 B8
Amherstburg Canada 42°6N 83°6W 72 D3
Amiata, Mte. Italy 42°53N 11°37E 22 C4
Amidon U.S.A. 46°29N 103°19W 80 B2
Amiens France 49°54N 2°16E 20 B5
Amindivi Is. India 11°23N 72°23E 45 J1
Amini I. India 11°6N 72°45E 45 J1
Aminuis Namibia 23°43S 19°21E 56 B2
Amīrābād Iran 33°20N 46°16E 46 C5
Amirante Is. Seychelles 6°0S 53°0E 24 J7
Amisk ⌂ Canada 56°43N 98°0W 71 B9
Amisk L. Canada 54°35N 102°15W 71 C8
Amistad, Presa de la Mexico 29°26N 101°3W 86 B4
Amistad ⌂ U.S.A. 29°32N 101°12W 84 G4
Amite U.S.A. 30°44N 90°30W 85 F9
Amla India 21°56N 78°7E 42 J8
Amlapura Indonesia 8°27S 115°37E 37 J18
Amlia I. U.S.A. 52°4N 173°30W 74 E5
Amlwch U.K. 53°24N 4°20W 12 D3
'Ammān Jordan 31°57N 35°52E 48 D4
'Ammān ✈ (AMM) Jordan 31°45N 36°2E 48 D5
Ammanford U.K. 51°48N 3°59W 13 F4
Ammassalik = Tasiilaq Greenland 65°40N 37°20W 4 C6
Ammochostos = Famagusta Cyprus 35°8N 33°55E 46 C2
Ammon U.S.A. 43°28N 111°58W 76 E8
Amnat Charoen Thailand 15°51N 104°38E 38 E5
Amnura Bangla. 24°37N 88°25E 43 G13
Amo Jiang → China 23°0N 101°50E 34 F3
Āmol Iran 36°23N 52°20E 47 B7
Amorgos Greece 36°50N 25°57E 23 F11
Amory U.S.A. 33°59N 88°29W 85 E10
Amos Canada 48°35N 78°5W 72 C4
Åmot Norway 59°57N 9°54E 9 G13
Amoy = Xiamen China 24°25N 118°4E 35 E12
Ampang Malaysia 3°8N 101°45E 39 L3
Ampani India 19°35N 82°38E 44 E6
Ampanihy Madag. 24°40S 44°45E 55 J8
Ampenan Indonesia 8°34S 116°4E 37 K18
Amper → Germany 48°29N 11°55E 16 D6
Amphitrite Group S. China Sea 16°50N 112°20E 36 A4
Amphoe Kathu Thailand 7°55N 98°21E 39 a
Amphoe Thalang Thailand 8°1N 98°20E 39 a
Amqui Canada 48°28N 67°27W 73 C6
Amrabad India 16°23N 78°50E 45 F4
Amravati India 20°55N 77°45E 44 D3
Amreli India 21°35N 71°17E 42 J4
Amritsar India 31°35N 74°57E 42 D6
Amroha India 28°53N 78°30E 43 E8
Amsterdam U.S.A. 42°56N 74°11W 83 D10
Amsterdam I. = Nouvelle Amsterdam, Î. Ind. Oc. 38°30S 77°30E 3 F13
Amstetten Austria 48°7N 14°51E 16 D8
Amudarya → Uzbekistan 43°58N 59°34E 26 E6
Amukta Pass U.S.A. 52°0N 171°0W 74 E5
Amund Ringnes I. Canada 78°20N 96°25W 69 B12
Amundsen Abyssal Plain S. Ocean 65°0S 125°0W 5 C14
Amundsen Basin Arctic 87°30N 80°0E 4 A
Amundsen Gulf Canada 71°0N 124°0W 68 C7
Amundsen Ridges S. Ocean 69°15S 123°0W 5 C14
Amundsen-Scott Antarctica 90°0S 166°0E 5 E
Amundsen Sea Antarctica 72°0S 115°0W 5 D15
Amuntai Indonesia 2°28S 115°25E 36 E5
Amur → Russia 52°56N 141°10E 27 D15
Amurang Indonesia 1°5N 124°40E 37 D6
Amursk Russia 50°14N 136°54E 27 D14
Amyderya = Amudarya → Uzbekistan 43°58N 59°34E 26 E6
An Bang, Dao = Amboyna Cay S. China Sea 7°50N 112°50E 36 C4
An Bien Vietnam 9°45N 105°0E 39 H5
An Hoa Vietnam 15°40N 108°5E 38 E7
An Khe Vietnam 13°57N 108°51E 38 F7
An Nabatīyah at Tahta Lebanon 33°23N 35°27E 48 B4
An Nabk Syria 34°2N 36°44E 48 A5
An Nafūd Si. Arabia 28°15N 41°0E 46 D4
An Najaf Iraq 32°3N 44°15E 46 C5
An Nāṣirīyah Iraq 31°0N 46°15E 46 D5
An Nhon = Binh Dinh Vietnam 13°55N 109°7E 38 F7
An Nu'ayrīyah Si. Arabia 27°30N 48°30E 47 E6
An Nu'mānīyah Iraq 32°32N 45°25E 46 C5
An Ros = Rush Ireland 53°31N 6°6W 10 C5
An Thoi, Quan Dao Vietnam 9°58N 104°0E 39 H5
Anabar → Russia 73°8N 113°36E 27 B12
Anaconda U.S.A. 46°8N 112°57W 76 C7
Anacortes U.S.A. 48°30N 122°37W 78 B4
Anadarko U.S.A. 35°4N 98°15W 84 D5
Anadolu Turkey 39°0N 30°0E 19 G5
Anadyr Russia 64°35N 177°20E 27 C18
Anadyr → Russia 64°55N 176°5E 27 C18
Anadyrskiy Zaliv Russia 64°0N 180°0E 27 C19
'Ānah Iraq 34°25N 42°0E 46 C4
Anaheim U.S.A. 33°50N 117°55W 79 M9
Anahim Lake Canada 52°28N 125°18W 70 C3
Anai Mudi India 10°12N 77°4E 45 J3
Anaimalai Hills India 10°20N 76°40E 45 J3
Anakapalle India 17°42N 83°6E 44 F6
Anakie Australia 23°32S 147°45E 62 C4
Analalava Madag. 14°35S 48°0E 55 G9
Anambar → Pakistan 30°15N 68°50E 42 D3
Anambas, Kepulauan Indonesia 3°20N 106°30E 36 D3
Anambas Is. = Anambas, Kepulauan Indonesia 3°20N 106°30E 36 D3
Anamosa U.S.A. 42°7N 91°17W 80 D8
Anamur Turkey 36°8N 32°58E 46 B2
Anan Japan 33°54N 134°40E 29 H7
Anand India 22°32N 72°59E 42 H5
Anandapuram India 14°5N 75°12E 45 G2
Anandpur India 21°16N 86°13E 44 D8
Anangu Pitjantjatjara ❂ Australia 27°0S 132°0E 61 E5
Anantapur India 14°39N 77°42E 45 G3
Anantnag India 33°45N 75°10E 43 C6
Ananyiv Ukraine 47°44N 29°58E 17 E15
Anápolis Brazil 16°15S 48°50W 93 G9
Anapu → Brazil 1°53S 50°53W 93 D8
Anār Iran 30°55N 55°13E 47 D7
Anārak Iran 33°25N 53°40E 47 C7
Anas → India 23°26N 74°0E 42 H5
Anatolia = Anadolu Turkey 39°0N 30°0E 19 G5
Añatuya Argentina 28°20S 62°50W 94 B3
Anatye ❂ Australia 22°29S 137°3E 62 C2
Anaunethad L. Canada 60°55N 104°25W 71 A8
Anbyŏn N. Korea 39°1N 127°35E 33 E14
Ancaster Canada 43°13N 79°59W 82 C5
Anchor Bay U.S.A. 38°48N 123°34W 78 G3
Anchorage U.S.A. 61°13N 149°54W 68 E2
Anchuthengu India 8°40N 76°46E 45 K3
Anci China 39°20N 116°40E 32 E9
Ancohuma, Nevado Bolivia 16°0S 68°50W 92 G5
Ancón Peru 11°50S 77°10W 92 F3
Ancona Italy 43°38N 13°30E 22 C5
Ancud Chile 42°0S 73°50W 96 E2
Ancud, G. de Chile 42°0S 73°0W 96 E2
Anda China 46°24N 125°19E 31 B14
Andacollo Argentina 37°10S 70°42W 94 D1
Andacollo Chile 30°14S 71°6W 94 C1
Andalgalá Argentina 27°40S 66°30W 94 B2
Åndalsnes Norway 62°35N 7°43E 8 E12
Andalucía □ Spain 37°35N 5°0W 21 D3
Andalusia = Andalucía □ Spain 37°35N 5°0W 21 D3
Andalusia U.S.A. 31°18N 86°29W 85 F11
Andaman & Nicobar Is. □ India 10°0N 93°0E 45 K11
Andaman Is. Ind. Oc. 12°30N 92°45E 45 H11
Andaman Sea Ind. Oc. 13°0N 96°0E 36 B1
Andamooka Australia 30°27S 137°9E 63 E2
Andapa Madag. 14°39S 49°39E 55 G9
Andara Namibia 18°2S 21°9E 56 A3
Andenes Norway 69°19N 16°18E 8 B17
Andenne Belgium 50°28N 5°5E 15 D5
Anderson Alaska, U.S.A. 64°25N 149°15W 74 C10
Anderson Calif., U.S.A. 40°27N 122°18W 76 F2
Anderson Ind., U.S.A. 40°10N 85°41W 81 E11
Anderson Mo., U.S.A. 36°39N 94°27W 80 G6
Anderson S.C., U.S.A. 34°31N 82°39W 85 D13
Anderson → Canada 69°42N 129°0W 68 D6
Anderson I. India 12°46N 92°43E 45 H11
Andes U.S.A. 42°12N 74°47W 83 D10
Andes, Cord. de los S. Amer. 20°0S 68°0W 92 H5
Andfjorden Norway 69°10N 16°20E 8 B17
Andhra, L. India 18°54N 73°32E 44 E1
Andhra Pradesh □ India 18°0N 79°0E 44 F4
Andijon Uzbekistan 41°10N 72°15E 30 C3
Andikíthira = Antikythira Greece 35°52N 23°15E 23 G10
Andīmeshk Iran 32°27N 48°21E 47 C6
Andizhan = Andijon Uzbekistan 41°10N 72°15E 30 C3
Andoany Madag. 13°25S 48°16E 55 G9
Andol India 17°51N 78°4E 44 F4
Andola India 16°57N 76°50E 44 F3
Andong S. Korea 36°40N 128°43E 33 F15
Andorra ■ Europe 42°30N 1°30E 20 E4
Andorra La Vella Andorra 42°31N 1°32E 20 E4
Andover U.K. 51°12N 1°29W 13 F6
Andover Kans., U.S.A. 37°43N 97°7W 80 G5
Andover Maine, U.S.A. 44°38N 70°45W 83 B14
Andover Mass., U.S.A. 42°40N 71°8W 83 D13
Andover N.J., U.S.A. 40°59N 74°45W 83 F10
Andover N.Y., U.S.A. 42°10N 77°48W 82 D7
Andover Ohio, U.S.A. 41°36N 80°34W 82 E4
Andøya Norway 69°10N 15°50E 8 B16
Andradina Brazil 20°54S 51°23W 93 H8
Andreanof Is. U.S.A. 51°30N 176°0W 74 E4
Andrews S.C., U.S.A. 33°27N 79°34W 85 E15
Andrews Tex., U.S.A. 32°19N 102°33W 84 E3
Ándria Italy 41°13N 16°17E 22 D7
Andros Greece 37°50N 24°57E 23 F11
Andros I. Bahamas 24°30N 78°0W 88 B4
Andros Town Bahamas 24°43N 77°47W 88 B4
Androth I. India 10°50N 73°41E 45 J1
Andselv Norway 69°4N 18°34E 8 B18
Andújar Spain 38°3N 4°5W 21 C3
Andulo Angola 11°25S 16°45E 54 G3
Anegada Br. Virgin Is. 18°45N 64°20W 89 e
Anegada Passage W. Indies 18°15N 63°45W 89 C7
Aneto, Pico de Spain 42°37N 0°40E 21 A6
Anfu China 27°21N 114°40E 35 D10
Ang Thong Thailand 14°35N 100°31E 38 E3
Ang Thong, Ko Thailand 9°37N 99°41E 39 b
Ang Thong, Mu Ko △ Thailand 9°40N 99°43E 39 b
Angamos, Punta Chile 23°1S 70°32W 94 A1
Angara → Russia 58°5N 94°20E 27 D10
Angarsk Russia 52°30N 104°0E 30 A9
Angas Hills Australia 23°0S 127°50E 60 D4
Angaston Australia 34°30S 139°8E 63 E2
Ånge Sweden 62°31N 15°35E 8 E16
Ángel, Salto = Angel Falls Venezuela 5°57N 62°30W 92 B6
Ángel de la Guarda, I. Mexico 29°20N 113°25W 86 B2
Angel Falls Venezuela 5°57N 62°30W 92 B6
Angeles Phil. 15°9N 120°33E 37 A6
Ängelholm Sweden 56°15N 12°53E 9 H15
Angels Camp U.S.A. 38°4N 120°32W 78 G6
Ångermanälven → Sweden 63°0N 17°20E 8 E17
Ångermanland Sweden 63°36N 17°45E 8 E17
Angers Canada 45°31N 75°29W 83 A9
Angers France 47°30N 0°35W 20 C3
Ängesån → Sweden 66°16N 22°47E 8 C20
Angikuni L. Canada 62°12N 99°59W 71 A9
Angkor Cambodia 13°22N 103°50E 38 F4
Angledool Australia 29°5S 147°55E 63 D4
Anglesey U.K. 53°17N 4°20W 12 D3
Anglesey, Isle of □ U.K. 53°16N 4°18W 12 D3
Angleton U.S.A. 29°10N 95°26W 84 G7
Angmagssalik = Tasiilaq Greenland 65°40N 37°20W 4 C6
Ango Dem. Rep. of the Congo 4°10N 26°5E 54 D5
Angoche Mozam. 16°8S 39°55E 55 H7
Angol Chile 37°56S 72°45W 94 D1
Angola Ind., U.S.A. 41°38N 85°0W 81 E11
Angola N.Y., U.S.A. 42°38N 79°2W 82 D5
Angola ■ Africa 12°0S 18°0E 55 G3
Angoulême France 45°39N 0°10E 20 D4
Angoumois France 45°50N 0°25E 20 D3
Angra do Heroismo Azores 38°39N 27°13W 52 a
Angra dos Reis Brazil 23°0S 44°10W 95 A7
Angtassom Cambodia 11°1N 104°41E 39 G5
Anguang China 45°15N 123°45E 33 B12
Anguilla ⊿ W. Indies 18°14N 63°5W 89 C7
Angul India 20°51N 85°6E 44 D7
Anguo China 38°28N 115°15E 32 E8
Angurugu Australia 14°0S 136°25E 62 A2
Angus Canada 44°19N 79°53W 82 B5
Angus □ U.K. 56°46N 2°56W 11 E6
Angwa → Zimbabwe 16°0S 30°23E 57 A5
Anhanduí → Brazil 21°46S 52°9W 95 A5
Anholt Denmark 56°42N 11°33E 9 H14
Anhua China 28°23N 111°12E 35 C8
Anhui □ China 32°0N 117°0E 35 B11
Anhwei = Anhui □ China 32°0N 117°0E 35 B11
Anichab Namibia 21°0S 14°46E 56 B1
Animas → U.S.A. 36°43N 108°13W 77 H9
Anin Myanmar 15°36N 97°50E 38 E1
Anjalankoski Finland 60°45N 26°51E 8 F22
Anjangaon India 21°10N 77°20E 44 D3
Anjar = Hawsh Mūssá Lebanon 33°45N 35°55E 48 B4
Anjar India 23°6N 70°10E 42 H4
Anjengo = Anchuthengu India 8°40N 76°46E 45 K3
Anji China 30°46N 119°40E 35 B12
Anjidiv I. India 14°40N 74°10E 45 G2
Anjou France 47°20N 0°15W 20 C3
Anjouan Comoros Is. 12°15S 44°20E 55 a
Anju N. Korea 39°36N 125°40E 33 E13
Ankaboa, Tanjona Madag. 21°58S 43°20E 55 J8
Ankang China 32°40N 109°1E 32 H5
Ankara Turkey 39°57N 32°54E 19 G5
Ankaratra Madag. 19°25S 47°12E 55 H9
Ankazoabo Madag. 22°18S 44°31E 55 J8
Ankeny U.S.A. 41°44N 93°36W 80 E7
Ankleshwar India 21°38N 73°3E 44 D1
Ankola India 14°40N 74°18E 45 G2
Anlong China 25°2N 105°27E 34 E5
Anlong Veng Cambodia 14°14N 104°5E 38 E5
Anlu China 31°15N 113°45E 35 B9
Anmyeondo S. Korea 36°25N 126°25E 33 F14
Ann, C. U.S.A. 42°38N 70°35W 83 D14
Ann Arbor U.S.A. 42°17N 83°45W 81 D12
Anna U.S.A. 37°28N 89°15W 80 G9
Annaba Algeria 36°50N 7°46E 52 A7
Annalee → Ireland 54°2N 7°24W 10 B4
Annam = Trung Phan Vietnam 17°0N 109°0E 38 D6
Annamitique, Chaîne Asia 17°0N 106°40E 38 D6
Annan U.K. 54°59N 3°16W 11 G5
Annan → U.K. 54°58N 3°16W 11 G5
Annapolis U.S.A. 38°59N 76°30W 81 F15
Annapolis Royal Canada 44°44N 65°32W 73 D6
Annapurna Nepal 28°34N 83°50E 43 E10
Annean, L. Australia 26°54S 118°14E 61 E2
Annecy France 45°55N 6°8E 20 D7
Annette I. U.S.A. 55°9N 131°28W 70 B2
Annigeri India 15°26N 75°26E 45 G2
Anning China 24°55N 102°26E 34 E4
Anniston U.S.A. 33°39N 85°50W 85 E12
Annobón Atl. Oc. 1°25S 5°36E 51 G4
Annotto B. Jamaica 18°17N 76°45W 88 a
Annville U.S.A. 40°20N 76°31W 83 F8
Anping Hebei, China 38°15N 115°30E 32 E8
Anping Liaoning, China 41°5N 123°30E 33 D12
Anpu Gang China 21°25N 109°50E 34 G7
Anqing China 30°30N 117°3E 35 B11
Anqiu China 36°25N 119°10E 33 F10
Anren China 26°43N 113°18E 35 D9
Ansai China 36°50N 109°20E 32 F5
Ansan S. Korea 37°21N 126°52E 33 F14
Ansbach Germany 49°28N 10°34E 16 D6
Anse Boileau Seychelles 4°43S 55°29E 55 b
Anse la Raye St. Lucia 13°55N 61°3W 89 f
Anse Royale Seychelles 4°44S 55°31E 55 b
Anshan China 41°5N 122°58E 33 D12
Anshun China 26°18N 105°57E 34 D5
Ansley U.S.A. 41°18N 99°23W 80 E4
Anson U.S.A. 32°45N 99°54W 84 E5
Anson B. Australia 13°20S 130°6E 60 B5
Ansongo Mali 15°25N 0°35E 52 E6
Ansonia U.S.A. 41°21N 73°5W 83 E11
Anstruther U.K. 56°14N 2°41W 11 E6
Ansudu Indonesia 2°11S 139°22E 37 E9
Antabamba Peru 14°40S 73°0W 92 F4
Antagarh India 20°6N 81°9E 44 D5
Antakya = Hatay Turkey 36°14N 36°10E 46 B3
Antalaha Madag. 14°57S 50°20E 55 G10
Antalya Turkey 36°52N 30°45E 19 G5
Antalya Körfezi Turkey 36°15N 31°30E 19 G5
Antananarivo Madag. 18°55S 47°31E 55 H9
Antarctic Pen. Antarctica 67°0S 60°0W 5 C18
Antarctica 90°0S 0°0 5 E3
Antep = Gaziantep Turkey 37°6N 37°23E 46 B3
Antequera Paraguay 24°8S 57°7W 94 A4
Antequera Spain 37°5N 4°33W 21 D3
Antero, Mt. U.S.A. 38°41N 106°15W 76 G10
Anthony Kans., U.S.A. 37°9N 98°2W 80 G4
Anthony N. Mex., U.S.A. 32°0N 106°36W 77 K10
Anti Atlas Morocco 30°0N 8°30W 52 C4
Anti-Lebanon = Sharqi, Al Jabal ash Lebanon 33°40N 36°10E 48 B5
Antibes France 43°34N 7°6E 20 E7
Anticosti, Î. d' Canada 49°30N 63°0W 73 C7
Antigo U.S.A. 45°9N 89°9W 80 C9
Antigonish Canada 45°38N 61°58W 73 C7
Antigua Guatemala 14°34N 90°41W 88 D1
Antigua W. Indies 17°0N 61°50W 89 C7
Antigua & Barbuda ■ W. Indies 17°20N 61°48W 89 C7
Antikythira Greece 35°52N 23°15E 23 G10
Antilla Cuba 20°40N 75°50W 88 B4
Antilles = West Indies Cent. Amer. 15°0N 65°0W 89 D7
Antioch U.S.A. 38°1N 121°48W 78 G5
Antioquia Colombia 6°40N 75°55W 92 B3
Antipodes Is. Pac. Oc. 49°45S 178°40E 64 M9
Antlers U.S.A. 34°14N 95°37W 84 D7
Antofagasta Chile 23°50S 70°30W 94 A1
Antofagasta □ Chile 24°0S 69°0W 94 A2
Antofagasta de la Sierra Argentina 26°5S 67°20W 94 B2
Antofalla Argentina 25°30S 68°5W 94 B2
Antofalla, Salar de Argentina 25°40S 67°45W 94 B2
Anton U.S.A. 33°49N 102°10W 84 E3
Antonina Brazil 25°26S 48°42W 95 B6
Antrim U.K. 54°43N 6°14W 10 B5
Antrim U.S.A. 40°7N 81°21W 82 F3
Antrim □ U.K. 54°56N 6°25W 10 B5
Antrim, Mts. of U.K. 55°3N 6°14W 10 A5
Antrim Plateau Australia 18°8S 128°20E 60 C4
Antsalova Madag. 18°40S 44°37E 55 H8
Antsirabe Madag. 19°55S 47°2E 55 H9
Antsiranana Madag. 12°25S 49°20E 55 G9
Antsohihy Madag. 14°50S 47°59E 55 G9
Antu China 42°30N 128°20E 33 C15
Antwerp = Antwerpen Belgium 51°13N 4°25E 15 C4
Antwerp U.S.A. 44°12N 75°37W 83 B9
Antwerpen Belgium 51°13N 4°25E 15 C4
Antwerpen □ Belgium 51°15N 4°40E 15 C4
Anupgarh India 29°10N 73°10E 42 E5
Anuppur India 23°6N 81°41E 43 H9
Anuradhapura Sri Lanka 8°22N 80°28E 45 K5
Anurrete ❂ Australia 20°50S 135°38E 62 C2
Anveh Iran 27°23N 54°11E 47 E7
Anvers = Antwerpen Belgium 51°13N 4°25E 15 C4
Anvers I. Antarctica 64°30S 63°40W 5 C17
Anwen China 29°4N 120°26E 35 C13
Anxi Fujian, China 25°2N 118°12E 35 E12
Anxi Gansu, China 40°30N 95°43E 30 C8
Anxian China 31°40N 104°25E 34 B5
Anxiang China 29°27N 112°11E 35 C9
Anxious B. Australia 33°24S 134°45E 63 E1
Anyang China 36°5N 114°21E 32 F8
Anyang S. Korea 37°23N 126°55E 33 F14
Anyer Indonesia 6°4S 105°53E 37 G11
Anyi Jiangxi, China 28°49N 115°25E 35 C10
Anyi Shanxi, China 35°2N 111°2E 32 G6
Anyuan China 25°9N 115°21E 35 E10
Anyue China 30°9N 105°50E 34 B5
Anza U.S.A. 33°35N 116°39W 79 M10
Anze China 36°10N 112°12E 32 F7
Anzhero-Sudzhensk Russia 56°10N 86°0E 26 D9
Ánzio Italy 41°27N 12°37E 22 D5
Ao Makham Thailand 7°50N 98°24E 39 a
Ao Phangnga △ Thailand 8°10N 98°32E 39 a
Aoga-Shima Japan 32°28N 139°46E 29 H9
Aohan Qi China 43°18N 119°43E 33 C10
Aoji N. Korea 42°31N 130°23E 33 C16
Aomen = Macau China 22°12N 113°33E 35 F9
Aomori Japan 40°45N 140°45E 28 D10
Aomori □ Japan 40°45N 140°40E 28 D10
tAonach, An = Nenagh Ireland 52°52N 8°11W 10 D3
Aonla India 28°16N 79°11E 43 E8
Aorai, Mt. Tahiti 17°34S 149°30W 59 d
Aoraki Mount Cook N.Z. 43°36S 170°9E 59 E3
Aoral, Phnum Cambodia 12°0N 104°15E 39 G5
Aosta Italy 45°45N 7°20E 20 D7
Aotearoa = New Zealand ■ Oceania 40°0S 176°0E 59 D6
Aoukâr Mauritania 17°40N 10°0W 52 E4
Aozou, Couloir d' Chad 22°0N 19°0E 53 D9
Apá → S. Amer. 22°6S 58°2W 94 A4
Apache U.S.A. 34°54N 98°22W 84 D5
Apache Junction U.S.A. 33°25N 111°33W 77 K8
Apalachee B. U.S.A. 30°0N 84°0W 85 G13
Apalachicola U.S.A. 29°43N 84°59W 85 G12
Apalachicola → U.S.A. 29°43N 84°58W 85 G12
Apaporis → Colombia 1°23S 69°25W 92 D5
Aparados da Serra △ Brazil 29°10S 50°8W 95 B5
Aparri Phil. 18°22N 121°38E 37 A6
Apatity Russia 67°34N 33°22E 8 C25
Apatula = Finke Australia 25°34S 134°35E 62 D1
Apatzingán Mexico 19°5N 102°21W 86 D4
Apeldoorn Neths. 52°13N 5°57E 15 B5
Apennines = Appennini Italy 44°30N 10°0E 22 B4
Api Nepal 30°0N 80°57E 30 F5
Apia Samoa 13°50S 171°50W 59 b
Apiacás, Serra dos Brazil 9°50S 57°0W 92 E7
Apies → S. Africa 25°15S 28°8E 57 C4
Apizaco Mexico 19°25N 98°8W 87 D5
Aplao Peru 16°0S 72°40W 92 G4
Apo, Mt. Phil. 6°53N 125°14E 37 C7
Apollonia = Sūsah Libya 32°52N 21°59E 53 B10
Apolo Bolivia 14°30S 68°30W 92 F5
Apopa El Salv. 13°48N 89°10W 88 D2
Aporé → Brazil 19°27S 50°57W 93 G8
Apostle Is. U.S.A. 47°0N 90°40W 80 B8
Apostle Islands ⌂ U.S.A. 46°55N 91°0W 80 B8
Apóstoles Argentina 28°0S 56°0W 95 B4
Apostolos Andreas, C. Cyprus 35°42N 34°35E 46 C2
Apoteri Guyana 4°2N 58°32W 92 C7
Appalachian Mts. U.S.A. 38°0N 80°0W 81 G14
Appennini Italy 44°30N 10°0E 22 B4
Apple Hill Canada 45°13N 74°46W 83 A10
Apple Valley U.S.A. 34°32N 117°14W 79 L9
Appleby-in-Westmorland U.K. 54°35N 2°29W 12 C5
Appledore U.K. 51°3N 4°13W 13 F3
Appleton U.S.A. 44°16N 88°25W 80 C9
Approuague → Fr. Guiana 4°30N 51°57W 93 C8
Aprília Italy 41°36N 12°39E 22 D5
Apsley Canada 44°45N 78°6W 82 B6
Apucarana Brazil 23°55S 51°33W 95 A5
Apure → Venezuela 7°37N 66°25W 92 B5
Apurímac → Peru 12°17S 73°56W 92 F4
Āq Qālā Iran 37°10N 54°30E 47 B7
Aqaba = Al 'Aqabah Jordan 29°31N 35°0E 48 F4
Aqaba, G. of Red Sea 29°0N 34°40E 46 D2
'Aqabah, Khalīj al = Aqaba, G. of Red Sea 29°0N 34°40E 46 D2
'Aqdā Iran 32°26N 53°37E 47 C7
'Aqrah Iraq 36°46N 43°45E 46 B4
Aqsay Kazakhstan 51°11N 53°0E 19 D9
Aqtaū Kazakhstan 43°39N 51°12E 19 F9
Aqtöbe Kazakhstan 50°17N 57°10E 19 D10
Aqtoghay Kazakhstan 46°57N 79°40E 26 E8
Aqua = Sokhumi Georgia 43°0N 41°0E 19 F7
Aquidauana Brazil 20°30S 55°50W 93 H7
Aquila Mexico 18°36N 103°30W 86 D4
Aquiles Serdán Mexico 28°36N 105°53W 86 B3
Aquin Haiti 18°16N 73°24W 89 C5
Aquitain, Bassin France 44°0N 0°30W 20 D3
Ar Horqin Qi China 43°45N 120°0E 33 C11
Ar Rafid Syria 32°57N 35°52E 48 C4
Ar Raḥḥālīyah Iraq 32°44N 43°23E 46 C4
Ar Ramādī Iraq 33°25N 43°20E 46 C4
Ar Ramthā Jordan 32°34N 36°0E 48 C5
Ar Raqqah Syria 35°59N 39°8E 46 C3
Ar Rashidiya = Er Rachidia Morocco 31°58N 4°20W 52 B5
Ar Rass Si. Arabia 25°50N 43°40E 46 E4
Ar Rawḍah Si. Arabia 21°16N 42°50E 49 C3
Ar Rayyan Qatar 25°17N 51°25E 47 E6
Ar Rifā'ī Iraq 31°50N 46°10E 46 D5

Ar Riyāḍ *Si. Arabia* 24°41N 46°42E **46 E5**
Ar Ru'ays *Qatar* 26°8N 51°12E **47 E6**
Ar Rukhaymīyah *Iraq* 29°22N 45°38E **46 D5**
Ar Rumaythah *Iraq* 31°31N 45°12E **46 D5**
Ar Ruşāfah *Syria* 35°45N 38°49E **46 C3**
Ar Ruşāfah *Iraq* 33°0N 40°15E **46 C4**
Ara *India* 25°35N 84°32E **43 G11**
Arab *U.S.A.* 34°19N 86°30W **85 D11**
'Arab, Baḥr el ➤
  South Sudan 9°0N 29°30E **53 G11**
Arab, Shatt al ➤ *Asia* 29°57N 48°34E **47 D6**
'Arabābād *Iran* 33°2N 57°41E **47 C8**
Arabia *Asia* 25°0N 45°0E **24 F6**
Arabian Desert = Sharqīya, Es
  Saḥrâ esh *Egypt* 27°30N 32°30E **53 C12**
Arabian Gulf = Persian Gulf
  Asia 27°0N 50°0E **47 E6**
Arabian Sea *Ind. Oc.* 16°0N 65°0E **24 G8**
Aracaju *Brazil* 10°55S 37°4W **93 F11**
Aracati *Brazil* 4°30S 37°44W **93 D11**
Araçatuba *Brazil* 21°10S 50°30W **95 A5**
Aracena *Spain* 37°53N 6°38W **21 D2**
Araçuai *Brazil* 16°52S 42°4W **93 G10**
'Arad *Israel* 31°15N 35°12E **48 D4**
Arad *Romania* 46°10N 21°20E **17 E11**
Arādān *Iran* 35°21N 52°30E **47 C7**
Arafura Sea *E. Indies* 9°0S 135°0E **58 B6**
Aragón □ *Spain* 41°25N 0°40W **21 B5**
Aragón ➤ *Spain* 42°13N 1°44W **21 A5**
Araguacema *Brazil* 8°50S 49°20W **93 E9**
Araguaia ➤ *Brazil* 5°21S 48°41W **93 E9**
Araguaína *Brazil* 7°12S 48°12W **93 E9**
Araguari *Brazil* 18°38S 48°11W **93 G9**
Araguari ➤ *Brazil* 1°15N 49°55W **93 C9**
Arain *India* 26°27N 75°2E **42 F6**
Arak *Algeria* 25°20N 3°45E **52 C6**
Arāk *Iran* 34°0N 49°40E **47 C6**
Arakan = Rakhine □
  Myanmar 19°0N 94°15E **41 K18**
Arakan Coast *Myanmar* 19°0N 94°0E **41 K19**
Arakan Yoma *Myanmar* 20°0N 94°40E **41 K19**
Arakkonam *India* 13°7N 79°43E **45 H4**
Araks = Aras, Rūd-e ➤
  Asia 40°5N 48°29E **46 B5**
Aral *Kazakhstan* 46°41N 61°45E **26 E7**
Aral Sea *Asia* 45°0N 58°20E **26 E7**
Aral Tengizi = Aral Sea
  Asia 45°0N 58°20E **26 E7**
Aralsk = Aral *Kazakhstan* 46°41N 61°45E **26 E7**
Aralskoye More = Aral Sea
  Asia 45°0N 58°20E **26 E7**
Aramac *Australia* 22°58S 145°14E **62 C4**
Aran ➤ *India* 19°55N 78°12E **44 E4**
Aran I. = Arranmore
  Ireland 55°0N 8°30W **10 A3**
Aran Is. *Ireland* 53°6N 9°38W **10 C2**
Aranda de Duero *Spain* 41°39N 3°42W **21 B4**
Arandān *Iran* 35°23N 46°55E **46 C5**
Arani *India* 12°43N 79°19E **45 H4**
Aranjuez *Spain* 40°1N 3°40W **21 B4**
Aranos *Namibia* 24°9S 19°7E **56 B2**
Aransas Pass *U.S.A.* 27°55N 97°9W **84 H6**
Aranyaprathet *Thailand* 13°41N 102°30E **38 F4**
Arapaho ➤ *U.S.A.* 40°18N 99°54W **80 E4**
Arapey Grande ➤
  Uruguay 30°55S 57°49W **94 C4**
Arapgir *Turkey* 39°5N 38°30E **46 B3**
Arapiraca *Brazil* 9°45S 36°39W **93 E11**
Arapongas *Brazil* 23°29S 51°28W **95 A5**
Ar'ar *Si. Arabia* 30°59N 41°2E **46 D4**
Araranguá *Brazil* 29°0S 49°30W **95 B6**
Araraquara *Brazil* 21°50S 48°0W **93 H9**
Ararás, Serra das *Brazil* 25°0S 53°10W **95 B5**
Ararat *Australia* 37°16S 142°58E **63 F3**
Ararat, Mt. = Ağrı Dağı
  Turkey 39°50N 44°15E **46 B5**
Araria *India* 26°9N 87°33E **43 F12**
Araripe, Chapada do
  Brazil 7°20S 40°0W **93 E11**
Araruama, L. de *Brazil* 22°53S 42°12W **95 A7**
Aras, Rūd-e ➤ *Asia* 40°5N 48°29E **46 B5**
Arauca *Colombia* 7°0N 70°40W **92 B4**
Arauca ➤ *Venezuela* 7°24N 66°35W **92 B5**
Arauco *Chile* 37°16S 73°25W **94 D1**
Aravalli Range *India* 25°0N 73°30E **42 G5**
Araxá *Brazil* 19°35S 46°55W **93 G9**
Araya, Pen. de *Venezuela* 10°40N 64°0W **92 A6**
Arba Minch *Ethiopia* 6°0N 37°30E **49 F2**
Arbat *Iraq* 35°25N 45°35E **46 C5**
Árbatax *Italy* 39°56N 9°42E **22 E3**
Arbīl *Iraq* 36°15N 44°5E **46 B5**
Arborfield *Canada* 53°6N 103°39W **71 C8**
Arborg *Canada* 50°54N 97°13W **71 C9**
Arbroath *U.K.* 56°34N 2°35W **11 E6**
Arbuckle *U.S.A.* 39°1N 122°3W **78 F4**
Arcachon *France* 44°40N 1°10W **20 D3**
Arcade *U.S.A.* 42°32N 78°25W **82 D6**
Arcadia *Fla., U.S.A.* 27°13N 81°52W **85 H14**
Arcadia *La., U.S.A.* 32°33N 92°55W **84 E8**
Arcadia *Pa., U.S.A.* 40°47N 78°51W **82 F6**
Arcata *U.S.A.* 40°52N 124°5W **76 F1**
Archangel = Arkhangelsk
  Russia 64°38N 40°36E **18 B7**
Archbald *U.S.A.* 41°30N 75°32W **83 E9**
Archer ➤ *Australia* 13°28S 141°41E **62 A3**
Archer B. *Australia* 13°20S 141°30E **62 A3**
Archer Bend = Mungkan
  Kandju △ *Australia* 13°35S 142°52E **62 A3**
Arches △ *U.S.A.* 38°45N 109°25W **76 G9**
Archipel-de-Mingan △
  Canada 50°13N 63°10W **73 B7**
Archipiélago Los Roques △
  Venezuela 11°50N 66°44W **89 D6**
Arckaringa Cr. ➤
  Australia 28°10S 135°22E **63 D2**
Arco *U.S.A.* 43°38N 113°18W **76 E7**
Arcos de la Frontera
  Spain 36°45N 5°49W **21 D3**
Arcot *India* 12°53N 79°20E **45 H4**
Arctic Bay *Canada* 73°1N 85°7W **69 C14**

Arctic Mid-Ocean Ridge
  Arctic 87°0N 90°0E **4 A**
Arctic Ocean *Arctic* 78°0N 160°0W **4 B18**
Arctic Red River = Tsiigehtchic
  Canada 67°15N 134°0W **68 D5**
Arctowski *Antarctica* 62°30S 58°0W **5 C18**
Arda ➤ *Bulgaria* 41°40N 26°30E **23 D12**
Ardabīl *Iran* 38°15N 48°18E **47 B6**
Ardabīl □ *Iran* 38°20N 48°0E **47 B6**
Ardakān = Sepīdān *Iran* 30°20N 52°5E **47 D7**
Ardakān *Iran* 32°19N 53°59E **47 C7**
Ardara *Ireland* 54°46N 8°25W **10 B3**
Ardee *Ireland* 53°52N 6°33W **10 C5**
Arden *Canada* 44°43N 76°56W **82 B8**
Arden *Calif., U.S.A.* 38°36N 121°33W **78 G5**
Arden *Nev., U.S.A.* 36°1N 115°14W **79 J11**
Ardenne *Belgium* 49°50N 5°5E **15 E5**
Ardennes = Ardenne
  Belgium 49°50N 5°5E **15 E5**
Arderin *Ireland* 53°2N 7°39W **10 C4**
Ardestān *Iran* 33°20N 52°25E **47 C7**
Ardfert *Ireland* 52°20N 9°47W **10 D2**
Ardglass *U.K.* 54°16N 5°36W **10 B6**
Ardivachar Pt. *U.K.* 57°23N 7°26W **11 D1**
Ardlethan *Australia* 34°22S 146°53E **63 E4**
Ardmore *Okla., U.S.A.* 34°10N 97°8W **84 D6**
Ardmore *Pa., U.S.A.* 40°2N 75°17W **83 F9**
Ardnamurchan, Pt. of
  U.K. 56°43N 6°14W **11 E2**
Ardnave Pt. *U.K.* 55°53N 6°20W **11 F2**
Ardrossan *Australia* 34°26S 137°53E **63 E2**
Ardrossan *U.K.* 55°39N 4°49W **11 F4**
Ards Pen. *U.K.* 54°33N 5°34W **10 B6**
Arecibo *Puerto Rico* 18°29N 66°43W **89 d**
Areia Branca *Brazil* 5°0S 37°0W **93 E11**
Arena, Pt. *U.S.A.* 38°57N 123°44W **78 G3**
Arenal *Honduras* 15°21N 86°50W **88 C2**
Arendal *Norway* 58°28N 8°46E **9 G13**
Arequipa *Peru* 16°20S 71°30W **92 G4**
Arévalo *Spain* 41°3N 4°43W **21 B3**
Arezzo *Italy* 43°25N 11°53E **22 C4**
Arga ➤ *Turkey* 38°21N 37°59E **46 B3**
Arganda del Rey *Spain* 40°19N 3°26W **21 B4**
Argarapa ◎ *Australia* 22°20S 134°58E **62 C1**
Argenta *Canada* 50°11N 116°56W **70 C5**
Argentan *France* 48°45N 0°1W **20 B3**
Argentário, Mte. *Italy* 42°24N 11°9E **22 C4**
Argentia *Canada* 47°18N 53°58W **73 C9**
Argentina ■ *S. Amer.* 35°0S 66°0W **96 D3**
Argentine Basin *Atl. Oc.* 45°0S 45°0W **96 F6**
Argentino, L. *Argentina* 50°10S 73°0W **96 G2**
Argeş ➤ *Romania* 44°5N 26°38E **17 F14**
Arghandab ➤ *Afghan.* 31°30N 64°15E **42 D1**
Argolikos Kolpos *Greece* 37°20N 22°52E **23 F10**
Argos *Greece* 37°40N 22°43E **23 F10**
Argostoli *Greece* 38°11N 20°29E **23 E9**
Arguello, Pt. *U.S.A.* 34°35N 120°39W **79 L6**
Argun ➤ *Russia* 53°20N 121°28E **31 A6**
Argungu *Nigeria* 12°40N 4°31E **52 F6**
Argus Pk. *U.S.A.* 35°52N 117°26W **79 K9**
Argyle, L. *Australia* 16°20S 128°40E **60 C4**
Argyle *Trin. & Tob.* 10°38N 61°17W **93 K15**
Argyll & Bute □ *U.K.* 56°13N 5°28W **11 E3**
Århus = Aarhus *Denmark* 56°8N 10°11E **9 H14**
Ariadnoye *Russia* 45°8N 134°25E **28 B7**
Ariamsvlei *Namibia* 28°9S 19°51E **56 C2**
Ariana, L' *Tunisia* 36°52N 10°12E **53 A8**
Arica *Chile* 18°32S 70°20W **92 G4**
Arica *Colombia* 2°0S 71°50W **92 D4**
Arid, C. *Australia* 34°1S 123°10E **61 F3**
Arida *Japan* 34°5N 135°8E **29 G7**
Aride *Seychelles* 4°13S 55°40E **55 b**
Ariège ➤ *France* 43°30N 1°25E **20 E4**
Arima *Trin. & Tob.* 10°38N 61°17W **93 K15**
Arinos ➤ *Brazil* 10°25S 58°20W **92 F7**
Ario de Rosales *Mexico* 19°12N 101°43W **86 D4**
Aripo, Mt. *Trin. & Tob.* 10°45N 61°15W **93 K15**
Aripuanã *Brazil* 9°25S 60°30W **92 E6**
Aripuanã ➤ *Brazil* 5°7S 60°25W **92 E6**
Ariquemes *Brazil* 9°55S 63°6W **92 E6**
Arisaig *U.K.* 56°55N 5°51W **11 E3**
Aristazabal I. *Canada* 52°40N 129°10W **70 C3**
Ariyalur *India* 11°8N 79°8E **45 J4**
Arizaro, Salar de
  Argentina 24°40S 67°50W **94 A2**
Arizona *Argentina* 35°45S 65°25W **94 D2**
Arizona □ *U.S.A.* 34°0N 112°0W **77 J8**
Arizpe *Mexico* 30°20N 110°10W **86 A2**
'Arjah *Si. Arabia* 24°43N 44°17E **46 E5**
Arjeplog *Sweden* 66°3N 17°54E **8 C17**
Arjeplouvve = Arjeplog
  Sweden 66°3N 17°54E **8 C17**
Arjona *Colombia* 10°14N 75°22W **92 A3**
Arjuna *Indonesia* 7°49S 112°34E **37 G15**
Arka *Russia* 60°15N 142°0E **27 C15**
Arkadelphia *U.S.A.* 34°7N 93°4W **84 D8**
Arkaig, L. *U.K.* 56°59N 5°10W **11 E3**
Arkalgud *India* 12°46N 76°3E **45 H3**
Arkalyk = Arqalyk
  Kazakhstan 50°13N 66°50E **26 D7**
Arkansas □ *U.S.A.* 35°0N 92°30W **84 D8**
Arkansas ➤ *U.S.A.* 33°47N 91°4W **84 E9**
Arkansas City *U.S.A.* 37°4N 97°2W **80 G5**
Arkaroola *Australia* 30°20S 139°22E **63 E2**
Arkhangelsk *Russia* 64°38N 40°36E **18 B7**
Arki *India* 31°9N 76°58E **42 D7**
Arklow *Ireland* 52°48N 6°10W **10 D5**
Arkport *U.S.A.* 42°24N 77°42W **82 D7**
Arkticheskiy, Mys *Russia* 81°10N 95°0E **27 A10**
Arkville *U.S.A.* 42°9N 74°37W **83 D10**
Arlanzón ➤ *Spain* 42°3N 4°17W **21 A3**
Arlbergpass *Austria* 47°9N 10°12E **16 E6**
Arlbergtunnel *Austria* 47°9N 10°12E **16 E6**
Arles *France* 43°41N 4°40E **20 E6**
Arlington *S. Africa* 28°1S 27°53E **57 C4**
Arlington *N.Y., U.S.A.* 41°42N 73°54W **83 E11**
Arlington *S. Dak., U.S.A.* 44°22N 97°8W **80 C6**
Arlington *Vt., U.S.A.* 43°5N 73°9W **83 C11**
Arlington *Wash., U.S.A.* 48°12N 122°8W **78 B4**
Arlington Heights
  U.S.A. 42°5N 87°59W **80 D10**

Arlit *Niger* 19°0N 7°38E **52 E7**
Arlon *Belgium* 49°42N 5°49E **15 E5**
Arlparra *Australia* 22°11S 134°30E **62 C1**
Arltunga *Australia* 23°26S 134°41E **62 C1**
Armadale *Australia* 32°9S 116°0E **61 F2**
Armagh *U.K.* 54°21N 6°39W **10 B5**
Armagh □ *U.K.* 54°18N 6°37W **10 B5**
Armando Bermudez △
  Dom. Rep. 19°3N 71°0W **89 C5**
Armavir *Russia* 45°2N 41°7E **19 E7**
Armenia *Colombia* 4°35N 75°45W **92 C3**
Armenia ■ *Asia* 40°20N 45°0E **19 F7**
Armidale *Australia* 30°30S 151°40E **63 E5**
Armori *India* 20°28N 79°59E **44 D4**
Armour *U.S.A.* 43°19N 98°21W **80 D4**
Armstrong *B.C., Canada* 50°25N 119°10W **70 C5**
Armstrong *Ont., Canada* 50°18N 89°4W **72 B2**
Armur *India* 18°48N 78°16E **44 E4**
Arnarfjörður *Iceland* 65°48N 23°40W **8 D2**
Arnaud ➤ *Canada* 59°59N 69°46W **69 F18**
Arnett *U.S.A.* 36°8N 99°46W **84 C5**
Arnhem *Neths.* 51°58N 5°55E **15 C5**
Arnhem, C. *Australia* 12°20S 137°30E **62 A2**
Arnhem B. *Australia* 12°20S 136°10E **62 A2**
Arnhem Land *Australia* 13°10S 134°30E **62 A1**
Arnhem Land ◎
  Australia 12°50S 134°50E **62 A1**
Arno ➤ *Italy* 43°41N 10°17E **22 C4**
Arno Bay *Australia* 33°54S 136°34E **63 E2**
Arnold *U.K.* 53°1N 1°7W **12 D6**
Arnold *Calif., U.S.A.* 38°15N 120°21W **78 G6**
Arnold *Mo., U.S.A.* 38°26N 90°23W **80 F8**
Arnot *Canada* 55°56N 96°41W **71 B9**
Arnøya *Norway* 70°9N 20°40E **8 A19**
Arnprior *Canada* 45°26N 76°21W **83 A8**
Arnsberg *Germany* 51°24N 8°5E **16 C5**
Arnsleben *Germany* 51°45N 11°29E **16 C6**
Aroa, Pte. *Moorea* 17°28S 149°46W **59 d**
Aroab *Namibia* 26°41S 19°39E **56 C2**
Aron *India* 25°57N 77°56E **42 G6**
Aros ➤ *Mexico* 29°9N 107°57W **86 B3**
Arqalyk *Kazakhstan* 50°13N 66°50E **26 D7**
Arrah = Ara *India* 25°35N 84°32E **43 G11**
Arrah *Côte d'Ivoire* 6°40N 3°58E **52 G5**
Arran *U.K.* 55°34N 5°12W **11 F3**
Arranmore *Ireland* 55°0N 8°30W **10 A3**
Arras *France* 50°17N 2°46E **20 A5**
Arrecife *Canary Is.* 28°57N 13°37W **52 C3**
Arrecifes *Argentina* 34°6S 60°9W **94 C3**
Arrée, Mts. d' *France* 48°26N 3°55W **20 B2**
Arriaga *Mexico* 16°14N 93°54W **87 D6**
Arrilalah *Australia* 23°43S 143°54E **62 C3**
Arrino *Australia* 29°30S 115°40E **61 E2**
Arrow, L. *Ireland* 54°3N 8°19W **10 B3**
Arrowtown *N.Z.* 44°57S 168°50E **59 F2**
Arroyo Grande *U.S.A.* 35°7N 120°35W **79 K6**
Ars *Iran* 37°9N 47°46E **46 B5**
Arsenault L. *Canada* 55°6N 108°32W **71 B7**
Arsenev *Russia* 44°10N 133°15E **28 B6**
Arsikere *India* 13°15N 76°15E **45 H3**
Arta *Greece* 39°8N 21°2E **23 E9**
Arteaga *Mexico* 18°28N 102°25W **86 D4**
Artem *Russia* 43°22N 132°13E **28 C6**
Artemivsk *Ukraine* 48°35N 38°0E **19 E6**
Artemovsk *Russia* 54°45N 93°35E **27 D10**
Artesia = Mosomane
  Botswana 24°2S 26°19E **56 B4**
Artesia *U.S.A.* 32°51N 104°24W **77 K11**
Arthur *Canada* 43°50N 80°32W **82 C4**
Arthur ➤ *Australia* 41°2S 144°40E **63 G3**
Arthur Cr. ➤ *Australia* 22°30S 136°25E **62 C2**
Arthur Pt. *Australia* 22°7S 150°3E **62 C5**
Arthur River *Australia* 33°20S 117°2E **61 F2**
Arthur's Pass *N.Z.* 42°54S 171°35E **59 E3**
Arthur's Pass △ *N.Z.* 42°56S 171°42E **59 E3**
Arthur's Town *Bahamas* 24°38N 75°42W **89 B4**
Artigas *Antarctica* 62°30S 58°0W **5 C18**
Artigas *Uruguay* 30°20S 56°30W **94 C4**
Artillery L. *Canada* 63°9N 107°52W **71 A7**
Artois *France* 50°20N 2°30E **20 A5**
Arts Bogd Uul *Mongolia* 44°40N 102°20E **32 B2**
Artsyz *Ukraine* 46°4N 29°26E **17 E15**
Artux *China* 39°40N 76°10E **30 D4**
Artvin *Turkey* 41°14N 41°44E **19 F7**
Artyk *Russia* 64°12N 145°6E **27 C15**
Aru, Kepulauan *Indonesia* 6°0S 134°30E **37 F8**
Aru Is. = Aru, Kepulauan
  Indonesia 6°0S 134°30E **37 F8**
Arua *Uganda* 3°1N 30°58E **54 D6**
Aruanã *Brazil* 14°54S 51°10W **93 F8**
Aruba ☒ *W. Indies* 12°30N 70°0W **89 D6**
Arué *Tahiti* 17°31S 149°30W **59 d**
Arun ➤ *Nepal* 26°55N 87°10E **43 F12**
Arun ➤ *U.K.* 50°49N 0°33W **13 G7**
Arunachal Pradesh □
  India 28°0N 95°0E **41 F19**
Aruppukkottai *India* 9°31N 78°8E **45 K4**
Arusha *Tanzania* 3°20S 36°40E **54 E7**
Aruvi ➤ *Sri Lanka* 8°48N 79°53E **45 K4**
Aruwimi ➤
  Dem. Rep. of the Congo 1°13N 23°36E **54 D4**
Arvada *Colo., U.S.A.* 39°48N 105°5W **76 G11**
Arvada *Wyo., U.S.A.* 44°39N 106°8W **76 D10**
Arvakalu *Sri Lanka* 8°20N 79°58E **45 K4**
Arvayheer *Mongolia* 46°15N 102°48E **30 B9**
Arvi *India* 20°59N 78°16E **44 D4**
Arviat *Canada* 61°6N 93°59W **71 A10**
Arvidsjaur *Sweden* 65°35N 19°10E **8 D18**
Arvika *Sweden* 59°40N 12°36E **9 G15**
Arvin *U.S.A.* 35°12N 118°50W **79 K8**
Arwal *India* 25°15N 84°41E **43 G11**
Arxan *China* 47°11N 119°57E **31 B12**
Arys *Kazakhstan* 42°26N 68°48E **26 E7**
Arzamas *Russia* 55°27N 43°55E **18 C7**
Arzanah *U.A.E.* 24°47N 52°34E **47 E7**
As Safā *Syria* 33°10N 37°0E **48 B6**
As Saffānīyah *Si. Arabia* 27°55N 48°50E **47 E6**
As Safirah *Syria* 36°5N 37°21E **46 B3**
Aş Şahm *Oman* 24°10N 56°53E **47 E8**
As Sājir *Si. Arabia* 25°11N 44°36E **46 E5**

As Salamīyah *Syria* 35°1N 37°2E **46 C3**
As Salmān *Iraq* 30°30N 44°32E **46 D5**
As Salṭ *Jordan* 32°2N 35°43E **48 C4**
As Sal'w'a *Qatar* 24°23N 50°50E **47 E6**
As Samāwah *Iraq* 31°15N 45°15E **46 D5**
As Sanamayn *Syria* 33°3N 36°10E **48 B5**
As Sila' *U.A.E.* 24°4N 51°45E **47 E6**
As Sukhnah *Syria* 34°52N 38°52E **46 C3**
As Sulaymānīyah *Iraq* 35°35N 45°29E **46 C5**
As Sulaymī *Si. Arabia* 26°17N 41°21E **46 E4**
As Sulayyil *Si. Arabia* 20°27N 45°34E **49 C4**
As Summān *Si. Arabia* 25°0N 47°0E **46 E5**
As Suwaydā *Syria* 32°40N 36°30E **48 C5**
As Suwaydā □ *Syria* 32°45N 36°45E **48 C5**
As Suwayq *Oman* 23°51N 57°26E **47 F8**
Aş Şuwayrah *Iraq* 32°55N 45°0E **46 C5**
Asab *Namibia* 25°30S 18°0E **56 C2**
Asad, Buḩayrat al *Syria* 36°0N 38°15E **46 C3**
Asahi *Japan* 35°43N 140°39E **29 G10**
Asahi-Gawa ➤ *Japan* 34°36N 133°58E **29 G6**
Asahigawa = Asahikawa
  Japan 43°46N 142°22E **28 C11**
Asahikawa *Japan* 43°46N 142°22E **28 C11**
Asaluyeh *Iran* 27°29N 52°37E **47 E7**
Asamankese *Ghana* 5°50N 0°40W **52 G5**
Asan ➤ *India* 26°37N 78°24E **43 F8**
Asansol *India* 23°40N 87°1E **43 H12**
Asau *Samoa* 13°27S 172°33W **59 b**
Asbesberge *S. Africa* 29°0S 23°0E **56 C3**
Asbestos *Canada* 45°47N 71°58W **73 C5**
Asbury Park *U.S.A.* 40°13N 74°1W **83 F10**
Ascensión *Mexico* 31°6N 107°59W **86 A3**
Ascensión, B. de la
  Mexico 19°40N 87°30W **87 D7**
Ascension I. *Atl. Oc.* 7°57S 14°23W **51 G2**
Aschaffenburg *Germany* 49°58N 9°6E **16 D5**
Aschersleben *Germany* 51°45N 11°29E **16 C6**
Áscoli Piceno *Italy* 42°51N 13°34E **22 C5**
Ascope *Peru* 7°46S 79°8W **92 E3**
Ascotán *Chile* 21°45S 68°17W **94 A2**
Aseb *Eritrea* 13°0N 42°40E **49 E3**
Asela *Ethiopia* 8°0N 39°0E **49 F2**
Asenovgrad *Bulgaria* 42°1N 24°51E **23 C11**
Aşgabat = Ashgabat
  Turkmenistan 37°58N 58°24E **47 B8**
Ash Fork *U.S.A.* 35°13N 112°29W **77 J7**
Ash Grove *U.S.A.* 37°19N 93°35W **80 G7**
Ash Shamāl □ *Lebanon* 34°25N 36°0E **48 A5**
Ash Shāmīyah *Iraq* 31°55N 44°35E **46 D5**
Ash Shāriqah *U.A.E.* 25°23N 55°26E **47 E7**
Ash Sharmah *Si. Arabia* 28°1N 35°16E **46 D2**
Ash Sharqāt *Iraq* 35°27N 43°16E **46 C4**
Ash Shaṭrah *Iraq* 31°30N 46°10E **46 D5**
Ash Shawbak *Jordan* 30°32N 35°34E **46 D2**
Ash Shiḩr *Yemen* 14°45N 49°36E **49 E4**
Ash Shināfīyah *Iraq* 31°35N 44°39E **46 D5**
Ash Shu'bah *Si. Arabia* 28°54N 44°44E **46 D5**
Ash Shumlūl *Si. Arabia* 26°31N 47°20E **46 E5**
Ash Shūr'a *Iraq* 35°58N 43°13E **46 C4**
Ash Shuwayfāt *Lebanon* 33°45N 35°30E **48 B4**
Asha *Russia* 55°0N 57°16E **18 D10**
Ashbourne *U.K.* 53°2N 1°43W **12 D6**
Ashburn *U.S.A.* 31°43N 83°39W **85 F13**
Ashburton *N.Z.* 43°53S 171°48E **59 E3**
Ashburton ➤ *Australia* 21°40S 114°56E **60 D1**
Ashcroft *Canada* 50°40N 121°20W **70 C4**
Ashdod *Israel* 31°49N 34°35E **48 D3**
Ashdown *U.S.A.* 33°40N 94°8W **84 E7**
Asheboro *U.S.A.* 35°43N 79°49W **85 D15**
Ashern *Canada* 51°11N 98°21W **71 C9**
Asherton *U.S.A.* 28°27N 99°46W **84 G5**
Asheville *U.S.A.* 35°36N 82°33W **85 D13**
Ashewat *Pakistan* 31°22N 68°32E **42 D3**
Asheweig ➤ *Canada* 54°17N 87°12W **72 B2**
Ashford *Australia* 29°15S 151°3E **63 D5**
Ashford *U.K.* 51°8N 0°53E **13 F8**
Ashgabat *Turkmenistan* 37°58N 58°24E **47 B8**
Ashibetsu *Japan* 43°31N 142°11E **28 C11**
Ashikaga *Japan* 36°28N 139°29E **29 F9**
Ashington *U.K.* 55°11N 1°33W **12 B6**
Ashizuri-Uwakai △
  Japan 32°56N 132°32E **29 H6**
Ashizuri-Zaki *Japan* 32°44N 133°0E **29 H6**
Ashkarkot *Afghan.* 33°3N 67°58E **42 C2**
Ashkhabad = Ashgabat
  Turkmenistan 37°58N 58°24E **47 B8**
Āshkhāneh *Iran* 37°26N 56°55E **47 B8**
Ashland *Kans., U.S.A.* 37°11N 99°46W **80 G4**
Ashland *Ky., U.S.A.* 38°28N 82°38W **81 F12**
Ashland *Maine, U.S.A.* 46°38N 68°24W **81 B19**
Ashland *Mont., U.S.A.* 45°36N 106°16W **76 D10**
Ashland *Ohio, U.S.A.* 40°52N 82°19W **82 F2**
Ashland *Oreg., U.S.A.* 42°12N 122°43W **76 E2**
Ashland *Pa., U.S.A.* 40°45N 76°22W **83 F8**
Ashland *Va., U.S.A.* 37°46N 77°29W **81 G15**
Ashland *Wis., U.S.A.* 46°35N 90°53W **80 B8**
Ashley *N. Dak., U.S.A.* 46°2N 99°22W **80 B4**
Ashley *Pa., U.S.A.* 41°12N 75°55W **83 E9**
Ashmore and Cartier Is.
  Ind. Oc. 12°15S 123°0E **60 B3**
Ashmore Reef *Australia* 12°14S 123°5E **60 B3**
Ashmyany *Belarus* 54°26N 25°52E **17 A13**
Ashokan Res. *U.S.A.* 41°56N 74°13W **83 E10**
Ashoknagar *India* 24°34N 77°43E **44 D3**
Ashqelon *Israel* 31°42N 34°35E **48 D3**
Ashta *India* 23°1N 76°43E **42 H7**
Ashtabula *U.S.A.* 41°52N 80°47W **82 E4**
Ashti *Maharashtra, India* 21°12N 78°11E **44 D4**
Ashti *Maharashtra, India* 18°50N 75°15E **44 E2**
Āshtīyān *Iran* 34°31N 50°0E **47 C6**
Ashton *S. Africa* 33°50S 20°5E **56 D3**
Ashton *U.S.A.* 44°4N 111°27W **76 D8**
Ashuanipi, L. *Canada* 52°45N 66°15W **73 B6**
Ashur = Assur *Iraq* 35°27N 43°15E **46 C4**
Ashville *U.S.A.* 40°34N 78°33W **82 F6**
Asia *Asia* 45°0N 75°0E **24 E9**

Asia, Kepulauan *Indonesia* 1°0N 131°13E **37 D8**
Asifabad *India* 19°20N 79°24E **44 E4**
Asinara *Italy* 41°4N 8°16E **22 D3**
Asinara, G. dell' *Italy* 41°0N 8°30E **22 D3**
Asino *Russia* 57°0N 86°0E **26 D9**
Asipovichy *Belarus* 53°19N 28°33E **17 B15**
'Asīr □ *Si. Arabia* 18°40N 42°30E **49 D3**
Asir, Ras *Somalia* 11°55N 51°10E **49 E5**
Aska *India* 19°2N 84°42E **44 E7**
Askham *S. Africa* 26°59S 20°47E **56 C3**
Askim *Norway* 59°35N 11°10E **9 G14**
Askja *Iceland* 65°3N 16°48W **8 D5**
Askøyna *Norway* 60°29N 5°10E **8 F11**
Asmara = Asmera
  Eritrea 15°19N 38°55E **49 D2**
Asmera *Eritrea* 15°19N 38°55E **49 D2**
Åsnen *Sweden* 56°37N 14°45E **9 H16**
Aso Kujū △ *Japan* 32°53N 131°6E **29 H5**
Aspatria *U.K.* 54°47N 3°19W **12 C4**
Aspen *U.S.A.* 39°11N 106°49W **76 G10**
Aspermont *U.S.A.* 33°8N 100°14W **84 E4**
Aspiring, Mt. *N.Z.* 44°23S 168°46E **59 F2**
Aspur *India* 23°58N 74°7E **42 H6**
Asquith *Canada* 52°8N 107°13W **71 C7**
Assab = Aseb *Eritrea* 13°0N 42°40E **49 E3**
Assal, L. *Djibouti* 11°40N 42°26E **49 E3**
Assam □ *India* 26°0N 93°0E **41 G18**
Assateague Island △
  U.S.A. 38°15N 75°10W **81 F16**
Assaye *India* 20°15N 75°53E **44 D2**
Asse *Belgium* 50°24N 4°10E **15 D4**
Assen *Neths.* 53°0N 6°35E **15 A6**
Assiniboia *Canada* 49°40N 105°59W **71 D7**
Assiniboine ➤ *Canada* 49°53N 97°8W **71 D9**
Assiniboine, Mt. *Canada* 50°52N 115°39W **70 C5**
Assis *Brazil* 22°40S 50°20W **95 A5**
Assisi *Italy* 43°4N 12°37E **22 C5**
Assur *Iraq* 35°27N 43°15E **46 C4**
Assynt, L. *U.K.* 58°10N 5°3W **11 C3**
Astana *Kazakhstan* 51°10N 71°30E **30 A3**
Āstāneh *Iran* 37°17N 49°59E **47 B6**
Astara *Azerbaijan* 38°30N 48°50E **47 B6**
Asterabad = Gorgān *Iran* 36°55N 54°30E **47 B7**
Asti *Italy* 44°54N 8°12E **20 D8**
Astipalea *Greece* 36°32N 26°22E **23 F12**
Astorga *Spain* 42°29N 6°8W **21 A2**
Astoria *U.S.A.* 46°11N 123°50W **78 D3**
Astrakhan *Russia* 46°25N 48°5E **19 E8**
Astrebla Downs
  Australia 24°12S 140°34E **62 C3**
Asturias □ *Spain* 43°15N 6°0W **21 A3**
Asunción *Paraguay* 25°10S 57°30W **94 B4**
Asunción Nochixtlán
  Mexico 17°28N 97°14W **87 D5**
Aswân *Egypt* 24°4N 32°57E **53 D12**
Aswan High Dam = Sadd el Aali
  Egypt 23°54N 32°54E **53 D12**
Asyûṭ *Egypt* 27°11N 31°4E **53 C12**
At Ṭafīlah *Jordan* 30°45N 35°30E **48 E4**
At Ṭafīlah □ *Jordan* 30°45N 35°30E **48 E4**
At Ṭā'if *Si. Arabia* 21°5N 40°27E **49 C3**
At Ta'mīm □ *Iraq* 35°30N 44°30E **46 C5**
Aṭ Ṭiraq *Si. Arabia* 27°19N 44°33E **46 E5**
Aṭ Ṭubayq *Si. Arabia* 29°30N 37°0E **46 D3**
Aṭ Ṭunayb *Jordan* 31°48N 35°57E **48 D4**
Atacama, Desierto de
  Chile 24°0S 69°20W **94 A2**
Atacama, Salar de *Chile* 23°30S 68°20W **94 A2**
Atakeye ◎ *Australia* 22°33S 133°45E **60 D5**
Atakpamé *Togo* 7°31N 1°13E **52 G6**
Atalaya *Peru* 10°45S 73°50W **92 F4**
Atami *Japan* 35°5N 139°4E **29 G9**
Atamyrat *Turkmenistan* 37°50N 65°12E **26 F7**
Atapupu *Indonesia* 9°0S 124°51E **37 F6**
Atâr *Mauritania* 20°30N 13°5W **52 D3**
Atari *Pakistan* 30°56N 74°2E **42 D6**
Atascadero *U.S.A.* 35°29N 120°40W **78 K6**
Atasū *Kazakhstan* 48°30N 71°0E **26 E8**
Atauro *Timor-Leste* 8°10S 125°30E **37 F7**
Atbara *Sudan* 17°42N 33°59E **53 E12**
'Atbara, Nahr ➤ *Sudan* 17°40N 33°56E **53 E12**
Atbasar *Kazakhstan* 51°48N 68°20E **26 D7**
Atchafalaya B. *U.S.A.* 29°25N 91°25W **84 G9**
Atchison *U.S.A.* 39°34N 95°7W **80 F6**
Āteshān *Iran* 35°35N 52°37E **47 C7**
Ath *Belgium* 50°38N 3°47E **15 D3**
Athabasca *Canada* 54°45N 113°20W **70 C6**
Athabasca ➤ *Canada* 58°40N 110°50W **71 B6**
Athabasca, L. *Canada* 59°15N 109°15W **71 B7**
Athabasca Sand Dunes △
  Canada 59°4N 108°43W **71 B7**
Athagarh *India* 20°32N 85°37E **44 D7**
Athboy *Ireland* 53°36N 6°56E **10 C5**
Athenry *Ireland* 53°18N 8°44W **10 C3**
Athens *Ala., U.S.A.* 34°48N 86°58W **85 D11**
Athens *Ga., U.S.A.* 33°57N 83°23W **85 E13**
Athens *N.Y., U.S.A.* 42°16N 73°49W **83 D11**
Athens *Ohio, U.S.A.* 39°20N 82°6W **81 F12**
Athens *Pa., U.S.A.* 41°57N 76°31W **83 E8**
Athens *Tenn., U.S.A.* 35°27N 84°36W **85 D12**
Athens *Tex., U.S.A.* 32°12N 95°51W **84 E7**
Atherley *Canada* 44°37N 79°20W **82 B5**
Atherton *Australia* 17°17S 145°30E **62 B4**
Athlone *Ireland* 53°25N 7°56W **10 C4**
Athmalik *India* 20°43N 84°32E **44 D7**
Athni *India* 16°44N 75°6E **44 F2**
Athol *U.S.A.* 42°36N 72°14W **83 D12**
Atholl, Forest of *U.K.* 56°51N 3°50W **11 E5**
Atholville *Canada* 47°59N 66°43W **73 C6**
Athos *Greece* 40°9N 24°22E **23 D11**
Athy *Ireland* 53°0N 7°0W **10 C5**
Ati *Chad* 13°13N 18°20E **53 F9**
Atik L. *Canada* 55°15N 96°0W **71 B9**
Atikaki △ *Canada* 51°30N 95°31W **71 C9**
Atikameg ➤ *Canada* 52°30N 82°46W **72 B3**
Atikokan *Canada* 48°45N 91°37W **72 C1**
Atikonak L. *Canada* 52°40N 64°32W **73 B7**
Atimaono *Tahiti* 17°46S 149°28W **59 d**

Atirampattinam *India* 10°28N 79°20E **45** J4
Atiu *Cook Is.* 20°0S 158°10W **65** J12
Atka *Russia* 60°50N 151°48E **27** C16
Atka I. *U.S.A.* 52°7N 174°30W **74** E5
Atkinson *U.S.A.* 42°32N 98°59W **80** D4
Atlanta *U.S.A.* 33°7N 94°10W **84** E7
Atlantic *U.S.A.* 41°24N 95°1W **80** E6
Atlantic City *U.S.A.* 39°21N 74°27W **81** F16
Atlantic-Indian Basin
Antarctica 60°0S 30°0E **5** B4
Atlantic Ocean 0°0 20°0W **2** D8
Atlantis *S. Africa* 33°34S 18°29E **56** D2
Atlas Mts. = Haut Atlas
Morocco 32°30N 5°0W **52** B4
Atlin *Canada* 59°31N 133°41W **70** B2
Atlin, L. *Canada* 59°26N 133°45W **70** B2
Atlin △ *Canada* 59°10N 134°30W **70** B2
Atmakur *Andhra Pradesh,*
India 14°37N 79°40E **45** G4
Atmakur *Andhra Pradesh,*
India 15°53N 78°35E **45** G4
Atmakur *Telangana, India* 18°45N 78°39E **44** E4
Atmore *U.S.A.* 31°2N 87°29W **85** F11
Atoka *U.S.A.* 34°23N 96°8W **84** D6
Atolia *U.S.A.* 35°19N 117°37W **79** K9
Atqasuk *U.S.A.* 70°28N 157°24W **74** A8
Atrai → *India* 24°7N 89°22E **43** G13
Atrak = Atrek →
Turkmenistan 37°35N 53°58E **47** B8
Atrauli *India* 28°2N 78°20E **42** E8
Atrek → *Turkmenistan* 37°35N 53°58E **47** B8
Atsuta *Japan* 43°24N 141°26E **28** C10
Attalla *U.S.A.* 34°1N 86°6W **85** D11
Attapeu *Laos* 14°48N 106°50E **38** E6
Attawapiskat *Canada* 52°56N 82°24W **72** B3
Attawapiskat → *Canada* 52°57N 82°18W **72** B3
Attawapiskat L. *Canada* 52°18N 87°54W **72** B2
Attica *Ind., U.S.A.* 40°18N 87°15W **80** E10
Attica *Ohio, U.S.A.* 41°4N 82°53W **82** E2
Attikamagen L. *Canada* 55°0N 66°30W **73** B6
Attleboro *U.S.A.* 41°57N 71°17W **83** E13
Attock *Pakistan* 33°52N 72°20E **42** C5
Attopu = Attapeu *Laos* 14°48N 106°50E **38** E6
Attu I. *U.S.A.* 52°55N 172°55E **74** E2
Attur *India* 11°35N 78°30E **45** J4
Atuel → *Argentina* 36°17S 66°50W **94** D2
Åtvidaberg *Sweden* 58°12N 16°0E **9** G17
Atwater *U.S.A.* 37°21N 120°37W **78** H6
Atwood *Canada* 43°40N 81°1W **82** C3
Atwood *U.S.A.* 39°48N 101°3W **80** F3
Atyraū *Kazakhstan* 47°5N 52°0E **19** E9
Au Sable → *U.S.A.* 44°25N 83°20W **82** B1
Au Sable → *U.S.A.* 44°25N 83°20W **81** C12
Au Sable Forks *U.S.A.* 44°27N 73°41W **83** B11
Au Sable Pt. *U.S.A.* 44°20N 83°20W **82** B1
Auas *Honduras* 15°29N 84°20W **88** C3
Auasberg *Namibia* 22°37S 17°13E **56** B2
Aubagne *France* 43°17N 5°37E **20** E6
Aube □ *France* 48°34N 3°43E **20** B5
Auberry *U.S.A.* 37°7N 119°29W **78** H7
Auburn *Ala., U.S.A.* 32°36N 85°29W **85** E12
Auburn *Calif., U.S.A.* 38°54N 121°4W **78** G5
Auburn *Ind., U.S.A.* 41°22N 85°4W **81** E11
Auburn *Maine, U.S.A.* 44°6N 70°14W **81** B18
Auburn *N.Y., U.S.A.* 42°56N 76°34W **83** D8
Auburn *Nebr., U.S.A.* 40°23N 95°51W **80** E6
Auburn *Pa., U.S.A.* 40°36N 76°6W **83** F8
Auburn *Wash., U.S.A.* 47°18N 122°14W **78** C4
Auburn Ra. *Australia* 25°15S 150°30E **63** D5
Auburndale *U.S.A.* 28°4N 81°48W **85** G14
Aubusson *France* 45°57N 2°11E **20** D5
Auch *France* 43°39N 0°36E **20** E4
Auchterarder *U.K.* 56°18N 3°41W **11** E5
Auchtermuchty *U.K.* 56°18N 3°13W **11** E5
Auckland *N.Z.* 36°52S 174°46E **59** B5
Auckland Is. *Pac. Oc.* 50°40S 166°5E **64** N8
Aude → *France* 43°13N 3°14E **20** E5
Auden *Canada* 50°14N 87°53W **72** B2
Audubon *U.S.A.* 41°43N 94°56W **80** E6
Augathella *Australia* 25°48S 146°35E **63** D4
Aughnacloy *U.K.* 54°25N 6°59W **10** B5
Aughrim *Ireland* 53°18N 8°19W **10** C3
Augrabies Falls *S. Africa* 28°35S 20°20E **56** C3
Augrabies Falls △
S. Africa 28°40S 20°22E **56** C3
Augsburg *Germany* 48°25N 10°52E **16** D6
Augusta *Australia* 34°19S 115°9E **61** F2
Augusta *Italy* 37°13N 15°13E **22** F6
Augusta *Ark., U.S.A.* 35°17N 91°22W **84** D9
Augusta *Ga., U.S.A.* 33°28N 81°58W **85** E14
Augusta *Kans., U.S.A.* 37°41N 96°59W **80** G6
Augusta *Maine, U.S.A.* 44°19N 69°47W **81** C19
Augusta *Mont., U.S.A.* 47°30N 112°24W **76** C7
Augustów *Poland* 53°51N 23°0E **17** B12
Augustus, Mt. *Australia* 24°20S 116°50E **61** D2
Augustus I. *Australia* 15°20S 124°30E **60** C3
Aujuittuq = Grise Fiord
Canada 76°25N 82°57W **69** B15
Aukštaitija △ *Lithuania* 55°15N 26°0E **9** J22
Aukum *U.S.A.* 38°34N 120°43W **78** G6
Aul *India* 20°41N 86°39E **44** D8
Aulavik △ *Canada* 73°42N 119°55W **68** C8
Auld, L. *Australia* 22°25S 123°50E **60** D3
Ault *U.S.A.* 40°35N 104°44W **76** F11
Aundah *India* 19°32N 77°3E **44** E3
Aundh *India* 17°33N 74°23E **44** F2
Aunis *France* 46°5N 0°50W **20** C3
Aunu'u *Amer. Samoa* 14°20S 170°31W **59** b
Auponhia *Indonesia* 1°58S 125°27E **37** E7
Aur, Pulau *Malaysia* 2°35N 104°10E **39** L5
Auraiya *India* 26°28N 79°33E **43** F8
Aurangabad *Bihar, India* 24°45N 84°18E **43** G11
Aurangabad *Maharashtra,*
India 19°50N 75°23E **44** E2
Aurich *Germany* 53°28N 7°28E **16** B4
Aurillac *France* 44°55N 2°26E **20** D5
Aurora *Canada* 44°0N 79°28W **82** C5
Aurora *S. Africa* 32°40S 18°29E **56** E2
Aurora *Colo., U.S.A.* 39°43N 104°49W **76** G11
Aurora *Ill., U.S.A.* 41°45N 88°19W **80** E9

Aurora *Mo., U.S.A.* 36°58N 93°43W **80** G7
Aurora *N.Y., U.S.A.* 42°45N 76°42W **83** D8
Aurora *Nebr., U.S.A.* 40°52N 98°0W **80** E5
Aurora *Ohio, U.S.A.* 41°21N 81°20W **82** E3
Aurukun *Australia* 13°20S 141°45E **62** A3
Aurukun ☉ *Australia* 13°36S 141°48E **62** A3
Aus *Namibia* 26°35S 16°12E **56** C2
Ausa *India* 18°15N 76°30E **44** E3
Ausable → *Canada* 43°19N 81°46W **82** C3
Auschwitz = Oświęcim
Poland 50°2N 19°11E **17** C10
Auski Roadhouse
Australia 22°22S 118°41E **60** D2
Austen Harbour *India* 12°55N 92°45E **45** H11
Austin *Minn., U.S.A.* 43°40N 92°58W **80** D7
Austin *Nev., U.S.A.* 39°30N 117°4W **76** G5
Austin *Pa., U.S.A.* 41°38N 78°6W **82** E6
Austin *Tex., U.S.A.* 30°17N 97°45W **84** F6
Austin, L. *Australia* 27°40S 118°0E **61** E2
Austin I. *Canada* 61°10N 94°0W **71** A10
Austra *Norway* 65°8N 11°55E **8** D14
Austral Is. = Tubuaï, Îs.
French Polynesia 25°0S 150°0W **65** K13
Austral Seamount Chain
Pac. Oc. 24°0S 150°0W **65** K13
Australia ■ *Oceania* 23°0S 135°0E **58** D6
Australian-Antarctic Basin
S. Ocean 60°0S 120°0E **5** C9
Australian Capital Territory □
Australia 35°30S 149°0E **63** F4
Australind *Australia* 33°17S 115°42E **61** F2
Austria ■ *Europe* 47°0N 14°0E **16** E8
Austvågøya *Norway* 68°20N 14°40E **8** B16
Autlán de Navarro
Mexico 19°46N 104°22W **86** D4
Autun *France* 46°58N 4°17E **20** C6
Auvergne *France* 45°20N 3°15E **20** D5
Auvergne, Mts. d' *France* 45°20N 2°55E **20** D5
Auxerre *France* 47°48N 3°32E **20** C5
Auyuittuq △ *Canada* 67°30N 66°0W **69** D18
Av-Dovurak *Russia* 51°17N 91°35E **27** D10
Ava *U.S.A.* 36°57N 92°40W **80** G7
Avachinskaya Sopka
Russia 53°15N 158°50E **27** D16
Avallon *France* 47°30N 3°53E **20** C5
Avalon *U.S.A.* 33°21N 118°20W **79** M8
Avalon Pen. *Canada* 47°30N 53°20W **73** C9
Avanigadda *India* 16°0N 80°56E **45** G5
Avanos *Turkey* 38°43N 34°51E **46** B2
Avaré *Brazil* 23°4S 48°58W **95** A6
Avawatz Mts. *U.S.A.* 35°40N 116°30W **79** K10
Aveiro *Brazil* 3°10S 55°5W **93** D7
Aveiro *Portugal* 40°37N 8°38W **21** B1
Āvej *Iran* 35°40N 49°15E **47** C6
Avellaneda *Argentina* 34°50N 58°10W **94** C4
Avellino *Italy* 40°54N 14°47E **22** D6
Avenal *U.S.A.* 36°0N 120°8W **78** K6
Aversa *Italy* 40°58N 14°12E **22** D6
Avery *U.S.A.* 47°15N 115°49W **76** C6
Aves, I. de *W. Indies* 15°45N 63°55W **89** C7
Aves, Is. las *Venezuela* 12°0N 67°30W **89** D6
Avesta *Sweden* 60°9N 16°10E **9** F17
Aveyron → *France* 44°5N 1°16E **20** D4
Avezzano *Italy* 42°2N 13°25E **22** C5
Aviá Terai *Argentina* 26°45S 60°50W **94** B3
Aviemore *U.K.* 57°12N 3°50W **11** D5
Avignon *France* 43°57N 4°50E **20** E6
Ávila *Spain* 40°39N 4°43W **21** B3
Avila Beach *U.S.A.* 35°11N 120°44W **79** K6
Avilés *Spain* 43°35N 5°57W **21** A3
Avis *U.S.A.* 41°11N 77°19W **82** E7
Avissawella *Sri Lanka* 6°56N 80°11E **45** L5
Avoca *U.S.A.* 42°25N 77°25W **82** D7
Avoca → *Australia* 35°40S 143°43E **63** F3
Avoca → *Ireland* 52°48N 6°10W **10** D5
Avola *Canada* 51°45N 119°19W **70** C5
Avola *Italy* 36°56N 15°7E **22** F6
Avon *U.S.A.* 42°55N 77°45W **82** D7
Avon → *Australia* 31°40S 116°7E **61** F2
Avon → *Bristol, U.K.* 51°29N 2°41W **13** F5
Avon → *Dorset, U.K.* 50°44N 1°46W **13** G6
Avon → *Warks., U.K.* 52°0N 2°8W **13** E5
Avon Park *U.S.A.* 27°36N 81°31W **85** H14
Avonlea *Canada* 50°0N 105°0W **71** D8
Avonmore *Canada* 45°10N 74°58W **83** A10
Avonmouth *U.K.* 51°30N 2°42W **13** F5
Avranches *France* 48°40N 1°20W **20** B3
Awa-Shima *Japan* 38°27N 139°14E **28** E9
A'waj → *Syria* 33°23N 36°20E **48** B5
Awaji-Shima *Japan* 34°30N 134°50E **29** G7
'Awālī *Bahrain* 26°0N 50°30E **47** E6
Awantipur *India* 33°55N 75°3E **43** C6
Awarja → *India* 17°5N 76°15E **44** F3
Awasa *Ethiopia* 7°2N 38°28E **49** F2
Awash *Ethiopia* 9°1N 40°10E **49** F3
Awatere → *N.Z.* 41°37S 174°10E **59** D5
Awbārī *Libya* 26°46N 12°57E **53** C8
Awbārī, Idehan *Libya* 27°10N 11°30E **53** C8
Awe, L. *U.K.* 56°17N 5°16W **11** E3
Awjilah *Libya* 29°8N 21°7E **53** C10
Axe → *U.K.* 50°42N 3°4W **13** F5
Axel Heiberg I. *Canada* 80°0N 90°0W **69** B14
Axim *Ghana* 4°51N 2°15W **52** H5
Axios → *Greece* 40°57N 22°35E **23** D10
Axminster *U.K.* 50°46N 3°0W **13** G4
Ayabaca *Peru* 4°40S 79°53W **92** D3
Ayabe *Japan* 35°20N 135°20E **29** G7
Ayacucho *Argentina* 37°5S 58°20W **94** D4
Ayacucho *Peru* 13°0S 74°0W **92** F4
Ayaguz = Ayaköz
Kazakhstan 48°10N 80°10E **30** B5
Ayakkum Hu *China* 37°30N 89°20E **30** D6
Ayaköz *Kazakhstan* 48°10N 80°10E **30** B5
Ayakudi *India* 10°28N 77°56E **45** J3
Ayamonte *Spain* 37°12N 7°24W **21** D2
Ayan *Russia* 56°30N 138°16E **27** D14
Ayaviri *Peru* 14°50S 70°35W **92** F4
Aydın *Turkey* 37°51N 27°51E **23** F12
Aydıngkol Hu *China* 42°40N 89°15E **30** C6
Ayer *U.S.A.* 42°34N 71°35W **83** D13
Ayer Hitam *Malaysia* 5°24N 100°16E **39** c

Ayer's Cliff *Canada* 45°10N 72°3W **83** A12
Ayers Rock = Uluru
Australia 25°23S 131°5E **61** E5
Ayeyarwady = Ayeyawady →
Myanmar 15°50N 95°6E **41** M19
Ayeyawady → *Myanmar* 15°50N 95°6E **41** M19
Aykhal *Russia* 66°0N 111°30E **27** C12
Aykino *Russia* 62°15N 49°56E **18** B8
Aylesbury *U.K.* 51°49N 0°49W **13** F7
Aylmer *Canada* 42°46N 80°59W **82** D4
Aylmer, L. *Canada* 64°5N 108°30W **68** E10
Ayn Dār *Si. Arabia* 25°55N 49°10E **47** E7
Ayn Zālah *Iraq* 36°45N 42°35E **46** B4
Ayolas *Paraguay* 27°10S 56°59W **94** B4
Ayon, Ostrov *Russia* 69°50N 169°0E **27** C17
'Ayoûn el 'Atroûs
Mauritania 16°38N 9°37W **52** E4
Ayr *Australia* 19°35S 147°25E **62** B4
Ayr *Canada* 43°17N 80°27W **82** C4
Ayr *U.K.* 55°28N 4°38W **11** F4
Ayr → *U.K.* 55°28N 4°38W **11** F4
Ayre, Pt. of *I. of Man* 54°25N 4°21W **12** C3
Ayton *Australia* 15°56S 145°22E **62** B4
Aytos *Bulgaria* 42°42N 27°16E **23** C12
Ayutla *Guatemala* 14°40N 92°10W **88** D1
Ayutla de los Libres
Mexico 16°54N 99°13W **87** D5
Ayutthaya = Phra Nakhon Si
Ayutthaya *Thailand* 14°25N 100°30E **38** E3
Ayvacık *Turkey* 39°36N 26°24E **23** E12
Ayvalık *Turkey* 39°20N 26°46E **23** E12
Az Zabadānī *Syria* 33°43N 36°5E **48** B5
Az Zāhirīyah *West Bank* 31°25N 34°58E **48** D3
Az Zahrān *Si. Arabia* 26°10N 50°7E **47** E6
Az Zarqā *Jordan* 32°5N 36°4E **48** C5
Az Zarqā' *U.A.E.* 24°53N 53°4E **47** E7
Az Zarqā □ *Jordan* 32°5N 36°4E **48** C5
Az Zāwiyah *Libya* 32°52N 12°56E **53** B8
Az Zībār *Iraq* 36°52N 44°4E **46** B5
Az Zubayr *Iraq* 30°26N 47°40E **46** D5
Az Zuqur *Iraq* 26°12N 44°52E **46** E5
Azad Kashmir □ *Pakistan* 33°50N 73°50E **43** C5
Azamgarh *India* 26°5N 83°13E **43** F10
Azangaro *Peru* 14°55S 70°13W **92** F4
Azaouad *Mali* 19°0N 3°0E **52** E5
Āzar Shahr *Iran* 37°45N 45°59E **46** B5
Azarān *Iran* 37°25N 47°16E **46** B5
Azārbāyjān = Azerbaijan ■
Asia 40°20N 48°0E **19** F8
Āzārbāyjān-e Gharbī □
Iran 37°0N 44°30E **46** B5
Āzārbāyjān-e Sharqī □
Iran 37°20N 47°0E **46** B5
Azare *Nigeria* 11°55N 10°10E **52** F8
A'zāz *Syria* 36°36N 37°4E **46** B3
Azbine = Aïr *Niger* 18°30N 8°0E **52** E7
Azerbaijan ■ *Asia* 40°20N 48°0E **19** F8
Azogues *Ecuador* 2°35S 78°0W **92** D3
Azores = Açores, Is. dos
Atl. Oc. 38°0N 27°0W **52** a
Azov *Russia* 47°3N 39°25E **19** E6
Azov, Sea of *Europe* 46°0N 36°30E **19** E6
Azovskoye More = Azov, Sea of
Europe 46°0N 36°30E **19** E6
Azraq ash Shīshān *Jordan* 31°50N 36°49E **48** D5
Aztec *U.S.A.* 36°49N 107°59W **77** H10
Azua de Compostela
Dom. Rep. 18°25N 70°44W **89** C5
Azuaga *Spain* 38°16N 5°39W **21** C3
Azuero, Pen. de *Panama* 7°30N 80°30W **88** E3
Azul *Argentina* 36°42S 59°43W **94** D4
Azumino *Japan* 36°20N 137°50E **29** F8
Azur, Côte d' *France* 43°25N 7°10E **20** E7
Azusa *U.S.A.* 34°8N 117°52W **79** L9
Azzel Matti, Sebkra
Algeria 26°10N 0°43E **52** C6

B

Ba Be △ *Vietnam* 22°25N 105°37E **38** A5
Ba Don *Vietnam* 17°45N 106°26E **38** D6
Ba Dong *Vietnam* 9°40N 106°33E **39** H6
Ba Ngoi *Vietnam* 11°54N 109°10E **39** G7
Ba Ria *Vietnam* 10°30N 107°10E **39** G6
Ba Tri *Vietnam* 10°2N 106°36E **39** G6
Ba Vì △ *Vietnam* 21°1N 105°22E **38** B5
Ba Xian = Bazhou *China* 39°8N 116°22E **32** E9
Baa *Indonesia* 10°50S 123°0E **60** B3
Baalbek = Ba'labakk
Lebanon 34°0N 36°10E **48** B5
Baardheere *Somalia* 2°20N 42°27E **49** G3
Baarle-Nassau *Belgium* 51°27N 4°56E **15** C4
Bab el Mandeb *Red Sea* 12°35N 43°25E **49** E3
Bābā, Koh-i- *Afghan.* 34°30N 67°0E **40** B5
Bābā Budan Hills *India* 13°30N 75°44E **45** H2
Baba Burnu *Turkey* 39°29N 26°2E **23** E12
Bābā Kalū *Iran* 30°7N 50°49E **47** D6
Babadag *Romania* 44°53N 28°44E **17** F15
Babaeski *Turkey* 41°26N 27°6E **23** D12
Babahoyo *Ecuador* 1°40S 79°30W **92** D3
Babai = Sarju → *India* 27°21N 81°23E **43** F9
Babai *Nepal* 28°9N 81°25E **43** E9
Babar *Indonesia* 8°0S 129°30E **37** F7
Babar *India* 31°7N 69°32E **42** D3
Babarkach *Pakistan* 29°45N 68°0E **42** E3
Babb *U.S.A.* 48°51N 113°27W **76** B7
Baberu *India* 25°33N 80°43E **43** G9
Babi Besar, Pulau
Malaysia 2°25N 103°59E **39** L4
Babian Jiang → *China* 22°55N 101°47E **34** F3
Bābil □ *Iraq* 32°30N 44°30E **46** C5
Babinda *Australia* 17°20S 145°56E **62** B4
Babine *Canada* 55°22N 126°37W **70** B3
Babine → *Canada* 55°45N 127°44W **70** B3
Babine L. *Canada* 54°48N 126°0W **70** C3
Babo *Indonesia* 2°30S 133°30E **37** E8
Bābol *Iran* 36°40N 52°50E **47** B7
Bābol Sar *Iran* 36°45N 52°45E **47** B7

Baboua *C.A.R.* 5°49N 14°58E **54** C2
Babruysk *Belarus* 53°10N 29°15E **17** B15
Babuhri *India* 26°49N 69°43E **42** F3
Babusar Pass *Pakistan* 35°12N 73°59E **43** B5
Babuyan Chan. *Phil.* 18°40N 121°30E **37** A6
Babuyan Is. *Phil.* 19°10N 121°40E **37** A6
Babylon *Iraq* 32°34N 44°22E **46** C5
Bac Can *Vietnam* 22°8N 105°49E **34** F5
Bac Giang *Vietnam* 21°16N 106°11E **34** G6
Bac Lieu *Vietnam* 9°17N 105°43E **39** H5
Bac Ninh *Vietnam* 21°13N 106°4E **34** G6
Bac Phan *Vietnam* 22°0N 105°0E **34** G5
Bacabal *Brazil* 4°15S 44°45W **93** D10
Bacalar *Mexico* 18°43N 88°27W **87** D7
Bacan, Kepulauan
Indonesia 0°35S 127°30E **37** E7
Bacarra *Phil.* 18°15N 120°37E **37** A6
Bacău *Romania* 46°35N 26°55E **17** E14
Bacerac *Mexico* 30°18N 108°50W **86** A3
Bach Long Vi, Dao
Vietnam 20°10N 107°40E **38** B6
Bach Ma △ *Vietnam* 16°11N 107°49E **38** D6
Bachhwara *India* 25°35N 85°54E **43** G11
Back → *Canada* 65°10N 104°0W **68** D11
Bacolod *Phil.* 10°40N 122°57E **37** B6
Bacuk *Malaysia* 6°4N 102°25E **39** J4
Bácum *Mexico* 27°33N 110°5W **86** B2
Bād *Iran* 33°41N 52°1E **47** C7
Bad → *U.S.A.* 44°21N 100°22W **80** C3
Bad Axe *U.S.A.* 43°48N 83°0W **82** C2
Bad Ischl *Austria* 47°44N 13°38E **16** E7
Bad Kissingen *Germany* 50°11N 10°4E **16** C6
Bada Barabil *India* 22°7N 85°24E **43** H11
Badagara = Vadakara
India 11°35N 75°40E **45** J2
Badain Jaran Shamo
China 40°23N 102°0E **30** C9
Badajós, L. *Brazil* 3°15S 62°50W **92** D6
Badajoz *Spain* 38°50N 6°59W **21** C2
Badakhshān □ *Afghan.* 36°30N 71°0E **40** A7
Badalia *China* 40°20N 116°0E **32** D9
Badalzai *Afghan.* 29°50N 65°35E **42** E1
Badami *India* 15°55N 75°41E **45** G2
Badampahar *India* 22°10N 86°10E **44** B8
Badanah *Si. Arabia* 30°58N 41°30E **46** D4
Badarinath *India* 30°45N 79°30E **43** D8
Badas, Kepulauan
Indonesia 0°45N 107°5E **36** D3
Baddo → *Pakistan* 28°0N 64°20E **40** F4
Bade *Indonesia* 7°10S 139°35E **37** F9
Baden *Austria* 48°1N 16°13E **16** D9
Baden *U.S.A.* 40°38N 80°14W **82** F4
Baden-Baden *Germany* 48°44N 8°13E **16** D5
Baden-Württemberg □
Germany 48°20N 8°40E **16** D5
Badgam *India* 34°1N 74°45E **43** B6
Badgastein *Austria* 47°7N 13°9E **16** E7
Badger *Canada* 49°0N 56°4W **73** C8
Badger *U.S.A.* 36°38N 119°1W **78** J7
Bādghīs □ *Afghan.* 35°0N 63°0E **40** B3
Badgingarra △ *Australia* 30°23S 115°22E **61** F2
Badin *Pakistan* 24°38N 68°54E **42** G3
Badlands *U.S.A.* 43°55N 102°30W **80** D2
Badlands △ *U.S.A.* 43°38N 102°56W **80** D2
Badme *Africa* 14°43N 37°48E **49** E2
Badnera *India* 20°48N 77°44E **44** D3
Badrah *Iraq* 33°6N 45°58E **46** C5
Badrain Jaran Shamo
China 40°40N 103°20E **32** D2
Badrinath *India* 30°44N 79°29E **43** D8
Badu *Australia* 10°7S 142°11E **62** a
Badulla *Sri Lanka* 7°1N 81°7E **45** L5
Badung, Bukit *Indonesia* 8°49S 115°10E **37** K18
Badung, Selat *Indonesia* 8°40S 115°22E **37** K17
Badvel *India* 14°45N 79°3E **45** G4
Baena *Spain* 37°37N 4°20W **21** D3
Baengnyeongdo
S. Korea 37°57N 124°40E **33** F13
Baeza *Spain* 37°57N 3°25W **21** D4
Bafatá *Guinea-Biss.* 12°8N 14°40W **52** F3
Baffin B. *N. Amer.* 72°0N 64°0W **69** B19
Baffin I. *Canada* 68°0N 75°0W **69** D17
Bafing → *Mali* 13°49N 10°50W **52** F3
Bafliyūn *Syria* 36°37N 36°59E **46** B3
Bafoulabé *Mali* 13°50N 10°55W **52** F3
Bafoussam *Cameroon* 5°28N 10°25E **54** C2
Bāfq *Iran* 31°40N 55°25E **47** D7
Bafra *Turkey* 41°34N 35°54E **19** F6
Bāft *Iran* 29°15N 56°38E **47** D8
Bafwasende
Dem. Rep. of the Congo 1°3N 27°5E **54** D5
Bagaha *India* 27°6N 84°5E **44** A7
Bagalkot *India* 16°10N 75°40E **45** F2
Bagamoyo *Tanzania* 6°28S 38°55E **54** F7
Bagan Datoh *Malaysia* 3°59N 100°47E **39** L3
Bagan Serai *Malaysia* 5°1N 100°32E **39** K3
Baganga *Phil.* 7°34N 126°33E **37** C7
Bagani *Namibia* 18°7S 21°41E **56** A3
Bagansiapiapi *Indonesia* 2°12N 100°50E **36** D2
Bagasra *India* 21°30N 71°0E **42** J4
Bagaud *India* 22°19N 75°53E **42** H6
Bagdad *U.S.A.* 34°35N 115°53W **79** L11
Bagdarin *Russia* 54°26N 113°36E **27** D12
Bagé *Brazil* 31°20S 54°15W **95** C5
Bagenalstown *Ireland* 52°42N 6°58W **10** D5
Bagepalli *India* 13°47N 77°47E **45** H3
Bageshwar *India* 29°51N 79°46E **43** E8
Bagevadi *India* 16°35N 75°58E **44** F2
Baggs *U.S.A.* 41°2N 107°39W **76** F10
Bagh *Pakistan* 33°59N 73°45E **43** C5
Baghain → *India* 25°32N 81°1E **43** G9
Bagheria *Italy* 38°5N 13°30E **22** E5
Baghlān *Afghan.* 36°12N 68°46E **40** A6
Baghlān □ *Afghan.* 36°0N 68°30E **40** B6
Bagley *U.S.A.* 47°32N 95°24W **80** B6
Baglung *Nepal* 28°16N 83°36E **43** E10
Bago *Myanmar* 17°20N 96°29E **41** L20
Bago □ *Myanmar* 19°0N 96°0E **41** K20
Bagodar *India* 24°5N 85°52E **43** G11
Bagrationovsk *Russia* 54°23N 20°39E **9** J19
Baguio *Phil.* 16°26N 120°34E **37** A6
Bahadurganj *India* 26°16N 87°49E **43** F12

Bahadurgarh *India* 28°40N 76°57E **42** E7
Bahama, Canal Viejo de
W. Indies 22°10N 77°30W **88** B4
Bahamas ■ *N. Amer.* 24°0N 75°0W **89** B5
Bahār *Iran* 34°54N 48°26E **47** C6
Baharampur *India* 24°2N 88°27E **43** G13
Baharu Pandan = Pandan
Malaysia 1°32N 103°46E **39** d
Bahawalnagar *Pakistan* 30°0N 73°15E **42** E5
Bahawalpur *Pakistan* 29°24N 71°40E **42** E4
Bäherden *Turkmenistan* 38°25N 57°26E **47** B8
Baheri *India* 28°45N 79°34E **43** E8
Bahgul → *India* 27°45N 79°36E **43** F8
Bahía = Salvador *Brazil* 13°0S 38°30W **93** F11
Bahía □ *Brazil* 12°0S 42°0W **93** F10
Bahía, Is. de la *Honduras* 16°45N 86°15W **88** C2
Bahía Blanca *Argentina* 38°35S 62°13W **94** D3
Bahía de Caráquez
Ecuador 0°40S 80°27W **92** D2
Bahía de Los Angeles
Mexico 28°56N 113°34W **86** B2
Bahía Honda *Cuba* 22°54N 83°10W **88** B3
Bahía Kino *Mexico* 28°47N 111°58W **86** B2
Bahía Laura *Argentina* 48°10S 66°30W **96** F3
Bahía Negra *Paraguay* 20°5S 58°5W **92** H7
Bahir Dar *Ethiopia* 11°37N 37°10E **49** E2
Bahmanzād *Iran* 31°15N 51°47E **47** D6
Bahraich *India* 27°38N 81°37E **43** F9
Bahrain ■ *Asia* 26°0N 50°35E **47** E6
Bahror *India* 27°51N 76°20E **42** F7
Bāhū Kalāt *Iran* 25°43N 61°25E **47** E9
Bai Bung, Mui = Ca Mau, Mui
Vietnam 8°38N 104°44E **39** H5
Bai Thuong *Vietnam* 19°54N 105°23E **38** C5
Baia Mare *Romania* 47°40N 23°35E **17** E12
Baião *Brazil* 2°40S 49°40W **93** D9
Baïbokoum *Chad* 7°46N 15°43E **53** G9
Baicheng *China* 45°38N 122°42E **33** B12
Baidoa = Baydhabo
Somalia 3°8N 43°30E **49** G3
Baie-Comeau *Canada* 49°12N 68°10W **73** C6
Baie-St-Paul *Canada* 47°28N 70°32W **73** C5
Baie Ste-Anne *Seychelles* 4°18S 55°45E **55** b
Baie-Trinité *Canada* 49°25N 67°20W **73** C6
Baie Verte *Canada* 49°55N 56°12W **73** C8
Baihar *India* 22°6N 80°33E **43** H9
Baihe *Hubei, China* 32°50N 110°5E **32** H6
Baihe *Jilin, China* 42°27N 128°9E **33** C15
Baijnath *India* 29°55N 79°37E **43** E8
Baikal, L. = Baykal, Oz.
Russia 53°0N 108°0E **27** D11
Baikonur = Bayqongyr
Kazakhstan 45°40N 63°20E **26** E7
Baikunthpur *India* 23°15N 82°33E **43** H10
Bailadila, Mt. *India* 18°43N 81°15E **44** E5
Baile Átha Cliath = Dublin
Ireland 53°21N 6°15W **10** C5
Baile Átha Fhirdhia = Ardee
Ireland 53°52N 6°33W **10** C5
Baile Átha Í = Athy *Ireland* 53°0N 7°0W **10** C5
Baile Átha Luain = Athlone
Ireland 53°25N 7°56W **10** C4
Baile Átha Troim = Trim
Ireland 53°33N 6°48W **10** C5
Baile Brigín = Balbriggan
Ireland 53°37N 6°11W **10** C5
Baile Sear = Baleshare
U.K. 57°31N 7°22W **11** D1
Băilești *Romania* 44°1N 23°20E **17** F12
Bailhongal *India* 15°55N 74°53E **45** G2
Bailieborough *Ireland* 53°56N 6°59W **10** C5
Baima *China* 33°0N 100°26E **34** A3
Bainbridge *Ga., U.S.A.* 30°55N 84°35W **85** F12
Bainbridge *N.Y., U.S.A.* 42°18N 75°29W **83** D9
Bainbridge Island
U.S.A. 47°38N 122°32W **78** C4
Baine *China* 42°0N 128°0E **31** C14
Baing *Indonesia* 10°14S 120°34E **37** F6
Bainiu *China* 32°50N 112°15E **32** H7
Bā'ir *Jordan* 30°45N 36°55E **48** E5
Baird Mts. *U.S.A.* 67°0N 160°0W **74** B8
Bairiki = Tarawa *Kiribati* 1°30N 173°0E **64** G9
Bairin Youqi *China* 43°30N 118°35E **33** C10
Bairin Zuoqi *China* 43°58N 119°15E **33** C10
Bairnsdale *Australia* 37°48S 147°36E **63** F4
Baisha *China* 34°20N 112°32E **32** G7
Baisha Li *China* 19°12N 109°20E **38** C7
Baishan = Hunjiang
China 41°54N 126°26E **33** C14
Baishan *China* 42°43N 127°14E **33** C14
Baitadi *Nepal* 29°35N 80°25E **43** E9
Baitarani → *India* 20°45N 86°48E **44** D8
Baiyin *China* 36°45N 104°14E **32** F3
Baiyü *China* 31°16N 98°50E **34** B2
Baiyu Shan *China* 37°15N 107°30E **32** F4
Baj Baj *India* 22°30N 88°5E **43** H13
Baja *Hungary* 46°12N 18°59E **17** E10
Baja, Pta. *Mexico* 29°58N 115°49W **86** B1
Baja California *Mexico* 31°10N 115°12W **86** A1
Baja California □ *Mexico* 30°0N 115°0W **86** B2
Baja California Sur □
Mexico 25°50N 111°50W **86** B2
Bajag *India* 22°40N 81°21E **43** H9
Bajana *India* 23°7N 71°49E **42** H4
Bajatrejo *Indonesia* 8°29S 114°19E **37** J17
Bajawa *Indonesia* 8°47S 120°59E **37** F6
Bajera *Indonesia* 8°31S 115°2E **37** J18
Bājgīrān *Iran* 37°36N 58°24E **47** B8
Bajimba, Mt. *Australia* 29°17S 152°6E **63** D5
Bajo Boquete *Panama* 8°46N 82°27E **88** E3
Bajo Nuevo *Caribbean* 15°40N 78°50W **88** C4
Bajoga *Nigeria* 10°57N 11°52E **53** F8
Bajool *Australia* 23°40S 150°35E **62** C5
Bakel *Senegal* 14°56N 12°20W **52** F3
Baker *Calif., U.S.A.* 35°16N 116°4W **79** K10
Baker *Mont., U.S.A.* 46°22N 104°17W **76** C11
Baker, L. *Canada* 64°0N 96°0W **68** E12
Baker, Mt. *U.S.A.* 48°50N 121°49W **76** B3

Baker City *U.S.A.* 44°47N 117°50W **76** D5
Baker I. *Pac. Oc.* 0°10N 176°35W **64** G10
Baker I. *U.S.A.* 55°20N 133°40W **70** B2
Baker L. *Australia* 26°54S 126°5E **61** E4
Baker Lake *Canada* 64°20N 96°3W **68** E12
Bakers Creek *Australia* 21°13S 149°7E **62** C4
Bakers Dozen Is. *Canada* 56°45N 78°45W **72** A4
Bakersfield *Calif., U.S.A.* 35°23N 119°1W **79** K8
Bakersfield *Vt., U.S.A.* 44°45N 72°48W **83** B12
Bakharden = Bäherden
  Turkmenistan 38°25N 57°26E **47** B8
Bākhtarān = Kermānshāh □
  Iran 34°23N 47°0E **46** C5
Bākhtarān = Kermānshāh □
  Iran 34°0N 46°30E **46** C5
Bakhtegān, Daryācheh-ye
  Iran 29°40N 53°50E **47** D7
Bakhtegān △ *Iran* 29°51N 53°40E **47** D7
Bakı *Azerbaijan* 40°29N 49°56E **47** A6
Bakkafjörður *Iceland* 66°2N 14°48W **8** C6
Bakkagerði *Iceland* 65°31N 13°49W **8** D7
Bakony *Hungary* 47°10N 17°30E **17** E9
Bakony Forest = Bakony
  Hungary 47°10N 17°30E **17** E9
Bakouma *C.A.R.* 5°40N 22°56E **54** C4
Bakswaho *India* 24°15N 79°18E **43** G8
Baku = Bakı *Azerbaijan* 40°29N 49°56E **47** A6
Bakutis Coast *Antarctica* 74°0S 120°0W **5** D15
Baky = Bakı *Azerbaijan* 40°29N 49°56E **47** A6
Bala *Canada* 45°1N 79°37W **82** A5
Bala *U.K.* 52°54N 3°36W **12** E4
Bala, L. *U.K.* 52°53N 3°37W **12** E4
Balabac I. *Phil.* 8°0N 117°0E **36** C5
Balabac Str. *E. Indies* 7°53N 117°5E **36** C5
Balabagh *Afghan.* 34°25N 70°12E **42** B4
Ba'labakk *Lebanon* 34°0N 36°10E **48** B5
Balabalangan, Kepulauan
  Indonesia 2°20S 117°30E **36** E5
Balad *Iraq* 34°0N 44°9E **46** C5
Balad Rūz *Iraq* 33°42N 45°5E **46** C5
Bālādeh *Fārs, Iran* 29°17N 51°56E **47** D6
Bālādeh *Māzandarān, Iran* 36°12N 51°48E **47** B6
Balaghat *India* 21°49N 80°12E **44** D5
Balaghat Ra. *India* 18°50N 76°30E **44** E3
Balaguer *Spain* 41°50N 0°50E **21** B6
Balaklava *Ukraine* 44°30N 33°30E **19** F5
Balakovo *Russia* 52°4N 47°55E **18** D8
Balamau *India* 27°10N 80°21E **43** F9
Balancán *Mexico* 17°48N 91°32W **87** D6
Balangir *India* 20°43N 83°35E **44** D6
Balapur *India* 20°40N 76°45E **44** D3
Balashov *Russia* 51°30N 43°10E **19** D7
Balasinor *India* 22°57N 73°23E **42** H5
Balasore = Baleshwar
  India 21°35N 87°3E **44** D8
Balaton *Hungary* 46°50N 17°40E **17** E9
Balbina, Represa de *Brazil* 2°0S 59°30W **92** D7
Balboa *Panama* 8°57N 79°34W **88** E4
Balbriggan *Ireland* 53°37N 6°11W **10** C5
Balcarce *Argentina* 38°0S 58°10W **94** D4
Balcarres *Canada* 50°50N 103°35W **71** C8
Balchik *Bulgaria* 43°28N 28°11E **23** C13
Balclutha *N.Z.* 46°15S 169°45E **59** G2
Balcones Escarpment
  U.S.A. 29°30N 99°15W **84** G5
Bald I. *Australia* 34°57S 118°27E **61** F2
Bald Knob *U.S.A.* 35°19N 91°34W **84** D9
Baldock L. *Canada* 56°33N 97°57W **71** B9
Baldwin *Mich., U.S.A.* 43°54N 85°51W **81** D11
Baldwin *Pa., U.S.A.* 40°21N 79°58W **82** F5
Baldwinsville *U.S.A.* 43°10N 76°20W **83** C8
Baldy Peak *U.S.A.* 33°54N 109°34W **77** K9
Baleares, Is. *Spain* 39°30N 3°0E **21** C7
Balearic Is. = Baleares, Is.
  Spain 39°30N 3°0E **21** C7
Balearic Sea *Spain* 40°0N 1°30E **21** B6
Baleine → *Canada* 58°15N 67°40W **73** A6
Baleine, Petite R. de la →
  Canada 56°0N 76°45W **72** A4
Baler *Phil.* 15°46N 121°34E **37** A6
Baleshare *U.K.* 57°31N 7°22W **11** D1
Baleshwar *India* 21°35N 87°3E **44** D8
Baley *Russia* 51°36N 116°37E **27** D12
Balfate *Honduras* 15°48N 86°25W **88** C2
Balgo *Australia* 20°9S 127°58E **60** D4
Balharshah *India* 19°50N 79°23E **44** E4
Bali *India* 25°11N 73°17E **42** G5
Bali *Indonesia* 8°20S 115°0E **37** J18
Bali □ *Indonesia* 8°20S 115°0E **37** J17
Bali, Selat *Indonesia* 8°18S 114°25E **37** J17
Bali Barat △ *Indonesia* 8°12S 114°35E **37** J17
Bali Sea *Indonesia* 8°0S 115°0E **37** J17
Baliapal *India* 21°40N 87°17E **43** J12
Baliguda *India* 20°12N 83°55E **44** D6
Balik Pulau *Malaysia* 5°21N 100°14E **39** c
Balıkesir *Turkey* 39°39N 27°53E **23** E12
Balikpapan *Indonesia* 1°10S 116°55E **36** E5
Balimbing *Phil.* 5°5N 119°58E **37** C5
Baling *Malaysia* 5°41N 100°55E **39** K3
Balkan Mts. = Stara Planina
  Bulgaria 43°15N 23°0E **23** C10
Balkanabat *Turkmenistan* 39°30N 54°22E **47** B7
Balkhash = Balqash
  Kazakhstan 46°50N 74°50E **26** E8
Balkhash, Ozero = Balqash Köli
  Kazakhstan 46°0N 74°50E **30** B3
Balkonda *India* 18°52N 78°21E **44** E4
Ballachulish *U.K.* 56°41N 5°8W **11** E3
Balladonia *Australia* 32°27S 123°51E **61** F3
Ballaghaderreen *Ireland* 53°55N 8°34W **10** C3
Ballarat *Australia* 37°33S 143°50E **63** F3
Ballard, L. *Australia* 29°20S 120°40E **61** E3
Ballari *India* 15°10N 76°56E **45** G3
Ballater *U.K.* 57°3N 3°3W **11** D5
Ballenas, Canal de
  Mexico 29°10N 113°29W **86** B2
Balleny Is. *Antarctica* 66°30S 163°0E **5** C11
Ballia *India* 25°46N 84°12E **43** G11
Ballina *Australia* 28°50S 153°31E **63** D5
Ballina *Ireland* 54°7N 9°9W **10** B2

Ballinasloe *Ireland* 53°20N 8°13W **10** C3
Ballincollig *Ireland* 51°53N 8°33W **10** E3
Ballinger *U.S.A.* 31°45N 99°57W **84** F5
Ballinrobe *Ireland* 53°38N 9°13W **10** C2
Ballinskelligs B. *Ireland* 51°48N 10°13W **10** E1
Ballston Spa *U.S.A.* 43°0N 73°51W **83** D11
Ballyboghil *Ireland* 53°32N 6°16W **10** C5
Ballybunion *Ireland* 52°31N 9°40W **10** D2
Ballycanew *Ireland* 52°37N 6°19W **10** D5
Ballycastle *U.K.* 55°12N 6°15W **10** A5
Ballyclare *U.K.* 54°46N 6°0W **10** B5
Ballycroy △ *Ireland* 54°5N 9°50W **10** B2
Ballydehob *Ireland* 51°34N 9°28W **10** E2
Ballygawley *U.K.* 54°27N 7°2W **10** B4
Ballyhaunis *Ireland* 53°46N 8°46W **10** C3
Ballymena *U.K.* 54°52N 6°17W **10** B5
Ballymoney *U.K.* 55°5N 6°31W **10** A5
Ballymote *Ireland* 54°5N 8°31W **10** B3
Ballynahinch *U.K.* 54°24N 5°54W **10** B6
Ballyporeen *Ireland* 52°16N 8°6W **10** D3
Ballyquintin Pt. *U.K.* 54°20N 5°30W **10** B6
Ballyshannon *Ireland* 54°30N 8°11W **10** B3
Balmaceda *Chile* 46°0S 71°50W **96** F2
Balmertown *Canada* 51°4N 93°41W **71** C10
Balmoral *Australia* 37°15S 141°48E **63** F3
Balmorhea *U.S.A.* 30°59N 103°45W **84** F3
Balneário Camboriú
  Brazil 26°59S 48°38W **95** B6
Balochistan = Baluchistan □
  Pakistan 27°30N 65°0E **40** F4
Balod *India* 20°44N 81°13E **44** D5
Balonne → *Australia* 28°47S 147°56E **63** D4
Balotra *India* 25°50N 72°14E **42** G5
Balqash *Kazakhstan* 46°50N 74°50E **26** E8
Balqash Köli *Kazakhstan* 46°0N 74°50E **30** B3
Balrampur *India* 27°30N 82°20E **43** F10
Balranald *Australia* 34°38S 143°33E **63** E3
Balsas → *Brazil* 7°15S 44°35W **93** E9
Balsas → *Mexico* 17°55N 102°10W **86** D4
Balsas del Norte *Mexico* 18°0N 99°46W **87** D5
Balta *Ukraine* 47°56N 29°45E **17** D15
Bălți *Moldova* 47°48N 27°58E **17** E14
Baltic Sea *Europe* 57°0N 19°0E **9** H18
Baltimore *Ireland* 51°29N 9°22W **10** E2
Baltimore *Md., U.S.A.* 39°17N 76°36W **81** F15
Baltimore *Ohio, U.S.A.* 39°51N 82°36W **82** G2
Baltimore-Washington Int. ✈
  (BWI) U.S.A. 39°10N 76°40W **81** F15
Baltinglass *Ireland* 52°56N 6°43W **10** D5
Baltit *Pakistan* 36°15N 74°40E **43** A6
Baltiysk *Russia* 54°41N 19°58E **9** J18
Balurghat *India* 25°15N 88°44E **43** G13
Balvi *Latvia* 57°8N 27°15E **9** H22
Balya *Turkey* 39°44N 27°35E **23** E12
Balykchy *Kyrgyzstan* 42°26N 76°12E **30** C4
Balyqshy *Kazakhstan* 47°4N 51°52E **19** E9
Bam *Iran* 29°7N 58°14E **47** D8
Bama *China* 24°8N 107°12E **34** E6
Bama *Nigeria* 11°33N 13°41E **53** F8
Bamaga *Australia* 10°50S 142°25E **62** A3
Bamaji L. *Canada* 51°9N 91°25W **72** B1
Bamako *Mali* 12°34N 7°55W **52** F4
Bambari *C.A.R.* 5°40N 20°35E **54** C4
Bambaroo *Australia* 18°50S 146°10E **62** B4
Bamberg *Germany* 49°54N 10°54E **16** D6
Bamberg *U.S.A.* 33°18N 81°2W **85** E14
Bamburgh *U.K.* 55°37N 1°43W **12** B6
Bamenda *Cameroon* 5°57N 10°11E **54** C2
Bamfield *Canada* 48°45N 125°10W **70** D3
Bāmīān □ *Afghan.* 35°0N 67°0E **40** B5
Bamiancheng *China* 43°15N 124°2E **33** C13
Bamou *Iran* 29°45N 52°35E **47** D7
Bampūr *Iran* 27°15N 60°21E **47** E9
Bampūr → *Iran* 27°24N 59°0E **47** E8
Ban Ao Tu Khun *Thailand* 8°9N 98°20E **39** a
Ban Ban *Laos* 19°31N 103°30E **38** C4
Ban Bang Hin *Thailand* 9°32N 98°35E **39** H2
Ban Bang Khu *Thailand* 7°57N 98°23E **39** a
Ban Bang Rong *Thailand* 8°3N 98°25E **39** a
Ban Bo Phut *Thailand* 9°33N 100°2E **39** b
Ban Chaweng *Thailand* 9°32N 100°3E **39** b
Ban Chiang *Thailand* 17°30N 103°10E **38** D4
Ban Chiang Klang
  Thailand 19°25N 100°55E **38** C3
Ban Choho *Thailand* 15°2N 102°9E **38** E4
Ban Dan Lan Hoi *Thailand* 17°0N 99°35E **38** D2
Ban Don = Surat Thani
  Thailand 9°6N 99°20E **39** H2
Ban Don *Vietnam* 12°53N 107°48E **38** F6
Ban Don, Ao → *Thailand* 9°20N 99°25E **39** H2
Ban Dong *Thailand* 19°30N 100°59E **38** C3
Ban Hong *Thailand* 18°18N 98°50E **38** C2
Ban Hua Thanon *Thailand* 9°26N 100°1E **39** b
Ban Kantang *Thailand* 7°25N 99°31E **39** J2
Ban Karon *Thailand* 7°51N 98°18E **39** a
Ban Kata *Thailand* 7°50N 98°18E **39** a
Ban Keun *Laos* 18°22N 102°35E **38** C4
Ban Khai *Thailand* 12°46N 101°18E **38** F3
Ban Kheun *Laos* 20°13N 101°7E **38** B3
Ban Khlong Khian *Thailand* 8°10N 98°26E **39** a
Ban Khlong Kua *Thailand* 6°57N 100°8E **39** J3
Ban Khuan *Thailand* 8°20N 98°25E **39** a
Ban Ko Yai Chim
  Thailand 11°17N 99°26E **39** G2
Ban Laem *Thailand* 13°13N 99°59E **38** F2
Ban Lamai *Thailand* 9°28N 100°3E **39** b
Ban Lao Ngam *Laos* 15°28N 106°10E **38** E6
Ban Le Kathe *Thailand* 15°49N 98°53E **38** E2
Ban Lo Po Noi *Thailand* 8°1N 98°34E **39** a
Ban Mae Chedi *Thailand* 19°11N 99°31E **38** C2
Ban Mae Nam *Thailand* 9°34N 100°0E **39** b
Ban Mae Sariang
  Thailand 18°10N 97°56E **38** C1
Ban Mê Thuột = Buon Ma Thuot
  Vietnam 12°40N 108°3E **38** F7
Ban Mi *Thailand* 15°3N 100°32E **38** E3
Ban Muang Mo *Laos* 19°4N 103°58E **38** C4
Ban Na Bo *Thailand* 9°19N 99°41E **39** b

Ban Na San *Thailand* 8°53N 99°52E **39** H2
Ban Na Tong *Laos* 20°56N 101°47E **38** B3
Ban Nam Bac *Laos* 20°38N 102°20E **38** B4
Ban Nammi *Laos* 17°7N 105°40E **38** D5
Ban Nong Bok *Laos* 17°5N 104°48E **38** D5
Ban Nong Pling *Thailand* 15°40N 100°10E **38** E3
Ban Pak Chan *Thailand* 10°32N 98°51E **39** G2
Ban Patong *Thailand* 7°54N 98°18E **39** a
Ban Phai *Thailand* 16°4N 102°44E **38** D4
Ban Phak Chit *Thailand* 8°0N 98°24E **39** a
Ban Pong *Thailand* 13°50N 99°55E **38** F2
Ban Rawai *Thailand* 7°47N 98°20E **39** a
Ban Ron Phibun *Thailand* 8°9N 99°51E **39** H2
Ban Sakhu *Thailand* 8°4N 98°18E **39** a
Ban Sanam Chai *Thailand* 7°33N 100°25E **39** J3
Ban Tak *Thailand* 17°2N 99°4E **38** D2
Ban Tako *Thailand* 14°5N 102°40E **38** E4
Ban Tha Nun *Thailand* 8°12N 98°18E **39** a
Ban Tha Rua *Thailand* 7°59N 98°22E **39** a
Ban Tha Yu *Thailand* 8°17N 98°22E **39** a
Ban Thong Krut *Thailand* 9°25N 99°57E **39** b
Ban Xien Kok *Laos* 20°54N 100°39E **38** B3
Ban Yen Nhan *Vietnam* 20°57N 106°2E **38** B6
Banaba *Kiribati* 0°45S 169°50E **64** H8
Banagher *Ireland* 53°11N 7°59W **10** C3
Banalia
  Dem. Rep. of the Congo 1°32N 25°5E **54** D5
Banam *Cambodia* 11°20N 105°17E **39** G5
Banana *Australia* 6°57N 93°54E **45** L11
Bananal, I. do *Brazil* 11°30S 50°30W **93** F8
Bananga *India* 6°57N 93°54E **45** L11
Banaras = Varanasi *India* 25°22N 83°0E **43** G10
Banas → *Gujarat, India* 23°45N 71°25E **42** H4
Banas → *Mad. P., India* 24°15N 81°30E **43** G9
Bānās, Ras *Egypt* 23°57N 35°59E **53** D13
Banbridge *U.K.* 54°22N 6°16W **10** B5
Banbury *U.K.* 52°4N 1°20W **13** E6
Banchory *U.K.* 57°3N 2°29W **11** D6
Bancroft *Canada* 45°3N 77°51W **82** A7
Band Bonī *Iran* 25°30N 59°33E **47** E8
Band Qīr *Iran* 31°39N 48°53E **47** D6
Banda *Mad. P., India* 24°3N 78°57E **43** G8
Banda *Maharashtra, India* 15°49N 73°52E **45** G1
Banda *Ut. P., India* 25°30N 80°26E **43** G9
Banda, Kepulauan
  Indonesia 4°37S 129°50E **37** E7
Banda Aceh *Indonesia* 5°35N 95°20E **36** C1
Banda Banda, Mt.
  Australia 31°10S 152°28E **63** E5
Banda Elat *Indonesia* 5°40S 133°5E **37** F8
Banda Is. = Banda, Kepulauan
  Indonesia 4°37S 129°50E **37** E7
Banda Sea *Indonesia* 6°0S 130°0E **37** F8
Bandai-Asahi △ *Japan* 37°38N 140°4E **28** F10
Bandai-San *Japan* 37°36N 140°4E **28** F10
Bandān *Iran* 31°23N 60°44E **47** D9
Bandanaira *Indonesia* 4°32S 129°54E **37** E7
Bandanwara *India* 26°9N 74°38E **42** F6
Bandar = Machilipatnam
  India 16°12N 81°8E **45** F5
Bandar-e Abbās *Iran* 27°15N 56°15E **47** E8
Bandar-e Anzalī *Iran* 37°30N 49°30E **47** B6
Bandar-e Bushehr = Büshehr
  Iran 28°55N 50°55E **47** D6
Bandar-e Chārak *Iran* 26°45N 54°20E **47** E7
Bandar-e Deylam *Iran* 30°30N 50°45E **47** D6
Bandar-e Emām Khomeynī
  Iran 30°30N 49°5E **47** D6
Bandar-e Lengeh *Iran* 26°35N 54°58E **47** E7
Bandar-e Maqām *Iran* 26°56N 53°29E **47** E7
Bandar-e Ma'shur *Iran* 30°35N 49°10E **47** D6
Bandar-e Rīg *Iran* 29°29N 50°38E **47** D6
Bandar-e Torkeman *Iran* 37°0N 54°10E **47** B7
Bandar Labuan *Malaysia* 5°20N 115°14E **36** C5
Bandar Lampung
  Indonesia 5°20S 105°10E **36** F3
Bandar Maharani = Muar
  Malaysia 2°3N 102°34E **39** L4
Bandar Penggaram = Batu Pahat
  Malaysia 1°50N 102°56E **39** M4
Bandar Seri Begawan
  Brunei 4°52N 115°0E **36** D5
Bandar Shahid Rajaee *Iran* 27°7N 56°4E **47** E8
Bandar Sri Aman
  Malaysia 1°15N 111°32E **36** D4
Bandeira, Pico da *Brazil* 20°26S 41°47W **95** A7
Bandera *Argentina* 28°55S 62°20W **94** B3
Banderas, B. de *Mexico* 20°40N 105°25W **86** C3
Bandhavgarh *India* 23°40N 81°2E **43** H9
Bandhavgarh △ *India* 23°45N 81°10E **44** C5
Bandi → *India* 26°12N 75°47E **42** F6
Bandia → *India* 19°2N 80°28E **44** E5
Bandikui *India* 27°3N 76°34E **42** F7
Bandipur △ *India* 11°45N 76°30E **45** J3
Bandırma *Turkey* 40°20N 28°0E **23** D13
Bandjarmasin = Banjarmasin
  Indonesia 3°20S 114°35E **36** E4
Bandon *Ireland* 51°44N 8°44W **10** E3
Bandon → *Ireland* 51°43N 8°37W **10** E3
Bandundu
  Dem. Rep. of the Congo 3°15S 17°22E **54** E3
Bandung *Indonesia* 6°54S 107°36E **37** G12
Bāneh *Iran* 35°59N 45°53E **46** C5
Banes *Cuba* 21°0N 75°42W **89** B4
Banff *Canada* 51°10N 115°34W **70** C5
Banff *U.K.* 57°40N 2°33W **11** D6
Banff △ *Canada* 51°30N 116°15W **70** C5
Bang Fai → *Laos* 16°57N 104°45E **38** D5
Bang Hieng → *Laos* 16°10N 105°10E **38** D5
Bang Krathum *Thailand* 16°34N 100°18E **38** D3
Bang Lang △ *Thailand* 5°58N 101°9E **39** K3
Bang Lang Res. *Thailand* 6°6N 101°17E **39** J3
Bang Mun Nak *Thailand* 16°2N 100°23E **38** D3
Bang Pa In *Thailand* 14°14N 100°30E **38** E3
Bang Rakam *Thailand* 16°45N 100°7E **38** D3
Bang Saphan *Thailand* 11°14N 99°28E **39** G2
Bang Thao *Thailand* 8°1N 98°18E **39** a
Banganduni I. *India* 21°34N 88°52E **43** J13
Bangalore = Bengaluru
  India 12°59N 77°40E **45** H3
Banganapalle *India* 15°19N 78°14E **45** G4

Banganga → *India* 27°6N 77°25E **42** F6
Bangaon *India* 23°0N 88°47E **43** H13
Bangassou *C.A.R.* 4°55N 23°7E **54** D4
Banggai *Indonesia* 1°34S 123°30E **37** E6
Banggai, Kepulauan
  Indonesia 1°40S 123°30E **37** E6
Banggai Arch. = Banggai,
  Kepulauan *Indonesia* 1°40S 123°30E **37** E6
Banggi, Pulau *Malaysia* 7°17N 117°12E **36** C5
Banghāzī *Libya* 32°11N 20°3E **53** B10
Bangka *Sulawesi, Indonesia* 1°50N 125°5E **37** D7
Bangka *Sumatera, Indonesia* 2°0S 105°50E **36** E3
Bangka, Selat *Indonesia* 2°30S 105°30E **36** E3
Bangka-Belitung □
  Indonesia 2°30S 107°0E **36** E3
Bangkalan *Indonesia* 7°2S 112°46E **37** G15
Bangkang *Myanmar* 22°4N 99°1E **34** F2
Bangkinang *Indonesia* 0°18N 101°5E **36** D2
Bangko *Indonesia* 2°5S 102°9E **36** E2
Bangkok, Bight of
  Thailand 12°55N 100°30E **38** F3
Bangla = Paschimbanga □
  India 23°0N 88°0E **43** H13
Bangladesh ■ *Asia* 24°0N 90°0E **41** H17
Bangli *Indonesia* 8°27S 115°21E **37** J18
Bangong Co *China* 33°45N 78°43E **43** C8
Bangor *Down, U.K.* 54°40N 5°40W **10** B6
Bangor *Gwynedd, U.K.* 53°14N 4°8W **12** D3
Bangor *Maine, U.S.A.* 44°48N 68°46W **81** C19
Bangor *Pa., U.S.A.* 40°52N 75°13W **83** F9
Bangued *Phil.* 17°40N 120°37E **37** A6
Bangui *C.A.R.* 4°23N 18°35E **54** D3
Bangweulu, L. *Zambia* 11°0S 30°0E **54** G6
Banhine △ *Mozam.* 22°49S 32°55E **57** B5
Bani *Dom. Rep.* 18°16N 70°22W **89** C5
Bani Sa'd *Iraq* 33°34N 44°32E **46** C5
Banihal Pass *India* 33°30N 75°12E **43** C6
Bāniyās *Syria* 35°10N 36°0E **46** C3
Banja Luka *Bos.-H.* 44°49N 17°11E **22** B7
Banjar *India* 31°38N 77°21E **42** D7
Banjar → *India* 22°36N 80°22E **43** H9
Banjarmasin *Indonesia* 3°20S 114°35E **36** E4
Banjul *Gambia* 13°28N 16°40W **52** F2
Banka *India* 24°53N 86°55E **43** G12
Bankipore *India* 25°35N 85°10E **41** G14
Bankot *India* 17°58N 73°3E **44** F1
Banks I. = Moa *Australia* 10°11S 142°16E **62** a
Banks I. *B.C., Canada* 53°20N 130°0W **70** C3
Banks I. *N.W.T., Canada* 73°15N 121°30W **68** C7
Banks Pen. *N.Z.* 43°45S 173°15E **59** E4
Banks Str. *Australia* 40°40S 148°10E **63** G4
Bankura *India* 23°11N 87°18E **43** H12
Banmankhi *India* 25°53N 87°11E **43** G12
Bann → *Armagh, U.K.* 54°30N 6°31W **10** B5
Bann → *L'derry., U.K.* 55°8N 6°41W **10** A5
Bannang Sata *Thailand* 6°16N 101°16E **39** J3
Banning *U.S.A.* 33°56N 116°53W **79** M10
Bannockburn *Canada* 44°39N 77°33W **82** B7
Bannockburn *U.K.* 56°5N 3°55W **11** E5
Bannu *Pakistan* 33°0N 70°18E **40** C7
Bano *India* 22°40N 84°55E **43** H11
Bansagar Dam *India* 24°11N 81°17E **44** B5
Bansgaon *India* 26°33N 83°21E **43** F10
Banská Bystrica
  Slovakia 48°46N 19°14E **17** D10
Banswara *India* 23°32N 74°24E **42** H6
Bantaeng *Indonesia* 5°32S 119°56E **37** F5
Banteay Prei Nokor
  Cambodia 11°56N 105°40E **39** G5
Banten □ *Indonesia* 6°30S 106°0E **37** G11
Bantry *Ireland* 51°41N 9°27W **10** E2
Bantry B. *Ireland* 51°37N 9°44W **10** E2
Bantva *India* 21°29N 70°12E **42** J4
Bantval *India* 12°55N 75°0E **45** H2
Banyak, Kepulauan
  Indonesia 2°10N 97°10E **36** D1
Banyo *Cameroon* 6°52N 11°45E **54** C2
Banyuwangi *Indonesia* 8°13S 114°21E **37** J17
Banzare Coast *Antarctica* 68°0S 125°0E **5** C9
Bao Ha *Vietnam* 22°11N 104°21E **34** F5
Bao Lac *Vietnam* 22°57N 105°40E **38** A5
Bao Loc *Vietnam* 11°32N 107°48E **39** G6
Bao'an *China* 22°34N 113°52E **31** a
Baocheng *China* 33°12N 106°56E **34** A6
Baode *China* 39°1N 111°5E **32** E6
Baodi *China* 39°38N 117°20E **33** E9
Baoding *China* 38°50N 115°28E **32** E8
Baoji *China* 34°20N 107°5E **32** G4
Baojing *China* 28°45N 109°41E **34** C7
Baokang *China* 31°54N 111°12E **35** B8
Baoshan *China* 25°10N 99°5E **34** E2
Baotou *China* 40°32N 110°2E **32** D6
Baoxing *China* 30°24N 102°50E **34** B4
Baoying *China* 33°17N 119°20E **33** H10
Baoyou = Ledong *China* 18°41N 109°5E **38** C7
Bap *India* 27°23N 72°18E **42** F5
Bapatla *India* 15°55N 80°30E **45** G5
Bāqerābād *Iran* 33°2N 51°58E **47** C6
Ba'qūbah *Iraq* 33°45N 44°50E **46** C5
Baquedano *Chile* 23°20S 69°52W **94** A2
Bar *Montenegro* 42°8N 19°6E **23** C8
Bar *Ukraine* 49°4N 27°40E **17** D14
Bar Bigha *India* 25°21N 85°47E **43** G11
Bar Harbor *U.S.A.* 44°23N 68°13W **81** C19
Bar-le-Duc *France* 48°47N 5°10E **20** B6
Bara *India* 25°16N 81°43E **43** G9
Bara Banki *India* 26°55N 81°12E **43** F9
Barabai *Indonesia* 2°32S 115°34E **36** E5
Baraboo *U.S.A.* 43°28N 89°45W **80** D9
Baracoa *Cuba* 20°20N 74°30W **89** B5
Baradā → *Syria* 33°33N 36°34E **48** B5
Baradero *Argentina* 33°52S 59°29W **94** C4
Baraga *U.S.A.* 46°47N 88°30W **80** B9
Barah → *India* 27°42N 77°5E **42** F7
Barahona *Dom. Rep.* 18°13N 71°7W **89** C5
Barail Range *India* 25°15N 93°20E **41** G18
Barakaldo *Spain* 43°18N 2°59W **21** A4
Barakar → *India* 24°7N 86°14E **43** G12
Barakot *India* 21°33N 84°59E **43** J11
Baralaba *Australia* 24°13S 149°50E **62** C4

Baralzon L. *Canada* 60°0N 98°3W **71** B9
Baramati *India* 18°11N 74°33E **44** E2
Baramba *India* 20°25N 85°23E **44** D7
Baramula *India* 34°15N 74°20E **43** B6
Baran *India* 25°9N 76°40E **42** G7
Baran → *Pakistan* 25°13N 68°17E **42** G3
Baranavichy *Belarus* 53°10N 26°0E **17** B14
Baranof *U.S.A.* 57°5N 134°50W **70** B2
Baranof I. *U.S.A.* 57°0N 135°0W **68** F4
Barapasi *Indonesia* 2°15S 137°5E **37** E9
Barasat *India* 22°46N 88°31E **43** H13
Barat Daya, Kepulauan
  Indonesia 7°30S 128°0E **37** F7
Baratang I. *India* 12°13N 92°45E **45** H11
Barataria B. *U.S.A.* 29°20N 89°55W **85** G10
Barauda *India* 23°33N 75°15E **42** H6
Baraut *India* 29°13N 77°7E **42** E7
Barbacena *Brazil* 21°15S 43°56W **95** A7
Barbados ■ *W. Indies* 13°10N 59°30W **89** g
Barbas, C. *W. Sahara* 22°20N 16°42W **52** D2
Barbastro *Spain* 42°2N 0°5E **21** A6
Barbeau Pk. *Canada* 81°54N 75°1W **69** A16
Barberton *S. Africa* 25°42S 31°2E **57** C5
Barberton *U.S.A.* 41°1N 81°39W **82** E3
Barbosa *Colombia* 5°57N 73°37W **92** B4
Barbourville *U.S.A.* 36°52N 83°53W **81** G12
Barbuda *W. Indies* 17°30N 61°40W **89** C7
Barcaldine *Australia* 23°43S 145°6E **62** C4
Barcellona Pozzo di Gotto
  Italy 38°9N 15°13E **22** E6
Barcelona *Venezuela* 10°10N 64°40W **92** A6
Barceloneta *Puerto Rico* 18°27N 66°32W **89** d
Barcelos *Brazil* 1°0S 63°0W **92** D6
Barco → *Australia* 25°30S 142°50E **62** D3
Bardaï *Chad* 21°25N 17°0E **53** D9
Bardas Blancas *Argentina* 35°49S 69°45W **94** D2
Bardawîl, Sabkhet el
  Egypt 31°10N 33°15E **48** D2
Barddhaman *India* 23°14N 87°39E **43** H12
Bardejov *Slovakia* 49°18N 21°15E **17** D11
Bardera = Baardheere
  Somalia 2°20N 42°27E **49** G3
Bardīyah *Libya* 31°45N 25°5E **53** B10
Bardoli *India* 21°12N 73°5E **44** D1
Bardsey I. *U.K.* 52°45N 4°47W **12** E3
Bardstown *U.S.A.* 37°49N 85°28W **81** G11
Bareilly *India* 28°22N 79°27E **43** E8
Barela *India* 23°6N 80°3E **43** H9
Barents Sea *Arctic* 73°0N 39°0E **4** B9
Barfleur, Pte. de *France* 49°42N 1°16W **20** B3
Bargara *Australia* 24°50S 152°25E **62** C5
Bargarh *India* 21°20N 83°37E **44** D6
Bargi Dam *India* 22°59N 80°0E **44** H8
Barguzin *Russia* 53°37N 109°37E **27** D11
Barh *India* 25°29N 85°46E **43** G11
Barhaj *India* 26°18N 83°44E **43** F10
Barharwa *India* 24°52N 87°47E **43** G12
Barhi *India* 24°15N 85°25E **43** G11
Bari *India* 26°39N 77°39E **42** F7
Bari *Italy* 41°8N 16°51E **22** D7
Bari Doab *Pakistan* 30°20N 73°0E **42** D5
Bari Sadri *India* 24°28N 74°30E **42** G6
Barīdī, Ra's *Si. Arabia* 24°17N 37°31E **46** E3
Barīm *Yemen* 12°39N 43°25E **50** E8
Barinas *Venezuela* 8°36N 70°15W **92** B4
Baring, C. *Canada* 70°0N 117°30W **68** D8
Baripada *India* 21°57N 86°45E **44** D8
Barisal *Bangla.* 22°45N 90°20E **41** H17
Barisal □ *Bangla.* 22°45N 90°20E **41** H17
Barisan, Pegunungan
  Indonesia 3°30S 102°15E **36** E2
Barito → *Indonesia* 4°0S 114°50E **36** E4
Baritú △ *Argentina* 23°43S 64°40W **94** A3
Barjūj, Wadi → *Libya* 25°26N 12°12E **53** C8
Bark L. *Canada* 45°27N 77°51W **82** A7
Barkakana *India* 23°37N 85°29E **43** H11
Barkam *China* 31°51N 102°28E **34** B4
Barker *U.S.A.* 43°20N 78°33W **82** C6
Barkley, L. *U.S.A.* 37°1N 88°14W **85** C10
Barkley Sound *Canada* 48°50N 125°10W **70** D3
Barkly East *S. Africa* 30°58S 27°33E **56** D4
Barkly Homestead
  Australia 19°52S 135°50E **62** B2
Barkly Tableland
  Australia 17°50S 136°40E **62** B2
Barkly West *S. Africa* 28°5S 24°31E **56** D3
Barkol Kazak Zizhixian
  China 43°37N 93°2E **30** C7
Bârlad *Romania* 46°15N 27°38E **17** E14
Bârlad → *Romania* 45°38N 27°32E **17** F14
Barlee, L. *Australia* 29°15S 119°30E **61** E2
Barlee, Mt. *Australia* 24°38S 128°13E **61** E4
Barletta *Italy* 41°19N 16°17E **22** D7
Barlovento *Cabo Verde* 17°0N 25°0W **52** b
Barlow L. *Canada* 62°0N 103°0W **71** A8
Barmedman *Australia* 34°9S 147°21E **63** E4
Barmer *India* 25°45N 71°20E **42** G4
Barmera *Australia* 34°15S 140°28E **63** E3
Barmouth *U.K.* 52°44N 4°4W **12** E3
Barna → *India* 25°21N 83°3E **43** G10
Barnagar *India* 23°7N 75°19E **42** H6
Barnala *India* 30°23N 75°33E **42** D6
Barnard Castle *U.K.* 54°33N 1°55W **12** C6
Barnaul *Russia* 53°20N 83°40E **26** D9
Barnesville *Ga., U.S.A.* 33°3N 84°9W **85** E12
Barnesville *Minn., U.S.A.* 46°43N 96°28W **80** B5
Barnet □ *U.K.* 51°38N 0°9W **13** F7
Barneveld *Neths.* 52°7N 5°36E **15** B5
Barnhart *U.S.A.* 31°8N 101°10W **84** F4
Barnsley *U.K.* 53°34N 1°27W **12** D6
Barnstable *U.S.A.* 41°42N 70°18W **81** E18
Barnstaple *U.K.* 51°5N 4°4W **13** F3
Barnstaple Bay = Bideford Bay
  U.K. 51°5N 4°20W **13** F3
Barnwell *U.S.A.* 33°15N 81°23W **85** E14
Baro *Nigeria* 8°35N 6°18E **52** G7
Baroda = Vadodara *India* 22°20N 73°10E **42** H5
Baroda *India* 25°29N 76°33E **42** G7
Baroe *S. Africa* 33°13S 24°33E **56** D3
Baron Ra. *Australia* 23°30S 127°45E **60** D4

Barong *China* 31°3N 99°20E **34 B2**
Barotseland *Zambia* 15°0S 24°0E **55 H4**
Barpali *India* 21°11N 83°35E **44 D6**
Barpeta *India* 26°20N 91°10E **41 F17**
Barqa *Libya* 27°0N 23°0E **53 C10**
Barques, Pt. Aux *U.S.A.* 44°4N 82°58W **82 B2**
Barquisimeto *Venezuela* 10°4N 69°19W **92 A5**
Barr Smith Range
  Australia 27°4S 120°20E **61 E3**
Barra *Brazil* 11°5S 43°10W **93 F10**
Barra *U.K.* 57°0N 7°29W **11 E1**
Barra, Pta. *Mozam.* 23°48S 35°32E **57 B6**
Barra, Sd. of *U.K.* 57°4N 7°25W **11 D1**
Barra de Navidad
  Mexico 19°12N 104°41W **86 D4**
Barra do Corda *Brazil* 5°30S 45°10W **93 E9**
Barra do Garças *Brazil* 15°54S 52°16W **93 G8**
Barra do Piraí *Brazil* 22°30S 43°50W **95 A7**
Barra Falsa, Pta. da
  Mozam. 22°58S 35°37E **57 B6**
Barra Hd. *U.K.* 56°47N 7°40W **11 E1**
Barra Mansa *Brazil* 22°35S 44°12W **95 A7**
Barraba *Australia* 30°21S 150°35E **63 E5**
Barranca *Lima, Peru* 10°45S 77°50W **92 F3**
Barranca *Loreto, Peru* 4°50S 76°50W **92 D3**
Barranca del Cobre △
  Mexico 27°18N 107°40W **86 B3**
Barrancabermeja *Colombia* 7°0N 73°50W **92 B4**
Barrancas *Venezuela* 8°55N 62°5W **92 B6**
Barrancos *Portugal* 38°10N 6°58W **21 C2**
Barranqueras *Argentina* 27°30S 59°0W **94 B4**
Barranquilla *Colombia* 11°0N 74°50W **92 A4**
Barraute *Canada* 48°26N 77°38W **72 C4**
Barre *Mass., U.S.A.* 42°25N 72°6W **83 D12**
Barre *Vt., U.S.A.* 44°12N 72°30W **83 B12**
Barreal *Argentina* 31°33S 69°28W **94 C2**
Barreiras *Brazil* 12°8S 45°0W **93 F10**
Barreirinhas *Brazil* 2°30S 42°50W **93 D10**
Barren, Nosy *Madag.* 18°25S 43°40E **55 H8**
Barren I. *India* 12°16N 93°51E **45 H11**
Barretos *Brazil* 20°30S 48°35W **93 H9**
Barrhead *Canada* 54°10N 114°24W **70 C6**
Barrie *Canada* 44°24N 79°40W **82 B5**
Barrier Ra. *Australia* 31°0S 141°30E **63 E3**
Barrière *Canada* 51°12N 120°7W **70 C4**
Barrington *U.S.A.* 41°44N 71°18W **83 E13**
Barrington L. *Canada* 56°55N 100°15W **71 B8**
Barrington Tops *Australia* 32°6S 151°28E **63 E5**
Barringun *Australia* 29°1S 145°41E **63 D4**
Barron *U.S.A.* 45°24N 91°51W **80 C8**
Barrow *U.S.A.* 71°18N 156°47W **74 A8**
Barrow → *Ireland* 52°25N 6°58W **10 D5**
Barrow, Pt. *U.S.A.* 71°23N 156°29W **74 A8**
Barrow Creek *Australia* 21°30S 133°55E **62 C1**
Barrow I. *Australia* 20°45S 115°20E **60 D2**
Barrow-in-Furness *U.K.* 54°7N 3°14W **12 C4**
Barrow I. *Australia* 14°20S 144°40E **62 A3**
Barrow Ra. *Australia* 26°0S 127°40E **61 E4**
Barrow Str. *Canada* 74°20N 95°0W **69 C13**
Barry *U.K.* 51°24N 3°16W **13 F4**
Barry's Bay *Canada* 45°29N 77°41W **82 A7**
Barsat *Pakistan* 36°10N 72°45E **43 A5**
Barsi *India* 18°10N 75°50E **44 E2**
Barsoi *India* 25°48N 87°57E **41 G15**
Barstow *U.S.A.* 34°54N 117°1W **79 L9**
Bartica *Guyana* 6°25N 58°40W **92 B7**
Bartle Frere *Australia* 17°27S 145°50E **62 B4**
Bartlesville *U.S.A.* 36°45N 95°59W **84 C7**
Bartlett *Calif., U.S.A.* 36°29N 118°2W **78 J8**
Bartlett *Tenn., U.S.A.* 35°12N 89°52W **85 D10**
Bartlett, L. *Canada* 63°5N 118°20W **70 A5**
Barton *U.S.A.* 44°45N 72°11W **83 B12**
Barton-upon-Humber
  U.K. 53°41N 0°25W **12 D7**
Bartow *U.S.A.* 27°54N 81°50W **85 H14**
Barú, Volcan *Panama* 8°55N 82°35W **88 E3**
Barung, Nusa *Indonesia* 8°30S 113°30E **37 H15**
Baruun Urt *Mongolia* 46°46N 113°15E **31 B11**
Baruunsuu *Mongolia* 43°43N 105°35E **32 C3**
Barwani *India* 22°2N 74°57E **42 H6**
Barysaw *Belarus* 54°17N 28°28E **17 A15**
Barzān *Iraq* 36°55N 44°3E **46 B5**
Bāsa'idū *Iran* 26°35N 55°20E **47 E7**
Basal *Pakistan* 33°33N 72°13E **42 C5**
Basankusu
  Dem. Rep. of the Congo 1°5N 19°50E **54 D3**
Basarabeasca *Moldova* 46°21N 28°58E **17 E15**
Basarabia = Bessarabia
  Moldova 47°0N 28°10E **17 E15**
Basavakalyan *India* 17°52N 76°57E **44 F3**
Basawa *Afghan.* 34°15N 70°50E **42 B4**
Bascuñán, C. *Chile* 28°52S 71°35W **94 B1**
Basel *Switz.* 47°35N 7°35E **20 C7**
Bashākerd, Kūhhā-ye
  Iran 26°42N 58°35E **47 E8**
Bashaw *Canada* 52°35N 112°58W **70 C6**
Bāshī *Iran* 28°41N 51°4E **47 D6**
Bashkir Republic =
  Bashkortostan □
  Russia 54°0N 57°0E **18 D10**
Bashkortostan □ *Russia* 54°0N 57°0E **18 D10**
Basilan I. *Phil.* 6°35N 122°0E **37 C6**
Basilan Str. *Phil.* 6°50N 122°0E **37 C6**
Basildon *U.K.* 51°34N 0°28E **13 F8**
Basim = Washim *India* 20°3N 77°0E **44 D3**
Basin *U.S.A.* 44°23N 108°2W **76 D9**
Basingstoke *U.K.* 51°15N 1°5W **13 F6**
Baskatong, Rés. *Canada* 46°46N 75°50W **72 C4**
Basle = Basel *Switz.* 47°35N 7°35E **20 C7**
Basmat *India* 19°15N 77°12E **44 E3**
Basoda *India* 23°52N 77°54E **42 H7**
Basque Provinces = País Vasco □
  Spain 42°50N 2°45W **21 A4**
Basra = Al Başrah *Iraq* 30°30N 47°50E **46 D5**
Bass Str. *Australia* 39°15S 146°30E **63 F4**
Bassano *Canada* 50°48N 112°20W **70 C6**
Bassano del Grappa *Italy* 45°46N 11°44E **22 B4**
Bassas da India *Ind. Oc.* 22°0S 39°0E **57 B6**
Basse-Pointe *Martinique* 14°52N 61°8W **88 c**
Basse-Terre *Guadeloupe* 16°0N 61°44W **88 b**

Basse Terre *Trin. & Tob.* 10°7N 61°19W **93 K15**
Bassein = Pathein
  Myanmar 16°45N 94°30E **41 L19**
Basses, Pte. des *Guadeloupe* 15°52N 61°17W **88 b**
Basseterre
  St. Kitts & Nevis 17°17N 62°43W **89 C7**
Bassett *U.S.A.* 42°35N 99°32W **80 D4**
Bassi *India* 30°44N 76°21E **42 D7**
Bastak *Iran* 27°15N 54°25E **47 E7**
Baştām *Iran* 36°29N 55°4E **47 B7**
Bastar *India* 19°15N 81°40E **44 E5**
Basti *India* 26°52N 82°55E **43 F10**
Bastia *France* 42°40N 9°30E **20 E8**
Bastogne *Belgium* 50°1N 5°43E **15 D5**
Bastrop *La., U.S.A.* 32°47N 91°55W **84 E9**
Bastrop *Tex., U.S.A.* 30°7N 97°19W **84 F6**
Basuo = Dongfang
  China 18°50N 108°33E **38 C7**
Bat Yam *Israel* 32°2N 34°44E **48 C3**
Bata *Eq. Guin.* 1°57N 9°50E **54 D1**
Bataan □ *Phil.* 14°40N 120°25E **37 B6**
Batabanó *Cuba* 22°41N 82°18W **88 B3**
Batabanó, G. de *Cuba* 22°30N 82°30W **88 B3**
Batac *Phil.* 18°3N 120°34E **37 A6**
Batagai *Russia* 67°38N 134°38E **27 C14**
Batala *India* 31°48N 75°12E **42 D6**
Batam *Indonesia* 1°10N 104°2E **39 d**
Batamay *Russia* 63°30N 129°15E **27 C13**
Batang *China* 30°1N 99°0E **34 B2**
Batang *Indonesia* 6°55S 109°45E **37 G13**
Batangafo *C.A.R.* 7°25N 18°20E **54 C3**
Batangas *Phil.* 13°35N 121°10E **37 B6**
Batanta *Indonesia* 0°55S 130°40E **37 E8**
Batatais *Brazil* 20°54S 47°37W **95 A6**
Batavia *U.S.A.* 43°0N 78°11W **82 D6**
Batchelor *Australia* 13°4S 131°1E **60 B5**
Batdambang *Cambodia* 13°7N 103°12E **38 F4**
Batemans B. *Australia* 35°40S 150°12E **63 F5**
Batemans Bay *Australia* 35°44S 150°11E **63 F5**
Batesburg-Leesville
  U.S.A. 33°54N 81°33W **85 E14**
Batesville *Ark., U.S.A.* 35°46N 91°39W **84 D9**
Batesville *Miss., U.S.A.* 34°19N 89°57W **85 D10**
Batesville *Tex., U.S.A.* 28°58N 99°37W **84 G5**
Bath *Canada* 44°11N 76°47W **83 B8**
Bath *U.K.* 51°23N 2°22W **13 F5**
Bath *Maine, U.S.A.* 43°55N 69°49W **81 D19**
Bath *N.Y., U.S.A.* 42°20N 77°19W **82 D7**
Bath & North East Somerset □
  U.K. 51°21N 2°27W **13 F5**
Batheay *Cambodia* 11°59N 104°57E **39 G5**
Bathsheba *Barbados* 13°13N 59°32W **89 g**
Bathurst *Australia* 33°25S 149°31E **63 E4**
Bathurst *Canada* 47°37N 65°43W **73 C6**
Bathurst *S. Africa* 33°30S 26°50E **56 D4**
Bathurst, C. *Canada* 70°34N 128°0W **68 C6**
Bathurst B. *Australia* 14°16S 144°25E **62 A3**
Bathurst Harb. *Australia* 43°15S 146°10E **63 G4**
Bathurst I. *Australia* 11°30S 130°10E **60 B5**
Bathurst I. *Canada* 76°0N 100°30W **69 B11**
Bathurst Inlet *Canada* 66°50N 108°1W **68 D10**
Batki *Fiji* 17°48S 179°10E **59 a**
Batlow *Australia* 35°31S 148°9E **63 F4**
Batman *Turkey* 37°55N 41°5E **46 B4**
Baṭn al Ghūl *Jordan* 29°36N 35°56E **48 F4**
Batna *Algeria* 35°34N 6°15E **52 A7**
Baton Rouge *U.S.A.* 30°27N 91°11W **84 F9**
Batong, Ko *Thailand* 6°32N 99°12E **39 J2**
Batopilas *Mexico* 27°1N 107°44W **86 B3**
Batouri *Cameroon* 4°30N 14°25E **54 D2**
Båtsfjord *Norway* 70°38N 29°39E **8 A23**
Battambang = Batdambang
  Cambodia 13°7N 103°12E **38 F4**
Batti Malv *India* 8°50N 92°51E **45 K11**
Batticaloa *Sri Lanka* 7°43N 81°45E **45 L5**
Battipáglia *Italy* 40°37N 14°58E **22 D6**
Battle *U.K.* 50°55N 0°30E **13 G8**
Battle → *Canada* 52°43N 108°15W **71 C7**
Battle Creek *U.S.A.* 42°19N 85°11W **81 D11**
Battle Ground *U.S.A.* 45°47N 122°32W **78 E4**
Battle Lake *U.S.A.* 46°17N 95°43W **80 B6**
Battle Mountain *U.S.A.* 40°38N 116°56W **76 F5**
Battleford *Canada* 52°45N 108°15W **71 C7**
Batu *Ethiopia* 6°55N 39°45E **49 F2**
Batu *Malaysia* 3°15N 101°40E **39 L3**
Batu, Kepulauan *Indonesia* 0°30S 98°25E **36 E1**
Batu Ferringhi *Malaysia* 5°28N 100°15E **39 c**
Batu Gajah *Malaysia* 4°28N 101°3E **39 K3**
Batu Is. = Batu, Kepulauan
  Indonesia 0°30S 98°25E **36 E1**
Batu Pahat *Malaysia* 1°50N 102°56E **39 M4**
Batu Puteh, Gunung
  Malaysia 4°15N 101°31E **39 K3**
Batuata *Indonesia* 6°12S 122°42E **37 F6**
Batugondang, Tanjung
  Indonesia 8°6S 114°29E **37 J17**
Batukaru, Gunung
  Indonesia 8°20S 115°5E **37 J18**
Batumi *Georgia* 41°39N 41°44E **19 F7**
Batur, Gunung *Indonesia* 8°14S 115°23E **37 J18**
Batura Sar *Pakistan* 36°30N 74°31E **43 A6**
Baturité *Brazil* 4°28S 38°45W **93 D11**
Baturaja *Indonesia* 8°19S 115°11E **37 J18**
Bau *Malaysia* 1°25N 110°9E **36 D4**
Baubau *Indonesia* 5°25S 122°38E **37 F6**
Bauchi *Nigeria* 10°22N 9°48E **52 F7**
Bauda *India* 20°50N 84°25E **44 D7**
Baudette *U.S.A.* 48°43N 94°36W **80 A6**
Bauer, C. *Australia* 32°44S 134°4E **63 E1**
Bauhinia *Australia* 24°35S 149°18E **62 C4**
Baukau = Baucau
  Timor-Leste 8°27S 126°27E **37 F7**
Bauld, C. *Canada* 51°38N 55°26W **69 G21**
Bauru *Brazil* 22°10S 49°0W **95 A6**
Bausi *India* 24°48N 87°1E **43 G12**
Bauska *Latvia* 56°24N 24°15E **9 H21**
Bautzen *Germany* 51°10N 14°26E **16 C8**

Bavānāt *Iran* 30°28N 53°27E **47 D7**
Bavaria = Bayern □
  Germany 48°50N 12°0E **16 D6**
Bavispe → *Mexico* 29°15N 109°11W **86 B3**
Bawdwin *Myanmar* 23°5N 97°22E **41 H20**
Bawean *Indonesia* 5°46S 112°35E **36 F4**
Bawku *Ghana* 11°3N 0°19W **52 F5**
Bawlake *Myanmar* 19°11N 97°21E **41 K20**
Bawolung *China* 28°50N 101°16E **34 C3**
Baxley *U.S.A.* 31°47N 82°21W **85 F13**
Baxter *U.S.A.* 46°21N 94°17W **80 B6**
Baxter Springs *U.S.A.* 37°2N 94°44W **80 G6**
Baxter State △ *U.S.A.* 46°5N 68°57W **81 B19**
Bay City *Mich., U.S.A.* 43°36N 83°54W **81 D12**
Bay City *Tex., U.S.A.* 28°59N 95°58W **84 G7**
Bay Is. = Bahía, Is. de la
  Honduras 16°45N 86°15W **88 C2**
Bay Minette *U.S.A.* 30°53N 87°46W **85 F11**
Bay Roberts *Canada* 47°36N 53°16W **73 C9**
Bay St. Louis *U.S.A.* 30°19N 89°20W **85 F10**
Bay Springs *U.S.A.* 31°59N 89°17W **85 F10**
Bay View *N.Z.* 39°25S 176°50E **59 C6**
Bayamo *Cuba* 20°20N 76°40W **88 B4**
Bayamón *Puerto Rico* 18°24N 66°9W **89 d**
Bayan Har Shan *China* 34°0N 98°0E **30 E8**
Bayan Hot = Alxa Zuoqi
  China 38°50N 105°40E **32 E3**
Bayan Lepas *Malaysia* 5°17N 100°16E **39 c**
Bayan Obo *China* 41°52N 109°59E **32 D5**
Bayan-Ovoo = Erdenetsogt
  Mongolia 42°55N 106°5E **32 C4**
Bayana *India* 26°55N 77°18E **42 F7**
Bayanaüyl *Kazakhstan* 50°45N 75°45E **26 D8**
Bayanhongor *Mongolia* 46°8N 102°43E **30 B9**
Bayard *N. Mex., U.S.A.* 32°46N 108°8W **77 K9**
Bayard *Nebr., U.S.A.* 41°45N 103°20W **80 E2**
Baybay *Phil.* 10°40N 124°55E **37 B6**
Baydaratskaya Guba
  Russia 69°0N 67°30E **26 C7**
Baydhabo *Somalia* 3°8N 43°30E **49 G3**
Bayern □ *Germany* 48°50N 12°0E **16 D6**
Bayeux *France* 49°17N 0°42W **20 B3**
Bayfield *Canada* 43°34N 81°42W **82 C3**
Bayfield *U.S.A.* 46°49N 90°49W **80 B8**
Bayındır *Turkey* 38°13N 27°39E **23 E12**
Baykal, Oz. *Russia* 53°0N 108°0E **27 D11**
Baykan *Turkey* 38°7N 41°44E **46 B4**
Baymak *Russia* 52°36N 58°19E **18 D10**
Baynes Mts. *Namibia* 17°15S 13°0E **56 A1**
Bayombong *Phil.* 16°30N 121°10E **37 A6**
Bayonne *France* 43°30N 1°28W **20 E3**
Bayovar *Peru* 5°50S 81°0W **92 E2**
Bayqonyr *Kazakhstan* 45°40N 63°20E **26 E7**
Bayram-Ali = Bayramaly
  Turkmenistan 37°37N 62°10E **47 B9**
Bayramaly *Turkmenistan* 37°37N 62°10E **47 B9**
Bayramiç *Turkey* 39°48N 26°36E **23 E12**
Bayreuth *Germany* 49°56N 11°35E **16 D6**
Bayrūt *Lebanon* 33°53N 35°31E **48 B4**
Bays, L. of *Canada* 45°15N 79°4W **82 A5**
Baysville *Canada* 45°9N 79°7W **82 A5**
Baytown *U.S.A.* 29°43N 94°59W **84 G7**
Bayuquan *China* 40°16N 122°9E **33 D12**
Baza *Spain* 37°30N 2°47W **21 D4**
Bazaruto, I. do *Mozam.* 21°40S 35°28E **57 B6**
Bazaruto △ *Mozam.* 21°42S 35°26E **57 B6**
Bazhong *China* 31°52N 106°46E **34 B6**
Bazhou *China* 39°8N 116°22E **32 E9**
Bazmān, Kūh-e *Iran* 28°4N 60°1E **47 D9**
Bé, Nosy *Madag.* 13°25S 48°15E **55 G9**
Beach *U.S.A.* 46°58N 104°0W **80 B2**
Beach City *U.S.A.* 40°39N 81°35W **82 F3**
Beachport *Australia* 37°29S 140°0E **63 F3**
Beachville *Canada* 43°5N 80°49W **82 C4**
Beachy Hd. *U.K.* 50°44N 0°15E **13 G8**
Beacon *Australia* 30°26S 117°52E **61 F2**
Beacon *U.S.A.* 41°30N 73°58W **83 E11**
Beaconsfield *Australia* 41°11S 146°48E **63 G4**
Beagle, Canal *S. Amer.* 55°0S 68°30W **96 H3**
Beagle Bay *Australia* 16°58S 122°40E **60 C3**
Beagle Bay ♁ *Australia* 16°53S 122°40E **60 C3**
Beagle G. *Australia* 12°15S 130°25E **60 B5**
Béal an Átha = Ballina
  Ireland 54°7N 9°9W **10 B2**
Béal Átha na Sluaighe =
  Ballinasloe *Ireland* 53°20N 8°13W **10 C3**
Beals Cr. → *U.S.A.* 32°10N 100°51W **84 E4**
Beamsville *Canada* 43°12N 79°28W **82 C5**
Bear → *Calif., U.S.A.* 38°56N 121°36W **78 G5**
Bear → *Utah, U.S.A.* 41°30N 112°8W **74 G17**
Bear I. = Bjørnøya *Arctic* 74°30N 19°0E **4 B8**
Bear I. *Ireland* 51°38N 9°50W **10 E2**
Bear L. *Canada* 55°8N 96°0W **71 B9**
Bear L. *U.S.A.* 41°59N 111°21W **76 F8**
Bear Lake *U.S.A.* 39°53N 75°3W **82 A5**
Beardmore *Canada* 49°36N 87°57W **72 C2**
Beardmore Glacier
  Antarctica 84°30S 170°0E **5 E11**
Beardstown *U.S.A.* 40°1N 90°26W **80 E8**
Bearma → *India* 24°20N 79°51E **43 G8**
Béarn *France* 43°20N 0°30W **20 E3**
Bearpaw Mts. *U.S.A.* 48°12N 109°30W **76 B9**
Bearskin Lake *Canada* 53°58N 91°2W **72 B1**
Beas → *India* 31°10N 74°59E **42 D6**
Beata, C. *Dom. Rep.* 17°40N 71°30W **89 C5**
Beatrice *U.S.A.* 40°16N 96°45W **80 E5**
Beatrice, C. *Australia* 14°20S 136°55E **62 A2**
Beatton → *Canada* 56°15N 120°45W **70 B4**
Beatton River *Canada* 57°26N 121°20W **70 B4**
Beatty *U.S.A.* 36°54N 116°46W **78 J10**
Beau Bassin *Mauritius* 20°13S 57°27E **55 d**
Beauce, Plaine de la
  France 48°10N 1°45E **20 B4**
Beauceville *Canada* 46°13N 70°46W **73 C5**
Beaudesert *Australia* 27°59S 153°0E **63 D5**
Beaufort *Malaysia* 5°30N 115°40E **36 C5**
Beaufort *N.C., U.S.A.* 34°43N 76°40W **85 D16**
Beaufort *S.C., U.S.A.* 32°26N 80°40W **85 E14**
Beaufort Sea *Arctic* 72°0N 140°0W **66 B5**

Beaufort West *S. Africa* 32°18S 22°36E **56 D3**
Beauharnois *Canada* 45°20N 73°52W **83 A11**
Beaulieu → *Canada* 62°3N 113°11W **70 A6**
Beauly *U.K.* 57°30N 4°28W **11 D4**
Beauly → *U.K.* 57°29N 4°27W **11 D4**
Beaumaris *U.K.* 53°16N 4°6W **12 D3**
Beaumont *Belgium* 50°15N 4°14E **15 D4**
Beaumont *Calif., U.S.A.* 33°57N 116°59W **79 M9**
Beaumont *Tex., U.S.A.* 30°5N 94°6W **84 F7**
Beaune *France* 47°2N 4°50E **20 C6**
Beaupré *Canada* 47°3N 70°54W **73 C5**
Beauraing *Belgium* 50°7N 4°57E **15 D4**
Beausejour *Canada* 50°5N 96°35W **71 C9**
Beauvais *France* 49°25N 2°8E **20 B5**
Beauval *Canada* 55°9N 107°37W **71 B7**
Beaver *Okla., U.S.A.* 36°49N 100°31W **84 C4**
Beaver *Pa., U.S.A.* 40°42N 80°19W **82 F4**
Beaver *Utah, U.S.A.* 38°17N 112°38W **76 G7**
Beaver → *B.C., Canada* 59°52N 124°20W **70 B4**
Beaver → *Ont., Canada* 55°55N 87°48W **72 A2**
Beaver → *Sask., Canada* 55°26N 107°45W **71 B7**
Beaver → *U.S.A.* 36°35N 99°30W **84 C5**
Beaver City *U.S.A.* 40°8N 99°50W **80 E4**
Beaver Creek *Canada* 63°0N 141°0W **68 E3**
Beaver Dam *U.S.A.* 43°28N 88°50W **80 D9**
Beaver Falls *U.S.A.* 40°46N 80°20W **82 F4**
Beaver Hill L. *Canada* 54°5N 94°50W **71 C10**
Beaver I. *U.S.A.* 45°40N 85°33W **81 C11**
Beavercreek *U.S.A.* 39°43N 84°11W **81 F11**
Beaverhill L. *Canada* 53°27N 112°32W **70 C6**
Beaverlodge *Canada* 55°11N 119°29W **70 B5**
Beaverstone → *Canada* 54°59N 89°25W **72 B2**
Beaverton *Canada* 44°26N 79°9W **82 B5**
Beaverton *U.S.A.* 45°29N 122°48W **78 E4**
Beawar *India* 26°3N 74°18E **42 F6**
Bebedouro *Brazil* 21°0S 48°25W **95 A6**
Bebera, Tanjung
  Indonesia 8°44S 115°51E **37 K18**
Bebington *U.K.* 53°22N 3°0W **12 D4**
Becán *Mexico* 18°34N 89°31W **87 D7**
Bécancour *Canada* 46°20N 72°26W **81 D17**
Beccles *U.K.* 52°27N 1°35E **13 E9**
Bečej *Serbia* 45°36N 20°3E **23 B9**
Béchar *Algeria* 31°38N 2°18W **52 B5**
Becharof L. *U.S.A.* 57°56N 156°23W **74 D8**
Becharre = Bsharri
  Lebanon 34°15N 36°0E **48 A5**
Beckley *U.S.A.* 37°47N 81°11W **81 G13**
Beddouza, C. *Morocco* 32°33N 9°9W **52 B4**
Bedford *Canada* 45°7N 72°59W **83 A12**
Bedford *S. Africa* 32°40S 26°10E **56 D4**
Bedford *U.K.* 52°8N 0°28W **13 E7**
Bedford *Ind., U.S.A.* 38°52N 86°29W **80 F10**
Bedford *Iowa, U.S.A.* 40°40N 94°44W **80 E6**
Bedford *Ohio, U.S.A.* 41°23N 81°32W **82 E3**
Bedford *Pa., U.S.A.* 40°1N 78°30W **82 F6**
Bedford *Va., U.S.A.* 37°20N 79°31W **81 G14**
Bedford □ *U.K.* 52°4N 0°28W **13 E7**
Bedford, C. *Australia* 15°14S 145°21E **62 B4**
Bedourie *Australia* 24°30S 139°30E **62 C2**
Bedti → *India* 14°50N 74°44E **45 G2**
Bedugul *Indonesia* 8°17S 115°10E **37 J18**
Bedum *Neths.* 53°18N 6°36E **15 A6**
Beebe Plain *Canada* 45°1N 72°9W **83 A12**
Beech Creek *U.S.A.* 41°5N 77°36W **82 E7**
Beechy *Canada* 50°53N 107°24W **71 C7**
Beed = Bir *India* 19°4N 75°46E **44 E2**
Beef I. *Br. Virgin Is.* 18°26N 64°30W **89 e**
Beenleigh *Australia* 27°43S 153°10E **63 D5**
Be'er Sheva *Israel* 31°15N 34°48E **48 D3**
Beersheba = Be'er Sheva
  Israel 31°15N 34°48E **48 D3**
Beestekraal *S. Africa* 25°23S 27°38E **57 C4**
Beeston *U.K.* 52°56N 1°14W **12 E6**
Beeton *Canada* 44°5N 79°47W **82 B5**
Beeville *U.S.A.* 28°24N 97°45W **84 G6**
Befale
  Dem. Rep. of the Congo 0°25N 20°45E **54 D4**
Bega *Australia* 36°41S 149°51E **63 F4**
Begusarai *India* 25°24N 86°9E **43 G12**
Behābād *Iran* 32°24N 59°47E **47 C8**
Behbehān *Iran* 30°30N 50°15E **47 D6**
Behchoko *Canada* 62°50N 116°3W **70 A5**
Behm Canal *U.S.A.* 55°10N 131°0W **70 B2**
Behshahr *Iran* 36°45N 53°35E **47 B7**
Bei Jiang → *China* 23°2N 112°58E **35 F9**
Bei Shan *China* 41°30N 96°0E **30 B8**
Bei'an *China* 48°10N 126°20E **31 B14**
Beibei *China* 29°47N 106°22E **34 C6**
Beichuan *China* 31°55N 104°33E **34 B5**
Beihai *China* 21°28N 109°6E **34 G7**
Beijing Capital Int. ✈ (PEK)
  China 40°5N 116°35E **32 D9**
Beijing Shi □ *China* 39°55N 116°20E **32 E9**
Beilen *Neths.* 52°52N 6°27E **15 B6**
Beiliu *China* 22°41N 110°21E **35 F8**
Beilpajah *Australia* 32°54S 143°52E **63 E3**
Beinn na Faoghla = Benbecula
  U.K. 57°26N 7°21W **11 D1**
Beipan Jiang → *China* 24°55N 106°5E **34 E6**
Beipiao *China* 41°52N 120°32E **33 D11**
Beira *Mozam.* 19°50S 34°52E **55 H6**
Beirut = Bayrūt *Lebanon* 33°53N 35°31E **48 B4**
Beiseker *Canada* 51°23N 113°32W **70 C6**
Beit Lāhīyā *Gaza Strip* 31°32N 34°30E **48 D3**
Beitaolaizhao *China* 44°58N 125°58E **33 B13**
Beitbridge *Zimbabwe* 22°12S 30°0E **55 J6**
Beizhen = Binzhou
  China 37°20N 118°2E **33 F10**
Beizhen *China* 41°38N 121°54E **33 D11**
Beizhengzhen *China* 44°31N 123°30E **33 B12**
Beja *Portugal* 38°2N 7°53W **21 C2**
Béja *Tunisia* 36°43N 9°12E **53 A7**
Bejaïa *Algeria* 36°42N 5°2E **52 A7**
Béjar *Spain* 40°23N 5°46W **21 B3**
Bejestān *Iran* 34°30N 58°5E **47 C8**
Bekaa Valley = Al Biqā
  Lebanon 34°10N 36°10E **48 A5**
Bekasi *Indonesia* 6°14S 106°59E **37 G12**
Bekily *Madag.* 24°13S 45°19E **57 C8**
Békéscsaba *Hungary* 46°40N 21°5E **17 E11**

Bekok *Malaysia* 2°20N 103°7E **39 L4**
Bela *India* 25°50N 82°0E **43 G10**
Bela *Pakistan* 26°12N 66°20E **42 F2**
Bela Bela *S. Africa* 24°51S 28°19E **57 B4**
Bela Crkva *Serbia* 44°55N 21°27E **23 B9**
Bela Vista *Brazil* 22°12S 56°20W **94 A4**
Bela Vista *Mozam.* 26°10S 32°44E **57 C5**
Belagavi *India* 15°55N 74°35E **45 G2**
Belalcázar *India* 24°2N 81°45E **43 G9**
Belarus ■ *Europe* 53°30N 27°0E **17 B14**
Belau = Palau ■ *Palau* 7°30N 134°30E **64 G5**
Belawan *Indonesia* 3°33N 98°32E **36 D1**
Belaya → *Russia* 54°40N 56°0E **18 C9**
Belaya Tserkov = Bila Tserkva
  Ukraine 49°45N 30°10E **17 D16**
Belaya Zemlya, Ostrova
  Russia 81°36N 62°18E **26 A7**
Belcher Is. *Canada* 56°15N 78°45W **72 A3**
Belden *U.S.A.* 40°2N 121°17W **78 E5**
Belebey *Russia* 54°7N 54°7E **18 D9**
Beled Weyne *Somalia* 4°30N 45°5E **49 G4**
Belém *Brazil* 1°20S 48°30W **93 D9**
Belén *Argentina* 27°40S 67°5W **94 B2**
Belén *Paraguay* 23°30S 57°6W **94 A4**
Belet Uen = Beledweyne
  Somalia 4°30N 45°5E **49 G4**
Belev *Russia* 53°50N 36°5E **18 D6**
Belfair *U.S.A.* 47°27N 122°50W **78 C4**
Belfast = eMakhazeni
  S. Africa 25°42S 30°2E **57 C5**
Belfast *U.K.* 54°37N 5°56W **10 B6**
Belfast *Maine, U.S.A.* 44°26N 69°1W **81 C19**
Belfast *N.Y., U.S.A.* 42°21N 78°7W **82 D6**
Belfast L. *U.K.* 54°40N 5°50W **10 B6**
Belfield *U.S.A.* 46°53N 103°12W **80 B2**
Belfort *France* 47°38N 6°50E **20 C7**
Belfry *U.S.A.* 45°9N 109°1W **76 D9**
Belgaum = Belagavi
  India 15°55N 74°35E **45 G2**
Belgium ■ *Europe* 50°30N 5°0E **15 D4**
Belgorod *Russia* 50°35N 36°35E **19 D6**
Belgorod-Dnestrovskiy = Bilhorod-
  Dnistrovskyy *Ukraine* 46°11N 30°23E **19 E5**
Belgrade = Beograd
  Serbia 44°50N 20°37E **23 B9**
Belgrade *U.S.A.* 45°47N 111°11W **76 D8**
Belgrano II *Antarctica* 77°52S 34°37W **5 D1**
Belhaven *U.S.A.* 35°33N 76°37W **85 D16**
Beli Drim → *Europe* 42°6N 20°25E **23 C9**
Belimbing *Indonesia* 8°24S 115°2E **37 J18**
Belinyu *Indonesia* 1°35S 105°50E **36 E3**
Beliton Is. = Belitung
  Indonesia 3°10S 107°50E **36 E3**
Belitung *Indonesia* 3°10S 107°50E **36 E3**
Belize ■ *Cent. Amer.* 17°0N 88°30W **87 D7**
Belize Barrier Reef *Belize* 17°9N 88°3W **87 D7**
Belize City *Belize* 17°25N 88°10W **87 D7**
Belkovskiy, Ostrov
  Russia 75°32N 135°44E **27 B14**
Bell → *Canada* 49°48N 77°38W **72 C4**
Bell I. *Canada* 50°46N 55°35W **73 B8**
Bell-Irving → *Canada* 56°12N 129°5W **70 B3**
Bell Peninsula *Canada* 63°50N 82°0W **69 E15**
Bell Ville *Argentina* 32°40S 62°40W **94 C3**
Bella Bella *Canada* 52°10N 128°10W **70 C3**
Bella Coola *Canada* 52°25N 126°40W **70 C3**
Bella Unión *Uruguay* 30°15S 57°40W **94 C4**
Bella Vista *Corrientes,
  Argentina* 28°33S 59°0W **94 B4**
Bella Vista *Tucuman,
  Argentina* 27°10S 65°25W **94 B2**
Bella Vista *U.S.A.* 36°28N 94°16W **80 G6**
Bellaire *U.S.A.* 40°1N 80°45W **82 F4**
Bellata *Australia* 29°53S 149°46E **63 D4**
Belle Fourche *U.S.A.* 44°40N 103°51W **80 C2**
Belle Fourche → *U.S.A.* 44°26N 102°18W **80 C2**
Belle Glade *U.S.A.* 26°41N 80°40W **85 H14**
Belle-Île *France* 47°20N 3°10W **20 C2**
Belle Isle *Canada* 51°57N 55°25W **73 B8**
Belle Isle, Str. of *Canada* 51°30N 56°30W **73 B8**
Belle Plaine *U.S.A.* 41°54N 92°17W **80 E7**
Belle River *Canada* 42°18N 82°43W **82 D2**
Bellefontaine *U.S.A.* 40°22N 83°46W **81 E12**
Bellefonte *U.S.A.* 40°55N 77°47W **82 F7**
Belleoram *Canada* 47°31N 55°25W **73 C8**
Belleplaine *Barbados* 13°15N 59°34W **89 g**
Belleville *Canada* 44°10N 77°23W **82 B7**
Belleville *Ill., U.S.A.* 38°31N 89°59W **80 F8**
Belleville *Kans., U.S.A.* 39°50N 97°38W **80 F5**
Belleville *N.J., U.S.A.* 40°47N 74°9W **83 F10**
Belleville *N.Y., U.S.A.* 43°46N 76°10W **83 C8**
Bellevue *Idaho, U.S.A.* 43°28N 114°16W **76 E6**
Bellevue *Nebr., U.S.A.* 41°9N 95°54W **80 E6**
Bellevue *Ohio, U.S.A.* 41°17N 82°51W **82 E2**
Bellevue *Wash., U.S.A.* 47°37N 122°12W **78 C4**
Bellin = Kangirsuk
  Canada 60°0N 70°0W **69 F18**
Bellingen *Australia* 30°25S 152°50E **63 E5**
Bellingham *U.S.A.* 48°46N 122°29W **78 B4**
Bellingshausen Abyssal Plain
  S. Ocean 65°0S 90°0W **5 C16**
Bellingshausen Sea
  Antarctica 66°0S 80°0W **5 C17**
Bellinzona *Switz.* 46°11N 9°1E **20 C8**
Bello *Colombia* 6°20N 75°33W **92 B3**
Bellows Falls *U.S.A.* 43°8N 72°27W **83 C12**
Bellpat *Pakistan* 29°0N 68°5E **42 E3**
Belluno *Italy* 46°9N 12°13E **22 A5**
Bellwood *U.S.A.* 40°36N 78°20W **82 F6**
Belmont *Canada* 42°53N 81°5W **82 D3**
Belmont *S. Africa* 29°28S 24°22E **56 D3**
Belmont *U.S.A.* 42°14N 78°2W **82 D6**
Belmonte *Brazil* 16°0S 39°0W **93 G11**
Belmopan *Belize* 17°18N 88°30W **87 D7**
Belmullet *Ireland* 54°14N 9°58W **10 B1**
Belo Horizonte *Brazil* 19°55S 43°56W **93 G10**
Belo-Tsiribihina *Madag.* 19°40S 44°30E **55 H8**
Belogorsk *Russia* 51°0N 128°20E **27 D13**
Beloit *Kans., U.S.A.* 39°28N 98°6W **80 F4**

Beloit Wis., U.S.A. 42°31N 89°2W 80 D9
Belokorovichi Ukraine 51°7N 28°2E 17 C15
Belomorsk Russia 64°35N 34°54E 18 B5
Belonia India 23°15N 91°30E 41 H17
Beloretsk Russia 53°58N 58°24E 18 D10
Belorussia = Belarus ■ Europe 53°30N 27°0E 17 B14
Belovo Russia 54°30N 86°0E 26 D9
Beloyarskiy Russia 63°42N 66°40E 26 C7
Beloye, Ozero Russia 60°10N 37°35E 18 B6
Beloye More Russia 66°30N 38°0E 18 A6
Belozersk Russia 60°1N 37°45E 18 B6
Belpre U.S.A. 39°17N 81°34W 81 F13
Belrain India 28°23N 80°55E 43 E9
Belt U.S.A. 47°23N 110°55W 76 C8
Beltana Australia 30°48S 138°25E 63 E2
Belterra Brazil 2°45S 55°0W 93 D8
Belton U.S.A. 31°3N 97°28W 84 F6
Belton L. U.S.A. 31°6N 97°28W 84 F6
Beltsy = Bălţi Moldova 47°48N 27°58E 17 E14
Belturbet Ireland 54°6N 7°26W 10 B4
Belukha Russia 49°50N 86°50E 30 B6
Beluran Malaysia 5°48N 117°35E 36 C5
Belushya Guba Russia 71°32N 52°19E 26 B6
Belvidere Ill., U.S.A. 42°15N 88°50W 80 D9
Belvidere N.J., U.S.A. 40°50N 75°5W 83 F9
Belyando → Australia 21°38S 146°50E 62 C4
Belyando Crossing Australia 21°32S 146°51E 62 C4
Belyuen Australia 12°34S 130°42E 60 B5
Belyy, Ostrov Russia 73°30N 71°0E 26 B8
Belyy Yar Russia 58°26N 84°39E 26 D9
Belzoni U.S.A. 33°11N 90°29W 85 E9
Bembéréke Benin 10°11N 2°43E 52 F6
Bemetara India 21°42N 81°32E 43 J9
Bemidji U.S.A. 47°28N 94°53W 80 B6
Ben Iran 32°32N 50°45E 47 C6
Ben Cruachan U.K. 56°26N 5°8W 11 E3
Ben Dearg U.K. 57°47N 4°56W 11 D4
Ben En △ Vietnam 19°37N 105°30E 38 C5
Ben Gardane Tunisia 33°11N 11°11E 53 B8
Ben Hope U.K. 58°25N 4°36W 11 C4
Ben Lawers U.K. 56°32N 4°14W 11 E4
Ben Lomond N.S.W., Australia 30°1S 151°43E 63 E5
Ben Lomond Tas., Australia 41°38S 147°42E 63 G4
Ben Lomond U.K. 56°11N 4°38W 11 E4
Ben Lomond △ Australia 41°33S 147°39E 63 G4
Ben Luc Vietnam 10°39N 106°29E 39 G6
Ben Macdhui U.K. 57°4N 3°40W 11 D5
Ben Mhor U.K. 57°15N 7°18W 11 D1
Ben More Argyll & Bute, U.K. 56°26N 6°1W 11 E2
Ben More Stirling, U.K. 56°23N 4°32W 11 E4
Ben More Assynt U.K. 58°8N 4°52W 11 C4
Ben Nevis U.K. 56°48N 5°1W 11 E3
Ben Quang Vietnam 17°3N 106°55E 38 D6
Ben Tre Vietnam 10°14N 106°23E 39 G6
Ben Vorlich U.K. 56°21N 4°14W 11 E4
Ben Wyvis U.K. 57°40N 4°35W 11 D4
Bena Nigeria 11°20N 5°50E 52 F7
Benaco, L. di = Garda, L. di Italy 45°40N 10°41E 22 B4
Benalla Australia 36°30S 146°0E 63 F4
Benares = Varanasi India 25°22N 83°0E 43 G10
Benavente Spain 42°2N 5°43W 21 A3
Benavides U.S.A. 27°36N 98°25W 84 H5
Benbecula U.K. 57°26N 7°21W 11 D1
Benbonyathe Hill Australia 30°25S 139°11E 63 E2
Bend U.S.A. 44°4N 121°19W 76 D3
Bender Beyla Somalia 9°30N 50°48E 49 F5
Bendery Moldova 46°50N 29°30E 17 E15
Bendigo Australia 36°40S 144°15E 63 F3
Benē Beraq Israel 32°6N 34°51E 48 C3
Benevento Italy 41°8N 14°45E 22 D6
Beng Mealea Cambodia 13°28N 104°14E 38 F5
Bengal, Bay of Ind. Oc. 15°0N 90°0E 41 M17
Bengaluru India 12°59N 77°40E 45 H3
Bengbu China 32°58N 117°20E 33 H9
Benghazi = Banghāzī Libya 32°11N 20°3E 53 B10
Bengkalis Indonesia 1°30N 102°10E 39 M4
Bengkulu Indonesia 3°50S 102°12E 36 E2
Bengkulu □ Indonesia 3°48S 102°16E 36 E2
Bengough Canada 49°25N 105°10W 71 D7
Benguela Angola 12°37S 13°25E 55 G2
Benguérua, I. Mozam. 21°58S 35°28E 57 B6
Beni Dem. Rep. of the Congo 0°30N 29°27E 54 D5
Beni → Bolivia 10°23S 65°24W 92 F5
Beni Mellal Morocco 32°21N 6°21W 52 B4
Beni Suef Egypt 29°5N 31°6E 53 C12
Beniah L. Canada 63°23N 112°17W 70 A6
Benidorm Spain 38°33N 0°9W 21 C5
Benin ■ Africa 10°0N 2°0E 52 G6
Benin, Bight of W. Afr. 5°0N 3°0E 52 H6
Benin City Nigeria 6°20N 5°31E 52 G7
Benito Juárez Argentina 37°40S 59°43W 94 D4
Benjamin Aceval Paraguay 24°58S 57°34W 94 A4
Benjamin Constant Brazil 4°40S 70°15W 92 D4
Benjamín Hill Mexico 30°9N 111°7W 86 A2
Benkelman U.S.A. 40°3N 101°32W 80 E3
Bennett Canada 59°51N 135°0W 70 B2
Bennett, L. Australia 22°50S 131°2E 60 D5
Bennetta, Ostrov Russia 76°21N 148°56E 27 B15
Bennettsville U.S.A. 34°37N 79°41W 85 D15
Bennington N.H., U.S.A. 43°0N 71°55W 83 D11
Bennington Vt., U.S.A. 42°53N 73°12W 83 D11
Benom Malaysia 3°50N 102°6E 39 L4
Benoni S. Africa 26°11S 28°18E 57 C4
Benque Viejo del Carmen Belize 17°5N 89°8W 87 D7
Benson Ariz., U.S.A. 31°58N 110°18W 77 L8
Benson Minn., U.S.A. 45°19N 95°36W 80 C6
Bent Iran 26°20N 59°31E 47 E8
Benteng Indonesia 6°10S 120°30E 37 F6
Bentinck I. Australia 17°3S 139°35E 62 B2
Bentinck I. Myanmar 11°45N 98°3E 39 G2
Bentley Subglacial Trench Antarctica 80°0S 115°0W 5 E15
Bento Gonçalves Brazil 29°10S 51°31W 95 B5
Benton Ark., U.S.A. 34°34N 92°35W 84 D8
Benton Calif., U.S.A. 37°48N 118°32W 78 H8
Benton Ill., U.S.A. 38°0N 88°55W 80 F9
Benton Pa., U.S.A. 41°12N 76°23W 83 E8
Benton Harbor U.S.A. 42°6N 86°27W 80 D10
Bentong Malaysia 3°31N 101°55E 39 L3
Bentonville U.S.A. 36°22N 94°13W 84 C7
Benue → Nigeria 7°48N 6°46E 52 G7
Benxi China 41°20N 123°48E 33 D12
Beo Indonesia 4°25N 126°50E 37 D7
Beograd Serbia 44°50N 20°37E 23 B9
Beolgyo S. Korea 34°51N 127°21E 33 G14
Beppu Japan 33°15N 131°30E 29 H5
Beqa Fiji 18°23S 178°8E 59 a
Beqaa Valley = Al Biqā Lebanon 34°10N 36°10E 48 A5
Ber Mota India 23°27N 68°34E 42 H3
Bera, Tasik Malaysia 3°5N 102°38E 39 L4
Berach → India 25°15N 75°2E 42 G6
Berastagi Indonesia 3°11N 98°31E 39 L2
Berat Albania 40°43N 19°59E 23 D8
Berau = Tanjungredeb Indonesia 2°9N 117°29E 36 D5
Berau, Teluk Indonesia 2°30S 132°30E 37 E8
Berber Sudan 18°0N 34°0E 53 E12
Berbera Somalia 10°30N 45°2E 49 E4
Berbérati C.A.R. 4°15N 15°40E 54 D3
Berbice → Guyana 6°20N 57°32W 92 B7
Berdichev = Berdychiv Ukraine 49°57N 28°30E 17 D15
Berdsk Russia 54°47N 83°2E 26 D9
Berdyansk Ukraine 46°45N 36°50E 19 E6
Berdychiv Ukraine 49°57N 28°30E 17 D15
Berea U.S.A. 37°34N 84°17W 81 G11
Berebere Indonesia 2°25N 128°45E 37 D7
Bereeda Somalia 11°45N 51°0E 49 E5
Berehove Ukraine 48°15N 22°35E 17 D12
Bereket Turkmenistan 39°16N 55°32E 47 B7
Berekum Ghana 7°29N 2°34W 52 G5
Berens → Canada 52°25N 97°2W 71 C9
Berens I. Canada 52°18N 97°18W 71 C9
Berens River Canada 52°25N 97°0W 71 C9
Beresford U.S.A. 43°5N 96°47W 80 D5
Berestechko Ukraine 50°22N 25°5E 17 C13
Bereza = Byaroza Belarus 52°31N 24°51E 17 B13
Berezhany Ukraine 49°26N 24°58E 17 D13
Berezina = Byarezina → Belarus 52°33N 30°14E 17 B16
Bereznik Russia 62°51N 42°40E 18 B7
Berezniki Russia 59°24N 56°46E 18 C10
Berezovo Russia 64°0N 65°0E 26 C7
Berga Spain 42°6N 1°48E 21 A6
Bergama Turkey 39°8N 27°11E 23 E12
Bérgamo Italy 45°41N 9°43E 20 D8
Bergaon India 20°41N 80°27E 44 D5
Bergen Neths. 52°40N 4°43E 15 B4
Bergen Norway 60°20N 5°20E 8 F11
Bergen U.S.A. 43°5N 77°57W 82 C7
Bergen op Zoom Neths. 51°28N 4°18E 15 C4
Bergerac France 44°51N 0°30E 20 D4
Bergholz U.S.A. 40°31N 80°53W 82 F4
Bergville S. Africa 28°52S 29°18E 57 C4
Berhala, Selat Indonesia 1°0S 104°15E 36 E2
Berhampore = Baharampur India 24°2N 88°27E 43 G13
Berhampur = Brahmapur India 19°15N 84°54E 44 E7
Bering Glacier U.S.A. 60°20N 143°30W 74 C11
Bering Sea Pac. Oc. 58°0N 171°0W 66 D2
Bering Strait Pac. Oc. 65°30N 169°0W 74 B6
Beringovskiy Russia 63°3N 179°19E 27 C18
Berisso Argentina 34°56S 57°50W 94 C4
Berja Spain 36°50N 2°56W 21 D4
Berkner I. Antarctica 79°30S 50°0W 5 D18
Berkshire U.S.A. 42°19N 76°11W 83 D8
Berkshire Downs U.K. 51°33N 1°29W 13 F6
Berlin Md., U.S.A. 38°20N 75°13W 81 F16
Berlin N.H., U.S.A. 44°28N 71°11W 83 B13
Berlin N.Y., U.S.A. 42°42N 73°23W 83 D11
Berlin Wis., U.S.A. 43°58N 88°57W 80 D9
Berlin L. U.S.A. 41°3N 81°0W 82 E4
Bermejo → Formosa, Argentina 26°51S 58°23W 94 B4
Bermejo → San Juan, Argentina 32°30S 67°30W 94 C2
Bermejo, Paso = Uspallata, P. de Argentina 32°37S 69°22W 94 C2
Bermen, L. Canada 53°35N 68°55W 73 B6
Bermuda ⊘ Atl. Oc. 32°18N 64°45W 67 F13
Bern Switz. 46°57N 7°28E 20 C7
Bernalillo U.S.A. 35°18N 106°33W 77 J10
Bernardo de Irigoyen Argentina 26°15S 53°40W 95 B5
Bernardsville U.S.A. 40°43N 74°34W 83 F10
Bernasconi Argentina 37°55S 63°44W 94 D3
Bernburg Germany 51°47N 11°44E 16 C6
Berne = Bern Switz. 46°57N 7°28E 20 C7
Berneray U.K. 57°43N 7°11W 11 D1
Bernier I. Australia 24°50S 113°12E 61 D1
Bernina, Piz Switz. 46°20N 9°54E 20 C8
Beroun Czechia 49°57N 14°5E 16 D8
Berri Australia 34°14S 140°35E 63 E3
Berriane Algeria 32°50N 3°46E 52 B6
Berry Australia 34°46S 150°43E 63 E5
Berry France 46°50N 2°0E 20 C5
Berry Is. Bahamas 25°40N 77°50W 88 A4
Berryessa, L. U.S.A. 38°31N 122°6W 78 G4
Berryville U.S.A. 36°22N 93°34W 84 C8
Berseba Namibia 26°0S 17°46E 56 C2
Bershad Ukraine 48°22N 29°31E 17 D15
Berthold U.S.A. 48°19N 101°44W 80 A3
Berthoud U.S.A. 40°19N 105°5W 76 F11
Bertoua Cameroon 4°30N 13°45E 54 D2
Bertraghboy B. Ireland 53°22N 9°54W 10 C2
Beruwala Sri Lanka 6°30N 80°0E 45 L4
Berwick U.S.A. 41°3N 76°14W 83 E8
Berwick-upon-Tweed U.K. 55°46N 2°0W 12 B6
Berwyn Mts. U.K. 52°54N 3°26W 12 E4
Besal Pakistan 35°4N 73°56E 43 B5
Besalampy Madag. 16°43S 44°29E 55 H8
Besançon France 47°15N 6°2E 20 C7
Besar Indonesia 2°40S 116°0E 36 E5
Besnard L. Canada 55°25N 106°0W 71 B7
Besni Turkey 37°41N 37°52E 46 B3
Besor, N. → Egypt 31°28N 34°22E 48 D3
Bessarabiya Moldova 47°0N 28°10E 17 E15
Bessarabka = Basarabeasca Moldova 46°21N 28°58E 17 E15
Bessemer Ala., U.S.A. 33°24N 86°58W 85 E11
Bessemer Mich., U.S.A. 46°29N 90°3W 80 B8
Bessemer Pa., U.S.A. 40°59N 80°30W 82 F4
Beswick Australia 14°34S 132°53E 60 B5
Beswick ☼ Australia 14°31S 132°51E 60 B5
Bet She'an Israel 32°30N 35°30E 48 C4
Bet Shemesh Israel 31°44N 35°0E 48 D4
Betanzos Spain 43°15N 8°12W 21 A1
Bétaré Oya Cameroon 5°40N 14°5E 54 C2
Bethal S. Africa 26°27S 29°28E 57 C4
Bethanien Namibia 26°31S 17°8E 56 C2
Bethany Canada 44°11N 78°34W 82 B6
Bethany Mo., U.S.A. 40°16N 94°2W 80 E6
Bethany Okla., U.S.A. 35°31N 97°38W 84 D6
Bethel Alaska, U.S.A. 60°48N 161°45W 74 C7
Bethel Conn., U.S.A. 41°22N 73°25W 83 E11
Bethel Maine, U.S.A. 44°25N 70°47W 83 B14
Bethel Vt., U.S.A. 43°50N 72°38W 83 C12
Bethel Park U.S.A. 40°19N 80°2W 82 F4
Bethlehem S. Africa 28°14S 28°18E 57 C4
Bethlehem U.S.A. 40°37N 75°23W 83 F9
Bethulie S. Africa 30°30S 25°59E 56 D4
Béthune France 50°30N 2°38E 20 A5
Betioky Madag. 23°48S 44°20E 55 J8
Betong Malaysia 1°24N 111°31E 36 D4
Betong Thailand 5°45N 101°5E 39 K3
Betoota Australia 25°45S 140°42E 62 D3
Betpaqdala Kazakhstan 45°45N 70°30E 30 B3
Betroka Madag. 23°16S 46°0E 55 J9
Betsiamites Canada 48°56N 68°40W 73 C6
Betsiamites → Canada 48°56N 68°38W 73 C6
Bettendorf U.S.A. 41°32N 90°30W 80 E8
Bettiah India 26°48N 84°33E 43 F11
Betul India 21°58N 77°59E 44 D3
Betws-y-Coed U.K. 53°5N 3°48W 12 D4
Beulah Mich., U.S.A. 44°38N 86°6W 80 C10
Beulah N. Dak., U.S.A. 47°16N 101°47W 80 B3
Beveren Belgium 51°12N 4°16E 15 C4
Beverley Australia 32°9S 116°56E 61 F2
Beverley U.K. 53°51N 0°26W 12 D7
Beverly U.S.A. 42°33N 70°53W 83 D14
Beverly Hills U.S.A. 28°55N 82°28W 85 G13
Bewas → India 23°59N 79°21E 43 H8
Bewdley Canada 44°5N 78°19W 82 B6
Bexhill U.K. 50°51N 0°29E 13 G8
Beyānlū Iran 36°0N 47°51E 46 C5
Beyneu Kazakhstan 45°18N 55°9E 19 E10
Beypazarı Turkey 40°10N 31°56E 19 F5
Beypore → India 11°10N 75°47E 45 J2
Beyşehir Gölü Turkey 37°41N 31°33E 46 B1
Béziers France 43°20N 3°12E 20 E5
Bezwada = Vijayawada India 16°31N 80°39E 44 F5
Bhabua India 25°3N 83°37E 43 G10
Bhachau India 23°20N 70°16E 42 H4
Bhadar → Gujarat, India 22°17N 72°20E 42 H5
Bhadar → Gujarat, India 21°27N 69°47E 42 J3
Bhadarwah India 32°58N 75°46E 43 C6
Bhadgaon = Bhaktapur Nepal 27°38N 85°24E 43 F11
Bhadohi India 25°25N 82°34E 43 G10
Bhadra India 29°8N 75°14E 42 E6
Bhadra → India 14°0N 75°20E 45 H2
Bhadrachalam India 17°40N 80°53E 44 F5
Bhadrak India 21°10N 86°30E 44 D8
Bhadran India 22°19N 72°6E 42 H5
Bhadravati India 13°49N 75°40E 45 H2
Bhag Pakistan 29°2N 67°49E 42 E2
Bhagalpur India 25°10N 87°0E 43 G12
Bhagirathi → Paschimbanga, India 23°25N 88°23E 43 H13
Bhagirathi → Uttarakhand, India 30°8N 78°35E 43 D8
Bhainsa India 19°10N 77°58E 44 E3
Bhakkar Pakistan 31°40N 71°5E 42 D4
Bhakra Dam India 31°30N 76°45E 42 D7
Bhaktapur Nepal 27°38N 85°24E 43 F11
Bhalki India 18°2N 77°13E 44 E3
Bhamo Myanmar 24°15N 97°15E 41 G20
Bhamragarh India 19°30N 80°40E 44 E5
Bhandara India 21°5N 79°42E 44 D4
Bhanpura India 24°31N 75°44E 42 G6
Bhanrer Ra. India 23°40N 79°45E 43 H8
Bhaptiahi India 26°19N 86°44E 43 F12
Bharat = India ■ Asia 20°0N 78°0E 40 K11
Bharati Antarctica 69°24S 76°11E 5 C6
Bharatpur Chhattisgarh, India 23°44N 81°46E 43 H9
Bharatpur Raj., India 27°15N 77°30E 42 F7
Bharatpur Nepal 27°34N 84°10E 43 F11
Bharno India 23°14N 84°53E 43 H11
Bharraig = Barra U.K. 57°0N 7°29W 11 E1
Bharraig, Caolas = Barra, Sd. of U.K. 57°4N 7°25W 11 D1
Bharuch India 21°47N 73°0E 44 D1
Bhatarsaigh = Vatersay U.K. 56°55N 7°32W 11 E1
Bhatghar L. India 18°10N 73°48E 44 E1
Bhatinda India 30°15N 74°57E 42 D6
Bhatkal India 13°58N 74°35E 45 H2
Bhatpara India 22°50N 88°25E 43 H13
Bhattu India 29°36N 75°19E 42 E6
Bhaun Pakistan 32°55N 72°40E 42 C5
Bhaunagar = Bhavnagar India 21°45N 72°10E 44 D1
Bhavani India 11°27N 77°43E 45 J3
Bhavnagar India 21°45N 72°10E 44 D1
Bhawanipatna India 19°55N 83°10E 44 E6
Bhawari India 25°42N 73°4E 42 G5
Bhayavadar India 21°51N 70°15E 42 J4
Bhearnaraigh = Berneray U.K. 57°43N 7°11W 11 D1
Bhera Pakistan 32°29N 72°57E 42 C5
Bheri → Nepal 28°47N 81°18E 43 E9
Bhikangaon India 21°52N 75°57E 42 J6
Bhilai = Bhilainagar-Durg India 21°13N 81°26E 44 D5
Bhilainagar-Durg India 21°13N 81°26E 44 D5
Bhilsa = Vidisha India 23°28N 77°53E 42 H7
Bhilwara India 25°25N 74°38E 42 G6
Bhima → India 16°25N 77°17E 44 F3
Bhimavaram India 16°30N 81°30E 45 F5
Bhimbar Pakistan 32°59N 74°3E 43 C6
Bhind India 26°30N 78°46E 43 F8
Bhinga India 27°43N 81°56E 43 F9
Bhinmal India 25°0N 72°15E 42 G5
Bhisho S. Africa 32°50S 27°23E 56 D4
Bhiwandi India 19°20N 73°0E 44 E1
Bhiwani India 28°50N 76°9E 42 E7
Bhogava → India 22°26N 72°20E 42 H5
Bhojpur Nepal 27°10N 87°3E 43 F12
Bhokardan India 20°16N 75°46E 44 D2
Bhola Bangla. 22°45N 90°35E 41 H17
Bholari Pakistan 25°19N 68°13E 42 G3
Bhongir India 17°30N 78°56E 44 F4
Bhopal India 23°20N 77°30E 42 H7
Bhopalpatnam India 18°52N 80°23E 44 E5
Bhor India 18°12N 73°53E 44 E1
Bhuban India 20°53N 85°50E 44 D7
Bhubaneshwar India 20°15N 85°50E 44 D7
Bhuj India 23°15N 69°49E 42 H3
Bhumiphol Res. Thailand 17°20N 98°40E 38 D2
Bhusawal India 21°3N 75°46E 44 D2
Bhutan ■ Asia 27°25N 90°30E 41 F17
Biafra, B. of = Bonny, Bight of Africa 3°30N 9°20E 54 D1
Biak Indonesia 1°10S 136°6E 37 E9
Biała Podlaska Poland 52°4N 23°6E 17 B12
Białogard Poland 54°2N 15°58E 16 A8
Białystok Poland 53°10N 23°10E 17 B12
Biaora India 23°56N 76°56E 42 H7
Biārjmand Iran 36°6N 55°53E 47 B7
Biaro Indonesia 2°5N 125°26E 37 D7
Biarritz France 43°29N 1°33W 20 E3
Bibai Japan 43°19N 141°52E 28 C10
Bibby I. Canada 61°55N 93°0W 71 A10
Biberach Germany 48°5N 9°47E 16 D5
Bibile Sri Lanka 7°10N 81°25E 45 L5
Bicester U.K. 51°54N 1°9W 13 F6
Bicheno Australia 41°52S 148°18E 63 G4
Bichia India 22°27N 80°42E 43 H9
Bickerton I. Australia 13°45S 136°10E 62 A2
Bid = Bir India 19°4N 75°46E 44 E2
Bida Nigeria 9°3N 5°58E 52 G7
Bidar India 17°55N 77°35E 44 F3
Biddeford U.S.A. 43°30N 70°28W 81 D18
Bideford U.K. 51°1N 4°13W 13 F3
Bideford Bay U.K. 51°5N 4°20W 13 F3
Bidhuna India 26°49N 79°31E 43 F8
Bīdokht Iran 34°20N 58°46E 47 C8
Bidor Malaysia 4°6N 101°15E 39 K3
Bidyadanga Australia 18°45S 121°43E 60 C3
Bié, Planalto de Angola 12°0S 16°0E 55 G3
Bieber U.S.A. 41°7N 121°8W 76 F3
Biel Switz. 47°8N 7°14E 20 C7
Bielefeld Germany 52°1N 8°33E 16 B5
Biella Italy 45°34N 8°3E 20 D8
Bielsk Podlaski Poland 52°47N 23°12E 17 B12
Bielsko-Biała Poland 49°50N 19°2E 17 D10
Bien Hoa Vietnam 10°57N 106°49E 39 G6
Bienne = Biel Switz. 47°8N 7°14E 20 C7
Bienville, L. Canada 55°5N 72°40W 72 A5
Biesbosch △ Neths. 51°45N 4°48E 15 C4
Biesiesfontein S. Africa 30°57S 17°58E 56 D2
Big → Canada 54°50N 58°55W 73 B8
Big B. Canada 55°43N 60°35W 73 A7
Big Bear City U.S.A. 34°16N 116°51W 79 L10
Big Bear Lake U.S.A. 34°15N 116°56W 79 L10
Big Belt Mts. U.S.A. 46°30N 111°25W 76 C8
Big Bend Eswatini 26°50S 31°58E 57 C5
Big Bend △ U.S.A. 29°20N 103°5W 84 G3
Big Black → U.S.A. 32°3N 91°4W 85 E9
Big Blue → U.S.A. 39°35N 96°34W 80 F5
Big Buddha Hong Kong, China 22°15N 113°54E 31 a
Big Creek U.S.A. 37°11N 119°14W 78 H7
Big Creek ⌂ Canada 51°18N 123°10W 70 C4
Big Cypress ⌂ U.S.A. 26°0N 81°10W 85 H14
Big Desert Australia 35°45S 141°10E 63 F3
Big Falls U.S.A. 48°12N 93°48W 80 A7
Big Fork → U.S.A. 48°31N 93°43W 80 A7
Big Horn Mts. = Bighorn Mts. U.S.A. 44°25N 107°0W 76 D10
Big I. Canada 61°7N 116°45W 70 A5
Big Lake U.S.A. 31°12N 101°28W 84 F4
Big Moose U.S.A. 43°49N 74°58W 83 C10
Big Muddy Cr. → U.S.A. 48°8N 104°36W 76 B11
Big Pine U.S.A. 37°10N 118°17W 78 H8
Big Piney U.S.A. 42°32N 110°7W 76 E8
Big Quill L. Canada 51°55N 104°30W 71 C8
Big Rapids U.S.A. 43°42N 85°29W 81 D11
Big Rideau L. Canada 44°40N 76°15W 83 B8
Big River Canada 53°50N 107°0W 71 C7
Big Run U.S.A. 40°57N 78°55W 82 F6
Big Sable Pt. U.S.A. 44°3N 86°1W 80 C10
Big Salmon → Canada 61°52N 134°55W 70 A2
Big Sand L. Canada 57°45N 99°45W 71 B9
Big Sandy U.S.A. 48°11N 110°7W 76 B8
Big Sandy → U.S.A. 38°25N 82°36W 81 F12
Big Sandy Cr. = Sandy Cr. → U.S.A. 41°51N 109°47W 76 F9
Big Sandy Cr. → U.S.A. 38°7N 102°29W 76 G12
Big Sioux → U.S.A. 42°29N 96°27W 80 D5
Big South Fork ⌂ U.S.A. 36°27N 84°47W 85 C12
Big Spring U.S.A. 32°15N 101°28W 84 E4
Big Stone City U.S.A. 45°18N 96°28W 80 C5
Big Stone Gap U.S.A. 36°52N 82°47W 81 G12
Big Stone L. U.S.A. 45°18N 96°27W 80 C5
Big Sur U.S.A. 36°15N 121°48W 78 J5
Big Timber U.S.A. 45°50N 109°57W 76 D9
Big Trout L. Canada 53°40N 90°0W 72 B2
Big Trout Lake Canada 53°45N 90°0W 72 B2
Biğa Turkey 40°13N 27°14E 23 D12
Bigadiç Turkey 39°22N 28°7E 23 E13
Biggar Canada 52°4N 108°0W 71 C7
Biggar U.K. 55°38N 3°32W 11 F5
Bigge I. Australia 14°35S 125°10E 60 B4
Biggenden Australia 25°31S 152°4E 63 D5
Biggleswade U.K. 52°5N 0°14W 13 E7
Biggs U.S.A. 39°25N 121°43W 78 F5
Bighorn U.S.A. 46°10N 107°27W 76 C10
Bighorn → U.S.A. 46°10N 107°28W 76 C10
Bighorn Canyon ⌂ U.S.A. 45°10N 108°0W 76 D10
Bighorn L. U.S.A. 44°55N 108°15W 76 D9
Bighorn Mts. U.S.A. 44°25N 107°0W 76 D10
Bigstone L. Canada 53°42N 95°44W 71 C9
Bihać Bos.-H. 44°49N 15°57E 16 F8
Bihar India 25°5N 85°40E 43 G11
Bihar □ India 25°0N 86°0E 43 G12
Bihariganj India 25°44N 86°59E 43 G12
Bihor, Munţii Romania 46°29N 22°47E 17 E12
Bijagós, Arquipélago dos Guinea-Biss. 11°15N 16°10W 52 F2
Bijaipur India 26°2N 77°20E 42 F7
Bijapur = Vijayapura India 16°50N 75°55E 44 F2
Bijapur India 18°50N 80°50E 44 E5
Bījār Iran 35°52N 47°35E 46 C5
Bijauri Nepal 28°6N 82°20E 43 E10
Bijawar India 24°38N 79°30E 43 G8
Bijeljina Bos.-H. 44°46N 19°14E 23 B8
Bijie China 27°20N 105°16E 34 D5
Bijnor India 29°27N 78°11E 42 E8
Bikaner India 28°2N 73°18E 42 E5
Bikapur India 26°30N 82°7E 43 F10
Bikeqi China 40°43N 111°20E 32 D6
Bikfayyā Lebanon 33°55N 35°41E 48 B4
Bikin Russia 46°50N 134°20E 28 A7
Bikin → Russia 46°51N 134°2E 28 A7
Bikini Atoll Marshall Is. 12°0N 167°30E 64 F8
Bikita Zimbabwe 20°6S 31°41E 57 B5
Bīkkū Bīttī Libya 22°0N 19°12E 53 D9
Bila Tserkva Ukraine 49°45N 30°10E 17 D16
Bilara India 26°14N 73°53E 42 F5
Bilaspur Chhattisgarh, India 22°2N 82°15E 43 H10
Bilaspur Punjab, India 31°19N 76°50E 42 D7
Bilauk Taungdan Thailand 13°0N 99°0E 38 F2
Bilauri Nepal 28°41N 80°21E 43 E9
Bilbao Spain 43°16N 2°56W 21 A4
Bilbo = Bilbao Spain 43°16N 2°56W 21 A4
Bildudalur Iceland 65°41N 23°36W 8 D2
Bílé Karpaty Europe 49°5N 18°0E 17 D9
Bilecik Turkey 40°5N 30°5E 19 F5
Bilgram India 27°11N 80°2E 43 F9
Bilhaur India 26°51N 80°5E 43 F9
Bilhorod-Dnistrovskyy Ukraine 46°11N 30°23E 19 E5
Bilibino Russia 68°3N 166°20E 27 C17
Bilimora India 20°45N 72°57E 44 D1
Billiluna Australia 19°37S 127°41E 60 C4
Billings U.S.A. 45°47N 108°30W 76 D9
Billiton Is. = Belitung Indonesia 3°10S 107°50E 36 E3
Bilma Niger 18°50N 13°30E 53 E8
Bilma, Grand Erg de Niger 18°30N 14°0E 53 E8
Biloela Australia 24°24S 150°31E 62 C5
Biloli India 18°46N 77°44E 44 E3
Biloxi U.S.A. 30°24N 88°53W 85 F10
Bilpa Morea Claypan Australia 25°0S 140°0E 62 D3
Biltine Chad 14°40N 20°50E 53 F10
Bim Son Vietnam 20°4N 105°51E 38 B5
Bima Indonesia 8°22S 118°49E 37 F5
Bimbo C.A.R. 4°15N 18°33E 54 D3
Bimini Is. Bahamas 25°42N 79°25W 88 A4
Bin Xian Heilongjiang, China 45°42N 127°32E 33 B14
Bin Xian Shaanxi, China 35°2N 108°4E 32 G5
Bina-Etawah India 24°13N 78°14E 42 G8
Binalong Australia 34°40S 148°39E 63 E4
Bīnālūd, Kūh-e Iran 36°30N 58°30E 47 B8
Binatang = Bintangau Malaysia 2°10N 111°40E 36 D4
Binche Belgium 50°26N 4°10E 15 D4
Binchuan China 25°42N 100°38E 34 E3
Bindki India 26°2N 80°36E 43 F9
Bindura Zimbabwe 17°18S 31°18E 55 H6
Bingara Australia 29°52S 150°36E 63 D5
Bingaram I. India 10°56N 72°17E 45 J1
Bingham U.S.A. 45°3N 69°53W 81 C19
Binghamton U.S.A. 42°6N 75°55W 83 D9
Bingöl Turkey 38°53N 40°29E 46 B4
Binh Dinh Vietnam 13°55N 109°7E 38 F7
Binh Son Vietnam 15°20N 108°40E 38 E7
Binhai China 34°2N 119°49E 33 G10
Binjai Indonesia 3°20N 98°30E 36 D3
Binka India 21°2N 83°48E 44 D6
Binnaway Australia 31°28S 149°24E 63 E4
Binongko Indonesia 5°57S 124°2E 37 F6
Binscarth Canada 50°37N 101°17W 71 C8
Bintan Indonesia 1°0N 104°0E 36 D2
Bintangau Malaysia 2°10N 111°40E 36 D4
Bintulu Malaysia 3°10N 113°0E 36 D4
Bintuni Indonesia 2°7S 133°32E 37 E8
Binyang China 23°12N 108°47E 34 F7
Binzert = Bizerte Tunisia 37°15N 9°50E 53 A7
Binzhou China 37°20N 118°2E 33 F10
Biobío □ Chile 37°35S 72°0W 94 D1
Biobío → Chile 36°49S 73°10W 94 D1
Bioko Eq. Guin. 3°30N 8°40E 54 D1
Bir India 19°4N 75°46E 44 E2
Bîr Abu Muḩammad Egypt 29°44N 34°14E 48 F3

Bi'r al Butayyihāt *Jordan*	29°47N 35°20E	**48** F4
Bi'r al Mārī *Jordan*	30°4N 35°33E	**48** E4
Bi'r al Qattār *Jordan*	29°47N 35°32E	**48** F4
Bîr Atrun *Sudan*	18°15N 26°40E	**53** E11
Bîr Beïda *Egypt*	30°25N 34°29E	**48** E3
Bîr el 'Abd *Egypt*	31°2N 33°0E	**48** D2
Bîr el Biarât *Egypt*	29°30N 34°43E	**48** F3
Bîr el Duweidar *Egypt*	30°56N 32°32E	**48** E1
Bîr el Garârât *Egypt*	31°3N 33°34E	**48** D2
Bîr el Heisi *Egypt*	29°22N 34°36E	**48** F3
Bîr el Jafir *Egypt*	30°50N 32°41E	**48** E1
Bîr el Mâlhi *Egypt*	30°38N 33°19E	**48** E2
Bîr el Thamâda *Egypt*	30°12N 33°27E	**48** E2
Bi'r Ghadir *Syria*	34°6N 37°3E	**48** A6
Bîr Hasana *Egypt*	30°29N 33°46E	**48** E2
Bîr Kaseiba *Egypt*	31°0N 33°17E	**48** E2
Bîr Lahfân *Egypt*	31°0N 33°51E	**48** E2
Bîr Madkûr *Egypt*	30°44N 32°33E	**48** E1
Bîr Mogreïn *Mauritania*	25°10N 11°25W	**52** C3
Bi'r Mutribah *Kuwait*	29°54N 47°17E	**46** D5
Bîr Qatia *Egypt*	30°58N 32°45E	**48** E1
Bîr Shalatein *Egypt*	23°5N 35°25E	**53** D13
Birāk *Libya*	27°31N 14°20E	**53** C8
Biratnagar *Nepal*	26°27N 87°17E	**43** F12
Birch → *Canada*	58°28N 112°17W	**70** B6
Birch Hills *Canada*	52°59N 105°25W	**71** C7
Birch I. *Canada*	52°26N 99°54W	**71** C9
Birch L. *N.W.T., Canada*	62°4N 116°33W	**70** A5
Birch L. *Ont., Canada*	51°23N 92°18W	**72** B1
Birch Mts. *Canada*	57°30N 113°10W	**70** B6
Birch River *Canada*	52°24N 101°6W	**71** C8
Birchip *Australia*	35°56S 142°55E	**63** F3
Bird *Canada*	56°30N 94°13W	**71** B10
Bird I. = Aves, I. de		
W. Indies	15°45N 63°55W	**89** C7
Bird I. *S. Georgia*	54°0S 38°3W	**96** G9
Birds Creek *Canada*	45°6N 77°52W	**82** A7
Birdsville *Australia*	25°51S 139°20E	**62** D2
Birdum Cr. → *Australia*	15°14S 133°0E	**60** C5
Birecik *Turkey*	37°2N 38°0E	**46** B3
Birein *Israel*	30°50N 34°28E	**48** E3
Birganj *Nepal*	27°1N 84°52E	**43** F11
Birigüi *Brazil*	21°18S 50°16W	**95** A5
Bîrjand *Iran*	32°53N 59°13E	**47** C8
Birkenhead *U.K.*	53°23N 3°2W	**12** D4
Bîrlad = Bârlad *Romania*	46°15N 27°38E	**17** E14
Birmingham *U.K.*	52°29N 1°52W	**13** E6
Birmingham *U.S.A.*	33°31N 86°48W	**85** E11
Birmingham Int. ✈ (BHX)		
U.K.	52°26N 1°45W	**13** E6
Birmitrapur *India*	22°24N 84°46E	**44** C7
Birni Nkonni *Niger*	13°55N 5°15E	**52** F7
Birnin Kebbi *Nigeria*	12°32N 4°12E	**52** F6
Birobidzhan *Russia*	48°50N 132°50E	**31** B15
Birr *Ireland*	53°6N 7°54W	**10** C4
Birrie → *Australia*	29°43S 146°37E	**63** D4
Birsilpur *India*	28°11N 72°15E	**42** F5
Birsk *Russia*	55°25N 55°30E	**18** C10
Birtle *Canada*	50°30N 101°5W	**71** C8
Birur *India*	13°30N 75°55E	**40** N9
Biržai *Lithuania*	56°11N 24°45E	**9** H21
Bisa *Indonesia*	1°15S 127°28E	**37** E7
Bisalpur *India*	28°14N 79°48E	**43** E8
Bisbee *U.S.A.*	31°27N 109°55W	**77** L9
Biscarrosse *France*	44°22N 1°20W	**20** D3
Biscay, B. of *Atl. Oc.*	45°0N 2°0W	**20** D1
Biscayne B. *U.S.A.*	25°40N 80°12W	**85** J14
Biscoe Is. *Antarctica*	66°0S 67°0W	**5** C17
Biscotasing *Canada*	47°18N 82°9W	**72** C3
Bishan *China*	29°33N 106°12E	**34** C6
Bishkek *Kyrgyzstan*	42°54N 74°46E	**30** C8
Bishnupur *India*	23°8N 87°20E	**43** H12
Bisho = Bhisho *S. Africa*	32°50S 27°23E	**56** D4
Bishoftu = Debre Zeyit		
Ethiopia	8°30N 39°0E	**49** F2
Bishop *Calif., U.S.A.*	37°22N 118°24W	**78** H8
Bishop *Tex., U.S.A.*	27°35N 97°48W	**84** H6
Bishop Auckland *U.K.*	54°39N 1°40W	**12** C6
Bishop's Falls *Canada*	49°2N 55°30W	**73** C8
Bishop's Stortford *U.K.*	51°52N 0°10E	**13** F8
Biskra *Algeria*	34°50N 5°44E	**52** B7
Bismarck *U.S.A.*	46°48N 100°47W	**80** B3
Bismarck Arch.		
Papua N. G.	2°30S 150°0E	**58** B7
Bison *U.S.A.*	45°31N 102°28W	**80** C2
Bisotūn *Iran*	34°23N 47°26E	**46** C5
Bissagos = Bijagós, Arquipélago		
dos *Guinea-Biss.*	11°15N 16°10W	**52** F2
Bissam Cuttack *India*	19°31N 83°31E	**44** E6
Bissau *Guinea-Biss.*	11°45N 15°45W	**52** F2
Bistcho L. *Canada*	59°45N 118°50W	**70** B5
Bistrița *Romania*	47°9N 24°35E	**17** E13
Bistrița → *Romania*	46°30N 26°57E	**17** E14
Biswan *India*	27°29N 81°2E	**43** F9
Bitam *Gabon*	2°5N 11°25E	**54** D2
Bitkine *Chad*	11°59N 18°13E	**53** F9
Bitlis *Turkey*	38°20N 42°3E	**46** B4
Bitola *Macedonia*	41°1N 21°20E	**23** D9
Bitolj = Bitola *Macedonia*	41°1N 21°20E	**23** D9
Bitra I. *India*	11°33N 72°9E	**45** J1
Bitter Creek *U.S.A.*	41°33N 108°33W	**76** F9
Bitterfontein *S. Africa*	31°1S 18°32E	**56** E2
Bitterroot → *U.S.A.*	46°52N 114°7W	**76** C6
Bitterroot Range *U.S.A.*	46°0N 114°20W	**76** D6
Bitterwater *U.S.A.*	36°23N 121°0W	**78** J6
Biu *Nigeria*	10°40N 12°3E	**53** F8
Biwa-Ko *Japan*	35°15N 136°10E	**29** G8
Biwabik *U.S.A.*	47°32N 92°21W	**80** B7
Bixby *U.S.A.*	35°57N 95°53W	**84** D7
Biyang *China*	32°38N 113°21E	**32** H7
Bizana *S. Africa*	30°50S 29°52E	**57** D4
Bizen *Japan*	34°43N 134°8E	**29** G7
Bizerte *Tunisia*	37°15N 9°50E	**53** A7
Bjargtangar *Iceland*	65°30N 24°30W	**8** D1
Bjelovar *Croatia*	45°56N 16°49E	**22** B7
Björneborg = Pori *Finland*	61°29N 21°48E	**8** F19
Bjørnevatn *Norway*	69°40N 30°0E	**8** B24
Bjørnøya *Arctic*	74°30N 19°0E	**4** B8
Black → *Da → Vietnam*	21°15N 105°20E	**34** G5
Black → *Canada*	44°42N 79°19W	**82** B5
Black → *Ariz., U.S.A.*	33°44N 110°13W	**77** K8
Black → *Ark., U.S.A.*	35°38N 91°20W	**84** D9
Black → *La., U.S.A.*	31°16N 91°50W	**84** F9
Black → *Mich., U.S.A.*	42°59N 82°27W	**82** D2
Black → *N.Y., U.S.A.*	43°59N 76°4W	**83** C8
Black → *Wis., U.S.A.*	43°57N 91°22W	**80** D8
Black Bay Pen. *Canada*	48°38N 88°21W	**72** C2
Black Birch L. *Canada*	56°53N 107°45W	**71** B7
Black Canyon of the Gunnison △		
U.S.A.	38°40N 107°35W	**76** G10
Black Diamond *Canada*	50°45N 114°14W	**70** C6
Black Duck → *Canada*	56°51N 89°2W	**72** A2
Black Forest = Schwarzwald		
Germany	48°30N 8°20E	**16** D5
Black Forest *U.S.A.*	39°0N 104°43W	**76** G11
Black Hd. *Ireland*	53°9N 9°16W	**10** C2
Black Hills *U.S.A.*	44°0N 103°45W	**80** D2
Black I. *Canada*	51°12N 96°30W	**71** C9
Black L. *Canada*	59°12N 105°15W	**71** B7
Black L. *Mich., U.S.A.*	45°28N 84°16W	**81** C11
Black L. *N.Y., U.S.A.*	44°31N 75°36W	**83** B9
Black Lake *Canada*	59°11N 105°20W	**71** B7
Black Mesa *U.S.A.*	36°58N 102°58W	**84** C3
Black Mt. = Mynydd Du		
U.K.	51°52N 3°50W	**13** F4
Black Mts. *U.K.*	51°55N 3°7W	**13** F4
Black Range *U.S.A.*	33°15N 107°50W	**77** K10
Black River *Jamaica*	18°0N 77°50W	**88** a
Black River *U.S.A.*	44°0N 75°47W	**83** C9
Black River Falls *U.S.A.*	44°18N 90°51W	**80** C8
Black Rock *Barbados*	13°7N 59°37W	**89** g
Black Rock Desert		
U.S.A.	41°10N 118°50W	**76** F4
Black Sea *Eurasia*	43°30N 35°0E	**19** F6
Black Tickle *Canada*	53°28N 55°45W	**73** B8
Black Volta → *Africa*	8°41N 1°33W	**52** G5
Black Warrior →		
U.S.A.	32°32N 87°51W	**85** E11
Blackall *Australia*	24°25S 145°45E	**62** C4
Blackball *N.Z.*	42°22S 171°26E	**59** E3
Blackbraes △ *Australia*	19°10S 144°10E	**62** B3
Blackbull *Australia*	17°55S 141°45E	**62** B3
Blackburn *U.K.*	53°45N 2°29W	**12** D5
Blackburn, Mt. *U.S.A.*	61°44N 143°26W	**74** C11
Blackburn with Darwen □		
U.K.	53°45N 2°29W	**12** D5
Blackdown Tableland △		
Australia	23°52S 149°8E	**62** C4
Blackfoot *U.S.A.*	43°11N 112°21W	**76** E7
Blackfoot → *U.S.A.*	46°52N 113°53W	**76** C7
Blackfoot Res. *U.S.A.*	42°55N 111°39W	**76** E8
Blackpool *U.K.*	53°49N 3°3W	**12** D4
Blackpool □ *U.K.*	53°49N 3°3W	**12** D4
Blackriver *U.S.A.*	44°46N 83°17W	**82** B1
Blacks Harbour *Canada*	45°3N 66°49W	**73** C6
Blacksburg *U.S.A.*	37°14N 80°25W	**81** G13
Blacksod B. *Ireland*	54°6N 10°0W	**10** B1
Blackstairs Mt. *Ireland*	52°33N 6°48W	**10** D5
Blackstone *U.S.A.*	37°5N 78°0W	**81** G14
Blackstone Ra. *Australia*	26°0S 128°30E	**61** E4
Blackwater = West Road →		
Canada	53°18N 122°53W	**70** C4
Blackwater *Australia*	23°35S 148°53E	**62** C4
Blackwater → *Meath,*		
Ireland	53°39N 6°41W	**10** C4
Blackwater → *Waterford,*		
Ireland	51°51N 7°52W	**10** D4
Blackwater → *U.K.*	54°31N 6°35W	**10** B5
Blackwell *U.S.A.*	36°48N 97°17W	**84** C6
Blackwells Corner		
U.S.A.	35°37N 119°47W	**79** K7
Blackwood *U.K.*	51°39N 3°12W	**13** F4
Bladensburg △ *Australia*	22°30S 142°59E	**62** C3
Blaenau Ffestiniog *U.K.*	53°0N 3°56W	**12** E4
Blaenau Gwent □ *U.K.*	51°48N 3°12W	**13** F4
Blåfjella-Skjækerfjella △		
Norway	64°15N 13°58E	**8** D15
Blagodarnyy *Russia*	45°7N 43°37E	**19** E7
Blagoevgrad *Bulgaria*	42°2N 23°5E	**23** C10
Blagoveshchensk		
Russia	50°20N 127°30E	**31** A14
Blahkiuh *Indonesia*	8°31S 115°12E	**37** J18
Blain *U.S.A.*	40°20N 77°31W	**82** F7
Blaine *Minn., U.S.A.*	45°10N 93°13W	**80** C7
Blaine *Wash., U.S.A.*	48°59N 122°45W	**78** B4
Blaine Lake *Canada*	52°51N 106°52W	**71** C7
Blair *U.S.A.*	41°33N 96°8W	**80** E6
Blair Athol *Australia*	22°42S 147°31E	**62** C4
Blair Atholl *U.K.*	56°46N 3°50W	**11** E5
Blairgowrie *U.K.*	56°35N 3°21W	**11** E5
Blairsden *U.S.A.*	39°47N 120°37W	**78** F6
Blairsville *U.S.A.*	40°26N 79°16W	**82** F5
Blakang Mati, Pulau		
Singapore	1°15N 103°50E	**39** d
Blake Pt. *U.S.A.*	48°11N 88°25W	**80** A9
Blakely *U.S.A.*	31°23N 84°56W	**85** F12
Blakely *Pa., U.S.A.*	41°28N 75°37W	**83** E9
Blambangan, Semenanjung		
Indonesia	8°42S 114°29E	**37** K17
Blanc, Mont *Europe*	45°48N 6°50E	**20** D7
Blanca, B. *Argentina*	39°10S 61°30W	**96** D4
Blanca, Cord. *Peru*	9°10S 77°35W	**92** E3
Blanca, Costa *Spain*	38°25N 0°10W	**21** C5
Blanca Peak *U.S.A.*	37°35N 105°29W	**77** H11
Blanche, C. *Australia*	33°1S 134°9E	**63** E1
Blanche, L. *S. Austral.,*		
Australia	29°15S 139°40E	**63** D2
Blanche, L. *W. Austral.,*		
Australia	22°25S 123°17E	**60** D3
Blanchisseuse		
Trin. & Tob.	10°48N 61°18W	**93** K15
Blanco *S. Africa*	33°55S 22°23E	**56** E3
Blanco *U.S.A.*	30°6N 98°25W	**84** F5
Blanco → *Argentina*	30°20S 68°42W	**94** C2
Blanco, C. *Costa Rica*	9°34N 85°8W	**88** E2
Blanco, C. *U.S.A.*	42°51N 124°34W	**76** E1
Blanda → *Iceland*	65°37N 20°9W	**8** D3
Blandford Forum *U.K.*	50°51N 2°9W	**13** G5
Blanding *U.S.A.*	37°37N 109°29W	**77** H9
Blanes *Spain*	41°40N 2°48E	**21** B7
Blankenberge *Belgium*	51°20N 3°9E	**15** C3
Blanquilla, I. *Venezuela*	11°51N 64°37W	**89** D7
Blanquillo *Uruguay*	32°53S 55°37W	**95** C4
Blantyre *Malawi*	15°45S 35°0E	**55** H7
Blarney *Ireland*	51°56N 8°33W	**10** E3
Blasdell *U.S.A.*	42°48N 78°50W	**82** D6
Blåvands Huk *Denmark*	55°33N 8°4E	**9** J13
Blaydon *U.K.*	54°58N 1°42W	**12** C6
Blayney *Australia*	33°32S 149°14E	**63** E4
Blaze, Pt. *Australia*	12°56S 130°11E	**60** B5
Blekinge *Sweden*	56°25N 15°20E	**9** H16
Blenheim *Canada*	42°20N 82°0W	**82** D3
Blenheim *N.Z.*	41°38S 173°57E	**59** D4
Bletchley *U.K.*	51°59N 0°44W	**13** F7
Blida *Algeria*	36°30N 2°49E	**52** A6
Bligh Water *Fiji*	17°0S 178°0E	**59** a
Blind River *Canada*	46°10N 82°58W	**72** C3
Bliss *Idaho, U.S.A.*	42°56N 114°57W	**76** E6
Bliss *N.Y., U.S.A.*	42°34N 78°15W	**82** D6
Blissfield *U.S.A.*	40°24N 81°58W	**82** F3
Blitar *Indonesia*	8°5S 112°11E	**37** H15
Block I. *U.S.A.*	41°11N 71°35W	**83** E13
Block Island Sd. *U.S.A.*	41°15N 71°40W	**83** E13
Bloemfontein *S. Africa*	29°6S 26°7E	**56** C4
Bloemhof *S. Africa*	27°38S 25°32E	**56** D4
Blois *France*	47°35N 1°20E	**20** C4
Blönduós *Iceland*	65°40N 20°12W	**8** D3
Blongas *Indonesia*	8°53S 116°2E	**37** K19
Bloodvein → *Canada*	51°47N 96°43W	**71** C9
Bloody Foreland *Ireland*	55°10N 8°17W	**10** A3
Bloomer *U.S.A.*	45°6N 91°29W	**80** C8
Bloomfield *Canada*	43°59N 77°14W	**82** C7
Bloomfield *Iowa, U.S.A.*	40°45N 92°25W	**80** E7
Bloomfield *N. Mex.,*		
U.S.A.	36°43N 107°59W	**77** H10
Bloomfield *Nebr., U.S.A.*	42°36N 97°39W	**80** D5
Bloomington *Ill., U.S.A.*	40°28N 89°0W	**80** E9
Bloomington *Minn.,*		
U.S.A.	39°10N 86°32W	**80** F10
Bloomington *Ind.,*		
U.S.A.	44°50N 93°17W	**80** C7
Bloomsburg *U.S.A.*	41°0N 76°27W	**83** F8
Bloomsbury *Australia*	20°48S 148°38E	**62** b
Blora *Indonesia*	6°57S 111°25E	**37** G14
Blossburg *U.S.A.*	41°41N 77°4W	**82** E7
Blouberg *S. Africa*	23°8S 28°59E	**57** C4
Blountstown *U.S.A.*	30°27N 85°3W	**85** F12
Blue Earth *U.S.A.*	43°38N 94°6W	**80** D6
Blue Hole △ *Belize*	17°9N 88°40W	**88** C2
Blue Mesa Res. *U.S.A.*	38°28N 107°20W	**76** G10
Blue Mountain Lake		
U.S.A.	43°51N 74°27W	**83** C10
Blue Mountain Pk. *Jamaica*	18°3N 76°36W	**88** a
Blue Mt. *U.S.A.*	40°30N 76°33W	**83** F8
Blue Mts. *Jamaica*	18°3N 76°36W	**88** a
Blue Mts. *Maine, U.S.A.*	44°50N 70°35W	**83** B14
Blue Mts. *Oreg., U.S.A.*	45°0N 118°20W	**76** D4
Blue Mud B. *U.S.A.*	35°56N 79°0W	**81** G14
Blue Mud Bay ☼ *Australia*	13°25S 136°2E	**62** A2
Blue Nile = Nîl el Azraq →		
Sudan	15°38N 32°31E	**53** E12
Blue Rapids *U.S.A.*	39°41N 96°39W	**80** F5
Blue Ridge *U.S.A.*	36°40N 80°50W	**81** G13
Blue River *Canada*	52°6N 119°13W	**70** C5
Bluefield *U.S.A.*	37°15N 81°17W	**81** G13
Bluefields *Nic.*	12°20N 83°50W	**88** D3
Bluevale *Canada*	43°51N 81°15W	**82** C3
Bluff *Australia*	23°35S 149°4E	**62** C4
Bluff *N.Z.*	46°37S 168°20E	**59** G2
Bluff *U.S.A.*	37°17N 109°33W	**77** H9
Bluff Knoll *Australia*	34°24S 118°15E	**61** F2
Bluff Pt. *Australia*	27°50S 114°5E	**61** E1
Bluffton *Ind., U.S.A.*	40°44N 85°11W	**81** E11
Bluffton *S.C., U.S.A.*	32°14N 80°52W	**85** E14
Blumenau *Brazil*	27°0S 49°0W	**95** B6
Blunt *U.S.A.*	44°31N 99°59W	**80** C4
Bly *U.S.A.*	42°24N 121°3W	**76** E3
Blyde River Canyon △		
S. Africa	24°37S 31°2E	**57** B5
Blyth *Canada*	43°44N 81°26W	**82** C3
Blyth *U.K.*	55°8N 1°31W	**12** B6
Blythe *U.S.A.*	33°37N 114°36W	**79** M12
Blytheville *U.S.A.*	35°56N 89°55W	**85** D10
Bo *S. Leone*	7°55N 11°50W	**52** G3
Bo Duc *Vietnam*	11°58N 106°50E	**39** G6
Bo Hai *China*	39°0N 119°0E	**33** E10
Bo Hai Haixia *Asia*	38°25N 121°10E	**33** E11
Bo Xian = Bozhou *China*	33°55N 115°41E	**32** H8
Boa Vista *Brazil*	2°48N 60°30W	**92** C6
Boa Vista *Cabo Verde*	16°0N 22°49W	**52** b
Boaco *Nic.*	12°29N 85°35W	**88** D2
Bo'ai *China*	35°10N 113°3E	**32** G7
Boane *Mozam.*	26°6S 32°19E	**57** D5
Boardman *U.S.A.*	41°2N 80°40W	**82** E4
Boath *India*	19°20N 78°20E	**44** E4
Bobadah *Australia*	32°19S 146°41E	**63** E4
Bobai *China*	22°17N 109°59E	**34** F7
Bobbili *India*	18°35N 83°30E	**44** E6
Bobcaygeon *Canada*	44°33N 78°33W	**82** B6
Boblad *India*	17°13N 75°26E	**44** F2
Bobo-Dioulasso		
Burkina Faso	11°8N 4°13W	**52** F5
Bobonong *Botswana*	21°58S 28°20E	**57** C4
Bóbr → *Poland*	52°4N 15°4E	**16** B8
Bobraomby, Tanjon' i		
Madag.	12°40S 49°10E	**55** G9
Bobruysk = Babruysk		
Belarus	53°10N 29°15E	**17** B15
Boby, Pic *Madag.*	22°12S 46°55E	**55** J9
Boca del Río *Mexico*	19°5N 96°4W	**87** D5
Boca do Acre *Brazil*	8°50S 67°27W	**92** E5
Boca Raton *U.S.A.*	26°21N 80°5W	**85** H14
Bocas del Dragón = Dragon's		
Mouths *Trin. & Tob.*	11°0N 61°50W	**93** K15
Bocas del Toro *Panama*	9°15N 82°20W	**88** E3
Bochnia *Poland*	49°58N 20°27E	**17** D11
Bochum = Senwabarana		
S. Africa	23°17S 29°7E	**57** B4
Bochum *Germany*	51°28N 7°13E	**16** C4
Bocoyna *Mexico*	27°52N 107°35W	**86** B3
Bodaybo *Russia*	57°50N 114°0E	**27** D12
Boddam *U.K.*	59°56N 1°17W	**11** B7
Boddington *Australia*	32°50S 116°30E	**61** F2
Bodega Bay *U.S.A.*	38°20N 123°3W	**78** G3
Boden *Sweden*	65°50N 21°42E	**8** D19
Bodensee *Europe*	47°35N 9°25E	**20** C8
Bodh Gaya *India*	24°41N 84°59E	**43** G11
Bodhan *India*	18°40N 77°44E	**44** E3
Bodinayakkanur *India*	10°2N 77°10E	**45** J3
Bodmin *U.K.*	50°28N 4°43W	**13** G3
Bodmin Moor *U.K.*	50°33N 4°36W	**13** G3
Bodø *Norway*	67°17N 14°24E	**8** C16
Bodrog → *Hungary*	48°11N 21°22E	**17** D11
Bodrum *Turkey*	37°3N 27°30E	**23** F12
Boende		
Dem. Rep. of the Congo	0°24S 21°12E	**54** E4
Boerne *U.S.A.*	29°47N 98°44W	**84** G5
Boesmans → *S. Africa*	33°42S 26°39E	**56** D4
Bogalusa *U.S.A.*	30°47N 89°52W	**85** F10
Bogan → *Australia*	30°20S 146°55E	**63** D4
Bogan Gate *Australia*	33°7S 147°49E	**63** E4
Bogantungan *Australia*	23°41S 147°17E	**62** C4
Bogata *U.S.A.*	33°28N 95°13W	**84** E7
Bogda Shan *China*	43°35N 89°40E	**30** C6
Boggabilla *Australia*	28°36S 150°24E	**63** D5
Boggabri *Australia*	30°45S 150°5E	**63** E5
Boggeragh Mts. *Ireland*	52°2N 8°55W	**10** D3
Boglan = Solhan *Turkey*	38°57N 41°3E	**46** B4
Bognes *Norway*	68°13N 16°5E	**8** B17
Bognor Regis *U.K.*	50°47N 0°40W	**13** G7
Bogo *Phil.*	11°3N 124°0E	**37** B6
Bogong, Mt. *Australia*	36°47S 147°17E	**63** F4
Bogor *Indonesia*	6°36S 106°48E	**37** G12
Bogotá *Colombia*	4°34N 74°0W	**92** C4
Bogotol *Russia*	56°15N 89°50E	**26** D9
Bogra *Bangla.*	24°51N 89°22E	**41** G16
Boguchanskoye Vdkhr.		
Russia	58°42N 99°9E	**27** D10
Boguchany *Russia*	58°40N 97°30E	**27** D10
Bogué *Mauritania*	16°45N 14°10W	**52** E3
Bohemian Forest = Böhmerwald		
Germany	49°8N 13°14E	**16** D7
Böhmerwald *Germany*	49°8N 13°14E	**16** D7
Bohol □ *Phil.*	9°50N 124°10E	**37** C6
Bohol Sea *Phil.*	9°0N 124°0E	**37** C6
Bohorok *Indonesia*	3°30N 98°12E	**39** L2
Böhöt *Mongolia*	45°13N 108°16E	**32** B5
Bohuslän *Sweden*	58°25N 12°0E	**9** G15
Boi, Pta. do *Brazil*	23°55S 45°15W	**95** A6
Boiaçu *Brazil*	0°27S 61°46W	**92** D6
Boigu *Australia*	9°16S 142°13E	**62** a
Boileau, C. *Australia*	17°40S 122°7E	**60** C3
Boipariguda *India*	18°46N 82°26E	**44** E6
Boise *U.S.A.*	43°37N 116°13W	**76** E5
Boise City *U.S.A.*	36°44N 102°31W	**84** C3
Boissevain *Canada*	49°15N 100°5W	**71** D8
Bojador, C. *W. Sahara*	26°0N 14°30W	**52** C3
Bojana → *Albania*	41°52N 19°22E	**23** D8
Bojnūrd *Iran*	37°30N 57°20E	**47** B8
Bojonegoro *Indonesia*	7°11S 111°54E	**37** G14
Bokaro *India*	23°46N 85°55E	**43** H11
Boké *Guinea*	10°56N 14°17W	**52** F3
Bokhara → *Australia*	29°55S 146°42E	**63** D4
Boknafjorden *Norway*	59°14N 5°40E	**9** G11
Bokor △ *Cambodia*	10°50N 104°1E	**39** G5
Bokoro *Chad*	12°25N 17°14E	**53** F9
Bokpyin *Myanmar*	11°18N 98°42E	**39** G2
Bokungu		
Dem. Rep. of the Congo	0°35S 22°50E	**54** E4
Bolan → *Pakistan*	28°38N 67°42E	**42** E2
Bolan Pass *Pakistan*	29°50N 67°20E	**40** E5
Bolaños → *Mexico*	21°12N 104°5W	**86** C4
Bolbec *France*	49°30N 0°30E	**20** B4
Boldājī *Iran*	31°56N 51°3E	**47** D6
Bole *China*	44°55N 81°37E	**30** C5
Bolekhiv *Ukraine*	49°0N 23°57E	**17** D12
Bolesławiec *Poland*	51°17N 15°37E	**16** C8
Bolgatanga *Ghana*	10°44N 0°53W	**52** F5
Bolgrad = Bolhrad		
Ukraine	45°40N 28°32E	**17** F15
Bolhrad *Ukraine*	45°40N 28°32E	**17** F15
Bolinao *Phil.*	16°23N 119°54E	**37** A5
Bolivar *Mo., U.S.A.*	37°37N 93°25W	**80** G7
Bolivar *N.Y., U.S.A.*	42°4N 78°10W	**82** D6
Bolivar *Tenn., U.S.A.*	35°12N 89°0W	**85** D10
Bolívar, Pico *Venezuela*	8°32N 71°2W	**89** E5
Bolivia ■ *S. Amer.*	17°6S 64°0W	**92** G6
Bolivian Plateau = Altiplano		
Bolivia	17°0S 68°0W	**92** G5
Bollnäs *Sweden*	61°21N 16°24E	**8** F17
Bollon *Australia*	28°2S 147°29E	**63** D4
Bolmen *Sweden*	56°55N 13°40E	**9** H15
Bolobo *Dem. Rep. of the Congo*	2°6S 16°20E	**54** E3
Bologna *Italy*	44°29N 11°20E	**22** B4
Bologoye *Russia*	57°55N 34°5E	**18** C5
Bolomba		
Dem. Rep. of the Congo	0°35N 19°0E	**54** D3
Bolonchén *Mexico*	20°1N 89°45W	**87** D7
Boloven, Cao Nguyen		
Laos	15°10N 106°30E	**38** E6
Bolpur *India*	23°40N 87°45E	**43** H12
Bolsena, L. di *Italy*	42°36N 11°56E	**22** C4
Bolshevik, Ostrov		
Russia	78°30N 102°0E	**27** B11
Bolshoy Anyuy →		
Russia	68°30N 160°49E	**27** C17
Bolshoy Begichev, Ostrov		
Russia	74°20N 112°30E	**27** B12
Bolshoy Kamen *Russia*	43°7N 132°19E	**28** C6
Bolshoy Kavkas = Caucasus		
Mountains *Eurasia*	42°50N 44°0E	**19** F7
Bolshoy Lyakhovskiy, Ostrov		
Russia	73°35N 142°0E	**27** B15
Bolshoy Tyuters, Ostrov		
Russia	59°51N 27°13E	**9** G22
Bolsward *Neths.*	53°3N 5°32E	**15** A5
Bolt Head *U.K.*	50°12N 3°48W	**13** G4
Bolton *Canada*	43°54N 79°45W	**82** C5
Bolton *U.K.*	53°35N 2°26W	**12** D5
Bolton Landing *U.S.A.*	43°32N 73°35W	**83** C11
Bolu *Turkey*	40°45N 31°35E	**19** F5
Bolungavík *Iceland*	66°9N 23°15W	**8** C2
Boluo *China*	23°3N 114°21E	**35** F10
Bolvadin *Turkey*	38°45N 31°4E	**46** B1
Bolzano *Italy*	46°31N 11°22E	**22** A4
Bom Jesus da Lapa		
Brazil	13°15S 43°25W	**93** F10
Boma *Dem. Rep. of the Congo*	5°50S 13°4E	**54** F2
Bombala *Australia*	36°56S 149°15E	**63** F4
Bombay *S. Africa*	44°56N 74°34W	**83** B10
Bombedor, Pta. *Venezuela*	9°53N 61°37W	**93** L15
Bomberai, Semenanjung		
Indonesia	3°0S 133°0E	**37** E8
Bomboma		
Dem. Rep. of the Congo	2°25N 18°55E	**54** D3
Bomi *China*	29°50N 95°45E	**30** F8
Bømlo *Norway*	59°37N 5°13E	**9** G11
Bompoka *India*	8°15N 93°13E	**45** K11
Bomu → *C.A.R.*	4°40N 22°30E	**54** D4
Bon, C. = Ra's at Tib *Tunisia*	37°1N 11°2E	**52** A7
Bon Acceuil *Mauritius*	20°10S 57°39E	**55** d
Bon Echo △ *Canada*	44°55N 77°16W	**82** B7
Bon Sar Pa *Vietnam*	12°24N 107°35E	**38** F6
Bonāb *Iran*	36°35N 48°41E	**47** B6
Bonaigarh *India*	21°50N 84°57E	**43** J11
Bonaire *W. Indies*	12°10N 68°15W	**89** D6
Bonampak *Mexico*	16°44N 91°5W	**87** D6
Bonang *Australia*	37°11S 148°41E	**63** F4
Bonanza *Nic.*	13°54N 84°35W	**88** D3
Bonaparte Arch.		
Australia	14°0S 124°30E	**60** B3
Bonar Bridge *U.K.*	57°54N 4°20W	**11** D4
Bonasse *Trin. & Tob.*	10°5N 61°54W	**93** K15
Bonaventure *Canada*	48°5N 65°32W	**73** C6
Bonavista *Canada*	48°40N 53°5W	**73** C9
Bonavista, C. *Canada*	48°42N 53°5W	**73** C9
Bonavista B. *Canada*	48°45N 53°25W	**73** C9
Bondo		
Dem. Rep. of the Congo	3°55N 23°53E	**54** D4
Bondokodi *Indonesia*	9°33S 119°0E	**60** A2
Bondoukou *Côte d'Ivoire*	8°2N 2°47W	**52** G5
Bondowoso *Indonesia*	7°55S 113°49E	**37** G15
Bone, Teluk *Indonesia*	4°10S 120°50E	**37** E6
Bonerate *Indonesia*	7°25S 121°5E	**37** F6
Bonerate, Kepulauan		
Indonesia	6°30S 121°10E	**37** F6
Bo'ness *U.K.*	56°1N 3°37W	**11** E5
Bonete, Cerro *Argentina*	27°55S 68°40W	**94** B2
Bong Son = Hoai Nhon		
Vietnam	14°28N 109°1E	**38** E7
Bongaigaon *India*	26°28N 90°34E	**30** F7
Bongandanga		
Dem. Rep. of the Congo	1°24N 21°3E	**54** D4
Bongor *Chad*	10°35N 15°20E	**53** F9
Bongos, Massif des *C.A.R.*	8°40N 22°25E	**54** C4
Bonham *U.S.A.*	33°35N 96°11W	**84** E6
Bonifacio *France*	41°24N 9°10E	**20** F8
Bonifacio, Bouches de		
Medit. S.	41°12N 9°15E	**22** D3
Bonin Is. = Ogasawara Gunto		
Pac. Oc.	27°0N 142°0E	**64** E6
Bonn *Germany*	50°46N 7°6E	**16** C4
Bonners Ferry *U.S.A.*	48°42N 116°19W	**76** B5
Bonney, L. *Australia*	37°50S 140°20E	**63** F3
Bonnie Rock *Australia*	30°29S 118°22E	**61** F2
Bonny, Bight of *Africa*	3°30N 9°20E	**54** D1
Bonnyrigg *U.K.*	55°53N 3°6W	**11** F5
Bonnyville *Canada*	54°20N 110°45W	**71** C6
Bonoi *Indonesia*	1°45S 137°41E	**37** E9
Bonsall *U.S.A.*	33°16N 117°14W	**79** M9
Bontang *Indonesia*	0°10N 117°30E	**36** D5
Bontebok △ *S. Africa*	34°5S 20°28E	**56** D3
Bonthe *S. Leone*	7°30N 12°33W	**52** G3
Bontoc *Phil.*	17°7N 120°58E	**37** A6
Bonython Ra. *Australia*	23°40S 128°45E	**60** D4
Boodjamulla △ *Australia*	18°15S 138°6E	**62** B2
Bookabie *Australia*	31°50S 132°41E	**61** F5
Booker *U.S.A.*	36°27N 100°32W	**84** C4
Booligal *Australia*	33°58S 144°53E	**63** E3
Böön Tsagaan Nuur		
Mongolia	45°35N 99°9E	**30** B8
Boonah *Australia*	27°58S 152°41E	**63** D5
Boone *Iowa, U.S.A.*	42°4N 93°53W	**80** D7
Boone *N.C., U.S.A.*	36°13N 81°41W	**85** C14
Booneville *Ark., U.S.A.*	35°8N 93°55W	**84** D8
Booneville *Miss., U.S.A.*	34°39N 88°34W	**85** D10
Boonville *Calif., U.S.A.*	39°1N 123°22W	**78** F3
Boonville *Ind., U.S.A.*	38°3N 87°16W	**80** F10
Boonville *Mo., U.S.A.*	38°58N 92°44W	**80** F7
Boonville *N.Y., U.S.A.*	43°29N 75°20W	**83** C9
Boorabbin △ *Australia*	31°30S 120°10E	**61** F3
Boorindal *Australia*	30°22S 146°11E	**63** E4
Boorowa *Australia*	34°28S 148°44E	**63** E4
Boosaaso *Somalia*	11°12N 49°18E	**49** E4
Boothia, Gulf of *Canada*	71°0N 90°0W	**68** C11
Boothia Pen. *Canada*	71°0N 94°0W	**68** C13
Bootle *U.K.*	53°28N 3°1W	**12** D4
Booué *Gabon*	0°5S 11°55E	**54** E2
Boquilla, Presa de la		
Mexico	27°31N 105°30W	**86** B3
Boquillas del Carmen		
Mexico	29°11N 102°58W	**86** B4
Bor *Serbia*	44°5N 22°7E	**23** B10
Bor *South Sudan*	6°10N 31°40E	**53** G12
Bor Mashash *Israel*	31°7N 34°50E	**48** D3
Bora Bora		
French Polynesia	16°30S 151°45W	**65** J12
Borah Peak *U.S.A.*	44°8N 113°47W	**76** D7
Boraha, Nosy *Madag.*	16°50S 49°55E	**55** H9
Borås *Sweden*	57°43N 12°56E	**9** H15
Borāzjān *Iran*	29°22N 51°10E	**47** D6
Borba *Brazil*	4°12S 59°34W	**92** D7
Borborema, Planalto da		
Brazil	7°0S 37°0W	**90** D7

Bord Khūn-e Now *Iran* 28°3N 51°28E **47** D6
Borda, C. *Australia* 35°45S 136°34E **63** F2
Bordeaux *France* 44°50N 0°36W **20** D3
Borden *Australia* 34°3S 118°12E **61** F2
Borden-Carleton *Canada* 46°18N 63°47W **73** C7
Borden I. *Canada* 78°30N 111°30W **69** B9
Borden Pen. *Canada* 73°0N 83°0W **69** C15
Border Ranges △
 Australia 28°24S 152°56E **63** D5
Borders = Scottish Borders □
 U.K. 55°35N 2°50W **11** F6
Bordertown *Australia* 36°19S 140°45E **63** F3
Borðeyri *Iceland* 65°12N 21°6W **8** D3
Bordj Flye Ste-Marie
 Algeria 27°19N 2°32W **52** C5
Bordj in Eker *Algeria* 24°9N 5°3E **52** D7
Bordj Mokhtar *Algeria* 21°20N 0°56E **52** D6
Bordj Omar Driss *Algeria* 28°10N 6°40E **52** C7
Borehamwood *U.K.* 51°40N 0°15W **13** F7
Borgampad *India* 17°39N 80°52E **44** F5
Borgarnes *Iceland* 64°32N 21°55W **8** D3
Børgefjellet *Norway* 65°20N 13°45E **8** D15
Borger *Neths.* 52°54N 6°44E **15** B6
Borger *U.S.A.* 35°39N 101°24W **84** D4
Borgholm *Sweden* 56°52N 16°39E **9** H17
Borhoyn Tal *Mongolia* 43°50N 111°58E **32** C6
Borigumma *India* 19°3N 82°33E **44** E6
Borikhane *Laos* 18°33N 103°43E **38** C4
Borisoglebsk *Russia* 51°27N 42°5E **19** D7
Borisov = Barysaw
 Belarus 54°17N 28°28E **17** A15
Borja *Peru* 4°20S 77°40W **92** D3
Borkou *Chad* 18°15N 18°50E **53** E9
Borkum *Germany* 53°34N 6°40E **16** B4
Borlänge *Sweden* 60°29N 15°26E **9** F16
Borley, C. *Antarctica* 66°15S 52°30E **5** C5
Borneo *E. Indies* 1°0N 115°0E **36** D5
Bornholm *Denmark* 55°10N 15°0E **9** J16
Borobudur △ *Indonesia* 7°36S 110°12E **37** G14
Borogontsy *Russia* 62°42N 131°8E **27** C14
Borohoro Shan *China* 44°6N 83°10E **30** B3
Boron *U.S.A.* 35°0N 117°39W **79** L9
Borongan *Phil.* 11°37N 125°26E **37** B7
Borovichi *Russia* 58°25N 33°55E **18** C5
Borrego Springs
 U.S.A. 33°15N 116°23W **79** M10
Borrisokane *Ireland* 53°0N 8°7W **10** D3
Borroloola *Australia* 16°4S 136°17E **62** B2
Borşa *Romania* 47°41N 24°50E **17** E13
Borsad *India* 22°25N 72°54E **42** H5
Bortala = Bole *China* 44°55N 81°37E **30** C5
Borth *U.K.* 52°29N 4°2W **13** E3
Borūjerd *Iran* 33°55N 48°50E **47** C6
Boryeong *S. Korea* 36°21N 126°36E **33** F14
Boryslav *Ukraine* 49°18N 23°28E **17** D12
Borzya *Russia* 50°24N 116°31E **31** A12
Bosa *Italy* 40°18N 8°30E **22** D3
Bosanska Gradiška = Gradiška
 Bos.-H. 45°10N 17°15E **22** B7
Boscastle *U.K.* 50°41N 4°42W **13** G3
Boscobelle *Barbados* 13°17N 59°35W **89** g
Bose *China* 23°53N 106°35E **34** F6
Boseong *S. Korea* 34°46N 127°5E **33** G14
Boshan *China* 36°28N 117°49E **33** F9
Boshof *S. Africa* 28°31S 25°13E **56** C4
Boshrūyeh *Iran* 33°50N 57°30E **47** C8
Bosna → *Bos.-H.* 45°4N 18°29E **23** B8
Bosna i Hercegovina = Bosnia-
 Herzegovina ■ *Europe* 44°0N 18°0E **22** B7
Bosnia-Herzegovina ■
 Europe 44°0N 18°0E **22** B7
Bosnik *Indonesia* 1°5S 136°10E **37** E9
Bosobolo
 Dem. Rep. of the Congo 4°15N 19°50E **54** D3
Bosque Farms *U.S.A.* 35°51N 106°42W **77** J10
Bosra = Buşra ash Shām
 Syria 32°30N 36°25E **48** C5
Bossangoa *C.A.R.* 6°35N 17°30E **54** C3
Bossier City *U.S.A.* 32°31N 93°44W **84** E8
Bossiesvlei *Namibia* 25°1S 16°44E **56** C2
Bosso *Niger* 13°43N 13°19E **53** F8
Bostan *Pakistan* 30°26N 67°2E **42** D2
Bostānābād *Iran* 37°50N 46°50E **46** B5
Bosten Hu *China* 41°55N 87°40E **30** C6
Boston *U.K.* 52°59N 0°2W **12** E7
Boston Bar *Canada* 49°52N 121°30W **70** D4
Boston Mts. *U.S.A.* 35°42N 93°15W **84** D8
Boswell *Canada* 49°28N 116°45W **70** D5
Boswell *U.S.A.* 40°10N 79°2W **82** F5
Botad *India* 22°15N 71°40E **42** H4
Botene *Laos* 17°35N 101°12E **38** D3
Bothaville *S. Africa* 27°23S 26°34E **56** C4
Bothnia, G. of *Europe* 62°0N 20°0E **8** F19
Bothwell *Australia* 42°20S 147°1E **63** G4
Bothwell *Canada* 42°38N 81°52W **82** D3
Botletle → *Botswana* 20°10S 23°15E **56** B3
Botoşani *Romania* 47°42N 26°41E **17** E14
Botou *Burkina Faso* 12°42N 1°59E **52** F6
Botou *China* 38°4N 116°34E **32** E9
Botshabelo *S. Africa* 29°14S 26°44E **56** C4
Botswana ■ *Africa* 22°0S 24°0E **56** C3
Bottineau *U.S.A.* 48°50N 100°27W **80** A3
Botucatu *Brazil* 22°55S 48°30W **95** A6
Botum Sakor △ *Cambodia* 11°55N 103°15E **39** G4
Botwood *Canada* 49°6N 55°23W **73** C8
Bou Saâda *Algeria* 35°11N 4°9E **52** A6
Bouaflé *Côte d'Ivoire* 7°1N 5°47W **52** G4
Bouaké *Côte d'Ivoire* 7°40N 5°2W **52** G4
Bouar *C.A.R.* 6°0N 15°40E **54** C3
Bouârfa *Morocco* 32°32N 1°58W **52** B5
Boucaut B. *Australia* 14°30S 135°42E **62** A2
Bouctouche *Canada* 46°30N 64°45W **73** C7
Bougainville, C. *Australia* 13°57S 126°4E **60** B4
Bougainville I. *Papua N. G.* 6°0S 155°0E **58** B8
Bougainville Reef
 Australia 15°30S 147°5E **62** B4
Bougie = Bejaïa *Algeria* 36°42N 5°2E **52** A7
Bougouni *Mali* 11°30N 7°20W **52** F4
Bouillon *Belgium* 49°44N 5°3E **15** E5
Boulder *Colo., U.S.A.* 40°1N 105°17W **76** F11

Boulder *Mont., U.S.A.* 46°14N 112°7W **76** C7
Boulder City *U.S.A.* 35°58N 114°49W **79** K12
Boulder Creek *U.S.A.* 37°7N 122°7W **78** H4
Boulder Dam = Hoover Dam
 U.S.A. 36°1N 114°44W **79** K12
Boulia *Australia* 22°52S 139°51E **62** C2
Boulogne-sur-Mer *France* 50°42N 1°36E **20** A4
Boulsa *Burkina Faso* 12°39N 0°34W **52** F5
Boultoum *Niger* 14°45N 10°25E **53** F8
Bouma △ *Fiji* 16°50S 179°52W **59** a
Boun Neua *Laos* 21°38N 101°54E **38** A3
Boun Tai *Laos* 21°23N 101°58E **38** B3
Bouna *Côte d'Ivoire* 9°10N 3°0W **52** G5
Boundary Peak *U.S.A.* 37°51N 118°21W **78** H8
Boundiali *Côte d'Ivoire* 9°30N 6°20W **52** G4
Bountiful *U.S.A.* 40°53N 111°52W **76** F8
Bounty Is. *Pac. Oc.* 48°0S 178°30E **64** M9
Bounty Trough *Pac. Oc.* 46°0S 178°0E **64** M9
Bourbonnais *France* 46°28N 3°0E **20** C5
Bourdel L. *Canada* 56°43N 74°10W **72** A5
Bourem *Mali* 17°0N 0°24W **52** E5
Bourg-en-Bresse *France* 46°13N 5°12E **20** C6
Bourg-St-Maurice *France* 45°35N 6°46E **20** D7
Bourgas = Burgas
 Bulgaria 42°33N 27°29E **23** C12
Bourges *France* 47°9N 2°25E **20** C5
Bourget *Canada* 45°26N 75°9W **83** A9
Bourgogne *France* 47°0N 4°50E **20** C6
Bourke *Australia* 30°8S 145°55E **63** E4
Bourne *U.K.* 52°47N 0°22W **12** E7
Bournemouth *U.K.* 50°43N 1°52W **13** G6
Bournemouth □ *U.K.* 50°43N 1°52W **13** G6
Bouse *U.S.A.* 33°56N 114°0W **79** M13
Bousso *Chad* 10°34N 16°52E **53** F9
Bouvet I. = Bouvetøya
 Antarctica 54°26S 3°24E **2** G10
Bouvetøya *Antarctica* 54°26S 3°24E **2** G10
Bovanenkovo *Russia* 70°22N 68°40E **26** B7
Bovill *U.S.A.* 46°51N 116°24W **76** C5
Bovril *Argentina* 31°21S 59°26W **94** C4
Bow → *Canada* 49°57N 111°41W **70** C6
Bow Island *Canada* 49°50N 111°23W **76** B8
Bowbells *U.S.A.* 48°48N 102°15W **80** A2
Bowdle *U.S.A.* 45°27N 99°39W **80** C4
Bowelling *Australia* 33°25S 116°30E **61** F2
Bowen *Argentina* 35°0S 67°31W **94** D2
Bowen *Australia* 20°0S 148°16E **62** J6
Bowen Mts. *Australia* 37°0S 147°50E **63** F4
Bowers Basin *Pac. Oc.* 53°45N 176°0E **4** D16
Bowers Ridge *Pac. Oc.* 54°0N 180°0E **4** D17
Bowie *Ariz., U.S.A.* 32°19N 109°29W **77** K9
Bowie *Tex., U.S.A.* 33°34N 97°51W **84** E6
Bowkān *Iran* 36°31N 46°12E **46** B5
Bowland, Forest of *U.K.* 54°0N 2°30W **12** D5
Bowling Green *Ky.,*
 U.S.A. 36°59N 86°27W **80** G10
Bowling Green *Ohio,*
 U.S.A. 41°23N 83°39W **81** E12
Bowling Green, C.
 Australia 19°19S 147°25E **62** B4
Bowling Green Bay △
 Australia 19°26S 146°57E **62** B4
Bowman *U.S.A.* 46°11N 103°24W **80** B2
Bowman I. *Antarctica* 65°0S 104°0E **5** C8
Bowmanville = Clarington
 Canada 43°55N 78°41W **82** C6
Bowmore *U.K.* 55°45N 6°17W **11** F2
Bowral *Australia* 34°26S 150°27E **63** E5
Bowraville *Australia* 30°37S 152°52E **63** E5
Bowron → *Canada* 54°3N 121°50W **70** C4
Bowron Lake △ *Canada* 53°10N 121°5W **70** C4
Bowser L. *Canada* 56°30N 129°30W **70** B3
Bowsman *Canada* 52°14N 101°12W **71** C8
Box Cr. → *Australia* 34°10S 143°50E **63** E3
Boxmeer *Neths.* 51°38N 5°56E **15** C5
Boxtel *Neths.* 51°36N 5°20E **15** C5
Boyang *China* 29°0N 116°38E **35** C11
Boyce *U.S.A.* 31°23N 92°40W **84** F8
Boyd L. *Canada* 52°46N 76°42W **72** B4
Boyle *Canada* 54°35N 112°49W **70** C6
Boyle *Ireland* 53°59N 8°18W **10** C3
Boyne → *Ireland* 53°43N 6°15W **10** C5
Boyne, Bend of the *Ireland* 53°41N 6°27W **10** C5
Boyne City *U.S.A.* 45°13N 85°1W **81** C11
Boynton Beach *U.S.A.* 26°32N 80°4W **85** H14
Boyoma, Chutes
 Dem. Rep. of the Congo 0°35N 25°23E **50** F6
Boysen Res. *U.S.A.* 43°25N 108°11W **76** E9
Boyuibe *Bolivia* 20°25S 63°17W **92** G6
Boyup Brook *Australia* 33°50S 116°23E **61** F2
Boz Dağları *Turkey* 38°20N 28°0E **23** E13
Bozburun *Turkey* 36°43N 28°4E **23** F13
Bozcaada *Turkey* 39°49N 26°3E **23** E12
Bozdoğan *Turkey* 37°40N 28°17E **23** F13
Bozeman *U.S.A.* 45°41N 111°2W **76** D8
Bozen = Bolzano *Italy* 46°31N 11°22E **22** A4
Bozhou *China* 33°55N 115°41E **32** H8
Bozoum *C.A.R.* 6°25N 16°35E **54** C3
Bozyazı *Turkey* 36°6N 33°0E **46** B2
Bra *Italy* 44°42N 7°51E **20** D7
Brabant □ *Belgium* 50°46N 4°30E **15** D4
Brabant L. *Canada* 55°58N 103°43W **71** B8
Brač *Croatia* 43°20N 16°40E **22** C7
Bracadale, L. *U.K.* 57°20N 6°30W **11** D2
Bracciano, L. di *Italy* 42°7N 12°14E **22** C5
Bracebridge *Canada* 45°2N 79°19W **82** A5
Bräcke *Sweden* 62°45N 15°26E **8** E16
Brackettville *U.S.A.* 29°19N 100°25W **84** G4
Bracknell *U.K.* 51°25N 0°43W **13** F7
Bracknell Forest □ *U.K.* 51°25N 0°44W **13** F7
Brad *Romania* 46°10N 22°50E **17** E12
Bradenton *U.S.A.* 27°30N 82°34W **85** H13
Bradford *Canada* 44°7N 79°34W **82** B5
Bradford *U.K.* 53°47N 1°45W **12** D6
Bradford *Pa., U.S.A.* 41°58N 78°38W **82** E6
Bradford *Vt., U.S.A.* 43°59N 72°9W **83** C12
Bradley *Ark., U.S.A.* 33°6N 93°39W **84** E8
Bradley *Calif., U.S.A.* 35°52N 120°48W **78** K6
Brady *U.S.A.* 31°9N 99°20W **84** F5
Braeside *Canada* 45°28N 76°24W **83** A8

Braga *Portugal* 41°35N 8°25W **21** B1
Bragado *Argentina* 35°2S 60°27W **94** D3
Bragança *Brazil* 1°0S 47°2W **93** D9
Bragança *Portugal* 41°48N 6°50W **21** B2
Bragança Paulista *Brazil* 22°55S 46°32W **95** A6
Brahestad = Raahe
 Finland 64°40N 24°28E **8** D21
Brahmanbaria *Bangla.* 23°58N 91°15E **41** H17
Brahmani → *India* 20°39N 86°46E **44** D8
Brahmapur *India* 19°15N 84°54E **44** E7
Brahmaputra → *Asia* 23°40N 90°35E **43** H13
Braich-y-pwll *U.K.* 52°47N 4°46W **12** E3
Braidwood *Australia* 35°27S 149°49E **63** F4
Brăila *Romania* 45°19N 27°59E **17** F14
Brainerd *U.S.A.* 46°22N 94°12W **80** B6
Braintree *U.K.* 51°53N 0°34E **13** F8
Braintree *U.S.A.* 42°13N 71°0W **83** D14
Brak → *S. Africa* 29°35S 22°55E **56** C3
Brakwater *Namibia* 22°28S 17°3E **56** B2
Bramhapuri *India* 20°36N 79°52E **44** D8
Brampton *Canada* 43°45N 79°45W **82** C5
Brampton *U.K.* 54°57N 2°44W **12** C5
Brampton I. *Australia* 20°49S 149°16E **62** b
Branco → *Brazil* 1°20S 61°50W **92** D6
Branco, C. *Brazil* 7°9S 34°47W **90** D7
Brandberg *Namibia* 21°10S 14°33E **56** B1
Brandberg △ *Namibia* 21°10S 14°30E **56** B1
Brandenburg = Neubrandenburg
 Germany 53°33N 13°15E **16** B7
Brandenburg *Germany* 52°25N 12°33E **16** B7
Brandenburg □ *Germany* 52°50N 13°0E **16** B6
Brandfort *S. Africa* 28°40S 26°30E **56** C4
Brandon *Canada* 49°50N 99°57W **71** D9
Brandon *U.S.A.* 43°48N 73°6W **83** C11
Brandon B. *Ireland* 52°17N 10°8W **10** D1
Brandon Mt. *Ireland* 52°15N 10°15W **10** D1
Brandsen *Argentina* 35°10S 58°15W **94** D4
Brandvlei *S. Africa* 30°25S 20°30E **56** D3
Branford *U.S.A.* 41°17N 72°49W **83** E12
Braniewo *Poland* 54°25N 19°50E **17** A10
Bransfield Str. *Antarctica* 63°0S 59°0W **5** C18
Branson *U.S.A.* 36°39N 93°13W **80** G7
Brantford *Canada* 43°10N 80°15W **82** C4
Bras d'Or L. *Canada* 45°50N 60°50W **73** C7
Brasher Falls *U.S.A.* 44°49N 74°47W **83** B10
Brasil = Brazil ■ *S. Amer.* 12°0S 50°0W **93** F9
Brasil, Planalto *Brazil* 18°0S 46°30W **90** E6
Brasiléia *Brazil* 11°0S 68°45W **92** F5
Brasília *Brazil* 15°47S 47°55W **93** G9
Brasília Legal *Brazil* 3°49S 55°36W **93** D7
Braslaw *Belarus* 55°38N 27°0E **9** J22
Braşov *Romania* 45°38N 25°35E **17** F13
Brasschaat *Belgium* 51°19N 4°27E **15** C4
Brassey, Banjaran
 Malaysia 5°0N 117°15E **36** D5
Brassey Ra. *Australia* 25°8S 122°15E **61** E3
Brasstown Bald *U.S.A.* 34°53N 83°49W **85** D13
Brastad *Sweden* 58°23N 11°30E **9** G14
Bratislava *Slovakia* 48°10N 17°7E **17** D9
Bratsk *Russia* 56°10N 101°30E **27** D11
Bratskoye Vdkhr.
 Russia 56°0N 101°40E **27** D11
Brattleboro *U.S.A.* 42°51N 72°34W **83** D12
Braunau am Inn *Austria* 48°15N 13°3E **16** D7
Braunschweig *Germany* 52°15N 10°31E **16** B6
Braunton *U.K.* 51°7N 4°10W **13** F3
Brava *Cabo Verde* 15°0N 24°40W **52** b
Brava, Costa *Spain* 41°30N 3°0E **21** B7
Bravo del Norte, Rio → Grande,
 Rio → *N. Amer.* 25°58N 97°9W **84** J6
Brawley *U.S.A.* 32°59N 115°31W **79** N11
Bray *Ireland* 53°13N 6°7W **10** C5
Bray, Mt. *Australia* 14°0S 134°30E **62** A1
Bray, Pays de *France* 49°46N 1°26E **20** B4
Brazeau → *Canada* 52°55N 115°14W **70** C5
Brazil *U.S.A.* 39°32N 87°8W **80** F10
Brazil ■ *S. Amer.* 12°0S 50°0W **93** F9
Brazilian Highlands = Brasil,
 Planalto *Brazil* 18°0S 46°30W **90** E6
Brazo Sur → *S. Amer.* 25°21S 57°42W **94** B4
Brazos → *U.S.A.* 28°53N 95°23W **84** G7
Brazzaville *Congo* 4°9S 15°12E **54** E3
Brčko *Bos.-H.* 44°54N 18°46E **23** B8
Bré = Bray *Ireland* 53°13N 6°7W **10** C5
Breaden, L. *Australia* 25°51S 125°28E **61** E4
Breaksea Sd. *N.Z.* 45°35S 166°35E **59** F1
Bream B. *N.Z.* 35°56S 174°28E **59** A5
Bream Hd. *N.Z.* 35°51S 174°36E **59** A5
Breas *Chile* 25°29S 70°24W **94** B1
Brebes *Indonesia* 6°52S 109°3E **37** G13
Brechin *Canada* 44°32N 79°10W **82** B5
Brechin *U.K.* 56°44N 2°39W **11** E6
Brecht *Belgium* 51°21N 4°38E **15** C4
Breckenridge *Colo.,*
 U.S.A. 39°29N 106°3W **76** G10
Breckenridge *Minn.,*
 U.S.A. 46°16N 96°35W **80** B5
Breckenridge *Tex., U.S.A.* 32°45N 98°54W **84** E5
Breckland *U.K.* 52°30N 0°40E **13** E8
Brecon *U.K.* 51°57N 3°23W **13** F4
Brecon Beacons *U.K.* 51°53N 3°26W **13** F4
Brecon Beacons △ *U.K.* 51°50N 3°30W **13** F4
Breda *Neths.* 51°35N 4°45E **15** C4
Bredasdorp *S. Africa* 34°33S 20°2E **56** D3
Bree *Belgium* 51°8N 5°35E **15** C5
Bregenz *Austria* 47°30N 9°45E **16** E5
Bregman *Germany* 53°43N 8°47E **16** B5
Bremen *Germany* 53°4N 8°47E **16** B5
Bremer Bay *Australia* 34°21S 119°20E **61** F2
Bremer I. *Australia* 12°5S 136°45E **62** A2
Bremerhaven *Germany* 53°33N 8°36E **16** B5
Bremerton *U.S.A.* 47°34N 122°37W **78** C4
Brenham *U.S.A.* 30°10N 96°24W **84** F6
Brennerpass *Austria* 47°2N 11°30E **16** E6
Brent *U.K.* 51°33N 0°16W **13** F7
Brentwood *U.K.* 51°37N 0°19E **13** F8
Brentwood *Calif., U.S.A.* 37°56N 121°42W **78** H5
Brentwood *N.Y., U.S.A.* 40°47N 73°15W **83** F11
Bréscia *Italy* 45°33N 10°15E **20** D9

Breskens *Neths.* 51°23N 3°33E **15** C3
Breslau = Wrocław *Poland* 51°5N 17°5E **17** C9
Bressanone *Italy* 46°43N 11°39E **22** A4
Bressay *U.K.* 60°9N 1°6W **11** A7
Brest *Belarus* 52°10N 23°40E **17** B12
Brest *France* 48°24N 4°31W **20** B1
Brest □ *Belarus* 52°30N 26°10E **17** B13
Brest-Litovsk = Brest
 Belarus 52°10N 23°40E **17** B12
Bretagne □ *France* 48°10N 3°0W **20** B2
Breton *Canada* 53°7N 114°28W **70** C6
Breton Sd. *U.S.A.* 29°35N 89°15W **85** G10
Brett, C. *N.Z.* 35°10S 174°20E **59** A5
Brevard *U.S.A.* 35°14N 82°44W **85** D13
Breves *Brazil* 1°40S 50°29W **93** D8
Brewarrina *Australia* 30°0S 146°51E **63** E4
Brewer *U.S.A.* 44°48N 68°46W **81** C19
Brewer, Mt. *U.S.A.* 36°44N 118°28W **78** J8
Brewster *N.Y., U.S.A.* 41°24N 73°36W **83** E11
Brewster *Ohio, U.S.A.* 40°43N 81°36W **82** F3
Brewster *Wash., U.S.A.* 48°6N 119°47W **76** B4
Brewster, Kap = Kangikajik
 Greenland 70°7N 22°0W **4** B6
Brewton *U.S.A.* 31°7N 87°4W **85** F11
Breyten *S. Africa* 26°16S 30°0E **57** C5
Bria *C.A.R.* 6°30N 21°58E **54** C4
Briançon *France* 44°54N 6°39E **20** D7
Bribie I. *Australia* 27°0S 153°10E **63** D5
Bribri *Costa Rica* 9°38N 82°50W **88** E3
Bridgefield *Barbados* 13°9N 59°36W **89** g
Bridgehampton *U.S.A.* 40°56N 72°19W **83** F12
Bridgend *U.K.* 51°30N 3°34W **13** F4
Bridgend □ *U.K.* 51°36N 3°36W **13** F4
Bridgenorth *Canada* 44°23N 78°23W **82** B6
Bridgeport *Calif., U.S.A.* 38°15N 119°14W **78** G7
Bridgeport *Conn., U.S.A.* 41°11N 73°12W **83** E11
Bridgeport *N.Y., U.S.A.* 43°9N 75°58W **83** C9
Bridgeport *Nebr., U.S.A.* 41°40N 103°6W **80** E2
Bridgeport *Tex., U.S.A.* 33°13N 97°45W **84** E6
Bridger *U.S.A.* 45°18N 108°55W **76** D9
Bridgeton *U.S.A.* 39°26N 75°14W **81** F16
Bridgetown *Australia* 33°58S 116°7E **61** F2
Bridgetown *Barbados* 13°6N 59°37W **89** g
Bridgetown *Canada* 44°55N 65°18W **73** D6
Bridgewater *Australia* 42°44S 147°14E **63** G4
Bridgewater *Canada* 44°25N 64°31W **73** D7
Bridgewater *Mass.,*
 U.S.A. 41°59N 70°58W **83** E14
Bridgewater *N.Y., U.S.A.* 42°53N 75°15W **83** D9
Bridgewater, C. *Australia* 38°23S 141°23E **63** F3
Bridgnorth *U.K.* 52°32N 2°25W **13** E5
Bridgton *U.S.A.* 44°3N 70°42W **83** B14
Bridgwater *U.K.* 51°8N 2°59W **13** F5
Bridgwater B. *U.K.* 51°15N 3°15W **13** F4
Bridlington *U.K.* 54°5N 0°12W **12** C7
Bridlington B. *U.K.* 54°4N 0°10W **12** C7
Bridport *Australia* 40°59S 147°23E **63** G4
Bridport *U.K.* 50°44N 2°45W **13** G5
Brig *Switz.* 46°18N 7°59E **20** C7
Brigg *U.K.* 53°34N 0°28W **12** D7
Brigham City *U.S.A.* 41°31N 112°1W **76** F7
Bright *Australia* 36°42S 146°56E **63** F4
Brighton *Australia* 35°5S 138°30E **63** F2
Brighton *Canada* 44°2N 77°44W **82** B7
Brighton *U.K.* 50°49N 0°7W **13** G7
Brighton *Trin. & Tob.* 10°15N 61°39W **93** K15
Brightside *Canada* 45°7N 76°29W **83** A8
Brilliant *U.S.A.* 40°15N 80°39W **82** F4
Brindisi *Italy* 40°39N 17°55E **23** D7
Brinkley *U.S.A.* 34°53N 91°12W **84** D9
Brinnon *U.S.A.* 47°41N 122°54W **78** C4
Brion, Î. *Canada* 47°46N 61°26W **73** C7
Brisay *Canada* 54°26N 70°31W **73** B5
Brisbane *Australia* 27°25S 153°2E **63** D5
Brisbane → *Australia* 27°24S 153°9E **63** D5
Bristol *U.K.* 51°26N 2°35W **13** F5
Bristol *Conn., U.S.A.* 41°40N 72°57W **83** E12
Bristol *Pa., U.S.A.* 40°6N 74°51W **83** F10
Bristol *R.I., U.S.A.* 41°40N 71°16W **83** E13
Bristol *Tenn., U.S.A.* 36°36N 82°11W **85** C13
Bristol *Vt., U.S.A.* 44°8N 73°4W **83** B11
Bristol, City of □ *U.K.* 51°27N 2°36W **13** F5
Bristol B. *U.S.A.* 58°0N 160°0W **74** D8
Bristol Channel *U.K.* 51°18N 4°30W **13** F3
Bristol I. *Antarctica* 58°45S 28°0W **5** B1
Bristol L. *U.S.A.* 34°28N 115°41W **79** L11
Bristow *U.S.A.* 35°50N 96°23W **84** D6
Britain = Great Britain
 Europe 54°0N 2°15W **6** E5
British Columbia □
 Canada 55°0N 125°15W **70** C3
British Indian Ocean Terr. =
 Chagos Arch. ☑ *Ind. Oc.* 6°0S 72°0E **3** E13
British Isles *Europe* 54°0N 4°0W **14** D5
British Mts. *N. Amer.* 68°50N 140°0W **74** B12
British Virgin Is. ☑
 W. Indies 18°30N 64°30W **89** e
Brits *S. Africa* 25°37S 27°48E **57** C4
Britstown *S. Africa* 30°37S 23°30E **56** D3
Britt *Canada* 45°46N 80°34W **72** C3
Brittany = Bretagne □
 France 48°10N 3°0W **20** B2
Brive-la-Gaillarde *France* 45°10N 1°32E **20** D4
Brixen = Bressanone
 Italy 46°43N 11°39E **22** A4
Brixham *U.K.* 50°23N 3°31W **13** G4
Brno *Czechia* 49°10N 16°35E **17** D9
Broach = Bharuch *India* 21°47N 73°0E **44** D1
Broad → *U.S.A.* 34°1N 81°4W **85** D14
Broad Arrow *Australia* 30°23S 121°15E **61** F3
Broad B. *U.K.* 58°14N 6°18W **11** C2
Broad Haven *Ireland* 54°20N 9°55W **10** B2
Broad Law *U.K.* 55°30N 3°21W **11** F5
Broad Pk. = Faichan Kangri
 India 35°48N 76°34E **43** B7
Broad Sd. *Australia* 22°0S 149°45E **62** C4
Broadalbin *U.S.A.* 43°4N 74°12W **83** C10

Broadback → *Canada* 51°21N 78°52W **72** B4
Broadhurst Ra. *Australia* 22°30S 122°30E **60** D3
Broads, The *U.K.* 52°45N 1°30E **12** E9
Broadus *U.S.A.* 45°27N 105°25W **76** D11
Brochet *Canada* 57°53N 101°40E **71** B8
Brochet, L. *Canada* 58°36N 101°35W **71** B8
Brock I. *Canada* 77°52N 114°19W **69** B9
Brocken *Germany* 51°47N 10°37E **16** C6
Brockport *U.S.A.* 43°13N 77°56W **82** C7
Brockton *U.S.A.* 42°5N 71°1W **83** D13
Brockville *Canada* 44°35N 75°41W **83** B9
Brockway *Mont.,*
 U.S.A. 47°18N 105°45W **76** C11
Brockway *Pa., U.S.A.* 41°15N 78°47W **82** E6
Brocton *U.S.A.* 42°23N 79°26W **82** D5
Brodeur Pen. *Canada* 72°30N 88°10W **69** C14
Brodick *U.K.* 55°35N 5°9W **11** F3
Brodnica *Poland* 53°15N 19°25E **17** B10
Brody *Ukraine* 50°5N 25°10E **17** C13
Brogan *U.S.A.* 44°15N 117°31W **76** D5
Broken Arrow *U.S.A.* 36°3N 95°48W **84** C7
Broken Bow *Nebr.,*
 U.S.A. 41°24N 99°38W **80** E4
Broken Bow *Okla., U.S.A.* 34°2N 94°44W **84** D7
Broken Bow Lake *U.S.A.* 34°9N 94°40W **84** D7
Broken Hill *Australia* 31°58S 141°29E **63** E3
Broken Ridge *Ind. Oc.* 30°0S 94°0E **64** L1
Broken River Ra. *Australia* 21°0S 148°22E **62** b
Bromo, Gunung
 Indonesia 7°56N 112°57E **37** H15
Bromo Tengger Semeru △
 Indonesia 7°56S 112°57E **37** H15
Bromsgrove *U.K.* 52°21N 2°2W **13** E5
Brønderslev *Denmark* 57°16N 9°57E **9** H13
Bronkhorstspruit
 S. Africa 25°46S 28°45E **57** C4
Brønnøysund *Norway* 65°28N 12°14E **8** D15
Brook Park *U.S.A.* 41°23N 81°48W **82** E4
Brookhaven *U.S.A.* 31°35N 90°26W **85** F9
Brookings *Oreg., U.S.A.* 42°3N 124°17W **76** E1
Brookings *S. Dak., U.S.A.* 44°19N 96°48W **80** C6
Brooklin *Canada* 43°55N 78°55W **82** C6
Brooklyn Park *U.S.A.* 45°6N 93°23W **80** C7
Brooks *Canada* 50°35N 111°55W **70** C6
Brooks Range *U.S.A.* 68°0N 152°0W **74** B9
Brooksville *U.S.A.* 28°33N 82°23W **85** G13
Brookton *Australia* 32°22S 117°0E **61** F2
Brookville *U.S.A.* 41°10N 79°5W **82** E5
Broom, L. *U.K.* 57°55N 5°15W **11** D3
Broome *Australia* 18°0S 122°15E **60** C3
Brora *U.K.* 58°0N 3°52W **11** C5
Brora → *U.K.* 58°0N 3°51W **11** C5
Brosna → *Ireland* 53°14N 7°58W **10** C4
Brothers *U.S.A.* 43°49N 120°36W **76** E3
Brough *U.K.* 54°32N 2°18W **12** C5
Brough Hd. *U.K.* 59°8N 3°20W **11** B5
Broughton Island = Qikiqtarjuaq
 Canada 67°33N 63°0W **69** D19
Brown, L. *Australia* 31°5S 118°15E **61** F2
Brown, Pt. *Australia* 32°32S 133°50E **63** E1
Brown City *U.S.A.* 43°13N 82°59W **82** C2
Brown Willy *U.K.* 50°35N 4°37W **13** G3
Brownfield *U.S.A.* 33°11N 102°17W **84** E3
Browning *U.S.A.* 48°34N 113°1W **76** B7
Brownsville *Oreg.,*
 U.S.A. 44°24N 122°59W **76** D2
Brownsville *Pa., U.S.A.* 40°1N 79°53W **82** F5
Brownsville *Tenn.,*
 U.S.A. 35°36N 89°16W **85** D10
Brownsville *Tex., U.S.A.* 25°54N 97°30W **84** J6
Brownville *U.S.A.* 44°0N 75°59W **83** C9
Brownwood *U.S.A.* 31°43N 98°59W **84** F5
Browse I. *Australia* 14°7S 123°33E **60** B3
Bruas *Malaysia* 4°30N 100°47E **39** K3
Bruay-la-Buissière *France* 50°29N 2°33E **20** A5
Bruce, Mt. *Australia* 22°37S 118°8E **60** D2
Bruce Pen. *Canada* 45°0N 81°30W **82** A3
Bruce Peninsula △
 Canada 45°14N 81°36W **82** A3
Bruce Rock *Australia* 31°52S 118°8E **61** F2
Bruck an der Leitha
 Austria 48°1N 16°47E **17** D9
Bruck an der Mur *Austria* 47°24N 15°16E **16** E8
Brue → *U.K.* 51°13N 2°59W **13** F5
Bruges = Brugge *Belgium* 51°13N 3°13E **15** C3
Brugge *Belgium* 51°13N 3°13E **15** C3
Bruin *U.S.A.* 41°3N 79°43W **82** E5
Brûk, W. el → *Egypt* 30°15N 33°50E **48** E2
Brûlé *Canada* 53°15N 117°58W **70** C5
Brûlé, L. *Canada* 53°35N 64°4W **73** B7
Brumado *Brazil* 14°14S 41°40W **93** F10
Brumunddal *Norway* 60°53N 10°56E **8** F14
Bruneau *U.S.A.* 42°53N 115°48W **76** E6
Bruneau → *U.S.A.* 42°56N 115°57W **76** E6
Brunei = Bandar Seri Begawan
 Brunei 4°52N 115°0E **36** D5
Brunei ■ *Asia* 4°50N 115°0E **36** D5
Brunner, L. *N.Z.* 42°37S 171°27E **59** E3
Brunssum *Neths.* 50°57N 5°59E **15** D5
Brunswick = Braunschweig
 Germany 52°15N 10°31E **16** B6
Brunswick *Ga., U.S.A.* 31°10N 81°30W **85** F14
Brunswick *Maine,*
 U.S.A. 43°55N 69°58W **81** D19
Brunswick *Md., U.S.A.* 39°19N 77°38W **81** F15
Brunswick *Mo., U.S.A.* 39°26N 93°8W **80** F7
Brunswick *Ohio, U.S.A.* 41°14N 81°51W **82** E3
Brunswick, Pen. de *Chile* 53°30S 71°30W **96** G2
Brunswick B. *Australia* 15°15S 124°50E **60** C3
Brunswick Junction
 Australia 33°15S 115°50E **61** F2
Brunt Ice Shelf *Antarctica* 75°30S 25°0W **5** D2
Brus Laguna *Honduras* 15°47N 84°35W **88** C3
Brush *U.S.A.* 40°15N 103°37W **76** F12
Brushton *U.S.A.* 44°50N 74°31W **83** B10
Brusque *Brazil* 27°5S 49°0W **95** B6
Brussels *Canada* 43°44N 81°15W **82** C3
Bruthen *Australia* 37°42S 147°50E **63** F4
Bryan *Ohio, U.S.A.* 41°28N 84°33W **81** E11

Bryan Tex., U.S.A. 30°40N 96°22W 84 F6
Bryan, Mt. Australia 33°30S 139°5E 63 E2
Bryansk Russia 53°13N 34°25E 18 D4
Bryce Canyon △ U.S.A. 37°30N 112°10W 77 H7
Bryne Norway 58°44N 5°38E 9 G11
Bryson City U.S.A. 35°26N 83°27W 85 D13
Bsharri Lebanon 34°15N 36°0E 48 A5
Bū Baqarah U.A.E. 25°35N 56°25E 47 E8
Bu Craa W. Sahara 26°45N 12°50W 52 C3
Bū Ḥasā U.A.E. 23°30N 53°20E 47 F7
Bua Fiji 16°48S 178°37E 59 a
Bua Yai Thailand 15°33N 102°26E 38 E4
Buan S. Korea 35°44N 126°44E 33 G14
Buapinang Indonesia 4°40S 121°30E 37 E6
Bubi → Zimbabwe 22°20S 31°7E 57 B5
Būbiyān Kuwait 29°45N 48°15E 47 D6
Buca Fiji 16°38S 179°52E 59 a
Bucaramanga Colombia 7°0N 73°0W 92 B4
Bucasia Australia 21°2S 149°10E 62 b
Buccaneer Arch.
  Australia 16°7S 123°20E 60 C3
Buccoo Reef Trin. & Tob. 11°10N 60°51W 93 J16
Buchach Ukraine 49°5N 25°25E 17 D13
Buchan U.K. 57°32N 2°21W 11 D6
Buchan Ness U.K. 57°29N 1°46W 11 D7
Buchanan Canada 51°40N 102°45W 71 C8
Buchanan Liberia 5°57N 10°2W 52 G3
Buchanan, L. Queens.,
  Australia 21°35S 145°52E 62 C4
Buchanan, L. W. Austral.,
  Australia 25°33S 123°2E 61 E3
Buchanan, L. U.S.A. 30°45N 98°25W 84 F5
Buchanan Cr. →
  Australia 19°13S 136°33E 62 B2
Buchans Canada 48°50N 56°52W 73 C8
Bucharest = Bucureşti
  Romania 44°27N 26°10E 17 F14
Bucheon S. Korea 37°28N 126°45E 33 F14
Buchon, Pt. U.S.A. 35°15N 120°54W 78 K6
Buck Hill Falls U.S.A. 41°11N 75°16W 83 E9
Buckeye Lake U.S.A. 39°55N 82°29W 82 G2
Buckhannon U.S.A. 39°0N 80°8W 81 F13
Buckhaven U.K. 56°11N 3°3W 11 E5
Buckhorn L. Canada 44°29N 78°23W 82 B6
Buckie U.K. 57°41N 2°58W 11 D6
Buckingham Canada 45°37N 75°24W 72 C4
Buckingham U.K. 51°59N 0°57W 13 F7
Buckingham B.
  Australia 12°10S 135°40E 62 A2
Buckingham Canal India 14°0N 80°5E 45 H5
Buckinghamshire □ U.K. 51°53N 0°55W 13 F7
Buckle Hd. Australia 14°26S 127°52E 60 B4
Buckleboo Australia 32°54S 136°12E 63 E2
Buckley U.K. 53°10N 3°5W 12 D4
Buckley → Australia 20°10S 138°49E 62 C2
Bucklin U.S.A. 37°33N 99°38W 80 G4
Bucks L. U.S.A. 39°54N 121°12W 78 F5
Bucureşti Romania 44°27N 26°10E 17 F14
Bucyrus U.S.A. 40°48N 82°59W 81 E12
Budalin Myanmar 22°20N 95°10E 41 H19
Budaun India 28°5N 79°10E 43 E8
Budd Coast Antarctica 68°0S 112°0E 5 C8
Bude U.K. 50°49N 4°34W 13 G3
Budennovsk Russia 44°50N 44°10E 19 F7
Budge Budge = Baj Baj
  India 22°30N 88°5E 43 H13
Budgewoi Australia 33°13S 151°34E 63 E5
Budjala
  Dem. Rep. of the Congo 2°50N 19°40E 54 D3
Budo-Sungai Padi △
  Thailand 6°19N 101°42E 39 J3
Buellton U.S.A. 34°37N 120°12W 79 L6
Buena Esperanza
  Argentina 34°45S 65°15W 94 C2
Buena Park U.S.A. 33°52N 117°59W 79 M9
Buena Vista Colo.,
  U.S.A. 38°51N 106°8W 76 G10
Buena Vista Va., U.S.A. 37°44N 79°21W 81 G14
Buena Vista Lake Bed
  U.S.A. 35°12N 119°18W 79 K7
Buenaventura Colombia 3°53N 77°4W 92 C3
Buenaventura Mexico 29°51N 107°29W 86 B3
Buenos Aires Costa Rica 9°10N 83°20W 88 E3
Buenos Aires □ Argentina 36°30S 60°0W 94 D4
Buenos Aires, L. = General
  Carrera, L. S. Amer. 46°35S 72°0W 96 F2
Buffalo Mo., U.S.A. 37°39N 93°6W 80 G7
Buffalo N.Y., U.S.A. 42°53N 78°53W 82 D6
Buffalo Okla., U.S.A. 36°50N 99°38W 84 C5
Buffalo S. Dak., U.S.A. 45°35N 103°33W 80 C2
Buffalo Wyo., U.S.A. 44°21N 106°42W 76 D10
Buffalo → Canada 60°5N 115°5W 70 A5
Buffalo → S. Africa 28°43S 30°37E 57 C5
Buffalo → U.S.A. 36°14N 92°36W 84 C8
Buffalo Head Hills
  Canada 57°25N 115°55W 70 B5
Buffalo L. Alta., Canada 52°27N 112°54W 70 C6
Buffalo L. N.W.T.,
  Canada 60°12N 115°25W 70 A5
Buffalo Narrows Canada 55°51N 108°29W 71 B7
Buffels → S. Africa 29°36S 17°3E 56 C2
Buford U.S.A. 34°7N 83°59W 85 D12
Bug = Buh → Ukraine 46°59N 31°58E 19 E5
Bug → Poland 52°31N 21°5E 17 B11
Buga Colombia 4°0N 76°15W 92 C3
Bugel, Tanjung Indonesia 6°26S 111°3E 37 G14
Bugsuk I. Phil. 8°12N 117°18E 36 C5
Bugulma Russia 54°33N 52°48E 18 D9
Buguruslan Russia 53°39N 52°26E 18 D9
Buh → Ukraine 46°59N 31°58E 19 E5
Buhera Zimbabwe 19°18S 31°29E 57 A5
Buhl U.S.A. 42°36N 114°46W 76 E6
Builth Wells U.K. 52°9N 3°24W 13 E4
Buir Nur Mongolia 47°50N 117°42E 31 B12
Buji China 22°37N 114°5E 31 a
Bujumbura Burundi 3°16S 29°18E 54 E5
Bukachacha Russia 52°55N 116°50E 27 D12
Bukavu
  Dem. Rep. of the Congo 2°20S 28°52E 54 E5
Bukhara = Buxoro
  Uzbekistan 39°48N 64°25E 26 F7

Bukhoro = Buxoro
  Uzbekistan 39°48N 64°25E 26 F7
Bukhtarma Res. = Zaysan Köli
  Kazakhstan 48°0N 83°0E 26 E9
Bukit Bendera Malaysia 5°25N 100°15E 39 c
Bukit Mertajam Malaysia 5°22N 100°28E 39 c
Bukit Nil Malaysia 1°22N 104°12E 39 d
Bukit Tengah Malaysia 5°22N 100°28E 39 c
Bukittinggi Indonesia 0°20S 100°20E 36 E2
Bukkapatnam India 14°14N 77°46E 45 G3
Bukoba Tanzania 1°20S 31°49E 54 E6
Būl, Kuh-e Iran 30°48N 52°45E 47 D7
Bula Indonesia 3°6S 130°30E 37 E8
Bulahdelah Australia 32°23S 152°13E 63 E5
Bulan Phil. 12°40N 123°52E 37 B6
Bulawayo Zimbabwe 20°7S 28°32E 55 J5
Buldan Turkey 38°2N 28°50E 23 E13
Buldana India 20°30N 76°18E 44 D3
Buldir I. U.S.A. 52°21N 175°56E 74 E3
Bulgan Mongolia 48°45N 103°34E 30 B9
Bulgar Russia 54°57N 49°4E 18 D8
Bulgaria ■ Europe 42°35N 25°30E 23 C11
Buli, Teluk Indonesia 0°48N 128°25E 37 D7
Buliluyan, C. Phil. 8°20N 117°15E 36 C5
Bulkley → Canada 55°15N 127°40W 70 B3
Bull Shoals L. U.S.A. 36°22N 92°35W 84 C8
Bullaring → Australia 17°39S 143°56E 62 B3
Bullhead City U.S.A. 35°8N 114°32W 79 K12
Büllingen Belgium 50°25N 6°16E 15 D6
Bullock Creek Australia 17°43S 144°31E 62 B3
Bulloo → Australia 28°43S 142°30E 63 D3
Bulloo L. Australia 28°43S 142°25E 63 D3
Bulls N.Z. 40°10S 175°24E 59 D5
Bulman Australia 13°39S 134°20E 62 A1
Bulnes Chile 36°42S 72°19W 94 D1
Bulsar = Valsad India 20°40N 72°58E 44 D1
Bultfontein S. Africa 28°18S 26°10E 56 C4
Bulukumba Indonesia 5°33S 120°11E 37 F6
Bulun Russia 70°37N 127°30E 27 B13
Bumba
  Dem. Rep. of the Congo 2°13N 22°30E 54 D4
Bumbah, Khalīj Libya 32°20N 23°15E 53 B10
Bumhpa Bum Myanmar 26°51N 97°14E 41 F20
Bunaken Indonesia 1°37N 124°46E 37 D6
Bunbury Australia 33°20S 115°35E 61 F2
Bunclody Ireland 52°39N 6°40W 10 D5
Buncrana Ireland 55°8N 7°27W 10 A4
Bundaberg Australia 24°54S 152°22E 63 C5
Bundey → Australia 21°46S 135°37E 62 C2
Bundi India 25°30N 75°35E 42 G6
Bundjalung △ Australia 29°16S 153°21E 63 D5
Bundoran Ireland 54°28N 8°18W 10 B3
Bung Kan Thailand 18°23N 103°37E 38 C4
Bungay U.K. 52°27N 1°28E 13 E9
Bungil Cr. → Australia 27°5S 149°5E 63 D4
Bungle Bungle = Purnululu △
  Australia 17°20S 128°20E 60 C4
Bungo-Suidō Japan 33°0N 132°15E 29 H6
Bungotakada Japan 33°35N 131°25E 29 H5
Bunia
  Dem. Rep. of the Congo 1°35N 30°20E 54 D6
Bunji Pakistan 35°45N 74°40E 43 B6
Bunkie U.S.A. 30°57N 92°11W 84 F8
Bunnell U.S.A. 29°28N 81°16W 85 G14
Buntok Indonesia 1°40S 114°58E 36 E4
Bunya Mts. △ Australia 26°51S 151°34E 63 D5
Bunyu Indonesia 3°35N 117°50E 36 D5
Buol Indonesia 1°15N 121°32E 37 D6
Buon Brieng Vietnam 13°9N 108°12E 38 F7
Buon Ho Vietnam 12°57N 108°18E 38 F7
Buon Ma Thuot Vietnam 12°40N 108°3E 38 F7
Buong Long Cambodia 13°44N 106°59E 38 F6
Buorkhaya, Mys
  Russia 71°50N 132°40E 27 B14
Buqayq Si. Arabia 26°0N 49°45E 47 E6
Bur Acaba = Buurhakaba
  Somalia 3°12N 44°20E 49 G3
Būr Safāga Egypt 26°43N 33°57E 46 E2
Būr Sa'īd Egypt 31°16N 32°18E 53 B12
Būr Sūdân Sudan 19°32N 37°9E 53 E13
Burakin Australia 30°31S 117°10E 61 F2
Burang China 30°15N 81°10E 30 E5
Burao = Burco Somalia 9°32N 45°32E 49 F4
Burāq Syria 33°11N 36°29E 48 B5
Burathum Nepal 28°4N 84°50E 43 E11
Buraydah Si. Arabia 26°20N 43°59E 46 E4
Burco Somalia 9°32N 45°32E 49 F4
Burda India 25°50N 77°35E 42 G7
Burdekin → Australia 19°38S 147°25E 62 B4
Burdur Turkey 37°45N 30°17E 19 G5
Burdwan = Barddhaman
  India 23°14N 87°39E 43 H12
Bure Ethiopia 10°40N 37°4E 49 E2
Bure → U.K. 52°38N 1°43E 12 E9
Bureskoye Vdkhr.
  Russia 50°16N 130°20E 27 D14
Bureya → Russia 49°27N 129°30E 27 E13
Burford Canada 43°7N 80°27W 82 C4
Burgas Bulgaria 42°33N 27°29E 23 C12
Burgeo Canada 47°37N 57°38W 73 C8
Burgersdorp S. Africa 31°0S 26°20E 56 D4
Burgess, Mt. Australia 30°50S 121°5E 61 F3
Burghead U.K. 57°43N 3°30W 11 D5
Burgos Spain 42°21N 3°41W 21 A4
Burgsvik Sweden 57°3N 18°19E 9 H18
Burgundy = Bourgogne
  France 47°0N 4°50E 20 C6
Burhaniye Turkey 39°30N 26°58E 23 E12
Burhanpur India 21°18N 76°14E 44 D3
Burhi Gandak → India 25°20N 86°37E 43 G12
Burhner → India 22°43N 80°31E 43 H9
Burias I. Phil. 12°55N 123°5E 37 B6
Burica, Pta. Costa Rica 8°3N 82°51W 88 E3
Burien U.S.A. 47°28N 122°20W 78 C4
Burin Canada 47°1N 55°14W 73 C8
Buriram Thailand 15°0N 103°0E 38 E4
Burkburnett U.S.A. 34°6N 98°34W 84 D5
Burke → Australia 23°12S 139°33E 62 C2
Burke Chan. Canada 52°10N 127°30W 70 C3
Burketown Australia 17°45S 139°33E 62 B2

Burkhan Khaldun
  Mongolia 48°45N 108°40E 31 B10
Burkina Faso ■ Africa 12°0N 1°0W 52 F5
Burk's Falls Canada 45°37N 79°24W 72 C4
Burleigh Falls Canada 44°33N 78°12W 82 B6
Burley U.S.A. 42°32N 113°48W 76 E7
Burlingame U.S.A. 37°35N 122°21W 78 H4
Burlington Canada 43°18N 79°45W 82 C5
Burlington Colo.,
  U.S.A. 39°18N 102°16W 76 G12
Burlington Iowa, U.S.A. 40°49N 91°14W 80 E8
Burlington Kans., U.S.A. 38°12N 95°45W 80 F7
Burlington N.C., U.S.A. 36°6N 79°26W 85 C15
Burlington N.J., U.S.A. 40°4N 74°51W 83 F10
Burlington Vt., U.S.A. 44°29N 73°12W 83 B11
Burlington Wash.,
  U.S.A. 48°28N 122°20W 78 B4
Burlington Wis., U.S.A. 42°41N 88°17W 80 D9
Burma = Myanmar ■
  Asia 21°0N 96°30E 41 J20
Burnaby I. Canada 52°25N 131°19W 70 C2
Burnet U.S.A. 30°45N 98°14W 84 F5
Burney U.S.A. 40°53N 121°40W 76 F3
Burnham U.S.A. 40°38N 77°34W 82 F7
Burnham-on-Sea U.K. 51°14N 3°0W 13 F5
Burnie Australia 41°4S 145°56E 63 G4
Burnley U.K. 53°47N 2°14W 12 D5
Burns U.S.A. 43°35N 119°3W 76 E4
Burns Junction U.S.A. 42°47N 117°51W 76 E5
Burns Lake Canada 54°14N 125°45W 70 C3
Burnside → Canada 66°51N 108°4W 68 D10
Burnside, L. Australia 25°22S 123°0E 61 E3
Burnsville U.S.A. 44°47N 93°17W 80 C7
Burnt River Canada 44°41N 78°42W 82 B6
Burntwood → Canada 56°8N 96°34W 71 B9
Burntwood L. Canada 55°22N 100°26W 71 B8
Burqān Kuwait 29°0N 47°57E 46 D5
Burqin China 47°43N 87°0E 30 B6
Burra Australia 33°40S 138°55E 63 E2
Burray U.K. 58°51N 2°54W 11 C6
Burren △ Ireland 53°9N 9°5W 10 C2
Burren Junction Australia 30°7S 148°58E 63 E4
Burrinjuck, L. Australia 35°0S 148°36E 63 F4
Burro, Serranías del
  Mexico 28°56N 102°5W 86 B4
Burrow Hd. U.K. 54°41N 4°24W 11 G4
Burrum Coast △
  Australia 25°13S 152°36E 63 D5
Burruyacú Argentina 26°30S 64°40W 94 B3
Burry Port U.K. 51°41N 4°15W 13 F3
Bursa Turkey 40°15N 29°5E 23 D13
Burstall Canada 50°39N 109°54W 71 C7
Burton Ohio, U.S.A. 41°28N 8° 8W 82 E3
Burton S.C., U.S.A. 32°26N 80°43W 85 E14
Burton, L. Canada 54°45N 78°20W 72 B4
Burton upon Trent U.K. 52°48N 1°38W 12 E6
Buru Indonesia 3°30S 126°30E 37 E7
Burūn, Râs Egypt 31°14N 33°7E 48 D2
Burundi ■ Africa 3°15S 30°0E 54 E6
Burutu Nigeria 5°20N 5°29E 52 G7
Burwell U.S.A. 41°47N 99°8W 80 E4
Burwick U.K. 58°45N 2°58W 11 C5
Bury U.K. 53°35N 2°17W 12 D5
Bury St. Edmunds U.K. 52°15N 0°43E 13 E8
Buryatia □ Russia 53°0N 110°0E 27 D12
Busan S. Korea 35°5N 129°0E 33 G15
Busaso = Boosaaso
  Somalia 11°12N 49°18E 49 E4
Buşayrah Syria 35°9N 40°26E 46 C4
Būshehr Iran 28°55N 50°55E 47 D6
Būshehr □ Iran 28°20N 51°45E 47 D6
Bushire = Būshehr Iran 28°55N 50°55E 47 D6
Businga
  Dem. Rep. of the Congo 3°16N 20°59E 54 D4
Buşra ash Shām Syria 32°30N 36°25E 48 C5
Busselton Australia 33°42S 115°15E 61 F2
Bussol, Proliv Russia 46°30N 151°0E 27 E16
Bussum Neths. 52°16N 5°10E 15 B5
Busto Arsizio Italy 45°37N 8°51E 20 D8
Busu Djanoa
  Dem. Rep. of the Congo 1°43N 21°23E 54 D4
Busuanga I. Phil. 12°10N 120°0E 37 B6
Busungbiu Indonesia 8°16S 114°58E 37 J17
Buta Dem. Rep. of the Congo 2°50N 24°53E 54 D4
Butare Rwanda 2°31S 29°52E 54 E5
Butaritari Kiribati 3°30N 174°0E 64 G9
Bute U.K. 55°48N 5°2W 11 F3
Bute Inlet Canada 50°40N 124°53W 70 C4
Butembo
  Dem. Rep. of the Congo 0°9N 29°18E 54 D5
Butha-Buthe Lesotho 28°47S 28°14E 57 C4
Butler Mo., U.S.A. 38°16N 94°20W 80 F6
Butler Pa., U.S.A. 40°52N 79°54W 82 F5
Buton Indonesia 5°0S 122°45E 37 E6
Butte Mont., U.S.A. 46°0N 112°32W 76 C7
Butte Nebr., U.S.A. 42°58N 98°51W 80 D4
Butte Creek → U.S.A. 39°12N 121°56W 78 F5
Butterworth = Gcuwa
  S. Africa 32°20S 28°11E 57 D4
Butterworth Malaysia 5°24N 100°23E 39 c
Buttevant Ireland 52°14N 8°40W 10 D3
Buttfield, Mt. Australia 24°45S 128°9E 61 D4
Button B. Canada 58°45N 94°23W 71 B10
Buttonwillow U.S.A. 35°24N 119°28W 79 K7
Butty Hd. Australia 33°54S 121°39E 61 F3
Butuan Phil. 8°57N 125°33E 37 C7
Butung = Buton Indonesia 5°0S 122°45E 37 E6
Buturlinovka Russia 50°50N 40°35E 19 D7
Butwal Nepal 27°33N 83°31E 43 F10
Buurhakaba Somalia 3°12N 44°20E 49 G3
Buxa Duar India 26°45N 89°35E 43 F13
Buxar India 25°34N 83°58E 43 G10
Buxoro Uzbekistan 39°48N 64°25E 26 F7
Buxtehude Germany 53°28N 9°39E 16 B5
Buxton U.K. 53°16N 1°54W 12 D6
Buy Russia 58°28N 41°28E 18 C7
Buyant-Uhaa Mongolia 44°55N 110°11E 32 B6
Buyo, L. de Côte d'Ivoire 6°16N 7°10W 52 G4
Büyük Menderes →
  Turkey 37°28N 27°11E 23 F12

Büyükçekmece Turkey 41°2N 28°35E 23 D13
Buyun Shan China 40°4N 122°43E 33 D12
Buzău Romania 45°10N 26°50E 17 F14
Buzău → Romania 45°26N 27°44E 17 F14
Buzen Japan 33°35N 131°5E 29 H5
Buzi → Mozam. 19°50S 34°43E 55 H6
Būzmeyin Turkmenistan 38°3N 58°12E 47 B8
Buzuluk Russia 52°48N 52°12E 18 D9
Buzzards Bay U.S.A. 41°45N 70°37W 83 E14
Byam Martin I. Canada 75°15N 104°15W 69 B11
Byarezina → Belarus 52°33N 30°14E 17 B16
Byaroza Belarus 52°31N 24°51E 17 B13
Byblos = Jubayl Lebanon 34°5N 35°39E 48 A4
Bydgoszcz Poland 53°10N 18°0E 17 B9
Byelorussia = Belarus ■
  Europe 53°30N 27°0E 17 B14
Byers U.S.A. 39°43N 104°14W 76 G11
Byesville U.S.A. 39°58N 81°32W 82 G3
Byfield △ Australia 22°52S 150°45E 62 C5
Bykhaw Belarus 53°31N 30°14E 17 B16
Bykhov = Bykhaw
  Belarus 53°31N 30°14E 17 B16
Bylas U.S.A. 33°8N 110°7W 77 K8
Bylot Canada 58°25N 94°8W 71 B10
Bylot I. Canada 73°13N 78°34W 69 C16
Byram U.S.A. 32°11N 90°15W 85 E9
Byrd, C. Antarctica 69°38S 76°7W 5 C17
Byrock Australia 30°40S 146°27E 63 E4
Byron, C. Australia 28°43S 153°37E 63 D5
Byron Bay Australia 28°43S 153°37E 63 D5
Byrranga, Gory Russia 75°0N 100°0E 27 B11
Byrranga Mts. = Byrranga, Gory
  Russia 75°0N 100°0E 27 B11
Byske Sweden 64°57N 21°11E 8 D19
Byskeälven → Sweden 64°57N 21°13E 8 D19
Bytom Poland 50°25N 18°54E 17 C10
Bytów Poland 54°10N 17°30E 17 A9

C

C.W. McConaughy, L.
  U.S.A. 41°14N 101°40W 80 E3
Ca → Vietnam 18°45N 105°45E 38 C5
Ca Mau Vietnam 9°7N 105°8E 39 H5
Ca Mau, Mui Vietnam 8°38N 104°44E 39 H5
Ca Na Vietnam 11°20N 108°54E 39 G7
Caacupé Paraguay 25°23S 57°5W 94 B4
Caaguazú □ Paraguay 26°5S 55°31W 95 B4
Caála Angola 12°46S 15°30E 55 G3
Caamaño Sd. Canada 52°55N 129°25W 70 C3
Caazapá Paraguay 26°8S 56°19W 94 B4
Caazapá □ Paraguay 26°10S 56°0W 95 B4
Cabanatuan Phil. 15°30N 120°58E 37 A6
Cabano Canada 47°40N 68°56W 73 C6
Cabazon U.S.A. 33°55N 116°47W 79 M10
Cabedelo Brazil 7°0S 34°50W 93 E12
Cabhán, An = Cavan
  Ireland 54°0N 7°22W 10 B4
Cabildo Chile 32°30S 71°5W 94 C1
Cabimas Venezuela 10°23N 71°25W 92 A4
Cabinda Angola 5°33S 12°11E 54 F2
Cabinda □ Angola 5°0S 12°30E 54 F2
Cabinet Mts. U.S.A. 48°10N 115°50W 76 B6
Cabo Blanco Argentina 47°15N 65°47W 96 F3
Cabo Frio Brazil 22°51S 42°3W 95 A7
Cabo Pantoja Peru 1°0S 75°10W 92 D3
Cabo Pulmo → Mexico 23°20N 109°28W 86 C3
Cabo San Lucas Mexico 22°53N 109°54W 86 C3
Cabo Verde ■ Atl. Oc. 16°0N 24°0W 52 b
Cabonga, Réservoir
  Canada 47°20N 76°40W 72 C4
Cabool U.S.A. 37°7N 92°6W 80 G7
Caboolture Australia 27°5S 152°58E 63 D5
Cabora Bassa Dam = Cahora
  Bassa, Lago de Mozam. 15°20S 32°50E 55 H6
Caborca Mexico 30°37N 112°6W 86 A2
Cabot, Mt. U.S.A. 44°30N 71°25W 83 B13
Cabot Hd. Canada 45°14N 81°17W 82 A3
Cabot Str. Canada 47°15N 59°40W 73 C8
Cabra Spain 37°30N 4°28W 21 D3
Cabra I. India 7°18N 93°50E 45 L11
Cabrera Spain 39°8N 2°57E 21 C7
Cabri Canada 50°35N 108°25W 71 C7
Cabriel → Spain 39°14N 1°3W 21 C5
Caçador Brazil 26°47S 51°0W 95 B5
Caçapava do Sul Brazil 30°30S 53°30W 95 C5
Cáceres Brazil 16°5S 57°40W 92 G7
Cáceres Spain 39°26N 6°23W 21 C2
Cache Bay Canada 46°22N 80°0W 72 C4
Cache Cr. → U.S.A. 38°42N 121°42W 78 G5
Cache Creek Canada 50°48N 121°19W 70 C4
Cachi Argentina 25°5S 66°10W 94 B2
Cachimbo, Serra do Brazil 9°30S 55°30W 93 E7
Cachinal de la Sierra
  Chile 24°58S 69°32W 94 A2
Cachoeira Brazil 12°30S 39°0W 93 F11
Cachoeira do Sul Brazil 30°3S 52°53W 95 C5
Cachoeiro de Itapemirim
  Brazil 20°51S 41°7W 95 A7
Cacoal Brazil 11°32S 61°18W 92 F6
Cacólo Angola 10°9S 19°21E 54 G3
Caconda Angola 13°48S 15°8E 55 G3
Cadney Park Australia 27°55S 134°3E 63 D1
Cadomin Canada 53°2N 117°20W 70 C5
Cadotte Lake Canada 56°26N 116°23W 70 B5
Cadoux Australia 30°46S 117°7E 61 F2

Caen France 49°10N 0°22W 20 B3
Caerdydd = Cardiff U.K. 51°29N 3°10W 13 F4
Caerfyrddin = Carmarthen
  U.K. 51°52N 4°19W 13 F3
Caergybi = Holyhead
  U.K. 53°18N 4°38W 12 D3
Caernarfon U.K. 53°8N 4°16W 12 D3
Caernarfon B. U.K. 53°4N 4°40W 12 D3
Caernarvon = Caernarfon
  U.K. 53°8N 4°16W 12 D3
Caerphilly U.K. 51°35N 3°13W 13 F4
Caerphilly □ U.K. 51°37N 3°12W 13 F4
Caesarea Israel 32°30N 34°53E 48 C3
Cactité Brazil 13°50S 42°32W 93 F10
Cafayate Argentina 26°2S 66°0W 94 B2
Cafu Angola 16°30S 15°8E 56 B2
Cagayan → Phil. 8°30N 124°0E 37 C6
Cagayan de Oro Phil. 8°30N 124°40E 37 C6
Cágliari Italy 39°13N 9°7E 22 E3
Cágliari, G. di Italy 39°8N 9°11E 22 E3
Caguán → Colombia 0°8S 74°18W 92 D4
Caguas Puerto Rico 18°14N 66°2W 89 d
Caha Mts. Ireland 51°45N 9°40W 10 E2
Cahama Angola 16°17S 14°19E 56 A1
Caherciveen Ireland 51°56N 10°14W 10 E1
Cahir Ireland 52°22N 7°56W 10 D4
Cahora Bassa, Lago de
  Mozam. 15°20S 32°50E 55 H6
Cahore Pt. Ireland 52°33N 6°12W 10 D5
Cahors France 44°27N 1°27E 20 D4
Cahul Moldova 45°50N 28°15E 17 F15
Cai Bau, Dao Vietnam 21°10N 107°27E 34 G6
Cai Be Vietnam 10°20N 106°2E 39 G6
Cai Nuoc Vietnam 8°56N 105°1E 39 H5
Caia Mozam. 17°51S 35°24E 55 H7
Caianda Angola 11°2S 23°31E 54 G4
Caibarién Cuba 22°30N 79°30W 88 B4
Caicara Venezuela 7°38N 66°10W 92 B5
Caicó Brazil 6°20S 37°0W 93 E11
Caicos Is. Turks & Caicos 21°40N 71°40W 89 B5
Caicos Passage W. Indies 22°45N 72°45W 89 B5
Caiguna Australia 32°16S 125°29E 61 F4
Caird Coast Antarctica 75°0S 25°0W 5 D1
Cairn Gorm U.K. 57°7N 3°39W 11 D5
Cairngorm Mts. U.K. 57°6N 3°42W 11 D5
Cairngorms △ U.K. 57°10N 3°50N 11 D5
Cairnryan U.K. 54°59N 5°1W 11 G3
Cairns Australia 16°57S 145°45E 62 B4
Cairns L. Canada 51°42N 94°30W 71 C10
Cairo Ga., U.S.A. 30°52N 84°13W 85 F12
Cairo Ill., U.S.A. 37°0N 89°11W 80 G9
Cairo N.Y., U.S.A. 42°18N 74°0W 83 D11
Caiseal = Cashel Ireland 52°30N 7°53W 10 D4
Caisleán an Bharraigh = Castlebar
  Ireland 53°52N 9°18W 10 C2
Caithness U.K. 58°25N 3°35W 11 C5
Caithness, Ord of U.K. 58°8N 3°36W 11 C5
Caja de Muertos, I.
  Puerto Rico 17°54N 66°32W 89 d
Cajamarca Peru 7°5S 78°28W 92 E3
Cajazeiras Brazil 6°52S 38°30W 93 E11
Calabar Nigeria 4°57N 8°20E 52 H7
Calabogie Canada 45°18N 76°43W 83 A8
Calabozo Venezuela 9°0N 67°28W 92 B5
Calábria □ Italy 39°0N 16°30E 22 E7
Calahorra Spain 42°18N 1°59W 21 A5
Calais France 50°57N 1°56E 20 A4
Calais U.S.A. 45°11N 67°17W 81 C20
Calakmul △ Mexico 18°14N 89°48W 87 D7
Calalaste, Cord. de
  Argentina 25°0S 67°0W 94 B2
Calama Brazil 8°0S 62°50W 92 E6
Calama Chile 22°30S 68°55W 94 A2
Calamar Colombia 10°15N 74°55W 92 A4
Calamian Group Phil. 11°50N 119°55E 37 B5
Calamocha Spain 40°50N 1°17W 21 B5
Calang Indonesia 4°37N 95°37E 36 D1
Calanscio, Sarīr Libya 27°30N 22°30E 53 C10
Calapan Phil. 13°25N 121°7E 37 B6
Călărași Romania 44°12N 27°20E 17 F14
Calatayud Spain 41°20N 1°40W 21 B5
Calauag Phil. 13°55N 122°15E 37 B6
Calavite, C. Phil. 13°26N 120°20E 37 B6
Calbayog Phil. 12°4N 124°38E 37 B6
Calca Peru 13°22S 72°0W 92 F4
Calcasieu L. U.S.A. 29°55N 93°18W 84 G8
Calcium U.S.A. 44°1N 75°50W 83 B9
Calcutta U.S.A. 40°40N 80°34W 82 F4
Caldas da Rainha Portugal 39°24N 9°8W 21 C1
Calder → U.K. 53°44N 1°22W 12 D6
Caldera Chile 27°5S 70°55W 94 B1
Caldwell Idaho, U.S.A. 43°40N 116°41W 76 E5
Caldwell Kans., U.S.A. 37°2N 97°37W 80 G5
Caldwell Tex., U.S.A. 30°32N 96°42W 84 F6
Caledon Canada 43°51N 79°51W 82 C5
Caledon S. Africa 34°14S 19°26E 56 E2
Caledon → S. Africa 30°31S 26°5E 56 D4
Caledon B. Australia 12°45S 137°0E 62 A2
Caledonia Canada 43°7N 79°58W 82 C5
Caledonia U.S.A. 42°58N 77°51W 82 D7
Calemba Angola 16°0S 15°44E 56 B2
Calen Australia 20°56S 148°48E 62 b
Caletones Chile 34°6S 70°27W 94 C1
Calexico U.S.A. 32°40N 115°30W 79 N11
Calf of Man I. of Man 54°3N 4°48W 12 C3
Calgary Canada 51°0N 114°10W 70 C6
Calhoun U.S.A. 34°30N 84°57W 85 D12
Cali Colombia 3°25N 76°35W 92 C3
Calicut = Kozhikode
  India 11°15N 75°43E 45 J2
Cálida, Costa Spain 37°30N 1°30E 21 D5
Caliente U.S.A. 37°37N 114°31W 77 H6
California Mo., U.S.A. 38°38N 92°34W 80 F7
California Pa., U.S.A. 40°4N 79°54W 82 F5
California □ U.S.A. 37°30N 119°30W 78 H7
California, Baja, T.N. = Baja
  California □ Mexico 30°0N 115°0W 86 A1
California, Baja, T.S. = Baja
  California Sur □
  Mexico 25°50N 111°50W 86 B2

California, G. de *Mexico* 27°0N 111°0W **86** B2
California City *U.S.A.* 35°10N 117°55W **79** K9
California Hot Springs
U.S.A. 35°51N 118°41W **79** K8
Calilegua △ *Argentina* 25°36S 64°50W **94** B3
Calingasta *Argentina* 31°15S 69°30W **94** C2
Calipatria *U.S.A.* 33°8N 115°31W **79** M11
Calistoga *U.S.A.* 38°35N 122°35W **78** G4
Calitzdorp *S. Africa* 33°33S 21°42E **56** E3
Callabonna, L. *Australia* 29°40S 140°5E **63** D3
Callan *Ireland* 52°32N 7°24W **10** D4
Callander *U.K.* 56°15N 4°13W **11** E4
Callicoon *U.S.A.* 41°46N 75°3W **83** E9
Calling Lake *Canada* 55°15N 113°12W **70** B6
Calliope *Australia* 24°0S 151°16E **62** C5
Calne *U.K.* 51°26N 2°0W **13** F6
Calola *Angola* 16°25S 17°48E **56** A2
Caloundra *Australia* 26°45S 153°10E **63** D5
Calpella *U.S.A.* 39°14N 123°12W **78** F3
Calpine *U.S.A.* 39°40N 120°27W **78** F6
Calstock *Canada* 49°47N 84°9W **72** C3
Caltagirone *Italy* 37°14N 14°31E **22** F6
Caltanissetta *Italy* 37°29N 14°4E **22** F6
Calulo *Angola* 10°1S 14°56E **54** G2
Calvert → *Australia* 16°17S 137°44E **62** B2
Calvert I. *Canada* 51°30N 128°0W **70** C3
Calvert Ra. *Australia* 24°0S 122°30E **60** D3
Calvi *France* 42°34N 8°45E **20** E8
Calvià *Spain* 39°34N 2°31E **21** C7
Calvillo *Mexico* 21°51N 102°43W **86** C4
Calvinia *S. Africa* 31°28S 19°45E **56** D2
Calwa *U.S.A.* 36°42N 119°46W **78** J7
Cam → *U.K.* 52°21N 0°16E **13** E8
Cam Lam = Ba Ngoi
Vietnam 11°54N 109°10E **39** G7
Cam Pha *Vietnam* 21°7N 107°18E **34** G6
Cam Ranh *Vietnam* 11°54N 109°12E **39** G7
Cam Xuyen *Vietnam* 18°15N 106°0E **38** C6
Camabatela *Angola* 8°20S 15°26E **54** F3
Camacupa *Angola* 11°58S 17°22E **55** G3
Camagüey *Cuba* 21°20N 77°55W **88** B4
Camaná *Peru* 16°30S 72°50W **92** G4
Camanche Res. *U.S.A.* 38°14N 121°1W **78** G6
Camaquã *Brazil* 30°51S 51°49W **95** C5
Camaquã → *Brazil* 31°17S 51°47W **95** C5
Camargo *Mexico* 26°19N 98°50W **87** B5
Camarillo *U.S.A.* 34°13N 119°2W **79** L7
Camarón, C. *Honduras* 16°0N 85°5W **88** C2
Camarones *Argentina* 44°50S 65°40W **96** E3
Camas *U.S.A.* 45°35N 122°24W **78** E4
Camas Valley *U.S.A.* 43°2N 123°40W **76** E2
Camballin *Australia* 17°59S 124°12E **60** C3
Cambará *Brazil* 23°2S 50°5W **95** A5
Cambay = Khambhat
India 22°23N 72°33E **42** H5
Cambay, G. of = Khambhat, G. of
India 20°45N 72°30E **40** J8
Cambodia ■ *Asia* 12°15N 105°0E **38** F5
Camborne *U.K.* 50°12N 5°19W **13** G2
Cambrai *France* 50°11N 3°14E **20** A5
Cambria *U.S.A.* 35°34N 121°5W **78** K5
Cambrian Mts. *U.K.* 52°3N 3°57W **13** E4
Cambridge *Canada* 43°23N 80°15W **82** C4
Cambridge *Jamaica* 18°18N 77°54W **88** a
Cambridge *N.Z.* 37°54S 175°29E **59** B5
Cambridge *U.K.* 52°12N 0°8E **13** E8
Cambridge *Minn., U.S.A.* 45°34N 93°13W **80** C7
Cambridge *N.Y., U.S.A.* 43°2N 73°22W **83** C11
Cambridge *Nebr., U.S.A.* 40°17N 100°10W **80** E3
Cambridge *Ohio, U.S.A.* 40°2N 81°35W **82** F3
Cambridge Bay *Canada* 69°10N 105°0W **68** D11
Cambridge G. *Australia* 14°55S 128°15E **60** B4
Cambridge Springs *U.S.A.* 41°48N 80°4W **82** E4
Cambridgeshire □ *U.K.* 52°25N 0°7W **13** E7
Cambuci *Brazil* 21°35S 41°55W **95** A7
Cambundi-Catembo
Angola 10°10S 17°35E **54** G3
Camdeboo △ *S. Africa* 32°15S 24°44E **56** E3
Camden *Australia* 34°1S 150°43E **63** B5
Camden *Ala., U.S.A.* 31°59N 87°17W **85** F11
Camden *Ark., U.S.A.* 33°35N 92°50W **84** E8
Camden *Maine, U.S.A.* 44°13N 69°4W **81** C19
Camden *N.J., U.S.A.* 39°55N 75°7W **83** G9
Camden *N.Y., U.S.A.* 43°20N 75°45W **83** C9
Camden *S.C., U.S.A.* 34°16N 80°36W **85** D14
Camden Sd. *Australia* 15°27S 124°25E **60** C3
Camdenton *U.S.A.* 38°1N 92°45W **80** F7
Camelford *U.K.* 50°37N 4°42W **13** G3
Cameron *Ariz., U.S.A.* 35°53N 111°25W **77** J8
Cameron *La., U.S.A.* 29°48N 93°19W **84** G8
Cameron *Mo., U.S.A.* 39°44N 94°14W **80** F6
Cameron *Tex., U.S.A.* 30°51N 96°59W **84** F6
Cameron Highlands
Malaysia 4°27N 101°22E **39** K3
Cameron Hills *Canada* 59°48N 118°0W **70** B5
Cameroon ■ *Africa* 6°0N 12°30E **53** G7
Cameroun, Mt. *Cameroon* 4°13N 9°10E **54** D1
Cametá *Brazil* 2°12S 49°30W **93** D9
Camilla *U.S.A.* 31°14N 84°12W **85** F12
Caminha *Portugal* 41°50N 8°50W **21** B1
Camino *U.S.A.* 38°44N 120°41W **78** G6
Cammal *U.S.A.* 41°24N 77°28W **82** E7
Camocim *Brazil* 2°55S 40°50W **93** D10
Camooweal *Australia* 19°56S 138°7E **62** B2
Camooweal Caves △
Australia 20°1S 138°11E **62** C2
Camopi *Fr. Guiana* 3°12N 52°17W **93** C8
Camorta *India* 8°8N 93°30E **45** K11
Camp Hill *U.S.A.* 40°14N 76°55W **82** F8
Camp Nelson *U.S.A.* 36°8N 118°39W **79** J8
Camp Pendleton *U.S.A.* 33°13N 117°24W **79** M9
Camp Verde *U.S.A.* 34°34N 111°51W **77** J8
Camp Wood *U.S.A.* 29°40N 100°1W **84** G4
Campana *Argentina* 34°10S 58°55W **94** C4
Campana, I. *Chile* 48°20S 75°20W **96** F1
Campánia □ *Italy* 41°0N 14°30E **22** D6
Campas del Tuyú △
Argentina 36°17S 56°50W **94** D4
Campbell *S. Africa* 28°48S 23°44E **56** D3
Campbell *Calif., U.S.A.* 37°17N 121°57W **78** H5
Campbell *Ohio, U.S.A.* 41°5N 80°37W **82** E4
Campbell I. *Pac. Oc.* 52°30S 169°0E **64** N8
Campbell L. *Canada* 63°14N 106°55W **71** A7
Campbell Plateau *S. Ocean* 50°0S 170°0E **5** A11
Campbell River *Canada* 50°5N 125°20W **70** C3
Campbellford *Canada* 44°18N 77°48W **82** B7
Campbellsville *U.S.A.* 37°21N 85°20W **81** G11
Campbellton *Canada* 47°57N 66°43W **73** C6
Campbelltown *Australia* 34°4S 150°49E **63** E5
Campbeltown *U.K.* 55°26N 5°36W **11** F3
Campeche *Mexico* 19°51N 90°32W **87** D6
Campeche □ *Mexico* 19°0N 90°30W **87** D6
Campeche, Banco *Mexico* 22°30N 88°0W **87** C7
Campeche, Golfo de
Mexico 19°30N 93°0W **87** D6
Camperdown *Australia* 38°14S 143°9E **63** F3
Camperville *Canada* 51°59N 100°9W **71** C8
Câmpina *Romania* 45°10N 25°45E **17** F13
Campina Grande *Brazil* 7°20S 35°47W **93** E11
Campinas *Brazil* 22°50S 47°0W **95** A6
Campo de los Alisos △
Argentina 27°15S 66°0W **94** B2
Campo Grande *Brazil* 20°25S 54°40W **93** H8
Campo Maior *Brazil* 4°50S 42°12W **93** D10
Campo Mourão *Brazil* 24°3S 52°22W **95** A5
Campobasso *Italy* 41°34N 14°39E **22** D6
Campos *Brazil* 21°50S 41°20W **95** A7
Campos Belos *Brazil* 13°10S 47°3W **93** F9
Campos Novos *Brazil* 27°21S 51°50W **95** B5
Camptonville *U.S.A.* 39°27N 121°3W **78** F5
Camptown *U.S.A.* 41°44N 76°14W **83** E8
Camrose *Canada* 53°0N 112°50W **70** C6
Camsell Portage *Canada* 59°37N 109°15W **71** B7
Çan *Turkey* 40°2N 27°3E **23** D12
Can Gio *Vietnam* 10°25N 106°58E **39** G6
Can Tho *Vietnam* 10°2N 105°46E **39** G5
Canaan *U.S.A.* 42°2N 73°20W **83** D11
Canacona *India* 15°1N 74°4E **45** G2
Canada ■ *N. Amer.* 60°0N 100°0W **68** G11
Canada Abyssal Plain
Arctic 80°0N 140°0W **4** B18
Canada Basin *Arctic* 75°0N 145°0W **4** B18
Cañada de Gómez
Argentina 32°40S 61°30W **94** C3
Canadian *U.S.A.* 35°55N 100°23W **84** D4
Canadian → *U.S.A.* 35°28N 95°3W **84** D7
Canadian Shield *Canada* 53°0N 75°0W **66** D12
Canajoharie *U.S.A.* 42°54N 74°35W **83** D10
Çanakkale *Turkey* 40°8N 26°24E **23** D12
Çanakkale Boğazı
Turkey 40°17N 26°32E **23** D12
Canal Flats *Canada* 50°10N 115°48W **70** C5
Canalejas *Argentina* 35°15S 66°34W **94** D2
Canals *Argentina* 33°35S 62°53W **94** C3
Canandaigua *U.S.A.* 42°54N 77°17W **82** D7
Canandaigua L. *U.S.A.* 42°47N 77°19W **82** D7
Cananea *Mexico* 31°0N 110°18W **86** A2
Canarias, Is. *Atl. Oc.* 28°30N 16°0W **52** C2
Canaries *St. Lucia* 13°55N 61°4W **89** f
Canarreos, Arch. de los
Cuba 21°35N 81°40W **88** B3
Canary Is. = Canarias, Is.
Atl. Oc. 28°30N 16°0W **52** C2
Canaseraga *U.S.A.* 42°27N 77°45W **82** D7
Canatlán *Mexico* 24°31N 104°47W **86** C4
Canaveral, C. *U.S.A.* 28°27N 80°32W **85** G14
Canaveral △ *U.S.A.* 28°28N 80°34W **85** G14
Canavieiras *Brazil* 15°39S 39°0W **93** G11
Canberra *Australia* 35°15S 149°8E **63** F4
Canby *Calif., U.S.A.* 41°27N 120°52W **76** F3
Canby *Minn., U.S.A.* 44°43N 96°16W **80** C5
Canby *Oreg., U.S.A.* 45°16N 122°42W **78** E4
Cancún *Mexico* 21°8N 86°44W **87** C7
Candela *Argentina* 27°29S 55°44W **95** B4
Candelaria *Argentina* 27°29S 55°44W **95** B4
Candelo *Australia* 36°47S 149°43E **63** F4
Candi Dasa *Indonesia* 8°30S 115°34E **37** J18
Candia = Iraklio *Greece* 35°20N 25°12E **23** G11
Candle L. *Canada* 53°50N 105°18W **71** C7
Candlemas I. *Antarctica* 57°3S 26°40W **5** B1
Cando *U.S.A.* 48°32N 99°12W **80** A4
Canea = Chania *Greece* 35°30N 24°4E **23** G11
Canelones *Uruguay* 34°32S 56°17W **95** C4
Cangas del Narcea *Spain* 43°10N 6°32W **21** A2
Cañete *Chile* 37°50S 73°30W **94** D1
Cangnan *China* 27°30N 120°23E **35** D13
Cangshan *China* 34°50N 118°2E **33** G10
Canguaretama *Brazil* 6°20S 35°5W **93** E11
Canguçu *Brazil* 31°22S 52°43W **95** C5
Canguçu, Serra do *Brazil* 31°20S 51°58W **95** C5
Cangxi *China* 31°47N 105°59E **34** B5
Cangyuan *China* 23°12N 99°14E **34** F2
Cangzhou *China* 38°19N 116°52E **32** F9
Caniapiscau → *Canada* 56°40N 69°30W **73** A6
Caniapiscau, L. *Canada* 54°10N 69°55W **73** B6
Canicattì *Italy* 37°21N 13°51E **22** F5
Canim Lake *Canada* 51°47N 120°54W **70** C4
Canindeyu □ *Paraguay* 24°10S 55°0W **95** A5
Canisteo *U.S.A.* 42°16N 77°36W **82** D7
Canisteo → *U.S.A.* 42°7N 77°8W **82** D7
Cañitas de Felipe Pescador
Mexico 23°36N 102°43W **86** C4
Çankırı *Turkey* 40°40N 33°37E **19** F5
Canmore *Canada* 51°7N 115°18W **70** C5
Cann River *Australia* 37°35S 149°7E **63** F4
Cannanore = Kannur
India 11°53N 75°27E **45** J2
Cannanore Is. *India* 10°30N 72°30E **45** J1
Cannes *France* 43°32N 7°1E **20** E7
Canning Town = Port Canning
India 22°23N 88°40E **43** H13
Cannington *Canada* 44°20N 79°2W **82** B5
Cannock *U.K.* 52°41N 2°1W **13** E5
Cannonball → *U.S.A.* 46°26N 100°35W **80** B3
Cannondale Mt.
Australia 25°13S 148°57E **62** D4
Cannonsville Res. *U.S.A.* 42°4N 75°22W **83** D9
Cannonvale *Australia* 20°17S 148°43E **62** b
Canoas *Brazil* 29°56S 51°11W **95** B5
Canoe L. *Canada* 55°10N 108°15W **71** B7
Canon City *U.S.A.* 38°27N 105°14W **76** G11
Cañon de Río Blanco △
Mexico 18°43N 97°15W **87** D5
Canonniers Pt. *Mauritius* 20°2S 57°32E **55** d
Canora *Canada* 51°40N 102°30W **71** C8
Canowindra *Australia* 33°35S 148°38E **63** E4
Canso *Canada* 45°20N 61°0W **73** C7
Canso, Str. of *Canada* 45°37N 61°22W **73** C7
Cantabria □ *Spain* 43°10N 4°0W **21** A4
Cantabrian Mts. = Cantábrica,
Cordillera *Spain* 43°0N 5°10W **21** A3
Cantábrica, Cordillera
Spain 43°0N 5°10W **21** A3
Cantal, Plomb du *France* 45°3N 2°45E **20** D5
Canterbury *Australia* 25°23S 141°53E **62** D3
Canterbury *U.K.* 51°16N 1°6E **13** F9
Canterbury Bight *N.Z.* 44°16S 171°55E **59** F3
Canterbury Plains *N.Z.* 43°55S 171°22E **59** E3
Cantil *U.S.A.* 35°18N 117°58W **79** K9
Canton *Ga., U.S.A.* 34°14N 84°29W **85** D12
Canton *Ill., U.S.A.* 40°33N 90°2W **80** E8
Canton *Miss., U.S.A.* 32°37N 90°2W **85** E9
Canton *Mo., U.S.A.* 40°8N 91°32W **80** E8
Canton *N.Y., U.S.A.* 44°36N 75°10W **83** B9
Canton *Ohio, U.S.A.* 40°48N 81°23W **82** F3
Canton *Pa., U.S.A.* 41°39N 76°51W **82** E8
Canton *S. Dak., U.S.A.* 43°18N 96°35W **80** D6
Canton L. *U.S.A.* 36°6N 98°35W **84** C5
Canudos *Brazil* 7°13S 58°5W **92** E7
Canumã → *Brazil* 3°55S 59°10W **92** D7
Canutama *Brazil* 6°30S 64°20W **92** E6
Canutillo *U.S.A.* 31°55N 106°36W **84** L1
Canvey Island *U.K.* 51°31N 0°37E **13** F8
Canyon *U.S.A.* 34°59N 101°55W **84** D4
Canyon De Chelly △
U.S.A. 36°10N 109°20W **77** H9
Canyonlands △ *U.S.A.* 38°15N 110°0W **77** G9
Canyons of the Ancients △
U.S.A. 37°30N 108°55W **77** H9
Canyonville *U.S.A.* 42°56N 123°17W **76** E2
Cao Bang *Vietnam* 22°40N 106°15E **34** F6
Cao He → *China* 40°10N 124°32E **33** D13
Cao Lanh *Vietnam* 10°27N 105°38E **39** G5
Cao Xian *China* 34°50N 115°35E **32** G8
Caofeidian *China* 38°56N 118°32E **33** E10
Cap-aux-Meules *Canada* 47°23N 61°52W **73** C7
Cap-Chat *Canada* 49°6N 66°40W **73** C6
Cap-de-la-Madeleine
Canada 46°22N 72°31W **72** C5
Cap-Haïtien *Haiti* 19°40N 72°20W **89** C5
Cap Pt. *St. Lucia* 14°7N 60°57W **89** f
Capac *U.S.A.* 43°1N 82°56W **82** C2
Capanaparo → *Venezuela* 7°1N 67°7W **92** B5
Cape → *Australia* 20°59S 146°51E **62** C4
Cape Arid △ *Australia* 33°58S 123°13E **61** F3
Cape Barren I. *Australia* 40°25S 148°15E **63** G4
Cape Breton Highlands △
Canada 46°50N 60°40W **73** C7
Cape Breton I. *Canada* 46°0N 60°30W **73** C7
Cape Charles *U.S.A.* 37°16N 76°1W **81** G15
Cape Coast *Ghana* 5°5N 1°15W **52** G5
Cape Cod △ *U.S.A.* 41°56N 70°6W **81** E18
Cape Coral *U.S.A.* 26°33N 81°57W **85** H14
Cape Crawford *Australia* 16°41S 135°43E **62** B2
Cape Dorset = Kinngait
Canada 64°14N 76°32W **69** E16
Cape Fear → *U.S.A.* 33°53N 78°1W **85** E15
Cape Girardeau *U.S.A.* 37°19N 89°32W **80** G9
Cape Hatteras △ *U.S.A.* 35°30N 75°28W **85** D17
Cape Hillsborough △
Australia 20°54S 149°2E **62** b
Cape Lambert *Australia* 20°36S 117°11E **60** D2
Cape Le Grand △
Australia 33°54S 122°26E **61** F3
Cape Lookout △ *U.S.A.* 35°45N 76°25W **85** D16
Cape May *U.S.A.* 38°56N 74°56W **81** F16
Cape May Point *U.S.A.* 38°56N 74°58W **81** F16
Cape Melville △
Australia 14°26S 144°28E **62** A3
Cape Range △ *Australia* 22°3S 114°0E **60** D1
Cape St. George *Canada* 48°28N 59°14W **73** C8
Cape Tormentine *Canada* 46°8N 63°47W **73** C7
Cape Upstart △ *Australia* 19°45S 147°48E **62** B4
Cape Verde Is. = Cabo Verde ■
Atl. Oc. 16°0N 24°0W **52** b
Cape Vincent *U.S.A.* 44°8N 76°20W **83** B8
Cape York Peninsula
Australia 12°0S 142°30E **62** A3
Capela *Brazil* 10°30S 37°0W **93** F11
Capella *Australia* 23°2S 148°1E **62** C4
Capesterre-Belle-Eau
Guadeloupe 16°4N 61°36W **88** b
Capesterre-de-Marie-Galante
Guadeloupe 15°53N 61°14W **88** b
Capim → *Brazil* 1°40S 47°47W **93** D9
Capitan *U.S.A.* 33°35N 105°35W **77** K11
Capitán Arturo Prat
Antarctica 63°0S 61°0W **5** C17
Capitol Reef △ *U.S.A.* 38°15N 111°10W **77** G8
Capitola *U.S.A.* 36°59N 121°57W **78** J5
Capodistria = Koper
Slovenia 45°31N 13°44E **16** F7
Caporetto = Kobarid
Slovenia 46°15N 13°30E **16** E7
Capraia *Italy* 43°2N 9°50E **20** C8
Capri *Italy* 40°33N 14°14E **22** D6
Capricorn Coast
Australia 23°16S 150°49E **62** C5
Capricorn Group
Australia 23°30S 151°55E **62** C5
Capricorn Ra. *Australia* 23°20S 116°50E **60** D2
Caprivi △ *Namibia* 17°55S 22°37E **56** A4
Caprivi Strip *Namibia* 18°0S 23°0E **56** A4
Captains Flat *Australia* 35°35S 149°27E **63** F4
Capulin Volcano △
U.S.A. 36°47N 103°58W **84** C3
Caquetá → *Colombia* 1°15S 69°15W **92** D5
Car Nicobar *India* 9°10N 92°47E **45** K11

Caracal *Romania* 44°8N 24°22E **17** F13
Caracas *Venezuela* 10°30N 66°55W **92** A5
Caracol *Belize* 16°45N 89°6W **88** C2
Caracol *Mato Grosso do Sul,
Brazil* 22°18S 57°1W **94** A4
Caracol *Piauí, Brazil* 9°15S 43°22W **93** E10
Carajás *Canada* 51°40N 102°30W **71** C8
Carajás *Brazil* 6°5S 50°23W **93** E8
Carajás, Serra dos *Brazil* 6°0S 51°30W **93** E8
Carangola *Brazil* 20°44S 42°5W **95** A7
Caransebeş *Romania* 45°28N 22°18E **17** F12
Caraquet *Canada* 47°48N 64°57W **73** C6
Caratasca, L. de
Honduras 15°20N 83°40W **88** C3
Caratinga *Brazil* 19°50S 42°10W **93** G10
Caraúbas *Brazil* 5°43S 37°33W **93** E11
Caravaca de la Cruz *Spain* 38°8N 1°52W **21** C5
Caravelas *Brazil* 17°45S 39°15W **93** G11
Caraveli *Peru* 15°45S 73°25W **92** G4
Caravelle, Presqu'ile de la
Martinique 14°46N 60°48W **88** c
Caraz *Peru* 9°3S 77°47W **92** E3
Carazinho *Brazil* 28°16S 52°46W **95** B5
Carballo *Spain* 43°13N 8°41W **21** A1
Carberry *Canada* 49°50N 99°25W **71** D9
Carbó *Mexico* 29°42N 110°58W **86** B2
Carbón, L. del *Argentina* 49°35S 68°21W **96** G3
Carbonara, C. *Italy* 39°6N 9°31E **22** E3
Carbondale *Colo.,
U.S.A.* 39°24N 107°13W **76** G10
Carbondale *Ill., U.S.A.* 37°44N 89°13W **80** G9
Carbondale *Pa., U.S.A.* 41°35N 75°30W **83** E9
Carbonear *Canada* 47°42N 53°13W **73** C9
Carbónia *Italy* 39°10N 8°30E **22** E3
Carcajou *Canada* 57°47N 117°6W **70** B5
Carcarana → *Argentina* 32°27S 60°48W **94** C3
Carcasse, C. *Haiti* 18°30N 74°28W **89** C5
Carcassonne *France* 43°13N 2°20E **20** E5
Carcross *Canada* 60°13N 134°45W **70** A2
Cardamon Hills *India* 9°30N 77°15E **45** K3
Cardamom Mts. = Kravanh, Chuor
Phnum *Cambodia* 12°0N 103°32E **39** G4
Cárdenas *Cuba* 23°0N 81°30W **88** B3
Cárdenas *San Luis Potosí,
Mexico* 22°0N 99°38W **87** C5
Cárdenas *Tabasco, Mexico* 17°59N 93°22W **87** D6
Cardiff *U.K.* 51°29N 3°10W **13** F4
Cardiff □ *U.K.* 51°31N 3°12W **13** F4
Cardiff-by-the-Sea
U.S.A. 33°1N 117°17W **79** M9
Cardigan *U.K.* 52°5N 4°40W **13** E3
Cardigan B. *U.K.* 52°30N 4°30W **13** E3
Cardinal *Canada* 44°47N 75°23W **83** B9
Cardona *Uruguay* 33°53S 57°18W **94** C4
Cardston *Canada* 49°15N 113°20W **70** D6
Cardwell *Australia* 18°14S 146°2E **62** B4
Careen L. *Canada* 57°0N 108°11W **71** B7
Carei *Romania* 47°40N 22°29E **17** E12
Carey *U.S.A.* 43°19N 113°57W **76** E7
Carey, L. *Australia* 29°0S 122°15E **61** E3
Carey L. *Canada* 62°12N 102°55W **71** A8
Carhué *Argentina* 37°10S 62°50W **94** D3
Caria *Turkey* 37°20N 28°10E **23** F13
Cariacica *Brazil* 20°16S 40°25W **93** H10
Caribbean Sea *W. Indies* 15°0N 75°0W **89** D5
Cariboo Mts. *Canada* 53°0N 121°0W **70** C4
Caribou *U.S.A.* 46°52N 68°1W **81** B19
Caribou → *Man.,
Canada* 59°20N 94°44W **71** B10
Caribou → *N.W.T.,
Canada* 61°27N 125°45W **70** A3
Caribou I. *Canada* 47°22N 85°49W **72** C2
Caribou Is. *Canada* 61°55N 113°15W **70** A6
Caribou L. *Man., Canada* 59°21N 96°10W **71** B9
Caribou L. *Ont., Canada* 50°25N 89°5W **72** B2
Caribou Mts. *Canada* 59°12N 115°40W **70** B5
Caribou River △ *Canada* 59°35N 96°35W **71** B9
Carichíc *Mexico* 27°56N 107°3W **86** B3
Carinda *Australia* 30°28S 147°41E **63** E4
Carinhanha *Brazil* 14°15S 44°46W **93** F10
Carinhanha → *Brazil* 14°20S 43°47W **93** F10
Carinthia = Kärnten □
Austria 46°52N 13°30E **16** E8
Caripito *Venezuela* 10°8N 63°6W **92** A6
Carleton, Mt. *Canada* 47°23N 66°53W **73** C6
Carleton Place *Canada* 45°8N 76°9W **83** A8
Carletonville *S. Africa* 26°23S 27°22E **56** C4
Carlin *U.S.A.* 40°43N 116°7W **76** F5
Carlingford L. *U.K.* 54°3N 6°9W **10** B5
Carlini Base *Antarctica* 62°30S 58°0W **5** C18
Carlinville *U.S.A.* 39°17N 89°53W **80** F9
Carlisle *U.K.* 54°54N 2°56W **12** C5
Carlisle *U.S.A.* 40°12N 77°12W **82** F7
Carlisle B. *Barbados* 13°5N 59°37W **89** g
Carlisle I. *Australia* 20°49S 149°18E **62** b
Carlos Casares *Argentina* 35°32S 61°20W **94** D3
Carlos Tejedor *Argentina* 35°25S 62°25W **94** D3
Carlow *Ireland* 52°50N 6°56W **10** D5
Carlow □ *Ireland* 52°43N 6°50W **10** D5
Carlsbad *Calif., U.S.A.* 33°10N 117°21W **79** M9
Carlsbad *N. Mex.,
U.S.A.* 32°25N 104°14W **77** K11
Carluke *U.K.* 55°45N 3°50W **11** F5
Carlyle *Canada* 49°40N 102°20W **71** D8
Carmacks *Canada* 62°5N 136°16W **68** E4
Carman *Canada* 49°30N 98°0W **71** D9
Carmarthen *U.K.* 51°52N 4°19W **13** F3
Carmarthen B. *U.K.* 51°40N 4°30W **13** F3
Carmarthenshire □ *U.K.* 51°55N 4°13W **13** F3
Carmaux *France* 44°3N 2°10E **20** D5
Carmel *U.S.A.* 41°26N 73°41W **83** E11
Carmel, Mt. = Ha Karmel, Har
Israel 32°44N 35°3E **48** C4
Carmel-by-the-Sea
U.S.A. 36°33N 121°55W **78** J5
Carmel Valley *U.S.A.* 36°29N 121°43W **78** J5
Carmelo *Uruguay* 34°0S 58°20W **94** C4
Carmen *Paraguay* 27°13S 56°12W **95** B4

Carmen, I. *Mexico* 25°57N 111°12W **86** B2
Carmen de Patagones
Argentina 40°50S 63°0W **96** E4
Carmensa *Argentina* 35°15S 67°40W **94** D2
Carmi *Canada* 49°36N 119°8W **70** D5
Carmi *U.S.A.* 38°5N 88°10W **80** F9
Carmila *Australia* 21°55S 149°24E **62** C4
Carmona *Costa Rica* 10°0N 85°15W **88** E2
Carmona *Spain* 37°28N 5°42W **21** D3
Carn Ban *U.K.* 57°7N 4°15W **11** D4
Carn Eige *U.K.* 57°17N 5°8W **11** D3
Carnamah *Australia* 29°41S 115°53E **61** E2
Carnarvon *Australia* 24°51S 113°42E **61** D1
Carnarvon *Canada* 45°3N 78°41W **82** A6
Carnarvon *S. Africa* 30°56S 22°8E **56** E3
Carnarvon △ *Australia* 24°54S 148°2E **62** C4
Carnarvon Ra. *Queens.,
Australia* 25°15S 148°30E **62** D4
Carnarvon Ra. *W. Austral.,
Australia* 25°20S 120°45E **61** E3
Carnatic *India* 9°40N 77°50E **45** K3
Carnation *U.S.A.* 47°39N 121°55W **78** C5
Carncastle *U.K.* 54°54N 5°53W **10** B6
Carndonagh *Ireland* 55°16N 7°15W **10** A4
Carnduff *Canada* 49°10N 101°50W **71** D8
Carnegie *U.S.A.* 40°24N 80°5W **82** F4
Carnegie, L. *Australia* 26°5S 122°30E **61** E3
Carnegie Ridge *Pac. Oc.* 1°0S 87°0W **65** H19
Carney I. *Antarctica* 74°0S 121°0W **5** D14
Carnic Alps = Karnische Alpen
Europe 46°36N 13°0E **16** E7
Carniche Alpi = Karnische Alpen
Europe 46°36N 13°0E **16** E7
Carnot *C.A.R.* 4°59N 15°56E **54** D3
Carnot, C. *Australia* 34°57S 135°38E **63** E2
Carnot B. *Australia* 17°20S 122°15E **60** C3
Carnoustie *U.K.* 56°30N 2°42E **11** E6
Carnsore Pt. *Ireland* 52°10N 6°22W **10** D5
Caro *U.S.A.* 43°29N 83°24W **81** D12
Caroga Lake *U.S.A.* 43°8N 74°28W **83** C10
Carolina *Brazil* 7°10S 47°30W **93** E9
Carolina *Puerto Rico* 18°23N 65°58W **89** d
Carolina *S. Africa* 26°5S 30°6E **57** C5
Caroline I. *Kiribati* 9°58S 150°13W **65** H12
Caroline Is. *Micronesia* 8°0N 150°0E **64** G6
Caroni → *Venezuela* 8°21N 62°43W **92** B6
Caronie = Nébrodi, Monti
Italy 37°54N 14°35E **22** F6
Caroona *Australia* 31°24S 150°26E **63** E5
Carpathians *Europe* 49°30N 21°0E **17** D11
Carpați Meridionali
Romania 45°30N 25°0E **17** F13
Carpentaria, G. of *Australia* 14°0S 139°0E **62** A2
Carpentras *France* 44°3N 5°2E **20** D6
Carpi *Italy* 44°47N 10°53E **22** B4
Carpinteria *U.S.A.* 34°24N 119°31W **79** L7
Carr Boyd Ra. *Australia* 16°15S 128°35E **60** C4
Carra, L. *Ireland* 53°41N 9°14W **10** C2
Carrabelle *U.S.A.* 29°51N 84°40W **85** G12
Carraig Mhachaire Rois =
Carrickmacross *Ireland* 53°59N 6°43W **10** C5
Carraig na Siúire =
Carrick-on-Suir *Ireland* 52°21N 7°24W **10** D4
Carranya ⌖ *Australia* 19°13S 127°46E **60** C4
Carrara *Italy* 44°5N 10°6E **20** D9
Carrauntoohill *Ireland* 52°0N 9°45W **10** D2
Carrick-on-Shannon
Ireland 53°57N 8°7W **10** C3
Carrick-on-Suir *Ireland* 52°21N 7°24W **10** D4
Carrickfergus *U.K.* 54°43N 5°49W **10** B6
Carrickmacross *Ireland* 53°59N 6°43W **10** C5
Carrieton *Australia* 32°25S 138°31E **63** E2
Carrigaline *Ireland* 51°48N 8°23W **10** E3
Carrillo *Mexico* 26°54N 103°55W **86** B4
Carrington *U.S.A.* 47°27N 99°8W **80** B4
Carrizal Bajo *Chile* 28°5S 71°20W **94** B1
Carrizalillo *Chile* 29°5S 71°30W **94** B1
Carrizo Cr. → *U.S.A.* 36°55N 103°55W **77** H12
Carrizo Plain △ *U.S.A.* 35°11N 119°47W **78** K7
Carrizo Springs *U.S.A.* 28°31N 99°52W **84** G5
Carrizozo *U.S.A.* 33°38N 105°53W **77** K11
Carroll *U.S.A.* 42°4N 94°52W **80** D6
Carrollton *Ga., U.S.A.* 33°35N 85°5W **85** D12
Carrollton *Ill., U.S.A.* 39°18N 90°24W **80** F8
Carrollton *Ky., U.S.A.* 38°41N 85°11W **81** F11
Carrollton *Mo., U.S.A.* 39°22N 93°30W **80** F7
Carrollton *Ohio, U.S.A.* 40°34N 81°5W **82** F3
Carron → *U.K.* 57°53N 4°22W **11** D4
Carron, L. *U.K.* 57°22N 5°35W **11** D3
Carrot → *Canada* 53°50N 101°17W **71** C8
Carrot River *Canada* 53°17N 103°35W **71** C8
Carruthers *Canada* 52°52N 109°16W **71** C7
Carson *Calif., U.S.A.* 33°49N 118°16W **79** M8
Carson *N. Dak., U.S.A.* 46°25N 101°34W **80** B3
Carson → *U.S.A.* 39°45N 118°40W **78** F8
Carson City *U.S.A.* 39°10N 119°46W **78** F7
Carson Sink *U.S.A.* 39°50N 118°25W **76** G4
Cartagena *Colombia* 10°25N 75°33W **92** A3
Cartagena *Spain* 37°38N 0°59W **21** D5
Cartago *Colombia* 4°45N 75°55W **92** C3
Cartago *Costa Rica* 9°50N 83°55W **88** E3
Carter Bar *U.K.* 55°21N 2°29W **11** F6
Cartersville *U.S.A.* 34°10N 84°48W **85** D12
Carterton *N.Z.* 41°2S 175°31E **59** D5
Carthage *Tunisia* 36°52N 10°20E **22** F4
Carthage *Ill., U.S.A.* 40°25N 91°8W **80** E8
Carthage *Mo., U.S.A.* 37°11N 94°19W **80** G6
Carthage *N.Y., U.S.A.* 43°59N 75°37W **83** C9
Carthage *Tex., U.S.A.* 32°9N 94°20W **84** E7
Cartier I. *Australia* 12°31S 123°29E **60** B3
Cartwright *Canada* 53°41N 56°58W **73** B8
Caruaru *Brazil* 8°15S 35°55W **93** E11
Carúpano *Venezuela* 10°39N 63°15W **92** A6
Caruthersville *U.S.A.* 36°11N 89°39W **80** G9
Carvoeiro *Brazil* 1°30S 61°59W **92** D6
Carvoeiro, C. *Portugal* 39°21N 9°24W **21** C1
Cary *U.S.A.* 35°47N 78°46W **85** D15
Cas-gwent = Chepstow
U.K. 51°38N 2°41W **13** F5

Casa de Piedra *Argentina* 38°5S 67°28W **94** D2
Casa de Piedra, Embalse
Argentina 38°5S 67°32W **94** D2
Casa Grande *U.S.A.* 32°53N 111°45W **77** K8
Casa Nova *Brazil* 9°25S 41°5W **93** E10
Casablanca *Chile* 33°20S 71°25W **94** C1
Casablanca *Morocco* 33°36N 7°36W **52** B4
Cascada de Basaseachic △
Mexico 28°9N 108°15W **86** B3
Cascade *Seychelles* 4°39S 55°29E **55** b
Cascade *Idaho, U.S.A.* 44°31N 116°2W **76** D5
Cascade *Mont., U.S.A.* 47°16N 111°42W **76** C8
Cascade Locks *U.S.A.* 45°40N 121°54W **78** E5
Cascade Ra. *U.S.A.* 47°0N 121°30W **78** D5
Cascade Res. *U.S.A.* 44°32N 116°3W **76** D5
Cascades, Pte. des *Réunion* 21°9S 55°51E **55** c
Cascais *Portugal* 38°41N 9°25W **21** C1
Cascavel *Brazil* 24°57S 53°28W **95** A5
Cáscina *Italy* 43°41N 10°33E **22** C4
Casco B. *U.S.A.* 43°45N 70°0W **81** D19
Caserta *Italy* 41°4N 14°20E **22** D6
Casey *Antarctica* 66°0S 76°0E **5** C8
Caseyr, Raas = Asir, Ras
Somalia 11°55N 51°10E **49** E5
Cashel *Ireland* 52°30N 7°53W **10** D4
Casiguran *Phil.* 16°22N 122°7E **37** A6
Casilda *Argentina* 33°10S 61°10W **94** C3
Casino *Australia* 28°52S 153°3E **63** D5
Casiquiare → *Venezuela* 2°1N 67°7W **92** C5
Casma *Peru* 9°30S 78°20W **92** E3
Casmalia *U.S.A.* 34°50N 120°32W **79** L6
Casnewydd = Newport
U.K. 51°35N 3°0W **13** F5
Caspe *Spain* 41°14N 0°1W **21** B5
Casper *U.S.A.* 42°51N 106°19W **76** E10
Caspian Depression *Eurasia* 47°0N 48°0E **19** E8
Caspian Sea *Eurasia* 43°0N 50°0E **19** F9
Cass City *U.S.A.* 43°36N 83°10W **82** C1
Cass Lake *U.S.A.* 47°23N 94°37W **80** B6
Cassadaga *U.S.A.* 42°20N 79°19W **82** D5
Casselman *Canada* 45°19N 75°5W **83** A9
Casselton *U.S.A.* 46°54N 97°13W **80** B5
Cassiar Mts. *Canada* 59°30N 130°30W **70** B2
Cassino *Italy* 41°30N 13°49E **22** D5
Cassville *U.S.A.* 36°41N 93°52W **80** G7
Castaic *U.S.A.* 34°30N 118°38W **79** L8
Castalia *U.S.A.* 41°24N 82°49W **82** E2
Castanhal *Brazil* 1°18S 47°55W **93** D9
Castara *Trin. & Tob.* 11°17N 60°42W **93** J16
Casteddu = Cágliari *Italy* 39°13N 9°7E **22** E3
Castell-Nedd = Neath
U.K. 51°39N 3°48W **13** F4
Castellammare di Stábia
Italy 40°42N 14°29E **22** D6
Castelli *Argentina* 36°7S 57°47W **94** D4
Castelló de la Plana *Spain* 39°58N 0°3W **21** C5
Castelo *Brazil* 20°33S 41°14W **95** A7
Castelo Branco *Portugal* 39°50N 7°31W **21** C2
Castelsarrasin *France* 44°2N 1°7E **20** E4
Castelvetrano *Italy* 37°41N 12°47E **22** F5
Casterton *Australia* 37°30S 141°30E **63** F3
Castile *U.S.A.* 42°38N 78°3W **82** D6
Castilla-La Mancha □
Spain 39°30N 3°30W **21** C4
Castilla y Leon □ *Spain* 42°0N 5°0W **21** B3
Castillos *Uruguay* 34°12S 53°52W **95** C5
Castle Dale *U.S.A.* 39°13N 111°1W **76** G8
Castle Douglas *U.K.* 54°56N 3°56W **11** G5
Castle Rock *Colo.,*
U.S.A. 39°22N 104°51W **76** G11
Castle Rock *Wash.,*
U.S.A. 46°17N 122°54W **78** D4
Castlebar *Ireland* 53°52N 9°18W **10** C2
Castlebay *U.K.* 56°57N 7°31W **11** E1
Castleblayney *Ireland* 54°7N 6°44W **10** B5
Castlecomer *Ireland* 52°48N 7°14W **10** D4
Castlederg *U.K.* 54°42N 7°36W **10** B4
Castleford *U.K.* 53°43N 1°21W **12** D6
Castlegar *Canada* 49°20N 117°40W **70** D5
Castleisland *Ireland* 52°14N 9°28W **10** D2
Castlemaine *Australia* 37°2S 144°12E **63** F3
Castlemaine *Ireland* 52°10N 9°42W **10** D2
Castlepollard *Ireland* 53°41N 7°19W **10** C4
Castlerea *Ireland* 53°46N 8°29W **10** C3
Castlereagh → *Australia* 30°12S 147°32E **63** E4
Castlereagh B. *Australia* 12°10S 135°10E **62** A2
Castleton *U.S.A.* 43°37N 73°11W **83** C11
Castleton-on-Hudson
U.S.A. 42°31N 73°45W **83** D11
Castletown *I. of Man* 54°5N 4°38W **12** C3
Castletown Bearhaven
Ireland 51°39N 9°55W **10** E2
Castor *Canada* 52°15N 111°50W **70** C6
Castor → *Canada* 53°24N 78°58W **72** B4
Castorland *U.S.A.* 43°53N 75°31W **83** C9
Castres *France* 43°37N 2°13E **20** E5
Castricum *Neths.* 52°33N 4°40E **15** B4
Castries *St. Lucia* 14°2N 60°58W **89** f
Castro *Brazil* 24°45S 50°0W **95** A6
Castro *Chile* 42°30S 73°50W **96** E2
Castro Alves *Brazil* 12°46S 39°33W **93** F11
Castro Valley *U.S.A.* 37°41N 122°5W **78** H4
Castroville *U.S.A.* 36°46N 121°45W **78** J5
Castuera *Spain* 38°43N 5°37W **21** C3
Cat Ba, Dao *Vietnam* 20°50N 107°0E **38** B6
Cat Ba △ *Vietnam* 20°47N 107°3E **38** B6
Cat I. *Bahamas* 24°30N 75°30W **89** B4
Cat L. *Canada* 51°40N 91°50W **72** B1
Cat Tien △ *Vietnam* 11°30N 107°30E **39** G6
Cat Lake *Canada* 51°40N 91°50W **72** B1
Cat Tien △ *Vietnam* 11°30N 107°30E **39** G6
Catacamas *Honduras* 14°54N 85°56W **88** D2
Cataguases *Brazil* 21°23S 42°39W **95** A7
Catalão *Brazil* 18°10S 47°57W **93** G9
Çatalca *Turkey* 41°8N 28°27E **23** D13
Catalina *Canada* 48°31N 53°4W **73** C9
Catalina *Chile* 25°13S 69°43W **94** B2
Catalina *U.S.A.* 32°30N 110°50W **77** K8
Catalonia = Cataluña □
Spain 41°40N 1°15E **21** B6
Cataluña □ *Spain* 41°40N 1°15E **21** B6

Catamarca *Argentina* 28°30S 65°50W **94** B2
Catamarca □ *Argentina* 27°0S 65°50W **94** B2
Catanduanes □ *Phil.* 13°50N 124°20E **37** B6
Catanduva *Brazil* 21°5S 48°58W **95** A6
Catánia *Italy* 37°30N 15°6E **22** F6
Catanzaro *Italy* 38°54N 16°35E **22** E7
Catarman *Phil.* 12°28N 124°35E **37** B6
Catatumbo-Bari △
Colombia 9°3N 73°12W **89** E5
Catchacoma *Canada* 44°44N 78°19W **82** B6
Cateel *Phil.* 7°47N 126°24E **37** C7
Catembe *Mozam.* 26°0S 32°33E **57** C5
Caterham *U.K.* 51°15N 0°4W **13** F7
Cathair na Mart = Westport
Ireland 53°48N 9°31W **10** C2
Cathcart *S. Africa* 32°18S 27°10E **56** D4
Cathedral City *U.S.A.* 33°47N 116°28W **79** M10
Cathlamet *U.S.A.* 46°12N 123°23W **78** D3
Catlettsburg *U.S.A.* 38°25N 82°36W **81** F12
Catoche, C. *Mexico* 21°35N 87°5W **87** C7
Catrilo *Argentina* 36°26S 63°24W **94** D3
Catrimani *Brazil* 0°27N 61°41W **92** C6
Catrimani → *Brazil* 0°28N 61°44W **92** C6
Catskill *U.S.A.* 42°14N 73°52W **83** D11
Catskill △ *U.S.A.* 42°8N 74°39W **83** D10
Catskill Mts. *U.S.A.* 42°10N 74°25W **83** D10
Catt, Mt. *Australia* 13°49S 134°23E **62** A1
Cattaraugus *U.S.A.* 42°20N 78°52W **82** D6
Catterick *U.K.* 54°23N 1°37W **12** C6
Catuala *Angola* 16°25S 19°2E **56** A2
Catuane *Mozam.* 26°48S 32°18E **57** C5
Caubvick, Mt. = Iberville, Mt. d'
Canada 58°50N 63°50W **69** F19
Cauca → *Colombia* 8°54N 74°28W **92** B4
Caucaia *Brazil* 3°40S 38°35W **93** D11
Caucasus Mountains
Eurasia 42°50N 44°0E **19** F7
Caucete *Argentina* 31°38S 68°20W **94** C2
Caungula *Angola* 8°26S 18°38E **54** F3
Cauquenes *Chile* 36°0S 72°22W **94** D1
Caura → *Venezuela* 7°38N 64°53W **92** B6
Causapscal *Canada* 48°19N 67°12W **73** C6
Cauvery → *India* 11°9N 78°52E **45** J4
Caux, Pays de *France* 49°38N 0°35E **20** B4
Cavalier *U.S.A.* 48°48N 97°37W **80** A5
Cavan *Ireland* 54°0N 7°22W **10** B4
Cavan □ *Ireland* 54°1N 7°16W **10** C4
Cave Creek *U.S.A.* 33°50N 111°57W **77** K8
Cavendish *Australia* 37°31S 142°2E **63** F3
Caviana, I. *Brazil* 0°10N 50°10W **93** C8
Cawndilla L. *Australia* 32°30S 142°15E **63** E3
Cawnpore = Kanpur
India 26°28N 80°20E **43** F9
Caxias *Brazil* 4°55S 43°20W **93** D10
Caxias do Sul *Brazil* 29°10S 51°10W **95** B5
Cay Sal Bank *Bahamas* 23°45N 80°0W **88** B4
Cayambe *Ecuador* 0°3N 78°8W **92** C3
Cayenne *Fr. Guiana* 5°5N 52°18W **93** B8
Cayey *Puerto Rico* 18°7N 66°10W **89** d
Cayman Brac *Cayman Is.* 19°43N 79°49W **88** C4
Cayman Is. ☑ *W. Indies* 19°40N 80°30W **88** C3
Cayman Trench *Caribbean* 17°0N 83°0W **66** H11
Cayuga *Canada* 42°59N 79°50W **82** D5
Cayuga *U.S.A.* 42°54N 76°44W **83** D8
Cayuga Heights *U.S.A.* 42°27N 76°29W **83** D8
Cayuga L. *U.S.A.* 42°41N 76°41W **83** D8
Cazenovia *U.S.A.* 42°56N 75°51W **83** D9
Cazombo *Angola* 11°54S 22°56E **55** G4
Ceadır-Lunga *Moldova* 46°3N 28°51E **17** E15
Ceanannus Mor = Kells
Ireland 53°44N 6°53W **10** C5
Ceará = Fortaleza *Brazil* 3°45S 38°35W **93** D11
Ceará □ *Brazil* 5°0S 40°0W **93** E11
Ceará-Mirim *Brazil* 5°38S 35°25W **93** E11
Ceatharlach = Carlow
Ireland 52°50N 6°56W **10** D5
Cébaco, I. de *Panama* 7°33N 81°9W **88** E3
Cebollar *Argentina* 29°10S 66°35W **94** B2
Cebu *Phil.* 10°18N 123°54E **37** B6
Cecil Plains *Australia* 27°30S 151°11E **63** D5
Cedar → *U.S.A.* 41°17N 91°21W **80** E8
Cedar City *U.S.A.* 37°41N 113°4W **77** H7
Cedar Creek Res. *U.S.A.* 32°11N 96°4W **84** E6
Cedar Falls *Iowa, U.S.A.* 42°32N 92°27W **80** D7
Cedar Falls *Wash.,*
U.S.A. 47°25N 121°45W **78** C5
Cedar Key *U.S.A.* 29°8N 83°2W **85** G13
Cedar L. *Canada* 53°10N 100°0W **71** C9
Cedar Park *U.S.A.* 30°30N 97°49W **84** F6
Cedar Rapids *U.S.A.* 41°59N 91°40W **80** E9
Cedartown *U.S.A.* 34°1N 85°15W **85** D12
Cedarvale *Canada* 55°1N 128°22W **70** B3
Cedarville *S. Africa* 30°23S 29°3E **57** D4
Cedral *Mexico* 23°50N 100°45W **86** C4
Cedro *Brazil* 6°34S 39°3W **93** E11
Cedros, I. *Mexico* 28°12N 115°15W **86** B1
Cedros B. *Trin. & Tob.* 10°16N 61°54W **93** K15
Ceduna *Australia* 32°7S 133°46E **63** E1
Ceel Gaal *Somalia* 10°58N 50°20E **49** E5
Ceel Waaq *Kenya* 2°9N 40°56E **54** D8
Ceeldheere *Somalia* 3°50N 47°8E **49** G4
Ceerigaabo *Somalia* 10°35N 47°20E **49** E4
Cefalù *Italy* 38°2N 14°1E **22** E6
Cegléd *Hungary* 47°11N 19°47E **17** E10
Ceheng *China* 24°58N 105°48E **34** E5
Cekik *Indonesia* 8°12S 114°27E **37** J17
Celaque △ *Honduras* 14°30N 88°43W **88** D2
Celaya *Mexico* 20°31N 100°37W **86** C4
Celbridge *Ireland* 53°20N 6°32W **10** C5
Celebes = Sulawesi
Indonesia 2°0S 120°0E **37** E6
Celebes Sea *Indonesia* 3°0N 123°0E **37** D6
Celina *U.S.A.* 40°33N 84°35W **81** E11
Celje *Slovenia* 46°16N 15°18E **16** E8
Celle *Germany* 52°37N 10°4E **16** B6
Celtic Sea *Atl. Oc.* 50°9N 9°34W **14** F2
Cenderawasih, Teluk
Indonesia 3°0S 135°20E **37** E9
Cengong *China* 27°13N 108°44E **34** D7

Centennial *U.S.A.* 39°34N 104°52W **76** G11
Center *N. Dak., U.S.A.* 47°7N 101°18W **80** B3
Center *Tex., U.S.A.* 31°48N 94°11W **84** F7
Centerburg *U.S.A.* 40°18N 82°42W **82** F2
Centerville *Calif., U.S.A.* 36°44N 119°30W **78** J7
Centerville *Iowa, U.S.A.* 40°44N 92°52W **80** E7
Centerville *Pa., U.S.A.* 40°3N 79°59W **82** F5
Centerville *Tenn., U.S.A.* 35°47N 87°28W **85** D11
Centerville *Tex., U.S.A.* 31°16N 95°59W **84** F7
Central = Tsentralnyy □
Russia 52°0N 40°0E **26** D4
Central □ *Botswana* 22°0S 26°30E **56** B4
Central, Cordillera *Colombia* 5°0N 75°0W **92** C4
Central, Cordillera
Costa Rica 10°10N 84°5W **88** D3
Central, Cordillera
Dom. Rep. 19°15N 71°0W **89** C5
Central, Cordillera
Puerto Rico 18°8N 66°35W **89** d
Central African Rep. ■
Africa 7°0N 20°0E **53** G9
Central America *America* 12°0N 85°0W **66** H11
Central Australia ۞
Australia 22°30S 128°30E **60** D4
Central Bedfordshire □
U.K. 52°5N 0°20W **13** E7
Central Butte *Canada* 50°48N 106°31W **71** C7
Central City *Colo.,*
U.S.A. 39°48N 105°31W **76** G11
Central City *Ky., U.S.A.* 37°18N 87°7W **80** G10
Central City *Nebr., U.S.A.* 41°7N 98°0W **80** E4
Central Desert ۞
Australia 19°56S 130°46E **60** C5
Central Japan Int. ✈ (NGO)
Japan 34°53N 136°45E **29** G8
Central Kalahari ۞
Botswana 22°36S 23°58E **56** B3
Central Makran Range
Pakistan 26°30N 64°15E **40** F4
Central Pacific Basin
Pac. Oc. 8°0N 175°0W **64** G10
Central Patricia *Canada* 51°30N 90°9W **72** B1
Central Point *U.S.A.* 42°23N 122°55W **76** E2
Central Russian Uplands
Europe 54°0N 36°0E **6** E13
Central Siberian Plateau
Russia 65°0N 105°0E **24** B12
Central Square *U.S.A.* 43°17N 76°9W **83** C8
Centralia *Canada* 43°17N 81°28W **82** C3
Centralia *Ill., U.S.A.* 38°32N 89°8W **80** F9
Centralia *Mo., U.S.A.* 39°13N 92°8W **80** F7
Centralia *Wash., U.S.A.* 46°43N 122°58W **78** D4
Centre de Flacq *Mauritius* 20°12S 57°43E **55** d
Centreville *N.Y., U.S.A.* 42°28N 78°14W **82** D6
Centreville *Pa., U.S.A.* 41°44N 79°45W **82** E5
Cenxi *China* 22°57N 110°57E **35** F8
Cephalonia = Kefalonia
Greece 38°15N 20°30E **23** E9
Cepu *Indonesia* 7°9S 111°35E **37** G14
Ceram = Seram *Indonesia* 3°10S 129°0E **37** E7
Ceram Sea = Seram Sea
Indonesia 2°30S 128°30E **37** E7
Ceredigion □ *U.K.* 52°16N 4°15W **13** E3
Ceres *Argentina* 29°55S 61°55W **94** B3
Ceres *S. Africa* 33°21S 19°18E **56** D2
Ceres *U.S.A.* 37°35N 120°57W **78** H6
Cerf *Seychelles* 4°38S 55°40E **55** b
Cerignola *Italy* 41°17N 15°53E **22** D6
Cerigo = Kythira *Greece* 36°8N 23°0E **23** F10
Çerkezköy *Turkey* 41°17N 28°0E **23** D12
Cerralvo, I. *Mexico* 24°15N 109°55W **86** C3
Cerritos *Mexico* 22°25N 100°16W **86** C4
Cerro Chato *Uruguay* 33°6S 55°8W **95** C4
Cerro Cofre de Perote △
Mexico 19°29N 97°3W **87** D5
Cerro Corá △ *Paraguay* 22°35S 56°2W **95** A4
Cerro de Pasco *Peru* 10°45S 76°10W **92** F3
Cerro el Copey △
Venezuela 10°59N 63°53W **89** D7
Cerro Hoya △ *Panama* 7°17N 80°45W **88** E3
Cerro Saroche △
Venezuela 10°8N 69°33W **89** D6
Cerventes *Australia* 30°31S 115°3E **61** F2
Cervera *Spain* 41°40N 1°16E **21** B6
Cesena *Italy* 44°8N 12°15E **22** B5
Cēsis *Latvia* 57°18N 25°15E **9** H21
Česká Rep. = Czechia ■
Europe 50°0N 15°0E **16** D8
České Budějovice *Czechia* 48°55N 14°25E **16** D8
Českomoravská Vrchovina
Czechia 49°30N 15°40E **16** D8
Çeşme *Turkey* 38°20N 26°23E **23** E12
Cessnock *Australia* 32°50S 151°21E **63** E5
Cetinje *Montenegro* 42°23N 18°59E **23** C8
Cetraro *Italy* 39°31N 15°55E **22** E6
Ceuta *N. Afr.* 35°52N 5°18W **21** E3
Cévennes *France* 44°10N 3°50E **20** D5
Ceyhan *Turkey* 37°4N 35°47E **46** B2
Ceylanpınar *Turkey* 36°50N 40°2E **46** B4
Ceylon = Sri Lanka ■ *Asia* 7°30N 80°50E **45** L5
Cha-am *Thailand* 12°48N 99°58E **38** F2
Chacabuco *Argentina* 34°40S 60°27W **94** C3
Chachapoyas *Peru* 6°15S 77°50W **92** E3
Chachoengsao *Thailand* 13°42N 101°5E **38** F3
Chachran *Pakistan* 28°55N 70°30E **42** E4
Chachro *Pakistan* 25°5N 70°15E **42** G4
Chaco □ *Argentina* 26°30S 61°0W **94** B3
Chaco □ *Paraguay* 26°0S 60°0W **94** A4
Chaco → *Argentina* 27°0S 59°30W **94** B4
Chaco △ *Argentina* 27°0S 59°30W **94** B4
Chaco Austral *S. Amer.* 27°0S 61°30W **96** B4
Chaco Boreal *S. Amer.* 22°0S 60°0W **92** H6
Chaco Central *S. Amer.* 24°0S 61°0W **96** A4
Chaco Culture △ *U.S.A.* 36°3N 107°58W **77** H10
Chacon, C. *U.S.A.* 54°42N 132°0W **70** C2
Chad ■ *Africa* 15°0N 17°15E **53** F8
Chad, L. = Tchad, L. *Chad* 13°30N 14°30E **53** F8
Chadileuvú → *Argentina* 37°46S 66°0W **94** D2
Chadron *U.S.A.* 42°50N 103°0W **80** D2
Chadyr-Lunga = Ceadır-Lunga
Moldova 46°3N 28°51E **17** E15

Chae Hom *Thailand* 18°43N 99°35E **38** C2
Chae Son △ *Thailand* 18°42N 99°20E **38** C2
Chaem → *Thailand* 18°11N 98°38E **38** C2
Chaeryŏng *N. Korea* 38°24N 125°36E **33** E13
Chagai Hills = Chāh Gay Hills
Afghan. 29°30N 64°0E **40** E3
Chagda *Russia* 58°45N 130°38E **27** D14
Chaghcharān *Afghan.* 34°31N 65°15E **40** B4
Chagos Arch. ☑ *Ind. Oc.* 6°0S 72°0E **3** E13
Chagres △ *Panama* 9°33N 79°37W **88** E4
Chaguanas *Trin. & Tob.* 10°30N 61°26W **93** K15
Chāh Ākhvor *Iran* 32°41N 59°40E **47** C8
Chāh Bahar *Iran* 25°20N 60°40E **47** E9
Chāh-e Kavīr *Iran* 34°29N 56°52E **47** C8
Chāhār Borjak *Afghan.* 30°17N 62°3E **40** D3
Ch'ang Chiang = Chang Jiang →
China 31°48N 121°10E **35** B13
Chang Jiang → *China* 31°48N 121°10E **35** B13
Changan *China* 22°48N 113°48E **35** a
Changanacheri *India* 9°25N 76°31E **45** K3
Changanassery = Changanacheri
India 9°25N 76°31E **45** K3
Changane → *Mozam.* 24°30S 33°30E **57** B5
Changbai *China* 41°25N 128°5E **33** D15
Changbai Shan *China* 42°20N 129°0E **33** C15
Changchiak'ou = Zhangjiakou
China 40°48N 114°55E **32** D8
Ch'angchou = Changzhou
China 31°47N 119°58E **35** B12
Changchun *China* 43°57N 125°17E **33** C13
Changchunling *China* 45°18N 125°27E **33** B13
Changde *China* 29°4N 111°35E **35** C8
Changdo-ri *N. Korea* 38°30N 127°40E **33** E14
Changfeng *China* 32°28N 117°10E **35** A11
Changge *China* 34°13N 113°46E **32** G7
Changhua *China* 30°12N 119°12E **35** B12
Changhua *Taiwan* 24°2N 120°30E **35** E13
Changhŭngni *N. Korea* 40°24N 128°19E **33** D15
Changji *China* 44°1N 87°19E **30** C6
Changjiang *China* 19°20N 108°55E **38** C7
Changjiang Shuiku
China 22°29N 113°27E **31** a
Changjin *N. Korea* 40°23N 127°15E **33** D14
Changjin-ho *N. Korea* 40°30N 127°15E **33** D14
Changle *China* 25°59N 119°27E **35** E12
Changli *China* 39°40N 119°13E **33** E10
Changlun *Malaysia* 6°25N 100°26E **39** J3
Changning *Hunan, China* 26°28N 112°22E **35** D9
Changning *Sichuan,*
China 28°40N 104°56E **34** C5
Changning *Yunnan, China* 24°45N 99°30E **34** E2
Changping *China* 40°14N 116°12E **32** D9
Changsha *China* 28°12N 113°0E **35** C9
Changshan *China* 28°55N 118°27E **35** C12
Changshan Qundao
China 39°11N 122°32E **33** E12
Changshou *China* 29°50N 107°4E **34** C6
Changshu *China* 31°38N 120°43E **35** B13
Changshun *China* 26°3N 106°25E **34** D6
Changtai *China* 24°35N 117°42E **35** E11
Changting *China* 25°50N 116°22E **35** E11
Changtu *China* 42°46N 124°6E **33** C13
Changuinola *Panama* 9°26N 82°31W **88** E3
Changwu *Guangxi Zhuangzu,*
China 23°25N 111°17E **35** F8
Changwu *Shaanxi, China* 35°10N 107°45E **32** G4
Changxing *China* 31°0N 119°55E **35** B12
Changyang *China* 30°30N 111°10E **35** B8
Changyi *China* 36°40N 119°30E **33** F10
Changyŏn *N. Korea* 38°15N 125°6E **33** E13
Changyuan *China* 35°15N 114°42E **32** G8
Changzhi *China* 36°10N 113°6E **32** F7
Changzhou *China* 31°47N 119°58E **35** B12
Chanhanga *Angola* 16°0S 14°8E **56** A1
Chania *Greece* 35°30N 24°4E **23** G11
Chanion, Kolpos *Greece* 35°33N 23°55E **23** G10
Chambersburg *U.S.A.* 39°56N 77°40W **81** F15
Channagiri *India* 14°2N 75°56E **45** G2
Channapatna *India* 12°40N 77°15E **45** H3
Channel Is. *U.K.* 49°19N 2°24W **13** H5
Channel Is. *U.S.A.* 33°40N 119°15W **79** M7
Channel Islands △
U.S.A. 34°0N 119°24W **79** L7
Channel-Port aux Basques
Canada 47°30N 59°9W **73** C8
Channel Tunnel *Europe* 51°0N 1°30E **13** F9
Channing *U.S.A.* 35°41N 102°20W **84** D3
Chantada *Spain* 42°36N 7°46W **21** A2
Chanthaburi *Thailand* 12°38N 102°12E **38** F4
Chantrey Inlet *Canada* 67°48N 96°20W **68** D12
Chanumla *India* 8°19N 93°5E **45** K11
Chanute *U.S.A.* 37°41N 95°27W **80** G6
Chao Hu *China* 31°30N 117°30E **35** B11
Chao Phraya →
Thailand 13°40N 100°31E **38** F3
Chao Phraya Lowlands
Thailand 15°30N 100°0E **38** E3
Chaocheng *China* 36°4N 115°37E **32** F8
Chaohu *China* 31°38N 117°50E **35** B11
Chaoyang *Guangdong,*
China 23°17N 116°30E **35** F11
Chaoyang *Liaoning,*
China 41°35N 120°22E **33** D11
Chaozhou *China* 23°42N 116°32E **35** F11
Chapaev *Kazakhstan* 50°25N 51°10E **19** D9
Chapais *Canada* 49°47N 74°51W **72** C5
Chapala, L. de *Mexico* 20°15N 103°0W **86** C4
Chapayevsk *Russia* 53°0N 49°40E **18** D8
Chapecó *Brazil* 27°14S 52°41W **95** B5
Chapel Hill *U.S.A.* 35°55N 79°4W **85** D15
Chapleau *Canada* 47°50N 83°24W **72** C3
Chaplin *Canada* 50°28N 106°40W **71** C7
Chaplin L. *Canada* 50°22N 106°36W **71** C7
Chappell *U.S.A.* 41°6N 102°28W **80** E2
Chapra = Chhapra *India* 25°48N 84°44E **43** G11
Chara *Russia* 56°54N 118°20E **27** D12
Charadai *Argentina* 27°35S 59°55W **94** B4
Charagua *Bolivia* 19°45S 63°10W **92** G6
Charambirá, Punta
Colombia 4°16N 77°32W **92** C3
Charaña *Bolivia* 17°30S 69°25W **92** G5
Charanwala *India* 27°51N 72°10E **42** F5
Charata *Argentina* 27°13S 61°14W **94** B3

Charcas *Mexico* 23°8N 101°7W **86** C4
Charcot I. *Antarctica* 70°0S 70°0W **5** C17
Chard *U.K.* 50°52N 2°58W **13** G5
Chardon *U.S.A.* 41°35N 81°12W **82** E3
Chardzhou = Türkmenabat
  Turkmenistan 39°6N 63°34E **47** B9
Charente ➤ *France* 45°57N 1°5W **20** D3
Chari ➤ *Chad* 12°58N 14°31E **53** F8
Chārīkār *Afghan.* 35°0N 69°10E **40** B6
Chariton *U.S.A.* 41°1N 93°19W **80** E7
Chariton ➤ *U.S.A.* 39°19N 92°58W **80** F7
Chärjew = Türkmenabat
  Turkmenistan 39°6N 63°34E **47** B9
Charkhari *India* 25°24N 79°45E **43** G8
Charkhi Dadri *India* 28°37N 76°17E **42** E7
Charleroi *Belgium* 50°24N 4°27E **15** D4
Charleroi *U.S.A.* 40°9N 79°57W **82** F5
Charles, C. *U.S.A.* 37°7N 75°58W **81** G16
Charles, Peak *Australia* 32°52S 121°11E **61** F3
Charles City *U.S.A.* 43°4N 92°41W **80** D7
Charles L. *Canada* 62°39N 74°15W **69** E17
Charles L. *Canada* 59°50N 110°33W **71** B6
Charles Town *U.S.A.* 39°17N 77°52W **81** F15
Charlesbourg *Canada* 46°51N 71°16W **81** B18
Charleston *Ill., U.S.A.* 39°30N 88°10W **80** F9
Charleston *Miss., U.S.A.* 34°1N 90°4W **85** D9
Charleston *Mo., U.S.A.* 36°55N 89°21W **80** G10
Charleston *S.C., U.S.A.* 32°46N 79°56W **85** E15
Charleston *W. Va.,*
  U.S.A. 38°21N 81°38W **81** F13
Charleston L. *Canada* 44°32N 76°0W **83** B9
Charleston Peak
  U.S.A. 36°16N 115°42W **79** J11
Charlestown *Ireland* 53°58N 8°48W **10** C3
Charlestown *S. Africa* 27°26S 29°53E **57** C4
Charlestown *Ind.,*
  U.S.A. 38°27N 85°40W **81** F11
Charlestown *N.H.,*
  U.S.A. 43°14N 72°25W **83** C12
Charlestown of Aberlour
  U.K. 57°28N 3°14W **11** D5
Charleville *Australia* 26°24S 146°15E **63** D4
Charleville *Ireland* 52°21N 8°40W **10** D3
Charleville-Mézières
  France 49°44N 4°40E **20** B6
Charlevoix *U.S.A.* 45°19N 85°16W **81** C11
Charlotte *Mich., U.S.A.* 42°34N 84°50W **81** D11
Charlotte *N.C., U.S.A.* 35°13N 80°50W **85** D14
Charlotte *Vt., U.S.A.* 44°19N 73°16W **83** B11
Charlotte Amalie
  U.S. Virgin Is. 18°21N 64°56W **89** e
Charlotte-Douglas Int. ✈ (CLT)
  U.S.A. 35°13N 80°56W **85** D14
Charlotte Harbor *U.S.A.* 26°57N 82°4W **85** H13
Charlotte L. *Canada* 52°12N 125°19W **70** C3
Charlottesville *U.S.A.* 38°2N 78°30W **81** F14
Charlottetown *Nfld. & L.,*
  Canada 52°46N 56°7W **73** B8
Charlottetown *P.E.I.,*
  Canada 46°14N 63°8W **73** C7
Charlotteville
  Trin. & Tob. 11°20N 60°33W **93** J16
Charlton *Australia* 36°16S 143°24E **63** F3
Charlton I. *Canada* 52°0N 79°20W **72** B4
Charny *Canada* 46°43N 71°15W **73** C5
Charolles *France* 46°27N 4°16E **20** C6
Charre *Mozam.* 17°13S 35°10E **55** H7
Charsadda *Pakistan* 34°7N 71°45E **42** B4
Charters Towers *Australia* 20°5S 146°13E **62** C4
Chartres *France* 48°29N 1°30E **20** B4
Chascomús *Argentina* 35°30S 58°0W **94** D4
Chase *Canada* 50°50N 119°41W **70** C5
Chashma Barrage
  Pakistan 32°27N 71°20E **42** C4
Chāt *Iran* 37°59N 55°16E **47** B7
Châteaubriant *France* 47°43N 1°23W **20** C3
Chateaugay *U.S.A.* 44°56N 74°5W **83** B10
Châteauguay, L. *Canada* 56°26N 70°3W **73** A5
Châteaulin *France* 48°11N 4°8W **20** B1
Châteauroux *France* 46°50N 1°40E **20** C4
Châteaux, Pte. des
  Guadeloupe 16°15N 61°10W **88** b
Châtellerault *France* 46°50N 0°30E **20** C4
Chatham = Miramichi
  Canada 47°2N 65°28W **73** C6
Chatham *Canada* 42°24N 82°11W **82** D2
Chatham *U.K.* 51°22N 0°32E **13** F8
Chatham *U.S.A.* 42°21N 73°36W **83** D11
Chatham Is. *Pac. Oc.* 44°0S 176°40W **64** M10
Chatham Rise *Pac. Oc.* 43°30S 180°0E **64** M10
Chatmohar *Bangla.* 24°15N 89°15E **43** G13
Chatra *India* 24°12N 84°56E **43** G11
Chatrapur *India* 19°22N 85°2E **44** E7
Chats, L. des *Canada* 45°30N 76°20W **83** A8
Chatsu *India* 26°36N 75°57E **42** F6
Chatsworth *Canada* 44°27N 80°54W **82** B4
Chāttagām = Chittagong
  Bangla. 22°19N 91°48E **41** H17
Chattahoochee *U.S.A.* 30°42N 84°51W **85** F12
Chattahoochee ➤
  U.S.A. 30°54N 84°57W **85** F12
Chattanooga *U.S.A.* 35°3N 85°19W **85** D12
Chatteris *U.K.* 52°28N 0°2E **13** E8
Chatturat *Thailand* 15°40N 101°51E **38** E3
Chau Doc *Vietnam* 10°42N 105°7E **39** G5
Chaukan Pass *Myanmar* 27°8N 97°10E **41** F20
Chaumont *France* 48°7N 5°8E **20** B6
Chaumont *U.S.A.* 44°4N 76°8W **83** B8
Chaunskaya G. *Russia* 69°0N 169°0E **27** C17
Chaura *India* 8°27N 93°2E **45** K11
Chautara *Nepal* 27°46N 85°42E **43** F11
Chautauqua L. *U.S.A.* 42°10N 79°24W **82** D5
Chauvin *Canada* 52°45N 110°10W **71** C6
Chavakachcheri *Sri Lanka* 9°39N 80°9E **45** K5
Chaves *Brazil* 0°15S 49°55W **93** D9
Chaves *Portugal* 41°45N 7°32W **21** B2
Chazy *U.S.A.* 44°53N 73°26W **83** B11
Cheb *Czechia* 50°9N 12°28E **16** C7

Cheboksary *Russia* 56°8N 47°12E **18** C8
Cheboygan *U.S.A.* 45°39N 84°29W **81** C11
Chech, Erg *Africa* 25°0N 2°15W **52** D5
Checheno-Ingush Republic =
  Chechenia □ *Russia* 43°30N 45°29E **19** F8
Chechenia □ *Russia* 43°30N 45°29E **19** F8
Chechnya = Chechenia □
  Russia 43°30N 45°29E **19** F8
Checotah *U.S.A.* 35°28N 95°31W **84** D7
Chedabucto B. *Canada* 45°25N 61°8W **73** C7
Cheduba I. *Myanmar* 18°45N 93°40E **41** K18
Cheektowaga *U.S.A.* 42°54N 78°45W **82** D6
Cheepie *Australia* 26°33S 145°0E **63** D4
Chegdomyn *Russia* 51°7N 133°1E **27** D14
Chegga *Mauritania* 25°27N 5°40W **52** C4
Chegutu *Zimbabwe* 18°10S 30°14E **55** H6
Chehalis *U.S.A.* 46°40N 122°58W **78** D4
Chehalis ➤ *U.S.A.* 46°57N 123°50W **78** D3
Cheju = Jeju *S. Korea* 33°31N 126°32E **33** H14
Cheju-do = Jeju-do
  S. Korea 33°29N 126°34E **33** H14
Cheju Str. = Jeju Haehyop
  S. Korea 33°50N 126°30E **33** H14
Chekiang = Zhejiang □
  China 29°0N 120°0E **35** C13
Chela, Sa. da *Angola* 16°20S 13°20E **56** A1
Chelan *U.S.A.* 47°51N 120°1W **76** C3
Chelan, L. *U.S.A.* 48°11N 120°30W **76** B3
Cheleken = Hazar
  Turkmenistan 39°34N 53°16E **19** G9
Cheleken Yarymadasy
  Turkmenistan 39°30N 53°15E **47** B7
Chelforó *Argentina* 39°0S 66°33W **96** D3
Chelkar = Shalqar
  Kazakhstan 47°48N 59°39E **26** E6
Chełm *Poland* 51°8N 23°30E **17** C12
Chełmno *Poland* 53°20N 18°30E **17** B10
Chelmsford *U.K.* 51°44N 0°29E **13** F8
Chelsea *Australia* 38°5S 145°8E **63** F4
Chelsea *U.S.A.* 43°59N 72°27W **83** C12
Cheltenham *U.K.* 51°54N 2°4W **13** F5
Chelyabinsk *Russia* 55°10N 61°24E **26** D7
Chelyuskin, C. = Chelyuskin, Mys
  Russia 77°30N 103°0E **27** B11
Chelyuskin, Mys *Russia* 77°30N 103°0E **27** B11
Chemainus *Canada* 48°55N 123°42W **78** B3
Chemba *Mozam.* 17°9S 34°53E **55** H6
Chemin Grenier *Mauritius* 20°29S 57°28E **55** d
Chemnitz *Germany* 50°51N 12°54E **16** C7
Chemult *U.S.A.* 43°14N 121°47W **76** E3
Chen, Gora *Russia* 65°16N 141°50E **27** C15
Chenab ➤ *Pakistan* 30°23N 71°2E **42** D4
Chenab Nagar *Pakistan* 31°45N 72°52E **42** D5
Chenango Forks *U.S.A.* 42°15N 75°51W **83** D9
Chenchiang = Zhenjiang
  China 32°11N 119°26E **35** A12
Cheney *U.S.A.* 47°30N 117°35W **76** C5
Cheng Xian *China* 33°43N 105°42E **32** H3
Chengbu *China* 26°18N 110°16E **35** D8
Chengchou = Zhengzhou
  China 34°45N 113°34E **32** G7
Chengde *China* 40°59N 117°58E **33** D9
Chengdong Hu *China* 32°15N 116°20E **35** A11
Chengdu *China* 30°38N 104°2E **34** B5
Chengdu Shuangliu Int. ✈ (CTU)
  China 30°35N 103°57E **34** B4
Chenggong *China* 24°52N 102°56E **34** E4
Chenggu *China* 33°10N 107°21E **34** A6
Chenghai *China* 23°30N 116°42E **35** F11
Chengjiang *China* 24°39N 103°0E **34** E4
Chengkou *China* 31°54N 108°31E **34** B7
Chengmai *China* 19°50N 109°58E **38** C7
Chengshan Jiao *China* 37°25N 122°44E **33** F12
Ch'engtu = Chengdu
  China 30°38N 104°2E **34** B5
Chengwu *China* 34°58N 115°50E **32** G8
Chengxi Hu *China* 32°15N 116°10E **35** A11
Chengyang *China* 36°18N 120°21E **33** F11
Chenjiagang *China* 34°23N 119°47E **33** G10
Chenkaladi *Sri Lanka* 7°47N 81°35E **45** L5
Chennai *India* 13°8N 80°19E **45** H5
Chenxi *China* 28°2N 110°12E **35** C8
Chenzhou *China* 25°47N 113°1E **35** E9
Cheò, Eilean a' = Skye
  U.K. 57°15N 6°10W **11** D2
Cheo Reo *Vietnam* 13°20N 108°25E **38** F7
Cheom Ksan *Cambodia* 14°13N 104°56E **38** E5
Cheonan *S. Korea* 36°48N 127°9E **33** F14
Cheongdo *S. Korea* 35°38N 128°42E **33** G15
Cheongju *S. Korea* 36°39N 127°27E **33** F14
Cheorwon *S. Korea* 38°15N 127°10E **33** E14
Chepén *Peru* 7°15S 79°23W **92** E3
Chepes *Argentina* 31°20S 66°35W **94** C2
Chepo *Panama* 9°10N 79°6W **88** E4
Chepstow *U.K.* 51°38N 2°41W **13** F5
Chequamegon B. *U.S.A.* 46°39N 90°51W **80** B8
Cher ➤ *France* 47°21N 0°29E **20** C4
Cheraw *U.S.A.* 34°42N 79°53W **85** D15
Cherbourg-Octeville
  France 49°39N 1°40W **20** B3
Cherdyn *Russia* 60°24N 56°29E **18** B10
Cheremkhovo *Russia* 53°8N 103°1E **30** A9
Cherepovets *Russia* 59°5N 37°55E **18** C6
Chergui, Chott ech *Algeria* 34°21N 0°25E **52** B6
Cherikov = Cherykaw
  Belarus 53°32N 31°20E **17** B16
Cheriyam I. *India* 10°9N 73°40E **45** J1
Cherkasy *Ukraine* 49°27N 32°4E **19** E5
Cherkessk *Russia* 44°15N 42°5E **19** F7
Cherla *India* 18°5N 80°49E **44** E5
Cherlak *Russia* 54°15N 74°55E **26** D8
Chernaya *Russia* 70°30N 89°10E **27** B9
Chernigov = Chernihiv
  Ukraine 51°28N 31°20E **18** C5
Chernihiv *Ukraine* 51°28N 31°20E **18** C5
Chernivtsi *Ukraine* 48°15N 25°52E **17** D13

Chernobyl = Chornobyl
  Ukraine 51°20N 30°15E **17** C16
Chernogorsk *Russia* 53°49N 91°18E **27** D10
Chernovtsy = Chernivtsi
  Ukraine 48°15N 25°52E **17** D13
Chernyakhovsk *Russia* 54°36N 21°48E **9** J19
Chernysheyskiy *Russia* 63°0N 112°30E **27** C12
Chichén-Itzá *Mexico* 20°37N 88°35E **87** C7
Cherokee *Iowa, U.S.A.* 42°45N 95°33W **80** D6
Cherokee *Okla., U.S.A.* 36°45N 98°21W **84** C5
Cherokee Village *U.S.A.* 36°18N 91°31W **84** C9
Cherokees, Grand Lake O' The
  U.S.A. 36°28N 94°55W **84** C7
Cherrapunji *India* 25°17N 91°47E **41** G17
Cherry Valley *U.S.A.* 42°48N 74°45W **83** D10
Cherskiy *Russia* 68°45N 161°18E **27** C17
Cherskogo Khrebet
  Russia 65°0N 143°0E **27** C15
Cherthala *India* 9°42N 76°20E **45** K3
Cherven *Belarus* 53°45N 28°28E **17** B15
Chervonohrad *Ukraine* 50°25N 24°10E **17** C13
Cherwell ➤ *U.K.* 51°44N 1°14W **13** F6
Cherykaw *Belarus* 53°32N 31°20E **17** B16
Chesapeake *U.S.A.* 36°49N 76°16W **81** G15
Chesapeake B. *U.S.A.* 38°0N 76°10W **81** F14
Cheshire East □ *U.K.* 53°15N 2°15W **12** D5
Cheshire West and Chester □
  U.K. 53°15N 2°40W **12** D5
Cheshskaya Guba *Russia* 67°20N 47°0E **18** A8
Chesil Beach *U.K.* 50°37N 2°33W **13** G5
Chesley *Canada* 44°17N 81°5W **82** B3
Chester *U.K.* 53°12N 2°53W **12** D5
Chester *Calif., U.S.A.* 40°19N 121°14W **76** F3
Chester *Ill., U.S.A.* 37°55N 89°49W **80** G9
Chester *Mont., U.S.A.* 48°31N 110°58W **76** B8
Chester *Pa., U.S.A.* 39°51N 75°22W **81** F16
Chester *S.C., U.S.A.* 34°43N 81°12W **85** D14
Chester *Vt., U.S.A.* 43°16N 72°36W **83** C12
Chester *W. Va., U.S.A.* 40°37N 80°34W **82** F4
Chester-le-Street *U.K.* 54°51N 1°34W **12** C6
Chesterfield *U.K.* 53°15N 1°25W **12** D6
Chesterfield, Îs. *N. Cal.* 19°52S 158°15E **58** C8
Chesterfield Inlet
  Canada 63°30N 90°45W **68** E13
Chesterton Ra. *Australia* 25°30S 147°27E **63** D4
Chesterton Range △
  Australia 26°16S 147°22E **63** D4
Chestertown *U.S.A.* 43°40N 73°48W **83** C11
Chesterville *Canada* 45°6N 75°14W **83** A9
Chesuncook L. *U.S.A.* 46°0N 69°21W **81** C19
Chetamale *India* 10°43N 92°33E **45** J11
Chéticamp *Canada* 46°37N 60°59W **73** C7
Chetlat I. *India* 11°42N 72°42E **45** J1
Chetumal *Mexico* 18°30N 88°20W **87** D7
Chetumal, B. de
  Cent. Amer. 18°40N 88°10W **87** D7
Chetwynd *Canada* 55°45N 121°36W **70** B4
Cheviot, The *U.K.* 55°29N 2°9W **12** B5
Cheviot Hills *U.K.* 55°20N 2°30W **12** B5
Cheviot Ra. *Australia* 25°20S 143°45E **62** D3
Chew Bahir *Ethiopia* 4°40N 36°50E **49** G2
Chewelah *U.S.A.* 48°17N 117°43W **76** B5
Cheyenne *Okla., U.S.A.* 35°37N 99°40W **84** D5
Cheyenne *Wyo., U.S.A.* 41°8N 104°49W **76** F11
Cheyenne ➤ *U.S.A.* 44°41N 101°18W **80** C3
Cheyenne Wells
  U.S.A. 38°49N 102°21W **76** G12
Cheyne B. *Australia* 34°35S 118°50E **61** F2
Cheyur *India* 12°21N 80°0E **45** H5
Chhabra *India* 24°40N 76°54E **42** G7
Chhaktala *India* 22°6N 74°11E **42** H6
Chhapra *India* 25°48N 84°44E **43** G11
Chhata *India* 27°42N 77°30E **42** F7
Chhatarpur *Jharkhand,*
  India 24°23N 84°11E **43** G11
Chhatarpur *Mad. P., India* 24°55N 79°35E **43** G8
Chhati *India* 20°47N 81°40E **44** D5
Chhattisgarh □ *India* 22°0N 82°0E **43** J10
Chhep *Cambodia* 13°45N 105°24E **38** F5
Chhindwara *Mad. P., India* 23°3N 79°29E **43** H8
Chhindwara *Mad. P., India* 22°2N 78°59E **43** H8
Chhinhdipada *India* 21°6N 84°52E **44** D7
Chhlong *Cambodia* 12°15N 105°58E **39** F5
Chhota Tawa ➤ *India* 22°14N 76°36E **42** H7
Chhoti Kali Sindh ➤
  India 24°2N 75°31E **42** G6
Chhuikhadan *India* 21°32N 80°59E **43** J9
Chhuk *Cambodia* 10°46N 104°28E **39** G5
Chi ➤ *Thailand* 15°11N 104°43E **38** E5
Chi Thanh *Vietnam* 13°17N 109°16E **38** F7
Chiai *Taiwan* 23°29N 120°25E **35** F13
Chiali *Taiwan* 23°9N 120°10E **35** F13
Chiang Dao *Thailand* 19°22N 98°58E **38** C2
Chiang Dao, Doi *Thailand* 19°23N 98°54E **38** C2
Chiang Kham *Thailand* 19°32N 100°18E **38** C3
Chiang Khan *Thailand* 17°52N 101°36E **38** D3
Chiang Khong *Thailand* 20°17N 100°24E **34** G4
Chiang Mai *Thailand* 18°47N 98°59E **38** C2
Chiang Rai *Thailand* 19°52N 99°50E **34** H4
Chiang Saen *Thailand* 20°16N 100°5E **34** G3
Chiapa de Corzo *Mexico* 16°42N 93°0W **87** D6
Chiapas □ *Mexico* 16°30N 92°30W **87** D6
Chiapas, Sa. Madre de
  Mexico 15°40N 93°0W **87** D6
Chiautla de Tapia
  Mexico 18°18N 98°36W **87** D5
Chiávari *Italy* 44°19N 9°19E **20** D8
Chiavenna *Italy* 46°19N 9°24E **20** C8
Chiba *Japan* 35°30N 140°7E **29** G10
Chiba □ *Japan* 35°30N 140°20E **29** G10
Chibabava *Mozam.* 20°17S 33°35E **57** B5
Chibemba *Cunene, Angola* 15°48S 14°8E **55** H2
Chibemba *Huila, Angola* 16°20S 15°20E **56** A2
Chibi *Zimbabwe* 20°18S 30°25E **57** B5
Chibia *Angola* 15°10S 13°42E **55** H2
Chibougamau *Canada* 49°56N 74°24W **72** C5
Chibougamau, L. *Canada* 49°50N 74°20W **72** C5
Chibuk *Nigeria* 10°52N 12°50E **53** F8
Chibuto *Mozam.* 24°40S 33°33E **57** C5
Chic-Chocs, Mts. *Canada* 48°55N 66°0W **73** C6

Chicacole = Srikakulam
  India 18°14N 83°58E **44** E6
Chicago Heights *U.S.A.* 41°30N 87°38W **80** E10
Chichagof I. *U.S.A.* 57°30N 135°30W **68** F4
Chichaoua *Morocco* 31°32N 8°44W **52** B4
Chichawatni *Pakistan* 30°32N 72°42E **42** D5
Chichén-Itzá *Mexico* 20°37N 88°35W **87** C7
Chicheng *China* 40°55N 115°55E **32** D8
Chichester *U.K.* 50°50N 0°47W **13** G7
Chichester Ra. *Australia* 22°12S 119°15E **60** D2
Chichibu *Japan* 35°59N 139°10E **29** F9
Chichibu-Tama-Kai △
  Japan 35°52N 138°42E **29** G9
Ch'ich'ihaerh = Qiqihar
  China 47°26N 124°0E **31** B13
Chicholi *India* 22°1N 77°40E **42** H8
Chickasaw △ *U.S.A.* 34°26N 97°0W **84** D6
Chickasha *U.S.A.* 35°3N 97°58W **84** D6
Chiclana de la Frontera
  Spain 36°26N 6°9W **21** D2
Chiclayo *Peru* 6°42S 79°50W **92** E3
Chico *U.S.A.* 39°44N 121°50W **78** F5
Chico ➤ *Chubut, Argentina* 44°0S 67°0W **96** E3
Chico ➤ *Santa Cruz,*
  Argentina 50°0S 68°30W **96** G3
Chicoa *Mozam.* 15°36S 32°20E **57** A5
Chicomo *Mozam.* 24°31S 34°6E **57** B5
Chicomostoc *Mexico* 22°28N 102°46W **86** C4
Chicontepec *Mexico* 20°58N 98°10W **87** C5
Chicopee *U.S.A.* 42°9N 72°37W **83** D12
Chicoutimi *Canada* 48°28N 71°5W **73** C5
Chicualacuala *Mozam.* 22°6S 31°42E **57** B5
Chidambaram *India* 11°20N 79°45E **45** J4
Chidenguele *Mozam.* 24°55S 34°11E **57** B5
Chidley, C. *Canada* 60°23N 64°26W **69** E19
Chiducuane *Mozam.* 24°35S 34°25E **57** B5
Chiede *Angola* 17°15S 16°22E **56** A2
Chiefs Pt. *Canada* 44°41N 81°18W **82** B3
Chiem Hoa *Vietnam* 22°12N 105°17E **38** A5
Chiemsee *Germany* 47°53N 12°28E **16** E7
Chiengmai = Chiang Mai
  Thailand 18°47N 98°59E **38** C2
Chiese ➤ *Italy* 45°8N 10°25E **20** D9
Chieti *Italy* 42°21N 14°10E **22** C6
Chifeng *China* 42°18N 118°58E **33** C10
Chignecto B. *Canada* 45°30N 64°40W **73** C7
Chiguana *Bolivia* 21°0S 67°58W **94** A2
Chigwell *U.K.* 51°37N 0°6E **13** F8
Chihli, G. of = Bo Hai
  China 39°0N 119°0E **33** E10
Chihuahua *Mexico* 28°38N 106°5W **86** B3
Chihuahua □ *Mexico* 28°30N 106°0W **86** B3
Chiili = Shïeli *Kazakhstan* 44°20N 66°15E **26** E7
Chik Bollapur *India* 13°25N 77°45E **45** H3
Chikalda *India* 21°24N 77°19E **44** D3
Chikhli *Ahmadabad, India* 20°45N 73°4E **44** D1
Chikhli *Maharashtra, India* 20°20N 76°18E **44** D3
Chikkamagaluru *India* 13°15N 75°45E **45** H2
Chiknayakanhalli *India* 13°26N 76°37E **45** H3
Chikodi *India* 16°26N 74°38E **45** F2
Chilapa *Mexico* 17°36N 99°10W **87** D5
Chilas *Pakistan* 35°25N 74°5E **43** B6
Chilaw *Sri Lanka* 7°30N 79°50E **45** L4
Chilcotin ➤ *Canada* 51°44N 122°23W **70** C4
Childers *Australia* 25°15S 152°17E **63** D5
Childress *U.S.A.* 34°25N 100°13W **84** D4
Chile ■ *S. Amer.* 35°0S 72°0W **96** D2
Chile Rise *Pac. Oc.* 38°0S 92°0W **65** L18
Chilecito *Argentina* 29°10S 67°30W **94** B2
Chilete *Peru* 7°10S 78°50W **92** E3
Chililabombwe *Zambia* 12°18S 27°43E **55** G5
Chilim *Pakistan* 35°5N 75°5E **43** B6
Chilin = Jilin *China* 43°44N 126°30E **33** C14
Chilka L. *India* 19°40N 85°25E **44** E7
Chilko ➤ *Canada* 52°0N 123°40W **70** C4
Chilko L. *Canada* 51°20N 124°10W **70** C4
Chillagoe *Australia* 17°7S 144°33E **62** B3
Chillán *Chile* 36°40S 72°10W **94** D1
Chillicothe *Ill., U.S.A.* 40°55N 89°29W **80** E9
Chillicothe *Mo., U.S.A.* 39°48N 93°33W **80** F7
Chillicothe *Ohio, U.S.A.* 39°20N 82°59W **81** F12
Chilliwack *Canada* 49°10N 121°54W **70** D4
Chilo *India* 27°25N 73°32E **42** F5
Chiloane, I. *Mozam.* 20°40S 34°55E **57** B5
Chiloé, I. de *Chile* 42°30S 73°50W **96** E2
Chilpancingo *Mexico* 17°33N 99°30W **87** D5
Chiltern Hills *U.K.* 51°40N 0°53W **13** F7
Chilton *U.S.A.* 44°2N 88°10W **80** C9
Chilung *Taiwan* 25°3N 121°45E **35** E13
Chilwa, L. *Malawi* 15°15S 35°40E **55** H7
Chimaltitán *Mexico* 21°35N 103°50W **86** C4
Chimán *Panama* 8°45N 78°40W **88** E4
Chimanimani *Zimbabwe* 19°48S 32°52E **57** A5
Chimanimani △ *Zimbabwe* 19°48S 33°0E **57** A5
Chimay *Belgium* 50°3N 4°20E **15** D4
Chimayo *U.S.A.* 36°0N 105°56W **77** J11
Chimborazo *Ecuador* 1°29S 78°55W **92** D3
Chimbote *Peru* 9°0S 78°35W **92** E3
Chimboy *Uzbekistan* 42°57N 59°47E **26** E6
Chimkent = Shymkent
  Kazakhstan 42°18N 69°36E **26** E7
Chimoio *Mozam.* 19°4S 33°30E **55** H6
Chimur *India* 20°30N 79°29E **44** D4
Chin □ *Myanmar* 22°0N 93°0E **41** J18
Chin Hills *Myanmar* 22°30N 93°30E **41** H18
Chin Ling Shan = Qinling Shandi
  China 33°50N 108°10E **32** H5
China *Mexico* 25°42N 99°14W **87** B5
China ■ *Asia* 30°0N 110°0E **31** E11
China, Great Plain of
  Asia 35°0N 115°0E **24** E13
China Lake *U.S.A.* 35°44N 117°37W **79** K9
Chinan = Jinan *China* 36°38N 117°1E **32** F9
Chinandega *Nic.* 12°35N 87°12W **88** D2
Chinati Peak *U.S.A.* 29°57N 104°29W **84** G2
Chincha Alta *Peru* 13°25S 76°7W **92** F3
Chinchaga ➤ *Canada* 58°53N 118°20W **70** B5
Chinchilla *Australia* 26°45S 150°38E **63** D5
Chincholi *India* 17°28N 77°20E **44** F3
Chinchorro, Banco
  Mexico 18°35N 87°22W **87** D7

Chinchou = Jinzhou
  China 41°5N 121°3E **33** D11
Chincoteague *U.S.A.* 37°56N 75°23W **81** G16
Chinde *Mozam.* 18°35S 36°30E **55** H7
Chindwin ➤ *Myanmar* 21°26N 95°15E **41** J19
Chineni *India* 33°2N 75°15E **43** C6
Chingola *Zambia* 12°31S 27°53E **55** G5
Ch'ingtao = Qingdao
  China 36°5N 120°20E **33** F11
Chinguetti *Mauritania* 20°25N 12°24W **52** D3
Chingune *Mozam.* 20°33S 34°58E **57** B5
Chinhanguanine *Mozam.* 25°21S 32°30E **57** C5
Chinhoyi *Zimbabwe* 17°20S 30°8E **55** H6
Chiniot *Pakistan* 31°45N 73°0E **42** D5
Chinipas *Mexico* 27°23N 108°32E **86** B3
Chinji *Pakistan* 32°42N 72°22E **42** C5
Chinju = Jinju *S. Korea* 35°12N 128°2E **33** G15
Chinko ➤ *C.A.R.* 4°50N 23°53E **54** D4
Chinle *U.S.A.* 36°9N 109°33W **77** H9
Chinmen *Taiwan* 24°26N 118°19E **35** E12
Chinmen Tao *Taiwan* 24°26N 118°22E **35** E12
Chinnamanur *India* 9°50N 77°24E **45** K3
Chinnampo = Namp'o
  N. Korea 38°52N 125°10E **33** E13
Chino *Japan* 35°59N 138°9E **29** G9
Chino *U.S.A.* 34°1N 117°41W **79** L9
Chino Valley *U.S.A.* 34°45N 112°27W **77** J7
Chinon *France* 47°10N 0°15E **20** C4
Chinook *U.S.A.* 48°35N 109°14W **76** B9
Chinook Trough *Pac. Oc.* 44°0N 175°0W **64** C10
Chinsura = Chunchura
  India 22°53N 88°27E **43** H13
Chintalapudi *India* 17°4N 80°59E **44** F5
Chintamani *India* 13°26N 78°3E **45** H4
Chióggia *Italy* 45°13N 12°17E **22** B5
Chíos *Greece* 38°27N 26°9E **23** E12
Chipata *Zambia* 13°38S 32°28E **55** G6
Chipindo *Angola* 13°49S 15°48E **55** G3
Chipinge *Zimbabwe* 20°13S 32°28E **55** J6
Chipley *U.S.A.* 30°47N 85°32W **85** F12
Chiplun *India* 17°31N 73°34E **44** F1
Chipman *Canada* 46°6N 65°53W **73** C6
Chippenham *U.K.* 51°27N 2°6W **13** F5
Chippewa ➤ *U.S.A.* 44°25N 92°5W **80** C7
Chippewa Falls *U.S.A.* 44°56N 91°24W **80** C8
Chipping Norton *U.K.* 51°56N 1°32W **13** F6
Chiputneticook Lakes
  N. Amer. 45°35N 67°35W **81** C20
Chiquián *Peru* 10°10S 77°0W **92** F3
Chiquibul □ *Belize* 16°49N 88°52W **88** C2
Chiquimula *Guatemala* 14°51N 89°37W **88** D2
Chiquinquira *Colombia* 5°37N 73°50W **92** B4
Chirala *India* 15°50N 80°26E **45** G5
Chirawa *India* 28°14N 75°42E **42** E6
Chirchiq *Uzbekistan* 41°29N 69°35E **26** E7
Chiredzi *Zimbabwe* 21°0S 31°38E **57** B5
Chiricahua △ *U.S.A.* 32°0N 109°20W **77** K9
Chiricahua Peak *U.S.A.* 31°51N 109°18W **77** L9
Chirikof I. *U.S.A.* 55°50N 155°40W **74** D8
Chiriquí, G. de *Panama* 8°0N 82°10W **88** E3
Chiriquí, L. de *Panama* 9°10N 82°0W **88** E3
Chirmiri *India* 23°15N 82°20E **43** H10
Chirripó Grande, Cerro
  Costa Rica 9°29N 83°29W **88** E3
Chirundu *Zimbabwe* 16°3S 28°50E **57** A4
Chisamba *Zambia* 14°55S 28°0E **55** G5
Chisapani *Nepal* 28°37N 81°16E **43** E9
Chisasibi *Canada* 53°50N 79°0W **72** B4
Ch'ishan *Taiwan* 22°44N 120°31E **35** F13
Chisholm *Canada* 54°55N 114°10W **70** C6
Chisholm *U.S.A.* 47°29N 92°53W **80** B7
Chishtian Mandi *Pakistan* 29°50N 72°55E **42** E5
Chishui *China* 28°30N 105°42E **34** C5
Chishui He ➤ *China* 28°49N 105°6E **34** C5
Chisimaio = Kismaayo
  Somalia 0°22S 42°32E **49** H3
Chişinău *Moldova* 47°2N 28°50E **17** E15
Chisos Mts. *U.S.A.* 29°5N 103°15W **84** G3
Chistopol *Russia* 55°25N 50°38E **18** C9
Chita *Russia* 52°0N 113°35E **31** A11
Chitapur *India* 17°10N 77°5E **44** F3
Chitose *Japan* 42°49N 141°39E **28** C10
Chitradurga *India* 14°14N 76°24E **45** H3
Chitrakot *India* 19°10N 81°40E **44** E5
Chitral *Pakistan* 35°50N 71°56E **40** B7
Chitravati ➤ *India* 14°45N 78°15E **45** G4
Chitré *Panama* 7°59N 80°27E **88** E3
Chittagong *Bangla.* 22°19N 91°48E **41** H17
Chittagong □ *Bangla.* 24°5N 91°0E **41** G17
Chittaurgarh *India* 24°52N 74°38E **42** G5
Chittoor *India* 13°15N 79°5E **45** H4
Chittur *India* 10°40N 76°45E **45** J3
Chitungwiza *Zimbabwe* 18°0S 31°6E **55** H6
Chiusi *Italy* 43°1N 11°57E **22** C4
Chivasso *Italy* 45°11N 7°53E **20** D7
Chivilcoy *Argentina* 34°55S 60°0W **94** C4
Chixi *China* 22°0N 112°58E **35** G9
Chkalov = Orenburg
  Russia 51°45N 55°6E **18** D10
Chloride *U.S.A.* 35°25N 114°12W **79** K12
Cho-do *N. Korea* 38°30N 124°40E **33** E13
Cho Phuoc Hai *Vietnam* 10°26N 107°18E **39** G6
Chobe △ *Botswana* 18°37S 24°23E **56** A4
Chocolate Mts. *U.S.A.* 33°15N 115°15W **79** M11
Choctawhatchee ➤
  U.S.A. 30°25N 86°8W **85** F11
Chodavaram *Andhra Pradesh,*
  India 17°50N 82°57E **44** F6
Chodavaram *Andhra Pradesh,*
  India 17°27N 81°46E **44** F5
Choele Choel *Argentina* 39°11S 65°40W **96** D3
Choghā Zanbil *Iran* 32°1N 48°32E **47** C6
Choiseul *St. Lucia* 13°47N 61°3W **89** f
Choiseul *Solomon Is.* 7°0S 156°40E **58** B8
Choix *Mexico* 26°43N 108°17W **86** B3
Chojnice *Poland* 53°42N 17°32E **17** B9
Chok Chai *Thailand* 14°44N 102°10E **38** E4
Chōkai-San *Japan* 39°6N 140°3E **28** E10
Choke Canyon Res.
  U.S.A. 28°30N 98°20W **84** G5
Chokurdakh *Russia* 70°38N 147°55E **27** B15

Chokwé Mozam. 24°32S 32°59E 57 B5
Cholame U.S.A. 35°44N 120°18W 78 K6
Cholet France 47°4N 0°52W 20 C3
Cholguan Chile 37°10S 72°39W 94 D1
Choloma Honduras 15°37N 87°57W 88 C2
Choluteca Honduras 13°20N 87°14W 88 D2
Choluteca → Honduras 13°0N 87°20W 88 D2
Chom Bung Thailand 13°37N 99°36E 38 F2
Chom Thong Thailand 18°25N 98°41E 38 C2
Choma Zambia 16°48S 26°59E 55 H5
Chomolungma = Everest, Mt.
  Nepal 28°5N 86°58E 43 E12
Chomun India 27°15N 75°40E 42 F6
Chomutov Czechia 50°28N 13°23E 16 C7
Chon Buri Thailand 13°21N 101°1E 38 F3
Chon Thanh Vietnam 11°24N 106°36E 39 G6
Chone Ecuador 0°40S 80°0W 92 D3
Chong Kai Cambodia 13°57N 103°35E 38 F4
Chong Mek Thailand 15°10N 105°27E 38 E5
Chong Phangan Thailand 9°39N 100°0E 39 b
Chong Samui Thailand 9°25N 99°50E 39 b
Chongde China 30°32N 120°26E 35 B13
Ch'ŏngjin N. Korea 41°47N 129°50E 33 D15
Chŏngju N. Korea 39°40N 125°5E 33 E13
Chongli China 40°58N 115°15E 32 D8
Chongming China 31°38N 121°23E 35 B13
Chongming Dao China 31°40N 121°30E 35 B13
Chŏngp'yŏng N. Korea 39°47N 127°23E 33 E14
Chongqing Chongqing,
  China 29°35N 106°25E 34 C6
Chongqing Sichuan,
  China 30°38N 103°40E 34 B4
Chongqing Jiangbei Int. ✈ (CKG)
  China 29°43N 106°38E 34 C6
Chongqing Shi □ China 30°0N 108°0E 34 C6
Chongren China 27°46N 116°3E 35 D11
Chonguene Mozam. 25°3S 33°49E 57 C5
Chongyi China 25°45N 114°29E 35 E10
Chongzuo China 22°23N 107°20E 34 F6
Chonogol Mongolia 45°54N 115°22E 32 B8
Chonos, Arch. de los Chile 45°0S 75°0W 96 F2
Chop Ukraine 48°26N 22°12E 17 D12
Chopda India 21°20N 75°15E 44 D2
Chopim → Brazil 25°35S 53°5W 95 B5
Chor Pakistan 25°31N 69°46E 42 G3
Chora Sfakion Greece 35°15N 24°9E 23 G11
Chorbat La India 34°42N 76°37E 43 B7
Chorley U.K. 53°39N 2°38W 12 D5
Chornobyl Ukraine 51°20N 30°15E 17 C16
Chorolque, Cerro Bolivia 20°59S 66°5W 94 A2
Chorregon Australia 22°40S 143°32E 62 C3
Chorro el Indio △
  Venezuela 7°43N 72°9W 89 E5
Chortkiv Ukraine 49°2N 25°46E 17 D13
Chorzów Poland 50°18N 18°57E 17 C10
Chos-Malal Argentina 37°20S 70°15W 94 D1
Ch'osan N. Korea 40°50N 125°47E 33 D13
Choszczno Poland 53°7N 15°25E 16 B8
Choteau U.S.A. 47°49N 112°11W 76 C7
Chotila India 22°23N 71°15E 42 H4
Chotta Udepur India 22°19N 74°1E 42 H6
Chowchilla U.S.A. 37°7N 120°16W 78 H6
Choybalsan Mongolia 48°4N 114°30E 31 B11
Choyr Mongolia 46°24N 108°30E 31 B10
Christchurch N.Z. 43°33S 172°47E 59 E4
Christchurch U.K. 50°44N 1°47W 13 G6
Christian I. Canada 44°50N 80°12W 82 B4
Christian Sd. U.S.A. 55°56N 134°40W 75 D13
Christiana S. Africa 27°52S 25°8E 56 C4
Christiansted
  U.S. Virgin Is. 17°45N 64°42W 89 C7
Christie B. Canada 62°32N 111°10W 71 A6
Christina → Canada 56°40N 111°3W 71 B6
Christmas Cr. →
  Australia 18°29S 125°23E 60 C4
Christmas I. = Kiritimati
  Kiribati 1°58N 157°27W 65 G12
Christmas I. Ind. Oc. 10°30S 105°40E 64 J2
Christopher, L. Australia 24°49S 127°42E 61 D4
Chū = Shū Kazakhstan 43°36N 73°42E 26 E8
Chu → Vietnam 19°53N 105°45E 38 C5
Chu Lai Vietnam 15°28N 108°45E 38 E7
Chu Mom Ray △
  Vietnam 14°29N 107°38E 38 E6
Chu Se Vietnam 13°40N 108°8E 38 F7
Chuadanga Bangla. 23°38N 88°51E 43 H13
Chuak, Ko Thailand 9°28N 99°41E 39 b
Ch'uanchou = Quanzhou
  China 24°55N 118°34E 35 E12
Chuankou China 34°20N 110°59E 32 G6
Chubbuck U.S.A. 42°55N 112°28W 76 E7
Chūbu □ Japan 36°45N 137°30E 29 F8
Chūbu-Sangaku △
  Japan 36°30N 137°40E 29 F8
Chubut → Argentina 43°20S 65°5W 96 E3
Chuçand = Khŭjand
  Tajikistan 40°17N 69°37E 26 E7
Chuchi L. Canada 55°12N 124°30W 70 B4
Chuda India 22°29N 71°41E 42 H4
Chudskoye, Ozero Russia 58°13N 27°30E 9 G22
Chugach Mts. U.S.A. 60°45N 147°0W 74 C10
Chūgoku □ Japan 35°0N 133°0E 29 G6
Chūgoku-Sanchi Japan 35°0N 133°0E 29 G6
Chugwater U.S.A. 41°46N 104°50W 76 F11
Chukchi Plateau Arctic 78°0N 165°0W 4 B17
Chukchi Sea Russia 68°0N 175°0W 27 C19
Chukotskiy, Mys Russia 64°14N 173°8W 74 C5
Chukotskiy Poluostrov
  Russia 66°0N 174°0W 74 B5
Chukotskoye Nagorye
  Russia 68°0N 175°0E 27 C18
Chula Vista U.S.A. 32°38N 117°5W 79 N9
Chulband → India 20°40N 79°54E 44 D4
Chulucanas Peru 5°8S 80°10W 92 E2
Chulym → Russia 57°43N 83°51E 26 D9
Chum Phae Thailand 16°40N 102°6E 38 D4
Chum Saeng Thailand 15°55N 100°15E 38 E3
Chumar India 32°40N 78°35E 43 C8
Chumbicha Argentina 29°0S 66°10W 94 B2
Chumikan Russia 54°40N 135°10E 27 D14

Chumphon Thailand 10°35N 99°14E 39 G2
Chuna → Russia 57°47N 94°37E 27 D10
Chun'an China 29°35N 119°3E 35 C12
Chuncheon S. Korea 37°58N 127°44E 33 F14
Chunchura India 22°53N 88°27E 43 H13
Chunggang-ŭp
  N. Korea 41°48N 126°48E 33 D14
Chunghwa N. Korea 38°52N 125°47E 33 E13
Chungju S. Korea 36°58N 127°58E 33 F14
Chungking = Chongqing
  China 29°35N 106°25E 34 C6
Chungli Taiwan 24°57N 121°13E 35 E13
Chungt'iaoshan = Zhongtiao Shan
  China 35°0N 111°10E 32 G6
Chungyang Shanmo
  Taiwan 23°10N 121°0E 35 F13
Chunian Pakistan 30°57N 74°0E 42 D6
Chunya Tanzania 8°30S 33°27E 54 F6
Chunyang China 43°38N 129°23E 33 C15
Chupara Pt. Trin. & Tob. 10°49N 61°22W 93 K15
Chuquibamba Peru 15°47S 72°44W 92 G4
Chuquicamata Chile 22°15S 69°0W 94 A2
Chur Switz. 46°52N 9°32E 20 C8
Churachandpur India 24°20N 93°40E 41 G18
Church Stretton U.K. 52°32N 2°48W 13 E5
Churchill Canada 58°47N 94°11W 71 B10
Churchill → Man.,
  Canada 58°47N 94°12W 71 B10
Churchill, C. Canada 58°46N 93°12W 71 B10
Churchill Falls Canada 53°36N 64°19W 73 B7
Churchill L. Canada 55°55N 108°20W 71 B7
Churchill Pk. Canada 58°10N 125°10W 70 B3
Churki India 23°50N 83°12E 43 H10
Churu India 28°20N 74°50E 42 E6
Churún Merú = Angel Falls
  Venezuela 5°57N 62°30W 92 B6
Chushal India 33°40N 78°40E 43 C8
Chuska Mts. U.S.A. 36°15N 108°50W 77 H9
Chusovoy Russia 58°22N 57°50E 18 C10
Chute-aux-Outardes
  Canada 49°7N 68°24W 73 C6
Chuuk = Truk Micronesia 7°25N 151°46E 64 G7
Chuvash Republic = Chuvashia □
  Russia 55°30N 47°0E 18 C8
Chuvashia □ Russia 55°30N 47°0E 18 C8
Chuwārtah Iraq 35°43N 45°34E 46 C5
Chuxiong China 25°2N 101°28E 34 E3
Chuy Uruguay 33°41S 53°27W 95 C5
Chuzhou China 32°19N 118°20E 35 A12
Ci Xian China 36°20N 114°25E 32 F8
Ciamis Indonesia 7°20S 108°21E 37 G13
Cianjur Indonesia 6°49S 107°8E 37 G12
Cianorte Brazil 23°37S 52°37W 95 A5
Cibola U.S.A. 33°17N 114°42W 79 M12
Cicia Fiji 17°45S 179°18W 59 a
Ciéagas del Cataumbo △
  Venezuela 9°25N 71°54W 89 E5
Ciechanów Poland 52°52N 20°38E 17 B11
Ciego de Ávila Cuba 21°50N 78°50W 88 B4
Ciénaga Colombia 11°1N 74°15W 92 A4
Cienfuegos Cuba 22°10N 80°30W 88 B3
Cieszyn Poland 49°45N 18°35E 17 D10
Cieza Spain 38°17N 1°23W 21 C5
Cihuatlán Mexico 19°14N 104°35W 86 D4
Cijara, Embalse de Spain 39°18N 4°52W 21 C3
Cijulang Indonesia 7°42S 108°27E 37 G13
Cilacap Indonesia 7°43S 109°0E 37 G13
Cili China 29°30N 111°8E 35 C8
Cill Airne = Killarney
  Ireland 52°4N 9°30W 10 D2
Cill Chainnigh = Kilkenny
  Ireland 52°39N 7°15W 10 D4
Cill Dara = Kildare Ireland 53°9N 6°55W 10 C5
Cill Droichid = Celbridge
  Ireland 53°20N 6°32W 10 C5
Cill Mhantáin = Wicklow
  Ireland 52°59N 6°3W 10 D5
Cilo Dağı Turkey 37°28N 43°55E 19 G7
Cima U.S.A. 35°14N 115°30W 79 K11
Cimarron Kans., U.S.A. 37°48N 100°21W 80 G3
Cimarron N. Mex.,
  U.S.A. 36°31N 104°55W 77 H11
Cimarron → U.S.A. 36°10N 96°16W 84 C6
Cimişlia Moldova 46°34N 28°44E 17 E15
Cimone, Mte. Italy 44°12N 10°42E 22 B4
Cinca → Spain 41°26N 0°21E 21 B6
Cincar Bos.-H. 43°55N 17°5E 22 C7
Cincinnati U.S.A. 39°9N 84°27W 81 F11
Cincinnatus U.S.A. 42°33N 75°54W 83 D9
Çine Turkey 37°37N 28°2E 23 F13
Ciney Belgium 50°18N 5°5E 15 D5
Cinque I. India 11°16N 92°42E 45 J11
Cinto, Mte. France 42°24N 8°54E 20 E8
Circle Alaska, U.S.A. 65°50N 144°4W 74 B11
Circle Mont., U.S.A. 47°25N 105°35W 76 C11
Circleville U.S.A. 39°36N 82°57W 81 F12
Cirebon Indonesia 6°45S 108°32E 37 G13
Cirencester U.K. 51°43N 1°57W 13 F6
Cisco U.S.A. 32°23N 98°59W 84 E5
Citlaltépetl = Orizaba, Pico de
  Mexico 18°58N 97°15W 87 D5
Citrus Heights U.S.A. 38°42N 121°17W 78 G5
Citrusdal S. Africa 32°35S 19°0E 56 E2
Città di Castello Italy 43°27N 12°14E 22 C5
Ciudad Acuña Mexico 29°18N 100°55W 86 B4
Ciudad Altamirano
  Mexico 18°20N 100°40W 86 D4
Ciudad Anáhuac Mexico 27°14N 100°7W 86 B4
Ciudad Bolívar Venezuela 8°5N 63°36W 92 B6
Ciudad Camargo
  Mexico 27°40N 105°10W 86 B3
Ciudad Cortés Costa Rica 8°55N 84°0W 88 E3
Ciudad del Carmen
  Mexico 18°38N 91°50W 87 D6
Ciudad del Este Paraguay 25°30S 54°50W 95 B5
Ciudad Delicias = Delicias
  Mexico 28°13N 105°28W 86 B3
Ciudad Frontera Mexico 26°56N 101°27W 86 B4

Ciudad Guayana Venezuela 8°0N 62°30W 92 B6
Ciudad Guerrero
  Mexico 28°33N 107°30W 86 B3
Ciudad Guzmán Mexico 19°41N 103°29W 86 D4
Ciudad Juárez Mexico 31°44N 106°29W 86 A3
Ciudad Lerdo Mexico 25°32N 103°32W 86 B4
Ciudad Madero Mexico 22°19N 97°50W 87 C5
Ciudad Mante Mexico 22°44N 98°59W 87 C5
Ciudad Obregón Mexico 27°29N 109°56W 86 B3
Ciudad Real Spain 38°59N 3°55W 21 C4
Ciudad Rodrigo Spain 40°35N 6°32W 21 B2
Ciudad Valles Mexico 21°59N 99°1W 87 C5
Ciudad Victoria Mexico 23°44N 99°8W 87 C5
Civitanova Marche Italy 43°18N 13°44E 22 C5
Civitavécchia Italy 42°6N 11°48E 22 C4
Cixi China 30°17N 121°9E 35 B13
Cizre Turkey 37°19N 42°10E 46 B4
Clackmannanshire □
  U.K. 56°10N 3°43W 11 E5
Clacton-on-Sea U.K. 51°47N 1°11E 13 F9
Claire, L. Canada 58°35N 112°5W 70 B6
Clairton U.S.A. 40°18N 79°53W 82 F5
Clallam Bay U.S.A. 48°15N 124°16W 78 B2
Clanton U.S.A. 32°51N 86°38W 85 E11
Clanwilliam S. Africa 32°11S 18°52E 56 E2
Clara Ireland 53°21N 7°37W 10 C4
Claraville U.S.A. 35°24N 118°20W 79 K8
Clare Australia 33°50S 138°37E 63 E2
Clare U.S.A. 43°49N 84°46W 81 D11
Clare □ Ireland 52°45N 9°0W 10 D3
Clare → Ireland 53°20N 9°2W 10 C2
Clare I. Ireland 53°47N 10°0W 10 C1
Claremont Calif., U.S.A. 34°6N 117°43W 79 L9
Claremont N.H., U.S.A. 43°23N 72°20W 83 C12
Claremont Pt. Australia 14°1S 143°41E 62 A3
Claremore U.S.A. 36°19N 95°36W 84 C7
Claremorris Ireland 53°45N 9°0W 10 C3
Clarence → Australia 29°25S 153°22E 63 D5
Clarence → N.Z. 42°10S 173°56E 59 E4
Clarence, I. Chile 54°0S 72°0W 96 G2
Clarence I. Antarctica 61°10S 54°0W 5 C18
Clarence Str. Australia 12°0S 131°0E 60 B5
Clarence Town Bahamas 23°6N 74°59W 89 B5
Clarendon Pa., U.S.A. 41°47N 79°6W 82 E5
Clarendon Tex., U.S.A. 34°56N 100°53W 84 D4
Clarenville Canada 48°10N 54°1W 73 C9
Claresholm Canada 50°2N 113°33W 70 D6
Clarie Coast Antarctica 68°0S 135°0E 5 C9
Clarinda U.S.A. 40°44N 95°2W 80 E6
Clarington Canada 43°55N 78°41W 82 C6
Clarion Iowa, U.S.A. 42°44N 93°44W 80 D7
Clarion Pa., U.S.A. 41°13N 79°23W 82 E5
Clarion → U.S.A. 41°7N 79°41W 82 E5
Clarion Fracture Zone
  Pac. Oc. 20°0N 120°0W 66 H7
Clark, Pt. Canada 44°4N 81°45W 82 B3
Clark Fork U.S.A. 48°9N 116°11W 76 B5
Clark Fork → U.S.A. 48°9N 116°15W 76 B5
Clarkdale U.S.A. 34°46N 112°3W 77 J7
Clarke City Canada 50°12N 66°38W 73 B6
Clarke Ra. Australia 40°32S 148°10E 63 G4
Clarke Ra. Australia 20°40S 148°30E 62 b
Clarks Fork Yellowstone →
  U.S.A. 45°39N 108°43W 76 D9
Clark's Harbour Canada 43°25N 65°38W 73 D6
Clark Hill L. = J. Strom Thurmond
  L., U.S.A. 33°40N 82°12W 85 E13
Clarks Summit U.S.A. 41°30N 75°42W 83 E9
Clarksburg U.S.A. 39°17N 80°30W 81 F13
Clarksdale U.S.A. 34°12N 90°35W 85 D9
Clarkston U.S.A. 46°25N 117°3W 76 C5
Clarksville Ark., U.S.A. 35°28N 93°28W 84 D8
Clarksville Tenn., U.S.A. 36°32N 87°21W 85 C11
Clarksville Tex., U.S.A. 33°37N 95°3W 84 E7
Clatskanie U.S.A. 46°6N 123°12W 78 D3
Claude U.S.A. 35°7N 101°22W 84 D4
Claveria Phil. 18°37N 121°4E 37 A6
Clay U.S.A. 38°17N 81°5W 81 F13
Clay Center U.S.A. 39°23N 97°8W 80 F5
Claypool U.S.A. 33°25N 110°51W 77 K8
Claysburg U.S.A. 40°17N 78°27W 82 F6
Claysville U.S.A. 40°7N 80°25W 82 F4
Clayton N. Mex., U.S.A. 36°27N 103°11W 77 H12
Clayton N.Y., U.S.A. 44°14N 76°5W 83 B8
Clear, C. Ireland 51°25N 9°32W 10 E2
Clear, L. Canada 45°26N 77°12W 82 A7
Clear Hills Canada 56°40N 119°30W 70 B5
Clear I. Ireland 51°26N 9°30W 10 E2
Clear L. U.S.A. 39°2N 122°47W 78 F4
Clear Lake Iowa, U.S.A. 43°8N 93°23W 80 D7
Clear Lake S. Dak., U.S.A. 44°45N 96°41W 80 C5
Clear Lake Res. U.S.A. 41°56N 121°5W 76 F3
Clearfield Pa., U.S.A. 41°2N 78°27W 82 E6
Clearfield Utah, U.S.A. 41°7N 112°2W 76 F7
Clearlake U.S.A. 38°57N 122°38W 78 G4
Clearwater Canada 51°38N 120°2W 70 C4
Clearwater U.S.A. 27°59N 82°48W 85 H13
Clearwater → Alta.,
  Canada 52°22N 114°57W 70 C6
Clearwater → Alta.,
  Canada 56°44N 111°23W 71 B6
Clearwater L. Canada 53°34N 99°49W 71 C9
Clearwater Lake △
  Canada 54°0N 101°0W 71 C8
Clearwater Mts. U.S.A. 46°5N 115°20W 76 C6
Clearwater River △
  Canada 56°55N 109°10W 71 B7
Cleburne U.S.A. 32°21N 97°23W 84 E6
Clee Hills U.K. 52°26N 2°35W 13 E5
Cleethorpes U.K. 53°33N 0°3W 12 D7
Cleeve Cloud U.K. 51°56N 2°0W 13 F6
Clemson U.S.A. 34°41N 82°50W 85 D13
Clerke Reef Australia 17°22S 119°20E 60 C2
Clermont Australia 22°49S 147°39E 62 C4
Clermont U.S.A. 28°33N 81°46W 85 G14
Clermont-Ferrand France 45°46N 3°4E 20 D5
Clervaux Lux. 50°4N 6°2E 15 D6
Clevedon U.K. 51°26N 2°52W 13 F5

Cleveland Miss., U.S.A. 33°45N 90°43W 85 E9
Cleveland Ohio, U.S.A. 41°29N 81°41W 82 E3
Cleveland Okla., U.S.A. 36°19N 96°28W 84 C6
Cleveland Tenn., U.S.A. 35°10N 84°53W 85 D12
Cleveland Tex., U.S.A. 30°21N 95°5W 84 F7
Cleveland, C. Australia 19°11S 147°1E 62 B4
Cleveland, Mt. U.S.A. 48°56N 113°51W 76 B7
Cleveland Heights U.S.A. 41°31N 81°33W 82 E3
Clevelândia Brazil 26°24S 52°23W 95 B5
Clew B. Ireland 53°50N 9°49W 10 C2
Clewiston U.S.A. 26°45N 80°56W 85 H14
Clifden Ireland 53°29N 10°1W 10 C1
Clifden N.Z. 46°1S 167°42E 59 G1
Cliffdell U.S.A. 46°56N 121°5W 78 D5
Cliffy Hd. Australia 35°1S 116°29E 61 G2
Clifton Australia 27°59S 151°53E 63 D5
Clifton Ariz., U.S.A. 33°3N 109°18W 77 K9
Clifton Colo., U.S.A. 39°7N 108°25W 76 G9
Clifton Tex., U.S.A. 31°47N 97°35W 84 F6
Clifton Beach Australia 16°46S 145°39E 62 B4
Clinch → U.S.A. 35°53N 84°29W 85 D12
Clingmans Dome
  U.S.A. 35°34N 83°30W 85 D13
Clint U.S.A. 31°35N 106°14W 84 F1
Clinton B.C., Canada 51°6N 121°35W 70 C4
Clinton Ont., Canada 43°37N 81°32W 82 C3
Clinton N.Z. 46°12S 169°23E 59 G2
Clinton Ark., U.S.A. 35°36N 92°28W 84 D8
Clinton Conn., U.S.A. 41°17N 72°32W 83 E12
Clinton Ill., U.S.A. 40°9N 88°57W 80 E9
Clinton Ind., U.S.A. 39°40N 87°24W 80 F10
Clinton Iowa, U.S.A. 41°51N 90°12W 80 E8
Clinton Mass., U.S.A. 42°25N 71°41W 83 D13
Clinton Miss., U.S.A. 32°20N 90°20W 85 E9
Clinton Mo., U.S.A. 38°22N 93°46W 80 F7
Clinton N.C., U.S.A. 35°0N 78°22W 85 D15
Clinton Okla., U.S.A. 35°31N 98°58W 84 D5
Clinton S.C., U.S.A. 34°29N 81°53W 85 D14
Clinton Tenn., U.S.A. 36°6N 84°8W 85 C12
Clinton Wash., U.S.A. 47°59N 122°21W 78 C4
Clinton, C. Australia 22°30S 150°45E 62 C5
Clinton Colden L.
  Canada 63°58N 107°27W 68 E10
Clipperton, Î. Pac. Oc. 10°18N 109°13W 65 F17
Clipperton Fracture Zone
  Pac. Oc. 19°0N 122°0W 65 G16
Clisham U.K. 57°58N 6°49W 11 D2
Clitheroe U.K. 53°53N 2°22W 12 D5
Clo-oose Canada 48°39N 124°49W 78 B2
Cloates, Pt. Australia 22°43S 113°40E 60 D1
Clocolan S. Africa 28°55S 27°34E 57 C4
Clodomira Argentina 27°35S 64°14W 94 B3
Cloghaneely Ireland 55°8N 8°5W 10 A3
Clogher Hd. Ireland 53°48N 6°14W 10 C5
Clonakilty Ireland 51°37N 8°53W 10 E3
Clonakilty B. Ireland 51°35N 8°51W 10 E3
Cloncurry Australia 20°40S 140°28E 62 C3
Cloncurry Ireland 53°25N 6°48W 10 C5
Cloncurry → Australia 18°37S 140°40E 62 B3
Clondalkin Ireland 53°19N 6°25W 10 C5
Clones Ireland 54°11N 7°15W 10 B4
Clonmel Ireland 52°21N 7°42W 10 D4
Cloppenburg Germany 52°50N 8°2E 16 B5
Cloquet U.S.A. 46°43N 92°28W 80 B7
Clorinda Argentina 25°16S 57°45W 94 B4
Cloud Peak U.S.A. 44°23N 107°11W 76 D10
Cloudcroft U.S.A. 32°58N 105°45W 77 K11
Cloverdale U.S.A. 38°48N 123°1W 78 G4
Clovis Calif., U.S.A. 36°49N 119°42W 78 J7
Clovis N. Mex., U.S.A. 34°24N 103°12W 77 J12
Cloyne Canada 44°49N 77°11W 82 B7
Cluain Meala = Clonmel
  Ireland 52°21N 7°42W 10 D4
Cluj-Napoca Romania 46°47N 23°38E 17 E12
Clunes Australia 37°20S 143°45E 63 F3
Clutha → N.Z. 46°20S 169°49E 59 G2
Clwyd → U.K. 53°19N 3°31W 12 D4
Clyde Canada 54°9N 113°39W 70 C6
Clyde N.Z. 45°12S 169°20E 59 F2
Clyde U.S.A. 43°5N 76°52W 82 C8
Clyde → U.K. 55°55N 4°30W 11 F4
Clyde, Firth of U.K. 55°22N 5°1W 11 F3
Clyde River Canada 70°30N 68°30W 69 C18
Clydebank U.K. 55°54N 4°23W 11 F4
Clymer N.Y., U.S.A. 42°1N 79°37W 82 D5
Clymer Pa., U.S.A. 40°40N 79°1W 82 D5
Coachella U.S.A. 33°41N 116°10W 79 M10
Coachella Canal
  U.S.A. 32°43N 114°57W 79 N12
Coahoma U.S.A. 32°18N 101°18W 84 E4
Coahuayana → Mexico 18°41N 103°45W 86 D4
Coahuila □ Mexico 27°0N 103°0W 86 B4
Coal → Canada 59°39N 126°57W 70 B3
Coalcomán Mexico 18°47N 103°9W 86 D4
Coaldale Canada 49°45N 112°35W 70 D6
Coalgate U.S.A. 34°32N 96°13W 84 D6
Coalinga U.S.A. 36°9N 120°21W 78 J6
Coalisland U.K. 54°33N 6°42W 10 B5
Coalville U.K. 52°44N 1°23W 12 E6
Coalville U.S.A. 40°55N 111°24W 76 F8
Coamo Puerto Rico 18°5N 66°22W 89 d
Coari Brazil 4°8S 63°7W 92 D6
Coast Mts. Canada 55°0N 129°20W 70 C3
Coast Ranges U.S.A. 39°0N 123°0W 78 G4
Coatbridge U.K. 55°52N 4°6W 11 F4
Coatepeque Guatemala 14°46N 91°55W 88 D1
Coatesville U.S.A. 39°59N 75°50W 83 G9
Coaticook Canada 45°10N 71°46W 83 A13
Coats I. Canada 62°30N 83°0W 69 E15
Coats Land Antarctica 77°0S 25°0W 5 D1
Coatzacoalcos Mexico 18°7N 94°25W 87 D6
Cobá Mexico 20°31N 87°5W 87 C7
Cobalt Canada 47°25N 79°42W 72 C4
Cobán Guatemala 15°30N 90°21W 88 C1
Cobar Australia 31°27S 145°48E 63 E4
Cobh Ireland 51°51N 8°17W 10 E3
Cóbh, An = Cobh Ireland 51°51N 8°17W 10 E3
Cobija Bolivia 11°0S 68°50W 92 F5
Cobleskill U.S.A. 42°41N 74°29W 83 D10
Coboconk Canada 44°39N 78°48W 82 B6

Cobourg Canada 43°58N 78°10W 82 C6
Cobourg Pen. Australia 11°20S 132°15E 60 B5
Cobram Australia 35°54S 145°40E 63 F4
Coburg Germany 50°15N 10°58E 16 C6
Coburg I. Canada 75°57N 79°26W 69 B16
Cocanada = Kakinada
  India 16°57N 82°11E 44 F6
Cochabamba Bolivia 17°26S 66°10W 92 G5
Cochin = Kochi India 9°58N 76°20E 45 K3
Cochin China = Nam Phan
  Vietnam 10°30N 106°0E 39 G6
Cochran U.S.A. 32°23N 83°21W 85 E13
Cochrane Alta., Canada 51°11N 114°30W 70 C6
Cochrane Ont., Canada 49°0N 81°0W 72 C3
Cochrane Chile 47°15S 72°33W 96 F2
Cochrane → Canada 59°0N 103°40W 71 B8
Cochrane, L. Chile 47°10S 72°0W 96 F2
Cockburn Australia 32°5S 141°0E 63 E3
Cockburn, Canal Chile 54°30S 72°0W 96 G2
Cockburn I. Canada 45°55N 83°22W 72 C3
Cockburn Ra. Australia 15°46S 128°0E 60 C4
Cockermouth U.K. 54°40N 3°22W 12 C4
Cocklebiddy Australia 32°0S 126°3E 61 F4
Cockpit Country, The
  Jamaica 18°15N 77°45W 88 a
Coco → Cent. Amer. 15°0N 83°8W 88 D3
Coco, I. del Pac. Oc. 5°25N 87°55W 65 G19
Coco Channel Asia 13°45N 93°10E 45 H11
Cocoa U.S.A. 28°21N 80°44W 85 G14
Cocobeach Gabon 0°59N 9°34E 54 D1
Cocos B. Trin. & Tob. 10°25N 61°2W 93 K15
Cocos I. = Coco, I. del
  Pac. Oc. 5°25N 87°55W 65 G19
Cocos Is. Ind. Oc. 12°10S 96°55E 64 J1
Cocos Ridge Pac. Oc. 4°0N 88°0W 65 G19
Cod, C. U.S.A. 42°5N 70°10W 81 D18
Codajás Brazil 3°55S 62°0W 92 D6
Codó Brazil 4°30S 43°55W 93 D10
Cody U.S.A. 44°32N 109°3W 76 D9
Coe Hill Canada 44°52N 77°50W 82 B7
Coelemu Chile 36°30S 72°48W 94 D1
Coen Australia 13°52S 143°12E 62 A3
Coeur d'Alene U.S.A. 47°41N 116°46W 76 C5
Coeur d'Alene L. U.S.A. 47°32N 116°49W 76 C5
Coevorden Neths. 52°40N 6°44E 15 B6
Coffeyville U.S.A. 37°2N 95°37W 80 G6
Coffin B. Australia 34°38S 135°28E 63 E2
Coffin Bay Australia 34°37S 135°29E 63 E2
Coffin Bay △ Australia 34°34S 135°19E 63 E2
Coffin Bay Peninsula
  Australia 34°32S 135°15E 63 E2
Coffs Harbour Australia 30°16S 153°5E 63 E5
Cognac France 45°41N 0°20W 20 D3
Cohocton U.S.A. 42°30N 77°30W 82 D7
Cohocton → U.S.A. 42°9N 77°6W 82 D7
Cohoes U.S.A. 42°46N 73°42W 83 D11
Cohuna Australia 35°45S 144°15E 63 F3
Coiba, I. de Panama 7°30N 81°40W 88 E3
Coig → Argentina 51°0S 69°10W 96 G3
Coigeach, Rubha U.K. 58°6N 5°26W 11 C3
Coihaique Chile 45°30S 71°45W 96 F2
Coimbatore India 11°2N 76°59E 45 J3
Coimbra Brazil 19°55S 57°48W 92 G7
Coimbra Portugal 40°15N 8°27W 21 B1
Coín Spain 36°40N 4°48W 21 D3
Coipasa, Salar de Bolivia 19°26S 68°9W 92 G5
Cojimies Ecuador 0°20N 80°0W 92 C3
Cojutepeque El Salv. 13°41N 88°54W 88 D2
Cokeville U.S.A. 42°5N 110°57W 76 E8
Colac Australia 38°21S 143°35E 63 F3
Colachel = Kolachel India 8°10N 77°15E 45 K3
Colatina Brazil 19°32S 40°37W 93 G10
Colbeck, C. Antarctica 77°6S 157°48W 5 D13
Colborne Canada 44°0N 77°53W 82 C7
Colby U.S.A. 39°24N 101°3W 80 F3
Colca → Peru 15°55S 72°43W 92 G4
Colchester U.K. 51°54N 0°55E 13 F8
Colchester U.S.A. 41°35N 72°20W 83 E12
Cold L. Canada 54°33N 110°5W 71 C7
Cold Lake Canada 54°27N 110°10W 71 C6
Coldstream Canada 50°13N 119°11W 70 C5
Coldstream U.K. 55°39N 2°15W 11 F6
Coldwater Canada 44°42N 79°40W 82 B5
Coldwater Kans., U.S.A. 37°16N 99°20W 80 G4
Coldwater Mich., U.S.A. 41°57N 85°0W 81 E11
Colebrook U.S.A. 44°54N 71°30W 83 B13
Coleman Canada 49°40N 114°30W 70 D6
Coleman U.S.A. 31°50N 99°26W 84 F5
Coleman → Australia 15°6S 141°38E 62 B3
Colenso S. Africa 28°44S 29°50E 57 C4
Coleraine Australia 37°36S 141°40E 63 F3
Coleraine U.K. 55°8N 6°41W 10 A5
Coleridge, L. N.Z. 43°17S 171°30E 59 E3
Coleroon → India 11°25N 79°50E 45 J4
Colesberg S. Africa 30°45S 25°5E 56 E4
Coleville U.S.A. 38°34N 119°30W 78 G7
Colfax Calif., U.S.A. 39°6N 120°57W 78 F6
Colfax La., U.S.A. 31°31N 92°42W 84 F8
Colfax Wash., U.S.A. 46°53N 117°22W 76 C5
Colhué Huapi, L.
  Argentina 45°30S 69°0W 96 F3
Coligny S. Africa 26°17S 26°15E 57 C4
Colima Mexico 19°14N 103°43W 86 D4
Colima □ Mexico 19°10N 104°0W 86 D4
Colima, Nevado de
  Mexico 19°30N 103°40W 86 D4
Colina Chile 33°13S 70°45W 94 C1
Colinas Brazil 6°0S 44°10W 93 E10
Coll U.K. 56°39N 6°34W 11 E2
Collahuasi Chile 21°5S 68°45W 94 A2
Collarenebri Australia 29°33S 148°34E 63 D4
College U.S.A. 64°52N 147°49W 74 C10
College Station U.S.A. 30°37N 96°21W 84 F6
Collie Australia 33°22S 116°8E 61 F2
Collier B. Australia 16°10S 124°15E 60 C3
Collier Ra. Australia 24°45S 119°10E 61 D2
Collier Range △ Australia 24°38S 119°1E 61 D2
Collierville U.S.A. 35°3N 89°40W 85 D10
Collina, Passo di Italy 44°2N 10°56E 22 B4

Collingwood *Canada* 44°29N 80°13W **82** B4
Collingwood *N.Z.* 40°41S 172°40E **59** D4
Collins *Canada* 50°17N 89°27W **72** B2
Collins Bay *Canada* 44°14N 76°36W **83** B8
Collinson Pen. *Canada* 69°58N 101°24W **68** D11
Collipulli *Chile* 37°55S 72°30W **94** D1
Collooney *Ireland* 54°11N 8°29W **10** B3
Colmar *France* 48°5N 7°20E **20** B7
Colo → *Australia* 33°25S 150°52E **63** E5
Cologne = Köln *Germany* 50°56N 6°57E **16** C4
Coloma *U.S.A.* 38°48N 120°53W **78** G6
Colomb-Béchar = Béchar
 Algeria 31°38N 2°18W **52** B5
Colombia ■ *S. Amer.* 3°45N 73°0W **92** C4
Colombian Basin *Caribbean* 14°0N 76°0W **88** D4
Colombo *Sri Lanka* 6°56N 79°58E **45** L4
Colón *B. Aires, Argentina* 33°53S 61°7W **94** C3
Colón *Entre Rios,*
 Argentina 32°12S 58°10W **94** C4
Colón *Cuba* 22°42N 80°54W **88** B3
Colón *Panama* 9°20N 79°54W **88** E4
Colón, Arch. de *Ecuador* 0°0 91°0W **90** D1
Colonia del Sacramento
 Uruguay 34°25S 57°50W **94** C4
Colonia Dora *Argentina* 28°34S 62°59W **94** B3
Colonial Beach *U.S.A.* 38°15N 76°58W **81** F15
Colonie *U.S.A.* 42°43N 73°50W **83** D11
Colonsay *Canada* 51°59N 105°52W **71** C7
Colonsay *U.K.* 56°5N 6°12W **11** E2
Colorado □ *U.S.A.* 39°30N 105°30W **76** G11
Colorado → *Argentina* 39°50S 62°8W **96** D4
Colorado → *N. Amer.* 31°45N 114°40W **77** L6
Colorado → *U.S.A.* 28°36N 95°59W **84** G7
Colorado City *U.S.A.* 32°24N 100°52W **84** E4
Colorado Plateau *U.S.A.* 37°0N 111°0W **77** H8
Colorado River Aqueduct
 U.S.A. 33°50N 117°23W **79** L12
Colorado Springs
 U.S.A. 38°50N 104°49W **76** G11
Colotlán *Mexico* 22°6N 103°16W **86** C4
Colstrip *U.S.A.* 45°53N 106°38W **76** D10
Colton *U.S.A.* 44°33N 74°56W **83** B10
Columbia *Ky., U.S.A.* 37°6N 85°18W **81** G11
Columbia *La., U.S.A.* 32°6N 92°5W **84** E8
Columbia *Miss., U.S.A.* 31°15N 89°50W **85** F10
Columbia *Mo., U.S.A.* 38°57N 92°20W **80** F7
Columbia *Pa., U.S.A.* 40°2N 76°30W **83** F8
Columbia *S.C., U.S.A.* 34°0N 81°2W **85** D14
Columbia *Tenn., U.S.A.* 35°37N 87°2W **85** D11
Columbia → *N. Amer.* 46°15N 124°5W **78** D2
Columbia, C. *Canada* 83°6N 69°57W **69** A18
Columbia, District of □
 U.S.A. 38°55N 77°0W **81** F15
Columbia, Mt. *Canada* 52°8N 117°20W **70** C5
Columbia Basin *U.S.A.* 46°45N 119°5W **76** C4
Columbia Falls *U.S.A.* 48°23N 114°11W **76** B6
Columbia Mts. *Canada* 52°0N 119°0W **70** C5
Columbia Plateau *U.S.A.* 44°0N 117°30W **76** D5
Columbiana *U.S.A.* 40°53N 80°42W **82** F4
Columbretes, Is. *Spain* 39°50N 0°50E **21** C6
Columbus *Ga., U.S.A.* 32°28N 84°59W **85** E12
Columbus *Ind., U.S.A.* 39°13N 85°55W **81** F11
Columbus *Kans., U.S.A.* 37°10N 94°50W **80** G6
Columbus *Miss., U.S.A.* 33°30N 88°25W **85** E10
Columbus *Mont., U.S.A.* 45°38N 109°15W **76** D9
Columbus *N. Mex.,*
 U.S.A. 31°50N 107°38W **77** L10
Columbus *Nebr., U.S.A.* 41°26N 97°22W **80** E5
Columbus *Ohio, U.S.A.* 39°58N 83°0W **81** F12
Columbus *Tex., U.S.A.* 29°42N 96°33W **84** G6
Colusa *U.S.A.* 39°13N 122°1W **78** F4
Colville *U.S.A.* 48°33N 117°54W **76** B5
Colville → *U.S.A.* 70°25N 150°30W **74** A9
Colville, C. *N.Z.* 36°29S 175°21E **59** B5
Colwood *Canada* 48°26N 123°29W **78** B3
Colwyn Bay *U.K.* 53°18N 3°44W **12** D4
Comácchio *Italy* 44°42N 12°11E **22** B5
Comalcalco *Mexico* 18°16N 93°13W **87** D6
Comallo *Argentina* 41°0S 70°5W **96** E2
Comanche *U.S.A.* 31°54N 98°36W **84** F5
Comandante Ferraz
 Antarctica 62°30S 58°0W **5** C18
Comayagua *Honduras* 14°25N 87°37W **88** D2
Combahee → *U.S.A.* 32°31N 80°31W **85** E14
Combarbalá *Chile* 31°11S 71°2W **94** C1
Combe Martin *U.K.* 51°12N 4°3W **13** F3
Comber *Canada* 42°14N 82°33W **82** D2
Comber *U.K.* 54°33N 5°45W **10** B6
Combermere *Canada* 45°22N 77°37W **82** A7
Comblain-au-Pont
 Belgium 50°29N 5°35E **15** D5
Comeragh Mts. *Ireland* 52°18N 7°34W **10** D4
Comet *Australia* 23°36S 148°38E **62** C4
Comilla *Bangla.* 23°28N 91°10E **41** H17
Comino, C. *Italy* 40°32N 9°49E **22** D3
Comitán de Domínguez
 Mexico 16°15N 92°8W **87** D6
Commerce *Ga., U.S.A.* 34°12N 83°28W **85** D13
Commerce *Tex., U.S.A.* 33°15N 95°54W **84** E7
Committee B. *Canada* 68°30N 86°30W **69** D14
Commodore, C. *Canada* 44°47N 80°54W **82** B4
Commonwealth B.
 Antarctica 67°0S 144°0E **5** C10
Commoron Cr. →
 Australia 28°22S 150°8E **63** D5
Communism Pk. = imeni Ismail
 Samani, Pik *Tajikistan* 39°0N 72°2E **26** F8
Como *Italy* 45°47N 9°5E **20** B8
Como, L. di *Italy* 46°0N 9°11E **20** B8
Comodoro Rivadavia
 Argentina 45°50S 67°40W **96** F3
Comorin, C. = Kannyakumari
 India 8°3N 77°40E **45** K3
Comoros ■ *Ind. Oc.* 12°10S 44°15E **55** a
Comox *Canada* 49°42N 124°55W **70** D4
Compiègne *France* 49°24N 2°50E **20** B5
Compostela *Mexico* 21°14N 104°55W **86** C4
Comprida, I. *Brazil* 24°50S 47°42W **95** A6
Compton *Canada* 45°14N 71°49W **83** A13

Compton *U.S.A.* 33°53N 118°13W **79** M8
Comrat *Moldova* 46°18N 28°40E **17** E15
Con Cuong *Vietnam* 19°2N 104°54E **38** C5
Con Dao △ *Vietnam* 8°42N 106°35E **39** H6
Con Son, Dao *Vietnam* 8°41N 106°37E **39** H6
Conakry *Guinea* 9°29N 13°49W **52** G3
Conara *Australia* 41°50S 147°26E **63** G4
Concarneau *France* 47°52N 3°56W **20** C2
Conceição da Barra
 Brazil 18°35S 39°45W **93** G11
Conceição do Araguaia
 Brazil 8°0S 49°2W **93** E9
Concepción *Argentina* 27°20S 65°35W **94** B2
Concepción *Bolivia* 16°15S 62°8W **92** G6
Concepción *Chile* 36°50S 73°0W **94** D1
Concepción *Paraguay* 23°22S 57°26W **94** A4
Concepción → *Mexico* 30°32N 113°2W **86** A2
Concepción, Est. de *Chile* 50°30S 74°55W **96** G2
Concepción, L. *Bolivia* 17°20S 61°20W **92** G6
Concepción, Pta.
 Mexico 26°53N 111°50W **86** B2
Concepción del Oro
 Mexico 24°38N 101°25W **86** C4
Concepción del Uruguay
 Argentina 32°35S 58°20W **94** C4
Conception, Pt. *U.S.A.* 34°27N 120°28W **79** L6
Conception B. *Canada* 47°45N 53°0W **73** C9
Conception B. *Namibia* 23°55S 14°22E **56** B1
Conception I. *Bahamas* 23°52N 75°9W **89** B4
Conchas Dam *U.S.A.* 35°22N 104°11W **77** J11
Concho *U.S.A.* 34°28N 109°36W **77** J9
Concho → *U.S.A.* 31°34N 99°43W **84** F5
Conchos → *Chihuahua,*
 Mexico 29°35N 104°25W **86** B4
Conchos → *Tamaulipas,*
 Mexico 24°55N 97°38W **87** B5
Concord *Calif., U.S.A.* 37°59N 122°2W **78** H4
Concord *N.C., U.S.A.* 35°25N 80°35W **85** D14
Concord *N.H., U.S.A.* 43°12N 71°32W **83** C13
Concordia *Antarctica* 75°6S 123°23E **5** D9
Concordia *Argentina* 31°20S 58°2W **94** C4
Concórdia *Amazonas,*
 Brazil 4°36S 66°36W **92** D5
Concórdia *Sta. Catarina,*
 Brazil 27°14S 52°1W **95** B5
Concordia *Mexico* 23°17N 106°4W **86** C3
Concordia *U.S.A.* 39°34N 97°40W **80** F5
Concrete *U.S.A.* 48°32N 121°45W **76** B3
Condamine *Australia* 26°56S 150°9E **63** D5
Conde *U.S.A.* 45°9N 98°6W **80** C4
Condeúba *Brazil* 14°52S 42°0W **93** F10
Condobolin *Australia* 33°4S 147°6E **63** E4
Condon *U.S.A.* 45°14N 120°11W **76** D3
Conegliano *Italy* 45°53N 12°18E **22** B5
Conejos *Mexico* 26°14N 103°53W **86** B4
Conemaugh → *U.S.A.* 40°28N 79°19W **82** F5
Confuso → *Paraguay* 25°9S 57°34W **94** B4
Conghua *China* 23°36N 113°31E **35** F9
Congjiang *China* 25°43N 108°52E **34** D7
Congleton *U.K.* 53°10N 2°13W **12** D5
Congo (Brazzaville) = Congo ■
 Africa 1°0S 16°0E **54** E3
Congo (Kinshasa) = Congo, Dem.
 Rep. of the ■ *Africa* 3°0S 23°0E **54** E4
Congo ■ *Africa* 1°0S 16°0E **54** E3
Congo → *Africa* 6°4S 12°24E **54** F2
Congo, Dem. Rep. of the ■
 Africa 3°0S 23°0E **54** E4
Congo Basin *Africa* 0°10S 24°30E **54** E4
Congonhas *Brazil* 20°30S 43°52W **95** A7
Congress *U.S.A.* 34°9N 112°51W **77** J7
Coniston *Canada* 46°29N 80°51W **72** C3
Conjeeveram = Kanchipuram
 India 12°52N 79°45E **45** H4
Conklin *Canada* 55°38N 111°5W **71** B6
Conklin *U.S.A.* 42°2N 75°49W **83** D9
Conn, L. *Ireland* 54°3N 9°15W **10** B2
Connaught □ *Ireland* 53°43N 9°12W **10** C2
Conneaut *U.S.A.* 41°57N 80°34W **82** E4
Conneautville *U.S.A.* 41°45N 80°22W **82** E4
Connecticut □ *U.S.A.* 41°30N 72°45W **83** E12
Connecticut → *U.S.A.* 41°16N 72°20W **83** E12
Connell *U.S.A.* 46°40N 118°52W **76** C4
Connellsville *U.S.A.* 40°1N 79°35W **82** F5
Connemara *Ireland* 53°29N 9°45W **10** C2
Connemara △ *Ireland* 53°32N 9°52W **10** C2
Connersville *U.S.A.* 39°39N 85°8W **81** F11
Connors Ra. *Australia* 21°40S 149°10E **62** C4
Conquest *Canada* 51°32N 107°14W **71** C7
Conrad *U.S.A.* 48°10N 111°57W **76** B8
Conran, C. *Australia* 37°49S 148°44E **63** F4
Conroe *U.S.A.* 30°19N 95°27W **84** F7
Consecon *Canada* 44°0N 77°31W **82** C7
Conselheiro Lafaiete
 Brazil 20°40S 43°48W **95** A7
Consett *U.K.* 54°51N 1°50W **12** C6
Consort *Canada* 52°1N 110°46W **71** C6
Constance = Konstanz
 Germany 47°40N 9°10E **16** E5
Constance, L. = Bodensee
 Europe 47°35N 9°25E **20** C8
Constanța *Romania* 44°14N 28°38E **17** F15
Constantine *Algeria* 36°25N 6°42E **52** A7
Constitución *Chile* 35°20S 72°30W **94** D1
Constitución *Uruguay* 31°0S 57°50W **94** C4
Constitución de 1857 △
 Mexico 32°4N 115°55W **86** A1
Consul *Canada* 49°20N 109°30W **71** D7
Contact *U.S.A.* 41°46N 114°45W **76** F6
Contai *India* 21°54N 87°46E **43** J12
Contamana *Peru* 7°19S 74°55W **92** E4
Contas → *Brazil* 14°17S 39°1W **93** F11
Contoocook *U.S.A.* 43°13N 71°45W **83** C13
Contra Costa *Mozam.* 25°9S 33°30E **57** C5
Contwoyto L. *Canada* 65°42N 110°50W **68** D9
Conway = Conwy *U.K.* 53°17N 3°50W **12** D4
Conway = Conwy → *U.K.* 53°17N 3°50W **12** D4
Conway *Australia* 20°24S 148°41E **62** b

Conway *Canada* 44°6N 76°54W **82** B8
Conway *Ark., U.S.A.* 35°5N 92°26W **84** D8
Conway *N.H., U.S.A.* 43°59N 71°7W **83** C13
Conway *S.C., U.S.A.* 33°51N 79°3W **85** E15
Conway, C. *Australia* 20°34S 148°46E **62** b
Conway, L. *Australia* 28°17S 135°35E **63** D2
Conwy *U.K.* 53°17N 3°50W **12** D4
Conwy □ *U.K.* 53°10N 3°44W **12** D4
Conwy → *U.K.* 53°17N 3°50W **12** D4
Cooch Behar = Koch Bihar
 India 26°22N 89°29E **41** F16
Cooinda *Australia* 13°15S 130°5E **60** B5
Cook *Australia* 30°37S 130°25E **61** F5
Cook *U.S.A.* 47°51N 92°41W **80** B7
Cook, B. *Chile* 55°10S 70°0W **96** H3
Cook, C. *Canada* 50°8N 127°55W **70** C3
Cook, Mt. = Aoraki Mount Cook
 N.Z. 43°36S 170°9E **59** E3
Cook Inlet *U.S.A.* 60°0N 152°0W **68** F1
Cook Is. ☑ *Pac. Oc.* 17°0S 160°0W **65** J12
Cook Strait *N.Z.* 41°15S 174°29E **59** D5
Cookeville *U.S.A.* 36°10N 85°30W **85** C12
Cookhouse *S. Africa* 32°44S 25°47E **56** D4
Cooks Harbour *Canada* 51°36N 55°52W **73** B8
Cookshire *Canada* 45°25N 71°38W **83** A13
Cookstown *Canada* 44°11N 79°42W **82** B5
Cookstown *U.K.* 54°38N 6°45W **10** B5
Cooktown *Australia* 15°30S 145°16E **62** B4
Coolabah *Australia* 31°1S 146°43E **63** E4
Cooladdi *Australia* 26°37S 145°23E **63** D4
Coolah *Australia* 31°48S 149°41E **63** E4
Coolamon *Australia* 34°46S 147°8E **63** E4
Coolgardie *Australia* 30°55S 121°8E **61** F3
Coolidge *U.S.A.* 32°59N 111°31W **77** K8
Coolidge Dam *U.S.A.* 33°10N 110°32W **77** K8
Cooma *Australia* 36°12S 149°8E **63** F4
Coon Rapids *U.S.A.* 45°9N 93°19W **80** C7
Coonabarabran
 Australia 31°14S 149°18E **63** E4
Coonamble *Australia* 30°56S 148°27E **63** E4
Coonana *Australia* 31°0S 123°0E **61** F3
Coonana ☉ *Australia* 30°51S 122°53E **61** F3
Coondapoor *India* 13°42N 74°40E **45** H2
Coonoor *India* 11°21N 76°45E **45** J3
Cooper *U.S.A.* 33°23N 95°42W **84** E7
Cooper Cr. → *Australia* 28°29S 137°46E **63** D2
Cooper Ridge *Pac. Oc.* 10°0N 150°30W **65** G12
Cooperstown *N. Dak.,*
 U.S.A. 47°27N 98°8W **80** B4
Cooperstown *N.Y.,*
 U.S.A. 42°42N 74°56W **83** D10
Coorabie *Australia* 31°54S 132°18E **61** F5
Coorong, The *Australia* 35°50S 139°20E **63** F2
Coorow *Australia* 29°53S 116°2E **61** E2
Cooroy *Australia* 26°22S 152°54E **63** D5
Coos Bay *U.S.A.* 43°22N 124°13W **76** E1
Coosa → *U.S.A.* 32°30N 86°16W **85** E11
Cootamundra *Australia* 34°36S 148°1E **63** E4
Cootehill *Ireland* 54°4N 7°5W **10** B4
Copahue Paso *Argentina* 37°49S 71°8W **94** D1
Copainalá *Mexico* 17°4N 93°18W **87** D6
Copake *U.S.A.* 42°7N 73°31W **83** D11
Copán *Honduras* 14°50N 89°9W **88** D2
Cope *U.S.A.* 39°40N 102°51W **76** G12
Copenhagen *U.S.A.* 43°54N 75°41W **83** C9
Copiapó *Chile* 27°30S 70°20W **94** B1
Copiapó → *Chile* 27°19S 70°56W **94** B1
Coplay *U.S.A.* 40°44N 75°29W **83** F9
Copp → *Argentina* 25°53S 61°41W **94** B3
Copp L. *Canada* 60°14N 114°40W **70** A6
Coppename → *Suriname* 5°48N 55°55W **93** B7
Copper Canyon = Barranca del
 Cobre △ *Mexico* 27°18N 107°40W **86** B3
Copper Center *U.S.A.* 61°58N 145°18W **74** C10
Copper Harbor *U.S.A.* 47°28N 87°53W **80** B10
Copperas Cove *U.S.A.* 31°8N 97°54W **84** F5
Coppermine = Kugluktuk
 Canada 67°50N 115°5W **68** D8
Coppermine → *Canada* 67°49N 116°4W **68** D8
Copperopolis *U.S.A.* 37°58N 120°38W **78** H6
Coquet → *U.K.* 55°20N 1°32W **12** B6
Coquille *U.S.A.* 43°11N 124°11W **76** E1
Coquimbo *Chile* 30°0S 71°20W **94** C1
Coquimbo □ *Chile* 31°0S 71°0W **94** C1
Coquitlam *Canada* 49°17N 122°45W **70** D4
Corabia *Romania* 43°48N 24°30E **17** G13
Coracora *Peru* 15°5S 73°45W **92** G4
Coraki *Australia* 28°59S 153°17E **63** D5
Coral *U.S.A.* 40°29N 79°10W **82** F5
Coral Bay *Australia* 23°8S 113°46E **60** D1
Coral Harbour *Canada* 64°8N 83°10W **69** E15
Coral Sea *Pac. Oc.* 15°0S 150°0E **58** C8
Coral Sea Basin *Pac. Oc.* 14°0S 152°0E **64** J7
Coral Sea Islands Terr. □
 Australia 20°0S 155°0E **58** C8
Coral Springs *U.S.A.* 26°16N 80°16W **85** H14
Corantijn = Courantyne →
 S. Amer. 5°50N 57°8W **92** B7

Corfield *Australia* 21°40S 143°21E **62** C3
Corfu = Kerkyra *Greece* 39°38N 19°50E **23** E8
Corfu *U.S.A.* 42°57N 78°24W **82** D6
Coria *Spain* 39°58N 6°33W **21** C2
Corigliano Cálabro *Italy* 39°36N 16°31E **22** E7
Coringa Is. *Australia* 16°58S 149°58E **62** B4
Corinth = Korinthos
 Greece 37°56N 22°55E **23** F10
Corinth *Miss., U.S.A.* 34°56N 88°31W **85** D10
Corinth *N.Y., U.S.A.* 43°15N 73°49W **83** C11
Corinth, G. of = Korinthiakos
 Kolpos *Greece* 38°16N 22°30E **23** E10
Corinto *Brazil* 18°20S 44°30W **93** G10
Corinto *Nic.* 12°30N 87°10W **88** D2
Cork *Ireland* 51°54N 8°29W **10** E3
Cork □ *Ireland* 51°57N 8°40W **10** E3
Cork Harbour *Ireland* 51°47N 8°16W **10** E3
Çorlu *Turkey* 41°11N 27°49E **23** D12
Cormack L. *Canada* 60°56N 121°37W **70** A4
Cormorant *Canada* 54°14N 100°35W **71** C8
Cormorant L. *Canada* 54°15N 100°50W **71** C8
Corn Is. = Maíz, Is. del
 Nic. 12°15N 83°4W **88** D3
Cornélio Procópio *Brazil* 23°7S 50°40W **95** A5
Corner Brook *Canada* 48°57N 57°58W **73** C8
Corneşti *Moldova* 47°21N 28°1E **17** E15
Corning *Ark., U.S.A.* 36°25N 90°35W **85** C9
Corning *Calif., U.S.A.* 39°56N 122°11W **76** G2
Corning *Iowa, U.S.A.* 40°59N 94°44W **80** E6
Corning *N.Y., U.S.A.* 42°9N 77°3W **82** D7
Cornwall *Canada* 45°2N 74°44W **83** A10
Cornwall *U.S.A.* 40°17N 76°25W **83** F8
Cornwall □ *U.K.* 50°26N 4°40W **13** G3
Cornwall I. *Canada* 77°37N 94°38W **69** B13
Cornwallis I. *Canada* 75°8N 95°0W **69** B13
Corny Pt. *Australia* 34°55S 137°0E **63** E2
Coro *Venezuela* 11°25N 69°41W **92** A5
Coroatá *Brazil* 4°8S 44°0W **93** D10
Corocoro *Bolivia* 17°15S 68°28W **92** G5
Coroico *Bolivia* 16°0S 67°50W **92** G5
Coromandel *N.Z.* 36°45S 175°31E **59** B5
Coromandel Coast *India* 12°30N 81°0E **45** H5
Corona *Calif., U.S.A.* 33°53N 117°34W **79** M9
Corona *N. Mex., U.S.A.* 34°15N 105°36W **77** J11
Coronado *U.S.A.* 32°41N 117°10W **79** N9
Coronado, B. de *Costa Rica* 9°0N 83°40W **88** E3
Coronados, Is. Los
 Mexico 32°26N 117°19W **79** N9
Coronation *Canada* 52°5N 111°27W **70** C6
Coronation Gulf *Canada* 68°25N 110°0W **68** D10
Coronation I. *Antarctica* 60°45S 46°0W **5** C18
Coronation Is. *Australia* 14°57S 124°55E **60** B3
Coronda *Argentina* 31°58S 60°56W **94** C3
Coronel *Chile* 37°0S 73°10W **94** D1
Coronel Bogado
 Paraguay 27°11S 56°18W **94** B4
Coronel Dorrego
 Argentina 38°40S 61°10W **94** D3
Coronel Oviedo *Paraguay* 25°24S 56°30W **94** B4
Coronel Pringles
 Argentina 38°0S 61°30W **94** D3
Coronel Suárez *Argentina* 37°30S 61°52W **94** D3
Coronel Vidal *Argentina* 37°28S 57°45W **94** D4
Coropuna, Nevado *Peru* 15°30S 72°41W **92** G4
Corowa *Australia* 35°58S 146°21E **63** F4
Corozal *Belize* 18°23N 88°23W **87** D7
Corozal □ *Belize* 18°30N 88°30W **87** D7
Corozal, Pt. *Trin. & Tob.* 10°45N 61°37W **93** K15
Corpus *Argentina* 27°10S 55°30W **94** B4
Corpus Christi *U.S.A.* 27°47N 97°24W **84** H6
Corpus Christi, L. *U.S.A.* 28°2N 97°52W **84** G6
Corraun Pen. *Ireland* 53°54N 9°54W **10** C2
Correntes → *La das Mozam.* 24°6S 35°34E **57** B6
Corrib, L. *Ireland* 53°27N 9°16W **10** C2
Corrientes *Argentina* 27°30S 58°45W **94** B4
Corrientes □ *Argentina* 28°0S 57°0W **94** B4
Corrientes → *Argentina* 30°42S 59°38W **94** C4
Corrientes → *Peru* 3°43S 74°35W **92** D4
Corrientes, C. *Colombia* 5°30N 77°34W **92** B3
Corrientes, C. *Cuba* 21°43N 84°30W **88** B3
Corrientes, C. *Mexico* 20°25N 105°42W **86** C3
Corrigan *U.S.A.* 31°0N 94°52W **84** F7
Corrigin *Australia* 32°20S 117°53E **61** F2
Corriverton *Guyana* 5°55N 57°20W **92** B7
Corry *U.S.A.* 41°55N 79°39W **82** E5
Corse *France* 42°0N 9°0E **20** F8
Corse, C. *France* 43°1N 9°25E **20** E8
Corsica = Corse □ *France* 42°0N 9°0E **20** F8
Corsicana *U.S.A.* 32°6N 96°28W **84** E6
Corte *France* 42°19N 9°11E **20** E8
Cortés, Mar de = California, G. de
 Mexico 27°0N 111°0W **86** B2
Cortez *U.S.A.* 37°21N 108°35W **77** H9
Cortland *N.Y., U.S.A.* 42°36N 76°11W **83** D8
Cortland *Ohio, U.S.A.* 41°20N 80°44W **82** E4
Çorum *Turkey* 40°30N 34°57E **19** F5
Corumbá *Brazil* 19°0S 57°30W **92** G7
Corunna = A Coruña
 Spain 43°20N 8°25W **21** A1
Corvallis *U.S.A.* 44°34N 123°16W **76** D2
Corvette, L. de la *Canada* 53°25N 74°3W **72** B5
Corvo *Azores* 39°43N 31°8W **52** a
Corydon *U.K.* 40°46N 93°19W **80** E7
Cosalá *Mexico* 24°23N 106°41W **86** C3
Cosamaloapan de Carpio
 Mexico 18°22N 95°48W **87** D5
Cosenza *Italy* 39°18N 16°15E **22** E7
Coshocton *U.S.A.* 40°16N 81°51W **82** F3
Cosmo Newberry
 Australia 28°0S 122°54E **61** E3
Cosmo Newberry ◇
 Australia 27°59S 122°53E **61** E3
Cosmonaut Sea *S. Ocean* 66°30S 40°0E **5** C5
Coso Junction *U.S.A.* 36°3N 117°57W **79** J9
Coso Pk. *U.S.A.* 36°13N 117°44W **79** J9
Cosquín *Argentina* 31°15S 64°30W **94** C3
Costa de la Luz *Spain* 36°15N 5°58W **21** D2
Costa del Azahar *Spain* 39°39N 0°13W **21** B6

Costa Rica ■ *Cent. Amer.* 10°0N 84°0W **88** E3
Costa Verde *Spain* 43°22N 4°14W **21** A3
Cosumnes → *U.S.A.* 38°16N 121°26W **78** G5
Cotabato *Phil.* 7°14N 124°15E **37** C6
Cotagaita *Bolivia* 20°45S 65°40W **94** A2
Côte d'Ivoire ■ *Africa* 7°30N 5°0W **52** G4
Coteau des Prairies
 U.S.A. 45°20N 97°50W **80** C5
Coteau du Missouri
 U.S.A. 47°0N 100°0W **80** B4
Cotentin *France* 49°15N 1°30W **20** B3
Cotonou *Benin* 6°20N 2°25E **52** G6
Cotopaxi *Ecuador* 0°40S 78°30W **92** D3
Cotswold Hills *U.K.* 51°42N 2°10W **13** F5
Cottage Grove *U.S.A.* 43°48N 123°3W **76** E2
Cottam *U.S.A.* 42°8N 82°45W **82** D2
Cottbus *Germany* 51°45N 14°20E **16** C8
Cottingham *U.K.* 53°48N 0°25W **12** D7
Cottonwood *U.S.A.* 34°45N 112°1W **77** J7
Cotulla *U.S.A.* 28°26N 99°14W **84** G5
Coudersport *U.S.A.* 41°46N 78°1W **82** E6
Couedic, C. du *Australia* 36°5S 136°40E **63** F2
Coulee City *U.S.A.* 47°37N 119°17W **76** C4
Coulee Dam Nat. Recr. Area =
 Lake Roosevelt △
 U.S.A. 48°5N 118°14W **76** B4
Coulman I. *Antarctica* 73°35S 170°0E **5** D11
Coulonge → *Canada* 45°52N 76°46W **72** C4
Coulterville *U.S.A.* 37°43N 120°12W **78** H6
Council *Alaska, U.S.A.* 64°53N 163°41W **74** C7
Council *Idaho, U.S.A.* 44°44N 116°26W **76** D5
Council Bluffs *U.S.A.* 41°16N 95°52W **80** E6
Council Grove *U.S.A.* 38°40N 96°29W **80** F5
Coupeville *U.S.A.* 48°13N 122°41W **78** B4
Courantyne → *S. Amer.* 5°50N 57°8W **92** B7
Courcelles *Belgium* 50°28N 4°22E **15** D4
Courtenay *Canada* 49°45N 125°0W **70** D4
Courtland *Canada* 42°51N 80°38W **82** D4
Courtland *U.S.A.* 38°20N 121°34W **78** G5
Courtrai = Kortrijk
 Belgium 50°50N 3°17E **15** D3
Courtright *Canada* 42°49N 82°28W **82** D2
Coushatta *U.S.A.* 32°1N 93°21W **84** E8
Coutts Crossing
 Australia 29°49S 152°55E **63** D5
Couva *Trin. & Tob.* 10°25N 61°27W **93** K15
Couvin *Belgium* 50°3N 4°29E **15** D4
Cove I. *Canada* 45°17N 81°44W **82** A3
Coventry *U.K.* 52°25N 1°28W **13** E6
Covilhã *Portugal* 40°17N 7°31W **21** B2
Covington *Ga., U.S.A.* 33°36N 83°51W **85** E13
Covington *Ky., U.S.A.* 39°5N 84°30W **81** F11
Covington *Tenn., U.S.A.* 35°34N 89°39W **85** D10
Covington *Va., U.S.A.* 37°47N 79°59W **81** G14
Cowal, L. *Australia* 33°40S 147°25E **63** E4
Cowan, L. *Australia* 31°45S 121°45E **61** F3
Cowan L. *Canada* 54°0N 107°15W **71** C7
Cowangie *Australia* 35°12S 141°26E **63** F3
Cowansville *Canada* 45°14N 72°46W **83** A12
Coward Springs
 Australia 29°24S 136°49E **63** D2
Cowcowing Lakes
 Australia 30°55S 117°20E **61** F2
Cowdenbeath *U.K.* 56°7N 3°21W **11** E5
Cowell *Australia* 33°39S 136°56E **63** E2
Cowes *U.K.* 50°45N 1°18W **13** G6
Cowichan L. *Canada* 48°53N 124°17W **78** B2
Cowlitz → *U.S.A.* 46°6N 122°55W **78** D4
Cowra *Australia* 33°49S 148°42E **63** E4
Coxilha Grande *Brazil* 28°18S 51°30W **95** B5
Coxim *Brazil* 18°30S 54°55W **93** G8
Cox's Bazar *Bangla.* 21°26N 91°59E **41** J17
Coyote Wells *U.S.A.* 32°44N 115°58W **79** N11
Coyuca de Benítez *Mexico* 17°2N 100°4W **87** D4
Coyuca de Catalán
 Mexico 18°20N 100°39W **86** D4
Cozad *U.S.A.* 40°52N 99°59W **80** E4
Cozumel *Mexico* 20°31N 86°55W **87** C7
Cozumel, Isla *Mexico* 20°30N 86°40W **87** C7
Crab Hill *Barbados* 13°19N 59°38W **89** g
Cracow = Kraków
 Poland 50°4N 19°57E **17** C10
Cracow *Australia* 25°17S 150°17E **63** D5
Cradle Mt.-Lake St. Clair △
 Australia 41°49S 147°56E **63** G4
Cradock *Australia* 32°6S 138°31E **63** E2
Cradock *S. Africa* 32°8S 25°36E **56** D4
Craig *U.S.A.* 40°31N 107°33W **76** F10
Craigavon *U.K.* 54°27N 6°23W **10** B5
Craik *Canada* 51°3N 105°49W **71** C7
Crailsheim *Germany* 49°8N 10°5E **16** D6
Craiova *Romania* 44°21N 23°48E **17** F12
Cramsie *Australia* 23°20S 144°15E **62** C3
Cranberry L. *U.S.A.* 44°11N 74°50W **83** B10
Cranberry Portage
 Canada 54°35N 101°23W **71** C8
Cranbrook *Australia* 34°18S 117°33E **61** F2
Cranbrook *Canada* 49°30N 115°46W **70** D5
Crandon *U.S.A.* 45°34N 88°54W **80** C9
Crane *Oreg., U.S.A.* 43°25N 118°35W **76** E4
Crane *Tex., U.S.A.* 31°24N 102°21W **84** F3
Crane, The *Barbados* 13°6N 59°27W **89** g
Cranganore *India* 10°13N 76°13E **45** J3
Cranston *U.S.A.* 41°47N 71°26W **83** E13
Crater L. *U.S.A.* 42°56N 122°6W **76** E2
Crater Lake △ *U.S.A.* 42°55N 122°10W **76** E2
Craters of the Moon △
 U.S.A. 43°25N 113°30W **76** E7
Crateús *Brazil* 5°10S 40°39W **93** E10
Crato *Brazil* 7°10S 39°25W **93** E11
Craven, L. *Canada* 54°20N 76°56W **72** B4
Crawford *U.S.A.* 42°41N 103°25W **80** D2
Crawfordsville *U.S.A.* 40°2N 86°54W **80** E10
Crawley *U.K.* 51°7N 0°11W **13** F7
Crazy Mts. *U.S.A.* 46°12N 110°20W **76** C8
Crean L. *Canada* 54°5N 106°9W **71** C7
Crediton *Canada* 43°17N 81°33W **82** C3
Crediton *U.K.* 50°47N 3°40W **13** G4
Cree → *Canada* 58°57N 105°47W **71** B7
Cree → *U.K.* 54°55N 4°25W **11** G4

Cree L. Canada 57°30N 106°30W 71 B7
Creede U.S.A. 37°51N 106°56W 77 H10
Creekside U.S.A. 40°40N 79°11W 82 F5
Creel Mexico 27°45N 107°38W 86 B3
Creemore Canada 44°19N 80°6W 82 B4
Creighton Canada 54°45N 101°54W 71 C8
Creighton U.S.A. 42°28N 97°54W 80 D5
Crema Italy 45°22N 9°41E 20 D8
Cremona Italy 45°7N 10°2E 20 D9
Cres Croatia 44°58N 14°25E 16 F8
Crescent City U.S.A. 41°45N 124°12W 76 F1
Crescent Group S. China Sea 16°30N 111°40E 36 A4
Crespo Argentina 32°2S 60°19W 94 C3
Cresson U.S.A. 40°28N 78°36W 82 F6
Crestline Calif., U.S.A. 34°14N 117°18W 79 L9
Crestline Ohio, U.S.A. 40°47N 82°44W 82 F2
Creston Canada 49°10N 116°31W 70 D5
Creston Calif., U.S.A. 35°32N 120°33W 78 K6
Creston Iowa, U.S.A. 41°4N 94°22W 80 E6
Crestview Calif., U.S.A. 37°46N 118°58W 78 H8
Crestview Fla., U.S.A. 30°46N 86°34W 85 F11
Crete = Kriti Greece 35°15N 25°0E 23 G11
Crete U.S.A. 40°38N 96°58W 80 E5
Creus, C. de Spain 42°20N 3°19E 21 A7
Creuse → France 47°0N 0°34E 20 C4
Crewe U.K. 53°6N 2°26W 12 D5
Crewkerne U.K. 50°53N 2°48W 13 G5
Crianlarich U.K. 56°24N 4°37W 11 E4
Criciúma Brazil 28°40S 49°23W 95 B6
Crieff U.K. 56°22N 3°50W 11 E5
Crimea □ Ukraine 45°30N 33°10E 19 E5
Crimean Pen. = Krymskyy Pivostriv Ukraine 45°0N 34°0E 19 F5
Crişul Alb → Romania 46°42N 21°17E 17 E11
Crişul Negru → Romania 46°42N 21°16E 17 E11
Crna → Macedonia 41°33N 21°59E 23 D9
Crna Gora = Montenegro ■ Europe 42°40N 19°20E 23 C8
Crna Gora Macedonia 42°10N 21°30E 23 C9
Crna Reka = Crna → Macedonia 41°33N 21°59E 23 D9
Croagh Patrick Ireland 53°46N 9°40W 10 C2
Croatia ■ Europe 45°20N 16°0E 16 F9
Crocker, Banjaran Malaysia 5°40N 116°30E 36 C5
Crockett U.S.A. 31°19N 95°27W 84 F7
Crocodile = Umgwenya → Mozam. 25°14S 32°18E 57 C5
Crocodile → S. Africa 24°12S 26°53E 56 B4
Crocodile Is. Australia 12°3S 134°58E 62 A1
Crohy Hd. Ireland 54°55N 8°26W 10 B3
Croix, L. la Canada 48°20N 92°15W 72 C1
Croker, C. Australia 10°58S 132°35E 60 B5
Croker, C. Canada 44°58N 80°59W 82 B4
Croker I. Australia 11°12S 132°32E 60 B5
Croker Islands Seas ✪ Australia 11°20S 132°30E 60 B5
Cromarty U.K. 57°40N 4°2W 11 D4
Cromer U.K. 52°56N 1°17E 12 E9
Cromwell N.Z. 45°3S 169°14E 59 F2
Cromwell U.S.A. 41°36N 72°39W 83 E12
Crook U.K. 54°43N 1°45W 12 C6
Crooked → Canada 54°50N 122°54W 70 C4
Crooked → U.S.A. 44°32N 121°16W 76 D3
Crooked I. Bahamas 22°50N 74°10W 89 B5
Crooked Island Passage Bahamas 22°55N 74°35W 89 B5
Crookston Minn., U.S.A. 47°47N 96°37W 80 B5
Crookston Nebr., U.S.A. 42°56N 100°45W 80 D3
Crookwell Australia 34°28S 149°24E 63 E4
Crosby U.K. 53°30N 3°3W 12 D4
Crosby N. Dak., U.S.A. 48°55N 103°18W 80 A2
Crosby Pa., U.S.A. 41°45N 78°23W 82 E6
Crosbyton U.S.A. 33°40N 101°14W 84 E4
Cross City U.S.A. 29°38N 83°7W 85 G13
Cross Fell U.K. 54°43N 2°28W 12 C5
Cross L. Canada 54°45N 97°30W 71 C9
Cross Lake Canada 54°37N 97°47W 71 C9
Cross Sound U.S.A. 58°0N 135°0W 68 F4
Crossett U.S.A. 33°8N 91°58W 84 E9
Crosshaven Ireland 51°47N 8°17W 10 E3
Crossmaglen U.K. 54°5N 6°36W 10 B5
Crossmolina Ireland 54°6N 9°20W 10 B2
Crossville U.S.A. 35°57N 85°2W 85 D12
Croswell U.S.A. 43°16N 82°37W 82 C2
Croton-on-Hudson U.S.A. 41°12N 73°55W 83 E11
Crotone Italy 39°5N 17°8E 22 E7
Crow → Canada 59°41N 124°20W 70 B4
Crow Agency U.S.A. 45°36N 107°28W 76 D10
Crow Hd. Ireland 51°35N 10°9W 10 E1
Crowell U.S.A. 33°59N 99°43W 84 E5
Crowley U.S.A. 30°13N 92°22W 84 F8
Crowley, L. U.S.A. 37°35N 118°42W 78 H8
Crown Point Ind., U.S.A. 41°25N 87°22W 80 E10
Crown Point N.Y., U.S.A. 43°57N 73°26W 83 C11
Crown Pt. Trin. & Tob. 11°18N 60°51W 93 J16
Crownpoint U.S.A. 35°41N 108°9W 77 J9
Crows Landing U.S.A. 37°23N 121°6W 78 H5
Crows Nest Australia 27°16S 152°4E 63 D5
Crowsnest Pass Canada 49°40N 114°40W 70 D6
Croydon Australia 18°13S 142°14E 62 B3
Croydon □ U.K. 51°22N 0°5W 13 F7
Crozet, Îs. Ind. Oc. 46°27S 52°0E 3 G12
Crusheen Ireland 52°57N 8°53W 10 D3
Cruz, C. Cuba 19°50N 77°50W 88 C4
Cruz Alta Brazil 28°45S 53°40W 95 B5
Cruz Bay U.S. Virgin Is. 18°20N 64°48W 89 e
Cruz del Eje Argentina 30°45S 64°50W 94 C3
Cruzeiro Brazil 22°33S 45°0W 95 A7
Cruzeiro do Oeste Brazil 23°46S 53°4W 95 A5
Cruzeiro do Sul Brazil 7°35S 72°35W 92 E4
Cry L. Canada 58°45N 129°0W 70 B3
Crystal Bay U.S.A. 39°15N 120°0W 78 F7
Crystal Brook Australia 33°21S 138°12E 63 E2
Crystal City U.S.A. 28°41N 99°50W 84 G5
Crystal Falls U.S.A. 46°5N 88°20W 80 B9
Crystal River U.S.A. 28°54N 82°35W 85 G13
Crystal Springs U.S.A. 31°59N 90°21W 85 F9
Csongrád Hungary 46°43N 20°12E 17 E11
Cu Lao Hon Vietnam 10°54N 108°18E 39 G7
Cua Rao Vietnam 19°16N 104°27E 38 C5
Cuamato Angola 17°2S 15°7E 56 A2
Cuamba Mozam. 14°45S 36°22E 55 G7
Cuando → Angola 17°30S 23°15E 55 H4
Cuangar Angola 17°36S 18°39E 56 A2
Cuango = Kwango → Dem. Rep. of the Congo 3°14S 17°22E 54 E3
Cuanza → Angola 9°21S 13°9E 54 F2
Cuarto → Argentina 33°25S 63°2W 94 C3
Cuatrociénegas Mexico 26°59N 102°5W 86 B4
Cuauhtémoc Mexico 28°25N 106°52W 86 B3
Cuba N. Mex., U.S.A. 36°1N 107°4W 77 H10
Cuba N.Y., U.S.A. 42°13N 78°17W 82 D6
Cuba ■ W. Indies 22°0N 79°0W 88 B4
Cubango → Africa 18°50S 22°25E 56 A3
Cuc Phuong △ Vietnam 20°17N 105°38E 38 B5
Cuchumatanes, Sierra de los Guatemala 15°35N 91°25W 88 C1
Cuckfield U.K. 51°1N 0°8W 13 F7
Cucuí Brazil 1°12N 66°50W 92 C5
Cucurpé Mexico 30°20N 110°43W 86 A2
Cúcuta Colombia 7°54N 72°31W 92 B4
Cuddalore India 11°46N 79°45E 45 J4
Cuddapah = Kadapa India 14°30N 78°47E 45 G4
Cuddapan, L. Australia 25°45S 141°26E 62 D3
Cue Australia 27°25S 117°54E 61 E2
Cuenca Ecuador 2°50S 79°9W 92 D3
Cuenca Spain 40°5N 2°10W 21 B4
Cuenca, Serranía de Spain 39°55N 1°50W 21 C5
Cuernavaca Mexico 18°55N 99°15W 87 D5
Cuero U.S.A. 29°6N 97°17W 84 G6
Cueva de la Quebrada del Toro △ Venezuela 10°46N 69°3W 89 D6
Cuevas del Almanzora Spain 37°18N 1°58W 21 D5
Cuevo Bolivia 20°15S 63°30W 92 H6
Cuiabá Brazil 15°30S 56°0W 93 G7
Cuiabá → Brazil 17°5S 56°36W 93 G7
Cuihangcun China 22°27N 113°32E 31 a
Cuijk Neths. 51°44N 5°50E 15 C5
Cuilco Guatemala 15°24N 91°58W 88 C1
Cuillin Hills U.K. 57°13N 6°15W 11 D2
Cuillin Sd. U.K. 57°4N 6°20W 11 D2
Cuilo = Kwilu → Dem. Rep. of the Congo 3°22S 17°22E 54 E3
Cuito → Angola 18°1S 20°48E 56 A3
Cuitzeo, L. de Mexico 19°55N 101°5W 86 D4
Cukai Malaysia 4°13N 103°25E 39 K4
Culbertson U.S.A. 48°9N 104°31W 76 B11
Culcairn Australia 35°41S 147°3E 63 F4
Culebra Puerto Rico 18°19N 65°18W 89 d
Culgoa → Australia 29°56S 146°20E 63 D4
Culgoa Flood Plain △ Australia 28°58S 147°5E 63 D4
Culiacán Mexico 24°50N 107°23W 86 C3
Culiacán → Mexico 24°30N 107°42W 86 C3
Culik Indonesia 8°21S 115°37E 37 J18
Culion Phil. 11°54N 119°58E 37 B6
Cullarin Ra. Australia 34°30S 149°30E 63 E4
Cullen U.K. 57°42N 2°49W 11 D6
Cullen Pt. Australia 11°57S 141°54E 62 A3
Cullera Spain 39°9N 0°17W 21 C5
Cullman U.S.A. 34°11N 86°51W 85 D11
Cullompton U.K. 50°51N 3°24W 13 G4
Culpeper U.S.A. 38°30N 78°0W 81 F14
Culuene → Brazil 12°56S 52°51W 93 F8
Culver, Pt. Australia 32°54S 124°43E 61 F3
Culverden N.Z. 42°47S 172°49E 59 E4
Cumaná Venezuela 10°30N 64°5W 92 A6
Cumberland B.C., Canada 49°40N 125°0W 70 D4
Cumberland Ont., Canada 45°29N 75°24W 83 A9
Cumberland U.S.A. 39°39N 78°46W 81 F14
Cumberland → U.S.A. 37°9N 88°25W 80 G9
Cumberland, L. U.S.A. 36°52N 85°9W 81 G11
Cumberland Gap ⌂ U.S.A. 36°36N 83°40W 81 G12
Cumberland I. U.S.A. 30°50N 81°25W 85 F14
Cumberland Is. Australia 20°35S 149°10E 62 b
Cumberland Island ⌂ U.S.A. 30°12N 81°24W 85 F14
Cumberland L. Canada 54°3N 102°18W 71 C8
Cumberland Pen. Canada 67°0N 64°0W 69 D19
Cumberland Plateau U.S.A. 36°0N 85°0W 85 D12
Cumberland Sd. Canada 65°30N 66°0W 69 D18
Cumbernauld U.K. 55°57N 3°58W 11 F5
Cumborah Australia 29°40S 147°45E 63 D4
Cumbres de Majalca △ Mexico 28°48N 106°30W 86 B3
Cumbres de Monterrey △ Mexico 25°26N 100°25W 86 B4
Cumbria □ U.K. 54°42N 2°52W 12 C5
Cumbrian Mts. U.K. 54°30N 3°0W 12 C5
Cumbum India 15°40N 79°10E 45 G4
Cuminá → Brazil 1°30S 56°0W 93 D7
Cummings Mt. U.S.A. 35°2N 118°34W 79 K8
Cummins Australia 34°16S 135°43E 63 E2
Cumnock Australia 32°59S 148°46E 63 E4
Cumnock U.K. 55°28N 4°17W 11 F4
Cumpas Mexico 30°2N 109°48W 86 B3
Cunco Chile 38°55S 72°2W 96 D2
Cuncumén Chile 31°53S 70°38W 94 C1
Cundeelee ✪ Australia 30°43S 123°25E 61 F3
Cunderdin Australia 31°37S 117°12E 61 F2
Cunene → Angola 17°20S 11°50E 56 A1
Cúneo Italy 44°23N 7°32E 20 D7
Cung Son Vietnam 13°2N 108°58E 38 F7
Çüngüş Turkey 38°13N 39°17E 46 B3
Cunnamulla Australia 28°2S 145°38E 63 D4
Cupar Canada 50°57N 104°10W 71 C8
Cupar U.K. 56°19N 3°1W 11 E5
Cupertino U.S.A. 37°19N 122°2W 78 H4
Cupica, G. de Colombia 6°25N 77°30W 92 B3
Curaçao W. Indies 12°10N 69°0W 89 D6
Curanilahue Chile 37°29S 73°28W 94 D1
Curaray → Peru 2°20S 74°5W 92 D4
Curepipe Mauritius 20°19S 57°31E 55 d
Curepto Chile 35°8S 72°1W 94 D1
Curiapo Venezuela 8°33N 61°5W 92 B6
Curicó Chile 34°55S 71°20W 94 C1
Curieuse Seychelles 4°15S 55°44E 55 b
Curitiba Brazil 25°20S 49°10W 95 B6
Curitibanos Brazil 27°18S 50°36W 95 B5
Curonian Lagoon = Kurshskiy Zaliv Russia 55°9N 21°6E 9 J19
Currabubula Australia 31°16S 150°44E 63 E5
Currais Novos Brazil 6°13S 36°30W 93 E11
Curral Velho Cabo Verde 16°8N 22°48W 52 b
Curralinho Brazil 1°45S 49°46W 93 D9
Currane, L. Ireland 51°49N 10°4W 10 E1
Currant U.S.A. 38°44N 115°28W 76 G6
Currawinya △ Australia 28°55S 144°27E 63 D3
Current → U.S.A. 36°15N 90°55W 84 C9
Currie Australia 39°56S 143°53E 63 F3
Currie U.S.A. 40°16N 114°45W 76 F6
Curtea de Argeş Romania 45°12N 24°42E 17 F13
Curtin Springs Australia 25°20S 131°45E 61 E5
Curtis U.S.A. 40°38N 100°31W 80 E3
Curtis Group Australia 39°30S 146°37E 63 F4
Curtis I. Australia 23°35S 151°10E 62 C5
Curuápanema → Brazil 2°25S 55°2W 93 D7
Curuçá Brazil 0°43S 47°50W 93 D9
Curuguaty Paraguay 24°31S 55°42W 95 A4
Çürüksu Çayi = Büyük Menderes → Turkey 37°28N 27°11E 23 F12
Curup Indonesia 3°26S 102°13E 36 E2
Cururupu Brazil 1°50S 44°50W 93 D10
Curuzú Cuatiá Argentina 29°50S 58°5W 94 B4
Curvelo Brazil 18°45S 44°27W 93 G10
Cusco Peru 13°32S 72°0W 92 F4
Cushendall U.K. 55°5N 6°4W 10 A5
Cushing U.S.A. 35°59N 96°46W 84 D6
Cushing, Mt. Canada 57°35N 126°57W 70 B3
Cusihuiriáchic Mexico 28°14N 106°50W 86 B3
Custer U.S.A. 43°46N 103°36W 80 D2
Cut Bank U.S.A. 48°38N 112°20W 76 B7
Cutchogue U.S.A. 41°1N 72°30W 83 E12
Cuthbert U.S.A. 31°46N 84°48W 85 F12
Cutler U.S.A. 36°31N 119°17W 78 J7
Cuttaburra → Australia 29°43S 144°22E 63 D3
Cuttack India 20°25N 85°57E 44 D7
Cuvier, C. Australia 23°14S 113°22E 61 D1
Cuvier I. N.Z. 36°27S 175°50E 59 B5
Cuxhaven Germany 53°51N 8°41E 16 B5
Cuyahoga Falls U.S.A. 41°8N 81°29W 82 E3
Cuyahoga Valley △ U.S.A. 41°24N 81°33W 82 E3
Cuyo Phil. 10°51N 121°2E 37 B6
Cuyuni → Guyana 6°23N 58°41W 92 B7
Cuzco = Cusco Peru 13°32S 72°0W 92 F4
Cuzco Bolivia 20°0S 66°50W 92 H5
Cwmbran U.K. 51°39N 3°2W 13 F4
Cyclades = Kyklades Greece 37°0N 24°30E 23 F11
Cygnet Australia 43°8S 147°1E 63 G4
Cynthiana U.S.A. 38°23N 84°18W 81 F11
Cypress Hills Canada 49°40N 109°30W 71 D7
Cypress Hills ⌂ Canada 49°40N 109°30W 71 D7
Cyprus ■ Asia 35°0N 33°0E 46 C2
Cyrenaica = Barqa Libya 27°0N 23°0E 53 C10
Cyrene Libya 32°53N 21°52E 53 B10
Czar Canada 52°27N 110°50W 71 C6
Czech Rep. = Czechia ■ Europe 50°0N 15°0E 16 D8
Czechia ■ Europe 50°0N 15°0E 16 D8
Częstochowa Poland 50°49N 19°7E 17 C10

D

Da → Vietnam 21°15N 105°20E 34 G5
Da Hinggan Ling China 48°0N 121°0E 31 B13
Da Lat Vietnam 11°56N 108°25E 39 G7
Da Nang Vietnam 16°4N 108°13E 38 D7
Da Qaidam China 37°50N 95°15E 30 D8
Da Yunhe → Hopei, China 39°10N 117°10E 33 E9
Da Yunhe → Jiangsu, China 34°25N 120°5E 33 H10
Da'an China 45°30N 124°7E 33 B13
Daan Viljoen ⌂ Namibia 22°2S 16°45E 56 B2
Daba Shan China 32°0N 109°0E 34 B7
Dabbagh, Jabal Si. Arabia 27°52N 35°45E 46 E2
Dabhoi India 22°10N 73°20E 42 H5
Dabie Shan China 31°20N 115°20E 35 B10
Dabola Guinea 10°50N 11°5W 52 F3
Dabu China 24°22N 116°41E 35 E11
Dabugam India 19°27N 82°26E 44 E6
Dabung Malaysia 5°23N 102°1E 39 K4
Dacca = Dhaka Bangla. 23°43N 90°26E 43 H14
Dachang China 32°13N 118°45E 35 A12
Dachaoshan Dam China 24°1N 100°22E 34 E3
Dachigam △ India 34°10N 75°0E 42 B6
Dacre Canada 45°22N 76°57W 82 A8
Dadanawa Guyana 2°50N 59°30W 92 C7
Dade City U.S.A. 28°22N 82°11W 85 G13
Dadhar Pakistan 29°28N 67°39E 42 E2
Đadra U.A.E. 25°32N 56°22E 47 E8
Dadra & Nagar Haveli □ India 20°5N 73°0E 44 D1
Dadri = Charkhi Dadri India 28°37N 76°17E 42 E7
Dadu Pakistan 26°45N 67°45E 42 F2
Dadu He → China 29°31N 103°46E 34 C4
Daegu S. Korea 35°50N 128°37E 33 G15
Daejeon S. Korea 36°20N 127°28E 33 F14
Daejeong S. Korea 33°8N 126°17E 33 H14
Daet Phil. 14°2N 122°55E 37 B6
Dafang China 27°9N 105°39E 34 D5
Dafeng China 33°3N 120°45E 33 H11
Dagana Senegal 16°30N 15°35W 52 E2
Dagestan □ Russia 42°30N 47°0E 19 F8
Daggett U.S.A. 34°52N 116°52W 79 L10
Daghestan Republic = Dagestan □ Russia 42°30N 47°0E 19 F8
Dağlıq Qarabağ = Nagorno-Karabakh □ Azerbaijan 39°55N 46°45E 46 B5
Dagö = Hiiumaa Estonia 58°50N 22°45E 9 G20
Dagu China 38°59N 117°40E 33 E9
Daguan China 27°43N 103°56E 34 D4
Dagupan Phil. 16°3N 120°20E 37 A6
Daguragu Australia 17°33S 130°30E 60 C5
Daguragu ✪ Australia 17°24S 130°48E 60 C5
Dahab Egypt 28°31N 34°31E 46 D2
Dahanu India 19°58N 72°44E 44 E1
Dahivadi India 17°43N 74°33E 44 F2
Dahlak Kebir Eritrea 15°50N 40°10E 49 D3
Dahlonega U.S.A. 34°32N 83°59W 85 D13
Dahod India 22°50N 74°15E 42 H6
Dahong Shan China 31°25N 113°0E 35 B9
Dahongliutan China 35°45N 79°20E 43 B8
Dahra Libya 29°30N 17°50E 53 C9
Dahūk Iraq 36°50N 43°1E 46 B3
Dai Hao Vietnam 18°1N 106°25E 38 C6
Dai-Sen Japan 35°22N 133°32E 29 G6
Dai Shan China 30°25N 122°10E 35 B14
Dai Xian China 39°4N 112°58E 32 E7
Daicheng China 38°42N 116°38E 32 E9
Daikondi = Dāykondī □ Afghan. 34°0N 66°0E 40 C5
Dailekh Nepal 28°50N 81°44E 43 E9
Daingean Ireland 53°18N 7°17W 10 C4
Daingean, An = Dingle Ireland 52°9N 10°17W 10 D1
Dainkog China 32°30N 97°58E 34 A1
Daintree Australia 16°20S 145°20E 62 B4
Daintree △ Australia 16°8S 145°2E 62 B4
Daiō-Misaki Japan 34°15N 136°45E 29 G8
Daisen Japan 39°27N 140°29E 28 E10
Daisen-Oki △ Japan 35°23N 133°34E 29 G6
Daisetsu-Zan Japan 43°30N 142°57E 28 C11
Daisetsu-Zan △ Japan 43°30N 142°55E 28 C11
Daitari India 21°10N 85°46E 44 D7
Daiyun Shan China 25°50N 118°15E 35 E12
Dajarra Australia 21°42S 139°30E 62 C2
Dajiawa China 37°9N 119°0E 33 F10
Dajin Chuan → China 31°16N 101°59E 34 B3
Dak Dam Cambodia 12°20N 107°21E 38 F6
Dak Nhe Vietnam 15°28N 107°48E 38 E6
Dak Pek Vietnam 15°4N 107°44E 38 E6
Dak Song Vietnam 12°19N 107°35E 39 F6
Dak Sui Vietnam 14°55N 107°43E 38 E6
Dakar Senegal 14°34N 17°29W 52 F2
Dakhla W. Sahara 23°50N 15°53W 52 D2
Dakhla, El Wâhât el Egypt 25°30N 28°50E 53 C11
Dakoank India 7°2N 93°43E 45 L11
Dakor India 22°45N 73°11E 42 H5
Dakota City U.S.A. 42°25N 96°25W 80 D5
Đakovica = Gjakovë Kosovo 42°22N 20°26E 23 C9
Dalachi China 36°48N 105°0E 32 F3
Dalai Nur China 43°20N 116°45E 32 C9
Dālakī Iran 29°26N 51°17E 47 D6
Dalälven → Sweden 60°12N 16°43E 9 F17
Dalaman → Turkey 36°41N 28°43E 23 F13
Dalandzadgad Mongolia 43°27N 104°30E 32 C3
Dalap-Uliga-Darrit = Majuro Marshall Is. 7°9N 171°12E 64 G9
Dalarna Sweden 61°0N 14°0E 8 F16
Dalay Mongolia 43°28N 103°30E 32 C2
Dālbandīn Pakistan 29°0N 64°23E 40 E4
Dalbeattie U.K. 54°56N 3°50W 11 G5
Dalbeg Australia 20°16S 147°18E 62 C4
Dalby Australia 27°10S 151°17E 63 D5
Dale City U.S.A. 38°38N 77°19W 81 F15
Dale Hollow L. U.S.A. 36°32N 85°27W 85 C12
Dalgān Iran 27°31N 59°19E 47 E8
Dalhart U.S.A. 36°4N 102°31W 84 C3
Dalhousie Canada 48°5N 66°26W 73 C6
Dalhousie India 32°38N 75°58E 42 C6
Dali Shaanxi, China 34°48N 109°58E 32 G5
Dali Yunnan, China 25°40N 100°10E 34 E3
Dalian China 38°50N 121°40E 33 E11
Daliang Shan China 28°0N 102°45E 34 D4
Daling He → China 40°55N 121°40E 33 D11
Dāliyat el Karmel Israel 32°43N 35°2E 48 C4
Dalkey Ireland 53°16N 6°6W 10 C5
Dallas U.S.A. 44°55N 123°19W 76 D2
Dallas-Fort Worth Int. ✈ (DFW) U.S.A. 32°54N 97°2W 84 E6
Dalles, The U.S.A. 45°36N 121°10W 76 D3
Dalmā U.A.E. 24°30N 52°20E 47 E7
Dalmacija Croatia 43°20N 17°0E 22 C7
Dalmas, L. Canada 53°30N 71°50W 73 B5
Dalmatia = Dalmacija Croatia 43°20N 17°0E 22 C7
Dalmau India 26°4N 81°2E 43 F9
Dalmellington U.K. 55°19N 4°23W 11 F4
Dalnegorsk Russia 44°32N 135°33E 28 B7
Dalnerechensk Russia 45°50N 133°40E 28 B6
Dalnevostochnyy □ Russia 67°0N 140°0E 27 C14
Daloa Côte d'Ivoire 7°0N 6°30W 52 G4
Dalou Shan China 28°15N 107°0E 34 C6
Dalry U.K. 55°42N 4°43W 11 F4
Dalrymple, L. Australia 20°40S 147°0E 62 C4
Dalrymple, Mt. Australia 21°1S 148°39E 62 b
Dalsland Sweden 58°50N 12°15E 9 G15
Daltenganj India 24°0N 84°4E 43 H11
Dalton Ga., U.S.A. 34°46N 84°58W 85 D12
Dalton Mass., U.S.A. 42°28N 73°11W 83 D11
Dalton Nebr., U.S.A. 41°25N 102°58W 80 E2
Dalton-in-Furness U.K. 54°10N 3°11W 12 C4
Dalvík Iceland 65°58N 18°32W 8 D4
Dálvvadis = Jokkmokk Sweden 66°35N 19°50E 8 C18
Dalwallinu Australia 30°17S 116°40E 61 F2
Daly → Australia 13°35S 130°19E 60 B5
Daly L. Canada 56°32N 105°39W 71 B7
Daly River Australia 13°46S 130°42E 60 B5
Daly River-Port Keats ✪ Australia 14°13S 129°36E 60 B4
Daly Waters Australia 16°15S 133°24E 62 B1
Dam Doi Vietnam 8°50N 105°12E 39 H5
Dam Ha Vietnam 21°21N 107°36E 38 B6
Daman India 20°25N 72°57E 44 D1
Daman & Diu □ India 20°25N 72°58E 44 D1
Dāmaneh Iran 33°1N 50°29E 47 C6
Damanganga → India 20°25N 72°56E 44 D1
Damanhûr Egypt 31°0N 30°30E 53 B12
Damant L. Canada 61°45N 105°5W 71 A7
Damar Indonesia 7°7S 128°40E 37 F7
Damara C.A.R. 4°58N 18°42E 54 D3
Damaraland Namibia 20°0S 15°0E 56 B2
Damascus = Dimashq Syria 33°30N 36°18E 48 B5
Damaturu Nigeria 11°45N 11°55E 54 B2
Damāvand Iran 35°57N 52°7E 47 C7
Damāvand, Qolleh-ye Iran 35°57N 52°7E 47 C7
Damba Angola 6°44S 15°20E 54 F3
Dâmboviţa → Romania 44°12N 26°26E 17 F14
Dambulla Sri Lanka 7°51N 80°39E 45 L5
Dame Marie Haiti 18°34N 74°26W 89 C5
Dāmghān Iran 36°10N 54°17E 47 B7
Damiel Spain 39°4N 3°37W 21 C4
Damietta = Dumyât Egypt 31°24N 31°48E 53 B12
Daming China 36°15N 115°6E 32 F8
Damīr Qābū Syria 36°58N 41°51E 46 B4
Dammam = Ad Dammām Si. Arabia 26°20N 50°5E 47 E6
Damodar → India 23°17N 87°35E 43 H12
Damoh India 23°50N 79°28E 43 H8
Dampier Australia 20°41S 116°42E 60 D2
Dampier, Selat Indonesia 0°40S 131°0E 37 E8
Dampier Arch. Australia 20°38S 116°32E 60 D2
Damrei, Chuor Phnum Cambodia 11°30N 103°0E 39 G4
Damyang S. Korea 35°19N 126°59E 33 G14
Dana Indonesia 11°0S 121°15E 37 F6
Dana Jordan 30°41N 35°37E 48 E4
Dana Nepal 28°32N 83°37E 43 E10
Dana, L. Canada 50°53N 77°20W 72 B4
Dana, Mt. U.S.A. 37°54N 119°12W 78 H7
Danakil Desert Ethiopia 12°45N 41°0E 49 E3
Danané Côte d'Ivoire 7°16N 8°9W 52 G4
Danba China 30°54N 101°48E 34 B3
Danbury U.S.A. 41°24N 73°28W 83 E11
Danby L. U.S.A. 34°13N 115°5W 79 L11
Dand Afghan. 31°28N 65°32E 42 D1
Dandeldhura Nepal 29°20N 80°35E 43 E9
Dandeli India 15°5N 74°30E 45 G2
Dandenong Australia 38°0S 145°15E 63 F4
Dandong China 40°10N 124°20E 33 D13
Danfeng China 33°45N 110°25E 32 H6
Dangan Liedao China 22°2N 114°8E 35 F10
Danger Is. = Pukapuka Cook Is. 10°53S 165°49W 65 J11
Danger Pt. S. Africa 34°40S 19°17E 56 D2
Dangla Shan = Tanggula Shan China 32°40N 92°10E 30 E7
Dangrek, Mts. = Dangrek, Phnom Thailand 14°20N 104°0E 38 E5
Dangrek, Phnom Thailand 14°20N 104°0E 38 E5
Dangriga Belize 17°0N 88°13W 87 D7
Dangshan China 34°27N 116°22E 32 G9
Dangtu China 31°32N 118°25E 35 B12
Dangyang China 30°52N 111°44E 35 B8
Daniel U.S.A. 42°52N 110°4W 76 E8
Daniel's Harbour Canada 50°13N 57°35W 73 B8
Danielskuil S. Africa 28°11S 23°33E 56 C3
Danielson U.S.A. 41°48N 71°53W 83 E13
Danilov Russia 58°16N 40°13E 18 C7
Daning China 36°28N 110°45E 32 F6
Danjiangkou China 32°31N 111°30E 35 A8
Danjiangkou Shuiku China 32°37N 111°30E 35 A8
Đank Oman 23°33N 56°16E 47 F8
Dankhar Gompa India 32°10N 78°10E 42 C8
Danleng China 30°1N 103°31E 34 B4
Danlí Honduras 14°4N 86°35W 88 D2
Danmark = Denmark ■ Europe 55°45N 10°0E 9 J14
Dannemora U.S.A. 44°43N 73°44W 83 B11
Dannevirke N.Z. 40°12S 176°8E 59 D6
Dannhauser S. Africa 28°0S 30°3E 57 C5
Dansville U.S.A. 42°34N 77°42W 82 D7
Danta India 24°11N 72°46E 42 G5
Dantan India 21°57N 87°20E 43 J12
Dante = Xaafuun Somalia 10°25N 51°16E 49 E5
Dantewara India 18°54N 81°21E 44 E5
Danube = Dunărea → Europe 45°20N 29°40E 17 F15
Danvers U.S.A. 42°34N 70°56W 83 D14
Danville Ill., U.S.A. 40°8N 87°37W 80 E10
Danville Ky., U.S.A. 37°39N 84°46W 81 G11
Danville Pa., U.S.A. 40°58N 76°37W 83 F8
Danville Va., U.S.A. 36°36N 79°23W 81 G14
Danville Vt., U.S.A. 44°25N 72°9W 83 B12
Danyang China 32°0N 119°31E 35 B12
Danzhai China 26°11N 107°48E 34 D6
Danzhou China 19°31N 109°33E 38 C7
Danzig = Gdańsk Poland 54°22N 18°40E 17 A10
Dao Xian China 25°36N 111°31E 35 E8
Daocheng China 29°0N 100°10E 34 C3
Dapaong Togo 10°55N 0°16E 52 F6
Dapoli India 17°46N 73°11E 44 F1
Daqing China 46°35N 125°0E 31 B13
Daqing Shan China 40°40N 111°0E 32 D6
Daqq-e Sorkh, Kavīr Iran 33°45N 52°50E 47 C7
Daqu Shan China 30°25N 122°20E 35 B14
Dar Banda Africa 8°0N 23°0E 50 F6
Dar el Beida = Casablanca Morocco 33°36N 7°36W 52 B4
Dar es Salaam Tanzania 6°50S 39°12E 54 F7
Dar Mazār Iran 29°14N 57°20E 47 D8
Dar'ā Syria 32°36N 36°7E 48 C5
Dar'ā □ Syria 32°55N 36°10E 48 C5
Dārāb Iran 28°50N 54°30E 47 D7
Daraban Pakistan 31°44N 70°20E 42 D4
Daraj Libya 30°10N 10°28E 53 B8
Dārān Iran 32°59N 50°24E 47 C6

Dārayyā Syria 33°28N 36°15E 48 B5
Darband Pakistan 34°20N 72°50E 42 B5
Darband, Kūh-e Iran 31°34N 57°8E 47 D8
Darbhanga India 26°15N 85°55E 43 F11
D'Arcy Canada 50°33N 122°29W 70 C4
Dardanelle Ark., U.S.A. 35°13N 93°9W 84 D8
Dardanelle Calif., U.S.A. 38°20N 119°50W 78 G7
Dardanelles = Çanakkale Boğazı
 Turkey 40°17N 26°32E 23 D12
Dārestān Iran 29°9N 58°42E 47 D8
Dârfûr Sudan 13°40N 24°0E 53 F10
Dargai Pakistan 34°25N 71°55E 42 B4
Dargaville N.Z. 35°57S 173°52E 59 A4
Darhan Mongolia 49°37N 106°21E 30 B10
Darhan Muminggan
 China 41°40N 110°28E 32 D6
Darıca Turkey 40°45N 29°23E 23 D13
Darién, G. del Caribbean 9°0N 77°0W 92 B3
Darién △ Panama 7°36N 77°57W 88 E4
Dariganga = Ovoot
 Mongolia 45°21N 113°45E 32 B7
Daringbadi India 19°54N 84°8E 44 E7
Darjeeling = Darjiling
 India 27°3N 88°18E 43 F13
Darjiling India 27°3N 88°18E 43 F13
Darkan Australia 33°20S 116°43E 61 F2
Darkhana Pakistan 30°39N 72°11E 42 D5
Darkhazīneh Iran 31°54N 48°39E 47 D6
Darkot Pass Pakistan 36°45N 73°26E 43 A5
Darling → Australia 34°4S 141°54E 63 E3
Darling Downs Australia 27°30S 150°30E 63 D5
Darling Ra. Australia 32°30S 116°20E 61 F2
Darlington U.K. 54°32N 1°33W 12 C6
Darlington U.S.A. 34°18N 79°52W 85 D15
Darlington □ U.K. 54°32N 1°33W 12 C6
Darlington, L. S. Africa 33°10S 25°9E 56 D4
Darlot, L. Australia 27°48S 121°35E 61 E3
Darłowo Poland 54°25N 16°25E 16 A9
Darmstadt Germany 49°51N 8°39E 16 D5
Darnah Libya 32°45N 22°45E 53 B10
Darnall S. Africa 29°23S 31°18E 57 D5
Darnley Australia 9°35S 143°46E 62 a
Darnley, C. Antarctica 68°0S 69°0E 5 C6
Darnley B. Canada 69°30N 123°30W 68 D7
Darr → Australia 23°39S 143°50E 62 C3
Darra Pezu Pakistan 32°19N 70°44E 42 C4
Darrequeira Argentina 37°42S 63°10W 94 D3
Darrington U.S.A. 48°15N 121°36W 76 B3
Darsi India 15°46N 79°44E 45 G4
Dart → U.K. 50°24N 3°39W 13 G4
Dartmoor U.K. 50°38N 3°57W 13 G4
Dartmoor △ U.K. 50°37N 3°59W 13 G4
Dartmouth Canada 44°40N 63°30W 73 D7
Dartmouth U.K. 50°21N 3°36W 13 G4
Dartmouth, L. Australia 26°4S 145°18E 63 D4
Darvel, Teluk = Lahad Datu, Telok
 Malaysia 4°50N 118°20E 37 D5
Darwen U.K. 53°42N 2°29W 12 D5
Darwendale Zimbabwe 17°41S 30°33E 57 A5
Darwha India 20°15N 77°45E 44 D3
Darwin Australia 12°25S 130°51E 60 B5
Darwin U.S.A. 36°15N 117°35W 79 J9
Darya Khan Pakistan 31°48N 71°6E 42 D4
Daryapur India 20°55N 77°20E 44 D3
Daryoi Amu = Amudarya →
 Uzbekistan 43°58N 59°34E 26 E6
Dās U.A.E. 25°20N 53°30E 47 E7
Dashen, Ras Ethiopia 13°8N 38°26E 49 E2
Dashetai China 41°0N 109°5E 32 D5
Dashiqiao China 40°38N 122°30E 33 D12
Dashköpri Turkmenistan 36°16N 62°8E 47 B9
Dasht → Pakistan 25°10N 61°40E 40 G2
Daska Pakistan 32°20N 74°20E 42 C6
Daşoguz Turkmenistan 41°49N 59°58E 26 E6
Dasuya India 31°49N 75°38E 42 D6
Datça Turkey 36°46N 27°40E 23 F12
Date Japan 42°28N 140°52E 28 C10
Datia India 25°39N 78°27E 43 G8
Datian China 25°40N 117°50E 35 E11
Datong Anhui, China 30°48N 117°44E 35 B11
Datong Qinghai, China 36°20N 102°50E 30 D9
Datong Shanxi, China 40°6N 113°18E 32 D7
Dattakhel Pakistan 32°54N 69°46E 42 C3
Dattapur = Dhamangaon
 India 20°48N 78°9E 44 D4
Datu, Tanjung Indonesia 2°5N 109°39E 36 D3
Datu Piang Phil. 7°2N 124°30E 37 C6
Datuk, Tanjong = Datu, Tanjung
 Indonesia 2°5N 109°39E 36 D3
Daud Khel Pakistan 32°53N 71°34E 42 C4
Daudnagar India 25°2N 84°24E 43 G11
Daugava → Latvia 57°4N 24°3E 9 H21
Daugavpils Latvia 55°53N 26°32E 9 J22
Daulatabad India 19°57N 75°15E 44 E2
Daulpur India 26°45N 77°59E 42 F7
Daund India 18°26N 74°40E 44 E2
Daung Kyun Myanmar 12°13N 98°4E 39 F1
Dauphin Canada 51°9N 100°5W 71 C8
Dauphin U.S.A. 40°22N 76°56W 82 F8
Dauphin L. Canada 51°20N 99°45W 71 C9
Dauphiné France 45°15N 5°25E 20 D6
Daurada, Costa Spain 41°12N 1°15E 21 B6
Dausa India 26°52N 76°20E 42 F7
Davangere India 14°25N 75°55E 45 G2
Davao Phil. 7°0N 125°40E 37 C7
Davao G. Phil. 6°30N 125°48E 37 C7
Dāvar Panāh = Sarāvān
 Iran 27°25N 62°15E 47 E9
Davenport Calif., U.S.A. 37°1N 122°12W 78 H4
Davenport Iowa, U.S.A. 41°32N 90°35W 80 E8
Davenport Wash., U.S.A. 47°39N 118°9W 76 C4
Davenport Ra. U.S.A. 20°28S 134°0E 62 C1
Davenport Range △
 Australia 20°36S 134°22E 62 C1
Daventry U.K. 52°16N 1°10W 13 E6
David Panama 8°30N 82°30W 88 E3
David City U.S.A. 41°15N 97°8W 80 E5
David Glacier Antarctica 75°20S 162°0E 5 D11
David Gorodok = Davyd Haradok
 Belarus 52°4N 27°8E 17 B14

Davidson Canada 51°16N 105°59W 71 C7
Davidson Mts. U.S.A. 68°41N 142°22W 74 B11
Davis Antarctica 68°34S 77°55E 5 C6
Davis U.S.A. 38°33N 121°44W 78 G5
Davis Dam U.S.A. 35°12N 114°34W 79 K12
Davis Mts. U.S.A. 30°50N 103°55W 84 F3
Davis Sea Antarctica 66°0S 92°0E 5 C7
Davis Str. N. Amer. 65°0N 58°0W 69 D19
Davos Switz. 46°48N 9°49E 20 C8
Davy L. Canada 58°53N 108°18W 71 B7
Davyd Haradok Belarus 52°4N 27°8E 17 B14
Dawei Myanmar 14°2N 98°12E 38 E2
Dawes Ra. Australia 24°40S 150°40E 62 C5
Dawlish U.K. 50°35N 3°28W 13 G4
Dawmat al Jandal
 Si. Arabia 29°55N 39°40E 46 D3
Dawna Ra. Myanmar 16°30N 98°30E 38 D2
Dawros Hd. Ireland 54°50N 8°33W 10 B3
Dawson U.S.A. 31°46N 84°27W 85 F12
Dawson, I. Chile 53°50S 70°50W 96 G2
Dawson B. Canada 52°53N 100°49W 71 C8
Dawson City Canada 64°10N 139°30W 68 E4
Dawson Creek Canada 55°45N 120°15W 70 B4
Dawson Inlet Canada 61°50N 93°25W 71 A10
Dawson Ra. Australia 24°30S 149°48E 62 C4
Dawu Hubei, China 31°34N 114°7E 35 B10
Dawu Sichuan, China 30°55N 101°0E 34 B3
Dax France 43°44N 1°3W 20 E3
Daxian China 31°15N 107°23E 34 B6
Daxin China 22°50N 107°11E 34 F6
Daxindian China 37°30N 120°50E 33 F11
Daxinggou China 43°25N 129°40E 33 C15
Daxue Shan Sichuan,
 China 30°30N 101°30E 34 B3
Daxue Shan Yunnan,
 China 23°42N 99°48E 34 F2
Dayao China 25°43N 101°20E 34 E3
Daye China 30°6N 114°58E 35 B10
Dayi China 30°41N 103°29E 34 B4
Dāykondī □ Afghan. 34°0N 66°0E 40 C5
Daylesford Australia 37°21S 144°9E 63 F3
Dayong = Zhangjiajie
 China 29°11N 110°30E 35 C8
Dayr az Zawr Syria 35°20N 40°5E 46 C4
Daysland Canada 52°50N 112°20W 70 C6
Dayton Nev., U.S.A. 39°14N 119°36W 78 F7
Dayton Ohio, U.S.A. 39°45N 84°12W 81 F11
Dayton Pa., U.S.A. 40°53N 79°15W 82 F5
Dayton Tenn., U.S.A. 35°30N 85°1W 85 D12
Dayton Wash., U.S.A. 46°19N 117°59W 76 C5
Dayton Wyo., U.S.A. 44°53N 107°16W 76 D10
Daytona Beach U.S.A. 29°13N 81°1W 85 G14
Dayu China 25°24N 114°22E 35 E10
Dayville U.S.A. 44°28N 119°32W 76 D4
Dazhu China 30°41N 107°15E 34 B6
Dazu China 29°40N 105°42E 34 C5
De Aar S. Africa 30°39S 24°0E 56 D3
De Funiak Springs
 U.S.A. 30°43N 86°7W 85 F11
De Grey → Australia 20°12S 119°13E 60 D2
De Haan Belgium 51°16N 3°2E 15 C3
De Hoop △ S. Africa 34°30S 20°28E 56 D3
De Kalb Junction U.S.A. 44°30N 75°16W 83 B9
De Land U.S.A. 29°2N 81°18W 85 G14
De Leon U.S.A. 32°7N 98°32W 84 E5
De Long Mts. U.S.A. 68°10N 163°30W 74 B7
De Panne Belgium 51°6N 2°34E 15 C2
De Pere U.S.A. 44°27N 88°4W 80 C9
De Queen U.S.A. 34°2N 94°21W 84 D7
De Quincy U.S.A. 30°27N 93°26W 84 F8
De Ruyters U.S.A. 42°45N 75°53W 83 D9
De Smet U.S.A. 44°23N 97°33W 80 C5
De Soto U.S.A. 38°8N 90°34W 80 F8
De Tour Village U.S.A. 46°0N 83°56W 81 B12
De Witt U.S.A. 34°18N 91°20W 84 D9
Dead Sea Asia 31°30N 35°30E 48 D4
Deadwood U.S.A. 44°23N 103°44W 80 C2
Deadwood L. Canada 59°10N 128°30W 70 B3
Deal U.K. 51°13N 1°25E 13 F9
Deal I. Australia 39°30S 147°20E 63 F4
Dealesville S. Africa 28°41S 25°44E 56 C4
De'an China 29°21N 115°46E 35 C10
Dean → Canada 52°49N 126°58W 70 C3
Dean, Forest of U.K. 51°45N 2°33W 13 F5
Dean Chan. Canada 52°30N 127°15W 70 C3
Deán Funes Argentina 30°20S 64°20W 94 C3
Dease → Canada 59°56N 128°32W 70 B3
Dease L. Canada 58°40N 130°5W 70 B2
Dease Lake Canada 58°25N 130°6W 70 B2
Death Valley U.S.A. 36°15N 116°50W 79 J10
Death Valley △ U.S.A. 36°29N 117°6W 79 J9
Death Valley Junction
 U.S.A. 36°20N 116°25W 79 J10
Deatnu = Tana →
 Norway 70°30N 28°14E 8 A23
Debagram India 23°41N 88°18E 43 H13
Debao China 23°21N 106°46E 34 F6
Debar Macedonia 41°31N 20°30E 23 D9
Debden Canada 53°30N 106°50W 71 C7
Dębica Poland 50°2N 21°25E 17 C11
Deborah East, L.
 Australia 30°45S 119°30E 61 F2
Deborah West, L.
 Australia 30°45S 119°5E 61 F2
Debre Markos Ethiopia 10°20N 37°40E 49 E2
Debre Tabor Ethiopia 11°50N 38°26E 49 E2
Debre Zeyit Ethiopia 8°50N 39°0E 49 F2
Debrecen Hungary 47°33N 21°42E 17 E11
Decatur Ala., U.S.A. 34°36N 86°59W 85 D11
Decatur Ill., U.S.A. 39°51N 88°57W 80 F9
Decatur Ind., U.S.A. 40°50N 84°56W 81 E11
Decatur Tex., U.S.A. 33°14N 97°35W 84 E5
Deccan India 18°0N 79°0E 44 F4
Deception Bay Australia 27°10S 153°5E 63 D5
Deception I. Antarctica 63°0S 60°15W 5 C17
Deception L. Canada 56°33N 104°13W 71 B8
Dechang China 27°25N 102°11E 34 D4
Dechhu India 26°46N 72°20E 42 F5
Děčín Czechia 50°47N 14°12E 16 C8

Deckerville U.S.A. 43°32N 82°44W 82 C2
Decorah U.S.A. 43°18N 91°48W 80 D8
Dedéagach = Alexandroupoli
 Greece 40°50N 25°54E 23 D11
Dee → Aberds., U.K. 57°9N 2°5W 11 D6
Dee → Dumf. & Gall., U.K. 54°51N 4°3W 11 G4
Dee → Wales, U.K. 53°22N 3°17W 12 D4
Deep B. Canada 61°15N 116°35W 70 A5
Deep Bay = Shenzhen Wan
 China 22°27N 113°55E 31 a
Deepwater Australia 29°25S 151°51E 63 D5
Deer → Canada 58°23N 94°13W 71 B10
Deer L. Canada 52°40N 94°20W 71 C10
Deer Lake Nfld. & L.,
 Canada 49°11N 57°27W 73 C8
Deer Lake Ont., Canada 52°36N 94°20W 71 C10
Deer Lodge U.S.A. 46°24N 112°44W 76 C7
Deer Park U.S.A. 47°57N 117°28W 76 C5
Deer River U.S.A. 47°20N 93°48W 80 B7
Deeragun Australia 19°16S 146°33E 62 B4
Defiance U.S.A. 41°17N 84°22W 81 E11
Degana India 26°50N 74°20E 42 F6
Dêgê China 31°44N 98°39E 34 B2
Dégelis Canada 47°30N 68°35W 73 C6
Deggendorf Germany 48°50N 12°57E 16 D7
Degh → Pakistan 31°3N 73°21E 42 D5
Deh Bīd Iran 30°39N 53°11E 47 D7
Deh Dasht Iran 30°47N 50°33E 47 D6
Deh-e Shīr Iran 31°29N 53°45E 47 D7
Dehaj Iran 30°42N 54°53E 47 D7
Dehak Iran 27°11N 62°37E 47 E9
Dehdez Iran 31°43N 50°17E 47 D6
Dehej India 21°44N 72°40E 42 J5
Dehestān Iran 28°30N 55°35E 47 D7
Dehgolān Iran 35°17N 47°25E 46 C5
Dehibat Tunisia 32°0N 10°47E 53 B8
Dehiwala Sri Lanka 6°50N 79°51E 45 L4
Dehlorān Iran 32°41N 47°16E 46 C5
Dehnow-e Kūhestān Iran 27°58N 58°32E 47 E8
Dehra Dun India 30°20N 78°4E 42 D8
Dehri India 24°50N 84°15E 43 G11
Dehua China 25°26N 118°14E 35 E12
Dehui China 44°30N 125°40E 33 B13
Deinze Belgium 50°59N 3°32E 15 D3
Deir al Balah Gaza Strip 31°25N 34°21E 48 D3
Dej Romania 47°10N 23°52E 17 E12
Dejiang China 28°18N 108°7E 34 C7
Deka → Zimbabwe 18°4S 26°42E 56 A4
DeKalb U.S.A. 41°56N 88°46W 80 E9
Dekese
 Dem. Rep. of the Congo 3°24S 21°24E 54 E4
Del Mar U.S.A. 32°58N 117°16W 79 N9
Del Norte U.S.A. 37°41N 106°21W 77 H10
Del Rio U.S.A. 29°22N 100°54W 84 G4
Delambre I. Australia 20°26S 117°5E 60 D2
Delano U.S.A. 35°46N 119°15W 79 K7
Delano Peak U.S.A. 38°22N 112°22W 76 G7
Delareyville S. Africa 26°41S 25°26E 56 C4
Delaronde L. Canada 54°3N 107°3W 71 C7
Delavan U.S.A. 42°38N 88°39W 80 D9
Delaware U.S.A. 40°18N 83°4W 81 E12
Delaware □ U.S.A. 39°0N 75°20W 81 F16
Delaware → U.S.A. 39°0N 75°10W 81 F16
Delaware B. U.S.A. 39°0N 75°10W 81 F16
Delaware Water Gap △
 U.S.A. 41°10N 74°55W 83 E10
Delay → Canada 56°56N 71°28W 73 A5
Delegate Australia 37°4S 148°56E 63 F4
Delevan U.S.A. 42°29N 78°29W 82 D6
Delft Neths. 52°1N 4°22E 15 B4
Delft I. Sri Lanka 9°30N 79°40E 45 K4
Delfzijl Neths. 53°20N 6°55E 15 A6
Delgado, C. Mozam. 10°45S 40°40E 54 G8
Delgerhet Mongolia 45°50N 110°30E 32 B6
Delgo Sudan 20°6N 30°40E 53 D12
Delhi India 28°38N 77°17E 42 E7
Delhi La., U.S.A. 32°28N 91°30W 84 E9
Delhi N.Y., U.S.A. 42°17N 74°55W 83 D10
Delia Canada 51°38N 112°23W 70 C6
Delice Turkey 39°54N 34°2E 19 G5
Delicias Mexico 28°13N 105°28W 86 B3
Delījān Iran 33°59N 50°40E 47 C6
Déline Canada 65°11N 123°25W 68 D7
Delingha China 37°23N 97°23E 30 D8
Delisle Canada 51°55N 107°8W 71 C7
Deliverance I. Australia 9°31S 141°34E 62 a
Dell City U.S.A. 31°56N 105°12W 84 F2
Dell Rapids U.S.A. 43°50N 96°43W 80 D5
Delmar U.S.A. 42°37N 73°47W 83 D11
Delmenhorst Germany 53°3N 8°37E 16 B5
Delonga, Ostrova
 Russia 76°40N 149°20E 27 B15
Deloraine Australia 41°30S 146°40E 63 G4
Deloraine Canada 49°15N 100°29W 71 D8
Delphi U.S.A. 40°36N 86°41W 80 E10
Delphos U.S.A. 40°51N 84°21W 81 E11
Delportshoop S. Africa 28°22S 24°20E 56 C3
Delray Beach U.S.A. 26°28N 80°4W 85 H14
Delta Colo., U.S.A. 38°44N 108°4W 76 G9
Delta Utah, U.S.A. 39°21N 112°35W 76 G7
Delta Dunărea △
 Romania 45°15N 29°25E 17 F15
Delta Junction U.S.A. 64°2N 145°44W 68 E2
Deltona U.S.A. 28°54N 81°16W 85 G14
Delungra Australia 29°39S 150°51E 63 D5
Delvada India 20°46N 71°2E 42 J4
Delvinë Albania 39°59N 20°6E 23 E9
Demak Indonesia 6°53S 110°38E 37 G14
Demanda, Sierra de la
 Spain 42°15N 3°0W 21 A4
Dembidolo Ethiopia 8°34N 34°50E 49 F1
Demchok India 32°42N 79°29E 43 C8
Demer → Belgium 50°57N 4°42E 15 D4
Deming N. Mex.,
 U.S.A. 32°16N 107°46W 77 K10
Deming Wash., U.S.A. 48°50N 122°13W 78 B4
Demini → Brazil 0°46S 62°56W 92 D6
Demirci Turkey 39°2N 28°38E 23 E13
Demirköy Turkey 41°49N 27°45E 23 D12
Demopolis U.S.A. 32°31N 87°50W 85 E11
Dempo Indonesia 4°2S 103°15E 36 E2

Den Bosch = 's-Hertogenbosch
 Neths. 51°42N 5°17E 15 C5
Den Burg Neths. 53°3N 4°47E 15 A4
Den Chai Thailand 17°59N 100°4E 38 D3
Den Haag = 's-Gravenhage
 Neths. 52°7N 4°17E 15 B4
Den Helder Neths. 52°57N 4°45E 15 B4
Den Oever Neths. 52°56N 5°2E 15 B5
Denair U.S.A. 37°32N 120°48W 78 H6
Denali U.S.A. 63°4N 151°0W 68 E1
Denau = Denov
 Uzbekistan 38°16N 67°54E 26 F7
Denbigh Canada 45°8N 77°15W 82 A7
Denbigh U.K. 53°12N 3°25W 12 D4
Denbighshire □ U.K. 53°8N 3°22W 12 D4
Dendang Indonesia 3°7S 107°56E 36 E3
Dendermonde Belgium 51°2N 4°5E 15 C4
Dengchuan China 25°59N 100°3E 34 E3
Dengfeng China 34°25N 113°2E 32 G7
Dengkou China 40°18N 106°55E 32 D4
Dengzhou China 32°34N 112°4E 35 A9
Denham Australia 25°56S 113°31E 61 E1
Denham, Mt. Jamaica 18°13N 77°32W 88 a
Denham Ra. Australia 21°55S 147°46E 62 C4
Denham Sd. Australia 25°45S 113°15E 61 E1
Denholm Canada 52°39N 108°1W 71 C7
Denia Spain 38°49N 0°8E 21 C6
Denial B. Australia 32°14S 133°32E 63 E1
Deniliquin Australia 35°30S 144°58E 63 F3
Denimoo = Fort Resolution
 Canada 61°10N 113°40W 70 A6
Denison Iowa, U.S.A. 42°1N 95°21W 80 D6
Denison Tex., U.S.A. 33°45N 96°33W 84 E6
Denison, C. Antarctica 67°0S 142°40E 5 C10
Denison Plains Australia 18°35S 128°0E 60 C4
Deniyaya Sri Lanka 6°21N 80°33E 45 L5
Denizli Turkey 37°42N 29°2E 19 G4
Denman Glacier Antarctica 66°45S 100°0E 5 C8
Denmark Australia 34°59S 117°25E 61 F2
Denmark ■ Europe 55°45N 10°0E 9 J14
Denmark Str. Atl. Oc. 66°0N 30°0W 66 C17
Dennery St. Lucia 13°55N 60°54W 89 f
Dennison U.S.A. 40°24N 81°19W 82 F3
Denny U.K. 56°1N 3°55W 11 E5
Denov Uzbekistan 38°16N 67°54E 26 F7
Denpasar Indonesia 8°39S 115°13E 37 K18
Denpasar ✈ (DPS)
 Indonesia 8°44S 115°10E 37 K18
Denton Mont., U.S.A. 47°19N 109°57W 76 C9
Denton Tex., U.S.A. 33°13N 97°8W 84 E6
D'Entrecasteaux, Pt.
 Australia 34°50S 115°57E 61 F2
D'Entrecasteaux △
 Australia 34°20S 115°33E 61 F2
D'Entrecasteaux Is.
 Papua N. G. 9°0S 151°0E 58 B8
Denver Colo., U.S.A. 39°42N 104°59W 76 G11
Denver Pa., U.S.A. 40°14N 76°8W 83 F8
Denver City U.S.A. 32°58N 102°50W 84 E3
Denver Int. ✈ (DEN)
 U.S.A. 39°52N 104°40W 76 G11
Deoband India 29°42N 77°43E 42 E7
Deobhog India 19°53N 82°44E 44 E6
Deodrug India 16°26N 76°54E 45 F3
Deogarh Odisha, India 21°32N 84°45E 44 D7
Deogarh Raj., India 25°32N 73°54E 42 G5
Deoghar India 24°30N 86°42E 43 G12
Deolali India 19°58N 73°50E 44 E1
Deoli = Devli India 25°50N 75°20E 42 G6
Deoli India 25°50N 75°20E 42 G6
Deora India 26°22N 70°55E 42 F4
Deoria India 26°31N 83°48E 43 F10
Deosai Mts. Pakistan 35°40N 75°0E 43 B6
Deosri India 26°46N 90°29E 43 F14
Depalpur India 22°51N 75°33E 42 H6
Deposit U.S.A. 42°4N 75°25W 83 D9
Depuch I. Australia 20°37S 117°44E 60 D2
Deputatskiy Russia 69°18N 139°54E 27 C14
Dêqên China 28°34N 98°51E 34 C2
Deqing China 23°8N 111°42E 35 F8
Dera Ghazi Khan Pakistan 30°5N 70°43E 42 D4
Dera Ismail Khan
 Pakistan 31°50N 70°50E 42 D4
Derabugti Pakistan 29°2N 69°9E 42 E3
Derawar Fort Pakistan 28°46N 71°20E 42 E4
Derbent Russia 42°5N 48°15E 19 F8
Derby Australia 17°18S 123°38E 60 C3
Derby U.K. 52°56N 1°28E 12 E6
Derby Conn., U.S.A. 41°19N 73°5W 83 E11
Derby Kans., U.S.A. 37°33N 97°16W 80 G6
Derby N.Y., U.S.A. 42°41N 78°58W 82 D6
Derby City □ U.K. 52°56N 1°28W 12 E6
Derby Line U.S.A. 45°0N 72°6W 83 B12
Derbyshire □ U.K. 53°11N 1°38W 12 D6
Derdepoort S. Africa 24°38S 26°24E 56 B4
Dereham U.K. 52°41N 0°57E 13 E8
Derg → U.K. 54°44N 7°26W 10 B4
Derg, L. Ireland 53°0N 8°20W 10 D3
Deridder U.S.A. 30°51N 93°17W 84 F8
Dermott U.S.A. 33°32N 91°26W 84 E9
Dêrong China 28°44N 99°9E 34 C2
Derry = Londonderry U.K. 55°0N 7°20W 10 B4
Derry = Londonderry □
 U.K. 55°0N 7°20W 10 B4
Derry N.H., U.S.A. 42°53N 71°19W 83 D13
Derry Pa., U.S.A. 40°20N 79°18W 82 F5
Derryveagh Mts. Ireland 54°56N 8°11W 10 B3
Derwent → Cumb., U.K. 54°39N 3°33W 12 C4
Derwent → Derby, U.K. 52°57N 1°28E 12 E6
Derwent → N. Yorks.,
 U.K. 53°45N 0°58W 12 D7
Derwent Water U.K. 54°35N 3°9W 12 C4
Des Moines Iowa, U.S.A. 41°35N 93°37W 80 E7
Des Moines N. Mex.,
 U.S.A. 36°46N 103°50W 77 H12
Des Moines Wash.,
 U.S.A. 47°24N 122°19W 78 C4
Des Moines → U.S.A. 40°23N 91°25W 80 E8
Desaguadero →
 Argentina 34°30S 66°46W 94 C2

Desaguadero → Bolivia 16°35S 69°5W 92 G5
Desaru Malaysia 1°31N 104°17E 39 d
Descanso, Pta. Mexico 32°21N 117°3W 79 N9
Deschaillons-sur-St-Laurent
 Canada 46°32N 72°7W 73 C5
Deschambault L.
 Canada 54°50N 103°30W 71 C8
Deschutes → U.S.A. 45°38N 120°55W 76 D3
Dese Ethiopia 11°5N 39°40E 49 E2
Deseado → Argentina 47°45S 65°54W 96 F3
Deseronto Canada 44°12N 77°3W 82 B7
Desert Center U.S.A. 33°43N 115°24W 79 M11
Desert Hot Springs
 U.S.A. 33°58N 116°30W 79 M10
Deshnok India 27°48N 73°21E 42 F5
Desierto Central de Baja
 California □ Mexico 29°40N 114°50W 86 B2
Desna → Ukraine 50°33N 30°32E 17 C16
Desolación, I. Chile 53°0S 74°0W 96 G2
Despeñaperros, Paso
 Spain 38°24N 3°30W 21 C4
Dessau Germany 51°51N 12°14E 16 C7
Dessye = Dese Ethiopia 11°5N 39°40E 49 E2
D'Estrees B. Australia 35°55S 137°45E 63 F2
Desuri India 25°18N 73°35E 42 G5
Det Udom Thailand 14°54N 105°5E 38 E5
Dete Zimbabwe 18°38S 26°50E 56 A4
Detmold Germany 51°56N 8°52E 16 C5
Detour, Pt. U.S.A. 45°40N 86°40W 80 C10
Detroit U.S.A. 42°19N 83°12W 82 D1
Detroit Lakes U.S.A. 46°49N 95°51W 80 B6
Deua △ Australia 35°32S 149°46E 63 F4
Deurne Neths. 51°27N 5°49E 15 C5
Deutsche Bucht Germany 54°15N 8°0E 16 A5
Deutschland = Germany ■
 Europe 51°0N 10°0E 16 C6
Deva Romania 45°53N 22°55E 17 F12
Devakottai India 9°55N 78°45E 45 K4
Devaprayag India 30°13N 78°35E 43 D8
Devarkonda India 16°42N 78°56E 44 F4
Deventer Neths. 52°15N 6°10E 15 B6
Deveron → U.K. 57°41N 2°32W 11 D6
Devgad I. India 14°48N 74°5E 45 G2
Devgadh Bariya India 22°40N 73°55E 42 H5
Devgarh India 16°23N 73°23E 45 F1
Devi → India 20°59N 86°24E 44 E8
Devikot India 26°42N 71°12E 42 F4
Devils Den U.S.A. 35°46N 119°58W 78 K7
Devils Hole = Death Valley △
 U.S.A. 36°29N 117°6W 79 J9
Devils Lake U.S.A. 48°7N 98°52W 80 A4
Devils Paw Canada 58°47N 134°0W 70 B2
Devils Postpile △ U.S.A. 37°37N 119°5W 78 H7
Devil's Pt. Sri Lanka 9°26N 80°6E 45 K5
Devils Tower U.S.A. 44°35N 104°42W 76 D11
Devils Tower △ U.S.A. 44°48N 104°55W 76 D11
Devine U.S.A. 29°8N 98°54W 84 G5
Devipattinam India 9°29N 78°54E 45 K4
Devizes U.K. 51°22N 1°58W 13 F6
Devli India 25°50N 75°20E 42 G6
Devon Canada 53°24N 113°44W 70 C6
Devon □ U.K. 50°50N 3°40W 13 G4
Devon I. Canada 75°10N 85°0W 69 B15
Devonport Australia 41°10S 146°22E 63 G4
Devonport N.Z. 36°49S 174°49E 59 B5
Devrukh India 17°3N 73°37E 44 F1
Dewas India 22°59N 76°3E 42 H7
Dewetsdorp S. Africa 29°33S 26°39E 56 C4
Dewey Puerto Rico 18°18N 65°18W 89 d
Dexing China 28°46N 117°30E 35 C11
Dexter Maine, U.S.A. 45°1N 69°18W 81 C19
Dexter Mo., U.S.A. 36°48N 89°57W 80 G9
Dexter N. Mex., U.S.A. 33°12N 104°22W 77 K11
Dey-Dey, L. Australia 29°12S 131°4E 61 E5
Deyang China 31°3N 104°27E 34 B5
Deyhūk Iran 33°15N 57°30E 47 C8
Deyyer Iran 27°55N 51°55E 47 E6
Dez → Iran 31°39N 48°52E 47 D6
Dezadeash L. Canada 60°28N 136°58W 70 A1
Dezfūl Iran 32°20N 48°30E 47 C6
Dezhneva, Mys Russia 66°5N 169°40W 27 C19
Dezhou China 37°26N 116°18E 32 F9
Dhadhar → India 24°56N 85°24E 43 G11
Dhahiriya = Az̧ Z̧āhirīyah
 West Bank 31°25N 34°58E 48 D3
Dhahran = Az̧ Z̧ahrān
 Si. Arabia 26°10N 50°7E 47 E6
Dhak Pakistan 32°25N 72°33E 42 C5
Dhaka Bangla. 23°43N 90°26E 43 H14
Dhaka □ Bangla. 23°30N 90°0E 43 H14
Dhamangaon India 20°48N 78°9E 44 D4
Dhamār Yemen 14°30N 44°20E 49 E3
Dhampur India 29°19N 78°33E 43 E8
Dhamra → India 20°47N 86°58E 44 D8
Dhamtari India 20°42N 81°35E 44 D5
Dhanbad India 23°50N 86°30E 43 H12
Dhangarhi Nepal 28°55N 80°40E 43 E9
Dhankuta Nepal 26°55N 87°40E 43 F12
Dhanora India 20°20N 80°22E 44 D5
Dhanpuri India 23°13N 81°33E 44 C5
Dhanushkodi India 9°11N 79°24E 45 K4
Dhar India 22°35N 75°26E 42 H6
Dharampur India 22°13N 75°18E 42 H6
Dharamsala = Dharmsala
 India 32°16N 76°23E 42 C7
Dharan Nepal 26°49N 87°16E 43 F12
Dharangaon India 21°1N 75°16E 44 D2
Dharapuram India 10°45N 77°34E 45 J3
Dhariwal India 31°57N 75°19E 42 D6
Dharla → Bangla. 25°46N 89°42E 43 G13
Dharmapuri India 12°10N 78°10E 45 H4
Dharmavaram India 14°29N 77°44E 45 G3
Dharmjaygarh India 22°28N 83°13E 43 H10
Dharmsala India 32°16N 76°23E 42 C7
Dharni India 21°33N 76°53E 44 D3
Dharur India 18°3N 76°8E 44 E3
Dharwad India 15°30N 75°4E 45 G2
Dhasan → India 25°48N 79°24E 43 G8
Dhaulagiri Nepal 28°39N 83°28E 43 E10
Dhebar, L. India 24°10N 74°0E 42 G6

Dhenkanal *India* 20°45N 85°35E **44 D7**
Dhī Qār □ *Iraq* 31°0N 46°15E **46 D5**
Dhībān *Jordan* 31°30N 35°46E **48 D4**
Dhilwan *India* 31°31N 75°21E **42 D6**
Dhimarkhera *India* 23°28N 80°22E **43 H9**
Dholka *India* 22°44N 72°29E **42 H5**
Dhond = Daund *India* 18°26N 74°40E **44 E2**
Dhone *India* 15°25N 77°53E **45 E3**
Dhoraji *India* 21°45N 70°37E **42 J4**
Dhorpatan *Nepal* 28°29N 83°4E **43 E10**
Dhrangadhra *India* 22°59N 71°31E **42 H4**
Dhrol *India* 22°33N 70°25E **42 H4**
Dhuburi *India* 26°2N 89°59E **41 F16**
Dhule *India* 20°58N 74°50E **44 D2**
Di Linh *Vietnam* 11°35N 108°4E **39 G7**
Di Linh, Cao Nguyen
    Vietnam 11°30N 108°0E **39 G7**
Diablo Range *U.S.A.* 37°20N 121°25W **78 J5**
Diafarabé *Mali* 14°9N 4°57W **52 F5**
Diamante *Argentina* 32°5S 60°40W **94 C3**
Diamante ↦ *Argentina* 34°30S 66°46W **94 C2**
Diamantina *Brazil* 18°17S 43°40W **93 G10**
Diamantina ↦
    Australia 26°45S 139°10E **63 D2**
Diamantina △ *Australia* 23°33S 141°23E **62 C3**
Diamantino *Brazil* 14°30S 56°30W **93 F7**
Diamond Bar *U.S.A.* 34°1N 117°48W **79 L9**
Diamond Harbour *India* 22°11N 88°14E **43 H13**
Diamond Is. *Australia* 17°25S 151°5E **62 B5**
Diamond Mts. *U.S.A.* 39°40N 115°50W **76 G6**
Diamond Springs
    U.S.A. 38°42N 120°49W **78 G6**
Dian Chi *China* 24°50N 102°43E **34 E4**
Dianbai *China* 21°33N 111°0E **35 G8**
Diancheng *China* 21°30N 111°4E **35 G8**
Dianjiang *China* 30°24N 107°20E **34 B6**
Diaoyu Dao = Senkaku-Shotō
    E. China Sea 25°45N 123°30E **29 M1**
Diaoyu Tai = Senkaku-Shotō
    E. China Sea 25°45N 123°30E **29 M1**
Diavolo, Mt. *India* 12°40N 92°56E **45 H11**
Diba = Dibbā al Ḥiṣn
    U.A.E. 25°45N 56°16E **47 E8**
Dibai *India* 28°13N 78°15E **42 E8**
Dibaya
    Dem. Rep. of the Congo 6°30S 22°57E **54 F4**
Dibaya-Lubue
    Dem. Rep. of the Congo 4°12S 19°54E **54 E3**
Dibbā al Ḥiṣn *U.A.E.* 25°45N 56°16E **47 E8**
Dibbeen △ *Jordan* 32°20N 35°45E **48 C4**
D'Iberville, Lac *Canada* 55°55N 73°15W **72 A5**
Dibete *Botswana* 23°45S 26°32E **56 B4**
Dibrugarh *India* 27°29N 94°55E **41 F19**
Dickens *U.S.A.* 33°37N 100°50W **84 E4**
Dickinson *U.S.A.* 46°53N 102°47W **80 B2**
Dickson *U.S.A.* 36°5N 87°23W **85 C11**
Dickson City *U.S.A.* 41°28N 75°36W **83 E9**
Didiéni *Mali* 13°53N 8°6W **52 F4**
Didsbury *Canada* 51°35N 114°10W **70 C6**
Didwana *India* 27°23N 74°36E **42 F6**
Diefenbaker, L. *Canada* 51°0N 106°55W **71 C7**
Diego de Almagro *Chile* 26°22S 70°3W **94 B1**
Diego Suarez = Antsiranana
    Madag. 12°25S 49°20E **55 G9**
Diekirch *Lux.* 49°52N 6°10E **15 E6**
Dien Ban *Vietnam* 15°53N 108°16E **38 E7**
Dien Bien Phu *Vietnam* 21°20N 103°0E **34 G4**
Dien Chau, Vinh *Vietnam* 19°0N 105°55E **38 C5**
Dien Khanh *Vietnam* 12°15N 109°6E **39 F7**
Dieppe *France* 49°54N 1°4E **20 B4**
Dierks *U.S.A.* 34°7N 94°1W **84 D7**
Diest *Belgium* 50°58N 5°4E **15 D5**
Dif *Somalia* 0°59N 40°58E **49 G3**
Differdange *Lux.* 49°31N 5°54E **15 E5**
Dig *India* 27°28N 77°20E **42 F7**
Digby *Canada* 44°38N 65°50W **73 D6**
Digges Is. *Canada* 62°40N 77°50W **69 E16**
Diggi *India* 26°22N 75°26E **42 F6**
Dighinala *Bangla.* 23°15N 92°5E **41 H18**
Dighton *U.S.A.* 38°29N 100°28W **80 F3**
Diglur *India* 18°34N 77°33E **44 E3**
Digne-les-Bains *France* 44°5N 6°12E **20 D7**
Digos *Phil.* 6°45N 125°20E **37 C7**
Digranes *Iceland* 66°4N 14°44W **8 C6**
Digras *India* 20°6N 77°45E **44 D3**
Digul ↦ *Indonesia* 7°7S 138°42E **37 F9**
Dihang = Brahmaputra ↦
    Asia 23°40N 90°35E **43 H13**
Dijlah, Nahr ↦ *Asia* 31°0N 47°25E **46 D5**
Dijon *France* 47°20N 5°3E **20 C6**
Dikhil *Djibouti* 11°8N 42°20E **49 E3**
Diksmuide *Belgium* 51°2N 2°52E **15 C2**
Dikson *Russia* 73°40N 80°5E **26 B9**
Dikti Oros *Greece* 35°8N 25°30E **23 G11**
Dila *Ethiopia* 6°21N 38°22E **49 F2**
Dili *Timor-Leste* 8°39S 125°34E **37 F7**
Diligent Strait *India* 12°11N 92°57E **45 H11**
Dilley *U.S.A.* 28°40N 99°10W **84 G5**
Dillingham *U.S.A.* 59°3N 158°28W **74 D8**
Dillon *Canada* 55°56N 108°35W **71 B7**
Dillon *Mont., U.S.A.* 45°13N 112°38W **76 D7**
Dillon *S.C., U.S.A.* 34°25N 79°22W **85 D15**
Dillon ↦ *Canada* 55°56N 108°56W **71 B7**
Dillsburg *U.S.A.* 40°7N 77°2W **82 F7**
Dilolo
    Dem. Rep. of the Congo 10°28S 22°18E **54 G4**
Dimapur *India* 25°54N 93°45E **30 F7**
Dimas *Mexico* 23°43N 106°47W **86 C3**
Dimashq *Syria* 33°30N 36°18E **48 B5**
Dimashq □ *Syria* 33°30N 36°30E **48 B5**
Dimbaza *S. Africa* 32°50S 27°14E **57 D4**
Dimboola *Australia* 36°28S 142°7E **63 F3**
Dîmbovița = Dâmbovița ↦
    Romania 44°12N 26°26E **17 F14**
Dimbulah *Australia* 17°8S 145°4E **62 B4**
Dimitrovgrad *Bulgaria* 42°5N 25°35E **23 C11**
Dimitrovgrad *Russia* 54°14N 49°39E **18 D8**
Dimitrovo = Pernik
    Bulgaria 42°35N 23°2E **23 C10**
Dimmitt *U.S.A.* 34°33N 102°19W **84 D3**

Dimona *Israel* 31°2N 35°1E **48 D4**
Dinagat I. *Phil.* 10°10N 125°40E **37 B7**
Dinajpur *Bangla.* 25°33N 88°43E **41 G16**
Dinan *France* 48°28N 2°2W **20 B2**
Dīnān Āb *Iran* 32°4N 56°49E **47 C8**
Dinant *Belgium* 50°16N 4°55E **15 D4**
Dinapur *India* 25°38N 85°5E **43 G11**
Dīnār, Kūh-e *Iran* 30°42N 51°46E **47 D6**
Dinara Planina *Croatia* 44°0N 16°30E **22 C7**
Dinard *France* 48°38N 2°6W **20 B2**
Dinaric Alps = Dinara Planina
    Croatia 44°0N 16°30E **22 C7**
Dinbych-y-Pysgod = Tenby
    U.K. 51°40N 4°42W **13 F3**
Dindi ↦ *India* 16°24N 78°15E **45 F4**
Dindigul *India* 10°25N 78°0E **45 J4**
Dindori *India* 22°57N 81°5E **43 H9**
Ding Xian = Dingzhou
    China 38°30N 114°59E **32 E8**
Dinga *Pakistan* 25°26N 67°10E **42 G2**
Ding'an *China* 19°42N 110°19E **38 C8**
Dingbian *China* 37°35N 107°32E **32 F4**
Dingle *Ireland* 52°9N 10°17W **10 D1**
Dingle B. *Ireland* 52°3N 10°20W **10 D1**
Dingle Pen. *Ireland* 52°12N 10°5W **10 D1**
Dingmans Ferry *U.S.A.* 41°13N 74°55W **83 E10**
Dingnan *China* 24°45N 115°0E **35 E10**
Dingo *Australia* 23°38S 149°19E **62 C4**
Dingtao *China* 35°5N 115°35E **32 G8**
Dingxi *China* 35°30N 104°33E **32 G3**
Dingxiang *China* 38°30N 112°58E **32 E7**
Dingyuan *China* 32°32N 117°41E **35 A11**
Dingzhou *China* 38°30N 114°59E **32 E8**
Dinh, Mui *Vietnam* 11°22N 109°1E **39 G7**
Dinh Lap *Vietnam* 21°33N 107°6E **34 G6**
Dinin ↦ *Ireland* 52°43N 7°18W **10 D4**
Dinira △ *Venezuela* 9°57N 70°6W **89 E6**
Dinokwe *Botswana* 23°29S 26°37E **56 B4**
Dinorwic *Canada* 49°41N 92°30W **71 D10**
Dinosaur = Canada 50°47N 111°30W **70 C6**
Dinosaur △ *U.S.A.* 40°30N 108°45W **76 F9**
Dinuba *U.S.A.* 36°32N 119°23W **78 J7**
Diourbel *Senegal* 14°39N 16°12W **52 F2**
Dipalpur *Pakistan* 30°40N 73°39E **42 D5**
Diplo *Pakistan* 24°35N 69°35E **42 G3**
Dipolog *Phil.* 8°36N 123°20E **37 C6**
Dir *Pakistan* 35°8N 71°59E **40 B7**
Dire Dawa *Ethiopia* 9°35N 41°45E **49 F3**
Dirfis Oros *Greece* 38°40N 23°54E **23 E10**
Diriamba *Nic.* 11°51N 86°19W **88 D2**
Dirk Hartog I. *Australia* 25°50S 113°5E **61 E1**
Dirranbandi *Australia* 28°33S 148°17E **63 D4**
Disa *India* 24°18N 72°10E **42 G5**
Disappointment, C.
    U.S.A. 46°18N 124°5W **78 D2**
Disappointment, L.
    Australia 23°20S 122°40E **60 D3**
Disaster B. *Australia* 37°15S 149°58E **63 F4**
Discovery B. *Australia* 38°10S 140°40E **63 F3**
Disko = Qeqertarsuaq
    Greenland 69°45N 53°30W **4 C5**
Disney Reef *Tonga* 19°17S 174°7W **59 c**
Diss *U.K.* 52°23N 1°7E **13 E9**
Disteghil Sar *Pakistan* 36°20N 75°12E **43 A6**
District of Columbia □
    U.S.A. 38°55N 77°0W **81 F15**
Distrito Federal □ *Brazil* 15°45S 47°45W **93 G9**
Distrito Federal □
    Mexico 19°15N 99°10W **87 D5**
Diu *India* 20°45N 70°58E **42 J4**
Divândarreh *Iran* 35°55N 47°2E **46 C5**
Divi Pt. *India* 15°59N 81°9E **45 G5**
Dividing Ra. *Australia* 27°45S 116°0E **61 E2**
Divinópolis *Brazil* 20°10S 44°54W **93 H10**
Divnoye *Russia* 45°55N 43°21E **19 E7**
Divo *Côte d'Ivoire* 5°48N 5°15W **52 G4**
Dīwāl Kol *Afghan.* 34°23N 67°52E **42 B2**
Dixie Mt. *U.S.A.* 39°55N 120°16W **78 F6**
Dixon *Calif., U.S.A.* 38°27N 121°49W **78 G5**
Dixon *Ill., U.S.A.* 41°50N 89°29W **80 E9**
Dixon Entrance *U.S.A.* 54°30N 132°0W **68 G5**
Dixville *Canada* 45°4N 71°46W **83 A13**
Diyālá □ *Iraq* 33°45N 44°50E **46 C5**
Diyālá ↦ *Iraq* 33°13N 44°30E **46 C5**
Diyarbakır *Turkey* 37°55N 40°18E **46 B4**
Diyodar *India* 24°8N 71°50E **42 G4**
Djamba *Angola* 16°45S 13°58E **56 A1**
Djambala *Congo* 2°32S 14°30E **54 E2**
Djanet *Algeria* 24°35N 9°32E **52 D7**
Djawa = Jawa *Indonesia* 7°0S 110°0E **36 F3**
Djelfa *Algeria* 34°40N 3°15E **52 B6**
Djerid, Chott *Tunisia* 33°42N 8°30E **52 B7**
Djerba, Î. de *Tunisia* 33°50N 10°48E **53 B8**
Djibouti *Djibouti* 11°30N 43°5E **49 E3**
Djibouti ■ *Africa* 12°0N 43°0E **49 E3**
Djolu *Dem. Rep. of the Congo* 0°35N 22°5E **54 D4**
Djougou *Benin* 9°40N 1°45E **52 G6**
Djoum *Cameroon* 2°41N 12°35E **54 D2**
Djourab, Erg du *Chad* 16°40N 18°50E **53 E9**
Djukbinj △ *Australia* 12°11S 131°2E **60 B5**
Djúpivogur *Iceland* 64°39N 14°17W **8 D6**
Dmitriya Lapteva, Proliv
    Russia 73°0N 140°0E **27 B15**
Dnepr = Dnipro ↦
    Ukraine 46°30N 32°18E **19 E5**
Dneprodzerzhinsk =
    Dniprodzerzhynsk
    Ukraine 48°32N 34°37E **19 E5**
Dnepropetrovsk = Dnipropetrovsk
    Ukraine 48°30N 35°0E **19 E6**
Dnestr = Dnister ↦
    Europe 46°18N 30°17E **17 E16**
Dnieper = Dnipro ↦
    Ukraine 46°30N 32°18E **19 E5**
Dniester = Dnister ↦
    Europe 46°18N 30°17E **17 E16**
Dnipro ↦ *Ukraine* 46°30N 32°18E **19 E5**

Dniprodzerzhynsk
    Ukraine 48°32N 34°37E **19 E5**
Dnipropetrovsk *Ukraine* 48°30N 35°0E **19 E6**
Dnister ↦ *Europe* 46°18N 30°17E **17 E16**
Dno *Russia* 57°50N 29°58E **9 H23**
Dnyapro = Dnipro ↦
    Ukraine 46°30N 32°18E **19 E5**
Do Gonbadān = Gachsārān
    Iran 30°15N 50°45E **47 D6**
Doaktown *Canada* 46°33N 66°8W **73 C6**
Doan Hung *Vietnam* 21°30N 105°10E **34 G5**
Doba *Chad* 8°40N 16°50E **53 G9**
Dobandi *Pakistan* 31°13N 66°50E **42 D2**
Dobbyn *Australia* 19°44S 140°2E **62 B3**
Dobele *Latvia* 56°37N 23°16E **9 H20**
Doberai, Jazirah *Indonesia* 1°25S 133°0E **37 E8**
Dobo *Indonesia* 5°45S 134°15E **37 F8**
Doboj *Bos.-H.* 44°46N 18°4E **23 B8**
Dobrich *Bulgaria* 43°37N 27°49E **23 C12**
Dobruja *Europe* 44°30N 28°15E **17 F15**
Dobrush *Belarus* 52°25N 31°22E **17 B16**
Doc, Mui *Vietnam* 17°58N 106°30E **38 D6**
Docker River = Kaltukatjara
    Australia 24°52S 129°5E **61 D4**
Doctor Arroyo *Mexico* 23°40N 100°11W **86 C4**
Doctor Pedro P. Peña
    Paraguay 22°27S 62°21W **94 A3**
Doda *India* 33°10N 75°34E **43 C6**
Doda, L. *Canada* 49°25N 75°13W **72 C4**
Doda Betta *India* 11°24N 76°44E **45 J3**
Dodballapur *India* 13°18N 77°32E **45 H3**
Dodecanese = Dodekanisa
    Greece 36°35N 27°0E **23 F12**
Dodekanisa *Greece* 36°35N 27°0E **23 F12**
Dodge City *U.S.A.* 37°45N 100°1W **80 G3**
Dodge L. *Canada* 59°50N 105°36W **71 B7**
Dodgeville *U.S.A.* 42°58N 90°8W **80 D8**
Dodoma *Tanzania* 6°8S 35°45E **54 F7**
Dodsland *Canada* 51°50N 108°45W **71 C7**
Dodson *U.S.A.* 48°24N 108°15W **76 B9**
Doesburg *Neths.* 52°1N 6°9E **15 B6**
Doetinchem *Neths.* 51°59N 6°18E **15 C6**
Dog Creek *Canada* 51°35N 122°14W **70 C4**
Dog L. *Man., Canada* 51°2N 98°31W **71 C9**
Dog L. *Ont., Canada* 48°18N 89°30W **72 C2**
Dogran *Pakistan* 31°48N 73°35E **42 D5**
Doğubayazıt *Turkey* 39°31N 44°4E **46 B5**
Doha = Ad Dawḥah
    Qatar 25°15N 51°35E **47 E6**
Doha Int. ✈ (DOH) *Qatar* 25°16N 51°34E **47 E6**
Dohazari *Bangla.* 22°10N 92°5E **41 H18**
Dohrighat *India* 26°16N 83°31E **43 F10**
Doi *Indonesia* 2°14N 127°49E **37 D7**
Doi Inthanon *Thailand* 18°35N 98°29E **38 C2**
Doi Inthanon △ *Thailand* 18°33N 98°34E **38 C2**
Doi Khuntan △ *Thailand* 18°33N 99°14E **38 C2**
Doi Luang *Thailand* 18°30N 101°0E **38 C3**
Doi Luang △ *Thailand* 19°22N 99°3E **38 C2**
Doi Phukha △ *Thailand* 19°8N 101°9E **38 C3**
Doi Saket *Thailand* 18°52N 99°9E **38 C2**
Doi Suthep Pui △
    Thailand 18°49N 98°53E **38 C2**
Doi Toa *Thailand* 17°55N 98°30E **38 D2**
Dois Irmãos, Sa. *Brazil* 9°0S 42°30W **93 E10**
Dokdo = Liancourt Rocks
    Asia 37°15N 131°52E **29 F5**
Dokkum *Neths.* 53°20N 5°59E **15 A5**
Dokri *Pakistan* 27°25N 68°7E **42 F3**
Dolak, Pulau *Indonesia* 8°0S 138°30E **37 F9**
Dolbeau-Mistassini
    Canada 48°53N 72°14W **73 C5**
Dole *France* 47°7N 5°31E **20 C6**
Dolgellau *U.K.* 52°45N 3°53W **12 E4**
Dolgelley = Dolgellau
    U.K. 52°45N 3°53W **12 E4**
Dolinsk *Russia* 47°21N 142°48E **27 E15**
Dollard *Neths.* 53°20N 7°10E **15 A7**
Dolo *Ethiopia* 4°11N 42°3E **49 G3**
Dolomites = Dolomiti
    Italy 46°23N 11°51E **22 A4**
Dolomiti *Italy* 46°23N 11°51E **22 A4**
Dolores *Argentina* 36°20S 57°40W **94 D4**
Dolores *Uruguay* 33°34S 58°15W **94 C4**
Dolores *U.S.A.* 37°28N 108°30W **77 H9**
Dolores ↦ *U.S.A.* 38°49N 109°17W **76 G9**
Dolphin, C. *Falk. Is.* 51°10S 59°0W **96 G5**
Dolphin and Union Str.
    Canada 69°5N 114°45W **68 D9**
Dom Pedrito *Brazil* 31°0S 54°40W **95 C5**
Domariaganj ↦ *India* 26°17N 83°44E **43 F10**
Dombarovskiy *Russia* 50°46N 59°32E **26 D6**
Dombås *Norway* 62°4N 9°8E **8 E13**
Dome Argus *Antarctica* 80°50S 76°30E **5 E6**
Dome C. *Antarctica* 75°12S 123°37E **5 D9**
Dome Fuji *Antarctica* 77°20S 39°45E **5 D5**
Domel I. = Letsôk-aw Kyun
    Myanmar 11°30N 98°25E **39 G2**
Domeyko *Chile* 29°0S 71°0W **94 B1**
Domeyko, Cordillera
    Chile 24°30S 69°0W **94 A2**
Dominador *Chile* 24°21S 69°20W **94 A2**
Dominica ■ *W. Indies* 15°20N 61°20W **89 C7**
Dominica Passage
    W. Indies 15°10N 61°20W **89 C7**
Dominican Rep. ■
    W. Indies 19°0N 70°30W **89 C5**
Domodóssola *Italy* 46°7N 8°17E **20 C8**
Domville, Mt. *Australia* 28°1S 151°15E **63 D5**
Don ↦ *India* 16°20N 76°15E **45 F3**
Don ↦ *Russia* 47°4N 39°18E **19 E6**
Don ↦ *Aberds., U.K.* 57°11N 2°5W **11 D6**
Don ↦ *S. Yorks., U.K.* 53°41N 0°52W **12 D7**
Don Benito *Spain* 38°53N 5°51W **21 C3**
Don Figuereoa Mts.
    Jamaica 18°5N 77°36W **88 a**
Don Sak *Thailand* 9°18N 99°41E **39 b**
Donaghadee *U.K.* 54°39N 5°33W **10 B6**
Donaghmore *Ireland* 52°52N 7°36W **10 D4**

Donald *Australia* 36°23S 143°0E **63 F3**
Donaldsonville *U.S.A.* 30°6N 90°59W **84 F9**
Donalsonville *U.S.A.* 31°3N 84°53W **85 F12**
Donau = Dunărea ↦
    Europe 45°20N 29°40E **17 F15**
Donauwörth *Germany* 48°43N 10°47E **16 D6**
Doncaster *U.K.* 53°32N 1°6W **12 D6**
Dondo *Angola* 9°45S 14°25E **54 F2**
Dondo, Teluk *Indonesia* 0°50N 120°30E **37 D6**
Dondra Head *Sri Lanka* 5°55N 80°40E **45 M5**
Donegal *Ireland* 54°39N 8°5W **10 B3**
Donegal □ *Ireland* 54°53N 8°0W **10 B4**
Donegal B. *Ireland* 54°31N 8°49W **10 B3**
Donets ↦ *Russia* 47°33N 40°55E **19 E7**
Donets Basin *Ukraine* 49°0N 38°0E **6 F13**
Donetsk *Ukraine* 48°0N 37°45E **19 E6**
Dong Ba Thin *Vietnam* 12°8N 109°13E **39 F7**
Dong Dang *Vietnam* 21°54N 106°42E **34 G6**
Dong Giam *Vietnam* 19°25N 105°31E **38 C5**
Dong Ha *Vietnam* 16°55N 107°8E **38 D6**
Dong Hoi *Vietnam* 17°29N 106°36E **38 D6**
Dong Jiang ↦ *China* 23°6N 114°0E **35 F10**
Dong Khe *Vietnam* 22°26N 106°27E **38 A6**
Dong Phayayen
    Thailand 14°20N 101°22E **38 E3**
Dong Van *Vietnam* 23°16N 105°22E **38 A5**
Dong Xoai *Vietnam* 11°32N 106°55E **39 G6**
Dong'an *China* 26°23N 111°12E **35 D8**
Dongara *Australia* 29°14S 114°57E **61 E1**
Dongargarh *India* 21°10N 80°40E **44 D5**
Dongbei *China* 45°0N 125°0E **33 D13**
Dongchuan *China* 26°8N 103°1E **34 D4**
Dongfang *China* 18°50N 108°33E **38 C7**
Dongfeng *China* 42°40N 125°34E **33 C13**
Donggala *Indonesia* 0°30S 119°40E **37 E5**
Donggan *China* 23°22N 105°9E **34 F5**
Donggang *China* 39°52N 124°10E **33 E13**
Dongguan *China* 22°58N 113°44E **35 F9**
Dongguang *China* 37°50N 116°30E **32 F9**
Donghae *S. Korea* 37°29N 129°7E **33 F15**
Donghai Dao *China* 21°0N 110°15E **35 G8**
Dongjingcheng *China* 44°5N 129°10E **33 B15**
Dongkou *China* 27°6N 110°35E **35 D8**
Donglan *China* 24°30N 107°21E **34 E6**
Dongliao He ↦ *China* 42°58N 123°32E **33 C12**
Dongliu *China* 30°13N 116°55E **35 B11**
Dongmen *China* 22°20N 107°48E **34 F6**
Dongning *China* 44°2N 131°5E **33 B16**
Dongnyi *China* 28°3N 100°1E **34 C3**
Dongola *Sudan* 19°9N 30°22E **53 E12**
Dongping *China* 35°55N 116°20E **32 G9**
Dongsha Dao
    S. China Sea 20°45N 116°43E **35 G11**
Dongshan *China* 23°43N 117°30E **35 F11**
Dongsheng = Ordos
    China 39°50N 110°0E **32 E6**
Dongtai *China* 32°51N 120°21E **33 H11**
Dongting Hu *China* 29°18N 112°45E **35 C9**
Dongtou *China* 27°51N 121°10E **35 D13**
Dongxiang *China* 28°11N 116°34E **35 C11**
Dongxing *China* 21°34N 108°0E **34 G7**
Dongyang *China* 29°13N 120°15E **35 C13**
Dongying *China* 37°37N 118°37E **33 F10**
Dongyinggang *China* 37°55N 118°58E **33 F10**
Dongzhi *China* 30°9N 117°0E **35 B11**
Donington, C. *Australia* 34°45S 136°0E **63 E2**
Doniphan *U.S.A.* 36°37N 90°50W **80 G8**
Dønna *Norway* 66°6N 12°30E **8 C15**
Donna *U.S.A.* 26°9N 98°4W **84 H5**
Donnaconna *Canada* 46°41N 71°41W **73 C5**
Donnelly's Crossing
    N.Z. 35°42S 173°38E **59 A4**
Donner Pass *U.S.A.* 39°19N 120°20W **78 F6**
Donnybrook *Australia* 33°34S 115°48E **61 F2**
Donnybrook *S. Africa* 29°59S 29°48E **57 C4**
Donora *U.S.A.* 40°11N 79°52W **82 F5**
Donostia = Donostia-San
    Sebastián *Spain* 43°17N 1°58W **21 A5**
Donostia-San Sebastián
    Spain 43°17N 1°58W **21 A5**
Donwood *Canada* 44°19N 78°16W **82 B6**
Doomadgee *Australia* 17°56S 138°49E **62 B2**
Doomadgee ◎ *Australia* 17°56S 138°49E **62 B2**
Doon ↦ *U.K.* 55°27N 4°39W **11 F4**
Doon Doon ◎ *Australia* 16°18S 128°14E **60 C4**
Dora, L. *Australia* 22°0S 123°0E **60 D3**
Dora Báltea ↦ *Italy* 45°11N 8°3E **20 D8**
Doran L. *Canada* 61°13N 108°6W **71 A7**
Dorchester *U.K.* 50°42N 2°27E **13 G5**
Dorchester, C. *Canada* 65°27N 77°27W **69 D16**
Dordabis *Namibia* 22°52S 17°38E **56 B2**
Dordogne ↦ *France* 45°2N 0°36W **20 D3**
Dordrecht *Neths.* 51°48N 4°39E **15 C4**
Dordrecht *S. Africa* 31°20S 27°3E **56 D4**
Doré L. *Canada* 54°46N 107°17W **71 C7**
Dori *Burkina Faso* 14°3N 0°2W **52 F5**
Doring ↦ *S. Africa* 31°54S 18°39E **56 D2**
Doringbos *S. Africa* 31°59S 19°16E **56 D2**
Dorking *U.K.* 51°14N 0°19W **13 F7**
Dornakal *India* 17°27N 80°10E **44 F5**
Dornbirn *Austria* 47°25N 9°45E **16 E5**
Dornie *U.K.* 57°17N 5°31W **11 D3**
Dornoch *Canada* 44°18N 80°51W **82 B4**
Dornoch *U.K.* 57°53N 4°2W **11 D4**
Dornoch Firth *U.K.* 57°51N 4°4W **11 D4**
Dornogovĭ □ *Mongolia* 44°0N 110°0E **32 C6**
Doro, Kavo *Greece* 38°9N 24°38E **23 E11**
Dorohoi *Romania* 47°56N 26°23E **17 E14**
Döröö Nuur *Mongolia* 48°0N 93°0E **30 B7**
Dorr *Iran* 33°17N 50°38E **47 C6**
Dorre I. *Australia* 25°13S 113°12E **61 E1**
Dorrigo *Australia* 30°20S 152°44E **63 E5**
Dorris *U.S.A.* 41°58N 121°55W **76 F3**
Dorset *Canada* 45°14N 78°54W **82 A6**
Dorset *Ohio, U.S.A.* 41°40N 80°40W **82 E4**
Dorset □ *U.K.* 50°45N 2°26W **13 G5**
Dortmund *Germany* 51°30N 7°28E **16 C4**

Dörtyol *Turkey* 36°50N 36°13E **46 B3**
Dorüneh *Iran* 35°10N 57°18E **47 C8**
Dos Bahías, C. *Argentina* 44°58S 65°32W **96 E3**
Dos Hermanas *Spain* 37°16N 5°55W **21 D3**
Dos Palos *U.S.A.* 36°59N 120°37W **78 J6**
Dosso *Niger* 13°0N 3°13E **52 F6**
Dothan *U.S.A.* 31°13N 85°24W **85 F12**
Doty *U.S.A.* 46°38N 123°17W **78 D3**
Douai *France* 50°21N 3°4E **20 A5**
Douala *Cameroon* 4°0N 9°45E **54 D1**
Douarnenez *France* 48°6N 4°21W **20 B1**
Double Island Pt.
    Australia 25°56S 153°11E **63 D5**
Double Mountain Fork ↦
    U.S.A. 33°16N 100°0W **84 E4**
Doubs ↦ *France* 46°53N 5°1E **20 C6**
Doubtful Sd. *N.Z.* 45°20S 166°49E **59 F1**
Doubtless B. *N.Z.* 34°55S 173°26E **59 A4**
Douglas *Canada* 45°31N 76°56W **82 A8**
Douglas *I. of Man* 54°10N 4°28W **12 C3**
Douglas *S. Africa* 29°4S 23°46E **56 C3**
Douglas *Ariz., U.S.A.* 31°21N 109°33W **77 L9**
Douglas *Ga., U.S.A.* 31°31N 82°51W **85 F13**
Douglas *Wyo., U.S.A.* 42°45N 105°24W **76 E11**
Douglas Apsley △
    Australia 41°45S 148°11E **63 G4**
Douglas Chan. *Canada* 53°40N 129°20W **70 C3**
Douglas Pt. *Canada* 44°19N 81°37W **82 B3**
Douglasville *U.S.A.* 33°45N 84°45W **85 E12**
Doumen *China* 22°10N 113°18E **35 F9**
Dounreay *U.K.* 58°35N 3°44W **11 C5**
Dourada, Serra *Brazil* 13°10S 48°45W **93 F9**
Dourados *Brazil* 22°9S 54°50W **95 A5**
Dourados ↦ *Brazil* 21°58S 54°18W **95 A5**
Dourados, Serra dos
    Brazil 23°30S 53°30W **95 A5**
Douro ↦ *Europe* 41°8N 8°40W **21 B1**
Dove ↦ *U.K.* 52°51N 1°36W **12 E6**
Dove Creek *U.S.A.* 37°46N 108°54W **77 H9**
Dover *Australia* 43°18S 147°2E **63 G4**
Dover *U.K.* 51°7N 1°19E **13 F9**
Dover *Del., U.S.A.* 39°10N 75°32W **81 F16**
Dover *N.H., U.S.A.* 43°12N 70°56W **83 C14**
Dover *N.J., U.S.A.* 40°53N 74°34W **83 F10**
Dover *Ohio, U.S.A.* 40°32N 81°29W **82 F3**
Dover, Pt. *Australia* 32°32S 125°32E **61 F4**
Dover, Str. of *Europe* 51°0N 1°30E **13 G9**
Dover-Foxcroft *U.S.A.* 45°11N 69°13W **81 C19**
Dover Plains *U.S.A.* 41°43N 73°35W **83 E11**
Dovey = Dyfi ↦ *U.K.* 52°32N 4°3W **13 E3**
Dovrefjell *Norway* 62°15N 9°33E **8 E13**
Dovrefjell-Sunndalsfjella △
    Norway 62°23N 9°11E **8 E13**
Dow Rūd *Iran* 33°28N 49°4E **47 C6**
Dowagiac *U.S.A.* 41°59N 86°6W **80 E10**
Dowerin *Australia* 31°12S 117°2E **61 F2**
Dowgha'i *Iran* 36°54N 58°32E **47 B8**
Dowlatābād *Kermān, Iran* 28°20N 56°40E **47 D8**
Dowlatābād *Khorāsān,*
    Iran 35°16N 59°29E **47 C8**
Down □ *U.K.* 54°23N 6°2W **10 B5**
Downey *U.S.A.* 42°26N 112°7W **76 E7**
Downham Market *U.K.* 52°37N 0°23E **13 E8**
Downieville *U.S.A.* 39°34N 120°50W **78 F6**
Downpatrick *U.K.* 54°20N 5°43W **10 B6**
Downpatrick Hd. *Ireland* 54°20N 9°21W **10 B2**
Downsville *U.S.A.* 42°5N 75°0W **83 D10**
Downton, Mt. *Canada* 52°42N 124°52W **70 C4**
Dowsārī *Iran* 28°25N 57°59E **47 D8**
Doyle *U.S.A.* 40°2N 120°6W **78 E6**
Doylestown *U.S.A.* 40°21N 75°10W **83 F9**
Dozois, Rés. *Canada* 47°30N 77°5W **72 C4**
Dra Khel *Pakistan* 27°58N 66°45E **42 F2**
Drâa, C. *Morocco* 28°47N 11°0W **52 C3**
Drâa, Hamada du *Algeria* 28°0N 6°0W **52 C4**
Drâa, Oued ↦ *Morocco* 28°40N 11°0W **52 C3**
Drachten *Neths.* 53°7N 6°5E **15 A6**
Drăgășani *Romania* 44°39N 24°17E **17 F13**
Dragichyn *Belarus* 52°15N 25°8E **17 B13**
Dragoman, Prokhod
    Bulgaria 42°58N 22°53E **23 C10**
Dragon's Mouths
    Trin. & Tob. 11°0N 61°50W **93 K15**
Draguignan *France* 43°32N 6°27E **20 E7**
Drain *U.S.A.* 43°40N 123°19W **76 E2**
Drake *U.S.A.* 47°55N 100°23W **80 B3**
Drake Passage *S. Ocean* 58°0S 68°0W **5 B17**
Drakensberg *S. Africa* 31°0S 28°0E **57 D4**
Drama *Greece* 41°9N 24°10E **23 D11**
Drammen *Norway* 59°42N 10°12E **9 G14**
Drangajökull *Iceland* 66°9N 22°15W **8 C2**
Dras *India* 34°25N 75°48E **43 B6**
Drau = Drava ↦ *Croatia* 45°33N 18°55E **23 B8**
Drava ↦ *Croatia* 45°33N 18°55E **23 B8**
Drayton *Canada* 43°46N 80°40W **82 C4**
Drayton Valley *Canada* 53°12N 114°58W **70 C6**
Drenthe □ *Neths.* 52°52N 6°40E **15 B6**
Dresden *Canada* 42°35N 82°11W **82 D2**
Dresden *Germany* 51°3N 13°44E **16 C7**
Dresden *U.S.A.* 42°41N 76°57W **82 D8**
Dreux *France* 48°44N 1°23E **20 B4**
Driffield *U.K.* 54°0N 0°26W **12 C7**
Driftwood *U.S.A.* 41°20N 78°8W **82 E6**
Driggs *U.S.A.* 43°44N 111°6W **76 E8**
Drin ↦ *Albania* 41°39N 19°38E **23 C8**
Drina ↦ *Bos.-H.* 44°53N 19°21E **23 B8**
Drøbak *Norway* 59°39N 10°39E **9 G14**
Drobeta-Turnu Severin
    Romania 44°39N 22°41E **17 F12**
Drochia *Moldova* 48°2N 27°48E **17 D14**
Drogheda *Ireland* 53°43N 6°22W **10 C5**
Drogichin = Dragichyn
    Belarus 52°15N 25°8E **17 B13**
Drogobych = Drohobych
    Ukraine 49°20N 23°30E **17 D12**
Drohobych *Ukraine* 49°20N 23°30E **17 D12**
Droichead Átha = Drogheda
    Ireland 53°43N 6°22W **10 C5**
Droichead na Bandan = Bandon
    Ireland 51°44N 8°44W **10 E3**

Droichead Nua = Newbridge
  Ireland 53°11N 6°48W 10 C5
Droitwich U.K. 52°16N 2°8W 13 E5
Drôme □ France 44°46N 4°46E 20 D6
Dromedary, C. Australia 36°17S 150°10E 63 F5
Dromore Down, U.K. 54°25N 6°9W 10 B5
Dromore Tyrone, U.K. 54°31N 7°28W 10 B4
Dromore West Ireland 54°15N 8°52W 10 B3
Dronfield U.K. 53°19N 1°27W 12 D6
Dronning Maud Land
  Antarctica 72°30S 12°0E 5 D3
Dronten Neths. 52°32N 5°43E 15 B5
Druk Yul = Bhutan ■
  Asia 27°25N 90°30E 41 F17
Drumbo Canada 43°16N 80°35W 82 C4
Drumcliff Ireland 54°20N 8°29W 10 B3
Drumheller Canada 51°25N 112°40W 70 C6
Drummond U.S.A. 46°40N 113°9W 76 C7
Drummond I. U.S.A. 46°1N 83°39W 81 B12
Drummond Pt. Australia 34°9S 135°16E 63 E2
Drummond Ra.
  Australia 23°45S 147°10E 62 C4
Drummondville Canada 45°55N 72°25W 72 C5
Drumright U.S.A. 35°59N 96°36W 84 D6
Druskininkai Lithuania 54°3N 23°58E 9 J20
Drut → Belarus 53°8N 30°5E 17 B16
Druzhina Russia 68°14N 145°18E 27 C15
Dry Harbour Mts. Jamaica 18°19N 77°24W 88 a
Dry Tortugas U.S.A. 24°38N 82°55W 85 J13
Dryander △ Australia 20°13S 148°34E 62 b
Dryden Canada 49°47N 92°50W 71 D10
Dryden U.S.A. 42°30N 76°18W 83 D8
Drygalski I. Antarctica 66°0S 92°0E 5 C7
Drygalski Ice Tongue
  Antarctica 75°24S 163°30E 5 D11
Drysdale → Australia 13°59S 126°51E 60 B4
Drysdale I. Australia 11°41S 136°0E 62 A2
Drysdale River △
  Australia 14°56S 127°2E 60 B4
Du Gué → Canada 57°21N 70°45W 72 A5
Du He → China 32°48N 110°40E 35 A8
Du Quoin U.S.A. 38°1N 89°14W 80 F9
Du'an China 23°59N 108°3E 34 F7
Duanesburg U.S.A. 42°45N 74°11W 83 D10
Duaringa Australia 23°42S 149°42E 62 C4
Duarte, Pico Dom. Rep. 19°2N 70°59W 89 D5
Dubǎsari Moldova 47°15N 29°0E 17 E15
Dubǎsari Vdkhr. Moldova 47°30N 29°0E 17 E15
Dubawnt → Canada 64°33N 100°6W 71 A8
Dubawnt L. Canada 63°8N 101°28W 71 A8
Dubbo Australia 32°11S 148°35E 63 E4
Dublin Ireland 53°21N 6°15W 10 C5
Dublin Ga., U.S.A. 32°32N 82°54W 85 E13
Dublin Tex., U.S.A. 32°5N 98°21W 84 E5
Dublin □ Ireland 53°24N 6°20W 10 C5
Dublin ✈ (DUB) Ireland 53°26N 6°15W 10 C5
Dubno Ukraine 50°25N 25°45E 17 C13
Dubois Idaho, U.S.A. 44°10N 112°14W 76 D7
DuBois Pa., U.S.A. 41°7N 78°46W 82 E6
Dubossary = Dubǎsari
  Moldova 47°15N 29°10E 17 E15
Dubovka Russia 49°5N 44°50E 19 E7
Dubrajpur India 23°48N 87°25E 43 H12
Dubréka Guinea 9°46N 13°31W 52 G3
Dubrovitsa = Dubrovytsya
  Ukraine 51°31N 26°35E 17 C14
Dubrovnik Croatia 42°39N 18°6E 23 C8
Dubrovytsya Ukraine 51°31N 26°35E 17 C14
Dubuque U.S.A. 42°30N 90°41W 80 D8
Duc Tho Vietnam 18°32N 105°35E 38 C5
Duchang China 29°18N 116°12E 35 C11
Duchesne U.S.A. 40°10N 110°24W 76 F8
Duchess Australia 21°20S 139°50E 62 C2
Ducie I. Pac. Oc. 24°40S 124°48W 65 K15
Duck → U.S.A. 36°2N 87°52W 85 C11
Duck Cr. → Australia 22°37S 116°53E 60 D2
Duck Lake Canada 52°50N 106°16W 71 C7
Duck Mountain △
  Canada 51°45N 101°0W 71 C8
Duckwall, Mt. U.S.A. 37°58N 120°7W 78 H6
Dudhi India 24°15N 83°10E 43 G10
Dudinka Russia 69°30N 86°13E 27 C9
Dudley U.K. 52°31N 2°5W 13 E5
Dudna → India 19°17N 76°54E 44 E3
Dudwa India 28°30N 80°41E 43 E9
Dudwa △ India 28°30N 80°40E 43 E9
Duero = Douro → Europe 41°8N 8°40W 21 B1
Dufftown U.K. 57°27N 3°8W 11 D5
Dugi Otok Croatia 44°0N 15°3E 16 G8
Duisburg Germany 51°26N 6°45E 16 C4
Duiwelskloof = Modjadjiskloof
  S. Africa 23°42S 30°10E 57 B5
Dujiangyan China 31°2N 103°38E 34 B4
Dūkdamīn Iran 35°59N 57°43E 47 C8
Dukelský Průsmyk
  Slovakia 49°25N 21°42E 17 D11
Dukhān Qatar 25°25N 50°50E 47 E6
Duki Pakistan 30°14N 68°25E 40 D6
Duku Nigeria 10°43N 10°43E 53 F8
Dukuza = Stanger
  S. Africa 29°27S 31°14E 57 C5
Dulan China 36°0N 97°11E 30 D8
Dulce U.S.A. 36°56N 107°0W 77 H10
Dulce → Argentina 30°32S 62°33W 94 C3
Dulce, G. Costa Rica 8°40N 83°20W 88 E3
Dulf Iraq 35°7N 45°51E 46 C5
Duliu China 39°2N 116°55E 32 E9
Dulles Int. ✈ (IAD)
  U.S.A. 38°57N 77°27W 81 F15
Dullewala Pakistan 31°50N 71°25E 42 D4
Dullstroom S. Africa 25°27S 30°37E 57 B5
Dulq Maghār Syria 36°22N 38°39E 46 B3
Duluth U.S.A. 46°47N 92°6W 80 B7
Dum Duma India 27°40N 95°40E 41 F19
Dūmā Syria 33°34N 36°24E 48 B5
Dumaguete Phil. 9°17N 123°15E 37 C6
Dumai Indonesia 1°35N 101°28E 36 D2
Dumaran Phil. 10°33N 119°50E 37 B5
Dumas Ark., U.S.A. 33°53N 91°29W 84 E9
Dumas Tex., U.S.A. 35°52N 101°58W 84 D4

Dumayr Syria 33°39N 36°42E 48 B5
Dumbarton U.K. 55°57N 4°33W 11 F4
Dumbleyung Australia 33°17S 117°42E 61 F2
Dumfries U.K. 55°4N 3°37W 11 F5
Dumfries & Galloway □
  U.K. 55°9N 3°58W 11 F5
Dumka India 24°12N 87°15E 43 G12
Dumoine → Canada 46°13N 77°51W 72 C4
Dumoine, L. Canada 46°55N 77°55W 72 C4
Dumont d'Urville
  Antarctica 66°40S 140°0E 5 C10
Dumont d'Urville Sea
  S. Ocean 63°30S 138°0E 5 C9
Dumyât Egypt 31°24N 31°48E 53 B12
Dún Dealgan = Dundalk
  Ireland 54°1N 6°24W 10 B5
Dún Garbhán = Dungarvan
  Ireland 52°5N 7°37W 10 D4
Dún Laoghaire Ireland 53°17N 6°8W 10 C5
Dún Laoghaire-Rathdown □
  Ireland 53°14N 6°11W 10 C5
Duna = Dunărea →
  Europe 45°20N 29°40E 17 F15
Dunagiri India 30°31N 79°52E 43 D8
Dunaj = Dunărea →
  Europe 45°20N 29°40E 17 F15
Dunakeszi Hungary 47°37N 19°8E 17 E10
Dunărea → Europe 45°20N 29°40E 17 F15
Dunaújváros Hungary 46°58N 18°57E 17 E10
Dunav = Dunărea →
  Europe 45°20N 29°40E 17 F15
Dunay Russia 42°52N 132°22E 28 C6
Dunback N.Z. 45°23S 170°36E 59 F3
Dunbar U.K. 56°0N 2°31W 11 E6
Dunblane U.K. 56°11N 3°58W 11 E5
Duncan Canada 48°45N 123°40W 78 B3
Duncan Ariz., U.S.A. 32°43N 109°6W 77 K9
Duncan Okla., U.S.A. 34°30N 97°57W 84 D6
Duncan, L. Canada 53°29N 77°58W 72 B4
Duncan L. Canada 62°51N 113°58W 70 A6
Duncan Passage India 11°0N 92°0E 45 J11
Duncan Town Bahamas 22°15N 75°45W 88 B4
Duncannon U.S.A. 40°23N 77°2W 82 F7
Duncansby Head U.K. 58°38N 3°1W 11 C5
Duncansville U.S.A. 40°25N 78°26W 82 F6
Dund-Us Mongolia 48°1N 91°38E 30 B7
Dundalk Canada 44°10N 80°24W 82 B4
Dundalk Ireland 54°1N 6°24W 10 B5
Dundalk U.S.A. 39°15N 76°31W 81 F15
Dundalk Bay Ireland 53°55N 6°15W 10 C5
Dundas = Uummannaq
  Greenland 77°33N 68°52W 69 B18
Dundas Canada 43°17N 79°59W 82 C5
Dundas, L. Australia 32°35S 121°50E 61 F3
Dundas I. Canada 54°30N 130°50W 70 C2
Dundas Str. Australia 11°15S 131°35E 60 B5
Dundee S. Africa 28°11S 30°15E 57 C5
Dundee U.K. 56°28N 2°59W 11 E6
Dundee U.S.A. 42°32N 76°59W 82 D8
Dundee City □ U.K. 56°30N 2°58W 11 E6
Dundgovĭ □ Mongolia 45°10N 106°0E 32 B4
Dundrum U.K. 54°16N 5°52W 10 B6
Dundrum B. U.K. 54°13N 5°47W 10 B6
Dunedin N.Z. 45°50S 170°33E 59 F3
Dunedin U.S.A. 28°1N 82°46W 85 G13
Dunfanaghy Ireland 55°11N 7°58W 10 A4
Dunfermline U.K. 56°5N 3°27W 11 E5
Dungannon Canada 43°51N 81°36W 82 C3
Dungannon U.K. 54°31N 6°46W 10 B5
Dungarpur India 23°52N 73°45E 42 H5
Dungarvan Ireland 52°5N 7°37W 10 D4
Dungarvan Harbour
  Ireland 52°4N 7°35W 10 D4
Dungeness U.K. 50°54N 0°59E 13 G8
Dungiven U.K. 54°56N 6°56W 10 B5
Dungloe Ireland 54°57N 8°21W 10 B3
Dungo, L. do Angola 17°15S 19°0E 56 A2
Dungog Australia 32°22S 151°46E 63 E5
Dungu
  Dem. Rep. of the Congo 3°40N 28°32E 54 D5
Dungun Malaysia 4°45N 103°25E 39 K4
Dunhua China 43°20N 128°14E 33 C15
Dunhuang China 40°8N 94°36E 30 C7
Dunk I. Australia 17°59S 146°29E 62 B4
Dunkeld Australia 33°25S 149°29E 63 E4
Dunkeld U.K. 56°34N 3°35W 11 E5
Dunkerque France 51°2N 2°20E 20 A5
Dunkery Beacon U.K. 51°9N 3°36W 13 F4
Dunkirk = Dunkerque
  France 51°2N 2°20E 20 A5
Dunkirk U.S.A. 42°29N 79°20W 82 D5
Dunleary = Dún Laoghaire
  Ireland 53°17N 6°8W 10 C5
Dunleer Ireland 53°50N 6°24W 10 C5
Dunmanus B. Ireland 51°31N 9°50W 10 E2
Dunmanway Ireland 51°43N 9°6W 10 E2
Dunmarra Australia 16°42S 133°25E 62 B1
Dunmore U.S.A. 41°25N 75°38W 83 E9
Dunmore East Ireland 52°9N 7°0W 10 D5
Dunmore Town
  Bahamas 25°30N 76°39W 88 A4
Dunn U.S.A. 35°19N 78°37W 85 D15
Dunnellon U.S.A. 29°3N 82°28W 85 G13
Dunnet Hd. U.K. 58°40N 3°21W 11 C5
Dunning U.S.A. 41°50N 100°6W 80 E3
Dunnville Canada 42°54N 79°36W 82 D5
Dunolly Australia 36°51S 143°44E 63 F3
Dunoon U.K. 55°57N 4°56W 11 F4
Duns U.K. 55°47N 2°20W 11 F6
Dunseith U.S.A. 48°50N 100°3W 80 A3
Dunshaughlin Ireland 53°31N 6°33W 10 C5
Dunsmuir U.S.A. 41°13N 122°16W 76 F2
Dunstable U.K. 51°53N 0°32W 13 F7
Dunstan Mts. N.Z. 44°53S 169°35E 59 F2
Dunster Canada 53°8N 119°50W 70 C5
Dunvegan U.K. 57°27N 6°35W 11 D2
Dunvegan L. Canada 60°8N 107°10W 71 A7
Duolun China 42°12N 116°28E 32 C9
Duong Dong Vietnam 10°13N 103°58E 39 G4
Dupree U.S.A. 45°4N 101°35W 80 C3

Dupuyer U.S.A. 48°13N 112°30W 76 B7
Durack → Australia 15°33S 127°52E 60 C4
Durack Ra. Australia 16°50S 127°40E 60 C4
Durack River Australia 15°32S 127°39E 60 C4
Durance → France 43°55N 4°45E 20 E6
Durand U.S.A. 44°38N 91°58W 80 C8
Durango Mexico 24°3N 104°39W 86 C4
Durango U.S.A. 37°16N 107°53W 77 H10
Durango □ Mexico 24°50N 105°20W 86 C4
Durant Miss., U.S.A. 33°4N 89°51W 85 E10
Durant Okla., U.S.A. 33°59N 96°25W 84 E6
Durazno Uruguay 33°25S 56°31W 94 C4
Durazzo = Durrës
  Albania 41°19N 19°28E 23 D8
Durban S. Africa 29°49S 31°1E 57 C5
Durban ✈ (DUR) S. Africa 29°37S 31°7E 57 C5
Durbuy Belgium 50°21N 5°28E 15 D5
Düren Germany 50°48N 6°29E 16 C4
Durg = Bhilainagar-Durg
  India 21°13N 81°26E 44 D5
Durgapur India 23°30N 87°20E 43 H12
Durham Canada 44°10N 80°49W 82 B4
Durham U.K. 54°47N 1°34W 12 C6
Durham Calif., U.S.A. 39°39N 121°48W 78 F5
Durham N.C., U.S.A. 35°59N 78°54W 85 D15
Durham N.H., U.S.A. 43°8N 70°56W 83 C14
Durham □ U.K. 54°42N 1°45W 12 C6
Durlas = Thurles Ireland 52°41N 7°49W 10 D4
Durmā Si. Arabia 24°37N 46°8E 46 E5
Durmitor Montenegro 43°10N 19°0E 23 C8
Durness U.K. 58°34N 4°45W 11 C4
Durrës Albania 41°19N 19°28E 23 D8
Durrow Ireland 52°51N 7°24W 10 D4
Dursey I. Ireland 51°36N 10°12W 10 E1
Dursley U.K. 51°40N 2°21W 13 F5
Dursunbey Turkey 39°35N 28°37E 23 E13
Durūz, Jabal ad Jordan 32°35N 36°40E 48 C5
D'Urville, Tanjung
  Indonesia 1°28S 137°54E 37 E9
D'Urville I. N.Z. 40°50S 173°55E 59 D4
Duryea U.S.A. 41°20N 75°45W 83 E9
Dushak Turkmenistan 37°13N 60°1E 47 B9
Dushan China 25°48N 107°30E 34 E6
Dushanbe Tajikistan 38°33N 68°48E 26 F7
Dushore U.S.A. 41°31N 76°24W 83 E8
Dusky Sd. N.Z. 45°47S 166°30E 59 F1
Dussejour, C. Australia 14°45S 128°13E 60 B4
Düsseldorf Germany 51°14N 6°47E 16 C4
Dutch Harbor U.S.A. 53°53N 166°32W 74 E6
Dutlwe Botswana 23°58S 23°46E 56 B3
Dutton Canada 42°39N 81°30W 82 D3
Dutton → Australia 20°44S 143°10E 62 C3
Dutywa S. Africa 32°8S 28°18E 57 D4
Duwayhin, Khawr
  U.A.E. 24°20N 51°25E 47 E6
Duyfken Pt. Australia 12°33S 141°38E 62 A3
Duyun China 26°18N 107°29E 34 D6
Dvina, Severnaya →
  Russia 64°32N 40°30E 18 B7
Dvinsk = Daugavpils
  Latvia 55°53N 26°32E 9 J22
Dvinskaya Guba Russia 65°0N 39°0E 18 B6
Dwarka India 22°18N 69°8E 42 H3
Dwellingup Australia 32°43S 116°4E 61 F2
Dwight Canada 45°20N 79°1W 82 A5
Dwight U.S.A. 41°5N 88°26W 80 E9
Dyatlovo = Dzyatlava
  Belarus 53°28N 25°28E 17 B13
Dyce U.K. 57°13N 2°12W 11 D6
Dyer, C. Canada 66°37N 61°16W 69 D19
Dyer Bay Canada 45°10N 81°20W 82 A3
Dyer Plateau Antarctica 70°45S 65°30W 5 D17
Dyersburg U.S.A. 36°3N 89°23W 85 C10
Dyfi → U.K. 52°32N 4°3W 13 E3
Dymer Ukraine 50°47N 30°18E 17 C16
Dysart Australia 22°32S 148°23E 62 C4
Dzaoudzi Mayotte 12°47S 45°16E 55 a
Dzavhan Gol →
  Mongolia 48°54N 93°23E 30 B7
Dzerzhinsk Russia 56°14N 43°30E 18 C7
Dzhalinda Russia 53°26N 124°0E 27 D13
Dzhambul = Taraz
  Kazakhstan 42°54N 71°22E 30 C3
Dzhankoy Ukraine 45°40N 34°20E 19 E5
Dzhezkazgan = Zhezqazghan
  Kazakhstan 47°44N 67°40E 26 E7
Dzhizak = Jizzax
  Uzbekistan 40°6N 67°50E 26 E7
Dzhugdzur, Khrebet
  Russia 57°30N 138°0E 27 D14
Dzhungarskiye Vorota =
  Dzungarian Gate Asia 45°10N 82°0E 30 B5
Działdowo Poland 53°15N 20°15E 17 B11
Dzibilchaltún Mexico 21°10N 89°35W 87 C7
Dzierżoniów Poland 50°45N 16°39E 17 C9
Dzilam de Bravo Mexico 21°24N 88°53W 87 C7
Dzūkija △ Lithuania 54°10N 24°30E 9 J21
Dzungarian Basin = Junggar Pendi
  China 44°30N 86°0E 30 C6
Dzungarian Gate Asia 45°10N 82°0E 30 B5
Dzüünbayan Mongolia 44°29N 110°2E 32 B6
Dzüünharaa Mongolia 48°52N 106°28E 30 B10
Dzüünmod Mongolia 47°45N 106°58E 30 B10
Dzyarzhynsk Belarus 53°40N 27°1E 17 B14
Dzyatlava Belarus 53°28N 25°28E 17 B13

E

E.C. Manning △ Canada 49°5N 120°45W 70 D4
Eabamet L. Canada 51°30N 87°46W 72 B2
Eabametoong Canada 51°30N 88°0W 72 B2
Éadan Doire = Edenderry
  Ireland 53°21N 7°4W 10 C4
Eads U.S.A. 38°29N 102°47W 76 G12
Eagar U.S.A. 34°6N 109°17W 77 J9
Eagle Alaska, U.S.A. 64°47N 141°12W 68 C3
Eagle Colo., U.S.A. 39°39N 106°50W 76 G10
Eagle → Canada 53°36N 57°26W 73 B8
Eagle Butte U.S.A. 45°0N 101°10W 80 C3
Eagle Grove U.S.A. 42°40N 93°54W 80 D7

Eagle L. Canada 49°42N 93°13W 71 D10
Eagle L. Calif., U.S.A. 40°39N 120°45W 76 F3
Eagle L. Maine, U.S.A. 46°20N 69°22W 81 B19
Eagle Lake Canada 45°8N 78°29W 82 A6
Eagle Lake Maine, U.S.A. 47°3N 68°36W 81 B19
Eagle Lake Tex., U.S.A. 29°35N 96°20W 84 G6
Eagle Mountain
  U.S.A. 33°49N 115°27W 79 M11
Eagle Nest U.S.A. 36°33N 105°16W 77 H11
Eagle Pass U.S.A. 28°43N 100°30W 84 G4
Eagle Pk. U.S.A. 38°10N 119°25W 78 G7
Eagle Pt. Australia 16°11S 124°23E 60 C3
Eagle River Mich., U.S.A. 47°25N 88°18W 80 B9
Eagle River Wis., U.S.A. 45°55N 89°15W 80 C9
Eaglehawk Australia 36°44S 144°15E 63 F3
Eagles Mere U.S.A. 41°25N 76°33W 83 E8
Ear Falls Canada 50°38N 93°13W 71 C10
Earlimart U.S.A. 35°53N 119°16W 79 K7
Earlville U.S.A. 42°44N 75°32W 83 D9
Earn → U.K. 56°21N 3°18W 11 E5
Earn, L. U.K. 56°23N 4°13W 11 E4
Earnslaw, Mt. N.Z. 44°32S 168°27E 59 F2
Earth U.S.A. 34°14N 102°24W 84 D3
Easley U.S.A. 34°50N 82°36W 85 D13
East Anglia U.K. 52°50N 1°0E 12 E9
East Angus Canada 45°30N 71°40W 73 C5
East Antarctica Antarctica 80°0S 90°0E 5 D7
East Aurora U.S.A. 42°46N 78°37W 82 D6
East Ayrshire □ U.K. 55°26N 4°11W 11 F4
East Bengal Bangla. 24°0N 90°0E 41 G17
East Beskids = Vychodné Beskydy
  Europe 49°20N 22°0E 17 D11
East Brady U.S.A. 40°59N 79°37W 82 F5
East Branch Clarion River L.
  U.S.A. 41°35N 78°35W 82 E6
East C. = Dezhneva, Mys
  Russia 66°5N 169°40W 27 C19
East C. N.Z. 37°42S 178°35E 59 B7
East Caroline Basin
  Pac. Oc. 4°0N 146°45E 64 G6
East Chicago U.S.A. 41°38N 87°27W 80 E10
East China Sea Asia 30°0N 126°0E 31 F14
East Coulee Canada 51°23N 112°27W 70 C6
East Dereham = Dereham
  U.K. 52°41N 0°57E 13 E8
East Dunbartonshire □
  U.K. 55°57N 4°13W 11 F4
East Falkland Falk. Is. 51°30S 58°30W 96 G5
East Grand Forks U.S.A. 47°56N 97°1W 80 B5
East Greenwich U.S.A. 41°40N 71°27W 83 E13
East Grinstead U.K. 51°7N 0°0 13 F8
East Hartford U.S.A. 41°46N 72°39W 83 E12
East Haydon Australia 18°0S 141°30E 62 B3
East Helena U.S.A. 46°35N 111°56W 76 C8
East Indies Asia 0°0 120°0E 24 J14
East Kavango □ Namibia 18°0S 20°15E 56 A3
East Kilbride U.K. 55°47N 4°11W 11 F4
East Lansing U.S.A. 42°44N 84°29W 81 D11
East Liverpool U.S.A. 40°37N 80°35W 82 F4
East London S. Africa 33°0S 27°55E 57 D4
East Lothian □ U.K. 55°58N 2°44W 11 F6
East Main = Eastmain
  Canada 52°10N 78°30W 72 B4
East Mariana Basin
  Pac. Oc. 12°0N 153°0E 64 F7
East Northport U.S.A. 40°53N 73°19W 83 F11
East Orange U.S.A. 40°46N 74°12W 83 F10
East Pacific Rise Pac. Oc. 15°0S 110°0W 65 J17
East Palestine U.S.A. 40°50N 80°33W 82 F4
East Pine Canada 55°48N 120°12W 70 B4
East Providence U.S.A. 41°49N 71°23W 83 E13
East Pt. Br. Virgin Is. 18°40N 64°18W 89 e
East Pt. Canada 46°27N 61°58W 73 C7
East Renfrewshire □ U.K. 55°46N 4°21W 11 F4
East Retford = Retford
  U.K. 53°19N 0°56W 12 D7
East Riding of Yorkshire □
  U.K. 53°55N 0°30W 12 D7
East Rochester U.S.A. 43°7N 77°29W 82 C7
East St. Louis U.S.A. 38°37N 90°9W 80 F8
East Schelde = Oosterschelde →
  Neths. 51°33N 4°0E 15 C4
East Sea = Japan, Sea of
  Asia 40°0N 135°0E 28 E7
East Siberian Sea Russia 73°0N 160°0E 27 B17
East Stroudsburg U.S.A. 41°1N 75°11W 83 E9
East Sussex □ U.K. 50°56N 0°19E 13 G8
East Tasman Plateau
  Pac. Oc. 43°30S 152°0E 64 M7
East Tawas U.S.A. 44°17N 83°29W 81 C12
East Timor = Timor-Leste ■
  Asia 8°50S 126°0E 37 F7
East Toorale Australia 30°27S 145°28E 63 E4
East Walker → U.S.A. 38°52N 119°10W 78 G7
East Windsor U.S.A. 40°17N 74°34W 83 F10
Eastbourne N.Z. 41°19S 174°55E 59 D5
Eastbourne U.K. 50°46N 0°18E 13 G8
Eastend Canada 49°32N 108°50W 71 D7
Easter Fracture Zone
  Pac. Oc. 25°0S 115°0W 65 K16
Easter I. = Pascua, I. de
  Chile 27°7S 109°23W 65 K17
Eastern Cape □ S. Africa 32°0S 26°0E 57 D4
Eastern Cr. → Australia 20°40S 141°35E 62 C3
Eastern Desert = Sharqîya, Es
  Sahrâ esh Egypt 27°30N 32°30E 53 C12
Eastern Ghats India 14°0N 78°50E 45 H4
Eastern Group = Lau Group
  Fiji 17°0S 178°30W 59 a
Eastern Group Australia 33°30S 124°30E 61 F3
Eastern Guruma ۞
  Australia 22°0S 117°30E 60 D2
Eastern Transvaal =
  Mpumalanga □ S. Africa 26°0S 30°0E 57 C5
Easterville Canada 53°8N 99°49W 71 C9
Easthampton U.S.A. 42°16N 72°40W 83 D12
Eastlake U.S.A. 41°40N 81°26W 82 E3
Eastland U.S.A. 32°24N 98°49W 84 E5
Eastleigh U.K. 50°58N 1°21W 13 G6
Eastmain Canada 52°10N 78°30W 72 B4

Eastmain → Canada 52°27N 78°26W 72 B4
Eastman Canada 45°18N 72°19W 83 A12
Eastman U.S.A. 32°12N 83°11W 85 E13
Easton Md., U.S.A. 38°47N 76°5W 81 F15
Easton Pa., U.S.A. 40°41N 75°13W 83 F9
Easton Wash., U.S.A. 47°14N 121°11W 78 C5
Eastport U.S.A. 44°56N 67°0W 81 C20
Eastsound U.S.A. 48°42N 122°55W 78 B4
Eatonia Canada 51°13N 109°25W 71 C7
Eatonton U.S.A. 33°20N 83°23W 85 E13
Eatontown U.S.A. 40°19N 74°4W 83 F10
Eatonville U.S.A. 46°52N 122°16W 78 D4
Eau Claire U.S.A. 44°49N 91°30W 80 C8
Eau Claire, L. à l' Canada 56°10N 74°25W 72 A5
Eauripik Rise Pac. Oc. 2°0N 142°0E 64 G6
Ebano Mexico 22°13N 98°24E 87 C5
Ebbw Vale U.K. 51°46N 3°12W 13 F4
Ebeltoft Denmark 56°12N 10°41E 9 H14
Ebensburg U.S.A. 40°29N 78°44W 82 F6
Eberswalde-Finow
  Germany 52°50N 13°49E 16 B7
Ebetsu Japan 43°7N 141°34E 28 C10
Ebey's Landing △
  U.S.A. 48°12N 122°41W 78 B4
Ebian China 29°11N 103°13E 34 C4
Ebinur Hu China 44°55N 82°55E 30 C5
Ebolowa Cameroon 2°55N 11°10E 54 D2
Ebonda
  Dem. Rep. of the Congo 2°12N 22°21E 54 D4
Ebre = Ebro → Spain 40°43N 0°54E 21 B6
Ebro → Spain 40°43N 0°54E 21 B6
Ecatepec de Morelos
  Mexico 19°36N 99°3W 87 D5
Ecbatana = Hamadān
  Iran 34°52N 48°32E 47 C6
Eceabat Turkey 40°11N 26°21E 23 D12
Ech Chéliff Algeria 36°10N 1°20E 52 A6
Echigo-Sammyaku
  Japan 36°50N 139°50E 29 F9
Echizen Japan 35°50N 136°10E 29 G8
Echizen-Misaki Japan 35°59N 135°57E 29 G7
Echo Bay N.W.T., Canada 66°5N 117°55W 68 B8
Echo Bay Ont., Canada 46°29N 84°4W 72 C3
Echoing → Canada 55°51N 92°5W 72 B1
Echternach Lux. 49°49N 6°25E 15 E6
Echuca Australia 36°10S 144°45E 63 F3
Écija Spain 37°30N 5°10W 21 D3
Eclipse I. Australia 35°5S 117°58E 61 G2
Eclipse Is. Australia 13°54S 126°19E 60 B4
Eclipse Sd. Canada 72°38N 79°0W 69 C16
Ecuador ■ S. Amer. 2°0S 78°0W 92 D3
Ed Da'ein Sudan 11°26N 26°9E 54 B5
Ed Damazin Sudan 11°46N 34°21E 53 F12
Ed Dâmer Sudan 17°27N 34°0E 53 E12
Ed Dar el Beida = Casablanca
  Morocco 33°36N 7°36W 52 B4
Ed Debba Sudan 18°0N 30°51E 53 E12
Ed Déffa Egypt 30°40N 26°30E 53 B11
Ed Dueim Sudan 14°0N 32°10E 53 F12
Edam Canada 53°11N 108°46W 71 C7
Edam Neths. 52°31N 5°3E 15 B5
Edapally India 11°19N 78°3E 45 J4
Eday U.K. 59°11N 2°47W 11 B6
Eddrachillis B. U.K. 58°17N 5°14W 11 C3
Eddystone U.K. 50°11N 4°16W 13 G3
Eddystone Pt. Australia 40°59S 148°20E 63 G4
Ede Neths. 52°4N 5°40E 15 B5
Edehon L. Canada 60°25N 97°15W 71 A9
Eden Australia 37°3S 149°55E 63 F4
Eden N.C., U.S.A. 36°29N 79°53W 85 C15
Eden N.Y., U.S.A. 42°39N 78°55W 82 D6
Eden Tex., U.S.A. 31°13N 99°51W 84 F5
Eden → U.K. 54°57N 3°1W 12 C4
Edenburg S. Africa 29°43S 25°58E 56 C4
Edendale S. Africa 29°39S 30°18E 57 C5
Edenderry Ireland 53°21N 7°4W 10 C4
Edenton U.S.A. 36°4N 76°39W 85 C16
Edenville S. Africa 27°37S 27°34E 57 C4
Eder → Germany 51°12N 9°28E 16 C5
Edessa Greece 40°48N 22°5E 23 D10
Edfu = Idfû Egypt 24°55N 32°49E 53 D12
Edgar U.S.A. 40°22N 97°58W 80 E5
Edgartown U.S.A. 41°23N 70°31W 83 E14
Edge Hill U.K. 52°8N 1°26W 13 E6
Edgefield U.S.A. 33°47N 81°56W 85 E14
Edgeley U.S.A. 46°22N 98°43W 80 B4
Edgemont U.S.A. 43°18N 103°50W 80 D2
Edgeøya Svalbard 77°45N 22°30E 4 B9
Édhessa = Edessa Greece 40°48N 22°5E 23 D10
Edievale N.Z. 45°49S 169°22E 59 F2
Edina U.S.A. 40°10N 92°11W 80 E7
Edinboro U.S.A. 41°52N 80°8W 82 E4
Edinburg U.S.A. 26°18N 98°10W 84 H5
Edinburgh, City of □ U.K. 55°57N 3°17W 11 F5
Edineţ Moldova 48°9N 27°18E 17 D14
Edirne Turkey 41°40N 26°34E 23 D12
Edison U.S.A. 48°33N 122°7W 78 B4
Edithburgh Australia 35°5S 137°43E 63 F2
Edmeston U.S.A. 42°42N 75°15W 83 D9
Edmond U.S.A. 35°39N 97°29W 84 D6
Edmonds U.S.A. 47°48N 122°22W 78 C4
Edmonton Australia 17°2S 145°46E 62 B4
Edmonton Canada 53°30N 113°30W 70 C6
Edmund L. Canada 54°45N 93°17W 72 B1
Edmundston Canada 47°23N 68°20W 73 C6
Edna U.S.A. 28°59N 96°39W 84 G6
Edremit Turkey 39°34N 27°0E 23 E12
Edremit Körfezi Turkey 39°30N 26°45E 23 E12
Edson Canada 53°35N 116°28W 70 C5
Eduardo Castex
  Argentina 35°50S 64°18W 94 D3
Eduardo Frei Montalva = Frei
  Antarctica 62°30S 58°0W 5 C18
Edward → Australia 35°5S 143°30E 63 F3
Edward, L. Africa 0°25S 29°40E 54 E5
Edward VII Land
  Antarctica 80°0S 150°0W 5 E13
Edwards Calif., U.S.A. 34°50N 117°40W 79 L9
Edwards N.Y., U.S.A. 44°20N 75°15W 83 B9

Edwards Plateau U.S.A. 30°45N 101°20W 84 F4
Edwardsville U.S.A. 41°15N 75°56W 83 E9
Edzná Mexico 19°39N 90°19W 87 D6
Edzo = Behchoko Canada 62°50N 116°3W 70 A5
Eeklo Belgium 51°11N 3°33E 15 C3
Eenhana Namibia 17°30S 16°23E 56 A2
Eesti = Estonia ■ Europe 58°30N 25°30E 9 G21
Effigy Mounds △ U.S.A. 43°5N 91°11W 80 D8
Effingham U.S.A. 39°7N 88°33W 80 F9
Égadi, Ísole Italy 37°55N 12°16E 22 F5
Egan Range U.S.A. 39°35N 114°55W 76 G6
Eganville Canada 45°32N 77°5W 82 A7
Eger = Cheb Czechia 50°9N 12°28E 16 C7
Eger Hungary 47°53N 20°27E 17 E11
Egersund Norway 58°26N 6°1E 9 G12
Egg L. Canada 55°5N 105°30W 71 B7
Éghezée Belgium 50°35N 4°55E 15 D4
Egilsstaðir Iceland 65°16N 14°25W 8 D6
Egio Greece 38°15N 22°5E 23 E10
Eglinton I. Canada 75°48N 118°30W 69 B8
Egmont Canada 49°45N 123°56W 70 D4
Egmont, C. N.Z. 39°16S 173°45E 59 C4
Egmont, Mt. = Taranaki, Mt.
  N.Z. 39°17S 174°5E 59 C5
Egmont △ N.Z. 39°17S 174°4E 59 C5
Egra India 21°54N 87°32E 43 J12
Eğridir Turkey 37°52N 30°51E 19 G5
Eğridir Gölü Turkey 37°53N 30°50E 46 B1
Egvekinot Russia 66°19N 179°50W 27 C19
Egypt ■ Africa 28°0N 31°0E 53 C12
Ehime □ Japan 33°30N 132°40E 29 H6
Ehrenberg U.S.A. 33°36N 114°31W 79 M12
Eibar Spain 43°11N 2°28W 21 A4
Eidsvold Australia 25°25S 151°12E 63 D5
Eidsvoll Norway 60°19N 11°14E 9 F14
Eielson U.S.A. 64°40N 147°4W 74 C10
Eifel Germany 50°15N 6°50E 16 C4
Eigg U.K. 56°54N 6°10W 11 E2
Eighty Mile Beach
  Australia 19°30S 120°40E 60 C3
Eil, L. U.K. 56°51N 5°16W 11 E3
Eildon, L. Australia 37°10S 146°0E 63 F4
Eilean Siar □ U.K. 57°30N 7°10W 11 D1
Einasleigh Australia 18°32S 144°5E 62 B3
Einasleigh → Australia 17°30S 142°17E 62 B3
Eindhoven Neths. 51°26N 5°28E 15 C5
Eire = Ireland ■ Europe 53°50N 7°52W 10 C4
Eiríksjökull Iceland 64°46N 20°24W 8 D3
Eiriosgaigh = Eriskay U.K. 57°4N 7°18W 11 D1
Eirunepé Brazil 6°35S 69°53W 92 E5
Eiseb → Namibia 20°33S 20°59E 56 B3
Eisenach Germany 50°58N 10°19E 16 C6
Eisenerz Austria 47°32N 14°54E 16 E8
Eivissa Spain 38°54N 1°26E 21 C6
Ejutla Mexico 16°34N 96°44W 87 D5
Ekalaka U.S.A. 45°53N 104°33W 76 D11
Ekaterinburg = Yekaterinburg
  Russia 56°50N 60°30E 26 D7
Ekenäs = Raasepori
  Finland 60°0N 23°26E 9 G20
Eketahuna N.Z. 40°38S 175°43E 59 D5
Ekibastuz Kazakhstan 51°50N 75°10E 26 D8
Eksjö Sweden 57°40N 14°58E 9 H16
Ekuma → Namibia 18°40S 16°2E 56 A2
Ekwan → Canada 53°12N 82°15W 72 B3
Ekwan Pt. Canada 53°16N 82°7W 72 B3
El Aaiún W. Sahara 27°9N 13°12W 52 C3
El Abanico Chile 37°20S 71°31W 94 D1
El 'Agrûd Egypt 30°14N 34°24E 48 E3
El Alamein Egypt 30°48N 28°58E 53 B11
El 'Aqaba, W. → Egypt 30°7N 33°54E 48 E2
El 'Arīḥā West Bank 31°52N 35°27E 48 D4
El 'Arîsh Egypt 31°8N 33°50E 48 D2
El 'Arîsh, W. → Egypt 31°8N 33°47E 48 D2
El Asnam = Ech Chéliff
  Algeria 36°10N 1°20E 52 A6
El Bayadh Algeria 33°40N 1°1E 52 B6
El Bluff Nic. 11°59N 83°40W 88 D3
El Cajon U.S.A. 32°48N 116°58W 79 N10
El Calafate Argentina 50°19S 72°15W 96 G2
El Campo U.S.A. 29°12N 96°16W 84 G6
El Capitan U.S.A. 37°44N 119°38E 78 H7
El Carbón Honduras 15°25N 85°32W 88 C2
El Carmen Colombia 9°43N 75°8W 92 B3
El Centro U.S.A. 32°48N 115°34W 79 N11
El Cerro Bolivia 17°30S 61°40W 92 G6
El Compadre Mexico 32°20N 116°14W 79 N10
El Cuy Argentina 39°55S 68°25W 96 D3
El Cuyo Mexico 21°31N 87°41W 87 C7
El Daheir Egypt 31°13N 34°10E 48 D3
El Descanso Mexico 32°12N 116°58W 79 N10
El Desemboque Mexico 30°33N 113°1W 86 A2
El Diviso Colombia 1°22N 78°14W 92 C3
El Djouf Mauritania 21°25N 6°40W 52 D4
El Dorado Mexico 24°17N 107°21W 86 C3
El Dorado Ark., U.S.A. 33°12N 92°40W 84 E8
El Dorado Kans., U.S.A. 37°49N 96°52W 80 G5
El Dorado Venezuela 6°55N 61°37W 92 B6
El Dorado Springs U.S.A. 37°52N 94°1W 80 G6
El Escorial Spain 40°35N 4°7W 21 B3
El Faiyûm Egypt 29°19N 30°50E 53 C12
El Fâsher Sudan 13°33N 25°26E 53 F11
El Ferrol = Ferrol Spain 43°29N 8°15W 21 A1
El Fuerte Mexico 26°25N 108°39W 86 B3
El Geneina = Al Junaynah
  Sudan 13°27N 22°45E 53 F10
El Gezira □ Sudan 15°0N 33°0E 53 F12
El Gogorrón △ Mexico 21°49N 100°57W 86 C4
El Goléa Algeria 30°30N 2°50E 52 B6
El Guácharo △ Venezuela 10°8N 63°21W 89 D7
El Guache △ Venezuela 9°45N 69°30W 89 E6
El Iskandarîya Egypt 31°13N 29°58E 53 B11
El Istiwa'iya Sudan 5°0N 28°0E 53 G11
El Jadida Morocco 33°11N 8°17W 52 B4
El Jardal Honduras 14°54N 88°50W 88 D2
El Kef □ Tunisia 36°0N 9°0E 52 A7
El Khârga Egypt 25°30N 30°33E 53 C12
El Khartûm Sudan 15°31N 32°35E 53 E12
El Khartûm Bahrî Sudan 15°40N 32°31E 53 E12

El Kuntilla Egypt 30°1N 34°45E 48 E3
El Leoncito △ Argentina 31°58S 69°10W 94 C2
El Lucero Mexico 30°37N 106°31W 86 A3
El Maestrazgo Spain 40°30N 0°25W 21 B5
El Mahalla el Kubra Egypt 31°0N 31°0E 53 B12
El Malpais △ U.S.A. 34°53N 108°0W 77 J10
El Mansûra Egypt 31°0N 31°19E 53 B12
El Ménia = El Goléa
  Algeria 30°30N 2°50E 52 B6
El Milagro Argentina 30°59S 65°59W 94 C2
El Minyâ Egypt 28°7N 30°33E 53 C12
El Obeid Sudan 13°8N 30°10E 53 F12
El Odaiya Sudan 12°8N 28°12E 53 F11
El Oro Mexico 19°51N 100°7W 87 D4
El Oued Algeria 33°20N 6°58E 52 B7
El Palmar △ Argentina 32°10S 58°31W 94 C4
El Paso U.S.A. 31°45N 106°29W 84 F1
El Paso de Robles = Paso Robles
  U.S.A. 35°38N 120°41W 78 K6
El Pinacate y Gran Desierto de
  Altar = Gran Desierto del
  Pinacate △ Mexico 31°51N 113°32W 86 A2
El Portal U.S.A. 37°41N 119°47W 78 H7
El Porvenir Mexico 31°15N 105°51W 86 A3
El Progreso Honduras 15°26N 87°51W 88 C2
El Puerto de Santa María
  Spain 36°36N 6°13W 21 D2
El Qantara Egypt 30°51N 32°20E 48 E1
El Quseima Egypt 30°40N 34°15E 48 E3
El Real de Santa María
  Panama 8°0N 77°40W 92 B3
El Reno U.S.A. 35°32N 97°57W 75 H20
El Rey △ Argentina 24°40S 64°34W 94 A3
El Rio U.S.A. 34°14N 119°10W 79 L7
El Rosario Mexico 30°1N 115°45W 86 A1
El Salto Mexico 23°47N 105°22W 86 C3
El Salvador ■ Cent. Amer. 13°50N 89°0W 88 D2
El Sauce Nic. 13°0N 86°40W 88 D2
El Suweis Egypt 29°58N 32°31E 53 C12
El Tamarāni, W. → Egypt 30°7N 34°43E 48 E3
El Thamad Egypt 29°40N 34°28E 48 F3
El Tigre Venezuela 8°44N 64°15W 92 B6
El Tîh, Gebel Egypt 29°40N 33°50E 48 F2
El Tofo Chile 29°22S 71°18W 94 B1
El Tránsito Chile 28°52S 70°17W 94 B1
El Tûr Egypt 28°14N 33°36E 46 D2
El Turbio Argentina 51°45S 72°5W 96 G2
El Uqsur Egypt 25°41N 32°38E 53 C12
El Vergel Mexico 26°28N 106°22W 86 B3
El Vigía Venezuela 8°38N 71°39W 92 B4
El Wabeira Egypt 29°34N 33°6E 48 F2
El Wuz Sudan 15°5N 30°7E 53 F12
Elamanchili India 17°33N 82°50E 44 F6
Elat Israel 29°30N 34°56E 48 F3
Elâzığ Turkey 38°37N 39°14E 46 B3
Elba Italy 42°46N 10°17E 22 C4
Elba U.S.A. 31°25N 86°4W 85 F11
Elbasan Albania 41°9N 20°9E 23 D9
Elbe U.S.A. 46°45N 122°10W 78 D4
Elbe → Europe 53°50N 9°0E 16 B5
Elbert, Mt. U.S.A. 39°7N 106°27W 76 G10
Elberton U.S.A. 34°7N 82°52W 85 D13
Elbeuf France 49°17N 1°2E 20 B4
Elbing = Elbląg Poland 54°10N 19°25E 17 A10
Elbistan Turkey 38°13N 37°15E 46 B3
Elbląg Poland 54°10N 19°25E 17 A10
Elbrus Russia 43°21N 42°30E 19 F7
Elburz Mts. = Alborz, Reshteh-ye
  Kūhhā-ye Iran 36°0N 52°0E 47 C7
Elche Spain 38°15N 0°42W 21 C5
Elcho I. Australia 11°55S 135°45E 62 A2
Elda Spain 38°29N 0°47W 21 C5
Elde → Germany 53°7N 11°15E 16 B6
Eldon Mo., U.S.A. 38°21N 92°35W 80 F7
Eldon Wash., U.S.A. 47°33N 123°3W 78 C3
Eldora U.S.A. 42°22N 93°5W 80 D7
Eldorado Argentina 26°28S 54°43W 95 B5
Eldorado Canada 44°35N 77°31W 82 B7
Eldorado Ill., U.S.A. 37°49N 88°26W 80 G9
Eldorado Tex., U.S.A. 30°52N 100°36W 84 F4
Eldoret Kenya 0°30N 35°17E 54 D7
Eldred U.S.A. 41°58N 78°23W 82 E6
Eleanora, Pk. Australia 32°57S 121°9E 61 F3
Elefantes → Africa 24°10S 32°40E 57 B5
Elektostal Russia 55°41N 38°32E 18 C6
Elemi Triangle = Ilemi Triangle
  Africa 5°0N 35°20E 54 D7
Elephant Butte Res.
  U.S.A. 33°9N 107°11W 77 K10
Elephant I. Antarctica 61°0S 55°0W 5 C18
Elephant Pass Sri Lanka 9°35N 80°25E 45 K5
Eleuthera I. Bahamas 25°0N 76°20W 88 B4
Elgin Canada 44°36N 76°13W 83 B8
Elgin U.K. 57°39N 3°19W 11 D5
Elgin Ill., U.S.A. 42°2N 88°17W 80 D9
Elgin N. Dak., U.S.A. 46°24N 101°51W 80 B3
Elgin Oreg., U.S.A. 45°34N 117°55W 76 D5
Elgin Tex., U.S.A. 30°21N 97°22W 84 F6
Elgon, Mt. Africa 1°10N 34°30E 54 D6
Elhovo Bulgaria 42°10N 26°35E 23 C12
Eliase Indonesia 8°21S 130°48E 37 F8
Elim Namibia 17°48S 15°31E 56 A2
Elista Russia 46°16N 44°14E 19 E7
Elizabeth Australia 34°42S 138°41E 63 E2
Elizabeth U.S.A. 40°39N 74°12W 83 F10
Elizabeth City U.S.A. 36°18N 76°14W 85 C16
Elizabethton U.S.A. 36°21N 82°13W 85 C13
Elizabethtown Ky.,
  U.S.A. 37°42N 85°52W 81 G11
Elizabethtown N.Y.,
  U.S.A. 44°13N 73°36W 83 B11
Elizabethtown Pa., U.S.A. 40°9N 76°36W 83 F8
Elk Poland 53°50N 22°21E 17 B12
Elk → Canada 49°11N 115°14W 70 C5
Elk City U.S.A. 35°25N 99°25W 84 D5
Elk Creek U.S.A. 39°36N 122°32W 78 F4
Elk Grove U.S.A. 38°25N 121°22W 78 G5

Elk Island △ Canada 53°35N 112°59W 70 C6
Elk Lake Canada 47°40N 80°25W 72 C3
Elk Point Canada 53°54N 110°55W 71 C6
Elk River Idaho, U.S.A. 46°47N 116°11W 76 C5
Elk River Minn., U.S.A. 45°18N 93°35W 80 C7
Elkedra → Australia 21°8S 136°22E 62 C2
Elkhart Ind., U.S.A. 41°41N 85°58W 81 E11
Elkhart Kans., U.S.A. 37°0N 101°54W 80 G3
Elkhorn Canada 49°59N 101°14W 71 D8
Elkhorn → U.S.A. 41°8N 96°19W 80 E5
Elkin U.S.A. 36°15N 80°51W 85 C14
Elkins U.S.A. 38°55N 79°51W 81 F14
Elkland U.S.A. 41°59N 77°19W 82 E7
Elko Canada 49°20N 115°10W 70 D5
Elko U.S.A. 40°50N 115°46W 76 F6
Elkton U.S.A. 43°49N 83°11W 82 C1
Ellas = Greece ■ Europe 40°0N 23°0E 23 E9
Ellef Ringnes I. Canada 78°30N 102°2W 69 B11
Ellen, Mt. U.S.A. 44°9N 72°56W 83 B12
Ellenburg U.S.A. 44°54N 73°48W 83 B11
Ellendale U.S.A. 46°0N 98°32W 80 B4
Ellensburg U.S.A. 46°59N 120°34W 76 C3
Ellenville U.S.A. 41°43N 74°24W 83 E10
Ellerton Barbados 13°7N 59°33W 89 g
Ellery, Mt. Australia 37°28S 148°47E 63 F4
Ellesmere I. Canada 79°30N 80°0W 69 B16
Ellesmere Port U.K. 53°17N 2°54W 12 D5
Ellice Is. = Tuvalu ■
  Pac. Oc. 8°0S 178°0E 58 B10
Ellicottville U.S.A. 42°17N 78°40W 82 D6
Ellington U.S.A. 42°13N 79°6W 82 D5
Elliot Australia 17°33S 133°32E 62 B1
Elliot S. Africa 31°22S 27°48E 57 D4
Elliot Lake Canada 46°25N 82°35W 72 C3
Elliotdale = Xhora
  S. Africa 31°55S 28°38E 57 D4
Ellis U.S.A. 38°56N 99°34W 80 F4
Ellisville U.S.A. 31°36N 89°12W 85 F10
Ellon U.K. 57°22N 2°4W 11 D6
Ellora India 20°1N 75°10E 44 D2
Ellore = Eluru India 16°48N 81°8E 44 F5
Ellsworth Kans., U.S.A. 38°44N 98°14W 80 F4
Ellsworth Maine, U.S.A. 44°33N 68°25W 81 C19
Ellsworth Land Antarctica 76°0S 89°0W 5 D16
Ellsworth Mts. Antarctica 78°30S 85°0W 5 D16
Ellwood City U.S.A. 40°52N 80°17W 82 F4
Elma Canada 49°52N 95°55W 71 D9
Elma U.S.A. 47°0N 123°25W 78 D3
Elmalı Turkey 36°44N 29°56E 19 G4
Elmhurst U.S.A. 41°53N 87°56W 80 E10
Elmira Canada 43°36N 80°33W 82 C4
Elmira U.S.A. 42°6N 76°48W 82 D8
Elmira Heights U.S.A. 42°8N 76°50W 82 D8
Elmore Australia 36°30S 144°37E 63 F3
Elmshorn Germany 53°43N 9°40E 16 B5
Elmvale Canada 44°35N 79°52W 82 B5
Elora Canada 43°41N 80°26W 82 C4
Eloy U.S.A. 32°45N 111°33W 77 K8
Elphin Canada 44°55N 76°37W 83 B8
Elpitiya Sri Lanka 6°17N 80°10E 45 L5
Elrose Canada 51°12N 108°0W 71 C7
Elsby △ Australia 14°55S 133°10E 60 B5
Elsie U.S.A. 45°52N 123°36W 78 E3
Elsinore = Helsingør
  Denmark 56°2N 12°35E 9 H15
Eltanin Fracture Zone System
  S. Ocean 54°0S 130°0W 5 B14
Eltham N.Z. 39°26S 174°19E 59 C5
Eluru India 16°48N 81°8E 44 F5
Elvas Portugal 38°50N 7°10W 21 C2
Elverum Norway 60°53N 11°34E 8 F14
Elvire → Australia 17°51S 128°11E 60 C4
Elvire, Mt. Australia 29°22S 119°36E 61 E2
Elwell, L. = Tiber Res.
  U.S.A. 48°19N 111°6W 76 B8
Elwood Ind., U.S.A. 40°17N 85°50W 81 E11
Elwood Nebr., U.S.A. 40°36N 99°52W 80 E4
Elx = Elche Spain 38°15N 0°42W 21 C5
Ely U.K. 52°24N 0°16E 13 E8
Ely Minn., U.S.A. 47°55N 91°51W 80 B8
Ely Nev., U.S.A. 39°15N 114°54W 76 G6
Elyria U.S.A. 41°22N 82°7W 82 E2
eMakhazeni S. Africa 25°42S 30°2E 57 C5
eMalahleni S. Africa 25°51S 29°14E 57 C4
Emāmrūd Iran 36°30N 55°0E 47 B7
eMbalenhle S. Africa 26°32S 29°4E 57 C4
Embarcación Argentina 23°10S 64°0W 94 A3
Embetsu Japan 44°44N 141°47E 28 B10
Embi Kazakhstan 48°50N 58°8E 26 E6
Embi → Kazakhstan 46°55N 53°28E 19 E9
Embro Canada 43°9N 80°54W 82 C4
Embrun France 44°34N 6°30E 20 D7
Emden Germany 53°21N 7°12E 16 B4
Emei Shan China 29°32N 103°46E 34 C4
Emeishan China 29°31N 103°23E 34 C4
Emerald Australia 23°32S 148°10E 62 C4
Emerald I. Canada 76°48N 114°10W 69 B9
Emerson Canada 49°0N 97°10W 71 D9
Emet Turkey 39°20N 29°15E 23 E13
Emgwenya S. Africa 25°40S 30°18E 57 C5
Emi Koussi Chad 19°45N 18°55E 53 E9
eMijindini Pakistan 22°20N 74°8E 42 C6
Emine, Nos Bulgaria 42°40N 27°56E 23 C12
Emissi, Tarso Chad 21°27N 18°36E 53 D9
eMkhondo = Piet Retief
  S. Africa 27°1S 30°50E 57 C5
Emlenton U.S.A. 41°11N 79°43W 82 E5
Emmaus S. Africa 29°2S 25°15E 56 C4
Emmaus U.S.A. 40°32N 75°30W 83 F9
Emmeloord Neths. 52°44N 5°46E 15 B5
Emmen Neths. 52°48N 6°57E 15 B6
Emmet Australia 24°45S 144°30E 62 C3
Emmetsburg U.S.A. 43°7N 94°41W 80 D6
Emmett Idaho, U.S.A. 43°52N 116°30W 76 E5
Emmett Mich., U.S.A. 42°59N 82°46W 82 D2
Emmiganuru = Yemmiganur
  India 15°44N 77°29E 45 G3
Emmonak U.S.A. 62°47N 164°31W 74 C7

Emo Canada 48°38N 93°50W 71 D10
Empalme Mexico 27°58N 110°51W 86 B2
Empangeni S. Africa 28°50S 31°52E 57 C5
Empedrado Argentina 28°0S 58°46W 94 B4
Emperor Seamount Chain
  Pac. Oc. 40°0N 170°0E 64 D9
Emperor Trough Pac. Oc. 43°0N 175°30E 64 C9
Emporia Kans., U.S.A. 38°25N 96°11W 80 F5
Emporia Va., U.S.A. 36°42N 77°32W 81 G15
Emporium U.S.A. 41°31N 78°14W 82 E6
Empress Canada 50°57N 110°0W 71 C7
Empty Quarter = Rub' al Khālī
  Si. Arabia 19°0N 48°0E 49 D4
Ems → Germany 53°20N 7°12E 16 B4
Emsdale Canada 45°32N 79°19W 82 A5
Emu China 43°40N 128°6E 33 C15
Emu Park Australia 23°13S 150°50E 62 C5
eMuziwezinto S. Africa 30°15S 30°45E 57 E5
'En 'Avrona Israel 29°43N 35°0E 48 F4
'En Boqeq Israel 31°12N 35°21E 47 D4
'En Gedi Israel 31°28N 35°25E 47 D4
En Nahud Sudan 12°45N 28°25E 53 F11
Ena Japan 35°25N 137°25E 29 G8
Enard B. U.K. 58°5N 5°20W 11 C3
Enarotali Indonesia 3°55S 136°21E 37 E9
Encampment U.S.A. 41°12N 106°47W 76 F10
Encantadas, Serra Brazil 30°40S 53°0W 95 C5
Encarnación Paraguay 27°15S 55°50W 95 B4
Encarnación de Díaz
  Mexico 21°31N 102°14W 86 C4
Encinitas U.S.A. 33°3N 117°17W 79 M9
Encino U.S.A. 34°39N 105°28W 77 J11
Encounter B. Australia 35°45S 138°45E 63 F2
Endako Canada 54°6N 125°2W 70 C3
Endau Rompin △
  Malaysia 2°27N 103°45E 39 L4
Ende Indonesia 8°45S 121°40E 37 F6
Endeavour Str. Australia 10°45S 142°0E 62 A3
Enderbury Kiribati 3°8S 171°5W 64 H10
Enderby Canada 50°35N 119°10W 70 C5
Enderby Abyssal Plain
  S. Ocean 60°0S 40°0E 5 C5
Enderby I. Australia 20°35S 116°30E 60 D2
Enderby Land Antarctica 66°0S 53°0E 5 C5
Enderlin U.S.A. 46°38N 97°36W 80 B5
Endicott U.S.A. 42°6N 76°4W 83 D8
Endicott Mts. U.S.A. 68°0N 152°0W 74 B9
Endwell U.S.A. 42°6N 76°2W 83 D8
Endyalgout I. Australia 11°40S 132°35E 60 B5
Eneabba Australia 29°49S 115°16E 61 E2
Enewetak Atoll
  Marshall Is. 11°30N 162°15E 64 F8
Enez Turkey 40°45N 26°5E 23 D12
Enfer, Pte. d' Martinique 14°22N 60°54W 88 c
Enfield Canada 44°56N 63°32W 73 D7
Enfield Conn., U.S.A. 41°58N 72°36W 83 E12
Enfield N.C., U.S.A. 36°11N 77°41W 85 C16
Enfield N.H., U.S.A. 43°39N 72°9W 83 C12
Engadin Switz. 46°45N 10°10E 20 C9
Engaño, C. Dom. Rep. 18°30N 68°20W 89 C6
Engaño, C. Phil. 18°35N 122°23E 37 A6
Engaru Japan 44°3N 143°31E 28 B11
Engcobo = Ngcobo
  S. Africa 31°37S 28°0E 57 D4
Engels Russia 51°28N 46°6E 19 D8
Engemann L. Canada 58°0N 106°55W 71 B7
Enggano Indonesia 5°20S 102°40E 36 F2
England U.S.A. 34°33N 91°58W 84 D9
England □ U.K. 53°0N 2°0W 13 E6
Englee Canada 50°45N 56°5W 73 B8
Englehart Canada 47°49N 79°52W 72 C4
English → Canada 49°12N 91°5W 71 C10
English Bazar = Ingraj Bazar
  India 24°58N 88°10E 43 G13
English Channel Europe 50°0N 2°0W 13 G6
English Company's Is., The
  Australia 11°50S 136°32E 62 A2
English River Canada 49°14N 91°0W 72 C1
Enid U.S.A. 36°24N 97°53W 84 C6
Eniwa Japan 43°0N 141°30E 28 C10
Enkhuizen Neths. 52°42N 5°17E 15 B5
Enle China 24°0N 101°9E 34 F3
Enna Italy 37°34N 14°16E 22 F6
Ennadai L. Canada 60°58N 101°20W 71 A8
Ennedi Chad 17°15N 22°0E 53 E10
Enngonia Australia 29°21S 145°50E 63 D4
Ennis Ireland 52°51N 8°59W 10 D3
Ennis Mont., U.S.A. 45°21N 111°44W 76 D8
Ennis Tex., U.S.A. 32°20N 96°38W 84 E6
Enniscorthy Ireland 52°30N 6°34W 10 D5
Enniskillen U.K. 54°21N 7°39W 10 B4
Ennistymon Ireland 52°57N 9°17W 10 D2
Enns → Austria 48°14N 14°32E 16 D8
Eno Finland 62°47N 30°10E 8 E24
Enosburg Falls U.S.A. 44°55N 72°48W 83 B12
Enping China 22°16N 112°21E 35 F9
Enriquillo, L. Dom. Rep. 18°20N 71°40W 89 C5
Enschede Neths. 52°13N 6°53E 15 B6
Ensenada Argentina 34°55S 57°55W 94 C4
Ensenada Mexico 31°52N 116°37W 86 A1
Ensenada de los Muertos
  Mexico 23°59N 109°51W 86 C2
Enshi China 30°18N 109°29E 34 B7
Entebbe Uganda 0°4N 32°28E 54 D6
Enterprise Canada 60°47N 115°45W 70 A5
Enterprise Ala., U.S.A. 31°19N 85°51W 85 F12
Enterprise Oreg., U.S.A. 45°25N 117°17W 76 D5
Entiako △ Canada 53°15N 125°0W 70 C3
Entre Ríos Bolivia 21°30S 64°25W 94 A3
Entre Ríos □ Argentina 30°30S 58°30W 94 C4
Entroncamento Portugal 39°28N 8°28W 21 C1
Enugu Nigeria 6°30N 7°30E 52 G7
Enumclaw U.S.A. 47°12N 121°59W 78 C5
Eochaill = Youghal
  Ireland 51°56N 7°52W 10 E4
Eólie, Ís. Italy 38°30N 14°57E 22 E6
Epe Neths. 52°21N 5°59E 15 B5
Épernay France 49°3N 3°56E 20 B5

Ephesus Turkey 37°55N 27°22E 23 F12
Ephraim U.S.A. 39°22N 111°35W 76 G8
Ephrata Pa., U.S.A. 40°11N 76°11W 83 F8
Ephrata Wash., U.S.A. 47°19N 119°33W 76 C4
Épinal France 48°10N 6°27E 20 B7
Epsom U.K. 51°19N 0°16W 13 F7
Epukiro Namibia 21°40S 19°9E 56 B2
Equatoria = El Istiwa'iya
  Sudan 5°0N 28°0E 53 G11
Equatorial Guinea ■ Africa 2°0N 8°0E 54 D1
Er Hai China 25°48N 100°11E 34 E3
Er Rachidia Morocco 31°58N 4°20W 52 B5
Er Rahad Sudan 12°45N 30°32E 53 F12
Er Rif Morocco 35°1N 4°1W 52 A5
Erandol India 20°56N 75°20E 44 D2
Erāwadī Myit = Ayeyawadī →
  Myanmar 15°50N 95°6E 41 M19
Erāwadī Myitwanya = Irrawaddy,
  Mouths of the
  Myanmar 15°30N 95°0E 41 M19
Erawan △ Thailand 14°25N 98°58E 38 E2
Erçek Turkey 38°39N 43°36E 46 B4
Erciyaş Dağı Turkey 38°30N 35°30E 46 B2
Érd Hungary 47°22N 18°56E 17 E10
Erdao Jiang → China 42°37N 128°0E 33 C14
Erdek Turkey 40°23N 27°47E 23 D12
Erdene = Ulaan-Uul
  Mongolia 44°N 100°49E 30 B9
Erdenet Mongolia 49°2N 104°5E 30 B9
Erdenetsogt Mongolia 42°55N 106°5E 32 C4
Erebus, Mt. Antarctica 77°35S 167°0E 5 D11
Erechim Brazil 27°35S 52°15W 95 B5
Ereğli Konya, Turkey 37°31N 34°4E 46 C2
Ereğli Zonguldak, Turkey 41°15N 31°24E 19 F5
Erenhot China 43°48N 112°2E 32 C7
Eresma → Spain 41°26N 4°45W 21 B3
Erfenisdam S. Africa 28°30S 26°50E 56 C4
Erfurt Germany 50°58N 11°2E 16 C6
Ergani Turkey 38°17N 39°49E 46 B3
Ergel Mongolia 43°8N 109°5E 32 C5
Ergeni Vozvyshennost
  Russia 47°0N 44°0E 19 E7
Érgli Latvia 56°54N 25°38E 9 H21
Ergun He = Argun →
  Russia 53°20N 121°28E 31 A13
Ergun Youqi China 50°15N 120°11E 31 A13
Erhlin Taiwan 23°54N 120°22E 35 F13
Eriboll, L. U.K. 58°30N 4°42W 11 C4
Érice Italy 38°2N 12°35E 22 E5
Erie U.S.A. 42°8N 80°5W 82 D4
Erie, L. N. Amer. 42°15N 81°0W 82 D4
Erie Canal U.S.A. 43°5N 78°43W 82 C7
Erieau Canada 42°16N 81°57W 82 D3
Erigavo = Ceerigaabo
  Somalia 10°35N 47°20E 49 E4
Eriksdale Canada 50°52N 98°7W 71 C9
Erimanthos Greece 37°57N 21°50E 23 F9
Erimo-Misaki Japan 41°50N 143°15E 28 D11
Erin Canada 43°45N 80°7W 82 C4
Erin Pt. Trin. & Tob. 10°3N 61°39W 93 K15
Erinpura India 25°9N 73°3E 42 G5
Eriskay U.K. 57°4N 7°18W 11 D1
Eritrea ■ Africa 14°0N 38°30E 49 D2
Erlangen Germany 49°36N 11°0E 16 D6
Erldunda Australia 25°14S 133°12E 62 D1
Ermelo Neths. 52°18N 5°35E 15 B5
Ermelo S. Africa 26°31S 29°59E 57 C4
Ermenek Turkey 36°38N 33°0E 46 C2
Ermoupoli Greece 37°28N 24°57E 23 F11
Ernakulam India 9°59N 76°22E 45 K3
Erne → Ireland 54°30N 8°16W 10 B3
Erne, Lower L. U.K. 54°28N 7°47W 10 B4
Erne, Upper L. U.K. 54°14N 7°32W 10 B4
Ernest Giles Ra. Australia 27°0S 123°45E 61 E3
Erode India 11°24N 77°45E 45 J3
Eromanga Australia 26°40S 143°11E 63 D3
Erongo Namibia 21°39S 15°58E 56 B2
Erongo □ Namibia 22°20S 15°5E 56 B2
Erramala Hills India 15°30N 78°15E 45 G4
Errentería Spain 43°19N 1°54W 21 A5
Errigal Ireland 55°2N 8°6W 10 A3
Errinundra △ Australia 37°20S 148°47E 63 F4
Erris Hd. Ireland 54°17N 10°0W 10 B1
Erskine U.S.A. 47°40N 96°0W 80 B6
Ertan Shuiku China 27°5N 101°52E 34 D3
Ertis = Irtysh → Russia 61°4N 68°52E 26 C7
Erwin U.S.A. 36°9N 82°25W 85 C13
Eryuan China 26°7N 99°57E 34 D2
Erzgebirge Germany 50°27N 12°55E 16 C7
Erzin Russia 50°15N 95°10E 27 D10
Erzincan Turkey 39°57N 39°30E 46 B3
Erzurum Turkey 39°57N 41°15E 46 B4
Es Sînâ' Egypt 29°0N 34°0E 48 F2
Esan-Misaki Japan 41°40N 141°10E 28 D10
Esashi Hokkaidō, Japan 44°56N 142°35E 28 B11
Esashi Hokkaidō, Japan 41°52N 140°7E 28 D10
Esbjerg Denmark 55°29N 8°29E 9 J13
Esbo = Espoo Finland 60°12N 24°40E 9 F21
Escalante U.S.A. 37°47N 111°36W 76 H8
Escalante → U.S.A. 37°24N 110°57W 77 H8
Escalón Mexico 26°45N 104°20W 86 B4
Escambia → U.S.A. 30°32N 87°11W 85 F11
Escanaba U.S.A. 45°45N 87°4W 80 C10
Escárcega Mexico 18°37N 90°43W 87 D6
Esch-sur-Alzette Lux. 49°32N 6°0E 15 E6
Escondido U.S.A. 33°7N 117°5W 79 M9
Escuinapa de Hidalgo
  Mexico 22°50N 105°50W 86 C3
Escuintla Guatemala 14°20N 90°48W 88 D1
Esenguly Turkmenistan 37°37N 53°59E 26 F6
Esfahān Iran 32°39N 51°43E 47 C6
Esfahān □ Iran 32°50N 51°50E 47 C6
Esfarāyen Iran 37°4N 57°30E 47 B8
Esfideh Iran 33°39N 59°46E 47 C8
Esh Sham = Dimashq
  Syria 33°30N 36°18E 48 B5
Esha Ness U.K. 60°29N 1°38W 11 A7
Eshan China 24°11N 102°24E 34 E4
Eshkol △ Israel 31°20N 34°30E 48 D3
Eshowe S. Africa 28°50S 31°30E 57 C5

Esigodini Zimbabwe 20°18S 28°56E 57 B4
Esil = Ishim → Russia 57°45N 71°10E 26 D8
Esk → Dumf. & Gall., U.K. 54°58N 3°2W 11 G5
Esk → N. Yorks., U.K. 54°30N 0°37W 12 C7
Eskån Iran 26°48N 63°9E 47 E9
Esker Siding Canada 53°53N 66°25W 73 B6
Eskifjörður Iceland 65°3N 13°55W 8 D7
Eskilstuna Sweden 59°22N 16°32E 9 G17
Eskimo Point = Arviat
  Canada 61°6N 93°59W 71 A10
Eskişehir Turkey 39°50N 30°30E 19 G5
Esla → Spain 41°29N 6°3W 21 B2
Eslāmābād-e Gharb Iran 34°10N 46°30E 46 C5
Eslāmshahr Iran 35°40N 51°10E 47 C6
Eşme Turkey 38°23N 28°58E 23 E13
Esmeraldas Ecuador 1°0N 79°40W 92 C3
Esna = Isna Egypt 25°17N 32°30E 53 C12
Esnagi L. Canada 48°36N 84°33W 72 C3
España = Spain ■ Europe 39°0N 4°0W 21 B4
Espanola Canada 46°15N 81°46W 72 C3
Espanola U.S.A. 35°59N 106°5W 77 J10
Esparza Costa Rica 9°59N 84°40W 88 E3
Esperance Australia 33°45S 121°55E 61 F3
Esperance B. Australia 33°48S 121°55E 61 F3
Esperance Harbour
  St. Lucia 14°4N 60°55W 89 f
Esperanza Antarctica 65°0S 55°0W 5 C18
Esperanza Argentina 31°29S 61°3W 94 C3
Esperanza Puerto Rico 18°6N 65°28W 89 d
Espichel, C. Portugal 38°22N 9°16W 21 C1
Espigão, Serra do Brazil 26°35S 50°30W 95 B5
Espinazo, Sierra del = Espinhaço,
  Serra do Brazil 17°30S 43°30W 93 G10
Espinhaço, Serra do
  Brazil 17°30S 43°30W 93 G10
Espinilho, Serra do Brazil 28°30S 55°0W 95 B5
Espírito Santo □ Brazil 20°0S 40°45W 93 H10
Espírito Santo do Pinhal
  Brazil 22°10S 46°46W 95 A6
Espíritu Santo Vanuatu 15°15S 166°50E 58 C9
Espíritu Santo, B. del
  Mexico 19°20N 87°35W 87 D7
Espíritu Santo, I.
  Mexico 24°30N 110°22W 86 C2
Espita Mexico 21°1N 88°19W 87 C7
Espoo Finland 60°12N 24°40E 9 F21
Espungabera Mozam. 20°29S 32°45E 57 B5
Esquel Argentina 42°55S 71°20W 96 E2
Esquimalt Canada 48°26N 123°25W 78 B3
Esquina Argentina 30°0S 59°30W 94 C4
Essaouira Morocco 31°32N 9°42W 52 B4
Essen Belgium 51°28N 4°28E 15 C4
Essen Germany 51°28N 7°2E 16 C4
Essendon, Mt. Australia 25°0S 120°29E 61 E3
Essequibo → Guyana 6°50N 58°30W 92 B7
Essex Canada 42°10N 82°49W 82 D2
Essex Calif., U.S.A. 34°44N 115°15W 79 L11
Essex N.Y., U.S.A. 44°19N 73°21W 83 B11
Essex □ U.K. 51°54N 0°27E 13 F8
Essex Junction U.S.A. 44°29N 73°7W 83 B11
Esslingen Germany 48°44N 9°18E 16 D5
Estación Camacho
  Mexico 24°25N 102°18W 86 C4
Estación Simón Mexico 24°42N 102°35W 86 C4
Estados, I. de Los
  Argentina 54°40S 64°30W 96 G4
Eştahbānāt Iran 29°8N 54°4E 47 D7
Estância Brazil 11°16S 37°26W 93 F11
Estancia U.S.A. 34°46N 106°4W 77 J10
Estārm Iran 28°21N 58°21E 47 D8
Estcourt S. Africa 29°0S 29°53E 57 C4
Este △ Dom. Rep. 18°14N 68°42W 89 C6
Estelí Nic. 13°9N 86°22W 88 D2
Esterhazy Canada 50°37N 102°5W 71 C8
Estevan Canada 49°10N 102°59W 71 D8
Estevan Group Canada 53°3N 129°38W 70 C3
Estherville U.S.A. 43°24N 94°50W 80 D6
Eston Canada 51°8N 108°40W 71 C7
Estonia ■ Europe 58°30N 25°30E 9 G21
Estreito Brazil 6°32S 47°25W 93 E9
Estrela, Serra da Portugal 40°10N 7°45W 21 B2
Estremoz Portugal 38°51N 7°39W 21 C2
Estrondo, Serra do Brazil 7°20S 48°0W 93 E9
Eswatini ■ Africa 26°30S 31°30E 57 C5
Esztergom Hungary 47°47N 18°44E 17 E10
Et Tidra Mauritania 19°45N 16°20W 52 E2
Etah India 27°35N 78°40E 43 F8
Étampes France 48°26N 2°10E 20 B5
Etanga Namibia 17°55S 13°0E 56 A1
Etawah India 26°48N 79°6E 43 F8
Etawney L. Canada 57°50N 96°50W 71 B9
Etchojoa Mexico 26°55N 109°38W 86 B3
Etelä-Konneveden △
  Finland 62°34N 26°39E 8 E22
eThekwini = Durban
  S. Africa 29°49S 31°1E 57 C5
Ethel U.S.A. 46°32N 122°46W 78 D4
Ethelbert Canada 51°32N 100°25W 71 C8
Ethiopia ■ Africa 8°0N 40°0E 49 F3
Ethiopian Highlands
  Ethiopia 10°0N 37°0E 49 F2
Etive, L. U.K. 56°29N 5°10W 11 E3
Etna Italy 37°50N 14°55E 22 F6
Etolin Strait U.S.A. 60°20N 165°15W 74 C6
Etosha △ Namibia 19°0S 16°0E 56 A2
Etosha Pan Namibia 18°40S 16°30E 56 A2
Etowah U.S.A. 35°20N 84°32W 85 D12
Etrek Turkmenistan 37°36N 54°46E 47 B7
Ettelbruck Lux. 49°51N 6°5E 15 E6
Ettrick Water → U.K. 55°31N 2°55W 11 F6
Etzná-Tixmucuy = Edzná
  Mexico 19°39N 90°19W 87 D6
Eua Tonga 21°22S 174°56W 59 c
Euboea = Evia Greece 38°30N 24°0E 23 E11
Eucla Australia 31°41S 128°52E 61 F4
Euclid U.S.A. 41°34N 81°32W 82 E3
Eucumbene, L. Australia 36°2S 148°40E 63 F4
Eudora U.S.A. 33°7N 91°16W 84 E9
Eufaula Ala., U.S.A. 31°54N 85°9W 85 F12
Eufaula Okla., U.S.A. 35°17N 95°35W 84 D7

Eufaula L. U.S.A. 35°18N 95°21W 84 D7
Eugene U.S.A. 44°5N 123°4W 76 D2
Eugowra Australia 33°22S 148°24E 63 E4
Eulo Australia 28°10S 145°3E 63 D4
Eungella △ Australia 20°57S 148°40E 62 b
Eunice La., U.S.A. 30°30N 92°25W 84 F8
Eunice N. Mex., U.S.A. 32°26N 103°10W 77 K12
Eupen Belgium 50°37N 6°3E 15 D6
Euphrates = Furāt, Nahr al →
  Asia 31°0N 47°25E 46 D5
Eureka Canada 80°0N 85°56W 69 B14
Eureka Calif., U.S.A. 40°47N 124°9W 76 F1
Eureka Kans., U.S.A. 37°49N 96°17W 80 G5
Eureka Mont., U.S.A. 48°53N 115°3W 76 B6
Eureka Nev., U.S.A. 39°31N 115°58W 76 G6
Eureka S. Dak., U.S.A. 45°46N 99°38W 80 C4
Eureka, Mt. Australia 26°35S 121°35E 61 E3
Eureka Sd. Canada 79°0N 85°0W 69 B15
Euroa Australia 36°44S 145°35E 63 F4
Europa, Île Ind. Oc. 22°20S 40°22E 57 B7
Europa, Picos de Spain 43°10N 4°49W 21 A3
Europa, Pt. Gib. 36°3N 5°21W 21 D3
Europe 50°0N 20°0E 6 E10
Europoort Neths. 51°57N 4°10E 15 C4
Euskadi = País Vasco □
  Spain 42°50N 2°45W 21 A4
Eustis U.S.A. 28°51N 81°41W 85 G14
Eutsuk L. Canada 53°20N 126°45W 70 C3
Evale Angola 16°33S 15°44E 56 A2
Evans U.S.A. 40°23N 104°41W 76 F11
Evans, L. Canada 50°50N 77°0W 72 B4
Evans City U.S.A. 40°46N 80°4W 82 F4
Evans Head Australia 29°7S 153°27E 63 D5
Evansburg Canada 53°36N 114°59W 70 C5
Evanston U.S.A. 41°16N 110°58W 76 F8
Evansville U.S.A. 37°58N 87°35W 80 G10
Evaz Iran 27°46N 53°59E 47 E7
Eveleth U.S.A. 47°28N 92°32W 80 B7
Evensk Russia 62°12N 159°30E 27 C16
Everard, L. Australia 31°30S 135°0E 63 E2
Everard Ranges Australia 27°5S 132°28E 61 E5
Everest, Mt. Nepal 28°5N 86°58E 43 E12
Everett Pa., U.S.A. 40°1N 78°23W 82 F6
Everett Wash., U.S.A. 47°59N 122°12W 78 C4
Everglades, The U.S.A. 25°50N 81°0W 85 J14
Everglades △ U.S.A. 25°30N 81°0W 85 J14
Everglades City U.S.A. 25°52N 81°23W 85 J14
Evergreen Ala., U.S.A. 31°26N 86°57W 85 F11
Evergreen Mont., U.S.A. 48°14N 114°17W 76 B6
Evesham U.K. 52°6N 1°56W 13 E6
Evia Greece 38°30N 24°0E 23 E11
Évje Norway 58°36N 7°51E 9 G12
Évora Portugal 38°33N 7°57W 21 C2
Evowghlī Iran 38°43N 45°13E 46 B5
Évreux France 49°3N 1°8E 20 B4
Evros → Greece 41°40N 26°34E 23 D12
Évry France 48°38N 2°27E 20 B5
Évvoia = Evia Greece 38°30N 24°0E 23 E11
Ewe, L. U.K. 57°49N 5°38W 11 D3
Ewing U.S.A. 42°16N 98°21W 80 D4
Ewo Congo 0°48S 14°45E 54 E2
Exaltación Bolivia 13°10S 65°20W 92 F5
Excelsior Springs U.S.A. 39°20N 94°13W 80 F6
Exe → U.K. 50°41N 3°29W 13 G4
Exeter Canada 43°21N 81°29W 82 C3
Exeter U.K. 50°43N 3°31W 13 G4
Exeter Calif., U.S.A. 36°18N 119°9W 78 J7
Exeter N.H., U.S.A. 42°59N 70°57W 83 D14
Exmoor U.K. 51°12N 3°45W 13 F4
Exmoor △ U.K. 51°8N 3°42W 13 F4
Exmouth Australia 21°54S 114°10E 60 D1
Exmouth U.K. 50°37N 3°25W 13 G4
Exmouth G. Australia 22°15S 114°15E 60 D1
Exmouth Plateau Ind. Oc. 19°0S 114°0E 64 J3
Expedition △ Australia 25°41S 149°7E 63 D4
Expedition Ra. Australia 24°30S 149°12E 62 C4
Extremadura □ Spain 39°30N 6°5W 21 C2
Exuma Sound Bahamas 24°30N 76°20W 88 B4
Eyasi, L. Tanzania 3°30S 35°0E 54 E7
Eye Pen. U.K. 58°13N 6°10W 11 C2
Eyemouth U.K. 55°52N 2°5W 11 F6
Eyjafjallajökull Iceland 63°38N 19°36W 8 E4
Eyjafjörður Iceland 66°15N 18°30W 8 C4
Eyl Somalia 8°0N 49°50E 49 F4
Eyre, L. = Kati Thanda-Lake Eyre
  Australia 29°30S 137°26E 58 D6
Eyre Mts. N.Z. 45°25S 168°25E 59 F2
Eyre Pen. Australia 33°30S 136°17E 63 E2
Eysturoy Faeroe Is. 62°13N 6°54W 8 E9
Eyvān = Jūy Zar Iran 33°50N 46°18E 46 C5
Eyvānkī Iran 35°24N 51°56E 47 C6
Ezhou China 30°23N 114°50E 35 B10
Ezhva Russia 61°48N 50°35E 18 B9
Ezine Turkey 39°48N 26°20E 23 E12

F
F.Y.R.O.M. = Macedonia ■
  Europe 41°53N 21°40E 23 D9
Faaa Tahiti 17°34S 149°35W 59 d
Faaone Tahiti 17°40S 149°21W 59 d
Fabala Guinea 9°44N 9°5W 52 G4
Fabens U.S.A. 31°30N 106°10W 84 F1
Fabius U.S.A. 42°50N 75°59W 83 D9
Fabriano Italy 43°20N 12°54E 22 C5
Fachi Niger 18°6N 11°34E 53 E8
Fada Chad 17°13N 21°34E 53 E10
Fada-n-Gourma
  Burkina Faso 12°10N 0°30E 52 F6
Faddeyevskiy, Ostrov
  Russia 76°0N 144°0E 27 B15
Fadghāmī Syria 35°53N 40°52E 46 C4
Faenza Italy 44°17N 11°53E 22 B4
Færoe Is. = Føroyar ☑
  Atl. Oc. 62°0N 7°0W 8 F9
Făgăraș Romania 45°48N 24°58E 17 F13
Fagersta Sweden 60°1N 15°46E 9 F16
Fagnano, L. Argentina 54°30S 68°0W 96 G3
Fahlīān Iran 30°11N 51°28E 47 D6
Fahraj Kermān, Iran 29°0N 59°0E 47 D8

Fahraj Yazd, Iran 31°46N 54°36E 47 D7
Fai Tsi Long Vietnam 21°0N 107°30E 34 G6
Faial Azores 38°34N 28°42W 52 a
Faichan Kangri India 35°48N 76°54E 43 B7
Fair Haven N.Y., U.S.A. 43°18N 76°42W 83 C8
Fair Haven Vt., U.S.A. 43°36N 73°16W 83 C11
Fair Hd. U.K. 55°14N 6°9W 10 A5
Fair Isle U.K. 59°32N 1°38W 14 B6
Fair Oaks U.S.A. 38°39N 121°16W 78 G5
Fairbanks U.S.A. 64°51N 147°43W 68 E2
Fairbury U.S.A. 40°8N 97°11W 80 E5
Fairfax U.S.A. 44°40N 73°1W 83 B11
Fairfield Calif., U.S.A. 38°15N 122°3W 78 G4
Fairfield Conn., U.S.A. 41°9N 73°16W 83 E11
Fairfield Idaho, U.S.A. 43°21N 114°44W 76 E6
Fairfield Ill., U.S.A. 38°23N 88°22W 80 F9
Fairfield Iowa, U.S.A. 40°56N 91°57W 80 E8
Fairfield Tex., U.S.A. 31°44N 96°10W 84 F6
Fairford Canada 51°37N 98°38W 71 C9
Fairhope U.S.A. 30°31N 87°54W 85 F11
Fairlie N.Z. 44°5S 170°49E 59 F3
Fairmead U.S.A. 37°5N 120°10W 78 H6
Fairmont Minn., U.S.A. 43°39N 94°28W 80 D6
Fairmont W. Va., U.S.A. 39°29N 80°9W 81 F13
Fairmount Calif., U.S.A. 34°45N 118°26W 79 L8
Fairmount N.Y., U.S.A. 43°5N 76°12W 83 C8
Fairplay U.S.A. 39°15N 106°2W 76 G10
Fairport U.S.A. 43°6N 77°27W 82 C7
Fairport Harbor U.S.A. 41°45N 81°17W 82 E3
Fairview Canada 56°5N 118°25W 70 B5
Fairview Mont., U.S.A. 47°51N 104°3W 76 C11
Fairview Okla., U.S.A. 36°16N 98°29W 84 C5
Fairweather, Mt. U.S.A. 58°55N 137°32W 70 B1
Faisalabad Pakistan 31°30N 73°5E 42 D5
Faith U.S.A. 45°2N 102°2W 80 C2
Faizabad India 26°45N 82°10E 43 F10
Faizpur India 21°14N 75°49E 44 D2
Fajardo Puerto Rico 18°20N 65°39W 89 d
Fajr, W. → Si. Arabia 29°10N 38°10E 46 D3
Fakenham U.K. 52°51N 0°51E 12 E8
Fakfak Indonesia 2°55S 132°18E 37 E8
Faku China 42°32N 123°21E 33 C12
Falaise France 48°54N 0°12W 20 B3
Falam Myanmar 23°0N 93°45E 41 H18
Falcón, Presa Mexico 26°35N 99°10W 87 B5
Falcon Lake Canada 49°42N 95°15W 71 D9
Falcon Res. U.S.A. 26°34N 99°10W 84 H5
Falconara Marittima
  Italy 43°37N 13°24E 22 C5
Falcone, C. del Italy 40°58N 8°12E 22 D3
Falconer U.S.A. 42°7N 79°13W 82 D5
Falefa Samoa 13°54S 171°31W 59 b
Falelatai Samoa 13°55S 171°59W 59 b
Falelima Samoa 13°32S 172°41W 59 b
Faleshty = Fălești
  Moldova 47°32N 27°44E 17 E14
Fălești Moldova 47°32N 27°44E 17 E14
Falfurrias U.S.A. 27°14N 98°9W 84 H5
Falher Canada 55°44N 117°15W 70 B5
Falkenberg Sweden 56°54N 12°30E 9 H15
Falkirk U.K. 56°0N 3°47W 11 F5
Falkirk □ U.K. 55°58N 3°49W 11 F5
Falkland U.K. 56°16N 3°12W 11 E5
Falkland Is. ☑ Atl. Oc. 51°30S 59°0W 96 G5
Falkland Sd. Falk. Is. 52°0S 60°0W 96 G5
Fall River U.S.A. 41°43N 71°10W 83 E13
Fallbrook U.S.A. 33°23N 117°15W 79 M9
Fallon U.S.A. 39°28N 118°47W 76 G4
Falls City U.S.A. 40°3N 95°36W 80 E6
Falls Creek U.S.A. 41°9N 78°48W 82 E6
Falmouth Jamaica 18°30N 77°40W 88 a
Falmouth U.K. 50°9N 5°5W 13 G2
Falmouth U.S.A. 41°33N 70°37W 83 E14
Falsa, Pta. Mexico 27°51N 115°3W 86 B1
False B. S. Africa 34°15S 18°40E 56 D2
False Pt. India 15°43N 80°50E 45 G5
False Pt. India 20°18N 86°48E 44 D8
Falso, C. Honduras 15°12N 83°21W 88 C3
Falster Denmark 54°45N 11°55E 9 J14
Fălticeni Romania 47°21N 26°20E 17 E14
Falun Sweden 60°37N 15°37E 8 F16
Famagusta Cyprus 35°8N 33°55E 46 C2
Famatina, Sierra de
  Argentina 27°30S 68°0W 94 B2
Family L. Canada 51°54N 95°27W 71 C9
Famoso U.S.A. 35°37N 119°12W 79 K7
Fan Xian China 35°55N 115°38E 32 G8
Fanad Hd. Ireland 55°17N 7°38W 10 A4
Fang Thailand 19°55N 99°13E 38 C2
Fang Xian China 32°3N 110°40E 35 A8
Fangchang China 31°5N 118°4E 35 B12
Fangcheng China 33°18N 112°59E 32 H7
Fangchenggang China 21°42N 108°21E 34 G7
Fangliao Taiwan 22°22N 120°38E 35 F13
Fangshan Beijing, China 39°41N 116°0E 32 E9
Fangshan Shanxi, China 38°3N 111°25E 32 E6
Fangzi China 36°33N 119°10E 33 F10
Fanjiatun China 43°40N 125°15E 33 C13
Fanling China 22°30N 114°8E 31 a
Fannich, L. U.K. 57°38N 4°59W 11 D4
Fannūj Iran 26°35N 59°38E 47 E8
Fanø Denmark 55°25N 8°25E 9 J13
Fano Italy 43°50N 13°1E 22 C5
Fanshi China 39°12N 113°20E 32 E7
Fao = Al Fāw Iraq 30°0N 48°30E 47 E6
Faqirwali Pakistan 29°27N 73°0E 42 E5
Far Dalnevostochnyy □
  Russia 60°0N 140°0E 27 C14
Far East Asia 40°0N 130°0E 24 E14
Faradje
  Dem. Rep. of the Congo 3°50N 29°45E 54 D5
Farafangana Madag. 22°49S 47°50E 55 J9
Farāh Afghan. 32°20N 62°7E 40 C3
Farāh □ Afghan. 32°25N 62°10E 40 C3
Faranah Guinea 10°3N 10°45W 52 F3
Farasān, Jazā'ir Si. Arabia 16°45N 41°55E 49 D3
Farasan Is. = Farasān, Jazā'ir
  Si. Arabia 16°45N 41°55E 49 D3
Fareham U.K. 50°51N 1°11W 13 G6
Farewell, C. = Nunap Isua
  Greenland 59°48N 43°55W 66 D15

Farewell, C. N.Z. 40°29S 172°43E 59 D4
Fargo U.S.A. 46°53N 96°48W 80 B5
Farg'ona Uzbekistan 40°23N 71°19E 26 E8
Fär'iah, W. al →
  West Bank 32°12N 35°27E 48 C4
Faribault U.S.A. 44°18N 93°16W 80 C7
Faridabad India 28°26N 77°19E 42 E6
Faridkot India 30°44N 74°45E 42 D6
Faridpur Bangla. 23°15N 89°55E 43 H13
Faridpur India 28°13N 79°33E 43 E8
Farīmān Iran 35°40N 59°49E 47 C8
Farleigh Australia 21°4S 149°8E 62 b
Farmerville U.S.A. 32°47N 92°24W 84 E8
Farmingdale U.S.A. 40°12N 74°10W 83 F10
Farmington Canada 55°54N 120°30W 70 B4
Farmington Calif.,
  U.S.A. 37°55N 120°59W 78 H6
Farmington Maine,
  U.S.A. 44°40N 70°9W 81 C18
Farmington Mo., U.S.A. 37°47N 90°25W 80 G8
Farmington N.H., U.S.A. 43°24N 71°4W 83 C13
Farmington N. Mex.,
  U.S.A. 36°44N 108°12W 77 H9
Farmington Utah,
  U.S.A. 40°59N 111°53W 76 F8
Farmington → U.S.A. 41°51N 72°38W 83 E12
Farmville U.S.A. 37°18N 78°24W 81 G14
Farne Is. U.K. 55°38N 1°37W 12 B6
Farnham Canada 45°17N 72°59W 83 A12
Farnham, Mt. Canada 50°29N 116°30W 70 C5
Faro Brazil 2°10S 56°39W 92 D7
Faro Canada 62°11N 133°22W 68 E5
Faro Portugal 37°2N 7°55W 21 D2
Fårö Sweden 57°55N 19°5E 9 H18
Farquhar, C. Australia 23°50S 113°36E 61 D1
Farrars Cr. → Australia 25°35S 140°43E 62 D3
Farrāshband Iran 28°57N 52°5E 47 D7
Farrell U.S.A. 41°13N 80°30W 82 E4
Farrokhī Iran 33°50N 59°31E 47 C8
Farrukhabad India 27°24N 79°34E 44 A4
Fārs □ Iran 29°30N 55°0E 47 D7
Farsala Greece 39°17N 22°23E 23 E10
Fārsī Iran 27°58N 50°11E 47 E6
Farson U.S.A. 42°7N 109°26W 76 E9
Farsund Norway 58°5N 6°55E 9 G12
Fartak, Râs Si. Arabia 28°5N 34°34E 46 D2
Fartak, Ra's Yemen 15°38N 52°15E 49 D5
Fartura, Serra da Brazil 26°21S 52°52W 95 B5
Fārūj Iran 37°14N 58°14E 47 B8
Farvel, Kap = Nunap Isua
  Greenland 59°48N 43°55W 66 D15
Farwell U.S.A. 34°23N 103°2W 84 B3
Fāryāb □ Afghan. 36°0N 65°0E 40 B4
Fasā Iran 29°0N 53°39E 47 D7
Fasano Italy 40°50N 17°22E 22 D7
Fastiv Ukraine 50°7N 29°57E 17 C15
Fastnet Rock Ireland 51°22N 9°37W 10 E2
Fastov = Fastiv Ukraine 50°7N 29°57E 17 C15
Fatagartuting, Tanjung
  Indonesia 2°46S 131°57E 37 E8
Fatehabad Haryana, India 29°31N 75°27E 42 E6
Fatehabad Ut. P., India 27°1N 78°19E 42 F8
Fatehgarh India 27°25N 79°35E 43 F8
Fatehpur Raj., India 28°0N 74°40E 42 F6
Fatehpur Ut. P., India 25°56N 81°13E 43 G9
Fatehpur Ut. P., India 27°10N 81°13E 43 F9
Fatehpur Sikri India 27°6N 77°40E 42 F6
Fathom Five △ Canada 45°17N 81°40W 82 A3
Fatima Canada 47°24N 61°53W 73 C7
Faulkton U.S.A. 45°2N 99°8W 80 C4
Faure I. Australia 25°52S 113°50E 61 E1
Fauresmith S. Africa 29°44S 25°17E 56 C4
Fauske Norway 67°17N 15°25E 8 C16
Favara Italy 37°19N 13°39E 22 F5
Favignana Italy 37°56N 12°20E 22 F5
Fawcett, Pt. Australia 11°46S 130°2E 60 B5
Fawn → Canada 52°22N 87°35W 72 A2
Fawnskin U.S.A. 34°16N 116°56W 79 L10
Faxaflói Iceland 64°29N 23°0W 8 D2
Faya-Largeau Chad 17°58N 19°6E 53 E9
Fayd Si. Arabia 27°1N 42°52E 46 E4
Fayette Ala., U.S.A. 33°41N 87°50W 85 E11
Fayette Mo., U.S.A. 39°9N 92°41W 80 F7
Fayette N.Y., U.S.A. 42°48N 76°48W 83 D8
Fayetteville Ark., U.S.A. 36°4N 94°10W 84 C7
Fayetteville N.C., U.S.A. 35°3N 78°53W 85 D15
Fayetteville N.Y., U.S.A. 43°1N 76°0W 83 D9
Fayetteville Tenn., U.S.A. 35°9N 86°34W 85 D11
Faylakah Kuwait 29°27N 48°20E 47 D6
Fazilka India 30°27N 74°2E 42 D6
Fazilpur Pakistan 29°18N 70°29E 42 E4
Fdérik Mauritania 22°40N 12°45W 52 D3
Feakle Ireland 52°56N 8°40W 10 D3
Feale → Ireland 52°27N 9°37W 10 D2
Fear, C. U.S.A. 33°50N 77°58W 85 E16
Feather → U.S.A. 38°47N 121°36W 78 G5
Feather Falls U.S.A. 39°36N 121°16W 78 F5
Featherston N.Z. 41°6S 175°20E 59 D5
Fécamp France 49°45N 0°22E 20 B4
Fedala = Mohammedia
  Morocco 33°44N 7°21W 52 B4
Federación Argentina 31°0S 57°55W 94 C4
Féderal Argentina 30°57S 58°48W 94 C5
Federal Way U.S.A. 47°18N 122°20W 78 C4
Fedeshküh Iran 28°49N 53°50E 47 D7
Fehmarn Germany 54°27N 11°7E 16 A6
Fehmarn Bælt Europe 54°35N 11°20E 9 J14
Fehmarn Belt = Fehmarn Bælt
  Europe 54°35N 11°20E 9 J14
Fei Xian China 35°18N 117°59E 33 G9
Feicheng China 36°14N 116°45E 32 F9
Feidong China 31°58N 117°28E 35 B11
Feijó Brazil 8°9S 70°21W 92 E4
Feilding N.Z. 40°13S 175°35E 59 D5
Feira de Santana Brazil 12°15S 38°57W 93 F11
Feixi China 31°43N 117°10E 35 B11
Feixiang China 36°30N 114°45E 32 F8

Félicité Seychelles 4°19S 55°52E 55 b
Felipe Carrillo Puerto
  Mexico 19°38N 88°3W 87 D7
Felixburg Zimbabwe 19°29S 30°51E 57 A5
Felixstowe U.K. 51°58N 1°23E 13 F9
Felton U.S.A. 37°3N 122°4W 78 H4
Femer Bælt = Fehmarn Bælt
  Europe 54°35N 11°20E 9 J14
Femunden Norway 62°10N 11°53E 8 E14
Femundsmarka △ Norway 62°18N 12°6E 8 E15
Fen He → China 35°36N 110°42E 32 G6
Fenelon Falls Canada 44°32N 78°45W 82 B6
Feng Xian Jiangsu, China 34°43N 116°35E 32 G9
Feng Xian Shaanxi, China 33°54N 106°40E 32 H4
Fengcheng Jiangxi,
  China 28°12N 115°48E 35 C10
Fengcheng Liaoning,
  China 40°28N 124°5E 33 D13
Fengdu China 29°57N 107°48E 34 C6
Fengfeng China 36°28N 114°8E 32 F8
Fenggang China 27°57N 107°42E 34 D6
Fenghua China 29°40N 121°25E 35 C13
Fenghuang China 27°57N 109°29E 34 D7
Fengjie China 31°3N 109°31E 34 B7
Fengkai China 23°24N 111°30E 35 F8
Fengkang Taiwan 22°12N 120°41E 35 F13
Fengle China 31°29N 112°29E 35 B9
Fenglin Taiwan 23°45N 121°26E 35 F13
Fengning China 41°10N 116°33E 32 D9
Fengqing China 24°38N 99°55E 34 E2
Fengqiu China 35°2N 114°25E 32 G8
Fengrun China 39°48N 118°8E 33 E10
Fengshan Guangxi Zhuangzu,
  China 24°39N 109°15E 34 E7
Fengshan Guangxi Zhuangzu,
  China 24°31N 107°3E 34 E6
Fengshan Taiwan 22°38N 120°21E 35 F13
Fengshun China 23°46N 116°10E 35 F11
Fengtai China 32°50N 116°40E 35 A11
Fengtongzhai △ China 30°32N 102°54E 34 B4
Fengxiang China 34°29N 107°25E 32 G4
Fengxin China 28°41N 115°18E 35 C10
Fengyang China 32°51N 117°29E 33 H9
Fengyi China 25°37N 100°20E 34 E3
Fengyüan Taiwan 24°15N 120°35E 35 E13
Fenoarivo Atsinanana
  Madag. 17°22S 49°25E 55 H9
Fens, The U.K. 52°38N 0°2E 12 E7
Fenton U.S.A. 42°48N 83°42W 81 D12
Fenxi China 36°40N 111°31E 32 F6
Fenyang China 37°18N 111°48E 32 F6
Fenyi China 27°45N 114°47E 35 D10
Feodosiya Ukraine 45°2N 35°16E 19 F5
Ferbane Ireland 53°16N 7°50W 10 C4
Ferdows Iran 33°58N 58°2E 47 C8
Ferfer Somalia 5°4N 45°9E 49 F4
Fergana = Farg'ona
  Uzbekistan 40°23N 71°19E 26 E8
Fergus Canada 43°43N 80°24W 82 C4
Fergus Falls U.S.A. 46°17N 96°4W 80 B5
Ferizaj Kosovo 42°23N 21°10E 23 C9
Ferkéssédougou
  Côte d'Ivoire 9°35N 5°6W 52 G4
Ferland Canada 50°19N 88°27W 72 B2
Ferlo, Vallée du Senegal 15°15N 14°15W 52 E3
Fermanagh □ U.K. 54°21N 7°40W 10 B4
Fermo Italy 43°9N 13°43E 22 C5
Fermont Canada 52°47N 67°5W 73 B6
Fermoy Ireland 52°9N 8°16W 10 D3
Fernández Argentina 27°55S 63°50W 94 B3
Fernandina Beach
  U.S.A. 30°40N 81°27W 85 F14
Fernando de Noronha
  Brazil 4°0S 33°10W 93 D12
Fernando Póo = Bioko
  Eq. Guin. 3°30N 8°40E 54 D1
Ferndale Canada 44°58N 81°17W 82 B3
Ferndale U.S.A. 48°51N 122°36W 78 B4
Fernie Canada 49°30N 115°5W 70 D5
Fernlees Australia 23°51S 148°7E 62 C4
Fernley U.S.A. 39°36N 119°15W 76 G4
Fernwood U.S.A. 43°16N 73°38W 83 C11
Feroke India 11°9N 75°46E 45 J2
Ferozepore = Firozpur
  India 30°55N 74°40E 42 D6
Ferrara Italy 44°50N 11°35E 22 B4
Ferreñafe Peru 6°42S 79°50W 92 E3
Ferret, C. France 44°38N 1°15W 20 D3
Ferriday U.S.A. 31°38N 91°33W 84 F9
Ferrol Spain 43°29N 8°15W 21 A1
Ferron U.S.A. 39°5N 111°8W 76 G8
Ferryland Canada 47°2N 52°53W 73 C9
Fertile U.S.A. 47°32N 96°17W 80 B5
Fès Morocco 34°0N 5°0W 52 B5
Fessenden U.S.A. 47°39N 99°38W 80 B4
Festus U.S.A. 38°13N 90°24W 80 F8
Fetești Romania 44°22N 27°51E 17 F14
Fethiye Turkey 36°36N 29°6E 19 G4
Fetlar U.K. 60°36N 0°52W 11 A8
Feuilles → Canada 58°47N 70°4W 69 F17
Fez = Fès Morocco 34°0N 5°0W 52 B5
Fezzan Libya 27°0N 13°0E 53 C8
Fianambal Argentina 27°45S 67°37W 94 B2
Fianarantsoa Madag. 21°26S 47°5E 55 J9
Ficksburg S. Africa 28°51S 27°53E 57 C4
Field → Australia 23°48S 138°0E 62 C2
Field I. Australia 12°5S 132°23E 60 B5
Fier Albania 40°43N 19°33E 23 D8
Fife □ U.K. 56°16N 3°1W 11 E5
Fife Ness U.K. 56°17N 2°35W 11 E6
Fifth Cataract Sudan 18°22N 33°50E 53 E12
Figeac France 44°37N 2°2E 20 D5
Figueira da Foz Portugal 40°7N 8°54W 21 B1
Figueres Spain 42°18N 2°58E 21 A7
Figuig Morocco 32°5N 1°11W 52 B5
Fiji ■ Pac. Oc. 17°20S 179°0E 59 a
Filabus Zimbabwe 20°34S 29°20E 57 B4
Filadelfia Paraguay 22°21S 60°2W 94 A3
Filchner Ice Shelf Antarctica 79°0S 40°0W 5 D1

Filey U.K. 54°12N 0°18W 12 C7
Filey B. U.K. 54°12N 0°15W 12 C7
Filiatra Greece 37°9N 21°35E 23 F9
Filingué Niger 14°21N 3°22E 52 F6
Filipstad Sweden 59°43N 14°9E 9 G16
Fillmore Calif., U.S.A. 34°24N 118°55W 79 L8
Fillmore Utah, U.S.A. 38°58N 112°20W 76 G7
Fimbul Ice Shelf S. Ocean 69°30S 1°0W 5 D2
Finch Canada 45°11N 75°7W 83 A9
Finch Hatton Australia 20°25S 148°39E 62 b
Findhorn → U.K. 57°38N 3°38W 11 D5
Findlay U.S.A. 41°2N 83°39W 81 E12
Fine U.S.A. 44°14N 75°8W 83 B9
Fingal □ Ireland 53°29N 6°14W 10 C5
Finger L. Canada 53°33N 93°30W 72 B1
Finger Lakes U.S.A. 42°40N 76°30W 83 D8
Fingoè Mozam. 15°55S 31°50E 55 G6
Finisterre, C. = Fisterra, C.
  Spain 42°50N 9°19W 21 A1
Finke Australia 25°34S 134°35E 62 D1
Finke Gorge △ Australia 24°8S 132°49E 60 D5
Finland ■ Europe 63°0N 27°0E 8 E22
Finland, G. of Europe 60°0N 26°0E 9 G22
Finlay → Canada 57°0N 125°10W 70 B3
Finley Australia 35°38S 145°35E 63 F4
Finley U.S.A. 47°31N 97°50W 80 B5
Finn → Ireland 54°51N 7°28W 10 B4
Finnigan, Mt. Australia 15°49S 145°17E 62 B4
Finniss, C. Australia 33°8S 134°51E 63 E1
Finnmark Norway 69°37N 23°57E 8 B20
Finnsnes Norway 69°14N 18°0E 8 B18
Finspång Sweden 58°43N 15°47E 9 G16
Fiora → Italy 42°20N 11°34E 22 C4
Fiordland △ N.Z. 45°46S 167°0E 59 F1
Fiq Syria 32°46N 35°41E 48 C4
Firat = Furāt, Nahr al →
  Asia 31°0N 47°25E 46 D5
Fire Island △ U.S.A. 40°38N 73°8W 83 F11
Firebag → Canada 57°45N 111°21W 71 B6
Firebaugh U.S.A. 36°52N 120°27W 78 J6
Firedrake L. Canada 61°25N 104°30W 71 A8
Firenze Italy 43°46N 11°15E 22 C4
Firk, Sha'ib → Iraq 30°59N 44°34E 46 D5
Firozabad India 27°10N 78°25E 43 F8
Firozpur India 30°55N 74°40E 42 D6
Firozpur-Jhirka India 27°48N 76°57E 42 F7
Fīrūzābād Iran 28°52N 52°35E 47 D7
Fīrūzkūh Iran 35°50N 52°50E 47 C7
Firvale Canada 52°27N 126°13W 70 C3
Fish → Namibia 28°7S 17°10E 56 D2
Fish → S. Africa 31°30S 20°16E 56 D3
Fish River Canyon
  Namibia 27°40S 17°35E 56 C2
Fisher B. Canada 51°35N 97°13W 71 C9
Fishers I. U.S.A. 41°15N 72°0W 83 E13
Fishguard U.K. 52°0N 4°58W 13 E3
Fishing L. Canada 52°10N 95°24W 71 C9
Fishkill U.S.A. 41°32N 73°54W 83 E11
Fisterra, C. Spain 42°50N 9°19W 21 A1
Fitchburg Mass., U.S.A. 42°35N 71°48W 83 D13
Fitchburg Wis., U.S.A. 42°58N 89°28W 80 D9
Fitz Roy Argentina 47°0S 67°0W 96 F3
Fitz Roy, Cerro Argentina 49°17S 73°5W 96 F2
Fitzgerald Canada 59°51N 111°36W 70 B6
Fitzgerald U.S.A. 31°43N 83°15W 85 F13
Fitzgerald River △
  Australia 33°53S 119°55E 61 F3
Fitzmaurice → Australia 14°45S 130°5E 60 B5
Fitzroy → Queens.,
  Australia 23°32S 150°52E 62 C5
Fitzroy → W. Austral.,
  Australia 17°31S 123°35E 60 C3
Fitzroy Crossing Australia 18°9S 125°38E 60 C4
Fitzwilliam I. Canada 45°30N 81°45W 82 A3
Fiume = Rijeka Croatia 45°20N 14°21E 16 F8
Five Points U.S.A. 36°26N 120°6W 78 J6
Fizi Dem. Rep. of the Congo 4°17S 28°55E 54 C5
Flagstaff U.S.A. 35°12N 111°39W 77 J8
Flagstaff L. U.S.A. 45°12N 70°18W 83 A14
Flaherty I. Canada 56°15N 79°15W 72 A4
Flåm Norway 60°50N 7°7E 8 F12
Flambeau → U.S.A. 45°18N 91°14W 80 C8
Flamborough Hd. U.K. 54°7N 0°5W 12 C7
Flaming Gorge △
  U.S.A. 41°10N 109°25W 76 F9
Flaming Gorge Res.
  U.S.A. 41°10N 109°25W 76 F9
Flamingo, Teluk Indonesia 5°30S 138°0E 37 F9
Flanders = Flandre Europe 50°50N 2°30E 15 B9
Flandre Europe 50°50N 2°30E 15 B9
Flandre-Occidentale = West-
  Vlaanderen □ Belgium 51°0N 3°0E 15 C2
Flandre-Orientale = Oost-
  Vlaanderen □ Belgium 51°5N 3°50E 15 C3
Flandreau U.S.A. 44°3N 96°36W 80 C5
Flanigan U.S.A. 40°10N 119°53W 78 F7
Flannan Is. U.K. 58°17N 7°36W 11 C1
Flåsjön Sweden 64°5N 15°40E 8 D16
Flat → Canada 61°33N 125°18W 70 A3
Flat I. Mauritius 19°53S 57°35E 55 d
Flat I. S. China Sea 10°49N 115°49E 36 B5
Flathead L. U.S.A. 47°51N 114°8W 76 B6
Flattery, C. Australia 14°58S 145°21E 62 A4
Flattery, C. U.S.A. 48°23N 124°29W 78 B2
Flatwoods U.S.A. 38°31N 82°43W 81 F12
Fleetwood U.K. 53°55N 3°1W 12 D4
Fleetwood U.S.A. 40°27N 75°49W 83 F9
Flekkefjord Norway 58°18N 6°39E 9 G12
Flemington U.S.A. 41°7N 77°28W 82 F7
Flensburg Germany 54°47N 9°27E 16 A5
Flers France 48°47N 0°33W 20 B3
Flesherton Canada 44°16N 80°33W 82 B4
Flesko, Tanjung Indonesia 0°29N 124°30E 37 D6
Fleurieu Pen. Australia 35°40S 138°5E 63 F2
Flevoland □ Neths. 52°30N 5°30E 15 B5
Flin Flon Canada 54°46N 101°53W 71 C8
Flinders → Australia 17°36S 140°36E 62 B3
Flinders B. Australia 34°19S 115°19E 61 F2
Flinders Group Australia 14°11S 144°15E 62 A3
Flinders I. S. Austral.,
  Australia 33°44S 134°41E 63 E1

Flinders I. Tas., Australia 40°0S 148°0E 63 G4
Flinders Ranges
  Australia 31°30S 138°30E 63 E2
Flinders Reefs Australia 17°37S 148°31E 62 B4
Flint U.K. 53°15N 3°8W 12 D4
Flint U.S.A. 43°1N 83°41W 81 D12
Flint → U.S.A. 30°57N 84°34W 85 F12
Flint I. Kiribati 11°26S 151°48W 65 J12
Flintshire □ U.K. 53°17N 3°17W 12 D4
Flodden U.K. 55°37N 2°8W 12 B5
Floodplains △ Sri Lanka 8°10N 81°10E 45 K5
Floodwood U.S.A. 46°56N 92°55W 80 B7
Flora U.S.A. 38°40N 88°29W 80 F9
Florala U.S.A. 31°0N 86°20W 85 F11
Florence = Firenze Italy 43°46N 11°15E 22 C4
Florence Ala., U.S.A. 34°48N 87°41W 85 D11
Florence Ariz., U.S.A. 33°2N 111°23W 77 K8
Florence Colo., U.S.A. 38°23N 105°8W 76 G11
Florence Oreg., U.S.A. 43°58N 124°7W 76 D1
Florence S.C., U.S.A. 34°12N 79°46W 85 D15
Florence, L. Australia 28°53S 138°9E 63 D2
Florencia Colombia 1°36N 75°36W 92 C3
Florennes Belgium 50°15N 4°35E 15 D4
Florenville Belgium 49°40N 5°19E 15 E5
Flores Azores 39°26N 31°13W 52 a
Flores Guatemala 16°59N 89°50W 88 C2
Flores Indonesia 8°35S 121°0E 37 F6
Flores I. Canada 49°20N 126°10W 70 D3
Flores Sea Indonesia 6°30S 120°0E 37 F6
Floreşti Moldova 47°53N 28°17E 17 E15
Floresville U.S.A. 29°8N 98°10W 84 G5
Floriano Brazil 6°50S 43°0W 93 E10
Florianópolis Brazil 27°30S 48°30W 95 B6
Florida Cuba 21°32N 78°14W 88 B4
Florida Uruguay 34°7S 56°10W 95 C4
Florida □ U.S.A. 28°0N 82°0W 85 G14
Florida, Straits of U.S.A. 25°0N 80°0W 88 B4
Florida B. U.S.A. 25°0N 80°45W 88 B3
Florida Keys U.S.A. 24°40N 81°0W 85 J14
Florin U.S.A. 38°30N 121°24W 78 G5
Florina Greece 40°48N 21°26E 23 D9
Florissant U.S.A. 38°47N 90°19W 80 F8
Florø Norway 61°35N 5°1E 8 F11
Flower Station Canada 45°10N 76°41W 83 A8
Flowerpot I. Canada 45°18N 81°38W 82 A3
Floydada U.S.A. 33°59N 101°20W 84 E4
Fluk Indonesia 1°42S 127°44E 37 E7
Flushing = Vlissingen
  Neths. 51°26N 3°34E 15 C3
Fly → Papua N. G. 8°25S 143°0E 58 B7
Flying Fish, C. Antarctica 72°6S 102°29W 5 D15
Foa Tonga 19°45S 174°19W 59 c
Foam Lake Canada 51°40N 103°32W 71 C8
Foça Turkey 38°39N 26°46E 23 E12
Fochabers U.K. 57°37N 3°6W 11 D5
Focşani Romania 45°41N 27°15E 17 F14
Fogang China 23°52N 113°30E 35 F9
Fóggia Italy 41°27N 15°34E 22 D6
Fogo Cabo Verde 15°5N 24°20W 52 b
Fogo Canada 49°43N 54°17W 73 C9
Fogo I. Canada 49°40N 54°5W 73 C9
Föhr Germany 54°43N 8°30E 16 A5
Foix France 42°58N 1°38E 20 E4
Folda Nord-Trøndelag,
  Norway 64°32N 10°30E 8 D14
Folda Nordland, Norway 67°38N 14°50E 8 C16
Foley Botswana 21°34S 27°21E 56 C4
Foley U.S.A. 30°24N 87°41W 85 F11
Foleyet Canada 48°15N 82°25W 72 C3
Folgefonna Norway 60°3N 6°23E 9 F12
Foligno Italy 42°57N 12°42E 22 C5
Folkestone U.K. 51°5N 1°12E 13 F9
Folkston U.S.A. 30°50N 82°0W 85 F13
Follansbee U.S.A. 40°19N 80°35W 82 F4
Folsom U.S.A. 38°40N 121°9W 78 G5
Folsom L. U.S.A. 38°42N 121°9W 78 G5
Fomboni Comoros Is. 12°18S 43°46E 55 a
Fond-du-Lac Canada 59°19N 107°12W 71 B7
Fond du Lac U.S.A. 43°47N 88°27W 80 D9
Fond-du-Lac → Canada 59°17N 106°0W 71 B7
Fonda U.S.A. 42°57N 74°22W 83 D10
Fondi Italy 41°21N 13°25E 22 D5
Fongafale Tuvalu 8°31S 179°13E 58 B10
Fonsagrada = A Fonsagrada
  Spain 43°8N 7°4W 21 A2
Fonseca, G. de
  Cent. Amer. 13°10N 87°40W 88 D2
Fontainebleau France 48°24N 2°40E 20 B5
Fontana U.S.A. 34°6N 117°26W 79 L9
Fontas → Canada 58°14N 121°48W 70 B4
Fonte Boa Brazil 2°33S 66°0W 92 D5
Fontenay-le-Comte
  France 46°28N 0°48W 20 C3
Fontenelle Res. U.S.A. 42°1N 110°3W 76 E8
Fontur Iceland 66°23N 14°32W 8 C6
Fonuafo'ou Tonga 20°19S 175°25W 59 c
Fonualei Tonga 18°1S 174°19W 59 c
Foochow = Fuzhou
  China 26°5N 119°16E 35 D12
Foping China 33°41N 108°0E 32 H5
Foraker, Mt. U.S.A. 62°58N 151°24W 74 C9
Forbes Australia 33°22S 148°5E 63 E4
Forbesganj India 26°17N 87°18E 43 F12
Ford City Calif., U.S.A. 35°9N 119°27W 79 K7
Ford City Pa., U.S.A. 40°46N 79°32W 82 F5
Førde Norway 61°27N 5°53E 8 F11
Fords Bridge Australia 29°41S 145°29E 63 D4
Fordyce U.S.A. 33°49N 92°25W 84 E8
Forel, Mt. Greenland 66°52N 36°55W 4 C6
Foremost Canada 49°26N 111°34W 70 D6
Forest Canada 43°6N 82°0W 82 C2
Forest U.S.A. 32°22N 89°29W 85 E10
Forest City Iowa, U.S.A. 43°16N 93°39W 80 D7
Forest City N.C., U.S.A. 35°20N 81°52W 85 D14
Forest City Pa., U.S.A. 41°39N 75°28W 83 E9
Forest Grove U.S.A. 45°31N 123°7W 78 E3
Forestburg Canada 52°35N 112°1W 70 C6
Foresthill U.S.A. 39°1N 120°49W 78 F6
Forestier Pen. Australia 43°0S 148°0E 63 G4
Forestville Canada 48°48N 69°2W 73 C6

Forestville Calif., U.S.A. 38°28N 122°54W 78 G4
Forestville N.Y., U.S.A. 42°28N 79°10W 82 D5
Forfar U.K. 56°39N 2°53W 11 E6
Forillon △ Canada 48°46N 64°12W 73 C7
Forks U.S.A. 47°57N 124°23W 78 C2
Forlì Italy 44°13N 12°3E 22 B5
Forman U.S.A. 46°7N 97°38W 80 B5
Formby Pt. U.K. 53°33N 3°6W 12 D4
Formentera Spain 38°43N 1°27E 21 C6
Formentor, C. de Spain 39°58N 3°13E 21 C7
Former Yugoslav Republic of
  Macedonia = Macedonia ■
  Europe 41°53N 21°40E 23 D9
Fórmia Italy 41°15N 13°37E 22 D5
Formosa = Taiwan ■
  Asia 23°30N 121°0E 35 F13
Formosa Argentina 26°15S 58°10W 94 B4
Formosa Brazil 15°32S 47°20W 93 G9
Formosa □ Argentina 25°0S 60°0W 94 B4
Formosa, Serra Brazil 12°0S 55°0W 93 F8
Forollhogna △ Norway 62°39N 10°41E 8 E14
Forres U.K. 57°37N 3°37W 11 D5
Forrest Australia 30°51S 128°6E 61 F4
Forrest, Mt. Australia 24°48S 127°45E 61 D4
Forrest City U.S.A. 35°1N 90°47W 85 D9
Forsayth Australia 18°33S 143°34E 62 B3
Forssa Finland 60°49N 23°38E 8 F20
Forst Germany 51°45N 14°37E 16 C8
Forster Australia 32°12S 152°31E 63 E5
Forsyth U.S.A. 46°16N 106°41W 76 C10
Fort Abbas Pakistan 29°12N 72°52E 42 E5
Fort Albany Canada 52°15N 81°35W 72 B3
Fort Assiniboine Canada 54°20N 114°45W 70 C6
Fort Augustus U.K. 57°9N 4°42W 11 D4
Fort Beaufort S. Africa 32°46S 26°40E 56 D4
Fort Benton U.S.A. 47°49N 110°40W 76 C8
Fort Bragg U.S.A. 39°26N 123°48W 76 G2
Fort Bridger U.S.A. 41°19N 110°23W 76 F8
Fort Chipewyan Canada 58°42N 111°8W 71 B6
Fort Clatsop = Lewis and Clark △
  U.S.A. 46°8N 123°53W 78 D3
Fort Collins U.S.A. 40°35N 105°5W 76 E11
Fort Coulonge Canada 45°50N 76°45W 72 C4
Fort Covington U.S.A. 44°59N 74°29W 83 B10
Fort Dauphin = Taolanaro
  Madag. 25°2S 47°0E 55 K9
Fort Davis U.S.A. 30°35N 103°54W 84 F3
Fort-de-France Martinique 14°36N 61°5W 88 c
Fort Defiance U.S.A. 35°45N 109°5W 77 J9
Fort Dodge U.S.A. 42°30N 94°11W 80 D6
Fort Edward U.S.A. 43°16N 73°35W 83 C11
Fort Erie Canada 42°54N 78°56W 82 D6
Fort Fairfield U.S.A. 46°46N 67°50W 81 B20
Fort Frances Canada 48°36N 93°24W 71 D10
Fort Franklin = Déline
  Canada 65°11N 123°25W 68 D7
Fort Garland U.S.A. 37°26N 105°26W 77 H11
Fort George = Chisasibi
  Canada 53°50N 79°0W 72 B4
Fort Good Hope Canada 66°14N 128°40W 68 D7
Fort Hancock U.S.A. 31°18N 105°51W 84 F2
Fort Hope = Eabametoong
  Canada 51°30N 88°0W 72 B2
Fort Irwin U.S.A. 35°16N 116°41W 79 K10
Fort Kent U.S.A. 47°15N 68°36W 81 B19
Fort Klamath U.S.A. 42°42N 122°0W 76 E3
Fort Laramie U.S.A. 42°13N 104°31W 76 E11
Fort Liard Canada 60°14N 123°30W 70 A4
Fort Liberté Haiti 19°42N 71°51W 89 C5
Fort Lupton U.S.A. 40°5N 104°49W 76 F11
Fort MacKay Canada 57°12N 111°41W 70 B6
Fort Macleod Canada 49°45N 113°30W 70 D6
Fort McMurray Canada 56°44N 111°7W 70 B6
Fort McPherson Canada 67°30N 134°55W 68 D5
Fort Madison U.S.A. 40°38N 91°27W 80 E8
Fort Meade U.S.A. 27°45N 81°48W 85 H14
Fort Morgan U.S.A. 40°15N 103°48W 76 F12
Fort Myers U.S.A. 26°39N 81°52W 85 H14
Fort Nelson Canada 58°50N 122°44W 70 B4
Fort Nelson → Canada 59°32N 124°0W 70 B4
Fort Norman = Tulita
  Canada 64°57N 125°30W 68 E6
Fort Payne U.S.A. 34°26N 85°43W 85 D12
Fort Peck U.S.A. 48°1N 106°27W 76 B10
Fort Peck Dam U.S.A. 48°0N 106°26W 76 C10
Fort Peck L. U.S.A. 48°0N 106°26W 76 C10
Fort Pierce U.S.A. 27°27N 80°20W 85 H14
Fort Pierre U.S.A. 44°21N 100°22W 80 C3
Fort Plain U.S.A. 42°56N 74°37W 83 D10
Fort Portal Uganda 0°40N 30°20E 54 D6
Fort Providence Canada 61°3N 117°40W 70 A5
Fort Qu'Appelle Canada 50°45N 103°50W 71 C8
Fort Resolution Canada 61°10N 113°40W 70 A6
Fort Ross U.S.A. 38°32N 123°13W 78 G3
Fort Rupert = Waskaganish
  Canada 51°30N 78°40W 72 B4
Fort St. James Canada 54°30N 124°10W 70 C4
Fort St. John Canada 56°15N 120°50W 70 B4
Fort Saskatchewan
  Canada 53°40N 113°15W 70 C6
Fort Scott U.S.A. 37°50N 94°42W 80 G6
Fort Severn Canada 56°0N 87°40W 72 A2
Fort Shevchenko
  Kazakhstan 44°35N 50°23E 19 F9
Fort Simpson Canada 61°45N 121°15W 70 A4
Fort Smith Canada 60°0N 111°51W 70 B6
Fort Smith U.S.A. 35°23N 94°25W 84 D7
Fort Stockton U.S.A. 30°53N 102°53W 84 F3
Fort Sumner U.S.A. 34°28N 104°15W 77 J11
Fort Thompson U.S.A. 44°3N 99°26W 80 C4
Fort Union △ U.S.A. 35°54N 105°1W 77 J11
Fort Valley U.S.A. 32°33N 83°53W 85 E13
Fort Vermilion Canada 58°24N 116°0W 70 B5
Fort Walton Beach
  U.S.A. 30°25N 86°36W 85 F11
Fort Ware Canada 57°26N 125°41W 70 B3
Fort Wayne U.S.A. 41°4N 85°9W 81 E11
Fort William U.K. 56°49N 5°7W 11 E3

Fort Yates U.S.A. 46°5N 100°38W 80 B3
Fort Yukon U.S.A. 66°34N 145°16W 68 D2
Fortaleza Brazil 3°45S 38°35W 93 D11
Forteau Canada 51°28N 56°58W 73 B8
Fortescue → Australia 21°0S 116°4E 60 D2
Fortescue River Roadhouse
  Australia 21°17S 116°8E 60 D2
Forth → U.K. 56°9N 3°50W 11 E5
Fortrose U.K. 57°35N 4°9W 11 D4
Fortuna Calif., U.S.A. 40°36N 124°9W 76 F1
Fortuna N. Dak., U.S.A. 48°55N 103°47W 80 A2
Fortune Canada 47°4N 55°50W 73 C8
Fortune B. Canada 47°30N 55°22W 73 C8
Forūr Iran 26°17N 54°32E 47 E7
Fosen Norway 63°50N 10°20E 8 E14
Fosnavåg Norway 62°22N 5°38E 8 E11
Fossano Italy 44°33N 7°43E 20 D7
Fossil U.S.A. 45°0N 120°9W 76 D3
Fossil Butte △ U.S.A. 41°50N 110°27W 76 F8
Foster Canada 45°17N 72°30W 83 A12
Foster → Canada 55°47N 105°49W 71 B7
Fosters Ra. Australia 21°35S 133°48E 62 C1
Fostoria U.S.A. 41°10N 83°25W 81 E12
Fougères France 48°21N 1°14W 20 B3
Foul Pt. Sri Lanka 8°35N 81°18E 45 K5
Foula U.K. 60°10N 2°5W 11 A6
Foulness I. U.K. 51°36N 0°55E 13 F8
Foulpointe Madag. 17°41S 49°31E 55 B8
Fountain U.S.A. 38°41N 104°42W 76 G11
Fountain Hills U.S.A. 33°37N 111°43W 77 K8
Fountain Springs
  U.S.A. 35°54N 118°51W 79 K8
Four Mountains, Is. of
  U.S.A. 53°0N 170°0W 74 E5
Fouriesburg S. Africa 28°38S 28°14E 57 C4
Fourni Greece 37°36N 26°32E 23 F12
Fourth Cataract Sudan 18°47N 32°3E 53 E12
Fouta Djallon Guinea 11°20N 12°10W 52 F3
Foux, Cap-à- Haiti 19°43N 73°27W 89 C5
Foveaux Str. N.Z. 46°42S 168°10E 59 G2
Fowey U.K. 50°20N 4°39W 13 G3
Fowler Calif., U.S.A. 36°38N 119°41W 78 J7
Fowler Colo., U.S.A. 38°8N 104°2W 76 G11
Fowler, Pt. Australia 32°2S 132°3E 61 F5
Fowlers B. Australia 31°59S 132°34E 61 F5
Fowman Iran 37°13N 49°19E 47 B6
Fox → Canada 56°3N 93°18W 71 B10
Fox Creek Canada 54°24N 116°48W 70 C5
Fox Is. U.S.A. 53°0N 168°0W 74 E6
Fox Lake Canada 58°28N 114°31W 70 B6
Fox Valley Canada 50°30N 109°25W 71 C7
Foxboro Canada 44°14N 77°26W 82 B7
Foxboro U.S.A. 42°4N 71°16W 83 D13
Foxdale Australia 20°22S 148°35E 62 b
Foxe Basin Canada 66°0N 77°0W 69 D16
Foxe Chan. Canada 65°0N 80°0W 69 E16
Foxe Pen. Canada 65°0N 76°0W 69 E16
Foxford Ireland 53°59N 9°7W 10 C2
Foxton N.Z. 40°29S 175°18E 59 D5
Foyle, Lough U.K. 55°7N 7°4W 10 A4
Foynes Ireland 52°37N 9°7W 10 D2
Foz do Cunene Angola 17°15S 11°48E 56 A1
Foz do Iguaçu Brazil 25°30S 54°30W 95 B5
Frackville U.S.A. 40°47N 76°14W 83 F8
Fraile Muerto Uruguay 32°31S 54°32W 95 C5
Framingham U.S.A. 42°18N 71°24W 83 D13
Franca Brazil 20°33S 47°30W 93 H9
Francavilla Fontana
  Italy 40°32N 17°35E 23 D7
France ■ Europe 47°0N 3°0E 20 C5
Frances Australia 36°41S 140°55E 63 F3
Frances → Canada 60°16N 129°10W 70 A3
Frances L. Canada 61°23N 129°30W 70 A3
Franceville Gabon 1°40S 13°32E 54 E2
Franche-Comté France 46°50N 5°55E 20 C6
Francis Case, L. U.S.A. 43°4N 98°34W 80 D4
Francisco Beltrão Brazil 26°5S 53°4W 95 B5
Francisco Ignacio Madero Coahuila,
  Mexico 25°48N 103°18W 86 B4
Francisco Ignacio Madero Durango,
  Mexico 24°26N 104°18W 86 C4
Francisco Ignacio Madero, Presa
  Mexico 28°10N 105°37W 86 B3
Francistown Botswana 21°7S 27°33E 57 B4
François Canada 47°35N 56°45W 73 C8
François L. Canada 54°0N 125°30W 70 C3
Francois Peron △
  Australia 25°42S 113°33E 61 E1
Francs Pk. U.S.A. 43°58N 109°20W 76 E9
Franeker Neths. 53°12N 5°33E 15 A5
Frank Hann △ Australia 32°52S 120°19E 61 F3
Frankford S. Africa 27°17S 28°30E 57 C4
Frankfort Ind., U.S.A. 40°17N 86°31W 80 E10
Frankfort Kans., U.S.A. 39°42N 96°25W 80 F5
Frankfort Ky., U.S.A. 38°12N 84°52W 81 F11
Frankfort N.Y., U.S.A. 43°2N 75°4W 83 C9
Frankfurt Brandenburg,
  Germany 52°20N 14°32E 16 B8
Frankfurt Hessen, Germany 50°7N 8°41E 16 C5
Fränkische Alb Germany 49°10N 11°23E 16 D6
Frankland → Australia 35°0S 116°48E 61 G2
Franklin Ky., U.S.A. 36°43N 86°35W 80 G10
Franklin La., U.S.A. 29°48N 91°30W 84 G9
Franklin Mass., U.S.A. 42°5N 71°24W 83 D13
Franklin N.H., U.S.A. 43°27N 71°39W 83 C13
Franklin N.Y., U.S.A. 42°20N 75°9W 83 D9
Franklin Nebr., U.S.A. 40°6N 98°57W 80 E4
Franklin Pa., U.S.A. 41°24N 79°50W 82 E5
Franklin Va., U.S.A. 36°41N 76°56W 81 G15
Franklin W. Va., U.S.A. 38°39N 79°20W 81 F14
Franklin B. Canada 69°45N 126°0W 68 D6
Franklin D. Roosevelt L.
  U.S.A. 48°18N 118°9W 76 B4
Franklin-Gordon Wild Rivers △
  Australia 42°39S 145°51E 63 G4
Franklin I. Antarctica 76°10S 168°30E 5 D11
Franklin I. Canada 45°24N 80°20W 82 A4
Franklin L. U.S.A. 40°25N 115°22W 76 F6

Franklin Mts. Canada 65°0N 125°0W 68 D6
Franklin Str. Canada 72°0N 96°0W 68 C12
Franklinton U.S.A. 30°51N 90°9W 85 F9
Franklinville U.S.A. 42°20N 78°27W 82 D6
Frankston Australia 38°8S 145°8E 63 F4
Fransfontein Namibia 20°12S 15°1E 56 B2
Frantsa Iosifa, Zemlya
  Arctic 82°0N 55°0E 26 A6
Franz Canada 48°25N 84°30W 72 C3
Franz Josef Land = Frantsa Iosifa,
  Zemlya Arctic 82°0N 55°0E 26 A6
Fraser U.S.A. 42°32N 82°57W 82 D2
Fraser → B.C., Canada 49°7N 123°11W 78 A3
Fraser → Nfld. & L.,
  Canada 56°39N 62°10W 73 A7
Fraser, Mt. Australia 25°35S 118°20E 61 E2
Fraser I. Australia 25°15S 153°10E 63 D5
Fraser Lake Canada 54°0N 124°50W 70 C4
Fraserburg S. Africa 31°55S 21°30E 56 E3
Fraserburgh U.K. 57°42N 2°1W 11 D6
Fraserdale Canada 49°55N 81°37W 72 C3
Fray Bentos Uruguay 33°10S 58°15W 94 C4
Fray Jorge △ Chile 30°42S 71°40W 94 C1
Frazier Downs ◇
  Australia 18°48S 121°42E 60 C3
Fredericia Denmark 55°34N 9°45E 9 J13
Frederick Md., U.S.A. 39°25N 77°25W 81 F15
Frederick Okla., U.S.A. 34°23N 99°1W 84 D5
Frederick S. Dak., U.S.A. 45°50N 98°31W 80 C4
Fredericksburg Pa.,
  U.S.A. 40°27N 76°26W 83 F8
Fredericksburg Tex.,
  U.S.A. 30°16N 98°52W 84 F5
Fredericksburg Va.,
  U.S.A. 38°18N 77°28W 81 F15
Fredericktown Mo.,
  U.S.A. 37°34N 90°18W 80 G8
Fredericktown Ohio,
  U.S.A. 40°29N 82°33W 82 F2
Frederico Westphalen
  Brazil 27°22S 53°24W 95 B5
Fredericton Canada 45°57N 66°40W 73 C6
Fredericton Junction
  Canada 45°41N 66°40W 73 C6
Frederikshåb = Paamiut
  Greenland 62°0N 49°43W 4 C5
Frederikshamn = Hamina
  Finland 60°34N 27°12E 8 F22
Frederikshavn Denmark 57°28N 10°31E 9 H14
Frederiksted
  U.S. Virgin Is. 17°43N 64°53W 89 C7
Fredonia Ariz., U.S.A. 36°57N 112°32W 77 H7
Fredonia Kans., U.S.A. 37°32N 95°49W 80 G6
Fredonia N.Y., U.S.A. 42°26N 79°20W 82 D5
Fredrikstad Norway 59°13N 10°57E 9 G14
Free State □ S. Africa 28°30S 27°0E 56 C4
Freehold U.S.A. 40°16N 74°17W 83 F10
Freeland U.S.A. 41°1N 75°54W 83 E9
Freels, C. Nfld. & L.,
  Canada 49°15N 53°30W 73 C9
Freels, C. Nfld. & L.,
  Canada 46°37N 53°32W 73 C9
Freeman Calif., U.S.A. 35°35N 117°53W 79 K9
Freeman S. Dak., U.S.A. 43°21N 97°26W 80 D5
Freeport Bahamas 26°30N 78°47W 88 A4
Freeport Ill., U.S.A. 42°17N 89°36W 80 D9
Freeport N.Y., U.S.A. 40°39N 73°35W 83 F11
Freeport Ohio, U.S.A. 40°12N 81°15W 82 F3
Freeport Pa., U.S.A. 40°41N 79°41W 82 F5
Freeport Tex., U.S.A. 28°57N 95°21W 84 G7
Freetown S. Leone 8°30N 13°17W 52 G3
Freeville U.S.A. 42°30N 76°20W 83 D8
Frégate, L. de la Canada 53°15N 74°45W 72 B5
Fregenal de la Sierra
  Spain 38°10N 6°39W 21 C2
Fregon Australia 26°45S 132°1E 61 E5
Frei Antarctica 62°30S 58°0W 5 C18
Freibourg = Fribourg
  Switz. 46°49N 7°9E 20 C7
Freiburg Germany 47°59N 7°51E 16 E4
Freire Chile 38°54S 72°38W 96 D2
Freirina Chile 28°30S 71°10W 94 B1
Freising Germany 48°24N 11°45E 16 D6
Freistadt Austria 48°30N 14°30E 16 D8
Fréjus France 43°25N 6°44E 20 E7
Fremantle Australia 32°7S 115°47E 61 F2
Fremont Calif., U.S.A. 37°32N 121°57W 78 H4
Fremont Mich., U.S.A. 43°28N 85°57W 81 D11
Fremont Nebr., U.S.A. 41°26N 96°30W 80 E5
Fremont Ohio, U.S.A. 41°21N 83°7W 81 E12
Fremont → U.S.A. 38°24N 110°42W 76 G8
French Camp U.S.A. 37°53N 121°16W 78 H5
French Cays = Plana Cays
  Bahamas 22°38N 73°30W 89 B5
French Creek → U.S.A. 41°24N 79°50W 82 E5
French Frigate Shoals
  U.S.A. 23°45N 166°10W 75 L6
French Guiana ☑ S. Amer. 4°0N 53°0W 93 C8
French Polynesia ☑
  Pac. Oc. 20°0S 145°0W 65 J13
French Riviera = Azur, Côte d'
  France 43°25N 7°10E 20 E7
Frenchman Cr. →
  N. Amer. 48°31N 107°10W 76 B10
Frenchman Cr. →
  U.S.A. 40°14N 100°50W 80 E3
Fresco → Brazil 7°15S 51°30W 93 E8
Freshfield, C. Antarctica 68°25S 151°10E 5 C10
Fresnillo Mexico 23°10N 102°53W 86 C4
Fresno U.S.A. 36°44N 119°47W 78 J7
Fresno Res. U.S.A. 48°36N 109°57W 76 B9
Frew → Australia 20°0S 135°38E 62 C2
Frewsburg U.S.A. 42°3N 79°10W 82 D5
Freycinet △ Australia 42°10S 148°25E 63 G4
Freycinet Pen. Australia 42°10S 148°25E 63 G4
Fria Guinea 10°27N 13°38W 52 F3
Fria, C. Namibia 18°0S 12°0E 56 B1
Friant U.S.A. 36°59N 119°43W 78 J7
Frías Argentina 28°40S 65°5W 94 B2
Fribourg Switz. 46°49N 7°9E 20 C7

Friday Harbor *U.S.A.* 48°32N 123°1W **78** B3
Friedens *U.S.A.* 40°3N 78°59W **82** F6
Friedrichshafen *Germany* 47°39N 9°30E **16** E5
Friendship *U.S.A.* 42°12N 78°8W **82** D6
Friesland □ *Neths.* 53°5N 5°50E **15** A5
Frigate *Seychelles* 4°35S 55°56E **55** b
Frio *→ U.S.A.* 28°26N 98°11W **84** G5
Frio, C. *Brazil* 22°50S 41°50W **90** F6
Friona *U.S.A.* 34°38N 102°43W **84** D3
Frisco *U.S.A.* 33°38N 96°49W **84** E6
Fritch *U.S.A.* 35°38N 101°36W **84** D4
Friza, Proliv *Russia* 45°30N 149°0E **27** E15
Frobisher B. *Canada* 62°30N 66°0W **69** E18
Frobisher Bay = Iqaluit
 Canada 63°44N 68°31W **69** E18
Frobisher L. *Canada* 56°20N 108°15W **71** B7
Frohavet *Norway* 64°0N 9°30E **8** E13
Frome *U.K.* 51°14N 2°19W **13** F5
Frome *→ U.K.* 50°41N 2°6W **13** G5
Frome, L. *Australia* 30°45S 139°45E **63** E2
Front Range *U.S.A.* 40°25N 105°45W **76** F11
Front Royal *U.S.A.* 38°55N 78°12W **81** F14
Frontenac *→ Canada* 44°32N 76°30W **83** B8
Frontera *Mexico* 18°32N 92°38W **87** D6
Fronteras *Mexico* 30°56N 109°31W **86** A3
Frosinone *Italy* 41°38N 13°19E **22** D5
Frostburg *U.S.A.* 39°39N 78°56W **81** F14
Frostisen *Norway* 68°14N 17°10E **8** B17
Frøya *Norway* 63°43N 8°40E **8** E13
Fruita *U.S.A.* 39°9N 108°44W **76** G9
Frunze = Bishkek
 Kyrgyzstan 42°54N 74°46E **30** C3
Frutal *Brazil* 20°0S 49°0W **93** H9
Frýdek-Místek *Czechia* 49°40N 18°20E **17** D10
Fryeburg *U.S.A.* 44°1N 70°59W **83** B14
Fu Jiang *→ China* 30°0N 106°16E **34** C6
Fu Xian = Wafangdian
 China 39°38N 121°58E **33** E11
Fu Xian *China* 36°0N 109°20E **32** G5
Fu'an *China* 27°11N 119°36E **35** D12
Fubian *China* 31°17N 102°22E **34** B4
Fucheng *China* 37°50N 116°10E **32** F9
Fuchou = Fuzhou *China* 26°5N 119°16E **35** D12
Fuchū *Japan* 34°34N 133°14E **29** G6
Fuchuan *China* 24°50N 111°5E **35** E8
Fuchun Jiang *→ China* 30°5N 120°5E **35** B13
Fuding *China* 27°20N 120°12E **35** D13
Fuengirola *Spain* 36°32N 4°41W **21** D3
Fuentes de Oñoro *Spain* 40°33N 6°52W **21** B2
Fuerte *→ Mexico* 25°54N 109°22W **86** B3
Fuerte Olimpo *Paraguay* 21°0S 57°51W **94** A4
Fuerteventura *Canary Is.* 28°30N 14°0W **52** C3
Fufeng *China* 34°22N 108°0E **32** G5
Fugong *China* 27°5N 98°47E **34** D2
Fugou *China* 34°3N 114°25E **32** G8
Fugu *China* 39°2N 111°3E **32** E6
Fuhai *China* 47°2N 87°25E **30** B6
Fuhaymī *Iraq* 34°16N 42°10E **46** C4
Fuidhaigh = Wiay *U.K.* 57°24N 7°13W **11** D1
Fuji *Japan* 35°9N 138°39E **29** G9
Fuji-Hakone-Izu △
 Japan 35°15N 138°45E **29** G9
Fuji-San *Japan* 35°22N 138°44E **29** G9
Fuji-Yoshida *Japan* 35°30N 138°46E **29** G9
Fujian □ *China* 26°0N 118°0E **35** E12
Fujin *China* 47°16N 132°1E **31** B15
Fujinomiya *Japan* 35°10N 138°40E **29** G9
Fujisawa *Japan* 35°22N 139°29E **29** G9
Fujiyama, Mt. = Fuji-San
 Japan 35°22N 138°44E **29** G9
Fukagawa *Japan* 43°43N 142°2E **28** C11
Fukien = Fujian □ *China* 26°0N 118°0E **35** E12
Fukuchiyama *Japan* 35°19N 135°9E **29** G7
Fukue *Japan* 32°41N 128°51E **29** H4
Fukue-Shima *Japan* 32°40N 128°45E **29** H4
Fukui *Japan* 36°5N 136°10E **29** F8
Fukui □ *Japan* 36°0N 136°12E **29** G8
Fukuoka *Japan* 33°39N 130°21E **29** H5
Fukuoka □ *Japan* 33°30N 131°0E **29** H5
Fukushima *Japan* 37°44N 140°28E **28** F10
Fukushima □ *Japan* 37°30N 140°15E **28** F10
Fukuyama *Japan* 34°35N 133°20E **29** G6
Fulaga *Fiji* 19°8S 178°33W **59** a
Fulda *Germany* 50°32N 9°40E **16** C5
Fulda *→ Germany* 51°25N 9°39E **16** C5
Fulford Harbour *Canada* 48°47N 123°27W **78** B3
Fuliang *China* 29°23N 117°14E **35** C11
Fuling *China* 29°39N 107°17E **34** C6
Fullerton *Calif., U.S.A.* 33°53N 117°56W **79** M9
Fullerton *Nebr., U.S.A.* 41°22N 97°58W **80** E5
Fulongquan *China* 44°20N 124°42E **33** B13
Fulton *Mo., U.S.A.* 38°52N 91°57W **80** F8
Fulton *N.Y., U.S.A.* 43°19N 76°25W **83** C8
Fumin *China* 25°10N 102°20E **34** E4
Funabashi *Japan* 35°45N 140°0E **29** G10
Funan *China* 32°39N 115°42E **35** A10
Funchal *Madeira* 32°38N 16°54W **52** B2
Fundación *Colombia* 10°31N 74°11W **92** A4
Fundão *Portugal* 40°8N 7°30W **21** B2
Fundy, B. of *Canada* 45°0N 66°0W **73** D6
Fundy △ *Canada* 45°35N 65°10W **73** D6
Funhalouro *Mozam.* 23°3S 34°25E **57** B5
Funing *Hebei, China* 39°53N 119°12E **33** E10
Funing *Jiangsu, China* 33°45N 119°50E **35** H10
Funing *Yunnan, China* 23°35N 105°45E **34** F5
Funiu Shan *China* 33°30N 112°20E **32** H7
Funtua *Nigeria* 11°30N 7°18E **52** F7
Fuping *Hebei, China* 38°48N 114°12E **32** E8
Fuping *Shaanxi, China* 34°42N 109°10E **32** G5
Fuqing *China* 25°41N 119°21E **35** E12
Fuquan *China* 26°40N 107°27E **34** D6
Furano *Japan* 43°21N 142°23E **28** C11
Furāt, Nahr al *→ Asia* 31°0N 47°25E **46** D5
Fūrg *Iran* 28°18N 55°13E **47** D7
Furnas, Represa de
 Brazil 20°50S 45°30W **95** A6
Furneaux Group
 Australia 40°10S 147°50E **63** G4
Furqlus *Syria* 34°36N 37°8E **48** A6
Fürstenwalde *Germany* 52°22N 14°3E **16** B8
Fürth *Germany* 49°28N 10°59E **16** D6
Furukawa = Ōsaki
 Japan 38°34N 140°58E **28** E10
Fury and Hecla Str.
 Canada 69°56N 84°0W **69** D15
Fusagasugá *Colombia* 4°21N 74°22W **92** C4
Fushan *Shandong, China* 37°30N 121°15E **33** F11
Fushan *Shanxi, China* 35°58N 111°51E **32** G6
Fushun *Liaoning, China* 41°50N 123°56E **33** D12
Fushun *Sichuan, China* 29°13N 104°52E **34** C5
Fusong *China* 42°20N 127°15E **33** C14
Fustic *Barbados* 13°16N 59°38W **89** g
Fusui *China* 22°40N 107°56E **34** F6
Futian *China* 22°32N 114°4E **31** a
Fuxian Hu *China* 24°30N 102°53E **34** E4
Fuxin *China* 42°5N 121°48E **33** C11
Fuyang *Anhui, China* 33°0N 115°48E **32** H8
Fuyang *Zhejiang, China* 30°5N 119°57E **35** B12
Fuyang He *→ China* 38°12N 117°0E **32** E9
Fuying Dao *China* 26°34N 120°9E **35** D13
Fuyong *China* 22°40N 113°49E **31** a
Fuyu *Heilongjiang, China* 47°49N 124°27E **31** B13
Fuyu *Jilin, China* 45°12N 124°43E **33** B13
Fuyuan *China* 25°40N 104°16E **34** E5
Fuzhou *China* 47°0N 89°28E **30** B6
Fuzhou = Linchuan
 China 27°57N 116°15E **35** D11
Fuzhou *China* 26°5N 119°16E **35** D12
Fyn *Denmark* 55°20N 10°30E **9** J14
Fyne, L. *U.K.* 55°59N 5°23W **11** F3

G

Gaalkacyo *Somalia* 6°30N 47°30E **49** F4
Gabba *Australia* 9°45S 142°38E **62** a
Gabela *Angola* 11°0S 14°24E **54** G2
Gabès *Tunisia* 33°53N 10°2E **53** B8
Gabès, G. de *Tunisia* 34°0N 10°30E **53** B8
Gabon ■ *Africa* 0°10S 10°0E **54** E2
Gaborone *Botswana* 24°45S 25°57E **56** B4
Gabriels *U.S.A.* 44°26N 74°12W **83** B10
Gäbrík *Iran* 25°44N 58°28E **47** E8
Gabrovo *Bulgaria* 42°52N 25°19E **23** C11
Gäch Sär *Iran* 36°7N 51°19E **47** B6
Gachsārān *Iran* 30°15N 50°45E **47** D6
Gad Hinglaj *India* 16°14N 74°21E **45** F2
Gadag *India* 15°30N 75°45E **45** G2
Gadap *Pakistan* 25°5N 67°28E **42** G2
Gadarwara *India* 22°50N 78°50E **43** H8
Gadhada *India* 22°0N 71°35E **42** J4
Gadra *Pakistan* 25°40N 70°38E **42** G4
Gadsden *U.S.A.* 34°1N 86°1W **85** D11
Gadwal *India* 16°10N 77°50E **45** F3
Gaffney *U.S.A.* 35°5N 81°39W **85** D14
Gafsa *Tunisia* 34°24N 8°43E **53** B7
Gagaria *India* 25°43N 70°46E **42** G4
Găgăuzia □ *Moldova* 46°10N 28°40E **17** E15
Gagnoa *Côte d'Ivoire* 6°56N 6°16W **52** G4
Gagnon *Canada* 51°50N 68°5W **73** B6
Gagnon, L. *Canada* 62°3N 110°27W **71** A6
Gahmar *India* 25°27N 83°49E **43** G10
Gahnpa = Ganta *Liberia* 7°15N 8°59W **52** G4
Gai Xian = Gaizhou
 China 40°22N 122°20E **33** D12
Gail *U.S.A.* 32°46N 101°27W **84** E4
Gaillimh = Galway *Ireland* 53°17N 9°3W **10** C2
Gaines *U.S.A.* 41°46N 77°35W **82** E7
Gainesville *Fla., U.S.A.* 29°40N 82°20W **85** G13
Gainesville *Ga., U.S.A.* 34°18N 83°50W **85** D13
Gainesville *Mo., U.S.A.* 36°36N 92°26W **80** G7
Gainesville *Tex., U.S.A.* 33°38N 97°8W **84** E6
Gairdner, L. *Australia* 31°30S 136°0E **63** E2
Gairloch *U.K.* 57°43N 5°41W **11** D3
Gairloch, L. *U.K.* 57°43N 5°45W **11** D3
Gaizhou *China* 40°22N 122°20E **33** D12
Gaj *→ Pakistan* 26°26N 67°21E **42** F2
Gajendragarh *India* 15°44N 75°58E **45** G2
Gakuch *Pakistan* 36°7N 73°45E **43** A5
Gal Oya △ *Sri Lanka* 7°0N 81°20E **45** L5
Gal Oya Res. *Sri Lanka* 7°5N 81°30E **45** L5
Galán, Cerro *Argentina* 25°55S 66°52W **94** B2
Galápagos = Colón, Arch. de
 Ecuador 0°0 91°0W **90** D1
Galapagos Fracture Zone
 Pac. Oc. 3°0N 110°0W **65** G17
Galapagos Rise *Pac. Oc.* 15°0S 95°0W **65** J18
Galashiels *U.K.* 55°37N 2°49W **11** F6
Galați *Romania* 45°27N 28°2E **17** F15
Galax *U.S.A.* 36°40N 80°56W **81** G13
Galbīn Govĭ *Mongolia* 43°0N 107°0E **32** C4
Galcaio = Gaalkacyo
 Somalia 6°30N 47°30E **49** F4
Galdhøpiggen *Norway* 61°38N 8°18E **8** F13
Galeana *Chihuahua,
 Mexico* 30°7N 107°38W **86** A3
Galeana *Nuevo León,
 Mexico* 24°50N 100°4W **86** A3
Galela *Indonesia* 1°50N 127°49E **37** D7
Galeota Pt. *Trin. & Tob.* 10°8N 60°59W **93** K16
Galera Pt. *Trin. & Tob.* 10°49N 60°54W **93** K16
Galesburg *U.S.A.* 40°57N 90°22W **80** E8
Galeton *U.S.A.* 41°44N 77°39W **82** E7
Galich *Russia* 58°22N 42°24E **18** C7
Galicia □ *Spain* 42°43N 7°45W **21** A2
Galilee = Hagalil *Israel* 32°53N 35°18E **48** C4
Galilee, L. *Australia* 22°20S 145°50E **62** C4
Galilee, Sea of = Yam Kinneret
 Israel 32°45N 35°35E **48** C4
Galina Pt. *Jamaica* 18°24N 76°58W **88** a
Galion *U.S.A.* 40°44N 82°47W **82** F2
Galiuro Mts. *U.S.A.* 32°30N 110°20W **77** K8
Galiwinku *Australia* 12°5S 135°34E **62** A2
Gallan Hd. *U.K.* 58°15N 7°2W **11** C1
Galle *Sri Lanka* 6°5N 80°10E **45** L5
Gállego *→ Spain* 41°39N 0°51W **21** B5
Gallegos *→ Argentina* 51°35S 69°0W **96** G3
Galley Hd. *Ireland* 51°32N 8°55W **10** E3
Gallinas, Pta. *Colombia* 12°28N 71°40W **92** A4
Gallipoli = Gelibolu
 Turkey 40°28N 26°43E **23** D12
Gallípoli *Italy* 40°3N 17°58E **23** D8
Gallipolis *U.S.A.* 38°49N 82°12W **81** F12
Gällivare *Sweden* 67°9N 20°40E **8** C19
Galloo I. *U.S.A.* 43°55N 76°25W **83** C8
Galloway *U.K.* 55°1N 4°29W **11** F4
Galloway, Mull of *U.K.* 54°39N 4°52W **11** G4
Gallup *U.S.A.* 35°32N 108°45W **77** J9
Galmudug *Somalia* 6°0N 48°0E **49** F4
Galoya *Sri Lanka* 8°10N 80°55E **45** K5
Galt *U.S.A.* 38°15N 121°18W **78** G5
Galty Mts. *Ireland* 52°22N 8°10W **10** D3
Galtymore *Ireland* 52°21N 8°11W **10** D3
Galugāh *Iran* 36°43N 53°48E **47** B7
Galva *U.S.A.* 41°10N 90°3W **80** E8
Galveston *U.S.A.* 29°18N 94°48W **84** G7
Galveston B. *U.S.A.* 29°36N 94°50W **84** G7
Gálvez *Argentina* 32°0S 61°14W **94** C3
Galway *Ireland* 53°17N 9°3W **10** C2
Galway □ *Ireland* 53°22N 9°1W **10** C2
Galway B. *Ireland* 53°13N 9°10W **10** C2
Gam *→ Vietnam* 21°55N 105°12E **38** B5
Gamagōri *Japan* 34°50N 137°14E **29** G8
Gambat *Pakistan* 27°17N 68°26E **42** F3
Gambhir *→ India* 26°58N 77°27E **42** F6
Gambia ■ *W. Afr.* 13°25N 16°0W **52** F2
Gambia *→ W. Afr.* 13°28N 16°34W **52** F2
Gambier, C. *Australia* 11°56S 130°57E **60** B5
Gambier, Îs.
 French Polynesia 23°8S 134°58W **65** K14
Gambier Is. *Australia* 35°3S 136°30E **63** F2
Gambo *Canada* 48°47N 54°13W **73** C9
Gamboli *Pakistan* 29°53N 68°24E **42** E3
Gamboma *Congo* 1°55S 15°52E **54** E3
Gamka *→ S. Africa* 33°18S 21°39E **56** D3
Gamkab *→ Namibia* 28°4S 17°54E **56** C2
Gamlakarleby = Kokkola
 Finland 63°50N 23°8E **8** E20
Gammon *→ Canada* 51°24N 95°44W **71** C9
Gammon Ranges △
 Australia 30°38S 139°8E **63** E2
Gampaha *Sri Lanka* 7°5N 79°59E **45** L4
Gampola *Sri Lanka* 7°10N 80°34E **45** L5
Gamtoos *→ S. Africa* 33°58S 25°1E **56** D4
Gamzigrad-Romuliana
 Serbia 43°53N 22°11E **23** C10
Gan Jiang *→ China* 29°15N 116°0E **35** C11
Ganado *U.S.A.* 35°43N 109°33W **77** J9
Gananoque *Canada* 44°20N 76°10W **83** B8
Ganāveh *Iran* 29°35N 50°35E **47** D6
Gäncä *Azerbaijan* 40°45N 46°20E **19** F8
Gancheng *China* 18°51N 108°37E **38** C7
Gand = Gent *Belgium* 51°2N 3°42E **15** C3
Ganda *Angola* 13°3S 14°35E **55** G2
Gandajika
 Dem. Rep. of the Congo 6°46S 23°58E **54** F4
Gandak *→ India* 25°39N 85°13E **43** G11
Gandava *Pakistan* 28°32N 67°32E **42** E2
Gander *Canada* 48°58N 54°35W **73** C9
Gander L. *Canada* 48°58N 54°35W **73** C9
Gandhi Sagar *India* 24°40N 75°40E **42** G6
Gandhinagar *India* 23°15N 72°45E **42** H5
Gandia *Spain* 38°58N 0°9W **21** C5
Ganedidalem = Gani
 Indonesia 0°48S 128°14E **37** E7
Ganga *→ India* 23°20N 90°30E **43** H14
Ganga Sagar *India* 21°38N 88°5E **43** J13
Gangakher *India* 18°57N 76°45E **44** E3
Gangan *→ India* 28°38N 78°58E **43** E8
Ganganagar *India* 29°56N 73°56E **42** E5
Gangapur *Maharashtra,
 India* 19°41N 75°1E **44** E2
Gangapur *Raj., India* 26°32N 76°49E **42** F7
Gangaw *Myanmar* 22°5N 94°5E **41** H19
Gangawati *India* 15°30N 76°36E **45** G3
Gangdisê Shan *China* 31°20N 81°0E **43** D9
Ganges = Ganga *→
 India* 23°20N 90°30E **43** H14
Ganges *Canada* 48°51N 123°31W **70** D4
Ganges, Mouths of the
 India 21°30N 90°0E **43** J14
Ganggyeong *S. Korea* 36°10N 127°0E **33** F14
Gangneung *S. Korea* 37°45N 128°54E **33** F15
Gangoh *India* 29°46N 77°18E **42** E7
Gangotri *India* 30°50N 79°10E **43** D8
Gangotri △ *India* 30°50N 79°10E **43** D8
Gangseong *S. Korea* 38°24N 128°30E **33** E15
Gangtok *India* 27°20N 88°37E **41** F16
Gangu *China* 34°40N 105°15E **32** G3
Gangyao *China* 44°12N 126°37E **33** B14
Gani *Indonesia* 0°48S 128°14E **37** E7
Ganj *India* 27°45N 78°57E **43** F8
Ganjam *India* 19°23N 85°4E **44** E7
Ganluo *China* 28°58N 102°59E **34** C4
Ganquan *China* 36°20N 109°20E **32** F5
Ganshui *China* 28°40N 106°40E **34** C6
Gansu □ *China* 36°0N 104°0E **32** G3
Ganta *Liberia* 7°15N 8°59W **52** G4
Gantheaume, C. *Australia* 36°4S 137°32E **63** F2
Gantheaume B. *Australia* 27°40S 114°10E **61** E1
Gantsevichi = Hantsavichy
 Belarus 52°49N 26°30E **17** B14
Ganyem = Genyem
 Indonesia 2°46S 140°12E **37** E10
Ganyu *China* 34°50N 119°8E **33** G10
Ganzhou *China* 25°51N 114°56E **35** E10
Gao *Mali* 16°15N 0°5W **52** E5
Gao Xian *China* 28°21N 104°32E **34** C5
Gao'an *China* 28°26N 115°17E **35** C10
Gaobeidian *China* 39°1N 115°59E **32** E8
Gaocheng *China* 38°2N 114°49E **32** E8
Gaochun *China* 31°19N 118°49E **35** B12
Gaohebu *China* 30°43N 116°49E **35** B11
Gaokeng *China* 27°40N 113°58E **35** D9
Gaolan Dao *China* 21°55N 113°10E **35** G9
Gaoligong Shan *China* 24°45N 98°45E **34** E2
Gaomi *China* 36°20N 119°42E **33** F10
Gaoping *China* 35°45N 112°55E **32** G7
Gaotang *China* 36°50N 116°15E **32** F9
Gaoua *Burkina Faso* 10°20N 3°8W **52** F5
Gaoual *Guinea* 11°45N 13°25W **52** F3
Gaoyang *China* 38°40N 115°45E **32** E8
Gaoyao *China* 23°3N 112°27E **35** F9
Gaoyou *China* 32°47N 119°26E **35** A12
Gaoyou Hu *China* 32°45N 119°20E **35** A11
Gaoyuan *China* 37°8N 117°58E **33** F9
Gaozhou *China* 21°58N 110°50E **35** G8
Gap *France* 44°33N 6°5E **20** D7
Gapat *→ India* 24°30N 82°28E **43** G10
Gapuwiyak *Australia* 12°25S 135°43E **62** A2
Gar *China* 32°10N 79°58E **30** E4
Gara, L. *Ireland* 53°57N 8°26W **10** C3
Garabogazköl Aylagy
 Turkmenistan 41°0N 53°30E **19** F9
Garachiné *Panama* 8°0N 78°12W **88** E4
Garagum *Turkmenistan* 39°30N 60°0E **47** B8
Garah *Australia* 29°5S 149°38E **63** D4
Garanhuns *Brazil* 8°50S 36°30W **93** E11
Garautha *India* 25°34N 79°18E **43** G8
Garawa ✿ *Australia* 16°43S 136°51E **62** B2
Garberville *U.S.A.* 40°6N 123°48W **76** F2
Garbiyang *India* 30°8N 80°54E **43** D9
Gard *→ France* 43°51N 4°37E **20** E6
Garda, L. di *Italy* 45°40N 10°41E **22** B4
Garde L. *Canada* 62°50N 106°13W **71** A7
Garden City *Ga., U.S.A.* 32°6N 81°9W **85** E14
Garden City *Kans.,
 U.S.A.* 37°58N 100°53W **80** G3
Garden City *Tex., U.S.A.* 31°52N 101°29W **84** F4
Garden Grove *U.S.A.* 33°47N 117°55W **79** M9
Gardēz *Afghan.* 33°37N 69°9E **42** C3
Gardiner *Maine, U.S.A.* 44°14N 69°47W **81** C19
Gardiner *Mont., U.S.A.* 45°2N 110°22W **76** D8
Gardiners I. *U.S.A.* 41°6N 72°6W **83** E12
Gardner *U.S.A.* 42°34N 71°59W **83** D13
Gardner Canal *Canada* 53°27N 128°8W **70** C3
Gardner Pinnacles
 U.S.A. 25°0N 167°55W **75** L6
Gardnerville *U.S.A.* 38°56N 119°45W **78** G7
Gardo = Qardho *Somalia* 9°30N 49°6E **49** F4
Garey *U.S.A.* 34°53N 120°19W **79** L6
Garfield *U.S.A.* 47°1N 117°9W **76** C5
Garforth *U.K.* 53°47N 1°24W **12** D6
Gargantua, C. *Canada* 47°36N 85°2W **81** B11
Gargett *Australia* 21°9S 148°46E **62** b
Garhchiroli *India* 20°10N 80°0E **44** D5
Garibaldi △ *Canada* 49°50N 122°40W **70** D4
Gariep, L. *S. Africa* 30°40S 25°40E **56** D4
Garies *S. Africa* 30°32S 17°59E **56** D2
Garig Gunak Barlu △
 Australia 11°25S 131°58E **60** B5
Garigliano *→ Italy* 41°13N 13°42E **22** D5
Garissa *Kenya* 0°25S 39°40E **54** E7
Garland *U.S.A.* 41°45N 112°10W **76** F7
Garmāb *→ Iran* 35°25N 56°45E **47** C8
Garmisch-Partenkirchen
 Germany 47°30N 11°6E **16** E6
Garmsār *Iran* 35°20N 52°25E **47** C7
Garner *U.S.A.* 43°6N 93°36W **80** D7
Garnett *U.S.A.* 38°17N 95°14W **80** F6
Garo Hills *India* 25°30N 90°30E **43** G14
Garoe = Garoowe *Somalia* 8°25N 48°33E **49** F4
Garonne *→ France* 45°2N 0°36W **20** D3
Garot *India* 24°19N 75°41E **42** G6
Garoua *Cameroon* 9°19N 13°21E **53** G8
Garrauli *India* 25°5N 79°22E **43** G8
Garrison *Mont., U.S.A.* 46°31N 112°49W **76** C7
Garrison *N. Dak., U.S.A.* 47°40N 101°25W **80** B3
Garrison Res. = Sakakawea, L.
 U.S.A. 47°30N 101°25W **80** B3
Garron Pt. *U.K.* 55°3N 5°59W **10** A6
Garry *→ U.K.* 56°44N 3°47W **11** E5
Garry, L. *Canada* 65°58N 100°18W **68** D11
Garrygala *Turkmenistan* 38°31N 56°29E **47** B8
Garson L. *Canada* 56°19N 110°2W **71** B6
Garstang *U.K.* 53°55N 2°46W **12** D5
Garu *India* 23°40N 84°14E **43** H11
Garub *Namibia* 26°37S 16°0E **56** C2
Garut *Indonesia* 7°14S 107°53E **37** G12
Garvie Mts. *N.Z.* 45°30S 168°50E **59** F2
Garwa = Garoua
 Cameroon 9°19N 13°21E **53** G8
Garwa *India* 24°11N 83°47E **43** G10
Gary *U.S.A.* 41°36N 87°20W **80** E10
Garzê *China* 31°38N 100°1E **34** B3
Garzón *Colombia* 2°10N 75°40W **92** C3
Gas-San *Japan* 38°32N 140°1E **28** E10
Gasan Kuli = Esenguly
 Turkmenistan 37°37N 53°59E **26** F6
Gascogne *France* 43°45N 0°20E **20** E4
Gascogne, G. de *Europe* 44°0N 2°0W **20** D2
Gascony = Gascogne
 France 43°45N 0°20E **20** E4
Gascoyne *→ Australia* 24°52S 113°37E **61** D1
Gascoyne Junction
 Australia 25°2S 115°17E **61** E2
Gashaka *Nigeria* 7°20N 11°29E **53** G8
Gasherbrum *Pakistan* 35°40N 76°40E **43** B7
Gashua *Nigeria* 12°54N 11°0E **53** F8
Gaspar Str. = Gelasa, Selat
 Indonesia 2°50S 107°0E **36** E3
Gasparillo *Trin. & Tob.* 10°18N 61°26W **93** K15
Gaspé *Canada* 48°52N 64°30W **73** C7
Gaspé, C. de *Canada* 48°48N 64°7W **73** C7
Gaspé Pen. = Gaspésie, Pén. de la
 Canada 48°45N 65°40W **73** C6
Gaspésie, Pén. de la
 Canada 48°45N 65°40W **73** C6
Gaspésie △ *Canada* 48°55N 66°10W **73** C6
Gasteiz = Vitoria-Gasteiz
 Spain 42°50N 2°41W **21** A4
Gastonia *U.S.A.* 35°16N 81°11W **85** D14
Gastre *Argentina* 42°20S 69°15W **96** E3
Gata, C. de *Spain* 36°41N 2°13W **21** D4
Gata, Sierra de *Spain* 40°20N 6°45W **21** B2
Gataga *→ Canada* 58°35N 126°59W **70** B3
Gatchina *Russia* 59°35N 30°9E **9** G24
Gatehouse of Fleet *U.K.* 54°53N 4°12W **11** G4
Gates *U.S.A.* 43°9N 77°42W **82** C7
Gateshead I. *Canada* 70°36N 100°26W **68** C11
Gatesville *U.S.A.* 31°26N 97°45W **84** F6
Gatineau *Canada* 45°29N 75°39W **83** A9
Gatineau *→ Canada* 45°27N 75°42W **72** C4
Gatineau △ *Canada* 45°40N 76°0W **72** C4
Gatton *Australia* 27°32S 152°17E **63** D5
Gatún, L. *Panama* 9°7N 79°56W **88** E4
Gatwick, London ✈ (LGW)
 U.K. 51°10N 0°11W **13** F7
Gatyana *S. Africa* 32°16S 28°31E **57** D4
Gau *Fiji* 18°2S 179°18E **59** a
Gauer L. *Canada* 57°0N 97°50W **71** B9
Gauhati = Guwahati
 India 26°10N 91°45E **41** F17
Gauja *→ Latvia* 57°10N 24°16E **9** H21
Gaujas △ *Latvia* 57°10N 24°50E **9** H21
Gaula *→ Norway* 63°21N 10°14E **8** E14
Gauri Phanta *India* 28°41N 80°36E **43** E9
Gauribidanur *India* 13°37N 77°32E **45** H3
Gaustatoppen *Norway* 59°48N 8°40E **9** G13
Gauteng □ *S. Africa* 26°0S 28°0E **57** C4
Gäv Koshī *Iran* 28°38N 57°12E **47** D8
Gāvakān *Iran* 29°37N 53°10E **47** D7
Gāvāter *Iran* 25°10N 61°31E **47** E9
Gāvbandī *Iran* 27°12N 53°4E **47** E7
Gavdos *Greece* 34°50N 24°5E **23** G11
Gaviota *U.S.A.* 34°29N 120°13W **79** L6
Gävkhūnī, Bāțlāq-e *Iran* 32°6N 52°52E **47** C7
Gävle *Sweden* 60°40N 17°9E **8** F17
Gawachab *Namibia* 27°4S 17°55E **56** C2
Gawilgarh Hills *India* 21°15N 76°45E **44** D3
Gawler *Australia* 34°30S 138°42E **63** E2
Gawler Ranges *Australia* 32°30S 135°45E **63** E2
Gaxun Nur *China* 42°22N 100°30E **30** C5
Gay *Russia* 51°27N 58°27E **18** D10
Gaya *India* 24°47N 85°4E **43** G11
Gaya *Niger* 11°52N 3°28E **52** F6
Gaylord *U.S.A.* 45°2N 84°41W **81** C11
Gayndah *Australia* 25°35S 151°32E **63** D5
Gaysin = Haysyn
 Ukraine 48°57N 29°25E **17** D15
Gayvoron = Hayvoron
 Ukraine 48°22N 29°52E **17** D15
Gaza *Gaza Strip* 31°30N 34°28E **48** D3
Gaza □ *Mozam.* 23°10S 32°45E **57** B5
Gaza Strip □ *Asia* 31°29N 34°25E **48** D3
Gazanjyk = Bereket
 Turkmenistan 39°16N 55°32E **47** B7
Gāzbor *Iran* 28°5N 58°51E **47** D8
Gaziantep *Turkey* 37°6N 37°23E **46** B3
Gazimağusa = Famagusta
 Cyprus 35°8N 33°55E **46** C2
Gbadolite
 Dem. Rep. of the Congo 4°17N 21°1E **54** D4
Gbarnga *Liberia* 7°19N 9°13W **52** G4
Gcoverega *Botswana* 19°8S 24°18E **56** A3
Gcuwa *S. Africa* 32°20S 28°11E **57** D4
Gdańsk *Poland* 54°22N 18°40E **17** A10
Gdansk B. = Gdańska, Zatoka
 Poland 54°30N 19°20E **17** A10
Gdańska, Zatoka *Poland* 54°30N 19°20E **17** A10
Gdov *Russia* 58°48N 27°55E **9** G22
Gdynia *Poland* 54°35N 18°33E **17** A10
Gebe *Indonesia* 0°5N 129°25E **37** D7
Gebze *Turkey* 40°47N 29°25E **23** D13
Gedaref *Sudan* 14°2N 35°28E **53** F13
Gede, Tanjung *Indonesia* 6°46S 105°12E **37** G11
Gediz *→ Turkey* 38°35N 26°48E **23** E12
Gedser *Denmark* 54°35N 11°55E **9** J14
Gedung, Pulau *Malaysia* 5°17N 100°23E **39** c
Geegully Cr. *→
 Australia* 18°32S 123°41E **60** C3
Geel *Belgium* 51°10N 4°59E **15** C4
Geelong *Australia* 38°10S 144°22E **63** F3
Geelvink B. = Cenderawasih,
 Teluk *Indonesia* 3°0S 135°20E **37** E9
Geelvink Chan. *Australia* 28°30S 114°0E **61** E1
Geesthacht *Germany* 53°26N 10°22E **16** B6
Geidam *Nigeria* 12°57N 11°57E **53** F8
Geikie *→ Canada* 57°45N 103°52W **71** B8
Geikie Gorge △ *Australia* 18°3S 125°41E **60** C4
Geistown *U.S.A.* 40°18N 78°52W **82** F6
Gejiu *China* 23°20N 103°10E **34** F4
Gel, Meydān-e *Iran* 29°4N 54°50E **47** D7
Gela *Italy* 37°4N 14°15E **22** F6
Gelang Patah *Malaysia* 1°27N 103°35E **39** d
Gelasa, Selat *Indonesia* 2°50S 107°0E **36** E3
Gelderland □ *Neths.* 52°5N 6°10E **15** B6
Geldrop *Neths.* 51°25N 5°32E **15** C5
Geleen *Neths.* 50°57N 5°49E **15** D5
Gelib = Jilib *Somalia* 0°29N 42°46E **49** G3
Gelibolu *Turkey* 40°28N 26°43E **23** D12
Gelsenkirchen *Germany* 51°32N 7°6E **16** C4
Gelugur *Malaysia* 5°22N 100°18E **39** c
Gemas *Malaysia* 2°37N 102°36E **39** L4
Gembloux *Belgium* 50°34N 4°43E **15** D4
Gemena
 Dem. Rep. of the Congo 3°13N 19°48E **54** D3
Gemerek *Turkey* 39°15N 36°10E **46** B3
Gemlik *Turkey* 40°26N 29°9E **23** D13
Gemsbok △ *Botswana* 25°5S 21°1E **56** C3
Genale *→ Ethiopia* 6°0N 39°30E
General Acha *Argentina* 37°20S 64°38W **94** D3
General Alvear *B. Aires,
 Argentina* 36°0S 60°0W **94** D4
General Alvear *Mendoza,
 Argentina* 35°0S 67°40W **94** D2
General Artigas
 Paraguay 26°52S 56°16W **94** B4
General Belgrano
 Argentina 36°35S 58°47W **94** D4
General Bernardo O'Higgins
 Antarctica 63°0S 58°3W **5** C18
General Cabrera
 Argentina 32°53S 63°52W **94** C3

General Carrera, L.
  S. Amer. 46°35S 72°0W **96 F2**
General Cepeda Mexico 25°21N 101°22W **86 B4**
General Guido Argentina 36°40S 57°50W **94 D4**
General Juan Madariaga
  Argentina 37°0S 57°0W **94 D4**
General La Madrid
  Argentina 37°17S 61°20W **94 D3**
General MacArthur
  Phil. 11°18N 125°28E **37 B7**
General Martin Miguel de Güemes
  Argentina 24°50S 65°0W **94 A3**
General Pico Argentina 35°45S 63°50W **94 D3**
General Pinedo Argentina 27°15S 61°20W **94 B3**
General Pinto Argentina 34°45S 61°50W **94 D3**
General Roca Argentina 39°2S 67°35W **96 D3**
General Santos Phil. 6°5N 125°14E **37 C7**
General Treviño Mexico 26°14N 99°29W **87 B5**
General Trías Mexico 28°21N 106°22W **86 B3**
General Viamonte
  Argentina 35°1S 61°3W **94 D3**
General Villegas Argentina 35°5S 63°0W **94 D3**
Genesee Idaho, U.S.A. 46°33N 116°56W **76 C5**
Genesee Pa., U.S.A. 41°59N 77°54W **82 E7**
Genesee → U.S.A. 43°16N 77°36W **82 C7**
Geneseo Ill., U.S.A. 41°27N 90°9W **80 E8**
Geneseo N.Y., U.S.A. 42°48N 77°49W **82 D7**
Geneva = Genève Switz. 46°12N 6°9E **20 C7**
Geneva Ala., U.S.A. 31°2N 85°52W **85 F12**
Geneva N.Y., U.S.A. 42°52N 76°59W **82 D8**
Geneva Nebr., U.S.A. 40°32N 97°36W **80 E6**
Geneva Ohio, U.S.A. 41°48N 80°57W **82 E4**
Geneva, L. = Léman, L.
  Europe 46°26N 6°30E **20 C7**
Genève Switz. 46°12N 6°9E **20 C7**
Gengma China 23°32N 99°20E **34 F2**
Genhe China 50°47N 121°31E **31 A13**
Genil → Spain 37°42N 5°19W **21 D3**
Genk Belgium 50°58N 5°32E **15 D5**
Gennargentu, Mti. del Italy 40°1N 9°19E **22 D3**
Genoa Australia 37°29S 149°35E **63 F4**
Genoa = Génova Italy 44°25N 8°57E **20 D8**
Genoa N.Y., U.S.A. 42°40N 76°32W **83 D8**
Genoa Nebr., U.S.A. 41°27N 97°44W **80 E5**
Genoa Nev., U.S.A. 39°2N 119°50W **78 F7**
Génova Italy 44°25N 8°57E **20 D8**
Génova, G. di Italy 44°0N 9°0E **22 C3**
Genriyetty, Ostrov
  Russia 77°6N 156°30E **27 B16**
Gent Belgium 51°2N 3°42E **15 C3**
Genteng Jawa Barat,
  Indonesia 7°22S 106°24E **37 G12**
Genteng Jawa Timur,
  Indonesia 8°22S 114°9E **37 J17**
Genyem Indonesia 2°46S 140°12E **37 E10**
Geochang S. Korea 35°41N 127°55E **33 G14**
Geographe B. Australia 33°30S 115°15E **61 F2**
Geographe Chan.
  Australia 24°30S 113°0E **61 D1**
Geoje S. Korea 34°51N 128°35E **33 G15**
Georga, Zemlya Russia 80°30N 49°0E **26 A5**
George S. Africa 33°58S 22°29E **56 D3**
George → Canada 58°49N 66°10W **73 A6**
George, L. N.S.W.,
  Australia 35°10S 149°25E **63 F4**
George, L. S. Austral.,
  Australia 37°25S 140°0E **63 F3**
George, L. W. Austral.,
  Australia 22°45S 123°40E **60 D3**
George, L. Fla., U.S.A. 29°17N 81°36W **85 G14**
George, L. N.Y., U.S.A. 43°37N 73°33W **83 C11**
George Bush Intercontinental,
  Houston ✈ (IAH)
  U.S.A. 29°59N 95°20W **84 G7**
George Gill Ra. Australia 24°22S 131°45E **60 D5**
George Pt. Australia 20°6S 148°36E **62 b**
George River = Kangiqsualujjuaq
  Canada 58°30N 65°59W **69 F18**
George Sound N.Z. 44°52S 167°25E **59 F1**
George Town Australia 41°6S 146°49E **63 G4**
George Town Bahamas 23°33N 75°47W **88 B4**
George Town Cayman Is. 19°20N 81°24W **88 C3**
George Town Malaysia 5°25N 100°20E **39 c**
George V Land Antarctica 69°0S 148°0E **5 C10**
George VI Sound Antarctica 71°0S 68°0W **5 D17**
George West U.S.A. 28°20N 98°7W **84 G5**
Georgetown = Janjanbureh
  Gambia 13°30N 14°47W **52 F3**
Georgetown Australia 18°17S 143°33E **62 B3**
Georgetown Ont., Canada 43°40N 79°56W **82 C5**
Georgetown P.E.I.,
  Canada 46°13N 62°24W **73 C7**
Georgetown Guyana 6°50N 58°12W **92 B7**
Georgetown Calif.,
  U.S.A. 38°54N 120°50W **78 G6**
Georgetown Colo.,
  U.S.A. 39°42N 105°42W **76 G11**
Georgetown Ky., U.S.A. 38°13N 84°33W **81 F11**
Georgetown N.Y., U.S.A. 42°46N 75°44W **83 D9**
Georgetown Ohio,
  U.S.A. 38°52N 83°54W **81 F12**
Georgetown S.C., U.S.A. 33°23N 79°17W **85 E15**
Georgetown Tex., U.S.A. 30°38N 97°41W **84 F6**
Georgia □ U.S.A. 32°50N 83°15W **85 E13**
Georgia ■ Asia 42°0N 43°0E **19 F7**
Georgia, Str. of N. Amer. 49°25N 124°0W **78 A3**
Georgia Basin S. Ocean 50°45S 35°30W **5 B1**
Georgian B. Canada 45°15N 81°0W **82 A4**
Georgian Bay Islands △
  Canada 44°53N 79°52W **82 B5**
Georgievka Kazakhstan 49°19N 84°34E **26 E9**
Georgina → Australia 23°30S 139°47E **62 C2**
Georgina I. Canada 44°22N 79°17W **82 B5**
Georgiyevsk Russia 44°12N 43°28E **19 F7**
Gera Germany 50°53N 12°4E **16 C7**
Geraardsbergen Belgium 50°45N 3°53E **15 D3**
Geral, Serra Brazil 26°25S 50°0W **95 B6**
Geral de Goiás, Serra Brazil 12°0S 46°0W **93 F9**
Geraldine U.S.A. 47°36N 110°16W **76 C8**
Geraldton Australia 28°48S 114°32E **61 E1**

Geraldton Canada 49°44N 87°10W **72 C2**
Gerdine, Mt. U.S.A. 61°35N 152°27W **74 C9**
Gereshk Afghan. 31°47N 64°35E **40 D4**
Gerik Malaysia 5°50N 101°15E **39 K3**
Gering U.S.A. 41°50N 103°40W **80 E2**
Gerlach U.S.A. 40°39N 119°21W **76 F4**
German Bight = Deutsche Bucht
  Germany 54°15N 8°0E **16 A5**
Germansen Landing
  Canada 55°43N 124°40W **70 B4**
Germantown U.S.A. 35°5N 89°49W **85 D10**
Germany ■ Europe 51°0N 10°0E **16 C6**
Germī Iran 39°1N 48°3E **47 B6**
Gernika-Lumo Spain 43°19N 2°40W **21 A4**
Gero Japan 35°48N 137°14E **29 G8**
Gerokgak Indonesia 8°11S 114°27E **37 J17**
Gerona = Girona Spain 41°58N 2°46E **21 B7**
Gerrard Canada 50°30N 117°17W **70 C5**
Gersoppa Falls India 14°12N 74°46E **45 G2**
Gertak Sanggul Malaysia 5°17N 100°12E **39 c**
Gertak Sanggul, Tanjung
  Malaysia 5°16N 100°11E **39 c**
Gerung Indonesia 8°43S 116°7E **37 K19**
Geser Indonesia 3°50S 130°54E **37 E8**
Gettysburg Pa., U.S.A. 39°50N 77°14W **81 F15**
Gettysburg S. Dak., U.S.A. 45°1N 99°57W **80 C4**
Getxo = Algorta Spain 43°21N 2°59W **21 A4**
Getz Ice Shelf Antarctica 75°0S 130°0W **5 D14**
Gevrai India 19°16N 75°45E **44 E2**
Geyser U.S.A. 47°16N 110°30W **76 C8**
Geyserville U.S.A. 38°42N 122°54W **78 G4**
Gezhouba Dam China 30°40N 111°20E **35 B8**
Ghadāf, W. al → Iraq 32°56N 43°30E **46 C4**
Ghadāmis Libya 30°11N 9°29E **53 B8**
Ghaggar → India 29°30N 74°53E **42 E6**
Ghaghara → India 25°45N 84°40E **43 G11**
Ghaghat → Bangla. 25°19N 89°38E **43 G13**
Ghagra India 23°17N 84°33E **43 H11**
Ghallamane Mauritania 23°15N 10°0W **52 D4**
Ghana ■ W. Afr. 8°0N 1°0W **52 G5**
Ghanpokhara Nepal 28°17N 84°14E **43 E11**
Ghansor India 22°39N 80°1E **43 H9**
Ghanzi Botswana 21°50S 21°34E **56 B3**
Ghanzi □ Botswana 22°30S 22°30E **56 B3**
Ghardaïa Algeria 32°20N 3°37E **52 B6**
Gharm Tajikistan 39°0N 70°20E **26 F8**
Gharyān Libya 32°10N 13°0E **53 B8**
Ghāt Libya 24°59N 10°11E **53 D8**
Ghatal India 22°40N 87°46E **43 H12**
Ghatampur India 26°8N 80°13E **43 F9**
Ghatgaon India 21°24N 85°53E **44 D7**
Ghatprabha → India 16°15N 75°20E **45 F2**
Ghats, Eastern India 14°0N 78°50E **45 H4**
Ghats, Western India 14°0N 75°0E **45 H2**
Ghatsila India 22°36N 86°29E **43 H12**
Ghaṭṭī Si. Arabia 31°16N 37°31E **46 D3**
Ghawdex = Gozo Malta 36°3N 14°15E **25 C1**
Ghazal, Bahr el → Chad 13°0N 15°47E **53 F9**
Ghazal, Bahr el →
  South Sudan 9°31N 30°25E **53 G12**
Ghaziabad India 28°42N 77°26E **42 E7**
Ghazipur India 25°38N 83°35E **43 G10**
Ghaznī Afghan. 33°30N 68°28E **42 C3**
Ghaznī □ Afghan. 32°10N 68°20E **40 C6**
Ghent = Gent Belgium 51°2N 3°42E **15 C3**
Gheorghe Gheorghiu-Dej = Onești
  Romania 46°17N 26°47E **17 E14**
Ghīnah, Wādī al →
  Si. Arabia 30°27N 38°14E **46 D3**
Ghizar → Pakistan 36°15N 73°43E **43 A5**
Ghod → India 18°30N 74°35E **44 F2**
Ghogha India 21°40N 72°20E **44 D1**
Ghotaru India 27°20N 70°1E **42 F4**
Ghotki Pakistan 28°5N 69°21E **42 E3**
Ghowr □ Afghan. 34°0N 64°20E **40 C4**
Ghughri India 22°39N 80°41E **43 H9**
Ghugus India 19°58N 79°12E **44 E4**
Ghulam Mohammad Barrage
  Pakistan 25°30N 68°20E **42 G3**
Ghūrīān Afghan. 34°17N 61°25E **40 B2**
Gia Dinh Vietnam 10°49N 106°42E **39 G6**
Gia Lai = Plei Ku Vietnam 13°57N 108°0E **38 F7**
Gia Nghia Vietnam 11°58N 107°42E **39 G6**
Gia Ngoc Vietnam 14°50N 108°58E **38 E7**
Gia Vuc Vietnam 14°42N 108°34E **38 E7**
Giamama = Jamaame
  Somalia 0°4N 42°44E **49 G3**
Gianitsa Greece 40°46N 22°24E **23 D10**
Giant Forest U.S.A. 36°36N 118°43W **78 J8**
Giant Sequoia △ U.S.A. 36°10N 118°35W **78 K8**
Giant's Causeway U.K. 55°16N 6°29W **10 A5**
Giant's Tank Sri Lanka 8°51N 80°2E **45 K5**
Gianyar Indonesia 8°32S 115°20E **37 K18**
Giarabub = Al Jaghbūb
  Libya 29°42N 24°38E **53 C10**
Giarre Italy 37°43N 15°11E **22 F6**
Gibara Cuba 21°9N 76°11W **88 B4**
Gibbon U.S.A. 40°45N 98°51W **80 E4**
Gibe II Ethiopia 8°0N 37°30E **49 F2**
Gibe III Ethiopia 7°0N 37°30E **49 F2**
Gibeon Namibia 25°9S 17°43E **56 C2**
Gibraltar ☑ Europe 36°7N 5°22W **21 D3**
Gibraltar, Str. of Medit. S. 35°55N 5°40W **21 E3**
Gibraltar Range △
  Australia 29°31S 152°19E **63 D5**
Gibson Desert Australia 24°0S 126°0E **60 D4**
Gibsons Canada 49°24N 123°32W **70 D4**
Gibsonville U.S.A. 39°46N 120°54W **78 F6**
Giddalur India 15°20N 78°57E **45 G4**
Giddings U.S.A. 30°11N 96°56W **84 F6**
Giebnegáisi = Kebnekaise
  Sweden 67°53N 18°33E **8 C18**
Giessen Germany 50°34N 8°41E **16 C5**
Gīfān Iran 37°54N 57°28E **47 B8**
Gift Lake Canada 55°53N 115°49W **70 B5**
Gifu Japan 35°30N 136°45E **29 G8**
Gifu □ Japan 35°40N 137°0E **29 G8**
Giganta, Sa. de la Mexico 26°0N 111°39W **86 B2**
Gigha U.K. 55°42N 5°44W **11 F3**
Giglio Italy 42°20N 10°52E **22 C4**

Gijón Spain 43°32N 5°42W **21 A3**
Gil I. Canada 53°12N 129°15W **70 C3**
Gila → U.S.A. 32°43N 114°33W **77 K6**
Gila Bend U.S.A. 32°57N 112°43W **77 K7**
Gila Bend Mts. U.S.A. 33°10N 113°0W **77 K7**
Gila Cliff Dwellings △
  U.S.A. 33°12N 108°16W **77 K9**
Gīlān □ Iran 37°0N 50°0E **47 B6**
Gilbert → Australia 16°35S 141°15E **62 B3**
Gilbert Is. Kiribati 1°0N 172°0E **58 A10**
Gilbert River Australia 18°9S 142°52E **62 B3**
Gilbert Seamounts
  Pac. Oc. 52°50N 150°10W **4 D18**
Gilead U.S.A. 44°24N 70°59W **83 B14**
Gilf el Kebir, Hadabat el
  Egypt 23°50N 25°50E **53 D11**
Gilford I. Canada 50°40N 126°30W **70 C3**
Gilgandra Australia 31°43S 148°39E **63 E4**
Gilgit India 35°50N 74°15E **43 B6**
Gilgit → Pakistan 35°44N 74°37E **43 B6**
Gilgit-Baltistan □ Pakistan 36°30N 73°0E **43 A5**
Gilimanuk Indonesia 8°10S 114°26E **37 J17**
Gillam Canada 56°20N 94°40W **71 B10**
Gillen, L. Australia 26°11S 124°38E **61 E3**
Gilles, L. Australia 32°50S 136°45E **63 E2**
Gillette U.S.A. 44°18N 105°30W **76 D11**
Gilliat Australia 20°40S 141°28E **62 C3**
Gillingham U.K. 51°23N 0°33E **13 F8**
Gilmer U.S.A. 32°44N 94°57W **84 E7**
Gilmore, L. Australia 32°29S 121°37E **61 F3**
Gilmour Canada 44°48N 77°37W **82 B7**
Gilroy U.S.A. 37°1N 121°34W **78 H5**
Gimcheon S. Korea 36°11N 128°4E **33 F15**
Gimhae S. Korea 35°14N 128°53E **33 G15**
Gimhwa S. Korea 38°17N 127°28E **33 E14**
Gimie, Mt. St. Lucia 13°54N 61°0W **89 f**
Gimje S. Korea 35°48N 126°45E **33 G14**
Gimli Canada 50°40N 97°0W **71 C9**
Gin → Sri Lanka 5°58N 80°7E **45 L5**
Gin Gin Australia 25°0S 151°58E **63 D5**
Gingee India 12°15N 79°25E **45 H4**
Gingin Australia 31°22S 115°54E **61 F2**
Gingindlovu S. Africa 29°2S 31°30E **57 C5**
Ginir Ethiopia 7°6N 40°40E **49 F3**
Giohar = Jawhar Somalia 2°48N 45°30E **49 G4**
Giona, Oros Greece 38°38N 22°14E **23 E10**
Gir → India 21°0N 71°0E **42 J4**
Gir Hills India 21°0N 71°0E **42 J4**
Girab India 26°2N 70°38E **42 F4**
Girâfi, W. → Egypt 29°58N 34°39E **48 F3**
Girard St. Lucia 13°59N 60°57W **89 D7**
Girard Kans., U.S.A. 37°31N 94°51W **80 G6**
Girard Ohio, U.S.A. 41°9N 80°42W **82 E4**
Girard Pa., U.S.A. 42°0N 80°19W **82 E4**
Girdle Ness U.K. 57°9N 2°3W **11 D6**
Giresun Turkey 40°55N 38°30E **19 F6**
Girga Egypt 26°17N 31°55E **53 C12**
Giri → India 30°28N 77°41E **42 D7**
Giridih India 24°10N 86°21E **43 G12**
Girne = Kyrenia Cyprus 35°20N 33°20E **46 C2**
Giron = Kiruna Sweden 67°52N 20°15E **8 C19**
Girona Spain 41°58N 2°46E **21 B7**
Gironde → France 45°32N 1°7W **20 D3**
Girraween △ Australia 28°46S 151°54E **63 D5**
Girringun △ Australia 18°15S 145°32E **62 B4**
Giru Australia 19°30S 147°5E **62 B4**
Girvan U.K. 55°14N 4°51W **11 F4**
Gisborne N.Z. 38°39S 178°5E **59 C7**
Gisenyi Rwanda 1°41S 29°15E **54 E5**
Gislaved Sweden 57°19N 13°32E **9 H15**
Gitega Burundi 3°26S 29°56E **54 E5**
Githio Greece 36°46N 22°34E **23 F10**
Giuba → Somalia 1°30N 42°35E **49 G3**
Giurgiu Romania 43°52N 25°57E **17 G13**
Giyani S. Africa 23°20N 30°43E **57 B5**
Gizab Afghan. 33°22N 66°17E **42 C1**
Gizhiga Russia 62°3N 160°30E **27 C17**
Gizhiginskaya Guba
  Russia 61°0N 158°0E **27 C16**
Giżycko Poland 54°2N 21°48E **17 A11**
Gjakovë Kosovo 42°22N 20°26E **23 C9**
Gjirokastër Albania 40°7N 20°10E **23 D9**
Gjoa Haven Canada 68°38N 95°53W **68 D12**
Gjøvik Norway 60°47N 10°43E **8 F14**
Glace Bay Canada 46°11N 59°58W **73 C8**
Glacier △ Canada 51°15N 117°30W **70 C5**
Glacier Bay U.S.A. 58°40N 136°0W **68 F4**
Glacier Bay △ U.S.A. 58°45N 136°30W **70 B1**
Glacier Peak U.S.A. 48°7N 121°7W **76 B3**
Gladewater U.S.A. 32°33N 94°56W **84 E7**
Gladstone Queens.,
  Australia 23°52S 151°16E **62 C5**
Gladstone S. Austral.,
  Australia 33°15S 138°22E **63 E2**
Gladstone Canada 50°13N 98°57W **71 C9**
Gladstone U.S.A. 45°51N 87°1W **80 C10**
Gladwin U.S.A. 43°59N 84°29W **81 D11**
Glagah Indonesia 8°13S 114°18E **37 J17**
Glâma = Glomma →
  Norway 59°12N 10°57E **9 G14**
Gláma Iceland 65°48N 23°0W **8 D2**
Glamis U.S.A. 32°55N 115°5W **79 N11**
Glamorgan, Vale of □
  U.K. 51°28N 3°25W **13 F4**
Glasco Kans., U.S.A. 39°22N 97°50W **80 F5**
Glasco N.Y., U.S.A. 42°3N 73°57W **83 D11**
Glasgow U.K. 55°51N 4°15W **11 F4**
Glasgow Ky., U.S.A. 37°0N 85°55W **81 G11**
Glasgow Mont., U.S.A. 48°12N 106°38W **76 B10**
Glasgow City □ U.K. 55°51N 4°12W **11 F4**
Glasgow Int. ✈ (GLA)
  U.K. 55°51N 4°21W **11 F4**
Glaslyn Canada 53°22N 108°21W **71 C7**
Glastonbury U.K. 51°9N 2°43W **13 F5**
Glastonbury U.S.A. 41°43N 72°37W **83 E12**
Glazov Russia 58°9N 52°40E **18 C9**
Gleichen Canada 50°52N 113°3W **70 C6**
Gleiwitz = Gliwice
  Poland 50°22N 18°41E **17 C10**

Glen U.S.A. 44°7N 71°11W **83 B13**
Glen Affric U.K. 57°17N 5°1W **11 D3**
Glen Canyon U.S.A. 37°30N 110°40W **77 H8**
Glen Canyon △ U.S.A. 37°15N 111°0W **77 H8**
Glen Canyon Dam
  U.S.A. 36°57N 111°29W **77 H8**
Glen Coe U.K. 56°40N 5°0W **11 E3**
Glen Cove U.S.A. 40°52N 73°38W **83 F11**
Glen Garry U.K. 57°3N 5°7W **11 D3**
Glen Innes Australia 29°44S 151°44E **63 D5**
Glen Lyon U.S.A. 41°10N 76°5W **83 E8**
Glen Mor U.K. 57°9N 4°37W **11 D4**
Glen Moriston U.K. 57°11N 4°52W **11 D4**
Glen Robertson Canada 45°22N 74°30W **83 A10**
Glen Spean U.K. 56°53N 4°40W **11 E4**
Glen Ullin U.S.A. 46°49N 101°50W **80 B3**
Glenamaddy Ireland 53°37N 8°33W **10 C3**
Glenbeigh Ireland 52°3N 9°58W **10 D2**
Glencoe Canada 42°45N 81°43W **82 D3**
Glencoe S. Africa 28°11S 30°11E **57 C5**
Glencoe U.S.A. 44°46N 94°9W **80 C6**
Glencolumbkille Ireland 54°43N 8°42W **10 B3**
Glendale U.S.A. 33°32N 112°11W **77 K7**
Glendive U.S.A. 47°7N 104°43W **76 C11**
Glendo U.S.A. 42°30N 105°2W **76 E11**
Gleneig → Australia 38°4S 140°59E **63 F3**
Glenfield U.S.A. 43°43N 75°24W **83 C9**
Glengad Hd. Ireland 55°20N 7°10W **10 A4**
Glengarriff Ireland 51°45N 9°34W **10 E2**
Glenmont U.S.A. 40°31N 82°6W **82 F2**
Glenmora U.S.A. 30°59N 92°35W **84 F8**
Glenmorgan Australia 27°14S 149°42E **63 D4**
Glenn U.S.A. 39°31N 122°1W **78 F4**
Glennallen U.S.A. 62°7N 145°33W **68 E2**
Glenns Ferry U.S.A. 42°57N 115°18W **76 E6**
Glenora Canada 44°2N 77°3W **82 B7**
Glenorchy Australia 42°49S 147°18E **63 G4**
Glenore Australia 17°50S 141°12E **62 B3**
Glenreagh Australia 30°2S 153°1E **63 E5**
Glenrock U.S.A. 42°52N 105°52W **76 E11**
Glenrothes U.K. 56°12N 3°10W **11 E5**
Glens Falls U.S.A. 43°19N 73°39W **83 C11**
Glenside U.S.A. 40°6N 75°9W **83 F9**
Glenties Ireland 54°48N 8°17W **10 B3**
Glenveagh △ Ireland 55°3N 8°1W **10 A3**
Glenville U.S.A. 38°56N 80°50W **81 F13**
Glenwood Canada 49°0N 54°58W **73 C9**
Glenwood Ark., U.S.A. 34°20N 93°33W **84 D8**
Glenwood Iowa, U.S.A. 41°3N 95°45W **80 E6**
Glenwood Minn., U.S.A. 45°39N 95°23W **80 C6**
Glenwood Wash., U.S.A. 46°1N 121°17W **78 D5**
Glenwood Springs
  U.S.A. 39°33N 107°19W **76 G10**
Glettinganes Iceland 65°30N 13°37W **8 D7**
Glin Ireland 52°34N 9°17W **10 D2**
Gliwice Poland 50°22N 18°41E **17 C10**
Globe U.S.A. 33°24N 110°47W **77 K8**
Głogów Poland 51°37N 16°5E **16 C9**
Glomma → Norway 59°12N 10°57E **9 G14**
Glorieuses, Îs. Ind. Oc. 11°30S 47°20E **55 G9**
Glossop U.K. 53°27N 1°56W **12 D6**
Gloucester Australia 32°0S 151°59E **63 E5**
Gloucester U.K. 51°53N 2°15W **13 F5**
Gloucester U.S.A. 42°37N 70°40W **83 D14**
Gloucester I. Australia 20°0S 148°30E **62 b**
Gloucester Island △
  Australia 20°0S 148°30E **62 b**
Gloucester Point U.S.A. 37°15N 76°30W **81 G15**
Gloucestershire □ U.K. 51°46N 2°15W **13 F5**
Gloversville U.S.A. 43°3N 74°21W **83 C10**
Glovertown Canada 48°40N 54°3W **73 C9**
Glusk Belarus 52°53N 28°41E **17 B15**
Glyn Ebwy = Ebbw Vale
  U.K. 51°46N 3°12W **13 F4**
Gmünd Austria 48°45N 15°0E **16 D8**
Gmunden Austria 47°55N 13°48E **16 E7**
Gniezno Poland 52°30N 17°35E **17 B9**
Gnowangerup Australia 33°58S 117°59E **61 F2**
Go Cong Vietnam 10°22N 106°40E **39 G6**
Goa India 15°33N 73°59E **45 G1**
Goa □ India 15°33N 73°59E **45 G1**
Goalen Hd. Australia 36°33S 150°4E **63 F5**
Goalpara India 26°10N 90°40E **41 F17**
Goaltor India 22°43N 87°10E **43 H12**
Goalundo Ghat Bangla. 23°50N 89°47E **43 H13**
Goat Fell U.K. 55°38N 5°11W **11 F3**
Goba Ethiopia 7°1N 39°59E **49 F2**
Goba Mozam. 26°15S 32°13E **57 D5**
Gobabis Namibia 22°30S 19°0E **56 B2**
Gobi Asia 44°0N 110°0E **32 C6**
Gobi Gurvan Saykhan △
  Mongolia 43°24N 101°24E **32 C2**
Gobichettipalayam India 11°31N 77°21E **45 J3**
Gobō Japan 33°53N 135°10E **29 H7**
Gochas Namibia 24°59S 18°55E **56 B2**
Godalming U.K. 51°11N 0°36W **13 F7**
Godavari → India 16°25N 82°18E **44 F6**
Godavari Pt. India 17°0N 82°20E **44 F6**
Godbout Canada 49°20N 67°38W **73 C6**
Godda India 24°50N 87°13E **43 G12**
Goderich Canada 43°45N 81°41W **82 C3**
Godfrey Ra. Australia 24°0S 117°0E **61 D2**
Godhavn = Qeqertarsuaq
  Greenland 69°15N 53°38W **4 C5**
Godhra India 22°49N 73°40E **42 H5**
Godoy Cruz Argentina 32°56S 68°52W **94 C2**
Gods → Canada 56°22N 92°51W **72 A1**
Gods L. Canada 54°40N 94°15W **72 B1**
Gods River Canada 54°50N 94°5W **71 C10**
Godthåb = Nuuk
  Greenland 64°10N 51°35W **67 C14**
Goeie Hoop, Kaap die = Good
  Hope, C. of S. Africa 34°24S 18°30E **56 D2**
Goéland, L. au Canada 49°50N 76°48W **72 C4**
Goélands, L. aux Canada 55°27N 64°17W **73 A7**
Goeree Neths. 51°50N 4°0E **15 C3**
Goes Neths. 51°30N 3°55E **15 C3**
Goffstown U.S.A. 43°1N 71°36W **83 C13**
Gogama Canada 47°35N 81°43W **72 C3**
Gogebic, L. U.S.A. 46°30N 89°35W **80 B9**

Gogra = Ghaghara →
  India 25°45N 84°40E **43 G11**
Gogrial South Sudan 8°30N 28°8E **53 G11**
Gohana India 29°8N 76°42E **42 E7**
Goharganj India 23°1N 77°41E **42 H7**
Goi → India 22°4N 74°46E **42 H6**
Goiabeiras Brazil 16°43S 49°20W **93 G9**
Goiânia Brazil 15°55S 50°10W **93 G8**
Goiás Brazil 12°10S 48°0W **93 F9**
Goiás □ Brazil 12°10S 48°0W **93 F9**
Goio-Erê Brazil 24°12S 53°1W **95 A5**
Gojō Japan 34°21N 135°42E **29 G7**
Gojra Pakistan 31°10N 72°40E **42 D5**
Gokak India 16°11N 74°52E **45 F2**
Gokarn India 14°33N 74°17E **45 G2**
Gökçeada Turkey 40°10N 25°50E **23 D11**
Gökova Körfezi Turkey 36°55N 27°50E **23 F12**
Göksu → Turkey 36°19N 34°5E **46 B2**
Göksun Turkey 22°26N 97°0E **41 H20**
Gokwe Zimbabwe 18°7S 28°58E **57 A4**
Gola India 28°3N 80°32E **43 E9**
Golakganj India 26°8N 89°52E **43 F13**
Golan Heights = Hagolan
  Syria 33°0N 35°45E **48 C4**
Golāshkerd Iran 27°59N 57°16E **47 E8**
Golconda India 17°24N 78°23E **44 F4**
Golconda U.S.A. 40°58N 117°30W **76 F5**
Gold U.S.A. 41°52N 77°50W **82 E7**
Gold Beach U.S.A. 42°25N 124°25W **76 E1**
Gold Coast W. Afr. 4°0N 1°40W **52 H5**
Gold Hill U.S.A. 42°26N 123°3W **76 E2**
Gold River Canada 49°46N 126°3W **70 D3**
Golden Canada 51°20N 116°59W **70 C5**
Golden B. N.Z. 40°40S 172°50E **59 D4**
Golden Gate Highlands △
  S. Africa 28°40S 28°40E **57 C4**
Golden Hinde Canada 49°40N 125°44W **70 D3**
Golden Lake Canada 45°34N 77°21W **82 A7**
Golden Rock India 10°45N 78°48E **45 J4**
Golden Spike △ U.S.A. 41°37N 112°33W **76 F7**
Golden Vale Ireland 52°33N 8°17W **10 D3**
Goldendale U.S.A. 45°49N 120°50W **76 D3**
Goldfield U.S.A. 37°42N 117°14W **77 H5**
Goldsand L. Canada 57°2N 101°8W **71 B8**
Goldsboro U.S.A. 35°23N 77°59W **85 D16**
Goldsmith U.S.A. 31°59N 102°37W **84 F3**
Goldthwaite U.S.A. 31°27N 98°34W **84 F5**
Goleniów Poland 53°35N 14°50E **16 B8**
Golestan □ Iran 37°20N 55°25E **47 B7**
Golestānak Iran 30°36N 54°14E **47 D7**
Goleta U.S.A. 34°27N 119°50W **79 L7**
Golfito Costa Rica 8°41N 83°5W **88 E3**
Golfo Aranci Italy 40°59N 9°38E **22 D3**
Golfo de Santa Clara
  Mexico 31°42N 114°30W **86 A2**
Goliad U.S.A. 28°40N 97°23W **84 G6**
Golmud China 36°25N 94°53E **30 D7**
Golpāyegān Iran 33°27N 50°18E **47 C6**
Golra Pakistan 33°37N 72°56E **42 C5**
Golspie U.K. 57°58N 3°59W **11 D5**
Goma Dem. Rep. of the Congo 1°37S 29°10E **54 E5**
Gomal Pass Pakistan 31°56N 69°20E **42 D3**
Gomati → India 25°32N 83°11E **43 G10**
Gombe Nigeria 10°19N 11°2E **53 F8**
Gomel = Homyel Belarus 52°28N 31°0E **17 B16**
Gomera Canary Is. 28°7N 17°14W **52 C2**
Gómez Palacio Mexico 25°34N 103°30W **86 B4**
Gomīshān Iran 37°4N 54°6E **47 B7**
Gomogomo Indonesia 6°39S 134°43E **37 F8**
Gomoh India 23°52N 86°10E **43 H12**
Gompa = Ganta Liberia 7°15N 8°59W **52 G4**
Gonābād Iran 34°15N 58°45E **47 C8**
Gonaïves Haiti 19°20N 72°42W **89 C5**
Gonâve, G. de la Haiti 19°29N 72°42W **89 C5**
Gonâve, Île de la Haiti 18°51N 73°3W **89 C5**
Gonbad-e Kāvūs Iran 37°20N 55°25E **47 B7**
Gonda India 27°9N 81°58E **43 F9**
Gondal India 21°58N 70°52E **42 J4**
Gonder Ethiopia 12°39N 37°30E **49 E2**
Gondia India 21°23N 80°10E **44 D5**
Gönen Turkey 40°6N 27°39E **23 D12**
Gong Xian China 28°23N 104°47E **34 C5**
Gong'an China 30°7N 112°12E **35 B9**
Gongbei China 22°12N 113°32E **31 a**
Gongchangling China 41°7N 123°27E **33 D12**
Gongga Shan China 29°40N 101°55E **34 C3**
Gonggar China 29°23N 91°7E **30 F7**
Gongguan China 21°48N 109°36E **34 G7**
Gonghe China 36°18N 100°32E **30 D9**
Gongju S. Korea 36°27N 127°7E **33 F14**
Gongola → Nigeria 9°30N 12°4E **53 G8**
Gongshan China 28°15N 98°58E **34 C2**
Gongtan China 28°55N 108°20E **34 C7**
Gongyi China 34°46N 112°58E **32 G7**
Gongzhuling China 43°30N 124°40E **33 C13**
Goniri Nigeria 11°30N 12°15E **53 F8**
Gonjo China 30°50N 98°17E **34 B2**
Gonzales Calif., U.S.A. 36°30N 121°26W **78 J5**
Gonzales Tex., U.S.A. 29°30N 97°27W **84 G6**
González Mexico 22°48N 98°25W **87 C5**
Good Hope, C. of S. Africa 34°24S 18°30E **56 D2**
Gooderham Canada 44°54N 78°21W **82 B6**
Goodhouse S. Africa 28°57S 18°13E **56 C2**
Gooding U.S.A. 42°56N 114°43W **76 E6**
Goodland U.S.A. 39°21N 101°43W **80 F3**
Goodlands Mauritius 20°2S 57°39E **55 d**
Goodlow Canada 56°20N 120°8W **70 B4**
Goodooga Australia 29°3S 147°28E **63 D4**
Goodsprings U.S.A. 35°49N 115°27W **79 K11**
Goole U.K. 53°42N 0°53W **12 D7**
Goolgowi Australia 33°58S 145°41E **63 E4**
Goomalling Australia 31°15S 116°49E **61 F2**
Goomeri Australia 26°12S 152°6E **63 D5**
Goondiwindi Australia 28°30S 150°21E **63 D5**
Goongarrie, L. Australia 30°3S 121°9E **61 F3**
Goongarrie △ Australia 30°7S 121°30E **61 F3**
Goonyella Australia 21°47S 147°58E **62 C4**

Goose → *Canada* 53°20N 60°35W **73** B7
Goose Creek *U.S.A.* 32°59N 80°2W **85** E14
Goose L. *U.S.A.* 41°56N 120°26W **76** F3
Gooty *India* 15°7N 77°41E **45** G3
Gop *India* 22°5N 69°50E **42** H3
Gopalganj *India* 26°28N 84°30E **43** F11
Göppingen *Germany* 48°42N 9°39E **16** D5
Gorakhpur *India* 26°47N 83°23E **43** F10
Goražde *Bos.-H.* 43°38N 18°58E **23** C8
Gorda, Pta. *U.S.A.* 14°20N 83°10W **88** D3
Gordan B. *Australia* 11°35S 130°10E **60** B5
Gordon *U.S.A.* 42°48N 102°12W **80** D2
Gordon → *Australia* 42°27S 145°30E **63** G4
Gordon Bay *Canada* 45°12N 79°57W **82** A5
Gordon L., *Alta., Canada* 56°30N 110°25W **71** B6
Gordon L. *N.W.T., Canada* 63°5N 113°11W **70** A6
Gordonvale *Australia* 17°5S 145°50E **62** B4
Goré *Chad* 7°59N 16°31E **53** G9
Gore *Ethiopia* 8°12N 35°32E **49** F2
Gore *N.Z.* 46°5S 168°58E **59** G2
Gore Bay *Canada* 45°57N 82°28W **72** C3
Gorey *Ireland* 52°41N 6°18W **10** D5
Gorg *Iran* 29°29N 59°43E **47** D8
Gorgān *Iran* 36°55N 54°30E **47** B7
Gorgona, I. *Colombia* 3°0N 78°10W **92** C3
Gorham *U.S.A.* 44°23N 71°10W **83** B13
Goribidnur = Gauribidanur
  India 13°37N 77°32E **45** H3
Goriganga → *India* 29°45N 80°23E **43** E9
Gorinchem *Neths.* 51°50N 4°59E **15** C4
Goris *Armenia* 39°31N 46°22E **25** G8
Gorizia *Italy* 45°56N 13°37E **22** B5
Gorkiy = Nizhniy Novgorod
  Russia 56°20N 44°0E **18** C7
Gorkovskoye Vdkhr.
  Russia 57°2N 43°4E **18** C7
Gorleston-on-Sea *U.K.* 52°35N 1°44E **13** E9
Görlitz *Germany* 51°9N 14°58E **16** C8
Gorlovka = Horlivka
  Ukraine 48°19N 38°5E **19** E6
Gorman *U.S.A.* 34°47N 118°51W **79** L8
Gorna Dzhumayo = Blagoevgrad
  Bulgaria 42°2N 23°5E **23** C10
Gorna Oryahovitsa
  Bulgaria 43°7N 25°40E **23** C11
Gorno-Altay □ *Russia* 51°0N 86°0E **26** D9
Gorno-Altaysk *Russia* 51°50N 86°5E **26** D9
Gornozavodsk *Russia* 46°33N 141°50E **27** E15
Gornyatski *Russia* 67°32N 64°3E **18** A11
Gornyy *Russia* 44°57N 133°59E **28** B6
Gorodenka = Horodenka
  Ukraine 48°41N 25°29E **17** D13
Gorodok = Horodok
  Ukraine 49°46N 23°32E **17** D12
Gorokhov = Horokhiv
  Ukraine 50°30N 24°45E **17** C13
Gorong, Kepulauan
  Indonesia 3°59S 131°25E **37** E8
Gorongose → *Mozam.* 20°30S 34°40E **57** B5
Gorongoza △ *Mozam.* 18°50S 34°29E **57** A5
Gorontalo *Indonesia* 0°35N 123°5E **37** D6
Gorontalo □ *Indonesia* 0°50N 122°20E **37** D6
Gort *Ireland* 53°3N 8°49W **10** C3
Gorumahisani *India* 22°20N 86°24E **44** C8
Goryeong *S. Korea* 35°44N 128°15E **33** G15
Gorzów Wielkopolski
  Poland 52°43N 15°15E **16** B8
Gosford *Australia* 33°23S 151°18E **63** E5
Goshen *Calif., U.S.A.* 36°21N 119°25W **78** J7
Goshen *Ind., U.S.A.* 41°35N 85°50W **81** E11
Goshen *N.Y., U.S.A.* 41°24N 74°20W **83** E10
Goshogawara *Japan* 40°48N 140°27E **28** D10
Goslar *Germany* 51°54N 10°25E **16** C6
Gospić *Croatia* 44°35N 15°23E **16** F8
Gosport *U.K.* 50°48N 1°9W **13** G6
Gosse → *Australia* 19°32S 134°37E **62** B1
Göta älv → *Sweden* 57°42N 11°54E **9** H14
Göta kanal *Sweden* 58°30N 15°58E **9** G16
Götaland *Sweden* 57°30N 14°30E **9** H16
Göteborg *Sweden* 57°43N 11°59E **9** H14
Gotha *Germany* 50°56N 10°42E **16** C6
Gothenburg = Göteborg
  Sweden 57°43N 11°59E **9** H14
Gothenburg *U.S.A.* 40°56N 100°10W **80** E3
Gotland *Sweden* 57°30N 18°33E **9** H18
Gotō = Fukue *Japan* 32°41N 128°51E **29** H4
Gotō-Rettō *Japan* 32°55N 129°5E **29** H4
Gotska Sandön *Sweden* 58°24N 19°15E **9** G18
Gōtsu *Japan* 35°0N 132°14E **29** G6
Göttingen *Germany* 51°31N 9°55E **16** C5
Gottwaldov = Zlín
  Czechia 49°14N 17°40E **17** D9
Goubangzi *China* 41°20N 121°52E **33** D11
Gouda *Neths.* 52°1N 4°42E **15** B4
Gouin, Rés. *Canada* 48°35N 74°40W **72** C5
Goulburn *Australia* 34°44S 149°44E **63** E4
Goulburn → *Australia* 36°36S 144°20E **63** F4
Goulburn Is. *Australia* 11°40S 133°20E **62** A1
Goundam *Mali* 16°27N 3°40W **52** E5
Gourits → *S. Africa* 34°21S 21°52E **56** D3
Gourock *U.K.* 55°57N 4°49W **11** F4
Gouverneur *U.S.A.* 44°20N 75°28W **83** B9
Gove Peninsula
  Australia 12°17S 136°49E **62** A2
Governador Valadares
  Brazil 18°15S 41°57W **93** G10
Governor's Harbour
  Bahamas 25°10N 76°14W **88** A4
Govindgarh *India* 24°23N 81°18E **43** G9
Gowan Ra. *Australia* 25°0S 145°0E **62** D4
Gowanda *U.S.A.* 42°28N 78°56W **82** D6
Gower *U.K.* 51°35N 4°10W **13** F3
Gowna, L. *Ireland* 53°51N 7°34W **10** C4
Goya *Argentina* 29°10S 59°10W **94** B4
Goyang *S. Korea* 37°39N 126°50E **33** F14
Goyder Lagoon *Australia* 27°3S 138°58E **63** D2
Goyllarisquizga *Peru* 10°31S 76°24W **92** F3
Goz Beïda *Chad* 12°10N 21°20E **53** F10
Gozo *Malta* 36°3N 14°15E **22** F6
Graaff-Reinet *S. Africa* 32°13S 24°32E **56** D3
Gračac *Croatia* 44°18N 15°57E **16** F8

Gracias a Dios, C.
  Honduras 15°0N 83°10W **88** D3
Graciosa *Azores* 39°4N 28°0W **52** a
Gradiška *Bos.-H.* 45°10N 17°15E **22** B7
Grado *Spain* 43°23N 6°4W **21** A2
Grady *U.S.A.* 34°49N 103°19W **77** J12
Grafham Water *U.K.* 52°19N 0°18W **13** E7
Grafton *Australia* 29°38S 152°58E **63** D5
Grafton *N. Dak., U.S.A.* 48°25N 97°25W **80** A5
Grafton *W. Va., U.S.A.* 39°21N 80°2W **81** F13
Graham *Canada* 49°20N 90°30W **72** C1
Graham *U.S.A.* 33°6N 98°35W **84** E5
Graham, Mt. *U.S.A.* 32°42N 109°52W **77** K9
Graham Bell, Ostrov = Greem-Bell,
  Ostrov *Russia* 81°0N 62°0E **26** A7
Graham I. *B.C., Canada* 53°40N 132°30W **70** C2
Graham I. *Nunavut,*
  Canada 77°25N 90°30W **69** B13
Graham Land *Antarctica* 65°0S 64°0W **5** C17
Grahamstown *S. Africa* 33°19S 26°31E **56** D4
Grahamsville *U.S.A.* 41°51N 74°33W **83** E10
Grain Coast *W. Afr.* 4°20N 10°0W **52** H3
Grajagan *Indonesia* 8°35S 114°13E **37** K17
Grajaú *Brazil* 5°50S 46°4W **93** E9
Grajaú → *Brazil* 3°41S 44°48W **93** D10
Grampian *U.S.A.* 40°58N 78°37W **82** F6
Grampian Highlands = Grampian
  Mts. *U.K.* 56°50N 4°0W **11** E5
Grampian Mts. *U.K.* 56°50N 4°0W **11** E5
Grampians, The
  Australia 37°15S 142°20E **63** F3
Gran Canaria *Canary Is.* 27°55N 15°35W **52** C2
Gran Chaco *S. Amer.* 25°0S 61°0W **94** B3
Gran Desierto del Pinacate
  Mexico 31°51N 113°32W **86** A2
Gran Paradiso *Italy* 45°33N 7°17E **20** D7
Gran Sasso d'Itália *Italy* 42°27N 13°42E **22** C5
Granada *Nic.* 11°58N 86°0W **88** D2
Granada *Spain* 37°10N 3°35W **21** D4
Granada *U.S.A.* 38°4N 102°19W **76** G12
Granard *Ireland* 53°47N 7°30W **10** C4
Granbury *U.S.A.* 32°27N 97°47W **84** E6
Granby *Canada* 45°25N 72°45W **83** A12
Granby *U.S.A.* 40°5N 105°56W **76** F11
Grand → *Canada* 42°51N 79°34W **82** D5
Grand → *Mo., U.S.A.* 39°23N 93°7W **80** F7
Grand → *S. Dak., U.S.A.* 45°40N 100°45W **80** C3
Grand-Anse = Portsmouth
  Dominica 15°34N 61°27W **89** C7
Grand Bahama I.
  Bahamas 26°40N 78°30W **88** A4
Grand Baie *Mauritius* 20°0S 57°35E **55** d
Grand Bank *Canada* 47°6N 55°48W **73** C8
Grand Bassam *Côte d'Ivoire* 5°10N 3°49W **52** G5
Grand Bend *Canada* 43°18N 81°45W **82** C3
Grand-Bourg *Guadeloupe* 15°53N 61°19W **88** b
Grand Canal = Da Yunhe →
  China 34°25N 120°5E **33** H10
Grand Canyon *U.S.A.* 36°3N 112°9W **77** H7
Grand Canyon △
  U.S.A. 36°15N 112°30W **77** H7
Grand Canyon-Parashant △
  U.S.A. 36°30N 113°45W **77** H7
Grand Cayman
  Cayman Is. 19°20N 81°20W **88** C3
Grand Coulee *U.S.A.* 47°57N 119°0W **76** C4
Grand Coulee Dam
  U.S.A. 47°57N 118°59W **76** C4
Grand Falls *Canada* 47°3N 67°44W **73** C6
Grand Falls-Windsor
  Canada 48°56N 55°40W **73** C8
Grand Forks *Canada* 49°0N 118°30W **70** D5
Grand Forks *U.S.A.* 47°55N 97°3W **80** B5
Grand Gorge *U.S.A.* 42°21N 74°29W **83** D10
Grand Haven *U.S.A.* 43°4N 86°13W **80** D10
Grand I. *Mich., U.S.A.* 46°31N 86°40W **80** B10
Grand I. *N.Y., U.S.A.* 43°0N 78°58W **82** D6
Grand Island *U.S.A.* 40°55N 98°21W **80** E4
Grand Isle *La., U.S.A.* 29°14N 90°0W **85** G9
Grand Isle *Vt., U.S.A.* 44°43N 73°18W **83** B11
Grand Junction *U.S.A.* 39°4N 108°33W **76** G9
Grand L. *N.B., Canada* 45°57N 66°7W **73** C6
Grand L. *Nfld. & L., Canada* 49°0N 57°30W **73** C8
Grand L. *Nfld. & L.,*
  Canada 53°40N 60°30W **73** B7
Grand L. *U.S.A.* 29°55N 92°47W **84** G8
Grand Lake *U.S.A.* 40°15N 105°49W **76** F11
Grand Manan I. *Canada* 44°45N 66°52W **73** D6
Grand Marais *Mich.,*
  U.S.A. 46°40N 85°59W **81** B11
Grand Marais *Minn.,*
  U.S.A. 47°45N 90°25W **72** C1
Grand-Mère *Canada* 46°36N 72°40W **72** C5
Grand Portage *U.S.A.* 47°58N 89°41W **80** B9
Grand Rapids *Canada* 53°12N 99°19W **71** C9
Grand Rapids *Mich.,*
  U.S.A. 42°58N 85°40W **81** D11
Grand Rapids *Minn.,*
  U.S.A. 47°14N 93°31W **80** B7
Grand St-Bernard, Col du
  Europe 45°50N 7°10E **20** D7
Grand Staircase-Escalante △
  U.S.A. 37°25N 111°33W **77** H8
Grand Teton *U.S.A.* 43°54N 110°50W **76** E8
Grand Teton △ *U.S.A.* 43°50N 110°50W **76** E8
Grand Union Canal *U.K.* 52°7N 0°53W **13** E7
Grande → *Jujuy, Argentina* 24°20S 65°2W **94** A2
Grande → *Mendoza,*
  Argentina 36°52S 69°45W **94** D2
Grande → *Bolivia* 15°51S 64°39W **92** G6
Grande → *Bahia, Brazil* 11°30S 44°30W **93** F10
Grande → *Minas Gerais,*
  Brazil 20°6S 51°4W **93** H8
Grande, B. *Argentina* 50°30S 68°20W **96** G3
Grande, Rio → *N. Amer.* 25°58N 97°9W **84** J6
Grande Anse *Seychelles* 4°18S 55°45E **55** b
Grande Baleine →
  Canada 55°16N 77°47W **72** A4
Grande Cache *Canada* 53°53N 119°8W **70** C5
Grande Comore
  Comoros Is. 11°35S 43°20E **55** a

Grande-Entrée *Canada* 47°30N 61°40W **73** C7
Grande Prairie *Canada* 55°10N 118°50W **70** B5
Grande-Rivière *Canada* 48°26N 64°30W **73** C7
Grande-Terre *Guadeloupe* 16°20N 61°25W **88** b
Grande Vigie, Pte. de la
  Guadeloupe 16°32N 61°27W **88** b
Grande-Vallée *Canada* 49°14N 65°8W **73** C6
Grandfalls *U.S.A.* 31°20N 102°51W **84** F3
Grands-Jardins △
  Canada 47°41N 70°51W **73** C5
Grandview *Canada* 51°10N 100°42W **71** C8
Grandview *U.S.A.* 46°15N 119°54W **76** C4
Graneros *Chile* 34°5S 70°45W **94** C1
Grangemouth *U.K.* 56°1N 3°42W **11** E5
Granger *U.S.A.* 41°35N 109°58W **76** F9
Grangeville *U.S.A.* 45°56N 116°7W **76** D5
Granisle *Canada* 54°53N 126°13W **70** C3
Granite City *U.S.A.* 38°42N 90°8W **80** F8
Granite Falls *U.S.A.* 44°49N 95°33W **80** C6
Granite L. *Canada* 48°8N 57°5W **73** C8
Granite Mt. *U.S.A.* 33°5N 116°28W **79** M10
Granite Pk. *U.S.A.* 45°10N 109°48W **76** D9
Graniteville *U.S.A.* 44°8N 72°29W **83** B12
Granity *N.Z.* 41°39S 171°51E **59** D3
Granja *Brazil* 3°7S 40°50W **93** D10
Granollers *Spain* 41°39N 2°18E **21** B7
Grant *U.S.A.* 40°50N 101°43W **80** E3
Grant, Mt. *U.S.A.* 38°34N 118°48W **76** G4
Grant City *U.S.A.* 40°29N 94°25W **80** E6
Grant I. *Australia* 11°10S 132°52E **60** B5
Grant Range *U.S.A.* 38°30N 115°25W **76** G6
Grantham *U.K.* 52°55N 0°38W **12** E7
Grantown-on-Spey *U.K.* 57°20N 3°36W **11** D5
Grants *U.S.A.* 35°9N 107°52W **77** J10
Grants Pass *U.S.A.* 42°26N 123°19W **76** E2
Grantsville *U.S.A.* 40°36N 112°28W **76** F7
Granville *France* 48°50N 1°35W **20** B3
Granville *N. Dak., U.S.A.* 48°16N 100°47W **80** A3
Granville *N.Y., U.S.A.* 43°24N 73°16W **83** C11
Granville *Ohio, U.S.A.* 40°4N 82°31W **82** F2
Granville L. *Canada* 56°18N 100°30W **71** B8
Graskop *S. Africa* 24°56S 30°49E **57** B5
Grass → *Canada* 56°3N 96°33W **71** B9
Grass Range *U.S.A.* 47°2N 108°48W **76** C9
Grass River △ *Canada* 54°40N 100°50W **71** C8
Grass Valley *Calif., U.S.A.* 39°13N 121°4W **78** F6
Grass Valley *Oreg.,*
  U.S.A. 45°22N 120°47W **76** D3
Grasse *France* 43°38N 6°56E **20** E7
Grassflat *U.S.A.* 41°0N 78°6W **82** E6
Grasslands △ *Canada* 49°11N 107°38W **71** D7
Grassy *Australia* 40°3S 144°5E **63** G3
Graulhet *France* 43°45N 1°59E **20** E4
Gravelbourg *Canada* 49°50N 106°35W **71** D7
's-Gravenhage *Neths.* 52°7N 4°17E **15** B4
Gravenhurst *Canada* 44°52N 79°20W **82** B5
Gravesend *Australia* 29°35S 150°20E **63** D5
Gravesend *U.K.* 51°26N 0°22E **13** F8
Gravois, Pointe-à- *Haiti* 18°2N 73°56W **89** C5
Grayling *U.S.A.* 44°40N 84°43W **81** C11
Grays *U.K.* 51°28N 0°21E **13** F8
Grays Harbor *U.S.A.* 46°59N 124°1W **78** D2
Grays L. *U.S.A.* 43°4N 111°26W **76** E8
Grays River *U.S.A.* 46°21N 123°37W **78** D3
Graz *Austria* 47°4N 15°27E **16** E8
Greasy L. *Canada* 62°55N 122°12W **70** A4
Great Abaco I. = Abaco I.
  Bahamas 26°25N 77°10W **88** A4
Great Artesian Basin
  Australia 23°0S 144°0E **62** C3
Great Australian Bight
  Australia 33°30S 130°0E **61** F5
Great Bahama Bank
  Bahamas 23°15N 78°0W **88** B4
Great Barrier I. *N.Z.* 36°11S 175°25E **59** B5
Great Barrier Reef
  Australia 18°0S 146°50E **62** B4
Great Barrier Reef △
  Australia 20°0S 150°0E **62** B4
Great Barrington
  U.S.A. 42°12N 73°22W **83** D11
Great Basalt Wall △
  Australia 19°52S 145°43E **62** B4
Great Basin *U.S.A.* 40°0N 117°0W **76** G5
Great Basin △ *U.S.A.* 38°56N 114°15W **76** G6
Great Basses *Sri Lanka* 6°11N 81°29E **45** L5
Great Bear → *Canada* 65°0N 126°0W **68** C7
Great Bear L. *Canada* 65°30N 120°0W **68** C8
Great Belt = Store Bælt
  Denmark 55°20N 11°0E **9** J14
Great Bend *Kans., U.S.A.* 38°22N 98°46W **80** F4
Great Bend *Pa., U.S.A.* 41°58N 75°45W **83** E9
Great Blasket I. *Ireland* 52°6N 10°32W **10** D1
Great Britain *Europe* 54°0N 2°15W **6** E5
Great Camanoe
  Br. Virgin Is. 18°30N 64°35W **89** e
Great Channel *Asia* 6°0N 94°0E **45** L11
Great Coco I. = Koko Kyunzu
  Myanmar 14°7N 93°22E **45** G11
Great Codroy *Canada* 47°51N 59°16W **73** C8
Great Divide, The = Great Dividing
  Ra. *Australia* 23°0S 146°0E **62** C4
Great Divide Basin *U.S.A.* 42°0N 108°0W **76** E9
Great Dividing Ra.
  Australia 23°0S 146°0E **62** C4
Great Driffield = Driffield
  U.K. 54°0N 0°26W **12** C7
Great Exuma I. *Bahamas* 23°30N 75°50W **88** B4
Great Falls *U.S.A.* 47°30N 111°17W **76** C8
Great Fish = Groot-Vis →
  S. Africa 33°28S 27°5E **56** D4
Great Guana Cay
  Bahamas 24°0N 76°20W **88** B4
Great Himalayan △ *India* 31°30N 77°30E **42** D7
Great Inagua I. *Bahamas* 21°0N 73°20W **89** B5
Great Indian Desert = Thar Desert
  India 28°0N 72°0E **42** F5
Great Karoo *S. Africa* 31°55S 21°0E **56** D3
Great Khingan Mts. = Da Hinggan
  Ling *China* 48°0N 121°0E **31** B13

Great Lake *Australia* 41°50S 146°40E **63** G4
Great Lakes *N. Amer.* 46°0N 84°0W **66** E11
Great Limpopo Transfrontier △
  Africa 23°0S 31°45E **57** B5
Great Malvern *U.K.* 52°7N 2°18W **13** E5
Great Miami → *U.S.A.* 39°7N 84°49W **81** F11
Great Nicobar *India* 7°0N 93°50E **45** L11
Great Ormes Head *U.K.* 53°20N 3°52W **12** D4
Great Ouse → *U.K.* 52°48N 0°21E **12** E8
Great Palm I. *Australia* 18°45S 146°40E **62** B4
Great Pedro Bluff *Jamaica* 17°51N 77°44W **88** a
Great Pee Dee →
  U.S.A. 33°21N 79°10W **85** E15
Great Plains *N. Amer.* 47°0N 105°0W **66** E9
Great Ruaha → *Tanzania* 7°56S 37°52E **54** F7
Great Sacandaga L.
  U.S.A. 43°6N 74°16W **83** C10
Great Saint Bernard Pass = Grand
  St-Bernard, Col du
  Europe 45°50N 7°10E **20** D7
Great Salt Desert = Kavīr, Dasht-e
  Iran 34°30N 55°0E **47** C7
Great Salt L. *U.S.A.* 41°15N 112°40W **76** F7
Great Salt Lake Desert
  U.S.A. 40°50N 113°30W **76** F7
Great Salt Plains L. *U.S.A.* 36°45N 98°8W **84** C5
Great Sand Dunes △
  U.S.A. 37°48N 105°45W **77** H11
Great Sandy △ *Australia* 26°13S 153°2E **63** D5
Great Sandy Desert
  Australia 21°0S 124°0E **60** D3
Great Sangi = Sangihe, Pulau
  Indonesia 3°35N 125°30E **37** D7
Great Sea Reef *Fiji* 16°15S 179°0E **59** a
Great Sitkin I. *U.S.A.* 52°3N 176°6W **74** E4
Great Skellig *Ireland* 51°47N 10°33W **10** E1
Great Slave L. *Canada* 61°23N 115°38W **70** A5
Great Smoky Mts. △
  U.S.A. 35°40N 83°40W **85** D13
Great Stour = Stour →
  U.K. 51°18N 1°22E **13** F9
Great Victoria Desert
  Australia 29°30S 126°30E **61** E4
Great Wall *Antarctica* 62°30S 58°0W **5** C18
Great Wall *China* 38°30N 109°30E **32** E5
Great Whernside *U.K.* 54°10N 1°58W **12** C6
Great Yarmouth *U.K.* 52°37N 1°44E **13** E9
Great Zab = Zāb al Kabīr →
  Iraq 36°1N 43°24E **46** B4
Greater Antilles *W. Indies* 17°40N 74°0W **89** C5
Greater London □ *U.K.* 51°31N 0°6W **13** F7
Greater Manchester □
  U.K. 53°30N 2°15W **12** D5
Greater Sudbury *Canada* 46°30N 81°0W **72** C3
Greater Sunda Is. *Indonesia* 7°0S 112°0E **36** F4
Gredos, Sierra de *Spain* 40°20N 5°0W **21** B3
Greece *U.S.A.* 43°13N 77°41W **82** C7
Greece ■ *Europe* 40°0N 23°0E **23** E9
Greeley *Colo., U.S.A.* 40°25N 104°42W **76** F11
Greeley *Nebr., U.S.A.* 41°33N 98°32W **80** E4
Greely Fd. *Canada* 80°30N 85°0W **69** A15
Greem-Bell, Ostrov *Russia* 81°0N 62°0E **26** A7
Green → *Ky., U.S.A.* 37°54N 87°30W **80** G10
Green → *Utah, U.S.A.* 38°11N 109°53W **76** G9
Green B. *U.S.A.* 45°0N 87°30W **80** C10
Green Bay *U.S.A.* 44°31N 88°0W **80** C9
Green C. *Australia* 37°13S 150°1E **63** F5
Green Cove Springs
  U.S.A. 29°59N 81°42W **85** G14
Green I. = Lütao
  Taiwan 22°40N 121°30E **35** F13
Green Lake *Canada* 54°17N 107°47W **71** C7
Green Mts. *U.S.A.* 43°45N 72°45W **83** C12
Green River *Utah,*
  U.S.A. 38°59N 110°10W **76** G8
Green River *Wyo.,*
  U.S.A. 41°32N 109°28W **76** F9
Green Valley *U.S.A.* 31°52N 110°56W **77** L8
Greenbank *U.S.A.* 48°6N 122°34W **78** B4
Greenbush *Mich., U.S.A.* 44°35N 83°19W **82** B1
Greenbush *Minn., U.S.A.* 48°42N 96°11W **80** A5
Greencastle *U.S.A.* 39°38N 86°52W **80** F10
Greene *U.S.A.* 42°20N 75°46W **83** D9
Greeneville *U.S.A.* 36°10N 82°50W **85** C13
Greenfield *Calif., U.S.A.* 36°19N 121°15W **78** J5
Greenfield *Calif., U.S.A.* 35°15N 119°0W **79** K8
Greenfield *Ind., U.S.A.* 39°47N 85°46W **81** F11
Greenfield *Iowa, U.S.A.* 41°18N 94°28W **80** E6
Greenfield *Mass., U.S.A.* 42°35N 72°36W **83** D12
Greenfield *Mo., U.S.A.* 37°25N 93°51W **80** G7
Greenland ☑ *N. Amer.* 66°0N 45°0W **67** C15
Greenland Sea *Arctic* 73°0N 10°0W **4** B7
Greenock *U.K.* 55°57N 4°46W **11** F4
Greenore *Ireland* 54°1N 6°9W **10** B5
Greenore Pt. *Ireland* 52°14N 6°19W **10** D5
Greenough *Australia* 28°58S 114°43E **61** E1
Greenough → *Australia* 28°51S 114°38E **61** E1
Greenough Pt. *Canada* 44°58N 81°26W **82** B3
Greenport *U.S.A.* 41°6N 72°22W **83** E12
Greensboro *Ga., U.S.A.* 33°35N 83°11W **85** E13
Greensboro *N.C., U.S.A.* 36°4N 79°48W **85** C15
Greensboro *Vt., U.S.A.* 44°36N 72°18W **83** B12
Greensburg *Ind., U.S.A.* 39°20N 85°29W **81** F11
Greensburg *Kans., U.S.A.* 37°36N 99°18W **80** G4
Greensburg *Pa., U.S.A.* 40°18N 79°33W **82** F5
Greenstone = Geraldton
  Canada 49°44N 87°10W **72** C2
Greenstone Pt. *U.K.* 57°55N 5°37W **11** D3
Greenvale *Australia* 18°59S 145°7E **62** B4
Greenville *Liberia* 5°1N 9°6E **52** H4
Greenville *Ala., U.S.A.* 31°50N 86°38W **85** F11
Greenville *Calif., U.S.A.* 40°8N 120°57W **78** E6
Greenville *Mich., U.S.A.* 43°11N 85°15W **81** D11
Greenville *Miss., U.S.A.* 33°24N 91°4W **85** E9
Greenville *Mo., U.S.A.* 37°8N 90°27W **80** G8
Greenville *N.C., U.S.A.* 35°37N 77°23W **85** D16
Greenville *N.H., U.S.A.* 42°46N 71°49W **83** D13
Greenville *N.Y., U.S.A.* 42°25N 74°1W **83** D10
Greenville *Ohio, U.S.A.* 40°6N 84°38W **81** E11

Greenville *Pa., U.S.A.* 41°24N 80°23W **82** E4
Greenville *S.C., U.S.A.* 34°51N 82°24W **85** D13
Greenville *Tex., U.S.A.* 33°8N 96°7W **84** E6
Greenwater Lake △
  Canada 52°32N 103°30W **71** C8
Greenwich *Conn., U.S.A.* 41°2N 73°38W **83** E11
Greenwich *N.Y., U.S.A.* 43°5N 73°30W **83** C11
Greenwich *Ohio, U.S.A.* 41°2N 82°31W **82** E2
Greenwood *Canada* 49°10N 118°40W **70** D5
Greenwood *Ark., U.S.A.* 35°13N 94°16W **84** D7
Greenwood *Ind., U.S.A.* 39°37N 86°7W **80** F10
Greenwood *Miss., U.S.A.* 33°31N 90°11W **85** E9
Greenwood *S.C., U.S.A.* 34°12N 82°10W **85** D13
Greenwood, Mt. *Australia* 13°48S 130°4E **60** B5
Gregory *U.S.A.* 43°14N 99°26W **80** D4
Gregory → *Australia* 17°53S 139°17E **62** B2
Gregory, L. *S. Austral.,*
  Australia 28°55S 139°0E **63** D2
Gregory, L. *W. Austral.,*
  Australia 20°0S 127°40E **60** D4
Gregory, L. *W. Austral.,*
  Australia 25°38S 119°58E **61** E2
Gregory △ *Australia* 15°38S 131°15E **60** C5
Gregory Downs
  Australia 18°35S 138°45E **62** B2
Gregory Ra. *Queens.,*
  Australia 19°30S 143°40E **62** B3
Gregory Ra. *W. Austral.,*
  Australia 21°20S 121°12E **60** D3
Greifswald *Germany* 54°5N 13°23E **16** A7
Greiz *Germany* 50°39N 12°10E **16** C7
Gremikha *Russia* 67°59N 39°47E **18** A6
Grenaa *Denmark* 56°25N 10°53E **9** H14
Grenada *U.S.A.* 33°47N 89°49W **85** E10
Grenada ■ *W. Indies* 12°10N 61°40W **89** D7
Grenadier I. *U.S.A.* 44°3N 76°22W **83** B8
Grenadines, The
  St. Vincent 12°40N 61°20W **89** D7
Grenen *Denmark* 57°44N 10°40E **9** H14
Grenfell *Australia* 33°52S 148°8E **63** E4
Grenfell *Canada* 50°30N 102°56W **71** C8
Grenoble *France* 45°12N 5°42E **20** D6
Grenville, C. *Australia* 12°0S 143°13E **62** A3
Grenville Chan. *Canada* 53°40N 129°46W **70** C3
Gresham *U.S.A.* 45°30N 122°25W **78** E4
Gresik *Indonesia* 7°13S 112°38E **37** G15
Gretna *U.K.* 55°0N 3°3W **11** F5
Grevenmacher *Lux.* 49°41N 6°26E **15** E6
Grey → *N.Z.* 42°27S 171°12E **59** E3
Grey, C. *Australia* 13°0S 136°35E **62** A2
Grey Is. *Canada* 50°50N 55°35W **69** G20
Grey Ra. *Australia* 27°0S 143°30E **63** D3
Greybull *U.S.A.* 44°30N 108°3W **76** D9
Greymouth *N.Z.* 42°29S 171°13E **59** E3
Greystones *Ireland* 53°9N 6°5W **10** C5
Greytown *N.Z.* 41°5S 175°29E **59** D5
Greytown *S. Africa* 29°1S 30°36E **57** C5
Gribbell I. *Canada* 53°23N 129°0W **70** C3
Gridley *U.S.A.* 39°22N 121°42W **78** F5
Griekwastad *S. Africa* 28°49S 23°15E **56** D3
Griffin *U.S.A.* 33°15N 84°16W **85** E12
Griffith *Australia* 34°18S 146°2E **63** E4
Griffith *Canada* 45°15N 77°10W **82** A7
Griffith I. *Canada* 44°50N 80°55W **82** B4
Grimailov = Hrymayliv
  Ukraine 49°20N 26°5E **17** D14
Grimes *U.S.A.* 39°4N 121°54W **78** F5
Grimsby *Canada* 43°12N 79°34W **82** C5
Grimsby *U.K.* 53°34N 0°5W **12** D7
Grímsey *Iceland* 66°33N 17°58W **8** C5
Grimshaw *Canada* 56°10N 117°40W **70** B5
Grimstad *Norway* 58°20N 8°35E **9** G13
Grindstone I. *U.S.A.* 44°17N 76°27W **83** B8
Grinnell *U.S.A.* 41°45N 92°43W **80** E7
Grinnell Pen. *Canada* 76°40N 95°0W **69** B13
Griomasaigh = Grimsay
  U.K. 57°29N 7°14W **11** D1
Gris-Nez, C. *France* 50°52N 1°35E **20** A4
Grise Fiord *Canada* 76°25N 82°57W **69** B15
Groais I. *Canada* 50°55N 55°35W **73** B8
Groblersdal *S. Africa* 25°15S 29°25E **57** C4
Grodno = Hrodna
  Belarus 53°42N 23°52E **17** B12
Grodzyanka = Hrodzyanka
  Belarus 53°31N 28°42E **17** B15
Groesbeck *U.S.A.* 31°31N 96°32W **84** F6
Grójec *Poland* 51°50N 20°58E **17** C11
Grong *Norway* 64°25N 12°8E **8** D15
Groningen *Neths.* 53°15N 6°35E **15** A6
Groningen □ *Neths.* 53°16N 6°40E **15** A6
Groom *U.S.A.* 35°12N 101°6W **84** D4
Groot → *S. Africa* 33°45S 24°36E **56** D3
Groot-Berg → *S. Africa* 32°47S 18°8E **56** E2
Groot-Brakrivier *S. Africa* 34°2S 22°18E **56** D3
Groot Karasberge
  Namibia 27°20S 18°40E **56** C2
Groot-Kei → *S. Africa* 32°41S 28°22E **57** D4
Groot-Vis → *S. Africa* 33°28S 27°5E **56** D4
Grootdrink *S. Africa* 28°33S 21°42E **56** D3
Groote Eylandt *Australia* 14°0S 136°40E **62** A2
Groote Peel △ *Neths.* 51°22N 5°49E **15** C5
Grootfontein *Namibia* 19°31S 18°6E **56** A2
Grootlaagte → *Africa* 20°55S 21°27E **56** A3
Grootvloer → *S. Africa* 30°0S 20°40E **56** D3
Gros C. *Canada* 61°59N 113°32W **70** A6
Gros Islet *St. Lucia* 14°5N 60°58W **89** f
Gros Morne → *Canada* 49°40N 57°50W **73** C8
Gros Piton *St. Lucia* 13°49N 61°5W **89** f
Gros Piton Pt. *St. Lucia* 13°49N 61°5W **89** f
Grosse Point *U.S.A.* 42°23N 82°54W **82** D2
Grosser Arber *Germany* 49°6N 13°8E **16** D7
Grosseto *Italy* 42°46N 11°8E **22** C4
Grossglockner *Austria* 47°5N 12°40E **16** E7
Groswater B. *Canada* 54°20N 57°40W **73** B8
Groton *Conn., U.S.A.* 41°21N 72°5W **83** E12
Groton *N.Y., U.S.A.* 42°36N 76°22W **83** D8
Groton *S. Dak., U.S.A.* 45°27N 98°6W **80** C4
Grouard Mission *Canada* 55°33N 116°9W **70** B5

Groulx, Mts. Canada 51°27N 68°41W 73 B6
Groundhog → Canada 48°45N 82°58W 72 C3
Grouw Neths. 53°5N 5°51E 15 A5
Grove City U.S.A. 41°10N 80°5W 82 E4
Grove Hill U.S.A. 31°42N 87°47W 85 F11
Groveland U.S.A. 37°50N 120°14W 78 H6
Grover Beach U.S.A. 35°7N 120°37W 79 K6
Groves U.S.A. 29°57N 93°54W 84 G8
Groveton U.S.A. 44°36N 71°31W 83 B13
Grovetown U.S.A. 33°27N 82°12W 85 E13
Groznyy Russia 43°20N 45°45E 19 F8
Grudziądz Poland 53°30N 18°47E 17 B10
Gruinard B. U.K. 57°56N 5°35W 11 D3
Grundy Center U.S.A. 42°22N 92°47W 80 D7
Gruver U.S.A. 36°16N 101°24W 84 C4
Gryazi Russia 52°30N 39°58E 18 D6
Gryazovets Russia 58°50N 40°10E 18 C7
Grytviken S. Georgia 54°19S 36°33E 96 G9
Gua India 22°18N 85°20E 43 H11
Guacanayabo, G. de Cuba 20°40N 77°20W 88 B4
Guachipas → Argentina 25°40S 65°30W 94 B2
Guadalajara Mexico 20°40N 103°20W 86 C4
Guadalajara Spain 40°37N 3°12W 21 B4
Guadalaviar = Turia → Spain 39°27N 0°19W 21 C5
Guadalcanal Solomon Is. 9°32S 160°12E 58 B9
Guadales Argentina 34°30S 67°55W 94 C2
Guadalete → Spain 36°35N 6°13W 21 D2
Guadalquivir → Spain 36°47N 6°22W 21 D2
Guadalupe = Guadeloupe ☑ W. Indies 16°15N 61°40W 88 b
Guadalupe Mexico 22°45N 102°31W 86 C4
Guadalupe U.S.A. 34°58N 120°34W 79 L6
Guadalupe → U.S.A. 28°27N 96°47W 84 G6
Guadalupe, Sierra de Spain 39°28N 5°30W 21 C3
Guadalupe de Bravo Mexico 31°23N 106°7W 86 A3
Guadalupe I. Pac. Oc. 29°0N 118°50W 66 G8
Guadalupe Mts. △ U.S.A. 31°40N 104°30W 84 F2
Guadalupe Peak U.S.A. 31°50N 104°52W 84 F2
Guadalupe y Calvo Mexico 26°6N 106°58W 86 B3
Guadarrama, Sierra de Spain 41°0N 4°0W 21 B4
Guadeloupe ☑ W. Indies 16°15N 61°40W 88 b
Guadeloupe △ Guadeloupe 16°10N 61°40W 88 b
Guadeloupe Passage W. Indies 16°50N 62°15W 89 C7
Guadiana → Portugal 37°14N 7°22W 21 D2
Guadix Spain 37°18N 3°11W 21 D4
Guafo, Boca del Chile 43°35S 74°0W 96 E2
Guàhàn = Guam ☑ Pac. Oc. 13°27N 144°45E 64 F6
Guaico Trin. & Tob. 10°35N 61°9W 93 K15
Guainía → Colombia 2°1N 67°7W 92 C5
Guaíra Brazil 24°5S 54°10W 95 A5
Guaíra □ Paraguay 25°45S 56°30W 94 B4
Guaire = Gorey Ireland 52°41N 6°18W 10 D5
Guaitecas, Is. Chile 44°0S 74°30W 96 E2
Guajará-Mirim Brazil 10°50S 65°20W 92 F5
Guajira, Pen. de la Colombia 12°0N 72°0W 92 A4
Gualán Guatemala 15°8N 89°22W 88 C2
Gualeguay Argentina 33°10S 59°14W 94 C4
Gualeguaychú Argentina 33°3S 59°31W 94 C4
Gualequay → Argentina 33°19S 59°39W 94 C4
Guam ☑ Pac. Oc. 13°27N 144°45E 64 F6
Guamini Argentina 37°1S 62°28W 94 D3
Guamúchil Mexico 25°28N 108°6W 86 B3
Guana I. Br. Virgin Is. 18°30N 64°30W 89 e
Guanabacoa Cuba 23°8N 82°18W 88 B3
Guanacaste, Cordillera de Costa Rica 10°40N 85°4W 88 D2
Guanacaste △ Costa Rica 10°57N 85°30W 88 D2
Guanacevi Mexico 25°56N 105°57W 86 B3
Guanahani = San Salvador I. Bahamas 24°0N 74°30W 89 B5
Guanaja Honduras 16°30N 85°55W 88 C2
Guanajay Cuba 22°56N 82°42W 88 B3
Guanajuato Mexico 21°1N 101°15W 86 C4
Guanajuato □ Mexico 21°0N 101°0W 86 C4
Guandacol Argentina 29°30S 68°40W 94 B2
Guandi Shan China 37°53N 111°29E 32 F6
Guane Cuba 22°10N 84°7W 88 B3
Guang'an China 30°28N 106°35E 34 B6
Guangchang China 26°50N 116°21E 35 D11
Guangde China 30°54N 119°25E 35 B12
Guangdong □ China 23°0N 113°0E 35 F9
Guangfeng China 28°20N 118°15E 35 C12
Guanghan China 30°58N 104°17E 34 B5
Guangling China 39°47N 114°22E 32 E8
Guangnan China 24°5N 105°4E 34 E5
Guangning China 23°40N 112°22E 35 F9
Guangrao China 37°5N 118°25E 33 F10
Guangshui China 31°37N 114°0E 35 B10
Guangshun China 26°8N 106°21E 34 D6
Guangwu China 37°48N 105°57E 32 F3
Guangxi Zhuangzu Zizhiqu □ China 24°0N 109°0E 34 F7
Guangyuan China 32°26N 105°31E 34 A5
Guangze China 27°30N 117°12E 35 D11
Guanica Puerto Rico 17°58N 66°55W 89 d
Guanipa → Venezuela 9°56N 62°26W 92 B6
Guanling China 25°56N 105°35E 34 E5
Guannan China 34°8N 119°21E 33 G10
Guantánamo Cuba 20°10N 75°14W 89 B4
Guantánamo B. Cuba 19°59N 75°10W 89 C4
Guantao China 36°42N 115°25E 32 F8
Guanting Shuiku China 40°14N 115°35E 32 D8
Guanyang China 25°30N 111°18E 35 E8
Guanyun China 34°20N 119°18E 33 G10
Guapay = Grande → Bolivia 15°51S 64°39W 92 G6
Guápiles Costa Rica 10°10N 83°46W 88 D3
Guapo B. Trin. & Tob. 10°12N 61°41W 93 K15
Guaporé Brazil 28°51S 51°54W 95 B5

Guaporé → Brazil 11°55S 65°4W 92 F5
Guaqui Bolivia 16°41S 68°54W 92 G5
Guaramacal △ Venezuela 9°13N 70°12W 89 E5
Guarapari Brazil 20°40S 40°30W 95 A7
Guarapuava Brazil 25°20S 51°30W 95 B5
Guaratinguetá Brazil 22°49S 45°9W 95 A6
Guaratuba Brazil 25°53S 48°38W 95 B6
Guarda Portugal 40°32N 7°20W 21 B2
Guardafui, C. = Asir, Ras Somalia 11°55N 51°10E 49 E5
Guárico □ Venezuela 8°40N 66°35W 92 B5
Guarujá Brazil 24°2S 46°25W 95 A6
Guarulhos Brazil 23°29S 46°33W 95 A6
Guasave Mexico 25°34N 108°27W 86 B3
Guasdualito Venezuela 7°15N 70°44W 92 B4
Guatemala Guatemala 14°40N 90°22W 88 D1
Guatemala ■ Cent. Amer. 15°40N 90°30W 88 C1
Guatemala Basin Pac. Oc. 11°0N 95°0W 65 F18
Guatemala Trench Pac. Oc. 14°0N 95°0W 66 H10
Guatopo △ Venezuela 10°5N 66°30W 89 D6
Guatuaro Pt. Trin. & Tob. 10°19N 60°59W 93 K16
Guaviare → Colombia 4°3N 67°44W 92 C5
Guaxupé Brazil 21°10S 47°5W 95 A6
Guayaguayare Trin. & Tob. 10°8N 61°2W 93 K15
Guayama Puerto Rico 17°59N 66°7W 89 d
Guayaquil Ecuador 2°15S 79°52W 92 D3
Guayaquil Mexico 29°59N 115°4W 86 B1
Guayaquil, G. de Ecuador 3°10S 81°0W 92 D2
Guaymas Mexico 27°56N 110°54W 86 B2
Gubbi India 13°19N 76°56E 45 H3
Gubin Russia 51°17N 37°32E 19 D6
Gubkin Russia 51°17N 37°32E 19 D6
Gubkinskiy Russia 64°27N 76°36E 26 C8
Gucheng China 32°20N 111°30E 35 A8
Gudalur India 11°30N 76°29E 45 J3
Gudbrandsdalen Norway 61°33N 10°10E 8 F14
Guddu Barrage Pakistan 28°30N 69°50E 42 E3
Gudivada India 16°30N 81°3E 45 F5
Gudiyattam India 12°57N 78°55E 45 H4
Gudur India 14°12N 79°55E 45 G4
Guecho = Algorta Spain 43°21N 2°59W 21 A4
Guékédou Guinea 8°40N 10°5W 52 G3
Guelmim Morocco 28°56N 10°0W 52 C3
Guelph Canada 43°35N 80°20W 82 C4
Guéret France 46°11N 1°51E 20 C4
Guerneville U.S.A. 38°30N 123°0W 78 G4
Guernica = Gernika-Lumo Spain 43°19N 2°40W 21 A4
Guernsey U.K. 49°26N 2°35W 13 H5
Guernsey U.S.A. 42°16N 104°45W 76 E11
Guerrara Algeria 32°51N 4°22E 52 B6
Guerrero □ Mexico 17°40N 100°0W 87 D5
Gügher Iran 29°28N 56°27E 47 D8
Gui Jiang → China 23°30N 111°15E 35 F8
Guia Lopes da Laguna Brazil 21°26S 56°7W 95 A4
Guiana Highlands S. Amer. 5°10N 60°40W 90 C4
Guichi China 30°39N 117°27E 35 B11
Guiding China 26°34N 107°11E 34 D6
Guidong China 26°7N 113°57E 35 D9
Guidónia-Montecélio Italy 42°1N 12°45E 22 C5
Guigang China 23°8N 109°35E 34 F7
Guijá Mozam. 24°27S 33°0E 57 B5
Guildford U.K. 51°14N 0°34W 13 F7
Guilford U.S.A. 41°17N 72°41W 83 E12
Guilin China 25°18N 110°15E 35 E8
Guillaume-Delisle, L. Canada 56°15N 76°17W 72 A4
Guimarães Portugal 41°28N 8°24W 21 B1
Guimaras □ Phil. 10°35N 122°37E 37 B6
Guinda U.S.A. 38°50N 122°12W 78 G4
Guinea Africa 8°0N 8°0E 50 F4
Guinea ■ W. Afr. 10°20N 11°30W 52 F3
Guinea, Gulf of Atl. Oc. 3°0N 2°30E 51 F4
Guinea-Bissau ■ Africa 12°0N 15°0W 52 F3
Güines Cuba 22°50N 82°0W 88 B3
Guingamp France 48°34N 3°10W 20 B2
Guiping China 23°21N 110°2E 35 F8
Güiria Venezuela 10°32N 62°18W 93 K14
Guiuan Phil. 11°5N 125°55E 37 B7
Guixi China 28°16N 117°15E 35 C11
Guiyang Guizhou, China 26°32N 106°40E 34 D6
Guiyang Hunan, China 25°46N 112°42E 35 E9
Guizhou □ China 27°0N 107°0E 34 D6
Gujar Khan Pakistan 33°16N 73°19E 42 C5
Gujarat □ India 23°20N 71°0E 42 H4
Gujiang China 27°11N 114°47E 35 D10
Gujiao China 37°54N 112°8E 32 F7
Gujō Japan 35°45N 136°57E 29 G8
Gujranwala Pakistan 32°10N 74°12E 42 C6
Gujrat Pakistan 32°40N 74°2E 42 C6
Gulbarga = Kalaburagi India 17°20N 76°50E 44 F3
Gulbene Latvia 57°8N 26°52E 9 H22
Guledagudda India 16°3N 75°48E 45 F2
Gulf, The = Persian Gulf Asia 27°0N 50°0E 47 E6
Gulfport U.S.A. 30°22N 89°6W 85 F10
Gulgong Australia 32°20S 149°49E 63 E4
Gulian China 52°56N 122°21E 31 A13
Gulin China 28°1N 105°50E 34 C5
Gulistan Pakistan 30°30N 66°35E 42 D2
Gulja = Yining China 43°58N 81°10E 30 C5
Gull Lake Canada 50°10N 108°29W 71 C7
Güllük Turkey 37°14N 27°35E 23 F12
Gulmarg India 34°3N 74°25E 43 B6
Gülshat Kazakhstan 46°45N 74°25E 28 E8
Gulu Uganda 2°48N 32°17E 54 D6
Gumal → Pakistan 31°40N 71°50E 42 D4
Gumbaz Pakistan 30°2N 69°0E 42 D3
Gumel Nigeria 12°39N 9°22E 52 F7
Gumla India 23°3N 84°33E 43 H11
Gumlu Australia 19°53S 147°41E 62 B4
Gumzai Indonesia 5°28S 134°42E 37 F8
Guna India 24°40N 77°19E 42 G7

Gunbalanya Australia 12°20S 133°4E 60 B5
Gundabooka △ Australia 30°30S 145°20E 63 E4
Gundarehi India 20°57N 81°17E 44 D5
Gundlakamma → India 15°30N 80°15E 45 G5
Gundlupet India 11°48N 76°41E 45 J3
Gunisao → Canada 53°56N 97°53W 71 C9
Gunisao L. Canada 53°33N 96°15W 71 C9
Gunjyal Pakistan 32°20N 71°55E 42 C4
Gunma □ Japan 36°30N 138°20E 29 F9
Gunnbjørn Fjeld Greenland 68°55N 29°47W 4 C6
Gunnedah Australia 30°59S 150°15E 63 E5
Gunnewin Australia 25°59S 148°33E 63 D4
Gunningbar Cr. → Australia 31°14S 147°6E 63 E4
Gunnison Colo., U.S.A. 38°33N 106°56W 76 G10
Gunnison Utah, U.S.A. 39°9N 111°49W 76 G8
Gunnison → U.S.A. 39°4N 108°35W 76 G9
Gunsan S. Korea 35°59N 126°45E 33 G14
Guntakal India 15°11N 77°27E 45 G3
Gunter Canada 44°52N 77°32W 82 B7
Guntersville U.S.A. 34°21N 86°18W 85 D11
Guntong Malaysia 4°36N 101°3E 39 K3
Guntur India 16°23N 80°30E 45 F5
Gunung Ciremay △ Indonesia 6°53S 108°24E 37 G13
Gunungapi Indonesia 6°45S 126°30E 37 F7
Gunungsitoli Indonesia 1°15N 97°30E 36 D1
Gunupur India 19°5N 83°50E 44 E6
Gunza Angola 10°50S 13°50E 54 G2
Guo He → China 32°59N 117°10E 33 H9
Guoyang China 33°32N 116°12E 32 H9
Gupis Pakistan 36°15N 73°20E 43 A5
Gurbantünggüt Shamo China 45°8N 87°20E 30 B6
Gurdaspur India 32°5N 75°31E 42 C6
Gurdon U.S.A. 33°55N 93°9W 84 E8
Gurgaon = Gurugram India 28°27N 77°1E 42 E7
Gurgueia → Brazil 6°50S 43°24W 93 E10
Gurha India 25°12N 71°39E 42 G4
Guri, Embalse de Venezuela 7°50N 62°52W 92 B6
Gurkha Nepal 28°5N 84°40E 43 E11
Gurla Mandhata = Naimona'nyi Feng China 30°26N 81°18E 43 D9
Gurley Australia 29°45S 149°48E 63 D4
Gurnet Point U.S.A. 42°1N 70°34W 83 D14
Gurugram India 28°27N 77°1E 42 E7
Gurun Malaysia 5°49N 100°27E 39 K3
Gürün Turkey 38°43N 37°15E 19 G6
Gurupá Brazil 1°25S 51°35W 93 D8
Gurupá, I. Grande de Brazil 1°25S 51°45W 93 D8
Gurupi Brazil 11°43S 49°4W 93 F9
Gurupi → Brazil 1°13S 46°6W 93 D9
Guruwe Zimbabwe 16°40S 30°42E 57 A5
Gurvan Sayhan Uul Mongolia 43°50N 104°0E 32 C3
Guryev = Atyraū Kazakhstan 47°5N 52°0E 19 E9
Gusau Nigeria 12°12N 6°40E 52 F7
Gushan China 39°50N 123°35E 33 E12
Gushgy = Serhetabat Turkmenistan 35°20N 62°18E 47 C9
Gushi China 32°11N 115°41E 35 A10
Gusinoozersk Russia 51°16N 106°27E 27 D11
Gustavus U.S.A. 58°25N 135°44W 70 B1
Gustine U.S.A. 37°16N 121°0W 78 H6
Güstrow Germany 53°47N 12°10E 16 B7
Gütersloh Germany 51°54N 8°24E 16 C5
Gutha Australia 28°58S 115°55E 61 E2
Guthalungra Australia 19°52S 147°50E 62 B4
Guthrie Canada 44°28N 79°32W 82 B5
Guthrie Okla., U.S.A. 35°53N 97°25W 84 H6
Guthrie Tex., U.S.A. 33°37N 100°19W 84 J4
Gutian China 26°32N 118°43E 35 D12
Guttenberg U.S.A. 42°47N 91°6W 80 D8
Gutu Zimbabwe 19°41S 31°9E 57 A5
Guwahati India 26°10N 91°45E 41 F17
Guy Fawkes River △ Australia 30°0S 152°20E 63 D5
Guyana ■ S. Amer. 5°0N 59°0W 92 C7
Guyane française = French Guiana ☑ S. Amer. 4°0N 53°0W 93 C8
Guyang China 41°0N 110°5E 32 D6
Guyenne France 44°30N 0°40E 20 D4
Guymon U.S.A. 36°41N 101°29W 84 C4
Guyra Australia 30°15S 151°40E 63 E5
Guyuan Hebei, China 41°37N 115°40E 32 D8
Guyuan Ningxia Huizu, China 36°0N 106°20E 32 F4
Güzelyurt = Morphou Cyprus 35°12N 32°59E 46 C2
Guzhang China 28°42N 109°58E 34 C7
Guzhen China 33°22N 117°18E 33 H9
Guzmán, L. de Mexico 31°20N 107°30W 86 A3
Gwa Myanmar 17°36N 94°34E 41 L19
Gwabegar Australia 30°37S 148°59E 63 E4
Gwädar Pakistan 25°10N 62°18E 40 G3
Gwaii Haanas △ Canada 52°21N 131°26W 70 C2
Gwalior India 26°12N 78°10E 42 F8
Gwanda Zimbabwe 20°55S 29°0E 55 H5
Gwangju S. Korea 35°9N 126°54E 33 G14
Gwangyang S. Korea 34°56N 127°41E 33 G14
Gwanju = Gwangju S. Korea 35°9N 126°54E 33 G14
Gweebarra B. Ireland 54°51N 8°23W 10 B3
Gweedore Ireland 55°3N 8°14W 10 A3
Gweru Zimbabwe 19°28S 29°45E 55 H5
Gwinn U.S.A. 46°19N 87°27W 80 B10
Gwydir → Australia 29°27S 149°48E 63 D4
Gwynedd □ U.K. 52°52N 4°10W 12 E3
Gyandzha = Gäncä Azerbaijan 40°45N 46°20E 19 F8
Gyaring Hu China 34°50N 97°40E 30 E8
Gydanskiy Poluostrov Russia 70°0N 78°0E 26 B8

Gyeonggi-man S. Korea 37°0N 125°30E 33 F13
Gyeongju S. Korea 35°51N 129°14E 33 G15
Gympie Australia 26°11S 152°38E 63 D5
Gyöngyös Hungary 47°48N 19°56E 17 E10
Győr Hungary 47°41N 17°40E 17 E9
Gypsum Pt. Canada 61°53N 114°35W 70 A6
Gypsumville Canada 51°45N 98°40W 71 C9
Gyula Hungary 46°38N 21°17E 17 E11
Gyumri Armenia 40°47N 43°50E 19 F7
Gyzylarbat = Serdar Turkmenistan 39°4N 56°23E 47 B8
Gyzyletrek = Etrek Turkmenistan 37°36N 54°46E 47 B7

H

Ha 'Arava → Israel 30°50N 35°20E 48 E4
Ha Coi Vietnam 21°26N 107°46E 34 G6
Ha Dong Vietnam 20°58N 105°46E 34 G5
Ha Giang Vietnam 22°50N 104°59E 34 F5
Ha Karmel, Har Israel 32°44N 35°3E 48 C4
Ha Karmel △ Israel 32°45N 35°5E 48 C4
Ha Long = Hong Gai Vietnam 20°57N 107°5E 34 G6
Ha Long, Vinh Vietnam 20°56N 107°3E 38 B6
Ha Tien Vietnam 10°23N 104°29E 39 G5
Ha Tinh Vietnam 18°20N 105°54E 38 C5
Ha Trung Vietnam 19°58N 105°50E 38 C5
Haaksbergen Neths. 52°9N 6°45E 15 B6
Ha'ano Tonga 19°41S 174°18W 59 c
Ha'apai Group Tonga 19°47S 174°27W 59 c
Haapiti Moorea 17°34S 149°52W 59 d
Haapsalu Estonia 58°56N 23°30E 9 G20
Haarlem Neths. 52°23N 4°39E 15 B4
Haast → N.Z. 43°50S 169°2E 59 E2
Haasts Bluff Australia 23°22S 132°0E 60 D5
Haasts Bluff ۞ Australia 23°39S 130°34E 60 D5
Hab → Pakistan 24°53N 66°41E 42 G3
Hab Nadi Chauki Pakistan 25°0N 66°50E 42 G2
Habaswein Kenya 1°2N 39°30E 54 B4
Habay Canada 58°50N 118°44W 70 B5
Habirag China 42°17N 115°42E 32 C8
Haboro Japan 44°22N 141°42E 28 B10
Habshān U.A.E. 23°50N 53°37E 47 F7
Hachijō-Jima Japan 33°5N 139°45E 29 H9
Hachinohe Japan 40°30N 141°29E 28 D10
Hachiōji Japan 35°40N 139°20E 29 G9
Hackettstown U.S.A. 40°51N 74°50W 83 F10
Hadali Pakistan 32°16N 72°11E 42 C5
Hadarba, Ras Sudan 22°4N 36°51E 53 D13
Hadarom □ Israel 31°0N 35°0E 48 E4
Hadd, Ra's al Oman 22°35N 59°50E 49 C6
Haddington U.K. 55°57N 2°47W 11 F6
Hadejia Nigeria 12°30N 10°5E 52 F7
Hadera Israel 32°27N 34°55E 48 C3
Hadera, N. → Israel 32°28N 34°52E 48 C3
Haderslev Denmark 55°15N 9°30E 9 J13
Hadgaon India 19°36N 77°44E 44 E3
Hadhramaut = Ḥaḍramawt □ Yemen 15°30N 49°30E 49 D4
Hadīboh Yemen 12°39N 54°2E 49 E5
Hadley B. Canada 72°31N 108°12W 68 C10
Hadong S. Korea 35°5N 127°44E 33 G14
Ḥaḍramawt □ Yemen 15°30N 49°30E 49 D4
Ḥadrāniyah Iraq 35°38N 43°14E 46 C4
Hadrian's Wall U.K. 55°0N 2°30W 12 B5
Hae, Ko Thailand 7°44N 98°22E 39 a
Haeju N. Korea 38°3N 125°45E 33 E13
Hä'ena Hawai'i 22°14N 159°34W 75 L8
Haenam S. Korea 34°34N 126°35E 33 G14
Haenertsburg S. Africa 24°0S 29°50E 57 B4
Haerhpin = Harbin China 45°48N 126°40E 33 B14
Hafar al Bāţin Si. Arabia 28°32N 45°52E 46 D5
Hafirat al 'Aydā Si. Arabia 26°26N 39°12E 46 E3
Hafit Oman 23°59N 55°49E 47 F7
Hafizabad Pakistan 32°5N 73°40E 42 C5
Haflong India 25°10N 93°5E 41 G18
Haft Gel Iran 31°30N 49°32E 47 D6
Hagalil Israel 32°53N 35°18E 48 C4
Hagari → India 15°30N 76°45E 45 G3
Hagemeister I. U.S.A. 58°39N 160°54W 74 D7
Hagen Germany 51°21N 7°27E 16 C4
Hagerman U.S.A. 33°7N 104°20W 77 K11
Hagerman Fossil Beds △ U.S.A. 42°48N 114°57W 76 E6
Hagerstown U.S.A. 39°39N 77°43W 81 F15
Hagersville Canada 42°58N 80°3W 82 D4
Hagfors Sweden 60°3N 13°45E 9 F15
Hagi Japan 34°30N 131°22E 29 G5
Hagolan Syria 33°0N 35°45E 48 C4
Hagondange France 49°16N 6°11E 20 B7
Hags Hd. Ireland 52°57N 9°28W 10 D2
Hague, C. de la France 49°44N 1°56W 20 B3
Hague, The = 's-Gravenhage Neths. 52°7N 4°17E 15 B4
Haguenau France 48°49N 7°47E 20 B7
Hai Duong Vietnam 20°56N 106°19E 34 G6
Hai'an Guangdong, China 20°15N 110°11E 35 G8
Hai'an Jiangsu, China 32°35N 120°27E 35 A13
Haicheng China 40°50N 122°45E 33 D12
Haida Gwaii Canada 53°20N 132°10W 70 C2
Haidar Khel Afghan. 33°58N 68°38E 42 C3
Haidargarh India 26°37N 81°22E 43 F9
Haidarâbâd = Hyderabad India 17°22N 78°29E 44 F4
Haifa = Ḥefa Israel 32°46N 35°0E 48 C4
Haifeng China 22°58N 115°10E 35 F10
Haikou China 20°1N 110°16E 38 B8
Ḥā'il Si. Arabia 27°28N 41°45E 46 E4
Ḥā'il □ Si. Arabia 26°40N 41°40E 46 E4
Hailar China 49°10N 119°38E 31 B11
Hailey U.S.A. 43°31N 114°19W 76 E6
Haileybury Canada 47°30N 79°38W 72 C4
Hailin China 44°37N 129°30E 33 B15
Hailing Dao China 21°35N 111°47E 35 G8
Hailun China 47°28N 126°50E 31 B14
Hailuoto Finland 65°3N 24°45E 8 D21

Haimen Guangdong, China 23°15N 116°38E 35 F11
Haimen Jiangsu, China 31°52N 121°10E 35 B13
Hainan □ China 19°0N 109°30E 38 C7
Hainan Dao China 19°0N 109°30E 38 C7
Hainan Str. = Qiongzhou Haixia China 20°10N 110°15E 38 B8
Hainaut □ Belgium 50°30N 4°0E 15 D4
Haines Alaska, U.S.A. 59°14N 135°26W 70 B1
Haines Oreg., U.S.A. 44°55N 117°56W 76 D5
Haines City U.S.A. 28°7N 81°38W 85 G14
Haines Junction Canada 60°45N 137°30W 70 A1
Haining China 30°28N 120°40E 35 B13
Haitan Dao China 25°30N 119°45E 35 E12
Haiti ■ W. Indies 19°0N 72°30W 89 C5
Haiya Sudan 18°20N 36°21E 53 E13
Haiyan Qinghai, China 36°59N 100°55E 32 F2
Haiyang China 36°47N 121°9E 33 F11
Haiyang Zhejiang, China 30°28N 120°58E 35 B13
Haiyuan Guangxi Zhuangzu, China 22°8N 107°35E 34 F6
Haiyuan Ningxia Huizu, China 36°35N 105°52E 32 F3
Haizhou China 34°37N 119°7E 33 G10
Haizhou Wan China 34°50N 119°20E 33 G10
Hajdúböszörmény Hungary 47°40N 21°30E 17 E11
Haji Ibrahim Iraq 36°40N 44°30E 46 B5
Hajipur India 25°45N 85°13E 43 G11
Ḥājjī 'Alī Qolī, Kavīr-e Iran 35°55N 54°50E 47 C7
Hajjah Yemen 15°42N 43°36E 49 D3
Ḥājjīābād Hormozgān, Iran 28°19N 55°55E 47 D7
Ḥājjīābād Khorāsān, Iran 33°37N 60°0E 47 C9
Ḥājjīābād-e Zarrīn Iran 33°9N 55°0E 47 C7
Hajnówka Poland 52°47N 23°35E 17 B12
Hakkâri Turkey 37°34N 43°44E 46 C5
Hakken-Zan Japan 34°10N 135°54E 29 G7
Hakkōda San Japan 40°40N 140°44E 28 D10
Hakodate Japan 41°45N 140°44E 28 D10
Hakos Namibia 23°13S 16°21E 56 C2
Hakskeenpan S. Africa 26°48S 20°13E 56 C3
Haku-San Japan 36°9N 136°46E 29 F8
Haku-San △ Japan 36°15N 136°45E 29 F8
Hakui Japan 36°53N 136°47E 29 F8
Hakusan Japan 36°31N 136°34E 29 F8
Hala Pakistan 25°43N 68°20E 40 G6
Ḥalab Syria 36°10N 37°15E 46 B3
Halabjah Iraq 35°10N 45°58E 46 C5
Halaib Sudan 22°12N 36°30E 53 D13
Halaib Triangle Africa 22°30N 35°20E 53 D13
Ḥālat 'Ammār Si. Arabia 29°10N 36°4E 46 D3
Halbā Lebanon 34°34N 36°6E 48 A5
Halberstadt Germany 51°54N 11°3E 16 C6
Halcombe N.Z. 40°8S 175°30E 59 D5
Halcon, Mt. Phil. 13°16N 121°0E 37 B6
Halde Fjäll = Haltiatunturi Finland 69°17N 21°18E 8 B19
Halden Norway 59°9N 11°23E 9 G14
Haldia Bangla. 22°1N 88°3E 43 H13
Haldwani India 29°31N 79°30E 43 E8
Hale → Australia 24°56S 135°53E 62 C2
Halesowen U.K. 52°27N 2°3W 13 E5
Halesworth U.K. 52°20N 1°31E 13 E9
Haleyville U.S.A. 34°14N 87°37W 85 D11
Half Dome U.S.A. 37°44N 119°32W 78 H7
Halfmoon Bay N.Z. 46°50S 168°5E 59 G2
Halfway → Canada 56°12N 121°32W 70 B4
Halia India 24°50N 82°19E 43 G10
Haliburton Canada 45°3N 78°30W 82 A6
Halifax Australia 18°32S 146°22E 62 B4
Halifax Canada 44°38N 63°35W 73 D7
Halifax U.K. 53°43N 1°52W 12 D6
Halifax U.S.A. 40°25N 76°55W 82 F8
Halifax B. Australia 18°50S 147°0E 62 B4
Halifax I. Namibia 26°38S 15°4E 56 C2
Halik Shan China 42°20N 81°30E 30 C5
Ḥalīl → Iran 27°40N 58°30E 47 E8
Halim △ Indonesia 6°42S 106°26E 37 G12
Halkida = Chalkida Greece 38°27N 23°42E 23 E10
Halkirk U.K. 58°30N 3°29W 11 C5
Hall Beach Canada 68°46N 81°12W 69 D15
Hall Pen. Canada 63°30N 66°0W 69 E18
Hall Pt. Australia 15°40S 124°23E 60 C3
Halland Sweden 57°8N 12°47E 9 H15
Ḥallāniyat, Jazā'ir al Oman 17°30N 55°58E 49 D6
Hallasan S. Korea 33°22N 126°32E 33 H14
Halle Germany 51°30N 11°56E 16 C6
Hällefors Sweden 59°47N 14°31E 9 G16
Hallett Australia 33°25S 138°55E 63 E2
Hallettsville U.S.A. 29°27N 96°57W 84 G6
Halley Antarctica 75°35S 26°39W 5 D1
Hallia → India 16°55N 79°20E 44 F4
Hallim S. Korea 33°24N 126°15E 33 H14
Hallingdalselva → Norway 60°23N 9°35E 8 F13
Hallingskarvet △ Norway 60°37N 7°45E 8 F12
Hallock U.S.A. 48°47N 96°57W 80 A5
Halls Creek Australia 18°16S 127°38E 60 C4
Halls Gap Australia 37°8S 142°34E 63 F3
Hallsberg Sweden 59°5N 15°7E 9 G16
Hallstead U.S.A. 41°58N 75°45W 83 E9
Halmahera Indonesia 0°40N 128°0E 37 D7
Halmahera Sea Indonesia 2°0N 130°0E 37 E7
Halong Bay = Ha Long, Vinh Vietnam 20°56N 107°3E 38 B6
Hälsingborg = Helsingborg Sweden 56°3N 12°42E 9 H15
Hälsingland Sweden 61°40N 16°5E 8 F17
Halstead U.K. 51°57N 0°40E 13 F8
Halti = Haltiatunturi Finland 69°17N 21°18E 8 B19
Halton □ U.K. 53°22N 2°45W 12 D5
Haltiatunturi Finland 69°17N 21°18E 8 B19
Haltwhistle U.K. 54°58N 2°26W 12 C5
Ḥālūl Qatar 25°40N 52°40E 47 E7
Halvad India 23°1N 71°11E 42 H4

Halvān *Iran* 33°57N 56°15E **47** C8
Hamab *Namibia* 28°7S 19°16E **56** C2
Hamada *Japan* 34°56N 132°4E **29** G6
Hamadān *Iran* 34°52N 48°32E **47** C6
Hamadān □ *Iran* 35°0N 49°0E **47** C6
Hamāh *Syria* 35°5N 36°40E **46** C3
Hamamatsu *Japan* 34°45N 137°45E **29** G8
Hamar *Norway* 60°48N 11°7E **8** F14
Hamāta, Gebel *Egypt* 24°17N 35°0E **46** E2
Hamatonbetsu *Japan* 45°10N 142°20E **28** B11
Hamber △ *Canada* 52°20N 118°0W **70** C5
Hamburg *Germany* 53°33N 9°59E **16** B5
Hamburg *Ark., U.S.A.* 33°14N 91°48W **84** E9
Hamburg *N.Y., U.S.A.* 42°43N 78°50W **82** D6
Hamburg *Pa., U.S.A.* 40°33N 75°59W **83** F9
Ḩamḑ, W. al → *Si. Arabia* 24°55N 36°20E **46** E3
Hamden *U.S.A.* 41°23N 72°54W **83** E12
Häme *Finland* 61°38N 25°10E **8** F21
Hämeenlinna *Finland* 61°0N 24°28E **8** F21
Hamelin Pool *Australia* 26°22S 114°20E **61** E1
Hamelin *Germany* 52°6N 9°21E **16** B5
Hamerkaz □ *Israel* 32°15N 34°55E **48** C3
Hamersley Ra. *Australia* 22°0S 117°45E **60** D2
Hamhŭng *N. Korea* 39°54N 127°30E **33** E14
Hami *China* 42°55N 93°25E **30** C7
Hamilton *Australia* 37°45S 142°2E **63** F3
Hamilton *Canada* 43°15N 79°50W **82** C5
Hamilton *N.Z.* 37°47S 175°19E **59** B5
Hamilton *U.K.* 55°46N 4°2W **11** F4
Hamilton *Ala., U.S.A.* 34°9N 87°59W **85** D11
Hamilton *Mont., U.S.A.* 46°15N 114°10W **76** C6
Hamilton *N.Y., U.S.A.* 42°50N 75°33W **83** D9
Hamilton *Ohio, U.S.A.* 39°24N 84°34W **81** F11
Hamilton *Tex., U.S.A.* 31°42N 98°7W **84** F5
Hamilton → *Queens., Australia* 23°30S 139°47E **62** C2
Hamilton → *S. Austral., Australia* 26°40S 135°19E **63** D2
Hamilton City *U.S.A.* 39°45N 122°1W **78** F4
Hamilton I. *Australia* 20°21S 148°56E **62** b
Hamilton Inlet *Canada* 54°0N 57°30W **73** B8
Hamilton Mt. *U.S.A.* 43°25N 74°22W **83** C10
Hamina *Finland* 60°34N 27°12E **8** F22
Hamirpur *H.P., India* 31°41N 76°31E **42** D7
Hamirpur *Ut. P., India* 25°57N 80°9E **43** G9
Hamlet *U.S.A.* 34°53N 79°42W **85** D15
Hamley Bridge *Australia* 34°17S 138°35E **63** E2
Hamlin = Hameln *Germany* 52°6N 9°21E **16** B5
Hamlin *N.Y., U.S.A.* 43°17N 77°55W **82** C7
Hamlin *Tex., U.S.A.* 32°53N 100°8W **84** E4
Hamm *Germany* 51°40N 7°50E **16** C4
Ḩammār, Hawr al *Iraq* 30°50N 47°10E **46** D5
Hammerfest *Norway* 70°39N 23°41E **8** A20
Hammond *Ind., U.S.A.* 41°38N 87°30W **80** L10
Hammond *La., U.S.A.* 30°30N 90°28W **85** F9
Hammond *N.Y., U.S.A.* 44°27N 75°42W **83** B9
Hammondsport *U.S.A.* 42°25N 77°13W **82** D7
Hammonton *U.S.A.* 39°39N 74°48W **81** F16
Hampden *N.Z.* 45°18S 170°50E **59** F3
Hampi *India* 15°18N 76°28E **45** G3
Hampshire □ *U.K.* 51°7N 1°23W **13** F6
Hampshire Downs *U.K.* 51°15N 1°10W **13** F6
Hampton *N.B., Canada* 45°32N 65°51W **73** C6
Hampton *Ont., Canada* 43°58N 78°45W **82** C6
Hampton *Ark., U.S.A.* 33°32N 92°28W **84** E8
Hampton *Iowa, U.S.A.* 42°45N 93°13W **80** D7
Hampton *N.H., U.S.A.* 42°57N 70°50W **83** D14
Hampton *S.C., U.S.A.* 32°52N 81°7W **85** E14
Hampton *Va., U.S.A.* 37°2N 76°21W **81** G15
Hampton Bays *U.S.A.* 40°53N 72°30W **83** F12
Hampton Tableland *Australia* 32°0S 127°0E **61** F4
Hamyang *S. Korea* 35°32N 127°42E **33** G14
Han = Hangang → *S. Korea* 37°50N 126°30E **33** F14
Han Jiang → *China* 23°25N 116°40E **35** F11
Han Pijesak *Bos.-H.* 44°5N 18°57E **23** B8
Han Shui → *China* 30°34N 114°17E **35** B10
Hanak *Si. Arabia* 25°32N 37°0E **46** E3
Hanamaki *Japan* 39°23N 141°7E **28** E10
Hanau *Germany* 50°7N 8°56E **16** C5
Hanbogd = Ihbulag *Mongolia* 43°11N 107°10E **32** C4
Hancheng *China* 35°31N 110°25E **32** G6
Hanchuan *China* 30°40N 113°50E **35** B9
Hancock *Mich., U.S.A.* 47°8N 88°35W **80** B9
Hancock *N.Y., U.S.A.* 41°57N 75°17W **83** E9
Hancock *Vt., U.S.A.* 43°55N 72°50W **83** C12
Handa *Japan* 34°53N 136°55E **29** G8
Handa I. *U.K.* 58°23N 5°11W **11** C3
Handan *China* 36°35N 114°28E **32** F8
Handwara *India* 34°21N 74°20E **43** B6
Hanegev *Israel* 30°50N 35°0E **48** E4
Hanford *U.S.A.* 36°20N 119°39W **78** J7
Hanford Reach △ *U.S.A.* 46°40N 119°30W **76** C4
Hang Chat *Thailand* 18°20N 99°21E **38** C2
Hangang → *S. Korea* 37°50N 126°30E **33** F14
Hangayn Nuruu *Mongolia* 47°30N 99°0E **30** B8
Hangchou = Hangzhou *China* 30°18N 120°11E **35** B13
Hanggin Houqi *China* 40°58N 107°4E **32** D4
Hanggin Qi *China* 39°52N 108°50E **32** E5
Hangu *China* 39°18N 117°53E **33** E9
Hangzhou *China* 30°18N 120°11E **35** B13
Hangzhou Wan *China* 30°15N 120°45E **35** B13
Hanh *Mongolia* 51°32N 100°35E **30** A9
Hanhongor *Mongolia* 43°55N 104°28E **32** C3
Hania = Chania *Greece* 35°30N 24°4E **23** G11
Ḩanīdh *Si. Arabia* 26°35N 48°38E **47** E6
Ḩanīsh *Yemen* 13°45N 42°46E **49** E3
Hanjiang *China* 25°26N 119°6E **35** E12
Hankinson *U.S.A.* 46°4N 96°54W **80** B6
Hankö *Finland* 59°50N 22°57E **9** G20
Hankou *China* 30°35N 114°30E **35** B10
Hanksville *U.S.A.* 38°22N 110°43W **76** G8
Hanle *India* 32°42N 79°4E **43** C8
Hanmer Springs *N.Z.* 42°32S 172°50E **59** E4
Hann → *Australia* 17°26S 126°17E **60** C4
Hann, Mt. *Australia* 15°45S 126°0E **60** C4
Hanna *Canada* 51°40N 111°54W **70** C6
Hanna *U.S.A.* 41°52N 106°34W **76** F10
Hannah B. *Canada* 51°40N 80°0W **72** B4
Hannibal *Mo., U.S.A.* 39°42N 91°22W **80** F8
Hannibal *N.Y., U.S.A.* 43°19N 76°35W **83** C8
Hannover *Germany* 52°22N 9°46E **16** B5
Hanoi *Vietnam* 21°5N 105°55E **34** G5
Hanover = Hannover *Germany* 52°22N 9°46E **16** B5
Hanover *Canada* 44°9N 81°2W **82** B3
Hanover *S. Africa* 31°4S 24°29E **56** D3
Hanover *N.H., U.S.A.* 43°42N 72°17W **83** C12
Hanover *Ohio, U.S.A.* 40°4N 82°16W **82** F2
Hanover *Pa., U.S.A.* 39°48N 76°59W **81** F15
Hanover, I. *Chile* 51°0S 74°50W **96** G2
Hans Lollik I. *U.S. Virgin Is.* 18°24N 64°53W **89** e
Hansdiha *India* 24°36N 87°5E **43** G12
Hanshou *China* 28°56N 111°50E **35** C8
Hansi *H.P., India* 32°27N 77°50E **42** C7
Hansi *Haryana, India* 29°10N 75°57E **42** E6
Hanson, L. *Australia* 31°0S 136°15E **63** E2
Hanting *China* 36°46N 119°12E **33** F10
Hantsavichy *Belarus* 52°49N 26°30E **17** B14
Hanumangarh *India* 29°35N 74°19E **42** E6
Hanyin *China* 32°54N 108°28E **32** H5
Hanyuan *China* 29°21N 102°40E **34** C4
Hanzhong *China* 33°10N 107°1E **34** A6
Hanzhuang *China* 34°33N 117°23E **33** G9
Haoxue *China* 30°3N 112°24E **35** B9
Haparanda *Sweden* 65°52N 24°8E **8** D21
Haparanda Skärgård △ *Sweden* 65°35N 23°44E **8** D20
Happy *U.S.A.* 34°45N 101°52W **84** D4
Happy Camp *U.S.A.* 41°48N 123°23W **76** F2
Happy Valley-Goose Bay *Canada* 53°15N 60°20W **73** B7
Hapsu *N. Korea* 41°13N 128°51E **33** D15
Hapur *India* 28°45N 77°45E **42** E7
Ḩaql *Si. Arabia* 29°10N 34°58E **48** F3
Har *Indonesia* 5°16S 133°14E **37** F8
Har-Ayrag *Mongolia* 45°47N 109°16E **32** B5
Har Hu *China* 38°20N 97°38E **30** D8
Har Us Nuur *Mongolia* 48°0N 92°0E **30** B7
Har Yehuda *Israel* 31°35N 34°57E **48** D3
Ḩaraḑ *Si. Arabia* 24°22N 49°0E **49** C4
Haramosh *Pakistan* 35°50N 74°54E **43** B6
Haranomachi = Minamisōma *Japan* 37°38N 140°58E **28** F10
Harar = Harer *Ethiopia* 9°20N 42°8E **49** F3
Harare *Zimbabwe* 17°43S 31°2E **55** H6
Harazé *Chad* 9°57N 20°48E **53** G10
Harbhanga *India* 20°38N 84°36E **44** J7
Harbin *China* 45°48N 126°40E **33** B14
Harbor Beach *U.S.A.* 43°51N 82°39W **82** C2
Harborcreek *U.S.A.* 42°9N 79°57W **82** D5
Harbour Breton *Canada* 47°29N 55°50W **73** C8
Harbour Deep *Canada* 50°25N 56°32W **73** B8
Harda *India* 22°27N 77°5E **42** H7
Hardangerfjorden *Norway* 60°5N 6°0E **9** F12
Hardangervidda *Norway* 60°7N 7°20E **8** F12
Hardap □ *Namibia* 24°0S 17°0E **56** B2
Hardap △ *Namibia* 24°29S 17°45E **56** B2
Hardap Dam *Namibia* 24°32S 17°50E **56** B2
Hardenberg *Neths.* 52°34N 6°37E **15** B6
Harderwijk *Neths.* 52°21N 5°38E **15** B5
Hardey → *Australia* 22°45S 116°8E **60** D2
Hardin *U.S.A.* 45°44N 107°37W **76** D10
Harding *S. Africa* 30°35S 29°55E **57** E4
Harding Ra. *Australia* 16°17S 124°55E **60** C3
Hardisty *Canada* 52°40N 111°18W **70** C6
Hardoi *India* 27°26N 80°6E **43** F9
Hardwar = Haridwar *India* 29°58N 78°9E **42** E8
Hardwick *U.S.A.* 44°30N 72°22W **83** B12
Hardwood Lake *Canada* 45°12N 77°26W **82** A7
Hardy, Pen. *Chile* 55°30S 68°20W **96** H3
Hardy, Pte. *St. Lucia* 14°6N 60°56W **89** f
Hare B. *Canada* 51°15N 55°45W **73** B8
Hareid *Norway* 62°22N 6°1E **8** E12
Harer *Ethiopia* 9°20N 42°8E **49** F3
Hargeisa *Somalia* 9°30N 44°2E **49** F3
Hari → *Indonesia* 1°16S 104°5E **36** E2
Haridwar *India* 29°58N 78°9E **42** E8
Harihar *India* 14°32N 75°44E **45** G2
Hariharpur Garhi *Nepal* 27°19N 85°29E **43** F11
Harim, Jabal al *Oman* 25°58N 56°14E **47** E8
Haringhata → *Bangla.* 22°0N 89°58E **41** J16
Haripad *India* 9°14N 76°28E **45** K3
Harīr, W. al → *Syria* 32°44N 35°59E **48** C4
Harīrūd → *Asia* 37°24N 60°38E **47** B9
Härjedalen *Sweden* 62°22N 13°5E **8** E15
Harlan *Iowa, U.S.A.* 41°39N 95°19W **80** E6
Harlan *Ky., U.S.A.* 36°51N 83°19W **81** G12
Harlech *U.K.* 52°52N 4°6W **12** E3
Harlem *U.S.A.* 48°32N 108°47W **76** B9
Harlingen *Neths.* 53°11N 5°25E **15** A5
Harlingen *U.S.A.* 26°12N 97°42W **84** H6
Harlow *U.K.* 51°46N 0°8E **13** F8
Harlowton *U.S.A.* 46°26N 109°50W **76** C9
Harnai *India* 17°48N 73°6E **44** F1
Harnai *Pakistan* 30°6N 67°56E **42** D2
Harney Basin *U.S.A.* 43°14N 119°8W **76** E4
Harney L. *U.S.A.* 43°14N 119°8W **76** E4
Harney Peak *U.S.A.* 43°52N 103°32W **80** D2
Härnösand *Sweden* 62°38N 17°55E **8** E17
Haroldswick *U.K.* 60°48N 0°50W **11** A8
Harp L. *Canada* 55°5N 61°50W **73** A7
Harpanahalli *India* 14°47N 76°2E **45** G3
Harper *Liberia* 4°25N 7°43W **52** H4
Harper, Mt. *U.S.A.* 64°14N 143°51W **74** C11
Harrai *India* 22°37N 79°13E **43** H8
Harrand *Pakistan* 29°28N 70°3E **42** E4
Harricana → *Canada* 50°56N 79°32W **72** B4
Harriman *U.S.A.* 35°56N 84°33W **85** D12
Harrington Harbour *Canada* 50°31N 59°30W **73** B8
Harris *U.K.* 57°50N 6°55W **11** D2
Harris, L. *Australia* 31°10S 135°10E **63** E2
Harris, Sd. of *U.K.* 57°44N 7°6W **11** D1
Harris Pt. *Canada* 43°6N 82°9W **82** C2
Harrisburg *Ill., U.S.A.* 37°44N 88°32W **80** G9
Harrisburg *Nebr., U.S.A.* 41°33N 103°44W **80** E2
Harrisburg *Pa., U.S.A.* 40°16N 76°53W **82** F8
Harrismith *S. Africa* 28°15S 29°8E **57** C4
Harrison *Ark., U.S.A.* 36°14N 93°7W **84** C8
Harrison *Maine, U.S.A.* 44°7N 70°39W **83** B14
Harrison *Nebr., U.S.A.* 42°41N 103°53W **80** D2
Harrison, C. *Canada* 54°55N 57°55W **73** B8
Harrison Bay *U.S.A.* 70°40N 151°0W **74** A9
Harrison L. *Canada* 49°33N 121°50W **70** D4
Harrisonburg *U.S.A.* 38°27N 78°52W **81** F14
Harriston *Canada* 43°57N 80°53W **82** C4
Harrisville *Mich., U.S.A.* 44°39N 83°17W **82** B1
Harrisville *N.Y., U.S.A.* 44°9N 75°19W **83** B9
Harrisville *Pa., U.S.A.* 41°8N 80°0W **82** E5
Harrodsburg *U.S.A.* 37°46N 84°51W **81** G11
Harrogate *U.K.* 54°0N 1°33W **12** C6
Harrow *Canada* 42°2N 82°55W **82** D2
Harrow □ *U.K.* 51°35N 0°21W **13** F7
Harrowsmith *Canada* 44°24N 76°40W **83** B8
Harry S. Truman Res. *U.S.A.* 38°16N 93°24W **80** F7
Harsin *Iran* 34°18N 47°33E **46** C5
Harstad *Norway* 68°48N 16°30E **8** B17
Harsud *India* 22°6N 76°44E **42** H7
Hart *U.S.A.* 43°42N 86°22W **80** D10
Hart, L. *Australia* 31°10S 136°25E **63** E2
Hartbees → *S. Africa* 28°45S 20°32E **56** C3
Hartford *Conn., U.S.A.* 41°46N 72°41W **83** E12
Hartford *Ky., U.S.A.* 37°27N 86°55W **80** G10
Hartford *S. Dak., U.S.A.* 43°38N 96°57W **80** D5
Hartford *Vt., U.S.A.* 43°40N 72°20W **83** C12
Hartford City *U.S.A.* 40°27N 85°22W **81** E11
Hartland *Canada* 46°20N 67°32W **73** C6
Hartland Pt. *U.K.* 51°1N 4°32W **13** F3
Hartlepool *U.K.* 54°42N 1°13W **12** C6
Hartlepool □ *U.K.* 54°42N 1°17W **12** C6
Hartley Bay *Canada* 53°25N 129°15W **70** C3
Hartmannberge *Namibia* 17°0S 13°0E **56** A1
Hartney *Canada* 49°30N 100°35W **71** D8
Harts → *S. Africa* 28°24S 24°17E **56** C3
Harts Range *Australia* 23°6S 134°55E **62** C1
Hartselle *U.S.A.* 34°27N 86°56W **85** D11
Hartshorne *U.S.A.* 34°51N 95°34W **84** D7
Hartstown *U.S.A.* 41°33N 80°23W **82** E4
Hartsville *U.S.A.* 34°23N 80°4W **85** D14
Hartswater *S. Africa* 27°34S 24°43E **56** C3
Hartwell *U.S.A.* 34°21N 82°56W **85** D13
Harunabad *Pakistan* 29°35N 73°8E **42** E5
Harur *India* 12°3N 78°29E **45** H4
Harvand *Iran* 28°25N 55°43E **47** D7
Harvey *Australia* 33°5S 115°54E **61** F2
Harvey *U.S.A.* 47°47N 99°56W **80** B4
Harwich *U.K.* 51°56N 1°17E **13** F9
Haryana □ *India* 29°0N 76°10E **42** E7
Haryn → *Belarus* 52°7N 27°17E **17** B14
Harz *Germany* 51°38N 10°44E **16** C6
Hasa *Si. Arabia* 25°50N 49°0E **47** E6
Ḩaṣā, W. al → *Jordan* 31°4N 35°29E **48** D4
Ḩasanābād *Iran* 32°8N 52°44E **47** C7
Hasanparti *India* 18°4N 79°32E **44** E4
Ḩasb, W. → *Iraq* 31°45N 44°17E **46** D5
Hasdo → *India* 21°44N 82°44E **43** J10
Hashimoto *Japan* 34°19N 135°37E **29** G7
Hashtjerd *Iran* 35°52N 50°40E **47** C6
Hashtpur = Tālesh *Iran* 37°58N 48°58E **47** B6
Haskell *U.S.A.* 33°10N 99°44W **84** E5
Haskovo *Bulgaria* 41°56N 25°30E **23** D11
Haslemere *U.K.* 51°5N 0°43W **13** F7
Hasselt *Belgium* 50°56N 5°21E **15** D5
Hassi Messaoud *Algeria* 31°51N 6°1E **52** B7
Hässleholm *Sweden* 56°10N 13°46E **9** H15
Hastings *N.Z.* 39°39S 176°52E **59** C6
Hastings *U.K.* 50°51N 0°35E **13** G8
Hastings *Mich., U.S.A.* 42°39N 85°17W **81** D11
Hastings *Minn., U.S.A.* 44°44N 92°51W **80** C7
Hastings *Nebr., U.S.A.* 40°35N 98°23W **80** E4
Hastings Ra. *Australia* 31°15S 152°14E **63** E5
Hat Lot *Vietnam* 21°15N 104°7E **38** B5
Hat Yai *Thailand* 7°1N 100°27E **39** J3
Hatanbulag = Ergel *Mongolia* 43°8N 109°5E **32** C5
Hatay *Turkey* 36°14N 36°10E **46** B3
Hatch *U.S.A.* 32°40N 107°9W **77** K10
Hatches Creek *Australia* 20°56S 135°12E **62** C2
Hateruma-Shima *Japan* 24°3N 123°47E **29** M1
Hatfield *Australia* 33°54S 143°49E **63** E3
Hatgal *Mongolia* 50°26N 100°9E **30** A9
Hathras *India* 27°36N 78°6E **42** F8
Hatia *Bangla.* 22°30N 91°5E **41** H17
Hatia *Nepal* 27°43N 87°21E **43** F12
Hato Mayor *Dom. Rep.* 18°46N 69°15W **89** C6
Hatra = Al Ḩaḑr *Iraq* 35°35N 42°44E **46** C4
Hatta *India* 24°7N 79°36E **43** G8
Hatta *U.A.E.* 24°48N 56°4E **47** E8
Hattah *Australia* 34°48S 142°17E **63** E3
Hattah Kulkyne △ *Australia* 34°16S 142°33E **63** E3
Hatteras, C. *U.S.A.* 35°14N 75°32W **85** D17
Hattiesburg *U.S.A.* 31°20N 89°17W **85** F10
Hatvan *Hungary* 47°40N 19°45E **17** E10
Hau → *Vietnam* 9°30N 106°13E **39** H6
Haugesund *Norway* 59°23N 5°13E **9** G11
Haukipudas *Finland* 65°12N 25°20E **8** D21
Haultain → *Canada* 55°51N 106°46W **71** B7
Hauraki G. *N.Z.* 36°35S 175°5E **59** B5
Haut Atlas *Morocco* 32°30N 5°0W **52** B4
Hautes-Fagnes = Hohes Venn *Belgium* 50°30N 6°5E **15** D6
Hauts Plateaux *Algeria* 35°0N 1°0E **52** B6
Havana = La Habana *Cuba* 23°8N 82°22W **88** B3
Havana *U.S.A.* 40°18N 90°4W **80** E8
Havant *U.K.* 50°51N 0°58W **13** G7
Havasor = Kızgı *Turkey* 38°18N 43°25E **46** B4
Havasu, L. *U.S.A.* 34°18N 114°28W **79** L12
Havelian *Pakistan* 34°2N 73°10E **42** B5
Havelock *Canada* 44°26N 77°53W **82** B7
Havelock *N.Z.* 41°17S 173°48E **59** D4
Havelock *U.S.A.* 34°53N 76°54W **85** D16
Havelock I. *India* 11°58N 93°0E **45** J11
Haverfordwest *U.K.* 51°48N 4°58W **13** F3
Haverhill *U.S.A.* 42°47N 71°5W **83** D13
Haveri *India* 14°53N 75°24E **45** G2
Haverstraw *U.S.A.* 41°12N 73°58W **83** E11
Havirga *Mongolia* 45°41N 113°5E **32** B7
Havířov *Czechia* 49°46N 18°20E **17** D10
Havlíčkův Brod *Czechia* 49°36N 15°33E **16** D8
Havre *U.S.A.* 48°33N 109°41W **76** B9
Havre-Aubert *Canada* 47°12N 61°56W **73** C7
Havre-St.-Pierre *Canada* 50°18N 63°33W **73** B7
Haw → *U.S.A.* 35°36N 79°3W **85** D15
Hawa'i *U.S.A.* 19°30N 155°30W **75** M8
Hawai'i □ *U.S.A.* 19°30N 156°30W **75** M8
Hawaiian Is. *Pac. Oc.* 20°30N 156°0W **65** E11
Hawaiian Ridge *Pac. Oc.* 24°0N 165°0W **65** E11
Hawarden *U.S.A.* 43°0N 96°29W **80** D5
Hawea, L. *N.Z.* 44°28S 169°19E **59** F2
Hawera *N.Z.* 39°35S 174°19E **59** C5
Hawi *U.S.A.* 20°14N 155°50W **75** L8
Hawick *U.K.* 55°26N 2°47W **11** F6
Hawk Junction *Canada* 48°5N 84°38W **72** C3
Hawke B. *N.Z.* 39°25S 177°20E **59** C6
Hawker *Australia* 31°59S 138°22E **63** E2
Hawke's Bay *Canada* 50°36N 57°10E **73** B8
Hawkesbury *Canada* 45°37N 74°37W **72** C5
Hawkesbury I. *Canada* 53°37N 129°3W **70** C3
Hawkesbury Pt. *Australia* 11°55S 134°5E **62** A1
Hawkinsville *U.S.A.* 32°17N 83°28W **85** E13
Hawley *Minn., U.S.A.* 46°53N 96°19W **80** B5
Hawley *Pa., U.S.A.* 41°28N 75°11W **83** E9
Ḩawrān, W. → *Iraq* 33°58N 42°34E **46** C4
Hawsh Mūssá *Lebanon* 33°45N 35°55E **48** B4
Hawthorne *U.S.A.* 38°32N 118°38W **76** G4
Hay *Australia* 34°30S 144°51E **63** E3
Hay → *Australia* 24°50S 138°0E **62** C2
Hay → *Canada* 60°50N 116°26W **70** A5
Hay I. *Canada* 44°53N 80°58W **82** B4
Hay L. *Canada* 58°50N 118°50W **70** B5
Hay-on-Wye *U.K.* 52°5N 3°8W **13** E4
Hay Point *Australia* 21°18S 149°17E **62** C4
Hay River *Canada* 60°51N 115°44W **70** A5
Hay Springs *U.S.A.* 42°41N 102°41W **80** D2
Hayachine-San *Japan* 39°34N 141°29E **28** E10
Hayastan = Armenia ■ *Asia* 40°20N 45°0E **19** F7
Ḩaydān, W. al → *Jordan* 31°29N 35°34E **48** D4
Hayden *U.S.A.* 40°30N 107°16W **76** F10
Haydon *U.S.A.* 44°23N 101°1W **80** C3
Hayes → *Canada* 57°3N 92°12W **72** A1
Hayes, Mt. *U.S.A.* 63°37N 146°43W **74** C10
Hayes Creek *Australia* 13°43S 131°22E **60** B5
Hayle *U.K.* 50°11N 5°26W **13** G2
Hayling I. *U.K.* 50°48N 0°59W **13** G7
Hayman I. *Australia* 20°4S 148°53E **62** b
Hayrabolu *Turkey* 41°12N 27°5E **23** D12
Hays *Canada* 50°6N 111°48W **70** C6
Hays *U.S.A.* 38°53N 99°20W **80** F4
Haysyn *Ukraine* 48°57N 29°25E **17** D15
Hayvoron *Ukraine* 48°22N 29°52E **17** D15
Hayward *Calif., U.S.A.* 37°40N 122°4W **78** H4
Hayward *Wis., U.S.A.* 46°1N 91°29W **80** B8
Haywards Heath *U.K.* 51°0N 0°5W **13** G7
Hazafon □ *Israel* 32°40N 35°20E **48** C4
Hazar *Turkmenistan* 39°34N 53°16E **19** G9
Hazarān, Kūh-e *Iran* 29°35N 57°20E **47** D8
Hazard *U.S.A.* 37°15N 83°12W **81** G12
Hazaribag *India* 23°58N 85°26E **43** H11
Hazaribag Road *India* 24°12N 85°57E **43** G11
Hazelton *Canada* 55°20N 127°42W **70** B3
Hazelton *U.S.A.* 46°29N 100°17W **80** B3
Hazen *U.S.A.* 47°18N 101°38W **80** B3
Hazen, L. *Canada* 81°47N 71°1W **69** A17
Hazlehurst *Ga., U.S.A.* 31°52N 82°36W **85** F13
Hazlehurst *Miss., U.S.A.* 31°52N 90°24W **85** F9
Hazlet *U.S.A.* 40°25N 74°12W **83** F10
Hazleton *U.S.A.* 40°57N 75°59W **83** F9
Hazlett, L. *Australia* 21°30S 128°48E **60** D4
Hazro *Turkey* 38°15N 40°47E **46** B4
He Xian = Hezhou *China* 24°27N 111°30E **35** E8
He Xian *China* 31°45N 118°20E **35** B6
Head of Bight *Australia* 31°30S 131°25E **61** F5
Head-Smashed-In Buffalo Jump *Canada* 49°42N 113°37W **70** D6
Healdsburg *U.S.A.* 38°37N 122°52W **78** G4
Healdton *U.S.A.* 34°14N 97°29W **84** D6
Healesville *Australia* 37°35S 145°30E **63** F4
Healy *U.S.A.* 63°52N 148°58W **74** C10
Heany Junction *Zimbabwe* 20°6S 28°54E **57** B4
Heard I. *Ind. Oc.* 53°6S 72°36E **3** G13
Hearne *U.S.A.* 30°53N 96°36W **84** F6
Hearst *Canada* 49°40N 83°41W **72** C3
Heart → *U.S.A.* 46°46N 100°50W **80** B4
Heart's Content *Canada* 47°54N 53°27W **73** C9
Heath, Pte. *Canada* 49°8N 61°40W **73** C7
Heavener *U.S.A.* 34°53N 94°36W **84** D7
Hebbronville *U.S.A.* 27°18N 98°41W **84** H5
Hebei □ *China* 39°0N 116°0E **32** E9
Hebel *Australia* 28°58N 147°24E **63** D4
Heber *U.S.A.* 32°44N 115°32W **79** N11
Heber Springs *U.S.A.* 35°30N 92°2W **84** D8
Hebgen L. *U.S.A.* 44°52N 111°20W **76** D8
Hebi *China* 35°57N 114°7E **32** G8
Hebrides *U.K.* 57°30N 7°0W **6** D4
Hebrides, Sea of the *U.K.* 57°5N 7°0W **11** D2
Hebron = Al Khalīl *West Bank* 31°32N 35°6E **48** D4
Hebron *Canada* 58°5N 62°30W **69** F19
Hebron *N. Dak., U.S.A.* 46°54N 102°3W **80** B2
Hebron *Nebr., U.S.A.* 40°10N 97°35W **80** E5
Hecate Str. *Canada* 53°10N 130°30W **70** C2
Heceta I. *U.S.A.* 55°46N 133°40W **70** B2
Hechi *China* 24°40N 108°2E **34** E7
Hechuan *China* 30°2N 106°12E **34** B6
Hecla *U.S.A.* 45°53N 98°9W **80** C4
Hecla I. *Canada* 51°10N 96°43W **71** C9
Hede *Sweden* 62°23N 13°30E **8** E15
Hedemora *Sweden* 60°18N 15°58E **9** F16
Heerde *Neths.* 52°24N 6°2E **15** B6
Heerenveen *Neths.* 52°57N 5°55E **15** B5
Heerhugowaard *Neths.* 52°40N 4°51E **15** B4
Heerlen *Neths.* 50°55N 5°58E **15** D5
Ḩefa *Israel* 32°46N 35°0E **48** C4
Ḩefa □ *Israel* 32°40N 35°0E **48** C4
Hefei *China* 31°52N 117°18E **35** B11
Hefeng *China* 29°55N 109°52E **34** C7
Hegang *China* 47°20N 130°19E **31** B15
Heglig *Sudan* 10°0N 29°24E **53** G11
Heichengzhen *China* 36°24N 106°3E **32** F4
Heidelberg *Germany* 49°24N 8°42E **16** D5
Heidelberg *S. Africa* 34°6S 20°59E **56** E3
Heihe *China* 50°10N 127°30E **31** A14
Heijing *China* 25°22N 101°44E **34** E3
Heilbron *S. Africa* 27°16S 27°59E **57** C4
Heilbronn *Germany* 49°9N 9°13E **16** D5
Heilongjiang □ *China* 48°0N 126°0E **31** B14
Heiloo *Neths.* 52°36N 4°42E **15** B4
Heilunkiang = Heilongjiang □ *China* 48°0N 126°0E **31** B14
Heimaey *Iceland* 63°26N 20°17W **8** E3
Heinola *Finland* 61°13N 26°2E **8** F22
Heinze Chaung *Myanmar* 14°42N 97°52E **38** E1
Heinze Kyun *Myanmar* 14°25N 97°45E **38** E1
Heishan *China* 41°40N 122°5E **33** D12
Heishui *Liaoning, China* 42°8N 119°30E **33** C10
Heishui *Sichuan, China* 32°4N 103°2E **34** A4
Hejaz = Ḩijāz *Si. Arabia* 24°0N 40°0E **46** E3
Hejian *China* 38°25N 116°5E **32** E9
Hejiang *China* 28°43N 105°46E **34** C5
Hejin *China* 35°35N 110°42E **32** G6
Hekimhan *Turkey* 38°50N 37°55E **46** B3
Hekla *Iceland* 63°56N 19°35W **8** E4
Hekou *Gansu, China* 36°10N 103°26E **32** F2
Hekou *Guangdong, China* 23°13N 112°45E **35** F9
Hekou *Yunnan, China* 22°30N 103°59E **34** F4
Helan Shan *China* 38°30N 105°55E **32** E3
Helen Atoll *Palau* 2°40N 132°0E **37** D8
Helena *U.S.A.* 46°36N 112°2W **76** C7
Helena -West Helena *U.S.A.* 34°32N 90°36W **85** D9
Helendale *U.S.A.* 34°44N 117°19W **79** L9
Helensburgh *U.K.* 56°1N 4°43W **11** E4
Helensville *N.Z.* 36°41S 174°29E **59** B5
Helenvale *Australia* 15°43S 145°14E **62** B4
Helgeland *Norway* 66°7N 13°29E **8** C15
Helgoland *Germany* 54°10N 7°53E **16** A4
Heligoland = Helgoland *Germany* 54°10N 7°53E **16** A4
Heligoland B. = Deutsche Bucht *Germany* 54°15N 8°0E **16** A5
Hell Hole Gorge △ *Australia* 25°31S 144°12E **62** D3
Hella *Iceland* 63°50N 20°24W **8** E3
Hellas = Greece ■ *Europe* 40°0N 23°0E **23** E9
Hellertown *U.S.A.* 40°35N 75°21W **83** F9
Hellespont = Çanakkale Boğazı *Turkey* 40°17N 26°32E **23** D12
Hellevoetsluis *Neths.* 51°50N 4°8E **15** C4
Hellín *Spain* 38°31N 1°40W **21** C5
Hells Canyon △ *U.S.A.* 45°30N 117°45W **76** D5
Helmand □ *Afghan.* 31°20N 64°0E **40** D4
Helmand → *Afghan.* 31°12N 61°34E **40** D2
Helmeringhausen *Namibia* 25°54S 16°57E **56** C2
Helmond *Neths.* 51°29N 5°41E **15** C5
Helmsdale *U.K.* 58°7N 3°39W **11** C5
Helmsdale → *U.K.* 58°8N 3°43W **11** C5
Helong *China* 42°40N 129°0E **33** C15
Helper *U.S.A.* 39°41N 110°51W **76** G8
Helsingborg *Sweden* 56°3N 12°42E **9** H15
Helsingør *Denmark* 56°2N 12°35E **9** H15
Helston *U.K.* 50°6N 5°17W **13** G2
Helvellyn *U.K.* 54°32N 3°1W **12** C4
Helvetinjärvi △ *Finland* 62°5N 23°47E **8** E20
Helwân *Egypt* 29°50N 31°20E **53** C12
Hemavati → *India* 12°30N 76°20E **45** H3
Hemel Hempstead *U.K.* 51°44N 0°28W **13** F7
Hemet *U.S.A.* 33°45N 116°58W **79** M10
Hemingford *U.S.A.* 42°19N 103°4W **80** D2
Hemis △ *India* 34°10N 77°15E **42** B7
Hemmingford *Canada* 45°3N 73°35W **83** A11
Hempstead *N.Y., U.S.A.* 40°42N 73°37W **83** F11
Hempstead *Tex., U.S.A.* 30°6N 96°5W **84** F6
Hemse *Sweden* 57°15N 18°22E **9** H18
Henan □ *China* 34°0N 114°0E **32** H8
Henares → *Spain* 40°24N 3°30W **21** B4
Henashi-Misaki *Japan* 40°37N 139°51E **28** D9
Henderson *Argentina* 36°18S 61°43W **94** D3
Henderson *Ky., U.S.A.* 37°50N 87°35W **80** G10
Henderson *N.C., U.S.A.* 36°20N 78°25W **85** C15
Henderson *N.Y., U.S.A.* 43°50N 76°10W **83** C8
Henderson *Nev., U.S.A.* 36°2N 114°58W **79** J12
Henderson *Tenn., U.S.A.* 35°26N 88°38W **85** D10
Henderson *Tex., U.S.A.* 32°9N 94°48W **84** E7
Henderson I. *Pac. Oc.* 24°22S 128°19W **65** K15
Hendersonville N.C., *U.S.A.* 35°19N 82°28W **85** D13
Hendersonville Tenn., *U.S.A.* 36°18N 86°37W **85** C11
Hendījān *Iran* 30°14N 49°43E **47** D6
Hendorābī *Iran* 26°40N 53°37E **47** E7
Heng Jiang → *China* 28°40N 104°25E **34** C5
Heng Xian *China* 22°40N 109°17E **34** F7
Hengām *Iran* 26°43N 55°53E **47** E7
Hengcheng *China* 38°18N 106°28E **32** E4
Hēngch'un *Taiwan* 22°0N 120°44E **35** F13
Hengdaohezi *China* 44°52N 129°0E **33** B15
Hengduan Shan *China* 28°30N 98°50E **34** C2
Hengelo *Neths.* 52°16N 6°48E **15** B6
Henggang *China* 22°39N 114°14E **31** a
Hengmen *China* 22°33N 113°35E **31** a
Hengshan *Hunan, China* 27°16N 112°45E **35** D9
Hengshan *Shaanxi, China* 37°58N 109°5E **32** F5

Hengshui *China* 37°41N 115°40E 32 F8
Hengyang *China* 26°59N 112°22E 35 D9
Henley-on-Thames *U.K.* 51°32N 0°54W 13 F7
Henlopen, C. *U.S.A.* 38°48N 75°6W 81 F16
Hennenman *S. Africa* 27°59S 27°1E 56 C4
Hennessey *U.S.A.* 36°6N 97°54W 84 C6
Henri Pittier △ *Venezuela* 10°26N 67°37W 89 D6
Henrietta *N.Y., U.S.A.* 43°4N 77°37W 82 C7
Henrietta *Tex., U.S.A.* 33°49N 98°12W 84 E5
Henrietta, Ostrov = Genriyetty, Ostrov *Russia* 77°6N 156°30E 27 B16
Henrietta Maria, C. *Canada* 55°9N 82°20W 72 A3
Henry *U.S.A.* 41°7N 89°22W 80 E9
Henry Ice Rise *Antarctica* 80°35S 62°0W 5 E17
Henry Lawrence I. *India* 12°9N 93°5E 45 H11
Henryetta *U.S.A.* 35°27N 95°59W 84 D7
Henryville *Canada* 45°8N 73°11W 83 A11
Hensall *Canada* 43°26N 81°30W 82 C3
Hentiesbaai *Namibia* 22°8S 14°18E 56 B1
Hentiyn Nuruu *Mongolia* 48°30N 108°30E 31 B10
Henty *Australia* 35°30S 147°3E 63 F4
Henzada = Hinthada *Myanmar* 17°38N 95°26E 41 L19
Heping *China* 24°29N 115°0E 35 E10
Heppner *U.S.A.* 45°21N 119°33W 76 D4
Hepu *China* 21°40N 109°12E 34 G7
Hepworth *Canada* 44°37N 81°9W 82 B3
Heqing *China* 26°37N 100°11E 34 D3
Hequ *China* 39°20N 111°15E 32 E6
Héraðsflói *Iceland* 65°42N 14°12W 8 D6
Héraðsvötn → *Iceland* 65°45N 19°25W 8 D4
Heraklion = Iraklio *Greece* 35°20N 25°12E 23 G11
Herald Cays *Australia* 16°58S 149°9E 62 B4
Herāt *Afghan.* 34°20N 62°7E 40 B3
Herāt □ *Afghan.* 35°0N 62°0E 40 B3
Herbert *Canada* 50°30N 107°10W 71 C7
Herbert → *Australia* 18°31S 146°17E 62 B4
Herbertabad *India* 11°43N 92°37E 45 J11
Herberton *Australia* 17°20S 145°25E 62 B4
Herbertsdale *S. Africa* 34°1S 21°46E 56 D3
Herceg-Novi *Montenegro* 42°30N 18°33E 23 C8
Herchmer *Canada* 57°22N 94°10W 71 B10
Herðubreið *Iceland* 65°11N 16°21W 8 D5
Hereford *U.K.* 52°4N 2°43W 13 E5
Hereford *U.S.A.* 34°49N 102°24W 84 D3
Herefordshire □ *U.K.* 52°8N 2°40W 13 E5
Herentals *Belgium* 51°12N 4°51E 15 C4
Herford *Germany* 52°7N 8°39E 16 B5
Herington *U.S.A.* 38°40N 96°57W 80 F5
Herkimer *U.S.A.* 43°2N 74°59W 83 D10
Herlen → *Asia* 48°48N 117°0E 31 B12
Herlong *U.S.A.* 40°8N 120°8W 78 E6
Herm *U.K.* 49°30N 2°28W 13 H5
Hermann *U.S.A.* 38°42N 91°27W 80 F8
Hermannsburg *Australia* 23°57S 132°45E 60 D5
Hermanus *S. Africa* 34°27S 19°12E 56 D2
Hermidale *Australia* 31°30S 146°42E 63 E4
Hermiston *U.S.A.* 45°51N 119°17W 76 D4
Hermon *Canada* 45°6N 77°37W 82 A7
Hermon *U.S.A.* 44°28N 75°14W 83 B9
Hermon, Mt. = Shaykh, J. ash *Lebanon* 33°25N 35°50E 48 B4
Hermosillo *Mexico* 29°10N 111°0W 86 B2
Hernád → *Hungary* 47°56N 21°8E 17 D11
Hernandarias *Paraguay* 25°20S 54°40W 95 B5
Hernandez *U.S.A.* 36°24N 120°46W 78 J6
Hernando *Argentina* 32°28S 63°40W 94 C3
Hernando *U.S.A.* 34°50N 90°0W 85 D10
Herndon *U.S.A.* 40°43N 76°51W 82 F8
Herne Bay *U.K.* 51°21N 1°8E 13 F9
Herning *Denmark* 56°8N 8°58E 9 H13
Heroica Caborca = Caborca *Mexico* 30°37N 112°6W 86 A2
Heroica Nogales = Nogales *Mexico* 31°19N 110°56W 86 A2
Heron Bay *Canada* 48°40N 86°25W 72 C2
Heron I. *Australia* 23°27S 151°55E 62 C5
Herreid *U.S.A.* 45°50N 100°4W 80 C3
Herrin *U.S.A.* 37°48N 89°2W 80 G9
Herriot *Canada* 56°22N 101°16W 71 B8
Herschel I. *Canada* 69°35N 139°5W 4 C1
Hershey *U.S.A.* 40°17N 76°39W 83 F8
Herstal *Belgium* 50°40N 5°38E 15 D5
Hertford *U.K.* 51°48N 0°4W 13 F7
Hertfordshire □ *U.K.* 51°51N 0°5W 13 F7
's-Hertogenbosch *Neths.* 51°42N 5°17E 15 C5
Hertzogville *S. Africa* 28°9S 25°30E 56 C4
Hervey B. *Australia* 25°0S 152°52E 62 C5
Herzliyya *Israel* 32°10N 34°50E 48 C3
Ḩeşār *Fārs, Iran* 29°52N 50°16E 47 D6
Ḩeşār *Markazī, Iran* 35°50N 49°12E 47 C6
Heshan *Guangdong, China* 22°34N 113°4E 35 F9
Heshan *Guangxi Zhuangzu, China* 23°50N 108°53E 34 F7
Heshui *China* 35°48N 108°0E 32 G5
Heshun *China* 37°22N 113°32E 32 F7
Hesperia *U.S.A.* 34°25N 117°18W 79 L9
Hesse = Hessen □ *Germany* 50°30N 9°0E 16 C5
Hessen □ *Germany* 50°30N 9°0E 16 C5
Hessle *U.K.* 53°44N 0°24W 12 D7
Hetauda *Nepal* 27°25N 85°2E 43 F11
Hetch Hetchy Aqueduct *U.S.A.* 37°29N 122°19W 78 H5
Hetta Enontekiö *Finland* 68°23N 23°37E 8 B20
Hettinger *U.S.A.* 46°0N 102°42W 80 B2
Heuksando *S. Korea* 34°40N 125°30E 33 G13
Heunghae *S. Korea* 36°12N 129°21E 33 F15
Heuvelton *U.S.A.* 44°37N 75°25W 83 B9
Hewitt *U.S.A.* 31°28N 97°12W 84 F6
Hexham *U.K.* 54°58N 2°4W 12 C5
Hexi *Yunnan, China* 24°9N 102°38E 34 E4
Hexi *Zhejiang, China* 27°58N 119°38E 35 D12
Hexigten Qi *China* 43°18N 117°30E 33 C9
Ḩeydarābād *Iran* 30°33N 55°38E 47 D7
Heysham *U.K.* 54°3N 2°53W 12 C5
Heyuan *China* 23°39N 114°40E 35 F10
Heywood *Australia* 38°8S 141°37E 63 F3
Heze *China* 35°14N 115°20E 32 G8
Hezhang *China* 27°8N 104°41E 34 D5
Hezhou *China* 24°27N 111°30E 35 E8
Hi Vista *U.S.A.* 34°45N 117°46W 79 L9
Hiawatha *U.S.A.* 39°51N 95°32W 80 F6
Hibbing *U.S.A.* 47°25N 92°56W 80 B7
Hibernia Reef *Australia* 12°0S 123°23E 60 B3
Hickman *U.S.A.* 36°34N 89°11W 80 G9
Hickory *U.S.A.* 35°44N 81°21W 85 D14
Hicks, Pt. *Australia* 37°49S 149°17E 63 F4
Hicks L. *Canada* 61°25N 100°0W 71 A9
Hicksville *U.S.A.* 40°46N 73°32W 83 F11
Hida-Gawa → *Japan* 35°26N 137°3E 29 G8
Hida-Sammyaku *Japan* 36°30N 137°40E 29 F8
Hidaka *Japan* 42°30N 142°10E 28 C11
Hidaka-Sammyaku *Japan* 42°35N 142°45E 28 C11
Hidalgo □ *Mexico* 20°30N 99°0W 87 C5
Hidalgo del Parral *Mexico* 26°56N 105°40W 86 B3
Hierro *Canary Is.* 27°44N 18°0W 52 C2
Higashiajima-San *Japan* 37°40N 140°10E 28 F10
Higashiōsaka *Japan* 34°39N 135°37E 29 G7
Higgins *U.S.A.* 36°7N 100°2W 84 C4
Higgins Corner *U.S.A.* 39°2N 121°5W 78 F5
High Bridge *U.S.A.* 40°40N 74°54W 83 F10
High Desert *U.S.A.* 43°40N 120°20W 76 E3
High Island Res. *China* 22°22N 114°21E 31 a
High Level *Canada* 58°31N 117°8W 70 B5
High Point *U.S.A.* 35°57N 80°0W 85 D15
High Prairie *Canada* 55°30N 116°30W 70 B5
High River *Canada* 50°30N 113°50W 70 C6
High Tatra = Tatry *Slovakia* 49°20N 20°0E 17 D11
High Veld *Africa* 27°0S 27°0E 50 J6
High Wycombe *U.K.* 51°37N 0°45W 13 F7
Highland □ *U.K.* 57°17N 4°21W 11 D4
Highland Park *U.S.A.* 42°11N 87°48W 80 D10
Highmore *U.S.A.* 44°31N 99°27W 80 C4
Highrock L. *Canada* 55°45N 100°30W 71 B8
Higüey *Dom. Rep.* 18°37N 68°42W 89 C6
Hiidenportti △ *Finland* 63°53N 29°0E 8 E23
Hiiumaa *Estonia* 58°50N 22°45E 9 G20
Ḩijārah, Şaḩrā' al *Iraq* 30°25N 44°30E 46 D5
Ḩijāz *Si. Arabia* 24°0N 40°0E 46 E3
Hijo = Tagum *Phil.* 7°33N 125°53E 37 C7
Hikari *Japan* 33°58N 131°58E 29 H5
Hikkaduwa *Sri Lanka* 6°8N 80°6E 45 L5
Hiko *U.S.A.* 37°32N 115°14W 78 H11
Hikone *Japan* 35°15N 136°10E 29 G8
Hikurangi *Gisborne, N.Z.* 37°55S 178°4E 59 C6
Hikurangi *Northland, N.Z.* 35°36S 174°17E 59 A5
Hildesheim *Germany* 52°9N 9°56E 16 B5
Hill → *Australia* 30°23S 115°3E 61 F2
Hill City *Idaho, U.S.A.* 43°18N 115°3W 76 E6
Hill City *Kans., U.S.A.* 39°22N 99°51W 80 F4
Hill City *Minn., U.S.A.* 46°59N 93°36W 80 B7
Hill City *S. Dak., U.S.A.* 43°56N 103°35W 80 D2
Hill Island L. *Canada* 60°30N 109°50W 71 A7
Hillaby, Mt. *Barbados* 13°12N 59°35W 89 g
Hillcrest *Barbados* 13°13N 59°31W 89 g
Hillegom *Neths.* 52°18N 4°35E 15 B4
Hillsboro *Kans., U.S.A.* 38°21N 97°12W 80 F5
Hillsboro *N. Dak., U.S.A.* 47°26N 97°3W 80 B5
Hillsboro *Ohio, U.S.A.* 39°12N 83°37W 81 F12
Hillsboro *Oreg., U.S.A.* 45°31N 122°59W 78 E4
Hillsboro *Tex., U.S.A.* 32°1N 97°8W 84 E6
Hillsborough *Grenada* 12°28N 61°28W 89 D7
Hillsborough *U.S.A.* 43°7N 71°54W 83 C13
Hillsborough Channel *Australia* 20°56S 149°15E 62 b
Hillsdale *Mich., U.S.A.* 41°56N 84°38W 81 E11
Hillsdale *N.Y., U.S.A.* 42°11N 73°32W 83 D11
Hillsport *Canada* 49°27N 85°34W 72 C2
Hillston *Australia* 33°30S 145°31E 63 E4
Hilo *U.S.A.* 19°44N 155°5W 75 M8
Hilton *U.S.A.* 43°17N 77°48W 82 C7
Hilton Head Island *U.S.A.* 32°13N 80°45W 85 E14
Hilversum *Neths.* 52°14N 5°10E 15 B5
Himachal Pradesh □ *India* 31°30N 77°0E 42 D7
Himalaya *Asia* 29°0N 84°0E 43 E11
Himalchuli *Nepal* 28°27N 84°38E 43 E11
Himatnagar *India* 23°37N 72°57E 42 H5
Himeji *Japan* 34°50N 134°40E 29 G7
Himi *Japan* 36°50N 136°55E 29 F8
Ḩimş *Syria* 34°40N 36°45E 48 A5
Ḩimş □ *Syria* 34°30N 37°0E 48 A6
Hin Khom, Laem *Thailand* 9°25N 99°56E 39 b
Hinche *Haiti* 19°9N 72°1W 89 C5
Hinchinbrook I. *Australia* 18°20S 146°15E 62 B4
Hinchinbrook Island △ *Australia* 18°14S 146°6E 62 B4
Hinckley *U.K.* 52°33N 1°22W 13 E6
Hinckley *U.S.A.* 46°1N 92°56W 80 B7
Hindaun *India* 26°44N 77°5E 42 F7
Hindmarsh, L. *Australia* 36°5S 141°55E 63 F3
Hindol *India* 20°40N 85°10E 44 D7
Hindu Bagh *Pakistan* 30°56N 67°50E 42 D2
Hindu Kush *Asia* 36°0N 71°0E 40 B7
Hindupur *India* 13°49N 77°32E 45 H3
Hines Creek *Canada* 56°20N 118°40W 70 B5
Hinesville *U.S.A.* 31°51N 81°36W 85 F14
Hinganghat *India* 20°30N 78°52E 44 D4
Hingham *U.S.A.* 48°33N 110°25W 76 B8
Hingir *India* 21°57N 83°41E 43 J10
Hingoli *India* 19°41N 77°15E 44 E3
Hinna = Imi *Ethiopia* 6°28N 42°10E 49 F3
Hinnøya *Norway* 68°35N 15°50E 8 B16
Hinojosa del Duque *Spain* 38°30N 5°9W 21 C3
Hinsdale *U.S.A.* 42°47N 72°29W 83 D12
Hinthada *Myanmar* 17°38N 95°26E 41 L19
Hinton *Canada* 53°26N 117°34W 70 C5
Hinton *U.S.A.* 37°40N 80°54W 81 G13
Hios = Chios *Greece* 38°27N 26°9E 23 E12
Hirado *Japan* 33°22N 129°33E 29 H4
Hirakud Dam *India* 21°32N 83°45E 44 D6
Hiran → *India* 23°6N 79°21E 43 H8
Hirapur *India* 24°22N 79°13E 43 G8
Hirara = Miyakojima *Japan* 24°48N 125°17E 29 M2
Hiratsuka *Japan* 35°19N 139°21E 29 G9
Hirekerur *India* 14°28N 75°23E 45 G2
Hiroo *Japan* 42°17N 143°19E 28 C11
Hirosaki *Japan* 40°34N 140°28E 28 D10
Hiroshima *Japan* 34°24N 132°30E 29 G6
Hiroshima □ *Japan* 34°50N 133°0E 29 G6
Hisar *India* 29°12N 75°45E 42 E6
Hisb, Sha'ib = Ḩasb, W. → *Iraq* 31°45N 44°17E 46 D5
Ḩismá *Si. Arabia* 28°30N 36°0E 46 D3
Hispaniola *W. Indies* 19°0N 71°0W 89 C5
Hīt *Iraq* 33°38N 42°49E 46 C4
Hita *Japan* 33°20N 130°58E 29 H5
Hitachi *Japan* 36°36N 140°39E 29 F10
Hitchin *U.K.* 51°58N 0°16W 13 F7
Hitiaa *Tahiti* 17°36S 149°18W 59 d
Hitoyoshi *Japan* 32°13N 130°45E 29 H5
Hitra *Norway* 63°30N 8°45E 8 E13
Hiva Oa *French Polynesia* 9°45S 139°0W 65 H14
Hixon *Canada* 53°25N 122°35W 70 C4
Ḩiyyon, N. → *Israel* 30°25N 35°10E 48 E4
Hjalmar L. *Canada* 61°33N 109°25W 71 A7
Hjälmaren *Sweden* 59°18N 15°40E 9 G16
Hjørring *Denmark* 57°29N 9°59E 9 H13
Hjort Trench *S. Ocean* 58°0S 157°30E 5 B10
Hkakabo Razi *Myanmar* 28°25N 97°23E 34 C1
Hkamti *Myanmar* 26°0N 95°39E 41 G19
Hlobane *S. Africa* 27°42S 31°0E 57 C5
Hluhluwe *S. Africa* 28°1S 32°15E 57 C5
Hluhluwe △ *S. Africa* 22°10S 32°5E 57 B5
Hlyboka *Ukraine* 48°5N 25°56E 17 D13
Ho *Ghana* 6°37N 0°27E 52 G6
Ho Chi Minh City = Thanh Pho Ho Chi Minh *Vietnam* 10°58N 106°40E 39 G6
Ho Hoa Binh *Vietnam* 20°50N 105°0E 34 G5
Ho Thac Ba *Vietnam* 21°42N 105°1E 38 A5
Ho Thuong *Vietnam* 19°32N 105°48E 38 C5
Hoa Binh *Vietnam* 20°50N 105°20E 34 G5
Hoa Hiep *Vietnam* 11°34N 105°51E 39 G5
Hoai Nhon *Vietnam* 14°28N 109°1E 38 E7
Hoang Lien △ *Vietnam* 21°30N 105°32E 38 B5
Hoang Lien Son *Vietnam* 22°0N 104°0E 34 F4
Hoang Sa, Dao = Paracel Is. *S. China Sea* 15°50N 112°0E 36 A4
Hoanib → *Namibia* 19°27S 12°46E 56 A2
Hoare B. *Canada* 65°17N 62°30W 69 D19
Hoarusib → *Namibia* 19°3S 12°36E 56 A2
Hobart *Australia* 42°50S 147°21E 63 G4
Hobart *U.S.A.* 35°1N 99°6W 84 D5
Hobbs *U.S.A.* 32°42N 103°8W 77 K12
Hobbs Coast *Antarctica* 74°50S 131°0W 5 D14
Hobe Sound *U.S.A.* 27°4N 80°8W 85 H14
Hobro *Denmark* 56°39N 9°46E 9 H13
Hoburgen *Sweden* 56°55N 18°7E 9 H18
Hobyo *Somalia* 5°25N 48°30E 49 F4
Hochfeld *Namibia* 21°28S 17°58E 56 B2
Hodaka-Dake *Japan* 36°17N 137°39E 29 F8
Hodeida = Al Ḩudaydah *Yemen* 14°50N 43°0E 49 E3
Hodgeville *Canada* 50°7N 106°58W 71 C7
Hodgson *Canada* 51°13N 97°36W 71 C9
Hódmezővásárhely *Hungary* 46°28N 20°22E 17 E11
Hodna, Chott el *Algeria* 35°26N 4°43E 52 A6
Hodonín *Czechia* 48°50N 17°10E 17 D9
Hoek van Holland *Neths.* 52°0N 4°7E 15 C4
Hoengseong *S. Korea* 37°29N 127°59E 33 F14
Hoeryong *N. Korea* 42°30N 129°45E 33 C15
Hoeyang *N. Korea* 38°43N 127°36E 33 E14
Hof *Germany* 50°19N 11°55E 16 C6
Hofmeyr *S. Africa* 31°39S 25°50E 56 D4
Höfn *Iceland* 64°15N 15°13W 8 D6
Hofors *Sweden* 60°31N 16°15E 9 F17
Hofsjökull *Iceland* 64°49N 18°48W 8 D4
Hōfu *Japan* 34°3N 131°34E 29 G5
Hogan Group *Australia* 39°13S 147°1E 63 F4
Hogarth, Mt. *Australia* 21°48S 136°58E 62 C2
Hoge Kempen △ *Belgium* 51°6N 5°35E 15 C5
Hoge Veluwe △ *Neths.* 52°5N 5°46E 15 B5
Hogenakai Falls *India* 12°6N 77°50E 45 H3
Hoggar = Ahaggar *Algeria* 23°0N 6°30E 52 D7
Hogsty Reef *Bahamas* 21°41N 73°48W 89 B5
Hoh → *U.S.A.* 47°45N 124°29W 78 C2
Hoh Xil Shan *China* 35°0N 89°0E 30 D6
Hohenwald *U.S.A.* 35°33N 87°33W 85 D11
Hoher Rhön = Rhön *Germany* 50°24N 9°58E 16 C5
Hohes Venn *Belgium* 50°30N 6°5E 15 D6
Hohhot *China* 40°52N 111°40E 32 D6
Hoi An *Vietnam* 15°53N 108°19E 38 E7
Hoi Xuan *Vietnam* 20°25N 105°9E 34 G5
Hoisington *U.S.A.* 38°31N 98°47W 80 F4
Hōjō *Japan* 33°58N 132°46E 29 H6
Hokianga Harbour *N.Z.* 35°31S 173°22E 59 A4
Hokitika *N.Z.* 42°42S 171°0E 59 E3
Hokkaidō □ *Japan* 43°30N 143°0E 28 C11
Hokuto *Japan* 41°49N 140°39E 28 D10
Holalkere *India* 14°2N 76°11E 45 G3
Holbrook *Australia* 35°42S 147°18E 63 F4
Holbrook *U.S.A.* 34°54N 110°10W 77 J8
Holcomb *U.S.A.* 42°54N 77°25W 82 D7
Holden *U.S.A.* 39°6N 112°16W 76 G7
Holdenville *U.S.A.* 35°5N 96°24W 84 D6
Holdrege *U.S.A.* 40°26N 99°23W 80 E4
Hole-Narsipur *India* 12°48N 76°16E 45 H3
Holetown *Barbados* 13°11N 59°38W 89 g
Holguín *Cuba* 20°50N 76°20W 88 B4
Hollams Bird I. *Namibia* 24°40S 14°30E 56 B1
Holland = Netherlands ■ *Europe* 52°0N 5°30E 15 C5
Holland *Mich., U.S.A.* 42°47N 86°7W 80 D10
Holland *N.Y., U.S.A.* 42°38N 78°32W 82 D6
Holland Centre *Canada* 44°23N 80°47W 82 B4
Holland Patent *U.S.A.* 43°14N 75°15W 83 C9
Hollandale *U.S.A.* 33°10N 90°51W 85 E9
Holley *U.S.A.* 43°14N 78°2W 82 C6
Hollidaysburg *U.S.A.* 40°26N 78°24W 82 F6
Hollis *U.S.A.* 34°41N 99°55W 84 D5
Hollister *Calif., U.S.A.* 36°51N 121°24W 78 J5
Hollister *Idaho, U.S.A.* 42°21N 114°35W 76 E6
Holly Hill *U.S.A.* 29°16N 81°3W 85 G14
Holly Springs *U.S.A.* 34°46N 89°27W 85 D10
Hollywood *Ireland* 53°6N 6°35W 10 B6
Holman = Ulukhaktok *Canada* 70°44N 117°44W 68 C8
Hólmavík *Iceland* 65°42N 21°40W 8 D3
Holmen *U.S.A.* 43°58N 91°15W 80 D8
Holmes Reefs *Australia* 16°27S 148°0E 62 B4
Holmsund *Sweden* 63°41N 20°20E 8 E19
Holon *Israel* 32°0N 34°46E 48 C3
Holroyd → *Australia* 14°10S 141°36E 62 A3
Holstebro *Denmark* 56°22N 8°37E 9 H13
Holsworthy *U.K.* 50°48N 4°22W 13 G3
Holton *Canada* 54°31N 57°12W 73 B8
Holton *U.S.A.* 39°28N 95°44W 80 F6
Holtville *U.S.A.* 32°49N 115°23W 79 N11
Holwerd *Neths.* 53°22N 5°54E 15 A5
Holy Cross *U.S.A.* 62°12N 159°46W 74 C8
Holy I. *Anglesey, U.K.* 53°17N 4°37W 12 D3
Holy I. *Northumberland, U.K.* 55°40N 1°47W 12 B6
Holyhead *U.K.* 53°18N 4°38W 12 D3
Holyoke *Colo., U.S.A.* 40°35N 102°18W 76 F12
Holyoke *Mass., U.S.A.* 42°12N 72°37W 83 D12
Holyrood *Canada* 47°27N 53°8W 73 C9
Homalin *Myanmar* 24°55N 95°0E 41 G19
Homand *Iran* 32°28N 59°37E 47 C8
Homathko → *Canada* 51°0N 124°56W 70 C4
Hombori *Mali* 15°20N 1°38W 52 E5
Home B. *Canada* 68°40N 67°10W 69 D18
Home Hill *Australia* 19°43S 147°25E 62 B4
Home Reef *Tonga* 18°59S 174°47W 59 c
Homedale *U.S.A.* 43°37N 116°56W 76 E5
Homer *Alaska, U.S.A.* 59°39N 151°33W 68 F1
Homer *La., U.S.A.* 32°48N 93°4W 84 E8
Homer *N.Y., U.S.A.* 42°38N 76°10W 83 D8
Homer City *U.S.A.* 40°32N 79°10W 82 F5
Homestead *Australia* 20°20S 145°40E 62 C4
Homestead *U.S.A.* 25°28N 80°29W 85 J14
Homestead △ *U.S.A.* 40°17N 96°50W 80 E5
Homnabad *India* 17°45N 77°11E 44 F3
Homoine *Mozam.* 23°55S 35°8E 57 B6
Homs = Ḩimş *Syria* 34°40N 36°45E 48 A5
Homyel *Belarus* 52°28N 31°0E 17 B16
Hon Chong *Vietnam* 10°25N 104°30E 39 G5
Hon Hai *Vietnam* 10°0N 109°0E 39 H7
Hon Me *Vietnam* 19°23N 105°56E 38 C5
Honan = Henan □ *China* 34°0N 114°0E 32 H8
Honavar *India* 14°17N 74°27E 45 G2
Honbetsu *Japan* 43°7N 143°37E 28 C11
Honcut *U.S.A.* 39°20N 121°32W 78 F5
Hondeklipbaai *S. Africa* 30°19S 17°17E 56 D2
Hondo *Japan* 32°27N 130°12E 29 H5
Hondo *U.S.A.* 29°21N 99°9W 84 G5
Hondo, Río → *Belize* 18°25N 88°21W 87 D7
Honduras ■ *Cent. Amer.* 14°40N 86°30W 88 D2
Honduras, G. de *Caribbean* 16°50N 87°0W 88 C2
Hønefoss *Norway* 60°10N 10°18E 9 F14
Honesdale *U.S.A.* 41°34N 75°16W 83 E9
Honey Harbour *Canada* 44°52N 79°49W 82 B5
Honey L. *U.S.A.* 40°15N 120°19W 78 E6
Honfleur *France* 49°25N 0°13E 20 B4
Hong → *Asia* 20°16N 106°34E 38 B5
Hong Gai *Vietnam* 20°57N 107°5E 34 G6
Hong He → *China* 32°25N 115°35E 32 H8
Hong Hu *China* 29°54N 113°24E 35 C9
Hong Kong □ *China* 22°11N 114°14E 31 a
Hong'an *China* 31°20N 114°40E 35 B10
Hongcheon *S. Korea* 37°44N 127°53E 33 F14
Honghai Wan *China* 22°40N 115°0E 35 F10
Honghe *China* 23°25N 102°25E 34 F4
Honghu *China* 29°50N 113°30E 35 C9
Hongjiang *China* 27°7N 109°59E 34 D7
Hongliu He → *China* 38°0N 109°50E 32 F5
Hongor *Mongolia* 45°45N 112°50E 32 B7
Hongseong *S. Korea* 36°37N 126°38E 33 F14
Hongshan *China* 36°38N 117°58E 33 F9
Hongshui He → *China* 23°48N 109°30E 34 F7
Hongtong *China* 36°16N 111°40E 32 F6
Honguedo, Détroit d' *Canada* 49°15N 64°0W 73 C7
Hongwon *N. Korea* 40°0N 127°56E 33 E14
Hongya *China* 29°57N 103°22E 34 C4
Hongyuan *China* 32°51N 102°40E 34 A4
Hongze Hu *China* 33°15N 118°35E 33 H10
Honiara *Solomon Is.* 9°27S 159°57E 58 B8
Honiton *U.K.* 50°47N 3°11W 13 G4
Honjō = Yurihonjō *Japan* 39°23N 140°3E 28 E10
Honnali *India* 14°15N 75°40E 45 G2
Honningsvåg *Norway* 70°59N 25°59E 8 A21
Honolulu *U.S.A.* 21°19N 157°52W 75 L8
Honshū *Japan* 36°0N 138°0E 29 F9
Hood, Mt. *U.S.A.* 45°23N 121°42W 76 D3
Hood, Pt. *Australia* 34°23S 119°34E 61 F2
Hood River *U.S.A.* 45°43N 121°31W 76 D3
Hoodsport *U.S.A.* 47°24N 123°9W 78 C3
Hoogeveen *Neths.* 52°44N 6°28E 15 B6
Hoogezand-Sappemeer *Neths.* 53°9N 6°45E 15 A6
Hooghly = Hugli → *India* 21°56N 88°4E 43 J13
Hooghly-Chinsura = Chunchura *India* 22°53N 88°27E 43 H13
Hook Hd. *Ireland* 52°7N 6°56W 10 D5
Hook I. *Australia* 20°4S 149°0E 62 b
Hook of Holland = Hoek van Holland *Neths.* 52°0N 4°7E 15 C4
Hooker *U.S.A.* 36°52N 101°13W 84 C4
Hooker Creek = Lajamanu *Australia* 18°23S 130°38E 60 C5
Hooker Creek ✪ *Australia* 18°6S 130°23E 60 C5
Hoonah *U.S.A.* 58°7N 135°27W 70 B1
Hooper Bay *U.S.A.* 61°32N 166°6W 74 C6
Hoopeston *U.S.A.* 40°28N 87°40W 80 E10
Hoopstad *S. Africa* 27°50S 25°55E 56 C4
Hoorn *Neths.* 52°38N 5°4E 15 B5
Hoover *U.S.A.* 33°24N 86°49W 85 E11
Hoover Dam *U.S.A.* 36°1N 114°44W 79 K12
Hooversville *U.S.A.* 40°9N 78°55W 82 F6
Hop Bottom *U.S.A.* 41°42N 75°46W 83 E9
Hope *Canada* 49°25N 121°25W 70 D4
Hope *Ariz., U.S.A.* 33°43N 113°42W 79 M13
Hope *Ark., U.S.A.* 33°40N 93°36W 84 E8
Hope, L. *S. Austral., Australia* 28°24S 139°18E 63 D2
Hope, L. *W. Austral., Australia* 32°35S 120°15E 61 F3
Hope, Pt. *U.S.A.* 68°21N 166°47W 66 C3
Hope I. *Canada* 44°55N 80°11W 82 B4
Hope Town *Bahamas* 26°35N 76°57W 88 A4
Hope Vale *Australia* 15°16S 145°20E 62 B4
Hope Vale ✪ *Australia* 15°8S 145°15E 62 B4
Hopedale *Canada* 55°28N 60°13W 73 A7
Hopedale *U.S.A.* 42°8N 71°33W 83 D13
Hopefield *S. Africa* 33°3S 18°22E 56 D2
Hopei = Hebei □ *China* 39°0N 116°0E 32 E9
Hopelchén *Mexico* 19°46N 89°51W 87 D7
Hopetoun *Vic., Australia* 35°42S 142°22E 63 F3
Hopetoun *W. Austral., Australia* 33°57S 120°7E 61 F3
Hopetown *S. Africa* 29°34S 24°3E 56 C3
Hopewell *U.S.A.* 37°18N 77°17W 81 G15
Hopkins, L. *Australia* 24°15S 128°35E 60 D4
Hopkinsville *U.S.A.* 36°52N 87°29W 80 G10
Hopland *U.S.A.* 38°58N 123°7W 78 G3
Hoquiam *U.S.A.* 46°59N 123°53W 78 D3
Horana *Sri Lanka* 6°43N 80°4E 45 L5
Hordern Hills *Australia* 20°15S 130°0E 60 D5
Horinger *China* 40°28N 111°48E 32 D6
Horizontina *Brazil* 27°37S 54°19W 95 B5
Horlick Mts. *Antarctica* 84°0S 102°0W 5 E15
Horlivka *Ukraine* 48°19N 38°5E 19 E6
Hormak *Iran* 29°58N 60°51E 47 D9
Hormoz *Iran* 27°35N 55°0E 47 E7
Hormoz, Jaz.-ye *Iran* 27°8N 56°28E 47 E8
Hormozgān □ *Iran* 27°30N 56°0E 47 E8
Hormuz, Kūh-e *Iran* 27°27N 55°10E 47 E7
Hormuz, Str. of *The Gulf* 26°30N 56°30E 47 E8
Horn *Austria* 48°39N 15°40E 16 D8
Horn → *Canada* 61°30N 118°1W 70 A5
Horn, Cape = Hornos, C. de *Chile* 55°50S 67°30W 96 H3
Horn Head *Ireland* 55°14N 8°0W 10 A3
Horn I. *Australia* 10°37S 142°17E 62 A3
Horn Plateau *Canada* 62°15N 119°15W 70 A5
Hornavan *Sweden* 66°15N 17°30E 8 C17
Hornbeck *U.S.A.* 31°20N 93°24W 84 F8
Hornbrook *U.S.A.* 41°55N 122°33W 76 F2
Horncastle *U.K.* 53°13N 0°7W 12 D7
Hornell *U.S.A.* 42°20N 77°40W 82 D7
Hornell L. *Canada* 62°20N 119°25W 70 A5
Hornepayne *Canada* 49°14N 84°48W 72 C3
Hornings Mills *Canada* 44°9N 80°12W 82 B4
Hornitos *U.S.A.* 37°30N 120°14W 78 H6
Hornos, C. de *Chile* 55°50S 67°30W 96 H3
Hornsby *Australia* 33°42S 151°2E 63 B5
Hornsea *U.K.* 53°55N 0°11W 12 D7
Horobetsu = Noboribetsu *Japan* 42°24N 141°6E 28 C10
Horodenka *Ukraine* 48°41N 25°29E 17 D13
Horodok *Khmelnytskyy, Ukraine* 49°10N 26°34E 17 D14
Horodok *Lviv, Ukraine* 49°46N 23°32E 17 D12
Horokhiv *Ukraine* 50°30N 24°45E 17 C13
Horqin Youyi Qianqi *China* 46°5N 122°3E 33 A12
Horqin Zuoyi Zhongqi *China* 44°8N 123°18E 33 B12
Horqueta *Paraguay* 23°15S 56°55W 94 A4
Horse Cr. → *U.S.A.* 41°57N 103°58W 76 F12
Horse I. *Canada* 53°20N 99°6W 71 C9
Horse Is. *Canada* 50°15N 55°50W 73 B8
Horsefly L. *Canada* 52°25N 121°0W 70 C4
Horseheads *U.S.A.* 42°10N 76°49W 82 D8
Horsens *Denmark* 55°52N 9°51E 9 J13
Horseshoe Lake *Canada* 45°17N 79°51W 82 A5
Horsham *Australia* 36°44S 142°13E 63 F3
Horsham *U.K.* 51°4N 0°20W 13 F7
Horta *Azores* 38°32N 28°38W 52 a
Horten *Norway* 59°25N 10°32E 9 G14
Horti *India* 17°7N 75°47E 44 F2
Horton *U.S.A.* 39°40N 95°32W 80 F6
Horton → *Canada* 69°56N 126°52W 68 D6
Horwood L. *Canada* 48°5N 82°20W 72 C3
Hosapete *India* 15°15N 76°20E 45 G3
Hosdrug = Kanhangad *India* 12°21N 74°58E 45 H2
Hosdurga *India* 13°49N 76°17E 45 H3
Ḩoseynābād *Khuzestān, Iran* 32°45N 48°20E 47 C6
Ḩoseynābād *Kordestān, Iran* 35°33N 47°8E 46 C5
Hoshangabad *India* 22°45N 77°45E 42 H7
Hoshiarpur *India* 31°30N 75°58E 42 D6
Hoskote *India* 13°4N 77°48E 45 H3
Hospet = Hosapete *India* 15°15N 76°20E 45 G3
Hoste, I. *Chile* 55°0S 69°0W 96 H3
Hosur *India* 12°43N 77°49E 45 H3
Hot *Thailand* 18°8N 98°29E 38 C2
Hot Creek Range *U.S.A.* 38°40N 116°20W 76 G5
Hot Springs *Ark., U.S.A.* 34°31N 93°3W 84 D8
Hot Springs *S. Dak., U.S.A.* 43°26N 103°29W 80 D2
Hot Springs △ *U.S.A.* 34°31N 93°3W 84 D8
Hotagen *Sweden* 63°59N 14°12E 8 E16
Hotan *China* 37°25N 79°55E 30 D4
Hotan He → *China* 40°22N 80°56E 30 C5
Hotazel *S. Africa* 27°17S 22°58E 56 C3
Hotchkiss *U.S.A.* 38°48N 107°43W 76 G10
Hotham, C. *Australia* 12°2S 131°18E 60 B5
Hoting *Sweden* 64°8N 16°15E 8 D17
Hotte, Massif de la *Haiti* 18°30N 73°45W 89 C5
Hottentotsbaai *Namibia* 26°8S 14°59E 56 C1
Hou Hai *China* 22°32N 113°56E 31 a
Houei Sai *Laos* 20°18N 100°26E 34 G3

Houffalize *Belgium* 50°8N 5°48E **15** D5
Houghton *Mich., U.S.A.* 47°7N 88°34W **80** B9
Houghton *N.Y., U.S.A.* 42°25N 78°10W **82** D6
Houghton L. *U.S.A.* 44°21N 84°44W **81** C11
Houghton-le-Spring *U.K.* 54°51N 1°28W **12** C6
Houhora Heads *N.Z.* 34°49S 173°9E **59** A4
Houlton *U.S.A.* 46°8N 67°51W **81** B20
Houma *China* 35°36N 111°20E **32** G6
Houma *U.S.A.* 29°36N 90°43W **85** G9
Housatonic → *U.S.A.* 41°10N 73°7W **83** E11
Houston *Canada* 54°25N 126°39W **70** C3
Houston *Mo., U.S.A.* 37°22N 91°58W **80** G8
Houston *Tex., U.S.A.* 29°45N 95°21W **84** G7
Houston George Bush
  Intercontinental ✈ (IAH)
  U.S.A. 29°59N 95°20W **84** G7
Hout = Mogwadi →
  S. Africa 23°4S 29°36E **57** B4
Houtkraal *S. Africa* 30°23S 24°5E **56** D3
Houtman Abrolhos
  Australia 28°43S 113°48E **61** E1
Hovd = Dund-Us *Mongolia* 48°1N 91°38E **30** B7
Hove *U.K.* 50°50N 0°10W **13** G7
Hovenweep △ *U.S.A.* 37°20N 109°0W **77** H9
Hoveyzeh *Iran* 31°27N 48°4E **47** D6
Hövsgöl *Mongolia* 43°37N 109°39E **32** C5
Hövsgöl Nuur *Mongolia* 51°0N 100°30E **30** A9
Howar, Wadi → *Sudan* 17°30N 27°8E **53** E11
Howard *Australia* 25°16S 152°32E **63** D5
Howard *Pa., U.S.A.* 41°1N 77°40W **82** F7
Howard *S. Dak., U.S.A.* 44°1N 97°32W **80** C5
Howe *U.S.A.* 43°48N 113°0W **76** E7
Howe, C. *Australia* 37°30S 150°0E **63** F5
Howe, West Cape
  Australia 35°8S 117°36E **61** G2
Howe I. *Canada* 44°16N 76°17W **83** B8
Howell *U.S.A.* 42°36N 83°56W **81** D12
Howick *Canada* 45°11N 73°51W **83** A11
Howick *S. Africa* 29°28S 30°14E **57** C5
Howick Group *Australia* 14°20S 145°30E **62** A4
Howitt, L. *Australia* 27°40S 138°40E **63** D2
Howland I. *Pac. Oc.* 0°48N 176°38W **64** G10
Howth *Ireland* 53°23N 6°7W **10** C5
Howth Hd. *Ireland* 53°22N 6°4W **10** C5
Höxter *Germany* 51°46N 9°22E **16** C5
Hoy *U.K.* 58°50N 3°15W **11** C5
Høyanger *Norway* 61°13N 6°4E **8** F12
Hoyerswerda *Germany* 51°26N 14°14E **16** C8
Hpa-an = Pa-an
  Myanmar 16°51N 97°40E **41** L20
Hpunan Pass *Asia* 27°30N 96°55E **41** F20
Hpyu = Pyu *Myanmar* 18°30N 96°28E **41** K20
Hradec Králové *Czechia* 50°15N 15°50E **16** C8
Hrodna *Belarus* 53°42N 23°52E **17** B12
Hrodzyanka *Belarus* 53°31N 28°42E **17** B15
Hron → *Slovakia* 47°49N 18°45E **17** E10
Hrvatska = Croatia ■
  Europe 45°20N 16°0E **16** F9
Hrymayliv *Ukraine* 49°20N 26°5E **17** D14
Hsenwi *Myanmar* 23°22N 97°55E **41** H20
Hsiamen = Xiamen
  China 24°25N 118°4E **35** E12
Hsian = Xi'an *China* 34°15N 109°0E **32** G5
Hsinchu *Taiwan* 24°48N 120°58E **35** E13
Hsinhailien = Lianyungang
  China 34°40N 119°11E **33** G10
Hsinkai = Bhamo
  Myanmar 24°15N 97°15E **41** G20
Hsinying *Taiwan* 23°21N 120°17E **35** F13
Hsopket *Myanmar* 23°11N 98°26E **34** F2
Hsüchou = Xuzhou
  China 34°18N 117°10E **33** G9
Htawei = Dawei *Myanmar* 14°2N 98°12E **38** E2
Hu Xian *China* 34°8N 108°42E **32** G5
Hua Hin *Thailand* 12°34N 99°58E **38** F2
Hua Muang *Laos* 20°13N 103°52E **38** B4
Hua Shan *China* 34°28N 110°4E **32** G6
Hua Xian *Henan, China* 35°30N 114°30E **32** G8
Hua Xian *Shaanxi, China* 34°30N 109°48E **32** G5
Hua'an *China* 25°1N 117°32E **35** E11
Huab → *Namibia* 20°52S 13°25E **56** A2
Huacheng *China* 24°4N 115°37E **35** E10
Huachinera *Mexico* 30°9N 108°55E **86** A3
Huacho *Peru* 11°10S 77°35W **92** F3
Huade *China* 41°55N 113°59E **32** D7
Huadian *China* 43°0N 126°40E **33** C14
Huai, Î. *Fr. Polynesia* 16°46S 150°58W **65** J12
Huai Hat △ *Thailand* 16°52N 104°17E **38** D5
Huai He → *China* 33°0N 118°30E **35** A12
Huai Kha Khaeng △
  Thailand 15°20N 98°55E **38** E2
Huai Nam Dang △
  Thailand 19°30N 98°30E **38** C2
Huai Yot *Thailand* 7°45N 99°37E **39** J2
Huai'an *Hebei, China* 40°30N 114°20E **32** D8
Huai'an *Jiangsu, China* 33°30N 119°10E **33** H10
Huaibei *China* 34°0N 116°48E **32** G9
Huaibin *China* 32°32N 115°27E **35** A10
Huaide = Gongzhuling
  China 43°30N 124°40E **33** C13
Huaidezhen *China* 43°48N 124°50E **33** C13
Huaihua *China* 27°32N 109°57E **34** D6
Huaiji *China* 23°55N 112°12E **35** F9
Huainan *China* 32°38N 116°58E **35** A11
Huaining *China* 30°24N 116°40E **35** B11
Huairen *China* 39°48N 113°20E **32** E7
Huairou *China* 40°20N 116°35E **32** D9
Huaiyang *China* 33°40N 114°52E **32** H8
Huaiyin *China* 33°30N 119°2E **33** H10
Huaiyuan *Anhui, China* 32°55N 117°10E **33** H9
Huaiyuan *Guangxi Zhuangzu,*
  China 24°31N 108°22E **34** E7
Huajuápan de León
  Mexico 17°48N 97°46W **87** D5
Hualapai Peak *U.S.A.* 35°5N 113°54W **79** K13
Hualien *Taiwan* 23°59N 121°36E **35** F13
Huallaga → *Peru* 5°15S 75°30W **92** E3
Huambo *Angola* 12°42S 15°54E **55** G3

Huan Jiang → *China* 34°28N 109°0E **32** G5
Huan Xian *China* 36°33N 107°7E **32** F4
Huancabamba *Peru* 5°10S 79°15W **92** E3
Huancane *Peru* 15°10S 69°44W **92** G5
Huancavelica *Peru* 12°50S 75°5W **92** F3
Huancayo *Peru* 12°5S 75°12W **92** F3
Huanchaca *Bolivia* 20°15S 66°40W **92** H5
Huang Hai = Yellow Sea
  China 35°0N 123°0E **33** G12
Huang He → *China* 37°55N 118°50E **33** F10
Huang Xian *China* 37°38N 120°30E **33** F11
Huangchuan *China* 32°15N 115°10E **35** A10
Huangdao *China* 36°0N 120°7E **33** G11
Huanggang *China* 30°29N 114°52E **35** B10
Huangguoshu *China* 26°0N 105°40E **34** E5
Huanghua *China* 38°22N 117°20E **33** E9
Huanghuagang *China* 38°20N 117°54E **33** E9
Huangling *China* 35°34N 109°15E **32** G5
Huanglong *China* 35°30N 109°59E **32** G5
Huanglong △ *China* 32°44N 103°50E **34** A4
Huanglongtan *China* 32°40N 110°33E **35** A8
Huangmei *China* 30°5N 115°56E **35** B10
Huangpi *China* 30°50N 114°22E **35** B10
Huangping *China* 26°52N 107°54E **34** D6
Huangshan *Anhui, China* 30°8N 118°9E **35** B12
Huangshan *Anhui,*
  China 29°42N 118°25E **35** C12
Huangshi *China* 30°10N 115°3E **35** B10
Huangsongdian *China* 43°45N 127°25E **33** C14
Huangyan *China* 28°38N 121°19E **35** C13
Huangyangsi *China* 26°33N 111°39E **35** D8
Huaning *China* 24°17N 102°56E **34** E4
Huanjiang *China* 24°50N 108°18E **34** E7
Huanren *China* 41°23N 125°20E **33** D13
Huantai *China* 36°58N 117°56E **33** F9
Huánuco *Peru* 9°55S 76°15W **92** E3
Huaping *China* 26°46N 101°25E **34** D3
Huaraz *Peru* 9°30S 77°32W **92** E3
Huarmey *Peru* 10°5S 78°5W **92** F3
Huarong *China* 29°29N 112°30E **35** C9
Huascarán, Nevado *Peru* 9°7S 77°37W **92** E3
Huasco *Chile* 28°30S 71°15W **94** B1
Huasco → *Chile* 28°27S 71°13W **94** B1
Huasna *U.S.A.* 35°6N 120°24W **79** K6
Huatabampo *Mexico* 26°50N 109°38W **86** B3
Huauchinango *Mexico* 20°12N 98°3W **87** C5
Huautla de Jiménez
  Mexico 18°8N 96°51W **87** D5
Huaxi *China* 26°25N 106°40E **34** D6
Huayin *China* 34°35N 110°5E **32** G6
Huaying *China* 30°8N 106°44E **34** B6
Huayuan *China* 28°37N 109°29E **34** C7
Huazhou *China* 21°33N 110°33E **35** G8
Hubballi *India* 15°22N 75°15E **45** G2
Hubbard *Ohio, U.S.A.* 41°9N 80°34W **82** E4
Hubbard *Tex., U.S.A.* 31°51N 96°48W **84** F6
Hubbard Glacier *Canada* 60°18N 139°22W **68** E4
Hubbart Pt. *Canada* 59°21N 94°41W **71** B10
Hubei □ *China* 31°0N 112°0E **35** B9
Hubli = Hubballi *India* 15°22N 75°15E **45** G2
Huch'ang *N. Korea* 41°25N 127°2E **33** D14
Hucknall *U.K.* 53°3N 1°13W **12** D6
Huddersfield *U.K.* 53°39N 1°47W **12** D6
Hudiksvall *Sweden* 61°43N 17°10E **8** F17
Hudson *Canada* 50°6N 92°9W **72** B1
Hudson *Mass., U.S.A.* 42°23N 71°34W **83** D13
Hudson *N.Y., U.S.A.* 42°15N 73°46W **83** D11
Hudson *Wis., U.S.A.* 44°58N 92°45W **80** C7
Hudson *Wyo., U.S.A.* 42°54N 108°35W **76** E9
Hudson → *U.S.A.* 40°42N 74°2W **83** F10
Hudson, C. *Antarctica* 68°21S 153°45E **5** C10
Hudson Bay *Nunavut,*
  Canada 60°0N 86°0W **69** F14
Hudson Bay *Sask.,*
  Canada 52°51N 102°23W **71** C8
Hudson Falls *U.S.A.* 43°18N 73°35W **83** C11
Hudson Mts. *Antarctica* 74°32S 99°20W **5** D16
Hudson Str. *Canada* 62°0N 70°0W **69** E18
Hudson's Hope *Canada* 56°0N 121°54W **70** B4
Hue *Vietnam* 16°30N 107°35E **38** D6
Huehuetenango
  Guatemala 15°20N 91°28W **88** C1
Huejúcar *Mexico* 22°21N 103°13W **86** C4
Huelva *Spain* 37°18N 6°57W **21** D2
Huentelauquén *Chile* 31°38S 71°33W **94** C1
Huerta, Sa. de la
  Argentina 31°10S 67°30W **94** C2
Huesca *Spain* 42°8N 0°25W **21** A5
Huetamo *Mexico* 18°35N 100°53W **86** D4
Hugh → *Australia* 25°1S 134°1E **62** D1
Hughenden *Australia* 20°52S 144°10E **62** C3
Hughesville *U.S.A.* 41°14N 76°44W **83** E8
Hugli → *India* 21°56N 88°4E **43** J13
Hugo *Colo., U.S.A.* 39°8N 103°28W **76** G12
Hugo *Okla., U.S.A.* 34°1N 95°31W **84** D7
Hugoton *U.S.A.* 37°11N 101°21W **80** G3
Hui Xian = Huixian
  China 35°27N 113°12E **32** G7
Hui Xian *China* 33°50N 106°4E **32** H4
Hui'an *China* 25°1N 118°43E **35** E12
Hui'anbu *China* 37°28N 106°38E **32** F4
Huichang *China* 25°32N 115°45E **35** E10
Huichapan *Mexico* 20°23N 99°39W **87** C5
Huichon *N. Korea* 40°10N 126°16E **33** D14
Huidong *Guangdong,*
  China 22°58N 114°43E **35** F10
Huidong *Sichuan, China* 26°34N 102°35E **34** D4
Huifa He → *China* 43°0N 127°50E **33** C14
Huila, Nevado del *Colombia* 3°0N 76°0W **92** C3
Huilai *China* 23°0N 116°18E **35** F11
Huili *China* 26°35N 102°17E **34** D4
Huimin *China* 37°27N 117°28E **33** F9
Huinan *China* 42°40N 126°2E **33** C14
Huinca Renancó
  Argentina 34°51S 64°22W **94** C3
Huining *China* 35°38N 105°0E **32** G3
Huinong *China* 39°5N 106°35E **32** E4
Huishui *China* 26°7N 106°38E **34** D6
Huiting *China* 34°5N 116°5E **32** G9
Huitong *China* 26°50N 109°45E **34** D7

Huixian *China* 35°27N 113°12E **32** G7
Huixtla *Mexico* 15°9N 92°28W **87** D6
Huize *China* 26°24N 103°15E **34** D4
Huizhou *China* 23°0N 114°23E **35** F10
Hukawng Valley
  Myanmar 26°30N 96°30E **41** F20
Hukeri *India* 16°14N 74°36E **45** F2
Hukou *China* 29°45N 116°21E **35** C11
Hukuntsi *Botswana* 23°58S 21°45E **56** B3
Hukuyfā' *Si. Arabia* 25°58N 40°45E **46** E4
Hulin *China* 45°48N 132°59E **31** B15
Hulin He → *China* 45°0N 122°10E **33** B12
Hull = Kingston upon Hull
  U.K. 53°45N 0°21W **12** D7
Hull *Canada* 45°26N 75°43W **83** A9
Hull → *U.K.* 53°44N 0°20W **12** D7
Hulst *Neths.* 51°17N 4°2E **15** C4
Huludao *China* 40°45N 120°50E **33** D11
Hulun Nur *China* 49°0N 117°30E **31** B12
Hulunbuir = Hailar
  China 49°10N 119°38E **31** B12
Huma, Tanjung *Malaysia* 5°29N 100°16E **39** c
Humacao *Puerto Rico* 18°9N 65°50W **89** d
Humahuaca *Argentina* 23°10S 65°25W **94** A2
Humaitá *Brazil* 7°35S 63°1W **92** E6
Humaitá *Paraguay* 27°2S 58°31W **94** B4
Humansdorp *S. Africa* 34°2S 24°46E **56** E3
Humbe *Angola* 16°40S 14°55E **56** B1
Humber → *U.K.* 53°42N 0°27W **12** D7
Humboldt *Canada* 52°15N 105°9W **71** C7
Humboldt *Iowa, U.S.A.* 42°44N 94°13W **80** D6
Humboldt *Tenn., U.S.A.* 35°50N 88°55W **85** D10
Humboldt → *U.S.A.* 39°59N 118°36W **76** G4
Humboldt Gletscher = Sermersuaq
  Greenland 79°30N 62°0W **69** B19
Hume *U.S.A.* 36°48N 118°54W **78** J8
Hume, L. *Australia* 36°0S 147°5E **63** F4
Humen *China* 22°50N 113°40E **31** a
Humenné *Slovakia* 48°55N 21°50E **17** D11
Humphreys, Mt. *U.S.A.* 37°17N 118°40W **78** H8
Humphreys Peak
  U.S.A. 35°21N 111°41W **77** J8
Humptulips *U.S.A.* 47°14N 123°57W **78** C3
Hūn *Libya* 29°2N 16°0E **53** C9
Hun Jiang → *China* 40°50N 125°38E **33** D13
Húnaflói *Iceland* 65°50N 20°50W **8** D3
Hunan □ *China* 27°30N 112°0E **35** D9
Hunchun *China* 42°52N 130°28E **33** C16
Hundewali *Pakistan* 31°55N 72°38E **42** D5
Hundred Mile House
  Canada 51°38N 121°18W **70** C4
Hunedoara *Romania* 45°40N 22°50E **17** F12
Hung Yen *Vietnam* 20°39N 106°4E **34** G6
Hunga Ha'apai *Tonga* 20°41S 175°7W **59** c
Hungary ■ *Europe* 47°20N 19°20E **17** E10
Hungary, Plain of *Europe* 47°0N 20°0E **6** F10
Hungerford *Australia* 28°58S 144°24E **63** D3
Hŭngnam *N. Korea* 39°49N 127°45E **33** E14
Hungt'ou Hsü = Lan Yü
  Taiwan 22°4N 121°25E **35** F13
Hunjiang *China* 41°54N 126°26E **33** D14
Hunsberge *Namibia* 27°45S 17°12E **56** D2
Hunsrück *Germany* 49°56N 7°27E **16** D4
Hunstanton *U.K.* 52°56N 0°29E **12** E8
Hunsur *India* 12°16N 76°16E **45** H3
Hunter *U.S.A.* 42°13N 74°13W **83** D10
Hunter I. *Australia* 40°30S 144°45E **63** G3
Hunter I. *Canada* 51°55N 128°0W **70** C3
Hunter Ra. *Australia* 32°45S 150°15E **63** E5
Hunterville *N.Z.* 39°56S 175°35E **59** C5
Huntingburg *U.S.A.* 38°18N 86°57W **80** F10
Huntingdon *U.K.* 52°20N 0°11W **13** E7
Huntingdon *U.S.A.* 40°30N 78°1W **82** F6
Huntington *Ind., U.S.A.* 40°53N 85°30W **81** E11
Huntington *N.Y., U.S.A.* 40°52N 73°26W **83** F11
Huntington *Oreg.,*
  U.S.A. 44°21N 117°16W **76** D5
Huntington *Utah,*
  U.S.A. 39°20N 110°58W **76** G8
Huntington *W. Va.,*
  U.S.A. 38°25N 82°27W **81** F12
Huntington Beach
  U.S.A. 33°40N 118°5W **79** M9
Huntly *N.Z.* 37°34S 175°11E **59** B5
Huntly *U.K.* 57°27N 2°47W **11** D6
Huntsville *Canada* 45°20N 79°14W **82** A5
Huntsville *Ala., U.S.A.* 34°44N 86°35W **85** D11
Huntsville *Tex., U.S.A.* 30°43N 95°33W **84** F7
Hunyuan *China* 39°42N 113°42E **32** E7
Hunza → *India* 35°54N 74°20E **43** B6
Huo Shan *China* 36°36N 111°42E **32** F6
Huo Xian = Huozhou
  China 36°36N 111°42E **32** F6
Huolin Gol *China* 45°32N 119°38E **33** B10
Huong Khe *Vietnam* 18°13N 105°41E **38** C5
Huonville *Australia* 43°0S 147°5E **63** G4
Huoqiu *China* 32°20N 116°12E **35** A11
Huoshan *China* 31°25N 116°20E **35** B11
Huoshao Dao = Lütao
  Taiwan 22°40N 121°30E **35** F13
Hupeh = Hubei □ *China* 31°0N 112°0E **35** B9
Ḩūr *Iran* 30°50N 57°7E **47** D8
Hurand *Iran* 38°51N 47°22E **46** B5
Ḩuraymīla *Si. Arabia* 25°8N 46°8E **46** E5
Hurd, C. *Canada* 45°13N 81°44W **82** A3
Hure Qi *China* 42°45N 121°45E **33** C11
Hurghada *Egypt* 27°15N 33°50E **53** C12
Hurley *N. Mex., U.S.A.* 32°42N 108°8W **77** K9
Hurley *Wis., U.S.A.* 46°27N 90°11W **80** B8
Huron *Calif., U.S.A.* 36°12N 120°6W **78** J6
Huron *Ohio, U.S.A.* 41°24N 82°33W **82** E2
Huron *S. Dak., U.S.A.* 44°22N 98°13W **80** C4
Huron, L. *U.S.A.* 44°30N 82°40W **82** B2
Huron East *Canada* 43°37N 81°18W **82** C3
Hurricane *U.S.A.* 37°11N 113°17W **77** H7
Húsavík *Iceland* 66°3N 17°21W **8** C5
Huşi *Romania* 46°41N 28°7E **17** E15
Hustadvika *Norway* 63°0N 7°0E **8** E12

Hustontown *U.S.A.* 40°3N 78°2W **82** F6
Hutchinson *Kans., U.S.A.* 38°5N 97°56W **80** F5
Hutchinson *Minn.,*
  U.S.A. 44°54N 94°22W **80** C6
Hutiao Xia *China* 27°13N 100°9E **34** D3
Hutte Sauvage, L. de la
  Canada 56°15N 64°45W **73** A7
Hutton, Mt. *Australia* 25°51S 148°20E **63** D4
Huwaki *Indonesia* 7°55S 126°30E **37** F7
Huy *Belgium* 50°31N 5°15E **15** D5
Huzhou *China* 30°51N 120°8E **35** B13
Huzurabad *India* 18°12N 79°25E **44** E4
Huzurnagar *India* 16°54N 79°53E **44** F4
Hvammstangi *Iceland* 65°24N 20°57W **8** D3
Hvar *Croatia* 43°11N 16°28E **22** C7
Hvítá → *Iceland* 64°30N 21°58W **8** D3
Hwacheon-Cheosuji
  S. Korea 38°5N 127°50E **33** E14
Hwang Ho = Huang He →
  China 37°55N 118°50E **33** F10
Hwange *Zimbabwe* 18°18S 26°30E **55** H5
Hwange △ *Zimbabwe* 19°0S 26°30E **56** A4
Hwlffordd = Haverfordwest
  U.K. 51°48N 4°58W **13** F3
Hyannis *Mass., U.S.A.* 41°39N 70°17W **81** E18
Hyannis *Nebr., U.S.A.* 42°0N 101°46W **80** E3
Hyargas Nuur *Mongolia* 49°0N 93°0E **30** B7
Hydaburg *U.S.A.* 55°15N 132°50W **70** B2
Hyde Park *U.S.A.* 41°47N 73°56W **83** E11
Hyden *Australia* 32°24S 118°53E **61** F2
Hyder *U.S.A.* 55°55N 130°5W **70** B2
Hyderabad *India* 17°22N 78°29E **44** F4
Hyderabad *Pakistan* 25°23N 68°24E **42** G3
Hydra *Greece* 37°20N 23°28E **23** F10
Hyères *France* 43°8N 6°9E **20** E7
Hyères, Îs. d' *France* 43°0N 6°20E **20** E7
Hyesan *N. Korea* 41°20N 128°10E **33** D15
Hyland → *Canada* 59°52N 128°12W **70** B3
Hyndman Peak *U.S.A.* 43°45N 114°8W **76** E6
Hyōgo □ *Japan* 35°15N 134°50E **29** G7
Hyrum *U.S.A.* 41°38N 111°51W **76** F8
Hysham *U.S.A.* 46°18N 107°14W **76** C10
Hythe *U.K.* 51°4N 1°5E **13** F9
Hyūga *Japan* 32°25N 131°35E **29** H5
Hyvinge = Hyvinkää
  Finland 60°38N 24°50E **8** F21
Hyvinkää *Finland* 60°38N 24°50E **8** F21

I

I-n-Gall *Niger* 16°51N 7°1E **52** E7
Iaco → *Brazil* 9°3S 68°34W **92** E5
Ialomiţa → *Romania* 44°42N 27°51E **17** F14
Iaşi *Romania* 47°10N 27°40E **17** E14
Ib → *India* 21°34N 83°48E **43** J10
Iba *Phil.* 15°22N 120°0E **37** A6
Ibadan *Nigeria* 7°22N 3°58E **52** G6
Ibagué *Colombia* 4°20N 75°20W **92** C3
Ibar → *Serbia* 43°43N 20°45E **23** C9
Ibaraki □ *Japan* 36°10N 140°10E **29** F10
Ibarra *Ecuador* 0°21N 78°7W **92** C3
Ibb *Yemen* 14°2N 44°10E **49** E3
Ibenga → *Congo* 2°19N 18°9E **54** D3
Ibera, L. *Argentina* 28°30S 57°9W **94** B4
Iberian Peninsula *Europe* 40°0N 5°0W **6** H5
Iberville *Canada* 45°19N 73°17W **83** A11
Iberville, Mt. d' *Canada* 58°50N 63°50W **69** F19
Ibiá *Brazil* 19°30S 46°30W **93** G9
Ibiapaba, Sa. da *Brazil* 4°0S 41°30W **93** D10
Ibicuí → *Brazil* 29°25S 56°47W **95** B4
Ibicuy *Argentina* 33°55S 59°10W **94** C4
Ibiza = Eivissa *Spain* 38°54N 1°26E **21** C6
Ibonma *Indonesia* 3°29S 133°31E **37** E8
Ibotirama *Brazil* 12°13S 43°12W **93** F10
Ibrāhīm → *Lebanon* 34°4N 35°38E **48** A4
'Ibrī *Oman* 23°14N 56°30E **49** C6
Ibu *Indonesia* 1°35N 127°33E **37** D7
Ibusuki *Japan* 31°12N 130°40E **29** J5
Ica *Peru* 14°0S 75°48W **92** F3
Iça → *Brazil* 2°55S 67°58W **92** D5
Içana *Brazil* 0°21N 67°19W **92** C5
Içana → *Brazil* 0°26N 67°19W **92** C5
İçel = Mersin *Turkey* 36°51N 34°36E **46** B2
Iceland ■ *Europe* 64°45N 19°0W **8** D4
Iceland Basin *Atl. Oc.* 61°0N 19°0W **4** C7
Icelandic Plateau *Arctic* 64°0N 10°0W **4** C7
Ichalkaranji *India* 16°40N 74°33E **44** F2
Ich'ang = Yichang
  China 30°40N 111°20E **35** B8
Ichchapuram *India* 19°10N 84°40E **44** E7
Ichhawar *India* 23°1N 77°1E **42** H7
Ichihara *Japan* 35°28N 140°5E **29** G10
Ichilo → *Bolivia* 15°57S 64°50W **92** G6
Ichinohe *Japan* 40°13N 141°17E **28** D10
Ichinomiya *Japan* 35°18N 136°48E **29** G8
Ichinoseki *Japan* 38°55N 141°8E **28** E10
Içoguz *Turkmenistan* 40°11N 58°24E **26** E6
Icy C. *U.S.A.* 70°20N 161°52W **66** B3
Ida Grove *U.S.A.* 42°21N 95°28W **80** D6
Idabel *U.S.A.* 33°54N 94°50W **84** E7
Idaho □ *U.S.A.* 45°0N 115°0W **76** D6
Idaho City *U.S.A.* 43°50N 115°50W **76** E6
Idaho Falls *U.S.A.* 43°30N 112°2W **76** E7
Idalia △ *Australia* 24°49S 144°36E **62** C3
Idar-Oberstein *Germany* 49°43N 7°16E **16** D4
Idensalmi = Iisalmi
  Finland 63°32N 27°10E **8** E22
Idfû *Egypt* 24°55N 32°49E **53** D12
Idi *Indonesia* 5°2N 97°37E **36** C1
Idi, Oros = Psiloritis, Oros
  Greece 35°15N 24°45E **23** G11
Idiofa *Dem. Rep. of the Congo* 4°55S 19°42E **54** E3
Idlib *Syria* 35°55N 36°36E **46** C3
Idra = Hydra *Greece* 37°20N 23°28E **23** F10
Idria *U.S.A.* 36°25N 120°41W **78** J6
Idutywa = Dutywa
  S. Africa 32°8S 28°18E **57** D4
Ieper *Belgium* 50°51N 2°53E **15** D2
Ierapetra *Greece* 35°1N 25°44E **23** G11

Iesi *Italy* 43°31N 13°14E **22** C5
Ifakara *Tanzania* 8°8S 36°41E **54** F7
'Ifāl, W. al → *Si. Arabia* 28°7N 35°3E **46** D2
Ife *Nigeria* 7°30N 4°31E **52** G6
Iffley *Australia* 18°53S 141°12E **62** B3
Iforas, Adrar des *Africa* 19°40N 1°40E **52** E6
Ifould, L. *Australia* 30°52S 132°6E **61** F5
Igarapava *Brazil* 20°3S 47°47W **93** H9
Igarka *Russia* 67°30N 86°33E **26** C9
Igatpuri *India* 19°40N 73°35E **44** K1
Iglésias *Italy* 39°19N 8°32E **22** E3
Igloolik = Iglulik
  Canada 69°20N 81°49W **69** D15
Igluligaarjuk = Chesterfield Inlet
  Canada 63°30N 90°45W **68** E13
Iglulik *Canada* 69°20N 81°49W **69** D15
Ignace *Canada* 49°30N 91°40W **72** C1
İğneada Burnu *Turkey* 41°53N 28°2E **23** D13
Igoumenitsa *Greece* 39°32N 20°18E **23** E9
Igrim *Russia* 63°12N 64°30E **26** C7
Iguaçu → *Brazil* 25°36S 54°36W **95** B5
Iguaçu, Cat. del *Brazil* 25°41S 54°26W **95** B5
Iguaçu △ *Brazil* 25°30S 54°0W **95** B5
Iguaçu Falls = Iguaçu, Cat. del
  Brazil 25°41S 54°26W **95** B5
Iguala *Mexico* 18°21N 99°32W **87** D5
Igualada *Spain* 41°37N 1°37E **21** B6
Iguassu = Iguaçu →
  Brazil 25°36S 54°36W **95** B5
Iguatu *Brazil* 6°20S 39°18W **93** E11
Iguazú △ *Argentina* 25°42S 54°22W **95** B5
Iguidi, Erg *Africa* 27°0N 6°0W **52** C4
Iharana *Madag.* 13°25S 50°0E **55** G10
Ihbulag *Mongolia* 43°11N 107°10E **32** C4
Iheya-Shima *Japan* 27°4N 127°58E **29** L3
Ihosy *Madag.* 22°24S 46°8E **55** J9
Ii *Finland* 65°19N 25°22E **8** D21
Ii-Shima *Japan* 26°43N 127°47E **29** L3
Iida *Japan* 35°35N 137°50E **29** G8
Iijoki → *Finland* 65°20N 25°20E **8** D21
Iisalmi *Finland* 63°32N 27°10E **8** E22
Iiyama *Japan* 36°51N 138°22E **29** F9
Iizuka *Japan* 33°38N 130°42E **29** H5
Ijâfene *Mauritania* 20°40N 8°0W **52** D4
Ijebu-Ode *Nigeria* 6°47N 3°58E **52** G6
IJmuiden *Neths.* 52°28N 4°35E **15** B4
Ijo älv = Iijoki → *Finland* 65°20N 25°20E **8** D21
IJssel → *Neths.* 52°35N 5°50E **15** B5
IJsselmeer *Neths.* 52°45N 5°20E **15** B5
Ijuí *Brazil* 28°23S 53°55W **95** B5
Ijuí → *Brazil* 27°58S 55°20W **95** B4
Ikare *Nigeria* 7°32N 5°40E **52** G7
Ikaria *Greece* 37°35N 26°10E **23** F12
Ikeda *Japan* 34°1N 133°48E **29** G6
Ikela *Dem. Rep. of the Congo* 1°6S 23°6E **54** E4
Iki *Japan* 33°45N 129°42E **29** H4
Ikopa → *Madag.* 16°45S 46°40E **55** H9
Ikparjuk = Arctic Bay
  Canada 73°1N 85°7W **69** C14
Iksan *S. Korea* 35°59N 127°0E **33** G14
Ikuntji = Haasts Bluff
  Australia 23°22S 132°0E **60** D5
Ilagan *Phil.* 17°7N 121°53E **37** A6
Īlām *Iran* 33°36N 46°36E **46** C5
Ilam *Nepal* 26°58N 87°58E **43** F12
Īlām □ *Iran* 33°0N 47°0E **46** C5
Ilan *Taiwan* 24°45N 121°44E **35** E13
Ilanskiy *Russia* 56°14N 96°3E **27** D10
Iława *Poland* 53°36N 19°34E **17** B10
Ilayangudi *India* 9°34N 78°37E **45** K4
Ile → *Kazakhstan* 45°53N 77°10E **26** E8
Île-à-la-Crosse *Canada* 55°27N 107°53W **71** B7
Île-à-la-Crosse, Lac
  Canada 55°40N 107°45W **71** B7
Île-de-France □ *France* 49°0N 2°20E **20** B5
Ilebo *Dem. Rep. of the Congo* 4°17S 20°55E **54** E4
Ilek *Russia* 51°32N 53°21E **26** D6
Ilek → *Russia* 51°30N 53°22E **18** D9
Ilemi Triangle *Africa* 5°0N 35°20E **54** B7
Ilesha *Nigeria* 7°37N 4°40E **52** G6
Ilford *Canada* 56°4N 95°35W **71** B9
Ilfracombe *Australia* 23°30S 144°30E **62** C3
Ilfracombe *U.K.* 51°12N 4°8W **13** F3
Ilha Grande, Represa
  Brazil 23°10S 53°5W **95** A5
Ilha Grande △ *Brazil* 23°10S 53°20W **95** A5
Ilhéus *Brazil* 14°49S 39°2W **93** F11
Ili = Ile → *Kazakhstan* 45°53N 77°10E **26** E8
Iliamna L. *U.S.A.* 59°30N 155°0W **74** D8
Iligan *Phil.* 8°12N 124°13E **37** C6
Ilion *U.S.A.* 43°1N 75°2W **83** D9
Ilkal *India* 15°57N 76°8E **45** G3
Ilkeston *U.K.* 52°58N 1°19W **12** E6
Ilkley *U.K.* 53°56N 1°48W **12** D6
Illampu = Ancohuma, Nevado
  Bolivia 16°0S 68°50W **92** G5
Illana B. *Phil.* 7°35N 123°45E **37** C6
Illapel *Chile* 32°0S 71°10W **94** C1
Iller → *Germany* 48°23N 9°58E **16** D6
Illes Balears = Baleares, Is.
  Spain 39°30N 3°0E **21** C7
Illimani, Nevado *Bolivia* 16°30S 67°50W **92** G5
Illinois □ *U.S.A.* 40°15N 89°30W **80** E9
Illinois → *U.S.A.* 38°58N 90°28W **80** F8
Illizi *Algeria* 26°31N 8°32E **52** C7
Ilma, L. *Australia* 29°13S 127°46E **61** E4
Ilmajoki *Finland* 62°44N 22°34E **8** E20
Ilmen, Ozero *Russia* 58°15N 31°10E **18** C5
Ilo *Peru* 17°40S 71°20W **92** G4
Iloilo *Phil.* 10°45N 122°33E **37** B6
Ilomantsi *Finland* 62°38N 30°57E **8** E24
Ilorin *Nigeria* 8°30N 4°35E **52** G6
Ilwaco *U.S.A.* 46°19N 124°3W **78** D2
Imabari *Japan* 34°4N 133°0E **29** G6
Imandra, Ozero *Russia* 67°30N 33°0E **8** C25
Imari *Japan* 33°15N 129°52E **29** H4
Imatra *Finland* 61°12N 28°48E **8** F23
imeni 26 Bakinskikh Komissarov
  = Neftçala *Azerbaijan* 39°19N 49°12E **47** B6

imeni 26 Bakinskikh Komissarov
  Turkmenistan 39°22N 54°10E **47 B7**
imeni Ismail Samani, Pik
  Tajikistan 39°0N 72°2E **26 F8**
Imeri, Serra Brazil 0°50N 65°25W **92 C5**
Imfolozi △ S. Africa 28°18S 31°50E **57 C5**
Imi Ethiopia 6°28N 42°10E **49 F3**
Imlay U.S.A. 40°40N 118°9W **76 F4**
Imlay City U.S.A. 43°2N 83°5W **82 D1**
Immingham U.K. 53°37N 0°13W **12 D7**
Immokalee U.S.A. 26°25N 81°25W **85 H14**
Imola Italy 44°20N 11°42E **22 B4**
Imperatriz Brazil 5°30S 47°29W **93 E9**
Impéria Italy 43°53N 8°3E **20 E8**
Imperial Canada 51°21N 105°28W **71 C7**
Imperial Calif., U.S.A. 32°51N 115°34W **79 N11**
Imperial Nebr., U.S.A. 40°31N 101°39W **80 E3**
Imperial Beach U.S.A. 32°35N 117°6W **79 N9**
Imperial Dam U.S.A. 32°55N 114°25W **79 N12**
Imperial Res. U.S.A. 32°53N 114°28W **79 N12**
Imperial Valley U.S.A. 33°0N 115°30W **79 N11**
Imperieuse Reef
  Australia 17°36S 118°50E **60 C2**
Impfondo Congo 1°40N 18°0E **54 D3**
Imphal India 24°48N 93°56E **41 G18**
İmroz = Gökçeada
  Turkey 40°10N 25°50E **23 D11**
Imuris Mexico 30°47N 110°52W **86 A2**
Imuruan B. Phil. 10°40N 119°10E **37 B5**
In Amenas Algeria 28°5N 9°33E **53 C7**
In Guezzam Algeria 19°37N 5°52E **52 E7**
In Salah Algeria 27°10N 2°32E **52 C6**
Ina Japan 35°50N 137°55E **29 G8**
Inagua △ Bahamas 21°5N 73°24W **89 B5**
Inangahua N.Z. 41°52S 171°59E **59 D3**
Inanwatan Indonesia 2°8S 132°10E **37 E8**
Iñapari Peru 11°0S 69°40W **92 F5**
Inari Finland 68°54N 27°1E **8 B22**
Inarijärvi Finland 69°0N 28°0E **8 B23**
Inawashiro-Ko Japan 37°29N 140°6E **28 F10**
†Inbhear Mór, An = Arklow
  Ireland 52°48N 6°10W **10 D5**
Inca Spain 39°43N 2°54E **21 C7**
Inca de Oro Chile 26°45S 69°54W **94 B2**
Incahuasi Argentina 27°2S 68°18W **94 B2**
Incahuasi Chile 29°12S 71°5W **94 B1**
İnce Burun Turkey 42°7N 34°56E **19 F5**
İncesu Turkey 38°38N 35°11E **46 B2**
Incheon S. Korea 37°27N 126°40E **33 F14**
İncirliova Turkey 37°50N 27°41E **23 F12**
Incline Village U.S.A. 39°10N 119°58W **78 F7**
Incomáti → Mozam. 25°46S 32°43E **57 C5**
Indalsälven → Sweden 62°36N 17°30E **8 E17**
Indaw Myanmar 24°15N 96°5E **41 G20**
Independence Calif.,
  U.S.A. 36°48N 118°12W **78 J8**
Independence Iowa,
  U.S.A. 42°28N 91°54W **80 D8**
Independence Kans.,
  U.S.A. 37°14N 95°42W **80 G6**
Independence Ky.,
  U.S.A. 38°57N 84°33W **81 F11**
Independence Mo., U.S.A. 39°6N 94°25W **80 F6**
Independence Fjord
  Greenland 82°10N 29°0W **4 A6**
Independence Mts.
  U.S.A. 41°20N 116°0W **76 F5**
Index U.S.A. 47°50N 121°33W **78 C5**
Indi India 17°10N 75°58E **44 F2**
India ■ Asia 20°0N 78°0E **40 K11**
Indian → U.S.A. 27°59N 80°34W **85 H14**
Indian Cabins Canada 59°52N 117°40W **70 B5**
Indian Harbour Canada 54°27N 57°13W **73 B8**
Indian Head Canada 50°30N 103°41W **71 C8**
Indian L. U.S.A. 43°46N 74°16W **83 C10**
Indian Lake U.S.A. 43°47N 74°16W **83 C10**
Indian Springs U.S.A. 36°35N 115°40W **79 J11**
Indiana U.S.A. 40°37N 79°9W **82 F5**
Indiana □ U.S.A. 40°0N 86°0W **81 F11**
Indianapolis U.S.A. 39°46N 86°9W **80 F10**
Indianola Iowa, U.S.A. 41°22N 93°34W **80 E7**
Indianola Miss., U.S.A. 33°27N 90°39W **85 E9**
Indiga Russia 67°38N 49°9E **18 A8**
Indigirka → Russia 70°48N 148°54E **27 B15**
Indio U.S.A. 33°43N 116°13W **79 M10**
Indira Gandhi Canal India 28°0N 72°0E **42 F5**
Indira Pt. India 6°44N 93°49E **45 L11**
Indira Sagar India 22°15N 76°40E **42 H7**
Indo-China Asia 15°0N 102°0E **24 G2**
Indonesia ■ Asia 5°0S 115°0E **36 F5**
Indore India 22°42N 75°53E **42 H6**
Indramayu Indonesia 6°20S 108°19E **37 G13**
Indravati → India 19°20N 80°20E **44 E5**
Indre → France 47°16N 0°11E **20 C4**
Indulkana Australia 26°58S 133°5E **63 D1**
Indus → Pakistan 24°20N 67°47E **42 G2**
Indus, Mouths of the
  Pakistan 24°0N 68°0E **42 H3**
İnebolu Turkey 41°55N 33°40E **19 F5**
Infiernillo, Presa del
  Mexico 18°35N 101°50W **86 D4**
Inga, Barrage d'
  Dem. Rep. of the Congo 5°35S 13°39E **54 F2**
Ingenio Santa Ana
  Argentina 27°25S 65°40W **94 B2**
Ingersoll Canada 43°4N 80°55W **82 C4**
Ingham Australia 18°43S 146°10E **62 B4**
Ingleborough U.K. 54°10N 2°22W **12 C5**
Inglewood Queens.,
  Australia 28°25S 151°2E **63 D5**
Inglewood Vic., Australia 36°29S 143°53E **63 F3**
Inglewood N.Z. 39°9S 174°14E **59 C5**
Ingólfshöfði Iceland 63°48N 16°39W **8 E5**
Ingolstadt Germany 48°46N 11°26E **16 D6**
Ingomar U.S.A. 46°35N 107°23W **76 C10**
Ingonish Canada 46°42N 60°18W **73 C7**
Ingraj Bazar India 24°58N 88°10E **43 G13**
Ingrid Christensen Coast
  Antarctica 69°30S 76°0E **5 C6**
Ingulec = Inhulec
  Ukraine 47°42N 33°14E **19 E5**

Ingushetia □ Russia 43°20N 44°50E **19 F8**
Ingwavuma S. Africa 27°9S 31°59E **57 C5**
Inhaca Mozam. 26°1S 32°57E **57 C5**
Inhaca Pen. Mozam. 26°13S 32°55E **57 C5**
Inhafenga Mozam. 20°36S 33°53E **57 B5**
Inhambane Mozam. 23°54S 35°30E **57 C6**
Inhambane □ Mozam. 22°30S 34°20E **57 B5**
Inharrime Mozam. 24°30S 35°0E **57 B6**
Inharrime → Mozam. 24°30S 35°0E **57 B6**
Inhulec Ukraine 47°42N 33°14E **19 E5**
Inírida → Colombia 3°55N 67°52W **92 C5**
Inis = Ennis Ireland 52°51N 8°59W **10 D3**
Inishbofin Ireland 53°37N 10°13W **10 C1**
Inisheer Ireland 53°3N 9°32W **10 C2**
Inishfree B. Ireland 55°4N 8°23W **10 A3**
Inishkea North Ireland 54°9N 10°11W **10 B1**
Inishkea South Ireland 54°7N 10°12W **10 B1**
Inishmaan Ireland 53°5N 9°35W **10 C2**
Inishmore Ireland 53°8N 9°45W **10 C2**
Inishmurray Ireland 54°26N 8°39W **10 B3**
Inishowen Pen. Ireland 55°14N 7°15W **10 A4**
Inishshark Ireland 53°37N 10°16W **10 C1**
Inishturk Ireland 53°42N 10°7W **10 C1**
Inishvickillane Ireland 52°3N 10°37W **10 D1**
Injinoo ۞ Australia 10°56S 142°15E **62 A3**
Injune Australia 25°53S 148°32E **63 D4**
Inklin → N. Amer. 58°50N 133°10W **70 B2**
Inland Kaikoura Ra.
  N.Z. 41°59S 173°41E **59 D4**
Inland Sea = Setonaikai
  Japan 34°20N 133°30E **29 G6**
Inle L. Myanmar 20°30N 96°58E **41 J20**
Inlet U.S.A. 43°45N 74°48W **83 C10**
Inn → Austria 48°35N 13°28E **16 D7**
Innamincka Australia 27°44S 140°46E **63 D3**
Inner Hebrides U.K. 57°0N 6°30W **11 E2**
Inner Mongolia = Nei Mongol
  Zizhiqu □ China 42°0N 112°0E **32 D7**
Inner Sound U.K. 57°30N 5°55W **11 D3**
Innerkip Canada 43°13N 80°42W **82 C4**
Innetalling I. Canada 56°0N 79°0W **72 A4**
Innisfail Australia 17°33S 146°5E **62 B4**
Innisfail Canada 52°2N 113°57W **70 C6**
In'noshima Japan 34°19N 133°10E **29 G6**
Innsbruck Austria 47°16N 11°23E **16 E6**
Inny → Ireland 53°32N 7°51W **10 C4**
Inongo
  Dem. Rep. of the Congo 1°55S 18°30E **54 E3**
Inoucdjouac = Inukjuak
  Canada 58°25N 78°15W **69 F16**
Inowrocław Poland 52°50N 18°12E **17 B10**
Inscription, C. Australia 25°29S 112°59E **61 E1**
Insein Myanmar 16°50N 96°5E **41 L20**
Inta Russia 66°5N 60°8E **18 A11**
Intendente Alvear
  Argentina 35°12S 63°32W **94 D3**
Interlaken Switz. 46°41N 7°50E **20 C7**
Interlaken U.S.A. 42°37N 76°44W **83 D8**
International Falls
  U.S.A. 48°36N 93°25W **80 A7**
Interview I. India 12°55N 92°43E **45 H11**
Intiyaco Argentina 28°43S 60°5W **94 B3**
Inukjuak Canada 58°25N 78°15W **69 F16**
Inútil, B. Chile 53°30S 70°15W **96 G2**
Inuvik Canada 68°16N 133°40W **68 D5**
Inveraray U.K. 56°14N 5°5W **11 E3**
Inverbervie U.K. 56°51N 2°17W **11 E6**
Invercargill N.Z. 46°24S 168°24E **59 G2**
Inverclyde □ U.K. 55°55N 4°49W **11 F4**
Inverell Australia 29°45S 151°8E **63 D5**
Invergordon U.K. 57°41N 4°10W **11 D4**
Inverloch Australia 38°38S 145°45E **63 F4**
Invermere Canada 50°30N 116°2W **70 C5**
Inverness Canada 46°15N 61°19W **73 C7**
Inverness U.K. 57°29N 4°13W **11 D4**
Inverness U.S.A. 28°50N 82°20W **85 G13**
Inverurie U.K. 57°17N 2°23W **11 D6**
Investigator Group
  Australia 34°45S 134°20E **63 E1**
Investigator Str. Australia 35°30S 137°0E **63 F2**
Inya Russia 50°28N 86°37E **26 D9**
Inyangani Zimbabwe 18°5S 32°50E **55 H6**
Inyantue Zimbabwe 18°33S 26°39E **56 A4**
Inyo Mts. U.S.A. 36°40N 118°0W **78 J9**
Inyokern U.S.A. 35°39N 117°49W **79 K9**
Inza Russia 53°55N 46°25E **18 D8**
Iō-Jima Japan 30°48N 130°18E **29 J5**
Ioannina Greece 39°42N 20°47E **23 E9**
Iola U.S.A. 37°55N 95°24W **80 G6**
Iona U.K. 56°20N 6°25W **11 E2**
Ione U.S.A. 38°21N 120°56W **78 G6**
Ionia U.S.A. 42°59N 85°4W **81 D11**
Ionian Is. = Ionioi Nisoi
  Greece 38°40N 20°0E **23 E9**
Ionian Sea Medit. S. 37°30N 17°30E **23 E7**
Ionioi Nisoi Greece 38°40N 20°0E **23 E9**
Iony, Ostrov Russia 56°24N 143°22E **27 D15**
Ios Greece 36°41N 25°20E **23 F11**
Iowa □ U.S.A. 42°18N 93°30W **80 D7**
Iowa → U.S.A. 41°10N 91°1W **80 E8**
Iowa City U.S.A. 41°40N 91°32W **80 E9**
Iowa Falls U.S.A. 42°31N 93°16W **80 D7**
Iowa Park U.S.A. 33°57N 98°40W **84 J5**
Ipameri Brazil 17°44S 48°9W **93 G9**
Ipatinga Brazil 19°32S 42°30W **93 G10**
Ipiales Colombia 0°50N 77°37W **92 C3**
Ipin = Yibin China 28°45N 104°32E **34 C5**
Ipixuna Brazil 7°0S 71°40W **92 E4**
Ipoh Malaysia 4°35N 101°5E **39 K3**
Ippy C.A.R. 6°5N 21°7E **54 C4**
Ipsala Turkey 40°55N 26°23E **23 D12**
Ipswich Australia 27°35S 152°40E **63 D5**
Ipswich U.K. 52°4N 1°10E **13 E9**
Ipswich Mass., U.S.A. 42°41N 70°50W **83 D14**
Ipswich S. Dak., U.S.A. 45°27N 99°2W **80 C4**
Ipu Brazil 4°23S 40°44W **93 D10**
Iqaluit Canada 63°44N 68°31W **69 E18**
Iqaluktuutiaq = Cambridge Bay
  Canada 69°10N 105°0W **68 D11**

Iquique Chile 20°19S 70°5W **92 H4**
Iquitos Peru 3°45S 73°10W **92 D4**
Irabu-Jima Japan 24°50N 125°10E **29 M2**
Iracoubo Fr. Guiana 5°30N 53°10W **93 B8**
Irafshān Iran 26°42N 61°56E **47 E9**
Iraklio Greece 35°20N 25°12E **23 G11**
Iráklion = Iraklio Greece 35°20N 25°12E **23 G11**
Irala Paraguay 25°55S 54°35W **95 B5**
Iran ■ Asia 33°0N 53°0E **47 C7**
Iran, Pegunungan
  Malaysia 2°20N 114°50E **36 D4**
Iran Ra. = Iran, Pegunungan
  Malaysia 2°20N 114°50E **36 D4**
Iranamadu Tank Sri Lanka 9°23N 80°29E **45 K5**
Īrānshahr Iran 27°15N 60°40E **47 E9**
Irapuato Mexico 20°41N 101°28W **86 C4**
Irati Brazil 25°25S 50°38W **95 B5**
Irazú, Volcan Costa Rica 9°59N 83°51W **88 D3**
Irbid Jordan 32°35N 35°48E **48 C4**
Irbid □ Jordan 32°30N 35°50E **48 C5**
Irbil = Arbīl Iraq 36°15N 44°5E **46 B5**
Irebu Dem. Rep. of the Congo 0°40S 17°46E **54 E3**
Ireland ■ Europe 53°50N 7°52W **10 C4**
Iri = Iksan S. Korea 35°59N 127°0E **33 G14**
Irian Jaya = Papua □
  Indonesia 4°0S 137°0E **37 E9**
Irian Jaya Barat □
  Indonesia 2°5S 132°50E **37 E8**
Iringa Tanzania 7°48S 35°43E **54 F7**
Irinjalakuda India 10°21N 76°14E **45 J3**
Iriomote △ Japan 24°29N 123°53E **29 M1**
Iriomote-Jima Japan 24°19N 123°48E **29 M1**
Iriona Honduras 15°57N 85°11W **88 C2**
Iriri → Brazil 3°52S 52°37W **93 D8**
Irish Sea Europe 53°38N 4°48W **12 D3**
Irkutsk Russia 52°18N 104°20E **30 A9**
Irma Canada 52°55N 111°14W **71 C6**
Irō-Zaki Japan 34°36N 138°51E **29 G9**
Iron Baron Australia 32°58S 137°11E **63 E2**
Iron Gate = Portile de Fier
  Europe 44°44N 22°30E **17 F12**
Iron Knob Australia 32°46S 137°8E **63 E2**
Iron Mountain U.S.A. 45°49N 88°4W **80 C9**
Iron Range △ Australia 12°34S 143°18E **62 A3**
Iron River U.S.A. 46°6N 88°39W **80 B9**
Irondequoit U.S.A. 43°13N 77°35W **82 C7**
Ironton Mo., U.S.A. 37°36N 90°38W **80 G8**
Ironton Ohio, U.S.A. 38°32N 82°41W **81 F12**
Ironwood U.S.A. 46°27N 90°9W **80 B8**
Ironwood Forest △
  U.S.A. 32°32N 111°28W **77 K8**
Iroquois Canada 44°51N 75°19W **83 B9**
Iroquois Falls Canada 48°46N 80°41W **72 C3**
Irpin Ukraine 50°30N 30°15E **17 C16**
Irrara Cr. → Australia 29°35S 145°31E **63 D4**
Irrawaddy = Ayeyawadi →
  Myanmar 15°50N 95°6E **41 M19**
Irrawaddy □ Myanmar 17°0N 95°0E **41 L19**
Irrawaddy, Mouths of the
  Myanmar 15°30N 95°0E **41 M19**
Irricana Canada 51°19N 113°37W **70 C6**
Irrunytju Australia 26°3S 128°56E **61 E4**
Irtysh → Russia 61°4N 68°52E **26 C7**
Irún Spain 43°20N 1°52W **21 A5**
Irunea = Pamplona-Iruña
  Spain 42°48N 1°38W **21 A5**
Irvine Canada 49°57N 110°16W **71 D6**
Irvine U.K. 55°37N 4°41W **11 F4**
Irvine Calif., U.S.A. 33°41N 117°46W **79 M9**
Irvine Ky., U.S.A. 37°42N 83°58W **81 G12**
Irvinestown U.K. 54°28N 7°39W **10 B4**
Irvona U.S.A. 40°46N 78°33W **82 F6**
Irwin → Australia 29°15S 114°54E **61 E1**
Irymple Australia 34°14S 142°8E **63 E3**
Isa Khel Pakistan 32°41N 71°17E **42 C4**
Isaac → Australia 22°55S 149°20E **62 C4**
Isabel U.S.A. 45°24N 101°26W **80 C3**
Isabel, I. Mexico 21°51N 105°55W **86 C3**
Isabela Phil. 6°40N 121°59E **37 C6**
Isabela Puerto Rico 18°30N 67°2W **89 d**
Isabela, Cord. Nic. 13°30N 85°25W **88 D2**
Isabella Ra. Australia 21°0S 121°4E **60 D3**
Isachsen, C. Canada 79°20N 105°20W **69 B10**
Isachsen Mt. Antarctica 72°8S 26°5E **5 D4**
Īsafjarðardjúp Iceland 66°10N 23°0W **8 C2**
Īsafjörður Iceland 66°5N 23°9W **8 C2**
Isagarh India 24°48N 77°51E **42 G7**
Isahaya Japan 32°52N 130°2E **29 H5**
Isan → India 26°51N 80°7E **43 F9**
Isana = Içana → Brazil 0°26N 67°19W **92 C5**
Isar → Germany 48°48N 12°57E **16 D7**
Ischia Italy 40°44N 13°57E **22 D5**
Ischigualasto △ Argentina 30°0S 66°0W **94 B2**
Isdell → Australia 16°27S 124°51E **60 C3**
Ise Japan 34°25N 136°45E **29 G8**
Ise-Shima △ Japan 34°25N 136°45E **29 G8**
Ise-Wan Japan 34°43N 136°43E **29 G8**
Isère → France 44°59N 4°51E **20 D6**
Isérnia Italy 41°36N 14°14E **22 D6**
Isfahan = Eşfahān Iran 32°39N 51°43E **47 C6**
Ishigaki Japan 24°20N 124°10E **29 M2**
Ishigaki-Shima Japan 24°20N 124°10E **29 M2**
Ishikari-Gawa →
  Japan 43°15N 141°23E **28 C10**
Ishikari-Sammyaku
  Japan 43°30N 143°0E **28 C11**
Ishikari-Wan Japan 43°25N 141°1E **28 C10**
Ishikawa □ Japan 36°30N 136°30E **29 L3**
Ishim Russia 56°10N 69°30E **26 D7**
Ishim → Russia 57°45N 71°10E **26 D8**
Ishinomaki Japan 38°32N 141°20E **28 E10**
Ishioka Japan 36°11N 140°16E **29 F10**
Ishkoman Pakistan 36°30N 73°50E **43 A5**
Isil Kul Russia 54°55N 71°16E **26 D8**
İsiolo Kenya 0°24N 37°33E **54 D7**
Isiro Dem. Rep. of the Congo 2°53N 27°40E **54 D5**

Isisford Australia 24°15S 144°21E **62 C3**
Iskar → Bulgaria 43°45N 24°25E **23 C11**
İskenderun Turkey 36°32N 36°10E **46 B3**
İskenderun Körfezi
  Turkey 36°40N 35°50E **19 G6**
Iskut → Canada 56°45N 131°49W **70 B2**
Isla → U.K. 56°32N 3°20W **11 E5**
Isla Coiba △ Panama 7°33N 81°36W **88 E3**
Isla de Salamanca △
  Colombia 10°59N 74°40W **89 D5**
Isla Gorge △ Australia 25°10S 149°57E **62 C4**
Isla Isabel △ Mexico 21°54N 105°58W **86 C3**
Isla Tiburón y San Estebán △
  Mexico 29°0N 112°27W **86 B2**
Isla Vista U.S.A. 34°25N 119°53W **79 L7**
Islam Headworks
  Pakistan 29°49N 72°33E **42 E5**
Islamabad Pakistan 33°40N 73°10E **42 C5**
Islamgarh Pakistan 27°51N 70°48E **42 F4**
Islamkot Pakistan 24°42N 70°13E **42 G4**
Islampur Bihar, India 25°9N 85°12E **43 G11**
Islampur Maharashtra,
  India 17°2N 74°20E **44 F2**
Islampur Paschimbanga,
  India 26°16N 88°12E **43 F13**
Island = Iceland ■ Europe 64°45N 19°0W **8 D4**
Island L. Canada 53°47N 94°25W **71 C10**
Island Lagoon Australia 31°30S 136°40E **63 E2**
Island Pond U.S.A. 44°49N 71°53W **83 B13**
Islands, B. of Canada 49°11N 58°15W **73 C8**
Islands, B. of N.Z. 35°15S 174°6E **59 A5**
Islay U.K. 55°46N 6°10W **11 F2**
Isle → France 44°55N 0°15W **20 D3**
Isle aux Morts Canada 47°35N 59°0W **73 C8**
Isle of Wight □ U.K. 50°41N 1°17W **13 G6**
Isle Royale △ U.S.A. 48°0N 88°55W **80 B9**
Isleton U.S.A. 38°10N 121°37W **78 G5**
Ismail = Izmayil Ukraine 45°22N 28°46E **17 F15**
Ismâ'iliya Egypt 30°37N 32°18E **53 B12**
Isna Egypt 25°17N 32°30E **53 C12**
Isojärvi △ Finland 61°40N 25°0E **8 F21**
Isparta Turkey 37°47N 30°30E **19 G5**
İspica Italy 36°47N 14°55E **22 F6**
Israel ■ Asia 32°0N 34°50E **48 D3**
Issoire France 45°32N 3°15E **20 D5**
Issyk-Kul = Balykchy
  Kyrgyzstan 42°26N 76°12E **30 C4**
Issyk-Kul, Ozero = Ysyk-Köl
  Kyrgyzstan 42°25N 77°15E **26 E8**
Istiea Greece 38°57N 23°9E **23 E10**
Isto, Mt. U.S.A. 69°12N 143°48W **74 A11**
Istokpoga, L. U.S.A. 27°23N 81°17W **85 H14**
Istra Croatia 45°10N 14°0E **16 F7**
Istres France 43°31N 4°59E **20 E6**
Istria = Istra Croatia 45°10N 14°0E **16 F7**
Itá Paraguay 25°29S 57°21W **94 B4**
Itaberaba Brazil 12°32S 40°18W **93 F10**
Itabira Brazil 19°37S 43°13W **93 G10**
Itabirito Brazil 20°15S 43°48W **95 A7**
Itabuna Brazil 14°48S 39°16W **93 F11**
Itacaunas → Brazil 5°21S 49°8W **93 E9**
Itacoatiara Brazil 3°8S 58°25W **92 D7**
Itaguaí Brazil 22°15S 43°46W **95 A7**
Itaipú, Represa de Brazil 25°30S 54°30W **95 B5**
Itäisen Suomenlahti △
  Finland 60°25N 27°15E **8 F22**
Itaituba Brazil 4°10S 55°50W **93 D7**
Itajaí Brazil 27°50S 48°39W **95 B6**
Itajubá Brazil 22°24S 45°30W **95 A6**
Itala △ S. Africa 27°30S 31°7E **57 C5**
Italy ■ Europe 42°0N 13°0E **22 C5**
Itamaraju Brazil 17°4S 39°32W **93 G11**
Itapecuru Mirim Brazil 3°24S 44°20W **93 D10**
Itaperuna Brazil 21°10S 41°54W **95 A7**
Itapetininga Brazil 23°36S 48°7W **95 A6**
Itapeva Brazil 23°59S 48°59W **95 A6**
Itapicuru → Bahia,
  Brazil 11°47S 37°32W **93 F11**
Itapicuru → Maranhão,
  Brazil 2°52S 44°12W **93 D10**
Itapipoca Brazil 3°30S 39°35W **93 D11**
Itapuá □ Paraguay 26°40S 55°40W **95 B4**
Itaquí Brazil 29°8S 56°30W **94 B4**
Itararé Brazil 24°6S 49°23W **95 A6**
Itarsi India 22°36N 77°51E **42 H7**
Itati Argentina 27°16S 58°15W **94 B4**
Itatiaia △ Brazil 22°25S 44°38W **95 A7**
Itchen → U.K. 50°55N 1°22W **13 G6**
Itezhi Tezhi, L. Zambia 15°30S 25°30E **55 H5**
Ithaca = Ithaki Greece 38°25N 20°40E **23 E9**
Ithaca U.S.A. 42°27N 76°30W **83 D8**
Ithaki Greece 38°25N 20°40E **23 E9**
Itiquira → Brazil 17°18S 56°44W **93 G7**
Itiyuro → Argentina 22°40S 63°50W **94 A3**
Itō Japan 34°58N 139°5E **29 G9**
Itoigawa Japan 37°2N 137°51E **29 F8**
Itonamas → Bolivia 12°28S 64°24W **92 F6**
Ittoqqortoormiit Greenland 70°20N 23°0W **4 B6**
Itu Brazil 23°17S 47°15W **95 A6**
Itu Aba I. S. China Sea 10°23N 114°21E **36 B4**
Ituiutaba Brazil 19°0S 49°25W **93 G9**
Itumbiara Brazil 18°20S 49°10W **93 G9**
Ituna Canada 51°10N 103°24W **71 C8**
Iturbe Argentina 23°0S 65°25W **94 A2**
Iturup, Ostrov Russia 45°0N 148°0E **27 E15**
Ituxi → Brazil 7°18S 64°51W **92 E6**
Itzehoe Germany 53°55N 9°31E **16 B5**
Ivaí → Brazil 23°18S 53°42W **95 A5**
Ivalo Finland 68°38N 27°35E **8 B22**
Ivalojoki → Finland 68°40N 27°40E **8 B22**
Ivanava Belarus 52°7N 25°29E **17 B13**
Ivanhoe Australia 32°56S 144°20E **63 E3**
Ivanhoe Calif., U.S.A. 36°23N 119°13W **78 J7**
Ivanhoe Minn., U.S.A. 44°28N 96°15W **80 C5**
Ivano-Frankivsk
  Ukraine 48°40N 24°40E **17 D13**
Ivanovo = Ivanava
  Belarus 52°7N 25°29E **17 B13**

Ivanovo Russia 57°5N 41°0E **18 C7**
Ivatsevichy Belarus 52°43N 25°21E **17 B13**
Ivdel Russia 60°42N 60°24E **18 B11**
Iveragh Pen. Ireland 51°52N 10°15W **10 E1**
Ivinheima → Brazil 23°14S 53°42W **95 A5**
Ivinhema Brazil 22°10S 53°37W **95 A5**
Ivory Coast = Côte d'Ivoire
  Africa 7°30N 5°0W **52 G4**
Ivory Coast W. Afr. 4°20N 5°0W **52 H4**
Ivrea Italy 45°28N 7°52E **20 D7**
Ivujivik Canada 62°24N 77°55W **69 E16**
Ivvavik △ Canada 69°6N 139°30W **68 D4**
Ivybridge U.K. 50°23N 3°56W **13 G4**
Iwaizumi Japan 39°50N 141°45E **28 E10**
Iwaki Japan 37°3N 140°55E **28 F10**
Iwakuni Japan 34°15N 132°8E **29 G6**
Iwamizawa Japan 43°12N 141°46E **28 C10**
Iwanai Japan 42°58N 140°30E **28 C10**
Iwata Japan 34°42N 137°51E **29 G8**
Iwate □ Japan 39°30N 141°30E **28 E10**
Iwate-San Japan 39°51N 141°0E **28 E10**
Iwo Nigeria 7°39N 4°9E **52 G6**
Iwŏn N. Korea 40°19N 128°39E **33 D15**
Ixiamas Bolivia 13°50S 68°5W **92 F5**
Ixopo S. Africa 30°11S 30°5E **57 E5**
Ixtepec Mexico 16°34N 95°6W **87 D5**
Ixtlán del Río Mexico 21°2N 104°22W **86 C4**
Iyo Japan 33°45N 132°45E **29 H6**
Izabal, L. de Guatemala 15°30N 89°10W **88 C2**
Izamal Mexico 20°56N 89°1W **87 C7**
Izena-Shima Japan 26°56N 127°56E **29 L3**
Izhevsk Russia 56°51N 53°14E **18 C9**
Izhma → Russia 65°19N 52°54E **18 A9**
Izmayil Ukraine 45°22N 28°46E **17 F15**
İzmir Turkey 38°25N 27°8E **23 E12**
İzmit = Kocaeli Turkey 40°45N 29°50E **19 F4**
İznik Gölü Turkey 40°27N 29°30E **23 D13**
Izra Syria 32°51N 36°15E **48 C5**
Izu-Hantō Japan 34°45N 139°0E **29 G9**
Izu-Shotō Japan 34°30N 140°0E **29 G10**
Izúcar de Matamoros
  Mexico 18°36N 98°28W **87 D5**
Izumi Japan 32°5N 130°22E **29 H5**
Izumi-Sano Japan 34°23N 135°18E **29 G7**
Izumo Japan 35°20N 132°46E **29 G6**
Izyaslav Ukraine 50°5N 26°50E **17 C14**

J

J.F.K. Int. ✈ (JFK)
  U.S.A. 40°38N 73°47W **83 F11**
J. Strom Thurmond L.
  U.S.A. 33°40N 82°12W **85 E13**
Ja-ela Sri Lanka 7°5N 79°53E **45 L4**
Jabalpur India 23°9N 79°58E **43 H8**
Jabālya Gaza Strip 31°32N 34°29E **48 D3**
Jabbūl Syria 36°4N 37°30E **46 B3**
Jabiru Australia 12°40S 132°53E **60 B5**
Jablah Syria 35°20N 36°0E **46 C3**
Jablonec nad Nisou
  Czechia 50°43N 15°10E **16 C8**
Jaboatão Brazil 8°7S 35°1W **93 E11**
Jaboticabal Brazil 21°15S 48°17W **95 A6**
Jaca Spain 42°35N 0°33W **21 A5**
Jacareí Brazil 23°20S 46°0W **95 A6**
Jacarèzinho Brazil 23°5S 49°58W **95 A6**
Jack River △ Australia 14°58S 144°19E **62 A3**
Jackman U.S.A. 45°37N 70°15W **81 C18**
Jacksboro U.S.A. 33°13N 98°10W **84 E5**
Jackson Barbados 13°7N 59°36W **89 g**
Jackson Ala., U.S.A. 31°31N 87°53W **85 F11**
Jackson Calif., U.S.A. 38°21N 120°46W **78 G6**
Jackson Ky., U.S.A. 37°33N 83°23W **81 G12**
Jackson Mich., U.S.A. 42°15N 84°24W **81 D11**
Jackson Minn., U.S.A. 43°37N 95°1W **80 D6**
Jackson Miss., U.S.A. 32°18N 90°12W **85 E9**
Jackson Mo., U.S.A. 37°23N 89°40W **80 G9**
Jackson N.H., U.S.A. 44°10N 71°11W **83 B13**
Jackson Ohio, U.S.A. 39°3N 82°39W **81 F12**
Jackson Tenn., U.S.A. 35°37N 88°49W **85 D10**
Jackson Wyo., U.S.A. 43°29N 110°46W **76 E8**
Jackson B. N.Z. 43°58S 168°42E **59 E2**
Jackson L. U.S.A. 43°52N 110°36W **76 E8**
Jacksons N.Z. 42°46S 171°32E **59 E3**
Jackson's Arm Canada 49°52N 56°47W **73 C8**
Jacksonville Ala., U.S.A. 33°49N 85°46W **85 E12**
Jacksonville Calif.,
  U.S.A. 37°52N 120°24W **78 H6**
Jacksonville Fla., U.S.A. 30°20N 81°39W **85 F14**
Jacksonville Ill., U.S.A. 39°44N 90°14W **80 F8**
Jacksonville N.C.,
  U.S.A. 34°45N 77°26W **85 D16**
Jacksonville Tex., U.S.A. 31°58N 95°17W **84 F7**
Jacksonville Beach
  U.S.A. 30°17N 81°24W **85 F14**
Jacmel Haiti 18°14N 72°32W **89 C5**
Jacob Lake U.S.A. 36°43N 112°13W **77 H7**
Jacobabad Pakistan 28°20N 68°29E **42 E3**
Jacobina Brazil 11°11S 40°30W **93 F10**
Jacques-Cartier, Dét. de
  Canada 50°0N 63°30W **73 C7**
Jacques-Cartier, Mt.
  Canada 48°57N 66°0W **73 C6**
Jacques-Cartier △
  Canada 47°15N 71°33W **73 C5**
Jacuí → Brazil 30°2S 51°15W **95 C5**
Jacumba U.S.A. 32°37N 116°11W **79 N10**
Jacundá → Brazil 1°57S 50°26W **93 D8**
Jadcherla India 16°46N 78°9E **44 F4**
Jade City Canada 59°12N 129°37W **70 B3**
Jade Dragon Snow Mt. = Yulong
  Xueshan China 27°6N 100°10E **34 D3**
Jade Mt. = Yü Shan
  Taiwan 23°25N 120°52E **35 F13**
Jaén Peru 5°25S 78°40W **92 E3**
Jaén Spain 37°44N 3°43W **21 D4**
Jafarabad India 20°52N 71°22E **42 J4**
Jaffa = Tel Aviv-Yafo
  Israel 32°4N 34°48E **48 C3**

Jaffa, C. *Australia* 36°58S 139°40E **63** F2
Jaffna *Sri Lanka* 9°45N 80°2E **45** K5
Jaffrey *U.S.A.* 42°49N 72°2W **83** D12
Jagadhri *India* 30°10N 77°20E **42** D7
Jagadishpur *India* 25°30N 84°21E **43** G11
Jagat *Nepal* 28°19N 84°53E **43** E11
Jagdalpur *India* 19°3N 82°0E **44** E6
Jagdaqi *China* 50°25N 124°7E **31** A13
Jagersfontein *S. Africa* 29°44S 25°27E **56** C4
Jaghīn → *Iran* 27°17N 57°13E **47** E8
Jagodina *Serbia* 44°5N 21°15E **23** C9
Jagraon *India* 30°50N 75°25E **42** D6
Jagtial *India* 18°50N 79°0E **44** E4
Jaguariaíva *Brazil* 24°10S 49°50W **95** A6
Jaguaribe → *Brazil* 4°25S 37°45W **93** D11
Jagüey Grande *Cuba* 22°35N 81°7W **88** B3
Jahanabad *India* 25°13N 84°59E **43** G11
Jahazpur *India* 25°37N 75°17E **42** G6
Jahrom *Iran* 28°30N 53°31E **47** D7
Jaigarh *India* 17°17N 73°13E **44** F1
Jaijon *India* 31°21N 76°9E **42** D7
Jailolo *Indonesia* 1°5N 127°30E **37** D7
Jailolo, Selat *Indonesia* 0°5N 129°5E **37** D7
Jaipur *India* 27°0N 75°50E **42** F6
Jais *India* 26°15N 81°32E **43** F9
Jaisalmer *India* 26°55N 70°54E **42** F4
Jaisinghnagar *India* 23°38N 78°34E **43** H8
Jaitaran *India* 26°12N 73°56E **42** F5
Jaithari *India* 23°14N 78°37E **43** H8
Jajarkot *Nepal* 28°42N 82°14E **43** E10
Jājarm *Iran* 36°58N 56°27E **47** B8
Jajpur *India* 20°53N 86°22E **44** D8
Jakam → *India* 23°54N 74°13E **42** H6
Jakarta Sukarno-Hatta Int. ✈ **(CGK)** *Indonesia* 6°7S 106°40E **37** G12
Jakhal *India* 29°48N 75°50E **42** E6
Jakhau *India* 23°13N 68°43E **42** H3
Jakobstad = Pietarsaari *Finland* 63°40N 22°43E **8** E20
Jal *U.S.A.* 32°7N 103°12W **77** K12
Jalājil *Si. Arabia* 25°40N 45°27E **46** E5
Jalālābād *Afghan.* 34°30N 70°29E **42** B4
Jalalabad *India* 27°41N 79°42E **43** F8
Jalalpur Jattan *Pakistan* 32°38N 74°11E **42** C6
Jalama *U.S.A.* 34°29N 120°29W **79** L6
Jalandhar *India* 31°20N 75°40E **42** D6
Jalapa *Guatemala* 14°39N 89°59W **88** D2
Jalapa Enríquez = Xalapa *Mexico* 19°32N 96°55W **87** D5
Jalasjärvi *Finland* 62°29N 22°47E **8** E20
Jalaun *India* 26°8N 79°25E **43** F8
Jaldhaka → *Bangla.* 26°16N 89°16E **43** F13
Jalesar *India* 27°29N 78°19E **42** F8
Jaleswar *Nepal* 26°38N 85°48E **43** F11
Jalgaon *India* 21°0N 75°42E **44** D2
Jalībah *Iraq* 30°35N 46°32E **46** D5
Jalingo *Nigeria* 8°55N 11°25E **53** G8
Jalisco □ *Mexico* 20°20N 103°40W **86** D4
Jalkot *Pakistan* 35°14N 73°24E **43** B5
Jalna *India* 19°48N 75°38E **44** E2
Jalón → *Spain* 41°47N 1°4W **21** B5
Jalor *India* 25°21N 72°37E **42** G5
Jalpa *Mexico* 21°38N 102°58W **86** C4
Jalpaiguri *India* 26°32N 88°46E **41** F16
Jalpan *Mexico* 21°14N 99°29W **87** C5
Jaluit I. *Marshall Is.* 6°0N 169°30E **64** G8
Jalūlā *Iraq* 34°16N 45°10E **46** C5
Jamaame *Somalia* 0°4N 42°44E **49** G3
Jamaica ■ *W. Indies* 18°10N 77°30W **88** a
Jamalpur *Bangla.* 24°52N 89°56E **41** G16
Jamalpur *India* 25°18N 86°28E **43** G12
Jamalpurganj *India* 23°2N 87°59E **43** H13
Jamanxim → *Brazil* 4°43S 56°18W **93** D7
Jambewangi *Indonesia* 8°17S 114°7E **37** J17
Jambi *Indonesia* 1°38S 103°30E **36** E2
Jambi □ *Indonesia* 1°30S 102°30E **36** E2
Jambongan, Pulau *Malaysia* 6°45N 117°20E **36** C5
Jambusar *India* 22°3N 72°51E **42** H5
James → *S. Dak., U.S.A.* 42°52N 97°18W **80** D5
James → *Va., U.S.A.* 36°56N 76°27W **81** G15
James B. *Canada* 54°0N 80°0W **72** B3
James Ranges *Australia* 24°10S 132°30E **60** D5
James Ross I. *Antarctica* 63°58S 57°50W **5** C18
James Ross Str. *Canada* 69°40N 96°10W **68** D12
Jamesabad *Pakistan* 25°17N 69°15E **42** G3
Jamestown *Australia* 33°10S 138°32E **63** E2
Jamestown *S. Africa* 31°6S 26°45E **56** D4
Jamestown *N. Dak., U.S.A.* 46°54N 98°42W **80** B4
Jamestown *N.Y., U.S.A.* 42°6N 79°14W **82** D5
Jamestown *Pa., U.S.A.* 41°29N 80°27W **82** E4
Jamīlābād *Iran* 34°24N 48°28E **47** C6
Jamira → *India* 21°35N 88°28E **43** J13
Jamkhandi *India* 16°30N 75°15E **44** F2
Jamkhed *India* 18°43N 75°19E **44** E2
Jammalamadugu *India* 14°51N 78°25E **45** G4
Jammu *India* 32°43N 74°54E **42** C6
Jammu & Kashmir □ *India* 34°25N 77°0E **43** B7
Jamnagar *India* 22°30N 70°6E **42** H4
Jamner *India* 20°45N 75°52E **44** D2
Jamni → *India* 25°13N 78°35E **43** G8
Jampur *Pakistan* 29°39N 70°40E **42** E4
Jamrud *Pakistan* 33°59N 71°24E **42** C4
Jämsä *Finland* 61°53N 25°10E **8** F21
Jamshedpur *India* 22°44N 86°12E **43** H12
Jamtara *India* 23°59N 86°49E **43** H12
Jämtland *Sweden* 63°31N 14°0E **8** E16
Jan L. *Canada* 54°56N 102°55W **71** C8
Jan Mayen *Arctic* 71°0N 9°0W **4** B7
Janakpur *Nepal* 26°42N 85°55E **44** A7
Janaúba *Brazil* 15°48S 43°19W **93** G10
Jand *Pakistan* 33°30N 72°6E **42** C5
Jandanku ✪ *Australia* 16°20S 135°45E **62** B2
Jandaq *Iran* 34°3N 54°22E **47** C7
Jandola *Pakistan* 32°20N 70°9E **42** C4
Jandowae *Australia* 26°45S 151°7E **63** D5
Janesville *U.S.A.* 42°41N 89°1W **80** D9
Jang Bogo *Antarctica* 74°37S 164°12E **5** D11
Jangamo *Mozam.* 24°6S 35°21E **57** B6
Janghai *India* 25°33N 82°19E **43** G10
Jangheung *S. Korea* 34°41N 126°52E **33** G14
Jangipur *India* 24°28N 88°4E **43** G12
Jangoon *India* 17°44N 79°5E **44** F4
Janjanbureh *Gambia* 13°30N 14°47W **52** F3
Janjgir *India* 22°1N 82°34E **43** J10
Janos *Mexico* 30°54N 108°10W **86** A3
Januária *Brazil* 15°25S 44°25W **93** G10
Janûb Sînî □ *Egypt* 29°30N 33°50E **48** F2
Janwada *India* 18°0N 77°29E **44** E3
Jaora *India* 23°40N 75°10E **42** H6
Japan ■ *Asia* 36°0N 136°0E **29** G8
Japan, Sea of *Asia* 40°0N 135°0E **28** E7
Japan Trench *Pac. Oc.* 32°0N 142°0E **64** D6
Japen = Yapen *Indonesia* 1°50S 136°0E **37** E9
Japla *India* 24°33N 84°1E **43** G11
Japurá → *Brazil* 3°8S 65°46W **92** D5
Jaquarão *Brazil* 32°34S 53°23W **95** C5
Jaqué *Panama* 7°27N 78°8W **88** E4
Jarābulus *Syria* 36°49N 38°1E **46** B3
Jaraguá do Sul *Brazil* 26°29S 49°4W **95** B6
Jarama → *Spain* 40°24N 3°32W **21** B4
Jaranwala *Pakistan* 31°15N 73°26E **42** D5
Jarash *Jordan* 32°17N 35°54E **48** C4
Jarash □ *Jordan* 32°17N 35°54E **48** C4
Jardim *Brazil* 21°28S 56°2W **94** A4
Jardín América *Argentina* 27°3S 55°14W **95** B4
Jardine River △ *Australia* 11°9S 142°21E **62** A3
Jardines de la Reina, Arch. de los *Cuba* 20°50N 78°50W **88** B4
Jargalang *China* 43°5N 122°55E **33** C12
Jari → *Brazil* 1°9S 51°54W **93** D8
Jarīr, W. al → *Si. Arabia* 25°38N 42°30E **46** E4
Jarosław *Poland* 50°2N 22°42E **17** C12
Jarrahdale *Australia* 32°24S 116°5E **61** F2
Jarrahi → *Iran* 30°49N 48°48E **47** D6
Jartai *China* 39°45N 105°48E **32** E3
Jarud Qi *China* 44°28N 120°50E **33** B11
Järvenpää *Finland* 60°29N 25°5E **8** F21
Jarvis *Canada* 42°53N 80°6W **82** D4
Jarvis I. *Pac. Oc.* 0°15S 160°5W **65** H11
Jarwa *India* 27°38N 82°30E **43** F10
Jasdan *India* 22°2N 71°12E **42** H4
Jashpurnagar *India* 22°54N 84°9E **43** H11
Jasidih *India* 24°31N 86°39E **43** G12
Jāsimīyah *Iraq* 33°45N 44°41E **46** C5
Jasin *Malaysia* 2°20N 102°26E **39** L4
Jāsk *Iran* 25°38N 57°45E **47** E8
Jasło *Poland* 49°45N 21°30E **17** D11
Jaso *India* 24°30N 80°29E **43** G9
Jasper *Alta., Canada* 52°55N 118°5W **70** C5
Jasper *Ont., Canada* 44°52N 75°57W **83** B9
Jasper *Ala., U.S.A.* 33°50N 87°17W **85** E11
Jasper *Fla., U.S.A.* 30°31N 82°57W **85** F13
Jasper *Ind., U.S.A.* 38°24N 86°56W **80** F10
Jasper *Tex., U.S.A.* 30°56N 94°1W **84** F7
Jasper △ *Canada* 52°50N 118°8W **70** C5
Jasrasar *India* 27°43N 73°49E **42** F5
Jászberény *Hungary* 47°30N 19°55E **17** E10
Jataí *Brazil* 17°58S 51°48W **93** G8
Jath *India* 17°3N 75°13E **44** F2
Jati *Pakistan* 24°20N 68°19E **42** G3
Jatibarang *Indonesia* 6°28S 108°18E **37** G13
Jatiluwih *Indonesia* 8°23S 115°8E **37** J18
Játiva = Xátiva *Spain* 38°59N 0°32W **21** C5
Jaú *Brazil* 22°10S 48°30W **95** A6
Jauja *Peru* 11°45S 75°15W **92** F3
Jaunpur *India* 25°46N 82°44E **43** G10
Java = Jawa *Indonesia* 7°0S 110°0E **36** F3
Java Sea *Indonesia* 4°35S 107°15E **36** E3
Java Trench *Ind. Oc.* 9°0S 105°0E **36** F3
Javadi Hills *India* 12°40N 78°40E **45** H4
Javla *India* 17°18N 75°9E **44** F2
Jawa *Indonesia* 7°0S 110°0E **36** F3
Jawa Barat □ *Indonesia* 7°0S 107°0E **37** G12
Jawa Tengah □ *Indonesia* 7°0S 110°0E **37** G14
Jawa Timur □ *Indonesia* 8°0S 113°0E **37** G15
Jawad *India* 24°36N 74°51E **42** G6
Jawhar *India* 19°55N 73°14E **44** E1
Jawhar *Somalia* 2°48N 45°30E **49** G4
Jawoyn ✪ *Australia* 14°16S 132°28E **60** B5
Jay Peak *U.S.A.* 44°55N 72°32W **83** B12
Jaya, Puncak *Indonesia* 3°57S 137°17E **37** E9
Jayanti *India* 26°45N 89°40E **41** F16
Jayapura *Indonesia* 2°28S 140°38E **37** E10
Jayawijaya, Pegunungan *Indonesia* 5°0S 139°0E **37** F9
Jaynagar *India* 26°43N 86°9E **43** F12
Jaypur = Jeypore *India* 18°50N 82°38E **44** E6
Jayrūd *Syria* 33°49N 36°44E **46** C3
Jayton *U.S.A.* 33°15N 100°34W **84** E4
Jāz Mūrīān, Hāmūn-e *Iran* 27°20N 58°55E **47** E8
Jazīreh-ye Shīf *Iran* 29°4N 50°54E **47** D6
Jazminal *Mexico* 24°52N 101°24W **86** C4
Jazzīn *Lebanon* 33°31N 35°35E **48** B4
Jean *U.S.A.* 35°47N 115°20W **79** K11
Jean Marie River *Canada* 61°32N 120°38W **70** A4
Jean-Rabel *Haiti* 19°50N 73°5W **89** C5
Jeanerette *U.S.A.* 29°55N 91°40W **84** G9
Jeanette, Ostrov = Zhannetty, Ostrov *Russia* 76°43N 158°0E **27** B16
Jeannette *U.S.A.* 40°20N 79°36W **82** F5
Jebāl Bārez, Kūh-e *Iran* 28°30N 58°20E **47** D8
Jebel, Bahr el → *South Sudan* 9°30N 30°25E **53** G12
Jebel Ali = Minā' Jabal 'Alī *U.A.E.* 25°2N 55°8E **47** E7
Jecheon *S. Korea* 37°8N 128°12E **33** F15
Jedburgh *U.K.* 55°29N 2°33W **11** F6
Jedda = Jiddah *Si. Arabia* 21°29N 39°10E **49** C2
Jeddore L. *Canada* 48°3N 55°55W **73** C8
Jędrzejów *Poland* 50°35N 20°15E **17** C11
Jefferson *Iowa, U.S.A.* 42°1N 94°23W **80** D6
Jefferson *Ohio, U.S.A.* 41°44N 80°46W **82** E4
Jefferson *Tex., U.S.A.* 32°46N 94°21W **84** E7
Jefferson, Mt. *Nev., U.S.A.* 38°47N 116°56W **76** G5
Jefferson, Mt. *Oreg., U.S.A.* 44°41N 121°48W **76** D3
Jefferson City *Mo., U.S.A.* 38°34N 92°10W **80** F7
Jefferson City *Tenn., U.S.A.* 36°7N 83°30W **85** C13
Jeffersontown *U.S.A.* 38°12N 85°35W **81** F11
Jeffersonville *U.S.A.* 38°17N 85°44W **81** F11
Jeffrey City *U.S.A.* 42°30N 107°49W **76** E10
Jega *Nigeria* 12°15N 4°23E **52** F6
Jeju *S. Korea* 33°31N 126°32E **33** H14
Jeju-do *S. Korea* 33°29N 126°34E **33** H14
Jeju Haehyop *S. Korea* 33°50N 126°30E **33** H14
Jēkabpils *Latvia* 56°29N 25°57E **9** H21
Jekyll I. *U.S.A.* 31°4N 81°25W **85** F14
Jelenia Góra *Poland* 50°50N 15°45E **16** C8
Jelgava *Latvia* 56°41N 23°49E **9** H20
Jemaluang *Malaysia* 2°16N 103°52E **39** L4
Jember *Indonesia* 8°11S 113°41E **37** H15
Jena *Germany* 50°54N 11°35E **16** C6
Jena *U.S.A.* 31°41N 92°8W **84** F8
Jengish Chokusu = Pobedy, Pik *Asia* 42°0N 79°58E **30** C4
Jenīn *West Bank* 32°28N 35°18E **48** C4
Jenkins *U.S.A.* 37°10N 82°38W **81** G12
Jenner *U.S.A.* 38°27N 123°7W **78** G3
Jennings *U.S.A.* 30°13N 92°40W **84** F8
Jeong-eup *S. Korea* 35°35N 126°50E **33** G14
Jeongseon *S. Korea* 37°20N 128°45E **33** F15
Jeonju *S. Korea* 35°50N 127°4E **33** G14
Jepara *Indonesia* 7°40S 109°14E **37** G14
Jeparit *Australia* 36°8S 142°1E **63** F3
Jequié *Brazil* 13°51S 40°5W **93** F10
Jequitinhonha *Brazil* 16°30S 41°0W **93** G10
Jequitinhonha → *Brazil* 15°51S 38°53W **93** G11
Jerada *Morocco* 34°17N 2°10W **52** B5
Jerantut *Malaysia* 3°56N 102°22E **39** L4
Jerejak, Pulau *Malaysia* 5°19N 100°19E **39** c
Jérémie *Haiti* 18°40N 74°10W **89** C5
Jerez, Pta. *Mexico* 22°58N 97°40W **87** C5
Jerez de García Salinas *Mexico* 22°39N 103°0W **86** C4
Jerez de la Frontera *Spain* 36°41N 6°7W **21** D2
Jerez de los Caballeros *Spain* 38°20N 6°45W **21** C2
Jericho = El Arīḩā *West Bank* 31°52N 35°27E **48** D4
Jericho *Australia* 23°38S 146°6E **62** C4
Jerid, Chott el = Djerid, Chott *Tunisia* 33°42N 8°30E **52** B7
Jerilderie *Australia* 35°20S 145°41E **63** F4
Jermyn *U.S.A.* 41°32N 75°33W **83** E9
Jerome *U.S.A.* 42°44N 114°31W **76** E6
Jerramungup *Australia* 33°55S 118°55E **61** F2
Jersey *U.K.* 49°11N 2°7W **13** H5
Jersey Shore *U.S.A.* 41°12N 77°15W **82** E7
Jerseyville *U.S.A.* 39°7N 90°20W **80** F8
Jervis B. *Australia* 35°8S 150°46E **63** F5
Jervis Inlet *Canada* 50°0N 123°57W **70** C4
Jesi = Iesi *Italy* 43°31N 13°14E **22** C5
Jessore *Bangla.* 23°10N 89°10E **41** H16
Jesup *U.S.A.* 31°36N 81°53W **85** F14
Jesús Carranza *Mexico* 17°26N 95°2W **87** D5
Jesús María *Argentina* 30°59S 64°5W **94** C3
Jetmore *U.S.A.* 38°4N 99°54W **80** F4
Jetpur *India* 21°45N 70°10E **42** J4
Jevnaker *Norway* 60°15N 10°26E **9** F14
Jewett *U.S.A.* 40°22N 81°2W **82** F3
Jewett City *U.S.A.* 41°36N 71°59W **83** E13
Jeyḩūnābād *Iran* 34°58N 48°59E **47** C6
Jeypore *India* 18°50N 82°38E **44** E6
Jha Jha *India* 24°46N 86°22E **43** G12
Jhaarkand = Jharkhand □ *India* 24°0N 85°50E **43** H11
Jhabua *India* 22°46N 74°36E **42** H6
Jhajjar *India* 28°37N 76°42E **42** E7
Jhal *Pakistan* 28°17N 67°27E **42** E2
Jhal Jhao *Pakistan* 26°20N 65°35E **40** F4
Jhalawar *India* 24°40N 76°10E **42** G7
Jhalida *India* 23°22N 85°58E **43** H11
Jhalrapatan *India* 24°33N 76°10E **42** G7
Jhang Maghiana *Pakistan* 31°15N 72°22E **42** D5
Jhang Sadr = Jhang Maghiana *Pakistan* 31°15N 72°22E **42** D5
Jhansi *India* 25°30N 78°36E **43** G8
Jhargram *India* 22°27N 86°59E **43** H12
Jharia *India* 23°45N 86°26E **43** H12
Jharkhand □ *India* 24°0N 85°50E **43** H11
Jharsuguda *India* 21°56N 84°5E **44** D7
Jhelum *Pakistan* 33°0N 73°45E **42** C5
Jhelum → *Pakistan* 31°20N 72°10E **42** D5
Jhilmilli *India* 23°24N 82°51E **43** H10
Jhudo *Pakistan* 24°58N 69°18E **42** G3
Jhunjhunu *India* 28°10N 75°30E **42** E6
Ji-Paraná *Brazil* 10°52S 62°57W **92** F6
Ji Xian *China* 36°7N 110°40E **32** F6
Jia Xian *Henan, China* 33°59N 113°12E **32** H7
Jia Xian *Shaanxi, China* 38°12N 110°28E **32** E6
Jiahe *China* 25°38N 112°19E **35** E9
Jiaji = Qionghai *China* 19°15N 110°26E **38** C8
Jialing Jiang → *China* 29°30N 106°20E **34** C6
Jiamusi *China* 46°40N 130°26E **31** B15
Ji'an *Jiangxi, China* 27°6N 114°59E **35** D10
Ji'an *Jilin, China* 41°5N 126°10E **33** D14
Jianchang *China* 40°55N 120°35E **33** D11
Jianchuan *China* 26°38N 99°55E **34** D2
Jiande *China* 29°23N 119°15E **35** C12
Jiang'an *China* 28°40N 105°3E **34** C5
Jiangbei *China* 29°40N 106°34E **34** C6
Jiangcheng *China* 22°36N 101°52E **34** F3
Jiangchuan *China* 24°8N 102°39E **34** E4
Jiangdi *China* 26°57N 103°37E **34** D4
Jiangdu *China* 32°27N 119°36E **35** A12
Jiange *China* 32°4N 105°32E **34** A5
Jianghua *China* 25°0N 111°47E **35** E8
Jiangjin *China* 29°14N 106°14E **34** C6
Jiangkou *China* 27°40N 108°49E **34** D7
Jiangle *China* 26°42N 117°23E **35** D11
Jiangmen *China* 22°32N 113°0E **35** F9
Jiangning *China* 31°55N 118°50E **35** B12
Jiangshan *China* 28°40N 118°37E **35** C12
Jiangsu □ *China* 33°0N 120°0E **33** H11
Jiangxi □ *China* 27°30N 116°0E **35** D11
Jiangyan *China* 32°30N 120°7E **35** A13
Jiangyin *China* 31°54N 120°17E **35** B13
Jiangyong *China* 25°20N 111°22E **35** E8
Jiangyou *China* 31°44N 104°43E **34** B5
Jiangyuan *China* 42°2N 126°34E **33** C14
Jianhe *China* 26°37N 108°31E **34** D7
Jianli *China* 29°46N 112°56E **35** C9
Jianning *China* 26°50N 116°50E **35** D11
Jian'ou *China* 27°3N 118°17E **35** D12
Jianping *China* 41°53N 119°42E **33** D10
Jianshi *China* 30°37N 109°38E **34** B7
Jianshui *China* 23°36N 102°43E **34** F4
Jianyang *Fujian, China* 27°20N 118°5E **35** D12
Jianyang *Sichuan, China* 30°24N 104°33E **34** B5
Jiao Xian = Jiaozhou *China* 36°18N 120°1E **33** F11
Jiaohe *Hebei, China* 38°2N 116°20E **32** E9
Jiaohe *Jilin, China* 43°40N 127°22E **33** C14
Jiaoling *China* 24°41N 116°12E **35** E11
Jiaonan *China* 35°52N 119°58E **33** G10
Jiaozhou *China* 36°18N 120°1E **33** F11
Jiaozhou Wan *China* 36°5N 120°10E **33** F11
Jiaozuo *China* 35°16N 113°12E **32** G7
Jiawang *China* 34°28N 117°26E **33** G9
Jiaxiang *China* 35°25N 116°20E **32** G9
Jiaxing *China* 30°49N 120°45E **35** B13
Jiayu *China* 29°55N 113°55E **35** C9
Jiayuguan *China* 39°49N 98°18E **30** D8
Jibuti = Djibouti ■ *Africa* 12°0N 43°0E **49** E3
Jicarón, I. *Panama* 7°10N 81°50W **88** E3
Jiddah *Si. Arabia* 21°29N 39°10E **49** C2
Jido *India* 29°2N 94°58E **41** E19
Jieshou *China* 33°18N 115°22E **32** H8
Jiexiu *China* 37°2N 111°55E **32** F6
Jieyang *China* 23°35N 116°21E **35** F11
Jigalong *Australia* 23°21S 120°47E **60** D3
Jigalong ✪ *Australia* 23°21S 120°46E **60** D3
Jigni *India* 25°45N 79°25E **43** G8
Jihlava *Czechia* 49°28N 15°35E **16** D8
Jihlava → *Czechia* 48°55N 16°36E **17** D9
Jijiga *Ethiopia* 9°20N 42°50E **49** F3
Jilib *Somalia* 0°29N 42°46E **49** G3
Jilin *China* 43°44N 126°30E **33** C14
Jilin □ *China* 44°0N 127°0E **33** C14
Jim Thorpe *U.S.A.* 40°52N 75°44W **83** F9
Jima *Ethiopia* 7°40N 36°47E **49** F2
Jimbaran, Teluk *Indonesia* 8°46S 115°9E **37** K18
Jiménez *Mexico* 27°8N 104°54W **86** B4
Jimeta *Nigeria* 9°17N 12°28E **54** C2
Jimo *China* 36°23N 120°30E **33** F11
Jin Jiang → *China* 28°24N 115°48E **35** C10
Jin Xian = Jinzhou *China* 38°55N 121°42E **33** E11
Jinan *China* 36°38N 117°1E **32** F9
Jinchang *China* 38°30N 102°10E **30** D9
Jincheng *China* 35°29N 112°50E **32** G7
Jinchuan *China* 31°30N 102°3E **34** B4
Jind *India* 29°19N 76°22E **42** E7
Jindabyne *Australia* 36°25S 148°35E **63** F4
Jinding *China* 22°22N 113°33E **31** a
Jindo *S. Korea* 34°28N 126°15E **33** G14
Jindřichův Hradec *Czechia* 49°10N 15°2E **16** D8
Jing He → *China* 34°27N 109°4E **32** G5
Jing Shan *China* 31°20N 111°35E **35** B8
Jing Xian *China* 30°38N 118°25E **35** B12
Jing'an *China* 28°50N 115°17E **35** C10
Jingbian *China* 37°20N 108°30E **32** F5
Jingchuan *China* 35°20N 107°20E **32** G4
Jingde *China* 30°15N 118°27E **35** B12
Jingdezhen *China* 29°20N 117°11E **35** C11
Jingdong *China* 24°23N 100°47E **34** E3
Jinggangshan *China* 26°58N 114°15E **35** D10
Jinggu *China* 23°35N 100°41E **34** F3
Jinghai *Guangdong, China* 22°59N 116°31E **35** F11
Jinghai *Tianjin, China* 38°55N 116°55E **32** E9
Jinghong *China* 22°0N 100°45E **34** G3
Jinghong Dam *China* 22°10N 100°46E **34** F3
Jingjiang *China* 32°2N 120°16E **35** A13
Jingle *China* 38°20N 111°55E **32** E6
Jingmen *China* 31°0N 112°10E **35** B9
Jingning *China* 35°30N 105°43E **32** G3
Jingpo Hu *China* 43°55N 128°55E **33** C15
Jingshan *China* 31°1N 113°7E **35** B9
Jingtai *China* 37°10N 104°6E **32** F3
Jingtang *China* 39°10N 119°5E **33** E10
Jingxi *China* 23°8N 106°27E **34** F6
Jingyang *China* 34°30N 108°50E **32** G5
Jingyu *China* 42°25N 126°45E **33** C14
Jingyuan *China* 36°30N 104°40E **32** F3
Jingzhou *Hubei, China* 30°21N 112°11E **35** B9
Jingzhou *Hunan, China* 26°33N 109°40E **34** D7
Jingziguan *China* 33°15N 111°0E **32** H6
Jinhua *China* 29°8N 119°38E **35** C12
Jining *Nei Monggol Zizhiqu, China* 41°5N 113°0E **32** D7
Jining *Shandong, China* 35°22N 116°34E **32** G9
Jinja *Uganda* 0°25N 33°12E **54** D6
Jinjang *Malaysia* 3°13N 101°39E **39** L3
Jinji *China* 37°58N 106°8E **32** F4
Jinjiang *Fujian, China* 24°43N 118°33E **35** E12
Jinjiang *Yunnan, China* 26°14N 100°34E **34** D3
Jinju *S. Korea* 35°12N 128°2E **33** G15
Jinkou *China* 30°20N 114°8E **35** B10
Jinkouhe *China* 29°18N 103°4E **34** C4
Jinmu Jiao *China* 18°9N 109°34E **38** C7
Jinnah Barrage *Pakistan* 32°58N 71°33E **42** C4
Jinning *China* 24°38N 102°38E **34** E4
Jinotega *Nic.* 13°6N 85°59W **88** D2
Jinotepe *Nic.* 11°50N 86°10W **88** D2
Jinping *Guizhou, China* 26°41N 109°10E **34** D7
Jinping *Yunnan, China* 22°45N 103°18E **34** F4
Jinping Bend Dams *China* 28°1N 101°39E **34** C3
Jinsha *China* 27°29N 106°12E **34** D6
Jinsha Jiang → *China* 28°50N 104°36E **34** C5
Jinshi *China* 29°40N 111°50E **35** C8
Jintan *China* 31°42N 119°36E **35** B12
Jintur *India* 19°37N 76°42E **44** E3
Jinxi *Jiangxi, China* 27°56N 116°45E **35** D11
Jinxi *Liaoning, China* 40°52N 120°50E **33** D11
Jinxian *China* 28°26N 116°17E **35** C11
Jinxiang *China* 35°5N 116°22E **32** G9
Jinyang *China* 27°28N 103°5E **34** D4
Jinyun *China* 28°35N 120°5E **35** C13
Jinzhai *China* 31°40N 115°53E **35** B10
Jinzhong *China* 37°42N 112°46E **32** F7
Jinzhou *Liaoning, China* 38°55N 121°42E **33** E11
Jinzhou *Liaoning, China* 41°5N 121°3E **33** D11
Jiparaná → *Brazil* 8°3S 62°52W **92** E6
Jipijapa *Ecuador* 1°0S 80°40W **92** D2
Jiquilpan *Mexico* 19°59N 102°43W **86** D4
Jirisan *S. Korea* 35°20N 127°44E **33** G14
Jiroft *Iran* 28°45N 57°50E **47** D8
Jishan *China* 35°34N 110°58E **32** G6
Jishou *China* 28°21N 109°43E **34** C7
Jishui *China* 27°12N 115°8E **35** D10
Jisr ash Shughūr *Syria* 35°49N 36°18E **46** C3
Jitarning *Australia* 32°48S 117°57E **61** F2
Jitra *Malaysia* 6°16N 100°25E **39** J3
Jiu → *Romania* 43°47N 23°48E **17** F12
Jiudengkou *China* 39°56N 106°40E **32** E4
Jiujiang *Guangdong, China* 22°50N 113°0E **35** F9
Jiujiang *Jiangxi, China* 29°42N 115°58E **35** C10
Jiuling Shan *China* 28°40N 114°40E **35** C10
Jiulong *China* 28°57N 101°31E **34** C3
Jiuquan *China* 39°50N 98°20E **30** D8
Jiutai *China* 44°10N 125°50E **33** B13
Jiuxincheng *China* 39°17N 115°59E **32** E8
Jiuzhaigou ⌓ *China* 33°8N 103°52E **34** A4
Jiwani *Pakistan* 25°1N 61°44E **40** G2
Jixi *Anhui, China* 30°5N 118°34E **35** B12
Jixi *Heilongjiang, China* 45°20N 130°50E **33** B16
Jiyang *China* 37°0N 117°12E **33** F9
Jiyuan *China* 35°7N 112°57E **32** G7
Jīzān *Si. Arabia* 17°0N 42°20E **49** D3
Jize *China* 36°54N 114°56E **32** F8
Jizhou *China* 37°35N 115°30E **32** F8
Jīzl, Wādī al → *Si. Arabia* 25°39N 38°25E **46** E3
Jizō-Zaki *Japan* 35°34N 133°20E **29** G6
Jizzax *Uzbekistan* 40°6N 67°50E **26** E7
Joaçaba *Brazil* 27°5S 51°31W **95** B5
João Pessoa *Brazil* 7°10S 34°52W **93** E12
Joaquín V. González *Argentina* 25°10S 64°0W **94** B3
Jobat *India* 22°25N 74°34E **42** H6
Jodhpur *India* 26°23N 73°8E **42** F5
Jodiya *India* 22°42N 70°18E **42** H4
Joensuu *Finland* 62°37N 29°49E **8** E23
Jōetsu *Japan* 37°12N 138°10E **29** F9
Jofane *Mozam.* 21°15S 34°18E **57** B5
Jog Falls = Gersoppa Falls *India* 14°12N 74°46E **45** G2
Jogbani *India* 26°25N 87°15E **43** F12
Jõgeva *Estonia* 58°45N 26°24E **9** G22
Jogjakarta = Yogyakarta *Indonesia* 7°49S 110°22E **37** G14
Johannesburg *U.S.A.* 35°22N 117°38W **79** K9
Johilla → *India* 23°37N 81°14E **43** H9
John Crow Mts. *Jamaica* 18°5N 76°25W **88** a
John Day *U.S.A.* 44°25N 118°57W **76** D4
John Day → *U.S.A.* 45°44N 120°39W **76** D3
John Day Fossil Beds ⌓ *U.S.A.* 44°33N 119°38W **76** D4
John D'or Prairie *Canada* 58°30N 115°8W **70** B5
John H. Kerr Res. *U.S.A.* 36°36N 78°18W **85** C15
John o' Groats *U.K.* 58°38N 3°4W **11** C5
Johnnie *U.S.A.* 36°25N 116°5W **79** J10
John's Ra. *Australia* 21°55S 133°23E **62** C1
Johnson *U.S.A.* 44°38N 72°41W **83** B12
Johnson City *Kans., U.S.A.* 37°34N 101°45W **80** G3
Johnson City *N.Y., U.S.A.* 42°7N 75°58W **83** D9
Johnson City *Tenn., U.S.A.* 36°19N 82°21W **85** C13
Johnson City *Tex., U.S.A.* 30°17N 98°25W **84** F5
Johnsonburg *U.S.A.* 41°29N 78°41W **82** E6
Johnsondale *U.S.A.* 35°58N 118°32W **79** K8
Johnsons Crossing *Canada* 60°29N 133°18W **70** A2
Johnston, L. *Australia* 32°25S 120°30E **61** F3
Johnston Atoll *Pac. Oc.* 17°10N 169°8W **65** F11
Johnston Falls = Mambilima Falls *Zambia* 10°31S 28°45E **54** G5
Johnstone Str. *Canada* 50°28N 126°0W **70** C3
Johnstown *Ireland* 52°45N 7°33W **10** D4
Johnstown *N.Y., U.S.A.* 43°0N 74°22W **83** C10
Johnstown *Ohio, U.S.A.* 40°9N 82°41W **82** F2
Johnstown *Pa., U.S.A.* 40°20N 78°55W **82** F6
Johor □ *Malaysia* 2°5N 103°20E **39** M4
Johor, Selat *Asia* 1°28N 103°47E **39** d
Johor Bahru *Malaysia* 1°28N 103°46E **39** d
Johor Port *Malaysia* 1°26N 103°53E **39** d
Jōhvi *Estonia* 59°22N 27°27E **9** G22
Joinville *Brazil* 26°15S 48°55W **95** B6
Joinville I. *Antarctica* 65°0S 55°30W **5** C18
Jojutla *Mexico* 18°37N 99°11W **87** D5
Jokkmokk *Sweden* 66°35N 19°50E **8** C18
Jökulsá á Bru → *Iceland* 65°40N 14°16W **8** D6
Jökulsá á Fjöllum → *Iceland* 66°10N 16°30W **8** C5
Jolfā *Āzarbājān-e Sharqī, Iran* 38°57N 45°38E **46** B5
Jolfā *Eşfahan, Iran* 32°58N 51°37E **47** C6
Joliet *U.S.A.* 41°32N 88°5W **80** E9
Joliette *Canada* 46°3N 73°24W **72** C5
Jolo *Phil.* 6°0N 121°0E **37** C6
Jolon *U.S.A.* 35°58N 121°9W **78** K5
Jombang *Indonesia* 7°33S 112°14E **37** G15
Jomda *China* 31°28N 98°12E **34** B2
Jonava *Lithuania* 55°8N 24°12E **9** J21
Jones Sound *Canada* 76°0N 85°0W **69** B15
Jonesboro *Ark., U.S.A.* 35°50N 90°42W **85** D9
Jonesboro *La., U.S.A.* 32°15N 92°43W **84** E8
Joniškis *Lithuania* 56°13N 23°35E **9** H20
Jönköping *Sweden* 57°45N 14°8E **9** H16

Jonquière Canada 48°27N 71°14W 73 C5
Joplin U.S.A. 37°6N 94°31W 80 G6
Jora India 26°20N 77°49E 42 F6
Jordan Mont., U.S.A. 47°19N 106°55W 76 C10
Jordan N.Y., U.S.A. 43°4N 76°29W 83 C8
Jordan ■ Asia 31°0N 36°0E 48 E5
Jordan → Asia 31°48N 35°32E 48 D4
Jordan Valley U.S.A. 42°59N 117°3W 76 E5
Jorhat India 26°45N 94°12E 41 F19
Jörn Sweden 65°4N 20°1E 8 D19
Jorong Indonesia 3°58S 114°56E 36 E4
Jørpeland Norway 59°3N 6°1E 9 G12
Jorquera → Chile 28°3S 69°58W 94 B2
Jos Nigeria 9°53N 8°51E 52 G7
José Batlle y Ordóñez Uruguay 33°20S 55°10W 95 C4
Joseph, L. Canada 45°10N 79°44W 82 A5
Joseph Bonaparte G. Australia 14°35S 128°50E 60 B4
Joseph L. Canada 52°45N 65°18W 73 B6
Joshinath India 30°34N 79°34E 43 D8
Joshinetsu-Kōgen △ Japan 36°42N 138°32E 29 F9
Joshua Tree U.S.A. 34°8N 116°19W 79 L10
Joshua Tree △ U.S.A. 33°55N 116°0W 79 M10
Jost Van Dyke I. Br. Virgin Is. 18°29N 64°47W 89 e
Jostedalsbreen Norway 61°40N 6°59E 8 F12
Jotunheimen Norway 61°35N 8°25E 8 F13
Joubertberge Namibia 18°30S 14°0E 56 A1
Jourdanton U.S.A. 28°55N 98°33W 84 G5
Jovellanos Cuba 22°40N 81°10W 88 B3
Ju Xian China 35°35N 118°20E 33 G10
Juan Aldama Mexico 24°19N 103°21W 86 C4
Juan Bautista Alberdi Argentina 34°26S 61°48W 94 C3
Juan de Fuca, Str of. N. Amer. 48°15N 124°0W 78 B3
Juan de Nova Ind. Oc. 17°3S 43°45E 57 A7
Juan Fernández, Arch. de Pac. Oc. 33°50S 80°0W 90 G2
Juan José Castelli Argentina 25°27S 60°57W 94 B3
Juan L. Lacaze Uruguay 34°26S 57°25W 94 C4
Juankoski Finland 63°3N 28°19E 8 E23
Juárez Mexico 27°37N 100°44W 86 B4
Juárez, Sa. de Mexico 32°0N 115°50W 86 A1
Juàzeiro Brazil 9°30S 40°30W 93 E10
Juàzeiro do Norte Brazil 7°10S 39°18W 93 E11
Juba South Sudan 4°50N 31°35E 53 H12
Juba → Somalia 1°30N 42°35E 49 G3
Jubail = Al Jubayl Si. Arabia 27°0N 49°50E 47 E6
Jubany = Carlini Base Antarctica 62°30S 58°0W 5 C18
Jubayl Lebanon 34°5N 35°39E 48 A4
Jubbah Si. Arabia 28°2N 40°56E 46 D4
Jubbal India 31°5N 77°40E 42 D7
Jubbulpore = Jabalpur India 23°9N 79°58E 43 H8
Jubilee L. Australia 29°0S 126°50E 61 E4
Juby, C. Morocco 28°0N 12°59W 52 C3
Júcar = Xúquer → Spain 39°5N 0°10W 21 C5
Júcaro Cuba 21°37N 78°51W 88 B4
Juchitán de Zaragoza Mexico 16°26N 95°1W 87 D5
Judea = Har Yehuda Israel 31°35N 34°57E 48 D3
Judith → U.S.A. 47°44N 109°39W 76 C9
Judith, Pt. U.S.A. 41°22N 71°29W 83 E13
Judith Gap U.S.A. 46°41N 109°45W 76 C9
Jugaipa Nic. 12°6N 85°26W 88 D2
Juiz de Fora Brazil 21°43S 43°19W 95 A7
Jujuy □ Argentina 23°20S 65°40W 94 A2
Julesburg U.S.A. 40°59N 102°16W 76 F12
Juli Peru 16°10S 69°25W 92 G5
Julia Cr. → Australia 20°0S 141°11E 62 C3
Julia Creek Australia 20°39S 141°44E 62 C3
Juliaca Peru 15°25S 70°10W 92 G4
Julian U.S.A. 33°4N 116°38W 79 M10
Julian, L. Canada 54°25N 77°57W 72 B4
Julianatop Suriname 3°40N 56°30W 93 C7
Julianehåb = Qaqortoq Greenland 60°43N 46°0W 4 C5
Julimes Mexico 28°25N 105°27W 86 B3
Jullundur = Jalandhar India 31°20N 75°40E 42 D6
Julu China 37°15N 115°2E 32 F8
Jumbo Pk. U.S.A. 36°12N 114°11W 79 J12
Jumentos Cays Bahamas 23°0N 75°40W 88 B4
Jumilla Spain 38°28N 1°19W 21 C5
Jumla Nepal 29°15N 82°13E 43 E10
Jumna = Yamuna → India 25°30N 81°53E 43 G9
Jumunjin S. Korea 37°55N 128°54E 33 F15
Junagadh India 21°30N 70°30E 42 J4
Junan China 35°12N 118°53E 33 G10
Junction Tex., U.S.A. 30°29N 99°46W 84 F5
Junction Utah, U.S.A. 38°14N 112°13W 77 G7
Junction B. Australia 11°52S 133°55E 62 A1
Junction City Kans., U.S.A. 39°2N 96°50W 80 F5
Junction City Oreg., U.S.A. 44°13N 123°12W 76 D2
Junction Pt. Australia 11°45S 133°50E 62 A1
Jundah Australia 24°46S 143°2E 62 C3
Jundiaí Brazil 24°30S 47°0W 95 A6
Juneau U.S.A. 58°18N 134°25W 70 B2
Junee Australia 34°53S 147°35E 63 E4
Jungar Qi China 39°49N 110°57E 32 E6
Jungfrau Switz. 46°32N 7°58E 20 C7
Junggar Pendi China 44°30N 86°0E 30 C6
Jungshahi Pakistan 24°52N 67°44E 42 G2
Juniata → U.S.A. 40°24N 77°1W 82 F7
Junín Argentina 34°33S 60°57W 94 C3
Junín de los Andes Argentina 39°45S 71°0W 96 D2
Jūniyah Lebanon 33°59N 35°38E 48 B4
Junkerdal △ Norway 66°50N 15°50E 8 C16
Junlian China 28°8N 104°29E 34 C5
Junnar India 19°12N 73°58E 44 E1
Juntas Chile 28°24S 69°58W 94 B2
Juntura U.S.A. 43°45N 118°5W 76 E4
Jur → South Sudan 8°45N 29°15E 53 G11
Jura = Jura, Mts. du Europe 46°40N 6°5E 20 C7
Jura = Schwäbische Alb Germany 48°20N 9°30E 16 D5
Jura U.K. 56°0N 5°50W 11 F3
Jura, Mts. du Europe 46°40N 6°5E 20 C7
Jura, Sd. of U.K. 55°57N 5°45W 11 F3
Jurassic Coast U.K. 50°42N 2°50W 13 G5
Jurbarkas Lithuania 55°4N 22°46E 9 J20
Jurien Bay Australia 30°18S 115°2E 61 F2
Jūrmala Latvia 56°58N 23°34E 9 H20
Jurong China 31°57N 119°9E 35 B12
Juruá → Brazil 2°37S 65°44W 92 D5
Juruena Brazil 13°0S 58°10W 92 F7
Juruena → Brazil 7°20S 58°3W 92 E7
Juruti Brazil 2°9S 56°4W 93 D7
Justo Daract Argentina 33°52S 65°12W 94 C2
Jutaí → Brazil 2°43S 66°57W 92 D5
Juticalpa Honduras 14°40N 86°12W 88 D2
Jutland = Jylland Denmark 56°25N 9°30E 9 H13
Juuka Finland 63°13N 29°17E 8 E23
Juventud, I. de la Cuba 21°40N 82°40W 88 B3
Jūy Zar Iran 33°50N 46°18E 46 C5
Juye China 35°22N 116°5E 32 G9
Jwaneng Botswana 24°45S 24°50E 55 J4
Jylland Denmark 56°25N 9°30E 9 H13
Jyväskylä Finland 62°14N 25°50E 8 E21

K

K2 Pakistan 35°58N 76°32E 43 B7
Kaakha = Kaka Turkmenistan 37°21N 59°36E 47 B8
Kaap Plateau S. Africa 28°30S 24°0E 56 C3
Kaapkruis Namibia 21°55S 13°57E 56 B1
Kabaena Indonesia 5°15S 122°0E 37 F6
Kabala S. Leone 9°38N 11°37W 52 G3
Kabale Uganda 1°15S 30°0E 54 E6
Kabalo Dem. Rep. of the Congo 6°0S 27°0E 54 F5
Kabambare Dem. Rep. of the Congo 4°41S 27°39E 54 E5
Kabanjahe Indonesia 3°6N 98°30E 36 D1
Kabankalan Phil. 9°59N 122°49E 37 C6
Kabara Fiji 18°59S 178°56W 59 a
Kabardino-Balkaria □ Russia 43°30N 43°30E 19 F7
Kabarega Falls = Murchison Falls Uganda 2°15N 31°30E 54 D6
Kabasalan Phil. 7°47N 122°44E 37 C6
Kabat Indonesia 8°16S 114°19E 37 J17
Kabbani → India 12°13N 76°54E 45 H3
Kabin Buri Thailand 13°57N 101°43E 38 F3
Kabinakagami L. Canada 48°54N 84°25W 72 C3
Kabinda Dem. Rep. of the Congo 6°19S 24°20E 54 F4
Kabompo → Zambia 14°11S 23°11E 55 G4
Kabongo Dem. Rep. of the Congo 7°22S 25°33E 54 F5
Kabrît, G. el Egypt 29°42N 33°16E 48 F2
Kabūd Gonbad Iran 37°5N 59°45E 47 B8
Kābul Afghan. 34°28N 69°11E 42 B3
Kābul □ Afghan. 34°30N 69°0E 40 B6
Kābul → Pakistan 33°55N 72°14E 42 C5
Kaburuang Indonesia 3°50N 126°30E 37 D7
Kabwe Zambia 14°30S 28°29E 55 G5
Kachchh, Gulf of India 22°50N 69°15E 42 H3
Kachchh, Rann of India 24°0N 70°0E 42 H4
Kachchhidhana India 21°44N 78°46E 43 J8
Kachikau Botswana 18°8S 24°26E 56 A3
Kachin □ Myanmar 26°0N 97°30E 34 D1
Kachīry Kazakhstan 53°10N 75°50E 26 D8
Kachnara India 23°50N 75°6E 42 H6
Kachot Cambodia 11°30N 103°3E 39 G4
Kaçkar Turkey 40°45N 41°10E 19 F7
Kadaiyanallur India 9°3N 77°22E 45 K3
Kadan Kyun Myanmar 12°30N 98°20E 38 F2
Kadanai → Afghan. 31°22N 65°45E 42 D1
Kadapa India 14°30N 78°47E 45 G4
Kadavu Fiji 19°0S 178°15E 59 a
Kadavu Passage Fiji 18°45S 178°0E 59 a
Kade Ghana 6°7N 0°56W 52 G5
Kadhimain = Al Kāẓimīyah Iraq 33°22N 44°18E 46 C5
Kadi India 23°18N 72°23E 42 H5
Kadina Australia 33°55S 137°43E 63 E2
Kadipur India 26°10N 82°23E 43 F10
Kadirabad India 19°51N 75°54E 44 E2
Kadiri India 14°12N 78°13E 45 G4
Kadirli Turkey 37°23N 36°5E 46 B3
Kadiyevka = Stakhanov Ukraine 48°35N 38°40E 19 E6
Kadmat I. India 11°14N 72°47E 45 J1
Kadoka U.S.A. 43°50N 101°31W 80 D3
Kadoma Zimbabwe 18°20S 29°52E 55 H5
Kâdugli Sudan 11°0N 29°45E 53 F11
Kaduna Nigeria 10°30N 7°21E 52 F7
Kadur India 13°34N 76°1E 45 H3
Kaédi Mauritania 16°9N 13°28W 52 E3
Kaeng Khoi Thailand 14°35N 101°0E 38 E3
Kaeng Krachan △ Thailand 12°57N 99°23E 38 F2
Kaeng Krung △ Thailand 9°30N 98°50E 39 H2
Kaeng Tana △ Thailand 15°25N 105°32E 38 E5
Kaesŏng N. Korea 37°58N 126°35E 33 F14
Kāf Si. Arabia 31°25N 37°29E 46 D3
Kafan = Kapan Armenia 39°18N 46°27E 46 B5
Kafanchan Nigeria 9°40N 8°20E 52 G7
Kafue Zambia 15°46S 28°9E 55 H5
Kafue → Zambia 15°30S 29°0E 55 H5
Kaga Afghan. 34°14N 70°10E 42 B4
Kaga Bandoro C.A.R. 7°0N 19°10E 54 C3
Kagawa □ Japan 34°15N 134°0E 29 G7
Kagera → Uganda 0°57S 31°47E 54 E6
Kağızman Turkey 40°5N 43°10E 46 B4
Kagoshima Japan 31°35N 130°33E 29 J5
Kagoshima □ Japan 31°30N 130°30E 29 J5
Kagul = Cahul Moldova 45°50N 28°15E 17 F15
Kahak Iran 36°6N 49°46E 47 B6
Kahan Pakistan 29°18N 68°54E 42 E3
Kahang Malaysia 2°12N 103°32E 39 L4
Kahayan → Indonesia 3°40S 114°0E 36 E4
Kahemba Dem. Rep. of the Congo 7°18S 18°55E 54 F3
Kahnūj Iran 27°55N 57°40E 47 E8
Kahoka U.S.A. 40°25N 91°44W 80 E8
Kaho'olawe U.S.A. 20°33N 156°37W 75 L8
Kahramanmaraş Turkey 37°37N 36°53E 46 B3
Kâhta Turkey 37°46N 38°36E 46 B3
Kahului U.S.A. 20°54N 156°28W 75 L8
Kahurangi △ N.Z. 41°10S 172°32E 59 D4
Kahuta Pakistan 33°35N 73°24E 42 C5
Kai, Kepulauan Indonesia 5°55S 132°45E 37 F8
Kai Besar Indonesia 5°35S 133°0E 37 F8
Kai Is. = Kai, Kepulauan Indonesia 5°55S 132°45E 37 F8
Kai Kecil Indonesia 5°45S 132°40E 37 F8
Kai Xian China 31°11N 108°21E 34 B7
Kaiapoi N.Z. 43°24S 172°40E 59 E4
Kaidu He → China 41°46N 86°31E 30 C6
Kaieteur Falls Guyana 5°1N 59°10W 92 B7
Kaifeng China 34°48N 114°21E 32 G8
Kaihua China 29°12N 118°20E 35 C12
Kaijiang China 31°7N 107°55E 34 B6
Kaikohe N.Z. 35°25S 173°49E 59 A4
Kaikoura N.Z. 42°25S 173°43E 59 E4
Kailash = Kangrinboqe Feng China 31°0N 81°25E 43 D9
Kaili China 26°33N 107°59E 34 D6
Kailu China 43°38N 121°18E 33 C11
Kailua Kona U.S.A. 19°39N 155°59W 75 M8
Kaimana Indonesia 3°39S 133°45E 37 E8
Kaimanawa Mts. N.Z. 39°15S 175°56E 59 C5
Kaimganj India 27°33N 79°24E 43 F8
Kaimur Hills India 24°30N 82°0E 43 G10
Kainab → Namibia 28°32S 19°34E 56 C2
Kainji Res. Nigeria 10°1N 4°40E 52 F6
Kainuu □ Finland 64°30N 29°7E 8 D23
Kaipara Harbour N.Z. 36°25S 174°14E 59 B5
Kaiping China 22°23N 112°42E 35 F9
Kaipokok B. Canada 54°54N 59°47W 73 B8
Kaira India 22°45N 72°50E 42 H5
Kairana India 29°24N 77°15E 42 E7
Kaironi Indonesia 0°47S 133°40E 37 E8
Kairouan Tunisia 35°45N 10°5E 53 A8
Kaiserslautern Germany 49°26N 7°45E 16 D4
Kaitaia N.Z. 35°8S 173°17E 59 A4
Kaitangata N.Z. 46°17S 169°51E 59 G2
Kaithal India 29°48N 76°26E 42 E7
Kaitu → Pakistan 33°10N 70°30E 42 C4
Kaiwi Channel U.S.A. 21°15N 157°30W 75 L8
Kaiyang China 27°4N 106°59E 34 D6
Kaiyuan Liaoning, China 42°28N 124°1E 33 C13
Kaiyuan Yunnan, China 23°40N 103°12E 34 F4
Kaiyuh Mts. U.S.A. 64°30N 158°0W 74 C8
Kajaani Finland 64°17N 27°46E 8 D22
Kajabbi Australia 20°0S 140°1E 62 C3
Kajana = Kajaani Finland 64°17N 27°46E 8 D22
Kajang Malaysia 2°59N 101°48E 39 L3
Kajo Kaji South Sudan 3°58N 31°40E 53 H12
Kaka Turkmenistan 37°21N 59°36E 47 B8
Kakabeka Falls Canada 48°24N 89°37W 72 C2
Kakadu △ Australia 12°0S 132°3E 60 B5
Kakamas S. Africa 28°45S 20°33E 56 C3
Kakamega Kenya 0°20N 34°46E 54 D6
Kakana India 9°7N 92°48E 45 K11
Kakanui Mts. N.Z. 45°10S 170°30E 59 F3
Kakdwip India 21°53N 88°11E 43 J13
Kake = Akiōta Japan 34°36N 132°19E 29 G6
Kake U.S.A. 56°59N 133°57W 70 B2
Kakegawa Japan 34°45N 138°1E 29 G9
Kakeroma-Jima Japan 28°8N 129°14E 29 K4
Kākhak Iran 34°9N 58°38E 47 C8
Kakhovka Ukraine 46°45N 33°30E 19 E5
Kakhovske Vdskh. Ukraine 47°5N 34°0E 19 E5
Kakinada India 16°57N 82°11E 44 F6
Kakisa Canada 60°56N 117°25W 70 A5
Kakisa → Canada 61°3N 118°10W 70 A5
Kakisa L. Canada 60°56N 117°43W 70 A5
Kakogawa Japan 34°46N 134°51E 29 G7
Kakwa → Canada 54°37N 118°28W 70 C5
Kāl Gūsheh Iran 30°59N 58°12E 47 D8
Kal Sefīd Iran 34°52N 47°23E 46 C5
Kala Oya → Sri Lanka 8°20N 79°45E 45 K4
Kalaallit Nunaat = Greenland ⊠ N. Amer. 66°0N 45°0W 67 C15
Kalabagh Pakistan 33°0N 71°28E 42 C4
Kalabahi Indonesia 8°13S 124°31E 37 F6
Kalaburagi India 17°20N 76°50E 44 F3
Kalach Russia 50°22N 41°0E 19 D7
Kaladan → Myanmar 20°20N 93°5E 41 J18
Kaladar Canada 44°37N 77°5W 82 B7
Kalahari Africa 24°0S 21°30E 56 B3
Kalahari Gemsbok △ S. Africa 25°30S 20°30E 56 C3
Kalajoki Finland 64°12N 24°10E 8 D21
Kalakamati Botswana 20°40S 27°25E 57 B4
Kalakan Russia 55°15N 116°45E 27 D12
K'alak'unlun Shank'ou = Karakoram Pass Asia 35°33N 77°50E 43 B7
Kalam Pakistan 35°34N 72°30E 43 B5
Kalama U.S.A. 46°1N 122°51W 78 E4
Kalamata Greece 37°3N 22°10E 23 F10
Kalamazoo U.S.A. 42°17N 85°35W 81 D11
Kalamazoo → U.S.A. 42°40N 86°10W 80 D10
Kalamb India 18°3N 74°48E 44 E2
Kalamnuri India 19°40N 77°20E 44 E3
Kalan = Tunceli Turkey 39°6N 39°31E 46 B3
Kalannie Australia 30°22S 117°5E 61 F2
Kalāntarī Iran 32°10N 54°8E 47 C7
Kalao Indonesia 7°21S 121°0E 37 F6
Kalaotoa Indonesia 7°20S 121°50E 37 F6
Kalasin Thailand 16°26N 103°30E 38 D4
Kālat Iran 25°29N 59°22E 47 E8
Kalat Pakistan 29°8N 66°31E 40 E5
Kalāteh Iran 36°33N 55°41E 47 B7
Kalāteh-ye Ganj Iran 27°31N 57°55E 47 E8
Kalbā U.A.E. 25°5N 56°22E 47 E8
Kalbarri Australia 27°40S 114°10E 61 E1
Kalbarri △ Australia 27°51S 114°30E 61 E1
Kalce Slovenia 45°54N 14°13E 16 F8
Kale Turkey 37°27N 28°49E 23 F13
Kalegauk Kyun Myanmar 15°33N 97°35E 38 E1
Kalemie Dem. Rep. of the Congo 5°55S 29°9E 54 F5
Kalewa Myanmar 23°10N 94°15E 41 H19
Kaleybar Iran 38°47N 47°2E 46 B5
Kalghatgi India 15°11N 74°58E 45 G2
Kalgoorlie-Boulder Australia 30°40S 121°22E 61 F3
Kali → India 27°6N 79°55E 43 F8
Kali Sindh → India 25°32N 76°17E 42 G6
Kaliakra, Nos Bulgaria 43°21N 28°30E 23 C13
Kalianda Indonesia 5°50S 105°45E 36 F3
Kalibo Phil. 11°43N 122°22E 37 B6
Kalimantan Indonesia 0°0 114°0E 36 E4
Kalimantan Barat □ Indonesia 0°0 110°30E 36 E4
Kalimantan Selatan □ Indonesia 2°30S 115°30E 36 E5
Kalimantan Tengah □ Indonesia 2°0S 113°30E 36 E4
Kalimantan Timur □ Indonesia 1°30N 116°30E 36 D5
Kálimnos Greece 37°0N 27°0E 23 F12
Kalimpong India 27°4N 88°35E 43 F13
Kalinadi → India 14°50N 74°7E 45 G2
Kaliningrad Russia 54°42N 20°32E 9 J19
Kalinkavichy Belarus 52°12N 29°20E 17 B15
Kalinkovichi = Kalinkavichy Belarus 52°12N 29°20E 17 B15
Kalispell U.S.A. 48°12N 114°19W 76 B6
Kalisz Poland 51°45N 18°8E 17 C10
Kaliveli Tank India 12°5N 79°50E 45 H4
Kalix Sweden 65°53N 23°12E 8 D20
Kalixälven → Sweden 65°50N 23°11E 8 D20
Kalka India 30°46N 76°57E 42 D7
Kalkarindji Australia 17°30S 130°47E 60 C5
Kalkaska U.S.A. 44°44N 85°11W 81 C11
Kalkfeld Namibia 20°57S 16°14E 56 B2
Kalkfontein Botswana 22°4S 20°57E 56 B3
Kalkrand Namibia 24°1S 17°35E 56 B2
Kallakkurichchi India 11°44N 79°1E 45 J4
Kallam India 18°36N 76°2E 44 E3
Kallavesi Finland 62°58N 27°30E 8 E22
Kallidaikurichi India 8°38N 77°31E 45 K3
Kallsjön Sweden 63°38N 13°0E 8 E15
Kalmar Sweden 56°40N 16°20E 9 H17
Kalmunai Sri Lanka 7°25N 81°49E 45 L5
Kalmykia □ Russia 46°5N 46°1E 19 E8
Kalna India 23°13N 88°25E 43 H13
Kalnai India 22°46N 83°30E 43 H10
Kalocsa Hungary 46°32N 19°0E 17 E10
Kalol Gujarat, India 22°37N 73°31E 42 H5
Kalol Gujarat, India 23°15N 72°33E 42 H5
Kalpeni I. India 10°5N 73°38E 45 J1
Kalpi India 26°8N 79°47E 43 F8
Kalpitiya Sri Lanka 8°14N 79°46E 45 K4
Kalputhi I. India 10°49N 72°10E 45 J1
Kalrayan Hills India 11°45N 78°40E 45 J4
Kalsubai India 19°35N 73°45E 44 E1
Kaltag U.S.A. 64°20N 158°43W 74 C8
Kaltukatjara Australia 24°52S 129°5E 61 D4
Kalu Pakistan 25°5N 67°39E 42 G2
Kaluga Russia 54°35N 36°10E 18 D6
Kalumburu Australia 13°55S 126°35E 60 B4
Kalumburu ✪ Australia 14°17S 126°38E 60 B4
Kalush Ukraine 49°3N 24°23E 17 D13
Kalutara Sri Lanka 6°35N 80°0E 45 L5
Kalwakurti India 16°41N 78°30E 44 F4
Kalya Russia 60°15N 59°59E 18 B10
Kalyan = Basavakalyan India 17°52N 76°57E 44 F3
Kalyan Maharashtra, India 20°30N 74°3E 44 D2
Kalyan Maharashtra, India 19°15N 73°9E 44 E1
Kalyandurg India 14°33N 77°6E 45 G3
Kalyansingapuram India 19°30N 83°19E 44 E6
Kama Japan 33°33N 130°49E 29 H5
Kama → Russia 55°45N 52°0E 18 C9
Kamaishi Japan 39°16N 141°53E 28 E10
Kamalapuram India 14°35N 78°39E 45 G4
Kamalia Pakistan 30°44N 72°42E 42 D5
Kaman India 27°39N 77°16E 42 F6
Kamanjab Namibia 19°35S 14°51E 56 A2
Kamarān Yemen 15°21N 42°35E 49 D3
Kamareddi India 18°19N 78°21E 44 E4
Kamativi Zimbabwe 18°20S 27°6E 56 A4
Kambalda West Australia 31°10S 121°37E 61 F3
Kambam India 9°45N 77°16E 45 K3
Kambangan, Nusa Indonesia 7°40S 108°10E 37 G13
Kambar Pakistan 27°37N 68°1E 42 F3
Kambarka Russia 56°15N 54°11E 18 C9
Kambove Dem. Rep. of the Congo 10°51S 26°33E 54 G5
Kamchatka, Poluostrov Russia 57°0N 160°0E 27 D17
Kamchatka Pen. = Kamchatka, Poluostrov Russia 57°0N 160°0E 27 D17
Kamchia → Bulgaria 43°4N 27°44E 23 C12
Kameda-Hantō Japan 41°50N 141°0E 28 D10
Kamen Russia 53°50N 81°30E 26 D9
Kamen-Rybolov Russia 44°46N 132°2E 28 B5
Kamenjak, Rt Croatia 44°47N 13°55E 16 F7
Kamenka Russia 65°58N 44°0E 18 A7
Kamenka Bugskaya = Kamyanka-Buzka Ukraine 50°8N 24°16E 17 C13
Kamensk Uralskiy Russia 56°25N 62°2E 26 D7
Kamenskoye Russia 62°45N 165°30E 27 C17
Kameoka Japan 35°0N 135°35E 29 G7
Kamet India 30°55N 79°35E 43 D8
Kamiah U.S.A. 46°14N 116°2W 76 C5
Kamieskroon S. Africa 30°9S 17°56E 56 D2
Kamilukuak L. Canada 62°22N 101°40W 71 A8
Kamin-Kashyrskyy Ukraine 51°39N 24°56E 17 C13
Kamina Dem. Rep. of the Congo 8°45S 25°0E 54 F5
Kaminak L. Canada 62°10N 95°0W 71 A10
Kaminoyama Japan 38°9N 140°17E 28 E10
Kamla → India 25°35N 86°36E 43 G12
Kamloops Canada 50°40N 120°20W 70 C4
Kamo Japan 37°39N 139°3E 28 F9
Kamoke Pakistan 32°4N 74°4E 42 C6
Kampala Uganda 0°20N 32°32E 54 D6
Kampar Malaysia 4°18N 101°9E 39 K3
Kampar → Indonesia 0°30N 103°8E 36 D2
Kampen Neths. 52°33N 5°53E 15 B5
Kampene Dem. Rep. of the Congo 3°36S 26°40E 54 E5
Kamphaeng Phet Thailand 16°28N 99°30E 38 D2
Kampong Cham Cambodia 12°0N 105°30E 39 G5
Kampong Chhnang Cambodia 12°20N 104°35E 39 F5
Kampong Pengerang Malaysia 1°22N 104°7E 39 d
Kampong Punggai Malaysia 1°27N 104°18E 39 d
Kampong Saom Cambodia 10°38N 103°30E 39 G4
Kampong Saom, Chaak Cambodia 10°50N 103°32E 39 G4
Kampong Tanjong Langsat Malaysia 1°28N 104°1E 39 d
Kampong Telok Ramunia Malaysia 1°22N 104°15E 39 d
Kampot Cambodia 10°36N 104°10E 39 G5
Kampuchea = Cambodia ■ Asia 12°15N 105°0E 38 F5
Kampung Air Putih Malaysia 4°15N 103°10E 39 K4
Kampung Jerangau Malaysia 4°50N 103°10E 39 K4
Kampung Raja Malaysia 5°45N 102°35E 39 K4
Kampungbaru = Tolitoli Indonesia 1°5N 120°50E 37 D6
Kamrau, Teluk Indonesia 3°30S 133°36E 37 E8
Kamsack Canada 51°34N 101°54W 71 C8
Kamsar Guinea 10°40N 14°36W 52 F3
Kamskoye Vdkhr. Russia 58°41N 56°7E 18 C10
Kamthi India 21°9N 79°19E 44 D4
Kamuchawie L. Canada 56°18N 101°59W 71 B8
Kamui-Misaki Japan 43°20N 140°21E 28 C10
Kamyanets-Podilskyy Ukraine 48°45N 26°40E 17 D14
Kamyanka-Buzka Ukraine 50°8N 24°16E 17 C13
Kāmyārān Iran 34°47N 46°56E 46 C5
Kamyshin Russia 50°10N 45°24E 19 D8
Kanaaupscow → Canada 54°2N 76°30W 72 B4
Kanab U.S.A. 37°3N 112°32W 77 H7
Kanab Cr. → U.S.A. 36°24N 112°38W 77 H7
Kanacea Lau Group, Fiji 17°15S 179°6W 59 a
Kanacea Taveuni, Fiji 16°59S 179°56E 59 a
Kanaga I. U.S.A. 51°45N 177°22W 74 E4
Kanagi Japan 40°54N 140°27E 28 D10
Kanairiktok → Canada 55°2N 60°18W 73 A7
Kanakapura India 12°33N 77°28E 45 H3
Kananga Dem. Rep. of the Congo 5°55S 22°18E 54 F4
Kanash Russia 55°30N 47°32E 18 C8
Kanaskat U.S.A. 47°19N 121°54W 78 C5
Kanastraíon, Ákra = Paliouri, Akra Greece 39°57N 23°45E 23 E10
Kanawha → U.S.A. 38°50N 82°9W 81 F12
Kanazawa Japan 36°30N 136°38E 29 F8
Kanchanaburi Thailand 14°2N 99°31E 38 E2
Kanchenjunga Nepal 27°50N 88°10E 43 F13
Kanchenjunga △ India 27°42N 88°8E 43 F13
Kanchipuram India 12°52N 79°45E 45 H4
Kandaghat India 30°59N 77°7E 42 D7
Kandahār Afghan. 31°32N 65°43E 40 D4
Kandahar India 18°52N 77°12E 44 E3
Kandahār □ Afghan. 31°0N 65°0E 40 D4
Kandalaksha Russia 67°9N 32°30E 8 C25
Kandalakshkiy Zaliv Russia 66°0N 35°0E 18 A6
Kandangan Indonesia 2°50S 115°20E 36 E5
Kandavu = Kadavu Fiji 19°0S 178°15E 59 a
Kandavu Passage = Kadavu Passage Fiji 18°45S 178°0E 59 a
Kandhkot Pakistan 28°16N 69°8E 42 E3
Kandhla India 29°18N 77°19E 42 E7
Kandi Benin 11°7N 2°55E 52 F6
Kandi India 23°58N 88°5E 43 H13
Kandiaro Pakistan 27°4N 68°13E 42 F3
Kandla India 23°0N 70°10E 42 H4
Kandos Australia 32°45S 149°58E 63 E4
Kandy Sri Lanka 7°18N 80°43E 45 L5
Kane U.S.A. 41°40N 78°49W 82 E6
Kane Basin Greenland 79°1N 70°0W 69 B18
Kang Botswana 23°41S 22°50E 56 B3
Kangān Fārs, Iran 27°50N 52°3E 47 E7
Kangān Hormozgān, Iran 25°48N 57°28E 47 E8
Kangar Malaysia 6°27N 100°12E 39 J3
Kangaroo I. Australia 35°45S 137°0E 63 F2
Kangaroo Mts. Australia 23°29S 141°51E 62 C3
Kangasala Finland 61°28N 24°4E 8 F21
Kangāvar Iran 34°40N 48°0E 47 C6
Kangding China 30°2N 101°57E 34 B3
Kangdong N. Korea 39°9N 126°5E 33 E14
Kangean, Kepulauan Indonesia 6°55S 115°23E 36 F5
Kangean Is. = Kangean, Kepulauan Indonesia 6°55S 115°23E 36 F5
Kanggye N. Korea 41°0N 126°35E 33 D14
Kangikajik Greenland 70°7N 22°0W 4 B6
Kangiqliniq = Rankin Inlet Canada 62°30N 93°0W 68 E13
Kangiqsualujjuaq Canada 58°30N 65°59W 69 F18
Kangiqsujuaq Canada 61°30N 72°0W 69 E17
Kangiqtugaapik = Clyde River Canada 70°30N 68°30W 69 C18

Kangirsuk Canada 60°0N 70°0W 69 F18
Kangkar Chemaran
　Malaysia 1°34N 104°12E 39 d
Kangkar Sungai Tiram
　Malaysia 1°35N 103°55E 39 d
Kangkar Teberau
　Malaysia 1°32N 103°51E 39 d
Kangping China 42°43N 123°18E 33 C12
Kangra India 32°6N 76°16E 42 C7
Kangrinboqe Feng China 31°0N 81°25E 43 D9
Kangto China 27°50N 92°35E 41 F18
Kanha △ India 22°15N 80°40E 43 H9
Kanhan → India 21°4N 79°34E 44 D4
Kanhangad India 12°21N 74°58E 45 H2
Kanhar → India 24°28N 83°8E 43 G10
Kaniapiskau = Caniapiscau →
　Canada 56°40N 69°30W 73 A6
Kaniapiskau, L. = Caniapiscau, L.
　Canada 54°10N 69°55W 73 B6
Kanigiri India 15°24N 79°31E 45 G4
Kanin, Poluostrov Russia 68°0N 45°0E 18 A8
Kanin Nos, Mys Russia 68°39N 43°32E 18 A7
Kanin Pen. = Kanin, Poluostrov
　Russia 68°0N 45°0E 18 A8
Kaniva Australia 36°22S 141°18E 63 F3
Kanjut Sar Pakistan 36°7N 75°25E 43 A6
Kankaanpää Finland 61°44N 22°50E 8 F20
Kankakee U.S.A. 41°7N 87°52W 80 E2
Kankakee → U.S.A. 41°23N 88°15W 80 E9
Kankan Guinea 10°23N 9°15W 52 F4
Kankendy = Xankändi
　Azerbaijan 39°52N 46°49E 46 B5
Kanker India 20°10N 81°40E 44 D5
Kankesanturai Sri Lanka 9°49N 80°2E 45 K5
Kankroli India 25°4N 73°53E 42 G5
Kanmaw Kyun Myanmar 11°40N 98°28E 39 G2
Kannapolis U.S.A. 35°30N 80°37W 85 D14
Kannauj India 27°3N 79°56E 43 F8
Kanniyakumari India 8°5N 77°34E 45 K3
Kannod India 22°45N 76°40E 40 H10
Kannur India 11°53N 75°27E 45 J2
Kannyakumari India 8°3N 77°40E 45 K3
Kano Nigeria 12°2N 8°30E 52 F7
Kan'onji Japan 34°7N 133°39E 29 G6
Kanowit Malaysia 2°14N 112°20E 36 D4
Kanoya Japan 31°25N 130°50E 29 J5
Kanpetlet Myanmar 21°10N 93°59E 41 J18
Kanpur India 26°28N 80°20E 43 F9
Kansas □ U.S.A. 38°30N 99°0W 80 F4
Kansas → U.S.A. 39°7N 94°37W 80 F6
Kansas City Kans., U.S.A. 39°7N 94°38W 80 F6
Kansas City Mo., U.S.A. 39°6N 94°35W 80 F6
Kansk Russia 56°20N 95°37E 27 D10
Kansu = Gansu □ China 36°0N 104°0E 32 G3
Kantaphor India 22°35N 76°34E 42 H7
Kantharalak Thailand 14°39N 104°39E 38 E5
Kanthi = Contai India 21°54N 87°46E 43 J12
Kantli → India 28°20N 75°30E 42 E6
Kantō □ Japan 36°15N 139°30E 29 F9
Kantō-Sanchi Japan 35°59N 138°50E 29 G9
Kanturk Ireland 52°11N 8°54W 10 D3
Kanuma Japan 36°34N 139°42E 29 F9
Kanus Namibia 27°50S 18°39E 56 C2
Kanye Botswana 24°55S 25°28E 56 C4
Kao Tonga 19°40S 175°1W 59 c
Kao Phara Thailand 8°3N 98°22E 39 a
Kaohsiung Taiwan 22°35N 120°16E 35 F13
Kaokoveld Namibia 19°15S 14°30E 56 A1
Kaolack Senegal 14°5N 16°8W 52 F2
Kaoshan China 44°38N 124°50E 33 B13
Kapa'a U.S.A. 22°5N 159°19W 75 L8
Kapadvanj India 23°5N 73°0E 42 H5
Kapan Armenia 39°18N 46°27E 46 B5
Kapanga
　Dem. Rep. of the Congo 8°30S 22°40E 54 F4
Kapchagai = Qapshaghay
　Kazakhstan 43°51N 77°14E 26 E8
Kapela = Velika Kapela
　Croatia 45°10N 15°5E 16 F8
Kapfenberg Austria 47°26N 15°18E 16 E8
Kapiri Mposhi Zambia 13°59S 28°43E 55 G5
Kāpīsā □ Afghan. 35°0N 69°20E 40 B6
Kapiskau → Canada 52°47N 81°55W 72 B3
Kapit Malaysia 2°0N 112°55E 36 D4
Kapiti I. N.Z. 40°50S 174°56E 59 D5
Kaplan U.S.A. 30°0N 92°17W 84 F8
Kapoe Thailand 9°34N 98°32E 39 H2
Kapoeta South Sudan 4°50N 33°35E 53 H12
Kaposvár Hungary 46°25N 17°47E 17 E9
Kapowsin U.S.A. 46°59N 122°13W 78 D4
Kapps Namibia 22°32S 17°18E 56 B2
Kapsan N. Korea 41°4N 128°19E 33 D15
Kapsukas = Marijampolė
　Lithuania 54°33N 23°19E 9 J20
Kaptai L. Bangla. 22°40N 92°20E 41 H18
Kapuas → Indonesia 0°25S 109°20E 36 E3
Kapuas Hulu, Pegunungan
　Malaysia 1°30N 113°30E 36 D4
Kapuas Hulu Ra. = Kapuas Hulu,
　Pegunungan Malaysia 1°30N 113°30E 36 D4
Kapunda Australia 34°20S 138°56E 63 E2
Kapuni N.Z. 39°29S 174°8E 59 C5
Kapurthala India 31°23N 75°25E 42 D6
Kapuskasing Canada 49°25N 82°30W 72 C3
Kapuskasing → Canada 49°49N 82°0W 72 C3
Kaputar, Mt. Australia 30°15S 150°10E 63 E5
Kara Russia 69°10N 65°0E 26 C7
Kara Bogaz Gol, Zaliv =
　Garabogazköl Aylagy
　Turkmenistan 41°0N 53°30E 19 F9
Kara Kala = Garrygala
　Turkmenistan 38°31N 56°29E 47 B8
Kara Kalpak Republic =
　Qoraqalpog'iston □
　Uzbekistan 43°0N 58°0E 26 E6
Kara Kum = Garagum
　Turkmenistan 39°30N 60°0E 47 B8
Kara Sea Russia 75°0N 70°0E 26 B8
Karabiğa Turkey 40°23N 27°17E 23 D12
Karabük Turkey 41°12N 32°37E 19 F5

Karaburun Turkey 38°41N 26°28E 23 E12
Karabutak = Qarabutaq
　Kazakhstan 50°0N 60°14E 26 E7
Karacabey Turkey 40°12N 28°21E 23 D13
Karacasu Turkey 37°43N 28°35E 23 F13
Karachey-Cherkessia □
　Russia 43°40N 41°30E 19 F7
Karad India 17°15N 74°10E 44 F2
Karaganda = Qaraghandy
　Kazakhstan 49°50N 73°10E 30 B3
Karagayly = Qaraghayly
　Kazakhstan 49°26N 76°0E 26 E8
Karaginskiy, Ostrov
　Russia 58°45N 164°0E 27 D17
Karagiye, Vpadina
　Kazakhstan 43°27N 51°45E 19 F9
Karagiye Depression = Karagiye,
　Vpadina Kazakhstan 43°27N 51°45E 19 F9
Karagola Road India 25°29N 87°23E 43 G12
Karaikal India 10°59N 79°50E 45 J4
Karaikkudi India 10°5N 78°45E 45 J4
Karaitivu I. Sri Lanka 9°45N 79°52E 45 K4
Karaj Iran 35°48N 51°0E 47 C6
Karajarri ☉ Australia 19°0S 122°30E 60 C3
Karak Malaysia 3°25N 102°2E 39 L4
Karakalpakstan =
　Qoraqalpog'iston □
　Uzbekistan 43°0N 58°0E 26 E6
Karakelong Indonesia 4°35N 126°50E 37 D7
Karakitang Indonesia 3°14N 125°28E 37 D7
Karakol Kyrgyzstan 42°30N 78°20E 30 C4
Karakoram Pass Asia 35°33N 77°50E 43 B7
Karakoram Ra. Pakistan 35°30N 77°0E 43 B7
Karakuwisa Namibia 18°56S 19°40E 56 A2
Karalon Russia 57°5N 115°50E 27 D12
Karama Jordan 31°57N 35°35E 48 D4
Karaman Turkey 37°14N 33°13E 46 B2
Karamay China 45°30N 84°58E 30 B5
Karambu Indonesia 3°53S 116°6E 36 E5
Karamea Bight N.Z. 41°22S 171°40E 59 D3
Karamnasa → India 25°31N 83°52E 43 G10
Karān Si. Arabia 27°43N 49°49E 47 E6
Karand Iran 34°16N 46°15E 46 C5
Karanganyar Indonesia 7°38S 109°37E 37 G13
Karanja Maharashtra,
　India 21°11N 78°24E 44 D4
Karanja Maharashtra,
　India 20°29N 77°31E 44 D3
Karanjia India 21°47N 85°58E 43 J11
Karas □ Namibia 27°0S 17°30E 56 C2
Karasburg Namibia 28°0S 18°44E 56 C2
Karasino Russia 66°50N 86°50E 26 C9
Karasjok Norway 69°27N 25°30E 8 B21
Karasuk Russia 53°44N 78°2E 26 D8
Karasuyama Japan 36°39N 140°9E 29 F10
Karatau, Khrebet = Qarataū
　Kazakhstan 43°30N 69°30E 26 E7
Karatax Shan China 35°57N 81°0E 30 D5
Karativu Sri Lanka 8°22N 79°47E 45 K4
Karatsu Japan 33°26N 129°58E 29 H5
Karaul Russia 70°6N 82°15E 26 B9
Karauli India 26°30N 77°4E 42 F7
Karawang Indonesia 6°30S 107°15E 37 G12
Karawanken Europe 46°30N 14°40E 16 E8
Karayazı Turkey 39°41N 42°9E 19 G7
Karazhal = Qarazhal
　Kazakhstan 48°2N 70°49E 26 E8
Karbalā' Iraq 32°36N 44°3E 46 C5
Karcag Hungary 47°19N 20°57E 17 E11
Karcha → Pakistan 34°45N 76°10E 43 B7
Karchana India 25°17N 81°56E 43 G9
Karditsa Greece 39°23N 21°54E 23 E9
Kärdla Estonia 59°0N 22°45E 9 G20
Kardzhali Bulgaria 41°38N 25°21E 23 D11
Kareeberge S. Africa 30°59S 21°50E 56 E3
Kareha → India 25°44N 86°21E 43 G12
Kareima Sudan 18°30N 31°49E 53 E12
Karelia □ Russia 65°30N 32°30E 18 A5
Karelian Republic = Karelia □
　Russia 65°30N 32°30E 18 A5
Karera India 25°32N 78°9E 42 G8
Kārevāndar Iran 27°53N 60°44E 47 E9
Kargasok Russia 59°3N 80°53E 26 D9
Kargat Russia 55°10N 80°15E 26 D9
Kargil India 34°32N 76°12E 43 B7
Kargopol Russia 61°30N 38°58E 18 B6
Kariān Iran 26°57N 57°14E 47 E8
Kariba, L. Zimbabwe 16°40S 28°25E 55 H5
Kariba Dam Zimbabwe 16°30S 28°35E 55 H5
Kariba Gorge Zambia 16°30S 28°50E 55 H5
Karibib Namibia 22°0S 15°56E 56 B2
Karijini △ Australia 23°8S 118°15E 60 D2
Karimata, Kepulauan
　Indonesia 1°25S 109°0E 36 E3
Karimata, Selat Indonesia 2°0S 108°40E 36 E3
Karimata Is. = Karimata,
　Kepulauan Indonesia 1°25S 109°0E 36 E3
Karimnagar India 18°26N 79°10E 44 E4
Karimun, Pulau Indonesia 1°3N 103°22E 39 d
Karimun Kecil, Pulau
　Indonesia 1°8N 103°22E 39 d
Karimunjawa, Kepulauan
　Indonesia 5°50S 110°30E 36 F4
Karin Somalia 10°50N 45°52E 49 E4
Kariya Japan 34°58N 137°1E 29 G8
Kariyangwe Zimbabwe 18°0S 27°38E 57 A4
Karjala Finland 62°0N 30°5E 8 F24
Karjat India 18°33N 75°0E 44 E2
Karkal India 13°15N 74°56E 45 H2
Karkaralinsk = Qarqaraly
　Kazakhstan 49°26N 75°30E 26 E8
Karkheh → Iran 31°2N 47°29E 46 D5
Karkinitska Zatoka
　Ukraine 45°56N 33°0E 19 E5
Karkinitskiy Zaliv = Karkinitska
　Zatoka Ukraine 45°56N 33°0E 19 E5
Karkuk = Kirkūk Iraq 35°30N 44°21E 46 C5

Karlantiipa North ☉
　Australia 19°27S 133°33E 60 C5
Karlantiipa South ☉
　Australia 20°31S 133°9E 60 D5
Karleby = Kokkola
　Finland 63°50N 23°8E 8 E20
Karlovac Croatia 45°31N 15°36E 16 F8
Karlovo Bulgaria 42°38N 24°47E 23 C11
Karlovy Vary Czechia 50°13N 12°51E 16 C7
Karlsbad = Karlovy Vary
　Czechia 50°13N 12°51E 16 C7
Karlsena, Mys Russia 77°0N 67°42E 26 B7
Karlshamn Sweden 56°10N 14°51E 9 H16
Karlskoga Sweden 59°28N 14°33E 9 G16
Karlskrona Sweden 56°10N 15°35E 9 H16
Karlsruhe Germany 49°0N 8°23E 16 D5
Karlstad Sweden 59°23N 13°30E 9 G15
Karlstad U.S.A. 48°35N 96°31W 80 A5
Karmala India 18°25N 75°12E 44 E2
Karmi'el Israel 32°55N 35°18E 48 C4
Karnak Egypt 25°43N 32°39E 53 C12
Karnal India 29°42N 77°2E 42 E7
Karnali = Ghaghara →
　India 25°45N 84°40E 43 G11
Karnali → Nepal 28°45N 81°16E 43 E9
Karnaphuli Res. = Kaptai L.
　Bangla. 22°40N 92°20E 41 H18
Karnaprayag India 30°16N 79°15E 43 D8
Karnataka □ India 13°15N 77°0E 45 H3
Karnes City U.S.A. 28°53N 97°54W 84 G6
Karnische Alpen Europe 46°36N 13°0E 16 E7
Kärnten □ Austria 46°52N 13°30E 16 E8
Karon, Ao Thailand 7°51N 98°17E 39 a
Karonga Malawi 9°57S 33°55E 54 F6
Karoo △ S. Africa 32°18S 22°27E 56 D3
Karoonda Australia 35°1S 139°59E 63 F2
Karor Pakistan 31°15N 70°59E 42 D4
Karora Sudan 17°44N 38°15E 53 E13
Karpathos Greece 35°37N 27°10E 23 G12
Karpinsk Russia 59°45N 60°1E 18 C11
Karpogory Russia 64°0N 44°27E 18 B7
Karpuz Burnu = Apostolos
　Andreas, C. Cyprus 35°42N 34°35E 46 C2
Karratha Australia 20°44S 116°52E 60 D2
Kars Turkey 40°40N 43°5E 19 F7
Karsakpay Kazakhstan 47°55N 66°40E 26 E7
Karshi = Qarshi
　Uzbekistan 38°53N 65°48E 26 F7
Karsiyang India 26°56N 88°18E 43 F13
Karsog India 31°23N 77°12E 42 D7
Kartapur India 31°27N 75°32E 42 D6
Karthaus U.S.A. 41°8N 78°9W 82 E6
Karufa Indonesia 3°50S 133°20E 37 E8
Karumba Australia 17°31S 140°50E 62 B3
Kārūn → Iran 30°26N 48°10E 47 D6
Karungu Kenya 0°50S 34°10E 54 E6
Karur India 10°59N 78°2E 45 J4
Karviná Czechia 49°53N 18°31E 17 D10
Karwan → India 27°26N 78°4E 42 F8
Karwar India 14°55N 74°13E 45 G2
Karwi India 25°12N 80°57E 43 G9
Karymskoye Russia 51°36N 114°21E 27 D12
Kasai →
　Dem. Rep. of the Congo 3°30S 16°10E 54 E3
Kasama Zambia 10°16S 31°9E 54 G6
Kasan-dong N. Korea 41°18N 126°55E 33 D14
Kasane Namibia 17°34S 24°50E 56 A3
Kasaragod India 12°30N 74°58E 45 H2
Kasba L. Canada 60°20N 102°10W 71 A8
Kāseh Garān Iran 34°5N 46°2E 46 C5
Kasempa Zambia 13°30S 25°44E 55 G5
Kasenga
　Dem. Rep. of the Congo 10°20S 28°45E 54 G5
Kasese Uganda 0°13N 30°3E 54 D6
Kasganj India 27°48N 78°42E 43 F8
Kashabowie Canada 48°40N 90°26W 72 C1
Kashaf Iran 35°58N 61°7E 47 C9
Kāshān Iran 34°5N 51°30E 47 C6
Kashechewan Canada 52°18N 81°37W 72 B3
Kashgar = Kashi China 39°30N 76°2E 30 D4
Kashi China 39°30N 76°2E 30 D4
Kashipur Odisha, India 19°16N 83°3E 44 E6
Kashipur Uttarakhand,
　India 29°15N 79°0E 43 E8
Kashiwazaki Japan 37°22N 138°33E 29 F9
Kashk-e Kohneh Afghan. 34°55N 62°30E 40 B3
Kashkūʼīyeh Iran 30°31N 55°40E 47 D7
Kāshmar Iran 35°16N 58°26E 47 C8
Kashmir Asia 34°0N 76°0E 43 C7
Kashmor Pakistan 28°28N 69°32E 42 E3
Kashun Noerh = Gaxun Nur
　China 42°22N 100°30E 32 B9
Kasiari India 22°8N 87°14E 43 H12
Kasimov Russia 54°55N 41°20E 18 D7
Kasiruta Indonesia 0°25S 127°12E 37 E7
Kaskaskia → U.S.A. 37°58N 89°57W 80 G9
Kaskattama → Canada 57°3N 90°4W 71 B10
Kaskinen Finland 62°22N 21°15E 8 E19
Kaskö = Kaskinen
　Finland 62°22N 21°15E 8 E19
Kaslo Canada 49°55N 116°55W 70 D5
Kasmere L. Canada 59°34N 101°10W 71 B8
Kasongo
　Dem. Rep. of the Congo 4°30S 26°33E 54 E5
Kasongo Lunda
　Dem. Rep. of the Congo 6°35S 16°49E 54 F3
Kasos Greece 35°20N 26°55E 23 G12
Kassalâ Sudan 15°30N 36°0E 53 E13
Kassandra Kolpos Greece 40°5N 23°30E 23 D10
Kassel Germany 51°18N 9°26E 16 C5
Kasson U.S.A. 44°2N 92°45W 80 C7
Kastamonu Turkey 41°25N 33°43E 19 F5
Kasterlee Belgium 51°15N 4°59E 15 C4
Kastoria Greece 40°30N 21°19E 23 D9
Kastrom Mefa'a = Umm al Rasas
　Jordan 31°30N 35°55E 48 D4
Kasumi Japan 35°38N 134°38E 29 G7
Kasur Pakistan 31°5N 74°25E 42 D6

Kata, Ao Thailand 7°48N 98°18E 39 J2
Kata Tjuta Australia 25°20S 130°50E 61 E5
Katahdin, Mt. U.S.A. 45°54N 68°56W 81 C19
Kataka = Cuttack India 20°25N 85°57E 44 D7
Katanga
　Dem. Rep. of the Congo 8°0S 25°0E 54 F5
Katangi India 21°56N 79°50E 44 D4
Katanning Australia 33°40S 117°33E 61 F2
Katchall India 7°57N 93°22E 45 L11
Katerini Greece 40°18N 22°37E 23 D10
Katghora India 22°30N 82°33E 43 H10
Katha Myanmar 24°10N 96°30E 41 G20
Katherîna, Gebel Egypt 28°30N 33°57E 46 D2
Katherine Australia 14°27S 132°20E 60 B5
Katherine Gorge = Nitmiluk □
　Australia 14°6S 132°15E 60 B5
Kathi India 21°47N 71°3E 42 J4
Kathiawar India 22°20N 71°0E 42 H4
Kathmandu Nepal 27°45N 85°20E 43 F11
Kathua India 32°23N 75°34E 42 C6
Kati Thanda-Lake Eyre
　Australia 29°30S 137°26E 58 D6
Kati Thanda-Lake Eyre (North)
　Australia 28°40S 137°20E 63 D2
Kati Thanda-Lake Eyre (South)
　Australia 29°18S 137°25E 63 D2
Katihar India 25°34N 87°36E 43 G12
Katima Mulilo Namibia 17°28S 24°13E 56 A3
Katingan = Mendawai →
　Indonesia 3°30S 113°0E 36 E4
Katiola Côte d'Ivoire 8°10N 5°10W 52 G4
Katiti ☉ Australia 25°1S 131°11E 61 E5
Katmandu = Kathmandu
　Nepal 27°45N 85°20E 43 F11
Katni India 23°51N 80°24E 43 H9
Katol India 21°17N 78°38E 44 D4
Katoomba Australia 33°41S 150°19E 63 E5
Katowice Poland 50°17N 19°5E 17 C10
Katrine, L. U.K. 56°15N 4°30W 11 E4
Katrineholm Sweden 59°0N 16°12E 9 G17
Katsina Nigeria 13°0N 7°32E 52 F7
Katsumoto Japan 33°51N 129°42E 29 H4
Katsuura Japan 35°10N 140°20E 29 G10
Katsuyama Japan 36°3N 136°30E 29 F8
Kattegat Denmark 56°40N 11°20E 9 H14
Katwa India 23°30N 88°5E 43 H13
Katwijk Neths. 52°12N 4°24E 15 B4
Kau-Ye Kyun Myanmar 11°1N 98°32E 39 G2
Kaua'i U.S.A. 22°3N 159°30W 75 L8
Kaudom △ Namibia 18°45S 20°51E 56 A3
Kaufman U.S.A. 32°35N 96°19W 84 E6
Kauhajoki Finland 62°25N 22°10E 8 E20
Kauhaneva-Pohjankangas △
　Finland 62°13N 22°20E 8 E20
Kaukauna U.S.A. 44°17N 88°17W 80 C9
Kaukauveld Namibia 20°0S 20°15E 56 B3
Ka'ula I. U.S.A. 21°40N 160°33W 75 L7
Kaunas Lithuania 54°54N 23°54E 9 J20
Kaunia Bangla. 25°46N 89°26E 43 G13
Kautokeino Norway 69°0N 23°4E 8 B20
Kauwapur India 27°31N 82°18E 43 F10
Kavacha Russia 60°16N 169°51E 27 C17
Kavalerovo Russia 44°15N 135°4E 28 B7
Kavali India 14°55N 80°1E 45 G5
Kavango = Cubango →
　Africa 18°50S 22°25E 56 A3
Kavār Iran 29°11N 52°44E 47 D7
Kavaratti India 10°34N 72°37E 45 J1
Kavaratti I. India 10°33N 72°38E 45 J1
Kavála Greece 40°57N 24°28E 23 D11
Kavi India 22°12N 72°38E 42 H5
Kavimba Botswana 18°2S 24°38E 56 A3
Kavīr, Dasht-e Iran 34°30N 55°0E 47 C7
Kavīr △ Iran 34°40N 52°0E 47 C7
Kaw Fr. Guiana 4°30N 52°15W 93 C8
Kawagama L. Canada 45°18N 78°45W 82 A6
Kawagoe Japan 35°55N 139°29E 29 G9
Kawaguchi Japan 35°52N 139°45E 29 G9
Kawah Ijen △ Indonesia 8°3S 114°14E 37 H15
Kawanoe = Shikokuchūō
　Japan 34°1N 133°34E 29 G6
Kawardha India 22°0N 81°17E 43 J9
Kawasi Indonesia 1°38S 127°28E 37 E7
Kawawachikamach
　Canada 54°48N 66°50W 73 B6
Kawerau N.Z. 38°7S 176°42E 59 C6
Kawhia N.Z. 38°4S 174°49E 59 C5
Kawhia Harbour N.Z. 38°5S 174°51E 59 C5
Kawio, Kepulauan
　Indonesia 4°30N 125°30E 37 D7
Kawthaung Myanmar 10°5N 98°36E 39 H2
Kawthoolei = Kayin □
　Myanmar 18°0N 97°30E 41 L20
Kawthule = Kayin □
　Myanmar 18°0N 97°30E 41 L20
Kaya Burkina Faso 13°4N 1°10W 52 F5
Kayah □ Myanmar 19°15N 97°15E 41 K20
Kayak I. U.S.A. 59°56N 144°23W 74 D11
Kayamkulam India 9°10N 76°33E 45 K3
Kayan → Indonesia 2°55N 117°35E 36 D5
Kaycee U.S.A. 43°43N 106°38W 76 E10
Kayeli Indonesia 3°20S 127°10E 37 E7
Kayenta U.S.A. 36°44N 110°15W 77 H8
Kayes Mali 14°25N 11°30W 52 F3
Kayin □ Myanmar 18°0N 97°30E 41 L20
Kayoa Indonesia 0°1N 127°28E 37 D7
Kayseri Turkey 38°45N 35°30E 19 G6
Kaysville U.S.A. 41°2N 111°56W 76 F8
Kayts Sri Lanka 9°41N 79°52E 45 K4
Kazachye Russia 70°52N 135°58E 27 B14
Kazakhstan ■ Asia 50°0N 70°0E 26 E8
Kazan Russia 55°50N 49°10E 18 C8
Kazan → Canada 64°2N 95°29W 71 A9
Kazan-Rettō Pac. Oc. 25°0N 141°0E 64 E6
Kazanlak Bulgaria 42°38N 25°20E 23 C11
Kazatin = Kozyatyn
　Ukraine 49°45N 28°50E 17 D15
Kāzerūn Iran 29°38N 51°40E 47 D6
Kazi Magomed = Qazımämmäd
　Azerbaijan 40°3N 49°0E 47 A6

Kazipet India 17°58N 79°30E 44 F4
Kazuno Japan 40°10N 140°45E 28 D10
Kazym → Russia 63°54N 65°50E 26 C7
Kea Greece 37°35N 24°22E 23 F11
Keady U.K. 54°15N 6°42W 10 B5
Kearney U.S.A. 40°42N 99°5W 80 E4
Kearney ☉ Australia 20°10S 128°4E 60 D4
Kearny U.S.A. 33°3N 110°55W 77 K8
Kearsarge, Mt. U.S.A. 43°22N 71°50W 83 C13
Keban Turkey 38°50N 38°50E 19 G6
Keban Baraji Turkey 38°41N 38°33E 46 B3
Kebnekaise Sweden 67°53N 18°33E 8 C18
Kebri Dehar Ethiopia 6°45N 44°17E 49 F3
Kebumen Indonesia 7°42S 109°40E 37 G13
Kechika → Canada 59°41N 127°12W 70 B3
Kecskemét Hungary 46°57N 19°42E 17 E10
Kedah □ Malaysia 5°50N 100°40E 39 K3
Kėdainiai Lithuania 55°15N 24°2E 9 J21
Kedarnath India 30°43N 79°4E 43 D8
Kedgwick Canada 47°40N 67°20W 73 C6
Kediri Indonesia 7°51S 112°1E 37 G15
Keeler U.S.A. 36°29N 117°52W 78 J9
Keeley L. Canada 54°54N 108°8W 71 C7
Keeling Is. = Cocos Is.
　Ind. Oc. 12°10S 96°55E 64 J1
Keelung = Chilung
　Taiwan 25°3N 121°45E 35 E13
Keene Canada 44°15N 78°10W 82 B6
Keene Calif., U.S.A. 35°13N 118°33W 79 K8
Keene N.H., U.S.A. 42°56N 72°17W 83 D12
Keene N.Y., U.S.A. 44°16N 73°46E 83 B11
Keep River △ Australia 15°49S 129°8E 60 C4
Keeper Hill Ireland 52°45N 8°16W 10 D3
Keerweer, C. Australia 14°0S 141°32E 62 A3
Keeseville U.S.A. 44°29N 73°30W 83 B11
Keetmanshoop Namibia 26°35S 18°8E 56 D2
Keewatin Canada 49°46N 94°34W 71 D10
Keewatin → Canada 56°29N 100°46W 71 B8
Kefalonia Greece 38°15N 20°30E 23 E9
Kefamenanu Indonesia 9°28S 124°29E 37 F6
Kefar Sava Israel 32°11N 34°54E 48 C3
Keffi Nigeria 8°55N 7°43E 52 G7
Keflavík Iceland 64°2N 22°35W 8 D2
Keg River Canada 57°54N 117°55W 70 B5
Kegalla Sri Lanka 7°15N 80°21E 45 L5
Kegaska Canada 50°9N 61°18W 73 B7
Keighley U.K. 53°52N 1°54W 12 D6
Keila Estonia 59°18N 24°25E 9 G21
Keimoes S. Africa 28°41S 20°59E 56 C3
Keitele Finland 63°10N 26°20E 8 E22
Keith Australia 36°6S 140°20E 63 F3
Keith U.K. 57°32N 2°57W 11 D6
Keiyasi Fiji 17°53S 177°46E 59 a
Kejimkujik △ Canada 44°25N 65°25W 73 D6
Kejserr Franz Joseph Fd.
　Greenland 73°30N 24°30W 4 B6
Kekri India 26°0N 75°10E 42 G6
Kelan China 38°43N 111°31E 32 E6
Kelang = Klang Malaysia 3°2N 101°26E 39 L3
Kelani Ganga → Sri Lanka 6°58N 79°50E 45 L4
Kelantan □ Malaysia 5°10N 102°0E 39 K3
Kelantan → Malaysia 6°13N 102°14E 39 K4
Kelkit → Turkey 40°45N 36°32E 19 F6
Kellerberrin Australia 31°36S 117°38E 61 F2
Kellett, C. Canada 72°0N 126°0W 4 B1
Kelleys I. U.S.A. 41°36N 82°42W 82 E2
Kellogg U.S.A. 47°32N 116°7W 76 C5
Kells Ireland 53°44N 6°53W 10 C5
Kélo Chad 9°10N 15°45E 53 G9
Kelowna Canada 49°50N 119°25W 70 D5
Kelsey Creek Australia 20°26S 148°31E 62 b
Kelseyville U.S.A. 38°59N 122°50W 78 G4
Kelso N.Z. 45°54S 169°15E 59 F2
Kelso U.K. 55°36N 2°26W 11 F6
Kelso U.S.A. 46°9N 122°54W 78 D4
Keluang = Kluang
　Malaysia 2°3N 103°18E 39 L4
Kelud Indonesia 7°56N 112°18E 37 H15
Kelvington Canada 52°10N 103°30W 71 C8
Kem Russia 65°0N 34°38E 18 B5
Kem → Russia 64°57N 34°41E 18 B5
Kema Indonesia 1°22N 125°8E 37 D7
Kemah Turkey 39°32N 39°5E 46 B3
Kemaman Malaysia 4°12N 103°18E 39 K4
Kemano Canada 53°35N 128°0W 70 C3
Kemasik Malaysia 4°25N 103°27E 39 K4
Kemerovo Russia 55°20N 86°5E 26 D9
Kemi Finland 65°44N 24°34E 8 D21
Kemi älv = Kemijoki →
　Finland 65°47N 24°32E 8 D21
Kemi träsk = Kemijärvi
　Finland 66°43N 27°22E 8 C22
Kemijärvi Finland 66°43N 27°22E 8 C22
Kemijoki → Finland 65°47N 24°32E 8 D21
Kemmerer U.S.A. 41°48N 110°32W 76 F8
Kemp, L. U.S.A. 33°46N 99°9W 84 E5
Kemp Land Antarctica 69°0S 55°0E 5 C5
Kempas Malaysia 1°33N 103°42E 39 d
Kempsey Australia 31°1S 152°50E 63 E5
Kempt, L. Canada 47°25N 74°22W 72 C5
Kempten Germany 47°45N 10°17E 16 E6
Kempton Australia 42°31S 147°12E 63 G4
Kemptville Canada 45°0N 75°38W 83 B9
Ken → India 25°13N 80°27E 43 G9
Kenai U.S.A. 60°33N 151°16W 68 E1
Kenai Mts. U.S.A. 60°0N 150°0W 74 D9
Kendai India 22°45N 82°37E 43 H10
Kendal Indonesia 6°56S 110°14E 37 G14
Kendal U.K. 54°20N 2°44W 12 C5
Kendall Australia 31°35S 152°44E 63 E5
Kendall → Australia 14°4S 141°35E 62 A3
Kendallville U.S.A. 41°27N 85°16W 81 E11
Kendari Indonesia 3°50S 122°30E 37 E6
Kendawangan Indonesia 2°32S 110°17E 36 E4
Kendi, Pulau Malaysia 5°13N 100°11E 39 c
Kendrapara India 20°35N 86°30E 44 D8
Kendrew S. Africa 32°32S 24°30E 56 E3
Kene Thao Laos 17°44N 101°10E 38 D3
Kenedy U.S.A. 28°49N 97°51W 84 G6

Kenema *S. Leone* 7°50N 11°14W **52** G3
Keng Kok *Laos* 16°26N 105°12E **38** D5
Keng Tawng *Myanmar* 20°45N 98°18E **41** J21
Keng Tung *Myanmar* 21°18N 99°39E **38** B2
Kenhardt *S. Africa* 29°19S 21°12E **56** C3
Kenitra *Morocco* 34°15N 6°40W **52** B4
Kenli *China* 37°30N 118°20E **33** F10
Kenmare *Ireland* 51°53N 9°36W **10** E2
Kenmare *U.S.A.* 48°41N 102°5W **80** A2
Kenmare River → *Ireland* 51°48N 9°51W **10** E2
Kennebago Lake *U.S.A.* 45°4N 70°40W **83** A14
Kennebec *U.S.A.* 43°54N 99°52W **80** D4
Kennebec → *U.S.A.* 43°45N 69°46W **81** D19
Kennebunk *U.S.A.* 43°23N 70°33W **83** C14
Kennedy *Zimbabwe* 18°52S 27°10E **56** A4
Kennedy Channel *Arctic* 80°50N 66°0W **69** A18
Kennedy Ra. *Australia* 24°45S 115°10E **61** D2
Kennedy Range △
  Australia 24°34S 115°2E **61** D2
Kennemerduinen △
  Neths. 52°27N 4°33E **15** B4
Kennet → *U.K.* 51°27N 0°57W **13** F7
Kenneth Ra. *Australia* 23°50S 117°8E **61** D2
Kennett *U.S.A.* 36°14N 90°3W **80** G8
Kennewick *U.S.A.* 46°12N 119°7W **76** C4
Kennisis Lake *Canada* 45°13N 78°36W **82** A6
Kenogami → *Canada* 51°6N 84°28W **72** B3
Kenora *Canada* 49°47N 94°29W **71** D10
Kenosha *U.S.A.* 42°35N 87°49W **80** D10
Kenozersky △ *Russia* 62°5N 38°10E **26** C1
Kensington *Canada* 46°28N 63°34W **73** C7
Kent *Ohio, U.S.A.* 41°9N 81°22W **82** E3
Kent *Tex., U.S.A.* 31°4N 104°13W **84** F2
Kent *Wash., U.S.A.* 47°22N 122°14W **78** C4
Kent □ *U.K.* 51°12N 0°40E **13** F8
Kent Group *Australia* 39°30S 147°20E **63** F4
Kent Pen. *Canada* 68°30N 107°0W **68** D10
Kentland *U.S.A.* 40°46N 87°27W **80** E10
Kenton *U.S.A.* 40°39N 83°37W **81** E12
Kentucky □ *U.S.A.* 37°0N 84°0W **81** G11
Kentucky → *U.S.A.* 38°41N 85°11W **81** F11
Kentucky L. *U.S.A.* 37°1N 88°16W **80** G9
Kentville *Canada* 45°6N 64°29W **73** C7
Kentwood *U.S.A.* 30°56N 90°31W **85** F9
Kenya ■ *Africa* 1°0N 38°0E **54** E7
Kenya, Mt. *Kenya* 0°10S 37°18E **54** E7
Kenyir, Tasik *Malaysia* 5°1N 102°54E **39** K4
Keo Neua, Deo *Vietnam* 18°23N 105°10E **38** C5
Keokuk *U.S.A.* 40°24N 91°24W **80** E8
Keoladeo △ *India* 27°0N 77°20E **42** F7
Keonjhargarh *India* 21°28N 85°35E **43** J11
Kep *Cambodia* 10°29N 104°19E **39** G5
Kep *Vietnam* 21°24N 106°16E **38** B6
Kep △ *Cambodia* 10°30N 104°18E **39** G5
Kepala Batas *Malaysia* 5°31N 100°26E **39** c
Kepi *Indonesia* 6°32S 139°19E **37** F9
Kerala □ *India* 11°0N 76°15E **45** J3
Kerama-Rettō *Japan* 26°5N 127°15E **29** L3
Keran *Pakistan* 34°35N 73°59E **43** B5
Kerang *Australia* 35°40S 143°55E **63** F3
Keraudren, C. *Australia* 19°58S 119°45E **60** C2
Kerch *Ukraine* 45°20N 36°20E **19** E6
Kerepakupai-Meru = Angel Falls
  Venezuela 5°57N 62°30W **92** B6
Kerguelen *Ind. Oc.* 49°15S 69°10E **3** G13
Kerian, Kuala *Malaysia* 5°10N 100°25E **39** c
Kericho *Kenya* 0°22S 35°15E **54** E7
Kerinci *Indonesia* 1°40S 101°15E **36** E2
Kerki = Atamyrat
  Turkmenistan 37°50N 65°12E **26** F7
Kerkrade *Neths.* 50°53N 6°4E **15** D6
Kerkyra *Greece* 39°38N 19°50E **23** E8
Kermadec Is. *Pac. Oc.* 30°0S 178°15W **58** E11
Kermadec Trench
  Pac. Oc. 30°30S 176°0W **64** L10
Kermān *Iran* 30°15N 57°1E **47** D8
Kerman *U.S.A.* 36°43N 120°4W **78** J6
Kermān □ *Iran* 30°0N 57°0E **47** D8
Kermān, Bīābān-e *Iran* 28°45N 59°45E **47** D8
Kermānshāh *Iran* 34°23N 47°0E **46** C5
Kermānshāh □ *Iran* 34°0N 46°30E **46** C5
Kermit *U.S.A.* 31°52N 103°6W **84** F3
Kern → *U.S.A.* 35°16N 119°18W **79** K7
Kernow = Cornwall □
  U.K. 50°26N 4°40W **13** G3
Kernville *U.S.A.* 35°45N 118°26W **79** K8
Keroh *Malaysia* 5°43N 101°1E **39** K3
Kerrera *U.K.* 56°24N 5°33W **11** E3
Kerrobert *Canada* 51°56N 109°8W **71** C7
Kerrville *U.S.A.* 30°3N 99°8W **84** F5
Kerry □ *Ireland* 52°7N 9°35W **10** D2
Kerry Hd. *Ireland* 52°25N 9°56W **10** D2
Kerulen = Herlen →
  Asia 48°48N 117°0E **31** B12
Kerzaz *Algeria* 29°29N 1°37W **52** C5
Kesagami → *Canada* 51°40N 79°45W **72** B4
Kesagami L. *Canada* 50°23N 80°15W **72** B3
Keşan *Turkey* 40°49N 26°38E **23** D12
Kesennuma *Japan* 38°54N 141°35E **28** E10
Keshit *Iran* 29°43N 58°17E **47** D8
Kesgi = Kosgi *India* 16°58N 77°42E **44** L10
Keskal *India* 20°5N 81°35E **44** D5
Kestenga *Russia* 65°50N 31°45E **8** D24
Keswick *U.K.* 54°36N 3°8W **12** C4
Ket → *Russia* 58°55N 81°32E **26** D9
Ketapang *Jawa Timur,*
  Indonesia 8°9S 114°23E **37** J17
Ketapang *Kalimantan Barat,*
  Indonesia 1°55S 110°0E **36** E4
Ketchikan *U.S.A.* 55°21N 131°39W **70** B2
Ketchum *U.S.A.* 43°41N 114°22W **76** E6
Keti Bandar *Pakistan* 24°8N 67°27E **42** G2
Ketri *India* 28°1N 75°50E **42** E6
Kętrzyn *Poland* 54°7N 21°22E **17** A11
Kettering *U.K.* 52°24N 0°43W **13** E7
Kettering *U.S.A.* 39°41N 84°10W **81** F11
Kettle → *Canada* 56°40N 89°34W **71** B11
Kettle Falls *U.S.A.* 48°37N 118°3W **76** B4
Kettle Point *Canada* 43°10N 82°1W **82** C2

Kettle Pt. *Canada* 43°13N 82°1W **82** C2
Kettleman City *U.S.A.* 36°1N 119°58W **78** J7
Keuka L. *U.S.A.* 42°30N 77°9W **82** D7
Keuruu *Finland* 62°16N 24°41E **8** E21
Kewanee *U.S.A.* 41°14N 89°56W **80** E9
Kewanee *Nepal* 27°57N 83°47E **43** F10
Kewaunee *U.S.A.* 44°27N 87°31W **80** C10
Keweenaw B. *U.S.A.* 47°0N 88°15W **80** B9
Keweenaw Pen. *U.S.A.* 47°15N 88°15W **80** B9
Keweenaw Pt. *U.S.A.* 47°25N 87°43W **80** B10
Key, L. *Ireland* 54°0N 8°15W **10** C3
Key Lake Mine *Canada* 57°5N 105°32W **71** B7
Key Largo *U.S.A.* 25°5N 80°27W **85** J14
Key West *U.S.A.* 24°33N 81°48W **88** B3
Keynsham *U.K.* 51°24N 2°29W **13** F5
Keyser *U.S.A.* 39°26N 78°59W **81** F14
Kezhma *Russia* 58°59N 101°9E **27** D11
Kezi *Zimbabwe* 20°58S 28°32E **57** B4
Kgalagadi △ *Botswana* 24°30S 22°0E **56** B3
Kgalagadi Transfrontier △
  Africa 25°10S 21°0E **56** C3
Khabarovsk *Russia* 48°30N 135°5E **31** B16
Khabr △ *Iran* 28°51N 56°22E **47** D8
Khābūr → *Syria* 35°17N 40°35E **46** C4
Khachmas = Xaçmaz
  Azerbaijan 41°31N 48°42E **19** F8
Khachrod *India* 23°25N 75°20E **42** H6
Khadro *Pakistan* 26°11N 68°50E **42** F3
Khadzhilyangar = Dahongliutan
  China 35°45N 79°20E **43** B8
Khaga *India* 25°47N 81°7E **43** G9
Khagaria *India* 25°30N 86°32E **43** G12
Khaipur *Pakistan* 29°34N 72°17E **42** E5
Khair *India* 27°57N 77°46E **42** F7
Khairabad *India* 27°33N 80°47E **43** F9
Khairagarh *India* 21°27N 81°2E **43** J9
Khairpur *Pakistan* 27°32N 68°49E **42** F3
Khairpur Nathan Shah
  Pakistan 27°6N 67°44E **42** F2
Khairwara *India* 23°58N 73°38E **42** H5
Khaisor → *Pakistan* 31°17N 68°59E **42** D3
Khajuraho *India* 24°51N 79°55E **43** G8
Khajuri Kach *Pakistan* 32°4N 69°51E **42** C3
Khakassia □ *Russia* 53°0N 90°0E **26** D9
Khalafābād *Iran* 30°54N 49°24E **47** D6
Khalilabad *India* 26°48N 83°5E **43** F10
Khalīlī *Iran* 27°38N 53°17E **47** E7
Khalkhāl *Iran* 37°37N 48°32E **47** B6
Khalkis = Chalkida
  Greece 38°27N 23°42E **23** E10
Khalmer Yu *Russia* 67°58N 65°1E **26** C7
Khalturin *Russia* 58°40N 48°50E **18** C8
Khalūf *Oman* 20°30N 58°0E **47** C6
Kham Keut *Laos* 18°15N 104°43E **38** C5
Khamaria *India* 23°5N 80°48E **43** H9
Khambhaliya *India* 22°14N 69°41E **42** H3
Khambhat *India* 22°23N 72°33E **42** H5
Khambhat, G. of *India* 20°45N 72°30E **40** J8
Khamgaon *India* 20°42N 76°37E **44** D3
Khamir *Iran* 26°57N 55°36E **47** E7
Khamir *Yemen* 16°2N 44°0E **49** D3
Khamīs Mushayţ
  Si. Arabia 18°18N 42°44E **49** D3
Khammam *India* 17°11N 80°6E **44** F5
Khamsa *Egypt* 30°27N 32°23E **48** E1
Khān → *Namibia* 22°37S 14°56E **56** B2
Khān Abū Shāmat *Syria* 33°39N 36°53E **48** B5
Khān Azād *Iraq* 33°7N 44°22E **46** C5
Khān Mujiddah *Iraq* 32°21N 43°48E **46** C4
Khān Shaykhūn *Syria* 35°26N 36°38E **46** C3
Khan Tengri, Pik *Asia* 42°12N 80°10E **30** C5
Khān Yūnis *Gaza Strip* 31°21N 34°18E **48** D3
Khanai *Pakistan* 30°30N 67°8E **42** D2
Khānaqīn *Iraq* 34°23N 45°25E **46** C5
Khānbāghī *Iran* 36°10N 55°25E **47** B7
Khandwa *India* 21°49N 76°22E **44** D3
Khandyga *Russia* 62°42N 135°35E **27** C14
Khanewal *Pakistan* 30°20N 71°55E **42** D4
Khangah Dogran
  Pakistan 31°50N 73°37E **42** D5
Khangchendzonga =
  Kanchenjunga △ *India* 27°42N 88°8E **43** F13
Khanh Duong *Vietnam* 12°44N 108°44E **38** F7
Khaniá = Chania *Greece* 35°30N 24°4E **23** G11
Khaniadhana *India* 25°1N 78°8E **42** G8
Khanka, L. *Asia* 45°0N 132°24E **28** B6
Khankendy = Xankändi
  Azerbaijan 39°52N 46°49E **46** B5
Khanna *India* 30°42N 76°16E **42** D7
Khanozai *Pakistan* 30°37N 67°19E **42** D2
Khanpur *Pakistan* 28°42N 70°35E **42** E4
Khanty-Mansiysk *Russia* 61°0N 69°0E **26** C7
Khao Khitchakut △
  Thailand 12°50N 102°10E **38** F4
Khao Laem △ *Thailand* 14°56N 98°31E **38** E2
Khao Laem Res. *Thailand* 14°50N 98°30E **38** E2
Khao Lak △ *Malaysia* 8°38N 98°18E **39** H2
Khao Luang △ *Thailand* 8°34N 99°42E **39** H2
Khao Nam Khang △
  Thailand 6°32N 100°35E **39** J3
Khao Phlu *Thailand* 9°29N 99°59E **39** b
Khao Pu -Khao Ya △
  Thailand 7°26N 99°57E **39** J2
Khao Sam Roi Yot △
  Thailand 12°13N 99°57E **39** F2
Khao Sok △ *Thailand* 8°55N 98°38E **39** H2
Khao Yai △ *Thailand* 14°21N 101°29E **38** E3
Khaoen Si Nakarin △
  Thailand 14°47N 99°0E **38** E2
Khapalu *Pakistan* 35°10N 76°20E **43** B7
Khapcheranga *Russia* 49°42N 112°24E **27** E12
Khaptao △ *Nepal* 29°20N 81°10E **43** E9
Kharaghoda *India* 23°11N 71°46E **42** H4
Kharagpur *India* 22°20N 87°25E **43** H12
Kharan Kalat *Pakistan* 28°34N 65°21E **40** E4
Kharānaq *Iran* 32°20N 54°45E **47** C7
Kharda *India* 18°40N 75°34E **44** E2
Khardung La *India* 34°20N 77°43E **43** B7
Kharg = Khārk, Jazīreh-ye
  Iran 29°15N 50°28E **47** D6

Khârga, El Wâhât el
  Egypt 25°10N 30°35E **53** C12
Khargon *India* 21°45N 75°40E **44** D2
Khari → *India* 25°54N 74°31E **42** G6
Kharian *Pakistan* 32°49N 73°52E **42** C5
Khārk, Jazīreh-ye *Iran* 29°15N 50°28E **47** D6
Kharkiv *Ukraine* 49°58N 36°20E **19** E6
Kharkov = Kharkiv
  Ukraine 49°58N 36°20E **19** E6
Kharovsk *Russia* 59°56N 40°13E **18** C7
Kharsawangarh *India* 22°48N 85°50E **43** H11
Kharta *Turkey* 40°55N 29°7E **23** D13
Khartoum = El Khartûm
  Sudan 15°31N 32°35E **53** E12
Khartum *Canada* 45°15N 77°5W **82** A7
Khasan *Russia* 42°25N 130°40E **28** C5
Khāsh *Iran* 28°15N 61°15E **47** D9
Khashm el Girba *Sudan* 14°59N 35°58E **53** F13
Khat, Laem *Thailand* 8°6N 98°26E **39** a
Khatanga *Russia* 72°0N 102°20E **27** B11
Khatanga → *Russia* 72°55N 106°0E **27** B11
Khatauli *India* 29°17N 77°43E **42** E7
Khatra *India* 22°59N 86°51E **43** H12
Khātūnābād *Iran* 30°1N 55°25E **47** D7
Khatyrka *Russia* 62°3N 175°15E **27** C18
Khavda *India* 23°51N 69°43E **42** H3
Khawr Fakkān *U.A.E.* 25°21N 56°22E **47** E8
Khaybar, Ḩarrat
  Si. Arabia 25°30N 39°45E **46** E4
Khāzimiyah *Iraq* 34°46N 43°37E **46** C4
Khe Bo *Vietnam* 19°8N 104°41E **38** C5
Khe Long *Vietnam* 21°29N 104°46E **38** B5
Khe Sanh *Vietnam* 16°37N 106°45E **38** D6
Khed *Maharashtra, India* 17°43N 73°27E **44** F1
Khed *Maharashtra, India* 18°51N 73°56E **44** E1
Khed Brahma *India* 24°7N 73°5E **42** G5
Khekra *India* 28°52N 77°20E **42** E7
Khemarak Phouminville = Krong
  Kaoh Kong *Cambodia* 11°37N 102°59E **39** G4
Khemisset *Morocco* 33°50N 6°1W **52** B4
Khemmarat *Thailand* 16°10N 105°15E **38** D5
Khenāmān *Iran* 30°27N 56°29E **47** D8
Khenchela *Algeria* 35°28N 7°11E **52** A7
Khersān → *Iran* 31°33N 50°22E **47** D6
Kherson *Ukraine* 46°35N 32°35E **19** E5
Kheta → *Russia* 71°54N 102°6E **27** B11
Khewari *Pakistan* 26°36N 68°52E **42** F3
Khilchipur *India* 24°2N 76°34E **42** G7
Khilok *Russia* 51°30N 110°45E **27** D12
Khíos = Chios *Greece* 38°27N 26°9E **23** E12
Khirsadoh *India* 22°11N 78°47E **43** H8
Khiuma = Hiiumaa
  Estonia 58°50N 22°45E **9** G20
Khiva = Xiva *Uzbekistan* 41°30N 60°18E **26** E7
Khiwa = Xiva *Uzbekistan* 41°30N 60°18E **26** E7
Khlong Khlung *Thailand* 16°12N 99°43E **38** D2
Khlong Lan △ *Thailand* 16°12N 99°13E **38** D2
Khlong Phanom △
  Thailand 8°45N 98°38E **39** H2
Khmelnik *Ukraine* 49°33N 27°58E **17** D14
Khmelnytskyy *Ukraine* 49°23N 27°0E **17** D14
Khmelnytskyy □
  Ukraine 49°50N 26°40E **17** D14
Khmer Rep. = Cambodia ■
  Asia 12°15N 105°0E **38** F5
Khoai, Hon *Vietnam* 8°26N 104°50E **39** H5
Khobar = Al Khubar
  Si. Arabia 26°17N 50°12E **47** E6
Khodoriv *Ukraine* 49°24N 24°19E **17** D13
Khodzent = Khüjand
  Tajikistan 40°17N 69°37E **26** E7
Khojak Pass *Afghan.* 30°51N 66°34E **42** D2
Khok Kloi *Thailand* 8°17N 98°19E **39** a
Khok Pho *Thailand* 6°43N 101°6E **39** J3
Khok Samrong *Thailand* 15°3N 100°43E **38** E3
Kholm *Russia* 57°10N 31°15E **18** C5
Kholmsk *Russia* 47°40N 142°5E **27** E15
Khomas □ *Namibia* 23°30S 17°0E **56** B2
Khomas Hochland
  Namibia 22°40S 16°0E **56** B2
Khomeyn *Iran* 33°40N 50°7E **47** C6
Khomeynī Shahr *Iran* 32°41N 51°31E **47** C6
Khomodino *Botswana* 22°46S 23°52E **56** B3
Khon Kaen *Thailand* 16°30N 102°47E **38** D4
Khong → *Cambodia* 13°32N 105°58E **38** F5
Khong Sedone *Laos* 15°34N 105°49E **38** E5
Khonuu *Russia* 66°30N 143°12E **27** C15
Khoper → *Russia* 49°30N 42°20E **19** E7
Khorāsān-e Janūb □ *Iran* 32°0N 59°0E **47** C8
Khorāsān-e Razavī □ *Iran* 35°0N 59°0E **47** C8
Khorāsān-e Shemālī □
  Iran 37°0N 57°0E **47** B8
Khorat = Nakhon Ratchasima
  Thailand 14°59N 102°12E **38** E4
Khorat, Cao Nguyen
  Thailand 15°30N 102°50E **38** E4
Khorixas *Namibia* 20°16S 14°59E **56** B1
Khorramābād *Khorāsān,*
  Iran 35°6N 57°57E **47** C8
Khorramābād *Lorestān,*
  Iran 33°30N 48°25E **47** C6
Khorramshahr *Iran* 30°29N 48°15E **47** D6
Khorugh *Tajikistan* 37°30N 71°36E **26** F8
Khosravī *Iran* 30°48N 51°28E **47** D6
Khosrowābād *Khuzestán,*
  Iran 30°10N 48°25E **47** D6
Khosrowābād *Kordestán,*
  Iran 35°31N 47°38E **46** C5
Khost *Pakistan* 30°13N 67°35E **42** D2
Khosūyeh *Iran* 28°32N 54°26E **47** D7
Khotang *Nepal* 27°1N 86°51E **43** F12
Khotyn *Ukraine* 48°31N 26°27E **17** D14
Khouribga *Morocco* 32°58N 6°57W **52** B4
Khowst *Afghan.* 33°22N 69°58E **42** C3
Khowst □ *Afghan.* 33°20N 70°0E **40** C6
Khoyniki *Belarus* 51°54N 29°55E **17** C15
Khram, Ko *Thailand* 12°55N 100°53E **38** F3
Khuan Wa *Thailand* 7°53N 98°17E **39** a
Khudzhand = Khüjand
  Tajikistan 40°17N 69°37E **26** E7

Khuff *Si. Arabia* 24°55N 44°53E **46** E5
Khūgīānī *Afghan.* 31°34N 66°32E **42** D2
Khuis *Botswana* 26°40S 21°49E **56** C3
Khuiyala *India* 27°9N 70°25E **42** F4
Khüjand *Tajikistan* 40°17N 69°37E **26** E7
Khukhan *Thailand* 14°42N 104°12E **38** E5
Khulna *Bangla.* 22°45N 89°34E **41** H16
Khulna □ *Bangla.* 22°25N 89°35E **41** H16
Khumago *Botswana* 20°26S 24°32E **56** B3
Khunjerab △ *Pakistan* 36°40N 75°30E **43** A6
Khunjerab Pass = Kinjirap Daban
  Asia 36°40N 75°25E **40** A9
Khūnsorkh *Iran* 27°9N 56°7E **47** E8
Khunti *India* 23°5N 85°17E **43** H11
Khūr *Iran* 32°55N 58°18E **47** C8
Khurai *India* 24°3N 78°23E **42** G8
Khurays *Si. Arabia* 25°6N 48°2E **47** E6
Khurda *India* 20°11N 85°37E **44** D7
Khurja *India* 28°15N 77°58E **42** E7
Khūrmāl *Iraq* 35°18N 46°2E **46** C5
Khurr, Wādī al *Iraq* 32°3N 43°52E **46** C4
Khūsf *Iran* 32°46N 58°53E **47** C8
Khushab *Pakistan* 32°20N 72°20E **42** C5
Khust *Ukraine* 48°10N 23°18E **17** D12
Khūzestān □ *Iran* 31°0N 49°0E **47** D6
Khvāf *Iran* 34°33N 60°8E **47** C9
Khvājeh *Iran* 38°9N 46°35E **46** B5
Khvānsār *Iran* 29°56N 54°8E **47** D7
Khvor *Iran* 33°45N 55°0E **47** C7
Khvorgū *Iran* 27°34N 56°27E **47** E8
Khvormūj *Iran* 28°40N 51°30E **47** D6
Khvoy *Iran* 38°35N 45°0E **46** B5
Khwae Noi → *Thailand* 14°1N 99°32E **38** E2
Khyber Pakhtunkhwa □
  Pakistan 34°0N 72°0E **42** C5
Khyber Pass *Afghan.* 34°10N 71°8E **42** B4
Kia *Fiji* 16°16S 179°7E **59** a
Kiadho → *India* 19°37N 77°40E **44** E3
Kiama *Australia* 34°40S 150°50E **63** E5
Kiamba *Phil.* 6°2N 124°46E **37** C6
Kiangsi = Jiangxi □
  China 27°30N 116°0E **35** D11
Kiangsu = Jiangsu □
  China 33°0N 120°0E **33** H11
Kibombo
  Dem. Rep. of the Congo 3°57S 25°53E **54** E5
Kibre Mengist *Ethiopia* 5°54N 38°59E **49** F2
Kıbrıs = Cyprus ■ *Asia* 35°0N 33°0E **46** C2
Kibwezi *Kenya* 2°27S 37°57E **54** E7
Kichha → *India* 28°41N 79°18E **43** E8
Kichmengskiy Gorodok
  Russia 59°59N 45°48E **18** B8
Kicking Horse Pass
  Canada 51°28N 116°16W **70** C5
Kidal *Mali* 18°26N 1°22E **52** E6
Kidderminster *U.K.* 52°24N 2°15W **13** E5
Kidnappers, C. *N.Z.* 39°38S 177°5E **59** C6
Kidsgrove *U.K.* 53°5N 2°14W **12** D5
Kidston *Australia* 18°52S 144°8E **62** B3
Kiel *Germany* 54°19N 10°8E **16** A6
Kiel Canal = Nord-Ostsee-Kanal
  Germany 54°12N 9°32E **16** A5
Kielce *Poland* 50°52N 20°42E **17** C11
Kielder Water *U.K.* 55°11N 2°31W **12** B5
Kieler Bucht *Germany* 54°35N 10°25E **16** A6
Kiev = Kyyiv *Ukraine* 50°30N 30°28E **17** C16
Kiffa *Mauritania* 16°37N 11°24W **52** E3
Kifrī *Iraq* 34°45N 45°0E **46** C5
Kigali *Rwanda* 1°59S 30°4E **54** E6
Kigoma-Ujiji *Tanzania* 4°55S 29°36E **54** E5
Kii-Sanchi *Japan* 34°20N 136°0E **29** G8
Kii-Suidō *Japan* 33°40N 134°45E **29** H7
Kikaiga-Shima *Japan* 28°19N 129°59E **29** K4
Kikiak = Rigolet *Canada* 54°10N 58°23W **73** B8
Kikinda *Serbia* 45°50N 20°30E **23** B9
Kikládhes = Kyklades
  Greece 37°0N 24°30E **23** F11
Kikuchi *Japan* 32°59N 130°47E **29** H5
Kikwit *Dem. Rep. of the Congo* 5°0S 18°45E **54** F3
Kilakkarai *India* 9°12N 78°47E **45** K4
Kilar *India* 33°6N 76°25E **42** C7
Kilbeggan *Ireland* 53°22N 7°30W **10** C4
Kilbrannan Sd. *U.K.* 55°37N 5°26W **11** F3
Kilbuck Mts. *U.S.A.* 60°36N 159°53W **74** C8
Kilchu *N. Korea* 40°57N 129°25E **33** D15
Kilcoy *Australia* 26°59S 152°30E **63** D5
Kildare *Ireland* 53°9N 6°55W **10** C5
Kildare □ *Ireland* 53°10N 6°50W **10** C5
Kildinstroy *Russia* 68°48N 33°6E **8** B25
Kilfinnane *Ireland* 52°21N 8°28W **10** D3
Kilgarvan *Ireland* 51°54N 9°27W **10** E2
Kilgore *U.S.A.* 32°23N 94°53W **84** E7
Kilifi *Kenya* 3°40S 39°48E **54** E7
Kilimanjaro *Tanzania* 3°7S 37°20E **54** E7
Kilindini *Kenya* 4°4S 39°40E **54** E7
Kilinochchi *Sri Lanka* 9°24N 80°25E **45** K5
Kilis *Turkey* 36°42N 37°6E **46** B3
Kiliya *Ukraine* 45°28N 29°16E **17** F15
Kilkee *Ireland* 52°41N 9°39W **10** D2
Kilkeel *U.K.* 54°7N 5°55W **10** B5
Kilkenny *Ireland* 52°39N 7°15W **10** D4
Kilkenny □ *Ireland* 52°35N 7°15W **10** D4
Kilkieran B. *Ireland* 53°20N 9°41W **10** C2
Kilkis *Greece* 40°58N 22°57E **23** D10
Killala *Ireland* 54°13N 9°13W **10** B2
Killala B. *Ireland* 54°16N 9°8W **10** B2
Killaloe *Ireland* 52°48N 8°28W **10** D3
Killaloe *Canada* 45°33N 77°25W **82** A7
Killarney *Australia* 28°20S 152°18E **63** D5
Killarney *Canada* 49°10N 99°40W **71** D9
Killarney *Ireland* 52°4N 9°30W **10** D2
Killarney △ *Ireland* 52°0N 9°33W **10** D2
Killary Harbour *Ireland* 53°38N 9°52W **10** C2
Killdeer *U.S.A.* 47°22N 102°45W **80** B2

Killeen *U.S.A.* 31°7N 97°44W **84** F6
Killin *U.K.* 56°28N 4°19W **11** E4
Killiney *Ireland* 53°15N 6°7W **10** C5
Killington Pk. *U.S.A.* 43°36N 72°49W **83** C12
Killini *Greece* 37°54N 22°25E **23** F10
Killíniq I. *Canada* 60°24N 64°37W **69** E19
Killorglin *Ireland* 52°6N 9°47W **10** D2
Killybegs *Ireland* 54°38N 8°26W **10** B3
Kilmarnock *U.K.* 55°37N 4°29W **11** F4
Kilmore *Australia* 37°25S 144°53E **63** F3
Kilmore Quay *Ireland* 52°10N 6°36W **10** D5
Kilosa *Tanzania* 6°48S 37°0E **54** F7
Kilrush *Ireland* 52°38N 9°29W **10** D2
Kilwa Kivinje *Tanzania* 8°45S 39°25E **54** F7
Kilwinning *U.K.* 55°39N 4°43W **11** F4
Kim *U.S.A.* 37°15N 103°21W **77** H12
Kimaam *Indonesia* 7°58S 138°53E **37** F9
Kimba *Australia* 33°8S 136°23E **63** E2
Kimball *Nebr., U.S.A.* 41°14N 103°40W **80** E2
Kimball *S. Dak., U.S.A.* 43°45N 98°57W **80** D4
Kimberley *Australia* 16°20S 127°0E **60** C4
Kimberley *B.C., Canada* 49°40N 115°59W **70** D5
Kimberley *Ont., Canada* 44°23N 80°32W **82** B4
Kimberley *S. Africa* 28°43S 24°46E **56** D3
Kimberly *U.S.A.* 42°32N 114°22W **76** E6
Kimch'aek *N. Korea* 40°40N 129°10E **33** D15
Kimhae = Gimhae
  S. Korea 35°14N 128°53E **33** G15
Kimmirut *Canada* 62°50N 69°50W **69** E18
Kimpese
  Dem. Rep. of the Congo 5°33S 14°26E **54** F2
Kimry *Russia* 56°55N 37°15E **18** C6
Kinabalu, Gunung
  Malaysia 6°3N 116°14E **36** C5
Kinaskan L. *Canada* 57°38N 130°8W **70** B2
Kinbasket L. *Canada* 52°0N 118°10W **70** C5
Kincardine *Canada* 44°10N 81°40W **82** B3
Kincolith *Canada* 55°0N 129°57W **70** C3
Kinde *U.S.A.* 43°56N 83°0W **82** C2
Kinder Scout *U.K.* 53°24N 1°52W **12** D6
Kindersley *Canada* 51°30N 109°10W **71** C7
Kindia *Guinea* 10°0N 12°52W **52** F3
Kindu
  Dem. Rep. of the Congo 2°55S 25°50E **54** E5
Kineshma *Russia* 57°30N 42°5E **18** C7
King, L. *Australia* 33°10S 119°35E **61** F2
King, Mt. *Australia* 25°10S 147°30E **62** D4
King Abdullah Economic City
  Si. Arabia 22°24N 39°5E **49** C2
King Christian I.
  Canada 77°48N 101°40W **69** B11
King City *U.S.A.* 36°13N 121°8W **78** J5
King Cr. → *Australia* 24°35S 139°30E **62** C2
King Edward →
  Australia 14°14S 126°35E **60** B4
King Edward Point
  S. Georgia 54°17S 36°30W **96** A5
King Frederick VI Land = Kong
  Frederik VI.s Kyst
  Greenland 63°0N 43°0W **4** C5
King George B. *Falk. Is.* 51°30S 60°30W **96** G4
King George I. *Antarctica* 60°0S 60°0W **5** C18
King George Is. *Canada* 57°20N 80°30W **69** F15
King George Sd. *Australia* 35°5S 118°0E **61** G2
King I. = Kadan Kyun
  Myanmar 12°30N 98°20E **38** F2
King I. *Australia* 39°50S 144°0E **63** F3
King I. *Canada* 52°10N 127°40W **70** C3
King Khalid Int. ✈ (RUH)
  Si. Arabia 24°57N 46°42E **46** E4
King Khalid Military City =
  Madinat al Malik Khälid al
  Askärïyah *Si. Arabia* 27°54N 45°31E **46** E5
King Leopold Ranges
  Australia 17°30S 125°45E **60** C4
King of Prussia *U.S.A.* 40°5N 75°23W **83** F9
King Sd. *Australia* 16°50S 123°20E **60** C3
King Sejong *Antarctica* 62°30S 58°0W **5** C18
King Shaka Int. ✈ (DUR)
  S. Africa 29°37S 31°7E **57** C5
King William I. *Canada* 69°10N 97°25W **68** D12
King William's Town
  S. Africa 32°51S 27°22E **56** D4
Kingaok = Bathurst Inlet
  Canada 66°50N 108°1W **68** D10
Kingaroy *Australia* 26°32S 151°51E **63** D5
Kingfisher *U.S.A.* 35°52N 97°56W **84** D6
Kingirbān *Iraq* 34°40N 44°54E **46** C5
Kingisepp = Kuressaare
  Estonia 58°15N 22°30E **9** G20
Kingisepp *Russia* 59°25N 28°40E **9** G23
Kingman *Ariz., U.S.A.* 35°12N 114°4W **79** K12
Kingman *Kans., U.S.A.* 37°39N 98°7W **80** G4
Kingoonya *Australia* 30°55S 135°19E **63** E2
Kingri *Pakistan* 30°27N 69°49E **42** D3
Kings → *U.S.A.* 36°3N 119°50W **78** J7
Kings Canyon *Australia* 24°15S 131°34E **60** D5
Kings Canyon △ *U.S.A.* 36°50N 118°40W **78** J8
King's Lynn *U.K.* 52°45N 0°24E **12** E8
Kings Park *U.S.A.* 40°53N 73°16W **83** F11
Kings Peak *U.S.A.* 40°46N 110°23W **76** F8
Kingsbridge *U.K.* 50°17N 3°47W **13** G4
Kingscote *Australia* 35°40S 137°38E **63** F2
Kingscourt *Ireland* 53°54N 6°48W **10** C5
Kingsford *U.S.A.* 45°48N 88°4W **80** C9
Kingsland *U.S.A.* 30°48N 81°41W **85** F14
Kingsport *U.S.A.* 36°33N 82°33W **85** C13
Kingston *Canada* 44°14N 76°30W **82** B8
Kingston *Jamaica* 17°55N 76°50W **88** a
Kingston *N.Z.* 45°20S 168°43E **59** F2
Kingston *N.H., U.S.A.* 42°56N 71°3W **83** D13
Kingston *N.Y., U.S.A.* 41°56N 73°59W **83** E11
Kingston *Pa., U.S.A.* 41°16N 75°54W **83** E9
Kingston *R.I., U.S.A.* 41°29N 71°30W **83** E13
Kingston Pk. *U.S.A.* 35°44N 115°54W **79** K11
Kingston South East
  Australia 36°51S 139°55E **63** F2
Kingston upon Hull *U.K.* 53°45N 0°21W **12** D7

Kingston upon Hull □
　U.K.　53°45N 0°21W **12** D7
Kingstown St. Vincent　13°10N 61°10W **89** D7
Kingstree U.S.A.　33°40N 79°50W **85** E15
Kingsville Canada　42°2N 82°45W **82** D2
Kingsville U.S.A.　27°31N 97°52W **84** H6
Kingussie U.K.　57°6N 4°2W **11** D4
Kingwood U.S.A.　30°2N 95°16W **84** F7
Kınık Turkey　39°6N 27°24E **23** E12
Kinistino Canada　52°57N 105°2W **71** C7
Kinjirap Daban Asia　36°40N 75°25E **40** M9
Kinkala Congo　4°18S 14°49E **54** E2
Kinki □ Japan　33°45N 136°0E **29** H8
Kinleith N.Z.　38°20S 175°56E **59** C5
Kinlochleven U.K.　56°43N 5°0W **11** E4
Kinmount Canada　44°48N 78°45W **82** B6
Kinna Sweden　57°32N 12°42E **9** H15
Kinnairds Hd. U.K.　57°43N 2°1W **11** D6
Kinnarodden = Nordkinn
　Norway　71°8N 27°40E **8** A22
Kinngait Canada　64°14N 76°32W **69** E16
Kinniyai Sri Lanka　8°29N 81°11E **45** K5
Kino Nuevo Mexico　28°52N 112°33W **86** B2
Kinoje → Canada　52°8N 81°25W **72** B3
Kinomoto Japan　35°30N 136°13E **29** G8
Kinoosao Canada　57°5N 102°1W **71** B8
Kinross U.K.　56°13N 3°25W **11** E5
Kinsale Ireland　51°42N 8°31W **10** E3
Kinsale, Old Hd. of Ireland 51°37N 8°33W **10** E3
Kinsha = Chang Jiang →
　China　31°48N 121°10E **35** B13
Kinshasa
　Dem. Rep. of the Congo　4°20S 15°15E **54** E3
Kinsley U.S.A.　37°55N 99°25W **80** G4
Kinsman U.S.A.　41°26N 80°35W **82** E4
Kinston U.S.A.　35°16N 77°35W **85** D16
Kintamani Indonesia　8°14S 115°19E **37** J18
Kintore U.K.　57°14N 2°20W **11** D6
Kintore Ra. Australia　23°15S 128°47E **60** D4
Kintyre U.K.　55°30N 5°35W **11** F3
Kintyre, Mull of U.K.　55°17N 5°47W **11** F3
Kinushseo → Canada　55°15N 83°45W **72** A3
Kinuso Canada　55°20N 115°25W **70** B5
Kinvarra Ireland　53°8N 8°56W **10** C3
Kinwat India　19°38N 78°12E **44** E4
Kinzua U.S.A.　41°52N 78°58W **82** E6
Kiosk Canada　46°6N 78°53W **72** C4
Kiowa Kans., U.S.A.　37°1N 98°29W **80** G4
Kiowa Okla., U.S.A.　34°43N 95°54W **84** D7
Kipahigan L. Canada　55°20N 101°55W **71** B8
Kiparissia Greece　37°15N 21°40E **23** F9
Kiparissiakos Kolpos
　Greece　37°25N 21°25E **23** F9
Kipawa, L. Canada　46°50N 79°0W **72** C4
Kipling Canada　50°6N 102°38W **71** C8
Kippure Ireland　53°11N 6°21W **10** C5
Kipushi
　Dem. Rep. of the Congo　11°48S 27°12E **55** G5
Kirandul India　18°33N 81°10E **44** E5
Kirensk Russia　57°50N 107°55E **27** D11
Kirghiz Range Asia　42°40N 73°40E **30** C3
Kirghizia = Kyrgyzstan ■
　Asia　42°0N 75°0E **26** E8
Kirgiziya Steppe Eurasia　50°0N 55°0E **19** E10
Kiri Buru India　22°0N 85°0E **44** D7
Kiribati ■ Pac. Oc.　3°0S 180°0E **58** B10
Kırıkkale Turkey　39°51N 33°32E **19** G5
Kirillov Russia　59°49N 38°24E **18** C6
Kirin = Jilin China　43°44N 126°30E **33** C14
Kirindi Oya → Sri Lanka　6°15N 81°20E **45** L5
Kirinyaga = Kenya, Mt.
　Kenya　0°10S 37°18E **54** E7
Kirirom △ Cambodia　11°18N 104°5E **39** G5
Kirishima Japan　31°44N 130°46E **29** J5
Kirishima Yaku △ Japan 31°24N 130°50E **29** J5
Kiritimati Kiribati　1°58N 157°27W **65** G12
Kirkby U.K.　53°30N 2°54W **12** D5
Kirkby-in-Ashfield U.K.　53°6N 1°14W **12** D6
Kirkby Lonsdale U.K.　54°12N 2°36W **12** C5
Kirkby Stephen U.K.　54°29N 2°21W **12** C5
Kirkcaldy U.K.　56°7N 3°9W **11** E5
Kirkcudbright U.K.　54°50N 4°2W **11** G4
Kirkenes Norway　69°40N 30°5E **8** B24
Kirkfield Canada　44°34N 78°59W **82** B6
Kirkintilloch U.K.　55°56N 4°8W **11** F4
Kirkjubæjarklaustur
　Iceland　63°47N 18°4W **8** E4
Kirkkonummi Finland　60°8N 24°26E **9** F21
Kirkland U.S.A.　47°40N 122°12W **78** C4
Kirkland Lake Canada　48°9N 80°2W **72** C3
Kırklareli Turkey　41°44N 27°15E **23** D12
Kirkpatrick, Mt.
　Antarctica　84°20S 166°25E **5** E11
Kirksville U.S.A.　40°12N 92°35W **80** E7
Kirkūk Iraq　35°30N 44°21E **46** C5
Kirkwall U.K.　58°59N 2°58W **11** C6
Kirkwood S. Africa　33°22S 25°15E **56** D4
Kirlampudi India　17°12N 82°12E **44** F6
Kirov Russia　58°35N 49°40E **18** C8
Kirovabad = Gäncä
　Azerbaijan　40°45N 46°20E **19** F8
Kirovo-Chepetsk Russia　58°28N 50°0E **18** C9
Kirovograd = Kirovohrad
　Ukraine　48°35N 32°20E **19** E5
Kirovohrad Ukraine　48°35N 32°20E **19** E5
Kirovsk Russia　67°32N 33°41E **18** A5
Kirovskiy Kamchatka,
　Russia　54°27N 155°42E **27** D16
Kirovskiy Primorsk,
　Russia　45°7N 133°30E **28** B6
Kirsanov Russia　52°35N 42°40E **18** D7
Kırşehir Turkey　39°14N 34°5E **46** B2
Kirthar △ Pakistan　25°45N 67°32E **42** F2
Kirthar Range Pakistan　27°0N 67°0E **42** F2
Kirtland U.S.A.　36°44N 108°21W **77** H9
Kiruna Sweden　67°52N 20°15E **8** C19
Kiryū Japan　36°24N 139°20E **29** F9
Kisangani
　Dem. Rep. of the Congo　0°35N 25°15E **54** D5

Kisar Indonesia　8°5S 127°10E **37** F7
Kisarazu Japan　35°23N 139°55E **29** G9
Kiselevsk Russia　54°5N 86°39E **26** D9
Kish = Qeys Iran　26°32N 53°58E **47** E7
Kishanganga → Pakistan 34°18N 73°28E **43** B5
Kishanganj India　26°3N 88°14E **43** F13
Kishangarh Raj., India　26°34N 74°52E **42** F6
Kishangarh Raj., India　27°50N 70°30E **42** F4
Kishinev = Chişinău
　Moldova　47°2N 28°50E **17** E15
Kishiwada Japan　34°28N 135°22E **29** G7
Kishtwar India　33°20N 75°48E **42** C6
Kisii Kenya　0°40S 34°45E **54** E6
Kiska I. U.S.A.　51°59N 177°30E **74** E3
Kiskőrös Hungary　46°37N 19°20E **17** E10
Kiskunfélegyháza
　Hungary　46°42N 19°53E **17** E10
Kiskunhalas Hungary　46°28N 19°37E **17** E10
Kislovodsk Russia　43°50N 42°45E **19** F7
Kismaayo Somalia　0°22S 42°32E **49** H3
Kiso-Gawa → Japan　35°20N 136°45E **29** G8
Kiso-Sammyaku Japan　35°45N 137°45E **29** G8
Kisofukushima Japan　35°52N 137°43E **29** G8
Kissidougou Guinea　9°5N 10°5W **52** G3
Kissimmee U.S.A.　28°18N 81°24W **85** G14
Kissimmee → U.S.A.　27°9N 80°52W **85** H14
Kississing L. Canada　55°10N 101°20W **71** B8
Kisumu Kenya　0°3S 34°45E **54** E6
Kit Carson U.S.A.　38°46N 102°48W **76** G12
Kita Mali　13°5N 9°25W **52** F4
Kitaibaraki Japan　36°50N 140°45E **29** F10
Kitakami Japan　39°20N 141°10E **28** E10
Kitakami-Gawa →
　Japan　38°25N 141°19E **28** E10
Kitakami-Sammyaku
　Japan　39°30N 141°30E **28** E10
Kitakata Japan　37°39N 139°52E **28** F9
Kitakyūshū Japan　33°50N 130°50E **29** H5
Kitale Kenya　1°0N 35°0E **54** D7
Kitami Japan　43°48N 143°54E **28** C11
Kitami-Sammyaku
　Japan　44°22N 142°43E **28** B11
Kitchener Canada　43°27N 80°29W **82** C4
Kitee Finland　62°5N 30°9E **8** E24
Kitega = Gitega Burundi　3°26S 29°56E **54** E5
Kithira = Kythira Greece　36°8N 23°0E **23** F10
Kíthnos = Kythnos
　Greece　37°26N 24°27E **23** F11
Kitikmeot Canada　67°0N 110°0W **68** D9
Kitimat Canada　54°3N 128°38W **70** C3
Kitinen → Finland　67°14N 27°27E **8** C22
Kitsuki Japan　33°25N 131°37E **29** H5
Kittakittaooloo, L.
　Australia　28°3S 138°14E **63** D2
Kittanning U.S.A.　40°49N 79°31W **82** F5
Kittatinny Mt. U.S.A.　41°19N 74°39W **83** F10
Kittery U.S.A.　43°5N 70°45W **83** C14
Kittilä Finland　67°40N 24°51E **8** C21
Kitui Kenya　1°17S 38°0E **54** E7
Kitwanga Canada　55°6N 128°4W **70** B3
Kitwe Zambia　12°54S 28°13E **55** G5
Kivalliq Canada　62°0N 97°30W **68** E12
Kivarli India　24°33N 72°46E **42** G5
Kivertsi Ukraine　50°50N 25°28E **17** C13
Kivu, L.
　Dem. Rep. of the Congo　1°48S 29°0E **54** E5
Kiwirrkurra Australia　22°49S 127°45E **60** D4
Kiwirrkurra ⊙ Australia 22°49S 127°45E **60** D4
Kiyev = Kyyiv Ukraine　50°30N 30°28E **17** C16
Kiyevskoye Vdkhr. = Kyyivske
　Vdskh. Ukraine　51°0N 30°25E **17** C16
Kizel Russia　59°3N 57°40E **18** C10
Kızıl Irmak → Turkey　41°44N 35°58E **19** F6
Kızıl Jilga China　35°26N 78°50E **43** B8
Kızıldağ △ Turkey　38°5N 31°20E **46** B1
Kızıltepe Turkey　37°12N 40°35E **46** B4
Kizlyar Russia　43°51N 46°40E **19** F8
Kizyl-Arvat = Serdar
　Turkmenistan　39°4N 56°23E **47** B8
Kjölur Iceland　64°50N 19°25W **8** D4
Kladno Czechia　50°10N 14°7E **16** C8
Klaeng Thailand　12°47N 101°39E **38** F3
Klagenfurt Austria　46°38N 14°20E **16** E8
Klaipėda Lithuania　55°43N 21°10E **9** J19
Klaksvík Færoe Is.　62°14N 6°35W **8** E9
Klamath → U.S.A.　41°33N 124°5W **76** F1
Klamath Falls U.S.A.　42°13N 121°46W **76** E3
Klamath Mts. U.S.A.　41°50N 123°20W **76** F2
Klamono Indonesia　1°8S 131°30E **37** E8
Klang Malaysia　3°2N 101°26E **39** L3
Klappan → Canada　58°0N 129°43W **70** B3
Klarälven → Sweden　59°23N 13°32E **9** G15
Klatovy Czechia　49°23N 13°18E **16** D7
Klawer S. Africa　31°44S 18°36E **56** D2
Klazienaveen Neths.　52°44N 7°0E **15** B6
Kleena Kleene Canada　52°0N 124°59W **70** C4
Klein-Karas Namibia　27°33S 18°7E **56** C2
Kleinbegin S. Africa　28°54S 21°40E **56** C3
Klerksdorp S. Africa　26°53S 26°38E **56** D4
Klerksk = Klyetsk Belarus 53°5N 26°45E **17** B14
Kletskiy Russia　49°16N 43°11E **19** E7
Klickitat U.S.A.　45°49N 121°9W **76** D3
Klickitat → U.S.A.　45°42N 121°17W **78** E5
Klinaklini → Canada　51°21N 125°40W **70** C3
Klip → S. Africa　27°3S 29°3E **57** C4
Klipdale S. Africa　34°19S 19°57E **56** E2
Klipplaat S. Africa　33°1S 24°22E **56** D3
Kłodzko Poland　50°28N 16°38E **17** C9
Klong Wang Chao △
　Thailand　16°20N 99°9E **38** D2
Kluane Canada　60°45N 139°30W **70** A1
Kluane L. Canada　61°15N 138°40W **68** E4
Kluang Malaysia　2°3N 103°18E **39** L4
Kluczbork Poland　50°58N 18°12E **17** C10
Klukwan U.S.A.　59°24N 135°54W **70** B1
Klungkung Indonesia　8°32S 115°24E **37** K18
Klyetsk Belarus　53°5N 26°45E **17** B14
Klyuchevskaya, Sopka
　Russia　55°50N 160°30E **27** D17

Klyuchi Russia　56°18N 160°51E **27** D17
Knaresborough U.K.　54°1N 1°28W **12** C6
Knee L. Man., Canada　55°3N 94°45W **72** A1
Knee L. Sask., Canada　55°51N 107°0W **71** B7
Knight Inlet Canada　50°45N 125°40W **70** C3
Knighton U.K.　52°21N 3°3W **13** E4
Knights Ferry U.S.A.　37°50N 120°40W **78** H6
Knights Landing U.S.A.　38°48N 121°43W **78** G5
Knob, C. Australia　34°32S 119°16E **61** F2
Knock Ireland　53°48N 8°55W **10** C3
Knockmealdown Mts.
　Ireland　52°14N 7°56W **10** D4
Knokke-Heist Belgium　51°21N 3°17E **15** C3
Knossós Greece　35°16N 25°10E **23** G11
Knowlton Canada　45°13N 72°31W **83** A12
Knox U.S.A.　41°18N 86°37W **80** E10
Knox Coast Antarctica　66°30S 108°0E **5** C8
Knoxville Iowa, U.S.A.　41°19N 93°6W **80** E7
Knoxville Tenn., U.S.A.　35°58N 83°55W **85** D13
Knud Rasmussen Land
　Greenland　78°0N 60°0W **69** B20
Knysna S. Africa　34°2S 23°2E **56** E3
Ko Kha Thailand　18°11N 99°24E **38** C2
Ko Tarutao △ Thailand　6°31N 99°26E **39** J2
Ko Yao Thailand　8°7N 98°35E **39** a
Koartac = Quaqtaq
　Canada　60°55N 69°40W **69** E18
Koba Indonesia　6°37S 134°37E **37** F8
Kobarid Slovenia　46°15N 13°30E **16** E7
Kobayashi Japan　31°56N 130°59E **29** J5
Kōbe Japan　34°41N 135°13E **29** G7
Kōbi-Sho E. China Sea　25°56N 123°41E **29** M1
Koblenz Germany　50°21N 7°36E **16** C4
Kobryn Belarus　52°15N 24°22E **17** B13
Kobuk → U.S.A.　66°54N 160°38W **74** B7
Kocaeli Turkey　40°45N 29°50E **19** F4
Kočani Macedonia　41°55N 22°25E **23** D10
Koch Bihar India　26°22N 89°29E **41** F16
Kochas India　25°15N 83°56E **43** G10
Kochi India　9°58N 76°20E **45** K3
Kōchi Japan　33°30N 133°35E **29** H6
Kōchi □ Japan　33°40N 133°30E **29** H6
Kochiu = Gejiu China　23°20N 103°10E **34** F4
Kodala India　19°38N 84°57E **44** E7
Kodarma India　24°28N 85°36E **43** G11
Koddiyar B. Sri Lanka　8°33N 81°15E **45** K5
Kodiak U.S.A.　57°47N 152°24W **74** D9
Kodiak I. U.S.A.　57°30N 152°45W **74** D9
Kodikkarai = Point Calimere
　India　10°17N 79°49E **45** J4
Kodinar India　20°46N 70°46E **42** J4
Kodinsk Russia　58°40N 99°10E **27** D10
Kodlipet India　12°48N 75°53E **45** H2
Kodungallur = Cranganore
　India　10°13N 76°13E **45** J3
Koedoesberge S. Africa　32°40S 20°11E **56** D3
Koes Namibia　26°0S 19°15E **56** C2
Koffiefontein S. Africa　29°30S 25°0E **56** D4
Kofiau Indonesia　1°11S 129°50E **37** E7
Koforidua Ghana　6°3N 0°17W **52** G5
Kōfu Japan　35°40N 138°30E **29** G9
Koga Japan　36°11N 139°43E **29** F9
Kogaluc → Canada　56°12N 61°44W **73** A7
Køge Denmark　55°27N 12°11E **9** J15
Kogon → Uzbekistan　39°43N 64°33E **26** F7
Koh-i-Khurd Afghan.　33°30N 65°59E **42** C1
Koh-i-Maran Pakistan　29°18N 66°50E **42** E2
Koh Ker Cambodia　13°47N 104°32E **38** F5
Koh Wai Thailand　11°54N 102°58E **39** H4
Kohat Pakistan　33°40N 71°29E **42** C4
Kohima India　25°35N 94°10E **41** G19
Kohkilūyeh va Būyer Aḥmadi □
　Iran　31°30N 50°30E **47** D6
Kohler Ra. Antarctica　77°0S 110°0W **5** D15
Kohlu Pakistan　29°54N 69°15E **42** E3
Kohtla-Järve Estonia　59°20N 27°20E **9** G22
Koi Sanjaq Iraq　36°5N 44°38E **46** B5
Koihoa India　8°12N 93°29E **45** K11
Koilkuntla India　15°14N 78°21E **45** G4
Koillismaa Finland　65°44N 28°36E **8** D23
Koin □ N. Korea　40°28N 126°18E **33** D14
Kojō N. Korea　38°58N 127°58E **33** E14
Kojonup Australia　33°48S 117°10E **61** F2
Kojūr Iran　36°23N 51°43E **47** B6
Kokand = Qo'qon
　Uzbekistan　40°31N 70°56E **26** E8
Kokang Myanmar　23°45N 98°30E **34** F2
Kokas Indonesia　2°42S 132°26E **37** E8
Kokchetav = Kökshetaū
　Kazakhstan　53°20N 69°25E **26** D7
Kokemäenjoki →
　Finland　61°32N 21°44E **8** F19
Kokkilai Sri Lanka　9°0N 80°57E **45** K5
Kokkola Finland　63°50N 23°8E **8** E20
Koko Kyunzu Myanmar　14°7N 93°22E **45** G11
Koko Nur = Qinghai Hu
　China　36°40N 100°10E **30** D9
Kokomo U.S.A.　40°29N 86°8W **80** E10
Kokopo Papua N. G.　4°22S 152°19E **64** H7
Koksan N. Korea　38°46N 126°40E **33** E14
Kökshetaū Kazakhstan　53°20N 69°25E **26** D7
Koksoak → Canada　58°30N 68°10W **69** F18
Kokstad S. Africa　30°32S 29°29E **57** D4
Kokubu = Kirishima
　Japan　31°44N 130°46E **29** J5
Kola Indonesia　5°35S 134°30E **37** F8
Kola Russia　68°45N 33°8E **8** B25
Kola Pen. = Kolskiy Poluostrov
　Russia　67°30N 38°0E **18** A6
Kolachel India　8°10N 77°15E **45** K3
Kolachi → Pakistan　27°8N 67°2E **42** F2
Kolahoi India　34°12N 75°22E **43** B6
Kolaka Indonesia　4°3S 121°46E **37** E6
Kolar India　13°12N 78°15E **45** H4
Kolar Gold Fields India　12°58N 78°16E **45** H4
Kolaras India　25°14N 77°36E **42** G6
Kolari Finland　67°20N 23°48E **8** C20
Kolasib India　24°15N 92°45E **41** G18
Kolayat India　27°50N 72°50E **42** F5
Kolda Senegal　12°55N 14°57W **52** F3

Kolding Denmark　55°30N 9°29E **9** J13
Kolepom = Dolak, Pulau
　Indonesia　8°0S 138°30E **37** F9
Kolguyev, Ostrov Russia　69°20N 48°30E **18** A8
Kolhapur India　16°43N 74°15E **44** F2
Kolin Czechia　50°2N 15°9E **16** C8
Kolkas rags Latvia　57°46N 22°37E **9** H20
Kollam India　8°50N 76°38E **45** K3
Kollegal India　12°9N 77°9E **45** H3
Kolleru L. India　16°40N 81°10E **44** F5
Kollum Neths.　53°17N 6°10E **15** A6
Kolmanskop Namibia　26°45S 15°14E **56** C2
Köln Germany　50°56N 6°57E **16** C4
Kolo Poland　52°14N 18°40E **17** B10
Kołobrzeg Poland　54°10N 15°35E **16** A8
Kolokani Mali　13°35N 7°45W **52** F4
Kolomna Russia　55°8N 38°45E **18** C6
Kolomyya Ukraine　48°31N 25°2E **17** D13
Kolonodale Indonesia　2°0S 121°19E **37** E6
Kolpashevo Russia　58°20N 83°5E **26** D9
Kolpino Russia　59°44N 30°39E **18** C5
Kolskiy Poluostrov Russia 67°30N 38°0E **18** A6
Kolskiy Zaliv Russia　69°23N 34°0E **8** B26
Kolwezi
　Dem. Rep. of the Congo　10°40S 25°25E **54** G5
Kolyma → Russia　69°30N 161°0E **27** C17
Kolymskoye Nagorye
　Russia　63°0N 157°0E **27** C16
Kolyma = Kolmyskoye Nagorye
　Russia　55°0N 167°0E **27** D17
Komandorskiye Is. =
　Komandorskiye Ostrova
　Russia　55°0N 167°0E **27** D17
Komandorskiye Ostrova
　Russia　55°0N 167°0E **27** D17
Komárno Slovakia　47°49N 18°5E **17** E10
Komatipoort S. Africa　25°25S 31°55E **57** C5
Komatsu Japan　36°25N 136°30E **29** F8
Komatsushima Japan　34°0N 134°35E **29** H7
Komi □ Russia　64°0N 55°0E **18** B10
Kommamur Canal India　16°0N 80°25E **45** G5
Kommunarsk = Alchevsk
　Ukraine　48°30N 38°45E **19** E6
Kommunizma, Pik = imeni Ismail
　Samani, Pik Tajikistan　39°0N 72°2E **26** F8
Komodo Indonesia　8°37S 119°20E **37** F5
Komoran, Pulau
　Indonesia　8°18S 138°45E **37** F9
Komoro Japan　36°19N 138°26E **29** F9
Komotiní Greece　41°9N 25°26E **23** D11
Kompasberg S. Africa　31°45S 24°32E **56** D3
Kompong Chhnang = Kampong
　Chhnang Cambodia　12°20N 104°35E **39** F5
Kompong Chikreng
　Cambodia　13°5N 104°18E **38** F5
Kompong Kleang
　Cambodia　13°6N 104°8E **38** F5
Kompong Luong
　Cambodia　11°49N 104°48E **39** G5
Kompong Pranak
　Cambodia　13°35N 104°55E **38** F5
Kompong Som = Kampong Saom
　Cambodia　10°38N 103°30E **39** G4
Kompong Som, Chhung =
　Kampong Saom, Chaak
　Cambodia　10°50N 103°32E **39** G4
Kompong Speu
　Cambodia　11°26N 104°32E **39** G5
Kompong Sralau
　Cambodia　14°5N 105°46E **38** E5
Kompong Thom
　Cambodia　12°35N 104°51E **38** F5
Kompong Trabeck
　Cambodia　13°6N 105°14E **38** F5
Kompong Trach
　Cambodia　11°25N 105°48E **39** G5
Kompong Tralach
　Cambodia　11°54N 104°47E **39** G5
Komrat = Comrat
　Moldova　46°18N 28°40E **17** E15
Komsberg S. Africa　32°40S 20°45E **56** D3
Komsomolets, Ostrov
　Russia　80°30N 95°0E **27** A10
Komsomolsk-na-Amur
　Russia　50°30N 137°0E **31** A16
Kon Ka Kinh △ Vietnam 14°19N 107°23E **38** E6
Kon Tum Vietnam　14°24N 108°0E **38** E7
Kon Tum, Plateau du
　Vietnam　14°30N 108°30E **38** E7
Konar □ Afghan.　34°30N 71°3E **40** B7
Konarak India　19°54N 86°7E **44** E8
Konārī Iran　28°13N 51°36E **47** D6
Konch India　26°0N 79°10E **43** G8
Kondagaon India　19°35N 81°35E **44** E5
Kondoa Tanzania　4°55S 35°50E **54** E7
Kondopoga Russia　62°12N 34°17E **18** B5
Kondratyevo Russia　57°22N 98°15E **27** D10
Kondukur India　15°12N 79°57E **45** G4
Köneürgench
　Turkmenistan　42°19N 59°10E **26** E6
Konevo Russia　62°8N 39°20E **18** B6
Kong = Khong →
　Cambodia　13°32N 105°58E **38** F5
Kong Côte d'Ivoire　8°54N 4°36W **52** G5
Kong, Koh Cambodia　11°20N 103°0E **39** G4
Kong Christian IX.s Land
　Greenland　68°0N 36°0W **4** C6
Kong Christian X.s Land
　Greenland　74°0N 29°0W **4** B6
Kong Frederik IX.s Land
　Greenland　67°0N 52°0W **4** C5
Kong Frederik VI.s Kyst
　Greenland　63°0N 43°0W **4** C5
Kong Frederik VIII.s Land
　Greenland　78°30N 26°0W **4** B6
Kong Oscar Fjord
　Greenland　72°20N 24°0W **4** B6
Konglu Myanmar　27°13N 97°57E **41** F20
Kongola Namibia　17°45S 23°20E **56** A3

Kongolo
　Dem. Rep. of the Congo　5°22S 27°0E **54** F5
Kongsberg Norway　59°39N 9°39E **9** G13
Kongsvinger Norway　60°12N 12°2E **9** F15
Kongur Shan China　38°34N 75°18E **30** D4
Konin Poland　52°12N 18°15E **17** B10
Konjic Bos.-H.　43°42N 17°58E **23** C7
Konkiep Namibia　26°49S 17°15E **56** C2
Konnur India　16°14N 74°49E **45** F2
Konosha Russia　61°0N 40°5E **18** B7
Kōnosu Japan　36°3N 139°31E **29** F9
Konotop Ukraine　51°12N 33°7E **19** D5
Konqi He → China　40°45N 90°10E **30** C6
Końskie Poland　51°15N 20°23E **17** C11
Konstanz Germany　47°40N 9°10E **16** E5
Kont Iran　26°55N 61°50E **47** E9
Konta India　17°48N 81°23E **44** F5
Kontagora Nigeria　10°23N 5°27E **52** F7
Kontiolahti Finland　62°46N 29°50E **8** E23
Konya Turkey　37°52N 32°35E **46** B2
Koocanusa, L. Canada　49°20N 115°15W **76** B6
Kookynie Australia　29°17S 121°22E **61** E3
Koolyanobbing Australia 30°48S 119°36E **61** E2
Koonibba Australia　31°54S 133°25E **63** E1
Koorawatha Australia　34°2S 148°33E **63** E4
Koorda Australia　30°48S 117°35E **61** F2
Kootenay → U.S.A.　49°19N 117°39W **70** D5
Kootenay △ Canada　51°0N 116°0W **70** C5
Kootenay L. Canada　49°45N 116°50W **76** B6
Kootjieskolk S. Africa　31°15S 20°21E **56** D3
Kopaonik Serbia　43°10N 20°50E **23** C9
Kopargaon India　19°51N 74°28E **44** E2
Kópavogur Iceland　64°6N 21°55W **8** D3
Koper Slovenia　45°31N 13°44E **16** F7
Kopervik Norway　59°17N 5°17E **9** G11
Kopet Dagh Asia　38°0N 58°0E **47** B8
Kopeysk Russia　55°7N 61°37E **26** D7
Kopi Australia　33°24S 135°40E **63** E2
Köping Sweden　59°31N 16°3E **9** G17
Koppa India　13°33N 75°21E **45** H2
Koppal India　15°23N 76°5E **45** G3
Koppeh Dāgh = Kopet Dagh
　Asia　38°0N 58°0E **47** B8
Koppies S. Africa　27°20S 27°30E **57** C4
Koprivnica Croatia　46°12N 16°42E **22** A7
Köprülü △ Turkey　37°20N 31°5E **46** B1
Kopychyntsi Ukraine　49°7N 25°58E **17** D13
Korab Macedonia　41°44N 20°40E **23** D9
Koral India　21°50N 73°12E **42** J5
Korangal India　17°6N 77°38E **44** F4
Koraput India　18°50N 82°40E **44** E6
Korba India　22°20N 82°45E **43** H10
Korbu, Gunung Malaysia 4°41N 101°18E **39** K3
Korçë Albania　40°37N 20°50E **23** D9
Korčula Croatia　42°56N 16°57E **22** C7
Kord Kūy Iran　36°48N 54°7E **47** B7
Kord Sheykh Iran　28°31N 52°53E **47** D7
Kordestān □ Iran　36°0N 47°0E **46** C5
Kordofân Sudan　13°0N 29°0E **53** F11
Korea, North ■ Asia　40°0N 127°0E **33** E14
Korea, South ■ Asia　36°0N 128°0E **33** G15
Korea Bay Korea　39°0N 124°0E **33** E13
Korea Strait Asia　34°0N 129°30E **33** H15
Koregaon India　17°40N 74°10E **44** F2
Korets Ukraine　50°40N 27°5E **17** C14
Korff Ice Rise Antarctica 79°0S 69°30W **5** D17
Korhogo Côte d'Ivoire　9°29N 5°28W **52** G4
Korinthiakos Kolpos
　Greece　38°16N 22°30E **23** E10
Kórinthos Greece　37°56N 22°55E **23** F10
Kōriyama Japan　37°24N 140°23E **28** F10
Korla China　41°45N 86°4E **30** C6
Kornešti = Cornești
　Moldova　47°21N 28°1E **17** E15
Koro Côte d'Ivoire　8°32N 7°30W **52** G4
Koro Fiji　17°19S 179°23E **59** a
Koro Sea Fiji　17°30S 179°45W **59** a
Korogwe Tanzania　5°5S 38°25E **54** F7
Korolevu Fiji　18°12S 177°46E **59** a
Koronadal Phil.　6°12N 124°51E **37** C6
Körös → Hungary　46°43N 20°12E **17** E11
Korosten Ukraine　50°54N 28°36E **17** C15
Korostyshev Ukraine　50°19N 29°4E **17** C15
Korovou Fiji　17°47S 178°32E **59** a
Koroyanitu △ Fiji　17°40S 177°35E **59** a
Korsakov Russia　46°36N 142°42E **27** E15
Korshunovo Russia　58°37N 110°10E **27** D12
Korsør Denmark　55°20N 11°9E **9** J14
Kortrijk Belgium　50°50N 3°17E **15** D3
Korwai India　24°7N 78°5E **42** G8
Koryakskoye Nagorye
　Russia　61°0N 171°0E **27** C18
Kos Greece　36°50N 27°15E **23** F12
Kosan N. Korea　38°52N 127°25E **33** E14
Kościan Poland　52°5N 16°40E **17** B9
Kosciusko U.S.A.　33°4N 89°35W **85** E10
Kosciuszko, Mt.
　Australia　36°27S 148°16E **63** F4
Kosgi Andhra Pradesh,
　India　16°58N 77°43E **44** F3
Kosgi Andhra Pradesh,
　India　15°51N 77°16E **45** G3
Kosha Sudan　20°50N 30°30E **53** D12
K'oshih = Kashi China　39°30N 76°2E **30** D4
Koshiki-Rettō Japan　31°45N 129°49E **29** J4
Kosi → India　28°41N 78°57E **43** E8
Košice Slovakia　48°42N 21°15E **17** D11
Koslan Russia　63°34N 49°14E **18** B8
Kosŏng N. Korea　38°40N 128°22E **33** E15
Kosovo ■ Europe　42°30N 21°0E **23** C9
Kosovska Mitrovica = Mitrovicë
　Kosovo　42°54N 20°52E **23** C9
Kossou, L. de Côte d'Ivoire　6°59N 5°31W **52** G4
Koster S. Africa　25°52S 26°54E **56** C4
Kôstî Sudan　13°8N 32°43E **53** F12
Kostomuksha Russia　64°41N 30°49E **8** D24
Kostopil Ukraine　50°51N 26°22E **17** C14
Kostroma Russia　57°50N 40°58E **18** C7
Kostrzyn Poland　52°35N 14°39E **16** B8

Koszalin *Poland* 54°11N 16°8E **16** A9
Kot Addu *Pakistan* 30°30N 71°0E **42** D4
Kot Kapura *India* 30°35N 74°50E **42** D6
Kot Moman *Pakistan* 32°13N 73°0E **42** C5
Kot Sultan *Pakistan* 30°46N 70°56E **42** D4
Kota *India* 25°14N 75°49E **42** G6
Kota Barrage *India* 25°6N 75°51E **42** G6
Kota Belud *Malaysia* 6°21N 116°26E **36** C5
Kota Bharu *Malaysia* 6°7N 102°14E **39** J4
Kota I. = Loaita I.
    S. China Sea 10°41N 114°25E **36** B4
Kota Kinabalu *Malaysia* 6°0N 116°4E **36** C5
Kota Tinggi *Malaysia* 1°44N 103°53E **39** M4
Kotaagung *Indonesia* 5°38S 104°29E **36** F2
Kotabaru *Indonesia* 3°20S 116°20E **36** E5
Kotabumi *Indonesia* 4°49S 104°54E **36** E2
Kotamobagu *Indonesia* 0°57N 124°31E **37** D6
Kotapad *India* 19°9N 82°21E **44** E6
Kotapinang *Indonesia* 1°53N 100°5E **39** M3
Kotcho L. *Canada* 59°7N 121°12W **70** B4
Kotdwara *India* 29°45N 78°32E **43** E8
Kotelnich *Russia* 58°22N 48°24E **18** C8
Kotelnikovo *Russia* 47°38N 43°8E **19** E7
Kotelnyy, Ostrov *Russia* 75°10N 139°0E **27** B14
Kothapet *India* 19°21N 79°28E **44** E4
Kothari →‎ *India* 25°20N 75°4E **42** G6
Kothi *Chhattisgarh, India* 23°21N 82°3E **43** H10
Kothi *Mad. P., India* 24°45N 80°40E **43** G9
Kotiro *Pakistan* 26°17N 67°13E **42** F2
Kotka *Finland* 60°28N 26°58E **8** F22
Kotlas *Russia* 61°17N 46°43E **18** B8
Kotli *Pakistan* 33°30N 73°55E **42** C5
Kotlik *U.S.A.* 63°2N 163°33W **74** C7
Kotma *India* 23°12N 81°54E **43** H9
Kotor *Montenegro* 42°25N 18°47E **23** C8
Kotovsk *Ukraine* 47°45N 29°35E **17** E15
Kotputli *India* 27°43N 76°12E **42** F7
Kotri *Pakistan* 25°22N 68°22E **42** G3
Kotri →‎ *India* 19°15N 80°35E **44** E5
Kottagudem *India* 17°30N 80°40E **44** F5
Kottayam *India* 9°35N 76°33E **45** K3
Kotto →‎ *C.A.R.* 4°14N 22°2E **54** D4
Kottur *India* 10°34N 76°56E **45** J3
Kotturu *India* 14°45N 76°10E **45** G3
Kotu Group *Tonga* 20°0S 174°45W **59** c
Kotuy →‎ *Russia* 71°54N 102°6E **27** B11
Kotzebue *U.S.A.* 66°53N 162°39W **74** B7
Kotzebue Sound *U.S.A.* 66°20N 163°0W **74** B7
Kouchibouguac △
    Canada 46°50N 65°0W **73** C6
Koudougou *Burkina Faso* 12°10N 2°20W **52** F5
Kougaberge *S. Africa* 33°48S 23°50E **56** D3
Kouilou →‎ *Congo* 4°10S 12°5E **54** E2
Koukdjuak →‎ *Canada* 66°43N 73°0W **69** D17
Koula Moutou *Gabon* 1°15S 12°25E **54** E2
Koulen = Kulen
    Cambodia 13°50N 104°40E **38** F5
Koumala *Australia* 21°38S 149°15E **62** C4
Koumra *Chad* 8°50N 17°35E **53** G9
Kountze *U.S.A.* 30°22N 94°19W **84** F7
Kourou *Fr. Guiana* 5°9N 52°39W **93** B8
Kouroussa *Guinea* 10°45N 9°45W **52** F4
Kousséri *Cameroon* 12°0N 14°55E **53** F8
Koutiala *Mali* 12°25N 5°23W **52** F4
Kouvola *Finland* 60°52N 26°43E **8** F22
Kovdor *Russia* 67°34N 30°24E **8** C24
Kovel *Ukraine* 51°11N 24°38E **17** C13
Kovrov *Russia* 56°25N 41°25E **18** C7
Kovur *Andhra Pradesh, India* 17°3N 81°39E **44** F5
Kovur *Andhra Pradesh,
    India* 14°30N 80°1E **45** G5
Kowanyama *Australia* 15°29S 141°44E **62** B3
Kowanyama ☼ *Australia* 15°20S 141°47E **62** B3
Kowŏn *N. Korea* 39°26N 127°14E **33** E14
Koyampattur = Coimbatore
    India 11°2N 76°59E **45** J3
Köyceğiz *Turkey* 36°57N 28°40E **23** F13
Koyukuk →‎ *U.S.A.* 64°55N 157°32W **74** C8
Koza = Okinawa *Japan* 26°19N 127°46E **29** L3
Kozan *Turkey* 37°26N 35°50E **46** B2
Kozani *Greece* 40°19N 21°47E **23** D9
Kozhikode *India* 11°15N 75°43E **45** J2
Kozhva *Russia* 65°10N 57°0E **18** A10
Kōzu-Shima *Japan* 34°13N 139°10E **29** G9
Kozyatyn *Ukraine* 49°45N 28°50E **17** D15
Kozyrevsk *Russia* 56°3N 159°51E **27** D16
Kpalimé *Togo* 6°57N 0°44E **52** G6
Kra, Isthmus of = Kra, Kho Khot
    Thailand 10°15N 99°30E **39** G2
Kra, Kho Khot *Thailand* 10°15N 99°30E **39** G2
Kra Buri *Thailand* 10°22N 98°46E **39** G2
Kraai →‎ *S. Africa* 30°40S 26°45E **56** D4
Krabi *Thailand* 8°4N 98°55E **39** H2
Kracheh = Kratie
    Cambodia 12°32N 106°10E **38** F6
Kragan *Indonesia* 6°43S 111°38E **37** G14
Kragerø *Norway* 58°52N 9°25E **9** G13
Kragujevac *Serbia* 44°2N 20°56E **23** B9
Krakatau = Rakata, Pulau
    Indonesia 6°10S 105°20E **37** G11
Krakatoa = Rakata, Pulau
    Indonesia 6°10S 105°20E **37** G11
Krakor *Cambodia* 12°32N 104°12E **38** F5
Kraków *Poland* 50°4N 19°57E **17** C10
Kraksaan *Indonesia* 7°43S 113°23E **37** G16
Kralanh *Cambodia* 13°35N 103°25E **38** F4
Kraljevo *Serbia* 43°44N 20°41E **23** C9
Kramatorsk *Ukraine* 48°50N 37°30E **19** E6
Kramfors *Sweden* 62°55N 17°48E **8** E17
Kranj *Slovenia* 46°16N 14°22E **16** E8
Krankskop *S. Africa* 28°0S 30°47E **57** C5
Krasavino *Russia* 60°58N 46°29E **18** B8
Krasieo Res. *Thailand* 14°49N 99°30E **38** E2
Kraskino *Russia* 42°44N 130°48E **30** C5
Kraśnik *Poland* 50°55N 22°15E **17** C12
Krasnoarmeysk *Russia* 51°0N 45°42E **26** D5
Krasnodar *Russia* 45°5N 39°0E **19** E6
Krasnokamensk *Russia* 50°3N 118°0E **27** D12
Krasnokamsk *Russia* 58°4N 55°48E **18** C10
Krasnoperekopsk *Ukraine* 46°0N 33°54E **19** E5

Krasnorechenskiy
    Russia 44°41N 135°14E **28** B7
Krasnoselkup *Russia* 65°20N 82°10E **26** C9
Krasnoturinsk *Russia* 59°46N 60°12E **18** C11
Krasnoufimsk *Russia* 56°36N 57°38E **18** C10
Krasnouralsk *Russia* 58°21N 60°3E **18** C11
Krasnovishersk *Russia* 60°23N 57°3E **18** B10
Krasnoyarsk *Russia* 56°8N 93°0E **27** D10
Krasnoyarskoye Vdkhr.
    Russia 56°0N 92°30E **27** D10
Krasnyy Kut *Russia* 50°50N 47°0E **19** D8
Krasnyy Luch *Ukraine* 48°13N 39°0E **19** E6
Krasnyy Yar *Russia* 46°43N 48°23E **19** E8
Kratie *Cambodia* 12°32N 106°10E **38** F6
Krau *Indonesia* 3°19S 140°5E **37** E10
Kravanh, Chuor Phnum
    Cambodia 12°0N 103°32E **39** G4
Krefeld *Germany* 51°20N 6°33E **16** C4
Kremen *Croatia* 44°28N 15°53E **16** F8
Kremenchuk *Ukraine* 49°5N 33°25E **19** E5
Kremenchuksk Vdskh.
    Ukraine 49°20N 32°30E **19** E5
Kremenets *Ukraine* 50°8N 25°43E **17** C13
Kremmling *U.S.A.* 40°4N 106°24W **76** F10
Krems an der Donau
    Austria 48°25N 15°36E **16** D8
Kretinga *Lithuania* 55°53N 21°15E **9** J19
Kribi *Cameroon* 2°57N 9°56E **54** D1
Krichev = Krychaw
    Belarus 53°40N 31°41E **17** B16
Kril'on, Mys *Russia* 45°53N 142°5E **28** B11
Krishna →‎ *India* 15°57N 80°59E **45** G5
Krishnagiri *India* 12°32N 78°16E **45** H4
Krishnanagar *India* 23°24N 88°33E **43** H13
Krishnaraja Sagar *India* 12°20N 76°30E **45** H3
Kristiansand *Norway* 58°8N 8°1E **9** G13
Kristianstad *Sweden* 56°2N 14°9E **9** H16
Kristiansund *Norway* 63°7N 7°45E **8** E12
Kristiinankaupunki
    Finland 62°16N 21°21E **8** E19
Kristinehamn *Sweden* 59°18N 14°7E **9** G16
Kristinestad = Kristiinankaupunki
    Finland 62°16N 21°21E **8** E19
Kriti *Greece* 35°15N 25°0E **23** G11
Krivoy Rog = Kryvyy Rih
    Ukraine 47°51N 33°20E **19** E5
Krk *Croatia* 45°8N 14°40E **16** F8
Krokodil = Umgwenya →‎
    Mozam. 25°14S 32°18E **57** C5
Krong Kaoh Kong
    Cambodia 11°37N 102°59E **39** G4
Kronprins Frederik Land
    Greenland 81°0N 45°0W **4** B5
Kronprins Olav Kyst
    Antarctica 69°0S 42°0E **5** C5
Kronprinsesse Märtha Kyst
    Antarctica 73°30S 10°0W **5** D2
Kronshtadt *Russia* 59°57N 29°51E **18** B4
Kroonstad *S. Africa* 27°43S 27°19E **56** C4
Kropotkin *Russia* 45°28N 40°28E **19** E7
Krosno *Poland* 49°42N 21°46E **17** D11
Krotoszyn *Poland* 51°42N 17°23E **17** C9
Kruger △ *S. Africa* 24°50S 31°40E **57** B5
Krugersdorp *S. Africa* 26°5S 27°46E **57** C4
Kruisfontein *S. Africa* 33°59S 24°43E **56** D3
Krupki *Belarus* 54°19N 29°8E **17** A15
Kruševac *Serbia* 43°35N 21°28E **23** C9
Kruzenshterna, Proliv
    Russia 48°0N 154°0E **27** E16
Krychaw *Belarus* 53°40N 31°41E **17** B16
Krymskiy Poluostrov = Krymskyy
    Pivostriv *Ukraine* 45°0N 34°0E **19** F5
Krymskyy Pivostriv
    Ukraine 45°0N 34°0E **19** F5
Kryvyy Rih *Ukraine* 47°51N 33°20E **19** E5
Ksar el Kebir *Morocco* 35°0N 6°0W **52** B4
Ksar es Souk = Er Rachidia
    Morocco 31°58N 4°20W **52** B5
Kuah *Malaysia* 6°19N 99°51E **39** J2
Kuala Belait *Malaysia* 4°35N 114°11E **36** D4
Kuala Berang *Malaysia* 5°5N 103°1E **39** K4
Kuala Dungun = Dungun
    Malaysia 4°45N 103°25E **39** K4
Kuala Kangsar *Malaysia* 4°46N 100°56E **39** K3
Kuala Kelawang *Malaysia* 2°56N 102°5E **39** L4
Kuala Kerai *Malaysia* 5°30N 102°12E **39** K4
Kuala Kubu Bharu
    Malaysia 3°34N 101°39E **39** L3
Kuala Lipis *Malaysia* 4°10N 102°3E **39** K4
Kuala Lumpur *Malaysia* 3°9N 101°41E **39** L3
Kuala Lumpur Int. ✈ (KUL)
    Malaysia 2°44N 101°42E **39** L3
Kuala Nerang *Malaysia* 6°16N 100°37E **39** J3
Kuala Pilah *Malaysia* 2°45N 102°15E **39** L4
Kuala Rompin *Malaysia* 2°49N 103°29E **39** L4
Kuala Selangor *Malaysia* 3°20N 101°15E **39** L3
Kuala Sepetang *Malaysia* 4°49N 100°28E **39** K3
Kuala Terengganu
    Malaysia 5°20N 103°8E **39** K4
Kualajelai *Indonesia* 2°58S 110°46E **36** E4
Kualakapuas *Indonesia* 2°55S 114°20E **36** E4
Kualakurun *Indonesia* 1°10S 113°50E **36** E4
Kualapembuang
    Indonesia 3°14S 112°38E **36** E4
Kualasimpang *Indonesia* 4°17N 98°3E **36** D1
Kuancheng *China* 40°37N 118°30E **33** D10
Kuandang *Indonesia* 0°56N 123°1E **37** D6
Kuandian *China* 40°45N 124°45E **33** D13
Kuangchou = Guangzhou
    China 23°5N 113°10E **35** F9
Kuantan *Malaysia* 3°49N 103°20E **39** L4
Kuba = Quba *Azerbaijan* 41°21N 48°32E **19** F8
Kuban →‎ *Russia* 45°20N 37°30E **19** E6
Kubokawa = Shimanto
    Japan 33°12N 133°8E **29** H6
Kubu *Indonesia* 8°16S 115°35E **37** J18
Kubutambahan *Indonesia* 8°5S 115°10E **37** J18
Kucar, Tanjung
    Indonesia 8°39S 114°34E **37** K18
Kuchaman *India* 27°13N 74°47E **42** F6

Kuchchaveli *Sri Lanka* 8°49N 81°6E **45** K5
Kuchinda *India* 21°44N 84°21E **43** J11
Kuching *Malaysia* 1°33N 110°25E **36** D4
Kuchino-eruba-Jima
    Japan 30°28N 130°12E **29** J5
Kuchino-Shima *Japan* 29°57N 129°55E **29** K4
Kuchinotsu *Japan* 32°36N 130°11E **29** H5
Kucing = Kuching
    Malaysia 1°33N 110°25E **36** D4
Kud →‎ *Pakistan* 26°5N 66°20E **42** F2
Kuda *India* 23°10N 71°15E **42** H4
Kudal *India* 16°2N 73°41E **45** F1
Kudalier →‎ *India* 18°35N 79°48E **44** E4
Kudat *Malaysia* 6°55N 116°55E **36** C5
Kudremukh *India* 13°15N 75°20E **45** H2
Kudus *Indonesia* 6°48S 110°51E **37** G14
Kudymkar *Russia* 59°1N 54°39E **18** C9
Kueiyang = Guiyang
    China 26°32N 106°40E **34** D6
Kufra Oasis = Al Kufrah
    Libya 24°17N 23°15E **53** D10
Kufstein *Austria* 47°35N 12°11E **16** E7
Kugaaruk = Pelly Bay
    Canada 68°38N 89°50W **69** D14
Kugluktuk *Canada* 67°50N 115°5W **68** D8
Kugong I. *Canada* 56°18N 79°50W **72** A4
Kūh Dasht *Iran* 33°32N 47°36E **46** C5
Kūhak *Iran* 27°12N 63°10E **47** E9
Kuhan *Pakistan* 28°19N 67°14E **42** E2
Kūhbonān *Iran* 31°23N 56°19E **47** D8
Kūhestak *Iran* 26°47N 57°2E **47** E8
Kuhin *Iran* 36°22N 49°40E **47** B6
Kūhīrī *Iran* 26°55N 61°2E **47** E9
Kuhmo *Finland* 64°7N 29°31E **8** D23
Kuhn Chae △ *Thailand* 19°8N 99°24E **38** C2
Kūhpāyeh *Esfahan, Iran* 32°44N 52°20E **47** C7
Kūhpāyeh *Kermān, Iran* 30°35N 57°15E **47** D8
Kūhrān, Kūh-e *Iran* 26°46N 58°12E **47** E8
Kui Buri *Thailand* 12°3N 99°52E **39** F2
Kuiburi △ *Thailand* 12°10N 99°37E **39** F2
Kuichong *China* 22°38N 114°25E **31** a
Kuiseb →‎ *Namibia* 22°59S 14°31E **56** B1
Kuito *Angola* 12°22S 16°55E **55** G3
Kuiu I. *U.S.A.* 57°45N 134°10W **70** B2
Kujang *N. Korea* 39°57N 126°1E **33** E14
Kuji *Japan* 40°11N 141°46E **28** D10
Kujū-San *Japan* 33°5N 131°15E **29** H5
Kukës *Albania* 42°5N 20°27E **23** C9
Kukup *Malaysia* 1°20N 103°27E **39** d
Kukup, Pulau *Malaysia* 1°18N 103°25E **39** d
Kula *Turkey* 38°32N 28°40E **23** E13
K'ula Shan *Bhutan* 28°14N 90°36E **30** F7
Kulachi *Pakistan* 31°56N 70°27E **42** D4
Kulai *Malaysia* 1°44N 103°35E **39** M4
Kulasekarappattinam *India* 8°20N 78°5E **45** K4
Kuldīga *Latvia* 56°58N 21°59E **9** H19
Kulen *Cambodia* 13°50N 104°40E **38** F5
Kulgam *India* 33°36N 75°2E **43** C6
Kulgera *Australia* 25°50S 133°18E **62** D1
Kulim *Malaysia* 5°22N 100°34E **39** K3
Kulin *Australia* 32°40S 118°2E **61** F2
Kulittalai *India* 10°55N 78°25E **45** J4
Kulkayu = Hartley Bay
    Canada 53°25N 129°15W **70** C3
Kullu *India* 31°58N 77°6E **42** D7
Kůlob *Tajikistan* 37°55N 69°50E **26** F7
Kulsary = Qulsary
    Kazakhstan 46°59N 54°1E **19** E9
Kulti *India* 23°43N 86°50E **43** H12
Kulunda *Russia* 52°35N 78°57E **26** D8
Kulungar *Afghan.* 34°0N 69°2E **42** C3
Kulwin *Australia* 35°2S 142°42E **63** F3
Kulyab = Kůlob *Tajikistan* 37°55N 69°50E **26** F7
Kuma →‎ *Russia* 44°55N 47°0E **19** F8
Kumaganum *Nigeria* 13°8N 10°38E **53** F8
Kumagaya *Japan* 36°9N 139°22E **29** F9
Kumai *Indonesia* 2°44S 111°43E **36** E4
Kumamba, Kepulauan
    Indonesia 1°36S 138°45E **37** E9
Kumamoto *Japan* 32°45N 130°45E **29** H5
Kumamoto □ *Japan* 32°55N 130°55E **29** H5
Kumanovo *Macedonia* 42°9N 21°42E **23** C9
Kumara *N.Z.* 42°37S 171°12E **59** E3
Kumarina Roadhouse
    Australia 24°41S 119°32E **61** D2
Kumasi *Ghana* 6°41N 1°38W **52** G5
Kumba *Cameroon* 4°36N 9°24E **54** D1
Kumbakonam = India* 10°58N 79°25E **45** J4
Kumbarilla *Australia* 27°15S 150°55E **63** D5
Kumbhalgarh △ *India* 25°10N 73°35E **42** G5
Kumbhraj *India* 24°22N 77°3E **42** G7
Kumbia *Australia* 26°41S 151°39E **63** D5
Kumbukkan Oya →‎
    Sri Lanka 6°35N 81°40E **45** L5
Kŭmch'on *N. Korea* 38°10N 126°29E **33** E14
Kume-Shima *Japan* 26°20N 126°47E **29** L3
Kumertau *Russia* 52°45N 55°57E **18** D10
Kumharsain *India* 31°19N 77°27E **42** D7
Kumo *Nigeria* 10°1N 11°12E **53** F8
Kumon Bum *Myanmar* 26°30N 97°15E **41** F20
Kumta *India* 14°29N 74°25E **45** G2
Kumtag Shamo *China* 39°40N 92°0E **30** D7
Kumul = Hami *China* 42°55N 93°25E **30** C7
Kuna *U.S.A.* 43°30N 116°25W **76** E5
Kunashir, Ostrov *Russia* 44°0N 146°0E **27** E15
Kunchha *Nepal* 28°8N 84°22E **43** E11
Kunda *Estonia* 59°30N 26°34E **9** G22
Kunda *India* 25°43N 81°31E **43** G9
Kundar →‎ *Pakistan* 31°56N 69°19E **42** D3
Kundian *Pakistan* 32°27N 71°28E **42** C4
Kundla *India* 21°21N 71°25E **42** J4
Kunene →‎ *Namibia* 17°20S 11°50E **56** B1
Kunga →‎ *Bangla.* 21°46N 89°30E **43** J13
Kungrad = Qŭnghirot
    Uzbekistan 43°2N 58°50E **26** E6
Kungsbacka *Sweden* 57°30N 12°5E **9** H15

Kungur *Russia* 57°25N 56°57E **18** C10
Kungurri *Australia* 21°4S 148°45E **62** b
Kunhar →‎ *Pakistan* 34°20N 73°30E **43** B5
Kuningan *Indonesia* 6°59S 108°29E **37** G13
Kunlong *Myanmar* 23°20N 98°50E **34** F2
Kunlun *Antarctica* 80°25S 77°7E **5** E6
Kunlun Shan *Asia* 36°0N 86°30E **30** D6
Kunlun Shankou *China* 35°38N 94°4E **30** D7
Kunming *China* 25°1N 102°41E **34** E4
Kunming Changshui Int. ✈ (KMG)
    China 24°59N 102°45E **34** E4
Kunmunya ◎ *Australia* 15°26S 124°42E **60** C3
Kunnamkulam *India* 10°38N 76°7E **45** J3
Kunnunurra *Australia* 15°40S 128°50E **60** C4
Kunwari →‎ *India* 26°26N 79°11E **43** F8
Kunya-Urgench = Köneürgench
    Turkmenistan 42°19N 59°10E **26** E6
Kuopio *Finland* 62°53N 27°35E **8** E22
Kupa →‎ *Croatia* 45°28N 16°24E **16** F9
Kupang *Indonesia* 10°19S 123°39E **37** F6
Kupreanof I. *U.S.A.* 56°50N 133°30W **70** B2
Kupyansk-Uzlovoi
    Ukraine 49°40N 37°43E **19** E6
Kuqa *China* 41°35N 82°30E **30** C5
Kür →‎ *Azerbaijan* 39°29N 49°15E **19** G8
Kür Dili *Azerbaijan* 39°3N 49°13E **47** B6
Kura = Kür →‎ *Azerbaijan* 39°29N 49°15E **19** G8
Kuranda *Australia* 16°48S 145°35E **62** B4
Kuranga *India* 22°4N 69°10E **42** H3
Kurashiki *Japan* 34°40N 133°50E **29** G6
Kurayn *Si. Arabia* 27°39N 49°50E **47** E6
Kurayoshi *Japan* 35°26N 133°50E **29** G6
Kürchatov *Kazakhstan* 50°45N 78°32E **26** D8
Kurduvadi *India* 18°8N 75°29E **44** E2
Kure *Japan* 34°14N 132°32E **29** G6
Kure I. *U.S.A.* 28°25N 178°25W **75** K4
Kuressaare *Estonia* 58°15N 22°30E **9** G20
Kurgan *Russia* 55°26N 65°18E **26** D7
Kuri *India* 26°37N 70°43E **42** F4
Kuria Maria Is. = Ḥallāniyat,
    Jazā'ir al *Oman* 17°30S 55°58E **49** D6
Kurichchi *India* 11°36N 77°35E **45** J3
Kuridala *Australia* 21°16S 140°29E **62** C3
Kurigram *Bangla.* 25°49N 89°39E **41** G16
Kurikka *Finland* 62°36N 22°24E **8** E20
Kuril Basin *Pac. Oc.* 47°0N 150°0E **4** E15
Kuril Is. = Kurilskiye Ostrova
    Russia 45°0N 150°0E **27** E16
Kuril-Kamchatka Trench
    Pac. Oc. 44°0N 153°0E **64** C7
Kurilsk *Russia* 45°14N 147°53E **27** E15
Kurilskiye Ostrova
    Russia 45°0N 150°0E **27** E16
Kurino *Japan* 31°57N 130°43E **29** J5
Kurinskaya Kosa = Kür Dili
    Azerbaijan 39°3N 49°13E **47** B6
Kurkheda *India* 20°37N 80°12E **44** D5
Kurlkuta ◎ *Australia* 24°0S 127°5E **60** D4
Kurnool *India* 15°45N 78°0E **45** G4
Kuro-Shima *Kagoshima,
    Japan* 30°50N 129°57E **29** J4
Kuro-Shima *Okinawa,
    Japan* 24°14N 124°1E **29** M2
Kurow *N.Z.* 44°44S 170°29E **59** F3
Kurram →‎ *Pakistan* 32°36N 71°20E **42** C4
Kurri Kurri *Australia* 32°50S 151°28E **63** E5
Kurrimine *Australia* 17°47S 146°6E **62** B4
Kurse Korhi *India* 20°14N 80°46E **44** D5
Kurseong = Karsiyang
    India 26°56N 88°18E **43** F13
Kurshskiy Zaliv *Russia* 55°9N 21°6E **9** J19
Kursk *Russia* 51°42N 36°11E **18** D6
Kuruçay *Turkey* 39°39N 38°29E **46** B3
Kurukshetra = Thanesar
    India 30°1N 76°52E **42** D7
Kuruktag *China* 41°0N 89°0E **30** C6
Kuruman *S. Africa* 27°28S 23°28E **56** C3
Kuruman →‎ *S. Africa* 26°56S 20°39E **56** C3
Kurume *Japan* 33°15N 130°30E **29** H5
Kurunegala *Sri Lanka* 7°30N 80°23E **45** L5
Kurya *Russia* 61°42N 57°9E **18** B10
Kus Gölü *Turkey* 40°10N 27°55E **23** D12
Kuşadası *Turkey* 37°52N 27°15E **23** F12
Kusamba *Indonesia* 8°34S 115°27E **37** K18
Kusatsu *Japan* 36°37N 138°36E **29** F9
Kusawa L. *Canada* 60°20N 136°13W **70** A1
Kushalgarh *India* 23°10N 74°27E **42** H6
Kushalnagar *India* 12°14N 75°57E **45** H2
Kushikino *Japan* 31°44N 130°16E **29** J5
Kushima *Japan* 31°29N 131°14E **29** J5
Kushimoto *Japan* 33°28N 135°47E **29** H7
Kushiro *Japan* 43°0N 144°25E **28** C12
Kushiro-Gawa →‎
    Japan 42°59N 144°23E **28** C12
Kushiro Shitsugen △
    Japan 43°9N 144°26E **28** C12
Kŭm-Shima *N. Korea* 38°10N 126°29E **33** E14
Kume-Shima *Japan* 26°20N 126°47E **29** L3
Kümertau *Russia* 52°45N 55°57E **18** D10
Kushk *Iran* 28°46N 56°51E **47** D8
Kushka = Serhetabat
    Turkmenistan 35°20N 62°18E **47** C9
Kushol *India* 33°40N 76°36E **43** C7
Kushtia *Bangla.* 23°55N 89°5E **41** H16
Kushva *Russia* 58°18N 59°45E **18** C10
Kuskokwim →‎ *U.S.A.* 60°5N 162°25W **74** C7
Kuskokwim B. *U.S.A.* 59°45N 162°25W **74** C7
Kuskokwim Mts. *U.S.A.* 62°30N 156°0W **74** C8
Kusmi *India* 23°17N 83°55E **43** H10
Kusŏng *N. Korea* 39°59N 125°25E **33** E13
Kussharo-Ko *Japan* 43°38N 144°21E **28** C12
Kustanay = Qostanay
    Kazakhstan 53°10N 63°35E **26** D7
Kut, Ko *Thailand* 11°40N 102°35E **39** G4
Kuta *Indonesia* 8°43S 115°11E **37** K18
Kutaraja = Banda Aceh
    Indonesia 5°35N 95°20E **36** C1
Kutch, Gulf of = Kachchh, Gulf of
    India 22°50N 69°15E **42** H3
Kutch, Rann of = Kachchh, Rann
    of *India* 24°0N 70°0E **42** H4

Kutiyana *India* 21°36N 70°2E **42** J4
Kutno *Poland* 52°15N 19°23E **17** B10
Kutru *India* 19°5N 80°46E **44** E5
Kutse *Botswana* 21°7S 22°16E **56** B3
Kuttabul *Australia* 21°5S 148°54E **62** b
Kutu *Dem. Rep. of the Congo* 2°40S 18°11E **54** E3
Kutum *Sudan* 14°10N 24°40E **53** F10
Kuujjuaq *Canada* 58°6N 68°15W **69** F18
Kuujjuarapik *Canada* 55°20N 77°35W **72** A4
Kuusamo *Finland* 65°57N 29°8E **8** D23
Kuusankoski *Finland* 60°55N 26°38E **8** F22
Kuwait = Al Kuwayt
    Kuwait 29°30N 48°0E **46** D5
Kuwait ■ *Asia* 29°30N 47°30E **46** D5
Kuwana *Japan* 35°5N 136°43E **29** G8
Kuwana →‎ *India* 26°25N 83°15E **43** F10
Kuybyshev = Samara
    Russia 53°8N 50°6E **18** D9
Kuybyshev *Russia* 55°27N 78°19E **26** D8
Kuybyshevskoye Vdkhr.
    Russia 55°2N 49°30E **18** C8
Kuye He →‎ *China* 38°23N 110°46E **32** E6
Küyeh *Iran* 38°45N 47°57E **46** B5
Kuyto, Ozero *Russia* 65°6N 31°20E **8** D24
Kuytun *China* 44°25N 85°0E **30** C6
Kuyumba *Russia* 60°58N 96°59E **27** C10
Kuzey Anadolu Dağları
    Turkey 41°0N 36°45E **19** F6
Kuzhitturai *India* 8°18N 77°11E **45** K3
Kuznetsk *Russia* 53°12N 46°40E **18** D8
Kuzomen *Russia* 66°22N 36°50E **18** A6
Kvænangen *Norway* 70°5N 21°15E **8** A19
Kvaløya *Norway* 69°40N 18°30E **8** B18
Kvarner *Croatia* 44°50N 14°10E **16** F8
Kvarnerič *Croatia* 44°43N 14°37E **16** F8
Kwabhaca *S. Africa* 30°51S 29°0E **57** D4
Kwai = Khwae Noi →‎
    Thailand 14°1N 99°32E **38** E2
Kwajalein *Marshall Is.* 9°5N 167°20E **64** G8
Kwakhanai *Botswana* 21°39S 21°16E **56** B3
Kwakoegron *Suriname* 5°12N 55°25W **93** B7
KwaMashu *S. Africa* 29°45S 30°58E **57** C5
Kwando →‎ *Africa* 18°27S 23°32E **56** A3
Kwangdaeri *N. Korea* 40°34N 127°33E **33** D14
Kwango →‎
    Dem. Rep. of the Congo 3°14S 17°22E **54** E3
Kwangsi-Chuang = Guangxi
    Zhuangzu Zizhiqu □
    China 24°0N 109°0E **34** F7
Kwangtung = Guangdong □
    China 23°0N 113°0E **35** F9
Kwataboahegan →‎
    Canada 51°9N 80°50W **72** B3
Kwatisore *Indonesia* 3°18S 134°50E **37** E8
KwaZulu Natal □ *S. Africa* 29°0S 30°0E **57** C5
Kweichow = Guizhou □
    China 27°0N 107°0E **34** D6
Kwekwe *Zimbabwe* 18°58S 29°48E **55** H5
Kweneng □ *Botswana* 24°0S 25°0E **56** C3
Kwidzyn *Poland* 53°44N 18°55E **17** B10
Kwilu →‎
    Dem. Rep. of the Congo 3°22S 17°22E **54** E3
Kwinana *Australia* 32°15S 115°47E **61** F2
Kwoka *Indonesia* 0°31S 132°27E **37** E8
Kyabra Cr. →‎ *Australia* 25°36S 142°55E **63** D3
Kyabram *Australia* 36°19S 145°4E **63** F4
Kyaikto *Myanmar* 17°20N 97°3E **38** D1
Kyaing Tong = Keng Tung
    Myanmar 21°18N 99°39E **38** B2
Kyakhta *Russia* 50°30N 106°25E **27** D11
Kyancutta *Australia* 33°8S 135°33E **63** E2
Kyaukpadaung *Myanmar* 20°52N 95°8E **41** J19
Kyaukpyu *Myanmar* 19°28N 93°30E **41** K18
Kyaukse *Myanmar* 21°36N 96°10E **41** J20
Kyburz *U.S.A.* 38°47N 120°18W **78** G6
Kyelang *India* 32°35N 77°2E **42** C7
Kyklades *Greece* 37°0N 24°30E **23** F11
Kyle *Canada* 50°50N 108°2W **71** C7
Kyle *U.S.A.* 29°59N 97°53W **84** F6
Kyle of Lochalsh *U.K.* 57°17N 5°44W **11** D3
Kymijoki →‎ *Finland* 60°30N 26°55E **8** F22
Kymmene älv = Kymijoki →‎
    Finland 60°30N 26°55E **8** F22
Kyneton *Australia* 37°10S 144°29E **63** F3
Kynuna *Australia* 21°37S 141°55E **62** C3
Kyō-ga-Saki *Japan* 35°45N 135°15E **29** G7
Kyoga, L. *Uganda* 1°35N 33°0E **54** D6
Kyogle *Australia* 28°40S 153°0E **63** D5
Kyŏngju = Gyeongju
    S. Korea 35°51N 129°14E **33** G15
Kyŏngsŏng *N. Korea* 41°35N 129°36E **33** D15
Kyonpyaw *Myanmar* 17°12N 95°10E **41** L19
Kyōto *Japan* 35°0N 135°45E **29** G7
Kyōto □ *Japan* 35°15N 135°45E **29** G7
Kypros = Cyprus ■ *Asia* 35°0N 33°0E **46** C2
Kyrenia *Cyprus* 35°20N 33°20E **46** C2
Kyrgyzstan ■ *Asia* 42°0N 75°0E **26** E8
Kyro älv = Kyrönjoki →‎
    Finland 63°14N 21°45E **8** E19
Kyrönjoki →‎ *Finland* 63°14N 21°45E **8** E19
Kystatyam *Russia* 67°20N 123°10E **27** C13
Kythira *Greece* 36°8N 23°0E **23** F10
Kythnos *Greece* 37°26N 24°27E **23** F11
Kyunhla *Myanmar* 23°25N 95°15E **41** H19
Kyuquot Sound *Canada* 50°2N 127°22W **70** D3
Kyūshū *Japan* 33°0N 131°0E **29** H5
Kyūshū □ *Japan* 33°0N 131°0E **29** H5
Kyūshū-Palau Ridge
    Pac. Oc. 20°0N 136°0E **64** E5
Kyūshū-Sanchi *Japan* 32°35N 131°17E **29** H5
Kyustendil *Bulgaria* 42°16N 22°41E **23** C10
Kyusyur *Russia* 70°19N 127°30E **27** B13
Kyyiv *Ukraine* 50°30N 30°28E **17** C16
Kyyivske Vdskh. *Ukraine* 51°0N 30°25E **17** C16
Kyzyl *Russia* 51°50N 94°30E **30** A7
Kyzyl Kum *Uzbekistan* 42°30N 65°0E **26** E7
Kyzyl-Kyya *Kyrgyzstan* 40°16N 72°8E **26** E8
Kyzyl Orda = Qyzylorda
    Kazakhstan 44°48N 65°28E **26** E7

L

La Alcarria *Spain* 40°31N 2°45W **21** B4
La Amistad △ *Cent. Amer.* 9°28N 83°18W **88** E3
La Asunción *Venezuela* 11°2N 63°51W **92** A6
La Baie *Canada* 48°19N 70°53W **73** C5
La Banda *Argentina* 27°45S 64°10W **94** B3
La Barca *Mexico* 20°17N 102°34W **86** C4
La Barge *U.S.A.* 42°16N 110°12W **76** E8
La Barra *Nic.* 12°54N 83°33W **88** D3
La Belle *U.S.A.* 26°46N 81°26W **85** H14
La Biche → *Canada* 59°57N 123°50W **70** B4
La Biche, L. *Canada* 54°50N 112°3W **70** C6
La Brea *Trin. & Tob.* 10°15N 61°37W **93** K15
La Calera *Chile* 32°50S 71°10W **94** C1
La Campana △ *Chile* 32°58S 71°14W **94** C1
La Carlota *Argentina* 33°30S 63°20W **94** C3
La Ceiba *Honduras* 15°40N 86°50W **88** C2
La Chaux-de-Fonds *Switz.* 47°7N 6°50E **20** C7
La Chorrera *Panama* 8°53N 79°47W **88** E4
La Cocha *Argentina* 27°50S 65°40W **94** B2
La Concepción *Panama* 8°31N 82°37W **88** E3
La Concordia *Mexico* 16°5N 92°38W **87** D6
La Coruña = A Coruña
  Spain 43°20N 8°25W **21** A1
La Crescent *U.S.A.* 43°50N 91°18W **80** D8
La Crete *Canada* 58°11N 116°24W **70** B5
La Crosse *Kans., U.S.A.* 38°32N 99°18W **80** F4
La Crosse *Wis., U.S.A.* 43°48N 91°15W **80** D8
La Cruz *Costa Rica* 11°4N 85°39W **88** D2
La Cruz *Mexico* 23°55N 106°54W **86** C3
La Désirade *Guadeloupe* 16°18N 61°3W **88** b
La Digue *Seychelles* 4°20S 55°51'E **55** b
La Esperanza *Cuba* 22°46N 83°44W **88** B3
La Esperanza *Honduras* 14°15N 88°10W **88** D2
La Estrada = A Estrada
  Spain 42°43N 8°27W **21** A1
La Fayette *U.S.A.* 34°42N 85°17W **85** D12
La Fé *Cuba* 22°2N 84°15W **88** B3
La Follette *U.S.A.* 36°23N 84°7W **85** C12
La Gi *Vietnam* 10°40N 107°45E **39** G6
La Grande *U.S.A.* 45°20N 118°5W **76** D4
La Grande → *Canada* 53°50N 79°0W **72** B4
La Grande 3, Rés. *Canada* 53°40N 75°10W **72** B4
La Grande 4, Rés. *Canada* 54°0N 73°15W **72** B5
La Grange *Calif., U.S.A.* 37°42N 120°27W **78** H6
La Grange *Ga., U.S.A.* 33°2N 85°2W **85** E12
La Grange *Ky., U.S.A.* 38°24N 85°23W **81** F11
La Grange *Tex., U.S.A.* 29°54N 96°52W **84** G6
La Guaira *Venezuela* 10°36N 66°56W **92** A5
La Guarda △ *Mexico* 29°20N 113°27W **86** B2
La Habana *Cuba* 23°8N 82°22W **88** B3
La Independencia *Mexico* 16°15N 92°1W **87** D6
La Isabela *Dom. Rep.* 19°58N 71°2W **89** C5
La Junta *U.S.A.* 37°59N 103°33W **76** H12
La Libertad = Puerto Libertad
  Mexico 29°55N 112°43W **86** B2
La Libertad *Guatemala* 16°47N 90°7W **88** C1
La Ligua *Chile* 32°30S 71°16W **94** C1
La Línea de la Concepción
  Spain 36°15N 5°23W **21** D3
La Loche *Canada* 56°29N 109°26W **71** B7
La Louvière *Belgium* 50°27N 4°10E **15** D4
La Lune *Trin. & Tob.* 10°3N 61°22W **93** K15
La Malbaie *Canada* 47°40N 70°10W **73** C5
La Malinche △ *Mexico* 19°15N 98°3W **87** D5
La Mancha *Spain* 39°10N 2°54W **21** C4
La Martre, L. *Canada* 63°15N 117°55W **70** A5
La Mercy ✈ (DUR)
  S. Africa 29°37S 31°7'E **57** C5
La Mesa *Mexico* 32°30N 116°57W **79** N10
La Mesa *U.S.A.* 32°46N 117°1W **79** N9
La Mesilla *U.S.A.* 32°16N 106°48W **77** K10
La Moure *U.S.A.* 46°21N 98°18W **80** B4
La Negra *Chile* 23°46S 70°18W **94** A1
La Oroya *Peru* 11°32S 75°54W **92** F3
La Palma *Canary Is.* 28°40N 17°50W **52** C2
La Palma *Panama* 8°15N 78°0W **88** E4
La Palma del Condado
  Spain 37°21N 6°38W **21** D2
La Paloma *Chile* 30°35S 71°0W **94** C1
La Pampa □ *Argentina* 36°50S 66°0W **94** D2
La Paragua *Venezuela* 6°50N 63°20W **92** B6
La Paz *Entre Ríos,*
  Argentina 30°50S 59°45W **94** C4
La Paz *San Luis, Argentina* 33°30S 67°20W **94** C2
La Paz *Bolivia* 16°20S 68°10W **92** G5
La Paz *Honduras* 14°20N 87°47W **88** D2
La Paz *Mexico* 24°10N 110°18W **86** C2
La Paz Centro *Nic.* 12°20N 86°41W **88** D2
La Pedrera *Colombia* 1°18S 69°43W **92** D5
La Pérade *Canada* 46°35N 72°12W **73** C5
La Perla *Mexico* 28°18N 104°32W **86** B4
La Perouse Str. *Asia* 45°40N 142°0E **28** B11
La Pesca *Mexico* 23°46N 97°47W **87** C5
La Piedad *Mexico* 20°21N 102°0W **86** C4
La Pine *U.S.A.* 43°40N 121°30W **76** E3
La Plata *Argentina* 35°0S 57°55W **94** C4
La Pocatière *Canada* 47°22N 70°2W **73** C5
La Porte *U.S.A.* 29°40N 95°1W **84** G7
La Purísima *Mexico* 26°10N 112°4W **86** B2
La Push *U.S.A.* 47°55N 124°38W **78** C2
La Quiaca *Argentina* 22°5S 65°35W **94** A2
La Rioja *Argentina* 29°20S 67°0W **94** B2
La Rioja □ *Argentina* 29°30S 67°0W **94** B2
La Rioja □ *Spain* 42°20N 2°20W **21** A4
La Robla *Spain* 42°50N 5°41W **21** A3
La Roche-en-Ardenne
  Belgium 50°11N 5°35E **15** D5
La Roche-sur-Yon *France* 46°40N 1°25W **20** C3
La Rochelle *France* 46°10N 1°9W **20** C3
La Roda *Spain* 39°13N 2°15W **21** C4
La Romaine *Canada* 50°13N 60°40W **73** B7
La Romana *Dom. Rep.* 18°27N 68°57W **89** C6
La Ronge *Canada* 55°5N 105°20W **71** B7
La Rumorosa *Mexico* 32°34N 116°6W **79** N10
La Salle *U.S.A.* 41°20N 89°6W **80** E9
La Sarre *Canada* 48°45N 79°15W **72** C4
La Scie *Canada* 49°57N 55°36W **73** C8
La Selva Beach *U.S.A.* 36°56N 121°51W **78** J5

La Serena *Chile* 29°55S 71°10W **94** B1
La Seu d'Urgell *Spain* 42°22N 1°23E **21** A6
La Seyne-sur-Mer *France* 43°7N 5°52E **20** E6
La Soufrière *St. Vincent* 13°20N 61°11W **89** D7
La Spézia *Italy* 44°7N 9°50E **20** D8
La Tagua *Colombia* 0°3N 74°40W **92** C4
La Tortuga, I. *Venezuela* 11°0N 65°22W **89** D6
La Trinité *Martinique* 14°45N 60°58W **88** c
La Tuque *Canada* 47°30N 72°50W **72** C5
La Unión *Chile* 40°10S 73°0W **96** E2
La Unión *El Salv.* 13°20N 87°50W **88** D2
La Unión *Mexico* 17°58N 101°49W **86** D4
La Urbana *Venezuela* 7°8N 66°56W **92** B5
La Vache Pt.
  Trin. & Tob. 10°47N 61°28W **93** K15
La Vall d'Uixó *Spain* 39°49N 0°15W **21** C5
La Vega *Dom. Rep.* 19°20N 70°30W **89** C5
La Vela de Coro
  Venezuela 11°27N 69°34W **92** A5
La Venta *Mexico* 18°5N 94°3W **87** D6
La Vergne *U.S.A.* 36°1N 86°35W **85** C11
La Villa Joiosa = Villajoyosa
  Spain 38°30N 0°12W **21** C5
Laascaanood = Las Anod
  Somalia 8°26N 47°19E **49** F4
Labasa *Fiji* 16°30S 179°27E **59** a
Labdah = Leptis Magna
  Libya 32°40N 14°12E **53** B8
Labe = Elbe → *Europe* 53°50N 9°0E **16** B5
Labé *Guinea* 11°24N 12°16W **52** F3
Laberge, L. *Canada* 61°11N 135°12W **70** A1
Labinsk *Russia* 44°40N 40°48E **19** F7
Labis *Malaysia* 2°22N 103°2E **39** L4
Laborie *St. Lucia* 13°45N 61°2W **89** f
Laboulaye *Argentina* 34°10S 63°30W **94** C3
Labrador *Canada* 53°20N 61°0W **73** B7
Labrador City *Canada* 52°57N 66°55W **73** B6
Labrador Sea *Atl. Oc.* 57°0N 54°0W **69** F21
Lábrea *Brazil* 7°15S 64°51W **92** E6
Labuan □ *Malaysia* 5°20N 115°12E **36** C4
Labuha *Indonesia* 0°30S 127°30E **37** E7
Labuhan *Indonesia* 6°22S 105°50E **37** G11
Labuhanbajo *Indonesia* 8°28S 119°54E **37** F6
Labuhanbilik *Indonesia* 2°31N 100°10E **39** L3
Labuk, Telok *Malaysia* 6°10N 117°50E **36** C5
Labyrinth, L. *Australia* 30°40S 135°11E **63** E2
Labytnangi *Russia* 66°39N 66°21E **18** A12
Lac-Bouchette *Canada* 48°16N 72°11W **73** C5
Lac-Édouard *Canada* 47°40N 72°16W **73** C5
Lac La Biche *Canada* 54°45N 111°58W **70** C6
Lac la Martre = Wha Ti
  Canada 63°8N 117°16W **68** E8
Lac La Ronge △ *Canada* 55°9N 104°41W **71** B7
Lac-Mégantic *Canada* 45°35N 70°53W **73** C5
Lac Thien *Vietnam* 12°25N 108°11E **38** F7
Lacanau *France* 44°58N 1°5W **20** D3
Lacantún → *Mexico* 16°36N 90°39W **87** D6
Laccadive Is. = Lakshadweep Is.
  India 10°0N 72°30E **45** J1
Lacepede B. *Australia* 36°40S 139°40E **63** F2
Lacepede Is. *Australia* 16°55S 122°0E **60** C3
Lacey *U.S.A.* 47°7N 122°49W **78** C4
Lachhmangarh *India* 27°50N 75°4E **42** F6
Lachi *Pakistan* 33°25N 71°20E **42** C4
Lachlan → *Australia* 34°22S 143°55E **63** E3
Lachute *Canada* 45°39N 74°21W **72** C5
Lackagh Hills *Ireland* 54°16N 8°10W **10** B3
Lackawanna *U.S.A.* 42°50N 78°50W **82** D6
Lackawaxen *U.S.A.* 41°29N 74°59W **83** E10
Lacolle *Canada* 45°5N 73°22W **83** A11
Lacombe *Canada* 52°30N 113°44W **70** C6
Lacona *U.S.A.* 43°39N 76°10W **83** C8
Laconia *U.S.A.* 43°32N 71°28W **83** C13
Ladakh Ra. *India* 34°0N 78°0E **43** C8
Ladismith *S. Africa* 33°28S 21°15E **56** E3
Lādīz *Iran* 28°55N 61°15E **47** D9
Ladnun *India* 27°38N 74°25E **42** F6
Ladoga, L. = Ladozhskoye Ozero
  Russia 61°15N 30°30E **8** F24
Ladozhskoye Ozero
  Russia 61°15N 30°30E **8** F24
Lady Elliott I. *Australia* 24°7S 152°42E **62** C5
Lady Frere *S. Africa* 31°42S 27°14E **56** D4
Lady Grey *S. Africa* 30°43S 27°13E **56** D4
Ladybrand *S. Africa* 29°9S 27°29E **56** D4
Ladysmith *Canada* 49°0N 123°49W **78** B3
Ladysmith *S. Africa* 28°32S 29°46E **57** C4
Ladysmith *U.S.A.* 45°28N 91°12W **80** C8
Lae *Papua N. G.* 6°40S 147°2E **58** B7
Laem Chabang *Thailand* 13°5N 100°53E **38** F3
Laem Ngop *Thailand* 12°10N 102°26E **39** F4
Laem Son △ *Thailand* 9°29N 98°24E **39** H2
Læsø *Denmark* 57°15N 11°5E **9** H14
Lafayette *Ind., U.S.A.* 40°25N 86°54W **80** E10
Lafayette *La., U.S.A.* 30°14N 92°1W **84** F8
Lafayette *Tenn., U.S.A.* 36°31N 86°2W **85** C11
Laferte → *Canada* 61°53N 117°44W **70** A5
Lafia *Nigeria* 8°30N 8°34E **52** G7
Lafleche *Canada* 49°45N 106°40W **71** D7
Laful *India* 7°10N 93°52E **45** L11
Lagan → *U.K.* 54°36N 5°55W **10** B6
Lagarfljót → *Iceland* 65°40N 14°18W **8** D6
Lagdo, L. de *Cameroon* 8°40N 14°0E **53** G8
Lågen → *Oppland, Norway* 61°8N 10°25E **8** F14
Lågen → *Vestfold, Norway* 59°3N 10°3E **9** G14
Lages *Brazil* 27°48S 50°20W **95** B5
Lagoa do Peixe △ *Brazil* 31°12S 50°55W **95** C5
Lagoa Vermelha *Brazil* 28°13S 51°32W **95** B5
Lagonoy G. *Phil.* 13°35N 123°50E **37** B6
Lagos *Nigeria* 6°25N 3°27E **52** G6
Lagos *Portugal* 37°5N 8°41W **21** D1
Lagos de Moreno
  Mexico 21°21N 101°55W **86** C4
Lagrange = Bidyadanga
  Australia 18°45S 121°43E **60** C3
Lagrange B. *Australia* 18°38S 121°42E **60** C3
Laguna *Brazil* 28°30S 48°50W **95** B6
Laguna, Sa. de la
  Mexico 23°35N 109°55W **86** C3

Laguna Beach *U.S.A.* 33°33N 117°47W **79** M9
Laguna de la Restinga △
  Venezuela 10°58N 64°0W **89** D6
Laguna de Lachuá △
  Guatemala 15°55N 90°40W **88** C1
Laguna del Laja △ *Chile* 37°27S 71°20W **94** D1
Laguna del Tigre △
  Guatemala 17°32N 90°56W **88** C1
Laguna Limpia *Argentina* 26°32S 59°45W **94** B4
Lagunas *Chile* 21°0S 69°45W **94** A2
Lagunas *Peru* 5°10S 75°35W **92** E3
Lagunas de Chacahua △
  Mexico 16°0N 97°43W **87** D5
Lagunas de Montebello △
  Mexico 16°4N 91°42W **87** D6
Lahad Datu *Malaysia* 5°0N 118°20E **37** D5
Lahad Datu, Telok
  Malaysia 4°50N 118°20E **37** D5
Lahan Sai *Thailand* 14°25N 102°52E **38** E4
Lahanam *Laos* 16°16N 105°16E **38** D5
Lahar *India* 26°12N 78°57E **43** F8
Laharpur *India* 27°43N 80°56E **43** F9
Lahat *Indonesia* 3°45S 103°30E **36** E2
Lahewa *Indonesia* 1°22N 97°12E **36** D1
Lähījān *Iran* 37°10N 50°6E **47** B6
Lahn → *Germany* 50°19N 7°37E **16** C4
Laholm *Sweden* 56°30N 13°2E **9** H15
Lahore *Pakistan* 31°32N 74°22E **42** D6
Lahri *Pakistan* 29°11N 68°13E **42** E3
Lährūd *Iran* 38°30N 47°52E **46** B5
Lahti *Finland* 60°58N 25°40E **8** F21
Lahtis = Lahti *Finland* 60°58N 25°40E **8** F21
Lahugala Kitulana △
  Sri Lanka 6°50N 81°40E **45** L5
Laï *Chad* 9°25N 16°18E **53** G9
Lai Chau *Vietnam* 22°5N 103°3E **34** F4
Lai'an *China* 32°28N 118°30E **35** A12
Laibin *China* 23°42N 109°14E **34** F7
Laifeng *China* 29°27N 109°20E **34** C7
Laila = Layla *Si. Arabia* 22°10N 46°40E **49** C4
Laingsburg *S. Africa* 33°9S 20°52E **56** D3
Lainioälven → *Sweden* 67°35N 22°40E **8** C20
Lairg *U.K.* 58°2N 4°24W **11** C4
Laiwu *China* 36°15N 117°40E **33** F9
Laixi *China* 36°50N 120°31E **33** F11
Laiyang *China* 36°59N 120°45E **33** F11
Laiyuan *China* 39°20N 114°40E **32** E8
Laizhou *China* 37°8N 119°57E **33** F10
Laizhou Wan *China* 37°30N 119°30E **33** F10
Lajamanu *Australia* 18°23S 130°38E **60** C5
Lak Sao *Laos* 18°11N 104°59E **38** C5
Lakaband *Pakistan* 31°2N 69°15E **42** D3
Lake *U.S.A.* 44°33N 110°24W **76** D8
Lake Alpine *U.S.A.* 38°29N 120°0W **78** G7
Lake Andes *U.S.A.* 43°9N 98°32W **80** D4
Lake Arthur *U.S.A.* 30°5N 92°41W **84** F8
Lake Bindegolly △
  Australia 28°0S 144°12E **63** D3
Lake Cargelligo *Australia* 33°15S 146°22E **63** E4
Lake Charles *U.S.A.* 30°14N 93°13W **84** F8
Lake City *Colo., U.S.A.* 38°2N 107°19W **76** G10
Lake City *Fla., U.S.A.* 30°11N 82°38W **85** G13
Lake City *Mich., U.S.A.* 44°20N 85°13W **81** C11
Lake City *Minn., U.S.A.* 44°27N 92°16W **80** C7
Lake City *Pa., U.S.A.* 42°1N 80°21W **82** D4
Lake City *S.C., U.S.A.* 33°52N 79°45W **85** E15
Lake Cowichan *Canada* 48°49N 124°3W **70** D4
Lake District △ *U.K.* 54°30N 3°21W **12** C4
Lake Elsinore *U.S.A.* 33°38N 117°20W **79** M9
Lake Eyre △ *Australia* 28°30S 137°31E **63** D2
Lake Gairdner △
  Australia 31°41S 135°51E **63** E2
Lake George *U.S.A.* 43°26N 73°43W **83** C11
Lake Grace *Australia* 33°7S 118°28E **61** F2
Lake Gregory ○
  Australia 20°12S 127°27E **60** D4
Lake Harbour = Kimmirut
  Canada 62°50N 69°50W **69** E18
Lake Havasu City
  U.S.A. 34°27N 114°22W **79** L12
Lake Hughes *U.S.A.* 34°41N 118°26W **79** L8
Lake Isabella *U.S.A.* 35°38N 118°28W **79** K8
Lake Jackson *U.S.A.* 29°3N 95°27W **84** G7
Lake King *Australia* 33°5S 119°45E **61** F2
Lake Lenore *U.S.A.* 52°24N 104°59W **71** C8
Lake Louise *Canada* 51°30N 116°10W **70** C5
Lake Mackay ○
  Australia 22°30S 129°0E **60** D4
Lake Mead △ *U.S.A.* 36°30N 114°22W **79** K12
Lake Meredith △
  U.S.A. 35°50N 101°50W **84** D4
Lake Mills *U.S.A.* 43°25N 93°32W **80** D7
Lake Placid *U.S.A.* 44°17N 73°59W **83** B11
Lake Pleasant *U.S.A.* 43°28N 74°25W **83** C10
Lake Providence *U.S.A.* 32°48N 91°10W **84** E9
Lake Roosevelt △ *U.S.A.* 48°5N 118°14W **76** B4
Lake St. Peter *Canada* 45°18N 78°2W **82** A6
Lake Stevens *U.S.A.* 48°1N 122°4W **78** C4
Lake Superior ○ *Canada* 47°45N 84°45W **72** C3
Lake Torrens △
  Australia 30°55S 137°40E **63** E2
Lake Village *U.S.A.* 33°20N 91°17W **84** E9
Lake Wales *U.S.A.* 27°54N 81°35W **85** H14
Lake Worth *U.S.A.* 26°37N 80°3W **85** H14
Lakeba *Fiji* 18°13S 178°47W **59** a
Lakeba Passage *Fiji* 18°0S 178°45W **59** a
Lakefield = Rinyirru △
  Australia 15°24S 144°26E **62** B3
Lakefield *Canada* 44°25N 78°16W **82** B6
Lakehurst *U.S.A.* 40°1N 74°19W **83** F10
Lakeland *Australia* 15°49S 144°57E **62** B3
Lakeland *U.S.A.* 28°3N 81°57W **85** G14
Lakemba = Lakeba *Fiji* 18°13S 178°47W **59** a
Lakeport *Calif., U.S.A.* 39°3N 122°55W **78** F4
Lakeport *Mich., U.S.A.* 43°7N 82°30W **82** C2
Lakes Entrance *Australia* 37°50S 148°0E **63** F4
Lakeside *Calif., U.S.A.* 32°52N 116°55W **79** N10
Lakeside *Nebr., U.S.A.* 42°3N 102°26W **80** D2
Lakeview *U.S.A.* 42°11N 120°21W **76** E3
Lakeville *U.S.A.* 44°39N 93°14W **80** C7

Laguna de la Restinga △
Lakewood *Colo., U.S.A.* 39°42N 105°4W **76** G11
Lakewood *N.J., U.S.A.* 40°6N 74°13W **83** F10
Lakewood *N.Y., U.S.A.* 42°6N 79°19W **82** D5
Lakewood *Ohio, U.S.A.* 41°28N 81°47W **82** E3
Lakewood *Wash.,*
  U.S.A. 47°11N 122°32W **78** C4
Lakha *India* 26°9N 70°54E **42** F4
Lakhimpur *India* 27°57N 80°46E **43** F9
Lakhisarai *India* 25°11N 86°5E **43** G12
Lakhnadon *India* 22°36N 79°36E **43** H8
Lakhnau = Lucknow
  India 26°50N 81°0E **43** F9
Lakhonpheng *Laos* 15°54N 105°34E **38** E5
Lakhpat *India* 23°48N 68°47E **42** H3
Lakin *U.S.A.* 37°57N 101°15W **80** G3
Lakitusaki → *Canada* 54°21N 82°25W **72** B3
Lakki *Pakistan* 32°36N 70°55E **42** C4
Lakonikos Kolpos
  Greece 36°40N 22°40E **23** F10
Lakor *Indonesia* 8°15S 128°17E **37** F7
Lakota *Côte d'Ivoire* 5°50N 5°30W **52** G4
Lakota *U.S.A.* 48°2N 98°21W **80** A4
Laksar *India* 29°46N 78°3E **42** E8
Laksefjorden *Norway* 70°45N 26°50E **8** A22
Lakselv *Norway* 70°2N 25°0E **8** A21
Laksettipet *India* 18°52N 79°13E **44** E4
Lakshadweep □ *India* 10°0N 72°30E **45** J1
Lakshadweep Is. *India* 10°0N 72°30E **45** J1
Lakshmanpur *India* 22°58N 83°3E **43** H10
Lakshmeshwar *India* 15°9N 75°28E **45** G2
Lakshmikantapur *India* 22°5N 88°20E **43** H13
Lala Musa *Pakistan* 32°40N 73°57E **42** C5
Lalaghat *India* 24°30N 92°40E **41** G18
L'Albufera *Spain* 39°20N 0°27W **21** C5
Lalganj *India* 25°52N 85°13E **43** G11
Lalgola *India* 24°25N 88°15E **43** G13
Lālī *Iran* 32°21N 49°6E **47** C6
Lalibela *Ethiopia* 12°3N 39°0E **49** E2
Lalin *China* 45°12N 127°0E **33** B14
Lalín *Spain* 42°40N 8°5W **21** A1
Lalin He → *China* 45°32N 125°40E **33** B13
Lalitapur *India* 24°42N 78°28E **43** G8
Lalitpur *Nepal* 27°40N 85°20E **43** F11
Lalkua *India* 29°5N 79°31E **43** E8
Lalsot *India* 26°34N 76°20E **42** F7
Lam Nam Nan △
  Thailand 17°55N 100°28E **38** D3
Lam Pao Res. *Thailand* 16°50N 103°15E **38** D4
Lama Kara *Togo* 9°30N 1°15E **52** G6
Lamae *Thailand* 9°51N 99°5E **39** H2
Lamaing *Myanmar* 15°25N 97°53E **38** E1
Lamar *Colo., U.S.A.* 38°5N 102°37W **76** G12
Lamar *Mo., U.S.A.* 37°30N 94°16W **80** G6
Lamas *Peru* 6°28S 76°31W **92** E3
Lamayuru *India* 34°25N 76°56E **43** B7
Lambaréné *Gabon* 0°41S 10°12E **54** E2
Lambasa = Labasa *Fiji* 16°30S 179°27E **59** a
Lambay I. *Ireland* 53°29N 6°1W **10** C5
Lambert's Bay *S. Africa* 32°5S 18°17E **56** E2
Lambeth *Canada* 42°54N 81°18W **82** D3
Lame Deer *U.S.A.* 45°37N 106°40W **76** D10
Lamego *Portugal* 41°5N 7°52W **21** B2
Lamèque *Canada* 47°45N 64°38W **73** C7
Lameroo *Australia* 35°19S 140°33E **63** F3
Lamesa *U.S.A.* 32°44N 101°58W **84** E4
Lamia *Greece* 38°55N 22°26E **23** E10
Lamington △ *Australia* 28°13S 153°12E **63** D5
Lamoille → *U.S.A.* 44°38N 73°13W **83** B11
Lamon B. *Phil.* 14°30N 122°20E **37** B6
Lamont *Canada* 53°46N 112°50W **70** C6
Lamont *Calif., U.S.A.* 35°15N 118°55W **79** K8
Lamont *Wyo., U.S.A.* 42°13N 107°29W **76** E10
Lampa *Peru* 15°22S 70°22W **92** G4
Lampang *Thailand* 18°16N 99°32E **38** C2
Lampasas *U.S.A.* 31°4N 98°11W **84** F5
Lampazos de Naranjo
  Mexico 27°1N 100°31W **86** B4
Lampedusa *Medit. S.* 35°36N 12°40E **22** G5
Lampeter *U.K.* 52°7N 4°4W **13** E3
Lamphun *Thailand* 18°40N 99°2E **38** C2
Lampione *Medit. S.* 35°33N 12°20E **22** G5
Lampman *Canada* 49°25N 102°50W **71** D8
Lampung □ *Indonesia* 5°30S 104°30E **36** F2
Lamta *India* 22°8N 80°7E **43** H9
Lamu *Kenya* 2°16S 40°55E **54** E8
Lamy *U.S.A.* 35°29N 105°53W **77** J11
Lan Xian *China* 38°15N 111°35E **32** E6
Lan Yü *Taiwan* 22°4N 121°25E **35** F13
Lāna'i *U.S.A.* 20°50N 156°55W **75** L8
Lanak La *China* 34°27N 79°32E **43** B8
Lanak'o Shank'ou = Lanak La
  China 34°27N 79°32E **43** B8
Lanark *Canada* 45°1N 76°22W **83** A8
Lanark *U.K.* 55°40N 3°47W **11** F5
Lanbi Kyun *Myanmar* 10°50N 98°20E **39** G2
Lancang → *China* 22°36N 99°58E **34** F2
Lancang Jiang → *China* 21°40N 101°10E **34** G3
Lancashire □ *U.K.* 53°50N 2°48W **12** D5
Lancaster *Canada* 45°10N 74°30W **83** A10
Lancaster *U.K.* 54°3N 2°48W **12** C5
Lancaster *Calif., U.S.A.* 34°42N 118°8W **79** L8
Lancaster *Ky., U.S.A.* 37°37N 84°35W **81** G11
Lancaster *N.H., U.S.A.* 44°29N 71°34W **83** B13
Lancaster *Ohio, U.S.A.* 39°43N 82°36W **81** F12
Lancaster *Pa., U.S.A.* 40°2N 76°19W **83** F8
Lancaster *S.C., U.S.A.* 34°43N 80°46W **85** D14
Lancaster *Wis., U.S.A.* 42°51N 90°43W **80** D8
Lancaster Sd. *Canada* 74°13N 84°0W **69** C15
Lancelin *Australia* 31°0S 115°18E **61** F2
Lanchow = Lanzhou
  China 36°1N 103°52E **32** F2
Lanciano *Italy* 42°14N 14°23E **22** C6
Lancun *China* 36°25N 120°10E **33** F11
Land Between the Lakes △
  U.S.A. 36°25N 88°0W **85** C11
Landeck *Austria* 47°9N 10°34E **16** E6
Lander *U.S.A.* 42°50N 108°44W **76** E9
Lander → *Australia* 22°0S 132°0E **60** D5
Landes *France* 44°0N 1°0W **20** D3

Landfall I. *India* 13°40N 93°2E **45** H11
Landi Kotal *Pakistan* 34°7N 71°6E **42** B4
Landisburg *U.S.A.* 40°21N 77°19W **82** F7
Landmannalaugar *Iceland* 63°59N 19°4W **8** D4
Land's End *U.K.* 50°4N 5°44W **13** G2
Landsborough Cr. →
  Australia 22°28S 144°35E **62** C3
Landshut *Germany* 48°34N 12°8E **16** D7
Lanesboro *U.S.A.* 41°57N 75°34W **83** E9
Lanett *U.S.A.* 32°52N 85°12W **85** E12
Lang Shan *China* 41°0N 106°30E **32** D4
Lang Son *Vietnam* 21°52N 106°42E **34** G6
Lang Suan *Thailand* 9°57N 99°4E **39** H2
La'nga Co *China* 30°45N 81°15E **43** D9
Langar *Iran* 35°23N 60°25E **47** C9
Langara I. *Canada* 54°14N 133°1W **70** C2
Langao *Iran* 37°11N 50°8E **47** B6
Langdai *China* 26°6N 105°21E **34** D5
Langdon *U.S.A.* 48°46N 98°22W **80** A4
Langeberg *S. Africa* 33°55S 21°0E **56** E3
Langeberge *S. Africa* 28°15S 22°33E **56** C3
Langeland *Denmark* 54°56N 10°48E **9** J14
Langenburg *Canada* 50°51N 101°43W **71** C8
Langfang *China* 39°30N 116°41E **32** E9
Langholm *U.K.* 55°9N 3°0W **11** F5
Langjökull *Iceland* 64°39N 20°12W **8** D3
Langkawi, Pulau *Malaysia* 6°25N 99°45E **39** J2
Langklip *S. Africa* 28°12S 20°20E **56** C3
Langkon *Malaysia* 6°30N 116°40E **36** C5
Langley *Canada* 49°7N 122°39W **78** A4
Langøya *Norway* 68°45N 14°50E **8** B16
Langreo *Spain* 43°18N 5°40W **21** A3
Langres *France* 47°52N 5°20E **20** C6
Langres, Plateau de *France* 47°45N 5°3E **20** C6
Langsa *Indonesia* 4°30N 97°57E **36** D1
Langtang △ *Nepal* 28°10N 85°30E **43** E11
Langtou *China* 40°1N 124°19E **33** D13
Langtry *U.S.A.* 29°49N 101°34W **84** G4
Langu *Thailand* 6°53N 99°47E **39** J2
Languedoc *France* 43°58N 3°55E **20** E5
Langwang *China* 22°38N 113°27E **31** a
Langxi *China* 31°10N 119°12E **35** B12
Langzhong *China* 31°38N 105°58E **34** B5
Lanigan *Canada* 51°51N 105°2W **71** C7
Lanjigarh *India* 19°43N 83°23E **44** E6
Lankao *China* 34°48N 114°50E **32** G8
Länkäran *Azerbaijan* 38°48N 48°52E **47** B6
Lannion *France* 48°46N 3°29W **20** B2
L'Annonciation *Canada* 46°25N 74°55W **72** C5
Lanping *China* 26°28N 99°15E **34** D2
Lansang △ *Thailand* 16°45N 99°0E **38** D2
Lansdale *U.S.A.* 40°14N 75°17W **83** F9
Lansdowne *Australia* 31°48S 152°30E **63** E5
Lansdowne *Canada* 44°24N 76°1W **83** B8
Lansdowne *India* 29°50N 78°41E **43** E8
Lansdowne House = Neskantaga
  Canada 52°14N 87°53W **72** B2
L'Anse *U.S.A.* 46°45N 88°27W **80** B9
L'Anse au Loup *Canada* 51°32N 56°50W **73** B8
L'Anse aux Meadows
  Canada 51°36N 55°32W **73** B8
Lansford *U.S.A.* 40°50N 75°53W **83** F9
Lanshan *China* 25°24N 112°10E **35** E9
Lanshantou *China* 35°5N 119°20E **33** G10
Länsi-Turunmaa *Finland* 60°18N 22°18E **9** F20
Lansing *U.S.A.* 42°44N 84°33W **81** D11
Lanta, Ko *Thailand* 7°35N 99°3E **39** J2
Lantian *China* 34°11N 109°20E **32** G5
Lanusei *Italy* 39°52N 9°34E **22** E3
Lanxi *China* 29°13N 119°28E **35** C12
Lanzarote *Canary Is.* 29°0N 13°40W **52** C3
Lanzhou *China* 36°1N 103°52E **32** F2
Lao Cai *Vietnam* 22°30N 103°57E **34** F4
Laoag *Phil.* 18°7N 120°34E **37** A6
Laoang *Phil.* 12°32N 125°8E **37** B7
Laoha He → *China* 43°25N 120°35E **33** C11
Laohekou *China* 32°22N 111°38E **35** A8
Laois □ *Ireland* 52°57N 7°27W **10** D4
Laon *France* 49°33N 3°35E **20** B5
Laona *U.S.A.* 45°34N 88°40W **80** C9
Laos ■ *Asia* 17°45N 105°0E **38** D5
Lapa *Brazil* 25°46S 49°44W **95** B6
Lapeer *U.S.A.* 43°3N 83°19W **81** D12
Lapland = Lappland *Europe* 68°7N 24°0E **8** B21
LaPorte *U.S.A.* 41°36N 86°43W **80** E10
Laporte *Pa., U.S.A.* 41°25N 76°30W **83** E8
Lappeenranta *Finland* 61°3N 28°12E **8** F23
Lappland *Europe* 68°7N 24°0E **8** B21
Lappo = Lapua *Finland* 62°58N 23°0E **8** E20
Laprida *Argentina* 37°34S 60°45W **94** D3
Lâpseki *Turkey* 40°20N 26°41E **23** D12
Laptev Sea *Russia* 76°0N 125°0E **27** B13
Lapua *Finland* 62°58N 23°0E **8** E20
L'Áquila *Italy* 42°22N 13°22E **22** C5
Lār *Iran* 27°40N 54°14E **47** E7
Lārak *Iran* 26°51N 56°21E **47** E8
Laramie *U.S.A.* 41°19N 105°35W **76** F11
Laramie Mts. *U.S.A.* 42°0N 105°30W **76** F11
Laranda = Karaman
  Turkey 37°14N 33°13E **46** C3
Laranjeiras do Sul *Brazil* 25°23S 52°23W **95** B5
Larantuka *Indonesia* 8°21S 122°55E **37** F6
Larat *Indonesia* 7°0S 132°0E **37** F8
Larder Lake *Canada* 48°5N 79°40W **72** C4
Laredo *U.S.A.* 27°30N 99°30W **84** H5
Laredo Sd. *Canada* 52°30N 128°53W **70** C3
Largo *U.S.A.* 27°54N 82°47W **85** H13
Largs *U.K.* 55°47N 4°52W **11** F4
Lariang *Indonesia* 1°26S 119°17E **37** E5
Lario, Il = Como, L. di *Italy* 46°0N 9°11E **20** D8
Larimore *U.S.A.* 47°54N 97°38W **80** B5
Larisa *Greece* 39°36N 22°27E **23** E10
Larkana *Pakistan* 27°32N 68°18E **42** F3
Larnaca *Cyprus* 34°55N 33°38E **46** C2
Larne *U.K.* 54°51N 5°51W **10** B6
Larned *U.S.A.* 38°11N 99°6W **80** F4
Larrimah *Australia* 15°35S 133°12E **60** C5
Larsen Ice Shelf *Antarctica* 67°0S 62°0W **5** C17
Larvik *Norway* 59°4N 10°2E **9** G14

Las Animas U.S.A. 38°4N 103°13W 76 G12
Las Anod Somalia 8°26N 47°19E 49 F4
Las Brenãs Argentina 27°5S 61°7W 94 B3
Las Cejas Argentina 26°53S 64°44W 94 B3
Las Cejas Argentina 26°53S 64°44W 96 B4
Las Chimeneas Mexico 32°8N 116°5W 79 N10
Las Cruces U.S.A. 32°19N 106°47W 77 K10
Las Flores Argentina 36°10S 59°7W 94 D4
Las Heras Argentina 32°51S 68°49W 94 C2
Las Lajas Argentina 38°30S 70°25W 96 D2
Las Lomitas Argentina 24°43S 60°35W 94 A3
Las Palmas Argentina 27°8S 58°45W 94 B4
Las Palmas → Mexico 32°31N 116°58W 79 N10
Las Palmas de Gran Canaria
Canary Is. 28°7N 15°26W 52 C2
Las Piedras Uruguay 34°44S 56°14W 95 C4
Las Pipinas Argentina 35°30S 57°19W 94 D4
Las Plumas Argentina 43°40S 67°15W 96 E3
Las Rosas Argentina 32°30S 61°35W 94 C3
Las Tablas Panama 7°49N 80°14W 88 E3
Las Toscas Argentina 28°21S 59°18W 94 B4
Las Tunas Cuba 20°58N 76°59W 88 B4
Las Varillas Argentina 31°50S 62°50W 94 C3
Las Vegas U.S.A. 35°36N 105°13W 77 J11
Lascano Uruguay 33°35S 54°12W 95 C5
Lash-e Joveyn Afghan. 31°45N 61°30E 40 D2
Lashburn Canada 53°10N 109°40W 71 C7
Lashio Myanmar 22°56N 97°45E 41 H20
Lashkar India 26°10N 78°10E 42 F8
Läsjerd Iran 35°24N 53°4E 47 C7
Lassen Pk. U.S.A. 40°29N 121°30W 76 F3
Lassen Volcanic △
U.S.A. 40°30N 121°20W 76 F3
Last Mountain L. Canada 51°5N 105°14W 71 C7
Lastchance Cr. →
U.S.A. 40°2N 121°15W 78 E5
Lastoursville Gabon 0°55S 12°38E 54 E2
Lastovo Croatia 42°46N 16°55E 22 C7
Lat Yao Thailand 15°45N 99°48E 38 E2
Latacunga Ecuador 0°50S 78°35W 92 D3
Latady I. Antarctica 70°45S 74°35W 5 D17
Latakia = Al Lādhiqīyah
Syria 35°30N 35°45E 46 C2
Latchford Canada 47°20N 79°50W 72 C4
Late Tonga 18°48S 174°39W 59 c
Latehar India 23°45N 84°30E 43 H11
Latham Australia 29°44S 116°20E 61 E2
Lathi India 27°43N 71°23E 42 F4
Lathrop Wells U.S.A. 36°39N 116°24W 79 J10
Latina Italy 41°28N 12°52E 22 D5
Latium = Lazio □ Italy 42°10N 12°30E 22 C5
Laton U.S.A. 36°26N 119°41W 78 J7
Latouche Treville, C.
Australia 18°27S 121°49E 60 C3
Latrobe Australia 41°14S 146°30E 63 G4
Latrobe U.S.A. 40°19N 79°23W 82 F5
Latur India 18°25N 76°40E 44 E3
Latvia ■ Europe 56°50N 24°0E 9 H21
Lau Group Fiji 17°0S 178°30W 59 a
Lauchhammer Germany 51°29N 13°47E 16 C7
Lauge Koch Kyst
Greenland 75°45N 57°45W 69 B20
Laughlin U.S.A. 35°10N 114°34W 79 K12
Lauhanvuori △ Finland 62°8N 22°4E 8 E20
Laukaa Finland 62°24N 25°56E 8 E21
Launceston Australia 41°24S 147°8E 63 G4
Launceston U.K. 50°38N 4°22W 13 G3
Laune → Ireland 52°7N 9°47W 10 D2
Launglon Bok Myanmar 13°50N 97°54E 38 F1
Laura Australia 15°32S 144°32E 62 B3
Laurel Miss., U.S.A. 31°41N 89°8W 85 F10
Laurel Mont., U.S.A. 45°40N 108°46W 76 D9
Laurel Hill U.S.A. 40°14N 79°6W 82 F5
Laurencekirk U.K. 56°50N 2°28W 11 E6
Laurens U.S.A. 34°30N 82°1W 85 D13
Laurentian Plateau Canada 52°0N 70°0W 73 B6
Lauria Italy 40°2N 15°50E 22 E6
Laurie L. Canada 56°35N 101°57W 71 B8
Laurinburg U.S.A. 34°47N 79°28W 85 D15
Laurium U.S.A. 47°14N 88°27W 80 B9
Lausanne Switz. 46°32N 6°38E 20 C7
Laut Indonesia 4°45N 108°0E 36 D3
Laut, Pulau Indonesia 3°40S 116°10E 36 E5
Laut Kecil, Kepulauan
Indonesia 4°45S 115°40E 36 E5
Lautoka Fiji 17°37S 177°27E 59 a
Lauwersmeer △ Neths. 53°22N 6°11E 15 A6
Lava Beds △ U.S.A. 41°40N 121°30W 76 F3
Lavagh More Ireland 54°46N 8°6W 10 B3
Laval France 48°4N 0°48W 20 B3
Lavalle Argentina 28°15S 65°15W 94 B2
Lāvān Iran 26°48N 53°22E 47 E7
Lavant Canada 45°3N 76°42W 83 A8
Lāvar Meydān Iran 30°20N 54°30E 47 D7
Laverton Australia 28°44S 122°29E 61 E3
Lavras Brazil 21°20S 45°0W 95 A7
Lavrio Greece 37°40N 24°4E 23 F11
Lavumisa Eswatini 27°20S 31°55E 57 C5
Law-Racoviţă Antarctica 69°23S 76°23E 5 C6
Lawak I. = Nanshan I.
S. China Sea 10°45N 115°49E 36 B5
Lawaki Fiji 17°40S 178°35E 59 a
Lawas Malaysia 4°55N 115°25E 36 D5
Lawele Indonesia 5°13S 122°57E 37 F6
Lawn Hill = Boodjamulla △
Australia 18°15S 138°6E 62 B2
Lawqah Si. Arabia 29°49N 42°45E 46 D4
Lawrence N.Z. 45°55S 169°41E 59 F2
Lawrence Ind., U.S.A. 39°50N 86°2W 80 F10
Lawrence Kans., U.S.A. 38°58N 95°14W 80 F6
Lawrence Mass., U.S.A. 42°43N 71°10W 83 D13
Lawrenceburg Ind.,
U.S.A. 39°6N 84°52W 81 F11
Lawrenceburg Tenn.,
U.S.A. 35°14N 87°20W 85 D11
Lawrenceville Ga.,
U.S.A. 33°57N 83°59W 85 E13
Lawrenceville Pa., U.S.A. 41°59N 77°8W 82 E7
Laws U.S.A. 37°24N 118°20W 78 H8
Lawton U.S.A. 34°37N 98°25W 84 D5
Lawu Indonesia 7°40S 111°13E 37 G14
Laxford, L. U.K. 58°24N 5°6W 11 C3
Laxiwa Dam China 36°4N 101°11E 30 D9
Layla Si. Arabia 22°10N 46°40E 49 C4
Laylān Iraq 35°18N 44°31E 46 C5
Laysan I. U.S.A. 25°50N 171°50W 75 K5
Layton U.S.A. 41°4N 111°58W 76 F8
Laytonville U.S.A. 39°41N 123°29W 76 G2
Lazarev Russia 52°13N 141°30E 27 D15
Lazarev Sea S. Ocean 67°30S 3°0W 5 C2
Lázaro Cárdenas
Mexico 17°55N 102°11W 86 D4
Lazio □ Italy 42°10N 12°30E 22 C5
Lazo Russia 43°25N 133°55E 28 C6
Le Bic Canada 48°20N 68°41W 73 C6
Le Creusot France 46°48N 4°24E 20 C6
Le François Martinique 14°38N 60°57W 88 c
Le Gosier Guadeloupe 16°14N 61°29W 88 b
Le Gris Gris Mauritius 20°31S 57°32E 55 d
Le Havre France 49°30N 0°5E 20 B4
Le Lamentin Martinique 14°35N 61°2W 88 c
Le Mans France 48°0N 0°10E 20 C4
Le Marin Martinique 14°27N 60°55W 88 c
Le Mars U.S.A. 42°47N 96°10W 80 D5
Le Mont-St-Michel France 48°40N 1°30W 20 B3
Le Moule Guadeloupe 16°20N 61°22W 88 b
Le Moyne, L. Canada 56°45N 68°47W 73 A6
Le Port Réunion 20°56S 55°18E 55 c
Le Prêcheur Martinique 14°50N 61°12W 88 c
Le Puy-en-Velay France 45°3N 3°52E 20 D5
Le Raysville U.S.A. 41°50N 76°10W 83 E8
Le Robert Martinique 14°40N 60°56W 88 c
Le Roy U.S.A. 42°58N 77°59W 82 D7
Le St-Esprit Martinique 14°34N 60°56W 88 c
Le Sueur U.S.A. 44°28N 93°55W 80 C7
Le Tampon Réunion 21°16S 55°32E 55 c
Le Thuy Vietnam 17°14N 106°49E 38 D6
Le Touquet-Paris-Plage
France 50°30N 1°36E 20 A4
Le Tréport France 50°3N 1°20E 20 A4
Le Verdon-sur-Mer France 45°33N 1°4W 20 D3
Lea → U.K. 51°31N 0°1E 13 F8
Leach Cambodia 12°21N 103°46E 39 F4
Lead U.S.A. 44°21N 103°46W 80 C2
Leader Canada 50°50N 109°30W 71 C7
Leadville U.S.A. 39°15N 106°18W 76 G10
Leaf → U.S.A. 30°59N 88°44W 85 F10
Leaf Rapids Canada 56°30N 99°59W 71 B9
League City U.S.A. 29°31N 95°6W 84 G7
Leamington Canada 42°3N 82°36W 82 D2
Leamington U.S.A. 39°32N 112°17W 76 G7
Leamington Spa = Royal
Leamington Spa U.K. 52°18N 1°31W 13 E6
Le'an China 27°22N 115°48E 35 D10
Leander U.S.A. 30°34N 97°52W 84 F5
Leandro Norte Alem
Argentina 27°34S 55°15W 95 B4
Leane, L. Ireland 52°2N 9°32W 10 D2
Learmonth Australia 22°13S 114°10E 60 D1
Leask Canada 53°5N 106°45W 71 C7
Leatherhead U.K. 51°18N 0°20W 13 F7
Leavdnja = Lakselv Norway 70°2N 25°0E 8 A21
Leavenworth Kans.,
U.S.A. 39°19N 94°55W 80 F6
Leavenworth Wash.,
U.S.A. 47°36N 120°40W 76 C3
Leawood U.S.A. 38°58N 94°37W 80 F6
Lebak Phil. 6°32N 124°5E 37 C6
Lebam U.S.A. 46°34N 123°33W 78 D3
Lebanon Ind., U.S.A. 40°3N 86°28W 80 E10
Lebanon Kans., U.S.A. 39°49N 98°33W 80 F4
Lebanon Ky., U.S.A. 37°34N 85°15W 81 G11
Lebanon Mo., U.S.A. 37°41N 92°40W 80 G7
Lebanon N.H., U.S.A. 43°39N 72°15W 83 C12
Lebanon Oreg., U.S.A. 44°32N 122°55W 76 D2
Lebanon Pa., U.S.A. 40°20N 76°26W 83 F8
Lebanon Tenn., U.S.A. 36°12N 86°18W 85 C11
Lebanon ■ Asia 34°0N 36°0E 48 B5
Lebec U.S.A. 34°51N 118°52W 79 L8
Lebel-sur-Quévillon
Canada 49°3N 76°59W 72 C4
Lebomboberge S. Africa 24°30S 32°0E 57 B5
Lębork Poland 54°33N 17°46E 17 A9
Lebowakgomo S. Africa 24°12S 29°30E 57 B4
Lebrija Spain 36°53N 6°5W 21 D2
Lebu Chile 37°40S 73°47W 94 D1
Lecce Italy 40°23N 18°11E 23 D8
Lecco Italy 45°51N 9°23E 20 D8
Lech → Germany 48°43N 10°56E 16 D6
Lechang China 25°10N 113°20E 35 E9
Lecontes Mills U.S.A. 41°5N 78°17W 82 E6
Łęczyca Poland 52°5N 19°15E 17 B10
Ledang, Gunung
Malaysia 2°22N 102°37E 39 L4
Ledong China 18°41N 109°5E 38 C7
Leduc Canada 53°15N 113°30W 70 C6
Lee U.S.A. 42°19N 73°15W 83 D11
Lee → Ireland 51°53N 8°56W 10 E3
Lee Vining U.S.A. 37°58N 119°7W 78 H7
Leech L. U.S.A. 47°10N 94°24W 80 B6
Leechburg U.S.A. 40°37N 79°36W 82 F5
Leeds U.K. 53°48N 1°33W 12 D6
Leeds U.S.A. 33°33N 86°33W 85 E11
Leek Neths. 53°10N 6°24E 15 A6
Leek U.K. 53°7N 2°1W 12 D5
Leeman Australia 29°57S 114°58E 61 E1
Leeper U.S.A. 41°22N 79°18W 82 E5
Leer Germany 53°13N 7°26E 16 B4
Leesburg U.S.A. 28°49N 81°53W 85 G14
Leesville U.S.A. 31°8N 93°16W 84 F8
Leeton Australia 34°33S 146°23E 63 E4
Leetonia U.S.A. 40°53N 80°45W 82 F4
Leeu Gamka S. Africa 32°47S 21°59E 56 D3
Leeuwarden Neths. 53°15N 5°48E 15 A5
Leeuwin, C. Australia 34°20S 115°9E 61 F2
Leeuwin Naturaliste △
Australia 34°6S 115°3E 61 F2
Leeward Is. Atl. Oc. 16°30N 63°30W 89 C7
Lefkada Greece 38°40N 20°43E 23 E9
Lefkosia = Nicosia
Cyprus 35°10N 33°25E 46 C2
Lefroy Canada 44°16N 79°34W 82 B5
Lefroy, L. Australia 31°21S 121°40E 61 F3
Legazpi Phil. 13°10N 123°45E 37 B6
Legendre I. Australia 20°22S 116°55E 60 D2
Leghorn = Livorno Italy 43°33N 10°19E 22 C4
Legian Indonesia 8°42S 115°10E 37 K18
Legionowo Poland 52°25N 20°50E 17 B11
Legnago Italy 45°11N 11°18E 22 B4
Legnica Poland 51°12N 16°10E 16 C9
Leh India 34°9N 77°35E 43 B7
Lehigh Acres U.S.A. 26°36N 81°39W 85 H14
Lehighton U.S.A. 40°50N 75°43W 83 F9
Lehututu Botswana 23°54S 21°55E 56 B3
Lei Shui → China 26°55N 112°35E 35 D9
Leiah Pakistan 30°58N 70°58E 42 D4
Leibo China 28°11N 103°34E 34 C4
Leicester U.K. 52°38N 1°8W 13 E6
Leicester City □ U.K. 52°38N 1°8W 13 E6
Leicestershire □ U.K. 52°41N 1°17W 13 E6
Leichhardt → Australia 17°35S 139°48E 62 B2
Leichhardt Ra. Australia 20°46S 147°40E 62 C4
Leiden Neths. 52°9N 4°30E 15 B4
Leie → Belgium 51°2N 3°45E 15 C3
Leimus Nic. 14°40N 84°3W 88 D3
Leine → Germany 52°43N 9°36E 16 B5
Leinster Australia 27°51S 120°36E 61 E3
Leinster □ Ireland 53°3N 7°8W 10 C4
Leinster, Mt. Ireland 52°37N 6°46W 10 D5
Leipzig Germany 51°18N 12°22E 16 C7
Leiria Portugal 39°46N 8°53W 21 C1
Leirvik Norway 59°47N 5°28E 9 G11
Leishan China 26°15N 108°20E 34 D7
Leisler, Mt. Australia 23°23S 129°20E 60 D4
Leith Hill U.K. 51°11N 0°22W 13 F7
Leitir Ceanainn = Letterkenny
Ireland 54°57N 7°45W 10 B4
Leitrim Ireland 54°0N 8°5W 10 B3
Leitrim □ Ireland 54°8N 8°0W 10 B4
Leixlip Ireland 53°22N 6°30W 10 C5
Leiyang China 26°27N 112°45E 35 D9
Leizhou China 20°52N 110°8E 35 G8
Leizhou Bandao China 21°0N 110°0E 34 G7
Leizhou Wan China 20°50N 110°20E 35 G8
Lek → Neths. 51°54N 4°35E 15 C4
Leka Norway 65°5N 11°35E 8 D14
Leland Mich., U.S.A. 45°1N 85°45W 81 C11
Leland Miss., U.S.A. 33°24N 90°54W 85 E9
Leleque Argentina 42°28S 71°0W 96 E2
Leling China 37°44N 117°13E 33 F9
Lelystad Neths. 52°30N 5°25E 15 B5
Léman, L. Europe 46°26N 6°30E 20 C7
Lembar Indonesia 8°45S 116°4E 37 K19
Lembongan, Nusa
Indonesia 8°40S 115°27E 37 K18
Lembuak Indonesia 8°36S 116°11E 37 K19
Lemesós = Limassol
Cyprus 34°42N 33°1E 46 C2
Lemhi Ra. U.S.A. 44°0N 113°0W 76 D7
Lemmenjoki △ Finland 68°40N 25°30E 8 B21
Lemmer Neths. 52°51N 5°43E 15 B5
Lemmon U.S.A. 45°57N 102°10W 80 C2
Lemon Grove U.S.A. 32°44N 117°1W 79 N9
Lemoore U.S.A. 36°18N 119°46W 78 J7
Lemvig Denmark 56°33N 8°20E 9 H13
Lena → Russia 72°52N 126°40E 27 B13
Lena Pillars = Lenskiy Stolby
Russia 60°55N 126°0E 27 C13
Lenadoon Pt. Ireland 54°18N 9°3W 10 B2
Lenggong Malaysia 5°6N 100°58E 39 K3
Lengshuijiang China 27°40N 111°26E 35 D8
Lengshuitan China 26°27N 111°35E 35 D8
Lengua de Vaca, Pta.
Chile 30°14S 71°38W 94 C1
Leninogorsk = Ridder
Kazakhstan 50°20N 83°30E 26 D9
Leninsk Russia 48°40N 45°15E 19 E8
Leninsk-Kuznetskiy
Russia 54°44N 86°10E 26 D9
Lenkoran = Länkäran
Azerbaijan 38°48N 48°52E 47 B6
Lenmalu Indonesia 1°45S 130°15E 37 E8
Lennox U.S.A. 43°21N 96°53W 80 D5
Lennoxville Canada 45°22N 71°51W 83 A13
Lenoir U.S.A. 35°55N 81°32W 85 D14
Lenoir City U.S.A. 35°48N 84°16W 85 D12
Lenore L. Canada 52°30N 104°59W 71 C8
Lenox U.S.A. 42°22N 73°17W 83 D11
Lens France 50°26N 2°50E 20 A5
Lensk Russia 60°48N 114°55E 27 C12
Lenskiy Stolby Russia 60°55N 126°0E 27 C13
Lentini Italy 37°17N 15°0E 22 F6
Lenwood U.S.A. 34°53N 117°7W 79 L9
Lenya Myanmar 11°33N 98°57E 39 G2
Leoben Austria 47°22N 15°5E 16 E8
Leodhais = Lewis U.K. 58°9N 6°40W 11 C2
Leola U.S.A. 45°43N 98°56W 80 C4
Leominster U.K. 52°14N 2°43W 13 E5
Leominster U.S.A. 42°32N 71°46W 83 D13
León Mexico 21°6N 101°41W 86 C4
León Nic. 12°27N 86°51W 88 D2
León Spain 42°38N 5°34W 21 A3
Leon U.S.A. 40°44N 93°45W 80 E7
Leon → U.S.A. 31°14N 97°28W 84 F6
León, Montes de Spain 42°30N 6°18W 21 A2
Leonardtown U.S.A. 38°17N 76°38W 81 F15
Leonardville Namibia 23°29S 18°49E 56 B2
Leone Amer. Samoa 14°23S 170°48W 59 b
Leongatha Australia 38°30S 145°58E 63 F4
Leonora Australia 28°49S 121°19E 61 E3
Leopoldina Brazil 21°28S 42°40W 95 A7
Leopoldsburg Belgium 51°7N 5°13E 15 C5
Leoti U.S.A. 38°29N 101°21W 80 F3
Leova Moldova 46°28N 28°15E 17 E15
Leoville Canada 53°39N 107°33W 71 C7
Lepel = Lyepyel Belarus 54°50N 28°40E 9 J23
Leping China 28°47N 117°7E 35 C11
Lépo, L. do Angola 17°0S 19°0E 56 A2
Leppävirta Finland 62°29N 27°46E 8 E22
Leptis Magna Libya 32°40N 14°12E 53 B8
Leribe Lesotho 28°51S 28°3E 57 C4
Lérida = Lleida Spain 41°37N 0°39E 21 B6
Lerwick U.K. 60°9N 1°9W 11 A7
Les Cayes Haiti 18°15N 73°46W 89 C5
Les Coteaux Canada 45°15N 74°13W 83 A10
Les Escoumins Canada 48°21N 69°24W 73 C6
Les Sables-d'Olonne
France 46°30N 1°45W 20 C3
Lesbos Greece 39°10N 26°20E 23 E12
Leshan China 29°33N 103°41E 34 C4
Leshukonskoye Russia 64°54N 45°46E 18 B8
Leskov I. Antarctica 56°0S 28°0W 5 B1
Leskovac Serbia 43°0N 21°58E 23 C9
Lesopilnoye Russia 46°44N 134°20E 28 A7
Lesotho ■ Africa 29°40S 28°0E 57 C4
Lesozavodsk Russia 45°30N 133°29E 28 B6
Lesse → Belgium 50°15N 4°54E 15 D4
Lesse et Lomme △ Belgium 50°8N 5°9E 15 D5
Lesser Antilles W. Indies 15°0N 61°0W 89 D7
Lesser Slave L. Canada 55°30N 115°25W 70 B5
Lesser Sunda Is. Indonesia 8°0S 120°0E 37 F6
Lessines Belgium 50°42N 3°50E 15 D3
Lestock Canada 51°19N 103°59W 71 C8
Lesuer I. Australia 13°50S 127°17E 60 B4
Lesueur △ Australia 30°11S 115°10E 61 F2
Lésvos = Lesbos Greece 39°10N 26°20E 23 E12
Leszno Poland 51°50N 16°30E 17 C9
Letaba S. Africa 23°59S 31°50E 57 B5
Letchworth Garden City
U.K. 51°59N 0°13W 13 F7
Lethbridge Canada 49°45N 112°45W 70 D6
Lethem Guyana 3°20N 59°50W 92 C7
Leti, Kepulauan Indonesia 8°10S 128°0E 37 F7
Leti Is. = Leti, Kepulauan
Indonesia 8°10S 128°0E 37 F7
Letiahau → Botswana 21°16S 24°0E 56 B3
Leticia Colombia 4°9S 70°0W 92 D5
Leting China 39°23N 118°55E 33 E10
Letjiesbos S. Africa 32°34S 22°16E 56 D3
Letlhakane Botswana 21°27S 25°30E 56 B4
Letlhakeng Botswana 24°0S 24°59E 56 B3
Letpadan Myanmar 17°45N 95°45E 41 L19
Letpan Myanmar 19°28N 94°10E 41 K19
Letsôk-aw Kyun
Myanmar 11°30N 98°25E 39 G2
Letterkenny Ireland 54°57N 7°45W 10 B4
Leucadia U.S.A. 33°4N 117°18W 79 M9
Leuchars U.K. 56°24N 2°53W 11 E6
Leuser, Gunung Indonesia 3°46N 97°12E 36 D1
Leuven Belgium 50°52N 4°42E 15 D4
Leuze-en-Hainaut Belgium 50°36N 3°37E 15 D3
Levanger Norway 63°45N 11°19E 8 E14
Levelland U.S.A. 33°35N 102°23W 84 E3
Leven U.K. 56°12N 3°0W 11 E6
Leven, L. U.K. 56°12N 3°22W 11 E5
Leveque C. Australia 16°20S 123°0E 60 C3
Levice Slovakia 48°13N 18°35E 17 D10
Levin N.Z. 40°37S 175°18E 59 D5
Lévis Canada 46°48N 71°9W 73 C5
Levis, L. Canada 62°37N 117°58W 70 A5
Levittown N.Y., U.S.A. 40°44N 73°31W 83 F11
Levittown Pa., U.S.A. 40°9N 74°51W 83 F10
Levka Oros Greece 35°18N 24°3E 23 G11
Levkás = Lefkada Greece 38°40N 20°43E 23 E9
Levskigrad = Karlovo
Bulgaria 42°38N 24°47E 23 C11
Levuka Fiji 17°34S 179°0E 59 a
Lewes U.K. 50°52N 0°1E 13 G8
Lewes U.S.A. 38°46N 75°9W 81 F16
Lewis U.K. 58°9N 6°40W 11 C2
Lewis → U.S.A. 45°51N 122°48W 78 E4
Lewis, Butt of U.K. 58°31N 6°16W 11 C2
Lewis and Clark △
U.S.A. 46°8N 123°53W 78 D3
Lewis Ra. Australia 20°3S 128°50E 60 D4
Lewis Range U.S.A. 48°5N 113°5W 76 B7
Lewis Run U.S.A. 41°52N 78°40W 82 E6
Lewisburg Pa., U.S.A. 40°58N 76°54W 82 F8
Lewisburg Tenn., U.S.A. 35°27N 86°48W 85 D11
Lewisburg W. Va.,
U.S.A. 37°48N 80°27W 81 G13
Lewisporte Canada 49°15N 55°3W 73 C8
Lewiston Idaho, U.S.A. 46°25N 117°1W 76 C5
Lewiston Maine, U.S.A. 44°6N 70°13W 81 C18
Lewiston N.Y., U.S.A. 43°11N 79°3W 82 C5
Lewistown Mont., U.S.A. 47°4N 109°26W 76 C9
Lewistown Pa., U.S.A. 40°36N 77°34W 82 F7
Lexington Ill., U.S.A. 40°39N 88°47W 80 E9
Lexington Ky., U.S.A. 38°3N 84°30W 81 F11
Lexington Mich., U.S.A. 43°16N 82°32W 82 C2
Lexington Mo., U.S.A. 39°11N 93°52W 80 F7
Lexington N.C., U.S.A. 35°49N 80°15W 85 D14
Lexington N.Y., U.S.A. 42°15N 74°22W 83 D10
Lexington Nebr., U.S.A. 40°47N 99°45W 80 E4
Lexington Ohio, U.S.A. 40°41N 82°35W 82 F2
Lexington S.C., U.S.A. 33°59N 81°11W 85 E14
Lexington Tenn., U.S.A. 35°39N 88°24W 85 D10
Lexington Va., U.S.A. 37°47N 79°27W 81 G14
Lexington Park U.S.A. 38°16N 76°27W 81 F15
Leyburn U.K. 54°19N 1°48W 12 C6
Leye China 24°48N 106°29E 34 E6
Leyland U.K. 53°42N 2°43W 12 D5
Leyte □ Phil. 11°0N 125°0E 37 B7
Lezhë Albania 41°47N 19°39E 23 D8
Lezhi China 30°19N 104°58E 34 B5
Lhasa China 29°25N 90°58E 30 F7
Lhazê China 29°5N 87°38E 30 F6
L'Hermite, I. Chile 55°50S 68°0W 96 H3
Lhokkruet Indonesia 4°55N 95°24E 36 D1
Lhokseumawe Indonesia 5°10N 97°10E 36 C1
Li Thailand 17°48N 98°57E 38 D2
Li Jiang → China 24°40N 110°40E 35 E8
Li Jiang △ China 24°38N 110°38E 35 E8
Li Shan China 35°30N 111°56E 32 G6
Li Shui → China 29°24N 112°1E 35 C9
Li Xian Gansu, China 34°10N 105°5E 32 G3
Li Xian Hebei, China 38°30N 115°35E 32 E8
Li Xian Hunan, China 29°36N 111°42E 35 C8
Liancheng China 25°42N 116°40E 35 E11
Liancourt Rocks Asia 37°15N 131°52E 29 F5
Lianga Phil. 8°38N 126°6E 37 C7
Liangcheng Nei Monggol Zizhiqu,
China 40°28N 112°25E 32 D7
Liangcheng Shandong,
China 35°32N 119°37E 33 G10
Liangdang China 33°56N 106°18E 32 H4
Lianghe China 24°50N 98°20E 34 E2
Lianghekou China 29°11N 108°44E 34 C7
Liangping China 30°38N 107°47E 34 B6
Liangpran Indonesia 1°4N 114°23E 36 D4
Lianhua China 27°3N 113°54E 35 D9
Lianhua Shan China 23°40N 115°48E 35 F10
Lianjiang Fujian, China 26°12N 119°27E 35 D12
Lianjiang Guangdong,
China 21°40N 110°20E 35 G8
Lianping China 24°26N 114°30E 35 E10
Lianshan China 24°38N 112°8E 35 E9
Lianshanguan China 40°53N 123°43E 33 D12
Lianshui China 33°42N 119°20E 33 H10
Lianyuan China 27°40N 111°38E 35 D8
Lianyungang China 34°40N 119°11E 33 G10
Lianzhou China 24°51N 112°22E 35 E9
Liao He → China 41°0N 121°50E 33 D11
Liaocheng China 36°28N 115°58E 32 F8
Liaodong Bandao China 40°0N 122°30E 33 E12
Liaodong Wan China 40°20N 121°10E 33 D11
Liaoning □ China 41°40N 122°30E 33 D12
Liaotung, G. of = Liaodong Wan
China 40°20N 121°10E 33 D11
Liaoyang China 41°15N 122°58E 33 D12
Liaoyuan China 42°58N 125°2E 33 C13
Liaozhong China 41°23N 122°50E 33 D12
Liard → Canada 61°51N 121°18W 70 A4
Liard River Canada 59°25N 126°5W 70 B3
Liari Pakistan 25°37N 66°30E 42 G2
Libanggaon Nepal 28°18N 82°38E 43 E10
Libau = Liepāja Latvia 56°30N 21°0E 9 H19
Libby U.S.A. 48°23N 115°33W 76 B6
Libenge
Dem. Rep. of the Congo 3°40N 18°55E 54 D3
Liberal U.S.A. 37°3N 100°55W 80 G3
Liberec Czechia 50°47N 15°7E 16 C8
Liberia Costa Rica 10°40N 85°30W 88 D2
Liberia ■ W. Afr. 6°30N 9°30W 52 G4
Libertador □ Chile 34°15S 70°45W 94 C1
Liberty Mo., U.S.A. 39°15N 94°25W 80 F6
Liberty N.Y., U.S.A. 41°48N 74°45W 83 E10
Liberty Pa., U.S.A. 41°34N 77°6W 82 E7
Liberty Tex., U.S.A. 30°3N 94°48W 84 F7
Liberty-Newark Int. ✕ (EWR)
U.S.A. 40°42N 74°10W 83 F10
Lībīya, Sahrā' Africa 25°0N 25°0E 53 C10
Libo China 25°22N 107°53E 34 E6
Libobo, Tanjung Indonesia 0°54S 128°28E 37 E7
Libode S. Africa 31°33S 29°2E 57 D4
Libong, Ko Thailand 7°15N 99°23E 39 J2
Libourne France 44°55N 0°14W 20 D3
Libramont Belgium 49°55N 5°23E 15 E5
Libreville Gabon 0°25N 9°26E 54 D1
Libya ■ N. Afr. 27°0N 17°0E 53 C9
Libyan Desert = Lībīya, Sahrâ'
Africa 25°0N 25°0E 53 C10
Libyan Plateau = Ed Déffa
Egypt 30°40N 26°30E 53 B11
Licantén Chile 35°55S 72°0W 94 D1
Licata Italy 37°6N 13°56E 22 F5
Licheng China 36°28N 113°20E 32 F7
Lichfield U.K. 52°41N 1°49W 13 E6
Lichinga Mozam. 13°13S 35°11E 55 G7
Lichtenburg S. Africa 26°8S 26°8E 56 C4
Lichuan Hubei, China 30°18N 108°57E 34 B7
Lichuan Jiangxi, China 27°18N 116°55E 35 D11
Licking → U.S.A. 39°6N 84°30W 81 F11
Lida Belarus 53°53N 25°15E 17 B13
Lidköping Sweden 58°31N 13°7E 9 G15
Liebig, Mt. Australia 23°18S 131°22E 60 D5
Liechtenstein ■ Europe 47°8N 9°35E 20 C8
Liège Belgium 50°38N 5°35E 15 D5
Liège □ Belgium 50°32N 5°35E 15 D5
Liegnitz = Legnica Poland 51°12N 16°10E 16 C9
Lieksa Finland 63°18N 30°2E 8 E24
Lienyünchiangshih =
Lianyungang China 34°40N 119°11E 33 G10
Lienz Austria 46°50N 12°46E 16 E7
Liepāja Latvia 56°30N 21°0E 9 H19
Lier Belgium 51°7N 4°34E 15 C4
Lierne △ Norway 64°20N 13°50E 8 D15
Lietuva = Lithuania ■
Europe 55°30N 24°0E 9 J21
Lièvre → Canada 45°31N 75°26W 72 C4
Liffey → Ireland 53°21N 6°13W 10 C5
Lifford Ireland 54°51N 7°29W 10 B4
Lifudzin Russia 44°21N 134°58E 28 B7
Lightning Ridge Australia 29°22S 148°0E 63 D4
Ligonier U.S.A. 40°15N 79°14W 82 F5
Liguria □ Italy 44°30N 8°50E 20 D8
Ligurian Sea Medit. S. 43°20N 9°0E 22 C3
Lihou Reefs and Cays
Australia 17°25S 151°40E 62 B5
Lihué Calel △ Argentina 38°0S 65°10W 94 D2
Lijiang China 26°55N 100°20E 34 D3
Lik → Laos 18°31N 102°30E 38 C4
Likasi
Dem. Rep. of the Congo 10°55S 26°48E 54 G5
L'Île-Rousse France 42°38N 8°57E 20 E8
Liling China 27°42N 113°29E 35 D9
Lille France 50°38N 3°3E 20 A5
Lille Bælt Denmark 55°20N 9°45E 9 J13
Lillehammer Norway 61°8N 10°30E 8 F14
Lillesand Norway 58°15N 8°23E 9 G13
Lillian Pt. Australia 27°40S 126°6E 61 E4
Lillooet Canada 50°44N 121°57W 70 C4
Lillooet → Canada 49°15N 121°57W 70 D4
Lilongwe Malawi 14°0S 33°48E 55 G6
Liloy Phil. 8°4N 122°39E 37 C6
Lim → Europe 43°45N 19°15E 23 C8
Lima Indonesia 3°39S 127°58E 37 E7
Lima Mont., U.S.A. 44°38N 112°36W 76 D7
Lima N.Y., U.S.A. 42°54N 77°36W 82 D7
Lima Ohio, U.S.A. 40°44N 84°6W 81 E11
Lima → Portugal 41°41N 8°50W 21 B1

Limassol *Cyprus* 34°42N 33°1E **46** C2
Limavady *U.K.* 55°3N 6°56W **10** A5
Limay → *Argentina* 39°0S 68°0W **96** D3
Limay Mahuida
  Argentina 37°10S 66°45W **94** D2
Limbang *Malaysia* 4°42N 115°6E **36** D5
Limbaži *Latvia* 57°31N 24°42E **9** H21
Limbdi *India* 22°34N 71°51E **42** H4
Limbe *Cameroon* 4°1N 9°10E **54** D1
Limburg *Germany* 50°22N 8°4E **16** C5
Limburg □ *Belgium* 51°2N 5°25E **15** C5
Limburg □ *Neths.* 51°20N 5°55E **15** C5
Limeira *Brazil* 22°35S 47°28W **95** A6
Limenas = Thasos
  Greece 40°40N 24°40E **23** D11
Limerick *Ireland* 52°40N 8°37W **10** D3
Limerick *U.S.A.* 43°41N 70°48W **83** C14
Limerick □ *Ireland* 52°30N 8°50W **10** D3
Limestone *U.S.A.* 42°2N 78°38W **82** D6
Limestone → *Canada* 56°31N 94°7W **71** B10
Limfjorden *Denmark* 56°55N 9°0E **9** H13
Limia = Lima → *Portugal* 41°41N 8°50W **21** B1
Limingen *Norway* 64°48N 13°35E **8** D15
Limmen ◇ *Australia* 15°15S 135°30E **62** B2
Limmen Bight *Australia* 14°40S 135°35E **62** A2
Limmen Bight →
  Australia 15°7S 135°44E **62** B2
Limnos *Greece* 39°50N 25°5E **23** E11
Limoges *Canada* 45°20N 75°16W **83** A9
Limoges *France* 45°50N 1°15E **20** D4
Limón *Costa Rica* 10°0N 83°2W **88** E3
Limon *U.S.A.* 39°16N 103°41W **76** G12
Limousin *France* 45°30N 1°30E **20** D4
Limoux *France* 43°4N 2°12E **20** E5
Limpopo □ *S. Africa* 24°5S 29°0E **57** B4
Limpopo → *Africa* 25°5S 33°30E **57** D5
Limuru *Kenya* 1°2S 36°35E **54** E7
Lin Xian *China* 37°57N 110°58E **32** F6
Lin'an *China* 30°15N 119°42E **35** B12
Linares *Chile* 35°50S 71°40W **94** D1
Linares *Mexico* 24°52N 99°34W **87** C5
Linares *Spain* 38°10N 3°40W **21** C4
Lincang *China* 23°58N 100°1E **34** F3
Lincheng *China* 37°25N 114°30E **32** F8
Linchuan *China* 27°57N 116°15E **35** D11
Lincoln = Beamsville
  Canada 43°12N 79°28W **82** C5
Lincoln *Argentina* 34°55S 61°30W **94** C3
Lincoln *N.Z.* 43°38S 172°30E **59** E4
Lincoln *U.K.* 53°14N 0°32W **12** D7
Lincoln *Calif., U.S.A.* 38°54N 121°17W **78** G5
Lincoln *Ill., U.S.A.* 40°9N 89°22W **80** E9
Lincoln *Kans., U.S.A.* 39°3N 98°9W **80** F4
Lincoln *Maine, U.S.A.* 45°22N 68°30W **81** C19
Lincoln *N.H., U.S.A.* 44°3N 71°40W **83** B13
Lincoln *N. Mex., U.S.A.* 33°30N 105°23W **77** K11
Lincoln *Nebr., U.S.A.* 40°49N 96°41W **80** E5
Lincoln City *U.S.A.* 44°57N 124°1W **76** D1
Lincoln Hav = Lincoln Sea
  Arctic 84°0N 55°0W **69** A21
Lincoln Sea *Arctic* 84°0N 55°0W **69** A21
Lincolnshire □ *U.K.* 53°14N 0°32W **12** D7
Lincolnshire Wolds *U.K.* 53°26N 0°13W **12** D7
Lincolnton *U.S.A.* 35°29N 81°16W **85** D14
Lind *U.S.A.* 46°58N 118°37W **76** C4
Linda *U.S.A.* 39°8N 121°34W **78** F5
Lindeman I. *Australia* 20°27S 149°3E **62** b
Lindeman Islands △
  Australia 20°28S 149°5E **62** b
Linden *Guyana* 6°0N 58°10W **92** B7
Linden *Ala., U.S.A.* 32°18N 87°48W **85** E11
Linden *Calif., U.S.A.* 38°1N 121°5W **78** G5
Linden *Tex., U.S.A.* 33°1N 94°22W **84** E7
Lindenhurst *U.S.A.* 40°41N 73°23W **83** F11
Lindesnes *Norway* 57°58N 7°3E **9** H12
Lindi *Tanzania* 9°58S 39°38E **54** F7
Lindi →
  Dem. Rep. of the Congo 0°33N 25°5E **54** D5
Lindley *U.S.A.* 42°1N 77°8W **82** D7
Lindos *Greece* 36°6N 28°4E **23** F13
Lindsay *Canada* 44°22N 78°43W **82** B6
Lindsay *Calif., U.S.A.* 36°12N 119°5W **78** J7
Lindsay *Okla., U.S.A.* 34°50N 97°38W **84** D6
Lindsborg *U.S.A.* 38°35N 97°40W **80** F5
Line Islands *Pac. Oc.* 7°0N 160°0W **65** H12
Linesville *U.S.A.* 41°39N 80°26W **82** E4
Linfen *China* 36°3N 111°30E **32** F6
Ling Xian *Hunan, China* 26°29N 113°48E **35** D9
Ling Xian *Shandong,*
  China 37°22N 116°30E **32** F9
Lingal *India* 16°17N 78°31E **45** F4
Linganamakki Res. *India* 14°6N 74°52E **45** G2
Lingao *China* 19°56N 109°42E **38** C7
Lingayen *Phil.* 16°1N 120°14E **37** A6
Lingayen G. *Phil.* 16°10N 120°15E **37** A6
Lingbao *China* 34°31N 110°51E **32** G6
Lingbi *China* 33°33N 117°33E **33** H9
Lingchuan *Guangxi Zhuangzu,*
  China 25°26N 110°21E **35** E8
Lingchuan *Shanxi, China* 35°45N 113°12E **32** G7
Lingding Yang *China* 22°25N 113°44E **31** a
Lingen *Germany* 52°31N 7°19E **16** B4
Lingga *Indonesia* 0°12S 104°37E **36** E2
Lingga, Kepulauan
  Indonesia 0°10S 104°30E **36** E2
Lingga Arch. = Lingga, Kepulauan
  Indonesia 0°10S 104°30E **36** E2
Linghai *China* 41°11N 121°22E **33** D11
Lingle *U.S.A.* 42°8N 104°21W **76** E11
Lingqiu *China* 39°28N 114°22E **32** E8
Lingshan *China* 22°25N 109°18E **34** F7
Lingshi *China* 36°48N 111°48E **32** F6
Lingshou *China* 38°20N 114°20E **32** E8
Lingshui *China* 18°27N 110°0E **38** C8
Lingsugur *India* 16°10N 76°31E **45** F3
Lingtai *China* 35°0N 107°40E **32** G4
Linguère *Senegal* 15°25N 15°5W **52** E2
Lingui *China* 25°12N 110°2E **35** E8
Lingwu *China* 38°6N 106°20E **32** E4
Lingyuan *China* 41°10N 119°15E **33** D10

Lingyun *China* 25°2N 106°35E **34** E6
Linhai *China* 28°50N 121°8E **35** C13
Linhares *Brazil* 19°25S 40°4W **93** G10
Linhe *China* 40°48N 107°20E **32** D4
Linjiang *China* 41°50N 127°0E **33** D14
Linkou *China* 45°15N 130°18E **33** B16
Linli *China* 29°27N 111°30E **35** C8
Linköping *Sweden* 58°28N 15°36E **9** G16
Linnansaari △ *Finland* 62°3N 28°40E **8** E23
Linnhe, L. *U.K.* 56°36N 5°25W **11** E3
Linosa *Medit. S.* 35°51N 12°50E **22** G5
Linqi *China* 35°45N 113°52E **32** G7
Linqing *China* 36°50N 115°42E **32** F8
Linqu *China* 36°25N 118°30E **33** F10
Linquan *China* 33°5N 115°17E **35** A10
Lins *Brazil* 21°40S 49°44W **95** A6
Linshu *China* 34°53N 118°38E **33** G10
Linshui *China* 30°21N 106°57E **34** B6
Lintao *China* 35°26N 103°58E **32** G2
Linton *Ind., U.S.A.* 39°2N 87°10W **80** F10
Linton *N. Dak., U.S.A.* 46°16N 100°14W **80** B3
Lintong *China* 34°20N 109°10E **32** G5
Linwood *Canada* 43°35N 80°43W **82** C4
Linwu *China* 25°19N 112°31E **35** E9
Linxi *Hebei, China* 39°42N 118°26E **33** E10
Linxi *Liaoning, China* 43°36N 118°2E **33** C10
Linxia *China* 35°36N 103°10E **30** D9
Linxiang *China* 29°28N 113°23E **35** C9
Linyanti → *Africa* 17°50S 25°5E **56** A4
Linyi *Shandong, China* 37°13N 116°54E **32** F9
Linyi *Shandong, China* 35°5N 118°21E **33** G10
Linying *China* 33°48N 113°56E **32** H7
Linz *Austria* 48°18N 14°18E **16** D8
Linzhenzhen *China* 36°30N 109°59E **32** F5
Linzhou *China* 36°4N 113°49E **32** F7
Linzi *China* 36°50N 118°20E **33** F10
Lion, G. du *France* 43°10N 4°0E **20** E6
Lions, G. of = Lion, G. du
  France 43°10N 4°0E **20** E6
Lion's Head *Canada* 44°58N 81°15W **82** B3
Lipa *Phil.* 13°57N 121°10E **37** B6
Lipari *Italy* 38°26N 14°58E **22** E6
Lipari, Is. = Eólie, Ís.
  Italy 38°30N 14°57E **22** E6
Lipcani *Moldova* 48°14N 26°48E **17** D14
Liperi *Finland* 62°31N 29°24E **8** E23
Lipetsk *Russia* 52°37N 39°35E **18** D6
Liping *China* 26°15N 109°7E **34** D7
Lipkany = Lipcani
  Moldova 48°14N 26°48E **17** D14
Lipovets *Ukraine* 49°12N 29°1E **17** D15
Lippe → *Germany* 51°39N 6°36E **16** C4
Lipscomb *U.S.A.* 36°14N 100°16W **84** C4
Liptrap, C. *Australia* 38°50S 145°55E **63** F4
Lipu *China* 24°30N 110°22E **35** E8
Lira *Uganda* 2°17N 32°57E **54** D6
Liria = Lliria *Spain* 39°37N 0°35W **21** C5
Lisala *Dem. Rep. of the Congo* 2°12N 21°38E **54** D4
Lisbon *N. Dak., U.S.A.* 46°27N 97°41W **80** B5
Lisbon *N.H., U.S.A.* 44°13N 71°55W **83** B13
Lisbon *N.Y., U.S.A.* 44°43N 75°19W **83** B9
Lisbon *Ohio, U.S.A.* 40°46N 80°46W **82** F4
Lisbon Falls *U.S.A.* 44°0N 70°4W **81** D18
Lisburn *U.K.* 54°31N 6°3W **10** B5
Lisburne, C. *U.S.A.* 68°53N 166°13W **74** B6
Liscannor B. *Ireland* 52°55N 9°24W **10** D2
Lisdoonvarna *Ireland* 53°2N 9°18W **10** C2
Lishe Jiang → *China* 24°15N 101°35E **34** E3
Lishi *China* 37°31N 111°8E **32** F6
Lishu *China* 43°20N 124°18E **33** C13
Lishui *Jiangsu, China* 31°38N 119°2E **35** B12
Lishui *Zhejiang, China* 28°28N 119°54E **35** C12
Lisianski I. *U.S.A.* 26°2N 174°0W **75** K5
Lisichansk = Lysychansk
  Ukraine 48°55N 38°30E **19** E6
Lisieux *France* 49°10N 0°12E **20** B4
Liski *Russia* 51°3N 39°30E **19** D6
Lismore *Australia* 28°44S 153°21E **63** D5
Lismore *Ireland* 52°8N 7°55W **10** D4
Lista *Norway* 58°7N 6°39E **9** G12
Lister, Mt. *Antarctica* 78°0S 162°0E **5** D11
Liston *Australia* 28°39S 152°6E **63** D5
Listowel *Canada* 43°44N 80°58W **82** C4
Listowel *Ireland* 52°27N 9°29W **10** D2
Litang *Guangxi Zhuangzu,*
  China 23°12N 109°8E **34** F7
Litang *Sichuan, China* 30°1N 100°17E **34** B3
Litang Qu → *China* 28°4N 101°32E **34** C3
Litani → *Lebanon* 33°20N 35°15E **48** B4
Litchfield *Calif., U.S.A.* 40°24N 120°23W **78** E6
Litchfield *Conn., U.S.A.* 41°45N 73°11W **83** E11
Litchfield *Ill., U.S.A.* 39°11N 89°39W **80** F9
Litchfield *Minn., U.S.A.* 45°8N 94°32W **80** C6
Litchfield △ *Australia* 13°14S 131°1E **60** B5
Lithgow *Australia* 33°25S 150°8E **63** E5
Lithino, Ákra *Greece* 34°55N 24°44E **23** G11
Lititz *U.S.A.* 40°9N 76°18W **83** F8
Litoměřice *Czechia* 50°33N 14°10E **16** C8
Little Abaco *Bahamas* 26°50N 77°30W **88** A4
Little Andaman I. *India* 10°45N 92°30E **45** J11
Little Barrier I. *N.Z.* 36°12S 175°8E **59** B5
Little Basses *Sri Lanka* 6°24N 81°43E **45** L5
Little Belt Mts. *U.S.A.* 46°40N 110°45W **76** C8
Little Bighorn Battlefield ◇
  U.S.A. 45°34N 107°25W **76** D10
Little Blue → *U.S.A.* 39°42N 96°41W **80** F5
Little Buffalo → *Canada* 61°0N 113°46W **70** A6
Little Cayman *Cayman Is.* 19°41N 80°3W **88** C3
Little Churchill →
  Canada 57°30N 95°22W **71** B9
Little Coco I. *Myanmar* 14°0N 93°13E **45** H11
Little Colorado →
  U.S.A. 36°12N 111°48W **77** H8
Little Current *Canada* 45°55N 82°0W **72** C3
Little Current → *Canada* 50°57N 84°36W **72** B3
Little Diomede I. *U.S.A.* 65°45N 168°56W **74** B6
Little Falls *Minn., U.S.A.* 45°59N 94°22W **80** C6
Little Falls *N.Y., U.S.A.* 43°3N 74°51W **83** C10
Little Fork → *U.S.A.* 48°31N 93°35W **80** A7

Little Grand Rapids
  Canada 52°0N 95°29W **71** C9
Little Humboldt →
  U.S.A. 41°1N 117°43W **76** F5
Little Inagua I. *Bahamas* 21°40N 73°50W **89** B5
Little Karoo *S. Africa* 33°45S 21°0E **56** E3
Little Khingan Mts. = Xiao
  Hinggan Ling *China* 49°0N 127°0E **31** B14
Little Lake *U.S.A.* 35°56N 117°55W **79** K9
Little Laut Is. = Laut Kecil,
  Kepulauan *Indonesia* 4°45S 115°40E **36** E5
Little Mecatina = Petit-
  Mécatina → *Canada* 50°40N 59°30W **73** B8
Little Minch *U.K.* 57°35N 6°45W **11** D2
Little Missouri →
  U.S.A. 47°36N 102°25W **80** B2
Little Nicobar *India* 7°20N 93°40E **45** L11
Little Ouse → *U.K.* 52°22N 1°12E **13** E9
Little Rann *India* 23°25N 71°25E **42** H4
Little Red → *U.S.A.* 35°11N 91°27W **84** D9
Little River *N.Z.* 43°45S 172°49E **59** E4
Little Rock *U.S.A.* 34°45N 92°17W **84** D8
Little Sable Pt. *U.S.A.* 43°38N 86°33W **80** D10
Little Sioux → *U.S.A.* 41°48N 96°4W **80** E5
Little Smoky → *Canada* 54°44N 117°11W **70** C5
Little Snake → *U.S.A.* 40°27N 108°26W **76** F9
Little Tobago
  Trin. & Tob. 11°18N 60°30W **93** J16
Little Valley *U.S.A.* 42°15N 78°48W **82** D6
Little Wabash → *U.S.A.* 37°55N 88°5W **80** G9
Little White → *U.S.A.* 43°40N 100°40W **80** D3
Little Zab = Zāb aş Şaghīr →
  Iraq 35°17N 43°29E **46** C4
Littlefield *U.S.A.* 33°55N 102°20W **84** E3
Littlehampton *U.K.* 50°49N 0°32W **13** G7
Littleton *U.S.A.* 44°18N 71°46W **83** B13
Liu He → *China* 40°55N 121°35E **33** D11
Liu Jiang → *China* 23°55N 109°30E **34** F7
Liuba *China* 33°38N 106°55E **34** A6
Liucheng *China* 24°38N 109°14E **34** E7
Liugou *China* 40°57N 118°15E **33** D10
Liuhe *China* 42°17N 125°43E **33** C13
Liuheng Dao *China* 29°40N 122°5E **35** C14
Liujiang *China* 24°26N 109°11E **34** E7
Liukang Tenggaja = Sabalana,
  Kepulauan *Indonesia* 6°45S 118°50E **37** F5
Liupan Shan *China* 35°39N 106°12E **32** G4
Liupanshui *China* 26°38N 104°48E **34** D5
Liuwa Plain *Zambia* 14°20S 22°30E **55** G4
Liuyang *China* 28°10N 113°37E **35** C9
Liuzhou *China* 24°22N 109°22E **34** E7
Liuzhuang *China* 33°12N 120°18E **33** H11
Livadia *Greece* 38°27N 22°54E **23** E10
Live Oak *Calif., U.S.A.* 39°17N 121°40W **78** F5
Live Oak *Fla., U.S.A.* 30°18N 82°59W **85** F13
Lively *Canada* 46°26N 81°9W **81** B13
Livermore *U.S.A.* 37°41N 121°47W **78** H5
Livermore, Mt. *U.S.A.* 30°38N 104°11W **84** F2
Livermore Falls *U.S.A.* 44°29N 70°11W **81** C18
Liverpool *Australia* 33°54S 150°58E **63** B5
Liverpool *Canada* 44°5N 64°41W **73** D7
Liverpool *U.K.* 53°25N 3°0W **12** D4
Liverpool *U.S.A.* 43°6N 76°13W **83** C8
Liverpool Bay *U.K.* 53°30N 3°20W **12** D4
Liverpool Ra. *Australia* 31°50S 150°30E **63** E5
Livingston *Guatemala* 15°50N 88°50W **88** C2
Livingston *S. Amer.* 55°54N 3°30W **11** F5
Livingston *Ala., U.S.A.* 32°35N 88°11W **85** E10
Livingston *Calif., U.S.A.* 37°23N 120°43W **78** H6
Livingston *Mont.,*
  U.S.A. 45°40N 110°34W **76** D8
Livingston *S.C., U.S.A.* 33°38N 81°7W **85** E14
Livingston *Tenn., U.S.A.* 36°23N 85°19W **85** C12
Livingston *Tex., U.S.A.* 30°43N 94°56W **84** F7
Livingston, L. *U.S.A.* 30°50N 95°10W **84** F7
Livingston Manor
  U.S.A. 41°54N 74°50W **83** E10
Livingstone *Zambia* 17°46S 25°52E **55** H5
Livny *Russia* 52°30N 37°30E **18** D6
Livonia *Mich., U.S.A.* 42°23N 83°23W **81** D12
Livonia *N.Y., U.S.A.* 42°49N 77°40W **82** D7
Livorno *Italy* 43°33N 10°19E **22** C4
Livramento *Brazil* 30°55S 55°30W **95** C4
Lixi *China* 26°23N 101°59E **34** D3
Lixian *China* 31°23N 103°13E **34** B4
Lixin *China* 33°8N 116°13E **35** A11
Liyang *China* 31°26N 119°28E **35** B12
Lizard I. *Australia* 14°42S 145°30E **62** A4
Lizard Pt. *U.K.* 49°57N 5°13W **13** H2
Ljubljana *Slovenia* 46°4N 14°33E **16** E8
Ljungan → *Sweden* 62°18N 17°23E **8** E17
Ljungby *Sweden* 56°49N 13°55E **9** H15
Ljusdal *Sweden* 61°46N 16°3E **8** F17
Ljusnan → *Sweden* 61°12N 17°8E **8** F17
Ljusne *Sweden* 61°13N 17°7E **8** F17
Llancanelo, Salina
  Argentina 35°40S 69°8W **94** D2
Llandeilo *U.K.* 51°53N 3°59W **13** F4
Llandovery *U.K.* 51°59N 3°48W **13** F4
Llandrindod Wells *U.K.* 52°14N 3°22W **13** E4
Llandudno *U.K.* 53°19N 3°50W **12** D4
Llanelli *U.K.* 51°41N 4°10W **13** F3
Llanes *Spain* 43°25N 4°50W **21** A3
Llanfair-ym-Muallt = Builth Wells
  U.K. 52°9N 3°25W **13** E4
Llangollen *U.K.* 52°58N 3°11W **12** E4
Llanidloes *U.K.* 52°27N 3°31W **13** E4
Llano *U.S.A.* 30°45N 98°41W **84** F5
Llano → *U.S.A.* 30°39N 98°26W **84** F5
Llano Estacado *U.S.A.* 33°30N 103°0W **84** E3
Llanos *S. Amer.* 5°0N 71°35W **92** C4
Llanos de Challe △ *Chile* 28°8S 71°0W **94** B1
Llanquihue, L. *Chile* 41°10S 72°50W **96** E1
Llanwrtyd Wells *U.K.* 52°7N 3°38W **13** E4
Llera de Canales *Mexico* 23°19N 99°1W **87** C5
Lleyn Peninsula *U.K.* 52°51N 4°36W **12** E3
Llico *Chile* 34°46S 72°5W **94** C1
Lleida *Spain* 41°37N 0°39E **21** B6
Lliria *Spain* 39°37N 0°35W **21** C5
Llobregat → *Spain* 41°19N 2°5E **21** B7

Lloret de Mar *Spain* 41°41N 2°53E **21** B7
Lloyd B. *Australia* 12°45S 143°27E **62** A3
Lloyd L. *Canada* 57°22N 108°57W **71** B7
Lloydminster *Canada* 53°17N 110°0W **71** C7
Llucmajor *Spain* 39°29N 2°53E **21** C7
Llullaillaco, Volcán
  S. Amer. 24°43S 68°30W **94** A2
Llullaillaco △ *Chile* 24°50S 68°51W **94** A2
Lo → *Vietnam* 21°18N 105°25E **38** B5
Loa *U.S.A.* 38°24N 111°39W **76** G8
Loa → *Chile* 21°26S 70°41W **94** A1
Loaita I. *S. China Sea* 10°41N 114°25E **36** B4
Loange →
  Dem. Rep. of the Congo 4°17S 20°2E **54** E4
Lobamba *Eswatini* 26°28S 31°12E **57** C5
Lobatse *Botswana* 25°12S 25°40E **56** C4
Loberia *Argentina* 38°10S 58°40W **94** D4
Lobito *Angola* 12°18S 13°35E **55** G2
Lobos *Argentina* 35°10S 59°0W **94** D4
Lobos, I. *Mexico* 27°20N 110°36W **86** B2
Loc Binh *Vietnam* 21°46N 106°54E **38** B6
Loc Ninh *Vietnam* 11°50N 106°34E **39** G6
Locarno *Switz.* 46°10N 8°47E **20** C8
Loch Garman = Wexford
  Ireland 52°20N 6°28W **10** D5
Loch Lomond and the Trossachs △
  U.K. 56°10N 4°40W **11** E4
Lochaber *U.K.* 56°59N 5°1W **11** E3
Locharbriggs *U.K.* 55°7N 3°35W **11** F5
Lochboisdale *U.K.* 57°9N 7°20W **11** D1
Loche, L. La *Canada* 56°30N 109°30W **71** B7
Lochem *Neths.* 52°9N 6°26E **15** B6
Loches *France* 47°7N 1°0E **20** C4
Lochgilphead *U.K.* 56°2N 5°26W **11** E3
Lochinver *U.K.* 58°9N 5°14W **11** C3
Lochmaddy *U.K.* 57°36N 7°10W **11** D1
Lochnagar *Australia* 23°33S 145°38E **62** C4
Lochnagar *U.K.* 56°57N 3°15W **11** E5
Lochy, L. *U.K.* 57°0N 4°53W **11** E4
Lock *Australia* 33°34S 135°46E **63** E2
Lock Haven *U.S.A.* 41°8N 77°28W **82** E7
Lockeford *U.S.A.* 38°10N 121°9W **78** G5
Lockeport *Canada* 43°47N 65°4W **73** D6
Lockerbie *U.K.* 55°7N 3°21W **11** F5
Lockhart *U.S.A.* 29°53N 97°40W **84** G6
Lockhart, L. *Australia* 33°15S 119°3E **61** F2
Lockhart River *Australia* 12°58S 143°30E **62** A3
Lockhart River ◇
  Australia 12°47S 143°20E **62** A3
Lockney *U.S.A.* 34°7N 101°27W **84** D4
Lockport *U.S.A.* 43°10N 78°42W **82** C6
Lod *Israel* 31°57N 34°54E **48** D3
Lodeinoye Pole *Russia* 60°44N 33°33E **18** B5
Lodge Bay *Canada* 52°14N 55°51W **73** B8
Lodge Grass *U.S.A.* 45°19N 107°22W **76** D10
Lodhran *Pakistan* 29°32N 71°30E **42** E4
Lodi *Italy* 45°19N 9°30E **20** D8
Lodi *Calif., U.S.A.* 38°8N 121°16W **78** G5
Lodi *Ohio, U.S.A.* 41°2N 82°1W **82** E3
Lodja *Dem. Rep. of the Congo* 3°30S 23°23E **54** E4
Lodwar *Kenya* 3°7N 35°36E **54** D7
Łódź *Poland* 51°45N 19°27E **17** C10
Loei *Thailand* 17°29N 101°35E **38** D3
Loeriesfontein *S. Africa* 31°0S 19°26E **56** E2
Lofoten *Norway* 68°30N 13°59E **8** B16
Logan *Iowa, U.S.A.* 41°39N 95°47W **80** E6
Logan *Ohio, U.S.A.* 39°32N 82°25W **81** F12
Logan *Utah, U.S.A.* 41°44N 111°50W **76** F8
Logan *W. Va., U.S.A.* 37°51N 81°59W **81** G13
Logan, Mt. *Canada* 60°34N 140°23W **68** B5
Logandale *U.S.A.* 36°36N 114°29W **79** J12
Logansport *Ind., U.S.A.* 40°45N 86°22W **80** E10
Logansport *La., U.S.A.* 31°58N 94°0W **84** F8
Logone → *Chad* 12°6N 15°2E **53** F9
Logroño *Spain* 42°28N 2°27W **21** A4
Lohardaga *India* 23°27N 84°45E **43** H11
Loharia *India* 23°45N 74°14E **42** H6
Loharu *India* 28°27N 75°49E **42** E6
Lohri Wah → *Pakistan* 27°27N 67°37E **42** F2
Loikaw *Myanmar* 19°40N 97°17E **41** K20
Loimaa *Finland* 60°50N 23°5E **8** F20
Loir → *France* 47°33N 0°32W **20** C3
Loire → *France* 47°16N 2°10W **20** C2
Loja *Ecuador* 3°59S 79°16W **92** D3
Loja *Spain* 37°10N 4°10W **21** D3
Loji = Kawasi *Indonesia* 1°38S 127°28E **37** E7
Lojung *China* 24°27N 109°36E **34** E7
Lokeren *Belgium* 51°6N 3°59E **15** C3
Lokgwabe *Botswana* 24°10S 21°50E **56** C3
Lokitaung *Kenya* 4°12N 35°48E **54** D7
Lokkan tekojärvi *Finland* 67°55N 27°35E **8** C22
Lokoja *Nigeria* 7°47N 6°45E **52** G7
Lokolo →
  Dem. Rep. of the Congo 1°43S 18°23E **54** E3
Lokoloko → *Dem. Rep. of the Congo* 2°19S 23°15E **54** E4
Lola, Mt. *U.S.A.* 39°26N 120°22W **78** F6
Lolland *Denmark* 54°45N 11°30E **9** J14
Lolo *U.S.A.* 46°45N 114°5W **76** C6
Lom *Bulgaria* 43°48N 23°12E **23** C10
Lom Kao *Thailand* 16°53N 101°14E **38** D3
Lom Sak *Thailand* 16°47N 101°15E **38** D3
Loma *U.S.A.* 34°3N 117°16W **79** L9
Loma Linda *U.S.A.* 34°3N 117°16W **79** L9
Lomaloma *Fiji* 17°17S 178°59W **59** a
Lomami →
  Dem. Rep. of the Congo 0°46N 24°16E **54** D4
Lomas de Zamora
  Argentina 34°45S 58°24W **94** C4
Lombadina *Australia* 16°31S 122°54E **60** C3
Lombárdia □ *Italy* 45°40N 9°30E **20** D8
Lombardy = Lombárdia □
  Italy 45°40N 9°30E **20** D8
Lomblen *Indonesia* 8°30S 123°32E **37** F6
Lombok *Indonesia* 8°45S 116°30E **36** F5
Lombok, Selat *Indonesia* 8°30S 115°50E **37** K18
Lomé *Togo* 6°9N 1°20E **52** G6
Lomela
  Dem. Rep. of the Congo 2°19S 23°15E **54** E4
Lomela → *Dem. Rep. of the Congo* 0°15S 20°40E **54** E4
Lommel *Belgium* 51°14N 5°19E **15** C5

Lomond *Canada* 50°24N 112°36W **70** C6
Lomond, L. *U.K.* 56°8N 4°38W **11** E4
Lomonosov Ridge *Arctic* 88°0N 140°0E **4** A
Lomphat *Cambodia* 13°30N 106°59E **38** F6
Lompobatang *Indonesia* 5°24S 119°56E **37** F5
Lompoc *U.S.A.* 34°38N 120°28W **79** L6
Łomża *Poland* 53°10N 22°2E **17** B12
Lon, Ko *Thailand* 7°47N 98°23E **39** a
Lonavale *India* 18°46N 73°29E **44** E1
Loncoche *Chile* 39°20S 72°50W **96** D2
Londa *India* 15°30N 74°30E **45** G2
London *Canada* 42°59N 81°15W **82** D3
London *Ky., U.S.A.* 37°8N 84°5W **81** G11
London *Ohio, U.S.A.* 39°53N 83°27W **81** F12
London, Greater □ *U.K.* 51°36N 0°5W **13** F7
London Gateway *U.K.* 51°31N 0°29E **13** F8
London Gatwick ✈ (LGW)
  U.K. 51°10N 0°11W **13** F7
London Stansted ✈ (STN)
  U.K. 51°54N 0°14E **13** F8
Londonderry *U.K.* 55°0N 7°20W **10** B4
Londonderry □ *U.K.* 55°0N 7°20W **10** B4
Londonderry, C.
  Australia 13°45S 126°55E **60** B4
Londonderry, I. *Chile* 55°0S 71°0W **96** H2
Londres *Argentina* 27°43S 67°7W **94** B2
Londres *Argentina* 27°43S 67°7W **96** B3
Londrina *Brazil* 23°18S 51°10W **95** A5
Lone Pine *U.S.A.* 36°36N 118°4W **78** J8
Lonely Mine *Zimbabwe* 19°30S 28°49E **57** A4
Long B. *U.S.A.* 33°35N 78°45W **85** E15
Long Beach *Calif.,*
  U.S.A. 33°46N 118°11W **79** M8
Long Beach *N.Y., U.S.A.* 40°35N 73°39W **83** F11
Long Beach *Wash.,*
  U.S.A. 46°21N 124°3W **78** D2
Long Branch *U.S.A.* 40°18N 74°0W **83** F11
Long Creek *U.S.A.* 44°43N 119°6W **76** D4
Long Eaton *U.K.* 52°53N 1°15W **12** E6
Long I. *Australia* 20°22S 148°51E **62** b
Long I. *Bahamas* 23°20N 75°10W **89** B4
Long I. *Canada* 54°50N 79°20W **72** B4
Long I. *Ireland* 51°30N 9°34W **10** E2
Long I. *U.S.A.* 40°45N 73°30W **83** F11
Long Island Sd. *U.S.A.* 41°10N 73°0W **83** E12
Long L. *Canada* 49°30N 86°50W **72** C2
Long L. *U.S.A.* 44°0N 74°23W **83** C10
Long Lake *U.S.A.* 43°58N 74°25W **83** C10
Long Point *Canada* 42°34N 80°25W **82** D4
Long Point B. *Canada* 42°40N 80°10W **82** D4
Long Prairie *U.S.A.* 45°59N 94°52W **80** C6
Long Prairie → *U.S.A.* 46°20N 94°36W **80** B6
Long Pt. *Ont., Canada* 42°35N 80°2W **82** D4
Long Pt. *Ont., Canada* 43°56N 76°53W **83** C8
Long Range Mts. *Canada* 49°30N 57°30W **73** C8
Long Reef *Australia* 14°1S 125°48E **60** B4
Long Sault *Canada* 45°2N 74°53W **83** A10
Long Str. = Longa, Proliv
  Russia 70°0N 175°0E **27** C18
Long Thanh *Vietnam* 10°47N 106°57E **39** G6
Long Xian *China* 34°55N 106°55E **32** G4
Long Xuyen *Vietnam* 10°19N 105°28E **39** G5
Longa, Proliv *Russia* 70°0N 175°0E **27** C18
Long'an *China* 23°10N 107°40E **34** F6
Longbenton *U.K.* 55°1N 1°31W **12** B6
Longboat Key *U.S.A.* 27°23N 82°39W **85** H13
Longchang *China* 29°18N 105°15E **34** C5
Longchuan *Guangdong,*
  China 24°5N 115°17E **35** E10
Longchuan *Yunnan, China* 24°23N 97°58E **34** E1
Longde *China* 35°30N 106°20E **32** G4
Longford *Australia* 41°32S 147°3E **63** G4
Longford *Ireland* 53°43N 7°49W **10** C4
Longford □ *Ireland* 53°42N 7°45W **10** C4
Longford, An = Longford
  Ireland 53°43N 7°49W **10** C4
Longhai *China* 24°25N 117°46E **35** E11
Longhua *Guangdong, China* 22°39N 114°0E **31** a
Longhua *Hebei, China* 41°18N 117°45E **33** D9
Longhua *China* 27°7N 111°2E **35** D8
Longiram *Indonesia* 0°5S 115°45E **36** E5
Longjing *China* 42°46N 129°25E **33** C15
Longkou *Jiangxi, China* 26°8N 115°10E **35** D10
Longkou *Shandong,*
  China 37°40N 120°18E **33** F11
Longlac *Canada* 49°45N 86°25W **72** C2
Longli *China* 26°25N 106°58E **34** D6
Longlin *China* 24°47N 105°20E **34** E5
Longling *China* 24°37N 98°39E **34** E2
Longmeadow *U.S.A.* 42°3N 72°34W **83** D12
Longmen *China* 23°43N 114°18E **35** F10
Longmen Shiku *China* 34°28N 112°28E **32** G7
Longming *China* 22°59N 107°7E **34** F6
Longmont *U.S.A.* 40°10N 105°6W **76** F11
Longnan *China* 24°55N 114°47E **35** E10
Longnawan *Indonesia* 1°51N 114°55E **36** D4
Longquan *China* 28°7N 119°10E **35** C12
Longreach *Australia* 23°28S 144°14E **62** C3
Longshan *China* 29°29N 109°25E **34** C7
Longsheng *China* 25°48N 110°0E **35** E8
Longtan Dam *China* 25°5N 107°0E **34** E6
Longtan Shuiku *China* 25°10N 106°50E **34** E6
Longview *Tex., U.S.A.* 32°30N 94°44W **84** E7
Longview *Wash., U.S.A.* 46°8N 122°57W **78** D4
Longxi *China* 34°53N 104°40E **32** G3
Longxue Dao *China* 22°41N 113°38E **31** a
Longyearbyen *Svalbard* 78°13N 15°40E **4** B8
Longyou *China* 29°1N 119°8E **35** C12
Longzhou *China* 22°22N 106°50E **34** F6
Lonoke *U.S.A.* 34°47N 91°54W **84** D9
Lonquimay *Chile* 38°26S 71°14W **96** D2
Lons-le-Saunier *France* 46°40N 5°31E **20** C6
Looe *U.K.* 50°22N 4°28E **13** G3
Lookout, C. *Canada* 55°18N 83°56W **72** A3
Lookout, C. *U.S.A.* 34°35N 76°32W **85** D16
Loon → *Alta., Canada* 57°8N 115°3W **70** B5
Loon → *Man., Canada* 55°53N 101°59W **71** B8
Loon Lake *Canada* 54°2N 109°10W **71** C7
Loongana *Australia* 30°52S 127°5E **61** F4

Loop Hd. *Ireland* 52°34N 9°56W **10** D2
Lop *China* 37°3N 80°11E **30** D5
Lop Nor = Lop Nur *China* 40°20N 90°10E **30** C7
Lop Nur *China* 40°20N 90°10E **30** C7
Lopatina, Gora *Russia* 50°47N 143°10E **27** D15
Lopatka, Mys *Russia* 50°52N 156°40E **27** D16
Lopburi *Thailand* 14°48N 100°37E **38** E3
Lopez *U.S.A.* 41°27N 76°20W **83** E8
Lopez, C. *Gabon* 0°47S 8°40E **54** E1
Lopphavet *Norway* 70°27N 21°15E **8** A19
Lora → *Afghan.* 31°35N 66°32E **40** D4
Lora, Hāmūn-i- *Pakistan* 29°38N 64°58E **40** E4
Lora Cr. → *Australia* 28°10S 135°22E **63** D2
Lora del Río *Spain* 37°39N 5°33W **21** D3
Lorain *U.S.A.* 41°28N 82°11W **82** E2
Loralai *Pakistan* 30°20N 68°41E **42** D3
Lorca *Spain* 37°41N 1°42W **21** D5
Lord Howe I. *Pac. Oc.* 31°33S 159°6E **58** E8
Lord Howe Rise *Pac. Oc.* 30°0S 162°30E **64** L8
Lord Loughborough I.
  Myanmar 10°25N 97°54E **39** G1
Lordsburg *U.S.A.* 32°21N 108°43W **77** K9
Lorestān □ *Iran* 33°30N 48°40E **47** C6
Loreto *Brazil* 7°5S 45°10W **93** E9
Loreto *Mexico* 26°0N 111°21W **86** B2
Lorient *France* 47°45N 3°23W **20** C2
Lormi *India* 22°17N 81°41E **43** H9
Lorn *U.K.* 56°26N 5°10W **11** E3
Lorn, Firth of *U.K.* 56°20N 5°40W **11** E3
Lorne *Australia* 38°33S 143°59E **63** F3
Lorraine *France* 48°53N 6°0E **20** B7
Los Alamos *Calif., U.S.A.* 34°44N 120°17W **79** L6
Los Alamos *N. Mex.,
  U.S.A.* 35°53N 106°19W **77** J10
Los Altos *U.S.A.* 37°23N 122°7W **78** H4
Los Andes *Chile* 32°50S 70°40W **94** C1
Los Angeles *Chile* 37°28S 72°23W **94** D1
Los Angeles Aqueduct
  U.S.A. 35°22N 118°5W **79** K9
Los Banos *U.S.A.* 37°4N 120°51W **78** H6
Los Blancos *Argentina* 23°40S 62°30W **94** A3
Los Cabos Int. ✈ (SJD)
  Mexico 23°9N 109°43W **86** C3
Los Cardones △ *Argentina* 25°8S 65°55W **94** B2
Los Chiles *Costa Rica* 11°2N 84°43W **88** D3
Los Gatos *U.S.A.* 37°14N 121°59W **78** H5
Los Haïtises △ *Dom. Rep.* 19°4N 69°36W **89** C6
Los Hermanos, Is.
  Venezuela 11°45N 64°25W **89** D7
Los Loros *Chile* 27°50S 70°6W **94** B1
Los Lunas *U.S.A.* 34°48N 106°44W **77** J10
Los Mochis *Mexico* 25°45N 108°57W **86** B3
Los Olivos *U.S.A.* 34°40N 120°7W **79** L6
Los Palacios *Cuba* 22°35N 83°15W **88** B3
Los Queñes *Chile* 35°1S 70°48W **94** D1
Los Reyes de Salgado
  Mexico 19°35N 102°29W **86** D4
Los Roques, Is. *Venezuela* 11°50N 66°45W **89** D6
Los Teques *Venezuela* 10°21N 67°2W **92** A5
Los Testigos, Is. *Venezuela* 11°23N 63°6W **92** A6
Los Vilos *Chile* 32°10S 71°30W **94** C1
Lošinj *Croatia* 44°30N 14°30E **16** F8
Loskop Dam *S. Africa* 25°23S 29°20E **57** C4
Lossiemouth *U.K.* 57°42N 3°17W **11** D5
Lostwithiel *U.K.* 50°24N 4°41W **13** G3
Lot → *France* 44°18N 0°20E **20** D4
Lota *Chile* 37°5S 73°10W **94** D1
Lotfābād *Iran* 37°32N 59°20E **47** B8
Lothair *S. Africa* 26°22S 30°27E **57** C5
Lotta → *Europe* 68°42N 31°6E **8** B24
Lotung *Taiwan* 24°41N 121°46E **35** E13
Loubomo *Congo* 4°9S 12°47E **54** E2
Loudi *China* 27°42N 111°59E **35** D8
Loudonville *U.S.A.* 40°38N 82°14W **82** F2
Louga *Senegal* 15°45N 16°5W **52** E2
Loughborough *U.K.* 52°47N 1°11W **12** E6
Lougheed I. *Canada* 77°26N 105°6W **69** B10
Loughrea *Ireland* 53°12N 8°33W **10** C3
Loughros More B. *Ireland* 54°48N 8°32W **10** B3
Louis Trichardt *S. Africa* 23°1S 29°43E **57** B4
Louis XIV, Pte. *Canada* 54°37N 79°45W **72** B4
Louisa *U.S.A.* 38°7N 82°36W **81** F12
Louisbourg *Canada* 45°55N 60°0W **73** C8
Louisburgh *Ireland* 53°46N 9°49W **10** C2
Louise I. *Canada* 52°55N 131°50W **70** C2
Louiseville *Canada* 46°20N 72°56W **72** C5
Louisiade Arch.
  Papua N. G. 11°10S 153°0E **58** C8
Louisiana *U.S.A.* 39°27N 91°3W **80** F8
Louisiana □ *U.S.A.* 30°50N 92°0W **84** F9
Louisville *Ky., U.S.A.* 38°15N 85°46W **81** F11
Louisville *Miss., U.S.A.* 33°7N 89°3W **85** E10
Louisville *Ohio, U.S.A.* 40°50N 81°16W **82** F3
Louisville Ridge *Pac. Oc.* 31°0S 172°30W **64** L10
Loulé *Portugal* 37°9N 8°0W **21** D1
Loup City *U.S.A.* 41°17N 98°58W **80** E4
Loups Marins, Lacs des
  Canada 56°30N 73°45W **72** A5
Lourdes *France* 43°6N 0°3W **20** E3
Lourdes-de-Blanc-Sablon
  Canada 51°24N 57°12W **73** B8
Louth *Australia* 30°30S 145°8E **63** E4
Louth *Ireland* 53°58N 6°32W **10** C5
Louth *U.K.* 53°22N 0°1W **12** D7
Louth □ *Ireland* 53°56N 6°34W **10** C5
Louvain = Leuven
  Belgium 50°52N 4°42E **15** D4
Louwsburg *S. Africa* 27°37S 31°7E **57** D5
Loveland *U.S.A.* 40°24N 105°5W **76** F11
Lovell *U.S.A.* 44°50N 108°24W **76** D9
Lovelock *U.S.A.* 40°11N 118°28W **76** F4
Loviisa *Finland* 60°28N 26°12E **8** F22
Lovina *Indonesia* 8°9S 115°1E **37** J18
Loving *U.S.A.* 32°17N 104°6W **77** K11
Lovington *U.S.A.* 32°57N 103°21W **77** K12
Lovisa = Loviisa *Finland* 60°28N 26°12E **8** F22
Low, L. *Canada* 52°29N 76°17W **72** B4
Low Pt. *Australia* 32°25S 127°25E **61** F4
Low Tatra = Nízké Tatry
  Slovakia 48°55N 19°30E **17** D10

Lowell *U.S.A.* 42°38N 71°19W **83** D13
Lowellville *U.S.A.* 41°2N 80°32W **82** E4
Löwen → *Namibia* 26°51S 18°17E **56** C2
Lower Alkali L. *U.S.A.* 41°16N 120°2W **76** F3
Lower Arrow L. *Canada* 49°40N 118°5W **70** D5
Lower California = Baja California
  Mexico 31°10N 115°12W **86** A1
Lower Hutt *N.Z.* 41°10S 174°55E **59** D5
Lower Lake *U.S.A.* 38°55N 122°37W **78** G4
Lower Manitou L.
  Canada 49°15N 93°0W **71** D10
Lower Post *Canada* 59°58N 128°30W **70** B3
Lower Red L. *U.S.A.* 47°58N 95°0W **80** B6
Lower Saxony = Niedersachsen □
  Germany 52°50N 9°0E **16** B5
Lower Tunguska = Tunguska,
  Nizhnyaya → *Russia* 65°48N 88°4E **27** C9
Lowestoft *U.K.* 52°29N 1°45E **13** E9
Lowgar □ *Afghan.* 34°0N 69°0E **40** B6
Lowick *I. Canada* 74°33N 97°30W **69** C12
Lowther I. *Canada* 74°33N 97°30W **69** C12
Lowville *U.S.A.* 43°47N 75°29W **83** C9
Loxton *Australia* 34°28S 140°31E **63** E3
Loxton *S. Africa* 31°30S 22°22E **56** D3
Loyalton *U.S.A.* 39°41N 120°14W **78** F6
Loyalty Is. = Loyauté, Îs.
  N. Cal. 20°50S 166°30E **58** D9
Loyang = Luoyang
  China 34°40N 112°26E **32** G7
Loyauté, Îs. *N. Cal.* 20°50S 166°30E **58** D9
Loyev = Loyew *Belarus* 51°56N 30°46E **17** C16
Loyew *Belarus* 51°56N 30°46E **17** C16
Ltalaltuma ☺ *Australia* 23°57S 132°25E **60** D5
Lü Shan *China* 29°30N 115°55E **35** C10
Lü Shan △ *China* 29°26N 115°52E **35** C10
Lu Wo *China* 22°33N 114°6E **31** a
Luachimo *Angola* 7°23S 20°48E **54** F4
Luajan → *India* 24°44N 85°1E **43** G11
Lualaba →
  Dem. Rep. of the Congo 0°26N 25°20E **54** D5
Lu'an *China* 31°45N 116°29E **35** B11
Luan Chau *Vietnam* 21°38N 103°24E **34** G4
Luan He → *China* 39°20N 119°5E **33** E10
Luan Xian *China* 39°40N 118°40E **33** E10
Luancheng *Guangxi Zhuangzu,
  China* 22°48N 108°55E **34** F7
Luancheng *Hebei, China* 37°53N 114°40E **32** F8
Luanda *Angola* 8°50S 13°15E **54** F2
Luang, Doi *Thailand* 18°30N 101°15E **38** C3
Luang, Thale *Thailand* 7°30N 100°15E **39** J3
Luang Nam Tha *Laos* 20°58N 101°30E **34** G3
Luang Prabang *Laos* 19°52N 102°10E **34** H4
Luangwa → *Zambia* 14°25S 30°25E **55** G6
Luangwa Valley *Zambia* 13°30S 31°30E **55** G6
Luangwe = Loange →
  Dem. Rep. of the Congo 4°17S 20°2E **54** E4
Luanne *China* 40°55N 117°40E **33** D9
Luanping *China* 40°53N 117°23E **33** D9
Luanshya *Zambia* 13°3S 28°28E **55** G5
Luapula → *Africa* 9°26S 28°33E **55** D9b
Luarca *Spain* 43°32N 6°32W **21** A2
Luashi
  Dem. Rep. of the Congo 10°50S 23°36E **54** G4
Luau *Angola* 10°40S 22°10E **54** G4
Lubana, Ozero = Lubānas Ezers
  Latvia 56°45N 27°0E **9** H22
Lubānas Ezers *Latvia* 56°45N 27°0E **9** H22
Lubang Is. *Phil.* 13°50N 120°12E **37** B6
Lubango *Angola* 14°55S 13°30E **55** G2
Lubbock *U.S.A.* 33°35N 101°51W **84** E4
Lübeck *Germany* 53°52N 10°40E **16** B6
Lubero = Luofu
  Dem. Rep. of the Congo 0°1S 29°15E **54** E5
Lubilash →
  Dem. Rep. of the Congo 6°2S 23°45E **54** F4
Lubicon L. *Canada* 56°23N 115°56W **70** B5
Lubin *Poland* 51°24N 16°11E **16** C9
Lublin *Poland* 51°12N 22°38E **17** C12
Lubnān = Lebanon ■ *Asia* 34°0N 36°0E **48** B5
Lubnān, Jabal *Lebanon* 33°45N 35°40E **48** B4
Lubny *Ukraine* 50°3N 32°58E **26** D4
Lubudi
  Dem. Rep. of the Congo 9°57S 25°58E **54** F5
Lubuklinggau *Indonesia* 3°15S 102°55E **36** E2
Lubuksikaping *Indonesia* 0°10N 100°15E **36** D2
Lubumbashi
  Dem. Rep. of the Congo 11°40S 27°28E **55** G5
Lubutu
  Dem. Rep. of the Congo 0°45S 26°30E **54** E5
Luc An Chau *Vietnam* 22°6N 104°43E **34** F5
Lucan *Canada* 43°11N 81°24W **82** C3
Lucan *Ireland* 53°22N 6°28W **10** C5
Lucania, Mt. *Canada* 61°1N 140°27W **68** E3
Lucas Channel = Main Channel
  Canada 45°21N 81°45W **82** A3
Lucca *Italy* 43°50N 10°29E **22** C4
Luce Bay *U.K.* 54°45N 4°48W **11** G4
Lucea *Jamaica* 18°27N 78°10W **88** a
Lucedale *U.S.A.* 30°56N 88°35W **85** F10
Lucena *Phil.* 13°56N 121°37E **37** B6
Lucena *Spain* 37°27N 4°31W **21** D3
Lučenec *Slovakia* 48°18N 19°42E **17** D10
Lucerne = Luzern *Switz.* 47°3N 8°18E **20** C8
Lucerne *U.S.A.* 39°6N 122°48W **78** F4
Lucerne Valley *U.S.A.* 34°27N 116°57W **79** L10
Lucheng *China* 36°20N 113°11E **32** F7
Luchuan *China* 22°21N 110°12E **35** F8
Lucinda *Australia* 18°32S 146°20E **62** B4
Luckenwalde *Germany* 52°5N 13°10E **16** B7
Luckhoff *S. Africa* 29°44S 24°43E **56** D3
Lucknow *Canada* 43°57N 81°31W **82** C3
Lucknow *India* 26°50N 81°0E **43** F9
Lüda = Dalian *China* 38°50N 121°40E **33** E11
Lüderitz *Namibia* 26°41S 15°8E **56** D2
Lüderitzbaai *Namibia* 26°36S 15°8E **56** D2
Ludhiana *India* 30°57N 75°56E **42** D6
Ludian *China* 27°10N 103°33E **34** D4
Luding Qiao *China* 29°53N 102°12E **34** C4
Ludington *U.S.A.* 43°57N 86°27W **80** D10
Ludlow *U.K.* 52°22N 2°42W **13** E5

Ludlow *Calif., U.S.A.* 34°43N 116°10W **79** L10
Ludlow *Pa., U.S.A.* 41°43N 78°56W **82** E6
Ludlow *Vt., U.S.A.* 43°24N 72°42W **83** C12
Ludvika *Sweden* 60°8N 15°14E **9** F16
Ludwigsburg *Germany* 48°53N 9°11E **16** D5
Ludwigshafen *Germany* 49°29N 8°26E **16** D5
Luena Flats *Zambia* 14°47S 23°17E **55** G4
Lüeyang *China* 33°22N 106°10E **34** A6
Lufeng *Guangdong,
  China* 22°57N 115°38E **35** F10
Lufeng *Yunnan, China* 25°0N 102°5E **34** E4
Lufira →
  Dem. Rep. of the Congo 9°30S 27°0E **54** F5
Lufkin *U.S.A.* 31°21N 94°44W **84** F7
Luga *Russia* 58°40N 29°55E **9** G23
Lugano *Switz.* 46°1N 8°57E **20** C8
Lugansk = Luhansk
  Ukraine 48°38N 39°15E **19** E6
Lugenda → *Mozam.* 11°25S 38°33E **55** G7
Lugh = Luuq *Somalia* 3°48N 42°34E **49** G3
Lugnaquilla *Ireland* 52°58N 6°28W **10** D5
Lugo *Italy* 44°25N 11°54E **22** B4
Lugo *Spain* 43°2N 7°35W **21** A2
Lugoj *Romania* 45°42N 21°57E **17** F11
Lugovoy = Qulan
  Kazakhstan 42°55N 72°43E **26** E8
Luhansk *Ukraine* 48°38N 39°15E **19** E6
Luhe *China* 32°19N 118°50E **35** A12
Luhuo *China* 31°21N 100°48E **34** B3
Lui → *Angola* 8°21S 17°33E **54** F3
Luiana *Angola* 17°25S 22°59E **56** A3
Luiana → *Angola* 17°24S 23°3E **55** H4
Luichow Pen. = Leizhou Bandao
  China 21°0N 110°0E **34** G7
Luimneach = Limerick
  Ireland 52°40N 8°37W **10** D3
Luing *U.K.* 56°14N 5°39W **11** E3
Luís Correia *Brazil* 3°0S 41°35W **93** D10
Luitpold Coast *Antarctica* 78°30S 32°0W **5** D1
Luiza *Dem. Rep. of the Congo* 7°40S 22°30E **54** F4
Luján *Argentina* 34°45S 59°5W **94** C4
Lujiang *China* 31°20N 117°15E **35** B11
Lukang *Taiwan* 24°1N 120°22E **35** E13
Lukanga Swamp *Zambia* 14°30S 27°40E **55** G5
Lukenie →
  Dem. Rep. of the Congo 3°0S 18°50E **54** E3
Lukla *Nepal* 27°42N 86°43E **43** F12
Łuków *Poland* 51°55N 22°23E **17** C12
Lülang Shan *China* 38°0N 111°15E **32** F6
Luleå *Sweden* 65°35N 22°10E **8** D20
Luleälven → *Sweden* 65°35N 22°10E **8** D20
Lüleburgaz *Turkey* 41°23N 27°22E **23** D12
Luliang *China* 25°0N 103°40E **34** E4
Luling *U.S.A.* 29°41N 97°39W **84** G6
Lulong *China* 39°53N 118°51E **33** E10
Lulonga →
  Dem. Rep. of the Congo 1°0N 18°10E **54** D3
Lulua →
  Dem. Rep. of the Congo 4°30S 20°30E **54** E4
Luma *Amer. Samoa* 14°16S 169°33W **59** b
Lumajang *Indonesia* 8°8S 113°13E **37** H15
Lumbala N'guimbo
  Angola 14°18S 21°18E **55** G4
Lumberton *N.C., U.S.A.* 34°37N 79°0W **85** D15
Lumberton *Tex., U.S.A.* 30°16N 94°12W **84** F7
Lumsden *Canada* 50°39N 104°52W **71** C8
Lumsden *N.Z.* 45°44S 168°27E **59** F2
Lumut *Malaysia* 4°13N 100°37E **39** K3
Lumut, Tanjung *Indonesia* 3°50S 105°58E **36** E3
Luna *India* 23°43N 69°16E **42** H3
Lunan *China* 24°40N 103°18E **34** E4
Lunavada *India* 23°8N 73°37E **42** H5
Lund *Sweden* 55°44N 13°12E **9** J15
Lundazi *Zambia* 12°20S 33°7E **55** G6
Lundu *Malaysia* 1°40N 109°50E **36** D3
Lundy *U.K.* 51°10N 4°41W **13** F3
Lune → *U.K.* 54°0N 2°51W **12** C5
Lüneburg *Germany* 53°15N 10°24E **16** B6
Lüneburg Heath = Lüneburger
  Heide *Germany* 53°10N 10°12E **16** B6
Lüneburger Heide
  Germany 53°10N 10°12E **16** B6
Lunenburg *Canada* 44°22N 64°18W **73** D7
Lunéville *France* 48°36N 6°30E **20** B7
Lunglei *India* 22°55N 92°45E **41** H18
Luni *India* 26°0N 73°6E **42** G5
Luni → *India* 24°41N 71°14E **42** G4
Luninets = Luninyets
  Belarus 52°15N 26°50E **17** B14
Luning *U.S.A.* 38°30N 118°11W **76** G4
Luninyets *Belarus* 52°15N 26°50E **17** B14
Lunkaransar *India* 28°29N 73°44E **42** E5
Luo He → *China* 34°35N 110°20E **32** G6
Luocheng *China* 24°48N 108°53E **34** E7
Luochuan *China* 35°45N 109°26E **32** G5
Luoci *China* 25°19N 102°18E **34** E4
Luodian *China* 25°24N 106°43E **34** E6
Luoding *China* 22°45N 111°40E **35** F8
Luofu *Dem. Rep. of the Congo* 0°10S 29°15E **54** E5
Luohe *China* 33°32N 114°2E **32** H8
Luojiang *China* 31°18N 104°33E **34** B5
Luonan *China* 34°5N 110°10E **32** G6
Luoning *China* 34°35N 111°40E **32** G6
Luoshan *China* 32°13N 114°30E **35** A10
Luotian *China* 30°46N 115°22E **35** B10
Luoxiao Shan *China* 26°30N 114°1E **35** D10
Luoyang *China* 26°28N 119°30E **35** D12
Luozigou *China* 43°42N 130°18E **33** C16
Lupeng *China* 24°53N 104°21E **34** E5
Luquan *Hebei, China* 38°4N 114°17E **32** E8
Luquan *Yunnan, China* 25°35N 102°40E **34** E4
Luque *Paraguay* 25°19S 57°25W **94** B4
Luquillo, Sierra de
  Puerto Rico 18°20N 65°47W **89** d
Luray *U.S.A.* 38°40N 78°28W **81** F14
Lurgan *U.K.* 54°27N 6°20W **10** B5
Lusaka *Zambia* 15°28S 28°16E **55** H5
Lusambo
  Dem. Rep. of the Congo 4°58S 23°28E **54** E4

Luseland *Canada* 52°5N 109°24W **71** C7
Lushan *Henan, China* 33°45N 112°55E **32** H7
Lushan *Sichuan, China* 30°12N 102°52E **34** B4
Lushi *China* 34°3N 111°3E **32** G6
Lushnjë *Albania* 40°55N 19°41E **23** D8
Lushui *China* 25°58N 98°44E **34** E2
Lüshun *China* 38°45N 121°15E **33** E11
Lusk *U.S.A.* 42°46N 104°27W **76** E11
Lūt, Dasht-e *Iran* 31°30N 58°0E **47** D8
Luta = Dalian *China* 38°50N 121°40E **33** E11
Lütao *Taiwan* 22°40N 121°30E **35** F13
Lutherstadt Wittenberg
  Germany 51°53N 12°39E **16** C7
Luton *U.K.* 51°53N 0°24W **13** F7
Luton □ *U.K.* 51°53N 0°24W **13** F7
Lutsel K'e *Canada* 62°24N 110°44W **71** A6
Lutsk *Ukraine* 50°50N 25°15E **17** C13
Lutto = Lotta → *Europe* 68°42N 31°6E **8** B24
Lützow Holmbukta
  Antarctica 69°10N 37°30E **5** C4
Lutzputs *S. Africa* 28°3S 20°40E **56** D3
Luuq *Somalia* 3°48N 42°34E **49** G3
Luverne *Ala., U.S.A.* 31°43N 86°16W **85** F11
Luverne *Minn., U.S.A.* 43°39N 96°13W **80** D5
Luvua →
  Dem. Rep. of the Congo 6°50S 27°30E **54** F5
Luvuvhu → *S. Africa* 22°25S 31°18E **57** B5
Luwuk *Indonesia* 0°56S 122°47E **37** E6
Luxembourg *Lux.* 49°37N 6°9E **15** E6
Luxembourg □ *Belgium* 49°58N 5°30E **15** E5
Luxembourg ■ *Europe* 49°45N 6°0E **15** E5
Luxembourg ✈ (LUX)
  Lux. 49°37N 6°10E **15** E6
Luxi *Hunan, China* 28°20N 110°7E **35** C8
Luxi *Yunnan, China* 24°40N 103°55E **34** E4
Luxi *Yunnan, China* 24°27N 98°36E **34** E2
Luxian *China* 29°25N 105°24E **34** C5
Luxor = El Uqsur *Egypt* 25°41N 32°38E **53** C12
Luyi *China* 33°50N 115°35E **32** H8
Luyksgestel
  Neths. 51°18N 5°23E **15** C5
Luykau = Loikaw
  Myanmar 19°40N 97°17E **41** K20
Luza *Russia* 60°39N 47°10E **18** B8
Luzern *Switz.* 47°3N 8°18E **20** C8
Luzhai *China* 24°29N 109°42E **34** E7
Luzhi *China* 26°21N 105°16E **34** D5
Luzhou *China* 28°52N 105°20E **34** C5
Luziânia *Brazil* 16°20S 48°0W **93** G9
Luzon *Phil.* 16°0N 121°0E **37** A6
Luzon Strait *Asia* 21°0N 120°40E **35** G13
Lviv *Ukraine* 49°50N 24°0E **17** D13
Lviv □ *Ukraine* 49°30N 23°45E **17** D12
Lvov = Lviv *Ukraine* 49°50N 24°0E **17** D13
Lyakhavichy *Belarus* 53°2N 26°32E **17** B14
Lyakhovskiye, Ostrova
  Russia 73°40N 141°0E **27** B15
Lyal I. *Canada* 44°57N 81°24W **82** B3
Lybster *U.K.* 58°18N 3°15W **11** C5
Lycksele *Sweden* 64°38N 18°40E **8** D18
Lydda = Lod *Israel* 31°57N 34°54E **48** D3
Lyddan I. *Antarctica* 74°0S 21°0W **5** D2
Lydenburg *S. Africa* 25°10S 30°29E **57** C5
Lydia *Turkey* 38°48N 28°19E **23** E13
Lyell *N.Z.* 41°48S 172°4E **59** D4
Lyell I. *Canada* 52°40N 131°35W **70** C2
Lyepyel *Belarus* 54°50N 28°40E **9** J23
Lykens *U.S.A.* 40°34N 76°42W **83** F8
Lyman *U.S.A.* 41°20N 110°18W **76** F8
Lyme B. *U.K.* 50°42N 2°53W **13** G4
Lyme Regis *U.K.* 50°43N 2°57W **13** G5
Lymington *U.K.* 50°45N 1°32W **13** G6
Łyna → *Poland* 54°37N 21°14E **17** A11
Lynchburg *U.S.A.* 37°25N 79°9W **81** G14
Lynd → *Australia* 16°28S 143°18E **62** B3
Lynd Ra. *Australia* 25°30S 149°20E **63** D4
Lynden *Canada* 43°14N 80°9W **82** C4
Lynden *U.S.A.* 48°57N 122°27W **78** B4
Lyndhurst *Australia* 30°15S 138°18E **63** E2
Lyndon → *Australia* 23°29S 114°6E **61** D1
Lyndonville *N.Y., U.S.A.* 43°20N 78°23W **82** C6
Lyndonville *Vt., U.S.A.* 44°31N 72°1W **83** B12
Lyngen *Norway* 69°45N 20°30E **8** B19
Lynher Reef *Australia* 15°27S 121°55E **60** C3
Lynn *U.S.A.* 42°28N 70°57W **83** D14
Lynn Canal *U.S.A.* 58°50N 135°15W **74** D22
Lynn Haven *U.S.A.* 30°15N 85°39W **85** F12
Lynn Lake *Canada* 56°51N 101°3W **71** B8
Lynnwood *U.S.A.* 47°49N 122°18W **78** C4
Lynton *U.K.* 51°13N 3°50W **13** F4
Lyntupy *Belarus* 55°4N 26°23E **9** J22
Lynx L. *Canada* 62°25N 106°15W **71** A7
Lyon *France* 45°46N 4°50E **20** D6
Lyonnais *France* 45°45N 4°15E **20** D6
Lyons = Lyon *France* 45°46N 4°50E **20** D6
Lyons *Ga., U.S.A.* 32°12N 82°19W **85** E13
Lyons *Kans., U.S.A.* 38°21N 98°12W **80** F4
Lyons *N.Y., U.S.A.* 43°5N 77°0W **82** C8
Lyons → *Australia* 25°2S 115°9E **61** E2
Lyons Falls *U.S.A.* 43°37N 75°22W **83** C9
Lys = Leie → *Belgium* 51°2N 3°45E **15** C3
Lysva *Russia* 58°7N 57°49E **18** C10
Lysychansk *Ukraine* 48°55N 38°30E **19** E6
Lytham St. Anne's *U.K.* 53°45N 3°0W **12** D4
Lyttelton *N.Z.* 43°35S 172°44E **59** E4
Lytton *Canada* 50°13N 121°31W **70** C4
Lyubertsy *Russia* 55°40N 37°51E **18** C6
Lyuboml *Ukraine* 51°11N 24°4E **17** C13

M

Ma → *Vietnam* 19°47N 105°56E **34** H5
Ma'adaba *Jordan* 31°43N 35°47E **48** D4
Maamba *Zambia* 17°17S 26°28E **56** A4
Ma'ān *Jordan* 30°12N 35°44E **48** E4
Ma'ān □ *Jordan* 30°0N 36°0E **48** E5
Maanselkä *Finland* 63°52N 28°32E **8** C23
Ma'anshan *China* 31°44N 118°29E **35** B12
Maarianhamina = Mariehamn
  Finland 60°5N 19°55E **9** F18
Ma'arrat an Nu'mān
  Syria 35°43N 36°43E **46** C3

Maas → *Neths.* 51°45N 4°32E **15** C4
Maaseik *Belgium* 51°6N 5°45E **15** C5
Maasin *Phil.* 10°8N 124°50E **37** B6
Maastricht *Neths.* 50°50N 5°40E **15** D5
Maave *Mozam.* 21°4S 34°47E **57** B5
Mababe Depression
  Botswana 18°50S 24°15E **56** A3
Mabalane *Mozam.* 23°37S 32°31E **57** B5
Mabel L. *Canada* 50°35N 118°43W **70** C5
Maberly *Canada* 44°50N 76°32W **83** B8
Mabian *China* 28°47N 103°37E **34** C4
Mablethorpe *U.K.* 53°20N 0°15E **12** D8
Mabuasehube △ *Botswana* 25°5S 21°10E **56** C3
Mabuiag *Australia* 9°57S 142°11E **62** a
Mac Bac *Vietnam* 9°46N 106°7E **39** H6
Macachín *Argentina* 37°10S 63°43W **94** D3
Macaé *Brazil* 22°20S 41°43W **95** A7
McAlester *U.S.A.* 34°56N 95°46W **84** D7
McAllen *U.S.A.* 26°12N 98°14W **84** H5
MacAlpine L. *Canada* 66°32N 102°45W **68** D11
Macamic *Canada* 48°45N 79°0W **72** C4
Macao = Macau *China* 22°12N 113°33E **35** F9
Macapá *Brazil* 0°5N 51°4W **93** C8
Macarao △ *Venezuela* 10°22N 67°7W **89** D6
McArthur → *Australia* 15°54S 136°40E **62** B2
McArthur, Port *Australia* 16°4S 136°23E **62** B2
Macau *Brazil* 5°15S 36°40W **93** E11
Macau *China* 22°12N 113°33E **35** F9
McBride *Canada* 53°20N 120°19W **70** C4
McCall *U.S.A.* 44°55N 116°6W **76** D5
McCamey *U.S.A.* 31°8N 102°14W **84** F3
McCammon *U.S.A.* 42°39N 112°12W **76** E7
McCauley I. *Canada* 53°40N 130°15W **70** C2
McCleary *U.S.A.* 47°3N 123°16W **78** C3
Macclenny *U.S.A.* 30°17N 82°7W **85** F13
Macclesfield *U.K.* 53°15N 2°8W **12** D5
Macclesfield Bank
  S. China Sea 16°0N 114°30E **36** A4
M'Clintock Chan.
  Canada 72°0N 102°0W **68** C11
McClintock Ra.
  Australia 18°44S 127°38E **60** C4
McCloud *U.S.A.* 41°15N 122°8W **76** F2
McCluer I. *Australia* 11°5S 133°0E **60** B5
McClure *U.S.A.* 40°42N 77°19W **82** F7
McClure, L. *U.S.A.* 37°35N 120°16W **78** H6
M'Clure Str. *Canada* 75°0N 119°0W **69** C8
McClusky *U.S.A.* 47°29N 100°27W **80** B3
McComb *U.S.A.* 31°15N 90°27W **85** F9
McCook *U.S.A.* 40°12N 100°38W **80** E3
McCreary *Canada* 50°47N 99°29W **71** C9
McCullough Mt.
  U.S.A. 35°35N 115°13W **79** K11
McCusker → *Canada* 55°32N 108°39W **71** B7
McDermitt *U.S.A.* 41°59N 117°43W **76** F5
Macdonald, L. *Australia* 23°30S 129°0E **60** D4
McDonald *U.S.A.* 40°22N 80°14W **82** F4
McDonald Is. *Ind. Oc.* 53°0S 73°0E **3** G13
MacDonnell Ranges
  Australia 23°40S 133°0E **60** D5
McDowell L. *Canada* 52°15N 92°45W **72** B1
Macduff *U.K.* 57°40N 2°31W **11** D6
Macedonia *U.S.A.* 41°19N 81°31W **82** E3
Macedonia □ *Greece* 40°39N 22°0E **23** D10
Macedonia ■ *Europe* 41°53N 21°40E **23** D9
Maceió *Brazil* 9°40S 35°41W **93** E11
Macerata *Italy* 43°18N 13°27E **22** C5
McFarland *U.S.A.* 35°41N 119°14W **79** K7
McFarlane → *Canada* 59°12N 107°58W **71** B7
Macfarlane, L. *Australia* 32°0S 136°40E **63** E2
McGehee *U.S.A.* 33°38N 91°24W **84** E9
McGill *U.S.A.* 39°23N 114°47W **76** G6
Macgillycuddy's Reeks
  Ireland 51°58N 9°45W **10** E2
McGraw *U.S.A.* 42°36N 76°8W **83** D8
McGregor *U.S.A.* 43°1N 91°11W **80** D8
McGregor Ra. *Australia* 27°0S 142°45E **63** D3
McGuire, Mt. *U.S.A.* 20°18S 148°23E **62** b
Mach *Pakistan* 29°50N 67°20E **42** E2
Māch Kowr *Iran* 25°48N 61°28E **47** E9
Machado = Jiparaná →
  Brazil 8°3S 62°52W **92** E6
Machagai *Argentina* 26°56S 60°2W **94** B3
Machakos *Kenya* 1°30S 37°15E **54** E7
Machala *Ecuador* 3°20S 79°57W **92** D3
Machanga *Mozam.* 20°59S 35°0E **57** B6
Machattie, L. *Australia* 24°50S 139°48E **62** C2
Macheke *Zimbabwe* 18°5S 31°51E **57** A5
Macheng *China* 31°12N 115°2E **35** B10
Macherla *India* 16°29N 79°26E **44** F4
Machgaon *India* 20°5N 86°17E **44** D8
Machhu → *India* 23°6N 70°46E **42** H4
Machiara △ *Pakistan* 34°40N 73°30E **42** B5
Machias *Maine, U.S.A.* 44°43N 67°28W **81** C20
Machias *N.Y., U.S.A.* 42°25N 78°29W **82** D6
Machichi → *Canada* 57°3N 92°6W **71** B10
Machilipatnam *India* 16°12N 81°8E **45** F5
Machipanga *Venezuela* 10°4N 72°34W **92** A4
Machu Picchu *Peru* 13°8S 72°30W **92** F4
Machynlleth *U.K.* 52°35N 3°50W **13** E4
Macia *Mozam.* 25°2S 33°8E **57** C5
McIlwraith Ra. *Australia* 13°50S 143°20E **62** A3
McInnes L. *Canada* 52°13N 93°45W **72** B1
McIntosh *U.S.A.* 45°55N 101°21W **80** C3
McIntosh L. *Canada* 55°45N 105°0W **71** B8
Macintosh Ra. *Australia* 27°39S 125°32E **61** E4
Macintyre → *Australia* 28°37S 150°47E **63** D5
Mackay *Australia* 21°8S 149°11E **62** K7
Mackay *U.S.A.* 43°55N 113°37W **76** E7
Mackay → *Canada* 57°10N 111°38W **70** B6
Mackay, L. *Australia* 22°30S 129°0E **60** D4
McKay Ra. *Australia* 23°0S 122°30E **60** D3
McKeesport *U.S.A.* 40°20N 79°51W **82** F5
McKellar *Canada* 45°30N 79°55W **82** A5
McKenna *U.S.A.* 46°56N 122°33W **78** D4
Mackenzie = Linden
  Guyana 6°0N 58°10W **92** B7
Mackenzie *Canada* 55°20N 123°5W **70** B4
McKenzie *U.S.A.* 36°8N 88°31W **85** C10

Mackenzie → *Australia* 23°38S 149°46E **62** C4
Mackenzie → *Canada* 69°10N 134°20W **68** D5
McKenzie → *U.S.A.* 44°7N 123°6W **76** D2
Mackenzie Bay *Canada* 69°0N 137°30W **66** C6
Mackenzie King I.
  Canada 77°45N 111°0W **69** B9
Mackenzie Mts. *Canada* 64°0N 130°0W **66** C6
Mackinac, Straits of
  U.S.A. 45°50N 84°40W **81** C11
Mackinaw City *U.S.A.* 45°47N 84°44W **81** C11
McKinlay *Australia* 21°16S 141°18E **62** C3
McKinlay → *Australia* 20°50S 141°28E **62** C3
McKinley, Mt. = Denali
  U.S.A. 63°4N 151°0W **68** E1
McKinley Sea *Arctic* 82°0N 0°0 **4** A7
McKinney *U.S.A.* 33°12N 96°37W **84** E6
McKittrick *U.S.A.* 35°18N 119°37W **79** K7
Macklin *Canada* 52°20N 109°56W **71** C7
Macksville *Australia* 30°40S 152°56E **63** E5
McLaughlin *U.S.A.* 45°49N 100°49W **80** C4
Maclean *Australia* 29°26S 153°16E **63** D5
McLean *U.S.A.* 35°14N 100°36W **84** D4
McLeansboro *U.S.A.* 38°6N 88°32W **80** F9
Maclear *S. Africa* 31°2S 28°23E **57** D4
Macleay → *Australia* 30°56S 153°0E **63** E5
McLennan *Canada* 55°42N 116°50W **70** B5
McLeod → *Canada* 54°9N 115°44W **70** C5
MacLeod, L. *Australia* 24°9S 113°47E **61** D1
MacLeod B. *Canada* 62°53N 110°0W **71** A7
MacLeod Lake *Canada* 54°58N 123°0W **70** C4
McLoughlin, Mt. *U.S.A.* 42°27N 122°19W **76** E2
McMechen *U.S.A.* 39°57N 80°44W **82** G4
McMinnville *Oreg.,*
  U.S.A. 45°13N 123°12W **76** D2
McMinnville *Tenn.,*
  U.S.A. 35°41N 85°46W **85** D12
McMurdo *Antarctica* 77°51S 166°37E **5** D11
McMurdo Sd. *Antarctica* 77°0S 170°0E **5** D11
McMurray = Fort McMurray
  Canada 56°44N 111°7W **70** B6
McMurray *U.S.A.* 48°19N 122°14W **78** B4
Maçobere *Mozam.* 21°13S 32°47E **57** B5
Macodoene *Mozam.* 23°32S 35°5E **57** B6
Macomb *U.S.A.* 40°27N 90°40W **80** E8
Mâcon *France* 46°19N 4°50E **20** C6
Macon *Ga., U.S.A.* 32°51N 83°38W **85** E13
Macon *Miss., U.S.A.* 33°7N 88°34W **85** E10
Macon *Mo., U.S.A.* 39°44N 92°28W **80** F7
Macoun L. *Canada* 56°32N 103°40W **71** B8
Macovane *Mozam.* 21°30S 35°2E **57** B6
McPherson *U.S.A.* 38°22N 97°40W **80** F5
McPherson Pk. *U.S.A.* 34°53N 119°53W **79** L7
McPherson Ra. *Australia* 28°15S 153°15E **63** D5
Macquarie → *Australia* 30°7S 147°24E **63** E4
Macquarie Harbour
  Australia 42°15S 145°23E **63** G4
Macquarie I. *Pac. Oc.* 54°36S 158°55E **64** N7
Macquarie Ridge *S. Ocean* 57°0S 159°0E **5** B10
MacRobertson Land
  Antarctica 71°0S 64°0E **5** D6
Macroom *Ireland* 51°54N 8°57W **10** E3
MacTier *Canada* 45°8N 79°47W **82** A5
Macuira △ *Colombia* 12°9N 71°21W **89** D5
Macumba → *Australia* 27°52S 137°12E **63** D2
Macuro *Venezuela* 10°42N 61°55W **93** K15
Macusani *Peru* 14°4S 70°29W **92** F4
Macuspana *Mexico* 17°46N 92°36W **87** D6
Macusse *Angola* 17°48S 20°23E **56** A3
Ma'dabā □ *Jordan* 31°43N 35°47E **48** D4
Madadeni *S. Africa* 27°43S 30°3E **57** C5
Madagascar ■ *Africa* 20°0S 47°0E **55** J9
Madā'in Sālih *Si. Arabia* 26°46N 37°57E **46** E3
Madakasira *India* 13°56N 77°16E **45** H3
Madama *Niger* 22°0N 13°40E **53** D8
Madame, I. *Canada* 45°30N 60°58W **73** C7
Madanapalle *India* 13°33N 78°28E **45** H4
Madang *Papua N. G.* 5°12S 145°49E **58** B7
Madaripur *Bangla.* 23°19N 90°15E **41** H17
Madawaska *Canada* 45°30N 78°0W **82** A7
Madawaska → *Canada* 45°27N 76°21W **82** A7
Madaya *Myanmar* 22°12N 96°10E **41** H20
Maddalena *Italy* 41°16N 9°23E **22** D3
Maddur *India* 12°36N 77°4E **45** H3
Madeira *Atl. Oc.* 32°50N 17°0W **52** B2
Madeira → *Brazil* 3°22S 58°45W **92** D7
Madeleine, Îs. de la
  Canada 47°30N 61°40W **73** C7
Madera *Mexico* 29°12N 108°7W **86** B3
Madera *Calif., U.S.A.* 36°57N 120°3W **78** J6
Madera *Pa., U.S.A.* 40°49N 78°26W **82** F6
Madgaon *India* 15°12N 73°58E **45** G1
Madha *India* 18°0N 75°30E **44** F2
Madhavpur *India* 21°15N 69°58E **42** J3
Madhepura *India* 26°11N 86°23E **43** F12
Madhira *India* 16°55N 80°22E **44** F5
Madhubani *India* 26°21N 86°7E **43** F12
Madhugiri *India* 13°40N 77°12E **45** H3
Madhupur *India* 24°16N 86°39E **43** G12
Madhya Pradesh □ *India* 22°50N 78°0E **42** J8
Madidi → *Bolivia* 12°32S 66°52W **92** F5
Madikeri *India* 12°30N 75°45E **45** H2
Madikwe △ *S. Africa* 27°38S 32°15E **57** C5
Madill *U.S.A.* 34°6N 96°46W **84** D6
Madimba
  Dem. Rep. of the Congo 4°58S 15°5E **54** E3
Ma'din *Syria* 35°45N 39°36E **46** C3
Madinat al Malik Khālid al
  Askarīyah *Si. Arabia* 27°54N 45°31E **46** E5
Madīnat Masdar *U.A.E.* 24°26N 54°37E **47** E7
Madingou *Congo* 4°10S 13°33E **54** E2
Madison *Calif., U.S.A.* 38°41N 121°59W **78** G5
Madison *Fla., U.S.A.* 30°28N 83°25W **85** F13
Madison *Ind., U.S.A.* 38°44N 85°23W **81** F11
Madison *Nebr., U.S.A.* 41°50N 97°27W **80** E6
Madison *Ohio, U.S.A.* 41°46N 81°3W **82** E3
Madison *S. Dak., U.S.A.* 44°0N 97°7W **80** C5
Madison *Wis., U.S.A.* 43°4N 89°24W **80** D9
Madison → *U.S.A.* 45°56N 111°31W **76** D8
Madison Heights *U.S.A.* 37°25N 79°8W **81** G14

Madisonville *Ky.,*
  U.S.A. 37°20N 87°30W **80** G10
Madisonville *Tex., U.S.A.* 30°57N 95°55W **84** F7
Madista *Botswana* 21°15S 25°6E **56** B4
Madiun *Indonesia* 7°38S 111°32E **37** G14
Madoc *Canada* 44°30N 77°28W **82** B7
Madoi *China* 34°46N 98°18E **30** E8
Madona *Latvia* 56°53N 26°5E **9** H22
Madrakah, Ra's al *Oman* 19°0N 57°50E **49** D6
Madras = Chennai *India* 13°8N 80°19E **45** H5
Madras = Tamil Nadu □
  India 11°0N 77°0E **45** J3
Madras *U.S.A.* 44°38N 121°8W **76** D3
Madre, L. *U.S.A.* 26°50N 97°30W **84** J6
Madre, Sierra *Phil.* 17°0N 122°0E **37** A6
Madre de Dios → *Bolivia* 10°59S 66°8W **92** F5
Madre de Dios, I. *Chile* 50°20S 75°10W **96** G1
Madre del Sur, Sierra
  Mexico 17°30N 100°0W **87** D5
Madre Occidental, Sierra
  Mexico 27°0N 107°0W **86** B3
Madre Oriental, Sierra
  Mexico 25°0N 100°0W **86** C5
Madri *India* 24°16N 73°32E **42** G5
Madrid *U.S.A.* 44°45N 75°8W **83** B9
Madura *Australia* 31°55S 127°0E **61** F4
Madura *Indonesia* 7°30S 114°0E **37** G15
Madura, Selat *Indonesia* 7°30S 113°20E **37** G15
Madura Oya △ *Sri Lanka* 7°20N 81°10E **45** L5
Madurai *India* 9°55N 78°10E **45** K4
Madurantakam *India* 12°30N 79°50E **45** H4
Mae Chan *Thailand* 20°9N 99°52E **38** B2
Mae Charim △ *Thailand* 18°17N 100°59E **38** C3
Mae Hong Son *Thailand* 19°16N 97°56E **38** C2
Mae Khlong → *Thailand* 13°24N 100°0E **38** F3
Mae Moei △ *Thailand* 17°26N 98°7E **38** D2
Mae Phang △ *Thailand* 19°7N 99°13E **38** C2
Mae Phrik *Thailand* 17°27N 99°7E **38** D2
Mae Ping △ *Thailand* 17°37N 98°51E **38** D2
Mae Ramat *Thailand* 16°58N 98°31E **38** D2
Mae Rim *Thailand* 18°54N 98°57E **38** C2
Mae Sai *Thailand* 20°20N 99°55E **34** G2
Mae Sot *Thailand* 16°43N 98°34E **38** D2
Mae Suai *Thailand* 19°39N 99°33E **34** H2
Mae Tha *Thailand* 18°28N 99°8E **38** C2
Mae Tup Res. *Thailand* 17°52N 98°45E **38** D2
Mae Wa △ *Thailand* 17°23N 99°16E **38** D2
Mae Wong △ *Thailand* 15°54N 99°12E **38** E2
Mae Yom △ *Thailand* 18°43N 100°15E **38** C3
Maebaru *Japan* 33°33N 130°12E **29** H5
Maebashi *Japan* 36°24N 139°4E **29** F9
Maelpaeg L. *Canada* 48°20N 56°30W **73** C8
Maestra, Sierra *Cuba* 20°15N 77°0W **88** B4
Maevatanana *Madag.* 16°56S 46°49E **55** H9
Mafadi *S. Africa* 29°12S 29°21E **57** C4
Mafeking = Mafikeng
  S. Africa 25°50S 25°38E **56** C4
Mafeking *Canada* 52°40N 101°10W **71** C8
Mafeteng *Lesotho* 29°51S 27°15E **56** C4
Maffra *Australia* 37°53S 146°58E **63** F4
Mafia I. *Tanzania* 7°45S 39°50E **54** F7
Mafikeng *S. Africa* 25°50S 25°38E **56** C4
Mafra *Brazil* 26°10S 49°55W **95** B6
Mafra *Portugal* 38°55N 9°20W **21** C1
Magadan *Russia* 59°38N 150°50E **27** D16
Magadi *India* 12°58N 77°14E **45** H3
Magaliesburg *S. Africa* 26°0S 27°32E **57** C4
Magallanes, Estrecho de
  Chile 52°30S 75°0W **96** G2
Magangué *Colombia* 9°14N 74°45W **92** B4
Magdagachi *Russia* 53°27N 125°48E **27** D13
Magdalen Is. = Madeleine, Îs. de la
  Canada 47°30N 61°40W **73** C7
Magdalena *Argentina* 35°5S 57°30W **94** D4
Magdalena *Bolivia* 13°13S 63°57W **92** F6
Magdalena *U.S.A.* 34°7N 107°15W **77** J10
Magdalena → *Colombia* 11°6N 74°51W **92** A4
Magdalena, B. *Mexico* 24°35N 112°0W **86** C2
Magdalena, I. *Mexico* 24°40N 112°15W **86** C2
Magdalena, Llano de
  Mexico 25°0N 111°25W **86** C2
Magdalena de Kino
  Mexico 30°38N 110°57W **86** A2
Magdeburg *Germany* 52°7N 11°38E **16** B6
Magdelaine Cays
  Australia 16°33S 150°18E **62** B5
Magee *U.S.A.* 31°52N 89°44W **85** F10
Magelang *Indonesia* 7°29S 110°13E **37** G14
Magellan's Str. = Magallanes,
  Estrecho de *Chile* 52°30S 75°0W **96** G2
Magenta, L. *Australia* 33°30S 119°2E **61** F2
Mageroya *Norway* 71°3N 25°40E **8** A21
Maggiore, L. *Italy* 45°57N 8°39E **20** D8
Maggotty *Jamaica* 18°9N 77°46W **88** a
Maghâgha *Egypt* 28°38N 30°50E **53** C12
Maghera *U.K.* 54°51N 6°41W **10** B5
Magherafelt *U.K.* 54°45N 6°37W **10** B5
Maghreb *N. Afr.* 32°0N 4°0W **50** C5
Magistralnyy *Russia* 56°16N 107°36E **27** D11
Magnetic Pole (North)
  Arctic 85°9N 149°0W **4** A1
Magnetic Pole (South)
  Antarctica 64°8S 138°8E **5** C9
Magnitogorsk *Russia* 53°27N 59°4E **18** D10
Magnolia *Ark., U.S.A.* 33°16N 93°14W **84** E8
Magnolia *Miss., U.S.A.* 31°9N 90°28W **85** F9
Mago *Fiji* 17°26S 179°8W **59** a
Magog *Canada* 45°18N 72°9W **83** A12
Magpie, L. *Canada* 51°0N 64°41W **73** B7
Magrath *Canada* 49°25N 112°50W **70** D6
Maguan *China* 23°0N 104°21E **34** F5
Maguarinho, C. *Brazil* 0°15S 48°30W **93** D9
Magude *Mozam.* 25°2S 32°40E **57** C5
Maḡusa = Famagusta
  Cyprus 35°8N 33°55E **46** C2
Maguse L. *Canada* 61°37N 95°10W **71** A9
Maguse Pt. *Canada* 61°20N 93°50W **71** A10
Magvana *India* 23°13N 69°22E **42** H3
Magway *Myanmar* 20°10N 95°0E **41** J19
Magyarország = Hungary ■
  Europe 47°20N 19°20E **17** E10

Maha Oya *Sri Lanka* 7°31N 81°22E **45** L5
Maha Sarakham
  Thailand 16°12N 103°16E **38** D4
Mahābād *Iran* 36°50N 45°45E **46** B5
Mahabaleshwar *India* 17°58N 73°43E **44** F1
Mahabalipuram *India* 12°37N 80°11E **45** H5
Mahabharat Lekh *Nepal* 28°30N 82°0E **43** E10
Mahabo *Madag.* 20°23S 44°40E **55** J8
Mahad *India* 18°6N 73°29E **44** E1
Mahadeo Hills *India* 22°20N 78°30E **43** H8
Mahadeopur *India* 18°48N 80°0E **44** E5
Mahaffey *U.S.A.* 40°53N 78°44W **82** F6
Mahajan *India* 28°48N 73°56E **42** E5
Mahajanga *Madag.* 15°40S 46°25E **55** H9
Mahakam → *Indonesia* 0°35S 117°17E **36** E5
Mahalapye *Botswana* 23°1S 26°51E **56** B4
Maḩallāt *Iran* 33°55N 50°30E **47** C6
Māhān *Iran* 30°5N 57°18E **47** D8
Mahanadi → *India* 20°20N 86°25E **44** D8
Mahananda → *India* 25°12N 87°52E **43** G12
Mahanoro *Madag.* 19°54S 48°48E **55** H9
Mahanoy City *U.S.A.* 40°49N 76°9W **83** F8
Maharashtra □ *India* 20°30N 75°30E **44** D2
Mahasamund *India* 21°6N 82°6E **44** D6
Mahasham, W. → *Egypt* 30°15N 34°10E **48** E3
Mahattat ash Shīdīyah
  Jordan 29°55N 35°55E **48** F4
Mahattat 'Unayzah
  Jordan 30°30N 35°47E **48** E4
Mahaweli Ganga →
  Sri Lanka 8°27N 81°13E **45** K5
Mahaxay *Laos* 17°22N 105°12E **38** D5
Mahbubabad *India* 17°42N 80°2E **44** F5
Mahbubnagar *India* 16°45N 77°59E **44** F3
Mahda *U.A.E.* 25°20N 56°15E **47** E7
Mahdia *Tunisia* 35°28N 11°0E **53** A8
Mahe *Jammu & Kashmir,*
  India 33°10N 78°32E **43** C8
Mahé *Puducherry, India* 11°42N 75°34E **45** J2
Mahé *Seychelles* 5°0S 55°30E **55** b
Mahé ✈ (SEZ) *Seychelles* 4°40S 55°31E **55** b
Mahébourg *Mauritius* 20°24S 57°42E **55** d
Mahendra Giri *India* 8°20N 77°30E **45** K3
Mahendragarh *India* 28°17N 76°14E **42** E7
Mahendranagar *Nepal* 28°55N 80°20E **43** E9
Mahenge *Tanzania* 8°45S 36°41E **54** F7
Maheno *N.Z.* 45°10S 170°50E **59** F3
Mahesana *India* 23°39N 72°26E **42** H5
Mahesh *India* 22°11N 75°35E **42** H6
Mahgawan *India* 26°29N 78°37E **43** F8
Mahi → *India* 22°15N 72°55E **42** H5
Mahia Pen. *N.Z.* 39°9S 177°55E **59** C6
Mahikeng = Mafikeng
  S. Africa 25°50S 25°38E **56** C4
Mahilyow *Belarus* 53°55N 30°18E **17** B16
Mahim *India* 19°39N 72°44E **44** E1
Mahina *Tahiti* 17°30S 149°27W **59** d
Mahinerangi, L. *N.Z.* 45°50S 169°56E **59** F2
Mahmud Kot *Pakistan* 30°16N 71°0E **42** D4
Mahnomen *U.S.A.* 47°19N 95°58W **80** B6
Maho *Sri Lanka* 7°49N 80°16E **45** L5
Mahoba *India* 25°15N 79°55E **43** G8
Mahón = Maó *Spain* 39°53N 4°16E **21** C8
Mahone Bay *Canada* 44°27N 64°23W **73** D7
Mahongo △ *Namibia* 18°0S 23°15E **56** B3
Mahopac *U.S.A.* 41°22N 73°45W **83** E11
Mahuva *India* 21°5N 71°48E **42** J4
Mai-Ndombe, L.
  Dem. Rep. of the Congo 2°0S 18°20E **54** E3
Mai Thon, Ko *Thailand* 7°40N 98°28E **39** a
Maicuru → *Brazil* 2°14S 54°17W **93** D8
Maidan Khula *Afghan.* 33°36N 69°50E **42** C3
Maidenhead *U.K.* 51°31N 0°42W **13** F7
Maidstone *Canada* 53°5N 109°20W **71** C7
Maidstone *U.K.* 51°16N 0°32E **13** F8
Maiduguri *Nigeria* 12°0N 13°20E **53** F8
Maigh Nuad = Maynooth
  Ireland 53°23N 6°34W **10** C5
Maihar *India* 24°16N 80°45E **43** G9
Maikala Ra. *India* 22°0N 81°0E **44** D5
Mailani *India* 28°17N 80°21E **43** E9
Mailsi *Pakistan* 29°48N 72°15E **42** E5
Main → *Germany* 50°0N 8°18E **16** C5
Main → *U.K.* 54°48N 6°18W **10** B5
Main Channel *Canada* 45°21N 81°45W **82** A3
Main Range △ *Australia* 28°11S 152°27E **63** D5
Main Ridge *Trin. & Tob.* 11°16N 60°40W **93** J16
Maindargi *India* 17°28N 76°18E **44** F3
Maine *France* 48°20N 0°15W **20** C3
Maine □ *U.S.A.* 45°20N 69°0W **81** C19
Maine → *Ireland* 52°9N 9°45W **10** D2
Maine, G. of *U.S.A.* 43°0N 68°30W **75** G26
Maingkwan *Myanmar* 26°15N 96°37E **41** F20
Mainistir na Corann = Midleton
  Ireland 51°55N 8°10W **10** E3
Maint, L. *Phil.* 9°31N 125°30E **37** C7
Mainland *Orkney, U.K.* 58°59N 3°8W **11** C5
Mainland *Shet., U.K.* 60°15N 1°22W **11** A7
Mainpuri *India* 27°18N 79°4E **43** F8
Mainz *Germany* 50°1N 8°14E **16** C5
Maio *Cabo Verde* 15°10N 23°10W **52** b
Maipú *Argentina* 36°52S 57°50W **94** D4
Maiquetía *Venezuela* 10°36N 66°57W **92** A5
Mairabari *India* 26°30N 92°22E **41** F18
Maisí *Cuba* 20°17N 74°9W **89** B5
Maisí, Pta. de *Cuba* 20°10N 74°10W **89** B5
Maitland *N.S.W.,*
  Australia 32°33S 151°36E **63** E5
Maitland *S. Austral.,*
  Australia 34°23S 137°40E **63** E2
Maitland → *Canada* 43°45N 81°43W **82** C3
Maitri *Antarctica* 70°0S 3°0W **5** D3
Maiyuan *China* 25°34N 117°28E **35** E11
Maíz, Is. del *Nic.* 12°15N 83°4W **88** D3
Maizuru *Japan* 35°25N 135°22E **29** G7
Majalengka *Indonesia* 6°50S 108°13E **37** G13

Majene *Indonesia* 3°38S 118°57E **37** E5
Majiang *China* 26°28N 107°32E **34** D6
Majorca = Mallorca *Spain* 39°30N 3°0E **21** C7
Mak, Ko *Thailand* 11°49N 102°29E **39** G4
Makaha *Zimbabwe* 16°51S 32°30E **57** A5
Makale *Indonesia* 3°6S 119°51E **37** E5
Makalu *Nepal* 27°55N 87°8E **43** F12
Makalu-Barun △ *Nepal* 27°45N 87°10E **43** F12
Makarikari = Makgadikgadi Salt
  Pans *Botswana* 20°40S 25°45E **56** B4
Makarov Basin *Arctic* 87°0N 150°0W **4** A
Makarovo *Russia* 57°40N 107°45E **27** D11
Makassar *Indonesia* 5°10S 119°20E **37** F5
Makassar, Selat *Indonesia* 1°0S 118°20E **37** E5
Makassar, Str. of = Makassar,
  Selat *Indonesia* 1°0S 118°20E **37** E5
Makat = Maqat
  Kazakhstan 47°39N 53°19E **19** E9
Makedonija = Macedonia ■
  Europe 41°53N 21°40E **23** D9
Makeni *S. Leone* 8°55N 12°5W **52** G3
Makeyevka = Makiyivka
  Ukraine 48°0N 38°0E **19** E6
Makgadikgadi △
  Botswana 20°27S 24°47E **56** B3
Makgadikgadi Salt Pans
  Botswana 20°40S 25°45E **56** B4
Makhachkala *Russia* 43°0N 47°30E **19** F8
Makhado = Louis Trichardt
  S. Africa 23°1S 29°43E **57** B4
Makham, Ao *Thailand* 7°51N 98°25E **39** a
Makhfar al Buşayyah *Iraq* 30°0N 46°10E **46** D5
Makhmūr *Iraq* 35°46N 43°35E **46** C4
Makhtal *India* 16°30N 77°31E **45** E3
Makian *Indonesia* 0°20N 127°20E **37** D7
Makinsk *Kazakhstan* 52°37N 70°26E **26** D8
Makira = San Cristóbal
  Solomon Is. 10°30S 161°0E **58** C9
Makiyivka *Ukraine* 48°0N 38°0E **19** E6
Makkah *Si. Arabia* 21°30N 39°54E **49** C2
Makkovik *Canada* 55°10N 59°10W **73** A8
Makó *Hungary* 46°14N 20°33E **17** E11
Makogai *Fiji* 17°28S 179°0E **59** a
Makokou *Gabon* 0°40N 12°50E **54** D2
Makrai *India* 22°2N 77°0E **42** H7
Makran Coast Range
  Pakistan 25°40N 64°0E **40** G4
Makrana *India* 27°2N 74°46E **42** F6
Makri *India* 19°46N 81°55E **44** E5
Mākū *Iran* 39°15N 44°31E **46** B5
Makunda *Botswana* 22°30S 20°7E **56** B3
Makung *Taiwan* 23°34N 119°34E **35** F12
Makurazaki *Japan* 31°15N 130°20E **29** J5
Makurdi *Nigeria* 7°43N 8°35E **52** G7
Makushin Volcano
  U.S.A. 53°53N 166°55W **74** E6
Makūyeh *Iran* 28°7N 53°9E **47** D7
Makwassie *S. Africa* 27°17S 26°0E **56** D4
Makwiro *Zimbabwe* 17°58S 30°25E **57** A5
Mal B. *Ireland* 52°50N 9°30W **10** D2
Mala = Mallow *Ireland* 52°8N 8°39W **10** D3
Mala △ *Australia* 21°39S 130°45E **60** D5
Mala, Pta. *Panama* 7°28N 80°2W **88** E3
Malabar Coast *India* 11°0N 75°0E **45** J1
Malacca, Straits of *Indonesia* 3°0N 101°0E **39** L3
Malad City *U.S.A.* 42°12N 112°15W **76** E7
Maladzyechna *Belarus* 54°20N 26°50E **17** A14
Málaga *Spain* 36°43N 4°23W **21** D3
Malagasy Rep. = Madagascar ■
  Africa 20°0S 47°0E **55** J9
Malahide *Ireland* 53°26N 6°9W **10** C5
Malaimbandy *Madag.* 20°20S 45°36E **55** J9
Malaita *Solomon Is.* 9°0S 161°0E **58** B9
Malakal *South Sudan* 9°33N 31°40E **53** G12
Malakand *Pakistan* 34°40N 71°55E **42** B4
Malakula *Vanuatu* 16°15S 167°30E **58** C9
Malakwal *Pakistan* 32°34N 73°13E **42** C5
Malamala *Indonesia* 3°21S 120°55E **37** E6
Malanda *Australia* 17°22S 145°35E **62** B4
Malang *Indonesia* 7°59S 112°45E **37** G15
Malangen *Norway* 69°24N 18°37E **8** B18
Malanje *Angola* 9°36S 16°17E **54** F3
Malappuram *India* 11°7N 76°11E **45** J3
Mälaren *Sweden* 59°30N 17°10E **9** G17
Malargüe *Argentina* 35°32S 69°30W **94** D2
Malartic *Canada* 48°9N 78°9W **72** C4
Malaryta *Belarus* 51°50N 24°3E **17** C13
Malaspina Glacier
  U.S.A. 59°50N 140°30W **74** D11
Malatya *Turkey* 38°25N 38°20E **46** B3
Malawi ■ *Africa* 11°55S 34°0E **55** G6
Malawi, L. *Africa* 12°30S 34°30E **55** G6
Malay Pen. *Asia* 7°25N 100°0E **39** J3
Malaya Vishera *Russia* 58°55N 32°25E **18** C5
Malaybalay *Phil.* 8°5N 125°7E **37** C7
Malāyer *Iran* 34°19N 48°51E **47** C6
Malaysia ■ *Asia* 5°0N 110°0E **36** D4
Malazgirt *Turkey* 39°10N 42°33E **46** B4
Malbon *Australia* 21°5S 140°17E **62** C3
Malbooma *Australia* 30°41S 134°11E **63** E1
Malbork *Poland* 54°3N 19°1E **17** B10
Malcolm *Australia* 28°51S 121°25E **61** E3
Malcolm, Pt. *Australia* 33°48S 123°45E **61** F3
Maldah *India* 25°2N 88°9E **43** G13
Maldegem *Belgium* 51°14N 3°26E **15** C3
Malden *U.S.A.* 36°34N 89°57W **80** G9
Malden I. *Kiribati* 4°3S 155°1W **65** H12
Maldives ■ *Ind. Oc.* 5°0N 73°0E **29** H9
Maldon *U.K.* 51°44N 0°42E **13** F8
Maldonado *Uruguay* 34°59S 55°0W **95** C5
Maldonado, Pta. *Mexico* 16°19N 98°33W **87** D5
Malé *Maldives* 4°0N 73°28E **29** J11
Malé Karpaty *Slovakia* 48°30N 17°20E **17** D9
Maleas, Akra *Greece* 36°28N 23°7E **23** F10
Malebo, Pool *Africa* 4°17S 15°20E **54** E3
Malegaon *India* 20°30N 74°38E **44** D2

Malek Kandī *Iran* 37°9N 46°6E **46** B5
Malema *Mozam.* 14°57S 37°20E **55** G7
Maler Kotla *India* 30°32N 75°58E **42** D6
Malha *Sudan* 15°8N 25°10E **53** E11
Malhargarh *India* 24°17N 74°59E **42** G6
Malheur → *U.S.A.* 44°4N 116°59W **76** D5
Malheur L. *U.S.A.* 43°20N 118°48W **76** E4
Mali ■ *Africa* 17°0N 3°0W **52** E5
Mali → *Myanmar* 25°42N 97°30E **41** G20
Mali Kyun *Myanmar* 13°0N 98°20E **38** F2
Malibu *U.S.A.* 34°2N 118°41W **79** L8
Maliku = Minicoy I. *India* 8°17N 73°2E **45** K1
Maliku *Indonesia* 0°39S 123°16E **37** E6
Malili *Indonesia* 2°42S 121°6E **37** E6
Malimba, Mts.
  Dem. Rep. of the Congo 7°30S 29°30E **54** F5
Malin Hd. *Ireland* 55°23N 7°23W **10** A4
Malin Pen. *Ireland* 55°20N 7°17W **10** A4
Malindi *Kenya* 3°12S 40°5E **54** E8
Malines = Mechelen
  Belgium 51°2N 4°29E **15** C4
Malino *Indonesia* 1°0N 121°0E **37** D6
Malipo *China* 23°7N 104°42E **34** F5
Malita *Phil.* 6°19N 125°39E **37** C7
Maliwun *Myanmar* 10°17N 98°40E **39** G2
Maliya *India* 23°5N 70°46E **42** H4
Malkapur *India* 20°53N 76°12E **44** D3
Malkara *Turkey* 40°53N 26°53E **23** D12
Malkhangiri = Malakanagiri
  India 18°21N 81°54E **44** E5
Mallacoota Inlet
  Australia 37°34S 149°40E **63** F4
Mallaig *U.K.* 57°0N 5°50W **11** D3
Mallawan *India* 27°4N 80°12E **43** F9
Mallawi *Egypt* 27°44N 30°44E **53** C12
Mallicolo = Malakula
  Vanuatu 16°15S 167°30E **58** C9
Mallorca *Spain* 39°30N 3°0E **21** C7
Mallorytown *Canada* 44°29N 75°53W **83** B9
Mallow *Ireland* 52°8N 8°39W **10** D3
Malmberget *Sweden* 67°11N 20°40E **8** C19
Malmédy *Belgium* 50°25N 6°2E **15** D6
Malmesbury *S. Africa* 33°28S 18°41E **56** D2
Malmivaara = Malmberget
  Sweden 67°11N 20°40E **8** C19
Malmö *Sweden* 55°36N 12°59E **9** J15
Malolo *Fiji* 17°45S 177°11E **59** a
Malolos *Phil.* 14°50N 120°49E **37** B6
Malombe L. *Malawi* 14°40S 35°15E **55** G7
Malone *U.S.A.* 44°51N 74°18W **83** B10
Malong *China* 25°24N 103°34E **34** E4
Maloti Mts. = Drakensberg
  S. Africa 31°0S 28°0E **57** D4
Måløy *Norway* 61°57N 5°6E **8** F11
Malpaso, Presa = Netzahualcóyotl,
  Presa *Mexico* 17°8N 93°35W **87** D6
Malpelo, I. de *Colombia* 4°3N 81°35W **92** C2
Malprabha → *India* 16°20N 76°5E **45** F3
Malpur *India* 23°21N 73°27E **42** H5
Malpura *India* 26°17N 75°23E **42** F6
Malsiras *India* 17°52N 74°55E **44** F2
Malta *Idaho, U.S.A.* 42°18N 113°22W **76** E7
Malta *Mont., U.S.A.* 48°21N 107°52W **76** B10
Malta ■ *Europe* 35°55N 14°26E **22** G6
Malta Freeport *Malta* 35°49N 14°32E **22** a
Maltahöhe *Namibia* 24°55S 17°0E **56** B2
Malton *U.K.* 54°8N 0°49W **12** C7
Maluku *Indonesia* 1°0S 127°0E **37** E7
Maluku □ *Indonesia* 3°0S 128°0E **37** E7
Maluku Sea = Molucca Sea
  Indonesia 0°0 125°0E **37** E6
Malur *India* 13°0N 77°55E **45** H3
Malvalli *India* 12°28N 77°8E **45** H3
Malvan *India* 16°2N 73°30E **45** G1
Malvern *U.S.A.* 34°22N 92°49W **84** D8
Malvern Hills *U.K.* 52°0N 2°19W **13** E5
Malvinas, Is. = Falkland Is. ☑
  Atl. Oc. 51°30S 59°0W **96** G5
Malyn *Ukraine* 50°46N 29°3E **17** C15
Malyy Lyakhovskiy, Ostrov
  Russia 74°7N 140°36E **27** B15
Malyy Taymyr, Ostrov
  Russia 78°6N 107°15E **27** B11
Mama *Russia* 58°18N 112°54E **27** D12
Mamanguape *Brazil* 6°50S 35°4W **93** E11
Mamarr Mitlā *Egypt* 30°2N 32°54E **48** E1
Mamasa *Indonesia* 2°55S 119°20E **37** E5
Mamberamo → *Indonesia* 2°0S 137°50E **37** E9
Mambilima Falls *Zambia* 10°31S 28°45E **54** G5
Mamburao *Phil.* 13°13N 120°39E **37** B6
Mameigwess L. *Canada* 52°35N 87°50W **72** B2
Mamili △ *Namibia* 18°2S 24°1E **56** A3
Mammoth *U.S.A.* 32°43N 110°39W **77** K8
Mammoth Cave △
  U.S.A. 37°8N 86°13W **80** G11
Mammoth Lakes
  U.S.A. 37°38N 118°59W **78** H8
Mamoré → *Bolivia* 10°23S 65°53W **92** F5
Mamou *Guinea* 10°15N 12°0W **52** F3
Mamoudzou *Mayotte* 12°48S 45°14E **55** a
Mamuju *Indonesia* 2°41S 118°50E **37** E5
Mamuno *Botswana* 22°16S 20°1E **56** C3
Man *Côte d'Ivoire* 7°30N 7°40W **52** G4
Man → *India* 17°17N 75°33E **44** F2
Man, I. of *India* 8°28N 93°36E **45** K11
Man, I. of *U.K.* 54°15N 4°30W **12** C3
Man-Bazar *India* 23°2N 86°39E **43** H12
Man Na *Myanmar* 23°27N 97°19E **41** H20
Mäna *U.S.A.* 22°2N 159°47W **75** L8
Mana → *Fr. Guiana* 5°45N 53°55W **93** B8
Manaar, G. of = Mannar, G. of
  Asia 8°30N 79°0E **45** K4
Manacapuru *Brazil* 3°16S 60°37W **92** D6
Manacor *Spain* 39°34N 3°13E **21** C7
Manado *Indonesia* 1°29N 124°51E **37** D6
Managua *Nic.* 12°6N 86°20W **88** D2
Managua, L. de *Nic.* 12°20N 86°30W **88** D2
Manakara *Madag.* 22°8S 48°1E **55** J9

Manali *India* 32°16N 77°10E **42** C7
Manama = Al Manāmah *Bahrain* 26°10N 50°30E **47** E6
Mananjary *Madag.* 21°13S 48°20E **55** J9
Manantavadi *India* 11°49N 76°1E **45** J3
Manantenina *Madag.* 24°17S 47°19E **55** J9
Manaos = Manaus *Brazil* 3°0S 60°0W **92** D7
Manapire → *Venezuela* 7°42N 66°7W **92** B5
Manapouri *N.Z.* 45°34S 167°39E **59** F1
Manapouri, L. *N.Z.* 45°32S 167°32E **59** F1
Manapparai *India* 10°36N 78°25E **45** J4
Manar → *India* 18°50N 77°20E **44** E3
Manār, Jabal *Yemen* 14°2N 44°17E **49** E3
Manas *China* 44°17N 86°10E **30** C6
Manas → *India* 26°12N 90°40E **41** F17
Manas He → *China* 45°38N 85°12E **30** B6
Manaslu *Nepal* 28°33N 84°33E **43** E11
Manasquan *U.S.A.* 40°8N 74°3W **83** F10
Manassa *U.S.A.* 37°11N 105°56W **77** H11
Manatí *Puerto Rico* 18°26N 66°29W **89** d
Manaus *Brazil* 3°0S 60°0W **92** D7
Manawan L. *Canada* 55°24N 103°14W **71** B8
Manbij *Syria* 36°31N 37°57E **46** B3
Manchegorsk *Russia* 67°54N 32°58E **26** C4
Manchester *U.K.* 53°29N 2°12W **12** D5
Manchester *Calif., U.S.A.* 38°58N 123°41W **78** G3
Manchester *Conn., U.S.A.* 41°47N 72°31W **83** E12
Manchester *Ga., U.S.A.* 32°51N 84°37W **85** E12
Manchester *Iowa, U.S.A.* 42°29N 91°27W **80** D8
Manchester *Ky., U.S.A.* 37°9N 83°46W **81** G12
Manchester *N.H., U.S.A.* 42°59N 71°28W **83** D13
Manchester *N.Y., U.S.A.* 42°56N 77°16W **82** D7
Manchester *Pa., U.S.A.* 40°4N 76°43W **83** F8
Manchester *Tenn., U.S.A.* 35°29N 86°5W **85** D11
Manchester *Vt., U.S.A.* 43°10N 73°5W **83** C11
Manchester Int. ✈ (MAN) *U.K.* 53°21N 2°17W **12** D5
Manchester L. *Canada* 61°28N 107°29W **71** A7
Manchhar L. *Pakistan* 26°25N 67°39E **42** F2
Manchuria = Dongbei *China* 45°0N 125°0E **33** D13
Manchurian Plain *China* 47°0N 124°0E **24** D14
Mand → *India* 21°42N 83°15E **43** J10
Mand → *Iran* 28°20N 52°30E **47** D7
Mandaguari *Brazil* 23°32S 51°42W **95** A5
Mandah = Töhöm *Mongolia* 44°27N 108°2E **32** B5
Mandal *Norway* 58°2N 7°25E **9** G12
Mandala, Puncak *Indonesia* 4°44S 140°20E **37** E10
Mandalay *Myanmar* 22°0N 96°4E **41** J20
Mandale = Mandalay *Myanmar* 22°0N 96°4E **41** J20
Mandalgarh *India* 25°12N 75°6E **42** G6
Mandalgovĭ *Mongolia* 45°45N 106°10E **32** B4
Mandalī *Iraq* 33°43N 45°28E **46** C5
Mandan *U.S.A.* 46°50N 100°54W **80** B3
Mandar, Teluk *Indonesia* 3°32S 119°21E **37** E5
Mandaue *Phil.* 10°20N 123°56E **37** B6
Mandeville *Jamaica* 18°2N 77°31W **88** a
Mandi *India* 31°39N 76°58E **42** D7
Mandi Burewala *Pakistan* 30°9N 72°41E **42** E5
Mandi Dabwali *India* 29°58N 74°42E **42** E6
Mandimba *Mozam.* 14°20S 35°40E **55** G7
Mandioli *Indonesia* 0°40S 127°20E **37** E7
Mandla *India* 22°39N 80°30E **43** H9
Mandorah *Australia* 12°32S 130°42E **60** B5
Mandra *Pakistan* 33°23N 73°12E **42** C5
Mandritsara *Madag.* 15°50S 48°49E **55** H9
Mandsaur *India* 24°3N 75°8E **42** G6
Mandurah *Australia* 32°36S 115°48E **61** F2
Mandvi *India* 22°51N 69°22E **42** H3
Mandya *India* 12°30N 77°0E **45** H3
Mandzai *Pakistan* 30°55N 67°6E **42** D2
Maneh *Iran* 37°39N 57°7E **47** B8
Maner → *India* 18°30N 79°40E **44** E4
Maneroo Cr. → *Australia* 23°21S 143°53E **62** C3
Manfalût *Egypt* 27°20N 30°52E **53** C12
Manfredónia *Italy* 41°38N 15°55E **22** D6
Mangabeiras, Chapada das *Brazil* 10°0S 46°30W **93** F9
Mangaia *Cook Is.* 21°55S 157°55W **65** K12
Mangalagiri *India* 16°26N 80°36E **45** F5
Mangalia *Romania* 43°50N 28°35E **17** G15
Mangalore = Mangaluru *India* 12°55N 74°47E **45** H2
Mangaluru *India* 12°55N 74°47E **45** H2
Mangalvedha *India* 17°31N 75°28E **44** F2
Mangan *India* 27°31N 88°32E **43** F13
Mangaon *India* 18°15N 73°20E **44** E1
Mangarrayi ⚙ *Australia* 15°5S 133°10E **62** B1
Mangawan *India* 24°41N 81°33E **43** G9
Mangaweka *N.Z.* 39°48S 175°47E **59** C5
Mangetti △ *Namibia* 18°43S 19°58E **56** A2
Manggar *Indonesia* 2°50S 108°10E **36** E3
Manggawitu *Indonesia* 4°8S 133°32E **37** E8
Mangghystaū Tübegi *Kazakhstan* 44°30N 52°30E **26** E6
Manggis *Indonesia* 8°29S 115°31E **37** J18
Mangkalihat, Tanjung *Indonesia* 1°2N 118°59E **37** D5
Mangkururrpa ⚙ *Australia* 20°35S 129°43E **60** D4
Mangla *Pakistan* 33°7N 73°39E **42** C5
Mangla Dam *Pakistan* 33°9N 73°44E **43** C5
Manglaur *India* 29°44N 77°49E **42** E7
Mangnai *China* 37°52N 91°43E **30** D7
Mangnai Zhen *China* 38°24N 90°14E **30** D7
Mango *Togo* 10°20N 0°30E **52** F6
Mango *Tonga* 20°17S 174°29W **59** c
Mangoche *Malawi* 14°25S 35°16E **55** G7
Mangoky → *Madag.* 21°29S 43°41E **55** J8
Mangole *Indonesia* 1°50S 125°55E **37** E6
Mangonui *N.Z.* 35°1S 173°32E **59** A4
Mangrol *Mad. P., India* 21°7N 70°7E **42** J4
Mangrol *Raj., India* 25°20N 76°31E **42** G6
Mangrul Pir *India* 20°19N 77°21E **44** D3
Mangshi = Luxi *China* 24°27N 98°36E **34** E2
Mangueira, L. da *Brazil* 33°0S 52°50W **95** C5
Mangui *China* 52°3N 122°3E **31** A13
Mangum *U.S.A.* 34°53N 99°30W **84** D5
Manguri *Australia* 28°58S 134°22E **63** A1
Mangyshlak, Poluostrov = Mangghystaū Tübegi *Kazakhstan* 44°30N 52°30E **26** E6
Manhattan *U.S.A.* 39°11N 96°35W **80** F5
Manhiça *Mozam.* 25°23S 32°49E **57** C5
Manica *Mozam.* 18°58S 32°59E **57** A5
Manica □ *Mozam.* 19°10S 33°45E **57** A5
Manicoré *Brazil* 5°48S 61°16W **92** E6
Manicouagan → *Canada* 49°30N 68°30W **73** C6
Manicouagan, Rés. *Canada* 51°5N 68°40W **73** B6
Manīfah *Si. Arabia* 27°44N 49°0E **47** E6
Manifold, C. *Australia* 22°41S 150°50E **62** C5
Maniganggo *China* 31°56N 99°10E **34** B2
Manigotagan *Canada* 51°6N 96°18W **71** C9
Manigotagan → *Canada* 51°7N 96°20W **71** C9
Manihari *India* 25°21N 87°38E **43** G12
Manihiki *Cook Is.* 10°24S 161°1W **65** J11
Manihiki Plateau *Pac. Oc.* 11°0S 164°0W **65** J11
Manikpur *India* 25°4N 81°7E **43** G9
Manila *U.S.A.* 40°59N 109°43W **76** F9
Manila B. *Phil.* 14°40N 120°35E **37** B6
Manilla *Australia* 30°45S 150°43E **63** E5
Maningrida *Australia* 12°3S 134°13E **62** A1
Manipa, Selat *Indonesia* 3°20S 127°25E **37** E7
Manipur □ *India* 25°0N 94°0E **41** G19
Manipur → *Myanmar* 23°45N 94°20E **41** H19
Manisa *Turkey* 38°38N 27°30E **23** E12
Manistee *U.S.A.* 44°15N 86°19W **80** C10
Manistee → *U.S.A.* 44°15N 86°21W **80** C10
Manistique *U.S.A.* 45°57N 86°15W **80** C10
Manitoba □ *Canada* 53°30N 97°0W **71** B9
Manitoba, L. *Canada* 51°0N 98°45W **71** C9
Manitou *Canada* 49°15N 98°32W **71** D9
Manitou, L. *Canada* 50°55N 65°17W **73** B6
Manitou Is. *U.S.A.* 45°8N 86°0W **80** C10
Manitou L. *Canada* 52°43N 109°43W **71** C7
Manitou Springs *U.S.A.* 38°52N 104°55W **76** G11
Manitoulin I. *Canada* 45°40N 82°30W **72** C3
Manitouwadge *Canada* 49°8N 85°48W **72** C2
Manitowoc *U.S.A.* 44°5N 87°40W **80** C10
Maniyachi *India* 8°51N 77°55E **45** K3
Manizales *Colombia* 5°5N 75°32W **92** B3
Manjacaze *Mozam.* 24°45S 34°0E **57** B5
Manjakandriana *Madag.* 18°55S 47°47E **55** H9
Manjhand *Pakistan* 25°50N 68°10E **42** G3
Manjimup *Australia* 34°15S 116°6E **61** F2
Manjlegaon *India* 19°9N 76°14E **44** E3
Manjra → *India* 18°49N 77°52E **44** E3
Mankato *Kans., U.S.A.* 39°47N 98°13W **80** F4
Mankato *Minn., U.S.A.* 44°10N 94°0W **80** C6
Mankayane *Eswatini* 26°40S 31°4E **57** C5
Mankera *Pakistan* 31°23N 71°26E **42** D4
Mankota *Canada* 49°25N 107°5W **71** D7
Mankulam *Sri Lanka* 9°8N 80°26E **45** K5
Manlay = Üydzin *Mongolia* 44°9N 107°0E **32** B4
Manmad *India* 20°18N 74°28E **44** D2
Mann Ranges *Australia* 26°6S 130°5E **61** E5
Manna *Indonesia* 4°25S 102°55E **36** E2
Mannahill *Australia* 32°25S 140°0E **63** E3
Mannar *Sri Lanka* 9°1N 79°54E **45** K4
Mannar, G. of *Asia* 8°30N 79°0E **45** K4
Mannar I. *Sri Lanka* 9°5N 79°45E **45** K4
Mannargudi *India* 10°45N 79°51E **45** J4
Mannheim *Germany* 49°29N 8°29E **16** D5
Manning *Canada* 56°53N 117°39W **70** B5
Manning *Oreg., U.S.A.* 45°45N 123°13W **78** E3
Manning *S.C., U.S.A.* 33°42N 80°13W **85** E14
Mannum *Australia* 34°50S 139°20E **63** E2
Manoharpur *India* 22°23N 85°12E **43** H11
Manokwari *Indonesia* 0°54S 134°0E **37** E8
Manombo *Madag.* 22°57S 43°28E **55** J8
Manono *Dem. Rep. of the Congo* 7°15S 27°25E **54** F5
Manono *Samoa* 13°50S 172°5W **59** b
Manorhamilton *Ireland* 54°18N 8°11W **10** B3
Manosque *France* 43°49N 5°47E **20** E6
Manotick *Canada* 45°13N 75°41W **83** A9
Manouane → *Canada* 49°30N 71°10W **73** C5
Manouane, L. *Canada* 50°45N 70°45W **73** B5
Manp'o *N. Korea* 41°6N 126°24E **33** D14
Manpojin = Manp'o *N. Korea* 41°6N 126°24E **33** D14
Manpur *Chhattisgarh, India* 23°17N 83°35E **43** H10
Manpur *Chhattisgarh, India* 20°22N 80°43E **44** D5
Manpur *Mad. P., India* 22°26N 75°37E **42** H6
Manresa *Spain* 41°48N 1°50E **21** B6
Mansa *Gujarat, India* 23°27N 72°45E **42** H5
Mansa *Punjab, India* 30°0N 75°27E **42** E6
Mansa *Zambia* 11°13S 28°55E **54** G5
Mansehra *Pakistan* 34°20N 73°15E **42** B5
Mansel I. *Canada* 62°0N 80°0W **69** E15
Mansfield *Australia* 37°4S 146°6E **63** F4
Mansfield *U.K.* 53°9N 1°11W **12** D6
Mansfield *La., U.S.A.* 32°2N 93°43W **84** E8
Mansfield *Mass., U.S.A.* 42°2N 71°13W **83** D13
Mansfield *Ohio, U.S.A.* 40°45N 82°31W **82** F2
Mansfield *Pa., U.S.A.* 41°48N 77°5W **82** E7
Mansfield, Mt. *U.S.A.* 44°33N 72°49W **83** B12
Manson Creek *Canada* 55°37N 124°32W **70** B4
Manta *Ecuador* 1°0S 80°40W **92** D2
Mantalingajan, Mt. *Phil.* 8°55N 117°45E **36** C5
Manteca *U.S.A.* 37°48N 121°13W **78** H5
Manteo *U.S.A.* 35°55N 75°40W **85** D17
Mantes-la-Jolie *France* 48°58N 1°41E **20** B4
Mantha *India* 19°40N 76°23E **44** E3
Manthani *India* 18°40N 79°35E **44** E4
Manti *U.S.A.* 39°16N 111°38W **76** G8
Mantiqueira, Serra da *Brazil* 22°0S 44°0W **95** A7
Manton *U.S.A.* 44°25N 85°24W **81** C11
Mántova *Italy* 45°9N 10°48E **22** B4
Mänttä Vilppula *Finland* 62°3N 24°40E **8** E21
Mantua = Mántova *Italy* 45°9N 10°48E **22** B4
Manú *Peru* 12°10S 70°51W **92** F4
Manú → *Peru* 12°16S 70°55W **92** F4
Manu'a Is. *Amer. Samoa* 14°13S 169°35W **59** b
Manuel Alves → *Brazil* 11°19S 48°28W **93** F9
Manui *Indonesia* 3°35S 123°5E **37** E6
Manukau *N.Z.* 37°0S 174°52E **59** B5
Manuripi → *Bolivia* 11°6S 67°36W **92** F5
Manvi *India* 15°57N 76°59E **45** G3
Manwan Dam *China* 24°44N 100°20E **34** E3
Manwath *India* 19°19N 76°32E **44** E3
Many *U.S.A.* 31°34N 93°29W **84** F8
Manyallaluk ⚙ *Australia* 14°16S 132°49E **60** B5
Manych-Gudilo, Ozero *Russia* 46°24N 42°38E **19** E7
Manyoni *Tanzania* 5°45S 34°55E **54** F6
Manzai *Pakistan* 32°12N 70°15E **42** C4
Manzanar ⌂ *U.S.A.* 36°44N 118°9W **78** J7
Manzanares *Spain* 39°2N 3°22W **21** C4
Manzanillo *Cuba* 20°20N 77°31W **88** B4
Manzanillo *Mexico* 19°3N 104°20W **86** D4
Manzanillo, Pta. *Panama* 9°30N 79°40W **88** E4
Manzano Mts. *U.S.A.* 34°40N 106°20W **77** J10
Manzarīyeh *Iran* 34°53N 50°50E **47** C6
Manzhouli *China* 49°35N 117°25E **31** B12
Manzini *Eswatini* 26°30S 31°25E **57** C5
Manzouli = Manzhouli *China* 49°35N 117°25E **31** B12
Manzur Vadisi △ *Turkey* 39°10N 39°30E **46** B3
Mao *Chad* 14°4N 15°19E **53** F9
Maó *Spain* 39°53N 4°16E **21** C8
Maoke, Pegunungan *Indonesia* 3°40S 137°30E **37** E9
Maolin *China* 43°58N 123°30E **33** C12
Maoming *China* 21°50N 110°54E **35** G8
Maopi T'ou *China* 21°56N 120°43E **35** G13
Maoxian *China* 31°41N 103°49E **34** B4
Maoxing *China* 45°28N 124°40E **33** B13
Mapam Yumco *China* 30°45N 81°28E **43** D9
Mapastepec *Mexico* 15°26N 92°54W **87** D6
Maphrao, Ko *Thailand* 7°56N 98°26E **39** a
Mapia, Kepulauan *Indonesia* 0°50N 134°20E **37** D8
Mapimí *Mexico* 25°49N 103°51W **86** B4
Mapimí, Bolsón de *Mexico* 27°0N 104°15W **86** B4
Maping *China* 31°34N 113°32E **35** B9
Mapinhane *Mozam.* 22°20S 35°0E **57** B6
Maple Creek *Canada* 49°55N 109°29W **71** D7
Maple Valley *U.S.A.* 47°25N 122°3W **78** C4
Mapleton *U.S.A.* 44°2N 123°52W **76** D2
Mapoon ⚙ *Australia* 11°44S 142°8E **62** A3
Mapuca *India* 15°36N 73°46E **45** G1
Mapuera → *Brazil* 1°5S 57°2W **92** D7
Mapulanguene *Mozam.* 24°29S 32°6E **57** B5
Mapungubwe △ *S. Africa* 22°12S 29°22E **57** B4
Maputo *Mozam.* 25°58S 32°32E **57** C5
Maputo □ *Mozam.* 26°0S 32°25E **57** C5
Maputo, B. de *Mozam.* 25°50S 32°45E **57** C5
Maputo ⌂ *Mozam.* 26°23S 32°48E **57** C5
Maqat *Kazakhstan* 47°39N 53°19E **19** E9
Maqên *China* 34°24N 100°6E **30** E9
Maqên Gangri *China* 34°55N 99°18E **30** E8
Maqiaohe *China* 44°40N 130°30E **33** B16
Maqnā *Si. Arabia* 28°25N 34°50E **46** D2
Maqteïr *Mauritania* 21°50N 11°40W **52** D3
Maqu *China* 33°52N 101°42E **30** E9
Maquan He = Brahmaputra → *Asia* 23°40N 90°35E **43** H13
Maquela do Zombo *Angola* 6°0S 15°15E **54** F3
Maquinchao *Argentina* 41°15S 68°50W **96** E3
Maquoketa *U.S.A.* 42°4N 90°40W **80** D8
Mar *Canada* 44°49N 81°12W **82** B3
Mar, Serra do *Brazil* 25°30S 49°0W **95** B6
Mar Chiquita, L. *Argentina* 30°40S 62°50W **94** C3
Mar del Plata *Argentina* 38°0S 57°30W **94** D4
Mar Menor *Spain* 37°40N 0°45W **21** D5
Maraã *Brazil* 1°52S 65°25W **92** D5
Maraa *Tahiti* 17°46S 149°34W **59** d
Marabá *Brazil* 5°20S 49°5W **93** E9
Maraboon, L. *Australia* 23°41S 148°0E **62** C4
Maracá, I. de *Brazil* 2°10N 50°30W **93** C8
Maracaibo *Venezuela* 10°40N 71°37W **92** A4
Maracaibo, L. de *Venezuela* 9°40N 71°30W **92** B4
Maracaju *Brazil* 21°38S 55°9W **95** A4
Maracas Bay Village *Trin. & Tob.* 10°46N 61°28W **93** K15
Maracay *Venezuela* 10°15N 67°28W **92** A5
Marādah *Libya* 29°15N 19°15E **53** C9
Maradi *Niger* 13°29N 7°20E **52** F7
Marāgheh *Iran* 37°30N 46°12E **46** B5
Marāh *Si. Arabia* 25°0N 45°35E **46** E5
Marajo, I. de *Brazil* 1°0S 49°30W **93** D9
Marākand *Iran* 38°51N 45°16E **46** B5
Marakele △ *S. Africa* 24°30S 27°30E **57** B4
Maralinga *Australia* 30°13S 131°32E **61** F5
Maralinga Tjarutja ⚙ *Australia* 29°30S 131°0E **61** E5
Marambio *Antarctica* 64°0S 56°0W **5** C18
Maran *Malaysia* 3°35N 102°45E **39** L4
Marana *U.S.A.* 32°27N 111°13W **77** K8
Maranboy *Australia* 14°40S 132°39E **60** B5
Marand *Iran* 38°30N 45°45E **46** B5
Marang *Malaysia* 5°12N 103°13E **39** K4
Maranguape *Brazil* 3°55S 38°50W **93** D11
Maranhão = São Luís *Brazil* 2°39S 44°15W **93** D10
Maranhão □ *Brazil* 5°0S 46°0W **93** E9
Maranoa → *Australia* 27°50S 148°37E **63** D4
Marañón → *Peru* 4°30S 73°35W **92** D4
Marão *Mozam.* 24°18S 34°2E **57** B5
Maraş = Kahramanmaraş *Turkey* 37°37N 36°53E **46** B3
Marathon *Australia* 20°51S 143°32E **62** C3
Marathon *Canada* 48°44N 86°23W **72** C2
Marathon *N.Y., U.S.A.* 42°27N 76°2W **83** D8
Marathon *Tex., U.S.A.* 30°12N 103°15W **84** F3
Maratua *Indonesia* 2°10N 118°35E **37** D5
Maraval *Trin. & Tob.* 10°42N 61°31W **93** K15
Maravatío *Mexico* 19°54N 100°27W **86** D4
Marāwih *U.A.E.* 24°18N 53°18E **47** E7
Marbella *Spain* 36°30N 4°57W **21** D3
Marble Bar *Australia* 21°9S 119°44E **60** D2
Marblehead *Mass., U.S.A.* 42°29N 70°51W **83** D14
Marblehead *Ohio, U.S.A.* 41°32N 82°44W **82** E2
Marburg *Germany* 50°47N 8°46E **16** C5
Marca, Pta. do *Angola* 16°31S 11°43E **55** H2
March *U.K.* 52°33N 0°5E **13** E8
Marche *France* 46°5N 1°20E **20** C4
Marche-en-Famenne *Belgium* 50°14N 5°19E **15** D5
Marchena *Spain* 37°18N 5°23W **21** D3
Marco Island *U.S.A.* 25°58N 81°44W **85** J14
Marcos Juárez *Argentina* 32°42S 62°5W **94** C3
Marcus Baker, Mt. *U.S.A.* 61°26N 147°45W **74** C10
Marcus I. = Minami-Tori-Shima *Pac. Oc.* 24°20N 153°58E **64** E7
Marcy, Mt. *U.S.A.* 44°7N 73°56W **83** B11
Mardan *Pakistan* 34°20N 72°0E **42** B5
Mardie *Australia* 21°12S 115°59E **60** D2
Mardin *Turkey* 37°20N 40°43E **46** B4
Maree, L. *U.K.* 57°40N 5°26W **11** D3
Mareeba *Australia* 16°59S 145°28E **62** B4
Mareetsane *S. Africa* 26°9S 25°25E **56** C4
Marek = Stanke Dimitrov *Bulgaria* 42°17N 23°9E **23** C10
Marengo *U.S.A.* 41°48N 92°4W **80** E7
Marfa *U.S.A.* 30°19N 104°1W **84** F2
Margao = Madgaon *India* 15°12N 73°58E **45** G1
Margaret → *Australia* 18°9S 125°41E **60** C4
Margaret Bay *Canada* 51°20N 127°35W **70** C3
Margaret L. *Canada* 58°56N 115°25W **70** B5
Margaret River *Australia* 33°57S 115°4E **61** F2
Margarita, I. de *Venezuela* 11°0N 64°0W **92** A6
Margaritovo *Russia* 43°25N 134°45E **28** C7
Margate *S. Africa* 30°50S 30°20E **57** D5
Margate *U.K.* 51°23N 1°23E **13** F9
Marg'ilon *Uzbekistan* 40°27N 71°42E **26** E8
Mārgow, Dasht-e *Afghan.* 30°40N 62°30E **40** D3
Marguerite *Canada* 52°30N 122°25W **70** C4
Mari El □ *Russia* 56°30N 48°0E **18** C8
Mari Indus *Pakistan* 32°57N 71°34E **42** C4
Mari Republic = Mari El □ *Russia* 56°30N 48°0E **18** C8
María Elena *Chile* 22°18S 69°40W **94** A2
María Grande *Argentina* 31°45S 59°55W **94** C4
Maria I. *N. Terr., Australia* 14°52S 135°45E **62** A2
Maria I. *Tas., Australia* 42°35S 148°0E **63** G4
Maria Island △ *Australia* 42°38S 148°5E **63** G4
Maria van Diemen, C. *N.Z.* 34°29S 172°40E **59** A4
Mariala △ *Australia* 25°57S 145°2E **63** D4
Marian *Australia* 21°9S 148°57E **62** b
Marian L. *Canada* 63°0N 116°15W **70** A5
Mariana Trench *Pac. Oc.* 13°0N 145°0E **64** F6
Marianna *Ark., U.S.A.* 34°46N 90°46W **85** D9
Marianna *Fla., U.S.A.* 30°46N 85°14W **85** F12
Marias → *U.S.A.* 47°56N 110°30W **76** C8
Marías, Is. *Mexico* 21°25N 106°28W **86** C3
Mariato, Punta *Panama* 7°12N 80°52W **88** E3
Maribor *Slovenia* 46°36N 15°40E **16** E8
Marico → *Africa* 23°35S 26°57E **56** B4
Maricopa *Ariz., U.S.A.* 33°4N 112°3W **77** K7
Maricopa *Calif., U.S.A.* 35°4N 119°24W **79** K7
Marié → *Brazil* 0°27S 66°26W **92** D5
Marie Byrd Land *Antarctica* 79°30S 125°0W **5** D14
Marie-Galante *Guadeloupe* 15°56N 61°16W **88** b
Mariecourt = Kangiqsujuaq *Canada* 61°30N 72°0W **69** E17
Mariehamn *Finland* 60°5N 19°55E **9** F18
Mariembourg *Belgium* 50°6N 4°31E **15** D4
Mariental *Namibia* 24°36S 18°0E **56** B2
Marienville *U.S.A.* 41°28N 79°8W **82** E5
Mariestad *Sweden* 58°43N 13°50E **9** G15
Marietta *Ga., U.S.A.* 33°57N 84°33W **85** E12
Marietta *Ohio, U.S.A.* 39°25N 81°27W **81** F13
Marieville *Canada* 45°26N 73°10W **83** A11
Mariinsk *Russia* 56°10N 87°20E **26** D9
Marijampolė *Lithuania* 54°33N 23°19E **9** J20
Marília *Brazil* 22°13S 50°0W **95** A6
Marín *Spain* 42°23N 8°42W **21** A1
Marina *U.S.A.* 36°41N 121°48W **78** J5
Marinduque *Phil.* 13°25N 122°0E **37** B6
Marine City *U.S.A.* 42°43N 82°30W **82** D2
Marinette *U.S.A.* 45°6N 87°38W **80** C10
Maringá *Brazil* 23°26S 52°2W **95** A5
Marion *Ala., U.S.A.* 32°38N 87°19W **85** E11
Marion *Ark., U.S.A.* 35°13N 90°12W **80** H8
Marion *Ill., U.S.A.* 37°44N 88°56W **80** G9
Marion *Ind., U.S.A.* 40°32N 85°40W **81** E11
Marion *Iowa, U.S.A.* 42°2N 91°36W **80** D8
Marion *Kans., U.S.A.* 38°21N 97°1W **80** F5
Marion *N.C., U.S.A.* 35°41N 82°1W **85** D13
Marion *Ohio, U.S.A.* 40°35N 83°8W **81** E12
Marion *S.C., U.S.A.* 34°11N 79°24W **85** D15
Marion *Va., U.S.A.* 36°50N 81°31W **81** G13
Marion, L. *U.S.A.* 33°28N 80°10W **85** E14
Mariposa *U.S.A.* 37°29N 119°58W **78** H7
Mariscal Estigarribia *Paraguay* 22°3S 60°40W **94** A3
Maritime Alps = Maritimes, Alpes *Europe* 44°10N 7°10E **20** D7
Maritimes, Alpes *Europe* 44°10N 7°10E **20** D7
Maritsa = Evros → *Greece* 41°40N 26°34E **23** D12
Mariupol *Ukraine* 47°5N 37°31E **19** E6
Mariusa △ *Venezuela* 9°24N 61°27W **89** E7
Marīvān *Iran* 35°30N 46°25E **46** C5
Marj 'Uyūn *Lebanon* 33°21N 35°34E **48** B4
Marka *Somalia* 1°48N 44°50E **49** G3
Markam *China* 29°42N 98°38E **34** C2
Markapur *India* 15°44N 79°19E **45** G4
Markazī □ *Iran* 34°0N 49°30E **47** C6
Markdale *Canada* 44°19N 80°39W **82** B4
Marked Tree *U.S.A.* 35°32N 90°25W **85** D9
Market Drayton *U.K.* 52°54N 2°29W **12** E5
Market Harborough *U.K.* 52°29N 0°55W **13** E7
Market Rasen *U.K.* 53°24N 0°20W **12** D7
Markham, Mt. *Antarctica* 83°0S 164°0E **5** E11
Markleeville *U.S.A.* 38°42N 119°47W **78** G7
Markovo *Russia* 64°40N 170°24E **27** C17
Marks *Russia* 51°45N 46°50E **18** D8
Marksville *U.S.A.* 31°8N 92°4W **84** F8
Marla *Australia* 27°19S 133°33E **63** D1
Marlbank *Canada* 44°26N 77°6W **82** B7
Marlboro *U.S.A.* 41°36N 73°59W **83** E11
Marlborough *Australia* 22°46S 149°52E **62** C4
Marlborough *U.K.* 51°25N 1°43W **13** F6
Marlborough *U.S.A.* 42°21N 71°33W **83** D13
Marlborough Downs *U.K.* 51°27N 1°53W **13** F6
Marlin *U.S.A.* 31°18N 96°54W **84** F6
Marlow *U.K.* 51°34N 0°46W **13** F7
Marlow *U.S.A.* 34°39N 97°58W **84** D6
Marmagao *India* 15°25N 73°56E **45** G1
Marmara *Turkey* 40°35N 27°34E **23** D12
Marmara, Sea of = Marmara Denizi *Turkey* 40°45N 28°15E **23** D13
Marmara Denizi *Turkey* 40°45N 28°15E **23** D13
Marmaris *Turkey* 36°50N 28°14E **23** F13
Marmion, Mt. *Australia* 29°16S 119°50E **61** E2
Marmion L. *Canada* 48°55N 91°20W **72** C1
Marmolada, Mte. *Italy* 46°26N 11°51E **22** A4
Marmora *Canada* 44°28N 77°41W **82** B7
Marne → *France* 48°47N 2°29E **20** B5
Maro Reef *U.S.A.* 25°25N 170°35W **75** K5
Maroantsetra *Madag.* 15°26S 49°44E **55** H9
Maroelaboom *Namibia* 19°15S 18°53E **56** A2
Marondera *Zimbabwe* 18°5S 31°42E **55** H6
Maroni → *Fr. Guiana* 5°30N 54°0W **93** B8
Maroochydore *Australia* 26°29S 153°5E **63** D5
Maroona *Australia* 37°27S 142°54E **63** F3
Maroua *Cameroon* 10°40N 14°20E **53** F8
Marovoay *Madag.* 16°6S 46°39E **55** H9
Marquard *S. Africa* 28°40S 27°28E **56** C4
Marquesas Fracture Zone *Pac. Oc.* 9°0S 125°0W **65** H15
Marquesas Is. = Marquises, Îs. *French Polynesia* 9°30S 140°0W **65** H14
Marquette *U.S.A.* 46°33N 87°24W **80** B10
Marquis *St. Lucia* 14°2N 60°54W **89** f
Marquises, Îs. *French Polynesia* 9°30S 140°0W **65** H14
Marra, Djebel *Sudan* 13°10N 24°22E **53** F10
Marracuene *Mozam.* 25°45S 32°35E **57** C5
Marrakech *Morocco* 31°9N 8°0W **52** B4
Marrawah *Australia* 40°55S 144°42E **63** G3
Marree *Australia* 29°39S 138°1E **63** D2
Marrimane *Mozam.* 22°58S 33°34E **57** B5
Marromeu *Mozam.* 18°15S 36°25E **57** A6
Marromeu ⌂ *Mozam.* 19°0S 36°0E **57** A6
Marrowie Cr. → *Australia* 33°23S 145°40E **63** E4
Marrupa *Mozam.* 13°8S 37°30E **55** G7
Mars Hill *U.S.A.* 46°31N 67°52W **81** B20
Marsá 'Alam *Egypt* 25°5N 34°54E **49** B1
Marsá Matrûh *Egypt* 31°19N 27°9E **53** B11
Marsabit *Kenya* 2°18N 38°0E **54** D7
Marsala *Italy* 37°48N 12°26E **22** F5
Marsden *Australia* 33°47S 147°32E **63** E4
Marseille *France* 43°18N 5°23E **20** E6
Marseilles = Marseille *France* 43°18N 5°23E **20** E6
Marsh I. *U.S.A.* 29°34N 91°53W **84** G9
Marshall *Ark., U.S.A.* 35°55N 92°38W **84** D8
Marshall *Mich., U.S.A.* 42°16N 84°58W **81** D11
Marshall *Minn., U.S.A.* 44°27N 95°47W **80** C6
Marshall *Mo., U.S.A.* 39°7N 93°12W **80** F7
Marshall *Tex., U.S.A.* 32°33N 94°23W **84** E7
Marshall → *Australia* 22°59S 136°59E **62** C2
Marshall Is. ■ *Pac. Oc.* 9°0N 171°0E **64** G9
Marshalltown *U.S.A.* 42°3N 92°55W **80** D7
Marshbrook *Zimbabwe* 18°33S 31°9E **57** A5
Marshfield *Mo., U.S.A.* 37°15N 92°54W **80** G7
Marshfield *Vt., U.S.A.* 44°20N 72°20W **83** B12
Marshfield *Wis., U.S.A.* 44°40N 90°10W **80** C8
Marshūn *Iran* 36°19N 49°23E **47** B6
Märsta *Sweden* 59°37N 17°52E **9** G17
Mart *U.S.A.* 31°33N 96°50W **84** F6
Martaban *Myanmar* 16°30N 97°35E **41** L20
Martaban, G. of = Mottama, G. of *Myanmar* 16°5N 96°30E **41** L20
Martapura *Kalimantan Selatan, Indonesia* 3°22S 114°47E **36** E4
Martapura *Sumatera Selatan, Indonesia* 4°19S 104°22E **36** E2
Marte R. Gómez, Presa *Mexico* 26°10N 99°0W **87** B5
Martelange *Belgium* 49°49N 5°43E **15** E5
Marthapal *India* 19°24N 81°37E **44** E5
Martha's Vineyard *U.S.A.* 41°25N 70°38W **83** E14
Martigny *Switz.* 46°6N 7°3E **20** C7
Martigues *France* 43°24N 5°4E **20** E6
Martin *Slovakia* 49°6N 18°58E **17** D10
Martin *S. Dak., U.S.A.* 43°11N 101°44W **80** D3
Martin *Tenn., U.S.A.* 36°21N 88°51W **85** C10
Martin L. *U.S.A.* 32°41N 85°55W **85** E12
Martina Franca *Italy* 40°42N 17°20E **22** D7
Martinborough *N.Z.* 41°14S 175°29E **59** D5
Martinez *Calif., U.S.A.* 38°1N 122°8W **78** G4
Martinez *Ga., U.S.A.* 33°31N 82°5W **85** E13
Martinique ⊠ *W. Indies* 14°40N 61°0W **88** c
Martinique Passage *W. Indies* 15°15N 61°0W **89** C7
Martinópolis *Brazil* 22°11S 51°12W **95** A5
Martins Bay *Barbados* 13°12N 59°29W **89** g
Martins Ferry *U.S.A.* 40°6N 80°44W **82** F4
Martinsburg *Pa., U.S.A.* 40°19N 78°20W **82** F6

Martinsburg *W. Va.*,
  U.S.A. 39°27N 77°58W **81** F15
Martinsville *Ind., U.S.A.* 39°26N 86°25W **80** F10
Martinsville *Va., U.S.A.* 36°41N 79°52W **81** G14
Marton *N.Z.* 40°4S 175°23E **59** D5
Martos *Spain* 37°44N 3°58W **21** D4
Martu ✧ *Australia* 22°30S 122°30E **60** D3
Marudi *Malaysia* 4°11N 114°19E **36** D4
Maruf *Afghan.* 31°30N 67°6E **40** D5
Marugame *Japan* 34°15N 133°40E **29** G6
Marunga *Angola* 17°28S 20°2E **56** A3
Maruwa ✧ *Australia* 22°30S 127°30E **60** D4
Marv Dasht *Iran* 29°50N 52°40E **47** D7
Marvast *Iran* 30°30N 54°15E **47** D7
Marvel Loch *Australia* 31°28S 119°29E **61** F2
Marwar *India* 25°43N 73°45E **42** G5
Mary *Turkmenistan* 37°40N 61°50E **47** B9
Maryborough = Portlaoise
  Ireland 53°2N 7°18W **10** C4
Maryborough *Queens.,*
  Australia 25°31S 152°37E **63** D5
Maryborough *Vic.,*
  Australia 37°3S 143°44E **63** F3
Maryfield *Canada* 49°50N 101°35W **71** D8
Maryland ☐ *U.S.A.* 39°0N 76°30W **81** F15
Maryland Junction
  Zimbabwe 17°45S 30°31E **55** H6
Maryport *U.K.* 54°44N 3°28W **12** C4
Mary's Harbour *Canada* 52°18N 55°51W **73** B8
Marystown *Canada* 47°10N 55°10W **73** C8
Marysville *Calif., U.S.A.* 39°9N 121°35W **76** G5
Marysville *Kans., U.S.A.* 39°51N 96°39W **80** F5
Marysville *Mich., U.S.A.* 42°54N 82°29W **82** D2
Marysville *Ohio, U.S.A.* 40°14N 83°22W **81** E12
Marysville *Wash., U.S.A.* 48°3N 122°11W **78** B4
Maryville *Mo., U.S.A.* 40°21N 94°52W **80** E6
Maryville *Tenn., U.S.A.* 35°46N 83°58W **85** D13
Masada *Israel* 31°18N 35°21E **48** D4
Masai *Malaysia* 1°29N 103°55E **39** d
Masai Steppe *Tanzania* 4°30S 36°30E **54** E7
Masaka *Uganda* 0°21S 31°45E **54** E6
Masalembo, Kepulauan
  Indonesia 5°35S 114°30E **36** F4
Masalima, Kepulauan
  Indonesia 5°4S 117°5E **36** F5
Masamba *Indonesia* 2°30S 120°15E **37** E6
Masan *S. Korea* 35°11N 128°32E **33** G15
Masandam, Ra's *Oman* 26°30N 56°30E **47** E8
Masasi *Tanzania* 10°45S 38°52E **54** G7
Masaya *Nic.* 12°0N 86°7W **88** D2
Masbate *Phil.* 12°21N 123°36E **37** B6
Mascara *Algeria* 35°26N 0°6E **52** A6
Mascarene Is. *Ind. Oc.* 22°0S 55°0E **50** J9
Mascota *Mexico* 20°32N 104°49W **86** C4
Masdar City = Madīnat Masdar
  U.A.E. 24°26N 54°37E **47** E7
Masela *Indonesia* 8°9S 129°51E **37** F7
Maseru *Lesotho* 29°18S 27°30E **56** C4
Mashābih *Si. Arabia* 25°35N 36°30E **46** E3
Mashan *China* 23°40N 108°11E **34** F7
Mashang *China* 36°48N 117°57E **33** F9
Mashatu ✧ *Botswana* 22°45S 29°5E **57** B4
Masherbrum *Pakistan* 35°38N 76°18E **43** B7
Mashhad *Iran* 36°20N 59°35E **47** B8
Mashīz *Iran* 29°56N 56°37E **47** D8
Māshkel, Hāmūn-i-
  Pakistan 28°20N 62°56E **47** D9
Mashki Chāh *Pakistan* 29°5N 62°30E **40** E3
Mashonaland *Zimbabwe* 16°30S 31°0E **55** H6
Mashonaland Central ☐
  Zimbabwe 17°30S 31°0E **57** A5
Mashonaland East ☐
  Zimbabwe 18°0S 32°0E **57** A5
Mashonaland West ☐
  Zimbabwe 17°30S 29°30E **57** A4
Mashrakh *India* 26°7N 84°48E **43** F11
Masi Manimba
  Dem. Rep. of the Congo 4°40S 17°54E **54** E3
Masig *Australia* 9°45S 143°24E **62** a
Masindi *Uganda* 1°40N 31°43E **54** D6
Maşīrah, Jazīrat *Oman* 21°0N 58°50E **49** C6
Maşīrah, Khalīj *Oman* 20°10N 58°10E **49** C6
Masisi
  Dem. Rep. of the Congo 1°23S 28°49E **54** E5
Masjed Soleyman *Iran* 31°55N 49°18E **47** D6
Mask, L. *Ireland* 53°36N 9°22W **10** C2
Maski *India* 15°56N 76°46E **45** G3
Maskin *Oman* 23°44N 56°52E **47** F8
Masoala, Tanjon' i
  Madag. 15°59S 50°13E **55** H10
Masohi = Amahai
  Indonesia 3°2S 128°55E **37** E7
Mason *Nev., U.S.A.* 38°56N 119°8W **78** G4
Mason *Tex., U.S.A.* 30°45N 99°14W **84** F5
Mason City *U.S.A.* 43°9N 93°12W **80** D7
Masqat *Oman* 23°37N 58°36E **49** C6
Massa *Italy* 44°1N 10°9E **20** D9
Massachusetts ☐ *U.S.A.* 42°30N 72°0W **83** D13
Massachusetts B.
  U.S.A. 42°25N 70°50W **83** D14
Massakory *Chad* 13°0N 15°49E **53** F9
Massangena *Mozam.* 21°34S 33°0E **57** B5
Massango *Angola* 8°2S 16°21E **54** F3
Massawa = Mitsiwa
  Eritrea 15°35N 39°25E **49** D2
Massena *U.S.A.* 44°56N 74°54W **83** B10
Massenya *Chad* 11°21N 16°9E **53** F9
Masset *Canada* 54°2N 132°10W **70** C2
Massiah Street *Barbados* 13°9N 59°29W **89** g
Massif Central *France* 44°55N 3°0E **20** D5
Massillon *U.S.A.* 40°48N 81°32W **82** F3
Massinga *Mozam.* 23°15S 35°22E **57** B6
Massingir *Mozam.* 23°51S 32°4E **57** B5
Masson-Angers *Canada* 45°32N 75°25W **83** A9
Masson I. *Antarctica* 66°10S 93°20E **5** C7
Mastanli = Momchilgrad
  Bulgaria 41°33N 25°23E **23** D11
Masterton *N.Z.* 40°56S 175°39E **59** D5
Mastic *U.S.A.* 40°47N 72°54W **83** F12
Mastuj *Pakistan* 36°20N 72°36E **43** A5

Mastung *Pakistan* 29°50N 66°56E **40** E5
Masty *Belarus* 53°27N 24°38E **17** B13
Masuda *Japan* 34°40N 131°51E **29** G5
Masuku = Franceville
  Gabon 1°40S 13°32E **54** E2
Masurian Lakes = Mazurski,
  Pojezierze *Poland* 53°50N 21°0E **17** B11
Masvingo *Zimbabwe* 20°8S 30°49E **55** J6
Maşyāf *Syria* 35°4N 36°20E **46** C3
Mata-au = Clutha ➤
  N.Z. 46°20S 169°49E **59** G2
Matabeleland *Zimbabwe* 18°0S 27°0E **55** H5
Matachewan *Canada* 47°56N 80°39W **72** C3
Matadi
  Dem. Rep. of the Congo 5°52S 13°31E **54** F2
Matagalpa *Nic.* 13°0N 85°58W **88** D2
Matagami *Canada* 49°45N 77°34W **72** C4
Matagami, L. *Canada* 49°50N 77°40W **72** C4
Matagorda B. *U.S.A.* 28°40N 96°12W **84** G6
Matagorda I. *U.S.A.* 28°15N 96°30W **84** G6
Mataiea *Tahiti* 17°46S 149°25W **59** d
Matak *Indonesia* 3°18N 106°16E **36** D3
Matale *Sri Lanka* 7°30N 80°37E **45** L5
Matam *Senegal* 15°34N 13°17W **52** E3
Matamoros *Coahuila,*
  Mexico 25°32N 103°15W **86** B4
Matamoros *Tamaulipas,*
  Mexico 25°53N 97°30W **87** B5
Ma'ţan as Sarra *Libya* 21°45N 22°0E **53** D10
Matane *Canada* 48°50N 67°33W **73** C6
Matang *China* 23°30N 104°7E **34** F5
Matanomadh *India* 23°33N 68°57E **42** H3
Matanzas *Cuba* 23°0N 81°40E **88** B3
Matapa *Botswana* 23°11S 24°39E **56** B3
Matapan, C. = Tenaro, Akra
  Greece 36°22N 22°27E **23** F10
Matapédia *Canada* 48°0N 66°59W **73** C6
Matara *Sri Lanka* 5°58N 80°30E **45** M5
Mataram *Indonesia* 8°35S 116°7E **37** K19
Matarani *Peru* 17°0S 72°10W **92** G4
Mataranka *Australia* 14°55S 133°4E **60** B5
Matarma, Râs *Egypt* 30°27N 32°44E **48** E1
Mataró *Spain* 41°32N 2°29E **21** B7
Matatiele *S. Africa* 30°20S 28°49E **57** D4
Matatila Dam *India* 25°0N 78°22E **44** B4
Mataura *N.Z.* 46°11S 168°51E **59** G2
Matavai, B. de *Tahiti* 17°30S 149°23W **59** d
Matehuala *Mexico* 23°39N 100°39W **86** C4
Mateke Hills *Zimbabwe* 21°48S 31°0E **55** J6
Matelot *Trin. & Tob.* 10°50N 61°7W **93** K15
Matera *Italy* 40°40N 16°36E **22** D7
Mathis *U.S.A.* 28°6N 97°50W **84** G6
Mathraki *Greece* 39°48N 19°31E **23** E8
Mathura *India* 27°30N 77°40E **42** F7
Mati *Phil.* 6°55N 126°15E **37** C7
Matiali *India* 26°56N 88°49E **43** F13
Matías Romero *Mexico* 16°53N 95°2W **87** D5
Matiri Ra. *N.Z.* 41°38S 172°20E **59** D4
Matjiesfontein *S. Africa* 33°14S 20°35E **56** D3
Matla ➤ *India* 21°40N 88°40E **43** J13
Matlamanyane *Botswana* 19°33S 25°57E **56** A4
Matli *Pakistan* 25°2N 68°39E **42** G3
Matlock *U.K.* 53°9N 1°33W **12** D6
Mato Grosso ☐ *Brazil* 14°0S 55°0W **93** F8
Mato Grosso, Planalto do
  Brazil 15°0S 55°0W **93** G8
Mato Grosso do Sul ☐
  Brazil 18°0S 55°0W **93** G8
Matochkin Shar, Proliv
  Russia 73°23N 55°12E **26** B6
Matola *Mozam.* 25°57S 32°27E **57** C5
Matopo Hills *Zimbabwe* 20°36S 28°20E **55** J5
Matosinhos *Portugal* 41°11N 8°42W **21** B1
Matroosberg *S. Africa* 33°23S 19°40E **56** D2
Maţruḥ *Oman* 23°37N 58°30E **49** C6
Matsu Tao *Taiwan* 26°8N 119°56E **35** D12
Matsue *Japan* 35°25N 133°10E **29** G6
Matsum, Ko *Thailand* 9°22N 99°55E **39** b
Matsumae *Japan* 41°26N 140°7E **28** D10
Matsumae-Hantō
  Japan 41°30N 140°15E **28** D10
Matsumoto *Japan* 36°15N 138°0E **29** F9
Matsusaka *Japan* 34°34N 136°32E **29** H4
Matsushima *Japan* 38°20N 141°10E **28** E10
Matsuura *Japan* 33°20N 129°49E **29** H4
Matsuyama *Japan* 33°45N 132°45E **29** H6
Mattagami ➤ *Canada* 50°43N 81°29W **72** B3
Mattancheri *India* 9°50N 76°15E **45** K3
Mattawa *Canada* 46°20N 78°45W **72** C4
Matterhorn *Switz.* 45°58N 7°39E **20** D7
Matthew Town *Bahamas* 20°57N 73°40W **89** B5
Matthews Ridge *Guyana* 7°37N 60°10W **92** B6
Mattice *Canada* 49°40N 83°20W **72** C3
Mattili *India* 18°33N 82°12E **44** E6
Mattituck *U.S.A.* 40°59N 72°32W **83** F12
Mattō = Hakusan *Japan* 36°31N 136°34E **29** F8
Mattoon *U.S.A.* 39°29N 88°23W **80** F9
Matuba *Mozam.* 24°28S 32°49E **57** B5
Matucana *Peru* 11°55S 76°25W **92** F3
Matugama *Sri Lanka* 6°31N 80°7E **45** L5
Matuku *Fiji* 19°10S 179°44E **59** a
Matūn = Khowst *Afghan.* 33°22N 69°58E **42** C3
Matura B. *Trin. & Tob.* 10°39N 61°1W **93** K15
Maturín *Venezuela* 9°45N 63°11W **92** B6
Mau *Mad. P., India* 26°17N 78°41E **43** F8
Mau *Ut. P., India* 25°56N 83°33E **43** G10
Mau *Ut. P., India* 25°17N 81°23E **43** G9
Mau Ranipur *India* 25°16N 79°8E **43** G8
Maubeuge *France* 50°17N 3°57E **20** A6
Maubin *Myanmar* 16°44N 95°39E **41** L19
Maud, Pt. *Australia* 23°6S 113°45E **60** D1
Maud Rise *S. Ocean* 66°0S 3°0E **5** C3
Maude *Australia* 34°29S 144°18E **63** E3
Maudin Sun *Myanmar* 16°0N 94°30E **41** M19
Maués *Brazil* 3°20S 57°45W **92** D7
Mauganj *India* 24°50N 81°55E **43** G9
Maughold Hd. *I. of Man* 54°18N 4°18W **12** C3
Maui *U.S.A.* 20°48N 156°20W **75** L8
Maulamyaing = Mawlamyine
  Myanmar 16°30N 97°40E **41** L20

Maule ☐ *Chile* 36°5S 72°30W **94** D1
Maumee *U.S.A.* 41°34N 83°39W **81** E12
Maumee ➤ *U.S.A.* 41°42N 83°28W **81** E12
Maumere *Indonesia* 8°38S 122°13E **37** F6
Maun *Botswana* 20°0S 23°26E **56** B3
Mauna Kea *U.S.A.* 19°50N 155°28W **75** M8
Mauna Loa *U.S.A.* 19°30N 155°35W **75** M8
Maunath Bhanjan = Mau
  India 25°56N 83°33E **43** G10
Maungmagan Kyunzu
  Myanmar 14°0N 97°48E **38** E1
Maupin *U.S.A.* 45°11N 121°5W **76** D3
Maurepas, L. *U.S.A.* 30°15N 90°30W **85** F9
Maurice, L. *Australia* 29°30S 131°0E **61** E5
Mauricie △ *Canada* 46°45N 73°0W **72** C5
Mauritania ■ *Africa* 20°50N 10°0W **52** E3
Mauritius ■ *Ind. Oc.* 20°0S 57°0E **55** d
Mauston *U.S.A.* 43°48N 90°5W **80** D8
Mavli *India* 24°45N 73°55E **42** G5
Mawai *India* 22°30N 81°4E **43** H9
Mawana *India* 29°6N 77°58E **42** E7
Mawand *Pakistan* 29°33N 68°38E **42** E3
Mawjib, W. al ➤ *Jordan* 31°28N 35°36E **48** D4
Mawkmai *Myanmar* 20°14N 97°37E **41** J20
Mawlaik *Myanmar* 23°40N 94°26E **41** H19
Mawlamyine *Myanmar* 16°30N 97°40E **41** L20
Mawqaq *Si. Arabia* 27°25N 41°8E **46** E4
Mawson *Antarctica* 67°30S 62°53E **5** C6
Mawson Coast *Antarctica* 68°30S 63°0E **5** C6
Max *U.S.A.* 47°49N 101°18W **80** B3
Maxcanú *Mexico* 20°35N 90°0W **87** C6
Maxesibeni *S. Africa* 30°49S 29°23E **57** D4
Maxhamish L. *Canada* 59°50N 123°17W **70** B4
Maxixe *Mozam.* 23°54S 35°17E **57** B6
Maxville *Canada* 45°17N 74°51W **83** A10
Maxwell *U.S.A.* 39°17N 122°11W **78** F4
Maxwelton *Australia* 20°43S 142°41E **62** C3
May, C. *U.S.A.* 38°56N 74°58W **81** F16
May Pen *Jamaica* 17°58N 77°15W **88** a
Maya ➤ *Russia* 60°28N 134°28E **27** D14
Maya, Costa *Mexico* 18°44N 87°42W **87** D7
Maya Mts. *Belize* 16°30N 89°0W **87** D7
Mayabandar *India* 12°56N 92°56E **45** H11
Mayaguana I. *Bahamas* 22°30N 72°44W **89** B5
Mayaguana Passage
  Bahamas 22°32N 73°15W **89** B5
Mayagüez *Puerto Rico* 18°12N 67°9W **89** d
Mayāmey *Iran* 36°24N 55°42E **47** B7
Mayang *China* 27°53N 109°49E **34** D7
Mayanup *Australia* 33°57S 116°27E **61** F2
Mayapán *Mexico* 20°29N 89°11W **87** C7
Mayari *Cuba* 20°40N 75°41W **89** B4
Mayaro *Trin. & Tob.* 10°17N 61°1W **93** K15
Mayaro B. *Trin. & Tob.* 10°14N 60°59W **93** K16
Mayavaram = Mayiladuthurai
  India 11°3N 79°42E **45** J4
Maybell *U.S.A.* 40°31N 108°5W **76** F9
Maybole *U.K.* 55°21N 4°42W **11** F4
Maydān *Iraq* 34°55N 45°37E **46** C5
Mayenne *France* 47°30N 0°32W **20** C3
Mayer *U.S.A.* 34°24N 112°14W **77** J7
Mayerthorpe *Canada* 53°57N 115°8W **70** C5
Mayfield *Ky., U.S.A.* 36°44N 88°38W **80** G9
Mayfield *N.Y., U.S.A.* 43°6N 74°16W **83** C10
Mayhill *U.S.A.* 32°53N 105°29W **77** K11
Mayiladuthurai *India* 11°3N 79°42E **45** J4
Maykop *Russia* 44°35N 40°10E **19** F7
Maymyo = Pyin-U-Lwin
  Myanmar 22°2N 96°28E **38** A1
Maynard *Mass., U.S.A.* 42°26N 71°27W **83** D13
Maynard *Wash., U.S.A.* 47°59N 122°55W **78** C4
Maynard Hills *Australia* 28°28S 119°49E **61** E2
Mayne ➤ *Australia* 23°40S 141°55E **62** C3
Maynooth *Canada* 45°13N 77°56W **82** A7
Maynooth *Ireland* 53°23N 6°34W **10** C5
Mayo *Canada* 63°38N 135°57W **68** E4
Mayo ☐ *Ireland* 53°53N 9°3W **10** C2
Mayon Volcano *Phil.* 13°15N 123°41E **37** B6
Mayor I. *N.Z.* 37°16S 176°17E **59** B6
Mayotte ☑ *Ind. Oc.* 12°50S 45°10E **55** a
Maysān ☐ *Iraq* 31°55N 47°15E **46** D5
Maysville *U.S.A.* 38°39N 83°46W **81** F12
Mayu *Indonesia* 1°30N 126°30E **37** D7
Mayuram = Mayiladuthurai
  India 11°3N 79°42E **45** J4
Mayville *N. Dak., U.S.A.* 47°30N 97°20W **80** B5
Mayville *N.Y., U.S.A.* 42°15N 79°30W **82** D5
Mazabuka *Zambia* 15°52S 27°44E **55** H5
Mazagán = El Jadida
  Morocco 33°11N 8°17W **52** B4
Mazagão *Brazil* 0°7S 51°16W **93** D8
Mazán *Peru* 3°30S 73°0W **92** D4
Mazapil ☐ *Iran* 36°30N 52°0E **47** B7
Mazapil *Mexico* 24°39N 101°34W **86** C4
Mazar *China* 36°32N 77°1E **30** D4
Mazara del Vallo *Italy* 37°39N 12°35E **22** F5
Mazarrón *Spain* 37°38N 1°19W **21** D5
Mazaruni ➤ *Guyana* 6°25N 58°35W **92** B7
Mazatán *Mexico* 29°0N 110°8W **86** B2
Mazatenango *Guatemala* 14°35N 91°30W **88** D1
Mazatlán *Mexico* 23°13N 106°25W **86** C3
Mažeikiai *Lithuania* 56°20N 22°20E **9** H20
Māzhān *Iran* 32°30N 59°0E **47** C8
Māzhān *Iran* 36°19N 56°56E **47** B8
Mazoe ➤ *Mozam.* 16°20S 33°30E **55** H6
Mazurski, Pojezierze
  Poland 53°50N 21°0E **17** B11
Mazyr *Belarus* 51°59N 29°15E **17** B15
Mba *Fiji* 17°33S 177°41E **59** a
Mbabane *Eswatini* 26°18S 31°6E **57** C5
Mbaïki *C.A.R.* 3°53N 18°1E **54** D3
Mbala *Zambia* 8°46S 31°24E **54** F6
Mbale *Uganda* 1°8N 34°12E **54** D6
Mbalmayo *Cameroon* 3°33N 11°33E **54** D2
Mbandaka
  Dem. Rep. of the Congo 0°1N 18°18E **54** D3
Mbanza Congo *Angola* 6°18S 14°16E **54** F2
Mbanza Ngungu
  Dem. Rep. of the Congo 5°12S 14°53E **54** F2

Mbarara *Uganda* 0°35S 30°40E **54** E6
Mbengga = Beqa *Fiji* 18°23S 178°8E **59** a
Mbeya *Tanzania* 8°54S 33°29E **54** F6
Mbhashe ➤ *S. Africa* 32°15S 28°54E **57** D4
Mbini = Río Muni ☐
  Eq. Guin. 1°30N 10°0E **54** D2
Mbizi *Zimbabwe* 21°23S 31°1E **57** B5
Mbombela *S. Africa* 25°29S 30°59E **57** C5
Mbomou = Bomu ➤
  C.A.R. 4°40N 22°30E **54** D4
Mbouda *Cameroon* 5°38N 10°15E **52** G8
M'boukou, L. de *Cameroon* 6°23N 12°50E **54** C2
Mbour *Senegal* 14°22N 16°54W **52** F2
Mbuji-Mayi
  Dem. Rep. of the Congo 6°9S 23°40E **54** F4
Mburucuyá *Argentina* 28°1S 58°14W **94** B4
Mburucuyá △ *Argentina* 28°1S 58°12W **94** B4
Mchinji *Malawi* 13°47S 32°58E **55** G6
Mdantsane *S. Africa* 32°56S 27°46E **57** D4
Mead, L. *U.S.A.* 36°0N 114°44W **79** J12
Meade *U.S.A.* 37°17N 100°20W **80** G3
Meade River = Atqasuk
  U.S.A. 70°28N 157°24W **74** A8
Meadow Lake *Canada* 54°10N 108°26W **71** C7
Meadow Lake △ *Canada* 54°27N 109°0W **71** C7
Meadow Valley Wash ➤
  U.S.A. 36°40N 114°34W **79** J12
Meadville *U.S.A.* 41°39N 80°9W **82** E4
Meaford *Canada* 44°36N 80°35W **82** B4
Meakan Dake *Japan* 45°15N 144°0E **28** C11
Mealy Mts. *Canada* 53°10N 58°0W **73** B8
Meander River *Canada* 59°2N 117°42W **70** B5
Meares, C. *U.S.A.* 45°37N 124°0W **76** D1
Mearim ➤ *Brazil* 3°4S 44°35W **93** D10
Meath ☐ *Ireland* 53°40N 6°57W **10** C5
Meath Park *Canada* 53°27N 105°22W **71** C7
Meaux *France* 48°58N 2°50E **20** B5
Mebechi-Gawa ➤
  Japan 40°31N 141°31E **28** D10
Mebulu, Tanjung
  Indonesia 8°50S 115°5E **37** K18
Mecca = Makkah
  Si. Arabia 21°30N 39°54E **49** C2
Mecca *U.S.A.* 33°34N 116°5W **79** M10
Mechanicsburg *U.S.A.* 40°13N 77°1W **82** F8
Mechanicville *U.S.A.* 42°54N 73°41W **83** D11
Mechelen *Belgium* 51°2N 4°29E **15** C4
Mecheria *Algeria* 33°35N 0°18W **52** B5
Mecklenburg *Germany* 53°33N 11°40E **16** B7
Mecklenburger Bucht
  Germany 54°20N 11°40E **16** A6
Meconta *Mozam.* 14°59S 39°50E **55** G7
Medak *India* 18°1N 78°15E **44** E4
Médanos de Coro △
  Venezuela 11°35N 69°44W **89** D6
Medanosa, Pta. *Argentina* 48°8S 66°0W **96** F3
Medawachchiya *Sri Lanka* 8°30N 80°30E **45** K5
Medchal *India* 17°37N 78°29E **44** F4
Médéa *Algeria* 36°12N 2°50E **52** A6
Medellín *Colombia* 6°15N 75°35W **92** B3
Medelpad *Sweden* 62°33N 16°30E **8** E17
Medemblik *Neths.* 52°46N 5°8E **15** B5
Medford *Oreg., U.S.A.* 42°19N 122°52W **76** E2
Medford *Wis., U.S.A.* 45°9N 90°20W **80** C8
Medgidia *Romania* 44°15N 28°19E **17** F15
Media Agua *Argentina* 31°58S 68°25W **94** C2
Media Luna *Argentina* 34°45S 66°44W **94** C2
Medianeira *Brazil* 25°17S 54°5W **95** B5
Mediaş *Romania* 46°9N 24°22E **17** E13
Medicine Bow *U.S.A.* 41°54N 106°12W **76** F10
Medicine Bow Mts.
  U.S.A. 40°40N 106°0W **76** F10
Medicine Hat *Canada* 50°0N 110°45W **71** D6
Medicine Lake *U.S.A.* 48°30N 104°30W **76** B11
Medicine Lodge *U.S.A.* 37°17N 98°35W **80** G4
Medina = Al Madīnah
  Si. Arabia 24°35N 39°52E **46** E3
Medina *N. Dak., U.S.A.* 46°54N 99°18W **80** B4
Medina *N.Y., U.S.A.* 43°13N 78°23W **82** C6
Medina *Ohio, U.S.A.* 41°8N 81°52W **82** E3
Medina ➤ *U.S.A.* 29°16N 98°29W **84** G5
Medina del Campo *Spain* 41°18N 4°55W **21** B3
Medina L. *U.S.A.* 29°32N 98°56W **84** G5
Medina Sidonia *Spain* 36°28N 5°57W **21** D3
Medinipur *India* 22°25N 87°21E **43** H12
Mediterranean Sea *Europe* 35°0N 15°0E **6** H7
Médoc *France* 45°10N 0°50W **20** D3
Medveditsa ➤ *Russia* 49°35N 42°41E **19** E7
Medvezhi, Ostrava
  Russia 71°0N 161°0E **27** B17
Medvezhyegorsk *Russia* 63°0N 34°25E **18** B5
Medway ☐ *U.K.* 51°25N 0°32E **13** F8
Medway ➤ *U.K.* 51°27N 0°46E **13** F8
Meekatharra *Australia* 26°32S 118°29E **61** E2
Meeker *U.S.A.* 40°2N 107°55W **76** F10
Meeteetse *U.S.A.* 44°9N 108°52W **76** D9
Mega *Ethiopia* 3°57N 38°19E **49** G2
Megara *Greece* 37°58N 23°22E **23** F10
Megasini *India* 21°38N 86°21E **43** J12
Meghalaya ☐ *India* 25°50N 91°0E **41** G17
Meghna ➤ *Bangla.* 22°50N 90°50E **41** H17
Mégion *Russia* 61°3N 76°6E **26** C8
Mégiscane, L. *Canada* 48°35N 75°55W **72** C5
Meharry, Mt. *Australia* 22°59S 118°35E **60** D2
Mehekar *India* 20°9N 76°34E **44** D3
Mehlville *U.S.A.* 38°31N 90°19W **80** F8
Mehndawal *India* 26°58N 83°5E **43** F10
Mehr Jān *Iran* 33°50N 55°6E **47** C7
Mehrābād *Iran* 37°24N 46°19E **46** C5
Mehrān *Iran* 33°7N 46°10E **46** C5
Mehrān ➤ *Iran* 26°45N 55°26E **47** E7
Mehrgarh *Pakistan* 29°30N 67°30E **42** E2
Mehrīz *Iran* 31°35N 54°28E **47** D7
Mei Jiang ➤ *China* 24°25N 116°35E **35** E11
Mei Xian *China* 34°18N 107°55E **34** G4
Meicheng *China* 29°29N 119°16E **35** C12
Meichengzhen *China* 29°9N 111°40E **35** C8
Meichuan *China* 30°8N 115°31E **35** B10

Meighen I. *Canada* 80°0N 99°30W **69** B12
Meigu *China* 28°16N 103°20E **34** C4
Meihekou *China* 42°32N 125°40E **33** C13
Meiktila *Myanmar* 20°53N 95°54E **41** J19
Meili Xue Shan *China* 28°30N 98°39E **34** C2
Meimyu = Pyin-U-Lwin
  Myanmar 22°2N 96°28E **38** A1
Meishan *China* 30°3N 103°23E **34** B4
Meissen *Germany* 51°9N 13°29E **16** C7
Meitan *China* 27°45N 107°29E **34** D6
Meizhou *China* 24°16N 116°6E **35** E11
Meja *India* 25°9N 82°7E **43** G10
Mejillones *Chile* 23°10S 70°30W **94** A1
Mekele *Ethiopia* 13°33N 39°30E **49** E2
Mekerghene, Sebkra
  Algeria 26°21N 1°30E **52** C6
Mekhtar *Pakistan* 30°30N 69°15E **40** D6
Meknès *Morocco* 33°57N 5°33W **52** B4
Mekong ➤ *Asia* 9°30N 106°15E **39** H6
Mekongga *Indonesia* 3°39S 121°15E **37** E6
Mekvari = Kür ➤
  Azerbaijan 39°29N 49°15E **19** G8
Melagiri Hills *India* 12°20N 77°30E **45** H3
Melaka *Malaysia* 2°15N 102°15E **39** L4
Melaka ☐ *Malaysia* 2°15N 102°15E **39** L4
Melanesia *Pac. Oc.* 4°0S 155°0E **64** H7
Melanesian Basin *Pac. Oc.* 0°5N 160°35E **64** G8
Melapalaiyam *India* 8°39N 77°44E **45** K3
Melaya *Indonesia* 8°17S 114°30E **37** J17
Melbourne *U.S.A.* 28°5N 80°37W **85** G14
Melchor Múzquiz
  Mexico 27°53N 101°31W **86** B4
Melchor Ocampo
  Mexico 24°51N 101°39W **86** C4
Melekeok *Palau* 7°27N 134°38E **64** G5
Mélèzes ➤ *Canada* 57°40N 69°29W **72** A5
Melfort *Canada* 52°50N 104°37W **71** C8
Melhus *Norway* 63°17N 10°18E **8** E14
Melilla *N. Afr.* 35°21N 2°57W **21** E4
Melipilla *Chile* 33°42S 71°15W **94** C1
Melissa *Canada* 45°24N 79°14W **82** A5
Melita *Canada* 49°15N 101°0W **71** D8
Melitopol *Ukraine* 46°50N 35°22E **19** E6
Melk *Austria* 48°13N 15°20E **16** D8
Mellansel *Sweden* 63°26N 18°19E **8** E18
Mellen *U.S.A.* 46°20N 90°40W **80** B8
Mellerud *Sweden* 58°41N 12°28E **9** G15
Mellette *U.S.A.* 45°9N 98°30W **80** C4
Melo *Uruguay* 32°20S 54°10W **95** C5
Melolo *Indonesia* 9°53S 120°40E **37** F6
Melouprey *Cambodia* 13°48N 105°16E **38** F5
Melrhir, Chott *Algeria* 34°13N 6°30E **52** B7
Melrose *Australia* 32°42S 146°57E **63** E4
Melrose *U.K.* 55°36N 2°43W **11** F6
Melrose *Minn., U.S.A.* 45°40N 94°49W **80** C6
Melrose *N. Mex., U.S.A.* 34°26N 103°38W **77** J12
Melstone *U.S.A.* 46°36N 107°52W **76** C10
Melton Mowbray *U.K.* 52°47N 0°54W **12** E7
Melun *France* 48°32N 2°39E **20** B5
Melung *Nepal* 27°31N 86°3E **43** F12
Melur *India* 10°2N 78°23E **45** J4
Melville *Canada* 50°55N 102°50W **71** C8
Melville, C. *Australia* 14°11S 144°30E **62** A3
Melville, L. *Canada* 53°30N 60°0W **73** B8
Melville B. *Australia* 12°0S 136°45E **62** A2
Melville B. *Greenland* 75°30N 63°0W **69** B19
Melville I. *Australia* 11°30S 131°0E **60** B5
Melville I. *Canada* 75°30N 112°0W **69** B8
Melville Pen. *Canada* 68°0N 84°0W **69** D15
Melvin, Lough *Ireland* 54°28N 8°10W **10** B3
Memba *Mozam.* 14°11S 40°30E **55** G8
Memboro *Indonesia* 9°30S 119°30E **60** A2
Memel = Klaipėda
  Lithuania 55°43N 21°10E **9** J19
Memel *S. Africa* 27°38S 29°36E **57** C4
Memmingen *Germany* 47°58N 10°10E **16** E6
Mempawah *Indonesia* 0°30N 109°5E **36** D3
Memphis *Mich., U.S.A.* 42°54N 82°46W **82** D2
Memphis *Tenn., U.S.A.* 35°8N 90°2W **85** D9
Memphis *Tex., U.S.A.* 34°44N 100°33W **84** D4
Memphrémagog, L.
  N. Amer. 45°8N 72°17W **83** B12
Mena *U.S.A.* 34°35N 94°15W **84** D7
Menado = Manado
  Indonesia 1°29N 124°51E **37** D6
Menai Strait *U.K.* 53°11N 4°13W **12** D3
Ménaka *Mali* 15°59N 2°18E **52** E6
Menan = Chao Phraya ➤
  Thailand 13°40N 100°31E **38** F3
Menard *U.S.A.* 30°55N 99°47W **84** F5
Menard Fracture Zone
  Pac. Oc. 43°0S 97°0W **65** M18
Mendaña Fracture Zone
  Pac. Oc. 16°0S 91°0W **65** J18
Mendawai ➤ *Indonesia* 3°30S 113°0E **36** E4
Mende *France* 44°31N 3°30E **20** D5
Mendeleyev Ridge *Arctic* 80°0N 178°0W **4** B17
Mendhar *India* 33°35N 74°10E **43** C6
Mendip Hills *U.K.* 51°17N 2°40W **13** F5
Mendocino *U.S.A.* 39°19N 123°48W **76** G2
Mendocino, C. *U.S.A.* 40°26N 124°25W **76** F1
Mendocino Fracture Zone
  Pac. Oc. 40°0N 142°0W **65** D13
Mendota *Calif., U.S.A.* 36°45N 120°23W **78** J6
Mendota *Ill., U.S.A.* 41°33N 89°7W **80** E9
Mendoyo *Indonesia* 8°23S 114°42E **37** J17
Mendoza *Argentina* 32°50S 68°52W **94** C2
Mendoza ☐ *Argentina* 33°0S 69°0W **94** C2
Mene Grande *Venezuela* 9°49N 70°56W **92** B4
Menemen *Turkey* 38°34N 27°3E **23** E12
Menen *Belgium* 50°47N 3°7E **15** D3
Mengcheng *China* 33°18N 116°31E **35** A11
Mengdingjie *China* 23°31N 98°58E **34** F2
Menggala *Indonesia* 4°30S 105°15E **36** E3
Menghai *China* 21°49N 100°25E **34** F3
Mengjin *China* 34°55N 112°45E **34** G7
Mengla *China* 22°21N 99°25E **34** F3
Menglian *China* 22°21N 99°31E **34** F2
Mengshan *China* 24°14N 110°55E **35** E8
Mengyin *China* 35°40N 117°58E **33** G9

Mengzhe *China* 22°2N 100°15E **34** F3
Mengzi *China* 23°20N 103°22E **34** F4
Menifee *U.S.A.* 33°41N 117°10W **79** M9
Menihek *Canada* 54°28N 56°36W **73** B6
Menihek L. *Canada* 54°0N 67°0W **73** B6
Menin = Menen *Belgium* 50°47N 3°7E **15** D3
Menindee *Australia* 32°20S 142°25E **63** E3
Menindee L. *Australia* 32°20S 142°25E **63** E3
Meningie *Australia* 35°50S 139°18E **63** F2
Menjangan, Pulau
  Indonesia 8°7S 114°31E **37** J17
Menlo Park *U.S.A.* 37°27N 122°12W **78** H4
Menngen ⊙ *Australia* 15°21S 131°16E **60** C5
Menominee *U.S.A.* 45°6N 87°37W **80** C10
Menominee → *U.S.A.* 45°6N 87°35W **80** C10
Menomonie *U.S.A.* 44°53N 91°55W **80** C8
Menongue *Angola* 14°48S 17°52E **55** G3
Menorca *Spain* 40°0N 4°0E **21** C8
Mentakab *Malaysia* 3°29N 102°21E **39** L4
Mentawai, Kepulauan
  Indonesia 2°0S 99°0E **36** E1
Menton *France* 43°50N 7°29E **20** E7
Mentor *U.S.A.* 41°40N 81°21W **82** E3
Menzies *Australia* 29°40S 121°2E **61** E3
Meob B. *Namibia* 24°25S 14°34E **56** B1
Meoqui *Mexico* 28°17N 105°29W **86** B3
Meppel *Neths.* 52°42N 6°12E **15** B6
Merak *Indonesia* 6°10N 106°26E **37** F12
Meramangye, L.
  Australia 28°25S 132°13E **61** E5
Meran = Merano *Italy* 46°40N 11°9E **22** A4
Merano *Italy* 46°40N 11°9E **22** A4
Merauke *Indonesia* 8°29S 140°24E **37** F10
Merbein *Australia* 34°10S 142°2E **63** E3
Merca = Marka *Somalia* 1°48N 44°50E **49** G3
Merced *U.S.A.* 37°18N 120°29W **78** H6
Merced → *U.S.A.* 37°21N 120°59W **78** H6
Merced Pk. *U.S.A.* 37°36N 119°24W **78** H7
Mercedes B. Aires,
  Argentina 34°40S 59°30W **94** C4
Mercedes Corrientes,
  Argentina 29°10S 58°5W **94** B4
Mercedes San Luis,
  Argentina 33°40S 65°21W **94** C2
Mercedes *Uruguay* 33°12S 58°0W **94** C4
Merceditas *Chile* 28°20S 70°35W **94** B1
Mercer *N.Z.* 37°16S 175°5E **59** B5
Mercer *U.S.A.* 41°14N 80°15W **82** E4
Mercer Island *U.S.A.* 47°34N 122°13W **78** C4
Mercury *U.S.A.* 36°40N 115°59W **79** J11
Mercy, C. *Canada* 65°0N 63°30W **69** E19
Mere *U.K.* 51°6N 2°16W **13** F5
Merebuk, Gunung
  Indonesia 8°13S 114°39E **37** J17
Meredith, C. *Falk. Is.* 52°15S 60°40W **96** G4
Meredith, L. *U.S.A.* 35°43N 101°33W **84** D4
Mergui *Myanmar* 12°26N 98°34E **38** F2
Mergui Arch. = Myeik Kyunzu
  Myanmar 11°30N 97°30E **39** G1
Mérida *Mexico* 20°58N 89°37W **87** C7
Mérida *Spain* 38°55N 6°25W **21** C2
Mérida *Venezuela* 8°24N 71°8W **92** B4
Mérida, Cord. de *Venezuela* 9°0N 71°0W **92** B4
Meriden *U.K.* 52°26N 1°38W **13** E6
Meriden *U.S.A.* 41°32N 72°48W **83** E12
Meridian *Calif., U.S.A.* 39°9N 121°55W **78** F5
Meridian *Idaho, U.S.A.* 43°37N 116°24W **76** E5
Meridian *Miss., U.S.A.* 32°22N 88°42W **85** E10
Merinda *Australia* 20°2S 148°11E **62** C4
Merir *Palau* 4°10N 132°30E **37** D8
Meririumã *Brazil* 1°15N 54°50W **93** C8
Merkel *U.S.A.* 32°28N 100°1W **84** E4
Meroe *India* 7°33N 93°33E **45** L11
Merowe Dam *Sudan* 18°35N 31°56E **53** E12
Merredin *Australia* 31°28S 118°18E **61** F2
Merrick *U.K.* 55°8N 4°28W **11** F4
Merrickville *Canada* 44°55N 75°50W **83** B9
Merrill *Oreg., U.S.A.* 42°1N 121°36W **76** E3
Merrill *Wis., U.S.A.* 45°11N 89°41W **80** C9
Merrimack → *U.S.A.* 42°49N 70°49W **83** D14
Merriman *U.S.A.* 42°55N 101°42W **80** D3
Merritt *Canada* 50°10N 120°45W **70** C4
Merritt Island *U.S.A.* 28°21N 80°42W **85** G14
Merriwa *Australia* 32°6S 150°22E **63** E5
Merry I. *Canada* 55°29N 77°31W **72** A4
Merryville *U.S.A.* 30°45N 93°33W **84** F8
Mersch *Lux.* 49°44N 6°7E **15** E6
Mersea I. *U.K.* 51°47N 0°58E **13** F8
Merseburg *Germany* 51°22N 11°59E **16** C6
Mersey → *U.K.* 53°25N 3°1W **12** D4
Merseyside □ *U.K.* 53°31N 3°2W **12** D4
Mersin *Turkey* 36°51N 34°36E **46** B2
Mersing *Malaysia* 2°25N 103°50E **39** L4
Merta *India* 26°39N 74°4E **42** F5
Merta Road *India* 26°43N 73°55E **42** F5
Merthyr Tydfil *U.K.* 51°45N 3°22W **13** F4
Merthyr Tydfil □ *U.K.* 51°46N 3°21W **13** F4
Mértola *Portugal* 37°40N 7°40W **21** D2
Mertz Glacier *Antarctica* 67°30S 144°45E **5** C10
Mertzon *U.S.A.* 31°16N 100°49W **84** F4
Meru *Kenya* 0°3N 37°40E **54** D7
Meru *Tanzania* 3°15S 36°46E **54** C4
Meru Betiri △ *Indonesia* 8°27S 113°51E **37** H15
Mesa *U.S.A.* 33°25N 111°50W **77** K8
Mesa Verde △ *U.S.A.* 37°11N 108°29W **77** H9
Mesgouez, L. *Canada* 51°20N 75°0W **72** B5
Meshed = Mashhad *Iran* 36°20N 59°35E **47** B8
Meshgīn Shahr *Iran* 38°30N 47°45E **46** B5
Meshoppen *U.S.A.* 41°36N 76°3W **83** E8
Mesilinka → *Canada* 56°6N 124°30W **70** B4
Mesolongi *Greece* 38°21N 21°28E **23** E9
Mesopotamia = Al Jazirah
  Iraq 33°30N 44°0E **46** C5
Mesopotamia *U.S.A.* 41°27N 80°57W **82** E4
Mesquite *Nev., U.S.A.* 36°48N 114°4W **77** H6
Mesquite *Tex., U.S.A.* 32°46N 96°36W **84** E6
Messaad *Algeria* 34°8N 3°30E **52** B6

Messalo → *Mozam.* 12°25S 39°15E **55** G7
Messene *Greece* 37°4N 22°1E **23** F10
Messina = Musina
  S. Africa 22°20S 30°5E **57** B5
Messina *Italy* 38°11N 15°34E **22** E6
Messina, Str. di *Italy* 38°15N 15°35E **22** F6
Messiniakos Kolpos
  Greece 36°45N 22°5E **23** F10
Mesta = Nestos →
  Europe 40°54N 24°49E **23** D11
Meta → *S. Amer.* 6°12N 67°28W **92** B5
Meta Incognita Pen.
  Canada 62°45N 68°30W **69** E18
Metabetchouan *Canada* 48°26N 71°52W **73** C5
Metaline Falls *U.S.A.* 48°52N 117°22W **76** B5
Metán *Argentina* 25°30S 65°0W **94** B3
Metcalfe *Canada* 45°14N 75°28W **83** A9
Metema *Ethiopia* 12°58N 36°12E **49** E2
Methven *N.Z.* 43°38S 171°40E **59** E3
Metlakatla *U.S.A.* 55°8N 131°35W **68** F5
Metropolis *U.S.A.* 37°9N 88°44W **80** G9
Metropolitana □ *Chile* 33°30S 70°50W **94** C1
Mettuppalaiyam *India* 11°18N 76°59E **45** J3
Mettur *India* 11°48N 77°47E **45** J3
Metu *Ethiopia* 8°18N 35°35E **49** F2
Metz *France* 49°8N 6°10E **20** B7
Meulaboh *Indonesia* 4°11N 96°3E **36** D1
Meureudu *Indonesia* 5°19N 96°10E **36** C1
Meuse → *Europe* 50°45N 5°41E **15** D5
Mexia *U.S.A.* 31°41N 96°29W **84** F6
Mexiana, I. *Brazil* 0°0 49°30W **93** D9
Mexicali *Mexico* 32°40N 115°30W **79** N11
Mexican Plateau *Mexico* 25°0N 104°0W **66** G9
Mexican Water *U.S.A.* 36°57N 109°32W **77** H9
Mexico *Maine, U.S.A.* 44°34N 70°33W **83** B14
Mexico *Mo., U.S.A.* 39°10N 91°53W **80** F8
Mexico *N.Y., U.S.A.* 43°28N 76°14W **83** C8
México □ *Mexico* 19°20N 99°30W **87** D5
Mexico ■ *Cent. Amer.* 25°0N 105°0W **86** C4
Mexico, G. of *Cent. Amer.* 25°0N 90°0W **87** C7
Mexico B. *U.S.A.* 43°35N 76°20W **83** C8
Meydān-e Naftūn *Iran* 31°56N 49°18E **47** D6
Meydani, Ra's-e *Iran* 25°24N 59°6E **47** E8
Meyers Chuck *U.S.A.* 55°45N 132°15W **70** B2
Meymaneh *Afghan.* 35°53N 64°38E **40** B4
Mezen *Russia* 65°50N 44°20E **18** A7
Mezen → *Russia* 65°44N 44°22E **18** A7
Mézenc, Mt. *France* 44°54N 4°11E **20** D6
Mezhdurechensk *Russia* 53°41N 88°3E **26** D9
Mezhdurechenskiy
  Russia 59°36N 65°56E **26** D7
Mezőkövesd *Hungary* 47°49N 20°35E **17** E11
Mezőtúr *Hungary* 47°1N 20°41E **17** E11
Mezquital *Mexico* 23°29N 104°23W **86** C4
Mfolozi → *S. Africa* 28°25S 32°26E **57** C5
Mhow *India* 22°33N 75°50E **42** H6
Miahuatlán *Mexico* 16°20N 96°36W **87** D5
Miami *Okla., U.S.A.* 36°53N 94°53W **84** C7
Miami *Tex., U.S.A.* 35°42N 100°38W **84** D4
Mian Xian *China* 33°10N 106°32E **34** A6
Mianchi *China* 34°48N 111°48E **32** G6
Miāndarreh *Iran* 35°37N 53°39E **47** C7
Miāndowāb *Iran* 37°0N 46°5E **46** B5
Miandrivazo *Madag.* 19°31S 45°29E **55** H9
Miāneh *Iran* 37°30N 47°40E **46** B5
Mianning *China* 28°32N 102°9E **34** C4
Mianwali *Pakistan* 32°38N 71°28E **42** C4
Mianyang *China* 31°22N 104°47E **34** B5
Mianzhu *China* 31°22N 104°7E **34** B5
Miao Ling *China* 26°5N 107°30E **34** D6
Miaodao Qundao
  China 38°10N 120°45E **33** E11
Miaoli *Taiwan* 24°37N 120°49E **35** E13
Miass *Russia* 54°59N 60°6E **18** D11
Mica *S. Africa* 24°10S 30°48E **57** B5
Michalovce *Slovakia* 48°47N 21°58E **17** D11
Michigan □ *U.S.A.* 44°0N 85°0W **81** C11
Michigan, L. *U.S.A.* 44°0N 87°0W **80** D10
Michigan City *U.S.A.* 41°43N 86°54W **80** E10
Michipicoten I. *Canada* 47°40N 85°40W **72** C2
Michoacán □ *Mexico* 19°10N 101°50W **86** D4
Michurin *Bulgaria* 42°9N 27°51E **23** C12
Michurinsk *Russia* 52°58N 40°27E **18** D7
Micoud *St. Lucia* 13°49N 60°54W **89** f
Micronesia *Pac. Oc.* 11°0N 160°0E **64** G7
Micronesia, Federated States of ■
  Pac. Oc. 9°0N 150°0E **64** G7
Mid-Indian Ridge *Ind. Oc.* 30°0S 75°0E **64** M1
Mid-Oceanic Ridge *Ind. Oc.* 42°0S 90°0E **64** M1
Mid-Pacific Seamounts
  Pac. Oc. 18°0N 177°0W **64** F10
Midai *Indonesia* 3°0N 107°47E **36** D3
Midale *Canada* 49°25N 103°20W **71** D8
Middelburg *Neths.* 51°30N 3°36E **15** C3
Middelburg *Eastern Cape,*
  S. Africa 31°30S 25°0E **56** D4
Middelburg *Mpumalanga,*
  S. Africa 25°49S 29°28E **57** C4
Middelpos *S. Africa* 31°55S 20°13E **56** E3
Middelwit *S. Africa* 24°51S 27°3E **56** C4
Middle Alkali L. *U.S.A.* 41°27N 120°5W **76** F3
Middle America Trench =
  Guatemala Trench
  Pac. Oc. 14°0N 95°0W **66** H10
Middle Andaman I.
  India 12°30N 92°30E **45** H11
Middle Bass I. *U.S.A.* 41°41N 82°48W **82** E2
Middle East *Asia* 35°0N 40°0E **24** E5
Middle Fork Feather →
  U.S.A. 38°33N 121°30W **78** F5
Middle I. *Australia* 34°6S 123°11E **61** F3
Middle Loup → *U.S.A.* 41°17N 98°24W **80** E4
Middleboro *U.S.A.* 41°54N 70°55W **83** E14
Middleburg *Fla., U.S.A.* 30°4N 81°52W **85** G14
Middleburg *Pa., U.S.A.* 40°47N 77°3W **82** F7
Middleburgh *U.S.A.* 42°36N 74°20W **83** D10
Middlebury *U.S.A.* 44°1N 73°10W **83** B11
Middlefield *U.S.A.* 41°27N 81°4W **82** E3
Middlemount *Australia* 22°50S 148°40E **62** C4
Middleport *N.Y., U.S.A.* 43°13N 78°29W **82** C6

Middleport *Ohio, U.S.A.* 39°0N 82°3W **81** F12
Middlesboro *U.S.A.* 36°36N 83°43W **81** G12
Middlesbrough *U.K.* 54°35N 1°13W **12** C6
Middlesbrough □ *U.K.* 54°28N 1°13W **12** C6
Middlesex *Belize* 17°2N 88°31W **88** C2
Middlesex *N.J., U.S.A.* 40°36N 74°30W **83** F10
Middlesex *N.Y., U.S.A.* 42°42N 77°16W **82** D7
Middleton *Australia* 22°22S 141°32E **62** C3
Middleton *Canada* 44°57N 65°4W **73** D6
Middleton Cr. →
  Australia 22°35S 141°51E **62** C3
Middleton I. *U.S.A.* 59°26N 146°20W **74** D10
Middleton *U.K.* 54°17N 6°51W **10** B5
Middletown *Calif.,*
  U.S.A. 38°45N 122°37W **78** G4
Middletown *Conn.,*
  U.S.A. 41°34N 72°39W **83** E12
Middletown *N.Y.,*
  U.S.A. 41°27N 74°25W **83** E10
Middletown *Ohio,*
  U.S.A. 39°31N 84°24W **81** F11
Middletown *Pa., U.S.A.* 40°12N 76°44W **83** F8
Midge Point *Australia* 20°38S 148°43E **62** b
Midhurst *Canada* 44°26N 79°43W **82** B5
Midhurst *U.K.* 50°59N 0°44W **13** G7
Midi, Canal du → *France* 43°45N 1°21E **20** E4
Midland *Australia* 31°54S 115°1E **61** F2
Midland *Canada* 44°45N 79°50W **82** B5
Midland *Calif., U.S.A.* 33°52N 114°48W **79** M12
Midland *Mich., U.S.A.* 43°37N 84°14W **81** D11
Midland *Pa., U.S.A.* 40°39N 80°27W **82** F4
Midland *Tex., U.S.A.* 32°0N 102°3W **84** F3
Midleton *Ireland* 51°55N 8°10W **10** E3
Midlothian *U.S.A.* 32°30N 97°0W **84** E6
Midlothian □ *U.K.* 55°51N 3°5W **11** F5
Midnapore = Medinipur
  India 22°25N 87°21E **43** H12
Midu *China* 25°18N 100°30E **34** E3
Midway Is. *Pac. Oc.* 28°13N 177°22W **75** K4
Midway Wells *U.S.A.* 32°41N 115°7W **79** N11
Midwest *U.S.A.* 42°0N 90°0W **75** G22
Midwest *Wyo., U.S.A.* 43°25N 106°16W **76** E10
Midwest City *U.S.A.* 35°27N 97°24W **84** D6
Midyat *Turkey* 37°25N 41°23E **46** B4
Midzör *Bulgaria* 43°24N 22°40E **23** C10
Mie □ *Japan* 34°30N 136°10E **29** G8
Międzychód *Poland* 52°35N 15°53E **16** B8
Międzyrzec Podlaski
  Poland 51°58N 22°45E **17** C12
Mielec *Poland* 50°15N 21°25E **17** C11
Mienga *Angola* 17°12S 19°48E **56** A2
Miercurea-Ciuc *Romania* 46°21N 25°48E **17** E13
Mieres *Spain* 43°18N 5°48W **21** A3
Mifflintown *U.S.A.* 40°34N 77°24W **82** F7
Mifraz Ḥefa *Israel* 32°52N 35°0E **48** C4
Migang Shan *China* 35°32N 106°13E **32** G4
Miguasha △ *Canada* 48°5N 66°26W **73** C6
Miguel Alemán, Presa
  Mexico 18°15N 96°32W **87** D5
Miguel Hidalgo, Presa
  Mexico 26°30N 108°34W **86** B3
Mihara *Japan* 34°24N 133°5E **29** G6
Mikhaylovgrad = Montana
  Bulgaria 43°27N 23°16E **23** C10
Mikhaylovka *Russia* 50°3N 43°5E **19** D7
Mikkeli *Finland* 61°43N 27°15E **8** F22
Mikkwa → *Canada* 58°25N 114°46W **70** B6
Míkonos = Mykonos
  Greece 37°30N 25°25E **23** F11
Mikun *Russia* 62°20N 50°0E **18** B9
Milaca *U.S.A.* 45°45N 93°39W **80** C7
Milagro *Ecuador* 2°11S 79°36W **92** D3
Milan *Mo., U.S.A.* 40°12N 93°7W **80** E7
Milan *Tenn., U.S.A.* 35°55N 88°46W **85** D10
Milâs *Turkey* 37°20N 27°50E **23** F12
Milazzo *Italy* 38°13N 15°15E **22** E6
Milbank *U.S.A.* 45°13N 96°38W **80** C5
Milbanke Sd. *Canada* 52°15N 128°35W **70** C3
Milden *Canada* 51°29N 107°32W **71** C7
Mildenhall *U.K.* 52°21N 0°32E **13** E8
Mildmay *Canada* 44°3N 81°7W **82** B3
Mildura *Australia* 34°13S 142°9E **63** E3
Mile *China* 24°24N 103°20E **34** E4
Miles *Australia* 26°40S 150°9E **63** D5
Miles City *U.S.A.* 46°25N 105°51W **76** C11
Milestone *Canada* 49°59N 104°31W **71** D8
Miletus *Turkey* 37°30N 27°18E **23** F12
Milford *Calif., U.S.A.* 40°10N 120°22W **78** E6
Milford *Conn., U.S.A.* 41°14N 73°3W **83** E11
Milford *Del., U.S.A.* 38°55N 75°26W **81** F16
Milford *Mass., U.S.A.* 42°8N 71°31W **83** D13
Milford *N.H., U.S.A.* 42°50N 71°39W **83** D13
Milford *N.Y., U.S.A.* 42°35N 74°56W **83** D10
Milford *Pa., U.S.A.* 41°19N 74°48W **83** E10
Milford *Utah, U.S.A.* 38°24N 113°1W **76** G7
Milford Haven *U.K.* 51°42N 5°7W **13** F2
Milford Sd. *U.S.A.* 44°45N 167°47E **59** F1
Milford Sound *N.Z.* 44°41S 167°55E **59** F1
Milḩ, Baḩr al = Razāzah, Buḩayrat
  ar *Iraq* 32°40N 43°35E **46** C4
Milikapiti *Australia* 11°26S 130°40E **60** B5
Miling *Australia* 30°30S 116°17E **61** F2
Milk River *Canada* 49°10N 112°5W **70** D6
Mill → *U.S.A.* 42°35N 83°23W **82** D1
Mill I. *Antarctica* 66°0S 101°30E **5** C8
Mill I. *Canada* 63°58N 77°47W **69** E16
Mill Valley *U.S.A.* 37°54N 122°32W **78** H4
Mill Lacs, L. des *Canada* 48°45N 90°35W **72** C1
Milledgeville *U.S.A.* 33°5N 83°14W **85** E13
Millen *U.S.A.* 32°48N 81°57W **85** E14
Millennium I. = Caroline I.
  Kiribati 9°58S 150°13W **65** H12
Miller *U.S.A.* 44°31N 98°59W **80** C4
Miller Lake *Canada* 45°6N 81°26W **82** A3
Millersburg *Ohio, U.S.A.* 40°33N 81°55W **82** F3

Millersburg *Pa., U.S.A.* 40°32N 76°58W **82** F8
Millerton *U.S.A.* 41°57N 73°31W **83** E11
Millerton L. *U.S.A.* 37°1N 119°41W **78** J7
Millet *St. Lucia* 13°55N 60°59W **89** f
Millheim *U.S.A.* 40°54N 77°29W **82** F7
Millicent *Australia* 37°34S 140°21E **63** F3
Millington *U.S.A.* 35°20N 89°53W **85** D10
Millinocket *U.S.A.* 45°39N 68°43W **81** C19
Millmerran *Australia* 27°53S 151°16E **63** D5
Millom *U.K.* 54°13N 3°16W **12** C4
Mills L. *Canada* 61°30N 118°20W **70** A5
Millsboro *U.S.A.* 40°0N 80°0W **82** G5
Millstream Chichester △
  Australia 21°35S 117°6E **60** D2
Millstreet *Ireland* 52°4N 9°4W **10** D2
Millville *N.J., U.S.A.* 39°24N 75°2W **81** F16
Millville *Pa., U.S.A.* 41°7N 76°32W **83** E8
Millwood L. *U.S.A.* 33°42N 93°58W **84** E8
Milne → *Australia* 21°10S 137°33E **62** C2
Milne Inlet *Canada* 72°30N 80°0W **69** B15
Milnor *U.S.A.* 46°16N 97°27W **80** B5
Milo *U.S.A.* 45°15N 68°59W **81** C19
Milos *Greece* 36°44N 24°25E **23** F11
Milparinka *Australia* 29°46S 141°57E **63** D3
Milpitas *U.S.A.* 37°26N 121°55W **78** H5
Milton *N.S., Canada* 44°4N 64°45W **73** D7
Milton *Ont., Canada* 43°31N 79°53W **82** C5
Milton *N.Z.* 46°7S 169°59E **59** G2
Milton *Calif., U.S.A.* 38°3N 120°51W **78** G6
Milton *Fla., U.S.A.* 30°38N 87°3W **85** F11
Milton *Pa., U.S.A.* 41°1N 76°51W **82** F8
Milton *Vt., U.S.A.* 44°38N 73°7W **83** B11
Milton-Freewater
  U.S.A. 45°56N 118°23W **76** D4
Milton Keynes *U.K.* 52°1N 0°44W **13** E7
Milton Keynes □ *U.K.* 52°1N 0°44W **13** E7
Miluo *China* 29°0N 112°59E **35** C9
Milverton *Canada* 43°34N 80°55W **82** C4
Milwaukee *U.S.A.* 43°2N 87°54W **80** D10
Milwaukee Deep *Atl. Oc.* 19°50N 68°0W **89** C6
Milwaukie *U.S.A.* 45°26N 122°38W **78** E4
Mimili *Australia* 27°0S 132°42E **61** E5
Mina Pirquitas *Argentina* 22°40S 66°30W **94** A2
Minago → *Canada* 54°33N 98°59W **71** C9
Minaki *Canada* 49°59N 94°40W **71** D10
Minamata *Japan* 32°10N 130°30E **29** H5
Minami-Arapusa △
  Japan 35°30N 138°9E **29** G9
Minami-Tori-Shima
  Pac. Oc. 24°20N 153°58E **64** E7
Minamiaizu *Japan* 37°12N 139°46E **29** F9
Minamiawaji *Japan* 34°10N 134°42E **29** G7
Minamisōma *Japan* 37°38N 140°58E **28** F10
Minas *Uruguay* 34°20S 55°10W **95** C4
Minas, Sierra de las
  Guatemala 15°9N 89°31W **88** C2
Minas Basin *Canada* 45°20N 64°12W **73** C7
Minas Gerais □ *Brazil* 18°50S 46°0W **93** G9
Minatitlán *Mexico* 17°59N 94°31W **87** D6
Minbu *Myanmar* 20°10N 94°52E **41** J19
Minchinabad *Pakistan* 30°10N 73°34E **42** D5
Mindanao *Phil.* 8°0N 125°0E **37** C7
Mindanao Sea = Bohol Sea
  Phil. 9°0N 124°0E **37** C6
Mindanao Trench *Pac. Oc.* 12°0N 126°6E **37** B7
Mindelo *Cabo Verde* 16°24N 25°0W **52** b
Minden *Canada* 44°55N 78°43W **82** B6
Minden *Germany* 52°17N 8°55E **16** B5
Minden *La., U.S.A.* 32°37N 93°17W **84** E8
Minden *Nev., U.S.A.* 38°57N 119°46W **78** G7
Mindibungu = Billiluna
  Australia 19°37S 127°41E **60** C4
Mindiptana *Indonesia* 5°55S 140°22E **37** F10
Mindoro *Phil.* 13°0N 121°0E **37** B6
Mindoro Str. *Phil.* 12°30N 120°30E **37** B6
Mine *Japan* 34°12N 131°7E **29** G5
Minehead *U.K.* 51°12N 3°29W **13** F4
Mineola *N.Y., U.S.A.* 40°44N 73°38W **83** F11
Mineola *Tex., U.S.A.* 32°40N 95°29W **84** E7
Mineral King *U.S.A.* 36°27N 118°36W **78** J8
Mineral Wells *U.S.A.* 32°48N 98°7W **84** E5
Miners Bay *Canada* 44°49N 78°46W **82** B6
Minersville *U.S.A.* 40°41N 76°16W **83** F8
Minerva *U.S.A.* 40°44N 81°6W **82** F3
Minerva Ohio, *U.S.A.* 40°44N 81°6W **82** F3
Minerva Reef *Pac. Oc.* 23°38S 178°50W **59** D11
Minfeng *China* 37°4N 82°46E **30** D5
Mingäçevir Su Anbarı =
  Mingächaurskoye Vdkhr. =
  Mingäçevir Su Anbarı
  Azerbaijan 40°57N 46°50E **19** F8
Mingela *Australia* 19°52S 146°38E **62** B4
Mingenew *Australia* 29°12S 115°21E **61** E2
Minggang *China* 32°24N 114°3E **35** A10
Mingin *Myanmar* 22°50N 94°30E **41** H19
Minglun *China* 28°12N 102°15E **34** C4
Mingshan *China* 30°6N 103°10E **34** B4
Mingteke Daban = Mintaka Pass
  Pakistan 37°0N 74°58E **43** A6
Mingxi *China* 26°18N 117°12E **35** D11
Mingyuegue *China* 43°2N 128°50E **33** C15
Minhe *China* 36°9N 102°49E **32** F2
Minho = Miño → *Spain* 41°52N 8°40W **21** A2
Minho *Portugal* 41°30N 8°16W **21** B2
Minhou *China* 26°0N 119°15E **35** E12
Minicoy I. *India* 8°17N 73°2E **45** K1
Minidoka *U.S.A.* 42°45N 113°29W **76** E7

Miniwgwal, L. *Australia* 29°31S 123°14E **61** E3
Minilya → *Australia* 23°45S 114°0E **61** D1
Minilya Roadhouse
  Australia 23°55S 114°0E **61** D1
Minipi L. *Canada* 52°25N 60°45W **73** B7
Minjilang *Australia* 11°8S 132°33E **60** B5
Mink L. *Canada* 61°54N 117°40W **70** A5
Minna *Nigeria* 9°37N 6°30E **52** G7
Minneapolis *Kans., U.S.A.* 39°8N 97°42W **80** F5
Minneapolis *Minn.,*
  U.S.A. 44°57N 93°16W **80** C7
Minneapolis-St. Paul Int. ✈ (MSP)
  U.S.A. 44°53N 93°13W **80** C7
Minnedosa *Canada* 50°14N 99°50W **71** C9
Minnesota □ *U.S.A.* 46°0N 94°15W **80** B6
Minnesota → *U.S.A.* 44°54N 93°9W **80** C7
Minnewaukan *U.S.A.* 48°4N 99°15W **80** A4
Minnipa *Australia* 32°51S 135°9E **63** E2
Minnitaki L. *Canada* 49°57N 92°10W **72** C1
Mino *Japan* 35°32N 136°55E **29** G8
Miño → *Spain* 41°52N 8°40W **21** A2
Minorca = Menorca *Spain* 40°0N 4°0E **21** C8
Minot *U.S.A.* 48°14N 101°18W **80** A3
Minqin *China* 38°38N 103°20E **32** E2
Minqing *China* 26°15N 118°50E **35** D12
Minsk *Belarus* 53°52N 27°30E **17** B14
Mińsk Mazowiecki
  Poland 52°10N 21°33E **17** B11
Mintabie *Australia* 27°15S 133°7E **63** D1
Mintaka Pass *Pakistan* 37°0N 74°58E **43** A6
Minto, L. *Canada* 57°13N 75°0W **72** A5
Minton *Canada* 49°10N 104°35W **71** D8
Minturn *U.S.A.* 39°35N 106°26W **76** G10
Minudasht *Iran* 37°17N 56°7E **47** B8
Minusinsk *Russia* 53°43N 91°20E **27** D10
Minutang *India* 28°15N 96°30E **41** E20
Minvoul *Gabon* 2°9N 12°8E **54** D2
Minya Konka = Gongga Shan
  China 29°40N 101°55E **34** C3
Minzhong *China* 22°37N 113°30E **31** a
Miquelon *Canada* 49°25N 76°27W **72** C4
Miquelon *St-P. & M.* 47°8N 56°22W **73** C8
Mīr Kūh *Iran* 26°22N 58°55E **47** E8
Mīr Shahdād *Iran* 26°15N 58°29E **47** E8
Mira *Italy* 45°26N 12°8E **22** B5
Mira por vos Cay
  Bahamas 22°9N 74°30W **89** B5
Mirador-Río Azul △
  Guatemala 17°45N 89°50W **88** C2
Miraj *India* 16°50N 74°45E **44** F2
Miram Shah *Pakistan* 33°0N 70°2E **42** C4
Miramar *Argentina* 38°15S 57°50W **94** D4
Miramar *Mozam.* 23°50S 35°35E **57** B6
Miramichi *Canada* 47°2N 65°28W **73** C6
Miramichi B. *Canada* 47°15N 65°0W **73** C7
Miranda *Brazil* 20°10S 56°15W **93** H7
Miranda → *Brazil* 19°25S 57°20W **93** G7
Miranda de Ebro *Spain* 42°41N 2°57W **21** A4
Miranda do Douro
  Portugal 41°30N 6°16W **21** B2
Mirandópolis *Brazil* 21°9S 51°6W **95** A5
Mirani *Australia* 21°8S 148°53E **62** b
Mirassol *Brazil* 20°46S 49°28W **95** A6
Mirbāṭ *Oman* 17°0N 54°45E **49** D5
Miri *Malaysia* 4°23N 113°59E **36** D4
Miriam Vale *Australia* 24°20S 151°33E **62** C5
Mirigama *Sri Lanka* 7°15N 80°8E **45** L5
Mirim, L. *S. Amer.* 32°45S 52°50W **95** C5
Miriuwung Gajerrong ⊙
  Australia 15°0S 128°45E **60** C4
Mīrjāveh *Iran* 29°1N 61°30E **47** D9
Mirny *Antarctica* 66°50S 92°30E **5** C14
Mirnyy *Russia* 62°33N 113°53E **27** C12
Mirokhan *Pakistan* 27°46N 68°6E **42** F3
Mirond L. *Canada* 55°6N 102°47W **71** B8
Mirpur *Pakistan* 33°32N 73°56E **43** C5
Mirpur Batoro *Pakistan* 24°44N 68°16E **42** G3
Mirpur Bibiwari *Pakistan* 28°33N 67°44E **42** E2
Mirpur Khas *Pakistan* 25°30N 69°0E **42** G3
Mirpur Sakro *Pakistan* 24°33N 67°41E **42** G2
Mirs Bay = Tai Pang Wan
  China 22°33N 114°24E **31** a
Mirtağ *Turkey* 38°23N 41°56E **46** B4
Mirtoo Sea *Greece* 37°0N 23°20E **23** F10
Miryang *S. Korea* 35°31N 128°44E **33** G15
Mirzapur *India* 25°10N 82°34E **43** G10
Mirzapur-cum-Vindhyachal =
  Mirzapur *India* 25°10N 82°34E **43** G10
Misantla *Mexico* 19°56N 96°50W **87** D5
Misawa *Japan* 40°41N 141°24E **28** D10
Miscou I. *Canada* 47°57N 64°31W **73** C7
Misha *India* 7°59N 93°20E **45** L11
Mish'āb, Ra's al
  Si. Arabia 28°15N 48°43E **47** E6
Mishan *China* 45°37N 131°48E **28** B5
Mishawaka *U.S.A.* 41°40N 86°11W **80** E10
Mishima *Japan* 35°10N 138°52E **29** G9
Misión *Mexico* 32°6N 116°53W **79** N10
Misiones □ *Argentina* 27°0S 55°0W **95** B5
Miskah *Si. Arabia* 24°49N 42°56E **46** E4
Miskitos, Cayos *Nic.* 14°26N 82°50W **88** D3
Miskolc *Hungary* 48°7N 20°50E **17** D11
Misool *Indonesia* 1°52S 130°10E **37** E8
Miṣr = Egypt ■ *Africa* 28°0N 31°0E **53** C12
Miṣrātah *Libya* 32°24N 15°3E **53** B9
Missanabie *Canada* 48°20N 84°6W **72** C3
Missinaibi → *Canada* 50°43N 81°29W **72** B3
Missinaibi L. *Canada* 48°23N 83°40W **72** C3
Mission *Canada* 49°10N 122°15W **70** D4
Mission *S. Dak., U.S.A.* 43°18N 100°39W **80** D3
Mission *Tex., U.S.A.* 26°13N 98°20W **84** H5
Mission Beach *Australia* 17°53S 146°6E **62** B4
Mission Viejo *U.S.A.* 33°36N 117°40W **79** M9
Missisa L. *Canada* 52°20N 85°7W **72** B2
Missisicabi → *Canada* 51°14N 79°31W **72** B4

Mississagi → *Canada* 46°15N 83°9W **72** C3
Mississippi □ *U.S.A.* 33°0N 90°0W **85** E10
Mississippi → *U.S.A.* 29°9N 89°15W **85** G10
Mississippi L. *Canada* 45°5N 76°10W **83** A8
Mississippi River Delta
  U.S.A. 29°10N 89°15W **85** G10
Mississippi Sd. *U.S.A.* 30°20N 89°0W **85** F10
Missoula *U.S.A.* 46°52N 114°1W **76** C6
Missouri □ *U.S.A.* 38°25N 92°30W **80** F7
Missouri → *U.S.A.* 38°49N 90°7W **80** F8
Missouri City *U.S.A.* 29°37N 95°32W **84** G7
Missouri Valley *U.S.A.* 41°34N 95°53W **80** E6
Mist *U.S.A.* 45°59N 123°15W **78** E3
Mistassibi → *Canada* 48°53N 72°13W **73** B5
Mistassini *Canada* 48°53N 72°12W **73** C5
Mistassini → *Canada* 48°42N 72°20W **73** C5
Mistassini, L. *Canada* 51°0N 73°30W **72** B5
Mistastin L. *Canada* 55°57N 63°20W **73** A7
Mistinibi, L. *Canada* 55°56N 64°17W **73** A7
Mistissini *Canada* 48°53N 72°12W **73** C5
Misty L. *Canada* 58°53N 101°40W **71** B8
Misurata = Miṣrātah
  Libya 32°24N 15°3E **53** B9
Mitchell *Australia* 26°29S 147°58E **63** D4
Mitchell *Canada* 43°28N 81°12W **82** D3
Mitchell *Nebr., U.S.A.* 41°57N 103°49W **80** E2
Mitchell *Oreg., U.S.A.* 44°34N 120°9W **76** D3
Mitchell *S. Dak., U.S.A.* 43°43N 98°2W **80** D4
Mitchell → *Australia* 15°12S 141°35E **62** B3
Mitchell, Mt. *U.S.A.* 35°46N 82°16W **85** D13
Mitchell-Alice Rivers △
  Australia 15°28S 142°5E **62** B3
Mitchell Ra. *Australia* 12°49S 135°36E **62** A2
Mitchelstown *Ireland* 52°15N 8°16W **10** D3
Mitha Tiwana *Pakistan* 32°13N 72°6E **42** C5
Mithi *Pakistan* 24°44N 69°48E **42** G3
Mithrao *Pakistan* 27°28N 69°40E **42** F3
Mitilini *Greece* 39°6N 26°35E **23** E12
Mitla Pass = Mamarr Mitlā
  Egypt 30°2N 32°54E **48** E1
Mito *Japan* 36°20N 140°30E **29** F10
Mitrovicë *Kosovo* 42°54N 20°52E **23** C9
Mitsamiouli *Comoros Is.* 11°20S 43°16E **55** a
Mitsiwa *Eritrea* 15°35N 39°25E **49** D2
Mitsukaidō *Japan* 36°1N 139°59E **29** F9
Mittagong *Australia* 34°28S 150°29E **63** E5
Mittimatalik = Pond Inlet
  Canada 72°40N 77°0W **69** C16
Mitú *Colombia* 1°15N 70°13W **92** C4
Mitumba, Mts.
  Dem. Rep. of the Congo 7°0S 27°30E **54** F5
Mitwaba
  Dem. Rep. of the Congo 8°2S 27°17E **54** F5
Mixteco → *Mexico* 18°11N 98°30W **87** D5
Miyagi □ *Japan* 38°15N 140°45E **28** E10
Miyāh, W. el → *Syria* 34°44N 39°57E **46** C3
Miyake-Jima *Japan* 34°5N 139°30E **29** G9
Miyako *Japan* 39°40N 141°59E **28** E10
Miyako-Jima *Japan* 24°45N 125°20E **29** M2
Miyako-Rettō *Japan* 24°24N 125°0E **29** M2
Miyakojima *Japan* 24°48N 125°17E **29** M2
Miyakonojō *Japan* 31°40N 131°5E **29** J5
Miyani *India* 21°50N 69°26E **42** J3
Miyanoura-Dake *Japan* 30°20N 130°31E **29** J5
Miyazaki *Japan* 31°56N 131°30E **29** J5
Miyazaki □ *Japan* 32°30N 131°30E **29** H5
Miyazu *Japan* 35°35N 135°10E **29** G7
Miyet, Bahr el = Dead Sea
  Asia 31°30N 35°30E **48** D4
Miyi *China* 26°47N 102°9E **34** D4
Miyoshi *Japan* 34°48N 132°51E **29** G6
Miyun *China* 40°28N 116°50E **32** D9
Miyun Shuiku *China* 40°30N 117°0E **33** D9
Mizdah *Libya* 31°30N 13°0E **53** B8
Mizen Hd. *Cork, Ireland* 51°27N 9°50W **10** E2
Mizen Hd. *Wicklow, Ireland* 52°51N 6°4W **10** D5
Mizhi *China* 37°47N 110°12E **32** F6
Mizoram □ *India* 23°30N 92°40E **41** H18
Mizpe Ramon *Israel* 30°34N 34°49E **48** E3
Mizuho *Antarctica* 70°30S 41°0E **5** D5
Mizusawa = Ōshū *Japan* 39°8N 141°8E **28** E10
Mjölby *Sweden* 58°20N 15°10E **9** G16
Mjosa *Norway* 60°40N 11°0E **8** F14
Mkhaya △ *Eswatini* 26°34S 31°45E **57** D5
Mkhuze △ *S. Africa* 29°27S 29°30E **57** C4
Mkomazi → *S. Africa* 30°12S 30°50E **57** D5
Mkuze *S. Africa* 27°10S 32°0E **57** C5
Mladá Boleslav *Czechia* 50°27N 14°53E **16** C8
Mlange = Mulanje, Mt.
  Malawi 16°2S 35°33E **55** H7
Mława *Poland* 53°9N 20°25E **17** B11
Mlawula △ *Eswatini* 26°12S 32°2E **57** C5
Mljet *Croatia* 42°43N 17°30E **22** C7
Mmabatho *S. Africa* 25°49S 25°30E **56** C4
Mo i Rana *Norway* 66°20N 14°7E **8** C16
Moa *Australia* 10°11S 142°16E **62** a
Moa → *Cuba* 20°40N 74°56W **89** B4
Moa *Indonesia* 8°0S 128°0E **37** F7
Moa → *S. Leone* 6°59N 11°36W **52** G3
Moab *U.S.A.* 38°35N 109°33W **76** G9
Moala *Fiji* 18°36S 179°53E **59** a
Moama *Australia* 36°7S 144°46E **63** F3
Moapa *U.S.A.* 36°40N 114°37W **79** J12
Moate *Ireland* 53°24N 7°44W **10** C4
Mobārakābād *Iran* 28°24N 53°20E **47** D7
Mobaye *C.A.R.* 4°25N 21°5E **54** D4
Moberly *U.S.A.* 39°25N 92°26W **80** F7
Moberly Lake *Canada* 55°50N 121°44W **70** B4
Mobile *U.S.A.* 30°41N 88°3W **85** F11
Mobile B. *U.S.A.* 30°30N 88°0W **85** F11
Mobridge *U.S.A.* 45°32N 100°26W **80** C3
Moc Chau *Vietnam* 20°50N 104°38E **38** B5
Moc Hoa *Vietnam* 10°46N 105°56E **39** G5
Moçambique = Mozambique ■
  Africa 19°0S 35°0E **55** H7
Moçambique *Mozam.* 15°3S 40°42E **55** H8
Mocanaqua *U.S.A.* 41°9N 76°8W **83** E8
Moce *Fiji* 18°40S 178°29W **59** a
Mochima △ *Venezuela* 10°30N 64°5W **89** D7

Mochudi *Botswana* 24°27S 26°7E **56** B4
Mocimboa da Praia
  Mozam. 11°25S 40°20E **54** G8
Moclips *U.S.A.* 47°14N 124°13W **78** C2
Mocoa *Colombia* 1°7N 76°35W **92** C3
Mococa *Brazil* 21°28S 47°0W **95** A6
Mocorito *Mexico* 25°29N 107°55W **86** B3
Moctezuma *Mexico* 29°48N 109°42W **86** B3
Moctezuma → *Mexico* 21°59N 98°34W **87** C5
Mocuba *Mozam.* 16°54S 36°57E **55** H7
Modane *France* 45°12N 6°40E **20** D7
Modasa *India* 23°30N 73°21E **42** H5
Modder → *S. Africa* 29°2S 24°37E **56** D3
Modderrivier *S. Africa* 29°2S 24°38E **56** C3
Módena *Italy* 44°40N 10°55E **22** B4
Modena *U.S.A.* 37°48N 113°56W **77** H7
Modesto *U.S.A.* 37°39N 121°0W **78** H6
Módica *Italy* 36°52N 14°46E **22** F6
Modimolle *S. Africa* 24°42S 28°22E **57** B4
Modjadjiskloof *S. Africa* 23°42S 30°10E **57** B5
Moe *Australia* 38°12S 146°19E **63** F4
Moengo *Suriname* 5°45N 54°20W **93** B8
Moenjodaro = Mohenjodaro
  Pakistan 27°19N 68°7E **42** F3
Moffat *U.K.* 55°21N 3°27W **11** F5
Moga *India* 30°48N 75°8E **42** D6
Mogadishu = Muqdisho
  Somalia 2°2N 45°25E **49** G4
Mogador = Essaouira
  Morocco 31°32N 9°42W **52** B4
Mogalakwena →
  S. Africa 22°38S 28°40E **57** B4
Mogami-Gawa → *Japan* 38°45N 140°0E **28** E10
Mogaung *Myanmar* 25°20N 97°0E **41** G20
Mogi-Mirim *Brazil* 22°29S 47°0W **93** H9
Mogilev = Mahilyow
  Belarus 53°55N 30°18E **17** B16
Mogilev-Podolskiy = Mohyliv-
  Podilskyy *Ukraine* 48°26N 27°48E **17** D14
Mogocha *Russia* 53°40N 119°50E **27** D12
Mogoditshane *Botswana* 24°37S 25°51E **56** B4
Mogok *Myanmar* 23°0N 96°40E **41** H20
Mogollon Rim *U.S.A.* 34°10N 110°50W **77** J8
Mogumber *Australia* 31°2S 116°3E **61** F2
Mogwadi → *S. Africa* 23°4S 29°36E **57** B4
Moháes *Hungary* 45°58N 18°41E **17** F10
Mohala *India* 20°35N 80°44E **44** D5
Mohales Hoek *Lesotho* 30°7S 27°26E **56** D4
Mohali = Ajitgarh *India* 30°47N 76°41E **42** D7
Mohall *U.S.A.* 48°46N 101°31W **80** A3
Moḥammadābād *Iran* 37°52N 59°5E **47** B8
Mohammedia *Morocco* 33°44N 7°21W **52** B4
Mohana *India* 19°27N 84°16E **44** E7
Mohana → *India* 24°43N 85°0E **43** G11
Mohanlalganj *India* 26°41N 80°58E **43** F9
Mohave, L. *U.S.A.* 35°12N 114°34W **79** K12
Mohawk → *U.S.A.* 42°47N 73°41W **83** D11
Mohéli *Comoros Is.* 12°20S 43°40E **55** a
Mohenjodaro *Pakistan* 27°19N 68°7E **42** F3
Moher, Cliffs of *Ireland* 52°58N 9°27W **10** D2
Mohicanville Res. *U.S.A.* 40°45N 82°9W **82** F2
Mohns Ridge *Arctic* 72°30N 5°0W **4** B7
Mohsenābād *Iran* 36°40N 59°35E **47** B8
Mohyliv-Podilskyy
  Ukraine 48°26N 27°48E **17** D14
Moidart, L. *U.K.* 56°47N 5°52W **11** E3
Moinabad *India* 17°44N 77°16E **44** L10
Moira → *Canada* 44°21N 77°24W **82** B7
Moisaküla *Estonia* 58°3N 25°12E **9** G21
Moisie *Canada* 50°12N 66°1W **73** B6
Moisie → *Canada* 50°14N 66°5W **73** B6
Mojave *U.S.A.* 35°3N 118°10W **79** K8
Mojave → *U.S.A.* 35°7N 115°32W **79** K11
Mojave Desert *U.S.A.* 35°0N 116°30W **79** L10
Moji das Cruzes *Brazil* 23°31S 46°11W **95** A6
Moji-Guaçu → *Brazil* 20°53S 48°10W **95** A6
Mojiang *China* 23°37N 101°35E **34** F3
Mojo *Bolivia* 21°48S 65°33W **94** A2
Mojokerto *Indonesia* 7°28S 112°26E **37** G15
Mokai *N.Z.* 38°32S 175°56E **59** C5
Mokala △ *S. Africa* 29°10S 24°10E **56** C3
Mokau *N.Z.* 38°42S 174°39E **59** C5
Mokelumne → *U.S.A.* 38°13N 121°28W **78** G5
Mokelumne Hill *U.S.A.* 38°18N 120°43W **78** G6
Mokhotlong *Lesotho* 29°22S 29°2E **57** C4
Mokokchung *India* 26°15N 94°30E **41** F19
Mokolo → *S. Africa* 23°14S 27°43E **57** B4
Mokopane *S. Africa* 24°10S 28°55E **57** B4
Mokpo *S. Korea* 34°50N 126°25E **33** G14
Mokra Gora *Europe* 42°50N 20°30E **23** C9
Mol *Belgium* 51°11N 5°5E **15** C5
Molakalmuru *India* 14°55N 76°50E **45** G3
Molchanovo *Russia* 57°40N 83°50E **26** D9
Mold *U.K.* 53°9N 3°8W **12** D4
Moldavia = Moldova ■
  Europe 47°0N 28°0E **17** E15
Moldavia *Romania* 46°30N 27°0E **17** E14
Molde *Norway* 62°45N 7°9E **8** E12
Moldova ■ *Europe* 47°0N 28°0E **17** E15
Moldoveanu, Vf.
  Romania 45°36N 24°45E **17** F13
Mole → *U.K.* 51°24N 0°21W **13** F7
Molepolole *Botswana* 24°28S 25°28E **56** B4
Molfetta *Italy* 41°12N 16°36E **22** D7
Moline *U.S.A.* 41°30N 90°31W **80** E8
Molinos *Argentina* 25°28S 66°15W **94** B2
Mollendo *Peru* 17°0S 72°0W **92** G4
Mollerin, L. *Australia* 30°30S 117°35E **61** F2
Molodechno = Maladzyechna
  Belarus 54°20N 26°50E **17** A14
Molodezhnaya *Antarctica* 67°40S 45°51E **5** C9
Moloka'i *U.S.A.* 21°8N 157°0W **75** L8
Molokai Fracture Zone
  Pac. Oc. 28°0N 125°0W **65** E15
Molong *Australia* 33°5S 148°54E **63** E4
Molopo → *Africa* 28°30S 20°12E **56** D3
Moloundou *Cameroon* 2°8N 15°15E **54** D3
Molson L. *Canada* 54°22N 96°40W **71** C9
Molteno *S. Africa* 31°22S 26°22E **56** E4

Molu *Indonesia* 6°45S 131°40E **37** F8
Molucca Sea *Indonesia* 0°0 125°0E **37** E6
Moluccas = Maluku
  Indonesia 1°0S 127°0E **37** E7
Moma *Mozam.* 16°47S 39°4E **55** H7
Mombasa *Kenya* 4°3S 39°40E **54** E7
Mombetsu *Japan* 44°21N 143°22E **28** B11
Momchilgrad *Bulgaria* 41°33N 25°23E **23** D11
Mompós *Colombia* 9°14N 74°26W **92** B4
Møn *Denmark* 54°57N 12°20E **9** J15
Mon □ *Myanmar* 16°0N 97°30E **41** L20
Mona, Canal de la = Mona
  Passage *W. Indies* 18°30N 67°45W **89** C6
Mona, Isla *Puerto Rico* 18°5N 67°54W **89** C6
Mona, Pta. *Costa Rica* 9°37N 82°36W **88** E3
Mona Passage *W. Indies* 18°30N 67°45W **89** C6
Monaca *U.S.A.* 40°41N 80°17W **82** F4
Monaco ■ *Europe* 43°46N 7°23E **20** E7
Monadhliath Mts. *U.K.* 57°10N 4°4W **11** D4
Monadnock, Mt. *U.S.A.* 42°52N 72°7W **83** D12
Monaghan *Ireland* 54°15N 6°57W **10** B5
Monaghan □ *Ireland* 54°11N 6°56W **10** B5
Monahans *U.S.A.* 31°36N 102°54W **84** F3
Monar, L. *U.K.* 57°26N 5°8W **11** D3
Monaragala *Sri Lanka* 6°52N 81°22E **45** L5
Monarch Mt. *Canada* 51°55N 125°57W **70** C3
Monashee Mts. *Canada* 51°0N 118°43W **70** C5
Monasterevin *Ireland* 53°8N 7°4W **10** C4
Monastir = Bitola
  Macedonia 41°1N 21°20E **23** D9
Monastir *Tunisia* 35°50N 10°49E **53** A8
Moncayo, Sierra del *Spain* 41°48N 1°50W **21** B5
Monchegorsk *Russia* 67°54N 32°58E **8** C25
Mönchengladbach
  Germany 51°11N 6°27E **16** C4
Monchique *Portugal* 37°19N 8°38W **21** D1
Moncks Corner *U.S.A.* 33°12N 80°1W **85** E14
Monclova *Mexico* 26°54N 101°25W **86** B4
Moncton *Canada* 46°7N 64°51W **73** C7
Mondego → *Portugal* 40°9N 8°52W **21** B1
Mondeodo *Indonesia* 3°34S 122°9E **37** E6
Mondlo *S. Africa* 27°59S 30°43E **57** C5
Mondovi *Italy* 44°23N 7°49E **20** D7
Mondrain I. *Australia* 34°9S 122°14E **61** F3
Moneague *Jamaica* 18°16N 77°7W **88** a
Monessen *U.S.A.* 40°9N 79°54W **82** F5
Monett *U.S.A.* 36°55N 93°55W **80** G7
Moneymore *U.K.* 54°41N 6°40W **10** B5
Monforte de Lemos *Spain* 42°31N 7°33W **21** A2
Mong Hpayak *Myanmar* 20°52N 99°55E **38** B2
Mong Hsat *Shan,*
  Myanmar 21°54N 98°30E **34** G2
Mong Hsat *Shan,*
  Myanmar 20°31N 99°15E **38** B2
Mong Kung *Myanmar* 21°35N 97°35E **41** J20
Mong Nai *Myanmar* 20°32N 97°46E **41** J20
Mong Ping *Myanmar* 21°22N 99°2E **34** G2
Mong Tai = Shan □
  Myanmar 21°30N 98°30E **41** J21
Mong Ton *Myanmar* 20°17N 98°45E **41** J21
Mong Yai *Myanmar* 22°21N 98°3E **41** H21
Mong Yang *Myanmar* 21°50N 99°41E **38** B2
Mongalla *South Sudan* 5°8N 31°42E **53** G12
Mongers, L. *Australia* 29°25S 117°5E **61** E2
Monghyr = Munger
  India 25°23N 86°30E **43** G12
Mongibello = Etna *Italy* 37°50N 14°55E **22** F6
Mongo *Chad* 12°14N 18°43E **53** F9
Mongolia ■ *Asia* 47°0N 103°0E **30** B9
Mongolia, Plateau of
  Asia 45°0N 105°0E **24** D12
Mongu *Zambia* 15°16S 23°12E **55** H4
Môngua *Angola* 16°43S 15°20E **56** B2
Monifieth *U.K.* 56°30N 2°48W **11** E6
Monkey Mia *Australia* 25°48S 113°43E **61** E1
Monkey River *Belize* 16°22N 88°29W **87** D7
Monkland *Canada* 45°11N 74°52W **83** A10
Monkoto
  Dem. Rep. of the Congo 1°38S 20°35E **54** E4
Monkton *Canada* 43°35N 81°5W **82** C3
Monmouth *U.K.* 51°48N 2°42W **13** F5
Monmouth *Ill., U.S.A.* 40°55N 90°39W **80** E8
Monmouth *Oreg.,*
  U.S.A. 44°51N 123°14W **76** D2
Monmouthshire □ *U.K.* 51°48N 2°54W **13** F5
Mono, Pta. *Nic.* 12°0N 83°30W **88** D3
Mono L. *U.S.A.* 38°1N 119°1W **78** H7
Monolith *U.S.A.* 35°7N 118°22W **79** K8
Monongahela *U.S.A.* 40°12N 79°56W **82** F5
Monópoli *Italy* 40°57N 17°18E **22** D7
Monos I. *Trin. & Tob.* 10°42N 61°44W **93** K15
Monroe *Ga., U.S.A.* 33°47N 83°43W **85** E13
Monroe *La., U.S.A.* 32°30N 92°7W **84** E8
Monroe *Mich., U.S.A.* 41°55N 83°24W **81** E12
Monroe *N.C., U.S.A.* 34°59N 80°33W **85** D14
Monroe *N.Y., U.S.A.* 41°20N 74°11W **83** E10
Monroe *Utah, U.S.A.* 38°38N 112°7W **76** G7
Monroe *Wash., U.S.A.* 47°51N 121°58W **78** C5
Monroe *Wis., U.S.A.* 42°36N 89°38W **80** D9
Monroe City *U.S.A.* 39°39N 91°44W **80** F8
Monroeton *U.S.A.* 41°43N 76°29W **83** E8
Monroeville *Ala., U.S.A.* 31°31N 87°20W **85** F11
Monroeville *Pa., U.S.A.* 40°26N 79°45W **82** F5
Monrovia *Liberia* 6°18N 10°47W **52** G3
Mons *Belgium* 50°27N 3°58E **15** D3
Monse *Indonesia* 4°7S 123°15E **37** E6
Mont-de-Marsan *France* 43°54N 0°31W **20** E3
Mont-Joli *Canada* 48°37N 68°10W **73** C6
Mont-Laurier *Canada* 46°35N 75°30W **72** C4
Mont-Louis *Canada* 49°15N 65°44W **73** C6
Mont-St-Michel, Le
  France 48°40N 1°30W **20** B3
Mont-Tremblant △
  Canada 46°30N 74°30W **72** C5
Montagu *S. Africa* 33°45S 20°8E **56** D3
Montagu I. *Antarctica* 58°25S 26°20W **5** B1

Montague *Canada* 46°10N 62°39W **73** C7
Montague, I. *Mexico* 31°45N 114°48W **86** A2
Montague, I. *U.S.A.* 60°0N 147°30W **74** D10
Montague Ra. *Australia* 27°15S 119°30E **61** E2
Montague Sd. *Australia* 14°28S 125°20E **60** B4
Montalbán *Spain* 40°50N 0°45W **21** B5
Montalvo *U.S.A.* 34°15N 119°12W **79** L7
Montana *Bulgaria* 43°27N 23°16E **23** C10
Montana □ *U.S.A.* 47°0N 110°0W **76** C9
Montaña *Peru* 6°0S 73°0W **92** E4
Montargis *France* 47°59N 2°43E **20** C5
Montauban *France* 44°2N 1°21E **20** D4
Montauk *U.S.A.* 41°3N 71°57W **83** E13
Montauk Pt. *U.S.A.* 41°4N 71°51W **83** E13
Montbéliard *France* 47°31N 6°48E **20** C7
Montceau-les-Mines
  France 46°40N 4°23E **20** C6
Montclair *U.S.A.* 40°49N 74°12W **83** F10
Monte Albán *Mexico* 17°2N 96°46W **87** D5
Monte Alegre *Brazil* 2°0S 54°0W **93** D8
Monte Azul *Brazil* 15°9S 42°53W **93** G10
Monte-Carlo *Monaco* 43°44N 7°25E **20** E7
Monte Caseros *Argentina* 30°10S 57°50W **94** C4
Monte Comán *Argentina* 34°40S 67°53W **94** C2
Monte Cristi *Dom. Rep.* 19°52N 71°39W **89** C5
Monte Lindo →
  Paraguay 23°56S 57°12W **94** A4
Monte Patria *Chile* 30°42S 70°58W **94** C1
Monte Quemado
  Argentina 25°53S 62°41W **94** B3
Monte Rio *U.S.A.* 38°28N 123°0W **78** G4
Monte Santu, C. di *Italy* 40°5N 9°44E **22** D3
Monte Vista *U.S.A.* 37°35N 106°9W **77** H10
Monteagudo *Argentina* 27°14S 54°8W **95** B5
Montebello *Canada* 45°40N 74°55W **72** C5
Montebello Is. *Australia* 20°30S 115°45E **60** D2
Montecarlo *Argentina* 26°34S 54°47W **95** B5
Montecito *U.S.A.* 34°26N 119°40W **79** L7
Montecristo *Italy* 42°20N 10°19E **22** C4
Montego Bay *Jamaica* 18°28N 77°55W **88** a
Montélimar *France* 44°33N 4°45E **20** D6
Montello *U.S.A.* 43°48N 89°20W **80** D9
Montemorelos *Mexico* 25°12N 99°49W **87** B5
Montenegro *Brazil* 29°39S 51°29W **95** B5
Montenegro ■ *Europe* 42°40N 19°20E **23** C8
Montepuez *Mozam.* 13°8S 38°59E **55** G7
Monterey *U.S.A.* 36°37N 121°55W **78** J5
Monterey B. *U.S.A.* 36°45N 122°0W **78** J5
Montería *Colombia* 8°46N 75°53W **92** B3
Monteros *Argentina* 27°11S 65°30W **94** B2
Monterrey *Mexico* 25°40N 100°19W **86** B4
Montes Azules △ *Mexico* 16°21N 91°3W **87** D6
Montes Claros *Brazil* 16°30S 43°50W **93** G10
Montesano *U.S.A.* 46°59N 123°36W **78** D3
Montesilvano *Italy* 42°29N 14°8E **22** C6
Montevideo *Uruguay* 34°50S 56°11W **95** C4
Montevideo *U.S.A.* 44°57N 95°43W **80** C6
Montezuma *U.S.A.* 41°35N 92°32W **80** E7
Montezuma Castle △
  U.S.A. 34°39N 111°45W **77** J8
Montgomery *U.K.* 52°34N 3°8W **13** E4
Montgomery *Ala.,*
  U.S.A. 32°23N 86°19W **85** E11
Montgomery *Pa., U.S.A.* 41°10N 76°53W **82** E8
Montgomery *W. Va.,*
  U.S.A. 38°11N 81°19W **81** F13
Montgomery City *U.S.A.* 38°59N 91°30W **80** F8
Monticello *Ark., U.S.A.* 33°38N 91°47W **84** E9
Monticello *Fla., U.S.A.* 30°33N 83°52W **85** F13
Monticello *Iowa, U.S.A.* 42°15N 91°12W **80** D8
Monticello *Ky., U.S.A.* 36°50N 84°51W **81** G11
Monticello *Minn., U.S.A.* 45°18N 93°48W **80** C7
Monticello *N.Y., U.S.A.* 41°39N 74°42W **83** E10
Monticello *Utah, U.S.A.* 37°52N 109°21W **77** H9
Montijo *Portugal* 38°41N 8°54W **21** C1
Montilla *Spain* 37°36N 4°40W **21** D3
Montluçon *France* 46°22N 2°36E **20** C5
Montmagny *Canada* 46°58N 70°34W **73** C5
Montmartre *Canada* 50°14N 103°27W **71** C8
Montmorillon *France* 46°26N 0°50E **20** C4
Monto *Australia* 24°52S 151°6E **62** C5
Montongbuwoh *Indonesia* 8°33S 116°4E **37** K19
Montoro *Spain* 38°1N 4°27W **21** C3
Montour Falls *U.S.A.* 42°21N 76°51W **82** D8
Montoursville *U.S.A.* 41°15N 76°55W **82** E8
Montpelier *Idaho, U.S.A.* 42°19N 111°18W **76** E8
Montpelier *Vt., U.S.A.* 44°16N 72°35W **83** B12
Montpellier *France* 43°37N 3°52E **20** E5
Montréal *Canada* 45°30N 73°33W **72** C5
Montréal L. *Canada* 54°20N 105°45W **71** C7
Montreal Lake *Canada* 54°3N 105°46W **71** C7
Montreux *Switz.* 46°26N 6°55E **20** C7
Montrose *U.K.* 56°44N 2°27W **11** E6
Montrose *Colo., U.S.A.* 38°29N 107°53W **76** G10
Montrose *Pa., U.S.A.* 41°50N 75°53W **83** E9
Monts, Pte. des *Canada* 49°20N 67°12W **73** C6
Montserrat ☑ *W. Indies* 16°40N 62°10W **89** C7
Monywa *Myanmar* 22°7N 95°11E **41** H19
Monze *Zambia* 16°17S 27°29E **55** H5
Monze, C. *Pakistan* 24°47N 66°37E **42** G2
Monzón *Spain* 41°52N 0°10E **21** B6
Mooers *U.S.A.* 44°58N 73°35E **83** B11
Mooi River *S. Africa* 28°45S 30°34E **57** C4
Mooi River → *S. Africa* 31°13N 29°45W **57** C4
Mookgopong *S. Africa* 24°31S 28°44E **57** B4
Moomba *Australia* 28°6S 140°12E **63** A3
Moonah → *Australia* 22°3S 138°33E **62** C2
Moonda, L. *Australia* 25°52S 140°25E **62** D3
Moonie *Australia* 27°46S 150°20E **63** D5
Moonie → *Australia* 29°19S 148°43E **63** D4
Moonta *Australia* 34°6S 137°32E **63** E2
Moora *Australia* 30°37S 115°58E **61** F2
Moorcroft *U.S.A.* 44°16N 104°57W **76** D11
Moore → *Australia* 31°22S 115°30E **61** F2
Moore, L. *Australia* 29°50S 117°35E **61** E2
Moore Falls *Canada* 44°48N 78°48W **82** B6
Moore Park *Australia* 24°43S 152°17E **62** C5
Moore Res. *U.S.A.* 44°20N 71°53W **83** B13

Moore River △ *Australia* 31°7S 115°39E **61** F2
Moorea *French Polynesia* 17°30S 149°50W **59** d
Moorefield *U.S.A.* 39°4N 78°58W **81** F14
Moorfoot Hills *U.K.* 55°44N 3°8W **11** F5
Moorhead *S. Africa* 33°6S 18°38E **56** D2
Moorhead *U.S.A.* 46°53N 96°45W **80** B6
Moorpark *U.S.A.* 34°17N 118°53W **79** L8
Moorreesburg *S. Africa* 33°6S 18°38E **56** E2
Moorrinya △ *Australia* 21°42S 144°58E **62** C3
Moose → *Canada* 51°20N 80°25W **72** B3
Moose *U.S.A.* 43°38N 75°24W **83** C9
Moose Creek *Canada* 45°15N 74°58W **83** A10
Moose Factory *Canada* 51°16N 80°32W **72** B3
Moose Jaw *Canada* 50°24N 105°30W **71** C7
Moose Jaw → *Canada* 50°34N 105°18W **71** C7
Moose Lake *Canada* 53°46N 100°8W **71** C8
Moose Lake *U.S.A.* 46°27N 92°46W **80** B7
Moose Mountain △
  Canada 49°48N 102°25W **71** D8
Moosehead L. *U.S.A.* 45°38N 69°40W **81** C19
Mooselookmeguntic L.
  U.S.A. 44°55N 70°49W **83** B14
Moosilauke, Mt. *U.S.A.* 44°3N 71°40W **83** B13
Moosomin *Canada* 50°9N 101°40W **71** C8
Moosonee *Canada* 51°17N 80°39W **72** B3
Moosup *U.S.A.* 41°43N 71°53W **83** E13
Mopane *S. Africa* 22°37S 29°52E **57** B4
Mopipi *Botswana* 21°6S 24°55E **56** B3
Mopti *Mali* 14°30N 4°0W **52** F5
Moqor *Afghan.* 32°50N 67°42E **42** C2
Moquegua *Peru* 17°15S 70°46W **92** G4
Mora *Sweden* 61°2N 14°38E **8** F16
Mora *Minn., U.S.A.* 45°53N 93°18W **80** C7
Mora *N. Mex., U.S.A.* 35°58N 105°20W **77** J11
Moradabad *India* 28°50N 78°50E **43** E8
Morafenobe *Madag.* 17°50S 44°53E **55** H8
Moramanga *Madag.* 18°56S 48°12E **55** H9
Moran *Kans., U.S.A.* 37°55N 95°10W **80** G6
Moran *Wyo., U.S.A.* 43°50N 110°31W **76** E8
Moranbah *Australia* 22°1S 148°6E **62** C4
Morang = Biratnagar
  Nepal 26°27N 87°17E **43** F12
Morant Bay *Jamaica* 17°53N 76°25W **88** a
Morant Cays *Jamaica* 17°22N 76°0W **88** C4
Morant Pt. *Jamaica* 17°55N 76°12W **88** a
Morar *India* 26°14N 78°14E **42** F8
Morar, L. *U.K.* 56°57N 5°40W **11** E3
Moratuwa *Sri Lanka* 6°45N 79°55E **45** L4
Morava → *Serbia* 44°36N 21°4E **23** B9
Morava → *Slovakia* 48°10N 16°59E **17** D9
Moravia *U.S.A.* 42°43N 76°25W **83** D8
Moravian Hts. = Českomoravská
  Vrchovina *Czechia* 49°30N 15°40E **16** D8
Morawa *Australia* 29°13S 116°0E **61** E2
Morawhanna *Guyana* 8°30N 59°40W **92** B7
Moray □ *U.K.* 57°31N 3°18W **11** D5
Moray Firth *U.K.* 57°40N 3°52W **11** D5
Morbi *India* 22°50N 70°42E **42** H4
Morden *Canada* 49°15N 98°10W **71** D9
Mordovian Republic =
  Mordvinia □ *Russia* 54°20N 44°30E **18** D7
Mordvinia □ *Russia* 54°20N 44°30E **18** D7
Moreau → *U.S.A.* 45°18N 100°43W **80** C3
Morebeng *S. Africa* 23°30S 29°55E **57** B4
Morecambe *U.K.* 54°5N 2°52W **12** C5
Morecambe B. *U.K.* 54°7N 3°0W **12** C4
Moree *Australia* 29°28S 149°54E **63** D4
Morehead *U.S.A.* 38°11N 83°26W **81** F12
Morehead City *U.S.A.* 34°43N 76°43W **85** D16
Morel → *India* 26°13N 76°36E **42** F7
Morelia *Mexico* 19°42N 101°7W **86** D4
Morella *Australia* 23°0S 143°52E **62** C3
Morella *Spain* 40°35N 0°5W **21** B5
Morelos *Mexico* 26°42N 107°40W **86** B3
Morelos □ *Mexico* 18°45N 99°0W **87** D5
Moremi △ *Botswana* 19°18S 23°10E **56** A3
Morena *India* 26°30N 78°4E **42** F8
Morena, Sierra *Spain* 38°20N 4°0W **21** C3
Moreno Valley *U.S.A.* 33°56N 117°14W **79** M10
Moresby I. *Canada* 52°30N 131°40W **70** C2
Moreton I. *Australia* 27°10S 153°25E **63** D5
Moreton Island △
  Australia 27°2S 153°24E **63** D5
Morgan *Australia* 41°2N 111°41W **76** F8
Morgan City *U.S.A.* 29°42N 91°12W **84** G9
Morgan Hill *U.S.A.* 37°8N 121°39W **78** H5
Morganfield *U.S.A.* 37°41N 87°55W **80** G10
Morgan's Port *U.S.A.* 29°40N 95°0W **84** G7
Morganton *U.S.A.* 35°45N 81°41W **85** D14
Morgantown *U.S.A.* 39°38N 79°57W **81** F14
Morgenzon *S. Africa* 26°45S 29°36E **57** C4
Morghak *Iran* 29°7N 57°54E **47** D8
Morhar → *India* 25°29N 85°11E **43** G11
Mori *Japan* 42°6N 140°35E **28** C10
Moriarty *U.S.A.* 34°59N 106°3W **77** J10
Morice L. *Canada* 53°50N 127°40W **70** C3
Morinville *Canada* 53°49N 113°41W **70** C6
Morioka *Japan* 39°45N 141°8E **28** E10
Moris *Mexico* 28°10N 108°32W **86** B3
Morlaix *France* 48°36N 3°52W **20** B2
Mormugao = Marmagao
  India 15°25N 73°56E **45** G1
Mornington *Australia* 38°15S 145°5E **63** F4
Mornington, I. *Chile* 49°50S 75°30W **96** F1
Mornington I. *Australia* 16°30S 139°30E **62** B2
Moro *Pakistan* 26°40N 68°0E **42** F2
Moro → *S. Africa* 26°40N 68°0E **42** F2
Moro G. *Phil.* 6°30N 123°0E **37** C6
Morocco ■ *N. Afr.* 32°0N 5°50W **52** B4
Morogoro *Tanzania* 6°50S 37°40E **54** F7
Moroleón *Mexico* 20°8N 101°12W **86** C4
Morombe *Madag.* 21°45S 43°22E **55** J8
Moron *Argentina* 34°39S 58°37W **94** C4
Morón *Cuba* 22°8N 78°39W **88** B4
Mörön *Mongolia* 49°38N 100°9E **30** B9
Morón de la Frontera
  Spain 37°6N 5°28W **21** D3
Morona → *Peru* 4°40S 77°10W **92** D3
Morondava *Madag.* 20°17S 44°17E **55** J8
Morongo Valley *U.S.A.* 34°3N 116°37W **79** L10
Moroni *Comoros Is.* 11°40S 43°16E **55** a

Moroni U.S.A. 39°32N 111°35W 76 G8
Morotai Indonesia 2°10N 128°30E 37 D7
Moroto Uganda 2°28N 34°42E 54 D6
Morpeth Canada 42°23N 81°50W 82 D3
Morpeth U.K. 55°10N 1°41W 12 B6
Morphou Cyprus 35°12N 32°59E 46 C2
Morrilton U.S.A. 35°9N 92°44W 84 D8
Morrinhos Brazil 17°45S 49°10W 93 G9
Morrinsville N.Z. 37°40S 175°32E 59 B5
Morris Canada 49°25N 97°22W 71 D9
Morris Ill., U.S.A. 41°22N 88°26W 80 E9
Morris Minn., U.S.A. 45°35N 95°55W 80 C6
Morris N.Y., U.S.A. 42°33N 75°15W 83 D9
Morris Pa., U.S.A. 41°35N 77°17W 82 E7
Morris, Mt. Australia 26°9S 131°4E 61 E5
Morris Jesup, Kap Greenland 83°40N 34°0W 66 A16
Morrisburg Canada 44°55N 75°7W 83 B9
Morristown Ariz., U.S.A. 33°51N 112°37W 77 K7
Morristown N.J., U.S.A. 40°48N 74°29W 83 F10
Morristown N.Y., U.S.A. 44°35N 75°39W 83 B9
Morristown Tenn., U.S.A. 36°13N 83°18W 85 C13
Morrisville N.Y., U.S.A. 42°53N 75°35W 83 D9
Morrisville Pa., U.S.A. 40°13N 74°47W 83 F10
Morrisville Vt., U.S.A. 44°34N 72°36W 83 B12
Morro, Pta. Chile 27°6S 71°0W 94 B1
Morro Bay U.S.A. 35°22N 120°51W 78 K6
Morrocoy △ Venezuela 10°48N 68°13W 89 D6
Morrosquillo, G. de Colombia 9°35N 75°40W 88 E4
Morrumbene Mozam. 23°31S 35°16E 57 B6
Morshansk Russia 53°28N 41°50E 18 D7
Morsi India 21°21N 78°0E 44 D4
Morteros Argentina 30°50S 62°0W 94 C3
Mortlach Canada 50°27N 106°4W 71 C7
Mortlake Australia 38°5S 142°50E 63 F3
Morton Tex., U.S.A. 33°44N 102°46W 84 E3
Morton Wash., U.S.A. 46°34N 122°17W 78 D4
Moruga Trin. & Tob. 10°4N 61°16W 93 K15
Morundah Australia 34°57S 146°19E 63 E4
Moruya Australia 35°58S 150°3E 63 F5
Morvan France 47°5N 4°3E 20 C6
Morven Australia 26°22S 147°5E 63 D4
Morvern U.K. 56°38N 5°44W 11 E3
Morwell Australia 38°10S 146°22E 63 F4
Morzhovets, Ostrov Russia 66°44N 42°35E 18 A7
Mosakahiken = Moose Lake Canada 53°46N 100°8W 71 C8
Moscos Is. Myanmar 14°0N 97°30E 38 F1
Moscow Idaho, U.S.A. 46°44N 117°0W 76 C5
Moscow Pa., U.S.A. 41°20N 75°31W 83 E9
Mosel → Europe 50°22N 7°36E 20 A7
Moselle = Mosel → Europe 50°22N 7°36E 20 A7
Moses Lake U.S.A. 47°8N 119°17W 76 C4
Mosgiel N.Z. 45°53S 170°21E 59 F3
Moshaweng → S. Africa 26°35S 22°50E 56 C3
Moshchnyy, Ostrov Russia 60°1N 27°50E 9 F22
Moshi Tanzania 3°22S 37°18E 54 E7
Moshupa Botswana 24°46S 25°29E 56 B4
Mosi-oa-Tunya = Victoria Falls Zimbabwe 17°58S 25°52E 55 H5
Mosjøen Norway 65°51N 13°12E 8 D15
Moskenesøya Norway 67°58N 13°0E 8 C15
Moskenstraumen Norway 67°47N 12°45E 8 C15
Mosomane Botswana 24°2S 26°19E 56 B4
Mosonmagyaróvár Hungary 47°52N 17°18E 17 E9
Mosquera Colombia 2°35N 78°24W 92 C3
Mosquero U.S.A. 35°47N 103°58W 77 J12
Mosquitia Honduras 15°20N 84°10W 88 C3
Mosquito Creek L. U.S.A. 41°18N 80°46W 82 E4
Mosquito L. Canada 62°35N 103°20W 71 A8
Mosquitos, G. de los Panama 9°15N 81°10W 88 E3
Moss Norway 59°27N 10°40E 9 G14
Moss Vale Australia 34°32S 150°25E 63 E5
Mossaka Congo 1°15S 16°45E 54 E3
Mossbank Canada 49°56N 105°56W 71 D7
Mossburn N.Z. 45°41S 168°15E 59 F2
Mosselbaai S. Africa 34°11S 22°8E 56 D3
Mossendjo Congo 2°55S 12°42E 54 E2
Mossgiel Australia 33°15S 144°5E 63 E3
Mossman Australia 16°21S 145°15E 62 B4
Mossoró Brazil 5°10S 37°15W 93 E11
Most Czechia 50°31N 13°38E 16 C7
Mostaganem Algeria 35°54N 0°5E 52 A6
Mostar Bos.-H. 43°22N 17°50E 23 C7
Mostardas Brazil 31°2S 50°51W 95 C5
Mostiska = Mostyska Ukraine 49°48N 23°4E 17 D12
Mosty = Masty Belarus 53°27N 24°38E 17 B13
Mostyska Ukraine 49°48N 23°4E 17 D12
Mosul = Al Mawşil Iraq 36°15N 43°5E 46 B4
Motagua → Guatemala 15°44N 88°14W 88 C2
Motala Sweden 58°32N 15°1E 9 G16
Motaze Mozam. 24°48S 32°52E 57 B5
Moth India 25°43N 78°57E 43 G8
Motherwell U.K. 55°47N 3°58W 11 F5
Motihari India 26°30N 84°55E 43 F11
Motozintla de Mendoza Mexico 15°22N 92°14W 87 D6
Motril Spain 36°31N 3°37W 21 D4
Mott U.S.A. 46°23N 102°20W 80 B2
Mottama, G. of Myanmar 16°5N 96°30E 41 L20
Motueka N.Z. 41°7S 173°1E 59 D4
Motueka → N.Z. 41°5S 173°1E 59 D4
Motul Mexico 21°6N 89°17W 87 C7
Mouchalagane → Canada 50°56N 68°41W 73 B6
Mouding China 25°20N 101°28E 34 E3
Moudros Greece 39°50N 25°18E 23 E11
Mouhoun = Black Volta → Africa 8°41N 1°33W 52 G5
Mouila Gabon 1°50S 11°0E 54 E2
Moulamein Australia 35°3S 144°1E 63 F3
Moule à Chique, C. St. Lucia 13°43N 60°57W 89 f
Moulins France 46°35N 3°19E 20 C5
Moulmein = Mawlamyine Myanmar 16°30N 97°40E 41 L20
Moulouya, O. → Morocco 35°5N 2°25W 52 B5
Moultrie U.S.A. 31°11N 83°47W 85 F13
Moultrie, L. U.S.A. 33°20N 80°5W 85 E14
Mound City Mo., U.S.A. 40°7N 95°14W 80 E6
Mound City S. Dak., U.S.A. 45°44N 100°4W 80 C3
Moundou Chad 8°40N 16°10E 53 G9
Moundsville U.S.A. 39°55N 80°44W 82 G4
Moung Cambodia 12°46N 103°27E 38 F4
Mount Airy U.S.A. 36°31N 80°37W 85 C14
Mount Albert Canada 44°8N 79°19W 82 B5
Mount Aspiring △ N.Z. 44°19S 168°47E 59 F2
Mount Barker S. Austral., Australia 35°5S 138°52E 63 F2
Mount Barker W. Austral., Australia 34°38S 117°40E 61 F2
Mount Barnett Roadhouse Australia 16°39S 125°57E 60 C4
Mount Brydges Canada 42°54N 81°29W 82 D3
Mount Burr Australia 37°34S 140°26E 63 F3
Mount Carleton ⌂ Canada 47°25N 66°55W 73 C6
Mount Carmel = Ha Karmel △ Israel 32°45N 35°5E 48 C4
Mount Carmel Ill., U.S.A. 38°25N 87°46W 80 F10
Mount Carmel Pa., U.S.A. 40°47N 76°26W 83 F8
Mount Clemens U.S.A. 42°35N 82°53W 82 D2
Mount Coolon Australia 21°25S 147°25E 62 C4
Mount Desert I. U.S.A. 44°21N 68°20W 81 C19
Mount Dora U.S.A. 28°48N 81°38W 85 G14
Mount Ebenezer Australia 25°6S 132°34E 61 E5
Mount Edziza ⌂ Canada 57°30N 130°45W 70 B2
Mount Field △ Australia 42°39S 146°35E 63 G4
Mount Fletcher S. Africa 30°40S 28°30E 57 D4
Mount Forest Canada 43°59N 80°43W 82 C4
Mount Frankland △ Australia 31°47S 116°37E 61 F2
Mount Frederick ✪ Australia 19°39S 129°18E 60 C4
Mount Gambier Australia 37°50S 140°46E 63 F3
Mount Garnet Australia 17°37S 145°6E 62 B4
Mount Holly U.S.A. 39°59N 74°47W 83 G10
Mount Holly Springs U.S.A. 40°7N 77°12W 82 F7
Mount Hope N.S.W., Australia 32°51S 145°51E 63 E4
Mount Hope S. Austral., Australia 34°7S 135°23E 63 E2
Mount Isa Australia 20°42S 139°26E 62 C2
Mount James ✪ Australia 24°51S 116°54E 61 D2
Mount Jewett U.S.A. 41°44N 78°39W 82 E6
Mount Kaputar △ Australia 30°16S 150°10E 63 E5
Mount Kisco U.S.A. 41°12N 73°44W 83 E11
Mount Laguna U.S.A. 32°52N 116°25W 79 N10
Mount Larcom Australia 23°48S 150°59E 62 C5
Mount Lofty Ranges Australia 34°35S 139°5E 63 E2
Mount Magnet Australia 28°2S 117°47E 61 E2
Mount Maunganui N.Z. 37°40S 176°14E 59 B6
Mount Molloy Australia 16°42S 145°20E 62 B4
Mount Morgan Australia 23°40S 150°25E 62 C5
Mount Morris U.S.A. 42°44N 77°52W 82 D7
Mount Pearl Canada 47°31N 52°47W 73 C9
Mount Penn U.S.A. 40°20N 75°54W 83 F9
Mount Perry Australia 25°13S 151°42E 63 D5
Mount Pleasant Iowa, U.S.A. 40°58N 91°33W 80 E8
Mount Pleasant Mich., U.S.A. 43°36N 84°46W 81 D11
Mount Pleasant Pa., U.S.A. 40°9N 79°33W 82 F5
Mount Pleasant S.C., U.S.A. 32°47N 79°52W 85 E15
Mount Pleasant Tenn., U.S.A. 35°32N 87°12W 85 D11
Mount Pleasant Tex., U.S.A. 33°9N 94°58W 84 E7
Mount Pleasant Utah, U.S.A. 39°33N 111°27W 76 G8
Mount Pocono U.S.A. 41°7N 75°22W 83 E9
Mount Rainier △ U.S.A. 46°55N 121°50W 78 D5
Mount Revelstoke △ Canada 51°5N 118°30W 70 C5
Mount Robson ⌂ Canada 53°0N 119°0W 70 C5
Mount St. Helens ⌂ U.S.A. 46°14N 122°11W 78 D4
Mount Selinda Zimbabwe 20°24S 32°43E 57 B5
Mount Shasta U.S.A. 41°19N 122°19W 76 F2
Mount Signal U.S.A. 32°39N 115°37W 79 N11
Mount Sterling Ill., U.S.A. 39°59N 90°45W 80 F8
Mount Sterling Ky., U.S.A. 38°4N 83°56W 81 F12
Mount Surprise Australia 18°10S 144°17E 62 B3
Mount Union U.S.A. 40°23N 77°53W 82 F7
Mount Upton U.S.A. 42°26N 75°23W 83 D9
Mount Vernon Ill., U.S.A. 38°19N 88°55W 80 F9
Mount Vernon Ind., U.S.A. 37°56N 87°54W 75 H22
Mount Vernon Ohio, U.S.A. 40°23N 82°29W 82 F2
Mount Vernon Wash., U.S.A. 48°25N 122°20W 78 B4
Mount William △ Australia 40°56S 148°14E 63 G4
Mountain Ash U.K. 51°40N 3°23W 13 F4
Mountain Center U.S.A. 33°42N 116°44W 79 M10
Mountain City Nev., U.S.A. 41°50N 115°58W 76 F6
Mountain City Tenn., U.S.A. 36°29N 81°48W 85 C14
Mountain Dale U.S.A. 41°41N 74°32W 83 E10
Mountain Grove U.S.A. 37°8N 92°16W 80 G7
Mountain Home Ark., U.S.A. 36°20N 92°23W 84 C8
Mountain Home Idaho, U.S.A. 43°8N 115°41W 76 E6
Mountain Iron U.S.A. 47°32N 92°37W 80 B7
Mountain Pass U.S.A. 35°29N 115°35W 79 K11
Mountain View Ark., U.S.A. 35°52N 92°7W 84 D8
Mountain View Calif., U.S.A. 37°23N 122°5W 78 H4
Mountain Zebra △ S. Africa 32°14S 25°27E 56 D4
Mountainair U.S.A. 34°31N 106°15W 77 J10
Mountbellew Ireland 53°28N 8°31W 10 C3
Mountlake Terrace U.S.A. 47°47N 122°18W 78 C4
Mountmellick Ireland 53°7N 7°20W 10 C4
Mountrath Ireland 53°0N 7°28W 10 D4
Moura Australia 24°35S 149°58E 62 C4
Moura Brazil 1°32S 61°38W 92 D6
Moura Portugal 38°7N 7°30W 21 C2
Mourdi, Dépression du Chad 18°10N 23°0E 53 E10
Mourilyan Australia 17°35S 146°3E 62 B4
Mourne → U.K. 54°52N 7°26W 10 B4
Mourne Mts. U.K. 54°10N 6°0W 10 B5
Mouscron Belgium 50°45N 3°12E 15 D3
Moussoro Chad 13°41N 16°35E 53 F9
Moutong Indonesia 0°28N 121°13E 37 D6
Movas Mexico 28°10N 109°25W 86 B3
Moville Ireland 55°11N 7°3W 10 A4
Mowandjum Australia 17°22S 123°40E 60 C3
Moy → Ireland 54°8N 9°8W 10 B2
Moya Comoros Is. 12°18S 44°18E 55 a
Moyale Kenya 3°30N 39°4E 54 D7
Moyen Atlas Morocco 33°0N 5°0W 52 B4
Moyo Indonesia 8°10S 117°40E 36 F5
Moyobamba Peru 6°0S 77°0W 92 E3
Møysalen △ Norway 68°32N 15°29E 8 B16
Moyyero → Russia 68°44N 103°42E 27 C11
Moyynqum Kazakhstan 44°12N 71°0E 30 C3
Moyynty Kazakhstan 47°10N 73°18E 26 E8
Mozambique = Moçambique Mozam. 15°3S 40°42E 55 H8
Mozambique ■ Africa 19°0S 35°0E 55 H7
Mozambique Chan. Africa 17°30S 42°30E 57 A7
Mozdok Russia 43°45N 44°48E 19 F7
Mozdūrān Iran 36°9N 60°35E 47 B9
Mozhnābād Iran 34°7N 60°6E 47 C9
Mozyr = Mazyr Belarus 51°59N 29°15E 17 B15
Mpanda Tanzania 6°23S 31°1E 54 F6
Mphoeng Zimbabwe 21°10S 27°51E 57 B4
Mpika Zambia 11°51S 31°25E 55 G6
Mpumalanga S. Africa 29°50S 30°33E 57 C5
Mpumalanga ☐ S. Africa 26°0S 30°0E 57 C5
Mpwapwa Tanzania 6°23S 36°30E 54 F7
Mqanduli S. Africa 31°49S 28°45E 57 D4
Msaken Tunisia 35°49N 10°33E 53 A8
M'sila Algeria 35°46N 4°30E 52 A6
Mstislavl = Mstsislaw Belarus 54°0N 31°50E 17 A16
Mstsislaw Belarus 54°0N 31°50E 17 A16
Mtamvuna = Mthamvuna → S. Africa 31°6S 30°12E 57 D5
Mthamvuna → S. Africa 31°6S 30°12E 57 D5
Mthatha S. Africa 31°36S 28°49E 57 D4
Mtubatuba S. Africa 28°30S 32°8E 57 C5
Mtwalume S. Africa 30°30S 30°38E 57 D5
Mtwara-Mikindani Tanzania 10°20S 40°20E 54 G8
Mu Gia, Deo Vietnam 17°40N 105°47E 38 D5
Mu Ko Chang △ Thailand 11°59N 102°22E 39 G4
Mu Ko Surin Thailand 9°30N 97°55E 39 H1
Mu Us Shamo China 39°0N 109°0E 32 E5
Muang Beng Laos 20°23N 101°46E 34 G3
Muang Chiang Rai = Chiang Rai Thailand 19°52N 99°50E 34 H2
Muang Et Laos 20°49N 104°1E 38 B5
Muang Hiam Laos 20°5N 103°22E 38 B4
Muang Hongsa Laos 19°43N 101°20E 38 C3
Muang Houn Laos 20°8N 101°23E 34 G3
Muang Kau Laos 15°6N 105°47E 38 E5
Muang Khao Laos 19°38N 103°32E 38 C4
Muang Khong Laos 14°7N 105°51E 38 E5
Muang Khoua Laos 21°5N 102°31E 34 G4
Muang Liap Laos 18°29N 101°40E 38 C3
Muang Mai Thailand 8°5N 98°21E 39 a
Muang May Laos 14°49N 106°56E 38 E6
Muang Na Mo Laos 21°3N 101°49E 34 G3
Muang Ngeun Laos 20°36N 101°3E 34 G3
Muang Ngoi Laos 20°43N 102°41E 34 G4
Muang Nong Laos 16°22N 106°30E 38 D6
Muang Ou Neua Laos 22°18N 101°48E 34 F3
Muang Ou Tay Laos 22°7N 101°48E 34 F3
Muang Pak Beng Laos 19°54N 101°8E 34 H3
Muang Phalane Laos 16°39N 105°34E 38 D5
Muang Phiang Laos 19°6N 101°32E 38 C3
Muang Phine Laos 16°32N 106°2E 38 D6
Muang Phonhong Laos 18°30N 102°25E 38 C4
Muang Saiapoun Laos 18°24N 101°31E 38 C3
Muang Sing Laos 21°11N 101°9E 34 G3
Muang Son Laos 20°27N 103°19E 38 B4
Muang Soui Laos 19°33N 102°52E 38 C4
Muang Va Laos 21°53N 102°19E 34 G4
Muang Va Laos 18°18N 101°20E 38 C3
Muang Xai Laos 20°42N 101°59E 34 G3
Muang Xamteu Laos 19°59N 104°38E 38 C5
Muar Malaysia 2°3N 102°34E 39 L4
Muarabungo Indonesia 1°28S 102°52E 36 E2
Muaraenim Indonesia 3°40S 103°50E 36 E2
Muarajuloi Indonesia 0°12S 114°3E 36 E4
Muarakaman Indonesia 0°2S 116°45E 36 E5
Muaratebo Indonesia 1°30S 102°26E 36 E2
Muaratembesi Indonesia 1°42S 103°8E 36 E2
Muarateweh Indonesia 0°58S 114°52E 36 E4
Mubarakpur India 26°6N 83°18E 43 F10
Mubarraz = Al Mubarraz Si. Arabia 25°30N 49°40E 47 E6
Mubi Nigeria 10°18N 13°16E 53 F8
Mucajaí → Brazil 2°25N 60°52W 92 C6
Muchinga Mts. Zambia 11°30S 31°30E 55 G6
Muchuan China 28°57N 103°55E 34 C5
Muck U.K. 56°50N 6°15W 11 E2
Muckadilla Australia 26°35S 148°23E 63 D4
Muckaty ✪ Australia 18°37S 133°52E 62 B1
Muckle Flugga U.K. 60°51N 0°54W 11 A8
Mucuri Brazil 18°0S 39°36W 93 G11
Mucusso Angola 18°1S 21°25E 56 A3
Mudanjiang China 44°38N 129°30E 33 B15
Mudanya Turkey 40°25N 28°50E 23 D13
Muddebihal India 16°20N 76°8E 45 F3
Muddus △ Sweden 66°58N 20°15E 8 C19
Muddy Cr. → U.S.A. 38°24N 110°42W 76 G8
Mudgee Australia 32°32S 149°31E 63 E4
Mudhol Karnataka, India 16°21N 75°17E 45 F2
Mudhol Telangana, India 18°58N 77°55E 44 E3
Mudigere India 13°8N 75°38E 45 H2
Mudjatik → Canada 56°1N 107°36W 71 B7
Mudukulattur India 9°21N 78°31E 45 K4
Mudumu △ Namibia 18°5S 23°29E 56 A3
Mueller Ranges Australia 18°18S 126°46E 60 C4
Muerto, Mar Mexico 16°10N 94°10W 87 D6
Mufu Shan China 29°20N 114°30E 35 C10
Mufulira Zambia 12°32S 28°15E 55 G5
Mughal Sarai India 25°18N 83°7E 43 G10
Mughayrā' Si. Arabia 29°17N 37°41E 46 D3
Mugi Japan 33°40N 134°25E 29 H7
Muğla Turkey 37°15N 28°22E 23 F13
Mugu Nepal 29°45N 82°30E 43 E10
Mugu Karnali → Nepal 29°38N 81°51E 43 E9
Muhammad, Râs Egypt 27°44N 34°16E 46 E2
Muhammad Qol Sudan 20°53N 37°9E 53 D13
Muhammadabad India 26°4N 83°25E 43 F10
Muḩāyil Si. Arabia 18°33N 42°3E 49 D3
Mühlhausen Germany 51°12N 10°27E 16 C6
Mühlig Hofmann fjell Antarctica 72°30S 5°0E 5 D3
Muhos Finland 64°47N 25°59E 8 D21
Muhu Estonia 58°36N 23°11E 9 G20
Muileann gCearr, An = Mullingar Ireland 53°31N 7°21W 10 C4
Muine Bheag = Bagenalstown Ireland 52°42N 6°58W 10 D5
Muineachán = Monaghan Ireland 54°15N 6°57W 10 B5
Muir, L. Australia 34°30S 116°40E 61 F2
Muir of Ord U.K. 57°32N 4°28W 11 D4
Mujeres, I. Mexico 21°13N 86°43W 88 B2
Muka, Tanjung Malaysia 5°28N 100°11E 39 c
Mukacheve Ukraine 48°27N 22°45E 17 D12
Mukachevo = Mukacheve Ukraine 48°27N 22°45E 17 D12
Mukah Malaysia 2°55N 112°5E 36 D4
Mukandwara India 24°49N 75°59E 42 G6
Mukdahan Thailand 16°32N 104°43E 38 D5
Mukdahan △ Thailand 16°26N 104°45E 38 D5
Mukden = Shenyang China 41°48N 123°27E 33 D12
Mukerian India 31°57N 75°37E 42 D6
Mukher India 18°42N 77°22E 44 E3
Mukinbudin Australia 30°55S 118°5E 61 F2
Muko Phetra △ Thailand 6°57N 99°33E 39 J2
Mukomuko Indonesia 2°30S 101°10E 36 E2
Muktinath Nepal 28°49N 83°53E 43 E10
Muktsar India 30°30N 74°30E 42 D6
Mukur = Moqor Afghan. 32°50N 67°42E 42 C2
Mukutuwa → Canada 53°10N 97°24W 71 C9
Mul India 20°4N 79°40E 44 D4
Mula Spain 38°3N 1°33W 21 C5
Mula → India 18°34N 74°21E 44 E2
Mula → Pakistan 27°57N 67°36E 42 F2
Mulanje, Mt. Malawi 16°2S 35°33E 55 H7
Mulbagal India 13°10N 78°24E 45 H4
Mulchatna → U.S.A. 59°40N 157°7W 74 D8
Mulchén Chile 37°45S 72°20W 94 D1
Mulde → Germany 51°53N 12°15E 16 C7
Mule Creek Junction U.S.A. 43°23N 104°13W 76 E11
Mulegé Mexico 26°53N 111°59W 86 B2
Muleshoe U.S.A. 34°13N 102°43W 84 D3
Mulgrave Canada 45°38N 61°31W 73 C7
Mulgrave I. = Badu Australia 10°7S 142°11E 62 a
Mulhacén Spain 37°4N 3°20W 21 D4
Mulhouse France 47°40N 7°20E 20 C7
Muli China 27°52N 101°8E 34 D3
Mulifanua Samoa 13°50S 171°59W 59 b
Muling China 44°35N 130°10E 33 B16
Mulki India 13°6N 74°48E 45 H2
Mull U.K. 56°25N 5°56W 11 E3
Mull, Sound of U.K. 56°30N 5°50W 11 E3
Mullach Íde = Malahide Ireland 53°26N 6°9W 10 C5
Mullaittivu Sri Lanka 9°15N 80°49E 45 K5
Mullen U.S.A. 42°3N 101°1W 80 D3
Mullengudgery Australia 31°43S 147°23E 63 B4
Mullens U.S.A. 37°35N 81°23W 81 G13
Muller, Pegunungan Indonesia 0°30N 113°30E 36 D4
Mullet Pen. Ireland 54°13N 10°2W 10 B1
Mullewa Australia 28°29S 115°30E 61 E2
Mulligan → Australia 25°0S 139°0E 62 D2
Mullingar Ireland 53°31N 7°21W 10 C4
Mullins U.S.A. 34°12N 79°15W 85 D15
Mullumbimby Australia 28°30S 153°30E 63 D5
Mulonga Plain Zambia 16°20S 22°40E 55 H4
Mulroy B. Ireland 55°15N 7°46W 10 A4
Mulshi L. India 18°30N 73°48E 44 E1
Multai India 21°50N 78°21E 44 D4
Multan Pakistan 30°15N 71°36E 42 D4
Mulug India 18°11N 79°57E 44 E4
Mulvane U.S.A. 37°29N 97°15W 80 G5
Mulwala, L. Australia 35°59S 146°1E 63 C4
Mun → Thailand 15°19N 105°30E 38 E5
Muna Indonesia 5°0S 122°30E 37 F6
Munabao India 25°45N 70°17E 42 G4
Munamagi Estonia 57°43N 27°4E 9 H22
Munaung Myanmar 18°45N 93°40E 41 K18
Munaung I. = Cheduba I. Myanmar 18°45N 93°40E 41 K18
Muncan Indonesia 8°34S 115°11E 37 K18
Muncar Indonesia 8°26S 114°20E 37 J17
Munchen-Gladbach = Mönchengladbach Germany 51°11N 6°27E 16 C4
Muncho Lake Canada 59°0N 125°50W 70 B3
Munch'ŏn N. Korea 39°14N 127°19E 33 E14
Muncie U.S.A. 40°12N 85°23W 81 E11
Muncoonie L. West Australia 25°12S 138°40E 62 D2
Mundabbera Australia 25°36S 151°18E 63 D5
Mundakayam India 9°30N 76°50E 45 K3
Mundal Sri Lanka 7°48N 79°48E 45 L4
Munday U.S.A. 33°27N 99°38W 84 E5
Münden Germany 51°25N 9°38E 16 C5
Mundiwindi Australia 23°47S 120°9E 60 D3
Mundo Novo Brazil 11°50S 40°29W 93 F10
Mundra India 22°54N 69°48E 42 H3
Mundrabilla Australia 31°52S 127°51E 61 F4
Muneru → India 16°45N 80°3E 44 F5
Mungallala Australia 26°28S 147°34E 63 D4
Mungallala Cr. → Australia 28°53S 147°5E 63 D4
Mungana Australia 17°8S 144°27E 62 B3
Mungaoli India 24°24N 78°7E 42 G8
Mungbere Dem. Rep. of the Congo 2°36N 28°28E 54 D5
Mungeli India 22°4N 81°41E 43 H9
Munger India 25°23N 86°30E 43 G12
Mungerannie Australia 28°1S 138°39E 63 A2
Mungilli ✪ Australia 25°14S 124°17E 61 E3
Mungkan Kandju △ Australia 13°35S 142°52E 62 A3
Mungkarta ✪ Australia 20°22S 134°2E 62 C1
Munising U.S.A. 46°25N 86°40W 80 B10
Munku-Sardyk Russia 51°45N 100°20E 27 D11
Munnsville U.S.A. 42°58N 75°35W 83 D9
Muñoz Gamero, Pen. Chile 52°30S 73°5W 96 G2
Munroe L. Canada 59°13N 98°35W 71 B9
Munsan S. Korea 37°51N 126°48E 33 F14
Münster Germany 51°58N 7°37E 16 C4
Munster ☐ Ireland 52°18N 8°44W 10 D3
Muntadgin Australia 31°45S 118°33E 61 F2
Muntok Indonesia 2°5S 105°10E 36 E3
Muong Nhie Vietnam 22°12N 102°28E 34 F4
Muong Sen Vietnam 19°24N 104°8E 38 C5
Muong Te Vietnam 22°24N 102°49E 34 F4
Muong Xia Vietnam 20°19N 104°50E 38 B5
Muonio Finland 67°57N 23°40E 8 C20
Muonio älv = Muonionjoki → Finland 67°11N 23°34E 8 C20
Muonioälven = Muonionjoki → Finland 67°11N 23°34E 8 C20
Muonionjoki → Finland 67°11N 23°34E 8 C20
Mupa → Mozam. 18°58S 35°54E 57 A6
Muping China 37°22N 121°36E 33 F11
Muqdisho Somalia 2°2N 45°25E 49 G4
Mur → Austria 47°18N 16°52E 17 E9
Murakami Japan 38°14N 139°29E 28 E9
Muralag = Prince of Wales I. Australia 10°40S 142°10E 62 A3
Murallón, Cerro Chile 49°48S 73°30W 96 F2
Murang'a Kenya 0°45S 37°9E 54 E7
Murashi Russia 59°30N 49°0E 18 C8
Murat → Turkey 38°46N 40°0E 19 G7
Muratlı Turkey 41°10N 27°29E 23 D12
Murayama Japan 38°30N 140°25E 28 E10
Murchison → Australia 27°45S 114°0E 61 E1
Murchison, Mt. Antarctica 73°25S 166°20E 5 D11
Murchison Falls Uganda 2°15N 31°30E 54 D6
Murchison Ra. Australia 20°0S 134°10E 62 C1
Murchison Roadhouse Australia 27°39S 116°14E 61 E2
Murcia Spain 38°5N 1°10W 21 D5
Murcia ☐ Spain 37°50N 1°30W 21 D5
Murdo U.S.A. 43°53N 100°43W 80 D3
Murdoch Pt. Australia 14°37S 144°55E 62 A3
Mureş → Romania 46°15N 20°13E 17 E11
Mureşul = Mureş → Romania 46°15N 20°13E 17 E11
Murewa Zimbabwe 17°39S 31°47E 57 A5
Murfreesboro N.C., U.S.A. 36°27N 77°6W 85 C16
Murfreesboro Tenn., U.S.A. 35°51N 86°24W 85 D11
Murgap Tajikistan 38°10N 74°2E 26 F8
Murgap → Turkmenistan 38°18N 61°12E 47 B9
Murgenella Australia 11°34S 132°56E 60 B5
Murgha Kibzai Pakistan 30°44N 69°25E 42 D3
Murghob = Murgap Tajikistan 38°10N 74°2E 26 F8
Murgon Australia 26°15S 151°54E 63 D5
Muri India 23°22N 85°52E 43 H11
Muria Indonesia 6°36S 110°53E 37 G14
Muriaé Brazil 21°8S 42°23W 95 A7
Müritz Germany 53°25N 12°42E 16 B7
Murliganj India 25°54N 86°59E 43 G12
Murmansk Russia 68°57N 33°10E 8 B25
Murmashi Russia 68°47N 32°42E 8 B25
Murom Russia 55°35N 42°3E 18 C7
Muroran Japan 42°25N 141°0E 28 C10
Muroto Japan 33°18N 134°9E 29 H7
Muroto-Misaki Japan 33°15N 134°10E 29 H7
Murphy U.S.A. 43°13N 116°33W 76 E5
Murphys U.S.A. 38°8N 120°28W 78 G6
Murray Australia 9°56S 144°2E 62 a

Murray *Ky., U.S.A.* 36°37N 88°19W **80 G9**
Murray *Utah, U.S.A.* 40°40N 111°53W **76 F8**
Murray → *Australia* 35°20S 139°22E **63 F2**
Murray, L. *U.S.A.* 34°3N 81°13W **85 D14**
Murray Bridge *Australia* 35°6S 139°14E **63 F2**
Murray Fracture Zone
  Pac. Oc. 35°0N 130°0W **65 D14**
Murray Harbour *Canada* 46°0N 62°28W **73 C7**
Murray River △
  Australia 34°23S 140°32E **63 E3**
Murraysburg *S. Africa* 31°58S 23°47E **56 D3**
Murree *Pakistan* 33°56N 73°28E **42 C5**
Murrieta *U.S.A.* 33°33N 117°13W **79 M9**
Murrumbidgee →
  Australia 34°43S 143°12E **63 E3**
Murrumburrah
  Australia 34°32S 148°22E **63 E4**
Murrurundi *Australia* 31°42S 150°51E **63 E5**
Murshidabad *India* 24°11N 88°19E **43 G13**
Murtazapur *India* 20°40N 77°25E **44 J10**
Murtle L. *Canada* 52°8N 119°38W **70 C5**
Murtoa *Australia* 36°35S 142°28E **63 F3**
Murud *India* 18°19N 72°58E **44 E1**
Mururoa
  French Polynesia 21°52S 138°55W **65 K14**
Murwara *India* 23°46N 80°28E **43 H9**
Murwillumbah *Australia* 28°18S 153°27E **63 D5**
Murzūq *Libya* 25°53N 13°57E **53 C8**
Murzuq, Idehān *Libya* 24°50N 13°51E **53 D8**
Mürzzuschlag *Austria* 47°36N 15°41E **16 E8**
Mus *India* 9°14N 92°47E **45 K11**
Muş *Turkey* 38°45N 41°30E **46 B4**
Mûsa, Gebel *Egypt* 28°33N 33°59E **46 D2**
Musa Khel *Pakistan* 30°59N 69°52E **42 D3**
Mûsa Qal'eh *Afghan.* 32°20N 64°50E **40 C4**
Musafirkhana *India* 26°22N 81°48E **43 F9**
Musala *Bulgaria* 42°13N 23°37E **23 C10**
Musala *Indonesia* 1°41N 98°28E **36 D1**
Musan *N. Korea* 42°12N 129°12E **33 C15**
Muscat = Masqat *Oman* 23°37N 58°36E **49 C6**
Muscatine *U.S.A.* 41°25N 91°3W **80 E8**
Muscle Shoals *U.S.A.* 34°45N 87°40W **85 D11**
Musgrave Harbour
  Canada 49°27N 53°58W **73 C9**
Musgrave Ranges
  Australia 26°0S 132°0E **61 E5**
Mushie
  Dem. Rep. of the Congo 2°56S 16°55E **54 E3**
Musi → *India* 16°41N 79°40E **44 F4**
Musi → *Indonesia* 2°20S 104°56E **36 E2**
Musina *S. Africa* 22°20S 30°5E **57 B5**
Musiri *India* 10°56N 78°27E **45 J4**
Muskeg → *Canada* 60°20N 123°20W **70 A4**
Muskegon *U.S.A.* 43°14N 86°16W **80 D10**
Muskegon → *U.S.A.* 43°14N 86°21W **80 D10**
Muskegon Heights
  U.S.A. 43°12N 86°16W **80 D10**
Muskogee *U.S.A.* 35°45N 95°22W **84 D7**
Muskoka, L. *Canada* 45°0N 79°25W **82 B5**
Muskoka Falls *Canada* 44°59N 79°17W **82 B5**
Muskwa → *Canada* 58°47N 122°48W **70 B4**
Muslimiyah *Syria* 36°19N 37°12E **46 B3**
Musoma *Tanzania* 1°30S 33°48E **54 E6**
Musquaro, L. *Canada* 50°38N 61°5W **73 B7**
Musquodoboit Harbour
  Canada 44°50N 63°9W **73 D7**
Musselburgh *U.K.* 55°57N 3°2W **11 F5**
Musselshell → *U.S.A.* 47°21N 107°57W **76 C10**
Mussende *Angola* 10°32S 16°5E **54 G3**
Mussoorie *India* 30°27N 78°6E **42 D8**
Mussuco *Angola* 17°2S 19°3E **56 A2**
Mustafakemalpaşa
  Turkey 40°2N 28°24E **23 D13**
Mustang *Nepal* 29°10N 83°55E **43 E10**
Musters, L. *Argentina* 45°20S 69°25W **96 F3**
Musudan *N. Korea* 40°50N 129°43E **33 D15**
Muswellbrook *Australia* 32°16S 150°56E **63 E5**
Mût *Egypt* 25°28N 28°58E **53 C11**
Mut *Turkey* 36°40N 33°28E **46 B2**
Mutanda *Mozam.* 21°0S 33°34E **57 B5**
Mutare *Zimbabwe* 18°58S 32°38E **55 H6**
Mutawintji △ *Australia* 31°10S 142°30E **63 E3**
Muting *Indonesia* 7°23S 140°20E **37 F10**
Mutki = Mirtağ *Turkey* 38°23N 41°56E **46 B4**
Mutoko *Zimbabwe* 17°24S 32°13E **57 A5**
Mutoray *Russia* 60°56N 101°0E **27 C11**
Mutsamudu *Comoros Is.* 12°10S 44°25E **55 a**
Mutsu *Japan* 41°5N 140°55E **28 D10**
Mutsu-Wan *Japan* 41°5N 140°55E **28 D10**
Muttaburra *Australia* 22°38S 144°29E **62 C3**
Mutton I. *Ireland* 52°49N 9°32W **10 D2**
Muttukuru *India* 14°16N 80°6E **45 G5**
Mutur *Sri Lanka* 8°27N 81°16E **45 K5**
Muweilih *Egypt* 30°42N 34°19E **48 E3**
Muy Muy *Nic.* 12°39N 85°36W **88 D2**
Müynoq *Uzbekistan* 43°44N 59°10E **26 E6**
Muyunkum, Peski = Moyynqum
  Kazakhstan 44°12N 71°0E **30 C3**
Muz Tag *China* 36°25N 87°25E **30 D6**
Muzaffarabad *Pakistan* 34°25N 73°30E **43 B5**
Muzaffargarh *Pakistan* 30°5N 71°14E **42 D4**
Muzaffarnagar *India* 29°26N 77°40E **42 E7**
Muzaffarpur *India* 26°7N 85°23E **43 F11**
Muzafirpur *Pakistan* 30°58N 69°42E **42 D3**
Muzhi *Russia* 65°25N 64°40E **18 A11**
Muztagh-Ata *China* 38°17N 75°7E **30 D4**
Mvuma *Zimbabwe* 19°16S 30°30E **55 H6**
Mwali = Mohéli
  Comoros Is. 12°20S 43°40E **55 a**
Mwanza
  Dem. Rep. of the Congo 7°55S 26°43E **54 F5**
Mwanza *Tanzania* 2°30S 32°58E **54 E6**
Mweelrea *Ireland* 53°39N 9°49W **10 C2**
Mweka
  Dem. Rep. of the Congo 4°50S 21°34E **54 E4**
Mwene-Ditu
  Dem. Rep. of the Congo 6°35S 22°27E **54 F4**
Mwenga
  Dem. Rep. of the Congo 3°1S 28°28E **54 E5**
Mweru, L. *Zambia* 9°0S 28°40E **54 F5**

Mwinilunga *Zambia* 11°43S 24°25E **55 G4**
My Son *Vietnam* 15°48N 108°7E **38 E7**
My Tho *Vietnam* 10°29N 106°23E **39 G6**
Myajlar *India* 26°15N 70°20E **42 F4**
Myanaung *Myanmar* 18°18N 95°22E **41 K19**
Myanmar ■ *Asia* 21°0N 96°30E **41 J20**
Myaungmya *Myanmar* 16°30N 94°40E **41 L19**
Mycenæ = Mykenes
  Greece 37°43N 22°46E **23 F10**
Myeik = Mergui
  Myanmar 12°26N 98°34E **38 F2**
Myeik Kyunzu *Myanmar* 11°30N 97°30E **39 G1**
Myerstown *U.S.A.* 40°22N 76°19W **83 F8**
Myingyan *Myanmar* 21°30N 95°20E **41 J19**
Myitkyina *Myanmar* 25°24N 97°26E **41 G20**
Mykenes *Greece* 37°43N 22°46E **23 F10**
Mykines *Færøe Is.* 62°7N 7°35W **8 E9**
Mykolayiv *Ukraine* 46°58N 32°0E **19 E5**
Mykonos *Greece* 37°30N 25°25E **23 F11**
Mymensingh *Bangla.* 24°45N 90°24E **41 G17**
Mynydd Du *U.K.* 51°52N 3°50W **13 F4**
Mýrdalsjökull *Iceland* 63°40N 19°6W **8 E4**
Myrtle Beach *U.S.A.* 33°42N 78°53W **85 E15**
Myrtle Creek *U.S.A.* 43°1N 123°17W **76 E2**
Myrtle Point *U.S.A.* 43°4N 124°8W **76 E1**
Myrtoan Sea = Mirtoo Sea
  Greece 37°0N 23°20E **23 F10**
Mysia *Turkey* 39°50N 27°0E **23 E12**
Mysore = Karnataka □
  India 13°15N 77°0E **45 H3**
Mysore = Mysuru *India* 12°17N 76°41E **45 H3**
Mystic *U.S.A.* 41°21N 71°58W **83 E13**
Mysuru *India* 12°17N 76°41E **45 H3**
Myszków *Poland* 50°45N 19°22E **17 C10**
Mytilene = Mitilini
  Greece 39°6N 26°35E **23 E12**
Mytishchi *Russia* 55°50N 37°50E **18 C6**
Mývatn *Iceland* 65°36N 17°0W **8 D5**
Mzimkulu → *S. Africa* 30°44S 30°28E **57 D5**
Mzimvubu → *S. Africa* 31°38S 29°33E **57 D4**
Mzuzu *Malawi* 11°30S 33°55E **54 G6**

N

Na Clocha Liatha = Greystones
  Ireland 53°9N 6°5W **10 C5**
Na Haeo △ *Thailand* 17°31N 100°58E **38 D3**
Na Hearadh = Harris
  U.K. 57°50N 6°55W **11 D2**
Na Hearadh, Caolas = Harris, Sd.
  of *U.K.* 57°44N 7°6W **11 D1**
Na Noi *Thailand* 18°19N 100°43E **38 C3**
Na Phao *Laos* 17°35N 105°44E **38 D5**
Na Sam *Vietnam* 22°3N 106°37E **34 F6**
Na Sceiri = Skerries *Ireland* 53°35N 6°6W **10 C5**
Na Thon *Thailand* 9°32N 99°56E **39 b**
Naab → *Germany* 49°1N 12°2E **16 D6**
Naantali *Finland* 60°29N 22°2E **9 F20**
Naas *Ireland* 53°12N 6°40W **10 C5**
Nababeep *S. Africa* 29°36S 17°46E **56 C2**
Nabadwip = Navadwip
  India 23°34N 88°20E **43 H13**
Nabawa *Australia* 28°30S 114°48E **61 E1**
Nabberu, L. *Australia* 25°50S 120°30E **61 E3**
Naberezhnyye Chelny
  Russia 55°42N 52°19E **18 C9**
Nabeul *Tunisia* 36°30N 10°44E **53 A8**
Nabha *India* 30°26N 76°14E **42 D7**
Nabid *Iran* 29°40N 57°38E **47 D8**
Nabire *Indonesia* 3°15S 135°26E **37 E9**
Nabisar *Pakistan* 25°8N 69°40E **42 G3**
Nabisipi → *Canada* 50°14N 62°13W **73 B7**
Nâblus = Nābulus
  West Bank 32°14N 35°15E **48 C4**
Naboomspruit *S. Africa* 24°32S 28°40E **57 B4**
Nabouwalu *Fiji* 17°0S 178°45E **59 a**
Nābulus *West Bank* 32°14N 35°15E **48 C4**
Nacala *Mozam.* 14°32S 40°34E **55 G8**
Nacaome *Honduras* 13°31N 87°30W **88 D2**
Naches *U.S.A.* 46°44N 120°42W **76 C3**
Naches → *U.S.A.* 46°38N 120°31W **78 D6**
Nachicapau, L. *Canada* 56°40N 68°5W **73 A6**
Nachingwea *Tanzania* 10°23S 38°49E **54 G7**
Nachna *India* 27°34N 71°41E **42 F4**
Nachuge *India* 10°47N 92°21E **45 J11**
Nacimiento, L. *U.S.A.* 35°46N 120°53W **78 K6**
Naco *Mexico* 31°19N 109°56W **86 A3**
Nacogdoches *U.S.A.* 31°36N 94°39W **84 F7**
Nácori Chico *Mexico* 29°40N 108°57W **86 B3**
Nacozari de García
  Mexico 30°25N 109°38W **86 A3**
Nacula *Fiji* 16°54S 177°27E **59 a**
Nada = Danzhou *China* 19°31N 109°33E **38 C7**
Nădendal = Naantali
  Finland 60°29N 22°2E **9 F20**
Nadi *Fiji* 17°42S 177°20E **59 a**
Nadiad *India* 22°41N 72°56E **42 H5**
Nador *Morocco* 35°14N 2°58W **52 B5**
Nadūshan *Iran* 32°2N 53°35E **47 C7**
Nadvirna *Ukraine* 48°37N 24°30E **17 D13**
Nadvoitsy *Russia* 63°52N 34°14E **18 B5**
Nadvornaya = Nadvirna
  Ukraine 48°37N 24°30E **17 D13**
Nadym *Russia* 65°35N 72°42E **26 C8**
Nadym → *Russia* 66°12N 72°0E **26 C8**
Nærbø *Norway* 58°40N 5°39E **9 G11**
Næstved *Denmark* 55°13N 11°44E **9 J14**
Nafarroa = Navarra □
  Spain 42°40N 1°40W **21 A5**
Nafpaktos *Greece* 38°24N 21°50E **23 E9**
Nafplio *Greece* 37°33N 22°50E **23 F10**
Naft-e Safid *Iran* 31°40N 49°17E **47 D6**
Naftshahr *Iran* 34°0N 45°30E **46 C5**
Nafud Desert = An Nafūd
  Si. Arabia 28°15N 41°0E **46 D4**
Naga *Phil.* 13°38N 123°15E **37 B6**
Nagagami → *Canada* 50°23N 84°20W **72 B3**
Nagahama *Japan* 35°23N 136°16E **29 G8**
Nagai *Japan* 38°6N 140°2E **28 E10**
Nagaland □ *India* 26°0N 94°30E **41 G19**

Nagano *Japan* 36°40N 138°10E **29 F9**
Nagano □ *Japan* 36°15N 138°0E **29 F9**
Nagaoka *Japan* 37°27N 138°51E **29 F9**
Nagaon *India* 26°20N 92°50E **41 F18**
Nagappattinam *India* 10°46N 79°51E **45 J4**
Nagar → *Bangla.* 24°27N 89°12E **43 G13**
Nagar Karnul *India* 16°29N 78°20E **45 F4**
Nagar Parkar *Pakistan* 24°28N 70°46E **42 G4**
Nagaram *India* 18°21N 80°26E **44 E5**
Nagarhole △ *India* 12°0N 76°10E **45 J3**
Nagari Hills *India* 13°3N 79°45E **45 H4**
Nagarjuna Sagar *India* 16°30N 79°13E **45 F4**
Nagasaki *Japan* 32°47N 129°50E **29 H4**
Nagasaki □ *Japan* 32°50N 129°40E **29 H4**
Nagato *Japan* 34°19N 131°5E **29 G5**
Nagaur *India* 27°15N 73°45E **42 F5**
Nagbhir *India* 20°34N 79°55E **44 D4**
Nagda *India* 23°27N 75°25E **42 H6**
Nagercoil *India* 8°12N 77°26E **45 K3**
Nagina *India* 29°30N 78°30E **43 E8**
Nagîneh *Iran* 34°20N 57°15E **47 C8**
Nagir *Pakistan* 36°12N 74°42E **43 A6**
Nagles Mts. *Ireland* 52°8N 8°30W **10 D3**
Nagod *India* 24°34N 80°36E **43 G9**
Nagoorin *Australia* 24°17S 151°15E **62 C5**
Nagorno-Karabakh □
  Azerbaijan 39°55N 46°45E **46 B5**
Nagornyy *Russia* 55°58N 124°57E **27 D13**
Nagoya *Japan* 35°10N 136°50E **29 G8**
Nagoya ✈ (NGO) *Japan* 34°53N 136°45E **29 G8**
Nagpur *India* 21°8N 79°10E **44 D4**
Nagqu *China* 31°29N 92°3E **30 E7**
Nagua *Dom. Rep.* 19°23N 69°50W **89 C6**
Naguabo *Puerto Rico* 18°13N 65°44W **89 d**
Nagurunguru ◉
  Australia 16°45S 129°45E **60 C4**
Nagykanizsa *Hungary* 46°28N 17°0E **17 E9**
Nagykőrös *Hungary* 47°5N 19°48E **17 E10**
Naha *Japan* 26°13N 127°42E **29 L3**
Nahan *India* 30°33N 77°18E **42 D7**
Nahanni → *Canada* 61°36N 125°41W **70 A4**
Nahanni Butte *Canada* 61°2N 123°31W **70 A4**
Nahargarh *Mad. P., India* 24°10N 75°14E **42 G6**
Nahargarh *Raj., India* 24°55N 76°50E **42 G7**
Nahariyya *Israel* 33°1N 35°5E **46 C2**
Nahāvand *Iran* 34°10N 48°22E **47 C6**
Nahuel Huapi, L.
  Argentina 41°0S 71°32W **96 E2**
Nahuelbuta △ *Chile* 37°44S 72°57W **94 D1**
Nai Yong *Thailand* 8°14N 98°22E **39 a**
Naicá *Mexico* 27°53N 105°31W **86 B3**
Naicam *Canada* 52°30N 104°30W **71 C8**
Naikoon △ *Canada* 53°55N 131°55W **70 C2**
Naikul *India* 21°20N 84°58E **44 D7**
Naimisharanya *India* 27°21N 80°30E **43 F9**
Naimona'nyi Feng *China* 30°26N 81°18E **43 D9**
Nain *Canada* 56°34N 61°40W **73 A7**
Nā'in *Iran* 32°54N 53°0E **47 C7**
Naini Tal *India* 29°30N 79°30E **43 E8**
Nainpur *India* 22°30N 80°10E **43 H9**
Nainwa *India* 25°46N 75°51E **42 G6**
Nairai *Fiji* 17°49S 179°15E **59 a**
Nairn *U.K.* 57°35N 3°53W **11 D5**
Nairobi *Kenya* 1°17S 36°48E **54 E7**
Naissaar *Estonia* 59°34N 24°29E **9 G21**
Naitaba *Fiji* 17°0S 179°19E **59 a**
Naivasha *Kenya* 0°40S 36°30E **54 E7**
Najaf = An Najaf *Iraq* 32°3N 44°15E **46 C5**
Najafābād *Iran* 32°40N 51°15E **47 C6**
Najd *Si. Arabia* 26°30N 42°0E **49 B3**
Najibabad *India* 29°40N 78°20E **42 E8**
Najin *N. Korea* 42°12N 130°15E **33 C16**
Najmah *Si. Arabia* 26°42N 50°6E **47 E6**
Najrān *Si. Arabia* 17°34N 44°18E **49 D3**
Naju *S. Korea* 35°3N 126°43E **33 G14**
Nakadōri-Shima *Japan* 32°57N 129°4E **29 H4**
Nakaminato *Japan* 36°21N 140°36E **29 F10**
Nakamura = Shimanto
  Japan 32°59N 132°56E **29 H6**
Nakano *Japan* 36°45N 138°22E **29 F9**
Nakano-Shima *Japan* 29°51N 129°52E **29 K4**
Nakashibetsu *Japan* 43°33N 144°59E **28 C12**
Nakfa *Eritrea* 16°40N 38°32E **49 D2**
Nakha Yai, Ko *Thailand* 8°3N 98°28E **39 a**
Nakhichevan = Naxçıvan
  Azerbaijan 39°12N 45°15E **46 B5**
Nakhichevan Rep. = Naxçıvan □
  Azerbaijan 39°25N 45°26E **46 B5**
Nakhl *Egypt* 29°55N 33°43E **48 F2**
Nakhl-e Taqī *Iran* 27°28N 52°36E **47 E7**
Nakhodka *Russia* 42°53N 132°54E **28 C6**
Nakhon Nayok *Thailand* 14°12N 101°13E **38 E3**
Nakhon Pathom *Thailand* 13°49N 100°3E **38 F3**
Nakhon Phanom
  Thailand 17°23N 104°43E **38 D5**
Nakhon Ratchasima
  Thailand 14°59N 102°12E **38 E4**
Nakhon Sawan *Thailand* 15°35N 100°10E **38 E3**
Nakhon Si Thammarat
  Thailand 8°29N 100°0E **39 H3**
Nakhon Thai *Thailand* 17°5N 100°44E **38 D3**
Nakhtarana *India* 23°20N 69°15E **42 H3**
Nakina *Canada* 50°10N 86°40W **72 B2**
Nakodar *India* 31°8N 75°31E **42 D6**
Naktong → *S. Korea* 35°7N 128°57E **33 G15**
Nakuru *Kenya* 0°15S 36°4E **54 E7**
Nakusp *Canada* 50°20N 117°45W **70 C5**
Nal *Pakistan* 27°40N 66°12E **42 F2**
Nal → *Pakistan* 25°20N 65°30E **42 G1**
Nalázi *Mozam.* 24°3S 33°20E **57 B5**
Nalchik *Russia* 43°30N 43°33E **19 F7**
Nalgonda *India* 17°6N 79°15E **44 F4**
Nalhati *India* 24°17N 87°52E **43 G12**
Naliya *India* 23°16N 68°50E **42 H3**
Nallamalai Hills *India* 15°30N 78°50E **45 M4**
Nam Can *Vietnam* 8°46N 104°59E **39 H5**
Nam-ch'on *N. Korea* 38°15N 126°26E **33 E14**
Nam Co *China* 30°30N 90°45E **30 E7**
Nam Dinh *Vietnam* 20°25N 106°5E **34 G6**
Nam Du, Quan Dao
  Vietnam 9°41N 104°21E **39 H5**

Nam Hka → *Myanmar* 21°34N 95°41E **34 G2**
Nam Loi → *Myanmar* 21°3N 98°27E **34 G3**
Nam Nao △ *Thailand* 16°44N 101°32E **38 D3**
Nam Ngum Res. *Laos* 18°35N 102°34E **38 C4**
Nam Phan *Vietnam* 10°30N 106°0E **39 G6**
Nam Phong *Thailand* 16°42N 102°52E **38 D4**
Nam Theun Res. *Laos* 17°51N 105°3E **38 D5**
Nam Tok *Thailand* 14°21N 99°4E **38 E2**
Nam Un Res. *Thailand* 17°13N 103°44E **38 D4**
Namacurra *Angola* 17°18S 15°50E **56 A2**
Namacurra *Mozam.* 17°30S 36°50E **57 A6**
Namak, Daryācheh-ye
  Iran 34°30N 52°0E **47 C7**
Namak, Kavir-e *Iran* 34°30N 57°30E **47 C8**
Namakkal *India* 11°13N 78°13E **45 J4**
Namakzār, Daryācheh-ye
  Iran 34°0N 60°30E **47 C9**
Namaland *Namibia* 26°0S 17°0E **56 C2**
Namangan *Uzbekistan* 41°0N 71°40E **30 C3**
Namapa *Mozam.* 13°43S 39°50E **55 G7**
Namaqua → *S. Africa* 30°0S 17°25E **56 D2**
Namaqualand *S. Africa* 30°0S 17°25E **56 D2**
Namber *Indonesia* 1°2S 134°49E **37 E8**
Nambour *Australia* 26°32S 152°58E **63 D5**
Namboomwalu = Nabouwalu
  Fiji 17°0S 178°45E **59 a**
Nambucca Heads
  Australia 30°37S 153°0E **63 E5**
Nambung △ *Australia* 30°30S 115°5E **61 F2**
Namcha Barwa *China* 29°40N 95°10E **30 F8**
Namche Bazar *Nepal* 27°51N 86°47E **43 F12**
Namchonjŏm = Nam-ch'on
  N. Korea 38°15N 126°26E **33 E14**
Namenalala *Fiji* 17°8S 179°9E **59 a**
Namew L. *Canada* 54°14N 101°56W **71 C8**
Namgia *India* 31°48N 78°40E **43 D8**
Namhkam *Myanmar* 23°50N 97°41E **34 E1**
Namib Desert *Namibia* 22°30S 15°0E **56 B2**
Namib-Naukluft △
  Namibia 24°40S 15°16E **56 B2**
Namibe *Angola* 15°7S 12°11E **55 H2**
Namibe □ *Angola* 16°35S 12°30E **56 A1**
Namibia ■ *Africa* 22°0S 18°9E **56 B2**
Namibwoestyn = Namib Desert
  Namibia 22°30S 15°0E **56 B2**
Naminüs = Lubango
  Angola 14°55S 13°30E **55 G2**
Naminüs = Lüderitz
  Namibia 26°41S 15°8E **56 C2**
Namjeju *S. Korea* 33°14N 126°33E **33 H14**
Namlea *Indonesia* 3°18S 127°5E **37 E7**
Namoi → *Australia* 30°12S 149°30E **63 E4**
Nampa *U.S.A.* 43°34N 116°34W **76 E5**
Namp'o *N. Korea* 38°52N 125°10E **33 E13**
Nampō-Shotō *Japan* 32°0N 140°0E **29 J10**
Nampula *Mozam.* 15°6S 39°15E **55 H7**
Namrole *Indonesia* 3°46S 126°46E **37 E7**
Namse Shankou *China* 30°0N 82°25E **43 E10**
Namsen → *Norway* 64°28N 11°37E **8 D14**
Namsos *Norway* 64°29N 11°30E **8 D14**
Namtok Chat Trakan △
  Thailand 17°17N 100°40E **38 D3**
Namtok Huay Yang △
  Thailand 11°35N 99°30E **39 G2**
Namtok Mae Surin △
  Thailand 18°55N 98°2E **38 C2**
Namtok Ngao △ *Thailand* 9°58N 98°46E **39 H2**
Namtok Phlew △
  Thailand 12°32N 102°13E **38 F4**
Namtok Yong △ *Thailand* 8°15N 99°45E **39 H2**
Namtsy *Russia* 62°43N 129°37E **27 C13**
Namtu *Myanmar* 23°5N 97°28E **41 H20**
Namu *Canada* 51°52N 127°50W **70 C3**
Namuka-i-Lau *Fiji* 18°53S 178°37W **59 a**
Namur *Belgium* 50°27N 4°52E **15 D4**
Namur □ *Belgium* 50°17N 5°0E **15 D4**
Namutoni *Namibia* 18°49S 16°55E **56 A2**
Namwon *S. Korea* 35°23N 127°23E **33 G14**
Namyang *N. Korea* 42°57N 129°52E **33 C15**
Namyit I. *S. China Sea* 10°11N 114°22E **36 C4**
Nan *Thailand* 18°48N 100°46E **38 C3**
Nan → *Thailand* 15°42N 100°9E **38 E3**
Nan Ling *China* 25°0N 112°30E **35 D9**
Nan Xian *China* 29°20N 112°22E **35 C9**
Nanaimo *Canada* 49°10N 124°0W **70 D4**
Nanakuli *U.S.A.* 21°24N 158°9W **75 L8**
Nanam *N. Korea* 41°44N 129°40E **33 D15**
Nan'an *China* 24°59N 118°21E **35 E12**
Nanango *Australia* 26°40S 152°0E **63 D5**
Nan'ao *China* 23°28N 117°5E **35 F11**
Nanao *Japan* 37°0N 137°0E **29 F8**
Nanbu *China* 31°18N 106°3E **34 B6**
Nanchang *China* 28°42N 115°55E **35 C10**
Nancheng *China* 27°33N 116°35E **35 D11**
Nanching = Nanjing
  China 32°2N 118°47E **35 A12**
Nanchong *China* 30°43N 106°2E **34 B6**
Nanchuan *China* 29°9N 107°6E **34 C6**
Nancowry *India* 7°59N 93°32E **45 L11**
Nancy *France* 48°42N 6°12E **20 B7**
Nanda Devi *India* 30°23N 79°59E **43 D8**
Nanda Devi △ *India* 30°30N 79°50E **43 D8**
Nanda Kot *India* 30°17N 80°5E **43 D9**
Nandan *Japan* 34°10N 134°42E **29 G7**
Nandan *China* 24°58N 107°29E **34 E6**
Nanded *India* 19°10N 77°20E **44 E3**
Nandewar Ra. *Australia* 30°15S 150°35E **63 E5**
Nandgaon *India* 20°19N 74°39E **44 D2**
Nandi = Nadi *Fiji* 17°42S 177°20E **59 a**
Nandi *Zimbabwe* 20°58S 31°44E **57 B5**
Nandigama *India* 16°47N 80°18E **45 F5**
Nandigram *India* 22°1N 87°58E **43 H12**
Nandikotkur *India* 15°52N 78°18E **45 G4**
Nandura *India* 20°52N 76°25E **44 D3**
Nandurbar *India* 21°20N 74°15E **44 D2**
Nandyal *India* 15°30N 78°30E **45 G4**
Nanfeng *Guangdong, China* 23°45N 111°47E **35 F8**
Nanfeng *Jiangxi, China* 27°12N 116°28E **35 D11**

Nang Rong *Thailand* 14°38N 102°48E **38 E4**
Nanga-Eboko *Cameroon* 4°41N 12°22E **54 D2**
Nanga Parbat *Pakistan* 35°10N 74°35E **43 B6**
Nangapinoh *Indonesia* 0°20S 111°44E **36 E4**
Nangarhār □ *Afghan.* 34°20N 70°0E **40 B7**
Nangatayap *Indonesia* 1°32S 110°34E **36 E4**
Nangong *China* 37°23N 115°22E **32 F8**
Nanguneri *India* 8°29N 77°40E **45 K3**
Nanhua *China* 25°2N 101°22E **34 E3**
Nanhuang *China* 36°58N 121°48E **33 F11**
Nanhui *China* 31°5N 121°44E **35 B13**
Nanisivik *Canada* 73°2N 84°33W **69 C15**
Nanjangud *India* 12°6N 76°43E **45 H3**
Nanji Shan *China* 27°27N 121°4E **35 D13**
Nanjian *China* 25°2N 100°25E **34 E3**
Nanjiang *China* 32°28N 106°51E **34 A6**
Nanjing *Fujian, China* 24°25N 117°20E **35 E11**
Nanjing *Jiangsu, China* 32°2N 118°47E **35 A12**
Nankana Sahib *Pakistan* 31°27N 73°38E **42 D5**
Nankang *China* 25°40N 114°45E **35 E10**
Nanking = Nanjing
  China 32°2N 118°47E **35 A12**
Nankoku *Japan* 33°39N 133°44E **29 H6**
Nanlang *China* 22°30N 113°32E **31 a**
Nanling *China* 30°55N 118°20E **35 B12**
Nannial *India* 19°4N 79°38E **44 E4**
Nanning *China* 22°48N 108°20E **34 F7**
Nannup *Australia* 33°59S 115°48E **61 F2**
Nanpan Jiang → *China* 25°10N 106°5E **34 E6**
Nanpara *India* 27°52N 81°33E **43 F9**
Nanping *Fujian, China* 26°38N 118°10E **35 D12**
Nanping *Henan, China* 29°55N 112°3E **35 C9**
Nanri Dao *China* 25°15N 119°25E **35 E12**
Nansei-Shotō = Ryūkyū-Rettō
  Japan 26°0N 126°0E **29 M3**
Nansen Basin *Arctic* 84°0N 50°0E **4 A10**
Nansen Sd. *Canada* 81°0N 91°0W **69 A13**
Nansha *China* 22°45N 113°34E **31 a**
Nansha Port *China* 22°40N 113°40E **31 a**
Nanshan *China* 18°19N 109°10E **38 C7**
Nanshan I. *S. China Sea* 10°45N 115°49E **36 B5**
Nantawarrinna ◉
  Australia 30°49S 138°58E **63 B2**
Nantes *France* 47°12N 1°33W **20 C3**
Nanticoke *U.S.A.* 41°12N 76°0W **83 E8**
Nanton *Canada* 50°21N 113°46W **70 C6**
Nantong *China* 32°1N 120°52E **35 A13**
Nantou *China* 22°32N 113°55E **31 a**
Nant'ou *Taiwan* 23°55N 120°41E **35 F13**
Nantucket *U.S.A.* 41°17N 70°6W **81 E18**
Nantucket I. *U.S.A.* 41°16N 70°5W **81 E18**
Nantwich *U.K.* 53°4N 2°31W **12 D5**
Nanty Glo *U.S.A.* 40°28N 78°50W **82 F6**
Nanuku Passage *Fiji* 16°45S 179°15W **59 a**
Nanuque *Brazil* 17°50S 40°21W **93 G10**
Nanusa, Kepulauan
  Indonesia 4°45N 127°1E **37 D7**
Nanutarra Roadhouse
  Australia 22°32S 115°30E **60 D2**
Nanxi *China* 28°54N 104°59E **34 C5**
Nanxiong *China* 25°6N 114°15E **35 E10**
Nanyang *China* 33°11N 112°30E **32 H7**
Nanyi Hu *China* 31°5N 119°0E **35 B12**
Nanyuki *Kenya* 0°2N 37°4E **54 D7**
Nanzhang *China* 31°45N 111°50E **35 B8**
Nanzhao *China* 33°30N 112°20E **32 H7**
Nao, C. de la *Spain* 38°44N 0°14E **21 C6**
Naococane, L. *Canada* 52°50N 70°45W **73 B5**
Naozhou Dao *China* 20°55N 110°20E **35 G8**
Napa *U.S.A.* 38°18N 122°17W **78 G4**
Napa → *U.S.A.* 38°10N 122°19W **78 G4**
Napanee *Canada* 44°15N 77°0W **82 B8**
Napanoch *U.S.A.* 41°44N 74°22W **83 E10**
Nape *Laos* 18°18N 105°6E **38 C5**
Nape Pass = Keo Neua, Deo
  Vietnam 18°23N 105°10E **38 C5**
Napier *N.Z.* 39°30S 176°56E **59 C6**
Napier Broome B.
  Australia 14°2S 126°37E **60 B4**
Napier Pen. *Australia* 12°4S 135°43E **62 A2**
Napierville *Canada* 45°11N 73°25W **83 A11**
Naples = Nápoli *Italy* 40°50N 14°15E **22 D6**
Naples *U.S.A.* 26°8N 81°48W **85 H14**
Napo *China* 23°20N 105°55E **34 F5**
Napo → *Peru* 3°20S 72°40W **92 D4**
Napoleon *N. Dak., U.S.A.* 46°30N 99°46W **80 B4**
Napoleon *Ohio, U.S.A.* 41°23N 84°8W **81 E11**
Nápoli *Italy* 40°50N 14°15E **22 D6**
Naqadeh *Iran* 36°57N 45°23E **46 B5**
Naqb, Ra's an *Jordan* 29°48N 35°44E **48 F4**
Naqqāsh *Iran* 35°40N 49°6E **47 C6**
Nara *Japan* 34°40N 135°49E **29 G7**
Nara *Mali* 15°10N 7°20W **52 E4**
Nara □ *Japan* 34°30N 136°0E **29 G8**
Nara Canal *Pakistan* 24°30N 69°20E **42 G3**
Nara Visa *U.S.A.* 35°37N 103°6W **77 J12**
Naracoorte *Australia* 36°58S 140°45E **63 F3**
Naradhan *Australia* 33°34S 146°17E **63 E4**
Naraini *India* 25°11N 80°29E **43 G9**
Naranjos *Mexico* 21°21N 97°41W **87 C5**
Narasannapeta *India* 18°25N 84°3E **44 E7**
Narasapur *India* 16°26N 81°40E **45 F5**
Narasaraopet *India* 16°14N 80°4E **45 F5**
Narathiwat *Thailand* 6°30N 101°48E **39 J3**
Narayangadh = Bharatpur
  Nepal 27°34N 84°10E **43 F11**
Narayanganj *Bangla.* 23°40N 90°33E **41 H17**
Narayanpet *India* 16°45N 77°30E **44 F3**
Narberth *U.K.* 51°47N 4°44W **13 F3**
Narbonne *France* 43°11N 3°0E **20 E5**
Narcondam I. *India* 13°20N 94°16E **45 H12**
Nardīn *Iran* 37°3N 55°59E **47 B7**
Nardò *Italy* 40°11N 18°2E **23 D8**
Narembeen *Australia* 32°7S 118°24E **61 F2**
Nares Str. *Arctic* 80°0N 70°0W **69 B19**
Naretha *Australia* 31°0S 124°45E **61 F3**
Narew → *Poland* 52°26N 20°41E **17 B11**
Nari → *Pakistan* 28°0N 67°40E **42 F2**

Narin *Afghan.* 36°5N 69°0E **40 A6**
Narita *Japan* 35°47N 140°19E **29 G10**
Nariva Swamp
  Trin. & Tob. 10°26N 61°4W **93 K15**
Narmada → *India* 21°38N 72°36E **42 J5**
Narmada Canal *India* 22°20N 73°45E **44 C1**
Narnaul *India* 28°5N 76°11E **42 E7**
Narodnaya *Russia* 65°5N 59°58E **18 A10**
Narooma *Australia* 36°14S 150°4E **63 F5**
Narowal *Pakistan* 32°6N 74°52E **42 C6**
Narrabri *Australia* 30°19S 149°46E **63 E4**
Narran → *Australia* 28°37S 148°12E **63 D4**
Narrandera *Australia* 34°42S 146°31E **63 E4**
Narrogin *Australia* 32°58S 117°14E **61 F2**
Narromine *Australia* 32°12S 148°12E **63 E4**
Narrow Hills △ *Canada* 54°0N 104°37W **71 C8**
Narsampet *India* 17°57N 79°58E **44 F4**
Narsimhapur *India* 22°54N 79°14E **43 H8**
Narsinghgarh *India* 23°45N 76°40E **42 H7**
Narsinghpur *India* 20°28N 85°5E **44 D7**
Narsipatnam *India* 17°40N 82°37E **44 F6**
Narutō = Sanmu *Japan* 34°11N 134°37E **29 G7**
Narva *Estonia* 59°23N 28°12E **18 C4**
Narva → *Russia* 59°27N 28°2E **9 G23**
Narva Bay = Narva Laht
  Estonia 59°35N 27°35E **9 G22**
Narva Laht *Estonia* 59°35N 27°35E **9 G22**
Narvik *Norway* 68°28N 17°26E **8 B17**
Narwana *India* 29°39N 76°6E **42 E7**
Narwinbi ☺ *Australia* 16°5S 136°17E **62 B2**
Naryan-Mar *Russia* 67°42N 53°12E **18 A9**
Narym *Russia* 59°0N 81°30E **26 D9**
Naryn *Kyrgyzstan* 41°26N 75°58E **30 C4**
Naryn Qum *Kazakhstan* 47°30N 49°0E **26 E5**
Nás, An = Naas *Ireland* 53°12N 6°40W **10 C5**
Nasa *Norway* 66°29N 15°23E **8 C16**
Nasau *Fiji* 17°19S 179°27E **59 a**
Nasca *Peru* 14°50S 74°57W **92 F4**
Nasca Ridge *Pac. Oc.* 20°0S 80°0W **65 K19**
Naseby *N.Z.* 45°1S 170°10E **59 F3**
Naselle *U.S.A.* 46°22N 123°49W **78 D3**
Naser, Buheirat en *Egypt* 23°0N 32°30E **53 D12**
Nashik = Nasik *India* 19°58N 73°50E **44 E1**
Nashua *Mont., U.S.A.* 48°8N 106°22W **76 B10**
Nashua *N.H., U.S.A.* 42°45N 71°28W **83 D13**
Nashville *Ark., U.S.A.* 33°57N 93°51W **84 E8**
Nashville *Ga., U.S.A.* 31°12N 83°15W **85 F13**
Nashville *Tenn., U.S.A.* 36°10N 86°47W **85 C11**
Nasik *India* 19°58N 73°50E **44 E1**
Nasirabad *India* 26°15N 74°45E **42 F6**
Nasirabad *Pakistan* 28°23N 68°24E **42 E3**
Nasiri = Ahvāz *Iran* 31°20N 48°40E **47 D6**
Nasiriyah = An Nāşiriyah
  Iraq 31°0N 46°15E **46 D5**
Naskaupi → *Canada* 53°47N 60°51W **73 B7**
Naşrābād *Iran* 34°8N 51°26E **47 C6**
Naşrīān-e Pā'īn *Iran* 32°52N 46°52E **46 C5**
Nass → *Canada* 55°0N 129°40W **70 C3**
Nassau *Bahamas* 25°5N 77°20W **88 A4**
Nassau *U.S.A.* 42°31N 73°37W **83 D11**
Nassau, B. *Chile* 55°20S 68°0W **96 H3**
Nasser, L. = Naser, Buheirat en
  Egypt 23°0N 32°30E **53 D12**
Nässjö *Sweden* 57°39N 14°42E **9 H16**
Nastapoka → *Canada* 56°55N 76°33W **72 A4**
Nastapoka, Is. *Canada* 56°55N 76°50W **72 A4**
Nasushiobara *Japan* 36°58N 140°3E **29 F10**
Nata *Botswana* 20°12S 26°12E **56 B4**
Nata → *Botswana* 20°14S 26°10E **56 B4**
Natal *Brazil* 5°47S 35°13W **93 E11**
Natal *Indonesia* 0°35N 99°7E **36 D1**
Natal Drakensberg = uKhahlamba
  Drakensberg △
  S. Africa 29°27S 29°30E **57 C4**
Naţanz *Iran* 33°30N 51°55E **47 C6**
Natashquan *Canada* 50°14N 61°46W **73 B7**
Natashquan → *Canada* 50°7N 61°50W **73 B7**
Natchez *U.S.A.* 31°34N 91°24W **84 F9**
Natchitoches *U.S.A.* 31°46N 93°5W **84 F8**
Natewa B. *Fiji* 16°35S 179°40E **59 a**
Nathalia *Australia* 36°1S 145°13E **63 F4**
Nathdwara *India* 24°55N 73°50E **42 G5**
Natimuk *Australia* 36°42S 142°0E **63 F3**
Nation → *Canada* 55°30N 123°32W **70 B4**
National City *U.S.A.* 32°40N 117°5W **79 N9**
Natitingou *Benin* 10°20N 1°26E **52 F6**
Natividad, I. *Mexico* 27°52N 115°11W **86 B1**
Natkyizin *Myanmar* 14°57N 97°59E **38 E1**
Natron, L. *Tanzania* 2°20S 36°0E **54 E7**
Natrona Heights *U.S.A.* 40°37N 79°44W **82 F5**
Natuashish *Canada* 55°55N 61°8W **73 A7**
Natukanaoka Pan
  Namibia 18°40S 15°45E **56 A2**
Natuna Besar, Kepulauan
  Indonesia 4°0N 108°15E **36 D3**
Natuna Is. = Natuna Besar,
  Kepulauan *Indonesia* 4°0N 108°15E **36 D3**
Natuna Selatan, Kepulauan
  Indonesia 2°45N 109°0E **36 D3**
Natural Bridge *U.S.A.* 44°5N 75°30W **83 B9**
Natural Bridges △
  U.S.A. 37°36N 110°0W **77 H9**
Naturaliste, C. *Tas.,*
  Australia 40°50S 148°15E **63 G4**
Naturaliste, C. *W. Austral.,*
  Australia 33°32S 115°0E **61 F2**
Naturaliste Plateau
  Ind. Oc. 34°0S 112°0E **64 L3**
Nau Qala *Afghan.* 34°5N 68°5E **42 B3**
Naugatuck *U.S.A.* 41°30N 73°3W **83 E11**
Naujaat = Repulse Bay
  Canada 66°30N 86°30W **69 D14**
Naumburg *Germany* 51°9N 11°47E **16 C6**
Naupada *India* 18°34N 84°18E **44 E7**
Nauru ■ *Pac. Oc.* 1°0S 166°0E **58 B9**
Naushahra = Nowshera
  Pakistan 34°0N 72°0E **40 C8**
Naushahro *Pakistan* 26°50N 68°7E **42 F3**
Naushon I. *U.S.A.* 41°29N 70°45W **83 E14**
Nausori *Fiji* 18°2S 178°32E **59 a**

Nauta *Peru* 4°31S 73°35W **92 D4**
Nautanwa *India* 27°20N 83°25E **43 F10**
Naute △ *Namibia* 26°55S 17°57E **56 C2**
Nautla *Mexico* 20°13N 96°47W **87 C5**
Nava *Mexico* 28°25N 100°45W **86 B4**
Navadwip *India* 23°34N 88°20E **43 H13**
Navahrudak *Belarus* 53°40N 25°50E **17 B13**
Navajo Res. *U.S.A.* 36°48N 107°36W **77 H10**
Navalgund *India* 15°34N 75°22E **45 G2**
Navalmoral de la Mata
  Spain 39°52N 5°33W **21 C3**
Navan *Ireland* 53°39N 6°41W **10 C5**
Navarin, Mys *Russia* 62°15N 179°5E **27 C18**
Navarino, I. *Chile* 55°0S 67°40W **96 H3**
Navarra □ *Spain* 42°40N 1°40W **21 A5**
Navarre *U.S.A.* 40°43N 81°31W **82 F3**
Navarro → *U.S.A.* 39°11N 123°45W **78 F3**
Navasota *U.S.A.* 30°23N 96°5W **84 F6**
Navassa I. *W. Indies* 18°30N 75°0W **89 C5**
Naver → *U.K.* 58°32N 4°14W **11 C4**
Navibandar *India* 21°26N 69°48E **42 J3**
Navidad *Chile* 33°57S 71°50W **94 C1**
Navirai *Brazil* 23°8S 54°13W **95 A5**
Naviti *Fiji* 17°7S 177°15E **59 a**
Navlakhi *India* 22°58N 70°28E **42 H4**
Năvodari *Romania* 44°19N 28°36E **17 F15**
Navoiy *Uzbekistan* 40°9N 65°22E **26 E7**
Navojoa *Mexico* 27°6N 109°26W **86 B3**
Navolato *Mexico* 24°47N 107°42W **86 C3**
Navsari *India* 20°57N 72°59E **44 D1**
Navua *Fiji* 18°12S 178°11E **59 a**
Nawa Kot *Pakistan* 28°21N 71°24E **42 E4**
Nawab Khan *Pakistan* 30°17N 69°12E **42 D3**
Nawabganj *Ut. P., India* 26°56N 81°14E **43 F9**
Nawabganj *Ut. P., India* 28°32N 79°40E **43 E8**
Nawabshah *Pakistan* 26°15N 68°25E **42 F3**
Nawada *India* 24°50N 85°33E **43 G11**
Nawakot *Nepal* 27°55N 85°10E **43 F11**
Nawalgarh *India* 27°50N 75°15E **42 F6**
Nawanshahr *India* 32°33N 74°48E **43 C6**
Nawapara *India* 20°46N 82°33E **44 D6**
Nawar, Dasht-i- *Afghan.* 33°52N 68°0E **42 C3**
Nawoiy = Navoiy
  Uzbekistan 40°9N 65°22E **26 E7**
Naxçıvan *Azerbaijan* 39°12N 45°15E **46 B5**
Naxçıvan □ *Azerbaijan* 39°25N 45°26E **46 B5**
Naxos *Greece* 37°8N 25°25E **23 F11**
Nay, Mui *Vietnam* 12°54N 109°26E **38 F7**
Nãy Band *Būshehr, Iran* 27°20N 52°40E **47 E7**
Nãy Band *Khorāsān, Iran* 32°20N 57°34E **47 C8**
Nay Pyi Taw = Naypyidaw
  Myanmar 19°44N 96°12E **30 H8**
Nayagarh *India* 20°8N 85°6E **44 D7**
Nayakhan *Russia* 61°56N 159°0E **27 C16**
Nayarit □ *Mexico* 22°0N 105°0W **86 C4**
Nayau *Fiji* 18°6S 178°10E **59 a**
Nayong *China* 26°50N 105°20E **34 D5**
Nayoro *Japan* 44°21N 142°28E **28 B11**
Naypyidaw *Myanmar* 19°44N 96°12E **30 H8**
Nayudupeta *India* 13°54N 79°54E **45 G4**
Nayyäl, W. → *Si. Arabia* 28°35N 39°4E **46 D3**
Nazaré *Brazil* 13°2S 39°0W **93 F11**
Nazareth = Nazerat
  Israel 32°42N 35°17E **48 C4**
Nazareth *U.S.A.* 40°44N 75°19W **83 F9**
Nazarovo *Russia* 57°2N 90°40E **27 D10**
Nazas *Mexico* 25°14N 104°8W **86 B4**
Nazas → *Mexico* 25°12N 104°12W **86 B4**
Nazca = Nasca *Peru* 14°50S 74°57W **92 F4**
Naze, The *U.K.* 51°53N 1°18E **13 F9**
Nazerat *Israel* 32°42N 35°17E **48 C4**
Nãzik *Iran* 39°1N 45°4E **46 B5**
Nazilli *Turkey* 37°55N 28°15E **23 F13**
Nazko *Canada* 53°1N 123°37W **70 C4**
Nazko → *Canada* 53°7N 123°34W **70 C4**
Nazret *Ethiopia* 8°32N 39°22E **49 F2**
Ndalatando *Angola* 9°12S 14°48E **54 F2**
Ndélé *C.A.R.* 8°25N 20°36E **54 C4**
Ndjamena *Chad* 12°10N 15°0E **53 F8**
Ndola *Zambia* 13°0S 28°34E **55 G5**
Ndomo △ *S. Africa* 26°52S 32°15E **57 C5**
Ndoto Mts. *Kenya* 2°0N 37°0E **54 D7**
Neagh, Lough *U.K.* 54°37N 6°25W **10 B5**
Neah Bay *U.S.A.* 48°22N 124°37W **78 B2**
Neale, L. *Australia* 24°15S 130°0E **60 D5**
Neales → *Australia* 28°8S 136°47E **63 D2**
Near Is. *U.S.A.* 52°30N 174°0E **74 E2**
Neath *U.K.* 51°39N 3°48W **13 F4**
Neath Port Talbot □ *U.K.* 51°42N 3°45W **13 F4**
Nebine Cr. → *Australia* 29°27S 146°56E **63 D4**
Nebitdag = Balkanabat
  Turkmenistan 39°30N 54°22E **47 B7**
Nebo *Australia* 21°42S 148°42E **62 C4**
Nebraska □ *U.S.A.* 41°30N 99°30W **80 E4**
Nebraska City *U.S.A.* 40°41N 95°52W **80 E6**
Nébrodi, Monti *Italy* 37°54N 14°35E **22 F6**
Necedah *U.S.A.* 44°2N 90°4W **80 C8**
Nechako → *Canada* 53°55N 122°42W **70 C4**
Neches → *U.S.A.* 29°58N 93°51W **84 D6**
Neckar → *Germany* 49°27N 8°29E **16 D5**
Necker I. *U.S.A.* 23°35N 164°42W **75 L7**
Necochea *Argentina* 38°30S 58°50W **94 D4**
Nederland = Netherlands ■
  Europe 52°0N 5°30E **15 C5**
Needles *Canada* 49°53N 118°7W **70 D5**
Needles *U.S.A.* 34°51N 114°37W **79 L12**
Needles, The *U.K.* 50°39N 1°35W **13 G6**
Neembucú □ *Paraguay* 27°0S 58°0W **94 B4**
Neemuch = Nimach
  India 24°30N 74°56E **42 G6**
Neenah *U.S.A.* 44°11N 88°28W **80 C9**
Neepawa *Canada* 50°15N 99°30W **71 C9**
Neftçala *Azerbaijan* 39°19N 49°12E **47 B6**
Neftegorsk *Russia* 53°1N 142°58E **27 D15**
Neftekumsk *Russia* 44°46N 44°50E **19 F7**
Neftyugansk *Russia* 61°5N 72°42E **26 C8**
Nefyn *U.K.* 52°56N 4°31W **12 E3**
Negapatam = Nagappattinam
  India 10°46N 79°51E **45 J4**
Negara *Indonesia* 8°22S 114°37E **37 J17**

Negaunee *U.S.A.* 46°30N 87°36W **80 B10**
Negele *Ethiopia* 5°20N 39°36E **49 F2**
Negeri Sembilan □
  Malaysia 2°45N 102°10E **39 L4**
Negev Desert = Hanegev
  Israel 30°50N 35°0E **48 E4**
Negombo *Sri Lanka* 7°12N 79°50E **45 L4**
Negotin *Serbia* 44°16N 22°37E **23 B10**
Negra, Pta. *Mauritania* 22°54N 16°18W **52 D2**
Negra, Pta. *Peru* 6°6S 81°10W **92 E2**
Negrais, C. = Maudin Sun
  Myanmar 16°0N 94°30E **41 M19**
Negril *Jamaica* 18°22N 78°20W **88 a**
Negro → *Argentina* 41°2S 62°47W **96 E4**
Negro → *Brazil* 3°0S 60°0W **92 D7**
Negro → *Uruguay* 33°24S 58°22W **94 C4**
Negros *Phil.* 9°30N 122°40E **37 C6**
Neguac *Canada* 47°15N 65°5W **73 C6**
Nehalem → *U.S.A.* 45°40N 123°56W **78 E3**
Nehâvand *Iran* 35°56N 49°31E **47 C6**
Nehbandān *Iran* 31°35N 60°5E **47 D9**
Nehe *China* 48°29N 124°50E **31 B13**
Nei Mongol Zizhiqu □
  China 42°0N 112°0E **32 D7**
Neiafu *Tonga* 18°39S 173°59W **59 c**
Neiges, Piton des *Réunion* 21°5S 55°29E **55 c**
Neijiang *China* 29°35N 104°55E **34 C5**
Neilingding Dao *China* 22°25N 113°48E **31 a**
Neill I. *India* 11°50N 93°3E **45 J11**
Neillsville *U.S.A.* 44°34N 90°36W **80 C8**
Neilton *U.S.A.* 47°25N 123°53W **78 C3**
Neiqiu *China* 37°15N 114°30E **32 F8**
Neiva *Colombia* 2°56N 75°18W **92 C3**
Neixiang *China* 33°10N 111°52E **32 H6**
Nejanilini L. *Canada* 59°33N 97°48W **71 B9**
Nejd = Najd *Si. Arabia* 26°30N 42°0E **49 B3**
Nekã *Iran* 36°39N 53°19E **47 B7**
Nekemte *Ethiopia* 9°4N 36°30E **49 F2**
Nekso *Denmark* 55°4N 15°8E **9 J16**
Nelamangala *India* 13°6N 77°24E **45 H3**
Nelia *Australia* 20°39S 142°12E **62 C3**
Neligh *U.S.A.* 42°8N 98°2W **80 D4**
Nelkan *Russia* 57°40N 136°4E **27 D14**
Nellikuppam *India* 11°46N 79°43E **45 J4**
Nellore *India* 14°27N 79°59E **45 G4**
Nelson *Canada* 49°30N 117°20W **70 D5**
Nelson *N.Z.* 41°18S 173°16E **59 D4**
Nelson *U.K.* 53°50N 2°13W **12 D5**
Nelson *Ariz., U.S.A.* 35°31N 113°19W **79 J7**
Nelson *Nev., U.S.A.* 35°42N 114°49W **79 K12**
Nelson → *Canada* 54°33N 98°2W **71 C9**
Nelson, C. *Australia* 38°26S 141°32E **63 F3**
Nelson, Estrecho *Chile* 51°30S 75°0W **96 G2**
Nelson Forks *Canada* 59°30N 124°0W **70 B4**
Nelson House *Canada* 55°47N 98°51W **71 B9**
Nelson L. *Canada* 55°48N 100°7W **71 B8**
Nelson Lakes △ *N.Z.* 41°55S 172°44E **59 D4**
Nelspoort *S. Africa* 32°7S 23°0E **56 E3**
Nelspruit = Mbombela
  S. Africa 25°29S 30°59E **57 C5**
Néma *Mauritania* 16°40N 7°15W **52 E4**
Neman = Nemunas →
  Lithuania 55°25N 21°10E **9 J19**
Nembrala *Indonesia* 10°53S 122°50E **60 B3**
Nemeiben L. *Canada* 55°20N 105°20W **71 B7**
Nemiscau *Canada* 51°18N 76°54W **72 B4**
Nemiscau, L. *Canada* 51°25N 76°40W **72 B4**
Nemunas → *Lithuania* 55°25N 21°10E **9 J19**
Nemuro *Japan* 43°20N 145°35E **28 C12**
Nemuro-Kaikyō *Japan* 43°30N 145°30E **28 C12**
Nen Jiang → *China* 45°28N 124°30E **33 B13**
Nenagh *Ireland* 52°52N 8°11W **10 D3**
Nenana *U.S.A.* 64°34N 149°5W **74 C10**
Nenasi *Malaysia* 3°9N 103°23E **39 L4**
Nene → *U.K.* 52°49N 0°11E **13 E8**
Nenjiang *China* 49°10N 125°10E **31 B14**
Neodesha *U.S.A.* 37°25N 95°41W **80 G6**
Neora Valley △ *India* 27°0N 88°45E **43 F13**
Neosho *U.S.A.* 36°52N 94°22W **80 G6**
Neosho → *U.S.A.* 36°48N 95°18W **84 C7**
Nepal ■ *Asia* 28°0N 84°30E **43 F11**
Nepalganj *Nepal* 28°5N 81°40E **43 E9**
Nepalganj Road *India* 28°1N 81°41E **43 E9**
Nephi *U.S.A.* 39°43N 111°50W **76 G8**
Nephin *Ireland* 54°1N 9°22W **10 B2**
Nephin Beg Range *Ireland* 54°0N 9°40W **10 C2**
Neptune *U.S.A.* 40°13N 74°2W **83 F10**
Neqâb *Iran* 36°42N 57°25E **47 B8**
Nerang *Australia* 27°58S 153°20E **63 D5**
Nerchinsk *Russia* 52°0N 116°39E **27 D12**
Néret, L. *Canada* 54°45N 70°44W **73 B5**
Neretva → *Croatia* 43°1N 17°27E **23 C7**
Neringa *Lithuania* 55°20N 21°5E **9 J19**
Neris → *Lithuania* 55°8N 24°16E **9 J21**
Neryungri *Russia* 57°38N 124°28E **27 D13**
Nescopeck *U.S.A.* 41°3N 76°12E **83 E8**
Neskantaga *Canada* 52°14N 87°53W **72 B2**
Neskaupstaður *Iceland* 65°9N 13°42W **8 D7**
Ness, L. *U.K.* 57°15N 4°32W **11 D4**
Ness City *U.S.A.* 38°27N 99°54W **80 F4**
Nesterov = Zhovkva
  Ukraine 50°4N 23°58E **17 C12**
Nestos → *Europe* 40°54N 24°49E **23 D11**
Nesvizh = Nyasvizh
  Belarus 53°14N 26°38E **17 B14**
Netanya *Israel* 32°20N 34°51E **48 C3**
Netarhat *India* 23°29N 84°16E **43 H11**
Nete → *Belgium* 51°7N 4°14E **15 C4**
Netherdale *Australia* 21°10S 148°33E **62 b**
Netherlands ■ *Europe* 52°0N 5°30E **15 C5**
Netherlands Antilles = ABC
  Islands *W. Indies* 12°15N 69°0W **89 D6**
Netrang *India* 21°39N 73°21E **42 J5**
Nettilling L. *Canada* 66°30N 71°0W **69 D17**
Netzahualcóyotl, Presa
  Mexico 17°8N 93°35W **87 D6**
Neubrandenburg
  Germany 53°33N 13°15E **16 B7**
Neuchâtel *Switz.* 47°0N 6°55E **20 C7**
Neuchâtel, Lac de *Switz.* 46°53N 6°50E **20 C7**

Neufchâteau *Belgium* 49°50N 5°25E **15 E5**
Neumayer III *Antarctica* 71°0S 68°30W **5 D2**
Neumünster *Germany* 54°4N 9°58E **16 A5**
Neunkirchen *Germany* 49°20N 7°9E **16 D4**
Neuquén *Argentina* 38°55S 68°0W **96 D3**
Neuquén □ *Argentina* 38°0S 69°50W **96 D2**
Neuruppin *Germany* 52°55N 12°48E **16 B7**
Neuse → *U.S.A.* 35°6N 76°29W **85 D16**
Neusiedler See *Austria* 47°50N 16°47E **17 E9**
Neustrelitz *Germany* 53°21N 13°4E **16 B7**
Neva → *Russia* 59°56N 30°20E **18 C5**
Nevada *Iowa, U.S.A.* 42°1N 93°27W **80 D7**
Nevada *Mo., U.S.A.* 37°51N 94°22W **80 G6**
Nevada City *U.S.A.* 39°16N 121°1W **78 F6**
Nevada □ *U.S.A.* 39°0N 117°0W **76 G5**
Nevado, Cerro *Argentina* 35°30S 68°32W **94 D2**
Nevado de Colima = Volcán de
  Colima △ *Mexico* 19°30N 103°40W **86 D4**
Nevado de Tres Cruces △
  Chile 27°13S 69°5W **94 B2**
Nevasa *India* 19°34N 75°0E **44 E2**
Nevel *Russia* 56°0N 29°55E **18 C4**
Nevelsk *Russia* 46°40N 141°51E **27 E15**
Nevers *France* 47°0N 3°9E **20 C5**
Nevertire *Australia* 31°50S 147°44E **63 E4**
Neville *Canada* 49°58N 107°39W **71 D7**
Nevinnomyssk *Russia* 44°40N 42°0E **19 F7**
Nevis *St. Kitts & Nevis* 17°0N 62°30W **89 C7**
Nevşehir *Turkey* 38°33N 34°40E **46 B2**
Nevyansk *Russia* 57°30N 60°13E **18 C11**
New → *U.S.A.* 38°10N 81°12W **81 F13**
New Aiyansh *Canada* 55°12N 129°4W **70 B3**
New Albany *Ind., U.S.A.* 38°18N 85°49W **81 F11**
New Albany *Miss.,*
  U.S.A. 34°29N 89°0W **85 D10**
New Albany *Pa., U.S.A.* 41°36N 76°27W **83 E8**
New Amsterdam *Guyana* 6°15N 57°36W **92 B7**
New Baltimore *U.S.A.* 42°41N 82°44W **82 D2**
New Bedford *U.S.A.* 41°38N 70°56W **83 E14**
New Berlin *N.Y., U.S.A.* 42°37N 75°20W **83 D9**
New Berlin *Pa., U.S.A.* 40°50N 76°57W **82 F8**
New Bern *U.S.A.* 35°7N 77°3W **85 D16**
New Bethlehem *U.S.A.* 41°0N 79°20W **82 F5**
New Bight *Bahamas* 24°19N 75°24W **89 B4**
New Bloomfield *U.S.A.* 40°25N 77°11W **82 F7**
New Boston *U.S.A.* 33°28N 94°25W **84 E7**
New Braunfels *U.S.A.* 29°42N 98°8W **84 G5**
New Brighton *N.Z.* 43°29S 172°43E **59 E4**
New Brighton *U.S.A.* 40°42N 80°19W **82 F4**
New Britain *Papua N. G.* 5°50S 150°20E **58 B8**
New Britain *U.S.A.* 41°40N 72°47W **83 E12**
New Brunswick *U.S.A.* 40°30N 74°27W **83 F10**
New Brunswick □
  Canada 46°50N 66°30W **73 C6**
New Caledonia ☑ *Pac. Oc.* 21°0S 165°0E **58 D9**
New Caledonia Trough
  Pac. Oc. 30°0S 165°0E **64 L8**
New Castile = Castilla-La
  Mancha □ *Spain* 39°30N 3°30W **21 C4**
New Castle *Ind., U.S.A.* 39°55N 85°22W **81 F11**
New Castle *Pa., U.S.A.* 41°0N 80°21W **82 F4**
New Chitose ✈ (CTS)
  Japan 42°46N 141°41E **28 C10**
New City *U.S.A.* 41°9N 73°59W **83 E11**
New Concord *U.S.A.* 39°59N 81°54W **82 G3**
New Cumberland *U.S.A.* 40°30N 80°36W **82 F4**
New Cuyama *U.S.A.* 34°57N 119°38W **79 L7**
New Denver *Canada* 50°0N 117°25W **70 D5**
New Don Pedro Res.
  U.S.A. 37°43N 120°24W **78 H6**
New England *U.S.A.* 43°0N 71°0W **75 G25**
New England *N. Dak.,*
  U.S.A. 46°32N 102°52W **80 B2**
New England Ra.
  Australia 30°20S 151°45E **63 E5**
New Forest △ *U.K.* 50°53N 1°34W **13 G6**
New Galloway *U.K.* 55°5N 4°9W **11 F4**
New Glasgow *Canada* 45°35N 62°36W **73 C7**
New Guinea *Oceania* 4°0S 136°0E **58 B6**
New Hamburg *Canada* 43°23N 80°42W **82 C4**
New Hampshire □
  U.S.A. 44°0N 71°30W **83 C13**
New Hampton *U.S.A.* 43°3N 92°19W **80 D7**
New Hanover *S. Africa* 29°22S 30°31E **57 C5**
New Hartford *U.S.A.* 43°4N 75°18W **83 C9**
New Haven *Conn.,*
  U.S.A. 41°18N 72°55W **83 E12**
New Haven *Mich., U.S.A.* 42°44N 82°48W **82 D2**
New Haven *N.Y., U.S.A.* 43°28N 76°18W **83 C8**
New Hazelton *Canada* 55°20N 127°30W **70 B3**
New Hebrides = Vanuatu ■
  Pac. Oc. 15°0S 168°0E **58 C9**
New Holland *U.S.A.* 40°6N 76°5W **83 F8**
New Iberia *U.S.A.* 30°1N 91°49W **84 F9**
New Ireland *Papua N. G.* 3°20S 151°50E **58 B8**
New Jersey □ *U.S.A.* 40°0N 74°30W **81 F16**
New Kensington *U.S.A.* 40°34N 79°46W **82 F5**
New Lexington *U.S.A.* 39°43N 82°13W **81 F12**
New Liskeard *Canada* 47°31N 79°41W **72 C4**
New London *Conn.,*
  U.S.A. 41°22N 72°6W **83 E12**
New London *Ohio, U.S.A.* 41°5N 82°24W **82 E2**
New London *Wis., U.S.A.* 44°23N 88°45W **80 C9**
New Madrid *U.S.A.* 36°36N 89°32W **80 G9**
New Martinsville
  U.S.A. 39°39N 80°52W **81 F13**
New Meadows *U.S.A.* 44°58N 116°18W **76 D5**
New Melones L. *U.S.A.* 37°57N 120°31W **78 H6**
New Mexico □ *U.S.A.* 34°30N 106°0W **77 J11**
New Milford *Conn.,*
  U.S.A. 41°35N 73°25W **83 E11**
New Milford *Pa., U.S.A.* 41°52N 75°44W **83 E9**
New Norcia *Australia* 30°57S 116°13E **61 F2**
New Norfolk *Australia* 42°46S 147°2E **63 G4**
New Philadelphia *U.S.A.* 40°30N 81°27W **82 F3**
New Plymouth *N.Z.* 39°4S 174°5E **59 C5**
New Plymouth *U.S.A.* 43°58N 116°49W **76 E5**
New Port Richey *U.S.A.* 28°16N 82°43W **85 G13**
New Providence
  Bahamas 25°25N 77°35W **88 A4**

New Quay *U.K.* 52°13N 4°21W **13 E3**
New Radnor *U.K.* 52°15N 3°9W **13 E4**
New Richmond *Canada* 48°15N 65°45W **73 C6**
New Richmond *U.S.A.* 45°7N 92°32W **80 C7**
New River Gorge △
  U.S.A. 37°53N 81°5W **81 G13**
New Roads *U.S.A.* 30°42N 91°26W **84 F9**
New Rochelle *U.S.A.* 40°55N 73°46W **83 F11**
New Rockford *U.S.A.* 47°41N 99°8W **80 B4**
New Romney *U.K.* 50°59N 0°57E **13 G8**
New Ross *Ireland* 52°23N 6°57W **10 D5**
New Salem *U.S.A.* 46°51N 101°25W **80 B3**
New Scone = Scone *U.K.* 56°25N 3°24W **11 E5**
New Siberian I. = Novaya Sibir,
  Ostrov *Russia* 75°10N 150°0E **27 B16**
New Siberian Is. = Novosibirskiye
  Ostrova *Russia* 75°0N 142°0E **27 B15**
New Smyrna Beach
  U.S.A. 29°1N 80°56W **85 G14**
New South Wales □
  Australia 33°0S 146°0E **63 E4**
New Tecumseth = Alliston
  Canada 44°9N 79°52W **82 B5**
New Town *U.S.A.* 47°59N 102°30W **80 B2**
New Ulm *U.S.A.* 44°19N 94°28W **80 C7**
New Waterford *Canada* 46°13N 60°4W **73 C7**
New Westminster
  Canada 49°13N 122°55W **78 A4**
New York □ *U.S.A.* 43°0N 75°0W **83 D9**
New York J.F. Kennedy Int. ✈
  (JFK) *U.S.A.* 40°38N 73°47W **83 F11**
New Zealand ■ *Oceania* 40°0S 176°0E **59 D6**
Newaj → *India* 24°24N 76°49E **42 G7**
Newark *Del., U.S.A.* 39°41N 75°46W **81 F16**
Newark *N.J., U.S.A.* 40°44N 74°10W **83 F10**
Newark *N.Y., U.S.A.* 43°3N 77°6W **82 C7**
Newark *Ohio, U.S.A.* 40°3N 82°24W **82 F2**
Newark Liberty Int. ✈ (EWR)
  U.S.A. 40°42N 74°10W **83 F10**
Newark-on-Trent *U.K.* 53°5N 0°48W **12 D7**
Newark Valley *U.S.A.* 42°14N 76°11W **83 D8**
Newberg *U.S.A.* 45°18N 122°58W **76 D2**
Newberry *Mich., U.S.A.* 46°21N 85°30W **81 B11**
Newberry *S.C., U.S.A.* 34°17N 81°37W **85 D14**
Newberry Springs
  U.S.A. 34°50N 116°41W **79 L10**
Newboro L. *Canada* 44°38N 76°20W **83 B8**
Newbridge *Ireland* 53°11N 6°48W **10 C5**
Newburgh *Canada* 44°19N 76°52W **82 B8**
Newburgh *U.S.A.* 41°30N 74°1W **83 E10**
Newbury *U.K.* 51°24N 1°20W **13 F6**
Newbury *N.H., U.S.A.* 43°19N 72°3W **83 C12**
Newbury *Vt., U.S.A.* 44°5N 72°4W **83 B12**
Newburyport *U.S.A.* 42°49N 70°53W **83 D14**
Newcastle *Australia* 33°0S 151°46E **63 E5**
Newcastle *N.B., Canada* 47°1N 65°38W **73 C6**
Newcastle *Ont., Canada* 43°55N 78°35W **72 D4**
Newcastle *Ireland* 52°27N 9°3W **10 D2**
Newcastle *S. Africa* 27°45S 29°58E **57 C4**
Newcastle *U.K.* 54°13N 5°54W **10 B6**
Newcastle *Calif., U.S.A.* 38°53N 121°8W **78 G5**
Newcastle *Wyo.,*
  U.S.A. 43°50N 104°11W **76 D11**
Newcastle Emlyn *U.K.* 52°2N 4°28W **13 E3**
Newcastle Ra. *Australia* 15°45S 130°15E **60 C5**
Newcastle-under-Lyme
  U.K. 53°1N 2°14W **12 D5**
Newcastle-upon-Tyne
  U.K. 54°58N 1°36W **12 C6**
Newcastle Waters
  Australia 17°30S 133°28E **62 B1**
Newcomb *U.S.A.* 43°58N 74°10W **83 C10**
Newcomerstown *U.S.A.* 40°16N 81°36W **82 F3**
Newdegate *Australia* 33°6S 119°0E **61 F2**
Newell *Australia* 16°20S 145°16E **62 B4**
Newell *U.S.A.* 44°43N 103°25W **80 C2**
Newenham, C. *U.S.A.* 58°39N 162°11W **74 D7**
Newfane *U.S.A.* 43°17N 78°43W **82 C6**
Newfield *U.S.A.* 42°18N 76°33W **83 D8**
Newfound L. *U.S.A.* 43°40N 71°47W **83 C13**
Newfoundland *Canada* 49°0N 55°0W **73 C8**
Newfoundland *U.S.A.* 41°18N 75°19W **83 E9**
Newfoundland & Labrador □
  Canada 52°0N 58°0W **73 B8**
Newhaven *U.K.* 50°47N 0°3E **13 G8**
Newkirk *U.S.A.* 36°53N 97°3W **84 C6**
Newlyn *U.K.* 50°6N 5°34W **13 G2**
Newman *Australia* 23°18S 119°45E **60 D2**
Newman *U.S.A.* 37°19N 121°1W **78 H5**
Newmarket *Canada* 44°3N 79°28W **82 B5**
Newmarket *Ireland* 52°13N 9°0W **10 D2**
Newmarket *U.K.* 52°15N 0°25E **13 E8**
Newmarket *U.S.A.* 43°5N 70°56W **83 C14**
Newnan *U.S.A.* 33°23N 84°48W **85 E12**
Newport *Ireland* 53°53N 9°33W **10 C2**
Newport *I. of W., U.K.* 50°42N 1°17W **13 G6**
Newport *Newport, U.K.* 51°35N 3°0W **13 F5**
Newport *Ark., U.S.A.* 35°37N 91°16W **84 D9**
Newport *Ky., U.S.A.* 39°5N 84°29W **81 F11**
Newport *N.H., U.S.A.* 43°22N 72°10W **83 C12**
Newport *N.Y., U.S.A.* 43°11N 75°1W **83 C9**
Newport *Oreg., U.S.A.* 44°39N 124°3W **76 D1**
Newport *Pa., U.S.A.* 40°29N 77°8W **82 F7**
Newport *Tenn., U.S.A.* 35°58N 83°11W **85 D13**
Newport *Vt., U.S.A.* 44°56N 72°13W **83 B12**
Newport *Wash., U.S.A.* 48°11N 117°3W **76 B5**
Newport □ *U.K.* 51°33N 3°1W **13 F4**
Newport Beach *U.S.A.* 33°37N 117°56W **79 M9**
Newport News *U.S.A.* 36°58N 76°25W **81 G15**
Newport Pagnell *U.K.* 52°5N 0°43W **13 E7**
Newquay *U.K.* 50°25N 5°6W **13 G2**
Newry *U.K.* 54°11N 6°21W **10 B5**
Newry Islands △
  Australia 20°51S 148°56E **62 b**
Newton *Ill., U.S.A.* 38°59N 88°10W **80 F9**
Newton *Iowa, U.S.A.* 41°42N 93°3W **80 E7**
Newton *Kans., U.S.A.* 38°3N 97°21W **80 F5**
Newton *Miss., U.S.A.* 32°19N 89°10W **85 E10**
Newton *N.C., U.S.A.* 35°40N 81°13W **85 D14**

Newton *N.J., U.S.A.* 41°3N 74°45W **83** E10
Newton *Tex., U.S.A.* 30°51N 93°46W **84** F8
Newton *U.K.* 50°32N 3°37W **13** G4
Newton Abbot *U.K.* 50°32N 3°37W **13** G4
Newton Aycliffe *U.K.* 54°37N 1°34W **12** C6
Newton Falls *N.Y., U.S.A.* 44°12N 74°59W **83** B10
Newton Falls *Ohio, U.S.A.* 41°11N 80°59W **82** E4
Newton Stewart *U.K.* 54°57N 4°30W **11** G4
Newtonmore *U.K.* 57°4N 4°8W **11** D4
Newtown *U.K.* 52°31N 3°19W **13** E4
Newtownabbey *U.K.* 54°40N 5°56W **10** B6
Newtownards *U.K.* 54°36N 5°42W **10** B6
Newtownbarry = Bunclody
Ireland 52°39N 6°40W **10** D5
Newtonstewart *U.K.* 54°43N 7°23W **10** B4
Newville *U.S.A.* 40°10N 77°24W **82** F7
Neya *Russia* 58°21N 43°49E **18** C7
Neyrīz *Iran* 29°15N 54°19E **47** D7
Neyshābūr *Iran* 36°10N 58°50E **47** B8
Neyveli *India* 11°32N 79°29E **45** J4
Neyyattinkara *India* 8°26N 77°5E **45** K3
Nezhin = Nizhyn *Ukraine* 51°5N 31°55E **19** D5
Nezperce *U.S.A.* 46°14N 116°14W **76** C5
Nga, Laem *Thailand* 7°55N 98°27E **39** a
Ngaanyatjarra ○
Australia 22°40S 127°0E **60** D4
Ngabang *Indonesia* 0°23N 109°55E **36** D3
Ngabordamlu, Tanjung
Indonesia 6°56S 134°11E **37** F8
N'Gage *Angola* 7°46S 15°15E **54** F3
Ngaliwurru Nungali ○
Australia 15°42S 130°4E **60** C5
Ngalurrtju ○ *Australia* 22°44S 132°5E **60** D5
Ngami Depression
Botswana 20°30S 22°46E **56** B3
Ngamring *China* 29°14N 87°10E **30** F6
Nganglong Kangri *China* 33°0N 81°0E **43** C9
Ngao *Thailand* 18°46N 99°59E **38** C2
Ngaoundéré *Cameroon* 7°15N 13°35E **54** C2
Ngapara *N.Z.* 44°57S 170°46E **59** F3
Ngarluma ○ *Australia* 21°30S 118°30E **60** D2
Ngawi *Indonesia* 7°24S 111°26E **37** G14
Ngcobo *S. Africa* 31°37S 28°0E **57** D4
Ngerulmud = Melekeok
Palau 7°27N 134°38E **64** G5
Nghia Lo *Vietnam* 21°33N 104°28E **34** G5
Ngoring Hu *China* 34°55N 97°5E **30** E8
Ngorongoro *Tanzania* 3°11S 35°32E **54** E7
Nguigmi *Niger* 14°20N 13°20E **53** F8
Nguiu *Australia* 11°46S 130°38E **60** B5
Ngukurr *Australia* 14°44S 134°44E **62** A1
Ngum → *Laos* 18°31N 102°32E **38** C4
Ngundu *Zimbabwe* 18°11S 31°15E **57** A5
Nguru *Nigeria* 12°56N 10°29E **53** F8
Nguyen Binh *Vietnam* 22°39N 105°56E **34** F5
Ngwaketse ○ *Botswana* 25°0S 25°0E **56** C3
Nha Bang *Vietnam* 10°37N 105°0E **39** G5
Nha Trang *Vietnam* 12°16N 109°10E **39** F7
Nhacoongo *Mozam.* 24°18S 35°14E **57** B6
Nhamundá → *Brazil* 2°12S 56°41W **93** D7
Nhangulaze, L. *Mozam.* 24°0S 34°30E **57** B5
Nharnuwangga, Wajarri and
Ngarlawangga ○
Australia 24°50S 118°0E **61** D2
Nhill *Australia* 36°18S 141°40E **63** F3
Nho Quan *Vietnam* 20°18N 105°45E **34** G5
Nhulunbuy *Australia* 12°10S 137°20E **62** A2
Niafounké *Mali* 16°0N 4°5W **52** E5
Niagara Falls *Canada* 43°7N 79°5W **82** C5
Niagara Falls *U.S.A.* 43°5N 79°4W **82** C6
Niagara-on-the-Lake
Canada 43°15N 79°4W **82** C5
Niah *Malaysia* 3°58N 113°46E **36** D4
Niamey *Niger* 13°27N 2°6E **52** F6
Niangara
Dem. Rep. of the Congo 3°42N 27°50E **54** D5
Niantic *U.S.A.* 41°20N 72°11W **83** E12
Nias *Indonesia* 1°0N 97°30E **36** D1
Niassa, L. = Malawi, L.
Africa 12°30S 34°30E **55** G6
Nibāk *Si. Arabia* 24°25N 50°50E **47** E7
Nicaragua ■ *Cent. Amer.* 11°40N 85°30W **88** D2
Nicaragua, L. de *Nic.* 12°0N 85°30W **88** D2
Nicastro *Italy* 38°59N 16°19E **22** E7
Nice *France* 43°42N 7°14E **20** E7
Niceville *U.S.A.* 30°31N 86°30W **85** F11
Nichicun, L. *Canada* 53°5N 71°0W **73** B5
Nichinan *Japan* 31°38N 131°23E **29** J5
Nicholás, Canal *Caribbean* 23°30N 80°5W **88** B3
Nicholas Channel = Nicholás,
Canal *Caribbean* 23°30N 80°5W **88** B3
Nicholasville *U.S.A.* 37°53N 84°34W **81** G11
Nichols *U.S.A.* 42°1N 76°22W **83** D8
Nicholson *Australia* 18°2S 128°54E **60** C4
Nicholson → *Australia* 17°31S 139°36E **62** B2
Nicholson L. *Canada* 62°40N 102°40W **71** A8
Nicholson Ra. *Australia* 27°15S 116°45E **61** E2
Nicholville *U.S.A.* 44°41N 74°39W **83** B10
Nicobar Is. *Ind. Oc.* 8°0N 93°30E **45** L11
Nicola *Canada* 50°12N 120°40W **70** C4
Nicolls Town *Bahamas* 25°8N 78°0W **88** A4
Nicosia *Cyprus* 35°10N 33°25E **46** C2
Nicoya *Costa Rica* 10°9N 85°27W **88** D2
Nicoya, G. de *Costa Rica* 10°0N 85°0W **88** E3
Nicoya, Pen. de *Costa Rica* 9°45N 85°40W **88** E2
Nidd → *U.K.* 53°59N 1°23W **12** D6
Niedersachsen □ *Germany* 52°50N 9°0E **16** B5
Niekerkshoop *S. Africa* 29°19S 22°51E **56** D3
Niemen = Nemunas →
Lithuania 55°25N 21°10E **9** J19
Nienburg *Germany* 52°39N 9°13E **16** B5
Nieu Bethesda *S. Africa* 31°51S 24°34E **56** D3
Nieuw Amsterdam
Suriname 5°53N 55°5W **93** B7
Nieuw Nickerie *Suriname* 5°53N 57°5W **93** B7
Nieuwoudtville *S. Africa* 31°23S 19°7E **56** D2
Nieuwpoort *Belgium* 51°8N 2°45E **15** C2
Niğde *Turkey* 37°58N 34°40E **46** B2

Nigel *S. Africa* 26°27S 28°25E **57** C4
Niger ■ *W. Afr.* 17°30N 10°0E **52** E7
Niger → *W. Afr.* 5°33N 6°33E **52** G7
Nigeria ■ *W. Afr.* 8°30N 8°0E **52** G7
Nighasin *India* 28°14N 80°52E **43** E9
Nightcaps *N.Z.* 45°57S 168°2E **59** F2
Nihon = Japan ■ *Asia* 36°0N 136°0E **29** G8
Nii-Jima *Japan* 34°20N 139°15E **29** G9
Niigata *Japan* 37°58N 139°0E **28** F9
Niigata □ *Japan* 37°15N 138°45E **29** F9
Niihama *Japan* 33°55N 133°16E **29** H6
Ni'ihau *Japan* 21°54N 160°9W **75** L7
Niimi *Japan* 34°59N 133°28E **29** G6
Niitsu *Japan* 37°48N 139°7E **28** F9
Nijil *Jordan* 30°32N 35°33E **48** E4
Nijkerk *Neths.* 52°13N 5°30E **15** B5
Nijmegen *Neths.* 51°50N 5°52E **15** C5
Nijverdal *Neths.* 52°22N 6°28E **15** B6
Nīk Pey *Iran* 36°50N 48°10E **47** B6
Nikaweratiya *Sri Lanka* 7°45N 80°7E **45** L5
Nikiniki *Indonesia* 9°49S 124°30E **60** A3
Nikkō *Japan* 36°45N 139°35E **29** F9
Nikkō □ *Japan* 36°56N 139°37E **29** F9
Nikolayev = Mykolaiv
Ukraine 46°58N 32°0E **19** E5
Nikolayevsk *Russia* 50°0N 45°35E **19** E8
Nikolayevsk-na-Amur
Russia 53°8N 140°44E **27** D15
Nikolskoye *Russia* 55°12N 166°0E **27** D17
Nikopol *Ukraine* 47°35N 34°25E **19** E5
Nīkshahr *Iran* 26°15N 60°10E **47** E9
Nikšić *Montenegro* 42°50N 18°57E **23** C8
Nīl, Nahr en → *Africa* 30°10N 31°6E **53** B12
Nīl el Abyad → *Sudan* 15°38N 32°31E **53** E12
Nīl el Azraq → *Sudan* 15°38N 32°31E **53** E12
Nila *Indonesia* 6°44S 129°31E **37** F7
Nilakkottai *India* 10°10N 77°52E **45** J3
Nilanga *India* 18°6N 76°46E **44** E3
Nile = Nīl, Nahr en →
Africa 30°10N 31°6E **53** B12
Niles *Mich., U.S.A.* 41°50N 86°15W **80** E10
Niles *Ohio, U.S.A.* 41°11N 80°46W **82** E4
Nileshwar *India* 12°15N 75°6E **45** H2
Nilgiri Hills *India* 11°30N 76°30E **45** J3
Nim Ka Thana *India* 27°44N 75°48E **42** F6
Nimach *India* 24°30N 74°56E **42** G6
Nimbahera *India* 24°37N 74°45E **42** G6
Nîmes *France* 43°50N 4°23E **20** E6
Nimfaíon, Ákra = Pines, Akra
Greece 40°5N 24°20E **23** D11
Nimmitabel *Australia* 36°29S 149°15E **63** F4
Nīnawá *Iraq* 36°25N 43°10E **46** B4
Nīnawá □ *Iraq* 36°15N 43°0E **46** B4
Nindigully *Australia* 28°21S 148°50E **63** D4
Nine Degree Channel *India* 9°0N 73°0E **45** K1
Ninepin Group *China* 22°16N 114°21E **31** a
Nineveh = Nīnawá *Iraq* 36°25N 43°10E **46** B4
Ning Xian *China* 35°30N 107°58E **32** G4
Ningaloo Marine ○
Australia 22°23S 113°32E **60** D1
Ning'an *China* 44°22N 129°20E **33** B15
Ningbo *China* 29°51N 121°28E **35** C13
Ningcheng *China* 41°32N 119°53E **33** D10
Ningde *China* 26°38N 119°23E **35** D12
Ningdu *China* 26°25N 115°59E **35** D10
Ninggang *China* 26°42N 113°55E **35** D9
Ningguo *China* 30°35N 119°0E **35** D12
Ninghai *China* 29°15N 121°27E **35** C13
Ninghua *China* 26°14N 116°45E **35** D11
Ningjin *China* 37°35N 114°57E **32** F8
Ningjing Shan *China* 31°0N 98°20E **34** C2
Ninglang *China* 27°0N 100°55E **34** D3
Ningling *China* 34°25N 115°22E **32** G8
Ningming *China* 22°8N 107°4E **34** F6
Ningnan *China* 27°5N 102°36E **34** D4
Ningpo = Ningbo
China 29°51N 121°28E **35** C13
Ningqiang *China* 32°47N 106°15E **32** H4
Ningshan *China* 33°21N 108°21E **34** A7
Ningsia Hui A.R. = Ningxia Huizu
Zizhiqu □ *China* 38°0N 106°0E **32** F4
Ningwu *China* 39°0N 112°18E **32** E7
Ningxia Huizu Zizhiqu □
China 38°0N 106°0E **32** F4
Ningxiang *China* 28°15N 112°30E **35** C9
Ningyang *China* 35°47N 116°45E **32** G9
Ningyuan *China* 25°37N 111°57E **35** E8
Ninh Binh *Vietnam* 20°15N 105°55E **34** G5
Ninh Giang *Vietnam* 20°44N 106°24E **34** B6
Ninh Hoa *Vietnam* 12°30N 109°7E **38** F7
Ninh Ma *Vietnam* 12°48N 109°21E **38** F7
Ninove *Belgium* 50°51N 4°2E **15** D4
Nioaque *Brazil* 21°5S 55°50W **95** A4
Niobrara *U.S.A.* 42°45N 98°2W **80** D4
Niobrara → *U.S.A.* 42°46N 98°3W **80** D4
Nioro du Sahel *Mali* 15°15N 9°30W **52** E4
Niort *France* 46°19N 0°29W **20** C3
Nipani *India* 16°20N 74°25E **45** G2
Nipawin *Canada* 53°20N 104°0W **71** C8
Nipigon *Canada* 49°0N 88°17W **72** C2
Nipigon, L. *Canada* 49°50N 88°30W **72** C2
Nipishish L. *Canada* 54°12N 60°45N **73** B7
Nipissing, L. *Canada* 46°20N 80°0W **72** C4
Nipomo *U.S.A.* 35°3N 120°29W **79** K6
Nippon = Japan ■ *Asia* 36°0N 136°0E **29** G8
Nipton *U.S.A.* 35°28N 115°16W **79** K11
Niquelândia *Brazil* 14°33S 48°23W **93** F9
Nīr *Iran* 38°2N 47°59E **46** B5
Nīr → *India* 17°58N 75°8E **44** F2
Nirasaki *Japan* 35°42N 138°27E **29** G9
Nirmal *India* 19°3N 78°20E **44** E4
Nirmali *India* 26°20N 86°35E **43** F12
Niš *Serbia* 43°19N 21°58E **23** C9
Niša *Turkmenistan* 37°59N 58°11E **47** B8
Nişāb *Si. Arabia* 29°11N 44°43E **46** D5
Nişāb *Yemen* 14°25N 46°29E **49** E4
Nishino'omote *Japan* 30°43N 130°59E **29** J5

Nishiwaki *Japan* 34°59N 134°58E **29** G7
Niskibi → *Canada* 56°29N 88°9W **72** A2
Nisqually → *U.S.A.* 47°7N 122°42W **78** C4
Nissum Bredning *Denmark* 56°40N 8°20E **9** H13
Nistru = Dnister →
Europe 46°18N 30°17E **17** E16
Nisutlin → *Canada* 60°14N 132°34W **70** A2
Nitchequon *Canada* 53°10N 70°58W **73** B5
Nith → *Canada* 43°12N 80°23W **82** C4
Nith → *U.K.* 55°14N 3°33W **11** F5
Nitmiluk △ *Australia* 14°6S 132°15E **60** B5
Nitra *Slovakia* 48°19N 18°4E **17** D10
Nitra → *Slovakia* 47°46N 18°10E **17** E10
Niue ☑ *Pac. Oc.* 19°2S 169°54W **65** J11
Niulan Jiang → *China* 27°30N 103°5E **34** D5
Niut *Indonesia* 0°55N 109°54E **36** D4
Niutou Shan *China* 29°5N 121°59E **35** C13
Niuzhuang *China* 40°58N 122°28E **33** D12
Nivala *Finland* 63°56N 24°57E **8** E21
Nivelles *Belgium* 50°35N 4°20E **15** D4
Nivernais *France* 47°15N 3°30E **20** C5
Niverville *Canada* 49°36N 97°3W **71** D9
Niwas *India* 23°3N 80°26E **43** H9
Nixa *U.S.A.* 37°3N 93°18W **80** G7
Nixon *U.S.A.* 29°16N 97°46W **84** G6
Nizam Sagar *India* 18°10N 77°58E **44** E3
Nizamabad *India* 18°45N 78°7E **44** E4
Nizamghat *India* 28°20N 95°45E **41** E19
Nizhne-Kolymsk
Russia 68°34N 160°55E **27** C17
Nizhnekamsk *Russia* 55°38N 51°49E **18** C9
Nizhneudinsk *Russia* 54°54N 99°3E **27** D10
Nizhnevartovsk *Russia* 60°56N 76°38E **26** C8
Nizhniy Bestyakh
Russia 61°57N 129°54E **27** C13
Nizhniy Novgorod *Russia* 56°20N 44°0E **18** C7
Nizhniy Tagil *Russia* 57°55N 59°57E **18** C10
Nizhyn *Ukraine* 51°5N 31°55E **19** D5
Nizip *Turkey* 37°5N 37°50E **46** B3
Nízké Tatry *Slovakia* 48°55N 19°30E **17** D10
Nizwá *Oman* 22°56N 57°32E **49** C6
Njazidja = Grande Comore
Comoros Is. 11°35S 43°20E **55** a
Njombe *Tanzania* 9°20S 34°50E **54** F6
Nkandla *S. Africa* 28°37S 31°5E **57** C5
Nkawkaw *Ghana* 6°36N 0°49W **52** G5
Nkhotakota *Malawi* 12°56S 34°15E **55** G6
Nkongsamba *Cameroon* 4°55N 9°55E **54** D1
Nkurenkuru *Namibia* 17°42S 18°32E **56** A2
Nmai → *Myanmar* 25°30N 97°25E **34** F2
Noakhali *Bangla.* 22°48N 91°10E **41** H17
Nobel *Canada* 45°25N 80°6W **82** A4
Nobeoka *Japan* 32°36N 131°41E **29** H5
Noblesville *U.S.A.* 40°3N 86°1W **80** E10
Noboribetsu *Japan* 42°24N 141°6E **28** C10
Noccundra *Australia* 27°50S 142°36E **63** D3
Nocera Inferiore *Italy* 40°44N 14°38E **22** D6
Nocona *U.S.A.* 33°47N 97°44W **84** E6
Noda *Japan* 35°56N 139°52E **29** G9
Nogales *Mexico* 31°19N 110°56W **86** A2
Nogales *U.S.A.* 31°21N 110°56W **77** L8
Nōgata *Japan* 33°48N 130°44E **29** H5
Noggerup *Australia* 33°32S 116°5E **61** F2
Noginsk *Russia* 64°30N 90°50E **27** C10
Nogliki *Russia* 51°50N 143°10E **27** D15
Nogoa → *Australia* 23°40S 147°55E **62** C4
Nogoyá *Argentina* 32°24S 59°48W **94** C4
Nohar *India* 29°11N 74°49E **42** E6
Nohta *India* 23°40N 79°34E **43** H8
Noires, Mts. *France* 48°11N 3°40W **20** B2
Noirmoutier, Î. de *France* 46°58N 2°10W **20** C2
Nojane *Botswana* 23°15S 20°14E **56** B3
Nojima-Zaki *Japan* 34°54N 139°53E **29** G9
Nok Kundi *Pakistan* 28°50N 62°45E **40** E3
Nok Ta Phao, Ko *Thailand* 9°23N 99°40E **39** b
Nokaneng *Botswana* 19°40S 22°17E **56** A3
Nokia *Finland* 61°30N 23°30E **8** F20
Nokomis *Canada* 51°35N 105°0W **71** C8
Nokomis L. *Canada* 57°0N 103°0W **71** B8
Nola *C.A.R.* 3°35N 16°4E **54** D3
Noma Omuramba →
Namibia 18°52S 20°53E **56** A3
Nombre de Dios *Panama* 9°34N 79°28W **88** E4
Nome *U.S.A.* 30°N 165°25W **74** C6
Nomgon *Mongolia* 42°50N 105°8E **32** C3
Nomo-Zaki *Japan* 32°35N 129°44E **29** H4
Nomuka *Tonga* 20°17S 174°48W **59** c
Nomuka Group *Tonga* 20°20S 174°48W **59** c
Nonacho L. *Canada* 61°42N 109°40W **71** A7
Nonda *Australia* 20°40S 142°28E **62** C3
Nong Chang *Thailand* 15°23N 99°51E **38** E2
Nong Han Res. *Thailand* 17°11N 104°9E **38** D5
Nong Het *Laos* 19°29N 103°59E **38** C4
Nong Khai *Thailand* 17°50N 102°46E **38** D4
Nong'an *China* 44°25N 125°5E **33** B13
Nongoma *S. Africa* 27°58S 31°35E **57** C5
Nongsa *Indonesia* 1°11N 104°8E **39** d
Nonoava *Mexico* 27°28N 106°44W **86** B3
Nonsan *S. Korea* 36°12N 127°5E **33** F14
Noonamah *Australia* 12°40S 131°4E **60** B5
Noondie, L. *Australia* 28°30S 119°30E **61** E2
Noonkanbah ○
Australia 18°30S 124°50E **60** C3
Noord Brabant □ *Neths.* 51°40N 5°0E **15** C5
Noord Holland □ *Neths.* 52°30N 4°45E **15** B4
Noordbeveland *Neths.* 51°35N 3°50E **15** C3
Noordoostpolder *Neths.* 52°45N 5°45E **15** B5
Noordwijk *Neths.* 52°14N 4°26E **15** B4
Noosa Heads *Australia* 26°25S 153°9E **63** D5
Nootka I. *Canada* 49°32N 126°42W **70** D3
Nopiming △ *Canada* 50°30N 95°37W **71** C9
Noralee *Canada* 53°59N 126°26W **70** C3
Noranda = Rouyn-Noranda
Canada 48°20N 79°0W **72** C4
Norco *U.S.A.* 33°56N 117°33W **79** M9
Nord-Ostsee-Kanal
Germany 54°12N 9°32E **16** A5
Nordaustlandet *Svalbard* 79°14N 23°0E **4** B9
Nordegg *Canada* 52°29N 116°5W **70** C5
Norderney *Germany* 53°42N 7°9E **16** B4

Norderstedt *Germany* 53°42N 10°1E **16** B5
Nordfjord *Norway* 61°55N 5°30E **8** F11
Nordfriesische Inseln
Germany 54°40N 8°20E **16** A5
Nordhausen *Germany* 51°30N 10°47E **16** C6
Nordkapp *Norway* 71°10N 25°50E **8** A21
Nordkapp *Svalbard* 80°31N 20°0E **4** A9
Nordkinn = Kinnarodden
Norway 70°55N 27°40E **8** A22
Nordkinn *Norway* 71°8N 27°40E **8** A22
Nordkinnhalvøya
Norway 70°55N 27°40E **8** A22
Nordrhein-Westfalen □
Germany 51°45N 7°30E **16** C4
Nordvik *Russia* 74°2N 111°32E **27** B12
Nore → *Ireland* 52°25N 6°58W **10** D4
Noreland *Canada* 44°43N 78°48W **82** B6
Norfolk = Simcoe
Canada 42°50N 80°23W **82** D4
Norfolk *N.Y., U.S.A.* 44°48N 74°59W **83** B10
Norfolk *Nebr., U.S.A.* 42°2N 97°25W **80** D5
Norfolk *Va., U.S.A.* 36°50N 76°17W **81** G15
Norfolk □ *U.K.* 52°39N 0°54E **13** E8
Norfolk Broads △ *U.K.* 52°45N 1°30E **13** E9
Norfolk I. *Pac. Oc.* 28°58S 168°3E **58** D9
Norfolk Ridge *Pac. Oc.* 29°0S 168°0E **64** K8
Norfork L. *U.S.A.* 36°15N 92°14W **84** C8
Norge = Norway ■ *Europe* 63°0N 11°0E **8** E14
Norilsk *Russia* 69°20N 88°6E **27** C9
Norma, Mt. *Australia* 20°55S 140°42E **62** C3
Normal *U.S.A.* 40°31N 88°59W **80** E9
Norman *U.S.A.* 35°13N 97°26W **84** H6
Norman → *Australia* 19°18S 141°51E **62** B3
Norman Wells *Canada* 65°17N 126°51W **68** D6
Normanby → *Australia* 14°23S 144°10E **62** A3
Normandie *France* 48°45N 0°10E **20** B4
Normandin *Canada* 48°49N 72°31W **72** C5
Normandy = Normandie
France 48°45N 0°10E **20** B4
Normanhurst, Mt.
Australia 25°4S 122°30E **61** E3
Normanton *Australia* 17°40S 141°10E **62** B3
Normétal *Canada* 49°0N 79°22W **72** C4
Norquay *Canada* 51°53N 102°5W **71** C8
Norquinco *Argentina* 41°51S 70°55W **96** E2
Norrbottens län □ *Sweden* 66°50N 20°0E **8** C19
Norris Point *Canada* 49°31N 57°53W **73** C8
Norristown *U.S.A.* 40°7N 75°21W **83** F9
Norrköping *Sweden* 58°37N 16°11E **9** G17
Norrland *Sweden* 62°15N 15°45E **8** E16
Norrtälje *Sweden* 59°46N 18°42E **9** G18
Norseman *Australia* 32°8S 121°43E **61** F3
Norsk *Russia* 52°30N 130°5E **27** D14
Norte, Serra do *Brazil* 11°20S 59°0W **92** F7
North, C. *Canada* 47°2N 60°20W **73** C7
North Adams *U.S.A.* 42°42N 73°7W **83** D11
North America 40°0N 100°0W **66** F10
North Andaman I. *India* 13°15N 92°55E **45** H11
North Arm *Canada* 62°0N 114°30W **70** A5
North Augusta *U.S.A.* 33°30N 81°59W **85** E14
North Australian Basin
Ind. Oc. 14°30S 116°30E **64** J3
North Ayrshire □ *U.K.* 55°45N 4°44W **11** F4
North Bass I. *U.S.A.* 41°40N 82°56W **82** E2
North Battleford *Canada* 52°50N 108°17W **71** C7
North Bay *Canada* 46°20N 79°30W **72** C4
North Belcher Is. *Canada* 56°50N 79°50W **72** A4
North Bend *Oreg.,
U.S.A.* 43°24N 124°14W **76** E1
North Bend *Pa., U.S.A.* 41°20N 77°42W **82** E7
North Bend *Wash.,
U.S.A.* 47°30N 121°47W **78** C5
North Bennington
U.S.A. 42°56N 73°15W **83** D11
North Berwick *U.K.* 56°4N 2°42W **11** E6
North Berwick *U.S.A.* 43°18N 70°44W **83** C14
North Brother I. *India* 10°59N 92°40E **45** J11
North Bruce *Canada* 44°22N 81°26W **82** B3
North C. *Canada* 47°5N 64°0W **73** C7
North C. *N.Z.* 34°23S 173°4E **59** A4
North Canadian →
U.S.A. 35°22N 95°37W **84** D7
North Canton *U.S.A.* 40°53N 81°24W **82** F3
North Cape = Nordkapp
Norway 71°10N 25°50E **8** A21
North Caribou L. *Canada* 52°50N 90°40W **72** B1
North Carolina □ *U.S.A.* 35°30N 80°0W **85** D15
North Cascades △
U.S.A. 48°45N 121°10W **76** B3
North Channel *Canada* 46°0N 83°0W **72** C3
North Channel *U.K.* 55°13N 5°52W **11** F3
North Charleston
U.S.A. 32°53N 79°58W **85** E15
North Chicago *U.S.A.* 42°19N 87°51W **80** D10
North Collins *U.S.A.* 42°35N 78°56W **82** D6
North Creek *U.S.A.* 43°42N 73°59W **83** C11
North Dakota □ *U.S.A.* 47°30N 100°15W **80** B4
North Downs *U.K.* 51°19N 0°21E **13** F8
North East □ *Botswana* 20°45S 27°30E **57** B4
North East Frontier Agency =
Arunachal Pradesh □
India 28°0N 95°0E **41** F19
North East Lincolnshire □
U.K. 53°34N 0°2W **12** D7
North Esk → *U.K.* 56°46N 2°24W **11** E6
North European Plain
Europe 55°0N 25°0E **6** D10
North Foreland *U.K.* 51°22N 1°28E **13** F9
North Fork *U.S.A.* 37°14N 119°21W **78** H7
North Fork American →
U.S.A. 38°57N 120°59W **78** G5
North Fork Feather →
U.S.A. 38°33N 121°30W **78** F5
North Fork Grand →
U.S.A. 45°47N 102°16W **80** C2
North Fork Red →
U.S.A. 34°24N 99°14W **84** D5

North Hd. *Australia* 30°14S 114°59E **61** F1
North Henik L. *Canada* 61°45N 97°40W **71** A9
North Highlands *U.S.A.* 38°40N 121°23W **78** G5
North I. *India* 10°8N 72°20E **45** J1
North I. *N.Z.* 38°0S 175°0E **59** C5
North I. *Seychelles* 4°25S 55°13E **55** b
North Kingsville *U.S.A.* 41°54N 80°42W **82** E4
North Knife → *Canada* 58°53N 94°45W **71** B10
North Koel → *India* 24°45N 83°50E **43** G10
North Korea ■ *Asia* 40°0N 127°0E **33** E14
North Lakhimpur *India* 27°14N 94°7E **41** F19
North Lanarkshire □
U.K. 55°52N 3°56W **11** F5
North Lincolnshire □
U.K. 53°36N 0°30W **12** D7
North Little Rock *U.S.A.* 34°45N 92°16W **84** D8
North Loup → *U.S.A.* 41°17N 98°24W **80** E4
North Magnetic Pole
Arctic 85°9N 149°0W **4** A1
North Mankato *U.S.A.* 44°10N 94°2W **80** C6
North Minch *U.K.* 58°5N 5°55W **11** C3
North Moose L. *Canada* 54°4N 100°12W **71** C8
North Myrtle Beach
U.S.A. 33°48N 78°42W **85** E15
North Nahanni →
Canada 62°15N 123°20W **70** A4
North Olmsted *U.S.A.* 41°25N 81°56W **82** E3
North Ossetia-Alaniya □
Russia 43°30N 44°30E **19** F7
North Pagai, I. = Pagai Utara,
Pulau *Indonesia* 2°35S 100°0E **36** E2
North Palisade *U.S.A.* 37°6N 118°31W **78** H8
North Paravur *India* 10°13N 76°14E **45** J3
North Platte *U.S.A.* 41°8N 100°46W **80** E3
North Platte → *U.S.A.* 41°7N 100°42W **80** E3
North Pole *Arctic* 90°0N 0°0 **4** A
North Portal *Canada* 49°0N 102°33W **71** D8
North Powder *U.S.A.* 45°2N 117°55W **76** D5
North Pt. *Barbados* 13°20N 59°37W **89** g
North Pt. *Trin. & Tob.* 11°21N 60°31W **93** J16
North Pt. *U.S.A.* 45°2N 83°16W **82** A1
North Reef I. *India* 13°5N 92°43E **45** H11
North Rhine Westphalia =
Nordrhein-Westfalen □
Germany 51°45N 7°30E **16** C4
North River *Canada* 53°49N 57°6W **73** B8
North Rona *Atl. Oc.* 59°7N 5°49W **14** B4
North Ronaldsay *U.K.* 59°22N 2°26W **11** B6
North Saskatchewan →
Canada 53°15N 105°5W **71** C7
North Sea *Europe* 56°0N 4°0E **6** D6
North Seal → *Canada* 58°50N 98°7W **71** B9
North Sentinel I. *India* 11°33N 92°15E **45** J11
North Slope ☆ *U.S.A.* 69°15N 152°0W **74** B9
North Somerset □ *U.K.* 51°24N 2°45W **13** F5
North Sydney *Canada* 46°12N 60°15W **73** C7
North Syracuse *U.S.A.* 43°8N 76°7W **83** C8
North Taranaki Bight
N.Z. 38°50S 174°15E **59** C5
North Thompson →
Canada 50°40N 120°20W **70** C4
North Tonawanda *U.S.A.* 43°2N 78°53W **82** C6
North Troy *U.S.A.* 45°0N 72°24W **83** B12
North Twin I. *Canada* 53°20N 80°0W **72** B4
North Tyne → *U.K.* 55°0N 2°8W **12** B5
North Uist *U.K.* 57°40N 7°15W **11** D1
North Vancouver *Canada* 49°19N 123°4W **78** A3
North Vernon *U.S.A.* 39°0N 85°38W **81** F11
North Wabasca L.
Canada 56°0N 113°55W **70** B6
North Walsham *U.K.* 52°50N 1°22E **12** E9
North West = Severo-Zapadnyy □
Russia 65°0N 40°0E **26** C4
North West □ *Botswana* 19°0S 22°30E **56** A3
North-West □ *S. Africa* 27°0S 25°0E **56** C4
North West C. *Australia* 21°45S 114°9E **60** D1
North West Christmas I. Ridge
Pac. Oc. 6°30N 165°0W **65** F11
North West Frontier = Khyber
Pakhtunkhwa □
Pakistan 34°0N 72°0E **42** C5
North West Highlands
U.K. 57°33N 4°58W **11** D4
North West River *Canada* 53°30N 60°10W **73** B7
North Wildwood *U.S.A.* 39°0N 74°48W **81** F16
North York Moors *U.K.* 54°23N 0°53W **12** C7
North York Moors △
U.K. 54°27N 0°51W **12** C7
North Yorkshire □ *U.K.* 54°15N 1°25W **12** C6
Northallerton *U.K.* 54°20N 1°26W **12** C6
Northam *Australia* 31°35S 116°42E **61** F2
Northam *S. Africa* 24°56S 27°18E **56** B4
Northampton *Australia* 28°27S 114°33E **61** E1
Northampton *U.K.* 52°15N 0°53W **13** E7
Northampton *Mass.,
U.S.A.* 42°19N 72°38W **83** D12
Northampton *Pa., U.S.A.* 40°41N 75°30W **83** F9
Northamptonshire □
U.K. 52°16N 0°55W **13** E7
Northbridge *U.S.A.* 42°9N 71°39W **83** D13
Northbrook *Canada* 44°44N 77°9W **82** B7
Northcliffe *Australia* 34°39S 116°7E **61** F2
Northeast Pacific Basin
Pac. Oc. 32°0N 145°0W **65** D13
Northeast Providence Channel
W. Indies 26°0N 76°0W **88** A4
Northern = Limpopo □
S. Africa 24°5S 29°0E **57** B4
Northern Areas = Gilgit-
Baltistan □ *Pakistan* 36°30N 73°0E **43** A5
Northern Cape □ *S. Africa* 30°0S 20°0E **56** C3
Northern Circars *India* 17°30N 82°30E **44** F6
Northern Dvina = Dvina,
Severnaya → *Russia* 64°32N 40°30E **18** B7
Northern Indian L.
Canada 57°20N 97°20W **71** B9
Northern Ireland □ *U.K.* 54°45N 7°0W **10** B5
Northern Light L. *Canada* 48°15N 90°39W **72** C1
Northern Marianas ☑
Pac. Oc. 17°0N 145°0E **64** F6

Northern Province □
  S. Africa 24°0S 29°0E 57 B4
Northern Range
  Trin. & Tob. 10°46N 61°15W 93 K15
Northern Sporades = Vóreioi
  Sporades Greece 39°15N 23°30E 23 E10
Northern Territory □
  Australia 20°0S 133°0E 60 D5
Northfield Minn., U.S.A. 44°27N 93°9W 80 C7
Northfield Vt., U.S.A. 44°9N 72°40W 83 B12
Northgate Canada 49°0N 102°16W 71 D8
Northland □ N.Z. 35°30S 173°30E 59 A4
Northome U.S.A. 47°52N 94°17W 80 B6
Northport Ala., U.S.A. 33°14N 87°35W 85 E11
Northport N.Y., U.S.A. 42°19N 73°22W 83 D11
Northport Wash., U.S.A. 48°55N 117°48W 76 B5
Northumberland □ U.K. 55°12N 2°0W 12 B6
Northumberland, C.
  Australia 38°5S 140°40E 63 F3
Northumberland Is.
  Australia 21°30S 149°50E 62 C4
Northumberland Str.
  Canada 46°20N 64°0W 73 C7
Northville Canada 43°10N 81°56W 82 C3
Northville U.S.A. 43°13N 74°11W 83 C10
Northwest Pacific Basin
  Pac. Oc. 32°0N 165°0E 64 D8
Northwest Providence Channel
  W. Indies 26°0N 78°0W 88 A4
Northwest Territories □
  Canada 63°0N 118°0W 68 E8
Northwich U.K. 53°15N 2°31W 12 D5
Northwood Iowa, U.S.A. 43°27N 93°13W 80 D7
Northwood N. Dak.,
  U.S.A. 47°44N 97°34W 80 B5
Norton Calif., U.S.A. 39°50N 99°53W 80 F4
Norton Sd. U.S.A. 63°50N 164°0W 74 C7
Norwalk Calif., U.S.A. 33°54N 118°4W 79 M8
Norwalk Conn., U.S.A. 41°7N 73°22W 83 E11
Norwalk Iowa, U.S.A. 41°29N 93°41W 80 E7
Norwalk Ohio, U.S.A. 41°15N 82°37W 82 E2
Norway Maine, U.S.A. 44°13N 70°32W 81 C18
Norway Mich., U.S.A. 45°47N 87°55W 80 C10
Norway ■ Europe 63°0N 11°0E 8 E14
Norway House Canada 53°59N 97°50W 71 C9
Norwegian B. Canada 77°30N 90°0W 69 B14
Norwegian Basin Atl. Oc. 68°0N 2°0W 4 C7
Norwegian Sea Atl. Oc. 66°0N 1°0E 6 B6
Norwich Canada 42°59N 80°36W 82 D4
Norwich U.K. 52°38N 1°18E 13 E9
Norwich Conn., U.S.A. 41°31N 72°5W 83 E12
Norwich N.Y., U.S.A. 42°32N 75°32W 83 D9
Norwood Canada 44°23N 77°59W 82 B7
Norwood U.S.A. 44°45N 95°30W 73 C8
Nosappu-Misaki Japan 45°26N 141°39E 28 C12
Noshiro Japan 40°12N 140°0E 28 D10
Noṣratābād Iran 29°55N 60°0E 47 D8
Noss Hd. U.K. 58°28N 3°3W 11 C5
Nossob → S. Africa 26°55S 20°45E 56 C3
Nosy Varika Madag. 20°35S 48°32E 55 J9
Noteć → Poland 52°44N 15°26E 16 B8
Notikewin → Canada 57°2N 117°38W 70 B5
Noto-Hantō Japan 37°15N 136°40E 29 F8
Notodden Norway 59°35N 9°17E 9 G13
Notre Dame B. Canada 49°45N 55°30W 73 C8
Notre-Dame-de-Koartac =
  Quaqtaq Canada 60°55N 69°40W 69 E18
Notre-Dame-des-Bois
  Canada 45°24N 71°4W 83 A13
Notre-Dame-d'Ivugivic = Ivujivik
  Canada 62°24N 77°55W 69 E16
Notre-Dame-du-Nord
  Canada 47°36N 79°30W 72 C4
Nottawasaga B. Canada 44°35N 80°15W 82 B4
Nottaway → Canada 51°22N 78°55W 72 B4
Nottingham U.K. 52°58N 1°10W 12 E6
Nottingham, City of □
  U.K. 52°58N 1°10W 12 E6
Nottingham I. Canada 63°20N 77°55W 69 E16
Nottinghamshire □ U.K. 53°10N 1°3W 12 D6
Nottoway → U.S.A. 36°33N 76°55W 81 G15
Notwane → Botswana 23°35S 26°58E 56 B4
Nouâdhibou Mauritania 20°54N 17°0W 52 D2
Nouâdhibou, Râs
  Mauritania 20°50N 17°0W 52 D2
Nouakchott Mauritania 18°9N 15°58W 52 E2
Nouméa N. Cal. 22°17S 166°30E 58 D9
Noupoort S. Africa 31°10S 24°57E 56 D3
Nouveau Comptoir = Wemindji
  Canada 53°0N 78°49W 72 B4
Nouvelle Amsterdam, Î.
  Ind. Oc. 38°30S 77°30E 3 F13
Nouvelle-Calédonie = New
  Caledonia ☑ Pac. Oc. 21°0S 165°0E 58 D9
Nova Esperança Brazil 23°8S 52°24W 95 A5
Nova Friburgo Brazil 22°16S 42°30W 95 A7
Nova Iguaçu Brazil 22°45S 43°28W 95 A7
Nova Iorque Brazil 7°0S 44°5W 93 E10
Nova Lamego
  Guinea-Biss. 12°19N 14°11W 52 F3
Nova Mambone Mozam. 21°0S 35°3E 57 B6
Nova Scotia □ Canada 45°10N 63°0W 73 C7
Nova Sofala Mozam. 20°7S 34°42E 57 C5
Nova Venécia Brazil 18°45S 40°24W 93 G10
Nova Zagora Bulgaria 42°32N 26°1E 23 C11
Novar Italy 45°28N 8°38E 20 D8
Novato U.S.A. 38°6N 122°35W 78 G4
Novaya Ladoga Russia 60°7N 32°16E 18 B5
Novaya Lyalya Russia 59°4N 60°45E 18 C11
Novaya Sibir, Ostrov
  Russia 75°10N 150°0E 27 B16
Novaya Zemlya Russia 75°0N 56°0E 26 B6
Nové Zámky Slovakia 48°2N 18°8E 17 D10
Novgorod = Velikiy Novgorod
  Russia 58°30N 31°25E 18 C5
Novgorod-Severskiy = Novhorod-
  Siverskyy Ukraine 52°2N 33°10E 18 D5
Novhorod-Siverskyy
  Ukraine 52°2N 33°10E 18 D5

Novi Lígure Italy 44°46N 8°47E 20 D8
Novi Pazar Serbia 43°12N 20°28E 23 C9
Novi Sad Serbia 45°18N 19°52E 23 B8
Novo Hamburgo Brazil 29°37S 51°7W 95 B5
Novo Mesto Slovenia 45°47N 15°12E 22 B6
Novoaltaysk Russia 53°30N 84°0E 26 D9
Novocherkassk Russia 47°27N 40°15E 19 E7
Novodvinsk Russia 64°25N 40°42E 18 B7
Novogrudok = Navahrudak
  Belarus 53°40N 25°50E 17 B13
Novohrad-Volynskyy
  Ukraine 50°34N 27°35E 17 C14
Novokachalinsk Russia 45°5N 132°0E 28 B5
Novokuybyshevsk Russia 53°7N 49°58E 18 D8
Novokuznetsk Russia 53°45N 87°10E 26 D9
Novolazarevskaya Antarctica 71°0S 12°0E 5 D3
Novomoskovsk Russia 54°5N 38°15E 18 D6
Novorossiysk Russia 44°43N 37°46E 19 F6
Novorybnoye Russia 72°50N 105°50E 27 B11
Novoselytsya Ukraine 48°14N 26°15E 17 D14
Novoshakhtinsk Russia 47°46N 39°58E 19 E6
Novosibirsk Russia 55°0N 83°5E 26 D9
Novosibirskiye Ostrova
  Russia 75°0N 142°0E 27 B15
Novotroitsk Russia 51°10N 58°15E 18 D10
Novouzensk Russia 50°32N 48°17E 19 D8
Novovolynsk Ukraine 50°45N 24°4E 17 C13
Novská Croatia 45°19N 17°0E 22 B7
Novvy Bor Russia 66°43N 52°19E 18 A9
Novyy Port Russia 67°40N 72°30E 26 C8
Novyy Urengoy Russia 65°48N 76°52E 26 C8
Nowa Sól Poland 51°48N 15°44E 16 C8
Nowata U.S.A. 36°42N 95°38W 84 C7
Nowbarān Iran 35°8N 49°42E 47 C6
Nowghāb Iran 33°53N 59°4E 47 C8
Nowgong = Nagaon
  India 26°20N 92°50E 41 F18
Nowgong India 25°4N 79°27E 43 G8
Nowra Australia 34°53S 150°35E 63 E5
Nowrangapur India 19°14N 82°33E 44 E6
Nowshera Pakistan 34°0N 72°0E 40 C8
Nowy Sącz Poland 49°40N 20°41E 17 D11
Nowy Targ Poland 49°29N 20°2E 17 D11
Nowy Tomyśl Poland 52°19N 16°10E 16 B9
Noxen U.S.A. 41°25N 76°4W 83 E8
Noyabr'sk Russia 64°34N 76°21E 26 C8
Noyon France 49°34N 2°59E 20 B5
Noyon Mongolia 43°2N 102°4E 32 C2
Nsanje Malawi 16°55S 35°12E 55 H7
Nsawam Ghana 5°50N 0°24W 52 G5
Ntaria = Australia 24°0S 132°41E 60 D5
Nu Jiang → China 29°58N 97°25E 34 E2
Nu Shan China 26°0N 99°20E 34 E2
Nuba Mts. = Nubah, Jibalan
  Sudan 12°0N 31°0E 53 F12
Nubah, Jibalan Sudan 12°0N 31°0E 53 F12
Nubia Africa 21°0N 32°0E 50 D7
Nubian Desert = Nûbîya, Es Sahrâ
  en Sudan 21°30N 33°30E 53 D12
Nûbîya, Es Sahrâ en
  Sudan 21°30N 33°30E 53 D12
Nuboai Indonesia 2°10S 136°30E 37 E9
Nubra → India 34°35N 77°35E 43 B7
Nueces → U.S.A. 27°51N 97°30W 84 H6
Nueltin L. Canada 60°30N 99°30W 71 A9
Nuestra Señora del Rosario de
  Caá-Catí Argentina 27°45S 57°36W 94 B4
Nueva Ciudad Guerrero
  Mexico 26°34N 99°12W 87 B5
Nueva Gerona Cuba 21°53N 82°49W 88 B3
Nueva Palmira Uruguay 33°52S 58°20W 94 C4
Nueva Rosita Mexico 27°57N 101°13W 86 B4
Nueva San Salvador
  El Salv. 13°40N 89°18W 88 D2
Nuéve de Julio Argentina 35°30S 61°0W 94 D3
Nuevitas Cuba 21°30N 77°20W 88 B4
Nuevo, G. Argentina 43°0S 64°30W 96 E4
Nuevo Casas Grandes
  Mexico 30°25N 107°55W 86 A3
Nuevo Laredo Mexico 27°30N 99°31W 87 B5
Nuevo León □ Mexico 25°20N 100°0W 86 C5
Nuevo Rocafuerte
  Ecuador 0°55S 75°27W 92 D3
Nugget Pt. N.Z. 46°27S 169°50E 59 G2
Nuhaka N.Z. 39°3S 177°45E 59 C6
Nukey Bluff Australia 32°26S 135°29E 63 E2
Nukhayb Iraq 32°4N 42°3E 46 C4
Nuku Hiva
  French Polynesia 8°54S 140°6W 65 H13
Nuku'alofa Tonga 21°10S 175°12W 59 c
Nukus Uzbekistan 42°27N 59°41E 26 E6
Nulato U.S.A. 64°43N 158°6W 74 C8
Nullagine Australia 21°53S 120°7E 60 D3
Nullagine → Australia 21°20S 120°20E 60 D3
Nullarbor Australia 31°28S 130°55E 61 F5
Nullarbor △ Australia 32°39S 130°0E 61 F2
Nullarbor Plain Australia 31°10S 129°0E 61 F4
Numalla, L. Australia 28°43S 144°20E 63 D3
Numan Nigeria 9°29N 12°3E 53 G8
Numata Japan 36°45N 139°4E 29 F9
Numaykoos Lake △
  Canada 57°52N 95°58W 71 B9
Numazu Japan 35°7N 138°51E 29 G9
Numbulwar Australia 14°15S 135°45E 62 A2
Numfoor Indonesia 1°0S 134°50E 37 E8
Numurkah Australia 36°5S 145°26E 63 F4
Nunaksaluk I. Canada 55°49N 60°20W 73 A7
Nunap Isua Greenland 59°48N 43°55W 66 D15
Nunatsiavut Canada 55°30N 62°0W 73 A7
Nunavik Canada 56°30N 71°0W 69 F17
Nunavik Greenland 66°0N 50°0W 69 C21
Nunavut □ Canada 66°0N 85°0W 69 D15
Nunda U.S.A. 42°35N 77°56W 82 D7
Nuneaton U.K. 52°32N 1°27W 13 E6
Nungarin Australia 31°12S 118°6E 61 F2
Nunivak I. U.S.A. 60°10N 166°30W 74 C6
Nunkun India 33°57N 76°2E 43 C7
Núoro Italy 40°20N 9°20E 22 D3
Nuozhadu Dam China 22°39N 100°25E 34 F3

Nūr Iran 36°33N 52°1E 47 B7
Nūrābād Hormozgān, Iran 27°47N 57°12E 47 E8
Nūrābād Lorestān, Iran 34°4N 47°58E 46 C5
Nuremberg = Nürnberg
  Germany 49°27N 11°3E 16 D6
Nuri Mexico 28°5N 109°22W 86 B3
Nuriootpa Australia 34°27S 139°0E 63 E2
Nuristan □ Afghan. 35°20N 71°0E 40 B7
Nurmes Finland 63°33N 29°10E 8 E23
Nürnberg Germany 49°27N 11°3E 16 D6
Nurpur Pakistan 31°53N 71°54E 42 D4
Nurran, L. = Terewah, L.
  Australia 29°52S 147°35E 63 D4
Nurrari Lakes Australia 29°1S 130°5E 61 E5
Nusa Dua Indonesia 8°48S 115°14E 37 K18
Nusa Tenggara Barat □
  Indonesia 8°50S 117°30E 36 F5
Nusa Tenggara Timur □
  Indonesia 9°30S 122°0E 37 F6
Nusaybin Turkey 37°3N 41°10E 19 G7
Nuşeirat Gaza Strip 31°27N 34°24E 48 D3
Nushki Pakistan 29°35N 66°0E 42 E2
Nuuk Greenland 64°10N 51°35W 67 C14
Nuupere, Pte. Moorea 17°36S 149°47W 59 d
Nuwakot Nepal 28°10N 83°55E 43 E10
Nuwara Eliya Sri Lanka 6°58N 80°48E 45 L5
Nuweiba' Egypt 28°59N 34°39E 46 D2
Nuwerus S. Africa 31°8S 18°24E 56 D2
Nuweveldberge S. Africa 32°10S 21°45E 56 E3
Nuyts, Pt. Australia 35°4S 116°38E 61 G2
Nuyts Arch. Australia 32°35S 133°20E 63 E1
Nxai Pan △ Botswana 19°50S 24°46E 56 A3
Nxaunxau Botswana 18°57S 21°4E 56 A3
Nyabing Australia 33°33S 118°9E 61 F2
Nyack U.S.A. 41°5N 73°55W 83 E11
Nyagan Russia 62°30N 65°38E 26 C7
Nyahururu Kenya 0°2N 36°27E 54 D7
Nyainqêntanglha Shan
  China 30°0N 90°0E 30 F7
Nyâlâ Sudan 12°2N 24°58E 53 F10
Nyalam China 28°32N 86°4E 30 F6
Nyandoma Russia 61°40N 40°12E 18 B7
Nyangana Namibia 18°0S 20°40E 56 A3
Nyasa, L. = Malawi, L.
  Africa 12°0S 34°30E 55 G6
Nyasvizh Belarus 53°14N 26°38E 17 B14
Nyaungdon = Yandoon
  Myanmar 17°0N 95°40E 41 L19
Nyazepetrovsk Russia 56°3N 59°36E 18 C10
Nybro Sweden 56°44N 15°55E 9 H16
Nyda Russia 66°40N 72°58E 26 C8
Nyeboe Land Greenland 82°0N 57°0W 69 A20
Nyingchi China 29°32N 94°25E 30 F7
Nyíregyháza Hungary 47°58N 21°47E 17 E11
Nykarleby = Uusikaarlepyy
  Finland 63°32N 22°31E 8 E20
Nykøbing Nordjylland,
  Denmark 56°48N 8°51E 9 H13
Nykøbing Sjælland,
  Denmark 54°56N 11°52E 9 J14
Nykøbing Sjælland,
  Denmark 55°55N 11°40E 9 J14
Nyköping Sweden 58°45N 17°1E 9 G17
Nylstroom = Modimolle
  S. Africa 24°42S 28°22E 57 B4
Nymagee Australia 32°7S 146°20E 63 E4
Nymboida △ Australia 29°38S 152°26E 63 D5
Nynäshamn Sweden 58°54N 17°57E 9 G17
Nyngan Australia 31°30S 147°8E 63 E4
Nyoma Rap India 33°10N 78°40E 43 C8
Nyoman = Nemunas →
  Lithuania 55°25N 21°10E 9 J19
Nysa Poland 50°30N 17°22E 17 C9
Nysa → Europe 52°4N 14°46E 16 B8
Nyslott = Savonlinna
  Finland 61°52N 28°53E 8 F23
Nyssa U.S.A. 43°53N 117°0W 76 E5
Nystad = Uusikaupunki
  Finland 60°47N 21°25E 8 F19
Nyunzu
  Dem. Rep. of the Congo 5°57S 27°58E 54 F5
Nyurba Russia 63°17N 118°28E 27 C12
Nzega Tanzania 4°10S 33°12E 54 C6
Nzérékoré Guinea 7°49N 8°48W 52 G4
Nzeto Angola 7°10S 12°52E 54 F2
Nzwani = Anjouan
  Comoros Is. 12°15S 44°20E 55 a

O

O Le Pupū Pu'e △ Samoa 13°59S 171°43W 59 b
Ō-Shima Hokkaidō, Japan 41°30N 139°22E 28 D9
Ō-Shima Shizuoka, Japan 34°44N 139°24E 29 G9
O.R. Tambo Int. ✈ (JNB)
  S. Africa 26°8S 28°15E 57 C4
Oa, Mull of U.K. 55°35N 6°20W 11 F2
Oacoma U.S.A. 43°48N 99°24W 80 D4
Oahe, L. U.S.A. 44°27N 100°24W 80 C3
Oahe Dam U.S.A. 44°27N 100°24W 80 C3
O'ahu U.S.A. 21°28N 157°58W 75 L8
Oak Harbor U.S.A. 48°18N 122°39W 78 B4
Oak Hill U.S.A. 37°59N 81°9W 81 G13
Oak Island U.S.A. 33°55N 78°10W 85 E15
Oak Ridge U.S.A. 36°1N 84°16W 85 C12
Oak View U.S.A. 34°24N 119°18W 79 L7
Oakan-Dake Japan 43°27N 144°10E 28 C12
Oakdale Calif., U.S.A. 37°46N 120°51W 78 H6
Oakdale La., U.S.A. 30°49N 92°40W 84 F8
Oakes U.S.A. 46°8N 98°6W 80 B4
Oakey Australia 27°25S 151°43E 63 D5
Oakfield U.S.A. 43°4N 78°16W 82 C6
Oakham U.K. 52°40N 0°43W 13 E7
Oakhurst U.S.A. 37°19N 119°40W 78 H7
Oakland U.S.A. 37°48N 122°16W 78 H4
Oakley Idaho, U.S.A. 42°15N 113°53W 76 E7
Oakley Kans., U.S.A. 39°8N 100°51W 80 F3
Oakover → Australia 21°0S 120°40E 60 D3

Oakridge U.S.A. 43°45N 122°28W 76 E2
Oakville Canada 43°27N 79°41W 82 C5
Oakville U.S.A. 46°51N 123°14W 78 D3
Oamaru N.Z. 45°5S 170°59E 59 F3
Oasis Calif., U.S.A. 37°29N 117°55W 78 H9
Oasis Calif., U.S.A. 33°28N 116°6W 79 M10
Oates Land Antarctica 69°0S 160°0E 5 C11
Oatman U.S.A. 35°1N 114°19W 79 K12
Oaxaca Mexico 17°3N 96°43W 87 D5
Oaxaca □ Mexico 17°0N 96°30W 87 D5
Ob → Russia 66°45N 69°30E 26 C7
Oba Canada 49°4N 84°7W 72 C3
Obama Japan 35°30N 135°45E 29 G7
Oban U.K. 56°25N 5°29W 11 E3
Obbia = Hobyo Somalia 5°25N 48°30E 49 F4
Oberá Argentina 27°21S 55°2W 95 B4
Oberhausen Germany 51°28N 6°51E 16 C4
Oberlin Kans., U.S.A. 39°49N 100°32W 80 F3
Oberlin La., U.S.A. 30°37N 92°46W 84 F8
Oberlin Ohio, U.S.A. 41°18N 82°13W 82 E2
Oberon Australia 33°45S 149°52E 63 E4
Obi, Kepulauan Indonesia 1°23S 127°45E 37 E7
Óbidos Brazil 1°50S 55°30W 92 D7
Obihiro Japan 42°56N 143°12E 28 C11
Obilatu Indonesia 1°25S 127°20E 37 E7
Obluchye Russia 49°1N 131°4E 27 E14
Obo C.A.R. 5°20N 26°32E 54 C5
Oboyan Russia 51°15N 36°21E 26 D4
Obozerskaya = Obozerskiy
  Russia 63°34N 40°21E 18 B7
Obozerskiy Russia 63°34N 40°21E 18 B7
Observatory Inlet
  Canada 55°10N 129°54W 70 B3
Obshchi Syrt Russia 52°0N 53°0E 6 E16
Obskaya Guba Russia 69°0N 73°0E 26 C8
Obuasi Ghana 6°17N 1°40W 52 G5
Ocala U.S.A. 29°11N 82°8W 85 G13
Ocampo Chihuahua,
  Mexico 28°11N 108°23W 86 B3
Ocampo Tamaulipas,
  Mexico 22°50N 99°20W 87 C5
Ocaña Spain 39°55N 3°30W 21 C4
Occidental, Cordillera
  Colombia 5°0N 76°0W 92 C3
Occidental, Grand Erg
  Algeria 30°20N 1°0E 52 B6
Ocean City Md., U.S.A. 38°20N 75°5W 81 F16
Ocean City N.J., U.S.A. 39°17N 74°35W 81 F16
Ocean City Wash., U.S.A. 47°4N 124°10W 78 C2
Ocean Falls Canada 52°18N 127°48W 70 C3
Ocean I. = Banaba
  Kiribati 0°45S 169°50E 64 H8
Ocean Park U.S.A. 46°30N 124°3W 78 D2
Oceano U.S.A. 35°6N 120°37W 79 K6
Oceanport U.S.A. 40°19N 74°3W 83 F10
Oceanside U.S.A. 33°12N 117°23W 79 M9
Ochil Hills U.K. 56°14N 3°40W 11 E5
Ocho Rios Jamaica 18°24N 77°6W 88 a
Ocilla U.S.A. 31°36N 83°15W 85 F13
Ocmulgee → U.S.A. 31°58N 82°33W 85 F13
Ocniţa Moldova 48°25N 27°30E 17 D14
Oconee → U.S.A. 31°58N 82°33W 85 F13
Oconomowoc U.S.A. 43°7N 88°30W 80 D9
Oconto U.S.A. 44°53N 87°52W 80 C10
Oconto Falls U.S.A. 44°52N 88°9W 80 C9
Ocosingo Mexico 16°53N 92°7W 87 D6
Ocotal Nic. 13°41N 86°31W 88 D2
Ocotlán Jalisco, Mexico 20°21N 102°46W 86 C4
Ocotlán Oaxaca, Mexico 16°48N 96°40W 87 D5
Ōdāḍahraun Iceland 65°5N 17°0W 8 D5
Ōdaejin N. Korea 41°34N 129°40E 28 D4
Odate Japan 40°16N 140°34E 28 D10
Odawara Japan 35°20N 139°6E 29 G9
Odda Norway 60°3N 6°35E 9 F12
Odei → Canada 56°6N 96°54W 71 B9
Ödemiş Turkey 38°15N 28°0E 23 E13
Odendaalsrus S. Africa 27°48S 26°45E 56 D4
Odense Denmark 55°22N 10°23E 9 J14
Oder → Europe 53°33N 14°38E 16 B8
Odesa Ukraine 46°30N 30°45E 19 E5
Odessa = Odesa Ukraine 46°30N 30°45E 19 E5
Odessa Canada 44°17N 76°43W 83 B8
Odessa Tex., U.S.A. 31°52N 102°23W 84 F3
Odessa Wash., U.S.A. 47°20N 118°41W 76 C4
Odiakwe Botswana 20°12S 25°17E 56 B4
Odienné Côte d'Ivoire 9°30N 7°34W 52 G4
Odintsovo Russia 55°40N 37°16E 18 C6
Odisha □ India 20°0N 84°0E 44 E7
O'Donnell U.S.A. 32°58N 101°50W 84 E4
O'Donnell Pt. Canada 45°5N 80°5W 82 A4
Odorheiu Secuiesc
  Romania 46°21N 25°21E 17 E13
Odra = Oder → Europe 53°33N 14°38E 16 B8
Odzi Zimbabwe 19°0S 32°20E 57 A5
Odzi → Zimbabwe 19°45S 32°23E 57 A5
Oecussi = Pante Macassar
  Timor-Leste 9°30S 123°58E 37 F6
Oeiras Brazil 7°0S 42°8W 93 E10
Oelrichs U.S.A. 43°11N 103°14W 80 D2
Oelwein U.S.A. 42°41N 91°55W 80 D8
Oenpelli = Gunbalanya
  Australia 12°20S 133°4E 60 B5
Ofanto → Italy 41°22N 16°13E 22 D7
Offa Nigeria 8°13N 4°42E 52 G6
Offaly □ Ireland 53°15N 7°30W 10 C4
Offenbach Germany 50°6N 8°44E 16 C5
Offenburg Germany 48°28N 7°56E 16 D4
Officer Cr. → Australia 27°46S 132°30E 61 E5
Ofolanga Tonga 19°38S 174°27W 59 c
Ofu Amer. Samoa 14°11S 169°41W 59 b
Ōfunato Japan 39°4N 141°43E 28 E10
Oga Japan 39°55N 139°50E 28 E9
Oga-Hantō Japan 39°58N 139°47E 28 E9
Ogaden Ethiopia 7°30N 45°30E 49 F3
Ōgaki Japan 35°21N 136°37E 29 G8
Ogallala U.S.A. 41°8N 101°43W 80 E3

Ogbomosho Nigeria 8°1N 4°11E 52 G6
Ogden U.S.A. 41°13N 111°58W 76 F8
Ogdensburg U.S.A. 44°42N 75°30W 83 B9
Ogea Driki Fiji 19°12S 178°27W 59 a
Ogea Levu Fiji 19°8S 178°24W 59 a
Ogeechee → U.S.A. 31°50N 81°3W 85 F14
Ogilby U.S.A. 32°49N 114°50W 79 N12
Óglio → Italy 45°2N 10°39E 22 B4
Ogmore Australia 22°37S 149°35E 62 C4
Ogoki Canada 51°38N 85°58W 72 B2
Ogoki → Canada 51°38N 85°57W 72 B2
Ogoki L. Canada 50°50N 87°10W 72 B2
Ogoki Res. Canada 50°45N 88°15W 72 B2
Ogooué → Gabon 1°0S 9°0E 54 E1
Ogowe = Ogooué → Gabon 1°0S 9°0E 54 E1
Ogre Latvia 56°49N 24°36E 9 H21
Ogurja Ada Turkmenistan 38°55N 53°2E 47 B7
Ohai N.Z. 45°55S 168°0E 59 F2
Ohakune N.Z. 39°24S 175°24E 59 C5
Ohangwena □ Namibia 17°30S 17°0E 56 A2
Ohata Japan 41°24N 141°10E 28 D10
Ohau, L. N.Z. 44°15S 169°53E 59 F2
Ohio □ U.S.A. 40°15N 82°45W 82 F2
Ohio → U.S.A. 36°59N 89°8W 80 G9
Ohře → Czechia 50°30N 14°10E 16 C8
Ohrid Macedonia 41°8N 20°52E 23 D9
Ohridsko Jezero Macedonia 41°8N 20°52E 23 D9
Ohrigstad S. Africa 24°39S 30°36E 57 B5
Oi Qu → China 28°37N 98°16E 34 C2
Oiapoque Brazil 3°50N 51°50W 93 C8
Oikou China 38°35N 117°42E 33 E9
Oil City U.S.A. 41°26N 79°42W 82 E5
Oil Springs Canada 42°47N 82°7W 82 D2
Oildale U.S.A. 35°25N 119°1W 79 K7
Oise → France 49°0N 2°4E 20 B5
Oistins Barbados 13°4N 59°33W 89 g
Oistins B. Barbados 13°4N 59°33W 89 g
Ōita Japan 33°14N 131°36E 29 H5
Ōita □ Japan 33°15N 131°30E 29 H5
Oiticica Brazil 5°3S 41°5W 93 E10
Ojai U.S.A. 34°27N 119°15W 79 L7
Ojhar India 20°6N 73°56E 44 D1
Ojinaga Mexico 29°34N 104°25W 86 B4
Ojiya Japan 37°18N 138°48E 29 F9
Ojo Caliente Mexico 22°34N 102°15W 86 C4
Ojo de Liebre, L. Mexico 27°45N 114°15W 86 B2
Ojos del Salado, Cerro
  Argentina 27°0S 68°40W 94 B2
Oka → Russia 56°20N 43°59E 18 C7
Okaba Indonesia 8°6S 139°42E 37 F9
Okahandja Namibia 22°0S 16°59E 56 B2
Okakarara Namibia 20°35S 17°27E 56 B2
Okanagan L. Canada 50°0N 119°30W 70 D5
Okandja Gabon 0°35S 13°45E 54 E2
Okanogan U.S.A. 48°22N 119°35W 76 B4
Okanogan → U.S.A. 48°6N 119°44W 76 B4
Okanogan Range
  N. Amer. 49°0N 119°55W 70 D5
Okaputa Namibia 20°5S 17°0E 56 B2
Okara Pakistan 30°50N 73°31E 42 D5
Okarukambe = Steinhausen
  Namibia 21°49S 18°20E 56 B2
Okaukuejo Namibia 19°10S 16°0E 56 A2
Okavango = Cubango →
  Africa 18°50S 22°25E 56 A3
Okavango Delta
  Botswana 18°45S 22°45E 56 A3
Okavango Swamp = Okavango
  Delta Botswana 18°45S 22°45E 56 A3
Okaya Japan 36°5N 138°10E 29 F9
Okayama Japan 34°40N 133°54E 29 G6
Okayama □ Japan 35°0N 133°50E 29 G6
Okazaki Japan 34°57N 137°10E 29 G8
Okeechobee U.S.A. 27°15N 80°50W 85 H14
Okeechobee, L. U.S.A. 27°0N 80°50W 85 H14
Okefenokee △ U.S.A. 30°45N 82°18W 85 F13
Okefenokee Swamp
  U.S.A. 30°40N 82°20W 85 F13
Okehampton U.K. 50°44N 4°0W 13 G4
Okha India 22°27N 69°4E 42 H3
Okha Russia 53°40N 143°0E 27 D15
Okhotsk Russia 59°20N 143°10E 27 D15
Okhotsk, Sea of Asia 55°0N 145°0E 27 D15
Okhotskiy Perevoz
  Russia 61°52N 135°35E 27 C14
Okhtyrka Ukraine 50°25N 35°0E 19 D5
Oki-Shotō Japan 36°5N 133°15E 29 F6
Okiep S. Africa 29°39S 17°53E 56 D2
Okinawa Japan 26°19N 127°46E 29 L3
Okinawa □ Japan 26°40N 128°0E 29 L4
Okinawa-Guntō Japan 26°40N 128°0E 29 L4
Okinawa-Jima Japan 26°32N 128°0E 29 L4
Okino-erabu-Shima
  Japan 27°21N 128°33E 29 L4
Oklahoma □ U.S.A. 35°20N 97°30W 84 D6
Oklahoma City U.S.A. 35°30N 97°30W 84 D6
Okmulgee U.S.A. 35°37N 95°58W 84 D7
Oknitsa = Ocniţa
  Moldova 48°25N 27°30E 17 D14
Okolona U.S.A. 34°0N 88°45W 85 E10
Okombahe Namibia 21°23S 15°22E 56 B2
Okotoks Canada 50°43N 113°58W 70 C6
Oksovskiy Russia 62°33N 39°57E 18 B6
Oktyabrsk = Qandyaghash
  Kazakhstan 49°28N 57°25E 19 E10
Oktyabrskiy = Aktsyabrski
  Belarus 52°38N 28°53E 17 B15
Oktyabrskiy Bashkortostan,
  Russia 54°28N 53°28E 18 D9
Oktyabrskiy Kamchatka,
  Russia 52°39N 156°14E 27 D16
Oktyabrskoy Revolyutsii, Ostrov
  Russia 79°30N 97°0E 27 B10
Okuru N.Z. 43°55S 168°55E 59 F2
Okushiri-Tō Japan 42°15N 139°30E 28 C9
Okwa → Botswana 22°30S 23°0E 56 B3
Ola Russia 59°35N 151°17E 27 D16
Ólafsfjörður Iceland 66°4N 18°39W 8 C4
Ólafsvík Iceland 64°53N 23°43W 8 D2

Olancha *U.S.A.* 36°17N 118°1W **79** J8
Olancha Pk. *U.S.A.* 36°16N 118°7W **79** J8
Olanchito *Honduras* 15°30N 86°30W **88** C2
Öland *Sweden* 56°45N 16°38E **9** H17
Olary *Australia* 32°18S 140°19E **63** E3
Olascoaga *Argentina* 35°15S 60°39W **94** D3
Olathe *U.S.A.* 38°53N 94°49W **80** F6
Olavarría *Argentina* 36°55S 60°20W **94** D3
Oława *Poland* 50°57N 17°20E **17** C9
Ólbia *Italy* 40°55N 9°31E **22** D3
Olcott *U.S.A.* 43°20N 78°42W **82** C6
Old Bahama Chan. = Bahama,
   Canal Viejo de
   W. Indies 22°10N 77°30W **88** B4
Old Baldy Pk. = San Antonio, Mt.
   U.S.A. 34°17N 117°38W **79** L9
Old Bridge *U.S.A.* 40°25N 74°22W **83** F10
Old Castile = Castilla y Leon □
   Spain 42°0N 5°0W **21** B3
Old Crow *Canada* 67°30N 139°55W **68** D4
Old Dale *U.S.A.* 34°8N 115°47W **79** L11
Old Forge *N.Y., U.S.A.* 43°43N 74°58W **83** C10
Old Forge *Pa., U.S.A.* 41°22N 75°45W **83** E9
Old Mapoon ◎ *Australia* 11°5S 142°22E **62** A3
Old Perlican *Canada* 48°5N 53°1W **73** C9
Old Speck Mt. *U.S.A.* 44°34N 70°57W **83** B14
Old Town *U.S.A.* 44°56N 68°39W **81** C19
Old Washington *U.S.A.* 40°2N 81°27W **82** F3
Old Wives L. *Canada* 50°5N 106°0W **71** C7
Oldbury *U.K.* 51°38N 2°33W **13** F5
Oldcastle *Ireland* 53°46N 7°10W **10** C4
Oldenburg *Germany* 53°9N 8°13E **16** B5
Oldenzaal *Neths.* 52°19N 6°53E **15** B6
Oldham *U.K.* 53°33N 2°7W **12** D5
Oldman → *Canada* 49°57N 111°42W **70** D6
Oldmeldrum *U.K.* 57°20N 2°19W **11** D6
Olds *Canada* 51°50N 114°10W **70** C6
Öldziyt *Mongolia* 44°40N 109°1E **32** B5
Olean *U.S.A.* 42°5N 78°26W **82** D6
Olekma → *Russia* 60°22N 120°42E **27** C13
Olekminsk *Russia* 60°25N 120°30E **27** C13
Oleksandriya *Ukraine* 50°37N 26°19E **17** C14
Olema *U.S.A.* 38°3N 122°47W **78** G4
Olenegorsk *Russia* 68°9N 33°18E **8** B25
Olenek *Russia* 68°28N 112°18E **27** C12
Olenek → *Russia* 73°0N 120°10E **27** B13
Oléron, Î. d' *France* 45°55N 1°15W **20** D3
Oleśnica *Poland* 51°13N 17°22E **17** C9
Olevsk *Ukraine* 51°12N 27°39E **17** C14
Olga, L. *Canada* 49°47N 77°15W **72** C4
Olgas, The = Kata Tjuta
   Australia 25°20S 130°50E **61** E5
Ölgiy *Mongolia* 48°56N 89°57E **30** B6
Olhão *Portugal* 37°3N 7°48W **21** D2
Olifants = Elefantes →
   Africa 24°10S 32°40E **57** B5
Olifants → *Namibia* 25°30S 19°30E **56** B2
Olifantshoek *S. Africa* 27°57S 22°42E **56** C3
Ólimbos, Óros = Olympos Oros
   Greece 40°6N 22°23E **23** D10
Olímpia *Brazil* 20°44S 48°54W **95** A6
Olinda *Brazil* 8°1S 34°51W **93** E12
Oliva *Argentina* 32°0S 63°38W **94** C3
Olivares, Cerro los
   Argentina 30°18S 69°55W **94** C2
Olive Branch *U.S.A.* 34°57N 89°49W **85** D10
Olivehurst *U.S.A.* 39°6N 121°34W **78** F5
Oliver *Canada* 49°13N 119°37W **70** D5
Oliver L. *Canada* 56°56N 103°22W **71** B8
Ollagüe *Chile* 21°15S 68°10W **94** A2
Olmaliq *Uzbekistan* 40°50N 69°35E **26** E7
Olney *Ill., U.S.A.* 38°44N 88°5W **80** F9
Olney *Tex., U.S.A.* 33°22N 98°45W **84** E5
Olomane → *Canada* 50°14N 60°37W **73** B7
Olomouc *Czechia* 49°38N 17°12E **17** D9
Olonets *Russia* 61°0N 32°54E **18** B5
Olongapo *Phil.* 14°50N 120°18E **37** B6
Olosega *Amer. Samoa* 14°10S 169°37W **59** b
Olosenga = Swains I.
   Amer. Samoa 11°11S 171°4W **65** J11
Olot *Spain* 42°11N 2°30E **21** A7
Olovyannaya *Russia* 50°58N 115°35E **27** D12
Oloy → *Russia* 66°29N 159°29E **27** C16
Olsztyn *Poland* 53°48N 20°29E **17** B11
Olt → *Romania* 43°43N 24°51E **17** G13
Olten *Switz.* 34°11N 102°8W **84** D3
Oltenița *Romania* 44°7N 26°42E **17** F14
Oluan Pi *Taiwan* 21°53N 120°51E **35** G13
Olymbos Oros *Greece* 40°6N 22°23E **23** D10
Olympia *Greece* 37°39N 21°39E **23** F9
Olympia *U.S.A.* 47°3N 122°53W **78** D4
Olympic △ *U.S.A.* 47°45N 123°43W **78** C3
Olympic Dam *Australia* 30°30S 136°55E **63** E2
Olympic Mts. *U.S.A.* 47°55N 123°45W **78** C3
Olympus *Cyprus* 34°56N 32°52E **46** C2
Olympus, Mt. = Olymbos Oros
   Greece 40°6N 22°23E **23** D10
Olympus, Mt. = Uludağ
   Turkey 40°4N 29°13E **23** D13
Olympus, Mt. *U.S.A.* 47°48N 123°43W **78** C3
Olyphant *U.S.A.* 41°27N 75°36W **83** E9
Olyutorskiy, Mys
   Russia 59°55N 170°27E **27** D18
Om → *Russia* 54°59N 73°22E **26** D8
Om Koi *Thailand* 17°48N 98°22E **38** D2
Ōma *Japan* 41°45N 141°5E **28** D10
Ōmachi *Japan* 36°30N 137°50E **29** F8
Omae-Zaki *Japan* 34°36N 138°14E **29** G9
Ōmagari = Daisen
   Japan 39°27N 140°29E **28** E10
Omagh *U.K.* 54°36N 7°19W **10** B4
Omagh □ *U.K.* 54°35N 7°15W **10** B4
Omaha *U.S.A.* 41°17N 95°58W **80** E6
Omaheke □ *Namibia* 21°30S 19°0E **56** B2
Omak *U.S.A.* 48°25N 119°31W **76** B4
Omalur *India* 11°44N 78°4E **45** J4
Oman ■ *Asia* 23°0N 58°0E **49** C6
Oman, G. of *Asia* 24°30N 58°30E **47** E8
Omaruru *Namibia* 21°26S 16°0E **56** B2

Omaruru → *Namibia* 22°7S 14°15E **56** B1
Omate *Peru* 16°45S 71°0W **92** G4
Ombai, Selat *Indonesia* 8°30S 124°50E **37** F6
Omboué *Gabon* 1°35S 9°15E **54** E1
Ombrone → *Italy* 42°42N 11°5E **22** C4
Omdurmân *Sudan* 15°40N 32°28E **53** E12
Omemee *Canada* 44°18N 78°33W **82** B6
Ometepe, I. de *Nic.* 11°32N 85°35W **88** D2
Ometepec *Mexico* 16°41N 98°25W **87** D5
Ominato *Japan* 41°17N 141°10E **28** D10
Omineca → *Canada* 56°3N 124°16W **70** B4
Omineca Mts. *Canada* 56°30N 125°30W **70** B3
Omitara *Namibia* 22°16S 18°2E **56** B2
Ōmiya = Saitama *Japan* 35°54N 139°38E **29** G9
Ommen *Neths.* 52°31N 6°26E **15** B6
Ömnögovĭ □ *Mongolia* 43°15N 104°0E **32** C3
Omo → *Ethiopia* 6°25N 36°10E **49** F2
Omolon → *Russia* 68°42N 158°36E **27** C16
Omono-Gawa → *Japan* 39°46N 140°3E **28** E10
Ompha *Canada* 45°0N 76°50W **83** B8
Omsk *Russia* 55°0N 73°12E **26** D8
Omsukchan *Russia* 62°32N 155°48E **27** C16
Ōmu *Japan* 44°34N 142°58E **28** B11
Ōmura *Japan* 32°56N 129°57E **29** H4
Omuramba Omatako →
   Namibia 17°45S 20°25E **56** A2
Omuramba Ovambo →
   Namibia 18°45S 16°59E **56** A2
Omusati □ *Namibia* 18°30S 15°0E **56** A1
Ōmuta *Japan* 33°5N 130°26E **29** H5
Omuthiya *Namibia* 17°43S 16°13E **56** A2
Onaga *U.S.A.* 39°29N 96°10W **80** F5
Onalaska *U.S.A.* 43°53N 91°14W **80** D8
Onancock *U.S.A.* 37°43N 75°45W **81** G16
Onangue, L. *Gabon* 0°57S 10°4E **54** E2
Onaping L. *Canada* 47°3N 81°30W **72** C3
Onavas *Mexico* 28°31N 109°35W **86** B3
Onawa *U.S.A.* 42°2N 96°6W **80** D5
Oncócua *Angola* 16°30S 13°25E **56** A1
Onda *Spain* 39°55N 0°17W **21** C5
Ondangwa *Namibia* 17°57S 16°4E **56** A2
Ondjiva *Angola* 16°48S 15°50E **56** A2
Öndörhaan *Mongolia* 47°19N 110°39E **31** B11
Öndverðarnes *Iceland* 64°52N 24°0W **8** D2
One Arm Point *Australia* 16°26S 123°3E **60** C3
One Arm Point ◎
   Australia 16°31S 122°53E **60** C3
One Tree *Australia* 34°11S 144°43E **63** E3
Oneata *Fiji* 18°26S 178°25W **59** a
Onega *Russia* 64°0N 38°10E **18** B6
Onega → *Russia* 63°58N 38°2E **18** B6
Onega, G. of = Onezhskaya Guba
   Russia 64°24N 36°38E **18** B6
Onega, L. = Onezhskoye Ozero
   Russia 61°44N 35°22E **18** B6
Oneida *U.S.A.* 43°6N 75°39W **83** C9
Oneida L. *U.S.A.* 43°12N 75°54W **83** C9
O'Neill *U.S.A.* 42°27N 98°39W **80** D4
Onekotan, Ostrov
   Russia 49°25N 154°45E **27** E16
Oneonta *U.S.A.* 42°27N 75°4W **83** D9
Oneşti *Romania* 46°17N 26°47E **17** E14
Onezhskaya Guba *Russia* 64°24N 36°38E **18** B6
Onezhskoye Ozero *Russia* 61°44N 35°22E **18** B6
Ongarue *N.Z.* 38°42S 175°19E **59** C5
Ongea Levu = Ogea Levu
   Fiji 19°8S 178°24W **59** a
Ongers → *S. Africa* 31°4S 23°13E **56** D3
Ongerup *Australia* 33°58S 118°28E **61** F2
Ongi *Mongolia* 45°27N 103°54E **32** B2
Ongjin *N. Korea* 37°56N 125°21E **33** F13
Ongkharak *Thailand* 14°8N 101°1E **38** E3
Ongniud Qi *China* 43°0N 118°38E **33** C10
Ongole *India* 15°33N 80°2E **45** G5
Ongon = Havirga
   Mongolia 45°41N 113°5E **32** B7
Ongwediva *Namibia* 17°47S 15°46E **56** A2
Onida *U.S.A.* 44°42N 100°4W **80** C3
Onilahy → *Madag.* 23°34S 43°45E **55** J8
Onitsha *Nigeria* 6°6N 6°42E **52** G7
Ono *Fiji* 18°55S 178°29E **59** a
Onoda *Japan* 33°59N 131°11E **29** G5
Onslow *Australia* 21°40S 115°12E **60** D2
Onslow B. *U.S.A.* 34°20N 77°15W **85** D16
Ontake-San *Japan* 35°53N 137°29E **29** G8
Ontario *Calif., U.S.A.* 34°4N 117°39W **79** M9
Ontario *Oreg., U.S.A.* 44°2N 116°58W **76** D5
Ontario □ *Canada* 48°0N 83°0W **72** B2
Ontario, L. *N. Amer.* 43°20N 78°0W **82** C7
Ontonagon *U.S.A.* 46°52N 89°19W **80** B9
Onyx *U.S.A.* 35°41N 118°14W **79** K8
Oodnadatta *Australia* 27°33S 135°30E **63** D2
Ooldea *Australia* 30°27S 131°50E **61** F5
Oombulgurri *Australia* 15°15S 127°45E **60** C4
Oombulgurri ◎
   Australia 15°10S 127°50E **60** C4
Oorindi *Australia* 20°40S 141°1E **62** C3
Oost-Vlaanderen □
   Belgium 51°5N 3°50E **15** C3
Oostende *Belgium* 51°15N 2°54E **15** C2
Oosterhout *Neths.* 51°39N 4°47E **15** C4
Oosterschelde → *Neths.* 51°33N 4°0E **15** C4
Oosterwolde *Neths.* 53°0N 6°17E **15** B6
Oostesschelde △ *Neths.* 51°40N 3°40E **15** C3
Oostvaardersplassen △
   Neths. 52°27N 5°22E **15** B5
Ootacamund = Udagamandalam
   India 11°30N 76°44E **45** J3
Ootsa L. *Canada* 53°50N 126°2W **70** C3
Ooty = Udagamandalam
   India 11°30N 76°44E **45** J3
Op Luang △ *Thailand* 18°12N 98°32E **38** C2
Opala *Dem. Rep. of the Congo* 0°40S 24°20E **54** E4
Opanake *Sri Lanka* 6°35N 80°40E **45** L5
Opasatika *Canada* 49°30N 82°50W **72** C3
Opasquia △ *Canada* 53°33N 93°5W **72** B1
Opava *Czechia* 49°57N 17°58E **17** D9
Opelika *U.S.A.* 32°39N 85°23W **85** E12
Opelousas *U.S.A.* 30°32N 92°5W **84** F8

Opémisca, L. *Canada* 49°56N 74°52W **72** C5
Opheim *U.S.A.* 48°51N 106°24W **76** B10
Ophthalmia Ra.
   Australia 23°15S 119°30E **60** D2
Opinaca → *Canada* 52°15N 78°2W **72** B4
Opinaca, Rés. *Canada* 52°39N 76°20W **72** B4
Opinnagau → *Canada* 54°12N 82°25W **72** B3
Opiscotéo, L. *Canada* 53°10N 68°10W **73** B6
Opobo *Nigeria* 4°35N 7°34E **52** H7
Opole *Poland* 50°42N 17°58E **17** C9
Oporto = Porto *Portugal* 41°8N 8°40W **21** B1
Opotiki *N.Z.* 38°1S 177°19E **59** C6
Opp *U.S.A.* 31°17N 86°16W **85** F11
Oppdal *Norway* 62°35N 9°41E **8** E13
Opportunity *U.S.A.* 47°39N 117°15W **76** C5
Opua *N.Z.* 35°19S 174°9E **59** A5
Opunake *N.Z.* 39°26S 173°52E **59** C4
Oracle *U.S.A.* 32°37N 110°46W **77** K8
Oradea *Romania* 47°2N 21°58E **17** E11
Öræfajökull *Iceland* 64°2N 16°39E **8** D5
Orai *India* 25°58N 79°30E **43** G8
Oral = Zhayyq →
   Kazakhstan 47°0N 51°48E **19** E9
Oral *Kazakhstan* 51°20N 51°20E **19** D9
Oran *Algeria* 35°45N 0°39W **52** A5
Orange *Australia* 33°15S 149°7E **63** E4
Orange *France* 44°8N 4°47E **20** D6
Orange *Calif., U.S.A.* 33°47N 117°51W **79** M9
Orange *Mass., U.S.A.* 42°35N 72°19W **83** D12
Orange *Tex., U.S.A.* 30°6N 93°44W **84** F8
Orange *Va., U.S.A.* 38°15N 78°7W **81** F14
Orange → *S. Africa* 28°41S 16°28E **56** C2
Orange, C. *Brazil* 4°20N 51°30W **93** C8
Orange Cove *U.S.A.* 36°38N 119°19W **78** J7
Orange Free State = Free State □
   S. Africa 28°30S 27°0E **56** C4
Orange Grove *U.S.A.* 27°58N 97°56W **84** H6
Orange Walk *Belize* 18°6N 88°33W **87** D7
Orangeburg *U.S.A.* 33°30N 80°52W **85** E14
Orangeville *Canada* 43°55N 80°5W **82** C4
Orango *Guinea-Biss.* 11°5N 16°0W **52** F2
Oranienburg *Germany* 52°45N 13°14E **16** B7
Oranje = Orange →
   S. Africa 28°41S 16°28E **56** C2
Oranjemund *Namibia* 28°38S 16°29E **56** C2
Oranjerivier *S. Africa* 29°40S 24°12E **56** D3
Oranjestad *Aruba* 12°32N 70°2W **89** D5
Orapa *Botswana* 21°15S 25°30E **55** J5
Oras *Phil.* 12°9N 125°28E **37** B7
Orbetello *Italy* 42°27N 11°13E **22** C4
Orbisonia *U.S.A.* 40°15N 77°54W **82** F7
Orbost *Australia* 37°40S 148°29E **63** F4
Orcadas *Antarctica* 60°44S 44°37W **5** C18
Orcas I. *U.S.A.* 48°42N 122°56W **78** B4
Orchard City *U.S.A.* 38°50N 107°58W **76** G10
Orchard Homes *U.S.A.* 46°55N 114°4W **76** C6
Orchid I. = Lan Yü
   Taiwan 22°4N 121°25E **35** F13
Orchila, I. *Venezuela* 11°48N 66°10W **89** D6
Orcutt *U.S.A.* 34°52N 120°27W **79** L6
Ord *U.S.A.* 41°36N 98°56W **80** E4
Ord → *Australia* 15°33S 128°15E **60** C4
Ord, Mt. *Australia* 17°20S 125°34E **60** C4
Ord Mts. *U.S.A.* 34°39N 116°45W **79** L10
Orderville *U.S.A.* 37°17N 112°38W **77** H7
Ordos = Mu Us Shamo
   China 39°0N 109°0E **32** E5
Ordos *China* 39°50N 110°0E **32** E6
Ordu *Turkey* 40°55N 37°53E **19** F6
Ordway *U.S.A.* 38°13N 103°46W **76** G12
Ore Mts. = Erzgebirge
   Germany 50°27N 12°55E **16** C7
Oregon *U.S.A.* 42°1N 89°20W **80** D9
Oregon □ *U.S.A.* 44°0N 121°0W **76** E3
Oregon City *U.S.A.* 45°21N 122°36W **78** E4
Oregon Dunes △ *U.S.A.* 43°40N 124°10W **76** E1
Orekhovo-Zuyevo *Russia* 55°50N 38°55E **18** C6
Orel *Russia* 52°57N 36°3E **18** D6
Orem *U.S.A.* 40°19N 111°42W **76** F8
Ören *Turkey* 37°3N 27°57E **23** F12
Orenburg *Russia* 51°45N 55°6E **18** D10
Orense = Ourense *Spain* 42°19N 7°55W **21** A2
Orepuki *N.Z.* 46°19S 167°46E **59** G1
Orestes Pereyra *Mexico* 26°31N 105°40W **86** B3
Orestiada *Greece* 41°30N 26°33E **23** D12
Orford Ness *U.K.* 52°5N 1°35E **13** E9
Organ Pipe Cactus △
   U.S.A. 32°0N 112°52W **77** K7
Orgaz *Spain* 39°39N 3°53W **21** C4
Orgeyev = Orhei
   Moldova 47°24N 28°50E **17** E15
Orhaneli *Turkey* 39°54N 28°59E **23** E13
Orhangazi *Turkey* 40°29N 29°18E **23** D13
Orhei *Moldova* 47°24N 28°50E **17** E15
Orhon Gol → *Mongolia* 50°21N 106°0E **30** A10
Oriental, Cordillera
   Colombia 6°0N 73°0W **92** B4
Oriental, Grand Erg *Algeria* 30°0N 6°30E **52** B7
Oriente *Argentina* 38°44S 60°37W **94** D3
Orihuela *Spain* 38°7N 0°55W **21** C5
Orillia *Canada* 44°40N 79°24W **82** B5
Orinoco → *Venezuela* 9°15N 61°30W **92** B6
Orion *Canada* 49°27N 110°49W **71** D6
Oriskany *U.S.A.* 43°10N 75°20W **83** C9
Orissa = Odisha □ *India* 20°0N 84°0E **44** E7
Orissaare *Estonia* 58°34N 23°5E **9** G20
Oristano *Italy* 39°54N 8°36E **22** E3
Oristano, G. di *Italy* 39°50N 8°29E **22** E3
Orizaba *Mexico* 18°51N 97°6W **87** D5
Orizaba, Pico de *Mexico* 18°58N 97°15W **87** D5
Orkanger *Norway* 63°18N 9°52E **8** E13
Orkhon = Orhon Gol →
   Mongolia 50°21N 106°0E **30** A10
Orkla → *Norway* 63°18N 9°51E **8** E13
Orkney *S. Africa* 26°58S 26°40E **56** C4
Orkney □ *U.K.* 59°2N 3°13W **11** B5

Orkney Is. *U.K.* 59°0N 3°0W **11** B6
Orland *U.S.A.* 39°45N 122°12W **78** F4
Orléanais *France* 48°0N 2°0E **20** C5
Orléans *France* 47°54N 1°52E **20** C4
Orleans *U.S.A.* 44°49N 72°12W **83** B12
Orléans, Î. d' *Canada* 46°54N 70°58W **73** C5
Ormara *Pakistan* 25°16N 64°33E **40** G4
Ormoc *Phil.* 11°0N 124°37E **37** B6
Ormond *N.Z.* 38°33S 177°56E **59** C6
Ormond Beach *U.S.A.* 29°17N 81°3W **85** G14
Ormskirk *U.K.* 53°35N 2°54W **12** D5
Ormstown *Canada* 45°8N 74°0W **83** A11
Örnsköldsvik *Sweden* 63°17N 18°40E **8** E18
Oro *N. Korea* 40°1N 127°27E **33** D14
Oro → *Mexico* 25°35N 105°2W **86** B3
Oro Grande *U.S.A.* 34°36N 117°20W **79** L9
Oro Valley *U.S.A.* 32°26N 110°58W **77** K8
Orocué *Colombia* 4°48N 71°20W **92** C4
Orofino *U.S.A.* 46°29N 116°15W **76** C5
Orohena, Mt. *Tahiti* 17°37S 149°28W **59** d
Orol Dengizi = Aral Sea
   Asia 45°0N 58°20E **26** E7
Oromocto *Canada* 45°54N 66°29W **73** C6
Orono *Canada* 43°59N 78°37W **82** C6
Orono *U.S.A.* 44°53N 68°40W **81** C19
Oronsay *U.K.* 56°1N 6°15W **11** E2
Oroquieta *Phil.* 8°32N 123°44E **37** C6
Orosei *Italy* 40°23N 9°42E **22** D3
Orosháza *Hungary* 46°32N 20°42E **17** E11
Orotukan *Russia* 62°16N 151°42E **27** C16
Oroville *Calif., U.S.A.* 39°31N 121°33W **78** F5
Oroville *Wash., U.S.A.* 48°56N 119°26W **76** B4
Oroville, L. *U.S.A.* 39°33N 121°29W **78** F5
Orroroo *Australia* 32°43S 138°38E **63** E2
Orrville *U.S.A.* 40°50N 81°46W **82** F3
Orsha *Belarus* 54°30N 30°25E **18** D5
Orsk *Russia* 51°12N 58°34E **26** D6
Orşova *Romania* 44°41N 22°25E **17** F12
Ortaca *Turkey* 36°49N 28°45E **23** F13
Ortegal, C. *Spain* 43°43N 7°52W **21** A2
Orthez *France* 43°29N 0°48W **20** E3
Ortigueira *Spain* 43°40N 7°50W **21** A2
Orting *U.S.A.* 47°6N 122°12W **78** C4
Ortles *Italy* 46°31N 10°33E **20** C8
Ortón → *Bolivia* 10°50S 67°0W **92** F5
Ortonville *U.S.A.* 45°19N 96°27W **80** C5
Orūmīyeh *Iran* 37°40N 45°0E **46** B5
Orūmīyeh, Daryācheh-ye
   Iran 37°50N 45°30E **46** B5
Oruro *Bolivia* 18°0S 67°9W **92** G5
Orust *Sweden* 58°10N 11°40E **9** G14
Oruzgān □ *Afghan.* 33°0N 66°0E **40** C5
Orvieto *Italy* 42°43N 12°7E **22** C5
Orwell *N.Y., U.S.A.* 43°35N 75°50W **83** C9
Orwell *Ohio, U.S.A.* 41°32N 80°52W **82** E4
Orwell → *U.K.* 51°59N 1°18E **13** F9
Orwigsburg *U.S.A.* 40°38N 76°6W **83** F8
Oryol = Orel *Russia* 52°57N 36°3E **18** D6
Osa *Russia* 57°17N 55°26E **18** C10
Osa, Pen. de *Costa Rica* 8°0N 84°0W **88** E3
Osage *U.S.A.* 43°17N 92°49W **80** D7
Osage → *U.S.A.* 38°36N 91°57W **80** F8
Osage City *U.S.A.* 38°38N 95°50W **80** F6
Ōsaki *Japan* 38°34N 140°58E **28** E10
Osawatomie *U.S.A.* 38°31N 94°57W **80** F6
Osborne *U.S.A.* 39°26N 98°42W **80** F4
Osceola *Ark., U.S.A.* 35°42N 89°58W **85** D10
Osceola *Iowa, U.S.A.* 41°2N 93°46W **80** E7
Oscoda *U.S.A.* 44°26N 83°20W **82** B1
Ösel = Saaremaa *Estonia* 58°30N 22°30E **9** G20
Osgoode *Canada* 45°8N 75°36W **83** A9
Osh *Kyrgyzstan* 40°37N 72°49E **30** C3
Oshakati *Namibia* 17°45S 15°40E **55** H3
Oshana □ *Namibia* 17°50S 15°40E **56** A2
Oshawa *Canada* 43°50N 78°50W **82** C6
Oshigambo *Namibia* 18°30S 17°0E **56** A2
Oshika-Hantō *Japan* 38°30N 141°30E **28** E10
Oshikoto □ *Namibia* 18°30S 17°0E **56** A2
Oshivelo *Namibia* 18°37S 17°10E **56** A2
Oshkosh *Nebr., U.S.A.* 41°24N 102°21W **80** E2
Oshkosh *Wis., U.S.A.* 44°1N 88°33W **80** C9
Oshmyany = Ashmyany
   Belarus 54°26N 25°52E **17** A13
Oshnovīyeh *Iran* 37°2N 45°6E **46** B5
Oshogbo *Nigeria* 7°48N 4°37E **52** G6
Oshtorīnān *Iran* 34°1N 48°38E **47** C6
Ōshū *Japan* 39°8N 141°8E **28** E10
Oshwe
   Dem. Rep. of the Congo 3°25S 19°28E **54** E3
Osijek *Croatia* 45°34N 18°41E **23** B8
Osipovichi = Asipovichy
   Belarus 53°19N 28°33E **17** B15
Osiyan *India* 26°43N 72°55E **42** F5
Osizweni *S. Africa* 27°49S 30°7E **57** D5
Oskaloosa *U.S.A.* 41°18N 92°39W **80** E7
Oskarshamn *Sweden* 57°15N 16°27E **9** H17
Oskélanéo *Canada* 48°5N 75°15W **72** C5
Öskemen *Kazakhstan* 50°0N 82°36E **26** D9
Oslo *Norway* 59°54N 10°43E **9** G14
Oslofjorden *Norway* 59°20N 10°35E **9** G14
Osmanabad *India* 18°5N 76°10E **44** E3
Osmaniye *Turkey* 37°5N 36°10E **46** B3
Osnabrück *Germany* 52°17N 8°3E **16** B5
Osogbo = Oshogbo *Nigeria* 7°48N 4°37E **52** G6
Osório *Brazil* 29°53S 50°17W **95** B5
Osorio, Vol. *Chile* 41°0S 72°30W **96** E2
Osoyoos *Canada* 49°0N 119°30W **70** D5
Osøyro *Norway* 60°9N 5°30E **8** F11
Ospika → *Canada* 56°20N 124°0W **70** B4
Osprey Reef *Australia* 13°52S 146°36E **62** A4
Oss *Neths.* 51°46N 5°32E **15** C5
Ossa, Mt. *Australia* 41°52S 146°3E **63** G4
Ossa, Oros *Greece* 39°47N 22°42E **23** E10
Ossabaw I. *U.S.A.* 31°50N 81°5W **85** F14
Ossining *U.S.A.* 41°10N 73°55W **83** E11
Ossipee *U.S.A.* 43°41N 71°7W **83** C13
Ossokmanuan L. *Canada* 53°25N 65°0W **73** B7
Ossora *Russia* 59°20N 163°13E **27** D17

Ostend = Oostende
   Belgium 51°15N 2°54E **15** C2
Oster *Ukraine* 50°57N 30°53E **17** C16
Österbotten = Pohjanmaa □
   Finland 62°58N 22°50E **8** E20
Osterburg *U.S.A.* 40°16N 78°31W **82** F6
Österdalälven → *Sweden* 60°30N 15°7E **8** F15
Österdalen *Norway* 61°40N 10°50E **8** F14
Östermyra = Seinäjoki
   Finland 62°40N 22°51E **8** E20
Österreich = Austria ■
   Europe 47°0N 14°0E **16** E8
Östersund *Sweden* 63°10N 14°38E **8** E16
Ostfriesische Inseln
   Germany 53°42N 7°0E **16** B4
Ostrava *Czechia* 49°51N 18°18E **17** D10
Ostróda *Poland* 53°42N 19°58E **17** B10
Ostroh *Ukraine* 50°20N 26°30E **17** C14
Ostrołęka *Poland* 53°4N 21°32E **17** B11
Ostrów Mazowiecka
   Poland 52°50N 21°51E **17** B11
Ostrów Wielkopolski
   Poland 51°36N 17°44E **17** C9
Ostrowiec-Świętokrzyski
   Poland 50°55N 21°22E **17** C11
Ostuni *Italy* 40°44N 17°35E **23** D7
Ōsumi-Kaikyō *Japan* 30°55N 131°0E **29** J5
Ōsumi-Shotō *Japan* 30°30N 130°0E **29** J5
Osuna *Spain* 37°14N 5°8W **21** D3
Oswegatchie → *U.S.A.* 44°42N 75°30W **83** B9
Oswego *U.S.A.* 43°27N 76°31W **83** C8
Oswego → *U.S.A.* 43°27N 76°30W **83** C8
Oswestry *U.K.* 52°52N 3°3W **12** E4
Oświęcim *Poland* 50°2N 19°11E **17** C10
Otago □ *N.Z.* 45°15S 170°0E **59** F2
Otago Harbour *N.Z.* 45°47S 170°42E **59** F3
Otaheite B. *Trin. & Tob.* 10°15N 61°30W **93** K15
Otaki *Japan* 34°12N 132°13E **29** G6
Otaki *N.Z.* 40°45S 175°10E **59** D5
Otaru *Japan* 43°10N 141°0E **28** C10
Otaru-Wan = Ishikari-Wan
   Japan 43°25N 141°1E **28** C10
Otavalo *Ecuador* 0°13N 78°20W **92** C3
Otavi *Namibia* 19°40S 17°24E **56** A2
Ōtawara *Japan* 36°50N 140°5E **29** F10
Otchinjau *Angola* 16°30S 13°56E **56** A1
Otego *U.S.A.* 42°23N 75°10W **83** D9
Otelnuk, L. *Canada* 56°9N 68°12W **73** A6
Othello *U.S.A.* 46°50N 119°10W **76** C4
Otish, Mts. *Canada* 52°22N 70°30W **73** B5
Otjinene *Namibia* 21°8S 18°46E **56** B2
Otjiwarongo *Namibia* 20°30S 16°33E **56** B2
Otjozondjupa □ *Namibia* 21°0S 17°0E **56** B2
Oto Tolu Group *Tonga* 20°21S 174°32W **59** c
Otoineppu *Japan* 44°44N 142°16E **28** B11
Otorohanga *N.Z.* 38°12S 175°14E **59** C5
Otoskwin → *Canada* 52°13N 88°6W **72** B2
Otra → *Norway* 58°9N 8°1E **9** G13
Otranto *Italy* 40°9N 18°28E **23** D8
Otranto, C. d' *Italy* 40°7N 18°30E **23** D8
Otranto, Str. of *Italy* 40°15N 18°40E **23** D8
Otse *S. Africa* 25°2S 25°45E **56** C4
Otsego L. *U.S.A.* 42°45N 74°53W **83** D10
Ōtsu *Japan* 35°0N 135°50E **29** G7
Ōtsuki *Japan* 35°36N 138°57E **29** G9
Ottapalam *India* 10°46N 76°23E **45** J3
Ottawa = Outaouais →
   Canada 45°27N 74°8W **72** C5
Ottawa *Canada* 45°26N 75°42W **83** A9
Ottawa *Ill., U.S.A.* 41°21N 88°51W **80** E9
Ottawa *Kans., U.S.A.* 38°37N 95°16W **80** F6
Ottawa Is. *Canada* 59°35N 80°10W **69** F15
Otter Cr. → *U.S.A.* 44°13N 73°17W **83** B11
Otter Lake *Canada* 45°17N 79°56W **82** A5
Otterville *Canada* 42°55N 80°36W **82** D4
Ottery St. Mary *U.K.* 50°44N 3°17W **13** G4
Ottosdal *S. Africa* 26°46S 25°59E **56** C4
Ottumwa *U.S.A.* 41°1N 92°25W **80** E7
Oturkpo *Nigeria* 7°16N 8°8E **52** G7
Otway, B. *Chile* 53°30S 74°0W **96** G2
Otway, C. *Australia* 38°52S 143°30E **63** F3
Otwock *Poland* 52°5N 21°20E **17** B11
Ou → *Laos* 20°4N 102°13E **38** B4
Ou-Sammyaku *Japan* 39°20N 140°35E **28** E10
Ouachita → *U.S.A.* 31°38N 91°49W **84** F9
Ouachita, L. *U.S.A.* 34°34N 93°12W **84** D8
Ouachita Mts. *U.S.A.* 34°30N 94°30W **84** D7
Ouagadougou
   Burkina Faso 12°25N 1°30W **52** F5
Ouahigouya *Burkina Faso* 13°31N 2°25W **52** F5
Ouahran = Oran *Algeria* 35°45N 0°39W **52** A5
Ouallene *Algeria* 24°41N 1°11E **52** D6
Ouarâne *Mauritania* 21°0N 10°30E **52** D3
Ouargla *Algeria* 31°59N 5°16E **52** B7
Ouarra → *C.A.R.* 5°5N 24°26E **54** C4
Ouarzazate *Morocco* 30°55N 6°50W **52** B4
Oubangi →
   Dem. Rep. of the Congo 0°30S 17°50E **54** E3
Ouddorp *Neths.* 51°50N 3°57E **15** C3
Oude → *Neths.* 52°12N 4°24E **15** B4
Oudenaarde *Belgium* 50°50N 3°37E **15** D3
Oudtshoorn *S. Africa* 33°35S 22°14E **56** D3
Ouessant, Î. d' *France* 48°28N 5°6W **20** B1
Ouesso *Congo* 1°37N 16°5E **54** D3
Ouest, Pte. de l' *Canada* 49°52N 64°40W **73** C7
Ouezzane *Morocco* 34°51N 5°35W **52** B4
Oughter, L. *Ireland* 54°1N 7°28W **10** B4
Oughterard *Ireland* 53°26N 9°18W **10** C2
Ouidah *Benin* 6°25N 2°0E **52** G6
Oujda *Morocco* 34°41N 1°55W **52** B5
Oulainen *Finland* 64°17N 24°47E **8** D21
Oulanka △ *Finland* 66°16N 29°25E **8** C23
Oulu *Finland* 65°1N 25°29E **8** D21
Oulujärvi *Finland* 64°25N 27°15E **8** D22
Oulujoki → *Finland* 65°1N 25°30E **8** D21
Oum Chalouba *Chad* 15°48N 20°46E **53** E10
Oum Hadjer *Chad* 13°18N 19°41E **53** F9
Ounasjoki → *Finland* 66°31N 25°40E **8** C21
Ounguati *Namibia* 21°54S 16°0E **56** B2
Ounianga Kébir *Chad* 19°4N 20°29E **53** E10

Our ➤ Lux. 49°55'N 6°5'E **15** E6
Ouray U.S.A. 38°1'N 107°40'W **77** G10
Ourense Spain 42°19'N 7°55'W **21** A2
Ouricuri Brazil 7°53'S 40°5'W **93** E10
Ourinhos Brazil 23°0'S 49°54'W **95** A6
Ouro Fino Brazil 22°16'S 46°25'W **95** A6
Ouro Prêto Brazil 20°20'S 43°30'W **95** A7
Ourthe ➤ Belgium 50°29'N 5°35'E **15** D5
Ouse ➤ E. Sussex, U.K. 50°47'N 0°4'E **13** G8
Ouse ➤ N. Yorks., U.K. 53°44'N 0°55'W **12** D7
Outaouais ➤ Canada 45°27'N 74°8'W **72** C5
Outapi Namibia 17°30'S 15°0'E **56** A2
Outardes ➤ Canada 49°24'N 69°30'W **73** C6
Outer Hebrides U.K. 57°30'N 7°15'W **11** D1
Outjo Namibia 20°5'S 16°7'E **56** B2
Outlook Canada 51°30'N 107°0'W **71** C7
Outokumpu Finland 62°43'N 29°1'E **8** E23
Ouyen Australia 35°1'S 142°22'E **63** F3
Ovalau Fiji 17°40'S 178°48'E **59** a
Ovalle Chile 30°33'S 71°18'W **94** C1
Ovamboland Namibia 18°30'S 16°0'E **56** A2
Overflakkee Neths. 51°44'N 4°10'E **15** C4
Overijssel □ Neths. 52°25'N 6°35'E **15** B6
Overland Park U.S.A. 38°58'N 94°40'W **80** F6
Overlander Roadhouse
  Australia 26°19'S 114°28'E **61** E1
Overton U.S.A. 36°33'N 114°27'W **79** J12
Övertorneå Sweden 66°23'N 23°38'E **8** C20
Ovid U.S.A. 42°41'N 76°49'W **83** D8
Oviedo Spain 43°25'N 5°50'W **21** A3
Ovišrags Latvia 57°33'N 21°44'E **9** H19
Ovoot Mongolia 45°21'N 113°45'E **32** B7
Övör Hangay □ Mongolia 45°0'N 102°30'E **32** B2
Øvre Anárjohka △
  Norway 68°30'N 24°40'E **8** B21
Øvre Årdal Norway 61°19'N 7°48'E **8** F12
Øvre Dividal △ Norway 68°43'N 19°50'E **8** B18
Øvre Pasvik △ Norway 69°6'N 28°54'E **8** B23
Ovruch Ukraine 51°25'N 28°45'E **17** C15
Owaka N.Z. 46°27'S 169°40'E **59** G2
Owambo = Ovamboland
  Namibia 18°30'S 16°0'E **56** A2
Owasco L. U.S.A. 42°50'N 76°31'W **83** D8
Owase Japan 34°7'N 136°12'E **29** G8
Owatonna U.S.A. 44°5'N 93°14'W **80** C7
Owbeh Afghan. 34°28'N 63°10'E **40** B3
Owego U.S.A. 42°6'N 76°16'W **83** D8
Owen Sound Canada 44°35'N 80°55'W **82** B4
Owen Stanley Ra.
  Papua N. G. 8°30'S 147°0'E **58** B7
Oweniny ➤ Ireland 54°8'N 9°34'W **10** B2
Owens ➤ U.S.A. 36°32'N 117°59'W **78** J9
Owens L. U.S.A. 36°26'N 117°57'W **79** J9
Owensboro U.S.A. 37°46'N 87°7'W **80** G10
Owl ➤ Canada 57°51'N 92°44'W **71** B10
Owo Nigeria 7°10'N 5°39'E **52** G7
Owosso U.S.A. 43°0'N 84°10'W **81** D11
Owyhee U.S.A. 41°57'N 116°6'W **76** F5
Owyhee ➤ U.S.A. 43°49'N 117°2'W **76** E5
Owyhee, L. U.S.A. 43°38'N 117°14'W **76** E5
Ox Mts. = Slieve Gamph
  Ireland 54°6'N 9°0'W **10** B3
Öxarfjörður Iceland 66°15'N 16°45'W **8** C5
Oxbow Canada 49°14'N 102°10'W **71** D8
Oxelösund Sweden 58°43'N 17°5'E **9** G17
Oxford N.Z. 43°18'S 172°11'E **59** E4
Oxford U.K. 51°46'N 1°15'W **13** F6
Oxford Mass., U.S.A. 42°7'N 71°52'W **83** D13
Oxford Miss., U.S.A. 34°22'N 89°31'W **85** D10
Oxford N.C., U.S.A. 36°19'N 78°35'W **85** C15
Oxford N.Y., U.S.A. 42°27'N 75°36'W **83** D9
Oxford Ohio, U.S.A. 39°31'N 84°45'W **81** F11
Oxford L. Canada 54°51'N 95°37'W **71** C9
Oxfordshire □ U.K. 51°48'N 1°16'W **13** F6
Oxnard U.S.A. 34°12'N 119°11'W **79** L7
Oxus = Amudarya ➤
  Uzbekistan 43°58'N 59°34'E **26** E6
Oya Malaysia 2°55'N 111°55'E **36** D4
Oyama Japan 36°18'N 139°48'E **29** F9
Oyem Gabon 1°34'N 11°31'E **54** D2
Oyen Canada 51°22'N 110°28'W **71** C6
Oykel ➤ U.K. 57°56'N 4°26'W **11** D4
Oymyakon Russia 63°25'N 142°44'E **27** C15
Oyo Nigeria 7°46'N 3°56'E **52** G6
Ōyūbari Japan 43°1'N 142°5'E **28** C11
Ozamiz Phil. 8°15'N 123°50'E **37** C6
Ozar = Ojhar India 20°6'N 73°56'E **44** D1
Ozark Ala., U.S.A. 31°28'N 85°39'W **85** F12
Ozark Ark., U.S.A. 35°29'N 93°50'W **84** D8
Ozark Mo., U.S.A. 37°1'N 93°12'W **80** G7
Ozark Plateau U.S.A. 37°20'N 91°40'W **80** G8
Ozarks, L. of the U.S.A. 38°12'N 92°38'W **80** F7
Özd Hungary 48°14'N 20°15'E **17** D11
Ozette, L. U.S.A. 48°6'N 124°38'W **78** B2
Ozieri Italy 40°35'N 9°0'E **22** D3
Ozona U.S.A. 30°43'N 101°12'W **84** F4
Ozuluama Mexico 21°40'N 97°51'W **87** C5

P

Pa-an Myanmar 16°51'N 97°40'E **41** L20
Pa Mong Dam Thailand 18°0'N 102°22'E **38** D4
Pa Sak ➤ Thailand 15°30'N 101°0'E **38** E3
Paamiut Greenland 62°0'N 49°43'W **4** C5
Paanayarvi △ Russia 66°16'N 30°8'E **8** C24
Paarl S. Africa 33°45'S 18°56'E **56** D2
Pab Hills Pakistan 26°30'N 66°45'E **42** F2
Pabaidh = Pabbay U.K. 57°46'N 7°14'W **11** D1
Pabbay U.K. 57°46'N 7°14'W **11** D1
Pabianice Poland 51°40'N 19°20'E **17** C10
Pabna Bangla. 24°1'N 89°18'E **41** G16
Pacaja ➤ Brazil 1°56'S 50°50'W **93** D8
Pacaraima, Sa. S. Amer. 4°0'N 62°30'W **92** C6
Pacasmayo Peru 7°20'S 79°35'W **92** E3
Pachitea ➤ Peru 8°46'S 74°33'W **92** E4
Pachmarhi India 22°28'N 78°26'E **43** H8
Pachora India 20°38'N 75°29'E **44** D2
Pachpadra India 25°58'N 72°10'E **42** G5
Pachuca Mexico 20°7'N 98°44'W **87** C5

Pacific Antarctic Ridge
  Pac. Oc. 43°0'S 115°0'W **5** B13
Pacific Grove U.S.A. 36°38'N 121°56'W **78** J5
Pacific Ocean 10°0'N 140°0'W **65** G14
Pacific Rim △ Canada 48°40'N 124°45'W **78** B2
Pacitan Indonesia 8°12'S 111°7'E **37** H14
Packwood U.S.A. 46°36'N 121°40'W **78** D5
Padaido, Kepulauan
  Indonesia 1°15'S 136°30'E **37** E9
Padampur India 20°59'N 83°4'E **44** D6
Padang Riau, Indonesia 1°30'N 102°30'E **39** M4
Padang Sumatera Barat,
  Indonesia 1°0'S 100°20'E **36** E2
Padang Endau Malaysia 2°40'N 103°38'E **39** L4
Padangpanjang Indonesia 0°40'S 100°20'E **36** E2
Padangsidempuan
  Indonesia 1°30'N 99°15'E **36** D1
Paddle Prairie Canada 57°57'N 117°29'W **70** B5
Paderborn Germany 51°42'N 8°45'E **16** C5
Paderoo India 18°5'N 82°40'E **44** E6
Padjelanta △ Sweden 67°20'N 16°35'E **8** C17
Padma India 24°12'N 85°22'E **43** G11
Pádova Italy 45°25'N 11°53'E **22** B4
Padra India 22°15'N 73°7'E **42** H5
Padrauna India 26°54'N 83°59'E **43** F10
Padre I. U.S.A. 27°0'N 97°25'W **84** H6
Padre Island △ U.S.A. 27°0'N 97°25'W **84** H6
Padstow U.K. 50°33'N 4°58'W **13** G3
Padua = Pádova Italy 45°25'N 11°53'E **22** B4
Paducah Ky., U.S.A. 37°5'N 88°37'W **80** G9
Paducah Tex., U.S.A. 34°1'N 100°18'W **84** D4
Padukka Sri Lanka 6°50'N 80°5'E **45** L5
Padwa India 18°27'N 82°47'E **44** E6
Paea Tahiti 17°41'S 149°35'W **59** d
Paektu-san N. Korea 41°59'N 128°4'E **33** D15
Paeroa N.Z. 37°23'S 175°41'E **59** B5
Pafúri Mozam. 22°28'S 31°17'E **57** B5
Pag Croatia 44°25'N 15°3'E **16** F8
Pagadian Phil. 7°55'N 123°30'E **37** C6
Pagai Selatan, Pulau
  Indonesia 3°0'S 100°15'E **36** E2
Pagai Utara, Pulau
  Indonesia 2°35'S 100°0'E **36** E2
Pagalu = Annobón Atl. Oc. 1°25'S 5°36'E **51** G4
Pagara India 24°22'N 80°1'E **43** G9
Pagasa I. = Thitu I.
  S. China Sea 11°3'N 114°17'E **36** B4
Pagastikós Kólpos Greece 39°15'N 23°0'E **23** E10
Pagatan Indonesia 3°33'S 115°59'E **36** E5
Page U.S.A. 36°57'N 111°27'W **77** H8
Paget, Mt. S. Georgia 54°26'S 36°31'W **96** G9
Paget I. India 13°26'N 92°50'E **45** H11
Pago Pago Amer. Samoa 14°16'S 170°43'W **59** b
Pagosa Springs U.S.A. 37°16'N 107°1'W **77** H10
Pagri China 27°45'N 89°10'E **30** F6
Pagwa River Canada 50°2'N 85°14'W **72** B2
Pāhala U.S.A. 19°12'N 155°29'W **75** M8
Pahang □ Malaysia 3°30'N 102°45'E **39** L4
Pahang ➤ Malaysia 3°30'N 103°9'E **39** L4
Pahiatua N.Z. 40°27'S 175°50'E **59** D5
Pahokee U.S.A. 26°50'N 80°40'W **85** H14
Pahrump U.S.A. 36°12'N 115°59'W **79** J11
Pahute Mesa U.S.A. 37°20'N 116°45'W **78** H10
Pai Thailand 19°19'N 98°27'E **38** C2
Paicines U.S.A. 36°44'N 121°17'W **78** J5
Paide Estonia 58°53'N 25°33'E **9** G21
Paignton U.K. 50°26'N 3°35'W **13** G4
Paihō Taiwan 23°21'N 120°25'E **35** F13
Päijänne Finland 61°30'N 25°30'E **8** F21
Pailani India 25°45'N 80°26'E **43** G9
Pailin Cambodia 12°46'N 102°36'E **38** F4
Painan Indonesia 1°21'S 100°34'E **36** E2
Painesville U.S.A. 41°43'N 81°15'W **82** E3
Paint Hills = Wemindji
  Canada 53°0'N 78°49'W **72** B4
Paint L. Canada 55°28'N 97°57'W **71** B9
Painted Desert U.S.A. 36°0'N 111°0'W **77** J8
Paintsville U.S.A. 37°49'N 82°48'W **81** G12
País Vasco □ Spain 42°50'N 2°45'W **21** A4
Paisley Canada 44°18'N 81°16'W **82** B3
Paisley U.K. 55°50'N 4°25'W **11** F4
Paisley U.S.A. 42°42'N 120°32'W **76** E3
Paita Peru 5°11'S 81°9'W **92** E2
Paithan India 19°29'N 75°23'E **44** E2
Paizhou China 30°12'N 113°55'E **35** B9
Pajares, Puerto de Spain 42°58'N 5°46'W **21** A3
Pak Lay Laos 18°15'N 101°27'E **38** C3
Pak Ou Laos 20°3'N 102°12'E **38** B4
Pak Phanang Thailand 8°21'N 100°12'E **39** H3
Pak Sane Laos 18°22'N 103°39'E **38** C4
Pak Song Laos 15°11'N 106°14'E **38** E6
Pak Suang Laos 19°58'N 102°15'E **34** H4
Pak Tam Chung China 22°24'N 114°19'E **31** a
Pak Thong Chai Thailand 14°43'N 102°1'E **38** E4
Pakala India 13°29'N 79°8'E **45** N4
Pakaur India 24°38'N 87°51'E **43** G12
Pakch'ŏn N. Korea 39°44'N 125°35'E **33** E13
Pakenham Canada 45°18'N 76°18'W **83** A8
Pakhuis S. Africa 32°9'S 19°5'E **56** D2
Pakistan ■ Asia 30°0'N 70°0'E **42** E4
Pakkading Laos 18°19'N 103°59'E **38** C4
Pakokku Myanmar 21°20'N 95°0'E **41** J19
Pakowki L. Canada 49°20'N 111°0'W **71** D6
Pakpattan Pakistan 30°25'N 73°27'E **42** D5
Paktiā □ Afghan. 33°0'N 69°15'E **40** C6
Paktīkā □ Afghan. 32°30'N 69°0'E **40** C6
Pakwach Uganda 2°28'N 31°27'E **54** D6
Pakxe Laos 15°5'N 105°52'E **38** E5
Pal Lahara India 21°27'N 85°11'E **43** J11
Pala Chad 9°25'N 15°5'E **53** G9
Pala U.S.A. 33°22'N 117°5'W **79** M9
Palacios U.S.A. 28°42'N 96°13'W **84** G6
Palagruža Croatia 42°24'N 16°15'E **22** C7
Palakkad India 10°46'N 76°42'E **45** P3
Palakol India 16°31'N 81°46'E **45** F5
Palalankwe India 10°52'N 92°29'E **45** J11
Palam India 19°0'N 77°0'E **44** E3
Palampur India 32°10'N 76°42'E **42** C7
Palana Australia 39°45'S 147°55'E **63** F4
Palana Russia 59°10'N 159°59'E **27** D16

Palanan Phil. 17°8'N 122°29'E **37** A6
Palanan Pt. Phil. 17°17'N 122°30'E **37** A6
Palandri Pakistan 33°42'N 73°40'E **43** C5
Palanga Lithuania 55°58'N 21°3'E **9** J19
Palangkaraya Indonesia 2°16'S 113°56'E **36** E4
Palani India 10°30'N 77°30'E **45** J3
Palani Hills India 10°14'N 77°33'E **45** J3
Palanpur India 24°10'N 72°25'E **42** G5
Palapye Botswana 22°30'S 27°7'E **56** B4
Palar ➤ India 12°27'N 80°13'E **45** H5
Palas Pakistan 35°4'N 73°14'E **43** B5
Palasponga India 21°47'N 85°34'E **43** J11
Palatka Russia 60°6'N 150°54'E **27** C16
Palatka U.S.A. 29°39'N 81°38'W **85** G14
Palau Palau 7°30'N 134°30'E **64** G5
Palau Sri Lanka 6°45'N 81°48'E **45** L5
Palauk Myanmar 13°10'N 98°40'E **38** F2
Palaw Myanmar 12°58'N 98°39'E **38** F2
Palawan Phil. 9°30'N 118°30'E **36** C5
Palayankottai India 8°45'N 77°45'E **45** K3
Paldiski Estonia 59°23'N 24°9'E **9** G21
Palembang Indonesia 3°0'S 104°50'E **36** E2
Palencia Spain 42°1'N 4°34'W **21** A3
Palenque Mexico 17°29'N 92°1'W **87** D6
Palermo Italy 38°7'N 13°22'E **22** E5
Palermo U.S.A. 39°26'N 121°33'W **78** F5
Palestina Chile 23°50'S 69°47'W **94** A2
Palestina Chile 23°50'S 69°47'W **96** A3
Palestine Asia 32°0'N 35°0'E **48** D4
Palestine U.S.A. 31°46'N 95°38'W **84** F7
Paletwa Myanmar 21°10'N 92°50'E **41** J18
Palghat = Palakkad India 10°46'N 76°42'E **45** J3
Palgrave, Mt. Australia 23°22'S 115°58'E **60** D2
Palhoça Brazil 27°38'S 48°40'W **95** B6
Pali India 25°50'N 73°20'E **42** G5
Palikir Micronesia 6°55'N 158°9'E **64** G7
Paliouri, Ákra Greece 39°57'N 23°45'E **23** E10
Palisades Res. U.S.A. 43°20'N 111°12'W **76** E8
Palitana India 21°32'N 71°49'E **42** J4
Palizada Mexico 18°15'N 92°5'W **87** D6
Palk Bay Asia 9°30'N 79°15'E **45** K4
Palk Strait Asia 10°0'N 79°45'E **45** K4
Palkānah Iraq 35°49'N 44°26'E **46** C5
Palkonda India 18°36'N 83°48'E **44** E6
Palkonda Ra. India 13°50'N 79°20'E **45** H4
Palkot India 22°53'N 84°39'E **43** H11
Pallanza = Verbánia Italy 45°56'N 8°33'E **20** D8
Pallarenda Australia 19°12'S 146°46'E **62** B4
Pallas-Yllästunturi △
  Finland 68°8'N 24°15'E **8** B21
Palleru ➤ India 16°45'N 80°2'E **44** F5
Pallinup ➤ Australia 34°27'S 118°50'E **61** F2
Pallu India 28°59'N 74°14'E **42** E6
Palm Bay U.S.A. 28°2'N 80°35'W **85** G14
Palm Beach U.S.A. 26°43'N 80°2'W **85** H14
Palm Coast U.S.A. 29°35'N 81°12'W **85** G14
Palm Desert U.S.A. 33°43'N 116°22'W **79** M10
Palm-Grove △ Australia 24°57'S 149°21'E **62** C4
Palm Is. Australia 18°40'S 146°35'E **62** B4
Palm Springs U.S.A. 33°50'N 116°33'W **79** M10
Palma, B. de Spain 39°30'N 2°39'E **21** C7
Palma de Mallorca Spain 39°35'N 2°39'E **21** C7
Palma Soriano Cuba 20°15'N 76°0'W **88** B4
Palmaner India 13°12'N 78°45'E **45** H4
Palmares Brazil 8°41'S 35°28'W **93** E11
Palmas Brazil 26°29'S 52°0'W **95** B5
Palmas, C. Liberia 4°27'N 7°46'W **52** H4
Pálmas, G. di Italy 39°0'N 8°30'E **22** E3
Palmdale U.S.A. 34°35'N 118°7'W **79** L8
Palmeira das Missões
  Brazil 27°55'S 53°17'W **95** B5
Palmeira dos Índios
  Brazil 9°25'S 36°37'W **93** E11
Palmer Antarctica 64°35'S 65°0'W **5** C17
Palmer U.S.A. 61°36'N 149°7'W **68** E2
Palmer ➤ Australia 16°0'S 142°26'E **62** B3
Palmer Arch. Antarctica 64°15'S 65°0'W **5** C17
Palmer Lake U.S.A. 39°7'N 104°55'W **76** G11
Palmer Land Antarctica 73°0'S 63°0'W **5** D18
Palmerston Australia 12°31'S 130°59'E **60** B5
Palmerston Canada 43°50'N 80°51'W **82** C4
Palmerston N.Z. 45°29'S 170°43'E **59** F3
Palmerston North N.Z. 40°21'S 175°39'E **59** D5
Palmerton U.S.A. 40°48'N 75°37'W **83** F9
Palmetto U.S.A. 27°31'N 82°34'W **85** H13
Palmi Italy 38°21'N 15°51'E **22** E6
Palmira Argentina 32°59'S 68°34'W **94** C2
Palmira Colombia 3°32'N 76°16'W **92** C3
Palmyra = Tudmur Syria 34°36'N 38°15'E **46** C3
Palmyra Mo., U.S.A. 39°48'N 91°32'W **80** F8
Palmyra N.J., U.S.A. 40°0'N 75°1'W **83** G9
Palmyra N.Y., U.S.A. 43°5'N 77°18'W **82** C7
Palmyra Pa., U.S.A. 40°18'N 76°36'W **83** F8
Palmyra Is. Pac. Oc. 5°52'N 162°5'W **65** G11
Palmyras Pt. India 20°46'N 87°° E **44** D8
Palo Alto U.S.A. 37°27'N 122°10'W **78** H4
Palo Seco Trin. & Tob. 10°4'N 61°36'W **93** K15
Palo Verde U.S.A. 33°26'N 114°44'W **79** M12
Palo Verde △ Costa Rica 10°21'N 85°21'W **88** D2
Palomar Mt. U.S.A. 33°22'N 116°50'W **79** M10
Palopo Indonesia 3°0'S 120°16'E **37** E6
Palos, C. de Spain 37°38'N 0°40'W **21** D5
Palos Verdes, Pt. U.S.A. 33°46'N 118°25'W **79** M8
Palos Verdes Estates
  U.S.A. 33°48'N 118°23'W **79** M8
Palu Indonesia 1°0'S 119°52'E **37** E5
Palu Turkey 38°45'N 40°0'E **46** B3
Paluma Ra. Australia 19°9'S 146°22'E **62** B4
Pálváncza Mexico 22°9'N 98°10'W **37** B1
Pamanukan Indonesia 6°16'S 107°49'E **37** G12
Paman I. India 9°15'N 79°20'E **45** K4
Pamekasan Indonesia 7°10'S 113°28'E **37** G15
Pamenang Indonesia 8°24'S 116°6'E **37** J19
Pamiers France 43°7'N 1°39'E **20** E4
Pamir Tajikistan 37°40'N 73°0'E **26** F8
Pamlico ➤ U.S.A. 35°20'N 76°28'W **85** D16
Pamlico Sd. U.S.A. 35°20'N 76°0'W **85** D17
Pampa U.S.A. 35°32'N 100°58'W **84** D4
Pampa de las Salinas
  Argentina 32°1'S 66°58'W **94** C2

Pampanua Indonesia 4°16'S 120°8'E **37** E6
Pampas Argentina 35°0'S 63°0'W **94** D3
Pampas Peru 12°20'S 74°50'W **92** F4
Pamplona Colombia 7°23'N 72°39'W **92** B4
Pamplona-Iruña Spain 42°48'N 1°38'W **21** A5
Pampoenpoort S. Africa 31°3'S 22°40'E **56** D3
Pan de Azúcar Chile 24°55'S 68°10'W **94** A2
Pan de Azúcar △ Chile 26°0'S 70°40'W **94** B1
Pan Xian China 25°46'N 104°38'E **34** E5
Pana U.S.A. 39°23'N 89°5'W **80** F9
Panaca U.S.A. 37°47'N 114°23'W **77** H6
Panadura Sri Lanka 6°47'N 79°53'E **45** L4
Panaitan Indonesia 6°36'S 105°12'E **37** G11
Panaji India 15°25'N 73°50'E **45** G1
Panamá Panama 9°0'N 79°25'W **88** E4
Panama Sri Lanka 6°45'N 81°48'E **45** L5
Panama ■ Cent. Amer. 8°48'N 79°55'W **88** E4
Panamá, G. de Panama 8°4'N 79°20'W **88** E4
Panama, Isthmus of
  Cent. Amer. 9°0'N 79°0'W **88** E4
Panama Basin Pac. Oc. 5°0'N 83°30'W **65** G19
Panama Canal Panama 9°10'N 79°37'W **88** E4
Panama City U.S.A. 30°10'N 85°40'W **85** F12
Panamint Range U.S.A. 36°20'N 117°20'W **79** J9
Panamint Springs
  U.S.A. 36°20'N 117°28'W **79** J9
Panão Peru 9°55'S 75°55'W **92** E3
Panare Thailand 6°51'N 101°30'E **39** J3
Panay Phil. 11°10'N 122°30'E **37** B6
Panay G. Phil. 11°0'N 122°30'E **37** B6
Pančevo Serbia 44°52'N 20°41'E **23** B9
Panch'iao Taiwan 25°1'N 121°27'E **35** E13
Panda Mozam. 24°2'S 34°45'E **57** C5
Pandan Malaysia 1°32'N 103°46'E **39** d
Pandan Phil. 11°45'N 122°10'E **37** B6
Pandan Tampoi = Tampoi
  Malaysia 1°30'N 103°39'E **39** d
Pandegelang Indonesia 6°25'S 106°5'E **37** G12
Pandhana India 21°42'N 76°13'E **42** J7
Pandharpur India 17°41'N 75°20'E **44** F2
Pandhurna India 21°36'N 78°35'E **44** D4
Pando Uruguay 34°44'S 56°0'W **95** C4
Pando, L. = Hope, L.
  Australia 28°24'S 139°18'E **63** D2
Pandora Costa Rica 9°43'N 83°3'W **88** E3
Panevėžys Lithuania 55°42'N 24°25'E **9** J21
Pang Sida △ Thailand 14°5'N 102°17'E **38** E4
Pangandaran Indonesia 7°40'S 108°39'E **37** G13
Pangandaran △
  Indonesia 7°43'S 108°42'E **37** G13
Pangani Tanzania 5°25'S 38°58'E **54** F7
Pangfou = Bengbu
  China 32°58'N 117°20'E **33** H9
Pangga, Tanjung
  Indonesia 8°54'S 116°2'E **37** K19
Panghsang = Bangkang
  Myanmar 22°4'N 99°1'E **34** F2
Pangjiabu China 40°38'N 115°26'E **32** D8
Pangkah, Tanjung
  Indonesia 6°51'S 112°33'E **37** G15
Pangkai Myanmar 22°49'N 98°39'E **34** F2
Pangkajene Indonesia 4°46'S 119°34'E **37** E5
Pangkalanbrandan
  Indonesia 4°1'N 98°20'E **36** D1
Pangkalanbuun Indonesia 2°41'S 111°37'E **36** E4
Pangkalpinang Indonesia 2°10'S 106°10'E **36** E3
Pangkor, Pulau Malaysia 4°13'N 100°34'E **39** K3
Pangnirtung = Pangnirtung
  Canada 66°8'N 65°43'W **69** D18
Pangnirtung Canada 66°8'N 65°43'W **69** D18
Pangody Russia 65°52'N 74°27'E **26** C8
Pangong Tso = Bangong Co
  China 33°45'N 78°43'E **43** C8
Panguitch U.S.A. 37°50'N 112°26'W **77** H7
Pangutaran Group Phil. 6°18'N 120°34'E **37** C6
Panhala India 16°49'N 74°7'E **44** F2
Panhandle U.S.A. 35°21'N 101°23'W **84** D4
Pani Mines India 22°29'N 73°50'E **42** H5
Panikota I. India 20°46'N 71°21'E **42** J4
Panipat India 29°25'N 77°2'E **42** E7
Panjal Range = Pir Panjal Range
  India 32°30'N 76°50'E **42** C7
Panjgur Pakistan 27°0'N 64°5'E **40** F4
Panjhra ➤ India 21°13'N 74°57'E **42** D2
Panjim = Panaji India 15°25'N 73°50'E **45** G1
Panjin China 41°3'N 122°2'E **33** D12
Panjnad ➤ Pakistan 28°57'N 70°30'E **42** E4
Panjnad Barrage Pakistan 29°22'N 71°15'E **42** E4
Panjwai Afghan. 31°26'N 65°27'E **42** D1
Panmunjom N. Korea 37°59'N 126°38'E **33** F14
Panna India 24°40'N 80°15'E **43** G9
Panna △ India 24°40'N 80°0'E **43** G8
Panna Hills India 24°40'N 81°15'E **43** G9
Pannawonica Australia 21°39'S 116°19'E **60** D2
Pano Akil Pakistan 27°51'N 69°7'E **42** F3
Panorama Brazil 21°21'S 51°51'W **95** A5
Panruti India 11°46'N 79°35'E **45** J4
Pansemal India 21°39'N 74°42'E **42** J6
Panshan = Panjin China 41°3'N 122°2'E **33** D12
Panshi China 42°58'N 126°5'E **33** C14
Pantanal Brazil 17°30'S 57°40'W **92** H7
Pantanos de Centla △
  Mexico 18°25'N 92°25'W **87** D6
Pantar Indonesia 8°28'S 124°10'E **37** F6
Pante Macassar
  Timor-Leste 9°30'S 123°58'E **37** F6
Pantelleria Italy 36°50'N 11°57'E **22** F4
Pánuco Mexico 22°3'N 98°10'W **87** C5
Panvel India 18°59'N 73°4'E **44** E1
Panzhihua China 26°33'N 101°44'E **34** D3
Paola U.S.A. 38°35'N 94°53'W **80** F7
Paonia U.S.A. 38°52'N 107°36'W **76** G10
Paopao Moorea 17°30'S 149°49'W **59** d
Paoting = Baoding
  China 38°50'N 115°28'E **32** E8
Paot'ou = Baotou China 40°32'N 110°2'E **32** D6
Paoua C.A.R. 7°9'N 16°20'E **54** C3
Pápa Hungary 47°22'N 17°30'E **17** E9
Papa Stour U.K. 60°20'N 1°42'W **11** A7

Papa Westray U.K. 59°20'N 2°55'W **11** B6
Papagayo ➤ Mexico 16°46'N 99°43'W **87** D5
Papagayo, G. de
  Costa Rica 10°30'N 85°50'W **88** D2
Papagni ➤ India 15°35'N 77°45'E **45** G3
Papakura N.Z. 37°4'S 174°59'E **59** B5
Papantla Mexico 20°27'N 97°19'W **87** C5
Papar Malaysia 5°45'N 116°0'E **36** C5
Papara Tahiti 17°43'S 149°31'W **59** d
Paparoa N.Z. 42°7'S 171°26'E **59** d
Papeete Tahiti 17°32'S 149°34'W **59** d
Papenoo Tahiti 17°30'S 149°25'W **59** d
Papenoo ➤ Tahiti 17°30'S 149°25'W **59** d
Papetoai Moorea 17°29'S 149°52'W **59** d
Paposo Chile 25°0'S 70°30'W **94** B1
Papua □ Indonesia 4°0'S 137°0'E **37** E9
Papua, G. of Papua N. G. 9°0'S 144°50'E **58** B7
Papua New Guinea ■
  Oceania 8°0'S 145°0'E **58** B7
Papudo Chile 32°29'S 71°27'W **94** C1
Papun Myanmar 18°2'N 97°30'E **41** K20
Papunya Australia 23°15'S 131°54'E **60** D5
Pará = Belém Brazil 1°20'S 48°30'W **93** D9
Pará □ Brazil 3°20'S 52°0'W **93** D8
Paraburdoo Australia 23°14'S 117°32'E **60** D2
Paracatu Brazil 17°10'S 46°50'W **93** G9
Paracel Is. S. China Sea 15°50'N 112°0'E **36** A4
Parachilna Australia 31°10'S 138°21'E **63** E2
Parachinar Pakistan 33°55'N 70°5'E **42** C4
Paradip India 20°15'N 86°35'E **44** D8
Paradise Canada 39°46'N 121°37'W **78** F5
Paradise ➤ Canada 53°27'N 57°19'W **73** B8
Paradise Hill Canada 53°32'N 109°28'W **71** C7
Paradise River Canada 53°27'N 57°17'W **73** B8
Paradise Valley U.S.A. 41°30'N 117°32'W **76** F5
Paragould U.S.A. 36°3'N 90°29'W **85** C9
Paragua ➤ Venezuela 6°55'N 62°55'W **92** B6
Paraguaçu ➤ Brazil 12°45'S 38°54'W **93** F11
Paraguaçu Paulista
  Brazil 22°22'S 50°35'W **95** A5
Paraguaná, Pen. de
  Venezuela 12°0'N 70°0'W **92** A4
Paraguari Paraguay 25°36'S 57°0'W **94** B4
Paraguarí □ Paraguay 26°0'S 57°10'W **94** B4
Paraguay ■ S. Amer. 23°0'S 57°0'W **94** A4
Paraguay ➤ Paraguay 27°18'S 58°38'W **94** B4
Paraíba = João Pessoa
  Brazil 7°10'S 34°52'W **93** E12
Paraíba □ Brazil 7°0'S 36°0'W **93** E11
Paraíba do Sul ➤ Brazil 21°37'S 41°3'W **95** A7
Paraíso Mexico 18°24'N 93°14'W **87** D6
Parak Iran 28°38'N 52°25'E **47** E7
Parakou Benin 9°25'N 2°40'E **52** G6
Paralkote India 19°47'N 80°41'E **44** E5
Paramaribo Suriname 5°50'N 55°10'W **93** B7
Páramos del Batallón y La Negra △
  Venezuela 8°2'N 71°55'W **89** E5
Paramushir, Ostrov
  Russia 50°24'N 156°0'E **27** D16
Paran ➤ Israel 30°20'N 35°10'E **48** E4
Paraná Argentina 31°45'S 60°30'W **94** C3
Paraná Brazil 12°30'S 47°48'W **93** F9
Paraná □ Brazil 24°30'S 51°0'W **95** A5
Paraná ➤ Argentina 33°43'S 59°15'W **94** C4
Paranaguá Brazil 25°30'S 48°30'W **95** B6
Paranaíba Brazil 19°40'S 51°11'W **93** G8
Paranaíba ➤ Brazil 20°6'S 51°4'W **93** H8
Paranal, Cerro Chile 24°38'S 70°24'W **94** A1
Paranapanema ➤ Brazil 22°40'S 53°9'W **95** A5
Paranapiacaba, Serra do
  Brazil 24°31'S 48°35'W **95** A6
Paranavaí Brazil 23°4'S 52°56'W **95** A5
Parang Maguindanao, Phil. 7°23'N 124°16'E **37** C6
Parang Sulu, Phil. 5°55'N 120°54'E **37** C6
Parângul Mare, Vf.
  Romania 45°20'N 23°37'E **17** F12
Paranthan Sri Lanka 9°26'N 80°24'E **45** K5
Paraparaumu N.Z. 40°57'S 175°3'E **59** D5
Parauapebas Brazil 6°4'S 49°54'W **93** E9
Parbati ➤ Mad. P., India 25°50'N 76°30'E **42** G7
Parbati ➤ Raj., India 26°54'N 77°53'E **42** F7
Parbhani India 19°8'N 76°52'E **44** E3
Parchim Germany 53°26'N 11°52'E **16** B6
Pardes Hanna-Karkur
  Israel 32°28'N 34°57'E **48** C3
Pardo ➤ Bahia, Brazil 15°40'S 39°0'W **93** G11
Pardo ➤ Mato Grosso,
  Brazil 21°46'S 52°9'W **95** A5
Pardoo Roadhouse
  Australia 20°6'S 119°3'E **60** D2
Pardubice Czechia 50°3'N 15°45'E **16** C8
Pare Indonesia 7°43'S 112°12'E **37** G15
Parecis, Serra dos Brazil 13°0'S 60°0'W **92** F7
Paren Russia 62°30'N 163°15'E **27** C17
Parenda India 18°16'N 75°28'E **44** E2
Parent Canada 47°55'N 74°35'W **72** C5
Parent, L. Canada 48°31'N 77°1'W **72** C4
Parepare Indonesia 4°0'S 119°40'E **37** E5
Parga Greece 39°15'N 20°29'E **23** E9
Pargas = Länsi-Turunmaa
  Finland 60°18'N 22°18'E **9** F20
Pargi India 17°11'N 77°53'E **44** E3
Parham Canada 44°39'N 76°43'W **83** B8
Paria ➤ U.S.A. 36°52'N 111°36'W **77** H8
Paria, G. de Venezuela 10°20'N 61°40'W **93** K14
Paria, Pen. de Venezuela 10°50'N 61°50'W **93** K14
Pariaguán Venezuela 8°51'N 64°34'W **92** B6
Paricutín, Cerro Mexico 19°28'N 102°15'W **86** D4
Parigi Indonesia 0°50'S 120°5'E **37** E6
Parika Guyana 6°50'N 58°20'W **92** B7
Parikkala Finland 61°33'N 29°31'E **8** F23
Parima, Serra Brazil 2°30'N 64°0'W **92** C6
Parinari Peru 4°35'S 74°25'W **92** D4
Pariñas, Pta. Peru 4°30'S 82°0'W **90** D2
Parintins Brazil 2°40'S 56°50'W **93** D7
Pariparit Kyun
  Myanmar 14°52'N 93°41'E **45** G11
Paris Canada 43°12'N 80°25'W **82** C4
Paris Idaho, U.S.A. 42°14'N 111°24'W **76** E8
Paris Ky., U.S.A. 38°13'N 84°15'W **81** F11

Paris *Tenn., U.S.A.* 36°18N 88°19W **85** C10
Paris *Tex., U.S.A.* 33°40N 95°33W **84** E7
Parish *U.S.A.* 43°25N 76°8W **83** C8
Parishville *U.S.A.* 44°38N 74°49W **83** B10
Pariti *Indonesia* 10°1S 123°45E **60** B3
Park *U.S.A.* 48°45N 122°18W **78** B4
Park City *U.S.A.* 37°48N 97°20W **80** G5
Park Falls *U.S.A.* 45°56N 90°27W **80** C8
Park Head *Canada* 44°36N 81°9W **82** B3
Park Hills *U.S.A.* 37°51N 90°51W **80** G8
Park Range *U.S.A.* 40°41N 106°41W **76** F10
Park Rapids *U.S.A.* 46°55N 95°4W **80** B6
Park River *U.S.A.* 48°24N 97°45W **80** A5
Park Rynie *S. Africa* 30°25S 30°45E **57** D5
Parkã *Bandar Iran* 25°55N 59°35E **47** E8
Parkano *Finland* 62°1N 23°0E **8** E20
Parker *Ariz., U.S.A.* 34°9N 114°17W **79** L12
Parker *Pa., U.S.A.* 41°5N 79°41W **82** E5
Parker Dam *U.S.A.* 34°18N 114°8W **79** L12
Parkersburg *U.S.A.* 39°16N 81°34W **81** F13
Parkes *Australia* 33°9S 148°11E **63** E4
Parkfield *U.S.A.* 35°54N 120°26W **78** K6
Parkhill *Canada* 43°15N 81°38W **82** C3
Parkland *U.S.A.* 47°9N 122°26W **78** C4
Parkston *U.S.A.* 43°24N 97°59W **80** D5
Parksville *Canada* 49°20N 124°21W **70** D4
Parkway *U.S.A.* 38°32N 121°26W **78** G5
Parla *Spain* 40°14N 3°46W **21** B4
Parlakimidi *India* 18°45N 84°5E **44** E7
Parli *India* 18°50N 76°35E **44** E3
Parma *Italy* 44°48N 10°20E **20** D9
Parma *Idaho, U.S.A.* 43°47N 116°57W **76** E5
Parma *Ohio, U.S.A.* 41°24N 81°43W **82** E3
Parnaguá *Brazil* 10°10S 44°38W **93** F10
Parnaíba *Brazil* 2°54S 41°47W **93** D10
Parnaíba → *Brazil* 3°0S 41°50W **93** D10
Parnassos *Greece* 38°35N 22°30E **23** E10
Parner *India* 19°0N 74°26E **44** E2
Pärnu *Estonia* 58°28N 24°33E **9** G21
Parola *India* 20°47N 75°7E **44** D2
Paroo → *Australia* 31°28S 143°32E **63** E3
Paros *Greece* 37°5N 25°12E **23** F11
Parowan *U.S.A.* 37°51N 112°50W **77** H7
Parral *Chile* 36°10S 71°52W **94** D1
Parramatta *Australia* 33°48S 151°1E **63** B5
Parras *Mexico* 25°25N 102°11W **86** B4
Parrett → *U.K.* 51°12N 3°1W **13** F4
Parris I. *U.S.A.* 32°20N 80°41W **85** E14
Parrsboro *Canada* 45°30N 64°25W **73** C7
Parry Channel *Canada* 74°15N 94°0W **69** B10
Parry I. *Canada* 45°18N 80°10W **82** A4
Parry Is. *Canada* 77°0N 110°0W **69** B10
Parry Sound *Canada* 45°20N 80°0W **82** A5
Parsnip → *Canada* 55°10N 123°2W **70** B4
Parsons *U.S.A.* 37°20N 95°16W **80** G6
Parsons Ra. *Australia* 13°30S 135°15E **62** A2
Partabpur *India* 20°0N 80°42E **44** E5
Partínico *Italy* 38°3N 13°7E **22** E5
Partizansk *Russia* 43°8N 133°9E **27** E14
Partridge I. *Canada* 55°59N 87°37W **72** A2
Partry Mts. *Ireland* 53°40N 9°28W **10** C2
Partur *India* 19°40N 76°14E **44** E3
Paru → *Brazil* 1°33S 52°38W **93** D8
Parur = North Paravar
  India 10°13N 76°14E **45** J3
Parvān □ *Afghan.* 35°0N 69°0E **40** B6
Parvatipuram *India* 18°50N 83°25E **44** E6
Parvatsar *India* 26°52N 74°49E **42** F6
Parys *S. Africa* 26°52S 27°29E **56** C4
Pas, The *Canada* 53°45N 101°15W **71** C8
Pasadena *Canada* 49°1N 57°36W **73** C8
Pasadena *U.S.A.* 29°43N 95°13W **84** G7
Pasaje → *Argentina* 25°39S 63°56W **94** B3
Pasar *Indonesia* 8°27S 114°54E **37** J17
Pasargadae *Iran* 30°11N 53°10E **47** D7
Pascagoula *U.S.A.* 30°21N 88°33W **85** F10
Pascagoula → *U.S.A.* 30°23N 88°37W **85** F10
Paşcani *Romania* 47°14N 26°45E **17** E14
Paschimbanga □ *India* 23°0N 88°0E **43** H13
Pasco *U.S.A.* 46°14N 119°6W **76** C4
Pasco I. *Australia* 20°57S 115°20E **60** D2
Pascoag *U.S.A.* 41°57N 71°42W **83** E13
Pascua, I. de *Chile* 27°7S 109°23W **65** K17
Pasfield L. *Canada* 58°24N 105°20W **71** B7
Pasir Mas *Malaysia* 6°2N 102°8E **39** J4
Pasir Putih *Malaysia* 5°50N 102°24E **39** K4
Paskūh *Iran* 27°34N 61°39E **47** E9
Pasley, C. *Australia* 33°52S 123°35E **61** F3
Pašman *Croatia* 43°58N 15°20E **16** G8
Pasni *Pakistan* 25°15N 63°27E **40** G3
Paso Bravo △ *Paraguay* 22°32S 57°55W **94** A4
Paso Cantinela *Mexico* 32°33N 115°47W **79** N11
Paso de Indios *Argentina* 43°55S 69°0W **96** E3
Paso de los Libres
  Argentina 29°44S 57°10W **94** B4
Paso de los Toros
  Uruguay 32°19S 56°30W **94** C4
Paso Robles *U.S.A.* 35°38N 120°41W **78** K6
Paspébiac *Canada* 48°3N 65°17W **73** C6
Pasrur *Pakistan* 32°16N 74°43E **42** C6
Passage East *Ireland* 52°14N 7°0W **10** D5
Passage West *Ireland* 51°52N 8°21W **10** E3
Passau *Germany* 48°34N 13°28E **16** D7
Passero, C. *Italy* 36°41N 15°10E **22** F6
Passo Fundo *Brazil* 28°10S 52°20W **95** B5
Passos *Brazil* 20°45S 46°37W **93** H9
Pastavy *Belarus* 55°4N 26°50E **9** J22
Pastaza → *Peru* 4°50S 76°52W **92** D3
Pasto *Colombia* 1°13N 77°17W **92** C3
Pasuruan *Indonesia* 7°40S 112°44E **37** G15
Patag I. = Flat I.
  S. China Sea 10°49N 115°49E **36** B5
Patagonia *Argentina* 45°0S 69°0W **96** F3
Patagonia *U.S.A.* 31°33N 110°45W **77** L8
Patambar *Iran* 29°45N 60°17E **47** D9
Patan = Lalitpur *Nepal* 27°40N 85°20E **43** F11
Patan = Somnath *India* 20°53N 70°22E **42** J4
Patan *Gujarat, India* 23°54N 72°14E **42** H5
Patan *Maharashtra, India* 17°22N 73°57E **44** F1

Patani *Indonesia* 0°20N 128°50E **37** D7
Pataudi *India* 28°18N 76°48E **42** E7
Patchewollock *Australia* 35°22S 142°12E **63** F3
Patchogue *U.S.A.* 40°46N 73°1W **83** F11
Patea *N.Z.* 39°45S 174°30E **59** C5
Patensie *S. Africa* 33°46S 24°49E **56** D3
Paternò *Italy* 37°34N 14°54E **22** F6
Paterson *U.S.A.* 40°54N 74°9W **83** F10
Paterson Ra. *Australia* 21°45S 122°10E **60** D3
Pathankot *India* 32°18N 75°45E **42** C6
Pathardi *India* 19°10N 75°11E **44** E2
Pathein *Myanmar* 16°45N 94°30E **41** L19
Pathfinder Res. *U.S.A.* 42°28N 106°51W **76** E10
Pathiu *Thailand* 10°42N 99°19E **39** G2
Pathri *India* 19°15N 76°27E **44** E3
Pathum Thani *Thailand* 14°1N 100°32E **38** E3
Pati *Indonesia* 6°45S 111°1E **37** G14
Patía → *Colombia* 2°13N 78°40W **92** C3
Patiala *Punjab, India* 30°23N 76°26E **42** D7
Patiala *Ut. P., India* 27°43N 79°1E **43** F8
Patkai Bum *India* 27°0N 95°30E **41** F19
Patmos *Greece* 37°21N 26°36E **23** F12
Patna *India* 25°35N 85°12E **43** G11
Patnagarh *India* 20°43N 83°9E **44** D6
Pato Branco *Brazil* 26°13S 52°40W **95** B5
Patong, Ao *Thailand* 7°54N 98°17E **39** a
Patos *Brazil* 6°55S 37°16W **93** E11
Patos, L. dos *Brazil* 31°20S 51°0W **95** C5
Patos, Río de los →
  Argentina 31°18S 69°25W **94** C2
Patos de Minas *Brazil* 18°35S 46°32W **93** G9
Patquia *Argentina* 30°2S 66°55W **94** C2
Patra *Greece* 38°14N 21°47E **23** E9
Patraikos Kolpos *Greece* 38°17N 21°30E **23** E9
Patras = Patra *Greece* 38°14N 21°47E **23** E9
Patrocínio *Brazil* 18°57S 47°0W **93** G9
Pattadakal *India* 16°1N 75°42E **45** F2
Pattani *Thailand* 6°48N 101°15E **39** J3
Pattaya *Thailand* 12°52N 100°55E **38** F3
Patten *U.S.A.* 46°0N 68°38W **81** B19
Patterson *Calif., U.S.A.* 37°28N 121°8W **78** H5
Patterson *La., U.S.A.* 29°42N 91°18W **84** G9
Patterson, Mt. *U.S.A.* 38°29N 119°20W **78** G7
Patti *Punjab, India* 31°17N 74°54E **42** D6
Patti *Ut. P., India* 25°55N 82°12E **43** G10
Pattoki *Pakistan* 31°5N 73°52E **42** D5
Patton *U.S.A.* 40°38N 78°39W **82** F6
Patuakhali *Bangla.* 22°20N 90°25E **41** H17
Patuanak *Canada* 55°55N 107°43W **71** B7
Patuca → *Honduras* 15°50N 84°18W **88** C3
Patuca, Punta *Honduras* 15°49N 84°14W **88** C3
Patuca △ *Honduras* 14°30N 85°30W **88** D2
Patur *India* 20°27N 76°56E **44** D3
Patvinsuo △ *Finland* 63°7N 30°45E **8** E24
Pátzcuaro *Mexico* 19°31N 101°38W **86** D4
Pau *France* 43°19N 0°25W **20** E3
Paudash *Canada* 44°59N 77°58W **82** B7
Pauk *Myanmar* 21°27N 94°30E **41** J19
Paul I. *Canada* 56°30N 61°20W **73** A7
Paul Smiths *U.S.A.* 44°26N 74°15W **83** B10
Paulatuk *Canada* 69°25N 124°0W **68** D7
Paulding Bay *S. Ocean* 66°0S 118°0E **5** C8
Paulistana *Brazil* 8°9S 41°9W **93** E10
Paulo Afonso *Brazil* 9°21S 38°15W **93** E11
Paulpietersburg *S. Africa* 27°23S 30°50E **57** C5
Pauls Valley *U.S.A.* 34°44N 97°13W **84** D6
Pauma Valley *U.S.A.* 33°16N 116°58W **79** M10
Pauni *India* 20°48N 79°40E **44** D4
Pauri *India* 30°9N 78°47E **43** D8
Pavagada *India* 14°6N 77°16E **45** G3
Pāveh *Iran* 35°3N 46°22E **46** C5
Pavia *Italy* 45°7N 9°8E **20** D8
Pavilion *U.S.A.* 42°52N 78°1W **82** D6
Pāvilosta *Latvia* 56°53N 21°14E **9** H19
Pavlodar *Kazakhstan* 52°33N 77°0E **26** D8
Pavlograd = Pavlohrad
  Ukraine 48°30N 35°52E **19** E6
Pavlohrad *Ukraine* 48°30N 35°52E **19** E6
Pavlovo *Russia* 55°58N 43°5E **18** C7
Pavlovsk *Russia* 50°26N 40°5E **19** E6
Pavlovskaya *Russia* 46°17N 39°47E **19** E6
Pawai, Pulau *Singapore* 1°11N 103°44E **39** d
Pawayan *India* 28°4N 80°6E **43** E9
Pawhuska *U.S.A.* 36°40N 96°20W **84** C6
Pawling *U.S.A.* 41°34N 73°36W **83** E11
Pawnee *U.S.A.* 36°20N 96°48W **84** C6
Pawnee City *U.S.A.* 40°7N 96°9W **80** E5
Pawtucket *U.S.A.* 41°53N 71°23W **83** E13
Paxi *Greece* 39°14N 20°12E **23** E9
Paxton *U.S.A.* 40°27N 88°6W **80** E9
Payakumbuh *Indonesia* 0°20S 100°35E **36** E2
Payette *U.S.A.* 44°5N 116°56W **76** D5
Payne Bay = Kangirsuk
  Canada 60°0N 70°0W **69** F18
Payne L. *Canada* 59°30N 74°30W **69** F17
Paynes Find *Australia* 29°15S 117°42E **61** E2
Paynesville *U.S.A.* 45°23N 94°43W **80** C6
Paysandú *Uruguay* 32°19S 58°8W **94** C4
Payson *Ariz., U.S.A.* 34°14N 111°20W **77** J8
Payson *Utah, U.S.A.* 40°3N 111°44W **76** F8
Paz → *Guatemala* 13°44N 90°10W **88** D1
Paz, B. la *Mexico* 24°9N 110°25W **86** C2
Pāzanān *Iran* 30°35N 49°59E **47** D6
Pazardzhik *Bulgaria* 42°12N 24°20E **23** C11
Pe Ell *U.S.A.* 46°34N 123°18W **78** D3
Peabody *U.S.A.* 42°31N 70°56W **83** D14
Peace → *Canada* 59°0N 111°25W **70** B6
Peace Point *Canada* 59°7N 112°27W **70** B6
Peace River *Canada* 56°15N 117°18W **70** B5
Peach Springs *U.S.A.* 35°32N 113°25W **77** J7
Peachland *Canada* 49°47N 119°45W **70** D5
Peachtree City *U.S.A.* 33°25N 84°35W **85** E12
Peak, The = Kinder Scout
  U.K. 53°24N 1°52W **12** D6
Peak Charles △ *Australia* 32°42S 121°10E **61** F3
Peak District △ *U.K.* 53°24N 1°46W **12** D6
Peak Hill *Australia* 32°47S 148°11E **63** E4
Peak Ra. *Australia* 22°50S 148°20E **62** C4

Peake Cr. → *Australia* 28°2S 136°7E **63** D2
Peale, Mt. *U.S.A.* 38°26N 109°14W **76** G9
Pearblossom *U.S.A.* 34°30N 117°55W **79** L9
Pearl → *U.S.A.* 30°11N 89°32W **85** F10
Pearl and Hermes Reef
  U.S.A. 27°55N 175°45W **75** K4
Pearl Banks *Sri Lanka* 8°45N 79°45E **45** K4
Pearl River = Zhu Jiang →
  China 22°45N 113°37E **35** F9
Pearl River *U.S.A.* 41°4N 74°2W **83** E10
Pearl River Bridge *China* 22°15N 113°48E **31** a
Pearsall *U.S.A.* 28°54N 99°6W **84** G5
Peary Chan. *Canada* 79°40N 101°30W **69** B11
Peary Land *Greenland* 82°40N 33°0W **4** A6
Pease → *U.S.A.* 34°12N 99°2W **84** D5
Peawanuck *Canada* 55°15N 85°12W **72** A2
Pebane *Mozam.* 17°10S 38°8E **55** H7
Pebas *Peru* 3°10S 71°46W **92** D4
Pebble Beach *U.S.A.* 36°34N 121°57W **78** J5
Peć = Pejë *Kosovo* 42°40N 20°17E **23** C9
Pechenga *Russia* 69°29N 31°4E **8** B24
Pechenizhyn *Ukraine* 48°30N 24°48E **17** D13
Pechora *Russia* 65°10N 57°11E **18** A10
Pechora → *Russia* 68°13N 54°15E **18** A9
Pechorskaya Guba *Russia* 68°40N 54°0E **18** A9
Pechory *Russia* 57°48N 27°40E **9** H22
Pecos *N. Mex., U.S.A.* 35°35N 105°41W **77** J11
Pecos *Tex., U.S.A.* 31°26N 103°30W **84** F3
Pecos → *U.S.A.* 29°42N 101°22W **84** G4
Pécs *Hungary* 46°5N 18°15E **17** E10
Pedasí *Panama* 7°32N 80°2W **88** E3
Pedda Bellala *India* 19°4N 78°4E **44** E4
Peddapalli *India* 18°40N 79°24E **44** E4
Peddapuram *India* 17°6N 82°8E **44** F6
Pedder, L. *Australia* 42°55S 146°10E **63** G4
Peddie *S. Africa* 33°14S 27°7E **57** D4
Pedernales *Dom. Rep.* 18°2N 71°44W **89** C5
Pedirka Desert *Australia* 26°47S 134°11E **63** A1
Pedra Azul *Brazil* 16°2S 41°17W **93** G10
Pedra Lume *Cabo Verde* 16°40N 22°52W **52** b
Pedreiras *Brazil* 4°32S 44°40W **93** D10
Pedro Afonso *Brazil* 9°0S 48°10W **93** E9
Pedro Cays *Jamaica* 17°5N 77°48W **88** C4
Pedro de Valdivia *Chile* 22°55S 69°38W **94** A2
Pedro Juan Caballero
  Paraguay 22°30S 55°40W **95** A4
Pee Dee = Great Pee Dee →
  U.S.A. 33°21N 79°10W **85** E15
Peebinga *Australia* 34°52S 140°57E **63** E3
Peebles *U.K.* 55°40N 3°11W **11** F5
Peekskill *U.S.A.* 41°17N 73°55W **83** E11
Peel I. of Man *U.K.* 54°13N 4°40W **12** C3
Peel → *Australia* 30°50S 150°29E **63** E5
Peel → *Canada* 67°0N 135°0W **68** D5
Peel Sd. *Canada* 73°0N 96°0W **68** C12
Peera Peera Poolanna L.
  Australia 26°30S 138°0E **63** D2
Peerless Lake *Canada* 56°37N 114°40W **70** B6
Peers *Canada* 53°40N 116°0W **70** C5
Pegasus Bay *N.Z.* 43°20S 173°10E **59** E4
Pegu = Bago *Myanmar* 17°20N 96°29E **41** L20
Pegu Yoma *Myanmar* 19°0N 96°0E **41** K20
Pehuajó *Argentina* 35°45S 62°0W **94** D3
Pei Xian *China* 34°44N 116°55E **32** G9
Peikang *Taiwan* 23°34N 120°18E **35** F13
Peine *Chile* 23°45S 68°8W **94** A2
Peine *Germany* 52°19N 10°14E **16** B6
Peipus, L. = Chudskoye, Ozero
  Russia 58°13N 27°30E **9** G22
Peixe *Brazil* 12°0S 48°40W **93** F9
Peixe → *Brazil* 21°31S 51°58W **93** H8
Pejë *Kosovo* 42°40N 20°17E **23** C9
Pekalongan *Indonesia* 6°53S 109°40E **37** G13
Pekan *Malaysia* 3°30N 103°25E **39** L4
Pekan Nenas *Malaysia* 1°31N 103°31E **39** d
Pekanbaru *Indonesia* 0°30N 101°15E **36** D2
Pekin *U.S.A.* 40°35N 89°40W **80** E9
Pekutatan *Indonesia* 8°25S 114°49E **37** J17
Pelabuhan Ratu, Teluk
  Indonesia 7°5S 106°30E **37** G12
Pelagie, Is. *Italy* 35°39N 12°33E **22** G5
Pelaihari *Indonesia* 3°55S 114°45E **36** E4
Pelée, Mt. *Martinique* 14°48N 61°10W **88** c
Pelée, Pt. *Canada* 41°54N 82°31W **72** D3
Pelee I. *Canada* 41°47N 82°40W **72** E3
Peleng *Indonesia* 1°20S 123°30E **37** E6
Pelentong *Malaysia* 1°32N 103°49E **39** d
Pelican *U.S.A.* 57°58N 136°14W **70** B1
Pelican L. *Canada* 52°28N 100°20W **71** C8
Pelican Narrows
  Canada 55°10N 102°56W **71** B8
Peljesac *Croatia* 42°55N 17°25E **22** C7
Pelkosenniemi *Finland* 67°6N 27°28E **8** C22
Pella *S. Africa* 29°1S 19°6E **56** C2
Pella *U.S.A.* 41°25N 92°55W **80** E7
Pello *Finland* 66°47N 23°59E **8** C20
Pelly → *Canada* 62°47N 137°19W **70** A1
Pelly Bay *Canada* 68°38N 89°50W **69** C11
Pelorus Sd. *N.Z.* 40°59S 173°59E **59** D4
Pelotas *Brazil* 31°42S 52°23W **95** C5
Pelotas → *Brazil* 27°28S 51°55W **95** B5
Pelvoux, Massif du *France* 44°52N 6°20E **20** D7
Pemalang *Indonesia* 6°53S 109°23E **37** G13
Pemanggil, Pulau
  Malaysia 2°37N 104°21E **39** L5
Pematangsiantar *Indonesia* 2°57N 99°5E **36** D1
Pemba *Mozam.* 12°58S 40°30E **55** G8
Pemba I. *Tanzania* 5°0S 39°45E **54** F7
Pemberton *Australia* 34°30S 116°0E **61** F2
Pemberton *Canada* 50°25N 122°50W **70** C4
Pembina → *Canada* 54°45N 114°17W **70** C6
Pembroke *Canada* 45°50N 77°7W **72** C4
Pembroke *U.K.* 51°41N 4°55W **13** F3
Pembrokeshire □ *U.K.* 51°52N 4°56W **13** F3
Pembrokeshire Coast △
  U.K. 51°50N 5°2W **13** F2
Pen *India* 18°45N 73°5E **44** E1
Pen-y-bont ar Ogwr = Bridgend
  U.K. 51°30N 3°34W **13** F4

Pen-y-Ghent *U.K.* 54°10N 2°14W **12** C5
Penal *Trin. & Tob.* 10°9N 61°29W **93** K15
Penang = Pinang *Malaysia* 5°25N 100°15E **39** c
Penápolis *Brazil* 21°30S 50°0W **95** A6
Peñarroya-Pueblonuevo
  Spain 38°19N 5°16W **21** C3
Penarth *U.K.* 51°26N 3°11W **13** F4
Peñas, C. de *Spain* 43°42N 5°52W **21** A3
Peñas, G. de *Chile* 47°0S 75°0W **96** F1
Pench → *India* 21°17N 79°10E **44** D4
Pench △ *India* 21°45N 79°20E **43** J8
Penchi'i = Benxi *China* 41°20N 123°48E **33** D12
Pend Oreille → *U.S.A.* 49°4N 117°37W **76** B5
Pend Oreille, L. *U.S.A.* 48°10N 116°21W **76** B5
Pendembu *S. Leone* 9°7N 11°14W **52** G3
Pender B. *Australia* 16°45S 122°42E **60** C3
Pendleton *U.S.A.* 45°40N 118°47W **76** D4
Pendra *India* 22°46N 81°57E **43** H9
Penedo *Brazil* 10°15S 36°36W **93** F11
Penelokan *Indonesia* 8°17S 115°22E **37** J18
Penetanguishene *Canada* 44°50N 79°55W **82** B5
Penfield *U.S.A.* 41°13N 78°35W **82** E6
Penfro = Pembroke *U.K.* 51°41N 4°55W **13** F3
Peng'an *China* 31°2N 106°22E **34** B6
Penganga → *India* 19°53N 79°9E **44** E4
P'enghu Ch'üntou
  Taiwan 23°34N 119°30E **35** F12
Penglai *China* 37°48N 120°42E **33** F11
Pengshan *China* 30°14N 103°58E **34** B4
Pengshui *China* 29°17N 108°12E **34** C7
Penguin *Australia* 41°8S 146°6E **63** G4
Pengxi *China* 30°44N 105°45E **34** B5
Pengze *China* 29°52N 116°32E **35** C11
Pengzhou *China* 31°4N 103°32E **34** B4
Peniche *Portugal* 39°19N 9°22W **21** C1
Penida, Nusa *Indonesia* 8°45S 115°30E **37** K18
Peninsular Malaysia □
  Malaysia 4°0N 102°0E **39** L4
Penitente, Serra do *Brazil* 8°45S 46°20W **93** E9
Penkridge *U.K.* 52°44N 2°6W **12** E5
Penmarch, Pte. de *France* 47°48N 4°22E **20** C1
Penn Hills *U.S.A.* 40°28N 79°52W **82** F5
Penn Yan *U.S.A.* 42°40N 77°3W **82** D7
Pennant *Canada* 50°32N 108°14W **71** C7
Penner → *India* 14°35N 80°10E **45** G5
Pennines *U.K.* 54°45N 2°27E **12** C5
Pennington *U.S.A.* 39°15N 121°47W **78** F5
Pennsburg *U.S.A.* 40°23N 75°29W **83** F9
Pennsylvania □ *U.S.A.* 40°45N 77°30W **81** E8
Penny *U.S.A.* 53°51N 121°20W **70** C4
Penobscot → *U.S.A.* 44°30N 68°48W **81** C19
Penobscot B. *U.S.A.* 44°35N 68°50W **81** C19
Penola *Australia* 37°25S 140°48E **63** F3
Penong *Australia* 31°56S 133°1E **61** F5
Penonomé *Panama* 8°31N 80°21W **88** E3
Penrhyn *Cook Is.* 9°0S 158°0W **65** H12
Penrith *Australia* 33°43S 150°38E **63** E5
Penrith *U.K.* 54°40N 2°45W **12** C5
Penryn *U.K.* 50°9N 5°7W **13** G2
Pensacola *U.S.A.* 30°25N 87°13W **85** F11
Pensacola Mts. *Antarctica* 84°0S 40°0W **5** E1
Pense *Canada* 50°25N 104°59W **71** C8
Penshurst *Australia* 37°49S 142°20E **63** F3
Penticton *Canada* 49°30N 119°38W **70** D5
Pentland *Australia* 20°32S 145°25E **62** C4
Pentland Firth *U.K.* 58°43N 3°10W **11** C5
Pentland Hills *U.K.* 55°48N 3°25W **11** F5
Penukonda *India* 14°5N 77°38E **45** G3
Penza *Russia* 53°15N 45°5E **18** D8
Penzance *U.K.* 50°7N 5°33W **13** G2
Penzhino *Russia* 63°30N 167°55E **27** C17
Penzhinskaya Guba
  Russia 61°30N 163°0E **27** C17
Peoria *Ariz., U.S.A.* 33°43N 112°14W **77** K7
Peoria *Ill., U.S.A.* 40°42N 89°36W **80** E9
Pepani → *S. Africa* 25°49S 22°47E **56** D3
Pepacton Res. *U.S.A.* 42°5N 74°58W **83** D10
Pera Hd. *Australia* 12°55S 141°37E **62** A3
Perabumulih *Indonesia* 3°27S 104°15E **36** E2
Perak □ *Malaysia* 5°0N 101°0E **39** K3
Perak → *Malaysia* 4°0N 100°50E **39** K3
Perämeri △ *Finland* 65°35N 24°22E **8** D21
Perancak *Indonesia* 8°24S 114°37E **37** J17
Percé *Canada* 48°31N 64°13W **73** C7
Perche, Collines du *France* 48°30N 0°40E **20** B4
Percival Lakes *Australia* 21°25S 125°0E **60** D4
Percy Is. *Australia* 21°39S 150°16E **62** C5
Perdido, Mte. *Spain* 42°40N 0°5E **21** A6
Perdu, Mt. = Perdido, Mte.
  Spain 42°40N 0°5E **21** A6
Pereira *Colombia* 4°49N 75°43W **92** C3
Peremul Par *India* 11°10N 72°4E **45** J1
Perenjori *Australia* 29°26S 116°16E **61** E2
Pereyaslav-Khmelnytskyy
  Ukraine 50°3N 31°28E **19** D5
Pérez, I. *Mexico* 22°24N 89°42W **87** C7
Pergamino *Argentina* 33°52S 60°30W **94** C3
Pergau → *Malaysia* 5°23N 102°2E **39** K3
Perham *U.S.A.* 46°36N 95°34W **80** B6
Perhentian, Kepulauan
  Malaysia 5°54N 102°42E **39** K4
Péribonka → *Canada* 48°45N 72°5E **73** C5
Péribonka, L. *Canada* 50°1N 71°10W **73** B5
Péribonka, La Centrale de
  Canada 49°30N 71°10W **73** C5
Perico *Argentina* 24°20S 65°5W **94** A2
Pericos *Mexico* 25°3N 107°42W **86** B3
Périgueux *France* 45°10N 0°42E **20** D4
Perijá, Sierra de *Colombia* 9°30N 73°3W **92** B4
Perijá △ *Venezuela* 8°17S 115°22E **92** B4
Peringat *Malaysia* 6°2N 102°17E **39** J4
Perito Moreno *Argentina* 46°36S 70°56W **96** F2
Periyakulam *India* 10°15N 77°15E **45** J3
Periyar → *India* 10°15N 76°10E **45** J3
Periyar, L. *India* 9°25N 77°10E **45** K3
Periyar △ *India* 9°25N 77°10E **45** K3
Perkasie *U.S.A.* 40°22N 75°18W **83** F9
Perlas, Arch. de las
  Panama 8°41N 79°7W **88** E4
Perlas, Punta de *Nic.* 12°30N 83°30W **88** D3
Perlis □ *Malaysia* 6°30N 100°15E **39** J2
Perm *Russia* 58°0N 56°10E **18** C10
Pernambuco = Recife
  Brazil 8°0S 35°0W **93** E12
Pernambuco □ *Brazil* 8°0S 37°0W **93** E11
Pernatty Lagoon
  Australia 31°30S 137°12E **63** E2
Pernik *Bulgaria* 42°35N 23°2E **23** C10
Peron Is. *Australia* 13°9S 130°4E **60** B5
Peron Pen. *Australia* 26°0S 113°10E **61** E1
Perow *Canada* 54°35N 126°10W **70** C3
Perpignan *France* 42°42N 2°53E **20** E5
Perris *U.S.A.* 33°47N 117°14W **79** M9
Perry *Fla., U.S.A.* 30°7N 83°35W **85** F13
Perry *Ga., U.S.A.* 32°28N 83°44W **85** E13
Perry *Iowa, U.S.A.* 41°51N 94°6W **80** E6
Perry *N.Y., U.S.A.* 42°42N 78°0W **82** D7
Perry *Okla., U.S.A.* 36°17N 97°14W **84** C6
Perryton *U.S.A.* 36°24N 100°48W **84** C4
Perryville *U.S.A.* 37°43N 89°52W **80** G9
Persepolis *Iran* 29°55N 52°50E **47** D7
Pershotravensk *Ukraine* 50°13N 27°40E **17** C14
Persia = Iran ■ *Asia* 33°0N 53°0E **47** C7
Persian Gulf *Asia* 27°0N 50°0E **47** E6
Perth *Australia* 31°57S 115°52E **61** F2
Perth *Canada* 44°55N 76°15W **83** B8
Perth *U.K.* 56°24N 3°26W **11** E5
Perth & Kinross □ *U.K.* 56°45N 3°55W **11** E5
Perth Amboy *U.S.A.* 40°30N 74°15W **83** F10
Perth-Andover *Canada* 46°44N 67°42W **73** C6
Perth Basin *Ind. Oc.* 30°0S 108°0E **64** L2
Peru *Ind., U.S.A.* 40°45N 86°4W **81** E11
Peru *N.Y., U.S.A.* 44°35N 73°32W **83** B11
Peru ■ *S. Amer.* 4°0S 75°0W **92** D4
Peru Basin *Pac. Oc.* 20°0S 95°0W **65** J18
Peru-Chile Trench *Pac. Oc.* 20°0S 72°0W **92** G3
Perugia *Italy* 43°7N 12°23E **22** C5
Pervomaysk *Ukraine* 48°10N 30°46E **19** E5
Pervouralsk *Russia* 56°59N 59°59E **18** C10
Pésaro *Italy* 43°54N 12°55E **22** C5
Pescadores = P'enghu Ch'üntou
  Taiwan 23°34N 119°30E **35** F12
Pescara *Italy* 42°28N 14°13E **22** C6
Peshawar *Pakistan* 34°2N 71°37E **42** B4
Peshkopi *Albania* 41°41N 20°25E **23** D9
Peshtigo *U.S.A.* 45°3N 87°45W **80** C10
Pesqueira *Brazil* 8°20S 36°42W **93** E11
Petah Tiqwa *Israel* 32°6N 34°53E **48** C3
Petaling Jaya *Malaysia* 3°4N 101°42E **39** L3
Petaluma *U.S.A.* 38°14N 122°39W **78** G4
Pétange *Lux.* 49°33N 5°55E **15** E5
Petaro *Pakistan* 25°31N 68°18E **42** G3
Petatlán *Mexico* 17°31N 101°16W **86** D4
Petauke *Zambia* 14°14S 31°20E **55** G6
Petén Itzá, L. *Guatemala* 16°58N 89°50W **88** C2
Peter I. *Br. Virgin Is.* 18°22N 64°35W **89** e
Peter I. Øy *Antarctica* 69°0S 91°0W **5** C16
Peter Pond L. *Canada* 55°55N 108°44W **71** B7
Peterbell *Canada* 48°36N 83°21W **72** C3
Peterborough *Australia* 32°58S 138°51E **63** E2
Peterborough *Canada* 44°20N 78°20W **82** B6
Peterborough *U.K.* 52°35N 0°15E **13** E7
Peterborough □ *U.K.* 52°35N 0°15W **13** E7
Peterculter *U.K.* 57°6N 2°16W **11** D6
Peterhead *U.K.* 57°31N 1°48W **11** D7
Peterlee *U.K.* 54°47N 1°20W **12** C6
Petermann ○ *Australia* 24°58S 130°0E **61** E4
Petermann Gletscher
  Greenland 80°30N 60°0W **69** A20
Petermann Ranges
  Australia 26°0S 130°30E **61** E4
Petersburg *Alaska,
  U.S.A.* 56°48N 132°58W **68** F3
Petersburg *Pa., U.S.A.* 40°34N 78°3W **82** F6
Petersburg *Va., U.S.A.* 37°14N 77°24W **81** G15
Petersburg *W. Va., U.S.A.* 39°1N 79°5W **81** F14
Petersfield *U.K.* 51°1N 0°56W **13** F7
Petit-Canal *Guadeloupe* 16°25N 61°31W **88** b
Petit-Goâve *Haiti* 18°27N 72°51W **89** C5
Petit Lac Manicouagan
  Canada 51°25N 67°40W **73** B6
Petit-Mécatina →
  Canada 50°40N 59°30W **73** B8
Petit-Mécatina, Î. du
  Canada 50°30N 59°25W **73** B8
Petit Piton *St. Lucia* 13°51N 61°5W **89** f
Petit-Saguenay *Canada* 48°15N 70°4W **73** C5
Petitcodiac *Canada* 45°57N 65°11W **73** C6
Petite Terre, Îles de la
  Guadeloupe 16°13N 61°9W **88** b
Petitot → *Canada* 60°14N 123°29W **70** A4
Petitsikapau L. *Canada* 54°37N 66°25W **73** B6
Petlad *India* 22°30N 72°45E **42** H5
Peto *Mexico* 20°8N 88°55W **87** C7
Petone *N.Z.* 41°13S 174°53E **59** D5
Petorca *Chile* 32°15S 70°56W **94** C1
Petoskey *U.S.A.* 45°22N 84°57W **81** C11
Petra *Jordan* 30°20N 35°22E **48** E4
Petra, Ostrov *Russia* 76°15N 118°30E **27** B12
Petra Velikogo, Zaliv
  Russia 42°40N 132°0E **28** C6
Petre, Pt. *Canada* 43°50N 77°9W **82** C7
Petrich *Bulgaria* 41°24N 23°13E **23** D10
Petrified Forest △ *U.S.A.* 35°0N 109°30W **77** J9
Petrikov = Pyetrikaw
  Belarus 52°11N 28°29E **17** B15
Petrolândia *Brazil* 9°5S 38°20W **93** E11
Petrolia *Canada* 42°54N 82°9W **82** D2
Petrolina *Brazil* 9°24S 40°30W **93** E10
Petropavl *Kazakhstan* 54°53N 69°13E **26** D7
Petropavlovsk = Petropavl
  Kazakhstan 54°53N 69°13E **26** D7
Petropavlovsk-Kamchatskiy
  Russia 53°3N 158°43E **27** D16
Petrópolis *Brazil* 22°33S 43°9W **95** A7
Petroşani *Romania* 45°28N 23°20E **17** F12
Petrovaradin *Serbia* 45°16N 19°55E **23** B8

Petrovsk Russia 52°22N 45°19E 18 D8
Petrovsk-Zabaykalskiy Russia 51°20N 108°55E 27 D11
Petrozavodsk Russia 61°41N 34°20E 18 B5
Petrus Steyn S. Africa 27°38S 28°8E 57 C4
Petrusburg S. Africa 29°4S 25°26E 56 C4
Peumo Chile 34°21S 71°12W 94 C1
Peureulak Indonesia 4°48N 97°45E 36 D1
Pevek Russia 69°41N 171°19E 27 C18
Pforzheim Germany 48°52N 8°41E 16 D5
Pha Taem △ Thailand 15°32N 105°30E 38 E5
Phagwara India 31°10N 75°40E 42 D6
Phala Botswana 23°45S 26°50E 56 B4
Phalaborwa S. Africa 23°57S 31°7E 57 B5
Phalera = Phulera India 26°52N 75°16E 42 F6
Phalodi India 27°12N 72°24E 42 F5
Phaltan India 17°59N 74°26E 44 F2
Phaluai, Ko Thailand 9°32N 99°41E 39 b
Phan Thailand 19°28N 99°43E 38 C2
Phan Rang -Thap Cham Vietnam 11°34N 109°0E 39 G7
Phan Ri Cua Vietnam 11°16N 108°40E 39 G7
Phan Si Pan Vietnam 22°18N 103°46E 38 A4
Phan Thiet Vietnam 11°1N 108°9E 39 G7
Phan Thiet, Vinh Vietnam 10°53N 108°5E 39 G7
Phan Wa, Laem Thailand 7°47N 98°25E 39 a
Phanat Nikhom Thailand 13°27N 101°11E 38 F3
Phangan, Ko Thailand 9°45N 100°0E 39 H3
Phangnga Thailand 8°28N 98°30E 39 H2
Phangnga, Ao Thailand 8°16N 98°33E 39 a
Phanom Sarakham Thailand 13°45N 101°21E 38 F3
Phaphund India 26°36N 79°28E 43 F8
Pharenda India 27°5N 83°17E 43 F10
Pharr U.S.A. 26°12N 98°11W 84 H5
Phatthalung Thailand 7°39N 100°6E 39 J3
Phayam, Ko Thailand 9°44N 98°25E 39 H2
Phayao Thailand 19°11N 99°55E 38 C2
Phelps U.S.A. 42°58N 77°3W 82 D7
Phelps L. Canada 59°15N 103°15W 71 B8
Phenix City U.S.A. 32°28N 85°1W 85 E12
Phet Buri = Phetchaburi Thailand 13°1N 99°55E 38 F2
Phetchabun Thailand 16°25N 101°8E 38 D3
Phetchabun, Thiu Khao Thailand 16°0N 101°20E 38 E3
Phetchaburi Thailand 13°1N 99°55E 38 F2
Phi Phi, Ko Thailand 7°45N 98°46E 39 J2
Phiafay Laos 14°48N 106°0E 38 E6
Phibun Mangsahan Thailand 15°14N 105°14E 38 E5
Phichai Thailand 17°22N 100°10E 38 D3
Phichit Thailand 16°26N 100°22E 38 D3
Philadelphia Miss., U.S.A. 32°46N 89°7W 85 E10
Philadelphia N.Y., U.S.A. 44°9N 75°43W 83 B9
Philadelphia Pa., U.S.A. 39°57N 75°9W 83 G9
Philadelphia Int. ✈ (PHL) U.S.A. 39°51N 75°18W 83 G9
Philip U.S.A. 44°2N 101°40W 80 C3
Philip Smith Mts. U.S.A. 68°0N 148°0W 74 B10
Philippeville Belgium 50°12N 4°33E 15 D4
Philippi U.S.A. 39°9N 80°3W 81 F13
Philippi L. Australia 24°20S 138°55E 62 C2
Philippine Basin Pac. Oc. 17°0N 132°0E 64 F5
Philippine Sea Pac. Oc. 18°0N 125°0E 64 F4
Philippine Trench = Mindanao Trench Pac. Oc. 12°0N 126°6E 37 B7
Philippines ■ Asia 12°0N 123°0E 37 B6
Philippolis S. Africa 30°15S 25°16E 56 D4
Philippopolis = Plovdiv Bulgaria 42°8N 24°44E 23 C11
Philipsburg Canada 45°2N 73°5W 83 A11
Philipsburg Mont., U.S.A. 46°20N 113°18W 76 C7
Philipsburg Pa., U.S.A. 40°54N 78°13W 82 F6
Philipstown = Daingean Ireland 53°18N 7°17W 10 C4
Philipstown S. Africa 30°28S 24°30E 56 D3
Phillip I. Australia 38°30S 145°12E 63 F4
Phillips U.S.A. 45°42N 90°24W 80 C8
Phillipsburg Kans., U.S.A. 39°45N 99°19W 80 F4
Phillipsburg N.J., U.S.A. 40°42N 75°12W 83 F9
Philmont U.S.A. 42°15N 73°39W 83 D11
Philomath U.S.A. 44°32N 123°22W 76 D2
Phimai Thailand 15°13N 102°30E 38 E4
Phitsanulok Thailand 16°50N 100°12E 38 D3
Phnom Kulen △ Cambodia 13°38N 104°15E 38 F5
Phnom Penh Cambodia 11°33N 104°55E 39 G5
Phnum Penh = Phnom Penh Cambodia 11°33N 104°55E 39 G5
Pho, Laem Thailand 6°55N 101°19E 39 J3
Phoenicia U.S.A. 42°5N 74°14W 83 D10
Phoenix Mauritius 20°17S 57°30E 55 d
Phoenix Ariz., U.S.A. 33°26N 112°4W 77 K7
Phoenix N.Y., U.S.A. 43°14N 76°18W 83 C8
Phoenix Is. Kiribati 3°30S 172°0W 64 H10
Phoenix Sky Harbour Int. ✈ (PHX) U.S.A. 33°26N 112°5W 77 K7
Phoenixville U.S.A. 40°8N 75°31W 83 F9
Phon Thailand 15°49N 102°36E 38 E4
Phong → Thailand 16°23N 102°56E 38 D4
Phong Nha -Ke Bang △ Vietnam 17°30N 106°10E 38 D6
Phong Saly Laos 21°42N 102°9E 34 G4
Phong Tho Vietnam 22°32N 103°21E 38 A4
Phonsavan Laos 19°27N 103°10E 38 C4
Phonum Thailand 8°49N 98°48E 39 H2
Phosphate Hill Australia 21°53S 139°58E 62 C2
Photharam Thailand 13°41N 99°51E 38 F2
Phra Nakhon Si Ayutthaya Thailand 14°25N 100°30E 38 E3
Phra Thong, Ko Thailand 9°5N 98°17E 39 H2
Phrae Thailand 18°7N 100°9E 38 C3
Phrom Phiram Thailand 17°2N 100°12E 38 D3
Phrom Thep, Laem Thailand 7°45N 98°19E 39 a
Phu Bia Laos 19°10N 103°0E 38 C4
Phu Chong -Na Yoi △ Thailand 14°25N 105°30E 38 E5
Phu Hin Rong Kla △ Thailand 17°0N 100°59E 38 D3
Phu Kao -Phu Phan Kham △ Thailand 16°53N 102°31E 38 D4
Phu Kradung △ Thailand 17°2N 101°44E 38 D3
Phu Loi Laos 20°14N 103°14E 38 B4
Phu Luang △ Thailand 17°15N 101°29E 38 D3
Phu Ly Vietnam 20°35N 105°50E 34 G5
Phu My Vietnam 14°15N 109°5E 38 E7
Phu Pha Man △ Thailand 16°44N 101°50E 38 D3
Phu Phan △ Thailand 17°0N 103°56E 38 D4
Phu Quoc, Dao Vietnam 10°20N 104°0E 39 G4
Phu Sa Dok Bua △ Thailand 16°11N 104°45E 38 D5
Phu Sang △ Thailand 19°35N 100°19E 38 C3
Phu Tho Vietnam 21°24N 105°13E 34 G5
Phu Wiang △ Thailand 16°39N 102°23E 38 D4
Phuc Yen Vietnam 21°16N 105°45E 34 G5
Phuket Thailand 7°53N 98°24E 39 a
Phuket, Ko Thailand 8°0N 98°22E 39 a
Phul India 30°19N 75°14E 42 D6
Phulad India 25°38N 73°49E 42 G5
Phulbani India 20°28N 84°14E 44 D7
Phulchari Bangla. 25°11N 89°37E 43 G13
Phulera India 26°52N 75°16E 42 F6
Phulpur India 25°31N 82°49E 43 G10
Phunphin Thailand 9°7N 99°12E 39 H2
Phuntsholing Bhutan 26°51N 89°23E 43 F13
Phuphrabat Thailand 17°40N 102°45E 38 D4
Phuthaditjhaba S. Africa 28°29S 28°48E 57 C4
Phyu = Pyu Myanmar 18°30N 96°28E 41 K20
Pia ☼ Australia 27°7S 116°23E 61 E2
Piacenza Italy 45°1N 9°40E 20 D8
Piai, Tanjung Malaysia 1°17N 103°30E 39 d
Pian Cr. → Australia 30°2S 148°12E 63 E4
Pianosa Italy 42°35N 10°5E 22 C4
Piao'ertun China 41°50N 123°47E 33 D12
Piapot Canada 49°59N 109°8W 71 D7
Piatra Neamţ Romania 46°56N 26°21E 17 E14
Piauí □ Brazil 7°0S 43°0W 93 E10
Piauí → Brazil 6°38S 42°42W 93 E10
Piave → Italy 45°32N 12°44E 22 B5
Pibor Post South Sudan 6°47N 33°3E 53 G12
Picardie France 49°50N 3°0E 20 B5
Picardy = Picardie France 49°50N 3°0E 20 B5
Picayune U.S.A. 30°32N 89°41W 85 F10
Pichhor India 25°58N 78°20E 43 G8
Pichilemu Chile 34°22S 72°0W 94 C1
Pichor India 25°11N 78°11E 42 G8
Pickerel L. Canada 48°40N 91°25W 72 C1
Pickering U.K. 54°15N 0°46W 12 C7
Pickering, Vale of U.K. 54°14N 0°45W 12 C7
Pickle Lake Canada 51°30N 90°12W 72 B1
Pickwick L. U.S.A. 35°4N 88°15W 85 D10
Pico Azores 38°28N 28°20W 52 a
Pico Bonito △ Honduras 15°34N 86°48W 88 C2
Pico Truncado Argentina 46°40S 68°0W 96 F3
Picos Brazil 7°5S 41°28W 93 E10
Picton Canada 44°1N 77°9W 82 B7
Picton N.Z. 41°18S 174°3E 59 D5
Pictou Canada 45°41N 62°42W 73 C7
Picture Butte Canada 49°55N 112°45W 70 D6
Pictured Rocks ⌓ U.S.A. 46°30N 86°30W 80 B10
Picún Leufú Argentina 39°30S 69°5W 96 D3
Pidurutalagala Sri Lanka 7°10N 80°50E 45 L5
Piedmont = Piemonte □ Italy 45°0N 8°0E 20 D7
Piedmont Ala., U.S.A. 33°55N 85°37W 85 E12
Piedmont S.C., U.S.A. 34°42N 82°28W 66 F11
Piedras Negras Mexico 28°42N 100°31W 86 B4
Pieksämäki Finland 62°18N 27°10E 8 E22
Pielinen Finland 63°15N 29°40E 8 E23
Pieljekaise △ Sweden 66°20N 16°45E 8 C17
Piemonte □ Italy 45°0N 8°0E 20 D7
Pienaarsrivier S. Africa 25°15S 28°18E 57 C4
Piercefield U.S.A. 44°13N 74°35W 83 B10
Pierceland Canada 54°20N 109°46W 71 C7
Pierpont U.S.A. 41°45N 80°34W 82 E4
Pierre U.S.A. 44°22N 100°21W 80 C3
Pierrefonds Canada 45°29N 73°51W 83 A11
Piet Retief S. Africa 27°1S 30°50E 57 C5
Pietarsaari Finland 63°40N 22°43E 8 E20
Pietermaritzburg S. Africa 29°35S 30°25E 57 C5
Pietersburg = Polokwane S. Africa 23°54S 29°25E 57 B4
Pietrosul, Vf. Maramureş, Romania 47°35N 24°43E 17 E13
Pietrosul, Vf. Suceava, Romania 47°12N 25°18E 17 E13
Pigeon I. India 14°2N 74°20E 45 G2
Pigeon L. Canada 44°27N 78°30W 82 B6
Piggott U.S.A. 36°23N 90°11W 85 C9
Pigüe Argentina 37°36S 62°25W 94 D3
Pihani India 27°36N 80°15E 43 F9
Pihlajavesi Finland 61°45N 28°45E 8 F23
Pijijiapan Mexico 15°42N 93°14W 87 D6
Pikangikum Canada 51°49N 94°0W 71 C10
Pikes Peak U.S.A. 38°50N 105°3W 76 G11
Piketberg S. Africa 32°55S 18°40E 56 D2
Pikeville U.S.A. 37°29N 82°31W 81 G12
Pikou China 39°18N 122°22E 33 E12
Pikwitonei Canada 55°35N 97°9W 71 B9
Piła Poland 53°10N 16°48E 17 B9
Pilanesberg △ S. Africa 25°15S 27°4E 56 C4
Pilani India 28°22N 75°33E 42 E6
Pilar Paraguay 26°50S 58°20W 94 B4
Pilaya → Bolivia 20°55S 64°4W 92 H6
Pilbara Australia 21°15S 118°16E 60 D2
Pilcomaya → Paraguay 25°21S 57°42W 94 B4
Pilgrim's Rest S. Africa 24°55S 30°44E 57 B5
Pilibhit India 28°40N 79°50E 43 E8
Pilica → Poland 51°52N 21°17E 17 C11
Pilipinas = Philippines ■ Asia 12°0N 123°0E 37 B6
Pilkhawa India 28°43N 77°42E 42 E7
Pilliga Australia 30°21S 148°54E 63 E4
Pilos Greece 36°55N 21°42E 23 F9
Pilot Mound Canada 49°15N 98°54W 71 D9
Pilot Point U.S.A. 33°24N 96°53W 84 E6
Pilot Rock U.S.A. 45°29N 118°50W 76 D4
Pima U.S.A. 32°54N 109°50W 77 K9
Pimba Australia 31°18S 136°46E 63 E2
Pimenta Bueno Brazil 11°35S 61°10W 92 F6
Pimentel Peru 6°45S 79°55W 92 E3
Pimpri Chinchwad India 18°37N 73°47E 44 E1
Pin Valley △ India 31°50N 77°50E 42 D7
Pinang Malaysia 5°25N 100°15E 39 c
Pinang □ Malaysia 5°20N 100°20E 39 K3
Pinar del Río Cuba 22°26N 83°40W 88 B3
Pınarhisar Turkey 41°37N 27°30E 23 D12
Pinatubo, Mt. Phil. 15°8N 120°21E 37 A6
Pinawa Canada 50°9N 95°50W 71 C9
Pinchang China 31°36N 107°3E 34 B6
Pincher Creek Canada 49°30N 113°57W 70 D6
Pinchi L. Canada 54°38N 124°30W 70 C4
Pinckneyville U.S.A. 38°5N 89°23W 80 F9
Pińczów Poland 50°32N 20°32E 17 C11
Pindar Australia 28°30S 115°47E 61 E2
Pindera Downs ☼ Australia 29°24S 142°37E 63 A3
Pindi Gheb Pakistan 33°14N 72°21E 42 C5
Pindos Oros Greece 40°0N 21°0E 23 E9
Pindus Mts. = Pindos Oros Greece 40°0N 21°0E 23 E9
Pine → B.C., Canada 56°8N 120°43W 70 B4
Pine → Sask., Canada 58°50N 105°38W 71 B7
Pine Bluff U.S.A. 34°13N 92°1W 84 D8
Pine Bluffs U.S.A. 41°11N 104°4W 76 F11
Pine City U.S.A. 45°50N 92°59W 80 C7
Pine Cr. → U.S.A. 41°10N 77°16W 82 E7
Pine Creek Australia 13°50S 131°50E 60 B5
Pine Falls Canada 50°34N 96°11W 71 C9
Pine Flat L. U.S.A. 36°50N 119°20W 78 J7
Pine Grove U.S.A. 40°33N 76°23W 83 F8
Pine Hill Australia 23°38S 146°57E 62 C4
Pine Island Glacier Antarctica 76°0S 100°0W 5 D15
Pine Pass Canada 55°25N 122°42W 70 B4
Pine Ridge U.S.A. 43°2N 102°33W 80 D2
Pine River Canada 51°45N 100°30W 71 C8
Pine River U.S.A. 46°43N 94°24W 80 B6
Pine Valley U.S.A. 32°50N 116°32W 79 N10
Pinecrest U.S.A. 38°12N 120°1W 78 G6
Pinedale Calif., U.S.A. 36°50N 119°48W 78 J7
Pinedale Wyo., U.S.A. 42°52N 109°52W 76 E9
Pinega → Russia 64°30N 44°19E 18 B8
Pinehouse L. Canada 55°32N 106°35W 71 B7
Pineimuta → Canada 52°8N 88°33W 72 B1
Pinerolo Italy 44°53N 7°21E 20 D7
Pines, Akra Greece 40°5N 24°20E 23 D11
Pinetop-Lakeside U.S.A. 34°9N 109°58W 77 J9
Pinetown S. Africa 29°48S 30°54E 57 C5
Pineville U.S.A. 31°19N 92°26W 84 F8
Ping → Thailand 15°42N 100°9E 38 E3
Pingaring Australia 32°40S 118°32E 61 F2
Pingba China 26°23N 106°12E 34 D6
Pingbian China 23°0N 103°45E 34 F4
Pingchuan China 27°35N 101°55E 34 D3
Pingding China 37°47N 113°38E 32 F7
Pingdingshan China 33°43N 113°27E 32 H7
Pingdu China 36°42N 119°59E 33 F10
Pingelly Australia 32°32S 117°5E 61 F2
Pingguo China 23°19N 107°36E 34 F6
Pinghe China 24°17N 117°21E 35 E11
Pinghu China 30°40N 121°2E 35 B13
Pingjiang China 28°45N 113°36E 35 C9
Pingle China 24°40N 110°40E 35 E8
Pingli China 32°27N 109°22E 34 A7
Pingliang China 35°35N 106°31E 32 G4
Pinglu China 39°31N 112°30E 32 E7
Pingluo China 38°52N 106°30E 32 E4
Pingnan Fujian, China 26°55N 119°0E 35 D12
Pingnan Guangxi Zhuangzu, China 23°33N 110°22E 35 F8
Pingquan China 41°1N 118°37E 33 D10
Pingrup Australia 33°32S 118°29E 61 F2
Pingshan China 28°39N 104°3E 34 C5
Pingtan China 25°31N 119°47E 35 E12
Pingtang China 25°49N 107°17E 34 E6
P'ingtung Taiwan 22°38N 120°30E 35 F13
Pingwu China 32°25N 104°30E 32 H3
Pingxiang Guangxi Zhuangzu, China 22°6N 106°46E 34 F6
Pingxiang Jiangxi, China 27°43N 113°48E 35 D9
Pingyao China 37°12N 112°10E 32 F7
Pingyi China 35°30N 117°35E 33 G9
Pingyin China 36°20N 116°25E 32 F9
Pingyuan Guangdong, China 24°37N 115°57E 35 E10
Pingyuan Shandong, China 37°10N 116°22E 32 F9
Pingyuanjie China 23°45N 103°48E 34 F4
Pinheiro Brazil 2°31S 45°5W 93 D9
Pinheiro Machado Brazil 31°34S 53°23W 95 C5
Pinhel Portugal 40°50N 7°1W 21 B2
Pini Indonesia 0°10N 98°40E 36 D1
Pinios → Greece 39°55N 22°41E 23 E10
Pinjarra Australia 32°37S 115°52E 61 F2
Pink Mountain Canada 57°3N 122°52W 70 B4
Pinnacle Is. = Senkaku-Shotō E. China Sea 25°45N 123°30E 29 M1
Pinnacles △ U.S.A. 36°25N 121°12W 78 J5
Pinnaroo Australia 35°17S 140°53E 63 F3
Pinon Hills U.S.A. 34°26N 117°39W 79 L9
Pinos Mexico 22°18N 101°34W 86 C4
Pinos, Mt. U.S.A. 34°49N 119°8W 79 L7
Pinos Pt. U.S.A. 36°38N 121°57W 77 H3
Pinrang Indonesia 3°46S 119°41E 37 E5
Pins, Pte. aux Canada 42°15N 81°51W 82 D3
Pinsk Belarus 52°10N 26°1E 17 B14
Pintados Chile 20°35S 69°40W 92 H5
Pinyang China 27°42N 120°31E 35 D13
Pinyug Russia 60°5N 48°0E 18 B8
Pioche U.S.A. 37°56N 114°27W 77 H6
Piombino Italy 42°55N 10°32E 22 C4
Pioner, Ostrov Russia 79°50N 92°0E 27 B10
Piopiotaki = Milford Sd. N.Z. 44°41S 167°47E 59 F1
Piorini, L. Brazil 3°15S 62°35W 92 D6
Piotrków Trybunalski Poland 51°23N 19°43E 17 C10
Pīp Iran 26°45N 60°10E 47 E9
Pipar India 26°25N 73°31E 42 F5
Pipar Road India 26°27N 73°27E 42 F5
Piparia Mad. P., India 22°45N 78°23E 42 H8
Piparia Mad. P., India 21°49N 77°37E 42 J7
Pipestone U.S.A. 44°0N 96°19W 80 D5
Pipestone → Canada 52°53N 89°23W 72 B2
Pipestone Cr. → Canada 49°38N 100°15W 71 D8
Piplan Pakistan 32°17N 71°21E 42 C4
Piploda India 23°37N 74°56E 42 H6
Pipmuacan, Rés. Canada 49°45N 70°30W 73 C5
Pippingarra Australia 20°27S 118°42E 60 D2
Piqua U.S.A. 40°9N 84°15W 81 E11
Piquiri → Brazil 24°3S 54°14W 95 A5
Pir Panjal Range India 32°30N 76°50E 42 C7
Pīr Sohrāb Iran 25°44N 60°54E 47 E9
Piracicaba Brazil 22°45S 47°40W 95 A6
Piracuruca Brazil 3°50S 41°50W 93 D10
Pirae Tahiti 17°31S 149°32W 59 d
Pirajuí Brazil 21°59S 49°29W 95 A6
Piram I. India 21°36N 72°21E 42 J5
Pirané Argentina 25°42S 59°6W 94 B4
Pīrānshahr Iran 36°41N 45°8E 46 B5
Pirapora Brazil 17°20S 44°56W 93 G10
Pirawa India 24°10N 76°2E 42 G7
Pirgos Greece 37°40N 21°27E 23 F9
Piribebuy Paraguay 25°26S 57°2W 94 B4
Pirimapun Indonesia 6°20S 138°24E 37 F9
Pirin Planina Bulgaria 41°40N 23°30E 23 D10
Pírineos = Pyrénées Europe 42°45N 0°18E 20 E4
Piripiri Brazil 4°15S 41°46W 93 D10
Pirlangimpi Australia 11°24S 130°26E 60 B5
Pirmasens Germany 49°12N 7°36E 16 D4
Pirot Serbia 43°9N 22°33E 23 C10
Piru Indonesia 3°4S 128°12E 37 E7
Piru U.S.A. 34°25N 118°48W 79 L8
Pisa Italy 43°43N 10°23E 22 C4
Pisagua Chile 19°40S 70°15W 92 G4
Pisco Peru 13°50S 76°12W 92 F3
Písek Czechia 49°19N 14°10E 16 D8
Pishan China 37°30N 78°33E 30 D4
Pīshīn Iran 26°6N 61°47E 47 E9
Pishin Pakistan 30°35N 67°0E 42 D2
Pishin Lora → Pakistan 29°9N 64°5E 42 E1
Pising Indonesia 5°8S 121°53E 37 F6
Pismo Beach U.S.A. 35°9N 120°38W 79 K6
Pissis, Cerro Argentina 27°45S 68°48W 94 B2
Pistóia Italy 43°55N 10°54E 22 C4
Pistol B. Canada 62°25N 92°37W 71 A10
Pisuerga → Spain 41°33N 4°52W 21 B3
Pit → U.S.A. 40°47N 122°6W 76 F2
Pitarpunga L. Australia 34°24S 143°30E 63 E3
Pitcairn I. Pac. Oc. 25°5S 130°5W 65 K14
Pitch L. Trin. & Tob. 10°14N 61°39W 93 K15
Piteå Sweden 65°20N 21°25E 8 D19
Piteälven → Sweden 65°20N 21°25E 8 D19
Piteşti Romania 44°52N 24°54E 17 F13
Pithapuram India 17°10N 82°15E 44 F6
Pithara Australia 30°20S 116°35E 61 F2
Pithora India 21°16N 82°31E 44 D6
Pithoragarh India 29°35N 80°13E 43 E9
Pithoro Pakistan 25°31N 69°23E 42 G3
Pitlochry U.K. 56°42N 3°44W 11 E5
Pitt I. Canada 53°30N 129°50W 70 C3
Pitti I. India 10°50N 72°38E 45 J1
Pittsburg Calif., U.S.A. 38°2N 121°53W 78 G5
Pittsburg Kans., U.S.A. 37°25N 94°42W 80 G6
Pittsburg Tex., U.S.A. 33°0N 94°59W 84 E7
Pittsburgh U.S.A. 40°26N 79°58W 82 F5
Pittsfield Ill., U.S.A. 39°36N 90°49W 80 F8
Pittsfield Maine, U.S.A. 44°47N 69°23W 81 C19
Pittsfield Mass., U.S.A. 42°27N 73°15W 83 D11
Pittsfield N.H., U.S.A. 43°18N 71°20W 83 C13
Pittston U.S.A. 41°19N 75°47W 83 E9
Pittsworth Australia 27°41S 151°37E 63 D5
Pituri → Australia 22°35S 138°30E 62 C2
Piura Peru 5°15S 80°38W 92 E2
Piuthan Nepal 28°7N 82°56E 43 E10
Pixian China 30°48N 103°52E 34 B4
Pixley U.S.A. 35°58N 119°18W 78 K7
Pizhou = Pei Xian China 34°44N 116°55E 32 G9
Pizhou China 34°18N 117°57E 33 G9
Placentia Canada 47°20N 54°0W 73 C9
Placentia B. Canada 47°0N 54°40W 73 C9
Placerville U.S.A. 38°44N 120°48W 78 G6
Placetas Cuba 22°15N 79°44W 88 B4
Plaine des Jarres Laos 19°27N 103°10E 38 C4
Plainfield N.J., U.S.A. 40°37N 74°25W 83 F10
Plainfield Ohio, U.S.A. 40°13N 81°43W 82 F3
Plainfield Vt., U.S.A. 44°17N 72°26W 83 B12
Plains Mont., U.S.A. 47°28N 114°53W 76 C6
Plains Tex., U.S.A. 33°11N 102°50W 84 E3
Plainview Nebr., U.S.A. 42°21N 97°47W 80 D5
Plainview Tex., U.S.A. 34°11N 101°43W 84 D4
Plainwell U.S.A. 42°27N 85°38W 81 D11
Plaistow U.S.A. 42°50N 71°6W 83 D13
Plaka, Akra Greece 35°11N 26°19E 23 G12
Plana Cays Bahamas 22°38N 73°30W 89 B5
Planada U.S.A. 37°16N 120°19W 78 H6
Plano U.S.A. 33°1N 96°42W 84 E6
Plant City U.S.A. 28°1N 82°7W 85 G13
Plaquemine U.S.A. 30°17N 91°14W 84 F9
Plasencia Spain 40°3N 6°8W 21 B2
Plaster City U.S.A. 32°47N 115°51W 79 N11
Plaster Rock Canada 46°53N 67°22W 73 C6
Plastun Russia 44°45N 136°19E 28 B8
Plata, Río de la → S. Amer. 34°45S 57°30W 94 C4
Plátani → Italy 37°23N 13°16E 22 F5
Platte U.S.A. 43°23N 98°51W 80 D4
Platte → Mo., U.S.A. 39°16N 94°50W 80 F6
Platte → Nebr., U.S.A. 41°4N 95°53W 80 E6
Platteville U.S.A. 42°44N 90°29W 80 D8
Plattsburgh U.S.A. 44°42N 73°28W 83 B11
Plattsmouth U.S.A. 41°1N 95°53W 80 E6
Plauen Germany 50°30N 12°8E 16 C7
Plavinas Latvia 56°35N 25°46E 9 H21
Playa del Carmen Mexico 20°37N 87°4W 87 C7
Playgreen L. Canada 54°0N 98°15W 71 C9
Pleasant Bay Canada 46°51N 60°48W 73 C7
Pleasant Hill U.S.A. 37°57N 122°4W 78 H4
Pleasant Mount U.S.A. 41°44N 75°26W 83 E9
Pleasanton Calif., U.S.A. 37°39N 121°52W 78 H5
Pleasanton Tex., U.S.A. 28°58N 98°29W 84 G5
Pleasantville N.J., U.S.A. 39°24N 74°32W 81 F16
Pleasantville Pa., U.S.A. 41°35N 79°34W 82 E5
Plei Ku Vietnam 13°57N 108°0E 38 F7
Plenty → Australia 23°25S 136°31E 62 C2
Plenty, B. of N.Z. 37°45S 177°0E 59 B6
Plentywood U.S.A. 48°47N 104°34W 76 B11
Plesetsk Russia 62°43N 40°20E 18 B7
Plessisville Canada 46°14N 71°47W 73 C5
Plétipi, L. Canada 51°44N 70°6W 73 B5
Pleven Bulgaria 43°26N 24°37E 23 C11
Plevna Canada 44°58N 76°59W 82 B8
Pljevlja Montenegro 43°21N 19°21E 23 C8
Płock Poland 52°32N 19°40E 17 B10
Plöckenstein Germany 48°46N 13°51E 16 D7
Ploieşti Romania 44°57N 26°5E 17 F14
Plonge, Lac la Canada 55°8N 107°20W 71 B7
Plovdiv Bulgaria 42°8N 24°44E 23 C11
Plover Cove Res. China 22°28N 114°15E 31 a
Plum U.S.A. 40°29N 79°47W 82 F5
Plum I. U.S.A. 41°11N 72°12W 83 E12
Plumas U.S.A. 39°45N 120°4W 78 F6
Plummer U.S.A. 47°20N 116°53W 76 C5
Plumridge Lakes Australia 29°26S 125°16E 61 E4
Plumtree Zimbabwe 20°27S 27°55E 55 J5
Plungė Lithuania 55°53N 21°59E 9 J19
Plymouth Trin. & Tob. 11°14N 60°48W 93 J16
Plymouth U.K. 50°22N 4°10W 13 G3
Plymouth Calif., U.S.A. 38°29N 120°51W 78 G6
Plymouth Ind., U.S.A. 41°21N 86°19W 80 E10
Plymouth Mass., U.S.A. 41°57N 70°40W 83 E14
Plymouth N.C., U.S.A. 35°52N 76°43W 85 D16
Plymouth N.H., U.S.A. 43°46N 71°41W 83 C13
Plymouth Pa., U.S.A. 41°14N 75°57W 83 E9
Plymouth Wis., U.S.A. 43°45N 87°59W 80 D10
Plympton-Wyoming = Wyoming Canada 42°57N 82°7W 82 D2
Plynlimon = Pumlumon Fawr U.K. 52°28N 3°46W 13 E4
Plyusa Russia 58°28N 29°27E 9 G23
Plzeň Czechia 49°45N 13°22E 16 D7
Pmere Nyente ☼ Australia 24°15S 136°10E 62 C2
Po → Italy 44°57N 12°4E 22 B5
Po Hai = Bo Hai China 39°0N 119°0E 33 E10
Po Toi China 22°10N 114°16E 31 a
Pobeda Russia 65°12N 146°12E 27 C15
Pobedy, Pik Asia 42°0N 79°58E 30 C4
Pocahontas Ark., U.S.A. 36°16N 90°58W 85 C9
Pocahontas Iowa, U.S.A. 42°44N 94°40W 80 D6
Pocatello U.S.A. 42°52N 112°27W 76 E7
Pocomoke City U.S.A. 38°5N 75°34W 81 F16
Poços de Caldas Brazil 21°50S 46°33W 95 A6
Podgorica Montenegro 42°30N 19°19E 23 C8
Podile India 15°37N 79°37E 45 G4
Podilska Vysochyna Ukraine 49°0N 28°0E 17 D14
Podolsk Russia 55°25N 37°30E 18 C6
Podporozhye Russia 60°55N 34°2E 18 B5
Pofadder S. Africa 29°10S 19°22E 56 C2
Pogranichnyy Russia 44°25N 131°24E 28 B5
Poh Indonesia 0°46S 122°51E 37 E6
Pohang S. Korea 36°1N 129°23E 33 F15
Pohjanmaa □ Finland 62°58N 22°50E 8 E20
Pohnpei Micronesia 6°55N 158°10E 64 G7
Pohri India 25°32N 77°22E 42 G6
Poinsett, C. Antarctica 65°42S 113°18E 5 C8
Point Arena U.S.A. 38°55N 123°41W 78 G3
Point Baker U.S.A. 56°21N 133°37W 70 B2
Point Calimere India 10°17N 79°49E 45 J4
Point Fortin Trin. & Tob. 10°10N 61°42W 93 K15
Point Hope U.S.A. 68°21N 166°47W 74 B6
Point L. Canada 65°15N 113°4W 68 D9
Point Lisas Trin. & Tob. 10°24N 61°29W 93 K15
Point Pedro Sri Lanka 9°50N 80°15E 45 K5
Point Pelee △ Canada 41°57N 82°31W 82 E2
Point Pleasant N.J., U.S.A. 40°5N 74°4W 83 F10
Point Pleasant W. Va., U.S.A. 38°51N 82°8W 81 F12
Point Reyes ⌓ U.S.A. 38°10N 122°55W 78 G2
Pointe-à-Pitre Guadeloupe 16°15N 61°32W 88 b
Pointe-au-Pic = La Malbaie Canada 47°40N 70°10W 73 C5
Pointe-Claire Canada 45°26N 73°50W 83 A11
Pointe-Gatineau Canada 45°27N 75°41W 83 A9
Pointe-Noire Congo 4°48S 11°53E 54 E2
Pointe-Noire Guadeloupe 16°14N 61°47W 88 b
Poipet Cambodia 13°39N 102°33E 38 F4
Poisonbush Ra. Australia 22°30S 121°30E 60 D3
Poissonnier Pt. Australia 19°57S 119°10E 60 C2
Poitiers France 46°35N 0°20E 20 C4
Poitou France 46°40N 0°10W 20 C3
Pojoaque U.S.A. 35°54N 106°1W 77 J10
Pokaran India 27°0N 71°50E 42 F4
Pokataroo Australia 29°30S 148°36E 63 D4
Pokhara Nepal 28°14N 83°58E 43 E10
Poko Dem. Rep. of the Congo 3°7N 26°52E 54 D5
Pokrovsk Russia 61°29N 129°0E 27 C13
Pola = Pula Croatia 44°54N 13°57E 16 F7
Polacca U.S.A. 35°50N 110°23W 77 J8
Polan Iran 25°30N 61°10E 47 E9
Poland U.S.A. 43°13N 75°3W 83 C9
Poland ■ Europe 52°0N 20°0E 17 C10
Polar Bear ⌓ Canada 55°0N 83°45W 72 A2
Polatsk Belarus 55°30N 28°50E 9 J23
Polavaram India 17°15N 81°38E 44 F5
Polcura Chile 37°17S 71°43W 94 D1

Polesye = Pripet Marshes
  Europe 52°10N 27°10E **17 B15**
Polevskoy Russia 56°26N 60°11E **18 C11**
Police Poland 53°33N 14°33E **16 B8**
Police, Pte. Seychelles 4°51S 55°32E **55 b**
Poligiros Greece 40°23N 23°25E **23 D10**
Polillo Is. Phil. 14°56N 122°0E **37 B6**
Polk U.S.A. 41°22N 79°56W **82 E5**
Pollachi India 10°35N 77°0E **45 J3**
Polnovat Russia 63°50N 65°54E **26 C7**
Polokwane S. Africa 23°54S 29°25E **57 B4**
Polokwane → S. Africa 22°25S 30°5E **57 B5**
Polonnaruwa Sri Lanka 7°56N 81°0E **45 L5**
Polonne Ukraine 50°6N 27°30E **17 C14**
Polonnoye = Polonne
  Ukraine 50°6N 27°30E **17 C14**
Polson U.S.A. 47°41N 114°9W **76 C6**
Poltava Ukraine 49°35N 34°35E **19 E5**
Põltsamaa Estonia 58°39N 25°58E **9 G21**
Polunochnoye Russia 60°52N 60°25E **26 C7**
Polur India 12°32N 79°11E **45 H4**
Põlva Estonia 58°3N 27°3E **9 G22**
Polyarny Russia 69°8N 33°20E **8 B25**
Polyarnyye Zori Russia 67°22N 32°30E **8 C25**
Polynesia Pac. Oc. 10°0S 162°0W **65 F11**
Polynésie française = French
  Polynesia ☑ Pac. Oc. 20°0S 145°0W **65 J13**
Pombal Portugal 39°55N 8°40W **21 C1**
Pomene Mozam. 22°53S 35°33E **57 B6**
Pomeroy Ohio, U.S.A. 39°2N 82°2W **81 F12**
Pomeroy Wash., U.S.A. 46°28N 117°36W **76 C5**
Pomézia Italy 41°40N 12°30E **22 D5**
Pomona Australia 26°22S 152°52E **63 D5**
Pomona U.S.A. 34°4N 117°45W **79 L9**
Pomorskie, Pojezierze
  Poland 53°40N 16°37E **17 B9**
Pompeys Pillar U.S.A. 45°59N 107°57W **76 D10**
Pompeys Pillar △ U.S.A. 46°0N 108°0W **76 D10**
Pompton Lakes U.S.A. 41°0N 74°17W **83 F10**
Ponape = Pohnpei
  Micronesia 6°55N 158°10E **64 G7**
Ponask L. Canada 54°0N 92°41W **72 B1**
Ponca U.S.A. 42°34N 96°43W **80 D5**
Ponca City U.S.A. 36°42N 97°5W **84 C6**
Ponce Puerto Rico 18°1N 66°37W **89 d**
Ponchatoula U.S.A. 30°26N 90°26W **85 F9**
Poncheville, L. Canada 50°10N 76°55W **72 B4**
Pond U.S.A. 35°43N 119°20W **79 K7**
Pond Inlet Canada 72°40N 77°0W **69 C16**
Pondicherry = Puducherry
  India 11°59N 79°50E **45 J4**
Ponds, I. of Canada 53°27N 55°52W **73 B8**
Ponferrada Spain 42°32N 6°35W **21 A2**
Ponnaiyar → India 11°50N 79°45E **45 J4**
Ponnani India 10°45N 75°59E **45 J2**
Ponneri India 13°20N 80°15E **45 H5**
Ponnuru India 16°5N 80°34E **45 F5**
Ponoka Canada 52°42N 113°40W **70 C6**
Ponorogo Indonesia 7°52S 111°27E **37 G14**
Ponoy Russia 67°0N 41°13E **18 A7**
Ponoy → Russia 66°59N 41°17E **18 A7**
Ponta Delgada Azores 37°44N 25°40W **52 a**
Ponta Grossa Brazil 25°7S 50°10W **95 B5**
Ponta Porã Brazil 22°20S 55°35W **95 A4**
Pontardawe U.K. 51°43N 3°51W **13 F3**
Pontarlier France 46°54N 6°20E **20 C7**
Pontchartrain, L. U.S.A. 30°5N 90°5W **85 F9**
Ponte Nova Brazil 20°25S 42°54W **95 A7**
Ponteix Canada 49°46N 107°29W **71 D7**
Pontevedra Spain 42°26N 8°40W **21 A1**
Pontiac Ill., U.S.A. 40°53N 88°38W **80 E9**
Pontiac Mich., U.S.A. 42°38N 83°18W **81 D12**
Pontian Kechil Malaysia 1°29N 103°23E **39 d**
Pontianak Indonesia 0°3S 109°15E **36 E3**
Pontine Is. = Ponziane, Ísole
  Italy 40°55N 12°57E **22 D5**
Pontine Mts. = Kuzey Anadolu
  Dağları Turkey 41°0N 36°45E **19 F6**
Pontivy France 48°5N 2°58W **20 B2**
Pontoise France 49°3N 2°5E **20 B5**
Ponton → Canada 58°27N 116°11W **70 B5**
Pontypool Canada 44°6N 78°38W **82 B6**
Pontypool U.K. 51°42N 3°2W **13 F4**
Pontypridd U.K. 51°36N 3°20W **13 F4**
Ponziane, Ísole Italy 40°55N 12°57E **22 D5**
Poochera Australia 32°43S 134°51E **63 E1**
Poole U.K. 50°43N 1°59W **13 G6**
Poole □ U.K. 50°43N 1°59W **13 G6**
Poona = Pune India 18°29N 73°57E **44 E1**
Poonamallee India 13°3N 80°10E **45 H5**
Pooncarie Australia 33°22S 142°31E **63 E3**
Poopelloe L. Australia 31°40S 144°0E **63 E3**
Poopó, L. de Bolivia 18°30S 67°35W **92 G5**
Popayán Colombia 2°27N 76°36W **92 C3**
Poperinge Belgium 50°51N 2°42E **15 D2**
Popiltah L. Australia 33°10S 141°42E **63 E3**
Popio L. Australia 33°10S 141°52E **63 E3**
Poplar U.S.A. 48°7N 105°12W **76 B11**
Poplar → Canada 53°0N 97°19W **71 C9**
Poplar Bluff U.S.A. 36°46N 90°24W **80 G8**
Poplarville U.S.A. 30°51N 89°32W **85 F10**
Popocatépetl, Volcán
  Mexico 19°2N 98°38W **87 D5**
Popokabaka
  Dem. Rep. of the Congo 5°41S 16°40E **54 F3**
Poprad Slovakia 49°3N 20°18E **17 D11**
Porali → Pakistan 25°58N 66°26E **42 G2**
Porbandar India 21°44N 69°43E **42 J3**
Porcher I. Canada 53°50N 130°30W **70 C2**
Porcupine → Canada 59°11N 104°46W **71 B8**
Porcupine → U.S.A. 66°34N 145°19W **68 D2**
Porcupine Gorge △
  Australia 20°22S 144°26E **62 C3**
Pordenone Italy 45°57N 12°39E **22 B5**
Pori Finland 61°29N 21°48E **8 F19**
Porkhov Russia 57°45N 29°38E **9 H23**
Porlamar Venezuela 10°57N 63°51W **92 A6**
Pormpuraaw Australia 14°59S 141°26E **62 A3**
Pormpuraaw ◎
  Australia 14°55S 141°47E **62 A3**

Poronaysk Russia 49°13N 143°0E **31 B17**
Poroshiri-Dake Japan 42°41N 142°52E **28 C11**
Porpoise B. Antarctica 66°0S 127°0E **5 C9**
Porsangerfjorden Norway 70°40N 25°40E **8 A21**
Porsgrunn Norway 59°10N 9°40E **9 G13**
Port Alberni Canada 49°14N 124°50W **70 D4**
Port Alfred S. Africa 33°36S 26°55E **56 D4**
Port Alice Canada 50°20N 127°25W **70 C3**
Port Allegany U.S.A. 41°48N 78°17W **82 E6**
Port Allen U.S.A. 30°27N 91°12W **84 F9**
Port Alma Australia 23°38S 150°53E **62 C5**
Port Alma Canada 42°10N 82°14W **82 D2**
Port Angeles U.S.A. 48°7N 123°27W **78 B3**
Port Antonio Jamaica 18°10N 76°26W **88 a**
Port Aransas U.S.A. 27°50N 97°4W **84 H6**
Port Arthur Australia 43°7S 147°50E **63 G4**
Port Arthur U.S.A. 29°54N 93°56W **84 G8**
Port au Choix Canada 50°43N 57°22W **73 B8**
Port au Port B. Canada 48°40N 58°50W **73 C8**
Port-au-Prince Haiti 18°40N 72°20W **89 C5**
Port Augusta Australia 32°30S 137°50E **63 E2**
Port Austin U.S.A. 44°3N 83°1W **82 B2**
Port Blair India 11°40N 92°45E **45 J11**
Port Blandford Canada 48°20N 54°10W **73 C9**
Port Bradshaw Australia 12°30S 137°20E **62 A2**
Port Broughton
  Australia 33°37S 137°56E **63 E2**
Port Bruce Canada 42°39N 81°0W **82 D4**
Port Burwell Canada 42°40N 80°48W **82 D4**
Port Campbell Australia 11°56N 92°37E **45 J11**
Port Canning India 22°23N 88°40E **43 H13**
Port Carling Canada 45°7N 79°35W **82 A5**
Port-Cartier Canada 50°2N 66°50W **73 B6**
Port Chalmers N.Z. 45°49S 170°30E **59 F3**
Port Charlotte U.S.A. 26°59N 82°6W **85 H13**
Port Chester U.S.A. 41°0N 73°40W **83 F11**
Port Clements Canada 53°40N 132°10W **70 C2**
Port Clinton U.S.A. 41°31N 82°56W **81 E12**
Port Colborne Canada 42°50N 79°10W **82 D5**
Port Coquitlam Canada 49°15N 122°45W **78 A4**
Port Cornwallis India 13°17N 93°5E **45 H11**
Port Credit Canada 43°33N 79°35W **82 C5**
Port Curtis Australia 23°57S 151°20E **62 C5**
Port Dalhousie Canada 43°13N 79°16W **82 C5**
Port Darwin Australia 12°24S 130°45E **60 B5**
Port Darwin Falk. Is. 51°50S 59°0W **96 G5**
Port Davey Australia 43°16S 145°55E **63 G4**
Port-de-Paix Haiti 19°50N 72°50W **89 C5**
Port Dickson Malaysia 2°30N 101°49E **39 L3**
Port Douglas Australia 16°30S 145°30E **62 B4**
Port Dover Canada 42°47N 80°12W **82 D4**
Port Edward Canada 54°12N 130°10W **70 C2**
Port Elgin Canada 44°25N 81°25W **82 B3**
Port Elizabeth S. Africa 33°58S 25°40E **56 D4**
Port Ellen U.K. 55°38N 6°11W **11 F2**
Port Erin I. of Man 54°5N 4°45W **12 C3**
Port Essington Australia 11°15S 132°10E **60 B5**
Port Ewen U.S.A. 41°54N 73°59W **83 E11**
Port Fairy Australia 38°22S 142°12E **63 F3**
Port Gamble U.S.A. 47°51N 122°34W **78 C4**
Port-Gentil Gabon 0°40S 8°50E **54 E1**
Port Germein Australia 33°1S 138°1E **63 E2**
Port Ghalib Egypt 25°20N 34°50E **46 E2**
Port Gibson U.S.A. 31°58N 90°59W **84 F9**
Port Glasgow U.K. 55°56N 4°41W **11 F4**
Port Harcourt Nigeria 4°40N 7°10E **52 H7**
Port Hardy Canada 50°41N 127°30W **70 C3**
Port Harrison = Inukjuak
  Canada 58°25N 78°15W **69 F16**
Port Hawkesbury
  Canada 45°36N 61°22W **73 C7**
Port Hedland Australia 20°25S 118°35E **60 D2**
Port Henry U.S.A. 44°3N 73°28W **83 B11**
Port Hood Canada 46°0N 61°32W **73 C7**
Port Hope Canada 43°56N 78°20W **82 C6**
Port Hope U.S.A. 43°57N 82°43W **82 C2**
Port Hope Simpson
  Canada 52°33N 56°18W **73 B8**
Port Hueneme U.S.A. 34°7N 119°12W **79 L7**
Port Huron U.S.A. 42°58N 82°26W **82 D2**
Port Jefferson U.S.A. 40°57N 73°3W **83 F11**
Port Jervis U.S.A. 41°22N 74°41W **83 E10**
Port Kenny Australia 33°10S 134°41E **63 E1**
Port Klang Malaysia 3°0N 101°35E **39 L3**
Port Láirge = Waterford
  Ireland 52°15N 7°8W **10 D4**
Port Lavaca U.S.A. 28°37N 96°38W **84 G6**
Port Leyden U.S.A. 43°35N 75°21W **83 C9**
Port Lincoln Australia 34°42S 135°52E **63 E2**
Port Loko S. Leone 8°48N 12°46W **52 G3**
Port-Louis Guadeloupe 16°28N 61°32W **88 b**
Port Louis Mauritius 20°10S 57°30E **55 d**
Port MacDonnell
  Australia 38°5S 140°48E **63 F3**
Port McNeill Canada 50°35N 127°6W **70 C3**
Port Macquarie
  Australia 31°25S 152°25E **63 E5**
Port Maria Jamaica 18°22N 76°54W **88 a**
Port Matilda U.S.A. 40°48N 78°3W **82 F6**
Port McNicoll Canada 44°44N 79°48W **82 B5**
Port Mellon Canada 49°32N 123°31W **70 D4**
Port-Menier Canada 49°51N 64°15W **73 C7**
Port Moody Canada 49°17N 122°51W **78 A4**
Port Morant Jamaica 17°54N 76°19W **88 a**
Port Moresby Papua N. G. 9°24S 147°8E **58 B7**
Port Muhammed Bin Qasim = Port
  Qasim Pakistan 24°46N 67°20E **42 G2**
Port Musgrave Australia 11°55S 141°50E **62 A3**
Port Neches U.S.A. 30°0N 93°59W **84 G8**
Port Nolloth S. Africa 29°17S 16°52E **56 C2**
Port Nouveau-Québec =
  Kangiqsualujjuaq
  Canada 58°30N 65°59W **69 F18**
Port of Climax Canada 49°10N 108°20W **71 D7**
Port of Coronach Canada 49°7N 105°31W **71 D7**
Port of Spain
  Trin. & Tob. 10°40N 61°31W **93 K15**
Port Orange U.S.A. 29°9N 80°59W **85 G14**
Port Orchard U.S.A. 47°32N 122°38W **78 C4**
Port Orford U.S.A. 42°45N 124°30W **76 E1**

Port Pegasus N.Z. 47°12S 167°41E **59 G1**
Port Perry Canada 44°6N 78°56W **82 B6**
Port Phillip B. Australia 38°10S 144°50E **63 F3**
Port Pirie Australia 33°10S 138°1E **63 E2**
Port Qasim Pakistan 24°46N 67°20E **42 G2**
Port Renfrew Canada 48°30N 124°20W **78 B2**
Port Roper Australia 14°45S 135°25E **62 A2**
Port Rowan Canada 42°40N 80°30W **82 D4**
Port Safaga = Bûr Safâga
  Egypt 26°43N 33°57E **46 E2**
Port Said = Bûr Sa'îd
  Egypt 31°16N 32°18E **53 B12**
Port St. Joe U.S.A. 29°49N 85°18W **85 G12**
Port St. Johns = Umzimvubu
  S. Africa 31°38S 29°33E **57 D4**
Port St. Lucie U.S.A. 27°18N 80°21W **85 H14**
Port Sanilac U.S.A. 43°26N 82°33W **82 C2**
Port Severn Canada 44°48N 79°43W **82 B5**
Port Shepstone S. Africa 30°44S 30°28E **57 D5**
Port Simpson Canada 54°30N 130°20W **70 C2**
Port Stanley = Stanley
  Falk. Is. 51°40S 59°51W **96 G5**
Port Stanley Canada 42°40N 81°10W **82 D3**
Port Sudan = Bûr Sûdân
  Sudan 19°32N 37°9E **53 E13**
Port Sulphur U.S.A. 29°29N 89°42W **85 G10**
Port Talbot U.K. 51°35N 3°47W **13 F4**
Port Townsend U.S.A. 48°7N 122°45W **78 B4**
Port-Vendres France 42°32N 3°8E **20 E5**
Port Vila Vanuatu 17°45S 168°18E **58 C9**
Port Vladimir Russia 69°25N 33°6E **8 B25**
Port Wakefield Australia 34°12S 138°10E **63 E2**
Port Washington
  U.S.A. 43°23N 87°53W **80 D10**
Porta Orientalis Romania 45°6N 22°18E **17 F12**
Portacloy Ireland 54°20N 9°46W **10 B2**
Portadown U.K. 54°25N 6°27W **10 B5**
Portaferry U.K. 54°23N 5°33W **10 B6**
Portage Pa., U.S.A. 40°23N 78°41W **82 F6**
Portage Wis., U.S.A. 43°33N 89°28W **80 D9**
Portage la Prairie
  Canada 49°58N 98°18W **71 D9**
Portageville U.S.A. 36°26N 89°42W **80 G9**
Portalegre Portugal 39°19N 7°25W **21 C2**
Portales U.S.A. 34°11N 103°20W **77 J12**
Portarlington Ireland 53°9N 7°14W **10 C4**
Portbou Spain 42°25N 3°9E **21 A7**
Porter L. N.W.T., Canada 61°41N 108°5W **71 A7**
Porter L. Sask., Canada 56°20N 107°20W **71 B7**
Porterville S. Africa 33°0S 19°0E **56 D2**
Porterville U.S.A. 36°4N 119°1W **78 J8**
Porth Tywyn = Burry Port
  U.K. 51°41N 4°15W **13 F3**
Porthcawl U.K. 51°29N 3°42W **13 F4**
Porthill U.S.A. 48°59N 116°30W **76 B5**
Porthmadog U.K. 52°55N 4°8W **12 E3**
Portile de Fier Europe 44°44N 22°30E **17 F12**
Portimão Portugal 37°8N 8°32W **21 D1**
Portishead U.K. 51°29N 2°46W **13 F5**
Portknockie U.K. 57°42N 2°51W **11 D6**
Portland N.S.W., Australia 33°20S 150°0E **63 E5**
Portland Vic., Australia 38°20S 141°35E **63 F3**
Portland Canada 44°42N 76°12W **83 B8**
Portland Conn., U.S.A. 41°34N 72°38W **83 E12**
Portland Maine, U.S.A. 43°39N 70°16W **81 D18**
Portland Mich., U.S.A. 42°52N 84°54W **81 D11**
Portland Oreg., U.S.A. 45°32N 122°37W **78 E4**
Portland Pa., U.S.A. 40°55N 75°6W **83 F9**
Portland Tex., U.S.A. 27°53N 97°20W **84 H6**
Portland, I. of U.K. 50°33N 2°26W **13 G5**
Portland B. Australia 38°15S 141°45E **63 F3**
Portland Bight Jamaica 17°52N 77°5W **88 a**
Portland Bill U.K. 50°31N 2°28W **13 G5**
Portland Canal U.S.A. 55°56N 130°0W **70 B2**
Portland Int. ✈ (PDX)
  U.S.A. 45°35N 122°36W **78 E4**
Portland Pt. Jamaica 17°42N 77°11W **88 a**
Portlaoise Ireland 53°2N 7°18W **10 C4**
Portmadoc = Porthmadog
  U.K. 52°55N 4°8W **12 E3**
Portmore Jamaica 17°53N 76°53W **88 a**
Porto France 42°16N 8°42E **20 E8**
Porto Portugal 41°8N 8°40W **21 B1**
Pôrto Alegre Brazil 30°5S 51°10W **95 C5**
Porto de Moz Brazil 1°41S 52°13W **93 D8**
Porto Empédocle Brazil 37°17N 13°32E **22 F5**
Porto Esperança Brazil 19°37S 57°29W **92 G7**
Porto Franco Brazil 6°20S 47°24W **93 E9**
Porto Inglês = Vila do Maio
  Cabo Verde 15°21N 23°10W **52 b**
Porto Mendes Brazil 24°30S 54°15W **95 A5**
Porto Murtinho Brazil 21°45S 57°55W **92 H7**
Porto Nacional Brazil 10°40S 48°30W **93 F9**
Porto-Novo Benin 6°23N 2°42E **52 G6**
Porto Primavera, Represa
  Brazil 22°10S 52°45W **95 A5**
Porto Santo, I. de
  Madeira 33°45N 16°25W **52 B2**
Porto São José Brazil 22°43S 53°10W **95 A5**
Porto Seguro Brazil 16°26S 39°5W **93 G11**
Pôrto Tôrres Italy 40°50N 8°24E **22 D3**
Porto União Brazil 26°10S 51°10W **95 B5**
Porto-Vecchio France 41°35N 9°16E **20 F8**
Porto Velho Brazil 8°46S 63°54W **92 E6**
Porto Walter Brazil 8°15S 72°40W **92 E4**
Portobelo Panama 9°35N 79°42E **88 E4**
Portoferráio Italy 42°48N 10°20E **22 C4**
Portola U.S.A. 39°49N 120°28W **78 F6**
Portoscuso Italy 39°12N 8°24E **22 E3**
Portoviejo Ecuador 1°7S 80°28W **92 D2**
Portpatrick U.K. 54°51N 5°7W **11 G3**
Portree U.K. 57°25N 6°12W **11 D2**
Portrush U.K. 55°12N 6°40W **10 A5**
Portsmouth Dominica 15°34N 61°27N **89 C7**
Portsmouth U.K. 50°48N 1°6W **13 G6**
Portsmouth N.H., U.S.A. 43°5N 70°45W **83 C14**
Portsmouth Ohio, U.S.A. 38°44N 82°57W **81 F12**
Portsmouth R.I., U.S.A. 41°36N 71°15W **83 E13**
Portsmouth Va., U.S.A. 36°58N 76°23W **81 G15**
Portsmouth □ U.K. 50°48N 1°6W **13 G6**

Portsoy U.K. 57°41N 2°41W **11 D6**
Portstewart U.K. 55°11N 6°43W **10 A5**
Porttipahdan tekojärvi
  Finland 68°5N 26°40E **8 B22**
Portugal ■ Europe 40°0N 8°0W **21 C1**
Portumna Ireland 53°6N 8°14W **10 C3**
Portville U.S.A. 42°3N 78°20W **82 D6**
Poruma Australia 10°2S 143°4E **62 a**
Porvenir Chile 53°10S 70°16W **96 G2**
Posadas Argentina 27°30S 55°50W **95 B4**
Posht-e Badam Iran 33°2N 55°23E **47 C7**
Poso Indonesia 1°20S 120°55E **37 E6**
Poso, Danau Indonesia 1°52S 120°35E **37 E6**
Posse Brazil 14°4S 46°18W **93 F9**
Possession I. Antarctica 72°4S 172°0E **5 D11**
Possum Kingdom L.
  U.S.A. 32°52N 98°26W **84 E5**
Post U.S.A. 33°12N 101°23W **84 E4**
Post Falls U.S.A. 47°43N 116°57W **76 C5**
Postavy = Pastavy Belarus 55°4N 26°50E **9 J22**
Poste-de-la-Baleine =
  Kuujjuarapik Canada 55°20N 77°35W **72 A4**
Postmasburg S. Africa 28°18S 23°5E **56 C3**
Postojna Slovenia 45°46N 14°12E **16 F8**
Poston U.S.A. 34°0N 114°24W **79 M12**
Postville Canada 54°54N 59°47W **73 B8**
Posyet Russia 42°39N 130°48E **28 C5**
Potchefstroom S. Africa 26°41S 27°7E **56 C4**
Poteau U.S.A. 35°3N 94°37W **84 D7**
Poteet U.S.A. 29°2N 98°35W **84 G5**
Potenza Italy 40°38N 15°48E **22 D6**
Poteriteri, L. N.Z. 46°5S 167°10E **59 G1**
Potgietersrus = Mokopane
  S. Africa 24°10S 28°55E **57 B4**
Poti Georgia 42°10N 41°38E **19 F7**
Potiskum Nigeria 11°39N 11°2E **53 F8**
Potomac → U.S.A. 38°0N 76°23W **81 F14**
Potosí Bolivia 19°38S 65°50W **92 G5**
Potosi Mt. U.S.A. 35°57N 115°29W **79 K11**
Pototan Phil. 10°54N 122°38E **37 B6**
Potrerillos Chile 26°30S 69°30W **94 B2**
Potsdam Germany 52°23N 13°4E **16 B7**
Potsdam U.S.A. 44°40N 74°59W **83 B10**
Pottangi India 18°34N 82°58E **44 E6**
Pottersville U.S.A. 43°43N 73°50W **83 C11**
Pottstown U.S.A. 40°15N 75°39W **83 F9**
Pottsville U.S.A. 40°41N 76°12W **83 F8**
Pottuvil Sri Lanka 6°55N 81°50E **45 L5**
P'otzu Taiwan 23°28N 120°15E **35 F13**
Pouce Coupé Canada 55°40N 120°10W **70 B4**
Poughkeepsie U.S.A. 41°42N 73°56W **83 E11**
Poulaphouca Res. Ireland 53°8N 6°30W **10 C5**
Poulsbo U.S.A. 47°44N 122°38W **78 C4**
Poultney U.S.A. 43°31N 73°14W **83 C11**
Poulton-le-Fylde U.K. 53°51N 2°58W **12 D5**
Pouso Alegre Brazil 22°14S 45°57W **95 A6**
Pouthisat Cambodia 12°34N 103°50E **38 F4**
Považská Bystrica
  Slovakia 49°8N 18°27E **17 D10**
Povenets Russia 62°50N 34°50E **18 B5**
Poverty B. N.Z. 38°43S 178°2E **59 C7**
Póvoa de Varzim Portugal 41°25N 8°46W **21 B1**
Povorotnyy, Mys Russia 42°40N 133°2E **28 C6**
Povungnituk = Puvirnituq
  Canada 60°2N 77°10W **69 E16**
Powassan Canada 46°5N 79°25W **72 C4**
Poway U.S.A. 32°58N 117°2W **79 N9**
Powder → U.S.A. 46°45N 105°26W **76 C11**
Powder River U.S.A. 43°2N 106°59W **76 E10**
Powell U.S.A. 44°45N 108°46W **76 D9**
Powell, L. U.S.A. 36°57N 111°29W **77 H8**
Powell River Canada 49°50N 124°35W **70 D4**
Powers U.S.A. 45°41N 87°32W **80 C10**
Pownal U.S.A. 42°45N 73°14W **83 D11**
Powys □ U.K. 52°20N 3°20W **13 E4**
Poyang Hu China 29°5N 116°20E **35 C11**
Poyarkovo Russia 49°36N 128°41E **27 E13**
Poza Rica Mexico 20°33N 97°27W **87 C5**
Požarevac Serbia 44°35N 21°18E **23 B9**
Pozo U.S.A. 35°20N 120°24W **78 K6**
Pozo Almonte Chile 20°10S 69°50W **92 H5**
Pozo Colorado Paraguay 23°30S 58°45W **94 A4**
Pozoblanco Spain 38°23N 4°51W **21 C3**
Pozzuoli Italy 40°49N 14°7E **22 D6**
Prachin Buri Thailand 14°0N 101°25E **38 F3**
Prachuap Khirikhan
  Thailand 11°49N 99°48E **39 G2**
Prado Brazil 17°20S 39°13W **93 G11**
Prahita → India 19°0N 79°55E **44 E4**
Praia Cabo Verde 15°2N 23°34W **52 b**
Prainha Brazil 1°45S 53°30W **93 D8**
Prainha Nova Brazil 7°10S 60°30W **92 E6**
Prairie Australia 20°50S 144°35E **62 C3**
Prairie City U.S.A. 44°28N 118°43W **76 D4**
Prairie Dog Town Fork Red →
  U.S.A. 34°34N 99°58W **84 D5**
Prairie du Chien U.S.A. 43°3N 91°9W **80 D8**
Prairies, L. of the
  Canada 51°16N 101°32W **71 C8**
Prambanan △ Indonesia 7°45S 110°28E **37 G14**
Pran Buri Thailand 12°23N 99°55E **38 F2**
Prapat Indonesia 2°41N 98°58E **36 D1**
Praslin Seychelles 4°18S 55°45E **55 b**
Prata Brazil 19°25S 48°54W **93 G9**
Pratabpur India 23°28N 83°15E **43 H10**
Pratapgarh Raj., India 24°2N 74°40E **42 G6**
Pratapgarh Ut. P., India 25°56N 81°59E **43 G9**
Pratas I. = Dongsha Dao
  S. China Sea 20°45N 116°43E **35 G11**
Prato Italy 43°53N 11°6E **22 C4**
Pratt U.S.A. 37°39N 98°44W **80 G4**
Prattville U.S.A. 32°28N 86°29E **85 J2**
Pravara → India 19°35N 74°45E **44 E2**
Pravia Spain 43°30N 6°12W **21 A2**
Praya Indonesia 8°39S 116°17E **36 F5**
Prayag = Allahabad
  India 25°25N 81°58E **43 G9**
Pre-delta △ Argentina 32°0S 60°40W **94 C3**

Preah Seihanu = Kampong Saom
  Cambodia 10°38N 103°30E **39 G4**
Preah Vihear Cambodia 14°23N 104°41E **38 E5**
Preble U.S.A. 42°44N 76°8W **83 D8**
Precipice △ Australia 25°18S 150°5E **63 D5**
Precordillera Argentina 30°0S 69°1W **94 C2**
Preeceville Canada 51°57N 102°40W **71 C8**
Preiji Latvia 56°18N 26°43E **9 H22**
Premont U.S.A. 27°22N 98°7W **84 H5**
Prentice U.S.A. 45°33N 90°17W **80 C8**
Preobrazheniye Russia 42°54N 133°54E **28 C6**
Preparis I. = Pariparit Kyun
  Myanmar 14°52N 93°41E **45 G11**
Preparis North Channel
  Ind. Oc. 15°27N 94°5E **45 G11**
Preparis South Channel
  Ind. Oc. 14°33N 93°30E **45 G11**
Přerov Czechia 49°28N 17°27E **17 D9**
Prescott Canada 44°45N 75°30W **83 B9**
Prescott Ariz., U.S.A. 34°33N 112°28W **77 J7**
Prescott Ark., U.S.A. 33°48N 93°23W **84 E8**
Prescott Valley U.S.A. 34°40N 112°18W **77 J7**
Preservation Inlet N.Z. 46°8S 166°35E **59 G1**
Presho U.S.A. 43°54N 100°3W **80 D3**
Presidencia de la Plaza
  Argentina 27°0S 59°50W **94 B4**
Presidencia Roque Saenz Peña
  Argentina 26°45S 60°30W **94 B3**
Presidente Epitácio Brazil 21°56S 52°6W **93 H8**
Presidente Hayes □
  Paraguay 24°0S 59°0W **94 A4**
Presidente Prudente
  Brazil 22°5S 51°25W **95 A5**
Presidio U.S.A. 29°34N 104°22W **84 G2**
Prešov Slovakia 49°0N 21°15E **17 D11**
Prespa, L. = Prespansko Jezero
  Macedonia 40°55N 21°0E **23 D9**
Prespansko Jezero
  Macedonia 40°55N 21°0E **23 D9**
Presque I. U.S.A. 42°10N 80°6W **82 D4**
Presque Isle U.S.A. 46°41N 68°1W **81 B19**
Prestatyn U.K. 53°20N 3°24W **12 D4**
Presteigne U.K. 52°17N 3°0W **13 E5**
Preston Canada 43°23N 80°21W **82 C4**
Preston U.K. 53°46N 2°42W **12 D5**
Preston Idaho, U.S.A. 42°6N 111°53W **76 E8**
Preston Minn., U.S.A. 43°40N 92°5W **80 D7**
Preston, C. Australia 20°51S 116°12E **60 D2**
Prestonsburg U.S.A. 37°40N 82°47W **81 G12**
Prestwick U.K. 55°29N 4°37W **11 F4**
Pretoria S. Africa 25°44S 28°12E **57 C4**
Preveza Greece 38°57N 20°45E **23 E9**
Prey Veng Cambodia 11°35N 105°29E **39 G5**
Pribaykalsky △ Russia 52°30N 106°0E **27 D11**
Pribilof Is. U.S.A. 57°0N 170°0W **74 D6**
Příbram Czechia 49°41N 14°2E **16 D8**
Price U.S.A. 39°36N 110°49W **76 G8**
Price, C. India 13°34N 93°3E **45 H11**
Price I. Canada 52°23N 128°41W **70 C3**
Prichard U.S.A. 30°44N 88°5W **85 F10**
Priekule Latvia 56°26N 21°35E **9 H19**
Prienai Lithuania 54°38N 23°57E **9 J20**
Prieska S. Africa 29°40S 22°42E **56 C3**
Priest L. U.S.A. 48°35N 116°52W **76 B5**
Priest River U.S.A. 48°11N 116°55W **76 B5**
Priest Valley U.S.A. 36°10N 120°39W **78 J6**
Prievidza Slovakia 48°46N 18°36E **17 D10**
Prikaspiyskaya Nizmennost =
  Caspian Depression
  Eurasia 47°0N 48°0E **19 E8**
Prilep Macedonia 41°21N 21°32E **23 D9**
Priluki = Pryluky
  Ukraine 50°30N 32°24E **19 D5**
Prime Hd. Antarctica 63°12S 58°57W **5 C18**
Prime Seal I. Australia 40°3S 147°43E **63 G4**
Primo Tapia Mexico 32°16N 116°54W **79 N10**
Primorskiy Kray □ Russia 45°0N 135°0E **28 B7**
Primrose L. Canada 54°55N 109°45W **71 C7**
Prince Albert Canada 53°15N 105°50W **71 C7**
Prince Albert S. Africa 33°12S 22°2E **56 D3**
Prince Albert △ Canada 54°0N 106°25W **71 C7**
Prince Albert Mts.
  Antarctica 76°0S 161°30E **5 D11**
Prince Albert Pen.
  Canada 72°30N 116°0W **68 C8**
Prince Albert Sd. Canada 70°25N 115°0W **68 C8**
Prince Alfred, C. Canada 74°20N 124°40W **4 B1**
Prince Charles I.
  Canada 67°47N 76°12W **69 D16**
Prince Charles Mts.
  Antarctica 72°0S 67°0E **5 D6**
Prince Edward Fracture Zone
  Ind. Oc. 46°0S 35°0E **3 A4**
Prince Edward I. □
  Canada 46°20N 63°20W **73 C7**
Prince Edward Is. Ind. Oc. 46°35S 38°0E **3 G11**
Prince George Canada 53°55N 122°50W **70 C4**
Prince of Wales, C.
  U.S.A. 65°36N 168°5W **74 B6**
Prince of Wales I.
  Australia 10°40S 142°10E **62 A3**
Prince of Wales I. Canada 73°0N 99°0W **68 C12**
Prince of Wales I.
  U.S.A. 55°47N 132°50W **68 F5**
Prince of Wales Icefield
  Canada 78°15N 79°0W **69 B16**
Prince of Wales Str.
  Canada 73°0N 117°0W **68 C8**
Prince Patrick I. Canada 77°0N 120°0W **69 B2**
Prince Regent Inlet
  Canada 73°0N 90°0W **68 C12**
Prince Rupert Canada 54°20N 130°20W **70 C2**
Prince William Sd.
  U.S.A. 60°40N 147°0W **68 E2**
Princes Town
  Trin. & Tob. 10°16N 61°23W **93 K15**
Princess Charlotte B.
  Australia 14°25S 144°0E **62 A3**
Princess Elizabeth Trough
  S. Ocean 64°10S 83°0E **5 C17**

154 Princess May Ranges INDEX TO WORLD MAPS

Princess May Ranges *Australia* 15°30S 125°30E **60** C4
Princess Royal I. *Canada* 53°0N 128°40W **70** C3
Princeton *Canada* 49°27N 120°30W **70** D4
Princeton *Calif., U.S.A.* 39°24N 122°1W **78** F4
Princeton *Ill., U.S.A.* 41°23N 89°28W **80** E9
Princeton *Ind., U.S.A.* 38°21N 87°34W **80** F10
Princeton *Ky., U.S.A.* 37°7N 87°53W **80** G10
Princeton *Mo., U.S.A.* 40°24N 93°35W **80** E7
Princeton *N.J., U.S.A.* 40°21N 74°39W **83** F10
Princeton *W. Va., U.S.A.* 37°22N 81°6W **81** G13
Príncipe *São Tomé & Principe* 1°37N 7°25E **50** F4
Principe da Beira *Brazil* 12°20S 64°30W **92** F6
Prineville *U.S.A.* 44°18N 120°51W **76** D3
Prins Harald Kyst *Antarctica* 70°0S 35°1E **5** D4
Prinsesse Astrid Kyst *Antarctica* 70°45S 12°30E **5** D3
Prinsesse Ragnhild Kyst *Antarctica* 70°15S 27°30E **5** D4
Prinzapolca *Nic.* 13°20N 83°35W **88** D3
Priozersk *Russia* 61°2N 30°7E **8** F24
Pripet = Prypyat ➔ *Europe* 51°20N 30°15E **17** C16
Pripet Marshes *Europe* 52°10N 27°10E **17** B15
Pripyat Marshes = Pripet Marshes *Europe* 52°10N 27°10E **17** B15
Pripyats = Prypyat ➔ *Europe* 51°20N 30°15E **17** C16
Prishtinë *Kosovo* 42°40N 21°13E **23** C9
Priština = Prishtinë *Kosovo* 42°40N 21°13E **23** C9
Privas *France* 44°45N 4°37E **20** D6
Privolzhskaya Vozvyshennost *Russia* 51°0N 46°0E **19** D8
Privolzhskiy □ *Russia* 56°0N 50°0E **26** D6
Prizren *Kosovo* 42°13N 20°45E **23** C9
Probolinggo *Indonesia* 7°46S 113°13E **37** G15
Proctor *U.S.A.* 43°40N 73°2W **83** C11
Proddatur *India* 14°45N 78°30E **45** G4
Profondeville *Belgium* 50°23N 4°52E **15** D4
Progreso *Coahuila, Mexico* 27°28N 100°59W **86** B4
Progreso *Yucatán, Mexico* 21°20N 89°40W **87** C7
Progress *Antarctica* 66°22S 76°22E **5** C12
Progress *Russia* 49°45N 129°37E **27** E13
Prokopyevsk *Russia* 54°0N 86°45E **26** D9
Prokuplje *Serbia* 43°16N 21°36E **23** C9
Prome = Pye *Myanmar* 18°49N 95°13E **41** K19
Prophet ➔ *Canada* 58°48N 122°40W **70** B4
Prophet River *Canada* 58°6N 122°43W **70** B4
Propriá *Brazil* 10°13S 36°51W **93** F11
Propriano *France* 41°41N 8°52E **20** F8
Proserpine *Australia* 20°21S 148°36E **62** b
Prosna ➔ *Poland* 52°6N 17°44E **17** B9
Prospect *U.S.A.* 43°18N 75°9W **83** C9
Prosser *U.S.A.* 46°12N 119°46W **76** C4
Prostějov *Czechia* 49°30N 17°9E **17** D9
Proston *Australia* 26°8S 151°32E **63** D5
Provence *France* 43°40N 5°46E **20** E6
Providence *Ky., U.S.A.* 37°24N 87°46W **80** G10
Providence *R.I., U.S.A.* 41°49N 71°24W **83** E13
Providence Bay *Canada* 45°41N 82°15W **72** C3
Providence Mts. *U.S.A.* 35°10N 115°15W **79** K11
Providencia, I. de *Caribbean* 13°25N 81°26W **88** D3
Provideniya *Russia* 64°23N 173°18W **27** C19
Provincetown *U.S.A.* 42°3N 70°11W **81** D18
Provins *France* 48°33N 3°15E **20** B5
Provo *U.S.A.* 40°14N 111°39W **76** F8
Provost *Canada* 52°25N 110°20W **71** C6
Prudhoe Bay *U.S.A.* 70°18N 148°22W **74** A10
Prudhoe I. *Australia* 21°19S 149°41E **62** C4
Prud'homme *Canada* 52°20N 105°54W **71** C7
Pruszków *Poland* 52°9N 20°49E **17** B11
Prut ➔ *Romania* 45°28N 28°10E **17** F15
Pruzhany *Belarus* 52°33N 24°28E **17** B13
Prydz B. *Antarctica* 69°0S 74°0E **5** C6
Pryluky *Ukraine* 50°30N 32°24E **19** D5
Pryor *U.S.A.* 36°19N 95°19W **84** C7
Prypyat ➔ *Europe* 51°20N 30°15E **17** C16
Prypyatsky △ *Belarus* 52°0N 28°0E **17** C14
Przemyśl *Poland* 49°50N 22°45E **17** D12
Przhevalsk = Karakol *Kyrgyzstan* 42°30N 78°20E **30** C4
Psara *Greece* 38°37N 25°38E **23** E11
Psiloritis, Oros *Greece* 35°15N 24°45E **23** G11
Pskov *Russia* 57°50N 28°25E **9** H23
Ptich = Ptsich ➔ *Belarus* 52°9N 28°52E **17** B15
Ptolemaida *Greece* 40°30N 21°43E **23** D9
Ptsich ➔ *Belarus* 52°9N 28°52E **17** B15
Pu Xian *China* 36°24N 111°6E **32** F6
Pua *Thailand* 19°11N 100°55E **38** C3
Puán *Argentina* 37°30S 62°45W **94** D3
Pu'an *China* 25°46N 104°57E **34** E5
Pu'apu'a *Samoa* 13°34S 172°9W **59** b
Pubei *China* 22°16N 109°31E **34** F7
Pucallpa *Peru* 8°25S 74°30W **92** E4
Pucheng *China* 27°59N 118°31E **35** D12
Puch'on = Bucheon *S. Korea* 37°28N 126°45E **33** F14
Pudasjärvi *Finland* 65°23N 26°53E **8** D22
Puding *China* 26°18N 105°44E **34** D5
Pudozh *Russia* 61°48N 36°32E **18** B6
Pudu = Suizhou *China* 31°42N 113°24E **35** B9
Puducherry *India* 11°59N 79°50E **45** J4
Pudukkottai *India* 10°28N 78°47E **45** J4
Puebla *Mexico* 19°3N 98°12W **87** D5
Puebla □ *Mexico* 18°50N 98°0W **87** D5
Pueblo *U.S.A.* 38°16N 104°37W **76** G11
Puelches *Argentina* 38°5S 65°51W **94** D2
Puelén *Argentina* 37°32S 67°38W **94** D2
Puente Alto *Chile* 33°32S 70°35W **94** C1
Puente-Genil *Spain* 37°22N 4°47W **21** D3
Pu'er *China* 23°0N 101°15E **34** F3
Puerca, Pta. *Puerto Rico* 18°13N 65°36W **89** d
Puerco ➔ *U.S.A.* 34°22N 107°50W **77** J10
Puerto Aisén *Chile* 45°27S 73°0W **96** F2
Puerto Ángel *Mexico* 15°40N 96°29W **87** D5
Puerto Arista *Mexico* 15°56N 93°48W **87** D6
Puerto Armuelles *Panama* 8°20N 82°51W **88** E3
Puerto Ayacucho *Venezuela* 5°40N 67°35W **92** B5
Puerto Barrios *Guatemala* 15°40N 88°32W **88** C2
Puerto Bermejo *Argentina* 26°55S 58°34W **94** B4
Puerto Bermúdez *Peru* 10°20S 74°58W **92** F4
Puerto Bolívar *Ecuador* 3°19S 79°55W **92** D3
Puerto Cabello *Venezuela* 10°28N 68°1W **92** A5
Puerto Cabezas *Nic.* 14°0N 83°30W **88** D3
Puerto Cabo Gracias á Dios *Nic.* 15°0N 83°10W **88** D3
Puerto Carreño *Colombia* 6°12N 67°22W **92** B5
Puerto Castilla *Honduras* 16°0N 86°0W **88** C2
Puerto Chicama *Peru* 7°45S 79°20W **92** E3
Puerto Coig *Argentina* 50°54S 69°15W **96** G3
Puerto Cortés *Honduras* 15°51N 88°0W **88** C2
Puerto Cumarebo *Venezuela* 11°29N 69°30W **92** A5
Puerto de los Angeles ⌂ *Mexico* 23°39N 105°45W **86** C3
Puerto del Rosario *Canary Is.* 28°30N 13°52W **52** C3
Puerto Deseado *Argentina* 47°55S 66°0W **96** F3
Puerto Escondido *Mexico* 15°50N 97°3W **87** D5
Puerto Heath *Bolivia* 12°34S 68°39W **92** F5
Puerto Inírida *Colombia* 3°53N 67°52W **92** C5
Puerto Juárez *Mexico* 21°11N 86°49W **87** C7
Puerto La Cruz *Venezuela* 10°13N 64°38W **92** A6
Puerto Leguízamo *Colombia* 0°12S 74°46W **92** D4
Puerto Lempira *Honduras* 15°16N 83°46W **88** C3
Puerto Libertad *Mexico* 29°55N 112°43W **86** B2
Puerto Limón *Colombia* 3°23N 73°30W **92** C4
Puerto Lobos *Argentina* 42°0S 65°3W **96** E3
Puerto Madryn *Argentina* 42°48S 65°4W **96** E3
Puerto Maldonado *Peru* 12°30S 69°10W **92** F5
Puerto Manatí *Cuba* 21°22N 76°50W **88** B4
Puerto Montt *Chile* 41°28S 73°0W **96** E2
Puerto Morazán *Nic.* 12°51N 87°11W **88** D2
Puerto Morelos *Mexico* 20°50N 86°52W **87** C7
Puerto Natales *Chile* 51°45S 72°15W **96** G2
Puerto Oscuro *Chile* 31°24S 71°35W **94** C1
Puerto Padre *Cuba* 21°13N 76°35W **88** B4
Puerto Páez *Venezuela* 6°13N 67°28W **92** B5
Puerto Peñasco *Mexico* 31°20N 113°33W **86** A2
Puerto Pinasco *Paraguay* 22°36S 57°50W **94** A4
Puerto Plata *Dom. Rep.* 19°48N 70°45W **89** C5
Puerto Princesa *Phil.* 9°46N 118°45E **37** C5
Puerto Quepos *Costa Rica* 9°29N 84°6W **88** E3
Puerto Rico ☒ *W. Indies* 18°15N 66°45W **89** d
Puerto Rico Trench *Atl. Oc.* 19°50N 66°0W **89** C6
Puerto San Julián *Argentina* 49°18S 67°43W **96** F3
Puerto Santa Cruz *Argentina* 50°0S 68°32W **96** G3
Puerto Sastre *Paraguay* 22°2S 57°55W **94** A4
Puerto Suárez *Bolivia* 18°58S 57°52W **92** G7
Puerto Vallarta *Mexico* 20°37N 105°15W **86** C3
Puerto Varas *Chile* 41°19S 72°59W **96** E2
Puerto Wilches *Colombia* 7°21N 73°54W **92** B4
Puertollano *Spain* 38°43N 4°7W **21** C3
Pueu *Tahiti* 17°44S 149°13W **59** d
Pueyrredón, L. *Argentina* 47°20S 72°0W **96** F2
Puffin I. *Ireland* 51°50N 10°24W **10** E1
Pugachev *Russia* 52°0N 48°49E **18** D8
Pugal *India* 28°30N 72°48E **42** E5
Puge *China* 27°20N 102°31E **34** D4
Puget Sound *U.S.A.* 47°50N 122°30W **78** C4
Pugŏdong *N. Korea* 42°5N 130°0E **33** C16
Pūgūnzī *Iran* 25°49N 59°10E **47** E8
Puigcerdà *Spain* 42°24N 1°50E **21** A6
Puijiang *China* 30°14N 103°30E **34** B4
Pujiang *China* 29°29N 119°54E **35** C12
Pujon-ho *N. Korea* 40°35N 127°35E **33** D14
Pukaki, L. *N.Z.* 44°4S 170°1E **59** F3
Pukapuka *Cook Is.* 10°53S 165°49W **65** J11
Pukaskwa △ *Canada* 48°20N 86°0W **72** C2
Pukatawagan *Canada* 55°45N 101°20W **71** B8
Pukchin *N. Korea* 40°12N 125°45E **33** D13
Pukch'ŏng *N. Korea* 40°14N 128°19E **33** D15
Pukekohe *N.Z.* 37°12S 174°55E **59** B5
Pukhrayan *India* 26°14N 79°51E **43** F8
Puksubaek-san *N. Korea* 40°42N 127°45E **33** D14
Pula *Croatia* 44°54N 13°57E **16** F7
Pulacayo *Bolivia* 20°25S 66°41W **92** H5
Pulandian *China* 39°25N 121°58E **33** E11
Pulaski *N.Y., U.S.A.* 43°34N 76°8W **83** C8
Pulaski *Tenn., U.S.A.* 35°12N 87°2W **85** D11
Pulaski *Va., U.S.A.* 37°3N 80°47W **81** G13
Pulau ➔ *Indonesia* 5°50S 138°15E **37** F9
Pulau Gili *Indonesia* 8°21S 116°1E **37** J19
Puławy *Poland* 51°23N 21°59E **17** C11
Pulga *U.S.A.* 39°48N 121°29W **78** F5
Pulgaon *India* 20°44N 78°21E **44** D4
Pulicat *India* 13°25N 80°19E **45** H5
Pulicat L. *India* 13°40N 80°15E **45** H5
Pulivendla *India* 14°25N 78°14E **45** G4
Puliyangudi *India* 9°11N 77°24E **45** K3
Pullman *U.S.A.* 46°44N 117°10W **76** C5
Pulog, Mt. *Phil.* 16°40N 120°50E **37** A6
Pultusk *Poland* 52°43N 21°6E **17** B11
Pumlumon Fawr *U.K.* 52°28N 3°46W **13** E4
Puná, I. *Ecuador* 2°55S 80°5W **92** D2
Punaauia *Tahiti* 17°37S 149°34W **59** d
Punakaiki *N.Z.* 42°7S 171°20E **59** E3
Punakha Dzong *Bhutan* 27°42N 89°52E **41** F16
Punalur *India* 9°0N 76°56E **45** K3
Punasar *India* 27°6N 73°6E **42** F5
Punata *Bolivia* 17°32S 65°50W **92** G5
Punch *India* 33°48N 74°4E **43** C6
Punch ➔ *Pakistan* 33°12N 73°40E **42** C5
Punda Maria *S. Africa* 22°40S 31°5E **57** B5
Pune *India* 18°29N 73°57E **44** E1
P'ungsan *N. Korea* 40°50N 128°9E **33** D15
Puning *China* 23°20N 116°12E **35** F11
Punjab □ *India* 31°0N 76°0E **42** D7
Punjab □ *Pakistan* 32°0N 72°30E **42** E6
Puno *Peru* 15°55S 70°3W **92** G4
Punpun ➔ *India* 25°31N 85°18E **43** G11
Punta, Cerro de *Puerto Rico* 18°10N 66°37W **89** d
Punta Alta *Argentina* 38°53S 62°4W **96** D4
Punta Arenas *Chile* 53°10S 71°0W **96** G2
Punta del Díaz *Chile* 28°0S 70°45W **94** B1
Punta Gorda *Belize* 16°10N 88°45W **87** D7
Punta Gorda *U.S.A.* 26°56N 82°3W **85** H13
Punta Prieta *Mexico* 28°58N 114°17W **86** B2
Puntarenas *Costa Rica* 10°0N 84°50W **88** E3
Puntland *Somalia* 9°0N 50°0E **49** F4
Punto Fijo *Venezuela* 11°50N 70°13W **92** A4
Punxsutawney *U.S.A.* 40°57N 78°59W **82** F6
Pupuan *Indonesia* 8°19S 115°0E **37** J18
Puqi *China* 29°40N 113°50E **35** C9
Puquio *Peru* 14°45S 74°10W **92** F4
Pur ➔ *Russia* 67°31N 77°55E **26** C8
Puracé, Vol. *Colombia* 2°21N 76°23W **92** C3
Puralia = Puruliya *India* 23°17N 86°24E **43** H12
Puranpur *India* 28°31N 80°9E **43** E9
Purbalingga *Indonesia* 7°23S 109°21E **37** G13
Purbeck, Isle of *U.K.* 50°39N 1°59W **13** G5
Purcell *U.S.A.* 35°1N 97°22W **84** D6
Purcell Mts. *Canada* 49°55N 116°15W **70** D5
Purdy *Canada* 45°19N 77°44W **82** A7
Puri *India* 19°50N 85°58E **44** E7
Purmerend *Neths.* 52°32N 4°58E **15** B4
Purna ➔ *India* 19°6N 77°2E **44** E3
Purnia *India* 25°45N 87°31E **43** G12
Purnululu △ *Australia* 17°20S 128°20E **60** C4
Pursat = Pouthisat *Cambodia* 12°34N 103°50E **38** F4
Purukcahu *Indonesia* 0°35S 114°35E **36** E4
Puruliya *India* 23°17N 86°24E **43** H12
Purus ➔ *Brazil* 3°42S 61°28W **92** D6
Puruvesi *Finland* 61°50N 29°30E **8** F23
Purvis *U.S.A.* 31°9N 89°25W **85** F10
Purwa *India* 26°28N 80°47E **43** F9
Purwakarta *Indonesia* 6°35S 107°29E **37** G12
Purwo, Tanjung *Indonesia* 8°44S 114°21E **37** K18
Purwodadi *Indonesia* 7°7S 110°55E **37** G14
Purwokerto *Indonesia* 7°25S 109°14E **37** G13
Puryŏng *N. Korea* 42°5N 129°43E **33** C15
Pus ➔ *India* 19°55N 77°55E **44** E3
Pusa *India* 25°59N 85°41E **43** G11
Pusad *India* 19°56N 77°36E **44** E3
Pusan = Busan *S. Korea* 35°5N 129°0E **33** G15
Pushkin *Russia* 59°45N 30°25E **9** G24
Pushkino *Russia* 51°16N 47°0E **19** D8
Put-in-Bay *U.S.A.* 41°39N 82°49W **82** E2
Putahow L. *Canada* 59°54N 100°40W **71** B8
Putao *Myanmar* 27°28N 97°30E **41** F20
Putaruru *N.Z.* 38°2S 175°50E **59** C5
Puteran *Indonesia* 7°5S 114°0E **37** G15
Putian *China* 25°23N 119°0E **35** E12
Putignano *Italy* 40°51N 17°7E **22** D7
Puting, Tanjung *Indonesia* 3°31S 111°46E **36** E4
Putnam *U.S.A.* 41°55N 71°55W **83** E13
Putorana, Gory *Russia* 69°0N 95°0E **27** C10
Putrajaya *Malaysia* 2°55N 101°40E **39** L3
Puttalam *Sri Lanka* 8°1N 79°55E **45** K5
Puttalam Lagoon *Sri Lanka* 8°15N 79°45E **45** K4
Puttgarden *Germany* 54°30N 11°10E **16** A6
Puttur *Andhra Pradesh, India* 13°27N 79°33E **45** H4
Puttur *Karnataka, India* 12°46N 75°12E **45** H2
Putumayo ➔ *S. Amer.* 3°7S 67°58W **92** D5
Putuo *China* 29°56N 122°20E **35** C14
Putussibau *Indonesia* 0°50N 112°56E **36** D4
Puvirnituq *Canada* 60°2N 77°10W **69** E16
Puy-de-Dôme *France* 45°46N 2°57E **20** D5
Puyallup *U.S.A.* 47°12N 122°18W **78** C4
Puyang *China* 35°40N 115°1E **32** G8
Pūzeh Rīg *Iran* 27°20N 58°40E **47** E8
Pweto *Dem. Rep. of the Congo* 8°25S 28°51E **54** F5
Pwllheli *U.K.* 52°53N 4°25W **12** E3
Pyaozero, Ozero *Russia* 66°5N 30°58E **8** C24
Pyapon *Myanmar* 16°20N 95°40E **41** L19
Pyasina ➔ *Russia* 73°30N 87°0E **27** B9
Pyatigorsk *Russia* 44°2N 43°6E **19** F7
Pyay = Pye *Myanmar* 18°49N 95°13E **41** K19
Pye *Myanmar* 18°49N 95°13E **41** K19
Pyeongtaek *S. Korea* 37°1N 127°4E **33** F14
Pyetrikaw *Belarus* 52°11N 28°29E **17** B15
Pyhäjoki ➔ *Finland* 64°28N 24°14E **8** D21
Pyhätunturi △ *Finland* 66°58N 27°5E **8** C22
Pyin-U-Lwin *Myanmar* 22°2N 96°28E **38** A1
Pyinmana *Myanmar* 19°45N 96°12E **41** K20
Pymatuning Res. *U.S.A.* 41°30N 80°28W **82** E4
Pyŏktong *N. Korea* 40°50N 125°50E **33** D13
P'yŏnggang *N. Korea* 38°24N 127°17E **33** E14
P'yŏngsong *N. Korea* 39°14N 125°52E **33** E13
P'yŏngyang *N. Korea* 39°0N 125°30E **33** E13
Pyote *U.S.A.* 31°32N 103°8W **84** F3
Pyramid L. *U.S.A.* 40°1N 119°35W **76** F4
Pyramid Pk. *U.S.A.* 36°25N 116°37W **79** J10
Pyrénées *Europe* 42°45N 0°18E **20** E4
Pyu *Myanmar* 18°30N 96°28E **41** K20

Q

Qaanaaq *Greenland* 77°30N 69°10W **69** B18
Qachasnek *S. Africa* 30°6S 28°42E **57** D4
Qa'el Jafr *Jordan* 30°20N 36°25E **48** E5
Qa'emābād *Iran* 31°44N 60°2E **47** D9
Qā'emshahr *Iran* 36°30N 52°53E **47** B7
Qagan Nur *Jilin, China* 45°15N 124°18E **33** B13
Qagan Nur *Nei Monggol Zizhiqu, China* 43°30N 114°55E **32** C8
Qahar Youyi Zhongqi *China* 41°12N 112°40E **32** D7
Qahremānshahr = Kermānshāh *Iran* 34°23N 47°0E **46** C5
Qaidam Pendi *China* 37°0N 95°0E **30** D8
Qajarīyeh *Iran* 31°1N 48°22E **47** D6
Qala-i-Jadid = Spīn Būldak *Afghan.* 31°1N 66°25E **42** D2
Qala Viala *Pakistan* 30°49N 67°17E **42** D2
Qala Yangi *Afghan.* 34°20N 66°30E **42** B2
Qal'at al Akhḑar *Si. Arabia* 28°4N 37°9E **46** E3
Qal'at Dīzah *Iraq* 36°11N 45°7E **46** B5
Qal'at Ṣāliḩ *Iraq* 31°31N 47°16E **46** D5
Qal'at Sukkar *Iraq* 31°51N 46°5E **46** D5
Qamani'tuaq = Baker Lake *Canada* 64°20N 96°3W **68** E12
Qamdo *China* 31°15N 97°6E **34** B1
Qamea *Fiji* 16°45S 179°45W **59** a
Qamruddin Karez *Pakistan* 31°45N 68°20E **42** D3
Qandahār = Kandahār *Afghan.* 31°32N 65°43E **40** D4
Qandahār = Kandahār □ *Afghan.* 31°0N 65°0E **40** D4
Qandyaghash *Kazakhstan* 49°28N 57°25E **19** E10
Qapān *Iran* 37°40N 55°47E **47** B7
Qapshaghay *Kazakhstan* 43°51N 77°14E **26** E8
Qaqortoq *Greenland* 60°43N 46°0W **4** C5
Qara Qash ➔ *China* 35°0N 78°30E **43** B8
Qarabutaq *Kazakhstan* 50°0N 60°14E **26** E7
Qaraghandy *Kazakhstan* 49°50N 73°10E **30** B3
Qaraghayly *Kazakhstan* 49°26N 76°0E **26** E8
Qārah *Si. Arabia* 29°55N 40°3E **46** D4
Qarataū *Ongtüstik Qazaqstan, Kazakhstan* 43°30N 69°30E **26** E7
Qarataū *Zhambyl, Kazakhstan* 43°10N 70°28E **26** E8
Qarazhal *Kazakhstan* 48°2N 70°49E **26** E8
Qarchak *Iran* 35°25N 51°34E **47** C6
Qardho *Somalia* 9°30N 49°6E **49** F4
Qareh ➔ *Iran* 39°25N 47°22E **46** B5
Qareh Tekān *Iran* 36°38N 49°29E **47** B6
Qarnein *U.A.E.* 24°56N 52°52E **47** E7
Qarqan He ➔ *China* 39°30N 88°30E **30** D6
Qarqaraly *Kazakhstan* 49°26N 75°30E **30** B4
Qarshi *Uzbekistan* 38°53N 65°48E **26** F7
Qartabā *Lebanon* 34°4N 35°50E **48** A4
Qārūh *Kuwait* 28°49N 48°46E **47** D6
Qaryat al Gharab *Iraq* 31°27N 44°48E **46** D5
Qaryat al 'Ulyā *Si. Arabia* 27°33N 47°42E **46** E5
Qasr 'Amra *Jordan* 31°48N 36°35E **46** D3
Qaşr-e Qand *Iran* 26°15N 60°45E **47** E9
Qaşr-e Shīrīn *Iran* 34°31N 45°35E **46** C5
Qasr Farâfra *Egypt* 27°0N 28°1E **53** C11
Qasuittuq = Resolute *Canada* 74°42N 94°54W **69** C13
Qatanā *Syria* 33°26N 36°4E **48** B5
Qatar ■ *Asia* 25°30N 51°15E **47** E6
Qatlīsh *Iran* 37°50N 57°19E **47** B8
Qattâra, Munkhafed el *Egypt* 29°30N 27°30E **53** C11
Qattâra Depression = Qattâra, Munkhafed el *Egypt* 29°30N 27°30E **53** C11
Qausuittuq △ *Canada* 76°0N 101°0W **69** B11
Qawām al Ḩamzah = Al Ḩamzah *Iraq* 31°43N 44°58E **46** D5
Qāyen *Iran* 33°40N 59°10E **47** C8
Qazaqstan = Kazakhstan ■ *Asia* 50°0N 70°0E **26** E8
Qazımämmäd *Azerbaijan* 40°3N 49°0E **47** A6
Qazvīn *Iran* 36°15N 50°0E **47** B6
Qazvīn □ *Iran* 36°20N 50°0E **47** B6
Qena *Egypt* 26°10N 32°43E **53** C12
Qeqertarsuaq *Qaasuitsup, Greenland* 69°45N 53°30W **4** C5
Qeqertarsuaq *Qaasuitsup, Greenland* 69°15N 53°38W **4** C5
Qeshlāq *Iran* 34°55N 46°28E **46** C5
Qeshm *Iran* 26°55N 56°10E **47** E8
Qeys *Iran* 26°32N 53°58E **47** E7
Qezel Owzen ➔ *Iran* 36°45N 49°22E **47** B6
Qezi'ot *Israel* 30°52N 34°26E **48** E3
Qi Xian *China* 34°40N 114°48E **32** G8
Qian Gorlos *China* 45°5N 124°42E **33** B13
Qian Hai *China* 22°32N 113°54E **31** a
Qian Xian *China* 34°31N 108°15E **32** G5
Qian'an *China* 40°0N 118°41E **33** E10
Qiancheng *China* 27°12N 109°50E **34** D7
Qianjiang *Guangxi Zhuangzu, China* 23°38N 108°58E **34** F7
Qianjiang *Hubei, China* 30°24N 112°55E **35** B9
Qianjiang *Sichuan, China* 29°33N 108°47E **34** C7
Qianjin *China* 47°34N 133°4E **31** B15
Qianshan *Anhui, China* 30°37N 116°35E **35** B11
Qianshan *Guangdong, China* 22°15N 113°31E **31** a
Qianwei *China* 29°13N 103°56E **34** C4
Qianxi *China* 27°3N 106°3E **34** D6
Qianyang *Hunan, China* 27°18N 110°10E **35** D8
Qianyang *Shaanxi, China* 34°40N 107°8E **32** G4
Qianyang *Zhejiang, China* 30°11N 119°25E **35** B12
Qi'ao *China* 22°25N 113°39E **31** a
Qi'ao Dao *China* 22°25N 113°38E **31** a
Qiaocun *China* 39°56N 112°55E **32** E7
Qiaojia *China* 26°56N 102°58E **34** D4
Qichun *China* 30°18N 115°25E **35** B10
Qidong *Hunan, China* 26°49N 112°7E **35** D9
Qidong *Jiangsu, China* 31°48N 121°38E **35** B13
Qiemo *China* 38°8N 85°32E **30** D6
Qijiang *China* 28°57N 106°35E **34** C6
Qijiaojing *China* 43°28N 91°36E **30** C7
Qikiqtaaluk = Baffin I. *Canada* 68°0N 75°0W **69** D17
Qikiqtarjuaq *Canada* 67°33N 63°0W **69** D19
Qila Saifullāh *Pakistan* 30°45N 68°17E **42** D3
Qilian Shan *China* 38°30N 96°0E **30** D8
Qimen *China* 29°50N 117°42E **35** C11
Qin He ➔ *China* 35°1N 113°22E **32** G7
Qin Jiang ➔ *Guangxi Zhuangzu, China* 21°53N 108°35E **34** F7
Qin Jiang ➔ *Jiangxi, China* 26°15N 115°55E **35** D10
Qin Ling = Qinling Shandi *China* 33°50N 108°10E **32** H5
Qin'an *China* 34°48N 105°40E **32** G3
Qing Xian *China* 38°35N 116°45E **32** E9
Qingcheng *China* 37°15N 117°40E **33** F9
Qingcheng Shan *China* 30°58N 103°31E **34** B4
Qingchuan *China* 32°36N 105°9E **32** H3
Qingdao *China* 36°5N 120°20E **33** F11
Qingfeng *China* 35°52N 115°8E **32** G8
Qinghai □ *China* 36°0N 98°0E **30** D8
Qinghai Hu *China* 36°40N 100°10E **30** D9
Qinghecheng *China* 41°28N 124°15E **33** D13
Qinghemen *China* 41°48N 121°25E **33** D11
Qingjian *China* 37°8N 110°8E **32** F6
Qingjiang = Huaiyin *China* 33°30N 119°2E **33** H10
Qingliu *China* 26°11N 116°48E **35** D11
Qinglong *China* 25°49N 105°12E **34** E5
Qingping *China* 26°39N 107°47E **34** D6
Qingshui *China* 34°48N 106°8E **32** G4
Qingshuihe *China* 39°55N 111°35E **32** E6
Qingtian *China* 28°12N 120°15E **35** C13
Qingtongxia *China* 38°2N 106°3E **32** E4
Qingtongxia Shuiku *China* 37°50N 105°58E **32** F3
Qingxi *China* 27°8N 108°43E **34** D7
Qingxu *China* 37°34N 112°22E **32** F7
Qingyang *Anhui, China* 30°38N 117°50E **35** B11
Qingyang *Gansu, China* 36°2N 107°55E **32** F4
Qingyi Jiang ➔ *China* 29°32N 103°44E **34** C4
Qingyuan *Guangdong, China* 23°40N 112°59E **35** F9
Qingyuan *Liaoning, China* 42°10N 124°55E **33** C13
Qingyuan *Zhejiang, China* 27°36N 119°3E **35** D12
Qingyun *China* 37°45N 117°20E **33** F9
Qingzhen *China* 26°31N 106°25E **34** D6
Qinhuangdao *China* 39°56N 119°30E **33** E10
Qinling Shandi *China* 33°50N 108°10E **32** H5
Qinshui *China* 35°40N 112°8E **32** G7
Qinyang = Jiyuan *China* 35°7N 112°57E **32** G7
Qinyang *China* 35°5N 112°56E **32** G7
Qinyuan *China* 36°29N 112°20E **32** F7
Qinzhou *China* 21°58N 108°38E **34** G7
Qionghai *China* 19°15N 110°26E **38** C8
Qionglai *China* 30°25N 103°31E **34** B4
Qionglai Shan *China* 31°0N 102°30E **34** B4
Qiongshan *China* 19°51N 110°26E **38** C8
Qiongzhou Haixia *China* 20°10N 110°15E **38** B8
Qiqihar *China* 47°26N 124°0E **31** B13
Qira *China* 37°0N 80°48E **30** D5
Qirāīya, W. ➔ *Egypt* 30°27N 34°0E **48** E3
Qiryat Ata *Israel* 32°47N 35°6E **48** C4
Qiryat Gat *Israel* 31°32N 34°46E **48** D3
Qiryat Mal'akhi *Israel* 31°44N 34°44E **48** D3
Qiryat Shemona *Israel* 33°13N 35°35E **48** B4
Qiryat Yam *Israel* 32°51N 35°4E **48** C4
Qishan *China* 34°25N 107°38E **32** G4
Qitai *China* 44°2N 89°35E **30** C6
Qitaihe *China* 45°48N 130°51E **28** B5
Qiubei *China* 24°2N 104°12E **34** E5
Qixia *China* 37°17N 120°52E **33** F11
Qiyang *China* 26°35N 111°50E **35** D8
Qızılağac Körfäzi *Azerbaijan* 39°9N 49°0E **47** B6
Qods *Iran* 35°45N 51°15E **47** C6
Qojūr *Iran* 36°12N 47°55E **46** B5
Qom *Iran* 34°40N 51°0E **47** C6
Qom □ *Iran* 34°40N 51°0E **47** C6
Qomolangma Feng = Everest, Mt. *Nepal* 28°5N 86°58E **43** E12
Qomsheh *Iran* 32°0N 51°55E **47** D6
Qoqek = Tacheng *China* 46°40N 82°58E **30** B5
Qoqon = Qo'qon *Uzbekistan* 40°31N 70°56E **26** E8
Qo'qon *Uzbekistan* 40°31N 70°56E **26** E8
Qoraqalpog'iston □ *Uzbekistan* 43°0N 58°0E **26** E6
Qorveh *Iran* 35°10N 47°48E **46** C5
Qosshaghyl *Kazakhstan* 46°40N 54°0E **19** E9
Qostanay *Kazakhstan* 53°10N 63°35E **26** D7
Qu Jiang ➔ *China* 30°1N 106°24E **34** B6
Qu Xian *China* 30°48N 106°58E **34** B6
Quabbin Res. *U.S.A.* 42°20N 72°20W **83** D12
Quairading *Australia* 32°0S 117°21E **61** F2
Quakertown *U.S.A.* 40°26N 75°21W **83** F9
Qualicum Beach *Canada* 49°22N 124°26W **70** D4
Quambatook *Australia* 35°49S 143°34E **63** F3
Quambone *Australia* 30°57S 147°53E **63** E4
Quamby *Australia* 20°22S 140°17E **62** C3
Quan Long = Ca Mau *Vietnam* 9°7N 105°8E **39** H5
Quanah *U.S.A.* 34°18N 99°44W **84** D5
Quang Ngai *Vietnam* 15°13N 108°58E **38** E7
Quang Tri *Vietnam* 16°45N 107°13E **38** D6
Quang Yen *Vietnam* 20°56N 106°52E **34** G6
Quannan *China* 24°45N 114°33E **35** E10
Quantock Hills *U.K.* 51°8N 3°10W **13** F4
Quanyang *China* 42°21N 127°32E **33** C14
Quanzhou *Fujian, China* 24°55N 118°34E **35** E12
Quanzhou *Guangxi Zhuangzu, China* 25°57N 111°5E **35** E8
Qu'Appelle ➔ *Canada* 50°33N 103°53W **71** C8
Quaqtaq *Canada* 60°55N 69°40W **69** E18
Quaraí *Brazil* 30°15S 56°20W **94** C4
Quartu Sant'Élena *Italy* 39°15N 9°10E **22** E3
Quartzsite *U.S.A.* 33°40N 114°13W **79** M12
Quatre Bornes *Mauritius* 20°15S 57°28E **55** d
Quatsino Sd. *Canada* 50°25N 127°58W **70** C3
Quba *Azerbaijan* 41°21N 48°32E **19** F8
Qūchān *Iran* 37°10N 58°27E **47** B8
Queanbeyan *Australia* 35°17S 149°14E **63** F4
Québec *Canada* 46°52N 71°13W **73** C5
Québec □ *Canada* 48°0N 74°0W **72** B6
Quebrada del Condorito △ *Argentina* 31°49S 64°40W **94** C3
Queen Alexandra Ra. *Antarctica* 85°0S 170°0E **5** E11
Queen Charlotte City *Canada* 53°15N 132°2W **70** C2
Queen Charlotte Is. = Haida Gwaii *Canada* 53°20N 132°10W **70** C2

Queen Charlotte Sd. *Canada* 51°0N 128°0W **70** C3
Queen Charlotte Strait *Canada* 50°45N 127°10W **70** C3
Queen Elizabeth Is. *Canada* 76°0N 95°0W **69** B13
Queen Elizabeth Land *Antarctica* 85°0S 60°0W **5** E17
Queen Mary Land *Antarctica* 70°0S 95°0E **5** D7
Queen Maud G. *Canada* 68°15N 102°30W **68** D11
Queen Maud Land = Dronning Maud Land *Antarctica* 72°30S 12°0E **5** D3
Queen Maud Mts. *Antarctica* 86°0S 160°0W **5** E12
Queens Channel *Australia* 15°0S 129°30E **60** C4
Queenscliff *Australia* 38°16S 144°39E **63** F3
Queensland □ *Australia* 22°0S 142°0E **62** C3
Queenstown *Australia* 42°4S 145°35E **63** G4
Queenstown *N.Z.* 45°1S 168°40E **59** F2
Queenstown *S. Africa* 31°52S 26°52E **56** D4
Queets *U.S.A.* 47°32N 124°19W **78** C2
Queguay Grande → *Uruguay* 32°9S 58°9W **94** C4
Queimadas *Brazil* 11°0S 39°38W **93** F11
Quelimane *Mozam.* 17°53S 36°58E **55** H7
Quellón *Chile* 43°7S 73°37W **96** E2
Quelpart = Jeju-do *S. Korea* 33°29N 126°34E **33** H14
Quemado *N. Mex., U.S.A.* 34°20N 108°30W **77** J9
Quemado *Tex., U.S.A.* 28°56N 100°37W **84** G4
Quemoy = Chinmen *Taiwan* 24°26N 118°19E **35** E12
Quemú-Quemú *Argentina* 36°3S 63°36W **94** D3
Quepem *India* 15°13N 74°3E **45** G2
Quequén *Argentina* 38°30S 58°30W **94** D4
Querétaro *Mexico* 20°36N 100°23W **86** C4
Querétaro □ *Mexico* 21°0N 99°55W **86** C5
Queshan *China* 32°55N 114°2E **35** A10
Quesnel *Canada* 53°0N 122°30W **70** C4
Quesnel → *Canada* 52°58N 122°29W **70** C4
Quesnel L. *Canada* 52°30N 121°20W **70** C4
Questa *U.S.A.* 36°42N 105°36W **77** H11
Quetico △ *Canada* 48°30N 91°45W **72** C1
Quetta *Pakistan* 30°15N 66°55E **42** D2
Quetzaltenango *Guatemala* 14°50N 91°30W **88** D1
Qufār *Si. Arabia* 27°26N 41°37E **46** E4
Qufu *China* 35°36N 116°58E **32** G9
Qui Nhon *Vietnam* 13°40N 109°13E **38** F7
Quibala *Angola* 10°46S 14°59E **54** G2
Quibaxe *Angola* 8°24S 14°27E **54** F2
Quibdó *Colombia* 5°42N 76°40W **92** B3
Quiberon *France* 47°29N 3°9W **20** C2
Quiet L. *Canada* 61°5N 133°5W **70** A2
Quiindy *Paraguay* 25°58S 57°14W **94** B4
Quilá *Mexico* 24°23N 107°13W **86** C3
Quilán, C. *Chile* 43°15S 74°30W **96** E2
Quilcene *U.S.A.* 47°49N 122°53W **78** C4
Quilimarí *Chile* 32°5S 71°30W **94** C1
Quilino *Argentina* 30°14S 64°29W **94** C3
Quillabamba *Peru* 12°50S 72°50W **92** F4
Quillagua *Chile* 21°40S 69°40W **94** A2
Quillota *Chile* 32°54S 71°16W **94** C1
Quilmes *Argentina* 34°43S 58°15W **94** C4
Quilon = Kollam *India* 8°50N 76°38E **45** K3
Quilpie *Australia* 26°35S 144°11E **63** D3
Quilpué *Chile* 33°5S 71°33W **94** C1
Quimilí *Argentina* 27°40S 62°30W **94** B3
Quimper *France* 48°0N 4°9W **20** B1
Quimperlé *France* 47°53N 3°33W **20** C2
Quinault → *U.S.A.* 47°21N 124°18W **78** C2
Quincy *Calif., U.S.A.* 39°56N 120°57W **78** F6
Quincy *Fla., U.S.A.* 30°35N 84°34W **85** F12
Quincy *Ill., U.S.A.* 39°56N 91°23W **80** F8
Quincy *Wash., U.S.A.* 47°14N 119°51W **76** C4
Quines *Argentina* 32°13S 65°48W **94** C2
Quintana Roo □ *Mexico* 19°40N 88°30W **87** D7
Quintana Roo △ *Quintana Roo, Mexico* 20°15N 87°45W **87** C7
Quintanar de la Orden *Spain* 39°36N 3°5W **21** C4
Quintero *Chile* 32°45S 71°30W **94** C1
Quirihue *Chile* 36°15S 72°35W **94** D1
Quirindi *Australia* 31°28S 150°40E **63** E5
Quirinópolis *Brazil* 18°32S 50°30W **93** G8
Quissanga *Mozam.* 12°24S 40°28E **55** G8
Quissico *Mozam.* 24°42S 34°44E **57** B5
Quitilipi *Argentina* 26°50S 60°13W **94** B3
Quitman *U.S.A.* 30°47N 83°34W **85** F13
Quito *Ecuador* 0°15S 78°35W **92** D3
Quixadá *Brazil* 4°55S 39°0W **93** D11
Qujing *China* 25°32N 103°41E **34** E4
Qulan *Kazakhstan* 42°55N 72°43E **26** E8
Qul'ân, Jazâ'ir *Egypt* 24°22N 35°31E **46** E2
Qulsary *Kazakhstan* 46°59N 54°1E **19** E9
Qumbu *S. Africa* 31°10S 28°48E **57** D4
Quneitra = Al Qunayṭirah *Syria* 33°5N 35°45E **48** B4
Qŭnghirot *Uzbekistan* 43°2N 58°50E **26** E6
Qu'nyido *China* 31°15N 98°6E **34** B2
Quoin I. *Australia* 14°54S 129°32E **60** B4
Quoin Pt. *S. Africa* 34°46S 19°37E **56** D2
Quorn *Australia* 32°25S 138°5E **63** E2
Qurnat as Sawdā' *Lebanon* 34°18N 36°6E **48** A5
Quṣaybā' *Si. Arabia* 26°53N 43°35E **46** E4
Qusaybah *Iraq* 34°24N 40°59E **46** C4
Quseir *Egypt* 26°7N 34°16E **46** E2
Quseir Amra = Qasr 'Amra *Jordan* 31°48N 36°35E **46** D3
Qūshchī *Iran* 37°59N 45°3E **46** B5
Qutang Gorge = Qutang Xia *China* 31°0N 109°40E **34** B7
Qutang Xia *China* 31°0N 109°40E **34** B7
Quthing *Lesotho* 30°25S 27°36E **57** D4
Qūṭīābād *Iran* 35°47N 48°30E **47** C6
Quttinirpaaq = Ellesmere I. *Canada* 79°30N 80°0W **69** B16
Quttinirpaaq △ *Canada* 82°13N 72°13W **69** A17
Quwo *China* 35°38N 111°25E **32** G6
Quyang *China* 38°35N 114°40E **32** E8
Quynh Nhai *Vietnam* 21°49N 103°33E **38** B4
Quyon *Canada* 45°31N 76°14W **83** A8
Quzhou *China* 28°57N 118°54E **35** C12
Quzi *China* 36°20N 107°20E **32** F4
Qyzylorda *Kazakhstan* 44°48N 65°28E **26** E7

R

Ra, Ko *Thailand* 9°13N 98°16E **39** H2
Raahe *Finland* 64°40N 24°28E **8** D21
Raalte *Neths.* 52°23N 6°16E **15** B6
Raas *Indonesia* 7°8S 114°33E **37** G16
Raasay *U.K.* 57°25N 6°4W **11** D2
Raasay, Sd. of *U.K.* 57°30N 6°8W **11** D2
Raasepori *Finland* 60°0N 23°26E **9** G20
Rába → *Hungary* 47°38N 17°38E **17** E9
Rabat *Malta* 35°53N 14°24E **22** G6
Rabat *Morocco* 34°2N 6°48W **52** B4
Rabaul *Papua N. G.* 4°24S 152°18E **58** B8
Rabbit Flat *Australia* 20°11S 130°1E **60** D5
Rabbit Lake Mine *Canada* 58°4N 104°5W **71** B8
Rabi *Fiji* 16°30S 179°59W **59** a
Rābigh *Si. Arabia* 22°50N 39°5E **49** C2
Râbniţa = Rîbniţa *Moldova* 47°45N 29°0E **17** E15
Rābor *Iran* 29°17N 56°55E **47** D8
Rabwah = Chenab Nagar *Pakistan* 31°45N 72°55E **42** D5
Race, C. *Canada* 46°40N 53°5W **73** C9
Rach Gia *Vietnam* 10°5N 105°5E **39** G5
Rach Soi *Vietnam* 9°57N 105°7E **39** H5
Racha Noi, Ko *Thailand* 7°30N 98°19E **39** J2
Racha Yai, Ko *Thailand* 7°36N 98°21E **39** J2
Rachid *Mauritania* 18°45N 11°35W **52** E3
Racibórz *Poland* 50°7N 18°18E **17** C10
Racine *U.S.A.* 42°44N 87°47W **80** D10
Rackerby *U.S.A.* 39°26N 121°22W **78** F5
Rădăuţi *Romania* 47°50N 25°59E **17** E13
Radcliff *U.S.A.* 37°51N 85°57W **81** G11
Radekhiv *Ukraine* 50°25N 24°32E **17** C13
Radekhov = Radekhiv *Ukraine* 50°25N 24°32E **17** C13
Radford *U.S.A.* 37°8N 80°34W **81** G13
Radhanpur *India* 23°50N 71°38E **42** H4
Radhwa, Jabal *Si. Arabia* 24°34N 38°18E **46** E3
Radisson *Qué., Canada* 53°47N 77°37W **72** B4
Radisson *Sask., Canada* 52°30N 107°20W **71** C7
Radium Hot Springs *Canada* 50°35N 116°2W **70** C5
Radnor Forest *U.K.* 52°17N 3°10W **13** E4
Radom *Poland* 51°23N 21°12E **17** C11
Radomsko *Poland* 51°5N 19°28E **17** C10
Radomyshl *Ukraine* 50°30N 29°12E **17** C15
Radstock, C. *Australia* 33°12S 134°20E **63** E1
Raduzhnyy *Russia* 62°5N 77°28E **26** C8
Radviliškis *Lithuania* 55°49N 23°33E **9** J20
Radville *Canada* 49°30N 104°15W **71** D8
Rae = Behchoko *Canada* 62°50N 116°3W **70** A5
Rae Bareli *India* 26°18N 81°20E **43** F9
Rae Isthmus *Canada* 66°40N 87°30W **69** D14
Raeren *Belgium* 50°41N 6°7E **15** D6
Raeside, L. *Australia* 29°20S 122°0E **61** E3
Raetihi *N.Z.* 39°25S 175°17E **59** C5
Rafaela *Argentina* 31°10S 61°30W **94** C3
Rafah *Gaza Strip* 31°18N 34°14E **48** D3
Rafḥā *Si. Arabia* 29°35N 43°35E **46** D4
Rafsanjān *Iran* 30°30N 56°5E **47** D8
Raft Pt. *Australia* 16°4S 124°26E **60** C3
Raga *South Sudan* 8°28N 25°41E **53** G11
Ragachow *Belarus* 53°8N 30°5E **17** B16
Ragama *Sri Lanka* 7°0N 79°50E **40** R11
Ragged, Mt. *Australia* 33°27S 123°25E **61** F3
Ragged Pt. *Barbados* 13°10N 59°26W **89** g
Raghunathpalli *India* 22°14N 84°48E **43** H11
Raghunathpur *India* 23°33N 86°40E **43** H12
Raglan *N.Z.* 37°55S 174°55E **59** B5
Ragusa *Italy* 36°55N 14°44E **22** F6
Raha *Indonesia* 4°55S 123°0E **37** E6
Rahaeng = Tak *Thailand* 16°52N 99°8E **38** D2
Rahat *Israel* 31°24N 34°45E **48** D3
Rahatgarh *India* 23°47N 78°22E **43** H8
Rahimyar Khan *Pakistan* 28°30N 70°25E **42** E4
Rāhjerd *Iran* 34°22N 50°22E **47** C6
Rahon *India* 31°3N 76°7E **42** D7
Rahuri *India* 19°23N 74°39E **44** E2
Rai, Hon *Vietnam* 9°48N 104°38E **39** H5
Raiatéa, Î. *French Polynesia* 16°50S 151°25W **65** J12
Raichur *India* 16°10N 77°20E **45** F3
Raiganj *India* 25°37N 88°10E **43** G13
Raigarh *India* 21°56N 83°25E **44** D6
Raighar *India* 19°51N 82°6E **44** E6
Raijua *Indonesia* 10°37S 121°36E **37** F6
Raikot *India* 30°41N 75°42E **42** D6
Railton *Australia* 41°25S 146°28E **63** G4
Rainbow Bridge ⌂ *U.S.A.* 37°5N 110°58W **77** H8
Rainbow Lake *Canada* 58°30N 119°23W **70** B5
Rainier *U.S.A.* 46°53N 122°41W **78** D4
Rainier, Mt. *U.S.A.* 46°52N 121°46W **78** D5
Rainy L. *Canada* 48°42N 93°10W **71** D10
Rainy River *Canada* 48°43N 94°29W **71** D10
Raippaluoto *Finland* 63°13N 21°14E **8** E19
Raipur *India* 21°17N 81°45E **44** D5
Rairakhol *India* 21°4N 84°21E **44** D7
Raisen *India* 23°20N 77°48E **42** H8
Raisio *Finland* 60°28N 22°11E **9** F20
Raj Nandgaon *India* 21°5N 81°5E **44** D5
Raj Nilgiri *India* 21°28N 86°46E **43** J12
Raja, Ujung *Indonesia* 3°40N 96°25E **36** D1
Raja Ampat, Kepulauan *Indonesia* 0°30S 130°0E **37** E8
Rajahmahendravaram *India* 17°1N 81°48E **44** F5
Rajahmundry = Rajahmahendravaram *India* 17°1N 81°48E **44** F5
Rajaji △ *India* 30°10N 78°20E **42** D8
Rajampet *India* 14°11N 79°10E **45** G4
Rajang → *Malaysia* 2°30N 112°0E **36** D4
Rajanpur *Pakistan* 29°6N 70°19E **42** E4
Rajapalaiyam *India* 9°25N 77°35E **45** K3
Rajapur *India* 16°40N 73°31E **44** F1
Rajasthan □ *India* 26°45N 73°30E **42** F5
Rajasthan Canal = Indira Gandhi Canal *India* 28°0N 72°0E **42** F5
Rajauri *India* 33°25N 74°21E **43** C6
Rajendranagar *India* 17°18N 78°27E **44** F4
Rajgarh *Mad. P., India* 24°2N 76°45E **42** G7
Rajgarh *Raj., India* 27°14N 76°38E **42** F7
Rajgarh *Raj., India* 28°40N 75°25E **42** E6
Rajghat Dam *India* 24°45N 78°20E **44** B4
Rajgir *India* 25°2N 85°25E **43** G11
Rajim *India* 20°58N 81°53E **44** D5
Rajkot *India* 22°15N 70°56E **42** H4
Rajmahal Hills *India* 24°30N 87°30E **43** G12
Rajpipla *India* 21°50N 73°30E **44** D1
Rajpur *India* 22°18N 74°21E **42** H6
Rajpura *India* 30°25N 76°32E **42** D7
Rajsamand = Kankroli *India* 25°4N 73°53E **42** G5
Rajshahi *Bangla.* 24°22N 88°39E **41** G16
Rajshahi □ *Bangla.* 25°0N 89°0E **43** G13
Rajula *India* 21°3N 71°26E **42** J4
Rajur *India* 20°7N 78°55E **44** D4
Rajura *India* 19°47N 79°22E **44** E4
Rakaia *N.Z.* 43°45S 172°1E **59** E4
Rakaia → *N.Z.* 43°36S 172°15E **59** E4
Rakan, Ra's *Qatar* 26°10N 51°20E **47** E6
Rakaposhi *Pakistan* 36°10N 74°25E **43** A6
Rakata, Pulau *Indonesia* 6°10S 105°20E **37** G11
Rakhine □ *Myanmar* 19°0N 94°15E **41** K18
Rakhiv *Ukraine* 48°3N 24°12E **17** D13
Rakhni *Pakistan* 30°4N 69°56E **42** D3
Rakhni → *Pakistan* 29°31N 69°36E **42** E3
Rakiraki *Fiji* 17°22S 178°11E **59** a
Rakitnoye *Russia* 45°36N 134°17E **28** B7
Rakiura = Stewart I. *N.Z.* 46°58S 167°54E **59** G1
Rakiura △ *N.Z.* 47°0S 167°50E **59** G1
Rakops *Botswana* 21°1S 24°28E **56** B3
Rakvere *Estonia* 59°20N 26°25E **9** G22
Raleigh *U.S.A.* 35°47N 78°39W **85** D15
Ralik Chain *Pac. Oc.* 8°0N 168°0E **64** G8
Ralls *U.S.A.* 33°41N 101°24W **84** E4
Ralston *U.S.A.* 41°30N 76°57W **82** E8
Ram → *Canada* 62°1N 123°41W **70** A4
Rama *Nic.* 12°9N 84°15W **88** D3
Ramachandrapuram *India* 16°50N 82°4E **44** F6
Ramagiri Udayagiri *India* 19°5N 84°18E **44** E7
Ramagundam *India* 18°55N 79°15E **44** E4
Ramakona *India* 21°43N 78°50E **43** J8
Raman *Thailand* 6°29N 101°18E **39** J3
Ramanathapuram *India* 9°25N 78°55E **45** K4
Ramanujganj *India* 23°48N 83°42E **43** H10
Ramas C. *India* 15°5N 73°55E **45** G1
Ramat Gan *Israel* 32°4N 34°48E **48** C3
Ramatlhabama *S. Africa* 25°37S 25°33E **56** C4
Ramban *India* 33°14N 75°12E **43** C6
Rambi = Rabi *Fiji* 16°30S 179°59W **59** a
Rambipuji *Indonesia* 8°12S 113°37E **37** H15
Ramdurg *India* 15°58N 75°22E **45** G2
Ramea *Canada* 47°31N 57°23W **73** C8
Ramechhap *Nepal* 27°25N 86°10E **43** F12
Ramelton *Ireland* 55°2N 7°39W **10** A4
Rameswaram *India* 9°17N 79°18E **45** K4
Ramganga → *India* 27°5N 79°58E **43** F8
Ramgarh *Jharkhand, India* 23°40N 85°35E **43** H11
Ramgarh *Raj., India* 27°16N 75°14E **42** F6
Ramgarh *Raj., India* 27°30N 70°36E **42** F4
Rāmhormoz *Iran* 31°15N 49°35E **47** D6
Ramiān *Iran* 37°3N 55°16E **47** B7
Ramingining *Australia* 12°19S 135°3E **62** A2
Ramla *Israel* 31°55N 34°52E **48** D3
Ramm = Rum *Jordan* 29°39N 35°26E **48** F4
Ramm, Jabal *Jordan* 29°35N 35°24E **48** F4
Ramnad = Ramanathapuram *India* 9°25N 78°55E **45** K4
Ramnagar *Jammu & Kashmir, India* 32°47N 75°18E **43** C6
Ramnagar *Uttarakhand, India* 29°24N 79°7E **43** E8
Râmnicu Sărat *Romania* 45°26N 27°3E **17** F14
Râmnicu Vâlcea *Romania* 45°9N 24°21E **17** F13
Ramona *U.S.A.* 33°2N 116°52W **79** M10
Ramore *Canada* 48°30N 80°25W **72** C3
Ramotswa *Botswana* 24°50S 25°52E **56** B4
Rampur *H.P., India* 31°26N 77°43E **42** D7
Rampur *Mad. P., India* 23°25N 73°53E **42** H5
Rampur *Odisha, India* 21°48N 83°58E **44** D6
Rampur *Ut. P., India* 28°50N 79°5E **43** E8
Rampur Hat *India* 24°10N 87°50E **43** G12
Rampura *India* 24°30N 75°27E **42** G6
Ramrama Tola *India* 21°52N 79°55E **43** J8
Ramree I. *Myanmar* 19°0N 93°40E **41** K19
Rāmsar *Iran* 36°53N 50°41E **47** B6
Ramsey *I. of Man* 54°20N 4°22W **12** C3
Ramsey *U.S.A.* 41°4N 74°9W **83** E10
Ramsey L. *Canada* 47°13N 82°15W **72** C3
Ramsgate *U.K.* 51°20N 1°25E **13** F9
Ramtek *India* 21°20N 79°15E **44** D4
Rana Pratap Sagar Dam *India* 24°58N 75°38E **42** G6
Ranaghat *India* 23°15N 88°35E **43** H13
Ranahu *Pakistan* 25°55N 69°45E **42** G3
Ranau *Malaysia* 6°2N 116°40E **36** C5
Rancagua *Chile* 34°10S 70°50W **94** C1
Rancheria → *Canada* 60°13N 129°7W **70** A3
Ranchester *U.S.A.* 44°54N 107°10W **76** D10
Ranchi *India* 23°19N 85°27E **43** H11
Rancho Cordova *U.S.A.* 38°36N 121°18W **78** G5
Rancho Cucamonga *U.S.A.* 34°10N 117°30W **79** L9
Randalstown *U.K.* 54°45N 6°19W **10** B5
Rander *India* 21°14N 72°47E **44** D1
Randers *Denmark* 56°29N 10°1E **9** H14
Randfontein *S. Africa* 26°8S 27°45E **57** C4
Randle *U.S.A.* 46°32N 121°57W **78** D5
Randolph *Mass., U.S.A.* 42°10N 71°2W **83** D13
Randolph *N.Y., U.S.A.* 42°10N 78°59W **82** D6
Randolph *Utah, U.S.A.* 41°40N 111°11W **76** F8
Randolph *Vt., U.S.A.* 43°55N 72°40W **83** C12
Randsburg *U.S.A.* 35°22N 117°39W **79** K9
Råneälven → *Sweden* 65°50N 22°20E **8** D20
Rangae *Thailand* 6°19N 101°44E **39** J3
Rangaunu B. *N.Z.* 34°51S 173°15E **59** A4
Rangeley *U.S.A.* 44°58N 70°39W **83** B14
Rangeley L. *U.S.A.* 44°55N 70°43W **83** B14
Rangely *U.S.A.* 40°5N 108°48W **76** F9
Ranger *U.S.A.* 32°28N 98°41W **84** E5
Rangia *India* 26°28N 91°38E **41** F17
Rangiora *N.Z.* 43°19S 172°36E **59** E4
Rangitaiki → *N.Z.* 37°54S 176°49E **59** B6
Rangitata → *N.Z.* 43°45S 171°15E **59** E3
Rangitoto ke te tonga = D'Urville I. *N.Z.* 40°50S 173°55E **59** D4
Rangkasbitung *Indonesia* 6°21S 106°15E **37** G12
Rangoon = Yangôn *Myanmar* 16°45N 96°20E **41** L20
Rangpur *Bangla.* 25°42N 89°22E **41** G16
Rangsang *Indonesia* 1°20N 103°5E **39** M4
Rani-ki-Vav *India* 23°51N 72°6E **42** H4
Ranibennur *India* 14°35N 75°30E **45** G2
Raniganj *Paschimbanga, India* 23°40N 87°5E **41** H15
Raniganj *Ut. P., India* 27°3N 82°13E **43** F9
Ranikhet *India* 29°39N 79°25E **43** E8
Ranippettai *India* 12°56N 79°23E **45** H4
Raniwara *India* 24°50N 72°10E **42** G5
Rāniyah *Iraq* 36°15N 44°53E **46** B5
Ranka *India* 23°59N 83°47E **43** H10
Ranken → *Australia* 20°31S 137°36E **62** C2
Rankin *U.S.A.* 31°13N 101°56W **84** F4
Rankin Inlet *Canada* 62°30N 93°0W **68** E13
Rankins Springs *Australia* 33°49S 146°14E **63** E4
Rannoch, L. *U.K.* 56°41N 4°20W **11** E4
Rannoch Moor *U.K.* 56°38N 4°48W **11** E4
Ranohira *Madag.* 22°29S 45°24E **55** J9
Ranong *Thailand* 9°56N 98°40E **39** H2
Ranpur *India* 20°5N 85°20E **44** D7
Rānsa *Iran* 33°39N 48°18E **47** C6
Ransiki *Indonesia* 1°30S 134°10E **37** E8
Rantau Abang *Malaysia* 4°52N 103°24E **39** K4
Rantauprapat *Indonesia* 2°15N 99°50E **36** D1
Rantemario *Indonesia* 3°15S 119°57E **37** E5
Ranthambore △ *India* 26°10N 76°30E **42** F7
Rantoul *U.S.A.* 40°19N 88°9W **80** E9
Raohe *China* 46°47N 134°0E **28** A7
Raoping *China* 23°42N 117°1E **35** F11
Raoyang *China* 38°15N 115°45E **32** E8
Rap, Ko *Thailand* 9°19N 99°58E **39** b
Rapa *French Polynesia* 27°35S 144°20W **65** K13
Rapa Nui = Pascua, I. de *Chile* 27°7S 109°23W **65** K17
Rapallo *Italy* 44°21N 9°14E **20** D8
Rapar *India* 23°34N 70°38E **42** H4
Rāpch *Iran* 25°40N 59°15E **47** E8
Rapel, Lago *Chile* 34°20S 71°14W **94** C1
Raper, C. *Canada* 69°44N 67°6W **69** D18
Rapid City *U.S.A.* 44°5N 103°14W **80** C2
Rapid River *U.S.A.* 45°55N 86°58W **80** C10
Rapla *Estonia* 59°1N 24°52E **9** G21
Rapti → *India* 26°18N 83°41E **43** F10
Raquette → *U.S.A.* 45°0N 74°42W **83** B10
Raquette Lake *U.S.A.* 43°49N 74°40W **83** C10
Rara △ *Nepal* 29°30N 82°10E **43** E10
Rarotonga *Cook Is.* 21°30S 160°0W **65** K12
Ra's al 'Ayn *Syria* 36°45N 40°12E **46** B4
Ra's Al Khair *Si. Arabia* 27°27N 49°18E **47** E6
Ra's al Khaymah *U.A.E.* 25°50N 55°59E **47** E7
Ra's aṭ Tib *Tunisia* 37°1N 11°2E **22** F4
Rasa, Pta. *Argentina* 36°20S 56°41W **94** D4
Raseiniai *Lithuania* 55°25N 23°5E **9** J20
Rashmi *India* 25°4N 74°22E **42** G6
Rasht *Iran* 37°20N 49°40E **47** B6
Rasi Salai *Thailand* 15°20N 104°9E **38** E5
Rasipuram *India* 11°30N 78°15E **45** J4
Raskot *Nepal* 29°14N 81°39E **43** E9
Rason L. *Australia* 28°45S 124°25E **61** E3
Rasra *India* 25°50N 83°50E **43** G10
Rasua Garhi *Nepal* 28°17N 85°23E **43** E11
Rasul *Pakistan* 32°42N 73°34E **42** C5
Rat → *Canada* 49°35N 97°10W **71** D9
Rat Buri = Ratchaburi *Thailand* 13°30N 99°54E **38** F2
Rat Islands *U.S.A.* 52°0N 178°0E **74** E3
Rat L. *Canada* 56°10N 99°40W **71** B9
Ratak Chain *Pac. Oc.* 1°0N 170°0E **64** G8
Ratangarh *India* 28°5N 74°35E **42** E6
Raṭāwī *Iraq* 30°38N 47°13E **46** D5
Ratchaburi *Thailand* 13°30N 99°54E **38** F2
Rath *India* 25°36N 79°37E **43** G8
Rath Luirc = Charleville *Ireland* 52°21N 8°40W **10** D3
Rathangan *Ireland* 53°14N 7°0W **10** C4
Rathdrum *Ireland* 52°56N 6°14W **10** D5
Rathenow *Germany* 52°37N 12°19E **16** B7
Rathkeale *Ireland* 52°32N 8°56W **10** D3
Rathlin I. *U.K.* 55°18N 6°14W **10** A5
Ratibor = Racibórz *Poland* 50°7N 18°18E **17** C10
Ratlam *India* 23°20N 75°0E **42** H6
Ratmanova, Ostrov *Russia* 65°46N 169°6W **74** B6
Ratnagiri *India* 16°57N 73°18E **44** F1
Ratnapura *Sri Lanka* 6°40N 80°20E **45** L5
Ratodero *Pakistan* 27°48N 68°18E **42** F3
Raton *U.S.A.* 36°54N 104°24W **77** H11
Rattaphum *Thailand* 7°8N 100°16E **39** J3
Rattray Hd. *U.K.* 57°38N 1°50W **11** D7
Ratz, Mt. *Canada* 57°23N 132°12W **70** B2
Raub *Malaysia* 3°47N 101°52E **39** L3
Rauch *Argentina* 36°45S 59°5W **94** D4
Raudales *Mexico* 17°27N 93°39W **87** D6
Raufarhöfn *Iceland* 66°27N 15°57W **8** C6
Raufoss *Norway* 60°44N 10°37E **8** F14
Raukumara Ra. *N.Z.* 38°5S 177°55E **59** C6
Rauma *Finland* 61°10N 21°30E **8** F19
Raumo = Rauma *Finland* 61°10N 21°30E **8** F19
Raung, Gunung *Indonesia* 8°8S 114°3E **37** J17
Raurkela *India* 22°14N 84°50E **43** H11
Rausu-Dake *Japan* 44°4N 145°7E **28** B12
Rava-Ruska *Ukraine* 50°15N 23°42E **17** C12
Rava Russkaya = Rava-Ruska *Ukraine* 50°15N 23°42E **17** C12
Ravalli *U.S.A.* 47°17N 114°11W **76** C6
Ravānsar *Iran* 34°43N 46°40E **46** C5
Rāvar *Iran* 31°20N 56°51E **47** D8
Ravena *U.S.A.* 42°28N 73°49W **83** D11
Ravenna *Italy* 44°25N 12°12E **22** B5
Ravenna *Nebr., U.S.A.* 41°1N 98°55W **80** E4
Ravenna *Ohio, U.S.A.* 41°9N 81°15W **82** E3
Ravensburg *Germany* 47°46N 9°36E **16** E5
Ravenshoe *Australia* 17°37S 145°29E **62** B4
Ravensthorpe *Australia* 33°35S 120°2E **61** F3
Ravenswood *Australia* 20°6S 146°54E **62** C4
Ravenswood *U.S.A.* 38°57N 81°46W **81** F13
Raver *India* 21°15N 76°2E **44** D3
Ravi → *Pakistan* 30°35N 71°49E **42** D4
Rawalpindi *Pakistan* 33°38N 73°8E **42** C5
Rawang *Malaysia* 3°20N 101°35E **39** L3
Rawene *N.Z.* 35°25S 173°32E **59** A4
Rawi, Ko *Thailand* 6°33N 99°14E **39** J2
Rawlinna *Australia* 30°58S 125°28E **61** F4
Rawlins *U.S.A.* 41°47N 107°14W **76** F10
Rawlinson Ra. *Australia* 24°40S 128°30E **61** D4
Rawson *Argentina* 43°15S 65°5W **96** E3
Raxaul *India* 26°59N 84°51E **43** F11
Ray *U.S.A.* 48°21N 103°10W **80** A2
Ray, C. *Canada* 47°33N 59°15W **73** C8
Ray Mts. *U.S.A.* 66°0N 152°0W **74** B9
Raya Ring, Ko *Thailand* 8°18N 98°29E **39** a
Rayachoti *India* 14°4N 78°50E **45** G4
Rayadurg *India* 14°40N 76°50E **45** G3
Rayagada *India* 19°15N 83°20E **44** E6
Raychikhinsk *Russia* 49°46N 129°25E **27** E13
Rāyen *Iran* 29°34N 57°26E **47** D8
Rayleigh *U.K.* 51°36N 0°37E **13** F8
Raymond *Canada* 49°30N 112°35W **70** D6
Raymond *Calif., U.S.A.* 37°13N 119°54W **78** H7
Raymond *N.H., U.S.A.* 43°2N 71°11W **83** C13
Raymond *Wash., U.S.A.* 46°41N 123°44W **78** D3
Raymondville *U.S.A.* 26°29N 97°47W **84** H6
Raymore *Canada* 51°25N 104°31W **71** C8
Rayón *Mexico* 29°43N 110°35W **86** B2
Rayong *Thailand* 12°40N 101°20E **38** F3
Raystown L. *U.S.A.* 40°25N 78°5W **82** F6
Rayville *U.S.A.* 32°29N 91°46W **84** E9
Raz, Pte. du *France* 48°2N 4°47W **20** C1
Razan *Iran* 35°23N 49°2E **47** C6
Razāzah, Buḥayrat ar *Iraq* 32°40N 43°35E **46** C4
Razdel'naya = Rozdilna *Ukraine* 46°50N 30°2E **17** E16
Razdolnoye *Russia* 43°30N 131°52E **28** C5
Razeh *Iran* 32°47N 48°9E **47** C6
Razgrad *Bulgaria* 43°33N 26°34E **23** C12
Razim, Lacul *Romania* 44°50N 29°0E **17** F15
Razmak *Pakistan* 32°45N 69°50E **42** C3
Razzaza, L. = Razāzah, Buḥayrat ar *Iraq* 32°40N 43°35E **46** C4
Re, Cu Lao *Vietnam* 15°22N 109°8E **38** E7
Ré, Î. de *France* 46°12N 1°30W **20** C3
Reading *U.K.* 51°27N 0°58W **13** F7
Reading *U.S.A.* 40°20N 75°56W **83** F9
Reading □ *U.K.* 51°27N 0°58W **13** F7
Realicó *Argentina* 35°0S 64°15W **94** D3
Ream *Cambodia* 10°34N 103°39E **39** G4
Ream △ *Cambodia* 10°30N 103°45E **39** G4
Reay Forest *U.K.* 58°22N 4°55W **11** C4
Rebecca, L. *Australia* 30°0S 122°15E **61** F3
Rebi *Indonesia* 6°23S 134°7E **37** F8
Rebiana, Sahrâ' *Libya* 24°30N 21°0E **53** D10
Reboly *Russia* 63°49N 30°47E **8** E24
Rebun-Tō *Japan* 45°23N 141°2E **28** B10
Recherche, Arch. of the *Australia* 34°15S 122°50E **61** F3
Rechna Doab *Pakistan* 31°35N 73°30E **42** D5
Rechytsa *Belarus* 52°21N 30°24E **17** B16
Recife *Brazil* 8°0S 35°0W **93** E12
Recife *Seychelles* 4°36S 55°42E **55** b
Reckong Peo *India* 31°32N 78°16E **42** D8
Reconquista *Argentina* 29°10S 59°45W **94** B4
Recreo *Argentina* 29°25S 65°10W **94** B2
Red = Hong → *Asia* 20°16N 106°34E **38** B5
Red → *U.S.A.* 31°1N 91°45W **84** F9
Red Bank *U.S.A.* 40°21N 74°5W **83** F10
Red Bay *Canada* 51°44N 56°25W **73** B8
Red Bluff *U.S.A.* 40°11N 122°15W **76** F2
Red Bluff Res. *U.S.A.* 31°54N 103°55W **77** L12
Red Cliffs *Australia* 34°19S 142°11E **63** E3
Red Cloud *U.S.A.* 40°5N 98°32W **80** E4
Red Creek *U.S.A.* 43°14N 76°45W **83** C8
Red Deer *Canada* 52°20N 113°50W **70** C6
Red Deer → *Alta., Canada* 50°58N 110°0W **71** C7
Red Deer → *Man., Canada* 52°53N 101°1W **71** C8
Red Deer L. *Canada* 52°55N 101°20W **71** C8
Red Hook *U.S.A.* 41°55N 73°53W **83** E11
Red Indian L. *Canada* 48°35N 57°0W **73** C8
Red L. *Canada* 51°3N 93°49W **71** C10
Red Lake *Canada* 51°3N 93°49W **71** C10
Red Lake Falls *U.S.A.* 47°53N 96°16W **80** B5
Red Lake Road *Canada* 49°59N 93°25W **71** C10
Red Lodge *U.S.A.* 45°11N 109°15W **76** D9
Red Mountain *U.S.A.* 35°37N 117°38W **79** K9
Red Oak *U.S.A.* 41°1N 95°14W **80** E6
Red River of the North → *N. Amer.* 49°0N 97°15W **80** A5
Red Rock *Canada* 48°55N 88°15W **72** C2
Red Rock, L. *U.S.A.* 41°22N 92°59W **80** E7
Red Rocks Pt. *Australia* 32°13S 127°32E **61** F4
Red Sea *Asia* 25°0N 36°0E **49** C2
Red Slate Mt. *U.S.A.* 37°31N 118°52W **78** H8

Red Sucker L. *Canada* 54°9N 93°40W **72** B1
Red Tower Pass = Turnu Roşu, P.
 Romania 45°33N 24°17E **17** F13
Red Wing *U.S.A.* 44°34N 92°31W **80** C7
Redang, Pulau *Malaysia* 5°49N 103°2E **39** K4
Redcar *U.K.* 54°37N 1°4W **12** C6
Redcar & Cleveland □
 U.K. 54°29N 1°0W **12** C7
Redcliff *Canada* 50°10N 110°50W **76** A8
Redcliffe *Australia* 27°12S 153°6E **63** D5
Redcliffe, Mt. *Australia* 28°30S 121°30E **61** E3
Reddersburg *S. Africa* 29°41S 26°10E **56** D4
Redding *U.S.A.* 40°35N 122°24W **76** F2
Redditch *U.K.* 52°18N 1°55W **13** E6
Redfield *U.S.A.* 44°53N 98°31W **80** C4
Redford *U.S.A.* 44°38N 73°48W **83** B11
Redhead *Trin. & Tob.* 10°44N 60°58W **93** K16
Redlands *U.S.A.* 34°4N 117°11W **79** M9
Redmond *Oreg., U.S.A.* 44°17N 121°11W **76** D3
Redmond *Wash., U.S.A.* 47°40N 122°7W **78** C4
Redon *France* 47°40N 2°6W **20** C2
Redonda *Antigua & B.* 16°58N 62°19W **89** C7
Redondela *Spain* 42°15N 8°38W **21** A1
Redondo Beach *U.S.A.* 33°50N 118°23W **79** M8
Redoubt Volcano
 U.S.A. 60°29N 152°45W **74** C9
Redruth *U.K.* 50°14N 5°14W **13** G2
Redvers *Canada* 49°35N 101°40W **71** D8
Redwater *Canada* 53°55N 113°6W **70** C6
Redwood *U.S.A.* 44°18N 75°48W **83** B9
Redwood △ *U.S.A.* 41°40N 124°5W **76** F1
Redwood City *U.S.A.* 37°30N 122°15W **78** H4
Redwood Falls *U.S.A.* 44°32N 95°7W **80** C7
Ree, L. *Ireland* 53°35N 8°0W **10** C3
Reed City *U.S.A.* 43°53N 85°31W **81** D11
Reed L. *Canada* 54°38N 100°30W **71** C8
Reedley *U.S.A.* 36°36N 119°27W **78** J7
Reedsburg *U.S.A.* 43°32N 90°0W **80** D8
Reedsport *U.S.A.* 43°42N 124°6W **76** E1
Reedsville *U.S.A.* 40°39N 77°35W **82** F7
Reefton *N.Z.* 42°6S 171°51E **59** E3
Reese → *U.S.A.* 40°48N 117°4W **76** F5
Refugio *U.S.A.* 28°18N 97°17W **84** G6
Regensburg *Germany* 49°1N 12°6E **16** D7
Reggâne = Zaouiet Reggâne
 Algeria 26°32N 0°3E **52** C6
Réggio di Calábria *Italy* 38°6N 15°39E **22** E6
Réggio nell'Emília *Italy* 44°43N 10°36E **22** B4
Reghin *Romania* 46°46N 24°42E **17** E13
Regina *Canada* 50°27N 104°35W **71** C8
Regina Beach *Canada* 50°47N 105°0W **71** C8
Registro *Brazil* 24°29S 47°49W **95** A6
Rehar → *India* 23°55N 82°40E **43** H10
Rehli *India* 23°38N 79°5E **43** H8
Rehoboth *Namibia* 23°15S 17°4E **56** B2
Rehovot *Israel* 31°54N 34°48E **48** D3
Reichenbach *Germany* 50°37N 12°17E **16** C7
Reid *Australia* 30°49S 128°26E **61** F4
Reidsville *U.S.A.* 36°21N 79°40W **85** C15
Reigate *U.K.* 51°14N 0°12W **13** F7
Reims *France* 49°15N 4°1E **20** B6
Reina Adelaida, Arch.
 Chile 52°20S 74°0W **96** G2
Reindeer → *Canada* 55°36N 103°11W **71** B8
Reindeer I. *Canada* 52°30N 98°0W **71** C9
Reindeer L. *Canada* 57°15N 102°15W **71** B8
Reinga, C. *N.Z.* 34°25S 172°43E **59** A4
Reinheimen △ *Norway* 62°10N 7°45E **8** E12
Reinosa *Spain* 43°2N 4°15W **21** A3
Reitz *S. Africa* 27°48S 28°29E **57** C4
Reivilo *S. Africa* 27°36S 24°8E **56** C3
Reliance *Canada* 63°0N 109°20W **71** A7
Remanso *Brazil* 9°41S 42°4W **93** E10
Remarkable, Mt.
 Australia 32°48S 138°10E **63** E2
Rembang *Indonesia* 6°42S 111°21E **37** G14
Remedios *Panama* 8°15N 81°50W **88** E3
Remeshk *Iran* 26°55N 58°50E **47** E8
Remich *Lux.* 49°32N 6°22E **15** E6
Rendang *Indonesia* 8°26S 115°25E **37** J18
Rendsburg *Germany* 54°17N 9°39E **16** A5
René-Levasseur, Î.
 Canada 51°20N 68°40W **73** B6
Renfrew *Canada* 45°30N 76°40W **83** A8
Renfrewshire □ *U.K.* 55°49N 4°38W **11** F4
Rengat *Indonesia* 0°30S 102°45E **36** E2
Rengo *Chile* 34°24S 70°50W **94** C1
Renhua *China* 25°5N 113°40E **35** E9
Renhuai *China* 27°48N 106°28E **34** D6
Reni = Taranagar *India* 28°43N 74°50E **42** E6
Reni *Ukraine* 45°28N 28°15E **17** F15
Renigunta *India* 13°38N 79°30E **45** H4
Renmark *Australia* 34°11S 140°43E **63** E3
Rennell Sd. *Canada* 53°23N 132°35W **70** C2
Renner Springs *Australia* 18°20S 133°47E **62** B1
Rennes *France* 48°7N 1°41W **20** B3
Rennick Glacier
 Antarctica 70°30S 161°45E **5** D11
Rennie L. *Canada* 61°32N 105°35W **71** A7
Reno *U.S.A.* 39°31N 119°48W **78** F7
Reno → *Italy* 44°38N 12°16E **22** B5
Renovo *U.S.A.* 41°20N 77°45W **82** E7
Renqiu *China* 38°43N 116°5E **32** E9
Renshou *China* 29°59N 104°9E **34** C5
Rensselaer *Ind., U.S.A.* 40°57N 87°9W **80** E10
Rensselaer *N.Y., U.S.A.* 42°38N 73°45W **83** D11
Renton *U.S.A.* 47°28N 122°12W **78** C4
Renukoot *India* 24°12N 83°2E **43** G10
Reotipur *India* 25°33N 83°45E **43** G10
Repalle *India* 16°2N 80°45E **45** F5
Republic *Mo., U.S.A.* 37°7N 93°29W **80** G7
Republic *Wash., U.S.A.* 48°39N 118°44W **76** B4
Republican → *U.S.A.* 39°4N 96°48W **80** F5
Repulse B. *Australia* 20°35S 148°46E **62** b
Repulse Bay *Canada* 66°30N 86°30W **69** D14
Requena *Peru* 5°5S 73°52W **92** E4
Requena *Spain* 39°30N 1°4W **21** C5
Reserve *U.S.A.* 33°43N 108°45W **77** K9

Resht = Rasht *Iran* 37°20N 49°40E **47** B6
Resistencia *Argentina* 27°30S 59°0W **94** B4
Reşiţa *Romania* 45°18N 21°53E **17** F11
Reso = Raisio *Finland* 60°28N 22°11E **9** F20
Resolute *Canada* 74°42N 94°54W **69** C13
Resolution I. *Canada* 61°30N 65°0W **69** E19
Resolution I. *N.Z.* 45°40S 166°40E **59** F1
Ressano Garcia *Mozam.* 25°25S 32°0E **57** C5
Reston *Canada* 49°33N 101°6W **71** D8
Retalhuleu *Guatemala* 14°33N 91°46W **88** D1
Retford *U.K.* 53°19N 0°56W **12** D7
Rethimno *Greece* 35°18N 24°30E **23** G11
Reti *Pakistan* 28°5N 69°48E **42** E3
Réunion ☑ *Ind. Oc.* 21°0S 56°0E **55** c
Reus *Spain* 41°10N 1°5E **21** B6
Reutlingen *Germany* 48°29N 9°12E **16** D5
Reval = Tallinn *Estonia* 59°22N 24°48E **9** G21
Revda *Russia* 56°48N 59°57E **18** D10
Revelganj *India* 25°50N 84°40E **43** G11
Revelstoke *Canada* 51°0N 118°10W **70** C5
Reventazón *Peru* 6°10S 80°58W **92** E2
Revillagigedo, Is. de
 Pac. Oc. 18°40N 112°0W **86** D2
Revillagigedo Archipelago △
 Mexico 19°0N 112°30W **86** D2
Rewa *India* 24°33N 81°25E **43** G9
Rewari *India* 28°15N 76°40E **42** E7
Rexburg *U.S.A.* 43°49N 111°47W **76** E8
Rey, I. del *Panama* 8°20N 78°30W **88** E4
Rey, L. del *Mexico* 27°1N 103°26W **86** B4
Rey Malabo *Eq. Guin.* 3°45N 8°50E **54** D1
Reyes, Pt. *U.S.A.* 38°0N 123°0W **78** H3
Reykjahlíð *Iceland* 65°40N 16°55W **8** D5
Reykjanes *Iceland* 63°48N 22°40W **8** E2
Reykjavík *Iceland* 64°10N 21°57W **8** D3
Reynolds Ra. *Australia* 22°30S 133°0E **60** D5
Reynoldsville *U.S.A.* 41°6N 78°53W **82** E6
Reynosa *Mexico* 26°7N 98°18W **87** B5
Rēzekne *Latvia* 56°30N 27°17E **9** H22
Rezvān *Iran* 27°34N 56°6E **47** E8
Rhayader *U.K.* 52°18N 3°29W **13** E4
Rhein → *Europe* 51°52N 6°2E **15** C6
Rhein-Main-Donau-Kanal
 Germany 49°1N 11°27E **16** D6
Rheine *Germany* 52°17N 7°26E **16** B4
Rheinland-Pfalz □ *Germany* 50°0N 7°0E **16** C4
Rhin = Rhein → *Europe* 51°52N 6°2E **15** C6
Rhine = Rhein → *Europe* 51°52N 6°2E **15** C6
Rhinebeck *U.S.A.* 41°56N 73°55W **83** E11
Rhineland-Palatinate =
 Rheinland-Pfalz □
 Germany 50°0N 7°0E **16** C4
Rhinelander *U.S.A.* 45°38N 89°25W **80** C9
Rhinns Pt. *U.K.* 55°40N 6°29W **11** F2
Rhir, Cap *Morocco* 30°38N 9°54W **52** B4
Rhode Island □ *U.S.A.* 41°40N 71°30W **83** E13
Rhodes *Greece* 36°15N 28°10E **23** F13
Rhodope Mts. = Rodopi Planina
 Bulgaria 41°40N 24°20E **23** D11
Rhön *Germany* 50°24N 9°58E **16** C5
Rhondda *U.K.* 51°39N 3°31W **13** F4
Rhondda Cynon Taff □
 U.K. 51°42N 3°27W **13** F4
Rhône → *France* 43°28N 4°42E **20** E6
Rhum = Rùm *U.K.* 57°0N 6°20W **11** E2
Rhydaman = Ammanford
Rhyl *U.K.* 53°20N 3°29W **12** D4
Riachão *Brazil* 7°20S 46°37W **93** E9
Riang, Laem *Thailand* 8°7N 98°27E **39** a
Riasi *India* 33°10N 74°50E **43** C6
Riau □ *Indonesia* 0°0 102°35E **36** E2
Riau, Kepulauan □
 Indonesia 0°30N 104°20E **36** D2
Riau Arch. = Riau, Kepulauan □
 Indonesia 0°30N 104°20E **36** D2
Ribadeo *Spain* 43°35N 7°5W **21** A2
Ribas do Rio Pardo
 Brazil 20°27S 53°46W **93** H8
Ribble → *U.K.* 53°52N 2°25W **12** D5
Ribe *Denmark* 55°19N 8°44E **9** J13
Ribeira Grande *Cabo Verde* 17°0N 25°4W **52** b
Ribeirão Prêto *Brazil* 21°10S 47°50W **95** A6
Riberalta *Bolivia* 11°0S 66°0W **92** F5
Ribniţa *Moldova* 47°45N 29°0E **17** E15
Riccarton *N.Z.* 43°32S 172°37E **59** E4
Rice *U.S.A.* 34°5N 114°51W **79** L12
Rice L. *Canada* 44°12N 78°10W **82** B6
Rice Lake *U.S.A.* 45°30N 91°44W **80** C8
Rich, C. *Canada* 44°43N 80°38W **82** B4
Richards Bay *S. Africa* 28°48S 32°6E **57** C5
Richardson → *Canada* 58°25N 111°14W **71** B6
Richardson Lakes
 U.S.A. 44°46N 70°58W **81** C18
Richardson Springs
 U.S.A. 39°51N 121°46W **78** F5
Riche, C. *Australia* 34°36S 118°47E **61** F2
Richey *U.S.A.* 47°39N 105°4W **76** C11
Richfield *U.S.A.* 38°46N 112°5W **76** G7
Richfield Springs *U.S.A.* 42°51N 74°59W **83** D10
Richford *U.S.A.* 45°0N 72°40W **83** B12
Richibucto *Canada* 46°42N 64°54W **73** C7
Richland *Ga., U.S.A.* 32°5N 84°40W **85** E12
Richland *Wash., U.S.A.* 46°17N 119°18W **76** C4
Richland Center *U.S.A.* 43°21N 90°23W **80** D8
Richlands *U.S.A.* 37°6N 81°48W **81** G13
Richmond *Australia* 20°43S 143°8E **62** C3
Richmond *N.Z.* 41°20S 173°12E **59** D4
Richmond *U.K.* 54°25N 1°43W **12** C6
Richmond *Calif., U.S.A.* 37°56N 122°21W **78** H4
Richmond *Ind., U.S.A.* 39°50N 84°53W **81** F11
Richmond *Ky., U.S.A.* 37°45N 84°18W **81** G11
Richmond *Mich., U.S.A.* 42°49N 82°45W **82** D2
Richmond *Tex., U.S.A.* 29°35N 95°46W **84** G7
Richmond *Utah, U.S.A.* 41°56N 111°48W **76** F8
Richmond *Vt., U.S.A.* 44°24N 72°59W **83** B12
Richmond Hill *Canada* 43°52N 79°27W **82** C5

Richmond Ra. *Australia* 29°0S 152°45E **63** D5
Richmondville *U.S.A.* 42°38N 74°33W **83** D10
Richtersveld △ *S. Africa* 28°15S 17°10E **56** C2
Richville *U.S.A.* 44°25N 75°23W **83** B9
Richwood *U.S.A.* 38°14N 80°32W **81** F13
Riddesburg *U.S.A.* 40°9N 78°15W **82** F6
Rideau → *Canada* 45°27N 75°42W **83** A9
Ridgecrest *U.S.A.* 35°38N 117°40W **79** K9
Ridgefield *Conn., U.S.A.* 41°17N 73°30W **83** E11
Ridgefield *Wash., U.S.A.* 45°49N 122°45W **78** E4
Ridgeland *Miss., U.S.A.* 32°26N 90°8W **85** E9
Ridgeland *S.C., U.S.A.* 32°29N 80°59W **85** E14
Ridgetown *Canada* 42°26N 81°52W **82** D3
Ridgewood *U.S.A.* 40°59N 74°7W **83** F10
Ridgway *U.S.A.* 41°25N 78°44W **82** E6
Riding Mountain △
 Canada 50°50N 100°0W **71** C9
Ridley, Mt. *Australia* 33°12S 122°7E **61** F3
Riebeek-Oos *S. Africa* 33°10S 26°10E **56** D4
Ried *Austria* 48°14N 13°30E **16** D7
Riesa *Germany* 51°17N 13°17E **16** C7
Riet → *S. Africa* 29°0S 23°54E **56** D3
Rietbron *S. Africa* 32°54S 23°10E **56** D3
Rietfontein *Namibia* 21°58S 20°58E **56** B3
Rieti *Italy* 42°24N 12°51E **22** C5
Rif = Er Rif *Morocco* 35°1N 4°1W **52** A5
Riffe L. *U.S.A.* 46°32N 122°26W **78** D4
Rifle *U.S.A.* 39°32N 107°47W **76** G10
Rift Valley *Africa* 7°0N 30°0E **50** G7
Riga *Latvia* 56°53N 24°8E **9** H21
Riga, G. of *Latvia* 57°40N 23°45E **9** H20
Rīgān *Iran* 28°37N 58°58E **47** D8
Rīgas Jūras Līcis = Riga, G. of
 Latvia 57°40N 23°45E **9** H20
Rigaud *Canada* 45°29N 74°18W **83** A10
Rigby *U.S.A.* 43°40N 111°55W **76** E8
Rīgestān *Afghan.* 30°15N 65°0E **40** D4
Riggins *U.S.A.* 45°25N 116°19W **76** D5
Rigolet *Canada* 54°10N 58°23W **73** B8
Rihand Dam *India* 24°9N 83°2E **43** G10
Riihimäki *Finland* 60°45N 24°48E **8** F21
Riiser-Larsen-halvøya
 Antarctica 68°0S 35°0E **5** C4
Riiser-Larsen Ice Shelf
 S. Ocean 74°0S 19°0W **5** D2
Riiser-Larsen Sea *S. Ocean* 67°30S 22°0E **5** C4
Riisitunturi △ *Finland* 66°27N 26°27E **8** C23
Rijeka *Croatia* 45°20N 14°21E **16** F8
Rijssen *Neths.* 52°19N 6°31E **15** B6
Rikuchū-Kaigan △
 Japan 39°20N 142°0E **28** E11
Rikuzentakata *Japan* 39°0N 141°40E **28** E10
Riley *U.S.A.* 43°32N 119°28W **76** E4
Rima → *Nigeria* 13°4N 5°10E **52** F7
Rimah, Wadi ar →
 Si. Arabia 26°5N 41°30E **46** E4
Rimau, Pulau *Malaysia* 5°15N 100°16E **39** c
Rimbey *Canada* 52°35N 114°15W **70** C6
Rimersburg *U.S.A.* 41°3N 79°30W **82** E5
Rímini *Italy* 44°3N 12°33E **22** B5
Rimouski *Canada* 48°27N 68°30W **73** C6
Rimrock *U.S.A.* 46°40N 121°7W **78** D5
Rinca *Indonesia* 8°45S 119°35E **37** F5
Rincón de Romos
 Mexico 22°14N 102°18W **86** C4
Rinconada *Argentina* 22°26S 66°10W **94** A2
Rind → *India* 25°53N 80°33E **43** G9
Ringas *India* 27°21N 75°34E **42** F6
Ringgold Is. *Fiji* 16°15S 179°25W **59** a
Ringkøbing *Denmark* 56°5N 8°15E **9** H13
Ringvassøya *Norway* 69°56N 19°15E **8** B18
Ringwood *U.S.A.* 41°7N 74°15W **83** E10
Rinjani, Gunung
 Indonesia 8°24S 116°28E **36** F5
Rinyirru △ *Australia* 15°24S 144°26E **62** B3
Rio Branco *Brazil* 9°58S 67°49W **92** E5
Río Branco *Uruguay* 32°40S 53°40W **95** C5
Río Bravo *Mexico* 25°59N 98°6W **87** B5
Río Bravo → *N. Amer.* 29°20N 102°45W **86** B4
Río Bravo del Norte →
 Mexico 25°57N 97°9W **87** B5
Rio Brilhante *Brazil* 21°48S 54°33W **95** A5
Río Claro *Brazil* 22°19S 47°35W **95** A6
Río Claro *Trin. & Tob.* 10°20N 61°10W **93** K15
Río Colorado *Argentina* 39°0S 64°0W **96** D4
Río Cuarto *Argentina* 33°10S 64°25W **94** C3
Rio das Pedras *Mozam.* 23°8S 35°28E **57** B6
Rio de Janeiro □ *Brazil* 22°50S 43°0W **95** A7
Rio de Janeiro *Brazil* 23°0S 43°12W **95** A7
Río do Sul *Brazil* 27°13S 49°37W **95** B6
Río Dulce △ *Guatemala* 15°43N 88°50W **88** C2
Río Gallegos *Argentina* 51°35S 69°15W **96** G3
Río Grande *Argentina* 53°50S 67°45W **96** G3
Río Grande *Brazil* 32°0S 52°20W **95** C5
Río Grande *Mexico* 23°50N 103°2W **86** C4
Río Grande *Puerto Rico* 18°23N 65°50W **89** d
Río Grande → *N. Amer.* 25°58N 97°9W **84** J6
Río Grande City *U.S.A.* 26°23N 98°49W **84** H5
Río Grande de Santiago →
 Mexico 21°36N 105°26W **86** C3
Rio Grande do Norte □
 Brazil 5°40S 36°0W **93** E11
Rio Grande do Sul □ *Brazil* 30°0S 53°0W **95** C5
Río Hato *Panama* 8°22N 80°10W **88** E3
Río Lagartos *Mexico* 21°36N 88°10W **87** C7
Río Largo *Brazil* 9°28S 35°50W **93** E11
Río Mulatos *Bolivia* 19°40S 66°50W **92** G5
Río Muni □ *Eq. Guin.* 1°30N 10°0E **54** D2
Río Negro *Brazil* 26°0S 49°55W **95** B6
Río Pardo *Brazil* 30°0S 52°30W **95** C5
Río Pilcomayo △ *Argentina* 25°5S 58°5W **94** B4
Ríos, Atol das *Brazil* 4°0S 34°1W **93** D12
Río Rancho *U.S.A.* 35°14N 106°41W **77** J10
Río Segundo *Argentina* 31°40S 63°59W **94** C3
Río Tercero *Argentina* 32°15S 64°8W **94** C3
Río Verde *Brazil* 17°50S 51°0W **93** G8
Río Verde *Mexico* 21°56N 100°0W **86** C5
Río Vista *U.S.A.* 38°10N 121°42W **78** G5
Ríobamba *Ecuador* 1°50S 78°45W **92** D3
Ríohacha *Colombia* 11°33N 72°55W **92** A4

Riosucio *Colombia* 7°27N 77°7W **92** B3
Riou L. *Canada* 59°7N 106°25W **71** B7
Ripley *Canada* 44°4N 81°35W **82** B3
Ripley *Calif., U.S.A.* 33°32N 114°39W **79** M12
Ripley *N.Y., U.S.A.* 42°16N 79°43W **82** D5
Ripley *Tenn., U.S.A.* 35°45N 89°32W **85** D10
Ripley *W. Va., U.S.A.* 38°49N 81°43W **81** F13
Ripon *U.K.* 54°9N 1°31W **12** C6
Ripon *Calif., U.S.A.* 37°44N 121°7W **78** H5
Ripon *Wis., U.S.A.* 43°51N 88°50W **80** D9
Rishā', W. ar → *Si. Arabia* 25°33N 44°5E **46** E5
Rishikesh *India* 30°7N 78°19E **42** D8
Rishiri-Rebun-Sarobetsu △
 Japan 45°26N 141°30E **28** B10
Rishiri-Tō *Japan* 45°11N 141°15E **28** B10
Rishon le Ziyyon *Israel* 31°58N 34°48E **48** D3
Rison *U.S.A.* 33°58N 92°11W **84** E8
Risør *Norway* 58°43N 9°13E **9** G13
Rita Blanca Cr. →
 U.S.A. 35°40N 102°29W **84** D3
Ritchie's Arch. *India* 12°14N 93°10E **45** H11
Ritter, Mt. *U.S.A.* 37°41N 119°12W **78** H7
Rittman *U.S.A.* 40°58N 81°47W **82** F3
Ritzville *U.S.A.* 47°8N 118°23W **76** C4
Riva del Garda *Italy* 45°53N 10°50E **22** B4
Rivadavia *B. Aires,
 Argentina* 35°29S 62°59W **94** D3
Rivadavia *Mendoza,
 Argentina* 33°13S 68°30W **94** C2
Rivadavia *Salta, Argentina* 24°5S 62°54W **94** A3
Rivadavia *Chile* 29°57S 70°35W **94** B1
Rivas *Nic.* 11°30S 85°50W **88** D2
Rivera *Argentina* 37°12S 63°14W **94** D3
Rivera *Uruguay* 31°0S 55°50W **95** C4
Riverbank *U.S.A.* 37°44N 120°56W **78** H6
Riverdale *U.S.A.* 36°26N 119°52W **78** J7
Riverhead *U.S.A.* 40°55N 72°40W **83** F12
Riverhurst *Canada* 50°55N 106°50W **71** C7
Rivers *Canada* 50°2N 100°14W **71** C8
Rivers Inlet *Canada* 51°42N 127°15W **70** C3
Riversdale *Canada* 44°5N 81°20W **82** B3
Riversdale *S. Africa* 34°7S 21°15E **56** D3
Riverside *U.S.A.* 33°59N 117°22W **79** M9
Riversleigh *Australia* 19°5S 138°40E **62** B2
Riverton *Australia* 34°10S 138°46E **63** E2
Riverton *Canada* 51°1N 97°0W **71** C9
Riverton *N.Z.* 46°21S 168°0E **59** G2
Riverton *U.S.A.* 43°2N 108°23W **76** E9
Riviera = Azur, Côte d'
 France 43°25N 7°10E **20** E7
Riviera *U.S.A.* 35°4N 114°35W **79** K12
Riviera di Levante *Italy* 44°15N 9°30E **20** D8
Riviera di Ponente *Italy* 44°10N 8°20E **20** D8
Rivière-au-Renard
 Canada 48°59N 64°23W **73** C7
Rivière-du-Loup *Canada* 47°50N 69°30W **73** C6
Rivière-Pentecôte *Canada* 49°57N 67°1W **73** C6
Rivière-Pilote *Martinique* 14°26N 60°53W **88** c
Rivière St-Paul *Canada* 51°28N 57°45W **73** B8
Rivière-Salée *Martinique* 14°31N 61°0W **88** c
Rivne *Ukraine* 50°40N 26°10E **17** C14
Rivne □ *Ukraine* 51°15N 26°30E **17** C14
Rívoli *Italy* 45°3N 7°31E **20** D7
Rívoli B. *Australia* 37°32S 140°3E **63** F3
Riyadh = Ar Riyāḍ
 Si. Arabia 24°41N 46°42E **46** E5
Rize *Turkey* 41°0N 40°30E **19** F7
Rizhao *China* 35°25N 119°30E **33** G10
Rizzuto, C. *Italy* 38°53N 17°5E **22** E7
Rjukan *Norway* 59°54N 8°33E **9** G13
Road Town *Br. Virgin Is.* 18°27N 64°37W **89** e
Roan Plateau *U.S.A.* 39°20N 109°20W **76** G9
Roanne *France* 46°3N 4°4E **20** C6
Roanoke *Ala., U.S.A.* 33°9N 85°22W **85** E12
Roanoke *Va., U.S.A.* 37°16N 79°56W **81** G14
Roanoke → *U.S.A.* 35°57N 76°42W **85** D17
Roanoke I. *U.S.A.* 35°53N 75°39W **85** D17
Roanoke Rapids *U.S.A.* 36°28N 77°40W **85** C16
Roatán *Honduras* 16°18N 86°35W **88** C2
Robāt Sang *Iran* 35°35N 59°10E **47** C8
Robāţkarīm *Iran* 35°5N 50°59E **47** C6
Robbins I. *Australia* 40°42S 145°0E **63** G4
Robe → *Australia* 21°42S 116°15E **60** D2
Robert Bourassa, Rés.
 Canada 53°40N 76°55W **72** B4
Robert Lee *U.S.A.* 31°54N 100°29W **84** F4
Robertsdale *U.S.A.* 40°11N 78°6W **82** F6
Robertsganj *India* 24°44N 83°4E **43** G10
Robertson *S. Africa* 33°46S 19°50E **56** D2
Robertson I. *Antarctica* 65°15S 59°30W **5** C18
Robertson Ra. *Australia* 23°15S 121°0E **60** D3
Robertstown *Australia* 33°58S 139°5E **63** E2
Roberval *Canada* 48°32N 72°15W **73** C5
Robeson Chan. *N. Amer.* 82°0N 61°30W **69** A19
Robinson *U.S.A.* 39°0N 87°44W **80** F10
Robinson → *Australia* 16°3S 137°16E **62** B2
Robinson Crusoe I.
 Pac. Oc. 33°38S 78°52W **90** F2
Robinson Ra. *Australia* 25°40S 119°0E **61** E2
Robinvale *Australia* 34°40S 142°45E **63** E3
Roblin *Canada* 51°14N 101°21W **71** C8
Roboré *Bolivia* 18°10S 59°45W **92** G7
Robson, Mt. *Canada* 53°10N 119°10W **70** C5
Robstown *U.S.A.* 27°47N 97°40W **84** H6
Roca, C. da *Portugal* 38°40N 9°31W **21** C1
Roca Partida, I. *Mexico* 19°1N 112°2W **86** D2
Rocas, Atol das *Brazil* 4°0S 34°1W **93** D12
Rocha *Uruguay* 34°30S 54°25W **95** C5
Rochdale *U.K.* 53°38N 2°9W **12** D5
Rochefort *Belgium* 50°9N 5°12E **15** D5
Rochefort *France* 45°56N 0°57W **20** D3
Rochelle *U.S.A.* 41°56N 89°4W **80** E9
Rocher River *Canada* 61°23N 112°44W **70** A6
Rochester *U.K.* 51°23N 0°31E **13** F8
Rochester *Ind., U.S.A.* 41°4N 86°13W **80** E10

Rochester *Minn., U.S.A.* 44°1N 92°28W **80** C7
Rochester *N.H., U.S.A.* 43°18N 70°59W **83** C14
Rochester *N.Y., U.S.A.* 43°10N 77°37W **82** C7
Rock → *Canada* 60°7N 127°7W **70** A3
Rock, The *Australia* 35°15S 147°2E **63** F4
Rock Creek *U.S.A.* 41°40N 80°52W **82** E4
Rock Falls *U.S.A.* 41°47N 89°41W **80** E8
Rock Hill *U.S.A.* 34°56N 81°1W **85** D14
Rock Island *U.S.A.* 41°30N 90°34W **80** E8
Rock Port *U.S.A.* 40°25N 95°31W **80** E6
Rock Sound *Bahamas* 24°54N 76°12W **88** B4
Rock Springs *Mont.,
 U.S.A.* 46°49N 106°15W **76** C10
Rock Springs *Wyo.,
 U.S.A.* 41°35N 109°14W **76** F9
Rock Valley *U.S.A.* 43°12N 96°18W **80** D5
Rockall *Atl. Oc.* 57°37N 13°42W **6** D3
Rockdale *Tex., U.S.A.* 30°39N 97°0W **84** F6
Rockdale *Wash., U.S.A.* 47°22N 121°28W **78** C5
Rockeby = Mungkan Kandju △
 Australia 13°35S 142°52E **62** A3
Rockefeller Plateau
 Antarctica 76°0S 130°0W **5** E14
Rockford *U.S.A.* 42°16N 89°6W **80** D9
Rockglen *Canada* 49°11N 105°57W **71** D7
Rockhampton *Australia* 23°22S 150°32E **62** C5
Rockingham *Australia* 32°15S 115°38E **61** F2
Rockingham *N.C.,
 U.S.A.* 34°57N 79°46W **85** D15
Rockingham *Vt., U.S.A.* 43°11N 72°29W **83** C12
Rockingham B. *Australia* 18°5S 146°10E **62** B4
Rocklake *U.S.A.* 48°47N 99°15W **80** A4
Rockland *Canada* 45°33N 75°17W **83** A9
Rockland *Idaho, U.S.A.* 42°34N 112°53W **76** E7
Rockland *Maine, U.S.A.* 44°6N 69°7W **81** C19
Rockland *Mich., U.S.A.* 46°44N 89°11W **80** B9
Rocklin *U.S.A.* 38°48N 121°14W **78** G5
Rockly B. *Trin. & Tob.* 11°9N 60°46W **93** J16
Rockmart *U.S.A.* 34°1N 85°3W **85** D12
Rockport *Mass., U.S.A.* 42°39N 70°37W **83** D14
Rockport *Tex., U.S.A.* 28°2N 97°3W **84** G6
Rocksprings *U.S.A.* 30°1N 100°13W **84** F4
Rockville *Conn., U.S.A.* 41°52N 72°28W **83** E12
Rockville *Md., U.S.A.* 39°5N 77°9W **81** F15
Rockwall *U.S.A.* 32°56N 96°28W **84** E6
Rockwell City *U.S.A.* 42°24N 94°38W **80** D6
Rockwood *Canada* 43°37N 80°8W **82** C4
Rockwood *Maine,
 U.S.A.* 45°41N 69°45W **81** C19
Rockwood *Tenn., U.S.A.* 35°52N 84°41W **85** D12
Rocky Ford *U.S.A.* 38°3N 103°43W **76** G12
Rocky Gully *Australia* 34°30S 116°57E **61** F2
Rocky Harbour *Canada* 49°36N 57°55W **73** C8
Rocky Island L. *Canada* 46°55N 83°0W **72** C3
Rocky Lane *Canada* 58°31N 116°22W **70** B5
Rocky Mount *U.S.A.* 35°57N 77°48W **85** D16
Rocky Mountain △
 U.S.A. 40°25N 105°45W **76** F11
Rocky Mountain House
 Canada 52°22N 114°55W **70** C6
Rocky Mts. *N. Amer.* 49°0N 115°0W **76** B6
Rocky Point *Namibia* 19°3S 12°30E **56** A2
Rod *Pakistan* 28°10N 63°5E **40** E3
Rødbyhavn *Denmark* 54°39N 11°22E **9** J14
Roddickton *Canada* 50°51N 56°8W **73** B8
Rodez *France* 44°21N 2°33E **20** D5
Ródhos = Rhodes *Greece* 36°15N 28°10E **23** F13
Rodna *Romania* 47°25N 24°50E **17** E13
Rodney *Canada* 42°34N 81°41W **82** D3
Rodney, C. *N.Z.* 36°17S 174°50E **59** B5
Rodopi Planina *Bulgaria* 41°40N 24°20E **23** D11
Rodrigues *Ind. Oc.* 19°45S 63°20E **3** E13
Roe → *U.K.* 55°6N 6°59W **10** A5
Roebling *U.S.A.* 40°7N 74°47W **83** F10
Roebourne *Australia* 20°44S 117°9E **60** D2
Roebuck B. *Australia* 18°5S 122°20E **60** C3
Roebuck Roadhouse
 Australia 17°59S 122°36E **60** C3
Roermond *Neths.* 51°12N 6°0E **15** C6
Roes Welcome Sd. *Canada* 65°0N 87°0W **69** E14
Roeselare *Belgium* 50°57N 3°7E **15** D3
Rogachev = Ragachow
 Belarus 53°8N 30°5E **17** B16
Rogagua, L. *Bolivia* 13°43S 66°50W **92** F5
Rogatyn *Ukraine* 49°24N 24°36E **17** D13
Rogers *U.S.A.* 36°20N 94°7W **84** C7
Rogers City *U.S.A.* 45°25N 83°49W **81** C12
Rogersville *Canada* 46°44N 65°26W **73** C6
Roggan → *Canada* 54°24N 79°25W **72** B4
Roggan L. *Canada* 54°8N 77°50W **72** B4
Roggeveen Basin
 Pac. Oc. 31°30S 95°30W **65** L18
Roggeveldberge *S. Africa* 32°10S 20°10E **56** D3
Rogoaguado, L. *Bolivia* 13°0S 65°30W **92** F5
Rogojampi *Indonesia* 8°19S 114°17E **37** J17
Roha *India* 18°26S 73°4E **44** E1
Rohnert Park *U.S.A.* 38°16N 122°40W **78** G4
Rohri *Pakistan* 27°45N 68°51E **42** F3
Rohri Canal *Pakistan* 26°15N 68°27E **42** F3
Rohtak *India* 28°55N 76°43E **42** E7
Roi Et *Thailand* 16°4N 103°40E **38** D4
Roja *Latvia* 57°29N 22°43E **9** H20
Rojas *Argentina* 34°10S 60°45W **94** C3
Rojo, C. *Mexico* 21°33N 97°20W **87** C5
Rokan → *Indonesia* 2°0N 100°50E **36** D2
Rokiškis *Lithuania* 55°55N 25°35E **9** J21
Rokua △ *Finland* 64°30N 26°15E **8** D22
Rolândia *Brazil* 23°18S 51°23W **95** A5
Rolla *Mo., U.S.A.* 37°57N 91°46W **80** G8
Rolla *N. Dak., U.S.A.* 48°52N 99°37W **80** A4
Rolleston *Australia* 24°28S 148°35E **62** C4
Rollingstone *Australia* 19°2S 146°24E **62** B4
Roma *Australia* 26°32S 148°49E **63** D4
Roma *Sweden* 57°32N 18°26E **9** H18
Roma-Los Saenz *U.S.A.* 26°24N 99°1W **84** H5
Romain, C. *U.S.A.* 33°0N 79°22W **85** E15
Romaine → *Canada* 50°18N 63°47W **73** B7
Roman *Romania* 46°57N 26°55E **17** E14

Romang *Indonesia* 7°30S 127°20E **37** F7
Români *Egypt* 30°59N 32°38E **48** E1
Romania ■ *Europe* 46°0N 25°0E **17** F12
Romano, Cayo *Cuba* 22°0N 77°30W **88** B4
Romans-sur-Isère *France* 45°3N 5°3E **20** D6
Romanzof C. *U.S.A.* 61°49N 166°6W **74** C6
Romblon *Phil.* 12°33N 122°17E **37** B6
Rome *Ga., U.S.A.* 34°15N 85°10W **85** D12
Rome *N.Y., U.S.A.* 43°13N 75°27W **83** C9
Rome *Pa., U.S.A.* 41°51N 76°21W **83** E8
Romney *U.S.A.* 39°21N 78°45W **81** F14
Romney Marsh *U.K.* 51°2N 0°54E **13** F8
Rømø *Denmark* 55°10N 8°30E **9** J13
Romorantin-Lanthenay
  France 47°21N 1°45E **20** C4
Rompin → *Malaysia* 2°49N 103°29E **39** L4
Romsdalen *Norway* 62°25N 7°52E **8** E12
Romsey *U.K.* 51°0N 1°29W **13** G6
Ron *India* 15°40N 75°44E **45** G2
Ron *Vietnam* 17°53N 106°27E **38** D6
Rona *U.K.* 57°34N 5°59W **11** D3
Ronan *U.S.A.* 47°32N 114°6W **76** C6
Roncador, Cayos
  Caribbean 13°32N 80°4W **88** D3
Roncador, Serra do
  Brazil 12°30S 52°30W **93** F8
Ronda *Spain* 36°46N 5°12W **21** D3
Rondane *Norway* 61°57N 9°50E **8** F13
Rondônia □ *Brazil* 11°0S 63°0W **92** F6
Rondonópolis *Brazil* 16°28S 54°38W **93** G8
Rondu *Pakistan* 35°32N 75°10E **43** B6
Rong, Koh *Cambodia* 10°45N 103°15E **39** G4
Rong Jiang → *China* 24°35N 109°20E **34** E7
Rong Xian *China* 22°50N 110°31E **35** F8
Rong'an *China* 25°14N 109°22E **34** E7
Rongcheng *China* 29°20N 105°32E **34** C5
Rongcheng *China* 37°9N 122°23E **33** F12
Ronge, L. la *Canada* 55°6N 105°17W **71** B7
Rongjiang *China* 25°57N 108°28E **34** E7
Rongshui *China* 25°5N 109°12E **34** E7
Rongxian *China* 29°23N 104°22E **34** C5
Rønne *Denmark* 55°6N 14°43E **9** J16
Ronne Ice Shelf *Antarctica* 77°30S 60°0W **5** D18
Ronsard, C. *Australia* 24°46S 113°10E **61** D1
Ronse *Belgium* 50°45N 3°35E **15** D3
Roodepoort *S. Africa* 26°11S 27°54E **57** C4
Roof Butte *U.S.A.* 36°28N 109°5W **77** H9
Rooiboklaagte → *Namibia* 20°50S 21°0E **56** B3
Rooniu, Mt. *Tahiti* 17°49S 149°12W **59** d
Roorkee *India* 29°52N 77°59E **42** E7
Roosendaal *Neths.* 51°32N 4°29E **15** C4
Roosevelt *U.S.A.* 40°18N 109°59W **76** F9
Roosevelt → *Brazil* 7°35S 60°20W **92** E6
Roosevelt, Mt. *Canada* 58°26N 125°20W **70** B3
Roosevelt I. *Antarctica* 79°30S 162°0W **5** D12
Roper → *Australia* 14°43S 135°27E **62** A2
Roper Bar *Australia* 14°44S 134°44E **62** A1
Roper River = St. Vidgeon's ◊
  Australia 14°47S 134°53E **62** A1
Roque Pérez *Argentina* 35°25S 59°24W **94** D4
Roquetas de Mar *Spain* 36°46N 2°36W **21** D4
Roraima □ *Brazil* 2°0N 61°30W **92** C6
Roraima, Mt. *Venezuela* 5°10N 60°40W **92** B6
Røros *Norway* 62°35N 11°23E **8** E14
Ros Comáin = Roscommon
  Ireland 53°38N 8°11W **10** C3
Ros Mhic Thriúin = New Ross
  Ireland 52°23N 6°57W **10** D5
Rosa, Monte *Europe* 45°57N 7°53E **20** D7
Rosalia *U.S.A.* 47°14N 117°22W **76** C5
Rosamond *U.S.A.* 34°52N 118°10W **79** L8
Rosário *Argentina* 33°0S 60°40W **94** C3
Rosário *Brazil* 3°0S 44°15W **93** D10
Rosario *Mexico* 22°58N 105°53W **86** C3
Rosario *Paraguay* 24°30S 57°35W **94** A4
Rosario de la Frontera
  Argentina 25°50S 65°0W **94** B3
Rosario de Lerma
  Argentina 24°59S 65°35W **94** A2
Rosário del Tala
  Argentina 32°20S 59°10W **94** C4
Rosário do Sul *Brazil* 30°15S 54°55W **95** C5
Rosarito *Baja Calif.,*
  Mexico 32°20N 117°2W **79** N9
Rosarito *Baja Calif.,*
  Mexico 28°38N 114°1W **86** B2
Roscoe *U.S.A.* 41°56N 74°55W **83** E10
Roscommon *Ireland* 53°38N 8°11W **10** C3
Roscommon □ *Ireland* 53°49N 8°23W **10** C3
Roscrea *Ireland* 52°57N 7°49W **10** D4
Rose → *Australia* 14°16S 135°45E **62** A2
Rose, L. *Bahamas* 21°0N 73°30W **89** B5
Rose Belle *Mauritius* 20°24S 57°36E **55** d
Rose Blanche *Canada* 47°38N 58°45W **73** C8
Rose Hill *Mauritius* 20°14S 57°27E **55** d
Rose Pt. *Canada* 54°11N 131°39W **70** C2
Rose Valley *Canada* 52°19N 103°49W **71** C8
Roseau *Dominica* 15°17N 61°24W **89** C7
Roseau *U.S.A.* 48°51N 95°46W **80** A6
Rosebery *Australia* 41°46S 145°33E **63** G4
Rosebud *S. Dak., U.S.A.* 43°14N 100°51W **80** D3
Rosebud *Tex., U.S.A.* 31°4N 96°59W **84** F6
Rosedale *U.S.A.* 33°51N 91°2W **85** E9
Rosehearty *U.K.* 57°42N 2°7W **11** D6
Roseires Res. *Sudan* 11°51N 34°23E **53** F12
Roseland *U.S.A.* 38°25N 122°43W **78** G4
Rosemary *Canada* 50°46N 112°5W **70** C6
Rosenberg *U.S.A.* 29°34N 95°49W **84** L7
Rosenheim *Germany* 47°51N 12°7E **16** E7
Roses, G. de *Spain* 42°10N 3°15E **21** A7
Rosetown *Canada* 51°35N 107°59W **71** C7
Roseville *Calif., U.S.A.* 38°45N 121°17W **78** G5
Roseville *Mich., U.S.A.* 42°30N 82°56W **82** D2
Roseville *Pa., U.S.A.* 41°51N 76°57W **83** E8
Rosewood *Australia* 27°38S 152°36E **63** D5
Roshkhvār *Iran* 34°58N 59°37E **47** C8
Rosignano Marittimo
  Italy 43°24N 10°28E **22** C4
Rosignol *Guyana* 6°15N 57°30W **92** B7

Roșiori de Vede *Romania* 44°9N 25°0E **17** F13
Roskilde *Denmark* 55°38N 12°3E **9** J15
Roslavl *Russia* 53°57N 32°55E **18** D5
Rosmead *S. Africa* 31°29S 25°8E **56** D4
Ross *Australia* 42°2S 147°30E **63** G4
Ross *N.Z.* 42°53S 170°49E **59** E3
Ross Dependency
  Antarctica 76°0S 170°0W **5** D12
Ross I. *Antarctica* 77°30S 168°0E **5** D11
Ross Ice Shelf *Antarctica* 80°0S 180°0E **5** E12
Ross L. *U.S.A.* 48°44N 121°4W **76** B3
Ross-on-Wye *U.K.* 51°54N 2°34W **13** F5
Ross River *Australia* 23°44S 134°30E **62** C1
Ross River *Canada* 62°30N 131°30W **70** A2
Ross Sea *Antarctica* 74°0S 178°0E **5** D11
Rossall Pt. *U.K.* 53°55N 3°3W **12** D4
Rossan Pt. *Ireland* 54°42N 8°47W **10** B3
Rossano *Italy* 39°36N 16°39E **22** E7
Rossburn *Canada* 50°40N 100°49W **71** C8
Rosseau *Canada* 45°16N 79°39W **82** A5
Rosseau, L. *Canada* 45°10N 79°35W **82** A5
Rosses, The *Ireland* 55°2N 8°20W **10** A3
Rossignol, L. *Canada* 52°43N 73°40W **72** B5
Rossignol L. *Canada* 44°12N 65°10W **73** D6
Rossiya = Russia ■
  Eurasia 62°0N 105°0E **27** C11
Rossland *Canada* 49°6N 117°50W **70** D5
Rosslare *Ireland* 52°17N 6°24W **10** D5
Rosslare Europort = Rosslare
  Harbour *Ireland* 52°15N 6°20W **10** D5
Rosslare Harbour *Ireland* 52°15N 6°20W **10** D5
Rossmore *Canada* 44°8N 77°23W **82** B7
Rosso *Mauritania* 16°40N 15°45W **52** E2
Rossosh *Russia* 50°15N 39°28E **19** D6
Røssvatnet *Norway* 65°45N 14°5E **8** D16
Røst *Norway* 67°32N 12°10E **8** C15
Rosthern *Canada* 52°40N 106°20W **71** C7
Rostock *Germany* 54°5N 12°8E **16** A7
Rostov *Don, Russia* 47°15N 39°45E **19** E6
Rostov *Yaroslavl, Russia* 57°14N 39°25E **18** C6
Roswell *Ga., U.S.A.* 34°2N 84°22W **85** D12
Roswell *N. Mex., U.S.A.* 33°24N 104°32W **77** K11
Rotan *U.S.A.* 32°51N 100°28W **84** E4
Rote *Indonesia* 10°50S 123°0E **37** F6
Rother → *U.K.* 50°59N 0°45E **13** G8
Rothera *Antarctica* 67°34S 68°8W **5** C17
Rotherham *U.K.* 53°26N 1°20W **12** D6
Rothes *U.K.* 57°32N 3°13W **11** D5
Rothesay *Canada* 45°23N 66°0W **73** C6
Rothesay *U.K.* 55°50N 5°3W **11** F3
Roti = Rote *Indonesia* 10°50S 123°0E **37** F6
Roto *Australia* 33°0S 145°30E **63** E4
Rotondo, Mte. *France* 42°14N 9°8E **20** E8
Rotorua *N.Z.* 38°9S 176°16E **59** C6
Rotorua, L. *N.Z.* 38°5S 176°18E **59** C6
Rotterdam *Neths.* 51°55N 4°30E **15** C4
Rotterdam *U.S.A.* 42°48N 74°1W **83** D10
Rottnest I. *Australia* 32°0S 115°27E **61** F2
Rottumeroog *Neths.* 53°33N 6°34E **15** A6
Rotuma *Fiji* 12°25S 177°5E **58** C10
Roubaix *France* 50°40N 3°10E **20** A5
Rouen *France* 49°27N 1°4E **20** B4
Rouleau *Canada* 50°10N 104°56W **71** C8
Roulpmaulpma ◊
  Australia 23°52S 133°0E **60** D5
Round I. *Mauritius* 19°51S 57°45E **55** d
Round Mountain *U.S.A.* 38°43N 117°4W **76** G5
Round Mt. *Australia* 30°26S 152°16E **63** E5
Round Rock *U.S.A.* 30°31N 97°41W **84** F6
Roundup *U.S.A.* 46°27N 108°33W **76** C9
Rousay *U.K.* 59°10N 3°2W **11** B5
Rouses Point *U.S.A.* 44°59N 73°22W **83** B11
Rouseville *U.S.A.* 41°28N 79°42W **82** E5
Rousse = Ruse *Bulgaria* 43°48N 25°59E **23** C12
Roussillon *France* 42°30N 2°35E **20** E5
Rouxville *S. Africa* 30°25S 26°50E **56** D4
Rouyn-Noranda *Canada* 48°20N 79°0W **72** C4
Rovaniemi *Finland* 66°29N 25°41E **8** C21
Rovereto *Italy* 45°53N 11°3E **22** B4
Rovigo *Italy* 45°4N 11°47E **22** B4
Rovinj *Croatia* 45°5N 13°40E **16** F7
Rovno = Rivne *Ukraine* 50°40N 26°10E **17** C14
Rovuma = Ruvuma →
  Tanzania 10°29S 40°28E **54** G8
Row'ān *Iran* 35°8N 48°51E **47** C6
Rowena *Australia* 29°48S 148°55E **63** D4
Rowley I. *Canada* 69°6N 77°52W **69** D16
Rowley Shoals *Australia* 17°30S 119°0E **60** C2
Roxas *Phil.* 11°36N 122°49E **37** B6
Roxboro *U.S.A.* 36°24N 78°59W **85** C15
Roxborough *Trin. & Tob.* 11°15N 60°35W **93** J16
Roxburgh *N.Z.* 45°33S 169°19E **59** F2
Roxbury *N.Y., U.S.A.* 42°17N 74°33W **83** D10
Roxbury *Pa., U.S.A.* 40°6N 77°39W **82** F7
Roxby Downs *Australia* 30°43S 136°46E **63** E2
Roy *Mont., U.S.A.* 47°20N 108°58W **76** C9
Roy *N. Mex., U.S.A.* 35°57N 104°12W **77** J11
Roy *Utah, U.S.A.* 41°10N 112°2W **76** F7
Roy Hill *Australia* 22°41S 119°57E **60** D2
Royal Bardia △ *Nepal* 28°20N 81°20E **43** E9
Royal Canal *Ireland* 53°30N 7°13W **10** C4
Royal Chitwan △
  Nepal 26°30N 84°30E **43** F11
Royal Geographical Society Is.
  Canada 68°56N 100°15W **68** D11
Royal Leamington Spa
  U.K. 52°18N 1°31W **13** E6
Royal Natal △ *S. Africa* 28°43S 28°51E **57** C4
Royal Tunbridge Wells
  U.K. 51°7N 0°16E **13** F8
Royale, Isle *U.S.A.* 48°0N 88°54W **80** B9
Royan *France* 45°37N 1°2W **20** D3
Royston *U.K.* 52°3N 0°0 **13** E7
Rozdilna *Ukraine* 46°50N 30°2E **17** E16
Rozhyshche *Ukraine* 50°54N 25°15E **17** C13
Rtishchevo *Russia* 52°18N 43°46E **18** D7
Ruacaná *Namibia* 17°27S 14°21E **56** A1
Ruahine Ra. *N.Z.* 39°55S 176°2E **59** C6

Ruapehu *N.Z.* 39°17S 175°35E **59** C5
Ruapuke I. *N.Z.* 46°46S 168°31E **59** G2
Ruâq, W. → *Egypt* 30°0N 33°49E **48** F2
Rub' al Khālī *Si. Arabia* 19°0N 48°0E **49** D4
Rubha a' Mhail *U.K.* 55°56N 6°8W **11** F2
Rubha Hunish *U.K.* 57°42N 6°20W **11** D2
Rubha Robhanais = Lewis, Butt of
  U.K. 58°31N 6°16W **11** C2
Rubicon → *U.S.A.* 38°53N 121°4W **78** G5
Rubio *Venezuela* 7°43N 72°22W **92** B4
Rudong *China* 32°20N 121°22E **35** A13
Rudyard *U.S.A.* 46°14N 84°36W **81** B11
Ruffling Pt. *Br. Virgin Is.* 18°44N 64°27W **89** e
Rufiji → *Tanzania* 7°50S 39°15E **54** F7
Rufino *Argentina* 34°20S 62°50W **94** C3
Rugao *China* 32°23N 120°31E **35** A13
Rugby *U.K.* 52°23N 1°16W **13** E6
Rugby *U.S.A.* 48°22N 100°0W **80** A4
Rügen *Germany* 54°22N 13°24E **16** A7
Ruhnu *Estonia* 57°48N 23°15E **9** H20
Ruhr → *Germany* 51°27N 6°43E **16** C4
Rui'an *China* 27°47N 120°40E **35** D13
Ruichang *China* 29°40N 115°35E **35** C10
Ruidoso *U.S.A.* 33°20N 105°41W **77** K11
Ruili *China* 24°6N 97°46E **34** E1
Rujm Tal'at al Jamā'ah
  Jordan 30°24N 35°30E **48** E4
Ruk *Pakistan* 27°50N 68°42E **42** F3
Rukhla *Pakistan* 32°27N 71°57E **42** C4
Ruki →
  Dem. Rep. of the Congo 0°5N 18°17E **54** E3
Rukumkot *Nepal* 28°37N 82°37E **43** E10
Rukwa □ *Tanzania* 8°0S 32°20E **54** F6
Rukwa, L. *Tanzania* 8°0S 32°20E **54** F6
Rulhieres, C. *Australia* 13°56S 127°22E **60** B4
Rum *Jordan* 29°39N 35°26E **48** F4
Rùm *U.K.* 57°0N 6°20W **11** E2
Rum Cay *Bahamas* 23°40N 74°58W **89** B5
Rum Jungle *Australia* 13°0S 130°59E **60** B5
Rumāh *Si. Arabia* 25°29N 47°10E **46** E5
Rumania = Romania ■
  Europe 46°0N 25°0E **17** F12
Rumaylah *Iraq* 30°47N 47°37E **46** D5
Rumaylah, 'Urūq ar
  Si. Arabia 22°0N 48°30E **49** C4
Rumbek *South Sudan* 6°54N 29°37E **53** G11
Rumford *U.S.A.* 44°33N 70°33W **83** B14
Rumia *Poland* 54°37N 18°25E **17** A10
Rumoi *Japan* 43°56N 141°39E **28** C10
Rumson *U.S.A.* 40°22N 74°0W **83** F11
Runan *China* 33°0N 114°30E **32** H8
Runanga *N.Z.* 42°25S 171°15E **59** E3
Runaway, C. *N.Z.* 37°32S 177°59E **59** B6
Runaway Bay *Jamaica* 18°27N 77°20W **88** a
Runcorn *U.K.* 53°21N 2°44W **12** D5
Rundu *Namibia* 17°52S 19°43E **56** A2
Rungwe *Tanzania* 9°11S 33°32E **54** F6
Rungwe, Mt. *Tanzania* 9°8S 33°40E **54** F6
Runton Ra. *Australia* 23°31S 123°6E **60** D3
Ruo Shui → *China* 41°0N 100°16E **30** C9
Ruokolahti *Finland* 61°17N 28°50E **8** F23
Ruoqiang *China* 38°55N 88°10E **30** D6
Rupa *India* 27°15N 92°21E **41** F18
Rupar = Rupnagar *India* 31°2N 76°38E **42** D7
Rupat *Indonesia* 1°45N 101°40E **36** D2
Rupen → *India* 23°28N 71°31E **42** H4
Rupert → *Canada* 51°29N 78°45W **72** B4
Rupert *U.S.A.* 42°37N 113°41W **76** E7
Rupert → *Canada* 51°29N 78°45W **72** B4
Rupert B. *Canada* 51°35N 79°0W **72** B4
Rupert House = Waskaganish
  Canada 51°30N 78°40W **72** B4
Rupnagar *India* 31°2N 76°38E **42** D7
Rupsa *India* 21°37N 87°1E **43** J12
Rurrenabaque *Bolivia* 14°30S 67°32W **92** F5
Ruschuk = Ruse
  Bulgaria 43°48N 25°59E **23** C12
Ruse *Bulgaria* 43°48N 25°59E **23** C12
Rush *Ireland* 53°31N 6°6W **10** C5
Rushan *China* 36°56N 121°30E **33** F11
Rushden *U.K.* 52°18N 0°35W **13** E7
Rushikulya → *India* 19°23N 85°5E **44** K14
Rushmore, Mt. *U.S.A.* 43°53N 103°28W **80** D2
Rushville *Ill., U.S.A.* 40°7N 90°34W **80** E8
Rushville *Ind., U.S.A.* 39°37N 85°27W **81** F11
Rushville *Nebr., U.S.A.* 42°43N 102°28W **80** D2
Russas *Brazil* 4°55S 37°50W **93** D11
Russell *Canada* 50°50N 101°20W **71** C8
Russell *Kans., U.S.A.* 38°54N 98°52W **80** F4
Russell *N.Y., U.S.A.* 44°27N 75°9W **83** B9
Russell *Pa., U.S.A.* 41°56N 79°8W **82** E5
Russell Cave △ *U.S.A.* 34°59N 85°49W **85** D12
Russell L. *Man., Canada* 56°15N 101°30W **71** B8
Russell L. *N.W.T., Canada* 63°5N 115°44W **70** A5
Russellkonda *India* 19°57N 84°42E **44** K14
Russellville *Ala., U.S.A.* 34°30N 87°44W **85** D11
Russellville *Ark., U.S.A.* 35°17N 93°8W **84** D8
Russellville *Ky., U.S.A.* 36°51N 86°53W **80** G10
Russia ■ *Eurasia* 62°0N 105°0E **27** C11
Russian → *U.S.A.* 38°27N 123°8W **78** G3
Russkaya Arktika △
  Russia 73°40N 55°55E **26** B6
Russkiy, Ostrov *Russia* 43°0N 131°50E **28** C5
Rustam Shahr *Pakistan* 26°58N 66°6E **42** F2
Rustavi *Georgia* 41°30N 45°0E **19** F8
Rustenburg *S. Africa* 25°41S 27°14E **56** C4
Ruston *U.S.A.* 32°32N 92°38W **84** E8
Ruteng *Indonesia* 8°35S 120°30E **37** F6

Rutenga *Zimbabwe* 21°15S 30°44E **57** B5
Ruth *U.S.A.* 43°42N 82°45W **82** C2
Rutherford *U.S.A.* 38°26N 122°24W **78** G4
Rutland *U.S.A.* 43°37N 72°58W **83** C12
Rutland □ *U.K.* 52°38N 0°40W **13** E7
Rutland I. *India* 11°25N 92°10E **45** J11
Rutland Water □ *U.K.* 52°39N 0°38W **13** E7
Rutledge → *Canada* 61°4N 112°0W **71** A6
Rutledge L. *Canada* 61°33N 110°47W **71** A6
Rutog *China* 33°27N 79°42E **30** E4
Rutshuru
  Dem. Rep. of the Congo 1°13S 29°25E **54** E5
Ruvuma → *Tanzania* 10°29S 40°28E **54** G8
Ruwais *U.A.E.* 24°5N 52°50E **47** E7
Ruwenzori *Africa* 0°30N 29°55E **54** D5
Ruya → *Zimbabwe* 16°27S 32°5E **57** A5
Ruyang *China* 34°9N 112°27E **32** G7
Ruyuan *China* 24°46N 113°16E **35** E9
Ruzhou *China* 34°11N 112°52E **32** G7
Ružomberok *Slovakia* 49°3N 19°17E **17** D10
Rwanda ■ *Africa* 2°0S 30°0E **54** E5
Ryan, L. *U.K.* 55°0N 5°2W **11** G3
Ryazan *Russia* 54°40N 39°40E **18** D6
Ryazhsk *Russia* 53°45N 40°3E **18** D7
Rybachiy Poluostrov
  Russia 69°43N 32°0E **8** B25
Rybachye = Balykchy
  Kyrgyzstan 42°26N 76°12E **30** C4
Rybinsk *Russia* 58°5N 38°50E **18** C6
Rybinskoye Vdkhr.
  Russia 58°30N 38°25E **18** C6
Rybnitsa = Rîbniţa
  Moldova 47°45N 29°0E **17** E15
Rycroft *Canada* 55°45N 118°40W **70** B5
Ryde *U.K.* 50°43N 1°9W **13** G6
Ryderwood *U.S.A.* 46°23N 123°3W **78** D3
Rye *U.K.* 50°57N 0°45E **13** G8
Rye → *U.K.* 54°11N 0°44W **12** C7
Rye Bay *U.K.* 50°52N 0°49E **13** G8
Rye Patch Res. *U.S.A.* 40°28N 118°19W **76** F4
Ryegate *U.S.A.* 46°18N 109°15W **76** C9
Ryley *Canada* 53°17N 112°26W **70** C6
Rylstone *Australia* 32°46S 149°58E **63** E4
Ryn Peski = Naryn Qum
  Kazakhstan 47°30N 49°0E **26** E5
Ryōtsu *Japan* 38°5N 138°26E **28** E9
Rypin *Poland* 53°3N 19°25E **17** B10
Ryūgasaki *Japan* 35°54N 140°11E **29** G10
Ryukyu Is. = Ryūkyū-Rettō
  Japan 26°0N 126°0E **29** M3
Ryūkyū-Rettō *Japan* 26°0N 126°0E **29** M3
Rzeszów *Poland* 50°5N 21°58E **17** C11
Rzhev *Russia* 56°20N 34°20E **18** C5

S

Sa Dec *Vietnam* 10°20N 105°46E **39** G5
Sa Kaeo *Thailand* 13°49N 102°4E **38** F4
Sa Pa *Vietnam* 22°20N 103°47E **38** A4
Sa'ādat Shahr *Iran* 30°10N 53°5E **47** D7
Sa'ādatābād *Hormozgān,*
  Iran 28°3N 55°53E **47** D7
Sa'ādatābād *Kermān, Iran* 29°40N 55°51E **47** D7
Saale → *Germany* 51°56N 11°54E **16** C6
Saalfeld *Germany* 50°38N 11°21E **16** C6
Saanich *Canada* 48°29N 123°26W **78** B3
Saar → *Europe* 49°41N 6°32E **15** E6
Saarbrücken *Germany* 49°14N 6°59E **16** D4
Saaremaa *Estonia* 58°30N 22°30E **9** G20
Saarijärvi *Finland* 62°43N 25°16E **8** E21
Sab 'Ābar *Syria* 33°46N 37°41E **46** C3
Saba *W. Indies* 17°38N 63°14W **89** C7
Šabac *Serbia* 44°48N 19°42E **23** B8
Sabadell *Spain* 41°28N 2°7E **21** B7
Sabah □ *Malaysia* 6°0N 117°0E **36** C5
Sabak Bernam *Malaysia* 3°46N 100°58E **39** L3
Sabalān, Kūhhā-ye *Iran* 38°15N 47°45E **46** B5
Sabalana, Kepulauan
  Indonesia 6°45S 118°50E **37** F5
Sabana de la Mar
  Dom. Rep. 19°7N 69°24W **89** C6
Sábanalarga *Colombia* 10°38N 74°55W **92** A4
Sabang *Indonesia* 5°50N 95°15E **36** C1
Sabari → *India* 17°35N 81°16E **44** F5
Sabarmati → *India* 22°18N 72°22E **42** H5
Sabattis *U.S.A.* 44°6N 74°40W **83** B10
Saberania *Indonesia* 2°5S 138°18E **37** E9
Sabhā *Libya* 27°9N 14°29E **53** C8
Sabi → *India* 28°29N 76°44E **42** E7
Sabie *S. Africa* 25°10S 30°48E **57** C5
Sabinas *Mexico* 27°51N 101°7W **86** B4
Sabinas → *Mexico* 27°37N 100°42W **86** B4
Sabinas Hidalgo *Mexico* 26°30N 100°10W **86** B4
Sabine → *U.S.A.* 29°59N 93°47W **84** G8
Sabine L. *U.S.A.* 29°53N 93°51W **84** G8
Sabine Pass *U.S.A.* 29°44N 93°54W **84** G8
Sablayan *Phil.* 12°50N 120°50E **37** B6
Sable *Canada* 55°30N 68°21W **73** A6
Sable, C. *Canada* 43°29N 65°38W **73** D6
Sable, C. *U.S.A.* 25°9N 81°8W **88** A3
Sable I. *Canada* 44°0N 60°0W **73** D8
Sabrina Coast *Antarctica* 68°0S 120°0E **5** C9
Sabulubek *Indonesia* 1°36S 98°40E **36** E1
Sabzevār *Iran* 36°15N 57°40E **47** B8
Sabzvārān = Jiroft *Iran* 28°45N 57°50E **47** D8
Sac City *U.S.A.* 42°25N 94°59W **80** D6
Săcele *Romania* 45°37N 25°41E **17** F13
Sacheon *S. Korea* 35°0N 128°6E **33** G15
Sachigo → *Canada* 55°6N 88°58W **72** A2
Sachigo, L. *Canada* 53°50N 92°12W **72** B1
Sachin *India* 21°5N 72°53E **44** D1
Sachsen □ *Germany* 50°55N 13°10E **16** C7
Sachsen-Anhalt □
  Germany 52°0N 12°0E **16** C7
Sackets Harbor *U.S.A.* 43°57N 76°7W **83** C8
Sackville *Canada* 45°54N 64°22W **73** C7
Saco *Maine, U.S.A.* 43°30N 70°27W **83** C14
Saco *Mont., U.S.A.* 48°28N 107°21W **76** B10

Sacramento *U.S.A.* 38°35N 121°29W **78** G5
Sacramento → *U.S.A.* 38°3N 121°56W **78** G5
Sacramento Mts.
  U.S.A. 32°30N 105°30W **77** K11
Sacramento Valley
  U.S.A. 39°30N 122°0W **78** G5
Sada-Misaki *Japan* 33°20N 132°5E **29** H6
Sadabad *India* 27°27N 78°3E **42** F8
Şa'dah *Yemen* 16°15N 43°37E **49** D3
Sadao *Thailand* 6°38N 100°26E **39** J3
Sadaseopet *India* 17°38N 77°59E **44** F3
Sadd el Aali *Egypt* 23°54N 32°54E **53** D12
Saddle Mt. *U.S.A.* 45°58N 123°41W **78** E3
Saddle Pk. *India* 13°9N 93°1E **45** H11
Sado *Japan* 38°0N 138°25E **28** F9
Sadra *India* 23°21N 72°43E **42** H5
Sadri *India* 25°11N 73°26E **42** G5
Sæby *Denmark* 57°21N 10°30E **9** H14
Saegertown *U.S.A.* 41°43N 80°9W **82** E4
Şafājah *Si. Arabia* 26°25N 39°0E **46** E3
Safed Koh = Sefid Kuh
  Afghan. 34°45N 63°0E **40** B3
Safenwil *Switz.* 47°19N 7°59E **20** C5
Säffle *Sweden* 59°8N 12°55E **9** G15
Safford *U.S.A.* 32°50N 109°43W **77** K9
Saffron Walden *U.K.* 52°1N 0°16E **13** E8
Safi *Morocco* 32°18N 9°20W **52** B4
Safid Dasht *Iran* 33°27N 48°11E **47** C6
Safid Kūh *Afghan.* 34°45N 63°0E **40** B3
Safid Rūd → *Iran* 37°23N 50°11E **47** B6
Safipur *India* 26°44N 80°21E **43** F9
Şāfītā *Syria* 34°48N 36°7E **46** C4
Safune *Samoa* 13°25S 172°21W **59** b
Şafwān *Iraq* 30°7N 47°43E **46** D5
Sag Harbor *U.S.A.* 41°0N 72°18W **83** F12
Saga *Japan* 33°15N 130°16E **29** H5
Saga □ *Japan* 33°15N 130°20E **29** H5
Sagae *Japan* 38°22N 140°17E **28** E10
Sagaing *Myanmar* 21°52N 95°59E **41** J19
Sagamore *U.S.A.* 40°46N 79°14W **82** F5
Saganaga L. *Canada* 48°14N 90°52W **80** A8
Saganthit Kyun
  Myanmar 11°56N 98°29E **39** G2
Sagar *Karnataka, India* 16°38N 76°48E **44** F3
Sagar *Karnataka, India* 14°14N 75°6E **45** G2
Sagar *Mad. P., India* 23°50N 78°44E **43** H8
Sagarmatha = Everest, Mt.
  Nepal 28°5N 86°58E **43** E12
Sagarmatha △ *Nepal* 27°55N 86°45E **43** F12
Saginaw *U.S.A.* 43°26N 83°56W **81** D12
Saginaw B. *U.S.A.* 43°50N 83°40W **81** D12
Saglouc = Salluit
  Canada 62°14N 75°38W **69** E16
Sagone *France* 42°7N 8°42E **20** E8
Sagua la Grande *Cuba* 22°50N 80°10W **88** B3
Saguache *U.S.A.* 38°5N 106°8W **76** G10
Saguaro △ *U.S.A.* 32°12N 110°38W **77** K8
Saguenay → *Canada* 48°22N 71°0W **73** C5
Sagunt *Spain* 39°42N 0°18W **21** C5
Sagunto = Sagunt *Spain* 39°42N 0°18W **21** C5
Sagwara *India* 23°41N 74°1E **42** H6
Sahagún *Spain* 42°18N 5°2W **21** A3
Saham al Jawlān *Syria* 32°45N 35°55E **48** C4
Sahand, Kūh-e *Iran* 37°44N 46°27E **46** B5
Sahara *Africa* 23°0N 5°0E **52** D6
Saharan Atlas = Sahárien, Atlas
  Algeria 33°30N 1°0E **52** B6
Saharanpur *India* 29°58N 77°33E **42** E7
Sahárien, Atlas *Algeria* 33°30N 1°0E **52** B6
Saharsa *India* 25°53N 86°36E **43** G12
Sahaswan *India* 28°5N 78°45E **43** E8
Saheira, W. el → *Egypt* 30°5N 33°25E **48** E2
Sahel *Africa* 16°0N 5°0E **52** E5
Sahibganj *India* 25°12N 87°40E **43** G12
Sāhilīyah *Iraq* 33°43N 42°42E **46** C4
Sahiwal *Pakistan* 30°45N 73°8E **42** D5
Şaḥneh *Iran* 34°29N 47°41E **46** C5
Sahrawi = Western Sahara ■
  Africa 25°0N 13°0W **52** D3
Sahuaripa *Mexico* 29°3N 109°14W **86** B3
Sahuarita *U.S.A.* 31°57N 110°58W **77** L8
Sahuayo de Díaz *Mexico* 20°4N 102°43W **86** C4
Sai → *India* 25°39N 82°47E **43** G10
Sai Buri *Thailand* 6°43N 101°45E **39** J3
Sai Thong △ *Thailand* 15°56N 101°10E **38** E3
Sai Yok △ *Thailand* 14°25N 98°40E **38** E2
Saibai I. *Australia* 9°25S 142°40E **62** a
Sa'id Bundas *South Sudan* 8°24N 24°48E **53** G10
Sa'īdābād = Sīrjān *Iran* 29°30N 55°45E **47** D7
Saïdābād *India* 36°8N 54°11E **47** B7
Saidpur *India* 25°33N 83°11E **43** G10
Saidpur *Bangla.* 25°48N 89°0E **41** G16
Saidu Sharif *Pakistan* 34°43N 72°24E **43** B5
Saigō *Japan* 36°12N 133°20E **29** F6
Saigon = Thanh Pho Ho Chi Minh
  Vietnam 10°58N 106°40E **39** G6
Saijō *Japan* 33°55N 133°11E **29** H6
Saikai △ *Japan* 33°12N 129°36E **29** H4
Saikhoa Ghat *India* 27°50N 95°40E **41** F19
Saiki *Japan* 32°58N 131°51E **29** H5
Sailana *India* 23°28N 74°55E **42** H6
Sailolof *Indonesia* 1°15S 130°46E **37** E8
Sailu *India* 19°28N 76°28E **44** E3
Saimaa *Finland* 61°15N 28°15E **8** F23
Saimaa Canal = Saimaan Kanava
  Finland 61°15N 28°15E **8** F23
Şa'in Dezh *Iran* 36°40N 46°25E **46** B5
St. Abb's Head *U.K.* 55°55N 2°8W **11** F6
St. Alban's *Canada* 47°51N 55°50W **73** C8
St. Albans *U.K.* 51°45N 0°19W **13** F7
St. Albans *Vt., U.S.A.* 44°49N 73°5W **83** B11
St. Albans *W. Va.,*
  U.S.A. 38°23N 81°50W **81** F13
St. Alban's Head *U.K.* 50°34N 2°4W **13** G5
St. Albert *Canada* 53°37N 113°32W **70** C6
St-André *Réunion* 20°57S 55°39E **55** c
St. Andrew's *Canada* 47°45N 59°15W **73** C8
St. Andrews *U.K.* 56°20N 2°47W **11** E6
St-Anicet *Canada* 45°8N 74°22W **83** A10
St. Annes *Canada* 49°40N 96°39W **71** D9
St. Anns B. *Canada* 46°22N 60°25W **73** C7
St. Ann's Bay *Jamaica* 18°26N 77°12W **88** a

St. Anthony *Canada* 51°22N 55°35W **73** B8
St. Anthony *U.S.A.* 43°58N 111°41W **76** E8
St-Antoine *Canada* 46°22N 64°45W **73** C7
St. Arnaud *Australia* 36°40S 143°16E **63** F3
St-Augustin *Canada* 51°13N 58°38W **73** B8
St-Augustin ➤ *Canada* 51°16N 58°40W **73** B8
St. Augustine *U.S.A.* 29°54N 81°19W **85** G14
St. Austell *U.K.* 50°20N 4°47W **13** G3
St. Barbe *Canada* 51°12N 56°46W **73** B8
St-Barthélemy ☑
  W. Indies 17°50N 62°50W **89** C7
St. Barts = St-Barthélemy ☑
  W. Indies 17°50N 62°50W **89** C7
St. Bees Hd. *U.K.* 54°31N 3°38W **12** C4
St. Bees I. *Australia* 20°56S 149°26E **62** b
St-Benoît *Réunion* 21°2S 55°43E **55** c
St. Bride's *Canada* 46°56N 54°10W **73** C9
St. Brides B. *U.K.* 51°49N 5°9W **13** F2
St-Brieuc *France* 48°30N 2°46W **20** B2
St. Catharines *Canada* 43°10N 79°15W **82** C5
St. Catherines I. *U.S.A.* 31°40N 81°10W **85** F14
St. Catherine's Pt. *U.K.* 50°34N 1°18W **13** G6
St-Chamond *France* 45°28N 4°31E **20** D6
St. Charles Ill., *U.S.A.* 41°54N 88°19W **80** E9
St. Charles Md., *U.S.A.* 38°36N 76°56W **81** F15
St. Charles Mo., *U.S.A.* 38°47N 90°29W **80** F8
St. Charles Va., *U.S.A.* 36°48N 83°4W **81** G12
St. Christopher-Nevis = St. Kitts &
  Nevis ■ *W. Indies* 17°20N 62°40W **89** C7
St. Clair *Mich., U.S.A.* 42°50N 82°30W **82** D2
St. Clair *Pa., U.S.A.* 40°43N 76°12W **83** F8
St. Clair ➤ *U.S.A.* 42°38N 82°31W **82** D2
St. Clair, L. *N. Amer.* 42°27N 82°39W **82** D2
St. Clairsville *U.S.A.* 40°5N 80°54W **82** F4
St. Clears *U.K.* 51°49N 4°31W **13** F3
St-Clet *Canada* 45°21N 74°13W **83** A10
St. Cloud *Fla., U.S.A.* 28°15N 81°17W **85** G14
St. Cloud *Minn., U.S.A.* 45°34N 94°10W **80** C6
St. Cricq, C. *Australia* 25°17S 113°6E **61** E1
St. Croix *U.S. Virgin Is.* 17°45N 64°45W **89** C7
St. Croix ➤ *U.S.A.* 44°45N 92°48W **80** C7
St. Croix Falls *U.S.A.* 45°24N 92°38W **80** C7
St. David's *Canada* 48°12N 58°52W **73** C8
St. David's *U.K.* 51°53N 5°16W **13** F2
St. David's Head *U.K.* 51°54N 5°19W **13** F2
St-Denis *Réunion* 20°52S 55°27E **55** c
St-Denis ✈ (RUN) *Réunion* 20°53S 55°32E **55** c
St-Dizier *France* 48°38N 4°56E **20** B6
St. Elias, Mt. *U.S.A.* 60°18N 140°56W **68** E3
St. Elias Mts. *N. Amer.* 60°33N 139°28W **70** A1
St-Étienne *France* 45°27N 4°22E **20** D6
St. Eugène *Canada* 45°30N 74°28W **83** A10
St. Eustatius *W. Indies* 17°20N 63°0W **89** C7
St-Félicien *Canada* 48°40N 72°25W **72** C5
St-Flour *France* 45°2N 3°6E **20** D5
St. Francis *U.S.A.* 39°47N 101°48W **80** F3
St. Francis ➤ *U.S.A.* 34°38N 90°36W **85** D9
St. Francis, C. *S. Africa* 34°14S 24°49E **56** D3
St. Francisville *U.S.A.* 30°47N 91°23W **84** F9
St-François, L. *Canada* 45°10N 74°22W **83** A10
St-Gabriel *Canada* 46°17N 73°24W **72** C5
St. Gallen = Sankt Gallen
  Switz. 47°26N 9°22E **20** C8
St-Gaudens *France* 43°6N 0°44E **20** E4
St. George *Australia* 28°1S 148°30E **63** D4
St. George *N.B., Canada* 45°11N 66°50W **73** C6
St. George *Ont., Canada* 43°15N 80°15W **82** C4
St. George *S.C., U.S.A.* 33°11N 80°35W **85** E14
St. George *Utah, U.S.A.* 37°6N 113°35W **77** H7
St. George, C. *Canada* 48°30N 59°16W **73** C8
St. George, C. *U.S.A.* 29°40N 85°5W **85** G12
St. George I. *U.S.A.* 56°35N 169°35W **74** D6
St. George Ra. *Australia* 18°40S 125°0E **60** C4
St. George's *Canada* 48°26N 58°31W **73** C8
St-Georges *Canada* 46°8N 70°40W **73** C5
St-Georges *Grenada* 12°5N 61°43W **89** D7
St. George's B. *Canada* 48°24N 58°53W **73** C8
St. Georges Basin *N.S.W.,
  Australia* 35°7S 150°36E **63** F5
St. Georges Basin *W. Austral.,
  Australia* 15°23S 125°2E **60** C4
St. George's Channel *Europe* 52°0N 6°0W **10** E6
St. George's Channel
  India 7°15N 93°43E **45** L11
St. Georges Hd. *Australia* 35°12S 150°42E **63** F5
St. Gotthard P. = San Gottardo, P.
  del *Switz.* 46°33N 8°33E **20** C8
St. Helena *Atl. Oc.* 15°58S 5°42W **50** H3
St. Helena *U.S.A.* 38°30N 122°28W **78** G4
St. Helena, Mt. *U.S.A.* 38°40N 122°36W **78** G4
St. Helena B. *S. Africa* 32°40S 18°10E **56** D2
St. Helens *Australia* 41°20S 148°15E **63** G4
St. Helens *U.K.* 53°27N 2°44W **12** D5
St. Helens *U.S.A.* 45°52N 122°48W **78** E4
St. Helens, Mt. *U.S.A.* 46°12N 122°12W **78** D4
St. Helier *U.K.* 49°10N 2°7W **13** H5
St-Hyacinthe *Canada* 45°40N 72°58W **72** C5
St. Ignace *U.S.A.* 45°52N 84°44W **81** C11
St. Ignace I. *Canada* 48°45N 88°0W **72** C2
St. Ignatius *U.S.A.* 47°19N 114°6W **76** C6
St. Ives *Cambs., U.K.* 52°20N 0°4W **13** E7
St. Ives *Corn., U.K.* 50°12N 5°30W **13** G2
St. James *U.S.A.* 43°59N 94°38W **80** D6
St-Jean ➤ *Canada* 50°17N 64°20W **73** B7
St-Jean, L. *Canada* 48°40N 72°0W **73** C5
St-Jean-Port-Joli *Canada* 47°15N 70°13W **73** C5
St-Jean-sur-Richelieu
  Canada 45°20N 73°20W **83** A11
St-Jérôme *Canada* 45°47N 74°0W **72** C5
St. John *Canada* 45°20N 66°8W **73** C6
St. John *U.S.A.* 38°0N 98°46W **80** F4
St. John ➤ *N. Amer.* 45°12N 66°5W **81** C20
St. John, C. *Canada* 50°0N 55°32W **73** C8
St. John I. *U.S. Virgin Is.* 18°20N 64°42W **89** e
St. John's *Antigua & B.* 17°6N 61°51W **89** C7
St. John's *Canada* 47°35N 52°40W **73** C9
St. Johns *Ariz., U.S.A.* 34°30N 109°22W **77** J9
St. Johns *Mich., U.S.A.* 43°0N 84°33W **81** D11
St. Johns ➤ *U.S.A.* 30°24N 81°24W **85** F14

St. John's Pt. *Ireland* 54°34N 8°27W **10** B3
St. Johnsbury *U.S.A.* 44°25N 72°1W **83** B12
St. Johnsville *U.S.A.* 43°0N 74°43W **83** C10
St. Joseph *Canada* 43°24N 81°42W **82** C3
St-Joseph *Martinique* 14°39N 61°4W **88** c
St-Joseph *Réunion* 21°22S 55°37E **55** c
St. Joseph *La., U.S.A.* 31°55N 91°14W **84** F9
St. Joseph *Mo., U.S.A.* 39°46N 94°50W **80** F6
St. Joseph ➤ *U.S.A.* 42°7N 86°29W **80** D10
St. Joseph, I. *Canada* 46°12N 83°58W **72** C3
St. Joseph, L. *Canada* 51°10N 90°35W **72** B1
St. Kilda *U.K.* 57°49N 8°34W **14** C2
St. Kitts & Nevis ■
  W. Indies 17°20N 62°40W **89** C7
St. Laurent *Canada* 50°25N 97°58W **71** C9
St. Lawrence *Australia* 22°16S 149°31E **62** C4
St. Lawrence *Canada* 46°54N 55°23W **73** C8
St. Lawrence ➤ *Canada* 49°30N 66°0W **73** C6
St. Lawrence, Gulf of
  Canada 48°25N 62°0W **73** C7
St. Lawrence I. *U.S.A.* 63°30N 170°30W **74** C5
St. Lawrence Islands △
  Canada 44°27N 75°52W **83** B9
St. Léonard *Canada* 47°12N 67°58W **73** C6
St-Leu *Réunion* 21°9S 55°18E **55** c
St. Lewis ➤ *Canada* 52°26N 56°11W **73** B8
St-Lô *France* 49°7N 1°5W **20** B3
St-Louis *Guadeloupe* 15°56N 61°19W **88** b
St-Louis *Réunion* 21°16S 55°25E **55** c
St-Louis *Senegal* 16°8N 16°27W **52** E2
St. Louis *U.S.A.* 38°37N 90°11W **80** F8
St. Louis ➤ *U.S.A.* 46°44N 92°9W **80** B7
St-Luc *Canada* 45°22N 73°18W **83** A11
St. Lucia ■ *W. Indies* 14°0N 60°57W **89** f
St. Lucia, L. *S. Africa* 28°5S 32°30E **57** C5
St. Lucia △ *S. Africa* 28°5S 32°27E **57** C5
St. Lucia Channel
  W. Indies 14°15N 61°0W **89** D7
St. Maarten ☑ *W. Indies* 18°2N 63°5W **89** C7
St. Magnus B. *U.K.* 60°25N 1°35W **11** A7
St-Malo *France* 48°39N 2°1W **20** B2
St-Marc *Haiti* 19°10N 72°41W **89** C5
St. Maries *U.S.A.* 47°19N 116°35W **76** C5
St-Martin ☑ *W. Indies* 18°5N 63°5W **89** C7
St. Martin, C. *Martinique* 14°52N 61°14W **88** c
St. Martin, L. *Canada* 51°40N 98°30W **71** C9
St. Martins *Barbados* 13°5N 59°28W **89** g
St. Mary Is. *India* 13°20N 74°35E **45** H2
St. Mary Pk. *Australia* 31°32S 138°34E **63** E2
St. Marys *Australia* 41°35S 148°11E **63** G4
St. Marys *Canada* 43°20N 81°10W **82** C3
St. Mary's *Corn., U.K.* 49°55N 6°18W **13** H1
St. Mary's *Orkney, U.K.* 58°54N 2°54W **11** C6
St. Marys *Ga., U.S.A.* 30°44N 81°33W **85** F14
St. Marys *Pa., U.S.A.* 41°26N 78°34W **82** E6
St. Mary's, C. *Canada* 46°50N 54°12W **73** C9
St. Mary's B. *Canada* 46°50N 53°50W **73** C9
St. Mary's Bay *Canada* 44°25N 66°10W **73** D6
St-Mathieu, Pte. *France* 48°20N 4°45W **20** B1
St. Matthew I. *U.S.A.* 60°24N 172°42W **74** C5
St-Maurice ➤ *Canada* 46°21N 72°31W **72** C5
St. Mawes *U.K.* 50°10N 5°2W **13** G2
St-Nazaire *France* 47°17N 2°12W **20** C2
St. Neots *U.K.* 52°14N 0°15W **13** E7
St-Omer *France* 50°45N 2°15E **20** A5
St-Pamphile *Canada* 46°58N 69°48W **73** C6
St-Pascal *Canada* 47°32N 69°48W **73** C6
St. Paul *Canada* 54°0N 111°17W **70** C6
St-Paul *Réunion* 20°59S 55°17E **55** c
St. Paul *Minn., U.S.A.* 44°56N 93°5W **80** C8
St. Paul *Nebr., U.S.A.* 41°13N 98°27W **80** E4
St. Paul ➤ *Canada* 51°27N 57°42W **73** B8
St. Paul, Î. *Ind. Oc.* 38°55S 77°34E **3** F13
St. Paul I. *Canada* 47°12N 60°9W **73** C7
St. Paul I. *U.S.A.* 57°10N 170°15W **74** D5
St. Peter *U.S.A.* 44°20N 93°57W **80** C7
St. Peter Port *U.K.* 49°26N 2°33W **13** H5
St. Peters *N.S., Canada* 45°40N 60°53W **73** C7
St. Peters *P.E.I., Canada* 46°25N 62°35W **73** C7
St. Petersburg *U.S.A.* 27°46N 82°40W **85** H13
St-Phillippe *Réunion* 21°21S 55°44E **55** c
St-Pie *Canada* 45°30N 72°54W **83** A12
St-Pierre *Martinique* 14°45N 61°10W **88** c
St-Pierre *Réunion* 21°19S 55°28E **55** c
St-Pierre, L. *Canada* 46°12N 72°52W **72** C5
St-Pierre-et-Miquelon ☑
  N. Amer. 46°55N 56°10W **73** C8
St-Quentin *Canada* 47°30N 67°23W **73** C6
St-Quentin *France* 49°50N 3°16E **20** B5
St. Regis *U.S.A.* 47°18N 115°6W **76** C6
St. Regis Falls *U.S.A.* 44°40N 74°32W **83** B10
St-Siméon *Canada* 47°51N 69°54W **73** C6
St. Simons I. *U.S.A.* 31°12N 81°15W **85** F14
St. Simons Island *U.S.A.* 31°9N 81°22W **85** F14
St. Stephen *Canada* 45°16N 67°17W **73** C6
St. Thomas *Canada* 42°45N 81°10W **82** D3
St. Thomas I.
  U.S. Virgin Is. 18°20N 64°55W **89** e
St-Tite *Canada* 46°45N 72°34W **72** C5
St-Trond = Sint-Truiden
  Belgium 50°48N 5°10E **15** D5
St-Tropez *France* 43°17N 6°38E **20** E7
St. Vidgeon's ◎ *Australia* 14°47S 134°53E **62** A1
St. Vincent = São Vicente
  Cabo Verde 17°0N 25°0W **52** b
St. Vincent, G. *Australia* 35°0S 138°0E **63** F2
St. Vincent & the Grenadines ■
  W. Indies 13°0N 61°10W **89** D7
St. Vincent Passage
  W. Indies 13°30N 61°0W **89** D7
St-Vith *Belgium* 50°17N 6°9E **15** D6
St. Walburg *Canada* 53°39N 109°12W **71** C7
Saintala *India* 20°26N 83°20E **44** D6
Ste-Agathe-des-Monts
  Canada 46°3N 74°17W **72** C5
Ste-Anne *Guadeloupe* 16°13N 61°24W **88** b
Ste-Anne *Seychelles* 4°36S 55°31E **55** b
Ste-Anne, L. *Canada* 50°0N 67°42W **73** B6
Ste-Anne-des-Monts
  Canada 49°8N 66°30W **73** C6

Ste. Genevieve *U.S.A.* 37°59N 9C°2W **80** G8
Ste-Marguerite ➤
  Canada 50°9N 66°36W **73** B6
Ste-Marie *Canada* 46°26N 71°0W **73** C5
Ste-Marie *Martinique* 14°48N 61°1W **88** c
Ste-Marie *Réunion* 20°53S 55°33E **55** c
Ste-Marie, Ile = Boraha, Nosy
  Madag. 16°50S 49°55E **55** H9
Ste-Rose *Guadeloupe* 16°20N 6°°45W **88** b
Ste-Rose *Réunion* 21°8S 55°45E **55** c
Ste. Rose du Lac *Canada* 51°4N 99°30W **71** C9
Saintes *France* 45°45N 0°37W **20** D3
Saintes, Îs. des *Guadeloupe* 15°50N 61°35W **88** b
Saintfield *U.K.* 54°28N 5°49W **10** B6
Saintonge *France* 45°40N 0°50W **20** D3
Saipal *Nepal* 29°50N 81°40E **43** E9
Saipan *N. Marianas* 15°12N 145°45E **64** F6
Sairang *India* 23°50N 92°45E **41** H18
Sairecábur, Cerro *Bolivia* 22°43S 67°54W **94** A2
Saïtah *Si. Arabia* 16°36N 42°56E **49** D3
Saitama *Japan* 35°54N 139°38E **29** G9
Saitama □ *Japan* 36°25N 139°30E **29** F9
Saiyid *Pakistan* 33°7N 73°2E **42** C5
Sajama *Bolivia* 18°7S 69°0W **92** G5
Sajószentpéter *Hungary* 48°12N 20°44E **17** D11
Sajum *India* 33°20N 79°0E **43** C8
Sak ➤ *S. Africa* 30°52S 2C°25E **56** D3
Sakaide *Japan* 34°19N 133°50E **29** G6
Sakaiminato *Japan* 35°38N 133°11E **29** G6
Sakākah *Si. Arabia* 30°0N 40°8E **46** D4
Sakakawea, L. *U.S.A.* 47°30N 101°25W **80** B3
Sakami ➤ *Canada* 53°40N 76°40W **72** B4
Sakami, L. *Canada* 53°15N 77°0W **72** B4
Sakartvelo = Georgia ■
  Asia 42°0N 43°0E **19** F7
Sakarya *Turkey* 40°48N 30°25E **19** F5
Sakashima-Guntō *Japan* 24°46N 124°0E **29** M2
Sakata *Japan* 38°55N 139°50E **28** E9
Sakchu *N. Korea* 40°23N 125°2E **33** D13
Sakha □ *Russia* 66°0N 130°0E **27** C14
Sakhalin *Russia* 51°0N 143°0E **27** D15
Sakhalinskiy Zaliv
  Russia 54°0N 141°0E **27** D15
Sakhi Gopal *India* 19°58N 85°50E **44** E7
Sakiai *Lithuania* 54°59N 23°2E **9** J20
Sakoli *India* 21°5N 79°59E **44** D4
Sakon Nakhon *Thailand* 17°10N 104°9E **38** D5
Sakrand *Pakistan* 26°10N 68°15E **42** F3
Sakri *Maharashtra, India* 26°13N 86°5E **43** F12
Sakri *Maharashtra, India* 21°2N 74°20E **44** D2
Sakrivier *S. Africa* 30°54S 20°28E **56** D3
Sakti *India* 22°2N 82°58E **43** H10
Sakuma *Japan* 35°3N 137°49E **29** G8
Sakurai *Japan* 34°30N 135°51E **29** G7
Sal *Cabo Verde* 16°45N 22°55W **52** b
Sal Rei *Cabo Verde* 16°11N 22°53W **52** b
Sala *Sweden* 59°58N 16°35E **9** G17
Sala Consilina *Italy* 40°23N 15°36E **22** D6
Sala-y-Gómez *Pac. Oc.* 26°28S 105°28W **65** K17
Sala-y-Gómez Ridge
  Pac. Oc. 25°0S 9E°0W **65** K18
Salaberry-de-Valleyfield
  Canada 45°15N 74°8W **83** A10
Salada, L. *Mexico* 32°20N 115°40W **77** K6
Saladas *Argentina* 28°15S 58°40W **94** B4
Saladillo *Argentina* 35°40S 59°55W **94** D4
Salado ➤ *B. Aires,
  Argentina* 35°44S 57°22W **94** D4
Salado ➤ *La Pampa,
  Argentina* 37°30S 67°0W **96** D3
Salado ➤ *Santa Fe,
  Argentina* 31°40S 60°41W **94** C3
Salado ➤ *Mexico* 26°52N 99°19W **84** H5
Salaga *Ghana* 8°31N 0°31W **52** G5
Šalāh *Syria* 32°40N 36°45E **48** C5
Salālah *Oman* 16°56N 53°59E **49** D5
Salamajärvi △ *Finland* 63°12N 24°50E **8** E21
Salamanca *Chile* 31°46S 70°59W **94** C1
Salamanca *Spain* 40°58N 5°39W **21** B3
Salamanca *U.S.A.* 42°10N 78°43W **82** D6
Salāmatābād *Iran* 35°39N 47°50E **46** C5
Salamina *Greece* 37°56N 23°30E **23** F10
Salar de Atacama *Chile* 23°30S 68°25W **94** A2
Salar de Uyuni *Bolivia* 20°30S 67°45W **92** H5
Salatiga *Indonesia* 7°19S 110°30E **37** G14
Salavat *Russia* 53°21N 55°55E **18** D10
Salaverry *Peru* 8°15S 79°0W **92** E3
Salawati *Indonesia* 1°7S 130°52E **37** E8
Salawin △ *Thailand* 18°18N 97°40E **38** C1
Salaya *India* 22°19N 69°35E **42** H3
Salayar *Indonesia* 6°7S 120°30E **37** F6
Salcombe *U.K.* 50°14N 3°47W **13** G4
Saldanha *S. Africa* 33°0S 17°58E **56** D2
Saldanha B. *S. Africa* 33°6S 18°0E **56** D2
Saldus *Latvia* 56°38N 22°30E **9** H20
Sale *Australia* 38°6S ¹47°6E **63** F4
Salé *Morocco* 34°3N 6°48W **52** B4
Sale *U.K.* 53°26N 2°19W **12** D5
Salekhard *Russia* 66°30N 66°35E **26** C7
Salelologa *Samoa* 13°41S 172°11W **59** b
Salem *India* 11°40N 78°11E **45** J4
Salem *Ill., U.S.A.* 38°38N 88°57W **80** F9
Salem *Ind., U.S.A.* 38°36N 86°6W **80** F10
Salem *Mass., U.S.A.* 42°31N 70°53W **83** D14
Salem *Mo., U.S.A.* 37°39N 91°32W **80** G8
Salem *N.H., U.S.A.* 42°45N 71°12W **83** D13
Salem *N.J., U.S.A.* 39°34N 75°28W **81** F16
Salem *N.Y., U.S.A.* 43°10N 73°20W **83** C11
Salem *Ohio, U.S.A.* 40°54N 80°52W **82** F4
Salem *Oreg., U.S.A.* 44°56N 123°2W **76** D2
Salem *S. Dak., U.S.A.* 43°44N 97°23W **80** D5
Salem *Va., U.S.A.* 37°18N 80°3W **81** G13
Salerno *Italy* 40°41N ¹4°47E **22** D6
Salford *U.K.* 53°30N 2°18W **12** D5
Salgótarján *Hungary* 48°5N 19°47E **17** D10
Salgueiro *Brazil* 8°4S 39°6W **93** E11
Salher *India* 20°40N 73°55E **44** D1
Salibabu *Indonesia* 3°51N 126°40E **37** D7
Salibea = Salybia
  Trin. & Tob. 10°43N 61°2W **93** K15

Salida *U.S.A.* 38°32N 106°0W **76** G11
Salihli *Turkey* 38°28N 28°8E **23** E13
Salihorsk *Belarus* 52°51N 27°27E **17** B14
Salima *Malawi* 13°47S 34°28E **55** G6
Salina *Italy* 38°34N 14°50E **22** E6
Salina *Kans., U.S.A.* 38°50N 97°37W **80** F5
Salina *Utah, U.S.A.* 38°58N 111°51W **76** G8
Salina Cruz *Mexico* 16°10N 95°12W **87** D5
Salinas *Brazil* 16°10S 42°10W **93** G10
Salinas *Ecuador* 2°10S 80°58W **92** D2
Salinas ➤ *Guatemala* 16°28N 90°31W **87** D6
Salinas ➤ *U.S.A.* 36°45N 121°48W **78** J5
Salinas, B. de *Nic.* 11°4N 85°45W **88** D2
Salinas, Pampa de las
  Argentina 31°58S 66°42W **94** C2
Salinas Ambargasta
  Argentina 29°0S 65°0W **94** B3
Salinas de Hidalgo
  Mexico 22°38N 101°43W **86** C4
Salinas Grandes *Argentina* 30°0S 65°0W **94** C3
Salinas Pueblo Missions △
  U.S.A. 34°6N 106°4W **77** J10
Salinas Valley *U.S.A.* 36°15N 121°15W **78** J5
Saline ➤ *Ark., U.S.A.* 33°10N 92°8W **84** E8
Saline ➤ *Kans., U.S.A.* 38°52N 97°30W **80** F5
Salinópolis *Brazil* 0°40S 47°20W **93** D9
Salisbury *Australia* 34°46S 138°38E **63** E2
Salisbury *U.K.* 51°4N 1°47W **13** F6
Salisbury *Md., U.S.A.* 38°22N 75°36W **81** F16
Salisbury *N.C., U.S.A.* 35°40N 80°29W **85** D14
Salisbury I. *Canada* 63°30N 77°0W **69** E16
Salisbury Plain *U.K.* 51°14N 1°55W **13** F6
Şalkhad *Syria* 32°29N 36°43E **48** C5
Salla *Finland* 66°50N 28°49E **8** C23
Salliq = Coral Harbour
  Canada 64°8N 83°10W **69** E15
Sallisaw *U.S.A.* 35°28N 94°47W **84** D7
Salluit *Canada* 62°14N 75°38W **69** E16
Salmās *Iran* 38°11N 44°47E **46** B5
Salmo *Canada* 49°10N 117°20W **70** D5
Salmon *U.S.A.* 45°11N 113°54W **76** D7
Salmon ➤ *Canada* 54°3N 122°40W **70** C4
Salmon ➤ *U.S.A.* 45°51N 116°47W **76** D5
Salmon Arm *Canada* 50°40N 119°15W **70** C5
Salmon Gums *Australia* 32°59S 121°38E **61** F3
Salmon Pt. *Canada* 43°52N 77°15W **82** C7
Salmon River Mts.
  U.S.A. 44°50N 115°30W **76** D6
Salmon River Res.
  U.S.A. 43°32N 75°55W **83** C9
Salo *Finland* 60°22N 23°10E **9** F20
Salome *U.S.A.* 33°47N 113°37W **79** M13
Salon *India* 26°2N 81°27E **43** F9
Salon-de-Provence *France* 43°39N 5°6E **20** E6
Salonica = Thessaloniki
  Greece 40°38N 22°58E **23** D10
Salonta *Romania* 46°49N 21°42E **17** E11
Salpausselkä *Finland* 61°3N 26°15E **8** F22
Salsacate *Argentina* 31°20S 65°5W **94** C2
Salsk *Russia* 46°28N 41°30E **19** E7
Salso ➤ *Italy* 37°6N 13°57E **22** F5
Salt ➤ *Canada* 60°0N 112°25W **70** B6
Salt ➤ *U.S.A.* 33°23N 112°19W **77** K7
Salt Fork Red ➤ *U.S.A.* 34°27N 99°21W **84** D5
Salt L. *Australia* 30°6S 142°8E **63** E3
Salt Lake City *U.S.A.* 40°45N 111°53W **76** F8
Salt Lake City Int. ✈ (SLC)
  U.S.A. 40°47N 111°58W **76** F7
Salt Range *Pakistan* 32°30N 72°25E **42** C5
Salta *Argentina* 24°57S 65°25W **94** A2
Salta □ *Argentina* 24°48S 65°30W **94** A2
Saltash *U.K.* 50°24N 4°14W **13** G3
Saltburn-by-the-Sea *U.K.* 54°35N 0°58W **12** C7
Saltcoats *U.K.* 55°38N 4°47W **11** F4
Saltee Is. *Ireland* 52°7N 6°37W **10** D5
Saltfjellet *Norway* 66°40N 15°15E **8** C16
Saltfjorden *Norway* 67°15N 14°10E **8** C16
Saltfjellet-Svartisen △
  Norway 66°45N 15°10E **8** C16
Saltillo *Mexico* 25°25N 101°0W **86** B4
Salto *Argentina* 34°20S 60°15W **94** C3
Salto *Uruguay* 31°27S 57°50W **94** C4
Salto ➤ *Italy* 42°26N 12°25E **22** C5
Salto del Guaíra *Paraguay* 24°3S 54°17W **95** A5
Salton City *U.S.A.* 33°18N 115°57W **79** M11
Salton Sea *U.S.A.* 33°15N 115°45W **79** M11
Saltsburg *U.S.A.* 40°29N 79°27W **82** F5
Saluda ➤ *U.S.A.* 34°1N 81°4W **85** D14
Salue Timpaus, Selat
  Indonesia 1°50S 123°50E **37** E6
Salūm *Egypt* 31°31N 25°7E **53** B11
Salur *India* 18°27N 83°18E **44** E6
Salvador *Brazil* 13°0S 38°30W **93** F11
Salvador *Canada* 52°10N 109°32W **71** C7
Salvador, El ■ *Cent. Amer.* 13°50N 89°0W **88** D2
Salvador, L. *U.S.A.* 29°43N 90°15W **85** G9
Salween ➤ *Myanmar* 16°31N 97°37E **41** L20
Salyan *Azerbaijan* 39°33N 48°59E **47** B6
Salybia *Trin. & Tob.* 10°43N 61°2W **93** K15
Salzach ➤ *Austria* 48°12N 12°56E **16** D7
Salzburg *Austria* 47°48N 13°2E **16** E7
Salzgitter *Germany* 52°9N 10°19E **16** B6
Salzwedel *Germany* 52°52N 11°10E **16** B6
Sam *India* 26°50N 70°31E **42** F4
Sam Neua *Laos* 20°29N 104°0E **38** B5
Sam Ngao *Thailand* 17°18N 99°0E **38** D2
Sam Rong, Laem *Thailand* 9°35N 100°4E **39** b
Sam Son *Vietnam* 19°44N 105°54E **38** C5
Sama de Langreo = Langreo
  Spain 43°18N 5°40W **21** A3
Samagaltay *Russia* 50°36N 95°3E **27** D10
Samak, Tanjung *Indonesia* 2°34S 110°30E **36** E4
Samales Group *Phil.* 6°0N 122°0E **37** C6
Samalkot *India* 17°3N 82°13E **44** F6
Samana *India* 30°10N 76°13E **42** D7
Samana Cays *Bahamas* 23°3N 73°45W **89** B5
Samangān □ *Afghan.* 36°15N 68°3E **40** B5

Samani *Japan* 42°7N 142°56E **28** C11
Samar *Phil.* 12°0N 125°0E **37** B7
Samara *Russia* 53°8N 50°6E **18** D9
Samarinda *Indonesia* 0°30S 117°9E **36** E5
Samarkand = Samarqand
  Uzbekistan 39°40N 66°55E **26** F7
Samarqand *Uzbekistan* 39°40N 66°55E **26** F7
Sāmarrā' *Iraq* 34°12N 43°52E **46** C4
Samastipur *India* 25°50N 85°50E **43** G11
Samba *India* 32°32N 75°10E **43** C6
Sambalpur *India* 21°28N 84°4E **44** D7
Sambar, Tanjung
  Indonesia 2°59S 110°19E **36** E4
Sambas *Indonesia* 1°20N 109°20E **36** D3
Sambhajinagar = Aurangabad
  India 19°50N 75°23E **44** E2
Sambhal *India* 28°35N 78°37E **43** E8
Sambhar *India* 26°52N 75°6E **42** F6
Sambhar L. *India* 26°55N 75°12E **42** F6
Sambir *Ukraine* 49°30N 23°10E **17** D12
Sambor *Cambodia* 12°46N 106°0E **38** F6
Sambor Prei Kuk
  Cambodia 12°46N 105°58E **38** F5
Samborombón, B.
  Argentina 36°5S 57°20W **94** D4
Samcheok *S. Korea* 37°26N 129°10E **33** F15
Samet, Ko *Thailand* 12°34N 101°27E **38** F3
Sammanturai *Sri Lanka* 7°36N 81°39E **45** L5
Samnah *Si. Arabia* 25°10N 37°15E **46** E3
Samo Alto *Chile* 30°22S 71°0W **94** C1
Samoa ■ *Pac. Oc.* 14°0S 172°0W **59** b
Samoan Is. *Pac. Oc.* 14°0S 171°0W **59** b
Samokov *Bulgaria* 42°18N 23°35E **23** C10
Samos *Greece* 37°45N 26°50E **23** F12
Samothráki = Mathraki
  Greece 39°48N 19°31E **23** E8
Samothraki *Greece* 40°28N 25°28E **23** D11
Sampacho *Argentina* 33°20S 64°50W **94** C3
Sampalan *Indonesia* 8°41S 115°34E **37** K18
Sampang *Indonesia* 7°11S 113°13E **37** G15
Sampit *Indonesia* 2°34S 113°0E **36** E4
Sampit, Teluk *Indonesia* 3°5S 113°3E **36** E4
Samrong *Cambodia* 14°15N 103°30E **38** E4
Samsø *Denmark* 55°50N 10°35E **9** J14
Samsun *Turkey* 41°15N 36°22E **19** F6
Samui, Ko *Thailand* 9°30N 100°0E **39** b
Samut Prakan *Thailand* 13°32N 100°40E **38** F3
Samut Sakhon *Thailand* 13°31N 100°13E **38** F3
Samut Songkhram
  Thailand 13°24N 100°1E **38** F3
Samwari *Pakistan* 28°30N 66°46E **42** E2
San Mali 13°15N 4°57W **52** F5
San ➤ *Cambodia* 13°32N 105°57E **38** F5
San ➤ *Poland* 50°45N 21°51E **17** C11
San Agustín, C. *Phil.* 6°20N 126°13E **37** C7
San Agustín de Valle Fértil
  Argentina 30°35S 67°30W **94** C2
San Ambrosio *Pac. Oc.* 26°28S 79°53W **90** F3
San Andreas *U.S.A.* 38°12N 120°41W **78** G6
San Andrés, I. de
  Caribbean 12°42N 81°46W **88** D3
San Andres Mts. *U.S.A.* 33°0N 106°30W **77** K10
San Andrés Tuxtla
  Mexico 18°27N 95°13W **87** D5
San Angelo *U.S.A.* 31°28N 100°26W **84** F4
San Anselmo *U.S.A.* 37°59N 122°34W **78** H4
San Antonio *Belize* 16°15N 89°2W **87** D7
San Antonio *Chile* 33°40S 71°40W **94** C1
San Antonio *N. Mex.,
  U.S.A.* 33°55N 106°52W **77** K10
San Antonio *Tex., U.S.A.* 29°25N 98°29W **84** G5
San Antonio ➤ *U.S.A.* 28°30N 96°54W **84** G6
San Antonio, C.
  Argentina 36°15S 56°40W **94** D4
San Antonio, C. de *Cuba* 21°50N 84°57W **88** B3
San Antonio, Mt.
  U.S.A. 34°17N 117°38W **79** L9
San Antonio de los Baños
  Cuba 22°54N 82°31W **88** B3
San Antonio de los Cobres
  Argentina 24°10S 66°17W **94** A2
San Antonio Oeste
  Argentina 40°40S 65°0W **96** E4
San Ardo *U.S.A.* 36°1N 120°54W **78** J6
San Augustine *U.S.A.* 31°32N 94°7W **84** F7
San Benedetto del Tronto
  Italy 42°57N 13°53E **22** C5
San Benedicto, I.
  Mexico 19°18N 110°49W **86** D2
San Benito *U.S.A.* 26°8N 97°38W **84** H6
San Benito ➤ *U.S.A.* 36°53N 121°34W **78** J5
San Benito Mt. *U.S.A.* 36°22N 120°37W **78** J6
San Bernardino *U.S.A.* 34°7N 117°19W **79** L9
San Bernardino Mts.
  U.S.A. 34°10N 116°45W **79** L10
San Bernardino Str.
  Phil. 12°30N 124°10E **37** B7
San Bernardo *Chile* 33°40S 70°50W **94** C1
San Bernardo, I. de
  Colombia 9°45N 75°50W **92** B3
San Blas *Mexico* 26°5N 108°46W **86** B3
San Blas, Arch. de
  Panama 9°50N 78°31W **88** E4
San Blas, C. *U.S.A.* 29°40N 85°21W **85** G12
San Borja *Bolivia* 14°50S 66°52W **92** F5
San Buenaventura = Ventura
  U.S.A. 34°17N 119°18W **79** L7
San Buenaventura
  Mexico 27°5N 101°32W **86** B4
San Carlos *Argentina* 33°50S 69°0W **94** C2
San Carlos *Chile* 36°10S 72°0W **94** D1
San Carlos *Baja Calif. S.,
  Mexico* 24°47N 112°7W **86** C2
San Carlos *Coahuila,
  Mexico* 29°1N 100°51W **86** B4
San Carlos *Nic.* 11°12N 84°50W **88** D3
San Carlos *Phil.* 10°29N 123°25E **37** B6
San Carlos *Uruguay* 34°46S 54°58W **95** C5
San Carlos *Venezuela* 9°40N 68°36W **92** B5
San Carlos de Bariloche
  Argentina 41°10S 71°25W **96** E2

San Carlos de Bolívar
  Argentina 36°15S 61°6W 94 D3
San Carlos del Zulia
  Venezuela 9°1N 71°55W 92 B4
San Carlos L. U.S.A. 33°11N 110°32W 77 K8
San Clemente Chile 35°30S 71°29W 94 D1
San Clemente U.S.A. 33°26N 117°37W 79 M9
San Clemente I. U.S.A. 32°53N 118°29W 79 N8
San Cristóbal Argentina 30°20S 61°10W 94 C3
San Cristóbal Dom. Rep. 18°25N 70°6W 89 C5
San Cristóbal Solomon Is. 10°30S 161°0E 58 C9
San Cristóbal Venezuela 7°46N 72°14W 92 B4
San Cristóbal de las Casas
  Mexico 16°45N 92°38W 87 D6
San Diego Calif., U.S.A. 32°42N 117°9W 79 N9
San Diego Tex., U.S.A. 27°46N 98°14W 84 H5
San Diego, C. Argentina 54°40S 65°10W 96 G3
San Diego de la Unión
  Mexico 21°28N 100°52W 86 C4
San Diego Int. ✈ (SAN)
  U.S.A. 32°44N 117°11W 79 N9
San Estanislao Paraguay 24°39S 56°26W 94 A4
San Felipe Chile 32°43S 70°42W 94 C1
San Felipe Mexico 31°1N 114°52W 86 A2
San Felipe Venezuela 10°20N 68°44W 92 A5
San Felipe ➤ U.S.A. 33°10N 115°49W 79 M11
San Félix Chile 28°56S 70°28W 94 B1
San Félix Pac. Oc. 26°23S 80°0W 90 F2
San Fernando Chile 34°30S 71°0W 94 C1
San Fernando Mexico 24°51N 98°10W 87 C5
San Fernando La Union,
  Phil. 16°40N 120°23E 37 A6
San Fernando Pampanga,
  Phil. 15°5N 120°37E 37 A6
San Fernando Spain 36°28N 6°17W 21 D2
San Fernando
  Trin. & Tob. 10°16N 61°28W 93 K15
San Fernando U.S.A. 34°17N 118°26W 79 L8
San Fernando de Apure
  Venezuela 7°54N 67°15W 92 B5
San Fernando de Atabapo
  Venezuela 4°3N 67°42W 92 C5
San Francisco Argentina 31°30S 62°5W 94 C3
San Francisco ➤
  U.S.A. 32°59N 109°22W 77 K9
San Francisco, C. de
  Colombia 6°18N 77°29W 90 C3
San Francisco, Paso de
  S. Amer. 27°0S 68°0W 94 B2
San Francisco de Macorís
  Dom. Rep. 19°19N 70°15W 89 C5
San Francisco del Monte de Oro
  Argentina 32°36S 66°8W 94 C2
San Francisco del Oro
  Mexico 26°52N 105°51W 86 B3
San Francisco Int. ✈ (SFO)
  U.S.A. 37°37N 122°22W 78 H4
San Gabriel Chile 33°47S 70°15W 94 C1
San Gabriel Chilac
  Mexico 18°19N 97°21W 87 D5
San Gabriel Mts. U.S.A. 34°17N 117°38W 79 L9
San Gavino Monreale
  Italy 39°33N 8°47E 22 E3
San German Puerto Rico 18°4N 67°4W 89 d
San Gorgonio Mt.
  U.S.A. 34°6N 116°50W 79 L10
San Gottardo, P. del Switz. 46°33N 8°33E 20 C8
San Gregorio Uruguay 32°37S 55°40W 95 C4
San Gregorio U.S.A. 37°20N 122°23W 78 H4
San Guillermo △
  Argentina 27°50S 69°45W 94 B2
San Ignacio Belize 17°10N 89°5W 87 D7
San Ignacio Bolivia 16°20S 60°55W 92 G6
San Ignacio Mexico 27°27N 112°51W 86 B2
San Ignacio Paraguay 26°52S 57°3W 94 B4
San Ignacio, L. Mexico 26°54N 113°13W 86 B2
San Ildefonso, C. Phil. 16°0N 122°1E 37 A6
San Isidro Argentina 34°29S 58°31W 94 C4
San Jacinto U.S.A. 33°47N 116°57W 79 M10
San Javier Misiones,
  Argentina 27°55S 55°5W 95 B4
San Javier Santa Fe,
  Argentina 30°40S 59°55W 94 C4
San Javier Bolivia 16°18S 62°30W 92 G6
San Javier Chile 35°40S 71°45W 94 D1
San Jerónimo Taviche
  Mexico 16°44N 96°35W 87 D5
San Joaquin U.S.A. 36°36N 120°11W 78 J6
San Joaquin ➤ U.S.A. 38°4N 121°51W 78 G5
San Joaquin Valley
  U.S.A. 37°20N 121°0W 78 J6
San Jon U.S.A. 35°6N 103°20W 77 J12
San Jorge Argentina 31°54S 61°50W 94 C3
San Jorge, B. Mexico 31°20N 113°20W 86 A2
San Jorge, G. Argentina 46°0S 66°0W 96 F3
San José Argentina 32°12S 58°15W 94 C4
San Jose Costa Rica 9°55N 84°2W 88 E3
San Jose Guatemala 14°0N 90°50W 88 D1
San Jose Mind. Occ., Phil. 12°27N 121°4E 37 B6
San Jose Nueva Ecija,
  Phil. 15°45N 120°55E 37 A6
San Jose U.S.A. 37°20N 121°53W 78 H5
San Jose ➤ U.S.A. 34°25N 106°45W 77 J10
San José, I. Mexico 25°0N 110°38W 86 C2
San Jose de Buenavista
  Phil. 10°45N 121°56E 37 B6
San José de Chiquitos
  Bolivia 17°53S 60°50W 92 G6
San José de Feliciano
  Argentina 30°26S 58°46W 94 C4
San José de Jáchal
  Argentina 30°15S 68°46W 94 C2
San José de Mayo
  Uruguay 34°27S 56°40W 94 C4
San José del Cabo Mexico 23°3N 109°41W 86 C3
San José del Guaviare
  Colombia 2°35N 72°38W 92 C4
San Juan Argentina 31°30S 68°30W 94 C2
San Juan Puerto Rico 18°28N 66°7W 89 d
San Juan Trin. & Tob. 10°39N 61°29W 93 K15

San Juan □ Argentina 31°9S 69°0W 94 C2
San Juan ➤ Argentina 32°20S 67°25W 94 C2
San Juan ➤ Nic. 10°56N 83°42W 88 D3
San Juan ➤ U.S.A. 37°16N 110°26W 77 H8
San Juan Bautista
  Paraguay 26°37S 57°6W 94 B4
San Juan Bautista
  U.S.A. 36°51N 121°32W 78 J5
San Juan Capistrano
  U.S.A. 33°30N 117°40W 79 M9
San Juan Cr. ➤ U.S.A. 35°40N 120°22W 78 J5
San Juan de Guadelupe
  Mexico 24°38N 102°44W 86 C4
San Juan de la Costa
  Mexico 24°20N 110°41W 86 C2
San Juan de los Lagos
  Mexico 21°15N 102°18W 86 C4
San Juan de los Morros
  Venezuela 9°55N 67°21W 92 B5
San Juan del Norte Nic. 10°58N 83°40W 88 D3
San Juan del Norte, B. de
  Nic. 11°0N 83°40W 88 D3
San Juan del Río Mexico 20°23N 100°0W 87 C5
San Juan del Sur Nic. 11°20N 85°51W 88 D2
San Juan I. U.S.A. 48°32N 123°5W 78 B3
San Juan Island △
  U.S.A. 48°35N 123°8W 78 B4
San Juan Mts. U.S.A. 37°30N 107°0W 77 H10
San Justo Argentina 30°47S 60°30W 94 C3
San Kamphaeng Thailand 18°45N 99°8E 38 C2
San Lázaro, C. Mexico 24°50N 112°18W 86 C2
San Leandro U.S.A. 37°42N 122°9W 78 H4
San Lorenzo Argentina 32°45S 60°45W 94 C3
San Lorenzo Ecuador 1°15N 78°50W 92 C3
San Lorenzo Paraguay 25°20S 57°32W 94 B4
San Lorenzo ➤ Mexico 24°15N 107°24W 86 C3
San Lorenzo, I. Mexico 28°38N 112°51W 86 B2
San Lorenzo, Mte.
  Argentina 47°40S 72°20W 96 F2
San Lucas = Cabo San Lucas
  Mexico 22°53N 109°54W 86 C3
San Lucas Bolivia 20°5S 65°7W 92 H5
San Lucas Mexico 27°10N 112°14W 86 B2
San Lucas U.S.A. 36°8N 121°1W 78 J5
San Lucas Argentina 33°20S 66°20W 94 C2
San Lucas, C. Mexico 22°52N 109°53W 86 C3
San Luis Cuba 22°17N 83°46W 88 B3
San Luis Guatemala 16°14N 89°27W 88 C2
San Luis Ariz., U.S.A. 32°29N 114°47W 77 K6
San Luis Colo., U.S.A. 37°12N 105°25W 77 H11
San Luis □ Argentina 34°0S 66°0W 94 C2
San Luis, I. Mexico 29°58N 114°26W 86 B2
San Luis, Sierra de
  Argentina 32°30S 66°10W 94 C2
San Luis de la Paz
  Mexico 21°18N 100°31W 86 C4
San Luis Obispo U.S.A. 35°17N 120°40W 79 K6
San Luis Potosí Mexico 22°9N 100°59W 86 C4
San Luis Potosí □ Mexico 23°0N 101°0W 86 C4
San Luis Res. U.S.A. 37°4N 121°5W 78 H5
San Luis Río Colorado
  Mexico 32°29N 114°58W 86 A2
San Manuel U.S.A. 32°36N 110°38W 77 K8
San Marcos Calif., U.S.A. 33°9N 117°10W 79 M9
San Marcos Tex., U.S.A. 29°53N 97°56W 84 G6
San Marcos, I. Mexico 27°13N 112°6W 86 B2
San Marino San Marino 43°55N 12°30E 16 G7
San Marino ■ Europe 43°56N 12°25E 22 C5
San Martín Antarctica 68°11S 67°0W 5 C17
San Martín Argentina 33°5S 68°28W 94 C2
San Martín ➤ Bolivia 13°8S 63°43W 92 F6
San Martín, L. Argentina 48°50S 72°50W 96 F2
San Martín de los Andes
  Argentina 40°10S 71°20W 96 E2
San Mateo U.S.A. 37°34N 122°19W 78 H4
San Matías Bolivia 16°25S 58°20W 92 G7
San Matías, G. Argentina 41°30S 64°0W 96 E4
San Miguel Brazil 28°35S 54°33W 95 B5
San Miguel El Salv. 13°30N 88°12W 88 D2
San Miguel Panama 8°27N 78°55W 88 E4
San Miguel ➤ U.S.A. 35°45N 120°42W 78 K6
San Miguel ➤ Bolivia 13°52S 63°56W 92 F6
San Miguel de Tucumán
  Argentina 26°50S 65°20W 94 B2
San Miguel del Monte
  Argentina 35°23S 58°50W 94 D4
San Miguel I. U.S.A. 34°2N 120°23W 79 L6
San Nicandro Gargánico
  Italy 41°50N 15°34E 22 D6
San Nicolás de los Arroyos
  Argentina 33°25S 60°10W 94 C3
San Nicolas I. U.S.A. 33°15N 119°30W 79 M7
San Onofre U.S.A. 33°22N 117°34W 79 M9
San Pablo Bolivia 21°43S 66°38W 94 A2
San Pablo U.S.A. 37°58N 122°21W 78 H4
San Pedro B. Aires,
  Argentina 33°40S 59°40W 94 C4
San Pedro Misiones,
  Argentina 26°30S 54°10W 95 B5
San Pedro Chile 33°54S 71°28W 94 C1
San Pedro Côte d'Ivoire 4°50N 6°33W 52 H4
San Pedro Mexico 23°55N 110°17W 86 C2
San Pedro □ Paraguay 24°0S 57°0W 94 A4
San Pedro ➤ Chihuahua,
  Mexico 28°21N 105°25W 86 B3
San Pedro ➤ Nayarit,
  Mexico 21°45N 105°30W 86 C3
San Pedro ➤ U.S.A. 32°59N 110°47W 77 K8
San Pedro, Pta. Chile 25°30S 70°38W 94 B1
San Pedro Channel
  U.S.A. 33°30N 118°25W 79 M8
San Pedro de Atacama
  Chile 22°55S 68°15W 94 A2
San Pedro de Jujuy
  Argentina 24°12S 64°55W 94 A3
San Pedro de las Colonias
  Mexico 25°45N 102°59W 86 B4
San Pedro de Macorís
  Dom. Rep. 18°30N 69°18W 89 C6
San Pedro del Norte Nic. 13°4N 84°33W 88 D3

San Pedro del Paraná
  Paraguay 26°43S 56°13W 94 B4
San Pedro Mártir, Sa. de
  Mexico 30°45N 115°13W 86 A1
San Pedro Ocampo = Melchor
  Ocampo Mexico 24°51N 101°39W 86 C4
San Pedro Pochutla
  Mexico 15°44N 96°28W 87 D5
San Pedro Sula Honduras 15°30N 88°0W 88 C2
San Pedro Tututepec
  Mexico 16°9N 97°38W 87 D5
San Pietro Italy 39°8N 8°17E 22 E3
San Rafael Argentina 34°40S 68°21W 94 C2
San Rafael Calif., U.S.A. 37°58N 122°32W 78 H4
San Rafael N. Mex.,
  U.S.A. 35°7N 107°53W 77 J10
San Rafael Mt. U.S.A. 34°41N 119°52W 79 L7
San Rafael Mts. U.S.A. 34°40N 119°50W 79 L7
San Ramón de la Nueva Orán
  Argentina 23°10S 64°20W 94 A3
San Remo Italy 43°49N 7°46E 20 E7
San Roque Argentina 28°25S 58°45W 94 B4
San Roque Spain 36°17N 5°21W 21 D3
San Rosendo Chile 37°16S 72°43W 94 D1
San Saba U.S.A. 31°12N 98°43W 84 F5
San Salvador El Salv. 13°40N 89°10W 88 D2
San Salvador de Jujuy
  Argentina 24°10S 64°48W 94 A3
San Salvador I. Bahamas 24°0N 74°30W 89 B5
San Sebastián = Donostia-San
  Sebastián Spain 43°17N 1°58W 21 A5
San Sebastián Argentina 53°10S 68°30W 96 G3
San Sebastián Puerto Rico 18°20N 66°59W 89 d
San Severo Italy 41°41N 15°23E 22 D6
San Simeon U.S.A. 35°39N 121°11W 78 K5
San Simon U.S.A. 32°16N 109°14W 77 K9
San Telmo Mexico 30°58N 116°6W 86 A1
San Tiburcio Mexico 24°8N 101°32W 86 C4
San Valentin, Mte. Chile 46°30S 73°30W 96 F2
San Vicente de Cañete
  Peru 13°8S 76°30W 92 F3
San Vicente de la Barquera
  Spain 43°23N 4°29W 21 A3
San Vito Costa Rica 8°50N 82°58W 88 E3
Sana = Ṣanʻāʾ Yemen 15°27N 44°12E 49 D3
Ṣanʻāʾ Yemen 15°27N 44°12E 49 D3
Sana ➤ Bos.-H. 45°3N 16°23E 16 F9
Sanaa = Ṣanʻāʾ Yemen 15°27N 44°12E 49 D3
Sanae IV Antarctica 70°20S 9°0W 5 D2
Sanaga ➤ Cameroon 3°35N 9°38E 54 D1
Sanak I. U.S.A. 54°25N 162°40W 74 E7
Sanalona, Presa Mexico 24°49N 107°7W 86 B3
Sanana Indonesia 2°4S 125°58E 37 E7
Sanand India 22°59N 72°25E 42 H5
Sanandaj Iran 35°18N 47°1E 46 C5
Sanandita Bolivia 21°40S 63°45W 94 A3
Sanawad India 22°11N 76°5E 42 H7
Sancha He ➤ China 26°48N 106°7E 34 D6
Sanchahe China 44°50N 126°2E 33 B14
Sánchez Dom. Rep. 19°15N 69°36W 89 C6
Sanchi India 23°28N 77°44E 42 H7
Sanchor India 24°45N 71°55E 42 G4
Sancti Spíritus Cuba 21°52N 79°33W 88 B4
Sancy, Puy de France 45°32N 2°50E 20 D5
Sand ➤ Polokwane ➤
  S. Africa 22°25S 30°5E 57 B5
Sand Hills U.S.A. 42°10N 101°30W 80 D3
Sand Lakes △ Canada 57°51N 98°32W 71 B9
Sand Springs U.S.A. 36°9N 96°7W 84 C6
Sanda Japan 34°53N 135°14E 29 G7
Sandakan Malaysia 5°53N 118°4E 36 C5
Sandan = Sambor
  Cambodia 12°46N 106°0E 38 F6
Sandanski Bulgaria 41°35N 23°16E 23 D10
Sanday U.K. 59°16N 2°31W 11 B6
Sandefjord Norway 59°10N 10°15E 9 G14
Sanders U.S.A. 35°13N 109°20W 77 J9
Sanderson U.S.A. 30°9N 102°24W 84 F3
Sandersville U.S.A. 32°59N 82°48W 85 E13
Sandfire Roadhouse
  Australia 19°45S 121°15E 60 C3
Sandfly L. Canada 55°43N 106°6W 71 B7
Sandfontein Namibia 23°48S 19°1E 56 C2
Sandheads, The India 21°10N 88°20E 43 J13
Sandia Peru 14°10S 69°30W 92 F5
Sandila India 27°5N 80°31E 43 F9
Sandnes Norway 58°50N 5°45E 9 G11
Sandnessjøen Norway 66°2N 12°38E 8 C15
Sandoa
  Dem. Rep. of the Congo 9°41S 23°0E 54 F4
Sandomierz Poland 50°40N 21°43E 17 C11
Sandover ➤ Australia 21°43S 136°32E 62 C2
Sandoway = Thandwe
  Myanmar 18°20N 94°30E 41 K19
Sandoy Færoe Is. 61°52N 6°46W 8 F9
Sandpoint U.S.A. 48°17N 116°33W 76 B5
Sandray U.K. 56°53N 7°31W 11 E1
Sandringham U.K. 52°51N 0°31E 12 E8
Sandstone Australia 27°59S 119°16E 61 E2
Sandu China 26°0N 107°52E 34 E6
Sandur India 15°6N 76°33E 45 F3
Sandusky Mich., U.S.A. 43°25N 82°50W 82 C2
Sandusky Ohio, U.S.A. 41°27N 82°42W 82 E2
Sandveld Namibia 21°25S 20°0E 56 B3
Sandviken Sweden 60°38N 16°46E 8 F17
Sandwich, C. Australia 18°14S 146°18E 62 B4
Sandwich B. Canada 53°40N 57°15W 73 B8
Sandwich B. Namibia 23°25S 14°20E 56 B1
Sandy Oreg., U.S.A. 45°24N 122°16W 78 E4
Sandy Pa., U.S.A. 41°6N 78°46W 82 E6
Sandy Utah, U.S.A. 40°32N 111°50W 76 F8
Sandy Bay Canada 55°31N 102°19W 71 B8
Sandy Bight Australia 33°50S 123°20E 61 F3
Sandy C. Queens.,
  Australia 24°42S 153°15E 62 C5
Sandy C. Tas., Australia 41°25S 144°45E 63 G3
Sandy Cay Bahamas 23°13N 75°18W 88 B4
Sandy Cr. ➤ U.S.A. 41°51N 109°47W 76 F9
Sandy Creek U.S.A. 43°38N 76°5W 83 C8

Sandy L. Canada 53°2N 93°0W 72 B1
Sandy Lake Canada 53°0N 93°15W 72 B1
Sandy Point India 10°32N 92°22E 45 J11
Sandy Valley U.S.A. 35°49N 115°38W 79 K11
Sånfjället △ Sweden 62°17N 13°35E 8 E15
Sanford Fla., U.S.A. 28°48N 81°16W 85 G14
Sanford Maine, U.S.A. 43°27N 70°47W 83 C14
Sanford N.C., U.S.A. 35°29N 79°10W 85 D15
Sanford, Mt. U.S.A. 62°13N 144°8W 68 E3
Sang-i-Masha Afghan. 33°8N 67°27E 42 C2
Sanga ➤ Congo 1°5S 17°0E 54 E3
Sanga Congo 1°5S 17°0E 54 E3
Sangamner India 19°37N 74°15E 44 E2
Sangān Iran 34°23N 60°15E 47 C9
Sangar Afghan. 32°56N 65°30E 42 C1
Sangar Russia 64°2N 127°31E 27 C13
Sangar Sarai Afghan. 34°27N 70°35E 42 B4
Sangareddi India 17°38N 78°7E 44 F4
Sangarh ➤ Pakistan 30°43N 70°44E 42 D4
Sangay Ecuador 2°0S 78°20W 92 D3
Sangeang Indonesia 8°12S 119°6E 37 F5
Sanger U.S.A. 36°42N 119°33W 78 J7
Sangerhausen Germany 51°28N 11°18E 16 C6
Sanggan He ➤ China 38°12N 117°15E 32 E9
Sanggau Indonesia 0°5N 110°30E 36 D4
Sanghar Pakistan 26°2N 68°57E 42 F3
Sangihe, Kepulauan
  Indonesia 3°0N 125°30E 37 D7
Sangihe, Pulau Indonesia 3°35N 125°30E 37 D7
Sangiran ➤ Indonesia 7°27S 110°50E 37 G14
Sangju S. Korea 36°25N 128°10E 33 F15
Sangkapura Indonesia 5°52S 112°40E 36 F4
Sangkha Thailand 14°37N 103°52E 38 E4
Sangkhla Buri Thailand 14°57N 98°28E 38 E2
Sangkulirang Indonesia 0°59N 117°58E 36 D5
Sangla Pakistan 31°43N 73°23E 42 D5
Sangli India 16°55N 74°33E 44 F2
Sangmélima Cameroon 2°57N 12°1E 54 D2
Sango Zimbabwe 18°44S 31°44E 57 A5
Sangole India 17°26N 75°12E 44 F2
Sangre de Cristo Mts.
  U.S.A. 37°30N 105°20W 77 H11
Sangre Grande
  Trin. & Tob. 10°35N 61°8W 93 K15
Sangrur India 30°14N 75°50E 42 D6
Sangudo Canada 53°50N 114°54W 70 C6
Sangue ➤ Brazil 11°1S 58°39W 92 F7
Sangzhi China 29°25N 110°12E 35 C8
Sanibel U.S.A. 26°27N 82°1W 85 H13
Sanikluaq Canada 56°32N 79°14W 72 A4
Sanin-Kaigan △ Japan 35°39N 134°37E 29 G7
Sanirajak = Hall Beach
  Canada 68°46N 81°12W 69 D15
Sanjawi Pakistan 30°17N 68°21E 42 D3
Sanjiang China 25°48N 109°37E 34 E7
Sanjo Japan 37°37N 138°57E 28 F9
Sankarankovil India 9°10N 77°35E 45 K3
Sankeshwar India 16°23N 74°32E 45 F2
Sankh ➤ India 22°15N 84°48E 43 H11
Sankt Gallen Switz. 47°26N 9°22E 20 C8
Sankt Michel = Mikkeli
  Finland 61°43N 27°15E 8 F22
Sankt Moritz Switz. 46°30N 9°51E 20 C8
Sankt Pölten Austria 48°12N 15°38E 16 D8
Sankuru ➤
  Dem. Rep. of the Congo 4°17S 20°25E 54 E4
Şanlıurfa Turkey 37°12N 38°50E 46 B3
Sanlúcar de Barrameda
  Spain 36°46N 6°21W 21 D2
Sanmen China 29°5N 121°35E 35 C13
Sanmenxia China 34°47N 111°12E 32 G6
Sanming China 26°15N 117°40E 35 D11
Sanmu Japan 34°11N 134°37E 29 G7
Sanndraigh = Sandray
  U.K. 56°53N 7°31W 11 E1
Sânnicolau Mare
  Romania 46°5N 20°39E 17 E11
Sannieshof S. Africa 26°30S 25°47E 56 D4
Sannīn, J. Lebanon 33°57N 35°52E 48 B4
Sanniquellie Liberia 7°19N 8°38W 52 G4
Sano Japan 36°19N 139°35E 29 F9
Sanok Poland 49°35N 22°10E 17 D12
Sanqianga △ China 28°54N 118°3E 35 C12
Sanquhar U.K. 55°22N 3°54W 11 F5
Sanremo = San Remo
  Italy 43°49N 7°46E 20 E7
Sans Souci Trin. & Tob. 10°50N 61°0W 93 K16
Sansha China 26°58N 120°12E 35 D13
Sanshui China 23°10N 112°56E 35 F9
Sansui China 26°58N 108°39E 34 D7
Sant Antoni de Portmany
  Spain 38°59N 1°19E 21 C6
Sant Feliu de Guíxols Spain 41°45N 3°1E 21 B7
Sant Jordi, G. de Spain 40°53N 1°2E 21 B6
Santa Ana Bolivia 13°50S 65°40W 92 F5
Santa Ana El Salv. 14°0N 89°31W 88 D2
Santa Ana Mexico 30°33N 111°7W 86 A2
Santa Ana U.S.A. 33°46N 117°52W 79 M9
Santa Ana de los Ríos de Cuenca =
  Cuenca Ecuador 2°50S 79°9W 92 D3
Santa Bárbara Chile 37°40S 72°1W 94 D1
Santa Bárbara Honduras 14°53N 88°14W 88 D2
Santa Bárbara Mexico 26°48N 105°49W 86 B3
Santa Bárbara U.S.A. 34°25N 119°42W 79 L7
Santa Barbara Channel
  U.S.A. 34°15N 120°0W 79 L7
Santa Barbara I. U.S.A. 33°29N 119°2W 79 M7
Santa Catalina, Gulf of
  U.S.A. 33°10N 117°50W 79 N9
Santa Catalina, I.
  Mexico 25°40N 110°47W 86 B2
Santa Catalina I.
  U.S.A. 33°23N 118°25W 79 M8
Santa Catarina □ Brazil 27°25S 48°30W 95 B6
Santa Catarina, I. de
  Brazil 27°30S 48°40W 95 B6
Santa Cecília Brazil 26°56S 50°18W 95 B5
Santa Clara Cuba 22°20N 80°0W 88 B4
Santa Clara Calif.,
  U.S.A. 37°21N 121°57W 78 H5

Santa Clara N.Y., U.S.A. 44°38N 74°27W 83 B10
Santa Clara Utah, U.S.A. 37°8N 113°39W 77 H7
Santa Clara ➤ Mexico 29°51N 107°6W 86 A3
Santa Clara de Olimar
  Uruguay 32°50S 54°54W 95 C5
Santa Clara Valley
  U.S.A. 36°50N 121°30W 78 J5
Santa Clarita U.S.A. 34°24N 118°33W 79 L8
Santa Clotilde Peru 2°33S 73°45W 92 D4
Santa Cruz Bolivia 17°43S 63°10W 92 G6
Santa Cruz Chile 34°38S 71°27W 94 C1
Santa Cruz Costa Rica 10°15N 85°35W 88 D2
Santa Cruz Phil. 14°20N 121°24E 37 B6
Santa Cruz U.S.A. 36°58N 122°1W 78 J4
Santa Cruz ➤ Argentina 50°10S 68°20W 96 G3
Santa Cruz de Mompox = Mompós
  Colombia 9°14N 74°26W 92 B4
Santa Cruz de Tenerife
  Canary Is. 28°28N 16°15W 52 C2
Santa Cruz del Norte
  Cuba 23°9N 81°55W 88 B3
Santa Cruz del Sur Cuba 20°44N 78°0W 88 B4
Santa Cruz do Rio Pardo
  Brazil 22°54S 49°37W 95 A6
Santa Cruz do Sul Brazil 29°42S 52°25W 95 B5
Santa Cruz I. U.S.A. 34°1N 119°43W 79 M7
Santa Cruz Is. Solomon Is. 10°30S 166°0E 58 C9
Santa Cruz Mts. Jamaica 17°58N 77°43W 88 a
Santa Elena Argentina 30°58S 59°47W 94 C4
Santa Elena, C.
  Costa Rica 10°54N 85°56W 88 D2
Santa Fé Argentina 31°35S 60°41W 94 C3
Santa Fe U.S.A. 35°41N 105°57W 77 J11
Santa Fé □ Argentina 31°50S 60°55W 94 C3
Santa Fé do Sul Brazil 20°13S 50°56W 93 H8
Santa Filomena Brazil 9°6S 45°50W 93 E9
Santa Inês Brazil 13°17S 39°48W 93 F11
Santa Inés, I. Chile 54°0S 73°0W 96 G2
Santa Isabel Argentina 36°10S 66°54W 94 D2
Santa Isabel do Morro
  Brazil 11°34S 50°40W 93 F8
Santa Lucía Corrientes,
  Argentina 28°58S 59°5W 94 B4
Santa Lucía San Juan,
  Argentina 31°30S 68°30W 94 C2
Santa Lucía Uruguay 34°27S 56°24W 94 C4
Santa Lucia Range
  U.S.A. 36°0N 121°20W 78 K5
Santa Luzia Cabo Verde 16°50N 24°35W 52 b
Santa Margarita
  Argentina 38°28S 61°35W 94 D3
Santa Margarita U.S.A. 35°23N 120°37W 78 K6
Santa Margarita ➤
  U.S.A. 33°13N 117°23W 79 M9
Santa Margarita, I.
  Mexico 24°27N 111°50W 86 C2
Santa María Argentina 26°40S 66°0W 94 B2
Santa Maria Azores 36°58N 25°6W 52 a
Santa Maria Brazil 29°40S 53°48W 95 B5
Santa Maria Cabo Verde 16°31N 22°53W 52 b
Santa Maria U.S.A. 34°57N 120°26W 79 L6
Santa María, B. de Mexico 25°4N 108°6W 86 B3
Santa María, Vol.
  Guatemala 14°45N 91°33W 88 D1
Santa Maria da Vitória
  Brazil 13°24S 44°12W 93 F10
Santa Maria di Léuca, C.
  Italy 39°47N 18°22E 23 E8
Santa Marta Colombia 11°15N 74°13W 92 A4
Santa Marta, Sierra Nevada de
  Colombia 10°55N 73°50W 92 A4
Santa Marta Grande, C.
  Brazil 28°43S 48°50W 95 B6
Santa Maura = Lefkada
  Greece 38°40N 20°43E 23 E9
Santa Monica Mts. △
  U.S.A. 34°4N 118°44W 79 L8
Santa Paula U.S.A. 34°21N 119°4W 79 L7
Santa Rosa La Pampa,
  Argentina 36°40S 64°17W 94 D3
Santa Rosa San Luis,
  Argentina 32°21S 65°10W 94 C2
Santa Rosa Brazil 27°52S 54°29W 95 B5
Santa Rosa Calif., U.S.A. 38°26N 122°43W 78 G4
Santa Rosa N. Mex.,
  U.S.A. 34°57N 104°41W 77 J11
Santa Rosa and San Jacinto Mts. △
  U.S.A. 33°28N 116°20W 79 M10
Santa Rosa de Copán
  Honduras 14°47N 88°46W 88 D2
Santa Rosa de Río Primero
  Argentina 31°8S 63°20W 94 C3
Santa Rosa del Sara
  Bolivia 17°7S 63°35W 92 G6
Santa Rosa I. Calif.,
  U.S.A. 33°58N 120°6W 79 M6
Santa Rosa I. Fla.,
  U.S.A. 30°20N 86°50W 85 F11
Santa Rosa Range
  U.S.A. 41°45N 117°40W 76 F5
Santa Rosalía Mexico 27°19N 112°17W 86 B2
Santa Sylvina Argentina 27°50S 61°10W 94 B3
Santa Tecla = Nueva San Salvador
  El Salv. 13°40N 89°18W 88 D2
Santa Teresa Argentina 33°25S 60°47W 94 C3
Santa Teresa Australia 24°8S 134°22E 62 C1
Santa Teresa Mexico 25°17N 97°51W 87 B5
Santa Teresa △ Uruguay 33°57S 53°31W 95 C5
Santa Teresita Argentina 36°32S 56°41W 94 D4
Santa Vitória do Palmar
  Brazil 33°32S 53°25W 95 C5
Santa Ynez ➤ U.S.A. 34°41N 120°36W 79 L6
Santa Ynez Mts. U.S.A. 34°30N 120°0W 79 L7
Santa Ysabel U.S.A. 33°7N 116°40W 79 M10
Santai China 31°5N 104°58E 34 B5
Santana, Coxilha de
  Brazil 30°50S 55°35W 95 C4
Santana do Livramento
  Brazil 30°55S 55°30W 95 C4

160 Santander INDEX TO WORLD MAPS

Santander *Spain* 43°27N 3°51W **21** A4
Santander Jiménez *Mexico* 24°13N 98°28W **87** C5
Santanilla, Is. *Honduras* 17°22N 83°57W **88** C3
Santaquin *U.S.A.* 39°59N 111°47W **76** G8
Santarém *Brazil* 2°25S 54°42W **93** D8
Santarém *Portugal* 39°12N 8°42W **21** C1
Santaren Channel *W. Indies* 24°0N 79°30W **88** B4
Santee *U.S.A.* 32°50N 116°58W **79** N10
Santee → *U.S.A.* 33°7N 79°17W **85** E15
Santiago = Río Grande de Santiago → *Mexico* 21°36N 105°26W **86** C3
Santiago = São Tiago *Cabo Verde* 15°0N 23°40W **52** b
Santiago *Brazil* 29°11S 54°52W **95** B5
Santiago *Panama* 8°0N 81°0W **88** E3
Santiago *Phil.* 16°41N 121°33E **37** A6
Santiago → *Peru* 4°27S 77°38W **92** D3
Santiago de Compostela *Spain* 42°52N 8°37W **21** A1
Santiago de Cuba *Cuba* 20°0N 75°49W **88** C4
Santiago de los Caballeros *Dom. Rep.* 19°30N 70°40W **89** C5
Santiago del Estero *Argentina* 27°50S 64°15W **94** B3
Santiago del Estero □ *Argentina* 27°40S 63°15W **94** B3
Santiago Ixcuintla *Mexico* 21°49N 105°13W **86** C3
Santiago Jamiltepec *Mexico* 16°17N 97°49W **87** D5
Santiago Papasquiaro *Mexico* 25°3N 105°25W **86** C3
Santiago Pinotepa Nacional *Mexico* 16°19N 98°1W **87** D5
Santiaguillo, L. de *Mexico* 24°48N 104°48W **86** C4
Santo Amaro *Brazil* 12°30S 38°43W **93** F11
Santo Anastácio *Brazil* 21°58S 51°39W **95** A5
Santo André *Brazil* 23°39S 46°29W **95** A6
Santo Ângelo *Brazil* 28°15S 54°15W **95** B5
Santo Antão *Cabo Verde* 16°52N 25°10W **52** b
Sant' Antíoco *Italy* 39°4N 8°27E **22** E3
Santo Antônio do Içá *Brazil* 3°5S 67°57W **92** D5
Santo Antônio do Leverger *Brazil* 15°52S 56°5W **93** G7
Santo Domingo *Dom. Rep.* 18°30N 69°59W **89** C6
Santo Domingo *Mexico* 25°29N 111°55W **86** B2
Santo Domingo *Nic.* 12°14N 84°59W **88** D3
Santo Domingo, Cay *Bahamas* 21°25N 75°45W **88** B4
Santo Domingo de los Colorados *Ecuador* 0°15S 79°9W **92** D3
Santo Domingo Pueblo *U.S.A.* 35°31N 106°22W **77** J10
Santo Domingo Tehuantepec = Tehuantepec *Mexico* 16°21N 95°13W **87** D5
Santo Tomás *Mexico* 31°33N 116°24W **86** A1
Santo Tomás *Peru* 14°26S 72°8W **92** F4
Santo Tomé *Argentina* 28°40S 56°5W **95** B4
Santo Tomé de Guayana = Ciudad Guayana *Venezuela* 8°0N 62°30W **92** B6
Santoña *Spain* 43°29N 3°27W **21** A4
Santorini *Greece* 36°23N 25°27E **23** F11
Santos *Brazil* 24°0S 46°20W **95** A6
Santos Dumont *Brazil* 22°55S 43°10W **95** A7
Santuario de Aves Laguna Colorada △ *Bolivia* 22°10S 67°45W **94** A2
Sanuki *Japan* 34°19N 134°10E **29** G7
Sanur *Indonesia* 8°41S 115°15E **37** K18
Sanwer *India* 22°59N 75°50E **42** H6
Sanxia Shuiku *China* 30°3N 107°58E **34** B6
Sanxiang *China* 22°21N 113°25E **31** a
Sanya *China* 18°14N 109°29E **38** C7
Sanyuan *China* 34°35N 108°58E **32** G5
São Bernardo do Campo *Brazil* 23°45S 46°34W **95** A6
São Borja *Brazil* 28°39S 56°0W **95** B4
São Carlos *Brazil* 22°0S 47°50W **95** A6
São Cristóvão *Brazil* 11°1S 37°15W **93** F11
São Domingos *Brazil* 13°25S 46°19W **93** F9
São Filipe *Cabo Verde* 15°2N 24°30W **52** b
São Francisco *Brazil* 16°0S 44°50W **93** G10
São Francisco → *Brazil* 10°30S 36°24W **93** F11
São Francisco do Sul *Brazil* 26°15S 48°36W **95** B6
São Gabriel *Brazil* 30°20S 54°20W **95** C5
São Gonçalo *Brazil* 22°48S 43°5W **95** A7
São João da Boa Vista *Brazil* 22°0S 46°52W **95** A6
São João da Madeira *Portugal* 40°54N 8°30W **21** B1
São João del Rei *Brazil* 21°8S 44°15W **95** A7
São João do Araguaia *Brazil* 5°23S 48°46W **93** E9
São João do Piauí *Brazil* 8°21S 42°15W **93** E10
São Joaquim *Brazil* 28°18S 49°56W **95** B6
São Joaquim △ *Brazil* 28°12S 49°37W **95** B6
São Jorge *Azores* 38°38N 28°3W **52** a
São José *Brazil* 27°38S 48°39W **95** B5
São José do Norte *Brazil* 32°1S 52°3W **95** C5
São José do Rio Preto *Brazil* 20°50S 49°20W **95** A6
São José dos Campos *Brazil* 23°7S 45°52W **95** A6
São Leopoldo *Brazil* 29°50S 51°10W **95** B5
São Lourenço *Brazil* 22°7S 45°3W **95** A6
São Lourenço → *Brazil* 17°53S 57°27W **93** G7
São Lourenço do Sul *Brazil* 31°22S 51°58W **95** C5
São Luís *Brazil* 2°39S 44°15W **93** D10
São Luís Gonzaga *Brazil* 28°25S 55°0W **95** B5
São Marcos → *Brazil* 18°15S 47°37W **93** G9
São Marcos, B. de *Brazil* 2°0S 44°0W **93** D10
São Mateus *Brazil* 18°44S 39°50W **93** G11
São Mateus do Sul *Brazil* 25°52S 50°23W **95** B5
São Miguel *Azores* 37°47N 25°30W **52** a
São Miguel do Oeste *Brazil* 26°45S 53°34W **95** B5
São Nicolau *Cabo Verde* 16°20N 24°20W **52** b
São Paulo □ *Brazil* 22°0S 49°0W **95** A6
São Paulo de Olivença *Brazil* 3°27S 68°48W **92** D5
São Roque, C. de *Brazil* 5°30S 35°16W **93** E11
São Sebastião, I. de *Brazil* 23°50S 45°18W **95** A6
São Sebastião do Paraíso *Brazil* 20°54S 46°59W **95** A6
São Tiago *Cabo Verde* 15°0N 23°40W **52** b
São Tomé *São Tomé & Príncipe* 0°10N 6°39E **50** F4
São Tomé, C. de *Brazil* 22°0S 40°59W **95** A7
São Tomé & Príncipe ■ *Africa* 0°12N 6°39E **51** F4
São Vicente *Brazil* 23°57S 46°23W **95** A6
São Vicente *Cabo Verde* 17°0N 25°0W **52** b
São Vicente, C. de *Portugal* 37°0N 9°0W **21** D1
Saona, I. *Dom. Rep.* 18°10N 68°40W **89** C6
Saône → *France* 45°44N 4°50E **20** D6
Saonek *Indonesia* 0°22S 130°55E **37** E8
Sapam, Ao *Thailand* 8°0N 98°26E **39** a
Saparua *Indonesia* 3°33S 128°40E **37** E7
Sape *Indonesia* 8°34S 118°59E **37** F5
Sapele *Nigeria* 5°50N 5°40E **52** G7
Sapelo I. *U.S.A.* 31°25N 81°12W **85** F14
Saposoa *Peru* 6°55S 76°45W **92** E3
Sapphire *Australia* 23°28S 147°43E **62** C4
Sappho *U.S.A.* 48°4N 124°16W **78** B2
Sapporo *Japan* 43°0N 141°21E **28** C10
Sapporo New Chitose ✈ (CTS) *Japan* 42°46N 141°41E **28** C10
Sapt Kosi → *Nepal* 26°32N 86°56E **43** F12
Sapudi *Indonesia* 7°6S 114°20E **37** G16
Sapulpa *U.S.A.* 35°59N 96°5W **84** D6
Saqqez *Iran* 36°15N 46°20E **46** B5
Sar Dasht *Āzarbāyjān-e Gharbī, Iran* 36°9N 45°28E **46** B5
Sar Dasht *Khuzestān, Iran* 32°32N 48°52E **47** C6
Sar-e Pol □ *Afghan.* 36°20N 65°50E **40** B4
Sar Gachīneh = Yāsūj *Iran* 30°31N 51°31E **47** D6
Sar Planina *Macedonia* 42°0N 21°0E **23** C9
Sara Buri = Saraburi *Thailand* 14°30N 100°55E **38** E3
Sarāb *Iran* 37°55N 47°40E **46** B5
Sarābādī *Iraq* 33°1N 44°48E **46** C5
Saraburi *Thailand* 14°30N 100°55E **38** E3
Saradiya *India* 21°34N 70°2E **42** J4
Saragossa = Zaragoza *Spain* 41°39N 0°53W **21** B5
Saraguro *Ecuador* 3°35S 79°16W **92** D3
Sarahs *Turkmenistan* 36°32N 61°13E **47** B9
Sarai Naurang *Pakistan* 32°50N 70°47E **42** C4
Saraikela *India* 22°42N 85°56E **43** H11
Saraipali *India* 21°20N 82°59E **44** D6
Sarajevo *Bos.-H.* 43°52N 18°26E **23** C8
Sarakhs = Sarahs *Turkmenistan* 36°32N 61°13E **47** B9
Saran, Gunung *Indonesia* 0°30S 111°25E **36** E4
Saranac Lake *U.S.A.* 44°20N 74°10W **83** B10
Saranac Lakes *U.S.A.* 44°20N 74°28W **83** B10
Sarandí del Yí *Uruguay* 33°18S 55°38W **95** C4
Sarandí Grande *Uruguay* 33°44S 56°20W **94** C4
Sarangani B. *Phil.* 6°0N 125°13E **37** C7
Sarangani Is. *Phil.* 5°25N 125°25E **37** C7
Sarangarh *India* 21°30N 83°5E **44** D6
Saransk *Russia* 54°10N 45°10E **18** D8
Sarapul *Russia* 56°28N 53°48E **18** C9
Sarasota *U.S.A.* 27°20N 82°32W **85** H13
Saratoga *Calif., U.S.A.* 37°16N 122°2W **78** H4
Saratoga *Wyo., U.S.A.* 41°27N 106°49W **76** F10
Saratoga △ *U.S.A.* 43°0N 73°38W **83** D11
Saratoga L. *U.S.A.* 43°1N 73°44W **83** C11
Saratoga Springs *U.S.A.* 43°5N 73°47W **83** C11
Saratok *Malaysia* 1°55N 111°17E **36** D4
Saratov *Russia* 51°30N 46°2E **19** D8
Sarāvān *Iran* 27°25N 62°15E **47** E9
Saravane *Laos* 15°43N 106°25E **38** E6
Sarawak □ *Malaysia* 2°0N 113°0E **36** D4
Saray *Turkey* 41°26N 27°55E **23** D12
Sarayköy *Turkey* 37°55N 28°54E **23** F13
Sarbāz *Iran* 26°38N 61°19E **47** E9
Sarbīsheh *Iran* 32°30N 59°40E **47** C8
Sarda → *India* 27°21N 81°23E **43** F9
Sardar Sarovar Dam *India* 21°50N 73°50E **44** D1
Sardarshahr *India* 28°30N 74°29E **42** E6
Sardegna □ *Italy* 40°0N 9°0E **22** D3
Sardhana *India* 29°9N 77°39E **42** E7
Sardinia = Sardegna □ *Italy* 40°0N 9°0E **22** D3
Sardis *Turkey* 38°28N 27°58E **23** E12
Sārdūīyeh = Dar Mazār *Iran* 29°14N 57°20E **47** D8
Sarek △ *Sweden* 67°22N 17°35E **8** C17
Saren *Indonesia* 8°26S 115°34E **37** J18
Sarera, G. of *Indonesia* 2°0S 135°0E **58** B6
Sargasso Sea *Atl. Oc.* 27°0N 72°0W **66** G13
Sargodha *Pakistan* 32°10N 72°40E **42** C5
Sarh *Chad* 9°5N 18°23E **53** G9
Sārī *Iran* 36°30N 53°4E **47** B7
Saria *India* 21°38N 83°22E **43** J10
Sariab *Pakistan* 30°6N 66°59E **42** D2
Sarıgöl *Turkey* 38°14N 28°41E **23** E13
Sarikei *Malaysia* 2°8N 111°30E **36** D4
Sarila *India* 25°46N 79°41E **43** G8
Sarina *Australia* 21°22S 149°13E **62** C4
Sarita *U.S.A.* 27°13N 97°47W **84** H6
Sariwŏn *N. Korea* 38°31N 125°46E **33** E13
Sarju → *India* 27°21N 81°23E **43** F9
Sark *U.K.* 49°25N 2°22W **13** H5
Sarkari Tala *India* 27°39N 70°52E **42** F4
Şarköy *Turkey* 40°36N 27°6E **23** D12
Sarlat-la-Canéda *France* 44°54N 1°13E **20** D4
Sarmi *Indonesia* 1°49S 138°44E **37** E9
Sarmiento *Argentina* 45°35S 69°5W **96** F3
Särna *Sweden* 61°41N 13°8E **8** F15
Sarnia *Canada* 42°58N 82°23W **82** D2
Sarolangun *Indonesia* 2°19S 102°42E **36** E2
Saronikos Kolpos *Greece* 37°45N 23°45E **23** F10
Saros Körfezi *Turkey* 40°30N 26°15E **23** D12
Sarpsborg *Norway* 59°16N 11°7E **9** G14
Sarqan *Kazakhstan* 45°24N 79°55E **30** B4
Sarre = Saar → *Europe* 49°41N 6°32E **15** E6
Sarreguemines *France* 49°5N 7°4E **20** B7
Sartell *U.S.A.* 45°37N 94°12W **80** C6
Sarthe → *France* 47°33N 0°31W **20** C3
Saruna → *Pakistan* 26°31N 67°7E **42** F2
Sarvar *India* 26°4N 75°0E **42** F6
Sarvestān *Iran* 29°20N 53°10E **47** D7
Sary-Tash *Kyrgyzstan* 39°44N 73°15E **26** F8
Saryshaghan *Kazakhstan* 46°12N 73°38E **26** E8
Sasan Gir *India* 21°10N 70°36E **42** J4
Sasaram *India* 24°57N 84°5E **43** G11
Sasebo *Japan* 33°10N 129°43E **29** H4
Saser Kangri *India* 34°50N 77°50E **43** B7
Saskatchewan □ *Canada* 54°40N 106°0W **71** C7
Saskatchewan → *Canada* 53°37N 100°40W **71** C8
Saskatoon *Canada* 52°10N 106°38W **71** C7
Saskylakh *Russia* 71°55N 114°1E **27** B12
Saslaya △ *Nic.* 13°45N 85°4W **88** D2
Sasolburg *S. Africa* 26°46S 27°49E **57** C4
Sasovo *Russia* 54°25N 41°55E **18** D7
Sassandra *Côte d'Ivoire* 4°55N 6°8W **52** H4
Sassandra → *Côte d'Ivoire* 4°58N 6°5W **52** H4
Sássari *Italy* 40°43N 8°34E **22** D3
Sassie *Australia* 10°2S 142°51E **62** a
Sassnitz *Germany* 54°29N 13°39E **16** A7
Sassuolo *Italy* 44°33N 10°47E **22** B4
Sastamala *Finland* 61°20N 22°54E **8** F20
Sasvad *India* 18°20N 74°2E **44** E2
Sasyk, Ozero *Ukraine* 45°45N 29°40E **17** F15
Sata-Misaki *Japan* 31°0N 130°40E **29** J5
Satadougou *Mali* 12°25N 11°25W **52** F3
Satakunta □ *Finland* 61°45N 23°0E **8** F20
Satara *India* 17°44N 73°58E **44** F1
Satara *S. Africa* 24°29S 31°47E **57** B5
Satbarwa *India* 23°55N 84°16E **43** H11
Satevó *Mexico* 27°57N 106°7W **86** B3
Satilla → *U.S.A.* 30°59N 81°29W **85** F14
Satka *Russia* 55°3N 59°1E **18** C10
Satluj = Sutlej → *Pakistan* 29°23N 71°3E **42** E4
Satmala Hills *Maharashtra, India* 20°15N 74°40E **44** D2
Satmala Hills *Telangana, India* 19°45N 78°45E **44** E4
Satna *India* 24°35N 80°50E **43** G9
Sátoraljaújhely *Hungary* 48°25N 21°41E **17** D11
Satpura △ *India* 22°40N 78°15E **42** H8
Satpura Ra. *India* 21°25N 76°10E **44** D3
Satsuma-Sendai *Japan* 31°50N 130°20E **29** J5
Satsunan-Shotō *Japan* 30°0N 130°0E **29** K5
Sattahip *Thailand* 12°41N 100°54E **38** F3
Sattenapalle *India* 16°25N 80°6E **45** F5
Satu Mare *Romania* 47°46N 22°55E **17** E12
Satui *Indonesia* 3°50S 115°27E **36** E5
Satun *Thailand* 6°43N 100°2E **39** J3
Satupa'itea *Samoa* 13°45S 172°18W **59** b
Saturnina → *Brazil* 12°15S 58°10W **92** F7
Sauce *Argentina* 30°5S 58°46W **94** C4
Sauceda *Mexico* 25°46N 101°19W **86** B4
Saucillo *Mexico* 28°1N 105°17W **86** B3
Sauda *Norway* 59°40N 6°20E **9** G12
Sauðarkrókur *Iceland* 65°45N 19°40W **8** D4
Saudi Arabia ■ *Asia* 26°0N 44°0E **46** B3
Sauerland *Germany* 51°12N 7°59E **16** C4
Saugeen → *Canada* 44°30N 81°22W **82** B3
Saugerties *U.S.A.* 42°5N 73°57W **83** D11
Saugus *U.S.A.* 34°25N 118°32W **79** L8
Sauk Centre *U.S.A.* 45°44N 94°57W **80** C6
Sauk Rapids *U.S.A.* 45°35N 94°10W **80** C6
Sault Ste. Marie *Canada* 46°30N 84°20W **72** C3
Sault Ste. Marie *U.S.A.* 46°30N 84°21W **81** B11
Saumlaki *Indonesia* 7°55S 131°20E **37** F8
Saumur *France* 47°15N 0°5W **20** C3
Saundatti *India* 15°47N 75°7E **45** G2
Saunders, C. *N.Z.* 45°53S 170°45E **59** F3
Saunders I. *Antarctica* 57°48S 26°28W **5** B1
Saunders Pt. *Australia* 27°52S 125°38E **61** E4
Saurimo *Angola* 9°40S 20°12E **54** F4
Savá *Honduras* 15°32N 86°15W **88** C2
Sava → *Serbia* 44°50N 20°26E **23** B9
Savage *U.S.A.* 47°27N 104°21W **76** C11
Savage I. = Niue ☒ *Pac. Oc.* 19°2S 169°54W **65** J11
Savage River *Australia* 41°31S 145°14E **63** G4
Savai'i *Samoa* 13°28S 172°24W **59** b
Savalou *Benin* 7°57N 1°58E **52** G6
Savanna *U.S.A.* 42°5N 90°8W **80** D8
Savanna-la-Mar *Jamaica* 18°10N 78°10W **88** a
Savannah *Ga., U.S.A.* 32°5N 81°6W **85** E14
Savannah *Mo., U.S.A.* 39°56N 94°50W **80** F6
Savannah *Tenn., U.S.A.* 35°14N 88°15W **85** D10
Savannah → *U.S.A.* 32°2N 80°53W **85** E14
Savannakhet *Laos* 16°30N 104°49E **38** D5
Savant L. *Canada* 50°16N 90°44W **72** B1
Savant Lake *Canada* 50°14N 90°40W **72** B1
Savantvadi *India* 15°55N 73°54E **45** G1
Savanur *India* 14°59N 75°21E **45** G2
Savarkundla = Kundla *India* 21°21N 71°25E **42** J4
Savda *India* 21°9N 75°56E **44** D2
Save → *Mozam.* 21°16S 34°0E **57** B5
Sāveh *Iran* 35°2N 50°20E **47** C6
Savelugu *Ghana* 9°38N 0°54W **52** G5
Savo *Finland* 62°45N 27°30E **8** E22
Savoie □ *France* 45°26N 6°25E **20** D7
Savolax = Savo *Finland* 62°45N 27°30E **8** E22
Savona *Italy* 44°17N 8°30E **20** D8
Savona *U.S.A.* 42°17N 77°13W **82** D7
Savonlinna *Finland* 61°52N 28°53E **8** F23
Savoy = Savoie □ *France* 45°26N 6°25E **20** D7
Savur *Turkey* 37°34N 40°53E **46** B4
Savusavu *Fiji* 16°34S 179°15E **59** a
Savusavu B. *Fiji* 16°45S 179°15E **59** a
Savuti *Botswana* 18°37S 24°5E **56** A3
Sawahlunto *Indonesia* 0°40S 100°52E **36** E2
Sawai *Indonesia* 3°0S 129°5E **37** E7
Sawai Madhopur *India* 26°0N 76°25E **42** G7
Sawaleke *Fiji* 17°59S 179°18E **59** a
Sawang Daen Din *Thailand* 17°28N 103°28E **38** D4
Sawankhalok *Thailand* 17°19N 99°50E **38** D2
Sawara *Japan* 35°55N 140°30E **29** G10
Sawatch Range *U.S.A.* 39°0N 106°30W **76** G10
Sawel Mt. *U.K.* 54°50N 7°2W **10** B4
Sawi *Thailand* 10°14N 99°5E **39** G2
Sawtooth ⌂ *U.S.A.* 44°0N 114°50W **76** D6
Sawtooth Range *U.S.A.* 44°3N 114°58W **76** D6
Sawu *Indonesia* 10°35S 121°50E **37** F6
Sawu Sea *Indonesia* 9°30S 121°50E **37** F6
Saxby → *Australia* 18°25S 140°53E **62** B3
Saxmundham *U.K.* 52°13N 1°30E **13** E9
Saxony = Sachsen □ *Germany* 50°55N 13°10E **16** C7
Saxony, Lower = Niedersachsen □ *Germany* 52°50N 9°0E **16** B5
Saxton *U.S.A.* 40°13N 78°15W **82** F6
Sayabec *Canada* 48°35N 67°41W **73** C6
Sayaboury *Laos* 19°15N 101°45E **38** C3
Sayán *Peru* 11°8S 77°12W **92** F3
Sayan, Vostochnyy *Russia* 54°0N 96°0E **27** D10
Sayan, Zapadnyy *Russia* 52°30N 94°0E **30** A7
Sayanogorsk *Russia* 53°5N 91°23E **27** D10
Saydā *Lebanon* 33°35N 35°25E **48** B4
Sayhandulaan = Öldziyt *Mongolia* 44°40N 109°1E **32** B5
Sayhūt *Yemen* 15°12N 51°10E **49** D5
Saylac *Somalia* 11°21N 43°30E **49** E3
Saynshand = Buyant-Uhaa *Mongolia* 44°55N 110°11E **32** B6
Sayre *Okla., U.S.A.* 35°18N 99°38W **84** D5
Sayre *Pa., U.S.A.* 41°59N 76°32W **83** E8
Sayreville *U.S.A.* 40°28N 74°22W **83** F10
Sayula *Mexico* 19°52N 103°36W **86** D4
Say'ūn *Yemen* 15°56N 48°47E **49** D4
Sayward *Canada* 50°21N 125°55W **70** C3
Sazanit *Albania* 40°30N 19°20E **23** D8
Sázava → *Czechia* 49°53N 14°24E **16** D8
Sazin *Pakistan* 35°35N 73°30E **43** B5
Scafell Pike *U.K.* 54°27N 3°14W **12** C4
Scalloway *U.K.* 60°9N 1°17W **11** A7
Scalpay *U.K.* 57°18N 6°0W **11** D3
Scandia *Canada* 50°20N 112°2W **70** C6
Scandicci *Italy* 43°45N 11°11E **22** C4
Scandinavia *Europe* 64°0N 12°0E **8** E15
Scapa Flow *U.K.* 58°53N 3°3W **11** C5
Scappoose *U.S.A.* 45°45N 122°53W **78** E4
Scarba *U.K.* 56°11N 5°43W **11** E3
Scarborough *Trin. & Tob.* 11°11N 60°42W **93** J16
Scarborough *U.K.* 54°17N 0°24W **12** C7
Scariff I. *Ireland* 51°44N 10°15W **10** E1
Scarp *U.K.* 58°1N 7°8W **11** C1
Scebeli = Shabeelle → *Somalia* 2°0N 44°0E **49** G3
Schaffhausen *Switz.* 47°42N 8°39E **20** C8
Schagen *Neths.* 52°49N 4°48E **15** B4
Schaghticoke *U.S.A.* 42°54N 73°35W **83** D11
Schefferville *Canada* 54°48N 66°50W **73** B6
Schelde → *Belgium* 51°15N 4°16E **15** C4
Schell Creek Ra. *U.S.A.* 39°25N 114°40W **76** G6
Schellsburg *U.S.A.* 40°3N 78°39W **82** F6
Schenectady *U.S.A.* 42°49N 73°57W **83** D11
Schenevus *U.S.A.* 42°33N 74°50W **83** D10
Schiedam *Neths.* 51°55N 4°25E **15** C4
Schiermonnikoog *Neths.* 53°30N 6°15E **15** A6
Schiermonnikoog △ *Neths.* 53°30N 6°15E **15** A6
Schio *Italy* 45°43N 11°21E **22** B4
Schleswig *Germany* 54°31N 9°34E **16** A5
Schleswig-Holstein □ *Germany* 54°30N 9°30E **16** A5
Schœlcher *Martinique* 14°36N 61°7W **88** c
Schoharie *U.S.A.* 42°40N 74°19W **83** D10
Schoharie Cr. → *U.S.A.* 42°57N 74°18W **83** D10
Schokland *Neths.* 52°38N 5°46E **15** B5
Scholls *U.S.A.* 45°24N 122°56W **78** E4
Schouten I. *Australia* 42°20S 148°20E **63** G4
Schouten Is. = Supiori *Indonesia* 1°0S 136°0E **37** E9
Schouwen *Neths.* 51°43N 3°45E **15** C3
Schreiber *Canada* 48°45N 87°20W **72** C2
Schroffenstein *Namibia* 27°11S 18°42E **56** C2
Schroon Lake *U.S.A.* 43°50N 73°46W **83** C11
Schuler *Canada* 50°20N 110°6W **71** C6
Schumacher *Canada* 48°30N 81°16W **72** C3
Schurz *U.S.A.* 38°57N 118°49W **76** G4
Schuyler *U.S.A.* 41°27N 97°4W **80** E5
Schuylerville *U.S.A.* 43°6N 73°35W **83** C11
Schuylkill → *U.S.A.* 39°53N 75°12W **83** G9
Schuylkill Haven *U.S.A.* 40°37N 76°11W **83** F8
Schwäbische Alb *Germany* 48°20N 9°30E **16** D5
Schwaner, Pegunungan *Indonesia* 1°0S 112°30E **36** E4
Schwarzrand *Namibia* 25°37S 16°50E **56** C2
Schwarzwald *Germany* 48°30N 8°20E **16** D5
Schwatka Mts. *U.S.A.* 67°20N 156°30W **74** B8
Schwedt *Germany* 53°3N 14°16E **16** B8
Schweinfurt *Germany* 50°3N 10°14E **16** C6
Schweiz = Switzerland ■ *Europe* 46°30N 8°0E **20** C8
Schweizer-Reneke *S. Africa* 27°11S 25°18E **56** C4
Schwenningen = Villingen-Schwenningen *Germany* 48°3N 8°26E **16** D5
Schwerin *Germany* 53°36N 11°22E **16** B6
Schwyz *Switz.* 47°2N 8°39E **20** C8
Sciacca *Italy* 37°31N 13°3E **22** F5
Scilla *Italy* 38°15N 15°43E **22** E6
Scilly, Isles of *U.K.* 49°56N 6°22W **13** H1
Scioto → *U.S.A.* 38°44N 83°1W **81** F12
Scituate *U.S.A.* 42°12N 70°44W **83** D14
Scobey *U.S.A.* 48°47N 105°25W **76** B11
Scone *Australia* 32°5S 150°52E **63** E5
Scone *U.K.* 56°25N 3°24W **11** E5
Scoresbysund = Ittoqqortoormiit *Greenland* 70°20N 23°0W **4** B6
Scotia *Calif., U.S.A.* 40°29N 124°6W **76** F1
Scotia *N.Y., U.S.A.* 42°50N 73°58W **83** D11
Scotia Sea *Antarctica* 56°5S 56°0W **5** B18
Scotland *Canada* 43°1N 80°22W **82** C4
Scotland □ *U.K.* 57°0N 4°0W **11** E5
Scott *Antarctica* 77°50S 166°45E **5** D11
Scott, C. *Australia* 13°30S 129°49E **60** B4
Scott City *U.S.A.* 38°29N 100°54W **80** F3
Scott Glacier *Antarctica* 66°15S 100°5E **5** C8
Scott I. *Antarctica* 67°0S 179°0E **5** C11
Scott Is. *Canada* 50°48N 128°40W **70** C3
Scott L. *Canada* 59°55N 106°18W **71** B7
Scott Reef *Australia* 14°0S 121°50E **60** B3
Scottburgh *S. Africa* 30°15S 30°47E **57** D5
Scottdale *U.S.A.* 40°6N 79°35W **82** F5
Scottish Borders □ *U.K.* 55°35N 2°50W **11** F6
Scotts Valley *U.S.A.* 37°3N 122°1W **78** H4
Scottsbluff *U.S.A.* 41°52N 103°40W **80** E2
Scottsboro *U.S.A.* 34°40N 86°2W **85** D11
Scottsburg *U.S.A.* 38°41N 85°47W **81** F11
Scottsdale *Australia* 41°9S 147°31E **63** G4
Scottsdale *U.S.A.* 33°40N 111°53W **77** K8
Scottsville *Ky., U.S.A.* 36°45N 86°11W **80** G10
Scottsville *N.Y., U.S.A.* 43°2N 77°47W **82** C7
Scottville *U.S.A.* 43°58N 86°17W **80** D10
Scranton *U.S.A.* 41°25N 75°40W **83** E9
Scugog, L. *Canada* 44°10N 78°55W **82** B6
Scunthorpe *U.K.* 53°36N 0°39W **12** D7
Scutari = Shkodër *Albania* 42°4N 19°32E **23** C8
Sea Is. *U.S.A.* 31°30N 81°7W **85** F14
Seabrook, L. *Australia* 30°55S 119°40E **61** F2
Seaford *U.K.* 50°47N 0°7E **13** G8
Seaford *U.S.A.* 38°39N 75°37W **81** F16
Seaforth *Australia* 20°55S 148°57E **62** b
Seaforth *Canada* 43°35N 81°25W **82** C3
Seaforth, L. *U.K.* 57°52N 6°36W **11** D2
Seagraves *U.S.A.* 32°57N 102°34W **84** E3
Seaham *U.K.* 54°50N 1°20W **12** C6
Seal → *Canada* 59°4N 94°48W **71** B10
Seal L. *Canada* 54°20N 61°30W **73** B7
Sealy *U.S.A.* 29°47N 96°9W **84** G6
Searchlight *U.S.A.* 35°28N 114°55W **79** K12
Searcy *U.S.A.* 35°15N 91°44W **84** D9
Searles L. *U.S.A.* 35°44N 117°21W **79** K9
Seascale *U.K.* 54°24N 3°29W **12** C4
Seaside *Calif., U.S.A.* 36°37N 121°50W **78** J5
Seaside *Oreg., U.S.A.* 46°0N 123°56W **78** E3
Seaspray *Australia* 38°25S 147°15E **63** F4
Seattle *U.S.A.* 47°36N 122°19W **78** C4
Seattle-Tacoma Int. ✈ (SEA) *U.S.A.* 47°27N 122°18W **78** C4
Seba *Indonesia* 10°29S 121°50E **60** B3
Sebago L. *U.S.A.* 43°52N 70°34W **83** C14
Sebago Lake *U.S.A.* 43°51N 70°34W **83** C14
Sebastián Vizcaíno, B. *Mexico* 28°0N 114°30W **86** B2
Sebastopol = Sevastopol *Ukraine* 44°35N 33°30E **19** F5
Sebastopol *U.S.A.* 38°24N 122°49W **78** G4
Sebewaing *U.S.A.* 43°44N 83°27W **81** D12
Sebha = Sabhā *Libya* 27°9N 14°29E **53** C8
Şebinkarahisar *Turkey* 40°22N 38°28E **19** F6
Sebring *Fla., U.S.A.* 27°30N 81°27W **85** H14
Sebring *Ohio, U.S.A.* 40°55N 81°2W **82** F3
Sebringville *Canada* 43°24N 81°4W **82** C3
Sebta = Ceuta *N. Afr.* 35°52N 5°18W **21** E3
Sebuku *Indonesia* 3°30S 116°25E **36** E5
Sechelt *Canada* 49°25N 123°42W **70** D4
Sechura, Desierto de *Peru* 6°0S 80°30W **92** E2
Secretary I. *N.Z.* 45°15S 166°56E **59** F1
Secunderabad *India* 17°28N 78°30E **44** F4
Security *U.S.A.* 38°45N 104°45W **76** G11
Sedalia *U.S.A.* 38°42N 93°14W **80** F7
Sedam *India* 17°11N 77°17E **44** E3
Sedan *France* 49°43N 4°57E **20** B6
Sedan *U.S.A.* 37°8N 96°11W **80** G5
Sedbergh *U.K.* 54°20N 2°31W **12** C5
Seddon *N.Z.* 41°40S 174°7E **59** D5
Seddonville *N.Z.* 41°33S 172°1E **59** D4
Sedé Boqér *Israel* 30°52N 34°47E **48** E3
Sedeh *Fārs, Iran* 30°45N 52°11E **47** D7
Sedeh *Khorāsān, Iran* 33°20N 59°14E **47** C8
Sederot *Israel* 31°32N 34°37E **48** D3
Sédhiou *Senegal* 12°44N 15°30W **52** F2
Sedley *Canada* 50°10N 104°0W **71** C8
Sedona *U.S.A.* 34°52N 111°46W **77** J8
Sedova, Pik *Russia* 73°29N 54°58E **26** B6
Sedro-Woolley *U.S.A.* 48°30N 122°14W **78** B4
Seeheim *Namibia* 26°50S 17°45E **56** C2
Seeis *Namibia* 22°29S 17°39E **56** B2
Seekoei → *S. Africa* 30°18S 25°1E **56** D4
Seeley's Bay *Canada* 44°29N 76°14W **83** B8
Seemandhra = Andhra Pradesh □ *India* 18°0N 79°0E **44** F4
Seferihisar *Turkey* 38°10N 26°50E **23** E12
Sefophe *Botswana* 22°11S 27°58E **57** B4
Seg-ozero *Russia* 63°20N 33°46E **18** B5
Segamat *Malaysia* 2°30N 102°50E **39** L4
Segesta *Italy* 37°56N 12°50E **22** F5
Seget *Indonesia* 1°24S 130°58E **37** E8
Segezha *Russia* 63°44N 34°19E **18** B5
Ségou *Mali* 13°30N 6°16W **52** F4
Segovia = Coco → *Cent. Amer.* 15°0N 83°8W **88** D3
Segovia *Spain* 40°57N 4°10W **21** B3
Segre → *Spain* 41°40N 0°43E **21** B6
Seguam I. *U.S.A.* 52°19N 172°30W **74** E5
Séguéla *Côte d'Ivoire* 7°55N 6°40W **52** G4
Seguin *U.S.A.* 29°34N 97°58W **84** G6
Segundo → *Argentina* 30°53S 62°44W **94** C3
Segura → *Spain* 38°3N 0°44W **21** C5
Seh Konj, Kūh-e *Iran* 30°6N 57°30E **47** D8
Seh Qal'eh *Iran* 33°40N 58°24E **47** C8
Sehitwa *Botswana* 20°30S 22°30E **56** B3
Sehlabathebe △ *Lesotho* 29°53S 29°7E **57** C4
Sehore *India* 23°10N 77°5E **42** H7
Sehwan *Pakistan* 26°28N 67°53E **42** F2
Seikan Tunnel *Japan* 41°28N 140°10E **28** D10

Seil U.K. 56°18N 5°38W 11 E3
Seiland Norway 70°25N 23°15E 8 A20
Seiling U.S.A. 36°9N 98°56W 84 C5
Seinäjoki Finland 62°40N 22°51E 8 E20
Seine → France 49°26N 0°26E 20 B4
Seistan = Sīstān Asia 30°50N 61°0E 47 D9
Seistan, Daryācheh-ye = Sīstān, Daryācheh-ye Iran 31°0N 61°0E 47 D9
Seitseminen △ Finland 61°55N 23°25E 8 F20
Sekayu Indonesia 2°51S 103°51E 36 E2
Sekondi-Takoradi Ghana 4°58N 1°45W 52 H5
Sekudai Malaysia 1°32N 103°39E 39 d
Sekuma Botswana 24°36S 23°50E 56 B3
Selah U.S.A. 46°39N 120°32W 76 C3
Selama Malaysia 5°12N 100°42E 39 K3
Selangor □ Malaysia 3°10N 101°30E 39 L3
Selaru Indonesia 8°9S 131°0E 37 F8
Selatan, Selat Malaysia 5°15N 100°20E 39 c
Selawik L. U.S.A. 66°30N 160°45W 74 B7
Selby U.K. 53°47N 1°5W 12 D6
Selby U.S.A. 45°31N 100°2W 80 C3
Selçuk Turkey 37°56N 27°22E 23 F12
Selden U.S.A. 39°33N 100°34W 80 F3
Sele → Italy 40°29N 14°56E 22 D6
Selebi-Phikwe Botswana 21°58S 27°48E 57 B4
Selemdzha → Russia 51°42N 128°53E 27 D13
Selenga = Selenge Mörön → Asia 52°16N 106°16E 30 A10
Selenge Mörön → Asia 52°16N 106°16E 30 A10
Seletan, Tanjung Indonesia 4°10S 114°40E 36 E4
Sélibabi Mauritania 15°10N 12°15W 52 E3
Seligman U.S.A. 35°20N 112°53W 77 J7
Selîma Sudan 21°22N 29°19E 53 D11
Selinda Spillway → Botswana 18°35S 23°10E 56 A3
Selinsgrove U.S.A. 40°48N 76°52W 82 F8
Selkirk Man., Canada 50°10N 96°55W 71 C9
Selkirk Ont., Canada 42°49N 79°56W 82 D5
Selkirk U.K. 55°33N 2°50W 11 F6
Selkirk I. = Horse I. Canada 53°20N 99°6W 71 C9
Selkirk Mts. Canada 51°15N 117°40W 68 G8
Sellafield U.K. 54°25N 3°29W 12 C4
Sells U.S.A. 31°55N 111°53W 77 L8
Selma Ala., U.S.A. 32°25N 87°1W 85 E11
Selma Calif., U.S.A. 36°34N 119°37W 78 J7
Selma N.C., U.S.A. 35°32N 78°17W 85 D15
Selmer U.S.A. 35°10N 88°36W 85 D10
Selpele Indonesia 0°1S 130°5E 37 E8
Selsey Bill U.K. 50°43N 0°47W 13 G7
Seltso Russia 53°22N 34°4E 18 D5
Selu Indonesia 7°32S 130°55E 37 F8
Selva Argentina 29°50S 62°0W 94 B3
Selva Lancandona = Montes Azules ⌓ Mexico 16°21N 91°3W 87 D6
Selvagens, Ilhas Madeira 30°5N 15°55W 52 B2
Selvas Brazil 6°30S 67°0W 92 E5
Selwyn L. Canada 60°0N 104°30W 71 B8
Selwyn Mts. Canada 63°0N 130°0W 68 E5
Selwyn Ra. Australia 21°10S 140°0E 62 C3
Seman → Albania 40°47N 19°30E 23 D8
Semarang Indonesia 7°0S 110°26E 37 G14
Semarapura = Klungkung Indonesia 8°32S 115°24E 37 K18
Sembung Indonesia 8°28S 115°11E 37 J18
Semeru Indonesia 8°4S 112°55E 37 H15
Semey Kazakhstan 50°30N 80°10E 30 A5
Seminoe Res. U.S.A. 42°9N 106°55W 76 E10
Seminole Okla., U.S.A. 35°14N 96°41W 84 D6
Seminole Tex., U.S.A. 32°43N 102°39W 84 E3
Seminole Draw → U.S.A. 32°27N 102°20W 84 E3
Semipalatinsk = Semey Kazakhstan 50°30N 80°10E 30 A5
Semirara Is. Phil. 12°0N 121°20E 37 B6
Semisopochnoi I. U.S.A. 51°55N 179°36E 74 E3
Semitau Indonesia 0°29N 111°57E 36 D4
Semmering P. Austria 47°41N 15°45E 16 E8
Semnān Iran 35°40N 53°23E 47 C7
Semnān □ Iran 36°0N 54°0E 47 C7
Semporna Malaysia 4°30N 118°33E 37 D5
Semuda Indonesia 2°51S 112°58E 36 E4
Sen → Cambodia 12°32N 104°28E 38 F5
Senā Iran 28°27N 51°36E 47 D6
Sena Madureira Brazil 9°5S 68°45W 92 E5
Senador Pompeu Brazil 5°40S 39°20W 93 E11
Senang, Pulau Singapore 1°11N 103°52E 39 d
Senanga Zambia 16°7S 23°16E 55 H4
Senatobia U.S.A. 34°37N 89°58W 85 D10
Sendai = Satsuma-Sendai Japan 31°50N 130°20E 29 J5
Sendai Japan 38°15N 140°53E 28 E10
Sendai-Wan Japan 38°15N 141°0E 28 E10
Sendhwa India 21°41N 75°6E 42 J6
Sendurjana India 21°32N 78°17E 44 D4
Seneca U.S.A. 34°41N 82°57W 85 D13
Seneca Falls U.S.A. 42°55N 76°48W 83 D8
Seneca L. U.S.A. 42°40N 76°54W 82 D8
Senecaville L. U.S.A. 39°55N 81°25W 82 G3
Senegal ■ W. Afr. 14°30N 14°30W 52 F3
Sénégal → W. Afr. 15°48N 16°32W 52 E2
Senegambia Africa 12°45N 12°0W 50 E2
Senekal S. Africa 28°20S 27°36E 57 C4
Senge Khambab = Indus → Pakistan 24°20N 67°47E 42 G2
Senggigi Indonesia 8°29S 116°2E 37 J19
Senhor-do-Bonfim Brazil 10°30S 40°10W 93 F10
Senigállia Italy 43°43N 13°13E 22 C5
Senj Croatia 45°0N 14°58E 16 F8
Senja Norway 69°25N 17°30E 8 B17
Senkaku-Shotō E. China Sea 25°45N 123°30E 29 M1
Senlis France 49°13N 2°35E 20 B5
Senmonorom Cambodia 12°27N 107°12E 38 F6
Senneterre Canada 48°25N 77°15W 72 C4
Seno Laos 16°35N 104°50E 38 D5
Senqu = Orange → S. Africa 28°41S 16°28E 56 C2
Sens France 48°11N 3°15E 20 B5
Senta Serbia 45°55N 20°3E 23 B9
Sentinel U.S.A. 32°52N 113°13W 77 K7
Senwabarana S. Africa 23°17S 29°7E 57 B4
Seo de Urgel = La Seu d'Urgell Spain 42°22N 1°23E 21 A6
Seogwipo S. Korea 33°13N 126°34E 33 H14
Seohara India 29°15N 78°33E 43 E8
Seonath → India 21°44N 82°28E 43 J10
Seondha India 26°9N 78°48E 43 F8
Seongnam S. Korea 37°26N 127°8E 33 F14
Seoni India 22°5N 79°30E 43 H8
Seoni Malwa India 22°27N 77°28E 42 H8
Seonsan S. Korea 36°14N 128°17E 33 F15
Seoriuarayan India 21°45N 82°34E 44 D6
Seosan S. Korea 36°47N 126°27E 33 F14
Sepang Malaysia 2°49N 101°44E 39 L3
Sepīdān Iran 30°20N 52°5E 47 D7
Sepo-ri N. Korea 38°57N 127°25E 33 E14
Sepone Laos 16°45N 106°13E 38 D6
Sept-Îles Canada 50°13N 66°22W 73 B6
Sequim U.S.A. 48°5N 123°6W 78 B3
Sequoia △ U.S.A. 36°30N 118°30W 78 J8
Seraing Belgium 50°35N 5°32E 15 D5
Seram Indonesia 3°10S 129°0E 37 E7
Seram Sea Indonesia 2°30S 128°30E 37 E7
Serampore = Shrirampur India 22°44N 88°21E 43 H13
Serang Indonesia 6°8S 106°10E 37 G12
Serasan Indonesia 2°29N 109°4E 36 D3
Serbia ■ Europe 43°20N 20°0E 23 B9
Serdar Turkmenistan 39°4N 56°23E 47 B8
Serdobsk Russia 52°28N 44°10E 18 D7
Seremban Malaysia 2°43N 101°53E 39 L3
Serengeti Plain Tanzania 2°40S 35°0E 54 E7
Sereth = Siret → Romania 45°24N 28°1E 17 F14
Sergeya Kirova, Ostrova Russia 77°30N 89°0E 27 B10
Sergino Russia 62°25N 65°12E 26 C7
Sergipe □ Brazil 10°30S 37°30W 93 F11
Sergiyev Posad Russia 56°20N 38°10E 18 C6
Serhetabat Turkmenistan 35°20N 62°18E 47 C9
Seria Brunei 4°37N 114°23E 36 D4
Serian Malaysia 1°10N 110°31E 36 D4
Serifos Greece 37°9N 24°30E 23 F11
Sérigny → Canada 56°47N 66°0W 73 A6
Seringapatam Reef Australia 13°38S 122°5E 60 B3
Seririt Indonesia 8°12S 114°56E 37 J17
Serkout Algeria 23°56N 6°47E 52 D7
Sermata Indonesia 8°15S 128°50E 37 F7
Sermersuaq Greenland 79°30N 62°0W 69 B19
Serov Russia 59°29N 60°35E 18 C11
Serowe Botswana 22°25S 26°43E 56 B4
Serpentine Lakes Australia 28°30S 129°10E 61 E4
Serpent's Mouth = Sierpe, Bocas de la Venezuela 10°0N 61°30W 93 L15
Serpukhov Russia 54°55N 37°28E 18 D6
Serra do Navio Brazil 0°59N 52°3W 93 C8
Serranía San Luís △ Paraguay 22°35S 57°22W 94 A4
Serranía San Rafael △ Paraguay 26°30S 56°0W 95 B4
Serres Greece 41°5N 23°31E 23 D10
Serrezuela Argentina 30°40S 65°20W 94 C2
Serrinha Brazil 11°39S 39°0W 93 F11
Sertanópolis Brazil 23°4S 51°2W 95 A5
Sêrtar China 32°20N 100°41E 34 A3
Serua Indonesia 6°18S 130°1E 37 F8
Serui Indonesia 1°53S 136°10E 37 E9
Serule Botswana 21°57S 27°20E 56 B4
Sesepe Indonesia 1°30S 127°59E 37 E7
Sesfontein Namibia 19°7S 13°39E 56 A1
Sesheke Zambia 17°29S 24°13E 56 A3
Setana Japan 42°26N 139°51E 28 C9
Sète France 43°25N 3°42E 20 E5
Sete Lagoas Brazil 19°27S 44°16W 93 G10
Seti → Nepal 28°59N 81°8E 43 E9
Sétif Algeria 36°9N 5°26E 52 A7
Seto Japan 35°14N 137°6E 29 G8
Setonaikai Japan 34°20N 133°30E 29 G6
Setonaikai △ Japan 34°15N 133°15E 29 G6
Settat Morocco 33°0N 7°40W 52 B4
Setting L. Canada 55°0N 98°38W 71 C9
Settle U.K. 54°5N 2°16W 12 C5
Settlement, The Br. Virgin Is. 18°43N 64°22W 89 e
Settlers S. Africa 25°2S 28°30E 57 C4
Setúbal Portugal 38°30N 8°58W 21 C1
Setúbal, B. de Portugal 38°40N 8°56W 21 C1
Seul, Lac Canada 50°20N 92°30W 72 B1
Sevan, Ozero = Sevana Lich Armenia 40°30N 45°20E 46 A5
Sevana Lich Armenia 40°30N 45°20E 46 A5
Sevastopol Ukraine 44°35N 33°30E 19 F5
Seven Sisters Canada 54°56N 128°10W 70 C3
Severn → Canada 56°2N 87°36W 72 A2
Severn → U.K. 51°35N 2°40W 13 F5
Severnaya Zemlya Russia 79°0N 100°0E 27 B11
Severnyye Uvaly Russia 60°0N 50°0E 18 C8
Severo-Kurilsk Russia 50°40N 156°8E 27 D16
Severo-Yeniseyskiy Russia 60°22N 93°1E 27 C10
Severo-Zapadnyy □ Russia 65°0N 40°0E 26 C4
Severobaykalsk Russia 55°39N 109°19E 27 D11
Severodvinsk Russia 64°27N 39°58E 18 B6
Severomorsk Russia 69°5N 33°27E 8 B25
Severouralsk Russia 60°9N 59°57E 18 B10
Seversk Russia 56°36N 84°49E 26 D9
Sevier → U.S.A. 39°4N 113°6W 76 G7
Sevier Desert U.S.A. 39°40N 112°45W 76 G7
Sevier L. U.S.A. 38°54N 113°9W 76 G7
Sevilla Spain 37°23N 5°58W 21 D2
Seville = Sevilla Spain 37°23N 5°58W 21 D2
Sevlievo Bulgaria 43°2N 25°6E 23 C11
Sewani India 28°58N 75°39E 42 E6
Seward Alaska, U.S.A. 60°7N 149°27W 68 E2
Seward Nebr., U.S.A. 40°55N 97°6W 80 E5
Seward Pa., U.S.A. 40°25N 79°1W 82 F5
Seward Peninsula U.S.A. 65°30N 166°0W 74 B6
Sewell Chile 34°10S 70°23W 94 C1
Sewer Indonesia 5°53S 134°40E 37 F8
Sewickley U.S.A. 40°32N 80°12W 82 F4
Sexsmith Canada 55°21N 118°47W 70 B5
Seychelles ■ Ind. Oc. 5°0S 56°0E 55 b
Seyðisfjörður Iceland 65°16N 13°57W 8 D7
Seydişehir Turkey 37°25N 31°51E 19 G5
Seydvān Iran 38°34N 45°2E 46 B5
Seyhan → Turkey 36°43N 34°53E 46 B2
Seym → Ukraine 51°27N 32°34E 19 D5
Seymour Australia 37°2S 145°10E 63 F4
Seymour S. Africa 32°33S 26°46E 57 D4
Seymour Conn., U.S.A. 41°24N 73°4W 83 E11
Seymour Ind., U.S.A. 38°58N 85°53W 81 F11
Seymour Tex., U.S.A. 33°35N 99°16W 84 E5
Sfântu Gheorghe Romania 45°52N 25°48E 17 F13
Sfax Tunisia 34°49N 10°48E 53 B8
Sha Tau Kok China 22°33N 114°13E 31 a
Sha Xi → China 26°35N 118°0E 35 D12
Sha Xian China 26°23N 117°45E 35 D11
Shaanxi □ China 35°0N 109°0E 32 G5
Shaba = Katanga Dem. Rep. of the Congo 8°0S 25°0E 54 F5
Shabeelle → Somalia 2°0N 44°0E 49 G3
Shabogamo L. Canada 53°15N 66°30W 73 B6
Shabunda Dem. Rep. of the Congo 2°40S 27°16E 54 E5
Shache China 38°20N 77°10E 30 D4
Shackleton Fracture Zone S. Ocean 60°0S 60°0W 5 B18
Shackleton Ice Shelf Antarctica 66°0S 100°0E 5 C8
Shackleton Inlet Antarctica 83°0S 160°0E 5 E11
Shādegān Iran 30°40N 48°38E 47 D6
Shadi China 26°7N 114°47E 35 D10
Shadi India 33°24N 77°14E 43 C7
Shadrinsk Russia 56°5N 63°32E 26 D7
Shadyside U.S.A. 39°58N 80°45W 82 G4
Shafter U.S.A. 35°30N 119°16W 79 K7
Shaftesbury U.K. 51°0N 2°11W 13 F5
Shaftsbury U.S.A. 43°0N 73°11W 83 D11
Shagram Pakistan 36°24N 72°20E 43 A5
Shah Alam Malaysia 3°5N 101°32E 39 L3
Shah Alizai Pakistan 29°25N 66°33E 42 E2
Shah Bunder Pakistan 24°13N 67°56E 42 G2
Shahabad Karnataka, India 17°10N 76°54E 44 F3
Shahabad Punjab, India 30°10N 76°55E 42 D7
Shahabad Raj., India 25°15N 77°11E 42 G7
Shahabad Ut. P., India 27°36N 79°56E 43 F8
Shahada India 21°33N 74°30E 44 D2
Shahadpur Pakistan 25°55N 68°35E 42 G3
Shahapur India 15°50N 74°34E 45 G2
Shahbā' Syria 32°52N 36°38E 48 C5
Shahdād Iran 30°30N 57°40E 47 D8
Shahdād, Namakzār-e Iran 30°20N 58°20E 47 D8
Shahdadkot Pakistan 27°50N 67°55E 42 F2
Shahdol India 23°19N 81°26E 43 H9
Shahe China 37°0N 114°32E 32 F8
Shahganj India 26°3N 82°44E 43 F10
Shahgarh India 27°15N 69°50E 42 F3
Shahid Rajaee Port = Bandar Shahid Rajaee Iran 27°7N 56°4E 47 E8
Shāhīn Shahr Iran 32°49N 51°32E 47 C6
Shahjahanpur India 27°54N 79°57E 43 F8
Shahpur = Salmās Iran 38°11N 44°47E 46 B5
Shahpur Karnataka, India 16°40N 76°48E 44 F3
Shahpur Mad. P., India 22°12N 77°58E 42 H7
Shahpur Baluchistan, Pakistan 28°46N 68°27E 42 E3
Shahpur Punjab, Pakistan 32°17N 72°26E 42 C5
Shahpur Chakar Pakistan 26°9N 68°39E 42 F3
Shahpura Mad. P., India 23°10N 80°45E 43 H9
Shahpura Raj., India 25°38N 74°56E 42 G6
Shahr-e Bābak Iran 30°7N 55°9E 47 D7
Shahr-e Kord Iran 32°15N 50°55E 47 C6
Shahr-I Sokhta Iran 30°34N 61°21E 47 D9
Shāhrakht Iran 33°38N 60°16E 47 C9
Shāhrezā = Qomsheh Iran 32°0N 51°55E 47 D6
Shahrig Pakistan 30°15N 67°40E 42 D2
Shāhrud = Emāmrūd Iran 36°30N 55°0E 47 B7
Shahukou China 40°20N 112°18E 32 D7
Shaikhabad Afghan. 34°2N 68°45E 42 B3
Shajapur India 23°27N 76°21E 42 H7
Shajing China 22°44N 113°48E 31 a
Shakargarh Pakistan 32°17N 75°10E 42 C6
Shakawe Botswana 18°28S 21°49E 56 A3
Shaker Heights U.S.A. 41°28N 81°32W 82 E3
Shakhtersk Russia 49°10N 142°8E 27 E15
Shakhty Russia 47°40N 40°16E 19 E7
Shakhunya Russia 57°40N 46°46E 18 C8
Shaki Nigeria 8°41N 3°21E 52 G6
Shakotan-Hantō Japan 43°10N 140°30E 28 C10
Shaksam Valley Asia 36°0N 76°20E 43 A7
Shallow Lake Canada 44°36N 81°5W 82 B3
Shalqar Kazakhstan 47°48N 59°39E 26 E6
Shaluli Shan China 30°40N 99°55E 34 B2
Shām Iran 26°39N 57°21E 47 E8
Shām, Bādiyat ash Asia 32°0N 40°0E 46 C3
Shamâl Sînî □ Egypt 30°30N 33°30E 48 E2
Shamattawa Canada 55°51N 92°5W 72 A1
Shamattawa → Canada 55°1N 85°23W 72 A2
Shamīl Iran 27°30N 56°55E 47 E8
Shamkūh Iran 35°47N 57°50E 47 C8
Shamli India 29°32N 77°18E 42 E7
Shammar, Jabal Si. Arabia 27°40N 41°0E 46 E4
Shamo = Gobi Asia 44°0N 110°0E 32 C6
Shamo, L. Ethiopia 5°45N 37°30E 49 F2
Shamokin U.S.A. 40°47N 76°34W 83 F8
Shamrock Canada 45°23N 76°50W 83 A8
Shamrock U.S.A. 35°13N 100°15W 84 D4
Shan □ Myanmar 21°30N 98°30E 41 J21
Shan Xian China 34°50N 116°5E 32 G9
Shanchengzhen China 42°20N 125°20E 33 C13
Shāndak Iran 28°28N 60°27E 47 D9
Shandan China 38°45N 101°15E 30 D9
Shandon U.S.A. 35°39N 120°23W 78 K6
Shandong □ China 36°0N 118°0E 33 G10
Shandong Bandao China 37°0N 121°0E 33 F11
Shandur Pass Pakistan 36°4N 72°31E 43 A5
Shang Xian = Shangzhou China 33°50N 109°58E 32 H5
Shangani Zimbabwe 19°41S 29°20E 57 A4
Shangani → Zimbabwe 18°41S 27°10E 55 H5
Shangbancheng China 40°50N 118°1E 33 D10
Shangcheng China 31°47N 115°26E 35 B10
Shangchuan Dao China 21°40N 112°50E 35 G9
Shangdu China 41°30N 113°30E 32 D7
Shanggao China 28°17N 114°55E 35 C10
Shanghai Shi □ China 31°0N 121°30E 35 B13
Shanghang China 25°2N 116°23E 35 E11
Shanghe China 37°20N 117°10E 33 F9
Shanglin China 23°27N 108°33E 34 F7
Shangnan China 33°32N 110°50E 32 H6
Shangqiu China 34°26N 115°36E 32 G8
Shangrao China 28°25N 117°59E 35 C11
Shangri-La = Zhongdian China 27°48N 99°42E 34 D2
Shangshui China 33°32N 114°35E 32 H8
Shangsi China 22°8N 107°58E 34 F6
Shangyi China 41°4N 113°57E 32 D7
Shangyou China 25°48N 114°32E 35 E10
Shangyu China 30°3N 120°52E 35 B13
Shangzhi China 45°22N 127°56E 33 B14
Shangzhou China 33°50N 109°58E 32 H5
Shanhetun China 44°33N 127°15E 33 B14
Shanklin U.K. 50°38N 1°11W 13 G6
Shannon N.Z. 40°33S 175°25E 59 D5
Shannon → Ireland 52°35N 9°30W 10 D2
Shannon ✈ (SNN) Ireland 52°42N 8°57W 10 D3
Shannon, Mouth of the Ireland 52°30N 9°55W 10 D2
Shannon △ Australia 34°35S 116°25E 61 F2
Shannonbridge Ireland 53°17N 8°3W 10 C3
Shansi = Shanxi □ China 37°0N 112°0E 32 F7
Shantar, Ostrov Bolshoy Russia 55°9N 137°40E 27 D14
Shantipur India 23°17N 88°25E 43 H13
Shantou China 23°18N 116°40E 35 F11
Shantung = Shandong □ China 36°0N 118°0E 33 G10
Shanwei China 22°48N 115°22E 35 F10
Shanxi □ China 37°0N 112°0E 32 F7
Shanyang China 33°31N 109°55E 32 H5
Shanyin China 39°25N 112°56E 32 E7
Shaodong China 27°15N 111°43E 35 D8
Shaoguan China 24°48N 113°35E 35 E9
Shaoshan China 27°55N 112°33E 35 D9
Shaowu China 27°22N 117°28E 35 D11
Shaoxing China 30°0N 120°35E 35 C13
Shaoyang China 27°14N 111°25E 35 D8
Shap U.K. 54°32N 2°40W 12 C5
Shapinsay U.K. 59°3N 2°51W 11 B6
Shaqra' Si. Arabia 25°15N 45°16E 46 E5
Sharafkhāneh Iran 38°11N 45°29E 46 B5
Sharavati → India 14°20N 74°25E 45 G2
Sharbot Lake Canada 44°46N 76°41W 83 B8
Shari Japan 43°55N 144°40E 28 C12
Sharjah = Ash Shāriqah U.A.E. 25°23N 55°26E 47 E7
Shark B. Australia 25°30S 113°32E 61 E1
Shark Bay △ Australia 25°30S 113°30E 61 E1
Sharm el Sheikh Egypt 27°53N 34°18E 53 C12
Sharon Canada 44°6N 79°26W 82 B5
Sharon Mass., U.S.A. 42°7N 71°11W 83 D13
Sharon Pa., U.S.A. 41°14N 80°31W 82 E4
Sharon Springs Kans., U.S.A. 38°54N 101°45W 80 F3
Sharon Springs N.Y., U.S.A. 42°48N 74°37W 83 D10
Sharp Pt. Australia 10°58S 142°43E 62 A3
Sharpe L. Canada 54°24N 93°40W 72 B1
Sharpsville U.S.A. 41°15N 80°29W 82 E4
Sharqi, Al Jabal ash Lebanon 33°40N 36°10E 48 B5
Sharqîya, Es Sahrâ esh Egypt 27°30N 32°30E 53 C12
Sharya Russia 58°22N 45°20E 18 C8
Shashemene Ethiopia 7°13N 38°33E 49 F2
Shashi Botswana 21°15S 27°27E 57 B4
Shasta, Mt. U.S.A. 41°25N 122°12W 76 F2
Shasta L. U.S.A. 40°43N 122°25W 76 F2
Shatsky Rise Pac. Oc. 34°0N 157°0E 64 D7
Shatt al Arab Asia 29°57N 48°34E 47 D6
Shaunavon Canada 49°35N 108°25W 71 D7
Shaver L. U.S.A. 37°9N 119°18W 78 H7
Shaw → Australia 20°21S 119°17E 60 D2
Shaw I. Australia 20°30S 149°2E 62 b
Shawanaga Canada 45°31N 80°17W 82 A4
Shawangunk Mts. U.S.A. 41°35N 74°30W 83 E10
Shawano U.S.A. 44°47N 88°36W 80 C9
Shawinigan Canada 46°35N 72°50W 72 C5
Shawmari, J. ash Jordan 30°35N 36°35E 48 E5
Shawnee U.S.A. 35°20N 96°55W 84 D6
Shay Gap Australia 20°30S 120°10E 60 D3
Shayang China 30°42N 112°29E 35 B9
Shaybārā Si. Arabia 25°26N 36°47E 46 E3
Shaykh, J. ash Lebanon 33°25N 35°50E 48 B4
Shaykh Miskīn Syria 32°49N 36°9E 48 C5
Shaykh Sa'd Iraq 32°34N 46°17E 46 C5
Shaykh 'Uthmān Yemen 12°52N 44°59E 49 E3
Shāzand Iran 33°56N 49°24E 47 C6
Shchūchīnsk Kazakhstan 52°56N 70°12E 26 D8
She Xian Anhui, China 29°50N 118°25E 35 C12
She Xian Hebei, China 36°30N 113°40E 32 F7
Shebele = Shabeelle → Somalia 2°0N 44°0E 49 G3
Sheboygan U.S.A. 43°46N 87°45W 80 D10
Shediac Canada 46°14N 64°32W 73 C7
Sheelin, L. Ireland 53°48N 7°20W 10 C4
Sheenjek → U.S.A. 66°45N 144°33W 74 B11
Sheep Haven Ireland 55°11N 7°52W 10 A4
Sheep Range U.S.A. 36°35N 115°15W 79 J11
Sheerness U.K. 51°26N 0°47E 13 F8
Sheet Harbour Canada 44°56N 62°31W 73 D7
Sheffield U.K. 53°23N 1°28W 12 D6
Sheffield Ala., U.S.A. 34°46N 87°41W 85 D11
Sheffield Mass., U.S.A. 42°5N 73°21W 83 D11
Sheffield Pa., U.S.A. 41°42N 79°3W 82 E5
Shegaon India 20°48N 76°47E 44 D3
Shehong China 30°54N 105°18E 34 B5
Sheikhpura India 25°9N 85°53E 43 G11
Shekhupura Pakistan 31°42N 73°58E 42 D5
Shekou China 22°30N 113°55E 31 a
Shelburne N.S., Canada 43°47N 65°20W 73 D6
Shelburne Ont., Canada 44°4N 80°15W 82 B4
Shelburne U.S.A. 44°23N 73°14W 83 B11
Shelburne B. Australia 11°50S 142°50E 62 A3
Shelburne Falls U.S.A. 42°36N 72°45W 83 D12
Shelby Mich., U.S.A. 43°37N 86°22W 80 D10
Shelby Miss., U.S.A. 33°57N 90°46W 85 E9
Shelby Mont., U.S.A. 48°30N 111°51W 76 B8
Shelby N.C., U.S.A. 35°17N 81°32W 85 D14
Shelby Ohio, U.S.A. 40°53N 82°40W 82 F2
Shelbyville Ill., U.S.A. 39°24N 88°48W 80 F9
Shelbyville Ind., U.S.A. 39°31N 85°47W 81 F11
Shelbyville Ky., U.S.A. 38°13N 85°14W 81 F11
Shelbyville Tenn., U.S.A. 35°29N 86°28W 85 D11
Sheldon U.S.A. 43°11N 95°51W 80 D6
Sheldrake Canada 50°20N 64°51W 73 B7
Shelikhova, Zaliv Russia 59°30N 157°0E 27 D16
Shelikof Strait U.S.A. 57°30N 155°0W 74 D9
Shell Lakes Australia 29°20S 127°30E 61 E4
Shellbrook Canada 53°13N 106°24W 71 C7
Shellharbour Australia 34°31S 150°51E 63 E5
Shelter I. U.S.A. 41°4N 72°20W 83 E12
Shelton Conn., U.S.A. 41°19N 73°5W 83 E11
Shelton Wash., U.S.A. 47°13N 123°6W 78 C3
Shen Xian China 36°15N 115°40E 32 F8
Shenandoah Iowa, U.S.A. 40°46N 95°22W 80 E6
Shenandoah Pa., U.S.A. 40°49N 76°12W 83 F8
Shenandoah Va., U.S.A. 38°29N 78°37W 81 F14
Shenandoah → U.S.A. 39°19N 77°44W 81 F15
Shenandoah △ U.S.A. 38°35N 78°22W 81 F14
Shenchi China 39°8N 112°10E 32 E7
Shencottah India 8°59N 77°18E 45 K3
Shendam Nigeria 8°49N 9°30E 52 G7
Shendî Sudan 16°46N 33°22E 53 E12
Shendurni India 20°39N 75°36E 44 D2
Shengfang China 39°3N 116°42E 32 E9
Shengzhou China 29°35N 120°50E 35 C13
Shenjingzi China 44°40N 124°30E 33 B13
Shenmu China 38°50N 110°29E 32 E6
Shennongjia China 31°43N 110°44E 35 B8
Shenqiu China 33°25N 115°5E 32 H8
Shensi = Shaanxi □ China 35°0N 109°0E 32 G5
Shenyang China 41°48N 123°27E 33 D12
Shenzhen China 22°32N 114°5E 35 F10
Shenzhen Bao'an Int. ✈ (SZX) China 22°41N 113°49E 31 a
Shenzhen Shuiku China 22°34N 114°8E 31 a
Shenzhen Wan China 22°27N 113°55E 31 a
Sheo India 26°11N 71°15E 42 F4
Sheopur Kalan India 25°40N 76°40E 42 G7
Shepetivka Ukraine 50°10N 27°10E 17 C14
Shepparton Australia 36°23S 145°26E 63 F4
Sheppey, I. of U.K. 51°25N 0°48E 13 F8
Shepton Mallet U.K. 51°11N 2°33W 13 F5
Sheqi China 33°12N 112°57E 32 H7
Sher Qila Pakistan 36°7N 74°2E 43 A6
Sherborne U.K. 50°57N 2°31W 13 G5
Sherbro I. S. Leone 7°30N 12°40W 52 G3
Sherbrooke N.S., Canada 45°8N 61°59W 73 C7
Sherbrooke Qué., Canada 45°28N 71°57W 83 A13
Sherburne U.S.A. 42°41N 75°30W 83 D9
Shergarh India 26°20N 72°18E 42 F5
Sherghati India 24°34N 84°47E 43 G11
Sheridan Ark., U.S.A. 34°19N 92°24W 84 D8
Sheridan Wyo., U.S.A. 44°48N 106°58W 76 D10
Sheringham U.K. 52°56N 1°13E 12 E9
Sherkin I. Ireland 51°28N 9°26W 10 E2
Sherkot India 29°22N 78°35E 43 E8
Sherlovaya Gora Russia 50°34N 116°15E 27 D12
Sherman N.Y., U.S.A. 42°9N 79°35W 82 D5
Sherman Tex., U.S.A. 33°38N 96°36W 84 E6
Sherpur India 25°34N 83°47E 43 G10
Sherridon Canada 55°8N 101°5W 71 B8
Shertallai = Cherthala India 9°42N 76°20E 45 K3
Sherwood Forest U.K. 53°6N 1°7W 12 D6
Sherwood Park Canada 53°31N 113°19W 70 C6
Sheslay → Canada 58°48N 132°5W 70 B2
Shethanei L. Canada 58°48N 97°50W 71 B9
Shetland □ U.K. 60°30N 1°30W 11 A7
Shetland Is. U.K. 60°30N 1°30W 11 A7
Shetrunji → India 21°19N 72°7E 42 J5
Sheung Shui China 22°31N 114°7E 31 a
Shevaroy Hills India 11°58N 78°12E 45 J4
Shevgaon India 19°21N 75°14E 44 E2
Shey-Phoksundo △ Nepal 29°30N 82°45E 43 E10
Sheyang China 33°48N 120°29E 33 H11
Sheyenne → U.S.A. 47°2N 96°50W 80 B5
Shiashkotan, Ostrov Russia 48°49N 154°6E 27 E16
Shibām Yemen 15°59N 48°36E 49 D4
Shibata Japan 37°57N 139°20E 28 F9
Shibecha Japan 43°17N 144°36E 28 C12
Shibetsu Hokkaidō, Japan 43°30N 145°10E 28 C12
Shibetsu Hokkaidō, Japan 44°10N 142°23E 28 B11
Shibing China 27°2N 108°7E 34 D7
Shibogama L. Canada 53°35N 88°15W 72 B2
Shibushi Japan 31°25N 131°8E 29 J5
Shicheng China 26°22N 116°20E 35 D11
Shickshinny U.S.A. 41°9N 76°9W 83 E8
Shickshock Mts. = Chic-Chocs, Mts. Canada 48°55N 66°0W 73 C6
Shidao China 36°50N 122°25E 33 F12
Shidian China 24°40N 99°5E 34 E2
Shido = Sanuki Japan 34°19N 134°10E 29 G7
Shiel, L. U.K. 56°48N 5°34W 11 E3
Shield, C. Australia 13°20S 136°20E 62 A2

Shīeli Kazakhstan 44°20N 66°15E 26 E7
Shifang China 31°8N 104°10E 34 B5
Shiga □ Japan 35°20N 136°0E 29 G8
Shigu China 26°51N 99°56E 34 D2
Shiguaigou China 40°52N 110°15E 32 D6
Shihchiachuang = Shijiazhuang China 38°2N 114°28E 32 E8
Shihezi China 44°15N 86°2E 30 C6
Shijiazhuang China 38°2N 114°28E 32 E8
Shijiu Hu China 31°25N 118°50E 35 B12
Shikarpur India 28°17N 78°7E 42 E8
Shikarpur Pakistan 27°57N 68°39E 42 F3
Shikohabad India 27°6N 78°36E 43 F8
Shikokochūō Japan 34°1N 133°34E 29 G6
Shikoku □ Japan 33°30N 133°30E 29 H6
Shikoku-Sanchi Japan 33°30N 133°30E 29 H6
Shikotan, Ostrov Asia 43°47N 146°44E 27 E15
Shikotsu-Ko Japan 42°45N 141°25E 28 C10
Shikotsu-Tōya △ Japan 44°4N 145°8E 28 C10
Shiliguri India 26°45N 88°25E 41 F16
Shiliu = Changjiang China 19°20N 108°55E 38 C7
Shilka Russia 52°0N 115°55E 27 D12
Shilka → Russia 53°20N 121°26E 27 D13
Shillelagh Ireland 52°45N 6°32W 10 D5
Shillington U.S.A. 40°18N 75°58W 83 F9
Shillong India 25°35N 91°53E 41 G17
Shilo West Bank 32°4N 35°18E 48 C4
Shilong China 23°5N 113°52E 35 F9
Shilou China 37°0N 110°48E 32 F6
Shimabara Japan 32°48N 130°20E 29 H5
Shimada Japan 34°49N 138°10E 29 G9
Shimane □ Japan 35°0N 132°30E 29 G6
Shimanovsk Russia 52°15N 127°30E 27 D13
Shimanto Kōchi, Japan 33°12N 133°8E 29 H6
Shimanto Kōchi, Japan 32°59N 132°56E 29 H6
Shimbiris Somalia 10°44N 47°14E 49 E4
Shimen China 29°35N 111°20E 35 C8
Shimenjie China 29°29N 116°48E 35 C11
Shimian China 29°17N 102°23E 34 C4
Shimizu Japan 35°0N 138°30E 29 G9
Shimla India 31°2N 77°9E 42 D7
Shimodate Japan 36°20N 139°55E 29 F9
Shimoga = Shivamogga India 13°57N 75°32E 45 H2
Shimokita-Hantō Japan 41°20N 141°0E 28 D10
Shimonoseki Japan 33°58N 130°55E 29 H5
Shimpuru Rapids Namibia 17°45S 19°55E 56 A2
Shimsha → India 13°15N 77°10E 45 H3
Shin, L. U.K. 58°5N 4°30W 11 C4
Shinan China 22°44N 109°53E 34 F7
Shinano-Gawa → Japan 36°50N 138°30E 29 F9
Shināş Oman 24°46N 56°28E 47 E8
Shīndand Afghan. 33°12N 62°8E 40 C3
Shinglehouse U.S.A. 41°58N 78°12W 82 E6
Shingū Japan 33°40N 135°55E 29 H7
Shingwidzi S. Africa 23°5S 31°25E 57 B5
Shinjō Japan 38°46N 140°18E 28 E10
Shinkolobwe Dem. Rep. of the Congo 11°10S 26°40E 54 G5
Shinshār Syria 34°36N 36°43E 48 A5
Shinyanga Tanzania 3°45S 33°27E 54 E6
Shio-no-Misaki Japan 33°25N 135°45E 29 H7
Shiogama Japan 38°19N 141°1E 28 E10
Shiojiri Japan 36°6N 137°58E 29 F8
Shipchenski Prokhod Bulgaria 42°45N 25°15E 23 C11
Shiphoirt, L. = Seaforth, L. U.K. 57°52N 6°36W 11 D2
Shiping China 23°45N 102°23E 34 F4
Shippagan Canada 47°45N 64°45W 73 C7
Shippensburg U.S.A. 40°3N 77°31W 82 F7
Shippenville U.S.A. 41°15N 79°28W 82 E5
Shiprock U.S.A. 36°47N 108°41W 77 H9
Shiqian China 27°32N 108°13E 34 D7
Shiqma, N. → Israel 31°37N 34°30E 48 D3
Shiquan China 33°5N 108°15E 34 A7
Shiquan He = Indus → Pakistan 24°20N 67°47E 42 G2
Shīr Kūh Iran 31°39N 54°3E 47 D7
Shira'awh Qatar 25°2N 52°14E 47 E7
Shiragami-Misaki Japan 41°24N 140°12E 28 D10
Shirakawa Fukushima, Japan 37°7N 140°13E 29 F10
Shirakawa Gifu, Japan 36°17N 136°56E 29 F8
Shirane-San Gumma, Japan 36°48N 139°22E 29 F9
Shirane-San Yamanashi, Japan 35°42N 138°9E 29 G9
Shiraoi Japan 42°33N 141°21E 28 C10
Shīrāz Iran 29°42N 52°30E 47 D7
Shire → Africa 17°42S 35°19E 55 H7
Shiren China 41°57N 126°34E 33 D14
Shiretoko △ Japan 44°15N 145°15E 28 B12
Shiretoko-Misaki Japan 44°21N 145°20E 28 B12
Shirinab → Pakistan 30°15N 66°28E 42 D2
Shiriya-Zaki Japan 41°25N 141°30E 28 D10
Shiroishi Japan 38°0N 140°37E 28 F10
Shirol India 16°47N 74°41E 44 F2
Shirpur India 21°21N 74°57E 44 D2
Shirshov Ridge Pac. Oc. 58°0N 170°0E 64 B8
Shīrvān Iran 37°30N 57°50E 47 B8
Shirwa, L. = Chilwa, L. Malawi 15°15S 35°40E 55 H7
Shishaldin Volcano U.S.A. 54°45N 163°58W 74 E7
Shishi China 24°44N 118°37E 35 E12
Shishou China 29°38N 112°22E 35 C9
Shitai China 30°12N 117°25E 35 B11
Shivamogga India 13°57N 75°32E 45 H2
Shivpuri India 25°26N 77°42E 42 G7
Shixian China 43°5N 129°50E 33 C15
Shixing China 24°46N 114°5E 35 E10
Shiyan Guangdong, China 22°42N 113°56E 31 a
Shiyan Hubei, China 32°35N 110°45E 35 A8
Shiyan Shuiku China 22°42N 113°54E 31 a
Shizhu China 29°58N 108°7E 34 C7
Shizong China 24°50N 104°0E 34 E5
Shizuishan China 39°15N 106°50E 32 E4
Shizuoka Japan 34°57N 138°24E 29 G9
Shizuoka □ Japan 35°15N 138°40E 29 G9
Shklov = Shklow Belarus 54°16N 30°15E 17 A16
Shklow Belarus 54°16N 30°15E 17 A16
Shkodër Albania 42°4N 19°32E 23 C8
Shkumbini → Albania 41°2N 19°31E 23 D8
Shmidta, Ostrov Russia 81°0N 91°0E 27 A10
Shō-Gawa → Japan 36°47N 137°4E 29 F8
Shoal L. Canada 49°33N 95°1W 71 D9
Shoal Lake Canada 50°30N 100°35W 71 C8
Shōdo-Shima Japan 34°30N 134°15E 29 G7
Sholapur = Solapur India 17°43N 75°56E 44 F2
Shōmrōn West Bank 32°15N 35°13E 48 C4
Shoranur India 10°46N 76°19E 45 J3
Shorapur India 16°31N 76°48E 45 F3
Shoreham U.S.A. 43°53N 73°18W 83 C11
Shoreham-by-Sea U.K. 50°50N 0°16W 13 G7
Shori → Pakistan 28°29N 69°44E 42 E3
Shorkot Pakistan 30°50N 72°0E 42 D4
Shorkot Road Pakistan 30°47N 72°15E 42 D5
Shortt's I. India 20°47N 87°4E 44 D8
Shoshone Calif., U.S.A. 35°58N 116°16W 79 K10
Shoshone Idaho, U.S.A. 42°56N 114°25W 76 E6
Shoshone L. U.S.A. 44°22N 110°43W 76 D8
Shoshone Mts. U.S.A. 39°20N 117°25W 76 G5
Shoshong Botswana 22°56S 26°31E 56 B4
Shoshoni U.S.A. 43°14N 108°7W 76 E9
Shou Xian China 32°37N 116°42E 35 A11
Shouchang China 29°18N 119°12E 35 C12
Shouguang China 37°52N 118°45E 33 F10
Shouning China 27°27N 119°31E 35 D12
Shouyang China 37°54N 113°8E 32 F7
Show Low U.S.A. 34°15N 110°2W 77 J8
Shqipëria = Albania ■ Europe 41°0N 20°0E 23 D9
Shreveport U.S.A. 32°31N 93°45W 84 E8
Shrewsbury U.K. 52°43N 2°45W 13 E5
Shri Mohangarh India 27°17N 71°18E 42 F4
Shrigonda India 18°37N 74°41E 44 E2
Shrirampur India 22°44N 88°21E 43 H13
Shropshire □ U.K. 52°36N 2°45W 13 E5
Shū Kazakhstan 43°36N 73°42E 26 E8
Shuangbai China 24°42N 101°38E 34 E3
Shuangcheng China 45°20N 126°15E 33 B14
Shuangfeng China 27°29N 112°11E 35 D9
Shuanggou China 34°2N 117°30E 33 G9
Shuangjiang China 23°26N 99°58E 34 F2
Shuangliao China 43°29N 123°30E 33 C12
Shuangshanzi China 40°20N 119°8E 33 D10
Shuangyang China 43°28N 125°40E 33 C13
Shuangyashan China 46°28N 131°5E 31 B15
Shucheng China 31°28N 116°57E 35 B11
Shuiji China 27°13N 118°20E 35 D12
Shujalpur India 23°18N 76°46E 42 H7
Shukpa Kunzang India 34°22N 78°22E 43 B8
Shulan China 44°28N 127°0E 33 B14
Shule China 39°25N 76°3E 30 D4
Shule He → China 40°20N 92°50E 30 C7
Shumagin Is. U.S.A. 55°7N 160°30W 74 D7
Shumen Bulgaria 43°18N 26°55E 23 C12
Shumikha Russia 55°10N 63°15E 26 D7
Shunān Japan 34°3N 131°50E 29 G5
Shunchang China 26°54N 117°48E 35 D11
Shunde China 22°42N 113°14E 35 F9
Shungnak U.S.A. 66°52N 157°9W 74 B8
Shuo Xian = Shuozhou China 39°20N 112°33E 32 E7
Shuozhou China 39°20N 112°33E 32 E7
Shuqrā' Yemen 13°22N 45°44E 49 E4
Shūr → Fārs, Iran 28°30N 55°0E 47 D7
Shūr → Kermān, Iran 30°52N 57°37E 47 D8
Shūr → Yazd, Iran 31°45N 55°15E 47 D7
Shūr Āb Iran 34°23N 51°11E 47 C6
Shūr Gaz Iran 29°10N 59°20E 47 D8
Shūrāb Iran 33°43N 56°29E 47 C8
Shūrjestān Iran 31°24N 52°25E 47 D7
Shurugwi Zimbabwe 19°40S 30°0E 55 H6
Shūsf Iran 31°50N 60°5E 47 D9
Shūshtar Iran 32°0N 48°50E 47 D6
Shuswap L. Canada 50°55N 119°3W 70 C5
Shute Harbour △ Australia 20°17S 148°47E 62 b
Shuyang China 34°10N 118°42E 33 G10
Shūzū Iran 29°52N 54°30E 47 D7
Shwebo Myanmar 22°30N 95°45E 41 H19
Shwegu Myanmar 24°15N 96°26E 41 G20
Shweli → Myanmar 23°45N 96°45E 41 H20
Shyamnagar India 13°21N 92°57E 45 H11
Shymkent Kazakhstan 42°18N 69°36E 26 E7
Shyok India 34°13N 78°12E 43 B8
Shyok → Pakistan 35°13N 75°53E 43 B6
Si Kiang = Xi Jiang → China 22°5N 113°20E 35 F9
Si Lanna △ Thailand 19°17N 99°12E 38 C2
Si Nakarin Res. Thailand 14°35N 99°0E 38 E2
Si-ngan = Xi'an China 34°15N 109°0E 32 G5
Si Phangnga Thailand 9°8N 98°29E 39 H2
Si Prachan Thailand 14°37N 100°9E 38 E3
Si Racha Thailand 13°10N 100°48E 38 F3
Si Sa Ket Thailand 15°8N 104°23E 38 E5
Siachen Glacier Asia 35°20N 77°30E 43 B7
Siahaf → Pakistan 29°3N 68°57E 42 E3
Siahan Range Pakistan 27°30N 64°40E 40 F4
Siak Sri Indrapura Indonesia 0°51N 102°0E 36 D2
Sialkot Pakistan 32°32N 74°30E 42 C6
Siam = Thailand ■ Asia 16°0N 102°0E 38 E4
Sian = Xi'an China 34°15N 109°0E 32 G5
Sian Ka'an △ Mexico 19°35N 87°40W 87 D7
Siantan Indonesia 3°10N 106°15E 36 D3
Sīāreh Iran 28°5N 60°14E 47 D9
Siargao I. Phil. 9°52N 126°3E 37 C7
Siasi Phil. 5°34N 120°50E 37 C6
Siau Indonesia 2°50N 125°25E 37 D7
Šiauliai Lithuania 55°56N 23°15E 9 J20
Siavonga Zambia 16°33S 28°42E 57 A4
Sibâi, Gebel el Egypt 25°45N 34°10E 46 E2
Sibang Indonesia 8°34S 115°13E 37 K18
Sibay Russia 52°42N 58°39E 18 D10
Sibayi, L. S. Africa 27°20S 32°45E 57 C5
Šibenik Croatia 43°48N 15°54E 22 C6
Siberia = Sibirskiy □ Russia 58°0N 90°0E 27 D10
Siberia Russia 60°0N 100°0E 24 B12
Siberut Indonesia 1°30S 99°0E 36 E1
Sibi Pakistan 29°30N 67°54E 42 E2
Sibirskiy □ Russia 58°0N 90°0E 27 D10
Sibirtsevo Russia 44°12N 132°26E 28 B5
Sibiti Congo 3°38S 13°19E 54 E2
Sibiu Romania 45°45N 24°9E 17 F13
Sibley U.S.A. 43°24N 95°45W 80 D6
Sibolga Indonesia 1°42N 98°45E 36 D1
Siborongborong Indonesia 2°13N 98°58E 39 L2
Sibsagar = Sivasagar India 27°0N 94°36E 41 F19
Sibu Malaysia 2°18N 111°49E 36 D4
Sibuco Phil. 7°20N 122°10E 37 C6
Sibuguey B. Phil. 7°50N 122°45E 37 C6
Sibut C.A.R. 5°46N 19°10E 54 C3
Sibutu Phil. 4°45N 119°30E 37 D5
Sibutu Passage E. Indies 4°50N 120°0E 37 D6
Sibuyan I. Phil. 12°25N 122°40E 37 B6
Sibuyan Sea Phil. 12°30N 122°20E 37 B6
Sicamous Canada 50°49N 119°0W 70 C5
Siccus → Australia 31°55S 139°17E 63 E2
Sichon Thailand 9°0N 99°54E 39 H2
Sichuan □ China 30°30N 103°0E 34 B5
Sichuan Pendi China 31°0N 105°0E 34 B5
Sicilia Italy 37°30N 14°30E 22 F6
Sicily = Sicilia Italy 37°30N 14°30E 22 F6
Sicily, Str. of Medit. S. 37°35N 11°56E 22 F4
Sico → Honduras 15°58N 84°58W 88 C3
Sicuani Peru 14°21S 71°10W 92 F4
Siddapur India 14°20N 74°53E 45 G2
Siddhapur India 23°56N 72°25E 42 H5
Siddipet India 18°5N 78°51E 44 E4
Sidhauli India 27°17N 80°50E 43 F9
Sidhi India 24°25N 81°53E 43 G9
Sidi-bel-Abbès Algeria 35°13N 0°39W 52 A5
Sidi Ifni Morocco 29°29N 10°12W 52 C3
Sidikalang Indonesia 2°45N 98°19E 39 L2
Sidlaw Hills U.K. 56°32N 3°2W 11 E5
Sidley, Mt. Antarctica 77°2S 126°2W 5 D14
Sidmouth U.K. 50°40N 3°15W 13 G4
Sidmouth, C. Australia 13°25S 143°36E 62 A3
Sidney Canada 48°39N 123°24W 78 B3
Sidney Mont., U.S.A. 47°43N 104°9W 76 C11
Sidney N.Y., U.S.A. 42°19N 75°24W 83 D9
Sidney Nebr., U.S.A. 41°8N 102°59W 80 E2
Sidney Ohio, U.S.A. 40°17N 84°9W 81 E11
Sidney Lanier, L. U.S.A. 34°10N 84°4W 85 D12
Sidoarjo Indonesia 7°27S 112°43E 37 G15
Sidon = Saydā Lebanon 33°35N 35°25E 48 B4
Sidra = Surt Libya 31°11N 16°39E 53 B9
Sidra, G. of = Surt, Khalīj Libya 31°40N 18°30E 53 B9
Siedlce Poland 52°10N 22°20E 17 B12
Sieg → Germany 50°46N 7°6E 16 C4
Siegen Germany 50°51N 8°0E 16 C5
Siem Pang Cambodia 14°7N 106°23E 38 E6
Siem Reap = Siemreab Cambodia 13°20N 103°52E 38 F4
Siemreab Cambodia 13°20N 103°52E 38 F4
Siena Italy 43°19N 11°21E 22 C4
Sieradz Poland 51°37N 18°41E 17 C10
Sierpe, Bocas de la Venezuela 10°0N 61°30W 93 L15
Sierra Blanca U.S.A. 31°11N 105°22W 84 F2
Sierra Blanca Peak U.S.A. 33°23N 105°49W 77 K11
Sierra City U.S.A. 39°34N 120°38W 78 F6
Sierra Colorada Argentina 40°35S 67°50W 96 E3
Sierra de Agalta △ Honduras 15°1N 85°48W 88 C2
Sierra de Bahoruco △ Dom. Rep. 18°10N 71°25W 89 C5
Sierra de La Culata △ Venezuela 8°45N 71°10W 89 E5
Sierra de Lancandón △ Guatemala 16°59N 90°23W 88 C1
Sierra de las Quijadas △ Argentina 32°29S 67°5W 94 C2
Sierra de San Luis △ Venezuela 11°20N 69°43W 89 D6
Sierra de San Pedro Mártir △ Mexico 31°10N 115°30W 86 A1
Sierra Gorda Chile 22°50S 69°15W 94 A2
Sierra Leone ■ W. Afr. 9°0N 12°0W 52 G3
Sierra Madre Mexico 16°0N 93°0W 87 D6
Sierra Madre Occidental Mexico 27°0N 107°0W 86 B3
Sierra Madre Oriental Mexico 25°0N 100°0W 86 C5
Sierra Mojada Mexico 27°18N 103°41W 86 B4
Sierra Nevada Spain 37°3N 3°15W 21 D4
Sierra Nevada U.S.A. 39°0N 120°30W 78 H8
Sierra Nevada △ Venezuela 8°35N 70°45W 89 E5
Sierra Nevada de Santa Marta △ Colombia 10°56N 73°36W 89 D5
Sierra Vista U.S.A. 31°33N 110°18W 77 L8
Sierraville U.S.A. 39°36N 120°22W 78 F6
Sifnos Greece 37°0N 24°45E 23 F11
Sifton Canada 51°21N 100°8W 71 C8
Sifton Pass Canada 57°52N 126°15W 70 B3
Sig Algeria 35°32N 0°12W 52 A5
Sigatoka Fiji 18°8S 177°32E 59 a
Sighetu-Marmaţiei Romania 47°57N 23°52E 17 E12
Sighişoara Romania 46°12N 24°50E 17 E13
Sigiriya Sri Lanka 7°57N 80°45E 45 L5
Sigli Indonesia 5°25N 96°0E 36 C1
Siglufjörður Iceland 66°12N 18°55W 8 C4
Signal de Botrang Belgium 50°29N 6°4E 15 D6
Signal Pk. U.S.A. 33°20N 114°2W 79 M12
Signy I. Antarctica 60°43S 45°36W 5 C18
Sigsig Ecuador 3°0S 78°50W 92 D3
Sigüenza Spain 41°3N 2°40W 21 B4
Siguiri Guinea 11°31N 9°10W 52 F4
Sigulda Latvia 57°10N 24°55E 9 H21
Siguniangshan China 31°15N 103°10E 34 B4
Sihawa India 20°19N 81°55E 44 D5
Sihong China 33°27N 118°16E 33 H10
Sihora India 23°29N 80°6E 43 H9
Sihui China 23°20N 112°40E 35 F9
Siikajoki → Finland 64°50N 24°43E 8 D21
Siilinjärvi Finland 63°4N 27°39E 8 E22
Sika India 22°26N 69°47E 42 H3
Sikanni Chief → Canada 57°47N 122°15W 70 B4
Sikao Thailand 7°34N 99°21E 39 J2
Sikar India 27°33N 75°10E 42 F6
Sikasso Mali 11°18N 5°35W 52 F4
Sikeston U.S.A. 36°53N 89°35W 80 G9
Sikhote Alin, Khrebet Russia 45°0N 136°0E 28 B8
Sikhote Alin Ra. = Sikhote Alin, Khrebet Russia 45°0N 136°0E 28 B8
Sikinos Greece 36°40N 25°8E 23 F11
Sikkim □ India 27°50N 88°30E 41 F16
Sil → Spain 42°27N 7°43W 21 A2
Silacayoapan Mexico 17°30N 98°9W 87 D5
Silawad India 21°54N 74°54E 42 J6
Silchar India 24°49N 92°48E 41 G18
Silent Valley △ India 11°10N 76°20E 45 J3
Siler City U.S.A. 35°44N 79°28W 85 D15
Sileru → India 17°49N 81°24E 44 F5
Silesia = Śląsk Poland 51°0N 16°30E 16 C9
Silgarhi Doti Nepal 29°15N 81°0E 43 E9
Silghat India 26°35N 93°0E 41 F18
Silhouette Seychelles 4°29S 55°12E 55 b
Silicon Valley = Santa Clara Valley U.S.A. 36°50N 121°30W 78 J5
Silifke Turkey 36°22N 33°58E 46 B2
Siliguri = Shiliguri India 26°45N 88°25E 41 F16
Siling Co China 31°50N 89°20E 30 E6
Silistra Bulgaria 44°6N 27°19E 23 B12
Silivri Turkey 41°4N 28°14E 23 D13
Siljan Sweden 60°55N 14°45E 8 F16
Silkeborg Denmark 56°10N 9°32E 9 H13
Silkwood Australia 17°45S 146°2E 62 B4
Sillajhuay, Cordillera Chile 19°46S 68°40W 92 G5
Sillamäe Estonia 59°24N 27°45E 9 G22
Sillod India 20°18N 75°39E 44 D2
Silloth U.K. 54°52N 3°23W 12 C4
Siloam Springs U.S.A. 36°11N 94°32W 84 C7
Silopi Turkey 37°15N 42°27E 46 B4
Šilutė Lithuania 55°21N 21°33E 9 J19
Silvan Turkey 38°7N 41°2E 46 B4
Silvani India 23°18N 78°25E 43 H8
Silvassa India 20°16N 73°1E 44 D1
Silver City U.S.A. 32°46N 108°17W 77 K9
Silver Cr. → U.S.A. 43°16N 119°13W 76 E4
Silver Creek U.S.A. 42°33N 79°10W 82 D5
Silver L. U.S.A. 38°39N 120°6W 78 G6
Silver Lake Calif., U.S.A. 35°21N 116°7W 79 K10
Silver Lake Oreg., U.S.A. 43°8N 121°3W 76 E3
Silvermine Mts. Ireland 52°47N 8°15W 10 D3
Silverton Colo., U.S.A. 37°49N 107°40W 77 H10
Silverton Tex., U.S.A. 34°28N 101°19W 84 D4
Silvies → U.S.A. 43°34N 119°2W 76 E4
Simaltala India 24°43N 86°33E 43 G12
Simanggang = Bandar Sri Aman Malaysia 1°15N 111°32E 36 D4
Simao China 22°47N 101°5E 34 F3
Simard, L. Canada 47°40N 78°40W 72 C4
Simav Turkey 39°4N 28°58E 23 E13
Simbirsk = Ulyanovsk Russia 54°20N 48°25E 18 D8
Simcoe Canada 42°50N 80°23W 82 D4
Simcoe, L. Canada 44°25N 79°20W 82 B5
Simdega India 22°37N 84°31E 43 H11
Simeria Romania 45°51N 23°1E 17 F12
Simeulue Indonesia 2°45N 95°45E 36 D1
Simferopol Ukraine 44°55N 34°3E 19 F5
Simi Greece 36°35N 27°50E 23 F12
Simi Valley U.S.A. 34°16N 118°47W 79 L8
Simikot Nepal 30°0N 81°50E 43 E9
Simla = Shimla India 31°2N 77°9E 42 D7
Simlipal △ India 21°45N 86°30E 43 J12
Simmie Canada 49°56N 108°6W 71 D7
Simmler U.S.A. 35°21N 119°59W 79 K7
Simo älv = Simojoki → Finland 65°35N 25°1E 8 D21
Simojoki → Finland 65°35N 25°1E 8 D21
Simojovel Mexico 17°12N 92°38W 87 D6
Simonette → Canada 55°9N 118°15W 70 B5
Simonstown S. Africa 34°14S 18°26E 56 D2
Simpang Empat Malaysia 5°27N 100°29E 39 c
Simplonpass Switz. 46°15N 8°3E 20 C8
Simpson Desert Australia 25°0S 137°0E 62 D2
Simpson Desert △ Australia 24°59S 138°21E 62 C2
Simpson Pen. Canada 68°34N 88°45W 69 D14
Simrishamn Sweden 55°33N 14°22E 9 J16
Simsbury U.S.A. 41°53N 72°48W 83 E12
Simushir, Ostrov Russia 46°50N 152°30E 27 E16
Sin Cowe I. S. China Sea 9°53N 114°19E 36 C4
Sina → India 17°30N 75°55E 44 F2
Sina Dhago Somalia 5°50N 47°0E 49 F4
Sinabang Indonesia 2°30N 96°24E 36 D1
Sinai = Es Sînâ' Egypt 29°0N 34°0E 48 F2
Sinai, Mt. = Mûsa, Gebel Egypt 28°33N 33°59E 46 D2
Sinaloa □ Mexico 25°0N 107°30W 86 C3
Sinaloa de Leyva Mexico 25°50N 108°14W 86 B3
Sinan China 27°56N 108°13E 34 D7
Sincelejo Colombia 9°18N 75°24W 92 B3
Sinch'ang N. Korea 40°7N 128°28E 33 D15
Sinch'ŏn N. Korea 38°17N 125°21E 33 E13
Sinclair U.S.A. 41°47N 107°7W 76 F10
Sinclair Mills Canada 54°5N 121°40W 70 C4
Sinclair's B. U.K. 58°31N 3°5W 11 C5
Sinclairville U.S.A. 42°16N 79°16W 82 D5
Sincorá, Serra do Brazil 13°10S 41°20W 93 F10
Sind = Sindh □ Pakistan 26°0N 69°0E 42 G3
Sind → Jammu & Kashmir, India 34°18N 74°45E 43 B6
Sind → Mad. P., India 26°26N 79°13E 43 F8
Sind Sagar Doab Pakistan 32°0N 71°30E 42 D4
Sindangan Phil. 8°10N 123°5E 37 C6
Sindangbarang Indonesia 7°27S 107°1E 37 G12
Sindewahi India 20°17N 79°39E 44 D4
Sindgi India 16°55N 76°14E 44 F3
Sindh = Indus → Pakistan 24°20N 67°47E 42 G2
Sindh □ Pakistan 26°0N 69°0E 42 G3
Sindhnur India 15°47N 76°46E 45 F3
Sindhuli Garhi Nepal 27°16N 85°58E 43 F11
Sindi India 20°48N 78°52E 44 D4
Sindri India 23°45N 86°42E 43 H12
Sines Portugal 37°56N 8°51W 21 D1
Sines, C. de Portugal 37°58N 8°53W 21 D1
Sing Buri Thailand 14°53N 100°25E 38 E3
Singa Sudan 13°10N 33°57E 53 F12
Singalila △ India 27°10N 88°5E 43 F13
Singanallur India 11°2N 77°1E 45 J3
Singapore, Straits of Asia 1°15N 104°0E 39 d
Singaraja Indonesia 8°7S 115°6E 37 J18
Singatoka = Sigatoka Fiji 18°8S 177°32E 59 a
Singida Tanzania 4°49S 34°48E 54 E6
Singkang Indonesia 4°8S 120°1E 37 E6
Singkawang Indonesia 1°0N 108°57E 36 D3
Singkep Indonesia 0°30S 104°25E 36 E2
Singkil Indonesia 2°17N 97°49E 39 L1
Singkuang Indonesia 1°3N 98°55E 39 L2
Singleton Australia 32°33S 151°10E 63 E5
Singleton, Mt. N. Terr., Australia 22°0S 130°46E 60 D5
Singleton, Mt. W. Austral., Australia 29°27S 117°15E 61 E2
Singoli India 25°0N 75°22E 42 G6
Singora = Songkhla Thailand 7°13N 100°37E 39 J3
Singrauli India 24°7N 82°23E 43 G10
Sinh Ton, Dao = Sin Cowe I. S. China Sea 9°53N 114°19E 36 C4
Sinharaja Sri Lanka 6°25N 80°30E 45 L5
Sinhgarh India 18°22N 73°45E 44 E1
Sinhŭng N. Korea 40°11N 127°34E 33 D14
Siniscóla Italy 40°34N 9°41E 22 D3
Sinjai Indonesia 5°7S 120°20E 37 F6
Sinjār Iraq 36°19N 41°52E 46 B4
Sinkat Sudan 18°55N 36°49E 53 E13
Sinkiang = Xinjiang Uygur Zizhiqu □ China 42°0N 86°0E 30 C6
Sinmak N. Korea 38°25N 126°14E 33 E14
Sinmi-do N. Korea 39°33N 124°53E 33 E13
Sinnamary Fr. Guiana 5°25N 53°0W 93 B8
Sinnar India 19°48N 74°0E 44 E2
Sinni → Italy 40°8N 16°41E 22 D7
Sinop Turkey 42°1N 35°11E 19 F6
Sinor India 21°55N 73°20E 42 J5
Sinp'o N. Korea 40°0N 128°13E 33 E15
Sinsk Russia 61°8N 126°48E 27 C13
Sint-Hubert Belgium 50°2N 5°23E 15 D5
Sint-Niklaas Belgium 51°10N 4°8E 15 C4
Sint-Truiden Belgium 50°48N 5°10E 15 D5
Sintang Indonesia 0°5N 111°35E 36 D4
Sinton U.S.A. 28°2N 97°31W 84 G6
Sintra Portugal 38°47N 9°25W 21 C1
Sinŭiju N. Korea 40°5N 124°24E 33 D13
Siocon Phil. 7°40N 122°10E 37 C6
Siófok Hungary 46°54N 18°3E 17 E10
Sion Switz. 46°14N 7°20E 20 C7
Sion Mills U.K. 54°48N 7°29W 10 B4
tSionainn, An = Shannon → Ireland 52°35N 9°30W 10 D2
Sioux Center U.S.A. 43°5N 96°11W 80 D5
Sioux City U.S.A. 42°30N 96°24W 80 D5
Sioux Falls U.S.A. 43°33N 96°44W 80 D5
Sioux Lookout Canada 50°10N 91°50W 72 B1
Sioux Narrows Canada 49°25N 94°10W 71 D10
Sipadan Malaysia 4°6N 118°38E 37 D5
Siparia Trin. & Tob. 10°8N 61°31W 93 K15
Siping China 43°8N 124°21E 33 C13
Sipiwesk L. Canada 55°5N 97°35W 71 B9
Siple I. Antarctica 73°40S 125°10W 5 D14
Sipra → India 23°55N 75°28E 42 H6
Sipsongpanna = Xishuangbanna China 22°5N 101°1E 34 F3
Sipur India 21°11N 85°9E 44 D7
Sipura Indonesia 2°18S 99°40E 36 E1
Siquia → Nic. 12°10N 84°20W 88 D3
Siquijor Phil. 9°12N 123°35E 37 C6
Siquirres Costa Rica 10°6N 83°30W 88 D3
Şīr Abu Nu'ayr U.A.E. 25°20N 54°20E 47 E7
Şīr Banī Yās U.A.E. 24°19N 52°37E 47 E7
Sir Edward Pellew Group Australia 15°40S 137°10E 62 B2
Sir Graham Moore Is. Australia 13°53S 126°34E 60 B4
Sir James MacBrien, Mt. Canada 62°7N 127°41W 68 E6
Sira India 13°41N 76°49E 45 H3
Sira → Norway 58°23N 6°34E 9 G12
Siracusa Italy 37°4N 15°17E 22 F6
Sirajganj Bangla. 24°25N 89°47E 43 G13
Sirathu India 25°39N 81°19E 43 G9
Sīrdān Iran 36°39N 49°12E 47 B6
Siren U.S.A. 45°47N 92°24W 80 C7
Siret → Romania 45°24N 28°1E 17 F14
Sirghāyā Syria 33°51N 36°8E 48 B5
Sirikit Res. Thailand 17°45N 100°34E 38 C3
Sirinat △ Thailand 8°6N 98°17E 39 a
Sīrjān Iran 29°30N 55°45E 47 D7
Sirkali = Sirkazhi India 11°15N 79°41E 45 J4
Sirkazhi India 11°15N 79°41E 45 J4
Sirmaur India 24°51N 81°23E 43 G9
Sirmilik △ Canada 72°50N 80°35W 69 C15
Sirohi India 24°52N 72°53E 42 G5
Sironj India 24°5N 77°39E 42 G7
Síros = Ermoupoli Greece 37°28N 24°57E 23 F11
Sirpur India 19°29N 79°36E 44 E4
Sirr, Nafud as Si. Arabia 25°33N 44°35E 46 E5
Sirretta Pk. U.S.A. 35°56N 118°19W 79 K8
Sīrrī Iran 25°55N 54°32E 47 E7
Sirsa India 29°33N 75°4E 42 E6
Sirsa → India 26°51N 79°4E 43 F8

Sirsi *India* 14°40N 74°49E **45** G2
Sirsilla *India* 18°23N 78°50E **44** E4
Sirte = Surt *Libya* 31°11N 16°39E **53** B9
Siruguppa *India* 15°38N 76°54E **45** F3
Sirur *India* 18°50N 74°23E **44** E2
Širvan *Azerbaijan* 39°59N 48°52E **47** B6
Sisak *Croatia* 45°30N 16°21E **16** F9
Sishen *S. Africa* 27°47S 22°59E **56** C3
Sishui *China* 35°42N 117°18E **33** G9
Sisipuk L. *Canada* 55°45N 101°50W **71** B8
Sisophon *Cambodia* 13°38N 102°59E **38** F4
Sisseton *U.S.A.* 45°40N 97°3W **80** C5
Sīstān *Asia* 30°50N 61°0E **47** D9
Sīstān, Daryācheh-ye *Iran* 31°0N 61°0E **47** D9
Sīstān va Balūchestān □
  Iran 27°0N 62°0E **47** E9
Sisters *U.S.A.* 44°18N 121°33W **76** D3
Sisters, The *Seychelles* 4°16S 55°52E **55** b
Siswa Bazar *India* 27°9N 83°46E **43** F10
Sitamarhi *India* 26°37N 85°30E **43** F11
Sitapur *India* 27°38N 80°45E **43** F9
Siteki *Eswatini* 26°32S 31°58E **57** C5
Sitges *Spain* 41°17N 1°47E **21** B6
Sitia *Greece* 35°13N 26°6E **23** G12
Sitito-Ozima Ridge *Pac. Oc.* 23°0N 143°0E **64** E6
Sitka *U.S.A.* 57°3N 135°20W **70** B1
Sitkaing = Sagaing □
  Myanmar 21°52N 95°59E **41** J19
Sitoti *Botswana* 23°15S 23°40E **56** B3
Sittang Myit →
  Myanmar 17°20N 96°45E **41** L20
Sittard *Neths.* 51°0N 5°52E **15** C5
Sittingbourne *U.K.* 51°21N 0°45E **13** F8
Sittoung = Sittang Myit →
  Myanmar 17°20N 96°45E **41** L20
Sittwe *Myanmar* 20°18N 92°45E **41** J18
Situbondo *Indonesia* 7°42S 113°56E **37** G16
Si'umu *Samoa* 14°1S 171°48W **59** b
Siuna *Nic.* 13°37N 84°45W **88** D3
Siuri *India* 23°50N 87°34E **43** H12
Sivaganga *India* 9°50N 78°28E **45** K4
Sivagiri *India* 9°16N 77°26E **45** K3
Sivakasi *India* 9°24N 77°47E **45** K3
Sīvand *Iran* 30°5N 52°55E **47** D7
Sivas *Turkey* 39°43N 36°58E **46** B3
Sivasagar *India* 27°0N 94°36E **41** F19
Sivasamudram *India* 12°16N 77°10E **45** H3
Siverek *Turkey* 37°50N 39°19E **46** B3
Sivomaskinskiy *Russia* 66°40N 62°35E **18** A11
Sivrihisar *Turkey* 39°30N 31°35E **19** G5
Sīwa *Egypt* 29°11N 25°31E **53** C11
Siwa, El Wâhât es *Egypt* 29°10N 25°30E **50** D6
Siwa Oasis = Sīwa, El Wâhât es
  Egypt 29°10N 25°30E **50** D6
Siwalik Range *Nepal* 28°0N 83°0E **43** F10
Siwan *India* 26°13N 84°21E **43** F11
Siwana *India* 25°38N 72°25E **42** G5
Six Cross Roads *Barbados* 13°7N 59°28W **89** g
Sixian *China* 33°30N 117°50E **33** H9
Sixmilebridge *Ireland* 52°44N 8°46W **10** D3
Sixth Cataract *Sudan* 16°20N 32°42E **53** E12
Siyabuswa *S. Africa* 25°7S 29°3E **57** C4
Siyah Kuh, Kavīr-e *Iran* 30°0N 55°0E **47** C7
Siyang *China* 33°42N 118°40E **33** H10
Siziwang Qi *China* 41°25N 111°40E **32** D6
Sjælland *Denmark* 55°30N 11°30E **9** J14
Sjumen = Shumen
  Bulgaria 43°18N 26°55E **23** C12
Skadarsko Jezero *Europe* 42°10N 19°20E **23** C8
Skaftafell *Iceland* 64°1N 17°0W **8** D5
Skagafjörður *Iceland* 65°54N 19°35W **8** D4
Skagastølstindane *Norway* 61°28N 7°52E **8** F12
Skagaströnd *Iceland* 65°50N 20°19W **8** D3
Skagen *Denmark* 57°43N 10°35E **9** H14
Skagerrak *Denmark* 57°30N 9°0E **9** H13
Skagit → *U.S.A.* 48°23N 122°22W **78** B4
Skagway *U.S.A.* 59°28N 135°19W **68** F4
Skala-Podilska *Ukraine* 48°50N 26°15E **17** D14
Skalat *Ukraine* 49°23N 25°55E **17** D13
Skåne *Sweden* 55°59N 13°30E **9** J15
Skaneateles *U.S.A.* 42°57N 76°26W **83** D8
Skaneateles L. *U.S.A.* 42°51N 76°22W **83** D8
Skardu *Pakistan* 35°20N 75°44E **43** B6
Skarvan og Roltdalen △
  Norway 63°16N 11°31E **8** E14
Skarżysko-Kamienna
  Poland 51°7N 20°52E **17** C11
Skeena → *Canada* 54°9N 130°5W **70** C2
Skeena Mts. *Canada* 56°40N 128°30W **70** B3
Skegness *U.K.* 53°9N 0°20E **12** D8
Skeleton Coast *Namibia* 20°0S 13°0E **55** J2
Skeleton Coast △ *Namibia* 20°0S 13°20E **56** B1
Skellefteå *Sweden* 64°45N 20°50E **8** D19
Skellefteälv → *Sweden* 64°45N 21°9E **8** D19
Skellefteham *Sweden* 64°40N 21°9E **8** D19
Skellig Michael = Great Skellig
  Ireland 51°47N 10°33W **10** E1
Skerries *Ireland* 53°35N 6°8W **10** C5
Skerries, The *U.K.* 53°25N 4°36W **12** D3
Ski *Norway* 59°43N 10°52E **9** G14
Skiathos *Greece* 39°12N 23°30E **23** E10
Skibbereen *Ireland* 51°33N 9°16W **10** E2
Skiddaw *U.K.* 54°39N 3°9W **12** C4
Skidegate *Canada* 53°15N 132°1W **70** C2
Skien *Norway* 59°12N 9°35E **9** G13
Skierniewice *Poland* 51°58N 20°10E **17** C11
Skihist, Mt. *Canada* 50°12N 121°54W **70** C4
Skikda *Algeria* 36°50N 6°58E **52** A7
Skipton *U.K.* 53°58N 2°3W **12** D5
Skirmish Pt. *Australia* 11°59S 134°17E **62** A1
Skíros = Skyros *Greece* 38°55N 24°34E **23** E11
Skive *Denmark* 56°33N 9°2E **9** H13
Skjálfandafljót → *Iceland* 65°59N 17°25W **8** D5
Skjálfandi *Iceland* 66°5N 17°30E **8** C5
Skole *Ukraine* 49°3N 23°30E **17** D12
Skopelos *Greece* 39°9N 23°47E **23** E10
Skopje *Macedonia* 42°1N 21°26E **23** C9
Skövde *Sweden* 58°24N 13°50E **9** G15
Skovorodino *Russia* 54°0N 124°0E **27** D13
Skowhegan *U.S.A.* 44°46N 69°43W **81** C19
Skull *Ireland* 51°32N 9°34W **10** E2

Skunk → *U.S.A.* 40°42N 91°7W **80** E8
Skuodas *Lithuania* 56°16N 21°33E **9** H19
Skvyra *Ukraine* 49°44N 29°40E **17** D15
Sky Harbour Int., Phoenix ✈
  (PHX) *U.S.A.* 33°26N 112°5W **77** K7
Skye *U.K.* 57°15N 6°10W **11** D2
Skykomish *U.S.A.* 47°42N 121°22W **76** C3
Slade Point *Australia* 21°4S 149°13E **62** b
Slade Pt. *Australia* 21°5S 149°13E **62** b
Slættaratindur *Færoe Is.* 62°18N 7°1W **8** E9
Slagelse *Denmark* 55°23N 11°19E **9** J14
Slane *Ireland* 53°42N 6°33W **10** C5
Slaney → *Ireland* 52°26N 6°33W **10** D5
Slangberge *S. Africa* 31°32S 20°48E **56** D3
Śląsk *Poland* 51°0N 16°30E **16** C9
Slate Is. *Canada* 48°40N 87°0W **72** C2
Slatina *Romania* 44°28N 24°22E **17** F13
Slatington *U.S.A.* 40°45N 75°37W **83** F9
Slaton *U.S.A.* 33°26N 101°39W **84** E4
Slave → *Canada* 61°18N 113°39W **70** A6
Slave Coast *W. Afr.* 6°0N 2°30E **52** G6
Slave Lake *Canada* 55°17N 114°43W **70** B6
Slave Pt. *Canada* 61°11N 115°56W **70** A5
Slavgorod *Russia* 53°1N 78°37E **26** D8
Slavonski Brod *Croatia* 45°11N 18°1E **23** B8
Slavuta *Ukraine* 50°15N 27°2E **17** C14
Slavyanka *Russia* 42°53N 131°21E **28** C5
Slavyansk = Slovyansk
  Ukraine 48°55N 37°36E **19** E6
Slawharad *Belarus* 53°27N 31°0E **17** B16
Slea Hd. *Ireland* 52°6N 10°27W **10** D1
Sleaford *U.K.* 53°0N 0°24W **12** D7
Sleaford B. *Australia* 34°55S 135°45E **63** E2
Sleeper Is. *Canada* 58°30N 81°0W **69** F15
Sleeping Bear Dunes △
  U.S.A. 44°50N 86°5W **80** C10
Sleepy Eye *U.S.A.* 44°18N 94°43W **80** C6
Slemon L. *Canada* 63°13N 116°4W **70** A5
Slide Mt. *U.S.A.* 42°0N 74°25W **83** E10
Slidell *U.S.A.* 30°17N 89°47W **85** F10
Slieve Aughty *Ireland* 53°4N 8°30W **10** C3
Slieve Bloom *Ireland* 53°4N 7°40W **10** C4
Slieve Donard *U.K.* 54°11N 5°55W **10** B6
Slieve Gamph *Ireland* 54°6N 9°0W **10** B3
Slieve Gullion *U.K.* 54°7N 6°26W **10** B5
Slieve League *Ireland* 54°40N 8°42W **10** B3
Slieve Mish *Ireland* 52°12N 9°50W **10** D2
Slievenamon *Ireland* 52°25N 7°34W **10** D4
Sligeach = Sligo *Ireland* 54°16N 8°28W **10** B3
Sligo *Ireland* 54°16N 8°28W **10** B3
Sligo *U.S.A.* 41°6N 79°29W **82** E5
Sligo □ *Ireland* 54°8N 8°42W **10** B3
Sligo B. *Ireland* 54°18N 8°40W **10** B3
Slippery Rock *U.S.A.* 41°4N 80°3W **82** E4
Slite *Sweden* 57°42N 18°48E **9** H18
Sliven *Bulgaria* 42°42N 26°19E **23** C12
Sloan *U.S.A.* 35°57N 115°13W **79** K11
Sloansville *U.S.A.* 42°45N 74°22W **83** D10
Slobodskoy *Russia* 58°40N 50°6E **18** C9
Slobozia *Romania* 44°34N 27°23E **17** F14
Slocan *Canada* 49°48N 117°28W **70** D5
Slonim *Belarus* 53°4N 25°19E **17** B13
Slough *U.K.* 51°30N 0°36W **13** F7
Slough □ *U.K.* 51°30N 0°36W **13** F7
Sloughhouse *U.S.A.* 38°26N 121°12W **78** G5
Slovak Rep. = Slovakia ■
  Europe 48°30N 20°0E **17** D10
Slovakia ■ *Europe* 48°30N 20°0E **17** D10
Slovakian Ore Mts. = Slovenské
  Rudohorie *Slovakia* 48°30N 20°0E **17** D10
Slovenia ■ *Europe* 45°58N 14°30E **16** F8
Slovenija = Slovenia ■
  Europe 45°58N 14°30E **16** F8
Slovenska = Slovakia ■
  Europe 48°30N 20°0E **17** D10
Slovenské Rudohorie
  Slovakia 48°45N 20°0E **17** D10
Slovyansk *Ukraine* 48°55N 37°36E **19** E6
Sluch → *Ukraine* 51°37N 26°38E **17** C14
Sluis *Neths.* 51°18N 3°23E **15** C3
Słupsk *Poland* 54°30N 17°3E **17** A9
Slurry *S. Africa* 25°49S 25°42E **56** C4
Slutsk *Belarus* 53°2N 27°31E **17** B14
Slyne Hd. *Ireland* 53°25N 10°10W **10** C1
Slyudyanka *Russia* 51°40N 103°40E **27** D11
Småland *Sweden* 57°15N 15°25E **9** H16
Smalltree L. *Canada* 61°0N 105°0W **71** A8
Smallwood Res. *Canada* 54°5N 64°30W **73** B7
Smarhon *Belarus* 54°20N 26°24E **17** A14
Smartt Syndicate Dam
  S. Africa 30°45S 23°10E **56** D3
Smartville *U.S.A.* 39°13N 121°18W **78** F5
Smeaton *Canada* 53°30N 104°49W **71** C8
Smederevo *Serbia* 44°40N 20°57E **23** B9
Smeralda, Costa *Italy* 41°5N 9°35E **22** D3
Smerwick Harbour
  Ireland 52°12N 10°23W **10** D1
Smethport *U.S.A.* 41°49N 78°27W **82** E6
Smidovich *Russia* 48°36N 133°49E **27** E14
Smith *Canada* 55°10N 114°0W **70** B6
Smith Center *U.S.A.* 39°47N 98°47W **80** F4
Smith I. *Canada* 60°45N 78°25W **69** E16
Smith I. *India* 13°20N 93°4E **45** H11
Smith Islands △ *Australia* 20°40S 149°9E **62** b
Smith River → *U.S.A.* 41°55N 124°0W **76** F2
Smith Sd. *N. Amer.* 78°25N 74°0W **69** B18
Smithburne → *Australia* 17°3S 140°57E **62** B3
Smithers *Canada* 54°45N 127°10W **70** C3
Smithfield *S. Africa* 30°9S 26°30E **57** D4
Smithfield *N.C., U.S.A.* 35°31N 78°21W **85** D15
Smithfield *Utah, U.S.A.* 41°50N 111°50W **76** F8
Smiths Falls *Canada* 44°55N 76°0W **83** B9
Smithton *Australia* 40°53S 145°6E **63** G4
Smithville *Canada* 43°6N 79°33W **82** C5
Smithville *U.S.A.* 30°1N 97°10W **84** F6
Smoke Creek Desert
  U.S.A. 40°30N 119°40W **76** F4
Smoky → *Canada* 56°10N 117°21W **70** B5

Smoky Bay *Australia* 32°22S 134°13E **63** E1
Smoky Hill → *U.S.A.* 39°4N 96°48W **80** F5
Smoky Hills *U.S.A.* 39°15N 99°30W **80** F4
Smoky Lake *Canada* 54°10N 112°30W **70** C6
Smøla *Norway* 63°23N 8°3E **8** E13
Smolensk *Russia* 54°45N 32°5E **18** D5
Smolikas, Oros *Greece* 40°9N 20°58E **23** D9
Smolyan *Bulgaria* 41°36N 24°38E **23** D11
Smooth Rock Falls
  Canada 49°17N 81°37W **72** C3
Smoothstone L. *Canada* 54°40N 106°50W **71** C7
Smorgon = Smarhon
  Belarus 54°20N 26°24E **17** A14
Smyley I. *Antarctica* 72°55S 78°0W **5** D17
Smyrna = İzmir *Turkey* 38°25N 27°8E **23** E12
Smyrna *U.S.A.* 39°18N 75°36W **81** F16
Snæfell *Iceland* 64°48N 15°34W **8** D6
Snaefell *I. of Man* 54°16N 4°27W **12** C3
Snæfellsjökull *Iceland* 64°49N 23°46W **8** D2
Snake → *U.S.A.* 46°12N 119°2W **76** C4
Snake I. *Australia* 38°47S 146°33E **63** F4
Snake Range *U.S.A.* 39°0N 114°20W **76** G6
Snake River Plain *U.S.A.* 42°50N 114°0W **76** E7
Snåsavatnet *Norway* 64°12N 12°0E **8** D15
Sneek *Neths.* 53°2N 5°40E **15** A5
Sneem *Ireland* 51°50N 9°54W **10** E2
Sneeuberge *S. Africa* 31°46S 24°20E **56** D3
Snelling *U.S.A.* 37°31N 120°26W **78** H6
Snežka *Europe* 50°41N 15°50E **16** C8
Snizort, L. *U.K.* 57°33N 6°28W **11** D2
Snøhetta *Norway* 62°19N 9°16E **8** E13
Snohomish *U.S.A.* 47°55N 122°6W **78** C4
Snoqualmie *U.S.A.* 47°31N 121°49W **78** C5
Snoqualmie Pass *U.S.A.* 47°25N 121°25W **78** C5
Snoul *Cambodia* 12°4N 106°26E **39** F6
Snover *U.S.A.* 43°27N 82°58W **82** C2
Snow Hill *U.S.A.* 38°11N 75°24W **81** F16
Snow Lake *Canada* 54°52N 100°3W **71** C8
Snow Mt. *Calif., U.S.A.* 39°23N 122°45W **78** F4
Snow Mt. *Maine, U.S.A.* 45°18N 70°48W **83** A14
Snow Shoe *U.S.A.* 41°2N 77°57W **82** E7
Snowbird L. *Canada* 60°45N 103°0W **71** A8
Snowdon *U.K.* 53°4N 4°5W **12** D3
Snowdonia △ *U.K.* 53°7N 3°59W **12** D4
Snowdrift = Łutsel K'e
  Canada 62°24N 110°44W **71** A6
Snowdrift → *Canada* 62°24N 110°44W **71** A6
Snowflake *U.S.A.* 34°30N 110°5W **77** J8
Snowtown *Australia* 33°46S 138°14E **63** E2
Snowville *U.S.A.* 41°58N 112°43W **76** F7
Snowy → *Australia* 37°46S 148°30E **63** F4
Snowy Mt. *U.S.A.* 43°42N 74°23W **83** C10
Snowy Mts. *Australia* 36°30S 148°20E **63** F4
Snug Corner *Bahamas* 22°33N 73°52W **89** B5
Snug Harbour *Canada* 45°22N 80°17W **82** A4
Snyatyn *Ukraine* 48°27N 25°38E **17** D13
Snyder *Okla., U.S.A.* 34°40N 98°57W **84** H5
Snyder *Tex., U.S.A.* 32°44N 100°55W **84** E4
Soalala *Madag.* 16°6S 45°20E **55** H9
Soan → *Pakistan* 33°1N 71°44E **42** C4
Sobat → *South Sudan* 9°22N 31°33E **53** G12
Sobhapur *India* 22°47N 78°17E **42** H8
Sobradinho, Represa de
  Brazil 9°30S 42°0W **93** E10
Sobral *Brazil* 3°50S 40°20W **93** D10
Soc Giang *Vietnam* 22°54N 106°1E **34** F6
Soc Trang *Vietnam* 9°37N 105°50E **39** H5
Socastee *U.S.A.* 33°41N 78°59W **85** E15
Soch'e = Shache *China* 38°20N 77°10E **30** D4
Sochi *Russia* 43°35N 39°40E **19** F6
Société, Îs. de la
  French Polynesia 17°0S 151°0W **65** J12
Society Is. = Société, Îs. de la
  French Polynesia 17°0S 151°0W **65** J12
Socompa, Portezuelo de
  Chile 24°27S 68°18W **94** A2
Socorro *N. Mex., U.S.A.* 34°4N 106°54W **77** J10
Socorro *Tex., U.S.A.* 31°39N 106°18W **84** F1
Socorro, I. *Mexico* 18°45N 110°58W **86** D2
Socotra *Yemen* 12°30N 54°0E **49** E5
Soda L. *U.S.A.* 35°10N 116°4W **79** K10
Soda Plains *India* 35°30N 79°0E **43** B8
Soda Springs *U.S.A.* 42°39N 111°36W **76** E8
Sodankylä *Finland* 67°29N 26°40E **8** C22
Soddy-Daisy *U.S.A.* 35°17N 85°10W **85** D12
Söderhamn *Sweden* 61°18N 17°10E **8** F17
Söderköping *Sweden* 58°31N 16°20E **9** G17
Södermanland *Sweden* 58°56N 16°55E **9** G17
Södertälje *Sweden* 59°12N 17°39E **9** G17
Sodiri *Sudan* 14°27N 29°0E **53** F11
Sodus *U.S.A.* 43°14N 77°4W **82** C7
Sodwana Bay △ *S. Africa* 27°35S 32°43E **57** C5
Soe *Indonesia* 9°52S 124°17E **60** A3
Soekmekaar = Morebeng
  S. Africa 23°30S 29°55E **57** B4
Soest *Neths.* 52°9N 5°19E **15** B5
Sofala □ *Mozam.* 19°30S 34°30E **57** A5
Sofia *Bulgaria* 42°45N 23°20E **23** C10
Sofia → *Madag.* 15°27S 47°23E **55** H9
Sofiya = Sofia *Bulgaria* 42°45N 23°20E **23** C10
Sōfu-Gan *Japan* 29°49N 140°21E **29** K10
Sogamoso *Colombia* 5°43N 72°56W **92** B4
Sogār *Iran* 25°53N 58°6E **47** E8
Sogndalsfjøra *Norway* 61°14N 7°5E **8** F12
Søgne *Norway* 58°5N 7°48E **9** G12
Sognefjorden *Norway* 61°10N 5°50E **8** F11
Soh *Iran* 33°26N 51°27E **47** C6
Sohâg *Egypt* 26°33N 31°43E **53** C12
Sohagpur *India* 22°42N 78°12E **42** H8
Sohar = Şuḥār *Oman* 24°20N 56°40E **47** E8
Sohela *India* 21°18N 83°24E **44** D6
Soheuksando *S. Korea* 34°4N 125°7E **33** G13
Soignies *Belgium* 50°35N 4°5E **15** D4
Soissons *France* 49°25N 3°19E **20** B5
Sojat *India* 25°55N 73°45E **42** G5
Sokal *Ukraine* 50°31N 24°15E **17** C13
Sokcho *S. Korea* 38°12N 128°36E **33** E15
Söke *Turkey* 37°48N 27°28E **23** F12
Sokhumi *Georgia* 43°0N 41°0E **19** F7

Sokodé *Togo* 9°0N 1°11E **52** G6
Sokol *Russia* 59°30N 40°5E **18** C7
Sokółka *Poland* 53°25N 23°30E **17** B12
Sokołów Podlaski
  Poland 52°25N 22°15E **17** B12
Sokoto *Nigeria* 13°2N 5°16E **52** F7
Sol, Costa del *Spain* 36°30N 4°30W **21** D3
Sol Iletsk *Russia* 51°10N 55°0E **18** D10
Solan *India* 30°55N 77°7E **42** D7
Solana Beach *U.S.A.* 32°58N 117°16W **79** N9
Solander I. *N.Z.* 46°34S 166°54E **59** G1
Solapur *India* 17°43N 75°56E **44** F2
Soldotna *U.S.A.* 60°29N 151°3W **68** E1
Soledad *Colombia* 10°55N 74°46W **92** A4
Soledad *U.S.A.* 36°26N 121°20W **78** J5
Soledad *Venezuela* 8°10N 63°34W **92** B6
Solent, The *U.K.* 50°45N 1°25W **13** G6
Solfonntaggen *Norway* 60°2N 6°57E **9** F12
Solhan *Turkey* 38°57N 41°3E **46** B4
Soligalich *Russia* 59°5N 42°10E **18** C7
Soligorsk = Salihorsk
  Belarus 52°51N 27°27E **17** B14
Solihull *U.K.* 52°26N 1°47W **13** E6
Solikamsk *Russia* 59°38N 56°50E **18** C10
Solimões = Amazonas →
  S. Amer. 0°5S 50°0W **93** D8
Solingen *Germany* 51°10N 7°5E **16** C4
Sollefteå *Sweden* 63°12N 17°20E **8** E17
Sóller *Spain* 39°46N 2°43E **21** C7
Solo → *Indonesia* 6°47S 112°22E **37** G15
Sologne *France* 47°40N 1°45E **20** C4
Solok *Indonesia* 0°45S 100°40E **36** E2
Sololá *Guatemala* 14°49N 91°10W **88** D1
Solomon, N. Fork →
  U.S.A. 39°29N 98°26W **80** F4
Solomon, S. Fork →
  U.S.A. 39°25N 99°12W **80** F4
Solomon Is. ■ *Pac. Oc.* 6°0S 155°0E **58** B8
Solomon Rise *Pac. Oc.* 1°0N 157°0E **64** G7
Solon *China* 46°32N 121°10E **31** B13
Solon Springs *U.S.A.* 46°22N 91°49W **80** B8
Solor *Indonesia* 8°27S 123°0E **37** F6
Solothurn *Switz.* 47°13N 7°32E **20** C7
Solovetskiye Ostrova
  Russia 65°5N 35°40E **18** B6
Šolta *Croatia* 43°24N 16°15E **22** C7
Solţānābād *Khorāsān, Iran* 34°13N 59°58E **47** C8
Solţānābād *Khorāsān, Iran* 36°29N 58°5E **47** B8
Solţāniyeh *Iran* 36°26N 48°47E **47** B6
Solunska Glava
  Macedonia 41°44N 21°31E **23** D9
Solvang *U.S.A.* 34°36N 120°8W **79** L6
Solvay *U.S.A.* 43°3N 76°13W **83** C8
Sölvesborg *Sweden* 56°5N 14°35E **9** H16
Solvychegodsk *Russia* 61°21N 46°56E **18** B8
Solway Firth *U.K.* 54°49N 3°35W **12** C4
Solwezi *Zambia* 12°11S 26°21E **55** G5
Sōma *Japan* 37°40N 140°50E **28** F10
Soma *Turkey* 39°10N 27°35E **23** E12
Somabhula *Zimbabwe* 19°42S 29°40E **57** A4
Somali Pen. *Africa* 7°0N 46°0E **50** F8
Somalia ■ *Africa* 7°0N 47°0E **49** F4
Somaliland □ *Somalia* 10°0N 46°0E **49** F4
Sombor *Serbia* 45°46N 19°9E **23** B8
Sombra *Canada* 42°43N 82°29W **82** D2
Sombrerete *Mexico* 23°38N 103°39W **86** C4
Sombrero *Anguilla* 18°37N 63°30W **89** C7
Sombrero Channel *India* 7°41N 93°35E **45** L11
Somdari *India* 25°47N 72°38E **42** G5
Somers *U.S.A.* 48°5N 114°13W **76** B6
Somerset *Ky., U.S.A.* 37°5N 84°36W **81** G11
Somerset *Mass., U.S.A.* 41°47N 71°8W **83** E13
Somerset *Pa., U.S.A.* 40°1N 79°5W **82** F5
Somerset □ *U.K.* 51°9N 3°0W **13** F5
Somerset East *S. Africa* 32°42S 25°35E **56** D4
Somerset I. *Canada* 73°30N 93°0W **68** C13
Somerset West *S. Africa* 34°8S 18°50E **56** D2
Somersworth *U.S.A.* 43°16N 70°52W **83** C14
Somerton *U.S.A.* 32°36N 114°43W **77** K6
Somerville *U.S.A.* 40°35N 74°38W **83** F10
Someş → *Romania* 47°49N 22°43E **17** D12
Somme → *France* 50°11N 1°38E **20** A4
Somnath *India* 20°53N 70°22E **42** J4
Somosierra, Puerto de
  Spain 41°4N 3°35W **21** B4
Somosomo *Fiji* 16°47S 179°58W **59** a
Somosomo Str. *Fiji* 16°0S 180°0E **59** a
Somoto *Nic.* 13°28N 86°37W **88** D2
Somport, Túnel de *Spain* 42°48N 0°31W **20** E3
Somvarpet *India* 12°36N 75°52E **45** H2
Son → *India* 25°42N 84°52E **43** G11
Son, Laem *Thailand* 7°59N 98°16E **39** a
Son Ha *Vietnam* 15°3N 108°34E **38** E7
Son La *Vietnam* 21°20N 103°50E **34** G4
Son Tay *Vietnam* 21°8N 105°30E **34** G5
Son Tinh *Vietnam* 15°10N 108°40E **38** E7
Soná *Panama* 8°0N 81°20W **88** E3
Sonamarg *India* 34°18N 75°21E **43** B6
Sonamukhi *India* 23°18N 87°27E **43** H12
Sonar → *India* 24°24N 79°56E **43** G8
Sönch'ŏn *N. Korea* 39°48N 124°55E **33** E13
Sondags → *S. Africa* 33°44S 25°51E **56** D4
Sønderborg *Denmark* 54°55N 9°49E **9** J13
Sóndrio *Italy* 46°10N 9°52E **20** C8
Sonepur *India* 20°55N 83°50E **44** D6
Song *Thailand* 18°28N 100°11E **38** C3
Song Cau *Vietnam* 13°27N 109°18E **38** F7
Song Ma *Vietnam* 20°56N 103°53E **34** G4
Song Xian *China* 34°12N 112°8E **32** G7
Songadh *India* 21°9N 73°33E **44** D1
Songan *Indonesia* 8°13S 115°24E **37** J18
Songea *Tanzania* 10°40S 35°40E **54** G7
Songgang *China* 22°46N 113°50E **31** a
Songhua Hu *China* 43°35N 126°50E **33** C14
Songhua Jiang →
  China 47°45N 132°30E **31** B15
Songjiang *China* 31°1N 121°12E **35** B13
Songjianghe *China* 42°10N 127°29E **33** C14

Sŏngjin = Kimch'aek
  N. Korea 40°40N 129°10E **33** D15
Songkan *China* 28°35N 106°52E **34** C6
Songkhla *Thailand* 7°13N 100°37E **39** J3
Songming *China* 25°12N 103°2E **34** E4
Songnim *N. Korea* 38°45N 125°39E **33** E13
Songo *Mozam.* 15°34S 32°38E **57** A5
Songpan *China* 32°40N 103°30E **34** A4
Songtao *China* 28°11N 109°10E **34** C7
Songxi *China* 27°31N 118°44E **35** D12
Songzi *China* 30°12N 111°45E **35** B8
Sonhat *India* 23°29N 82°31E **43** H10
Sonid Youqi *China* 42°45N 112°48E **32** C7
Sonid Zuoqi *China* 43°50N 113°42E **32** C7
Sonipat *India* 29°0N 77°5E **42** E7
Sonkach *India* 22°59N 76°21E **42** H7
Sonmiani *Pakistan* 25°25N 66°40E **42** G2
Sonmiani B. *Pakistan* 25°15N 66°30E **42** G2
Sono → *Brazil* 9°58S 48°11W **93** E9
Sonoma *U.S.A.* 38°18N 122°28W **78** G4
Sonora *Calif., U.S.A.* 37°59N 120°23W **78** H6
Sonora *Tex., U.S.A.* 30°34N 100°39W **84** F4
Sonora → *Mexico* 29°20N 110°40W **86** B2
Sonora □ *Mexico* 29°5N 110°55W **86** B2
Sonoran Desert *U.S.A.* 33°40N 113°30W **79** L12
Sonoyta *Mexico* 31°51N 112°50W **86** A2
Sonsonate *El Salv.* 13°43N 89°44W **88** D2
Soochow = Suzhou
  China 31°19N 120°38E **35** B13
Sooke *Canada* 48°13N 123°43W **78** B3
Soomaaliya = Somalia ■
  Africa 7°0N 47°0E **49** F4
Sop Hao *Laos* 20°33N 104°27E **34** G5
Sop Prap *Thailand* 17°53N 99°20E **38** D2
Sopi *Indonesia* 2°34N 128°28E **37** D7
Sopot *Poland* 54°27N 18°31E **17** A10
Sopron *Hungary* 47°45N 16°32E **17** E9
Sopur *India* 34°18N 74°27E **43** B6
Sør-Rondane *Antarctica* 72°0S 25°0E **5** D4
Sorab *India* 14°23N 75°6E **45** G2
Sorada *India* 19°45N 84°26E **44** E7
Sorah *Pakistan* 27°13N 68°56E **42** F3
Soraon *India* 25°37N 81°51E **43** G9
Sord = Swords *Ireland* 53°28N 6°13W **10** C5
Sorel-Tracy *Canada* 46°0N 73°10W **72** C5
Sórgono *Italy* 40°1N 9°6E **22** D3
Soria *Spain* 41°43N 2°32W **21** B4
Soriano *Uruguay* 33°24S 58°19W **94** C4
Sorkh, Kuh-e *Iran* 35°40N 58°30E **47** C8
Soroca *Moldova* 48°8N 28°12E **17** D15
Sorocaba *Brazil* 23°31S 47°27W **95** A6
Sorochinsk *Russia* 52°26N 53°10E **18** D9
Soroki = Soroca *Moldova* 48°8N 28°12E **17** D15
Sorong *Indonesia* 0°55S 131°15E **37** E8
Soroti *Uganda* 1°43N 33°35E **54** D6
Sørøya *Norway* 70°40N 22°30E **8** A20
Sørøysundet *Norway* 70°25N 23°0E **8** A20
Sorrell *Australia* 42°47S 147°34E **63** G4
Sorrento *Italy* 40°37N 14°22E **22** D6
Sorsele *Sweden* 65°31N 17°30E **8** D17
Sorsogon *Phil.* 13°0N 124°0E **37** B6
Sortavala *Russia* 61°42N 30°41E **8** F24
Sortland *Norway* 68°42N 15°25E **8** B16
Sørvágen *Norway* 67°53N 13°1E **8** C15
Soscumica, L. *Canada* 50°15N 77°27W **72** B4
Sosnogorsk *Russia* 63°37N 53°51E **18** B9
Sosnowiec *Poland* 50°20N 19°10E **17** C10
Sossus Vlei *Namibia* 24°45S 15°23E **56** B2
Sôsura *N. Korea* 42°16N 130°36E **33** C16
Sot → *India* 27°27N 79°37E **43** F8
Sotavento *Cabo Verde* 15°0N 24°0W **52** b
Sotkamo *Finland* 64°8N 28°23E **8** D23
Soto la Marina *Mexico* 23°46N 98°13W **87** C5
Soto la Marina →
  Mexico 23°45N 97°45W **87** C5
Sotuta *Mexico* 20°36N 89°1W **87** C7
Souanké *Congo* 2°10N 14°3E **54** D2
Souda, Órmos *Greece* 35°25N 24°10E **23** G11
Souderton *U.S.A.* 40°19N 75°19W **83** F9
Soufrière *Guadeloupe* 16°5N 61°40W **88** b
Soufrière *St. Lucia* 13°51N 61°3W **89** f
Soufrière Bay *Dominica* 15°13N 61°22W **89** f
Soukhouma *Laos* 14°38N 105°48E **38** E5
Sound, The *U.K.* 50°20N 4°10W **13** G3
Sound I. *India* 13°27N 92°59E **45** H11
Sources, Mt. aux *Lesotho* 28°45S 28°50E **57** C4
Soure *Brazil* 0°35S 48°30W **93** D9
Souris *Man., Canada* 49°40N 100°20W **71** D8
Souris *P.E.I., Canada* 46°21N 62°15W **73** C7
Souris → *N. Amer.* 49°40N 99°34W **80** A4
Sousse *Tunisia* 35°50N 10°38E **53** A8
Sout → *S. Africa* 31°5S 18°24E **56** E2
South Africa ■ *Africa* 32°0S 23°0E **56** D3
South America 10°0S 60°0W **90** E5
South Andaman *India* 11°45N 92°10E **45** J11
South Aulatsivik I.
  Canada 56°45N 61°30W **73** A7
South Australia □
  Australia 32°0S 139°0E **63** E2
South Australian Basin
  Ind. Oc. 38°0S 126°0E **64** L4
South Ayrshire □ *U.K.* 55°18N 4°41W **11** F4
South Baldy Pk. *U.S.A.* 34°6N 107°11W **77** J10
South Bass I. *U.S.A.* 41°39N 82°49W **82** E2
South Bend *Ind., U.S.A.* 41°41N 86°15W **80** E10
South Bend *Wash.,
  U.S.A.* 46°40N 123°48W **78** D3
South Boston *U.S.A.* 36°42N 78°54W **81** G14
South Branch *Canada* 47°55N 59°2W **73** C8
South Brook *Canada* 49°26N 56°5W **73** C8
South Brother I. *India* 10°56N 92°37E **45** J11
South Bruny I. *Australia* 43°20S 147°15E **63** G4
South Carolina □ *U.S.A.* 34°0N 81°0W **85** E14
South Charleston
  U.S.A. 38°22N 81°44W **81** F13
South China Sea *Asia* 10°0N 113°0E **36** C4
South Cumberland Is. △
  Australia 20°42S 149°11E **62** b
South Dakota □ *U.S.A.* 44°15N 100°0W **80** C4
South Dayton *U.S.A.* 42°21N 79°3W **82** D5

South Deerfield *U.S.A.* 42°29N 72°37W **83 D12**
South Downs *U.K.* 50°52N 0°25W **13 G7**
South Downs △ *U.K.* 50°50N 0°50W **13 G7**
South Dublin □ *Ireland* 53°16N 6°24W **10 C5**
South East □ *Botswana* 25°0S 25°40E **56 C4**
South East L. *Australia* 43°40S 146°50E **63 G4**
South East Is. *Australia* 34°17S 123°30E **61 F3**
South Esk → *U.K.* 56°43N 2°31W **11 E6**
South Fiji Basin *Pac. Oc.* 26°0S 175°0E **64 K9**
South Foreland *U.K.* 51°8N 1°24E **13 F9**
South Fork American →
　U.S.A. 38°57N 120°59W **78 G5**
South Fork Feather →
　U.S.A. 39°17N 121°36W **78 F5**
South Fork Grand →
　U.S.A. 45°43N 102°17W **80 C2**
South Fork Milk →
　U.S.A. 48°4N 106°19W **76 B10**
South Fork Republican →
　U.S.A. 40°3N 101°31W **80 E3**
South Georgia *Antarctica* 54°30S 37°0W **96 G9**
South Gloucestershire □
　U.K. 51°32N 2°28W **13 F5**
South Hadley *U.S.A.* 42°16N 72°35W **83 D12**
South Haven *U.S.A.* 42°24N 86°16W **80 D10**
South Henik L. *Canada* 61°30N 97°20W **71 A9**
South Horr *Kenya* 2°12N 36°56E **54 D7**
South I. *India* 10°3N 72°17E **45 J1**
South I. *N.Z.* 44°0S 170°0E **59 F3**
South Indian Lake
　Canada 56°47N 98°56W **71 B9**
South Invercargill *N.Z.* 46°26S 168°23E **59 G2**
South Knife → *Canada* 58°55N 94°37W **71 B10**
South Koel → *India* 22°32N 85°14E **43 H11**
South Korea ■ *Asia* 36°0N 128°0E **33 G15**
South Lake Tahoe
　U.S.A. 38°57N 119°59W **78 G6**
South Lanarkshire □
　U.K. 55°37N 3°53W **11 F5**
South Loup → *U.S.A.* 41°4N 98°39W **80 E4**
South Magnetic Pole
　Antarctica 64°8S 138°8E **5 C9**
South Milwaukee
　U.S.A. 42°55N 87°52W **80 D10**
South Molton *U.K.* 51°1N 3°51W **13 F4**
South Moose L. *Canada* 53°49N 100°1W **71 C8**
South Nahanni →
　Canada 61°3N 123°21W **70 A4**
South Nation → *Canada* 45°34N 75°6W **83 A9**
South Natuna Is. = Natuna
　Selatan, Kepulauan
　Indonesia 2°45N 109°0E **36 D3**
South Negril Pt. *Jamaica* 18°16N 78°22W **88 a**
South Orkney Is. *Antarctica* 63°0S 45°0W **5 C18**
South Ossetia □ *Georgia* 42°21N 44°2E **19 F7**
South Otselic *U.S.A.* 42°38N 75°46W **83 D9**
South Pagai, I. = Pagai Selatan,
　Pulau *Indonesia* 3°0S 100°15E **36 E2**
South Paris *U.S.A.* 44°14N 70°31W **83 B14**
South Pittsburg *U.S.A.* 35°1N 85°42W **85 D12**
South Platte → *U.S.A.* 41°7N 100°42W **80 E3**
South Pole *Antarctica* 90°0S 0°0 **5 E**
South Porcupine *Canada* 48°30N 81°12W **72 C3**
South Portland *U.S.A.* 43°38N 70°15W **81 D18**
South Pt. *Barbados* 13°2N 59°32W **89 g**
South Pt. *U.S.A.* 44°52N 83°19W **82 B1**
South River *Canada* 45°52N 79°23W **72 C4**
South River *U.S.A.* 40°27N 74°23W **83 F10**
South Ronaldsay *U.K.* 58°48N 2°58W **11 C6**
South Sandwich Is.
　Antarctica 57°0S 27°0W **5 B1**
South Sandwich Trench
　Atl. Oc. 56°0S 24°0W **5 B1**
South Saskatchewan →
　Canada 53°15N 105°5W **71 C7**
South Seal → *Canada* 58°48N 98°8W **71 B9**
South Sentinel I. *India* 10°59N 92°14E **45 J11**
South Shetland Is.
　Antarctica 62°0S 59°0W **5 C18**
South Shields *U.K.* 55°0N 1°25W **12 C6**
South Sioux City *U.S.A.* 42°28N 96°24W **80 D6**
South Sister *U.S.A.* 44°4N 121°51W **76 D3**
South Sudan ■ *Africa* 8°0N 30°0E **53 G11**
South Taranaki Bight
　N.Z. 39°40S 174°5E **59 C5**
South Tasman Rise
　S. Ocean 48°0S 146°0E **5 A10**
South Thompson →
　Canada 50°40N 120°20W **70 C4**
South Twin I. *Canada* 53°7N 79°52W **72 B4**
South Tyne → *U.K.* 54°59N 2°8W **12 C5**
South Uist *U.K.* 57°20N 7°15W **11 D1**
South Valley *U.S.A.* 35°1N 106°41W **77 J10**
South Wellesley Is.
　Australia 16°58S 139°17E **62 B2**
South West C. *Australia* 43°34S 146°3E **63 G4**
South West C. *N.Z.* 47°17S 167°28E **59 G1**
South Williamsport
　U.S.A. 41°13N 77°0W **82 E8**
South Yorkshire □ *U.K.* 53°27N 1°36W **12 D6**
Southampton *Canada* 44°30N 81°25W **82 B3**
Southampton *U.K.* 50°54N 1°23W **13 G6**
Southampton *U.S.A.* 40°53N 72°23W **83 F12**
Southampton □ *U.K.* 50°54N 1°23W **13 G6**
Southampton I. *Canada* 64°30N 84°0W **69 E15**
Southaven *U.S.A.* 34°59N 90°0W **85 D9**
Southbank *Canada* 54°2N 125°46W **70 C3**
Southbridge *N.Z.* 43°48S 172°16E **59 E4**
Southbridge *U.S.A.* 42°5N 72°2W **83 D12**
Southend *Canada* 56°19N 103°22W **71 B8**
Southend-on-Sea *U.K.* 51°32N 0°44E **13 F8**
Southend-on-Sea □ *U.K.* 51°32N 0°44E **13 F8**
Southern = Yuzhnyy □
　Russia 44°0N 40°0E **26 E5**
Southern Alps *N.Z.* 43°41S 170°11E **59 E3**
Southern Cross *Australia* 31°12S 119°15E **61 F2**
Southern Indian L.
　Canada 57°10N 98°30W **71 B9**
Southern Lau Group *Fiji* 18°40S 178°40W **59 a**
Southern Ocean 62°0S 60°0E **5 C6**
Southern Pines *U.S.A.* 35°11N 79°24W **85 D15**

Southern Uplands *U.K.* 55°28N 3°52W **11 F5**
Southington *U.S.A.* 41°36N 72°53W **83 E12**
Southland □ *N.Z.* 45°30S 168°0E **59 F1**
Southold *U.S.A.* 41°4N 72°26W **83 E12**
Southport *Australia* 27°58S 153°25E **63 D5**
Southport *U.K.* 53°39N 3°0W **12 D4**
Southport *U.S.A.* 42°3N 76°49W **82 D8**
Southwest △ *Australia* 43°8S 146°5E **63 G4**
Southwest Pacific Basin
　Pac. Oc. 40°0S 140°0W **5 A12**
Southwold *U.K.* 52°20N 1°41E **13 E9**
Southwood △ *Australia* 27°48S 150°8E **63 D5**
Soutpansberg *S. Africa* 23°0S 29°30E **57 B4**
Sovetsk *Kaliningrad, Russia* 55°6N 21°50E **9 J19**
Sovetsk *Kirov, Russia* 57°38N 48°53E **18 C8**
Sovetskaya Gavan
　Russia 48°58N 140°18E **27 E15**
Sowma'eh Sarā *Iran* 37°17N 49°18E **47 B6**
Sōya-Kaikyō = La Perouse Str.
　Asia 45°40N 142°0E **28 B11**
Sōya-Misaki *Japan* 45°30N 141°55E **28 B10**
Soyo *Angola* 6°13S 12°20E **54 F2**
Sozh → *Belarus* 51°57N 30°48E **17 B16**
Spa *Belgium* 50°29N 5°53E **15 D5**
Spain ■ *Europe* 39°0N 4°0W **21 B4**
Spalding *Australia* 33°30S 138°37E **63 E2**
Spalding *U.K.* 52°48N 0°9W **12 E7**
Spanaway *U.S.A.* 47°6N 122°26W **78 C4**
Spangler *U.S.A.* 40°39N 78°48W **82 F6**
Spanish *Canada* 46°12N 82°20W **72 C3**
Spanish Fork *U.S.A.* 40°7N 111°39W **76 F8**
Spanish Town
　Br. Virgin Is. 18°26N 64°26W **89 e**
Spanish Town *Jamaica* 18°0N 76°57W **88 a**
Sparks *U.S.A.* 39°32N 119°45W **78 F7**
Sparta = Sparti *Greece* 37°5N 22°25E **23 F10**
Sparta *Mich., U.S.A.* 43°10N 85°42W **81 D11**
Sparta *N.J., U.S.A.* 41°2N 74°38W **83 E10**
Sparta *Wis., U.S.A.* 43°56N 90°49W **80 D8**
Spartanburg *U.S.A.* 34°56N 81°57W **85 D14**
Sparti *Greece* 37°5N 22°25E **23 F10**
Spartivento, C. *Calabria,*
　Italy 37°55N 16°4E **22 F7**
Spartivento, C. *Sard., Italy* 38°53N 8°50E **22 F3**
Sparwood *Canada* 49°44N 114°53W **70 D6**
Spassk-Dalniy *Russia* 44°40N 132°48E **28 B6**
Spatha, Akra *Greece* 35°42N 23°43E **23 G10**
Spatsizi → *Canada* 57°42N 128°7W **70 B3**
Spatsizi Plateau Wilderness △
　Canada 57°40N 128°0W **70 B3**
Spean → *U.K.* 56°55N 4°59W **11 E4**
Spearfish *U.S.A.* 44°30N 103°52W **80 C2**
Spearman *U.S.A.* 36°12N 101°12W **84 C4**
Speculator *U.S.A.* 43°30N 74°22W **83 C10**
Speightstown *Barbados* 13°15N 59°39W **89 g**
Spence Bay = Taloyoak
　Canada 69°32N 93°32W **68 D13**
Spencer *Idaho, U.S.A.* 44°22N 112°11W **76 D7**
Spencer *Iowa, U.S.A.* 43°9N 95°9W **80 D6**
Spencer *N.Y., U.S.A.* 42°13N 76°30W **83 D8**
Spencer *Nebr., U.S.A.* 42°53N 98°42W **80 D4**
Spencer, C. *Australia* 35°20S 136°53E **63 F2**
Spencer B. *Namibia* 25°30S 14°47E **56 C1**
Spencer G. *Australia* 34°0S 137°20E **63 E2**
Spencerville *Canada* 44°51N 75°33W **83 B9**
Spences Bridge *Canada* 50°25N 121°20W **70 C4**
Spennymoor *U.K.* 54°42N 1°36W **12 C6**
Spenser Mts. *N.Z.* 42°15S 172°45E **59 E4**
Sperrgebiet △ *Namibia* 27°38S 15°56E **56 C2**
Sperrin Mts. *U.K.* 54°50N 7°0W **10 B5**
Spey → *U.K.* 57°40N 3°6W **11 D5**
Speyer *Germany* 49°29N 8°25E **16 D5**
Spezand *Pakistan* 29°59N 67°0E **42 E2**
Spiddal *Ireland* 53°15N 9°18W **10 C2**
Spīn Būldak *Afghan.* 31°1N 66°25E **42 D2**
Spinifex ◎ *Australia* 28°30S 128°30E **61 E4**
Spirit Lake *U.S.A.* 46°15N 122°9W **78 D4**
Spirit River *Canada* 55°45N 118°50W **70 B5**
Spiritwood *Canada* 53°24N 107°33W **71 C7**
Spithead *U.K.* 50°45N 1°10W **13 G6**
Spitsbergen = Svalbard
　Arctic 78°0N 17°0E **4 B8**
Spjelkavik *Norway* 62°28N 6°22E **8 E12**
Split *Croatia* 43°31N 16°26E **22 C7**
Split L. *Canada* 56°8N 96°15W **71 B9**
Split Lake *Canada* 56°8N 96°15W **71 B9**
Spofford *U.S.A.* 29°10N 100°25W **84 G4**
Spokane *U.S.A.* 47°40N 117°24W **76 C5**
Spoleto *Italy* 42°44N 12°44E **22 C5**
Spooner *U.S.A.* 45°50N 91°53W **80 C8**
Sporyy Navolok, Mys
　Russia 75°50N 68°40E **26 B7**
Sprague *U.S.A.* 47°18N 117°59W **76 C5**
Spratly I. *S. China Sea* 8°38N 111°55E **36 C4**
Spratly Is. *S. China Sea* 8°20N 112°0E **36 C4**
Spray *U.S.A.* 44°50N 119°48W **76 D4**
Spree → *Germany* 52°32N 13°12E **16 B7**
Sprengisandur *Iceland* 64°52N 18°7W **8 D4**
Spring City *U.S.A.* 40°11N 75°33W **83 F9**
Spring Creek *U.S.A.* 40°44N 115°35W **76 F6**
Spring Garden *U.S.A.* 39°52N 120°47W **78 F6**
Spring Hall *Barbados* 13°18N 59°36W **89 g**
Spring Hill *U.S.A.* 28°27N 82°41W **85 G13**
Spring Mts. *U.S.A.* 36°0N 115°45W **79 J11**
Spring Temple Buddha
　China 33°46N 112°27E **32 H7**
Spring Valley *U.S.A.* 32°44N 116°59W **79 N10**
Springbok *S. Africa* 29°42S 17°54E **56 C2**
Springboro *U.S.A.* 41°48N 80°22W **82 E4**
Springdale *Canada* 49°30N 56°6W **73 C8**
Springdale *U.S.A.* 36°11N 94°8W **84 C7**
Springer *U.S.A.* 36°22N 104°36W **77 H11**
Springerville *U.S.A.* 34°8N 109°17W **77 J9**
Springfield *Canada* 42°50N 80°56W **82 D4**
Springfield *N.Z.* 43°19S 171°56E **59 E3**
Springfield *Colo.,*
　U.S.A. 37°24N 102°37W **77 H12**
Springfield *Ill., U.S.A.* 39°48N 89°39W **80 F9**
Springfield *Mass., U.S.A.* 42°6N 72°35W **83 D12**
Springfield *Mo., U.S.A.* 37°13N 93°17W **80 G7**

Springfield *Ohio, U.S.A.* 39°55N 83°49W **81 F12**
Springfield *Oreg., U.S.A.* 44°3N 123°1W **76 D2**
Springfield *Tenn., U.S.A.* 36°31N 86°53W **85 C11**
Springfield *Vt., U.S.A.* 43°18N 72°29W **83 C12**
Springfontein *S. Africa* 30°15S 25°40E **56 D4**
Springhill *Canada* 45°40N 64°4W **73 C7**
Springhill *U.S.A.* 33°0N 93°28W **84 E8**
Springhouse *Canada* 51°56N 122°7W **70 C4**
Springlands = Corriverton
　Guyana 5°55N 57°20W **92 B7**
Springs *S. Africa* 26°13S 28°25E **57 C4**
Springsure *Australia* 24°8S 148°6E **62 C4**
Springvale *U.S.A.* 43°28N 70°48W **83 C14**
Springville *Calif., U.S.A.* 36°8N 118°49W **78 J8**
Springville *N.Y., U.S.A.* 42°31N 78°40W **82 D6**
Springville *Utah, U.S.A.* 40°10N 111°37W **76 F8**
Springwater *U.S.A.* 42°38N 77°35W **82 D7**
Spruce-Creek *U.S.A.* 40°36N 78°9W **82 F6**
Spruce Knob-Seneca Rocks △
　U.S.A. 38°50N 79°30W **81 F14**
Spruce Mt. *U.S.A.* 44°12N 72°19W **83 B12**
Sprucedale *Canada* 45°29N 79°28W **82 A5**
Spur *U.S.A.* 33°28N 100°52W **84 E4**
Spurn Hd. *U.K.* 53°35N 0°8E **12 D8**
Spuzzum *Canada* 49°37N 121°23W **70 D4**
Squam L. *U.S.A.* 43°45N 71°32W **83 C13**
Squamish *Canada* 49°45N 123°10W **70 D4**
Square Islands *Canada* 52°47N 55°47W **73 B8**
Squires, Mt. *Australia* 26°14S 127°28E **61 E4**
Srbija = Serbia ■ *Europe* 43°20N 20°0E **23 B9**
Sre Ambel *Cambodia* 11°8N 103°46E **39 G4**
Sre Khtum *Cambodia* 12°10N 106°52E **39 F6**
Sre Umbell = Sre Ambel
　Cambodia 11°8N 103°46E **39 G4**
Srebrenica *Bos.-H.* 44°6N 19°18E **23 B8**
Sredinnyy Khrebet
　Russia 57°0N 160°0E **27 D17**
Sredinnyy Ra. = Sredinnyy
　Khrebet *Russia* 57°0N 160°0E **27 D17**
Srednekolymsk *Russia* 67°27N 153°40E **27 C16**
Śrem *Poland* 52°6N 17°2E **17 B9**
Sremska Mitrovica *Serbia* 44°59N 19°38E **23 B8**
Srepok → *Cambodia* 13°33N 106°16E **38 F6**
Sretensk *Russia* 52°10N 117°40E **27 D12**
Sri Aman = Bandar Sri Aman
　Malaysia 1°15N 111°32E **36 D4**
Sri Kalahasti *India* 13°45N 79°44E **45 H4**
Sri Lanka ■ *Asia* 7°30N 80°50E **45 L5**
Sri Pada = Adam's Peak
　Sri Lanka 6°48N 80°30E **45 L5**
Sriharikota I. *India* 13°40N 80°20E **45 H5**
Srikakulam *India* 18°14N 83°58E **44 E6**
Srinagar *India* 34°5N 74°50E **43 B6**
Srivardhan *India* 18°4N 73°3E **44 E1**
Srivilliputtur *India* 9°31N 77°40E **45 K3**
Srono *Indonesia* 8°24S 114°16E **37 J17**
Srungavarapukota *India* 18°7N 83°10E **44 E6**
Staaten → *Australia* 16°24S 141°17E **62 B3**
Staaten River △
　Australia 16°15S 142°40E **62 B3**
Stabbursdalen △ *Norway* 70°5N 24°15E **8 A21**
Stade *Germany* 53°35N 9°29E **16 B5**
Stadskanaal *Neths.* 53°4N 6°55E **15 A6**
Staffa *U.K.* 56°27N 6°21W **11 E2**
Stafford *U.K.* 52°49N 2°7W **12 E5**
Stafford *U.S.A.* 37°58N 98°36W **80 G4**
Stafford Springs *U.S.A.* 41°57N 72°18W **83 E12**
Staffordshire □ *U.K.* 52°53N 2°10W **12 E5**
Staines-upon-Thames
　U.K. 51°26N 0°29W **13 F7**
Stakhanov *Ukraine* 48°35N 38°40E **19 E6**
Stalowa Wola *Poland* 50°34N 22°3E **17 C12**
Stalybridge *U.K.* 53°28N 2°3W **12 D5**
Stamford *Australia* 21°15S 143°46E **62 C3**
Stamford *U.K.* 52°39N 0°29W **13 E7**
Stamford *Conn., U.S.A.* 41°3N 73°32W **83 E11**
Stamford *N.Y., U.S.A.* 42°25N 74°38W **83 D10**
Stamford *Tex., U.S.A.* 32°57N 99°48W **84 E5**
Stampriet *Namibia* 24°20S 18°28E **56 B2**
Stamps *U.S.A.* 33°22N 93°30W **84 E8**
Standerton *S. Africa* 26°55S 29°7E **57 C4**
Standish *U.S.A.* 43°59N 83°57W **81 D12**
Stanford *S. Africa* 34°26S 19°29E **56 E2**
Stanford *U.S.A.* 47°9N 110°13W **76 C8**
Stanger *S. Africa* 29°27S 31°14E **57 C5**
Stängelsån →
　Finland 61°30N 26°1E **8 F22**
Stanislaus → *U.S.A.* 37°40N 121°14W **78 H5**
Stanke Dimitrov *Bulgaria* 42°17N 23°9E **23 C10**
Stanley *Australia* 40°46S 145°19E **63 G4**
Stanley *Falk. Is.* 51°40S 59°51W **96 G5**
Stanley *U.K.* 54°53N 1°41W **12 C6**
Stanley *Idaho, U.S.A.* 44°13N 114°56W **76 D6**
Stanley *N. Dak., U.S.A.* 48°19N 102°23W **80 A2**
Stanley *N.Y., U.S.A.* 42°48N 77°6W **82 D7**
Stanley Mission *Canada* 55°25N 104°33W **71 B8**
Stanley Res. *India* 11°50N 77°40E **45 J3**
Stannards *U.S.A.* 42°5N 77°55W **82 D7**
Stanovoy Khrebet *Russia* 55°0N 130°0E **27 D14**
Stanovoy Ra. = Stanovoy Khrebet
　Russia 55°0N 130°0E **27 D14**
Stansmore Ra. *Australia* 21°23S 128°33E **60 D4**
Stansted, London ✈ (STN)
　U.K. 51°54N 0°14E **13 F8**
Stanthorpe *Australia* 28°36S 151°59E **63 D5**
Stanton *U.S.A.* 32°8N 101°48W **84 E4**
Stanwood *U.S.A.* 48°15N 122°23W **78 B4**
Staples *Canada* 42°10N 82°35W **82 D2**
Staples *U.S.A.* 46°21N 94°48W **80 B7**
Stapleton *U.S.A.* 41°29N 100°31W **80 E3**
Star City *Canada* 52°50N 104°20W **71 C8**
Star Lake *U.S.A.* 44°10N 75°2W **83 B9**
Stara Planina *Bulgaria* 43°15N 23°0E **23 C10**
Stara Zagora *Bulgaria* 42°26N 25°39E **23 C11**
Starachowice *Poland* 51°3N 21°2E **17 C11**
Staraya Russa *Russia* 57°58N 31°23E **18 C5**
Starbuck I. *Kiribati* 5°37S 155°55W **65 H12**
Starcke △ *Australia* 14°56S 145°2E **62 A4**
Stargard Szczeciński
　Poland 53°20N 15°0E **16 B8**
Staritsa *Russia* 56°33N 34°55E **18 C5**

Starke *U.S.A.* 29°57N 82°7W **85 G13**
Starkville *U.S.A.* 33°28N 88°49W **85 E10**
Starogard Gdański
　Poland 53°59N 18°30E **17 B10**
Starokonstantinov =
　Starokonstyantyniv
　Ukraine 49°48N 27°10E **17 D14**
Starokonstyantyniv
　Ukraine 49°48N 27°10E **17 D14**
Start Pt. *U.K.* 50°13N 3°39W **13 G4**
Staryy Chartoriysk
　Ukraine 51°15N 25°54E **17 C13**
Staryy Oskol *Russia* 51°19N 37°55E **19 D6**
State College *U.S.A.* 40°48N 77°52W **82 F7**
Stateline *U.S.A.* 38°57N 119°56W **78 G7**
Staten, I. = Estados, I. de Los
　Argentina 54°40S 64°30W **96 G4**
Staten I. *U.S.A.* 40°35N 74°9W **83 F10**
Statesboro *U.S.A.* 32°27N 81°47W **85 E14**
Statesville *U.S.A.* 35°47N 80°53W **85 D14**
Statia = St. Eustatius
　W. Indies 17°20N 63°0W **89 C7**
Stauffer *U.S.A.* 34°45N 119°3W **79 L7**
Staunton *Ill., U.S.A.* 39°1N 89°47W **80 F9**
Staunton *Va., U.S.A.* 38°9N 79°4W **81 F14**
Stavanger *Norway* 58°57N 5°40E **9 G11**
Staveley *N.Z.* 43°40S 171°32E **59 E3**
Stavelot *Belgium* 50°23N 5°55E **15 D5**
Stavern *Norway* 59°0N 10°1E **9 G14**
Stavoren *Neths.* 52°53N 5°22E **15 B5**
Stavropol *Russia* 45°5N 42°0E **19 E7**
Stawell *Australia* 37°5S 142°47E **63 F3**
Stawell → *Australia* 20°20S 142°55E **62 C3**
Stayner *Canada* 44°25N 80°5W **82 B4**
Stayton *U.S.A.* 44°48N 122°48W **76 D2**
Steamboat Springs
　U.S.A. 40°29N 106°50W **76 F10**
Steele *U.S.A.* 46°51N 99°55W **80 B4**
Steelton *U.S.A.* 40°14N 76°50W **82 F8**
Steen River *Canada* 59°40N 117°12W **70 B5**
Steens Mt. *U.S.A.* 42°35N 118°40W **76 E4**
Steenwijk *Neths.* 52°47N 6°7E **15 B6**
Steep Pt. *Australia* 26°8S 113°8E **61 E1**
Steep Rock *Canada* 51°30N 98°48W **71 C9**
Stefanie L. = Chew Bahir
　Ethiopia 4°40N 36°50E **49 G2**
Stefansson Bay *Antarctica* 67°20S 59°8E **5 C5**
Stefansson I. *Canada* 73°20N 105°45W **69 C10**
Steiermark □ *Austria* 47°26N 15°0E **16 E8**
Steilacoom *U.S.A.* 47°10N 122°36W **78 C4**
Steilrandberge *Namibia* 17°45S 13°20E **56 A1**
Steinbach *Canada* 49°32N 96°40W **71 D9**
Steinhausen *Namibia* 21°49S 18°20E **56 B2**
Steinkjer *Norway* 64°1N 11°31E **8 D14**
Steinkopf *S. Africa* 29°18S 17°43E **56 C2**
Stellarton *Canada* 45°32N 62°30W **73 C7**
Stellenbosch *S. Africa* 33°58S 18°50E **56 D2**
Stendal *Germany* 52°36N 11°53E **16 B6**
Steornabhaigh = Stornoway
　U.K. 58°13N 6°23W **11 C2**
Stepanakert = Xankändi
　Azerbaijan 39°52N 46°49E **46 B5**
Stephens Creek *Australia* 31°50S 141°30E **63 E3**
Stephens I. *Canada* 54°10N 130°45W **70 C2**
Stephens L. *Canada* 56°32N 95°0W **71 B9**
Stephenville *Canada* 48°31N 58°35W **73 C8**
Stephenville *U.S.A.* 32°13N 98°12W **84 E5**
Steppe *Asia* 50°0N 50°0E **24 C7**
Sterkstroom *S. Africa* 31°32S 26°32E **56 D4**
Sterling *Colo., U.S.A.* 40°37N 103°13W **76 F12**
Sterling *Ill., U.S.A.* 41°48N 89°42W **80 E9**
Sterling *Kans., U.S.A.* 38°13N 98°12W **80 F4**
Sterling City *U.S.A.* 31°51N 101°0W **84 F4**
Sterling Heights *U.S.A.* 42°35N 83°2W **81 D12**
Sterling Run *U.S.A.* 41°25N 78°12W **82 E6**
Sterlitamak *Russia* 53°40N 56°0E **18 D10**
Stettin = Szczecin *Poland* 53°27N 14°27E **16 B8**
Stettiner Haff *Germany* 53°47N 14°15E **16 B8**
Stettler *Canada* 52°19N 112°40W **70 C6**
Steubenville *U.S.A.* 40°22N 80°37W **82 F4**
Stevenage *U.K.* 51°55N 0°13W **13 F7**
Stevens Point *U.S.A.* 44°31N 89°34W **80 C9**
Stevenson *U.S.A.* 45°42N 121°53W **78 E5**
Stevenson → *Australia* 27°6S 135°33E **63 D2**
Stevenson L. *Canada* 53°55N 96°0W **71 C9**
Stevensville *U.S.A.* 46°30N 114°5W **76 C6**
Stewart *Canada* 55°56N 129°57W **70 B3**
Stewart *U.S.A.* 39°5N 119°46W **78 F7**
Stewart → *Canada* 63°19N 139°26W **68 E4**
Stewart, C. *Australia* 11°57S 134°56E **62 A1**
Stewart, I. *Chile* 54°50S 71°15W **96 G2**
Stewart I. *N.Z.* 46°58S 167°54E **59 G1**
Stewarts Point *U.S.A.* 38°39N 123°24W **78 G3**
Stewiacke *Canada* 45°9N 63°22W **73 C7**
Steynsburg *S. Africa* 31°15S 25°49E **56 D4**
Steyr *Austria* 48°3N 14°25E **16 D8**
Steytlerville *S. Africa* 33°17S 24°19E **56 D3**
Stigler *U.S.A.* 35°15N 95°8W **84 D7**
Stikine → *Canada* 56°40N 132°30W **70 B2**
Stilfontein *S. Africa* 26°51S 26°50E **56 D4**
Stillwater *N.Z.* 42°27S 171°20E **59 E4**
Stillwater *Minn., U.S.A.* 45°3N 92°49W **80 C7**
Stillwater *N.Y., U.S.A.* 42°55N 73°41W **83 D11**
Stillwater *Okla., U.S.A.* 36°7N 97°4W **84 C6**
Stillwater Range *U.S.A.* 39°50N 118°5W **76 G4**
Stillwater Res. *U.S.A.* 43°54N 75°3W **83 C9**
Stilwell *U.S.A.* 35°49N 94°38W **84 D7**
Stînga Nistrului = Transnistria □
　Moldova 47°20N 29°15E **17 E15**
Štip *Macedonia* 41°42N 22°10E **23 D10**
Stirling *Canada* 44°18N 77°33W **82 B7**
Stirling *U.K.* 56°8N 3°57W **11 E5**
Stirling □ *U.K.* 56°12N 4°18W **11 E4**
Stirling Ra. *Australia* 34°23S 118°0E **61 F2**
Stirling Range △
　Australia 34°26S 118°20E **61 F2**
Stittsville *Canada* 45°15N 75°55W **83 A9**
Stjernøya *Norway* 70°20N 22°40E **8 A20**
Stjørdalshalsen *Norway* 63°29N 10°51E **8 E14**
Stockerau *Austria* 48°24N 16°12E **16 D9**
Stockport *U.K.* 53°25N 2°9W **12 D5**

Stocksbridge *U.K.* 53°29N 1°35W **12 D6**
Stockton *Calif., U.S.A.* 37°58N 121°17W **78 H5**
Stockton *Kans., U.S.A.* 39°26N 99°16W **80 F4**
Stockton *Mo., U.S.A.* 37°42N 93°48W **80 G7**
Stockton-on-Tees *U.K.* 54°35N 1°19W **12 C6**
Stockton-on-Tees □ *U.K.* 54°35N 1°19W **12 C6**
Stockton Plateau
　U.S.A. 30°30N 102°30W **84 F3**
Stoeng Treng *Cambodia* 13°31N 105°58E **38 F5**
Stoer, Pt. of *U.K.* 58°16N 5°23W **11 C3**
Stoke-on-Trent *U.K.* 53°1N 2°11W **12 D5**
Stoke-on-Trent □ *U.K.* 53°1N 2°11W **12 D5**
Stokes △ *Australia* 33°45S 121°11E **61 F3**
Stokes Bay *Canada* 45°0N 81°28W **82 B3**
Stokes Pt. *Australia* 40°10S 143°56E **63 G4**
Stokes Ra. *Australia* 15°50S 130°50E **60 C5**
Stokksnes *Iceland* 64°14N 14°58W **8 D6**
Stokmarknes *Norway* 68°34N 14°54E **8 B16**
Stolac *Bos.-H.* 43°5N 17°59E **23 C7**
Stolbovoy, Ostrov
　Russia 74°44N 135°14E **27 B14**
Stolbtsy = Stowbtsy
　Belarus 53°30N 26°43E **17 B14**
Stolin *Belarus* 51°53N 26°50E **17 C14**
Stone *U.K.* 52°55N 2°9W **12 E5**
Stoneboro *U.S.A.* 41°20N 80°7W **82 E4**
Stonehaven *U.K.* 56°59N 2°12W **11 E6**
Stonehenge *Australia* 24°22S 143°17E **62 C3**
Stonehenge *U.K.* 51°9N 1°45W **13 F6**
Stonewall *Canada* 50°10N 97°19W **71 C9**
Stony I. *U.S.A.* 43°53N 76°19W **83 C8**
Stony L. *Man., Canada* 58°51N 98°40W **71 B9**
Stony L. *Ont., Canada* 44°30N 78°5W **82 B6**
Stony Point *U.S.A.* 41°14N 73°59W **83 E11**
Stony Pt. *U.S.A.* 43°50N 76°18W **83 C8**
Stony Rapids *Canada* 59°16N 105°50W **71 B7**
Stony Tunguska = Tunguska,
　Podkamennaya →
　Russia 61°50N 90°13E **27 C10**
Stonyford *U.S.A.* 39°23N 122°33W **78 F4**
Stora Lulevatten *Sweden* 67°10N 19°30E **8 C18**
Stora Sjöfallet △ *Sweden* 67°36N 17°45E **8 C17**
Storavan *Sweden* 65°45N 18°10E **8 D18**
Stord *Norway* 59°52N 5°23E **9 G11**
Store Bælt *Denmark* 55°20N 11°0E **9 J14**
Storkerson Pen.
　Canada 72°30N 106°30W **68 C10**
Storm B. *Australia* 43°10S 147°30E **63 G4**
Storm Lake *U.S.A.* 42°39N 95°13W **80 D6**
Stormberge *S. Africa* 31°16S 26°17E **56 D4**
Stormsrivier *S. Africa* 33°59S 23°52E **56 D3**
Stornoway *U.K.* 58°13N 6°23W **11 C2**
Storozhinets = Storozhynets
　Ukraine 48°14N 25°45E **17 D13**
Storozhynets *Ukraine* 48°14N 25°45E **17 D13**
Storrs *U.S.A.* 41°49N 72°15W **83 E12**
Storsjön *Sweden* 63°9N 14°30E **8 E16**
Storuman *Sweden* 65°5N 17°10E **8 D17**
Storuman, L. *Sweden* 65°13N 16°50E **8 D17**
Stouffville *Canada* 43°58N 79°15W **82 C5**
Stoughton *Canada* 49°40N 103°0W **71 D8**
Stour → *Dorset, U.K.* 50°43N 1°47W **13 G6**
Stour → *Kent, U.K.* 51°18N 1°22E **13 F9**
Stour → *Suffolk, U.K.* 51°57N 1°4E **13 F9**
Stourbridge *U.K.* 52°28N 2°8W **13 E5**
Stout L. *Canada* 52°0N 94°40W **71 C10**
Stove Pipe Wells Village
　U.S.A. 36°35N 117°11W **79 J9**
Stow *U.S.A.* 41°10N 81°27W **82 E3**
Stowbtsy *Belarus* 53°30N 26°43E **17 B14**
Stowmarket *U.K.* 52°12N 1°0E **13 E9**
Strabane *U.K.* 54°50N 7°27W **10 B4**
Strahan *Australia* 42°9S 145°20E **63 G4**
Stralsund *Germany* 54°18N 13°4E **16 A7**
Strand *S. Africa* 34°9S 18°48E **56 D2**
Stranda *Møre og Romsdal,*
　Norway 62°19N 6°58E **8 E12**
Stranda *Nord-Trøndelag,*
　Norway 63°33N 10°14E **8 E14**
Strangford L. *U.K.* 54°30N 5°37W **10 B6**
Stranorlar *Ireland* 54°48N 7°46W **10 B4**
Stranraer *U.K.* 54°54N 5°1W **11 G3**
Strasbourg *Canada* 51°4N 104°55W **71 C8**
Strasbourg *France* 48°35N 7°42E **20 B7**
Stratford *Canada* 43°23N 81°0W **82 C4**
Stratford *N.Z.* 39°20S 174°19E **59 C5**
Stratford *Calif., U.S.A.* 36°11N 119°49W **78 J7**
Stratford *Conn., U.S.A.* 41°12N 73°8W **83 E11**
Stratford *Tex., U.S.A.* 36°20N 102°4W **84 C3**
Stratford-upon-Avon
　U.K. 52°12N 1°42W **13 E6**
Strath Spey *U.K.* 57°9N 3°49W **11 D5**
Strathalbyn *Australia* 35°13S 138°53E **63 F2**
Strathaven *U.K.* 55°40N 4°5W **11 F4**
Strathcona △ *Canada* 49°38N 125°40W **70 D3**
Strathmore *Canada* 51°5N 113°18W **70 C6**
Strathmore *U.K.* 56°37N 3°7W **11 E5**
Strathmore *U.S.A.* 36°9N 119°4W **78 J7**
Strathnaver *Canada* 53°20N 122°33W **70 C4**
Strathpeffer *U.K.* 57°35N 4°32W **11 D4**
Strathroy *Canada* 42°58N 81°38W **82 D3**
Strathy Pt. *U.K.* 58°36N 4°1W **11 C4**
Strattanville *U.S.A.* 41°12N 79°19W **82 E5**
Stratton *U.S.A.* 39°19N 102°36W **80 F3**
Stratton Mt. *U.S.A.* 43°4N 72°55W **83 C12**
Straubing *Germany* 48°52N 12°34E **16 D7**
Straumnes *Iceland* 66°26N 23°8W **8 C2**
Strawberry → *U.S.A.* 40°10N 110°24W **76 F8**
Streaky B. *Australia* 32°48S 134°13E **63 E1**
Streaky Bay *Australia* 32°51S 134°18E **63 E1**
Streator *U.S.A.* 41°8N 88°50W **80 E9**
Streetsboro *U.S.A.* 41°14N 81°21W **82 E3**
Streetsville *Canada* 43°35N 79°42W **82 C5**
Streng → *Cambodia* 13°12N 103°37E **38 F4**
Strezhevoy *Russia* 60°42N 77°34E **26 C8**
Strimonas → *Greece* 40°46N 23°51E **23 D10**
Strokestown *Ireland* 53°47N 8°5W **10 C3**
Stroma *U.K.* 58°41N 3°7W **11 C5**
Strómboli *Italy* 38°47N 15°13E **22 E6**
Stromeferry *U.K.* 57°21N 5°33W **11 D3**

Stromness U.K. 58°58N 3°17W 11 C5
Stromsburg U.S.A. 41°7N 97°36W 80 E5
Strömstad Sweden 58°56N 11°10E 9 G14
Strömsund Sweden 63°51N 15°33E 8 E16
Strongsville U.S.A. 41°19N 81°50W 82 E3
Stronsay U.K. 59°7N 2°35W 11 B6
Stroud U.K. 51°45N 2°13W 13 F5
Stroud Road Australia 32°18S 151°57E 63 E5
Stroudsburg U.S.A. 40°59N 75°12W 83 F9
Struer Denmark 56°30N 8°35E 9 H13
Strugi Krasnyye Russia 58°21N 29°1E 9 G23
Strumica Macedonia 41°28N 22°41E 23 D10
Struthers U.S.A. 41°4N 80°39W 82 E4
Stryker U.S.A. 48°41N 114°46W 76 B6
Stryy Ukraine 49°16N 23°48E 17 D12
Strzelecki Cr. → Australia 29°37S 139°59E 63 D2
Strzelecki Desert Australia 29°30S 140°0E 63 D3
Stuart Fla., U.S.A. 27°12N 80°15W 85 H14
Stuart Nebr., U.S.A. 42°36N 99°8W 80 D4
Stuart → Canada 54°0N 123°35W 70 C4
Stuart Bluff Ra. Australia 22°50S 131°52E 60 D5
Stuart I. U.S.A. 63°35N 162°30W 74 C7
Stuart L. Canada 54°30N 124°30W 70 C4
Stuart Ra. Australia 29°10S 134°56E 63 D1
Stull L. Canada 54°24N 92°34W 72 B1
Stung Treng = Stoeng Treng Cambodia 13°31N 105°58E 38 F5
Stupart → Canada 56°0N 93°25W 72 A1
Sturge I. Antarctica 67°26S 164°47E 5 C11
Sturgeon B. Canada 52°0N 97°50W 71 C9
Sturgeon Bay U.S.A. 44°50N 87°23W 80 C10
Sturgeon Falls Canada 46°25N 79°57W 72 C4
Sturgeon L. Alta., Canada 55°6N 117°32W 70 B5
Sturgeon L. Ont., Canada 50°0N 90°45W 72 C1
Sturgeon L. Ont., Canada 44°28N 78°43W 82 B6
Sturgis Canada 51°56N 102°36W 71 C8
Sturgis Mich., U.S.A. 41°48N 85°25W 81 E11
Sturgis S. Dak., U.S.A. 44°25N 103°31W 80 C2
Sturt △ Australia 27°17S 141°37E 63 D3
Sturt Cr. → Australia 19°8S 127°50E 60 C4
Sturt Stony Desert Australia 28°30S 141°0E 63 D3
Stutterheim S. Africa 32°33S 27°28E 56 D4
Stuttgart Germany 48°48N 9°11E 16 D5
Stuttgart U.S.A. 34°30N 91°33W 84 D9
Stuyvesant U.S.A. 42°23N 73°45W 83 D11
Stykkishólmur Iceland 65°2N 22°40W 8 D2
Styria = Steiermark □ Austria 47°26N 15°0E 16 E8
Su Xian = Suzhou China 33°41N 116°59E 32 H9
Suakin Sudan 19°8N 37°20E 53 E13
Suamico U.S.A. 44°38N 88°2W 80 C9
Suan N. Korea 38°42N 126°22E 33 E14
Suana Indonesia 8°44S 115°36E 37 K18
Suar India 29°2N 79°3E 43 E8
Şubā Si. Arabia 27°10N 35°40E 46 E2
Subang Indonesia 6°34S 107°45E 37 G12
Subansiri → India 26°48N 93°50E 41 F18
Subarnagiri India 19°50N 83°51E 44 E6
Subarnarekha → India 22°34N 87°24E 43 H12
Subayhah Si. Arabia 30°2N 38°50E 46 D3
Subi Indonesia 2°58N 108°50E 36 D3
Subotica Serbia 46°6N 19°39E 23 A8
Suceava Romania 47°38N 26°16E 17 E14
Suchan = Partizansk Russia 43°8N 133°9E 27 E14
Suchil Mexico 23°39N 103°54W 86 C4
Suchou = Suzhou China 31°19N 120°38E 35 B13
Süchow = Xuzhou China 34°18N 117°10E 33 G9
Suck → Ireland 53°17N 8°3W 10 C3
Sucre Bolivia 19°0S 65°15W 92 G5
Sucuriú → Brazil 20°47S 51°38W 93 H8
Sud, Pte. du Canada 49°3N 62°14W 73 C7
Sud-Ouest, Pte. Canada 49°23N 63°36W 73 C7
Sud Ouest, Pte. Mauritius 20°28S 57°18E 55 d
Sudan U.S.A. 34°4N 102°31W 84 D3
Sudan ■ Africa 15°0N 30°0E 53 E11
Sudbury U.K. 52°2N 0°45E 13 E8
Sudd South Sudan 8°20N 30°0E 53 G12
Sudeten Mts. = Sudety Europe 50°20N 16°45E 17 C9
Sudety Europe 50°20N 16°45E 17 C9
Suðuroy Færoe Is. 61°32N 6°50W 8 F9
Sudirman, Pegunungan Indonesia 4°30S 137°0E 37 E9
Sudong, Pulau Singapore 1°13N 103°44E 39 d
Sueca Spain 39°12N 0°21W 21 C5
Suemez I. U.S.A. 55°15N 133°20W 70 B2
Suez = El Suweis Egypt 29°58N 32°31E 53 C12
Suez, G. of = Suweis, Khalîg el Egypt 28°40N 33°0E 53 C12
Suez Canal = Suweis, Qanâ es Egypt 31°0N 32°20E 53 B12
Suffield Canada 50°12N 111°10W 70 C6
Suffolk U.S.A. 36°44N 76°35W 81 G15
Suffolk □ U.K. 52°16N 1°0E 13 E9
Sugaing = Sagaing Myanmar 21°52N 95°59E 41 J19
Sugar Grove U.S.A. 41°59N 79°20W 82 E5
Sugarcreek U.S.A. 41°25N 79°52W 82 E5
Sugarive → India 26°16N 86°24E 43 F12
Sugluk = Salluit Canada 62°14N 75°38W 69 E16
Şuḩār Oman 24°20N 56°40E 47 E8
Sühbaatar Mongolia 50°17N 106°10E 30 A10
Sühbaatar □ Mongolia 45°30N 114°0E 32 B8
Suheli Par India 10°5N 72°17E 45 J1
Suhl Germany 50°36N 10°42E 16 C6
Sui Pakistan 28°37N 69°19E 42 E3
Sui Xian China 34°25N 115°2E 32 G8
Suichang China 28°29N 119°15E 35 C12
Suichuan China 26°20N 114°32E 35 D10
Suide China 37°30N 110°12E 32 F6
Suifenhe China 44°25N 131°10E 33 B16
Suihua China 46°32N 126°55E 31 B14
Suijiang China 28°40N 103°59E 34 C4
Suining Hunan, China 26°35N 110°10E 35 D8
Suining Jiangsu, China 33°56N 117°58E 33 H9
Suining Sichuan, China 30°26N 105°35E 34 B5
Suiping China 33°10N 113°59E 32 H7
Suir → Ireland 52°16N 7°9W 10 D4
Suisse = Switzerland ■ Europe 46°30N 8°0E 20 C8
Suisun City U.S.A. 38°15N 122°2W 78 G4
Suixi China 21°19N 110°18E 35 G8
Suiyang Guizhou, China 27°58N 107°18E 34 D6
Suiyang Heilongjiang, China 44°30N 130°56E 33 B16
Suizhong China 40°21N 120°20E 33 D11
Suizhou China 31°42N 113°24E 35 B9
Sujangarh India 27°42N 74°31E 42 F6
Sujiatun China 41°39N 123°20E 33 D12
Sukabumi Indonesia 6°56S 106°50E 37 G12
Sukadana Indonesia 1°10S 110°0E 36 E4
Sukagawa Japan 37°17N 140°23E 29 F10
Sukamade Indonesia 8°30S 113°52E 37 H15
Sukaraja Indonesia 2°28S 110°25E 36 E4
Sukarno-Hatta Int., Jakarta ✕ (CGK) Indonesia 6°7S 106°40E 37 G12
Sukawati Indonesia 8°35S 115°17E 37 K18
Sukch'ŏn N. Korea 39°22N 125°35E 33 E13
Sukhona → Russia 61°15N 46°39E 18 C6
Sukhothai Thailand 17°1N 99°49E 38 D2
Sukhumi = Sokhumi Georgia 43°0N 41°0E 19 F7
Sukkur Pakistan 27°42N 68°54E 42 F3
Sukkur Barrage Pakistan 27°40N 68°50E 42 F3
Sukma India 18°24N 81°45E 44 E5
Sukri → India 25°4N 71°43E 42 G4
Sukumo Japan 32°56N 132°44E 29 H6
Sukunka → Canada 55°45N 121°15W 70 B4
Sula, Kepulauan Indonesia 1°45S 125°0E 37 E7
Sulaco → Honduras 15°2N 87°44W 88 C2
Sulaiman Range Pakistan 30°30N 69°50E 42 D3
Sūlār Iran 31°53N 51°54E 47 D6
Sulawesi Indonesia 2°0S 120°0E 37 E6
Sulawesi Barat □ Indonesia 3°0S 119°0E 37 E5
Sulawesi Sea = Celebes Sea Indonesia 3°0N 123°0E 37 D6
Sulawesi Selatan □ Indonesia 2°30S 120°0E 37 E6
Sulawesi Tengah □ Indonesia 1°30S 121°0E 37 E6
Sulawesi Tenggara □ Indonesia 3°50S 122°0E 37 E6
Sulawesi Utara □ Indonesia 1°0N 124°0E 37 D6
Sulima S. Leone 6°58N 11°32W 52 G3
Sulina Romania 45°10N 29°40E 17 F15
Sulitjelma Norway 67°9N 16°3E 8 C17
Sullana Peru 4°52S 80°39W 92 D2
Sullivan Ill., U.S.A. 39°36N 88°37W 80 F9
Sullivan Ind., U.S.A. 39°6N 87°24W 80 F10
Sullivan Mo., U.S.A. 38°13N 91°10W 80 F8
Sullivan Bay Canada 50°55N 126°50W 70 C3
Sullivan I. = Lanbi Kyun Myanmar 10°50N 98°20E 39 G2
Sullom Voe U.K. 60°27N 1°20W 11 A7
Sulphur La., U.S.A. 30°14N 93°23W 84 F8
Sulphur Okla., U.S.A. 34°31N 96°58W 84 D6
Sulphur Pt. Canada 60°56N 114°48W 70 A6
Sulphur Springs U.S.A. 33°8N 95°36W 84 E7
Sultan Canada 47°36N 82°47W 72 C3
Sultan U.S.A. 47°52N 121°49W 78 C5
Sultanābād = Arāk Iran 34°0N 49°40E 47 C6
Sultanpur Mad. P., India 23°9N 77°56E 42 H8
Sultanpur Punjab, India 31°13N 75°11E 42 D6
Sultanpur Ut. P., India 26°18N 82°4E 43 F10
Sulu Arch. Phil. 6°0N 121°0E 37 C6
Sulu Sea E. Indies 8°0N 120°0E 37 C6
Sulūq Libya 31°44N 20°14E 53 B10
Suluru India 13°42N 80°1E 45 H5
Sulzberger Ice Shelf Antarctica 78°0S 150°0W 5 E13
Sumalata Indonesia 1°0N 122°31E 37 D6
Sumampa Argentina 29°25S 63°29W 94 B3
Sumatera Indonesia 0°40N 100°20E 36 D2
Sumatera Barat □ Indonesia 1°0S 101°0E 36 E2
Sumatera Selatan □ Indonesia 3°0S 104°0E 36 E2
Sumatera Utara □ Indonesia 2°30N 98°0E 36 D1
Sumatra = Sumatera Indonesia 0°40N 100°20E 36 D2
Sumba Indonesia 9°45S 119°35E 37 F5
Sumba, Selat Indonesia 9°0S 118°40E 37 F5
Sumbawa Indonesia 8°26S 117°30E 36 F5
Sumbawa Besar Indonesia 8°30S 117°26E 36 F5
Sumbawanga □ Tanzania 8°0S 31°30E 54 F6
Sumbe Angola 11°10S 13°48E 54 G2
Sumburgh Hd. U.K. 59°52N 1°17W 11 B7
Sumdeo India 31°26N 78°44E 43 D8
Sumdo China 35°6N 78°41E 43 B8
Sumedang Indonesia 6°52S 107°55E 37 G12
Šumen = Shumen Bulgaria 43°18N 26°55E 23 C12
Sumenep Indonesia 7°1S 113°52E 37 G15
Sumgait = Sumqayıt Azerbaijan 40°34N 49°38E 19 F8
Summer L. U.S.A. 42°50N 120°45W 76 E3
Summerland Canada 49°32N 119°41W 70 D5
Summerside Canada 46°24N 63°47W 73 C7
Summersville U.S.A. 38°17N 80°51W 81 F13
Summerville Ga., U.S.A. 34°29N 85°21W 85 D12
Summerville S.C., U.S.A. 33°1N 80°11W 85 E14
Summit Lake Canada 54°20N 122°40W 70 C4
Summit Peak U.S.A. 37°21N 106°42W 77 H10
Sumner Iowa, U.S.A. 42°51N 92°6W 80 D7
Sumner Wash., U.S.A. 47°12N 122°14W 78 C4
Sumoto Japan 34°21N 134°54E 29 G7
Šumperk Czechia 49°59N 16°59E 17 D9
Sumqayıt Azerbaijan 40°34N 49°38E 19 F8
Sumter U.S.A. 33°55N 80°21W 85 E14
Sumy Ukraine 50°57N 34°50E 19 D5
Sun City S. Africa 25°17S 27°3E 56 C4
Sun City Center U.S.A. 27°43N 82°21W 85 H13
Sun Kosi → Nepal 26°59N 87°8E 43 F12
Sun Lakes U.S.A. 33°10N 111°52W 77 K8
Sun Valley U.S.A. 43°42N 114°21W 76 E6
Sunagawa Japan 43°29N 141°55E 28 C10
Sunan N. Korea 39°15N 125°40E 33 E13
Sunart, L. U.K. 56°42N 5°43W 11 E3
Sunburst U.S.A. 48°53N 111°55W 76 B8
Sunbury Australia 37°35S 144°44E 63 F3
Sunbury U.S.A. 40°52N 76°48W 83 F8
Sunchales Argentina 30°58S 61°35W 94 C3
Suncheon S. Korea 34°52N 127°31E 33 G14
Suncho Corral Argentina 27°55S 63°27W 94 B3
Sunch'on N. Korea 39°25N 125°56E 33 E13
Suncook U.S.A. 43°8N 71°27W 83 C13
Sunda, Selat Indonesia 6°20S 105°30E 36 F3
Sunda Is. Indonesia 5°0S 105°0E 64 H2
Sunda Str. = Sunda, Selat Indonesia 6°20S 105°30E 36 F3
Sunda Trench = Java Trench Ind. Oc. 9°0S 105°0E 36 F3
Sundance Canada 56°32N 94°4W 71 B10
Sundance U.S.A. 44°24N 104°23W 76 D11
Sundar Nagar India 31°32N 76°53E 42 D7
Sundarbans Asia 22°0N 89°0E 41 J16
Sundarbans △ India 22°0N 88°45E 43 J13
Sundargarh India 22°4N 84°5E 44 C7
Sundays = Sondags → S. Africa 33°44S 25°51E 56 D4
Sunderland Canada 44°16N 79°4W 82 B5
Sunderland U.K. 54°55N 1°23W 12 C6
Sundown △ Australia 28°49S 151°38E 63 D5
Sundre Canada 51°49N 114°38W 70 C6
Sundsvall Sweden 62°23N 17°17E 8 E17
Sungai Acheh Malaysia 5°8N 100°30E 39 c
Sungai Kolok Thailand 6°2N 101°58E 39 J3
Sungai Lembing Malaysia 3°55N 103°3E 39 L4
Sungai Petani Malaysia 5°37N 100°30E 39 K3
Sungaigerong Indonesia 2°59S 104°52E 36 E2
Sungailiat Indonesia 1°51S 106°8E 36 E3
Sungaipenuh Indonesia 2°1S 101°20E 36 E2
Sungari = Songhua Jiang → China 47°45N 132°30E 31 B15
Sunghua Chiang = Songhua Jiang → China 47°45N 132°30E 31 B15
Sunland Park U.S.A. 31°50N 106°40W 77 L10
Sunndalsøra Norway 62°40N 8°33E 8 E13
Sunnyside U.S.A. 46°20N 120°0W 76 C4
Sunnyvale U.S.A. 37°23N 122°2W 78 H4
Suntar Russia 62°15N 117°30E 27 C12
Suomenselkä Finland 62°52N 24°0E 8 E21
Suomi = Finland ■ Europe 63°0N 27°0E 8 E22
Suomussalmi Finland 64°54N 29°10E 8 D23
Suoyarvi Russia 62°3N 32°20E 18 B5
Supai U.S.A. 36°15N 112°41W 77 H7
Supaul India 26°10N 86°40E 43 F12
Superior Ariz., U.S.A. 33°18N 111°6W 77 K8
Superior Mont., U.S.A. 47°12N 114°53W 76 C6
Superior Nebr., U.S.A. 40°1N 98°4W 80 E4
Superior Wis., U.S.A. 46°44N 92°6W 80 B7
Superior, L. N. Amer. 47°0N 87°0W 72 C2
Suphan Buri Thailand 14°14N 100°10E 38 E3
Suphan Dağı Turkey 38°54N 42°48E 46 B4
Supiori Indonesia 1°0S 136°0E 37 E9
Supung Shuiku China 40°35N 124°50E 33 D13
Sūq ash Shuyūkh Iraq 30°53N 46°28E 46 D5
Sūq Suwayq Si. Arabia 24°23N 38°27E 46 E3
Suqian China 33°54N 118°8E 33 H10
Suquṭra = Socotra Yemen 12°30N 54°0E 49 E5
Şūr Lebanon 33°19N 35°16E 48 B4
Şūr Oman 22°34N 59°32E 49 C6
Sur, Pt. U.S.A. 36°18N 121°54W 78 J5
Sura → Russia 56°6N 46°0E 18 C8
Surab Pakistan 28°25N 66°15E 42 E2
Surabaja = Surabaya Indonesia 7°17S 112°45E 37 G15
Surabaya Indonesia 7°17S 112°45E 37 G15
Surakarta Indonesia 7°35S 110°48E 37 G14
Surat Australia 27°10S 149°6E 63 D4
Surat India 21°12N 72°55E 44 D1
Surat Thani Thailand 9°6N 99°20E 39 H2
Suratgarh India 29°18N 73°55E 42 E5
Surathkal India 12°58N 74°46E 45 H2
Şuraymilā Si. Arabia 25°7N 46°7E 46 E5
Surendranagar India 22°45N 71°40E 42 H4
Surf U.S.A. 34°41N 120°36W 79 L6
Surfers Paradise Australia 28°0S 153°25E 63 D5
Surgana India 20°34N 73°37E 44 D1
Surgut Russia 61°14N 73°20E 26 C8
Suriapet India 17°10N 79°40E 44 F4
Surigao Phil. 9°47N 125°29E 37 C7
Surin Thailand 14°50N 103°34E 38 E4
Surinam = Suriname ■ S. Amer. 4°0N 56°0W 93 C7
Suriname ■ S. Amer. 4°0N 56°0W 93 C7
Suriname → Suriname 5°50N 55°15W 93 B7
Surjagarh India 19°36N 80°25E 44 E5
Sūrmaq Iran 31°3N 52°48E 47 D7
Surprise U.S.A. 33°38N 112°19W 77 K7
Surrey Canada 49°7N 122°45W 78 A4
Surrey □ U.K. 51°15N 0°31W 13 F7
Sursand India 26°39N 85°43E 43 F11
Sursar → India 26°14N 87°3E 43 F12
Surt Libya 31°11N 16°39E 53 B9
Surt, Khalīj Libya 31°40N 18°30E 53 B9
Surtanahu Pakistan 26°22N 70°0E 42 F4
Surtsey Iceland 63°20N 20°30W 8 E3
Suruga-Wan Japan 34°45N 138°30E 29 G9
Sūsah Libya 32°52N 21°59E 53 B10
Susaki Japan 33°22N 133°17E 29 H6
Sūsangerd Iran 31°35N 48°6E 47 D6
Susanville U.S.A. 40°25N 120°39W 76 F3
Susner India 23°57N 76°5E 42 H7
Susong China 30°10N 116°5E 35 B11
Susquehanna U.S.A. 41°57N 75°36W 83 E9
Susquehanna → U.S.A. 39°33N 76°5W 83 G8
Susques Argentina 23°35S 66°25W 94 A2
Sussex Canada 45°45N 65°37W 73 C6
Sussex U.S.A. 41°13N 74°37W 83 E10
Sussex, East □ U.K. 51°0N 0°20E 13 G8
Sussex, West □ U.K. 51°0N 0°30W 13 G7
Sustut → Canada 56°20N 127°30W 70 B3
Susuman Russia 62°47N 148°10E 27 C15
Susunu Indonesia 3°7S 133°39E 37 E8
Susurluk Turkey 39°54N 28°8E 23 E13
Sutay Uul Asia 46°35N 93°38E 30 B7
Sutherland S. Africa 32°24S 20°40E 56 D3
Sutherland U.K. 58°12N 4°50W 11 C4
Sutherland U.S.A. 41°10N 101°8W 80 E3
Sutherland Falls N.Z. 44°48S 167°46E 59 F1
Sutherlin U.S.A. 43°23N 123°19W 76 E2
Suthri India 23°3N 68°55E 42 H3
Sutlej → Pakistan 29°23N 71°3E 42 E4
Sutter U.S.A. 39°10N 121°45W 78 F5
Sutter Buttes U.S.A. 39°12N 121°49W 78 F5
Sutter Creek U.S.A. 38°24N 120°48W 78 G6
Sutton Canada 45°6N 72°37W 83 A12
Sutton Nebr., U.S.A. 40°36N 97°52W 80 E5
Sutton W. Va., U.S.A. 38°40N 80°43W 81 F13
Sutton → Canada 55°15N 83°45W 72 A3
Sutton Coldfield U.K. 52°35N 1°49W 13 E6
Sutton in Ashfield U.K. 53°8N 1°16W 12 D6
Sutton L. Canada 54°15N 84°42W 72 B3
Suttor → Australia 21°36S 147°2E 62 C4
Suttsu Japan 42°48N 140°14E 28 C10
Sutwik I. U.S.A. 56°34N 157°12W 74 D8
Suva Fiji 18°6S 178°30E 59 a
Suva Planina Serbia 43°10N 22°5E 23 C10
Suvorov Is. = Suwarrow Is. Cook Is. 13°15S 163°5W 65 J11
Suwałki Poland 54°8N 22°59E 17 A12
Suwannaphum Thailand 15°33N 103°47E 38 E4
Suwannee → U.S.A. 29°17N 83°10W 85 G13
Suwanose-Jima Japan 29°38N 129°43E 29 K4
Suwarrow Is. Cook Is. 13°15S 163°5W 65 J11
Suweis, Khalîg el Egypt 28°40N 33°0E 53 C12
Suweis, Qanâ es Egypt 31°0N 32°20E 53 B12
Suwon S. Korea 37°17N 127°1E 33 F14
Suzdal Russia 56°29N 40°26E 18 C7
Suzhou Anhui, China 33°41N 116°59E 32 H9
Suzhou Jiangsu, China 31°19N 120°38E 35 B13
Suzu Japan 37°25N 137°17E 29 F8
Suzu-Misaki Japan 37°31N 137°21E 29 F8
Suzuka Japan 34°55N 136°36E 29 G8
Svalbard Arctic 78°0N 17°0E 4 B8
Svalbard Radio = Longyearbyen Svalbard 78°13N 15°40E 4 B8
Svappavaara Sweden 67°40N 21°3E 8 C19
Svartisen Norway 66°40N 13°59E 8 C15
Svay Chek Cambodia 13°48N 102°58E 38 F4
Svay Rieng Cambodia 11°9N 105°45E 39 G5
Svealand Sweden 60°20N 15°0E 9 F16
Sveg Sweden 62°2N 14°21E 8 E16
Svendborg Denmark 55°4N 10°35E 9 J14
Sverdrup Chan. Canada 79°56N 96°25W 69 B12
Sverdrup Is. Canada 79°0N 97°0W 66 B10
Sverige = Sweden ■ Europe 57°0N 15°0E 9 H16
Svetlaya Russia 46°33N 138°18E 28 A9
Svetlogorsk = Svyetlahorsk Belarus 52°38N 29°46E 17 B15
Svir → Russia 60°30N 32°48E 18 B5
Svishtov Bulgaria 43°36N 25°23E 23 C11
Svislach Belarus 53°3N 24°2E 17 B13
Svizzera = Switzerland ■ Europe 46°30N 8°0E 20 C8
Svobodnyy Russia 51°20N 128°0E 27 D13
Svolvær Norway 68°15N 14°34E 8 B16
Svyetlahorsk Belarus 52°38N 29°46E 17 B15
Swabian Alps = Schwäbische Alb Germany 48°20N 9°30E 16 D5
Swaffham U.K. 52°39N 0°42E 13 E8
Swains I. Amer. Samoa 11°11S 171°4W 65 J11
Swainsboro U.S.A. 32°36N 82°20W 85 E13
Swakop → Namibia 22°38S 14°36E 56 B2
Swakopmund Namibia 22°37S 14°30E 56 B1
Swale → U.K. 54°5N 1°20W 12 C6
Swamihalli India 14°52N 76°38E 45 G3
Swan → Australia 32°3S 115°45E 61 F2
Swan → Canada 52°30N 100°45W 71 C8
Swan Hill Australia 35°20S 143°33E 63 F3
Swan Hills Canada 54°43N 115°24W 70 C5
Swan Is. = Santanilla, Is. Honduras 17°22N 83°57W 88 C3
Swan L. Man., Canada 52°30N 100°40W 71 C8
Swan L. Ont., Canada 54°16N 91°11W 72 B1
Swan Ra. U.S.A. 48°0N 113°45W 76 C7
Swan River Canada 52°10N 101°16W 71 C8
Swanage U.K. 50°36N 1°58W 13 G6
Swansea Australia 42°8S 148°4E 63 G4
Swansea U.K. 51°37N 3°57W 13 F4
Swansea □ U.K. 51°38N 4°3W 13 F3
Swartberge S. Africa 33°20S 22°0E 56 D3
Swartmodder S. Africa 28°1S 20°32E 56 C3
Swartnossob → Namibia 23°8S 18°42E 56 B2
Swartruggens S. Africa 25°39S 26°42E 56 C4
Swastika Canada 48°7N 80°6W 72 C3
Swat → Pakistan 34°40N 72°5E 43 B5
Swatow = Shantou China 23°18N 116°40E 35 F11
Swaziland = Eswatini ■ Africa 26°30S 31°30E 57 C5
Sweden ■ Europe 57°0N 15°0E 9 H16
Sweet Grass U.S.A. 48°59N 111°58W 76 B8
Sweet Home U.S.A. 44°24N 122°44W 76 D2
Sweetwater Nev., U.S.A. 38°27N 119°9W 78 G7
Sweetwater Tenn., U.S.A. 35°36N 84°28W 85 D12
Sweetwater Tex., U.S.A. 32°28N 100°25W 84 E4
Sweetwater → U.S.A. 42°31N 107°2W 76 E10
Swellendam S. Africa 34°1S 20°26E 56 D3
Świdnica Poland 50°50N 16°30E 17 C9
Świdnik Poland 51°13N 22°39E 17 C12
Świebodzin Poland 52°15N 15°31E 16 B8
Świecie Poland 53°25N 18°30E 17 B10
Swift Current Canada 50°20N 107°45W 71 C7
Swift Current → Canada 50°38N 107°44W 71 C7
Swilly, L. Ireland 55°12N 7°33W 10 A4
Swindon U.K. 51°34N 1°46W 13 F6
Swindon □ U.K. 51°34N 1°46W 13 F6
Swinemünde = Świnoujście Poland 53°54N 14°16E 16 B8
Swinford Ireland 53°57N 8°58W 10 C3
Świnoujście Poland 53°54N 14°16E 16 B8
Switzerland ■ Europe 46°30N 8°0E 20 C8
Swords Ireland 53°28N 6°13W 10 C5
Swoyerville U.S.A. 41°18N 75°53W 83 E9
Sydenham → Canada 42°33N 82°25W 82 D2
Sydney Canada 46°7N 60°7W 73 C7
Sydney L. Canada 50°41N 94°25W 71 C10
Sydney Mines Canada 46°18N 60°15W 73 C7
Sydprøven = Alluitsup Paa Greenland 60°30N 45°35W 4 C5
Sydra, G. of = Surt, Khalīj Libya 31°40N 18°30E 53 B9
Sykesville U.S.A. 41°3N 78°50W 82 E6
Syktyvkar Russia 61°45N 50°40E 18 B9
Sylacauga U.S.A. 33°10N 86°15W 85 E11
Sylarna Sweden 63°2N 12°13E 8 E15
Sylhet Bangla. 24°54N 91°52E 41 G17
Sylhet □ Bangla. 24°50N 91°50E 41 G17
Sylt Germany 54°54N 8°22E 16 A5
Sylvan Beach U.S.A. 43°12N 75°44W 83 C9
Sylvan Lake Canada 52°20N 114°3W 70 C6
Sylvania Ga., U.S.A. 32°45N 81°38W 85 E14
Sylvania Ohio, U.S.A. 41°43N 83°42W 81 E12
Sylvester U.S.A. 31°32N 83°50W 85 F13
Sym Russia 60°20N 88°18E 26 C9
Synnot Ra. Australia 16°30S 125°20E 60 C4
Syöte △ Finland 65°44N 27°58E 8 D22
Syowa Antarctica 68°50S 12°0E 5 C5
Syracuse Kans., U.S.A. 37°59N 101°45W 80 G3
Syracuse N.Y., U.S.A. 43°3N 76°9W 83 C8
Syracuse Nebr., U.S.A. 40°39N 96°11W 80 E5
Syrdarya → Kazakhstan 46°3N 61°0E 26 E7
Syria ■ Asia 35°0N 38°0E 46 C3
Syrian Desert = Shām, Bādiyat ash Asia 32°0N 40°0E 46 C3
Syros = Ermoupoli Greece 37°28N 24°57E 23 F11
Syzran Russia 53°12N 48°30E 18 D8
Szczecin Poland 53°27N 14°27E 16 B8
Szczecinek Poland 53°43N 16°41E 17 B9
Szczeciński, Zalew = Stettiner Haff Germany 53°47N 14°15E 16 B8
Szczytno Poland 53°33N 21°0E 17 B11
Szechuan = Sichuan □ China 30°30N 103°0E 34 B5
Szechuan Basin = Sichuan Pendi China 31°0N 105°0E 34 B5
Szeged Hungary 46°16N 20°10E 17 E11
Székesfehérvár Hungary 47°15N 18°25E 17 E10
Szekszárd Hungary 46°22N 18°42E 17 E10
Szentes Hungary 46°39N 20°21E 17 E11
Szolnok Hungary 47°10N 20°15E 17 E11
Szombathely Hungary 47°14N 16°38E 17 E9

T

Ta Khli Thailand 15°15N 100°21E 38 E3
Ta Lai Vietnam 11°24N 107°23E 39 G6
Ta Phraya △ Thailand 14°11N 102°49E 38 E4
Taal Volcano Phil. 14°7N 120°59E 37 B6
Taamisaari = Raasepori Finland 60°0N 23°26E 9 G20
Tabacal Argentina 23°15S 64°15W 94 A3
Tabaco Phil. 13°22N 123°44E 37 B6
Ţābah Si. Arabia 26°55N 42°38E 46 E4
Tabanan Indonesia 8°32S 115°8E 37 K18
Ţabas Khorāsān, Iran 32°48N 60°12E 47 C9
Ţabas Yazd, Iran 33°35N 56°55E 47 C8
Tabasará, Serranía de Panama 8°35N 81°40W 88 E3
Tabasco □ Mexico 18°0N 92°40W 87 D6
Tabāsīn Iran 31°12N 57°54E 47 D8
Tabatinga Brazil 4°16S 69°56W 92 D5
Tabatinga, Serra da Brazil 10°30S 44°0W 93 F10
Taber Canada 49°47N 112°8W 70 D6
Tablas I. Phil. 12°25N 122°2E 37 B6
Table, Pte. de la Réunion 21°14S 55°48E 55 c
Table B. Canada 53°40N 56°25W 73 B8
Table I. Myanmar 14°12N 93°22E 45 G11
Table Rock L. U.S.A. 36°36N 93°19W 80 G7
Tabletop, Mt. Australia 23°24S 147°11E 62 C4
Tábor Czechia 49°25N 14°39E 16 D8
Tabora Tanzania 5°2S 32°50E 54 F6
Tabou Côte d'Ivoire 4°30N 7°20W 52 H4
Tabrīz Iran 38°7N 46°20E 46 B5
Tabuaeran Kiribati 3°51N 159°22W 65 G12
Tabūk Si. Arabia 28°23N 36°36E 46 D3
Tabūk □ Si. Arabia 27°40N 36°50E 46 E3
Tacámbaro de Codallos Mexico 19°14N 101°28W 86 D4
Tacheng China 46°40N 82°58E 30 B5
Tach'i Taiwan 24°53N 121°17E 35 E13
Tachia Taiwan 24°25N 120°28E 35 E13
Tachilek Myanmar 20°26N 99°52E 38 B2
Tach'ing Shan = Daqing Shan China 40°40N 111°0E 32 D6
Tacloban Phil. 11°15N 124°58E 37 B6
Tacna Peru 18°0S 70°20W 92 G4
Tacoma U.S.A. 47°14N 122°26W 78 C4
Tacuarembó Uruguay 31°45S 56°0W 95 C4
Tademaït, Plateau du Algeria 28°30N 2°30E 52 C6
Tādepallegudem India 16°50N 81°30E 44 F5
Tadjourah Djibouti 11°50N 42°55E 49 E3
Tadmor N.Z. 41°27S 172°45E 59 D4
Tadoba △ India 20°30N 78°20E 44 D4
Tadoule L. Canada 58°36N 98°20W 71 B9
Tadoussac Canada 48°11N 69°42W 73 C6
Tadpatri India 14°55N 78°1E 45 G4
Tadzhikistan = Tajikistan ■ Asia 38°30N 70°0E 26 F8
Taegu = Daegu S. Korea 35°50N 128°37E 33 G15
Taegwan N. Korea 40°13N 125°12E 33 D13
Taejŏn = Daejeon S. Korea 36°20N 127°28E 33 F14
Taen, Ko Thailand 9°22N 99°57E 39 b
Tafalla Spain 42°30N 1°41W 21 A5
Tafermaar Indonesia 6°47S 134°10E 37 F8
Tafí Viejo Argentina 26°43S 65°17W 94 B2
Tafīhān Iran 29°25N 52°39E 47 D7
Tafresh Iran 34°45N 49°57E 47 C6
Taft Iran 31°45N 54°14E 47 D7
Taft Phil. 11°57N 125°30E 37 B7

Taft *U.S.A.* 35°8N 119°28W **79 K7**
Taftan *Pakistan* 29°0N 61°30E **40 E2**
Taftān, Kūh-e *Iran* 28°40N 61°0E **47 D9**
Tafwap *India* 7°23N 93°43E **45 L11**
Taga *Samoa* 13°46S 172°28W **59 b**
Taga Dzong *Bhutan* 27°5N 89°55E **41 F16**
Taganrog *Russia* 47°12N 38°50E **19 E6**
Tagbilaran *Phil.* 9°39N 123°51E **37 C6**
Tagish *Canada* 60°19N 134°16W **70 A2**
Tagish L. *Canada* 60°10N 134°20W **70 A2**
Tagliamento → *Italy* 45°38N 13°6E **22 B5**
Taguatinga *Brazil* 12°27S 46°22W **93 F10**
Tagum *Phil.* 7°33N 125°53E **37 C7**
Tagus = Tejo → *Europe* 38°40N 9°24W **21 C1**
Tahakopa *N.Z.* 46°30S 169°23E **59 G2**
Tahan, Gunung *Malaysia* 4°34N 102°17E **39 K4**
Tahat *Algeria* 23°18N 5°33E **52 D7**
Tāherī *Iran* 27°43N 52°20E **47 E7**
Tahiti *French Polynesia* 17°37S 149°27W **59 d**
Tahiti, I. *Tahiti* 17°37S 149°27W **59 d**
Tahlequah *U.S.A.* 35°55N 94°58W **84 D7**
Tahoe, L. *U.S.A.* 39°6N 120°2W **78 G6**
Tahoe City *U.S.A.* 39°10N 120°9W **78 F6**
Tahoka *U.S.A.* 33°10N 101°48W **84 E4**
Taholah *U.S.A.* 47°21N 124°17W **78 C2**
Tahoua *Niger* 14°57N 5°16E **52 F7**
Tahrūd *Iran* 29°26N 57°49E **47 D8**
Tahsis *Canada* 49°55N 126°40W **70 D3**
Tahta *Egypt* 26°44N 31°32E **53 C12**
Tahulandang *Indonesia* 2°27N 125°23E **37 D7**
Tahuna *Indonesia* 3°38N 125°30E **37 D7**
Tai Hu *China* 31°5N 120°10E **35 B13**
Tai Pang Wan *China* 22°33N 114°24E **31 a**
Tai Po *China* 22°27N 114°10E **31 a**
Tai Rom Yen △ *Thailand* 8°45N 99°30E **39 H2**
Tai Shan *China* 36°25N 117°20E **33 F9**
Tai'an *China* 36°12N 117°8E **33 F9**
Taiarapu, Presqu'île de
  Tahiti 17°47S 149°14W **59 d**
Taibai Shan *China* 33°57N 107°45E **32 H4**
Taibus Qi *China* 41°54N 115°22E **32 D8**
Taicang *China* 31°30N 121°5E **35 B13**
T'aichung *Taiwan* 24°9N 120°37E **35 E13**
Taieri → *N.Z.* 46°3S 170°12E **59 G3**
Taigu *China* 37°28N 112°30E **32 F7**
Taihang Shan *China* 36°0N 113°30E **32 G7**
Taihape *N.Z.* 39°41S 175°48E **59 C5**
Taihe *Anhui, China* 33°20N 115°42E **32 H8**
Taihe *Jiangxi, China* 26°47N 114°52E **35 D10**
Taihu *China* 30°22N 116°20E **35 B11**
Taijiang *China* 26°39N 108°21E **34 D7**
Taikang *China* 34°5N 114°50E **32 G8**
Tailem Bend *Australia* 35°12S 139°29E **63 F2**
T'ailuko *Taiwan* 24°9N 121°37E **35 E13**
Taimyr Peninsula = Taymyr,
  Poluostrov *Russia* 75°0N 100°0E **27 B11**
Tain *U.K.* 57°49N 4°4W **11 D4**
T'ainan *Taiwan* 23°0N 120°10E **35 F13**
Taining *China* 26°54N 117°9E **35 D11**
Taipa *China* 22°10N 113°35E **31 a**
T'aipei *Taiwan* 25°4N 121°29E **35 E13**
Taiping *China* 30°15N 118°6E **35 B12**
Taiping *Malaysia* 4°51N 100°44E **39 K3**
Taiping Dao = Itu Aba I.
  S. China Sea 10°23N 114°21E **36 B4**
Taipingchuan *China* 44°23N 123°11E **33 B12**
Taipingzhen *China* 33°35N 111°42E **32 H6**
Taishan *China* 22°14N 112°41E **35 F9**
Taishun *China* 27°30N 119°42E **35 D12**
Taitao, Pen. de *Chile* 46°30S 75°0W **96 F2**
T'aitung *Taiwan* 22°43N 121°4E **35 F13**
Taivalkoski *Finland* 65°33N 28°12E **8 D23**
Taiwan ■ *Asia* 23°30N 121°0E **35 F13**
Taiwan Strait *Asia* 24°40N 120°0E **35 E12**
Taixing *China* 32°11N 120°0E **35 A13**
Taiyiba *Israel* 32°36N 35°27E **48 C4**
Taiyuan *China* 37°52N 112°33E **32 F7**
Taizhou *Jiangsu, China* 32°28N 119°55E **35 A12**
Taizhou *Zhejiang, China* 28°40N 121°24E **35 C13**
Taizhou Liedao *China* 28°30N 121°55E **35 C13**
Ta'izz *Yemen* 13°35N 44°2E **49 E3**
Taj Mahal *India* 27°10N 78°2E **42 F8**
Tājābād *Iran* 30°2N 54°24E **47 D7**
Tajikistan ■ *Asia* 38°30N 70°0E **26 F8**
Tajima = Minamiaizu
  Japan 37°12N 139°46E **29 F9**
Tajo = Tejo → *Europe* 38°40N 9°24W **21 C1**
Tak *Thailand* 16°52N 99°8E **38 D2**
Takāb *Iran* 36°24N 47°7E **46 B5**
Takachiho *Japan* 32°42N 131°18E **29 H5**
Takachu *Botswana* 22°37S 21°58E **56 B3**
Takada *Japan* 37°7N 138°15E **29 F9**
Takahagi *Japan* 36°43N 140°45E **29 F10**
Takaka *N.Z.* 40°51S 172°50E **59 D4**
Takamaka *Seychelles* 4°50S 55°30E **55 b**
Takamatsu *Japan* 34°20N 134°5E **29 G7**
Takaoka *Japan* 36°47N 137°0E **29 F8**
Takapuna *N.Z.* 36°47S 174°47E **59 B5**
Takasaki *Japan* 36°20N 139°0E **29 F9**
Takatsuki *Japan* 34°51N 135°37E **29 G7**
Takayama *Japan* 36°18N 137°11E **29 F8**
Take-Shima *Japan* 30°49N 130°26E **29 J5**
Takefu = Echizen *Japan* 35°50N 136°10E **29 G8**
Takengon *Indonesia* 4°45N 96°50E **36 D1**
Takeo *Cambodia* 10°59N 104°47E **39 G5**
Takeo *Japan* 33°12N 130°1E **29 H5**
Takeshima = Liancourt Rocks
  Asia 37°15N 131°52E **29 F5**
Tākestān *Iran* 36°0N 49°40E **47 C6**
Taketa *Japan* 32°58N 131°24E **29 H5**
Takh *India* 33°6N 77°32E **43 C7**
Takhmau *Cambodia* 11°29N 104°57E **39 G5**
Takht-e Soleyman *Iran* 36°36N 47°14E **46 B5**
Takht-Sulaiman *Pakistan* 31°40N 69°58E **42 D3**
Takikawa *Japan* 43°33N 141°54E **28 C10**
Takla L. *Canada* 55°15N 125°45W **70 B3**
Takla Landing *Canada* 55°30N 125°50W **70 B3**
Taklamakan *China* 38°0N 83°0E **30 D5**
Taklamakan Shamo =
  Taklamakan *China* 38°0N 83°0E **30 D5**
Taksimo *Russia* 56°20N 114°52E **27 D12**

Taku → *Canada* 58°30N 133°50W **70 B2**
Takua Thung *Thailand* 8°24N 98°27E **39 a**
Tal Halāl *Iran* 28°54N 55°1E **47 D7**
Tala *Uruguay* 34°21S 55°46W **95 C4**
Talagang *Pakistan* 32°55N 72°25E **42 C5**
Talagante *Chile* 33°40S 70°50W **94 C1**
Talaimannar *Sri Lanka* 9°6N 79°43E **45 K4**
Talamanca, Cordillera de
  Cent. Amer. 9°20N 83°20W **88 E3**
Talampaya △ *Argentina* 29°43S 67°42W **94 B2**
Talara *Peru* 4°38S 81°18W **92 D2**
Talas *Kyrgyzstan* 42°30N 72°13E **26 E8**
Talāta *Egypt* 30°36N 32°20E **48 E1**
Talaud, Kepulauan
  Indonesia 4°30N 126°50E **37 D7**
Talaud Is. = Talaud, Kepulauan
  Indonesia 4°30N 126°50E **37 D7**
Talavera de la Reina
  Spain 39°55N 4°46W **21 C3**
Talayan *Phil.* 6°52N 124°24E **37 C6**
Talbandh *India* 22°3N 86°20E **43 H12**
Talbot, C. *Australia* 13°48S 126°43E **60 B4**
Talbragar → *Australia* 32°12S 148°37E **63 E4**
Talca *Chile* 35°28S 71°40W **94 D1**
Talcahuano *Chile* 36°40S 73°10W **94 D1**
Talcher *India* 21°0N 85°18E **44 D7**
Taldy Kurgan = Taldyqorghan
  Kazakhstan 45°10N 78°45E **30 B4**
Taldyqorghan *Kazakhstan* 45°10N 78°45E **30 B4**
Tālesh *Iran* 37°58N 48°58E **47 B6**
Tālesh, Kūhhā-ye *Iran* 37°42N 48°55E **47 B6**
Talguppa *India* 14°13N 74°56E **45 G2**
Tali Post *South Sudan* 5°55N 30°44E **53 G12**
Taliabu *Indonesia* 1°50S 125°0E **37 E6**
Talibon *Phil.* 10°9N 124°20E **37 B6**
Talihina *U.S.A.* 34°45N 95°3W **84 D7**
Talikota *India* 16°29N 76°17E **45 F3**
Talipparamba *India* 12°3N 75°21E **45 H2**
Taliwang *Indonesia* 8°50S 116°55E **36 F5**
Talkot *Nepal* 29°37N 81°19E **43 E9**
Talladega *U.S.A.* 33°26N 86°6W **85 E11**
Tallahassee *U.S.A.* 30°27N 84°17W **85 F12**
Tallangatta *Australia* 36°15S 147°19E **63 F4**
Tallering Pk. *Australia* 28°6S 115°37E **61 E2**
Talli *Pakistan* 29°32N 68°8E **42 E3**
Tallinn *Estonia* 59°22N 24°48E **9 G21**
Tallmadge *U.S.A.* 41°6N 81°27W **82 E3**
Tallulah *U.S.A.* 32°25N 91°11W **84 E9**
Talnakh *Russia* 69°29N 88°22E **27 C9**
Taloda *India* 21°34N 74°11E **44 D2**
Taloyoak *Canada* 69°32N 93°32W **68 D13**
Talpa de Allende
  Mexico 20°23N 104°51W **86 C4**
Talparo *Trin. & Tob.* 10°30N 61°17W **93 K15**
Talsi *Latvia* 57°10N 22°30E **9 H20**
Taltal *Chile* 25°23S 70°33W **94 B1**
Taltson → *Canada* 61°24N 112°46W **70 A6**
Talwood *Australia* 28°29S 149°29E **63 D4**
Talyawalkra Cr. →
  Australia 32°28S 142°22E **63 E3**
Tam Dao △ *Vietnam* 21°45N 105°45E **38 B5**
Tam Ky *Vietnam* 15°34N 108°29E **38 E7**
Tam Quan *Vietnam* 14°35N 109°3E **38 E7**
Tama *U.S.A.* 41°58N 92°35W **80 E7**
Tama Abu, Banjaran
  Malaysia 3°50N 115°5E **36 D5**
Tamale *Ghana* 9°22N 0°50W **52 G5**
Taman Negara △
  Malaysia 4°38N 102°26E **39 K4**
Tamano *Japan* 34°29N 133°59E **29 G6**
Tamanrasset *Algeria* 22°50N 5°30E **52 D7**
Tamaqua *U.S.A.* 40°48N 75°58W **83 F9**
Tamar → *U.K.* 50°27N 4°15W **13 G3**
Tamarin *Mauritius* 20°19S 57°20E **55 d**
Tamashima *Japan* 34°32N 133°40E **29 G6**
Tamatave = Toamasina
  Madag. 18°10S 49°25E **55 H9**
Tamaulipas □ *Mexico* 24°0N 98°45W **87 C5**
Tamaulipas, Sierra de
  Mexico 23°30N 98°20W **87 C5**
Tamazula *Mexico* 24°57N 106°57W **86 C3**
Tamazunchale *Mexico* 21°16N 98°47W **87 C5**
Tambacounda *Senegal* 13°45N 13°40W **52 F3**
Tambaram *India* 12°55N 80°7E **45 H5**
Tambelan, Kepulauan
  Indonesia 1°0N 107°30E **36 D3**
Tambellup *Australia* 34°4S 117°37E **61 F2**
Tambo *Australia* 24°54S 146°14E **62 C4**
Tambo de Mora *Peru* 13°30S 76°8W **92 F3**
Tambora *Indonesia* 8°12S 118°5E **36 F5**
Tambov *Russia* 52°45N 41°28E **18 D7**
Tambuku *Indonesia* 7°8S 113°40E **37 G15**
Tâmega → *Portugal* 41°5N 8°21W **21 B1**
Tamenglong *India* 25°0N 93°35E **41 G18**
Tamiahua, L. de *Mexico* 21°35N 97°35W **87 C5**
Tamil Nadu □ *India* 11°0N 77°0E **45 J3**
Tamluk *India* 22°18N 87°58E **43 H12**
Tammerfors = Tampere
  Finland 61°30N 23°50E **8 F20**
Tampa *U.S.A.* 27°56N 82°27W **85 H13**
Tampa, Tanjung
  Indonesia 8°55S 116°12E **37 K19**
Tampa B. *U.S.A.* 27°50N 82°30W **85 H13**
Tampere *Finland* 61°30N 23°50E **8 F20**
Tampico *Mexico* 22°13N 97°51W **87 C5**
Tampin *Malaysia* 2°28N 102°13E **39 L4**
Tampoi *Malaysia* 1°30N 103°39E **39 d**
Tamsagbulag *Mongolia* 47°14N 117°21E **31 B12**
Tamu *Myanmar* 24°13N 94°12E **41 G19**
Tamworth *Australia* 31°7S 150°58E **63 E5**
Tamworth *Canada* 44°29N 77°0W **82 B8**
Tamworth *U.K.* 52°39N 1°41W **13 E6**
Tan An *Vietnam* 10°32N 106°25E **39 G6**
Tan Chau *Vietnam* 10°48N 105°12E **39 G5**
Tan Hiep *Vietnam* 10°27N 106°21E **39 G6**
Tan Yen *Vietnam* 24°4N 105°3E **38 A5**
Tana → *Kenya* 2°32S 40°31E **54 E8**
Tana → *Norway* 70°30N 28°14E **8 A23**

Tana, L. *Ethiopia* 13°5N 37°30E **49 E2**
Tanabe *Japan* 33°44N 135°22E **29 H7**
Tanafjorden *Norway* 70°45N 28°25E **8 A23**
Tanaga I. *U.S.A.* 51°48N 177°53W **74 E4**
Tanah Merah *Malaysia* 5°48N 102°9E **39 K4**
Tanahbala *Indonesia* 0°30S 98°30E **36 E1**
Tanahgrogot *Indonesia* 1°55S 116°15E **36 E5**
Tanahjampea *Indonesia* 7°10S 120°35E **37 F6**
Tanahmasa *Indonesia* 0°12S 98°39E **36 E1**
Tanahmerah *Indonesia* 6°5S 140°16E **37 F10**
Tanakpur *India* 29°5N 80°7E **43 E9**
Tanamalwila *Sri Lanka* 6°26N 81°8E **45 L5**
Tanami Desert *Australia* 18°50S 132°0E **60 C5**
Tanana *U.S.A.* 65°10N 152°4W **74 B9**
Tanana → *U.S.A.* 65°10N 151°58W **68 D1**
Tananarive = Antananarivo
  Madag. 18°55S 47°31E **55 H9**
Tánaro → *Italy* 44°55N 8°40E **20 D8**
Tancheng *China* 34°25N 118°20E **33 G10**
Tanch'ŏn *N. Korea* 40°27N 128°54E **33 D15**
Tanda *Ut. P., India* 26°33N 82°35E **43 F10**
Tanda *Ut. P., India* 28°57N 78°56E **43 E8**
Tandag *Phil.* 9°4N 126°9E **37 C7**
Tandaué *Angola* 16°58S 18°5E **56 A2**
Tandil *Argentina* 37°15S 59°6W **94 D4**
Tandil, Sa. del *Argentina* 37°30S 59°0W **94 D4**
Tandlianwala *Pakistan* 31°3N 73°9E **42 D5**
Tando Adam *Pakistan* 25°45N 68°40E **42 G3**
Tando Allahyar *Pakistan* 25°28N 68°43E **42 G3**
Tando Bago *Pakistan* 24°47N 68°58E **42 G3**
Tando Mohommed Khan
  Pakistan 25°8N 68°32E **42 G3**
Tandou L. *Australia* 32°40S 142°5E **63 E3**
Tandoureh △ *Iran* 37°50N 59°0E **47 B8**
Tandragee *U.K.* 54°21N 6°24W **10 B5**
Tandula → *India* 21°6N 81°14E **44 D5**
Tandula Tank *India* 20°40N 81°12E **44 D5**
Tandur *Telangana, India* 19°11N 79°30E **44 E4**
Tandur *Telangana, India* 17°14N 77°35E **44 E3**
Tane-ga-Shima *Japan* 30°30N 131°0E **29 J5**
Tanen Tong Dan = Dawna Ra.
  Myanmar 16°30N 98°30E **38 D2**
Tanezrouft *Algeria* 23°9N 0°11E **52 D6**
Tang, Koh *Cambodia* 10°16N 103°7E **39 G4**
Tang, Ra's-e *Iran* 25°21N 59°52E **47 E8**
Tang Krasang *Cambodia* 12°34N 105°3E **38 F5**
Tanga *Tanzania* 5°5S 39°2E **54 F7**
Tangalla *Sri Lanka* 6°1N 80°48E **45 L5**
Tanganyika, L. *Africa* 6°40S 30°0E **54 F6**
Tangasseri *India* 8°53N 76°35E **45 K3**
Tanger *Morocco* 35°50N 5°49W **52 A4**
Tangerang *Indonesia* 6°11S 106°37E **37 G12**
Tangra *China* 39°2N 117°40E **33 E9**
Tanggula Shan *China* 32°40N 92°10E **30 E7**
Tanggula Shankou *China* 32°42N 92°27E **30 E7**
Tanghe *China* 32°47N 112°50E **32 H7**
Tanghla Range = Tanggula Shan
  China 32°40N 92°10E **30 E7**
Tangi *India* 19°56N 85°24E **44 D7**
Tangier = Tanger
  Morocco 35°50N 5°49W **52 A4**
Tangjia *China* 22°22N 113°35E **31 a**
Tangjia Wan *China* 22°21N 113°36E **31 a**
Tangorin *Australia* 21°47S 144°12E **62 C3**
Tangra Yumco *China* 31°0N 86°38E **30 E6**
Tangshan *China* 39°38N 118°10E **33 E10**
Tangtou *China* 35°28N 118°30E **33 G10**
Tangxi *China* 29°3N 119°25E **35 C12**
Tangyan He → *China* 28°54N 108°19E **34 C7**
Tangyin *China* 35°54N 114°21E **32 G8**
Taniantaweng Shan
  China 31°20N 98°0E **34 B2**
Tanimbar, Kepulauan
  Indonesia 7°30S 131°30E **37 F8**
Tanimbar Is. = Tanimbar,
  Kepulauan *Indonesia* 7°30S 131°30E **37 F8**
Tanintharyi = Taninthayi
  Myanmar 12°6N 99°3E **39 F2**
Taninthayi *Myanmar* 12°6N 99°3E **39 F2**
Tanjay *Phil.* 9°30N 123°5E **37 C6**
Tanjore = Thanjavur
  India 10°48N 79°12E **45 J4**
Tanjung *Kalimantan Selatan,
  Indonesia* 2°10S 115°25E **36 E5**
Tanjung *Nusa Tenggara Barat,
  Indonesia* 8°21S 116°9E **37 J19**
Tanjung Malim *Malaysia* 3°42N 101°31E **39 L3**
Tanjung Pelepas *Malaysia* 1°21N 103°33E **39 d**
Tanjung Tokong *Malaysia* 5°30N 100°18E **39 c**
Tanjungbalai *Indonesia* 2°55N 99°44E **36 D1**
Tanjungbatu *Indonesia* 2°23N 118°3E **36 D5**
Tanjungkarang Telukbetung =
  Bandar Lampung
  Indonesia 5°20S 105°10E **36 F3**
Tanjungpandan *Indonesia* 2°43S 107°38E **36 E3**
Tanjungpinang *Indonesia* 1°5N 104°30E **36 D2**
Tanjungredeb *Indonesia* 2°9N 117°29E **36 D5**
Tanjungselor *Indonesia* 2°55N 117°25E **36 D5**
Tank *Pakistan* 32°14N 70°25E **42 C4**
Tankhala *India* 21°58N 73°47E **42 J5**
Tankwa-Karoo △
  S. Africa 32°14S 19°50E **56 E2**
Tannersville *U.S.A.* 41°3N 75°18W **83 E9**
Tannu Ola *Asia* 51°0N 94°0E **27 D10**
Tannum Sands *Australia* 23°57S 151°22E **62 C5**
Tanout *Niger* 14°50N 8°55E **52 F7**
Tanshui *Taiwan* 25°10N 121°28E **35 E13**
Tansing *Nepal* 27°52N 83°33E **43 F10**
Tanta *Egypt* 30°45N 30°57E **53 B12**
Tantoyuca *Mexico* 21°21N 98°14W **87 C5**
Tantung = Dandong
  China 40°10N 124°20E **33 D13**
Tanuku *India* 16°45N 81°44E **44 L5**
Tanunda *Australia* 34°30S 139°0E **63 E2**
Tanur *India* 11°1N 75°52E **45 J2**
Tanzania ■ *Africa* 6°0S 34°0E **54 F6**
Tanzhou *China* 22°16N 113°28E **31 a**
Tanzilla → *Canada* 58°8N 130°43W **70 B2**
Tao, Ko *Thailand* 10°5N 99°52E **39 G2**

Tao'an = Taonan
  China 45°22N 122°40E **33 B12**
Tao'er He → *China* 45°45N 124°5E **33 B13**
Taohua Dao *China* 29°50N 122°20E **35 C14**
Taolanaro *Madag.* 25°2S 47°0E **55 K9**
Taole *China* 38°48N 106°40E **32 E4**
Taonan *China* 45°22N 122°40E **33 B12**
Taos *U.S.A.* 36°24N 105°35W **77 H11**
Taoudenni *Mali* 22°40N 3°55W **52 D5**
Taoyuan *China* 28°55N 111°16E **35 C8**
Taoyuan *Taiwan* 25°0N 121°4E **35 E13**
Tapa *Estonia* 59°15N 25°50E **9 G21**
Tapa Shan = Daba Shan
  China 32°0N 109°0E **34 B7**
Tapachula *Mexico* 14°54N 92°17W **87 E6**
Tapah *Malaysia* 4°12N 101°15E **39 K3**
Tapajós → *Brazil* 2°24S 54°41W **93 D8**
Tapaktuan *Indonesia* 3°15N 97°10E **36 D1**
Tapanahoni → *Suriname* 4°20N 54°25W **93 C8**
Tapanui *N.Z.* 45°56S 169°18E **59 F2**
Tapauá → *Brazil* 5°40S 64°21W **92 E6**
Tapes *Brazil* 30°40S 51°23W **95 C5**
Tapeta *Liberia* 6°29N 8°52W **52 G4**
Taphan Hin *Thailand* 16°13N 100°26E **38 D3**
Tapi → *India* 21°8N 72°41E **44 D1**
Tapirapecó, Serra
  Venezuela 1°10N 65°0W **92 C6**
Taplejung *Nepal* 27°1N 86°16E **43 F12**
Tapo-Capara △ *Venezuela* 7°55N 71°15W **89 E5**
Tapti → *India* 21°8N 72°41E **44 D1**
Tapuae-o-Uenuku *N.Z.* 42°0S 173°39E **59 E4**
Tapul Group *Phil.* 5°35N 120°50E **37 C6**
Tapurucuará *Brazil* 0°24S 65°2W **92 D5**
Taqtaq *Iraq* 35°53N 44°35E **46 C5**
Taquara *Brazil* 29°36S 50°46W **95 B5**
Taquari → *Brazil* 19°15S 57°17W **92 G7**
Tara *Canada* 44°28N 81°9W **82 B3**
Tara *Russia* 56°55N 74°24E **26 D8**
Tara → *Montenegro* 43°21N 18°51E **23 C8**
Tara → *Russia* 56°42N 74°36E **26 D8**
Tarābulus *Lebanon* 34°31N 35°50E **48 A4**
Tarābulus *Libya* 32°49N 13°7E **53 B8**
Tarābulus *Libya* 31°0N 13°0E **53 B8**
Taradehi *India* 23°18N 79°21E **43 H8**
Tarakan *Indonesia* 3°20N 117°35E **36 D5**
Tarama-Jima *Japan* 24°39N 124°42E **29 M2**
Taran, Mys *Russia* 54°56N 19°59E **9 J18**
Taranagar *India* 28°43N 74°50E **42 E6**
Taranaki □ *N.Z.* 39°25S 174°30E **59 C5**
Taranaki, Mt. *N.Z.* 39°17S 174°5E **59 C5**
Tarancón *Spain* 40°1N 3°1W **21 B4**
Taransay *U.K.* 57°54N 7°0W **11 D1**
Táranto *Italy* 40°28N 17°14E **22 D7**
Táranto, G. di *Italy* 40°8N 17°20E **22 D7**
Tarapacá *Colombia* 2°56S 69°46W **92 D5**
Tarapacá □ *Chile* 20°45S 69°30W **94 A2**
Tarapoto *Peru* 6°30S 76°20W **92 E3**
Tarashcha *Ukraine* 49°30N 30°31E **17 D16**
Tarauacá *Brazil* 8°6S 70°48W **92 E4**
Tarauacá → *Brazil* 6°42S 69°48W **92 E5**
Taravao *Tahiti* 17°43S 149°18W **59 d**
Taravao, Isthme de
  Tahiti 17°43S 149°19W **59 d**
Tarawa *Kiribati* 1°30N 173°0E **64 G9**
Tarawera *N.Z.* 39°2S 176°36E **59 C6**
Tarawera, L. *N.Z.* 38°13S 176°27E **59 C6**
Taraz *Kazakhstan* 42°54N 71°22E **30 C3**
Tarazona *Spain* 41°55N 1°43W **21 B5**
Tarbagatay, Khrebet
  Kazakhstan 48°0N 83°0E **30 B5**
Tarbat Ness *U.K.* 57°52N 3°47W **11 D5**
Tarbela Dam *Pakistan* 34°8N 72°52E **42 B5**
Tarbert *Ireland* 52°34N 9°22E **10 D2**
Tarbert *Argyll & Bute, U.K.* 55°52N 5°25W **11 F3**
Tarbert *W. Isles, U.K.* 57°54N 6°49W **11 D2**
Tarbes *France* 43°15N 0°3E **20 E4**
Tarboro *U.S.A.* 35°54N 77°32W **85 D16**
Tarcoola *Australia* 30°44S 134°36E **63 E1**
Tarcoon *Australia* 30°15S 146°43E **63 E4**
Taree *Australia* 31°50S 152°30E **63 E5**
Tarfaya *Morocco* 27°55N 12°55W **52 C3**
Targovishte *Bulgaria* 43°17N 26°38E **23 C12**
Târgoviște *Romania* 44°55N 25°27E **17 F13**
Târgu Jiu *Romania* 45°5N 23°19E **17 F12**
Târgu Mureş *Romania* 46°31N 24°38E **17 E13**
Tarif *U.A.E.* 24°3N 53°46E **47 E7**
Tarifa *Spain* 36°1N 5°36W **21 D3**
Tarija *Bolivia* 21°30S 64°40W **94 A3**
Tarija □ *Bolivia* 21°30S 63°30W **94 A3**
Tariku → *Indonesia* 2°55S 138°26E **37 E9**
Tarim *Yemen* 16°3N 49°0E **49 D4**
Tarim Basin = Tarim Pendi
  China 40°0N 84°0E **30 C5**
Tarim He → *China* 39°30N 88°30E **30 C6**
Tarim Pendi *China* 40°0N 84°0E **30 C5**
Taritatu → *Indonesia* 2°54S 138°27E **37 E9**
Tarka → *S. Africa* 32°10S 26°0E **56 E4**
Tarka La *Bhutan* 27°12N 89°44E **43 F13**
Tarkastad *S. Africa* 32°0S 26°16E **56 E4**
Tarko Sale *Russia* 64°55N 77°50E **26 C8**
Tarkwa *Ghana* 5°20N 2°0W **52 G5**
Tarlac *Phil.* 15°29N 120°35E **37 A6**
Tarma *Peru* 11°25S 75°45W **92 F3**
Tarn → *France* 44°5N 1°6E **20 E4**
Târnăveni *Romania* 46°19N 24°13E **17 E13**
Tarnobrzeg *Poland* 50°35N 21°41E **17 C11**
Tarnowskie Góry *Poland* 50°27N 18°54E **17 C10**
Tārom *Iran* 28°11N 55°46E **47 D7**
Taroom *Australia* 25°36S 149°48E **63 D4**
Taroudannt *Morocco* 30°30N 8°52W **52 B4**
Tarpon Springs *U.S.A.* 28°9N 82°45W **85 G13**
Tarrafal *Cabo Verde* 15°18N 23°39W **52 b**
Tarragona *Spain* 41°5N 1°17E **21 B6**
Tarraleah *Australia* 42°17S 146°26E **63 G4**
Tarrasa = Terrassa *Spain* 41°34N 2°1E **21 B7**
Tarrytown *U.S.A.* 41°4N 73°52W **83 E11**

Tarsus *Turkey* 36°58N 34°55E **46 B2**
Tartagal *Argentina* 22°30S 63°50W **94 A3**
Tărtăş *Estonia* 58°20N 26°44E **9 G22**
Ţarţūs *Syria* 34°55N 35°55E **46 C2**
Tarumizu *Japan* 31°29N 130°42E **29 J5**
Tarutao = Ko Tarutao △
  Thailand 6°31N 99°26E **39 J2**
Tarutao, Ko *Thailand* 6°33N 99°40E **39 J2**
Tarutung *Indonesia* 2°0N 98°54E **36 D1**
Taseko → *Canada* 52°8N 123°45W **70 C4**
Tasgaon *India* 17°2N 74°39E **44 F2**
Tash-Kömür *Kyrgyzstan* 41°40N 72°10E **26 E8**
Tashauz = Daşoguz
  Turkmenistan 41°49N 59°58E **26 E6**
Tashi Chho Dzong = Thimphu
  Bhutan 27°31N 89°45E **41 F16**
Tashk, Daryācheh-ye
  Iran 29°45N 53°35E **47 D7**
Tashkent = Toshkent
  Uzbekistan 41°20N 69°10E **26 E7**
Tashtagol *Russia* 52°47N 87°53E **26 D9**
Tasiilaq *Greenland* 65°40N 37°20W **4 C6**
Tasikmalaya *Indonesia* 7°18S 108°12E **37 G13**
Tāsjön *Sweden* 64°15N 15°40E **8 D16**
Taskan *Russia* 62°59N 150°20E **27 C16**
Tasman B. *N.Z.* 40°59S 173°25E **59 D4**
Tasman Basin *Pac. Oc.* 46°0S 158°0E **64 M7**
Tasman Mts. *N.Z.* 41°3S 172°25E **59 D4**
Tasman Pen. *Australia* 43°10S 148°0E **63 G4**
Tasman Sea *Pac. Oc.* 36°0S 160°0E **58 F9**
Tasmania □ *Australia* 42°0S 146°30E **63 G4**
Tasmanian Wilderness World
  Heritage Area △
  Australia 43°0S 146°0E **63 G4**
Tassili n' Ajjer *Algeria* 25°47N 8°1E **52 C7**
Tassili-oua-n-Ahaggar
  Algeria 20°41N 5°30E **52 D7**
Tat Ton △ *Thailand* 15°57N 102°2E **38 E4**
Tata *Morocco* 29°46N 7°56W **52 C4**
Tatabánya *Hungary* 47°32N 18°25E **17 E10**
Tataouine *Tunisia* 32°57N 10°29E **53 B8**
Tatar Republic = Tatarstan □
  Russia 55°30N 51°30E **18 C9**
Tatarbunary *Ukraine* 45°50N 29°39E **17 F15**
Tatarsk *Russia* 55°14N 76°0E **26 D8**
Tatarskiy Proliv *Russia* 50°0N 141°0E **27 E15**
Tatarstan □ *Russia* 55°30N 51°30E **18 C9**
Tatatua, Pte. *Tahiti* 17°44S 149°8W **59 d**
Tateyama *Japan* 35°0N 139°50E **29 G9**
Tathlina L. *Canada* 60°33N 117°39W **70 A5**
Tathra *Australia* 36°44S 149°59E **63 F4**
Tatinnai L. *Canada* 60°55N 97°40W **71 A9**
Tatla Lake *Canada* 52°0N 124°20W **70 C4**
Tatnam, C. *Canada* 57°16N 91°0W **71 B10**
Tatra = Tatry *Slovakia* 49°20N 20°0E **17 D11**
Tatry *Slovakia* 49°20N 20°0E **17 D11**
Tatshenshini →
  Canada 59°28N 137°45W **70 B1**
Tatshenshini-Alsek △
  Canada 59°55N 137°45W **70 B1**
Tatsuno *Japan* 34°52N 134°33E **29 G7**
Tatta = Thatta *Pakistan* 24°42N 67°55E **42 G2**
Tatuī *Brazil* 23°25S 47°53W **95 A6**
Tatum *U.S.A.* 33°16N 103°19W **77 K12**
Tat'ung = Datong *China* 40°6N 113°18E **32 D7**
Tatvan *Turkey* 38°31N 42°15E **46 B4**
Ta'ū *Amer. Samoa* 14°15S 169°30W **59 b**
Taubaté *Brazil* 23°0S 45°36W **95 A6**
Tauern *Austria* 47°15N 12°40E **16 E7**
Taumarunui *N.Z.* 38°53S 175°15E **59 C5**
Taumaturgo *Brazil* 8°54S 72°51W **92 E4**
Taung *S. Africa* 27°33S 24°47E **56 D3**
Taungdwingyi *Myanmar* 20°1N 95°40E **41 J19**
Taunggyi *Myanmar* 20°50N 97°0E **41 J20**
Taungoo = Taunggoo
  Myanmar 19°0N 96°30E **41 K20**
Taungup *Myanmar* 18°51N 94°14E **41 K19**
Taunsa *Pakistan* 30°42N 70°39E **42 D4**
Taunsa Barrage *Pakistan* 30°42N 70°50E **42 D4**
Taunton *U.K.* 51°1N 3°5W **13 F4**
Taunton *U.S.A.* 41°54N 71°6W **83 E13**
Taunus *Germany* 50°13N 8°34E **16 C5**
Taupo *N.Z.* 38°41S 176°7E **59 C6**
Taupo, L. *N.Z.* 38°46S 175°55E **59 C5**
Tauragé *Lithuania* 55°14N 22°16E **9 J20**
Tauranga *N.Z.* 37°42S 176°11E **59 B6**
Tauranga Harb. *N.Z.* 37°30S 176°5E **59 B6**
Taureau, Rés. *Canada* 46°46N 73°50W **72 C5**
Taurianova *Italy* 38°21N 16°1E **22 E7**
Taurus Mts. = Toros Dağları
  Turkey 37°0N 32°30E **46 B2**
Tautira *Tahiti* 17°44S 149°9W **59 d**
Tauyskaya Guba
  Russia 59°20N 150°20E **27 D16**
Tavan Bogd Uul *Mongolia* 49°10N 87°49E **30 B6**
Tavastehus = Hämeenlinna
  Finland 61°0N 24°28E **8 F21**
Tavda *Russia* 58°7N 65°8E **26 D7**
Tavda → *Russia* 57°47N 67°18E **26 D7**
Taverner B. *Canada* 67°12N 72°25W **69 D17**
Taveuni *Fiji* 16°51S 179°58W **59 a**
Tavira *Portugal* 37°8N 7°40W **21 D2**
Tavistock *Canada* 43°19N 80°50W **82 C4**
Tavistock *U.K.* 50°33N 4°9W **13 G3**
Tavoy = Dawei *Myanmar* 14°2N 98°12E **38 E2**
Tavua *Fiji* 17°37S 177°5E **59 a**
Tavuki *Fiji* 19°7S 178°8E **59 a**
Taw → *U.K.* 51°4N 4°4W **13 F3**
Tawa → *India* 22°48N 77°48E **44 C4**
Tawa Res. *India* 22°35N 78°5E **44 C4**
Tawas City *U.S.A.* 44°16N 83°31W **81 C12**
Tawau *Malaysia* 4°20N 117°55E **36 D5**
Tawi-tawi I. *Phil.* 5°10N 120°0E **37 C6**
Tawu *Taiwan* 22°22N 120°54E **35 F13**
Taxco *Mexico* 18°33N 99°36W **87 D5**
Taxila *Pakistan* 33°42N 72°52E **42 C5**
Taxkorgan Tajik Zizhixian
  China 37°49N 75°14E **30 D4**
Tay → *U.K.* 56°37N 3°38W **11 E5**

Tay, Firth of U.K. 56°25N 3°8W **11 E5**
Tay, L. Australia 32°55S 120°48E **61 F3**
Tay, L. U.K. 56°32N 4°8W **11 E4**
Tay ○ U.K. 56°43N 3°59W **11 E5**
Tay Ninh Vietnam 11°20N 106°5E **39 G6**
Tayabamba Peru 8°15S 77°16W **92 E3**
Taygetos Oros Greece 37°0N 22°23E **23 F10**
Taylakova Russia 59°13N 74°0E **26 D8**
Taylor Canada 56°13N 120°40W **70 B4**
Taylor Nebr., U.S.A. 41°46N 99°23W **80 E4**
Taylor Pa., U.S.A. 41°23N 75°43W **83 E9**
Taylor Tex., U.S.A. 30°34N 97°25W **84 F6**
Taylor, Mt. U.S.A. 35°14N 107°37W **77 J10**
Taylorville U.S.A. 39°33N 89°18W **80 F9**
Taymā Si. Arabia 27°35N 38°45E **46 E3**
Taymyr, Oz. Russia 74°20N 102°0E **27 B11**
Taymyr, Poluostrov Russia 75°0N 100°0E **27 B11**
Taypaq Kazakhstan 49°0N 51°47E **19 E9**
Tayport U.K. 56°27N 2°52W **11 E6**
Tayrona △ Colombia 11°20N 74°2W **89 D5**
Tayshet Russia 55°58N 98°1E **27 D10**
Taytay Phil. 10°45N 119°30E **37 B6**
Tăyyebād Iran 34°45N 60°45E **47 C9**
Tăyyebād □ Iran 34°44N 60°44E **47 C9**
Taz → Russia 67°32N 78°40E **26 C8**
Taza Morocco 34°16N 4°6W **52 B5**
Tāza Khurmātū Iraq 35°18N 44°20E **46 C5**
Tazawa-Ko Japan 39°43N 140°40E **28 E10**
Tazin → Canada 59°48N 109°55W **71 B7**
Tazin L. Canada 59°44N 108°42W **71 B7**
Tazovskiy Russia 67°30N 78°44E **26 C8**
Tbilisi Georgia 41°43N 44°50E **19 F7**
Tchad = Chad ■ Africa 15°0N 17°15E **53 F8**
Tchad, L. Chad 13°30N 14°30E **53 F8**
Tch'eng-tou = Chengdu China 30°38N 104°2E **34 B5**
Tchentlo L. Canada 55°15N 125°0W **70 B4**
Tchibanga Gabon 2°45S 11°0E **54 E2**
Tchogha Zanbil = Choghā Zanbīl Iran 32°1N 48°32E **47 C6**
Tch'ong-k'ing = Chongqing China 29°35N 106°25E **34 C6**
Tczew Poland 54°8N 18°50E **17 A10**
Te Anau, L. N.Z. 45°15S 167°45E **59 F1**
Te Aroha N.Z. 37°32S 175°44E **59 C5**
Te Awamutu N.Z. 38°1S 175°20E **59 C5**
Te Ika-a-Māui = North I. N.Z. 38°0S 175°0E **59 C5**
Te Kuiti N.Z. 38°20S 175°11E **59 C5**
Te Puke N.Z. 37°46S 176°22E **59 B6**
Te Waewae B. N.Z. 46°13S 167°33E **59 G1**
Te Waipounamu = South I. N.Z. 44°0S 170°0E **59 F3**
Teague U.S.A. 31°38N 96°17W **84 F6**
Teahupoo Tahiti 17°50S 149°16W **59 d**
Teapa Mexico 17°33N 92°57W **87 D6**
Tebakang Malaysia 1°6N 110°30E **36 D4**
Teberau → Malaysia 1°30N 103°42E **39 d**
Tébessa Algeria 35°22N 8°8E **52 A7**
Tebicuary → Paraguay 26°36S 58°16W **94 B4**
Tebingtinggi Riau, Indonesia 1°0N 102°45E **36 E2**
Tebingtinggi Sumatera Utara, Indonesia 3°20N 99°9E **36 D1**
Tecate Mexico 32°34N 116°38W **79 N10**
Tecka Argentina 43°29S 70°48W **96 E2**
Tecomán Mexico 18°55N 103°53W **86 D4**
Tecopa U.S.A. 35°51N 116°13W **79 K10**
Tecoripa Mexico 28°37N 109°57W **86 B3**
Tecuala Mexico 22°23N 105°27W **86 C3**
Tecuci Romania 45°51N 27°27E **17 F14**
Tecumseh Canada 42°19N 82°54W **82 D2**
Tecumseh Mich., U.S.A. 42°0N 83°57W **81 D12**
Tecumseh Okla., U.S.A. 35°15N 96°56W **84 D6**
Tedzhen = Tejen Turkmenistan 37°23N 60°31E **26 F7**
Tees → U.K. 54°37N 1°10W **12 C6**
Tees B. U.K. 54°40N 1°9W **12 C6**
Teeswater Canada 43°59N 81°17W **82 C3**
Tefé Brazil 3°25S 64°50W **92 D6**
Tegal Indonesia 6°52S 109°8E **37 G13**
Tegallalang Indonesia 8°27S 115°17E **37 J18**
Tegalsari Indonesia 8°25S 114°8E **37 J17**
Tegid, L. = Bala, L. U.K. 52°53N 3°37W **12 E4**
Tegucigalpa Honduras 14°5N 87°14W **88 D2**
Tehachapi U.S.A. 35°8N 118°27W **79 K8**
Tehachapi Mts. U.S.A. 35°0N 118°30W **79 L8**
Tehoru Indonesia 3°23S 129°30E **37 E7**
Tehrān Iran 35°30N 51°30E **47 C6**
Tehri India 30°23N 78°29E **43 D8**
Tehuacán Mexico 18°27N 97°23W **87 D5**
Tehuantepec Mexico 16°21N 95°13W **87 D5**
Tehuantepec, G. de Mexico 15°50N 95°12W **87 D5**
Tehuantepec, Istmo de Mexico 17°15N 94°30W **87 D6**
Teifi → U.K. 52°5N 4°41W **13 E3**
Teign → U.K. 50°32N 3°32W **13 G4**
Teignmouth U.K. 50°33N 3°31W **13 G4**
Teinainano = Tarawa Kiribati 1°30N 173°0E **64 G9**
Tejakula Indonesia 8°8S 115°20E **37 J18**
Tejen Turkmenistan 37°23N 60°31E **26 F7**
Tejen → Turkmenistan 37°24N 60°38E **47 B9**
Tejo → Europe 38°40N 9°24W **21 C1**
Tejon Pass U.S.A. 34°49N 118°53W **79 L8**
Tekamah U.S.A. 41°47N 96°13W **80 E5**
Tekapo, L. N.Z. 43°53S 170°33E **59 E3**
Tekax Mexico 20°12N 89°17W **87 C7**
Tekeli Kazakhstan 44°50N 79°0E **26 E8**
Tekeze Dam Ethiopia 13°10N 38°45E **49 E2**
Tekirdağ Turkey 40°58N 27°30E **23 D12**
Tekkali India 18°37N 84°15E **44 E7**
Tekoa U.S.A. 47°14N 117°4W **76 C5**
Tel → India 20°50N 83°54E **44 D6**
Tel Aviv ✈ (TLV) Israel 32°5N 34°49E **48 C3**
Tel Aviv-Yafo Israel 32°4N 34°48E **48 C3**

Tel Lakhish Israel 31°34N 34°51E **48 D3**
Tel Megiddo Israel 32°35N 35°11E **48 C4**
Tela Honduras 15°40N 87°28W **88 C2**
Telanaipura = Jambi Indonesia 1°38S 103°30E **36 E2**
Telangana □ India 17°30N 78°30E **44 F4**
Telavi Georgia 42°0N 45°30E **19 F8**
Telegraph Creek Canada 58°0N 131°10W **70 B2**
Telekhany = Tsyelyakhany Belarus 52°30N 25°46E **17 B13**
Telemark Norway 59°15N 7°40E **9 G12**
Telén Argentina 36°15S 65°31W **94 D2**
Teleng Iran 25°47N 61°3E **47 E9**
Teles Pires → Brazil 7°21S 58°3W **92 E7**
Telescope Pk. U.S.A. 36°10N 117°5W **79 J9**
Telford U.K. 52°40N 2°27W **13 E5**
Telford and Wrekin □ U.K. 52°45N 2°27W **12 E5**
Telkwa Canada 54°41N 127°5W **70 C3**
Tell City U.S.A. 37°57N 86°46W **80 G10**
Teller U.S.A. 65°16N 166°22W **74 B6**
Tellicherry = Thalassery India 11°45N 75°30E **45 J2**
Telluride U.S.A. 37°56N 107°49W **77 H10**
Teloloapán Mexico 18°21N 99°51W **87 D5**
Telpos Iz Russia 63°16N 59°13E **18 B10**
Telsen Argentina 42°30S 66°50W **96 E3**
Telšiai Lithuania 55°59N 22°14E **9 J20**
Teluk Anson = Teluk Intan Malaysia 4°3N 101°0E **39 K3**
Teluk Bahang Malaysia 5°28N 100°13E **39 c**
Teluk Betung = Bandar Lampung Indonesia 5°20S 105°10E **36 F3**
Teluk Intan Malaysia 4°3N 101°0E **39 K3**
Teluk Kumbar Malaysia 5°18N 100°14E **39 c**
Telukbutun Indonesia 4°13N 108°12E **36 D3**
Telukdalam Indonesia 0°33N 97°50E **36 D1**
Tema Ghana 5°41N 0°0 **52 G5**
Temagami, L. Canada 47°0N 80°10W **72 C3**
Temax Mexico 21°9N 88°56W **87 C7**
Tembe S. Africa 25°20S 28°17E **57 C4**
Tembagapura Indonesia 4°20S 137°0E **37 E9**
Tembe → S. Africa 26°51S 32°24E **57 C5**
Temblor Range U.S.A. 35°20N 119°50W **79 K7**
Teme → U.K. 52°11N 2°13W **13 E5**
Temecula U.S.A. 33°30N 117°9W **79 M9**
Temengor, Tasik Malaysia 5°24N 101°18E **39 K3**
Temerloh Malaysia 3°27N 102°25E **39 L4**
Teminabuan Indonesia 1°26S 132°1E **37 E8**
Temir Kazakhstan 49°1N 57°14E **19 E10**
Temirtau Kazakhstan 50°5N 72°56E **30 A3**
Témiscamie → Canada 50°59N 73°5W **73 B5**
Temiscaming Canada 46°44N 79°5W **72 C4**
Témiscamingue, L. Canada 47°10N 79°25W **72 C4**
Temosachic Mexico 28°57N 107°51W **86 B3**
Tempe U.S.A. 33°24N 111°54W **77 K8**
Tempiute U.S.A. 37°39N 115°38W **78 H11**
Temple U.S.A. 31°6N 97°21W **84 F6**
Temple B. Australia 12°15S 143°3E **62 A3**
Templemore Ireland 52°47N 7°51W **10 D4**
Templeton U.S.A. 35°33N 120°42W **78 K6**
Templeton → Australia 21°0S 138°40E **62 C2**
Tempoal de Sánchez Mexico 21°31N 98°23W **87 C5**
Temuco Chile 38°45S 72°40W **96 D2**
Temuka N.Z. 44°14S 171°17E **59 F3**
Ten Degree Channel India 10°0N 92°30E **45 K11**
Tenabo Mexico 20°3N 90°14W **87 C6**
Tenaha U.S.A. 31°57N 94°15W **84 F7**
Tenakee Springs U.S.A. 57°47N 135°13W **70 B1**
Tenali India 16°15N 80°35E **45 F5**
Tenancingo Mexico 18°58N 99°38W **87 D5**
Tenango del Valle Mexico 19°7N 99°33W **87 D5**
Tenasserim = Taninthayi Myanmar 12°6N 99°3E **39 F2**
Tenasserim □ Myanmar 14°0N 98°30E **38 F2**
Tenasserim → Myanmar 12°24N 98°37E **38 F2**
Tenby U.K. 51°40N 4°42W **13 F3**
Tenda, Colle di France 44°7N 7°36E **20 D7**
Tendaho Ethiopia 11°48N 40°54E **49 E3**
Tendō Japan 38°20N 140°30E **28 E10**
Tendukhera India 23°24N 79°33E **43 H8**
Ténéré, Erg du Niger 17°35N 10°55E **53 E8**
Tenerife Canary Is. 28°15N 16°35W **52 C2**
Teng Xian Guangxi Zhuangzu, China 23°21N 110°56E **35 F8**
Teng Xian Shandong, China 35°5N 117°10E **33 G9**
Tengah, Kepulauan Indonesia 7°5S 118°15E **36 F5**
Tengchong China 25°0N 98°28E **34 E2**
Tengchowfu = Penglai China 37°48N 120°42E **33 F11**
Tenggarong Indonesia 0°24S 116°58E **36 E5**
Tengger Shamo China 38°0N 104°10E **32 F3**
Tenggol, Pulau Malaysia 4°48N 103°41E **39 K4**
Tengiz Köli Kazakhstan 50°30N 69°0E **30 A2**
Tengzhou China 35°4N 117°9E **33 G9**
Teniente Enciso △ Paraguay 21°5S 61°8W **94 A3**
Tenino U.S.A. 46°51N 122°51W **78 D4**
Tenkasi India 8°55N 77°20E **45 K3**
Tennant Creek Australia 19°30S 134°15E **62 B1**
Tennessee □ U.S.A. 36°0N 86°30W **85 C10**
Tennessee → U.S.A. 37°4N 88°34W **85 C10**
Tenojoki = Tana → Norway 70°30N 28°14E **8 A23**
Tenom Malaysia 5°4N 115°57E **36 C5**
Tenosique Mexico 17°29N 91°26W **87 D6**
Tenryū-Gawa → Japan 35°39N 137°48E **29 G8**
Tenterden U.K. 51°4N 0°42E **13 F8**
Tenterfield Australia 29°0S 152°0E **63 D5**
Teófilo Otoni Brazil 17°50S 41°30W **93 G10**
Tepa Indonesia 7°52S 129°31E **37 F7**
Tepalcatepec → Mexico 18°35N 101°59W **86 D4**
Tepehuanes Mexico 25°21N 105°44W **86 B3**
Tepetongo Mexico 22°28N 103°9W **86 C4**

Tepic Mexico 21°30N 104°54W **86 C4**
Teplice Czechia 50°40N 13°48E **16 C7**
Tequila Mexico 20°54N 103°47W **86 C4**
Ter → Spain 42°2N 3°12E **21 A7**
Ter Apel Neths. 52°53N 7°5E **15 B7**
Téra Niger 14°0N 0°45E **52 F6**
Teraina Kiribati 4°43N 160°25W **65 G12**
Téramo Italy 42°39N 13°42E **22 C5**
Terang Australia 38°15S 142°55E **63 F3**
Terang, Teluk Indonesia 6°58N 106°10E **37 K19**
Terceira Azores 38°43N 27°13W **52 a**
Tercero → Argentina 32°58S 61°47W **94 C3**
Terdal India 16°33N 75°3E **44 F2**
Terebovlya Ukraine 49°18N 25°44E **17 D13**
Terek → Russia 44°0N 47°30E **19 F8**
Terengganu □ Malaysia 4°55N 103°0E **39 K4**
Terepaima △ Venezuela 9°58N 69°17W **89 E6**
Teresina Brazil 5°9S 42°45W **93 E10**
Terewah, L. Australia 29°52S 147°35E **63 D4**
Teridgerie Cr. → Australia 30°25S 148°50E **63 E4**
Termas de Río Hondo Argentina 27°29S 64°52W **94 B3**
Términi Imerese Italy 37°59N 13°42E **22 F5**
Términos, L. de Mexico 18°37N 91°33W **87 D6**
Termiz Uzbekistan 37°15N 67°15E **26 F7**
Térmoli Italy 42°0N 15°0E **22 C6**
Ternate Indonesia 0°45N 127°25E **37 D7**
Terneuzen Neths. 51°20N 3°50E **15 C3**
Terney Russia 45°3N 136°37E **28 B8**
Terni Italy 42°34N 12°37E **22 C5**
Ternopil Ukraine 49°30N 25°40E **17 D13**
Ternopil □ Ukraine 48°10N 25°10E **17 D13**
Ternopol = Ternopil Ukraine 49°30N 25°40E **17 D13**
Terowie Australia 33°8S 138°55E **63 E2**
Terra Bella U.S.A. 35°58N 119°3W **79 K7**
Terra Nova △ Canada 48°33N 53°55W **73 C9**
Terrace Canada 54°30N 128°35W **70 C3**
Terrace Bay Canada 48°47N 87°5W **72 C2**
Terracina Italy 41°17N 13°15E **22 D5**
Terralba Italy 39°43N 8°39E **22 E3**
Terrassa Spain 41°34N 2°1E **21 B7**
Terre Haute U.S.A. 39°28N 87°25W **80 F10**
Terrebonne B. U.S.A. 29°5N 90°35W **85 G9**
Terrenceville Canada 47°40N 54°44W **73 C9**
Terry U.S.A. 46°47N 105°19W **76 C11**
Terryville U.S.A. 41°41N 73°3W **83 E11**
Terschelling Neths. 53°25N 5°20E **15 A5**
Teruel Spain 40°22N 1°8W **21 B5**
Tervola Finland 66°6N 24°49E **8 C21**
Teryaweynya L. Australia 32°18S 143°22E **63 E3**
Teshio Japan 44°53N 141°44E **28 B10**
Teshio-Gawa → Japan 44°53N 141°45E **28 B10**
Tesiyn Gol → Mongolia 50°40N 93°20E **30 A7**
Teslin Canada 60°10N 132°43W **70 A2**
Teslin → Canada 61°34N 134°35W **70 A2**
Teslin L. Canada 60°15N 132°57W **70 A2**
Tessalit Mali 20°12N 1°0E **52 D6**
Tessaoua Niger 13°47N 7°56E **52 F7**
Test → U.K. 50°56N 1°29W **13 G6**
Testigos, Is. Los Venezuela 11°23N 63°7W **89 D7**
Tetachuck L. Canada 53°18N 125°55W **70 C3**
Tetas, Pta. Chile 23°31S 70°38W **94 A1**
Tete Mozam. 16°13S 33°33E **55 H6**
Teterev → Ukraine 51°1N 30°5E **17 C16**
Teteven Bulgaria 42°58N 24°17E **23 C11**
Tethul → Canada 60°35N 112°12W **70 A6**
Tetiyev Ukraine 49°22N 29°38E **17 D15**
Tetlit Zheh = Fort McPherson Canada 67°30N 134°55W **68 D5**
Teton → U.S.A. 47°56N 110°31W **76 C8**
Tétouan Morocco 35°35N 5°21W **52 A4**
Tetovo Macedonia 42°1N 20°59E **23 C9**
Tetufera, Mt. Tahiti 17°40S 149°26W **59 d**
Teuco → Argentina 25°35S 60°11W **94 B3**
Teulon Canada 50°23N 97°16W **71 C9**
Teun Indonesia 6°59S 129°8E **37 F7**
Teuri-Tō Japan 44°26N 141°19E **28 B10**
Teutoburger Wald Germany 52°5N 8°22E **16 B5**
Tevere → Italy 41°44N 12°14E **22 D5**
Teverya Israel 32°47N 35°32E **48 C4**
Teviot → U.K. 55°29N 2°38W **11 F6**
Tewantin Australia 26°27S 153°3E **63 D5**
Tewkesbury U.K. 51°59N 2°9W **13 F5**
Texada I. Canada 49°40N 124°25W **70 D4**
Texarkana Ark., U.S.A. 33°26N 94°2W **84 E7**
Texarkana Tex., U.S.A. 33°26N 94°3W **84 E7**
Texas Australia 28°49S 151°9E **63 D5**
Texas □ U.S.A. 31°40N 98°30W **84 F5**
Texas City U.S.A. 29°24N 94°54W **84 G7**
Texel Neths. 53°5N 4°50E **15 A4**
Texline U.S.A. 36°23N 103°2W **84 C3**
Texoma, L. U.S.A. 33°50N 96°34W **84 E6**
Teyateyaneng Lesotho 29°7S 27°34E **55 K5**
Tezin Afghan. 34°24N 69°30E **42 B3**
Teziutlán Mexico 19°49N 97°21W **87 D5**
Tezpur India 26°40N 92°45E **41 F18**
Tezzeron L. Canada 54°43N 124°30W **70 C4**
Tha-anne → Canada 60°31N 94°37W **71 A10**
Tha Deua Laos 17°57N 102°53E **38 D4**
Tha Deua Laos 19°26N 101°50E **38 C3**
Tha Li Thailand 17°48N 101°0E **38 D3**
Tha Pla Thailand 17°48N 100°44E **38 D3**
Tha Rua Thailand 14°34N 100°44E **38 E3**
Tha Sala Thailand 8°40N 99°56E **39 H2**
Tha Song Yang Thailand 17°34N 97°55E **38 D1**
Thaba Putsoa Lesotho 29°45S 28°0E **57 D4**
Thaba-Tseka Lesotho 29°32S 28°36E **57 C4**
Thabana Ntlenyana Lesotho 29°30S 29°16E **57 C4**
Thabazimbi S. Africa 24°40S 27°21E **57 B4**
Thādiq Si. Arabia 25°18N 45°52E **46 E5**
Thai Binh Vietnam 20°35N 106°1E **34 G6**
Thai Muang Thailand 8°24N 98°16E **39 H2**
Thai Nguyen Vietnam 21°35N 105°55E **34 G5**
Thailand ■ Asia 16°0N 102°0E **38 E4**
Thailand, G. of Asia 11°30N 101°0E **39 G3**
Thakhek Laos 17°25N 104°45E **38 D5**

Thal Pakistan 33°28N 70°33E **42 C4**
Thal Desert Pakistan 31°10N 71°30E **42 D4**
Thala La = Hkakabo Razi Myanmar 28°25N 97°23E **34 C1**
Thalabarivat Cambodia 13°33N 105°57E **38 F5**
Thalang = Amphoe Thalang Thailand 8°1N 98°20E **39 a**
Thalara Nepal 29°29N 80°59E **43 E9**
Thalassery India 11°45N 75°30E **45 J2**
Thale Sap Songkhla Thailand 7°12N 100°28E **39 J3**
Thallon Australia 28°39S 148°49E **63 D4**
Thalu, Ko Thailand 9°26N 99°54E **39 b**
Tham Lot Thailand 19°34N 98°16E **38 C2**
Thamarīt Oman 17°39N 54°2E **49 D5**
Thames N.Z. 37°7S 175°34E **59 B5**
Thames → Canada 42°20N 82°25W **82 D2**
Thames → U.K. 51°29N 0°34E **13 F8**
Thames → U.S.A. 41°18N 72°5W **83 E12**
Thames Estuary U.K. 51°29N 0°52E **13 F8**
Thamesford Canada 43°4N 81°0W **82 C4**
Thamesville Canada 42°33N 81°59W **82 D3**
Than India 22°34N 71°11E **42 H4**
Than Kyun Myanmar 9°49N 98°4E **39 H1**
Than Uyen Vietnam 22°0N 103°54E **34 G4**
Thana Gazi India 27°25N 76°19E **42 F7**
Thandla India 23°0N 74°34E **42 H6**
Thandwe Myanmar 18°20N 94°30E **41 K19**
Thane India 19°12N 72°59E **44 E1**
Thanesar India 30°1N 76°52E **42 D7**
Thanet, I. of U.K. 51°21N 1°20E **13 F9**
Thangool Australia 24°38S 150°42E **62 C5**
Thanh Hoa Vietnam 19°48N 105°46E **38 C5**
Thanh Hung Vietnam 9°55N 105°43E **39 H5**
Thanh Pho Ho Chi Minh Vietnam 10°58N 106°40E **39 G6**
Thanh Thuy Vietnam 22°55N 104°51E **38 A5**
Thanjavur India 10°48N 79°12E **45 J4**
Thanlwin = Salween → Myanmar 16°31N 97°37E **41 L20**
Thano Bula Khan Pakistan 25°22N 67°50E **42 G2**
Thanya Buri Thailand 14°1N 100°45E **38 E3**
Thaoge → Botswana 20°27S 22°36E **56 B3**
Thaolintoa L. Canada 61°30N 96°25W **71 A9**
Thap Lan △ Thailand 14°15N 102°16E **38 E4**
Thap Sakae Thailand 11°30N 99°37E **39 G2**
Thap Than Thailand 15°27N 99°54E **38 E2**
Thar Desert India 28°0N 72°0E **42 F5**
Tharad India 24°30N 71°44E **42 G4**
Thargomindah Australia 27°58S 143°46E **63 D3**
Tharthār, Buḩayrat ath Iraq 34°0N 43°15E **46 C4**
Tharthar, L. = Tharthār, Buḩayrat ath Iraq 34°0N 43°15E **46 C4**
Tharthār, W. ath → Iraq 34°32N 43°4E **46 C4**
Thasos Greece 40°40N 24°40E **23 D11**
That Khe Vietnam 22°16N 106°28E **34 F6**
Thatcher Ariz., U.S.A. 32°51N 109°46W **77 K9**
Thatcher Colo., U.S.A. 37°33N 104°7W **77 H11**
Thaton Myanmar 16°55N 97°22E **41 L20**
Thatta Pakistan 24°42N 67°55E **42 G2**
Thaungdut Myanmar 24°30N 94°40E **41 G19**
Thayawthadangy Kyun Myanmar 12°19N 98°0E **38 F1**
Thayer U.S.A. 36°31N 91°33W **80 G8**
Thayetmyo Myanmar 19°20N 95°10E **41 K19**
Thazi Myanmar 21°0N 96°5E **41 J20**
Thbeng Meanchey Cambodia 13°49N 104°58E **38 F5**
The Bahamas ■ N. Amer. 24°0N 75°0W **89 B5**
The Broads U.K. 52°45N 1°30E **12 E9**
The Everglades U.S.A. 25°50N 81°0W **85 J14**
The Gambia ■ W. Afr. 13°25N 16°0W **52 F2**
The Gulf = Persian Gulf Asia 27°0N 50°0E **47 E6**
The Hague = 's-Gravenhage Neths. 52°7N 4°17E **15 B4**
The Pas Canada 53°45N 101°15W **71 C8**
The Wash U.K. 52°58N 0°20E **12 E8**
The Weald U.K. 51°4N 0°20E **13 F8**
Thebes = Thiva Greece 38°19N 23°19E **23 E10**
Thebes Egypt 25°40N 32°35E **53 C12**
Thedford U.S.A. 41°59N 100°35W **80 E3**
Theebine Australia 25°57S 152°34E **63 D5**
Thekulthili L. Canada 61°3N 110°0W **71 A7**
Thelon → Canada 64°16N 96°4W **71 A8**
Theodore Australia 24°55S 150°3E **62 C5**
Theodore Canada 51°26N 102°59W **71 C8**
Theodore U.S.A. 30°33N 88°10W **85 F10**
Theodore Roosevelt △ U.S.A. 47°0N 103°25W **80 B2**
Theodore Roosevelt L. U.S.A. 33°40N 111°10W **77 K8**
Thepha Thailand 6°52N 100°58E **39 J3**
Theresa U.S.A. 44°13N 75°48W **83 B9**
Thermaïkos Kolpos Greece 40°15N 22°45E **23 D10**
Thermopolis U.S.A. 43°39N 108°13W **76 E9**
Thermopylæ Greece 38°48N 22°35E **23 E10**
Thessalon Canada 46°20N 83°30W **72 C3**
Thessalonica, Gulf of = Thermaïkos Kolpos Greece 40°15N 22°45E **23 D10**
Thessaloniki Greece 40°38N 22°58E **23 D10**
Thetford U.K. 52°25N 0°45E **13 E8**
Thetford Mines Canada 46°8N 71°18W **73 C5**
Theun → Laos 18°19N 104°0E **38 C5**
Theunissen S. Africa 28°26S 26°43E **56 C4**
Thévenard Canada 32°9S 133°38E **63 E1**
Thibodaux U.S.A. 29°48N 90°49W **85 G9**
Thicket Portage Canada 55°19N 97°42W **71 B9**
Thief River Falls U.S.A. 48°7N 96°10W **80 A5**
Thiel Mts. Antarctica 85°15S 91°0W **5 E16**
Thiers France 45°52N 3°33E **20 D5**
Thiès Senegal 14°50N 16°51W **52 F2**
Thika Kenya 1°1S 37°5E **54 E7**
Thimphu Bhutan 27°31N 89°45E **41 F16**

Thina → S. Africa 31°18S 29°13E **57 D4**
Þingvallavatn Iceland 64°11N 21°9W **8 D3**
Thionville France 49°20N 6°10E **20 B7**
Thira = Santorini Greece 36°23N 25°27E **23 F11**
Third Cataract Sudan 19°42N 30°20E **53 E12**
Thirsk U.K. 54°14N 1°19W **12 C6**
Thiruvananthapuram India 8°41N 77°0E **45 K3**
Thiruvarur India 10°46N 79°38E **45 J4**
Thisted Denmark 56°58N 8°40E **9 H13**
Thistle I. Australia 35°0S 136°8E **63 F2**
Thithia = Cicia Fiji 17°45S 179°18W **59 a**
Thitu I. S. China Sea 11°3N 114°17E **36 B4**
Thiva Greece 38°19N 23°19E **23 E10**
Þjórsá → Iceland 63°47N 20°48W **8 E3**
Thlewiaza → Canada 60°29N 94°40W **71 A10**
Thmar Puok Cambodia 13°57N 103°4E **38 F4**
Tho Chu, Dao Vietnam 9°20N 103°28E **39 H4**
Tho Vinh Vietnam 19°16N 105°42E **38 C5**
Thoa → Canada 60°31N 109°47W **71 A7**
Thoen Thailand 17°43N 99°12E **38 D2**
Thoeng Thailand 19°41N 100°12E **38 C3**
Thomas U.S.A. 35°45N 98°45W **84 D5**
Thomas, L. Australia 26°4S 137°58E **63 D2**
Thomas Hubbard, C. Canada 82°0N 94°25W **69 A13**
Thomaston U.S.A. 32°53N 84°20W **85 E12**
Thomasville Ala., U.S.A. 31°55N 87°44W **85 F11**
Thomasville Ga., U.S.A. 30°50N 83°59W **85 F13**
Thomasville N.C., U.S.A. 35°53N 80°5W **85 D14**
Thompson Canada 55°45N 97°52W **71 B9**
Thompson U.S.A. 41°52N 75°31W **83 E9**
Thompson → Canada 50°15N 121°24W **70 C4**
Thompson → U.S.A. 39°46N 93°37W **80 F7**
Thompson Falls U.S.A. 47°36N 115°21W **76 C6**
Thompson Pk. U.S.A. 41°0N 123°2W **76 F2**
Thompson Springs U.S.A. 38°58N 109°43W **76 G9**
Thompsontown U.S.A. 40°33N 77°14W **82 F7**
Thomson U.S.A. 33°28N 82°30W **85 E13**
Thomson → Australia 25°11S 142°53E **62 C3**
Thong Yang Thailand 9°28N 99°56E **39 b**
Thoothukudi = Tuticorin India 8°50N 78°12E **45 K4**
Thornaby on Tees U.K. 54°33N 1°18W **12 C6**
Thornbury Canada 44°34N 80°26W **82 B4**
Thorne U.K. 53°37N 0°57W **12 D7**
Thornton Canada 44°16N 79°43W **82 B5**
Thornton U.S.A. 39°52N 104°58W **76 G11**
Thorold Canada 43°7N 79°12W **82 C5**
Þórshöfn Iceland 66°12N 15°20W **8 C6**
Thouin, C. Australia 20°20S 118°10E **60 D2**
Thousand Islands U.S.A. 44°20N 76°0W **83 B9**
Thousand Oaks U.S.A. 34°10N 118°50W **79 L8**
Thrace Europe 41°0N 27°0E **23 D12**
Three Forks U.S.A. 45°54N 111°33W **76 D8**
Three Gorges Dam China 30°45N 111°15E **35 B8**
Three Gorges Res. = Sanxia Shuiku China 30°3N 107°58E **34 B6**
Three Hills Canada 51°43N 113°15W **70 C6**
Three Hummock I. Australia 40°25S 144°55E **63 G3**
Three Pagodas Pass Asia 15°20N 98°30E **38 E2**
Three Points, C. Ghana 4°42N 2°6W **52 H5**
Three Rivers Calif., U.S.A. 36°26N 118°54W **78 J8**
Three Rivers Tex., U.S.A. 28°28N 98°11W **84 G5**
Three Springs Australia 29°32S 115°45E **61 E2**
Thrissur India 10°30N 76°18E **45 J3**
Throssell, L. Australia 27°33S 124°10E **61 E3**
Throssell Ra. Australia 22°3S 121°43E **60 D3**
Thrushton △ Australia 27°47S 147°40E **63 D4**
Thu Dau Mot Vietnam 10°58N 106°39E **39 G6**
Thua → Kenya 1°31S 39°30E **54 E7**
Thuamal Rampur India 19°23N 82°56E **44 K6**
Thuan Hoa Vietnam 8°58N 105°30E **39 H5**
Thubun Lakes Canada 61°30N 112°0W **71 A6**
Thuin Belgium 50°20N 4°17E **15 D4**
Thule = Qaanaaq Greenland 77°30N 69°10W **69 B18**
Thule Air Base = Uummannaq Greenland 77°33N 68°52W **69 B18**
Thun Switz. 46°45N 7°38E **20 C7**
Thunder B. U.S.A. 45°0N 83°20W **82 B1**
Thunder Bay Canada 48°20N 89°15W **72 C2**
Thung Salaeng Luang △ Thailand 16°43N 100°50E **38 D3**
Thung Song Thailand 8°10N 99°40E **39 H2**
Thungyai △ Thailand 15°20N 98°58E **38 E2**
Thunkar Bhutan 27°55N 91°0E **41 F17**
Thuong Tra Vietnam 16°2N 107°42E **38 D6**
Thüringer Wald Germany 50°35N 11°0E **16 C6**
Thuringowa △ Australia 19°18S 146°43E **62 B4**
Thurles Ireland 52°41N 7°49W **10 D4**
Thurrock □ U.K. 51°31N 0°23E **13 F8**
Thurso Canada 45°36N 75°15W **72 C4**
Thurso U.K. 58°36N 3°32W **11 C5**
Thurso → U.K. 58°36N 3°32W **11 C5**
Thurston I. Antarctica 72°0S 100°0W **5 D16**
Thutade L. Canada 57°0N 126°55W **70 B3**
Ti-Tree Australia 22°5S 133°22E **62 C1**
Tian Shan Asia 40°30N 76°0E **30 C4**
Tianchang China 32°40N 119°0E **35 A12**
Tiandeng China 23°6N 107°7E **34 F6**
Tiandong China 23°36N 107°8E **34 F6**
Tian'e China 25°1N 107°9E **34 E6**
Tianhe China 24°48N 108°40E **34 E7**
Tianjin China 39°7N 117°12E **33 E9**
Tianjin Shi □ China 39°15N 117°12E **33 E9**
Tianjun China 38°0N 98°30E **30 D8**
Tianlin China 24°21N 106°12E **34 E6**
Tianmen China 30°39N 113°9E **35 B9**
Tianquan China 30°7N 102°43E **34 B4**
Tianshifu China 41°16N 124°22E **33 D13**
Tianshui China 34°32N 105°40E **32 G3**
Tiantai China 29°10N 121°2E **35 C13**
Tianya China 18°18N 109°20E **38 C7**

Tianyang *China* 23°42N 106°53E **34 F6**
Tianyar *Indonesia* 8°12S 115°30E **37 J18**
Tianzhen *China* 40°24N 114°5E **32 D8**
Tianzhu *China* 26°54N 109°11E **34 D7**
Tianzhuangtai *China* 40°43N 122°5E **33 D12**
Tiarei *Tahiti* 17°32S 149°20W **59 d**
Tiaret *Algeria* 35°20N 1°21E **52 A6**
Tibagi *Brazil* 24°30S 50°24W **95 A5**
Tibagi → *Brazil* 22°47S 51°1W **95 A5**
Tibatí, Sarīr *Libya* 22°50N 18°30E **53 D9**
Tibati *Cameroon* 6°22N 12°30E **54 C2**
Tiber = Tevere → *Italy* 41°44N 12°14E **22 D5**
Tiber Res. *U.S.A.* 48°19N 111°6W **76 B8**
Tiberias = Teverya *Israel* 32°47N 35°32E **48 C4**
Tiberias, L. = Yam Kinneret
  Israel 32°45N 35°35E **48 C4**
Tibesti *Chad* 21°0N 17°30E **53 D9**
Tibet = Xizang Zizhiqu □
  China 32°0N 88°0E **30 E6**
Tibet, Plateau of *Asia* 32°0N 86°0E **24 E10**
Tibnī *Syria* 35°36N 39°50E **46 C3**
Tibooburra *Australia* 29°26S 142°1E **63 D3**
Tibrikot *Nepal* 29°3N 82°48E **43 E10**
Ticino → *Italy* 45°9N 9°14E **20 D8**
Ticonderoga *U.S.A.* 43°51N 73°26W **83 C11**
Ticul *Mexico* 20°24N 89°32W **87 C7**
Tidaholm *Sweden* 58°12N 13°58E **11 F7**
Tiddim *Myanmar* 23°28N 93°45E **41 H18**
Tiden *India* 7°15N 93°33E **45 L11**
Tidioute *U.S.A.* 41°41N 79°24W **82 E5**
Tidjikja *Mauritania* 18°29N 11°35W **52 E3**
Tidore *Indonesia* 0°40N 127°25E **37 D7**
Tiefa *China* 42°28N 123°26E **33 C12**
Tiegang Shuiku *China* 22°37N 113°53E **31 a**
Tiel *Neths.* 51°53N 5°26E **15 C5**
Tieli *China* 46°57N 128°3E **31 B14**
Tieling *China* 42°20N 123°55E **33 C12**
Tielt *Belgium* 51°0N 3°20E **15 C3**
Tien Shan = Tian Shan
  Asia 40°30N 76°0E **30 C4**
Tien-tsin = Tianjin *China* 39°7N 117°12E **33 E9**
Tien Yen *Vietnam* 21°20N 107°24E **38 B6**
T'ienching = Tianjin
  China 39°7N 117°12E **33 E9**
Tienen *Belgium* 50°48N 4°57E **15 D4**
Tientsin = Tianjin *China* 39°7N 117°12E **33 E9**
Tieri *Australia* 23°2S 148°21E **62 C4**
Tierra Amarilla *Chile* 27°28S 70°18W **94 B1**
Tierra Amarilla *U.S.A.* 36°42N 106°33W **77 H10**
Tierra Colorada *Mexico* 17°11N 99°32W **87 D5**
Tierra de Campos *Spain* 42°10N 4°50W **21 A3**
Tierra del Fuego, I. Grande de
  Argentina 54°0S 69°0W **96 G3**
Tiétar → *Spain* 39°50N 6°1W **21 C3**
Tieté → *Brazil* 20°40S 51°35W **95 A5**
Tiffin *U.S.A.* 41°7N 83°11W **81 E12**
Tifton *U.S.A.* 31°27N 83°31W **85 F13**
Tifu *Indonesia* 3°39S 126°24E **37 E7**
Tiger Leaping Gorge = Hutiao Xia
  China 27°13N 100°9E **34 D3**
Tighina = Bendery
  Moldova 46°50N 29°30E **17 E15**
Tigil *Russia* 57°49N 158°40E **27 D16**
Tigiria *India* 20°29N 85°31E **44 D7**
Tignish *Canada* 46°58N 64°2W **73 C7**
Tigre → *Peru* 4°30S 74°10W **92 D4**
Tigre → *Venezuela* 9°20N 62°30W **92 B6**
Tigris = Dijlah, Nahr →
  Asia 31°0N 47°25E **46 D5**
Tigyaing *Myanmar* 23°45N 96°10E **41 H20**
Tihāmah *Asia* 15°3N 41°55E **49 D3**
Tiilikka △ *Finland* 63°40N 28°15E **8 E23**
Tijara *India* 27°56N 76°31E **42 F7**
Tijuana *Mexico* 32°32N 117°1W **79 N9**
Tikal *Guatemala* 17°13N 89°24W **88 C2**
Tikal △ *Guatemala* 17°23N 89°34W **88 C2**
Tikamgarh *India* 24°44N 78°50E **43 G8**
Tikchik Lakes *U.S.A.* 60°0N 159°0W **74 D8**
Tikhoretsk *Russia* 45°56N 40°5E **19 E7**
Tikhvin *Russia* 59°35N 33°30E **18 C5**
Tikirarjuaq = Whale Cove
  Canada 62°10N 92°34W **71 A10**
Tikrīt *Iraq* 34°35N 43°37E **46 C4**
Tiksi *Russia* 71°40N 128°45E **27 B13**
Tila' al 'Alī *Jordan* 32°0N 35°52E **48 D4**
Tilamuta *Indonesia* 0°32N 122°23E **37 D6**
Tilburg *Neths.* 51°31N 5°6E **15 C5**
Tilbury *Canada* 42°17N 82°23W **82 D2**
Tilbury *U.K.* 51°27N 0°22E **13 F8**
Tilcara *Argentina* 23°36S 65°23W **94 A2**
Tilden *U.S.A.* 42°3N 97°50W **80 D5**
Tilhar *India* 28°0N 79°45E **43 F8**
Tilichiki *Russia* 60°27N 166°5E **27 C17**
Till → *U.K.* 55°41N 2°13W **12 B5**
Tillamook *U.S.A.* 45°27N 123°51W **76 D2**
Tillanchong I. *India* 8°30N 93°37E **45 K11**
Tillsonburg *Canada* 42°53N 80°44W **82 D4**
Tilos *Greece* 36°27N 27°27E **23 F12**
Tilpa *Australia* 30°57S 144°24E **63 E3**
Tilt → *U.K.* 56°46N 3°51W **11 E5**
Tilton *U.S.A.* 43°27N 71°36W **83 C13**
Tiltonsville *U.S.A.* 40°10N 80°41W **82 F4**
Timanskiy Kryazh *Russia* 65°58N 50°5E **18 A9**
Timaru *N.Z.* 44°23S 171°14E **59 F3**
Timber Creek *Australia* 15°40S 130°29E **60 C5**
Timber Lake *U.S.A.* 45°26N 101°5W **80 C4**
Timber Mt. *U.S.A.* 37°6N 116°28W **78 H10**
Timbué, Ponta *Mozam.* 18°47S 36°22E **57 A6**
Timbuktu = Tombouctou
  Mali 16°50N 3°0W **52 E5**
Timika *Indonesia* 4°43S 136°32E **37 E9**
Timimoun *Algeria* 29°14N 0°16E **52 C6**
Timiris, Râs *Mauritania* 19°21N 16°30W **52 E2**
Timișkaming, L. =
  Témiscamingue, L.
  Canada 47°10N 79°25W **72 C4**
Timișoara *Romania* 45°43N 21°15E **17 F11**
Timmins *Canada* 48°28N 81°25W **72 C3**
Timok → *Serbia* 44°10N 22°40E **23 B10**
Timoleague *Ireland* 51°39N 8°46W **10 E3**

Timor *Asia* 9°0S 125°0E **37 F7**
Timor-Leste ■ *Asia* 8°50S 126°0E **37 F7**
Timor Sea *Ind. Oc.* 12°0S 127°0E **60 B4**
Tin Can Bay *Australia* 25°56S 153°0E **63 D5**
Tin Mt. *U.S.A.* 36°50N 117°10W **78 J9**
Tin Shui Wai *China* 22°28N 114°0E **31 a**
Tina = Thina → *S. Africa* 31°18S 29°13E **57 E4**
Tīna, Khalīg el *Egypt* 31°10N 32°40E **48 D1**
Tinaca Pt. *Phil.* 5°30N 125°25E **37 C7**
Tindal *Australia* 14°31S 132°22E **60 B5**
Tindivanam *India* 12°15N 79°41E **45 H4**
Tindouf *Algeria* 27°42N 8°10W **52 C4**
Tinfunque △ *Paraguay* 23°55S 60°17W **94 A3**
Ting Jiang → *China* 24°45N 116°35E **35 E11**
Tinggi, Pulau *Malaysia* 2°18N 104°7E **39 L5**
Tingo María *Peru* 9°10S 75°54W **92 E3**
Tingrela *Côte d'Ivoire* 10°27N 6°25W **52 F4**
Tingri *China* 28°34N 86°38E **30 F6**
Tinh Bien *Vietnam* 10°36N 104°57E **39 G5**
Tinian *N. Marianas* 15°0N 145°38E **64 F6**
Tinnevelly = Tirunelveli
  India 8°45N 77°45E **45 K3**
Tinogasta *Argentina* 28°5S 67°32W **94 B2**
Tinos *Greece* 37°33N 25°8E **23 F11**
Tinpahar *India* 24°59N 87°44E **43 G12**
Tintina *Argentina* 27°2S 62°45W **94 B3**
Tintinara *Australia* 35°48S 140°2E **63 F3**
Tiobraid Árann = Tipperary
  Ireland 52°28N 8°10W **10 D3**
Tioga *N. Dak., U.S.A.* 48°24N 102°56W **80 A2**
Tioga *Pa., U.S.A.* 41°55N 77°8W **82 E7**
Tioman, Pulau *Malaysia* 2°50N 104°10E **39 L5**
Tionesta *U.S.A.* 41°30N 79°28W **82 E5**
Tipperary *Ireland* 52°28N 8°10W **10 D3**
Tipperary □ *Ireland* 52°37N 7°55W **10 D4**
Tipton *Calif., U.S.A.* 36°4N 119°19W **78 J7**
Tipton *Iowa, U.S.A.* 41°46N 91°8W **80 E8**
Tipton *Mt., U.S.A.* 35°32N 114°12W **79 K12**
Tiptonville *U.S.A.* 36°23N 89°29W **85 C10**
Tiptur *India* 13°15N 76°26E **45 H3**
Tīrān *Iran* 32°45N 51°8E **47 C6**
Tiranë *Albania* 41°18N 19°49E **23 D8**
Tirari Desert *Australia* 28°22S 138°7E **63 D2**
Tiraspol *Moldova* 46°55N 29°35E **17 E15**
Tire *Turkey* 38°5N 27°45E **23 E12**
Tirebolu *Turkey* 40°58N 38°45E **19 F6**
Tiree *U.K.* 56°31N 6°55W **11 E2**
Tiree, Passage of *U.K.* 56°30N 6°30W **11 E2**
Tirgoviște = Târgoviște
  Romania 44°55N 25°27E **17 F13**
Tîrgu Jiu = Târgu Jiu
  Romania 45°5N 23°19E **17 F12**
Tîrgu Mureș = Târgu Mureș
  Romania 46°31N 24°38E **17 E13**
Tirich Mir *Pakistan* 36°15N 71°55E **40 A7**
Tiritiri o te Moana = Southern
  Alps *N.Z.* 43°41S 170°11E **59 E3**
Tirna → *India* 18°4N 76°57E **44 E3**
Tírnavos *Greece* 39°45N 22°18E **23 E10**
Tirodi *India* 21°40N 79°44E **44 D4**
Tirol □ *Austria* 47°3N 10°43E **16 E6**
Tirrukkovil *Sri Lanka* 7°7N 81°51E **45 L5**
Tirso → *Italy* 39°53N 8°32E **22 E3**
Tirtagangga *Indonesia* 8°24S 115°35E **37 J18**
Tiruchchendur *India* 8°30N 78°11E **45 K4**
Tiruchchirappalli *India* 10°45N 78°45E **45 J4**
Tirukkoyilur *India* 11°57N 79°12E **45 J4**
Tirumangalam *India* 9°49N 77°58E **45 K3**
Tiruvalla *India* 9°23N 76°34E **45 K3**
Tiruvallar *India* 13°9N 79°57E **45 H4**
Tiruvannamalai *India* 12°15N 79°5E **45 H4**
Tiruvettipuram *India* 12°39N 79°33E **45 H4**
Tiruvottiyur *India* 13°10N 80°22E **45 H5**
Tisa → *India* 32°50N 76°9E **42 C7**
Tisa → *Serbia* 45°15N 20°17E **23 B9**
Tisdale *Canada* 52°50N 104°0W **71 C8**
Tishomingo *U.S.A.* 34°14N 96°41W **84 D6**
Tisza = Tisa → *Serbia* 45°15N 20°17E **23 B9**
Tit-Ary *Russia* 71°55N 127°2E **27 B13**
Tithwal *Pakistan* 34°21N 73°50E **43 B5**
Titicaca, L. *S. Amer.* 15°30S 69°30W **92 G5**
Titiwa *Nigeria* 12°14N 12°53E **53 F8**
Titlagarh *India* 20°15N 83°11E **44 D6**
Titule
  Dem. Rep. of the Congo 3°15N 25°31E **54 D5**
Titusville *Fla., U.S.A.* 28°37N 80°49W **85 G14**
Titusville *Pa., U.S.A.* 41°38N 79°41W **82 E5**
Tivaouane *Senegal* 14°56N 16°45W **52 F2**
Tiverton *Canada* 44°16N 81°32W **82 B3**
Tiverton *U.K.* 50°54N 3°29W **13 G4**
Tívoli *Italy* 41°58N 12°45E **22 D5**
Tiwi ⊙ *Australia* 11°33S 130°42E **60 B5**
Tizi-Ouzou *Algeria* 36°42N 4°3E **52 A6**
Tizimín *Mexico* 21°9N 88°9W **87 C7**
Tiznit *Morocco* 29°48N 9°45W **52 C4**
Tjeggelvas *Sweden* 66°37N 17°45E **8 C17**
Tjeggelvas = Tjeggelvas
  Sweden 66°37N 17°45E **8 C17**
Tjirebon = Cirebon
  Indonesia 6°45S 108°32E **37 G13**
Tjirrkarli ⊙ *Australia* 26°0S 125°28E **61 E4**
Tjiluring *Indonesia* 8°25S 114°13E **37 J17**
Tjörn *Sweden* 58°0N 11°35E **9 H14**
Tjukayirla Roadhouse
  Australia 27°9S 124°34E **61 E3**
Tjurabalan ⊙ *Australia* 19°50S 128°0E **60 C4**
Tlacotalpan *Mexico* 18°37N 95°40W **87 D5**

Tlahualilo de Zaragoza
  Mexico 26°7N 103°27W **86 B4**
Tlaquepaque *Mexico* 20°39N 103°19W **86 C4**
Tlaxcala *Mexico* 19°19N 98°14W **87 D5**
Tlaxcala □ *Mexico* 19°25N 98°10W **87 D5**
Tlaxiaco *Mexico* 17°25N 97°35W **87 D5**
Tlemcen *Algeria* 34°52N 1°21W **52 B5**
Tlokweng *Botswana* 24°40S 25°58E **56 B4**
To Bong *Vietnam* 12°45N 109°16E **38 F7**
Toad → *Canada* 59°25N 124°57W **70 B3**
Toad River *Canada* 58°51N 125°14W **70 B3**
Toamasina *Madag.* 18°10S 49°25E **55 H9**
Toay *Argentina* 36°43S 64°38W **94 D3**
Toba *China* 31°19N 97°42E **34 B1**
Toba *Japan* 34°30N 136°51E **29 G8**
Toba, Danau *Indonesia* 2°30N 98°30E **36 D1**
Toba Kakar *Pakistan* 31°30N 69°0E **42 D3**
Toba Tek Singh *Pakistan* 30°55N 72°25E **42 D5**
Tobago *Trin. & Tob.* 11°10N 60°30W **93 J16**
Tobelo *Indonesia* 1°45N 127°56E **37 D7**
Tobercurry *Ireland* 54°3N 8°44W **10 B3**
Tobermory *Canada* 45°12N 81°40W **82 A3**
Tobermory *U.K.* 56°38N 6°5W **11 E2**
Tobi *Palau* 2°40N 131°10E **37 D8**
Tobi-Shima *Japan* 41°12N 139°34E **28 E9**
Tobin, L. *Australia* 21°45S 125°49E **60 D4**
Tobin L. *Canada* 53°35N 103°30W **71 C8**
Toboali *Indonesia* 3°0S 106°25E **36 E3**
Toboli *Indonesia* 0°38S 120°5E **37 E6**
Tobolsk *Russia* 58°15N 68°10E **26 D7**
Tobol → *Russia* 58°10N 68°12E **26 D7**
Tobruk = Tubruq *Libya* 32°7N 23°55E **53 B10**
Tobyhanna *U.S.A.* 41°11N 75°25W **83 E9**
Tobyl = Tobol → *Russia* 58°10N 68°12E **26 D7**
Tocantinópolis *Brazil* 6°20S 47°25W **93 E9**
Tocantins □ *Brazil* 10°0S 48°0W **93 F9**
Tocantins → *Brazil* 1°45S 49°10W **93 D9**
Toccoa *U.S.A.* 34°35N 83°19W **85 D13**
Tochi → *Pakistan* 32°49N 70°41E **42 C4**
Tochigi *Japan* 36°25N 139°45E **29 F9**
Tochigi □ *Japan* 36°45N 139°45E **29 F9**
Toco *Trin. & Tob.* 10°49N 60°57W **93 K16**
Toconao *Chile* 23°11S 68°1W **94 A2**
Tocopilla *Chile* 22°5S 70°10W **94 A1**
Tocumwal *Australia* 35°51S 145°31E **63 F4**
Tocuyo → *Venezuela* 11°3N 68°23W **92 A5**
Todd → *Australia* 24°52S 135°48E **62 C2**
Todeli *Indonesia* 1°40S 124°29E **37 E6**
Todgarh *India* 25°42N 73°58E **42 G5**
Todos os Santos, B. de
  Brazil 12°48S 38°38W **93 F11**
Todos Santos *Mexico* 23°26N 110°13W **86 C2**
Toe Hd. *U.K.* 57°50N 7°8W **11 D1**
Tofield *Canada* 53°25N 112°40W **70 C6**
Töfsingdalen △ *Sweden* 62°10N 12°28E **8 E15**
Tofua *Tonga* 19°45S 175°5W **59 c**
Tōgane *Japan* 35°33N 140°22E **29 G10**
Togian, Kepulauan
  Indonesia 0°20S 121°50E **37 E6**
Togliatti *Russia* 53°32N 49°24E **18 D8**
Togo ■ *W. Afr.* 8°30N 1°35E **52 G6**
Togtoh *China* 40°15N 111°10E **32 D6**
Tohiea, Mt. *Moorea* 17°33S 149°49W **59 d**
Tōhoku □ *Japan* 39°50N 141°45E **28 E10**
Tōhōm *Mongolia* 44°27N 108°2E **32 B5**
Toibalewe *India* 10°32N 92°45E **45 J11**
Toinya *South Sudan* 6°17N 29°46E **53 G11**
Toiyabe Range *U.S.A.* 39°30N 117°0W **76 G5**
Tojikiston = Tajikistan ■
  Asia 38°30N 70°0E **26 F8**
Tōjō *Japan* 34°53N 133°16E **29 G6**
Tok *U.S.A.* 63°20N 142°59W **68 E3**
Tokachi-Dake *Japan* 43°17N 142°5E **28 C11**
Tokachi-Gawa →
  Japan 42°44N 143°42E **28 C11**
Tokala *Indonesia* 1°30S 121°40E **37 E6**
Tōkamachi *Japan* 37°8N 138°43E **29 F9**
Tokanui *N.Z.* 46°34S 168°56E **59 G2**
Tokara-Rettō *Japan* 29°37N 129°2E **29 K4**
Tokarahi *N.Z.* 44°56S 170°39E **59 L3**
Tokashiki-Shima *Japan* 26°11N 127°21E **29 L3**
Tokat *Turkey* 40°22N 36°35E **19 F6**
Tŏkch'ŏn *N. Korea* 39°45N 126°18E **33 E14**
Tokdo = Liancourt Rocks
  Asia 37°15N 131°52E **29 F5**
Tokeland *U.S.A.* 46°42N 123°59W **78 D3**
Tokelau Is. ☑ *Pac. Oc.* 9°0S 171°45W **64 H10**
Tokmak *Kyrgyzstan* 42°49N 75°15E **26 E8**
Toko Ra. *Australia* 23°5S 138°20E **62 C2**
Tokoro-Gawa → *Japan* 44°7N 144°5E **28 B12**
Toku *Tonga* 18°10S 174°11W **59 c**
Tokuno-Shima *Japan* 27°56N 128°55E **29 L4**
Tokushima *Japan* 34°4N 134°34E **29 G7**
Tokushima □ *Japan* 33°55N 134°0E **29 H7**
Tokuyama = Shunan
  Japan 34°3N 131°50E **29 G5**
Tolaga Bay *N.Z.* 38°21S 178°20E **59 C7**
Tolbukhin = Dobrich
  Bulgaria 43°37N 27°49E **23 C12**
Toledo *Brazil* 24°44S 53°45W **95 A5**
Toledo *Spain* 39°50N 4°2E **21 C3**
Toledo *Ohio, U.S.A.* 41°39N 83°33W **81 E12**
Toledo *Oreg., U.S.A.* 44°37N 123°55W **76 D2**
Toledo *Wash., U.S.A.* 46°26N 122°51W **78 D4**
Toledo, Montes de *Spain* 39°33N 4°20W **21 C3**
Toledo Bend Res. *U.S.A.* 31°11N 93°34W **84 F8**
Tolga *Australia* 17°15S 145°29E **62 B4**
Toliara *Madag.* 23°21S 43°40E **55 J8**
Tolima *Colombia* 4°40N 75°19W **92 C3**
Tolitoli *Indonesia* 1°5N 120°50E **37 D6**
Tollhouse *U.S.A.* 37°1N 119°24W **78 H7**
Tolmachevo *Russia* 58°56N 29°51E **9 G23**
Tolo, Teluk *Indonesia* 2°20S 122°10E **37 E6**
Toluca *Mexico* 19°17N 99°40W **87 D5**
Tolyatti = Togliatti
  Russia 53°32N 49°24E **18 D8**
Tom Burke *S. Africa* 23°5S 28°0E **57 B4**
Tom Price *Australia* 22°40S 117°48E **60 D2**
Tomah *U.S.A.* 43°59N 90°30W **80 D8**
Tomahawk *U.S.A.* 45°28N 89°44W **80 C9**

Tomakomai *Japan* 42°38N 141°36E **28 C10**
Tomales *U.S.A.* 38°15N 122°53W **78 G4**
Tomales B. *U.S.A.* 38°15N 123°58W **78 G3**
Tomanivi *Fiji* 17°37S 178°1E **59 a**
Tomar *Portugal* 39°36N 8°25W **21 C1**
Tomaszów Mazowiecki
  Poland 51°30N 20°2E **17 C10**
Tomatlán *Mexico* 19°56N 105°15W **86 D3**
Tombador, Serra do *Brazil* 12°0S 58°0W **92 F7**
Tombigbee → *U.S.A.* 31°8N 87°57W **85 F11**
Tombouctou *Mali* 16°50N 3°0W **52 E5**
Tombstone *U.S.A.* 31°43N 110°4W **77 L8**
Tombua *Angola* 15°55S 11°55E **56 A1**
Tomé *Chile* 36°36S 72°57W **94 D1**
Tome *Japan* 38°40N 141°20E **28 E10**
Tomelloso *Spain* 39°10N 3°2W **21 C4**
Tomini *Indonesia* 0°30N 120°30E **37 D6**
Tomini, Teluk *Indonesia* 0°10S 121°0E **37 E6**
Tomintoul *U.K.* 57°15N 3°23W **11 D5**
Tomkinson Ranges
  Australia 26°11S 129°5E **61 E4**
Tommot *Russia* 59°4N 126°20E **27 D13**
Tomnop Ta Suos
  Cambodia 11°20N 104°15E **39 G5**
Tomo → *Colombia* 5°20N 67°48W **92 B5**
Toms Place *U.S.A.* 37°34N 118°41W **78 H8**
Toms River *U.S.A.* 39°58N 74°12W **83 G10**
Tomsk *Russia* 56°30N 85°5E **26 D9**
Tomür Feng = Pobedy, Pik
  Asia 42°0N 79°58E **30 C4**
Tonalá *Chiapas, Mexico* 16°4N 93°45W **87 D6**
Tonalá *Jalisco, Mexico* 20°37N 103°14W **86 C4**
Tonantins *Brazil* 2°45S 67°45W **92 D5**
Tonasket *U.S.A.* 48°42N 119°26W **76 B4**
Tonawanda *U.S.A.* 43°1N 78°53W **82 D6**
Tonb *U.A.E.* 26°15N 55°15E **47 E7**
Tonbridge *U.K.* 51°11N 0°17E **13 F8**
Tondano *Indonesia* 1°35N 124°54E **37 D6**
Tondi *India* 9°45N 79°4E **45 K4**
Tone → *Australia* 34°25S 116°25E **61 F2**
Tone-Gawa → *Japan* 35°44N 140°51E **29 F9**
Tonekābon *Iran* 36°45N 51°12E **47 B6**
Tong Xian *China* 39°55N 116°35E **32 E9**
Tong-yeong *S. Korea* 34°50N 128°20E **33 G15**
Tonga ■ *Pac. Oc.* 19°50S 174°30W **59 c**
Tonga Trench *Pac. Oc.* 18°0S 173°0W **64 J10**
Tongareva = Penrhyn
  Cook Is. 9°0S 158°0W **65 H12**
Tongariro △ *N.Z.* 39°8S 175°33E **59 C5**
Tongatapu *Tonga* 21°10S 175°10W **59 c**
Tongatapu Group *Tonga* 21°0S 175°0W **59 c**
Tongbai *China* 32°20N 113°23E **35 A9**
Tongcheng *Anhui, China* 31°4N 116°56E **35 B11**
Tongcheng *Hubei, China* 29°15N 113°50E **35 C9**
Tongchuan *China* 35°6N 109°3E **32 G5**
Tongdao *China* 26°10N 109°42E **34 D7**
Tongeren *Belgium* 50°47N 5°28E **15 D5**
Tonggu *China* 28°31N 114°20E **35 C10**
Tonggu Jiao *China* 22°22N 113°37E **31 a**
Tongguan *China* 34°40N 110°25E **32 G6**
Tonghai *China* 24°0N 102°53E **34 E4**
Tonghua *China* 41°42N 125°58E **33 D13**
Tongjiang *Heilongjiang,*
  China 47°40N 132°27E **31 B15**
Tongjiang *Sichuan, China* 31°58N 107°11E **34 B6**
Tongjosŏn-man
  N. Korea 39°30N 128°0E **33 E15**
Tongking, G. of = Tonkin, G. of
  Asia 20°0N 108°0E **38 C7**
Tongliang *China* 29°50N 106°3E **34 C6**
Tongliao *China* 43°38N 122°18E **33 C12**
Tongling *China* 30°55N 117°48E **35 B11**
Tonglu *China* 29°45N 119°37E **35 C12**
Tongnan = Anyue *China* 30°9N 105°50E **34 B5**
Tongoy *Chile* 30°16S 71°31W **94 C1**
Tongren *Guizhou, China* 27°43N 109°11E **34 D7**
Tongren *Qinghai, China* 35°25N 102°5E **30 D9**
Tongres = Tongeren
  Belgium 50°47N 5°28E **15 D5**
Tongsa Dzong *Bhutan* 27°31N 90°31E **41 F17**
Tongshi *China* 18°30N 109°20E **38 C7**
Tongue *U.K.* 58°29N 4°25W **11 C4**
Tongue → *U.S.A.* 46°25N 105°52W **76 C11**
Tongwei *China* 35°0N 105°5E **32 G3**
Tongxiang *China* 30°39N 120°34E **35 B13**
Tongxin *China* 36°59N 105°58E **32 F3**
Tongyang *N. Korea* 39°9N 126°53E **33 E14**
Tongyu *China* 44°45N 123°4E **33 B12**
Tongzhou *China* 32°12N 121°2E **35 A13**
Tongzi *China* 28°9N 106°49E **34 C6**
Tonj *South Sudan* 7°20N 28°44E **53 G11**
Tonk *India* 26°6N 75°54E **42 F6**
Tonkawa *U.S.A.* 36°41N 97°18W **84 C6**
Tonkin = Bac Phan
  Vietnam 22°0N 105°0E **34 G5**
Tonkin, G. of *Asia* 20°0N 108°0E **38 C7**
Tonlé Sap *Cambodia* 13°0N 104°0E **38 F5**
Tono *Japan* 39°19N 141°32E **28 E10**
Tonopah *U.S.A.* 38°4N 117°14W **77 G5**
Tonosi *Panama* 7°20N 80°20W **88 E3**
Tons → *Haryana, India* 30°30N 77°39E **42 D7**
Tons → *Ut. P., India* 24°15N 83°42E **43 G10**
Tønsberg *Norway* 59°19N 10°25E **9 G14**
Tonto △ *U.S.A.* 33°54N 111°27W **77 K8**
Tonumea *Tonga* 20°30S 174°30W **59 c**
Toobanna *Australia* 18°42S 146°9E **62 B4**
Toodyay *Australia* 31°34S 116°28E **61 F2**
Tooele *U.S.A.* 40°32N 112°18W **76 F7**
Toompine *Australia* 27°15S 144°19E **63 D3**
Toora *Australia* 38°39S 146°23E **63 F4**
Toora-Khem *Russia* 52°28N 96°17E **27 D10**
Toowoomba *Australia* 27°32S 151°56E **63 D5**
Top Springs *Australia* 16°37S 131°51E **60 C5**
Topaz *U.S.A.* 38°41N 119°30W **78 G7**
Topeka *U.S.A.* 39°3N 95°40W **80 F7**
Topley *Canada* 54°49N 126°18W **70 C3**
Topocalma, Pta. *Chile* 34°10S 72°2W **94 C1**
Topock *U.S.A.* 34°46N 114°29W **79 L12**

Topol'čany *Slovakia* 48°35N 18°12E **17 D10**
Topolobampo *Mexico* 25°36N 109°3W **86 B3**
Topozero, Ozero *Russia* 65°35N 32°0E **8 D25**
Toppenish *U.S.A.* 46°23N 120°19W **76 C3**
Torata *Peru* 17°23S 70°1W **92 G4**
Torbalı *Turkey* 38°10N 27°21E **23 E12**
Torbat-e Ḥeydārīyeh *Iran* 35°15N 59°12E **47 C8**
Torbat-e Jām *Iran* 35°16N 60°35E **47 C9**
Torbay *Canada* 47°40N 52°42W **73 C9**
Torbay □ *U.K.* 50°26N 3°31W **13 G4**
Tordesillas *Spain* 41°30N 5°0W **21 B3**
Torfaen □ *U.K.* 51°43N 3°3W **13 F4**
Torgau *Germany* 51°34N 13°0E **16 C7**
Torhout *Belgium* 51°5N 3°7E **15 C3**
Tori-Shima *Japan* 30°29N 140°19E **29 J10**
Torilla Pen. *Australia* 22°29S 150°5E **62 C5**
Torino *Italy* 45°3N 7°40E **20 D7**
Torit *South Sudan* 4°27N 32°31E **53 H12**
Torkamān *Iran* 37°35N 47°23E **46 B5**
Tormes → *Spain* 41°18N 6°29W **21 B2**
Tornado Mt. *Canada* 49°55N 114°40W **70 D6**
Torneå = Tornio *Finland* 65°50N 24°12E **8 D21**
Torneälven → *Europe* 65°50N 24°12E **8 D21**
Torneträsk *Sweden* 68°24N 19°15E **8 B18**
Torngat Mountains Nat. Park △
  Canada 59°0N 63°40W **69 F19**
Torngat Mts. *Canada* 59°0N 63°40W **69 F19**
Tornio *Finland* 65°50N 24°12E **8 D21**
Tornionjoki = Torneälven →
  Europe 65°50N 24°12E **8 D21**
Tornquist *Argentina* 38°8S 62°15W **94 D3**
Toro, Cerro del *Chile* 29°10S 69°50W **94 B2**
Toro Pk. *U.S.A.* 33°34N 116°24W **79 M10**
Toronto *Canada* 40°28N 80°36W **82 F4**
Toropets *Russia* 56°30N 31°40E **18 C5**
Tororo *Uganda* 0°45N 34°12E **54 D6**
Toros Dağları *Turkey* 37°0N 32°30E **46 B2**
Torpa *India* 22°57N 85°6E **43 H11**
Torquay *U.K.* 50°27N 3°32W **13 G4**
Torrance *U.S.A.* 33°50N 118°20W **79 M8**
Torre de Moncorvo
  Portugal 41°12N 7°8W **21 B2**
Torre del Greco *Italy* 40°47N 14°22E **22 D6**
Torrejón de Ardoz *Spain* 40°27N 3°29W **21 B4**
Torrelavega *Spain* 43°20N 4°5W **21 A3**
Torremolinos *Spain* 36°38N 4°30W **21 D3**
Torrens, L. *Australia* 31°0S 137°50E **63 E2**
Torrens Cr. → *Australia* 22°23S 145°9E **62 C4**
Torrens Creek *Australia* 20°48S 145°3E **62 C4**
Torrent *Spain* 39°27N 0°28W **21 C5**
Torreón *Mexico* 25°33N 103°26W **86 B4**
Torres *Brazil* 29°21S 49°44W **95 B5**
Torres *Mexico* 28°46N 110°47W **86 B2**
Torres Strait *Australia* 9°50S 142°20E **62 a**
Torres Vedras *Portugal* 39°5N 9°15W **21 C1**
Torrevieja *Spain* 37°59N 0°42W **21 D5**
Torrey *U.S.A.* 38°18N 111°25W **76 G8**
Torridge → *U.K.* 51°0N 4°13W **13 G3**
Torridon, L. *U.K.* 57°35N 5°50W **11 D3**
Torrington *Conn., U.S.A.* 41°48N 73°7W **83 E11**
Torrington *Wyo., U.S.A.* 42°4N 104°11W **76 E11**
Tórshavn *Færoe Is.* 62°5N 6°56W **8 E9**
Tortola *Br. Virgin Is.* 18°19N 64°45W **89 e**
Tortosa *Spain* 40°49N 0°31E **21 B6**
Tortosa, C. *Spain* 40°41N 0°52E **21 B6**
Tortue, Î. de la *Haiti* 20°5N 72°57W **89 B5**
Tortuguero △ *Costa Rica* 10°31N 83°29W **88 D3**
Torŭd *Iran* 35°25N 55°5E **47 C7**
Toruń *Poland* 53°2N 18°39E **17 B10**
Tory Hill *Canada* 44°58N 78°16W **82 B6**
Tory I. *Ireland* 55°16N 8°13W **10 A3**
Tosa *Japan* 33°24N 133°23E **29 H6**
Tosa-Shimizu *Japan* 32°52N 132°58E **29 H6**
Tosa-Wan *Japan* 33°15N 133°30E **29 H6**
Toscana □ *Italy* 43°25N 11°0E **22 C4**
Toshka, Buheirat en
  Egypt 22°50N 31°0E **53 D12**
Toshkent *Uzbekistan* 41°20N 69°10E **26 E7**
Tostado *Argentina* 29°15S 61°50W **94 B3**
Tosu *Japan* 33°22N 130°31E **29 H5**
Toteng *Botswana* 20°22S 22°58E **56 B3**
Totma *Russia* 60°0N 42°40E **18 C7**
Totnes *U.K.* 50°26N 3°42W **13 G4**
Totness *Suriname* 5°53N 56°19W **93 B7**
Totonicapán *Guatemala* 14°58N 91°12W **88 D1**
Totoya, I. *Fiji* 18°57S 179°50W **59 a**
Totten Glacier *Antarctica* 66°45S 116°10E **5 C8**
Tottenham *Australia* 32°14S 147°21E **63 E4**
Tottenham *Canada* 44°1N 79°49W **82 B5**
Tottori *Japan* 35°30N 134°15E **29 G7**
Tottori □ *Japan* 35°30N 134°12E **29 G7**
Toubkal, Djebel *Morocco* 31°0N 8°0W **52 B4**
Tougan *Burkina Faso* 13°11N 2°58W **52 F5**
Touggourt *Algeria* 33°6N 6°4E **52 B7**
Toul *France* 48°40N 5°53E **20 B6**
Touliu *Taiwan* 23°42N 120°31E **35 F13**
Toulon *France* 43°10N 5°55E **20 E6**
Toulouse *France* 43°37N 1°27E **20 E4**
Toummo *Niger* 22°45N 14°8E **53 D8**
Tounan *Taiwan* 23°40N 120°28E **35 F13**
Toungoo *Myanmar* 19°0N 96°30E **41 K20**
Touraine *France* 47°20N 0°30E **20 C4**
Touran = Tūrān △ *Iran* 35°45N 56°30E **47 C8**
Tourcoing *France* 50°42N 3°10E **20 A5**
Tournai *Belgium* 50°35N 3°25E **15 D3**
Tournon-sur-Rhône *France* 45°4N 4°50E **20 D6**
Tours *France* 47°22N 0°40E **20 C4**
Toussaint, Mt. *C.A.R.* 9°7N 21°14E **54 C4**
Touws → *S. Africa* 33°45S 21°11E **56 E3**
Touwsrivier *S. Africa* 33°20S 20°2E **56 E3**
Towada *Japan* 40°37N 141°13E **28 D10**
Towada-Hachimantai △
  Japan 40°20N 140°55E **28 D10**
Towada-Ko *Japan* 40°28N 140°55E **28 D10**
Towanda *U.S.A.* 41°46N 76°27W **83 E8**
Tower *U.S.A.* 47°48N 92°17W **80 B7**
Towerhill Cr. →
  Australia 22°28S 144°35E **62 C3**
Towner *U.S.A.* 48°21N 100°25W **80 A3**
Townsend *U.S.A.* 46°19N 111°31W **76 C8**

Townshend I. *Australia* 22°10S 150°31E **62** C5
Townsville *Australia* 19°15S 146°45E **62** B4
Towraghondī *Afghan.* 35°13N 62°16E **40** B3
Towson *U.S.A.* 39°24N 76°36W **81** F15
Towuti, Danau *Indonesia* 2°45S 121°32E **37** E6
Tōya-Ko *Japan* 42°35N 140°51E **28** C10
Toyama *Japan* 36°40N 137°15E **29** F8
Toyama □ *Japan* 36°45N 137°30E **29** F8
Toyama-Wan *Japan* 37°0N 137°30E **29** F8
Toyapakeh *Indonesia* 8°41S 115°29E **37** K18
Toyohashi *Japan* 34°45N 137°25E **29** G8
Toyokawa *Japan* 34°48N 137°27E **29** G8
Toyonaka *Japan* 34°50N 135°28E **29** G7
Toyooka *Japan* 35°35N 134°48E **29** G7
Toyota *Japan* 35°3N 137°7E **29** G8
Tozeur *Tunisia* 33°56N 8°8E **52** B7
Trá Lí = Tralee *Ireland* 52°16N 9°42W **10** D2
Trá Mhór = Tramore
  Ireland 52°10N 7°10W **10** D4
Tra On *Vietnam* 9°58N 105°55E **39** H5
Tra Vinh *Vietnam* 9°50N 106°15E **39** H6
Trabzon *Turkey* 41°0N 39°45E **19** F6
Tracadie *Canada* 47°30N 64°55W **73** C7
Tracy *Canada* 46°1N 73°9W **72** C5
Tracy *Calif., U.S.A.* 37°44N 121°26W **78** H5
Tracy *Minn., U.S.A.* 44°14N 95°37W **80** C6
Trafalgar, C. *Spain* 36°10N 6°2W **21** D2
Trail *Canada* 49°5N 117°40W **70** D5
Trainor L. *Canada* 60°24N 120°17W **70** A4
Trakai △ *Lithuania* 54°30N 25°10E **9** J21
Tralee *Ireland* 52°16N 9°42W **10** D2
Tralee B. *Ireland* 52°17N 9°55W **10** D2
Tramore *Ireland* 52°10N 7°10W **10** D4
Tramore B. *Ireland* 52°9N 7°10W **10** D4
Tran Ninh, Cao Nguyen
  Laos 19°30N 103°10E **38** C4
Tranås *Sweden* 58°3N 14°59E **9** G16
Trancas *Argentina* 26°11S 65°20W **94** B2
Trang *Thailand* 7°33N 99°38E **39** J2
Trangan *Indonesia* 6°40S 134°20E **37** F8
Trangie *Australia* 32°4S 148°0E **63** E4
Trani *Italy* 41°17N 16°25E **22** D7
Tranoroa *Madag.* 24°42S 45°4E **55** J9
Tranqueras *Uruguay* 31°13S 55°45W **95** C4
Transantarctic Mts.
  Antarctica 85°0S 170°0W **5** E12
Transilvania *Romania* 46°30N 24°0E **17** E12
Transilvanian Alps = Carpații
  Meridionali *Romania* 45°30N 25°0E **17** F13
Transnistria □ *Moldova* 47°20N 29°15E **17** E15
Transylvania = Transilvania
  Romania 46°30N 24°0E **17** E12
Trápani *Italy* 38°1N 12°29E **22** E5
Trapper Pk. *U.S.A.* 45°54N 114°18W **76** D6
Traralgon *Australia* 38°12S 146°34E **63** F4
Trasimeno, L. *Italy* 43°8N 12°6E **22** C5
Trat *Thailand* 12°14N 102°33E **39** F4
Tratani → *Pakistan* 29°19N 68°20E **42** E3
Traun *Austria* 48°14N 14°15E **16** D8
Travellers L. *Australia* 33°20S 142°0E **63** E3
Travemünde *Germany* 53°57N 10°52E **16** B6
Travers, Mt. *N.Z.* 42°1S 172°45E **59** E4
Traverse City *U.S.A.* 44°46N 85°38W **81** C11
Travis, L. *U.S.A.* 30°24N 97°55W **84** F6
Travnik *Bos.-H.* 44°17N 17°39E **23** B7
Trawbreaga B. *Ireland* 55°20N 7°25W **10** A4
Trébbia → *Italy* 45°4N 9°41E **20** D8
Třebíč *Czechia* 49°14N 15°55E **16** D8
Trebinje *Bos.-H.* 42°44N 18°22E **23** C8
Trebonne *Australia* 18°37S 146°5E **62** B4
Trefaldwyn = Montgomery
  U.K. 52°34N 3°8W **13** E4
Trefynwy = Monmouth
  U.K. 51°48N 2°42W **13** F5
Tregaron *U.K.* 52°14N 3°56W **13** E4
Tregrosse Is. *Australia* 17°41S 150°43E **62** B5
Treherne *Canada* 49°38N 98°42W **71** D9
Treinta y Tres *Uruguay* 33°16S 54°17W **95** C5
Trelawney *Zimbabwe* 17°30S 30°30E **57** A5
Trelew *Argentina* 43°10S 65°20W **96** E3
Trelleborg *Sweden* 55°20N 13°10E **9** J15
Tremadog Bay *U.K.* 52°51N 4°18W **12** E3
Tremonton *U.S.A.* 41°43N 112°10W **76** F7
Tremp *Spain* 42°10N 0°52E **21** A6
Trenche → *Canada* 47°46N 72°53W **72** C5
Trenčín *Slovakia* 48°52N 18°4E **17** D10
Trenggalek *Indonesia* 8°3S 111°43E **37** H14
Trenque Lauquen
  Argentina 36°5S 62°45W **94** D3
Trent → *Canada* 44°6N 77°34W **82** B7
Trent → *U.K.* 53°41N 0°42W **12** D7
Trento *Italy* 46°4N 11°8E **22** A4
Trenton *Canada* 44°10N 77°34W **82** B7
Trenton *Mo., U.S.A.* 40°5N 93°37W **80** E7
Trenton *N.J., U.S.A.* 40°14N 74°46W **83** F10
Trenton *Nebr., U.S.A.* 40°11N 101°1W **80** E3
Trepassey *Canada* 46°43N 53°25W **73** C9
Tres Arroyos *Argentina* 38°26S 60°20W **94** D3
Três Corações *Brazil* 21°44S 45°15W **95** A6
Três Lagoas *Brazil* 20°50S 51°43W **93** H8
Tres Lomas *Argentina* 36°27S 62°51W **94** D3
Tres Montes, C. *Chile* 46°50S 75°30W **96** F1
Tres Pinos *U.S.A.* 36°48N 121°19W **78** J5
Três Pontas *Brazil* 21°23S 45°29W **95** A6
Tres Puentes *Chile* 27°50S 70°15W **94** B1
Tres Puntas, C. *Argentina* 47°0S 66°0W **96** F3
Três Rios *Brazil* 22°6S 43°15W **95** A7
Tres Valles *Mexico* 18°15N 96°8W **87** D5
Tresco *U.K.* 49°57N 6°20W **13** H1
Treviso *Italy* 45°40N 12°15E **22** B5
Triabunna *Australia* 42°30S 147°55E **63** G4
Triangle *Zimbabwe* 21°2S 31°28E **57** B5
Tribal Areas □ *Pakistan* 33°0N 70°0E **42** C4
Tribulation, C. *Australia* 16°5S 145°29E **62** B4
Tribune *Canada* 38°28N 101°45W **80** F3
Trichinopoly = Tiruchirappalli
  India 10°45N 78°45E **45** J4
Trichur = Thrissur *India* 10°30N 76°18E **45** J3
Trichy = Tiruchirappalli
  India 10°45N 78°45E **45** J4
Trida *Australia* 33°1S 145°1E **63** E4
Trier *Germany* 49°45N 6°38E **16** D4
Trieste *Italy* 45°40N 13°46E **22** B5
Triglav *Slovenia* 46°21N 13°50E **16** E7
Trikala *Greece* 39°34N 21°47E **23** E9
Trikora, Puncak
  Indonesia 4°15S 138°45E **37** E9
Trim *Ireland* 53°33N 6°48W **10** C5
Trimbak *India* 19°56N 73°33E **44** E1
Trimmu Dam *Pakistan* 31°10N 72°8E **42** D5
Trincomalee *Sri Lanka* 8°38N 81°15E **45** K5
Trindade *Atl. Oc.* 20°20S 29°50W **2** F8
Trindade *Brazil* 16°40S 49°30W **93** G9
Trinidad *Bolivia* 14°46S 64°50W **92** F6
Trinidad *Cuba* 21°48N 80°0W **88** B4
Trinidad *Paraguay* 27°7S 55°47W **95** B4
Trinidad *Trin. & Tob.* 10°30N 61°15W **93** K15
Trinidad *Uruguay* 33°30S 56°50W **94** C4
Trinidad *U.S.A.* 37°10N 104°31W **77** H11
Trinidad & Tobago ■
  W. Indies 10°30N 61°20W **93** K15
Trinity *Canada* 48°59N 53°55W **73** C9
Trinity *U.S.A.* 30°57N 95°22W **84** F7
Trinity → *Calif., U.S.A.* 41°11N 123°42W **76** F2
Trinity → *Tex., U.S.A.* 29°45N 94°43W **84** G7
Trinity B. *Canada* 48°20N 53°10W **73** C9
Trinity Hills *Trin. & Tob.* 10°7N 61°7W **93** K15
Trinity Is. *U.S.A.* 56°33N 154°25W **74** D9
Trinity Range *U.S.A.* 40°10N 118°40W **76** F4
Trinkat *India* 8°5N 93°30E **45** K11
Trinkitat *Sudan* 18°45N 37°51E **53** E13
Trinway *U.S.A.* 40°9N 82°1W **82** F2
Triolet *Mauritius* 20°4S 57°32E **55** d
Tripoli = Tarābulus
  Lebanon 34°31N 35°50E **48** A4
Tripoli = Tarābulus *Libya* 32°49N 13°7E **53** B8
Tripoli *Greece* 37°31N 22°25E **23** F10
Tripolitania = Tarābulus
  Libya 31°0N 13°0E **53** B8
Tripura □ *India* 24°0N 92°0E **41** H18
Trisul *India* 30°19N 79°47E **43** D8
Triton I. *S. China Sea* 15°47N 111°12E **36** A4
Trivandrum =
  Thiruvananthapuram
  India 8°41N 77°0E **45** K3
Trnava *Slovakia* 48°23N 17°35E **17** D9
Trochu *Canada* 51°50N 113°13W **70** C6
Trodely I. *Canada* 52°15N 79°26W **72** B4
Troglav *Croatia* 43°56N 16°36E **22** C7
Troilus, L. *Canada* 50°50N 74°35W **72** B5
Trois-Pistoles *Canada* 48°5N 69°10W **73** C6
Trois-Rivières *Canada* 46°25N 72°34W **72** C5
Trois-Rivières *Guadeloupe* 15°57N 61°40W **88** b
Troitsk *Russia* 54°10N 61°35E **26** D7
Troitsko Pechorsk
  Russia 62°40N 56°10E **18** B10
Troll *Antarctica* 72°0S 2°30E **5** D3
Trölladyngja *Iceland* 64°54N 17°16W **8** D5
Trollhättan *Sweden* 58°17N 12°20E **9** G15
Trollheimen *Norway* 62°46N 9°1E **8** E13
Trombetas → *Brazil* 1°55S 55°35W **93** D7
Tromsø *Norway* 69°40N 18°56E **8** B18
Tron *Thailand* 17°28N 100°7E **38** D3
Trona *U.S.A.* 35°46N 117°23W **79** K9
Tronador, Mte. *Argentina* 41°10S 71°50W **96** E2
Trøndelag *Norway* 64°17N 11°50E **8** D14
Trondheim *Norway* 63°36N 10°25E **8** E14
Trondheimsfjorden
  Norway 63°35N 10°30E **8** E14
Troon *U.K.* 55°33N 4°39W **11** F4
Tropic *U.S.A.* 37°37N 112°5W **77** H7
Trostan *U.K.* 55°3N 6°10W **10** A5
Trou Gras Pt. *St. Lucia* 13°51N 60°53W **89** f
Trout → *Canada* 61°19N 119°51W **70** A5
Trout L. *N.W.T., Canada* 60°40N 121°14W **70** A4
Trout L. *Ont., Canada* 51°20N 93°15W **71** C10
Trout Lake *Canada* 56°30N 114°32W **70** B6
Trout Lake *U.S.A.* 46°0N 121°32W **78** E5
Trout River *Canada* 49°29N 58°8W **73** C8
Trout Run *U.S.A.* 41°23N 77°3W **82** E7
Trouville-sur-Mer *France* 49°21N 0°5E **20** B4
Trowbridge *U.K.* 51°18N 2°12W **13** F5
Troy *Turkey* 39°57N 26°12E **23** E12
Troy *Ala., U.S.A.* 31°48N 85°58W **85** F12
Troy *Kans., U.S.A.* 39°47N 95°5W **80** F6
Troy *Mo., U.S.A.* 38°59N 90°59W **80** F8
Troy *N.Y., U.S.A.* 42°44N 73°41W **83** D11
Troy *Ohio, U.S.A.* 40°2N 84°12W **81** E11
Troy *Pa., U.S.A.* 41°47N 76°47W **83** E8
Troyes *France* 48°19N 4°3E **20** B6
Truchas Pk. *U.S.A.* 35°58N 105°39W **77** J11
Trujillo *Honduras* 16°0N 86°0W **88** C2
Trujillo *Peru* 8°6S 79°0W **92** E3
Trujillo *Spain* 39°28N 5°55W **21** C3
Trujillo *U.S.A.* 35°32N 104°42W **77** J11
Trujillo *Venezuela* 9°22N 70°38W **92** B4
Truk *Micronesia* 7°25N 151°46E **64** G7
Trumann *U.S.A.* 35°41N 90°31W **85** D9
Trumansburg *U.S.A.* 42°33N 76°40W **83** D8
Trumbull, Mt. *U.S.A.* 36°25N 113°19W **77** H7
Trundle *Australia* 32°53S 147°35E **63** E4
Trung Lon, Hon *Vietnam* 8°36N 106°8E **39** H6
Trung Phan *Vietnam* 16°0N 108°0E **38** D6
Truong Sa, Dao = Spratly I.
  S. China Sea 8°38N 111°55E **36** C4
Truro *Canada* 45°21N 63°14W **73** C7
Truro *U.K.* 50°16N 5°4W **13** G2
Truskavets *Ukraine* 49°17N 23°30E **17** D12
Trutch *Canada* 57°44N 122°57W **70** B4
Truth or Consequences
  U.S.A. 33°8N 107°15W **77** K10
Trutnov *Czechia* 50°37N 15°54E **16** C8
Tryonville *U.S.A.* 41°42N 79°48W **82** E5
Tsandi *Namibia* 17°42S 14°50E **56** A1
Tsaratanana *Madag.* 16°47S 47°39E **55** G9
Tsau *Botswana* 20°8S 22°22E **56** B3

Tsavo *Kenya* 2°59S 38°28E **54** E7
Tsentralnyy □ *Russia* 52°0N 40°0E **26** D4
Tses *Namibia* 25°58S 18°8E **56** C2
Tsetserleg *Mongolia* 47°36N 101°32E **30** B9
Tsévié *Togo* 6°25N 1°20E **52** G6
Tshabong *Botswana* 26°2S 22°29E **56** C3
Tshane *Botswana* 24°5S 21°54E **56** B3
Tshela *Dem. Rep. of the Congo* 4°57S 13°4E **54** E2
Tshesebe *Botswana* 21°51S 27°32E **57** B4
Tshikapa
  Dem. Rep. of the Congo 6°28S 20°48E **54** F4
Tshwane = Pretoria
  S. Africa 25°44S 28°12E **57** C4
Tshwane *Botswana* 22°24S 22°1E **56** B3
Tsigara *Botswana* 20°22S 25°54E **56** B4
Tsihombe *Madag.* 25°10S 45°41E **55** K9
Tsiigehtchic *Canada* 67°15N 134°0W **68** D5
Ts'il-os △ *Canada* 51°9N 123°59W **70** C4
Tsimlyansk Res. = Tsimlyanskoye
  Vdkhr. *Russia* 48°0N 43°0E **19** E7
Tsimlyanskoye Vdkhr.
  Russia 48°0N 43°0E **19** E7
Tsinan = Jinan *China* 36°38N 117°1E **32** F9
Tsineng *S. Africa* 27°5S 23°5E **56** C3
Tsinghai = Qinghai □
  China 36°0N 98°0E **30** D8
Tsingtao = Qingdao
  China 36°5N 120°20E **33** F11
Tsirigo = Kythira *Greece* 36°8N 23°0E **23** F10
Tsitsikamma △ *S. Africa* 34°3S 23°40E **56** D3
Tskhinvali *Georgia* 42°14N 44°1E **19** F7
Tsna → *Russia* 54°55N 41°58E **18** D7
Tso Moriri, L. *India* 32°50N 78°20E **43** C8
Tsobis *Namibia* 19°27S 17°30E **56** A2
Tsodilo Hills *Botswana* 18°49S 21°43E **56** A3
Tsogttsetsiy = Baruunsuu
  Mongolia 43°43N 105°35E **32** C3
Tsolo *S. Africa* 31°18S 28°37E **57** D4
Tsomo *S. Africa* 32°0S 27°42E **57** D4
Tsu *Japan* 34°45N 136°25E **29** G8
Tsu L. *Canada* 60°40N 111°52W **70** A6
Tsuchiura *Japan* 36°5N 140°15E **29** F10
Tsugaru-Hantō *Japan* 41°0N 140°30E **28** D10
Tsugaru-Kaikyō *Japan* 41°35N 141°0E **28** D10
Tsumeb *Namibia* 19°9S 17°44E **56** A2
Tsumis *Namibia* 23°39S 17°29E **56** B2
Tsuruga *Japan* 35°45N 136°2E **29** G8
Tsurugi-San *Japan* 33°51N 134°6E **29** H7
Tsuruoka *Japan* 38°44N 139°50E **28** E9
Tsushima *Gifu, Japan* 35°10N 136°43E **29** G8
Tsushima *Nagasaki,*
  Japan 34°20N 129°20E **29** G4
Tsuyama *Japan* 35°3N 134°0E **29** G7
Tsyelyakhany *Belarus* 52°30N 25°46E **17** B13
Tuaim = Tuam *Ireland* 53°31N 8°51W **10** C3
Tual *Indonesia* 5°38S 132°44E **37** F8
Tualatin *U.S.A.* 45°23N 122°45W **78** E4
Tuam *Ireland* 53°31N 8°51W **10** C3
Tuamotu, Îs.
  French Polynesia 17°0S 144°0W **65** J13
Tuamotu Arch. = Tuamotu, Îs.
  French Polynesia 17°0S 144°0W **65** J13
Tuamotu Ridge *Pac. Oc.* 20°0S 138°0W **65** K14
Tuan Giao *Vietnam* 21°35N 103°25E **38** B4
Tuanfeng *China* 30°38N 114°52E **35** B10
Tuanxi *China* 27°28N 107°8E **34** D6
Tuao *Phil.* 17°45N 121°22E **37** A6
Tuapse *Russia* 44°5N 39°10E **19** F6
Tuatapere *N.Z.* 46°8S 167°41E **59** G1
Tuba City *U.S.A.* 36°8N 111°14W **77** H8
Tuban *Indonesia* 6°54S 112°3E **37** G15
Tubani *Botswana* 24°46S 24°18E **56** B3
Tubarão *Brazil* 28°30S 49°0W **95** B6
Tūbās *West Bank* 32°20N 35°22E **48** C4
Tubas → *Namibia* 22°54S 14°35E **56** B2
Tübingen *Germany* 48°31N 9°4E **16** D5
Tubou *Fiji* 18°13S 178°48W **59** a
Tubruq *Libya* 32°7N 23°55E **53** B10
Tubuai, Îs.
  French Polynesia 25°0S 150°0W **65** K13
Tuc Trung *Vietnam* 11°1N 107°12E **39** G6
Tucacas *Venezuela* 10°48N 68°19W **92** A5
T'uch'ang *Taiwan* 24°35N 121°0E **35** E13
Tuchitua *Canada* 60°55N 129°13W **70** A3
Tuchodi → *Canada* 58°17N 123°42W **70** B4
Tucson *U.S.A.* 32°13N 110°58W **77** K8
Tucumán □ *Argentina* 26°48S 66°2W **94** B2
Tucumcari *U.S.A.* 35°10N 103°44W **77** J12
Tucupita *Venezuela* 9°2N 62°3W **92** B6
Tucuruí *Brazil* 3°42S 49°44W **93** D9
Tucuruí, Represa de *Brazil* 4°0S 49°30W **93** D9
Tudela *Spain* 42°4N 1°39W **21** A5
Tudmur *Syria* 34°36N 38°15E **46** C3
Tudor, L. *Canada* 55°50N 65°25W **73** A6
Tug Hill Plateau *U.S.A.* 43°45N 75°50W **83** C9
Tugela → *S. Africa* 29°14S 31°30E **57** D5
Tugela Falls *S. Africa* 28°42S 29°51E **57** C4
Tuguegarao *Phil.* 17°35N 121°42E **37** A6
Tugur *Russia* 53°44N 136°45E **27** D14
Tui *Spain* 42°3N 8°39W **21** A1
Tukangbesi, Kepulauan
  Indonesia 6°0S 124°0E **37** F6
Tukarak I. *Canada* 56°15N 78°45W **72** A4
Tukayyid *Iraq* 29°47N 45°36E **46** D5
Tuktoyaktuk *Canada* 69°27N 133°2W **68** D5
Tuktut Nogait △ *Canada* 69°15N 122°0W **68** D7
Tukums *Latvia* 56°58N 23°10E **9** H20
Tukuyu *Tanzania* 9°17S 33°35E **54** F6
Tula *Hidalgo, Mexico* 20°3N 99°21W **87** C5
Tula *Tamaulipas, Mexico* 23°0N 99°43W **87** C5
Tula *Russia* 54°13N 37°38E **18** D6
Tulach Mhór = Tullamore
  Ireland 53°16N 7°31W **10** C4
Tulancingo *Mexico* 20°5N 98°22W **87** C5
Tulare *U.S.A.* 36°13N 119°21W **78** J7
Tulare Lake Bed *U.S.A.* 36°0N 119°48W **78** K7
Tularosa *U.S.A.* 33°5N 106°1W **77** K10
Tulbagh *S. Africa* 33°16S 19°6E **56** D2
Tulcán *Ecuador* 0°48N 77°43W **92** C3
Tulcea *Romania* 45°13N 28°46E **17** F15

Tulchyn *Ukraine* 48°41N 28°49E **17** D15
Tūleh *Iran* 34°35N 52°33E **47** C7
Tulemalu L. *Canada* 62°58N 99°25W **71** A9
Tulia *U.S.A.* 34°32N 101°46W **84** D4
Tulita *Canada* 64°57N 125°30W **68** E7
Tŭlkarm *West Bank* 32°19N 35°2E **48** C4
Tulla *Ireland* 52°53N 8°46W **10** D3
Tullahoma *U.S.A.* 35°22N 86°13W **85** D11
Tullamore *Australia* 32°39S 147°36E **63** E4
Tullamore *Ireland* 53°16N 7°31W **10** C4
Tulle *France* 45°16N 1°46E **20** D4
Tullow *Ireland* 52°49N 6°45W **10** D5
Tully *Australia* 17°56S 145°55E **62** B4
Tully *U.S.A.* 42°48N 76°7W **83** D8
Tulsa *U.S.A.* 36°10N 95°55W **84** C7
Tulsequah *Canada* 58°39N 133°35W **70** B2
Tuluá *Colombia* 4°6N 76°11W **92** C3
Tulum *Mexico* 20°13N 87°27E **87** C7
Tulun *Russia* 54°32N 100°35E **27** D11
Tulungagung *Indonesia* 8°5S 111°54E **37** H14
Tuma → *Nic.* 13°6N 84°35W **88** D3
Tumacacori △ *U.S.A.* 31°35N 111°6W **77** L8
Tumaco *Colombia* 1°50N 78°45W **92** C3
Tumakuru *India* 13°18N 77°6E **45** H3
Tumatumari *Guyana* 5°20N 58°55W **92** B7
Tumba *Sweden* 59°12N 17°48E **9** G17
Tumba, L.
  Dem. Rep. of the Congo 0°50S 18°0E **54** E3
Tumbarumba *Australia* 35°44S 148°0E **63** F4
Tumbaya *Argentina* 23°50S 65°26W **94** A2
Tumbes *Peru* 3°37S 80°27W **92** D2
Tumbler Ridge *Canada* 55°8N 121°0W **70** B4
Tumby Bay *Australia* 34°21S 136°8E **63** E2
Tumd Youqi *China* 40°30N 110°30E **32** D6
Tumen *China* 43°0N 129°50E **28** C4
Tumen Jiang → *China* 42°20N 130°35E **33** C16
Tumeremo *Venezuela* 7°18N 61°30W **92** B6
Tumkur = Tumakuru
  India 13°18N 77°6E **45** H3
Tump *Pakistan* 26°7N 62°16E **40** F3
Tumpat *Malaysia* 6°11N 102°10E **39** J4
Tumsar *India* 21°26N 79°45E **44** D4
Tumu *Ghana* 10°56N 1°56W **52** F5
Tumucumaque, Serra
  Brazil 2°0N 55°0W **93** C8
Tumut *Australia* 35°16S 148°13E **63** F4
Tumwater *U.S.A.* 47°1N 122°54W **78** C4
Tuna *India* 22°59N 70°5E **42** H4
Tunapuna *Trin. & Tob.* 10°38N 61°24W **93** K15
Tunas de Zaza *Cuba* 21°39N 79°34W **88** B4
Tunbridge Wells = Royal
  Tunbridge Wells *U.K.* 51°7N 0°16E **13** F8
Tunceli *Turkey* 39°6N 39°31E **46** B3
Tunchang *China* 19°21N 110°5E **38** C8
Tuncurry *Australia* 32°17S 152°29E **63** E5
Tundla *India* 27°12N 78°17E **42** F8
Tundzha → *Bulgaria* 41°40N 26°35E **23** C11
Tunga → *India* 15°0N 75°50E **45** G2
Tungabhadra → *India* 15°57N 78°15E **45** G4
Tungabhadra Dam *India* 15°0N 75°50E **45** G2
Tungla *Nic.* 13°24N 84°21W **88** D3
Tungsha Tao = Dongsha Dao
  S. China Sea 20°45N 116°43E **35** G11
Tungshih *Taiwan* 24°12N 120°43E **35** E13
Tungsten *Canada* 61°57N 128°16W **70** A3
Tunguska, Nizhnyaya →
  Russia 65°48N 88°4E **27** C9
Tunguska, Podkamennaya →
  Russia 61°50N 90°13E **27** C10
Tuni *India* 17°22N 82°36E **44** F6
Tunica *U.S.A.* 34°41N 90°23W **85** D9
Tunis *Tunisia* 36°50N 10°11E **53** A8
Tunisia ■ *Africa* 33°30N 9°10E **53** A7
Tunja *Colombia* 5°33N 73°25W **92** B4
Tunkhannock *U.S.A.* 41°32N 75°57W **83** E9
Tunkinsky △ *Russia* 51°30N 102°0E **27** D11
Tunliu *China* 36°13N 112°52E **32** F7
Tunnel Creek △
  Australia 17°41S 125°18E **60** C4
Tunnsjøen *Norway* 64°45N 13°25E **8** D15
Tunungayualok I. *Canada* 56°0N 61°0W **73** A7
Tunuyán *Argentina* 33°35S 69°0W **94** C2
Tunuyán → *Argentina* 33°33S 67°30W **94** C2
Tunxi = Huangshan
  China 29°42N 118°25E **35** C12
Tuo Jiang → *China* 28°50N 105°35E **34** C5
Tuolumne *U.S.A.* 37°58N 120°15W **78** H6
Tuolumne → *U.S.A.* 37°36N 121°13W **78** H5
Tūp Āghāj *Iran* 36°3N 47°50E **46** B5
Tupã *Brazil* 21°57S 50°28W **95** A5
Tupelo *U.S.A.* 34°16N 88°43W **85** D10
Tupinambarana, I. *Brazil* 3°0S 58°0W **92** D7
Tupiza *Bolivia* 21°30S 65°40W **94** A2
Tupman *U.S.A.* 35°18N 119°21W **79** K7
Tupper *Canada* 55°32N 120°1W **70** B4
Tupper L. *U.S.A.* 44°10N 74°32W **83** B10
Tupper Lake *U.S.A.* 44°14N 74°28W **83** B10
Tupungato, Cerro
  S. Amer. 33°15S 69°50W **94** C2
Tuquan *China* 45°18N 121°38E **33** B11
Túquerres *Colombia* 1°5N 77°37W **92** C3
Tura *Russia* 64°20N 100°17E **27** C11
Turabah *Si. Arabia* 28°20N 43°15E **46** D4
Tūrān *Iran* 35°39N 56°42E **47** C8
Turan *Russia* 51°55N 95°0E **27** D10
Tūrān □ *Iran* 35°45N 56°50E **47** C8
Ţurayf *Si. Arabia* 31°41N 38°39E **46** D3
Turda *Romania* 46°34N 23°47E **17** E12
Turek *Poland* 52°3N 18°30E **17** B10
Turén *Venezuela* 9°17N 69°6W **92** B5
Turfan = Turpan *China* 43°58N 89°10E **30** C6
Turfan Basin = Turpan Pendi
  China 42°40N 89°25E **30** C6
Turfan Depression = Turpan Pendi
  China 42°40N 89°25E **30** C6
Turgeon → *Canada* 50°0N 78°56W **72** C4
Turgutlu *Turkey* 38°30N 27°43E **23** E12
Turgwe → *Zimbabwe* 21°31S 32°15E **57** C5
Turia → *Spain* 39°27N 0°19W **21** C5
Turiaçu *Brazil* 1°40S 45°19W **93** D9
Turiaçu → *Brazil* 1°36S 45°19W **93** D9

Turin = Torino *Italy* 45°3N 7°40E **20** D7
Turkana, L. *Africa* 3°30N 36°5E **54** D7
Turkestan = Türkistan
  Kazakhstan 43°17N 68°16E **26** E7
Turkey ■ *Eurasia* 39°0N 36°0E **19** G6
Turkey Creek = Warmun
  Australia 17°2S 128°12E **60** C4
Türkistan *Kazakhstan* 43°17N 68°16E **26** E7
Türkmenabat
  Turkmenistan 39°6N 63°34E **47** B9
Türkmenbashi
  Turkmenistan 40°5N 53°5E **47** A7
Turkmenistan ■ *Asia* 39°0N 59°0E **26** F6
Turks & Caicos Is. ☑
  W. Indies 21°20N 71°20W **89** B5
Turks Island Passage
  Turks & Caicos 21°25N 71°19W **89** B5
Turku *Finland* 60°30N 22°19E **9** F20
Turkwel → *Kenya* 3°6N 36°6E **54** D7
Turlock *U.S.A.* 37°30N 120°51W **78** H6
Turnagain *Australia* 9°34S 142°17E **62** a
Turnagain → *Canada* 59°12N 127°35W **70** B3
Turneffe Is. *Belize* 17°20N 87°50W **87** D7
Turner *U.S.A.* 48°51N 108°24W **76** B9
Turner Pt. *Australia* 11°47S 133°32E **62** A1
Turner Valley *Canada* 50°40N 114°17W **70** C6
Turners Falls *U.S.A.* 42°36N 72°33W **83** D12
Turnhout *Belgium* 51°19N 4°57E **15** C4
Turnor L. *Canada* 56°35N 108°35W **71** B7
Turnovo = Veliko Tarnovo
  Bulgaria 43°5N 25°41E **23** C11
Turnu Măgurele
  Romania 43°46N 24°56E **17** G13
Turnu Roşu, P. *Romania* 45°33N 24°17E **17** F13
Turpan *China* 43°58N 89°10E **30** C6
Turpan Pendi *China* 42°40N 89°25E **30** C6
Turriff *U.K.* 57°32N 2°27W **11** D6
Tursāq *Iraq* 33°27N 45°47E **46** C5
Turtle Head I. *Australia* 10°56S 142°37E **62** a
Turtle Lake *Canada* 53°36N 108°38W **71** C7
Turtle Lake *U.S.A.* 47°31N 100°53W **80** B3
Turtleford *Canada* 53°23N 108°57W **71** C7
Turuépano △ *Venezuela* 10°34N 62°43W **89** D7
Turukhansk *Russia* 65°21N 88°5E **27** C9
Tuscaloosa *U.S.A.* 33°12N 87°34W **85** E11
Tuscany = Toscana □
  Italy 43°25N 11°0E **22** C4
Tuscarawas → *U.S.A.* 40°24N 81°25W **82** F3
Tuscarora Mt. *U.S.A.* 40°55N 77°55W **82** F7
Tuscola *Ill., U.S.A.* 39°48N 88°17W **80** F9
Tuscola *Tex., U.S.A.* 32°12N 99°48W **84** E5
Tuscumbia *U.S.A.* 34°44N 87°42W **85** D11
Tuskegee *U.S.A.* 32°25N 85°42W **85** E12
Tuticorin *India* 8°50N 78°12E **45** K4
Tutóia *Brazil* 2°45S 42°20W **93** D10
Tutong *Brunei* 4°47N 114°40E **36** D4
Tutrakan *Bulgaria* 44°2N 26°40E **23** B12
Tuttle Creek L. *U.S.A.* 39°15N 96°36W **80** F6
Tuttlingen *Germany* 47°58N 8°48E **16** E5
Tutuala *Timor-Leste* 8°25S 127°15E **37** F7
Tutuila *Amer. Samoa* 14°19S 170°50W **59** b
Tutume *Botswana* 20°30S 27°5E **55** J5
Tuul Gol → *Mongolia* 48°30N 104°25E **30** B9
Tuva □ *Russia* 51°30N 95°0E **27** D10
Tuvalu ■ *Pac. Oc.* 8°0S 178°0E **58** B10
Tuvuca *Fiji* 17°40S 178°48W **59** a
Tuxpan *Mexico* 20°57N 97°24W **87** C5
Tuxtla Gutiérrez *Mexico* 16°45N 93°7W **87** D6
Tuy = Tui *Spain* 42°3N 8°39W **21** A1
Tuy Duc *Vietnam* 12°15N 107°27E **39** F6
Tuy Phong *Vietnam* 11°14N 108°43E **39** G7
Tuya L. *Canada* 59°7N 130°35W **70** B2
Tuyen Hoa *Vietnam* 17°50N 106°10E **38** D6
Tuyen Quang *Vietnam* 21°50N 105°10E **34** G5
Tūysarkān *Iran* 34°33N 48°27E **47** C6
Tuz Gölü *Turkey* 38°42N 33°18E **19** G5
Tūz Khurmātū *Iraq* 34°56N 44°38E **46** C5
Tuzigoot △ *U.S.A.* 34°46N 112°2W **77** J7
Tuzla *Bos.-H.* 44°34N 18°41E **23** B8
Tver *Russia* 56°55N 35°59E **18** C6
Twain *U.S.A.* 40°1N 121°3W **78** E5
Twain Harte *U.S.A.* 38°2N 120°14W **78** G6
Twee River *Namibia* 25°27S 19°27E **56** C2
Tweed *Canada* 44°29N 77°19W **82** B7
Tweed → *U.K.* 55°45N 2°0W **11** F6
Tweed Heads *Australia* 28°10S 153°31E **63** D5
Tweedsmuir △ *Canada* 53°0N 126°20W **70** C3
Twentynine Palms
  U.S.A. 34°8N 116°3W **79** L10
Twillingate *Canada* 49°42N 54°45W **73** C9
Twin Bridges *U.S.A.* 45°33N 112°20W **76** D7
Twin Falls *Canada* 53°30N 64°32W **73** B7
Twin Falls *U.S.A.* 42°34N 114°28W **76** E6
Twin Valley *U.S.A.* 47°16N 96°16W **80** B5
Twinsburg *U.S.A.* 41°19N 81°26W **82** E3
Twitchell Res. *U.S.A.* 34°59N 120°19W **79** L6
Two Harbors *U.S.A.* 47°2N 91°40W **80** B8
Two Hills *Canada* 53°43N 111°52W **70** C6
Two Rivers *U.S.A.* 44°9N 87°34W **80** C10
Two Rocks *Australia* 31°30S 115°35E **61** F2
Twofold B. *Australia* 37°8S 149°59E **63** F4
Twyfelfontein *Namibia* 20°34S 14°28E **56** A1
Tyachiv *Ukraine* 48°1N 23°35E **17** D12
Tychy *Poland* 50°9N 18°59E **17** C10
Tyler *Minn., U.S.A.* 44°17N 96°8W **80** C5
Tyler *Tex., U.S.A.* 32°21N 95°18W **84** E7
Tynda *Russia* 55°10N 124°43E **27** D13
Tyndall *U.S.A.* 43°0N 97°50W **80** D5
Tyne → *U.K.* 54°59N 1°32W **12** C6
Tyne & Wear □ *U.K.* 55°6N 1°17W **12** B6
Tynemouth *U.K.* 55°1N 1°26W **12** B6
Tyre = Sūr *Lebanon* 33°19N 35°16E **48** B4
Tyrifjorden *Norway* 60°2N 10°8E **9** F14
Tyrol = Tirol □ *Austria* 47°3N 10°43E **16** E6
Tyrone *U.S.A.* 40°40N 78°14W **82** F6
Tyrone □ *U.K.* 54°38N 7°11W **10** B4
Tyrrell → *Australia* 35°26S 142°51E **63** F3
Tyrrell, L. *Australia* 35°20S 142°50E **63** F3
Tyrrell L. *Canada* 63°7N 105°27W **71** A7
Tyrrhenian Sea *Medit. S.* 40°0N 12°30E **22** E5

Tysfjorden Norway 68°7N 16°25E **8 B17**
Tyulgan Russia 52°22N 56°12E **18 D10**
Tyumen Russia 57°11N 65°29E **26 D7**
Tywi → U.K. 51°48N 4°21W **13 F3**
Tywyn U.K. 52°35N 4°5W **13 E3**
Tzaneen S. Africa 23°47S 30°9E **57 B5**
Tzukong = Zigong
  China 29°15N 104°48E **34 C5**

U

U.S.A. = United States of
  America ■ N. Amer. 37°0N 96°0W **75 H20**
U.S. Virgin Is. ☑ W. Indies 18°20N 65°0W **89 e**
Uaimh, An = Navan
  Ireland 53°39N 6°41W **10 C5**
Uanle Uen = Wanleweyne
  Somalia 2°37N 44°54E **49 G3**
Uatumã → Brazil 2°26S 57°37W **92 D7**
Uaupés Brazil 0°8S 67°5W **92 D5**
Uaupés → Brazil 0°2N 67°16W **92 C5**
Uaxactún Guatemala 17°25N 89°29W **88 C2**
Ubá Brazil 21°8S 43°0W **95 A7**
Ubaitaba Brazil 14°18S 39°20W **93 F11**
Ubangi = Oubangi →
  Dem. Rep. of the Congo 0°30S 17°50E **54 E3**
Ubauro Pakistan 28°15N 69°45E **42 E3**
Ubayyiḍ, W. al → Iraq 32°34N 43°48E **46 C4**
Ube Japan 33°56N 131°15E **29 H5**
Úbeda Spain 38°3N 3°23W **21 C4**
Uberaba Brazil 19°50S 47°55W **93 G9**
Uberlândia Brazil 19°0S 48°20W **93 G9**
Ubly U.S.A. 43°42N 82°55W **82 C2**
Ubolratna Res. Thailand 16°45N 102°30E **38 E4**
Ubombo S. Africa 27°31S 32°4E **57 C5**
Ubon Ratchathani
  Thailand 15°15N 104°50E **38 E5**
Ubort → Belarus 52°6N 28°30E **17 B15**
Ubud Indonesia 8°30S 115°16E **37 J18**
Ubundu
  Dem. Rep. of the Congo 0°22S 25°30E **54 E5**
Ucayali → Peru 4°30S 73°30W **92 D4**
Uchab Namibia 19°47S 17°42E **56 A2**
Uchiura-Wan Japan 42°25N 140°40E **28 C10**
Uchquduq Uzbekistan 41°50N 62°50E **26 E7**
Uchur → Russia 58°48N 130°35E **27 D14**
Ucluelet Canada 48°57N 125°32W **70 D3**
Uda → Russia 54°42N 135°14E **27 D14**
Uda Walawe △ Sri Lanka 6°20N 81°0E **45 L5**
Udachnyy Russia 66°25N 112°24E **27 C12**
Udagamandalam India 11°30N 76°44E **45 J3**
Udainagar India 22°33N 76°13E **42 H7**
Udaipur India 24°36N 73°44E **42 G5**
Udaipur Garhi Nepal 27°0N 86°35E **43 F12**
Udala India 21°35N 86°34E **43 J12**
Udayagiri Andhra Pradesh,
  India 14°52N 79°19E **45 G4**
Udayagiri Odisha, India 20°8N 84°23E **44 D7**
Uddevalla Sweden 58°21N 11°55E **9 G14**
Uddjaure Sweden 65°56N 17°49E **8 D17**
Udegeyskaya Legenda △
  Russia 45°45N 135°30E **28 B7**
Uden Neths. 51°40N 5°37E **15 C5**
Udgir India 18°25N 77°5E **44 E3**
Udhampur India 33°0N 75°5E **43 C6**
Údine Italy 46°3N 13°14E **22 A5**
Udintsev Fracture Zone
  S. Ocean 57°0S 145°0W **5 B13**
Udmurtia □ Russia 57°30N 52°30E **18 C9**
Udon Thani Thailand 17°29N 102°46E **38 D4**
Udong Cambodia 11°48N 104°45E **39 G5**
Udskaya Guba Russia 54°50N 135°45E **27 D14**
Udu Pt. Fiji 16°9S 179°57W **59 a**
Udumalaippettai India 10°35N 77°15E **45 J3**
Udupi India 13°25N 74°42E **45 H2**
Udva India 20°5N 73°0E **44 D1**
Udzungwa Range Tanzania 9°30S 35°10E **54 F7**
Ueda Japan 36°24N 138°16E **29 F9**
Uedineniya, Os. Russia 78°0N 85°0E **4 B12**
Uele →
  Dem. Rep. of the Congo 3°45N 24°45E **54 D4**
Uelen Russia 66°10N 170°0W **27 C19**
Uelzen Germany 52°57N 10°32E **16 B6**
Ufa Russia 54°45N 55°55E **18 D10**
Ufa → Russia 54°40N 56°0E **18 D10**
Ugab → Namibia 20°55S 13°30E **56 B1**
Ugalla → Tanzania 5°8S 30°42E **54 F6**
Uganda ■ Africa 2°0N 32°0E **54 D6**
Ugie S. Africa 31°10S 28°13E **57 D4**
Uglegorsk Russia 49°5N 142°2E **27 E15**
Ugljan Croatia 44°12N 15°10E **16 F8**
Ugolnye Kopi Russia 64°44N 177°42E **27 C18**
Uhlenhorst Namibia 23°45S 17°55E **56 C2**
Uhrichsville U.S.A. 40°24N 81°21W **82 F3**
Uibhist a Deas = South Uist
  U.K. 57°20N 7°15W **11 D1**
Uibhist a Tuath = North Uist
  U.K. 57°40N 7°15W **11 D1**
Uig U.K. 57°35N 6°21W **11 D2**
Uíge Angola 7°30S 14°40E **54 F2**
Uiha Tonga 19°54S 174°25W **59 c**
Uijeongbu S. Korea 37°44N 127°2E **33 F14**
Ŭiju N. Korea 40°15N 124°35E **33 D13**
Uinta Mts. U.S.A. 40°45N 110°30W **76 F8**
Uis Namibia 21°8S 14°49E **56 B1**
Uiseong S. Korea 36°21N 128°42E **33 F15**
Uitenhage S. Africa 33°40S 25°28E **56 D4**
Uithuizen Neths. 53°24N 6°41E **15 A6**
Ujh → India 32°10N 75°18E **42 C6**
Ujhani India 28°0N 79°6E **43 F8**
Uji-guntō Japan 31°15N 129°25E **29 J4**
Ujjain India 23°9N 75°43E **42 H6**
Ujung Kulon △
  Indonesia 6°46S 105°19E **37 G11**
Ujung Pandang = Makassar
  Indonesia 5°10S 119°20E **37 F5**
Uka Russia 57°50N 162°0E **27 D17**
Ukai Sagar India 21°20N 73°43E **44 D1**
Uke-Shima Japan 28°2N 129°14E **29 K4**
uKhahlamba Drakensberg △
  S. Africa 29°27S 29°30E **57 C4**

Ukhrul India 25°10N 94°25E **41 G19**
Ukhta Russia 63°34N 53°41E **18 B9**
Ukiah U.S.A. 39°9N 123°13W **78 F3**
Ukkusiksalik △ Canada 65°20N 89°30W **68 D14**
Ukmergė Lithuania 55°15N 24°45E **9 J21**
Ukraine ■ Europe 49°0N 32°0E **19 E5**
Ukwi Botswana 23°29S 20°30E **56 B3**
Ulaan Nuur Mongolia 44°30N 103°40E **32 B2**
Ulaan-Uul Mongolia 46°4N 100°49E **30 B9**
Ulaanbaatar Mongolia 47°55N 106°53E **30 B10**
Ulaangom Mongolia 50°5N 92°10E **30 A7**
Ulaanjirem Mongolia 45°5N 105°30E **32 B3**
Ulak I. U.S.A. 51°22N 178°57W **74 E4**
Ulan Bator = Ulaanbaatar
  Mongolia 47°55N 106°53E **30 B10**
Ulan Ude Russia 51°45N 107°40E **31 A10**
Ulanhad = Chifeng
  China 42°18N 118°58E **33 C10**
Ulanhot = Horqin Youyi Qianqi
  China 46°5N 122°3E **33 A12**
Ulansuhai Nur China 40°53N 108°51E **32 D5**
Ulcinj Montenegro 41°58N 19°10E **23 D8**
Ulco S. Africa 28°21S 24°15E **56 C3**
Ule älv = Oulujoki →
  Finland 65°1N 25°30E **8 D21**
Ule träsk = Oulujärvi
  Finland 64°25N 27°15E **8 D22**
Uleåborg = Oulu Finland 65°1N 25°29E **8 D21**
Ulefoss Norway 59°17N 9°16E **9 G13**
Ulhasnagar India 19°15N 73°10E **44 E1**
Uliastay Mongolia 47°56N 97°28E **30 B8**
Uljin S. Korea 36°59N 129°24E **33 F15**
Ulladulla Australia 35°21S 150°29E **63 F5**
Ullal India 12°48N 74°51E **45 H2**
Ullapool U.K. 57°54N 5°9W **11 D3**
Ulleungdo S. Korea 37°30N 130°30E **29 F5**
Ullswater Canada 45°12N 79°29W **82 A5**
Ullswater U.K. 54°34N 2°52W **12 C5**
Ulm Germany 48°23N 9°58E **16 D5**
Ulmarra Australia 29°37S 153°4E **63 D5**
Ulricehamn Sweden 57°46N 13°26E **9 H15**
Ulsan S. Korea 35°20N 129°15E **33 G15**
Ulsta U.K. 60°30N 1°9W **11 A7**
Ulster □ U.K. 54°35N 6°30W **10 B5**
Ulubat Gölü Turkey 40°9N 28°35E **23 D13**
Uludağ Turkey 40°4N 29°13E **23 D13**
Ulukhaktok Canada 70°44N 117°44W **68 C8**
Ulundi S. Africa 28°20S 31°25E **57 C5**
Ulungur He → China 47°1N 87°24E **30 B6**
Ulungur Hu China 47°20N 87°10E **30 B6**
Uluru Australia 25°23S 131°5E **61 E5**
Uluru-Kata Tjuta △
  Australia 25°19S 131°1E **61 E5**
Uluwatu Indonesia 8°50S 115°5E **37 K18**
Ulva U.K. 56°29N 6°13W **11 E2**
Ulverston U.K. 54°13N 3°5W **12 C4**
Ulverstone Australia 41°11S 146°11E **63 G4**
Ulya Russia 59°10N 142°0E **27 D15**
Ulyanovsk Russia 54°20N 48°25E **18 D8**
Ulyasutay = Uliastay
  Mongolia 47°56N 97°28E **30 B8**
Ulysses Kans., U.S.A. 37°35N 101°22W **80 G3**
Ulysses Pa., U.S.A. 41°54N 77°46W **82 E7**
Ulysses, Mt. Canada 57°20N 124°5W **70 B4**
Umala Bolivia 17°25S 68°5W **92 G5**
'Umān = Oman ■ Asia 23°0N 58°0E **49 C6**
Uman Ukraine 48°40N 30°12E **17 D16**
Umaria India 23°35N 80°50E **43 H9**
Umarkhed India 19°37N 77°46E **44 E3**
Umarkot Pakistan 25°15N 69°40E **42 G3**
Umarpada India 21°27N 73°30E **42 J5**
Umatilla U.S.A. 45°55N 119°21W **76 D4**
Umba Russia 66°42N 34°11E **18 A5**
Umbagog L. U.S.A. 44°46N 71°3W **83 B13**
Umbakumba Australia 13°47S 136°50E **62 A2**
Umbrella Mts. N.Z. 45°35S 169°5E **59 F2**
Umeå Sweden 63°45N 20°20E **8 E19**
Umeälven → Sweden 63°45N 20°20E **8 E19**
Umera Indonesia 0°12S 129°37E **37 E7**
Umgwenya → Mozam. 25°14S 32°18E **57 C5**
Umiujaq Canada 56°33N 76°33W **72 A4**
Umkomaas S. Africa 30°13S 30°48E **57 D5**
Umlazi S. Africa 29°59S 30°54E **55 L6**
Umm ad Daraj, J. Jordan 32°18N 35°48E **48 C4**
Umm al Qaywayn U.A.E. 25°30N 55°35E **47 E7**
Umm al Qittayn Jordan 32°18N 36°40E **48 C5**
Umm al Rasas 31°30N 35°55E **48 D5**
Umm Bāb Qatar 25°12N 50°48E **47 E6**
Umm Durman = Omdurmân
  Sudan 15°40N 32°28E **53 E12**
Umm el Fahm Israel 32°31N 35°9E **48 C4**
Umm el Ketef, Khalig
  Egypt 23°40N 35°35E **46 F2**
Umm Keddada Sudan 13°33N 26°35E **53 F11**
Umm Lajj Si. Arabia 25°0N 37°23E **46 E3**
Umm Qasr Iraq 30°1N 47°58E **46 D5**
Umm Ruwaba Sudan 12°50N 31°20E **53 F12**
Umm Sa'id Qatar 25°0N 51°33E **47 E6**
Umm Tais Qatar 26°7N 51°15E **47 E6**
Umnak I. U.S.A. 53°15N 168°20W **74 E6**
Umniati → Zimbabwe 16°49S 28°45E **55 H5**
Umpqua → U.S.A. 43°40N 124°12W **76 E1**
Umred India 20°51N 79°18E **44 D4**
Umreth India 22°41N 73°4E **42 H5**
Umtata = Mthatha
  S. Africa 31°36S 28°49E **57 D4**
Umuarama Brazil 23°45S 53°20W **95 A5**
Umvukwe Ra. Zimbabwe 16°45S 30°45E **55 H6**
Umzimvubu S. Africa 31°38S 29°33E **57 D4**
Umzinto = eMuziwezinto
  S. Africa 30°15S 30°45E **57 D5**
Una Brazil 20°46N 71°8E **42 J4**
Una → Bos.-H. 45°0N 16°20E **16 F9**
Unadilla U.S.A. 42°20N 75°19W **83 D9**
Unalakleet U.S.A. 63°52N 160°47W **74 C7**
Unalaska U.S.A. 53°53N 166°32W **74 E6**
Unalaska I. U.S.A. 53°35N 166°50W **74 E6**
'Unayzah Si. Arabia 26°6N 43°58E **46 E4**
'Unayzah, J. Asia 32°12N 39°18E **46 C3**

Uncía Bolivia 18°25S 66°40W **92 G5**
Uncompahgre Peak
  U.S.A. 38°4N 107°28W **76 G10**
Uncompahgre Plateau
  U.S.A. 38°20N 108°15W **76 G9**
Undara Volcanic △
  Australia 18°14S 144°41E **62 B3**
Underbool Australia 35°10S 141°51E **63 F3**
Underwood Canada 44°18N 81°29W **82 B3**
Ungarie Australia 33°38S 146°56E **63 E4**
Ungarra Australia 34°12S 136°2E **63 E2**
Ungava, Pén. d' Canada 60°0N 74°0W **69 F17**
Ungava B. Canada 59°30N 67°30W **69 F18**
Ungeny = Ungheni
  Moldova 47°11N 27°51E **17 E14**
Unggi = N. Korea 42°16N 130°28E **33 C16**
Ungheni Moldova 47°11N 27°51E **17 E14**
Unguja = Zanzibar
  Tanzania 6°12S 39°12E **54 F7**
União da Vitória Brazil 26°13S 51°5W **95 B5**
Unimak I. U.S.A. 54°45N 164°0W **74 E7**
Unimak Pass. U.S.A. 54°15N 164°30W **74 E7**
Union Miss., U.S.A. 32°34N 89°7W **85 E10**
Union Mo., U.S.A. 38°27N 91°0W **80 F8**
Union S.C., U.S.A. 34°43N 81°37W **85 D14**
Union City Calif., U.S.A. 37°36N 122°1W **78 H4**
Union City Pa., U.S.A. 41°54N 79°51W **82 E5**
Union City Tenn., U.S.A. 36°26N 89°3W **85 C10**
Union Dale U.S.A. 41°43N 75°29W **83 E9**
Union Gap U.S.A. 46°33N 120°28W **76 C3**
Union Springs Ala.,
  U.S.A. 32°9N 85°43W **85 E12**
Union Springs N.Y.,
  U.S.A. 42°50N 76°41W **83 D8**
Uniondale S. Africa 33°39S 23°7E **56 D3**
Uniontown U.S.A. 39°54N 79°44W **81 F14**
Unionville U.S.A. 40°29N 93°1W **80 E7**
United Arab Emirates ■
  Asia 23°50N 54°0E **47 F7**
United Kingdom ■ Europe 53°0N 2°0W **14 E6**
United States of America ■
  N. Amer. 37°0N 96°0W **75 H20**
Unity Canada 52°30N 109°5W **71 C7**
University Park U.S.A. 32°17N 106°45W **77 K10**
University Place U.S.A. 47°14N 122°33W **78 C4**
Unjha India 23°46N 72°24E **42 H5**
Unnao India 26°35N 80°30E **43 F9**
Unst U.K. 60°44N 0°53W **11 A8**
Unuk → Canada 56°5N 131°3W **70 B2**
Unzen-Amakusa △
  Japan 32°15N 130°10E **29 H5**
Uong Bi Vietnam 21°2N 106°47E **38 B6**
Uotsuri-Shima
  E. China Sea 25°45N 123°29E **29 M1**
Uozu Japan 36°48N 137°24E **29 F8**
Upata Venezuela 8°1N 62°24W **92 B6**
Upemba, L.
  Dem. Rep. of the Congo 8°30S 26°20E **54 F5**
Upernavik Greenland 72°49N 56°20W **69 B5**
Upington S. Africa 28°25S 21°15E **56 C3**
Upleta India 21°46N 70°16E **42 J4**
'Upolu Samoa 13°58S 172°0W **59 b**
Upper Alkali L. U.S.A. 41°47N 120°8W **76 F3**
Upper Arrow L. Canada 50°30N 117°50W **70 C5**
Upper Daly ۞ Australia 14°26S 131°3E **60 B5**
Upper Darby U.S.A. 39°55N 75°16W **81 F16**
Upper Foster L. Canada 56°47N 105°20W **71 B7**
Upper Hutt N.Z. 41°8S 175°5E **59 D5**
Upper Klamath L.
  U.S.A. 42°25N 121°55W **76 E3**
Upper Lake U.S.A. 39°10N 122°54W **78 F4**
Upper Liard Canada 60°3N 128°54W **70 A3**
Upper Manzanilla
  Trin. & Tob. 10°31N 61°4W **93 K15**
Upper Missouri Breaks △
  U.S.A. 47°50N 109°55W **76 C9**
Upper Musquodoboit
  Canada 45°10N 62°58W **73 C7**
Upper Red L. U.S.A. 48°8N 94°45W **80 A6**
Upper Sandusky U.S.A. 40°50N 83°17W **81 E12**
Upper Volta = Burkina Faso ■
  Africa 12°0N 1°0W **52 F5**
Uppland Sweden 59°59N 17°48E **9 G17**
Uppsala Sweden 59°53N 17°38E **9 G17**
Upshi India 33°48N 77°52E **43 C7**
Upton U.S.A. 44°6N 104°38W **76 D11**
Uqsuqtuuq = Gjoa Haven
  Canada 68°38N 95°53W **68 D12**
Ur Iraq 30°55N 46°25E **46 D5**
Urad Qianqi China 40°40N 108°30E **32 D5**
Uraga Japan 42°9N 142°47E **28 C11**
Urakawa Japan 42°9N 142°47E **28 C11**
Ural = Zhayyq →
  Kazakhstan 47°0N 51°48E **19 E9**
Ural Australia 33°21S 146°12E **63 E4**
Ural Mts. = Uralskie Gory
  Eurasia 60°0N 59°0E **18 C10**
Uralla Australia 30°37S 151°29E **63 E5**
Uralsk = Oral Kazakhstan 51°20N 51°20E **19 D9**
Uralskie Gory Eurasia 60°0N 59°0E **18 C10**
Uralskiy □ Russia 64°0N 70°0E **26 C7**
Urambo Tanzania 5°4S 32°0E **54 F6**
Urandangi Australia 21°32S 138°14E **62 C2**
Uranium City Canada 59°34N 108°37W **71 B7**
Urapuntja = Utopia
  Australia 22°14S 134°33E **62 C1**
Uraricoera → Brazil 3°2N 60°30W **92 C6**
Urasoe Japan 26°15N 127°43E **29 L3**
Uravakonda India 14°57N 77°12E **45 G3**
Urawa = Saitama □ Japan 35°54N 139°38E **29 G9**
Uray Russia 60°5N 65°15E **26 C7**
'Uray'irah Si. Arabia 25°57N 48°53E **47 E6**
Urbana Ill., U.S.A. 40°7N 88°12W **80 E9**
Urbana Ohio, U.S.A. 40°7N 83°45W **81 E12**
Urbandale U.S.A. 41°38N 93°43W **80 E7**
Urbino Italy 43°43N 12°38E **22 C5**
Urbión, Picos de Spain 42°1N 2°52W **21 A4**
Urcos Peru 13°40S 71°38W **92 F4**
Urdinarrain Argentina 32°37S 58°52W **94 C4**
Ure → U.K. 54°5N 1°20W **12 C6**

Urengoy Russia 65°58N 78°22E **26 C8**
Ures Mexico 29°26N 110°24W **86 B2**
Urewera △ N.Z. 38°29S 177°7E **59 C6**
Urfa = Şanlıurfa Turkey 37°12N 38°50E **46 B3**
Urganch Uzbekistan 41°40N 60°41E **26 E7**
Urgench = Urganch
  Uzbekistan 41°40N 60°41E **26 E7**
Ürgüp Turkey 38°38N 34°56E **46 B2**
Urho Kekkonen △
  Finland 68°20N 27°40E **8 B22**
Uri India 34°8N 74°2E **43 B6**
Uribia Colombia 11°43N 72°16W **92 A4**
Uriondo Bolivia 21°41S 64°41W **94 A3**
Urique Mexico 27°13N 107°55W **86 B3**
Urk Neths. 52°39N 5°36E **15 B5**
Urla Turkey 38°20N 26°47E **23 E12**
Urmia = Orūmīyeh Iran 37°40N 45°0E **46 B5**
Uroševac = Ferizaj
  Kosovo 42°23N 21°10E **23 C9**
Uroyan, Montanas de
  Puerto Rico 18°12N 66°50W **89 d**
Urrampinyi Iltjiltarri ۞
  Australia 24°20S 132°10E **60 D5**
Uruaçu Brazil 14°30S 49°10W **93 F9**
Uruapan Mexico 19°24N 102°3W **86 D4**
Urubamba → Peru 10°43S 73°48W **92 F4**
Urucará Brazil 2°32S 57°45W **92 D7**
Uruçuí Brazil 7°20S 44°28W **93 E10**
Uruguai → Brazil 26°0S 53°30W **95 B5**
Uruguaiana Brazil 29°50S 57°0W **94 B4**
Uruguay ■ S. Amer. 32°30S 56°30W **94 C4**
Uruguay → S. Amer. 34°12S 58°18W **94 C4**
Urumchi = Ürümqi China 43°45N 87°45E **30 C6**
Uruna ۞ Australia 24°3S 133°1E **60 D5**
Urup, Ostrov Russia 46°0N 151°0E **27 E16**
Ürzhar Kazakhstan 47°5N 81°38E **26 E9**
Ürziceni Romania 44°40N 26°15E **17 F14**
Usa → Russia 66°16N 59°49E **18 A10**
Uşak Turkey 38°43N 29°28E **19 G4**
Usakos Namibia 21°54S 15°31E **56 B2**
Usedom Germany 53°55N 14°2E **16 B8**
Useless Loop Australia 26°8S 113°23E **61 E1**
Ushakova, Ostrov Russia 82°0N 80°0E **27 A8**
Ushant = Ouessant, Î. d'
  France 48°28N 5°6W **20 B1**
Ushibuka Japan 32°11N 130°1E **29 H5**
Ushtöbe Kazakhstan 45°16N 78°0E **26 E8**
Ushuaia Argentina 54°50S 68°23W **96 G3**
Ushumun Russia 52°47N 126°32E **27 D13**
Usinsk Russia 66°0N 57°27E **18 A10**
Usk Canada 54°38N 128°26W **70 C3**
Usk → U.K. 51°33N 2°58W **13 F5**
Uska India 27°12N 83°7E **43 F10**
Usman Russia 52°5N 39°48E **18 D6**
Usolye-Sibirskoye
  Russia 52°48N 103°40E **27 D11**
Uspallata, P. de Argentina 32°37S 69°22W **94 C2**
Ussuriysk Russia 43°48N 131°59E **28 C5**
Ussurka Russia 45°12N 133°31E **28 B6**
Ust-Chaun Russia 68°47N 170°30E **27 C18**
Ust-Ilimsk Russia 58°3N 102°39E **27 D11**
Ust-Ishim Russia 57°45N 71°10E **26 D8**
Ust-Kamchatsk Russia 56°10N 162°28E **27 D17**
Ust-Kamenogorsk = Öskemen
  Kazakhstan 50°0N 82°36E **26 D9**
Ust-Khayryuzovo
  Russia 57°15N 156°45E **27 D16**
Ust-Kut Russia 56°50N 105°42E **27 D11**
Ust-Kuyga Russia 70°1N 135°43E **27 B14**
Ust-Maya Russia 60°30N 134°28E **27 C14**
Ust-Mil Russia 59°40N 133°11E **27 D14**
Ust-Nera Russia 64°35N 143°15E **27 C15**
Ust-Nyukzha Russia 56°34N 121°37E **27 D13**
Ust-Olenek Russia 73°0N 120°5E **27 B12**
Ust-Omchug Russia 61°9N 149°38E **27 C15**
Ust-Port Russia 69°40N 84°26E **26 C9**
Ust' Shchugor Russia 64°16N 57°36E **18 B10**
Ust-Tsilma Russia 65°28N 52°11E **18 A9**
Ust-Urt = Ustyurt Plateau
  Asia 44°0N 55°0E **26 E6**
Ust-Usa Russia 66°2N 56°57E **18 A10**
Ust-Vorkuta Russia 67°24N 64°0E **18 A11**
Ústí nad Labem Czechia 50°41N 14°3E **16 C8**
Ústica Italy 38°42N 13°11E **22 E5**
Ustinov = Izhevsk Russia 56°51N 53°14E **18 C9**
Ustyurt Plateau Asia 44°0N 55°0E **26 E6**
Usu China 44°27N 84°40E **30 C5**
Usuki Japan 33°8N 131°49E **29 H5**
Usulután El Salv. 13°25N 88°28W **88 D2**
Usumacinta → Mexico 18°24N 92°38W **87 D6**
Usumbura = Bujumbura
  Burundi 3°16S 29°18E **54 E5**
Usutuo → Mozam. 26°48S 32°7E **57 C5**
Uta Indonesia 4°33S 136°0E **37 E9**
Utah □ U.S.A. 39°20N 111°30W **76 G8**
Utah L. U.S.A. 40°12N 111°48W **76 F8**
Utara, Selat Malaysia 5°28N 100°20E **39 c**
Utarni India 26°5N 71°58E **42 F4**
Utatlan Guatemala 15°2N 91°11W **88 C1**
Ute Creek → U.S.A. 35°21N 103°50W **77 J12**
Utena Lithuania 55°27N 25°40E **9 J21**
Uthai Thani Thailand 15°22N 100°3E **38 E3**
Uthal Pakistan 25°44N 66°40E **42 G2**
Utiariti Brazil 13°0S 58°10W **92 F7**
Utica N.Y., U.S.A. 43°6N 75°14W **83 C9**
Utica Ohio, U.S.A. 40°14N 82°27W **82 F2**
Utikuma L. Canada 55°50N 115°30W **70 B5**
Utila Honduras 16°6N 86°56W **88 C2**
Utkela India 20°8N 83°22E **44 D6**
Utnur India 19°22N 78°46E **44 E4**
Utopia Australia 22°14S 134°33E **62 C1**
Utraula India 27°19N 82°25E **43 F10**
Utrecht Neths. 52°5N 5°8E **15 B5**
Utrecht S. Africa 27°38S 30°20E **57 C5**
Utrecht □ Neths. 52°6N 5°7E **15 B5**
Utrera Spain 37°12N 5°48W **21 D3**
Utsjoki Finland 69°51N 26°59E **8 B22**
Utsunomiya Japan 36°30N 139°50E **29 F9**
Uttar Pradesh □ India 27°0N 80°0E **43 F9**

Uttaradit Thailand 17°36N 100°5E **38 D3**
Uttarakhand □ India 30°0N 79°30E **43 D8**
Utterson Canada 45°12N 79°19W **82 A5**
Uttoxeter U.K. 52°54N 1°52W **12 E6**
Utuado Puerto Rico 18°16N 66°42W **89 d**
Uummannaq Qaasuitsup,
  Greenland 70°58N 52°17W **4 B5**
Uummannaq Qaasuitsup,
  Greenland 77°33N 68°52W **69 B18**
Uummannarsuaq = Nunap Isua
  Greenland 59°48N 43°55W **66 D15**
Uusikaarlepyy Finland 63°32N 22°31E **8 E20**
Uusikaupunki Finland 60°47N 21°25E **8 F19**
Uva Russia 56°59N 52°13E **18 C9**
Uvalde U.S.A. 29°13N 99°47W **84 G5**
Uvat Russia 59°5N 68°50E **26 D7**
Uvinza Tanzania 5°5S 30°24E **54 F6**
Uvira Dem. Rep. of the Congo 3°22S 29°3E **54 E5**
Uvs Nuur Mongolia 50°20N 92°30E **30 A7**
'Uwairidh, Ḥarrat al
  Si. Arabia 26°50N 38°0E **46 E3**
Uwajima Japan 33°10N 132°35E **29 H6**
Uweinat, Jebel Sudan 21°54N 24°58E **53 D10**
Uxbridge Canada 44°6N 79°7W **82 B5**
Uxin Qi China 38°50N 109°5E **32 E5**
Uxmal Mexico 20°22N 89°46W **87 C7**
Üydzin Mongolia 44°9N 107°0E **32 B4**
Uyo Nigeria 5°1N 7°53E **52 G7**
Uyūn Mûsa Egypt 29°53N 32°40E **48 F1**
Uyuni Bolivia 20°28S 66°47W **92 H5**
Uzbekistan ■ Asia 41°30N 65°0E **26 E7**
Uzboy → Turkmenistan 39°30N 55°0E **47 B7**
Uzen, Mal → Kazakhstan 49°4N 49°44E **19 E8**
Uzerche France 45°25N 1°34E **20 D4**
Uzh → Ukraine 51°15N 30°12E **17 C16**
Uzhgorod = Uzhhorod
  Ukraine 48°36N 22°18E **17 D12**
Uzhhorod Ukraine 48°36N 22°18E **17 D12**
Užice Serbia 43°55N 19°50E **23 C8**
Uzunköprü Turkey 41°16N 26°43E **23 D12**

V

Vaal → S. Africa 29°4S 23°38E **56 C3**
Vaal Dam S. Africa 27°0S 28°14E **57 C4**
Vaalwater S. Africa 24°15S 28°8E **57 B4**
Vaasa Finland 63°6N 21°38E **8 E19**
Vác Hungary 47°49N 19°10E **17 E10**
Vacaria Brazil 28°31S 50°52W **95 B5**
Vacaville U.S.A. 38°21N 121°59W **78 G5**
Vach → Russia 60°45N 76°45E **26 C8**
Vache, Î. à Haiti 18°2N 73°35W **89 C5**
Vacoas Mauritius 20°18S 57°29E **55 d**
Vada India 19°39N 73°8E **44 E1**
Vadakara India 11°35N 75°40E **45 J2**
Vadnagar India 23°47N 72°40E **42 H5**
Vadodara India 22°20N 73°10E **42 H5**
Vadsø Norway 70°3N 29°50E **8 A23**
Vaduj India 17°36N 74°27E **44 F2**
Vaduz Liech. 47°8N 9°31E **20 C8**
Vadvetjåkka △ Sweden 68°30N 18°28E **8 B18**
Værøy Norway 67°40N 12°40E **8 C15**
Vágar Færoe Is. 62°5N 7°15W **8 E9**
Vågsfjorden Norway 68°50N 16°50E **8 B17**
Váh → Slovakia 47°43N 18°7E **17 D9**
Vahsel B. Antarctica 75°0S 35°0W **5 D1**
Váhtjer = Gällivare
  Sweden 67°9N 20°40E **8 C19**
Vaiaku = Fongafale
  Tuvalu 8°31S 179°13E **58 B10**
Vaigai → India 9°15N 79°10E **45 K4**
Vaihiria, L. Tahiti 17°40S 149°25W **59 d**
Vaijapur India 19°58N 74°45E **44 E2**
Vaikam India 9°45N 76°24E **45 K3**
Vail U.S.A. 39°40N 106°20W **76 G10**
Vaippar → India 9°0N 78°25E **45 K4**
Vairao Tahiti 17°47S 149°17W **59 d**
Vaisali → India 26°28N 78°53E **43 F8**
Vaitogi Amer. Samoa 14°24S 170°44W **59 b**
Vajpur India 21°24N 73°17E **42 H5**
Vakarai Sri Lanka 8°8N 81°26E **45 K5**
Vakh → Russia 60°45N 76°45E **26 C8**
Val d'Or Canada 48°7N 77°47W **72 C4**
Val Marie Canada 49°15N 107°45W **71 D7**
Valaam Russia 61°22N 30°57E **8 F24**
Valahia Romania 44°35N 25°0E **17 F13**
Valaichenai Sri Lanka 7°54N 81°32E **45 K5**
Valandovo Macedonia 41°19N 22°34E **23 D10**
Valatie U.S.A. 42°24N 73°40W **83 D11**
Valcheta Argentina 40°40S 66°8W **96 E3**
Valdai Hills = Valdayskaya
  Vozvyshennost Russia 57°0N 33°30E **18 C5**
Valdayskaya Vozvyshennost
  Russia 57°0N 33°30E **18 C5**
Valdepeñas Spain 38°43N 3°25W **21 C4**
Valdés, Pen. Argentina 42°30S 63°45W **96 E4**
Valdez U.S.A. 61°7N 146°16W **68 E2**
Valdivia Chile 39°50S 73°14W **96 D2**
Valdivia Abyssal Plain
  S. Ocean 62°30S 70°0E **5 C6**
Valdosta U.S.A. 30°50N 83°17W **85 F13**
Valdres Norway 61°5N 9°5E **8 F13**
Vale U.S.A. 43°59N 117°15W **76 E5**
Vale of Glamorgan □
  U.K. 51°28N 3°25W **13 F4**
Valemount Canada 52°50N 119°15W **70 C5**
Valença Brazil 13°20S 39°5W **93 F11**
Valença do Piauí Brazil 6°20S 41°45W **93 E10**
Valence France 44°57N 4°54E **20 D6**
Valencia Spain 39°27N 0°23W **21 C5**
Valencia Trin. & Tob. 10°39N 61°11W **93 K15**
Valencia U.S.A. 34°48N 106°43W **77 J10**
Valencia Venezuela 10°11N 68°0W **92 A5**
Valencia □ Spain 39°20N 0°40W **21 C5**
Valencia, G. de Spain 39°30N 0°20E **21 C6**
Valencia de Alcántara
  Spain 39°25N 7°14W **21 C2**
Valencia I. Ireland 51°54N 10°22W **10 E1**
Valenciennes France 50°20N 3°34E **20 A5**
Valentim, Sa. do Brazil 6°0S 43°30W **93 E10**
Valentin Russia 43°8N 134°17E **28 C7**

Valentine Nebr., U.S.A. 42°52N 100°33W 80 D3
Valentine Tex., U.S.A. 30°35N 104°30W 84 F2
Valera Venezuela 9°19N 70°37W 92 B4
Valga Estonia 57°47N 26°2E 9 H22
Valier U.S.A. 48°18N 112°16W 76 B7
Valjevo Serbia 44°18N 19°53E 23 B8
Valkeakoski Finland 61°16N 24°2E 8 F21
Valkenswaard Neths. 51°21N 5°29E 15 C5
Vall de Uxó = La Vall d'Uixó
  Spain 39°49N 0°15W 21 C5
Valladolid Mexico 20°41N 88°12W 87 C7
Valladolid Spain 41°38N 4°43W 21 B3
Valle de la Pascua
  Venezuela 9°13N 66°0W 92 B5
Valle de las Palmas
  Mexico 32°20N 116°43W 79 N10
Valle de Santiago
  Mexico 20°23N 101°12W 86 C4
Valle de Zaragoza
  Mexico 27°25N 105°50W 86 B3
Valle Fértil, Sierra del
  Argentina 30°20S 68°0W 94 C2
Valle Hermoso Mexico 25°35N 97°40W 87 B5
Valle Nacional Mexico 17°47N 96°18W 87 D5
Valledupar Colombia 10°29N 73°15W 92 A4
Vallejo U.S.A. 38°7N 122°14W 78 G4
Vallenar Chile 28°30S 70°50W 94 B1
Valletta Malta 35°54N 14°31E 22 G6
Valley Center U.S.A. 33°13N 117°2W 79 M9
Valley City U.S.A. 46°55N 98°0W 80 B5
Valley Falls Oreg., U.S.A. 42°29N 120°17W 76 E3
Valley Falls R.I., U.S.A. 41°54N 71°24W 83 E13
Valley of Flowers △ India 30°50N 79°40E 43 D8
Valley Springs U.S.A. 38°12N 120°50W 78 G6
Valley View U.S.A. 40°39N 76°33W 83 F8
Valley Wells U.S.A. 35°27N 115°46W 79 K11
Valleyview Canada 55°5N 117°17W 70 B5
Vallimanca, Arroyo
  Argentina 35°40S 59°10W 94 D4
Valls Spain 41°18N 1°15E 21 B6
Valmiera Latvia 57°37N 25°29E 9 H21
Valognes France 49°30N 1°28W 20 B3
Valona = Vlorë Albania 40°32N 19°28E 23 D8
Valozhyn Belarus 54°3N 26°30E 17 A14
Valparai India 10°22N 76°58E 45 J3
Valparaíso Chile 33°2S 71°40W 94 C1
Valparaíso Mexico 22°46N 103°34W 86 C4
Valparaíso U.S.A. 41°28N 87°4W 80 E10
Valparaíso □ Chile 33°2S 71°40W 94 C1
Valpoy India 15°32N 74°8E 45 G2
Vals → S. Africa 27°23S 26°30E 56 C4
Vals, Tanjung Indonesia 8°26S 137°25E 37 F9
Valsad India 20°40N 72°58E 44 D1
Valverde del Camino
  Spain 37°35N 6°47W 21 D2
Vambori India 19°17N 74°44E 44 E2
Vammala = Sastamala
  Finland 61°20N 22°54E 8 F20
Vamsadhara → India 18°21N 84°8E 44 E7
Van Turkey 38°30N 43°20E 46 B4
Van, L. = Van Gölü Turkey 38°30N 43°0E 46 B4
Van Alstyne U.S.A. 33°25N 96°35W 84 E6
Van Blommestein Meer
  Suriname 4°45N 55°5W 93 C7
Van Buren Canada 47°10N 67°55W 73 C6
Van Buren Ark., U.S.A. 35°26N 94°21W 84 D7
Van Buren Maine,
  U.S.A. 47°10N 67°58W 81 B20
Van Buren Mo., U.S.A. 37°0N 91°1W 80 G8
Van Canh Vietnam 13°37N 109°0E 38 F7
Van Diemen, C. N. Terr.,
  Australia 11°9S 130°24E 60 B5
Van Diemen, C. Queens.,
  Australia 16°30S 139°46E 62 B2
Van Diemen G. Australia 11°45S 132°0E 60 B5
Van Gölü Turkey 38°30N 43°0E 46 B4
Van Horn U.S.A. 31°3N 104°50W 84 F2
Van Ninh Vietnam 12°42N 109°14E 38 F7
Van Rees, Pegunungan
  Indonesia 2°35S 138°15E 37 E9
Van Tivu India 8°51N 78°15E 45 K4
Van Wert U.S.A. 40°52N 84°35W 81 E11
Van Yen Vietnam 21°4N 104°42E 34 G5
Van Zylsrus S. Africa 26°52S 22°4E 56 C3
Vanadzor Armenia 40°48N 44°30E 19 F7
Vanavara Russia 60°22N 102°16E 27 C11
Vancouver Canada 49°15N 123°10W 78 A3
Vancouver U.S.A. 45°38N 122°40W 78 E4
Vancouver, C. Australia 35°2S 118°11E 61 G2
Vancouver I. Canada 49°50N 126°0W 78 B2
Vancouver Int. ✈ (YVR)
  Canada 49°10N 123°10W 78 A3
Vandalia Ill., U.S.A. 38°58N 89°6W 80 F9
Vandalia Mo., U.S.A. 39°19N 91°29W 80 F8
Vandavasi India 12°30N 79°30E 45 H4
Vandeloos B. Sri Lanka 8°0N 81°45E 45 L5
Vandenberg Village
  U.S.A. 34°43N 120°28W 79 L6
Vanderbijlpark S. Africa 26°42S 27°54E 57 D4
Vandergrift U.S.A. 40°36N 79°34W 82 F5
Vanderhoof Canada 54°0N 124°0W 70 C4
Vanderkloof Dam S. Africa 30°4S 24°40E 56 D3
Vanderlin I. Australia 15°44S 137°2E 62 B2
Vänern Sweden 58°47N 13°30E 9 G15
Vänersborg Sweden 58°26N 12°19E 9 G15
Vang Vieng Laos 18°58N 102°32E 38 C4
Vanganimtan Madag. 23°21S 47°36E 55 J9
Vanguard Canada 49°55N 107°20W 71 D7
Vanino Russia 48°50N 140°5E 27 E15
Vanivilasa Sagara India 13°45N 76°30E 45 H3
Vaniyambadi India 12°46N 78°44E 45 H4
Vankleek Hill Canada 45°32N 74°40W 83 A10
Vännäs Sweden 63°58N 19°48E 8 E18
Vannes France 47°40N 2°47W 20 C2
Vannøya Norway 70°6N 19°50E 8 A18
Vanrhynsdorp S. Africa 31°36S 18°44E 56 D2
Vansada India 20°47N 73°25E 44 D1
Vansbro Sweden 60°32N 14°15E 9 F16
Vansittart B. Australia 14°3S 126°17E 60 B4
Vansittart I. Canada 65°50N 84°0W 69 D15

Vanua Balavu Fiji 17°12S 178°55W 59 a
Vanua Levu Fiji 16°33S 179°15E 59 a
Vanua Vatu Fiji 18°22S 179°15W 59 a
Vanuatu ■ Pac. Oc. 15°0S 168°0E 58 C9
Vanwyksvlei S. Africa 30°18S 21°49E 56 D3
Vapi India 20°22N 72°54E 44 D1
Vapnyarka Ukraine 48°32N 28°45E 17 D15
Var → France 43°39N 7°12E 20 E7
Varada → India 15°0N 75°40E 45 G2
Varāmīn Iran 35°20N 51°39E 47 C6
Varāmīn Iran 35°18N 51°35E 47 B6
Varangerfjorden Norway 70°3N 29°25E 8 A23
Varangerhalvøya
  Norway 70°25N 29°30E 8 A23
Varaždin Croatia 46°20N 16°20E 16 E9
Varberg Sweden 57°6N 12°20E 9 H15
Vardak □ Afghan. 34°0N 68°0E 40 B6
Vardar = Axios →
  Greece 40°57N 22°35E 23 D10
Varde Denmark 55°38N 8°29E 9 J13
Vardø Norway 70°23N 31°5E 8 A24
Varella, Mui = Nay, Mui
  Vietnam 12°54N 109°26E 38 F7
Varėna Lithuania 54°12N 24°30E 9 J21
Varese Italy 45°48N 8°50E 20 D8
Varginha Brazil 21°33S 45°25W 95 A6
Varillas Chile 24°0S 70°10W 94 A1
Varkaus Finland 62°19N 27°50E 8 E22
Varna Bulgaria 43°13N 27°56E 23 C12
Varna → India 16°48N 74°32E 44 F2
Värnamo Sweden 57°10N 14°3E 9 H16
Värnjärga = Varangerhalvøya
  Norway 70°25N 29°30E 8 A23
Vars Canada 45°21N 75°21W 83 A9
Varysburg U.S.A. 42°46N 78°19W 82 D6
Varzaneh Iran 32°25N 52°40E 47 C7
Vasa = Vaasa Finland 63°6N 21°38E 8 E19
Vasa Barris → Brazil 11°10S 37°10W 93 F11
Vasai-Virar India 19°28N 72°48E 44 E1
Vascongadas = País Vasco □
  Spain 42°50N 2°45W 21 A4
Vasht = Khāsh Iran 28°15N 61°15E 47 D9
Vasilevichi Belarus 52°15N 29°50E 17 B16
Vasilkov = Vasylkiv
  Ukraine 50°7N 30°15E 17 C16
Vaslui Romania 46°38N 27°42E 17 E14
Vassar Canada 49°10N 95°55W 71 D9
Vassar U.S.A. 43°22N 83°35W 81 D12
Västerås Sweden 59°37N 16°38E 9 G17
Västerbotten Sweden 64°36N 20°4E 8 D19
Västerdalälven → Sweden 60°30N 15°7E 8 F16
Västervik Sweden 57°43N 16°33E 9 H17
Västmanland Sweden 59°45N 16°20E 9 G17
Vasto Italy 42°8N 14°40E 22 C6
Vasylkiv Ukraine 50°7N 30°15E 17 C16
Vat Phou Laos 14°51N 105°49E 38 E5
Vatersay U.K. 56°55N 7°32W 11 E1
Vatiu = Atiu Cook Is. 20°0S 158°10W 65 J12
Vatnajökull Iceland 64°30N 16°48W 8 D5
Vatnajökull △ Iceland 64°24N 16°48W 8 D5
Vatra-Dornei Romania 47°22N 25°22E 17 E13
Vatrak → India 23°9N 73°2E 42 H5
Vättern Sweden 58°25N 14°30E 9 G16
Vatu Vara Fiji 17°26S 179°31W 59 a
Vatulele Fiji 18°33S 177°37E 59 a
Vaudreuil-Dorion
  Canada 45°23N 74°3W 83 A10
Vaughn Mont., U.S.A. 47°33N 111°33W 76 C8
Vaughn N. Mex.,
  U.S.A. 34°36N 105°13W 77 J11
Vaujours L. Canada 55°27N 74°15W 72 A5
Vaupés = Uaupés →
  Brazil 0°2N 67°16W 92 C5
Vaupés □ Colombia 1°0N 71°0W 92 C4
Vauxhall Canada 50°5N 112°9W 70 C6
Vav India 24°22N 71°31E 42 G4
Vava'u Tonga 18°36S 174°0W 59 c
Vava'u Group Tonga 18°40S 174°0W 59 c
Vavuniya Sri Lanka 8°45N 80°50E 45 K5
Vawkavysk Belarus 53°9N 24°30E 17 B13
Vaxjö Sweden 56°52N 14°50E 9 H16
Vayalpad India 13°39N 78°38E 45 H4
Vaygach, Ostrov Russia 70°0N 60°0E 26 C7
Veaikevárri = Svappavaara
  Sweden 67°40N 21°3E 8 C19
Vechte → Neths. 52°34N 6°6E 15 B6
Vedaranniyam India 10°25N 79°50E 45 J4
Vedea → Romania 43°42N 25°41E 17 G13
Vedia Argentina 34°30S 61°31W 94 C3
Veendam Neths. 53°5N 6°52E 15 A6
Veenendaal Neths. 52°2N 5°34E 15 B5
Vefsna → Norway 65°48N 13°10E 8 D15
Vega Norway 65°40N 11°55E 8 D14
Vega U.S.A. 35°15N 102°26W 84 D3
Vega Baja Puerto Rico 18°27N 66°23W 89 d
Vegreville Canada 53°30N 112°5W 70 C6
Vejer de la Frontera Spain 36°15N 5°59W 21 D3
Vejle Denmark 55°43N 9°30E 9 J13
Velachha India 21°26N 73°1E 44 D1
Velanai I. Sri Lanka 9°45N 79°45E 45 K4
Velas, C. Costa Rica 10°21N 85°52W 88 D2
Velasco, Sierra de
  Argentina 29°20S 67°10W 94 B2
Velddrif S. Africa 32°42S 18°11E 56 D2
Velebit Planina Croatia 44°50N 15°20E 16 F8
Veles Macedonia 41°46N 21°47E 23 D9
Vélez-Málaga Spain 36°48N 4°5W 21 D3
Vélez Rubio Spain 37°41N 2°5W 21 D4
Velhas → Brazil 17°13S 44°49W 93 G10
Velika Kapela Croatia 45°10N 15°5E 16 F8
Velikaya → Russia 57°48N 28°10E 18 C4
Velikaya Kema Russia 45°30N 137°12E 28 B8
Veliki Ustyug Russia 60°47N 46°20E 18 B8
Velikiy Novgorod Russia 58°30N 31°25E 18 C5
Velikiye Luki Russia 56°25N 30°32E 18 C5
Veliko Tarnovo Bulgaria 43°5N 25°41E 23 C11
Velikonda Range India 14°45N 79°10E 45 G4
Vellar → India 11°30N 79°36E 45 J4
Velletri Italy 41°41N 12°47E 22 D5
Vellore India 12°57N 79°10E 45 H4

Velsk Russia 61°10N 42°0E 18 B7
Veluwezoom △ Neths. 52°5N 6°0E 15 B6
Velva U.S.A. 48°4N 100°56W 80 A3
Venado Mexico 22°56N 101°6W 86 C4
Venado Tuerto Argentina 33°50S 62°0W 94 C3
Vendée □ France 46°50N 1°35W 20 C3
Vendôme France 47°47N 1°3E 20 C4
Venézia Italy 45°27N 12°21E 22 B5
Venézia, G. di Italy 45°15N 13°0E 22 B5
Venezuela ■ S. Amer. 8°0N 66°0W 92 B5
Venezuela, G. de
  Venezuela 11°30N 71°0W 92 A4
Vengurla India 15°53N 73°45E 45 G1
Vengurla Rocks India 15°55N 73°22E 45 G1
Venice = Venézia Italy 45°27N 12°21E 22 B5
Venice U.S.A. 27°6N 82°27W 85 H13
Venkatagiri India 14°0N 79°35E 45 G4
Venkatapuram India 18°20N 80°30E 44 E5
Venlo Neths. 51°22N 6°11E 15 C6
Vennachar Junction
  Canada 45°5N 77°14W 82 A7
Vennesla Norway 58°15N 7°59E 9 G12
Venray Neths. 51°31N 6°0E 15 C6
Ventana, Sa. de la
  Argentina 38°0S 62°30W 94 D3
Ventersburg S. Africa 28°7S 27°9E 56 C4
Ventersdorp S. Africa 30°47S 25°48E 56 D4
Ventnor U.K. 50°36N 1°12W 13 G6
Ventotène Italy 40°47N 13°25E 22 D5
Ventoux, Mt. France 44°10N 5°17E 20 D6
Ventspils Latvia 57°25N 21°32E 9 H19
Ventuarí → Venezuela 3°58N 67°2W 92 C5
Ventucopa U.S.A. 34°50N 119°29W 79 L7
Ventura U.S.A. 34°17N 119°18W 79 L7
Vénus, Pte. Tahiti 17°29S 149°29W 59 d
Venus B. Australia 38°40S 145°42E 63 F4
Venustiano Carranza
  Mexico 30°25N 115°53W 86 A1
Venustiano Carranza, Presa
  Mexico 27°30N 100°37W 86 B4
Vera Argentina 29°30S 60°20W 94 B3
Vera Spain 37°15N 1°51W 21 D5
Veracruz Mexico 19°11N 96°8W 87 D5
Veracruz □ Mexico 19°0N 96°15W 87 D5
Veraval India 20°53N 70°27E 42 J4
Verbánia Italy 45°56N 8°33E 20 D8
Vercelli Italy 45°19N 8°25E 20 D8
Verdalsøra Norway 63°48N 11°30E 8 E14
Verde → Argentina 41°56S 65°5W 96 E3
Verde → Goiás, Brazil 18°1S 50°14W 93 G8
Verde → Mato Grosso do Sul,
  Brazil 21°25S 52°20W 93 H8
Verde → Chihuahua,
  Mexico 26°39N 107°11W 86 B3
Verde → Jalisco, Mexico 20°42N 103°14W 86 C4
Verde → Oaxaca, Mexico 15°59N 97°50W 87 D5
Verde → Paraguay 23°9S 57°37W 94 A4
Verde → U.S.A. 33°33N 111°40W 77 K8
Verde, Cay Bahamas 23°0N 75°5W 88 B4
Verden Germany 52°55N 9°14E 16 B5
Verdi U.S.A. 39°31N 119°59W 78 F7
Verdun France 49°9N 5°24E 20 B6
Vereeniging S. Africa 26°38S 27°57E 57 C4
Verga, C. Guinea 10°30N 14°10W 52 F3
Vergara Uruguay 32°56S 53°57W 95 C5
Vergemont Cr. →
  Australia 24°16S 143°16E 62 C3
Vergennes U.S.A. 44°10N 73°15W 83 B11
Veria Greece 40°34N 22°12E 23 D10
Verín Spain 41°57N 7°27W 21 B2
Verkhnetulomskoye Vdkhr.
  Russia 68°36N 31°12E 8 B24
Verkhnevilyuysk
  Russia 63°27N 120°18E 27 C13
Verkhniy Baskunchak
  Russia 48°14N 46°44E 19 E8
Verkhoyansk Russia 67°35N 133°25E 27 C14
Verkhoyansk Ra. =
  Verkhoyanskiy Khrebet
  Russia 66°0N 129°0E 27 C13
Verkhoyanskiy Khrebet
  Russia 66°0N 129°0E 27 C13
Vermilion Canada 53°20N 110°50W 71 C6
Vermilion U.S.A. 41°25N 82°22W 82 E2
Vermilion → Canada 53°22N 110°51W 71 C6
Vermilion B. U.S.A. 29°42N 92°0W 84 G9
Vermilion Bay Canada 49°51N 93°34W 71 D10
Vermilion Cliffs Nat. Monument △
  U.S.A. 36°54N 112°5W 77 H8
Vermilion L. U.S.A. 47°53N 92°26W 80 B7
Vermillion U.S.A. 42°47N 96°56W 80 D5
Vermillion → Canada 38°38N 72°56W 72 C5
Vermont □ U.S.A. 44°0N 73°0W 83 C12
Vernadsky Antarctica 65°0S 64°0W 5 C17
Verne → U.S.A. 30°27N 109°32W 76 F9
Vernalis U.S.A. 37°36N 121°17W 78 H5
Verner Canada 46°25N 80°8W 72 C3
Verneukpan S. Africa 30°0S 21°0E 56 E3
Vernon Canada 50°20N 119°15W 70 C5
Vernon U.S.A. 34°9N 99°17W 84 D5
Vernonia U.S.A. 45°52N 123°11W 78 E3
Vero Beach U.S.A. 27°38N 80°24W 85 H14
Verona Italy 44°29N 76°42W 83 B8
Verona Italy 45°27N 10°59E 22 B4
Vert, C. Senegal 14°45N 17°30W 52 F2
Verulam S. Africa 29°38S 31°2E 57 C5
Verviers Belgium 50°37N 5°52E 15 D5
Veselovskoye Vdkhr.
  Russia 46°58N 41°25E 19 E7
Vesoul France 47°40N 6°11E 20 C7
Vesterålen Norway 68°45N 15°0E 8 B16
Vestfjorden Norway 67°55N 14°0E 8 C15
Vestmannaeyjar Iceland 63°27N 20°15W 8 E3
Vestspitsbergen Svalbard 78°40N 17°0E 4 B8
Vestvågøy Norway 68°18N 13°50E 8 B15
Vesuvio Italy 40°49N 14°26E 22 D6
Vesuvius, Mt. = Vesuvio
  Italy 40°49N 14°26E 22 D6

Veszprém Hungary 47°8N 17°57E 17 E9
Vetapalem India 15°47N 80°18E 45 G5
Vetlanda Sweden 57°24N 15°3E 9 H16
Vetlugu → Russia 56°36N 46°4E 18 C8
Vettore, Mte. Italy 42°49N 13°16E 22 C5
Veurne Belgium 51°5N 2°40E 15 C2
Veys Iran 31°30N 49°0E 47 D6
Vezhen Bulgaria 42°50N 24°20E 23 C11
Vi Thanh Vietnam 9°42N 105°26E 39 H5
Viacha Bolivia 16°39S 68°18W 92 G5
Viamão Brazil 30°5S 51°0W 95 C5
Viana Brazil 3°13S 44°55W 93 D10
Viana do Alentejo
  Portugal 38°17N 7°59W 21 C2
Viana do Castelo Portugal 41°42N 8°50W 21 B1
Vianópolis Brazil 16°40S 48°35W 93 G9
Viaréggio Italy 43°52N 10°14E 22 C4
Vibo Valéntia Italy 38°40N 16°6E 22 E7
Viborg Denmark 56°27N 9°23E 9 H13
Vic Spain 41°58N 2°19E 21 B7
Vicenza Italy 45°33N 11°33E 22 B4
Vich = Vic Spain 41°58N 2°19E 21 B7
Vichada → Colombia 4°55N 67°50W 92 C5
Vichy France 46°9N 3°26E 20 C5
Vicksburg Ariz.,
  U.S.A. 33°45N 113°45W 79 M13
Vicksburg Miss., U.S.A. 32°21N 90°53W 85 E9
Victor India 21°0N 71°30E 42 J4
Victor Harbor Australia 35°30S 138°37E 63 F2
Victoria Argentina 32°40S 60°10W 94 C3
Victoria Canada 48°30N 123°25W 78 B3
Victoria Chile 38°13S 72°20W 96 D2
Victoria Seychelles 4°38S 55°28E 55 b
Victoria Kans., U.S.A. 38°52N 99°9W 80 F4
Victoria Tex., U.S.A. 28°48N 97°0W 84 G6
Victoria → Australia 37°0S 144°0E 63 F3
Victoria → Australia 15°10S 129°40E 60 C4
Victoria, Grand L.
  Canada 47°31N 77°30W 72 C4
Victoria, L. Africa 1°0S 33°0E 54 E6
Victoria, L. Australia 33°57S 141°15E 63 E3
Victoria, Mt. Myanmar 21°14N 93°55E 41 J18
Victoria Beach Canada 50°40N 96°35W 71 C9
Victoria de Durango = Durango
  Mexico 24°3N 104°39W 86 C4
Victoria de las Tunas = Las Tunas
  Cuba 20°58N 76°59W 88 B4
Victoria Falls Zimbabwe 17°58S 25°52E 55 H5
Victoria Harbour Canada 44°45N 79°45W 82 B5
Victoria I. Canada 71°0N 111°0W 68 C9
Victoria L. Canada 48°20N 57°27W 73 C8
Victoria Ld. Antarctica 75°0S 160°0E 5 D11
Victoria Pk. Belize 16°48N 88°37W 87 D7
Victoria River Australia 16°25S 131°0E 60 C5
Victoria Str. Canada 69°31N 100°30W 68 D11
Victoria West S. Africa 31°25S 23°4E 56 D3
Victoriaville Canada 46°4N 71°56W 73 C5
Victorica Argentina 36°20S 65°30W 94 D2
Victorville U.S.A. 34°32N 117°18W 79 L9
Vicuña Chile 30°0S 70°50W 94 C1
Vicuña Mackenna
  Argentina 33°53S 64°25W 94 C3
Vidal U.S.A. 34°7N 114°31W 79 L12
Vidalia U.S.A. 32°13N 82°25W 85 E13
Viddolatno = Vindelälven →
  Sweden 63°55N 19°50E 8 E18
Vidisha India 23°28N 77°53E 42 H7
Vidzy Belarus 55°23N 26°37E 9 J22
Viedma Argentina 40°50S 63°0W 96 E4
Viedma, L. Argentina 49°30S 72°30W 96 F2
Vielsalm Belgium 50°17N 5°54E 15 D5
Vieng Pou Kha Laos 20°41N 101°4E 34 G3
Vienna Canada 42°41N 80°48W 82 D4
Vienna Ill., U.S.A. 37°25N 88°54W 80 G9
Vienna Mo., U.S.A. 38°11N 91°57W 80 F8
Vienne France 45°31N 4°53E 20 D6
Vienne → France 47°13N 0°5E 20 C4
Vientiane Laos 17°58N 102°36E 38 D4
Vientos, Paso de los
  Caribbean 20°0N 74°0W 89 C5
Vieques Puerto Rico 18°8N 65°25W 89 d
Vierge Pt. St. Lucia 13°49N 60°53W 89 f
Vierzon France 47°13N 2°5E 20 C5
Viet Quang Vietnam 22°30N 104°48E 34 F5
Viet Tri Vietnam 21°18N 105°25E 38 B5
Vietnam ■ Asia 19°0N 106°0E 38 C5
Vieux Fort St. Lucia 13°46N 60°58W 89 f
Vigan Phil. 17°35N 120°28E 37 A6
Vigévano Italy 45°19N 8°51E 20 D8
Vigia Brazil 0°50S 48°5W 93 D9
Vigo Spain 42°12N 8°41W 21 A1
Vihowa Pakistan 31°8N 70°30E 42 D4
Vihowa → Pakistan 31°8N 70°41E 42 D4
Vijayadurg India 16°30N 73°25E 44 F1
Vijayapura India 16°50N 75°55E 44 F2
Vijayawada India 16°31N 80°39E 44 F5
Vijosë → Albania 40°37N 19°24E 23 D8
Vík Iceland 63°25N 19°1W 8 E4
Vikarabad India 17°20N 77°54E 44 E3
Vikeke = Viqueque
  Timor-Leste 8°52S 126°23E 37 F7
Viking Canada 53°7N 111°50W 70 C6
Vikna Norway 64°55N 10°58E 8 D14
Vila Bela da Santíssima Trindade
  Brazil 15°0S 59°57W 92 G7
Vila da Ribeira Brava
  Cabo Verde 16°32N 24°25W 52 b
Vila do Bispo Portugal 37°5N 8°53W 21 D1
Vila do Maio Cabo Verde 15°21N 23°10W 52 b
Vila Franca de Xira
  Portugal 38°57N 8°59W 21 C1
Vila Gomes da Costa
  Mozam. 24°20S 33°37E 57 C5
Vila Nova de Gaia Portugal 41°8N 8°37W 21 B1
Vila Real Portugal 41°17N 7°48W 21 B2
Vila-Real Spain 39°55N 0°3W 21 C5

Vila Real de Santo António
  Portugal 37°10N 7°28W 21 D2
Vila Velha Brazil 20°20S 40°17W 95 A7
Vilagarcía de Arousa
  Spain 42°34N 8°46W 21 A1
Vilaine → France 47°30N 2°27W 20 C2
Vilanandro, Tanjona
  Madag. 16°11S 44°27E 55 H8
Vilanculos Mozam. 22°1S 35°17E 57 B6
Vilanova i la Geltrú Spain 41°13N 1°40E 21 B6
Vilcheka, Ostrov Russia 80°0N 58°31E 26 B6
Vilcheka, Zemlya Russia 80°30N 60°30E 4 A11
Vileyka Belarus 54°30N 26°53E 17 A14
Vilhelmina Sweden 64°35N 16°39E 8 D17
Vilhena Brazil 12°40S 60°5W 92 F6
Viliya = Neris → Lithuania 55°8N 24°16E 9 J21
Viljandi Estonia 58°28N 25°30E 9 G21
Vilkitskogo, Proliv
  Russia 78°0N 103°0E 27 B11
Vilkovo = Vylkove
  Ukraine 45°28N 29°32E 17 F15
Villa Abecia Bolivia 21°0S 68°18W 94 A2
Villa Ana Argentina 28°28S 59°40W 94 B4
Villa Ángela Argentina 27°34S 60°45W 94 B3
Villa Bella Bolivia 10°25S 65°22W 92 F5
Villa Cañás Argentina 34°0S 61°35W 94 C3
Villa Constitución
  Argentina 33°15S 60°20W 94 C3
Villa de Arriaga Mexico 21°56N 101°20W 86 C4
Villa de María Argentina 29°55S 63°43W 94 B3
Villa de Méndez Mexico 25°7N 98°34W 87 B5
Villa Dolores Argentina 31°58S 65°15W 94 C2
Villa Gesell Argentina 37°0S 56°55W 94 D4
Villa Guillermina
  Argentina 28°15S 59°29W 94 B4
Villa Hayes Paraguay 25°5S 57°20W 94 B4
Villa Hidalgo Mexico 24°15N 99°26W 87 C5
Villa Iris Argentina 38°12S 63°12W 94 D3
Villa Las Estrellas = Frei
  Antarctica 62°30S 58°0W 5 C18
Villa María Argentina 32°20S 63°10W 94 C3
Villa Mazán Argentina 28°40S 66°30W 94 B2
Villa Montes Bolivia 21°10S 63°30W 94 A3
Villa Ocampo Argentina 28°30S 59°20W 94 B4
Villa Ocampo Mexico 26°27N 105°31W 86 B3
Villa Ojo de Agua
  Argentina 29°30S 63°44W 94 B3
Villa San Martín
  Argentina 28°15S 64°9W 94 B3
Villa Unión Mexico 23°12N 106°14W 86 C3
Villacarrillo Spain 38°7N 3°3W 21 C4
Villach Austria 46°37N 13°51E 16 E7
Villagrán Mexico 24°29N 99°29W 87 C5
Villaguay Argentina 32°0S 59°0W 94 C4
Villahermosa Mexico 17°59N 92°55W 87 D6
Villajoyosa Spain 38°30N 0°12W 21 C5
Villalba Spain 43°26N 7°40W 21 A2
Villanueva U.S.A. 35°16N 105°22W 77 J11
Villanueva de la Serena
  Spain 38°59N 5°50W 21 C3
Villanueva y Geltrú = Vilanova i la
  Geltrú Spain 41°13N 1°40E 21 B6
Villarreal = Vila-Real
  Spain 39°55N 0°3W 21 C5
Villarrica Chile 39°15S 72°15W 96 D2
Villarrica Paraguay 25°40S 56°30W 94 B4
Villarrobledo Spain 39°18N 2°36W 21 C4
Villavicencio Argentina 32°28S 69°0W 94 C2
Villavicencio Colombia 4°9N 73°37W 92 C4
Villaviciosa Spain 43°32N 5°27W 21 A3
Villazón Bolivia 22°0S 65°35W 94 A2
Ville-Marie Canada 47°20N 79°30W 72 C4
Ville Platte U.S.A. 30°41N 92°17W 84 F8
Villena Spain 38°39N 0°52W 21 C5
Villeneuve-d'Ascq France 50°38N 3°9E 20 A5
Villeneuve-sur-Lot France 44°24N 0°42E 20 D4
Villiers S. Africa 27°2S 28°36E 57 C4
Villingen-Schwenningen
  Germany 48°3N 8°26E 16 D5
Villmanstrand = Lappeenranta
  Finland 61°3N 28°12E 8 F23
Villupuram India 11°59N 79°31E 45 J4
Vilna Canada 54°7N 111°55W 70 C6
Vilnius Lithuania 54°38N 25°19E 9 J21
Vilyuchinsk Russia 52°55N 158°24E 27 D16
Vilyuy → Russia 64°24N 126°26E 27 C13
Vilyuysk Russia 63°40N 121°35E 27 C13
Vilyuyskoye Vdkhr.
  Russia 63°0N 112°0E 27 C12
Viña del Mar Chile 33°0S 71°30W 94 C1
Vinarós Spain 40°30N 0°27E 21 B6
Vincennes U.S.A. 38°41N 87°32W 80 F10
Vincennes Bay S. Ocean 66°0S 109°0E 5 C8
Vincent U.S.A. 34°33N 118°11W 79 L8
Vinchina Argentina 28°45S 68°15W 94 B2
Vindelälven → Sweden 63°55N 19°50E 8 E18
Vindeln Sweden 64°12N 19°43E 8 D18
Vindhya Ra. India 22°50N 77°0E 42 H7
Vineland U.S.A. 39°29N 75°2W 81 F16
Vinh Vietnam 18°45N 105°38E 38 C5
Vinh Long Vietnam 10°16N 105°57E 39 G5
Vinh Moc Vietnam 17°4N 107°2E 38 D6
Vinh Yen Vietnam 21°21N 105°35E 38 B5
Vinita U.S.A. 36°39N 95°9W 84 C7
Vinkovci Croatia 45°19N 18°48E 23 B8
Vinnitsa = Vinnytsya
  Ukraine 49°15N 28°30E 17 D15
Vinnytsya Ukraine 49°15N 28°30E 17 D15
Vinnytsya □ Ukraine 49°20N 28°15E 17 D15
Vinson Massif Antarctica 78°35S 85°25W 5 D16
Vinton Calif., U.S.A. 39°48N 120°10W 78 F6
Vinton Iowa, U.S.A. 42°10N 92°1W 80 D7
Vinton La., U.S.A. 30°11N 93°35W 84 F8
Vinukonda India 16°4N 79°45E 45 F4
Violet Valley ۞ Australia 17°10S 127°55E 60 C4
Vioolsdrif S. Africa 28°46S 17°59E 56 D2
Viqueque Timor-Leste 8°52S 126°23E 37 F7
Virac Phil. 13°30N 124°20E 37 B6
Virachey Cambodia 13°59N 106°49E 38 E6
Virachey △ Cambodia 14°14N 106°55E 38 E6
Virago Sd. Canada 54°0N 132°30W 70 C2

Virajpet = Virarajendrapet
  India 12°10N 75°50E **45** H2
Viramgam India 23°5N 72°0E **42** H5
Virananşehir Turkey 37°13N 39°45E **46** B3
Virarajendrapet India 12°10N 75°50E **45** H2
Virawah Pakistan 24°31N 70°46E **42** G4
Virden Canada 49°50N 100°56W **71** D8
Vire France 48°50N 0°53W **20** B3
Vírgenes, C. Argentina 52°19S 68°21W **96** G3
Virgin → U.S.A. 36°28N 114°21W **77** H6
Virgin Gorda Br. Virgin Is. 18°30N 64°26W **89** e
Virgin Is. (British) ☑
  W. Indies 18°30N 64°30W **89** e
Virgin Is. (U.S.) ☑ W. Indies 18°20N 65°0W **89** e
Virgin Islands △
  U.S. Virgin Is. 18°21N 64°43W **89** C7
Virginia S. Africa 28°8S 26°55E **56** C4
Virginia U.S.A. 47°31N 92°32W **80** B7
Virginia □ U.S.A. 37°30N 78°45W **81** G14
Virginia Beach U.S.A. 36°49N 76°9W **81** F16
Virginia City Mont.,
  U.S.A. 45°18N 111°56W **76** D8
Virginia City Nev.,
  U.S.A. 39°19N 119°39W **78** F7
Virginia Falls Canada 61°38N 125°42W **70** A3
Virginiatown Canada 48°9N 79°36W **72** C4
Viroqua U.S.A. 43°34N 90°53W **80** D8
Virovitica Croatia 45°51N 17°21E **22** B7
Virpur India 21°51N 70°42E **42** J4
Virton Belgium 49°35N 5°32E **15** E5
Virudhunagar India 9°30N 77°58E **45** K3
Vis Croatia 43°4N 16°10E **22** C7
Visalia U.S.A. 36°20N 119°18W **78** J7
Visayan Sea Phil. 11°30N 123°30E **37** B6
Visby Sweden 57°37N 18°18E **9** H18
Viscount Melville Sd.
  Canada 74°10N 108°0W **69** C10
Visé Belgium 50°44N 5°41E **15** D5
Vise, Ostrov Russia 79°33N 76°50E **26** B8
Višegrad Bos.-H. 43°47N 19°17E **23** C8
Viseu Brazil 1°10S 46°5W **93** D9
Viseu Portugal 40°40N 7°55W **21** B2
Vishakhapatnam India 17°45N 83°20E **44** L13
Visnagar India 23°45N 72°32E **42** H5
Viso, Mte. Italy 44°38N 7°5E **20** D7
Visokoi I. Antarctica 56°43S 27°15W **5** B1
Vista U.S.A. 33°12N 117°14W **79** M9
Vistula = Wisła →
  Poland 54°22N 18°55E **17** A10
Vita India 17°17N 74°33E **44** F2
Vitebsk = Vitsyebsk
  Belarus 55°10N 30°15E **18** C5
Viterbo Italy 42°25N 12°6E **22** C5
Viti Levu Fiji 17°30S 177°30E **59** a
Vitigudino Spain 41°1N 6°26W **21** B2
Vitim Russia 59°28N 112°35E **27** D12
Vitim → Russia 59°26N 112°34E **27** D12
Vitória Brazil 20°20S 40°22W **93** H10
Vitória da Conquista
  Brazil 14°51S 40°51W **93** F10
Vitória de Santo Antão
  Brazil 8°10S 35°20W **93** E11
Vitoria-Gasteiz Spain 42°50N 2°41W **21** A4
Vitsyebsk Belarus 55°10N 30°15E **18** C5
Vittória Italy 36°57N 14°32E **22** F6
Vittório Véneto Italy 45°59N 12°18E **22** B5
Viveiro Spain 43°39N 7°38W **21** A2
Vivian U.S.A. 32°53N 93°59W **84** E8
Viwa Fiji 17°10S 177°58E **59** a
Vizcaíno, Desierto de
  Mexico 27°30N 113°45W **86** B2
Vizcaíno, Sierra Mexico 27°30N 114°0W **86** B2
Vize Turkey 41°34N 27°45E **23** D12
Vizianagaram India 18°6N 83°30E **44** E6
Vlaardingen Neths. 51°55N 4°21E **15** C4
Vladikavkaz Russia 43°0N 44°35E **19** F7
Vladimir Russia 56°15N 40°30E **18** C6
Vladimir Volynskiy = Volodymyr-
  Volynskyy Ukraine 50°50N 24°18E **17** C13
Vladivostok Russia 43°10N 131°53E **28** C5
Vlieland Neths. 53°16N 4°55E **15** A4
Vlissingen Neths. 51°26N 3°34E **15** C3
Vlorë Albania 40°32N 19°28E **23** D8
Vltava → Czechia 50°21N 14°30E **16** D8
Vo Dat Vietnam 11°9N 107°31E **39** G6
Vodlozersky △ Russia 62°40N 37°5E **26** C1
Voe U.K. 60°21N 1°16W **11** A7
Vogelkop = Doberai, Jazirah
  Indonesia 1°25S 133°0E **37** E8
Vogelsberg Germany 50°31N 9°12E **16** C5
Voghera Italy 44°59N 9°1E **20** D8
Vohibinany Madag. 18°49S 49°4E **55** H9
Vohimarina = Iharana
  Madag. 13°25S 50°0E **55** G10
Vohimena, Tanjon' i
  Madag. 25°36S 45°8E **55** K9
Vohipeno Madag. 22°22S 47°51E **55** J9
Voi Kenya 3°25S 38°32E **54** E7
Voiron France 45°22N 5°35E **20** D6
Voisey B. Canada 56°15N 61°50W **73** A7
Vojmsjön Sweden 65°0N 16°24E **8** D17
Vojvodina □ Serbia 45°20N 20°0E **23** B9
Volborg U.S.A. 45°51N 105°41W **76** D11
Volcán de Colima △
  Mexico 19°30N 103°40W **86** D4
Volcano Is. = Kazan-Rettō
  Pac. Oc. 25°0N 141°0E **64** E6
Volda Norway 62°9N 6°5E **8** E12
Volga = Privolzhskiy □
  Russia 56°0N 50°0E **26** D6
Volga → Russia 46°0N 48°30E **19** E8
Volga Hts. = Privolzhskaya
  Vozvyshennost Russia 51°0N 46°0E **19** D8
Volgodonsk Russia 47°33N 42°5E **19** E7
Volgograd Russia 48°40N 44°25E **19** E7
Volgogradskoye Vdkhr.
  Russia 50°0N 45°20E **19** D8
Volkhov → Russia 60°8N 32°20E **18** B5
Volkovysk = Vawkavysk
  Belarus 53°9N 24°30E **17** B13
Volksrust S. Africa 27°24S 29°53E **57** C4

Volochanka Russia 71°0N 94°28E **27** B10
Volodymyr-Volynskyy
  Ukraine 50°50N 24°18E **17** C13
Vologda Russia 59°10N 39°45E **18** C6
Volos Greece 39°24N 22°59E **23** E10
Volosovo Russia 59°27N 29°32E **9** G23
Volovets Ukraine 48°43N 23°11E **17** D12
Volozhin = Valozhyn
  Belarus 54°3N 26°30E **17** A14
Volsk Russia 52°5N 47°22E **18** D8
Volta → Ghana 5°46N 0°41E **50** F4
Volta, L. Ghana 7°30N 0°0 **52** G6
Volta Redonda Brazil 22°31S 44°5W **95** A7
Voltaire, C. Australia 14°16S 125°35E **60** B4
Volterra Italy 43°24N 10°51E **22** C4
Volturno → Italy 41°1N 13°55E **22** D5
Volyn □ Ukraine 51°15N 24°30E **17** C13
Volzhskiy Russia 48°56N 44°46E **19** E7
Vomo Fiji 17°30S 177°15E **59** a
Vopnafjörður Iceland 65°45N 14°50W **8** D6
Voreios Sporades Greece 39°15N 23°30E **23** E10
Vorkuta Russia 67°48N 64°20E **18** A11
Vormsi Estonia 59°1N 23°13E **9** G20
Voronezh Russia 51°40N 39°10E **19** D6
Võrts järv Estonia 58°16N 26°3E **9** G22
Võru Estonia 57°48N 26°54E **9** H22
Vosges France 48°20N 7°10E **20** B7
Voss Norway 60°38N 6°26E **8** F12
Vostochnyy Port Russia 42°44N 133°4E **28** C6
Vostok Antarctica 78°30S 106°50E **5** D8
Vostok I. Kiribati 10°5S 152°23W **65** J12
Votkinsk Russia 57°0N 53°55E **18** C9
Votkinskoye Vdkhr.
  Russia 57°22N 55°12E **18** C10
Vouga → Portugal 40°41N 8°40W **21** B1
Voyageurs △ U.S.A. 48°32N 93°0W **80** A7
Voynitsa Russia 65°10N 30°20E **8** D24
Voyvozh Russia 62°56N 54°56E **18** B10
Vozhe, Ozero Russia 60°45N 39°0E **18** B6
Voznesensk Ukraine 47°35N 31°21E **19** E5
Voznesenye Russia 61°0N 35°28E **18** B6
Vrangel Russia 42°43N 133°5E **28** C6
Vrangelya, Ostrov Russia 71°0N 180°0E **27** B18
Vranje Serbia 42°34N 21°54E **23** C9
Vratsa Bulgaria 43°15N 23°30E **23** C10
Vrbas → Bos.-H. 45°8N 17°29E **22** B7
Vrede S. Africa 27°24S 29°6E **57** C4
Vredefort S. Africa 27°0S 27°22E **56** D4
Vredenburg S. Africa 32°56S 18°0E **56** D2
Vredendal S. Africa 31°41S 18°35E **56** D2
Vriddhachalam India 11°30N 79°20E **45** J4
Vrindavan India 27°37N 77°40E **42** F7
Vršac Serbia 45°8N 21°30E **23** B9
Vryburg S. Africa 26°55S 24°45E **56** C3
Vryheid S. Africa 27°45S 30°47E **57** C5
Vu Liet Vietnam 18°43N 105°23E **38** C5
Vukovar Croatia 45°21N 18°59E **23** B8
Vuktyl Russia 63°52N 57°20E **26** C6
Vulcan Canada 50°25N 113°15W **70** C6
Vulcan Romania 45°23N 23°17E **17** F12
Vulcăneşti Moldova 45°41N 28°18E **17** F15
Vulcano Italy 38°24N 14°58E **22** E6
Vulkaneshty = Vulcăneşti
  Moldova 45°41N 28°18E **17** F15
Vung Tau Vietnam 10°21N 107°4E **39** G6
Vunidawa Fiji 17°50S 178°21E **59** a
Vunisea Fiji 19°3S 178°10E **59** a
Vuntut △ Canada 68°25N 139°41W **68** B4
Vyara India 21°8N 73°28E **44** D1
Vyartsilya Russia 62°8N 30°45E **8** E24
Vyatka = Kirov Russia 58°35N 49°40E **18** C8
Vyatka → Russia 55°37N 51°28E **18** C9
Vyatskiye Polyany Russia 56°14N 51°5E **18** C9
Vyazemskiy Russia 47°32N 134°45E **27** E14
Vyazma Russia 55°10N 34°15E **18** C5
Vyborg Russia 60°43N 28°47E **8** F23
Vychegda → Russia 61°18N 46°36E **18** B8
Vychodné Beskydy
  Europe 49°20N 22°0E **17** D11
Vyg-ozero Russia 63°47N 34°29E **18** B5
Vylkove Ukraine 45°28N 29°32E **17** F15
Vynohradiv Ukraine 48°9N 23°2E **17** D12
Vypin India 10°10N 76°15E **45** J3
Vyrnwy, L. U.K. 52°48N 3°31W **12** E4
Vyshniy Volochek Russia 57°30N 34°30E **18** C5
Vyshzha = imeni 26 Bakinskikh
  Komissarov
  Turkmenistan 39°22N 54°10E **47** B7
Vyškov Czechia 49°17N 17°0E **17** D9
Vytegra Russia 61°0N 36°27E **18** B6

W

W.A.C. Bennett Dam
  Canada 56°2N 122°6W **70** B4
Wa Ghana 10°7N 2°25W **52** F5
Waal → Neths. 51°37N 5°0E **15** C5
Waalwijk Neths. 51°42N 5°4E **15** C5
Waanyi-Garawa ☉
  Australia 18°2S 137°33E **62** B2
Wabakimi △ Canada 50°43N 89°29W **72** B2
Wabana Canada 47°40N 53°0W **73** C9
Wabasca → Canada 58°22N 115°20W **70** B5
Wabasca-Desmarais
  Canada 55°57N 113°56W **70** B6
Wabash U.S.A. 40°48N 85°49W **81** E11
Wabash → U.S.A. 37°48N 88°2W **80** G9
Wabigoon L. Canada 49°44N 92°4W **71** D10
Wabowden Canada 54°55N 98°38W **71** C9
Wabu Hu China 32°20N 116°50E **35** A11
Wabuk Pt. Canada 55°20N 85°5W **72** A2
Wabush Canada 52°55N 66°52W **73** B6
Waco U.S.A. 31°33N 97°9W **84** F6
Waconichi, L. Canada 50°8N 74°0W **72** B5
Wad Hamid Sudan 16°30N 32°45E **53** E12
Wad Medanî Sudan 14°28N 33°30E **53** F12
Wad Thana Pakistan 27°22N 66°23E **42** F2
Wadayama Japan 35°19N 134°52E **29** G7
Waddeneilanden Neths. 53°25N 5°10E **15** A5
Waddenzee Neths. 53°6N 5°10E **15** A5
Waddington U.S.A. 44°52N 75°12W **83** B9

Waddington, Mt.
  Canada 51°23N 125°15W **70** C3
Wall U.S.A. 44°0N 102°8W **80** C2
Walla Walla U.S.A. 46°4N 118°20W **76** C4
Wallace Idaho, U.S.A. 47°28N 115°56W **76** C6
Wallace N.C., U.S.A. 34°44N 77°59W **85** D16
Wallaceburg Canada 42°34N 82°23W **82** D2
Wallachia = Valahia
  Romania 44°35N 25°0E **17** F13
Wallal Australia 26°32S 146°7E **63** D4
Wallam Cr. → Australia 28°40S 147°20E **63** D4
Wallambin, L. Australia 30°57S 117°35E **61** F2
Wallangarra Australia 28°56S 151°58E **63** D5
Wallangra Australia 29°56S 150°49E **63** D5
Wallaroo Australia 33°56S 137°39E **63** E2
Wallasey U.K. 53°25N 3°2W **12** D4
Wallenpaupack, L.
  U.S.A. 41°25N 75°15W **83** E9
Wallingford Conn.,
  U.S.A. 41°27N 72°50W **83** E12
Wallingford Vt., U.S.A. 43°28N 72°58W **83** C12
Wallis & Futuna, Îs. ☑
  Pac. Oc. 13°18S 176°10W **58** C11
Wallowa U.S.A. 45°34N 117°32W **76** D5
Wallowa Mts. U.S.A. 45°20N 117°30W **76** D5
Walls U.K. 60°14N 1°33W **11** A7
Walls of Jerusalem △
  Australia 41°56S 146°15E **63** G4
Wallula U.S.A. 46°5N 118°54W **76** C4
Wallumbilla Australia 26°33S 149°9E **63** D4
Walmsley L. Canada 63°25N 108°36W **71** A7
Walney, I. of U.K. 54°6N 3°15W **12** C4
Walnut Canyon △
  U.S.A. 35°15N 111°20W **77** J8
Walnut Creek U.S.A. 37°54N 122°4W **78** H4
Walnut Ridge U.S.A. 36°4N 90°57W **85** C9
Walpole Australia 34°58S 116°44E **61** F2
Walpole U.S.A. 42°9N 71°15W **83** D13
Walpole-Nornalup △
  Australia 35°0S 116°45E **61** G2
Walsall U.K. 52°35N 1°58W **13** E6
Walsenburg U.S.A. 37°38N 104°47W **77** H11
Walsh U.S.A. 37°23N 102°17W **77** H12
Walsh → Australia 16°31S 143°42E **62** B3
Walsingham Canada 42°40N 80°31W **82** D4
Waltair India 17°44N 83°23E **44** F6
Walter F. George Res.
  U.S.A. 31°38N 85°4W **85** F12
Walterboro U.S.A. 32°55N 80°40W **85** E14
Walters U.S.A. 34°22N 98°19W **84** D5
Waltman U.S.A. 43°4N 107°12W **76** E10
Walton U.S.A. 42°10N 75°8W **83** D9
Walton-on-the-Naze U.K. 51°51N 1°17E **13** F9
Walvis Bay Namibia 23°0S 14°28E **56** B1
Walvisbaai = Walvis Bay
  Namibia 23°0S 14°28E **56** B1
Wamba
  Dem. Rep. of the Congo 2°10N 27°57E **54** D5
Wambardi ☉ Australia 16°2S 130°55E **60** C5
Wamego U.S.A. 39°12N 96°18W **80** F5
Wamena Indonesia 4°4S 138°57E **37** E9
Wampana Karlantijpa ☉
  Australia 17°45S 132°10E **60** C5
Wampaya ☉ Australia 17°20S 135°0E **62** B2
Wampsville U.S.A. 43°4N 75°42W **83** C9
Wamsutter U.S.A. 41°40N 107°58W **76** F10
Wamulan Indonesia 3°27S 126°7E **37** E7
Wan Tup Myanmar 21°13N 98°42E **34** G2
Wan Xian China 38°47N 115°7E **32** E8
Wana Pakistan 32°20N 69°32E **42** C3
Wanaaring Australia 29°38S 144°9E **63** D3
Wanaka N.Z. 44°42S 169°9E **59** F2
Wanaka, L. N.Z. 44°33S 169°7E **59** F2
Wan'an China 26°26N 114°49E **35** D10
Wanapitei L. Canada 46°45N 80°40W **72** C3
Wandel Sea = McKinley Sea
  Arctic 82°0N 0°0 **4** A7
Wandhari Pakistan 27°42N 66°48E **42** F2
Wanding China 24°28N 98°7E **34** D2
Wandoan Australia 26°5S 149°55E **63** D4
Wandur Marine △ India 11°30N 92°30E **45** J11
Wanfu China 38°0N 122°38E **33** D12
Wang → Thailand 17°8N 99°2E **38** D2
Wang Noi Thailand 14°13N 100°44E **38** E3
Wang Saphung Thailand 17°18N 101°46E **38** D3
Wang Thong Thailand 16°50N 100°26E **38** D3
Wanganella Australia 35°6S 144°49E **63** F3
Wanganui N.Z. 39°56S 175°3E **59** C5
Wangaratta Australia 36°21S 146°19E **63** F4
Wangary Australia 34°35S 135°29E **63** E2
Wangcang China 32°18N 106°20E **34** A6
Wangcheng China 28°22N 112°47E **35** C9
Wangcun China 36°41N 117°41E **33** F9
Wangdu China 38°40N 115°7E **32** E8
Wangerooge Germany 53°47N 7°54E **16** B4
Wangiwangi Indonesia 5°22S 123°37E **37** F6
Wangjiang China 30°10N 116°42E **35** B11
Wangmo China 25°11N 106°5E **34** E6
Wangqing China 43°12N 129°42E **33** C15
Wani India 20°5N 78°55E **44** D4
Wanimiyn ☉ Australia 15°55S 130°49E **60** C5
Wanjina Wunggurr Wilinggin ☉
  Australia 16°0S 127°0E **60** C4
Wankaner India 22°35N 71°0E **42** H4
Wanless Canada 54°11N 101°21W **71** C8
Wanleweyne Somalia 2°37N 44°54E **49** G3
Wanneroo Australia 31°42S 115°46E **61** F2
Wannian China 28°42N 117°4E **35** C11
Wanning China 18°48N 110°22E **38** C8
Wannoo Billabong Roadhouse
  Australia 27°25S 115°49E **61** E2
Wanon Niwat Thailand 17°38N 103°46E **38** D4
Wanqinsha China 22°43N 113°33E **31** a
Wanquan China 40°50N 114°40E **32** D8
Wanrong China 35°25N 110°50E **32** G6
Wanshan China 27°30N 109°12E **34** D7
Wanshan Qundao China 21°57N 113°45E **31** a
Wansheng China 28°57N 106°58E **34** C6
Wanstead N.Z. 40°18S 176°28E **59** D6
Wantage U.K. 51°35N 1°25W **13** F6
Wanxian China 30°42N 108°20E **34** B7
Wanyuan China 32°4N 108°3E **34** A7
Wanzai Guangdong, China 22°12N 113°31E **31** a
Wanzai Jiangxi, China 28°7N 114°30E **35** C10

Wapakoneta U.S.A. 40°34N 84°12W **81** E11
Wapato U.S.A. 46°27N 120°25W **76** C3
Wapawekka L. Canada 54°55N 104°40W **71** C8
Wapikopa L. Canada 52°56N 87°53W **72** B2
Wapiti → Canada 55°5N 118°18W **70** B5
Wappingers Falls
  U.S.A. 41°36N 73°55W **83** E11
Wapsipinicon → U.S.A. 41°44N 90°19W **80** E8
Wapusk △ Canada 57°46N 93°22W **71** B10
Warakurna Australia 24°59S 128°17E **61** D4
Warangal India 17°58N 79°35E **44** F4
Waraseoni India 21°45N 80°2E **43** J9
Waratah Australia 41°30S 145°30E **63** G4
Waratah B. Australia 38°54S 146°5E **63** F4
Warburton Vic.,
  Australia 37°47S 145°42E **63** F4
Warburton W. Austral.,
  Australia 26°8S 126°35E **61** E4
Warburton ☉ Australia 28°4S 137°28E **63** D2
Warburton → Australia 28°4S 137°28E **63** D2
Warburton Groove
  Australia 28°18S 137°8E **63** A2
Warburton Ra. Australia 25°55S 126°28E **61** E4
Ward N.Z. 41°49S 174°11E **59** D5
Ward → Australia 26°28S 146°6E **63** D4
Ward Mt. U.S.A. 37°12N 118°54W **78** H8
Warden S. Africa 27°50S 29°0E **57** C4
Wardha India 20°45N 78°39E **44** D4
Wardha → India 19°57N 79°11E **44** E4
Wardsville Canada 42°39N 81°45W **82** D2
Ware U.K. 51°49N 0°0 **13** F8
Ware U.S.A. 42°16N 72°14W **83** D12
Waregem Belgium 50°53N 3°27E **15** D3
Wareham U.S.A. 41°46N 70°43W **83** E14
Waremme Belgium 50°43N 5°15E **15** D5
Warialda Australia 29°29S 150°33E **63** D5
Warin Chamrap
  Thailand 15°12N 104°53E **38** E5
Warkopi Indonesia 1°12S 134°9E **37** E8
Warm Springs U.S.A. 38°10N 116°20W **77** G5
Warman Canada 52°19N 106°30W **71** C7
Warmbad = Bela Bela
  S. Africa 24°51S 28°19E **57** B4
Warmbad Namibia 28°25S 18°42E **56** D2
Warminster U.K. 51°12N 2°10W **13** F5
Warminster U.S.A. 40°12N 75°6W **83** F9
Warmun Australia 17°2S 128°12E **60** C4
Warner Mts. U.S.A. 41°40N 120°15W **76** F3
Warner Robins U.S.A. 32°37N 83°36W **85** E13
Waroona Australia 32°50S 115°58E **61** F2
Warora India 20°14N 79°1E **44** D4
Warrabri ☉ Australia 21°1S 134°19E **62** C1
Warracknabeal Australia 36°9S 142°26E **63** F3
Warragul Australia 38°10S 145°58E **63** F4
Warrego → Australia 30°24S 145°21E **63** E4
Warrego Ra. Australia 24°58S 146°0E **62** C4
Warren Australia 31°42S 147°51E **63** E4
Warren Ark., U.S.A. 33°37N 92°4W **84** E8
Warren Mich., U.S.A. 42°28N 83°1W **81** D12
Warren Minn., U.S.A. 48°12N 96°46W **80** A5
Warren Ohio, U.S.A. 41°14N 80°49W **82** E4
Warren Pa., U.S.A. 41°51N 79°9W **82** E5
Warrenpoint U.K. 54°6N 6°15W **10** B5
Warrensburg Mo., U.S.A. 38°46N 93°44W **80** F7
Warrensburg N.Y.,
  U.S.A. 43°29N 73°46W **83** C11
Warrenton S. Africa 28°9S 24°47E **56** C3
Warrenton U.S.A. 46°10N 123°56W **78** D3
Warri Nigeria 5°30N 5°41E **52** G7
Warrington U.K. 53°24N 2°35W **12** D5
Warrington U.S.A. 30°23N 87°17W **85** F11
Warrington □ U.K. 53°24N 2°35W **12** D5
Warrnambool Australia 38°25S 142°30E **63** F3
Warroad U.S.A. 48°54N 95°19W **80** A6
Warruwi Australia 11°36S 133°20E **62** A1
Warsak Dam Pakistan 34°11N 71°19E **42** B4
Warsaw Ind., U.S.A. 41°14N 85°51W **81** E11
Warsaw N.Y., U.S.A. 42°45N 78°8W **82** D6
Warsaw Ohio, U.S.A. 40°20N 82°0W **82** F3
Warta → Poland 52°35N 14°39E **16** B8
Warthe = Warta →
  Poland 52°35N 14°39E **16** B8
Waru Indonesia 3°30S 130°36E **37** E8
Warud India 21°30N 78°16E **44** D4
Warumungu ☉
  Australia 19°15S 134°44E **62** B1
Warwick Australia 28°10S 152°1E **63** D5
Warwick U.K. 52°18N 1°35W **13** E6
Warwick N.Y., U.S.A. 41°16N 74°22W **83** E10
Warwick R.I., U.S.A. 41°42N 71°28W **83** E13
Warwickshire □ U.K. 52°14N 1°38W **13** E6
Wasaga Beach Canada 44°31N 80°1W **82** B4
Wasagaming Canada 50°39N 99°58W **71** C9
Wasatch Ra. U.S.A. 40°0N 111°30W **76** F8
Wasbank S. Africa 28°15S 30°9E **57** C5
Wasco Calif., U.S.A. 35°36N 119°20W **79** K7
Wasco Oreg., U.S.A. 45°36N 120°42W **76** D3
Waseca U.S.A. 44°5N 93°30W **80** C7
Wasgomuwa △ Sri Lanka 7°45N 81°0E **45** L5
Wash, The U.K. 52°58N 0°20E **12** E8
Washburn N. Dak.,
  U.S.A. 47°17N 101°2W **80** B2
Washburn Wis., U.S.A. 46°40N 90°54W **80** B8
Washim India 20°3N 77°0E **44** D3
Washington U.K. 54°55N 1°30W **12** C6
Washington Ga., U.S.A. 33°44N 82°44W **85** E13
Washington Ind., U.S.A. 38°40N 87°10W **80** F10
Washington Iowa, U.S.A. 41°18N 91°42W **80** E8
Washington Mo., U.S.A. 38°33N 91°1W **80** F8
Washington N.C., U.S.A. 35°33N 77°3W **85** D16
Washington N.J., U.S.A. 40°46N 74°59W **83** F10
Washington Pa., U.S.A. 40°10N 80°15W **82** F4
Washington Utah, U.S.A. 37°8N 113°31W **77** H7
Washington □ U.S.A. 47°30N 120°30W **76** C3
Washington, Mt.
  U.S.A. 44°16N 71°18W **83** B13
Washington Court House
  U.S.A. 39°32N 83°26W **81** F12

Washington Dulles Int. ✈ (IAD) U.S.A. 38°57N 77°27W 81 F15
Washington I. U.S.A. 45°23N 86°54W 80 C10
Washougal U.S.A. 45°35N 122°21W 78 E4
Washpool △ Australia 29°22S 152°20E 63 D5
Wasian Indonesia 1°47S 133°19E 37 E8
Wasilla U.S.A. 61°35N 149°26W 68 E2
Wasior Indonesia 2°43S 134°30E 37 E8
Wasiri Indonesia 7°30S 126°30E 37 F7
Wāsiţ □ Iraq 32°50N 45°50E 46 C5
Waskaganish Canada 51°30N 78°40W 72 B4
Waskaiowaka L. Canada 56°33N 96°23W 71 B9
Waskesiu Lake Canada 53°55N 106°5W 71 C7
Wasserkuppe Germany 50°29N 9°55E 16 C5
Wasur △ Indonesia 8°41S 140°44E 37 F10
Waswanipi Canada 49°40N 76°29W 72 C4
Waswanipi, L. Canada 49°35N 76°40W 72 C4
Watampone Indonesia 4°29S 120°25E 37 E6
Watarrka △ Australia 24°20S 131°30E 60 D5
Water Park Pt. Australia 22°56S 150°47E 62 C5
Water Valley U.S.A. 34°10N 89°38W 85 D10
Waterberg Plateau ⌓ Namibia 20°25S 17°18E 56 B2
Waterberge S. Africa 24°10S 28°0E 57 B4
Waterbury Conn., U.S.A. 41°33N 73°3W 83 E11
Waterbury Vt., U.S.A. 44°20N 72°46W 83 B12
Waterbury L. Canada 58°10N 104°22W 71 B8
Waterdown Canada 43°20N 79°53W 82 C5
Waterford Canada 42°56N 80°17W 82 D4
Waterford Ireland 52°15N 7°8W 10 D4
Waterford Calif., U.S.A. 37°38N 120°46W 78 H6
Waterford Pa., U.S.A. 41°57N 79°59W 82 E5
Waterford □ Ireland 52°10N 7°40W 10 D4
Waterford Harbour Ireland 52°8N 6°58W 10 D5
Waterhen L. Canada 52°10N 99°40W 71 C9
Waterloo Ont., Canada 43°30N 80°32W 82 C4
Waterloo Qué., Canada 45°22N 72°32W 83 A12
Waterloo Ill., U.S.A. 38°20N 90°9W 80 F8
Waterloo Iowa, U.S.A. 42°30N 92°21W 80 D7
Waterloo N.Y., U.S.A. 42°54N 76°52W 82 D8
Watersmeet U.S.A. 46°16N 89°11W 80 B9
Waterton Lakes △ Canada 48°45N 115°0W 70 D6
Watertown Conn., U.S.A. 41°36N 73°7W 83 E11
Watertown N.Y., U.S.A. 43°59N 75°55W 83 C9
Watertown S. Dak., U.S.A. 44°54N 97°7W 80 C5
Watertown Wis., U.S.A. 43°12N 88°43W 80 D9
Waterval-Boven = Emgwenya S. Africa 25°40S 30°18E 57 C5
Waterville Canada 45°16N 71°54W 83 A13
Waterville Maine, U.S.A. 44°33N 69°38W 81 C19
Waterville N.Y., U.S.A. 42°56N 75°23W 83 D9
Waterville Pa., U.S.A. 41°19N 77°21W 82 E7
Waterville Wash., U.S.A. 47°39N 120°4W 76 C3
Watervliet U.S.A. 42°44N 73°42W 83 D11
Wates Indonesia 7°51S 110°10E 37 G14
Watford Canada 42°57N 81°53W 82 D3
Watford U.K. 51°40N 0°24W 13 F7
Watford City U.S.A. 47°48N 103°17W 80 B2
Wathaman → Canada 57°16N 102°59W 71 B8
Wathaman L. Canada 56°58N 103°44W 71 B8
Watheroo Australia 30°15S 116°5E 61 F2
Watheroo △ Australia 30°19S 115°48E 61 F2
Wating China 35°40N 106°38E 32 G4
Watkins Glen U.S.A. 42°23N 76°52W 82 D8
Watling I. = San Salvador I. Bahamas 24°0N 74°30W 89 B5
Watonga U.S.A. 35°51N 98°25W 84 D5
Watrous Canada 51°40N 105°25W 71 C7
Watrous U.S.A. 35°48N 104°59W 77 J11
Watsa Dem. Rep. of the Congo 3°4N 29°30E 54 D5
Watseka U.S.A. 40°47N 87°44W 80 E10
Watson Canada 52°10N 104°30W 71 C8
Watson Lake Canada 60°6N 128°49W 70 A3
Watsontown U.S.A. 41°5N 76°52W 82 E8
Watsonville U.S.A. 36°55N 121°45W 78 J5
Wattiwarriganna Cr. → Australia 28°57S 136°10E 63 D2
Watuata = Batuata Indonesia 6°12S 122°42E 37 F6
Watubela, Kepulauan Indonesia 4°28S 131°35E 37 E8
Watubela Is. = Watubela, Kepulauan Indonesia 4°28S 131°35E 37 E8
Wau South Sudan 7°45N 28°1E 53 G11
Waubamik Canada 45°27N 80°1W 82 A4
Waubay U.S.A. 45°20N 97°18W 80 C5
Wauchope N.S.W., Australia 31°28S 152°45E 63 E5
Wauchope N. Terr., Australia 20°36S 134°15E 62 C1
Wauchula U.S.A. 27°33N 81°49W 85 H14
Waukarlycarly, L. Australia 21°18S 121°56E 60 D3
Waukegan U.S.A. 42°22N 87°50W 80 D10
Waukesha U.S.A. 43°1N 88°14W 80 D9
Waukon U.S.A. 43°16N 91°29W 80 D8
Waupaca U.S.A. 44°21N 89°5W 80 C9
Waupun U.S.A. 43°38N 88°44W 80 D9
Waurika U.S.A. 34°10N 98°0W 84 D6
Wausau U.S.A. 44°58N 89°38W 80 C9
Wautoma U.S.A. 44°4N 89°18W 80 C9
Wauwatosa U.S.A. 43°2N 88°0W 80 D9
Wave Hill = Kalkarindji Australia 17°30S 130°47E 60 C5
Wave Rock ⌓ Australia 32°26S 118°53E 61 F2
Waveney → U.K. 52°35N 1°39E 13 E9
Waverley N.Z. 39°46S 174°37E 59 C5
Waverly Iowa, U.S.A. 42°44N 92°29W 80 D7
Waverly N.Y., U.S.A. 42°1N 76°32W 83 E8
Wavre Belgium 50°43N 4°38E 15 D4
Wâw = Wau South Sudan 7°45N 28°1E 53 G11
Wāw al Kabīr Libya 25°20N 16°43E 53 C9
Wawa Canada 47°59N 84°47W 72 C3
Wawanesa Canada 49°36N 99°40W 71 D9
Wawona U.S.A. 37°32N 119°39W 78 H7
Waxahachie U.S.A. 32°24N 96°51W 84 E6
Way, L. Australia 26°45S 120°16E 61 E3
Waya Fiji 17°19S 177°10E 59 a
Waycross U.S.A. 31°13N 82°21W 85 F13
Wayland U.S.A. 42°34N 77°35W 82 D7
Wayne Nebr., U.S.A. 42°14N 97°1W 80 D5
Wayne W. Va., U.S.A. 38°13N 82°27W 81 F12
Waynesboro Ga., U.S.A. 33°6N 82°1W 85 E13
Waynesboro Miss., U.S.A. 31°40N 88°39W 85 F10
Waynesboro Pa., U.S.A. 39°45N 77°35W 81 F15
Waynesboro Va., U.S.A. 38°4N 78°53W 81 F14
Waynesburg U.S.A. 39°54N 80°11W 81 F13
Waynesville U.S.A. 35°28N 82°58W 85 D13
Waynoka U.S.A. 36°35N 98°53W 84 C5
Wazirabad Pakistan 32°30N 74°8E 42 C6
Waziristan Pakistan 33°0N 70°0E 42 C4
We Indonesia 5°51N 95°18E 36 C1
Weald, The U.K. 51°4N 0°20E 13 F8
Wear → U.K. 54°55N 1°23W 12 C6
Weatherford Okla., U.S.A. 35°32N 98°43W 84 D5
Weatherford Tex., U.S.A. 32°46N 97°48W 84 E6
Weaverville U.S.A. 40°44N 122°56W 76 F2
Webb City U.S.A. 37°9N 94°28W 80 G6
Webequie Canada 52°59N 87°21W 72 B2
Webster Mass., U.S.A. 42°3N 71°53W 83 D13
Webster N.Y., U.S.A. 43°13N 77°26W 82 C7
Webster S. Dak., U.S.A. 45°20N 97°31W 80 C5
Webster City U.S.A. 42°28N 93°49W 80 D7
Webster Springs U.S.A. 38°29N 80°25W 81 F13
Weda Indonesia 0°21N 127°50E 37 D7
Weda, Teluk Indonesia 0°20N 128°0E 37 D7
Weddell Abyssal Plain S. Ocean 65°0S 20°0W 5 C2
Weddell I. Falk. Is. 51°50S 61°0W 96 G4
Weddell Sea Antarctica 72°30S 40°0W 5 D1
Wedderburn Australia 36°26S 143°33E 63 F3
Wedgeport Canada 43°44N 65°59W 73 D6
Wee Waa Australia 30°11S 149°26E 63 E4
Weed U.S.A. 41°25N 122°23W 76 F2
Weed Heights U.S.A. 38°59N 119°13W 78 G7
Weedsport U.S.A. 43°2N 76°33W 83 C8
Weedville U.S.A. 41°17N 78°30W 82 E6
Weenen S. Africa 28°48S 30°7E 57 C5
Weerribben △ Neths. 52°47N 5°58E 15 B5
Weert Neths. 51°15N 5°43E 15 C5
Wei He → Hebei, China 36°10N 115°45E 32 F8
Wei He → Shaanxi, China 34°38N 110°15E 32 G6
Weichang China 41°58N 117°49E 33 D9
Weichuan China 34°20N 113°59E 32 G7
Weiden Germany 49°41N 12°10E 16 D7
Weifang China 36°44N 119°7E 33 F10
Weihai China 37°30N 122°6E 33 F12
Weihui China 35°25N 114°3E 32 G8
Weimar Germany 50°58N 11°19E 16 C6
Weinan China 34°31N 109°29E 32 G5
Weining China 26°50N 104°17E 34 D5
Weipa Australia 12°40S 141°50E 62 A3
Weir → Australia 28°20S 149°50E 63 D4
Weir → Canada 56°54N 93°21W 71 B10
Weir River Canada 56°49N 94°6W 71 B10
Weirton U.S.A. 40°24N 80°35W 82 F4
Weiser U.S.A. 44°15N 116°58W 76 D5
Weishan Shandong, China 34°47N 117°5E 33 G9
Weishan Yunnan, China 25°12N 100°20E 34 E3
Weishan Hu China 34°35N 117°14E 33 G9
Weixi China 27°10N 99°10E 34 D2
Weixin China 27°48N 105°3E 34 D5
Weiyuan Gansu, China 35°7N 104°10E 32 G3
Weiyuan Sichuan, China 29°35N 104°36E 34 C5
Weizhou Dao China 21°0N 109°5E 34 G7
Wejherowo Poland 54°35N 18°12E 17 A10
Wekusko L. Canada 54°40N 99°50W 71 C9
Welch U.S.A. 37°26N 81°35W 81 G13
Welford △ Australia 25°5S 143°16E 62 D3
Weligama Sri Lanka 5°58N 80°25E 45 M5
Welkom S. Africa 28°0S 26°46E 56 C4
Welland Canada 43°0N 79°15W 82 D5
Welland → U.K. 52°51N 0°5W 13 E7
Wellawaya Sri Lanka 6°44N 81°6E 45 L5
Wellesley Is. Australia 16°42S 139°30E 62 B2
Wellesley Islands ✪ Australia 16°32S 139°23E 62 B2
Wellingborough U.K. 52°19N 0°41W 13 E7
Wellington Australia 32°35S 148°59E 63 E4
Wellington Canada 43°57N 77°20W 82 C7
Wellington N.Z. 41°19S 174°46E 59 D5
Wellington S. Africa 33°38S 19°1E 56 D2
Wellington Somst., U.K. 50°58N 3°13W 13 G4
Wellington Telford & Wrekin, U.K. 52°42N 2°30W 13 E5
Wellington Colo., U.S.A. 40°42N 105°0W 76 F11
Wellington Kans., U.S.A. 37°16N 97°24W 80 G5
Wellington Nev., U.S.A. 38°45N 119°23W 78 G7
Wellington Ohio, U.S.A. 41°10N 82°13W 82 E2
Wellington Tex., U.S.A. 34°51N 100°13W 84 D4
Wellington, I. Chile 49°30S 75°0W 96 F2
Wellington, L. Australia 38°6S 147°20E 63 F4
Wellington Chan. Canada 75°0N 93°0W 69 C13
Wells U.K. 51°13N 2°39W 13 F5
Wells Maine, U.S.A. 43°20N 70°35W 83 C14
Wells N.Y., U.S.A. 43°24N 74°17W 83 C10
Wells Nev., U.S.A. 41°7N 114°58W 76 F6
Wells, L. Australia 26°44S 123°15E 61 E3
Wells, Mt. Australia 17°25S 127°8E 60 C4
Wells Gray △ Canada 52°30N 120°15W 70 C4
Wells-next-the-Sea U.K. 52°57N 0°51E 12 E8
Wells River U.S.A. 44°9N 72°4W 83 B12
Wellsboro U.S.A. 41°45N 77°18W 82 E7
Wellsburg U.S.A. 40°16N 80°37W 82 F4
Wellsville N.Y., U.S.A. 42°7N 77°57W 82 D7
Wellsville Ohio, U.S.A. 40°36N 80°39W 82 F4
Wellsville Utah, U.S.A. 41°38N 111°56W 76 F8
Wellton U.S.A. 32°40N 114°8W 77 K6
Wels Austria 48°9N 14°1E 16 D8
Welshpool U.K. 52°39N 3°8W 13 E4
Welwyn Garden City U.K. 51°48N 0°12W 13 F7
Wem U.K. 52°52N 2°44W 12 E5
Wemindji Canada 53°0N 78°49W 72 B4
Wemyss Canada 44°52N 76°23W 83 B8
Wen Xian Gansu, China 32°43N 104°36E 32 H3
Wen Xian Henan, China 34°55N 113°5E 32 G7
Wenatchee U.S.A. 47°25N 120°19W 76 C3
Wenchang China 19°38N 110°42E 38 C8
Wencheng China 27°46N 120°4E 35 D13
Wenchi Ghana 7°46N 2°8W 52 G5
Wenchow = Wenzhou China 28°0N 120°38E 35 D13
Wenchuan China 31°22N 103°35E 34 B4
Wenden U.S.A. 33°49N 113°33W 79 M13
Wendeng China 37°15N 122°5E 33 F12
Wendesi Indonesia 2°30S 134°17E 37 E8
Wendover U.S.A. 40°44N 114°2W 76 F6
Weng'an China 27°5N 107°25E 34 D6
Wengcheng China 24°22N 113°50E 35 E9
Wengyuan China 24°20N 114°9E 35 E10
Wenling China 28°21N 121°20E 35 C13
Wenlock → Australia 12°2S 141°55E 62 A3
Wenshan China 23°20N 104°18E 34 F5
Wenshang China 35°45N 116°30E 32 G9
Wenshui China 37°26N 112°1E 32 F7
Wensleydale U.K. 54°17N 2°0W 12 C6
Wensu China 41°15N 80°10E 30 C5
Wensum → U.K. 52°40N 1°15E 12 E8
Wentworth Australia 34°2S 141°54E 63 E3
Wentzel L. Canada 59°2N 114°28W 70 B6
Wenut Indonesia 3°11S 133°19E 37 E8
Wenxi China 35°20N 111°10E 32 G6
Wenzhou China 28°0N 120°38E 35 D13
Weott U.S.A. 40°20N 123°55W 76 F2
Wepener S. Africa 29°42S 27°3E 56 C4
Werda Botswana 25°24S 23°15E 56 C3
Weri Indonesia 3°10S 132°38E 37 E8
Werra → Germany 51°24N 9°39E 16 C5
Werrimull Australia 34°25S 141°38E 63 E3
Werris Creek Australia 31°18S 150°38E 63 E5
Weser → Germany 53°36N 8°28E 16 B5
Weslaco U.S.A. 26°10N 97°58W 84 H6
Weslemkoon L. Canada 45°2N 77°25W 82 A7
Wesleyville Canada 49°9N 53°33W 73 C9
Wesleyville U.S.A. 42°9N 80°1W 82 D4
Wessel, C. Australia 10°59S 136°46E 62 A2
Wessel Is. Australia 11°10S 136°45E 62 A2
Wessex U.K. 51°0N 2°0W 13 F5
Wessington Springs U.S.A. 44°5N 98°34W 80 C4
West U.S.A. 31°48N 97°6W 84 F6
West → U.S.A. 42°52N 72°33W 83 D12
West Allis U.S.A. 43°1N 88°0W 80 D9
West Antarctica Antarctica 80°0S 90°0W 5 D15
West Baines → Australia 15°38S 129°59E 60 C4
West Bank □ Asia 32°6N 35°13E 48 C4
West Bend U.S.A. 43°25N 88°11W 80 D9
West Bengal = Paschimbanga □ India 23°0N 88°0E 43 H13
West Berkshire □ U.K. 51°25N 1°17W 13 F6
West Beskids = Západné Beskydy Europe 49°30N 19°0E 17 D10
West Branch U.S.A. 44°17N 84°14W 81 C11
West Branch Susquehanna → U.S.A. 40°53N 76°48W 83 F8
West Bromwich U.K. 52°32N 1°59W 13 E6
West Burra U.K. 60°5N 1°21W 11 A7
West Canada Cr. → U.S.A. 43°1N 74°58W 83 C10
West Caroline Basin Pac. Oc. 4°0N 138°0E 64 G5
West Chazy U.S.A. 44°49N 73°28W 83 B11
West Chester U.S.A. 39°58N 75°36W 83 G9
West Coast △ Namibia 21°53S 14°14E 56 B1
West Coast △ S. Africa 33°13S 18°0E 56 D2
West Columbia U.S.A. 29°9N 95°39W 84 G7
West Covina U.S.A. 34°4N 117°54W 79 L9
West Des Moines U.S.A. 41°35N 93°43W 80 E7
West Dunbartonshire □ U.K. 55°59N 4°30W 11 F4
West End Bahamas 26°41N 78°58W 88 A4
West Falkland Falk. Is. 51°40S 60°0W 96 G4
West Fargo U.S.A. 46°52N 96°54W 80 B5
West Fiji Basin Pac. Oc. 17°0S 173°0E 64 J9
West Fjord = Vestfjorden Norway 67°55N 14°0E 8 C16
West Fork Trinity → U.S.A. 32°48N 96°54W 84 E6
West Frankfort U.S.A. 37°54N 88°55W 80 G9
West Grand L. U.S.A. 45°14N 67°51W 81 C20
West Hartford U.S.A. 41°45N 72°44W 83 E12
West Haven U.S.A. 41°17N 72°57W 83 E12
West Hazleton U.S.A. 40°58N 76°0W 83 F9
West Hurley U.S.A. 41°59N 74°7W 83 E10
West I. India 13°35N 92°54E 45 H11
West Ice Shelf Antarctica 67°0S 85°0E 5 C7
West Indies Cent. Amer. 15°0N 65°0W 89 D7
West Jordan U.S.A. 40°36N 111°56W 76 F8
West Kavango □ Namibia 18°0S 18°30E 56 A2
West Linn U.S.A. 45°21N 122°36W 78 E4
West Lorne Canada 42°36N 81°36W 82 D3
West Lothian □ U.K. 55°54N 3°36W 11 F5
West MacDonnell △ Australia 23°38S 132°59E 60 D5
West Mariana Basin Pac. Oc. 15°0N 137°0E 64 F5
West Memphis U.S.A. 35°8N 90°10W 85 D9
West Midlands □ U.K. 52°26N 2°0W 13 E6
West Mifflin U.S.A. 40°21N 79°52W 82 F5
West Milford U.S.A. 41°8N 74°22W 83 E10
West Milton U.S.A. 41°1N 76°50W 82 E8
West Monroe U.S.A. 32°31N 92°9W 84 E8
West Newton U.S.A. 40°14N 79°46W 82 F5
West Odessa U.S.A. 31°50N 102°30W 84 F3
West Palm Beach U.S.A. 26°43N 80°3W 85 H14
West Plains U.S.A. 36°44N 91°51W 80 G8
West Point Miss., U.S.A. 33°36N 88°39W 85 E10
West Point N.Y., U.S.A. 41°24N 73°58W 83 E11
West Point Nebr., U.S.A. 41°51N 96°43W 80 E5
West Point Va., U.S.A. 37°32N 76°48W 81 G15
West Point L. U.S.A. 33°8N 85°0W 85 E12
West Pt. = Ouest, Pte. de l' Canada 49°52N 64°40W 73 C7
West Pt. Australia 35°1S 135°56E 63 F2
West Road → Canada 53°18N 122°53W 70 C4
West Rutland U.S.A. 43°36N 73°3W 83 C11
West Schelde = Westerschelde → Neths. 51°25N 3°25E 15 C3
West Seneca U.S.A. 42°51N 78°48W 82 D6
West Siberian Plain Russia 62°0N 75°0E 24 B9
West Sussex □ U.K. 50°55N 0°30W 13 G7
West-Terschelling Neths. 53°22N 5°13E 15 A5
West Valley City U.S.A. 40°42N 111°58W 76 F8
West Virginia □ U.S.A. 38°45N 80°30W 81 F13
West-Vlaanderen □ Belgium 51°0N 3°0E 15 D2
West Walker → U.S.A. 38°54N 119°9W 78 G7
West Wyalong Australia 33°56S 147°10E 63 E4
West Yellowstone U.S.A. 44°40N 111°6W 76 D8
West Yorkshire □ U.K. 53°45N 1°40W 12 D6
Westall, Pt. Australia 32°55S 134°4E 63 E1
Westbrook U.S.A. 43°41N 70°22W 81 D18
Westbury Australia 41°30S 146°51E 63 G4
Westby U.S.A. 48°52N 104°3W 76 B11
Westend U.S.A. 35°42N 117°24W 79 K9
Westerland Germany 54°54N 8°17E 16 A5
Westerly U.S.A. 41°22N 71°50W 83 E13
Western Australia □ Australia 25°0S 118°0E 61 E2
Western Cape □ S. Africa 34°0S 20°0E 56 D3
Western Dvina = Daugava → Latvia 57°4N 24°3E 9 H21
Western Ghats India 14°0N 75°0E 45 H2
Western Isles = Eilean Siar □ U.K. 57°30N 7°10W 11 D1
Western Sahara ■ Africa 25°0N 13°0W 52 D3
Western Samoa = Samoa ■ Pac. Oc. 14°0S 172°0W 59 b
Western Sierra Madre = Madre Occidental, Sierra Mexico 27°0N 107°0W 86 B3
Westernport U.S.A. 39°29N 79°3W 81 F14
Westerschelde → Neths. 51°25N 3°25E 15 C3
Westerwald Germany 50°38N 7°56E 16 C4
Westfield Mass., U.S.A. 42°7N 72°45W 83 D12
Westfield N.Y., U.S.A. 42°20N 79°35W 82 D5
Westfield Pa., U.S.A. 41°55N 77°32W 82 E7
Westhill U.K. 57°9N 2°19W 11 D6
Westhope U.S.A. 48°55N 101°1W 80 A3
Westland Bight N.Z. 42°55S 170°5E 59 E3
Westland Tai Poutini △ N.Z. 43°16S 170°16E 59 E2
Westlock Canada 54°9N 113°55W 70 C6
Westmar Australia 27°55S 149°44E 63 D4
Westmeath □ Ireland 53°33N 7°34W 10 C4
Westminster Calif., U.S.A. 33°45N 118°0W 79 M8
Westminster Colo., U.S.A. 39°50N 105°2W 76 G11
Westminster Md., U.S.A. 39°34N 76°59W 81 F15
Westmont U.S.A. 40°19N 78°58W 82 F6
Westmoreland Barbados 13°13N 59°37W 89 g
Westmorland U.S.A. 33°2N 115°37W 79 M11
Weston Oreg., U.S.A. 45°49N 118°26W 76 D4
Weston W. Va., U.S.A. 39°2N 80°28W 81 F13
Weston I. Canada 52°33N 79°36W 72 B4
Weston-super-Mare U.K. 51°21N 2°58W 13 F5
Westover U.S.A. 40°45N 78°40W 82 F6
Westport Canada 44°40N 76°25W 83 B8
Westport Ireland 53°48N 9°31W 10 C2
Westport N.Z. 41°46S 171°37E 59 D3
Westport N.Y., U.S.A. 44°11N 73°26W 83 B11
Westport Oreg., U.S.A. 46°8N 123°23W 78 D3
Westport Wash., U.S.A. 46°53N 124°6W 78 D2
Westray Canada 53°36N 101°24W 71 C8
Westray U.K. 59°18N 3°0W 11 B5
Westree Canada 47°26N 81°34W 72 C3
Westville U.S.A. 39°8N 120°42W 78 F6
Westwood U.S.A. 40°18N 121°0W 76 F3
Wetar Indonesia 7°48S 126°30E 37 F7
Wetaskiwin Canada 52°55N 113°24W 70 C6
Wete Tanzania 5°4S 39°43E 54 F7
Wetherby U.K. 53°56N 1°23W 12 D6
Wethersfield U.S.A. 41°42N 72°40W 83 E12
Wetteren Belgium 51°0N 3°53E 15 D3
Wetzlar Germany 50°32N 8°31E 16 C5
Wewoka U.S.A. 35°9N 96°30W 84 D6
Wexford Ireland 52°20N 6°28W 10 D5
Wexford □ Ireland 52°20N 6°25W 10 D5
Wexford Harbour Ireland 52°20N 6°25W 10 D5
Weyburn Canada 49°40N 103°50W 71 D8
Weymouth Canada 44°30N 66°1W 73 D6
Weymouth U.K. 50°37N 2°28W 13 G5
Weymouth U.S.A. 42°13N 70°58W 83 D14
Weymouth, C. Australia 12°37S 143°27E 62 A3
Wha Ti Canada 63°8N 117°16W 68 E8
Whakaari N.Z. 37°30S 177°13E 59 B6
Whakatane N.Z. 37°57S 177°1E 59 B6
Whale = Baleine → Canada 58°15N 67°40W 73 A6
Whale B. Myanmar 11°37N 98°38E 39 G2
Whale Cove Canada 62°10N 92°34W 71 A10
Whales, B. of Antarctica 78°0S 160°0W 5 D12
Whalsay U.K. 60°22N 0°59W 11 A8
Whangamata N.Z. 37°12S 175°53E 59 B5
Whangamomona N.Z. 39°8S 174°44E 59 C5
Whanganui △ N.Z. 39°17S 174°53E 59 C5
Whangarei N.Z. 35°43S 174°21E 59 A5
Whangarei Harb. N.Z. 35°45S 174°28E 59 A5
Wharekauri = Chatham Is. Pac. Oc. 44°0S 176°40W 64 M10
Wharfe → U.K. 53°51N 1°9W 12 D6
Wharfedale U.K. 54°6N 2°1W 12 C5
Wharton N.J., U.S.A. 40°54N 74°35W 83 F10
Wharton Pa., U.S.A. 41°31N 78°1W 82 E6
Wharton Tex., U.S.A. 29°19N 96°6W 84 G6
Wharton Basin Ind. Oc. 22°0S 99°0E 64 K1
Wheatland Calif., U.S.A. 39°1N 121°25W 78 F5
Wheatland Wyo., U.S.A. 42°3N 104°58W 76 E11
Wheatley Canada 42°6N 82°27W 82 D2
Wheaton Md., U.S.A. 39°3N 77°3W 81 F15
Wheaton Minn., U.S.A. 45°48N 96°30W 80 C5
Wheelbarrow Pk. U.S.A. 37°26N 116°5W 78 H10
Wheeler Oreg., U.S.A. 45°41N 123°53W 76 D2
Wheeler Tex., U.S.A. 35°27N 100°16W 84 D4
Wheeler → Canada 57°2N 67°13W 73 A6
Wheeler L. U.S.A. 34°48N 87°23W 85 D11
Wheeler Pk. N. Mex., U.S.A. 36°34N 105°25W 77 H11
Wheeler Pk. Nev., U.S.A. 38°57N 114°15W 76 G6
Wheeler Ridge U.S.A. 35°0N 118°57W 79 L8
Wheelersburg U.S.A. 38°44N 82°51W 81 F12
Wheeling U.S.A. 40°4N 80°43W 82 F4
Whernside U.K. 54°14N 2°24W 12 C5
Whiddy I. Ireland 51°41N 9°31W 10 E2
Whim Creek Australia 20°50S 117°49E 60 D2
Whiskey Jack L. Canada 58°23N 101°55W 71 B8
Whiskeytown-Shasta-Trinity ⌓ U.S.A. 40°45N 122°15W 76 F2
Whistleduck Cr. → Australia 20°15S 135°18E 62 C2
Whistler Canada 50°7N 122°58W 70 C4
Whitby Canada 43°52N 78°56W 82 C6
Whitby U.K. 54°29N 0°37W 12 C7
White → Ark., U.S.A. 33°57N 91°5W 84 E9
White → Ind., U.S.A. 38°25N 87°45W 80 F10
White → S. Dak., U.S.A. 43°42N 99°27W 80 D4
White → Tex., U.S.A. 33°14N 100°56W 84 E4
White → Utah, U.S.A. 40°4N 109°41W 76 F9
White → Vt., U.S.A. 43°37N 72°20W 83 C12
White → Wash., U.S.A. 47°12N 122°15W 78 C4
White, L. Australia 21°9S 128°56E 60 D4
White B. Canada 50°0N 56°35W 73 C8
White Bird U.S.A. 45°46N 116°18W 76 D5
White Butte U.S.A. 46°23N 103°18W 80 B2
White City U.S.A. 42°26N 122°51W 76 E2
White Cliffs Australia 30°50S 143°10E 63 E3
White Hall U.S.A. 39°26N 90°24W 80 F8
White Haven U.S.A. 41°4N 75°47W 83 E9
White Horse, Vale of U.K. 51°37N 1°30W 13 F6
White I. = Whakaari N.Z. 37°30S 177°13E 59 B6
White L. Canada 45°18N 76°31W 83 A8
White L. U.S.A. 29°44N 92°30W 84 G8
White Lake Canada 45°21N 76°29W 83 A8
White Mountain Peak U.S.A. 37°38N 118°15W 78 H8
White Mts. Calif., U.S.A. 37°30N 118°15W 78 H8
White Mts. N.H., U.S.A. 44°15N 71°15W 83 B13
White Mts. △ Australia 20°43S 145°12E 62 C4
White Nile = Nîl el Abyad → Sudan 15°38N 32°31E 53 E12
White Otter L. Canada 49°5N 91°55W 72 C1
White Pass U.S.A. 46°38N 121°24W 78 D5
White Plains U.S.A. 41°2N 73°46W 83 E11
White River Canada 48°35N 85°20W 72 C2
White River U.S.A. 43°34N 100°45W 80 D3
White Rock Canada 49°2N 122°48W 78 A4
White Rock U.S.A. 35°50N 106°12W 77 J10
White Rocks Nat. Recr. Area ⌓ U.S.A. 43°22N 72°55W 83 C12
White Russia = Belarus ■ Europe 53°30N 27°0E 17 B14
White Sands ⌓ U.S.A. 32°46N 106°20W 77 K10
White Sea = Beloye More Russia 66°30N 38°0E 18 A6
White Sulphur Springs Mont., U.S.A. 46°33N 110°54W 76 C8
White Sulphur Springs W. Va., U.S.A. 37°48N 80°18W 81 G13
White Swan U.S.A. 46°23N 120°44W 78 D6
Whitecliffs N.Z. 43°26S 171°55E 59 E3
Whitecourt Canada 54°10N 115°45W 70 C5
Whiteface Mt. U.S.A. 44°22N 73°54W 83 B11
Whitefield U.S.A. 44°23N 71°37W 83 B13
Whitefish U.S.A. 48°25N 114°20W 76 B6
Whitefish B. U.S.A. 46°40N 84°55W 72 C3
Whitefish L. Canada 62°41N 106°48W 71 A7
Whitefish Pt. U.S.A. 46°45N 84°59W 81 B11
Whitegull, L. = Goélands, L. aux Canada 55°27N 64°17W 73 A7
Whitehall Mich., U.S.A. 43°24N 86°21W 80 D10
Whitehall Mont., U.S.A. 45°52N 112°6W 76 D7
Whitehall N.Y., U.S.A. 43°33N 73°24W 83 C11
Whitehall Wis., U.S.A. 44°22N 91°19W 80 C8
Whitehaven U.K. 54°33N 3°35W 12 C4
Whitehorse Canada 60°43N 135°3W 70 A1
Whitemark Australia 40°7S 148°3E 63 G4
Whiteriver U.S.A. 33°50N 109°58W 77 K9
Whitesand → Canada 60°9N 115°45W 70 A5
Whitesands S. Africa 34°23S 20°50E 56 D3
Whitesboro N.Y., U.S.A. 43°7N 75°18W 83 C9
Whitesboro Tex., U.S.A. 33°39N 96°54W 84 E6
Whiteshell ⌓ Canada 50°0N 95°40W 71 D9
Whiteville U.S.A. 34°20N 78°42W 85 D15
Whitewater U.S.A. 42°50N 88°44W 80 D9
Whitewater Baldy U.S.A. 33°20N 108°39W 77 K9
Whitewater L. Canada 50°50N 89°10W 72 B2
Whitewood Australia 21°28S 143°30E 62 C3
Whitewood Canada 50°20N 102°20W 71 C8
Whithorn U.K. 54°44N 4°26W 11 G4
Whitianga N.Z. 36°47S 175°41E 59 B5
Whitman U.S.A. 42°5N 70°56W 83 D14
Whitmore Mts. Antarctica 82°35S 104°30W 5 E15
Whitney Canada 45°31N 78°14W 82 A6
Whitney, Mt. U.S.A. 36°35N 118°18W 78 J8
Whitney Point U.S.A. 42°20N 75°58W 83 D9
Whitstable U.K. 51°21N 1°3E 13 F9
Whitsunday I. Australia 20°15S 149°4E 62 b
Whitsunday Islands △ Australia 20°15S 149°0E 62 b
Whittier U.S.A. 60°47N 148°41W 74 C10
Whittlesea Australia 37°27S 145°9E 63 F4
Wholdaia L. Canada 60°43N 104°20W 71 A8
Whyalla Australia 33°2S 137°30E 63 E2
Wiang Kosai △ Thailand 17°54N 99°29E 38 D2
Wiang Sa Thailand 18°34N 100°45E 38 C3
Wiarton Canada 44°40N 81°10W 82 B3
Wiay U.K. 57°24N 7°13W 11 D1
Wibaux U.S.A. 46°59N 104°11W 76 C11
Wichian Buri Thailand 15°39N 101°7E 38 E3
Wichita U.S.A. 37°42N 97°20W 80 G5
Wichita Falls U.S.A. 33°54N 98°30W 84 E5
Wick U.K. 58°26N 3°5W 11 C5
Wickenburg U.S.A. 33°58N 112°44W 77 K7

Wickepin *Australia* 32°50S 117°30E **61 F2**
Wickham *Australia* 20°42S 117°11E **60 D2**
Wickham, C. *Australia* 39°35S 143°57E **63 F3**
Wickliffe *U.S.A.* 41°36N 81°28W **82 E3**
Wicklow *Ireland* 52°59N 6°3W **10 D5**
Wicklow ☐ *Ireland* 52°57N 6°25W **10 D5**
Wicklow Hd. *Ireland* 52°58N 6°0W **10 D6**
Wicklow Mts. *Ireland* 52°58N 6°26W **10 C5**
Wicklow Mts. △ *Ireland* 53°6N 6°21W **10 C5**
Widgeegoara Cr. →
  Australia 28°51S 146°34E **63 D4**
Widgiemooltha *Australia* 31°30S 121°34E **61 F3**
Widnes *U.K.* 53°23N 2°45W **12 D5**
Wieluń *Poland* 51°15N 18°34E **17 C10**
Wiener Neustadt *Austria* 47°49N 16°16E **16 E9**
Wiesbaden *Germany* 50°4N 8°14E **16 C5**
Wigan *U.K.* 53°33N 2°38W **12 D5**
Wiggins *Colo., U.S.A.* 40°14N 104°4W **76 F11**
Wiggins *Miss., U.S.A.* 30°51N 89°8W **85 F10**
Wight, I. of *U.K.* 50°41N 1°17W **13 G6**
Wigston *U.K.* 52°35N 1°6W **13 E6**
Wigton *U.K.* 54°50N 3°10W **12 C4**
Wigtown *U.K.* 54°53N 4°27W **11 G4**
Wigtown B. *U.K.* 54°46N 4°15W **11 G4**
Wik and Wikway People ◇
  Australia 13°55S 142°28E **62 A3**
Wilber *U.S.A.* 40°29N 96°58W **80 E5**
Wilberforce *Canada* 45°2N 78°13W **82 A6**
Wilberforce, C. *Australia* 11°54S 136°35E **62 A2**
Wilburton *U.S.A.* 34°55N 95°19W **84 D7**
Wilcox *U.S.A.* 41°35N 78°41W **82 E6**
Wildomar *U.S.A.* 33°36N 117°16W **79 M9**
Wildrose *U.S.A.* 36°14N 117°11W **79 J9**
Wildspitze *Austria* 46°53N 10°53E **16 E6**
Wilge → *S. Africa* 27°3S 28°20E **57 C4**
Wilhelm II Coast *Antarctica* 68°0S 90°0E **5 C7**
Wilhelmshaven *Germany* 53°31N 8°7E **16 B5**
Wilhelmstal *Namibia* 21°58S 16°21E **56 B2**
Wilis *Indonesia* 7°51S 111°48E **37 G15**
Wilkes-Barre *U.S.A.* 41°15N 75°53W **83 E9**
Wilkes Land *Antarctica* 69°0S 120°0E **5 D9**
Wilkie *Canada* 52°27N 108°42W **71 C7**
Wilkins Ice Shelf
  Antarctica 70°30S 72°0W **5 C17**
Wilkinsburg *U.S.A.* 40°26N 79°52W **82 F5**
Wilkinson Lakes
  Australia 29°40S 132°39E **61 E5**
Willandra Creek →
  Australia 33°22S 145°52E **63 E4**
Willapa B. *U.S.A.* 46°40N 124°0W **78 D3**
Willapa Hills *U.S.A.* 46°35N 123°25W **78 D3**
Willard *U.S.A.* 41°3N 82°44W **82 E2**
Willare Bridge Roadhouse
  Australia 17°43S 123°38E **60 C3**
Willcox *U.S.A.* 32°15N 109°50W **77 K9**
Willemstad *Curaçao* 12°5N 68°55W **89 D6**
William → *Canada* 59°8N 109°19W **71 B7**
William 'Bill' Dannelly Res.
  U.S.A. 32°6N 87°24W **85 F11**
William Creek *Australia* 28°58S 136°22E **63 D2**
Williams *Australia* 33°2S 116°52E **61 F2**
Williams *Ariz., U.S.A.* 35°15N 112°11W **77 J7**
Williams *Calif., U.S.A.* 39°9N 122°9W **78 F4**
Williams Harbour
  Canada 52°33N 55°47W **73 B8**
Williams Lake *Canada* 52°10N 122°10W **70 C4**
Williamsburg *Ky.,*
  U.S.A. 36°44N 84°10W **81 G11**
Williamsburg *Pa., U.S.A.* 40°28N 78°12W **82 F6**
Williamsburg *Va.,*
  U.S.A. 37°16N 76°43W **81 G15**
Williamson *N.Y., U.S.A.* 43°14N 77°11W **82 C7**
Williamson *W. Va.,*
  U.S.A. 37°41N 82°17W **81 G12**
Williamsport *U.S.A.* 41°15N 77°1W **82 E7**
Williamston *U.S.A.* 35°51N 77°4W **85 D16**
Williamstown *Ky.,*
  U.S.A. 38°38N 84°34W **81 F11**
Williamstown *Mass.,*
  U.S.A. 42°43N 73°12W **83 D11**
Williamstown *N.Y.,*
  U.S.A. 43°26N 75°53W **83 C9**
Willimantic *U.S.A.* 41°43N 72°13W **83 E12**
Willingboro *U.S.A.* 40°3N 74°54W **81 E16**
Williston *S. Africa* 31°20S 20°53E **56 E3**
Williston *Fla., U.S.A.* 29°23N 82°27W **85 G13**
Williston *N. Dak., U.S.A.* 48°9N 103°37W **80 A2**
Williston L. *Canada* 56°0N 124°0W **70 B4**
Willits *U.S.A.* 39°25N 123°21W **76 G2**
Willmar *U.S.A.* 45°7N 95°3W **80 C6**
Willmore Wilderness ◠
  Canada 53°45N 119°30W **70 C5**
Willoughby *U.S.A.* 41°39N 81°24W **82 E3**
Willow Bunch *Canada* 49°20N 105°35W **71 D7**
Willow L. *Canada* 62°10N 119°8W **70 A5**
Willow Wall, The *China* 42°10N 122°0E **33 C12**
Willowick *U.S.A.* 41°38N 81°28W **82 E3**
Willowlake → *Canada* 62°42N 123°8W **70 A4**
Willowmore *S. Africa* 33°15S 23°30E **56 E3**
Willows *U.S.A.* 39°31N 122°12W **78 F4**
Willowvale = Gatyana
  S. Africa 32°16S 28°31E **57 E4**
Wills, L. *Australia* 21°25S 128°51E **60 D4**
Wills Cr. → *Australia* 22°43S 140°2E **62 C3**
Willsboro *U.S.A.* 44°21N 73°24W **83 B11**
Willunga *Australia* 35°15S 138°30E **63 F2**
Wilmington *Australia* 32°39S 138°7E **63 E2**
Wilmington *Del., U.S.A.* 39°45N 75°33W **81 F16**
Wilmington *N.C.,*
  U.S.A. 34°14N 77°55W **85 D16**
Wilmington *Ohio,*
  U.S.A. 39°27N 83°50W **81 F12**
Wilmington *Vt., U.S.A.* 42°52N 72°52W **83 D12**
Wilmslow *U.K.* 53°19N 2°13W **12 D5**
Wilpattu △ *Sri Lanka* 8°20N 79°50E **45 K4**
Wilpena → *Australia* 31°25S 139°29E **63 E2**
Wilsall *U.S.A.* 45°59N 110°38W **76 D8**
Wilson *N.C., U.S.A.* 35°44N 77°55W **85 D16**
Wilson *N.Y., U.S.A.* 43°19N 78°50W **82 C6**
Wilson *Pa., U.S.A.* 40°41N 75°15W **83 F9**

Wilson → *Australia* 16°48S 128°16E **60 C4**
Wilson Bluff *Australia* 31°41S 129°0E **61 F4**
Wilson Inlet *Australia* 35°0S 117°22E **61 G2**
Wilsons Promontory
  Australia 38°59S 146°23E **63 F4**
Wilton *U.S.A.* 47°10N 100°47W **80 B3**
Wilton → *Australia* 14°45S 134°33E **62 A1**
Wiltshire ☐ *U.K.* 51°18N 1°53W **13 F6**
Wiltz *Lux.* 49°57N 5°55E **15 E5**
Wiluna *Australia* 26°36S 120°14E **61 E3**
Wimborne Minster *U.K.* 50°48N 1°59W **13 G6**
Wimmera → *Australia* 36°8S 141°56E **63 F3**
Winburg *S. Africa* 28°30S 27°2E **56 C4**
Winchendon *U.S.A.* 42°41N 72°3W **83 D12**
Winchester *U.K.* 51°4N 1°18W **13 F6**
Winchester *Conn., U.S.A.* 41°53N 73°9W **83 E11**
Winchester *Idaho,*
  U.S.A. 46°14N 116°38W **76 C5**
Winchester *Ind., U.S.A.* 40°10N 84°59W **81 E11**
Winchester *Ky., U.S.A.* 37°59N 84°11W **81 G11**
Winchester *N.H., U.S.A.* 42°46N 72°23W **83 D12**
Winchester *Tenn., U.S.A.* 35°11N 86°7W **85 D11**
Winchester *Va., U.S.A.* 39°11N 78°10W **81 F14**
Wind → *U.S.A.* 43°12N 108°12W **76 E9**
Wind Cave △ *U.S.A.* 43°32N 103°17W **80 D2**
Wind River Range
  U.S.A. 43°0N 109°30W **76 E9**
Windamere, L. *Australia* 32°48S 149°51E **63 B4**
Windau = Ventspils
  Latvia 57°25N 21°32E **9 H19**
Windber *U.S.A.* 40°14N 78°50W **82 F6**
Windermere *U.K.* 54°23N 2°55W **12 C5**
Windhoek *Namibia* 22°35S 17°4E **56 B2**
Windidda ◇ *Australia* 26°23S 122°12E **61 E3**
Windjana Gorge △
  Australia 17°51S 125°0E **60 C3**
Windom *U.S.A.* 43°52N 95°7W **80 D6**
Windorah *Australia* 25°24S 142°36E **62 D3**
Window Rock *U.S.A.* 35°41N 109°3W **77 J9**
Windrush → *U.K.* 51°43N 1°24W **13 F6**
Windsor *Australia* 33°37S 150°50E **63 E5**
Windsor *N.S., Canada* 44°59N 64°5W **73 D7**
Windsor *Ont., Canada* 42°18N 83°0W **82 D2**
Windsor *U.K.* 51°29N 0°36W **13 F7**
Windsor *Calif., U.S.A.* 38°33N 122°49W **78 G4**
Windsor *Colo., U.S.A.* 40°29N 104°54W **76 F11**
Windsor *Conn., U.S.A.* 41°50N 72°39W **83 E12**
Windsor *Mo., U.S.A.* 38°32N 93°31W **80 F7**
Windsor *N.Y., U.S.A.* 42°5N 75°37W **83 D9**
Windsor *Vt., U.S.A.* 43°29N 72°24W **83 C12**
Windsor & Maidenhead ☐
  U.K. 51°29N 0°40W **13 F7**
Windsorton *S. Africa* 28°16S 24°44E **56 C3**
Windward Is. *W. Indies* 13°0N 61°0W **89 D7**
Windward Passage = Vientos,
  Paso de los *Caribbean* 20°0N 74°0W **89 C5**
Winefred L. *Canada* 55°30N 110°30W **71 B6**
Winfield *U.S.A.* 37°15N 96°59W **80 G5**
Wingate Mts. *Australia* 14°25S 130°40E **60 B5**
Wingellina = Irrunytju
  Australia 26°3S 128°56E **61 E4**
Wingham *Australia* 31°48S 152°22E **63 E5**
Wingham *Canada* 43°55N 81°20W **82 C3**
Winisk → *Canada* 55°17N 85°5W **72 A2**
Winisk L. *Canada* 52°55N 87°22W **72 B2**
Wink *U.S.A.* 31°45N 103°9W **84 F3**
Winkler *Canada* 49°10N 97°56W **71 D9**
Winlock *U.S.A.* 46°30N 122°56W **78 D4**
Winneba *Ghana* 5°25N 0°36W **52 G5**
Winnebago, L. *U.S.A.* 44°0N 88°26W **80 D9**
Winnecke Cr. →
  Australia 18°35S 131°34E **60 C5**
Winnemucca *U.S.A.* 40°58N 117°44W **76 F5**
Winnemucca L. *U.S.A.* 40°7N 119°21W **76 F4**
Winner *U.S.A.* 43°22N 99°52W **80 D4**
Winnett *U.S.A.* 47°0N 108°21W **76 C9**
Winnfield *U.S.A.* 31°56N 92°38W **84 F8**
Winnibigoshish, L.
  U.S.A. 47°27N 94°13W **80 B7**
Winnipeg *Canada* 49°54N 97°9W **71 D9**
Winnipeg → *Canada* 50°38N 96°19W **71 C9**
Winnipeg, L. *Canada* 52°0N 97°0W **71 C9**
Winnipeg Beach *Canada* 50°30N 96°58W **71 C9**
Winnipegosis *Canada* 51°39N 99°55W **71 C9**
Winnipegosis L. *Canada* 52°30N 100°0W **71 C9**
Winnipesaukee, L.
  U.S.A. 43°38N 71°21W **83 C13**
Winnisquam L. *U.S.A.* 43°33N 71°31W **83 C13**
Winnsboro *La., U.S.A.* 32°10N 91°43W **84 E9**
Winnsboro *S.C., U.S.A.* 34°23N 81°5W **85 D14**
Winnsboro *Tex., U.S.A.* 32°58N 95°17W **84 E7**
Winokapau, L. *Canada* 53°15N 62°50W **73 B7**
Winona *Minn., U.S.A.* 44°3N 91°39W **80 C8**
Winona *Miss., U.S.A.* 33°29N 89°44W **85 E10**
Winooski *U.S.A.* 44°29N 73°11W **83 B11**
Winooski → *U.S.A.* 44°32N 73°17W **83 B11**
Winschoten *Neths.* 53°9N 7°3E **15 A7**
Winsford *U.K.* 53°12N 2°31W **12 D5**
Winslow = Bainbridge Island
  U.S.A. 47°38N 122°32W **78 C4**
Winslow *U.S.A.* 35°2N 110°42W **77 J8**
Winsted *U.S.A.* 41°55N 73°4W **83 E11**
Winston-Salem *U.S.A.* 36°6N 80°15W **85 C14**
Winter Garden *U.S.A.* 28°34N 81°35W **85 G14**
Winter Haven *U.S.A.* 28°1N 81°44W **85 G14**
Winter Park *U.S.A.* 28°36N 81°20W **85 G14**
Winterhaven *U.S.A.* 32°44N 114°38W **79 N12**
Winters *U.S.A.* 38°32N 121°58W **78 G5**
Winterset *U.S.A.* 41°20N 94°1W **80 E6**
Wintersville *U.S.A.* 40°23N 80°42W **82 F4**
Winterswijk *Neths.* 51°58N 6°43E **15 C6**
Winterthur *Switz.* 47°30N 8°44E **20 C8**
Winthrop *U.S.A.* 48°28N 120°10W **76 B3**
Winton *Australia* 22°24S 143°3E **62 C3**
Winton *N.Z.* 46°8S 168°20E **59 G2**

Wisconsin → *U.S.A.* 43°0N 91°15W **80 D8**
Wisconsin Rapids *U.S.A.* 44°23N 89°49W **80 C9**
Wisdom *U.S.A.* 45°37N 113°27W **76 D7**
Wiseman *U.S.A.* 67°25N 150°6W **74 B8**
Wishaw *U.K.* 55°46N 3°54W **11 F5**
Wishek *U.S.A.* 46°16N 99°33W **80 B4**
Wisła → *Poland* 54°22N 18°55E **17 A10**
Wisłany, Zalew *Poland* 54°20N 19°50E **17 A10**
Wismar *Germany* 53°54N 11°29E **16 B6**
Wisner *U.S.A.* 41°59N 96°55W **80 E5**
Witbank = eMalahleni
  S. Africa 25°51S 29°14E **57 C4**
Witches Gorge = Wu Xia
  China 31°2N 110°10E **35 B8**
Witdraai *S. Africa* 26°58S 20°48E **56 C3**
Witham *U.K.* 51°48N 0°40E **13 F8**
Witham → *U.K.* 52°59N 0°2W **12 E7**
Withernsea *U.K.* 53°44N 0°1E **12 D8**
Witjira △ *Australia* 26°22S 135°33E **62 D2**
Witless Bay *Canada* 47°17N 52°50W **73 C9**
Witney *U.K.* 51°48N 1°28W **13 F6**
Witnossob → *Namibia* 23°55S 18°45E **56 C3**
Witriver *S. Africa* 25°20S 31°0E **57 C5**
Wittenberge *Germany* 53°0N 11°45E **16 B6**
Wittenoom *Australia* 22°15S 118°20E **60 D2**
Witvlei *Namibia* 22°23S 18°32E **56 B2**
Wiwon *N. Korea* 40°54N 126°3E **33 D14**
Wkra → *Poland* 52°27N 20°44E **17 B11**
Władysławowo *Poland* 8°5S 112°25E **37 H15**
Włocławek *Poland* 52°40N 19°3E **17 B10**
Włodawa *Poland* 51°33N 23°31E **17 C12**
Wodian *China* 32°50N 112°35E **32 H7**
Wodonga *Australia* 36°5S 146°50E **63 F4**
Woinbogoin *China* 32°51N 96°39E **34 A2**
Wokam *Indonesia* 5°45S 134°28E **37 F8**
Woking *U.K.* 51°19N 0°34W **13 F7**
Wokingham *U.K.* 51°24N 0°49W **13 F7**
Wokingham ☐ *U.K.* 51°25N 0°51W **13 F7**
Wolf → *Canada* 60°17N 132°33W **70 A2**
Wolf Creek *U.S.A.* 47°0N 112°4W **76 C7**
Wolf L. *Canada* 60°24N 131°40W **70 A2**
Wolf Point *U.S.A.* 48°5N 105°39W **76 B11**
Wolfe Creek Crater △
  Australia 19°10S 127°47E **60 C4**
Wolfe I. *Canada* 44°7N 76°20W **83 B8**
Wolfeboro *U.S.A.* 43°35N 71°13W **83 C13**
Wolfsberg *Austria* 46°50N 14°52E **16 E8**
Wolfsburg *Germany* 52°25N 10°48E **16 B6**
Wolin *Poland* 53°50N 14°37E **16 B8**
Wollaston, Is. *Chile* 55°40S 67°30W **96 H3**
Wollaston L. *Canada* 58°7N 103°10W **71 B8**
Wollaston Lake *Canada* 58°3N 103°33W **71 B8**
Wollaston Pen. *Canada* 69°30N 115°0W **68 D9**
Wollongong *Australia* 34°25S 150°54E **63 E5**
Wolmaransstad *S. Africa* 27°12S 25°59E **56 D4**
Wolseley *S. Africa* 33°26S 19°7E **56 D2**
Wolsey *U.S.A.* 44°25N 98°28W **80 C4**
Wolstenholme, C.
  Canada 62°35N 77°30W **66 C12**
Wolvega *Neths.* 52°52N 6°0E **15 B6**
Wolverhampton *U.K.* 52°35N 2°7W **13 E5**
Wondai *Australia* 26°20S 151°49E **63 D5**
Wongalarroo L. *Australia* 31°32S 144°0E **63 E3**
Wongan Hills *Australia* 30°51S 116°37E **61 F2**
Wonju *S. Korea* 37°22N 127°58E **33 F14**
Wonosari *Indonesia* 7°58S 110°36E **37 G14**
Wonosobo *Indonesia* 7°22S 109°54E **37 G13**
Wonowon *Canada* 56°44N 121°48W **70 B4**
Wŏnsan *N. Korea* 39°11N 127°27E **33 E14**
Wonthaggi *Australia* 38°37S 145°37E **63 F4**
Wood Buffalo △ *Canada* 59°0N 113°41W **70 B6**
Wood Is. *Australia* 16°24S 123°19E **60 C3**
Woodah, I. *Australia* 13°27S 136°10E **62 A2**
Woodbridge *U.K.* 52°6N 1°20E **13 E9**
Woodburn *Australia* 29°6S 153°23E **63 A5**
Woodend *Australia* 37°20S 144°33E **63 F3**
Woodford *Australia* 26°58S 152°47E **63 D5**
Woodfords *U.S.A.* 38°47N 119°50W **78 G7**
Woodlake *U.S.A.* 36°25N 119°6W **78 J7**
Woodland *Calif., U.S.A.* 38°41N 121°46W **78 G5**
Woodland *Maine, U.S.A.* 45°9N 67°25W **81 C20**
Woodland *Pa., U.S.A.* 41°0N 78°21W **82 F6**
Woodland *Wash., U.S.A.* 45°54N 122°45W **78 E4**
Woodland Caribou ◠
  Canada 51°0N 94°45W **71 C10**
Woodlands, The *U.S.A.* 30°9N 95°29W **84 F7**
Woodonga *Australia* 36°10S 146°50E **63 F4**
Woodridge *Canada* 49°20N 96°9W **71 D9**
Woodroffe, Mt. *Australia* 26°20S 131°45E **61 E5**
Woods, L. *Australia* 17°50S 133°30E **62 B1**
Woods, L. of the
  N. Amer. 49°15N 94°45W **71 D10**
Woods Bay *Canada* 45°8N 79°59W **82 A5**
Woodstock *Australia* 19°35S 146°50E **62 B4**
Woodstock *N.B., Canada* 46°11N 67°37W **73 C6**
Woodstock *Ont., Canada* 43°10N 80°45W **82 C4**
Woodstock *U.K.* 51°51N 1°20W **13 F6**
Woodstock *Ill., U.S.A.* 42°19N 88°27W **80 D9**
Woodstock *N.Y., U.S.A.* 42°2N 74°7W **83 D10**
Woodstock *Vt., U.S.A.* 43°37N 72°31W **83 C12**
Woodsville *U.S.A.* 44°9N 72°2W **83 B13**
Woodville *N.Z.* 40°20S 175°53E **59 D5**
Woodville *Miss., U.S.A.* 31°6N 91°18W **84 F9**
Woodville *Tex., U.S.A.* 30°47N 94°25W **84 F7**
Woodward *U.S.A.* 36°26N 99°24W **84 C5**
Woody → *Canada* 52°31N 100°51W **71 C8**
Woody I. *S. China Sea* 16°50N 112°20E **36 A4**
Woolacombe *U.K.* 51°10N 4°13W **13 F3**
Woolamai, C. *Australia* 38°30S 145°23E **63 F4**
Wooler *U.K.* 55°33N 2°1W **12 B5**
Woolgoolga *Australia* 30°6S 153°11E **63 E5**
Woomera *Australia* 31°5S 136°56E **63 E2**
Woonsocket *R.I., U.S.A.* 42°0N 71°31W **83 E13**
Woonsocket *S. Dak.,*
  U.S.A. 44°3N 98°17W **80 C4**

Wooramel → *Australia* 25°47S 114°10E **61 E1**
Wooramel Roadhouse
  Australia 25°45S 114°17E **61 E1**
Wooroonooran △
  Australia 16°25S 146°1E **62 B4**
Wooster *U.S.A.* 40°48N 81°56W **82 F3**
Worcester *S. Africa* 33°39S 19°27E **56 D2**
Worcester *U.K.* 52°11N 2°12W **13 E5**
Worcester *Mass., U.S.A.* 42°16N 71°48W **83 D13**
Worcester *N.Y., U.S.A.* 42°36N 74°45W **83 D10**
Worcestershire ☐ *U.K.* 52°13N 2°10W **13 E5**
Workington *U.K.* 54°39N 3°33W **12 C4**
Worksop *U.K.* 53°18N 1°7W **12 D6**
Workum *Neths.* 52°59N 5°26E **15 B5**
Worland *U.S.A.* 44°1N 107°57W **76 D10**
Worms *Germany* 49°37N 8°21E **16 D5**
Worsley *Canada* 56°31N 119°8W **70 B5**
Wortham *U.S.A.* 31°47N 96°28W **84 F6**
Worthing *Barbados* 13°5N 59°58W **89 g**
Worthing *U.K.* 50°49N 0°21W **13 G7**
Worthington *Minn.,*
  U.S.A. 43°37N 95°36W **80 D6**
Worthington *Pa., U.S.A.* 40°50N 79°38W **82 F5**
Wosi *Indonesia* 0°15S 128°0E **37 E7**
Wotjalum ◇ *Australia* 16°30S 123°45E **60 C3**
Wotjobaluk ◇ *Australia* 37°0S 142°0E **63 C3**
Wou-han = Wuhan
  China 30°31N 114°18E **35 B10**
Wousi = Wuxi *China* 31°33N 120°18E **35 B13**
Wowoni *Indonesia* 4°5S 123°5E **37 E6**
Wrangel I. = Vrangelya, Ostrov
  Russia 71°0N 180°0E **27 B18**
Wrangell *U.S.A.* 56°28N 132°23W **70 B2**
Wrangell Mts. *U.S.A.* 61°30N 142°0W **68 C5**
Wrath, C. *U.K.* 58°38N 5°1W **11 C3**
Wray *U.S.A.* 40°5N 102°13W **76 F12**
Wrekin, The *U.K.* 52°41N 2°32W **13 E5**
Wrens *U.S.A.* 33°12N 82°23W **85 E13**
Wrexham *U.K.* 53°3N 3°0W **12 D4**
Wrexham ☐ *U.K.* 53°1N 2°58W **12 D5**
Wright *Fla., U.S.A.* 30°27N 86°38W **85 F11**
Wright *Wyo., U.S.A.* 43°45N 105°28W **76 E11**
Wright Pt. *Canada* 43°48N 81°44W **82 C3**
Wrightmyo *India* 11°47N 92°43E **45 J11**
Wrightson, Mt. *U.S.A.* 31°42N 110°51W **77 L8**
Wrightwood *U.S.A.* 34°22N 117°38W **79 L9**
Wrigley *Canada* 63°16N 123°37W **68 E7**
Wrocław *Poland* 51°5N 17°5E **17 C9**
Września *Poland* 52°21N 17°36E **17 B9**
Wu Jiang → *China* 29°40N 107°20E **34 C6**
Wu Kau Tang *China* 22°30N 114°14E **31 a**
Wu Xia *China* 31°2N 110°10E **35 B8**
Wu'an *China* 36°40N 114°15E **32 F8**
Wubalawun ◇ *Australia* 15°28S 133°1E **60 C5**
Wubin *Australia* 30°6S 116°37E **61 F2**
Wubu *China* 37°28N 110°42E **32 F6**
Wuchang *China* 44°55N 127°5E **33 B14**
Wuchuan *Guangdong,*
  China 21°33N 110°43E **35 G8**
Wuchuan *Guizhou, China* 28°25N 108°3E **34 C7**
Wuchuan *Nei Monggol Zizhiqu,*
  China 41°5N 111°28E **32 D6**
Wuda *China* 39°29N 106°42E **32 E4**
Wudang Shan *China* 32°23N 111°2E **35 A8**
Wudi *China* 37°40N 117°35E **33 F9**
Wuding He → *China* 37°2N 110°23E **32 F6**
Wudinna *Australia* 33°0S 135°22E **63 E2**
Wudu *China* 33°22N 104°54E **34 H3**
Wufeng *China* 30°12N 110°42E **35 B8**
Wugang *China* 26°44N 110°35E **35 D8**
Wugong Shan *China* 27°30N 114°0E **35 D9**
Wuguishan *China* 22°25N 113°25E **31 a**
Wuhai *China* 39°39N 106°48E **32 E4**
Wuhan *China* 30°31N 114°18E **35 B10**
Wuhe *China* 33°10N 117°50E **35 H9**
Wuhsi = Wuxi *China* 31°33N 120°18E **35 B13**
Wuhu *China* 31°22N 118°21E **35 B12**
Wujiang *China* 31°10N 120°33E **35 B13**
Wukari *Nigeria* 7°51N 9°42E **52 G7**
Wulajie *China* 44°6N 126°33E **33 B14**
Wulanbulang *China* 41°5N 110°55E **32 D6**
Wular L. *India* 34°20N 74°30E **43 B6**
Wulian *China* 35°40N 119°12E **33 G10**
Wulian Feng *China* 27°48N 103°36E **34 D4**
Wuliang Shan *China* 24°30N 100°40E **34 E3**
Wuliaru *Indonesia* 7°27S 131°0E **37 F8**
Wuling Shan *China* 30°0N 110°0E **35 C8**
Wulingyuan ◠ *China* 29°20N 110°30E **35 C8**
Wulong *China* 29°22N 107°43E **34 C6**
Wulong △ *China* 31°8N 103°5E **34 B4**
Wulumuchi = Ürümqi
  China 43°45N 87°45E **30 C6**
Wumeng Shan *China* 26°48N 104°0E **34 D5**
Wuming *China* 23°12N 108°0E **34 F7**
Wuning *China* 29°17N 115°5E **35 C10**
Wunna → *India* 20°18N 78°48E **44 D4**
Wunnummin L. *Canada* 52°55N 89°10W **72 B2**
Wuntho *Myanmar* 23°55N 95°45E **41 H19**
Wupatki △ *U.S.A.* 35°35N 111°20W **77 J8**
Wuping *China* 25°5N 116°5E **35 E11**
Wuppertal *Germany* 51°16N 7°12E **16 C4**
Wuppertal *S. Africa* 32°13S 19°12E **56 E2**
Wuqing *China* 39°23N 117°4E **33 E9**
Wurralibi ◇ *Australia* 13°11S 135°46E **62 A2**
Wurtsboro *U.S.A.* 41°35N 74°29W **83 E10**
Würzburg *Germany* 49°46N 9°55E **16 D5**
Wushan *China* 34°43N 104°53E **34 G3**
Wushi *China* 41°9N 79°13E **30 C4**
Wutai *China* 38°40N 113°12E **32 E7**
Wutai Shan *China* 39°3N 113°32E **32 E7**
Wuting = Huimin *China* 37°27N 117°28E **33 F9**
Wutonghaolai *China* 42°50N 120°5E **33 C11**
Wutongqiao *China* 29°22N 103°50E **34 C4**
Wuwei *Anhui, China* 31°18N 117°54E **35 B11**
Wuwei *Gansu, China* 37°57N 102°34E **30 D9**

Wuxi *Jiangsu, China* 31°33N 120°18E **35 B13**
Wuxi *Sichuan, China* 31°23N 109°35E **34 B7**
Wuxiang *China* 36°49N 112°50E **32 F7**
Wuxuan *China* 23°34N 109°35E **34 F7**
Wuxue *China* 29°52N 115°30E **35 C10**
Wuyang *China* 33°25N 113°35E **32 H7**
Wuyi *Hebei, China* 37°46N 115°56E **32 F8**
Wuyi *Zhejiang, China* 28°52N 119°50E **35 C12**
Wuyi Shan *China* 27°0N 117°0E **35 D11**
Wuyishan *China* 27°45N 118°0E **35 D12**
Wuyishan △ *China* 27°55N 117°54E **35 D11**
Wuyuan *Jiangxi, China* 29°15N 117°50E **35 C11**
Wuyuan *Nei Monggol Zizhiqu,*
  China 41°2N 108°20E **32 D5**
Wuzhai *China* 38°54N 111°48E **32 E6**
Wuzhi Shan *China* 18°45N 109°30E **38 C7**
Wuzhishan = Tongshi
  China 18°50N 109°20E **38 C7**
Wuzhong *China* 38°2N 106°12E **32 E4**
Wuzhou *China* 23°30N 111°18E **35 F8**
Wyaaba Cr. → *Australia* 16°27S 141°35E **62 B3**
Wyalkatchem *Australia* 31°8S 117°22E **61 F2**
Wyalusing *U.S.A.* 41°40N 76°16W **83 E8**
Wyandotte *U.S.A.* 42°12N 83°9W **81 D12**
Wyandra *Australia* 27°12S 145°56E **63 D4**
Wyangala, L. *Australia* 33°54S 149°0E **63 E4**
Wyara, L. *Australia* 28°42S 144°14E **63 D3**
Wycheproof *Australia* 36°5S 143°17E **63 F3**
Wycliffe Well *Australia* 20°48S 134°14E **62 C1**
Wye → *U.K.* 51°38N 2°40W **13 F5**
Wyemandoo *Australia* 28°28S 118°29E **61 E2**
Wymondham *U.K.* 52°35N 1°7E **13 E9**
Wymore *U.S.A.* 40°7N 96°40W **80 E5**
Wyndham *Australia* 15°33S 128°3E **60 C4**
Wyndham *N.Z.* 46°20S 168°51E **59 G2**
Wynne *U.S.A.* 35°14N 90°47W **85 D9**
Wynyard *Australia* 41°5S 145°44E **63 G4**
Wynyard *Canada* 51°45N 104°10W **71 C8**
Wyola L. *Australia* 29°8S 130°17E **61 E5**
Wyoming *Canada* 42°57N 82°7W **82 D2**
Wyoming ☐ *U.S.A.* 43°0N 107°30W **76 E10**
Wyomissing *U.S.A.* 40°20N 75°59W **83 F9**
Wyong *Australia* 33°14S 151°24E **63 E5**
Wytheville *U.S.A.* 36°57N 81°5W **81 G13**

X

Xaafuun *Somalia* 10°25N 51°16E **49 E5**
Xaafuun, Ras *Somalia* 10°27N 51°24E **49 E5**
Xaçmaz *Azerbaijan* 41°31N 48°42E **19 F8**
Xai-Xai *Mozam.* 25°6S 33°31E **57 C5**
Xaignabouri = Sayaboury
  Laos 19°15N 101°45E **38 C3**
Xainza *China* 30°58N 88°35E **30 E6**
Xalapa *Mexico* 19°32N 96°55W **87 D5**
Xangongo *Angola* 16°45S 15°5E **56 B2**
Xankändi *Azerbaijan* 39°52N 46°49E **46 B5**
Xanthi *Greece* 41°10N 24°58E **23 D11**
Xanxerê *Brazil* 26°53S 52°23W **95 B5**
Xapuri *Brazil* 10°35S 68°35W **92 F5**
Xar Moron He →
  China 43°25N 120°35E **33 C11**
Xátiva *Spain* 38°59N 0°32W **21 C5**
Xau, L. *Botswana* 21°15S 24°44E **56 B3**
Xavantina *Brazil* 21°15S 52°48W **95 A5**
Xebert *China* 44°2N 122°0E **33 B12**
Xenia *U.S.A.* 39°41N 83°56W **81 F12**
Xhora *S. Africa* 31°55S 28°38E **57 D4**
Xhumo *Botswana* 21°7S 24°35E **56 B3**
Xi Jiang → *China* 22°5N 113°20E **35 F9**
Xi Ujimqin Qi *China* 44°32N 117°40E **33 B9**
Xi Xian *Henan, China* 32°20N 114°43E **35 A10**
Xi Xian *Shanxi, China* 36°41N 110°58E **32 F6**
Xia Xian *China* 35°8N 111°12E **32 G6**
Xiachengzi *China* 44°40N 130°18E **33 B16**
Xiachuan Dao *China* 21°40N 112°40E **35 G9**
Xiaguan *China* 25°32N 100°16E **34 E3**
Xiajin *China* 36°56N 116°0E **32 F9**
Xi'an *China* 34°15N 109°0E **32 G5**
Xian Xian *China* 38°12N 116°6E **32 E9**
Xian Xianyang Int. ✕ (XIY)
  China 34°27N 108°45E **32 G5**
Xianfeng *China* 29°40N 109°8E **34 C7**
Xiang Jiang → *China* 28°55N 112°50E **35 C9**
Xiang Khouang *Laos* 19°17N 103°25E **38 C4**
Xiangcheng *Henan,*
  China 33°50N 113°27E **32 H7**
Xiangcheng *Sichuan,*
  China 28°53N 99°47E **34 C2**
Xiangdu *China* 23°13N 106°58E **34 F6**
Xiangfan *China* 32°2N 112°8E **35 A9**
Xianggang = Hong Kong ☐
  China 22°11N 114°14E **31 a**
Xiangjiaba Dam *China* 28°37N 104°17E **34 C5**
Xiangning *China* 35°58N 110°50E **32 G6**
Xiangquan *China* 36°30N 113°1E **32 F7**
Xiangquan He = Sutlej →
  Pakistan 29°23N 71°3E **42 E4**
Xiangshan *China* 29°29N 121°51E **35 C13**
Xiangshui *China* 34°12N 119°33E **33 G10**
Xiangtan *China* 27°43N 112°28E **35 D9**
Xiangxiang *China* 27°43N 112°28E **35 D9**
Xiangyang *China* 32°1N 112°8E **35 A9**
Xiangyin *China* 28°38N 112°54E **35 C9**
Xiangzhou *China* 23°58N 109°40E **34 F7**
Xianju *China* 28°51N 120°44E **35 C13**
Xianshui He → *China* 30°10N 101°9E **34 B3**
Xiantao *China* 30°25N 113°25E **35 B9**
Xianyang *China* 34°20N 108°40E **32 G5**
Xiao Hinggan Ling *China* 49°0N 127°0E **31 B14**
Xiao Xian *China* 34°15N 116°55E **32 G9**
Xiaofeng *China* 30°52N 119°32E **35 B12**
Xiaogan *China* 30°52N 113°55E **35 B9**
Xiaojin *China* 30°59N 102°21E **34 B4**
Xiaolan *China* 22°38N 113°13E **31 a**
Xiaoshan *China* 30°12N 120°18E **35 B13**

Xiaowan Dam *China* 24°42N 100°5E **34 E3**
Xiaowutai Shan *China* 39°51N 114°59E **32 E8**
Xiaoyi *China* 37°8N 111°48E **32 F6**
Xiapu *China* 26°54N 119°59E **35 D12**
Xiashan = Zhanjiang
  China 21°15N 110°20E **35 G8**
Xiawa *China* 42°35N 120°38E **33 C11**
Xiayi *China* 34°15N 116°10E **32 G9**
Xichang *China* 27°51N 102°19E **34 D5**
Xichong *China* 30°57N 105°54E **34 B5**
Xichou *China* 23°25N 104°42E **34 E5**
Xichuan *China* 33°0N 111°30E **32 H6**
Xide *China* 28°8N 102°19E **34 C4**
Xiemahe *China* 31°38N 111°12E **35 B8**
Xifei He → *China* 32°45N 116°40E **32 H9**
Xifeng *Gansu, China* 35°40N 107°40E **32 G4**
Xifeng *Guizhou, China* 27°7N 106°42E **34 D6**
Xifeng *Liaoning, China* 42°42N 124°45E **33 C13**
Xifengzhen = Xifeng
  China 35°40N 107°40E **32 G4**
Xigazê *China* 29°5N 88°45E **30 F6**
Xihe *China* 34°2N 105°20E **32 G3**
Xihua *China* 33°45N 114°30E **32 H8**
Xili Shuiku *China* 22°36N 113°57E **31 a**
Xiliao He → *China* 43°32N 123°35E **33 C12**
Xilin *China* 24°30N 105°6E **34 E5**
Xiling Gorge = Xiling Xia
  China 30°54N 110°48E **35 B8**
Xiling Xia *China* 30°54N 110°48E **35 B8**
Xilinhot *China* 43°52N 116°2E **32 C9**
Xiluodu Dam *China* 28°12N 103°34E **34 C4**
Ximeng *China* 22°50N 99°27E **34 F2**
Ximiao *China* 40°59N 100°12E **30 C9**
Xin Jiang → *China* 28°45N 116°35E **35 C11**
Xin Xian = Xinzhou
  China 38°22N 112°46E **32 E7**
Xin'anjiang Shuiku □
  China 29°33N 118°56E **35 C12**
Xinavane *Mozam.* 25°2S 32°47E **57 C5**
Xinbin *China* 41°40N 125°2E **33 D13**
Xincai *China* 32°43N 114°58E **35 A10**
Xinchang *China* 29°28N 120°52E **35 C13**
Xincheng *Guangxi Zhuangzu,*
  China 24°5N 108°39E **34 E7**
Xincheng *Jiangxi, China* 26°48N 114°6E **35 D10**
Xinfeng *Guangdong,*
  China 24°5N 114°16E **35 E10**
Xinfeng *Jiangxi, China* 27°7N 116°11E **35 D11**
Xinfeng *Jiangxi, China* 25°27N 114°58E **35 E10**
Xinfengjiang Shuiku □
  China 23°52N 114°30E **35 F10**
Xing Xian *China* 38°27N 111°7E **32 E6**
Xing'an *Guangxi Zhuangzu,*
  China 25°38N 110°40E **35 E8**
Xingan *Jiangxi, China* 27°46N 115°20E **35 D10**
Xingcheng *China* 40°40N 120°45E **33 D11**
Xinghe *China* 40°55N 113°52E **32 D7**
Xinghua *China* 32°58N 119°48E **33 H10**
Xinghua Wan *China* 25°15N 119°20E **35 E12**
Xinglong *China* 40°25N 117°30E **33 D9**
Xingning *China* 24°3N 115°42E **35 E10**
Xingping *China* 34°20N 108°28E **32 G5**
Xingren *China* 25°24N 105°11E **34 E5**
Xingshan *China* 31°15N 110°45E **35 B8**
Xingtai *China* 37°3N 114°32E **32 F8**
Xingu → *Brazil* 1°30S 51°53W **93 D8**
Xingwen *China* 28°22N 104°50E **34 C5**
Xingxingxia *China* 41°47N 95°0E **30 C7**
Xingyang *China* 34°45N 112°52E **32 G7**
Xingyi *China* 25°3N 104°59E **34 E5**
Xinhe *China* 37°30N 115°15E **32 F8**
Xinhua *China* 27°42N 111°13E **35 D8**
Xinhuang *China* 27°21N 109°12E **34 D7**
Xinhui *China* 22°25N 113°0E **35 F9**
Xining *China* 36°34N 101°40E **30 D9**
Xinji *China* 37°55N 115°13E **32 F8**
Xinjian *China* 28°37N 115°40E **35 C10**
Xinjiang *China* 35°34N 111°11E **32 G6**
Xinjiang Uygur Zizhiqu □
  China 42°0N 86°0E **30 C6**
Xinjin = Pulandian
  China 39°25N 121°58E **33 E11**
Xinjin *China* 30°24N 103°47E **34 B4**
Xinkai He → *China* 43°32N 123°35E **33 C12**
Xinken *China* 22°39N 113°34E **31 a**
Xinle *China* 38°25N 114°40E **32 E8**
Xinlitun *China* 42°0N 122°8E **33 D12**
Xinlong *China* 30°57N 100°12E **34 B3**
Xinmi *China* 34°30N 113°25E **32 G7**
Xinmin *China* 41°59N 122°50E **33 D12**
Xinning *China* 26°28N 110°50E **35 D8**
Xinshao *China* 27°21N 111°26E **35 D8**
Xintai *China* 35°55N 117°45E **33 G9**
Xintian *China* 25°55N 112°13E **35 E9**
Xinwan *China* 22°47N 113°40E **31 a**
Xinxiang *China* 35°18N 113°50E **32 G7**
Xinxing *China* 22°35N 112°15E **35 F9**
Xinyang *China* 32°6N 114°3E **35 A10**
Xinye *China* 32°30N 112°21E **35 A9**
Xinyi *Guangdong, China* 22°25N 111°0E **35 F8**
Xinyi *Nei Monggol Zizhiqu,*
  China 34°23N 118°21E **33 G10**
Xinzhan *China* 43°50N 127°18E **33 C14**
Xinzheng *China* 34°20N 113°45E **32 G7**
Xinzhou *Hainan, China* 19°43N 109°17E **38 C7**
Xinzhou *Hubei, China* 30°50N 114°48E **35 B10**
Xinzhou *Shanxi, China* 38°22N 112°46E **32 E7**
Xiongyuecheng *China* 40°12N 122°5E **33 D12**
Xiping *Henan, China* 33°22N 114°5E **32 H8**
Xiping *Henan, China* 33°25N 111°8E **32 H6**
Xiping *Zhejiang, China* 28°16N 119°29E **35 C12**
Xique-Xique *Brazil* 10°50S 42°40W **93 F10**
Xisha Qundao = Paracel Is.
  S. China Sea 15°50N 112°0E **36 A4**
Xishuangbanna *China* 22°5N 101°1E **34 F3**
Xishui *Guizhou, China* 28°19N 106°9E **34 C6**
Xishui *Hubei, China* 30°30N 115°15E **35 B10**
Xiu Shui → *China* 29°13N 116°0E **35 C10**

Xiuning *China* 29°45N 118°10E **35 C12**
Xiuren *China* 24°27N 110°12E **35 E8**
Xiushan *China* 28°25N 108°57E **34 C7**
Xiushui *China* 29°2N 114°33E **35 C10**
Xiuwen *China* 26°49N 106°32E **34 D6**
Xiuyan *China* 40°18N 123°11E **33 D12**
Xiva *Uzbekistan* 41°30N 60°18E **26 E7**
Xixabangma Feng *China* 28°20N 85°40E **43 E11**
Xixia *China* 33°25N 111°29E **32 H6**
Xixiang *Guangdong, China* 22°34N 113°52E **31 a**
Xixiang *Shaanxi, China* 33°0N 107°44E **32 H4**
Xixón = Gijón *Spain* 43°32N 5°42W **21 A3**
Xiyang *China* 37°38N 113°38E **32 F7**
Xizang Zizhiqu □ *China* 32°0N 88°0E **30 E6**
Xochob *Mexico* 19°21N 89°48W **87 D7**
Xu Jiang → *China* 28°0N 116°25E **35 D11**
Xuan Loc *Vietnam* 10°56N 107°14E **39 G6**
Xuan'en *China* 30°0N 109°30E **34 C7**
Xuanhan *China* 31°18N 107°38E **34 B6**
Xuanhua *China* 40°40N 115°2E **32 D8**
Xuanwei *China* 26°15N 103°59E **34 C5**
Xuanzhou *China* 30°56N 118°43E **35 B12**
Xuchang *China* 34°2N 113°48E **32 G7**
Xuefeng Shan *China* 27°5N 110°35E **35 D8**
Xuejiaping *China* 31°39N 110°16E **35 B8**
Xun Jiang → *China* 23°35N 111°30E **35 F8**
Xun Xian *China* 35°42N 114°33E **32 G8**
Xundian *China* 25°36N 103°15E **34 E4**
Xunwu *China* 24°54N 115°37E **35 E10**
Xunyang *China* 32°48N 109°22E **32 H5**
Xunyi *China* 35°8N 108°20E **32 G5**
Xupu *China* 27°53N 110°32E **35 D8**
Xúquer → *Spain* 39°5N 0°10W **21 C5**
Xushui *China* 39°2N 115°40E **32 E8**
Xuwen *China* 20°20N 110°10E **35 G8**
Xuyi *China* 32°55N 118°32E **35 A12**
Xuyong *China* 28°10N 105°22E **34 C5**
Xuzhou *China* 34°18N 117°10E **33 G9**

Y

Y Drenewydd = Newtown
  U.K. 52°31N 3°19W **13 E4**
Y Fenni = Abergavenny
  U.K. 51°49N 3°1W **13 F4**
Y Gelli Gandryll = Hay-on-Wye
  U.K. 52°5N 3°8W **13 E4**
Y Trallwng = Welshpool
  U.K. 52°39N 3°8W **13 E4**
Ya Xian = Sanya *China* 18°14N 109°29E **38 C7**
Yaamba *Australia* 23°8S 150°22E **62 C5**
Ya'an *China* 29°58N 103°5E **34 C4**
Yaapeet *Australia* 35°45S 142°3E **63 F3**
Yablonovyy Khrebet
  Russia 53°0N 114°0E **27 D12**
Yablonovyy Ra. = Yablonovyy
  Khrebet *Russia* 53°0N 114°0E **27 D12**
Yabrai Shan *China* 39°40N 103°0E **32 E2**
Yabrūd *Syria* 33°58N 36°39E **48 B5**
Yabucoa *Puerto Rico* 18°3N 65°53W **89 d**
Yacambú △ *Venezuela* 9°42N 69°27W **89 E6**
Yacata *Fiji* 17°15S 179°31W **59 a**
Yacheng *China* 18°22N 109°6E **38 C7**
Yacuiba *Bolivia* 22°0S 63°43W **94 A3**
Yacuma → *Bolivia* 13°38S 65°23W **92 F5**
Yadgir *India* 16°45N 77°5E **44 L10**
Yadkin → *U.S.A.* 35°23N 80°4W **85 D14**
Yadua *Fiji* 16°49S 178°18E **59 a**
Yaeyama-Rettō *Japan* 24°30N 123°40E **29 M1**
Yagasa Cluster *Fiji* 18°57S 178°28W **59 a**
Yagodnoye *Russia* 62°33N 149°40E **27 C15**
Yahk *Canada* 49°6N 116°10W **70 D5**
Yahuma
  Dem. Rep. of the Congo 1°0N 23°10E **54 D4**
Yaita *Japan* 36°48N 139°56E **29 F9**
Yajiang *China* 30°2N 100°57E **34 B3**
Yakeshi *China* 49°17N 120°44E **31 B13**
Yakima *U.S.A.* 46°36N 120°31W **76 C3**
Yakima → *U.S.A.* 46°15N 119°14W **76 C4**
Yakishiri-Jima *Japan* 44°26N 141°25E **28 B10**
Yakobi I. *U.S.A.* 58°0N 136°30W **70 B1**
Yakovlevka *Russia* 44°26N 133°28E **28 B6**
Yaku-Shima *Japan* 30°20N 130°30E **29 J5**
Yakumo *Japan* 42°15N 140°16E **28 C10**
Yakutat *U.S.A.* 59°33N 139°44W **68 F4**
Yakutat B. *U.S.A.* 59°45N 140°45W **74 D11**
Yakutia = Sakha □
  Russia 66°0N 130°0E **27 C14**
Yakutsk *Russia* 62°5N 129°50E **27 C13**
Yala *Thailand* 6°33N 101°18E **39 J3**
Yala △ *Sri Lanka* 6°20N 81°30E **45 L5**
Yalata *Australia* 31°59S 132°26E **61 F5**
Yalata ○ *Australia* 31°35S 132°7E **61 F5**
Yalboroo *Australia* 20°50S 148°40E **62 b**
Yale *U.S.A.* 43°8N 82°48W **82 C2**
Yalgorup △ *Australia* 32°39S 115°38E **61 F2**
Yalinga *C.A.R.* 6°33N 23°10E **54 C4**
Yalkabul, Pta. *Mexico* 21°32N 88°37W **87 C7**
Yalleroi *Australia* 24°3S 145°42E **62 C4**
Yalobusha → *U.S.A.* 33°33N 90°10W **85 E9**
Yalong → *China* 18°12N 109°42E **38 C7**
Yalong Jiang → *China* 26°40N 101°55E **34 D3**
Yalova *Turkey* 40°41N 29°15E **23 D13**
Yalpirakinu ○ *Australia* 22°24S 132°15E **60 D5**
Yalta *Ukraine* 44°30N 34°10E **19 F5**
Yalu Jiang → *China* 39°55N 124°19E **33 E13**
Yam *Australia* 9°54S 142°46E **62 a**
Yam Ha Melah = Dead Sea
  Asia 31°30N 35°30E **48 D4**
Yam Kinneret *Israel* 32°45N 35°35E **48 C4**
Yamada = Kama *Japan* 33°33N 130°49E **29 H5**
Yamada *Japan* 38°15N 140°15E **28 E10**
Yamagata *Japan* 38°30N 140°0E **28 E10**
Yamagata □ *Japan* 38°30N 140°0E **28 E10**
Yamaguchi *Japan* 34°10N 131°32E **29 G5**
Yamaguchi □ *Japan* 34°20N 131°40E **29 G5**
Yamal, Poluostrov *Russia* 71°0N 70°0E **26 B8**
Yamal Pen. = Yamal, Poluostrov
  Russia 71°0N 70°0E **26 B8**
Yamanashi □ *Japan* 35°40N 138°40E **29 G9**
Yamantau, Gora *Russia* 54°15N 58°6E **18 D10**
Yamato Ridge *Sea of Japan* 39°20N 135°0E **28 E7**

Yamba *Australia* 29°26S 153°23E **63 D5**
Yambarran Ra.
  Australia 15°10S 130°25E **60 C5**
Yambio *South Sudan* 4°35N 28°16E **53 H11**
Yambol *Bulgaria* 42°30N 26°30E **23 C12**
Yamburg *Russia* 68°21N 77°8E **26 C8**
Yamdena *Indonesia* 7°45S 131°20E **37 F8**
Yame *Japan* 33°13N 130°35E **29 H5**
Yamethin *Myanmar* 20°29N 96°18E **41 J20**
Yamma Yamma, L.
  Australia 26°16S 141°20E **63 D3**
Yamoussoukro
  Côte d'Ivoire 6°49N 5°17W **52 G4**
Yampa → *U.S.A.* 40°32N 108°59E **77 F9**
Yampi Sd. *Australia* 16°8S 123°38E **60 C3**
Yampil *Moldova* 48°15N 28°15E **17 D15**
Yampol = Yampil
  Moldova 48°15N 28°15E **17 D15**
Yamu, Laem *Thailand* 7°59N 98°26E **39 a**
Yamuna → *India* 25°30N 81°53E **43 G9**
Yamunanagar *India* 30°7N 77°17E **42 D7**
Yamzho Yumco *China* 28°48N 90°35E **30 F7**
Yan Oya → *Sri Lanka* 9°0N 81°10E **45 K5**
Yana → *Russia* 71°30N 136°0E **27 B14**
Yanagawa *Japan* 33°10N 130°24E **29 H5**
Yanai *Japan* 33°58N 132°7E **29 H6**
Yan'an *China* 36°35N 109°26E **32 F5**
Yanaul *Russia* 56°25N 55°0E **18 C10**
Yanbian *China* 26°47N 101°31E **34 D3**
Yanbu 'al Baḥr *Si. Arabia* 24°5N 38°5E **46 E3**
Yanchang *China* 36°43N 110°1E **32 F6**
Yancheng *Henan, China* 33°35N 114°0E **32 H8**
Yancheng *Jiangsu, China* 33°23N 120°8E **33 H11**
Yanchep *Australia* 31°33S 115°37E **61 F2**
Yanchi *China* 37°48N 107°20E **32 F4**
Yanchuan *China* 36°51N 110°10E **32 F6**
Yanco Cr. → *Australia* 35°14S 145°35E **63 F4**
Yandang Shan *China* 28°0N 120°25E **35 D13**
Yandeyarra ○ *Australia* 21°17S 118°24E **60 D2**
Yandicoogina *Australia* 22°49S 119°12E **60 D2**
Yandoon *Myanmar* 17°0N 95°40E **41 L19**
Yanfeng *China* 25°52N 101°8E **34 E3**
Yang Xian *China* 33°15N 107°30E **34 A6**
Yang-yang *S. Korea* 38°4N 128°38E **35 E15**
Yangambi
  Dem. Rep. of the Congo 0°47N 24°24E **54 D4**
Yangbi *China* 25°41N 99°58E **34 E2**
Yangcheng *China* 35°28N 112°22E **32 G7**
Yangch'ü = Taiyuan
  China 37°52N 112°33E **32 F7**
Yangchun *China* 22°11N 111°48E **35 F8**
Yanggao *China* 40°21N 113°55E **32 D7**
Yanggu *China* 36°8N 115°43E **32 F8**
Yangjiang *China* 21°50N 111°59E **35 G8**
Yangliuqing *China* 39°2N 117°5E **33 E9**
Yangōn *Myanmar* 16°45N 96°20E **41 L20**
Yangping *China* 31°12N 111°25E **35 B8**
Yangpingguan *China* 32°58N 106°5E **34 A6**
Yangquan *China* 37°58N 113°31E **32 F7**
Yangshan *Guangdong,*
  China 24°30N 112°40E **35 E9**
Yangshan *Shanghai,*
  China 30°37N 122°4E **35 B14**
Yangshuo *China* 24°48N 110°29E **35 E8**
Yangtse = Chang Jiang →
  China 31°48N 121°10E **35 B13**
Yangtze Kiang = Chang Jiang →
  China 31°48N 121°10E **35 B13**
Yangxin *China* 29°50N 115°12E **35 C10**
Yangyuan *China* 40°1N 114°10E **32 D8**
Yangzhong *China* 32°22N 119°23E **35 A12**
Yangzhou *China* 32°21N 119°26E **35 A12**
Yanhe *China* 28°31N 108°29E **34 C7**
Yanji *China* 42°59N 129°30E **33 C15**
Yanjin *China* 28°5N 104°18E **34 C5**
Yanjing *China* 29°27N 98°30E **34 C2**
Yankton *U.S.A.* 42°53N 97°23W **80 D5**
Yankunytjatjara-Antakirinja ○
  Australia 27°20S 134°30E **63 A1**
Yanqi *China* 42°5N 86°35E **30 C6**
Yanqing *China* 40°30N 115°58E **32 D8**
Yanshan *Hebei, China* 38°4N 117°22E **33 E9**
Yanshan *Jiangxi, China* 28°15N 117°41E **35 C11**
Yanshan *Yunnan, China* 23°35N 104°20E **34 F5**
Yanshou *China* 45°28N 128°22E **33 B15**
Yantai *China* 37°34N 121°22E **33 F11**
Yantian *China* 22°35N 114°16E **31 a**
Yanting *China* 31°11N 105°24E **34 B5**
Yantongshan *China* 43°17N 126°0E **33 C14**
Yanuca *Fiji* 18°24S 178°0E **59 a**
Yanwa *China* 27°35N 98°55E **34 D2**
Yanyuan *China* 27°25N 101°30E **34 D3**
Yanzhou *China* 35°35N 116°49E **32 G9**
Yao Xian *China* 34°55N 108°59E **32 G5**
Yao Yai, Ko *Thailand* 8°7N 98°37E **39 a**
Yao'an *China* 25°31N 101°18E **34 E3**
Yaoundé *Cameroon* 3°50N 11°35E **54 D2**
Yaowan *China* 34°15N 118°3E **33 G10**
Yap *Pac. Oc.* 9°30N 138°10E **64 G5**
Yapen *Indonesia* 1°50S 136°0E **37 E9**
Yapen, Selat *Indonesia* 1°20S 136°10E **37 E9**
Yapero *Indonesia* 4°59S 137°11E **37 E9**
Yappar → *Australia* 18°22S 141°16E **62 B3**
Yapuparra ○ *Australia* 27°30S 126°30E **61 E4**
Yaqaga *Fiji* 16°35S 178°36E **59 a**
Yaqui → *Mexico* 27°37N 110°39W **86 B2**
Yar Çalli = Naberezhnyye Chelny
  Russia 55°42N 52°19E **18 C9**
Yar-Sale *Russia* 66°50N 70°50E **26 C8**
Yaraka *Australia* 24°53S 144°3E **62 C3**
Yare → *U.K.* 52°35N 1°38E **13 E9**
Yaremcha *Ukraine* 48°27N 24°33E **17 D13**
Yarensk *Russia* 62°11N 49°15E **18 B8**
Yarí → *Colombia* 0°20S 72°20W **92 D4**
Yarkand = Shache *China* 38°20N 77°10E **30 D4**
Yarkant He → *China* 40°26N 80°59E **30 C5**
Yarker *Canada* 44°23N 76°46W **83 B8**
Yarkhun → *Pakistan* 36°17N 72°30E **43 A5**

Yarlung Ziangbo Jiang =
  Brahmaputra → *Asia* 23°40N 90°35E **43 H13**
Yarmouth *Canada* 43°50N 66°7W **73 D6**
Yarmūk → *Syria* 32°42N 35°40E **48 C4**
Yarqa, W. → *Egypt* 30°0N 33°49E **48 F2**
Yarra Yarra Lakes
  Australia 29°40S 115°45E **61 E2**
Yarram *Australia* 38°29S 146°39E **63 F4**
Yarraman *Australia* 26°50S 152°0E **63 D5**
Yarras *Australia* 31°25S 152°20E **63 E5**
Yarrie *Australia* 20°40S 120°12E **60 D3**
Yartsevo *Russia* 60°20N 90°0E **27 C10**
Yarumal *Colombia* 6°58N 75°24W **92 B3**
Yasawa *Fiji* 16°47S 177°31E **59 a**
Yasawa Group *Fiji* 17°0S 177°23E **59 a**
Yaselda *Belarus* 52°7N 26°28E **17 B14**
Yasin *Pakistan* 36°24N 73°23E **43 A5**
Yasinski, L. *Canada* 53°16N 77°35W **72 B4**
Yasinya *Ukraine* 48°16N 24°21E **17 D13**
Yasothon *Thailand* 15°50N 104°10E **38 E5**
Yass *Australia* 34°49S 148°54E **63 E4**
Yāsūj *Iran* 30°31N 51°31E **47 D6**
Yatağan *Turkey* 37°20N 28°10E **23 F13**
Yates Center *U.S.A.* 37°53N 95°44W **80 G6**
Yathkyed L. *Canada* 62°40N 98°0W **71 A9**
Yatsushiro *Japan* 32°30N 130°40E **29 H5**
Yauco *Puerto Rico* 18°2N 66°51W **89 d**
Yaval *India* 21°10N 75°42E **44 J9**
Yavari → *Peru* 4°21S 70°2W **92 D4**
Yávaros *Mexico* 26°42N 109°31W **86 B3**
Yavatmal *India* 20°20N 78°15E **44 J11**
Yavne *Israel* 31°52N 34°45E **48 D3**
Yavoriv *Ukraine* 49°55N 23°20E **17 D12**
Yavorov = Yavoriv
  Ukraine 49°55N 23°20E **17 D12**
Yawatahama *Japan* 33°27N 132°24E **29 H6**
Yawri B. *S. Leone* 8°22N 13°0W **52 G3**
Yaxi *China* 27°33N 106°41E **34 D6**
Yaxian = Sanya *China* 18°14N 109°29E **38 C7**
Yazd *Iran* 31°55N 54°27E **47 D7**
Yazd □ *Iran* 32°0N 55°0E **47 D7**
Yazd-e Khvāst *Iran* 31°31N 52°7E **47 D7**
Yazman *Pakistan* 29°8N 71°45E **42 E4**
Yazoo → *U.S.A.* 32°22N 90°54W **85 E9**
Yazoo City *U.S.A.* 32°51N 90°25W **85 E9**
Ybycuí △ *Paraguay* 26°5S 56°46W **94 B4**
Ybytyruzú △ *Paraguay* 25°51S 56°11W **95 B4**
Ye *Myanmar* 15°15N 97°15E **38 E1**
Ye Xian *China* 33°35N 113°25E **32 H7**
Yebyu *Myanmar* 14°15N 98°13E **38 E2**
Yecheng *China* 37°54N 77°26E **30 D4**
Yecheon *S. Korea* 36°39N 128°23E **33 F15**
Yecla *Spain* 38°35N 1°5W **21 C5**
Yécora *Mexico* 28°20N 108°58W **86 B3**
Yedintsy = Edineţ
  Moldova 48°9N 27°18E **17 D14**
Yegros *Paraguay* 26°20S 56°25W **94 B4**
Yehbuah *Indonesia* 8°23S 114°45E **37 J17**
Yehuda, Midbar *Israel* 31°35N 35°15E **48 D4**
Yei *South Sudan* 4°9N 30°40E **53 H12**
Yekaterinburg *Russia* 56°50N 60°30E **26 D7**
Yekateriny, Proliv
  Russia 44°30N 146°30E **27 E15**
Yelandur *India* 12°6N 77°0E **45 H3**
Yelarbon *Australia* 28°33S 150°38E **63 D5**
Yelets *Russia* 52°40N 38°30E **18 D6**
Yelin = Lingshui *China* 18°27N 110°0E **38 C8**
Yelizavetgrad = Kirovohrad
  Ukraine 48°35N 32°20E **19 E5**
Yelizovo *Russia* 53°11N 158°23E **27 D16**
Yell *U.K.* 60°35N 1°5W **11 A7**
Yell Sd. *U.K.* 60°33N 1°15W **11 A7**
Yellamanchilli = Elamanchili
  India 17°33N 82°50E **44 F6**
Yellandu *India* 17°39N 80°23E **44 F5**
Yellapur *India* 14°58N 74°43E **45 G2**
Yellareddi *India* 18°12N 78°2E **44 E4**
Yellow = Huang He →
  China 37°55N 118°50E **33 F10**
Yellow Sea *China* 35°0N 123°0E **33 G12**
Yellowhead Pass
  Canada 52°53N 118°25W **70 C5**
Yellowknife *Canada* 62°27N 114°29W **70 A6**
Yellowknife → *Canada* 62°31N 114°19W **70 A6**
Yellowstone *U.S.A.* 47°59N 103°59W **76 C12**
Yellowstone → *U.S.A.* 44°40N 110°30W **76 D8**
Yellowstone L. *U.S.A.* 44°27N 110°22W **76 D8**
Yelsk *Belarus* 51°50N 29°10E **17 C15**
Yemen ■ *Asia* 15°0N 44°0E **49 E3**
Yemmiganur *India* 15°44N 77°29E **45 G3**
Yen Bai *Vietnam* 21°42N 104°52E **34 G5**
Yenbo = Yanbu 'al Baḥr
  Si. Arabia 24°5N 38°5E **46 E3**
Yenda *Australia* 34°13S 146°14E **63 E4**
Yenice *Turkey* 39°55N 27°17E **23 E12**
Yenisey → *Russia* 71°50N 82°40E **26 B9**
Yeniseysk *Russia* 58°27N 92°13E **27 D10**
Yeniseyskiy Zaliv *Russia* 72°20N 81°0E **26 B9**
Yenyuka *Russia* 57°57N 121°15E **27 D13**
Yeo → *U.K.* 51°2N 2°49W **13 G5**
Yeo, L. *Australia* 28°0S 124°30E **61 E3**
Yeo I. *Canada* 45°24N 81°48W **82 A3**
Yeola *India* 20°2N 74°30E **44 D2**
Yeong-wol *S. Korea* 37°11N 128°28E **33 F15**
Yeongcheon *S. Korea* 35°58N 128°56E **33 G15**
Yeongdeok *S. Korea* 36°24N 129°22E **33 F15**
Yeongdong *S. Korea* 36°6N 127°46E **33 F14**
Yeongju *S. Korea* 36°50N 128°40E **33 F15**
Yeosu *S. Korea* 34°47N 127°45E **33 G14**
Yeotmal = Yavatmal
  India 20°20N 78°15E **44 J11**
Yeovil *U.K.* 50°57N 2°38W **13 G5**
Yeppoon *Australia* 23°5S 150°47E **62 C5**
Yerbent *Turkmenistan* 39°19N 58°36E **47 B8**
Yerbogachen *Russia* 61°16N 108°0E **27 C11**
Yerevan *Armenia* 40°10N 44°31E **46 A5**
Yerington *U.S.A.* 38°59N 119°10W **76 G4**
Yerla → *India* 16°50N 74°30E **44 F2**
Yermo *U.S.A.* 34°54N 116°50W **79 L10**

Yeropol *Russia* 65°15N 168°40E **27 C17**
Yershov *Russia* 51°23N 48°27E **19 D8**
Yes Tor *U.K.* 50°41N 4°0W **13 G4**
Yesan *S. Korea* 36°41N 126°51E **33 F14**
Yeso *U.S.A.* 34°26N 104°37W **77 J11**
Yessey *Russia* 68°29N 102°10E **27 C11**
Yetman *Australia* 28°56S 150°48E **63 D5**
Yeu, Î. d' *France* 46°42N 2°20W **20 C2**
Yevpatoriya *Ukraine* 45°15N 33°20E **19 E5**
Yeysk *Russia* 46°40N 38°12E **19 E6**
Yezd = Yazd *Iran* 31°55N 54°27E **47 D7**
Ygatimi *Paraguay* 24°5S 55°40W **95 A4**
Yhati *Paraguay* 25°45S 56°35W **94 B4**
Yhú *Paraguay* 25°0S 56°0W **95 B4**
Yi → *Uruguay* 33°7S 57°8W **94 C4**
Yi 'Allaq, G. *Egypt* 30°21N 33°31E **48 E2**
Yi He → *China* 34°10N 118°8E **33 G10**
Yi Xian *Anhui, China* 29°55N 117°57E **35 C11**
Yi Xian *Hebei, China* 39°20N 115°30E **32 E8**
Yi Xian *Liaoning, China* 41°30N 121°22E **33 D11**
Yibin *China* 28°45N 104°32E **34 C5**
Yicheng *Henan, China* 31°41N 112°12E **35 B9**
Yicheng *Shanxi, China* 35°42N 111°40E **32 G6**
Yichuan *China* 36°2N 110°10E **32 F6**
Yichun *Heilongjiang,*
  China 47°44N 128°52E **31 B14**
Yichun *Jiangxi, China* 27°48N 114°22E **35 D10**
Yidu *China* 36°43N 118°28E **33 F10**
Yidun *China* 30°22N 99°21E **34 B2**
Yifeng *China* 28°22N 114°45E **35 C10**
Yihuang *China* 27°30N 116°12E **35 D11**
Yijun *China* 35°28N 109°8E **32 G5**
Yıldız Dağları *Turkey* 41°48N 27°36E **23 D12**
Yilehuli Shan *China* 51°20N 124°20E **31 A13**
Yiliang *Yunnan, China* 27°38N 104°2E **34 D5**
Yiliang *Yunnan, China* 24°56N 103°11E **34 E4**
Yilong *China* 31°34N 106°23E **34 B6**
Yima *China* 34°44N 111°53E **32 G6**
Yimen *China* 24°40N 102°10E **34 E4**
Yimianpo *China* 45°7N 128°2E **33 B15**
Yin Xu *China* 36°7N 114°18E **32 F8**
Yi'nan *China* 35°31N 118°24E **33 G10**
Yinchuan *China* 38°30N 106°15E **32 E4**
Yindarlgooda, L.
  Australia 30°40S 121°52E **61 F3**
Yining *China* 43°58N 81°10E **30 C5**
Yiningarra ○ *Australia* 20°53S 129°27E **60 D4**
Yinjiang *China* 28°1N 108°21E **34 C7**
Yinmabin *Myanmar* 22°10N 94°55E **41 H19**
Yipinglang *China* 25°10N 101°52E **34 E3**
Yirga Alem *Ethiopia* 6°48N 38°22E **49 F2**
Yirrkala *Australia* 12°14S 136°56E **62 A2**
Yishan *China* 24°28N 108°38E **34 E7**
Yishui *China* 35°47N 118°30E **33 G10**
Yitong *China* 43°13N 125°20E **33 C13**
Yiwu *China* 29°20N 120°3E **35 C13**
Yixing *China* 31°21N 119°48E **35 B12**
Yiyang *Henan, China* 34°27N 112°10E **32 G7**
Yiyang *Hunan, China* 28°35N 112°18E **35 C9**
Yiyang *Jiangxi, China* 28°22N 117°20E **35 C11**
Yizhang *China* 25°27N 112°57E **35 E9**
Yizheng *China* 32°18N 119°10E **35 A12**
Yli-Kitka *Finland* 66°8N 28°30E **8 C23**
Ylitornio *Finland* 66°19N 23°39E **8 C20**
Ylivieska *Finland* 64°4N 24°28E **8 D21**
Yoakum *U.S.A.* 29°17N 97°9W **84 G6**
Yog Pt. *Phil.* 14°6N 124°12E **37 B6**
Yogyakarta *Indonesia* 7°49S 110°22E **37 G14**
Yogyakarta □ *Indonesia* 7°48S 110°22E **37 G14**
Yoho △ *Canada* 51°25N 116°30W **70 C5**
Yojoa, L. de *Honduras* 14°53N 88°0W **88 D2**
Yok Don △ *Vietnam* 12°50N 107°40E **38 F6**
Yokadouma *Cameroon* 3°26N 14°55E **54 D2**
Yokkaichi *Japan* 34°55N 136°38E **29 G8**
Yoko *Cameroon* 5°32N 12°20E **54 C2**
Yokohama *Japan* 35°27N 139°28E **29 G9**
Yokosuka *Japan* 35°20N 139°40E **29 G9**
Yokote *Japan* 39°20N 140°30E **28 E10**
Yola *Nigeria* 9°10N 12°29E **53 G8**
Yolaina, Cordillera de
  Nic. 11°30N 84°0W **88 D3**
Yolöten *Turkmenistan* 37°18N 62°21E **47 B9**
Yom → *Thailand* 15°35N 100°1E **38 E3**
Yonago *Japan* 35°25N 133°19E **29 G6**
Yonaguni-Jima *Japan* 24°27N 123°0E **29 M1**
Yŏnan *N. Korea* 37°55N 126°11E **33 F14**
Yonezawa *Japan* 37°57N 140°4E **28 F10**
Yong Peng *Malaysia* 2°0N 103°3E **39 M4**
Yong Sata *Thailand* 7°8N 99°41E **39 J2**
Yongamp'o *N. Korea* 39°56N 124°23E **33 E13**
Yong'an *China* 25°59N 117°25E **35 E11**
Yongchang *China* 38°17N 102°7E **30 D9**
Yongcheng *China* 33°55N 116°20E **32 H9**
Yongchuan *China* 29°17N 105°57E **34 C5**
Yongchun *China* 25°16N 118°20E **35 E12**
Yongde *China* 24°5N 99°25E **34 E2**
Yongdeng *China* 36°38N 103°25E **32 F2**
Yongfeng *China* 27°20N 115°22E **35 D10**
Yongfu *China* 24°59N 109°59E **35 E8**
Yonghe *China* 36°46N 110°38E **32 F6**
Yŏnghŭng *N. Korea* 39°31N 127°18E **33 E14**
Yongji *Jilin, China* 43°33N 126°13E **33 C14**
Yongji *Shanxi, China* 34°52N 110°28E **32 G6**

Yongjia *China* 28°10N 120°45E **35 C13**
Yongkang *Yunnan, China* 24°9N 99°20E **34 E2**
Yongkang *Zhejiang, China* 28°55N 120°2E **35 C13**
Yongnian *China* 36°47N 114°29E **32 F8**
Yongning *Guangxi Zhuangzu, China* 22°44N 108°28E **34 F7**
Yongning *Ningxia Huizu, China* 38°15N 106°14E **32 E4**
Yongping *China* 25°27N 99°38E **34 E2**
Yongren *China* 26°4N 101°40E **34 D3**
Yongshan *China* 28°11N 103°35E **34 C4**
Yongsheng *China* 26°38N 100°46E **34 D3**
Yongshun *China* 29°2N 109°51E **34 C7**
Yongtai *China* 25°49N 118°58E **35 E12**
Yongxin = Jinggangshan *China* 26°58N 114°15E **35 D10**
Yongxing *China* 26°9N 113°8E **35 D9**
Yongxing Dao = Woody I. *S. China Sea* 16°50N 112°20E **36 A4**
Yongxiu *China* 29°2N 115°42E **35 C10**
Yongzhou *China* 26°17N 111°37E **35 D8**
Yonibana *S. Leone* 8°30N 12°19W **52 G3**
Yonne → *France* 48°23N 2°58E **20 B5**
York *Australia* 31°52S 116°47E **61 F2**
York *U.K.* 53°58N 1°6W **12 D6**
York *Ala., U.S.A.* 32°29N 88°18W **85 E10**
York *Nebr., U.S.A.* 40°52N 97°36W **80 E5**
York *Pa., U.S.A.* 39°58N 76°44W **81 F15**
York, C. *Australia* 10°42S 142°31E **62 A3**
York, City of □ *U.K.* 53°58N 1°6W **12 D6**
York, Kap *Greenland* 75°55N 66°25W **69 B18**
York, Vale of *U.K.* 54°15N 1°25W **12 C6**
York Pen. *Australia* 15°0S 125°5E **60 C4**
Yorke Pen. *Australia* 34°50S 137°40E **63 E2**
Yorkshire Dales △ *U.K.* 54°12N 2°10W **12 C5**
Yorkshire Wolds *U.K.* 54°8N 0°31W **12 C7**
Yorkton *Canada* 51°11N 102°28W **71 C9**
Yorkville *U.S.A.* 38°52N 123°13W **78 G3**
Yoro *Honduras* 15°9N 87°7W **88 C2**
Yoron-Jima *Japan* 27°2N 128°26E **29 L4**
Yos Sudarso, Pulau = Dolak, Pulau *Indonesia* 8°0S 138°30E **37 F9**
Yosemite △ *U.S.A.* 37°45N 119°40W **78 H7**
Yosemite Village *U.S.A.* 37°45N 119°35W **78 H7**
Yoshino-Kumano △ *Japan* 34°12N 135°55E **29 H8**
Yoshkar Ola *Russia* 56°38N 47°55E **18 C8**
Yotvata *Israel* 29°55N 35°2E **48 F4**
You Jiang → *China* 22°50N 108°6E **34 F6**
You Xian *China* 27°1N 113°17E **35 D9**
Youbou *Canada* 48°53N 124°13W **78 B2**
Youghal *Ireland* 51°56N 7°52W **10 E4**
Youghal B. *Ireland* 51°55N 7°49W **10 E4**
Young *Australia* 34°19S 148°18E **63 E4**
Young *Canada* 51°47N 105°45W **71 C7**
Young *Uruguay* 32°44S 57°36W **94 C4**
Young I. *Antarctica* 66°25S 162°24E **5 C11**
Younghusband, L. *Australia* 30°50S 136°5E **63 E2**
Younghusband Pen. *Australia* 36°0S 139°25E **63 F2**
Youngstown *Canada* 51°35N 111°10W **71 C6**
Youngstown *N.Y., U.S.A.* 43°15N 79°3W **82 C5**
Youngstown *Ohio, U.S.A.* 41°6N 80°39W **82 E4**
Youngsville *U.S.A.* 41°51N 79°19W **82 E5**
Youngwood *U.S.A.* 40°14N 79°34W **82 F5**
Youxi *China* 26°10N 118°13E **35 D12**
Youyang *China* 28°47N 108°42E **34 C7**
Youyu *China* 40°10N 112°20E **32 D7**
Yozgat *Turkey* 39°51N 34°47E **19 G5**
Ypacaraí △ *Paraguay* 25°18S 57°19W **94 B4**
Ypané → *Paraguay* 23°29S 57°19W **94 A4**
Ypres = Ieper *Belgium* 50°51N 2°53E **15 D2**
Yr Wyddgrug = Mold *U.K.* 53°9N 3°8W **12 D4**
Yreka *U.S.A.* 41°44N 122°38W **76 F2**
Ystad *Sweden* 55°26N 13°50E **9 J15**
Ystradgynlais *U.K.* 51°47N 3°46W **13 F4**
Ysyk-Köl = Balykchy *Kyrgyzstan* 42°26N 76°12E **30 C4**
Ysyk-Köl *Kyrgyzstan* 42°25N 77°15E **26 E8**
Ythan → *U.K.* 57°19N 1°59W **11 D7**
Ytyk-Kyuyel *Russia* 62°30N 133°45E **27 C14**
Yu Jiang → *China* 23°22N 110°3E **34 F7**
Yü Shan *Taiwan* 23°25N 120°52E **35 F13**
Yu Xian = Yuzhou *China* 34°10N 113°28E **32 G7**
Yu Xian *Hebei, China* 39°50N 114°35E **32 E8**
Yu Xian *Shanxi, China* 38°5N 113°20E **32 E7**
Yuan Jiang = Hong → *Asia* 20°16N 106°34E **38 B5**
Yuan Jiang → *Hunan, China* 28°55N 111°50E **35 C8**
Yuan Jiang → *Yunnan, China* 22°20N 103°59E **34 F4**
Yuan'an *China* 31°3N 111°34E **35 B8**
Yuanjiang *Hunan, China* 28°47N 112°21E **35 C9**
Yuanjiang *Yunnan, China* 23°20N 102°0E **34 F4**
Yüanli *Taiwan* 24°27N 120°39E **35 E13**
Yüanlin *Taiwan* 23°58N 120°30E **35 F13**
Yuanling *China* 28°29N 110°22E **35 C8**
Yuanmou *China* 25°42N 101°53E **34 E3**
Yuanping *China* 38°42N 112°46E **32 E7**
Yuanqu *China* 35°18N 111°40E **32 G6**
Yuanyang *Henan, China* 35°3N 113°58E **32 G7**
Yuanyang *Yunnan, China* 23°10N 102°58E **34 F4**
Yuba → *U.S.A.* 39°8N 121°36W **78 F5**
Yuba City *U.S.A.* 39°8N 121°37W **78 F5**
Yūbari *Japan* 43°4N 141°59E **28 C10**
Yūbetsu *Japan* 44°13N 143°50E **28 B11**
Yucatán □ *Mexico* 20°50N 89°0W **87 C7**
Yucatán, Canal de *Caribbean* 22°0N 86°30W **88 B2**
Yucatán, Península de *Mexico* 19°30N 89°0W **66 H11**
Yucatan Basin *Cent. Amer.* 19°0N 86°0W **87 D7**
Yucatan Channel = Yucatán, Canal de *Caribbean* 22°0N 86°30W **88 B2**
Yucca *U.S.A.* 34°52N 114°9W **79 L12**
Yucca Valley *U.S.A.* 34°8N 116°27W **79 L10**

Yucheng *China* 36°55N 116°32E **32 F9**
Yuci = Jinzhong *China* 37°42N 112°46E **32 F7**
Yudu *China* 25°59N 115°30E **35 E10**
Yuechi *China* 30°34N 106°25E **34 B6**
Yuen Long *China* 22°26N 114°2E **31 a**
Yuendumu *Australia* 22°16S 131°49E **60 D5**
Yuendumu ۞ *Australia* 22°21S 131°40E **60 D5**
Yueqing *China* 28°9N 120°59E **35 C13**
Yueqing Wan *China* 28°5N 121°20E **35 C13**
Yuexi *Anhui, China* 30°50N 116°20E **35 B11**
Yuexi *Sichuan, China* 28°37N 102°26E **34 C4**
Yueyang *China* 29°21N 113°5E **35 C9**
Yugan *China* 28°43N 116°37E **35 C11**
Yugorenok *Russia* 59°47N 137°40E **27 D14**
Yugyd Va △ *Russia* 62°25N 58°45E **26 C6**
Yuhuan *China* 28°9N 121°12E **35 C13**
Yühuan Dao *China* 28°5N 121°15E **35 C13**
Yujiang *China* 28°10N 116°43E **35 C11**
Yukon *U.S.A.* 35°31N 97°45W **84 D6**
Yukon □ *Canada* 63°0N 135°0W **68 E5**
Yukon → *U.S.A.* 62°32N 163°54W **74 C7**
Yukon Flats *U.S.A.* 66°40N 145°45W **74 B10**
Yukta *Russia* 63°26N 105°42E **27 C11**
Yukuhashi *Japan* 33°44N 130°59E **29 H5**
Yulara *Australia* 25°10S 130°55E **61 E5**
Yule → *Australia* 20°41S 118°17E **60 D2**
Yuleba *Australia* 26°37S 149°24E **63 D4**
Yüli *Taiwan* 23°20N 121°18E **35 F13**
Yulin *Guangxi Zhuangzu, China* 22°40N 110°8E **35 F8**
Yulin *Hainan, China* 18°10N 109°31E **38 C7**
Yulin *Shaanxi, China* 38°20N 109°30E **32 E5**
Yulong Xueshan *China* 27°6N 100°10E **34 D3**
Yuma *Ariz., U.S.A.* 32°43N 114°37W **79 N12**
Yuma *Colo., U.S.A.* 40°8N 102°43W **76 F12**
Yuma, B. de *Dom. Rep.* 18°20N 68°35W **89 C6**
Yumen *China* 39°50N 97°30E **30 D8**
Yun Gui Gaoyuan *China* 26°0N 104°0E **34 E3**
Yun Ling Shan *China* 27°0N 100°20E **34 E3**
Yun Xian *Hubei, China* 32°50N 110°46E **32 H6**
Yun Xian *Yunnan, China* 24°27N 100°8E **34 E3**
Yuna *Australia* 28°20S 115°0E **61 E2**
Yunan *China* 23°12N 111°30E **35 F8**
Yuncheng *Henan, China* 35°36N 115°57E **32 G8**
Yuncheng *Shanxi, China* 35°2N 111°0E **32 G6**
Yunfu *China* 22°50N 112°5E **35 F9**
Yungang Shiku *China* 40°6N 113°7E **32 D7**
Yungas *Bolivia* 17°0S 66°0W **92 G5**
Yungay *Chile* 37°10S 72°5W **94 D1**
Yunhe *China* 28°8N 119°33E **35 C12**
Yunkai Dashan *China* 22°30N 111°0E **35 F8**
Yunkanjini ۞ *Australia* 22°33S 131°6E **60 D5**
Yunling Shan *China* 28°30N 98°50E **34 D2**
Yunlong *China* 25°57N 99°13E **34 E2**
Yunmeng *China* 31°2N 113°43E **35 B9**
Yunnan □ *China* 25°0N 102°0E **34 E4**
Yunta *Australia* 32°34S 139°36E **63 E2**
Yunxi *China* 33°0N 110°22E **32 H6**
Yunxiao *China* 23°59N 117°18E **35 F11**
Yunyang *Chongqing, China* 31°2N 108°51E **34 B7**
Yunyang *Henan, China* 33°26N 112°42E **35 A9**
Yupanqui Basin *Pac. Oc.* 19°0S 101°0W **65 J17**
Yuping *China* 27°13N 108°56E **34 D7**
Yuqing *China* 27°13N 107°53E **34 D6**
Yuraygir △ *Australia* 29°45S 153°15E **63 D5**
Yurga *Russia* 55°42N 84°51E **26 D9**
Yurihonjō *Japan* 39°23N 140°3E **28 E10**
Yurimaguas *Peru* 5°55S 76°7W **92 E3**
Yurubí △ *Venezuela* 10°26N 68°42W **89 D6**
Yuscarán *Honduras* 13°58N 86°45W **88 D2**
Yushan *China* 28°42N 118°10E **35 C12**
Yushe *China* 37°4N 112°58E **32 F7**
Yushu *Jilin, China* 44°43N 126°38E **33 B14**
Yushu *Qinghai, China* 33°5N 96°55E **30 E8**
Yutai *China* 35°0N 116°45E **32 G9**
Yutian *Hebei, China* 39°53N 117°45E **33 E9**
Yutian *Sinkiang-Uigur, China* 36°52N 81°42E **30 D5**
Yuxarı Qarabağ = Nagorno-Karabakh □ *Azerbaijan* 39°55N 46°45E **46 B5**
Yuxi *China* 24°30N 102°35E **34 E4**
Yuyao *China* 30°3N 121°10E **35 B13**
Yuzawa *Japan* 39°10N 140°30E **28 E10**
Yuzhno-Kurilsk *Russia* 44°1N 145°51E **27 E15**
Yuzhno-Sakhalinsk *Russia* 46°58N 142°45E **31 B17**
Yuzhnyy □ *Russia* 44°0N 40°0E **26 E5**
Yuzhou *China* 34°10N 113°28E **32 G7**
Yvetot *France* 49°37N 0°44E **20 B4**

Z

Zāb al Kabīr → *Iraq* 36°1N 43°24E **46 B4**
Zāb aş Şaghīr → *Iraq* 35°17N 43°29E **46 C4**
Zabaykalsk *Russia* 49°40N 117°25E **27 E12**
Zabaykalsky △ *Russia* 53°40N 109°0E **27 D11**
Zabol *Iran* 31°0N 61°32E **47 D9**
Zābol □ *Afghan.* 32°0N 67°0E **40 D5**
Zāboli *Iran* 27°10N 61°35E **47 E9**
Zabrze *Poland* 50°18N 18°50E **17 C10**
Zacapa *Guatemala* 14°59N 89°31W **88 D2**
Zacapu *Mexico* 19°50N 101°43W **86 D4**
Zacatecas *Mexico* 22°47N 102°35W **86 C4**
Zacatecas □ *Mexico* 23°30N 103°0W **86 C4**
Zacatecoluca *El Salv.* 13°29N 88°51W **88 D2**
Zachary *U.S.A.* 30°39N 91°9W **84 F9**
Zacoalco de Torres *Mexico* 20°14N 103°35W **86 C4**
Zacualtipán *Mexico* 20°39N 98°36W **87 C5**
Zadar *Croatia* 44°8N 15°14E **16 F8**
Zadetkyi Kyun *Myanmar* 10°0N 98°25E **39 G2**
Zafarqand *Iran* 33°11N 52°29E **47 C7**
Zafra *Spain* 38°26N 6°30W **21 C2**
Żagań *Poland* 51°39N 15°22E **16 C8**
Zagaoua *Chad* 15°30N 22°24E **53 E10**
Zagazig *Egypt* 30°40N 31°30E **53 B12**
Zāgheh *Iran* 33°30N 48°42E **47 C6**
Zagreb *Croatia* 45°50N 15°58E **16 F9**

Zāgros, Kūhhā-ye *Iran* 33°45N 48°5E **47 C6**
Zagros Mts. = Zāgros, Kūhhā-ye *Iran* 33°45N 47°0E **47 C6**
Zāhedān *Fārs, Iran* 28°46N 53°52E **47 D7**
Zāhedān *Sīstān va Balūchestān, Iran* 29°30N 60°50E **47 D9**
Zahlah *Lebanon* 33°52N 35°50E **48 B4**
Zahrān al Janub *Si. Arabia* 17°40N 43°30E **49 D3**
Zaïre = Congo → *Africa* 6°4S 12°24E **54 F2**
Zaječar *Serbia* 43°53N 22°18E **23 C10**
Zaka *Zimbabwe* 20°20S 31°29E **57 B5**
Zakamensk *Russia* 50°23N 103°17E **27 D11**
Zakhodnaya Dzvina = Daugava → *Latvia* 57°4N 24°3E **9 H21**
Zākhū *Iraq* 37°10N 42°50E **46 B4**
Zakinthos = Zakynthos *Greece* 37°47N 20°54E **23 F9**
Zakopane *Poland* 49°18N 19°57E **17 D10**
Zakynthos *Greece* 37°47N 20°54E **23 F9**
Zalaegerszeg *Hungary* 46°53N 16°47E **17 E9**
Zalantun *China* 48°0N 122°43E **31 B13**
Zalari *Russia* 53°33N 102°30E **27 D11**
Zalău *Romania* 47°12N 23°3E **17 E12**
Zaleshchiki = Zalishchyky *Ukraine* 48°45N 25°45E **17 D13**
Zalingei *Sudan* 12°51N 23°29E **53 F10**
Zalishchyky *Ukraine* 48°45N 25°45E **17 D13**
Zama L. *Canada* 58°45N 119°5W **70 B5**
Zambeze → *Africa* 18°35S 36°20E **55 H7**
Zambezi = Zambeze → *Africa* 18°35S 36°20E **55 H7**
Zambezi *Zambia* 13°30S 23°15E **55 G4**
Zambezi □ *Namibia* 17°30S 24°30E **56 A3**
Zambia ■ *Africa* 15°0S 28°0E **55 H5**
Zamboanga *Phil.* 6°59N 122°3E **37 C6**
Zamora *Mexico* 19°59N 102°16W **86 D4**
Zamora *Spain* 41°30N 5°45W **21 B3**
Zamość *Poland* 50°43N 23°15E **17 C12**
Zamtang *China* 32°26N 101°6E **34 A3**
Zanda *China* 31°32N 79°50E **30 E4**
Zandvoort *Neths.* 52°22N 4°32E **15 B4**
Zanesville *U.S.A.* 39°56N 82°1W **82 G2**
Zangābād *Iran* 31°46N 61°44E **46 B5**
Zanjān *Iran* 36°40N 48°35E **47 B6**
Zanjān □ *Iran* 37°20N 49°30E **47 B6**
Zanjān → *Iran* 37°8N 47°47E **47 B6**
Zante = Zakynthos *Greece* 37°47N 20°54E **23 F9**
Zanthus *Australia* 31°2S 123°34E **61 F3**
Zanzibar *Tanzania* 6°12S 39°12E **54 F7**
Zaouiet El-Kala = Bordj Omar Driss *Algeria* 28°10N 6°40E **52 C7**
Zaouiet Reggâne *Algeria* 26°32N 0°3E **52 C6**
Zaoyang *China* 32°10N 112°45E **35 A9**
Zaozhuang *China* 34°50N 117°35E **33 G9**
Zap Suyu = Zāb al Kabīr → *Iraq* 36°1N 43°24E **46 B4**
Zapadnaya Dvina = Daugava → *Latvia* 57°4N 24°3E **9 H21**
Západné Beskydy *Europe* 49°30N 19°0E **17 D10**
Zapala *Argentina* 39°0S 70°5W **96 D2**
Zapaleri, Cerro *Bolivia* 22°49S 67°11W **94 A2**
Zapata *U.S.A.* 26°55N 99°16W **84 H5**
Zapolyarnyy *Russia* 69°26N 30°51E **8 B24**
Zapopán *Mexico* 20°43N 103°24W **86 C4**
Zaporizhzhya *Ukraine* 47°50N 35°10E **19 E6**
Zaporozhye = Zaporizhzhya *Ukraine* 47°50N 35°10E **19 E6**
Zara *Turkey* 39°58N 37°43E **46 B3**
Zaragoza *Coahuila, Mexico* 28°29N 100°55W **86 B4**
Zaragoza *Nuevo León, Mexico* 23°58N 99°46W **87 C5**
Zaragoza *Spain* 41°39N 0°53W **21 B5**
Zarand *Kermān, Iran* 30°46N 56°34E **47 D8**
Zarand *Markazī, Iran* 35°18N 50°25E **47 C6**
Zaranj *Afghan.* 30°55N 61°55E **40 D2**
Zarasai *Lithuania* 55°40N 26°20E **9 J22**
Zárate *Argentina* 34°7S 59°0W **94 C4**
Zard, Kūh-e *Iran* 32°22N 50°4E **47 C6**
Zāreh *Iran* 35°7N 49°9E **47 C6**
Zaria *Nigeria* 11°0N 7°40E **52 F7**
Zarneh *Iran* 33°55N 46°10E **46 C5**
Zarqā', Nahr az → *Jordan* 32°10N 35°37E **48 C4**
Zarrīn *Iran* 32°46N 54°37E **47 C7**
Zaruma *Ecuador* 3°40S 79°38W **92 D3**
Żary *Poland* 51°37N 15°10E **16 C8**
Zarzis *Tunisia* 33°31N 11°2E **53 B8**
Zaskar → *India* 34°13N 77°20E **43 B7**
Zaskar Mts. *India* 33°15N 77°30E **43 C7**
Zastron *S. Africa* 30°18S 27°7E **56 D4**
Zavāreh *Iran* 33°29N 52°28E **47 C7**
Zave *Zimbabwe* 17°6S 30°1E **57 A5**
Zavodovski I. *Antarctica* 56°0S 27°45W **5 B1**
Zawiercie *Poland* 50°30N 19°24E **17 C10**
Zāwiyat al Baydā = Al Baydā *Libya* 32°50N 21°44E **53 B10**
Zāyā *Iraq* 33°33N 44°13E **46 C5**
Zāyandeh → *Iran* 32°35N 52°0E **47 C7**
Zaysan *Kazakhstan* 47°28N 84°52E **30 B5**
Zaysan Köli *Kazakhstan* 48°0N 83°0E **26 E9**
Zayü *China* 28°48N 97°27E **41 E20**
Zbarazh *Ukraine* 49°43N 25°44E **17 D13**
Zdolbuniv *Ukraine* 50°30N 26°15E **17 C14**
Zduńska Wola *Poland* 51°37N 18°59E **17 C10**
Zeballos *Canada* 49°59N 126°50W **70 D3**
Zebediela *S. Africa* 24°20S 29°17E **57 B4**
Zeebrugge *Belgium* 51°19N 3°12E **15 C3**
Zeehan *Australia* 41°52S 145°25E **63 G4**
Zeeland □ *Neths.* 51°30N 3°50E **15 C3**
Zeerust *S. Africa* 25°31S 26°4E **56 C4**
Zefat *Israel* 32°58N 35°29E **48 C4**
Zehak *Iran* 30°53N 61°42E **47 D9**
Zeil, Mt. *Australia* 23°30S 132°23E **60 D5**
Zeila = Saylac *Somalia* 11°21N 43°30E **49 E3**
Zeist *Neths.* 52°5N 5°15E **15 B5**
Zeitz *Germany* 51°2N 12°7E **16 C7**
Zelenogorsk *Russia* 60°12N 29°43E **8 F23**

Zelenograd *Russia* 56°1N 37°12E **18 C6**
Zelienople *U.S.A.* 40°48N 80°8W **82 F4**
Zempoala *Mexico* 19°27N 96°23W **87 D5**
Zemun *Serbia* 44°51N 20°25E **23 B9**
Zengcheng *China* 23°13N 113°52E **35 F9**
Zenica *Bos.-H.* 44°10N 17°57E **23 B7**
Žepče *Bos.-H.* 44°28N 18°2E **23 B8**
Zeya *Russia* 53°48N 127°14E **27 D13**
Zeya → *Russia* 51°42N 128°53E **27 D13**
Zêzere → *Portugal* 39°28N 8°20W **21 C1**
Zghartā *Lebanon* 34°21N 35°53E **48 A4**
Zgorzelec *Poland* 51°10N 15°0E **16 C8**
Zhabinka *Belarus* 52°13N 24°2E **17 B13**
Zhambyl = Taraz *Kazakhstan* 42°54N 71°22E **30 C3**
Zhangaözen *Kazakhstan* 43°18N 52°48E **19 F9**
Zhangbei *China* 41°10N 114°45E **32 D8**
Zhangguangcai Ling *China* 45°0N 129°0E **33 B15**
Zhangjiabian *China* 22°33N 113°28E **31 a**
Zhangjiagang *China* 31°55N 120°30E **35 B13**
Zhangjiajie *China* 29°11N 110°30E **35 C8**
Zhangjiakou *China* 40°48N 114°55E **32 D8**
Zhangping *China* 25°17N 117°23E **35 E11**
Zhangpu *China* 24°8N 117°35E **35 E11**
Zhangshu *China* 28°4N 115°29E **35 C10**
Zhangye *China* 38°50N 100°23E **30 D9**
Zhangzhou *China* 24°30N 117°35E **35 E11**
Zhanhua *China* 37°40N 118°8E **33 F10**
Zhanjiang *China* 21°15N 110°20E **35 G8**
Zhannetty, Ostrov *Russia* 76°43N 158°0E **27 B16**
Zhanyi *China* 25°38N 103°48E **34 E4**
Zhanyu *China* 44°30N 122°30E **33 B12**
Zhao Xian *China* 37°43N 114°45E **32 F8**
Zhao'an *China* 23°41N 117°10E **35 F11**
Zhaocheng *China* 36°22N 111°38E **32 F6**
Zhaodong *China* 46°4N 125°59E **31 B13**
Zhaojue *China* 28°1N 102°49E **34 C4**
Zhaoping *China* 24°11N 110°48E **35 E8**
Zhaoqing *China* 23°0N 112°20E **35 F9**
Zhaotong *China* 27°20N 103°44E **34 D4**
Zhaoyang Hu *China* 35°4N 116°47E **32 G9**
Zhaoyuan *Heilongjiang, China* 45°27N 125°0E **33 B13**
Zhaoyuan *Shandong, China* 37°20N 120°23E **33 F11**
Zhari Namco *China* 31°6N 85°36E **30 E6**
Zhashkiv *Ukraine* 49°15N 30°5E **17 D16**
Zhashui *China* 33°40N 109°8E **32 H5**
Zhayylma *Kazakhstan* 51°37N 61°33E **26 D7**
Zhayyq → *Kazakhstan* 47°0N 51°48E **19 E9**
Zhdanov = Mariupol *Ukraine* 47°5N 37°31E **19 E6**
Zhecheng *China* 34°7N 115°20E **32 G8**
Zhegao *China* 31°46N 117°45E **35 B11**
Zhejiang □ *China* 29°0N 120°0E **35 C13**
Zheleznodorozhnyy *Russia* 62°35N 50°55E **18 B9**
Zheleznogorsk-Ilimskiy *Russia* 56°34N 104°8E **27 D11**
Zhen'an *China* 33°27N 109°9E **34 A7**
Zhenba *China* 32°34N 107°58E **34 A6**
Zhenfeng *China* 25°22N 105°40E **34 E5**
Zheng'an *China* 28°32N 107°27E **34 C6**
Zhengding *China* 38°8N 114°32E **32 E8**
Zhenghe *China* 27°20N 118°50E **35 D12**
Zhengyang *China* 32°37N 114°22E **35 A10**
Zhengyangguan *China* 32°30N 116°29E **35 A11**
Zhengzhou *China* 34°45N 113°34E **32 G7**
Zhenhai *China* 29°59N 121°42E **35 C13**
Zhenjiang *China* 32°11N 119°26E **35 A12**
Zhenkang *China* 23°58N 99°0E **34 F2**
Zhenlai *China* 45°50N 123°5E **33 B12**
Zhenning *China* 26°4N 105°45E **34 D5**
Zhenping *Henan, China* 33°10N 112°16E **32 H7**
Zhenping *Shaanxi, China* 31°59N 109°31E **34 A7**
Zhenxiong *China* 27°27N 104°50E **34 D5**
Zhenyuan *Gansu, China* 35°35N 107°30E **34 G4**
Zhenyuan *Guizhou, China* 27°4N 108°21E **34 D7**
Zhenyuan *Yunnan, China* 23°51N 100°59E **34 F3**
Zherong *China* 27°15N 119°52E **35 D12**
Zhetiqara *Kazakhstan* 52°11N 61°12E **26 D7**
Zhezqazghan *Kazakhstan* 47°44N 67°40E **26 E7**
Zhicheng *China* 30°25N 111°30E **35 B8**
Zhidan *China* 36°48N 108°48E **32 F5**
Zhigansk *Russia* 66°48N 123°27E **27 C13**
Zhijiang *Hubei, China* 30°28N 111°45E **35 B8**
Zhijiang *Hunan, China* 27°27N 109°42E **34 D7**
Zhijin *China* 26°38N 105°28E **34 D5**
Zhilinda *Russia* 70°0N 114°20E **27 C12**
Zhitomir = Zhytomyr *Ukraine* 50°20N 28°40E **17 C15**
Zhlobin *Belarus* 52°55N 30°0E **17 B16**
Zhmerynka *Ukraine* 49°2N 28°2E **17 D15**
Zhob *Pakistan* 31°20N 69°31E **42 D3**
Zhob → *Pakistan* 32°4N 69°50E **42 C3**
Zhodzina *Belarus* 54°5N 28°17E **17 A15**
Zhokhova, Ostrov *Russia* 76°4N 152°40E **27 B16**
Zhongba *China* 29°39N 84°10E **30 F5**
Zhongdian *China* 27°48N 99°42E **34 D2**
Zhongdong *China* 24°30N 109°40E **34 E7**
Zhongjian Dao = Triton I. *S. China Sea* 15°47N 111°12E **36 A4**
Zhongning *China* 37°29N 105°40E **32 F3**
Zhongshan *Antarctica* 69°0S 39°50E **5 C6**
Zhongshan *Guangdong, China* 22°26N 113°20E **35 F9**
Zhongshan *Guangxi Zhuangzu, China* 24°29N 111°18E **35 E8**
Zhongshankong *China* 22°35N 113°29E **31 a**
Zhongtiao Shan *China* 35°0N 111°10E **32 G6**

Zhongwei *China* 37°30N 105°12E **32 F3**
Zhongxian *China* 30°18N 107°58E **34 B6**
Zhongxiang *China* 31°12N 112°34E **35 B9**
Zhongyang *China* 37°20N 111°11E **32 F6**
Zhosaly *Kazakhstan* 45°29N 64°4E **26 E7**
Zhoucun *China* 36°47N 117°48E **33 F9**
Zhoukoudian *China* 39°41N 115°56E **32 E8**
Zhouning *China* 27°12N 119°20E **35 D12**
Zhoushan *China* 30°1N 122°6E **35 B14**
Zhoushan Dao *China* 30°5N 122°10E **35 B14**
Zhovkva *Ukraine* 50°4N 23°58E **17 C12**
Zhu Jiang → *China* 22°45N 113°37E **35 F9**
Zhuanghe *China* 39°40N 123°0E **33 E13**
Zhucheng *China* 36°0N 119°57E **33 G10**
Zhugqu *China* 33°40N 104°30E **32 H3**
Zhuhai *China* 22°17N 113°34E **35 F9**
Zhuji *China* 29°40N 120°10E **35 C13**
Zhujiang Kou *China* 22°20N 113°45E **31 a**
Zhumadian *China* 32°59N 114°2E **35 A10**
Zhuo Xian = Zhuozhou *China* 39°28N 115°58E **32 E8**
Zhuolu *China* 40°20N 115°12E **32 D8**
Zhuozhou *China* 39°28N 115°58E **32 E8**
Zhuozi *China* 41°0N 112°25E **32 D7**
Zhushan *China* 32°15N 110°13E **34 A8**
Zhuxi *China* 32°25N 109°40E **34 A7**
Zhuzhou *China* 27°49N 113°12E **35 D9**
Zhytomyr *Ukraine* 50°20N 28°40E **17 C15**
Zhytomyr □ *Ukraine* 50°50N 28°10E **17 C15**
Zi Shui → *China* 28°40N 112°40E **35 C9**
Ziarat *Pakistan* 30°25N 67°49E **42 D2**
Zibo *China* 36°47N 118°3E **33 F10**
Zichang *China* 37°18N 109°40E **32 F5**
Zidi = Wandhari *Pakistan* 27°42N 66°48E **42 F2**
Zielona Góra *Poland* 51°57N 15°31E **16 C8**
Zierikzee *Neths.* 51°40N 3°55E **15 C3**
Zigong *China* 29°15N 104°48E **34 C5**
Ziguéy *Chad* 14°43N 15°50E **53 F9**
Ziguinchor *Senegal* 12°35N 16°20W **52 F2**
Zihuatanejo *Mexico* 17°39N 101°33W **86 D4**
Zijin *China* 23°33N 115°8E **35 F10**
Žilina *Slovakia* 49°12N 18°42E **17 D10**
Zillah *Libya* 28°30N 17°33E **53 C9**
Zima *Russia* 54°0N 102°5E **27 D11**
Zimapán *Mexico* 20°45N 99°21W **87 C5**
Zimbabwe ■ *Africa* 19°0S 30°0E **55 H6**
Zimnicea *Romania* 43°40N 25°22E **17 G13**
Zinave △ *Mozam.* 21°35S 33°40E **57 B5**
Zinder *Niger* 13°48N 9°0E **52 F7**
Zion △ *U.S.A.* 37°15N 113°5W **77 H7**
Zirreh, Gowd-e *Afghan.* 29°45N 62°0E **40 E3**
Zitácuaro *Mexico* 19°24N 100°22W **86 D4**
Zitong *China* 31°37N 105°10E **34 B5**
Zitundo *Mozam.* 26°48S 32°47E **57 C5**
Ziway, L. *Ethiopia* 8°0N 38°50E **49 F2**
Zixi *China* 27°45N 117°4E **35 D11**
Zixing *China* 25°59N 113°21E **35 E9**
Ziyang *Shaanxi, China* 32°32N 108°31E **32 H5**
Ziyang *Sichuan, China* 30°6N 104°40E **34 B5**
Ziyuan *China* 26°2N 110°4E **35 D8**
Ziyun *China* 25°45N 106°5E **34 E6**
Zizhong *China* 29°48N 104°47E **34 C5**
Zlatograd *Bulgaria* 41°22N 25°7E **23 D11**
Zlatoust *Russia* 55°10N 59°40E **18 C10**
Zlín *Czechia* 49°14N 17°40E **17 D9**
Zmeinogorsk *Kazakhstan* 51°10N 82°13E **26 D9**
Znojmo *Czechia* 48°50N 16°2E **16 D9**
Zobeyrī *Iran* 34°10N 46°40E **46 C5**
Zoetermeer *Neths.* 52°3N 4°30E **15 B4**
Zogang *China* 29°55N 97°42E **34 C1**
Zohreh → *Iran* 30°16N 51°15E **47 D6**
Zolochiv *Ukraine* 49°45N 24°51E **17 D13**
Zomba *Malawi* 15°22S 35°19E **55 H7**
Zongo *Dem. Rep. of the Congo* 4°20N 18°35E **54 D3**
Zonguldak *Turkey* 41°28N 31°50E **19 F5**
Zongyang *China* 30°58N 117°7E **35 B11**
Zorritos *Peru* 3°43S 80°40W **92 D2**
Zou Xiang *China* 35°30N 116°58E **32 G9**
Zouar *Chad* 20°30N 16°32E **53 D8**
Zouérate = Zouïrât *Mauritania* 22°44N 12°21W **52 D3**
Zouïrât *Mauritania* 22°44N 12°21W **52 D3**
Zoutkamp *Neths.* 53°20N 6°18E **15 A6**
Zov Tigra △ *Russia* 43°25N 134°10E **28 C7**
Zrenjanin *Serbia* 45°22N 20°23E **23 B9**
Zufār *Oman* 17°40N 54°0E **49 D5**
Zug *Switz.* 47°10N 8°31E **20 C8**
Zugspitze *Germany* 47°25N 10°59E **16 E6**
Zuid-Holland □ *Neths.* 52°0N 4°35E **15 C4**
Zuidbeveland *Neths.* 51°30N 3°50E **15 C3**
Zuidhorn *Neths.* 53°15N 6°23E **15 A6**
Zula *Eritrea* 15°17N 39°40E **49 D2**
Zumbo *Mozam.* 15°35S 30°26E **55 H6**
Zumpango *Mexico* 19°48N 99°6W **87 D5**
Zunhua *China* 40°18N 117°58E **33 D9**
Zuni Pueblo *U.S.A.* 35°4N 108°51W **77 J9**
Zunyi *China* 27°42N 106°53E **34 D6**
Zuo Jiang → *China* 22°50N 108°6E **34 F6**
Zuoquan *China* 37°1N 113°22E **32 F7**
Zuozhou *China* 22°27N 107°27E **34 F6**
Zurbāṭīyah *Iraq* 33°9N 46°3E **46 C5**
Zürich *Switz.* 47°22N 8°32E **20 C8**
Zutphen *Neths.* 52°9N 6°12E **15 B6**
Zuurberg △ *S. Africa* 33°12S 25°32E **56 E4**
Zuwārah *Libya* 32°58N 12°1E **53 B8**
Zūzan *Iran* 34°22N 59°53E **47 C8**
Zvishavane *Zimbabwe* 20°17S 30°2E **55 J6**
Zvolen *Slovakia* 48°33N 19°10E **17 D10**
Zwettl *Austria* 48°35N 15°9E **16 D8**
Zwickau *Germany* 50°44N 12°30E **16 C7**
Zwolle *Neths.* 52°31N 6°6E **15 B6**
Zwolle *U.S.A.* 31°38N 93°39W **84 F8**
Żyrardów *Poland* 52°3N 20°28E **17 B11**
Zyryan *Kazakhstan* 49°43N 84°20E **26 E9**
Zyryanka *Russia* 65°45N 150°51E **27 C16**
Zyryanovsk = Zyryan *Kazakhstan* 49°43N 84°20E **26 E9**
Żywiec *Poland* 49°42N 19°10E **17 D10**